C0-CDZ-850

INTERNATIONAL MAPS AND ATLASES IN PRINT

INTERNATIONAL MAPS AND ATLASES IN PRINT

SECOND EDITION

Edited by KENNETH L. WINCH

BOWKER London & New York

First published 1974 in Great Britain by Bowker Publishing Company Limited, Epping, Essex and in the United States of America by R. R. Bowker Co., 1180 Avenue of the Americas, New York, NY 10036.

Second edition 1976

ISBN 0 85935 036 3

Library of Congress catalog card number ~~73-13336~~

Typeset by Millford Reprographics International Limited, Luton

Printed in Great Britain by R. MacLehose & Co. Ltd, Glasgow

Contents

Preface

The second edition of this carto-bibliography, which had its origins in the Stanford Reference Catalogue, incorporates a number of improvements including a wide-ranging revision of the map and atlas entries.

The complete book has been reset to improve clarity of the text and its subdivisions. Foreign-language accents, excluded from the first edition, have been included and a large number of the map index diagrams have been renewed or updated.

I should like to express my sincere thanks to the many publishers who made corrections to their existing entries and provided detailed information of new publications which form the basis of this second revised edition. My thanks also go to Mr Geoffry Allen who gave valuable advice on various foreign-language matters including transliteration, spellings and accents.

It is important that this book should be as close to user requirements as possible and so I would welcome any comments, criticism or additional information which would be helpful in making subsequent editions easier to use or more complete.

K. L. Winch

Acknowledgements

The editor wishes to acknowledge, with thanks, the permission granted by the many official and commercial mapping agencies to reproduce their map index diagrams, and to emphasize that copyright is strictly reserved. In particular, the following authorizations are noted :

Director of Federal Surveys, Lagos, Nigeria
Index diagrams 669/1-6
Department of Geological Surveys and Mines, Botswana
Index diagram 681/2
Government Printer of the Republic of South Africa. Copyright Authority No 4163
Index diagrams 68/1; 680/1-6
Civil Survey Officer, Survey of Ghana
Index diagrams 667/1, 2
United States Geological Survey, Washington, USA
Index diagrams 73/1, 2
Department of National Development, Canberra, ACT
Index diagrams 94/1-4, 955/1, 2; 99/1
NERC Copyright
Index diagrams 420/4; 411/1; 416/3
Institut Géographique Militaire de Belgique
Index diagrams 493/1, 2
Administration du Cadastre et de la Topographie, Grand Duché de Luxembourg
Index diagram 435.9/1
JRO Verlag, Munchen
Index diagrams 430.1/1, 2, 10
Generalstabens Litografiska Anstalts Forlag
Index diagram 485/1
Sahab Geographic and Drafting Institute, Tehran
Index diagram 55/1
Surveyor General of Rhodesia
Index diagrams 689.1/1, 2
Department of Lands and Surveys, Uganda
Index diagrams 676.1/1, 3
Director of Surveys, Jamaica
Index diagram 729.2/2
Ordnance Survey, Southampton
Index diagrams 410/8, 9, 10; 420/3, 6
Her Majesty's Stationery Office
Index diagrams
458.2/1, 512.317/1; 534/1; 564.3/1; 664/1; 665.1/1; 667/3; 669/5; 676.1/2; 676.2/3; 677/4; 678/2; 681/1; 683/1; 686/1; 689.4/2; 689.7/2; 696/1; 698.2/1; 728.2/1; 729.2/1, 3; 729.61/1; 729.82/1; 729.87/1; 729.9/1; 881/1; 961.1/1; 99/4; 99.1/1

Introduction

International Maps and Atlases in Print has been designed as a practical user's guide to currently available world mapping.

Evidence of available maps is at present rather dispersed, existing in bibliographies which are either incomplete or out of date, agents' and publishers' catalogues, journal bibliographies, library accession lists etc. It is, therefore, the purpose of this present work to bring together these various sources into a single volume which may act as a reliable bibliography of cartographic information.

Every effort has been made to include information of all maps known to be at present on sale, but with the great wealth of official and commercial cartography it is inevitable that certain material has had to be excluded – either through lack of detailed information or insufficient publicity.

SCOPE

Information is given of maps and atlases published throughout the world covering every country and also space and the planets. Aeronautical and nautical navigation charts and maps produced for advertising or internal use e.g. oil company road maps, have been excluded.

ARRANGEMENT

The arrangement is by the world region and country notation of the Universal Decimal Classification – Auxiliaries of Place (as set out in the English full edition (FID 179) Suppt. 1 1972 to British Standard 1000 (9) 1972 with certain amendments). UDC key maps have been prepared to illustrate this system and enable any particular country or region to be found easily. The key maps are on the following pages :

Europe 40
Asia 234
Africa 314
North and Central America 422
South America 504
Australia and Oceania 534
Polar Regions 576

Within each country the publications are divided into MAPS and ATLASES and each of these categories is subdivided according to subject matter under the following headings :

Maps

A1	GENERAL MAPS: ROADS Single or multi-sheet road maps of the complete country or region
A2	GENERAL MAPS: LOCAL General regional maps, road, walking, environs etc.
B	TOWN PLANS
C	OFFICIAL SURVEYS
D	POLITICAL & ADMINISTRATIVE Boundary, planning and outline
E1	PHYSICAL: RELIEF Including moulded plastic relief maps
E2	PHYSICAL: LAND FEATURES Landforms, geomorphology, hydrology
F	GEOLOGY
G	EARTH RESOURCES Minerals, soils, geophysical, magnetic
H	BIOGEOGRAPHY Land use, vegetation, animal life
J	CLIMATE
K	HUMAN GEOGRAPHY Population, social and cultural

Maps

L	ECONOMIC Industry, trade, agriculture, rail, air and water communications
M	HISTORICAL Including facsimiles and pictorial maps
N	MATHEMATICAL Geodetic, triangulation and levelling data

Atlases

These follow the same arrangement as maps with the following additions :

W1	WORLD ATLAS: REFERENCE
W2	WORLD ATLAS: SCHOOL EDITION
W3	WORLD ATLAS: LOCAL EDITION
O1	NATIONAL ATLAS: REFERENCE
O2	NATIONAL ATLAS: SCHOOL EDITION
P	REGIONAL

In certain cases the numerical suffixes have been omitted where they are unnecessary.

Within these subject groups, maps are generally arranged in enlarging scale order, starting with small-scale maps of the country or region and progressing to more detailed maps on more than one sheet. In some cases this order has been changed so that maps of a particular type can be grouped together, e.g. outline or plastic relief maps.

CONTENT

As much bibliographical detail as was available at the time of compilation has been given for each publication. The format has been based, with some amendment, on the second draft of a proposed British Standard for a map entry. The order is as follows :

Maps

1	Title
2	Scale
3	Series designation
4	Numbers of sheets and index reference
5	Edition
6	Author or editor
7	Place of publication
8	Publisher
9	Year of publication
10	Size in centimetres (width followed by depth)
11	Additional information (including general description, projection etc.)
12	List of sheets
13	Price in currency of origin

Atlases

1	Title
2	Volume number or section name
3	Author or editor
4	Edition
5	Place of publication
6	Publisher
7	Year of publication
8	Size of volume in centimetres (width followed by depth)
9	Number of pages
10	Additional information
11	Price in currency of origin

Those items underlined are used for a cross-reference.

Nearly 400 index diagrams of multi-sheet series have been reproduced showing the up-to-date status of publication. These are fully indexed to the text and will be found after page 595. An alphabetical index of countries, regions and islands is included to assist in finding any particular area, or alternatively the UDC key maps provide locations at a glance.

AVAILABILITY OF MAPS AND ATLASES

All maps and atlases included in this book are available at the time of inclusion, but warning should be given that availability constantly changes and any publication may, without notice, go out of print or become unobtainable because of a reprint or for some other reason.

Maps and atlases can be obtained through an appropriate trade agent. The principal retail specialists in this field are:

Stanfords International Map Centre
12-14 Long Acre
London
WC2E 9LP
England

The principal wholesale specialists are:

Geo Center International Landkartenhaus
7 Stuttgart 80 (Vaihingen)
Postfach 800830
Federal Republic of Germany

who will also supply certain maps direct to the public where these are not generally available. Maps can also in some cases be obtained direct from the publisher.

Prices, where given, are quoted in the currency of origin and serve as a guide only. They do not include local taxes or conversion charges; if ordering through a supplier prices would obviously be higher to cover these costs.

HOW TO USE THIS BIBLIOGRAPHY

To find any particular country simply look up the name in the alphabetical index at the end of the volume or locate it on the UDC key maps (see above, 'Arrangement') to find the appropriate UDC number.

For a map of a specific district, first turn to the country in which it is situated and then select the particular type of map required (see above, 'Arrangement'). It should be noted, however, that an alternative related subject category may have to be referred to so that the most appropriate map may be obtained. For example, the best road map of an area may well be classified as an official survey or physical map. If the map required is one sheet from a multi-sheet series consult the reference given in the text to the index diagram so that the correct sheet number may be found.

When ordering maps or atlases from any source it is important that full details regarding the publication are given.

Map Scale Conversion Table

Representative Fraction	Inches to the mile / Miles to the inch		Centimetres to metres / Centimetres to kilometres
1:10, 000	6¼	(6.34) inches to 1 mile	1 centimetre : 100 metres
1:10, 560	6	(6.00) inches to 1 mile	1 centimetre : 105.6 metres
1:15, 000	4¼	(4.22) inches to 1 mile	1 centimetre : 150 metres
1:25, 000	2½	(2.53) inches to 1 mile	1 centimetre : 250 metres
1:50, 000	1¼	(1.27) inches to 1 mile	1 centimetre : 500 metres
1:63, 360	1	(1.00) inches to 1 mile	1 centimetre : 633.6 metres
1:100, 000	1½	(1.58) miles to 1 inch	1 centimetre : 1 kilometre
1:126, 720	2	(2.00) miles to 1 inch	1 centimetre : 1.26 kilometres
1:150, 000	2¼	(2.37) miles to 1 inch	1 centimetre : 1.5 kilometres
1:175, 000	2¾	(2.76) miles to 1 inch	1 centimetre : 1.75 kilometres
1:200, 000	3¼	(3.16) miles to 1 inch	1 centimetre : 2 kilometres
1:250, 000	4	(3.95) miles to 1 inch	1 centimetre : 2.5 kilometres
1:253, 440	4	(4.00) miles to 1 inch	1 centimetre : 2.53 kilometres
1:300, 000	4¾	(4.73) miles to 1 inch	1 centimetre : 3 kilometres
1:400, 000	6¼	(6.31) miles to 1 inch	1 centimetre : 4 kilometres
1:500, 000	8	(7.89) miles to 1 inch	1 centimetre : 5 kilometres
1:600, 000	9½	(9.47) miles to 1 inch	1 centimetre : 6 kilometres
1:633, 600	10	(10.00) miles to 1 inch	1 centimetre : 6.33 kilometres
1:750, 000	11¾	(11.84) miles to 1 inch	1 centimetre : 7.5 kilometres
1:760, 320	12	(12.00) miles to 1 inch	1 centimetre : 7.6 kilometres
1:800, 000	12¾	(12.63) miles to 1 inch	1 centimetre : 8 kilometres
1:900, 000	14¼	(14.20) miles to 1 inch	1 centimetre : 9 kilometres
1:1, 000, 000	15¾	(15.78) miles to 1 inch	1 centimetre : 10 kilometres

Centimetres to Inches Conversion Table

cm	in
1	0.4
2	0.8
3	1.2
4	1.6
5	2
6	2.4
7	2.8
8	3.2
9	3.6
10	4
20	8
30	12
40	16
50	20
60	24
70	28
80	32
90	36
100	40
110	44
200	80

Abbreviations of Publishers' Names

AAG	Association of American Geographers, Washington
AAPG	American Association of Petroleum Geologists, Tulsa, Ok.
AAGS	Association of African Geological Surveys, Paris
ADAC	Allgemeiner Deutscher Automobil Club
Ag	Instituto Geografico Agostini, Novara
AGS	American Geographical Society, New York
AMC	American Map Co., New York
AMS	Army Map Service, Washington
ASS	Austrian Staff Survey - see BEV
Bart	John Bartholomew and Son Ltd, Edinburgh
BB	Bundesanstalt für Bodenforschung, Bad Godesberg
BEV	Bundesamt für Eich- und Vermessungswesen, Wien
BfLR	Bundesanstalt für Landeskunde und Raumforschung, Bad Godesberg
BMR	Bureau of Mineral Resources, Canberra
BPC	BPC Publishing Ltd., London
BRGM	Bureau de Recherches Géologiques et Minières, Orléans
Cart	Cartografia, Budapest
Carti	Cartimex, Bucarest
CGF	Service de la Carte Géologique de la France
CGS	Commission Géologique et Geotechnique Suisse (Schweizerischen Geologischen und Geotechnischen Kommission)
CNRS	Éditions du Centre National de la Recherche Scientifique, Paris
CSLO	Crown Lands and Survey Office, Hong Kong
DBP	Dewan Bahasa dan Pustaka Malaysia, Kuala Lumpur
DCLS	Dept. of Crown Lands and Survey - Australian States
DCT	Direction du Cadastre et de la Topographie, Luxembourg
DEMR	Dept. of Energy, Mines and Resources, Ottawa
DGGM	Direccion General de Geografía y Meteorologia, Mexico
DGU	Danmarks Geologiske Undersøgelse
DLFWR	Dept. of Lands, Forests and Water Resources, Victoria, BC
DMLS	Dept. of Mines, Lands and Surveys, Suva, Fiji
DMS	Directorate of Military Surveys, Feltham
DND	Dept. of National Development, Canberra
Doc	La Documentation Française, Paris
DOS	Directorate of Overseas Surveys, Tolworth
ECAFE	Economic Committee for Asia and the Far East
ECSC	European Coal and Steel Community
F - B	Freytag - Berndt Artaria, Wien
FH	Firestone-Hispania, Madrid
GB	Geologische Bundesanstalt, Wien
Ger	Geographers' Map Co Ltd, Sevenoaks
GI	Geodaetisk Institut, København
Gia	Geographia Ltd, London
GL	Geologische Landesamt - each German State
GLA	Generalstabens Litografiska Anstalt, Stockholm
GSA	Geological Society of America, New York
GSC	Geological Survey of Czechoslovakia
GSC	Geological Survey of Canada, Ottawa
GSI	Geographical Survey Institute, Tokyo
GSNI	Geological Survey of Northern Ireland, Belfast
GUGK	Glavnoe Upravlenie Geodezii i Kartografii, Moscow
IBGE	Instituto Brasileiro de Geografia e Estatistica, Rio de Janeiro
IEGMLRA	Imperial Ethiopian Government Ministry of Land Reform and Administration, Addis Ababa
IGC	Instituto Geográfico e Cadastral, Lisboa
IGM	Instituto Geológico y Minero, Madrid
IGM	Istituto Geografico Militare, Firenze
IGMB	Institut Géographique Militaire de Belgique, Bruxelles
IGN	Institut Géographique National, Paris
IGN	Instituto Geográfico Nacional - Central and South American countries
IGS	Institute of Geological Sciences, London
IGSR	Institute of Geological and Subsurface Research, Athens
JIO	Junta de Investigacoes do Ultramar, Lisboa
JLZ	Jugoslavenski Leksikografski Zavod, Zagreb
Kart	Kartografie, Praha
K & F	Kummerly & Frey AG, Bern
KNA	Kongelik Norsk Automobil Forlaget
KNT	Koninklijke Nederlandsche Toeristenbond, 's Gravenhage
KY	Kanaat Yayinlari, Istanbul
LAC	Litografia Artistica Cartografica, Firenze
LI	Landmaelingar Íslands, Reykjavik
LV	Land karten-verlag VEB Berlin, DDR
Lv	Landvermessungsamt - each West German State
La	Landeamt
Maan	Maanmittaushallituksen Kartanmyynti, Helsinki
MOD	Ministry of Defence, Tolworth
MP	Map Productions
NGD	National Geographical Directorate, Dalat, Vietnam

NGO	Norges Geografiske Oppmaling, Oslo
NGS	National Geographic Society, Washington
NGU	Norsk Geologiske Undersøkelse, Oslo
NP	Norsk Polarinstitut, Oslo
OAV	Osterreichischer Alpenverein, Innsbruck
OF	Orell Füssli Graphic Arts Ltd, Zurich
ORSTROM	Office de Recherche Scientifique et Technique d'Outre-Mer, Paris
OS	Ordnance Survey, Southampton
OSNI	Ordnance Survey of Northern Ireland, Belfast
OUP	Oxford University Press
PCGN	Permanent Committee on Geographical Names, London
PPWK	Państwowe Przedsiębiorstwo Wydawnictw Kartograficznych Warsaw
PUP	Províncias Ultramaras Portugueses, Lisboa
Rijks	Rijks Geologische Dienst, Haarlem
SDC	Survey Department, Ceylon
SETPH	Secrétariat d'État aux Travaux Publics et à l'Habitat, Tunis
SGE	Servicio Geográfico del Ejército, Madrid
SGI	Servizio Geologico d'Italia, Roma
SGP	Serviços Geológicos de Portugal, Lisboa
SGU	Sveriges Geologiska Undersøkning, Stockholm
SI	Survey of India, Dehra Dun
SII	Servizio Idografico d'Italia, Roma
SK	Survey of Kenya, Nairobi
SRA	Svenska Reproduktions AB, Stockholm
ST	Service Topographique Fédéral, Berne
TC1	Touring Club Italiano, Milano
TD	Topografische Dienst, Delft
UP	University Press - various
USGK	Ustřední Sprava Geodezie a Kartografie, Prague
USGS	United States Geological Survey, Washington
USN	United States Navy
USNOO	United States Naval Oceanographic Office, Washington
UUG	Ustřední Ustav Geologický, Prague
VVK	Verwaltungvermessungs- und Kartenwesen, Berlin, DDR
WMO	World Meteorological Organisation

Abbreviations used in Descriptions of Maps

acc.	According to
app.	Approximately
ARE.	Arab Republic of Egypt
C.	Century
c.	Circa (about)
cart.	Cartography, cartographer
Ch.	Chinese
col.	Coloured
com.	Commerce, commercial
CR.	Cloth with rollers (mounting)
CRV.	Cloth with rollers, varnished
Dan.	Danish
dept.	Department
devt.	Development
dir.	Director, Direction
Dut.	Dutch
Ed.	Edition, editor
Eng.	English
Fin.	Finnish
Fl.	Flemish
Fr.	French
ft.	Foot, feet
gen.	General
geog.	Geography, geographical
geol.	Geological
Gk.	Greek
grvt.	Government
Heb.	Hebrew
Hung.	Hungarian
hyd.	Hydrographic
inc.	Including
info.	Information
Inst.	Institute, Instant etc.
Int.	International
intro.	Introduction
is.	Island(s)
It.	Italian
Jap.	Japanese
km	Kilometre(s)
lang.	Language
Lt.	Latin
m	Metre(s)

Mdx.	Middlesex
misc.	Miscellaneous
Mt.	Mountain(ous)
Nor.	Norwegian
Pol.	Polish
pop.	Population
Port.	Portuguese
pp.	Pages
prof.	Professor
proj.	Projection
q.v.	Quod vide (which see)
ref.	Reference
rep.	Reprint (ed)
rev.	Revised or Revision
Rus.	Russian
Scan.	Scandinavian
serv.	Service
Sl.	Slovak
Sp.	Spanish
supp.	Supplement
Surv.	Survey
them.	Thematic
topog.	Topography
UTM	Universal Transverse Mercator
vol.	Volume
YB	Yearbook

World and Oceans

100 World

C OFFICIAL SURVEYS

KARTA MIRA
1:2, 500, 000
See index 100/2
Co-publication of the Official Surveys of Bulgaria, Czechoslovakia, East Germany, Poland, Hungary, Romania and the USSR
100 x 80 average
A map of the whole world on 234 sheets in progress. A standard style is used for the whole map, whose projections vary with latitude to give minimum distortions. Certain reduced size overlap sheets have been published to provide continuity on latitudes where the projection changes. The maps show full topog. detail with national and regional administrative boundaries, graded town stamps, waterways with limits of navigation, contours, isobaths and layer colouring. The lettering on the maps is in Latin script and in the native language of each country or in a transcription. The legend is in English and Russian and there is a list of administrative divisions with a reference diagram.
Sheets in series :

1 North Pole, 1972
2 Banks Island, 1968
3 Thule, 1969
4 Upernavik, 1969
5 Svalbard
6 Dickson, 1973
7 New Siberian Islands, 1973
8 Fairbanks, 1973
9 Dawson, 1971
10 Foxe Basin, 1971
11 Godthaab, 1971
12 Reykjavik, 1969
13 Murmansk, 1967
14 Arkhangelsk
15 Norilsk
16 Verkhoyansk
17 Anadyr
18 Anchorage
19 Whitehorse, 1971
20 Chesterfield Inlet, 1971
21 Julianehaab, 1971
22 Lerwick (overlap), 1969
23 Helsinki, 1967
24 Syktyvkar
25 Khanti-Mansiisk
26 Yakutsk
27 Seimchan
28 Dutch Harbor, 1967
29 Juneau, 1967
30 Vancouver, 1969
31 Winnipeg, 1968
32 Labrador, 1968
33 Newfoundland, 1969
34 Rockall, 1966
35 London, 1965
36 Warsaw, 1972
37 Moscow
38 Novosibirsk
39 Krasnoyarsk
40 Chita
41 Khabarovsk
42 Petropavlovsk-Kamchatski
43 N Pacific Basin - NW Part, 1969
44 N Pacific Basin - N Part, 1969
45 N Pacific Basin - NE Part, 1969
46 San Francisco, 1967
47 St Louis, 1966
48 New York, 1968
49 Boston, 1966
50 Grand Newfoundland Banks, 1967
51 Azores, 1967
52 Madrid, 1964
53 Rome, 1965
54 Sofia, 1968
55 Tbilisi
56 Tashkent
57 Alma-Ata
58 Ulan Bator, 1969
59 Peking, 1973
60 Seoul
61 Kurilsk, 1969
62 Pacific Ocean - NW Part, 1969
63 Midway Islands, 1969
64 Murray Escarpment, 1969
65 Erben Tablemount, 1969
66 Los Angeles, 1966
67 Houston, 1966
67A Houston, 1966
68 Atlanta, 1966
68A Miami, 1966
69 Bermuda Islands, 1966
70 N Atlantic Ridge - N Part, 1966
71 Canary Basin, 1967
72 Casablanca, 1968
73 Tripoli, 1968
74 Cairo, 1968
75 Baghdad
76 Karachi
77 Delhi, 1971
78 Chungking
79 Shanghai
80 Tokyo, 1971
81 Marcus Island, 1969
82 Mellish Seamount, 1969
83 Johnston Island, 1969
84 Honolulu, 1968
85 Eastern Pacific Basin - N Part, 1969
86 Islas Revilla Gigedo, 1966
87 Mexico, 1968
88 Havana (La Habana), 1968
89 Puerto Rico, 1967
90 N Atlantic Ridge - S Part, 1969
91 Cape Verde Islands, 1967
92 Dakar, 1968
93 Niamey, 1968
94 Khartoum, 1968
95 Mecca, 1969
96 Arabian Sea, 1969
97 Bombay, 1968
98 Bangkok
99 Canton
100 Philippine Basin, 1969
101 Mariana Islands, 1969
102 Wake Island, 1969
103 Howland Island, 1971
104 Christmas Island, 1967
105 E Pacific Basin - S Part, 1967
106 Clipperton, 1967
107 Bindloe Island, 1967
108 Bogota, 1964
108A Bogota (overlap), 1968
109 Caracas, 1966
110 Cayenne, 1964
110A Cayenne (overlap), 1968
111 St Peter & St Paul Rocks, 1964
112 Accra, 1969
113 Lagos, 1969
114 Kisangani, 1969
115 Addis Ababa, 1969
116 Arabian-Indian Ridge, 1968
117 Colombo, 1968
118 Singapore
119 Brunei
120 Palau Islands, 1970
120A Palau Islands, 1970
121 Truk Islands, 1969
122 Marshall Islands, 1969
123 Phoenix Is, 1968
124 Manihiki, 1968
125 Marquesas Islands, 1968
126 E Pacific Rise - N Part, 1967
127 Albemarle Island, 1968
128 Quito, 1966
129 Manaus, 1966
130 Belém, 1965
131 Recife, 1965
132 Ascension, 1966
133 Kinshasha (Leopoldville), 1966
134 Lubumbashi (Elisabethville), 1966
135 Nairobi, 1966
136 Seychelles, 1973
137 Diego Garcia, 1973
138 Djakarta
139 Surabaja
140 Ambon
141 Solomon Islands
142 Nauru Islands, 1970
143 Samoa Islands, 1968
144 Tahiti, 1968
145 Mangareva, 1968
146 E Pacific Rise - Middle Part, 1967
147 Peruvian Basin, 1967
148 Lima, 1966
149 La Paz, 1966
150 Rio de Janiero, 1966
151 Ilha-da-Trinidade, 1966
152 St Helena, 1966
153 Windhoek, 1967
154 Salisbury, 1967
155 Tananarive, 1966
156 Mascarene Is, 1973
157 Central Indian Basin, 1973
158 Cocos (Keeling) Islands, 1971
159 Port Hedland
160 Darwin
161 Coral Sea
162 New Hebrides, 1968
163 Kermadec Islands, 1968
164 Rapa, 1967
165 Pitcairn Island, 1968
166 Easter Island, 1967
167 Sala-y-Gomez, 1967
168 Juan Fernandez Islands, 1966
169 Buenos Aires, 1966
170 Porto Alegre, 1966
171 Rio-Grande-Plateau, 1969
172 South Atlantic Ridge, 1969
173 Luderitz, 1966
174 Johannesburg, 1967
175 Fort Dauphin, 1966
176 Central Indian Ridge, 1973
177 Central Indian Ridge
178 Broken Ridge, 1971
179 Perth, 1969
180 Adelaide, 1969
181 Sydney, 1969
182 Whangarei, 1968
183 Chatham Islands, 1968
184 Maria Theresa Reef, 1967
185 South Pacific Basin - NE Part, 1968
186 Eastern Pacific Rise - S Part, 1969
187 Chile Rise, 1967
188 Concepcion, 1966
189 Mar Del Plata, 1966
190 Argentine Basin - Western Part, 1966
191 Argentine Basin - Eastern Part, 1970
192 Tristan Da Cunha Group, 1970
193 Cape Basin, 1969
194 Agulhas Basin, 1973
195 Crozet Islands, 1973

196 Crozet Basin, 1973
197 Amsterdam Island
198 Australian - Antarctic Rise, 1971
199 South Australian Basin - W Part, 1971
200 South Australian Basin - E Part, 1968
201 Melbourne, 1969
202 Wellington, 1969
203 South Pacific Basin - SW Part, 1967
204 South Pacific Rise - Western Part, 1967
205 South Pacific Rise - Eastern Part, 1967
206 Southeast Pacific Antarctic Basin - N Part, 1967
207 Tierra Del Fuego, 1966
208 South Georgia, 1966
209 South Sandwich Islands, 1970
210 Bouvet Island, 1970
211 African-Antarctic Ridge, 1973
212 African Antarctic Basin, 1973
213 Kerguelen Islands, 1973
214 Australian Antarctic Basin - W Part, 1973
215 Australian Antarctic Basin - E Part, 1971
216 Mill Ridge, 1971
217 Macquarie Island, 1972
218 Scott Island, 1971
219 Southeast Pacific Basin - S Part, 1971
220 Charcot Island, 1971
221 Antarctic Peninsula, 1973
222 Cape Norvegia, 1971
223 Princess Ragnhild Coast, 1972
224 Enderby Land, 1972
225 Pravda Coast, 1972
226 Wilkes Island, 1972
227 George V Coast
228 Roosevelt Island
229 Ellsworth Land, 1972
230 Shackleton Range, 1972
231 Queen Maud Land, 1972
232 Plateau Sovetskoye, 1972
233 Ross Island, 1972
234 South Pole, 1972

INTERNATIONAL MAP OF THE WORLD
1:1, 000, 000
see index 100/1 A and B
Responsibility of each national survey office also published by :
Washington : Defense Mapping Agency (AMS)
Tolworth : Dir. of Military Survey
Washington : American Geographical Society
Various sizes
International topographical series begun in 1913 with the aim of each country mapping its own territory in a uniform scale and style. Specifications include contours with layer colouring, spot heights, water features, road and rail communications, boundaries and settlement. Publication has been irregular and is not yet complete but certain agencies have undertaken to map large areas of the world themselves which often provide the best coverage at this scale.

D POLITICAL & ADMINISTRATIVE

CROWN QUARTO HAND MAP OF THE WORLD
London : Philip, 1973
20 x 14
Political col. principal names and railways.
Paper flat - per 10 copies £1.50

IMPERIAL QUARTO HAND MAP OF THE WORLD
London : Philip, 1975
29 x 20
Political col, principal towns and railways.
10 copies £1.50

THE WORLD
PS 17
Tehran : Sahab
50 x 35
Political students map showing boundaries and major cities with physical and location insets. In Persian. Rls 4

PLANISFERIO
Barcelona : Editorial Teide
50 x 33
Hand map showing state boundaries, major cities. S.Ptas 2
Also : Planisferio politico at 1 pta (33 x 25)

STUDENT MAP OF THE WORLD
No 1800/Rev 1
New York : UN, 1969
61 x 46
Col. map of member states of the UN, with various information.

MAPA POLITYCZNA ŚWIATA
1:66, 000, 000
Warszawa : PPWK, 1972
69 x 42
Hand map showing political information and boundaries. Physical map on reverse.
Zl 5

PLANIGLOBY : MAPA FIZYCZNA I POLITYCZNA
1:60, 000, 000
PPWK
see WORLD 100 E1.

PLANISPHERE
1:50, 000, 000
No 4033
Bern : K & F
79 x 44
Political col. map of the World.
Atlantic centred on Van der Grinten proj, world times in accordance with grid, geog. and statistical information on reverse.

POLITICHESKAYA KARTA MIRA
1:50, 000, 000
Moskva : GUGK
Political wall map in Russian.

UMRISSKARTE DER WELT
1:50, 000, 000
No 0831
Bern : K & F
82 x 48
Base map of the continents with political col.

STANFORD'S GENERAL MAP OF THE WORLD
1:49, 000, 000
London : Stanford, 1975
92 x 57
Political col. towns graded by pop, boundaries, canals, shipping routes, Mercator proj, Atlantic centred, pictorial border.
Paper 45p

WORLD ROUTE CHART
1:45, 000, 000
Bart, 1972
see WORLD 100 L.

PHILIP'S POLITICAL SMALLER WALL MAP OF THE WORLD
1:40, 000, 000
London : Philip, 1974
101 x 77
Countries, railways, shipping routes, towns graded by pop. Gall's Proj, available Pacific or Atlantic centred.
Paper flat £1.50

WORLD RELATIONS - POLITICAL
1:40, 000, 000
Philip
see WORLD 100 E1

MAPA POLITYCZNO KOMUNIKACYJNA
1:40, 000, 000
Warszawa : PPWK, 1972
80 x 60
Political coloured world map with communications. Zl 12

THE WORLD, PROJECT MAP
Sydney : Gregory
73 x 55
Col. social study map for schools, showing relief, climatic and economic information - with 12 project cards in col.
A $ 0.30

THE WORLD
No 100
Sydney : Gregory
76 x 101
Map in col, indexed, pop. indicated; Europe and Antarctica inset. A $ 0.65

PHILIP'S INTERNATIONAL MAP OF THE WORLD
1:40, 000, 000
London : Philip, 1974
100 x 68
Bold political col. school wall map, principal towns. Mercator's Proj.
Each 50p

PLANISFERO POLITICO
1:40, 000, 000
Milano : TCI
106 x 65
Col. map showing political divisions and internat. organisations. In Italian.
L 1200

THE WORLD
1:38, 750, 000
Washington : NGS, 1970
108 x 70
Political col. wall map, col. boundaries, towns and communications.
Paper US $2.00
Plastic US $3.00
Enlarged ed.
172 x 109 US $5.00

DAILY EXPRESS MAP OF THE WORLD
1:35, 000, 000
London : Philip, 1976
114 x 82
Political col, principal road, rail and shipping routes, towns and insets of Mediterranean and Polar Regions. Mercator's Proj.
Mounted CRV £3.00

THE WORLD TODAY
Edinburgh : Johnston & Bacon
114 x 82
Politically coloured wall map with illus, time-zones, flags and statistics.
In folder 35p

VÄRLDEN
1:33, 000, 000
Stockholm : GLA
122 x 84
Political col. map in Swedish.

Flat	S.Kr 18.50
Rollers	S.Kr 59.00
Board	S.Kr 69.50

Ed. with flags as pictorial border.

Flat	S.Kr 21.00
Board	S.Kr 73.50

PLANISFERIO POLITICO
Barcelona : Editorial Teide
115 x 88
Political wall map of the world in Spanish.
For schools. S.Ptas 275

MAPAMUNDI
Barcelona : Editorial Teide
115 x 88
School wall map of the world in Spanish.
S.Ptas 275

EL MUNDO
Barcelona : Editorial Teide
115 x 88
School wall map of the world in Spanish.
S.Ptas 275

MAPPEMONDE
No 24
Paris : Hatier
120 x 100
School wall map; political and economic map on reverse.

SUPERIOR WALL MAP OF THE WORLD
Maplewood, NJ : Hammond
127 x 83
Political col. wall map for schools.
US $2.00

PLANISPHÈRE
Map No 322
Eds Vidal Lablache and H Varon
Paris : Armand Colin
120 x 100
School wall map showing political features of the world.

IMPERIAL MAP OF THE WORLD
1:37, 000, 000
Chicago : Rand McNally
132 x 88
Col. political map, Americas centred.
US $1.00

DIE ERDE : POLITISCHE UBERSICHTS-KARTE
1:35, 000, 000
2nd Edition
Gotha : Haack, 1973
96 x 60
Haack hand map with supp: Die Lander der Eide (the Countries of the World) 19pp text.
M 6.00

WELTKARTE
1:33, 000, 000
Stuttgart : Mair
126 x 84
Political-physical wall map, showing countries land relief, text. Communications, poles and time zones inset.

Flat	DM 5.80
Mounted CR	DM 28.50

LE MONDE POLITIQUE
1:33, 000, 000
Paris : IGN, 1974
124 x 77
Political map of the World in cols. Names in international spellings. F.Fr 16.67

WELTKARTE
1:33, 000, 000
Bern : Hallwag, 1969/70
122 x 80
Political col, main roads, rail and shipping lines. Atlantic centred.

CARTE DU MONDE
1:32, 000, 000
No 4023
Bern : K & F
123 x 78
Political col, relief shading, shipping routes, border of nat. flags. Van der Grinten's proj, Atlantic centred. Legend in Eng, Fr, Ger.

DAILY TELEGRAPH MAP OF THE WORLD
1:32, 000, 000
London : Gia
96 x 68
Political divisions, shipping and main rail routes, time zones. Mercator's proj, Far East and Pacific centred.
50p

POLITICAL WORLD MAPS
Various scales
Indianapolis : Cram
School wall maps available at different levels and depths :

Armadillo Primary		
1:20, 562, 500	129 x 130	US $23.00
1:16, 250, 000	162 x 132	US $26.25
Armadillo Beginners		
1:20, 562, 500	129 x 130	US $23.00
1:16, 250, 000	162 x 132	US $26.25
Armadillo Political		
1:16, 250,000	162 x 132	US $27.25
Level C Political-Physical (Mercator)		
1:32, 500, 000	129 x 127	US $23.00
Level C Political-Physical (Globular)		
1:35, 625, 000	129 x 128	US $23.00
Level C Political-Physical (US Centred)		
1:31, 250, 000	129 x 128	US $23.00
Excello Political Wall Map		
1:41, 875, 000	111 x 116	US $12.50
Excello North Polar World		
1:31, 250, 000	111 x 116	US $12.50

PLANISPHÈRE NO 2 (POLITIQUE)
St Germain-en-Laye : Éditions MDI
126 x 92
Political wall map for schools.
Plastic finish, double sided. Map "Économique" on reverse. Also in English or German.

THE WORLD
1:30, 000, 000
Edinburgh : Bart, 1973
100 x 61
Political colouring, relief shaded with boundaries, main roads, railways, airports and ports. 75p

LÄNDERKARTE WELT, POLITISCH
1:30, 000, 000
München : JRO
123 x 73
Political coloured map showing countries. Mercator's proj. Communications, relief shading.

shading.	DM 9.80
Mounted CR	DM 45.00

PLANISFERO POLITICO
1:30, 000, 000
Novara : Ag
140 x 75
School wall map in political colouring.

	L 2, 000
Mounted	L 4, 000

POLITICHESKAYA KARTA MIRA
1:30, 000, 000
Moskva : GUGK
Political wall map in Russian.

SVETA, POLITIČKA
1:30,000,000
In 2 sheets
Beograd : Geokarta
137 x 95 complete
2 sheet map, showing political divisions and communications.
Cloth mounted Dn 100

WELTKARTE
No. 484
Hamburg : Falk
168 x 75
World political wall map, physical map on reverse. DM 21.50

MAP OF THE WORLD
Michigan : Hearne Bros.
167 x 122
Col. school wall map, political boundaries, relief shading, mechanical index. Mercator proj. Americas centred.
US $ 152.50

STATER OG STORBYER
1:25,000,000
In 2 sheets
København : GI
155 x 122
Political map of the World showing countries and large towns in Danish.

WELTKARTE
1:31,000,000
No. 501
Frankfurt : Ravenstein
140 x 79
Political col map on Kreis proj. Shows rail, shipping, air routes

Paper	DM 18.50
Mounted CR	DM 108.00

POLITICAL WORLD MAPS
Various scales
Chicago : Denoyer Geppert
Politically col. wall maps
Maps available:
100091-14 Beginners
1:25,000,000 162 x 111 US $ 24.00
101091-14 Beginners Geog. Terms
1:25,000,000 162 x 111 US $ 24.00
108991-10 Giant Political World
1:18,750,000 218 x 162 US $ 42.50
108091-14 Prime Meridian Centred
1:25,000,000 162 x 111 US $ 24.00

PHILIP'S POLITICAL LARGE WALL MAP OF THE WORLD
1:24,000,000
London : Philip 1974
185 x 120
Boundaries, communications, Mercator's proj, Atlantic or Pacific centred
CR £15.00
Cloth dissected to fold £17.00

LE MONDE (PLANISPHÈRE)
1:23,000,000
Bruxelles : Mantnieks
182 x 121
Politically col. wall map with some relief shading. Van Grinten proj. Available in French or English eds.

POLITICAL MAP OF THE WORLD – PLANISPHERE
1:23,000,000
No 4003
Bern: K & F, 1966
178 x 104
2 sheet map, political col. relief shading, road, rail and shipping routed. Van der Grinten's proj, Atlantic centred.

NEW COMMERCIAL MAP OF THE WORLD
1:22,500,000
In 2 sheets
London : Philip, 1975
167 x 128
Political col. wall map, shipping routes, boundaries, Mercator's proj, Atlantic centred.
Paper £4.50
Mounted CRV £25.00

NIEUWE WERELDKAART
1:22,500,000
Groningen : Wolters-Noordhoff
234 x 160
Pacific centred map, showing direction of ocean currents. Insets of voyages of discovery, Polar regions, population.
Fl. 247.50

MAPA POLITYCZNA SWIATA
1:22,000,000
Warszawa : PPWK, 1972
180 x 120
Political school wall map, showing boundaries, political colouring.
Zl 130

SVETA
1:20,000,000
In 4 sheets
Beograd : Geokarta 1973
School wall map of the World with Cyrillic and Latin lettering.

WANDKARTE WELT
1:20,000,000
No 33
Munchen : JRO
94 x 114
Political col. wall map, Mercator's proj, communications.
DM 50
Mounted CR DM 134

MAGNA-GRAPHIC MAP OF THE WORLD-POLITICAL WITH GRID
1:19,000,000
Ed E Putnam Parker
Chicago : Weber Costello
167 x 129
Political colouring with lines of lat. and long. Pacific and Atlantic oceans condensed. Insets, Available mounted in various styles.

DIE STAATEN DER ERDE
1:18,000,000
Braunschweig : Westermann
202 x 130
Political col. wall map showing 1965 boundaries, principal air and sea routes. Pop. areas indicated.

POLAR WELTKARTE
1:18,000,000
In 2 sheets
No 34
Munchen : JRO
177 x 123
Col. political map, North Pole centred. Azimuthal Proj. Antarctic regions inset.
Flat DM 48.00
CR DM 131.00

MAPAMUNDI POLITICO
Madrid : Aguilar
130 x 200
Politically coloured school wall map.
Paper S.Ptas 250
Cloth S.Ptas 550

DIE STAATEN DER ERDE
1:16,000,000
No 301
Ed Haack and Painke
Darmstadt : Perthes
310 x 133
Countries in colour. German text. Atlantic centred. Shipping routes and distances. DM 128.00

MAAILMA
1:15,000,000
Helsinki : Wsoy
246 x 160
School wall map of the World in Finnish
FMK 100

POLITICHESKAYA KARTA MIRA
1:15,000,000
In 4 sheets
Moskva : GUGK
Political world wall map in Russian.

DIE ERDE, POLITISCHE ÜBERSICHT
1:15,000,000
Gotha : Haack, 1968
244 x 142
Political col. wall map for schools with rivers, railways, major cities.

DIE STAATEN DER ERDE
1:15,000,000
H238
Munchen : List
250 x 150
Harms political col. wall map for schools.
DM 164

LUINGE WERELDKAART
1:13,500,000
7th edition
Groningen : Wolters-Noordhof
220 x 140
Political col. wall map. Atlantic in centre. Simplified information, main railways, shipping routes and principal towns. Also ocean currents and poles inset. Legend in Dutch.
Fl. 158.00

Outline

CROWN QUARTO OUTLINE MAP OF THE WORLD
London : Philip
20 x 14
Black and white.

IMPERIAL QUARTO OUTLINE MAP OF THE WORLD
London : Philip
29 x 20
Black and white

MAPPAMONDO
Novara : Ag
Small outline map of the world.
L 40

UMRISSKARTE DER WELT
1:150,000,000
No 0833
Bern K & F
30 x 23
Outline map of the continents with boundaries

UMRISSKARTE DER WELT
1:120,000,000
No 0842
Bern : K & F
Outline map on Briesemeister proj without boundaries.

THE WORLD – OUTLINE
1:70,000,000
DOS 951
Edition 20
Tolworth : DOS : 1975
59 x 27
Interrupted Sinusoidal Proj, black outline, international boundaries, main towns, Commonwealth member countries etc. in red.
15p

LARGE OUTLINE MAP OF THE WORLD
1:40 000 000
London : Philip
101 x 74
In black and white showing boundaries and position of major towns No names. Gall's projection.
£1.25

WORLD MAP – OUTLINE
1:40,000,000
Washington : Defense Mapping Agency
101 x 61
Mercator's Proj. With or without blue water tint US $0.40
Also at :
1:60,000,000 76 x 53 US $0.25
1:135,000,000 35 x 26 US $0.15

PHILIP'S MAP BUILDING (BLACKBOARD) MAP OF THE WORLD
1:40,000,000
London : Philip
101 x 78
Coastline, inter-state boundaries printed in yellow on blackboard paper. Gall's Proj.
On cloth with rollers £4.00

GEOGRAPHIA PLANNING AND RECORD MAP OF THE WORLD
1:50,000,000
London : Gia
109 x 59
Outline map showing international boundaries and cities. 30p
Also available in reduced size edition
39 x 30, folded.
Set of 10 75p

OUTLINE WORLD MAPS
Various scales
Indianapolis : Cram
Outline maps for various purposes and levels.
Maps available :
Armadillo Political Outline Map
1:16,250,000 163 x 132 US $27.50
Political Outline (Mercator)
1:32 500,000 129 x 129 US $23.00
Desk Outline Map 43 x 30 US $0.60
Armadillo Desk Outline Map
43 x 30 US $0.60
Slated Outline (Blackboard) US $16.00

UMRISSKARTE DER WELT
1:32,000,000
No 0830
Bern : K & F
130 x 95
Outline map with rivers and boundaries.

WORLD OUTLINE SLATED
1:25,000,000
No 165091
Chicago : Denoyer-Geppert
152 x 129
Blackboard school map, yellow and blue on black. Also available Americas centred 165791
US $28.50

VITO-GRAPHIC CHALKBOARD MAP OF THE WORLD
1:21,000,000
Ref : VS 1
Chicago : Weber Costello Co
163 x 102
Land areas in green, meridians, parallels and outlines in yellow, water areas in blue.
On cloth – various mounted styles.
Also available with US VS1-2 or Canada VS1-9 on reverse side.

WORLD – OUTLINE SERIES
1:5,000,000
DMS Series 1105
In 28 sheets, see index 100/10
Tolworth : DMS
Various sizes
Black and white outline map showing national boundaries, principal towns and rivers. Millers Cylindrical Projection.
Each 20p

E1 PHYSICAL: RELIEF

PLANISFERIO FISICO
Barcelona : Editorial Teide
33 x 25
Physical world hand map for schools, without boundaries, in Spanish.
Ptas 1

PLANISFERO
Novara : Ag
33 x 26
Physical map with political map and economic details on reverse. In Italian.
L 450

SWIAT
1:80,000,000
Warszawa : PPWK, 1972
61 x 32
Physical hand map, Mercator's Proj. in Polish.
Zl 1

MAPA FIZYCZNA ŚWIATA
1:66,000,000
Warszawa : PPWK, 1972
61 x 43
Physical hand map, showing relief details. Political map on reverse.
Zl 5

MAPA FIZYCZNA ŚWIATA
1:66,000,000
Warszawa : PPWK, 1972
60 x 41
Physical hand map. Mollweide projection.
Zl 1

PLANIGLOBY : MAPA FIZYCZNA I POLITYCZNA
1:60,000,000
Warszawa : PPWK, 1972
69 x 42
Double-sided world map, physical and political school hand map.
Zl 5

TRI-GRAPHIC MAP OF THE WORLD
1:41,250,000
Ref TRI-1
Chicago : Weber Costello
137 x 101
Physical layer colouring with graphic relief shading and political boundaries. Mercator projection. Available mounted in various styles.

PHYSICAL MAP OF THE WORLD
1:40,600,000
Washington : AGS, 1968
106 x 66
Contoured, layer col, communications, boundaries, towns. Miller Cylindrical proj. Atlantic centred.

PHILIP'S PHYSICAL SMALLER WALL MAP OF THE WORLD
1:40,000,000
London : Philip
101 x 77
Layer col, communications and boundaries. Gall's proj.
Paper flat £1.50
Mounted CR £5.50
Mounted on cloth dissected to fold £7.00

PHILIP'S GRAPHIC RELIEF MAP OF THE WORLD
1:40,000,000
London : Philip
101 x 74
Col. to show forests, meadowlands, deserts, semi-deserts, hill shading. No town names.
Paper flat £1.50
Mounted CR £5.50
Mounted on cloth dissected to fold £7.00

PHILIP'S CLEAR PHYSICAL MAP OF THE WORLD
1:40,000,000
London : Philip, 1973
101 x 78
Bold layer colouring for land and sea. International boundaries, continents, islands, seas and physical features named. Insets of Polar regions.
£1.50

WORLD RELATIONS
1:40.000.000
London : Philip
101 x 77
Series of 8 maps on Gall's Projection, with polar regions inset. Showing :
Relief of Land
Political
Summer Climate
Winter Climate
Temperature
Rainfall
Natural Vegetation
Density of Population
Mounted CR £5.50
Mounted on cloth dissected £7.00
Set of 8 maps mounted on roller £30.00

PHYSICAL MAP OF THE WORLD
1:38,750,000
Washington : NGS
108 x 70
Physical col. wall map.
Paper US $2.00
Plastic US $3.00

MAPPAMONDO FISICO
1:30,000,000
Novara : Ag
140 x 100
School wall map showing land and sea relief, political boundaries. L 2,200
Mounted L 5,000

PHYSICAL WORLD MAPS
Various scales
Chicago : Denoyer-Geppert
School wall maps available at different levels and depths :

102191-14 Simplified
1:31,250,000 162 x 111 US $24.00
120091-14 Visual Relief
1:35,000,000 162 x 111 US $27.50
120791-14 Visual Relief (Americas centred)
1:35,000,000 162 x 111 US $27.50
110091 Visual Relief
1:37,500,000 147 x 111 US $18.75
135091-14 Large Physical-Political
1:25,000,000 162 x 111 US $27.00
135791-14 Large Physical-Political (Americas centred)
1:25,000,000 162 x 111 US $27.00
130091-10 Classroom Physical-Political
1:37,500,000 147 x 111 US $15.50
130071-10 Classroom Physical Political–E Hemisphere
1:18,750,000 147 x 111 US $15.50
130081-14 Classroom Physical Political–W Hemisphere
1:18,750,000 147 x 111 US $15.50
103531 Relief of Land
1:39,062,500 111 x 91 US $10.00

LÄNDERKARTE WELT, PHYSISCH
1:30,000,000
No 1
Munchen : JRO
123 x 64
Col. physical map with relief contours, ocean depths, no international boundaries.
DM 9.80
Mounted CR DM 40.00

VÄRLDEN
1:30,000,000
Stockholm : GLA 1973
136 x 86
Mercator's Proj. Land areas green, relief shading, in Swedish.
Flat S.Kr 12.50
Rollers S.Kr 67.00
Boards S.Kr 69.50

THE WORLD
1:30,000,000
London : Collins - Longman, 1973
134 x 71
Coloured physical wall map for schools, with political detail.
40p

PLANISFERIO FISICO - POLITICO MAPA MURAL
1:28,900,000
Barcelona : Ed. Vicens Vives, 1976
126 x 88
Physical - political map in Spanish on plasticised paper.
S.Ptas 500

PLANISPHÈRE NO 1
St Germain-en-Laye : Éditions MDI
126 x 92
Physical wall map for schools, plastic finish. Map "Faune et Végétation" on reverse. Also in English ed.

WORLD PORTRAIT MAP
Chicago : Rand McNally
132 x 86
Physically col. Inc. principal cities, geog. boundaries.
Folded US $1.00

POLAR AIR AGE WORLD
1:25,000,000
No 107571-00
Chicago : Denoyer-Geppert
147 x 111
Classroom physical-political map showing communications and boundaries.
Rollers US $15.50

DIE ERDE
1:24,000,000
Darmstadt : Perthes
146 x 90
Physical wall map for schools in the series "Kleiner Geographischer Wandatlas".
Available in 6 lang. editions.

PHILIP'S PHYSICAL LARGE WALL MAP OF THE WORLD
1:24,000,000
London : Philip 1975
173 x 95
Orographical col; hill shading, political boundaries, railways, ocean routes.
Winkel's Proj. A.
Atlantic centred. Arctic regions inset.
Mounted CR £15.00
Mounted on cloth dissected to fold £17.00

PLANISPHÈRE
1:23,000,000
Bruxelles : Mantnieks
180 x 125
Physical wall map of the world for schools. Shows relief of land and sea, direction of ocean currents, political boundaries in red. Also available in English, French, Dutch and Spanish.

CARTE DU MONDE
1:23,000,000
No 4013
In 2 sheets
Bern : K & F, 1966
178 x 104
Physical, layer col, relief shading, roads, railways. Van der Grinten's proj. Atlantic centred.

A FÖLD FELSZÍNE
1:22,500 000
2nd rev. ed. in 4 sheets
Budapest : Cart
Physical map in Hungarian.

MAPA FIZYCZNA ŚWIATA
1:22,000,000
In 2 sheets
Warszawa : PPWK, 1971
184 x 110
Physical school wall map, col, with contours, Mollweide's proj.

VÄRLDEN
1:20,000,000
Stockholm : GLA, 1971
195 x 140
Physical map, col. by land types.
Rollers S.Kr 185.00
Board S.Kr 275.00

SVETA - FIZIČKA
1:20,000,000
In 4 sheets
Beograd : Geokarta
Physical wall map with lettering in cyrillic and latin.
Cloth mounted Dn 150

WORLD MAP
1:20,000,000
AMS Series 1125
In 3 sheets
Washington : Defense Mapping Agency
76 x 147 each
Contoured, layer colouring with boundaries and principal towns.
Polar Regions inset.

WELTKARTE
No 484
Hamburg : Falk
168 x 75
Political world wall map, physical map on reverse.
DM 21.50

PHYSICAL WORLD MAPS
Various scales
Indianapolis : Cram
Col. school wall maps available at different levels and depths.
Armadillo Simplified Physical-Political
1:20,562,500 129 x 127 US $23.00
1:16,250,000 162 x 132 US $27.25
Level B Simplified Physical-Political Homolosine Proj.
1:32,500,000 129 x 129 US $23.00
Level C Armadillo Physical-Political
1:20,562,500 129 x 127 US $23.00
1:16,250,000 162 x 132 US $27.25
Level D Astro-vue
1:16,250,000 162 x 132 US $25.50
Physical Outline Map (Homolosine)
1:31,250,000 129 x 129 US $27.50
Excello Physical Wall Map
1:41,250,000 111 x 137 US $12.50

MAGNA-GRAPHIC MAP OF THE WORLD - CONTOUR - RELIEF WITH GRID MAP
1:19,000,000
Ed E Putnam Parker
Chicago : Weber Costello
167 x 129
Physical colouring with political boundaries and lines of lat. and long. Available mounted in various styles.

MAGNA-GRAPHIC MAP OF THE WORLD - BEGINNER'S MAP
1:19,000,000
Ed E Putnam Parker
Chicago : Weber Costello
167 x 129
Essential information emphasised, relief and political boundaries shown. Insets include geographic terms. Available mounted in various styles.

MAPAMUNDI FISICO
Madrid : Aguilar
200 x 130
Physical wall map for schools, in Spanish.
Paper Ptas 100
Cloth Ptas 550

VÄRLDEN
1:17,500,000
In 3 sheets
Stockholm : GLA, 1971
240 x 130
Physical map, Mercator's proj. in Swedish.
Flat S.Kr 140.00
Rollers S.Kr 195.00
Board S.Kr 240.00

DIE ERDE
1:16,000,000
No 190
Ed Haack and Painke
Darmstadt : Perthes
220 x 135
Physically col. wall map, boundaries, towns, ocean currents and depths. Eds. also in Eng, Fr. Dut. Dan, SW, Nor. Fin.
DM 128.00

PHYSICAL MAP OF THE WORLD
1:16,000,000
No 4043
In 4 sheets
Bern : K & F
252 x 152 complete
Shows relief by layer colouring and shading; boundaries, major roads and railways, towns, graded by pop, ocean depths.

DIE ERDE, PHYSISCH
1:15,000,000
Gotha : Haack, 1970
240 x 138
Physical wall map, hill shading, ocean depths, land elevations.

DIE ERDE
1:15,000,000
H212
Munchen : List
245 x 150
Harms physical wall map for schools. Shows relief of land and oceans, main cities and railways.
DM 164.00

PHYSISCHE ERDKARTE MIT MEERSBODENRELIEF
1:15,000,000
W701
München : List
250 x 160
Wenschow physical wall map for schools with relief of land and sea, by layer cols. and land relief shading.
DM 164.00

THE WORLD
1:15,000,000
Tehran : Sahab
245 x 260
Physical wall map with political divisions. In Persian. Printed in co-operation with Westermann.

PHYSISCHE WELTKARTE
1:12,000,000
No 101
Ed Haack and Painke
Darmstadt : Perthes
280 x 174
Atlantic centred, physical wall map, layer cols, communications, boundaries.
DM 150.00

PHYSICAL MAP OF THE WORLD
1:11,000,000
AMS Series 1101
In 9 sheets, see index 100/11
Washington : AMS, 1971
363 x 255 complete
Contours, layer col, relief shading, principal communications, boundaries and major towns. Mercator's proj. Available as a set which can be joined as wall map or in separate sheets.

CARTE GÉNÉRALE DU MONDE
1:10,000,000
In 12 sheets, see index 100/4
Paris : IGN
400 x 95 complete - 100 x 59/77 each
Contoured, layer tinted and relief shaded, with roads, railways and rivers, boundaries, towns, villages and geographical features. Available as a set which can be joined as one or in separate sheets.

THE WORLD
1:5,000,000
In 18 sheets, see index 100/3
New York : AGS
Various sizes
A physical and political map of the continental areas of the World, showing political and major administrative boundaries, roads tracks, railways and airports, towns graded by population, water features, ice caps, swamps and deserts, coral reefs, land and sea contours in metres and layer colouring on land.
Three projections are used; a special Miller Oblated Stereographic for Europe, Africa, Asia and Australia, Bipolar Oblique Conical Conformal for the Americas and Polar Stereographic for Antarctica. Each of the groups may be joined as a unit. Outline edition available.
Also published by AMS and DMS with different numbering system. Series 1106.

CARTE GÉNÉRALE DES CONTINENTS
1:5,000,000
In 5 parts, 35 sheets, see index 100/5
Paris : IGN
Various sizes
Physical map series covering continental land areas. Contoured, layer col, railways and roads, water features, internal admin. boundaries, towns classified by admin. status.
Each F.Fr 20.83

DEUTSCHE WELTKARTE (DWK)
1:5,000,000
In 32 sheets, see index 100/9
Mannheim : Biblio. Inst, Mayer Verlag
50 x 94
Topographical series in progress. Contoured, layer coloured and relief shaded with sea depths shown by bathymetric tints. Communications, boundaries, towns and villages. With each sheet is an overlay map showing rivers, national and provincial boundaries and major towns which are indexed alphabetically.
1 Europa - Nord
2 Europa - Sud
4 Südwestasien
26 Mittelamerika
Each DM 9.90

Moulded Relief Maps

RAISED RELIEF MAP OF THE WORLD
New York : Hagstrom
68 x 50
Moulded plastic raised relief map, physical col.
US $2.95

GEO-PHYSICAL WORLD
1:50,000,000
Chicago : Rand McNally
86 x 56
3-D moulded plastic relief map; vegetation col; political divs; ocean floor in shaded relief.
US $9.95

RELIEF MAP OF THE WORLD
1:50,000,000
No 198492
Chicago : Denoyer-Geppert
86 x 55
Moulded vinyl relief map, physical col.
US $7.95

TACTUAL RAISED RELIEF MAP OF THE WORLD
No 198091
Chicago : Denoyer-Geppert
129 x 94
Moulded plastic relief map, physical col. in steel frame.
US $49.50

VÄRLDEN : PLASTRELIEF
1:34,000,000
Stockholm : GLA
130 x 95
Plastic relief map, physical col. In Swedish.
S.Kr 215.00

PHILIP'S PLASTIC RELIEF MODEL MAP OF THE WORLD
1:34,000,000
London : Philip, 1969
130 x 94
Moulded relief map, contours, layer col, political boundaries, place names, principal communications.
Mercator's proj. Atlantic centred.
Self framed £20.00

RAISED RELIEF MAP OF THE WORLD
1:27,498,240
NR98
Chicago : Nystrom, 1975
144 x 97
Plastic moulded map, physical layer colouring, principal communications and boundaries.
Unframed US $46.00
Framed US $74.00

WORLD PLASTIC RELIEF MAP
1:1,000,000
AMS Series 1301P, see index 100/1 B
Washington : Defense Mapping Agency
81 x 94 each
Moulded plastic relief map series following sheet lines of standard 1:1M series. Maps contoured with road and rail communications and settlement, vertical exaggeration 4:1. Series in progress, certain sheets not scheduled for publication due to lack of relief.

Eastern Hemisphere

POŁKULA ZACHODNIA, MAPA FIZYCZNA
1:40,000,000
Warszawa : PPWK, 1972
52 x 49
Physical map of the Eastern Hemisphere.
Zl 1

VYCHODNÍ POLOKOULE
1:25,000,000
Praha : Kart, 1970
Relief map of the Eastern Hemisphere.
Kcs 280

ISTOČNA POLULOPTA
1:25,000,000
In 2 sheets
Beograd : Geokarta
127 x 93
Eastern hemisphere, with latin and cyrillic lettering.
Cloth mounted Dn 100

KARTA POLUSHARIE - VOSTOK
1:22,000,000
Moskva : GUGK
Physical map of Eastern Hemisphere in Russian.

MAP OF THE EASTERN HEMISPHERE
1:17,200,000
Michigan : Hearne Bros.
167 x 122
Col. school wall map, political boundaries, relief shading, mechanical index. Azimuthal proj, covering Europe, Asia, Africa, Australasia.Mounted on spring roller.
US $152.50

WORLD TRAVEL MAP - EURASIA
1:15,000,000
Edinburgh : Bart, 1970
90 x 69
Physical map with contours and layer col, towns and principal communications.
75p

ÖSTLICHE HALBKUGEL
1:12,000,000
Braunschweig : Westermann
163 x 176
School physical wall map of the Eastern Hemisphere. Layer col, hill shading, cities graded by pop, spot heights, international boundaries.

DIE ÖSTLICHE ERDHÄLFTE
1:10,000,000
H223
München : List
205 x 170
Harms physical wall map of the Eastern Hemisphere; cities graded by pop, relief of land and sea, boundaries, main communications.
DM 164.00

ITÄINEN PALLONPUOLI
1:10,000,000
Helsinki : Wsoy
205 x 170
School wall map of the Eastern Hemisphere, in Finnish.
FMK 100

Western Hemisphere

POLKULA ZACHODNIA
1:40,000,000
Warszawa : PPWK 1972
52 x 49
Physical hand map of the Western Hemisphere.
Zl 1

ZAPADNI POLOKOULE
1:25,000,000
Praha : Kart, 1970
Relief map of the Western Hemisphere.
Kcs 255

ZAPADNI POLULOPTA
1:25,000,000
In 2 sheets
Beograd : Geokarta
127 x 93
2 sheet wall map of the Western Hemisphere with lettering in cyrillic and latin.
Cloth mounted DN 100

KARTA POLUSHARIE - ZAPAD
1:22,000,000
Moskva : GUGK
Physical map of Western Hemisphere, in Russian.

MAP OF THE WESTERN HEMISPHERE
1:17,208,000
Michigan : Hearne Bros.
167 x 122
Col. school wall map, political boundaries, relief shading, mechanical index. Azimuthal proj, covering Americas, New Zealand, Greenland, Pacific Islands.
US $152.50

THE AMERICAS
1:12,500,000
New York : AGS, 1953
90 x 135
Physical map with thematic insets.

WESTLICHE HALBKUGEL
1:12,000,000
Braunschweig : Westermann
163 x 176
Physical school wall map showing land relief, international boundaries, cities graded by pop.

DIE WESTLICHEN ERDTEILE
1:10,000,000
No 103
Haack and Painke
Darmstadt : Perthes
172 x 218
Wall map of United States, part of Greenland, Pacific Ocean areas.
Van der Grintens Projection. Also in Eng, Dut, Nor, Fin.

LÄNTINEN PALLONPUOLI
1:10,000,000
Helsinki : Wsoy
210 x 170
School wall map of the Western Hemisphere in Finnish.
FMK 100

E2 PHYSICAL : LAND FEATURES

LANDFORMS OF THE WORLD
Richard E Murphy
1:50,000,000
Florida : AAG, 1968
86 x 70
Col. map showing morphology of the earth, with landforms classified, insets etc.
US $3.00

WORLD SEISMICITY 1961-1969
1:35,000,000
Ref NEIC - 3005
Washington : US Dept. of Commerce, 1970
116 x 74
World outline map, Miller's Modified Mercator proj. Sea in light blue, land areas beige, epicentres in colour by depth. Americas centred.

CARTE GÉNÉRALE BATHYMÉTRIQUE DES OCÉANS
1:10,000,000
Prepared : Int. Hydrographic Bureau, Monaco.
In 24 sheets, see index 26/1
Paris : IGN
100 x 59
Bathymetric contours, and layer cols, with depth soundings in metres. New 5th edition sheets in preparation.
The first sheet 5.05 N.Africa and Middle East has been published.

F GEOLOGY

DIE BAUELEMENTE DER ERDE
1:18,000,000
Braunschweig : Westermann
202 x 132
Col. wall map showing structural elements of the earth - foldings, volcanic structures, sedimentary rocks etc.

GEOLOGY OF THE EARTH
1:16,000,000
No 800 in 2 sheets
Ed Dr Klaus Fahlbusch
Darmstadt : Perthes, 1969
201 x 140
Col. showing Continental shelf areas, layered bathymetry. Inset - Paleographic map of the Jurassic (European) region.
Legend and title in Ger, Emg, Sp.

ERDE, GEOLOGIE
1:15,000,000
Braunschweig : Westermann
240 x 140
Geological school wall maps. With text.

ERDE, GEOLOGIE
1:15,000,000
Gotha : Haack, 1969
240 x 138
Col. geol. wall map, showing principal rocks and their locations, deposits etc.

ERDE, TEKTONIK
1:15,000,000
Gotha : Haack, 1969
240 x 168
Col. tectonic wall map, Polar regions inset.

ERDE TEKTONIK
1:15,000,000
Braunschweig : Westermann
240 x 140
Col. tectonic wall map col. by structural types with text.

G EARTH RESOURCES

CARTE DES PRINCIPAUX GITES MONDIAUX DE PIERRES PRÉCIEUSES ET AUTRES GEMMES
1:40,000.000
by H J Schubnel
Orleans : BRGM, 1969
Map showing world distribution of precious stones and minerals on geotechnic base. In Fr, Eng, or Ger.
F.Fr 30.00

CARTE MINIÈRE DU GLOBE
1:20,000,000
By P Laffite and P Rouveyrol
In 2 parts
Orleans : BRGM
180 x 108 complete size
2 world maps showing distribution of minerals on a tectonic base map. 1-12 col. sheets showing Au, Ba, Co, Cr, Cu, diamond, F, Hg, Mo, Ni, Pb and Zn and Ag. Pt, St, Sn, U, W deposits.
With text, the set F.Fr 50.00
II- 2 sheets showing Al, asbestos, B2, O_3, BeO, Fl, K_2O, Li_2, O, magnesite, Mn (NG, $Ta)_2$, O_5, S, talc, Ti O_2 V, Zr.
With text F.Fr 50.00

WORLD MINING COPPER MAP
2nd edition
Ed. R J M Wyllie
San Francisco : Miller Freeman Pubn's, 1976
124 x 86
Showing locations of every known important porphyry copper and molybdenum mining operation throughout the world. With insets of the important producing areas of S.W. and N.W. North America, Andes, Pacific Fire Belt and Copperbelt. Geochronology diagram, tables of copper production, copper smelters named and located.
Folded US $9.50
Rolled US $10.50

WORLD COAL MAP
1st edition
San Francisco : Miller Freeman Pubn's, 1975
127 x 89
4 colour map showing the coal resources of the world in more than 65 countries. Coals are classified with estimated resources, major trade routes, and resources, production and trade statistics.
Folded US $16.50
Rolled US $18.00

SOIL MAP OF THE WORLD
1:5,000,000
In 19 sheets, see index 100/6
Paris : UNESCO/Rome : FAO, 1971+
115 x 82 each
Coloured series in progress, legend Eng, Fr, Sp, Rus. Shows dominant soil groups with boundaries, texture, dominant landscape slope.
Each F.Fr 50.00

CARTA MAGNETICA DEL BACINO DEL MEDITERRANEO
1:6,000,000
Firenze : IGM
Shows lines of equal magnetic declination as at January 1950.

H BIOGEOGRAPHY

WORLD RELATIONS NATURAL VEGETATION
1:40,000,000
Philip
see WORLD 100 E1.

KLIMA- OG PLANTEBAELTER
1:25,000,000
GI
see WORLD 100 J.

ZOOGEOGRAFICHESKAYA KARTA MIRA
1:20,000,000
In 4 sheets
Moskva : GUGK, 1972
180 x 130
School wall map of zoogeographic regions, showing animal world etc. In Russian.

PRIRODNIE ZONY MIRA
1:20,000,000
In 2 sheets
Moskva : GUGK, 1973
180 x 120
School wall map showing natural regions.
34 kop

KARTA RASTITEL'NOSTI MIRA
1:20,000,000
In 4 sheets
Moskva : GUGK, 1968
180 x 130 complete
Col. vegetation map in Rus.

DIE LANDSCHAFTSGÜRTEL DER ERDE
1:20,000,000
Gotha : Haack, 1968
211 x 125
Col. school wall map, showing land-use and agricultural areas, vegetation etc.

VEGETATIONSGEBIETE DER ERDE
1:18,000,000
Braunschweig : Westermann, 1967
205 x 130
Col. vegetation wall map for schools, showing cultivated, irrigated areas, permafrost areas, agricultural products etc.

ERDE, VEGETATION
1:15,000,000
Gotha : Haack, 1966
240 x 140
Col. wall map showing major vegetation types by col. and symbols.
DM 142.00

DIE LANDSCHAFTSGÜRTEL DER ERDE
1:12,000,000
Darmstadt : Perthes
280 x 170
School wall map showing world land classification and utilisation.
DM 150.00

PLANISPHÈRE NO 1
Éditions MDI
'Faune et Végétation' on reverse.
see WORLD 100 E1.

WORLD MAP OF FISHERIES
København : Scandinavian Fishing YB, 1971
97 x 60
Illustrated col. land and sea map showing location of fish and crustaceans by numbers with ref. to the key book, supplied with the map.
D.Kr 75.00

VEGETATION MAP OF THE MEDITERRANEAN REGION
1:5,000,000
Paris : UNESCO/Rome : FAO, 1970
100 x 75 each
2 sheet map covering temperate regions of Europe and Central Asia, tropical Africa; shows 105 main vegetation types, with geog. names where useful. With brochure.
Each sheet with text £4.50

J CLIMATE

WORLD RELATIONS - CLIMATE
1:40,000,000
Philip
see WORLD 100 E1.

KLIMA DER ERDE
1:30,000,000
W723
München : List
245 x 160
Wenschow col. climatic wall map for schools; 4 maps showing mean January and July temperatures, mean annual precipitation climatic types.
DM 164.00

DIE ATMOSPHARE DER ERDE
1:30,000,000
In 12 sheets
Darmstadt : Perthes
130 x 90
School wall map showing air pressure, cloud and wind during January and July periods. In Ger and Eng.
Each DM 39.00

NEDBØRSFORHOLD OG HAVSTRØMME
1:25,000,000
In 2 sheets
København : GI
155 x 123
Col. wall map showing rainfall and ocean currents. Text in Dan, Eng.

KLIMA- OG PLANTEBAELTER
1:25,000,000
In 2 sheets
Kobenhavn : GI
155 x 122
Showing climatic zones and vegetation belts: tropical, subtropical, temperature and polar zones. Legend in Dan. and Eng.

CLIMATES OF THE EARTH
1:22,800,000
by G T Trewartha
Chicago : Rand McNally
145 x 81
Col. wall map showing climatic zones based on Koppen's classification.

STREFY KLIMATYCZNE Z ŚWIATA
1:22,000,000
Ed V Okolowicz
Warszawa : PPWK, 1971
Map of world climatic zones.

ERDE, TEMPERATUREN
1:20,000,000
Gotha : Haack, 1965
184 x 220
2 maps on 1 sheet showing average January and July temperatures; isotherms, ocean surface temperature, currents, floating ice.

KLIMATICHESKAYA KARTA MIRA
1:20,000,000
In 4 sheets
Moskva : GUGK, 1969
180 x 120 complete
Col. wall map showing yearly rainfall, isotherms for January and July, wind etc.

ERDE, LUFTDRUCK UND WINDE
1:20,000,000
Gotha : Haack, 1967
184 x 220
Col. wall map, 2 maps showing January and July pressure and winds, intensity of major systems, isobars.

KARTA KLIMATICHESKIKH POYASOV I OBLASTEI
1:20,000,000
In 2 sheets
Moskva : GUGK, 1973
School map of climatic zones and districts.

DIE KLIMATE DER ERDE
1:18,000,000
Braunschweig : Westermann
202 x 130
Climatic wall map showing 11 climatic types.
DM 128.00

KLIMA DER ERDE
1:16,000,000
Darmstadt : Perthes
220 x 148
Climatic wall map for schools, Winkels projection. Legend in Eng. and Ger.
DM 128.00

JAHRESZEITENKLIMATE DER ERDE
1:16,000,000
Ed Prof Drs Troll and Pffaffen
Hamburg : Schroedel, 1969
232 x 156
Col. school wall map showing how climatic factors affect the plant world.
DM 128.00

DIE ERDE, KLIMAZONEN
1:15,000,000
Gotha : Haack, 1966
240 x 140
Col. wall map showing climatic zones according to Koeppen-Geiger classification. Precipitation and temperature data.

ERDE, NIEDERSCHLAGE
1:15,000,000
Gotha : Haack, 1965
240 x 180
Map of mean annual rainfall; isohyets, climatographs on map, snowfall etc.

BIOCLIMATIC MAP OF THE MEDITERRANEAN REGION
1:5,000,000
In 2 sheets
Paris : UNESCO-FAO, 1963
75 x 100
In 17 cols, 4 maps of homologous regions (1:10,000,000). Leg. Eng and Fr, also explanatory notes. Synthesises climate features (especially warmth and water) in relation to living creatures.
£2.50

K HUMAN GEOGRAPHY

MONDMAPO
1:42,000,000
Beograd : Geokarta, 1968
Reproduced for the Internacia Instituto por Oficialigo de Esperanto. Physical map, showing major topog. features. Standardised Esperanto spellings for 850 important geog. names.

WORLD RELATIONS – DENSITY OF POPULATION
1:40,000,000
Philip
see WORLD 100 E1.

PANORAMA OF WORLD LITERATURE
No 161091-14
Chicago : Denoyer-Geppert
162 x 111
Pictorial wall map for schools.
Spring rollers US $24.00

DIE ERDE : LEBENSRAUM DES MENSCHEN
No scale
Braunschweig : Westermann
190 x 139
Pictorial wall map showing pop. types, agriculture and economy, famous buildings, etc.

BEVOLKERUNG DER ERDE
1:30,000,000
W726
München : List
245 x 160
Wenschow wall map; 4 maps showing pop. density, languages, religions, cultural regions and migrations.
DM 164.00

CARTE DU MONDE MUSULMAN
1:28,000,000
Rabat: Dir. de la Cons. Foncière et des Travaux Topog.
90 x 60
Map of the Muslim world - in preparation.

BEFOLKNINGSFORDELING
1:25,000,000
In 2 sheets
København : GI
162 x 124
Wall map in Dan. and Eng. showing pop. distribution by col. and town stamps.

KARTE DER RELIGIONEN UND MISSIONEN DER ERDE
1:23,000,000
Ed Prof. D M Schlunk and Dr H Quiring
No 4053
Bern : K+F
135 x 78
Distribution of world religions and missions shown by symbols.
Paper folded.

KARTA NARODOV MIRA
1:20,000,000
In 4 sheets
Moskva : GUGK, 1968
180 x 130 complete
Col. wall map, illus. world races and pop.

DIE BEVÖLKERUNG DER ERDE, VERTEILUNG UND WACHSTUM
1:15,000,000
Munchen : List
Harms wall map, showing world pop. distribution, with graphs to indicate rate of growth.
DM 115.00

BEVOLKERUNGSDICHTE DER ERDE
1:15,000,000
Braunschweig : Westermann
236 x 142
Pop. wall map, with graph of world pop. growth, 1600–2000 AD.

PICTORIAL MAP OF MEDITERRANEAN MYTHOLOGY AND CLASSICAL LITERATURE
No 161361-14
Chicago : Denoyer-Geppert
162 x 111
Pictorial wall map for schools.
Spring rollers US $24.00

L ECONOMIC

GREAT CIRCLE DISTANCES AND AZIMUTHS FROM WELLINGTON TO ALL PARTS OF THE WORLD
1:90,000,000
2nd edition
NZMS 47
Wellington : NZMS, 1953
63 x 54
Land areas named. Graticules at 10° intervals, equidistant azimuthal proj.
NZ $0.30

STANDARD TIME ZONES
1:39,000,000
Washington : Govt. Printing Office, 1970
89 x 137
Col chart
US $1.00

POLAR AIR AGE WORLD
1:25,000,000
No 107571
Chicago : Denoyer-Geppert
111 x 147
Shows main air routes, land use, south Polar area inset at same scale. Table of distances.
Mounted CR US $15.50

WORLD MAP OF THE SUGAR INDUSTRY
1:22,000,000
In 3 sheets
Ratzeburg : Licht, 1971
202 x 122
Col. map showing location of beet and cane factories. In Eng.
DM 110.00

WIRTSCHAFTS- UND LANDSCHAFTSGÜRTEL DER ERDE
1:18,000,000
München : List
200 x 135
Harms economic wall map showing industrial and agricultural regions of the world.
DM 135.00

WIRTSCHAFT DER ERDE
1:15,000,000
München : List
250 x 160
Wenschow school wall map showing economic links; statistical info.
DM 142.00

BERGBAU- UND INDUSTRIE-GEBIETE DER ERDE
1:15,000,000
Gotha : Haack, 1967
241 x 145
Col. wall map showing mining and industrial areas of the world by symbols.

LANDWIRTSCHAFTSGEBIETE DER ERDE
1:15,000,000
Gotha : Haack, 1957
240 x 140
Col. wall map showing major agricultural areas of the world and their products : cotton, coffee, crops etc.

DIE ERDE : WIRTSCHAFT
1:14,375,000
Hamburg : Flemming
228 x 165
Col. wall map showing location of principal minerals, agricultural raw materials, industrial and cultivated areas.

PLANISPHÈRE NO 2 (POLITIQUE)
Editions MDI
Economic map on reverse.
see WORLD 100 D.

PLANISPHÈRE NO 3 (POPULATION)
Editions MDI
'Voies de communication' on reverse.
see WORLD 100 K.

M HISTORICAL

GESCHIEDKUNDIGE WANDKARTEN
Maes en van den Broeck Namur : Ad Wesmael Charlier
Historical wall maps in Flemish mounted on linen with wooden rods.
Maps available :
I De Griekse Wereld
135 x 185, in 3 cols. B.Fr 660
II De Franse Revolutie
135 x 185, in 4 cols. B.Fr 849
III De Wereld omstreeks 500 voor Christus
135 x 185, in 4 cols. B.Fr 925
IV De Wereld in de Iste eeuw
135 x 185, in 4 cols. B.Fr 925
V De Wereld omstreeks 500
135 x 185, in 4 cols. B.Fr 925
VI De Wereld omstreeks 800
135 x 185, in 4 cols. B.Fr 925
VII De Knelpunten sedert 1945
135 x 185, in 4 cols. B.Fr 925

CARTES MURALES HISTORIQUES
Louis André
Various scales
Paris : Delagrave
100 x 130
Series of historical wall maps in French.
1-2 Monde Oriental — Grèce ancienne
3-4 Monde Grec — Empire d'Alexandre
5-6 Italie ancienne — Monde romain
7-8 Monde arabe — Empire de Charlemagne
9-10 Les Croisades — Formation Territoriale de la France
11-12 Grandes Explorations et Découvertes du XVe - XIXe siecle — L'Europe à la fin du XVe siècle
13-14 La Crise religieuses aux XVIe et XVIIe siècles — La Prépondérance franco-súedoise en 1661
15-16 La France en 1789 — L'Europe en 1815
17-18 Les Nationalités depuis 1815 — Le Dévelopment Économique depuis le XIXe siècle
19-20 L'Asie et L'Amérique — Le Partage d'Afrique
By J M d'Hoop
Each 105 x 125
21-22 L'Europe en 1914 — L'Europe après la Prèmiere Guerre Mondiale
23-24 L'Europe Hitlérienne — L'Extrême-Orient aux XIXe et XXe siècles
Supplied double-sided on stout card
F.Fr 45.00
The following maps are available individually on paper : No's 8, 9, 17, 18, 19, 20, 21.
F.Fr 17.80

CARTES MURALES HISTORIQUES
Various scales
Paris : Armand Colin
120 x 100
Series of school historical wall maps, double sided, on plastic surface.
Maps available :
503 Grèce Antique
Monde Grec Antique on reverse
505 Athènes Classique Ve and IVe siècles
Rome sous la République - on reverse
507 Rome Impériale
Monde Romain Antique - on reverse
509 Invasions barbares de la fin du IVe au VIIe siècle
L'Empire Byzantin du Vie au XIe siècle - on reverse
511 Empire Carolingien
La France au XVe siècle - on reverse
513 L'Expansion Chrétienne XIe–XIIIe siècles
Les Grandes Découvertes - on reverse
517 La France a la Mort de Saint Louis (1270)
L'Europe au Temps de Charles V (1535) - on reverse
519 La Renaissance
La Crise religieuse au XVIe siècle - on reverse
521 La France de 1559 a 1610
La France de 1610–1715 - on reverse
523 L'Europe de 1610 a 1660
Rivalités coloniales au XVIIIe siècle - on reverse
525 L'Europe de 1763 a 1792
La France a la fin de l'Ancien Régime - on reverse
537 L'Europe en 1878
L'Europe en 1914 - on reverse
541 La Guerre en Europe 1914-18
Le Front Occidental 1914-18 - on reverse
545 La 2e Guerre Mondiale : Victoires allemandes 1939-1942
La France dans la 2e Guerre Mondiale 1939-45 - on reverse
547 La 2e Guerre Mondiale : L'Effondrement de l'Axe 1943-45
La 2e Guerre Mondiale : Extrême-Orient et Pacifique 1941-45 - on reverse
549 L'URSS 1921-1941
Les Démocraties Populaires d'Europe (1945-60) - on reverse

CARTES HISTORIQUES
J Bouillon
Various scales
St Germain-en-Laye : Éditions MDI
126 x 92
Plastic-coated, double-sided historical wall maps for schools. In French.
Maps available :
1532 Les Luttes Franco-Anglaises en Amérique et aux Indes - Empires Coloniaux et Grand Commerce
1522 La Découverte du Monde - L'Exploration des Poles
1548 (Reverse) Les Victoires allemandes (1939-42)
1550 Les Victoires alliées 1943-45 — La Guerre du Pacifique 1941-45

PUTZGER GESCHICHTSWANDKARTEN
Bielefeld : Cornelsen, Velhagen and Klasing
Col. historical wall maps in German.
Maps available :
Die Welt im 19 Jahrhundert
1:21,500,000 137 x 189 DM 145.00
Die Welt im 20 Jahrhundert
1:18,300,000 194 x 196 DM 152.00

WELTGESCHICHTE DER NEUZEIT
1:55,000,000
Hamburg : Flemming
212 x 162
Historical wall map; 4 maps on 1 sheet showing world :
1450 - 1650
1830
1914
1950

HISTORICAL WALL MAPS
Gotha : Haack
Col. historical wall maps in German.
Maps available :
Grosse geographische Entdeckungen und Koloniale Groberungen 1462-1648
1:15,000,000, 1968, 240 x 142.
Shows geog. discoveries and colonial conquests.
Die Territoriale Aufteilung der Welt 1876-1914, 1:15,000,000, 1966, 240 x 144. Shows territorial divisions.

BREASTED-HUTH-HARDING WORLD HISTORY MAPS
Various scales
Chicago : Denoyer-Geppert
112 x 81
Series of col. historical wall maps printed on manilla. Available in various mounted styles.
Maps available:
20411 Ancient World
204021 Ancient Orient and Palestine
204031 Oriental Empires
204041 The Achaean World
204051 Ancient Greece
204061 Greek and Phoenician Colonies and Commerce
204071 Boetia and Attica
204081 Athens
204091 Sequence Map of Greece
204101 Alexander's Empire
204111 Ancient Italy
204121 Growth of Roman Power in Italy
204131 Rome
204141 Conquest of the Mediterranean
204151 Caesar's Gaul
204161 Roman Empire, Time of Augustus
204211 Barbarian Migrations
204421 The World in 1914
204501 League of Nations 1920-30
204521 The World, 1918-37
200361 The World in 1965

DENOYER-GEPPERT WORLD HISTORY MAPS
Various scales.
Chicago : Denoyer-Geppert
162 x 112
Col. historical wall maps.
Maps available :
World Origin of Man to 3000 BC
Changing Ways of Living, 3000 BC to AD1
The Bronze Age and Ancient Empires to 550 BC
Ancient Empires to 200 BC
Ancient Empires c AD 100
Barbarian Invasions and World Religions to AD 600
Moslem Ascendancy to AD 1100
Mongol Ascendancy to AD 1300
The World 1763-1848
Background of World War I
Background of World War II
World War II and Aftermath to 1950
World Relationships, July 1, 1963

WORLD HISTORY MAPS
Chicago : Weber Costello Co
139 x 106
Series of clear, coloured wall maps, each including approx. 7 insets.
Available mounted in various styles.
Maps available :
138– 800 Ancient World to About 275 BC
818 Roman World to About 150 AD
826 Medieval World in the 13th Century
834 Growth of Known World to 1800 AD
891 World in 1914
909 World in 1939
925 World in 1968

PALMER WORLD HISTORY MAPS
Various scales
Chicago : Rand McNally
50 x 46
Col. school historical wall maps.
Maps available :
Growth of Civilisation – Eurasia 3000 BC - 200 AD
Ancient World, 7th CBC
Age of Discovery (15th - 16th C)
The World about 1900 - empires, explorations etc.
World War II – 1942
The World after World War II

HISTORY MAPS
Indianapolis : Cram
Col. school wall maps.
Maps available :
Ancient Peoples
Ancient Empires
Greek and Phoenician Colonies 500 BC
The Spread of Christianity in the Middle Ages
Colonial Empires in 1763
Colonial Empires in 1815
Colonial Possessions of the World Powers 1914
The Nations at War in 1918
The World War 1914-1918
World War II, Pacific Theater
Each US $13.75

ELEMENTARY HISTORY MAPS
Indianapolis : Cram
132 x 100
Large scale historical wall maps.
Maps available :
Voyages and Discoveries to 1610
Political World
US $8.85

HISTORICAL WALL MAPS
Moskva : GUGK
Series of historical school wall maps in Russian.
Maps available :
States of the Ancient World
1:12,000,000
The Conquests of Alexander of Macedon in the 4th C
1:3,500,000
Great Geographical Discoveries and Colonial Uprisings in the 17th-18th C, 1973
1:20,000,000
The Growth of Territories and States in antiquity, 1973
1:12,000,000
Geographical Discovery and Colonial Settings in the Mid 15th-17th C, 1973
1:20,000,000
Important Geographical Discoveries and Colonial Settlements from the mid 17th-18th C, 1973
1:20,000,000
Colonial Ownership in the 18th C to the first period of modern history, 1973
1:20,000,000
First World War, 1914-18, 1973
1:3,000,000
Second World War, 1939-45
a) War Action in Europe and North Africa (1/9/39 - 18/11/42) and Great War of Soviet Union (22/6/41-18/11/42), 1973
1:6,000,000
b) Great National War of the Soviet Union. War action in Europe and North Africa (19/11/42-9/5/45), 1973
1:6,000,000
c) General Course of the Second World War (1/9/39-2/9/45) 1973
1:21,000,000

HISTORICAL WALL MAPS
Praha : Kart
Col. historical maps in Czech.
Maps available :
Svet po I svetové válce (The World after World War I) Kcs 115
Druhá svetová válka (The Second World War) Kcs 165

WIELKIE ODKRYCIA GEOGRAFICZNE I ZABONY KOLONIALNE OD POCZATKU XV DO POLOWY XVII WIEKU
1:22,000,000
Warszawa : PPWK, 1972
190 x 120
School wall map, showing the Voyages of Discovery and Colonial Settlements in the 15th-17th C.
Zl 140

CLASSICAL LANDS OF THE MEDITERRANEAN
1:2,697,500
Washington : NGS
81 x 55
Col. map with insets of ancient civilisations, descriptive notes.
Paper US $2.00
Plastic US $3.00

DAS FRÜHE CHRISTENTUM : WORLD RELIGIOUS WALL MAP
1:200,000
No 610
Darmstadt : Perthes
206 x 174
Wall map illustrating early chrstianity, with insets :
Journey of St Paul (1:2,000,000) and Spread of Christianity (1:4,500,000)
DM 142

WALL ATLAS OF THE BIBLE LANDS
London : Philip
917 x 94
Each map fully col.
Maps available:
1 The Distribution of Nations. Illustrates the book of Genesis.
2 Egypt, The Sinai Peninsula and the Promised Land. Illustrates the book of Exodus.
3 Canaan as Divided Among the Twelve Tribes Illustrates the Book of Joshua and Judges
4 The Holy Land in the Time of the Kings
5 Syria and Mesopotamia : Illustrates the Jewish Captivities
6 Palestine in the Time of Christ
7 The Journeys of St Paul : The Roman Empire Two maps on one sheet
8 Modern Palestine.
£1.50
Mounted on cloth, with covers or dissected
£7.00

TABULA IMPERII ROMANI – INTERNATIONAL MAP OF THE ROMAN EMPIRE
1:1,000,000
See index 100/8
Series of maps prepared by various national authorities based upon sheet lines of the International Map of the World. They show evidence of Roman occupation and settlement together with place names and boundaries. Some sheets have a descriptive text.
Sheets available :
London : Soc. of Antiquaries
NHI 33 Lepcis Magna, 1954
NHI 34 Cyrene, 1954
NG 36 Coptos, 1958
Rome : Unione Accademia Nazionale
NL 32 Mediolanum (Milan), 1966 with text 148pp
NL 33 Tergeste (Trieste), 1961 with text 78pp
NL 34 Aquincum-Sarmizegetusa-Sirmium (Budapest), 1968, with text 123pp
Southampton : Ordnance Survey
NM, NN, NO 30 and adjacent pt. sheets, Roman Britain, 1956, with text £2.00

WORLD
Maplewood : Hammond
62 x 41
Set of reproduction maps :
Double-hemisphere World Map by John Speed, 1651
Europe, Blaeu's Grooten Atlas (1648–65)
Africa, Blaeu's Grooten Atlas (1648-65)
North and South America, Johannes Baptista Hommann, 1732
US $3.95

NOVA TOTIUS TERRARUM ORBIS GEOGRAPHICA AC HYDROGRAPHICA TABULA
Gotha : Haack, 1971
70 x 54
Reproduction Blaeu map from the 16th C. With explanation in German, French, Russian and English.
M 26.00

THE WORLD, BY FREDERICK DE WIT, 1680
London : RGS - Edinburgh: Bart.
46 x 38
Coloured reproduction map of the world in two hemispheres.
£1.50

MERCATOR – WELTKARTE, 1633
Leipzig : Edition Leipzig, 1972
4th edition
81 x 57
Facsimile map.
M 12.00

MAPPEMONDE DE SEBASTIEN CABOT, 1544
1:17,500,000
Paris : Livre Club Diderot (Éditions les Yeux Ouverts), 1971
130 x 95
Coloured reproduction of the original in the Bibliothèque Nationale, Paris. 16pp notes, text booklet with original Latin and Spanish commentary.

CARTE DU MONDE CONNU EN 1688
Paris : IGN
95 x 60
Map by the Sieur Jaugeon. Shows world in 2 hemispheres, with allegorical representations of the constellations, definitions of geog. terms. Offset ed.
F.Fr 41.67

ATLASES
W1 WORLD : REFERENCE

Arranged by country of publication

Belgium

ATLAS DE GEOGRAPHIE
Jose A Sporck and Luc Pierard
Bruxelles : Asedi, 1968
22 x 32
Belgian atlas covering world and space, continents and individual countries in 250 maps. With index of 17,500 names. 67 maps for Belgium.
B.Fr 420

China

THE GRAND ATLAS OF THE WORLD
Ed Chang-Chi-Yun
Taiwan : Chinese Geog. Inst, 1965+
In 5 vols
27 x 39
World atlas in Chi. and Eng. Vols available :
1 Atlas of East China 1965, Not inc. China
2 Atlas of West Asia and USSR
3 Atlas of Europe and Africa, 1970
In preparation:
Vol 4 The Americas
Vol 5 The Pacific, Poles and General Maps of the World

Denmark

GYLDENDALS ATLAS
Ed. M. Rentsch
København : Gyldendal, 1970
23 x 28
294pp
Including 176pp of coloured relief maps including many thematic insets and 23pp Scandinavian section. Danish edition of G.Philip University Atlas.
D.Kr 177.00

POLITIKENS VERDENATLAS
Ed Prof. Axel Schou
København : Politiken
World atlas in colour with physical relief maps, 96pp large scale maps, index.
D.Kr 50.75

France

GRAND ATLAS BORDAS
Ed Pierre Serryn
Paris : Bordas, 1971
30 x 40
330pp
224pp maps: physical, political, economic. Index of 50,000 names, multilingual. Inc. principal world economic resources.
F.Fr 153.50

ATLAS WEBER
Cartography – Neguri Editorial, SA. Bilbao
Paris : Weber, SA., 1975
24 x 28
Includes 79pp of detailed physical maps with many large scale insets. Thematic section covers world history, demography and economy followed by a descriptive text to each map in French.
S.Fr. 170.00

ATLAS CLASSIQUE
Ed Robert Kienast and A-J-C Bertrand
2nd edition
Paris : Delagrave, 1974
25 x 21
80pp mainly physical maps, with some them. maps. Special emphasis on France. Index of over 12,000 names.
F.Fr 36.00

ATLAS INTERNATIONAL LAROUSSE, POLITIQUE ET ECONOMIQUE
Paris : Larousse
33 x 50
272pp
166 political and economic maps; 300 statistical tables; index 38,000 names; text in Eng. Fr, Sp.

ATLAS GÉNÉRAL LAROUSSE
Eds. G Reynaud-Dulaurier, H Fullard, H C Darby
Paris : Larousse, 1973
24 x 30
312pp
184pp maps - physical, political and thematic; city plans; index, 50,000 names. Including 20pp supplement of current information.

ATLAS MODERNE LAROUSSE
Paris : Larousse, 1969
22 x 30
144pp col. maps, physical with some them. Index of 20,000 names.

Germany

ATLAS INTERNATIONAL
2nd edition
Ed. Dr W Bormann
Gütersloh : Bertelsmann, 1975
38 x 39
580pp
171pp physical and thematic maps, 40pp text. Internat. lettering. 240pp Index over 170 000 names. Atlas vol. from 'Bertelsmann Lexikothek'.
DM 236.00

DER GROSSER BERTELSMANN-WELTATLAS
Ed Dr W Bormann
Gütersloh : Bertelsmann, Jubilee ed, 1972
24 x 32
440pp
Contains 100pp of physical, political world maps; with 20pp covering Europe and 40pp of thematic maps. 240pp index, text section with illus.
DM 136.00
Ordinary edition available in Finnish as 'Suuri Maailmankartasto', 1965
FMK 75.00

HAUSATLAS
Gütersloh : Bertelsmann, 1971 (1960)
24 x 32
320pp
Political and physical maps; geographical section; c 800 illus; text; index 60,000 names.
DM 49.80

LÄNDERLEXICON-WELTATLAS
Ed Werner Ludewig
Gütersloh : Bertelsmann, 1973
11 x 17
448pp
Atlas and gazetteer in 1 vol, with index (144pp). 185 col. maps with town plans.
DM 14.80

NEUER ATLAS DER WELT
Gütersloh : Bertelsmann, 1969
24 x 32
224pp
62pp col. maps; index 60,000 names; section covering economy, pop, govt., communications.
DM 26.00

MEYERS GROSSER WELTATLAS
Mannheim : Bibliographisches Inst.
26 x 37
557pp
195pp col. maps; 36pp section on the Heavens; index 120,000 names. Political, physical and thematic maps on new interconnective projection for land and ocean areas.
DM 98.00

WELTATLAS
Vol. 10 of "Das Grosse Duden-Lexicon"
Mannheim : Bibliographisches Inst/Duden Verlag, 1969
25 x 37
490pp
172pp col. maps; 140pp geog. profile; index 120,000 names, political and physical maps.
DM 89.00

MEYERS UNIVERSALATLAS
Mannheim : Bibliographisches Inst, 1970
26 x 37
248pp
61pp physical col. maps; 360 col. plates; index 55,000 names, gazetteer.
DM 39.00

GROSSER WELTATLAS
Berlin : Columbus, 1965
30 x 42
196pp
Physical maps hachured, also political and thematic plates. Index 110,000 names.
DM 98.00

HAUSATLAS
Berlin : Columbus, 1966
28 x 42
196pp
Political maps with hachured relief. Intro. Index 48,000 names.
DM 48.00

KLEINER WELTATLAS
Wien : F - B
9 x 15
60pp
22 maps, 42pp text.
A.Sch. 130

HANDATLAS
München : Goldmann, 1968
29 x 41
v 111 x 160pp
General world atlas including 14 historical maps; index 70,000 names.
DM 75.00

HAACK GROSSER WELTATLAS
In 7 parts + Index
Gotha : Haack, 1966
26 x 33
207pp
In loose-leaf folder. Contains political maps, communications networks, physical maps, natural features, city plans.
Index vol. (16 x 24) 720pp with 180,000 names.
Complete set DM 210
Maps can be bought separately for
Each DM 2.50

WELTATLAS
Gotha : Haack, 1972
26 x 34
189pp
100pp maps, text; index 100,000 names. Political and relief maps, col. photographs.
M 80.00

HAUSATLAS
3rd Edition
Gotha : Haack, 1973
25 x 34
298pp
72pp political and physical maps; 139pp text with them. maps, graphs, photographs; index 45,000 names.
M 30.00

KLEINER ATLAS : DIE ERDE
4th edition
Gotha : Haack, 1974
10 x 16
272pp
Political and relief maps with surface col; index 20,000 names. Statistical information.
M 9.80

WELTATLAS
Bern : Hallwag, 1967
24 x 32
56pp
39pp political maps, index 20,000 names; details of national flags.
DM 9.50

DER NEUER HERDER HANDATLAS
Marburg : Herder, 1966
41 x 55
208pp
Physical and them. maps, illus. and tables; index 85,000 names.
DM 195.00
Linen DM 175.00

GROSSER WELTATLAS
Marburg : Herder, 1968
27 x 40
250pp
142pp maps - physical, relief with contours and layer col; 100pp index of 90,000 names.
DM 85.00

HIRTS TASCHENTATLAS
1st edition
Kiel : Ferdinand Hirt, 1972
11 x 16
178pp
Pocket atlas with political and physical maps, 72pp index, text and statistical tables.
DM 9.80

GROSSER JRO-WELTATLAS
No 250
München : JRO-Verlag, 1966
37 x 45
404pp
Containing 85pp world political and physical maps; 36 large scale maps of Germany, Austria and Switzerland (each part has its own index); 25pp of them. maps; text; tables and illus.
DM 195.00
Supp. 1970/1 DM 29.00
1972 DM 29.00

GROSSER JRO-WELTATLAS
No 241
München : JRO-Verlag, 1966
31 x 44
280pp
92pp political and physical maps of the world with them. maps; 36pp large scale maps of Germany, Austria and Switzerland; 32pp text; 52 col. illus; 2 part index 160,000 names.
DM 98.50

HAUSATLAS
No 263
München : JRO-Verlag, 1973
22 x 30
332pp
124pp physical, political, them. maps, index 85,000 names, tables, statistics, gazetteer.
DM 59.50

WELTATLAS, HANDAUSGABE
No 260
München : JRO-Verlag, 1972
22 x 30
232pp
Physical, political, them. maps, index of 50,000 names, tables and statistics.
DM 36.00

TASCHEN-WELTATLAS
No 270
München : JRO-Verlag
12 x 17
196pp
74pp col. maps: 56pp text; index 17,000 names.
DM 9.80

ALEXANDER WELTATLAS
1st edition
Editor H.Schulze
Stuttgart : Ernst Klett Verlag, 1976
24 x 33
World Atlas with emphasis on Germany, having numerous thematic maps covering structure, climate, land use, industry, communications and population, also town studies and political groupings. German text.
DM 26.80

KNAURS GROSSER WELTATLAS
München : Droemer Knaur
Ger. lang. ed. of the Times Atlas of the World.
DM 295.00

WELT TASCHENATLAS
München : Kompass
Pocket atlas, physical, political map at scales 1:5 - 33,000,000
DM 3.80

R.V-ATLAS
UNSERE WELT HEUTE
Ed. R. Goock
Cartography Kart. Inst. Bertelsmann
Stuttgart : Reise-und Verkehrsverlag, 1975
27 x 36
Contains a series of regional physical maps, each illustrated by coloured land, aircraft and satellite photographs, thematic maps and brief descriptive text. Index
DM 69.00

NEUER WELTATLAS
Zurich : Stauffacher - Verlag. AG.
27 x 34
444pp
230pp maps - relief maps of Germany, Austria, Switzerland, and the world, thematic, political and geographical maps; index of 10,000 names. Maps taken from Haack Grosser Weltatlas.
DM 98.00

HAUSATLAS
Braunschweig : Westermann, 1967
24 x 34
238pp
423 maps, many of which them, 150 col. illus, inc. plates, diagrams, statistics, index 30,000 names.
DM 48.00

Great Britain

WORLD ATLAS
9th edition
Edinburgh : Bart, 1974
26 x 38
168pp
Physical atlas showing map relief, layer colouring, communications, boundaries, towns. Index of 24,000 names. Introductory maps in black and blue.
£5.50

MINI ATLAS
Edinburgh : Bart, 1974
10 x 14
162pp
Political maps of the world, with index of 4,000 names.
95p

THE COLLINS WORLD ATLAS
London : Collins, 1970
21 x 27
180pp
Large scale general maps; political divisions; relief and structure; climate; economics.
£3.50

THE DAILY TELEGRAPH ATLAS
Ed D L Baker
London : Collins, 1974
20 x 26
144pp
78pp coloured maps (printed GLA Stockholm); physical maps show relief, major roads and railways, towns; political maps showing borders; supplement of space exploration and world statistics; index to 20,000 entries. £1.95

GRAPHIC ATLAS
London : Collins
21 x 27
136pp
64pp col. maps; 8pp illus; 64pp index; additional maps and statistics.
£2.50

WORLD WIDE ATLAS
London : Collins
21 x 27
48pp
40pp col. pages; index. 50p

COLLINS POCKET ATLAS
London : Collins, 1971
12 x 18
160pp
96pp 4-col. physical and political maps; 16pp social and economical maps; index.
£1.00
School ed. 70p

THE FABER ATLAS
Ed D J Sinclair
5th edition
Oxford : Geo. Pub. Co. 1971 (rev. ed)
24 x 32
210pp
154pp political, relief, economic maps, aerial photos, plans of large urban areas, 44pp index. £3.50

POCKET ATLAS OF THE WORLD
London : Gia. 1976
8 x 13
67pp of maps showing International boundaries, principal railways, roads and rivers, also thematic section and 41pp index.
95p

THE ATLAS OF THE EARTH
Ed Tony Loftas
London : Mitchell Beazley/Philip, 1972
28 x 38
448pp
In 3 sections : The Good Earth - a pictorial encyclopaedia guide to the human and biological environment, inc. earth structure, life, resources; World Atlas - 187pp col. physical and thematic maps and 100pp index to places.
In slip case £13.95

THE OXFORD WORLD ATLAS
Ed. Saul B Cohen
Oxford : OUP, 1973
26 x 38
200pp app.
Arranged into topical sections : 13pp physical-structural maps of the oceans and continental areas. 16pp Human Environment maps covering settlement and economic factors, 40pp topog. maps of selected areas, 8pp urban and 46pp of thematic maps. Gazetteer. £9.75
Wire bound, limp cover edition
£4.75

THE NEW OXFORD ATLAS
Oxford : OUP, 1975
27 x 38
208pp
105pp of coloured maps, including series of physical maps of the world. 6 physical-environment maps and a 16pp section of thematic maps of the World and U.K. Index. £6.75

OXFORD HOME ATLAS OF THE WORLD
4th edition
Oxford : OUP, 1960, rep. with rev. 1976
144pp
112pp maps in colour, 32pp gazetteer.
£2.95

LITTLE OXFORD ATLAS
4th edition
Oxford : OUP, 1962. rep. with rev 1972
19 x 25
70pp
66pp coloured maps, with gazetteer.
£1.50

PENGUIN WORLD ATLAS
Ed P. Hall
Cartography : Clarendon Press, Oxford
Harmondsworth : Penguin Books Ltd. 1974
15 x 21
Coloured atlas including maps of the oceans, physical and human environment, topography, the world and also urban plans.
£1.50

THE INTERNATIONAL ATLAS
London : Philip
see THE INTERNATIONAL ATLAS
Chicago : Rand McNally

THE ATLAS OF THE EARTH
London : Philip
see THE ATLAS OF THE EARTH
London : Mitchell Beazley.

THE LIBRARY ATLAS
11th edition
Ed H Fullard and H C Darby
London : Philip, 1975
23 x 28
320pp
208pp physical maps with hill shading, with maps on geol, climate, volcanoes, soil, pop. 32pp economic maps, index of 50,000 names.
£5.75

THE UNIVERSITY ATLAS
15th edition
Ed H Fullard and H C Darby
London : Philip, 1975
23 x 29
288pp
Physical Ref. atlas, hill shading, climate graphs, some them. maps, index of 50,000 names.
£5.25

PHILIP'S CONCORDE WORLD ATLAS
Ed H Fullard
London : Philip, 1975
23 x 29
217pp
128pp physical and political maps; towns classified by size, boundaries, main communication routes, water features.
83pp index. £4.75

PRACTICAL ATLAS
Ed H Fullard
London : Philip, 1974
23 x 29
iv, 80pp
Political ref. atlas, showing political and admin. boundaries, communications, inc. shipping routes with distances. Index of 35,000 names.
£3.50

COMMERCIAL COURSE ATLAS
Ed H Fullard
London : Philip, 1974
23 x 28
120pp
64pp physical and political maps, 24pp economic maps, showing world distribution of resources, minerals, industry, land usage, agriculture. £1.20

MODERN HOME ATLAS
London : Philip, 1973
23 x 28
54pp
Political maps with index. £1.25

POCKET ATLAS OF THE WORLD
Ed H Fullard
London : Philip, 1971
12 x 20
96pp
Political maps with 24pp index.
85p

PRENTICE-HALL WORLD ATLAS
Joseph E Williams
Hemel Hempstead : Prentice-Hall International, 1963
137pp
In 3 sections : systematic world geography; world economic maps; physical maps. Index.

THE TIMES COMPREHENSIVE ATLAS OF THE WORLD
5th edition
London : Times Books (in collaboration with Bart, Edinburgh), 1975
30 x 45
x1, 359pp
244pp physical and political maps. Index of over 200,000 names. 40pp prelim. section incl. thematic and celestial maps.
£26.00

THE TIMES CONCISE ATLAS OF THE WORLD
2nd edition
London : Times Books, 1975
28 x 38
272pp
40pp prelims, 148pp col. maps, 84pp index of 90,000 names. Mainly physical maps with physical and economic prelims.
Contained in slip case £12.50

Hungary

KÉPES POLITIKAI ÉS GAZDASÁGI VILÁGATLASZ
Budapest : Cart, 1971
by Prof. Dr S Rado
25 x 34
Illus. political and economic world atlas, 185pp with over 400 col. maps; geog. and economic data; index 65,000 names; flags, astronomical maps; c 48pp plates. Shows space conquests, political boundaries etc.

KIS VILAGÁTLASZ
3rd edition
Budapest : Cart, 1971
10 x 18
292pp
Pocket world atlas, 96pp col. maps, 196pp statistical data and index.
Paper bound

Indonesia

ATLAS NASIONAL TENTANG, INDONESIA
Jakarta : Ganaco
24 x 38
Indonesian atlas; 29 topical world maps (rainfall, population) 22pp for Indonesia, 21pp for the rest of the world.

Italy

ATLANTE INTERNAZIONALE ITALIANO
8th edition
Milano : TCI, 1968
In 2 vols.
Vol 1 Atlas - 32 x 50
Vol 2 Index - 18 x 25
Large physical atlas containing 173pp maps using local spelling prepared at a series of comparable scales with many large scale local maps. Index of 1032pp containing 250,000 entries.
L 60,000

ATLANTE GEOGRAFICO GENERALE ZANICHELLI
Ed D Insolera and G Musiani Zaniboni
Bologna : Zanichelli, 1973
23 x 32
228pp
Physical and political maps, Italian section, European and world maps; thematic maps, 50 col. illus. and photos.
L 4,800

IL NUOVO ATLANTE MONDIALE
V Bonapace and G Motta
3rd edition
Novara : Ag, 1971
26 x 36
400pp app
160pp physical and political maps, 1000 coloured illus; index 30,000 names. Inc. geog. dictionary and statistical section.
L 12,000

Japan

NEW WORLD ATLAS
Comp Keiji Tanaka
Tokyo : Zenkoku Kyoiku Tosho, 1968
28 x 42
app 182pp
46 double page maps, 16 single page ones, mostly physical with contours, index of 60,000 names in Eng. Jap. Also in Ch and European editions.
£20.60

WORLD ATLAS
Ed Kaoru Tanaka and E B Espenshade
Tokyo : Heibonsha
see WORLD ATLAS
Chicago : Rand McNally

POCKET WORLD ATLAS
Tokyo : Heibonsha
11 x 16
254pp
Includes 82pp of coloured maps. In Japanese
Y 1,250

SEKAIRYOKOCHIZU – Travel Atlas of the World
1st edition
Tokyo : Geikoku-Shoin, 1974
14 x 19
474pp
Collection of travel maps of the countries of the world with 85 city maps, regional maps and factual information.
Y 2,500

Mexico

ATLAS UNIVERSAL Y DE MEXICO
Jorge Hernandez Millares
Mexico City : Editorial ECLAL
40pp
Coloured world atlas.
P 16.00

Netherlands

WINKLER PRINS WERELD ATLAS
Amsterdam : Elsevier, 1969
27 x 33
136pp col. maps, land-use and geog. section; supplementary text; index 50,000 names.

Norway

GYLDENDALS VERDENS ATLAS
Chief Eds H Fullard and H C Darby
Norwegian Ed G Wicklund-Hansen
Oslo : Gyldendal Norsk Forlag, 1974
23 x 28
Including 176pp of coloured relief maps, many thematic insets and 23pp Scandinavian section. Norwegian edition of G.Philip University Atlas.

Spain

GRAN ATLAS AGUILAR
3 vols
Madrid : Aguilar, 1970
33 x 50
684pp
Vol I Europe and North Asia, 262 mainly physical maps
Vol II South Asia, Africa. Ocean regions, Americas, 251 maps inc. 61 double ones
Vol III Index vol, 393,000 names, geog. dictionary, 1970
S.Ptas 7,500

EL ATLAS DE NUESTRO TIEMPO
7th edition
Cartography : Readers Digest – J Bartholomew
Madrid : Selecciones de Reader's Digest, 1976
47 x 34
260pp
Detailed physical world atlas with emphasis on Spain S.Ptas 1,490

NUEVO ATLAS MUNDIAL
Madrid : Aguilar
393pp
100pp mainly physical maps; 600 plates; index 60,000 names.

ATLAS UNIVERSAL AGUILAR
Madrid : Aguilar, 1968
376pp
192pp physical maps, many large scale; col. illus; index 200,000 names.

ATLAS BACHILLERATO – UNIVERSAL Y DE ESPAÑA
Madrid : Aguilar, 1970
25 x 35
Physical-political atlas of the world with special emphasis on Spain. 97pp maps, 15pp index.

GRAN ATLAS GEOGRAFICO UNIVERSAL
1st edition
Barcelona : Ediciones Nauto, S.A., 1974
23 x 32
212pp
Political and economic coverage for each country of the world with 50pp thematic section, drawings and photographs. Index of 15,000 names. S.Ptas 1,500

Sweden

VÄRLDEN I ETT NOTSKAL
Stockholm : GLA
242pp
World in a nutshell. Pocket sized ref. atlas: 92pp maps, 60pp index.
S.Kr 13.50

VÅR VÄRLD ATLAS
Stockholm : GLA
21 x 29
192pp
Our World Atlas. 80pp col. maps, 72pp index, factual information and illus.
Cloth S.Kr 59.00

STORA INTERNATIONELLA ATLASEN
Stockholm : GLA
28 x 37
556pp
285 physical and political them. maps, index, 160,000 names.
Cloth S.Kr 335

Switzerland

TASCHENWELTALAS
Bern : K & F
12 x 17
40pp
32pp maps, 8pp text in Ger and Fr.
DM 4.50

USA

MODERN WORLD ATLAS
Indianapolis : Cram
31 x 24
408pp
US bias, with world physical, historical maps. Index. US $12.95

THE WORLD: ITS GEOGRAPHY IN MAPS
Chicago : Denoyer-Geppert
21 x 28
96pp
43pp col. maps, political and physical. Index of 4,800 names.
Paper cover US $2.50

VISUAL RELIEF ATLAS OF WORLD CONTINENTS
Chicago : Denoyer-Geppert
21 x 28
Col. relief atlas; 10 double page maps covering the continents, with table of political divisions. Pop. data, 9pp index.

ENCYCLOPAEDIA BRITANNICA INTERNATIONAL ATLAS
Chicago : Encyclopaedia Britannica Inc.
see INTERNATIONAL WORLD ATLAS
Rand McNally/Philip

WORLD ATLAS, HALLMARK EDITION
Maplewood, NJ : Hammond
In 2 vols.
24 x 31
676pp
In Vol. I, 192pp foreign maps and index, 128pp US maps, index, census (1970) figures. Vol II – cross ref. index, them. maps.
In slip case US $39.95

MEDALLION WORLD ATLAS
Maplewood, NJ : Hammond
24 x 31
672pp
322pp political and them. maps, index 120,000 names; section on life and environment.
US $24.95

AMBASSADOR WORLD ATLAS
Maplewood, NJ : Hammond
24 x 31
492pp
Contains political, topog, economic, biblical and historical maps. 100,000 names in index. US $14.95

CITATION WORLD ATLAS
Maplewood, NJ : Hammond
24 x 31
360pp
Col. foreign and US maps, political, topog, economic. 25,000 name index, gazetteer section. US $10.95

PANORAMIC WORLD ATLAS
Maplewood, NJ : Hammond
24 x 31
206pp
Shaded relief maps of each continent; historical, pop, ocean, exploration maps.
US $8.95

GLOBEMASTER WORLD ATLAS
Maplewood, NJ : Hammond, 1971
21 x 28
104pp
Contains 60 foreign maps, 64 road and travel maps for the US.
US $2.95

INTERNATIONAL WORLD ATLAS
Maplewood, NJ : Hammond
24 x 31
200pp
264 world maps; national flags, gazetteer of 48,000 names, index sections.
US $6.95

COMPARATIVE WORLD ATLAS
Maplewood, NJ : Hammond
24 x 31
48pp
Comparative maps for each continent, political, physical, vegetation, pop. climate; land types in pictures. 81 maps.
US $1.28

THE HEYDEN NEW WORLD ATLAS
New York : Heyden, 1970
30 x 23
250pp app
142pp maps divided by continent. Political, physical, general maps; no thematic maps. Gazetteer of 50,000, glossary of terms. £4.50

MAN'S DOMAIN – A THEMATIC ATLAS OF THE WORLD
Ed N J W Thrower
2nd edition
New York : McGraw Hill, 1970
25 x 34
80pp
Paper covered atlas; climate, agriculture, minerals, physical and other them. maps. Index.

NATIONAL GEOGRAPHIC ATLAS OF THE WORLD
3rd edition
Washington : NGS, 1970
31 x 48
331pp
140pp col political maps for reference, physical data, description of countries etc.
Descriptive text. US $18.75
De luxe ed US $24.50

THE INTERNATIONAL ATLAS
Ed Russell L Voisin et al
Chicago : Rand McNally (London : Philip), 1970
29 x 38
liv, 503pp
Result of internat. co-operation. Distinctive col. 278pp maps mainly physical with town plans, col. plates, index of 160,000 entries.
Text in 4 langs. £18.00

Also available in Finnish edition "Atlas – Kansainvalinen suurkartasto" 1969-70.
FMK 280

NEW COSMOPOLITAN WORLD ATLAS
Chicago : Rand McNally, 1972
30 x 37
420pp
Contains global and space-eye views, 200 world maps (with all 50 US), comparative maps of population, religion etc, historical section for world and N America, space maps and text; political information, index of 82,000 names.

PREMIER WORLD ATLAS : NEW PORTRAIT EDITION
Chicago : Rand McNally, 1971
30 x 37
350pp
Political and physical maps: 50 col. illus; index 82,000 names; world facts; people and places. US $12.95

WORLD ATLAS : FAMILY EDITION
Chicago : Rand McNally
25 x 31
342pp
131pp maps in colour; political and physical, 26 historical plates; photos and illus; index 98pp; space section. World facts and glossary. US $9.95
De luxe ed US $12.95

STANDARD WORLD ATLAS
Chicago : Rand McNally, 1970
25 x 31
264pp
131pp coloured maps, inc. 89pp of US and North America; space; world data; discoveries and exploration since 600 BC, 26pp historical maps; 98pp index.
US $6.95

GOODE'S WORLD ATLAS
Ed E B Espenshade Jr
15th edition
Chicago : Rand McNally, 1975
25 x 29
372pp
113pp physical maps, contoured with layer col, topical and local maps. Geog. statistics and index of 30,000 names. Special emphasis on the Americas.

WORLD ATLAS
Ed Kaoru Tanaka and E B Espenshade
Chicago : Rand McNally/Tokyo : Heibonsha
25 x 29
274pp
109pp col. maps, inc. 64pp from "Goodes' World Atlas", 45pp maps Japan, Korea, China, ed. Japanese Cart Inst. 160pp index. In Japanese, index bilingual.
Y 3,000

RAND McNALLY WORLDMASTER ATLAS - REFERENCE EDITION
Chicago : Rand McNally, 1971
24 x 31
246pp
39pp of prelims followed by a collection of political world maps including 61pp for the Americas (separate page for most states) and 26pp for the rest of the world. Index to places. Paper covers. US $4.95

CONTINENTAL WORLD ATLAS
Chicago : Rand McNally
18 x 27
180pp col. maps; statistical material; American index; index 25,000 names.
US $5.95

PICTORIAL WORLD ATLAS
Chicago : Rand McNally
23 x 28
160pp
Facts about "today's world"; economic and social data; communications; political maps with emphasis on US.
US $4.95

CURRENT EVENTS WORLD ATLAS
Chicago : Rand McNally
23 x 32
32pp
Large size col. maps of major countries; political boundaries; text. US $0.69

WORLD ATLAS
Chicago : Rand McNally
24 x 32
30pp
Political maps of continents and major geographical areas. For world events; list of principal cities and population.

READER'S DIGEST GREAT WORLD ATLAS
New York : Reader's Digest Assoc, 1974
28 x 38
179pp
World map section, countries, relief showing landscape picture of the Earth, pop. details, climate, vegetation, natural features.

USSR

ATLAS MIRA
Ed A N Baranov
Moskva : GUGK, 1967
33 x 50
250pp
330 physical maps, contoured and layered; large scale regional maps and town plans; names in Lat. script, text and legend in Eng. Separate gazetteer vol. Russian edition also available.

Yugoslavia

ATLAS SVIJETA
Ed P Mardesić and O Oppitz
4th edition
Zagreb : Jugoslavenski Leksikografski Zavod, 1969
21 x 30
170pp
Contains mainly physical maps with index of 60,000 names and textual information.

ATLASES
W2 WORLD : SCHOOL

Arranged by country of publication

Argentina

COLORATLAS MUNDI
Buenos Aires : Ed Kapelusz, 1971
23 x 32
150pp app
School atlas with political, physical maps, them. information. Index. 30pp Spanish text.
US $5.90

Australia

ROBINSON'S PRIMARY WORLD ATLAS
Brisbane : Jacaranda Press
Physical world maps
A $1.15

Belgium

ALGEMENE ATLAS
Namur : Wesmael Charlier, 1976
32pp
General world atlas in Flemish containing 220 coloured maps. B.Fr 465

VEREENVOUDIGDE ATLAS
M De Roeck and J Tilmont
Namur : Wesmael Charlier, 1972
Flemish simplified world atlas containing 100 coloured maps. B.Fr 126

Brazil

NOVO ATLAS DE GEOGRÁFIA
J Monteiro and F D'Oliveira
Rio de Janeiro : Livraria·Francisco Alves, SA
World atlas for schools in Portuguese.
Cr $20.00

Czechoslovakia

ŠKOLNÍ ZEMĚPISNÝ ATLAS SVĚTA
Praha : Kart, 1967
21 x 29
School world atlas containing physical maps, and also climatic, economic, sociological maps. 28pp index.
Kcs 7.50

ATLAS SVĚTA
Praha : Kart, 1972
School atlas, also for reference purposes. 94pp continental and country maps, with topog. supplement and map of Czechoslovakia at 1:1,500,000. Index of 12,500 names. Kcs 75

Denmark

ATLAS UDEN NAVNE
Ed W F Hellner
20th edition
København : Gyldendal, 1963
28pp
School world atlas, 24 pages of maps.
D.Kr 12.00

ATLAS FOR FOLKESKOLEN
Ed W F Hellner and P Juel Jensen
33rd edition
København : Gyldendal, 1975
40pp
Primary school atlas, containing 34pp maps.
D.Kr 21.00

ATLAS 2
Ed W F Hellner
5th edition
København : Gyldendal, 1972
65pp
Atlas for 8th, 10th classes. 36pp maps.
D.Kr 33.50

ATLAS 1
3rd edition
København : Gyldendal, 1975
75pp
Primary school atlas, with 48pp maps.
D.Kr 26.00

GYLDENDALS RELIEFATLAS
Ed Poul Homelund and Ib Kejlbo
2nd edition
København : Gyldendal, 1969
126pp
School relief atlas with 70pp maps.
D.Kr 121.00

Finland

JOKA KODIN MAAILMANKARTASTO
Helsinki : Wsoy
180pp
Elementary school atlas, with 89pp maps (political), index of 20,000 names.
FMK 39

KOULON OMATOIMIKARTAT 1 & 2
by Eino Tahvonen and Tahvo Kontuniemi
Helsinki : WSOY
In 2 vols.
2 colour base maps for schools.
Vol I Europpa, 1970, 64 maps
FMK 2.25
Vol II Kaukomaat (other countries) 1971, 64 maps FMK 2.45

France

ATLAS GENERAL BORDAS
Ed Serryn, Blasselle and Bonnet
Paris : Bordas, 1970
23 x 32
168pp
206 maps (prepared by Holzel); index of 20,000 names. For students at school and college. F.Fr 34.43
Also published as Atlas Historique et Géographique with 32pp historical maps.
F.Fr 46.52

PETIT ATLAS BORDAS
Rene Cauet, Pierre Serryn and Marc Vincent
Paris : Bordas, 1970
23 x 32
80pp
48pp maps with index of 11,000 names.
F.Fr 16.75

ATLAS HACHETTE
Ed P Gourou
Paris : Hachette, 1971
23 x 23
224pp
School atlas with political and economic maps, text in margins, index of 15,000 names. 330 maps. F.Fr 90.00

NOUVEL ATLAS DU MONDE
Ed P Gourou
Paris : Hachette, 1966
24 x 31
114pp maps; 30pp index; them. and economic maps. F.Fr 28.60

Germany

MEYER'S KINDER-WELTATLAS
2nd edition
Mannheim : Bibliographisches Inst. Meyer Verlag
19 x 22
132pp
Elementary atlas for children. 29 col. pictorial maps with text.
DM 8.90

ATLAS DER ERDKUNDE
15th edition
Gotha : Haack
21 x 30
For secondary schools. 109 maps. 24pp index. DM 8.50

PETER ENTDECKT DIE WELT
3rd edition
Gotha : Haack
29 x 27
32pp
Peter discovers the World. Children's pictorial atlas, showing basic world areas, with topog. information.
M 6.80

UNSER ATLAS
4th edition
21 x 30
36pp
School atlas. M 3.50

ATLAS FÜR DIE 4 UND 5 KLASSE
4th edition
Gotha : Haack, 1971
21 x 29
24pp
School atlas. M 1.85

ATLAS ZUR ERDKUNDE
Ed Prof Dr Lautensach
Heidelberg : Keysersche
22 x 31
192pp
168pp physical maps; 34pp index.
DM 24.80

HARMS WELTATLAS
Ed Drs Eggers and List
München : Paul List Verlag
21 x 30
55pp
101 maps, inc. 73 thematic plates.
DM 8.20

Local editions:
Baden-Wurttemberg 95pp DM 12.40
Nordrhein-Westfalen 105pp DM 12.60
Bayerische Schule 67pp DM 9.20

WENSCHOW WELTATLAS
München : Paul List Verlag
24 x 32
44pp
Physical, economic, historical, geol. maps. 72pp. With 16 illus. DM 5.80

ATLAS UNSERE WELT
Ed Prof Dr Wilhelm Groteluschen Erich Otremba and Willi Walter Puls
Bielefeld : Velhagen and Klasing und Schroedel, 1970/1
23 x 32
184pp
144pp physical and economic maps; index 20,000 names with text and illus. For schools. DM 21.80
Eds. available for each of the W German States, 134pp each DM 15.80
Berlin DM 13.80

DIERKE WELTATLAS
10th edition
Ed D F Mayer
Braunschweig : Westermann, 1975
22 x 30
234pp
200 maps with index of 36,000 names. Physical relief maps, with maps showing climate, vegetation, religion, geology etc.
DM 30.00

WESTERMANN SCHULATLAS; GROSSE AUSGABE
3rd edition
Braunschweig : Westermann, 1972
21 x 30
183pp
152pp maps inc. 290 them. maps; index of 15,000 names. Aerial photographs, diagrams.
DM 20.00

WESTERMANN SCHULATLAS
Braunschweig : Westermann
21 x 30
132pp
96pp physical and thematic maps.
DM 12.00

Great Britain

ATLAS ADVANCED
1st edition
London : Collins - Longmans, 1968
23 x 28
232pp
160pp col. maps - hill shading, layer col; insets urban areas; economic graphs; index 25,000. For sixth forms and university.
£2.50

STUDY ATLAS
19th edition
London : Collins - Longman, 1972
22 x 28
152pp
64pp col. maps; index 6,000; prelims and statistics; 26 col. plates. Revised to include recent political and economic changes.
Limp covers 90p
Also : Visible Regions Atlas — as above, without exercises 60p

COLLINS CLEAR SCHOOL ATLAS
London : Collins
18 x 22
64pp
48pp col. physical, political, climatic, economic maps; also vegetation and pop; 16pp statistics and index.
35p

COLLINS' CHILDREN'S ATLAS
London : Collins
21 x 27
64pp
Coverage of British Isles and World, historical and biblical maps.
55p

ATLAS FOUR
J D Thompson
1st edition
London : Collins - Longman, 1973
22 x 27
180pp
174pp coloured physical maps with regional and thematic plates. £1.95

ATLAS THREE
1st edition
London : Collins - Longman, 1973
128pp
For ages to 16. With special emphasis on Britain - land use, industry, social and historic aspects. £1.50

ATLAS TWO
3rd edition
London : Collins - Longman, 1973
76pp
57 coloured maps including 19 of British Isles, 16 Continent, 14 the World, 8 historical, index. Metric edition.
£1.10

ATLAS ONE
2nd edition
London : Collins - Longman, 1970
32pp
First atlas for children. Metric ed.
50p

DIMENSION 3 ATLAS
1st edition
Edinburgh : Johnston & Bacon, 1969
21 x 27
72pp
Political, physical, economic atlas for middle schools. Includes exploration and space, index, 3pp world statistics.
95p

WORLD STUDY ATLAS
Edinburgh : Johnston and Bacon, 1974
20 x 27
64pp
Geographical atlas with pictorial maps covering geog, history, science etc. Graphic presentation of relief on physical maps. For 10-12 year olds. 95p

BACON'S JUNIOR SCHOOL ATLAS
Edinburgh : Johnston and Bacon
19 x 25
32pp
Simple atlas in colour, covering the world - physical, animals, industry, sea and air routes, also Great Britain and Ireland and the rest of the World.
Limp covers 35p

MY SECOND ATLAS
Edinburgh : Johnston and Bacon
21 x 27
64pp
For middle schools. 17pp for the British Isles. Coloured maps showing visual relief, physical, political, farming, mineral and climate details. Index. 70p

FIRST SCHOOL ATLAS
Edinburgh : Johnston and Bacon
21 x 27
24pp
For primary schools with maps graded from a town to the world, including a page on space and col. plates. 45p

NELSON JUNIOR ATLAS
Ed Prof J Wreford Watson
London : Nelson
28 x 43
50pp
44pp coloured physical and political maps. Index.
Limp 80p

THE OXFORD SCHOOL ATLAS
3rd edition
Oxford : OUP, 1960 rep. with rev. 1976
19 x 25
142pp
112pp coloured maps; many thematic ones; showing metric details. 30pp gazetteer, tables etc. £1.50
General edition as "The Oxford Home Atlas of the World" £2.95

THE SHORTER OXFORD SCHOOL ATLAS
Oxford : OUP, 1962, rep. with rev. 1974
3rd edition
19 x 25
70pp
Revised, metricated ed. 66pp maps in colour with gazetteer. 95p
General edition, available as "The Little Oxford Atlas" £1.50

WHEATON– PERGAMON SECONDARY SCHOOL ATLAS
Ed S Knight
Oxford : Pergamon Press, 1966
21 x 27
110pp app
Metric school atlas; 10pp maps for Great Britain at 1:1,000,000 showing land use and special topics. World physical and human geography. 32pp gazetteer.
Soft 75p
Hard covers 90p

PERGAMON GENERAL WORLD ATLAS
Ed S Knight
Oxford : Pergamon Press, 1966
21 x 27
135pp app
First metric edition school atlas; 95 maps for continental and world areas, 10pp maps for Great Britain at 1:1,000,000 showing land use detail. Physical relief and human geographical maps for the world. 40pp gazetteer. Hard covers 65p

WHEATON ATLAS FOR THE MIDDLE SCHOOL
Ed L R Hawkes
Oxford : Pergamon, 1968
27 x 22
48pp
Emphasis on the British Isles. Maps, photographs, diagrams, natural resources, pop, other thematic aspects. 90p

WHEATON PRIMARY ATLAS
Ed L R Hawkes
Oxford : Pergamon, 1971
29 x 22
32pp
Col. maps covering climate, social aspects of Great Britain; photographs and maps of other continents.
£2.40
Set of Geography Work Cards to accompany the atlas. 40p

MODERN SCHOOL ATLAS
Ed H Fullard
London : Philip, 1975
23 x 29
144pp
Continental maps, with hill shading, principal roads, 100 col. plates, 8pp climatic graphs, index of 18,000 names.
£1.50

NEW SCHOOL ATLAS
London : Philip, 1975
23 x 28
96pp
64pp coloured plates, 100 physical and political maps, climatic graphs, index of 13,000 names. £1.15

ELEMENTARY ATLAS
Ed H Fullard
107th edition
London : Philip, 1973
23 x 28
52pp
90 physical, political maps, climate and vegetation graphs, index. 75p
Also available as the "Secondary School Atlas".

MIDDLE SCHOOL ATLAS
Ed H Fullard
London : Philip, 1976
23 x 28
32pp
Historical and geographical maps of the British Isles (10pp) and World (5pp). Also physical maps of the continents and Introductory section and index.
Limp covers 50p

VENTURE ATLAS
Ed H Fullard
London : Philip, 1974
23 x 28
49pp
Layer col, hill shading on physical maps, some political maps, thematic aspects. 7pp index - gazetteer. 75p

VISUAL ATLAS
London : Philip, 1971
19 x 23
56pp
47 coloured plates with 59 maps, physical world and index. With thematic maps of the British Isles.
50p

FIRST VENTURE ATLAS
London : Philip, 1973
19 x 23
24pp
Coloured contoured maps, with 3 D relief, and coloured photographs.
35p

PRIMARY ATLAS
Ed H Fullard
London : Philip, 1972
23 x 28
18pp
Clear format atlas, relief and land use of the British Isles, world section.
40p

Hungary

MALÝ ŠKOLSKÝ ATLAS
Bratislava : Slovenska Kartografia, 1970
Small school atlas in Slovak and Hung.
16pp maps.

FÖLDRAJZI ATLASZ KÖZÉPISKOLAK SZÁMÁRA
Budapest : Cart
23 x 28
62pp
World atlas for secondary schools in 8 cols.

FÖLDRAJZI ATLASZ AZ ÁLTALÁNOS ISKOLAK SZÁMÁRA
Budapest : Cart, 1971
23 x 28
32pp
World Atlas for primary schools in 8 cols.

Iceland

LANDA-BREFABÓK
Reykjavik : Rikisútgafa Namsbóka (State Educ. Pub. Dept), 1970
18 x 25
56pp
World geographic atlas 41pp physical and thematic maps (inc. 13 of Iceland). Index.

Indonesia

ATLAS UNTUK SEKOLAH LANDJUTEN
Jakarta : Jambatan, 1964
25 x 32
56pp maps – physical and thematic, 9pp index.

ATLAS INDONESIA AND DUNIA
Eds C Latif and M J Ridwan
Jakarta : Pembina, 1974
24 x 32
28pp
School atlas of the world with 14pp section on Indonesia including plans and photographs.

Iran

ATLAS-E-JAHAN DAR ASFE-FAZA
Tehran : Sahab
'Atlas of the World in the Space Age' – School atlas in Persian.

ATLAS-E-DANESHAMUZ
Tehran : Sahab
'Students' atlas in Persian.
Rls 36

ATLAS-E-NOKHOSTIN
Tehran : Sahab
'The First Atlas' School atlas in Persian.
Rls 60

ATLAS-E-NOAMUZ
Tehran ' Sahab
'Beginners' School atlas in Persian.
Rls 30

Ireland

CERTIFICATE ATLAS FOR IRISH SCHOOLS
Dublin : Educational Company of Ireland
110pp maps and diagrams in colour; 8pp for Ireland, covering physical and 16 thematic aspects. £1.65

IRISH SCHOOL AND COLLEGE ATLAS
Dublin : Educational Company of Ireland
32pp coloured maps, showing layers and contours. Climatic maps for each continental area. 82½p

IRISH STUDENTS ATLAS
by E Butler
Dublin : Educational Company of Ireland
22 x 28
66pp app
48pp coloured maps, 16pp text, index and tables. £1.39

A FIRST ATLAS FOR IRISH SCHOOLS
Ed K Hurley
Dublin : The Educational Co of Ireland, 1975
20 x 25
World atlas with 6pp section on plans and maps with photographs. Map of Ireland in Irish. 66p

A SECOND ATLAS FOR IRISH SCHOOLS
Ed P O Duinin
Dublin : The Education Co of Ireland, 1975
20 x 25
World atlas with special emphasis on Ireland. 95p

IRISH PRIMARY SCHOOL ATLAS
Dublin : Educational Company of Ireland
20pp maps in colour 51½p

Italy

ATLANTE GEOGRAFICO METODICO
Ed G Motta and V Bonapace
Novara : Ag
17 x 34
160pp
Col. political and physical, 32pp index. Shows main road and rail communications, thematic maps cover land use, industry, mineral resources; and economic statistics.
L 4,200

GEOATLANTE
V Bonapace
Novara : Ag
21 x 30
School atlas showing geographical land detail in 96 coloured maps. With index of 24,000 names.
L 2,000

Japan

HYOJUN KOTO CHIZU
- Standard Atlas for High School Students
2nd edition
Tokyo : Teikoku - Shoin, 1976
18 x 26
146pp
World atlas in Japanese
Paper Y 920

SHINSYO KOTO CHIZU
- New detailed Atlas for High School Students
Tokyo : Teikoku - Shoin, 1976
18 x 26
150pp
World atlas in Japanese
Paper Y 920

CHU GAKKO SHAKAIKA CHIZU
- Social Study Atlas for Middle School Pupils
Tokyo : Teikoku - Shoin, 1976
18 x 26
142pp
World atlas in Japanese.
Paper Y 750

SHO GAKKO SHAKAIKA CHIZUCHO
- Social Study Atlas for Primary School Pupils.
2nd edition
Tokyo : Teikoku - Shoin, 1976
18 x 26
66pp
World atlas in Japanese
Paper Y 520

Norway

CAPPELENS NORGES ATLAS FOR SKOLEN
Oslo : Cappelen, 1972
21 x 30
24pp maps, many thematic; 13pp index.

Poland

ATLAS GEOGRAFICZNY V-VIII kl
Warszawa : PPWK, 1972
22 x 30
Atlas for 5th - 8th forms. Physical, political and economic maps for the continents; mineral, climatic and other them. maps for Poland. Zl 20

ATLAS GEOGRAFICZNY LICEALNY
10th edition
Warszawa : PPWK, 1972/3
22 x 33
120pp maps, index 15,000 names. Contains a physical map of Poland at 1:25,000,000, 50 economic and other thematic maps.
Zl 80
Plastic edition Zl 110

Spain

ATLAS BASICO UNIVERSAL
Ed U Bonapace
Barcelona : Editorial Teide, 1972
22 x 31
xvi 64pp
General school atlas, covering general geog, astronomy, geol, climate, 24 physical-political maps, 8 maps for Spain, 26 for Europe and other Continents
S.Ptas 150

ATLAS GENERAL BASICO AGUILAR
32nd edition
Madrid : Aguilar, 1973
25 x 35
118pp
97pp mainly physical maps, with 15pp index. Spiral bound. S.Ptas 180

ATLAS BASICO AGUILAR
Madrid : Aguilar, 1975
23 x 31
64pp
General atlas including thematic plates and 5,000 name index. S.Ptas 150

Sweden

SKOLANS VÄRLDATLAS
Stockholm : Kartographie Generalstabens, 1967
21 x 30
64pp maps; 32pp index, in Scandinavian. Other Scandinavian editions available.

Switzerland

SCHWEIZERISCHER MITTELSCHUL-ATLAS
by Prof Dr E Imhof
Zürich : Lehrmittelverlag des Kanton Zürich
156pp
Them, relief and detail maps of the World and Switzerland; no index; also Fr. and It. eds. S.Fr 24.00

USA

STUDENT QUICK REFERENCE ATLAS OF THE WORLD
Indianapolis : Cram
22 x 30
36pp
School reference atlas.
US $1.00

HEADLINE WORLD ATLAS
Maplewood, NJ : Hammond, 1971
21 x 28
52pp
60 political topog. economic maps showing all countries and world divisions; gazetteer, index. US $1.00

NEW COSMOPOLITAN SCHOOL ATLAS
Chicago : Rand McNally
29 x 36
420pp
200pp col. maps - political, physical, then, historical, index 82,000 names.
US $16.95

REGIONAL ATLAS
(abridged ed 'Goode's World Atlas)
12th edition
Chicago : Rand McNally
65pp
50pp col. maps; index, tables listing world pop. and statistics. US $2.75

CLASSROOM ATLAS
6th edition
Chicago : Rand McNally
84pp
Col. maps, political information.
US $1.40

A WORLD OF MAPS
1st edition
Chicago : Rand McNally
48pp
New col. maps. Teachers' edition also available. US $2.00

USSR

UCHENYI ATLAS MIRA
Moskva : GUGK, 1968
24 x 34
180pp
World Educational Atlas, 147pp maps (inc. USSR). 29pp index.

GEOGRAFICHESKIY ATLAS MATERIALOV DLYA 6 GO KLASSA
Moskva : GUGK, 1970
36pp
Atlas of the continents for the 6th class.

GEOGRAFICHESKIY ATLAS DLYA UCHITELEY SREDNEY SHKOLY
Moskva : GUGK, 1968
26 x 38
151pp maps (inc. 60 for USSR) – physical and them. 34pp index.

MALYY ATLAS MIRA
Ed V N Salmanova and L N Kolosova
Moskva : GUGK, 1971
11 x 19
Little World Atlas. Small political col. atlas in pocket format.

GEOGRAFICHESKIY ATLAS CHASTEY SVETA I ZARUBEZHNYKH GOSUDARSTV DLR 6 GO – 7 GO KLASSOV
Moskva : GUGK
22 x 28
48pp
Geographical atlas of the world and universe for 6th - 7th years.

Yugoslavia

ATLAS SVETA
Beograd : Geokarta
High School atlas with 104 maps. In Cyrillic and Latin lettering.
Dn 45

ATLAS SVETA
Beograd : Geokarta
Elementary school atlas with 46 maps. In Cyrillic and Latin lettering.
Dn 75.00

ATLASES
W3 WORLD : LOCAL EDITIONS

Arranged by continents

Africa

MODERN STUDENTS ATLAS FOR AFRICA
Ed H Fullard
London : Philip, 1972
23 x 28
World atlas with map supplement for Africa. Available in Eng. or Afrikaans eds.

MODERN COLLEGE ATLAS FOR AFRICA
Ed H Fullard
10th edition
London : Philip, 1974
23 x 29
168pp
A world atlas for students of Africa with 34pp African supplement of thematic maps and physical atlas of the world. Also available in Afrikaans. 90p

SCHOOL ATLAS FOR EAST AFRICA
Ed H Fullard
London : Philip, 1974
23 x 28
32pp 25p

EAST AFRICAN MODERN SCHOOL ATLAS
Ed H Fullard
London : Philip
23 x 28
Standard modern school atlas with E African map supplement.
90p

THE OXFORD ATLAS FOR EAST AFRICA
Oxford : OUP, 1966, rep. with rev. 1971
19 x 26
84pp 67pp maps – 13 for East Africa, 36 continental topographic maps, 15 general world maps. 14pp index, gazetteers for world and Africa. £1.20

NEW SCHOOL ATLAS FOR WEST AFRICA
Ed H Fullard
London : Philip
23 x 28 75p

LARGE-PRINT ATLAS FOR SOUTHERN AFRICA
Ed H Fullard
London : Philip
23 x 28
48pp maps. 58p

PHILIP'S STUDENTS' ATLAS FOR SOUTHERN AFRICA
Ed H Fullard
London : Philip
23 x 28 80p

PHILIP'S COLLEGE ATLAS FOR SOUTHERN AFRICA
Ed H Fullard
London : Philip
23 x 28
116 coloured plates, with 16 pages of special maps of Southern Africa and index.
90p

JUTA'S SPRINGBOK LARGE PRINT ATLAS FOR SOUTHERN AFRICA
Ed H Fullard
London : Philip
Available in English and Afrikaans editions.

THE FIRST KENYA ATLAS
Ed H Fullard
London : Philip
World atlas with map supplement for Kenya and E Africa.

THE OXFORD ATLAS FOR NIGERIA
Oxford : OUP, 1968, rep. with rev. 1975
26 x 19
88pp
72pp maps, 16pp index, gazetteer. Covers Nigeria, Africa and the world.
£1.50

ATLAS FOR WEST CAMEROON
1st edition
London : Collins – Longman, 1971
21 x 26
33pp
10pp maps West Cameroon; world political, physical, thematic maps.
45p

THE NEW JUNIOR ATLAS FOR SOUTH AFRICA
Salisbury : M O Collins (Pyt) Ltd
22 x 30
A 32pp world atlas for lower Secondary Schools US $2.40

Americas

THE HOLT WORLD ATLAS
Ed Jean de Varennes and Jean Lavallee
Toronto : Holt-Blond, 1970
26 x 34
158pp
Thematic and physical maps; 36pp devoted to Canada. Resources section with distribution maps and statistical tables, 11pp index. School atlas. Available in Fr. ed "Atlas General Holt".

LARROUSSE ATLAS CANADIEN
Ed B Brouillette
Paris : Larrousse, 1971
23 x 28
160pp
Physical and them. maps, 40pp for Canada.

NELSON'S WORLD ATLAS
Ed J Wreford Watson
Ontario : Nelson, 1974
World atlas with Canadian supplement.
C $4.65

THE CANADIAN OXFORD ATLAS OF THE WORLD
2nd edition
Oxford : OUP, 1957
26 x 38
246pp
132pp detailed maps for Canada; relief, land use, topog/admin. maps for the continents. Appendix and gazetteer.
£6.30

THE CANADIAN OXFORD SCHOOL ATLAS
3rd edition
Toronto : OUP, 1972
20 x 23
190pp
School atlas of the world with Canadian supplement including 128pp of coloured maps.

PHILIP'S SENIOR ATLAS FOR CANADA
Ed H Fullard
London : Philip
23 x 28
96 pages including 56 pages of maps.
90p

COLLINS CARIBBEAN SCHOOL ATLAS
London : Collins
18 x 22
56pp
40pp col. maps, inc. 13 of Caribbean; 16pp index. 25p

ATLAS FOR JAMAICA AND THE WESTERN CARIBBEAN
1st edition
London : Collins - Longman, 1971
21 x 26
57pp
16pp Caribbean region maps; 23pp world physical, political, them. maps; index.
50p

ATLAS FOR THE EASTERN CARIBBEAN
1st edition
London : Collins - Longman, 1971
21 x 26
57pp
World atlas; 16pp maps covering Caribbean region; 23pp maps, physical, political, thematic; index. 50p

CARIBBEAN PRIMARY ATLAS
Ed H Fullard
London : Philip
23 x 28
World atlas with map supplement for Caribbean.

VISUAL ATLAS FOR THE WEST INDIES
Ed H Fullard
London : Philip
19 x 23 40p

CARIBBEAN MODERN SCHOOL ATLAS
Ed H Fullard
London : Philip
23 x 28 90p

ATLAS GEOGRAFICO ESCOLAR
6th edition
Rio de Janeiro : Fundacao Nacional de Material Escolar, 1970
61pp
Covers Brazil in economic, physical, thematic maps, world in political maps. School atlas.

ATLAS BACHILLERATO UNIVERSAL Y DE COLOMBIA
Ed D Antonio Lopez
Madrid : Aguilar, S A 1971
25 x 35
120pp
World atlas, with section on Colombia, 8pp thematic maps.

Asia

CEYLON ATLAS
Ed H Fullard
London : Philip
World atlas with map supplement for Ceylon; available in Sinhalese and Tamil editions.

MODERN SCHOOL ATLAS - HONG KONG EDITION
Ed H Fullard
London : Philip
23 x 28
Includes supplement of Hong Kong maps.

SECONDARY ATLAS FOR MALAYSIA AND SINGAPORE
Ed J A Johnson
Brisbane : Jacaranda, 1971
22 x 28
106pp
Atlas for secondary schools, 30pp maps for S E Asia; index. Bahasa-Malaysian edition also available — 'Atlas Sekdan Menegah Malaysia'.

SENIOR ATLAS FOR MALAYSIA AND SIGNAPORE
Ed H Fullard
London : Philip
World atlas with map supplement for Malaysia.

MALAYSIAN MODERN SCHOOL ATLAS
Ed H Fullard
London : Philip
23 x 28
Includes supplement of maps of Malaysia.

THE OXFORD SCHOOL ATLAS FOR PAKISTAN
Oxford : OUP, 1966
19 x 25
60pp
50pp maps; 8pp gazetteer. £1.25

Australia and New Zealand

ROBINSON'S WORLD ATLAS
Brisbane : Jacaranda Press
For home or secondary school use. Emphasis on Australia.
A $2.95

JACARANDA ATLAS
Ed V G Honour
Brisbane : Jacaranda, 1969
23 x 28
152pp
124 plates, physical and thematic maps. 20pp index. Australian bias. School atlas.
A $3.20

THE JACARANDA JUNIOR WORLD ATLAS
Brisbane : Jacaranda
Primary atlas for schools, with eds. for:
Queensland
New South Wales
Victoria
Western Australia
South Australia
Tasmania
Each A $1.50

NEW AUSTRALIAN ATLAS
Ed H Fullard
London : Philip
World atlas with map supplement for Australia.

MODERN COMMONWEALTH ATLAS
Ed H Fullard
London : Philip
World atlas with map supplement for Commonwealth and Australia.

PHILIP'S PRIMARY ATLAS FOR AUSTRALIAN SCHOOLS
Ed H Fullard
London : Philip
23 x 28
Primary world atlas with map supplement for Australia.

OXFORD SOCIAL STUDIES ATLAS FOR NEW ZEALAND
Oxford : OUP, 1963
19 x 25
36pp
Physical world atlas with 6pp N.Z. supplement. Gazetteer. 33p

Europe

ÖSTERREICHER SCHULATLAS
Wien : F - B, 1971
23 x 32
Atlas for high schools. 90pp physical and thematic maps (25pp for Austria), 15 aerial photographs. 16pp supplement on Austrian economy.

ATLAS BELGIE EN DEN WERELD
J van den Branden and M Nouboers
Amsterdam : Meulenhof, 1972
23 x 32
150pp app
Middle school atlas; 114pp maps, mainly physical with emphasis on Belgium, some thematic ones. 27pp index.

KANSAKOULON KARTASTO
Arvi Ulvinen, et al
Helsinki : Wsoy, 1969
38pp
Primary school atlas, covering the Northern countries. FMK 4.70

HARMS ATLAS DEUTSCHLAND UND DIE WELT
Ed Drs Eggers and List
München : List, 1969
24 x 32
125pp
164 maps; 100 graphs and thematic diagrams; index of 12,000 names. Available for different regions of Germany, also.
DM 13.40

HARMS WELTATLAS BADEN-WURTTEMBERG
München : List
93pp
128 maps, plans and pictures.
DM 10.80

HARMS WELTATLAS FÜR DIE BAYERISCHE SCHULE
München : List
21 x 29
67pp
127 maps, 95 thematic plates.
DM 7.60

COLLINS BRITISH ISLES AND WORLD ATLAS
London : Collins
18 x 22
28pp
24pp col. maps, emphasis on British Isles; 4pp text. 15p

FIRST VENTURE ATLAS : BRITISH ISLES EDITION
London : Philip
19 x 23
32pp
Coloured contoured maps, 3-D relief, with 8pp regional British maps.
45p

WORLD ATLAS FOR IRELAND
Ed H Fullard
London : Philip
World atlas with supplement of maps covering Ireland.

IL NUOVO ATLANTE DELLA SCUOLA MEDIA
Ed U Bonapace
Novara : Ag
21 x 30
Middle school atlas with emphasis on Italy: also covering Europe and the rest of the World, in 64 coloured maps. With astronomical section and index of 17,000 names.
L 1,600

NEDERLAND EN DE WERELD
3rd edition
Amsterdam : Meulenhoff, 1967
132pp
School atlas comprising 195 maps of the world including 68 thematic maps of the Netherlands. Index. Text in Dutch.

DE GROTE BOSATLAS
by Prof Dr F J Ormeling
48th edition
Groningen : Wolters - Noordhoff
1976
24 x 37
164pp maps. School world atlas for the Netherlands. Index of 32pp.
Fl. 46.00

DE KLEINEBOSATLAS
Ed Prof Dr F J Ormeling
Groningen : Wolters-Noordhoff, 1974
23 x 30
School world atlas for the Netherlands. 64pp col maps. 16pp index.
Fl. 18.75

DE BOS-BASISATLAS
Groningen : Wolters-Noordhoff, 1976
23 x 30
59pp
Primary-school atlas of the world for the Netherlands. 5pp index.
Fl. 16.75

ATLAS METÓDICO DE GEOGRAFIA UNIVERSAL Y DE ESPAÑA
Barcelona : Editorial Teide
18 x 25
16pp
Maps and text covering Spain, western Europe and Spanish America. For school children aged 11-12.
S.Ptas 16

ATLAS BACHILLERATO UNIVERSAL Y DE ESPAÑA
28th edition
Madrid : Aguilar, 1970
25 x 35
118pp
World geog. section: regional geog. section; Spanish section including physical, political and thematic maps. Indexed.
S.Ptas 170

ATLAS MODERNO UNIVERSAL
Maplewood, NJ : Hammond
21 x 28
47pp
Sp. lang. atlas, covering the world; gazetteer, index of major cities.
Paper US $1.25

ATLASES
D POLITICAL AND ADMINISTRATIVE

OBSERVER ATLAS OF WORLD AFFAIRS: A GUIDE TO MAJOR TENSIONS AND CONFLICTS
Ed A Wilson
London : Mitchell Beazley/George Philip, 1971
20 x 28
112pp
20 political and physical coloured maps, numerous diagrams, graphs etc.
£2.50

EN DELAD VÄRLD
Stockholm : GLA, 1971
'A Divided World' — atlas covering the period after 1945 — world political atlas.
S.Kr. 24.50

KÉPES POLITIKAI ÉS GAZDASÁGI VILÁGATLASZ
Ed Prof Dr S Rado
Budapest : Cart, 1971
25 x 34
340pp
Col. political and economic, and other thematic maps. Statistics, text. Index 101pp.

ATLASES
E2 PHYSICAL - LAND FEATURES

MEYERS GROSSER PHYSISCHER WELTATLAS
Mannheim : Bibliog. Inst. Meyer
In 8 vols
21 x 30
International high school atlas covering various aspects of physical geog. each in a separate vol, with legends in Ger, Eng, Fr, Sp and Rus.
Vols available :
Vol 1 Atlas zur Bodenkunde. Ed Prof Dr R Ganssen. Covers soil, climate. DM 48.00
Vol 2 Atlas zur Geologie — Ed Prof Dr E Bederke. Covers geol. earthquakes, etc. DM 48.00
Vol 3 Atlas zur Ozeanographie. Ed Prof Dr G Dietrich. Covers physical, chemical oceanography by indiv. oceans. DM 68.00
Vol 4 Atlas zur Physischen Geographie (Orographie). Ed Dr K Wagner, 1971. Contour maps of the world. DM 68.00
Volumes covering Geomorphology, Climatology, Biogeography and the Heavens in preparation.

ATLAS OF WORLD PHYSICAL FEATURES
R E Snead
London : Wiley, 1972
120pp
New atlas showing world landforms (erosion and weathering) in 103 maps. Text covers distribution of Earth features. University level. £1.75 app

THE SOUTHERN HEMISPHERE GLACIER ATLAS
John H Mercer
Natick, Mass : US Army Earth Sciences Laboratory, 1967
327pp
15pp maps covering 6 regions : Andes, New Guinea, E Africa Sub-Antarctic Is, New Zealand, Antarctica. Text is description and bibliog. of mt. glacier areas.

ATLASES
F GEOLOGY

MEYERS GROSSER PHYSISCHER WELTATLAS
Bibliog. Inst. Meyer Verlag
see WORLD 100 E2.

ATLASES
G EARTH RESOURCES

MEYERS GROSSER PHYSISCHER WELTATLAS
Bibliog. Inst. Meyer Verlag
see WORLD 100 E2

ATLASES
H BIOGEOGRAPHY

WELTFORSTATLAS
Ed Prof Dr Claus Wiebeck
Starnberg : Fritz Haller, 1951-1970
Hamburg : Paul Parey, 1971+
75 x 60 each
In 67 maps. Series of maps and cartograms covering forest distribution, vegetation types, silviculture, timber trade and production. Trade statistics diagrams. Maps in Ger, Eng, Fr, Sp. Some maps now out of print, being reprinted.

Each sheet separately	DM 33.00
Each sheet on subscription	DM 30.00
Binder for complete work	DM 58.00
Complete work including 67 maps and binder	DM 2,068.00

ATLAS OF WILDLIFE
Jacqueline Wayman
London : Heinemann, 1972
22 x 31
128pp
Shows wildlife distribution by symbols and silhouette in 32 relief maps. In 9 sections, covering major world areas. With full text and illustrations. £2.50

THE MITCHELL BEAZLEY ATLAS OF WILDLIFE
London : Mitchell Beazley, 1974
27 x 37
208pp
Describing environment and habitats of wildlife with over 1500 original paintings, photographs, sketches, maps and diagrams.
£9.50

ATLAS OF ANIMAL MIGRATION
Ed Cathy Jarman
London : Heinemann
22 x 31
128pp
Describes migrations of birds, mammals, fishes, reptiles, amphibians and insects with maps, col. illustrations and text.
£2.50

THE WORLD ATLAS OF BIRDS
Consultant editor : Sir Peter Scott
London : Mitchell Beazley, 1974
23 x 29
272pp
Containing 500 full-colour bird paintings with detailed studies of each species with information on behaviour, evolution, migration and the mechanics of flight. There is also a 40pp classification section, 130 coloured maps and nearly 300 line drawings. £10.95

ATLASES
J CLIMATE

WORLD SURVEY OF CLIMATOLOGY
In 15 vols
Ed H E Landsberg
Amsterdam : Elsevier
Series of handbooks describing world climatology in maps, text and diagrams.
Vols in series :

1 General Climatology 1 ed H Flohn
2* General Climatology 2 ed H Flohn
3 General Climatology 3 ed H Flohn
4* Climate of the Free Atmosphere, ed D F Rex
5* Climates of Northern and Western Europe, ed C C Wallen
6 Climates of Central and Southern Europe, ed C C Wallen
7 Climates of the Soviet Union ed P E Lydolph
8 Climates of Northern and Eastern Asia, ed H Arakawa
9* Climates of Southern and Western Asia, ed H Arakawa
10* Climates of Africa, ed J F Griffiths
11 Climates of North America ed R A Bryson
12 Climates of Central and South America, ed W Schwerdtfeger
13* Climates of Australia and New Zealand, ed J Gentilli
14* Climates of the Polar Regions ed S Orvig
15 Climates of the Oceans, ed H Thomsen

* Vols. currently published.

KLIMADIAGRAMM WELTATLAS
In 3 sections
by Drs H Walter and H Leith
Jena : Gustav Fischer
42 x 60
Including 9000 climate graphs of stations throughout the World with other maps and sketches. Published in 3 sections :

1 Ger. text with abstracts in Eng, Fr, Rus, Sp. 1960. 11 maps, 65 supplementary. Covers : Spanish Peninsula, West Europe, Near East, India, Africa, South America, Australia. M 120.00
2 1964. 12 maps; 91 supplementary. Covers Central Europe, Western Europe (British Isles), Eastern Europe, South East Asia, New Zealand M 65.00
3 1967, 10 maps, 48 supplementary; 8pp test. Far East, Ocean Islands, N Polar Regions, North & Central America M 65.00

PHYSICAL ATLAS OF METEOROLOGY
by Drs J G Bartholomew and A J Herbertson
Edinburgh : Bart, 1899
30 x 46
400 col. maps; 34 double plates; 70pp text. £15.00

WORLD – CLIMATIC ATLAS
by H E Landsberg
Heidelberg : Akademie der Wissenschaften
Berlin : Springer Verlag
20 x 30
Folder containing 28 pages of text in Ger. and Eng, and 5 col. climatic maps in a pocket.

700 MB ATLAS FOR THE NORTHERN HEMISPHERE
E W Wahl and J F Lahey
Madison : Univ. Wisconsin Press, 1969
22 x 28
Shows in 147pp coloured maps, 5-day mean heights, standard deviations and changes for the 700 mb pressure surface. US $5.00

ATLASES
K HUMAN GEOGRAPHY

ATLAS OF ANTHROPOLOGY
by Robert F Spencer and Eldon Johnson
Iowa : Wm Brown and Co, 1969
2nd edition
61pp
Culture, language, tribal groups, 61pp text. Spiral bound. US $2.75

ATLAS HIERARCHICUS
by H Emmerich
Mödling : St Gabriel Verlag, 1976
30 x 44
Atlas of the catholic church, containing 54pp maps, 30 in col. showing world catholic church provinces, diocese, seminaries, high schools, churches etc. Text in 5 langs. and statistical tables of each district. A.Sch. 975.00

ATLAS OF MAN AND RELIGION
Ed Rev G K Hawes and Stanley Knight
Oxford : Religious Educ. Press, 1970
22 x 28
127pp
50 maps showing man in religious and social context. In 5 sections : The World We Live In; The Impact of Christianity on Western Civilisation; the Biblical Background of Christianity; the United Nations and its Agencies; the World Council of Churches. For schools. No index. 75p

ATLAS OF DISEASES
New York : AGS
96 x 63
Showing relation between labour and health, devt. of backward areas, distribution of pathological conditions.

1 World Distribution of Poliomyelitis, 1900–1950
2 World Distribution of Cholera, 1816–1950
3 World Distribution of Malaria Vectors
4 World Distribution of Helminthiases
5 World Distribution of Dengue and Yellow Fever
6 World Distribution of Plague, 1900–1952
7 World distribution of Leprosy, 1952
8 Study in Human Starvation. 1 Sources of Selected Foods
9 Out of print
10 World Distribution of Rickettsial Diseases. 1 Louse-borne and Flea-borne Typhus
11 World Distribution of Rickettsial Diseases. 2 Tick-borne and Mite-borne forms
12 World Distribution of Rickettsial Diseases. 3 Tick and Mite Vectors
13 Explored areas of Arthropod-borne Viral Infections (Yellow Fever and Dengue excepted)
14 World Distribution of Leishmaniase
15 World Distribution of Spirochetal Diseases 1 Yaws, Pinta, Bejal
16 World Distribution of Spirochetal Diseases. 2 Relapsing Fevers
17 World Distribution of Spirochetal Diseases. 3 Leptospiroses

Each plate US $2.00

ATLASES
L ECONOMIC

GRANDE ATLANTE GEOGRAFICO ECONOMICO
by L Visintin and V Bonapace
Novara : Ag, 1966
27 x 40
247 plates of maps, 104pp index. Covering geol; industry etc, with thematic maps of all kinds. L 24,000

WELTWIRTSCHAFTSATLAS
München : JRO
In 2 vols.
29 x 30
Loose leaf atlas in binder (sheet size 24 x 30) in 174 parts covering world, continents, individual countries; small scale maps of physical and economic features, population, statistical maps, diagrams and tables. Monthly updating supplements.

Inc. annual supp.	DM 398.00
Other supp.	DM 58.00
Out of date pages	DM 30.00

DIE STAATEN DER ERDE UND IHRE WIRTSCHAFT
Gotha : Haack, 1969/70, 9th ed.
25 x 34
192pp
100pp maps; 96pp text, 1p index.
Physical-political atlas, showing economy. M 24.00

OXFORD ECONOMIC ATLAS OF THE WORLD
4th edition
Oxford : OUP, 1972
26 x 38
242pp
77pp coloured economic and thematic maps, including minerals, trade and demography with statistical supplement, gazetteer of centres of economic activity.

Boards	£9.75
Paper	£4.75

WIRTSCHAFTSGEOGRAPHISCHER WELTATLAS
Prof Dr H Boesch
2nd edition
München : List
90pp
21 col. maps; 36 diagrams; 80 col. illus.
Covering economic geog. of the world.
DM 28.00

ATLAS NATURBILD UND WIRTSCHAFT
Ed Prof Dr G Grosjean
see WORLD 100 H.

ATLAS OF ECONOMIC DEVELOPMENT
Ed Norton Ginsberg
Chicago : UP, 1961
36 x 24
119pp
Shows details of world economy; each map with page of text covering economic potential, resources, international relationships, etc. US $9.50

ATLANTE DELLA PRODUZIONE E DEI COMMERCI
U Bonapace and G Motta
Novara : Ag
21 x 30
Atlas illustrating world commerce with directory, trade routes, exploitation of land and major products. Analyses state economies by country or groups of countries. L 2,700

ATLAS UNIVERSAL GEO-ECONÓMICO
Barcelona : Editorial Teide, 1972
22 x 31
xvi, 128pp
School atlas showing economic geog.
58 physical-political maps, 70 of economic details. Indexed. Ptas 350

KULTUR-GEOGRAFISK ATLAS
In 2 vols.
J Humlum
København : Gyldendal, 1975
Atlas of economic geog. in 2 vols. for schools.
Vol 1 Atlas, 7th ed, 1975, 160pp, 136pp maps D.Kr 138.00
Vol 2 Text, 7th ed, 1972, 792pp. D.Kr 246.00

ATLANTE GENERALE ILLUSTRATO ZANICHELLI
Ed D Insolera and G Musiani Zaniboni
Bologna : Zanichelli, 1975
25 x 35
186pp
Physical, political atlas with 14pp Italian section, thematic maps, 128 coloured illustrations.

WORLD ATLAS OF SHIPPING – SEA AND SHIPPING SECTION Ed W D Edwart
WORLD ATLAS Ed H Fullard
1st edition
London : Philip, 1972
23 x 29
276pp
64pp illustrated introduction to the sea and shipping followed by 128 page political atlas.
£6.95

LLOYDS MARITIME ATLAS
London : Lloyds, 1975
19 x 25
70pp
116pp maps, 33pp index. Covers shipping centres and ports of the world.
£4.50

THE TRAVELLER'S WORLD REFERENCE ATLAS –
A businessman's guide to 129 countries
Compiled by Dan Hillman
1st edition
Edinburgh : Johnston & Bacon, 1973
21 x 27
38pp of facts for each country including area, principal cities, ports, climate, economy, travel information and requirements, social customs and other essential information. 8pp of basic political maps.
£1.50

WORLD ATLAS OF AGRICULTURE
Pre. under aegis of Int. Assoc. of Agric. Economists
In 4 vols
Novara : Ag
34 x 48
246pp
Consists of 62 col. maps showing land use and ag. economy. Maps issued on publication of Monograph which describes in detail the agriculture of each region.
Monographs :
1 Europe, USSR, Asia Minor, 1969
2 South and East Asia, Oceania, 1973
3 Americas, 1970
4 Africa, 1976

ATLAS DES CULTURES VIVRIERES : ATLAS OF FOOD CROPS
Jacques Bertin et al
Paris : Centre de Recherches Historiques, 1971
32 x 42
41pp text
18 double maps (61 x 40) at 1:55,000,000 covering the history of crop production in the world. Text in English and French.

WORLD ATLAS OF WINE
Hugh Johnson
London : Mitchell Beazley/Philip
1971
23 x 29
272pp
Over 150 maps and 300 colour plates, covering wine growing districts, vintages, individual vineyards, history etc.
In slip case. £8.50

FILATELISTICKÝ ATLAS ZNAMKOVÝCH ZEMÍ
Praha : Kart, 1972
Philatelic atlas of the Stamp Countries.
Kcs 25

ATLASES
M HISTORICAL

Arranged under country of publication

Belgium

ATLAS D'HISTOIRE UNIVERSELLE
Revised by F Hayt
Namur : Ad Wesmael Charlier
20 x 26
138 pages comprising 113 coloured maps and an index.
Paper covers B.Fr 220
Bound boards B.Fr 235

Czechoslovakia

ŠKOLSKÝ ATLAS SVĚTOVÝCH DĚJIN
6th edition
Praha : Kart, 1972
95pp
World history school atlas, 52pp maps, showing world history from ancient times to 1965. With instruction section for teachers. 25pp index. 7th edition.
Kcs 34

Denmark

GYLDENDALS HISTORISKE ATLAS
Ed Johan S Rosing
2nd edition
København : Gyldendal, 1973
78pp
School historical atlas, with 56pp maps.
D.Kr 71.00

HISTORISK ATLAS
København : Politiken
108 coloured maps. D.Kr 30.50

GYLDENDALS BIBEL ATLAS
Ed K & G Tolderlund-Hansen and H Fullard
København : Gyldendal, 1972
27pp including 16pp of maps
Danish edition of Philips' New Scripture Atlas. D.Kr 17.75

France

ATLAS HISTORIQUE
Pierre Serryn and Rene Blasselle
Paris : Bordas, 1970
23 x 32
80pp
32pp historical maps, 48pp text and index.
Covers the period 2000 BC – end of World War 2. F.Fr 25.12

Germany

GROSSER HISTORISCHE WELTATLAS
In 3 vols.
München : Bayerischer Schulbuch-Verlag
24 x 34
3 vols, covering from earliest to modern times. Small scale maps with some town plans and transparent overlays. Text vols. in preparation.
Part I Vorgeschichte und Altertum 56pp col. maps, 19pp index. 5th ed, 1972 DM 35.00; Text DM 24.80
Part II Mittelalter 77pp maps, 57pp index, 1970 DM 35.00
Part III Neuzeit 97pp maps, 32pp index, 1970 DM 35.00

BSV GESCHICHTSATLAS
Ed W Böhm, E Deuerlein
1st edition
Munchen : Bayerischer Schulbuch-Verlag, 1974
24 x 34
49pp of maps including 152 col. maps.
Historical atlas of the world combining coloured maps. 175 photo's and descriptive text.
DM 11.80

HISTORISCHER WELTATLAS
Ed F W Putzger
Bielefeld : Cornelsen – Velhagen and Klasing
160pp
194 historical maps, 48pp index.

ORBIS TERRARUM ANTIQUUS
Albert van Kampen
4th edition
Gotha : Haack
30 x 26
Classical atlas for students of ancient history and langs. Foreword in Latin.
M 7.00

ATLAS ZUR KIRCHENGESCHICHTE DIE CHRISTLICHEN KIRCHEN IN GESCHICHTE UND GEGENWART
Ed H Jedin et al
Freiburg : Herder, 1970
23 x 34
274pp
257 coloured maps; tables. Covers the history of the Christian Churches in coloured and monochrome maps. With detailed text.
DM 158

HARMS GESCHICHTS – UND KULTURATLAS
60th edition
München : List
19 x 25
136pp
196 maps, 81 illus. historical atlas for secondary schools. DM 13.80

HARMS GESCHICHTSATLAS
München : List
21 x 30
49pp
81 col. maps, 220 illus. world history atlas.
DM 7.80
Also available in German Lander eds. for Bayern and Baden-Württemberg.
DM 8.60

PIPERS WELTGESCHICHTE IN KARTEN, DATEN, BILDERN
Ed H & R Bukor, H Kinder, W Hilgemann
München : R Piper & Co, 1970
700pp
Piper's World History in Maps, Data, Pictures. Historical atlas with 473 col. maps, diagrams, text; covers people, places, eras. DM 56.00

VÖLKER, STAATEN UND KULTUREN
Braunschweig : Westermann
99pp
266 historical maps; index, from Man's cultural beginnings. DM 18.00

WESTERMANN'S GROSSER ATLAS ZUR WELTGESICHTE
Ed Prof Dr H E Stier
Braunschweig : Westermann, 1969
22 x 28
160pp
530 maps: from the evolution of man to 1963. With text. DM 38.00

Great Britain

SHEPHERD'S HISTORICAL ATLAS
9th edition
London : Philip, 1966 (1970 reprint)
18 x 27
354pp
226pp coloured maps covering ancient, classical, mediaeval and modern history, from 2100 BC – 1969 AD. 115pp index.
£13.50

MUIR'S HISTORICAL ATLAS : ANCIENT, MEDIAEVAL AND MODERN
Ed H Fullard and R F Treharne
6th edition
London : Philip, 1973
23 x 28
172pp
Ancient and Classical atlas, Mediaeval and Modern History Atlas in 1 volume.
£3.95

INTERMEDIATE HISTORICAL ATLAS
Prepared under the direction of the Historical Association
London : Philip
19 x 23
52pp
Maps from 1500 BC to AD 1969. Physical detail only added when relevant to history of period concerned. 40 pages of col. maps, 8 pages of index. 60p

INTERMEDIATE HISTORICAL ATLAS – WEST AFRICA EDITION
London : Philip
19 x 23
Identical to the Intermediate Historical Atlas with the addition of 8 pages of specialised maps of Africa.
£1.00

THE ATLAS OF WORLD HISTORY
London : Rupert Hart Davis, 1970+
In 8 vols.
Coloured and black, white and blue maps with text and geographic index.
Vol I "From the Beginning to Alexander the Great" Colin and Sarah McEvedy, 1970 62pp maps etc. £1.50
Vol 3 "The Dark Ages" Colin and Sarah McEvedy, 1972, 62pp maps. £1.80
Further vols. in preparation.

AN ATLAS OF WORLD HISTORY
Susan Ault and Frank Baker
Oxford : Basil Blackwell
70pp app
School atlas; 62pp 3 colour maps – 24 for Britain, 22 for the World, 16 for thematic historical elements. 80p
Library edition £1.75

PENGUIN ATLAS OF WORLD HISTORY
Vol. 1 from the Beginning to the Eve of the French Revolution.
Translated from the German.
Ed H Kinder and W Hilgemann
Harmondsworth : Penguin Books Ltd., 1974
11 x 18
Coloured historical atlas with text.
£1.00

PERGAMON GENERAL HISTORICAL ATLAS
A C Cave and B S Trinder
Oxford : Pergamon Press
21 x 27
88pp
Secondary school atlas covering pre- and ancient history. Greek and Roman civilisations and up to present day. Political and cultural history emphasised. In colour.
Hard covers £1.40

HISTORY TEACHING ATLAS
C K Brampton
Oxford : Pergamon Press
School atlas covering political history to the period after Second World War.
Limp 95p
Hard covers £1.30

MUIR'S NEW SCHOOL HISTORICAL ATLAS
Ed H Fullard and R F Treharne
London : Philip, 1966
23 x 28
72pp
School atlas covering the period from the Roman Empire to the 2 World Wars.
56pp maps, 12pp index.
75p

ATLAS OF BRITISH AND WORLD HISTORY
T A Rennard
Oxford : Pergamon
School atlas emphasising British history in relation to world from ancient times to present day. Indexed.
35p

JEWISH HISTORY ATLAS
by Martin Gilbert
London : Weidenfeld & Nicolson, 1969
18 x 25
134pp
112pp black and white maps. History from earliest times to 6 Day War in 1967. No text. Bibliog. and index.
£1.75

FIRST WORLD WAR ATLAS
Ed Martin Gilbert
London : Weidenfeld & Nicolson, 1970
18 x 25
159pp
Introduction by Field Marshall Montgomery. Atlas has black and white maps covering military, naval, diplomatic, economic, human aspects of the war.
Bibliog, index. £2.75

WORLD ATLAS OF MILITARY HISTORY
Ed Arthur Banks
Vol I : To 1500
London : Seeley Service, 1974
19 x 25
188pp including 154 black and white maps. The first of 4 volumes.
£3.95

ATLAS OF MARITIME HISTORY
Ed C Lloyd
London : Country Life, 1975
25 x 34
144pp
Includes 75pp of coloured maps and 160 black and white illustrations. Survey of world maritime history from 3000 BC to the present day.
£10.75

RECENT HISTORY ATLAS 1860–1960
Ed Martin Gilbert, Cart: John Flower
London : Weidenfeld & Nicolson, 1970
Atlas traces historical devt. from 1860.

THE NEW CAMBRIDGE MODERN HISTORY ATLAS
Ed H C Darby and H Fullard
Cambridge : UP, 1971
15 x 23
342pp
To accompany the "New Cambridge Modern History". 288pp maps, covering the period from the Renaissance. Indexed.
£12.50
Paperback £4.40

PENGUIN ATLAS OF MODERN HISTORY (TO 1815)
Ed Colin McEvedy
Harmondsworth : Penguin, 1972
22 x 18
Col. historical atlas with text.
£1.50

ATLAS OF MODERN HISTORY
Prep. by Atlas Sub-Committee of the Historical Association
London : Philip, 1970
23 x 28
72pp
Maps covering the world in the 18th, 19th, 20th Centuries. £1.35

ATLAS OF DISCOVERY
by Gail Roberts
London : Aldus Books, 1974
192pp
The history of exploration described with coloured route maps and descriptive text.
£4.00

MUIR'S HISTORICAL ATLAS, MEDIAEVAL AND MODERN
Ed H Fullard and R F Treharne
11th edition
London : Philip, 1969
23 x 28
136pp
Covering the world to 1964, emphasising political details. 213 coloured maps, index 24pp. £2.95

PENGUIN ATLAS OF MEDIAEVAL HISTORY
Ed Colin McEvedy
Harmondsworth : Penguin Books, 1961
22 x 18
Col. historical atlas with text.
£1.50

MUIR'S ATLAS OF ANCIENT AND CLASSICAL HISTORY
Ed H Fullard and R F Treharne
London : Philip, 1965 (1966)
23 x 28
36pp
47 coloured maps covering the 16th C BC to the Barbarian Invasions of AD 395. With 4 black and white plans. Index
Limp 80p
Boards £1.00

ANCIENT HISTORY ATLAS 1700 BC – AD 565
Michael Grant
London : Weidenfeld & Nicolson, 1971
87pp
Classical atlas covering politics, economy, culture, religion etc. Maps in black and white.

ATLAS OF ANCIENT HISTORY
Ed Colin McEvedy
Harmondworth : Penguin Books, 1967
22 x 18
Col. historical atlas with text.
£1.50

ARCHAEOLOGICAL ATLAS OF THE WORLD
Ed D & R Whitehouse
London : Thames and Hudson
18 x 25
272pp
Includes 103 two-colour distribution maps covering the world and pinpointing 5,000 pre- and proto-historic sites, cultures and their influence. The atlas is arranged regionally and has explanatory notes and bibliography accompanying each map.
£5.75

SCRIPTURE ATLAS – AFRIKAANS EDITION
Ed H Fullard
London : Philip
23 x 28

Hungary

KÉPES TÖRTENELMI ATLASZ
Budapest : Cart
20 x 27
24pp
Coloured illus. historical atlas for primary schools.

TÓRTENELMI ATLASZ
Budapest : Cart
23 x 28
32pp
12 cols. historical atlas for secondary schools.

Italy

ATLANTE STORICO ZANICHELLI
Bologna : Zanichelli
21 x 29
114 historical maps with index.
Plastic cover L 2,600
Linen bound L 3,800

ATLANTE E CHRONOLOGIA DELLA STORIA DEL MONDO
Bologna : Zanichelli
21 x 29
Contains "Atlante Storico" and "Sinossi di Storia Universale". Covers period from 4000 BC in maps and chronological history.
Plastic L 5,800
Cloth L 6,400

ATLANTE STORICO PER LA SCUOLA MEDIA
Ed E Dettore
Novara : Ag
In 3 vols.
23 x 30
Middle school world history atlas.
Vol 1 Dalle Antiche civilta ai regni romano barbarico 78 maps and 18 coloured plates
Vol 2 Dai regni romano-barbarici al Congresso di Vienna, 51 maps and 20 coloured plates
Vol 3 Dal Congresso di Vienna ad oggi, 47 maps and 23 coloured plates.
Each L 1,400

PICCOLO ATLANTE STORICO
Ed M Baratta et al
Novara : Ag
17 x 24
Coloured atlas with 58 plates covering the ancient world to the present day.
L 1,800

ATLANTE STORICO
Ed G Motta
Novara : Ag, 1972
26 x 33
World atlas covering ancient history, the Middle Ages and the Modern Period.
8 coloured plates.
L 3,000

Japan

SHINSEN SEKAISHI SEIZU – New World Atlas of History for High School Students
7th edition
Tokyo : Teikoku - Shoin, 1976
26 x 18
66pp
In Jap, with emphasis on relation between Europe and Orient and chronological table of world history.
Y 300

SHOMITSU SEKAISHI CHIZU – Detailed World Atlas of History for High School Students
4th edition
Tokyo : Teikoku - Shoin, 1976
26 x 18
92pp
In Jap. Emphasis on civilisation, economics and modern times.
Y 350

MEI KAI SEKAISHI SEIZU – Concise World Atlas of History for High School Students
3rd edition
Tokyo : Teikoku - Shoin, 1976
18 x 26
78pp
Historical atlas including chronological table of world history. In Japanese.
Y 280

Poland

ATLAS DO HISTORII STAROŻYTNEJ
by L Piotrowicz
Warszawa : PPWK
20 x 30
Ancient historical atlas for schools, covering the early period in the East to the Roman Empire and Constantinople.
Zl 12

Spain

ATLAS DE HISTORIA UNIVERSAL
111th edition
J Vicens Vives
Barcelona : Editorial Teide
18 x 25
112pp
School atlas, 77 world history maps with explanatory text.
S.Ptas 150

Switzerland

HISTORISCHER ATLAS ZUR WELT-UND SCHWEIZERGESCHICHTE
F W Putzger
7th edition
Aarau : Verlag Sauerlandes, 1969
viii, 146pp
Atlas covering Swiss and World history; 8 maps for Switzerland.
S.Fr 18.80

BILDERATLAS ZUR KULTUR-GESCHICHTE
Alfred Bölliger
Aarau : Verlag Sauerlandes
In 3 vols.
Picture-cultural history atlas in 3 parts :
1 Alterum (Ancient time) 1968, From Man's Beginnings to the 4th C AD S.Fr 15.80
2 Mittelalter und Renaissance, 1951 S.Fr 6.00
3 Neuzeit (Modern History) 1942 S.Fr 4.20

USA

HISTORICAL ATLAS OF THE WORLD
New York : Barnes and Noble/
ATLAS OF WORLD HISTORY
Edinburgh : W & R Chambers, 1970
Eds Bjørklund and Holmbøe
144pp
New edition of the atlas produced by Cappelen, Oslo, 1962. 108 maps covering world history from 3,000 BC. Divided into Ancient Times; Middle Ages; Recent Times; Twentieth Century.

WORLD HISTORY ATLAS
Indianapolis : Cram
22 x 30
School history atlas in 32pp maps.
US $1.00

THE WORLD; ITS HISTORY IN MAPS
Ed H McNeill
Chicago : Denoyer-Geppert, 1963
22 x 28
96pp
16pp double page maps showing world history from the origin of man to modern times. With text, calendar of events, historical index. US $2.50

ATLAS OF WORLD HISTORY
Maplewood, NJ : Hammond
24 x 31
48pp
Covers ancient world to the Post War era.
US $12.50
Paper US $1.28

ATLAS OF WORLD HISTORY
Ed R R Palmer
Chicago : Rand McNally
19 x 27
216pp
128 maps, 196pp in colour, from beginnings of civilisation to the end of World War II, 60pp text.
US $7.95

HISTORICAL ATLAS OF THE WORLD
Ed R R Palmer
Chicago : Rand McNally
26 x 34
40pp
Inc. 49 maps from Atlas of World History, covers period from the beginnings of history to the 1960s.
US $0.95

AN OUTLINE ATLAS OF WORLD HISTORY
R R Sellman
New York : St Martin's Press, 1970
127pp
Historical atlas with 150 maps, 12pp index, with text and notes.
US $6.50

USSR

ATLAS VSEMIRNOI ISTORII
Moskva : GUGK
In 3 vols
32 x 50
Vol I Drevnego mira i srednich vekov (The Ancient World and Middle Ages), 1972. 158pp col. maps. Other vols. in preparation.

ATLAS ISTORII DREVNEGO MIRA DLYA V KLASSA SREDNEI SHKOLE
Moskva : GUGK
20 x 26
12pp
Historical atlas of the Ancient World for 5th Classes in middle schools. 17 maps.

FACSIMILES

THEATRUM ORBIS TERRARUM
Amsterdam : Theatrum Orbis Terrarum
A series of facsimile eds. of old and rare atlases, pilot books and seamen's guides, illustrating the progress of geographical and cartographical knowledge from the time of Ptolemy to the 17th century. Each vol. printed in black and white and accompanied by a Bibliog. Note prepared by an acknowledged specialist.
Volumes available :

Berlinghieri, Francesco – 'Geographia' Florence, 1482 (1966)
XVI, 372 pages, including 31 copper engraved maps. Bibliog. Note by R A Skelton
29 x 44
Buckram Fl 200.00

Bordone, Benedetto – 'Libro . . . de tutte l'Isole del Monde'. Venice, 1528 (1966)
XII, 168 pages, including 111 maps in the text. Bibliographical Note by R A Skelton.
22 x 32
Buckram FL 100.00

Johnson, William (Willem Jansz Blaeu) – 'The Light of Navigation'. Amsterdam, 1612 (1964)
Two parts in one volume. XIV, 298pp, including 39 double-page folding charts and 2 full-page charts. Bibliog. Note by R A Skelton. 30 x 26
Buckram Fl 190.00

Jode, Gerard de – 'Speculum Orbis Terrarum'. Antwerp 1578 (1965)
XVI, 280 pages including 65 double-page maps. Bibliog. Note by R A Skelton.
29 x 44
Buckram Fl 200.00

Ortelius, Abraham – Theatrum Orbis Terrarum, Antwerp, 1570 (1964).
XII, 184 pages incl. 53 double-page engraved maps. Bibliog. Note by R A Skelton. 29 x 44
Buckram Fl 180.00

Ptolemaeus, Claudius - Cosmographia. Bologna, 1477 (1963)
XIV 224 pages, including 26 double-page engraved maps. Bibliog. Note by R A Skelton. 29 x 44
Buckram Fl 155.00

Ptolemaeus, Claudius - Cosmographia, Roma, 1478 (1966).
XII, 248 pages, including 27 double-page maps. Bibliog. Note by R A Skelton.
29 x 44
Buckram Fl 200.00

Ptolemaeus, Claudius - Cosmographia, Ulm, 1482 (1963)
XII, 180 pages, including 19 double-page woodcut maps. Bibliog. Note by R A Skelton.
21 x 29
Buckram Fl 180.00

Ptolemaeus, Claudius - Geographia Strassburg, 1513 (1966)
Two parts in one volume. XXIV, 362 pages, including 46 double-page and one full page map in colours. Bibliog. Note by R A Skelton.
32 x 46
Buckram Fl 275.00

Ptolemaeus, Claudius, ed S Munster – 'Geographia'. Basle, 1540 (1966)
XII, 44 pages, including 48 woodcut maps. Bibliog. Note by R A Skelton. 22 x 32
Buckram Fl 145.00

Speed, John – 'A Prospect of the most famous parts of the World'. London, 1627 (1966)
XVI, 124 pages, including 22 double-page engraved maps. Bibliog. Note by R A Skelton. 29 x 44
Buckram Fl 120.00

Waghenaer, Lucas Jansz – 'Spieghel der Zeevaerdt'. Leydon, 1584-1585 (1964).
Two parts in one volume. XII, 196, 98 pages, including 44 double-page charts. Bibliog. Note by R A Skelton. 29 x 44
Buckram Fl 180.00

Waghenaer, Lucas Jansz – 'Thresoor der Zeevaert'. Leyden, 1592 (1965).
XVI, 360 pages, including 22 double-page folding charts. Bibliog. Note by R A Skelton. 30 x 25
Buckram Fl 140.00

Waghenaer, Lucas Jansz – 'The Mariners Mirrour'. London 1588 (1966)
Two parts in one volume. XII, 230 pages, including 45 double-page charts. Bibliog. Note by R A Skelton. 29 x 44
Buckram Fl 175.00

Coronelli, Vincenzo Mainz – 'Libro dei Globi' Venice 1693/1710.
XXIV, 292 pages, including 7 double page and 127 single page engravings of globes and globe gores, and 5 plates, including a portrait of Coronelli. Bibliog. Note by Dr H Wallis. 34 x 50
Buckram Fl 225.00

Ortelius, Abraham – 'The Theatre of the Whole World'. London 1606.
674 pages, including 157 double-page maps, 6 plates and a portrait of Ortelius. Bibliog. Note by R A Skelton. 30 x 48
Buckram Fl 380.00

Quad, Mathias – 'Geographisch Handtbuch Cologne 1600'
XXIV, 336 pages including 82 double-page maps. Bibliog. Note by W Bonacker (in German).
20 x 28
Buckram Fl 160.00

Mercator–Hondius–Janssonius – 'Atlas or A Geographicke Description . . .' Amsterdam, 1636
2 volumes, XXIV, 498 pages, including 195 double-page engraved maps. Bibliog. Note by R A Skelton. 30 x 46
Buckram Fl 580.00

Braun & Hogenberg – 'Civitates Orbis Terrarum' (The Towns of the World). 1572–1618, 1965
Folio. 3 volumes, 1612 pages, including 363 double-page plates. Preface by R V Tooley. Introduction and indexes by R A Skelton
Buckram Fl 700.00

Fisher W and Thornton J. 'The English Pilot – The Fourth Book'. London 1689.
XXIV, 148 pages with 19 double-page charts. Bibliog. Note by C Verner.
30 x 50
Buckram Fl 160.00

26 World Oceans

C OFFICIAL SERIES

KARTA MIRA
1:2,500,000
Eastern European and Soviet Survey Offices
Covers complete world including ocean areas.
see WORLD 100C and index 100/2

D POLITICAL & ADMINISTRATIVE

WELTKARTE : NAMEN UND NAUTISCHE GRENZEN DER OZEANE UND MEERE
1:45,000,000
Rostock : Seehydrographischer Dienst der DDR, 1969
World map showing sea and ocean names and boundaries.

E1 PHYSICAL : RELIEF

THE FLOOR OF THE WORLD OCEAN
by Richard E Harrison
1:50,000,000
Annals Map Supplement No 2
Florida : AAG
53 x 74
Shows relief, by shading, depths in feet, land areas. US $2.50

DEUTSCHE MEERESKARTE
1:25,000,000
In 3 sheets
Mannheim : Bibliographisches Inst. Meyers Verlag
German map of the oceans, showing depths, coastal areas with contours.
Sheets :

Atlantischer Ozean	56 x 88
Indischer Ozean	51 x 54
Pazifischer Ozean	71 x 87

DM 48 set

WORLD OCEANOGRAPHIC CHART
1:12,233,000
In 12 sheets
Washington : USN, 1961
370 x 254
Detailed map showing bathymetric contours 13 layer tints. Relief of land in brown with relief shading, ports, selected shipping routes.
Mercator's Proj.

CARTE GÉNÉRALE BATHYMETRIQUE DES OCEANS (GENERAL BATHYMETRIC CHART OF THE OCEANS GEBCO)
1:10,000,000
In 24 sheets, see index 26/1
Monaco : Int. Hyd. Bureau
109 x 74 each
Shows ocean depths by soundings in metres, layer col. for depths and height of land. 5th edition series in preparation.
Each F.Fr 30.00

OCEANIC REGIONS ADJACENT TO CANADA
1:6,750,000
No 800
Ottawa : Canadian Hydrog. Service
Coloured map illustrating the Bathymetry of the oceans by layer colours.

G EARTH RESOURCES

WORLD SUBSEA MINERAL RESOURCES : PRELIMINARY MAPS
V E McKelvey and F F H Wong
Misc. Geol. Inv. Map 1-632
Washington : USGS, 1970
23 x 30 (folder size)
1 map at 1:60,000,000 (73 x 60),
3 at 1:39,000,000 (108 x 85).
Showing basic geol. and physiographic features with potential minerals.
With 17pp text.

ATLASES
A1 GENERAL

SERIAL ATLAS OF THE MARINE ENVIRONMENT
New York : AGS
Number of map-based reports on all aspects of the Oceans.
Volumes published :

1 Sea Surface Temperature Regime in the Western North Atlantic, 1953-1954, by Robert L Pyle US $4.00
2 North Atlantic Temperatures at a Depth of 200 Meters, by Elizabeth H Schroeder US $8.00
3 A Geographic Study of the Clam, Spisula polynyma, by J Lockwood Chamberlin and Franklin Stearns US $8.00
also, bound US $9.00
4 Surface Water Types of the North Sea, and their Characteristics, by Taivo Laevastu US $4.00
5 North American Sea Stars (Echinodermata: Asteroidea) from North Alaska to the Strait of Belle Isle, by Edward H Grainger US $6.50
6 Euphausiids and Pelagic Amphipods; Distribution in North Atlantic and Arctic Waters, by Maxwell J Dunbar US $7.00
7 Surface Circulation on the Continental Shelf off Eastern North America between Newfoundland and Florida, by Dean F Bumpus and Louis M Lauzier US $5.00
8 Zooplankton Indicator Species in the North Sea, by James H Fraser; The Trace Elements, by Robert Johnston US $4.00
9 Meteorology of the North Sea, by Frank E Lumb US $4.00
10 Autumn Distribution of Groundfish Species in the Gulf of Maine and Adjacent Waters, 1955-1961, by Raymond L. Fritz US $5.00
11 Inorganic Nutrients in the North Sea, by Robert Johnston and Peter G W Jones US $4.50
12 Distribution of Decapod Crustacea in the Northwest Atlantic, by Hubert J Squires US $3.50
13 Distribution of the Euphausiid Crustacean Meganyctiphanes norvegica (M Sars), by John Mauchline and Leonard R Fisher US $5.00
also, bound US $9.00
14 Distribution of North Atlantic Pelagic Birds, by Robert Cushman Murphy US $8.00
15 Monthly Sea Temperature Structure from the Florida Keys to Cape Cod, by Lionel A Walford and Robert I Wicklund US $15.00
16 Mean Monthly Sea Surface Temperatures and Zonal Anomalies of the Tropical Atlantic, by Paul A Mazeika US $8.00
17 Shellfish of the North Sea, by Pieter Korringa US $9.00
18 The Wildlife Wetlands and Shellfish Areas of the Atlantic Coastal Zone, by George P Spinner US $12.00
19 The Water Masses of the North Atlantic Ocean; a Volumetric Census of Temperature and Salinity, by W R Wright and L V Worthington US $10.00
20 Gulf of Mexico Deep-Sea Fauna: Decapoda and Euphausiacea, by Willis E Pequegnat, Linda H Pequegnat, and others US $12.00
21 Average Monthly Sea-Water Temperatures Nova Scotia to Long Island 1940-1959, by John B Colton and Ruth R Stoddard US $12.00
22 Chemistry, primary, productivity and bentric algae of the Gulf of Mexico by S Z El-Sayed and others, 1972

ATLASES
E1 PHYSICAL

ATLAS ZUR OZEANOGRAPHIE
Meyers Grosser Physicher Weltatlas
Meyer, 1968
see WORLD ATLASES E1

SONOGRAPHS OF THE SEA FLOOR: A PICTURE ATLAS
R H Belderson and others
Amsterdam : Elsevier, 1972
200pp app
163 sonographs based on new side-scan sonar technique; covers rock structure, sedimentary patterns and relief, examples of mobile and stable floors, marine life etc.
Bibliog. Dfl 80.00

ATLASES
H BIOGEOGRAPHY

ATLAS OF THE LIVING RESOURCES OF THE SEAS
Prepared by the FAO Dept. of Fisheries
3rd edition
Rome : FAO, 1972
29 x 25
154pp
63pp maps in 3 colours (4 folded insets), 7pp index, 12pp text. Covers fish, crustaceans, plancton, use of resources.
US $4.80

261 Atlantic Ocean

E1 PHYSICAL

ATLANTIC OCEAN, DOUBLE PORTRAIT
1:30,412,800
Washington : NGS, 1968
48 x 63
Graphically shows Atlantic floor on one side, with conventional map on the other.
US $1.00

ATLANTICHESKIY OKEAN
1:20,000,000
Moskva : GUGK, 1973
Col. study map with geog. description.

ATLANTICHESKIY OKEAN
1:10,000,000
Moskva : GUGK
Col. bathymetric map.

PHYSIOGRAPHIC DIAGRAM OF THE NORTH ATLANTIC OCEAN
1:5,000,000
by B C Heezen and M Tharp
New York : GSA, 1958
150 x 79
Relief of sea floor shown by graphic hachuring; depth in metres, echo-sounding traverses. US $2.50

PHYSIOGRAPHIC DIAGRAMS OF THE SOUTH ATLANTIC OCEAN, THE CARIBBEAN SEA, THE SCOTIA SEA AND THE EASTERN MARGIN OF THE SOUTH PACIFIC OCEAN
1:11,000,000
by B C Heezen and M Tharp
New York : GSA, 1962
148 x 125
Relief of sea floor shown by graphic hachuring; depths in metres: topog. diagram with explanatory sheet. US $2.50

OCÉAN ATLANTIQUE ET POLE NORD
No 25
Paris : Hatier
100 x 120
Plastic map showing ocean depths, sea and air currents, fishing, navigation routes, ports etc.

MAP SHOWING RELATION OF LAND AND SUBMARINE TOPOGRAPHY, NOVA SCOTIA TO FLORIDA
1:1,000,000
Misc. Geol. Inv. 1-451
In 3 sheets
Ed Elazar Uchupi
Washington : USGS, 1965
70 x 95 US $1.50 set

BATHYMETRIC MAPS : EASTERN CONTINENTAL MARGINS, USA
1:1,000,000
In 3 sheets
Tulsa : Am. Assoc. Petroleum Geologists, 1970
Sea floor contours 6-25 fathoms at 1 fathom intervals. 25-100 at 5f intervals, 100+ at 25f, layer col.

Sheet 1 Atlantic Ocean North of Cape Hatteras 150 x 108
Sheet 2 Atlantic Ocean South of Cape Hatteras 150 x 108
Sheet 3 Northern Gulf of Mexico 176 x 82

BATHYMETRIC MAPS OF OFFSHORE CANADA (ATLANTIC)
Various scales
Ottawa : Canadian Hydrog. Service
Maps available :
801 Bay of Fundy to Gulf of St Lawrence 1:1,000,000
802 Newfoundland Shelf 1:1,000,000
810 Relief diagram of the Continental Margin of Eastern North America 1:1,000,000, 1971 2 sheets (accompanies Marine Science Paper No 9)
811 Gulf of St Lawrence 1:1,000,000
813 Labrador Shelf 1:1,500,000
mid Atlantic Ridge Near 45°N — Bathymetry and Magnetic Maps 1:362 070, 1972 (accompanying Marine Science Paper 11)

NATURAL RESOURCE SERIES
1:250,000
Ottawa : Canadian Hydrog. Service
Series of col. maps in progress designed to cover offshore areas of Canada. Each sheet is available in 3 editions :
A Bathymetry
B Gravity (Free Air Anomaly)
C Magnetic (Total Field)
also available : Plotting base which is a print of the bathymetric edition in grey.
Currently published for the mouth of the St Lawrence River, Nova Scotia and Newfoundland Banks.
Each C$2.00

F GEOLOGY

THE SUB PLEISTOCENE GEOLOGY OF THE BRITISH ISLES AND THE ADJACENT CONTINENTAL SHELF
1:2,500,000
IGS
see BRITISH ISLES 41F

GEOLOGICAL MAPS OF OFFSHORE AREAS OF CANADA (ATLANTIC)
Various scales
Ottawa : Canadian Hydrog. Service
No 811G Gulf of St Lawrence - Surficial Geology 1:1,000,000, 1973 (accompanies a Fisheries Board Publication)
812G Scotian Shelf - Bedrock Geology 1:1,000,000 1973
4039G Yarmouth to Browns Bank — Surficial Geology 1:300,000 1971 (accompanies Marine Science paper 2)
4040G Halifax to Sable Island — Surficial Geology 1:300,000 1970 (accompanies Marine Science paper No 1)
4041G Banquereau and Misaine Bank — Surficial Geology 1:300,000 1971 (accompanies Marine Science Paper 3)
4023G Northumberland Strait — Surficial Geology 1:300,000 1972 (accompanies Marine Science Paper 5)
10356 The Coatline of Chedabucto Bay - Sediment types and shore line features 1:75,000 1971 (accompanies Marine Science Paper 4)
Each C$2.00

L ECONOMIC

FISHING BANKS IN THE NORTH ATLANTIC
København : Scandinavian Fishing Y.B.
Outline chart showing the most important fishing grounds and the fish caught there.
D.Kr 20.00

ATLASES
E1 PHYSICAL

ATLANTIC OCEAN ATLAS OF TEMPERATURE AND SALINITY PROFILES AND DATA FROM THE INTERNATIONAL GEOPHYSICAL YEAR OF 1957-1958
Woods Hole Oceanographic Inst. Atlas Series Vol. I
Ed F C Fuglister
Woods Hole, Mass : Woods Hole Oceanographic Inst, 1960
44 x 31
Detailed collection of profiles, charts and tables. $11.00

NORTH ATLANTIC OCEAN ATLAS OF POTENTIAL TEMPERATURE AND SALINITY IN THE DEEP WATER, INCLUDING TEMPERATURE, SALINITY AND OXYGEN PROFILES FROM THE ERIKA DAN CRUISE OF 1962
Woods Hole Oceanographic Inst. Atlas Series Vol. 2.
L V Worthington and W R Wright
Woods Hole, Mass : Woods Hole Oceanographic Inst, 1970
44 x 31
42 maps
Maps at 1:38,000,000, with profiles and tables.
US $22.00

ICITA OCEANOGRAPHIC ATLAS
Ed A G Koleshikov
Prepared by Int. Co-operative Investigations of the Tropical Atlantic (ICITA)
Paris : UNESCO
45 x 61
Joint international project to prepare and publish the physical, chemical, geological, biological and meteorological data collected during ICITA.
Parts published :
Vol I Physical Oceanography 289pp, 1974. Contains 332 charts with 56pp brochure. £16.80

262 Mediterranean Sea

A1 GENERAL MAPS : ROADS

SHELL REISEKARTE MITTELMEER
1:4,500,000
Stuttgart : Mair, 1970
128 x 50
Col. road map covering Mediterranean area incl. Canary Is. and Madeira. Travel information, places of interest, shipping lines, legend in 12 languages.
DM 4.80

A2 GENERAL MAPS : LOCAL

MITTELMEERINSELN
1:5,000,000
Bern : Hallwag, 1971
94 x 41
General map in 3 cols. of the Mediterranean region, marking shipping routes in red with sailing time, with insets at scales of 1:200,000 - 1:1,000,000 of Majorca, Corsica, Sardinia, Sicily, Ibiza, Menorca, Elba, Malta and Gozo, Cyprus, Crete and Rhodes.

E1 PHYSICAL : RELIEF

PAESI DEL MEDITERRANEO
1:5,000,000
No 24/14
Novara : Ag
100 x 70
Physical col. wall map, layered and relief shaded.
L 400

PHILIP'S REGIONAL WALL MAP OF MEDITERRANEAN LANDS
1:4,000,000
London : Philip
117 x 96
Physical school wall map, layer col. communications and boundaries.
Paper £1.50
Cloth, rollers £5.50
Cloth, folded £7.00

BASSIN MÉDITERRANÉEN
1:3,800,000
No 1401
Ed F Le Meur
St Germain-en-Laye : Editions MDI, 1975
126 x 92
Double sided wall map, physical with economic map on the reverse. Also available in arabic edition.

MITTELMEERLÄNDER
1:2,000,000
Eds Haack - Painke
Darmstadt : Perthes
280 x 165
Includes S Europe, N Africa, Middle East. Physical school wall map, layer coloured and hachured.

MITTELMEERLÄNDER
1:2,000,000
H 228
Munchen : List, 1970
230 x 160
Harms wall map for schools, physical col. covering Mediterranean region, communications and cities graded by population.
DM 164.00

MITTELMEERLÄNDER UND VORDERER ORIENT
1:2,000,000
Braunschweig : Westermann
262 x 138
Physical school wall map of the Mediterranean and Near East. Relief shading, layer col. communications and cities graded by population.

MEDITERRANÉE
No 28
Paris : Hatier
100 x 120
Plastic wall map for schools, showing ocean depths, sea and air currents, navigation routes, ports, etc.

F GEOLOGY

CARTE GÉOLOGIQUE ET STRUCTURALE DES BASSINS TERTIAIRES DU DOMAINE MÉDITERRANÉEN
1:2,500,000
In 2 sheets
Paris : Editions Technip, 1974
113 x 95
Coloured map indicating detailed geology and structure of the mediterranean region with cross sections and legend.
F.Fr 190.00
Commentary 34pp. In French
F.Fr 20.00

G EARTH RESOURCES

CARTA MAGNETICA DEL BACINO DEL MEDITERRANEO
1:6,000,000
Firenze : IGM, 1950
Map showing lines of equal magnetic declination at the 1st of January 1950.
L 460

CARTE MAGNÉTIQUE DE MÉDITERRANÉE OCCIDENTALE
1:1,000,000
Paris : BRGM
Available in 2 editions. Intensity of Total Field and Anomalies of Total Field.
Each F.Fr 26.00

H BIOGEOGRAPHY

VEGETATION MAP OF THE MEDITERRANEAN REGION
1:5,000,000
Arid Zone Research XXX
Paris : UNESCO - FAO, 1970
212 x 79 complete
Showing vegetation zones in colour with text 90pp. Legends in English and French.
F.Fr 48.00

BIOCLIMATIC MAP OF THE MEDITERRANEAN REGION
1:5,000,000
In 2 sheets
Paris : UNESCO : FAO, 1963
212 x 79 complete
Showing bioclimatic zones in colour with text 58pp. 4 insets. Legends in English and French.
F.Fr 40.00

L ECONOMIC

BASSIN MÉDITERRANÉEN-ÉCONOMIQUE
1:3,800,000
Editions MDI, 1975
see MEDITERRANEAN SEA 262 E1

ATLASES
E1 PHYSICAL

MEDITERRANEAN SEA ATLAS OF TEMPERATURE, SALINITY, OXYGEN PROFILES AND DATA FROM CRUISES OF R/V ATLANTIS AND R/V CHAIN
Woods Hole Oceanographic Inst. Atlas Series. Vol 3.
Eds A R Miller, P Tchernia, H Charnock
Woods Hole, Mass : Woods Hole Oceanographic Inst., 1970
44 x 31
Detailed collection of profiles, charts and tables. Includes 'Distribution of Nutrient Chemical Properties' by D A McGill. Text in French and English.
US $30.00

ATLASES
H BIOGEOGRAPHY

ATLAS DES PRINCIPAUX FORAMINIFÉRES PLANCTONIQUES DU BASSIN MEDITERRANÉEN (OLIGOCÉNE A QUATERNAIRE)
G and J-J Bizon
Paris : Éditions Technip, 1972
18 x 24
328pp
Shows principal foraminifera planktons in the Oligocene to Quaternary periods. 70 species, each species having map, plates and description. 400 illus.

265 Pacific Ocean

D POLITICAL & ADMINISTRATIVE

PACIFIC OCEAN
1:36,432,000
Washington : NGS
67 x 101
Political col. wall map, boundaries in colour, detailed names of towns and island groups.
Paper US $2.00
Plastic US $3.00

PACIFIC OCEAN AND MAIN ISLAND GROUPS
1:28,187,500 (at Equator)
No 502
Sydney : Gregory
101 x 76
Col. map showing Alaska, South Shetland Is, India, American Coastland. Main Is. groups inset, air and shipping routes, main products.
A $0.75

PACIFIC OCEAN
1:25,000,000
Suva : DMLS, 1967
91 x 76
General geographical map, showing position of Fiji Islands in relation to other island groups. F$0.75

WESTERN PACIFIC
1:6,300,000
DOS 17/35
Tolworth : DOS, 1948
Shows location of island territories, with chief towns. 15p

PACIFIC OCEAN
1:4,960,400
Suva : DMLS, 1967
160 x 99
General geog. map in 2 sheets, dyeline print. F $4.20 each

E1 PHYSICAL : RELIEF

PACIFIC OCEAN, DOUBLE PORTRAIT
1:36,432,000
Washington : NGS, 1969
48 x 63
Graphically portrays Pacific floor on one side, with conventional detailed map on the reverse. US $1.00

TIKHIY OKEAN
1:22,500,000
Moskva : GUGK, 1973
Col. study map, with geog. description.

THE PACIFIC AND ADJACENT AREAS
1:20,000,000
NZMS 243
1st edition
Wellington : NZMS, 1969
86 x 121
Land and sea relief shown by col. Covers Pacific Basin and adjacent areas from India to E North America and Alaska, down to Macquarie Is.
US $1.50

PACIFIC OCEAN AREA
1:15,000,000
No 108211-14
Chicago : Denoyer-Geppert
162 x 111
Wall map of Pacific Ocean, showing depths, currents, continents of Australia, N America, part of S America.
CR US $26.00

STILLEHAV–OMRADET
(THE PACIFIC)
1:12,000,000
København : GI, 1970
147 x 117
2 sheet wall map showing elevation and depths by col. With or without names.
D.Kr 80.00

OCÉANIE
1:9,000,000
No 1062
St Germain-en-Laye : Editions MDI, 1970
126 x 90
Double sided wall map, physical map of Oceania with economic map of Australia and N.Z. on reverse. Available in French, English and Arabic editions.

OCÉAN PACIFIQUE
No scale given
No 26
Paris : Hatier
100 x 120
School wall map on plastic showing ocean depths, sea and air currents, fishing, navigation routes, ports etc.

PHYSIOGRAPHIC DIAGRAM OF THE WESTERN PACIFIC OCEAN
by Bruce C Heezen and Mairie Tharp
1:10,000,000
Boulder, Col : GSA, 1971
120 x 91
Hand drawn map illustrating the configuration of the sea bed. Areas of relief are hachured and roughly graded according to elevation, heights and names are given. Includes Borneo, Southern Japan, Hawaii, Tahiti, Australia and NZ.
US $3.00

PHYSIOGRAPHIC DIAGRAM OF THE SOUTH ATLANTIC OCEAN, THE CARIBBEAN SEA, THE SCOTIA SEA AND EASTERN MARGIN OF THE SOUTH PACIFIC OCEAN
1:10,000,000
see also ATLANTIC 261 E1

BATHYMETRY OF THE NORTH PACIFIC
T E Chase and others
1:6,500,000
La Jolla, Cal : Inst. Marine Resources, Univ. Calif, 1970
Bathymetric chart with diagrammatic abyssal topography. US $20.00

BATHYMETRIC MAP OF THE PACIFIC COAST (OF CANADA)
1:1,000,000
No 181
Ottawa : Canadian Hydrog. Service Map indicating sea depths by layer colouring.

F GEOLOGY

TEKTONICHESKAYA KARTA TIKHOOKEANSKOGO SEGMENTA ZEMLI
1:10,000,000
In 6 sheets
Moskva : Academy of Sciences/GUGK
1970
83 x 108 each
Col. tectonic map of the Pacific segment of the earth : shows seismology, structure, isobaths. Pacific Seamounts inset. With text, also available in Eng.

TECTONIC MAP OF THE SOUTHWEST PACIFIC
(At Lat 46°S)
1:10,000,000
Misc. Series 20, 1st edition
D J Cullen
Wellington : NZ Oceanographic Inst. Dept. Sci. and Indust. Research, 1970
39 x 57
Col. map showing folding, structures, geophysical details of NZ and environs.

L ECONOMIC

PACIFIC OCEAN : VEGETATION, LAND USE AND ECONOMY
1:27,500,000
2 maps :
No 77 Vegetation and Land Use - cultivation, irrigation, forests etc.
No 78 Economic - agriculture, fisheries, minerals. Inset - industry.
Tehran : Sahab
90 x 60
Coloured maps with legend in English and Persian. Rls 100

ATLASES
E1 PHYSICAL

WORLD OCEAN ATLAS
Vol I PACIFIC OCEAN
Ed S G Gorshkov
Moscow : USSR Ministry of Naval Defence, 1976
35 x 46
350pp
A thorough oceanic study of the Pacific, containing a detailed collection of coloured maps including studies of the history of ocean exploration, ocean bed, climate, hydrology, hydrochemistry, biogeography, reference and navigation — geographical charts. Each section is provided with descriptive explanations in Russian. Index.
£150.00

OCEANOGRAPHIC ATLAS OF THE PACIFIC OCEAN
by Richard A Barkley
Honolulu : Univ. Hawaii Press, 1969
31 x 45
176pp
Summary of 50 years observations of temperature, salinity, dissolved oxygen. Details of depth and sampling. 122 black and white maps, 17 col. sections, 17pp histograms of frequency values. Bibliog.
US $30.00

EASTROPAC ATLAS
Washington : Govt. Printing Office
In 11 vols.
Covers marine life and resources, physical factors of Eastern Tropical Pacific Ocean.
Vol 1 Physical, oceanographic and meteorological data from principal participating ships.
Feb – Mar 1967 1971
88 plates vii pp US $4.75
Vol 2 Biological and nutrient chemistry data
Feb – Mar 1967 1971
88 plates vii pp US $4.75
Vol 3 Physical, oceanographic and meteorological data
Apr – July 1967 US $4.75
Vol 4 Biological and nutrient chemistry data
Aug – Sept 1967 1970
viii, 12pp
121 illus. leaves US $4.75
Vol 5 Physical, oceanographic and meteorological data
Aug – Sept 1967 US $4.75
Vol 6 Biological and nutrient chemistry data
Aug – Sept 1967 US $4.75
Vol 7 Physical, oceanographic and meteorlogical data
Oct 1967 – Jan 1968 US $4.75
Vol 8 Biological and nutrient chemistry data
Oct 1967 – Jan 1968 US $4.75
Vol 9 Physical, oceanographic and meteorological data
Feb – Mar 1968 US $4.75
Vol 10 Biological and nutrient chemistry data
Feb – Mar 1968 US $4.75
Vol 11 Data from Latin American cooperating ships and ships of opportunity. All cruises
Feb 1967 – March 1968.
In prep.

MARINE ATLAS OF THE PACIFIC COASTAL WATERS OF SOUTH AMERICA
M R Stevenson and others
Berkley : Univ. California Press, 1970
31 x 44
99 charts, 20pp text in Eng. and Sp.
Covers climate, chemical structure, marine environment; changes in fish population and wind strength. Loose leaf binder.
US $25.00

ATLAS OF THE GREAT BARRIER REEF
Prof W H G Maxwell
Amsterdan : Elsevier, 1968
vii, 258pp
Maps, diagrams, aerial photos, text: covers bathymetry, geol, hydrology.

ATLASES
K HUMAN GEOGRAPHY

SPRACHENATLAS DES INDOPAZIFISCHEN RAUMES
Richard Salzner
Wiesbaden : Otto Harrassowitz, 1960
viii, 140pp
1 vol in 2 parts. Language atlas of the Indo-Pacific area, including 64 multi-coloured maps.
DM 180

ATLASES
P REGIONAL

ATLAS OF THE SOUTH WEST PACIFIC
I G Ord
2nd edition
Brisbane : Jacaranda Press, 1968
69pp
61pp maps, 9pp gazetteer.

267 Indian Ocean

E1 PHYSICAL

INDIYSKIY OKEAN
1:15,000,000
Moskva : GUGK, 1973
Col. study map with geog. description.

PHYSIOGRAPHIC DIAGRAM OF THE INDIAN OCEAN, THE RED SEA, THE SOUTH CHINA SEA, THE SULU SEA AND THE CELEBES SEA
by B C Heezen and M Tharp
1:11,000,000
New York : GSA, 1964
165 x 126
Relief of sea floor shown by graphic hachuring; depths in metres, with explanatory sheet.
US $2.50

THE BATHYMETRY OF THE GULF OF ADEN
1:2,000,000
prepared by the Experimental Cartography Unit of the Royal College of Art
London : RGS, 1968
75 x 86
Col. map prepared by automatic cartography showing sounding tracks, feature names. 5 sheets originally planned but only sheet 3 covering the Gulf of Aden has and will be published.
£1.00

OCÉAN INDIEN ET POLE SUD
No scale given
No 27
Paris : Hatier
100 x 120
Plastic school wall map showing ocean depths, sea and air currents, fishing, navigation routes, ports etc.

F GEOLOGY

THE INDIAN OCEAN, THE GEOLOGY OF ITS BORDERING LANDS AND THE CONFIGURATION OF ITS FLOOR
J F Pepper and G M Everhart
1:13,650,000
Geol. Inv. I-380
Washington : USGS, 1963
77 x 110
Geological map of offshore areas, bathymetric contours at 100, 1,000, 2,000, 2,500, 3,000 fathoms. With booklet.
US $1.25

ATLASES
E1 PHYSICAL

OCEANOGRAPHIC ATLAS OF INTERNATIONAL INDIAN OCEAN EXPEDITION
Ed V Klaus Wyrtki, National Science Foundation, 1971
Washington : Govt. Printing Office, 1971
xi, 531pp
Illustrated atlas with overlay; includes charts and diagrams.
US $30.00

ATLASES
F GEOLOGY

INTERNATIONAL GEOLOGICAL AND GEOPHYSICAL ATLAS OF THE INDIAN OCEAN
Ed G B Udintsev
Moscow : GUGK, 1976
37 x 66
168pp
Compilation of scientific data prepared 1972-75.
£50.00

ATLASES
J CLIMATE

METEOROLOGICAL ATLAS OF THE INTERNATIONAL INDIAN OCEAN EXPEDITION
Washington : Govt. Printing Office, 1972
Maps at 1:40,000,000 depicting results and data from the expedition.
Vol 1 The Surface Climates of 1963 and 1964
by C S Ramage and others.
xiii, 144 col. maps. US $17.25
Vol 2 Upper Air
by C S Ramage and C V R Roman
xiii, 121 col. maps. US $14.75

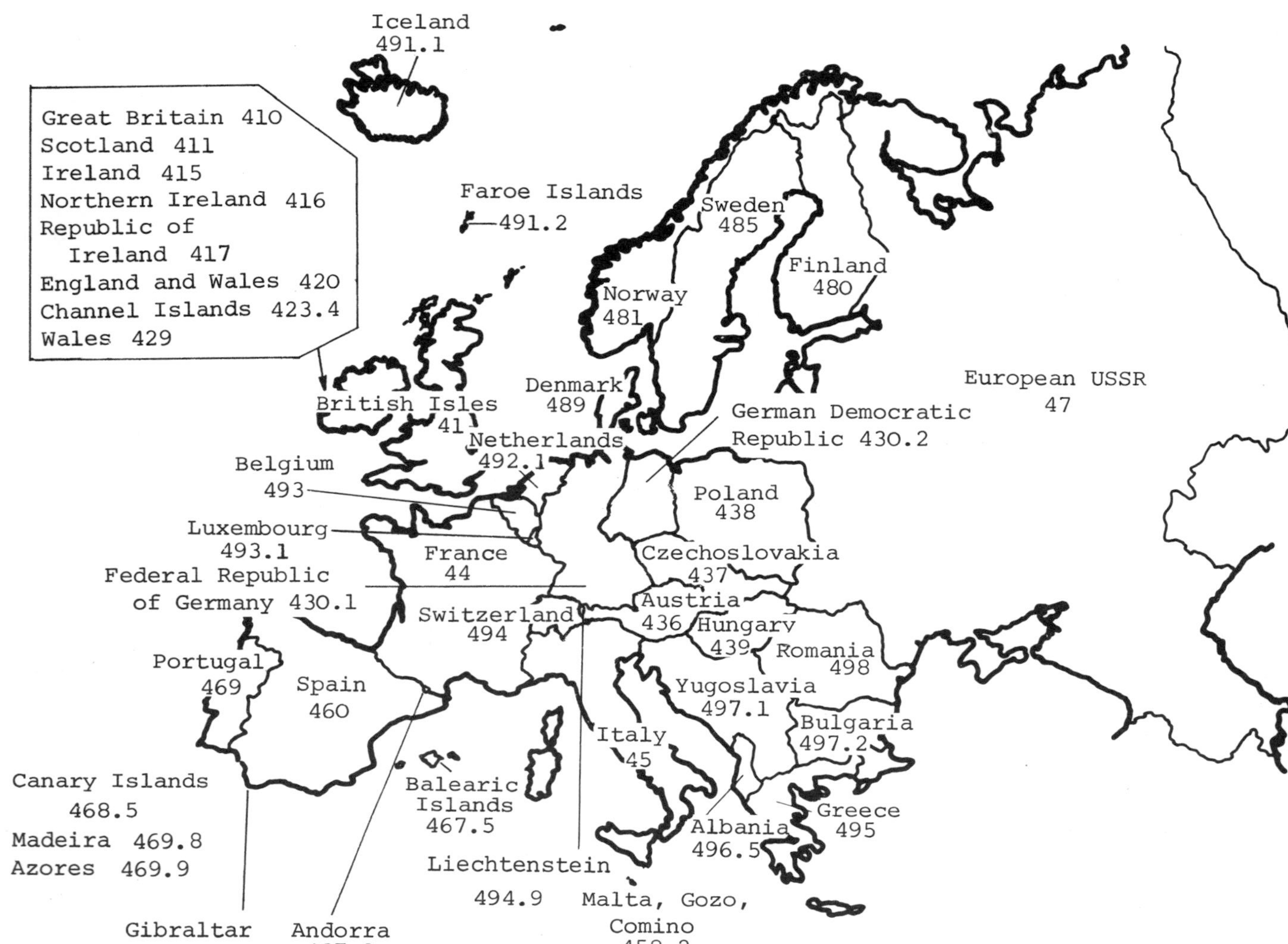

Regions

Europe 4
Iberian Peninsula 46
Scandinavia 48
Germany 430
Benelux Countries 492
Balkans 497

Europe

4 Europe

A1 GENERAL MAPS: ROADS

SHELL REISEKARTE EUROPA
1:4,500,000
Stuttgart : Mair
Col. road map, roads classified and numbered, distances in km. Places of tourist interest, motoring information.
DM 5.80

EUROPA BILVÄGAR
1:4,500,000
Stockholm : GLA
Roads numbered, classified; tourist information. S. Kr 13.50

EUROPA - FERNROUTEN
1:4,000,000
No 1180
Bern : K & F, 1972/3
88 x 101
Long distance road map showing main highways, link roads, distances in km, route numbers, international boundaries. Legend Eng, Fr, Ger. Covers the whole of Europe incl. Scandinavia east to Moscow.

EUROPE
1:3.750,000
London : Foldex
Shows roads classified, relief shading; patent fold. 45p

EUROPA AUTOKARTEN
1:3,500,000
No 390
Hamburg : Falk
Road map of Europe, mountains relief shaded and forest regions. Falk patent folding system. Index.
Plastic DM 8.60
In cover DM 5.60

EUROPA, STRASSEN ÜBERSICHTSKARTE
1:3,500,000
No 99
Stuttgart : RV
123 x 97
Relief shading, political boundaries in green, roads numbered. Legend Eng, Fr, Ger, Sw, Dut, It. DM 8.80

AUTOKARTA EUROPE
1:3,400,000
Beograd : Geokarta
General road map. Dn 15

DIE GROSSEN EUROPÄISCHEN VERBINDUNGSWEGE
1:3,170,000
Bern : Hallwag/Zurich : Reader's Digest, 1970
111 x 83
Main road map of Europe showing main and link roads, distances in km, state boundaries, political colouring.

MAPA SAMOCHODOWY EUROPY
1:3,000,000
Warszawa : PPWK, 1971
116 x 88
Col. road map of Europe in Polish.
Zl 30

EUROPA
1:3,000,000
Novara : Ag
Road map with 25 city plans inset.
(In plastic) L 700

EUROPA STRASSENKARTE - PHYSISCHE AUSGABE
1:2,750,000
In 2 sheets
Bern : K & F, 1973/4
North No 1150, South No 1151
126 x 90 each
Main and secondary roads with route numbers and distances in km, state boundaries, railways; relief shaded.
North sheet:
Iceland - Scandinavia - British Isles south to Brussels
South sheet:
British Isles - S Scandinavia (inset) USSR border south to Mediterranean
Also available in Political ed. (countries in colour)
North No 1155
South No 1156

EUROPÄISCHE STRASSENKARTE
1:2,600,000
No 869
Frankfurt : Ravenstein, 1976
130 x 98
Main routes numbered, political boundaries in yellow; hill shading. DM 8.80

MITTEL- UND WESTEUROPA
1:2,500,000
No 1960
München : JRO
123 x 88
Covers England - Czechoslovakia, Scandinavia inset at 1:5,000,000, Greece at 1:2,500,000. Shows roads, railways, air-routes etc. For journey planning purposes. DM 6.80

ROAD MAP OF EUROPE
1:2,000,000
In 6 sheets, see index 4/1
Wien : F-B
Various sizes
Main and secondary roads, numbers, spot heights, hill shading, state boundaries.
Sheets available:
Scandinavien und Finnland, 88 x 107
Östeuropa, 88 x 124
Westeuropa, mit Spanien und Portugal, 88 x 124
Mittel-europa, mit Italien, 88 x 124
Nordafrika und Westliches Mittelmeer
Kleinasien und Östliches Mittelmeer

MITTELEUROPA
1:2,000,000
No 870
Frankfurt : Ravenstein
72 x80
Detailed road map of central Europe.
DM 7.80

NYUGAT EURÓPA AUTOTÉRKEPÉ
1:2,000,000
Budapest : Cart
82 x 117
Col. road map of W Europe. Legend in 8 langs

AUTOMAPA STŘEDNÍ EVROPY
1:1,500,000
Praha : Kart
Roads classified and numbered, distances in km, motoring and tourist details.
Kcs 14

EURO-FALK
1:1,500,000
No 387
Hamburg : Falk
Road map with patent fold. DM 9.80

ROAD MAPS OF EUROPE
1:1,000,000
See index 4/2
Bern : K & F
Various sizes
All classes of roads, distances, scenic routes, railways, places of tourist interest.
Sheets available:
1130 Alpine Countries
1132 France
1136 Great Britain & Ireland
1134 Greece & Aegean
1146 Southern Scandinavia
1148 Germany
1140 Yugoslavia
1144 Spain and Portugal
1138 Italy
1142 Central Europe
1147 Finnland
1175 Eastern Europe
1176 DDR - Polen - CSSR
1177 Türkei

HALLWAG ROAD MAPS OF EUROPE
1:1,000,000
Bern : Hallwag
Various sizes
Showing all classes of roads, distances and route numbers, railways and camping sites. Relief shaded.
Maps available:
Central Europe
Austria
Benelux (1:600,000)
Czechoslovakia - Hungary
Finland
France
Germany
Germany North (1:602,000)
Germany South (1:602,000)
Great Britain
Greece
Italy
Mediterranean Isles
Rumania - Bulgaria
Scandinavia
Spain and Portugal
Switzerland (1:300,000)
Yugoslavia

GRANDES ROUTES
1:1,000,000
In 5 sheets, see index 4/3
Paris : Michelin, 1972
Main and secondary roads, road conditions, distances, car ferries, railways, airports and state boundaries.
Sheets available:
986 Great Britain & Ireland (1:900,000)
987 Germany, Benelux, Austria
988 Italy, Switzerland
989 France
990 Spain & Portugal

RV LÄNDERKARTEN
1:800,000
Stuttgart : RV
Various sizes
All classes of roads, route numbers, distances in km, spot heights in metres, hill shading, railways, youth hostels, camping sites, scenic routes and airports. Text in 4 langs.
Sheets available:

70 Schweiz-Tirol (1:400,000)
80 Deutschland
82 Österreich (1:450,000)
83 DDR (1:500,000)
84 Griechenland
85 Spanien und Portugal
86 Benelux (1:500,000)
87 Alpen
88 Italien
89 Frankreich
90 Jugoslavien
91 Süd-Skandinavien
92 Polen
94 Grossbritannien (1:625,000)
95 Rumanien
97 Turkei mit Naher Osten (1:800,000 and 1:2,500,000)
98 Südosteuropa (1:2,500,000)
99 Europa (1:3,500,000)
100 Naher Osten (1:2,500,000)
101 Danemark (1:300,000)
202 Deutschland (1:700,000)

CARTA STRADALE D'EUROPA
1:500,000
In 35 sheets, see index 4/4
Milano : TCI
All classes of roads, conditions, distances in km, spot heights, contour layer col, railways, car ferries.

LES CARTES BLEUES
1:500,000
In 27 sheets, see index 4/6
Paris : Bordas-Hachette
Roads classified with distances, railways, relief shading, tourist information. Series in progress.
Sheets published:

1 Paris - Normandie - Bretagne
2 Paris - Belgique - Vallée du Rhin
3 Paris - Suisse - Milan
4 Bordeaux - Lyon - Marseille
5 Marseille - Côte d'Azur - Rome - Venise
6 Rome - Naples - Tarente - Messine
7 Naples - Reggio - Sicile - Sardaigne - Tunis
8 Santander - Toulouse - Madrid - Barcelona - Iles Baléares
10 Badajoz - Valence - Seville - Gibraltar
21 Francfort - Prague - Munich - Vienne - Graz
22 Cracovis - Lvov - Vienne - Budapest - Cluj
24 Trieste - Zagreb - Belgrade - Dubrovnik
25 Sofia - Bucarest - Constantsa
26 Skopje - Tirana - Salonique - Athènes
27 Istanbul - Izmir - Rhodes - Crete

A2 GENERAL MAPS: LOCAL

EUROPA POLUDNIOWOWSCHODNIA - MAPA SAMACHODOWA
1:2,000,000
Warszawa : PPWK, 1971
Road map of SW Europe with 7 towns inset.

WORLD TRAVEL MAP OF CENTRAL EUROPE
1:1,250,000
Edinburgh : Bart
75 x 87
Road map, route numbers and distances, extends from London to Venice and Berlin to the Riviera. 75p

ALPENLÄNDER
1:1,000,000
No 1130
Bern : K & F
112 x 71
Covers Austria, S E France, N Italy (to Perugia). Roads classified and numbered, distances in km, hill shading, railways, ferries, camping sites, motels.

ZENTRALEUROPA (ALPENLÄNDER)
1:1,000,000
Bern : Hallwag, 1972
108 x 80
Main, secondary roads, distances in km, spot heights in metres, tourist details.

ALPENLÄNDER; AUTOKARTE
1:1,000,000
München : Kompass
Road map with route numbers and distances, places of interest. DM 1.90

NORTH ITALIAN LAKES, SWITZERLAND, TIROL AND THE RIVIERA
1:1,000,000
London : Foldex
Shows roads classified, relief shading; patent fold. 45p

THE ALPS AND ALPINE LAKES
1:1,000,000
London : Foldex
Showing roads classified, relief shading. Patent folding. 45p

ALPEN : SHELL REISEKARTE
1:850,000
Stuttgart : Mairs
Col. road map, roads classified and numbered, distances in km, places of tourist interest, camping sites, motoring information. Legend in 12 langs. DM 4.80

DIE ALPEN
1:800,000
No 87
Stuttgart : RV
113 x 88
Covers Switzerland, Austria, Northern Italy and Rhone Valley. Main and secondary roads, numbered, distances in km, other communications, places of interest, camping sites, motels. DM 8.80

ALPENLÄNDER
1:750,000
No 1775
München : JRO
123 x 88
Col. road map covering Switzerland, Austria, North Italy, Bavaria, Fr. Alps. Roads classified and numbered, distances in km, relief shading, places of interest. DM 6.80

ALPENSTRASSEN
1:500,000
No 1110
Bern : K & F, 1971
128 x 68
Covers Munich - Turin, Geneva - Salzburg. Roads classified and numbered, distances in km, spot heights, hill shading, places of interest, camping sites etc.

ZENTRALALPEN
1:450,000
No 1482
München : JRO
98 x 68
Col. map. Roads classified and numbered, distances in km, places of interest, internat. boundaries, railways. Covers area E Switzerland, Oberbayern, Voralberg, Tyrol, Salzburg. DM 4.80
Also available:
No 1439 Passefahrtenkarte Innsbruck bis Zurich; part of map 1482, showing mountain passes. DM 2.50

ZENTRALALPEN
No 534
München : JRO
68 x 51
Col. birds eye view map, showing land relief and formation, roads, settlements etc. DM 1.90
Also, enlarged ed, 115 x 87, No 535 DM 4.80

CROSSING THE CHANNEL : A DAILY TELEGRAPH LEISURE MAP
1:500,000
London : Geographia, 1972
103 x 41
Principal roads away from Channel ports; depth shown by col. Reverse has illus. of ferries, hovercraft, aircraft and street plans of Channel ports; historical notes. Legend Ger, Fr, Eng. 30p

SHELL REISEKARTE MITTELMEER
1:4,500,000
Stuttgart : Mairs, 1970
128 x 50
Col. road map covering Mediterranean Area, inc. Canary Is and Madeira. Travel information, places of interest, shipping lines; legend in 12 langs. DM 4.80

OSTEUROPA
1:3,000,000
Bern : Hallwag, 1971
67 x 80
Oslo-Moscow, Genoa-Ankara. Main and secondary roads, distances in km, mt. passes, heights in metres, state boundaries.

SÜD-OST EUROPA
1:2,500,000
No 98
Stuttgart : RV
96 x 70
Roads classified and numbered, with distances, inc. Southern Turkey. DM 6.80

KELET - EURÓPA AUTOTÉRKÉPE
1:1,950,000
Budapest : Cart
82 x 117
Col. road map of E Europe with legend in 9 langs.

EUROPE DE L'EST
1:1,950,000
Geneve : Nagel, 1972
Road map of Eastern Europe

PŘEHLEDNE AUTOMAPY SOCIALISTICKYCH KRAJIN
Praha : Kart, 1972
Comprehensive map of Socialist Countries. Covers Bulgaria, Yugoslavia, DDR, Hungary, Poland, Rumania, USSR North and South. In 4 sheets with title sheet contained in bag. Shows road networks, important camping sites. Legend Eng, Ger, Rus and Hung. Kcs 5

C OFFICIAL SURVEYS

THE WORLD
1:5,000,000
AGS
Sheet 1 covers Europe
See WORLD 100C and index 100/3.

WORLD - DEUTSCHE WELTKARTE
1:5,000,000
Meyer
Sheets 1 & 2
See WORLD 100C

CARTE DES CONTINENTS
1:5,000,000
IGN
4 sheets cover Europe
See WORLD 100C and index 100/5

EUROPE
1:2,000,000
Series 1209
In 6 sheets, see index 4/6
Feltham : DMS, 1971
108 x 158 each
Planning wall map, based on AGS world series, 1:5,000,000. Physical details, contours and layer col, communications and boundaries.
Each £1.50

THE WORLD
1:1,000,000
DMA Series 1301
Tolworth : MOD
See WORLD 100C and index 100/1.

ÜBERSICHTSKARTE VON MITTELEUROPA
1:750,000
In 54 sheets
Wien : BEV, c 1900-30
Coloured pre-war topog. map series, Bonne's projection.
Each A. Sch 10
Also, series on Albers projection, 12 sheets available.
Each A. Sch 10

THE WORLD
1:500,000
DMS Series 1404
Tolworth : MOD
See WORLD 100C and index 100/7.

ÜBERSICHTSKARTE VON MITTELEUROPA
1:300,000
See index 430/1
Frankfurt : Inst. für Angewandte Geodäsie
Pre-war series covering an area from Paris - Smolensk. In black and white, or 5-6 colour editions, showing general topog. information.
Monochrome DM 1.40
Coloured ed. DM 2.00

GENERALKARTE VON MITTELEUROPA
1:200,000
In 265 sheets, see index 436/1
Wien : BEV
48 x 66 each
Coloured pre-war map series, covering Zurich, Odessa, Stettin-Mediterranean. Vegetation green, relief hachures in brown, topog. detail, lettering in black. Present Austrian roads overprinted in red and yellow.
Roads overprinted A. Sch 15.00
Other sheets A. Sch 12.00
List of symbols A. Sch 8.00

D POLITICAL & ADMINISTRATIVE

EUROPA, MAPA FIZYCZNA I POLITYCZNA
1:12,000,000
PPWK
See EUROPE 4 E1.

EUROPAKARTE
1:8,500,000
No 502
Frankfurt : Ravenstein
70 x 65
Political col. map DM 6.80

EUROPE
Tehran : Sahab
30 x 45
Political student map with physical and location insets. In Persian.

EUROPE
1:8,000,000
Tehran : Sahab
60 x 90
Boundaries, settlements. Physical, economic and pictorial insets. Chart of political and economic info. In Persian.

DAILY TELEGRAPH MAP OF EUROPE
1:6,635,000
London : Gia, 1971
89 x 69
Political col; major roads and railways : 7 political insets; major towns named.
50p

EUROPE
1:6,375,000
Washington : NGS
67 x 76
Political col. wall map.
Paper US S2.00
Plastic US S3.00
Enlarged ed. (127 x 144) US S5.00

EUROPA
1:6,000,000
Wien : FB
106 x 83
Political col. wall map with communications.
DM 4.20

DIE STAATEN EUROPAS
1:6,000,000
Darmstadt : Perthes
110 x 100
Col. wall map (Kleine Geographischer Wandatlas) showing political divisions.
DM 48.00

PHILIP'S INTERNATIONAL MAP OF EUROPE
1:6,000,000
London : Philip, 1971
101 x 76
Bold political col. wall map; chief railways and towns. 50p

COMPARATIVE WALL ATLAS : EUROPE - POLITICAL
1:6,000,000
Philip
See EUROPE 4 E1.

EUROPE, SUPERIOR WALL MAP
Maplewood : Hammond
71 x 63
Col. Political map in folder. US S2.00

EUROPA POLÍTICA
Barcelona : Editorial Teide
88 x 115
Political wall map for schools in Spanish.
S. Ptas 175

POLITICAL SMALLER WALL MAPS OF EUROPE
1:6,000,000
London : Philip, 1971
101 x 80
Political col, with communications, town stamps graded by pop.
Paper flat £1.50
Mounted CR £5.50
Mounted on cloth, dissected to fold £7.00

STANFORD'S GENERAL MAP OF EUROPE
1:6,000,000
London : Stanford, 1973
91 x 74
Political col, pictorial border.
Paper folded 50p
Mounted CRV £6.50

EUROPA
1:5,000,000
Bern : Hallwag
110 x 95
Political col, international nomenclature.

EUROPE PHYSIQUE
1:5,000,000
Armand Colin
With polical map on reverse.
See EUROPE 4 E1.

EUROPA
1:5,000,000
Novara : Ag
100 x 140
Political map. L 1,600

EUROPA
1:5,000,000
Stuttgart : Mair
110 x 96
Political col, communications.
DM 5.80

EUROPA - GESAMTKARTE
1:5,000,000
No 4151
Bern : K & F
106 x 91
Political col, with communications; main cities named; border of national flags.

LÄNDERKARTE EUROPA
1:5,000,000
No. 11
München : JRO
119 x 88
Political col. map, with boundaries, communications, relief shading.
DM 9.80
Mounted CR DM 50.00

BARTHOLOMEW WORLD TRAVEL MAP EUROPE, POLITICAL
1:5,000,000
Edinburgh : Bart, 1970
70 x 94
White based map: principal cities shown, with main rail and shipping routes. Boundaries shown in col. Palestine and east Med. inset.
75p

EUROPE NO 3 (POLITIQUE)
1:5,000,000
No 1057
St Germain-en-Laye : Editions MDI
126 x 92
Plastic coated political wall map for schools, with agricultural map on reverse. Also in English ed.

MAP OF EUROPE
1:4.976,000
Michigan : Hearne Bros
167 x 122
Col. school wall map, political boundaries, relief shading, mechanical index.
US $152.50

EUROPE : POLITICAL GEOGRAPHY WALL MAP
1:4.687,500
No 107021
Chicago : Denoyer-Geppert
Political col. school wall map, showing boundaries, communications, water features, pop.
CR US $19.25

POLITICAL MAPS OF EUROPE
Indianapolis : Cram
Series of political col. school wall maps available at different levels and depths.

Level B – Simplified	1:4,677,500
129 x 122	US $23.00
Level C – Detailed	1:4,677,500
129 x 122	US $23.00
Political Outline	1:4,677,500
129 x 122	US $27.50
Desk Outline Map	No scale
43 x 30	US $0.60
Excello Political Wall Map	1:5,312,500
100 x 137	US $12.50

EUROPA
1:4.500.000
Stockholm : GLA, 1970
102 x 118
General map with political col.
Flat S.Kr 13.50
Boards S.Kr 76.00

EUROPA
1:4,000,000
Madrid : Aguilar
130 x 200
Political coloured school map.
Paper S.Ptas 100
Cloth S.Ptas 550

EUROPA POLITICA
1:4,000,000
Novara : Ag
155 x 140
2 sheet wall map for schools (First Series) showing state boundaries, major communications, towns graded by pop.
L 3,000
Mounted L 6,500

IMPERIAL MAP OF EUROPE
1:4.000.000
Chicago : Rand McNally
106 x 71
Countries shown by col. Index on political map. US $1.00

EUROPE POLITIQUE
No 14
Paris : Hatier
100 x 120
Political col. school wall map.

POLITICKÁ MAPA EVROPY
1:4.000,000
Praha : Kart, 1972
General school wall map of Europe, showing political boundaries, major roads and railways, shipping lines and airports. Border of national flags. Kcs 25

EUROPE
1:4,000,000
Bruxelles : Mantnieks
119 x 160
Politically coloured wall map in French or English eds. Bonne projection. Available mounted in various styles.

NEW COMMERCIAL MAP OF EUROPE
1:3,500,000
In 2 sheets
London : Philip, 1969
154 x 127
Politically col. wall map showing shipping routes and principal ports.
Set £4.50
Mounted CRV £25.00

POLITICAL LARGE WALL MAPS : EUROPE
1:3,000,000
London : Philip
173 x 155
Political divisions in col. communications, town stamps graded by pop.
Mounted CR £15.00
Mounted on cloth dissected to fold £17.00

EUROPA, POLITISCHE ÜBERSICHT
1:3,000,000
Gotha : Haack
207 x 191
Political wall map, col. by countries, cities graded by pop, communications, relief.

EUROPA, STAATEN
1:3,000,000
Braunschweig : Westermann
199 x 187
Political wall map col. by countries; cities graded by pop, main roads and railways, relief shown by hachures.

STAATEN EUROPAS
1:3.000.000 W722
München : List
210 x 170
Wenschow col. wall map, showing political divisions, relief, major communications and cities.
DM156.00

WOLTERS WANDKAART VAN EUROPA
Groningen : Wolters-Noordhof
200 x 169
Politically col. wall map, with relief indicated. Major towns shown.
Fl. 178.75

EUROPPA
1:2,800,000
Helsinki : WSOY
206 x 198
School wall map in Finnish
FMK 100

EUROPE, POLITICAL
Indianapolis : Cram
School political wall map also showing pop. density, National wealth, communications.
US $13.75

EUROPA
Various scales
Barcelona : Editorial Teide
25 x 33 (33 x 25)
Hand maps, showing boundaries, principal cities etc.
Maps available :
Europa (33 x 50) S.Ptas 2
Europa Política
Europa Norteoccidental
Francia y Benelux
Alemania, Polonia, Checoslovaquia
Europa Central
Europa Danubiana y Meridional
Europa
Europa Occidental
Europa Meridional
Each S.Ptas 1

EUROPA
1:20,000,000
Novara : Ag
Small outline map of Europe
L 40

LARGE OUTLINE MAP OF EUROPE
1:6,000,000
London : Philip, 1968
101 x 80
Marking in black, coastlines and national boundaries.
£1.25

MAP BUILDING SHEETS (BLACKBOARD MAPS) : EUROPE
1:6,000,000
London : Philip, 1968
101 x 80
Coastlines and national boundaries in yellow on blackboard paper.
Information can be added in chalk and erased.
CR £4.00

UMRISSKARTE EUROPA
1:5,000,000
No 0834
Bern : K & F
117 x 96
Base outline map with rivers and boundaries.
No 0835, with political boundaries.

EUROPE, OUTLINE SLATED
1:4,687,500
No 165021
Chicago : Denoyer-Geppert
112 x 129
Blackboard map showing countries, blue and yellow on black.
US $19.95

THE WORLD
1:5,000,000
DMS Series 1105
MOD
Sheets 12 and 13 cover Europe.
See WORLD 100D and index 100/10.

VITO-GRAPHIC CHALKBOARD OUTLINE MAP OF EUROPE
1:3,500,000
Ref : VS7
Chicago : Weber Costello Co
152 x 137
Land areas in green, meridians, parallels and outlines in yellow, water areas in blue.
On cloth — various mounted styles.

West Europe

HAACK - HANDKARTEN - EUROPA; WESTLICHER UND SÜDWESTLICHER TEIL
1:3,000,000
2nd ed
Gotha : Haack
60 x 100
Col. hand map showing boundaries, with relief shading, communications.
With 64pp text. M 7.20

WESTERN EUROPE
1:2,437,500
Washington : NGS
73 x 95
Political col. wall map.
Paper US $2.00
Plastic US $3.00

ZÁPADNÍ EVROPA
1:1,250,000
Praha : Kart, 1969
General school wall map of Western Europe.
Kcs 150

BELGIO, OLANDOE DANIMARCA
1:2,000,000
Novara : Ag
Small outline map of N W Europe.
L 40

Central Europe and Alps

EUROPA : MITTLERER UND SUDOSTLICHER TEIL
1:3,000,000
2nd ed
Gotha : Haack
60 x 88
Col. hand map with boundaries, communications and relief shading.
84pp text. M 7.00

STREDNÍ EVROPA
1:1,250,000
Praha : Kart, 1968
General school wall map of Central Europe.
Kcs 90

ALPI
1:3,000,000
Novara : Ag
Small outline map of the Alpine countries.
L 40

EUROPA CENTRALE
1:5,000,000
Novara : Ag
Small hand map for schools, showing outlines of the countries. L 40

Eastern Europe

HAACK HANDKARTEN - EUROPA : OSTSEELANDER
1:3,000,000
2nd ed
Gotha : Haack
60 x 88
Col. hand map with boundaries, communications and relief shading.
56pp text. M 6.60

JIHOVÝCHODNÍ EVROPA A ITALIE
1:1,250,000
Praha : Kart, 1969
General school wall map of S E Europe and Italy. Kcs 180

UMRISSKARTE DER DONAULANDER
1:3,000,000
No 0823
Bern : K & F
46 x 37
Base map with rivers and boundaries.

E1 PHYSICAL: RELIEF

EUROPA FISICA
Barcelona : Editorial Teide
25 x 33
Physical hand map S.Ptas 1

UMRISSKARTE EUROPA
1:28,000,000
No 0836
Bern : K & F
23 x 15
Base map with hydrography and hachuring.

EUROPA, MAPA FIZYCZNA I POLITYCZNA
1:12,000,000
Warszawa : PPWK, 1972
52 x 47
Double sided school wal; hydrographic and topographic features, relief shown on physical map, political boundaries on reverse.
Z1 5

EUROPA MAPA FIZYCZNA
1:12,000,000
Warszawa : PPWK, 1972
51 x 45
Physical hand map with contours.
Z1 I

EUROPE AND THE MIDDLE EAST
1:11,000,000
London : RGS, 1941
91 x 59
Six colour map showing relief and international boundaries. Also in Arabic edition.
£1.00

EUROPA FISICA
Barcelona : Editorial Teide
88 x 115
Physical wall map for schools.
S.Ptas 275

EUROPA AND NÄHER OSTEN
1:7,500,000
Munchen : List
125 x 100
Wenschow col. physical wall map for schools, layer cols, relief shading, communications and towns.

PHYSICAL SMALLER WALL MAPS: EUROPE
1:6,000,000
London : Philip, 1971
101 x 80
Physical features shown by 'layer tinting', political boundaries in red.
Paper flat £1.50
Mounted CR £5.50
Mounted on cloth dissected to fold £7.00
Arabic edition also available.

COMPARATIVE WALL ATLAS : EUROPE
1:6,000,000
London : Philip, 1970
101 x 80
A set of five maps portraying following geog. factors: Relief of Land : Political and Communications
Climate: Summer Conditions, Winter Conditions, Rainfall, Isobars, Winds, Actual Temperature and Sea Level Isotherms.
Natural Vegetation
Political
Density of Population
Mounted CR £5.50
Mounted on cloth dissected to fold £7.00

GRAPHIC RELIEF WALL MAPS: EUROPE
1:6,000,000
London : Philip, 1975
101 x 80
Hill shaded, col. to simulate predominant vegetation cover, giving graphic aerial impression.
Paper £1.50
Mounted CR £5.50
Mounted on cloth dissected to fold £7.00

KLEINE EUROPA KARTE
1:6,000,000
Darmstadt : Perthes
110 x 100
Small Physical map of Europe.
DM 48

TRI-GRAPHIC MAP OF EUROPE
1:5,000,000
TRI-7
Chicago : Weber Costello Co
137 x 101
Physical layer colouring with graphic relief shading and political boundaries.
Available mounted in various styles.

EUROPE PHYSIQUE
No 13
Paris : Hatier
120 x 100
School Wall map.

EUROPE PHYSIQUE
1:5,000,000
Map No 312
Ed. Vidal-Lablache and H. Varon
Paris: Armand Colin

120 x 100
School wall map, with political map on reverse.

KLEINE PHYSIKALISCHE EUROPAKARTE
1:5,000,000
Wien : FB
125 x 115
Small physical map, layer coloured.

ZAPADNAYA EVROPA, FIZICHESKAYA UCHEBNAYA KARTA
1:5,000,000
Moskva : GUGK, 1970
School geog. wall map in Russian.

EUROPE NO 1 (PHYSIQUE)
1:5,000,000
No 1055
St Germain-en-Laye : Editions MDI
126 x 92
Plastic coated physical wall map for schools, with physical outline map on reverse. Also in English ed.

EUROPE
1:4,687,500
No 130021
Chicago : Denoyer-Geppert
111 x 147
Classroom physical-political map showing land detail, boundaries, pop.
Rollers US $15.50

EUROPE, VISUAL RELIEF
1:4,687,500
No 110021
Chicago : Denoyer-Geppert
111 x 147
Physical wall school map showing relief of land and sea, boundaries.
US $18.75
Reduced size ed. available as desk map, No. 301521, US $3.30 per 25 copies, 28 x 43 each

PHYSICAL MAPS OF EUROPE
Indianapolis : Cram
Series of physical col, school wall maps available at different levels and depths.

Level B Simplified	1:4,677,500
129 x 129	US $23.00
Level C Detailed	1:4,677,500
129 x 129	US $23.00
Physical Outline	1:4,677,500
129 x 129	US $27.50
Excello Physical Wall Map	1:5,000,000
100 x 137	US $12.50

EUROPA
1:4,000,000
In 4 sheets
Beograd : Geokarta
164 x 138 complete
Physical wall map in cyrillic and latin lettering
Cloth mounted Dn 150

EUROPA
1:4,000,000
Madrid : Aguilar
130 x 200
Physical coloured school wall map, with hypsometric tints and altitude indicated.
Cloth map.

EVROPA
1:4,000,000
Praha : Kart, 1968
Relief map. Kcs 330

EUROPA : FISICO-POLITICA
1:4,000,000
In 2 sheets
Novara : Ag
150 x 140
School wall map, showing relief shading, communications, towns graded by pop, rivers. First series.
L 3,000
Mounted L 6,500
Second series:
1:3,500,000 186 x 210 (In 4 sheets)
L 4,000
Mounted L 8,500
Third series:
1:5,000,000 100 x 140 L 2,200
Mounted L 5,000

EURÓPA DOMBORZATA ÉS VÍZEI
1:4,000,000
In 4 sheets
Budapest : Cart, 1970
Physical wall map of Europe.

EUROPA FISICA
1:4,000,000
In 2 sheets
Novara : Ag
155 x 140
Map for schools, showing relief of land and sea, cities graded by pop.
First series: L 3,000
Mounted L 6,500
Second series:
1:3,000,000 (In 4 sheets) 204 x 190
L 4,000
Mounted L 8,500

INTERNATIONALE KARTE VON EUROPA
1:3,500,000
In 4 sheets
Berlin : Schaffmann & Kluge
Relief col; communications and political boundaries.
DM 42.00
CR DM 136.50

EUROPA
1:3,000,000
Groningen : Wolters-Noordhoff
210 x 170
Physical wall map for schools, showing land relief, settlements, boundaries, main communications, some economic features.
Fl 201.75

EUROPE
1:3,000,000
Bruxelles : Mantnieks
183 x 180
Physical wall map for schools, showing relief of land and sea in colour, political boundaries in red.

EUROPA
1:3,000,000
Braunschweig : Westermann
202 x 162
Physical col. wall map, showing relief, internat. boundaries, cities graded by pop.

EUROPA MIT MEERESBODENRELIEF
1:3,000,000
W711
Munchen : List
210 x 170
Wenschow col. relief wall map of land and sea areas. In Ger. Eng, Fr, Sw. It. eds.
DM 164.00

PHYSIKALISCHE KARTE EUROPA
1:3,000,000
Wien : FB
210 x 180
Physical col. wall map.

PHYSICAL LARGE WALL MAPS: EUROPE
1:3,000,000
London : Philip
173 x 155
Orographically col, hill shading, political boundaries, railways and ocean routes.
Mounted CR £15.00
Mounted on cloth dissected to fold £17.00

PHYSIKALISCHE KARTE EUROPA
1:3,000,000
Hamburg : Flemming
206 x 166
Physical col. wall map; layer col, hill shading, boundaries, railways, cities graded by pop.

EUROPA
1:3,000,000
In 4 sheets
København : GI
193 x 153
Physical wall map, layer colours, communications. Available either with or without place names.

EUROPA
1:3,000,000
Gotha : Haack, 1967
213 x 187
Physical col. wall map for schools, land relief, sea depths, boundaries, rivers.

PHYSIKALISCHE KARTE EUROPA
1:2,800,000
H205
München : List
210 x 195
Harms school wall map in col; political boundaries in red; relief shading.
DM164.00

EUROPA : REISEN-AUSGABE
1:2,000,000
Darmstadt : Perthes
300 x 300
Physical wall map with road and rail communications.
DM 400

EUROPA
1:20,000,000
Novara : Ag
33 x 26
Moulded plastic relief map with political map and physico-politico-economic details on reverse.
L 450

CARTE EN RELIEF EUROPE-AFRIQUE
1:5,000,000
Paris : IGN
61 x 87
Physical layered col. plastic relief map. Inc. Southern Scandinavia and Northern Africa.
F.Fr. 83.33

EUROPE
1:5,000,000
No 198021
Chicago : Denoyer-Geppert
121 x 91
Tactual raised relief map, vertical exaggeration 1/25. In steel frame.
US $49.50

EUROPA - FISICO-POLITICA
1:5,000,000
Novara : Ag
131 x 100
Moulded plastic relief map for schools, with political boundaries. Metal corners.
L 20,000

RAISED RELIEF MAP OF EUROPE
1:4,521,000
NR2
Chicago : Nystrom 1974
112 x 98
Plastic moulded map, physical layer colouring, principal communications and boundaries.
Unframed US $46.00
Framed US $74.00

RAISED RELIEF MAP OF EUROPE
New York : Hagstrom
50 x 68
3-D Plastic raised relief map, physical colouring. $2.95

Western Europe

WORLD TRAVEL MAP OF WESTERN EUROPE
1:3,000,000
Edinburgh : Bart, 1974
80 x 101
Contoured and layer col. with road and rail communications, international boundaries. Extends from Spain to Italy to Southern Scandinavia.
75p

SREDNYAYA I YUZHNAYA EVROPA
1:2,500,000
Moskva : GUGK, 1973
2 sheet physical school map of Central and Southern Europe.
32 kop

WESTEUROPA
1:2,000,000
Gotha : Haack
160 x 215
Physical wall map, relief shading of land and sea, boundaries, drainage.

NORDSEELÄNDER
1:1,625,000
Hamburg : Flemming
99 x 137
Physical col. school wall map, covering N Sea countries, inc. Iceland. Layer col, relief shading, boundaries.

SÜDWESTEUROPA
1:1,625,000
Hamburg : Flemming
96 x 137
Physical col. wall map, layer col, relief shading, cities graded by pop, boundaries, railways.

WESTEUROPA
1:1,000,000
W724
München : List
170 x 245
Wenschow physical wall map of W Europe.
DM 164.00

NORDSEELÄNDER
1:900,000
Braunschweig : Westermann
230 x 214
Physical school wall map, North Sea centred, covering Great Britain, Benelux Countries, N France and Germany, S Scandinavia. Relief shading, communications, cities graded by pop.

Central Europe and Alps

RELIEF MITTELEUROPA IN SCHRAFFENDARSTELLUNG
1:2,500,000
Bonn-Bad Godesberg : Inst. fur Landeskunde
61 x 53
1 colour relief map of Central Europe with hachuring, showing boundaries and water features.
DM 0.90
Also available at 1:3,000,000, 51 x 47, showing water features only
DM 0.65

MIDDEN-EUROPA
1:1,500,000
Groningen : Wolters-Noordhoff
107 x 85
Physical school wall map; relief shading, boundaries, communications.
FL. 44.75

MITTELEUROPA UND WESTLICHES OSTEUROPA
1:1,500,000
München : List
210 x 150
Harms physical wall map of Central Europe.
DM 164.00

STŘEDNÍ EVROPA
1:1.500,000
Praha : Kart, 1970
Physical/political reference map of Central Europe in series "Poznavame Svet" (getting to know the world).
With thematic text volume.
Kcs 18

REGIONAL WALL MAP OF CENTRAL EUROPE
1:1,250,000
London : Philip, 1971
107 x 86
Contoured and layer col. with communications, towns and boundaries. Extends from Bornholm to Ljubljana, Amsterdam to Grodno.
Mounted CR £5.50
Cloth dissected to fold £7.00

MITTELEUROPA
1:1,000,000
W709
München : List
240 x 175
Wenschow physical wall map for schools. Also available in Swedish ed.
DM 164.00

EUROPE CENTRALE
1:1,000,000
No 1064
Ed. P Serryn
St. Germain-en-Laye: Éditions MDI, 1973
126 x 92
Double sided physical wall map of the Balkan Peninsula with Poland-Czechoslovakia on the reverse.

MITTELEUROPA PHYSIKALISCH
1:900,000
Braunschweig : Westermann
223 x 214
Physical col. wall map for schools; layer col, cities graded by pop, land types indicated, drainage emphasised.

MITTELEUROPA
1:750,000
Gotha : Haack, 1967
201 x 214
Physical col. school wall map for the area English Channel - Carpathians. Shows relief, with political boundaries.

PAYS ALPINS ET DANUBE
1:700,000
No 1063
Ed. P. Serryn
St. Germain-en-Laye: Editions MDI, 1974
92 x 126
Double sided physical wall map of Alpine countries with Danube region on the reverse.

LE ALPI
1:500,000
Novara : Ag
200 x 120
2 sheet map, showing physical relief, political boundaries, major communications, cities graded by pop.
L 3,000
Mounted L 6,500

DIE ALPENLÄNDER
1:450,000
Gotha : Haack, 1962
216 x 168
Physical school wall map showing relief of the Alpine area.

DIE ALPEN
1:400,000
W733
München : List
245 x 165
Wenschow physical wall map covering Fr. Austrian, Italian, Germ. Alps. Cities graded by pop, communications, boundaries. Political map inset. DM 164.00

EUROPA CENTRALE
1:5,000,000
Novara : Ag
33 x 26
Plastic relief map covering Germany and the Alps. Physical, political and economic details on reverse.
L 450

ALPI
1:1,000,000
Novara : Ag
91 x 84
Plastic relief map with metal corners.
L 15,000

Eastern Europe

OOST-EUROPA
1:4,000,000
Groningen : Wolters — Noordhoff
107 x 85
Physical school wall map; relief shading, boundaries, communications.
Fl 44.75

WORLD TRAVEL MAP OF EASTERN EUROPE
1:2,500,000

41 British Isles

See also:

410 GREAT BRITAIN
411 SCOTLAND
415 IRELAND
416 NORTHERN IRELAND
417 REPUBLIC OF IRELAND
420 ENGLAND AND WALES
423.4 CHANNEL ISLANDS
429 WALES

A1 GENERAL MAPS: ROADS

SHELL REISEKARTE GROSSBRITANNIEN UND IRLAND
1:1,500,000
Stuttgart : Mair
Col. road map; roads classified and numbered, places of tourist interest, accommodation, motoring information. Legend in 12 langs. S W England inset at 1:750,000. DM 4.80

GRAN BRETAGNA E IRLANDA
1:1,000,000
Novara : Agostini
Tourist road map. L 700

GROSSBRITANNIEN, MIT IRLAND
1:1,000,000
Bern : Hallwag
98 x 102
Shaded relief map showing all classes of roads, distances in miles, railways, important camping sites, airports and car ferries.

GROSSBRITANNIEN - IRLAND
1:1,000,000
No 1136
Bern : K & F, 1972
86 x 96
Relief shaded showing all classes of roads, distances in km, places of interest, spot heights, ferries, motels, beaches and camping sites. Orkney, Shetland Islands, London, Channel Isles inset. Legend Eng, Fr, Ger, It.

BRITISCHE INSELN
1:1,000,000
No 898
Frankfurt : Ravenstein, 1976
91 x 104
Detailed route map, roads classified with distances in km. DM 8.80

BRITISH ISLES MOTORING MAP
1:1.000,000
Edinburgh : Bart, 1972
83 x 95
Road map, contour col; main and secondary roads, heights in feet, car ferries, airports, hill shading and distances in miles. Inset map of the counties and distance chart.
Paper folded 30p
Cloth folded 50p

BP PLANNING MAP OF GREAT BRITAIN AND IRELAND
1:1,000,000
London : Philip
58 x 92
Main and secondary roads, distances in miles, car ferries, county boundaries, airports, principal railways and canals, continental car ferry routes, road signs and a distance chart. Ireland and Scotland on reverse side at same scale. 40p

MICHELIN MOTORING MAP OF GREAT BRITAIN AND IRELAND
1:900,000
No 986
Paris : Michelin
97 x 107
All classes of roads, widths, distances in miles, road numbers, car ferries, important airports, places of interest and county boundaries. Insets of Orkney and Shetland Islands, and various town plans.

NU-WAY ROAD SERIES
Various scales
In 3 sheets
London : Johnston & Bacon
Roads and motorways classified with table of distances, inset plans of principal towns and index to place names.
Maps available:
England and Wales
1:633,600 114 x 89 35p
Scotland
1:506,880 102 x 76 40p
Ireland
1:506,880 102 x 76 35p

BACON'S REVERSIBLE MAPS
Various scales
In 4 sheets
London : Johnston & Bacon
102 x 76 each
Double sided maps with roads classified including motorways and primary routes and large scale plans of principal cities.
Sheets available:
1 S England and Wales 1:500,000
London Map 1:63,360
2 S England and Wales 1:500,000
N England and Wales 1:500,000
3 S Scotland 1:380,160
N Scotland 1:380,160
4 N Ireland 1:316,800
S Ireland 1:316,800
Paper in plastic wallet. 45p each

SHELL ROAD MAPS OF GREAT BRITAIN AND IRELAND
1:250,000
1:387,160 (Ireland)
In 9 sheets
London : Philip, 1971/2
Various sizes
Main and secondary roads, numbers, distances in miles, car ferries, spot heights in feet, railways, tourist attractions, county boundaries. Printed on both sides.
30p
Complete set in case £2.70

A2 GENERAL MAPS: LOCAL

YOUR GUIDE MAPS
Various scales
London : Johnston & Bacon
89 x 66
Series of contour coloured maps showing scenic routes, other roads and railways and places of interest which are described and illustrated in the margin text.
Maps available:
1 North West Scotland 1:380,160
2 Central Scotland 1:380,160
3 Wales 1:380,160
4 Shakespeare's Country and the Cotswolds 1:158,400
5 The West Country 1:380,160
6 The Isle of Wight 1:63,360
7 Dublin and Around 1:15,840 – 1:316,800
8 South-West Ireland 1:316,800
9 Northumbria 1:380,160
each 50p

ROCKALL
1:50,000
London : RGS, 1975
42 x 59
Topographic and bathymetric map of the island compiled from hydrographic surveys and air photographs. £1.00

C OFFICIAL SURVEYS

KARTA MIRA
1:2,500,000
WK
Sheet 35 covers British Isles
See WORLD 100C and index 100/2

D POLITICAL & ADMINISTRATIVE

VELIKOBRITANIYA I IRLANDIYA
1:1,500,000
Moskva : GUGK, 1973
Col. study map showing admin. divisions and centres, water features, settlements, communications, boundaries, economic details, pop, Geog. description.

COUNTY MAP OF THE BRITISH ISLES
1:1,200,000
London : Gia, 1968
71 x 96
Counties in colour. 60p

REFERENCE MAP OF GREAT BRITAIN AND IRELAND
1:1,000,000
London : Philip, 1968
86 x 106
Counties in colour with inset of statistical information concerning administrative areas and population.
Paper flat £1.00
Mounted CRV £4.00

NATIONAL MAP OF THE BRITISH ISLES
1:1,000,000
London : Philip, 1974
83 x 104
Simplified map; counties in bold col, rivers, major towns. 50p

GRAPHIC RELIEF WALL MAP OF THE BRITISH ISLES
1:1,000,000

London : Philip, 1972
78 x 102
Col. to simulate predominant land use with hill shading.
Paper flat £1.50
Mounted CR £5.50
Mounted on cloth dissected to fold £7.00

EXCELLO POLITICAL MAP OF THE BRITISH ISLES
1:1,000,000
Indianapolis : Cram
137 x 100
Political col. wall map for schools.
$12.50

POLITICAL LARGE WALL MAP OF THE UNITED KINGDOM AND IRELAND
1:750,000
London : Philip
122 x 180
Counties shown in colour with railways and town populations indicated by symbols.
Mounted CR £15.00
Mounted on cloth dissected to fold, with eyelets £17.00

LIBRARY MAP OF THE BRITISH ISLES
1:633,600
London : Stanford, 1969
148 x 170
Counties in colour with railways and canals.
Paper flat £4.50
Mounted CR £11.50

ILES BRITANNIQUES
No 58
Paris : Hatier
100 x 120
School wall map; political and economic map on reverse.

ISLAS BRITANICAS
Barcelona : Editorial Teide
25 x 33
School hand map showing boundaries, major cities. S. Ptas 1

ISOLE BRITANNICHE
1:5,000,000
Novara : Agostini
Small outline hand map for schools.
L 40

UMRISSKARTE DER BRITISCHEN INSELN
1:3,000,000
No 0818
Bern : K & F
33 x 44
Outline map with rivers and boundaries.

PLANNING AND RECORD MAP NO 2 BRITISH ISLES
1:1,500,000
London : Gia
60 x 84
Outline map showing county boundaries, principal cities and towns. 25p
Also available in reduced size edition, 30 x 39 – for 10 75p

LARGE OUTLINE MAP OF GREAT BRITAIN AND IRELAND
1:1,000,000
London : Philip, 1969
80 x 102
County boundaries; positions of major towns, with principal contours.
£1.25

MAP BUILDING SHEETS ('BLACK–BOARD MAPS') OF GREAT BRITAIN AND IRELAND
1:1,000,000
London : Philip, 1969
80 x 102
Outline map printed in yellow on black-board paper.
CR £4.00

SALES PROMOTION MAP OF THE BRITISH ISLES
1:663,600
SP1
London : Stanford, 1968
134 x 158
Major towns shown with county boundaries emphasised in red.
Paper flat £4.50
Mounted CR £11.50

E1 PHYSICAL: RELIEF

PHYSICAL SMALLER WALL MAP OF GREAT BRITAIN AND IRELAND
1:1,500,000
London : Philip
84 x 109
Physical features depicted by layer colouring without hill shading.
Paper £1.50
Mounted CR £5.50
Mounted on cloth dissected to fold £7.00

VERENIGO KONINKRUK EN IERLAND
1:1,500,000
Groningen : Wolters-Noordhoff
107 x 85
Physical wall map for schools. Relief colouring, communications, boundaries.
Fl 44.75

WIELKÀ BRYTANIA-IRLANDIA
1:1,500,000
Warszawa : PPWK
69 x 79
Layer col, text on reverse in Polish. In series "Przegladowa Mapa Europy"
Physical wall map.

VELKÁ BRITÁNIE, IRSKO A STATY BENELUXU
1:1.500,000
Praha : Kart, 1963
92 x 96
Layer col. text in Czech. Inc. British Isles and Benelux. Physical, political reference map in series "Poznaváme Svet" (getting to know the world). Kcs 16

VELIKOBRITANIYA I IRLANDIYA - SPRAVOCHNAYA KARTA
1:1,500,000
Moskva : GUGK
Reference map of GB and Ireland.

THE BRITISH ISLES
1:1,250,000
Novara : Agostini
86 x 115
School wall map, showing relief shading, county boundaries and county towns underlined, towns graded by pop, major roads and railways. In English.
L 1750
Mounted L 3500

COMPARATIVE WALL ATLAS OF THE BRITISH ISLES - RELIEF OF LAND
1:1,500,000
London : Philip
82 x 101
Coloured wall map, layer coloured.
Mounted CR £5.50
Mounted dissected to fold £7.00

GRAPHIC RELIEF WALL MAP OF THE BRITISH ISLES
1:1,000,000
London : Philip, 1972
78 x 102
Col. to simulate predominant land use with hill shading.
Paper flat £1.50
Mounted CR £5.50
Mounted on cloth dissected to fold £7.00

VELIKOBRITANIYA I IRLANDIYA, FIZICHESKAYA KARTA
1:1,000,000
Moskva : GUGK, 1976
2 sheet physical wall map.

ILES BRITANNIQUES NO 1 (PHYSIQUE)
1:1,000,000
No 1150
St Germain-en-Laye : Éditions MDI
92 x 126
Plastic coated physical wall map for schools Agricultural map on reverse. Also available in English.

BRITISH ISLES
1:875,000
No 130121
Chicago : Denoyer-Geppert
111 x 147
Classroom physical-political map showing land detail, boundaries, pop. etc.
Rollers US $15.50

PHYSICAL LARGE WALL MAP OF GREAT BRITAIN AND IRELAND
1:750,000
London : Philip
122 x 180
Orographically coloured, with hill shading, boundaries and railways.
Mounted CR £15.00
Mounted on cloth dissected to fold, with eyelets £17.00

BRITISCHE INSELN
1:750,000
Gotha : Haack
162 x 172
Physical wall map for schools. Shows land relief, bathymetric col, communications, cities graded by pop. Shetland Isles inset.
M 142

BRITISCHE INSELN
1:700,000
H220
München : Paul List
175 x 215
Harms wall map with relief shading; communications; headings also in English.
DM 164.00

BRITISCHE INSELN
1:600,000
Braunschweig : Westermann
183 x 134

Physical col. wall map with large towns named. Communications, boundaries. Also available in English. DM 128

ISOLE BRITANNICHE
1:5,000,000
Novara : Agostini
26 x 33
Plastic relief map with physical, political and economic details on reverse.
L 450

INGHILTERRA
1:1,250,000
Novara : Agostini
97 x 122
Moulded plastic relief map, in frame with metal corners. L 20,000

E2 PHYSICAL: LAND FEATURES

TERRAIN MAP OF THE BRITISH ISLES
1:2,000,000
Williamsburg, Mass : Robert Frank Collins, 1969
50 x 61
Black and white map depicting relief by hachures and shading with town names and rivers. Inset map shows county boundaries.

F GEOLOGY

THE SUB-PLEISTOCENE GEOLOGY OF THE BRITISH ISLES AND THE ADJACENT CONTINENTAL SHELF
1:2,500,000
London : IGS, 1972
64 x 81
Col. map showing geol. periods and systems, rock types, faults, geol. boundaries. Covers British Isles and N W Coast of Europe. Contours on Pleistocene base in sea areas.
£1.05

GEOLOGICAL MAP OF THE BRITISH ISLES
1:1,584,000
5th edition
London : IGS, 1969
57 x 82
Col. map produced by the Geological Survey of Great Britain.
coloured 50p
uncoloured 45p

TECTONIC MAP OF GREAT BRITAIN AND NORTHERN IRELAND
1:1,584,000
London : IGS, 1966
57 x 82
Col. map produced by the Geological Survey of Great Britain. 55p

G EARTH RESOURCES

SMOOTHED AEROMAGNETIC MAP OF THE BRITISH ISLES
1:1,584,000
London : IGS, 1970
64 x 96
Showing contour values representing smoothed total force magnetic anomalies in gammas, indicating positive and negative levels by col, and magnetic 'highs' and 'lows'. 50p

K HUMAN GEOGRAPHY

ILES BRITANNIQUES NO 2
1:1,000,000
Editions MDI
Population map.
see BRITISH ISLES 41L

LITERARY-PICTORIAL MAP OF THE BRITISH ISLES
No 161121-14
Chicago : Denoyer-Geppert
111 x 162
Pictorial wall map for schools.
Spring rollers US $19.25

SHAKESPEARE'S BRITAIN
No scale given
Washington : NGS
48 x 63
Based on 300yr old map, with sites from the plays marked. US $1.00

L ECONOMIC

VELIKOBRITANIYA I IRLANDIYA - EKONOMICHESKAYA KARTA
1:1,000,000
Moskva : GUGK, 1973
2 sheet economic map of GB and Ireland.

ILES BRITANNIQUES NO 2
1:1,000,000
No 1151
St Germain-en-Laye : Éditions MDI
92 x 126
Plastic coated school wall map showing mines and industry. Population map on reverse. Also available in English.

ILES BRITANNIQUES NO 1 (PHYSIQUE)
1:1,000,000
Éditions MDI
Agricultural map on reverse.
see BRITISH ISLES 41 E1

BRITISCHE INSELN : WIRTSCHAFT UND VERKEHR
Braunschweig : Westermann
96 x 127
Col. pictorial wall map for schools, showing economy and communications.

M HISTORICAL MAPS

EARLY MAP REPRODUCTIONS
Blaeu's Theatrum Orbis Terrarum - Atlas Novus
Plate : British Isles 1635
Edinburgh : Bart, 1966
This important atlas was published in a number of volumes during the 17th Century and coloured reproductions of certain individual plates are available.
£1.50

CATHEDRALS & ABBEYS MAP OF THE BRITISH ISLES
Edinburgh : Bart, 1972
76 x 102
Showing nearly 400 cathedrals and abbeys.
50p

BRITISH ISLES
1:1,774,080
Washington : NGS
67 x 82
Pictorial map showing famous British people. US $ 2.00

ATLASES
W3 WORLD: LOCAL EDITION

COLLINS BRITISH ISLES AND WORLD ATLAS
Wm Collins
see WORLD ATLASES 100 W2

ATLASES
A1 GENERAL: ROADS

ESSO ROAD ATLAS OF GREAT BRITAIN AND IRELAND
London : Philip, 1973/4
20 x 29
260pp
Road maps classifying motorways, primary routes, 'A' and 'B', minor roads, those under construction, route numbers and mileages. Maps of GB 1:316,800; Ireland 1:380,160, also motorway strip maps, town plans and special London section.
Board covers £3.50

NEW BOOK OF THE ROAD
prepared: Readers Digest Assoc. Ltd. — A.A.
London : Hodder and Stoughton, 1974
17 x 29
416pp
Includes 127pp of road maps scale 1:250,000 showing all classes of roads with places of interest, 109 town plans, motorway strip maps and gazetteer of 30,000 places. Introductory chapters on car maintenance, first aid, leisure maps and pictorial guides.
£5.50

THE MOTORIST'S TOURING MAPS AND GAZETTEER
18th edition
London : The Hamlyn Group, 1974
163pp
Set of road maps for the British Isles. Roads classified incl. Motorways and facilities, railways, contours, sport sites etc. England and Wales and mainland Scotland 1:253,440, Scottish Islands 1:760,320, Ireland 1:1,000,000 with 1:253,440 insets of Dublin and Belfast. 21 throughway plans of major towns.
Index. £2.25

BRITISH ISLES POCKET ATLAS
1:1,000,000
London : Gia, 1976
8 x 13
Collection of 5 colour maps showing boundaries, national parks and touring areas with main roads and motorways marked and numbered. 75p

HANDY ROAD ATLAS OF GREAT BRITAIN AND IRELAND
1:633,600
Edinburgh : Johnston & Bacon
13 x 18
72pp
Roads classified with plans of 25 major towns. 40p

POCKET ROAD ATLAS OF GREAT BRITAIN AND IRELAND
1:1,000,000
Edinburgh : Johnston & Bacon
8 x 13
64pp
Small road atlas showing main and secondary roads.
Laminated card cover 30p

ATLASES
F GEOLOGY

PALAEOGEOGRAPHICAL ATLAS OF THE BRITISH ISLES AND ADJACENT PARTS OF EUROPE
Ed L J Wills
Glasgow : Blackie
29 x 32
Describing selected geological periods with 54 maps, each with explanatory text. £5.50

ATLASES
H BIOGEOGRAPHY

ATLAS OF BRITISH FLORA
Ed F H Perring and S M Walters
London : T Nelson
25 x 38
432pp
Includes distribution maps of 1700 flowering plants and ferns together with 12 transparent overlays for comparative study including climate, topography and geology. £5.50

CRITICAL SUPPLEMENT TO THE ATLAS OF BRITISH FLORA
Ed F H Perring and P D Sell
London : T Nelson
27 x 38
168pp
Includes 391 distribution maps of micro species and sub-species, varieties and hybrids excluded from the original atlas.
£4.50

PROVISIONAL ATLAS OF THE INSECTS OF THE BRITISH ISLES
Ed John Heath
Abbots Ripton (Huntingdon) : Monks Wood Experimental Station, 1970
23 x 30
57pp
European Invertebrate Survey
Part I Lepidoptera Rhopalocera (butterflies). Distribution maps showing 56 species with 1 general map. 50p

ATLASES
J CLIMATE

BRITISH WEATHER IN MAPS
James A Taylor and R A Yates
2nd edition
London : Macmillan, 1967
304pp
Analysis of Meteorological Office Daily Weather Reports, with maps. Covers weather classification and climate types. For undergraduates. £2.50

ATLASES
K HUMAN GEOGRAPHY

A LITERARY ATLAS AND GAZETTEER OF THE BRITISH ISLES
Micahel Hardwick
Newton Abbot : David & Charles, 1973
18 x 24
Covers 4,500 literary entries of who wrote what where, arranged by counties and towns, and keyed into relevant maps.
£2.75

ATLASES
L ECONOMIC

WATERWAYS ATLAS OF THE BRITISH ISLES
2nd edition
Eds Cranfield and Bonfiel
London : Cranfield and Bonfiel, 1975
19 x 23
Indicating the navigable waterways of the country in colour. £1.05

BRITISH RAIL PRE-GROUPING ATLAS AND GAZETTEER
1:500,000
Shepperton : Ian Allan
17 x 25
84pp
Showing railways before amalgamation.
Spiral binding £1.38

ATLASES
M HISTORICAL

BRITISH HISTORY ATLAS
Martin Gilbert
London : Weidenfeld & Nicholson, 1968
118pp maps in black and white covering political, social, economic, religious development. Some world maps, showing the Empire with detailed maps of small sample areas.

HISTORICAL TOWNS : MAPS AND PLANS OF TOWNS AND CITIES IN THE BRITISH ISLES, WITH HISTORICAL COMMENTARIES FROM EARLIER TIMES TO CIRCA 1800
Ed M D Lobel
Oxford : Lovell Johns/London : Cook, Hammond, Kell, 1969
31 x 41
151pp
The British part of an international project to trace the development of towns and cities. Each town will be mapped at 1:2,500 showing it as it was in 1800 with the addition of medieval and earlier features together with additional maps and descriptive account.
Volumes published:
Vol I, 1969, including Banbury, Glasgow, Caernarvon, Gloucester, Hereford, Reading, Nottingham, Salisbury. £5.25

EARLY MAPS OF THE BRITISH ISLES, AD 1000-1579
London RGS
55 x 42
20 facsimile maps in portfolio.
Introduction and notes by G R Crone.
£3.00

CAMDEN'S BRITANNIA, 1695
Introduction by Stuart Piggott
Newton Abbot : David & Charles, 1970
40 x 25
Facsimile atlas covering English counties, Scotland and Ireland with account of history and archaeology; comments on present conditions. £35.00

THE COUNTY MAPS FROM WILLIAM CAMDEN'S BRITANNIA 1695 BY R MORDEN
Introduction by J B Harley
Newton Abbot : David & Charles, 1972
40 x 24
Comprising 50 facsimile maps compiled by Robert Morden including maps of each of the English Counties, North and South Wales, British Islands and England, Scotland and Ireland. In addition special antiquity maps of Roman and Saxon Britain.
£6.75

ATLAS OF THE BRITISH ISLES BY PIETER VAN DEN KEERE
Lympne Castle : Harry Margary, 1972
21 x 16
96pp
Black and white facsimile maps for each county from the atlas pub. 1605. 33 maps for England and Wales, 6 for Scotland, 5 for Ireland. £2.00

ATLASES
O NATIONAL

ATLAS OF BRITAIN AND NORTHERN IRELAND
Ed G E Blackman and others
Oxford : OUP, 1963
39 x 52
234pp
A geographical survey of Britain's total resources, physical, economic and demographic. Illustrated by 200 pages of statistical maps relating to geology, soils, water, sea and coasts, climate, vegetation, forestry, industry, agriculture, fisheries, population, housing, communications etc. with special reference section, regional maps and gazetteer. £40.00

410 Great Britain

See also:

41 BRITISH ISLES
411 SCOTLAND
420 ENGLAND AND WALES
423.4 CHANNEL ISLANDS
429 WALES

A1 GENERAL MAPS: ROADS

LEISURE MAP OF GREAT BRITAIN
1:1.100,000
Smarden, Kent : Estate Pubn's. 1976
90 x 63
Road map featuring places of tourist and historic interest. 50p

GREAT BRITAIN ROAD MAP
1:1,000,000
Sevenoaks : Gers
71 x 98
Road map with route numbers, county boundaries and index to towns and villages inset. Northern Ireland also included. 50p

GREAT BRITAIN - NATIONAL ROUTE MAP
1:1,000,000
London : Map Productions
78 x 103
Road map in col. showing all classes of roads and numbers. Northern tip of Scotland inset, also 7 major conurbations (scale 1:316,800), ferries, airports, urban areas, National Parks and forests. 70p

GREAT BRITAIN: MOTORWAYS AND MAIN ROADS MAP
1:950,000
London : Gia
68 x 101
Roads classified and numbered, distances in miles, spot heights in feet, car ferries, airports, county boundaries. Main urban areas inset. Legend Eng, Fr, Ger.
50p

THE DAILY TELEGRAPH TOURISTS MAP GREAT BRITAIN
1:800,000
London : Gia, 1971 (rev. ed.)
71 x 86
General road map, route numbers, slight relief shading, air and sea routes. Scotland inset on smaller scale. 7 inset maps show historic houses, National Parks, sunshine, rainfall, distances, touring areas and land types. 50p

REVERSIBLE ROAD MAP OF GREAT BRITAIN
1:760,320
London : Johnston & Bacon
74 x 74
Double sided map showing all classes of roads with 8 inset plans of major cities.
35p

GEOGRAPHER'S REVERSIBLE ROAD MAP OF GREAT BRITAIN
1:675, 840
Sevenoaks : Gers
97 x 71
Main and secondary roads, numbered, railways, canals, county boundaries, car ferries, airports, mileage chart. England and Wales to Westmorland on one side, continuation northwards on reverse; Northern Ireland and an inset of Orkney and Shetland Islands. 60p

DEVELOPMENT OF THE TRUNK ROAD NETWORK
Improvement schemes over £500,000.
1:750,000
London : Dept. of the Environment, 1976
North 86 x 71, South 86 x 86
Map in black and white, with existing and projected motorways in blue and other roads and relevant schemes in red. Inset of London area. Each 85p

GREAT BRITAIN
1:633,600
In 2 sheets
London : Foldex
Two double-sided sheets showing roads classified, relief shading, patent fold.
each 30p

ORDNANCE SURVEY ROUTE PLANNING MAP OF GREAT BRITAIN
1:625,000
In 2 sheets
Southampton : OS
78 x 98 complete
Main, secondary and minor roads, route numbers, mileage between towns, motorways, new stretches show dates of opening. Insets of motorway junctions with limited access. Railways, airports, car ferries, canals shown; relief indicated by layer col. Revised annually.
Legend Eng, Fr, Ger.
South Sheet:
north to Scarborough and Kendal; mileage chart; large scale diagrams of principal towns.
North Sheet:
Continuation northwards, Orkney and Shetland Islands inset; with a mileage chart; large scale diagrams of principal towns.
each sheet:
Paper folded - double sided 95p
Paper flat - separate sheets 65p

GROSSBRITANNIEN GROSSE AUTOKARTE
1:625,000
No 94
Stuttgart : RV, 1974
103 x 85
OS Route Planning Map (q.v.) printed as a double-sided map; legend Eng, Fr, Ger.
DM 8.80

THE TOURIST ROUTE MAP
1:570,240
In 3 sheets: Scotland, England N and England S.
Edinburgh : Barts, 1973
96 x 72 each sheet
Roads classified with route numbers and distances, places of interest. Inset plans of major towns. 40p

TOURING MAP OF ENGLAND, WALES AND SOUTHERN SCOTLAND
1:570,240
London : Gia
69 x 97
Roads classified including motorways and primary routes and index to places of interest. 50p

A to Z GREAT BRITAIN ROAD MAP SERIES
1:316,800
In 8 sheets, see index 410/1
Sevenoaks : Gers, 1970/1
111 x 85 each
All classes of roads; motorways; access points and service areas, also those proposed or under construction. Distances, gradients, railways and stations, ferries, canals, county boundaries etc. Places of interest. Separate index to places.
each 75p
Scotland (reversible) £1.30

DUNLOP WIDTH OF ROAD MAPS OF GREAT BRITAIN
1:316,800
In 6 sheets, see index 410/2
London : Gia, 1967/72
Main and secondary roads, route numbers, distances in miles, road widths, car ferries, airports, places of interest, county boundaries. Sketch town plan insets and index on reverse.
Sheets 1, 2, 4, 5 88 x 71
Sheet 3 106 x 78
Sheet 6 (1:400,000) 111 x 92
each 45p

PRIMARY ROUTES MAP
1:300,000
In 6 sheets, see index 410/3
London : Gia
102 x 87
All classes of roads classified distinctly in col, numbered, distances marked.
each 50p

BRITISCHE STRASSENKARTE
1:300,000
In 6 sheets.
Frankfurt : Ravenstein, 1976
Detailed series of road maps covering Great Britain, each map has an index to places.
Sheets:

281	S.E. England	102 x 81
282	S.W. England	102 x 75
283	North & Central England	109 x 81
284	Wales & Midlands	102 x 81
285	S. Scotland & Borders	102 x 75
286	North & Central Scotland 1:375,000	106 x 81
each		DM 6.80

G T MAP OF BRITAIN
1:250,000
In 10 sheets, see index 410/4
Edinburgh : Bart, 1969/72
98 x 70
All roads classified, route numbers and distances. View points, railways, canals, youth hostels, golf courses, woods and beaches marked. Relief shaded.
65p

GREAT BRITAIN
1:250,000
In 12 sheets
London : Foldex
Road map series, showing roads classified and numbered, relief shading. Available individually or as double sheets in the following sheets:

1 S E Counties
2 S W Counties
3 Eastern Counties
4 S Wales and W Midlands
5 E Midlands to S Coast
6 N Wales
7 N Midlands (E to W Coast)
8 N England (E to W Coast)
9 S Scotland
10 Mid Scotland
11 Mid Scotland
12 North Scotland

each 35p
(double-sided sheets) 65p

RAC REGIONAL MOTORING MAPS
1:190,080 England
1:253,440 Scotland
In 11 sheets, see index 410/5
London : Map Productions
92 x 87
Series of road maps indicating Motorways: existing, under construction and projected; Primary routes and other roads, distances, gradients, ferries, railways, places of interest, RAC services; principal towns inset showing through-routes, one-way streets and parking.
95p each

SUPER MOTORISTS MAPS OF GREAT BRITAIN
1:190,080
In 27 sheets, see index 410/6
London : Gia, 1969+
Various sizes
Main and secondary routes, distances in miles, route numbers; other communications, spot heights, tourist details.
National Grid over-print. 60p—85p each

THE HALF-INCH SERIES OF GREAT BRITAIN
1:126,720
In 62 sheets, see index 410/7
Edinburgh : Bart
78 x 50
Contoured, layer col. series. Main and secondary roads, tracks and footpaths, spot heights in feet, airports, canals, youth hostels, places of interest and county boundaries. Being replaced by new 1:100,000 series.
Paper folded 30p each

A2 GENERAL MAPS: LOCAL

'TO AND THROUGH' SERIES
1:250,000
Edinburgh : Bart
66 x 76
Double-sided maps; road map of town environs; large scale map of town centre with visible landmarks and principal through roads on reverse.

1 London, 1972
2 Manchester, Liverpool, Leeds and Sheffield, 1970
3 Birmingham 1971
4 Edinburgh, Glasgow, 1972

75p

30 MILES AROUND
1:126,720
In 15 sheets
London : Johnston & Bacon
89 x 58
Series of large scale maps, contoured and layer coloured showing major and minor roads, tracks, inns, youth hostels etc.
Maps available:
Birmingham : (Cannock to Stratford/ Ludlow to Rugby)
Bournemouth : (Amesbury to coast/ Sherborne to Havant)
Cornwall
Cotswolds : (Malvern to Wantage/ Hereford to Oxford)
Devon
Edinburgh : (Forth to Selkirk/ Grangemouth to Berwick)
Glasgow : (Loch Earn to Prestwick/ Dunoon to Falkirk)
Lake District : (Carlisle to Fleetwood/ coast to Appleby)
Lincoln : (Hull to Nottingham/ Mansfield to coast)
North Wales (Wallasey to Oswestry/ Holyhead to Chester)
Norwich and The Broads (Thetford to coast/coast to Ipswich)
The Peak (Wakefield to Coalville/ Stoke to Mansfield)
Somerset : (Bristol to coast/ Exmouth to Sherborne)
S W Scotland : (Ayr to coast/coast to Dumfries)
Yorkshire Coast : (Saltburn to Barton/ Goole to coast)
25p

C OFFICIAL SURVEYS

INTERNATIONAL MAP OF THE WORLD
1:1,000,000
Sheets NO 30 and NN 30
Southampton : OS
81 x 144
2 sheets cover Great Britain and N Ireland conforming in style to the 'Bonn Specification' of the UN, showing communications, boundaries populated area classified by size.
95p each
see also WORLD 100C and index 100/1.

ORDNANCE SURVEY QUARTER INCH MAP
1:250,000
In 17 sheets, see index 410/8
Fifth series
Southampton : OS
75 x 60
Contoured, layer col. series. Main and secondary roads, route numbers, airports, railways, heights in feet, places of interest, county boundaries.
Paper flat outline 80p
Paper flat col. 80p
Paper folded col. 80p
see also GREAT BRITAIN ATLASES 410C.

ORDNANCE SURVEY TOURIST MAP SERIES
1:63,360
Southampton : OS
Covering principal tourist areas; showing relief generally by contours, layer tints and shading. Rights of way, footpaths, antiquities, youth hostels, National Trust properties, features of interest to holidaymakers.
Maps available:
Dartmoor 101 x 77, 1967.
New Forest, 97 x 79, 1966
Exmoor, 101 x 79, 1967
Peak District, 74 x 98, 1963
North York Moors, 97 x 70, 1966
Lake District, 76 x 91, 1971
Loch Lomond and the Trossachs 77 x 91, 1972
Cairngorms, 76 x 91, 1964
Ben Nevis and Glencoe, 76 x 91, 1959
Paper folded 95p
Paper flat 85p

ORDNANCE SURVEY 1:50,000 MAP SERIES OF GREAT BRITAIN
1:50,000
In 204 sheets, see index 410/9
Southampton: OS 1974 –
100 x 89
A new series of topographical maps derived from the former O.S. 1" to mile series. The First Series sheets have been photographically enlarged to the new scale (approx. 1¼" to 1 mile) and include the new county and metropolitan county boundaries and show motorways in blue and incorporate newly designed colour system. Contours have been converted to metric values. The second series sheets generally have resurveyed metric contours, county and district boundaries and tourist information. Parish boundaries have been excluded from coloured editions but are shown on Second Series outline editions.
coloured, paper flat 80p
coloured, paper folded £1.15
outline, paper flat £1.00

ORDNANCE SURVEY 2½" MAP OF GREAT BRITAIN
1:25,000
In 1400 sheets, see index 410/10
Second series
Southampton : OS
New series to eventually replace Provisional Series. All classes of roads, public rights of way in Eng. and Wales, heights in feet, 25ft contour intervals, vegetation, National Trust areas, county boundaries. Provisional Series sheets are withdrawn as corresponding Second Series sheets published.
Large sheets : (97 x 56)
Paper flat outline 70p
Paper flat coloured 70p
Paper folded col. £1.00
Small sheets : (48 x 56)
Paper flat outline 50p
Paper flat coloured 50p
Paper folded col. 75p

ORDNANCE SURVEY 2½" MAP OF GREAT BRITAIN (PROVISIONAL SERIES)
1:25,000
In 2,027 sheets, see index 410/10
First edition
Southampton: OS, 1945–56
48 x 56 each
Covering the whole of Great Britain excl. Highlands and Islands of Scotland; gradually being superseded by Second Series (q.v.). No further revision except for important changes such as motorways, by-pass roads etc. to be added when sheets are rep. All classes of roads, footpaths, railways, National Trust areas, spot heights in feet, contours at 25ft intervals and county boundaries.

Paper flat outline 50p each
Paper flat coloured 50p each
Paper folded coloured 65p each

OUTDOOR LEISURE MAPS
1:25,000
Southampton : OS
Series of large scale walking maps based on standard 1:25,000 First Series with some revision. Contoured with paths and rights of way also camp and caravan sites, youth hostels, Information Centres and viewpoints.
Maps available:
The Dark Peak – Kinder Scout, Bleaklow, Black Hill, 85 x 103, 1972
The Three Peaks – Whernside, Ingleborough, Pen-y-Ghent, 80 x 104, 1973
The English Lakes – 4 sheets 104 x 84, 1974
Malham and Upper Wharfedale 85 x 104 1976
Maps available based on Second Series mapping
The High Tops of the Cairngorms 84 x 103
Brighton and Sussex Vale 80 x 104
Paper flat or folded, each £1.65
The Cuillin and Torridon Hills – Two maps printed back to back 103 x 84
Paper flat or folded, each £1.90
Paper flat or folded, each £1.50

ISLES OF SCILLY
1:25,000
Southampton : OS, 1964
80 x 60
Topog. map of complete island group. Contoured, showing field boundaries, historic sites etc.
Paper flat 50p
Paper folded 65p

ORDNANCE SURVEY SIX-INCH MAP
1:10,560
See Index 410/10
Southampton : OS
47 x 47
Covering whole of Great Britain. England and Wales and much of Scotland now covered by National Grid sheets. Rest of Scotland still covered by pre-war County sheets but these are being replaced by National Grid Sheets. Most of the National Grid sheets are square with sides representing 5km (being quarter sheets of the 1:25,000 OS series) but some of the coastal sheets are a little larger. As part of the metrication programme, the 1:10,560 series are being replaced by 1:10,000 maps.
Contouring (when available) will be at 10 metres in mountainous districts and 5 metres for other areas.
Paper flat sheets:
County (full sheets) 90p
County (quarter sheets) 70p
National Grid £1.90

ORDNANCE SURVEY 1:2500 PLANS
1:2500
Southampton : OS
Various sizes
Covering all of Great Britain, except mountain and moorland areas. Available in 2 editions : pre World War 2 'County Series' and post-war 'National Grid plans' which are now superseding the earlier series. New NG sheets represent an area of 1 square km but are generally available in 2 square km sheets.
County series £1.35
1 x 1 km £4.20
2 x 1 km £6.00

Also available as 35mm microfilm transparencies £2.10 plus VAT or photo-printouts at true scale £1.70 each

ORDNANCE SURVEY 1:1250 SCALE PLANS
1:1250
Southampton : OS
40 x 40
Plans at this scale cover most towns and urban areas with pop. of about 20,000 and over. Each plan represents an area of 500 metres square with National Grid at 100 metre intervals.
Paper flat, each £4.20
Also available as 35mm microfilm transparencies
each £1.20 plus VAT
or photo-printouts at true scale, each £1.70.

SUSI – The Supply of Unpublished Survey Information
1:2,500, 1:1,250
Southampton : OS
Using microfilm techniques a system is now in operation whereby large scale survey information which has been prepared for departmental use within the Ordnance Survey and other purposes, but not published, can also be supplied to customers. Forms in which this information is available:
Printouts each £3.75
Printouts-newly commissioned each £9.00
Microfilm 35mm each £4.50 plus VAT
Microfilms-newly commissioned each £11.50

D POLITICAL & ADMINISTRATIVE

THE TIMES BUSINESS PLANNING MAP OF GREAT BRITAIN
app 1:1,260,000
Edinburgh : Bart, 1970
85 x 105
Inset Greater London and major conurbations; index to principal towns; shows communications, county and ITV boundaries, ports, Legend Eng, Fr. and Ger.
Linen, laminated £3.00

GREAT BRITAIN COUNTIES IN COLOUR
1:1,000,000
London : Map Productions, 1975
73 x 88
Each county separate col; towns classified by pop; conurbations and N Scotland inset; incl. Northern Ireland; roads, local govt. areas marked. £1.00

GREAT BRITAIN : COUNTIES MAP
1:1,000,000 app.
Sevenoaks : Geographers
71 x 97
Counties in col; index to towns and villages; canals and rivers.
45p

GENERAL MAP OF GREAT BRITAIN
1:633,360
London : Stanford, 1975
84 x 108
Scotland inset, scale 1:760,320
Counties in colour with railways, canals; decorative border.
Paper 50p
Mounted CRV £6.50

ADMINISTRATIVE AREAS MAP OF GREAT BRITAIN
1:625,000
In 2 sheets
Southampton : OS, 1975
98 x 78
Interim edition showing county and district boundaries effective 1.4.74 in England, and 16.5.75 in Scotland. Also former county borough, urban and rural districts. New edition pub. annually in April.
each 75p

ADMINISTRATIVE AREAS – GREAT BRITAIN
1:1,250,000
London: Dept. of the Environment, 1974
54 x 82
Coloured administrative map 86p

PLANNING AND RECORD MAP NO 3 GREAT BRITAIN
1:1,250,000
London : Gia
60 x 84
Outline map showing county boundaries, cities and towns.
30p
Also available : reduced size edition
30 x 39 for 10 - 75p

OS OUTLINE BASE MAP OF GREAT BRITAIN
1:1,250,000
Southampton : OS, 1975
53 x 89
Black and white, main towns, communications, counties, Nat. Grid overprinted.
Paper 30p

SALES MANAGERS' AND POPULATION MAP OF GREAT BRITAIN
1:633,600
London : Gia
89 x 117
Shows by symbols and type faces business possibilities of every part of the country by means of pop. With separate index for ref.
Paper flat £2.75
CR £12.00
Mounted on board with cellulose finish £14.00

SALES PROMOTION MAP OF GREAT BRITAIN
1:633,600
SP6
London : Stanford
91 x 117
Printed in black with county boundaries in blue, principal roads in red.
Northern Scotland has been omitted and an inset shows Northern Ireland.
Paper flat £2.75
Mounted CR £4.00

OUTLINE MAP OF GREAT BRITAIN
1:625,000
In 2 sheets
Southampton : OS, 1969
98 x 78
Outline ed. of OS Route Planning map in black only.
Paper flat each £70p

E1 PHYSICAL: RELIEF

GRANDE-BRETAGNE
1:1,000,000
TC 41 (No 1610)
St Germain-en-Laye : Éditions MDI
92 x 126
Plastic coated physical wall map of Great Britain for schools. Map of USSR on reverse at 1:7,000,000

GREAT BRITAIN – PHYSICAL
1:625,000
2 sheets
Southampton : OS
98 x 156 complete
Relief of land, drainage, names of mountains, hills, rivers etc.
Each sheet each 70p

E2 PHYSICAL : LAND FEATURES

HYDROMETRICAL AREAS OF GREAT BRITAIN
1:633,600
In 2 sheets
Reading : Water Resources Board
98 x 156
Area boundaries in col. on grey base.

F GEOLOGY

SOLID GEOLOGY OF GREAT BRITAIN
1:625,000
2nd Edition
In 2 sheets
Southampton : OS, 1957, rev. '66
98 x 78 each
shows by col. and symbol geol. systems and stratigraphical sub-divisions of the country.
Paper flat, col. each 75p
Paper folded, col. each 85p
Paper flat outline, each 35p
Also available with the sheet lines of the 1" : 1 mile Geological Series overprinted:
Paper flat 85p
Paper folded 95p

SIX INCH GEOLOGICAL MAPS
1:10,560
London : IGS
National Grid – 47 x 47
County Series Quarter Sheets – 57 x 43
Prepared for the Coalfields and other important economic areas.
A Quarter sheets (County series)
uncoloured, each 60p
Full sheets (County series)
uncoloured 75p
being replaced by National Grid sheets, uncoloured.
each 85p
B Colour printed maps of the London District
quarter sheets, each 25p

G EARTH RESOURCES

AEROMAGNETIC MAP OF GREAT BRITAIN AND NORTHERN IRELAND
1:625,000
In 2 sheets
1st edition,
London : IGS, 1965
99 x 80
Contours representing total force magnetic anomalies in gammas, classified by col.
Col. flat sheet 1 £1.35
sheet 2 75p
Col. folded sheet 1 £1.65
sheet 2 £1.00
Uncol. on Permatrace sht 1 £4.00
sht 2 £2.00

H BIOGEOGRAPHY

GUIDE MAP TO YOUR FORESTS
1:1,000,000
London : Forestry Commission, 1975
61 x 97
Base map showing road system with locations of forests, forest parks, information centres, trails, camping and picnic sites marked. Pictorial guide to Forestry Commission services on reverse. 40p

LAND CLASSIFICATION
1:625,000
In 2 sheets
Southampton : OS 1944
108 x 85
Maps in cols. showing 10 categories of land use, available only from DOE Map Library
each 80p

LAND UTILISATION
1:625,000
In 2 sheets
Southampton : OS, 1944
108 x 85
Showing 6 categories of land use based on surveys 1931-39. Available only from DOE Map Library
each 80p

THE SECOND LAND UTILISATION SURVEY OF GREAT BRITAIN
1:25,000
see index 410/11
Ed A Coleman
London : Second Land Use Surv.
89 x 57 each
New series showing 70 categories of land use, 14 of which cover industry. In colour, following OS 1:25,000 sheet lines.
Each £1.10
Handbook to series 25p

J CLIMATE

RAINFALL ANNUAL AVERAGE 1916-50
1:625,000
In 2 sheets
Southampton : OS, 1967
108 x 85
Map in cols., only available from DOE Map Library each 80p

K HUMAN GEOGRAPHY

POPULATION DENSITY 1951
1:625,000
In 2 sheets
Southampton : OS, 1960
108 x 85
Coloured population map. Only available direct from DOE Map Library.
each 80p

POPULATION CHANGE 1951-61
1:625,000
In 2 sheets
Southampton : OS, 1966
108 x 85
Coloured population map. Only available from DOE Map Library.
each 80p

NATIONAL TRUST PROPERTIES
1:625,000
London : National Trust, 1974
Contour col. map covering England and Wales; insets of Northern Ireland at 1:760,320; London, Surrey and the Lake District at 1:316,800. All National Trust Properties shown in red and named.
50p

L ECONOMIC

ASSISTED AREAS AT 14.8.74
1:1,125,000
London : Dept. Environment, 1975
51 x 82
Assisted areas for industrial development as defined by Dept. of Industry.
75p

BRITISH RAIL SYSTEM MAP
1:475,000
2nd edition
London : Gia, 1969
109 x 202
3 maps contained in a card folder illus. railway system of the country on a plain white base map with locations of collieries, generating stations, cement works, docks, gas and steel works and oil refineries shown by conventional signs.
£1.05

RAILWAY HISTORY MAP OF BRITAIN
Edinburgh : Bart, 1971
65 x 74
Col. map; rail routes according to district, border of company badges; engines etc. illus. 40p

CHEFFINS MAP OF THE ENGLISH AND SCOTCH RAILWAYS, 1845
1:962,500
Burtle (Somerset) : P R Sparkes, 1971
Reproduction of the 1845 map.
£2.00

WATERWAYS MAP OF THE BRITISH WATERWAYS BOARD
1:440,000 app
London : BWB, 1968
75 x 95
Waterways in blue, class. according to width; facilities; Scotland, Birmingham, River Authority areas inset. 38p

Edinburgh : Bart, 1970
72 x 94
Contoured, layer col, with road and rail communications. Covers area from Baltic to Black Sea, Amsterdam to Istanbul.
75p

ZUIDOOST-EUROPA
1: 2,000,000
Groningen : Wolters-Noordhoff
85 x 107
Physical school wall map; relief shading, boundaries, communications.
Fl. 44.75

SÜDOSTEUROPA
1:1,625,000
Hamburg : Flemming
137 x 99
Physical col. wall map, layer col, relief shading, cities graded by pop. boundaries etc.

OSTMITTELEUROPA
1:1,000,000
München : List
170 x 235
Wenschow physical wall map for schools. Political map inset showing lang. distribution.
DM 164.00

ITALIEN UND SUDOSTEUROPA
1:1,000,000
W728
München : List
225 x 175
Wenschow physical wall map for schools.
DM 164.00

DONAURAUM UND BALKAN-HALBINSEL
1:900,000
Braunschweig : Westermann
183 x 228
Physical wall map of Danube lands and the Balkan Peninsular. Layer col, hill shading, communications, cities graded by pop.

DIE SOZIALISTISCHEN LÄNDER MITTEL- UND SÜDOSTEUROPAS
1:750,000
Gotha : Haack
Covering Socialist Countries of E Europe. Physical col. school wall map, showing relief by layer col, international boundaries, cities graded by pop.

DONAULÄNDER
1:750,000
Gotha : Haack
263 x 168
Col. physical school wall map, showing Danube Drainage Basin, covering areas Corsica — Black Sea. Relief shown by hachures.

REGIONE DANUBIANA
1:5,000,000
Novara : Ag
33 x 26
Moulded plastic relief map for schools, covering Yugoslavia, Romania and Bulgaria. Physical, political and economic details on reverse.
L 450

EUROPA CENTRO-ORIENTALE
1:5,000,000
Novara : Ag
33 x 26
Moulded plastic relief map covering Poland, Czechoslovakia and Hungary. Physical, political and economic details on reverse.
L 450

F GEOLOGY

INTERNATIONAL GEOLOGICAL MAP OF EUROPE AND THE MEDITERRANEAN REGION
1:5,000,000
In 2 sheets
Paris : UNESCO/B-B, 1971 (1972)
79 x 121 West
84 x 121 East
Col. geol. map covering Europe, N Africa and W Asia. Shows quaternary cover, stratigraphic sub-division, representation of facies, metamorphic and magmatic rocks in colour and symbol. Legend Eng. and Fr. Multilingual text 67pp.
Complete £5.00

GEOLOGIC MAP OF EUROPE
1:5,000,000
Maplewood : Hammond
95 x 60
Geol. map in brown monochrome depicting rock types by various hatchings and stipples. Northern Scandinavia excluded. Legend. Text on reverse side.

EUROPA - GEOLOGI
1:5,000,000
Stockholm : GLA, 1956
128 x 100
Simplified geol. school wall map in cols.

EUROPA, GEOLOGISCHE ÜBERSICHT
1:3,000,000
Gotha : Haack
205 x 190
Geol. wall map in col.
Mounted CR

INTERNATIONAL TECTONIC MAP OF EUROPE AND THE MEDITERRANEAN REGION
by Bogdanoff et al
1:2,500,000
2nd edition
In 20 sheets
Paris : UNESCO/Moskva : Academy of Sciences, USSR, 1972+
63 x 63 each
Series in preparation, also covering W Asia and N Africa. Shows old platforms, folded regions, general tectonics etc. Legends in French, explanatory text in English and French, text vol. in Eng. or French.

INTERNATIONAL QUATERNARY MAP OF EUROPE
1:2,500,000
In 15 sheets, see index 4/7
Paris : UNESCO/Hannover : B-B, 1967+
60 x 50 each
Series in progress. Shows stratigraphic and lithogenic subdivisions, volcanic rocks and other deposits, specialised geological and geomorphological features, quaternary localities, bathymetry and recent deposits on ocean bottom. Legends in German, brochure for each sheet in 4 langs. General explanatory brochure.
Each £2.40

METAMORPHIC MAP OF EUROPE
1:2,500,000
Prepared: sub-commission for the Cartography of the Metamorphic Belts of the World.
Paris : UNESCO, 1973
Coloured geological series in 17 sheets with brochure F.Fr. 200

CARTE GÉOLOGIQUE INTERNATIONALE DE L'EUROPE
1:1,500,000
2nd Edition
In 49 sheets, see index 4/8
Paris : UNESCO - B-B, 1964+
63 x 63 each
Geological series in progress. Shows pleistocene cover for major areas, magmatic rocks by age and chemical composition, metamorphic rocks by age of primary rock, of metamorphism and by grade.
Various prices

CARTE HYDROGÉOLOGIQUE INTERNATIONALE DE L'EUROPE
1:1,500,000
In 35 sheets, see index 4/8
Paris : UNESCO/Hannover : B-B, 1970+
90 x 67
Shows nature and extent of major water-bearing features, availability of ground water, shown by colour, stratigraphy and lithology in grey and black symbols, other hydrographic phenomena. Each has explanatory booklet. Legend in Eng, Fr. Rus, Sp.
Sheets published:
C5 and booklet £4.20
Model map and booklet
(30 x 21) £1.80

THE SUB-PLEISTOCENE GEOLOGY OF THE BRITISH ISLES AND THE ADJACENT CONTINENTAL SHELF
1:2,500,000
see BRITISH ISLES 41 F

GEOLOGISCHE KARTE VON MITTELEUROPA
1:2,000,000
Hannover : B-B, 1972 (with German State geol. surveys)
75 x 60
Col. geological map of Central Europe. DM12.00

GEOLOGISCHE KARTE VON MITTELEUROPA
1:900,000
Braunschweig : Westermann
200 x 186
Col. geol. wall map of Central Europe for schools. 45 geol. formations shown.

TECTONIC MAP OF THE CARPATHIAN-BALKAN MOUNTAIN SYSTEM AND ADJACENT AREAS
1:1,000,000
In 9 sheets
Paris: UNESCO/Bratislava : Geol. Inst. of Dionyz Stur.
150 x 135
Detailed map in colour incl. legend with text in English.
set F.Fr. 200

G EARTH RESOURCES

CARTA MAGNETICA DEL BACINO DEL MEDITERRANEO
1:6,000,000
Madrid : IGM
Showing lines of equal magnetic declination on 1st January 1959.

EUROPA, BODENVERHÄLTNISSE
1:3,000,000
Braunschweig : Westermann
Col. soil wall map of Europe.

CARTE MÉTALLOGÉNIQUE DE L'EUROPE
1:2,500,000
In 9 sheets, see index 4/9
Paris : UNESCO/Orleans : BRGM, 1968+
68 x 96 each
Metallogenetic map of Europe. Col. geol. base map, showing orogenic regions, simplified stratigraphy, lithology, tectonic and geophysical features with detailed information on mineral deposits, age etc. Each country, main structural region and mineral deposit is coded for reference in an accompanying leaflet.
Complete F.Fr. 616.60
Each Sheet F.Fr. 74.10

CARTE INTERNATIONALE DES GISEMENTS DE FER DE L'EUROPE (INTERNATIONALE KARTE DER EISENERZLAGERSTÄTTEN VON EUROPA)
Prepared for the International Geol. Congress
1:2,500,000
In 16 sheets, see index 4/7
Hannover : B-B, 1970+
Shows European iron bearing strata; minerals indicated on subdued geological-tectonic map. Series in progress.

CARTE INTERNATIONALE DES DÉPÔTS HOUILLERS EN EUROPE
1:2,500,000
In 16 sheets
Moskva : GUGK/Congres Geol. Internat, 1967/8
70 x 55 each
Col. map series showing European coal deposits. Pub. in Rus, also internat. eds. through co-operation with 19 European Geol. Surveys.

INTERNATIONAL MAP OF NATURAL GAS FIELDS IN EUROPE
1:2,500,000
In 9 sheets
Hannover : B-B/Geneva : UN Commission for Europe Committee on Gas, 1972.
80 x 70 each
Natural oil and gas fields overprinted in red and green. Title and legend in English, French and Russian.
Complete DM 220

SOIL MAP OF EUROPE
1:2,500,000
Prep. R Tavener, R Dudal, D Osmond, F Moorman
Paris : FAO, 1965
66 x 85
6 maps folded in box with separate explanatory text of 120pp inc. history of soil mapping in Europe.

H BIOGEOGRAPHY

EUROPE, VEGETATION
1:8,000,000
Tehran : Sahab
60 x 90
Map in Eng and Persian, showing variety of vegetation, cultivation, irrigation, oases, forests etc.
Rls 80

WESTLICHES EUROPA : VEGETATION UND BODENNÜTZUNG
No 9921
München : JRO
96 x 120
Pictorial wall map showing vegetation and land use.
DM 48.00

WESTLICHES EUROPA : BODENSCHATZE
Np 9922
Munchen : JRO
96 x 120
Pictorial wall map for schools, illustrating the produce of the soil.
DM 48.00

OSTLICHES EUROPA : VEGETATION UND BODENNUTZUNG
No 9925
München : JRO
96 x 130
Pictorial school wall map, illustrating vegetation and land use.
DM 48.00

ÖSTLICHES EUROPA: BODENSCHATZE
No 9926
München : JRO
96 x 130
Pictorial school wall map illustrating products of the land.
DM 48.00

EUROPA, KLIMA UND VEGETATION
1:6,000,000
Westermann
see EUROPE 4 J.

COMPARATIVE WALL ATLAS: EUROPE – NATURAL VEGETATION
1:6,000,000
Philip
see EUROPE 4 E1.

EUROPA, KLIMA UND VEGETATION
1:6,000,000
Haack
see EUROPE 4 J.

EUROPA : WILDTIERE UND WILDPFLANZEN
Braunschweig : Westermann
96 x 127
Pictorial wall map showing mammals, birds, fish and vegetation types in their native regions.
English ed. Europe : Wild Animals, Natural Vegetation, published by Denoyer-Geppert US $5.00

VEGETATION MAP OF THE MEDITERRANEAN REGION
1:5,000,000
FAO – UNESCO
see MEDITERRANEAN SEA 262 H.

DIVISIONS PHYTOGÉOGRAPHIQUES DE L'ENSEMBLE DE LA CHAÎNE ALPINE.
VÉGÉTATION POTENTIELLE DES ALPES SUD-OCCIDENTALES
1:400,000
Ed. P. Ozenda
Two maps from Vol. IV Doc. pour la Carte de la Végétation des Alpes, 1966.
Grenoble : Univ. Scientifique et Médicale de Grenoble. Analysis of the phytogeographic regions of the Alps and study of the vegetation potential of S.W. Alps. With 198pp text.

J CLIMATE

EUROPE
1:9,312,500
No 109021
Chicago : Denoyer-Geppert
111 x 162
4 thematic maps on 1 sheet. Shows Climate and Frost Free Days.
Rollers US $15.50

EUROPA, KLIMA UND VEGETATION
1:6,000,000
Braunschweig : Westermann
245 x 183
Col. wall map for schools showing climate on vegetation col. base.

EUROPA, KLIMA UND VEGETATION
1:6,000,000
Gotha : Haack
245 x 183
4 maps showing temperatures and air pressure in January, and July, mean annual rainfall, natural zones of vegetation and zones of cultivated land.

COMPARATIVE WALL ATLAS: EUROPE – CLIMATE
1:6,000,000
Philip
see EUROPE 4 E1.

KLIMATICHESKAYA KARTA EVROPY
1:4,000,000
In 4 sheets
Moskva : GUGK, 1969
150 x 148 complete
Col. climatic map showing wind, rainfall, isotherms etc.

BIOCLIMATIC MAP OF THE MEDITERRANEAN REGION
1:5,000,000
FAO-UNESCO
see MEDITERRANEAN SEA 262 J.

K HUMAN GEOGRAPHY

EUROPE
1:9,312,500
No 109021
Chicago : Denoyer-Geppert
111 x 162
4 them. maps on 1 sheet. Shows European pop. density.
Rollers US $15.50

COMPARATIVE WALL ATLAS: EUROPE – DENSITY OF POPULATION
1:6,000,000
Philip
see EUROPE 4 E1.

RESORTS MAP OF WESTERN EUROPE
1:2,500,000
Berkhamsted : Geog. Pub, 1962
91 x 80
Shows number of visitors to resorts with insets of popular regions.
75p

BEVÖLKERUNGSDICHTE – BEVÖLKERUNGSTENTWICKLUNG
1: 500,000
by Prof I B F Kormoss
Prepared for the 1968 "Conference des Regions de l'Europe du Nord Ouest"
Bruges : Conference de Communaute Europeenes
112 x 137 each
Set of 2 maps, both in 2 sheets, Population Density and Population Evolution, covers Netherlands, Belgium, Luxembourg, N W France, W Germany. Statistics for 1951-61.
Legend in 4 langs.
Per set £12.50

KARTA NARODOV EVROPY
1:4,000,000
In 4 sheets
Moskva : GUGK
150 x 148
Map of the Nationalities and Races of Europe. School map, covering language, races, groups etc. In Rus.

MUSIC IN EUROPE
No 161021
Chicago : Denoyer-Geppert
162 x 137
Pictorial school wall map of European composers and musical history.
Spring Rollers US $24.00

EUROPA : KULTUR
Braunschweig : Westermann
96 x 127
Col. pictorial wall map for schools with important people, buildings etc. illustrated.
Am. ed : Denoyer–Geppert
US $5.00

L ECONOMIC

EUROPE : ECONOMIC ACTIVITIES
1:9,312,500
No 109021
Chicago : Denoyer-Geppert
111 x 162
4 them. maps on 1 sheet. Shows socio-economic relationships.
Rollers US $15.50

EUROPA : WIRTSCHAFT
1:7,500,000
München : List
220 x 170
Harms pictorial economic wall map for schools.

EUROPE NO 3 (POLITIQUE)
1:5,000,000
Éditions MDI
Agricultural map on reverse
see EUROPE 4D.

STANFORDS MARKETING MAP OF WESTERN EUROPE
1:3,500,000
London : Stanford, 1969
94 x 122
Showing road, rail and water communications; populated areas, principal towns, with statistical data of EEC and EFTA countries.
£2.50

EUROPA : VERKEHR UND WIRTSCHAFT
Braunschweig : Westermann
96 x 127
Col. pictorial wall map for schools, showing types of manufactured products, resources, communications.

MAP SHOWING LOCATION OF ECSC IRON AND STEEL WORKS
No 10468
Luxembourg : EEC Publications Office
480 x 336
Shows location of European Coal and Steel works as at 1st January 1964, showing types of plants. In German, Fr. Italian, Dutch. £1.25

EUROPE, ECONOMIC
Indianapolis : Cram
School wall map, showing foreign trade agriculture, minerals and petroleum.
US $13.75

WIRTSCHAFTLICHE NÜTZUNG EUROPAS
1:3,000,000
Hamburg : Flemming
206 x 166
Economic wall map, showing proportional production. DM 142

EUROPA, WIRTSCHAFT
1:3,000,000
H275
München : Paul List
220 x 170
Economic wall map for schools.
DM 156.00

WIRTSCHAFT EUROPAS
1:3,000,000
Prof. Dr Haefke
Darmstadt : Perthes
220 x 165
Col. economic wall map indicating industrial areas, conurbations etc. by symbols. DM 128

EUROPA, WIRTSCHAFT
1:3,000,000
Hamburg : Flemming
208 x 167
Economic wall map showing forest and cultivated areas, production and commodities.

EUROPA, WIRTSCHAFT
1:3,000,000
Berlin : Velhagen & Klasing und Hermann Schroedel
232 x 166
Economic wall map.

EUROPA : WIRTSCHAFT
1:3,000,000
Prof. Otremba
Braunschweig : Westermann
194 x 189
Economic wall map for schools, showing industrial and agricultural regions, proportion of employed persons, types of industry etc.
DM 142

KARTE DER FLUGPLÄTZE EUROPAS
1:3,000,000
Frankfurt : Deutscher Aero Club, 1967.
118 x 166
Chart of European aerodromes. Hill-shaded outline map of Europe and N. Africa, showing boundaries and capitals, with aerodromes classified by type and usage. In Ger. Eng, Fr. Sp.

EUROPA : EISENBAHNKARTE
1:2,500,000
No 4171
Bern : K & F, 1972
129 x 92
Political col. map with railways classified. Legend in Fr and Gr.

WIRTSCHAFTSLEISTUNG UND HANDELSVERFLECHTUNG IN EWG/EFTA
1:2,500,000
Prof Dr Otremba
Hamburg : Flemming
195 x 190
Wall map showing production and trade in the EEC and EFTA.
DM 142

EUROPA, BERGBAU UND INDUSTRIE
1:2,500,000
Gotha: Haack
230 x 180
School wall map showing mining and industrial areas by symbols. Place names graded by pop.

WESTEUROPA IM AUFBAU
1:2,000,000
München : List
260 x 200
2 maps, showing economic structure and pop. of W Europe. Harms school wall map.

WESTLICHES EUROPA : VERWALTUNG, WIRTSCHAFT UND VERKEHR
No 9924
München : JRO
96 x 120
Pictorial school wall map illustrating admin. economy and communications.
DM 48.00

ÖSTLICHES EUROPA : VERWALTUNG, WIRTSCHAFT UND VERKEHR
No 9928
München : JRO
96 x 130
Pictorial school wall map, illustrating admin. economy and communications.
DM 48.00

WESTLICHES EUROPA : INDUSTRIE
No 9923
München : JRO
96 x 120
Pictorial school wall map illustrating industrial product. DM 48.00

ÖSTLICHES EUROPA : INDUSTRIE
No 9927
München : JRO
96 x 130

Pictorial school wall map illustrating industrial product. DM 48.00

HOSPODARSKÁ MAPA
1:1,250,000
Praha : Kart
Economic wall maps of Europe.
Maps available:
Severní Evropa (Northern)
1970 in 4 sheets Kcs 165
Západní Evropa (West)
1971 in 4 sheets Kcs 180
Jihovýchodní Evropa a Italie (S E Europe and Italy)
1970 in 4 sheets Kcs 180
Střední Evropa (Central)
1968 Kcs 120

ALLEMAGNE - POLOGNE - AUTRICHE, PHYSIQUE
1:1,100,000
Armand : Colin
Political and industrial map on reverse.
see EUROPE 4 E1.

MITTELEUROPA : LANDWIRTSCHAFT UND FISCHEREI
Braunschweig : Westermann
96 x 127
Col. pictorial wall map for schools, illustrating agriculture and fishing products for Central Europe.

MITTELEUROPAISCHE WASSER-STRASSEN
1:1,000,000
Duisberg : Binnenschiffahrts - Verlag, 1972
114 x 85
Central Europe — inland waterways — Germany (as far as Berlin), N France, Benelux. Col. map with insets.
DM 13.00

VOIES NAVIGABLES DE L'EUROPE DE L'OUEST
1:1,000,000
Paris : IGN, 1975
92 x 89
Layer coloured map classifying canal capacities, length and number of locks for each waterway. With large scale insets and statistics.

SOZIALISTISCHE LÄNDER MITTEL- UND SÜDOSTEUROPAS BERGBAU UND INDUSTRIE
1:750,000
Gotha : Haack
206 x 228
School wall map showing mining and industrial areas of Central and S E European Socialist countries. Mineral deposits located, other natural resources, towns graded by pop.

M HISTORICAL

CARTES HISTORIQUES
J Bouillon
Various Scales
St-Germain-en-Laye : Éditions MDI
92 x 126
Plastic-coated, double-sided historical wall maps for schools.
1520 La Guerre de Cent Ans, 1 and 2 1:1,700,000
1528 La Réforme religieuse au XVIe siècle en Europe, 1:1,170,000
1536 L'Empire de Napoléon 1:3,000,000
1538 L'Europe après le Congrès de Vienne (1815) 1:3,400,000
1540 L'Unité allemande et l'Unité Italienne
1544 La Guerre de 1914-18/Les Fronts français — L'Europe de 1914, 1:4,000,000
1546 La Guerre de 1914-18/Les Fronts Européens, 1:4,000,000 — L'Europe de 1918-1923, 1:5,000,000
1548 L'Europe de 1937-1939/ L'Europe de 1945-1948, 1:5,000,000

HISTORISCHE WANDKARTEN
Various scales
Hamburg : Flemming
Col. historical wall maps in German.
Maps available :
1 Alte Greichenland 1:750,000 228 x 127
2 Vom Römischen Weltreich zum Karolingerreich, 4 maps at 1:4,375,000, 203 x 182
3 Die Germanische Volkwanderung 1:3,000,000 203 x 162
4 Bildung und Verfall Mitteläterlichen Reiches, 4 maps at 1:4,375,000 203 x 182
5 Bildung der Modernen Staaten, 4 maps at 1:4,735,000 203 x 182
6 Europa in XX Jahrhundert, 4 maps at 1:4,375,000, 203 x 182
7 Die Ausbreitung des Christentums 3 maps at 1:4,375,000, 203 x 182
8 Tausend Jahre Abendlandischer Geschichte, 9 maps, 193 x 172

HISTORISCHER WANDKARTEN
1:3,000,000
Gotha : Haack
198 x 162
Col. historical wall maps.
Maps available:
Europa im 8 Jahrhundert (Century)
" 10 "
" 12 "
" 13/14 "
" 16 "
" 17 "
" 18 "
Europa zur Zeit der französische Revolution und der Napoleonischen Kriege (Fr. Rev. and Napoleonic Wars)
Europa im Zeitalter Napoleon I (at the time of Napoleon I)
Europa zwischen den beiden Weltkriegen (between the World Wars)
With text.

HISTORISCHE WANDKARTEN
1:3,800,000
by W Hillgemann
Darmstadt : Perthes
156 x 140
Col. historical wall maps in German.
Maps available:
Europa : Bündnissysteme Bismarck, 1871-1890
Europa : Bündnisse 1892-1914
Europa : Krise der Demokratie, 1918-37
Europa : Expansion Hitlers, 1937-45
Europa: Integrationspolitik, 1945-1967

HISTORISCHER WANDKARTEN
1:2,000,000
Darmstadt : Perthes
Col. historical wall maps in German.
Maps available :
Europa zur Zeit der Germanischen Völkerwanderung und Staatenbildung 375-580 AD (shows migration and settling of Germanic tribes)
Europa vor dem I Weltkrieg 1870-1914 (before the First World War)
Europa nach dem I Weltkrieg, 1918-1932 (after First World War)
Europa nach dem 2 Weltkrieg, 1945-1970 (after Second World War)

PUTZGER GESCHICHTSWAND-KARTEN
Bielefeld : Cornelsen, Velhagen & Klasing
Col.historical wall maps in German.
Maps available:
Europa im Hochmittelalter (um 1000)
1:2,500,000 196 x 147
Mittel- und Westeuropa zur Zeit der Staufer, Italien im 10 und 11 Jahrhundert
1:1,500,000 206 x 159
Reformation und Katholische Erneuerung (Renovation)
1:1,000,000 136 x 212
Europa im 16 Jahrhundert (um 1550)
1:2,500,000 197 x 154
Europa im Zeitalter des Absolutismus (um 1740)
1:2,500,000 197 x 154
Europa im Zeitalter Napoleons (1812)
1:2,500,000 197 x 154
Mitteleuropa 1815-1866 Restauration und Revolution
1:875,000 197 x 146
Sprachen (languages) Mittel-, Ost- und Südosteuropas um 1910
1:1,700,000 138 x 218
Europa nach dem Wiener Kongress, 1815
1,3,500,000 197 x 154
Europa vor dem Ersten Weltkrieg, 1914
1:2,500,000 197 x 154
Mitteleuropa nach dem Ersten Weltkrieg Weimarer Republik
1:875,000 197 x 146
Europa zwischen den Weltkriegen (1919-39)
1:2,700,000 190 x 149
Mitteleuropa seit dem Zweiten Weltkrieg
1:875,000 197 x 146
Various prices

HISTORISCHE WANDKARTEN
Braunschweig : Westermann
Col. historical wall maps in German.
Maps available :
No 298 Das Römische Reich
1:2,500,000 211 x 203
No 308 Völkerwanderung und Staatenbildung vom 4 bis zum 8 Jahrhundert (Migrations and formations of states)
1:4,000,000 199 x 203
No 309 Das Reich Karls des Grossen
No 310 Europa in der Zeit der Ottonen und Salier
205 x 140
No 326 Europa zur Zeit der Hohenstaufen 205 x 139
No 328 Europa im 14 Jahrhundert
203 x 138
No 329 Europa im 15 Jahrhundert
206 x 140
No 302 Europa im 16 Jahrhundert
204 x 140
No 324 Mitteleuropa im 16 Jahrhundert 201 x 139

No 303 Mittel- und Osteuropa nach dem 30 - jährigen Kriege (after the 30 years war) 202 x 140
No 301 Europa im 18 Jahrhundert 205 x 140
No 300 Deutschland 1789 und Europa bis 1815 207 x 140
No 297 Europa von 1815 bis 1871 205 x 140
No 283 Europa von 1871 bis 1914 209 x 139
No 304 Der I Weltkrieg 1914-18 207 x 194
No 284 Europa 1918 bis 1945 210 x 140
No 299 Der 2 Weltkrieg 1939-1945 207 x 187

TÖRTÉNELMI FALITÉRKÉPEK
In 2 sheets each
Budapest : Cart
119 x 168
Historical wall maps in Hungarian.
Maps available:
Európa a IX-XI században 1:4,000,000
Nagy Károly Korában (the time of Charlemagne) 1:3,500,000
a XII-XIII században 1:4,000,000
a XIV-XV században 1:3,000,000
a XVI században 1:3,500,000
a XVII század kozépen (mid 17th C) 1:3,500,000
a XVIII században 1:3,500,000
1815-1849 1:3,500,000
a XIX sz második felébén (2nd half 19th C)
Európa az I Világháború idején (During World War I)
Európa az II Világháború idején.

CARTE STORICHE
Various scales
Novara : Ag
Various sizes
Historical wall maps:
Europa Napoleonica 1:3,000,000 200 x 140 2 sheets L 3,500
Europa Politica Durante e Dopo La Guerra 1914-18 (During and After World War I) 1:4,000,000 150 x 140 2 sheets L 3,500

BREASTED-HUTH-HARDING HISTORICAL MAPS
Chicago : Denoyer-Geppert
110 x 80
Series of col. wall maps printed on manilla.
Maps available:
204221 Europe at the time of Charlemagne
204231 Europe, Time of the Crusades, 1097
204271 Europe in 1360
204291 Europe, Time of Charles V, 1519
204321 Europe in 1648 after the Treaty of Westphalia
204331 Europe in 1740
204351 Europe at the time of Napoleon 1812
204361 Europe after 1815
204391 Modern Italy and Central Europe
204401 Growth of Prussia and Modern Germany
204411 The Balkan States
204431 Europe 1914
204441 Economic Europe
204451 Peoples of Europe, Languages
204461 Northern France, Belgium and the Rhine
204471 Europe 1918-1937
204481 Central Europe 1918-1922

HISTORY MAPS
Indianapolis : Cram
Col. school wall maps.
Maps available:
The Mediterranean World in 164 BC
The Migrations to 486 AD
Europe after the Migrations
Europe at the Death of Charlemagne
Crusading Europe 1095-1291
Europe, Commercial and Industrial About 1453
Europe and the Near East in 1519
Christians and Mohammedans in 1600
Europe in 1648
Europe and the Near East, 1740
Europe under Napoleon, 1810
Europe after the Congress of Vienna, 1815
Europe after the Congress of Berlin, 1875
The Races of Europe
Europe after the Treaties of 1919-1924
Europe, September 1, 1938
World War II, European Theater
Each US $13.75

PALMER WORLD HISTORY MAPS
Various scales
Chicago : Rand McNally
50 x 46
Col. wall maps for :
Europe and the Crusader States (1140)
Europe in 1360
Europe about 1560
Europe in 1721
Europe in 1810
Europe in 1815
Expansion of Russia in Europe and European invasions of Russia, 1533, 1598, 1914
Europe in 1914
Europe in 1922-1940
Europe after World War II

WORLD HISTORY MAPS
Chicago : Weber Costello Co 139 x 106
Series of clear, coloured wall maps each including approx 7 inset maps.
Maps available:
138-842 Europe in 1648
859 Europe in 1763
867 Europe in 1815
875 Europe in 1914
883 Europe in 1936
Available mounted in various styles.

SCHOOL HISTORICAL WALL MAPS
Moskva : GUGK
Col. historical wall maps in Russian.
Maps available:
Europe in Early times 1:5,000,000
Europe in the 5th-7th C 1:3,000,000
Europe in the 9th-15th C 1:3,500,000
Europe in the 16th-17th C 1:3,500,000
Europe in the early years 1:5,000,000
Europe 1815-49 1:3,500,000
Europe 1850-60 1:3,500,000
Europe 1870-1914 1:3,500,000
First World War, 1914-18 1:3,000,000
W Europe after World War I, 1918-23 1:3,500,000
Europe in the 14th-15th C 1:3,500,000
Eastern Roman (Byzantine) Empire and Slavia, in the 6th-9th C, 1973 1:4,000,000
Europe in the Period of Directorate (1789-94) 1973 1:3,500,000
Europe c1799-1815, 1973 1:3,500,000

HISTORIA DE EUROPA
Barcelona : Editorial Teide
88 x 115
Historical wall map for schools in Spanish
S.Ptas 275

DER UMBRUCH EUROPAS IM 20 JAHRHUNDERT
1:4,000,000 H 296
München : List
240 x 180
Harms wall map; Reorganisation of Europe in the 20th Century. 4 maps showing Europe before and after the 1st World War; before and after the 2nd World War; migration since 1937; division in 1962/3.
DM 164.00

DIE MILITÄRISCHEN OPERATIONEN IN EUROPA, 1939-1945
1:5,000,000
No 149
Bern : K & F
124 x 89
Col. map with explanations in Eng. Fr and Ger.

POLACY NA FRONTACH II WOJNY ŚWIATOWEJ
1:4,000,000
Warszawa : PPWK
166 x 160
Historical wall map of Europe during the Second World War.
Zl 130

CENTRAL EUROPE 1914 TO THE PRESENT DAY
1:2,000,000
No 210051
Chicago : Denoyer-Geppert
198 x 203
School historical wall map in 4 parts: 1914-1920, 1920-1937, 1937-1945, 1945-1966.
CR US $42.50

EUROPA W LATACH 1848-49
1:3,500,000
by J Janczak
Warszawa : PPWK, 1972
186 x 120
Historical wall map for schools, showing the political situation in Europe in 1848-9.
Zl 140

EUROPA : NEUORDNUNG DURCH DEN WIENER KONGRESS 1815-1829
1:3,800,000
by W Hilgemann
Darmstadt : Perthes
156 x 140
Europe after the Congress of Vienna.
DM 76.00

EUROPA : DIE JULI-REVOLUTION UND IHRE FOLGEN 1830-1847
1:3,800,000
by W Hilgemann
Darmstadt : Perthes
156 x 140
Shows the July Revolution and its Consequences. DM 76.00

EUROPA : DIE UMGESTALTUNG DURCH NAPOLEON I, 1799-1815
1:3,800,000
by W Hilgemann
Darmstadt : Perthes
156 x 140
Napoleon's Empire : historical wall map for schools DM 76.00

EUROPA W XVI WIEKU
1:4,000,000
Warszawa : PPWK, 1972
167 x 116
Historical school wall map showing Europe in the 16th C. Zl 140

SLOWANIE W IX WIEKU
1:3,000,000
by T Ladogorski
Warszawa : PPWK, 1972
125 x 115
In 2 sheets, showing formation of Slav states.
School wall map. Zl 140

DEUTSCHLAND UND ITALIEN
911-1125 and
DEUTSCHLAND UND ITALIEN
1125-1273
1:1,000,000
by Haack and Herzberg
Darmstadt : Perthes
172 x 215
Historical wall map for schools.

EUROPA W IX-XI WIEKU
1:4,000,000
by B Kaczmarski
Warszawa : PPWK
184 x 120
Historical wall map of Europe in the 9th - 11th C. Zl 140

GALLIEN, GERMANIEN, BRITANNIEN
ZUR RÖMERZEIT
1:1,000,000
Prof. Dr Lauffer
Darmstadt : Perthes
146 x 176
Col. historical wall map for schools showing Gaul, Germany and Britain at the time of the Romans.

UNTERGANG DES RÖMISCHEN
WELTREICHES – GERMANISCHE
VOLKERWANDERUNG
by Hachen berg and Tackenberg
Berlin : Velhagen & Klasing
Showing decline of the Roman Empire and the wanderings of the Germanic Tribes.

EUROPA ZUR JÜNGEREN STEINZEIT
1:3,000,000
by Prof. Dr Narr
Darmstadt : Perthes
210 x 140
Early Stone-Age historical wall map.
DM 128

EARLY MAP REPRODUCTIONS
From Joan Blaeu's Theatrum Orbis Terrarum
Atlas Novus
Plate: Europe 1606
Edinburgh : Bart
61 x 52
Colour reproduction from the 1648 atlas
£1.50

EUROPE
Maplewood : Hammond
62 x 41
Set of 4 reproduction maps:
Navigation Chart of Europe, Pieter Goos, 1668
Great Britain and Ireland, John Speed Atlas c 1676
France, W.J. Blaeu, c 1664
Italy, Janssonius, 1650 US $3.95

UNIVERSE EUROPE MARITIME, 1586
København : GI
Facsimile print in black and white.
D.Kr. 30.00

CARTA ITINERARIA EUROPAE-
WALDSEEMÜLLER-KARTE
Published 1520 in Strasbourg by Martin Waldseemüller No 649
Bonn-Bad Godesberg : Kirschbaum Verlag
99 x 77
Facsimile map in colours with 24 page explanation DM 60.00

EUROPE : A PICTORIAL AND
HISTORICAL MAP
Edinburgh : Bart, 1972
70 x 93
Plain map, with col. illus. of famous buildings, people etc; national flags in border. 40p

ATLASES
A1 GENERAL: ROADS

ROAD ATLAS OF EUROPE
Edinburgh : Bart, 1974
22 x 30
136 pp
96 pp maps showing 4 classes of roads, distances and road conditions, strip maps of popular tourist areas, through-way town plans, distance chart. £2.25

AUTOATLAS BERTELSMANN:
DEUTSCHLAND, EUROPA
Bertelsmann 1973
see FED. REP. OF GERMANY
430. 1 ATLASES A1

ATLAS ROUTIER ET TOURISTIQUE
1,500,000
Paris : Bordas – Hachette, 1970
24 x 28
Same detail as "Les Cartes Bleues". Covers France, Belgium, Luxembourg, Switzerland. 76pp maps showing road networks, distances, tourist information etc.

AUTOATLAS EUROPA
1:2,000,000
Wien : F-B
58 road maps of Europe showing distances and route numbers, with sheets covering N Africa and Near East. 96pp index.
DM 12.80

EUROPEAN MOTORING ATLAS AND
GUIDE
1:2,000,000
London : Gia
22 x 29
88pp
32 selected routes with motorways, distances in km, scenic routes, descriptive notes. 32pp road maps, gasetteer to popular regions, tourist information, town plans. Index.
Hard cover £1.20

GRIEGS VEIATLAS OVER EUROPA
Bergen : J. Griegs Forlag.
Road atlas of Europe with maps scale 1:4,000,000 and 1:1,500,000 for Scandinavia. N.Kr. 35.00

AUTROPA ATLAS
1:3,125,000
Bern : Hallwag, 1970
15 x 25
15pp detailed road maps section, 54 town plans. 23pp index.

STRASSENATLAS EUROPA
1:1,500,000 – 1:4,000,000
Zürich: OF and Rand McNally, 1976
22 x 28
75pp of maps
Road atlas of Europe with central region on larger scale and legend in 6 languages. Index. S.Fr. 11.00

EUROPA AUTO ATLAS
Bern : Hallwag, 1971/2
16 x 26
92pp maps covering most of Europe, inc. Poland and Rumania, generally at the scale of 16 miles to 1". Inc. 54 town plans. 96pp index.
Hard cover £2.75

EUROPA TOURING
Bern : Hallwag
988 pp
184pp maps (1:3,000,000) 84 city plans special tourist maps and info; with descriptions of 1100 European towns and touring areas with details of accommodation and travel information.

GROSSER JRO STRASSENATLAS –
DEUTSCHLAND, ALPENLÄNDER,
EUROPA
1:300,000/1:750,000
JRO, 1973
see FED. REP. OF GERMANY
430.1 ATLASES A1

AUTO EUROPA
Bern : K & F
16 x 26
243pp
146pp detailed maps at 16 and 40 miles to 1", distance chart, 44 col. town plans. 97pp index.

EUROPA
Bern : K & F
14 x 23
140 detailed fold-out maps; tourist information. No index. Maps scale: 1:500,000, 1:1,000,000 and 1:2,500,000.

SHELL – ATLAS EUROPA
Stuttgart : Mair
17 x 27
250pp app
Detailed maps with tourist info.
114pp maps at 1:1,500,000. 134pp index. DM 15.80

CONTINENTAL ATLAS –
DEUTSCHLAND UND EUROPA
1:500,000 – 1:2,000,000
Mair
see FED. REP. OF GERMANY
430. 1 ATLASES A1

DER GROSSE SHELL ATLAS:
DEUTSCHLAND, EUROPA
Mairs, 1972
see FED. REP. OF GERMANY
430. 1 ATLASES A1.

ROAD ATLAS OF EUROPE
1:1,000,000
London, Philip, 1972
20 x 28
239pp
157pp of col. road maps, route numbers, class and distances marked, river, sea and rail ferries also railways, airports, buildings and places of interest. Relief shaded.
77pp index.

RAC ROAD ATLAS OF EUROPE
Chicago : Rand McNally, 1972
21 x 28

104pp
66pp road maps, scale 1:1,500,000 with N Scandinavia and W USSR and Bulgaria at 1:4,000,000. 18 large scale city plans; 4pp information and 24pp index. £1.25

POCKET ROAD ATLAS OF EUROPE
1:4,000,000
London : Gia, 1976
3 x 13
Shows distances in miles, car ferry routes, international boundaries and main roads with route numbers. Comprehensive index.
75p

DER AKTUELLE AUTO-ATLAS DEUTSCHLAND UND EUROPA : STRASSEN
No 802
Ravenstein, 1973
see GERMANY 430 ATLASES A1

REISEATLAS DEUTSCHLAND UND EUROPA
1:400,000 – 1:750,000
Ravenstein, 1971
see FED. REP. OF GERMANY, 430. 1 ATLASES A1

STRASSENATLAS – DEUTSCHLAND UND EUROPA
1:500,000 – 1:3,500,000
RV, 1973-74
see FED. REP. OF GERMANY 430. 1 ATLASES A1

AVTOMOBIL'NIE MARSHRUTY EVROPEYSKAYA CHASTE
Moskva : GUGK, 1973
17 x 27
39pp
Atlas of European routes.

ATLASES
B TOWN PLANS

44 STADTDURCHFÄHRTSPLANE
Bern : K & F
14 x 23
47pp
Small atlas containing 44 col. town plans of major cities in Europe. No street index.

ATLASES
H BIOGEOGRAPHY

ATLAS FLORAE EUROPAE
Helsinki : Committee for Mapping the Flora of Europe and Societas Biologica Fennica Vanamas, 1974
in 5 vols
21 x 28
Series covering the Vascular Plants of Europe, showing distribution of plants etc, with maps and texts. Vol. I Pteridophyta (Psilotaceae-Azollaceae) Ed Jaakko Jalas and Juha Suominen, 1972, 121pp.
Fmk 46.10

Vol. 2, Gymnospermae (Pinaceae to Ephedraceae) Fmk 20.20
In preparation:
Vol. 3, Angiospermae (Salicaceae-Balanophoraceae)
Vol. 4, Angiospermae, cont. (Polygonaceae to Basellaceae)
Vol. 5, Angiospermae, cont. (Caryophyllaceae).

AGRO-ECOLOGICAL ATLAS OF CEREAL GROWING IN EUROPE
Wageningen : Centre for Ag. Pub. and Documentation (PUDOC)
In 4 vols
43 x 45
Vol 1
Agro-climatic atlas of Europe. Ed P Thran, 1965, 36pp text, 128 maps. Shows temperature, precipitation etc. Text in Eng.
120 f
Vol. 2
Atlas of the Cereal-Growing Areas in Europe. Ed S Broekhuizen, 1969, 156pp text, 60 maps. Soil types in relation to cereal growing. Eng. Fr., Ger. 150 f
Vol. 3
Atlas of Cereal Diseases and Pests in Europe (in preparation)
Vol. 4
Atlas of Ecological Characteristics of European Cereals (in preparation)

ATLASES
J CLIMATE

CLIMATIC ATLAS OF EUROPE
Paris : UNESCO/WMO and Budapest: Cart, 1970
60 x 42
27 maps covering mean annual and monthly temperature and precipitation totals, annual temperature amplitude. Observation 1931-60. At scales of 1:10,000,000 (60 x 70) and 1:5,000,000 (120 x 70). With foreword and introduction in Eng, Fr., Rus, Sp. Loose-leaf binding.
£15.00

ATLASES
L ECONOMIC

ATLAS SOZIALÖKONOMISCHER REGIONEN EUROPAS (ATLAS OF SOCIAL AND ECONOMIC REGIONS OF EUROPE)
Ed Prof. Dr D Häring & Dr W Menges
Baden-Baden : Nomos, 1968+
In 12 instalments
45 x 63 (maps)
Series of 75 maps in folder, covering work, transport, economy, social services, population, education. Loose-leaf binder with separate sheet maps. Legend in German, French and English
Instalments 1-12 DM 738.00

OXFORD REGIONAL ECONOMIC ATLAS OF WESTERN EUROPE
Oxford : OUP, 1971
19 x 26
xix, 160
96pp col. maps. Thematic section includes physical and climatic background, population, agriculture, fuel and mineral resources, industry and transport. Topographic map coverage provided, 31 urban plans and gazetteer of 15,000 names.
Paper £3.50p

OXFORD REGIONAL ECONOMIC ATLAS OF THE USSR AND EASTERN EUROPE
OUP
see USSR ATLASES 57 L

ATLAS OF EUROPE – A PROFILE OF WESTERN EUROPE
Edinburgh: J. Bartholomew, London: F. Warne, 1974
21 x 31
128pp
Including 80pp of thematic maps, diagrams and explanatory notes covering, economic and political aspects of the grouping. 15pp of physical maps and statistical notes glossary and index.
£4.95

ECONOMIC ATLAS OF WESTERN EUROPE
Aylesbury : Ginn & Co Ltd. 1974
21 x 29
144 pp
Covers continental western Europe, excluding Switzerland, Portugal, British Isles and Scandinavia. After a preliminary section there follows a series of distribution maps on population, employment, finance, trade and major industries. National statistical tables. Legend in 4 languages.

ATLANTE DELL'EUROPA OCCIDENTALE
Ed Jean Dollfus
Novara : Ag
25 x 33
48pp
Atlas covering physical, economic and historical matters, 35pp maps, with illus. in black and white.
L 1,500

ATLANTE DELLE REGIONI D'EUROPA
Ed V Bonapace
Novara : Ag
21 x 25
80pp
Covers geog. of the various states with economy, culture and history. List of organisations. 16 geog. maps, 22 economic ones, in colour.
L 1,500

THE EUROPEAN COMMUNITY IN MAPS
1:9,000,000
Bruxelles : Europ. Com. Info. Service, 1970
22 x 28
12 col. maps in folder showing the 6 Community members, inc. most of England and Wales. Shows pop, land use, agriculture, transport, industry, etc.

VÄR VÄRLD : EUROPA
Stockholm : GLA
Political – economic atlas with col. maps and diagrams with facing page of explanatory text.
25.50 S Kr

ATLAS OF WESTERN EUROPEAN PULP AND PAPER INDUSTRY
1st Edition
compiled by editors of Pulp and Paper International
San Francisco: Miller Freeman Pubn's. 1976
36 x 51
Shows all pulp, paper and paperboard mills in Western Europe over 5,000 tons capacity. Symbols show size as well as type of mill, with index to mills. Consists of 9 separate maps which can be removed from the binder and assembled into a wall map.
US. $25.00

ATLASES
M HISTORICAL

ATLAS OF EUROPEAN HISTORY
Ed Edward W Fox
New York : OUP, 1958 (1969)
19 x 25
95pp
Covers European history (including Middle East and Holy Land) from Old Babylonian Empire (c 2100 BC) – AD 1955. 64 maps in colour, with gazetteer of topographical and historical sites. £3.50

ATLAS OF EUROPEAN POLITICAL HISTORY
Ed. P.G. Dickson Jones
Glasgow: Blackie, 1973
32pp
Includes 44 single colour maps covering the period from mid 17th century to modern times. Index. 66p

HISTORIA E MESJETËS PER KLASËN E VI TE SHKOLLES TETËVJECARE: HARTA
Various scales
Tirane : Hamid Shijaku, 1970
21 x 29
Booklet with 16 historical wall maps of Europe and Asia for schools in Albanian.

HARTA PËR TEKSTIN E HISTORISË SË KOHËS SE VJETËR KLASA V BOTIMI I - IV TË (1800C - 100 BC)
Various scales
Tiranë: "Hamid Shijaku", 1969
21 x 29
11 maps covering all or parts of Eurasia at different periods. In booklet. Albanian text.

ATLASES
P REGIONAL

ATLAS OF CENTRAL EUROPE
Prep. Bertelsmann Cartographic Inst, Gutersloh
London : John Murray
School atlas of large scale maps (1:1,000,000) covering Central Europe; index of 37,000 names.
£2.75

ATLAS DER DONAULÄNDER
Ed Dr Josef Breu
Wien : Österreichisches Ost-und Südost-Europa-Institut, 1970+
69 x 53
50 col. maps (68 x 99) generally 1:2,000,000. Text sheets – Ger, Eng, Fr. Rus. Covers Czechoslovakia, Poland, USSR, Rumania, Hungary, Austria, Yugoslavia, Bulgaria. To be published in annual instalments, each containing 5 maps with text.

Part 1 5 map sheets with text
No. 111 Topographical Map, A (Isohypses)
No 112 Topographical Map, B (Hypsometrical Tints)
121 Hypsographical Map
122 Relief
251 Administrative Districts
Part 2 5 map sheets with text
No. 214 Development of Cities and Towns 1930–1960
216 Age Structure
221 Distribution of Population by Economic Activity
No. 332 Electricity
341 Industries : General Survey
Part 3 5 map sheets with Text
215 Birth and Death Rates, Natural Population Increase
242 Illiteracy
342 Metallurgical Industry, Mechanical Engineering, Metal Manufacture, Electrical Engineering
343 Wood, Paper, Pulp and Printing Industries
344 Construction Materials, Glass, Ceramics and Chemical Industry
Part 4 5 map sheets with text
No. 142 Annual Rainfall
171 Natural Vegetation
241 Educational Standard
345 Leather, Textile and Clothing Industries
346 Food products and tobacco industries

each part A.Sch. 500.00
Binder (69 x 53) A.Sch. 290.00

WATTENMEER
Neumünster : Karl Wachholtz, 1976
25 x 30
368pp
A geographic description of the Friesian and other islands off the north-west European coast from Den Helder to Esbjerg. Includes over 300 4 colour maps and diagrams with descriptive text and 3 fold-out maps
DM 85

38 x 30
Covers Northern Ireland, showing contours with layer colouring, land features, motorways, and other communications. 10p

F GEOLOGY

GEOLOGICAL MAP OF NORTHERN IRELAND
1:250,000
Sheet 1 of 5 sheet map of Ireland
1st Edition
Belfast : Geol. Surv. of N.I. 1976
92 x 64
Coloured geological map.

ONE INCH TO ONE MILE GEOLOGICAL MAPS
1:63,360
In 205 sheets, see index 416/3
Belfast : Geol. Surv. NI
46 x 30 each
Old series in black and white (generally) to cover whole country. Some Northern sheets with relief hachures. Geol. detail shown by symbols; some cross sections. New coloured series in preparation published in both solid and drift editions.
Sheets published:
7 Giant's Causeway, 1968
8 Ballycastle, 1963
29 Carrickfergus, 1968
34 Ballygowley 1:50,000 – in press
35 Dungannon, 1961
36 Belfast, 1966
45 Enniskillen – in press
Old series outline 80p
New series coloured 80p

GEOLOGY OF BELFAST AND DISTRICT
SPECIAL ENGINEERING GEOLOGY SHEET
1:21,120
Belfast : Geol. Surv. NI, 1971
71 x 91
Coloured geological map, rocks shown by symbols. Summary of soil and rock characteristics. With plan of rock-head, contours in city area on reverse.
£1.65

NORTHERN IRELAND GEOLOGICAL SERIES
1:10,560
Belfast : Geol. Surv. NI
In black and white on County series sheet lines – quarter sheets
Sheets published:
Tyrone 46 SE, 47 NW, SW, 54 NE (Coalisland)
Antrim 5 SW, SE, 9 NW (Ballycastle)
Each 60p
Special maps of Development Areas available as dyeline prints:
Ballymena Sheet (composite of Antrim 32 SW, SE, 33 SW, 37 NW, NE, 38 NW)
Antrim Sheet (Part of Antrim 50)
Cookstown Sheet (Part of Londonderry 48, 49, Tyrone 29, 30, 31, 38, 39)
Each 40p

G EARTH RESOURCES

MINERAL DEPOSIT MAP (PROVISIONAL)
1:253,440
Belfast : Geol. Surv. NI, 1970
90 x 62
Black and white sun print of ¼ inch base map; mineral deposits shown by symbols, classified by type. 40p

QUARRY MAP OF NORTHERN IRELAND
1:253,440
Belfast: Geol. Sur. NI. 1975
90 x 62
Black and white dyeline print of ¼" base map. Locations of quarries and material worked indicated by symbols. 40p

AEROMAGNETIC MAP OF NORTHERN IRELAND
1:253,440
Belfast : Geol. Surv. NI, 1971
90 x 62
Geophysical map in colour. 75p

GRAVITY ANOMALY MAP OF NORTHERN IRELAND
1:253,440
Belfast : Geol. Surv. NI, 1967
90 x 62
Geophysical map in colour. 75p

H BIOGEOGRAPHY

THE LAND UTILISATION MAP
1:63,360
In 11 sheets
Belfast : OSNI
Coloured map series, based on survey 1938/9. Land classified in 6 headings: arable; grass; heath and moorland; orchards; gardens, etc; agriculturally unproductive; woodland.
Each, flat 25p

DUNDRUM NATURE RESERVE
1:12,500
Glasgow : Dept of Geog., Univ. of Glasgow. 1972
41 x 24
Coloured map of the reserve.

417 Republic Of Ireland

See also:

41 BRITISH ISLES
415 IRELAND
416 NORTHERN IRELAND

A2 GENERAL MAPS: LOCAL

SOUTH WEST IRELAND
1:400,000
Maidenhead: Fairey Surveys, 1975
59 x 58 sheet size 61 x 89
Coloured, shaded relief tourist map. All classes of roads with 45 categories of tourist information marked. Insets of Killarney region and plans of Limerick and Cork.
On reverse 1:700,000 road map of the whole of Ireland.
Paper folded 75p

B TOWN PLANS

IRELAND – TOWN PLANS
Various scales
Large scale plans with index to streets.
Plans available:

Cork (OS)	30p
Dublin (OS)	30p
Dublin (Map Productions)	25p
Dublin – Central (Gia)	25p
Dublin – Greater (Gia)	95p
Wickford (Barnett)	15p

C OFFICIAL SURVEYS

ONE INCH DISTRICT MAPS
1:63,360
Dublin : OS
Special tourist area maps, layer col; contours; spot heights in feet; all classes of road, numbers; footpaths; railways; youth hostels.
Maps available:
Cork, 69 x 52, 1967
Dripsey to Midleton, Bandon to Kinsdale
Dublin, 52 x 66, 1966
Ratoath to Rush, Blessington to Bray
Killarney, 52 x 69, 1968
Lough Caragh to Killarney, South to Adrigole
Wicklow, 69 x 57, 1970
Blessington to Bray, South to Rathdrum
Each 30p

ORDNANCE SURVEY SIX INCH SERIES OF THE REPUBLIC OF IRELAND
1:10,560
Dublin : OS
Detailed County series covering the whole country showing full topographical information.
Each 50p

ORDNANCE SURVEY TWENTY FIVE INCH SERIES
1:2,500
Dublin : OS
Large scale series covering the majority of the country but excluding mountain and moorland areas.
Each 50p

D POLITICAL & ADMINISTRATIVE

ADMINISTRATIVE PLAN OF DUBLIN
1:25,000
Dublin : OS
Showing County Borough Boundaries and Dun Laoire Borough Boundary in red with built up areas in grey. 25p

F GEOLOGY

IRELAND – GEOLOGY
SOLID GEOLOGY OF NORTH WEST AND CENTRAL DONEGAL
1:63,360
Map 1 – 1st edition
M O Spencer and W S Pitcher
Essex : W S Pitcher and M O Spencer, 1972
92 x 116
Prepared for 'The Geology of Donegal: a Study of Granite Emplacement and Unroofing' Wiley Interscience.
£1.50

G EARTH RESOURCES

IRELAND, GENERAL SOIL MAP
1:575,000
Dublin : Publications Section, An Foras Taluntais, 1969
With 15pp explanatory text.
£1.00

COUNTY SOIL MAPS
1:126,720
Dublin : Pubn's. Section, An Foras Taluntais
Series of soil Bulletins each containing 2 or 3 maps.
Bulletins:
1. Wexford – Soil, Soil Suitability, Drainage
16. Limerick – Soil, Soil Suitability, Drainage, Glacial
17. Carlow – Soil, Soil Suitability
22. Kildare – Soil, Soil Suitability
23. Clare – Soil, Soil Suitability
29. Leitrim – Soil, Ground Capacity, Forestry Potential

Each £3.00

RESOURCE SURVEYS
Dublin : Pubn's Section, An Foras Taluntais
Series of soil maps contained in Bulletin.
Bulletins published:
5. West Cork – Includes 5 soil maps of parishes 1:126,720
20. Donegal Part I – Soil, Soil Suitability maps 1:63,360

Each £2.00

RESEARCH FARM BULLETINS
various scales
Dublin : Pubn's Section, An Foras Taluntais
Series of soil surveys with explanatory text.
Bulletins published:
2. Animal Production Research Centre, Grange, Co. Meath 1:2500
3. Vegetable & Glasshouse Crops, Research Centre, Kinsealy, Malahide, Co. Dublin 1:2500
4. National Sheep Research Centre, Creagh, Ballinrobe, Co. Mayo 1:2500
7. Economic Test Farm, Herbertstown, Co. Limerick 1:2500
10. Dept. Agric. College Farm, Ballyhaise Co. Cavan 1:2947
13. Field Station, Ballintubber, Co. Roscommon 1:2500
14. Soil Physics Field Station, Ballinamore, Co. Leitrim 1:2500
15. Soft Fruits Research Centre, Clonroche, Co. Wexford 1:2500
18. John F. Kennedy Park, Slievecoiltia, Co. Wexford 1:2500
19. Economic Test Farm, Drumboylan, Co. Roscommon 1:2500
21. Field Station, Mullinahone, Co. Tipperary 1:2500
24. Soils of Anascaul Pilot Area 1:14729
25. Survey of some sub-peat Mineral Soils 1:20000
27. Pomology Research Centre, Dungarvan, Co. Waterford 1:2500
28. Survey of Kilpatrick and Derry-brennan Farms 1:2500
30. A survey of Cutover Peats and Underlying Mineral Soils, Bord na Mona, Cnoc Dioluin Group 1:21120

ATLASES
W3 WORLD: LOCAL EDITION

CERTIFICATE ATLAS FOR IRISH SCHOOLS
Educational Company of Ireland.
See WORLD ATLASES 100W

ATLASES
L ECONOMIC

AN AGRICULTURAL ATLAS OF COUNTY GALWAY
c. 1,000,000
Compiled by Social Sciences Research Centre, Univ. College, Galway
J H Johnson and B S Mac Aodha
Dublin : Scepter Publishers, 1967
In 2 vols.
14 x 21
Research Paper No. 4 Atlas
44pp of black and white distribution maps.
Research Paper No. 5 Notes
22pp explanatory notes to each of the Plates in the atlas.
Each 50p

ATLASES
M HISTORICAL

JUNIOR HISTORICAL ATLAS OF IRELAND

T P O'Neill
Dublin : Educational Company of Ireland
24 2 colour maps covering Irish history from 1 AD to the present day.
33p

ATLASES
P REGIONAL

THE GALWAY GAELTACHT SURVEY
Ed. B S Mac Aodha
Galway : Social Science Research Centre, Univ. College, 1969
In 2 vols.
49 x 37
2 volume planning atlas for County Galway.
Vol. 1 Text : 40pp in English and Gaelic, Illus.
Vol. 2 44pp coloured maps, showing population, economy and admin..
Set £6.00

420 England and Wales

See also:

41 BRITISH ISLES
410 GREAT BRITAIN

A1 GENERAL MAPS: ROADS

BARTHOLOMEW'S TOURING MAP OF ENGLAND AND WALES
1:760,320
Edinburgh : Bart, 1974
70 x 91
A contour coloured map with main and secondary roads, route numbering, car ferries, airports, railways, canals, county boundaries and heights in feet. Inset map showing main road mileages.
Paper folded 65p

A-Z SIGHT-SEEING MAP ENGLAND AND WALES
1:750,000
Sevenoaks : Geographers, 1972
90 x 116
Roads with distances marking places of interest and classifying buildings into historical periods. Insets of 28 town plans; index. 75p

ENGLAND
1:750,000
No 891
Frankfurt : Ravenstein
80 x 100
Col. map showing all classes of roads, route numbers, distances in km, communications, motoring information.
DM 8.80

ENGLAND AND WALES ROAD MAP
1:730,000
Sevenoaks : Ger.
72 x 88
Roads classified with route numbers, county boundaries and railways. Index to towns and villages inset. 45p

NATIONAL ROUTE MAP OF ENGLAND AND WALES
1:633,360
London : Map Productions
81 x 107
Clear road map showing primary routes, motorways, main and other routes all distinguished in colour with distances. Insets of London, Birmingham and Manchester.
95p

NU-WAY ROAD MAP – ENGLAND AND WALES
1:633,600
Johnston & Bacon
see BRITISH ISLES 41 A1

THE TOURIST ROUTE MAP
1:570,240
In 2 sheets – England N, England S
Edinburgh : Barts, 1973
96 x 72 each sheet
Roads classified with route numbers and distances. Places of interest. Inset plans of London, Birmingham and Bristol on S Sheet, Newcastle-upon-Tyne, Teesside, Manchester, Liverpool, Leeds and Sheffield on N Sheet.
Each 65p

BACON'S REVERSIBLE MAPS
Sheet 1 S England and Wales/London Map
Sheet 2 S England and Wales/
N England and Wales
1:500,000
Johnston & Bacon
see BRITISH ISLES 41 A1

A2 GENERAL MAPS: LOCAL

NORTHERN ENGLAND – COAST TO COAST
1:380,160
London : Johnston & Bacon
109 x 57
All classes of road shown with inset map of Isle of Man. 35p

SOUTHERN ENGLAND : KENT TO CORNWALL
1:380,160
London : Johnston & Bacon, 1973
109 x 51
Showing all classes of roads, camping and recreational sites and plans of principal towns. Covers the whole of southern England and Wales south of Oxford.
45p

RAC LEISURE SPECIAL MAPS
1:316,800
London : Map Productions, 1974
102 x 76
Regional road map series including detailed tourist planning information with coloured illustrations and town plans of principal resorts.
Sheets published:
Wales
East Coast
Thames Valley
South Coast
Each 95p

EAST ANGLIA ROAD MAP
1:253,440
Sevenoaks : Ger
76 x 102
Roads classified with route numbers and distances. 45p

50 MILES AROUND MANCHESTER – LIVERPOOL
1:253,440
Sevenoaks : Ger
89 x 114
Roads classified with route numbers and distances. 45p

MANCHESTER–LIVERPOOL MAIN ROAD MAP
1:63,360
Sevenoaks : Gers
114 x 89
Showing principal routes through the city. In colours with index. 55p

50 MILES AROUND BIRMINGHAM
1:253,440
Sevenoaks : Ger
102 x 76
Roads classified with route numbers and distances. 45p

BIRMINGHAM MAIN ROAD MAP
1:63,360
Sevenoaks : Gers
114 x 89
Showing principal routes through the city. In colours with index. 50p

ROAD MAP OF LONDON AND SOUTH EAST ENGLAND
1:316,800
London : Philip
81 x 69
Covering Coventry to Diss, Bournemouth to Dover. All classes of roads, route numbers, main railways and canals, airports, car ferries, spot heights in ft, National Parks and county boundaries. Map of London and 10 mile radius. 1:79,200 40p

RAC LOCAL MAPS
1:100,000
London : Map Productions, 1974-
99 x 71
New series of road maps of England and Wales in progress. Coloured in accordance with official route signposting. Gazetteer on reverse marking places of interest.
Each 95p

DUNLOP 'MOTORING ABOUT' MAPS
1:63,360 – 1:95,040
London : Gia
107 x 81
Clear series of road maps classifying all principal roads including motorways, main through routes, dual carriageways etc, each numbered and showing mileages. Index on reverse side.
Sheets available:
London 1:63,360 50p
Birmingham and West Midlands 1:95,040 40p

LONDON AND HOME COUNTIES MOTORING MAP
1:253,440
Edinburgh : Bart
86 x 76
All classes of roads with route numbers and distances. Covers from Gloucester and Bedford to the coast. 65p

RUND UM LONDON
1:200,000 – 1:12,000
No 287
Frankfurt: Ravenstein, 1976
114 x 89
Road map round and about London with suburbs on one side and plan of city centre on reverse. With street index.
DM 8.80

ENGLAND -- LEISURE MAP SERIES
1:200,000
Smarden, Kent : Estate Pubn's
Series of road maps featuring places of tourist and historic interest edited by the respective regional tourist authority.
Revised annually.

Maps published.
1. South East England 90 x 64
2. South of England 90 x 64
3. Wessex 90 x 64
4. Devon and Cornwall 103 x 73
each 65p
5. Isle of Wight 83 x 63
40p

LONDON TO THE SOUTH EAST COAST
LONDON TO THE SOUTH COAST
1:158,400
Sevenoaks : Ger
97 x 71 each
Two detailed road maps of SE England, having roads classified with route numbers, distances and gradients and places of interest. With index to towns and villages.
each 65p

LONDON ROAD MAPS
Various scales
London : Foldex
Col. road maps of London and the London region with roads classified.
Maps available:
Greater London Thoroughfares 1:84,480
Greater London and S E England 1:100,000
Greater London and South Coast 1:200,000
Greater London and South Wales and S E Anglia 1:300,000
Greater London and London 1:400,000 each 30p

TO AND THROUGH MAP OF LONDON
1:253,440 – 1:56,320
Edinburgh : Bart
86 x 76
Motorist's map of London, scale 1:56,320 showing the best through routes railways and boundaries with 1:253,440 contour coloured road map of the Home Counties. 75p

LONDON ROUND AND ABOUT
1:200,000
London : Gia
102 x 76
Road map of London extending from Reading – Southend – Bedford – Haywards Heath. All classes of roads with distances, National Grid and features of interest with index to places. On the reverse side is Geographia Big Ben map of London 1:12,000 95p

35 MILES AROUND LONDON ROAD MAP
1:126,720
Sevenoaks : Ger
114 x 86
Buckingham – Halstead – Alton – Tenterden. All classes of roads, distances in miles, airports, car ferries, canals, railways spot heights in feet, county boundaries and an index. 50p

30 MILES AROUND LONDON
1:84,480
London : Gia
102 x 127
Leighton Buzzard – Coggeshall – Alton – Biddenden. Main and secondary roads, through routes, ring roads, route numbering and county boundaries. 95p

LONDON AND SUBURBS
1:63,360
London : Stanford
94 x 56
Double sided map showing approaches to the city with principal through roads. On the reverse is a 1:12,672 map of the city centre.
30p

LONDON ROUTEFINDER
1:63,000
London : R Nicholson Pubn's, 1976
64 x 55
Showing main routes through the capital, including commuter and G B Motorway maps. 45p

DUNLOP MOTORING ABOUT LONDON
1:63,360
London : Gia
107 x 81
Berkhamsted – Epping – Chertsey – Farningham. Main and secondary roads, through and connecting routes, ring roads, road numbers, distances in miles, mainline and underground railways and stations. With index. 50p

A TO Z MAIN ROAD MAP OF LONDON
1:63,360
Sevenoaks : Ger
102 x 76
Main and secondary roads, route numbering, railways and stations, canals and county boundaries. Fully indexed. 50p

RAC GREATER LONDON REGION
1:63, 360
London : Map Productions
102 x 76
Double sided map showing motorways, primary routes and other principal roads. Extends to include Berkhamsted, Harlow, Tilbury, Sevenoaks, Guildford and Windsor, with gazetteer and index to districts.
85p

LONDON
1:40,000 – 1:10,000
Braunschweig : Westermann
102 x 144
Wall map showing two maps of London:
London and Environs (1:40,000) showing roads, parks, areas
London : City Centre (1:10,000) street-plan. Eng. ed.
DM 73

BARNETT'S COUNTY AND REGIONAL ROAD MAPS
Various scales
Barking : G I Barnett
Series of county roadmaps.
Maps available:

Berkshire	15p
Buckinghamshire	12½p
Essex	30p
Hertfordshire	40p
Kent and E Sussex	30p
London Central and Greater	20p
Norfolk	15p
Suffolk	20p
Sussex	30p

THE INNS OF CORNWALL
THE INNS OF DEVONSHIRE
1:250,000
Edinburgh : Barts
54 x 74
2 maps "Showing the whereabouts of the licenses houses in the rural areas and the names of several inns and taverns within the towns. Drawn and compiled by K C Jordan". Major roads (not named) in red on fawn base map. Pub names shown.
Decorative border.
Paper 40p

GEOGRAPHER'S TOURING MAPS – DEVON – CORNWALL
1:158,400
Sevenoaks : Gers
102 x 76 each
Two maps showing main and secondary roads, footpaths, route numbers and distances also camping sites and places of interest.
each 40p

YOUR GUIDE MAPS – SHAKESPEARE COUNTRY
1:158,400
Johnston & Bacon
see BRITISH ISLES 41 A2

COUNTY ROAD MAPS
Various scales
Sevenoaks : Ger
Series of detailed road maps.
Maps available:

Essex	1:142,560	89 x 55	35p
Kent	1:126,720	89 x 56	45p
Surrey	1:126,720	56 x 45	25p
Sussex - East	1:189,000	89 x 55	45p
Sussex - West	1:189,000	89 x 55	45p

GEOGRAPHIA VISITORS MAP OF THE ISLE OF MAN
1:79,200
London : Gia
Tourist information: roads, footpaths, places of interest. 35p

ISLE OF WIGHT HOLIDAY MAP
1:60,000
London : Gia, 1972
66 x 45
Index, roads, bus routes, footpaths, other tourist info. marked: places of interest, nature trails and walks on reverse.
45p

ISLE OF WIGHT
1:63,360
London : Johnston & Bacon
70 x 46
Layer coloured walking map, roads, footpaths and index of place names. 20p

A TO Z VISITOR'S MAP OF THE ISLE OF WIGHT
1:42,240
Sevenoaks : Ger
87 x 53
Relief shown by contours; layer col; roads and paths, bus routes indicated, features of tourist interest. Index. 6 major towns street plan inset. 40p

THE LAKE DISTRICT
1:63,360
Edinburgh : Bart
83 x 76
Contoured with layer colouring, roads and footpaths, short history on cover.
Paper 65p
Cloth 75p

B TOWN PLANS

ENGLAND AND WALES – TOWN PLANS
Various Scales
Publishers:

Barn — Barking : G I Barnett
Bart — Edinburgh : Bartholomew
BPC — London : BPC Publishing
Bur — Cheltenham : Ed J Burrow
Gers — Sevenoaks : Geographers
Gia — London : Geographia
Quail — Exeter : Quail Map Co

Series of plans in colour or black and white with street index. Plans followed by RD cover the whole Rural District and therefore are on a smaller scale. LB indicates London Borough.

Abbotts Langley *see* Kings Langley 15p
Aldeburgh (Barn) 30p
Aldershot (Barn) 30p
Altrincham & Sale (Gers) 20p
Amersham, *see* Chesham
Ascot, Bracknell & Wokingham RD (Barn) 30p
Ashford (Kent) (Barn) 10p
Ashton-under-Lyne (Gers) 25p
Aveley & W Thurrock (Barn) 30p
Aylesbury/Wendover/Tring (Barn) 30p
Banbury (Barn) 20p
Banstead/Tadworth (Barn) 30p
Barking LB (Barn) 30p
Barnet LB (Barn) 20p
Barnet-Enfield (Ger) 25p
Barnsley (Gia) 25p
Basildon, Billericay and Wickford (Gia) 20p
Basildon New Town (Barn) 30p
Basingstoke (Gia) 35p
Basingstoke (Barn) 30p
Bath (Ger) 25p
Bath (Gia) 25p
Beaconsfield (Barn) 24p
Bedford (Barn) 25p
Bedworth *see* Nuneaton
Benfleet (Barn) 30p
Berkhamsted & Tring (Barn) 18p
Berwick-on-Tweed (Bur) 15p
Bexhill *see* Hastings
Bexley LB (Barn) 30p
Bexley (Gers) 25p
Billericay (Barn) 25p
Birkenhead (Gia) 23p
Birmingham Central (Gia) 30p
Birmingham Greater (Gia) 75p
Birmingham Premier (Gers) 75p
Birmingham Inner (Gers) 20p
Biships Stortford & Sawbridge (Barn) 24p
Blackburn (Gia) 25p
Blackpool & Lytham St Annes (Gia) 25p
Bletchley/Leighton Buzzard RD (Barn) 24p
Bognor Regis including Pagham (Gia) 25p
Bolton (Gia) 25p
Bolton (Gers) 25p
Boston (Barn) 30p
Bournemouth & Poole (Gia) 35p
Bournemouth, Poole, Broadstone, Wimborne, Christchurch and Ferndown (Gia) 60p
Bournemouth (Ger) 65p
Bracknell New Town (Barn) 24p
Bradford Central (Gia) 25p
Bradford (Gia) 75p
Bradford Premier (Gers) 75p
Braintree (Barn) 30p
Brentwood (Barn) 24p
Bridgwater (Bur) 13p
Bridport (Quail) 10p
Brighton & Hove (Gia) 30p
Brighton /Hove/Shoreham (Barn) 30p
Bristol (Ger) 75p
Bristol Central (Ger) 25p
Bristol Greater (Gia) 95p
Bristol Central (Gia) 25p
Broadstairs/Margate/Ramsgate (Barn) 20p
Bromley (Ger) 25p
Bromley Orpington (Barn) 24p
Burnley (Gia) 24p
Bury (Gers) 25p
Bury (Gia) 17p
Bury St Edmunds (Barn) 30p
Bushey *see* Watford
Cambridge (Gia) 20p
Cambridge (Heffers) 25p
Cambridge (Barn) 24p
Camborne & Redruth (Quail) 7½p
Canterbury (Gers) 20p
Canterbury (Gia) 20p
Canterbury/Whitstable (Barn) 15p
Canvey Island (Barn) 30p
Cardiff including Penarth (Gia) 42p
Cardiff Central (Gia) 24p
Carlisle (Bur) 15p
Caterham (Barn) 24p
Chatham — *see* Medway Towns
Chelmsford/Ingatestone/Mountnessing (Barn) 30p
Chelmsford (Barn) 30p
Cheltenham (Ger) 25p
Cheltenham (Gia) 25p
Chertsey (Barn) 20p
Chesham/Amersham (Barn) 24p
Cheshunt (Barn) 30p
Chester (Gia) 25p
Chesterfield (Gia) 20p
Chichester (Gia) 25p
Chigwell (Barn) 30p
Chislehurst/Sidcup (Barn) 12½p
Clacton-on-Sea/Walton/Frinton (Barn) 30p
Clacton-on-Sea (Barn) 30p
Cleethorpes — *see* Grimsby
Colchester/Mersea/Brightlingsea/ Wivenhoe (Barn) 30p
Colchester — (Barn) 24p
Cookham/Maidenh'd RD (Barn) 15p
Corby New Town (Barn) 10p
Coulsdon/Purley (Barn) 12½p
Coventry (Gia) 40p
Coventry (Gers) 35p
Coventry (Barn) 30p
Crawley New Town (Barn) 24p
Crewe (Bur) 12½p
Croydon (Gers) 25p
Croydon LB (Barn) 30p
Cwmbran (Gia) 25p
Dagenham (Barn) 30p
Darlington (Gia) 23p
Dartford/Swanley/Stone (Barn) 24p
Derby (Gia) 45p
Derby (Barn) 30p
Doncaster (Gia) 30p
Dorchester, Dorset (Barn) 30p
Dorking/ Leatherhead RD (Barn) 30p
Douglas – *see* Isle of Man
Dudley (Gers) 15p
Dunstable (Barn) 20p
Durham (Gia) 25p
Ealing (Gers) 20p
Eastbourne (Gia) 25p
Eastbourne/Hailsham (Barn) 24p
East Grinstead RD (Barn) 30p
Edinburgh (Bart) 20p
Edinburgh (Miniplans) 20p
Edinburgh (Gia) 50p
Edinburgh Central (Gia) 25p
Egham/Staines (Barn) 20p
Elstree/Boreham Wood (Barn) 24p
Enfield LB (Barn) 30p
Epping/Ongar (Barn) 30p
Epsom & Ewell (Barn) 20p
Esher (Bur) 13p
Exeter (Gia) 35p
Fareham/Gosport/Porchester (Barn) 24p
Farnham/Aldershot/Fleet/ Farnborough (Barn) 24p
Felixstowe (Barn) 24p
Fleet (Barn) 12½p
Folkestone (Gers) 20p
Folkestone/Dover/Hythe (Gia) 20p
Frimley & Camberley (Barn) 30p
Gloucester (Ger) 25p
Gloucester (Gia) 30p
Gosport/Fareham/Portchester (Barn) 24p
Grantham (Barn) 30p
Gravesend (Barn) 30p
Gravesend/Rochester RD (Barn) 30p
Grays & Tilbury (Barn) 24p
Grimsby, Cleethorpes & Immingham (Gia) 45p
Grimsby,Cleethorpes (Barn) 30p
Halifax (Gia) 30p
Harlow New Town (Barn) 30p
Harpenden (Barn) 24p
Harrogate & Knaresborough (Gia) 30p
Harrow/Ruislip/Edgware (Gers) 25p
Hastings & Bexhill (Gia) 30p
Hastings/Bexhill/Battle (Barn) 30p
Hatfield (Barn) 24p
Hatfield/Welwyn Garden City/ Potters Bar/St Albans (Barn) 30p
Havant/Waterlooville/Hayling Island (Barn) 20p
Haverhill (Barn) 15p
Havering LB (Barn) 30p
Hayes (Gers) 25p
Haywards Heath/Cuckfield/ Burgess Hill RD (Barn) 30p
Hemel Hempstead (Barn) 24p
Henley-on-Thames 30p
Hertford (Barn) 30p
High Wycombe (Barn) 30p
High Wycombe/Amersham (Barn) 30p
Hillingdon LB (Bur) 25p
Hitchin (Barn) 30p
Hoddesdon (Barn) 24p
Horsham (Barn) 30p
Hounslow/Feltham/Twickenham (Gers) 25p
Huddersfield (Gia) 30p
Hull (Gia) 30p
Ilford & Romford (Gers) 20p
Ipswich/Martlesham/Holbrook (Barn) 20p
Ipswich (Barn) 30p
Isle of Man Street Plans (Gia) 35p
Islington LB (Bur) 25p
Kenilworth (Barn) 30p
Kensington & Chelsea (Bur) 15p
Kettering (Barn) 30p
Kidderminster (Gia) 18p
Kings Langley (Barn) 30p
Kings Lynn (Barn) 30p
Kingston-on-Thames (Barn) 15p
Kingston-on-Thames (Gers) 25p
Kingston-upon-Hull (Gia) 50p
Lambeth (Bur) 15p
Lancaster (Gia) 30p
Leamington Spa *see* Warwick
Leeds Premier (Gers) 75p
Leeds Central (Gia) 25p
Leicester (Gia) 60p
Leicester (Barn) 24p
Letchworth/Baldock/Hitchin (Barn) 30p
Lewes/Newhaven/Seaford (Barn) 24p
Lincoln (Gia) 25p
Lincoln (Barn) 30p
Liskeard (Quail) 8p
Liverpool Central (Gia) 35p
Liverpool Premier Map (Gers) 75p
Liverpool/Birkenhead/Wallasey (Gers) 25p
Llanelli (Bur) 12½p
Loughborough (Barn) 30p
Lowestoft (Barn) 30p
Luton (Barn) 25p
Luton/Dunstable (Barn) 25p
Macclesfield (Eas) 10p
Maidenhead (Barn) 15p
Maidenhead/Cookham/Marlow (Barn) 30p
Maidstone (Gia) 30p
Maidstone (Barn) 30p
Maidstone/Bearstead/ (Barn) 18p
Maidstone/Wateringbury/Paddock Wood (Barn) 18p

Maldon (Barn)	18p
Manchester Premier (Gers)	75p
Manchester & Salford City Centres (Ger)	25p
Manchester & Salford Central (Gia)	25p
Manchester Greater (Gia)	95p
Mansfield (Bur)	15p
Margate, Ramsgate and Broadstairs (Gers)	20p
Margate, Ramsgate and Broadstairs (Gia)	20p
Margate/Ramsgate/Broadstairs (Barn)	20p
Medway Towns (Gia) (Rochester/Chatham/Gillingham/Strood/Rainham etc)	45p
Melton Mowbray (Barn)	30p
Merton LB (Bur)	30p
Neath (Bur)	12½p
Newbury Rural (Barn)	30p
Newcastle-upon-Tyne & Gateshead (Gia)	65p
Newcastle-upon-Tyne (Gia)	30p
Newham LB (Barn)	20p
Newmarket (Barn)	30p
Newport, Mon (Gia)	25p
Newton Abbot, Teignmouth, Dawlish (Quail)	40p
Northampton (Barn)	30p
Northampton (Gia)	45p
Norwich (Barn)	30p
Norwich/Wymondham Rural (Barn)	15p
Norwich (Gia)	30p
Nottingham (Barn)	30p
Nottingham (Gia)	23p
Nottingham (Gia)	50p
Nuneaton (Barn)	24p
Oldham (Gia)	17p
Oldham (Gers)	25p
Orpington (Barn)	24p
Oxford (Gers)	25p
Oxford (Gia)	30p
Oxford/Abingdon/Dorchester/Steventon Rural (Barn)	30p
Oxted & Limpsfield (Quail)	8p
Peterborough (Barn)	30p
Plymouth (Gia)	50p
Plymouth (Gers)	25p
Portsmouth/Southsea/Cosham (Gia)	30p
Portsmouth (Ger)	65p
Portsmouth/Southsea (Barn)	24p
Potters Bar (Barn)	30p
Preston (Gia)	35p
Queenborough in Sheppey (Barn)	30p
Ramsgate *see* Margate	
Rayleigh (Barn)	30p
Reading (Gia)	22p
Reading (Gers)	20p
Reading (Barn)	18p
Redbridge LB (Barn)	30p
Redcar – *see* Tees-side	
Reigate/Redhill/Caterham/Banstead/Coulsdon (Barn)	24p
Richmond LB (Bur)	15p
Rickmansworth & Chorleywood (Barn)	25p
Rochdale (Gia)	18p
Rochdale (Gers)	25p
Rochford (Barn)	24p
Romford & Harold Hill (Barn)	20p
Rotherham (Gia)	35p
Rugby (Barn)	30p
Ruislip & Northwood (Barn)	15p
Runcorn (Gers)	20p
Rye/Winchelsea/Hastings (Barn)	12½p
St. Albans (Barn)	24p
St Helens (Gers)	25p
Sale and Altrincham – *see* Altrincham	
Scarborough (Gia)	22p
Scunthorpe (Barn)	30p
Sevenoaks (Gers)	30p
Sheffield Central (Gia)	35p
Sheffield Greater (Gia)	95p
Sheppey / Sittingbourne (Barn)	24p
Shrewsbury (Gia)	30p
Sittingbourne & Milton/Sheppey RD (Barn)	24p
Slough/Windsor/Gerrards Cross (Barn)	30p
Slough (Gia)	15p
Slough, Maidenhead & Windsor (Gers)	25p
Solihull (Gers)	25p
Southampton & Eastleigh (Gia)	30p
Southampton (Ger)	65p
Southampton (Barn)	30p
South Devon Street Atlas (Quail)	17½p
Southend-on-Sea (Barn)	20p
Southwark LB (Bur)	23p
Spalding (Barn)	30p
Stafford (Gia)	25p
Staines (Stfd)	10p
Staines (Ger)	25p
Staines/Egham (Barn)	20p
Stanford-le-Hope (Barn)	24p
Stevenage (Barn)	30p
Stockport (Gia)	18p
Stockport (Gers)	15p
Stockton-on-Tees (Gia)	15p
Stoke-on-Trent & Newcastle-under-Lyme (Gia)	50p
Stratford-upon-Avon (Gers)	20p
Sudbury/Halstead (Barn)	15p
Sunbury-on-Thames (Bur)	13p
Sunderland (Gia)	35p
Sutton LB (Barn)	30p
Sutton/Epsom/Ewell (Gers)	20p
Swansea (Gia)	45p
Swindon (Gia)	25p
Swindon (Gers)	20p
Tamworth (Barn)	30p
Tavistock/Plymstock/Saltash/East and West Looe (BPC)	12½p
Taunton (Gers)	15p
Tees-side (Gia)	50p
Teignmouth (Quail)	
Tonbridge (Barn)	18p
Torbay, Torquay, Brixham and Paignton (Gia)	30p
Torbay (Ger)	20p
Tower Hamlets LB (Bur)	15p
Tunbridge Wells (Barn)	24p
Wakefield (Gia)	23p
Wallasey – *see* Birkenhead	
Walsall (Gia)	15p
Walsall (Gers)	20p
Waltham Abbey (Barn)	20p
Waltham Forest LB (Barn)	30p
Walton-on-the-Naze/Frinton/Clacton	30p
Walton & Weybridge (Barn)	20p
Wandsworth LB (Bur)	15p
Ware (Barn)	24p
Warley (Gers)	15p
Warrington (Gia)	25p
Warwick & Leamington (Gia)	20p
Warwick/L'ton Spa (Barn)	30p
Watford, R'worth Bushey (Gia)	25p
Watford & Bushey (Barn)	30p
Wellingborough (Barn)	30p
Welwyn Garden City (Barn)	20p
West Bromwich (Gers)	15p
West Midlands (Gia)	75p
Westminster LB (Bur)	20p
Weston-super-Mare (Gia)	20p
Weymouth (Gers)	25p
Wickford (Barn)	30p
Widnes (Gia)	25p
Wigan (Gia)	35p
Wigan (Gers)	25p
Wimbledon (Gers)	25p
Winchester (Barn)	20p
Windsor & Eton (Barn)	30p
Wisbech (Barn)	30p
Witham/Tiptree (Barn)	18p
Woking (Barn)	30p
Wokingham (Barn)	24p
Wolverhampton (Gia)	20p
Wolverhampton (Gers)	25p
Woodbridge, Felixstowe, Harwich (Barn)	20p
Worcester (Gia)	22p
Worthing & L'hampton (Gia)	25p
Yarmouth/Gorleston (Barn)	30p
Yeovil (Barn)	30p
York (Gia)	35p

LONDON – TOWN PLANS

Various scales

Publishers:

Hall	Bern: Hallwag
Map Prodn.	London : Map Productions
Stanf.	London : Stanford
Falk	Hamburg : Falk
J & B	London : Johnston & Bacon
FC	London : Francis Chichester
Vp	London : Viewpoint UK
Nich.	London : Nicholson

Large scale plans, generally coloured and naming all principal streets and in some cases buildings. With street index.

Plans available:

CITY OF LONDON

City of London Map (Gia)
1:4,000 89 x 51 — 45p

A to Z Map of the City (Ger)
1:3,520 90 x 58 — 25p

CENTRAL LONDON

Super Scale Map of London (Ger)
1:7,040 140 x 97 — 85p

Ruby Map of London and Suburbs (J & B)
1:35,200 81 x 76 — 25p

London Large Scale Map (J & B)
1:27,550 97 x 76 — 30p

Master Map of Greater London
(In 9 sheets – see index 420/1)(Gers)
1:21,120 101 x 76 each — 50p

London Street Map (double-sided) (Gia)
1:20,000 35 x 48 — £1.25

Plan of London (Bart)
1:16,896 102 x 77 — 40p

New Map of Central London (J & B)
1:16,000 — 30p

London : Two maps (J & B) same map as 'New Map' with map on reverse at 1:63,360 — 50p

London (Hall)
1:16,000 63 x 56 — 65p

What's in London ? (Nich)
1:15,000 app 73 x 42 — 35p

London (Ravenstein)
1:14,000 app 62 x 98 — DM 8.80

London Streets (Map Prodn.)
1:14,000 61 x 99 — 30p

Nicholson's London Map (Nich)
1:12,500 89 x 54 — 45p

Two London Maps (Nich)
same map as 'Nicholson's London Map' with 1:63,360 map on reverse — 50p

Inner London (Stanf)
1:12,672 95 x 56 — 17p

London Official Visitors Map (Map Prodn)
1:12,672 48 x 76 — 25p

London and Suburbs (Stanf)
same as 'Inner London' map with 1:63,360 map on reverse — 30p

Big Ben Map of London (Gia)
1:12,000 86 x 56 — 50p

London Round & About (Gia)
same as 'Big Ben Map' with 1:200,000 map on reverse — 60p

London City (Falk)
1:11,000 patent fold — DM 4.80

Visitor's London Map (Gers)
1:10,560 89 x 56 — 25p

One Way London (Gia)
1:10,560 92 x 65 — 45p

Sight Seeing Map of London (Gers)
1:10,560 89 x 38 20p
International Map of London (Gia)
1:10,560 100 x 66 50p
Map of London (Gers)
1:10,000 89 x 57 25p
Heart of London Map (FC)
1:8,448 61 x 40 30p
Pocketbook of Central London (Bart)
1:7,040 89 x 56 40p
London : City & West End (Foldex)
1:4,000 35p
London's West End Map (Vp)
1:3,000 app 30p
London (Miniplan) 20p
Handy Map of Central London 15p

D POLITICAL & ADMINISTRATIVE

COUNTY MAP OF ENGLAND AND WALES
1:792,000
London : Gia
69 x 87
Counties in colour; railways, canals. 60p

COUNTIES AND DISTRICTS, LOCAL GOVERNMENT ACT 1972
1:750,000
London : Dept. of the Environment, 1974
82 x 93
Administrative areas map of England and Wales as at 1972, Also available with areas effective up to 1974. 80p

COUNTY BUSINESS MAP OF ENGLAND AND WALES
1:633,600
Edinburgh : Bart
82 x 103
Detailed map with counties in col; main and secondary roads, footpaths and steamer routes 30p

COMMERCIAL MAP OF ENGLAND AND WALES
1:390,160
London : Philip, 1969
142 x 189
Inc. Southern Scotland up to Edinburgh and Glasgow; counties in colour.
Paper flat £4.50
Mounted CRV £11.50

THE YORKSHIRE BUSINESS AND ADMINISTRATIVE MAP
1:253,440
Edinburgh : Bart, 1970
60 x 75
Admin. map marking each Riding in colour with towns and villages marked.
Paper 30p
Cloth 40p

ENGLAND AND WALES – ADMINISTRATIVE AREAS
1:100,000
Southampton : OS
Various sizes
Showing Parliamentary Constituencies, Counties, Districts and Civil Parishes. Available for each County on one or sometimes more sheets according to size.
Each £1.30

ENGLAND AND WALES – PETTY SESSIONS AREAS
1:100,000
Southampton : OS
Various sizes
The counties of England and Wales are covered by separate maps, sometimes in more than one sheet. Based on the Administrative Area Series without Parliamentary Constituencies with instead the boundaries of Judicial Areas. each £1.65

LONDON POSTAL DISTRICTS
1:63,360
London : Stanford
58 x 51
Postal Districts bounded and numbered in red with regional divisions in colour. 25p

GREATER LONDON POSTAL DISTRICTS AND BOROUGH BOUNDARIES
1:63,360
London : Gia, 1971
Shows administrative borough boundaries, London Inner and Outer Postal Region boundaries; County boundaries each in colour on a black and white main street map. Index on reverse to streets, districts, LT, and BR railway stations, postal and Administrative districts. 65p

POSTAL DISTRICTS MAP OF LONDON
1:63,360
Sevenoaks : Ger.
98 x 72
London Postal Districts with numbers and postal region boundaries in blue, county boundaries, main roads and motorways, mainline and underground railways with stations and canals. Fully indexed.
Coloured or outline 45p

A TO Z GREATER LONDON BOROUGH BOUNDARIES
1:63,360
Sevenoaks : Gers,
97 x 73
Watford-Brentwood-Woking-Sevenoaks. Showing the Borough boundaries and names with the GLC boundary on a black and white base map showing main and secondary roads 40p

ADMINISTRATIVE AREAS – LONDON
1:63,360
Southampton : OS
112 x 91
Boundaries of Greater London Council, London Boroughs and City of London in red; parliamentary boundaries in blue. £1.30

JUDICIAL AND LOCAL GOVERNMENT AREAS – METROPOLITAN POLICE DISTRICT
1:63,360
Southampton : OS
112 x 84
Using GLC Administrative map without Parliamentary Constituencies as a base it has the Judicial Areas within the Met. Police District in Blue. £1.65

ADMINISTRATIVE AREAS – LONDON
1:25,000
In 25 sheets, see index 420/2
Southampton : OS
48 x 55
Showing all administrative boundaries from GLC down to London Borough Wards in red on a grey outline base.
each 75p

PLANNING AND RECORD MAP NO 4 ENGLAND AND WALES
1:950,000
London : Gia
60 x 54
Outline map showing county boundaries cities and towns. 30p
Also available : reduced size edition
30 x 39 75p for 10

PHILIPS LARGE OUTLINE MAP OF ENGLAND AND WALES
1:640,000
London : Philip 1969
79 x 101
Counties black on white. 50p

MAP BUILDING SHEETS ('BLACKBOARD MAPS') OF ENGLAND AND WALES
1:640,000
London : Philip, 1969
79 x 101
Printed in yellow on blackboard paper and showing coastline and interstate boundaries.
CR £1.85

SALES MANAGER'S MAP OF ENGLAND AND WALES
1:380,000
SP7
London : Philip, 1969
140 x 178
Printed in black with county boundaries and roads in colour and showing railways, shipping routes, (distances in nautical miles) motorways, statistical data.
Mounted CR £11.50

E1 PHYSICAL – RELIEF

PHYSICAL SMALLER WALL MAP OF ENGLAND AND WALES
1:575,000
London : Philip
84 x 109
Physical features depicted by layer colouring with boundaries in red and towns indicated by initial letter only.
Paper flat £1.50
CR £5.50
Mounted on cloth dissected to fold £7.00

PHYSICAL LARGE WALL MAP OF ENGLAND AND WALES
1:375,000
London : Philip
157 x 178
Orographically coloured with hill shading, boundaries and railways.
CR £15.00
Mounted on cloth dissected to fold £17.00

E2 PHYSICAL – LAND FEATURES

A PHYSIOGRAPHIC MAP OF THE OXFORD REGION
1:63,360
Comp. R Webster & P Beckett
Oxford: Soil Science Lab, Dept. of Agricultural Science, 1965
84 x 97
Water detail in blue; physiographic regions in red (with index to regions on reverse); notes.

M HISTORICAL

BREASTED-HUTH-HARDING HISTORY MAPS
Chicago : Denoyer-Geppert
112 x 81
Series of col. wall maps.
Maps available:
204251 Saxon and Norman England
204311 Tudor and Stuart England, 1513-1649
204371 British Isles; Parliamentary Reform
204381 Industrial England, 1700 and 1911

SOUTHERN BRITAIN IN THE IRON AGE
1:625,000
Southampton : OS, 1967 (rep. of 1962 ed)
100 x 77
British history for 5 centuries before Roman Conquest. Shows sites of hill forts, lake villages, farmsteads, other settlements. Coloured over-print shows Belgic influence in latter part of period. Flat or folded with text. Covers Eng and Wales south of Lake District.
Flat 80p
With text in book form £2.00

ANCIENT BRITAIN
1:625,000
In 2 sheets
2nd edition
Southampton : OS, 1967
100 x 77 each sheet
Two sheets, North and South. Showing important antiquities from the earliest time to 1066AD, incl. neolithic, bronze and iron ages and Roman period. Maps are obtainable separate or with text and index.
Flat sheet without text each 80p
Map and text in book form each £1.50

ROMAN BRITAIN
1:1,000,000
3rd edition
Southampton : OS, 1956
76 x 98
Illus. Britain under Roman occupation from 43AD to 410AD. Showing land and water communications, urban settlements, agricultural and industrial activities etc. Explanatory text incl. chronological table and index.
Flat sheet without text 80p
Map and text in book form £2.00

BRITAIN IN THE DARK AGES
1:1,000,000
Southampton : OS, 1966
75 x 103
Covering the period from the end of the Roman occupation in Britain to the time of King Alfred (approximately 410AD to 870AD). Showing towns, villages and other sites of historical importance of Celtic, Saxon and Pictish origin. With a 64 page explanatory text including an index (1971).
Flat sheet without text 80p
Map and text in book form £2.00

BRITAIN BEFORE THE NORMAN CONQUEST (871–1066AD)
1:625,000
In 2 sheets
Southampton : OS, 1973
98 x 156 complete
Layered relief map with coloured symbols marking Celtic, Scandinavian and Anglo-Saxon place names, towns, royal and religious buildings, earthworks and much more evidence of the period. A 68pp text describes the history and settlement of the period and includes a complete index to places, sites, buildings etc.
Hard covers, maps contained in pocket £3.00

MONASTIC BRITAIN
1:625,000
In 2 sheets
2nd edition
Southampton : OS – North (1955)
South (1954)
100 x 74 each sheet
Showing British Monasticism from Norman Conquest to Dissolution in 1539; incl. all houses of monks, cells, hermitages, large chantries etc. where their sites can be determined. Each sheet has own explanatory text; and are available separately or together complete with text.
Flat sheet, each 80p
Map and text in book form, each £1.50

HADRIAN'S WALL
1:31,680
Ed. 2
Southampton : OS, 1972
100 x 77
Showing entire length of wall in 5 separate sections; forts, mile-castles, turrets etc. on the wall and roads, bridges, camps, quarries, civil settlements etc. in the immediate vicinity. Brief bibliography; index.
Flat sheet without text 95p
Folded in cover £1.00

ANTONINE WALL
1:25,000
Southampton : OS, 1969
100 x 77
Whole length of wall from the Firth of Forth to the mouth of the River Clyde. Surviving parts in black, parts disappeared in red. Forts; camps; civil settlements; temples and other Roman features. Brief history and bibliog. 3 strip maps.
Paper folded or flat £1.00

POSTAL HISTORY MAP OF BRITAIN
Edinburgh : Bart, 1971
70 x 96
Col. wall map; showing postmen's uniforms; devt. of the pillar box and other items of postal history. Around border are reproductions of famous stamps issued since 1840. 50p

BODLEIAN MAP OF GREAT BRITAIN
Southampton : OS
61 x 108
Reproduction of Bodleian Library Mediaeval Map of Great Britain, 1325-1350AD. In black with ancient names transcribed and overprinted in red.
Flat 75p

HISTORICAL MAPS OF GREAT BRITAIN
Various scales
In 40 sheets
Grimsby : Roy Faiers, 1967-70
38 x 51
Set of historical maps covering the English Counties, Scottish Lowlands and Highlands, North Wales, Channel Islands. With notes and illus. on each sheet.

ATLASES
A1 GENERAL: ROADS

HAMLYN ROAD ATLAS OF GREAT BRITAIN
1st edition
Cartography – Bartholomew
London : The Hamlyn Group, 1976
21 x 30
192pp
Includes 110pp of road maps, scale 4 mls : 1 inch covering Great Britain plus route planning maps, motorway strip maps, 38 pages of town plans, selective tourist gazetteer and Index. £3.95

'SHELL' ROAD ATLAS OF GREAT BRITAIN
London : Philip, 1976
22 x 28
150pp
62pp sectional maps at 1:316,800. All classes of roads route numbers, car ferries, distances in miles, spot heights in feet, railways, airports, principal canals, county boundaries, places of interest. London section with 9pp maps at scale 1:84,450, showing approaches to London. 7pp of maps at 1:30,000 and map of Central London at 1:12,670. Indexed.
Hard cover £2.25

'NATIONAL' ROAD ATLAS OF GREAT BRITAIN
London : Philip, 1976
22 x 28
176pp
The same as 'Shell' Road Atlas but with 30pp section of city centre and town plans showing all classes of roads, railways, car parks, one way streets, places of interest etc. £2.75

3 MILES TO 1" ROAD ATLAS OF GREAT BRITAIN
7th edition
Edinburgh : Johnston & Bacon, 1973
15 x 22
372pp
Contour col. maps; 1st and 2nd class roads in red, route numbers, 25 town plans, 46pp index of 19,000 entries, and open-out map of through routes in Great Britain; plan of London, road and motorway signs, motorway plan and table of distances.
£1.95

ROAD ATLAS OF BRITAIN
Edinburgh : Bart, 1974
21 x 30
112pp
88pp contour col. maps, scale 1:316,800 showing all classes of roads, numbers, distances in miles, car ferries, airports, railways, canals, county boundaries and map continuations. 15pp throughway town plans, index, road traffic signs, mileage chart. £1.90

GREAT BRITAIN – ROUTE PLANNING
London : Map Productions
22 x 28
136pp
32pp section of Route Planning maps at 1:625,000; all classes of roads, motorways, places of interest, index of over 6,000 places. Motorway strip maps and through route maps of London and other principal cities. 64pp touring section arranged regionally, incl. road conditions, places of interest and town plans. £1.75

GB MOTORING ATLAS
London : Gia
20 x 27
64pp
1:500,000 col. maps with sections at 1:18,750 for congested urban areas and small scale route planning maps. Gridded and indexed with the national grid.
£1.95

GREAT BRITAIN TOURING ATLAS AND GUIDE
8th edition
London : Gia
23 x 28
78pp
32pp sectional maps at 1:570,240, showing all classes of roads, mileages, airports, ferries, spot heights in feet and county boundaries. Each double page map has an accompanying text showing places of interest and tourist attractions. Also includes 22 pages of strip maps showing principal routes between towns with mileages, an 8 page Visitor's Guide to London, a selected list of gardens open to the public, a distance chart and a 14 page index.
£1.50
De Luxe edition £2.50

A AND B ROADS AND MOTORWAYS ATLAS OF GREAT BRITAIN
1:380,160
4th edition
Edinburgh : Johnston & Bacon 1973
26 x 33 folded
Main and secondary roads with route numbers and distances including motorways and dual carriageways also motor organisation telephone boxes. Inset plans of 42 towns. 95p

DUNLOP MOTORWAYS ATLAS
London : Map Productions
11 x 28
48pp
Small atlas containing detailed set of national road maps, strip maps of all the motorways incl. interchanges and services and 23 plans of major towns.
45p

MOTORWAY ATLAS OF GREAT BRITAIN
Ed Stuart Bladon
Edinburgh : Barts, 1972
30 x 21
48pp
Containing regional road maps and strip maps for each motorway 1:316,800 with plans of complex interchanges and details of services. £1.00

ATLASES
C OFFICIAL SURVEYS

OS QUARTER INCH ATLAS OF GREAT BRITAIN
Southampton : OS
44 x 72
Loose leaf atlas; containing 17 foldout sheets of the ¼" series (1:250,000); gazetteer contains 33,000 names appearing on the sheets. Nat. Grid location.
£17.00

ATLASES
E1 PHYSICAL: RELIEF

BARTHOLOMEW'S HALF-INCH LOOSE LEAF ATLAS OF GREAT BRITAIN
Edinburgh : Bart
50 x 61
Containing 62 ½" : 1 mile topographical maps mounted on linen and folded in half to fit a loose leaf binder. Replacement copies of revised individual plates can be supplied.
Atlas and binder £26.00
Replacement pages, each 30p

ATLASES
F GEOLOGY

STANFORDS' GEOLOGICAL ATLAS OF GREAT BRITAIN
Ed T Eastwood
London : Ed Stanford, 1966
17 x 24
296pp
Area in 29 selected geol. areas, each with black and white geol. map at 1:750,000, description, cross sections, brief bibliog. 18pp fossil illus. £3.25

ATLASES
H BIOGEOGRAPHY

SHELL NATURE LOVERS ATLAS OF ENGLAND, SCOTLAND AND WALES
London : M Joseph
14 x 22
Divided into 16 regional sections with maps 1:750,000, showing main and secondary roads, county boundaries, rivers and lakes. The entries locate nearly 700 places of interest including national parks and forests, islands and seabird sanctuaries, areas of outstanding beauty, field study centres, wildfowl refuges, archaeological and geological sites and zoological and botanical gardens which are marked on the map and indexed.
38p

WARNES NATURAL HISTORY ATLAS OF GREAT BRITAIN
by A Darlington
London : Warne, 1969
20 x 25
112pp
Illus. given of 10 vertebrates, 10 insects and 10 plants commonly associated with 6 different common land types; map section indicates extent of subsoil regions.
£1.75

ATLASES
K HUMAN GEOGRAPHY

NATIONAL ATLAS OF DISEASE MORTALITY IN THE UNITED KINGDOM
2nd Edition
Ed G Melvyn Howe
London : Nelson, 1970
28 x 21
197pp
Contains maps at various scales covering areas of illness.

ATLASES
L ECONOMIC

MAJOR SUBURBAN SHOPPING CENTRES ATLAS AND STATISTICAL HANDBOOK
by Drs D Thorpe and C J Thomas and P T Kiven
Research Report No 1a and b
Manchester : Manchester Business School, 1971
Atlas 30 x 42, 49 black and white maps (2½" OS based) showing residential areas, devt. 1919-69. "A" roads and borough boundaries; no. of shops indicated.
Handbook details on establishments.
132pp, 22 x 33
Set £9.00

ATLASES
M HISTORICAL

THE 'PLACES TO VISIT' ATLAS
London : the National Trust
1st edition 19 x 25
Over 6,000 places of architectural, historical and scenic interest in England, Wales, Scotland and Northern Ireland. England, Wales and Scotland – 61pp contour col. maps, 1:300,000, Northern Ireland, 1:633,600. Outer Hebrides Orkney and Shetland 1:600,000.
Main and secondary roads, railways, canals, county boundaries. Each double page section is followed by its own gazetteer so that the numbered sites can be quickly identified. Index. £2.50

411 Scotland

See also:

41 BRITISH ISLES
410 GREAT BRITAIN

A1 GENERAL MAPS: ROADS

TOURING MAP OF SCOTLAND
1:760,320
Edinburgh : Bart, 1972
51 x 78
Contoured, layer col; all classes of roads classified, numbered. Railways, canals, county boundaries, inset of road distances.
Paper folded 65p

COUNTY BUSINESS MAP OF SCOTLAND
1:633,600
Edinburgh : Bart, 1970
54 x 72
A very detailed administrative map showing the counties in colour, main and secondary roads and footpaths.
30p

SCHOTTLAND
1:507,000
No 892
Frankfurt : Ravenstein
63 x 95
Col. map; roads classified and numbered, distances in km; motoring and tourist details, other communications.
DM 8.80

SCOTLAND – TOURIST ROUTE MAP
1:570,240
Edinburgh : Bart, 1973
70 x 95
Roads classified with route numbers and distances, places of interest. Inset plans of Glasgow, Edinburgh, Aberdeen.
65p

NU-WAY ROAD MAP – SCOTLAND
1:506,880
Johnston & Bacon
see BRITISH ISLES 41 A1.

SCOTLAND MOTORWAYS AND MAIN ROAD MAP
1:500,000
London : Gia
73 x 94
All roads classified with distances and showing car ferries, railways, canals and shipping routes. Counties in colour
50p

RAC ROAD MAP OF SCOTLAND
1:500,000
London : Map Productions
73 x 98
All classes of roads shown with route numbers, distances and gradients. Relief shaded and showing principal airports, ferries, boundaries and National Parks.
Urban areas inset. 95p

BACONS REVERSIBLE MAPS
Sheet 3 S SCOTLAND/N SCOTLAND
1:380,160
Johnston & Bacon
see BRITISH ISLES 41 A1

A TO Z GREAT BRITAIN ROAD MAP SERIES – SCOTLAND (REVERSIBLE)
1:316,800
Ger
see GREAT BRITAIN 410 A1

THE VISITOR'S MAP OF SCOTLAND
London : Johnston & Bacon, 1972
101 x 76
Political map of Scotland, counties in colour surrounded by coats of arms of 36 towns and cities, 62 views and 16 pieces of silver jewellery.
Folded 50p
Rolled 65p

A2 GENERAL MAPS: LOCAL

YOUR GUIDE MAPS – NORTH WEST SCOTLAND
1:380,160
Johnston & Bacon
see BRITISH ISLES 41 A2.

TO AND THROUGH SERIES – EDINBURGH AND GLASGOW
1:250,000
Bart, 1972
see GREAT BRITAIN 410 A2.

30 MILES AROUND – EDINBURGH, GLASGOW, S.W SCOTLAND
1:126,720
Johnston & Bacon
see GREAT BRITAIN 410 A2

THE PENTLAND HILLS
1:42,240
Edinburgh : Bart
91 x 76
Contoured with layer colouring, roads, paths, rights of way. Covering from Edinburgh to Dunsyre and Eddleston.
Paper 30p
Cloth 50p

CAIRNGORM RECREATION MAP
1:35,000
Glasgow : Dept. of Geog., Univ. of Glasgow, 1974
75 x 50
Map showing location of recreation facilities.
50p

MAP OF THE BLACK CUILLINS OF SKYE
1:20,000
Scottish Mountaineering Trust
Reading : West Col Productions
51 x 64
The map shows the names of the climbs and is intended primarily for use in conjunction with the SMT Guide to Skye.
Paper folded 20p

RHUM
1:10,000
In 4 sheets
Glasgow : Dept. of Geog. Univ. of Glasgow, 1972
72 x 72 each sheet
Topographical map of the island with U.K. National Grid.

EXPLORING IONA
1:10,560
Edinburgh : Bart, 1972
64 x 46
Black and white map with relief by contours depicting surface and coastal detail with list of places of interest. Both English and Gaelic names given.
25p

YTHAN ESTUARY
1:7,500
Glasgow : Dept. of Geog., Univ. of Glasgow 1972
92 x 75
Topographic map of the region with U.K. National Grid.

B TOWN PLANS

SCOTLAND TOWN PLANS
various scales
Publishers :

Bart-Edinburgh	Bartholomew
Bur-Cheltenham	Ed J Burrow
Gia – London	Geographia
Miniplans - London	Miniplans

Plans generally in black and white with index to streets.
Maps available:

Aberdeen (Bart)	15p
Aberdeen (Gia)	30p
Airdrie (Bur)	15p
Ayr (Bur)	15p
Dumbarton (Bur)	15p
Dundee (Gia)	25p
Edinburgh (Bart)	40p
Edinburgh (Miniplans)	20p
Edinburgh Visitors Map (Gia)	15p
Edinburgh (Gia)	35p
Edinburgh Central (Gia)	20p
Edinburgh (Map Prodns)	25p
Glasgow (Bart)	40p
Glasgow (Gia)	60p
Glasgow Central (Gia)	25p
Glasgow Greater (Gia)	£1.25
Inverness (Gia)	25p
Motherwell & Wishaw (Bur)	15p
Perth (Gia)	20p
Stirling (Bur)	20p

C OFFICIAL SURVEYS

ORDNANCE SURVEY TOURIST MAP SERIES
– LOCH LOMOND AND THE TROSSACHS
– CAIRNGORMS
– BEN NEVIS AND GLENCOE
1:63,360
OS
see GREAT BRITAIN 410 C.

D POLITICAL & ADMINISTRATIVE

POLITICAL SMALLER WALL MAP OF SCOTLAND
1:500,000
London : Philip, 1965
79 x 104
Counties in col, railways, town pop. indicated.
Paper £1.50
CR £5.50

ADMINISTRATIVE AREAS OF SCOTLAND
1:250,000 – 1:100,000
In 5 sheets plus 2 area maps.
Southampton : OS see index 411/3
Various sizes
Also the new Scottish regions, island areas, districts, electoral divisions and civil parishes. Two larger scale sheets cover the central Lowland region.
Each £1.30

E1 PHYSICAL : RELIEF

PHYSICAL SMALLER WALL MAP OF SCOTLAND
1:500,000
London : Philip, 1965
79 x 104
Physical features shown by layer col. without hill shading, boundaries and towns indicated by initial only.
Paper flat £1.50
Mounted CR £5.50
Mounted on cloth dissected to fold £7.00

F GEOLOGY

GEOLOGICAL MAP OF SCOTLAND
1:253,440
In 17 sheets, see index 411/1
London : IGS
74 x 52
Series of coloured maps in progress.
Sheets published:
1/2 1963
3 1948
5 1948
6 1948
9 1948
10 1969
12 1948
13 1949
15 1948
16 1948
17 1948

GEOLOGICAL MAP OF SCOTLAND – NEW SERIES
1:63,360
In 131 sheets approx, see index 411/1
London : IGS
64 x 46
Col. sheets on 3rd edition sheet lines, with National Grid overprinted. Available in either 'Solid' (basic geology) or 'Drift' (superficial deposits) editions or a combination of both according to region covered. New sheets are being issued at the metric scale of 1:50,000 which will eventually replace the earlier series.
flat each £1.15
folded each £1.25

SCOTLAND GEOLOGY – SPECIAL SHEETS
1:63,360 – 1:50,000
London : IGS
Various sizes
Series of special area maps, coloured and available in 'Solid' (basic geology) or 'Drift' (superficial deposits) editions or a combination of both. New sheets published at the metric scale of 1:50,000.
Sheets available:
Glasgow district (Solid) and (Drift)
Assynt district (Solid with some Drift)
Arran 1:50,000 (Solid) and (Drift)
Northern Skye (Solid) and (Drift)
flat each £1.15
folded each £1.25
Northern Shetland (Solid) and (Drift) each 90p
Western Shetland (Solid) and (Drift) each 90p

GLASSICAL AREAS IN BRITISH GEOLOGY
1:25,000
London : IGS
Col. geol. maps based on OS topog. sheet lines and available in either 'Solid' (basic geology) or 'Drift' (superficial deposits) editions or combination of both.
Sheets available:
Edinburgh District – pts of sheets
NT 16, 17, 26, 27, 36, 37 (S & D)
Flat or folded £1.15

G EARTH RESOURCES

THE SOILS OF NORTH EAST SCOTLAND
1:250,000
Craigiebuckler : Macaulay Inst. for Soil Research
Col. soil map 40p

SOIL SURVEY OF SCOTLAND
1:63,360
See index 411/2
Craigiebuckler : Macaulay Inst. for Soil Research
Series in progress showing soil information overprinted on 1" base maps, 3rd edition. With memoirs. 75p

SOIL SURVEY OF SCOTLAND – LAND USE CAPABILITY
1:63,360
See index 411/2
Craigiebuckler : Macaulay Inst. for Soil Research
64 x 46
Col. series showing land use capability
Sheets published:
8 pt 7 Carrick pt Girvan
24 pt 32 Peebles and Edinburgh
39 pt 31 Stirling
48, 49 Perth and Arbroath
pts 83, 84, 93, 94 Black Isle
94 Cromarty and Invergordon
110, 116, pt 117 Latheron and Wick
each 75p

SOIL SURVEY OF SCOTLAND
1:25,000
Craigiebuckler : Macaulay Inst. for Soil Research, 1969
Col. maps, sheets available:
Soils of Candacraig and Glenbuchat
Soils of the Island of Rhum
each 75p

H BIOGEOGRAPHY

GAME FISHING MAP OF SCOTLAND
1:500,000
Ed. Dr D H Maling
Glasgow : Wm Collins, 1976
100 x 106
£1.50

ISLE OF RHUM – VEGETATION
1:20,000
Taunton : Nature Conservancy Council, 1970
76 x 102
Contours, roads, footpaths; land type, vegetation indicated by col.
£1.00

MOUTH OF THE RIVER ENDRICK–VEGETATION
1:10,000
Glasgow : Dept. of Geog. Univ. of Glasgow 1972
69 x 82
Coloured map depicting distribution of vegetation types for part of the Loch Lomond Nature Reserve.

ACHRAY FOREST
1:20,000
Glasgow : Dept. of Geog., Univ. of Glasgow, 1975
41 x 24
Coloured map of the forest
25p

LOCH A MHACHAIR – VEGETATION
1:5,000
Glasgow : Dept. of Geog. Univ. of Glasgow, 1972
27 x 37
Coloured vegetation map

J CLIMATE

ASSESSMENT OF CLIMATIC CONDITIONS IN SCOTLAND
1:625,000
Aberdeen : Macaulay Inst. for Soil Research, 1970
92 x 81
Set of 3 maps, each with transparent grid overlay and explanatory pamphlet.
1 Based on Accumulated Temperature and Potential Water Deficit
2 Based on Exposure and Accumulated Frost
3 Based on the Bio-Climatic Sub-regions each 85p

K HUMAN GEOGRAPHY

SCOTLAND : POPULATION DISTRIBUTION ON THE NIGHT OF APRIL 23rd 1961
1:500,000
Edinburgh : Collins, 1965
71 x 91
Indicating population by the dot method.
£1.75

M HISTORICAL

HISTORICAL MAP OF SCOTLAND
Edinburgh : Bart
51 x 68
Brightly coloured map, illustrating battles, castles, places and characters well known in history. Surrounding the map are the Coats of Arms of cities and towns.
Paper, each 50p
Cloth, each 60p

BONNIE PRINCE CHARLIE MAPS
Edinburgh : Bart
44 x 76
Double sided; with reproduction map of the wanderings of Prince Charlie drawn by Colonel Grante who took part in the '45' Rebellion and an up-to-date map of Scotland with the Prince's journeys marked on the reverse. 25p

CLAN MAP : 'SCOTLAND OF OLD'
Edinburgh : Bart, 1961
46 x 51
Shows the areas of over 330 different Scottish clans and families in colour. The map is surrounded by 174 clan crests with the Coats-of-Arms of their chiefs.
Paper folded 50p

CLAN MAP OF THE SCOTTISH HIGHLANDS
London : Johnston & Bacon
101 x 76
Coloured map of Scotland showing the clan districts and surrounded by 18 figures in ancient and modern Highland dress, 65 tartans with the chief's arms and flag of Scotland.
Paper flat 50p
Paper folded 35p
Cloth flat 70p
Cloth folded 50p

EARLY MAP REPRODUCTIONS FROM ATLAS NOVUS BY BLAEU
Various scales
Edinburgh : Bart
61 x 50
Col. reproductions from this 17th Century atlas.
Maps available:
Scotland 1635
North Scotland 1662
Aberdeen and Banff 1654
Dumbarton & Loch Lomond 1654
Kingdom of Fife 1662
Galloway 1662
Inverness and Cairngorms 1654
Isle of Islay 1662
Isle of Mull 1662
Kyle and Mid Ayrshire 1662
The Lothians 1632
Orkney and Shetland 1654
Renfrewshire 1654
Stirlingshire 1654
Teviotdale 1654
Each £1.50

A NEW DESCRIPTION OF THE SHYRES LOTHIAN AND LINLITQUO
1:145,000 app
Edinburgh : Bart/Royal Scottish Geog. Soc, 1969
34 x 52
Facsimile of Mercator's map from the 1630 Mercator-Hondius atlas.

THE PLAN OF EDENBURGH EXACTLY DONE FROM THE ORIGINAL OF YE FAMOUS DE WIT
1:2,350
Edinburgh : Bart, 1971
42 x 105
Facsimile of the 1700 map by Andrew Johnston.

THE NORTH PROSPECT OF THE CITY OF EDENBURGH
1:1.770
Edinburgh : Bart, 1971
40 x 107
Facsimile of the Map by Andrew Johnston, 1700.

ATLASES
B TOWN PLANS

TOWN STREET ATLASES
London : Gia
14 x 21 each
Detailed street atlases in black and white with index to streets.
Available for:

Edinburgh	1:14,080	55p
Glasgow	1:15,840	85p

AN ATLAS OF EDINBURGH
Edinburgh : Geographical Association (Edinburgh branch) 1964
37 x 26
39pp
Social and geographical survey portrayed in black and white maps, diagrams and descriptive text.

ATLASES
E1 PHYSICAL

'BARTHOLOMEWS' HALF-INCH LOOSE-LEAF ATLAS OF SCOTLAND
Edinburgh : Bart
50 x 60 (binder)
24 ½" topographical maps mounted on linen, folded to fit a loose leaf binder. Replacement copies of revised plates can be supplied separately.
Atlas and binder £11.00
Replacement pages, each 30p

ATLASES
M HISTORICAL

THE MAPPING OF SCOTLAND
Edinburgh : Bart, 1971
21 x 30
32pp
Pub. for the 4th Internat. Conference on the History of Cartography. Facsimiles, from earliest known maps to those of the 19th Century.
£1.00

415 Ireland

See also:

416 NORTHERN IRELAND
417 REPUBLIC OF IRELAND

A1 GENERAL MAPS: ROADS

TOURING MAP OF IRELAND
1:760,320
Edinburgh : Bart
46 x 68
Main and secondary roads with road numbering, contour col, spot heights in feet, county boundaries, customs, frontier stations and railways. Inset showing main tourist areas with mileages. 65p

IRELAND
633,600
London : Foldex
Shows roads classified, relief shading, patent fold. 30p

MOTORWAYS MAIN ROAD AND COUNTY MAP OF IRELAND
1:570,240
London : Gia, 1971
67 x 82
Motorways, trunk and other roads, distances in miles, heights in feet, railways, main airports, frontier posts, customs stations, car ferries, national boundaries and counties in colour. Also approved routes between Northern Ireland and the Republic. Counties in colour. 45p

IRELAND
1:570,000 app
No 893
Frankfurt : Ravenstein, 1976
69 x 86
Col. map; roads classified and numbered, distances, motoring and tourist details, other communications.
DM 8.80

NU-WAY ROAD MAP – IRELAND
1:506,880
Johnston & Bacon
see BRITISH ISLES 41 A1

RAC NATIONAL MAP OF IRELAND
1:500,000
73 x 99
Road map showing all classes of roads; distances in miles; rivers, ferries and information offices. Inset plans of 8 major cities; 11pp gazetteer to places of interest.
95p

SHELL ROAD MAP OF IRELAND
1:350,000
Sheet 9
London : Philip, 1971
88 x 55
Double sided map; main and secondary roads, route numbering, distances in miles, car ferries, spot heights, railways, airports, youth hostels, tourist attractions and county boundaries. 30p

BACONS REVERSIBLE MAPS
Sheet 4 N IRELAND/S IRELAND
1:316,800
Johnston & Bacon
see BRITISH ISLES 41 A1

THE VISITOR'S MAP OF IRELAND
London : Johnston & Bacon
76 x 102
County road map of Ireland surrounded by 36 coats of arms of main towns, 64 col. views and items of interest.
Paper folded 40p
Paper flat 55p

IRELAND
1:250,000
In 4 sheets
London : Foldex
Shows roads classified, relief shading etc. in patent fold. Available for:
1 South
2 Dublin and South Central
3 Dublin and North Central
4 North
Each 35p
(2 double sided sheets) 55p

IRELAND TRAVEL MAP
1:250,000
In 5 sheets, see index 415/2
Edinburgh : Bart
79 x 51
Contoured and layer col. maps showing all classes of roads, tracks, footpaths, spot heights in feet, railways, youth hostels, canals, state and county boundaries.
Paper folded, each 50p

YOUR GUIDE MAPS – SOUTH WEST IRELAND 1:316,800
– DUBLIN AND AROUND 1:15,840-1:316,800
Johnston & Bacon
see BRITISH ISLES 41 A2

C OFFICIAL SURVEYS

QUARTER INCH MAP OF IRELAND
1:250,000
In 5 sheets, see index 415/1
Dublin : OS
60 x 80 each
Contour col. maps: all classes of roads, railways, county boundaries, antiquities and youth hostels.
Sheets available:
1 North West, 1972, 3rd edition
2 North East, 1974, 4th edition
3 West, 1974, 4th edition
4 South East, 1976, 6th edition
5 South West, 1974, 5th edition

IRELAND TOURIST MAP
1:250,000
In 4 sheets
Belfast and Dublin : OS, 1972
New map in progress designed jointly by the two Irish Survey Depts. and Tourist Boards. Principally designed for tourists, it is contoured and layer coloured and gives detail of camping and caravan sites, antiquities, national parks and other items of recreational or tourist interest.
Sheet available:
Sheet 1 covering N Ireland and adjacent areas.

IRELAND HALF INCH MAP
1:126,720
In 25 sheets, see index 415/3
Dublin : OS, 1968
68 x 46
All classes of roads, railways, contour col, youth hostels and county boundaries.
Each 30p

D POLITICAL & ADMINISTRATIVE

COUNTY BUSINESS MAP OF IRELAND
1:633,600
Edinburgh : Bart, 1969
52 x 72
All motorways, main and secondary roads, customs and frontier stations, spot heights in feet and counties in colour.
30p

ADMINISTRATIVE MAP OF IRELAND
1:253,440
In 4 sheets
Dublin : OS, 1961
Showing County, County Borough, Urban District and Electoral Division boundaries in black on a white background.
Set 80p

OUTLINE MAP OF IRELAND
1:633,600
Dublin : OS, 1962
Showing coastline and County boundaries in black on a white background.
15p

F GEOLOGY

GEOLOGICAL MAP OF IRELAND
1:750,000
3rd edition
Dublin : OS, 1962
48 x 61
Col. geol. map inc. horizontal cross section. 50p

GEOLOGICAL SURVEY OF IRELAND
1:253,440
In 16 sheets
Belfast and Dublin : Geol. Surveys Col. series to cover all of Ireland. Only 2 sheets of the original early edition are available for the Republic, the remainder are out of print. Sheets covering Northern Ireland recently reprinted.
Sheets available :
2 Parts of Antrim, Londonderry and Donegal with southern part of Kintyre, 1952 70p
5 Parts of Tyrone, Antrim, Armagh, Monaghan and Down
70p
11 Dublin and country to the south as far as Arklow and Castlecomer, 1913 15p

16 Cork, Youghal and Clonakilty 15p

GEOLOGICAL SURVEY OF IRELAND
1:63,360
In 205 sheets, see index 415/4
Dublin : Geol. Surveys
46 x 30 each
Early series to cover the whole country; generally in black and white, some northern sheets with relief hachures. Geological information indicated by symbols, some cross sections. Certain sheets in colour with contours including cross sections.
Each 60p

K HUMAN GEOGRAPHY

IRISH FAMILY NAMES MAP
London : Johnston & Bacon
76 x 102
Coloured map of Ireland showing origins of Irish families surrounded by 192 coats of arms.
Paper folded 35p
Paper flat 50p

MONASTIC IRELAND
1:625,000
2nd edition
Dublin : OS, 1965
58 x 74
Showing diocesan and other boundaries; locations of various religious orders; index. 38p

M HISTORICAL

HISTORICAL MAP OF IRELAND
Edinburgh : Bart, 1969
56 x 73
Brightly col. map. illustrating battles, castles, places and characters well known in history. Surrounding the map are the Coats of Arms of cities and towns.
Paper 50p
Cloth £1.00

EARLY MAP REPRODUCTIONS FROM BLAEU'S 'THEATRUM ORBIS TERRARUM – ATLAS NOVUS'
Plates : Ireland, 1662, Ulster, 1662
Edinburgh : Bart
61 x 51
This important atlas was published in a number of volumes during the 17th Century and coloured reproductions of certain individual plates are available.

ATLASES
K HUMAN GEOGRAPHY

LINGUISTIC ATLAS AND SURVEY OF IRISH DIALECTS
In 4 volumes
Wagner and O'Baoill
Dublin : Inst. for Advanced Studies
Regional atlas of Irish dialects with notes.

ATLASES
L ECONOMIC

IRELAND – RAILWAYS
A RAILWAY ATLAS OF IRELAND
S Maxwell Hajducki
1st edition
Newton Abbot : David & Charles
1972
18 x 25
40pp maps showing rail system of Ireland as at 1925 with index, gazetteer and introduction.
In Ireland £2.25
Elsewhere £4.95

ATLASES
M HISTORICAL

AN ATLAS OF IRISH HISTORY
Ed Ruth Dudley Edwards
London: Methuen 1973
15 x 23
240pp
Descriptive text including 75 black and white maps £4.50
paperback £1.80

HIBERNIAE DELINEATIO
Sir William Petty, 1685
Newcastle-u-Tyne : Frank Graham, 1968
46 x 59
37 maps, based upon existing cadastral surveys of Ireland

HIBERNIAE DELINEATIO 1685 – GEOGRAPHICAL DESCRIPTION OF THE KINGDOM OF IRELAND, 1688
by Sir William Petty
Dublin : Irish UP
Facsimile atlas £10.50

MAPS OF THE ROADS OF IRELAND (1783)
G Taylor and A Skinner
Dublin : Irish UP
15 x 24
344 pp
Facsimile atlas, 289 plates £7.35

ULSTER AND OTHER IRISH MAPS C1600
Ed G A Hayes McCoy
Dublin : Stationery Office, for the Irish Manuscript Commission, 1964
33 x 49
51pp
23 map facsimiles; explanation; index.
£6.00

416 Northern Ireland

See also:

415 IRELAND
417 REPUBLIC OF IRELAND

A1 GENERAL MAPS: ROADS

ROAD MAP OF NORTHERN IRELAND
1:250,000
London : Gia
87 x 55
Motorways and all classes of roads; route numbering; railways, customs and frontier stations, spot heights in feet and county boundaries. 30p

B TOWN PLANS

BELFAST
1:15,000
London : Gia
81 x 96
Coloured plan with index to streets. 60p

BELFAST AND SURROUNDING DISTRICTS
1:10,560
In 4 sheets
Belfast : OSNI, 1938
71 x 91 each
Covers the County Borough. Land and water features, contours, parks etc. roads and buildings.
Provisional ed.
Each, flat 40p
Photographic reduction available at 1:21,120 25p

C OFFICIAL SURVEYS

THE QUARTER INCH MAP
1:253,440
2nd edition
Belfast : OSNI
101 x 77
Topog. map in col. Shows main and secondary roads, railways, contours, national boundaries, antiquities, forest areas green. Also available in outline edition.
Flat 23p
Folder in cover 30p
Outline ed. (flat) 23p

THE NORTHERN IRELAND TOURIST MAP
1:250,000
Belfast: OSNI
105 x 80
Sheet 1 of a projected 4 sheet map of Ireland. Road map in colours showing information on camping and caravan sites, sailing and fishing facilities, antiquities, forest parks and National Trust properties.
Paper flat or folded 18p

THE HALF INCH MAP (SECOND SERIES)
1:126,720
In 4 sheets, see index 416/1
Belfast : OSNI, 1968
94 x 63 each
Coloured, topog. map showing land features, roads classified, contours and layer colouring, forest areas etc. Outline ed, land features black, contours blue.
Flat (both eds) 25p
Folded in cover 33p

THE ONE INCH MAP
1:63,360
3rd series
In 9 sheets, see index 416/2
Belfast : OSNI, 1971
Various sizes
Contoured maps, showing land features, roads classified, forest areas, layer colouring, youth hostels. Also in outline ed – land features black, water blue.
Flat (both eds) 23p
Folded in cover 30p

ORDNANCE SURVEY SIX INCH COUNTY SERIES
1:10,560
Belfast : OSNI
Detailed series covering Northern Ireland, showing topog. information, and contours. Being replaced by the new Irish Grid series.
each £1.00

ORDNANCE SURVEY SIX INCH IRISH GRID SERIES
1:10,560 – 1:10,000
In 286 sheets, see index 416/4
Belfast : OSNI
New series designed to replace the earlier County series with detailed land information and contours. From 1971 it was decided that all sheets should be issued at the metric scale of 1:10,000 and in 2 editions:
1 detail in black, without contours
2 detail in grey with contours in red
These will eventually replace the 1:10,560 series.
Each edition 60p

PROVISIONAL MAPS
1:10,560
Belfast : OSNI
Special series for certain selected towns, revised from air photographs and existing large-scale maps.
Each 40p

THE ORDNANCE SURVEY 1:2,500 COUNTY SERIES
1:2,500
Belfast : OSNI
Based on individual sheet lines for each of the 6 counties. Covers cultivated areas only and shows permanent land features. Series being replaced by Irish Grid series on national sheet lines.
Each 60p

ORDNANCE SURVEY 1:2,500 IRISH GRID SERIES
1:2,500
See index 416/4
Belfast : OSNI
Detailed topog. series in progress covering the country on a standard national grid. This series supersedes the earlier county editions.
Each full sheets £2.00
quarter sheets £1.20

ORDNANCE SURVEY FIFTY INCH IRISH GRID SERIES OF NORTHERN IRELAND
1:1,250
Belfast : OSNI
A new detailed survey covering those towns with a population of more than 10,000, plus some smaller towns. The Irish Grid series in in preparation and for those towns which are not yet published, direct enlargements of the 1:2,500 County sheets can be supplied.
Either series, each £2.00

D POLITICAL & ADMINISTRATIVE

NORTHERN IRELAND LOCAL GOVERNMENT AREAS
1:250,000
Belfast : OSNI
78 x 65
Showing districts and ward boundaries with names as at 1972. Belfast and Londonderry inset.
Dyeline print 20p

PARLIAMENTARY CONSTITUENCY MAP OF NORTHERN IRELAND
1:253,440
Belfast : OSNI, 1959
Showing District Electoral Divisions in black, NI Parliamentary Constituencies in green on grey background. Inset of parliamentary constituencies in County Borough of Belfast.
Dyeline print 20p

LOCAL GOVERNMENT DISTRICT MAPS
1:63,360 – 1:25,000
In 15 sheets
Belfast: OSNI
Series of maps showing the revised local government boundaries, 1972. They show townlands and wards on a local government district basis with coloured boundaries on a grey topographical base. Includes plan of Belfast City at 1:25,000.
each 50p.

BELFAST AND DISTRICT – PARLIAMENTARY MAP OF BELFAST AND DISTRICT – UNITED KINGDOM CONSTITUENCIES
1:21,120
Belfast : OSNI, 1970
71 x 91
Dyeline print of parliamentary constituency boundary changes, 1970 20p

E1 PHYSICAL: RELIEF

THE ULSTER YEAR BOOK MAP
1:500,000
Belfast : OSNI

F GEOLOGY

GEOLOGICAL MAP OF ENGLAND AND WALES
1:253,440
In 24 sheets, see index 420/3
London : IGS
74 x 52
Series of coloured maps in progress.
Sheets published:
1/2, 1951
3, 1959
9/10, 1968
12, 1936
21/25, 1971
22, 1953
each 55p

GEOLOGICAL MAP OF ENGLAND AND WALES – NEW SERIES
1:63,360 – 1:50,000
In 359 sheets approx, see index 420/3
London : IGS
64 x 46
Col. sheets on 3rd edition sheet lines with National Grid overprinted. Available in either 'Solid' (basic geology) or 'Drift' (superficial deposits) editions or a combination of both according to region covered. New sheets are now being issued at the metric scale of 1:50,000 which will eventually replace the earlier series.
flat £1.15
folded £1.25

ENGLAND AND WALES GEOLOGY – SPECIAL SHEETS
1:63,360
London : IGS
Various Sizes
Series of special area maps, coloured and available in Solid (basic geology) or 'Drift' (superficial deposits) editions or a combination of both.
Sheets available:
Isle of Man (Drift)
Isle of Wight (Drift)
Anglesey (Solid and Drift)
Bristol District (Solid and Drift)
flat £1.15
folded £1.25

CLASSICAL AREAS IN BRITISH GEOLOGY
1:25,000
See index 410/10
London : IGS
Col. geol. maps based on 2½" OS sheet lines, available in either 'Solid' (basic geology) or 'Drift' (superficial deposits) editions or combinations of both.
Maps available:
NY 57 Bewcastle (S), 1969
NY 57 Bewcastle (D), 1969
NY 82 Part 92 Middleton-in-Teesdale (S & D) 1974
SD 74/84 Clitheroe & Gisburn (S with D) 1970
SK 18 Part 17 Edale & Castleton (S & D), 1969
Parts of SK25, 26, 35 & 36 Matlock (S & D), 1971
Cross Fell Inlier Special Sheet (S & D), 1973
flat or folded £1.35
Central Snowdonia Special Sheet (S & D) 1972
flat or folded £1.25
SM 72 St. Davids (S & D) 1973
*SO 48 Craven Arms (S & D), 1969
*SO 49 Church Stretton (S & D) 1968
*SO 59 Wenlock Edge (S & D), 1969
SP 83 (& Parts of 73, 74, 84, 93 & 94) Milton Keynes (S & D) 1971
ST 45 Cheddar (S & D) 1969
ST 47 Clevedon & Portishead (S & D) 1969
Parts of SO 20, 30, ST 29, 39 Usk-Cwmbran, 1971
TL 81 Witham (in press)
Parts of TF 00, 10, 20, TL09, 19, 29 Peterborough (S & D) 1973
flat or folded £1.35
TQ 22 Cuckfield and West Hoathly (S & D) 1975
* Explanatory Handbook available
Paper flat or folded £1.15

HYDROGEOLOGICAL MAPS OF ENGLAND AND WALES
Various scales
London : IGS
Col. maps showing hydrological information on a geological base map.
Maps available:
North and East Lincolnshire inc. Hydrometric areas 29, 30 and pts. 31, 1:126,720 £2.10
Northern East Anglia including Hydrometric areas 33, 34, 1:126,720 – in press
Dartford (Kent) District including parts of Hydrometric areas 37 and 40, 1:63,360 95p
The Chalk and Lower Greensand of Kent including Hydrometric Area 40, 1:126,720 in 2 sheets
1 Chalk, regional, hydrological characteristics with notes
2 Folkestone Beds and Hythe Beds. set £3.00

G EARTH RESOURCES

GENERALIZED SOIL MAP OF ENGLAND AND WALES
1:2,000,000
Harpenden : Rothamsted Exp. Station
Coloured soil map 60p

TYPES OF SOIL WATER REGIME
1:2,000,000
Harpenden : Rothamsted Exp. Station
Coloured hydrological map. 60p

SOIL MAP OF ENGLAND AND WALES
1:1,000,000
Compiled by Soil Survey
Southampton : OS, 1975
53 x 65 –sheet size 100 x 88
Coloured map with Natn'l Grid, depicting soil types in colour. Detailed analysis of soil groups in margin.
paper flat £1.00
folded in cover £2.00

SOIL SURVEY OF ENGLAND AND WALES – SPECIAL SHEETS
Various scales
Harpenden : Rothamsted Exp. Station
Col. soil maps accompanied by explanatory Bulletins.
Sheets available:
The soils of the West Midlands 1:625,000, 1964 25p
Soil Association Map of the County of Lancashire 1:250,000, 1972 30p
Soil Map of Berkshire 30p
Soil Map of Hertfordshire 1:250,000 10p
Luton and Bedford – outline 1:63,360 25p
Saffron Walden – outline 1:63,360 25p
Farringdon 1:25,000 25p
Teign Valley 1:25,000 25p

SOIL SURVEY OF ENGLAND AND WALES
1:63,360
See index 420/4
Harpenden : Rothamsted Experimental Station
64 x 46
Soil information overprinted in col. on 1 inch maps, 3rd edition sheet lines. With accompanying Memoirs. 75p
Composite sheets £1.00

SOIL SURVEY OF ENGLAND AND WALES – LAND USE CAPABILITY
1:63,360
See index 420/4
Harpenden : Rothamsted Experimental Station
64 x 46
Special edition of soil survey maps showing land use potential in colour.
Sheets published:
142 Melton Mowbray
166 Church Stretton
253 Abingdon 30p each

SOIL SURVEY OF ENGLAND AND WALES
1:25,000
See index
Harpenden : Rothamsted Experimental Station, 1966+
Series generally in black and white on OS National Grid sheet lines some with explanatory 'Soil Survey Records'. Published in 3 editions. Soil Maps
SD 58 Sedgwick
SE 32pts. 22,42 Castleford
SE 36 Boroughbridge
SE 60* Armthorpe
SE 64 Escrick
SE 65 York East
SE 74 Barmby Moor
SE 76 Westow
SJ 37 Ellesmere Port
SJ 65 Crewe West
SJ 82* Eccleshall
SK 05 Onecote
SK 17* Tideswell
SK 32/42 Melbourne
SK 66 Ollerton
SK 85* Newark on Trent
SM 90 Pembroke
SM 91 Haverfordwest
SN 41 Llangendeirne
SO 09 Caerws
SO 34 Staunton on Wye
SO 52 Ross-on-Wye
SO 53 Hereford - South
SO 82 Norton
SO 87 Kidderminster
SP 05 Alcester
SP 36 Leamington Spa
SS 73, 74, 83, 84 Exmoor Forest
ST 10* Honiton
SU 70,80 Chichester - coloured
SU 88 Marlow
SU 90 Bognor Regis - coloured
SZ 79,89 Selsey Bill - coloured
TQ 00,10 Worthing - coloured

TF 16** Woodhall Spa
TG 13/14*
Barningham/Sheringham
TM 49** Beccles
TQ 59** Harold Hill
TQ 92, TR 02 pts, TQ 91, 93, TR 01, 03, 13 Romney Marsh coloured
35p
TQ 99* Burnham on Crouch
TR 04* Ashford
TR 35* Deal
Special Sheet : The Breckland Forest
Sheet 1 Swaffham
Sheet 2 Brandon
Sheet 3 Thetford
* Land Use Capability Map also available
** Land Use Capability Map and Soil Drainage Map also available
each 25p

SPECIAL SOIL SURVEY – CHATTERIS
1:10,560
Compiled by Soil survey
Southampton : OS
Soil survey of Chatteris area. Cambridgeshire based on aerial mosaic base covering the OS 10 km square TL 38 in 4 sheets.
each 50p

H BIOGEOGRAPHY

COUNTRYSIDE MAP OF ENGLAND AND WALES
1:760,320
Edinburgh : Bart, 1971
70 x 91
Green base map with relief layer colouring, proposed and existing National Parks and Areas of Outstanding Beauty also forest parks, youth hostels, National Nature Reserves, National Park Information Centres and long distance footpaths.
50p

L ECONOMIC

BRITISH RAIL SYSTEM MAP, LONDON AREA
1:63,360
2nd edition
London : Gia, 1970
101 x 76
Col. map illus. transport systems; stations classified; index to stations.
75p

COMMUTERS' MAP OF 60 MILES AROUND LONDON
1:250,000
London : John Swann
91 x 84
Distances; routes, times for British Rail and underground services.
40p

STANFORD'S CANOEING MAP OF ENGLAND AND WALES
1:887,040
London : Stanford, 1973
62 x 74
Rivers and canals and the approximate limits of navigation by canoe or light craft.
35p

THE INLAND WATERWAYS OF ENGLAND
1:750,000 app
St Ives (Hunts): Imray, Laurie, Norie and Wilson, 1972
Shows canal and river details in colour with distances. Reverse has large scale outlines of the Thames, Fens, Broads, Birmingham, N-W and N-E systems.
60p

STANFORD'S INLAND CRUISING MAP OF ENGLAND FOR LARGER CRAFT
1:500,000
London : Stanford, 1973
70 x 69
Navigable rivers, locks with dimensions, railways, main roads, and a mileage chart of canal through-ways. 4 inset maps at larger scales.
85p

CHART OF THE RIVER DEBEN
1:375,000
St Ives (Hunts): Imray, Laurie, Norie and Wilson
Waterways map, with plan of Woodbridge Haven. Folded in wallet 65p

CHART OF THE RIVER ORE AND ALDE
1:375,000
St Ives (Hunts): Imray, Laurie, Norie and Wilson
Waterways map, with plan of Orfordhaven. In wallet. 65p

GRAFHAM WATER (HUNTS)
1:375,000
Y80
St Ives (Hunts) : Imray, Laurie, Norie and Wilson
61 x 43
Waterways map. 50p

THE UPPER REACHES OF THE RIVER MEDWAY
1:250,000
St Ives (Hunts) : Imray, Laurie, Norie and Wilson
Waterways map. 50p

THE UPPER REACHES OF THE GREAT OUSE
1:250,000
St Ives (Hunts): Imray, Laurie, Norie and Wilson
Covers the area St Neots to Bedford.
20p

RIVER WEY NAVIGATION
1:187,500
St Ives (Hunts) : Imray, Laurie, Norie and Wilson
Waterways map. 50p

THE RIVER NENE
1:187,500
St Ives (Hunts) : Imray, Laurie, Norie and Wilson
Waterways map. 50p

THE KENNET AND AVON WATERWAY
Nicholas Hammond
1:187,500
St Ives (Hunts) : Imray, Laurie, Norie and Wilson
Waterways map covering the western area – Avonmouth-Devizes.
80p

THE ENCLOSED WATERS OF THE RIVERS CAM AND GREAT OUSE
1:20,000
St Ives (Hunts) : Imray, Laurie, Norie and Wilson, 1967
119 x 18
Printed both sides, with locks, depths widths details, road directions near rivers, etc. 50p

STANFORD'S MAP OF THE RIVER THAMES : RICHMOND TO LECHLADE
1:42,240
London : Stanford, 1975
95 x 39
Strip map showing locks, weirs, towing paths and ferries, railways, motorways and main roads, general information and dimensions of locks. 75p

NICHOLSON'S GUIDE TO THE THAMES – FROM SOURCE TO SEA
London : Nicholson, 1969
11 x 23
158pp
98pp detailed strip maps of the river, places of interest, eating, drinking and accommodation, natural history and motoring on the same page.
Paper covers 62½p
Hard back £1.25

STANFORD'S MAP OF THE NORFOLK BROADS AND RIVERS
1:48,274
London : Stanford, 1973
56 x 88
Showing navigable rivers and broads, distances along rivers, main and secondary roads, shopping facilities, boat houses and yards. Inset of Fenland Waterways 1:380,160. 75p

MAPS OF THE NORFOLK BROADS
1:250,000 – 1,63,360
Edinburgh : Bart, 1973
71 x 39
Double sided map having detailed map of the Broads system with river distances speeds services and places of interest with road map of East Anglia including London on the reverse. 50p

TYPES OF FARM MAP OF ENGLAND AND WALES
1:625,000
Pinner : Min. of Agriculture, Fisheries and Food
Map in preparation 1976/77.

TYPE OF FARM MAPS FOR REGIONS IN ENGLAND AND WALES
1:250,000
See index 420/6
In 9 sheets.
Pinner : Min. of Agriculture, Fish and Food.
119 x 84 each
Regional maps based on 1968 Agricultural Census, showing 9 types of farming : Predominantly Dairying; Mainly Dairying; Livestock – Cattle; Livestock – Sheep; Pigs and Poultry: Cropping – Cereals; Cropping – General; Horticulture; Mixed. Dot distributions overprinted on OS. 1:250,000 base maps.
Available in 2 editions:
1 Size of Farm (acres)
2 Size of Farm Business (standard man-days)
Maps are published showing all types of farms or separately for each category for 8 Ministry Regions: Northern, Yorks and Lancs, E Midland, W Midland, S West (2 sheets), Eastern, S Eastern and Wales.

Explanatory note to the series 1974.
All farm categories £1.00
Separate categories 15p–25p

LAND CLASSIFICATION MAP OF ENGLAND AND WALES
1:625,000
Pinner : Min. of Agriculture, Fisheries and Food.
Map in preparation 1976/77.

LAND CLASSIFICATION MAP OF ENGLAND AND WALES
1:250,000
In 7 sheets
Pinner : Min. of Agriculture, Fisheries and Food.
Series of maps in preparation 1976/77.

AGRICULTURAL LAND CLASSIFICATION MAP OF ENGLAND AND WALES
1:63,360
See Index 420/7
In 113 sheets Provisional edition
Pinner : Ministry Agriculture, Fisheries, Food, 1965-1974
63 x 71 each
Coloured map series in progress based on OS 1" series (7th series). Classifies land use by 5 grades of agricultural land, urban land, non-agricultural land. Also shows communications and settlement.
Explanatory note, 1968.
Each £1.12
Series of separate sheet reports are in progress.

CONTRACTING COALFIELD: SERIES OF MAPS TO SHOW THE PAST AND PRESENT EXTENT OF COAL WORKING IN COUNTY DURHAM BY W ARTHUR MOYES
Newcastle-upon-Tyne : Frank Graham, 1972.
16pp including 6 maps.

M HISTORICAL

HISTORY MAPS
Indianapolis : Cram
Col. school wall maps.
Maps available :
Early English Kingdoms
Norman Conquest in England
Each $13.75

HISTORICAL MAP OF ENGLAND AND WALES
Edinburgh : Bart , 1971
51 x 69
Brightly coloured map, illustrating battles, castles, places and characters well known in history. Surrounding the map are the Coats of Arms of cities and towns.
Paper 50p
Cloth 60p

ARMADA MAPS
Edinburgh : Bart, 1971
Rep. of 1590 map 'Expeditionis Hispanorum in Angliam vera Descript by Robert Adams; on reverse modern route map with col. illus. and notes on people and objects in the Armada.
Paper 25p

FOOTBALL HISTORY MAP OF ENGLAND AND WALES
1:970,000
Edinburgh : Bart, 1971
59 x 51
Coloured map showing major events and places in football. Badges, club information, dates and notes in margin.

ENGLAND AND WALES
Kettering : J.L. Carr
46 x 76
Coloured pictorial map depicting principal figures and events of the country's history, architecture and traditions. £1.85

COUNTY MAPS
Kettering : J.L. Carr
46 x 76 approx.
Coloured pictorial maps to show the "essence" of a county – history, architecture, traditions. Available for the following counties:
Bedfordshire
Berkshire
Buckinghamshire
Cambridgeshire
Cheshire
Cornwall
Cumberland
Derbyshire
Devon
Dorset
Durham
Essex
Gloucestershire
Hampshire
Herefordshire
Hertfordshire
Huntingdonshire
Kent
Lancashire
Leicestershire
Lincolnshire
Middlesex
Norfolk
Northamptonshire
Northumberland
Nottinghamshire
Oxfordshire
Rutland
Shropshire
Somerset
Staffordshire
Suffolk
Surrey
Sussex
Warwickshire
Westmorland
Wiltshire
Worcestershire
Yorkshire each £1.85

HISTORICAL MAP OF LONDON
Edinburgh : Bart, 1969
76 x 37
Illus. people and places of importance from Roman to Modern Times with a border of the Trade Guild's Coats of Arms.
Paper folded 50p
Cloth folded 60p

PICTORIAL MAP OF LONDON
London : Pictorial Maps
121 x 96
Col. pictorial map of London depicting main sites and characters in history. Border illus. by heraldic design.
£2.25
Reduced edition 61 x 48 £1.25

DAILY TELEGRAPH PICTORIAL MAP OF LONDON
London : Gia
81 x 49
Col. map illus. the main places and events of interest to visitors.
Decorative border 50p

CHILDREN'S MAP OF LONDON
Edinburgh : Bart
62 x 41
Coloured map illustrating with nursery rhymes, poems and coats of arms the history of the capital.
Paper folded 25p
Cloth folded 40p

THE FIRST EDITION OF THE ONE INCH ORDNANCE SURVEY : A REPRINT COVERING ENGLAND AND WALES IN 97 SHEETS
1:63,360
In 87 sheets, see index 420/9
Ed J B Harley
Newton Abbot : David & Charles, 1969/71
102 x 76 each
Facsimile of the 1st edition (1805-73) copper engraved in black and white. Includes revision, especially of railway material. Bibliographical note for each sheet.
Each £1.00
Set £90.00

ORDNANCE SURVEY ONE-INCH MAP OF THE SOUTHAMPTON AREA, 1810
1:63,360
Southampton : OS
83 x 67
Reproduction of 1st edition series, with changes such as railways, about 1840. Covers Lymington – Chichester – Winchester
Flat £1.20

SAXTON'S COUNTY MAPS OF ENGLAND AND WALES
London : British Museum
63 x 50 average
Litho offset prints in colour.
Maps available:
Map of England and Wales – 1579
Caernarvonshire and Anglesey (Snowdonia) – 1578
Cheshire – 1577
Cornwall – 1576
Cumberland and Westmorland (Lake District 1576)
Denbighshire and Flintshire – (One map) – 1577
Derbyshire – 1577
Devonshire – 1575
Dorset – 1575
Durham – 1576
Essex – 1576
Glamorganshire – 1578
Gloucestershire – 1577
Hampshire – 1575
Herefordshire – 1577
Hertfordshire – 1577
Kent, Surrey, Sussex and Middlesex (one map) – 1575
Lancashire – 1577
Lincolnshire and Nottinghamshire (one map) – 1576
Monmouthshire – 1577
Montgomeryshire and Merionethshire (one map) – 1578
Norfolk (the Broads) – 1574
Northamptonshire, Bedfordshire, Cambridgeshire, Huntingdonshire and Rutland (one map) – 1576
Northumberland – 1576
Oxfordshire, Buckinghamshire and Berkshire (one map) – 1574
Pembrokeshire – 1578
Radnorshire, Brecknockshire, Cardiganshire and Carmarthenshire (one map) – 1578
Shropshire – 1577
Somerset – 1575

Staffordshire – 1577
Suffolk – 1575
Warwickshire and Leicestershire
(one map) – 1576
Wiltshire – 1576
Worcestershire – 1577
Yorkshire – 1577
60p each

JOHN SPEED'S ENGLAND (1611)
Ed J Arlott
London : Dent
In 4 volumes
50 x 63
Colour reproductions of Speed's maps, with list of hundreds and Speed's text on reverse. Vols. 1 and 2 out of print. Individual maps available as follows:

Part I

Hampshire
Dorset
Wiltshire
Herefordshire
The Isle of Wight
Cornwall
Gloucestershire
Devonshire
Somerset
Monmouthshire

Part 2

Kent
Berkshire
Suffolk
Buckinghamshire
Sussex
Middlesex
Norfolk
Surrey
Essex
Hertfordshire

Part 3

Shropshire
Leicestershire
Staffordshire
Worcestershire
Warwickshire
Huntingdonshire
Cambridgeshire
Oxfordshire
Northamptonshire
Rutland
Bedfordshire

Part 4

Cumberland
County Durham
Cheshire
Nottinghamshire
Westmorland
Lancashire
Derbyshire
Lincolnshire
Northumberland
Yorkshire (North and East Ridings)
Yorkshire (West Riding)
Bound vols. (3 & 4) each £4.50
Individual maps £1.25

EARLY MAP REPRODUCTIONS FROM BLAEU'S 'THEATRUM ORBIS TERRARUM – ATLAS NOVUS'
Edinburgh : Bart, 1966–
61 x 45
Reproductions in colour from this important atlas of 1648.
Maps available:
England and Wales 1635
Counties : all dated 1635
Cambridge
Cheshire
Cornwall
Cumberland and Lake District
Derbyshire
Essex
Gloucestershire
Hampshire
Hertfordshire
Kent
Lancashire
Middlesex
Norfolk
Nottinghamshire
Oxford
Staffordshire
Surrey
Sussex
Worcestershire and Warwickshire
Yorkshire
each £1.50

JOHN NORDEN'S MANUSCRIPT MAPS OF CORNWALL AND ITS NINE HUNDREDS
Intro. by William Ravenhill
Exeter : University, 1972
Facsimile map

BENJAMIN DONN : A MAP OF THE COUNTY OF DEVON, 1765
Exeter : Devon & Cornwall Record Society/the University of Exeter, 1965
29 x 34
45pp
Facsimile volume comprising an introduction; 1 general map of county; 24 double pp maps in atlas format. Scale 1inch to 1 mile; shows topog. features, with text by Dr. Ravenhill. £3.00

A REPRODUCTION OF A MAP OF THE COUNTY OF ESSEX, 1777
John Chapman and Peter André
Chelmsford : Essex County Council, 1970
32 x 25
Facsimile reproduction half scale (1": 1 mile) 25 plates with introduction.

SYMONSON'S MAP OF KENT "A NEW DESCRIPTION OF KENT"
Southampton : OS
97 x 76
Reproduction of Philip Symonson's map of 1596, published by Stent, showing churches pictorially.
Flat 75p

A TOPOGRAPHICAL MAP OF THE COUNTY OF KENT IN TWENTY-FIVE SHEETS ON A SCALE OF TWO INCHES TO A MILE . . . 1769 BY ANDREWS AND DURY
Lympne Castle (Kent): H Margary 1968.
41 x 51
25 folded pp maps in black and white: buildings, "everything remarkable in the County"; local divisions.
Case bound £12.00
Loose sheets £7.00

YATES MAP OF THE COUNTY OF LANCASHIRE, 1786
Intro by Dr J B Harley
Liverpool : Historic Society of Lancashire and Cheshire, 1968
42pp
Facsimile map divided into 29 sections at reduced scale, with text.

A MAP OF THE COUNTY OF MIDDLESEX
by John Rocque, 1754
London : London & Middlesex Archaeological Society, 1971
96 x 66 : 95 x 67
2 sheet facsimile map. £1.00

HODGKINSON'S MAP OF SUFFOLK, 1783
Ed D P Drummond
Ipswich : Suffolk Records Soc, 1972
20pp facsimile reproduction contained in paper folio. £2.25

JOHN NORDEN'S MAP OF SURREY, 1594
London : RGS
64 x 39
Facsimile reproduction £1.25

JOHN NORDEN'S MAP OF SUSSEX, 1595
London : RGS
64 x 39
Facsimile reproduction £1.25

MAP OF WILTSHIRE, 1773 BY ANDREWS AND DURY
Devizes : Wiltshire Archaeological & Natural History Society, 1952
Facsimile reproduction.

A PLAN OF THE BOROUGH AND PORT OF BOSTON IN 1741
Boston, Lincs : Richard Kay Pubn's., 1974
Reproduction of earliest known map of the Borough with pictorial insets and descriptive legend. £1.00

CHART OF THE WASH, 1693
Boston : Richard Kay Pubn's., 1975
36 x 46
Reproduction of earliest known chart of the Wash. £1.00

THE BOROUGH OF SOUTHAMPTON 1846
1:1,250 app
In 3 sheets
Southampton : Civic Record Office, 1970
52 x 78 each
Set of 3 sheets in colour from a detailed plan of Southampton made in 1846 by the O.S. These sheets cover the old medieval town and the area east of St. Mary's Church.
£3.30
Educational bodies £2.80

GLC REPRODUCTION MAPS
Various scales
London : Greater London Council
Series of facsimiles taken from early maps in the GLC archives. In black and white unless stated otherwise.
Maps available:

100 Elizabethan London
Braun & Hogenberg 1572 (from Civitates Orbis Terrarum)
50 x 36 37p

101 London in the 17th Century
Jacob de la Feville 1690
Amsterdam, 61 x 53 50p

102 London in the 18th Century
John Rocque 1769, centre sheet from survey of London and environs 76 x 56
50p

103 London in 1832
United Kingdom Newspaper (with engravings of principal buildings)
76 x 53 37p

104 Middlesex in the 17th Century
John Ogilby, 1672, 51 x 41
37p

105 Middlesex in the 18th Century
John Warburton 1749, 71 x 55
50p
106 Greater London in the 18th Century, John Rocque 1769 (environs in 1 sheet)
66 x 53 50p
170 Elizabethan Middlesex. John Norden 1593 (from Speculum Britanniae pt. 1) in colour 25 x 20 50p
171 Elizabethan Middlesex, Braun & Hogenberg 1572, same as No 100 but in colour, 50 x 36 £1.00

THE CITY OF LONDON THROUGH 5 CENTURIES
Edinburgh : Johnston & Bacon, 1972
76 x 102
6 facsimile maps from the 16th-20th Century; with prints and photographs.
60p

'AN EXACT SURVEY OF THE CITY'S OF LONDON AND WESTMINSTER YE BOROUGH OF SOUTHWARK AND THE COUNTRY NEAR 10 MILES ROUND LONDON'
by John Roque 1746
1:11,520 (5½" : 1 mile)
In 16 sheets
Lympne Castle (Kent) : H Margery/ Chichester: Phillimore & Co, 1971
82 x 55
Facsimile reproduction in black and white.

Unbound	£6.00
Bound	£12.00
Paper covers	£7.50

'A PLAN OF THE CITIES OF LONDON AND WESTMINSTER AND BOROUGH OF SOUTHWARK WITH THE CONTIGUOUS BUILDINGS FROM AN ACTUAL SURVEY' – 24 SHEETS IN 1746
by John Roque
1:2,437 (26" : 1 mile)
In 26 sheets
Lympne Castle (Kent) : H Margery/ Chichester : Phillimore & Co, 1971
82 x 55
Facsimile reproduction in black and white with 44pp index and introduction to streets.

Unbound	£7.00
Paper covers	£8.50
Bound	£14.00

HORWOOD'S 1799 PLAN OF LONDON, WESTMINSTER, SOUTHWARK AND PARTS ADJOINING, SHOWING EVERY HOUSE
In 32 sheets
London : Topographical Society, Pub No 106, 1966
59 x 52
Facsimile reproduction.

MAP OF THE PARISH OF HAMMERSMITH, 1853
1:6,336
Oxford : OUP (for Hammersmith Local History Group)
51 x 34
10pp facsimile map.

JOHN COE'S MAP OF WALTHAMSTOW IN 1822
13½in : 1 mile
Walthamstow : Antiquarian Society, 1966
12pp
Map produced in 1822 for Poor Law Assessment rate. 8 plate half-scale reproduction, showing all roads, buildings etc. 12pp Notes by A D Law, 40pp duplicated index.

A SERIES OF ACCURATE MAPS OF THE PRINCIPAL LAKES OF CUMBERLAND, WESTMORLAND AND LANCASHIRE
by Peter Crosthwaite
Newcastle-u-Tyne : Frank Graham, 1968
Facsimile of map from survey 1783-94. Map of each lake at 3 inches to the mile; not covering much of the fell area. Notes by William Rollinson.

ATLASES
A2 GENERAL : LOCAL

LONDON AND THE SOUTH EAST
London : Map Productions, 1972
16 x 23
144pp
Containing 90pp map section scale 1:100,000 covering the whole of S E England – Bedford-Ipswich-High Wycombe - Havant to the coast, showing motorways, major and minor roads, motor association services, ferries and airports with 17pp enlarged section 1:14,080 of central London. Separate index to each section.

Paper covers	£1.00
With plastic jacket	£1.25

BARNETTS LOCAL ATLASES
Barking : Barnett
Series of atlases containing road maps and town plans in black and white.
Available for:

Berkshire ABC Atlas and gazetteer	50p
Essex ABC Atlas and gazetteer	90p
Hertfordshire ABC Atlas	75p
Kent ABC Atlas	75p
Leicester ABC Atlas	60p

ROUND AND ABOUT SURREY STREET ATLAS
London : Stanford
18 x 28
County atlas comprising 180 pages of sectional maps at 1:21,120, showing all classes of roads, footpaths, county boundaries, railways and underground stations etc. Also includes a map of the major administrative boundaries, 6 town plans, a Surrey street index.
Laminated hard cover £3.25

COUNTY ATLAS SERIES
Smarden, Kent : Estate Pubn's.
11 x 15
Containing town centre plans for all towns in the county with index to streets, road map, Population gazetteer, admin. districts and postcode districts. Atlases available:

Cornwall	080A	48pp	65p
Kent	030C	64pp	75p
Sussex	076A	64pp	65p

ATLASES
B TOWN PLANS

MASTER ATLAS OF GREATER LONDON
Sevenoaks : Gers
20 x 29
287 pp
159pp sectional maps 1:21,120 showing main and secondary roads, bus routes, railway underground and police stations, postal districts, GLC and Borough boundaries. Same area as 9 sheet Master Map of London – Chorleywood, Brentwood, Tilbury, Kemsing, Woking but certain less populated areas have been omitted to allow Gravesend, Woking, Slough, Eton and Windsor to be included. Same index references are used so they may be used in conjunction or independently. List of shopping centres and their early closing days, cinemas, theatres, hospitals, places of interest and a plan of the Underground.
£4.95

LONDON ATLAS
7th edition
Sevenoaks : Gers
17 x 25
270pp
Watford – Romford – Weybridge – Eynsford. 141pp sectional maps 1:19,500; mainline and underground railways, bus routes, Borough boundaries, and postal districts, public parks etc. Maps of the West End cinemas and theatres, underground map. Index of 40,000 entries. £2.95

FRANCIS CHICHESTER'S MAP AND GUIDE OF LONDON
London : Francis Chichester Ltd.
9 x 14
119pp
Pocket sized atlas; 40pp street maps; Postal District map, gourmets guide; bus plan and car parks; index to streets and subjects.
£1.05

AA GREATER LONDON STREET ATLAS
1:12,500 – 1:23,000
London : AA/Gia
21 x 28
246pp Atlas section with 32pp section of information for the tourist. 132pp index.

A TO Z LONDON – DELUXE EDITION
Sevenoaks : Gers
15 x 23
271pp
Extended edition of the pocket version covering Watford-Romford-Eynsford-Epsom-Uxbridge. Detailed black and white maps, at 1:21,120, with comprehensive index.
Paper covers £1.50

A-Z ATLAS OF LONDON AND THE SUBURBS
Sevenoaks : Gers
11 x 18
288pp
120pp black and white maps scale 1:23,000 showing Harrow-Dagenham-Enfield-Croydon. All streets named; mainline and underground railways and stations, maps of theatres and cinemas in the West End and an underground railway map. Fully indexed.
50p
Library Edition 85p

LONDON STREET BY STREET
London : Gia
11 x 18
272pp
129pp black and white maps scale 1:21,120; Greenford-Barking-Barnet-Croydon. Naming all streets; mainline and underground stations, bus routes and map continuations; pictorial map of the City and West End, maps of museums, art galleries, theatres, cinemas, and a London guide. 45p

A TO Z CENTRAL LONDON ATLAS AND STREET GUIDE
Sevenoaks : Gers
13 x 19
80pp
48pp col. maps, 1:10,560, showing main roads, numbered bus routes, mainline and underground stations, postal districts; special maps of bus routes, underground, theatres, cinemas, main roads out of London and places of interest. Fully indexed.
50p

NICHOLSON'S LONDON STREET FINDER
3rd Edition
London : Nicholson, 1975
13 x 20
156 pp
Pocket street atlas of London and suburbs in black and white. Area covered: Bushey Heath - Enfield - Romford - Bromley - Croydon - Hounslow 1:21,120. Central London 1:13,072. Index. 50p
Available with central London section in colour 75p
Also available in a larger format edition 16 x 24. Central London 1:10,500 and Outer London 1:16,000 2nd Ed.
Paper £1.95
Cloth £2.95

CENTRAL LONDON MAP AND INDEX
1:12,500
London : R. Nicholson Pubn's. 1975
11 x 18
24pp
Covering 30 square miles of central London in 2 colours marking one-way streets. Theatre, cinema, shopping and underground maps. 25p.

POCKET ATLAS OF CENTRAL LONDON
1:15,840
London : Johnston & Bacon
9 x 14
Small atlas of London streets with separate throughway maps. Bus routes, theatres and underground system are included.
30p

A-Z SUPER SCALE ATLAS OF INNER LONDON
1:7,040
Sevenoaks : Geographers
Includes 59pp of fully coloured maps with 22pp street index. Extends to Camden Town, Hoxton, Bermondsey, The Oval, West Kensington, Notting Hill and Kilburn.
95p

LONDON POCKET ATLAS AND GUIDE
London : Gia. 1976
8 x 13
Coloured map section of Inner London with Tourist guide.

OLIVER'S GUIDE TO THE CITY OF LONDON
London : Oliver's Guides, 1976-77
22 x 30
Annual pub. containing 8pp maps covering City of London based on OS maps at the scale of 1:3,000. Index to street names and principal companies with their addresses and phone nos. £2.00

TOWN STREET ATLASES
Various scales
London : Gia/Sevenoaks : Gers
14 x 22 average
Detailed street atlases in black and white with index to streets.

Atlases available:
A-Z BIRMINGHAM (Gers) 50p
Library edition 85p
BIRMINGHAM AND W MIDLANDS (Inc. Coventry and Nuneaton) (Gia) 50p
A-Z BRISTOL, BATH, CARDIFF, CHELTENHAM, GLOUCESTER, NEWPORT, WESTON-SUPER-MARE (Gers) 45p
BRISTOL, BATH AND WESTON-SUPER-MARE (Gia) 50p
A-Z LEEDS AND BRADFORD (Gers) 50p
LEEDS (Gia) 45p
A-Z LIVERPOOL (Gers) 50p
MANCHESTER, GREATER (Gia) 55p
A-Z MANCHESTER (Gers) 50p
SHEFFIELD AND ROTHERHAM (Gia) 45p
STOKE ON TRENT, NEWCASTLE UNDER LYME (Gia) 55p
TYNESIDE (Newcastle, Gateshead, Sunderland etc) (Gia) 60p

STREET ATLAS SERIES
1:15,840 generally
Smarden, Kent : Estate Pubn's
11 x 15
Two colour atlases with street index.
Volumes available:

Ashford	022B	16pp	30p
Basildon-Brentwood	079A	32pp	45p
Brighton	043B	32pp	40p
Bromley	038A	40pp	35p
Chichester-Bognor Regis	0711A	16pp	35p
Crawley and Mid Sussex	059A	16pp	40p
Dartford-Gravesend	034B	32pp	40p
Dover-Folkestone	028A	32pp	30p
Sittingbourne-Faversham-Sheerness in Swale	031A	16pp	25p
Thanet-Canterbury-Herne Bay-Whitstable	040A	32pp	35p
Tunbridge Wells-Tonbridge	009B	32pp	40p
Worthing-Littlehampton	054A	32pp	35p
Fareham-Gosport	0701A	32pp	40p
Hastings-Eastbourne	042A	32pp	45p
Island Towns (Isle of Wight)	012B	16pp	30p
Maidstone	006B	32pp	35p
Medway-Gillingham	005B	32pp	40p
Portsmouth-Havant	069A	32pp	40p
Rye and Romney Marsh	029A	32pp	30p
Sevenoaks	058A	32pp	30p
Southend-on-Sea	078A	32pp	45p

ATLASES
E1 PHYSICAL - RELIEF

BARTHOLOMEW'S HALF-INCH LOOSE-LEAF ATLAS OF ENGLAND AND WALES
Edinburgh : Bart
50 x 60 (binder)
Containing 39 1:126,720 topographical maps mounted on linen, folded to fit loose-leaf binder. Replacement copies of revised plates can be supplied separately.
Atlas and binder £17.00
Replacement pages, each 30p

SURVEY ATLAS OF ENGLAND AND WALES
2nd edition
Edinburgh : Bart, 1939
46 x 30
Bartholomew's half-inch maps, with maps on geology and climate, town plans etc. with short index. 181 double page plates, 36pp text.
Bound in quarter morocco £25.00

ATLASES
H BIOGEOGRAPHY

ATLAS OF THE BREEDING BIRDS OF THE WEST MIDLANDS
Ed J Lord and D J Munns
Glasgow : Collins/West Midland Bird Club, 1970
13 x 20
276pp
Based on field survey of Warwickshire, Worcestershire, Staffordshire 1966-68. Showing species distribution by 10km OS National Grid squares with description on facing page.
£1.30

AN ATLAS OF THE BRYOPHYTES FOUND IN KENT
by A G Side
Maidstone : Transactions of the Kent Field Club, Vol. 4, 1970.
14 x 21
140pp
Indicates distribution of mosses and liverworts by 10km squares, ecological notes on each species.
£1.50

TYPE OF FARMING MAPS OF ENGLAND AND WALES
1:1,140,480
London : HMSO, 1968
20 x 30
Booklet with 11 black and white maps showing types of holdings. 1965 data. Notes. 40p

ATLASES
K HUMAN GEOGRAPHY

AN ATLAS OF POPULATION CHANGE 1952-66
THE YORKSHIRE AND HUMBERSIDE PLANNING REGION
by Dr D G Symes & E G Thomas
Hull : The University miscellaneous series No 8, 1968
21 x 34
16 folded population distribution maps in black and red; statistics and sources. With transparent overlay, containing geographical names.
Spiral bound £1.50

CHARACTER OF A CONURBATION: A COMPUTER ATLAS OF BIRMINGHAM AND THE BLACK COUNTRY
K E Rosing & P A Wood
London : Hodder & Stoughton, 1971
128pp
Analysis of 2 surveys in 1966; 1 for City of Birmingham, 1 for West Midland Conurbation. In 2 parts – study section and atlas. (22 paired maps). Covers social factors. £3.50

A SOCIAL ATLAS OF LONDON
by J W Shepherd, E J Westaway, T R Lee
Oxford : OUP, 1974
19 x 25
100pp
Showing the historical development of London with distribution of social and ethnic groups and resources.
boards £3.95
paper £1.75

ATLASES
L ECONOMIC

AN AGRICULTURAL ATLAS OF ENGLAND AND WALES
2nd Edition
Ed. J T Coppock
London : Faber and Faber, 1976
19 x 25
267pp
Includes 233 maps showing distribution of crops and livestock with descriptive text and analysis of statistics.
£12.00

NORTH WEST REGIONAL ATLAS
1:500,000
2nd Edition
London : Dept. of the Environment, 1975
31 x 42
Initial complement of 19 maps of various subjects including admin. boundaries, river/air pollution, housing and household conditions, roads and railways. New and revised sheets to be added at intervals.
Binder with 19 maps £8.37

ATLAS OF LONG-TERM IRRIGATION NEEDS FOR ENGLAND AND WALES
by W H Hogg
London : HMSO, 1969
Planning atlas of water requirements.
£2.07½

NORTH GLOUCESTERSHIRE SUB REGIONAL STUDY
1:253,440 (average scale)
N R Collins and others
Gloucester : Gloucestershire County Council, 1970
21 x 30
17 socio-administrative maps with 5 figures.

KINGSTON UPON HULL AND HALTEMPRICE. SOCIAL AREA ANALYSIS PART 1 – ATLAS
1:53,000
Hull : Univ. Geog. Dept., 1970
34 x 21
11 maps covering various social factors with 2 overlays. 25pp text. £1.20

NICHOLSONS GUIDES TO THE WATERWAYS
London : Nicholson
11 x 23
Series of detailed guides containing large scale strip maps 1:316,800 based on Ordnance Survey maps; with descriptive notes, incl. interesting features, places of interest and facilities. 75p
Guides published:
1 South East 1972
2 North West 1973
3 South West Area 1974
4 North East Area 1974
5 Midlands 1975
paper £1.50
cloth £2.95

THAMES GUIDE
Ed P Atterbury
London : R Nicholson Pubn's. 1969
11 x 23
48pp
Contains 98pp of detailed strip maps of the river side 1:125,000 based on O.S. maps. With detailed marginal notes.
paper £2.25
cloth £2.95
Also available in sections:
Thames – Oxford to Sonning 1975 £1.25
Thames – Sonning to Walton 1975 £1.25
Thames – Hampton Court to Greenwich 1975 £1.25

ATLASES
M HISTORICAL

THE ROYAL ENGLISH ATLAS : EIGHTEENTH-CENTURY COUNTY MAPS OF ENGLAND AND WALES
by Emanuel Bowen and Thomas Kitchin
Newton Abbot : David & Charles, 1971
30 x 47
14pp (44 maps)
Facsimile of 1763-1828 editions in British Museum of 44 engraved maps : 'The Royal English Atlas being a New and Accurate Set of Maps of all the Counties of South Britain. Drawn from Surveys . . . . Exhibiting all the Cities, Towns, Villages, Churches, Chapels etc.' £15.00

BRITANNIA. VOLUME THE FIRST: OR AN ILLUSTRATION OF THE KINGDOM OF ENGLAND AND WALES 1675
by John Ogilby
TOT series Y, vol. 2.
Amsterdam : Theatrum Orbis Terrarum, 1970
xxi, 200pp
100 plates. Facsimile atlas of the strip road maps with introduction by Dr J B Harley. Maps printed in black and white.
D.Fl. 360

OGILBY'S ROAD MAPS OF ENGLAND AND WALES, 1675
Reading : Osprey, 1971
27 x 40
420pp
Facsimile reproduction from the Britannia; 1st chart of English roads; established Eng. mile as 1760 yards. £10.00

BRITANNIA DEPICTA OR OGILBY IMPROVED, 1720
by Emanuel Bowen
Intro by Dr J B Harley
Newcastle-upon-Tyne : Frank Graham 1970
273pp
Facsimile copy of Bowen's Britannia Depicta (half scale version of Ogilby's Britannia) showing roads and topography.
£2.50

250 YEARS OF MAPMAKING IN THE COUNTY OF SUSSEX
Introduction R A Skelton
Lympne Castle (Kent) : Harry Margary, 1970
64 x 48
Selection of maps from 1579-1825
In 28 sheets, at various scales.
Facsimile eds.
Loose sheets £8.00
Card bound £9.00
Case bound £15.00

ORFORD NESS : A SELECTION OF MAPS MAINLY BY JOHN NORDEN
Cambridge : Heffer, 1966
31 x 25
22 maps (12 in colour)
A collection of 10 previously unpublished maps by Norden with other earlier and later maps of the neighbourhood of Orford. Produced as a tribute to Prof. J A Steers on his retirement. Includes a note on John Norden and a detailed bibliography of the writings of Prof. Steers. £4.20

PLANS OF ENGLISH TOWNS 1810
by G Cole and J Roper
Monmouth : Brian Stevens Historic Prints, 1970
21 plans from J Roper's "The British Atlas" of 1810. With title page, introductory note.
£1.00

AN ATLAS OF BOSTON
1st edition
Eds. F Molyneaux and N Wright
Boston, Lincs: Richard Kay Pubn's. 1974
21 x 30
Includes 9 reproductions of early maps with 15 original plans relevant to the history and development of the town.
£3.60

THE TOWN PLANS OF CHICHESTER 1595-1898
David J Butler
Chichester : West Sussex Council, 1972
28pp
10 plans reproduced in booklet, beginning with the inset on John Norden's Map of Sussex, 1595. With text and bibliog. list of street names. 50p

MAPS OF MANCHESTER, 1650-1848
Manchester : City of Manchester Cultural Committee, 1969.
55 x 43
6 facsimile maps in folder. £2.25

LONDON IN MAPS
by Philippa Glanville
London : Connoisseur, 1972
22 x 38
212pp
69 map plates, col. and black and white, covering London from the 13th C until the present day.
Descriptive text, bibliog. £15.00

SOUTHAMPTON MAPS – FROM ELIZABETHAN TIMES
Edited by E Welch
Southampton : Civic Record Office, 1964
46 x 36
A portfolio of 24 maps, 2 in colour showing the historical development of Southampton, with a separate introduction of 92pp including many illustrations £3.00
10 of the maps are available separately
each 15p

ATLASES
O NATIONAL

ATLAS OF PLANNING MAPS OF ENGLAND AND WALES (DESK ATLAS)
1:1,875,000 generally
London : Dept of the Environment, 1955
34 x 41
Atlas in 2 vols. currently containing 130 maps covering many socio-economic subjects including employment, housing and housing conditions and other planning topics.
Set £46.25
each individually 70p

ATLASES
P REGIONAL

ATLASES OF LONDON AND THE LONDON REGION
Ed Emrys Jones and D J Sinclair
Oxford : Pergamon, 1968
57 x 88
In 70 sheets, folded, coloured of London and the South East; covers social and environmental studies, physical, historical, admin. social maps (120 maps).
Complete £40.00

MERSEYSIDE IN MAPS
Ed J A Patmore and A G Hodgkiss (cart) (Liverpool University)
London : Collins – Longman, 1970 for Liverpool University
18 x 24
64pp
Reference atlas with maps of physical background, settlement evolution, transport, population and industry of the region. With analytical text.
£1.40

423.4 Channel Islands

A1 GENERAL MAPS : ROADS

CHANNEL ISLANDS
Various scales
Edinburgh : Bart
50 x 70
Maps of each of the major islands in the group, generally layer col. with roads, footpaths and all important topographical detail.
Paper 65p

A2 GENERAL MAPS : LOCAL

QUAIL MAP OF ALDERNEY
1:10,500
2nd Edition
Exeter : Quail Map Co, 1974
30 x 20
Black and white plan of island showing footpaths, bus route and topographical features. Brief factual guide on reverse.
15p

C OFFICAL SURVEYS

JERSEY – OFFICIAL MAP
1:25,000
Borehamwood : Hunting Surveys Ltd, 1968
84 x 60
Contoured; layer col, all classes of roads also tracks and footpaths. Woodland areas green; field boundaries and topographical detail.
85p

SARK
1:10,560
Series M 824
Feltham : Ministry of Defence
58 x 76
Showing island roads and those privately maintained, cliff paths, tracks, footpaths, woodland areas, spot heights and contours in feet.
25p

ALDERNEY
1:10,560
Series M 824
Feltham : Ministry of Defence
76 x 61
Showing roads, tracks, paths, spot heights and contours in feet and post offices. 25p

HERM AND JETHOU
1:10,000
Series M 824
Feltham : Ministry of Defence
43 x 62
Detailed topographical map showing contours and woodland in colour. Field boundaries, places and features named and offshore rocks depicted.
25p

M HISTORICAL

PHILIP DUMARESQ'S MAP OF JERSEY
1734.
London : RGS, 1970
46 x 38
A reproduction in colour of the map originally published in 1694.
£1.50

429 Wales

See also:

420 ENGLAND AND WALES
410 GREAT BRITAIN
41 BRITISH ISLES

A1 GENERAL MAPS: ROADS

WALES AND THE MARCHES
1:250,000
Southampton : OS, 1971
78 x 95
Anglesey – Liverpool and Pembroke – Bristol. Main and secondary roads, railways, ferries, airports, youth hostels, spot heights in feet, 200ft contour intervals, places of interest and county boundaries. Relief shading.
Paper folded 95p
Paper flat 85p

WALES – ROAD PROGRAMME MAP —Schemes costing over £250,000
1:250,000
Ref: W/TC/Rd/6/32
Cardiff : Welsh Office, 1976
96 x 97 96p

A2 GENERAL MAPS: LOCAL

30 MILES AROUND – NORTH WALES
1:126,720
Johnston & Bacon
see GREAT BRITAIN 410 A2.

SNOWDONIA NATIONAL PARK
1:126,720
Southampton : OS 1968 (1966)
71 x 86
Holyhead to Llandudno, Aberdaron to Machynlleth. Contour col, main and secondary roads, road numbers, railways, airports, ferries, youth hostels, places of interest, county boundaries.
Paper folded 95p
Paper flat 85p

VISITORS MAP OF GOWER PENINSULA
1:63,360
London : Gia
General map in black and white, showing roads, footpaths and tourist detail. 20p

THE MORAINES OF THE CWM IDWAL NATIONAL NATURE RESERVE
Brathay, Ambleside : Brathay Field Study Centre, 1971
56 x 39
Glacial map for the area. Field Studies Report No. 15.

K HUMAN GEOGRAPHY

WALES – MAJOR RECREATIONAL FACILITIES
1:385,000
Ref. W/O/R/7/8/
Cardiff: Welsh Office, 1975
52 x 71
Facilities marked by symbols 75p

WALES – HEALTH FACILITIES
Cardiff: Welsh Office, 1975
66 x 74
Series of maps for each of the eight new Welsh counties each 86p

D POLITICAL AND ADMINISTRATIVE

WALES – GENERAL REFERENCE MAP
1:385,000
Ref: W/T/G/7/39
Cardiff: Welsh Office, 1975
52 x 71
Showing county and district boundaries. 75p

WALES
1:250,000
Southampton : OS, 1973
82 x 96
Shows new counties and districts in red on a grey base. It is also available with both old and new counties. each £1.50

WALES – COUNTIES AND DISTRICTS
1:250,000
Ref: W/2G/AA/6/18
Cardiff: Welsh Office, 1974
83 x 97
Administrative map 91p

WALES
1:250,000
Ref: W/E/E/6/1
Cardiff: Welsh Office 1975
83 x 97
Showing counties and districts. Dept. of Employment local office areas and assisted areas. 91p

M HISTORICAL

HISTORICAL MAP OF WALES AND MONMOUTH
Edinburgh : Bart, 1966
56 x 70
Brightly coloured map, illustrating battles, castles, places and characters well-known in history. Surrounding the map are the Coats of Arms of cities and towns.
Paper, each 50p
Cloth, each 60p

EARLY MAP REPRODUCTION FROM BLAEU'S 'THEATRUM ORBIS TERRARUM – ATLAS NOVUS'
Plate : Wales 1648
Edinburgh : Bart, 1966+
61 x 51
This important atlas was published in a number of volumes during the 17th Century and coloured reproductions of certain individual plates are available. £1.50

SAXTONS COUNTY MAPS OF ENGLAND AND WALES
British Museum
see ENGLAND AND WALES 420 M.

ATLASES
M HISTORICAL

ATLAS HANESYDDOL CYMRU (HISTORICAL ATLAS OF WALES)
Editor J Idwal Jones
2nd revised edition
Cardiff : University of Wales Press 1972
19 x 24
137pp
Black and white sketch maps with facing page of descriptive text describing the social, religious and economic history from earliest times to the present day. Text throughout in Welsh. £1.50

ATLASES
O NATIONAL

WELSH OFFICE ATLAS
Cardiff : Welsh Office, 1974
44 x 55
Series of coloured thematic maps of Wales contained in a screw binder.
Sheets published to date:

1 General Reference Map
2 Administrative Areas (Pre 1974)
2A Administrative Areas (Post 1974)
3 Parliamentary Constituencies
4 Population – Total Change 1965-70
5 Population – National Change 1965-70
6 Population – Net Migration 1965-70
7 Forestry
8 Traffic Volumes 1965
8A Traffic Volumes 1972
9 Rate support Grants
10 Local Office Areas and Assisted Areas
11 Water Resources
12 Energy Facilities
13 Derelict Land 1971/72

each 45p
set of 15 maps £7.85

ATLASES
P REGIONAL

AN ATLAS OF ANGLESEY
Editor Melville Richards
1st edition
Llangefni : Anglesey Community Council 1972.
23 x 29
160pp
Divided into 59 chapters each dealing with a specific topic ranging from physical background, history and trade, to education, language and place names. Each subject depicted by black and white maps (two in colour) and photographs. £2.50

430 Germany

A1 GENERAL MAPS: ROADS

DEUTSCHLAND
1:1,000,000
No 875
Frankfurt : Ravenstein
80 x 100
Roads classified and numbered, distances in km, other communications, places of tourist interest.
DM 6.80

SHELL REISEKARTE DEUTSCHLAND
1:1,000,000
Stuttgart : Mair, 1972
63 x 38
Inc. E. Germany. Reversible col. map, showing main roads, places of tourist interest, etc. Legend in 12 languages.
DM 4.80

GERMANIA E AUSTRIA
1:1.000,000
Novara : Agostini
98 x 98
Coloured road and tourist map.
L 700

DEUTSCHLAND
1:800,000
No 80
Stuttgart : RV
Col. road map route numbers, distances and showing places of tourist interest.
DM 8,80

DEUTSCHLAND
1:800,000
No 868
Frankfurt: Ravenstein
88 x 112
Detailed road map of East and West Germany with index to places.
DM 8.80

NÉMET DEMOKRATIKUS KÖZTÁRSASÁG, NÉMET SZÖVETSÉGI KÖZTÁRSASÁG, NYUGAT-BERLIN AUTOTÉRKÉPE
1:800,000
Budapest : Cart, 1971
Road map of East and West Germany. Insets of E and W Berlin and other main towns.

DEUTSCHLAND STRASSENKARTE
1:750,000
1st edition, No. 36
Bruxelles : R de Rouck
110 x 61
Double sided map, roads classified with distances, index to places.
50 B fr

AUTOKARTE
1:700,000
Berlin : Schaffmann & Kluge
100 x 124
Shows State boundaries; 14 city through plans
DM 6.80

VERKEHRSWANDKARTE DEUTSCHLAND
1:500,000
No 3566, in 2 sheets
München : JRO
138 x 199
Col. wall map showing communications - road and rail etc. Available mounted as 1 sheet, or as 2 separate sheets. Index.
DM 67
Mounted CR DM 172
Index DM 25

SHELL REISEKARTE
In 2 sheets : Nord-deutschland and Sud-deutschland
1:550,000
Stuttgart : Mair
Road map in col. Roads classified and numbered, distances in km; places of tourist interest, motoring details.
Each DM 4.80

NORDDEUTSCHLAND
1:500,000
No 1122
Bern : K & F, 1972/3
125 x 89
Inc. E. Germany. Arnheim – Stettin, Köln – S Denmark. Roads classified, railways; size of towns. places of interest, boundaries.

C OFFICIAL SURVEYS

DEUTSCHLAND IN DER GRENZEN VON 1937
1:1,000,000
Frankfurt: Inst. für Angewandte Geodäsie
100 x 140
Contoured, layer coloured map with road and rail communications, showing Germany with borders as at 1937. 12 colours.
DM 9.50
Also available in following editions:
OH – Orohydrographic ed. DM 8.50
V – Verwaltungsgrenzen – admin boundaries DM 9.00

INTERNATIONAL MAP OF THE WORLD
1:1,000,000
Frankfurt am Main : Inst für Angewandte Geodäsie
Sheets : NN 32 Hamburg
NM 32 München
see WORLD 100C and index 100/1A

INTERNATIONAL MAP OF THE WORLD (UBERSICHTSKARTE)
1:1,000,000
Frankfurt am Main: Inst für Angewandte Geodäsie
Set of 6 maps not fully conforming to IMW standards completing the coverage of Germany and adjacent areas in this style.
Sheets:

NL	32pt	Mittl Alpengebiet
	33pt	Ostl Alpengebiet
NM	33	Wien
	34	Oberschlesien
NN	33	Berlin
NN	34	Ostpreussen

Each DM 3,90
The same sheets also available in Morphological editions:

1	Water only
2	Contours and layer colours only
3	Water, contours and layers colours
4	Water and contours
5	Topography with communications, water and contours

Each DM 3.30

ÜBERSICHTSKART VON MITTELEUROPA
1:300,000
See Index 430/1
Frankfurt am Main : Inst für Angewandt Geodäsie
Old series covering from Rouen – Smolensk – Helsinki – Klagenfurt.
Relief by hachures, principal roads in red, woodland in green. Available in 2 editions :
A 1 or 2 colours DM 1.40
B 5 or 6 colours DM 2,00

TOPOGRAPHISCHE ÜBERSICHTSKARTE DES DEUTSCHEN REICHES
1:200,000
See index 430/2
Frankfurt am Main : Inst für Angewandte Geodäsie
Old topographical series, in black and white with contours in brown and water in blue, covering area pre 1937 Germany.
Normal edition DM 1.90
Morphologic edition (contours and water only) DM 1.60

KARTE DES DEUTSCHEN REICHES
1:100,000
KDR 100
See index 430/3 and 4
Frankfurt am Main : Inst für Angewandte Geodäsie (pre 1937 Germany)
Landvermessüngsamts (W Germany)
Black and white topog. series produced end 19th Century. Being superseded by TK 100.
Relief by hachuring.

Ed C Quarter sheet	DM 0.80
Ed D1 Half sheet	DM 1.70
Ed D1 Large sheet	DM 2,70
Ed D2 Large sheet, 5 colours	DM 3.20

D POLITICAL & ADMINISTRATIVE

DEUTSCHLANDSKARTE
1:1,800,000
No 250
Hof (Saale): Fritsch
School map showing pre-1937 boundaries.
DM 2.00

WANDATLAS DEUTSCHLAND
1:1,250,000
Frankfurt : Keyers
113 x 84
Political wall map with 1937 boundaries.
DM 30

DEUTSCHLAND
1:1,250,000
Novara : Agostini
100 x 140
Political wall map. L 1,600

KARTE DER DEUTSCHEN LÄNDER
1:1,000,000

Frankfurt : Schwarz
85 x 94
Political col. map showing district (Kreise) boundaries, road and rail communications. With gazetteer. Ruhr area inset at 1:500,000.
Available in the following eds :
Representative areas DM 6
New Post areas DM 7
Political by States DM 7
Industrial and Trade Divisions DM 9.50
Waterways DM 9,50

"KLEINER GEOGRAPHISCHER WANDATLAS" – DEUTSCHLAND
1:1,000,000
Darmstadt : Perthes
136 x 100
Political wall map.

SCHULWANDKARTE DEUTSCHLAND
1:750,000
No 9432
München : JRO
185 x 123
Political col. wall map showing 1937 boundaries.
Mounted CR DM 128

ALLEMAGNE NO 1 (PHYSIQUE)
1:750,000
Political map on reverse
see GERMANY 430 E1

POLITISCHE ÜBERSICHTS DEUTSCHLAND
1:700,000
No 237
Braunschweig : Westermann, 1971
204 x 194
Political wall map covering the whole of Germany, inc. former States.

DEUTSCHLAND UND NACHBAR-LÄNDER
1:700,000
Braunschweig : Westermann
204 x 104
Political school wall map, covering much of Central Europe; National and provincial capitals underlined, cities graded by pop, communications.

KLEINE ORGANISATIONSKARTE
1:2,000,000
Berlin : Schaffmann & Kluge
37 x 51
Planning map showing boundaries with 3 regional insets. DM 2.50

ORGANISATIONS- UND VERKEHRS-KARTE VON WEST-UND MITTEL-DEUTSCHLAND
1:1,000,000
Berlin : Gea Verlag
75 x 105
Col. map showing State admin. boundaries.

VERWALTUNGSKARTE
1:1,000,000
No 74
Stuttgart : RV
80 x 97
Administrative map showing boundaries in colour. DM 5,80
Also available in smaller edition at 1:2,100,000 DM 3,80

VERWAL TUNGSGRENZENKARTE VON DEUTSCHLAND
1:1,000,000
Bonn - Bad Godesberg, 1960
Coloured map of admin. districts, with natural land divisions. List of natural region authorities on reverse. DM 4

VERKEHRSKARTE DEUTSCHLAND
1:1,000,000
Berlin : Gea Verlag
140 x 110
Pre 1937 borders. Col. admin. map on white background. Communications.
Paper DM 8,40
Mounted CR DM 82,50

DEUTSCHLAND – VERWALTUNGS-GLIEDERUNG
1:900,000
H 235
München : Paul List Verlag, 1971
160 x 120
Harms administrative wall map, showing boundaries and town pop. with the borders as of 1937. DM 112.00

DEUTSCHLAND
1:800,000
No 400
Frankfurt : Ravenstein, 1975
86 x 120
Planning map with principal towns, boundaries and communications. Index to places DM 12.80
Also available with postal boundaries over-printed DM 13.80

ARBEITSKARTE DEUTSCHLAND
1:750,000
No 9773
München : JRO
185 x 123
2 colour base map, with plastic writing surface. DM 108

VERWALTUNGSKARTE DEUTSCHLAND
1:750,000
No 3772
München : JRO
88 x 116
Political col. map showing district boundaries and autobahn. With gazetteer. DM 12.80
Mounted CR DM 52

BÜRO- UND VERWALTUNGSKARTE
1:700,000
Berlin : Schaffmann & Kluge
100 x 140
Col. admin. map showing national and local boundaries. DM 13,80
Mounted CR DM 62,80

ARBEITSKARTE FÜR MARKT- UND ABSATZFORSCHUNG
1:500,000
No 72/73
Stuttgart : RV
120 x 166 complete
2 sheet map for market and distribution research purposes. Showing admin. boundaries, towns etc. in col. on white background. In 2 eds: With communications each DM 22
Without DM 17

BÜRO- UND VERKEHRSKARTE
1:500,000
Goppingen : Wohrle
113 x 165
Col. admin. map on white background. Extends to Berlin, showing roads and boundaries.
Paper DM 16
Mounted CR DM 105,50

DEUTSCHE VERKEHRS- UND VERTRETERBEZIRKSKARTE
1:500,000
In 4 sheets
Frankfurt : Ravenstein
70 x 98 each
Planning map with communications, admin. boundaries on white background map. With gazetteer, inc list of districts (Bezirke) and their populations.
Sheets:
81 Dusseldorf – Hamburg
82 Braunschweig – Berlin
83 Frankfurt – Stuttgart
84 Erfurt – München
Each sheet DM 18.00
Gazetteer DM 8.00
Also available with postal districts over-printed each DM 19.00

DEUTSCHLAND
1:500,000
No 3565, in 2 sheets
München : JRO
138 x 199
Shows boundaries, districts (Landkreise), roads, railways and stations. DM 60
Mounted DM 165
Also available with old postal districts overprinted (No 3567) each DM 36

POSTLEITGEBIETE
1:1,000,000
No 11
Frankfurt : Schwarz
85 x 94
Col. map showing postal areas and boundaries. DM 7

POSTLEITKARTE
1:750,000
No 3774
München : JRO
88 x 116
Postal zones map for E and W Germany.
Folded DM 12,80
Mounted CR DM 52

POSTLEITKARTE
1:700,000
Berlin : Schaffmann & Kluge
100 x 140
Col. map of postal districts on green background. DM 17,50
Mounted CR DM 66,50

WANDKARTE DEUTSCHLAND MIT ALTEN POSTLEITGEBIETEN
1:500,000
No 3567
München : JRO
138 x 199
Col. wall map with former postal districts DM 36
Mounted CR DM 141

UMRISSKARTE DEUTSCHLAND
1:3,000,000
No. 0816
Bern : K & F
46 x 38
Outline map with rivers and borders.

E1 PHYSICAL : RELIEF

WANDATLAS DEUTSCHLAND
1:1,250,000
München : Keysers
113 x 84
Physical wall map. DM 30

GERMANIA FISICO-POLITICA
1:1,250,000
Novara : Agostini
140 x 100
School wall map showing relief of land and sea, water features, major communications, political boundaries, towns graded by pop. L 2,200
Mounted L 5,000
Also available in German edition.

NIEMIECKA REPUBLIKA DEMO-KRATYCZNA NIEMIECKA REPUBLIKA FEDERALNA
1:1,000,000
Warszawa : PPWK, 1972/3
69 x 90
Physical general wall map covering E and W Germany. Shows contours, communications etc. Pol. text on reverse. In series "Mapa Przegla-dowa Europy" (Review Maps of Europe) Zl 12

'KLEINER GEOGRAPHISCHER WANDATLAS' SERIES – DEUTSCHLAND
1:1,000,000
Darmstadt : Perthes
136 x 100
Physical wall map. DM 48

ALLEMAGNE No 1 (PHYSIQUE)
1:750,000
No 1156
St Germain-en-Laye : Éditions MDI
92 x 126
Plastic coated physical wall map for schools. Political and industrial map on reverse.

ALLEMAGNE
1:750,000
TC 43 (No 1612)
St Germain-en-Laye: Éditions MDI
92 x 126
Plastic coated physical wall map for schools. Scandinavia on reverse at 1:1,700,000

DEUTSCHLAND
1:750,000
No 9771
München : JRO
185 x 123
Physical col. wall map of E and W Germany, with 'Arbeitskarte" (2 col. map with plastic surface for writing on) on reverse. DM 138
No 9772 – as above, without "Arbeitskarte" DM 128

DEUTSCHLAND
1:700,000
H 201
München : Paul List Verlag
200 x 220
Harms physical wall map, layer col. and relief shaded, boundaries and towns. German borders as at 1937 and including Benelux, Alps, N Italy and Czechoslovakia. DM 142

DEUTSCHLAND
1:600,000
W818
München : Paul List Verlag
250 x 170
Wenschow physical wall map, layer col, relief shading, principal communications, boundaries and towns. Boundaries as at 1937 including W Poland, W Czechoslovakia and Benelux. DM 164.00

DEUTSCHLAND
1:600,000
No 9782
München : JRO
258 x 175
Physical colour wall map on linen. DM 164.00

MITTEL- UND OSTDEUTSCHLAND
1:400,000
W817
München : Paul List Verlag
245 x 170
Wenschow physical wall map, layer col, with relief shading, principal communications, boundaries and towns. Covering central and eastern Germany to include E Russia. DM 164.00

GERMANIA
1:1,250,000
Novara : Agostini
122 x 97
Plastic moulded relief map in frame with metal corners. L 20,000

E2 PHYSICAL : LAND FEATURES

NATURRÄUMLICHE GLIEDERUNG DEUTSCHLANDS
1:200,000
See Index 430/5
Bad Godesberg : Inst. für Landeskunde
56 x 37
Series in progress, showing natural divisions of Germany; based on geomorphology, vegetation, soils, climate, drainage. With text. DM 7.35
Double sheets DM 8.75

G EARTH RESOURCES

KARTE DER ERDMAGNETISCHEN MISSWEISUNG
1:1,000,000
Berlin : Dietrich Reimer, 1954
75 x 108
Coloured map showing magnetic declination for the 1954 period. DM 24

J CLIMATE

VERHÄLTNIS VON SOMMER- ZU WINTERNIEDERSCHLAG (RELATION BETWEEN SUMMER AND WINTER RAINFALL)
1:1,000,000
Offenbach : Deutscher Wetterdienst, 1964
70 x 95
Col. climatic map, taking study from 1891-1930. In folder DM 6.80

MITTLERE NIEDERSCHLAGSSUMEN (MM) FÜR DIE BUNDESREPUBLIK DEUTSCHLAND, JAHR UND HYDROLOGISCHE HALBJAHRE, ZEITRAUM 1891-1930
Ed. H. Schirmer
Offenback : Deutscher Wetterdienst, 1960
Average annual rainfall and run off for period 1891 - 1930 3 Maps and 3pp Text DM 12.30

KARTENWERK : MITTLERE JAHRSSUMMEN DES NIEDERSCHLAGS (MM) FÜR DAS GEBIET DER BUNDESREPUBLIK, ZEITRAUM 1891-1930
1:200,000
Ed. H. Schirmer
Offenbach : Deutscher Wetterdienst 1955
Collection of 46 maps showing average annual rainfall in Germany for the period 1891-1930 DM 13.50

K HUMAN GEOGRAPHY

KATHOLISCHE BEVÖLKERUNG IN DEN DEUTSCHEN DIOZESEN
1:1,000,000
Paderborn : Bonifacius
54 x 63
Col. map of the catholic population with political and ecclesiastical boundaries.

BISTÜMER DER KATHOLISCHEN KIRCHE IN DER BRD UND DDR (DIOCESES IN EAST AND WEST GERMANY)
1:1,000,000
Bonn – Bad Godesberg : Inst. für Landeskunde, 1969
Map in colour, showing Catholic dioceses at 1967.

L ECONOMIC

DEUTSCHLAND, WIRTSCHAFT
1:600,000
Braunschweig : Westermann
196 x 240
Showing main industries, mineral resources, agriculture, main communications. School wall map.

VERKEHRSWANDKARTE
1:500,000
No 3566
München : JRO
138 x 199
Col. wall map showing road, rail, air communications network and state boundaries. DM 67
Mounted CR DM 172
Index Col. DM 25

M HISTORICAL

HISTORISCHER WANDKARTEN
Darmstadt : Perthes
Series of col. historical wall maps.
Maps available :
900 Das Frankenreich 486-911
1:1,000,000
901 Deutschland und Italien im Zeitalter der sächsischen und salischen Kaiser 911-1125
1:1,000,000

902 Deutschland und Italien im Zeitalter der Hohenstaufen 1125-1273, 1:1,000,000
903 Deutschland im Spätmittelalter 1273-1437, 1:1,000,000
904 Deutschland im Zeitalter der Reformation 1438-1555, 1:750,000
905 Deutschland im Zeitalter der Gegenreformation 1555-1648 1:750,000
906 Deutschland im Zeitalter des Reichszerfalls 1648-1739
907 Deutschland zur Zeit Friedrichs des Grossen und der Französischen Revolution 1740-1801, 1:750,000
908 Deutschland zur Zeit der Napoleonischen Kriege 1802-1814, 1:750,000
909 Deutschland im Zeitalter nationaler einigung und sozialer Bewegung 1815-1918, 1:750,000
910 Die Weimarer Republik 1918-33 1:600,000
911 Deutschland unter der Hitler-Diktatur 1933-1945, 1:600,000
912 Deutschland nach dem 2 Weltkrieg 1945-65, 1:600,000

Varying sizes and prices.

HISTORISCHER WANDKARTEN
Various scales
Braunschweig : Westermann
Series of col. historical wall maps.
Maps available:
309 Das Reich Karls des Grossen 1:2,000,000 206 x 139
324 Mitteleuropa im 16 Jahrhundert 1:1,000,000 201 x 139
303 Mittel- und Osteuropa nach dem 30-jahrigen Kriege 1:1,000,000 202 x 140
300 Deutschland 1789 und Europa bis 1815 1:750,000 207 x 140
237 Deutschland und Nachbarlander (political) 1:700,000 204 x 194

HISTORISCHER WANDKARTEN
1:750,000
Gotha : Haack
220 x 180
Large col. historical wall maps.
Maps available:
Zur Deutschen Geschichte im 10 und 11 Jahrhundert (Ger. hist. 10th, 11th C) With text. 1:1,000,000 160 x 170
Zur Deutschen Geschichte 1815-1871 With text.
Deutschland 1871-1914. With text.
Zur Deutschen Geschichte 1918-1939 With Text.

BREASTED-HUTH-HARDING HISTORICAL WALL MAPS
Chicago : Denoyer-Geppert
112 x 81
Col. wall maps printed on stout manilla for schoolroom use.
204301 Germany at the time of the Reformation, 1547.
204401 Growth of Prussia and Modern Germany

PUTZGER HISTORICAL WALL MAPS
Bielefeld : Cornelsen, Velhagen & Klasing
Col. historical wall maps.
Maps available:
Die mittelalterliche deutsche Ostsiedlung (German Eastern settlements in the Middle Ages) 1:900,000, 138 x 193
Österreich und Preussen bis 1795 1:2,500,000, 196 x 137
Südwestdeutschland um 1789 1:750,000, 152 x 223

HISTORISCHE WANDKARTEN
1:81,250
Hamburg : Flemming
202 x 162
2 historical wall maps :
Deutschland im 17 Jahrhundert
Deutschland im 19 Jahrhundert

DEUTSCHLAND 1789
1:1,000,000
München : List
155 x 145
Harms historical wall map in colour with text in German.
DM 92.00

VIERMAL DEUTSCHLAND IM 20 JAHRHUNDERT
1:1,500,000
H 295
München : Paul List Verlag
240 x 180
4 col. historical maps of Germany as one wall map, depicting the changing borders in 1871-1918, 1919-1933, 1933-1945, 1945.

DEUTSCHLAND 1789
1:1,000,000
H 298
München : Paul List Verlag
155 x 145
Col. historical wall map with separate explanatory text in German.

UNIFICATION OF GERMANY
Indianapolis : Cram
School wall map showing German Confederation 1815-1866 and German Empire 1866-1871. US $13.75

UNIFICATION OF GERMANY
Chicago : Rand McNally
50 x 46
Col. historical wall map, showing Bismarck's Empire.

CARTE MURALE ISSAC : L'UNITÉ ALLEMANDE
Paris : Hachette
90 x 90
Col. wall map illustrating German unifcation in the 19th C.

DEUTSCHLAND IM XX JAHRHUNDERT
No 9402
München : JRO
96 x 120
Historical wall map of 20th C Germany for schools.
Mounted CR DM 56
No 9422, 133 x 175 (enlarged version) DM 108

JUNGSCHE STRASSENKARTE VON DEUTSCHLAND – 'TOTIUS GERMANIAE NOVUM ITINERARIUM STUDIO ET OPERE JUNGIORUM ELABORATUM'
By J G Jung, G C Jung, Rothenberg, 1641
Bonn-Bad Godesberg: Kirschbaum Verlag
60 x 45
Facsimile in black and white of the Jung's road map of Germany 1641. Covering central Europe and includes an explanatory text by W Bonacker. DM 18.80

ATLASES
A1 GENERAL: ROADS

ARAL AUTOBUCH
Dortmund : Aral, 1970/1
648pp
Road book covering both States: motorways, European roads, town plans with street indexes, places of tourist interest.
DM 28

DER AKTUELLE AUTO-ATLAS DEUTSCHLAND UND EUROPA: STRASSEN
No 802
Frankfurt : Ravenstein, 1976
21 x 28
Road atlas of Germany 1:400,000 with smaller scale maps for central and western Europe with details for motorists and tourists. New ed. each year.
DM 7.50

DIE BEIDEN DEUTSCHEN STAATEN
Berlin : VEB Lv
156pp
Pocket atlas of West and East Germany; 40pp maps with tables and index.
DM 5.80

DEUTSCHLAND, TASCHENATLAS
1:1,000,000
K 610
München : Kompass
Pocket road atlas covering East and West Germany. DM 18.50

ATLASES
J CLIMATE

KLIMA-ATLANTEN
Offenbach: Deutscher Wetterdienst
Series of climatic atlases for the german provinces (Land)
Volumes published:

Hessen	1950 75 maps 9 diagrams 20pp text DM 22.50
Bayern	1952 79 maps 8 diagrams 23pp text DM 47.00
Baden-Württemberg	1953 75 maps 9 diagrams 37pp text DM 30.00
Rheinland-Pfalz	1957 77 maps 9 diagrams 37pp text DM 32.00
Nordrhein-Westfalen	1960 77 maps 10 diagrams 38pp text DM 44.00
Niedersachsen	1964 77 maps 8 diagrams 38pp text DM 63.00
Schleswig-Holstein, Hamburg und Bremen	1967 63 maps 11 diagrams 43pp text DM 92.00

ATLASES
K HUMAN GEOGRAPHY

ATLAS DER DEUTSCHEN VOLKSKUNDE
Ed Matthias Zender
Marburg : Elwert, 1959-76
in 8 parts
Folk tradition atlas based on work done in 1929-35. 4 parts available – maps, covering population and social customs, feasts, charms, village life, women at work etc. With texts for each section.
Part 1 maps 1-12, 1958;
Part 2 maps 13-24, 1959;
Part 3 maps 25-36, 1963;
Part 4 maps 37-48, 1965
Part 5 maps 41-60, 1974;

Part 6 in preparation c. 110.00 DM.
Map sections 1-5 each DM 56.00
Texts:
1. Everyday life, festivals past and present 1967 DM 66.00
2. Word Geography of names for coffin, 1967 DM 32.00
3. Motives and motivations of sayings and beliefs 1974 DM 270.00

DEUTSCHER SPRACHATLAS
Marburg: N.G. Elwert Verlag
Series of language atlases showing distribution of word variations.
1. Siebenbürgisch – deutscher Sprachatlas
   Editors K. K. Klein and L. E. Schmitt
   Vol. 1 Sound and Form Atlas Part 1
   60 maps 1962 DM 68.00
   Part 2 93 maps 1964 DM 105.40
   Vol. II Word Atlas – in preparation
   Vol. III Text Volume – in preparation
2. Luxemburgischer Sprachatlas
   Editor L E Schmitt
   Vol. I Sound and Form Atlas 175 maps
   1963 DM 170.00
   Vol. II Word Atlas in preparation
3. Tirolischer Sprachatlas
   Editors K.K. Klein and L E Schmitt
   Vol. I Vowels 75 maps 1965 DM 100.00
   Vol.II Consonance, vowel types, accidence
   98 maps 1969 DM 135.00
   Vol. III Word Atlas, 110 Maps 1971
   DM 180.00
4. Schlesischer Sprachatlas
   Editor L E Schmitt
   Vol. I Sound and Form Atlas 98 maps
   1967 DM 220.00
   Vol.II Word Atlas 91 maps 1965
   DM 96.00
5. Linguistic Atlas of Texas German
   Editor G G Gilbert
   146 maps 1972 DM 222.00

WESTJIDDISCHER SPRACHATLAS
Editor F J Beranek
Marburg: N G Elwert Verlag 1965
224pp with 109 maps
Distribution atlas of Yiddish language.
DM 88.00

ATLASES
M HISTORICAL

BLAEU'S ATLAS VON DEUTSCHLAND
Gutersloh : Bertelsmann, 1972
32 x 53
418pp
Volume 3 of Joan Blaeu's Grosser Weltatlas; facsimile ed. 94 double page maps, mainly in col, 3 folded maps. Numbered editions.
Leather bound DM 495

HISTORISCH – GEOGRAPHISCHER ATLAS DES PREUSSENLANDES
Ed H & G Mortensen, Reinhard Wenskus
Wiesbaden : Franz Steiner, 1967+
56 x 63 (map size)
In 4-5 parts, historical and geographic survey of the former Prussian Empire.

Part 1	3 maps, 1968	DM 112
Part 2	4 maps, 1970	DM 84
Part 3	4 maps, 1971	DM 92
Part 4	3 maps, 1976	DM 180.00

HÄNSISCHE HANDELSTRASSEN
Hugo Weczerka
Koln : Bohlau Verlag, 1962
History of Hanseatic trade routes. Vol. 8, part 1 contains atlas of 50 maps showing the trading pattern of the League.

430.1 Federal Republic of Germany

See also : 430 GERMANY

A1 GENERAL MAPS : ROADS

ROAD MAP OF GERMANY
1:1,000,000
Bern : Hallwag, 1972
67 x 101
All classes of roads, distances in km, spot heights in metres, railways, car ferries, principal car camping sites, state boundaries and hill shading.

GERMANY - BENELUX.- AUSTRIA
1:1,000,000
Ref 987
Paris : Michelin, 1971
109 x 98
All classes of roads, road conditions and widths, distances in km, scenic routes and state boundaries.

DEUTSCHLAND
1:1,000,000
No 61
Stuttgart : RV
70 x 95
Road map showing motorways, main and secondary roads. DM 4.80

DEUTSCHLAND
1:1,000,000
No 1148
Bern : K & F, 1972/3
77 x 92
Political col. map; roads classified and numbered, distances in km, scenic routes, other communications, motels, camping sites.

DEUTSCHLAND
1:1,000,000
No 185
München : JRO
68 x 88
10 cols, classifies and numbers roads, distances in km, relief shading, tourist details. DM 4.80

GERMANY
1:1,000,000
London : Foldex
Shows roads classified, relief shading; patent folding. 45p

DEUTSHLAND AUTOKARTE
1:1,000,000
No 303
München : Kompass
67 x 96
Shows boundaries, railways. DM 4.90

GROSSE DEUTSCHLANDKARTE
1:800,000
No 80
Stuttgart : RV, 1972/3
84 x 119
Roads classified and numbered, distances in km, contour colouring, hill shading, railways, accommodation, places of interest. DM 7.80

DEUTSCHLAND STRASSENKARTE
1:750,000
No 1771
München : JRO
85 x 116
Classifies roads with route numbers; railways; relief shading; places of tourist interest. DM 6.80
Mounted CR DM 46
Index DM 3

DEUTSCHLAND
1:550,000
In 2 sheets
Bern : Hallwag, 1971/2
94 x 67 each
All classes of roads, numbered with distances; places of interest, state and national boundaries. North and South sheets. Legend Eng, Fr, Ger.

CARTA STRADALE D'EUROPA
1:500,000
In 2 sheets
Nos 18 and 19
Milano : TCI
114 x 76
All classes or roads, distances in km, spot heights, railways, car ferries, state boundaries and contour colouring.
Each L 1350
see also EUROPE 4 A1

ÜBERSICHTLICHE VERKEHRSKARTEN DER BUNDESREPUBLIK DEUTSCHLAND
1:500,000
In 3 sheets
München : JRO
Roads classified and numbered, railways and stations, relief shading, spot heights in metres.
1541 Süddeutschland, 117 x 88 DM 6.80
1542 Nord- und Westdeutschland 88 x 117 DM 6.80
1543 Bayern (part of 1541) 78 x 88 DM 4.80

DEUTSCHE STRASSENKARTE
1:400,000
In 4 sheets
Frankfurt : Ravenstein
84 x 50 each sheet
Col. series showing roads classified and numbered, distances in km, motoring details. Reversible.
Sheets available :
601 Nordblatt
602 Westblatt
603 Südwestblatt
604 Südblatt
Each DM 5.40

JRO GROSSRAUM-STRASSENKARTEN VON DEUTSCHLAND
1:300,000
See index 430. 1/1, 2
München : JRO
123 x 88
Col. map series covering the whole of W Germany. Roads classified and numbered, distances in km, boundaries, railways.
1301 München
1302 Stuttgart
1303 Nürnberg
1304 Frankfurt - Mannheim
1305 Dusseldorf - Köln
1306 Hannover - Bremen
1307 Hamburg - Kiel
Each DM 6.80

SPECIAL LOCALISED ROAD MAPS COVERING POPULAR TOURING AREAS:
1311 Baden-Wurttemberg, 88 x 123 DM 6.80
1369 Bayern, 123 x 145 (Nos 1301 and 1303 together) DM 14

SMALLER FORMAT SERIES WITH TOURIST INFORMATION – POCKET SIZE
1321 Oberbayern - Tirol 98 x 68
1322 Ostbayern 68 x 98
1323 Schwarzwald - Vogesen 98 x 68
1324 Der Main, 98 x 68
1325 Rheinland - Pfalz - Saarland 68 x 98
Each DM 4.80

DEUTSCHE STRASSENKARTE
1:250,000
In 9 sheets, see index 430. 1/3
Frankfurt : Ravenstein
Col. road map series, numbered with distances.
Sheets :
201 Neckar - Schwarzwald - Bodensee 80 x 100 Index DM 7.80
202 Mittelrhein - Pfalz - Saar 100 x 80 DM 7.20
203 Ruhrgebiet 80 x 100 DM 7.20
204 Schleswig - Holstein 80 x 100 DM 7.20
208 Hessen 80 x 100 Index DM 7.80
214 Harz - Heide - Weser 88 x 100 Index DM 7.80
236 Oberbayern - Nordtirol 100 x 80 DM 7.20
237 Nordostbayern mit Bayerischern Wald 100 x 88 DM 7.20

DEUTSCHE GENERALKARTE
1:200,000
In 26 sheets
see index 430. 1/4
Stuttgart : Mair
80 x 43
All classes of roads, footpaths, recommended hiking routes, distances in km, spot heights in metres, car ferries, railways, airports, scenic routes, youth hostels, camping sites, points of interest, state frontiers, hill shading. DM 4.50

SÜDDEUTSCHLAND
1:500,000
No 1122
Bern : K & F 1970
128 x 92
Koblenz to Hof and Basle to Salzburg. All classes of roads, road numbering, scenic routes, distances in km, car ferries, railways, camping sites, motels and state frontiers.

BODENSEE-SCHWARZWALD-ELSASS-VOGESEN
1:250,000
No 1104
Bern : K & F
129 x 92
Road map with relief shading, all classes of roads, distances, scenic routes and places of interest.

MICHELIN ROAD MAP OF GERMANY (RHINELAND)
1:200,000
In 5 sheets, see index 430. 1/5
Paris : Michelin, 1971/2
All classes of roads, distances in km, spot heights, railways, airports and scenic routes. Legend in Ger, easily identified symbols.

RV STRASSEN- UND TOURENKARTEN
1:200,000
Stuttgart : RV
Various sizes
Roads classified and numbered, scenic routes, places of interest, paths, youth hostels, camping sites.
Available for :
50 60 km um Stuttgart DM 6.80
51 Oberbayern – Tirol – Dolomiten DM 7.80
52 60 km um Mannheim – Ludwigshafen – Heidelberg DM 6.80
53 Stuttgart – Schwarzwald – Bodensee DM 6.80
54 Elsass Vogesen DM 6.80
55 Frankfurt – Würzburg – Stuttgart DM 6.80

REISEKARTEN
1:200,000
Bonn : Stollfuss
Tourist maps, showing roads, camping, youth hostels, places of interest, etc.
Available for :
Sauerland, 1972 DM 4.50
Eifel-Mosel, 1972 DM 4.20
Westerwald-Taunus DM 3.80

STRASSENKARTEN
1:150,000
Köln : Gleumes
Road maps available in the following sheets:
Eifel – Mosel
Köln, Bonn, Aachen und Umgebung
Mittelrheingebiet
Mosel – Hunsrück – Luxemburg
Münsterland
Niederrhein DM 3.80
Rhein – Ruhrgebiet
Sauerland – Siegerland
Teutoburgerwald und Weserbergland
Each DM 5

Baden Württemberg

STRASSENKARTE DES LANDES BADEN-WÜRTTEMBERG
1:200,000
Stuttgart : Baden-Württemberg Lv
107 x 77 each
2 sheet col. road map; boundaries, district towns, roads and motorways classified by col. DM 4

STRASSEN- UND ENTFERNUNGSKARTE DES LANDES BADEN-WÜRTTEMBERG
1:200,000
Stuttgart : Baden-Württemberg Lv
107 x 77 each
2 sheets col. map showing boundaries, road numbers and classification, distances on main and secondary roads.

STRASSENBAUMTSKARTE BADEN-WÜRTTEMBERG
1:100,000
In 29 sheets
Stuttgart : Baden-Württemberg Lv
Board of Work road maps in 5 and 7 col. editions.
5 col. eds. DM 2.50
7 col. eds DM 3.30

ENTFERNUNGSKARTE VON BADEN
1:100,000
Stuttgart : Baden-Württemberg Lv
In 8 sheets
80 x 80
Col. map showing distances on main and secondary roads.
Each DM 2.50

Bayern

STRASSENKARTE VON BAYERN
1:500,000
München : Bayern Lv, 1971
77 x 81
Col. road map based on relief ed. of Übersichtskarte, 1:500,000
DM 5.50

STRASSENKARTE MIT ENTFERNUNGSANGABEN
1:500,000
München : Bayern Lv, 1971
77 x 81
Distances for all roads overprinted on "Strassenkarte von Bayern"
DM 5.50

STRASSEN- UND VERWALTUNGSKARTE VON BAYERN
1:250,000
In 5 sheets
München : Bayerische Lv
Road and admin. area map. Roads of all types overprinted in red, boundaries of admin. areas in blue.
Each DM 3.30
North sheet DM 1.30

Nordrhein-Westfalen

STRASSENKARTE NORDRHEIN-WESTFALEN
1:500,000
Bad Godesberg : Nordrhein-Westfalen Lv
Col. road map DM 4.50

NORDRHEIN-WESTFALEN : STRASSENKARTE MIT ENTFERNUNGSANGABEN
1:250,000
Bad Godesberg : Nordrhein-Westfalen Lv
Col. map showing roads classified, with distances for all areas.
DM 8.00

Saarlandes

AMTLICHE KARTE DER KLASSIFIZIERTEN STRASSEN DES SAARLANDES
1:100,000
Saarbrucken : Saarlandes Lv, 1970
84 x 60
Official map showing road classification – national and state roads, numbered, in col. with distances in km.

ENTFERNUNGSKARTE DES SAARLANDES
1:75,000
Saarbrucken : Saarlandes Lv, 1972
110 x 83
Col. map showing distances on roads and projected roads to be completed.
DM 5

Schleswig-Holstein

STRASSENKARTE VON SCHLESWIG-HOLSTEIN
1:250,000
Kiel-Wik : Schleswig Holstein Lv.
Col. road map. DM 4.50

ENTFERNUNGSKARTEN SCHLESWIG-HOLSTEIN
1:75,000
Kiel-Wik : Schleswig-Holstein Lv
In 2 sheets, North and South : In grey and black, showing road numbers and distances.
Each DM 3.80

A2 GENERAL MAPS : LOCAL

FRANKEN UND OBERPFALZ
1:600,000
Hof (Saale) : Fritsch
School map. DM 1.20

REGIERUNSBEZIRK OBERFRANKEN
1:400,000
No 251
Hof (Saale) : Fritsch
School map. DM 2.00

SCHULWANDKARTE OBERFRANKEN
1:100,000
No 299
Hof (Saale) : Fritsch
School wall map DM 80.00

FRITSCHS AUTO-WANDERKARTEN
1:100,000
Hof (Saale) : Fritsch
Various sizes
Walking and driving maps, available for :
1 Frankenwald und Fichtelgebirge DM 4.20
2 Fränkische Schweiz und Frankenalb DM 4.00
3 Oberpfalzer Wald und Steinwald DM 4.00
4 Unteres Altmühltal-Regensburg DM 4.20
5 Bayerischer Wald DM 4.20
6 Unteres Inntal-Burghausen DM 4.20
7 München DM 4.80

F & B WANDERKARTEN
1:100,000
Geografa
see AUSTRIA 436 A2

RV WANDERKARTE
Various scales
Stuttgart : RV
Various sizes
Walking maps, showing main and secondary roads, distances in km, paths, railways, accommodation, places of tourist interest.
Available for :

RV2 Ruhpolding, 1:30,000 DM 5.80
RV3 Tegernsee 1:30,000 DM 5.80
RV4 Garmisch - Partenkirchen/Mitten Wald 1:39,000 DM 5.80
RV9 Bodensee, 1:75,000 DM 5.80
RV10 Allgäuer Alpen, 1:75,000 DM 5.80
RV11 Schwarzwald, Nordblatt 1:75,000 DM 5.80
RV12 Schwarzwald, Mittelblatt 1:75,000 DM 5.80
RV13 Schwarzwald, Südblatt 1:75,000 DM 5.80
RV14 Odenwald, 1:75,000 DM 6.80
RV15 Pfälzerwald, 1:75,000 DM 6.80
RV17 Freiburg im Breisgau 1:75,000 DM 4.80
RV20 Mittlerer Schwarzwald 1:50,000 DM 4.80
RV24 Feldberg-Schluchsee 1:50,000 DM 4.80
RV25 Hegall 1:50,000 DM 6.80
RV34 Stromberg 1:50,000 DM 5.80
RV35 Enzkreis 1:50,000 DM 5.80
RV36 Stuttgart 1:75,000 DM 6.80
RV37 Schönbuch 1:50,000 DM 4.80
RV38 Welzheimerund Murrhardter Wald 1:50,000 DM 5.80
RV39 Schwäbische Alb, Westteil 1:100,000 DM 4.80
RV40 Schwäbische Alb, Ostteil 1:100,000 DM 4.80
RV41 Ulm, 1:50,000 DM 5.80
RV42 Mittlere Schwäbische Alb 1:50,000 DM 5.80
RV44 Göppingen 1:50,000 DM 5.80
RV46 Heidenheim 1:50,000 DM 4.80
RV49 Saarland 1:75,000 DM 7.80
RV64 München Süd 1:150,000 DM 6.80
RV220 Grunewald und Havelseen 1:20,000 DM 5.80
RV223 Naturpark Harz 1:50,000 DM 5.50
RV224 Harz with guide 1:100,000 DM 2.80
RV225 Bad Harzburg und Umgebung 1:25,000 DM 3.80
RV227 Hahnenklee-Bockswiese und Umgebung 1:25,000 DM 3.80
RV228 Altenau und Umgebung 1:25,000 DM 3.80
RV229 Bad Sachsa und Umgebung 1:25,000 DM 4.50
RV230 Bad Lauterberg und Umgebung 1:25,000 DM 3.80
RV231 Braunlage - St Andreasberg 1:25,000 DM 3.80
RV232 Clausthal - Zellerfeld 1:25,000 DM 3.80
RV238 Lüneburger Heide 1:100,000 DM 5.80
RV239 Wilseder Berg 1:25,000 DM 3.80
RV240 Naturpark Südheide 1:25,000 DM 3.80
RV241 Harburger Berge 1:25,000 DM 3.80
RV245 Bergisches Land, Süd 1:75,000 DM 5.80
RV246 Bergisches Land, Nord 1:75,000 DM 5.80

WANDERKARTEN
Various scales
Koln : Gleumes
Various sizes
Walking and driving maps, available for :

Bergisches Land 1:75,000 DM 3.80
Das Oberbergische Land 1:100,000 DM 3.80
Dusseldorf und Umgeburg 1:75,000 DM 3.20
Eifel-Mosel 1:150,000 DM 4.80
Koblenz 1:100,000 DM 3.00
Konigsforst 1:50,000 DM 3.50
Lahntal 1:100,000 DM 3.00
Mittlehrheingebiet DM 4.20
Mittelrhein/Rheintaunus DM 3.20
Mosel-Hunsruck-Luxemburg 1:150,000 DM 4.80
Munsterland 1:150,000 DM 3.80
Niederrhein North DM 3.80
South DM 3.80
Rheingebiet Koblenz-Bonn 1:100,000 DM 3.20
Sauerland;Siegerland 1:150,000 DM 4.80
Siebengebirge 1:30,000 DM 2.00
Siegtal 1:100,000 DM 2.20
Taunus und Rheingau 1:100,000 DM 3.50
Teutoburgerwald und Weserbergland 1:150,000 DM 4.80
Westerwald, West and East sheets
Each DM 3.20

WANDER- UND AUSFLUGSKARTE
Various scales
Munchen : JRO
Various sizes
Col. tourist and excursion maps, for holiday areas, places of interest and natural beauty, roads, paths. Some with ski routes, and relief shading. Available for :

701 Berchtesgadener Land 1:75,000 46 x 64 DM 1.90
702 Chiemgau 1:75,000 59 x 85 DM 3.00
703 Rund um den Wendelstein 1:75,000 69 x 58 DM 3.00
705 Bad Tolz, Kochel- und Walchensee 1:75,000 58 x 73 DM 3.00
706 Werdenfelser Land 1:75,000 58 x 58 DM 3.00
707 Oberallgau 1:75,000 71 x 62 DM 3.00
711 Ostallgau 1:75,000 68 x 50 DM 3.00
712 Westallgau 1:75,000 79 x 58 DM 3.00
713 Inn- und Chiemgau 1:100,000 75 x 65 DM 3.00
717 Bodensee 1:150,000 84 x 50 DM 3.00
720 Bayerischer Wald (double sided) 1:100,000 72 x 68 DM 4.00
725 Starnberger und Ammersee 1:75,000 56 x 65 DM 3.50
726 Rupertwinkel - Berchtesgadener Land 1:75,000 75 x 65 DM 3.00
729 Schwarzwald 1:150,000 88 x 116 DM 5.80
740 Westharz 1:75,000 52 x 58 DM 3.00

WANDERKARTEN
Various scales
Frankfurt : Ravenstein
Various sizes
Coloured road and tourist map series, available in the following sheets :

903 Rhein- und Lahntaunus 1:50,000 80 x 100 DM 7.20
904 Hoch- und Mitteltaunus 1:50,000 80 x 100 DM 7.20
905 Hoch- und Osttaunus 1:50,000 80 x 50 DM 7.20
906 Waldungen Frankfurt - Darmstadt 1:50,000 80 x 50 DM 4.80
909 Odenwald 1:150,000 70 x 100 DM 7.80
910 Odenwald 1:100,000 77 x 80 DM 6.80
911 Spessart 1:100,000 66 x 80 DM 6.80
913 Rhön 1:100,000 77 x 92 DM 6.80
915 Heidelberg-Hirschhorn 1:25,000 90 x 75 DM 6.80
972 Naturpark Bergstrasse-Odenwald 1:100,000 66 x 69 DM 4.80
973 Rheingau 1:50,000 80 x 50 DM 4.80
974 Hochtaunus 1:50,000 80 x 50 DM 4.80
975 Hochspessart 1:75,000 80 x 50 DM 2.50
976 Südschwarzwald 1:100,000 92 x 70 DM 4.80
977 Nordschwarzwald 1:100,000 99 x 68 DM 4.80

WANDERKARTEN
1:50,000
München : Kompass
Various sizes
Tourist map series for forest areas.
Available for :

162 Westlicher Taunus DM 4.80
163 Östlicher Taunus DM 4.80
167 Nördliche Steigerwald DM 3.20
168 Südliche Steigerwald DM 3.20
169 Nördlicher Rangau DM 3.20
171 Fränkische Schweiz DM 3.20
172 Hersbrücker Land in der Frankenalb DM 3.20
192 Nördlicher Oberpfalzer Wald DM 3.20
193 Mittlerer Oberpfalzer Wald DM 3.20
194 Südlicher Oberpfalzer Wald DM 3.20
195 Nördlicher Bayerischer Wald DM 3.20
196 Mittlerer Bayerischer Wald DM 3.20
197 Südlicher Bayerischer Wald DM 3.20
198 Westliches Mühlviertel DM 3.20

see also AUSTRIA 436 A2.

WANDERKARTEN
1:50,000 ; 1:35,000
Hof (Saale) : Fritsch
Various sizes
50 Oberes Maintal – Coburg – Lichtenfels – Staffelstein DM 4.00
51 Kronach – Westl. Frankenwald DM 3.50
52 Fichtelgebirge und Steinwald (with guide on reverse) DM 4.00
53 Innere Fränkische Schweiz (with plans of caves) DM 3.00
54 Steinwald DM 3.00
55 Mittl. Oberpfalzer Wald – Vohenstrauss DM 3.00
56 Nördl. Bayer. Wald – Hoher Bogen DM 3.00
57 Vorderer Bayer. Wald – Donauwaldgau DM 3.00
58 Kelheim – Riedenburg 1:35,000 DM 2.80
59 Rachel-Lusen – Nationalpark Bayer. Wald (1:35,000) DM 3.00
60 Mittl. Bayer. Wald – Arber – Dreisessel DM 4.00

WANDERKARTEN
Various scales
Bonn : Stollfuss
Various sizes
Col. map series, showing road, paths, camping details, places of interest.
Available for :
Bergisches Land :
Oberbergisches Land 1:50,000 DM 3.40
Eifel:
Ahrtal 1:50,000 DM 2.80
Brohltal — Laacher See 1:50,000 DM 2.80
Nordost-Eifel 1:100,000 DM 3.60
Nordwest-Eifel 1:100,000 DM 3.60
Bad Bertrich, Maare, Mittelmosel 1:50,000 DM 3.40
Hunsruck:
Hunsruck 1:100,00 DM 3.80
Nahetal 1:100,000 DM 3.40
Lahn:
Lahntal 1:100,000 DM 2.80
Mosel:
Moseltal 1:100,000 DM 2.80
Niederrhein:
Mönchengladbach und Umgebung 1:50,000 DM 3.40
Odenwald:
Lindenfels im Naturpark Odenwald 1:30,000 DM 2.80
Rhein:
Bingen, Rüdesheim und Umgebung 1:50,000 DM 2.40
Bonn und Umgebung 1:50,000 DM 2.40
Koblenz und Umgebung 1:50,000 DM 3.80
Naturpark Siebengebirge 1:25,000 DM 3.40
Teutoburger Wald:
Bielefeld und Umgebung 1:50,000 DM 3.80
Münster und Umgebung 1:50,000 DM 3.80

WANDERKARTEN
Various scales
Kassel : Grothus
Series of large scale walking maps. Available for:
Kassel und Umgebung 1:50,000 DM 4.80
Sood-Allend 1:50,000 DM 2.80
Reinhardswald 1:50,000 DM 3.80
Grosse Knüllkarte 1:50,000 DM 4.80
Grosse Sollingkarte 1:50,000
Karte Meissner 1:25,000 DM 1.50
Bad Hersfeld 1:30,000 DM 1.50
Willingen 1:15,000 DM 2.80
Usseln 1:15,000 DM 2.80
Kellerwald 1:25,000 DM 3.50

HEIMATKARTEN
1:100,000/1:75,000
Hof (Saale) : Fritsch
Various sizes
Local tourist maps for the following areas:
201 Nordwest-Oberfranken (districts Coburg – Lichtenfels – Staffelstein) DM 3.00
202 Nordost-Oberfranken (districts Hof – Rehau – Munchberg) DM 3.00
203 Südwest-Oberfranken (districts Bamberg – Hochstadt – Forchheim – Ebermannstadt) DM 3.00
204 Südost-Oberfranken (districts Bayreuth – Pegnitz) DM 3.00
205 Frankenwald (districts Naila – Kronach) DM 3.00
206 districts Kulmbach – Stadtsteinach DM 3.00
207 districts Wunsiedel – Fichtelgebirge DM 3.00
248 Tetschen – Bodenbach (Sudetenland) DM 3.00
249 Mies – Marienbad – Pilsen (Sudetenland - 2 languages) DM 3.80

HEIMATKARTEN
Various scales
Kassel : Grothus
Series of large scale local maps showing roads, paths, towns and villages.
Available for :
Biedenkopf
Eschwege, with town plan
Frankenberg, with town plan
Fritzlar-Homberg
Fulda, with town plan DM 2.50
Hanau, with town plan
Hersfeld und Rotenburg DM 2.50
Hofgeismar
Kassel
Kassel-Melsung-Wirtzenhausen DM 2.50
Waldeck DM 2.50
Ziegenhain DM 2.20
Limburg/Oberlahn
Each DM 2.00

ENVIRONS MAPS
1:250,000
Hamburg : Falk
Road maps covering the environs of large cities and tourist area.
Available for :
Rund um Hamburg No 332
Rund um Hannover, Braunschweig, Kassel No 334
Rund um Rhein und Ruhr, No 336
Rund um Frankfurt, No 337
Rund um Saar und Mosel, No 338 (1:300,000)
Rund um München, No 339
Each DM 3.90

UMGEBUNGSKARTE
1:100,000
Official state surveys
Various sizes
Baden-Württemberg :
Umgebung des Bodensees 75 x 32 DM 2.70
Tübingen – Reutlingen – Urach mit weiterer Umgebung 65 x 67 DM 2.60
Bayern :
München und Umgebung 79 x 84 DM 4.90
Umgebung von Nürnberg und die Fränkische Schweiz DM 3.20
Steigerwald DM 2.60
Niedersachsen :
Braunschweig, 74 x 59 DM 4.30
Hannover, 90 x 72 (col) DM 4.30
(2 col) DM 3.30
Westharz, 54 x 46 DM 2.90
Goslar, 1972 DM 3.90
Rheinland-Pfalz :
Umgebungskarte von Mainz-Wiesbaden DM 3.20
Schleswig-Holstein :
Umgebungskarte Hamburg, 1970 103 x 76 DM 3.80

UMGEBUNGSKARTEN
Various scales
Frankfurt : Ravenstein
Various sizes
Coloured district maps, available for:
920 Bad Orb 1:35,000 49 x 50 DM 3.80
922 Bad Nauheim-Friedberg 1:50,000 54 x 69 DM 4.80
957 Rhein-Main-Gebiet 1:100,000 100 x 80 DM 7.20 (About 50km round Frankfurt/Main)

KIEL UND UMGEBUNG
1:75,000
Kiel-Wik : Schleswig Holstein Lv
Col. topog. map on UTM grid. DM 3.80

RUND UM LÜBECK
1:50,000
Lübeck : Lübecker Nachrichten, 1976
Tourist map of the environs of Lübeck DM 4.50

OFFIZIELLE WANDERKARTE KREIS HERZOGTUM LAUENBURG
1:50,000
Lübeck : Lübecker Nachrichten, 1975
Official walking map of the Lauenburg Duchy DM 4.50

KREIS- UND GEBIETSKARTEN
1:75,000/1:100,000
Stuttgart – Bad Cannstatt :
Stadte-Verlag
Various sizes
Motoring and touring maps for various parts of W Germany with indexes of towns and villages.
Maps available :
Aalen
Ahrweiler
Alfeld
Altenkirchen
Alzenau
Alzey-Worms
Ammerland
Ansbach
Arnsberg
Backnang
Bad Dürkheim
Bad Kreuznach
Bad Tolz
Balingen
Bayreuth
Bergheim
Bergstrasse
Biberach
Bielefeld
Boblingen
Borken
Breisgau
Bruchsal
Buchen
Budingen
Buhl
Burgdorf
Calw
Coburg
Crailsheim
Dachau
Darmstadt
Detmold
Dieburg
Dietholztal
Dillingen
Dinkelsbuhl
Donaueschingen
Donauworth
Donnersberg
Duren
Ehingen
Emmendingen
Erbach
Erkelenz
Esslingen
Euskirchen
Fallingbostel
Forchheim
Freising
Freudenstadt
Friedberg/Bay
Friedburg/H
Fritzlar-Homberg
Furstenfeldbruck
Fussen
Fulda
Garmisch-Partenkirchen
Gelnhausen
Germersheim
Giessen
Gifhorn
Goppingen
Gottingen
Grevenbroich
Gross-Gerau
Gunzenhausen
Halle
Hameln-Pyrmont
Hanau
Hechingen
Heidelberg
Heidenheim
Heilbronn
Hochschwarzwald
Hof
Hohenlohe
Holzminden
Homburg
Horb
Idyllische Strasse
Illertissen
Kaiserslautern
Karlsruhe
Kassel
Kaufbeuren
Kehl
Kempen-Krefeld
Kempton
Kitzingen
Kleve
Konstanz
Kronach
Kunzelsau
Kulmbach
Lahr
Landau-Bergzabern
Landsberg
Leonberg
Lichtenfels
Limburg
Lindau
Lorrach
Ludwigsburg
Ludwigshafen
Luneburg
Maintaunus
Mainz-Bingen
Mannheim
Marburg
Marktoberdorf
Mayen-Koblenz
Memmingen
Mergentheim
Merzig-Wadern
Meschede
Miesbach
Minden
Mosbach
Mullheim
Munsingen
Neuwied
Nienburg
Nordlingen
Northeim
Nurtingen
Oberberg. Kreis
Ohringen
Offenbach
Offenburg
Olpe
Osterode
Ottweiler
Paderborn
Peine
Pforzheim
Pirmasens
Rastatt m. Baden-Baden
Ravensburg
Recklinghausen
Reutlingen
Rheingau
Rhein-Hunsruck-Kreis
Rhein-Berg. Kreis
Rhein-Sieg-Kreis
Rosenheim
Rotenburg
Rothenburg o.d.T.
Rottweil
Saarbrucken
Saarlouis
Sackingen
St Ingbert
St Wendel
Saulgau
Schongau
Schwabach
Schwab. Gmund
Schwab. Hall
Schwarzwald-Baar
Schweinfurt
Siegen
Sigmaringen
Sinsheim
Soest
Soltau
Sonthofen
Springe
Staffelstein
Starnberg
Stockach
Tauberkreis
Tettnang
Traunstein
Trier-Saarburg
Tubingen
Tuttlingen
Uberlingen
Ulm
Unna
Unterwesterwald
Vaihingen
Villingen
Waiblingen
Waldeck
Waldshut
Wangen
Warburg
Weilheim
Weissenburg
Wetzlar
Wolfach
Wolfratshausen

UMGEBUNGSKARTE
1:50,000
State Official Surveys
Various sizes
Environs maps based on topog. 1:50,000 series.
Baden-Württemberg :
Stuttgart und Umgebung
90 x 72 DM 5
Umgebung des Bodensees (2 sheets)
79 x 62 DM 5.30
Isny und Umgebung
63 x 56 DM 3.90
Bayern :
Ammersee und Umgebung DM 3.90
Starnberger See und Umgebung DM 3.90
Regensburg West DM 4.10
Regensburg Ost DM 4.10
Berchtesgadener Alpen DM 4.90
Werdenfelser Land DM 4.40
Eilangen und Umgebung DM 4.40
Chiemsee und Umgebung DM 3.90
Allgaüer Alpen DM 4.90
Karwendelgebirge DM 4.40
Fussen und Umgebung DM 4.90
Mangfallgebirge DM 4.40
Würzburg und Umgebung DM 5.20
Bad Tolz - Lenggries und Umgebung DM 3.20
Bad Worishofen und Umgebung DM 2.00
Nordhein-Westfalen :
Wanderkarten SK 50 W
Saarland :
Wanderkarten TK 50 W
Umgebungskarte
Schleswig-Holstein :
Hamburg DM 3.80
Neumünster und Umgebung
90 x 75 DM 3.80
Lübecker Bucht DM 3.80

WILBAD MIT UMGEBUNG
1:20,000
Stuttgart : Baden-Württemberg Lv
59 x 62
Col. topog. map of Wildbad and Environs. Walking routes in red.
DM 4.60

GROSSRAUM HANNOVER
1:200,000
Hannover : Niedersachsen Lv
40 x 40
General map of the Greater Hannover area. Available in the following eds:
2 col. without topog. DM 2.70
Col. with topog. DM 3.30

VERBAND GROSSRAUM HANNOVER
1:50,000
In 3 sheets
Hannover : NLvL
Touring map for Greater Hannover showing roads, paths, places of interest.
Sheet 1 — Deister, Suntal, Osterwald, 1972
86 x 67
Sheets 2 and 3 to be published 1973.

UMGEBUNGSKARTEN
1:50,000/1:25,000
Hof (Saale) : Fritsch
Various sizes
District maps
Maps available :
101 Ludwigstadt – Lauenstein
1:35,000 DM 2.00
102 Wallenfels – Steinwiesen
1:35,000 DM 2.00
103 Bad Steben – Geroldsgrun
1:40,000 DM 2.00
104 Naila – Lichtenberg
1:40,000 DM 2.00
105 Nordhalben – Teuschnitz
1:40,000 DM 2.00
106 Schwarzenbach a. W.
1:35,000 DM 2.00
107 Wirsberg – Marktschorgast
1:50,000 DM 2.00
108 Bad Berneck
1:35,000 DM 2.00
109 Fichtelberg
1:35,000 DM 2.00
110 Warmensteinach – Ober-warmensteinach
1:35,000 DM 2.00
111 Bischofsgrün
1:35,000 DM 2.00
112 Kosseine – Luisenburg
1:50,000 DM 2.00
113 Mehlmeisel
1:35,000 DM 2.00
114 Tannesberg
1:40,000 DM 2.00
115 Waldmünchen
1:50,000 DM 2.00
116 Schönseer Ländchen
1:50,000 DM 2.00
117 Bodenmais – Arber
1:35,000 DM 2.00
118 Viechtach
1:40,000 DM 2.00
119 Bayer, Eisenstein - Falkenstein
1:35,000 DM 2.00
120 Zwiesel
1:40,000 DM 2.00
121 Lamer Winkel
1:40,000 DM 2.00
122 Zeller Tal
1:35,000
(Arnbruck - Drachselsried)
(1973) DM 2.00

UMGEBUNGSKARTEN
1:25,000
State Official Surveys
Various sizes
District maps based on topog. series 1:25,000
Baden-Württemberg :
Badenweiler 72 x 75 DM 4.50
Feldberg-Hinterzrten-Titisee
61 x 70 DM 3.50
Freudenstadt-Kniebis-Pfalzgrafenweiler
78 x 107 DM 5.00
Gegenbach 60 x 64 DM 3.80
Langenburg 54 x 56 DM 3.90
Loffingen 55 x 65 DM 3.50
Mainhardt 65 x 60 DM 3.60
Murrhardt 54 x 67 DM 2.60
Neustadt-Lenzkirch
61 x 70 DM 3.80
Schramberg 70 x 80 DM 4.40
St Blasien 91 x 78 DM 4.60
St Margen und St Peter
54 x 66 DM 3.50
Urach 63 x 63 DM 3.00
Bayern :
Bad Kissingen und Umgebung DM 2.80
Tegernsee und Umgebung DM 2.80
Königssee DM 3.90
Hesse :
Eibach - Michelstadt - Bad König
DM 4.50
Giessen - Wetzlar Rheingau (walking routes)
DM 4.50
Wiesbaden und Umgebung (walking routes)
DM 6.60
Hochtaunus (walking routes) DM 6.60
Darmstadt und Umgebung DM 4.50
Niedersachsen :
Bad Pyrmont (walking routes)
46 x 52 DM 3.30
Göttingen (walking routes)
86 x 68 DM 5.10
Hameln 64 x 63 DM 4.70
Stadt Salzgitter 71 x 88 DM 3.90
Stade 44 x 44 DM 3.70
Nordrhein-Westfalen :
Series SK 50 U various prices
Rheinland-Pfalz Bad Bergzabern und Umgebung (walking routes)
DM 3.90
Bad Münster am Stein und Umgebung
DM 2.80
Neustadt a.d.W.u. Umgebung (walking routes) DM 3.70
Bad Dürkheim und Umgebung (walking routes) DM 3.90
Wanderkarte Laacher See DM 0.80
Umgebungskarte Schönecken (walking routes) DM 3.00
Mittleres Kylltal (walking routes)
DM 3.00
Ahnweileram Trifels und Umgebung, 1972
62 x 86 DM 4.40
Schleswig-Holstein :
Insel Fohr DM 2.00
Der Sachsenwald DM 3.20
Insel Amrum DM 2.00
Ostseebader DM 3.20
Kieler Forde, 1972,
75 x 104 DM 3.20
Lübecker Bucht, 1972
63 x 90 DM 3.80

UMGEBUNGSKARTE
1:10,000
Hannover : Niedersachsen Lv
District maps based on topog. series 1:10,000
UK 10 : Braunlage (Harz) 69 x 75
DM 2.80

PANORAMAKARTEN
Munchen : JRO
Various sizes
Series of 'birdseye view' maps, showing land types, roads, settlements, physical features. Relief shown.
501 Berchtesgadener Land
70 x 42 DM 1.50
504 Inntal 60 x 42 DM 1.50
505 Schliersee, Bayerischzell
60 x 42 DM 1.50
507 Bad Tolz, Lenggries
60 x 42 DM 1.50
508 Kochel - Walchensee, Mittenwald
60 x 42 DM 1.50
509 Werdenfelser Land
60 x 42 DM 1.50
510 Ostallgau 60 x 42 DM 1.50
511 Oberallgau
60 x 42 DM 1.50
513 Ostbayerische Alpen
96 x 22 DM 2.50
514 Bayerische Alpen
123 x 22 DM 2.50
515 Allgaüer Alpen
106 x 22 DM 2.50
516 Deutsche Alpen
298 x 22 DM 6.00
523 Schwarzwald
42 x 62 DM 1.50
525 Südschwarzwald
73 x 58 DM 1.50
527 Freudenstadt
60 x 42 DM 1.50
528 Cheimsee 60 x 42 DM 1.50
530 Oberbayern, Schwabern
76 x 51 DM 1.90
531 Oberbayern, Schwabern
123 x 84 DM 4.80
538 Harz 61 x 42 DM 1.50
539 Sauerland 60 x 41 DM 1.50
540 Weserbergland
41 x 59 DM 1.50
543 Bayerischer Wald
62 x 42 DM 1.50
551 Der Rhein
21 x 136 DM 1.90

BILDLANDKARTEN
Bonn : Stollfuss
Various sizes
Coloured pictorial maps of popular tourist areas, with guides. Available for:
Die Grosse Rheinfahrt (Basel-Rotterdam), Ger, Eng, Fr, Dut. eds. 26 x 240. 16pp text. DM 5.80
Die Grosse Moselfahrt mit Saartal (Saarlouis-Koblenz), Ger, Eng, Fr eds. 26 x 175, 16pp text. DM 5.80
Bildlandkarte Mittelrhein-Mosel-Lahn, 1:150,000, 86 x 88 DM 5.80
Bildlandkarte Schwarzwald 1:200,000, 87 x 96 DM 5.80
Rhein-Bildkarte (Mainz-Nordsee) 26 x 173 DM 4.20

RHEINPANORAMA
17th edition
Bonn : Stollfuss
24 x 138
Pictorial map of the Rhine from Mainz to Koln (Cologne), showing canoe stations, camping sites, boat houses, footpaths, tracks, ferries, steamer landing stages. Available in 6 languages. DM 3.50

DER RHEIN
Koln : Gleumes
19 x 239
Pictorial col. map with guide in English. Distances shown in km, canoe stations, canoe-tenting facilities, car ferries, camping sites and landing stages. Folded for easy reference.

DER RHEINLAUF
Bonn : Stollfuss
Coloured pictorial guide map of the Rhine with illus. text, places of interest and accommodation. In Germ Eng, Fr, Dut editions.
Each DM 3.80

DER MOSELLAUF
Bonn : Stollfuss
25 x 106
From Trier to Koblenz, inc. Saar Valley and Mettlach. Pictorial map in colour showing tenting and camping places, passenger and car ferries, footpaths and distances in km. Available in 4 languages.
DM 3.80

DER AHRLAUF
Bonn : Stollfuss
Col. pictorial map of the course of the river Ahr. With tourist details, text etc.
DM 3.20
Also available for the 'Weserlauf'
DM 3.00

DER WESERLAUF
No 60760
Bonn : Stollfuss
Physical-pictorial map of the course of the River Weser. DM 3.00

Baden-Württemberg

WANDERKARTE FREIBURG/ BREISGAU
1:50,000
Stuttgart : Baden-Württemberg Lv, 1970
85 x 70
Col. map, relief shading, walking and touring routes.

WILDBAD, DOBEL, HERRENALB, GERNSBACH
1:35,000
Stuttgart : Baden-Württemberg Lv, 1972
67 x 58
'Wanderkarte' showing roads, paths, places of interest. DM 3.80

TOPOGRAPHISCHE KARTE
1:30,000
Stuttgart : Baden Württemberg Lv
Enlarged from 1:50,000 series : walking notes added.
Maps available :
Nagold - Simmersfeld - Dornstretten - Horb, 77 x 84 DM 4.50
Wildbad - Dobal - Herrenalb - Gernsbach, 68 x 70 DM 3.80

Bayern

ÜBERSICHTSKARTE VON BAYERN
1:800,000
Munchen : Bayerische Lv
Col. general map. Overprint on Amtsbezirksgrenzen. DM 5.00

ÜBERSICHTSKARTE VON BAYERN
1:500,000
UK 500
Munchen : Bayerische Lv, 1971
77 x 81
General map in col. In 3 editions : Standard ed, Relief shading ed.
Each DM 5.50

BAYERISCHER WALD-WANDER- UND SKIKARTE
1:100,000
Munchen : Bayerische Lv
Map showing Bavarian woods, walking routes, ski routes. DM 3.60

Hessen

KARTE VON HESSEN
1:200,000
Wiesbaden : Hessische Lv
Col. general map showing roads, classified and numbered, relief shading.
DM 5.50

TOPOGRAPHISCHE ÜNBERSICHTS-KARTE DES ODENWALDES
1:100,000
Wiesbaden : Hessische Lv fur Bodenforschung, 1907
Topog. map. DM 5.00

Niedersachsen

TOPOGRAPHISCHE ÜBERSICHTS-KARTE DES DEUTSCHEN REICHES
1:200,000
Hannover : Niedersächsiches Lv
3 col. topog. map of Niedersachsen centralised from 1: 200,000 topog. series (TUK 200) DM 1.90

WANDERKARTEN
1:50,000
Hannover : Niedersächsiches Lv
Various sizes
Walking maps based on Topog. series 1:50,000. Contours, relief shading, paths etc. In the following sheets :

Naturschutzgebiet Lüneburger Heide	48 x 58	DM 4.40
Neuenhaus	47 x 46	DM 3.20
Osnabrück	47 x 46	DM 3.90
Rotenburg (Han)	83 x 76	DM 5.50
Wintersportkarte Harz	75 x 92	DM 5.10

WANDERKARTEN
1:25,000
Hannover : Niedersächsiches Lv
Maps based on Topog. 1:25,000 series with walking routes marked; contours, woods, relief shading.
Sheets available :
Hitzacker und Umgebung 2 col. map
50 x 51 DM 2.70
Harburger Berge (Schwarze Berge) col. map 55 x 88 DM 5.30

Nordrhein-Westfalen

ÜBERSICHTSKARTE NORDRHEIN-WESTFALEN
1:500,000
Bad Godesberg : Nordrhein-Westfalen Lv, 1968
65 x 65
Coloured general map of the State, showing relief. DM 4.50

SKIWANDERKARTE HOCHSAUERLAND
1:50,000
Aarau : Verlag Sauerlander
Topog. map, contoured, marking ski routes and facilities. DM 4.20

Rheinland-Pfalz

ÜBERSICHTSKARTE VON RHEINLAND-PFALZ
1:250,000
Koblenz : Rheinland Pfalz Lv, 1970
80 x 105
Col. map showing roads, railways, contours, relief shading, spot heights.
DM 5.50

HUNSRUCK
1:250,000
Koblenz : Rheinland Pfalz Lv, 1970
81 x 62
Tourist map based on Topog. series. In col.

ÜBERSICHTSKARTE RHEINLAND-PFALZ
1:100,000
In 6 sheets
Koblenz : Rheinland Pfalz Lv
Col. general map showing roads, relief topog. detail.
Complete DM 36.00

EIFELKARTENWERK
1:50,000
In 6 sheets
Bonn : Stollfuss/Eifelvereins
Series for tourists, covering the Eifel area, prepared by the Eifel Club.
Sheets

1, 2	Nordeifel mit Naturpark
3	Arhtal-Nurburg-Laacher See - Mayen
4	Hollerath - Kronenburg - Prum - Malmedy - St Vith
5	Gerolstein - Daun - Manderscheid - Bad Bertrich - Wittlich. New ed in prep.
6	Deutsch - Luxemburgischer Naturpark - Bitburg - Neuerberg - Vianden - Echternach

Each DM 3.80
(sheet 1) DM 7.00

EIFEL WANDERKARTE
1:50,000
In 5 sheets
Koblenz : Rheinland Pfalz Lv, 1970
75 x 110
Sheets 1 & 2 covering the Nordeifel with natural park area. Vegetation, col. relief shading, contours.

LAACHER SEE WANDERKARTE
1:25,000
Koblenz : Rheinland-Pfalz Lv, 1970
20 x 24
Col. touring and walking map with relief shading. 4 lang. text on reverse.

KARTE DES NURBURGRINGES
1:20,000
Koblenz : Rheinland Pfalz Lv
Col. map. DM 2.00

RINGWALLE AUF DEM DONNERSBERG
1:5,000
Koblenz : Rheinland Pfals Lv
Col. general map. DM 4.60

Saarlandes

KARTES DES SAARLANDES
1:100,000
Saarbrucken : Saarlandes Lv, 1972
Based on TK 100 with relief shading, boundaries, main roads in col.

Schleswig-Holstein

ÜBERSICHTSKARTE VON SCHLESWIG-HOLSTEIN
1:250,000
Kiel : Schleswig-Holstein Lv, 1972
85 x 77
Coloured topographic map, showing vegetation, roads, relief shading, boundaries. DM 3.80

NORDFRIEDSISCHE INSELN
1:100,000
No 402
Hamburg : Falk
Road map with plans. DM 3.90

LAUENBURGISCHE SEEN
1:40,000
Kiel-Wik : Schleswig-Holstein Lv, 1971
74 x 103
Col. topog map with contours.
DM 3.80

INSEL SYLT
1:35,000
Kiel - Wik : Schleswig-Holstein Lv
Col. general map with plan of Westerland at 1:12,000.

HOLSTEINISCHE SCHWEIZ
1:30,000
Kiel; Wik : Schleswig Holstein Lv
Col. topog. map.
DM 3.20

INSEL FEHMARN
1:30,000
Kiel - Wik : Schleswig Holstein Lv
Col. topog. map. DM 3.20

B TOWN PLANS

TOWN PLANS
Various scales
Publishers abbreviations :

ABK	A Burckhardt
Be	Becker
Bo	Bollmann
E	Ernst
Falk	Falk Verlag
Fr	Fritsch
G	Grösschen
Groth	Grothus
Hw	Hallwag
Ju	Juncker
Kau	Kaupert
Komp	Kompass
Kro	Kronig
Lv	see VEB
Off	Official State Surveys (Lv)
Po	Posser
Re	Reco
RS	R Schwarz
Sch	Schwabenwerk
Schu	Schunemann
Sta	Stadte (Wagner & Mitterhuber)
Ull	Ullstein
VEB	VEB Lv
VV	Verkehrsverein
West	Westermann

Plans available:

Aachen			
	1:15,000	Off	DM 3.30
	1:15,000	Komp	DM 2.50
	1:17,000	Falk	DM 2.90
Aachen pictorial			
		Bo	DM 4.10
Aalen/Wttbg			
	1:10,000	Off	DM 3.20
	1:10,000	Sta	DM 1.95
Achern			
	1:6,000	Sta	DM 2.10
Ahlen/Westf			
	1:10,000	Sta	DM 2.40
Aibling, Bad			
	1:10,000	Sta	DM 2.10
Aichach			
	1:7,500	Sta	DM 1.95
Alfeld (Leine)			
	1:10,000	VV	DM 3.20
Alpirsfach			
	1:12,000	Sta	DM 2.25
	1:10,000	Re	DM 2.25
Alsfeld			
	1:7,000	Sta	DM 1.80
	1:10,000	Re	DM 2.50
Altena			
	1:10,000	Re	DM 2.50
Altensteig			
	1:6,000	Sta	DM 1.95
Altotting-Neuotting			
	1:10,000	Sta	DM 2.40
Alzey			
	1:5,000	Off	DM 1.50
Amberg/Opf			
	1:10,000	Sta	DM 2.10
Andernach			
	1:8,000	Sta	DM 2.40
Ansbach			
	1:10,000	Sta	DM 2.40
Arnsberg			
	1:10,000	VV	DM 2.40
Arzberg			
	1:7,500	Sta	DM 1.95
Aschaffenberg			
	1:15,000	Re	DM 2.50
	1:12,500	Sta	DM 2.10
	1:10,000	Off	DM 3.20
Asperg			
	1:7,500	Sta	DM 1.80
Auerbach/Opf			
	1:7,500	Sta	DM 1.65
Augsburg			
	1:15/33,000	Falk	DM 3.90
	1:12,500 small ed.		
		Off	DM 3.70
	1:12,500 large ed.		
		Off	DM 7.20
	1:15,000	E	DM 2.50
	Pictorial	Bo	DM 4.80
Aurich			
	1:10,000	Re	DM 2.50
Backnang			
	1:10,000	Sta	DM 2.40
Baden-Baden			
	1:10,000	Off	DM 4.00
Balingen			
	1:7,500	Sta	DM 2.40
Baltrum			
	1:5,000	Off	DM 2.50
Bamberg			
	1:10,000	Sta	DM 2.25
	1:10,000	Fr	DM 2.30
	Pictorial	Bo	DM 4.10
Bayreuth			
	1:12,500	Sta	DM 2.10
	1:10,000	Re	DM 2.50
	Pictorial	Bo	DM 4.10
Beckum			
	1:12,500	Sta	DM 2.10
Bensberg			
	1:20,000	Stollfuss	DM 3.80
	1:20,000	Sta	DM 3.80
	1:15,000	Off	DM 6.20
Bensheim			
	1:10,000	Re	DM 2.00
	1:12,000	Sta	DM 2.10
Bergisch-Gladbach			
	1:15,000	Off	DM 4.30
	1:15,000	Sta	DM 2.40
Berkheim/b Esslingen			
	1:7,500	Sta	DM 1.80
Berlin - Central			
	1:25/33,000	Falk	DM 2.90
Berlin - complete, incl. East			
	1:25/35,000	Falk	DM 4.80
Berlin - Central			
	1:25,000	RS	DM 1.60
Berlin			
	1:25,000	Sch	DM 2.00
	1:25,000 Wall map		
		Sch	DM 52.00
	1:30,000	RS	DM 3.20
	1:30,000	RS	DM 3.80
Berlin - complete (incl. East)			
	1:30,000	RS	DM 4.50
	1:28,000	Mair	DM 4.80
Berlin - West, top. UK			
	1:50,000	Off	DM 10.10
Berlin - Taschenplan			
	1:27,000	Sch	DM 4.50
Berlin - Tasche, Atlas			
	1:25,000	Ull	DM 8.80
Berlin - West, Kauperts Street guide with plan			
	1:27,000	Ka	DM 9.50
Berlin - Wall map Greater Berlin			
	1:20,000		
	165 x 240	Sch+Kl	DM 52.00
Berlin - Wall map Greater Berlin			
	1:25,000		
	204 x 142	RS	DM 30.00
Berlin - School wall map			
	1:40,000		
	110 x 140	West	DM 65.00
Berneck, Bad, pictorial			
		VV	DM 0.80
Bersenbruck			
	1:6,000	Re	DM 2.25
Besigheim			
	1:7,000	Sta	DM 1.65
Beuel			
	1:12,000	Stollfuss	DM 2.80
Beuel/Rhein			
	1:15,000	Sta	DM 1.95
Biberach/R			
	1:10,000	Sta	DM 2.40
Bielefeld			
	1:15,000	Off	DM 3.20
	1:15/38,000	Falk	DM 2.90
	Pictorial	Bo	DM 4.10
Bietigheim			
	1:10,000	Sta	DM 2.40
Bingen			
	1:20,000	VV	DM 2.20
	1:10,000	Re	DM 2.25
Bissingen			
	1:7,500	Sta	DM 1.80

Place	Scale	Publisher	Price
Blaubeuren			
	1:8,000	Sta	DM 2.10
Boblingen			
	1:10,000	Sta	DM 2.40
Bocholt			
	1:15,000	Off	DM 4.50
	1:12,500	Sta	DM 2.25
Bochum			
	1:23,000	Falk	DM 4.50
	1:15,000	Off	DM 4.50
Bockhorn-Neuenburg-Zetel/Oldbg.			
	1:10,000	We	DM 1.50
Bockum-Hovel			
	1:10,000	Off	DM 7.00
Bonn			
	1:16,000	Gleumes	DM 2.60
Bonn-Grossraum			
	1:15,000	Stollfuss	DM 4.20
Bonn			
	1:20,000	Mair	DM 4.80
	1:12,000 kl	Ausgabe Stollfuss	DM 2.80
	1:12,000 Gr	Ausgabe, m Beuel Stollfuss	DM 4.20
	1:17,500	Falk	DM 4.50
Bonn - Beuel-B Godesberg			
	1:22,500	Komp	DM 2.50
Borken			
	1:10,000	Off	DM 3.20
Borkum			
	1:7,500	Off	DM 1.50
Bottrop			
	1:23,000	Falk	DM 3.20
	1:15,000	Po	DM 4.20
Brackwede			
	1:10,000	Off	DM 3.20
	1:10,000	Sta	DM 1.80
Brackenheim/Wttbg			
	1:7,500	Sta	DM 0.75
Brake			
	1:10,000	Off	DM 2.40
Braunlage			
		Off	DM 2.50
Braunschweig			
	1:12,500	West	DM 2.40
	1:14,600/22,000	Falk	DM 4.50
	Pictorial	Bo	DM 4.10
Braunschweig with Sennestadt			
	Pictorial	Bo	DM 4.80
Bredstadt			
	1:10,000	ABK	DM 1.20
Bremen			
	1:16/26,000	Falk	DM 4.50
	1:22,000 Generalstadtplan m		
Bremerhaven			
	1:20,000	Schu	DM 3.90
	Pictorial	Bo	DM 4.80
Bremen - Central			
	1:12,000	Mair	DM 4.80
Bremerhavn			
	1:20/30,000	Falk	DM 2.90
	1:15,000	Off	DM 3.00
Bremervorde			
	1:7,350	Off	DM 4.20
Bretten			
	1:6,000	Sta	DM 2.40
Bruchsal			
	1:10,000	Sta	DM 2.10
Bruhl			
	1:15,000	Off	DM 2.00
Bruhl/b. Mannheim			
	1:10,000	Sta	DM 1.95
Buchen			
	1:5,500	Sta	DM 2.10
Buhl/Baden			
	1:7,500	Sta	DM 2.40
Buren			
	1:4,000	Off	DM 3.20
Burghausen			
	1:10,000	Sta	DM 2.40

Place	Scale	Publisher	Price
Burstadt			
	1:8,000	Sta	DM 1.80
Butzbach			
	1:7,500	Sta	DM 1.80
Calw			
	1:8,000	Sta	DM 2.40
Castrop-Rauxel			
	1:23,000	Falk	
	1:15,000	Sta	DM 2.40
	1:15,000	Off	DM 5.00
Celle			
	Pictorial	Bo	DM 4.80
Cham			
	1:7,500	VV	DM 2.00
Cloppenburg			
	1:10,000	Off	DM 3.20
Coburg			
	1:10,000	Sta	DM 2.40
	1:10,000	Fr	DM 2.30
Coesfeld			
	1:10,000	Off	DM 4.10
Crailsheim			
	1:8,000	Sta	DM 2.40
Cuxhaven			
	1:15,000	Re	
Dachau			
	1:12,000	Sta	DM 1.80
	1:10,000	Komp	DM 2.50
Darmstadt			
	1:23,000	Falk	DM 2.90
	1:20,000	Sta	DM 2.40
	1:15,000	Off	DM 4.20
	1:15,000	Off	DM 6.00
Datteln			
	1:20,000	Off	DM 4.40
Deggendorf			
	1:10,000	Sta	DM 2.40
Delmenhorst			
	1:15,000	Re	DM 2.80
	1:10,000	Off	DM 3.00
Denkendorf			
	1:7,500	Sta	DM 1.65
Detmold			
	1:25,000	Re	DM 3.50
	1:20,000	Re	DM 3.20
Dieburg			
	1:8,500	Re	DM 2.50
	1:7,500	Sta	DM 1.95
Diepholz			
	1:8,000	Sta	DM 2.10
Diessen			
	1:7,500	Kron	DM 1.60
Diez/Lahn			
	1:7,500	Sta	DM 1.80
Dillenburg			
	1:8,000	Sta	DM 2.40
	1:8,000	Sta	DM 2.40
Dillingen/Donau			
	1:7,500	Sta	DM 2.40
Dillingen/Saar			
	1:10,000	Off	DM 1.80
Dingolfing			
	1:10,000	Sta	DM 2.40
Dinkelsbühl			
	1:5,000	Brunnen	DM 3.20
	Pictorial	Bo	DM 4.80
Dinslaken			
	1:20,000	Off	DM 3.20
Ditzingen			
	1:7,500	Sta	DM 2.10
Donaueschingen			
	1:10,000	Sta	DM 2.25
Donauworth			
	1:7,500	Sta	DM 2.40
Donnersberg			
	1:5,000	Off	DM 4.60
Donzdorf/Wurtt			
	1:6,000	Sta	DM 1.65
Dormagen			
	1:12,000	Sta	DM 1.80

Place	Scale	Publisher	Price
Dorsten			
	1:15,000	Off	DM 4.00
	1:15,000	Sta	DM 2.40
Dortmund			
	1:16/32,000	Falk	DM 4.50
	1:20,000	Off	DM 3.90
	1:17,500	Gr	DM 4.00
	1:23,000	Mair	DM 4.80
	Pictorial	Bo	DM 4.80
Dossenheim/b Heidelbg			
	1:7,500	Sta	DM 1.80
Driburg			
	1:8,000	VV	DM 4.30
Duderstadt			
	1:5,000	Sta	DM 2.10
Dudweiler/Saar			
	1:10,000	Re	DM 2.00
Duisburg			
	1:23,000	Falk	DM 4.50
	1:20,000	Off	DM 3.70
	1:20,000	Mair	DM 4.80
Dulken			
	1:10,000	Sta	DM 1.95
Dulmen			
	1:10,000	Sta	DM 2.25
	1:10,000	Sta	DM 2.25
Düren			
	1:10,000	Off	DM 2.50
	Pictorial	Bo	DM 4.10
Durkheim, Bad			
	1:10,000	Sta	DM 2.25
Düsseldorf			
	1:18,500- 28,500	Falk	DM 4.50
	1:16,500 small ed	Gl	DM 2.50
	1:16,500 large ed	Gl	DM 7.00
	1:25,000	Mair	DM 4.80
	1:20,000	Stollfuss	DM 4.20
	Pictorial	Bo	DM 4.80
	1:22,500	Komp	DM 2.50
Eberbach/N			
	1:7,500	Sta	DM 2.25
Ebersbach/Fils			
	1:10,000	Sta	DM 1.80
Ebingen			
	1:10,000	Sta	DM 2.40
Eckernforde			
	1:11,000	ABK	DM 2.50
	1:10,000	Re	DM 2.50
Ehingen/D			
	1:7,500	Sta	DM 2.10
Eichstatt			
	1:7,000	Sta	DM 2.40
Einbeck			
	1:8,500	VV	DM 2.50
Eislingen/Fils			
	1:10,000	Sta	DM 1.95
Ellwangen			
	1:10,000	Sta	DM 2.10
Elmshorn			
	1:15/26,000	Falk	DM 3.20
	1:12,000	ABK	DM 2.50
	1:10,000	Re	DM 2.50
Emden			
	1:10,000	Off	DM 3.00
Emmendingen			
	1:6,000	Sta	DM 2.40
Ems, Bad			
	1:10,000	Sta	DM 2.25
Emsdetten			
	1:10,000	Off	DM 4.00
Ennepetal			
	1:15,000	Sta	DM 2.40
Eppingen			
	1:7,500	Sta	DM 1.65
Erding			
	1:10,000	Sta	DM 2.25
Erklenz			
	1:5,000	Off	DM 4.00

Erlangen
1:12,500 Sta DM 2.40
1:10,000 Ju DM 3.70
Eschwege
1:11,500 Off DM 3.20
1:12,000 Sta DM 2.40
Eschweiler
1:10,000 Off DM 3.50
Essen
1:23,000 Falk DM 4.50
1:25,000 Gr DM 3.50
1:20,000 Off DM 3.80
1:20,000 Mair DM 4.80
1:17,500 Komp DM 2.50
Pictorial Bo DM 4.80
Essen - Gruga-Gelande
Pictorial Bo DM 5.50
Esslingen
1:10,000 Off DM 3.20
Ettlingen
1:8,000 Sta DM 2.10
Euskirchen
1:12,000 Sta DM 2.40
Eutin
1:11,000 ABK DM 2.50
Faurndau
1:7,500 Sta DM 1.65
Fellbach
1:7,500 Sta DM 2.10
Flensburg
1:22,000 Falk DM 2.90
1:14,000 ABK DM 2.50
Forchheim
1:10,000 Sta DM 2.40
1:10,000 Sta DM 2.40
Frankenthal/Pfalz
1:12,000 Sta DM 2.10
Frankfurt/Main
1:12,500, Central
Falk DM 2.00
1:16,500/26,000
Falk DM 4.50
1:9,000 Rav DM 4.80
1:22,000 Mair DM 4.80
1:18,000 Komp DM 2.50
1:15,000 small ed
Rav DM 2.50
1:15,000 road plan
Rav DM 4.80
Frankfurt/Main with Offenbach
1:15,000 Rav DM 8.80
Frankfurt/Main with Offenbach
Pictorial Bo DM 4.80
Freiburg
1:17,500 Komp DM 2.50
Freiburg/Br
1:16,000 Falk DM 2.90
1:10,000 small ed
Off DM 1.00
1:10,000 large ed
Off DM 3.00
1:18,000 Sta DM 2.10
Friedrichsthal/Saar
1:10,000 Sta DM 1.95
Freilassing
1:10,000 Sta DM 2.10
Freising
1:10,000 Sta DM 2.10
Freudenstadt
1:7,500 Sta DM 2.40
Friedberg/Hessen
1:7,500 Sta DM 2.25
Friedberg/Bayern
1:10,000 Sta DM 2.40
Friedrichshafen
1:10,000 Off DM 4.80
1:15,000 Sta DM 2.70
Friedrichshall, Bad
1:10,000 Sta DM 1.65
Fulda
1:12,000 Sta DM 2.25

Furstenfeldbruck
1:12,500 Kro DM 3.00
1:7,500 Kro DM 2.50
1:5,000 Kro DM 3.00
Furth/Bayern
1:15,000 Sta DM 2.40
see also Nurnberg
Furth i Wald
1:10,000 Off DM 5.50
1:6,000 Sta DM 2.10
Furtwangen
1:7,500 Sta DM 1.95
Fussen
1:10,000 Sta DM 2.40
Gaggenau
1:12,500 Sta DM 2.40
Garmisch-Partenkirchen
1:10,000 Sta DM 2.10
Gauting
1:12,000 Sta DM 1.95
Geesthacht
1:15,000 Off DM 2.50
Geislingen/Steige
1:8,000 Sta DM 2.70
Gelnhausen
1:6,500 Re DM 2.25
Gelsenkirchen
1:23,000 Falk DM 3.90
with Bottrop-Gladbach
Gelsenkirchen
1:20 000 Off DM 4.80
Gengenbach
1:7,500 Sta DM 1.95
Gerestried
1:12,500 Sta DM 1.65
Gerlingen
1:7,500 Off DM 3.50
1:10,000 Sta DM 1.80
Germersheim
1:5,000 Off DM 1.00
Gernsbach
1:7,500 Sta DM 1.95
Gersthofen
1:10,000 Sta DM 1.95
Giengen/Brenz
1:7,000 Sta DM 1.80
Giessen
1:12,000 Off DM 2.40
1:12,500 Sta DM 2.10
Gilching/Kra Stanrberg
1:7,500 Sta DM 1.80
Gladbeck
1:15,000 Off DM 6.00
1:15,000 Sta DM 2.40
Godesberg, Bad
1:15,000 Sta DM 2.10
Goggingen
1:10,000 Sta DM 1.95
Goppingen
1:10,000 Off DM 5.60
Goppingen ca
1:10,000 Sta DM 2.10
Goslar
1:10,000 Off DM 5.00
Pictorial Bo DM 4.80
Göttingen
1:10,000 Off DM 3.30
Grafelfing
1:10,000 Sta DM 1.95
Grevenbroich
1:15,000 Sta DM 2.40
Griesheim
1:10,000 Sta DM 1.95
Gronau
1:15,000 Off DM 3.00
Gross-Gerau
1:7,000 Sta DM 2.40
Grunwald
1:10,000 Sta DM 2.40
Gunzburg
1:10,000 Sta DM 2.25

Gummersbach
1:15,000 Sta DM 2.40
Gunzenhausen
1:7,500 Sta DM 2.10
Gütersloh
Pictorial Bo DM 4.10
Hagen
1:23,000 Falk DM 2.90
Hagen/Westf
1:20,000 Off DM 4.50
Pictorial Bo DM 4.80
Hamburg
1:25,000-35,000 large ed
Falk DM 4.50
1:18,500-25 000
Falk DM 2.00
1:17,000-40 000
Falk DM 8.90
Hamburg
1:25,000 Mair DM 4.80
1:20,000 Sch+Kl DM 2.20
1:20,000 road map
Sch+Kl DM 8.60
Pictorial Bo DM 4.80
Hamein
1:10,000 Off DM 4.50
Hamm
1:12,500 Sta DM 2.40
Hammelburg
1:6,000 Sta DM 1.95
Hanau
1:10,000 Off DM 3.25
1:10,000 Sta DM 2.10
Hannover
1:20,000/30,000
Falk DM 4.50
1:18,500/25,000
Falk DM 2.00
1:20,000 Generalstadplan
Mair DM 4.80
1:20,000 Off DM 4.80
1:22,500 Komp DM 2.50
Bildplan Bo DM 4.80
Hann, Munden
1:7,500 Groth DM 2.50
Haslach
1:7,500 Sta DM 2.10
Hassfurt
1:7,000 Sta DM 2.10
Hasloch/Pfalz
1:8,000 Sta DM 4.60
Hattingen/Ruhr
1:7,000 Off DM 4.00
Haunstetten
1:7,500 Sta DM 1.80
Hausen/b Offenbach
1:10,000 Re DM 1.00
Hechingen
1:7,500 Sta DM 2.40
Hessen/Westf.
1:12,500 Sta DM 1.80
Heide
1:12,500 Re DM 2.50
1:8,000 ABK DM 2.50
Heidelberg
1:7,500 Off DM 4.20
1:15,000 Off DM 3.20
1:16 000 Falk DM 2.90
1:18,000 Sta DM 2.10
Heidenheim
1:10,000 Off DM 4.80
Pictorial Bo DM 4.80
Heilbronn
1:10,000 Off DM 3.60
Pictorial Bo DM 4.80
Heiligenhaus
1:10,000 Off DM 3.00
Hemer
1:10,000 Off DM 4.50
Hennef/Sieg
1:15,000 Re DM 1.50

Place	Scale	Publisher	Price
Heppenheim			
	1:10,000	Sta	DM 2.10
Herborn			
	1:7,000	Sta	DM 2.10
Herdecke			
	1:12,500	Sta	DM 1.80
Herford			
	1:20,000	Off	DM 4.80
Herne			
	1:15,000	Off	DM 4.00
	1:12,500	Sta	DM 2.40
	Pictorial	Bo	DM 4.80
Herrenberg			
	1:7,500	Sta	DM 1.80
Herrsching			
	1:10,000	Sta	DM 2.10
Hersbruck			
	1:6,000	Sta	DM 2.10
Hersfeld, Bad			
	1:12,000	Be	DM 1.50
	1:12,500	Sta	DM 2.10
Herten			
	1:15,000	Off	DM 4.00
Hilden			
	1:7,500	Off	DM 5.00
Hildesheim			
	1:12,500	Re	DM 3.80
	Pictorial	Bo	DM 4.10
Hochstadt			
	1:5,000	Off	DM 3.80
Hockenheim			
	1:10,000	Sta	DM 2.25
Hof			
	1:10,000	Sta	DM 1.80
Hof/Saale			
	1:10,000	Fr	DM 2.30
Hofgeismar			
	1:5,000	Groth	DM 2.00
Hofheim (T)			
	1:7,500	Sta	DM 2.25
Hohenlimburg			
	1:10,000	Off	DM 4.60
Holzkirchen			
	1:7,500	Sta	DM 1.95
Holzminden			
	1:10,000	Weserl	DM 2.00
Homburg/Saar			
	1:12,500	Re	DM 2.25
Hoxter			
	1:20,000	Re	DM 2.80
Hoxter-Corvey			
	1:10,000	Off	DM 4.20
Huckelhoven-Ratheim			
	1:15,000	Sta	DM 1.80
Hunfeld			
	1:10,000	Off	DM 2.00
Husum			
	1:12,500	ABK	DM 2.50
	1:10,000	Re	DM 2.80
Ibbenburen			
	1:10,000	Off	DM 3.50
Idar-Oberstein			
	1:12,500	Sta	DM 2.40
Illertissen			
	1:10,000	Sta	DM 1.95
Immenstadt			
	1:8,000	Sta	DM 2.40
Ingelheim			
	1:9,000	Re	DM 1.00
Ingolstadt			
	1:12,500	Sta	DM 3.20
Isny/Allgau			
	1:7,500	Sta	DM 1.95
Itzehoe			
	1:10,000	Re	DM 2.50
Jever			
	1:12,500	Sta	DM 2.10
Julich			
	1:8,000	Off	DM 1.50
Kamp-Lintfort			
	1:15,000	Off	DM 2.50
Kandern			
	1:7,500	Sta	DM 1.20
Karlsruhe			
	1:14,000-30,000	Falk	DM 4.50
	1:15,000	VV	DM 4.00
	1:15,000	Off	DM 4.00
	Pictorial	Bo	DM 4.80
Kassel			
	1:18,500	Sta	DM 2.40
	1:15,000	Groth	DM 4.40
	1:15,000-27,000	Falk	DM 4.50
Kaufbeuren-Neugablonz			
	1:10,000	Sta	DM 2.70
Kehl			
	1:10,000	Sta	DM 2.40
Kiel			
	1:14,000 (Olympiakarte)	Falk	DM 2.00
	1:20,000	Re	DM 3.00
	Pictorial	Bo	DM 4.10
Kelheim/Donau			
	1:10,000	Sta	DM 2.10
Kelkheim			
	1:8,000	Re	DM 1.00
Kelsterbach/Main			
	1:7,500	Off	DM 2.60
Kempten/Allgau			
	1:10,000	Sta	DM 1.95
Ketsch/b. Schwetzingen			
	1:10,000	Sta	DM 1.80
Kettwig			
	1:10,000	Off	DM 2.50
Kevelaer/Rhld			
	1:10,000	Re	DM 1.30
Kiel			
	1:14,000/50,000	Falk	DM 3.90
	1:20,000	ABK	DM 3.00
	1:17,500	Off	DM 5.00
	Pictorial	Bo	DM 4.10
Kircheim/Teck			
	1:10,000	Sta	DM 2.40
Kirchhellen			
	1:20,000	Sta	DM 1.80
Kirn			
	1:8,000	Sta	DM 1.95
Kissingen, Bad			
	1:10,000	Sta	DM 2 40
Kitzingen			
	1:10,000	Sta	DM 2.40
Kieve			
	1:20,000	Off	DM 3.00
Koblenz			
	1:20,000	Stollfuss	DM 4.50
	1:12,500	Sta	DM 2.40
Köln			
	1:19,000/33,000	Falk	DM 4.50
	1:15,000 small ed	Gl	DM 2.90
	1:22,000	Mair	DM 4.80
	1:20,000	Stollfuss	DM 4.50
	1:20,000	Gr	DM 7.50
	Pictorial	Bo	DM 4.80
	1:22,500	Komp	DM 2.50
Kongen/Neckar			
	1:7 500	Sta	DM 1.80
Konigswinter			
	1:10,000	Re	DM 2.50
Kolbermoor			
	1:12,500	Sta	DM 1.65
Konstanz			
	1:15,000	Off	DM 4.00
Korbach			
	1:8,000	Sta	DM 2.25
Korntal			
	1:6,000	Sta	DM 2.10
Kornwestheim			
	1:7,500	Sta	DM 1.95
Krefeld			
	1:20,000	Gl	DM 3.80
	1:20,000	Stollfuss	DM 3.80
	1:20,000-35,000	Falk	DM 4.50
	Pictorial	Bo	DM 4.80
Kreuznach, Bad			
	1:10,000	Sta	DM 2.40
Kronach		Sta	DM 2.25
Kronberg/T			
	1:6,000	Re	DM 2.00
Krumbach			
	1:7,500	Sta	DM 2.10
Kuchen/Fils			
	1:5,000	Sta	DM 1.80
Kunzelsau			
	1:8,000	Sta	DM 2.10
Kulmbach			
	1:8,000	Sta	DM 2.40
Lage/Lippe			
	1:5,000	Off	DM 4.90
Lahnstein			
	1:12,500	Sta	DM 2.25
Lahr			
	1:10,000	Sta	DM 2.40
Lampertheim/Hessen			
	1:10 000	Sta	DM 1.80
Landau/Pfalz			
	1:5,000	Kau	DM 3.50
	1:10,000	Sta	DM 2.10
Landsberg/Lech			
	1:7,500	Sta	DM 2.40
Landshut/Isar			
	1:12,000	Sta	DM 1.80
	1:12,000	Re	DM 1.80
Landstuhl			
	1:7,500	Off	DM 3.00
Langen b. Ffm			
	1:8,000	Re	DM 2.00
Langenberg/Rhld			
	1:10,000	Off	DM 3.20
Langenfeld/Rld			
	1:15,000	Off	DM 3.00
Langenhagen			
	1:10,000	Off	DM 3.20
Lauenberg			
	1:15,000	Re	DM 2.50
Lauf/Pegnitz			
	1:10,000	Fr	DM 1.60
Lauf			
	1:5,000	Sta	DM 2.10
Lauffen/N			
	1:7,500	Sta	DM 1.80
Laupheim			
	1:7,500	Sta	DM 1.80
Lauterbach			
	1:7,500	Sta	DM 1.80
	1:6,500	Re	DM 2.25
Leer/Ostfr.			
	1:10,000	Re	DM 2.25
Leinfelden-Musberg			
	1:7,500	Off	DM 1.60
Lemgo			
	1:20,000	Re	DM 2.80
Lemgo/Lippe			
	1:10,000	Off	DM 2.50
Lenggries			
	1:10,000	Sta	DM 2.10
Leonberg			
	1:10,000	Sta	DM 2.10
Letmathe			
	1:10,000	Off	DM 3.50
Leverkusen			
	1:15,000	Falk	DM 2.90
Limburg/L			
	1:7,500	Sta	DM 2.10
Lindau/B			
	1:15,000	Sta	DM 2.40
Lindenberg			
	1:10 000	Sta	DM 2.10

Lingen
1:10,000 Re DM 2.80
Linz/Rhein o.M. Re DM 1.00
Lohr a.M.
1:5,000 Re DM 2.50
Lorrach
1:10,000 Sta DM 2.70
Lübeck u. Travemunde
1:15-25,000 Falk DM 2.90
Lübeck
Pictorial Bo DM 4.10
Ludenscheid
1:10,000 Off DM 4.80
Ludwigsburg
1:10,000 Off DM 4.20
1:15,000 Off DM 1.80
Ludwigshafen
1:15,000 Off DM 5.00
Lüneburg
1:10,000/18,000
Falk DM 2.00
1:10,000 Off DM 3.30
1:10,000 Re DM 1.80
Pictorial Bo DM 4.10
Lunen
1:20,000 Off DM 4.50
1:18,000 Sta DM 2.40
Lutjenburg-Hohwacht
1:10,000 ABK DM 0.75
Mainz
1:15,000 Stollfuss DM 4.00
Pictorial Bo DM 4.10
Mainz-Wiesbaden
1:20,000-35,000
Falk DM 3.90
1:22,000 Mair DM 3.90
Mannheim
1:15,000 Off DM 4.60
1:16,500/33,000
Falk DM 4.50
Marbach/N
1:7,500 Sta DM 2.10
Marburg
1:10,000 Sta DM 1.80
1:10,000 Becker DM 1.50
Markgroningen
1:8,000 Sta DM 1.50
Marktheidenfeld
1:7,000 Sta DM 1.95
Marktoberdorf
1:10,000 Sta DM 2.10
Marktredwitz
1:7,500 Sta DM 2.40
Markt Schwaben
1:10,000 Sta DM 1.80
Marl
1:20,000 Off DM 3.60
Mayen/Eifel
1:10,000 Sta DM 2.25
Meinerzhagen
1:7,500 Sta DM 1.50
Melsungen
1:8,000 Groth DM 2.40
Memmingen
1:8,000 Sta DM 2.70
Menden
1:10,000 Off DM 2.50
Meppen
1:10,000 Re DM 2.50
Mergentheim, Bad
1:6,000 Sta DM 2.40
Mering b. Augsburg
1:10,000 Sta DM 1.65
Merzig
1:10,000 Sta DM 1.95
Meschede
1:6,000 Off DM 3.20
Mettmann
1:5,000 Bo DM 2.70
Metzingen
1:7,500 Sta DM 1.95

Miesbach
1:6,000 Sta DM 1.95
Mittenberg
1:7,500 Sta DM 2.10
Mindelheim
1:7,500 Sta DM 2.40
Minden
1:12,500 Re DM 2.80
Minden/W
1:10,000 Brunns DM 3.90
Mittenwald
1:10,000 Sta DM 2.10
Moers
1:10,000 Off DM 4.00
Mitterteich/Franken
1:7,500 Sta DM 1.80
MönchenGladbach u. Rheydt
1:10,000 Gl DM 4.00
1:18,000 Stollfuss DM 4.00
Pictorial Bo DM 6.80
Montabaur
1:5,000 Re DM 2.25
Moosburg/Bayern
1:8,000 Sta DM 1.95
Mosbach/B
1:10,000 Sta DM 2.40
Muhlacker
1:7,500 Sta DM 1.65
Muhldorf/Obb
1:8,000 Sta DM 2.40
Mulheim/Ruhr
1:23,000 Falk DM 4.50
1:20,000 Off DM 4.50
Munchberg
1:8,000 Sta DM 1.80
München - Central
1:20,000 Komp DM 1.30
1:22,500 Komp DM 4.90
1:22,000 Mair DM 4.80
München - with suburbs
1:19-33,000 Falk DM 4.50
1:22,000 JRO DM 6.80
1:22,000 Komp DM 4.90
Stadtatlas
1:22,500 Komp DM 9.80
1:6,000 Hw DM 3.80
1:20,000 Falk Olympiaplan
DM 2.00
Fleis Offizieller Olympia - Stadtplan
1:22,500
1:22,500 Olympia
Komp DM 4.80
Pictorial JRO DM 8.50
Pictorial Mair
Olympia DM 4.80
München Bildplan Weber DM 5.50
München Bildkarte Weber DM 1.25
München wall map in 4 sheets
1:15,000 Komp DM 44.50
Pictorial Bo DM 4.80
Munderkingen
1:7,500 Sta DM 1.80
Munsingen
1:5,000 Sta DM 2.40
Münster/W
1:16,500-22,000
Falk DM 2.90
1:15,000 Off DM 3.80
Pictorial Bo DM 4.10
Murnau/Staffelsee
1:10,000 Sta DM 2.25
Murrhardt
1:10,000 Sta DM 1.80
Nagold
1:10,000 Sta DM 2.10
Naila
1:7,500 Sta DM 1.95
Nauheim, Bad
1:8,000 Sta DM 2.40
Neckargmund
1:10,000 Ko DM 1.80

Neckarsulm
1:10,000 Sta DM 1.95
Neheim-Husten
1:15,000 Off DM 3.60
Neuburg/Donau
1:7,500 Sta DM 1.95
Neuenkirchen
1:12,500 Re DM 2.50
Neuhausen a.d.f.
1:7,500 Sta DM 1.65
Neumarkt/Opf
1:8,000 Re DM 1.80
1:10,000 Sta DM 2.10
Neumunster
1:20,000 ABK DM 3.00
1:10,000 Re DM 2.80
Neunkirchen/Saar
1:12,500 Re DM 2.60
Neuss
1:18,000 Sta DM 2.40
1:15,000 Off DM 4.10
1:16,500 Gl DM 2.50
Pictorial Bo DM 4.10
Neustadt/Aisch
1:5,000 Fr DM 2.10
Neustadt, Bad (Saale)
1:6,000 Raab DM 2.20
Neustadt/Coburg
1:7,500 Sta DM 2.10
Neustadt/Holstein
1:10,000 ABK DM 2.50
Neustadt/Schwarzwald
1:10,000 Sta DM 1.95
Neustadt/Weinstr.
1:10,000 Sta DM 2.70
Neuwied
1:10,000 Sta DM 2.10
Neviges
1:7,500 VV DM 3.20
Niederlahnstein-Oberlahnstein-Braubach
1:12,500 Sta DM 1.95
Norden
1:10,000 Off DM 3.00
1:10,000 Sta DM 2.10
Nordenham
1:10,000 Off DM 2.40
Nordlingen
1:8,000 Sta DM 2.40
Nürnberg
1:22,000 Mair DM 4.80
1:20,000 atlas
E DM 5.90
Nurnberg-Furth
1:16-24,000 Falk DM 4.50
1:20,000 Off DM 5.20
1:10,000 wall map in 4 sheets
Off DM 19.20
1:22,000 Komp DM 2.50
Pictorial Bo DM 4.80
Nurtingen
1:10,000 Sta DM 2.40
Nussloch
1:7,500 Sta DM 1.65
Oberhausen/Mulheim
1:25,000 Mair DM 4.80
Oberhausen
1:15,000 Off DM 4.00
Oberlahnstein
1:12,500 Sta DM 1.95
Oberndorf/N
1:8,000 Sta DM 1.65
Oberstorf/Allg
1:7,500 Sta DM 2.25
Oberursel/T
1:10,000 Sta DM 1.50
Ochsenfurt
1:7,500 Sta DM 1.95
Oer-Erkenschwick
1:10,000 Off DM 2.00

Place / Scale	Publisher	Price
Offenbach/Main		
1:15,000	Rav	DM 4.00
1:15,000	Off	DM 3.50
Offenbach		
1:15,000	Re	DM 2.90
Pictorial	Bo	DM 4.10
Offenburg/B		
1:10,000	Off	DM 6.00
1:8,000	Sta	DM 2.40
Ohningen		
1:6,000	Sta	DM 2.40
Oldenburg		
Pictorial	Bo	DM 4.10
Oldesloe, Bad		
1:10,000	Re	DM 2.80
Opladen		
1:12,500	Sta	DM 1.80
Osnabruck		
1:15,000-28,500	Falk	DM 2.90
Pictorial	Bo	DM 4.10
Osterode/H		
1:10,000	Sta	DM 2.40
Paderborn		
1:15,000	Re	DM 2.80
1:8,000-15,000	VV	DM 3.60
Passau		
1:10,000	Sta	DM 2.40
Pegnitz		
1:6,000	Sta	DM 1.95
Peine		
1:15,000	Sta	DM 2.40
1:12,500	Re	DM 2.50
Peissenberg		
1:10,000	Sta	DM 1.80
Peitling		
1:7,500	Sta	DM 1.65
Penzberg		
1:10,000	Sta	DM 1.80
Pfarrkirchen o.M.	Re	DM 1.00
1:7,500	Sta	DM 1.95
Pforzheim		
1:12,500	Off	DM 4.50
Pfronten	VV	DM 1.80
Pfullingen		
1:7,500	Sta	DM 1.50
Pinneberg		
1:15,000	Re	DM 2.80
Pirmasens		
1:15,000	St	DM 2.70
Plattling		
1:8,000	Sta	DM 1.65
Plettenberg/West		
1:20,000	Off	DM 3.30
Plochingen		
1:7,500	Sta	DM 1.80
Plon 1:11,000	ABK	DM 2.50
Porz		
1:16,500/25,000	Falk	DM 2.90
Radevormwald o.M.	VV	DM 2.50
Radolfzell		
1:10,000	Sta	DM 2.40
Rastatt		
1:10,000	Sta	DM 2.40
Ratingen		
1:10,000	Off	DM 4.00
Ravensburg		
1:8,000	Sta	DM 2.40
1:7,500	Off	DM 3.40
Recklinghausen		
1:23,000	Falk	DM 4.50
1:15,000	Off	DM 3.00
Reichenbach/Fils		
1:7,000	Sta	DM 1.95
Regen		
1:7,500	Off	DM 1.50
Regensburg		
1:12,500	Bosse	DM 2.50
1:12,000	Sta	DM 2.70
1:10,000	Off	DM 4.20
Rehau		
1:10,000	Sta	DM 1.95
Reichenhall		
1:10,000	Sta	DM 1.95
Remscheid		
1:16,000	Stollfuss	DM 3.80
Pictorial	Bo	DM 4.10
Rendsburg		
1:12,500	Re	DM 2.80
Reutlingen		
1:10,000	Off	DM 4.40
Rheinberg		
1:12,500	Sta	DM 1.80
Rheinfelden/Baden		
1:10,000	Sta	DM 2.10
Rheinhausen		
1:17,000	Off	DM 4.80
Rheinhausen		
1:12,000	Sta	DM 1.80
Rheinkamp		
1:15,000	Off	DM 3.50
Rheydt siehe Monchen-Gladbach		
Riedlingen		
1:7,500	Sta	DM 1.65
Rielasingen		
1:10,000	Sta	DM 1.65
Rodenkirchen beikoln		
1:12,500	Off	DM 5.90
Rosenheim		
1:12,500	Kro	DM 2.50
1:10,000	Sta	DM 2.10
Rothenburg o.b.T.		
1:7,500	Sta	DM 2.40
Pictorial	Bo	DM 4.80
Rottenburg/N.		
1:7,500	Sta	DM 2.40
Rottweil		
1:10,000	Sta	DM 2.40
Ruhpolding		
1:10,000	Sta	DM 1.95
Ruhrgebiet-Atlas		
1:50,000	Falk	DM 12.80
Rumeln-Kaldenhausen		
1:10,000	Sta	DM 1.80
Russelsheim		
1:10,000	Sta	DM 2.25
Saarbrücken		
1:11-22,000	Falk	DM 2.90
1:12,500	Off	DM 6.00
Pictorial	Bo	DM 4.10
Saarlouis		
1:10,000	Off	DM 3.50
Sackingen		
1:7,500	Sta	DM 2.40
Salach		
1:7,500	Sta	DM 0.60
St Georgen		
1:7,500	Sta	DM 2.40
St Ingbert		
1:10,000	Re	DM 2.50
St Wendel		
1:10,000	Re	DM 1.80
Saulgau		
1:7,000	Sta	DM 2.10
Schiefbahn/b. Monchengladbach		
1:10,000	Sta	DM 1.80
Schelklingen		
1:7,500	Sta	DM 1.65
Schleissbeim		
1:10,000	Sta	DM 1.95
Schleswig		
1:12,750	ABK	DM 2.50
1:12,000	Re	DM 2.80
Schliersee		
1:12,500	Sta	DM 1.80
Schluchtern	VV	DM 0.50
Schmiden		
1:7,500	Sta	DM 1.65
Schongau		
1:10,000	Sta	DM 2.40
Schopfheim		
1:7,500	Sta	DM 1.65
Schoningen		
1:7,500	Sta	DM 2.10
Schorndorf		
1:8,000	Sta	DM 1.95
Schramberg		
1:8,000	Sta	DM 2.10
Schwabach		
1:8,000	Sta	DM 2.40
Schwab. Gmund		
1:20,000	Sta	DM 2.40
1:12,500	Off	DM 2.50
Schwab. Hall		
1:10,000	Sta	DM 2.70
1:10,000	Off	DM 2.80
Schwabmunchen		
1:10,000	Sta	DM 1.80
Schwandorf		
1:9,000	Re	DM 1.80
Schweinfurt		
1:10,000	Sta	DM 2.00
Schwartau, Bad		
1:10,000	Off	DM 4.00
Schwelm-Gevelsberg		
1:23,000	Falk	DM 2.50
Schwelm		
1:10,000	Off	DM 4.60
Schwenningen		
1:7,500	Sta	DM 1.95
Schwerte		
1:10,000	Off	DM 4.00
Schwetzingen		
1:8,000	Sta	DM 2.40
Seesen/Harz		
1:7,500	Off	DM 2.60
Segeberg, Bad		
1:10,000	Re	DM 2.80
Selb		
1:7,500	Sta	DM 2.40
Sennestadt		
1:5,000	Off	DM 5.00
Siegburg		
1:12,000	Stollfuss	DM 3.20
Siegen		
1:17,000	Sta	DM 2.40
Pictorial	Bo	DM 4.10
Sigmaringen		
1:7,500	Sta	DM 2.10
Sindellfingen		
1:8,000	Sta	DM 1.50
1:10,000	Off	DM 2.00
Singen/Hoh.		
1:10,000	Sta	DM 2.40
Sinsheim		
1:7,500	Sta	DM 2.10
Soest		
1:10,000	Off	DM 4.00
1:10,000	Sta	DM 2.40
Pictorial	Bo	DM 4.10
Solingen		
1:23,000	Falk	DM 2.90
Solingen-Haan		
1:15,000	GI	DM 3.80
1:15,000	Stollfuss	DM 3.80
Sonthofen		
1:10,000	Sta	DM 2.40
Spaichingen		
1:5,000	Sta	DM 1.80
Speyer		
1:10,000	Sta	DM 2.10
Sprendlingen		
1:9,000	Re	DM 2.00
Stade		
Pictorial	Bo	DM 4.80
Stockach		
1:7,500	Sta	DM 1.80

Place	Scale	Publisher	Price
Straubing			
	1:10,000	Sta	DM 1.95
Stuttgart			
	Pictorial	Bo	DM 4.80
	1:15,000	Komp	DM 2.50
	1:15,000	Off	DM 5.40
Stuttgart central			
	1:14,000	Off	DM 2.70
	1:16-22,000	Falk	DM 2.50
	1:16-26,000	Falk	DM 4.80
Sulzbach-Rosenberg			
	1:10,000	Sta	DM 2.40
Sulzbach/Saar			
	1:10,000	Re	DM 2.00
Sussen			
	1:5,000	Sta	DM 2.50
Tailfingen			
	1:10,000	Sta	DM 2.40
Tauberbischofsheim			
	1:5,000	Sta	DM 1.95
Tettnang			
	1:10,000	Sta	DM 1.95
Tolz, Bad			
	1:7,500	Sta	DM 2.40
Traunstein			
	1:7,000	Sta	DM 2.25
Treysa/Hessen o.M.		Gro	DM 1.50
Trier			
	1:10,000	Stollfuss	DM 3.60
	1:20,000	Re	DM 2.80
	1:23,500	Falk	DM 2.90
	Pictorial	Bo	DM 4.80
Trossingen			
	1:7,500	Sta	DM 1.80
Tubingen			
	1:10,000	Off	DM 7.00
Tuttlingen			
	1:7,500	Sta	DM 2.40
	1:5,000	Off	DM 1.95
Tutzing			
	1:12,500	Sta	DM 1.95
Uebach-Palenberg			
	1:15,000	Off	DM 3.00
Ueberlingen			
	1:10,000	Sta	DM 2.40
Uhingen			
	1:8,000	Sta	DM 0.60
Ulm/Donau-Neu-Ulm			
	1:10,000	Off	DM 4.00
	Pictorial	Bo	DM 4.80
Unna/Westf.		Off	DM 2.60
Urach			
	1:7,500	Sta	DM 1.95
Vaihingen			
	1:5,500	Sta	DM 1.80
Vechta			
	1:15,000	Off	DM 3.50
Velbert			
	1:7,500	Off	DM 6.50
Verden/Aller			
	1:15,000	Re	DM 1.80
Viernheim			
	1:10,000	Sta	DM 1.50
Viersen			
	1:12,500	Sta	DM 2.40
Vilbel, Bad			
	1:10,000	Sta	DM 1.80
Villingen			
	1:10,000	Sta	DM 2.40
Vilsbiburg			
	1:5,000	Kro	DM 1.90
Volklingen			
	1:10,000	Off	DM 3.20
Waiblingen			
	1:7,500	Sta	DM 2.40
Waldkirch/Br sg.			
	1:6,000	Sta	DM 2.40
Waldshut			
	1:10,000	Sta	DM 2.40
Walldorf/Baden			
	1:10,000	Sta	DM 1.80
Walldorff/Hessen			
	1:5,000	Re	DM 1.50
Walsrode			
	1:14,000	Gro	DM 1.30
Walsum			
	1:10,000	Off	DM 4.50
Waltrop			
	1:20,000	Off	DM 4.00
Wangen/Allgau			
	1:10,000	Sta	DM 2.40
Wanne-Eickel			
	1:10,000	Off	DM 4.50
Wasseralfingen			
	1:7,500	Sta	DM 1.65
Wasserburg/Inn			
	1:7,500	Sta	DM 2.10
Wattenscheid			
	1:15,000	Off	DM 4.50
Wedel			
	1:10,000	Re	DM 2.50
Wehr/Baden			
	1:10,000	Sta	DM 1.95
Weiden/Opf.			
	1:12,500	Sta	DM 2.40
Weil/Rhein		Sta	DM 2.10
Weilheim/Obb			
	1:10,000	Sta	DM 2.40
Weingarten/Wurtt			
	1:8,000	Sta	DM 2.40
Weinheim/Bergstr.			
	1:10,000	Sta	DM 2.25
Weinsberg			
	1:8,000	Sta	DM 2.10
Weissenburg/Bayern			
	1:10,000	Sta	DM 2.40
Weissenhorn			
	1:7,500	Sta	DM 1.65
Wendlingen/N.			
	1:10,000	Sta	DM 1.95
Werdohl			
	1:10,000	Off	DM 3.00
Werl			
	1:5,000	Off	DM 3.00
Wermelskirchen			
	1:10,000	Off	DM 3.50
Wernau/Neckar			
	1:7,500	Sta	DM 1.50
Wertheim/M.			
	1:10,000	Sta	DM 2.10
	1:10,000	Re	DM 2.00
Wesel			
	1:15,000	Sta	DM 2.70
Westerholt			
	1:5,000	Off	DM 3.20
Wetzlar			
	1:12,000	Sta	DM 1.95
Wiesbaden			
	1:12,500	Gro	DM 3.90
	1:15,000	Off	DM 5.90
Wiesbaden Mainz			
	1:20,000-35,000	Falk	DM 4.50
Wiesbaden			
	1:22,000	Mair	DM 4.80
	Pictorial	Bo	DM 4.10
Wiesental/b. Bruchsal			
	1:7,500	Sta	DM 1.80
Wildungen, Bad		Gro	DM 1.20
	1:10,000	Sta	DM 1.95
Willich			
	1:15,000	Sta	DM 1.80
Willingen			
	1:15,000	Gro	DM 2.40
Wimpfen, Bad			
	1:10,000	Sta	DM 2.10
Winnenden			
	1:7,000	Sta	DM 2.10
Wipperfurth o.M.		Off	DM 1.30
Witten			
	1:20,000	Gro	DM 3.30
	1:18,000	Sta	DM 2.40
Witten			
	Pictorial	Bo	DM 4.80
Wittlich			
	1:10,000	Sta	DM 2.40
Witzenhausen			
	1:10,000	Off	DM 0.60
Wolfenbüttel			
	Pictorial	Bo	DM 4.10
Wolfrathausen			
	1:15,000	Sta	DM 2.10
Wolfsburg			
	1:15,000	Sta	DM 2.10
	1:16,000-25,000	Falk	DM 2.50
Worishofen, Bad			
	1:12,500	Sta	DM 1.95
Worms			
	1:10,000	Off	DM 4.00
Wunsiedal			
	1:6,000	Sta	DM 2.10
Wuppertal			
	1:20,000	Off	DM 3.20
	1:18,000-34,000	Falk	DM 4.50
Wurzburg			
	1:15,000	Sta	DM 2.25
Zweibrucken			
	1:10,000	Off	DM 2.25
	1:12,000	Sta	DM 2.40

STADTPLANWERK RUHRGEBIET
Various Scales
In 127 sheets
Essen : Siedlungsverband Ruhrkohlenbezirk
Various Sizes
Street map series of the Ruhr District. Buildings in grey, water features blue, writing in black.

Scale	Size
1:10,000	162 x 92
1:15,000	68 x 41
1:20,000	51 x 30

C OFFICIAL SURVEYS

WEST GERMANY – OFFICIAL SURVEYS
Large scale surveys, regional and admin. mapping is carried out by the Land Survey Office (Landesvermessungsamt) of each individual state ie Baden Wurttemberg, Bayern, Hessen, Niedersachsen, Nordrhein-Westfalen, Rheinland Pfalz, Saarlandes, Schleswig-Holstein. Cadastral Plans by State Cadastral Offices (Katasteramter) and small scale National Series by Institute of Applied Geodesy (Institut for Angewandte Geodasie).

ZUSAMMENSTELLUNG DER WICHTIGSTEN ZEICHEN FUR DIE NEUEN TOPOGRAPHISCHEN KARTEN
1:25,000-1:200,000
Stuttgart : Baden-Wurttenberg Lv
Showing conventional signs and symbols used in Topog. series
1:25,000-1:200,000 DM 2.00

ÜBERSICHTSKARTE VON MITTELEUROPA
1:300,000
Inst. fur Angewandte Geodäsie
see GERMANY 430 C.

TOPOGRAPHISCHE
UBERSICHTSKARTE
1:200,000
In 44 sheets, see index 430. 1/6
Frankfurt : Inst. für Angewandte
Geodäsie, 1972
45 x 45
Topog. series, contoured in brown, water in blue, vegetation in green. The 12 sheets for Bayern are published by Bayern Lv and are in a slightly different style.
Available in 3 editions :
Normal edition DM 3.20
Shaded Relief
(Schummerung) DM 3.90
Oro-hydrographic (contours
and water and relief
shading only) DM 3.20

TOPOGRAPHISCHE UBERSICHTS-
KARTE DES DEUTSCHEN REICHES
1:200,000
Inst. für Angewandte Geodäsie
see GERMANY 430 C

TOPOGRAPHISCHE KARTE
1:100,000
TK 100, see Index 430. 1/7
Official State Surveys (Lv), 1954+
50 x 50 (app)
Topog. series in progress. Available in 5 eds; Normalausgabe (contours brown, vegetation green, water blue), Schummerungsausgabe (with hill shading), Orohydrographische Ausgabe (contours brown, relief shading grey, water blue), Strassenausgabe (roads in red).
Normal and Orohydrographic
editions DM 3.20
Schummerung DM 3.90

KARTE DES DEUTSCHEN REICHES
1:100,000
Inst. für Angewandte Geodäsie/
Landvermessungsamt
see GERMANY 430 C.

TOPOGRAPHISCHE KARTE
1:50,000
TK 50, see index 430. 1/8
Official State Surveys (Lv), 1957+
Topog. series available in 4 eds:
Normalausgabe (5/6 col),
Schummerungsausgabe (5-7 col. with hill shading). Orohydrographische Ausgabe (showing only water in blue, contours brown). Wanderwegausgabe (with footpaths in red)
Normal DM 3.20
Sch. DM 3.90
Orohyd. DM 3.20
Wand. DM 3.90

MUSTERBLATT FUR DIE
TOPOGRAPHISCHE KARTE
1:50,000
Stuttgart : Baden-Württemberg Lv
Conventional sign sheet showing symbols used in 1:50,000 Topog. series.
DM 4.60

TOPOGRAPHISCHE KARTE
1:25,000
TK 25, see index 430. 1/9
Official State Surveys (Lv)
44 x 48
Basic edition in black and white with water blue and contours brown.
Some sheets available with woodland areas in green or in 'Oro-hydrographic' edition showing blue water and brown contours only, also in black and white without water and contours in colour.
Standard editions DM 3.20
Orohydrographic DM 2.60
1 colour DM 2.60

ZEICHENERKLÄRUNG
1:25,000
Stuttgart : Baden-Württemberg, Lv
Conventional sign charts showing topog. map symbols for the 1:25,000 series.
Württemberg alt (to 1921) 57 x 56
Württemberg neu (from 1922) 56 x 52
Baden alt (to 1925) 61 x 57
Baden neu (from 1925) 61 x 57
Each DM 3.20

TOPOGRAPHISCHE KARTE
1:10,000
68 x 68
Photo-enlargement of 1:25,000
topog. series. Sold in ¼ sheets.
Baden Württemberg Lv:
1 col. ed. DM 4.00
Bayern Lv :
Photog. print DM 50
4 sheets DM 15
Hessen Lv :
Blueprint DM 3.90
Nordrhein-Westfalen Lv:
Blueprint DM 4.00
Rheinland-Pfalz Lv:
Blueprint DM 4.00
Saarlandes Lv:
Blueprint DM 4.00

DEUTSCHE GRUNDKARTE
1:5,000 or 1:2,500
Katasteramt, 1926+
Published with or without relief by each individual State, showing detailed topographic detail.
Baden-Württemberg :
1:5,000 58 x 57
2 or 3 col. ed. contours
brown etc.
Standard sheet DM 9.00
Half sheet DM 4.50
Blueprint DM 4.50
Niedersachsen :
1:5,000 40 x 40
Blueprint with contours
DM 6.00
Blueprint without contours
DM 5.00
Nordrhein-Westfalen : 40 x 40
(1:2,500)
Blueprint DM 8.00
(1:5,000)
1 col. ed. DM 6.00
2 col. ed. DM 6.00
Rheinland - Pfalz :
1:5,000 40 x 40
1 col. ed. DM 5.00
Col. ed. DM 6.00
Blueprint DM 5.00
Saarland :
1:5,000 40 x 40
2 col. ed.
Blueprint
1 col. ed.
Schleswig-Holstein :
1:5,000
Blueprint DM 5.00
Blueprint with contours
DM 6.00

KATASTERPLANKARTE
1:5,000
Stuttgart : Baden-Württemberg Lv
58 x 57
Cadastral planning maps available in 1-col. or blueprint sheets. DM 7.00

HOHENFLURKARTEN BAYERN
1:2,500 and 1:5,000
München : Bayerische Lv
Topog. land series, showing field boundaries, land type, vegetation cover in black, contours in brown.
1 col. ed. DM 18
2 col. ed. DM 30
Contour ed. DM 10

KATASTERKARTEN
Munchen : Bayerische Lv
Cadastral maps available in 3 eds :
Flurkarten : 1:1,000, 1:1,250
1:2,500, 1:3,000
Showing property sites and
boundaries, for agricultural and
urban areas
Without field boundaries DM 8
With field boundaries, 1 col. DM 10
With field boundaries, 2 col. DM 22
Schätzungskarten :
Land valuation maps
1 col. ed. DM 12
2 col. ed. DM 24

KATASTERPLANKARTE
1:5,000
Hannover : Niedersachsen Lv
Blueprint cadastral plans of
Niedersachsen. DM 4.00

PFÄLZISCHE HOHENFLURKARTE
1:5,000
Koblenz : Rheinland-Pfalz Lv
Cadastral series showing land property areas.
1909/12 series, each DM 5.00
with contours DM 6.00
1 col. print DM 5.00
Col. eds. DM 6.00

LUFTBILDKARTE
1:5,000
Koblenz : Rheinland-Pfalz Lv
Orthophoto maps on sheet lines of Deutsche Grundkarte, 1:5,000.
Blueprint ed. DM 5.00

LUFTBILDAUSWERTUNG
1:5,000
Hannover : Niedersachsen Lv
Series of air photos in blueprint ed. available as base map or with contours.
DM 5.00

KATASTERPLANKARTE
1:2,500
Hannover : Niedersachsen Lv
Cadastral plans in blueprint ed. for planning purposes. DM 8.00

D POLITICAL & ADMINISTRATIVE

FEDERATIVNAYA RESPUBLIKA
GERMANII
1:1,000,000
Moskva : GUGK, 1973
Col. study map showing water features, settlements, admin. divisions and centres, communications, boundaries, economic details, pop. Geog. description. kop 30

KREISGRENZENKARTE DER BUNDESREPUBLIK DEUTSCHLAND
1:1,000,000
Bad Godesberg : Instituf für Landeskunde, 1970
Shows boundaries of admin. districts.
In 3 cols. DM 4.50
Also at 1:1,500,000 DM 3.00

DEUTSCHE ORGANISATIONS- UND VERTRETERBEZIRKSKARTE
1:1,000,000
Frankfurt : Revenstein
70 x 98
Series of business planning maps with various boundaries overprinted on subdued base map of towns and communications. Berlin inset.
Maps in series:
80 Admin. boundaries DM 7.80
801H Admin. and Chamber of Commerce boundaries DM 14.80
80N Admin. and 'Nielsen' regions DM 12.80
80P Admin. and Postal regions with 2 figure postal numbers DM 8.80
89 Organisation and Planning base map DM 5.60

GEMEINDEGRENZENKARTE
1:1,000,000
Bonn - Bad Godesberg : Inst. für Landeskunde, 1964
4 colour map showing the parish districts of W Germany : boundaries of 6.6.1961 DM 4.50
Edition also available without district names DM 4.50

GEMEINDEGRENZENKARTE
1:1,000,000
Bonn - Bad Godesberg : Inst. für Landeskunde, 1971
Coloured map of W. Germany showing parish admin. areas, boundaries of 27.5.70 DM 4.50

DIE FINANZAMTSBEZIRKE IN DER BUNDESREPUBLIK DEUTSCHLAND
1:1,000,000
Bonn - Bad Godesberg : Inst. für Landeskunde, 1959
Map showing in colour the Revenue Offices as at 1.10.58. List of offices and head offices on reverse. DM 6.00

OBERFINANZDIREKTIONS- UND FINANZAMTSBEZIRKE
1:1,000,000
Bonn - Bad Godesberg : Inst. für Landeskunde, 1968
4 colour map showing Chief Finance Offices and Inland Revenue districts, as at 1.1.67. DM 9.00

GLIEDERUNG UND BEZIRKE DER ORDENTLICHEN GERICHTE
1:1,000,000
Bonn - Bad Godesberg : Inst. für Landeskunde, 1968
4 colour map showing judicial areas and divisions as at 1.1.67. DM 9.00

KARTE DER WAHLKREISE FUR DIE WAHL ZUM FUNFTEN (UND SECHSTEN) BUNDESTAG
1:1,000,000
Bonn - Bad Godesberg : Inst. für Landeskunde, 1964
Coloured map showing electoral districts for the 5th (and 6th) Bundestag elections. With insets of large city electoral wards, and list on reverse. DM 3.50

DIE ARBEITSAMTSBEZIRKE IN DER BUNDESREPUBLIK DEUTSCHLAND
1:1,000,000
Bonn - Bad Godesberg : Inst. für Landeskunde, 1960
5 colour map showing Labour Exchange areas as at 1.7.59, 15 insets, and list of State Labour Exchanges, etc. on reverse. DM 11.50

ORGANISATIONSKARTE DEUTSCHLAND
1:750,000
No 3773
München : JRO
88 x 116
Planning map showing principal communications and admin. boundaries. Col. on white background, with gazetteer. DM 12.80
Mounted CR DM 52

VERWALTUNGSGRENZEN UND POSTLEITEINHEITEN
1:1,000,000
Bonn - Bad Godesberg : Inst. für Landeskunde, 1966
Coloured map showing admin. boundaries and postal areas. List of postal areas. DM 6.00
Map as above, but only showing postal districts DM 6.00

POSTLEITZAHLENKARTE
1:500,000
In 2 sheets
Munchen : JRO
88 x 116
Showing postal areas, in large numbers, smaller postal districts - old and new numbers. In red on white background map. With gazetteer.
Sheets :
3568 North
3569 South
Each DM 12.80
Mounted CR DM 52
Gazetteer DM 8.00

ORGANISATIONSKARTE BRD
1:500,000
In 2 sheets
München : JRO
88 x 117
Showing admin. boundaries and communications on white background.
Sheets :
No 3561 Süddeutschland
No 3562 Westdeutschland
Each DM 12.80
Mounted CR DM 52

ORGANISATIONSWANDKARTE
1:300,000
In 2 sheets
München : JRO
Various sizes
Wall map for planning purposes : showing admin. areas, and communications.
Sheets :
3386 Nordwestdeutschland 126 x 195
3387 Süddeutschland 190 x 130
Each DM 60
Mounted CR DM 154

ORGANISATIONSKARTE
1:300,000
In 9 sheets, see index 430. 1/10
München : JRO
Various sizes
Planning maps with admin. boundaries and communications in 5 cols. on white background.
Sheets available :
3301 München 123 x 88
3303 Nürnberg 123 x 88
3304 Frankfurt-Mannheim, Rheinlandpfalz, Saarland 123 x 88
3305 Düsseldorf-Koln, Nordrhein-Westfalen 123 x 88
3306 Hannover-Bremen, Niedersachsen 123 x 98
3307 Hamburg-Kiel, Schleswig-Holstein 88 x 123
3311 Baden-Württemberg 88 x 123
Each DM 12.80
3364 Hessen 75 x 88 DM 8.80
3369 Bayern (Sheets 3301, 3303) 123 x 145 DM 25.60

BÜROKARTE BUNDESREPUBLIK DEUTSCHLAND
1:300,000
In 4 sheets
Frankfurt : Ravenstein
Communications; boundaries; tables. Admin. and planning maps.
No 6 Niedersachsen 114 x 111 DM 18
12 Süddeutschland 160 x 124 DM 24
17 Schleswig-Holstein 69 x 85 DM 10
60 Westdeutschland 99 x 135 DM 18

GEMEINDEGRENZENKARTE (PARISH BOUNDARIES)
1:300,000
In 25 sheets
Bad Godesberg : Bundesforschungsanstalt für Landeskunde und Raumordnung, 1970
70 x 50 each
Map of Parish boundaries with names in 4 cols.
Each DM 2.70

DEUTSCHE LÄNDERKARTE
1:250,000
In 9 sheets
Frankfurt : Ravenstein
State wall maps showing communications and boundaries in colour.
401 Schleswig-Holstein und Hamburg 80 x 100
402 Niedersachsen Hamburg und Bremen 140 x 100
404 Niedersachsen-Ost 88 x 124
405 Nordrhein-Westfalen 109 x 88

406 Rheinland-Pfalz und Saarland 80 x 100
407 Baden-Württemberg 88 x 124
408 Hessen 80 x 100
409 Bayern-Nord 124 x 88
410 Bayern-Süd 124 x 88
Each DM 16.00
Map no 402 DM 28.00

DEUTSCHE ORGANISATIONS KARTE
1:250,000
In 9 sheets, see index 430. 1/11
Stuttgart : Mair, 1968+
Col. on white background showing all administrative boundaries, postal districts and numbers, and centres of pop.
Sheets published :

Bayern-Württemberg	96 x 108
Bayern- Nord	120 x 98
Bayern- Süd	132 x 98
Hessen	84 x 108
Niedersachsen - Nord	132 x 98
Niedersachsen - Süd	72 x 62
Nordrhein- Westfalen	108 x 98
Rheinland Pfalz - Saarland	84 x 99
Schleswig-Holstein	84 x 80

DM 12

BEZIRKSKARTEN
1:200,000
In 15 sheets, see index 430. 1/12
Frankfurt : Ravenstein, No 100- 113
Various sizes
Col. regional series with communications, admin. boundaries.
According to size DM 10.00 - 19.00

KREISKARTENWERK
1:100,000
115 sheets, see index 430. 1/13
München : Ernst
Comprehensive series of district maps, roads classified with footpaths, admin. boundaries and places of interest.

Baden Württemberg

GEMEINDE- UND KREISKARTE VON BADEN-WÜRTTEMBERG
1:350,000
Stuttgart : Baden-Württemberg Lv, 1974
70 x 81
Map showing new district and regional admin. areas in red and green at 1.1.74
6 col. ed. DM 4.20

KREISKARTE VON BADEN WÜRTTEMBERG
1:250,000
Stuttgart : Baden-Württemberg, 1973
125 x 103
Black and white map of admin. areas. DM 5.30
Also available at :
1:1,000,000 28 x 32 DM 0.50
1:1,300,000 DIN A4 DM 0.50

KARTE DER GEMEINDEGRENZEN - BADEN
1:200,000
Stuttgart : Baden-Württemberg Lv
General base maps showing regional admin. boundaries.
Sheets available :
Reg-Bezirk Südbaden, 1973 93 x 86 DM 2.70
Nordbaden, 1973 93 x 70 DM 2.50

MARKUNGSKARTE DER REG-BEZIRKE NORDWÜRTTEMBERG UND SÜDWURTTEMBERG - HOHENZOLLERN
1:200,000
Stuttgart : Baden-Württemberg Lv, 1970
90 x 118
Black and white map showing admin. districts. Enlargement of 1:350,000 map. DM 4.00

VERWALTUNGS- UND VERKEHRS-KARTE BADEN-WÜRTTEMBERG
1:100,000
In 12 sheets
Stuttgart : Baden-Württemberg Lv, 1973
7 col. map showing boundaries, district towns, road numbers, autobahns, secondary roads, various types of road classified by col.
Each DM 3.30
Also available at 1:200 000 in 2 sheets, 1973 (107 x 77 each) DM 4.00

SCHUL- UND KREISKARTEN
1:100,000
Stuttgart : Baden-Württemberg Lv
Col. district maps for schools; available for :
Kreise Biberach
Calw
Ehingen
Freudenstadt
Horb
Munsingen
Ravensberg
Reutlingen
Rottwell
Tettnang
Tübingen
Wangen
Each DM 2.50

Bayern

VERWALTUNGSKARTE VON BAYERN
1:800,000
München : Bayerische Lv
Map showing administrative boundaries. DM 1.30
Also at 1:1,200,000 DM 1.30

BAYERN, GEMEINDEGRENZENZKARTE
1:500,000
München : Bayerische Lv, 1972
80 x 90
Monochrome admin. map, with new boundaries and overprint of parishes.
52pp key index.
Complete DM 10.50

ORGANISATIONSKARTE - BAYERN
1:500,000
No 3563
München : JRO
78 x 88
Showing admin. boundaries in red, with communications in black on white background. DM 10.80
Also available in various mounted styles.

AMTSBEZIRKSUBERSICHTSKARTE VON BAYERN
1:100,000
In 38 sheets
München : Bayerische Lv, 1972
2 col. map showing local govt. boundaries in col, and index to locality plans.
Each DM 5

VERWALTUNGSKARTE VON BAYERN
1:100,000
München : Bayerische Lv
Series showing admin. areas. Based on Karte des Deutschen Reichs sheet lines, showing city, district boundaries in red overprint.
Sheet DM 3.20
Half sheet DM 1.60
Quarter sheet DM 0.90

Hessen

KREISGRENZKARTE VON HESSEN
1:500,000
Wiesbaden : Hessische Lv
Black and white map showing admin. districts (Kreise). DM 0.80
Also available at :
1:750,000 DM 0.50
and 1:1,000,000 DM 0.50

VERWALTUNGSKARTE VON HESSEN
1:200 000
Wiesbaden : Hessische Lv
Admin. areas map of Hesse, showing communications, admin. boundaries.
3 col. ed. (planning) DM 2
5 col. ed. (general) DM 4

GEMEINDEGRENZEKARTE VON HESSEN
1:200,000
Wiesbaden : Hessische Lv. 1972
94 x 143
2 col. map showing admin. areas and boundaries. DM 2.00

VERWALTUNGSKARTE DER REGIERUNGSBEZIRKE DARMSTADT, KASSEL, WIESBADEN
1:200,000
Wiesbaden : Hessische Lv
District map showing boundaries as at 29.4.1968.
3 col. ed. (planning map) DM 1.50
5 col. ed. (general map) DM 3.00

GEMEINDEGRENZENÜBERSICHT HESSEN
1:100,000
Wiesbaden : Hessische Lv
Black and white map showing and naming admin. areas. DM 0.80

Niedersachsen

NIEDERSACHSEN-PLANUNGSKARTE
1:500,000
Hannover : Niedersächsiche Lv, 1970
83 x 59
Col. planning map showing industrial, agricultural, park regions etc.

VERKEHRS- UND VERWALTUNGS-KARTE VON NIEDERSACHSEN
1:500,000
Hannover : Niedersächsische Lv
70 x 63
Communications map showing admin. areas.
Col. DM 4.80
Subdued col. DM 4.80

LÄNDER- UND PROVINZKARTEN NIEDERSACHSEN
1:300,000
Hannover : Niedersächsische Lv
96 x 111
Col. map showing provinces.
DM 8.00

NIEDERSACHSEN - JRO ORGANISATIONSKARTE
1:300,000
3306
München : JRO
135 x 100
Col. map of state and district boundaries, showing communications. DM 12.80

KARTE DER GEMEINDEGRENZEN - NIEDERSACHSEN
1:200,000
In 12 sheets
Hannover : Niedersächsische Lv
34 x 28
General base maps showing regional admin. boundaries.
Standard sheets :
1 col. DM 1.40
Col. DM 1.90
Also available as 6 double sheets, 45 x 30
1 col. DM 1.90
Col. DM 2.70

RICHTWERK-ÜBERSICHTSKARTE VON NIEDERSACHSEN
1:200,000
Hannover : Niedersächsische Lv
Administrative diagram.

KREISKARTE NIEDERSACHSEN
1:100,000
In 44 sheets
Hannover : Niedersächsische Lv
Various sizes
Col. district maps (Kreise) on Karte des Deutschen Reichs base.
Various prices.

KREISKARTEN - NIEDERSACHSEN
1:50,000
Hannover : Niedersächsische Lv
83 x 76
District map series.
Sheets available :
Rotenberg, col. or orohydrographic editions.
Each DM 4.70

Nordrhein-Westfalen

VERWALTUNGSKARTE NORDRHEIN-WESTFALEN
1:500,000
Bad Godesberg : Nordrhein-Westfalen Lv, 1970
53 x 53
3 col. admin map with district (Kreise) boundaries. Also 4 col. ed. DM 3.50

VERWALTUNGSGRENZENKARTE DES LANDES NORDRHEIN-WESTFALEN
1:500,000
Bad Godesberg : Nordrhein Westfalen Lv
3 col. admin map showing district boundaries. DM 3.00

VERWALTUNGSKARTE NORDRHEIN-WESTFALEN
1:250,000
Bad Godesberg : Nordrhein Westfalen Lv
Col. map of admin. areas.
DM 8.00

NORDRHEIN-WESTFALEN IN SEINER GLIEDERUNG NACH ZENTRALÖRTLICHEN BEREICHEN
1:250,000
Bad Godesberg : Inst. für Landeskunde, 1970
107 x 106
Col. map showing zones of local centres. With 42pp text. DM 15.70

REGIERUNGSBEZIRKS – ÜBERSICHTSKARTEN
1:200,000
Bad Godesberg : Nordrhein-Westfalen Lv
Various sizes
District boundary maps for : Aachen, Koln, Dusseldorf, Arnsberg, Detmold, Munster.

NORDRHEIN-WESTFALEN – STUMME KARTE
1:200,000
H 260
München : Paul List Verlag
140 x 155
Outline wall map, mounted on linen with laminated surface for adding extra information. DM 92

REGIERUNGSBEZIRKS-ÜBERSICHTSKARTEN NORDRHEIN-WESTFALEN
1:100,000
Bad Godesberg : Nordrhein-Westfalen Lv
Administrative map series.

KREISKARTEN - NORDRHEIN-WESTFALEN
1:50,000
Bad Godesberg : Nordrhein-Westfalen Lv
Various sizes
District map series in 94 sheets, printed in either 5 or 6 colours.
According to size DM 4.00 - 7.00

Rheinland-Pfalz

KARTE DER GEMEINDEGRENZEN - RHEINLAND PFALZ
1:200,000
In 2 sheets
Koblenz : Rheinland Pfalz Lv
100 x 130
General base map showing regional admin. boundaries. DM 3.80

STADT UND LANDKREIS KAISERLAUTERN
1:75,000
Koblenz : Rheinland Pfalz Lv
Col. map of the city and admin. area with boundaries as at 7.6.1969, enlargement of 1:100,000 topog. map (TK 100)
DM 3.20

KREISKARTE - RHEINLAND PFALZ
1:50,000
Koblenz : Rheinland Pfalz Lv
District map series.
Maps available :
Landkreis Bitburg
Landkreis Simmern
Landkreis Pirmasens
Unterlannkreis
Each DM 4.00

Saarlandes

VERWALTUNGSKARTE DES SAARLANDES
1:200,000
Saarbrücken : Saarlandes Lv, 1971
Outline map showing admin. areas and chief towns in black.
Also available at 1:100,000 in blueprint edition.

KREIS UND UMGEBUNGSKARTEN - SAARLANDES
1:50,000
In 7 sheets
Saarbrücken : Saarlandes Lv, 1970
Special district map ed. showing 'Kreis' boundaries in purple. Prov. ed. pending boundary changes.

Schleswig - Holstein

GEMEINDEGRENZENKARTE VON SCHLESWIG-HOLSTEIN
1:250,000
Kiel - Wik : Schleswig Holstein Lv
Black and white map showing local admin. boundaries. Also available showing sheet lines of 1:5,000 series.
Each DM 3.20
Also available at 1:600,000 DM 1.00

KREISÜBERSICHTSKARTE SCHLESWIG-HOLSTEIN
1:250,000
Kiel-Wik : Schleswig-Holstein Lv, 1970
85 x 78
Col. general map showing admin. areas.
DM 3.20

KREISKARTEN SCHLESWIG-HOLSTEIN
1:100,000
In 3 sheets
Kiel-Wik : Schleswig-Holstein Lv
Col. map showing admin areas.
Each DM 3.80

KREISKARTEN SCHLESWIG- HOLSTEIN
1:75,000
In 9 sheets
Kiel-Wik : Schleswig-Holstein Lv
Col. series showing admin. boundaries in blue on topog. base map.
Each sheet DM 3.80

GEMEINDEBEZIRKSKARTEN SCHLESWIG-HOLSTEIN
1:75,000
In 9 sheets
Kiel-Wik : Schleswig-Holstein Lv
Col. map showing local govt. districts.
Each DM 3.80

E1 · PHYSICAL : RELIEF

DEUTSCHLAND PHYSIKALISCH
1:1,000,000
No 18
München : JRO
91 x 87
Physical map of Germany to the boundaries of 1937, contoured, layer col. and hill shaded, showing rivers and towns graded by pop.

FEDERATIVNAYA RESPUBLIKA GERMANIA
1:1,000,000
Moskva : GUGK
Reference map.

HARMS HANDKARTEN
Various scales
München : List
Series of small size physical maps for school use. Col. relief shading.
Maps available :
010 Deutschland und seine Nachbarländer physical
1:2,500,000 DM 1.60
014 Baden-Württemberg, physical
1:600,000 DM 1.60
019 Niedersachsen, physical
1:750,000 DM 1.20
016 Rheinhessen-Pfalz, physical
1:250,000 DM 1.60
3409 Regierungbezirke Unterfranken (Wenschow)
1:300,000 DM 1.60

WESTERMANN WANDKARTEN
Various scales
Braunschweig : Westermann
Series of physical coloured wall maps, layer coloured, communications and boundaries.
Maps available :
238 Deutschland, physikalisch
1:700,000 213 x 234
359 Norddeutschland
1:150,000 245 x 167
385 Schleswig-Holstein
1:150,000 190 x 210
265 Freie und Hansestadt Hamburg und Umbegung
1:50,000 228 x 175
286 Niedersachsen
1:200,000 202 x 180
392 Nordrhein-Westfalen
1:150,000 193 x 183
287 Das Rheinland
1:175,000 147 x 216
362 Saarland
1:50,000 158 x 139
393 Hessen
1:150,000 150 x 216
360 Südwestdeutschland
1:150,000 195 x 228
361 Süddeutschland (Bayern)
1:250,000 235 x 200
600 Unser Wetter (Zyklone und Antizyklone) 210 x 180
288 Berlin mit Sonderkarte "Berlin Innere Stadt"
1:40,000 110 x 140

WANDKARTEN
Various scales
Darmstadt : Perthes
Physical wall maps, layer coloured, hachured relief, communications, boundaries and settlement.
Maps available :
180 Deutschland
1:600,000 226 x 167 DM 142
181 Norddeutschland
1:450,000 280 x 170 DM 150
182 Deutsche Mittelgebirge (South Germany)
1:450,000 226 x 165 DM 142
183 Bundesrepublik : Nordwest-deutschland
1:200,000 202 x 225 DM 150
184 Bundesrepublik : Westdeutschland
1:200,000 202 x 225 DM 150
185 Bundesrepublik : Süddeutschland
1:200,000 202 x 225 DM 150

WENSCHOW WANDKARTEN
Various scales
München : Paul List Verlag
Regional physical school wall maps, graphic relief shading.
Maps available :
W257 Bayern
1:200,000 195 x 220 DM 182
W259 Hessen
1:150,000 140 x 200 DM 156
W816 Nordwestdeutschland
1:250,000 220 x 230 DM 164
W810 Regierungsbezirk Mittelfranken
1:100,000 180 x 170 DM 115
W813 Regierungsbezirk Niederbayern
1:100,000 185 x 170 DM 115
W812 Regierungsbezirk Oberbayern
1:100,000 195 x 220 DM 128
W814 Regierungsbezirk Oberpfalz
1:100,000 140 x 185 DM 115
W815 Regierungsbezirk Schwaben
1:100,000 170 x 220 DM 128
W811 Regierungsbezirk Unterfranken
1:100,000 200 x 155 DM 115
W805 Südbayern
1:200,000 170 x 140 DM 135
W806 Süddeutschland
1:250,000 240 x 170 DM 164

HARMS WANDKARTEN
Various scales
München : Paul List Verlag
Series of physical col. wall maps, layer cols, graphic relief shading.
Maps available :
H256 Niedersachsen
1:150,000 220 x 206 DM 182
H254 Nordrhein-Westfalen
1:150,000 200 x 160 DM 182
H241 Rheinhessen/Pfalz
1:75,000 210 x 175 DM 156
H258 Rheinland-Pfalz und Saarland Reliefkarte
1:150,000 140 x 200 DM 168
H255 Schleswig-Holstein
1:100,000 200 x 220 DM 182
H240 Südwestdeutschland
1:150,000 170 x 205 DM 164

RELIEFKARTE DES LANDES BADEN-WURTTEMBERG
1:600,000
Stuttgart : Baden-Württemberg Lv
44 x 50
3 col. relief map of the State. DM 2
Also at 1:1,000,000 26 x 30 DM 1.10

KARTENRELIEF DES LANDES NORDRHEIN-WESTFALEN
1:500,000
Bad Godesberg : Nordrhein Westfalen Lv
65 x 65
Raised plastic relief map in col.
DM 33.00

LERNKARTE - TOPOGRAPHISCHES GRUNDWISSEN
Darmstadt : Perthes
Basic maps, showing rivers, principal towns, land relief.
480 Lernkarte von Deutschland
1:600,000 220 x 167
490 Lernkarte von Schleswig-Holstein und Hamburg
1:200,000 146 x 180
491 Lernkarte von Niedersachsen und Bremen
1:250,000 172 x 140
492 Lernkarte von Nordrhein-Westfalen
1:150,000 202 x 205
493 Lernkarte von Hessen
1:150,000 146 x 200
494 Lernkarte von Rheinland Pfalz und Saarland
1:150,000 148 x 200
494 Lernkarte von Baden-Wurttemberg
1:200,000 146 x 200
496 Lernkarte von Bayern
1:250,000 172 x 185
Various prices.

E2 PHYSICAL : LAND FEATURES

GEWÄSSERKARTE VON SUDWEST-DEUTSCHLAND
1:600,000
Stuttgart : Baden Württemberg Lv
58 x 65
2 col. map showing water features of SW Germany. DM 2.00

ÜBERSICHTSKARTE DER GRUNDWASSERBESCHAFFENHEIT IN HESSEN
1:300,000
Wiesbaden : Hessische Lv fur Boden-forschung, 1966
Map of ground water conditions in Hesse, with text. DM 10.00

GRUNDWASSERHÖFFIGKEIT
1:500,000
Kiel-Wik : Schleswig-Holstein Lv, 1955
Ground water map with text; Schleswig Hostein area. DM 3.60

MOORKARTE VON BADEN-WÜRTTEMERG
1:50,000
Stuttgart : Baden-Württemberg Lv
Map of marshy lands, following sheet lines of Topog. series 1:50,000. In col, marshy areas in green. Series in progress.
Sheets published :
L7922, L7924, L8120, L8122, L8124, L8324, L8320
Each sheet DM 7.20

F GEOLOGY

GEOLOGISCHE KARTE DER BUNDESREPUBLIK DEUTSCHLAND
1:1,000,000
Hannover : B-B
In preparation

GEOLOGISCHE KARTE
1:25,000
See index 430. 1/14
State Geological Depts.
Series in progress since 1914. On official topog. series sheet lines.
(with text) DM 13.50

GEOTEKTONISCHE ÜBERSICHTS-KARTE DER SUDWESTDEUTSCHEN GROSSSCHELLE
1:1,000,000
Stuttgart : Baden-Württemberg Geol. Lv
Tectonic map on geological base map.
DM 8.00

GEOLOGISCHE RELIEFKARTE - SÜDWESTDEUTSCHLAND
1:200,000
H246
München : Paul List Verlag
140 x 200
Harms col. geological wall map
DM 128
Also available, reduced size edition, 1:850,000 (046) DM 1.60

GEOLOGISCHE ÜBERSICHTSKARTE VON SÜDWESTDEUTSCHLAND
1:600,000
Stuttgart : Baden-Wurttemberg Geol. Lv, 1954
50 x 56
Geol. general map covering Frankfurt-Donauworth - Zurich - Saarbrucken.
Cross section. DM 13.50

GEOTEKTONISCHE KARTE VON NORDWESTDEUTSCHLAND
1:100,000
See index 430/3
Hannover : Amt für Bodenforschung, 1947-49
Geotectonic series on sheet lines of Karte des Deutschen Reiches - Large sheets.
The following sheets still available with texts :
7, 8, 60, 61, 70, 71, 72, 73, 74
Each DM 14.50

Baden-Württemberg

GEOLOGISCHE SCHULKARTE VON BADEN-WÜRTTEMBERG
1:1,000,000
Stuttgart : Baden-Württemberg Geol. Lv, 1972
41 x 47
School geol. map. With text. DM 1.50

GEOLOGISCHE ÜBERSICHTSKARTE VON BADEN-WÜRTTEMBERG
1:200,000
In 4 sheets
Stuttgart : Baden-Württemberg Geol. Lv, 1962
88 x 111 complete
Col. geol. general map. Western edge of state excluded.
Complete DM 43

ÜBERSICHTSKARTE DES ILLER-RISS GEBIETS
1:100,000
Baden-Württemberg Geol. Lv
General geological map. With text.
DM 10.40

GEOLOGISCHE ÜBERSICHTSKARTE KREIS BALINGEN
1:100,000
Stuttgart : Baden-Württemberg Geol. Lv
Geol. map with text for Balingen district.
DM 10.60

GEOGNOSTISCHE KARTE VON WÜRTTEMBERG
1:50,000
Stuttgart : Baden-Württemberg Geol. Lv
Map of land structure, with accompanying text. DM 16.12

GEOLOGISCHE KARTE DER LANDKREISS KONSTANZ MIT UMGEBUNG
1:50,000
Stuttgart : Baden-Württemberg Geol. Lv
102 x 70
Geological map covering surroundings of Lake Constance, with 286pp text.
DM 16.40

GEOLOGISCHE KARTE VON STUTTGART UND UMGEBUNG
1:50,000
Stuttgart : Baden-Württemberg Geol. Lv
Geol. map of Stuttgart and environs with text. DM 12.00

GEOLOGISCHE EXKURSIONSKARTE DES KAISERSTUHLS
1:25,000
Stuttgart : Baden-Württemberg Lv 1956
59 x 64
Geol. map of the Kaiserstuhl region of the Rhine Valley. With text. DM 13.50

Bayern

GEOLOGISCHE KARTE VON BAYERN
1:800,000
München : Bayerische Geol. Lv
56 x 60
Col. geol. map DM 2.00

GEOLOGISCHE KARTE VON BAYERN
1:500,000
München : BayerischesGeol. Lv
94 x 89
Col. geol. map with sections and text.
DM 16.00

TEKTONISCHE KARTE FRANKISCHE ALB
1:300,000
München : Bayerische Geol. Lv
42 x 65
3 col. tectonic map with 81pp text.
Complete DM 28

GEOLOGISCHE ÜBERSICHTSKARTE DAS RIES UND UMGEBUNG
1:100,000
München : Bayerische Geol. Lv
82 x 62
Col. geol. map with 478pp text.

AUGSBURG UND UMGEBUNGEN
1:50,000
München : Bayerische Geol. Lv
Geological map of Augsburg and environs, with text. DM 8.00

GEOLOGISCHE-HYDROLOGISCHE KARTE VON MÜNCHEN
1:50,000
München : Bayerische Geol. Lv
Col. map with overlay and text. DM 6.00

Berlin

GEOLOGISCHE KARTE VON BERLIN
1:10,000
In 27 sheets
Berlin : Staatliche Geol. Kommission
85 x 70 each
Geol. series in progress.
Each DM 7.20

Hessen

HYDROGEOLOGISCHE ÜBERSICHTSKARTE VON HESSEN
1:600,000
Wiesbaden : Hessische Lv für Bodenforschung, 1955
42 x 59
Hydrogeol. map DM 3.00

GEOLOGISCHE ÜBERSICHTSKARTE DER DILL-MULDE, DER NORD-ÖSTLICHEN LAHN-MULDE UND DES HORRE-ZUGES
1:100,000
Wiesbaden : Hessische Lv für Bodenforschung, 1958
General geological map. DM 1.00

GEOLOGISCHE KARTE DER UMGEBUNG VON BIEBER IM NORDWESTLICHEN SPESSART
by D Diederich
1:25,000
Wiesbaden : Hessische Lv für Bondenforschung, 1959/60
DM 2.20

GEOLOGISCHE KARTE DES SÜDLICHEN KELLERWALD-GEBIRGES
1:25,000
Wiesbaden : Hessische Lv für Bodenforschung, 1961
Geological map of the South Kellerwald mountains. DM 5.00

GEOLOGISCHE KARTE DER LAHNMULDE IM GEBIET DIEZ-LAURENBURG
1:25,000
Wiesbaden : Hessische Lv für Bodenforschung, 1958 DM 2.60

GEOLOGISCHE SPEZIALKARTE DER GEGEND SÜDLICH LANGENAUBACH
1:5,000
Wiesbaden : Hessische Lv für Bodenforschung, 1956 DM 3.00

Niedersachsen

GEOLOGISCHE KARTE DES EMSLANDES
1:100,000
Hannover : B-B, 1960
Large sheet No 58 on sheet lines of Karte des Deutschen Reiches; set of 5 maps showing: surface geology; soil; hydro-geography; stratigraphy; geotectonics.
With text. DM 60.00

GEOLOGISCHE WANDERKARTE HARZ
1:100,000
Berlin : Schaffmann & Kluge, 1971
49 x 59
Col. map with cross section. Text on reverse.
DM 7.80

Nordrhein-Westfalen

GEOLOGISCHE ÜBERSICHT VON NORDRHEIN-WESTFALEN
1:2,500,000
Krefeld : Nordrhein-Westfalen Geol. Lv
Small postcard size map.
10 copies : DM 3.00

ÜBERSICHTSKARTE VON NORDRHEIN-WESTFALEN
1:100,000
Krefeld : Nordrhein-Westfalen Geol. Lv
Col. map series available in geological, soil and hydrogeological eds.
Maps published :
Sheet C4302 Bocholt, 1968, 3 sheets and text. DM 40
C4306 Recklinghausen, 1973, 3 sheets and text, in preparation
C4310 Münster, 1962, 3 sheets and text, DM 30
Individual sheets with complete text. DM 14

GEOLOGISCHE ÜBERSICHTSKARTE DES NIEDERRHEINISCH-WESTFÄLISCHEN KARBONS
1:100,000
Krefeld : Nordrhein-Westfalen Geol. Lv, 1971
168 x 120 complete
2 sheet map showing coal and minerals. Geol. cross section and stratigraphical table on reverse.
Complete DM 20

GEOLOGISCHE ÜBERSICHTSKARTE DES RHEINISCH - WESTFALISCHEN STEINKOHLENGEBIET (COAL MINING AREA)
1:100,000
Krefeld : Nordrhein-Westfalen Geol. Lv, 1958
With description of surface deposits. DM 8.00

HYDROGEOLOGISCHE KARTE DES KREISES PADERBORN
1:50,000
Krefeld : Nordrhein Westfalen Geol. Lv
2 sheet map of the Paderborn District with text. DM 20

HYDROGEOLOGISCHE KARTE VON NORDRHEIN-WESTFÄLEN
1:25,000
Krefeld : Nordrhein Westfalen Geol. Lv
Map series on topog. sheet lines in progress to be published in 3 styles: A Base, B Geological profile, C Hydrogeological profile.
Sheets and styles published:
4603 A, 1961, 4904 A, 1960, 5004 A, 1959, 5005 A, 1959, 5104 A, 1962, 5106 A, 1963, 5205 A, 1963, 5206 A, 1958.
Each sheet DM 4.00

GEOLOGISCHE KARTE DER RHEINISCH-WESTFÄLISCH STEINKOHLENGEBIETES
1:10,000
In 52 sheets
Krefeld : Nordrhein-Westfalen Geol. Lv
Geol. series covering the Rhine-Westphalia industrial area. With 5 detailed text vols. Most sheets either include or have separate cross sections.

Rheinland-Pfalz

HYDROGEOLOGISCHE KARTE VON RHEINLAND-PFALZ
1:500,000
Koblenz : Rheinland Pfalz Geol Lv
Col. hydrogeol. map. DM 6.00

GEOLOGISCHE ÜBERSICHTSKARTE PFALZ
1:300,000
Mainz : Rheinland Pfalz Geol. Lv, 1969
47 x 37
Col. geol. map from Pfalz Atlas. DM 4.50

GEOLOGISCHE ÜBERSICHTSKARTE DES BERGAMTSBEZIRKS BAD KREUZNACH
1:200,000
Mainz : Rheinland Pfalz Geol Lv, 1971
75 x 81
2 col. general geol. map with mineral beds. DM 8.00

GEOLOGISCHES ÜBERSICHTSKARTE DER EIFEL
1:200,000
60806
Bonn : Stollfuss
70 x 70
Generalised geol. map with text. DM 4.80

GEOLOGISCHE KARTE OBERPFALZ
1:100,000
Mainz : Rheinland Pfalz Geol. Lv, 1969
73 x 51
Col. geol. map, 187pp text. DM 34

Saarlandes

GEOLOGISCHE KARTE DES SAARLANDES
1:100,000
Saarbrücken : Geol. Inst. der Universitat Saarlandes, 1964
84 x 63
Geol. map in 11 col, with text. DM 9.00

GEOLOGISCHE KARTE DES SAARLANDES
1:50,000
Saarbrücken : Saarlandes Geol. La, 1955
144 x 114
2 sheet col. geol. map, with inset structural sketch. Legend on reverse.
Out of print, new edition 1978.

Schleswig-Holstein

GEOLOGISCHE ÜBERSICHTSKARTE
1:500,000
Kiel - Wik : Schleswig-Holstein Geol. Lv, 1958
Col. geological map. DM 5.00

LAGERSTÄTTEN
1:500,000
Kiel-Wik : Schleswig-Holstein Geol. Lv
Map of strata in Schleswig-Holstein. DM 3.60

INSEL FEHMARN - GEOLOGISCHE KARTE
1:50,000
Kiel-Wik : Schleswig-Holstein Geol. Lv
Col. geol. map including photographic map, 1:25,000 DM 8.00

INSEL FEHMARN - HYDRO-GEOLOGISCHE KARTE
1:50,000
Kiel-Wik : Schleswig-Holstein Geol. Lv
Col. hydrogeologic map. DM 8.00

FLENSBURG - HYDROGEOLOGISCHE KARTE
1:50,000
Kiel-Wik : Schleswig-Holstein Geol. Lv
Col. hydrogeologic map covering official topog. sheets L1122 and L1222. DM 12.00

INGENIEURGEOLOGISCHE PLANUNGSATLAS - WIRTSCHAFTS-RAUM BRUNSBUTTEL
1:50,000
Kiel-Wik : Schleswig-Holstein Geol. Lv
Engineering geology map of the Brunsbuttel industrial area. DM 12.00

INGENIEURGEOLOGISCHE PLANUNGSKARTE
1:10,000
Kiel-Wik : Schleswig-Holstein Geol. Lv
Engineering geology maps with text.
Sheets available:
1 Bad St Peter-Ording incl. cross section. DM 30
2 Brunsbuttel - in preparation.

INGENIEURGEOLOGISCHE PLANUNGSKARTE - ST MICHAELISDONN
1:2,000
Kiel-Wik : Schleswig-Holstein Geol. Lv
Col. engineering geology map with boreholes. DM 12.00

INGENIEURGEOLOGISCHE PLANUNGSKARTE
1:5,000
Kiel-Wik : Schleswig-Holstein Geol. Lv
Series of col. engineering geology maps.
Sheets available :
1 Flugplatz Kattenkirchen (sheets 1-4) DM 30
2 Industriegebiet Brunsbuttel, boreholes, section etc. DM 45
3 St Michaelisdonn E & W with section DM 40
4 Lubeck-Sud with section in preparation

KARTE DER HOLOZÄNMÄCHTIGKEIT
1:25,000
Kiel-Wik : Schleswig-Holstein Geol. Lv
Series of maps showing alluvial deposits on official topog. sheet lines.
Sheets published:
1520, 1622, 1820, 1621, 1921.
Each DM 8.00

GEOLOGISCHE KARTE DER INSEL SYLT
1:25,000
In 2 sheets
Kiel-Wik : Schleswig-Holstein Geol Lv, 1952
54 x 80 each sheet
Col. geol. map DM 30

GEOLOGISCHE BAUGRUND-ÜBERSICHTSKARTE VON HAMBURG
1:50,000
C 39
Hamburg : Geologisches La, 1971
107 x 83
Geol. planning map of Hamburg for building projects. DM 9.00

HYDROGEOLOGISCHE KARTE DES HAMBURGER RAUMS
1:50,000
Hamburg : Geologisches La, 1976
107 x 83
Hydrogeological map of the Hamburg region with profile section on reverse side. DM 15.00

GEOLOGISCHE BAUGRUND-PLANUNGSKARTE VON HAMBURG
1:10,000
C 26
In 33 sheets
Hamburg : Geologisches La, 1950
85 x 60
Series of geol. planning maps for building works. 11 sheets out of print.
Each DM 9.00

G EARTH RESOURCES

ÜBERSICHTSKARTE DER ÖFFENTLICHE GASVERSORGUNG IN DER BRD
1:1,000,000
Mainz : Kohlhammer
Distribution of public gas supply in Western Germany.

BODENKARTE DER BUNDESREPUBLIK DEUTSCHLAND
1:1,000,000
Hannover : B-B, 1963
58 x 88
Coloured map showing soil types. DM 4.00

BODENKARTE DEUTSCHLAND
1:25,000
See index 430. 1/14
Geologische : Landvermessungsamt (State geological survey offices)
Series of col. soil maps on official topog. sheet lines. Some sheets have an explanatory text.
According to edition DM 12 - 28

DIE SALZSTRUKTUREN NORDWEST-DEUTSCHLAND
1:500,000
Hannover : B-B, 1972
74 x 78
Monochrome map showing salt deposits in surface soil layers and strata depths. DM 2.40

Bayern

BODENKÜNDLICHE ÜBERSICHTS-KARTE VON BAYERN
1:500,000
Munchen : Bayerisches Geol Lv, 1955
86 x 92
Coloured soil and soil usage map with inset climatic map at 1:2,500,000 with 168pp text. DM 10

KARTE DER GEWINNUNGSSTELLEN NATÜRLICHER BAUSTOFFE IN BAYERN
1:500,000
Munchen : Bayerische Geol Lv
Map showing location of natural building materials in Bavaria. DM 4.00

BODENGÜTEKARTE VON BAYERN
1:100,000
Munchen : Bayerisches Lv
75 x 102
Series of col. maps indicating soil quality on Administrative base map.
Each sheet DM 9.00

BODENSCHÄTZUNGS-ÜBERSICHTS-KARTEN DER REGIERUNGS-BEZIRKE NIEDERBAYERN
1:100,000
In 3 sheets
München : Bayerische Geol. Lv
Soil map of land valuation.
Sheets :
I Westlicher Teil, 1965 DM 16
II Nordostlicher Teil, 1961 DM 10
III Südöstlicher Teil, 1963 DM 16

Hessen

BODENÜBERSICHTSKARTE VON HESSEN
1:600,000
Wiesbaden : Hessisches Landesamt für Bodenforschung, 1958
General soil map of Hesse DM 3.00

BODENKUNDLICHE UBERSICHTS-KARTE VON HESSEN
1:300,000
Wiesbaden : Hessisches Lv für Bodenforschung, 1961
65 x 91
Text out of print. Soil map. DM 8.00
As above, with topog. detail DM 2.50

Niedersachsen

BODENKARTE DER WEDEMARK
1:25,000
Hannover : B-B, 1950
Col. soil map DM 6.00

BODENKARTE VON NIEDERSACHSEN
1:5,000
Hannover : B-B 1967
Soil map series in progress, with insets :
I Land use and soil improvement
II Ground water
New sheets for coastal marshes (after 1967) are geological-soil maps with soil amelioration overlay and text.
Each DM 15.00
Sheet with text DM 11.00
Without text DM 8.00

BODENKARTE (NIEDERSACHSEN)
1:5,000
Hannover : Niedersachsen Lv, 1964+
Soil map series, providing basis for land valuation.
With contours DM 7.00
Without contours DM 6.00

BODEN- UND MOORKARTE DES EMSLANDES
1:5,000
In 583 sheets
Hannover : B-B, 1953-66
Series showing soil types and marshy areas of the Ems district.

Nordrhein-Westfalen

BODENÜBERSICHTSKARTE VON NORDRHEIN-WESTFALEN
1:300,000
Bad Godesberg : Nordrhein-Westfalen Geol Lv, 1953
97 x 76
Col. soil map with text. DM 12.00

ÜBERSICHTSKARTE VON NORDRHEIN-WESTFALEN
1:100,000
Nordrhein-Westfalen Geol. Lv
see FED. REP. OF GERMANY 430. 1F

BODENKARTE VON NORDRHEIN-WESTFALEN
1:50 000
Krefeld : Nordrhein-Westfalen Geol. Lv, 1969
80 x 62
Soil map series on official topog. sheet lines.
Sheets published :
L3906 Vreden 1973
L3910 Burgsteinfurt 1973
L4704 Krefeld 1969
L4902 Erkelenz 1973
L4904 Mönchengladbach, 1972
L4906 Neuss 1972
L5106 Koln 1973
Each sheet DM 10.00

BODENKARTE DES KREISES WIEDENBRUCK
1:50,000
Krefeld : Nordrhein-Westfalen Geol. Lv, 1972
Soil map with text. DM 8.00

Rheinland-Pfalz

BODENÜBERSICHTSKARTE VON RHEINLAND-PFALZ
1:500,000
Koblenz : Rheinland Pfalz Geol. Lv
43 x 60
Soil map without text (atlas plate). DM 9.00

ÜBERSICHTSKARTE DER BODENTYPEN-GESELLSCHAFTEN VON RHEINLAND-PFALZ
Ed W T Stohr
1:250,000
Mainz : Rheinland Pfalz Geol. Lv.
86 x 108
Map of soil groups. DM 20

Schleswig-Holstein

BODENTYPEN UND BODENARTEN VON SCHLESWIG-HOLSTEIN
1:500,000
Kiel-Wik : Schleswig-Holstein Geol Lv, 1973
Soil type map with text. DM 5.00

HAMME-WUMME BODEN-UBERSICHTSKARTE
1:100,000
Hannover - Buchholz : Amt fur Bodenforschung, 1969
95 x 96
Col. map showing soils of the Hamme and Wumme river plain. With 96pp text, 1970.
Complete DM 42.20

DIE BODEN DER EIDERNIEDERUNG
1:100,000
Kiel-Wik : Schleswig-Holstein Geol. Lv, 1970
56 x 48
Col. soil map of the Eider river plain.
DM 8.00

INSEL FEHMARN - BODENKARTE
1:50,000
Kiel-Wik : Schleswig-Holstein Geol. Lv
Col. soil map of Fehmarn Island.
DM 8.00

H BIOGEOGRAPHY

WALDFLÄCHE IN DEN GEMEINDEN DER BRD
1:1,000,000
Mainz : Kohlhammer, 1960
Forested areas by parish. DM 9.50

Baden-Württemberg

VEGETATIONSKUNDLICHE ÜBERSICHTSKARTE DES LANDKREIS TUBINGEN
1:50,000
Stuttgart : Baden-Württemberg Lv 1969
87 x 73
Col. vegetation map on topog. base.
DM 11.00

VEGETATIONSKUNDLICHE KARTE BADEN-WÜRTTEMBERG
1:25,000
See index 430. 1/9
Stuttgart : Baden-Württemberg Lv
Col. vegetation type series in progress following official topog. sheet lines. With explanations.
Sheets published :
6526, 6617, 6916, 7416, 7521, 7617, 7624, 8115, 8123, 8225, 8226, 8326.
Per sheet DM 10.60

Bayern

NATURPARK RHON - SÜDBLATT
1:50,000
In 2 sheets
München : Bayerisches Lv
Topog. map of the Nature Park based on official series with walking routes marked. Covering southern half of the park. For north sheet see Hessen park maps.
Each DM 5.50

NATIONALPARK BAYERISCHER WALD
1:35,000
Hof Saale : Fritsch Wandkarte
Map of Bavarian Forest National Park with short guide.

Hessen

NATÜRLICHE VEGETATION UND WUCHSRAUME IN HESSEN
1:600,000
Wiesbaden - Hessisches Lv für Bodenforschung, 1959
Map of natural vegetation and growing areas in Hesse. DM 3.00

NATURPARK KARTE
1:50,000
Wiesbaden : Hessisches Lv
Various sizes
Nature park maps based on topog. series, contours, walking routes, relief shading etc.
Maps available :

Habichtswald	DM 4.50
Munden	DM 4.50
Meissner-Kaufunger Wald	DM 4.50
Hoher Vogelsberg	DM 4.50
Rhon, Nordblatt	DM 4.50
Spessart, Nordwest	DM 4.50
Spessart, Nordost	DM 4.50
Diemelsee	DM 4.50

Odenwald in preparation

Niedersachsen

NATURPARK SÜDHEIDE
1:50,000
Hannover : Niedersächsisches Lv
69 x 75
Topog. map of the Nature Park based on official series with relief shown and walking routes marked. DM 5.50

Nordrhein-Westfalen

NATURPARK KARTE
1:50,000
Bad - Godesberg : Nordrhein-Westfalen Lv
Topog. maps of the nature parks, col. based on official series, contoured with walking routes marked.
Maps available :

Arnsberger Wald	94 x 54	DM 5.50
Ebbegebirge in preparation		
Hohe Mark	106 x 82	DM 5.50
Homert	84 x 72	DM 5.00
Kottenforst-Ville (South sheet)	73 x 80	DM 5.00
"	(north sheet in prep.)	
Nordeifel	90 x 115	DM 7.00
Rothaargebirge (2 sheets) (each)	80 x 78	DM 5.50
Schwalm-Nette	62 x 82	DM 4.50

NATURPARK ARNSBERGER WALD
1:50,000
Iserlohn : Sauerland Verlag
Map of nature park, showing vegetation cover, paths, etc. DM 5.00

NATURPARK ROTHAARGEBIRGE
1:50,000
Iserlohn : Sauerländische Gebirgsverein, 1971
95 x 90 each
2 sheet map of nature park : contours, relief shading, vegetation cover, paths etc.
Each DM 4.60

Rheinland-Pfalz

NATURSCHUTZ-UND LANDSCHAFTS-SCHUTZGEBIETE IN RHEINLAND-PFALZ
1:250,000
Koblenz : Rheinland Pfalz Lv, 1970
79 x 100
Col. map showing land and nature reserve areas in the State. List of reserves on reverse. DM 7.50

NATURPARK KARTE
1:50,000
Koblenz : Rheinland-Pfalz
Topog. maps of Nature Parks based on official series, relief shown, also walking routes and paths. Maps available :
Deutsch - Luxemburgische Naturpark
Naturpark Nassau
Naturpark Rhein-Westerwald
Each DM 4.00

Schleswig-Holstein

DIE MOORE
1:500,000
Kiel-Wik : Schleswig Holstein Geol. Lv
Marsh areas of Schleswig-Holstein
DM 5.00

J CLIMATE

DIE BIOKLIMATISCHEN ZONEN IN DER BRD
1:1,500,000
Hannover : Forschungs- und Sitzungsberichte der Akademic fur Raumforschung and Landesplannung, 1972
50 x 65
Wooded and other vegetation areas overprinted on map of bioclimatic regions.
DM 8.50

K HUMAN GEOGRAPHY

BEVÖLKERUNGSDICHTE IN DEN KREISEN 1961
1:2,000,000
Stuttgart : Kohlhammer
Population density plate from 'Bundesrepublik Deutschland in Karten' showing the density of population by districts.

L ECONOMIC

RESEAU D'INTERCONNEXION/ VERBUNDNETZ
1:3,000,000
Heidelberg : Deutsche Verbundgesellschaft, 1972
Map showing electrical and communications link-ups.

KAUFKRAFTKARTE NIELSEN-GEBIETE (PURCHASING POWER MAP)
1:2,500,000
Frankfurt : Schwartz
30 x 41
Purchasing power map also showing postal districts. Available in larger ed.
1:1,000,000. 70 x 98

KAUFKRAFTKARTE DER BUNDES-REPUBLIK
1:1,000,000
Munich : Moderne Industries, 1970
76 x 99
Purchasing power by districts in relation to the mean. Coloured.

WASSERSPORTKARTE DEUTSCHLAND
1:1,000,000
No 62
Stuttgart : RV, 1971
74 x 90
Col. watersport map showing river courses, suitable for boats. Holstein Lake area inset at 1:400,000 DM 10.80

INDUSTRIE UND HANDELSKAMMER BEZIRKE (CHAMBER OF COMMERCE DISTRICTS)
No 14
1:1,000,000
Frankfurt : Schwarz
85 x 95
Map of Chamber of Commerce districts incl. West Berlin.

LANDWIRTSCHAFTLICHE BODEN-NÜTZUNGSSYTEME DER BRD
1:1,000,000
Stuttgart : Kohlhamer, 1960
Agricultural soil yield map of West Germany. DM 9.50

DEUTSCHLAND - LANDWIRTSCHAFT
1:900,000
H 271
Munchen : Paul List Verlag
155 x 120
Harms agricultural wall map with land types shown in colour with locations of products indicated by pictorial symbols.

DEUTSCHLAND, BERGBAU UND INDUSTRIE
1:900,000
H272
Munchen : Paul List Verlag
155 x 120
Harms economic wall map of mining and industry showing locations by pictorial symbols. Boundaries as at 1937.

PLANUNG DEUTSCHE VERBUNDNETZ
1:600,000
Heidelberg : Deutsche Verbundnetz-gesellschaft, 1972
115 x 150
Col. map of power networks. DM 40
Smaller ed. at 1:1,500,000,
40 x 60 DM 14

DIE AGRARSTURKTUR IN DEN GEMEINDEN DER BRD
In 4 sheets
1:600,000
Braunschweig : Westermann, 1960
Village agricultural structure.
DM 3.60

BADEN-WÜRTTEMBERG, VERKEHRSMENGENKARTE
1:250,000
Stuttgart : Baden-Württemberg Lv, 1971
100 x 136
Showing traffic density during a 24 hour period, based on Road Map.
DM 18

RHEINLAND PFALZ UND SAARLAND - WIRTSCHAFTSKARTE
1:150,000
H248
Munchen : Paul List Verlag
140 x 200
Harms coloured economic wall map showing location of products by pictorial symbols. DM 135

RHEINISCH-WESTFÄLISCHES INDUSTRIEGEBIET
1:50,000
No 30 0402
Braunschweig : Westermann, 1971
138 x 218
2 wall maps on 1 sheet, showing settlements, land use, communications and industry and mining. DM 108

M HISTORICAL

Baden-Württemberg

CHOROGRAPHIA DUCATAUS WIRTEMBERGICI
Georg Gadner and Johannes Ottinger
Stuttgart : Baden-Württemberg Lv
Facsimile map from the 1596 Gadner Atlas. 28 single col. maps and 1 col. map.
Case with 29 maps DM 80

LANDTAFEL VON WANGEN IM ALLGAU
Johannes Andreas Rauch
1:22,000
Stuttgart : Baden Württemberg Lv
Facsimile of the map of 1647.
DM 2.70

LANDTAFEL VON LINDAU
Johannes Andreas Rauch
1:20,460
Stuttgart : Baden Württemberg Lv
Facsimile of the map of 1647
DM 2.70

PLAN DER STADT STUTTGART
1:4,500
Stuttgart : Baden Württemberg Lv
Shows Stuttgart in 1855.
DM 9.20

Bayern

KARTE VON BAYERN
München : Bayerisches Lv
Facsimile of Finckh's map of 1655/84 in 28 sheets forming 1 large and 1 small general map.
Single sheets DM 15
Large scale general map DM 25

KARTE VON OBER- UND NIEDERBAYERN
München : Bayerisches Lv
Facsimile of Weinerus' map of 1579 in 22 sheets + 1 general map.
Set DM 25

KARTE VON OBER- UND NIEDERBAYERN
München : Bayerisches Lv, 1964
Facsimile of Aventin's map of 1523.
1964 reproduction of 1899 facsimile.
1 col. ed. DM 7
Col. ed. DM 15

KARTE VON ST MICHEL
1:86,400 app.
München : Bayerisches Lv
Sheets : Munchen und Umgebung, Pfaffenhofen und Umgebung. Facsimile of 1768 map.
Each DM 50

PLAN DES ENGLISCHEN GARTENS MÜNCHEN
München : Bayerisches Lv
Facsimile plan of 1806. DM 50

Hessen

KARTE VON DEM GROSSHER ZOGTUM HESSEN
1:50,000
In 31 sheets
Wiesbaden : Hessisches Lv
Facsimile map of the Grand Duchy of Hessen.

KARTE VON DEM KÜRFURSTENTUM HESSEN
1:50,000
In 40 sheets
Wiesbaden : Hessisches Lv
Map of the Electorate of Hessen, facsimile edition.

KARTE VON HERZOGTUM NASSAU
1:20,000
In 51 sheets
Wiesbaden : Hessisches Lv
Facsimile map of the Grand Duchy of Nassau.

KASSEL UM 1840
Kassel : Grothus-Verlag
Facsimile map of Kassel in 1840
DM 15

Niedersachsen

KURHANNOVERSCHE LANDES-AUFNAHME DES 18 JAHRHUNDERTS
1:21,333.$^1/_3$
In 165 sheets
Hannover : Niedersächsisches Lv
74 x 50 each
Facsimile map of Hannover state in the 18th C.
Each DM 2.70

Rheinland

TOPOGRAPHISCHE KARTE VON RHEINLAND UND WESTFALEN
1:80,000
Nordrhein-Westfalen, Rheinland Pfalz, Saarlandes Lv
Compiled 1841-55, topog. series, with hachures. Facsimile.
Each DM 2.60

TOPOGRAPHISCHE AUFNAHME DES 'PREUSSISCHEN TOPOGRAPHISCHEN BUREAUS'
1:25,000
Nordrhein-Westfalen, Niedersächsisches, Saarlandes Lv
Facsimile of map :
1836-42 Westfalen, 1843-50 Rheinprovinz
Available in the following eds :
1 col. blueprint DM 5.50
1 col. photoprint DM 10.00
Col. sheets DM 4.50
(few sheets for Westfalen)

KARTENAUFNAHME DER RHEINLANDE
1:25,000
Nordrhein-Westfalen, Rheinland Pfalz, Saarlandes Lv
Topog. series at 1:20,000, 1803-1820, compiled by Tranchot and Muffling.
In col.
Each sheet DM 3.60

ÜBERSICHTSKARTE DER ARCHÄOLOGISCHEN DENKMALER IM RHEINLAND
Ed A Herrnbrodt
1:200,000
Berlin : Schaffmann & Kluge, 1969
81 x 93
Lists archaeol. sites in the Rheinland : pre-Roman, Roman. Mediaeval also museums. Overprinted on topog. base.
Index on reverse. DM 6.50

WIRTSCHAFTSKARTE DE REGIERUNGSBEZIRKE DÜSSELDORF UND KLEVE UM 1820
by H E Kleindin
1:200,000
Bonn : Univ. Geog. Inst, 1970
Economic map of the Dusseldorf & Kleve area in 1820.

Saarlandes

KARTE DER RÖMISCHEN SIEDLUNGEN UND STRASSEN AN DER MITTLEREN SAAR
1:100,000
Ed : State Konservatoire of the Saar
Saarbrücken : Inst. für Landeskunde des Saarlandes 1962
Shows Roman settlements and remains in the Central Saar district DM 4.00

Schleswig-Holstein

SCHLESWIG-HOLSTEIN UND HAMBURG, KULTURKARTE
1:250,000
Kiel-Wik : Schleswig Hostein Lv, 1972
104 x 77
Red overprint on topog. map, showing historical and cultural buildings and areas, museums etc. With 56pp guide
DM 7.80

N MATHEMATICAL

DAS DEUTSCHE HAUPTDREIECKSNETZ
1:1,000,000
Stuttgart : Baden-Wurttemberg Lv
90 x 102
Col. map showing triangulation network.
DM 3.10

NIVELLEMENTSNETZE NORDRHEIN-WESTFALEN
1:250,000
Bad Godesberg : Nordrhein-Westfalen Lv
Col. map showing levelling network in Nordrhein-Westfalen. DM 3.00

TRIGONOMETRISCHE NETZVERDICHTUNG, NORDRHEIN-WESTFALEN
1:250,000
Bad Godesberg : Nordrhein-Westfalen Lv
Col. map, showing trigonometric network.
DM 3.00

NIVELLEMENTNETZ I UND II ORDNUNG IN RHEINLAND-PFALZ
1:300,000
Koblenz : Rheinland Pfalz Lv
Col. map showing levelling network.
DM 5.00

DREIECKNETZ I UND II ORDNUNG IN RHEINLAND-PFALZ
1:300,000
Koblenz : Rheinland Pfalz Lv
Col. map showing 3rd triangulation.
DM 5.00

ATLASES
W3 WORLD : LOCAL EDITION

HARMS ATLAS DEUTSCHLAND UND DIE WELT
Harms Weltatlas Baden-Württemberg
Harms Weltatlas für die Bayerische Schule
see WORLD ATLASES 100 W3

ATLASES
A1 GENERAL : ROADS

DEUTSCHER GENERALATLAS
Stuttgart : Mairs
29 x 38
450 pp
105 pages of maps covering West Germany, scale 1:200,000 showing all classes of roads and other topographical detail with hill shading. 18 pages of European road maps on a reduced scale, 15 town plans, 9 special feature maps and 261 pages of index. DM 98

CONTINENTAL ATLAS
Stuttgart : Mair, 1976/77
611 pp
Road planning maps at 1:500,000 (Germany, Austria, Switzerland, N Italy, Benelux) 1:300,000 (motorways), 1:2,000,000 (Europe). 150 pp motoring information. DM 26.80

DER GROSSE SHELL ATLAS : DEUTSCHLAND/EUROPA
Stuttgart : Mair, 1976/77
17 x 27
526pp
Road maps at 1:500,000 (Germany and Europe), 1:4,500,000 (European planning maps), 1:850,000 (Alps), 1:200,000 (City areas). Town plans, tourist details and accommodation distance tables, index, motoring information. DM 26.80

AUTOATLAS BERTELSMANN : DEUTSCHLAND, EUROPA
Gütersloh : Bertelsmann
16 x 26
386pp
Roads and other tourist info. - hotels, camping etc. 136pp maps, text, 52 large town maps, 108pp index, with 66,000 names. DM 24.80

READER'S DIGEST ADAC AUTOREISEBUCH - ATLAS VON DEM ALPEN BIS ZUR NORDSEE
Stuttgart : Verlag das Beste
22 x 30
440pp
107pp maps. Text, illus. city plans etc. 1:250,000 scale. DM 42.50

SHELL-ATLAS DEUTSCHLAND
1:500,000
Stuttgart : Mair
Road atlas with 29 city plans, hotel and camping information. Index. Covers W and Central Germany. DM 13.80
Leather DM 18.00

AUTO ATLAS BUNDESREPUBLIK
1:650,000
No 350
Hamburg : Falk
Detailed road maps of Germany with insets; also European countries at smaller scale. 7 through town plans.
DM 4.80
Plastic DM 8.60

STRASSENATLAS - DEUTSCHLAND UND EUROPA
Stuttgart : R. V.
16 x 26
Detailed road atlas, roads classified with distances, also railways, ferries, forests, national parks and places of interest.
W Germany, Switzerland and Austria covered on scale 1:500,000, Western Europe scale 1:3,500,000. 92pp col. maps. 70pp index and notes. DM 7.90

GROSSER JRO STRASSENATLAS : DEUTSCHLAND, ALPENLANDER EUROPA
1:750,000/1:4,000,000
München : JRO
No 166
21 x 30
120pp
Larger scale maps for Central Europe, showing main roads, places of interest, distances in km. Rest of Europe; major roads and places of interest. Through-town plans also. DM 14.00

JRO STRASSENATLAS : DEUTSCHLAND, ALPENLANDER EUROPA
München : JRO
No 165
21 x 30
88pp
65pp road maps at 1:400,000 and 1:750,000 for W Germany, Netherlands, Alpine Countries, Italy; 1:1,500,000 for Central Germany and Denmark; 1:5,000,000 for the rest of Europe. Motorways, secondary roads, motoring information. Index of West Germany, tables. DM 7.50

REISE-ATLAS : DEUTSCHLAND UND EUROPA
1:400,000 - 1:750,000
No 801
Frankfurt : Ravenstein, 1976
21 x 28
67pp
46 large scale maps of Germany, Switzerland, Austria; smaller scales for the rest of Europe. 7pp index, abbreviations, distance charts. DM 8.50

SCHWARZWALD - WANDERATLAS
1:100,000
Frankfurt : Ravenstein
13 x 20
Touring atlas of the Northern part of the Black Forest. DM 4.80

ATLASES
B TOWN PLANS

STÄDTE-BILDATLAS
Braunschweig : Bollman - Bildplan
In 3 vols.
38 x 24
108pp
Vols. contain 25 town plans (not all from Germany) of the Bollman-Bildplan style: oblique town views showing individual buildings. With text. Vol 1. DM 44

HAMBURGER STRASSEN- UND VERKEHRS ATLAS
Berlin : Schaffmann, 1971
24 x 23
116pp
Clear street atlas, 78pp maps; index; many symbols. DM 9.80

RHEIN - MAIN - STÄDTE ATLAS
Berlin : Schaffmann, 1971
24 x 23
128pp
Covers main towns from Mainz - Frankfurt - Darmstadt. 46pp index. 78pp maps at 1:10,000, Bad Homburg 1:15,000
DM 14.80

RUHRGEBIET STÄDTEATLAS
1:50,000
No 375
Hamburg : Falk
Town plan atlas of towns in the Ruhr area.
DM 12.80

STADTKERNATLAS SCHLESWIG-HOLSTEIN
Editor Hartwig Beseler
Neumünster : Karl Wachholtz, 1976
25 x 34
220pp
40 towns in the Province are described by a coloured aerial photograph and analysis map scale 1:5,000 and an oblique air photograph together with other photographs of streets of interest or historic buildings. A descriptive text is provided for each town. DM 49

ATLASES
D POLITICAL & ADMINISTRATIVE

NORDRHEIN-WESTFALEN – VERWALTUNGSATLAS
1:500,000
Düsseldorf : Statist. Landesamt, 1971
26 x 34
In 28 maps (65 x 50)
Coloured admin. maps for planning purposes. List of parishes and districts.
DM 60

ATLASES
F GEOLOGY

PALÄOGRAPHISCHER ATLAS DER UNTERKREIDE VON NORDWEST-DEUTSCHLAND
Hannover : B-B, 1967/9
315pp
Palaeographic Atlas of the Lower Chalk of N W Germany including 189pp of maps, scale 1:200,000 including information of mineral wells. 10 at 1:500,000 and 6 at 1:1,500,000 covering adjacent areas of Central Europe. In 2 map volumes with separate text. DM 115

ATLASES
K HUMAN GEOGRAPHY

DEUTSCHER SPRACHATLAS
N G Elwert Verlag
Series of German language atlases.
see Germany 430 Atlases K.

ATLAS DER CELLER MUNDART
Editor R Mehlem
Marburg: N G Elwert Verlag
398pp with 184 maps
Atlas of the Celler dialect of Niedersächsen.
DM 92.00

ATLASES
L ECONOMIC

BLV ATLAS : DIE LANDWIRTSCHAFT DER BRD
Ed Dipl-Volkswirt Inge Kloppenburg
1st edition
München : Bayerischer Landwirtschaftsverlag GmbH, 1968
33 x 44
Loose-leaf atlas in ring-binder of agricultural economy, containing app. 90 maps and graphs, diagrams, explanations.
In 9 sections : Nature of the land and unit value; Pop and work ability; Work structure; land use and cultivation; harvests; cattle rearing and milk yield; tractor ownership; fertilizers, general matters.
DM 190

ATLAS DER DEUTSCHEN AGRARLANDSCHAFT
Ed Prof Dr Otremba
Wiesbaden : Franz Steiner
In 4 parts
Loose leaf atlas in 4 folios. Various scales describing agrarian economy - livestock, land use, crops, cereals etc.

Vol I, 12 maps, 16pp text	DM 64.00
Vol II, 12 maps, 16pp text	DM 64.00
Vol III, 12 maps, 16pp text, 1969	DM 64.00
Vol IV, 18 maps, text, 1971	DM 64.00
Binder	DM 22.00
Maps	DM 256.00
Complete	DM 278.00

ATLASES
M HISTORICAL

HARMS GESCHICHTSATLAS
Paul List Verlag
Bayern edition
Baden-Württemberg edition
see WORLD ATLASES 100 M

BAYERISCHER GESCHICHTSATLAS
Ed Max Spindler
München : Bayerischer Schulebuch-Verlag, 1969
24 x 34
viii, 170pp
46pp maps, 83 text, 39pp index : Covering history of Bavaria from prehistoric times to the modern economy of W Germany. DM 48.00
School ed. available viii, 85pp, 46pp maps, 29pp index DM 24.80
Text volume DM 12.80

HISTORISCHER ATLAS VON BADEN-WÜRTTEMBERG
Stuttgart : Baden-Württemberg Lv with Kommission für geschichtliche Landeskunde in B-W, 1972
46 x 52 each
In 70 maps
Historical atlas issued in annual parts. In progress.

GESCHICHTLICHER ATLAS VON HESSEN
Ed E E Stengal and F Uhlhorn
Marburg : Arbeitsgemeinschaft der Historischen Kommissionen in Hessen, 1960
Atlas covers geog. climate, economy besides political and social history.
100 maps. School ed. also available.

GESCHICHTLICHER ATLAS FÜR DAS LAND AN DER SAAR
Ed M Born, E Meynen, H Walter Herrmann
In 7 parts
Saarbrücken : Inst. für Landeskunde Saarlandes, 1966+
50 x 44
Thematic historical atlas covering physical, social and cultural aspects, tracing developments to the present day. The first 3 parts, each of 12 plates, have been published, the remaining 4 are in preparation.

Parts 1 & 2
Subscription price each DM 18.00
Separately each DM 24.00
Part 3 Subscription price each DM 27.00
Separately each DM 36.00

RHEINISCHE STÄDTEATLAS
Ed Dr Edith Ennen
Mainz : Inst. für geschichtliche Landeskunde des Rheinlands, 1972+
Atlas published in instalments, covering various Rhine towns. Each town has a cadastral plan at 1:2,500 (1816 series), example of 1840 sheet and present day aerial photograph at 1:100,000. With text sheet illus. Part I covers : Lechenich, Bruhl, Meckenheim, Rheinbach, Zulpich, Bonn.

ATLASES
O NATIONAL

DIE BUNDESREPUBLIK DEUTSCHLAND IN KARTEN
Various scales
Prepared by Inst. für Landeskunde
Stuttgart : Kohlhammer
In 92 sheets
Loose leaf atlas sheets, coming under the following headings :
1 Allgemeine Übersichten und Verwaltungs-gliederung (general maps, admin areas) 9 maps
2 Natur (physical geog) 7 maps
3 Bevölkerung, Gesundheits - und Bildungswesen (pop, social aspects) 31 maps
4 Wirtschaft (economy, trade, agriculture) 41 maps
5 Raumgliederung (land cover and divisions) 6 maps
Each DM 9.50
Complete DM 720

DER DEUTSCHER PLANUNGSATLAS
Ed Karl Haubner, Hans Kraus and Werner Witt
Hannover : Gebrüder Janecke
Comprehensive series of atlases prepared by each state (Land). Provides complete survey of country's social, economic and physical background. In 10 vols.

I Nordrhein-Westfalen
Ed Herbert Reiners, 1971
In preparation, parts published :
Part 1 - Boden (soils) DM 20
2 - Gemeindegrenzen, 1961 DM 12
3 - Vegetation DM 20

II Niedersachsen und Bremen
1:800,000
48 x 42
108 maps
not available.

III Schleswig-Holstein
1:500,000
52 x 41
108 maps
not available.

IV Hessen
1:600,000
42 x 59
90 maps
not available.

V Bayern
1:800,000
58 x 60
73 maps
not available.

VI Baden-Württemberg
1969
80 maps, scale 1:600,000 or 1:2,000,000 with text DM 280

VII Rheinland-Pfalz
1:500,000
42 x 59
93 maps DM 250

VIII Hamburg, 1971/2
In preparation 1971/2, 60-70 maps,
Part 1 - DM 24; 2 - DM 12;
3 - DM 24; 5 - DM 18; 7 - DM 24

IX Berlin
1:25,000 - 1:100,000
101 maps
not available

X Saarland
1:200,000
1st section 47 sheets - not available
2nd section - in preparation.

LUFTBILDATLAS DER BUNDESREPUBLIK DEUTSCHLAND
Ed Dr Uwe Muuss
München : List 1972
24 x 34
180pp
About 80 col. aerial maps with other illus. and a selection of maps from the official state series illustrating selected landscape.
DM 48

ATLASES
P REGIONAL

WATTENMEER
Karl Wachholtz, 1976
Atlas of Friesian and other offshore islands.
see EUROPE 4 - ATLASES P

BAYERN : TOPOGRAPHISCHER ATLAS
Ed Geog. Inst. der Bayerischen Universitaten und Hochschulen
München : Bayerische Lv/Paul List Verlag, 1968
329pp
150 map sheets, covering land forms: based on official topog. series and the geography of the region described in text and pictures. DM 46

TOPOGRAPHISCHER ATLAS NORDRHEIN-WESTFALEN
Ed Prof Dr Adolf Schuttler and Ltd Reg Dir Prof Georg Krauss
Bad Godesberg : Nordrhein-Westfalen Lv, 1968
25 x 34
345pp
Based on official topog. series, divided into regional sections. 138 maps with text; covering individual and characteristic land areas. DM 38

PFALZATLAS
Ed W Alter
Speyer : Pfalzische Gesellschaft zur Förderung der Wissenschaften, 1963+
In 2 vols.
Economic, social and historical atlas of the region. Issued in instalments, with booklets.

LUFTBILDATLAS BADEN-WURTTEMBERG
Fritz Fezer and Dr Uwe Muuss
München : List/Wachholtz, 1971
24 x 34
180pp
72 col. aerial phtos, in col. with text.
DM 48

LUFTBILDATLAS BAYERN
Ed Prof Dr Hans Fehn und Lothar Beckel
München : List, 1973
24 x 34
180pp
72 col. aerial photos.
Subscription price to 15/10/73
DM 39.80

TOPOGRAPHISCHER ATLAS NIEDERSACHSEN UND BREMEN
Editor : Hans-Heinrich Seedorf
Neumünster : Karl Wachholtz Verlag, 1976
25 x 34
274pp
Includes 111 maps, extracts from official map series and descriptive text which together describes the appearance and development of the regions landscape.
DM 78

LUFTBILDATLAS NIEDERSACHSEN
Wilhelm Groteluschen and Uwe Muuss
2nd edition
Neumünster : Karl Wachholtz, 1975
24 x 34
200pp
86 aerial photographs with description of each. Comp. 1965-6, covers varying land forms of the region. DM 49.80

LUFTBILDATLAS NORDRHEIN-WESTFALEN
Uwe Muuss and Adolf Schuttler
Neumünster : Karl Wachholtz, 1969
24 x 34
186pp
Compiled 1967-9. 80 col. aerial photos, showing land formations with descriptive details. DM 49.80

NEUER LUFTBILDATLAS RHEINLAND-PFALZ
W Sperling and E Strunk
Neumünster : Karl Wachholtz, 1972
24 x 34
187pp
72 aerial photos, showing selected land formations. DM 49.80

LUFTBILDATLAS SCHLESWIG-HOLSTEIN
Christian Degan and Uwe Muuss
Neumünster : Karl Wachholtz
In 2 parts
Part I 1965, 185pp - Landscape forms shown by aerial photos
Part II (with Klaus Hingst) 1968, 176pp - additional aerial photos taken 1965-8.
Each DM 49.80

UNSERE WELT : GRUNDATLAS NORDRHEIN-WESTFALEN
Ed Werner G Mayer and Prof Dr Erika Wagner
Berlin : Cornelsen, Velhagen and Klasing
23 x 32
40pp
Col. atlas covering the Nordrhein-Westfalen area; school atlas for social studies and geog. With brief ref. to Europe and the world. DM 7.80

HARMS ATLAS FOR THE LÄNDER
München : List
24 x 32
145pp average, incl. approx. 216 maps. State atlases for schools. Volumes published:
Baden-Wurttemberg by Prof D F Pfrommer
Bayern by Dr W Bayer
Hessen by Prof Dr K E Fick
Niedersachsen by G Siebels
Nordrhein-Westfalen by Prof Dr Th. Schreiber
Rheinland-Pfalz by P Bins
Saarland
Schleswig-Holstein by G Pieske
Each DM 15.60

HARMS ATLAS NIEDERBAYERN
by R Dandorfer and Dr H Bleibrunner
München : List, 1973
24pp
Regional school atlas. Col. maps and plans. DM 8.00

HARMS HEIMATATLAS SCHWABEN
Ed A Gropper and F Lutz
München : List
29 x 21
24pp
Regional school atlas. 26 maps and town plans. DM 8.00

HARMS ATLAS MANNHEIM
München : List
153pp
Regional school atlas. 194 maps, index. DM 16.20

HARMS BERLINER GRUND-SCHULATLAS
Ed G Weissner
München : List
21 x 29
65pp
Regional school atlas. 71 maps and plans, 10 photos, many line drawings. DM 7.60

HARMS ATLAS KÖLN UND UMGEBUNG
Ed C H Lubbert
München : List
36pp
Regional school atlas. 49 maps with sketches and pictures. DM 7.40

GRUNDSCHULATLAS MANNHEIM
Ed K H Frank, M Gobel and K Riemer
München : List
21 x 30
Regional school atlas. 36pp maps, plans, graphs, photos. DM 6.20

HARMS MÜNCHENER ATLAS
by B Hirschbold and H Leiderer
New ed.
München : List
21 x 30
38pp
Regional school atlas. 25 maps and plans. 46 line drawings. DM 8.00

HARMS ATLAS NÜRNBERG-FURTH-ERLANGEN
Ed Ernst Feist et al
München : List Verlag
21 x 29
36pp
Regional school atlas. 40 maps and photos. DM 6.80

HARMS HEIMATATLAS WUPPERTAL
Ed G Voigt
München : List
21 x 29
18pp
Local school atlas. 20 maps and drawings. DM 6.40

430.2 German Democratic Republic

See also : 430 GERMANY

A1 GENERAL MAPS : ROADS

NĚMECKÁ DEMOKRATICKÁ REPUBLICKA
1:1,500,000
Praha : Kart
Roads classified and numbered, distances in km, motoring and tourist information.
Kcs 10

DDR – POLEN – CSSR
1:1,000,000
No 1176
Bern : K & F
129 x 92
Roadmap showing all classes of roads, distances, scenic routes, railways, places of interest. Covers Malmö-Brest (USSR) – Budapest – Bremerhaven.

DDR, REISEKARTE
1:750,000
Stuttgart : Mair, 1972/3
72 x 68
Roads classified and numbered, distances in km, places of tourist interest, other communications, relief shading, boundaries. M 4.80

AUTOKARTE DER DDR
1:600,000
Berlin : LV, 1971
60 x 83
8 col, roads classified, railways, boundaries. Legend Eng, Ger, Rus. Also available in Polish ed : Mapa Samochodowa Niemieckiej Republiki Demokratycznej 1972; Czech ed: Automapa Nemecká Demokratická Republiky, 1971 : English ed: Road Map of the GDR; French ed : Carte Automobile de la Rep Democratique Allemande.
Each M 5.50

DEUTSCHE DEMOKRATISCHE REPUBLIK
1:600,000
No 889
Frankfurt : Ravenstein
67 x 100
Detailed route map, roads classified and numbered with distances in km.
DM 6.80

REISELAND DDR (TOURIST COUNTY GDR)
1:600,000
Berlin : LV, 1972
60 x 83
Gives main roads and other communications; winter sports centres, recreation areas, excursion routes, places of interest. Hill shading. With notes. Also in English, French eds.
Each M 4.50

SEHENSWÜRDIGKEITEN DER DDR
1:600,000
2nd edition
Berlin : LV, 1973
65 x 98
Places of interest shown by col. symbols. Legend in 8 langs, with index. Roads, railways. M 4.50

GERMANSKAYA DEMOKRATISCHESKAYA RESPUBLIKA
Moskva : GUGK
Road map with geog. guide.

VERKEHRSKARTE DER DDR
1:200,000
In 9 sheets, see index 430. 2/1
Berlin : LV, 1971/2
Showing admin. boundaries, city through plans, index, road information; Legend Eng, Ger, Rus.
Each sheet M 4.50
In case M 40.50

A2 GENERAL MAPS : LOCAL

D.D.R. TOURISTEN-UND WANDERKARTEN
Various scales
In 7 sheets, see index 430. 2/2
Berlin : LV
In and Around Environs of Berlin
Tourist maps with parks, towns etc.
Legend Eng, Ger, Rus. See index.

Hoher Flaming - Havelseen	1:120,000	M 2.50
Berlin - Nord	1:100,000	M 3
Berlin – Süd	1:100,000	M 3
Naherholungsgebiet Berlin	1:100,000	M 1
Berliner Gewasser	1:50,000	M 2.50
Märkische Schweiz	1:30,000	M 1.50
Müggelsee und Dahme (pictorial map)	1:50,000	M 1.50

NÖRDLICHER TEIL DER DDR
Various scales
See index 430. 2/2
Berlin : LV
Tourist maps of Northern region German Dem. Rep., with legend in Eng, Ger, Rus.
Available for :

Mecklenburger Seenplatte	1:120,000	M 3
Rugen - Hiddensee	1:100,000	M 2.50
Usedom - Haffküste	1:100,000	M 2.50
Darss - Fischland (walking map)	1:50,000	M 2.50

SÜDLICHER TEIL DER DDR
Various scales
See index 430. 2/2
Berlin : LV
Tourist maps of Southern region German Dem. Rep. with town maps inset.
Available for :

Harz	1:100,000	M 2.50
Thüringer Wald	1:100,000	M 3
Gera - Plauen	1:120,000	M 3
Mulde - Zschopau	1:120,000	M 2.50
Untere Saale und Mulde	1:120,000	M 3
Dresden	1:100,000	M 2.50
Westlicher Thüringer Wald	1:50,000	M 2.50
Umgebung von Eisenach	1:50,000	M 1.25
Umgebung von Friedrichroda-Finstterbergen	1:50,000	M 1.25
Mittlerer Thüringer Wald	1:50,000	M 2.50
Oberhof und Umgebung	1:30,000	M 1.25
Schwarzatal	1:50,000	M 2.50
Saaletalsperren	1:50,000	M 2.50
Vogtland - Aschberggebiet	1:50,000	M 3
Westerzgebirge	1:50,000	M 2.50
Mittleres Erzgebirge	1:50,000	M 3.00
Osterzgebirge	1:50,000	M 2.50
Dresdener Heide-Seifersdorfer Tal	1:30,000	M 2
Sächsische Schweiz	1:30,000	M 3
Zittauer Gebirge	1:30,000	M 1.50

B TOWN PLANS

TOWN PLANS
Various scales
Berlin : LV
Coloured plans with index to streets.
Plans available :

Bautzen, 1:10,000	M 1.20
Berlin - East, 1:30,000	M 2.50
Bernburg, 1:10,000	M 1.20
Borna/Bez. Leipzig, 1:10,000	M 2.20
Cottbus, 1:10,000	M 1.50
Dresden, 1:20,000	M 2.30
Elster, Bad 1:10,000	M 1.20
Frankfurt/Oder, 1:15,000	M 1.50
Görlitz, 1:15,000	M 1.20
Halle/Saale, 1:20,000	M 2.00
Jena, 1:5,000	M 1.50
Karl-Marx-Stadt, 1:20,000	M 2.00
Leipzig, 1:15,000	M 2.40
Magdeburg, 1:20,000	M 1.50
Meissen, 1:13,000	M 1.20
Neubrandenburg, 1:10,000	M 1.50

Potsdam, 1:20,000 M 2.00
Strausberg 1:15,000 M 1.50
Weimar, 1:10,000 M 2.00
Zittau, 1:10,000 M 1.20
Zwickau, 1:13,000 M 1.50

C OFFICIAL SURVEYS

ÜBERSICHTSKARTE VON MITTELEUROPA
1:300,000
Inst. für Angewendte Geodäsie
see GERMANY 430 C

TOPOGRAPHISCHE ÜBERSICHTS-KARTE DES DEUTSCHEN REICHES
1:200,000
Inst. für Angewandte Geodäsie
see GERMANY 430 C

KARTE DES DEUTSCHEN REICHES
1:100,000
Inst. für Angewandte Geodäsie
see GERMANY 430 C

D POLITICAL & ADMINISTRATIVE

GERMANSKAYA DEMOKRATICHES-KAYA RESPUBLIKA - POLITIKO - ADMINISTRATIVNAYA KARTA
1:750,000
Moskva : GUGK, 1973
Political administration map of DDR.

VERWALTUNGSKARTE DER DEUTSCHEN DEMOKRATISCHEN REPUBLIK
2nd edition
1:600,000
Berlin : LV, 1972
65 x 98
Admin. map; showing district boundaries with index and text. Legend in 3 langs.
M 4.50

BEZIRKSKARTE DER DDR
1:200,000
In 12 sheets
Berlin : LV
55 x 85 each
Col. map series of each district and including the Kreis (County) boundaries within each; road and rail communications; legend Eng, Ger, Rus, with index to places on reverse side.

1 Rostock, 1972
2 Schwerin, 1971
3 Neubrandenburg, 1971
4 Berlin - Potzdam, 1972
5 Berlin - Frankfurt (Oder), 1971 M 3.50
6 Cottbus, 1972 M 3.50
7 Magdeburg, 1971
8 Halle, 1973
9 Dresden, 1973 M 3.50
10 Leipzig - Karl-Marx-Stadt, 1972
11 Gera - Suhl, 1973
12 Erfurt - Suhl, 1973

Each M 4

E1 PHYSICAL : RELIEF

POLAND, CZECHOSOLVAKIA, EAST GERMANY
1:1,000,000
Moskva : GUGK, 1973
Col. physical map in 2 sheets.

DEUTSCHE DEMOKRATISCHE REPUBLIK
1:250,000
Gotha : Haack
165 x 237
Physical wall map, showing relief by layer col, cities graded by pop, communications, physical features.

E2 PHYSICAL : LAND FEATURES

GEOMORPHOLOGISCHE ÜBERSICHTSKARTE : BERLIN - POTSDAM, FRANKFURT - EBERSWALDE
1:200,000
Ed Prof Dr J F Gellert & Dr E Scholz
Gotha : Haack, 1970/1
36 x 36 each
2 col. maps with 48pp text. To show geog. basic features.
Text and maps in case M 26

F GEOLOGY

GEOLOGISCHE ÜBERSICHTSKARTE VON THÜRINGEN
1:500,000
Gotha : Haack, 1971
60 x 45
General geological map covering the districts of Erfurt, Gera, Suhl.
M 6.30

H BIOGEOGRAPHY

KARTE DER NATURLICHEN VEGETATION DER DDR
1:500,000
Berlin : Akademie Verlag, 1964
31 x 43
Col. map showing principal types of vegetation. With text.

K HUMAN GEOGRAPHY

BEVÖLKERUNGSDICHTE DER GEMEINDEN DER DDR AM 31.12.1964
1:750,000
Berlin : LV
Population density by parish as at 31.12.64.

L ECONOMIC

POL'SHA, CHEKOSLOVAKIYA GERMANSKAYA DEMOKRATICHES-KAYA RESPUBLIKA
1:1,000,000
GUGK, 1971
Economic map.
see POLAND 438 L.

DEUTSCHE DEMOKRATISCHE REPUBLIK, BERGBAU UND INDUSTRIE
1:250,000
Gotha : Haack
165 x 237
School wall map showing mining and industrial areas, mineral resources, communications.

DEUTSCHE DEMOKRATISCHE REPUBLIK, VERKEHR
1:250,000
Gotha : Haack
165 x 237
School wall map, showing communications.

ATLASES
A1 GENERAL : ROADS

REISEATLAS DER DDR
1:500,000
4th edition
Berlin : LV, 1970
15 x 25
176pp
12 area maps of DDR at 1:500,000; 13 tourist maps 1:200,000; 26 through-city plans; 7 maps of other socialist European countries; index. M 14.00

VERKEHRSATLAS
1:500,000
Gotha : Haack, 1972
220pp app
10 x 16
Showing general communications maps of the DDR, 32 through town plans. Tourist information in 109pp text. Legend Ger, Eng, Rus. Haack "Kleiner Atlas" series. 57pp index. 2nd edition.
Plastic covers M 7.60

ATLASES
L ECONOMIC

AGRARATLAS ÜBER DAS GEBIET DER DDR BY R MATZ
1:200,000
Gotha : Haack
64 x 100 (map size)
67 maps, showing soil cultivation. Also available for the 10 districts of DDR at 29.35 M each M 150

ATLASES
M HISTORICAL

HISTORISCHER HANDATLAS VON BRANDENBURG UND BERLIN
Ed Prof Dr Heinz Quirin
Berlin : Walter de Gruyter, 1962+
Series of facsimile maps etc. covering history, economics, cultural affairs.
Issued in parts with text and map. 34 parts now complete.

ATLASES
O NATIONAL

ATLAS DDR
Gotha : VEB Haack/Deutsche Akademie der Wissenschaften
55 x 84 (map size)
102 maps at scale 1:750,000 - 1:2,000,000
Thematic maps - natural, economic, industrial, pop, communications, climate, education ed. In 2 parts : Part 1 end 1972, Sheets in binder. Legends Ger, Rus, Eng, Fr, Sp.
Complete M 450

436 Austria

A1 GENERAL MAPS : ROADS

ÖSTERREICH
1:1,000,000
Bern : Hallwag
94 x 39
All classes of roads, distances in km, hill shading, ferries, airports, camping sites and railways.

GERMANIA E AUSTRIA
1:1,000,000
Novara : Ag
Tourist road map, route numbers and distances. L 700

SHELL REISEKARTE ÖSTERREICH
1:850,000
Stuttgart : Mair
70 x 48
Classifies roads with views and tourist attractions. Legend in 12 languages.
DM 4.80

ÖSTERREICH
1:650,000
No 392
Hamburg : Falk
Roads classified; index; patent Falk folding. DM 4.80

AUSZTRIA AUTOTÉRKÉPE
1:650,000
Budapest : Cart, 1970
100 x 50
Col. road map with legend in 6 langs, inc. Eng.

ÖSTERREICH
1:625,000
No 871
Frankfurt : Ravenstein
99 x 69
Roads classified, distances in km; other communications, places of interest.
DM 7.80

ÖSTERREICH
1:600,000
Wien : F & B
99 x 75
All classes of roads, distances in km, road numbers, spot heights in m, hill shading, railways, airports, camp sites, car ferries, state boundaries.

HALLWAG ALPINA I - EASTERN ALPS
1:600,000
Bern : Hallwag
112 x 84
Covering most of Austria, south Bavaria and the Dolomites. All classes of roads, distances and route numbers, car ferries, camping sites, places of interest and mountain railways.

HALLWAG ALPINA III - CENTRAL ALPS
1:600,000
Bern : Hallwag
112 x 84
Covering Switzerland, western Austria and northern Italy. All classes of roads, distances in km, hill shading, caping sites, car ferries and railways.

SCHUTZHÜTTEN DER OST ALPEN
1:600,000
Innsbruck : OAV
100 x 65
Map of the Eastern Alps showing location of mountain huts which are listed separately.

ÖSTERREICH
1:500,000
No 116
Bern : K & F
127 x 90
Road map with hill shading, all classes of roads, ferries and camp sites. Town plan insets of Vienna, Innsbruck, Salzburg and Munich.

CARTA STRADALE D'EUROPA
1:500,000
Sheet 28 Austria
Milano : TCI
77 x 117
Layer col, all classes of roads, distances in km, railways, ferries, State, Regional and Provincial boundaries.
see also EUROPE 4 A1

AUSTRIA
1:450,000
London : Foldex
Showing roads classified, relief shading; patent folding. 45p

ÖSTERREICH UND NÖRDLICHES ITALIEN
1:450,000
No 1436
Munchen : JRO
123 x 88
Roads classified and numbered, distances in km, places of interest. DM 6.80

SÜDOSTBAYERN, TIROL
1:450,000
No 1440
München : JRO
60 x 43
Roads classified and numbered, distances in km, places of interest (section from map 1436). DM 6.80

GROSSE AUTOKARTE ÖSTERREICH
1:400,000
No 82
Stuttgart : RV
137 x 83
Showing all classes of roads, footpaths, railways, mountain passes, places of interest, hostels and camping sites. DM 6.80

KOMPASS AUTOKARTE
1:250,000
Munchen : Kompass
Detailed road maps, covering nearly all of the country. Relief highlighted by shading and spot heights. All classes of roads and tracks, distances, route numbers. Filling stations, gradients, railways, mountain passes, motels, camping sites, youth hostels, first aid posts and places of interest.
Sheets:
Oberbayern - Tirol - Dolomiten
118 x 84 DM 4.90
Ostosterreich
133 x 96 DM 5.80

OBERBAYERN - TIROL - DOLOMITEN
1:200,000
No 51
(Bregenz-Salzburg-Munich-Bolzano)
Stuttgart : RV
105 x 97
Road map showing motorways, classes of roads, numbers, distances, gradients, tracks, railways, mountain lifts. Hotels, restaurants, mountain huts, youth hostels, motels, camping sites; other features of tourist interest.

GENERALKARTE ÖSTERREICH
1:200,000
In 9 sheets, see index 436/11
Stuttgart : Mair (with F & B) 1971/2
91 x 47 each
Series showing roads classified and numbered, distances in km, spot heights, other communications, places of interest, camping sites, state frontiers, hill shading etc. With special sheet Sudtirol.
Each DM 3.50

STRASSENKARTE ÖSTERREICH
1:200,000
In 4 sheets
Wien : Holzel
104 x 48 each sheet
Tourist map with roads classified, distances, scenic routes, places of interest. Sheets : West, Central, South and East.
Each sheet DM 5.80

A2 GENERAL MAPS : LOCAL

WANDERKARTEN (TOURIST AND WALKING MAPS)
1:100,000
see index 436/2
Wien : FB, 1969
76 x 71
Detailed series for walking and skiing giving contour lines, roads, footpaths, tracks, ski-lifts, mountain railways, huts, rivers, camping sites and state boundaries.

1 Wienerwald
2 Schneeberg, Raxalpe Semmeringgebiet
3 Otscher, Mariazell
4 Hochschwab und Murztal
5 Unteres Ennstal
6 Ennstaler Alpen (Gesause)
7 Wachau, Kamptal
8 Ostl. Salzkammergut (Totes Gebirge)
9 Westl. Salzkammergut
10 Berchtesgadener Land- Salzburger Kalkalpen
11 Waldviertel und Strudengau
12 Glockner - und Venedigergruppe
13 Grazer Bergland, Hochlantsch
14 Julische Alpen
15 Zillertaler Alpen
16 Westl. Dolomiten
17 Ostl. Dolomiten
18 Lienzer Dolomiten, Schobergruppe
19 Goldberg - Ankogel, Radstadter Tauern
20 Schladminger Tauern
21 Seetaler Alpen, Murtal

22 Drau - und Gailtal
23 Karntner Seen - Saualpe
24 Stubaier Alpen
25 Otztaler Alpen
26 Muhlviertal und Bohmerwald
27 Leithagebirge, Neusiedler See
28 Dachstein und Salzkammergutseen
30 Kaisergebirge, Chiemgauer Alpen
31 Tegernseer - Schlierseer Berge und Rofangebirge
32 Karwendelgebirge
33 Umgebung von Innsbruck
34 Wettersteingebirge
35 Lechtaler - und Allgauer Alpen
36 Bregenzer Wald
37 Ratikon, Silvretta - und Verwallgruppe
38 Kitzbuheler Alpen und Pinzgau
39 Umgebung von Salzburg
40 Umgebung von Linz - Wels - Steyr
41 Graz - Koralpe - Eibiswald
42 Oststeiermark und Mittleres Burgenland
43 Hausruck und Kobernausser Wald
44 Bad Gliechenberg und Riegersburg
45 Bozen - Meran und Umgebung
46 Ortlegruppe
47 Ostkarawanken und Steiner Alpen
49 Gardasee
50 Brenta - Adamello - und Presanellagruppe
51 Bernina und Engadiner Alpen
52 Vinschgau Umgebungskarte von Wien
Each DM 4.60

WANDER UND AUFSFLUGSKARTE
Various scales
München : JRO
Various sizes
Col. tourist and excursion maps for holiday areas: places of interest and natural beauty, roads, paths etc. Some with ski-routes and relief shading. Available for :
704 Tegernseer Tal
1:75,000 46 x 67 DM 3.00
721 Salzkammergut
1:150,000 58 x 44 DM 1.90
728 Garmisch-Partenkirchen und Innsbruck
1:100,000 88 x 62 DM 3.50
730 Karntner Seegebiet
1:75,000 88 x 46 DM 3.00

UMGEBUNGSKARTE
1:50,000
see index 436/2
Wien : F-B
85 x 60
Series of regional maps in progress; showing roads, footpaths, contours, spot heights in metres, ski-lifts and railways, tourist accommodation, etc.
Sheets available :
121 Gerlospass - Krimml - Neunkirchen - Mittersill - Felber Tauern
122 Zell am See - Kaprun - Grossglockner - Heilingenblut
123 Matrei/Ostt - Hinterbichl - Grossvenediger - Defereggen
181 Lienz - Heiligenblut - Schobergruppe - Matrei - Östt - Kals
221 Millstatter See - Spittal/Drau - Gmund - Greifenburg
222 Randenthein - Turracher Hohe - Flattnitz
223 Weissensee - Oberdrauburg - Kotschach-Mauten - Hermager
224 Villach - Faaker See - Paternion - Tarvis
231 St Veit - Feldkirchen - Gurktal - Hochosterwitz - Magdalensberg
232 Volkermarkt - Klopeiner See - Wolfsberg - Saualpe
233 Klagenfurt - Worthersee - Villach - Ossaicher See - Rosenthal
234 Klagenfurt - Loiblpass - Klopeiner See - Eisenkappl - Bad Vellach
361 Bregenz - Dornbirn - Nordlicher Bregenzerwald
362 Feldkirch - Sudlicher Bregenzerwald - Grosses Walsertal
363 Sonthofen - Obestorf - Kleines Walsertal
371 Feldkirch - Bludenz - Schruns
372 Landeck - Ischgl - Arlberg - Flexenpass
373 Silvretta - Hochalpenstrasse - Schruns - Ischgl
282 Kitzbuhel - Pass Thurn - Fieberbrunn - Leogang - Saalbach - Zell am See
Each DM 3.20
Special Regional maps:
Dachstein DM 3.20
Sonnblick-Ankogel DM 3.20
Wienerwald DM 5.80

KOMPASS WANDERKARTEN
1:50,000
See index 436/3
München : Kompass
Various sizes
Series covering main tourist and climbing areas of Austria and Italian Dolomites. Contours, hill shading, footpaths, camp sites, mountain tracks, land detail.
Sheets available :
K1a Bodensee, westlicher Teil DM 3.20
K1b Bodensee, östlicher Teil DM 3.20
K1c Bodensee, Gesamtgebiet 1:750,000
K2 Westallgau - Westliche Nagelfluhkette DM 2.80
K3 Allgauer Alpen - Kleines Walsertal DM 3.20
K4 Fussen - Tannheimer Gruppe DM 2.80
K5 Wettersteingebirge DM 3.20
K6 Walchensee - Wallgau - Krun DM 2.80
K7 Murnau - Kochel - Staffelsee DM 3.20
K8 Tegernsee - Schliersee DM 3.20
K9 Kaisergebirge DM 3.20
K10 Chiemsee - Waginger See DM 3.20
K11 Reit im Winkl DM 2.80
K12 Ruhpolding DM 2.80
K13 Loferer Steinberge DM 3.20
K14 Berchtesgadener Alpen DM 3.20
K15 Tennengebirge - Hochkonig DM 3.20
K17 Salzburger Seengebiet DM 3.20
K18 Nordliches Salzkammergut DM 3.20
K20 Sudliches Salzkammergut DM 3.20
K21 Feldkirch - Vaduz (in prep) DM 3.80
K22 Bregenzerwald DM 3.20
K24 Lechtaler Alpen - Hornbachkette DM 3.20
K25 Ehrwald - Lermoos DM 3.20
K26 Karwendelgebirge DM 3.20
K27 Achensee-Rofangebirge DM 3.20
K28 Nordliches Zillertal DM 3.20
K29 Kitzbuheler Alpen DM 3.20
K29s Kitzbuheler Alpen DM 3.20
K30 Sallfelden - Leoganger Steinberge DM 3.20
K31 Radstadt - Schladming DM 3.20
K32 Ratikon - Bludenz - Montafon DM 3.20
K33 Arlberg - Nordliche Verwallgruppe DM 3.20
K33s Arlberg - Nordliche Verwallgruppe DM 3.20
K34 Landeck - Nordliche Samnaungruppe DM 3.20
K35 Telfs - Kuhtai - Sellraintal DM 3.20
K36 Innsbruck - Brenner DM 3.80
K37 Zillertaler Alpen - Tuxer Voralpen DM 3.20
K38 Venedigergruppe-Oberpinzgau DM 3.20
K39 Glocknergruppe - Zell am See DM 3.20
K40 Gasteiner Tal - Goldberggruppe DM 3.20
K41 Silvretta - Verwallgruppe DM 3.20
K42 Nauders - Reschenpasse DM 3.20
K43 Otztaler Alpen DM 3.80
K44 Sterzing/Vipiteno DM 3.20
K45 Deferegger Alpen DM 3.20
K46 Matrei (Osttirol)-Lasorlinggruppe DM 3.20
K47 Lienzer Dolomiten DM 3.20
K48 Kals - Granatspitz DM 3.20
K49 Mallnitz - Obervellach DM 3.20
K50 Heiligenblut - Dollach DM 3.20
K52 Vinschgau/Val Venosta DM 3.80
K53 Meran/Merano DM 3.80
K54 Bozen/Bolzano DM 3.80
K55 Cortina d'Ampezzo DM 3.80
K56 Brixen/Bressanone DM 3.80
K57 Bruneck/Brunico - Toblach DM 3.20
K58 Sextener Dolomiten DM 3.20
K59 Sellagruppe - Marmolata DM 3.20
K59s Sellagruppe - Marmolata DM 3.20
K60 Gailtaler Alpen DM 3.20
K61 Worther - Faaker - Ossiacher See DM 3.20
K62 Feldkirchen - Glantal DM 3.20
K63 Millstatter See - Nockgebiet DM 3.20
K64 Villacher Alpe - Unteres Drautal DM 3.20
K65 Klopeiner See DM 3.20
K66 Maltatal - Liesertal DM 3.20
K67 Radstadter Tauern - Lungau DM 3.20
K68 Ausseer Land - Tauplitzalm DM 3.20
K69 Hinterstoder - Windischgarsten DM 3.20
K70 Gesause - Ennstaler Alpen DM 3.20
K71 Adamello - La Presanella DM 3.20
K72 Ortler/Ortles/Gran Zebru DM 3.20
K73 Gruppo di Brenta DM 3.80
K74 Tramin/Termeno - Salurn/Salorno DM 3.20
K75 Trento - Levico - Lavarone DM 3.20
K76 Pale di San Martino DM 3.20
K78 Asiago - Cette Comuni DM 3.20
K80 Grossarital - Kleinarital DM 3.20
K81 Worgl - Hopfgarten DM 3.20
K82 Tauferer - Ahrntal - Valle di Tures DM 3.20
K83 Stubaier Alpen - Serleskamm DM 3.20
K85 Massiccio del Monte Bianco DM 3.80

K86 Gran Paradiso - Valle d'Aosta DM 3.80
K87 Breuil - Cervinia - Zermatt DM 3.80
K90 Lago Maggiore - Lago di Varese DM 3.80
K91 Lago di Como - Lago di Lugano DM 3.80
K92 Chiavenna - Bergell DM 3.80
K93 Bernina - Sondrio DM 3.80
K94 Edolo - Aprica DM 3.20
K96 Livigno - Bormio - Corna di Campo DM 3.20
K101 Rovereto - Monte Pasubio DM 3.20
K102 Lago di Garda - Monte Baldo DM 3.80
K132 Seetaler Alpen - Murtal DM 3.20
K133 Friesach - Metnitzer Alpen DM 3.20
K134 Glantal - St Veit - Wimitzer Berge DM 3.20
K147 Sylt with street plan DM 3.20
K148 Amrum - Fohr - Langeness DM 3.20
K150 Holsteinische Schweiz DM 3.20
K155 Harz, westlicher Teil DM 3.80
K162 Westlicher Taunus DM 4.80
K163 Ostlicher Taunus DM 4.80
K167 Nordlicher Steigerwald DM 3.20
K168 Sudlicher Steigerwald DM 3.20
K169 Nordlicher Rangau DM 3.20
K171 Frankische Schweiz DM 3.20
K172 Hersbrucker Land in der Frankenalb DM 3.20
K180 Starnberger See - Ammersee DM 3.80
K181 Rosenheim - Bad Aibling DM 3.80
K192 Nordlicher Oberpfalzer Wald DM 3.20
K193 Mittlerer Oberpfalzer Wald DM 3.20
K194 Sudlicher Oberpfalzer Wald DM 3.20
K195 Nordlicher Bayerischer Wald DM 3.20
K196 Mittlerer Bayerischer Wald DM 3.20
K197 Sudlicher Bayerischer Wald DM 3.20
K198 Westliches Muhlviertel DM 3.20
K207 Wachau DM 3.80

GEBIETSKARTEN
Various scales
Wien : BEV
Various sizes
Series of official topog. maps for various tourist areas, contoured with footpaths, some marked in colour, roads and places of interest.
Maps available :
Hochschwab
1:50,000 with walking routes A.Sch 42
Hohe Wand
1:40,000 with walking routes A.Sch 15
Innsbruck
1:25,000 with paths, folded A.Sch 45
Innsbruck
1:25,000 with paths, flat A.Sch 40
Innsbruck
1:25,000, flat A.Sch 33
Lienzer Dolomiten
1:25,000 A.Sch 31
Mariazell
1:40,000 with paths A.Sch 21
Schneeberg und Rax
1:25,000 with paths A.Sch 37
Schneeberg und Rax
1:25,000 without roads A.Sch 29
6 large sheets of Wien
1:25,000 each A.Sch 20
Umgebung (environs) von Wien
1:50,000 with paths, in cover A.Sch 45
1:50,000 with paths, flat A.Sch 40
1:50,000 roads in red, in cover A.Sch 43
1:50,000 roads in red, flat A.Sch 38
1:50,000 flat A.Sch 33
Umgebungskarte Mayrhofen (Zillertal)
1:50,000 with paths A.Sch 42

WANDERKARTEN
1:50,000 - 1:25,000
Salzburg : O Müller Verlag
Series of large scale walking maps marking footpaths. Sheets in series - 1:50,000 unless otherwise stated.
1 Salzburg-Umgebung 1:30,000 A.Sch 28
2 Saalfelden-Leogang 1:30,000 A.Sch 28
3 Salzkammergut - Seen A.Sch 28
4 Mattsee A.Sch 30
5 Wagrain A.Sch 28
5a Radstädter Tauern - Obertauern 1:25,000 A.Sch 28
6 Saalbach A.Sch 28
7 Zell am See A.Sch 28
11 Bad Ischl A.Sch 28
12 Bad Schallerbach A.Sch 28
21 St Johann i.T. 1:25,000 A.Sch 28
21a Pillersee - Fieberbrunn 1:25,000 A.Sch 28
22 Wilder Kaiser A.Sch 28
23 Zillertaler Alpen A.Sch 28
30 Kärntner Seen A.Sch 28
31 Millstätter See A.Sch 28
32 Faaker See 1:30,000 A.Sch 28
33 Bad Kleinkirchheim 1:25,000 A.Sch 30
34 Attersee - Traunsee A.Sch 28
34a Attersee A.Sch 30
35 Heiligenblut 1:25,000 A.Sch 28
36 Lungau A.Sch 28
37 Oberndorf - Tirol 1:25,000 A.Sch 25
38 Lienz 1:30,000 A.Sch 28
39 Südkärnten Klopeiner See - Turner See 1:30,000 A.Sch 28
40 Matrei- Osttirol 1:30,000 A.Sch 28
41 Brixen im Thale - Kirchberg 1:30,000 A.Sch 28
42 Inneres Montafon St Gallenkirch-Gaschurn - Partenen - Gargellent 1:30,000 A.Sch 28
43 Rofan-Alpbantal 1:30,000 A.Sch 28
44 Wörther See 1:25,000 A.Sch 30
45 Ossiacher See 1:25,000 A.Sch 30
46 Oberes Drautal 1:30,000 A.Sch 30
47 Weissensee 1:30,000 A.Sch 30

ALPENVEREINSKARTEN
1:25,000
see index 436/4
Innsbruck : Osterreichisher Alpenverein
Various sizes
Contoured climbing map series, covering mountainous and Alpine areas. Shows ski routes, alpine huts, rivers, waterfalls. Legend in German. See index.
Sheets available :
2/1 Allgauer Alpen West A.Sch 36
2/2 Allgauer Alpen East A.Sch 36
3/2 Lechtaler Alpen, Arlbert, with ski-routes A.Sch 36
4/1 Wetterstein - Mieminger Gebirge A.Sch 36
4/2 Wetterstein - Mieminger Gebirge, Central A.Sch 36
4/3 Wetterstein - Mieminger Gebirge, East A.Sch 36
5/1 Karwendel A.Sch 36
5/2 Karwendel, Central A.Sch 36
5/3 Karwendel, East A.Sch 36
6 Rofangebirge
8 Kaisergebirge A.Sch 36
9/1 Loferer Steinberge (tourist map) A.Sch 33
10/2 Hochkönig-Hagengebirge
14 Dachstein A.Sch 36
15/1 Totes Gebirge, Schonberg - Wilden Kogel A.Sch 36
15/2 Totes Gebirge, Gr Priel - Tauplitz A.Sch 36
15/3 Totes Gebirge, Warscheneckgruppe A.Sch 36
16 Gesauseberge A.Sch 36
26 Silvretta, with Ski-routes A.Sch 36
30/1 Otztaler Alpen, Gurgl, with ski-routes, paper A.Sch 36
Syntosil A.Sch 45
30/2 Otztaler Alpen, Weissekugel, with and without ski-routes A.Sch 36
30/3 Otztaler Alpen, Kauner Grat - Geigenkamm A.Sch 36
30/4 Otztaler Alpen, Nauders, with ski-routes A.Sch 33
31/1 Stubaier Alpen, Hochstubai, with ski-routes
Paper A.Sch 36
31/1 Stubaier Alpen, Hochstubai, with ski-routes and guide on reverse
Paper A.Sch 48
Syntosil A.Sch 60
31/2 Stubaier Alpen, Sellrain, with ski-routes A.Sch 36
31/3 Brennergebiet, 1:50,000
Summer ed. A.Sch 36
Winterausgabe, ed with ski-routes,
Paper A.Sch 42
Syntosil A.Sch 45
35/1 Zillertaler Alpen A.Sch 36
35/2 Zillertaler Alpen, Central A.Sch 36
35/3 Zillertaler Alpen, East with ski-routes A.Sch 36
35/3 Zillertaler Alpen, East, with ski-routes and guide on reverse A.Sch 48
Syntosil A.Sch 60
36 Venedigergruppe A.Sch 36
39 Granatspitzgruppe A.Sch 36
40 Glocknergruppe A.Sch 36
41 Schobergruppe A.Sch 36
42 Sonnblick, with and without ski-routes
Paper A.Sch 36
Syntosil A.Sch 45

42 Sonnblick, ski-routes and guide on reverse
Paper A.Sch 48
Syntosil A.Sch 60
45 Schladminger Tauern, 1:50,000, with ski-routes A.Sch 33
52/1b Sellagruppe (Summer ed) A.Sch 36
52/1b Sellagruppe (Winter ed) with ski-routes A.Sch 36
52/1c Palagruppe A.Sch 36
52/2 Dolomiten, East 1:100,000 A.Sch 33
56 Lienzer Dolomiten A.Sch 36
60 Steinernes Meer A.Sch 36
61 Niedere Tauern II East Radstadter and West Schladminger (Tauern) 1:50,000 A.Sch 36
Schutzhuttenkarte 1:600,000 A.Sch 33
Skikarte, Innsbruck and Umgebung, guide on reverse
Paper A.Sch 48
Syntosil A.Sch 60

KOMPASS UMGEBUNGSKARTEN
1:15,000 ; 1:30,000
See index 436/3
Munchen : Kompass
Various sizes
Large scale series of local maps covering popular touring areas, contoured with relief shading, roads, footpaths and tourist information.
Sheets published :
562 Seefeld (Tirol)
563 Villach
564 Kitzbuhel
566 Badgarstein
569 Innsbruck Igls
570 Kufstein
571 Oberstaufen
572 Oberaudorf
Each A.Sch 23

SALZKAMMERGUT : PANORAMAKARTE
No 526
Munchen : JRO
62 x 42
"Birds eye view" pictorial map, showing land types, roads, settlements, relief, physical features. DM 1.50

B TOWN PLANS

TOWN PLANS
Various scales
Publishers - see below
Col. town plans each with index to streets.
Plans available:

Graz
F-B 1:15,000 A.Sch 34
1:15,000 smaller ed. A.Sch 23
Bollman pictorial DM 5.50

Innsbruck
Kompass 1:12,500 DM 2.20
F-B 1:10,000 A.Sch 23

Linz
Kompass 1:17,500 DM 2.20
F-B 1:12,000 A.Sch 34

Salzburg
F-B 1:15,000 A.Sch 23
O.Muller 1:10,000
Greater A.Sch 40
Central A.Sch 25
Small A.Sch 13

Wien
Kompass 1:22,500 DM 2.20
Falk 1:18,000/35,000 DM 4.80
Hallwag 1:12,500 DM 4.50
F-B 1:25,000 A.Sch 38
F-B 1:15,000 (Traffic plan) A.Sch 38
F-B 1:20,000 A.Sch 27
F-B 1:20,000 (Central area) A.Sch 17
Kart Kcs 16

C OFFICIAL SURVEYS

INTERNATIONALE WELTKARTE (ÜBERSICHTSKARTE)
1:1,000,000
Frankfurt : Inst. für Angewandte Geodäsie
3 sheets to cover Austria
see GERMANY 430 C
WORLD 100 C and index 100/1.

ÜBERSICHTSKARTE VON MITTELEUROPA
1:750,000
In 54 sheets
BEV 1900-1930
see EUROPE 4C.

ÜBERSICHTSKARTE VON MITTELEUROPA
1:750,000
In 12 sheets
BEV 1937
see EUROPE 4C.

GENERALKARTE VON MITTELEUROPA
1:200,000
In 265 sheets, see index 436/1
BEV
23 sheets cover Austria
see EUROPE 4C.
Special editions for sheets covering Austria :
a) base detail and names in light grey and water in light blue
b) relief in light grey and water in light blue.
Each A.Sch 22

ÖSTERREICHISCHE KARTE
1:200,000
In 23 sheets, see index 436/5
Wien : BEV 1968 +
Topog. map series in progress, contoured with roads, railways, paths, vegetation in green and detailed land information.
With roads in red A.Sch 23
Without roads in red A.Sch 20
Special sheet : Burgenland A.Sch 42

ÖSTERREICHISCHE KARTE
1:50,000
In 213 sheets, see index 436/6
Wien : BEV
Topog. map series in progress, contoured with roads, paths and land detail in col. which will replace the earlier Provisional edition which is in black and white, relief by hachures with colour overprint.
Available in 4 editions :
Standard edition
with walking routes in red A.Sch 25
with roads in red A.Sch 22
without colour overprints A.Sch 20
Provisional edition
black and white with green woodland and walking routes in red A.Sch 16
black and white with green woodland only A.Sch 10
Conventional signs sheets for standard ed:
1962 ed A.Sch 13
1964 ed A.Sch 15
Conventional sign sheets for Provisional ed: A.Sch 5

ÖSTERREICHISCHE KARTE
1:25,000
800 sheets, see index 436/7
Wien : BEV
Topog. series in progress showing relief by shading and contours (in brown), vegetation green, water features blue, spot heights in m.
Each A.Sch 13
Symbol sheet A.Sch 10

ALTE ÖSTERREICHISCHE LANDESAUFNAHME
1:25,000
In 388 sheets, see index 436/8
Wien : BEV, 1920
Old topog. map series in black and white, relief by hachures. Many sheets now out of print.
Each A.Sch 10

D POLITICAL & ADMINISTRATIVE

AUSTRIYA
1:750,000
Moskva : GUGK, 1973
Col. general map showing water features, settlements, administrative divisions and centres, communications, boundaries, economic details, pop. Short geog. description. kop 30

ÜBERSICHTSKARTE VON ÖSTERREICH : POLITISCHE AUSGABE
1:500,000
Wien : BEV, 1973
124 x 84
Col. map showing admin. boundaries, col. by districts; communications. Separate index vol.
Folded with index A.Sch 53
Without index A.Sch 33

ÜBERSICHTSKARTE VON ÖSTERREICH VERMESSUNGS-BEZIRKE
1:500,000
Wien : BEV, 1972
123 x 72
Showing admin. districts and boundaries, hydrography. With index to parishes. A.Sch 30

BURO-UND STRASSENKARTE ÖSTERREICH
1:400,000
Wien : F-B
160 x 124
Political col; boundaries and borders; list of administrative divisions. A.Sch 98

ÜBERSICHTSKARTE DER BUNDESLÄNDER
1:200,000
In 7 sheets
Wien : BEV
Provincial series in black with water features blue, political boundaries purple.
Sheets :
Oberösterreich, Steiermark, Tirol
Each A.Sch 56
Burgenland, Kärnten, Salzburg, Voralberg
Each A.Sch 32

E1 PHYSICAL : RELIEF

ÖSTERREICH
1:1,000,000
Wien : F-B
65 x 49
Physical map, contoured with layer colouring and hill shading, communications and boundaries.

ÖSTERREICH
1:800,000
Wien : F-B
81 x 49
Contoured with layer colours, road and rail communications. DM 2.20

ÜBERSICHTSKARTE VON ÖSTERREICH
1:500,000
Wien : BEV
General topog. map, contoured with relief shading, roads and boundaries.
Folded, with index A.Sch 59
Folded without index A.Sch 39
Index A.Sch 16

ÜBERSICHTSKARTE
1:500,000
Wien : BEV
122 x 85
General map available in 2 editions:
a) base information and names in light grey and water in light blue
b) layer colours in light brown shades and water in light blue
Each A.Sch 36

ÖSTERREICH
1:350,000
No 9791
Munchen : JRO
185 x 123
Physical col. wall map, with 2 col. "Arbeitskarte" (base map, with plastic writing surface) on reverse. DM 138
No 9792 As above without Arbeitskarte DM 128

REPUBLIK ÖSTERREICH
1:300,000
Wien : F-B
235 x 190
Physical col. wall map.

NIEDERÖSTERREICH
1:150,000
Wien : F-B
170 x 152
Col. physical wall map with communications and boundaries.

OBERÖSTERREICH
1:100,000
Wien : F-B
185 x 160
Col. physical wall map with communications and boundaries.

STEIERMARK
1:150,000
Wien : F-B
162 x 160
Col. physical wall map with communications and boundaries.

TIROL UND VORARLBERG
1:150,000
Wien : F-B
205 x 175
Col. contoured physical wall map with communications and boundaries.

AUSTRIA
1:2,500,000
Novara : Ag
33 x 26
Plastic relief map for schools with political, physical and economic details on reverse.
L 450

PLASTIK RELIEFKARTEN VON ÖSTERREICH
Wien : F-B
Moulded relief map with layered relief col. showing roads, railways and principal sights with town pop. classified by symbol.
Maps available :
Osterreich - Ostalpen
1:800,000
83 x 50
Wien und Niederosterreich
1:400,000
60 x 64
Each A.Sch 260

F GEOLOGY

GEOLOGISCHE ÜBERSICHTSKARTE DER REPUBLIK ÖSTERREICH MIT TEKTONISCHER GLIEDERUNG
1:1,000,000
Wien : GB, 1971
94 x 52
Geol. map with tectonic information and section. A.Sch 110

HYDROGEOLOGISCHE KARTE DER REPUBLIK ÖSTERREICH
1:1,000,000
Wien : GB, 1970
65 x 47
Col. hydrogeol. map. A.Sch 140

GEOLOGISCHE KARTE DER REPUTLIK ÖSTERREICH UND DER NACHBARGEBIETE
1:500,000
by H Vetters
Wien : GB, 1968
129 x 91 complete
Geological map in 2 sheets with text in German Set A.Sch 400

GEOLOGISCHE KARTEN DER REPUBLIK ÖSTERREICH - GEBIETSKARTEN
1:75,000
Index 436/9
1:10,000 1:25,000, 1:50,000
1:100,000
Index 436/10
Wien : GB
Series of coloured geol. maps, some with explanatory texts in German.
Maps available :
BURGENLAND
Mattersburg-Deutschkreutz
1:50,000 (1957) A.Sch 270
Text A.Sch 65
KÄRNTEN
5253 Hüttenberg-Eberstein
1:75,000 (1931) A.Sch 270
Karnische und Julische Alpen (Karawankenkarte)
1:75,000 4 sheets with text (1895) A.Sch 400
5353 Blatt Völkermarkt A.Sch 50
5354 Blatt Unterdrauburg A.Sch 200
5453 Blatt Eisenkappel A.Sch 200
5454 Blatt Prassberg A.Sch 200
Text A.Sch 50
Umgebung von Klagenfurt
1:50,000 (1962) A.Sch 360
Sonnblickgruppe
1:50,000 (1962) A.Sch 360
Text (1964) A.Sch 250
200 Arnoldstein
1:50,000 (1976) In press
201/210 Villach-Assling
1:50,000 (1976) In press
Nassfeld-Gartnerkofel-Gebiet
1:25,000 (1959) A.Sch 160
Text (1963) A.Sch 180
2 Saualpe
1:25,000 (1977) In press
NIEDERÖSTERREICH
4657 Gänserndorf
1:75,000 (1954) A.Sch 270
Text (1968) together with sheet Nordöstl Weinviertel
A.Sch 320
4454 Litshau-Gmünd
1:75,000 (1950) A.Sch 270
4855 Schneeberg-St Ägid a N
1:75,000 (1931) A.Sch 270
Text A.Sch 50
4557 Nordöstl. Weinviertel
1:75,000 (1961) A.Sch 270
Text (1968) together with sheet Gänserndorf A.Sch 320
Text of the Geol. Karte d Umgebung v Wien (1954) map out of print
A.Sch 125
Umgebung von Korneuberg und Stockerau
1:50,000 (1957) A.Sch 180
Text (1962) A.Sch 65
17 Grosspertholz
1:50,000 (1977) In press
18 Weitra
1:50,000 (1977) In press
Hohe Wand-Gebiet
1:25,000 (1964) A.Sch 330
Text (1967) A.Sch 300
Schwechattal-Lindkogel-Gebiet W Baden (Niederösterreich)
1:10,000 (1970) A.Sch 250
Text A.Sch 120
OBERÖSTERREICH
Übersichtskarte des Kristallins in westl. Mühlviertel und im Sauwald
1:100,000 (1965) A.Sch 330
Text (1968) A.Sch 180

4750 Mattighofen
1:75,000 (1928) A.Sch 270
4749 Tittmoning
1:75,000 (1929) A.Sch 40
Trauntal
1:50,000 (1977) In press
Wolfgangsee-Gebiet
1:25,000 (1972). With text (1973) A.Sch 380
SALZBURG
5049 Kitzbühel-Zell am See
1:75,000 (1935) A.Sch 270
Umgebung von Gastein
1:50,000 (1956) A.Sch 360
Text (1957) A.Sch 145
Geol. panorama A.Sch 50
Salzburg
1:50,000 (1955) A.Sch 270
Umgebung der Stadt Salzburg
1:50,000 (1969) A.Sch 270
151 Krimml
1:50,000 (1977) In press
Adnet und Umgebung
1:10,000 (1960) A.Sch 200
STEIERMARK
Grazer Bergland
1:100,000 (1960) A.Sch 330
Text (1974) A.Sch 230
4953 Admont-Hieflau
1:75,000 (1933) A.Sch 270
5054 Leoben-Bruck a.d. Mur
1:75,000 (1932) A.Sch 270
5355 Marburg
1:75,000 (1931) A.Sch 70
Text A.Sch 50
4955 Mürzzushlag
1:75,000 (1936) A.Sch 270
5354 Unterdrauburg
1:75,000 (1929) A.Sch 270
Oberzeiring-Kalwang
1:50,000 (1967) A.Sch 360
Stadl-Murau
1:50,000 (1958) A.Sch 360
Text A.Sch 85
160 Neumarkt
1:50,000 (1977) In press
Weizer Bergland
1:25,000 (1958) A.Sch 270
TIROL
4947 Achenkirchen-Benedictbeuren
1:75,000 (1912) A.Sch 50
Text A.Sch 50
5746 Öztal
1:75,000 (1929) A.Sch 270
Text A.Sch 50
5246 Sölden - St Leonhard
1:75,000 (1932) A.Sch 200
Westliche Deferegger Alpen
1:26,000 (1972) A.Sch 330
VORARLBERG
5144 Stuben
1:75,000 (1937) A.Sch 270
Rötikon
1:25,000 (1965) A.Sch 420
Walgau
1:25,000 (1967) A.Sch 360
1 Oberes voralberger Rheintal
1:25,000 (1977) In press

G EARTH RESOURCES

KARTE DER LAGERSTÄTTEN
1:1,000,000
Wien : GB, 1964
Map of minerals and related strata.
A.Sch 140

ÜBERSICHTSKARTE MINERAL- UND HEILQUELLEN IN ÖSTERREICH
1:500,000
Wien : GB, 1966
Explanatory text, 101pp inc. index with map of mineral and healing springs.
A.Sch 150

H BIOGEOGRAPHY

DIVISIONS PHYTOGÉOGRAPHIQUES DE L'ENSEMBLE DE LA CHAÎNE ALPINE
VÉGÉTATION POTENTIELLE DES ALPES SUDOCCIDENTALES
1:400,000
2 maps from Vol. IV Doc. pour la Carte de la Végétation des Alpes. Univ. Scientifique et Médicale de Grenoble. 1966
See EUROPE 4 H.

KARTE DER AKTUELLEN VEGETATION VON TIROL
1:100,000
Ed Dr Schiechtl
Innsbruck : Geobotanischen Inst.
76 x 56
Coloured vegetation map series; legend in German and French.
Sheets published :
6 Innsbruck - Stubaier Alpen
7 Zillertaler und Tuxer Alpen

VEGETATIONSKARTE DES BERG UND HUELGELLANDES VON WEIZ (STEIERMARK)
1:50,000
Ed F Pratt
Contained in Vol. IX Doc. pour la Carte de la Végétation des Alpes.
Grenoble : Univ. Scientifique et Médicale de Grenoble. 1971
Coloured vegetation map of an area 20 km around Graz.

DIE PFLANZENDECKE DER KOMPERDELLALM IN TIROL
1:10,000
Ed H Wagner
Contained in Vol. III Doc. pour la Carte de la Vegetation des Alpes.
Grenoble : Univ. Scientifique et Médicale de Grenoble, 1965.
Detailed phytosociologic study of the vegetation of the Kompedell alpine pasture, Tyrol, with descriptive text in German and French summary.

L ECONOMIC

WIRTSCHAFTSKARTE VON OSTERREICH
1:500,000
Wien : Österreichisches Geselischafts- und Wirtschafts Museum, 1970
122 x 86
Economic map coloured according to land type indicating mines and mineral production also chemicals and other economic products. Production shown by size of symbol. Insets of 3 local town areas.
A.Sch 58

M HISTORICAL

ÖSTERREICH UND PREUSSEN BIS 1795
1:2,500,000
Bielefeld : Cornelsen, Velhagen and Klasing
196 x 137
Putzger historical wall map.

ÖSTERREICH PANORAMAKARTE
München : JRO
No 542
121 x 71
Col. pictorial map showing Austrian landscape depicted from a bird's eye view.

ATLASES
W3 WORLD ATLASES : LOCAL EDITIONS

ÖSTERREICHER SCHULATLAS F-B
see WORLD 100 ATLASES W3

ATLASES
A1 GENERAL : ROADS

ÖSTERREICH AUTOATLAS
1:200,000
Wien : F-B, 1970
15 x 27
111pp
Road atlas; maps showing main roads and motorways, hill shading, distance chart, through-town plans, index. 11 general maps at 1:600,000; covering Central Europe, 11 maps at 1:2,000,000

ÖSTERREICH; TASCHENATLAS
1:625,000
Munchen : Kompass
Pocket road atlas. DM 2.40

ATLASES
A2 GENERAL : LOCAL

WIENER WALD ATLAS
1:50,000
Wien : F-B, 1968
17 sheets
Tourist atlas of the Vienna Woods including col. maps with paths; tourist key word index; 25 selected car trips.
A.Sch 59

ATLASES
B TOWN PLANS

GROSSEN BUCHPLAN WIEN
Wien : F-B, 1972
14 x 21
70pp street atlas of Vienna, through traffic map and index.

ATLASES
D POLITICAL & ADMINISTRATIVE

PLANUNGSATLAS LAVANTTAL
In 2 vols
Klagenfurt : Amt der Karuther Landesregierung
Planning atlas of administrative development with 50 maps and illus.
Text vol.
complete DM 110

ATLASES
K HUMAN GEOGRAPHY

ÖSTERREICHISCHER VOLKS-KUNDEATLAS
Wien : H. Bohlaus, 1959-77
In 6 vols
33 x 65
929pp
Atlas of Austrian folklore, 143 maps, 32 picture charts and text.
Each vol. DM 90

TIROLISCHER SPRACHATLAS
Editors K K Klein and L E Schmitt
Part 3 of Deutscher Sprachatlas
Marburg : N G Elwert Verlag
Language atlas of the Tirol
Vol. I Vowels, 75 maps 1965 DM 100
II Consonance, vowel types, accidence 98 maps 1969 DM 135
III World Atlas, 110 maps 1971 DM 180

ATLASES
M HISTORICAL

KIRCHENHISTORISCHER ATLAS VON ÖSTERREICH
Ed Ernst Bernleithner
In 2 vols. Vol I, 1966; Vol II, 1972
Wien : Dom-Verlag
64 x 40
12 maps in each vol. illus various aspects of Catholic Church in Austria.
2nd Vol. 1972

HISTORISCHER ATLAS DER ÖSTERREICHISCHE ALPENLÄNDER
Wien : BEV
Arranged into 2 parts, the one containing detailed parish maps of the country and the other depicting Austrian diocese.
A.Sch 120

ATLAS DER HISTORISCHEN SCHUTZZONEN IN ÖSTERREICH
Vol I Städte und Märkte
1st edition
Wien : H Böhlau, 1970
34 x 32
Historical atlas of defence zones in Austria. The first volume deals with towns and trading centres. Second volume is in preparation. DM 156

ATLASES
O NATIONAL

ATLAS DER REPUBLIK ÖSTERREICH
Ed Hans Bobek
1:1,000,000
Wien : Österreichische Akademie der Wissenschaften 1961+
In 6 sections
73 x 47 each sheet
National atlas showing all major features of Austrian life - social, economic, geographical, physical, geological etc. App 85 maps, issued in parts. Parts I, II, III, IV, V available in binder. Each volume has transparent overlay showing admin. centres and boundaries.

LUFTBILDATLAS OSTERREICH
Ed Dr Leopold Scheidl and Lothar Beckel
Wien : F-B/Wachholtz, 1969
24 x 34
180pp
80 col. aerial photographs illus. natural, economic, cultural regions of Austria.
DM 45

ATLASES
P REGIONAL

LINZER ATLAS
Linz/Donau : Stadtmuseum, 1961+
Local atlas of thematic maps covering various aspects of the city and environs.
Part I
Die Boden des Linzer Raumes, 1961
Part II
Linz an der Donau im Kartenbild, 1963
Part III
Wanderwege um Linz, 1967
Part IV
Die Pflanzensoziologische Kartierung des Gemeindegebietes Linz/Donau, 1964
Part V
Abschnitte des phanologischen Jahresablauges im Gebiet von Linz/Donau, 1966
Part VI
Geologische Karte

SALZBURG - ATLAS
Salzburg : O Muller, 1955
66 col. map sheets of the town and environs. 138 single maps, 136pp text with diagrams and tables. DM 120

KÄRNTNER HEIMATLAS
Klagenfurt : Karntner Druckerie
Regional atlas of Carinthia province arranged in 3 parts. Looseleaf atlas with 48 map sheets. DM 37.50

ATLAS VON NIEDERÖSTERREICH (UND WIEN)
Ed Dr Erik Arnberger
Wien : F-B 1951-1959
Atlas containing 123 pages of col. maps covering political, physical, climatic, social, economic and cultural matters concerning Lower Austria. Map scale generally 1:500,000 with descriptive text.
Loose leaf edition 58 x 46 A.Sch 996
Half linen bound with screw binder
59 x 47 A.Sch 1,300
Half leather bound with screw binder
59 x 47 A.Sch 1,500
Half leather bound in half format
46 x 30 A.Sch 1,750

ATLAS VON OBERÖSTERREICH
1:500,000 and 1:1,000,000
Linz : Inst. für Landeskunde von Oberösterreich
80 map sheets, 66 already appeared (In 4 parts)
4 text vols. all pub.
Provincial atlas of Upper Austria containing 80 maps of physical social and economic maps arranged into 4 sections each with separate text volume.

ATLAS DER STEIERMARK
Ed Prof Dr Manfred Straka
Graz : Akademische Druck- und Verlagsanstalt, 1963-70
Various sizes
Atlas of Styria province published in 6 sections and arranged into 10 parts covering physical structure, climate and vegetation, soils, population, history, agriculture, economy and culture.
Text volume in preparation.

TIROL ATLAS
Ed E Troger
Inst. für Landeskunde der Universität
87 x 66 (map size)
To be published in approx. 12 parts to cover all aspects of the Tirol's history, geography and economy on maps scale 1:300,000 and 1:600,000. Sections 1 and 2 published with loose leaf screw binder.

NEUER SCHULATLAS FÜR SÜDTIROL
Produced by F-B
Bozen : Verlagsanstalt Athesia, 1971/2
22 x 31
88pp
For middle and high schools, 97 maps, 11 line drawings. Physical maps; 25pp for Sudtirol, Alps and Italy. No index.

437 Czechoslovakia

A1 GENERAL MAPS : ROADS

MAPA AUTOKEMPINKŮ ČSSR
1:1,000,000
Praha : Kart
General road map with camping sites marked.
Kcs 6

ČESKOSLOVENSKO
1:1,000,000
Bratislava : Slovenská Kartografia
General road map, with route numbers and distances. Legend Eng, Rus, Fr, Ger.

TSCHECHOSLOWAKEI-UNGARN
1:1,000,000
Bern : Hallwag, 1971
80 x 80
Coburg to Lublin, Padua to Resita.
All classes of roads, road numbers, distances in km, hill shading, spot heights in m, railways, ferries, important camping sites and state frontiers.

DDR - POLEN - CSSR
1:1,000,000
No 1176
Bern : K & F
129 x 92
Road map showing all classes of roads, distances, scenic routes, railways, places of interest. Covers: Malmö-Brest (USSR) - Budapest - Bremerhaven.

CSEHSZLOVÁKIA AUTOTÉRKÉPE
1:800,000
Budapest : KV, 1972
Roads classified with route numbers and distances. Inset maps of Praha, Bratislava. Legend in 6 langs.

TSECHEOSLOWAKEI
1:800,000
No 252
Köln : Polyglott
General touring map, roads classified, distances in km.

AUTOMAPA ČSSR
1:750,000
7th edition
Praha : Kart 1973
105 x 52
Roads classified and numbered, distances in km. Other communications, motoring details, camping sites. Pictorial guide on reverse. Also in French and German editions.
Kcs 7

ČESKOSLOVENSKO
1:600,000
No 879
Stuttgart : Ravenstein, 1976
97 x 66
Roads classified and numbered, distances in km. Other communications and places of tourist interest. Relief shaded, eastern section inset.
DM 7.80

TSCHECHOSLOWAKEI
1:600,000
Wien : F & B, 1971
111 x 72
All classes of roads, route numbers, distances in km, spot heights in m, railways, car ferries, camping sites, airports and state boundaries.

MAPA KULTURNÍCH PAMATEK CSSR
1:500,000
Praha : Kart
Map of cultural monuments and sites.
Kcs 17

A2 GENERAL MAPS : LOCAL

PŘÍRUČNÍ AUTOMAPY
1:200,000
Praha : Kart
Various sizes
Series of regional road maps showing all classes of roads and places of interest.
Maps available :
Praha
Brno
České Budejovice
Ostrava
Střední Povltavi (Central Vltava Basin)
Plzen
Jihlava
Krusné hory (Ore Mountains)
Luzické hory (Lusation Mountains)
Krkonose (Giant Mountains)
Sumava (Bohemian Forest)
Jeseniky (Ash Mountains)
Gottwaldov
Orlické hory (Eagle Mountains) Kcs 6
Střední Polabi (Central Elbe Basin)
Bratislava Kcs 7
Tatry Kcs 7
Each Kcs 4

TURSITICKÝCH MAP ČSSR
1:100,000 (unless stated otherwise)
Praha : Kart
Detailed tourist map series showing places of interest.
Maps available :
Bardejov - Dukla - Domasa Kcs 8
Bochynsko (Region of Bechyne) Kcs 7
Beskydy (The Beskides) Kcs 6
Bielé Karpaty
Bratislavský Jesný Park (Bratislava Forest Park) 1:20,000 Kcs 8
Brnenská přehradá a Velka cena ČSSR (Brno Dam and The Great Prize of the CSSR) Kcs 7
Českomoravská vrchovina - jih (The Bohemian-Moravian Uplands - South) Kcs 6
Českomoravská vrchovina - sever (The Bohemian-Moravian Uplands - North) Kcs 5.50
Českobudejovickó - jih (Region of České Budejovice - Southern Part) Kcs 6.50
Děčinsko (Region of Děčín) Kcs 5
Hradecko (Region of Hradec Kralové) Kcs 7
Jeseniky (The Ash Mountains) Kcs 6
Krkonose (The Giant Mountains) (1:50,000) Kcs 10
Kromerizsko (Region of Kromeriz) Kcs 6
Krusné hory (The Ore Mountains) Kcs 6
Lipenská přehrada (Lipno Dam) Kcs 4
Malá Fatra (The Small Fatra)
Malé Karpaty (Small Carpathians)
Nižké Tatry (Low Tatra) Kcs 12
Oderské vrchy (The Odra Highlands) Kcs 6
Okoli Brna (Brno Outskirts) Kcs 6
Okoli Prahy (Prague Outskirts) Kcs 7
Okoli Svratky (The Svratka Basin) Kcs 6
Orlická přehrada (Orlik Dam) Kcs 3.50
Orlické hory (The Eagle Mountains) Kcs 6
Orava - Orava - Oravaská Priehrada (Orava Dam) Kcs 8
Ostravsko (Region of Ostrava) Kcs 7
Pardubice - Litomysl - Chrudim Kcs 6
Pavlovské vrchy (The Pavlov Highlands) Kcs 6
Pieniny - Spisská Magura (Pienines) Kcs 8
Plzensko - jih (Region of Plzen - Southern Part) Kcs 6
Pizensko - sever (Region of Plzen - Northern Part) Kcs 6
Podkrkonosi a Jiráskův kraj (The Giant Mountains Slopes and Jirsek's Native Region) Kcs 7
Pojizeri (The Jizera Basin) Kcs 5
Slansko (Region of Slany) Kcs 6
Slapská přehrada (Slapy Dam) Kcs 3.50
Slovenský Kras (Slovak Kras Mts) Kcs 6
Strakonicko (Region of Strakonice) Kcs 7
Strázovské Vrchy (Strážov Mts) Kcs 6
Střední Povltavi (The Central Vltava Basin) Kcs 5
Sumava (Bohemian Forest) Kcs 7.50
Třebíčsko a Znojemsko (Region of Trebic and Znojmoj) Kcs 6
Velká Fatra (Great Fatra) Kcs 7
Vysoké Tatry (High Tatras) (1:50,000) Kcs 7
Zapadočeské lázně (West Bohemian Spas) Kcs 5
Zdarské vrchy (The Zdar Highlands) Kcs 5

TOURIST MAPS
Various scales
Bratislava : Slovenská Kart
Regional touring maps showing roads and paths.
Available for :
Orava - Oravská Priehrada, 1971
Vysoké Tatry (High Tatras) 1:50,000, 1972
Nitra, 1971

SKIING MAPS
1:100,000
Praha : Kart
Available for the following areas :
Beskydy Kcs 6
Jeseniky Kcs 6
Krkonose Kcs 5

VRATNA - MARTINSKÉ HOLE
1:50,000
Bratislava : Slovenska Kart, 1972
Folded skiing map, showing relief and topog. detail in colour.
Kcs 10

B TOWN PLANS

TOWN PLANS
Kart
Various sizes
Col. plans with street index.
Available for :

Brno, 1:15,000	Kcs 10
České Budejovice, 1:10,000	Kcs 4
Děčín	Kcs 6
Hradec Kralové	Kcs 6
Jihlava	Kcs 4
Marianské Lazne, 1:10,000	Kcs 6
Olomouc, 1:10,000	Kcs 4.50
Ostrava	Kcs 10
Podebrady, 1:10,000	Kcs 5
Plzen, 1:10,000	Kcs 3
Praha, 1:15,000	Kcs 8

TOWN PLANS
Bratislava : Slovenská Kartografia, 1971
Col. plans with street index.
Maps available :
Dunajská Streda
Komarno
Roznava

BRATISLAVA - ORIENTAČNÝ PLAN
1:10,000
Praha : Kart, 1972
117 x 81
Col. 1 sheet map, suitable for planning; shows streets and traffic network. Historical information: insets. Also available in ed. for motorists.
Kcs 7

KOŠICE - ORIENTAČNÝ PLAN
1:10,000
2nd rev. ed.
Praha : Kart, 1972
66 x 52
Street and traffic data; cultural and tourist info. Insets. Kcs 8

PRAHA ORIENTAČNÍ PLAN
1:15,000
Praha : Kart, 1971
80 x 63
Orientation street plan of Prague with information. In book form. Kcs 20

PRAHA - PLAN KULTURNÍCH PAMÁTEK
Praha : Kart
Plan of cultural monuments in Prague.
Kcs 5

PRAHA - PANORAMATICKY POHLED Z PETRINA
No scale
Praha : Kart
Panoramic view from the Petrin Hill.
Kcs 3.50

ORIENTAČNÝ PLAN TRENČÍNA A TRENČIANSKYCH TEPLIC
Bratislava : Slovenska Kart, 1972
42 x 44
Town plan with tourist information, directory of institutions and text.
Kcs 8

C OFFICIAL SURVEYS

INTERNATIONAL MAP OF THE WORLD
1:1,000,000
DMS
see WORLD 100C and index 100/1.

THE WORLD
1:500,000
DMS series 1404
see WORLD 100C and index 100/7.

ÜBERSICHTSKARTE VON MITTELEUROPA
1:750,000
In 54 sheets
BEV
see EUROPE 4 C.

GENERALKARTE VON MITTELEUROPA
1:200,000
BEV
33 sheets cover Czechoslovakia.
see EUROPE 4 C and index 436/1.

D POLITICAL & ADMINISTRATIVE

CHEKHOSLOVAKIYA - SPRAVOCHNAYA KARTA
1:1,000,000
Moskva : GUGK
Reference map showing towns and boundaries.

E1 PHYSICAL : RELIEF

POLAND, CZECHOSLOVAKIA, E GERMANY
1:1,000,000
Moskva : GUGK, 1973
2 sheet col. physical map. kop 26

OBECNE ZEMEPISNA MAPA
1:1,000,000
Praha : USGK, 1970
83 x 52
Contours, relief shading, communications. Physical map.

CZECHOSLOWACJA
1:1,000,000
Warszawa : PPWK, 1968
80 x 46
Contours, communications, text on reverse. Physical map in series "Przegladowa Mapa Europy" (Review Maps of Europe).

ČESKOSLOVENSKO
1:750,000
Praha : Kart
111 x 63
Physical reference map, with thematic text section. In series "Poznavame Svet" (Getting to know the World). Kcs 17.50

CSSR FYSICKÁ MAPA
1:500,000
Praha : Kart, 1969
175 x 105
Physical wall map; contours, hill shading, communications. Kcs 110

PLASTICKÁ MAPA SLOVENSKA SOCIALISTIČKA REPUBLIKA
1:750,000
Praha : Kart, 1972
66 x 44
Physical plastic relief map, col, showing geog. features, inc. water, road and rail communications, boundaries, size of pop. areas. Hypsometric col. Kcs 95

PLASTICKÁ MAPA ČSSR
1:500,000
Bratislava : Slovenská Kart, 1972
Plastic relief map, showing settlement, boundaries, railways. In Slovak.
Kcs 320

E2 PHYSICAL : LAND FEATURES

GEOMORPHOLOGICAL MAP OF THE PALOVSKÉ VRCHY HILLS AND THEIR SURROUNDINGS
1:50,000
Comp. Dr B Balatka and others
Praha : Kart, 1968.

F GEOLOGY

PŘEHLEDNÁ GEOLOGICKÁ MAPA CSSR
Comp. J Svoboda
1:1,000,000
Praha : UUG, 1964
80 x 43
Synoptic geol. map in col. Legend Eng, Fr, Ger, Rus.

GEOLOGICKÁ MAPA CSSR (ODKRYTA)
1:1,000,000
Praha : UUG, 1966
80 x 45
Col. geol. map with superficial deposits omitted.

MAPA KVARTERU A ZVĚTRAL-INOVÉHO PLASTE ČSSR
1:1,000,000
Compiled K Zebera
Praha : UUG, 1966
80 x 45
Map of Quaternary and Residual Deposits with inset maps of Quaternary rock cover 1:4,000,000 and Ostrava region 1:500,000

TEKTONICKÁ MAPA ČSSR
1:1,000,000
Praha : UUG, 1966
80 x 45
Col. tectonic map compiled according to specifications of Tectonic map of Europe.

HYDROGEOLOGICKÁ MAPA ČSSR
1:1,000,000
Compiled O Franko and others
Praha : UUG, 1966
80 x 45
Rocks classified by age, permeability and lithological composition with distribution of springs. Inset showing water capacity of rocks 1:2,000,000

GEOLOGICKÁ MAPA ČSSR
1:500,000
2 sheets
Praha : UUG, 1967
95 x 105 each sheet
Geol. wall map based on 1:200,000 Geol. series. Available in English ed.

GEOLOGICKÁ MAPA ČSSR
1:500,000
Praha : Kart
Geol. wall map. Kcs 105

REGIONAL ENGINEERING GEOLOGY OF CZECHOSLOVAK CARPATHIANS
1:500,000
Ed M Matula
Bratislava : Slovak Acad. of Sciences, 1969
Set of geol. maps with separate text volume.
216pp

GEOLOGICKA MAPA CSSR : MAPA PŘEDČTVRTOHORNÍCH ÚTVARŮ
(: PRE—QUATERNARY FORMATIONS)
Ed V Zoubek
In 33 sheets, see index 437/1
1:200,000
Praha : UUG, 1960-4
68 x 92 each sheet
Map of the Pre-Quaternary Formations. Comp. 1955-60. Each sheet has geol. sections, stratigraphical diagrams.

OSTRAU-KARWINER STEINKOHLEN-BECKEN, WESTBESKIDEN UND SUDE TISCHES RANDGEBIET
1:100,000
Wien : GB, 1932
Austrian geol. map. A.Sch 300

GEOLOGISCHE KARTE TSCHECHOSLOWAKEI
1:75,000
Wien : GB, 1898-1921
Old Austria geol. series.
Sheets available :
Austerlitz (1898)
Brünn (1912)
Brüsau - Gewitsch (1914)
Deutschbrod (1909)
Freudenthal (1898)
Gross-Meseritsch (1905)
Iglau (1912)
Josefstadt - Nachod (1921)
Landskron - Mährisch Trübau (1900)
Mährisch Neustadt - Mährisch Schönberg (1905)
Olmütz (1898)
Policka - Neustadtl (1914)
Prossnitz - Wischau (1898)
Trebitsch - Kromau (1905)
Each A.Sch 270

GEOLOGICKÁ MAPA KRKONOSSKÉHO NARODNIHO PARKU
1:50,000
Praha : UUG, 1968
85 x 68
Col. map of Krkonose National Reservation showing geomorphology and geology. Text on reverse.

GEOLOGISCHE KARTE DES MITTELBÖHMISCHEN SILURS UND DEVONS (CENTRAL BOHEMIAN SILURIAN AND DEVONIAN)
1:25,000
In 2 sheets
Praha : UUG, 1960
68 x 76 each sheet
Col. geol. map.

G EARTH RESOURCES

MAPA LOŽISEK NEROSTNÝCH SUROVIN ČSSR
1:1,000,000
Compiled A Dudek and others
Praha : UUG, 1966
80 x 45
Mineral deposits map in colour.

METALOGENETICKÁ MAPA ČSSR
1:1,000,000
Compiled by J Ilavsky and others
Praha : UUG, 1966
80 x 45
Showing stratigraphical, lithological, tectonic and geophysical basis of ore deposits. Inset of metallogenetic units 1:4,000,000

AEROMAGNETICKÁ MAPA ČSSR
1:1,000,000
Compiled by O Mah
Praha : UUG 1966
30 x 45
Based on map surveyed 1957-59 showing magnetic field deviations with inset of normal density diagram 1:4,000,000.

AEROMAGNETICKÁ MAPA ČSSR : MAPA PROFILŮ TOTALNÍ INTENZITY (TOTAL INTENSITY PROFILES)
MAPA IZANOMAL TOTALNÍ INTENZITY (TOTAL INTENSITY CONTOURS)
Comp. J Masin
1:200,000
In 33 sheets
Praha : UUG, 1965
64 x 58
Aeromagnetic map - in 2 editions on same sheet lines as 1:200,000 Geol. series.

H BIOGEOGRAPHY

MAPA VYUZITI PUDY ČSSR
1:500,000
In 2 sheets
Praha : USGK
174 x 90
Col. map showing land use.

GEOBOTANICKÁ MAPA ČSSR
1:200,000
In 22 sheets
Praha : Academia
Coloured Geobotanical map showing details of vegetation with insets on each sheet (1:1,000,000): hypsometric, climate and geology. Separate text volume describing survey by R Mikyska and others (1968). Kcs 300
Text book Kcs 30

MAPA PŘIRODNÍCH RESERVACÍ
1:1,000,000
Praha : Kart, 1966
Map of nature reserves, text on reverse.

L ECONOMIC

POL'SHA, CHEKHOSLOVAKIYA, GERMANSKAYA DEMOKRATICHES-KAYA RESPUBLIKA
1:1,000,000
GUGK
Economic map.
see POLAND 438L.

SLOVAKIA - LOCALISATION OF INDUSTRY
1:250,000
In 2 sheets
Pub. for the Chair of Economic Geog. Univ. Komensky
Bratislava : Slovenská Kart, 1970
46 x 37
Location of industry in Slovakia, 1967.

M HISTORICAL

SKOLNÍ NASTENNÉ HISTORICKÉ MAPY
Praha : Kart
Large col. historical school wall maps.
Maps available :
Praveké osidlení ČSSR (Primaeval inhabitation) Kcs 100
Český stát za Přemyslovců (under the Premysl Dynasty) Kcs 115
Husitske revoluční hnuti (Hussite Revolutionary Movement, 1430s) Kcs 70
Velká Morava (Greater Moravia) Kcs 145
Druha svetová valka (World War II) Kcs 169

25 let OSVOBOZENÍ ČESKOSLOVENSKA
Praha : Kart
Map showing 25 years of Czech liberation. Kcs 8

JUTTNERŮV PLAN PRAHY Z ROKU 1816
1:4,320
Praha : Kart
110 x 102
Map of Royal Prague in 1816 in 2 sheets. Based on trigonometric and topographic plan of Joseph Juttner, 1811-16. With 21pp text in Czech. Kcs 29.50

MAPA STARÉHO A ŽIDOVSKÉHO MĚSTA PRAŽSKÉHO
Praha : Kart
Map of Prague's Old Town and Jewish Town. Facsimile. Kcs 18

ATLASES
A1 GENERAL : ROADS

MAPA HRADŮ A ZAMKŮ ČSSR
1:750,000
Praha : Kart, 1970
13 x 22
88pp
Tourist atlas, 18pp maps, 40pp text, 38pp index. Maps of manors and castles; roads, relief shading, spot heights.

MAPA KULTURNÍCH PAMÁTEK ČSSR
1:500,000
Praha : USGK
Tourist atlas showing cultural sites; 44pp maps and illus. 135pp text in Czech. Legend Eng, Fr, Ger, Rus.

AUTOATLAS ČSSR
1:400,000
3rd edition
Praha : Kart, 1973
14 x 24
165pp
Shows road networks, distances in km, railways, border crossings, other motor information. Enlarged maps of certain areas. Explanation in 5 langs.
Kcs 29

ATLASES
B TOWN PLANS

PRAHA
1:15,000
Praha : Kartograficke nakladatelstvi
1970
150pp app
Street atlas, 86pp maps plus text and index to city.

ATLASES
D POLITICAL & ADMINISTRATIVE

MAPOVÝ LEXIKON OBCÍ ČSSR
1:200,000
Praha : Kart, 1968
22 x 30
Atlas of admin. districts - 100pp maps in col.

ATLASES
F GEOLOGY

GEOLOGICAL MAP ATLAS OF CZECHOSLOVAKIA
Ed O Kodym Jr
1:1,000,000
Praha : UUG, 1966
44 x 50
Contains 7 maps, with text.

1 Geologická Mapa ČSSR (odktyta) Geol. map with superficial deposits omitted. 80 x 45
2 Mapa Kvarteru a Zvětralinového Plaste ČSSR (Quaternary and Residual deposits) Insets. 80 x 45
3 Aeromagnetická mapa CSSR 45 x 30
4 Hydrogeologická Mapa CSSR, rocks classified; inset of water bearing capacity 80 x 45
5 Mapa Ložisek Nerosnych Surovin CSSR (mineral deposits) 80 x 45
6 Metalogenetická Mapa CSSR 80 x 45
7 Tektonická Mapa CSSR, 81 x 44 Prep. according to principles for Tectonic Map of Europe

ATLASES
K HUMAN GEOGRAPHY

ATLAS OBYVATELSTVA ČSSR
Praha : USGK, 1962
15 x 22
Population atlas containing 25 maps; statistical tables and diagrams, from 19th C onwards.

ATLAS DER SUDETENDEUTSCHEN UMGANSSPRACHE
Vol. 1
Editor F J Beranek
Marburg : N G Elwert Verlag 1970
222pp with 100 maps
Atlas of coloquial Sudentenland German.
DM 54

ATLASES
M HISTORICAL

ATLAS ČESKOSLOVENSKYCH DĚJIN
Praha : Kart
44 x 50
239pp
Czech historical atlas; maps, diagrams, kartograms. Social, cultural, economic history. Index. Text Eng, Ger, Rus.
Kcs 195

ŠKOLSKÝ ATLAS ČESKOSLOVENSKÝCH DĚJIN
9th edition
Bratislava : Slovenská Kartografia, 1973
21 x 31
75pp
School historical atlas, 44pp maps. Covers period to 1945. 15pp geographical and historical index, 15pp text.
Kcs 23.50

ATLASES
O NATIONAL

ATLAS ČESKOSLOVENSKÉ SOCIALISTICKÉ REPUBLIKY
Ed Antonín Götz
Praha : Cart, 1966
48 x 51
Comprehensive national atlas containing 433 double maps in colour - natural features, economy, cultural, social aspects. Summaries and map legends Eng and Rus. Text in Czech. With gazetteer.
Kcs 230

ATLAS ČESKOSLOVENSKEJ SOCIALISTICKEJ REPUBLIKY
Bratislava : Slovenska Kart, 1973
22 x 30
42 maps
Small atlas containing physical and thematic maps of the country. Index.

SUBOR MAPA POZNAVÁME SVĚT ČESKOSLOVENSKO
Praha : USGK
8 sheets in case. Political and physical at 1:750,000. 6 thematic at 1:2,250,000 With 67pp text. (Getting to know the world series).

ŠKOLNÍ ZEMPĚPISNÝ ATLAS ČSSR
Praha : Kart, 1972
8th edition
Czech school atlas. 35 maps, 6pp text, 15pp index. General and thematic maps.
Kcs 25

438 Poland

A1 GENERAL MAPS : ROADS

AUTOMAP POLSKO
1:1,500,000
Praha : Kart
Roads classified and numbered; distances in km, motoring and tourist information.
Kcs 10

MAPA SAMOCHODOWY POLSKI
1:1,000,000
Warszawa : PPWK, 1975
77 x 70
All classes of roads, distances in km, road numbers, railways and state boundaries. 23 through-way town plans and distance chart on reverse. New ed. annually.
Paper folded Zl 10

POLEN, AUTOKARTE
1:1,000,000
No 886
Frankfurt : Ravenstein, 1976
93 x 67
Principal roads numbered and classified, other roads and communications, tourist information, distances table. Insets of 4 large cities. Relief shading.
DM 7.80

LENGYELORSZAG AUTOTERKEPE
1:1,000,000
Budapest : KV, 1972
Road map with route numbers and distances. Insets of Sopot, Gdansk, Warszawa, Krakow. Legend in 6 languages.

DDR - POLEN - CSSR
1:1,000,000
No 1176
Bern : K & F
129 x 92
Road map showing all classes of roads, distances, scenic routes, railways, places of interest. Covers: Malmö - Brest (USSR) - Budapest - Bremerhaven

MAPA CAMPINGÓW
1:1,000,000
Warszawa : PPWK, 1971
72 x 66
Map of Polish camping sites, with other information for tourists. Zl 10

TOURIST MAP OF POLAND
1:750,000
Warszawa : PPWK, 1971
Road map in Rus, Hung, Czech.
20 town plans inset.

A2 GENERAL MAPS : LOCAL

MAPS OF ANTIQUITIES
1:400,000
Warszawa : PPWK
Various sizes
Col. tourist maps showing centres of history and remains; with roads.
Maps available:
Mapa zabytkow wojewodztwa bialostockiego (Map of relics in the Bialystok Vovoidship) 60 x 54
Mapa zabytkow wojewodztwa bydgoskiego (Bydgoszcz) 47 x 67
Mapa zabytkow wojewodztwa lodzkiego (Lodz) 47 x 67
Each Zl 10

MAPY TURYSTYCZNE
Various scales
Warszawa : PPWK
Series of tourist maps showing roads and footpaths, local boundaries, tourist routes and places of interest.
Maps available :

Map	Scale	Size	Price
Beskid Niski	1:125,000	67 x 47	Zl 10
Beskid Slaski i Zywiecki	1:125,000	51 x 43	Zl 10
Beskid Wyspowy	1:125,000	63 x 39	Zl 10
Bieszczady	1:125,000	55 x 47	Zl 10
Gory Izerskie	1:75,000	54 x 52	Zl 10
Gory Walbrzyskie	1:75,000	62 x 51	Zl 10
Karkonosze	1:75,000	70 x 62	Zl 10
Karpaty Mapa Obszaru Konwencji turystycznej	1:220,000	75 x 49	Zl 10
Okolice Krakowa	1:200,000	61 x 58	Zl 10
Okolice Wroclawia	1:175,000	57 x 40	Zl 10
Pieninski Park Narodowy	1:22,500	66 x 38	Zl 10
Pobrzeze Baltyku	1:400,000	95 x 57	Zl 15
Pobrzeze Gdanskie	1:220,000	61 x 41	Zl 10
Tatry	1:75,000	89 x 56	Zl 20
Tatry i Pieniny	1:75,000	83 x 70	Zl 10
Tatryanski Park Narodowy	1:30,000	98 x 62	Zl 15
Wielkie Jeziora Mazurskie	1:120,000	72 x 60	Zl 10

B TOWN PLANS

PLANY MIAST
Various scales
Warszawa : PPWK
Coloured plans with street index.
Plans available :

Plan	Year	Size	Price
Bydgoszcz		72 x 50	
Plan Gdanska	1972	64 x 48	Zl 10
Plan Gydni i Sopotu	1972	72 x 53	Zl 10
Plan Gliwic	1972	66 x 47	Zl 10
Plan Katowic	1972	77 x 57	Zl 10
Plan Kielce		70 x 63	
Plan Kozalina		70 x 63	
Plan Krakowa	1972	96 x 74	Zl 12.50
Plan Lublina	1973	60 x 55	Zl 10
Plan Lodzi	1972	84 x 79	Zl 12.50
Olsztyna		78 x 53	
Plan Opola		73 x 33	
Plan Poznania	1972	90 x 83	Zl 12.50
Plan Rzeszawa		69 x 49	
Plan Szlezecina	1972	67 x 59	Zl 10
Plan Warszawy	1972	83 x 81	Zl 12.50
Wroclawia	1972	96 x 66	
Plan Zakopanego	1972	72 x 51	Zl 10

C OFFICIAL SURVEYS

INTERNATIONAL MAP OF THE WORLD
1:1,000,000
see WORLD 100C and index 100/1.

THE WORLD
1:500,000
DMS Series 1404
11 sheets cover Poland
see WORLD 100C and index 100/7.

UBERSICHTSKARTE VON MITTELEUROPA
1:300,000
Frankfurt : Inst. fur Angewandte Geodasie
see GERMANY 430 C and index 430/1.

GENERALKARTE VON MITTEL-EUROPA
1:200,000
BEV
39 sheets cover Poland (incomplete)
see EUROPE 4 C and index 436/1.

D POLITICAL & ADMINISTRATIVE

POL'SHA
1:2,500,000
Moskva : GUGK, 1973
Col. study map showing water features, settlements, admin.districts and centres, communications, boundaries, economic details, pop. Geog. description.

MAPA ADMINISTRACYJNA
1:2,000,000
Warszawa : PPWK, 1975
49 x 38
Col. by provinces showing new boundaries.
Zl 1

MAPA FIZYCZNA I ADMINISTRACYJNA
1:2,000,000 and 1:1,000,000
PPWK
see POLAND 438 E1

HARMS HANDKARTEN - SCHLESIEN
1:1,000,000
012
Munchen : Paul List Verlag
Small hand map of Silesia, political col. principal boundaries and towns.
DM 0.50

POLSKA RZECZPOSPOLITA LUDOWA
1:500,000
In 4 sheets
Warszawa : PPWK, 1972
94 x 86 each
Polish Peoples Republic col. school wall map, with inset of communications. Shows political and administrative boundaries, with economic and historical details.
ZI 150

POLSKA - MAPA ADMINISTRACYJNA
1:500,000
In 4 sheets
Warszawa : PPWK, 1972
170 x 150 complete
Political coloured wall map showing voivodships, 8 town plans inset. With 170pp index.

MAPA WOJEWÓDZTWA POLSKA
1:500,000
In 17 sheets
Warszawa : PPWK, 1972
Various sizes
Each covers a voivodship or province. Main and secondary roads, railways, layer col, contours, spot heights in metres, pop. by symbols, provincial and state bouncaries. Statistical and other information on reverse. Text in Polish.
Each ZI 10

LÄNDER- UND PROVINZKARTEN
1:300,000
Frankfurt : Inst. fur Angewandte Geodasie
Regional maps showing communications, towns and villages available for the following former provinces:

Brandenburg	DM 8
Oberschlesien	DM 5
Ostpreussen	DM 8
Pommern	DM 8
Schlesien	DM 8

E1 PHYSICAL : RELIEF

MAPA FIZYCZNA
1:2,000,000
Warszawa : PPWK, 1972
49 x 38
Layer col, with contours. ZI 1

MAPA FIZYCZNA I ADMINISTRACYJNA
1:2,000,000
Warszawa : PPWK, 1965
49 x 38
Double sided sheet: layer coloured physical map on one; col. admin. map on other.
ZI 5

POLSKA, MAPA FIZYCZNA I ADMINISTRACYJNA
1:1,000,000
Warszawa : PPWK, 1970
87 x 74
Double sided map, layer col one side; provincial map on reverse. ZI 20

POLAND, CZECHOSLOVAKIA, E GERMANY
1:1,000,000
Moskva : GUGK, 1973
2 sheet col. physical map ZI 0.26

MAPA FIZYCZNA POLSKA
1:700,000
Warszawa : PPWK, 1970
142 x 110
Physical col. wall map in 2 sheets.
ZI 120

POLSKA, MAPA FIZYCZNA
1:500,000
In 4 sheets
Warszawa : PPWK, 1972
168 x 183
Physical school wall map, showing elementary morphology, contours, communications, water features.
ZI 170

MAPA FIZYCZNE
1:250,000
Warszawa : PPWK
Physical series of wall maps, with contours, water and communications, mineral resources, industrial centres.
Maps available:

Wielko-Polska			
	2 sheets	166 x 119	1966
Masowiecka-Podlasie			
Mazury i Warmia			
	2 sheets		
Pomorze			
	2 sheets	180 x 120	1962
Szlask			
	2 sheets	164 x 110	
Malo-Polska			
	2 sheets	180 x 110	1964
Karpaty Polski			
	2 sheets	164 x 98	1964

MAPA FIZYCZNA, PLASTYCZNA
1:1,250,000
Warszawa : PPWK
86 x 75
Moulded plastic raised relief map, layer coloured with communications and towns graded by population.

E2 PHYSICAL : LAND FEATURES

POLSKA : MAPA GEOMORFOLOGICZNA
1:500,000
In 4 sheets
Warszawa : PPWK, 1972
183 x 168
Geomorphological wall map for schools, in colour. ZI 170

F GEOLOGY

POLSKA MAPA GEOLOGICZNA
1:1,000,000
Warszawa : Inst. Geol. 1966
71 x 65
Geol map without Cenozoic deposits; inc. Lower Palaeocene. Legend and description in Eng, Rus, Pol
ZI 114.80

POLSKA GEOLOGIA - STRATYGRAFIA
1:700,000
by E Ruhle, St Soktowski, M Tyska
In 2 sheets
Warszawa : PPWK, 1973
120 x 115
Col geol. wall map.

MAPA KRUSZYWA NATURALNEGO W POLSCE 438 mF
1:500,000
J Pawlowska and Z Siliwonczuk
In 4 sheets
Warszawa : Inst. Geol, 1971
158 x 145 complete
Coloured map of loose natural rock material, with 137pp text. In Polish.
ZI 281

UPPER SILESIAN REGION - UPPER CARBONIFEROUS DEPOSITS
1:300,000
Warszawa : Inst. Geol, 1964
Series of 14 maps, showing thickness of strata, beds and seams.
ZI 541.10

GEOLOGICAL MAP OF THE LOWER SILESIAN REGION
1:200,000
Warszawa : Inst. Geol, 1967
117 x 85
Without quaternary formations.
Legend in Eng. ZI 70

GEOLOGISCHE KARTE POLEN
1:75,000
Wien : GB
2 geol. sheets from an early Austrian survey.
Sheets :
Alt Lublau - Szczawnica, 1921
Neumarkt - Zakopane, 1912
Each A.Sch 270

GEOLOGICAL MAP OF THE PIENINY KLIPPEN BELT
1:10,000
by K Birkenmajer
Warszawa : Inst. Geol.
Col. geol. map.
Sheets available :

5	Czorsztyn, 1963	ZI 304.60
16	Niedzica, 1960	ZI 427

GEOLOGICAL MAP OF THE TATRA MOUNTAINS
1:10,000
In 15 sheets
Warszawa : Inst. Geol, 1958+
Col. geol. map.

G EARTH RESOURCES

POLSKA MAPA MINERALO-GICZNA
1:1,000,000
Warszawa : Inst. Geol, 1969
70 x 67
Mineral map on geol, base. Legend Pol, Rus, Eng. ZI 237.30

MAP OF MINERAL DEPOSITS OF POLAND
R Osika
1:500,000
In 4 sheets
Warszawa : Inst. Geol, 1971
190 x 160 complete
Coloured mineral map in English, with mineral regions inset. ZI 444

H BIOGEOGRAPHY

POLSKA MAPA UŻYTKOWANIA ZIEMI
by F Uhorczak
1:1,000,000
Warszawa : Instytut Geografii Polskiej
1957
31 x 31
Land use map comprising 9 maps in folder, covering water, meadows and pasture, forests, arable land, settlement and combinations of these. 36pp text in Polish. (Eng summary)

PARKI I REZERWATY PRZYNODY POLSKIE (NATURE PARKS AND RESERVES)
1:1,000,000
Warszawa : PPWK
Col. map showing also woods, traffic, spot heights. 12 insets. Text in Eng, Pol on reverse.

L ECONOMIC

POLSKA ; MAPA GOSPODARCZA (ECONOMIC MAP)
1:1,250,000
Warszawa : PPWK
60 x 56
Economic wall map for schools.
ZI 3

POL'SHA, CHEKHOSLOVAKIYA, GERMANSKAYA DEMOCRATICHES-KAYA RESPUBLIKA
1:1,000,000
Moskva : GUGK, 1971
Economic wall map for schools.

POLSKA, MAPA
1:700,000
Warszawa : PPWK, 1968
125 x 118
Col. economic wall map, showing land use, industry, agriculture etc.

POLSKA : MAPA GOSPODARCZA
1:500,000
Warszawa : PPWK, 1972
183 x 168
Economic wall map for schools, indicating industries by coloured symbols. Description in Polish. ZI 170

WOJEWÓDZTWO WARSZAWSKIE, MAPA GOSPODARCZA
1:200,000
Warszawa : PPWK
180 x 140
Economic wall map of the Warsaw area.

M HISTORICAL

DIE TEILUNG POLENS 1772-1795 - POLEN IM 20 JAHRHUNDERT
1:1,200,000
Bielefeld : Cornelsen, Velhagen & Klasing
138 x 218
Putzger historical wall map of the partition of Poland and Poland in the 20th C.
DM 145

POLSKA W OKRESIE ROZBIOROW
by Z Rzepa
1:1,000,000
Warszawa : PPWK, 1972
166 x 120
Historical wall map showing Poland at time of its fragmentation. ZI 140

WALKI ZBROJNE Z NAJEŹDŹCĄ HITLEROWSKIM NA ZIEMIACH POLSKI : W LATACH WOJNY
1939-45
1:600,000
Warszawa : PPWK, 1972
150 x 120
The battles and invasion of Hitler's forces on Polish lands during the war period. Historical wall map for schools.
ZI 120
Also at 1:1,500,000 hand map, 60 x 51
ZI 3

WALKA Z NAJEŹDŹCĄ I ZBRODNIE HITLEROWSKIE W WOJEWODZTWIE GDANSKIM W LATACH 1939-45
1:150,000
Warszawa : PPWK, 1968
135 x 99
Armed struggles against the Nazi Invasion and Nazi Crimes in the Gdansk region. School historical wall map. ZI 120

ZBRODNIE HITLEROWSKIE NA ZIEMIACH POLSKI W LATACH 1939-45
1:1,500,000
Warszawa : PPWK
58 x 48
Hitler's invasion of Poland. ZI 3

HISTORISCHE WANDKARTEN
1:750,000
Darmstadt : Perthes
Series of col. historical wall maps.
Maps available :
920 Brandenburg - Preussen - Territoriale Entwicklung bis 1807
921 Preussen - Territoriale Entwicklung 1815-1945
140 x 202 DM 128

ATLASES
W3 WORLD ATLASES : LOCAL EDITION

ATLAS GEOGRAFICZNY DLA KLASY IV
Warszawa : PPWK, 1972
20 x 26
Polish school atlas for the 4th Class, with maps and coloured illus. ZI 9

ATLASES
A1 GENERAL : ROADS

ATLAS SAMOCHODOWY POLSKI
1:500,000
Warszawa : PPWK, 1973
13 x 23
201pp
Maps showing all classes roads, distances in km, motoring and tourist information, double page maps. ZI 62

ATLASES
B TOWN PLANS

STREET ATLAS OF WARSZAWA
Warszawa : PPWK, 1971
37pp maps for the town. 1 general map.

ATLASES
F GEOLOGY

GEOLOGICAL ATLAS OF POLAND
1:2,000,000
Warszawa : Inst. Geol, 1959-65
In 13 parts, approx 630 maps.
Each part has short text, list of refs, etc.

Part 1	Methods and Materials, M Pajchlowa, 1965	ZI 313.50
Part 2	Precambrian, Eocambrian and Cambrian, O Juskowiak et al 1963	ZI 404.40
Part 3	Ordovician, H Tomczyk, 1959	ZI 199
Part 4	Silurian, H Tomczyk, 1960	ZI 320
Part 5	Devonian, M Pajchlowa, 1959	ZI 314.40
Part 6	Carboniferous, K Bojkowski, 1960	ZI 250.60
Part 7	Permian, J Milewicz and K Pawlowska, 1961	ZI 257.20
Part 8	Triassic, H Senkowiczowa and A Szyperco-Sliwczynska, 1961	ZI 366
Part 9	Jurassic, R Dadlez et al, 1964	ZI 747.10
Part 10	Cretaceous, W Pozaryski, 1962	ZI 337.30
Part 11	Tertiary, B Aren, 1964	ZI 293
Part 12	Quaternary, J E Mojski and E Ruhle, 1965	ZI 523.95
Part 13	Cretaceous and Early Tertiary in the Polish External Carpathians, S Gucik et al, 1962	ZI 727.90

GEOLOGICAL ATLAS OF POLAND
1:2,000,000
Ed J Znosko
Warszawa : Inst. Geol, 1968
36 x 34 (map size)
Contains 10 tables, showing geol. cross sections, and rock types.
In wallet ZI 495

ATLAS GEOLOGIQUE DE POLOGNE
1:2,000,000
Warszawa : Inst. Geol, 1956
5 maps covering geol, quaternary deposits, gravimetry. Special ed. for the 20th Internat. Geol. Congress in Mexico, 1956.
ZI 100

GEOLOGICAL ATLAS OF THE POLISH CARPATHIAN FORELAND
1:500,000
P Karnkowski and S Oltuszyk
Warszawa : Inst. Geol, 1968
31 x 21
17 maps showing the surface and thickness of various rock types. 23pp text.
ZI 681

GEOLOGICAL ATLAS OF THE LOWER SILESIAN COAL BASIN PART II
K Augustyniak
1:100,000
Warszawa : Inst. Geol, 1970
30 x 21
14 maps covering carboniferous divisions, lithologic structure, coarse-clastic materials. 15pp text.
ZI 1373

ATLASES
G EARTH RESOURCES

ATLAS MINERALLOGNICZNY POLSKI
1:2,000,000
Ed R Osika
Warszawa : Inst. Geol, 1970
59 x 42 (map size)
7 maps; anthracogenic, bitumogenic, metallogenic, halogenic, petrogenic, hydrochemical, mineralogenic regionalisation. Maps in plastic wallet with 16pp text in Polish
ZI 266.50

ATLASES
H BIOGEOGRAPHY

ATLAS ROZMIESZCZENIA DRZEW I KRZEWAV POLSCE (ATLAS OF DISTRIBUTION OF PLANTS AND SHRUBS)
Warszawa : Panstwowe Wydawnictwo Naukowe
29 maps. Text Pol, Rus, Eng.

ATLASES
K HUMAN GEOGRAPHY

POLSKI ATLAS ETNOGRAFICZNY
To be published in 4 volumes - 3 currently published :
Part I 1964, Part II 1965, Part III 1968
Editor : Josef Gajek, Polish Academy of Sciences
Warszawa : PPWK
33 x 50
I Maps 1-57; II Maps 58-129;
III Maps 130-190
Gridded maps generally 1:2m or 1:1.4m on double folding sheets showing distributions of cultural matters incl. building implements, farming methods etc, and their names. In British text with list of contents in English. Separate sheets contained in card wallets.

MALY ATLAS GWAR POLSKICH (CONCISE ATLAS OF POLISH VERNACULARS)
Wroclaw : Ossolineum
In 13 volumes
23 x 49
Contains maps, text, showing various linguistic phenomena.

ATLAS JEZYKOWY KASUBS ZCZYNY I DIALEKTOW SASIEDNICH
Ed Zdzislaw Stiebar - director
Wroclaw : Ossolineum
A linguistic atlas of the Cashubian region and neighbouring dialects.

ATLAS GWAROWY WOJ. KIELECKIEGO KAROL DEJINA, ZESZYT 6
Wroclaw : Ossolineum, 1968
6, 42pp
Dialectal Atlas of the Kielce Voivodship, part 6, containing maps no 681-800.
ZI 40

ATLAS GWAR MAZOWIECKICH
Komitet Jezykoznawstwa
Wroclaw : Ossolineum, 1971
Vol. 1 of the Atlas of the Mazovian Dialects, 50 maps and text.
ZI 85

ATLAS JEZYKOWY SLASKA
Alfred Zaręba
Krakow : Śląski Inst. Naukowy w Katowiach, 1969+
In 7 vols.
Linguistic atlas of Silesia in publication. In 1500 maps app. with explanatory text.

ATLASES
M HISTORICAL

MALY ATLAS HISTORYCZNY
By Cz Nanke, L Piotrowicz and Wl Semkowicz
Warszawa : PPWK, 1972
20 x 30
School atlas of Polish history, with thematic maps.
ZI 12

ATLASES
O NATIONAL

POLISH NATIONAL ATLAS
Wroclaw : Ossolineum, 1973+
In 4 parts
Atlas in course of publication. To include 600 coloured maps in 125 plates, covering geog. environment, population, agriculture and forestry, mining and industry, communications and trade. Living and cultural conditions etc. With index and booklet in English and Russian.
(subscription price)
ZI 750

ATLAS STATYSTYCZNY
Warszawa : Główny Urząd Statystyczny, 1970
28 x 28
213pp
197pp col. maps, graphs, tables, showing economic, social, commercial life, 16pp table of contents in Pol, Eng, Rus.

POLSKA : ATLAS GEOGRAFICZNY
Warszawa : PPWK, 1971
21 x 32
38pp
120 maps of economy, physical geog. etc. Illus.
ZI 25

ATLASES
P REGIONAL

ATLAS WOJEWÓDZTWA KATOWICKIEGO
Ed J Szaflarski et al
Katowice : Slaski Inst. Naukowy & PPWK, 1971
Atlas of the Katowice Voivodship.

ATLAS WOJEWODZTWA KIELECKIEGO
Warszawa : Wydawnictwa Geologiczne
1070
24 x 33
46pp
40pp col. maps of Kielce Voivodship.

439 Hungary

A1 GENERAL MAPS : ROADS

MAĎARSKO (HUNGARY) AUTOMAPA
1:1,500,000
Praha : Kart
Roads classified and numbered, distances in km, motoring and tourist details.
kcs 8

TSCHECHOSLAWAKEI-UNGARN
1:1,000,000
Hallwag
see CZECHOSLOVAKIA 437 A1

ROAD MAP OF HUNGARY
1:650,000
Budapest : Cart, 1971
Roads classified with route numbers and distances. Budapest and Balaton inset.

UNGARN
1:600,000
Wien : FB, 1971
98 x 64
All classes of roads, distances in km, route numbering, hill shading, spot heights in metres, railways, camping sites, airports and state frontiers.

MAGYARORSZÁG ÚTTÉRKÉPE
1:525,000
Budapest : Cart
98 x 67
Main and secondary roads, distances in km, spot heights in metres, road numbering, forest areas and state boundaries. Includes 15 through-way town plans on the reverse.

UNGARN
1:525,000
No 880
Stuttgart : Ravenstein, 1974
98 x 67
Detailed road map showing all classes of roads, route numbers, distances. Filling stations, hotels, camping sites and places of interest indicated by symbols. 10 insets of principal towns.
Paper folded DM 7.80

A2 GENERAL MAPS : LOCAL

TURISTATÉRKÉPEK
Various scales
Budapest : Cart
Series of col. tourist maps, contoured and showing roads, footpaths and places of interest.
Maps available:
Balaton
1:95,000 33 x 98
Cserhát
1:100,000 50 x 70
Aggrelek és Jósvafö környéke
1:70,000 50 x 70
Soproni-hegység
1:25,000 59 x 42
Budai-hegység
1:30,000 59 x 84
Gerecse
1:60,000 38 x 56
Bakony hegység
1:25,000 59 x 84
Börzsöny hegység
1:25,000 59 x 84
Bükk hegység
1:25,000 59 x 84
Mátra hegység
1:25,000 50 x 70
Mecsek hegység
1:25,000 59 x 84
Pilis hegység
1:25,000 50 x 70
Velencei-tó es környéke
1:25,000 50 x 70
Vértes-hegység
1:25,000 59 x 84
Zempléni-hegység
1:25,000 59 x 84

MADÁRTÁVLATI TÉRKÉPEK
Budapest : Cart
35 x 50
Col. pictorial birds-eye-view maps.
Maps available:
Visegrad
Tihanyi-Felsziget (Tihany peninsula)
Badacsony és Környéke
Margitsziget (Margaret Is-Budapest)
A Budai Vár (Buda Castle Hill)

B TOWN PLANS

VÁROSTÉRKÉPEK
Various scales
Budapest : Cart
Town plans with index to streets.
Maps available:

Ajka	25 x 35
Baja	25 x 35
Békéscsaba	50 x 35
Cegléd	50 x 35
Debrecen	50 x 35
Dunaújváros	25 x 35
Eger	50 x 35
Esztergom	50 x 35
Gyöngyös	50 x 35
Györ	50 x 35
Hajduszoboszlö	50 x 35
Hatvan	25 x 35
Hódmezövásárhely	50 x 35
Kalocsa	25 x 35
Kaposvár	50 x 35
Karcag	25 x 35
Kazincbarcika	25 x 35
Kecskemét	50 x 35
Keszthely	25 x 35
Kiskunfélegyháza	25 x 35
Komárom	25 x 35
Komló	25 x 35
Miskolc	50 x 35
Mohács	25 x 35
Mosonmagyaróvár	25 x 35
Nagykanizsa	25 x 35
Nyíreghyháza	50 x 35
Orosháza	50 x 35
Oroszlány	25 x 35
Ózd	25 x 35
Pápa	25 x 35
Salgótarján	25 x 35
Sopron	50 x 35
Szeged	50 x 35
Székesfehérvár	50 x 35
Szekszárd	25 x 35
Szentendre	25 x 35
Szentes	25 x 35
Szolnok	50 x 35
Szombathely	50 x 35
Tata	25 x 35
Tatabánya	25 x 35
Vác	50 x 35
Varpalota	25 x 35
Veszprém	50 x 35
Zalaegerszeg	25 x 35

BUDAPEST
Budapest : Cart
119 x 84
Official Town plan with index and tourist information. Text in Hungarian.

BUDAPEST BELSŐ TERÜLETE
Budapest : Cart, 1965
70 x 50
Folded street map of central Budapest.

BUDAPEST
In 6 sheets
Budapest : Cart
250 x 230
Col. street wall map with pictorial symbols.

BUDAPEST TÁVLATI TÉRKÉPE
Budapest : Cart and Publishing House of the Arts Foundation
119 x 84
2 col. map perspective view map of Budapest

C OFFICIAL SURVEYS

INTERNATIONAL MAP OF THE WORLD
1:1,000,000
DMS 1301
see WORLD 100C and index 100/1.

THE WORLD
1:500,000
DMS Series 1404
see WORLD 100C and index 100/7.

ÜBERSICHTSKARTE VON MITTELEUROPA
1:300,000
Inst. für Angewandte Geodäsie
see GERMANY 430C and index 430/1.

GENERALKARTE VON MITTELEUROPA
1:200,000
BEV
22 sheets to cover Hungary.
see EUROPE 4C and index 436/1.

D POLITICAL & ECONOMIC

VENGRIYA
1:750,000
Moskva : GUGK
Col. study map showing water features, settlements, admin. divisions and centres. communications, boundaries, economic details, pop, Geog. descriptions.
30 kop

A MAGYAR NÉPKÖZTÁRSASGÁG ÁLLAMIGAZGATÁSI TÉRKÉPE (ADMINISTRATIVE)
1:500,000
Budapest : Cart, 1969
84 x 119
General map col. by admin. districts. Index on reverse.

MAGYARORSZÁG MUNKATÉRKÉPE
1:500,000
Budapest : Cart
119 x 84
Outline planning map with towns and regional boundaries in blue.

MEGYEI MUNKATÉRKÉPEK – BORSOD-ABAÚJ-ZEMPLÉN, VAS
1:250,000
Budapest : Cart
119 x 84
Planning and record outline of the counties of Borsod-Abaúj-Zemplén and Vas showing regional and county boundaries in blue with names.

MEGYEI KÉZITÉRKÉPEK
1:250,000
Budapest : Cart
various sizes
Series of county hand maps, showing various types of local boundaries, and communications. In col.
Maps available:
Fejér
Pest
Szabolcs-Szatmár
Szolnok

MAP OF THE DIOCESE OF VÂC
1:250,000
Budapest : Cart
64 x 98
Monochrome map showing parishes and deaconries with boundaries and major roads, as at 1969.

MAGYARORSZÁG MEGYEI
Budapest : Cart
84 x 119
Series of Hungarian county maps.
Maps available:

Baranya	1:132,000
Bács-Kiskun	1:135,000
Békés	1:135,000
Borsod-Abaúj-Zemplén	1:135,000
Csongrád	1:132,000
Fejér	1:100,000
Győr-Sopron	1:135,000
Hajdú-Bihar	1:138,000
Heves	1:136,000
Komárom	1:111,000
Nógrád	1:105,000
Pest	1:135,000
Somogy	1:156,000
Szabolcs-Szatmár	1:135,000
Szolnok	1:145,000
Tolna	1:110,000
Vas	1:100,000
Veszprém	1:137,000
Zala	1:100,000

BUDAPEST MUNKATÉRKÉPE
Budapest : Cart
119 x 84
Outline planning map of Budapest with street outlines in blue with street names in light grey.

E1 PHYSICAL : RELIEF

WĘGRY
1:1,000,000
Warszawa : PPWK, 1972
50 x 45
Physical map, contours, communications, text in Pol. In series "Przegladowa Mapa Europy" (Reivew Maps of Europe).
ZI 121

MAGYARORSZÁG DOMBORZATA ÉS VIZEI
1:350,000
Budapest : Cart, 1970
149 x 100
Col. physical wall map in 2 sheets; contours, hill shading, layer col; showing rivers and also principal mineral deposits.

E2 PHYSICAL : LAND FEATURES

GEOMORPHOLOGICAL MAP OF HUNGARY
by Márton Pécsi
1:1,000,000
Budapest : Akadémiai Kiadó
Detailed col. map, legend in Eng. 45pp text with diagrams, profiles.

F GEOLOGY

GEOLOGICAL MAP OF THE PALEOZOIC AND MESOZOIC BASEMENT OF HUNGARY
1:500,000
Budapest : Hung. Geol. Inst, 1967
112 x 73
Col. general geol. map of the area, showing subsurface formations. Legend Eng and Russian.

MAGYARORSZÁG FÖLDTANI TÉRKÉPE
1:300,000
In 4 sheets
Budapest : Hung. Geol. Inst, 1956
200 x 140 complete
Geol. wall map, with explanatory booklet in Eng, Fr., Ger., Rus.

BUDAPEST
1:200,000
Budapest : Hung; Geol. Inst, 1968
90 x 68
Geol. map series covering Budapest, available in 5 editions:
Földtani változat (Subsurface)
Gazdas ág földtani változat (Economic geol)
Talajvízszint (Ground water level)
Talajvízkemia (Ground water hydrochemical)
Építésföldtani változat (Engineering Geol).

GEOLOGICAL MAP OF HUNGARY – SHEET VESZPRÉM
1:200,000
Budapest : Hung. Geol. Inst.
Economic geol. map, with explanation in Eng.

ALFÖLD TALAJVÍZTÉRKÉPE
1:200,000
In 4 sheets
by András Rónai
Budapest : Hung. Geol. Inst, 1961
170 x 165 complete
Ground water map of the Great Hungarian Plain showing average depths of ground water. Legend and text in Hung, booklet in Eng.

BÜKKHEGYSÉG FÖLDTANI TÉRKÉPE
1:100,000
Budapest : Hung. Geol. Inst. 1963
84 x 119
Col. surface geol. map of the Bukk Mts. Text in Ger.

BÜKKHEGYSÉG KÖRNYÉKI HELVETI KÉPZODMÉNYEK MÉLYFÖLDTANI TÉRKÉPE
1:100,000
Budapest : Hung. Geol. Inst. 1966
84 x 119
Col. subsurface map of the Helvetian formations in the Bukk Mts. In Hung; text and profiles on reverse.

GEOLOGICAL SERIES
Various scales
Budapest : Hung. Geol. Inst.
Col. geol map series showing geol. and mineral info. In preparation.
Maps available:
Bakony-Hegység (Mountains) 10 sheets
1:25,000 98 x 68 each
Dorogi-Medence (Basin) 17 sheets
1:10,000
Matra-Hegység 29 sheets
1:10,000
Mecsek-Hegység 30 sheets
1:10,000
Tokaji-Hegység 22 sheets
1:25,000

A BALATON KÖRNYTÉKÉNEK ÉPÍTÉSFÖLDTANI TÉRKÉPES-OROZATA (ENGINEERING GEOL' MAP SERIES OF THE ENVIRONS OF LAKE BALATON)
1:10,000
Budapest : Hung. Geol. Inst.
Part I. Tihany 1969, 85 x 59, 9 maps with text and legend sheets in Eng.

G EARTH RESOURCES

LOCATION OF MINERAL RAW MATERIALS
1:500,000
Budapest : Hung. Geol. Inst, 1967
105 x 76
General mineral map showing exploitation possibilities.

H BIOGEOGRAPHY

KERECSEND ÉS MAKLÁR FÖLD-HASZNOSITASI TÉRKÉPE
Ed Dr Gyorgy Enyedi
1:25,000
No 1792
Budapest : Geog. Research Inst.
Hungarian Academy Sciences, 1969
47 x 68
Land use map of Kerecsend and Maklár, in English and Hungarian.

L ECONOMIC

MAGYARORSZÁG GAZDASÁGI TERKEPE (ECONOMIC MAP)
1:550,000
Budapest : Cart
100 x 70
Showing major industrial areas etc.

MAGYARORSZÁG FONTOSABB LÉTESÍTMÉNYEI 1945–1965
1:500,000
Budapest : Cart, 1965
108 x 70
Important establishments in Hungary 1945-1965
Outline map of Hungary, with col. pictorial symbols depicting industrial establishments, mines, oilwells etc. cultural and scientific institutes, sports centres, hospitals etc. In Hungarian.

A MAGYAR NÉPKÖZTÁRSASÁG MEGYEI, IPARA ES KÖZLEKEDESE
1:350,000
Budapest : Cart
119 x 168
Counties, Industry and Communications of the Hungarian Peoples Republic
Politically col. wall map in 2 sheets, showing counties, towns graded by pop, waterways, roads, railways and principal industries.

M HISTORICAL

TÖRTÉNELMI FALITÉRKÉPEK
In 2 sheets each
Budapest : Cart
119 x 168
Col. historical wall maps
Maps available:
Magyarország a korai feudalizmus idejen (devt. of Feudal System) 1:700,000
a XIII sz. középétol
a XV sz. középétol (13th-15th C) 1:750,000
a XV században (15thC) 1:750,000
1526-1606 1:650,000
a XVII században (17thC) 1:750,000
a XVIII században (18thC) 1:650,000
Az Ostrak-Magyar Monarchia 1914-ben (Austro-Hungarian dual monarchy 1914) 1:1,000,000

TABULA IMPERII ROMANI
1:1,000,000
Sheet NL 34 – Budapest
see WORLD 100M and index 100/8.

RECONQUEST OF THE FORTRESS BUDA
Budapest : Cart
5 facsimile extracts showing the reconquest of the fortress from the Turks:
1 Hallarth, View from the North 1684 67 x 45
2 Hallarth, View from the East 1684 67 x 55
3 Hooge, 1686 64 x 54
4 Rossi, sketch of the Assault on September 2, 1686 47 x 39
5 Rossi; Birds' eye view from the East 61 x 28

ATLASES
W3 WORLD ATLAS : LOCAL EDITION

FÖLDRAJZI ATLASZ A KÖZÉP IS-KOLAK SZAMARA
10th rev. ed.
Budapest : Cart, 1971
60pp
Secondary school atlas

FÖLDRAJZI ATLASZ AZ ÁLTALÁNOS ISKOLÁK SZÁMÁRA
16th ed.
Budapest : Cart, 1972
32pp
Primary school atlas

ATLASES
A1 GENERAL : ROADS

MAGYARORSZÁG AUTOATLASZA
1:360,000
Budapest : Cart, 1973
15 x 21
137pp
Detailed road maps and town plans. Index distance table. Legend Eng. Fr, Ger., Hung, Rus.

ATLASES
B TOWN PLANS

GUIDE AND ATLAS OF BUDAPEST
Budapest : Cart, 1971
14 x 27
127pp
38pp col. maps of the city with text and index. Sightseeing and accommodation details, traffic, motoring, etc.

ATLASES
F GEOLOGY

ALFOLD FOLDTANI ATLASZA
1:100,000
In 34 sheets
Budapest : Hung. Geol. Inst.
(Geol. Atlas of the Great Hungarian Plain)
Sheet 1 Szolnok by Dr András Rónai 1969
Many col. geol. maps with 15pp text in English. Includes 21 variant maps of the area.

MAGYAROSZÁG VÍZFÖLDTANI ATLASZA
Budapest : Geol. Inst. Hungary, 1962
57 x 42
Hydrogeol. atlas containing 73 col. maps; 45 at scale 1:1.000,000, 28 at 1:100,000/200,000. With text in Eng, Fr, Rus or Ger.

ATLASES
J CLIMATE

MAGYARORSZÁG ÉGHAJLATI ATLASZA
Ed Dr József Kakas
Budapest : Akadémiai Kiadó, 1967
Climatic atlas of Hungary.
Vol. 1, 1960, 20pp text, 130 col. maps on 78 plates 34 x 51 – out of print
Vol. 2, 1967, 263pp tables. 1 map in supplement 21 x 29

ATLASES
K HUMAN GEOGRAPHY

MAGYAR NYELVJÁRÁSOK ATLASZA
In 6 vols.
Ed Lóránd Benko, László Deme
Budapest : Akadémiai Kiadó
49 x 34
Atlas of Hungarian Dialects, legend in Hungarian and French. Loose Leaf maps with explanatory text contained in portfolio.
Volumes published:
Vol 1, 1968, 10pp text, 193 maps
Vol 2, 1970, 10pp text, 195 maps

ATLASES
M HISTORICAL

TÖRTÉNELMI ATLASZ
Budapest : Cart, 1971
23 x 29
33pp
33pp maps covering world history with reference to Hungary and central Europe from earliest times to 1966.

CARTOGRAFIA HUNGARICA I
In 10 maps
Ed Klars Nemes
Budapest : Cart, 1972
Various sizes
10 fascimile maps of Hungary from 1528-1696 in portfolio (34 x 50).
With 14pp text in Hungarian, Ger, Eng.
Maps include :
1 Tabula Hungarie by Lazarus (1528) 54 x 78
2 Hungariae Totius by M Zinthius (1567) 48 x 30
3 Hungaria Descripta by W Lazius (1570) 50 x 35
4 Ungariae Loca Praecipua by Sambucus (1579) 50 x 34
5 Hungaria by G Mercator (1585) 45 x 37
6 The Mappe of Hungri by J Speede (1626) 44 x 35
7 Hungaria Regnum by W & J Blaeu (1647) 50 x 41
8 Neue Land Tafel von Hungarn by J Sandrart (1664) 53 x 35
9 Le Royaume de Hongrie (1689) by N Sanson 87 x 58
10 Le Royaume de Hongrie (1696) by H Iallot 55 x 45
Part II - to be published 1973.

ATLASES
O NATIONAL

MAGYARORSZÁG NEMZETI ATLASZA
Budapest : Cart, 1967
29 x 41
112pp
A comprehensive National Atlas containing about 280 maps on 100 map plates, with introductions to each section and legends in English.
The work covers :
Physical :
geomagnetism, structure, geology, minerals, geomorphology, climate, drainage, vegetation, soils, landscape.
Population :
density, language, changes, settlement.

Agriculture :
land, reform, cultivation, irrigation, crops, wine, fruit, forests, livestock.
Industry :
mining, production, food, labour.
Transport and Communications.
Trade, Tourism, Foreign trade, and International relations.
Cultural and Social patterns.
Administration.
Administrative map of Hungary as a supplement 1:500, 000 with list of districts and legend in Eng. and gazetteer of places on reverse.
Bound in hard covers.

ATLASES
P REGIONAL

A DEL-ALFOLD ATLASZA
Part 1
Budapest : Cart, 1968
35 x 50
124 sheets
Regional Atlas of SW Hungary. Part 1 of a series "Regional Atlases of Hungary", 234 maps scale 1:500, 000/1:1, 000, 000 covering physical, economic and social nature with diagrams and text.

44 France

A1 GENERAL MAPS: ROADS

PETITE CARTE DES GRANDES ROUTES ET DES DEPARTEMENTS
1:2, 500, 000
No 150
Paris : Michelin, 1976
40 x 40
Main roads, distances in km, hill shading, distance chart. Paris inset.

TRAVELLER'S MAP OF FRANCE
1:1, 875, 000
Washington : NGS, 1971
58 x 83
Shows historic land marks, 8 city plans inset, index, descriptive notes.
Paper US $2.00
Plastic US $3.00

FRANKREICH
1:1, 700, 000
Koln : Polyglott
Classifies roads with distances. Inc. Corsica.
DM 3.20

SHELL REISEKARTE FRANKREICH
1:1, 500, 000
Stuttgart : Mair
Col road map; roads classified and numbered, distances in km, places of tourist interest, accommodation, motoring information. Inset at 1:750, 000. Legend in 12 langs.
DM 4.80

CARTE FRANCE-GUIDAGE AVEC TOUS LES CHEFS-LIEUX DE CANTON
1:1, 100, 000
Paris: Éditions Ponchet
120 x 90
Map showing road, rail and air communications, administrative districts and index of major towns. Legend in 5 languages.
F.Fr 9.00

FRANKREICH
1:1, 000, 000
Bern : Hallwag
95 x 101
All classes of roads, distances in km, spot heights in metres, hill shading, car ferries, railways, airports and the main car camping sites. Corsica inset.

FRANKREICH
1:1, 000, 000
No 1132
Bern : K & F
100 x 98
All classes of roads, distances in km, hill shading, car ferries, scenic routes, railways and camping sites. Paris, Marseilles, Lyons and Corsica inset.

FRANCE : GRANDES ROUTES
1:1, 000, 000
No 989
Paris : Michelin, 1976
107 x 96
All classes of roads, route numbers and conditions, distances in km, car ferries and airports. Corsica and environs of Paris inset. Legend in Fr.
Also in 2 sheet style : 998 North and 999 South
107 x 48 each sheet
and reversible style :
Sheet 916 - printed north on one side, south on reverse
107 x 48 each sheet

WORLD TRAVEL MAP OF FRANCE AND THE LOW COUNTRIES
1:1, 000, 000
In 2 sheets
Edinburgh : Bart
94 x 47 each sheet
All classes of roads, road numbers, distances in km, railways and contour col.
North - the Low Countries and Northern France south to Tours with inset of Paris
South - Southern France north to Tours including Western Alps and Corsica
Paper flat or folded 40p each

FRANCIAORSZÁG AUTOTÉRKÉPE
1:1, 000, 000
Budapest : Cart, 1971
Road map with route numbers and distances. Paris and Cote d'Azur inset. Legend in 6 langs.

FRANKREICH
1:1, 000, 000
No 890
Stuttgart : Ravenstein, 1975
101 x 49
Double sided road map; roads classified and numbered; distances in km; other communications, items of tourist interest.
DM 8.80

FRANKREICH
1:1, 000, 000
No 1858
Munchen : JRO
88 x 99
Green base with roads in red, water and route numbers in blue, with distances and other tourist info. DM 6.80

FRANCE
1:1, 000, 000
London : Foldex
Shows roads classified, relief shading; patent folding. Includes Corsica.
55p

FRANCIA
1:1, 000, 000
Novara : Ag
Tourist road map. L 700

FRANKREICH
1:800, 000
No 89
Stuttgart : RV
67 x 119
All classes of roads, numbers, distances in km, hill shading, spot heights in metres, railways, youth hostels, camping sites, scenic routes. 11 town plans inset, handbook of tourist information for motorist, text in German. (Printed both sides ie East and West)
DM 6.80

FRANKREICH
1:800, 000
No 386
Hamburg : Falk
Classifies and numbers roads, with distances. Index. DM 7.80

FRANKREICH (MIT BELGIEN)
1:750, 000
No 1776
Munchen : JRO
123 x 88
Classifies roads with distances and other motoring details. 2 sided map. Relief shading, airports. DM 9.80
Also available in 2 separate sheets
1777 Nordfrankreich - Belgien
1778 Sudfrankreich - Schweiz - Nordwestitalien
Each DM 6.80

FRANZÖSISCHE STRASSENKARTE
1:550, 000
In 4 sheets
Frankfurt : Ravenstein
Detailed road map of France in 4 sheets, roads classified with distances.
605 North-West 120 x 98
606 North-East 106 x 98
607 South-West 120 x 98
608 South-East 100 x 98
each DM 6.80

FRANKREICH - BENELUX
1:500, 000
In 4 sheets
Bern : K & F
All classes of roads, road numbers, distances in km, car ferries, railways, airports, scenic routes, places of interest, state and regional frontiers.
Sheets :
1181 Bretagne - Normandie 126 x 89
1182 Benelux - Champagne 87 x 127
1183 Massif Central - Pyrénées 127 x 89
1184 Riviera - Bourgogne 88 x 105

CARTA STRADALE D'EUROPA
1:500, 000
In 4 sheets
Milano : TCI
75 x 111 each sheet
All classes of roads, road conditions, distances in km, spot heights in metres, contour layer col, railways and car ferries.

F

Sheets :
4 North West France
6 Eastern France and Switzerland 1971
7 South East France and North West Italy, 1972
8 South West France, 1969
Each 95p
see also EUROPE 4 A1.

FRANZÖSISCHE STRASSENKARTE
1:250, 000
In 16 sheets, see index 44/1
Frankfurt : Ravenstein
Various sizes
Col. road map series, available in the following sheets :

251	Nordfrankreich	133 x 98
252	Normandie	133 x 98
253	Bretagne	133 x 98
254	Region Paris	133 x 98
255	Elsass-Lothringen	133 x 98
256	Loire Tal	133 x 98
557	Mittelfrankreich	133 x 98
258	Jura-Burgund	133 x 98
259	Charante-Périgord	120 x 98
260	Auvergne	133 x 98
261	Rhône-Alpen	120 x 98
262	Südwestfrankreich	133 x 98
263	Languedoc-Rousillon	133 x 98
264	Provence-Côte d'Azur	120 x 98
265	Korsika	67 x 98
270	L'Ile de la France 1:150, 000	126 x 94
Each		DM 6.80

FRANCE
1:250, 000
In 11 sheets
London : Foldex
Large scale road map; roads classified, relief shading. Patent folding.
Each 55p

CARTE DE FRANCE
1:200, 000
In 37 sheets, see index 44/2
Paris : Michelin, 1971/2
108 x 47 each sheet
All classes of roads and road conditions, distances in km, spot heights, places of interest and airports. Legend in French with easily understood symbols.
Also special sheets:
87 Alsace
91 Environs de Lyons
92 Jura-Savoie
93 Vallée du Rhone
1:100, 000
195 Environs de Nice, 110 x 99

A2 GENERAL MAPS: LOCAL

ALPINA III
1:600, 000
Bern : Hallwag
112 x 84
Road map covering the Riviera, Provence, Savoy and Piedmont incl. the region from Moulins to Davos and Perpignan to Leghorn. All classes of roads, distances in km, road conditions, railways, hill shading, spot heights, car ferries, airports and important car camping sites.

SHELL GENERALKARTE - FRENCH RIVIERA
1:200, 000
Stuttgart : Mair, 1971/2
102 x 50
Detailed road map showing all classes of roads with distances. Autoroute services, tolls and gradients. Air, sea and rail ferries, railways, nature reserves, places and buildings of interest, youth hostels, airports etc. Avignon-Marseilles-Castellane-Italian border.

VOSGES
1:200, 000
No 54
Stuttgart : RV
70 x 95
All classes of roads, numbered, distances in km, hill shading, spot heights in metres, tourist details. Inc. Western Black Forest; extends from Saarbrucken to Basel.

CARTE TOURISTIQUE, CERDAGNE-CAPCIR
1:50, 000
Paris : IGN, 1971
110 x 89
Col. tourist map of the region east of Andorra. Contoured with tourist information. F.Fr 15.00

CARTES DE CAMPS ET CHAMPS DE TIR
1:50, 000
Paris : IGN
Maps of camps and firing ranges. In black, enlargement of 1:80, 000 series with hachuring. 1922 type in colours with relief and UTM grid.
Causse
La Courtine
Meucon
Camps de Champagne
Type 1922 4.80 fr
Mailly Type 1922
St Cyr-Coetquidan
Type 1922
Camp de Canjvers
Type 1922
Coëtquidan 1960 F.Fr 5.83
Champagne 1966 F.Fr 5.83
Canjeurs 1972 F.Fr 5.83

CARTES DE CAMPS ET CHAMPS DE TIR
1:25, 000
Paris : IGN
Maps of Camps and Firing ranges.
Topographic maps in 1 or more sheets. Col. or in black and white.
Relief and contours shown.
Maps published:
Courtine, La (1 sheet) in cols.
Larzac, Le (1 sheet) in cols.
Larzac 1966 F.Fr 5.83
La Courtine 1967 F.Fr 5.83

CARTES DE SAVOIE ET DAUPHINE
1:25, 000 - 1:50, 000
See index 44/3
Grenoble : Didier-Richard
Series of large scale topog. maps based on French official surveys, contoured, relief shaded with roads and footpaths marked in colour.
Maps published:
1 Massif du Vercors
1:50, 000 70 x 100
2 Massifs de Belledonne et Taillefer
1:25, 000 70 x 100
3 Massifs de Chartreuse et Sept Laux
1:50, 000 100 x 65
4 Massifs du Haut Dauphiné
1:50, 000 100 x 120
5 Massifs du Queyras et Hte Ubaye
1:50, 000 100 x 120
6 Massif des Bornes Bauges
1:50, 000 123 x 100
7 Marzine les Gets
1:25, 000 123 x 100
8 Massif et Parc National Vanoise
1:50, 000 125 x 100
9 Les Trois Vallées (Allues, Courcheval, Belleville) 1:25, 000
10 Massifs du Mont Blanc et Beaufortin
1:50, 000 123 x 100
11 Massif des Aravis
1:25, 000 70 x 100
12 Massif du Chablais et Faucigny
1:50, 000
13 Massif du Gapençais
1:50, 000 100 x 123
14 Alpes de Provence - in preparation
15 Mercantour, Vallee des Merveilles - in preparation

MASSIF DU MONT BLANC
1:25, 000
In 2 sheets
Edition 2
Paris : IGN, 1975
118 x 86 each
Contoured, relief shaded with roads classified, railways, tracks, vegetation also tourist information - accommodation, marked paths and refuges. Index to features and places inset. F.Fr 25.00

CARTE DE LA RÉGION DU MONT BLANC
1:10, 000
In 24 sheets, 9 only available, see index 44/4
Paris : IGN
Various sizes
Contoured relief map series, showing in 10 colours land surface features, vegetation and ice with relief shading.
Large sheet F.Fr 16.67
Small sheet F.Fr 12.50

PANORAMA DE LA CHAINE DU MONT BLANC
No scale
Lyon : Francis Bererd
Panoramic map of the Mont Blanc mountain range. With guide. F.Fr 2.50

CARTES DES ILES
Various scales
Paris : IGN
Various sizes
Maps of the French offshore islands. Show major buildings, bathymetry, places of interest, roads and paths, etc. Sheets available :

Golfe du Morbinan		
1:50, 000	1975	89 x 88
Ile de Noirmoutier		
1:50, 000	1975	67 x 77
Ile-d'Yeu		
1:20, 000	1975	44 x 110
Ile de Re		
1:40, 000	1971	44 x 77
Ile d'Oleron		
1:50, 000	1975	67 x 77
Ile de Porquerolles		
1:15, 000	1969	44 x 84

MICHELIN 150km AUTOUR DE PARIS
1:200, 000
Sheet 97
Paris : Michelin, 1976
118 x 50
All classes of roads, distances in km, spot heights in metres, railways, airports and places of interest.
Printed on both sides of sheet, ie North and South Paris.

CARTE DE L'ÎLE DE FRANCE ROUTIERE ET TOURISTIQUE
1:180, 000
Paris : Éditions Ponchet
120 x 90
Road map of Paris and its environs with index of 2, 800 names of Communes and places of interest. F.Fr. 9.00

120 KILOMETRES AROUND PARIS
1:150, 000
London : Foldex
Large scale road map with relief shading; patent folding. 55p

CARTE DES ENVIRONS DE PARIS
1:100, 000
Edition 4
Paris : IGN 1976
122 x 100
Tourist map covering the surrounding area of Paris : Chartres, Fontainbleu, Pontoise. Contoured, relief shading, with roads, footpaths and tourist information.
F.Fr 4.17

MICHELIN ENVIRONS DE PARIS
1:100, 000
Sheet 96
Paris : Michelin, 1976
109 x 96
Detailed map from Les Andelys to Senlis and Chartres to Fontainebleu; Forest of Compiegne inset. Showing all classes of roads with distances in km, spot heights, railways and places of interest. Legend in French.

PARIS : BANLIEUE
1:70, 000
Paris : Leconte
54 x 74
Map of the Paris suburbs, showing one-way streets.

SORTIE DE PARIS
1:50, 000
Sheet 100
Paris : Michelin, 1976
75 x 48
All classes of roads, distances in km, spot heights in metres, places of interest, scenic routes, railways and an index. North to South, Enghien les Bains to Fresne, West to East, St Germain en Laye and Versailles to Chelles.

CARTE BANLIEUE-GUIDAGE
1:50, 000
Paris : Éditions Ponchet
120 x 90
Road map of the Paris Region, showing auto-routes, all principal roads, administrative boundaries and places of interest.
Legend in 5 languages.
F.Fr 9.00

TOWN PLANS
Various scales
Paris : Blay (unless otherwise stated)
Various sizes

Agen	
1:10, 000	75 x 53
Aix-en-Provence	
1:7, 500	53 x 63
Aix-les-Bains	
1:7, 000	53 x 43
Albi	
1:7, 000	63 x 49
Alençon	
1:9, 000	53 x 43
Alès	
1:6, 750	72 x 54
Amiens	
1:10, 000	73 x 53
Angers	
1:11, 000	73 x 53
Angoulême	
1:7, 500	63 x 49
Annecy	
1:7, 200	53 x 43
Arcachon	
1:12, 500	53 x 43
Arles	
1:6, 000	53 x 43
Arras	
1:9, 000	73 x 53
Auxerre	
1:8, 000	73 x 53
Avignon	
1:6, 300	63 x 53
La Baule	
1:11, 000	37 x 75
Bayonne-Biarritz-Anglet	
1:13, 000	73 x 53
Beauvais	
1:8, 500	53 x 43
Belfort	
1:10, 000	58 x 84
Besançon	
1:10, 000	73 x 54
Béziers	
1:6, 750	61 x 51
Blois	
1:10, 000	63 x 53
Bordeaux	
17, 000	108 x 72
Boulogne - Billancourt	
1:10, 000	42 x 34
Boulogne sur Mer	
1:9, 000	63 x 49
Bourg en Bresse	
1:7, 500	43 x 53
Bourges	
1:10, 000	53 x 43
Brest	
1:15, 000	63 x 48
Brive	
1:9, 300	74 x 53
Caen	
1:10, 000	73 x 53
Cahors	
1:6, 000	43 x 53
Calais	
1:9, 500	73 x 53
Cambrai	
1:10, 000	54 x 43
Cannes	
1:11, 250	63 x 48
Guide Pol - Cannes et Environs	
1:15, 000	F.Fr 6.50
Carcassone	
1:7, 100	53 x 43
Castres	
1:7, 500	53 x 43
Chalon sur Saone	
1:8, 500	63 x 48
Chalon sur Marne	
1:8, 500	53 x 63
Chambéry	
1:10, 000	53 x 73
Charleville Mézières	
1:8, 000	73 x 53
Chartres	
1:9, 000	73 x 53
Chateauroux	
1:9, 000	53 x 43
Chatellerault	
1:11, 000	72 x 53
Cherbourg	
1:10, 000	63 x 48
Cholet	
1:8, 300	53 x 43
Clermont Ferrand	
1:7, 900	73 x 53
Cognac	
1:7, 000	53 x 43
Colmar	
1:8, 000	63 x 48
Compiègne	
1:10, 000	53 x 43
Dax	
1:7, 500	43 x 53
Dieppe	
1:6, 000	53 x 43
Dijon	
1:10, 000	54 x 53
Douai	
1:10, 000	43 x 53
Dreux	
1:8, 500	53 x 43
Dunkerque	
1:12, 500	92 x 63
Épernay	
1:7, 500	53 x 43
Évreux	
1:10, 000	53 x 43
Fontainebleu	
1:7, 000	53 x 43
Grenoble	
1:12, 500	64 x 93
Le Havre	
1:14, 000	53 x 73
Leval	
1:8, 000	63 x 53
Lens Liévin	
1:12, 000	73 x 53
Lille	
1:12, 000	93 x 63
Limoges	
1:10, 000	63 x 53
Lorient	
1:8, 500	63 x 53
Lourdes	
1:7, 000	53 x 43
Lyon	
1:17, 715	82 x 57
Lyon et Banlieue Guide Pol	
1:16, 000	F.Fr 10.00
as wall map	F.Fr 30.00

Mâcon
1:10, 000 73 x 53
Le Mans
1:10, 000 73 x 53
Marseille
1:15, 600 74 x 54
Marseille Guide Pol
1:14, 000 F.Fr 10.00
without text F.Fr 4.00
Menton
1:12, 000 63 x 48
Metz
1:12, 700 76 x 73
Monaco - Monte Carlo
1:8, 000 42 x 27
Montauban
1:10, 000 53 x 73
Montluçon
1:9, 000 63 x 48
Montpellier
1:8, 500 71 x 63
Moulins
1:8, 000 63 x 48
Mulhouse
1:11, 000 63 x 53
Nancy
1:12, 000 53 x 63
Nantes
1:13, 000 82 x 57
Narbonne
1:6, 000 53 x 43
Nevers
1:8, 000 63 x 48
Nice
1:15, 000 73 x 53
Nice Guide Pol
1:12, 000 F.Fr 4.10
Nîmes
1:12, 500 82 x 57
Niort
1:7, 000 73 x 53
Orléans
1:10, 000 53 x 63
Paris (Foldex)
1:33, 000
Paris (Hallwag)
1:23, 000
Paris (Leconte)
1:17, 500
Paris (Ravenstein) No 311
1:14, 000 95 x 40 DM 8.80
Paris
1:14, 000 92 x 72
Paris (Falk)
1:12,000/28,000 DM 4.80
Paris (Falk)
1:12, 000/28, 000 DM 2.50
Plans par Arondissement Leconte
1:12, 000 series
Paris (Miniplan) 20p
Paris (Miniplan De Luxe ed)
25p
Paris par arondissement (ed Ponchet)
Region Parisienne (ed Ponchet)
Banlieue-Guidage (ed Ponchet)
1:50, 000
Reseaux Paris (ed Ponchet) (Metro and bus maps)
Reseau Banlieue (ed Ponchet) (bus and Metro maps)
Paris Auto (ed Ponchet)
1:11, 200 (blue parking zone, one-way streets)
Paris Éclair (Leconte)
1:10, 000 (by arondissements)
Guide Banlieue (Leconte)
1:2, 000
Pau
1:10, 000 73 x 53
Périgeux
1:10, 000 52 x 30
Perpignan
1:8, 000 71 x 78
Poitiers
1:9, 000 53 x 63
Le Puy
1:5, 000 54 x 74
Quimper
1:10, 000 53 x 44
Reims
1:12, 500 58 x 84
Rennes
1:13, 000 73 x 53
Roanne
1:12, 000 63 x 48
Rochefort
1:8, 000 53 x 43
La Rochelle
1:10, 000 82 x 53
Roubaix - Tourcoing
1:12, 000 53 x 73
Rouen
1:11, 000 81 x 57
Saint Brieuc
1:9, 000 73 x 54
Saintes
1:7, 000 53 x 43
St Étienne
1:16, 000 82 x 56
St Germain en Laye
1:6, 500 53 x 43
St Jean de Luz
1:7, 100 53 x 43
St Malo
1:11, 000 73 x 53
St Nazaire
1:12, 500 59 x 64
St Quentin
1:7, 500 63 x 48
Saumur
1:10, 000 63 x 53
Sens
1:7, 500 46 x 53
Sète
1:7, 150 63 x 48
Strasbourg
1:11, 500 83 x 58
Tarbes
1:7, 500 53 x 63
Toulon
1:10, 000 73 x 53
Toulouse
1:13, 000 93 x 63
Tours
1:8, 500 54 x 62
Troyes
1:10, 000 53 x 63
Valence
1:7, 700 74 x 55
Valenciennes
1:10, 000 53 x 73
Vannes
1:10, 000 63 x 48
Versailles
1:14, 000 62 x 42
Vichy
1:7, 000 54 x 74
Vierzon
1:10, 000 53 x 43

PARIS
1:40, 000
Braunschweig : Westermann
110 x 140
Col. wall map of the Paris region, showing relief and main roads, with enlarged Paris Central plan inset at 1:10, 000.

PARIS ET SA BANLIEUE
Hatier
On reverse of France Physique, Economique, Touristique
see FRANCE 44 E1

PARIS - AUTO S 75
1:11, 000
Paris : Éditions Ponchet
120 x 90
Street map of Paris showing one-way streets, green and blue zones, and parking facilities.
F.Fr 9.00

PARIS - SÉRIE BANLIEUE-ORIENTATION
1:15, 000
In 14 sheets, see index 44/5
Paris : Éditions Ponchet
120 x 90
Collection of street plans of the Paris Region, col. with street index.
each F.Fr 9.00

CARTE DE LA RÉGION PARISIENNE
1:5, 000
See index 44/7
Paris : IGN
95 x 65
Large scale plan of Paris in 2 col. ed. series in progress with admin. boundaries, lettering and water detail in black, and contours in brown. Inc. street names and indicates public and admin. buildings.
Each sheet F.Fr 20.83

C OFFICIAL SURVEYS

INTERNATIONAL MAP OF THE WORLD
1:1, 000, 000
see WORLD 100C and index 100/1.

THE WORLD
1:500, 000
DMS Series 1404
19 sheets cover France
see WORLD 100C and index 100/7.

CARTE DE FRANCE
1:500, 000
Series 1404
In 10 sheets, see index 44/7
Paris : IGN
Series of topographical maps based on DMS Series 1404. Contoured, layer coloured and showing communications and settlement. In progress.

CARTE DE FRANCE
1:250, 000
In 45 sheets, see index 44/6
Paris : IGN
60 x 44 each
Topog. map series in 2 eds.
Standard ed: roads, distances in km, settlements, contours, vegetation in green, departmental boundaries. Also military and aviation ed. with UTM grid and aeronautical overprint.
Each F.Fr 8.33

CARTES TOURISTIQUES (SÉRIE ROUGE)
1:250, 000
In 17 sheets, see index 44/9
Paris : IGN
Various sizes
"Carte de l'environment culturel et touristique" series covering the whole of France excluding Corsica showing all classes of road, route nos and distances. Towns graded by pop. with various landmarks, relief shading and tourist details of all kinds shown by symbols.
Each F.Fr 5.83

CARTE DE FRANCE
1:100, 000
Paris : IGN
In 293 sheets, see index 44/10
55 x 40
Multi-sheet topog. series. Contoured, roads numbered, railways, boundaries, vegetation cover. Available in standard ed, military ed with UTM grid overprinted in violet with legend in English or oro-hydrographic eds. with contours in brown and water in blue only.
Each F.Fr 8.33

CARTE POUR LE TOURISME (SÉRIE VERTE)
1:100, 000
In 74 sheets, see index 44/11
89 x 121 (89 x 132)
New enlarged sheet series completed for the whole of France, in same style as standard 1:100, 000 series. Tourist series contoured and showing road and motoring information.
Each F.Fr 6.67

CARTE DE FRANCE
1:50, 000
see index 44/12
Paris : IGN
55 x 40 each
Multi sheet topog. series in progress. Contours, relief shading, vegetation in green, roads and other features in black. Old Type M (Militaire) for areas not covered by new series. In black and white with vegetation, contours, roads and rivers overprinted in colours.
New series, Type 1922 F.Fr 8.33
Type Militaire incl. Corsica F.Fr 5.00

CARTE DE FRANCE
1:25, 000
see index 44/13
Paris : IGN, 1967+
56 x 40
Topographical series in progress available in either Standard ed. contoured with roads, paths, boundaries and land detail with woodland in green or Military ed, which has UTM grid overprinted in violet with legend in English (covering mainly area north of line Le Havre-Genève)
Per sheet F.Fr 8.33

CARTE DE FRANCE
1:20, 000
see index 44/13
Paris : IGN
70 x 50 double sheet, 35 x 50 single
Old series (Edition Ancienne) being replaced by new 1:25, 000 topog. series. Series incomplete and no new sheets are being published at this scale. For some areas unpublished at either 1:20, 000 or 1:25, 000 photo-copies of provisional (stereominute) editions can be supplied at 1:10, 000, 1:20, 000 or reduced to 1:25, 000.
Each F.Fr 5.00

CARTES DES ALPES MARITIME
1:5, 000
Paris : IGN, 1971
Large scale series of plans in progress currently published for the Cannes-Antibes area and surroundings.
each F.Fr 20.83

COMMUNE DE NICE
1:5, 000
In 10 sheets
Paris : IGN
Large scale plan of the district.
each F.Fr 23.33

D POLITICAL & ADMINISTRATIVE

REGIONE FRANCESE
1:5, 000, 000
Novara : Ag
Small hand map showing outlines.
L 40

UMRISSKARTE FRANKREICH
1:3,000, 000
No 0817
Bern : K & F
37 x 42
Outline map with rivers and boundaries.

FRANCE
1:3, 000, 000
No 127
Paris : Taride
Administrative base map in black and white.

PETITE FRANCE DEPARTMENTS
1:2, 000, 000
No 124
Paris : Taride
66 x 56
Col. map showing boundaries and railways.

CARTE DES PROVINCES ET PAYS DE FRANCE
1:1,820, 000
A Jarry and Ch Poisson
Paris : Girard et Barrere
62 x 67
Illustrating provinces in colours.

FRANCE
1:1, 500, 000
Paris : Blondel
68 x 68
Col. map of departements with other admin. boundaries.

CARTE ADMINISTRATIVE DE LA FRANCE
1:1, 400, 000
Paris : IGN, 1969
106 x 73
Showing departments, cantons and arrondissements in brown on a blue base.
F.Fr 11.67
Also available with planning regions overprinted: Region de Programme ed.

CARTE DÉPARTMENTALE DE LA FRANCE
1:1, 400, 000
Paris : IGN, 1973
106 x 73
7 colour map showing departments in colour and including principal routes and rivers. F.Fr 11.67

FRANCE DÉPARTMENTS
1:1, 260, 000
Paris : Taride
100 x 90
Col. map showing railways, admin. boundaries, at dept. and local level.

FRANCE
1:1, 187, 500
Paris : Forest
127 x 101
Showing provinces of 1789, with present communications.

FRANCE-CARTE MUETTE
Ed. A Gibert
Map No 1
Paris : Delagrave
105 x 125
Blank outline map of France with physical coloured map on reverse.
F.Fr 45.00

FRANCE CONTOUR - DÉPARTEMENTS
1:1, 170, 000
St Germain-en-Laye : Éditions MDI
92 x 126
Plastic coated outline wall map showing Departement areas. Base map on reverse.

LA FRANCE : COLLECTION J ANSCOMBE
1:1, 170, 000
1301 Administrative - Chemins de Fer
see FRANCE 44 E1

COURS D'EAU ET COTES
1:1, 100, 000
Paris : Armand Colin
Political map on reverse
see FRANCE 44 E2

CARTE DE LA FRANCE-ADMINISTRATIVE
1:1, 100, 000
Paris: Éditions Ponchet
120 x 90
Showing boundaries of Canton, Arrondissements, Départements and Régions with index of Préfectures, Sous-Préfectures and chief towns of the cantons with postal code. F.Fr 9.00

FRANCE POLITIQUE
1:1, 000, 000
No 12
Paris : Hatier
100 x 120
School political col. wall map. Shows pop. by departments; Paris and 1789 provinces as insets.

FRANCE
1:1, 000, 000
Paris : Forest
127 x 101
Political wall map, commercial information, depts in col, communications.

FRANCE ET RÉGIONS NATURELLES DE LA FRANCE
Various scales
Paris : Hatier
120 x 100
Series of physical-political wall maps with economic map on reverse.
Maps available :
2 Massif Central
3 Pyrénées et Bassin d'Aquitaine
4 Région Alpestre
5 Jura et Couloir Rhodanien
6 Midi Méditerranéen et Corse
7 Région du Nord
9-9bis Bassin Parisien - double sheet (Hinged) 200 x 120 reverse side blank.

DÉPARTEMENTS
1:200, 000
Paris : Leconte
54 x 74
General map of each département.

CARTES DÉPARTEMENT - ORIENTATION
1:180, 000
In 91 sheets
Paris : Éditions Ponchet
Series of maps covering each individual département showing administrative districts, roads, plans of principal towns and has an index of communes.
each F.Fr 6.00

DÉPARTEMENT DE L'ISERE : CARTE ADMINISTRATIVE
1:200, 000
Paris : IGN, 1970
73 x 70
Col. map showing admin. areas.
F.Fr 9.17

CARTE DE LA RÉGION PARISIENNE
1:150, 000
Paris : Éditions Ponchet
110 x 98
Administrative map of the Paris region with all boundaries marked and index to communes with their population.
F.Fr 9.00

CARTE DU SCHÉMA DIRECTEUR D'AMÉNAGEMENT ET D'URBANISME DE LA RÉGION DE PARIS
1:100, 000
Paris : Inst. AURP, 1965
105 x 96
Control map for planning and layout of the Paris region. Classifies by col., various planned use areas.
With text vol. F.Fr 15.00
Supplementary maps at
1:500,000 F.Fr 10.00

COMMUNAUTÉ URBAINE DE LYON
1:50, 000
Paris : IGN, 1970
Admin. boundaries in red, on topog. 1:50, 000 base. F.Fr 10.00

E1 PHYSICAL: RELIEF

TERRAIN MAP OF FRANCE
1:2, 000, 000
Williamsburg, Mass : Robert Frank Collins, 1968
51 x 61
Physical map showing relief by hachures.

CARTE DE FRANCE (IGN)
1:1, 750, 000
Paris : IGN, 1969
67 x 67
Contoured and layered, col. roads, railways and rivers. F.Fr 8.33

LA FRANCE : COLLECTION J ANSCOMBRE
1:1, 170, 000
St Germain-en-Laye : Éditions MDI
92 x 126 each
Double-sided plastic coated wall maps for schools. Available as :
1251 Relief - Régions Géologiques (1:1, 100, 000)
1250 Physique
1270 Climat - Blé (cereals)
1271 Vigne - Variations du Climat
1272 Légumes (vegetables), Fruits, Fleurs - Cultures Industrielles
1273 Gros Élevage (horses, cattle) - Forêts
1274 Petit Élevage (fishing etc) Industries Alimentaire (food)
1300 Population
1301 Administrative - Chemins de Fer (railways)
1302 Sources d'Energie - Industries

FRANKRIJK
1:1, 500, 000
Groningen : Wolters-Nordhoff
105 x 87
Physical wall map for schools.
Relief colouring, communications, boundaries. F.Fr 44.75

FRANCIE A SVYCARSKO
1:1, 500, 000
Praha : Kart
Physical/political reference map in "Poznaváme Svet" series (Getting to know the world). With thematic text volume.
Kcs 19

REGIONAL WALL MAP OF FRANCE AND THE LOW COUNTRIES
1:1, 250, 000
London : Philip
91 x 117
Col. physically with communications and boundaries and inset of Corsica.
Paper £1.50
CR £5.80
Cloth dissected to fold £7.00

FRANCE
1:1, 150, 000
Bruxelles : Mantnieks
91 x 125
Physical wall map for schools, showing relief by layer and bathymetric colouring, geog. regions named, major cities indicated, water features. Also available in English.

FRANCE
1:1, 250, 000
Novara : Ag
86 x 115
School wall map, with relief shading, departmental boundaries, towns graded by pop, major roads and railways. In French.
L 1, 750
Mounted L 3, 500

FRANCE - RELIEF DU SOL
1:1, 100, 000
Map No 303
Eds. Vidal Lablache and H Varon
Paris : Armand Colin
120 x 100
Relief wall map; Inset : relief of Europe.

LA FRANCE
1:1, 100, 000
Map No 301
Eds. Vidal Lablane and H Varon
Paris : Armand Colin
120 x 100
Relief wall map, showing geog. structure. Outline map on reverse.

FRANCE PHYSIQUE
Map No 1
Ed. A Gibert
Paris : Delagrave
105 x 125
Physical wall map of France with blank outline map on reverse
F.Fr 45.00

CARTE DE FRANCE
1:1, 000, 000
Paris : IGN, 1972
101 x 125
Covering the whole of France.
Shows planimetric details in black, roads in red, contours, vegetation cover green, settlements yellow, hypsometric tints.
F.Fr 16.67

CROQUIS HYPSOMÉTRIQUE DE LA FRANCE
1:1, 000, 000
Paris : IGN, 1966 (Rep. 1955 ed)
98 x 120
Map showing relief by 6 hypsometric tints. Shows rivers, but no towns or names.
F.Fr 12.50

FRANCE
1:1, 000, 000
Paris : Forest
127 x 101
Physical wall map to show land elevations, boundaries of natural regions.

FRANCE PHYSIQUE
1:1, 000, 000
No 11
Paris : Hatier
100 x 120
School physical col. wall map showing land forms.

FRANCE PHYSIQUE, ECONOMIQUE, TOURISTIQUE
1:1, 000, 000
No 48
Paris : Hatier
100 x 120
School wall map "Paris et sa Banlieue" on reverse.

FRANKREICH UND DIE BENELUX-STAATEN
1:750, 000
Gotha : Haack
156 x 200
Physical wall map of France and the Benelux countries, including central and southern England, Corsica inset. Communications, cities graded by pop.

FRANKREICH
1:600, 000
Braunschweig : Westermann
210 x 202
Col. wall map showing geog. features, large towns in red. Available in Eng, Fr, Dut, Sw eds. Relief shading, communications, boundaries.

FRANCIA
1:5, 000, 000
Novara : Ag
33 x 26
Plastic relief map, with physical, political and economic details on reverse. For schools.
L 450

FRANCIA
1:1, 250, 000
Novara : Ag
97 x 122
Moulded plastic relief map in frame with metal corners. L 20, 000

RÉGIONS FRANÇAISES PHYSIQUES
Various scales
No 1700 or 1342 (plastic coated)
St German-en-Laye : Éditions MDI
80 x 92
Double sided wall map containing 10 regional maps of France. For schools.
Région du Nord
Bassin Parisien
Pays de la Loire
Bassin Aquitain/Pyrénées
Massif Central
Région de l'Est
Normandie
Bretagne/Vendée
Alpes/Jura/Saône/Rhône
Région Méditerraneene

LA FRANCE
Various scales
St Germain-en-Laye : Éditions MDI
TC 20 (No 1631)
80 x 92
8 maps on one sheet with blackboard surface for schools. Showing:
1 Contours de la France
2 Relief et hydrographic
3 Les côtes
4 La Seine
5 La Loire
6 La Garonne
7 Le Rhône et le Rhin
8 Les Chemins de Fer

LES RÉGIONS FRANÇAISES
St Germain-en-Laye : Éditions MDI
92 x 126
Plastic coated school wall maps.
Physical, with economic-administrative map on reverse.
Available for:
1467 Lorraine
1498 Rhône-Alpes
1468 Bretagne
1448 Nord
1475 Région Parisienne
1478 Auvergne

RELIEFS DE FRANCE
Varying scales
Paris : IGN
Various sizes
Moulded plastic relief maps; height exaggeration shown by vertical scale.
Produced for mt. regions.
Maps published :
France
1:1, 750, 000 65 x 88 F.Fr 83.33
1:1, 000, 000 103 x 115 F.Fr 140.00
Aquitaine-Causses-Pyrenees
1:500, 000 75 x 104 1972
F.Fr 145.83
Massif Central
1:500, 000 75 x 104 1972
F.Fr 145.83
Languedoc-Cevennes-Provence
1:500, 000 104 x 75 1972
F.Fr 145.83
Vosges-Alsace
1:250, 000 70 x 65 1972
F.Fr 104.17
Sillon Rhodanien-Alpes
1:500, 000 F.Fr 145.83
Ardennes-Vosges-Jura F.Fr 145.83

RELIEFS DE FRANCE
1:200, 000
Paris : IGN
80 x 55
Moulded plastic relief maps.
Special sheets published :
Annecy-Genève et Grenoble
94 x 78
Grenoble et Gap 94 x 78
Berne et Grand St Bernard
94 x 78
Corse 116 x 64 F.Fr 195.83
Côtes du Nord 87 x 62 F.Fr 104.17

RELIEFS DE FRANCE - COUPURES SPECIALES
1:100, 000
Paris : IGN
Moulded plastic relief maps in same style as official topog. series.
Sheets published :
Haut Jura 80 x 60
Mont Blanc-Aravis 84 x 62
Lac Léman 81 x 58
Environs de Marseille 105 x 76
Maures Estérel 114 x 76
Bugey-Bauges-Genevois 82 x 99
Visges Sud 63 x 71
Côte d'Azur 109 x 77
Massif de la Vanoise 105 x 99
Pays Basque 105 x 76
Pyrénées Occidentales 105 x 76
Pyrénées Centrales 105 x 76
Each F.Fr 104.17

RELIEFS DE FRANCE - COUPURES SPECIALES
1:50, 000
Paris : IGN
Moulded plastic relief maps in same style as official topog. series.
Sheets published:
Massif de L'Oisans 116 x 80
Environs de Grenoble 115 x 82
Each F.Fr 104.17
Massif du Mont Blanc 115 x 82
F.Fr 250.00

E2 PHYSICAL: LAND FEATURES

CARTE DE VULNERABILITÉ À LA POLLUTION DES NAPPES D'EAU SOUTERRAINE DE LA FRANCE
By M Albinet
1:1, 000, 000
Paris : BRGM, 1970
100 x 101
Col. map indicating the present state of underground water pollution, and future areas likely to be affected, showing speed of pollution etc. F.Fr 26.00

CARTE DU DÉBIT MOYEN DES NAPPES D'EAU SOUTERRAINE DE LA FRANCE
By O Bouillien
1:1, 000, 000
Paris : BRGM
Average flow of subterranean water.
F.Fr 26.00

CARTE DES EAUX SOUTERRAINES
1:50, 000
Paris : BRGM
Map of underground water. Sheet for Douai available. F.Fr 26.00

ÉTAT D'AVANCEMENT DES PROFILS EN LONG DES COURS D'EAU
1:1, 000, 000
Paris : IGN
Shows against a background of rivers, streams and canals, sections of water courses at various scales.
F.Fr 5.00

F GEOLOGY

LA FRANCE
Ed. J Anscombre
1:1, 100, 000
Éditions MDI
Régions Géologiques
Plastic surfaced geological wall map with relief map of France on reverse.

GÉOLOGIE
1:1, 100, 000
Map No 339
Ed. Vidal Lablache and H Varon
Paris : Armand Colin
120 x 100
School wall map showing geol. with 4 enlarged regional maps at 1:320, 000 on reverse.

CARTE GÉOLOGIQUE DE LA FRANCE
1:1, 000, 000
5th ed. in 2 sheets
Paris : CGF, 1969
116 x 117
Col. geol. map.
Each sheet folded F.Fr 30.00
Complete, flat F.Fr 46.00

FRANCE GÉOLOGIQUE
No 15
Paris : Hatier
100 x 120
Col. school wall map.

CARTE DE LA SURFACE PIÉZOMÉTRIQUE DE LA NAPPE DE LA CRAIE EN PICARDY
By J C Roux and M Tirat
1:1, 000, 000
Orleans : BRGM, 1967
106 x 77
Piezometric map of the compressed strata of the Craie chalk basin of Picardy.
F.Fr 26.00

CARTE GÉOLOGIQUE DE LA FRANCE
1:320,000
See index 44/15
Orleans : BRGM, 1967+
Ord. geol. series in col. being reprinted.
Sheets available:
3-8 Lille-Dunkerque (2nd ed 1962)
9 Mézières (2nd ed 1953)
11-16 Brest-Lorient (2nd ed 1970)
12-7 Rennes-Cherbourg
13 Paris
15-20 Strasbourg-Mulhouse (1st ed 1956)
17 Nantes
18 Bourges (2nd ed 1968)
19 Dijon (2nd ed 1970)
21 La Rochelle (2nd ed 1967)
22 Clermont (2nd ed 1967)
25 Bordeaux (2nd ed 1967)
30 Toulouse (1st ed 1963)
Each F.Fr 37.00

CARTE GÉOLOGIQUE DE FRANCE
1:80, 000
See index 44/14
Paris : BRGM, 1903+
Full sheet : 79 x 50
Half sheet : 44 x 49
Col. geol. series in progress, overprinted on early hachured ed. (Carte dite d'Etat Major)
Each F.Fr 33.00

CARTE GÉOLOGIQUE DE FRANCE
1:50, 000
See index 44/14
Paris : BRGM, 1922+
55 x 40
Col. geol. series based on topog.
Type 1922 series with descriptive test to each sheet in Fr.
Each F.Fr 26.00

CARTE GÉOLOGIQUE EN RELIEF DE CHAMBÉRY
1:50, 000
Paris : IGN/BRGM
54 x 69
Map printed on plastic, combining 3-dimensional plastic relief with geol. and land conformation. Legend in Fr.
F.Fr 125.00

CARTE GÉOLOGIQUE DU MASSIF DU MONT BLANC
1:20, 000
In 14 sheets, see index 44/17
Paris : CNRS
Full sheets : 68 x 49
Half sheets : 34 x 49
Geol. map in col. With text.
Each F.Fr 23.70
Double sheet F.Fr 35.50

CARTE GÉOLOGIQUE DE LA MARGE CONTINENTALE FRANÇAISE
1:250, 000, 1:100, 000
Orléans : BRGM
Col. geol. series covering coastal areas and adjacent sea floor.
At 1:250,000, see index 44/19
I Geology :
Penmarc'h (Brittany) with text, 1970
F.Fr 30.00
Boulogne-sur-mer-Rouen) 1 text for
Caen-Wight) both sheets
each F.Fr 50.00
At 1:100,000, see index 44/18
II Marine deposits (Nature des Dépôts Meubles sous Marins)
Marseille (with text) F.Fr 30.00
Argeles-sur-Mer F.Fr 30.00

CARTE SÉDIMENTOLOGIQUE SOUS-MARINE DES CÔTES DE FRANCE
1:100,000, see index 44/18
Paris : IGN
96 x 64
Map series showing sea floor deposits.
In col.
Sheets available :
Pont Croix, 1969
Briquebec, 1968
St Nazaire, 1968
St Vaast la Holgue, 1967
Brest, 1968
Plabennec, 1975
Lorient, 1972
Ile d'Yeu, 1971
Each F.Fr 41.67

LA DÉCOUVERTE DES PAYSAGES GÉOLOGIQUES ENTRE PARIS ET AVALLON
1:200, 000
Orléans : BRGM
Small geol. map based on Michelin road map showing geol. landscape between Paris and Avallon. With 28pp brochure suggesting itineraries. F.Fr 5.00

CARTE PIÉZOMÉTRIQUE DE LA NAPPE CAPTIVE DES SABLES ÉOCÈNES EN GIRONDE POUR L'ANNÉE 1965
1:200, 000
Orleans : BRGM, 1967
105 x 90
Col. map of the compacted Eocene sand strata of the Gironde with 6 insets.
F.Fr 26.00

TOIT DU CÉNOMANIEN
By G Lecointre
1:200, 000
Orleans : BRGM
Geol. map covering SW Paris Basin, Touraine and surroundings.
F.Fr 30.00

GEOLOGICAL MAP OF THE PYRENEES
1:200, 000
In 2 sheets
Ed H J Zwart
Leiden : Geol. Inst. Leiden Univ. 1972
106 x 77 each sheet
Coloured map covering both sides of the border from the Mediterranean to the Atlantic.

VOSGES MOYENNES : CARTE GÉOLOGIQUE DES TERRAINS CRISTALLINS ET CRISTALLO-PHYLLIENS
1:100, 000
Strasbourg : Bulletin du Service de la Carte Geologique d'Alsace et de Lorraine, 1967
77 x 59
Col. crystalline map. Text vol. 16pp in Fr.

CARTE GÉOLOGIQUES DES MASSIFS DU CANIGOU ET DE LA CARANCA
1:50, 000
Orléans : BRGM, 1970
Col. geol. map with "Memoire" by G Guitard F.Fr 200.00

GEOLOGICAL MAP OF THE CENTRAL PYRENEES
1:50, 000
Leiden : Geol. Inst. Leiden Univ.
90 x 57
Col. map in 10 sheets; indicates folds and presence of economic minerals. Contained in "Overdruck vit Leidse Geologische Mededelingen"
Ed L V de Sitter and H J Zwart, 1959
Sheets include :
1 Garonne, 1962
2 Salat, 1962
3 Ariège, 1958
4 Valle de Aran, 1960
5 Pallaresa, 1959
6 Aston, 1965
7 Lys-Caillaouas-Esera, 1968
8 Ribagorzana 1967
9 In Press
10 Sègre-Valira, 1969

CARTES GÉOLOGIQUES DES FORMATIONS SUPERFICIELLES
1:25, 000, 1:50, 000
Orléans : BRGM, 1969+
Col. geol. maps showing superficial deposits.
Maps available :
1:25, 000
Saint-Bonnet-de-Joux (1969)
F.Fr 26.00
1:50, 000
Creil (1969) F.Fr 26.00
Sens (1971) F.Fr 26.00
Saint-Bonnet-de-Joux - in preparation
Montereau - in preparation

COUPES LITHOSTRATIGRAPHIQUES INTERPRÉTATIVES DANS LA TERTIAIRE NORD-AQUITAIN
By J-M Marionnaud
In 2 sheets
Orléans : BRGM, 1969
Geol. sections of the Tertiary strata of Nord Aquitaine.
Complete F.Fr 52.00

CARTE HYDROGÉOLOGIQUE DU BASSIN DE PARIS
1:500, 000
In 2 sheets
Orléans : BRGM, 1968
84 x 106 each
Shows various stages of Jurassic, Cretaceous, Tertian and Quaternary, Lithological character of outcrops, hydrological features.
Text on reverse. F.Fr 60.00

CARTE HYDROGÉOLOGIQUE DES GRANDS CAUSSES
1:200, 000
Orléans : BRGM
95 x 74
Hydrogeological map with 22pp text by H Paloc. F.Fr 50.00

REGION CHAMPAGNE-ARDENNES
1:100, 000
In 3 sheets
Orléans : BRGM
Hydrogeol. map.
Each sheet F.Fr 21.00

CARTE HYDROGÉOLOGIQUE DE LA FRANCE
By H Paloc
1:80, 000
Orléans : BRGM, 1967
Hydrogeologic map of the karst limestone area of north Montpelier region.
F.Fr 120.00

CARTE HYDROGÉLOGIQUE AU BASSIN DE L'AUTHION
1:50, 000
In 2 sheets
Orléans : BRGM
218 x 95
With text. F.Fr 60.00

CARTE HYDROGÉOLOGIQUE DE LA FRANCE
1:50, 000
Paris : BRGM
Col. hydrogeological series on same sheet lines as official topog. series.
Sheets published :
Paris
Auxerre
Valenciennes
Sète
Laon
Beauvais
Altkirch
Amiens
Creil
Douai
Évreux
La Crau (Istres-Eyguieres)
Région Grenobloise
Each F.Fr 26.00

G EARTH RESOURCES

UTILISATION AGRICOLE DU SOL DE FRANCE : SECONDE MOITIÉ XXe SIÈCLE
1:1,400, 000
Paris : CNRS, 1970
75 x 85
Map showing soil use in second half of the 20th C. In col. F.Fr 30.80

CARTE PÉDOLOGIQUE DE LA FRANCE
By J Dupuis
1:1, 000, 000
In 2 sheets
Paris : Inst. Nat. de la Recherche Agronomique, 1967
Soils map in colour. With 56pp text.
F.Fr 58.85

CARTE PÉDOLOGIQUE DE LA FRANCE
1:250, 000
Paris : Inst. Nat. de la Recherche Agronomique
74 x 56
Sheet published :
Paris 1973

CARTE PÉDOLOGIQUE DE FRANCE
1:100, 000
Paris : Inst. Nat. de la Recherche Agronomique
Soil series in progress. Sheets available for :
Vichy, 1969, with 58pp text
Argeles-sur-Mer, Perpignan, 1970
114pp text
Moulins, 1972
Condom, 1972
Dijon, 1973 F.Fr 57.75

CARTE DES SOLS D'AISNE
1:5, 000
See index 44/16
Laon : Service de Cartographie des Sols
Soil map series in progress, showing texture of soils, economy and production, limestone areas, etc. See index for sheets pub. With memoirs.
Each F.Fr 80.00

CARTE DES GISEMENTS DE FER DE LA FRANCE
By O Horon et al
1:1, 000, 000
In 2 sheets
Paris : BRGM
Iron bearing areas. Insets at 1:320, 000 for congested areas. F.Fr 30.00

CARTE DES GITES MINERAUX
1:320, 000
Paris : BRGM
Col. maps of mineral bearing strata on same sheet lines as Geol. Series.
Sheets available :
Brest
Cherbourg-Rennes
Vosges
Avignon
Lyon
Nantes
Marseille
Rodez
Corse
Bayonne
Dijon
Ardennes
Per sheet F.Fr 26.00

NATURE DES DÉPÔTS MEUBLES SOUS MARINS
1:100, 000
Orléans : BRGM
Series covering part of the Mediterranean Coast, showing nature of the changing marine deposits.
see FRANCE 44 F

CARTES DES SUBSTANCES UTILES
1:50, 000
Paris : BRGM, 1969+
Showing location of economic minerals.
Sheets available :
Nimes F.Fr 26.00

CARTE DES COURBES D'ÉGALE DÉCLINAISON MAGNÉTIQUE
1:1, 400, 000
Paris : IGN
60 x 60
Map showing lines of equal magnetic declination. In 2 eds : values in either degrees 1970, or grades (1975).
Each F.Fr 5.00

CARTE MAGNÉTIQUE DE LA FRANCE
1:1, 000, 000
Orléans : BRGM
In 2 sheets
Detailed anomalies of total field. Av. values 1 km. South sheet, based on geol. col. map available. F.Fr 26.00

CARTE MAGNÉTIQUE
1:1, 000, 000
In 2 sheets
Orléans : BRGM
Available in 2 eds. Intensity of the Total Field and Anomalies of the Total Field (Av. values at 10 km)
Each F.Fr 26.00

CARTE MAGNÉTIQUE DE MÉDITERRANÉE OCCIDENTALE
1:1, 000, 000
Orléans : BRGM
2 sheet map (North and South Zones) available in 2 eds: intensity of field, and anomalies of total field.
Each sheet F.Fr 26.00

CARTE MAGNÉTIQUE DU GOLFE DE GASCOGNE
1:1, 000, 000
Orléans : BRGM
Available in 2 eds. Intensity of total field and Anomalies of total field.
Each F.Fr 26.00

PROFILS MAGNÉTIQUES RABATTUS
1:200, 000
In 92 sheets
Orléans : BRGM
Series of maps showing magnetic profiles.
Each sheet F.Fr 26.00

CARTE MAGNÉTIQUE DÉTAILLEE
1:80, 000
See index 44/14
Orléans : BRGM
Series in progress on same sheet lines as geol. series.
71 Strasbourg
106 Angers
109 Gien
111 Avallon
120 Loches
121 Valençay
123 Nevers
124 Château-Chinon
132 Châtellerault
133 Châteauroux
135 Saint-Pierre
With text F.Fr 26.00

CARTE GRAVIMÉTRIQUE DE LA FRANCE
1:320, 000
Orléans : BRGM
Series in progress on same sheet lines as geol. series.
Maps published :
1:320, 000
Poitou-Vendee F.Fr 26.00
Poitou-Marches F.Fr 26.00
1:320, 000 on Geol. base
Nos.
7-12 Cherbourg-Rennes (density of 2.7) F.Fr 26.00
11-16 Brest-Lorient (density of 2.7) F.Fr 26.00
17 Nantes (density of 2.7) F.Fr 26.00
18 Bourges (density of 2.3) F.Fr 26.00
21 La Rochelle (density of 2.3) F.Fr 26.00
13 Paris with text (density of 2.3) F.Fr 30.00
Also at 1:200, 000 and 1:80, 000 following the Geol. Series outlines.
Per sheet F.Fr 10.00

CARTE GRAVIMÉTRIQUE DE LA FRANCE
1:200, 000
Orléans : BRGM
Series in progress on same sheet lines as topog. series.
Maps published :
2-3-4, 5-10, 7, 8, 9, 11-18, 12-21-29, 13-22, 14, 15, 16, 17, 19,23, 24, 25, 26, 28-36, 30, 31, 32, 33, 34, 37, 38, 39, 40, 44, 45, 46, 50, 56, 63 F.Fr 10.00

CARTE GRAVIMÉTRIQUE DE LA FRANCE
1:80, 000
See index 44/14
Orléans : BRGM
Series in progress on same sheet lines as geol. maps.
Each F.Fr 10.00

H BIOGEOGRAPHY

LA FRANCE : COLLECTION
J Anscombre
1:1, 700, 000
Éditions MDI
Vigne : Forets
see FRANCE 44 E1

FRANCE FORESTIÈRE
1:1, 000, 000
No 30
Paris : Hatier
100 x 120
School wall map. France Agricole on reverse. Showing green forests on background map, with principal forests named, and percentage cover given for each department.

CARTES DES PARCS NATIONAUX
Various scales
Paris : IGN, 1970-
Various sizes
Maps of the National parks, showing natural life, physical features, sporting areas etc.
Maps available :
Pyrénées (4 sheets)
1:25, 000 1970-2 121 x 66
(available in walking and skiing ed)
F.Fr 15.00
Port-Cros
1:12, 500 1973 F.Fr 4.17
Cévennes
1:100, 000 1972 121 x 89
F.Fr 15.00

PARCS NATURELS RÉGIONAUX
Various scales
Paris : IGN
Maps of regional nature parks, with information for the sportsman, tourist and nature lover.
Maps available:
St Armand Raismes
1:25, 000 1970 121 x 89
F.Fr 9.76
Vercors
1:50, 000 1972 89 x 133
F.Fr 12.20
Lorraine
1:100, 000 1972 133 x 89
Brière
1:50, 000 1975 99 x 89
Monts du Cantal
1:100, 000 1972 55 x 46
La Forêt de l'Orient
1:50, 000 1973 110 x 89
Le Morvan
1:200, 000 1976 121 x 89
Corsica
1:100, 000 1973 89 x 121
Haut Languedoc
1:100, 000 1973 121 x 89
Camargue
1:50, 000 1973 121 x 89
Londes de Gascogne
1:100, 000 1976 121 x 89
Le Pilat
1:50, 000 1976
each F.Fr 15.00

CARTES DES FORÊTS
1:25, 000
Paris : IGN
Various sizes
Topog. forest maps, contoured, with land detail - woodland, forest areas, nature reserves, recreational facilities etc. Available for :
Fontainebleau 1975 110 x 100
Rambouillet 1974 99 x 89
Compiègne (et de Laigue)
1971 121 x 89
Retz, Villers-Cotterets
1971 110 x 89
Chantilly (Halatte, Ermenonville)
1975 121 x 89
Crecy (1:20, 000)
1972 99 x 67
Hez-Froidment et du Parc
St Quentin 1974 121 x 89
Bouconne 1976
St Gobain et Corcy-Bass 1976
Forêt d'Orléans 3 sheets 1976
Each F.Fr 7.92

CARTE DE LA FRANCE VINICOLE
Paris : Carte Larmat
65 x 87
Coloured map showing wine-growing areas.
F.Fr 24.90

CARTES DES VINS DE BORDEAUX
No 12
Paris : Carte Larmat
Wine growing areas map.
F.Fr 9.95
Also available for the individual vineyards:
16 Côte de Bourg, Bourgeais
25 x 31 F.Fr 4.00
16b Premieres Côtes de Blaye-Blayais
25 x 31 F.Fr 4.00
16t Blayais, Côtes de Blaye, Bourgeais, Cote de Bourg
45 x 65 F.Fr 6.00
17 Carte geologique du Vignoble Girondin
24 x 38 F.Fr 4.00
18 Cerons
25 x 31 F.Fr 4.00
19 Côte de Canon-Fronsac
25 x 31 F.Fr 4.00
20 Premières Côtes de Bordeaux
31 x 60 F.Fr 4.00
21 Entre Deux-Mers, Graves de Vayres, Ste Foy-Bordeaux
31 x 50 F.Fr 4.00
21b ditto
45 x 65 F.Fr 6.00
23 Graves, Graves superieures
31 x 60 F.Fr 4.00
24 Graves, Graves superieures, Cerons
45 x 65 F.Fr 6.00
25 Loupiac, Ste Croix du Mont, Premieres Côte de Bordeaux-St Macaire
45 x 65 F.Fr 6.00
25b ditto
25 x 31 F.Fr 4.00
26 Médoc
25 x 31 F.Fr 4.00
27 Haut Médoc
31 x 60 F.Fr 4.00
29 Pomerol, Lalande de Pomerol, Néac
31 x 49 F.Fr 6.00
31 Lusac-St-Émilion, Montagne St Ém, Parsac-St-Ém, Puisseguin-St-Ém, St Georges-St-Ém, Sables St Émilion
25 x 31 F.Fr 4.00
32 Sauternes et Barsac
31 x 60 F.Fr 4.00

CARTES DES VINS DE BOURGOGNE
Paris : Carte Larmat
65 x 87
Map of the Burgundy wine growing areas : (Côte de Nuits, Côte de Beaune, Côte chalonnaise, Chablis, Beaujolais, Mâconnais) F.Fr 14.95
Also available for individual areas :
15b Côte de Beaune
90 x 35 F.Fr 10.00
15n Côte de Nuits
90 x 35 F.Fr 10.00
15 Le jeu des 2 cartes : Côte de Beaune et Côte de Nuits
F.Fr 18.00
15c Chablis
50 x 65 F.Fr 10.00

CARTES DES VINS DE CHAMPAGNE
Paris : Carte Larmat
50 x 65
Coloured map of Champagne growing areas F.Fr 6.00
Also available for smaller areas :
38 Bar Séquanais et Bar s/Aubois
45 x 65 F.Fr 6.00
40 Montagne de Reims
46 x 102 F.Fr 6.00
41 Montagne de Reims et Vallée de l'Ardre
45 x 65 F.Fr 6.00

COGNAC
Paris : Carte Larmat
Various sizes
Maps of cognac producing areas :
48 Bois ordinaires et Bois communs dit a terroir
45 x 65 F.Fr 6.00
49 Bons Bois
45 x 65 F.Fr 6.00
50 Fins Bois
45 x 65 F.Fr 6.00
51 Grande Champagne
45 x 65 F.Fr 6.00
52 Petite Champagne
45 x 65 F.Fr 6.00

COTEAUX DE LA LOIRE
Paris : Carte Larmat
Various sizes
Maps showing the Loire wine-growing areas:
44 Bourgueil, St Nicolas de Bourgueil, Chinon-Mont-Louis, Jasnieres
45 x 65 F.Fr 6.00
45 Côteaux de Touraine
45 x 65 F.Fr 6.00
46 Pouilly, Sancerre, Quincy, Reuilly
45 x 65 F.Fr 6.00

BRETAGNE ET RÉGIONS DES BOCAGES
No 10
Paris : Hatier
100 x 120
School wall map in "France et Regions Naturelles de la France" series. Scrublands of Brittany.

CARTE DE LA VÉGÉTATION DE LA FRANCE
1:200, 000
Toulouse : Service de la Carte de Veg. de la France
Various sizes
Multi-sheet series, with insets of comparative information. With brief text.
Each F.Fr 55.00
Half sheets F.Fr 36.30

CARTE DE LA VÉGÉTATION DES ALPES
1:100, 000, 1:75, 000, 1:50, 000
See index 44/20
Editor Prof. P Ozenda
Grenoble: Univ. Scientifique et Médicale de Grenoble, 1963
Series of coloured vegetation maps generally following sheet lines of official French surveys. Each sheet is very detailed and has an accompanying descriptive text.
The maps and texts are published in a series of volumes 'Documents pour lar Carte de la Végétation des Alpes' together with reports and maps of other vegetation studies.
The volume number is given below in roman numerals.
Sheets Published :
1 XXXII-36 La Chapelle-en-Vercors 1:100, 000 (I)

2 XXIII-37 Saint-Bonnet 1:100, 000 (I)
3 XXXV-36 Briançon 1:100, 000 (I)
4 Forêts de Haute Maurienne (Carte phytosociologique) 1: 75, 000 (V)
5 XXXV-31 Bourg-Saint-Maurice/XXXV-32 Moûtiers (V) combined sheet 1:75,000
6 XXXII-34 Grenoble 1: 50, 000 (II)
7 XXXIII-34 Domène 1: 50, 000 (II)
8 XXXV-38 Embrun Est 1: 50, 000 (III)
9 XXXI-39 Nyons 1: 50, 000 (III)
10 XXXI-34 Beaurepaire 1: 50, 000 (V)
11 XXXII-35 Vif 1: 50, 000 (VI)
12 XXXIII-35 Vizille 1: 50, 000 (VI)
13 Valle Grana (Alpi Cozie) 1: 50, 000 (VI)
14 Valle Gesso (Alpi Marittime) 1: 50, 000 (VII)
15 XXXIV-42 Moustiers-Sainte-Marie 1: 50, 000 (VII)
16 XXXI-40 Vaison-La-Romaine 1: 50, 000 (VII)
17 XXXIV-40 La Javie 1: 50, 000 (VIII)
18 XXXIII-33 Montmélian 1: 50, 000 (IX)
19 XXXIII-40 Sisteron 1: 50, 000 (X)
20 XXXII-31 Belley 1: 50, 000 (X)
21 XXXII-32 La Tour-du-Pin (Carte écologique) 1: 50, 000 (X)
22 XXXIV-31 Annecy-Ugine in preparation (XI)
23 XXXVI-30 Chamonix (carte écologique) 1: 50, 000 (XVI)
24 XXXV-30 Cluses (carte écologique) 1: 50, 000 (XVI)

The numbers 1-24 refer to the map location index.

CARTE FORESTIÈRE DE LA FRANCE
1:100, 000
see index 44/10
Paris : IGN
95 x 60 each
Multi-sheet series on same lines as topog. 1:100, 000 series. Shows forest types, ownership and employment; 2 comparative insets of soils and climate.
F.Fr 20.00

CARTE SCHÉMATIQUE DES GROUPEMENTS VÉGÉTAUX TERRESTRES, BIOCENOSES ET BIOTOPES MARINS DU CAP CORSE
By R Molinier
1:80, 000
Paris : CNRS, 1961
Col. sketch map of land vegetation grouping, biocoenosis, and marine biotopes of the Cap Corse region.
With text F.Fr 39.80

FORÊT DOMANIALE DE LA SAINTE-BAUME
By R Molinier
1:20, 000
Paris : CNRS, 1955
91 x 120
Col. forest map. F.Fr 20.40

COL DU LAUTARET ET VERSANT SUD DU GRAND GALIBIER
1:20, 000
Paris : CNRS, 1956
36 x 52
Ecological map, with text.
F.Fr 6.50

CARTE ÉCOLOGIQUE DES ALPES OCCIDENTALES
1:100, 000
Grenoble: Univ. Scientifique et Médicale de Grenoble
New series of ecological maps in preparation for the western alps of France.
Sheets published :
6 Grenoble with text.

ÉTUDE ÉCOLOGIQUES DU MARAIS DE LAVOURS (AIN)
1:50, 000
Editors G Ain & G Pautou
Contained in Vol VII Doc. pour la Carte de la Végétation des Alpes, 1969
Grenoble: Univ. Scientifique et Médicale de Grenoble.
Ecologic map of the Lavours marsh (Ain) with descriptive text.

CARTE ÉCOLOGIQUE DE PONTARLIER S O
1:20, 000
By M Guinochet
Paris : CNRS, 1955
75 x 106
Ecological map based on official topog. sheet lines. F.Fr 20.40

CARTE ÉCOLOGIQUE DE CLERMONT-FERRAND S O
By G Lemee
1:20, 000
Paris : CNRS, 1959
75 x 106
Ecological map based on official topog. sheet lines. F.Fr 39.80

CARTE PHYTO-ÉCOLOGIQUE DE AIX S O
By R Molinier
1:20, 000
Paris : CNRS, 1952
75 x 106
Ecological plant map of the SE quarter of 1:50, 000 official topog. sheet.

CARTE DES GROUPEMENTS VÉGÉTAUX DE LA CHAUTAGNE (SAVOIE)
1:10, 000
Editors G Pautou and others
Contained in Vol IX Doc. pour la Carte de la Végétation, 1971
Grenoble: Univ. Scientifique et Médicale de Grenoble
Coloured map of vegetation groupings of the La Chautagne region.

CARTE PHYTO-ÉCOLOGIQUE - CARTE DE L'OCCUPATION DES TERRES DE SOLOGNE
1:10, 000
Paris : CNRS, 1964
Plant ecology map with 192pp text, illus.
F.Fr 109.70

CARTE DES COLLINES SOUS-VOSGIENNES DES ENVIRONS D'OBERNOI (BAS-RHIN)
By L R Theuret
1:10, 000
Paris : CNRS, 1963
Ecological map of the hills around Obernoi in the Lower Rhine region.
With text. F.Fr 24.70

K HUMAN GEOGRAPHY

CARTE DES VARIATIONS DE LA POPULATION DES VILLES DE PLUS DE 8, 000 HABITANTS
1:2, 800, 000
By P George
Paris : CNRS
Col. maps showing population change.
In 2 maps : Between 1936-1954, published 1967 and Between 1954-1962, published 1968.

CARTE DE LA VARIATION DE POPULATION DE LA FRANCE PAR CANTONS - 1806-1962
1:1, 000, 000
By P George and M Mangolte
In 6 sheets
Paris : CNRS, 1969
Showing regional pop. change from 1806-1962.

CARTE DE LA REPARTITION DE LA POPULATION DE LA FRANCE - 1962
1:1,000,000
By P George
In 6 sheets
Paris : CNRS, 1967
40 x 57 each

L ECONOMIC

LA FRANCE GÉOGRAPHIE PHYSIQUE ET HUMAINE
1:2,500,000
Paris : Michelin, 1971
44 x 50
Col. economic map indicating agriculture and land use, population and industrial centres. With inset maps of regions and on reverse small maps showing relief, climate, population, agriculture, energy and iron production all with accompanying notes and diagrams.

LA FRANCE : COLLECTION J ANSCOMBRE
1:1,700,000
Editions MDI
Cereals, agricultural crops, livestock, industry and energy.
see FRANCE 44 E1

EKONOMICHESKAYA KARTA
1:1,250,000
Moskva : GUGK
Single sheet economic map of France.

FRANCE INDUSTRIELLE
No 32
Paris : Hatier
100 x 120
School wall map. France Minerale on reverse.

FRANCE : AGRICULTURE, INDUSTRIE, COMMERCE
1:1,187,500
Paris : Forest
127 x 101
Indicating industrial areas of various types — agriculture, mineral resources, wine-growing.

FRANCE AGRICOLE
No 30
Paris : Hatier
100 x 120
School wall map. France Forestiere on reverse.

PARIS
1:21,120
St-Germain-en-Laye : Éditions MDI
122 x 101
Coloured wall map, showing major industries in the suburbs and capital, with insets of important information.

FRANCE VOIES NAVIGABLES
1:1,000,000
Paris : Girard et Barrere
110 x 120
Showing all classes of waterways, locks, distances etc.

CARTE DES PLANS D'EAU ET VOIES NAVIGABLES POUR LA FRANCE - CARTE ESSO DE NAVIGATION
Grenoble : Arthaud
Map of navigable waterways.
F.Fr 12.50

FRANCE - CÔTES ET VOIES NAVIGABLES
Various scales
No 1701 or 1344 (plastic coated)
St Germain-en-Laye : Éditions MDI
80 x 92
Regional double-sided wall maps of coastal areas and navigable waters.
Available for :
1 La Seine et ses affluents - Côtes de la Manche et Mer du Nord
2 La Loire - Côtes de l'Atlantique
3 La Garonne - Côtes de la Méditerranée
4 La Rhône - France hydrographie
5 Le Rhin - Les voies navigables

CARTES DE NAVIGATION FLUVIALE
1:40, 000
by Clerc Rampal
Grenoble : Éd B Arthaud
Series of col. navigation maps of French rivers
Maps published :
Seine - Paris a la Mer par le canal Tancarville
Seine - Paris a Montereau
Marne
Yonne - d'Auxerre a Montereau
Saône - Lyon a St Jean de Losne
Saône - St Jean de Losne a Corre

CARTE DES CHEMINS DE FER FRANÇAIS
1:800, 000
In 4 sheets
Paris : IGN, 1974
98 x 65 each
Map showing railway stations and termini, with enlarged insets of congested areas.
Each F.Fr 11.67

PLAN DU RESEAU SNCF GRANDE BANLIEUE
1:100, 000
Paris : Éditions Ponchet
130 x 100
Official French National Railways plan of the rail network of the outer suburbs of Paris with index to communes and stations.
F.Fr 23.20

PLAN DU RESEAU URBAIN DU METRO
Prepared for Régie Autonome des Transport Parisiens
Paris : Éditions Ponchet
130 x 100
Official plan in 12 colours with metro and RER suburban services and bus connections.
F.Fr 23.20

PLAN DU RESEAU SNCF PROCHE BANLIEUE
Paris : Éditions Ponchet
Official French National Railways plan of Inner suburbs rail network of Paris, including local RER Services.
F.Fr 23.20

CARTE DE PARIS
1:15, 000
Paris : Éditions Ponchet
90 x 65
Arrondisement boundaries and metro, suburban (RER) and national (SNCF) rail systems marked. F.Fr 4.40

PLAN DU RESEAU BANLIEUE DES AUTO BUS-RER, METRO
Prepared for Régie Autonome des Transports Parisiens
1:37,000
Paris : Éditions Ponchet
130 x 100
Official plan of the bus routes of the Paris suburbs with roads, metro and suburban rail services. F.Fr 23.20

PLAN DU RESEAU URBAIN DES AUTOBUS
Prepared for Régie Autonome des Transports Parisiens
Paris : Éditions Ponchet
130 x 100
Official plan in 9 colours of the bus routes of central Paris. F.Fr 22.60

PLAN DU RESEAU DES AUTOCARS DE LA REGION PARISIENNE
Prepared for Ass. Prof. des Transporteurs publics Rout. de roy.
Paris : Éditions Ponchet
Official plan of the private coach routes with indexes to operating companies.
F.Fr 23.20

FRANCE ET RÉGIONS NATURELLES DE LA FRANCE
Hatier
Economic maps on reverse.
see FRANCE 44 D

M HISTORICAL

CARTES HISTORIQUES
J Bouillon
Various scales
St Germain-en-Laye : Éditions MDI
92 x 126
Plastic coated, double-sided historical wall maps for schools.
1506 France. Sites Préhistoriques - La Gaule Préromaine (Caesar's conquests)
1508 La Gaule Romaine - La Gaule Mérovingienne - Les Invasions barbares
1510 L'Empire de Charlemagne (1:2,100,000) — Les Invasions des IXe et Xe siècles (1:4,500,000)
1516 (Reverse) Les Centres Culturels en France (1:1, 120, 000)
1518 La France Romane - La France Gothique
1528 Les Luttes religieuses en France - 1:1, 170, 000
1536 La Révolution Française 1789-1795 (1:1, 760, 000)
1538 La Révolution Françaises 1795-1801 (1:1,760, 000)
1540 La Guerre de 1870/Le Siège de Paris/ La Commune

BREASTED-HUTH-HARDING HISTORICAL MAPS
Various scales
Chicago : Denoyer-Geppert
112 x 81
Series of large col. wall maps printed on manilla.
204261 England and France 1154-1453
204151 Caesar's Gaul
204461 Northern France, Belgium and the Rhine (World War I)

FRANKSKOE GOSUDARSTVO v V - NACHALE IX vv
1:4, 000, 000
Moskva : GUGK, 1973
Historical wall map of the Frankish State in the 5th - 9th C. kop 30
Also : France in the Period of the Bourgeois Republic 1789-1794.
1973
1:2, 500, 000

DAS REICH KARLS DES GROSSEN (814)
1:1, 600, 000
Bielefeld : Cornelsen, Velhagen and Klasing
182 x 142
Putzger historical wall map of Kingdom of Charlemagne
Also : Entwicklung der franzosischen Ostgrenze 1493-1801 (Devt. Fr Borders)
1:550, 000 128 x 205

CAESAR'S CONQUEST OF GAUL
58-50 BC
Indianapolis : Cram
School historical wall map showing Gaul and Caesar's other campaigns.
US $13.75

GALLIEN, GERMANIEN, BRITANNIEN ZUR RÖMERZEIT (GAUL, GERMANY, BRITAIN UNDER THE ROMANS)
1:1, 000, 000
Darmstadt : Perthes
146 x 175
Col. wall map with names in Latin and German. DM 128

GALLIA
1:750, 000
Gotha : Haack, 1954
170 x 157
Historical wall map of Fr, Belgian, Swiss territories in Roman times.
Names in Latin.

CARTE DE LA FRANCE
1:345, 600
In 14 Sheets
Paris : IGN
92 x 60
Reduction of Cassini's map and the "Carte des Pays-Bas Autrichiens" (see Belgium 493M) shows cantons, arrondissements, départements 1816-1821. Copper engraving.
Each F.Fr 60.00

CARTE DES MONTS PYRÉNÉES ET PARTIE DES ROYAUMES DE FRANCE ET D'ESPAGNE
1:216, 000
In 8 sheets
Paris : IGN
55 x 47 each
Copper engraved map of the Pyrénées, by Roussel in 1730.

Each, copper engraving	F.Fr 55.00
Complete	F.Fr 383.00
Offset ed.	F.Fr 27.50
Complete	F.Fr 191.67

CARTE TOPOGRAPHIQUE DE L'ILE DE CORSE
1:100, 000
In 6 sheets
Paris : IGN
50 x 83 each
Tranchot's map of 1824 showing topog. details. With decorative border.

Each	F.Fr 60.00
Complete	F.Fr 308.33
Each, offset ed.	F.Fr 32.50
Complete	F.Fr 170.00

CARTE GÉOMÉTRIQUE DE LA FRANCE (CARTE DE CASSINI)
1:86, 400
In 180 sheets
Paris : IGN
154 sheets at 56 x 90
Facsimile of the map conpiled 1683-1815
Black and white topog. series.

Each	F.Fr 60.00
Half sheet	F.Fr 50.00
Offset sheets	F.Fr 32.50
Offset half sheets	F.Fr 23.33

CARTE GÉOMÉTRIQUE DU HAUT-DAUPHINÉ
1:86, 400 app
In 9 sheets
Paris : IGN
45 x 65
Series compiled 1749-54 by Villaret. Illus. title sheet - animals, people etc. Copper engraving. Topog. details.
Each F.Fr 60.00

CARTE TOPOGRAPHIQUE DE LA GUYENNE
1:43, 000 app
In 51 sheets
Paris : IGN
35 sheets at 56 x 90, 16 half sheets at 56 x 45. Topog. series of the Aquitaine region compiled 1762-83, 1804-13. Copper plates incomplete for the sheets Condom and Villeneuve d'Agen. Copper engraving.

Each	F.Fr 60.00
Half sheet	F.Fr 50.00
Incomplete plates	F.Fr 50.00

PLAN DE PARIS
Paris : IGN
80 x 55
Plan of Paris in 1618 by the Dutch engraver Visscher.

Copper engraving	F.Fr 70.00
Offset ed.	F.Fr 41.67

PARIS 1618
Paris : Girard et Barrers
75 x 105
Facsimile map of the town of Paris by Visscher, with index to major buildings and decorative side borders showing characteristic citizens.

CARTE DES CHASSES DU ROI (CARTE TOPOGRAPHIQUE DES ENVIRONS DE VERSAILLES)
1:28, 800 app
Paris : IGN
47 x 45 each
Map of the environs of Versailles, in cadastral detail. Compiled 1765-68, - 1773. Copper plates engraved 1807.

Copper engraving	F.Fr 65.00
Offset ed	F.Fr 36.67

CARTE DE LA FRANCE ILLUSTRÉE
1:1, 000, 000 app
Paris : Andre Lescot
94 x 94
Col. pictorial map with some relief shading. Departement boundaries in red, with representative pictures for each region. Corsica inset.

N MATHEMATICAL

CARTE DE LA NOUVELLE TRIANGULATION DE LA FRANCE
1:1, 400, 000
Paris : IGN
106 x 73
Shows the advance of the New Triangulation of the 1st, 2nd, 3rd and 4th order. New ed 1st Jan every year. F.Fr 8.00

CARTE DE NIVELLEMENT GÉNÉRAL DE LA FRANCE
1:1, 400, 000
Paris : IGN
106 x 33
General levelling map, new ed 1st Jan every year. Shows the advance of networks of the 1st, 2nd, 3rd and 4th orders.
F.Fr 8.00

ATLASES
A1 ROADS

ATLAS DES GRANDES ROUTES DE FRANCE
1:1, 000, 000
No 999a
Paris : Michelin 1971
11 x 25
38pp
This is the Michelin Main Road Map of France in atlas form.

ATLAS DES AUTOROUTES DE FRANCE
1:200, 000
Paris : Michelin
11 x 25
54pp
Strip road maps covering 1500 km of French autoroutes: road connections, distances, gradients, maximum bridge heights, toll gates, parking, recreational and mechanical facilities, petrol stations etc.

LE GUIDE DE LA ROUTE
Paris : Readers Digest
17 x 29
Detailed road maps cover France, Belgium and Alps at 1:500, 000 (8 miles to 1") and the rest of Europe on a smaller scale, also town plans and a complete index to places. The text describes the car, its maintenance and items of interest to be seen in the countryside. Legend in French.

ATLAS ROUTIER ET TOURISTIQUE - FRANCE, BELGIQUE, LUXEMBOURG, SUISSE
1:500, 000
Paris : Bordas/Taride
22 x 29
76pp col. maps, roads classified, route numbers and distances, railways, ferries and places of tourist interest. No index.

ATLAS ROUTIER
1:500, 000
Paris : Hachette
Road atlas incorporating the 'Les Cartes Bleues' map series in atlas form. Inc. Belgium and Switzerland. No index.

ATLASES
B TOWN PLANS

PARIS PAR ARRONDISSEMENT
Paris : Éditions Ponchet
Atlas of the Paris arrondissement with index to streets and public buildings. Detailed street maps showing one way streets. Contained in plastic wallet.
F.Fr 23.00

ATLASES
D POLITICAL & ADMINISTRATIVE

ATLAS DES DÉPARTEMENTS FRANÇAIS
Paris : Éditions Oberthur, Service AT
21 x 26
Double map for each Department (35 x 23) with information on demography, plan of capital town on the reverse. Also, admin. road maps of France, other thematic maps, overseas territories etc.
F.Fr 34.39
Combines with "La Nomenclature des Communes" (gazetteer) to form "Index-Atlas". F.Fr 44.61

GUIDE BANLIEUE-ORIENTATION
Paris : Éditions Ponchet
Atlas of the Paris Region containing 275 coloured plans of the Communes, new towns and airports 1:15, 000 scale.
Index to roads, numerous facts concerning the administration and life of each commune and a general plan of the whole area covered. Contained in plastic wallet.
F.Fr 46.80

ATLASES
E2 PHYSICAL: LAND FEATURES

ATLAS DES EAUX SOUTERRAINES DE LA FRANCE
Orléans : BRGM/Paris : la Délégation à l'aménagement du territoire et à l'action regionale, 1969
28 x 28
360pp
152 maps divided among 21 large areas showing the state of underground waters with cross sections and mineral sources.
Text and bibliog. F.Fr 210.00

ATLASES
F GEOLOGY

GÉOLOGIE DU BASSIN D'AQUITAINE
Orléans : BRGM
45 x 60
26 coloured geol. maps of the Aqüitaine basin, text in Fr and Eng. To be published June 1973. F.Fr 550.00

ATLAS DES NAPPES AQUIFÈRES DU DISTRICT DE LA RÉGION PARISIENNE
Orléans : BRGM, 1970
In 20 plates
88 x 68
Study of underground water resources in 60 maps, covering 5 periods : Oligocene, Eocene Upper, Eocene Lower, Chalk and Albien. General, geol. and hydrogeological maps at differing scales. 160pp text.
F.Fr 230.00

ATLAS GÉOLOGIQUE DU GISEMENT DE FER DE LORRAINE
Metz : Inst. de Recherches de la Sidérugie
41 x 62 (map size)
26 col. geol. mineral atlas with profiles.
F.Fr 100.00

ATLASES
J CLIMATE

ATLAS CLIMATIQUE DE LA FRANCE
Ed Jean Bessemoulin
Paris : Direction de la Météorologie Nationale, 1969
33 x 53
45 double map plates, covering regions, atmospheric pressure, temperature etc. Tables and diagrams in accompanying texts.

ATLASES
K HUMAN GEOGRAPHY

LES ATLAS LINGUISTIQUES DE LA FRANCE PAR RÉGIONS
Paris : CNRS
Series of linguistic atlases in progress.
Vols. available :
Atlas linguistique et ethnographique du Lyonnais
Ed P Gardette 31 x 45 bound
in 5 vols. Covering agriculture, domestic life, wild life.
In 1320 maps. Text vol. with tables, statistics. Index vol.
Vol 1, 1967 (1st ed 1950)
F.Fr 150.50
Vol 2, 1970 (1st ed 1952)
F.Fr 150.50
Vol 3, 1956 (out of print)
Vol 4, 1969, 188pp F.Fr 39.50
Vol 5, in press

Atlas linguistique et ethnographique de la Gascogne
J Seguy
32 x 50
Covering wild life, industry, agriculture, social factors, food, language, etc. In 6 vols.
Vol 1, 2nd ed, 1965 F.Fr 94.60
Vol 2, 2nd ed 1967 F.Fr 100.00
Vol 3, 2nd ed 1968 F.Fr 120.40
Vol 5, 1972 F.Fr 150.50

L'Atlas Linguistique et ethnographique du Massif Central
by P Nauton
32 x 50
In 5 vols. Covers nature, social aspects, index, etc.
Vol 1, 1959 F.Fr 236.50
Vol 2, 1959 (out of print)
Vol 3, 1961 F.Fr 100.00
Vol 4, 1963 F.Fr 28.00

L'Atlas linguistique et ethnographique des Pyrénées orientales
by H Guiter
32 x 50
1 vol, 1956, 586 maps.
F.Fr 200.00

Atlas linguistique et ethnographique de la Champagne et de la Brie
by H Bourcelot
32 x 50
In 4 vols, covering the land, weather, nature, social aspects etc.
Vol 1, 1966 F.Fr 150.50
Vol 2, 1969 F.Fr 160.20

Atlas linguistique et ethnographique de l'Alsace
by E Beyer and R Matzen
52 x 29
In 6 vols covering various aspects of society, nature, agriculture, grammatical factors, domestic life.
In Fr and Ger.
Vol 1, 1969 264pp F.Fr 139.80

Atlas linguistique et ethnographique du Centre
by P Duboisson
32 x 50
Covering cultural and linguistic matter
Vol 1, 1971 F.Fr 236.50

Atlas linguistique et ethnographique de l'Ouest
by G Massignom and B Horiot
32 x 50
Covering nature, agriculture, domestic life.
Vol 1, 1971 320pp F.Fr 236.50

Atlas linguistique et ethnographique du Jura et des Alpes du Nord
by J B Martin and G Tuaillon
32 x 50
In 4 vols. Covering various atmospheric phenomena, agriculture, domestic activities, farm life. Index vol.
Vol 1, 1971, 320pp F.Fr 279.50

Atlas linguistique et ethnographique du Franco-Provençale
M Tuaillon and N Martin
Vol 1, 1971, 321 maps F.Fr 279.50

Atlas linguistique et ethnographique de la Franche-Comte.
Mme Doudaine (In press)

Atlas linguistique et ethnographique de la Lorraine Germanophone
M Philip (In press)

ATLASES
L ECONOMIC

ATLAS ÉCONOMIQUE ET SOCIAL POUR L'AMÉNAGEMENT DU TERRITOIRE
1:2, 500, 000
In 5 vols
Paris : La Doc, 1969+
45 x 55
To show relation of various regions of France to the rest of the country and to be used in conjunction with the regional atlases.
Vol 1 Démographie, 1968, 52pp
Vol 2 Agriculture, 1970, 96pp covering soil use, text
Vol 3 Industrie - in preparation
Vol 4 Infrastructures, 1967, 48pp
Vol 5 Vie sociale et culturelle - in preparation
Each vol. F.Fr 70.00

COLLECTION ATLAS D'ATTRACTION URBAINE
Paris : Gauthier-Villars, 1967+
Regional collection of marketing features of various rural and urban areas; reasons for peoples attraction to urban areas.

ATLAS D'ATTRACTION URBAINE
Paris : Gauthier-Villars, 1973
Atlas showing commercially attractive areas of the Alsace region.
Result of regional enquiry.
F.Fr 80.00

ATLAS DE LA FRANCE RURALE
Jean Duplex
Paris : 1968
Foundation Nationale des Sciences Politiques
34 x 30
180pp
Covers agricultural economy, rural population etc. 63 maps. In series "Foundation Nationale des Science Politiques". F.Fr 80.00

ATLASES
M HISTORICAL

ATLAS HISTORIQUE ET CULTUREL DE LA FRANCE
by Jacques Boussard
Amsterdam : Elsevier
25 x 35
248pp
Covers Prehistoric - Technical eras.
Over 900 illus and 95 maps - art - history - civilisation. With descriptive text.

'LE THÉATRE FRANCOYS'
Maurice Bougereau, published Tours 1594
Amsterdam : Theatrum Orbis Terrarum
29 x 44
This rare volume which constitutes the first national atlas of France available here in facsimile. The maps are by Gabriel Tavernier and others. 90 pages including 16 double-page maps with bibliographical notes by F de Dainville S. J.

ATLAS HISTORIQUE, PROVENCE, COMITAT, ORANGE, NICE, MONACO
Edouard Baratier, Georges Duby, Ernest Hildesheimer
Paris : Armand Colin, 1969
26 x 32
221pp
Historical atlas of S. East France with 326 maps in a box and 247pp text.

LES ARMÉES FRANCAISES DANS LA 2 ÈME GUERRE MONDIALE CAMPAGNE 1939-1940. ATLAS DES SITUATIONS QUOTIDIENNES DES ARMÉES ALLIÉES
Paris : Atélier d'Impressions de l'Armée, 1967 (1964)
47 folded maps, each with text for selected days from 2nd Sept, 1939 - 25th June, 1940. Shows how allied positions altered daily.

LE DAUPHINÉ ET SES CONFINS VUS PAR L'INGÉNIEUR D'HENRI IV JEAN DE BEINS
Editor R P F de Dainville S.J.
Genève : Librairie Droz/Paris : Librairie Minard, 1968
35 x 25
93pp
76 facsimile plates in portfolio, showing de Beins' maps of the extent of the Kingdom circa 1600. With index to areas covered, 93pp text by François de Dainville S.J.
F.Fr 70.00

ATLAS ADMINISTRATIF DE L'EMPIRE FRANCAIS
Ed F de Dainville and J Tulard
Genève : Librairie Droz, 1973
30 maps on 20 sheets, of a map of 1812 with descriptive text contained in folder.
F.Fr 50.00

ATLASES
O NATIONAL

GRAND ATLAS DE LA FRANCE
Paris : Readers Digest, 1969
28 x 41
244pp
Covering all aspects of the country: relief and vegetation, geol, sociological and economic factors, overseas territories, series of col. plates, statistical section to large scale (19N) map section index.

ATLASES
P REGIONAL

ATLAS DE L'AQUITAINE
Paris : Editions Technip, 1973
In 67 plates
Regional atlas, to be published in 2 parts. Consists of atlas sheets, with descriptive text. Plates divided into 7 sections, covering : geographic physique; population; agriculture; communications; activities secondaires et tertiaires (industry), logement et equipements sociaux; les villes (city statistics). F.Fr 290.00

ATLAS DE L'EST
Ed E Juillard
Nancy : Berger-Levrault, 1969
40 x 37
New edition to conform with other regional atlases. 58 maps in 1-4 col. covering geog, demography, rural and industrial life, communications, resources, social aspects. Based on 1962 and 1968 censuses.
F.Fr 230.00

ATLAS LANGUEDOC-ROUSSILLON
Ed Raymond Dugrand
1:750, 000/1:1, 250, 000
Paris : Berger-Levrault, 1969
45 x 56
In 2 parts : Part 1 with 31 sheets and explanations. Part 2, 34 sheets. Physical and thematic maps covering economy, communications, pop, etc. and descriptive text.

ATLAS RÉGIONAL DES PAYS DE LA LOIRE
Paris : Éditions Technip, 1972
In 63 plates
Atlas covering the Loire lands. In 2 parts: 1st part of 23 plates published in 6 sections : Generalities - Geographie physique; Le milieu humain; Les activities agricoles; Les activities industrielles; Les activities tertiaires (social services); Les villes (cities).
Both parts F.Fr 480.00

L'ATLAS MIDI-PYRÉNÉES
Ed Prof Taillefer
Paris : Berger-Levrault
In 3 vols :
Collection of maps covering various aspects of the physical, cultural and economic geography of the region, approx. 20 maps per section at scale 1:750, 000 with explanation sheets.
Vol 1, 1970
Vol 2, 1971
Vol 3, in preparation

ATLAS DE NORMANDIE
1:50, 000/1:1, 000, 000
Caen : Univ. Inst. Geog, 1966-70
In 3 parts with app. 65pp thematic maps and explanations. Covering pop, industry, climate, communications etc. in single sheets.
Complete F.Fr 250.00

ATLAS DU BASSIN PARISIEN
Paris : Groupe Interministeriel pour l'amenagement du Bassin Parisien, 1970
43 x 32
31 maps covering physical and administrative matters for planning purposes.
F.Fr 130.00

ATLAS DE PARIS ET DE LA RÉGION PARISIENNE
Ed J Beaujeau-Garnier and J Bastie
Prep. by l'Association Universitaire de Recherches Géographiques et Cartographiques
Paris : Berger-Levrault, 1968
28 x 19
964pp
92 sheets 67 x 55 containing 400 maps of the whole region - City and Greater Paris. General, topographical, planning, pop, transport and power, agriculture, industry, social aspects and the role of Paris.

ATLAS DE LA RÉGION RHÔNE-ALPES
Lyon : Assoc. pour l'Atlas de la Région R-A, 1972
In 3 parts
38 x 55
Part 1 only available, 26 maps covering wine and other industries. Whole atlas will contain 75 sheets. Part 2 will cover industry, demography, social and urban aspects; Part 3, communications, tourism etc.

45 Italy

See also: 4 EUROPE

A1 GENERAL MAPS: ROADS

TRAVELLER'S MAP OF ITALY
1:1, 875, 000
Washington : NGS, 1970
58 x 83
Historic landmarks, city plans, index descriptive notes.

ITALIEN
1:1, 500, 000
No 385
Hamburg : Falk
Falk patent folded road map; roads classified and numbered, distances in km, places of interest. DM 6.80

ITALIEN
1:1, 500, 000
No 203
Koln : Polyglott
57 x 76
Classifies roads, distances in km, with camp sites. DM 3.20

ITALIE
1:1, 500, 000
Praha : Kart
Roads classified and numbered, distances in km, motoring and tourist information. Kcs 12.50

CARTA PANORAMICA E STRADALE ITALIA
1:1, 400, 000
Udine : Tabacco
84 x 96
Coloured map with relief shading, roads in red, places of tourist interest, photos around border. Legend It, Fr, Ger. L 580

OLASZORSZÁG AUTOTÉRKÉPE
1:1, 250, 000
Budapest : Cart, 1970
70 x 100
Col. road map in 6 langs.

CARTA STRADALE D'ITALIA
1:1, 000, 000
Firenze : IGM, 1962
107 x 146 complete
2 sheet road map showing relief by hypsometric tints, distances in km, roads classified.
Each L 860

ITALIA
1:1, 000, 000
Novara : Ag
Tourist road map with 21 city insets. L 700

ITALIEN
1:1, 000, 000
Bern : Hallwag
84 x 101
All classes of roads with distances in km, spot heights in metres, hill shading, railways, car ferries and main car camping sites. Insets of Rome, Venice and Milan.

ITALIEN
1:1, 000, 000
No 1138
Bern : K & F
87 x 129
All classes of roads, distances in km, hill shading, railways, car ferries, camping sites and motels. Inset plans of Rome, Florence, Milan, Genoa, Naples, Turin and Palermo.

ITALIE - SUISSE GRANDES ROUTES
1:1, 000, 000
No 988
Paris : Michelin
109 x 99
All classes of roads, road conditions, widths and route numbers, distances in km, scenic routes, car ferries, airports and state boundaries.

ITALY
1:1, 000, 000 - 1:600, 000
London : Foldex
Two road maps; roads classified, relief shading; patent fold.
Each 45p

CARTA AUTOMOBILISTICA D'ITALIA
1:800, 000
In 2 sheets
Milano : TCI
86 x 80
Road map, revised annually. 2 sheets :
C92 Italia Settentrionale e Centrale fino a sud di Roma
C93 Roma, Italia Meridionale e Insulare
Each L 850

ITALIEN
1:800, 000
No 88
Stuttgart : RV
82 x 92
All classes of roads, numbers, conditions and distances, railways, airports, motels and camping sites. Printed on both sides, North and South; insets of Sardinia, Corsica and 11 town plans.
Paper folded DM 6.80

ITALIEN
1:800, 000
No 878
Stuttgart : Ravenstein
80 x 100
Double-sided road map, classifying roads, with distances in km, also other communications and places of interest.
DM 7.80

ITALIA - CARTA STRADALE
1:750, 000
In 4 sheets
Novara : Ag
175 x 175 complete
Road map in plastic cover with legend in Italian, German, English, French and Spanish. L 700

ITALIEN
1:650, 000
Wien : FB, 1973
Roads classified with route numbers and distances and places of interest.

CARTE GENERALE D'ITALIA
1:500, 000
In 4 sheets, see index 45/1
Milano : TCI
All classes of roads, distances in km, railways, layer colouring.
Legend in Italian. Also includes an index.
Varying sizes,
paper folded, each L 1200

ITALIA : CARTA STRADALE
1:500, 000
In 4 sheets
Novara : Ag
Road map, with route numbers and distances. With 22 city plans inset.
L 900

SHELL REISEKARTE ITALIEN
1:500, 000
Stuttgart : Mairs
87 x 48
Double-sided col. map, showing all classes of roads, relief shading, places of interest etc. Legend in 12 langs. Insets 1:750, 000, 1:850, 000. DM 4.80

LES CARTES BLEUES
1:500, 000
In 3 sheets
Paris : Hachette
Classifies roads, distances in km, tourist details.
Sheets :
5 Marseille - Cote d'Azur - Rome -Venice
6 Rome - Naples - Tarente - Messine
7 Naples - Reggio - Sicile - Sandaigue - Tunis

CARTA AUTOMOBILISTICA D'ITALIA
1:200, 000
In 28 sheets, see index 45/2
Milano : TCI
132 x 90 each sheet
All classes of roads, distances in km, spot heights, towns of tourist interest, railways and hill shading. Legend in It.
Each L 700

GRANDI CARTI
1:200, 000
Milano : TCI
132 x 89
Series covering tourist areas, based on an assemblage of 2 or more 200, 000 road map series, with increased tourist info. In 6 col.
Sheets published :
D11 Milano e sue mete turistiche
D12 Dolmeti, Alto Adige, Carnia, Garda, Venezia
D13 Da Torino e Milano alla Riviera Ligure
D14 Rome e le sue mete turistiche
D15 Mete turistiche in Toscana e Umbria
D16 Planura padana da Milano all' Adriatico
Each L 1450

A2 GENERAL MAPS: LOCAL

STRASSENKARTE ITALIEN - ALPENLANDER
1:750, 000
No 1774
Munchen : JRO
123 x 88
Double sided road map, with roads numbered and classified. Other tourist details, relief shading. DM 9.80

CARTA TURISTICA DELLE DOLOMITI
1:650, 000
Novara : Ag
70 x 50
Tourist road map of the Dolomites with relief shading. L 400

CARTA PANORAMICA E STRADALE DOLOMITI
1:650, 000
Udine : Tabacco
60 x 80
Panoramic relief map of the Dolomites, showing roads, settlements etc. Coloured photos of the area form a border with description in Italian and German. Reverse has road map of the area.
L 350
In same style covering Monte Bianco, Cervino - M Rosa, Alpi Italo - Franco - Svizzere.

CARTA AUTOMOBILISTICA DEL PIEMONTE, LOMBARDIA, LIGURIA
1:600, 000
Udine : Tabacco
77 x 68
Coloured map covering the area from the Border to Lake Geneva.
L 250

NORD ITALIEN
1:600, 000
Bern : Hallwag, 1972
109 x 81
Col. road map, showing road types, numbers, distances; relief shading; camping sites and other tourist information.
85p

ALPINA III - CENTRAL ALPS
1:600, 000
Bern : Hallwag
112 x 84
Covering Switzerland, Western Austria and Italy as far south as Florence. All classes of roads, distances in km, hill shading, railways, car ferries and car camping sites.

SCHWEIZ - NORDITALIEN
1:600, 000
F-B
see SWITZERLAND 494 A1.

NORDITALIEN
1:500, 000
No 1118
Bern : K & F
86 x 129
From Swiss border to Rome. All classes of roads, distances in km, hill shading, places of interest, car ferries, camping sites and motels.

SÜDITALIEN
1:500, 000
No 1124
Bern : K & F
86 x 126
From Rome south; inc. inset of Sardinia at 1:687, 500. All classes of roads, distances in km, places of interest, car ferries, camping sites and motels.
Paper folded

ÖSTERREICH UND NÖRDLICHES ITALIEN
1:450, 000
No 1436
JRO
see AUSTRIA 436 A1

OBERITALIEN
1:400, 000
No 1481
Munchen : JRO
123 x 88
Col. map of N Italy. Roads classified and numbered, distances in km, places of interest, railways, boundaries.
DM 6.80

SCHWEIZ - TIROL
1:400, 000
RV
see SWITZERLAND 494 A1.

LE VENEZIE - CARTE STRADALE
1:350, 000
Novara : Ag
Tourist road map of Venice and surroundings
L 400

LE AUTOSTRADE D'ITALIA
1:300, 000
Milano : TCI
Motorway strip maps showing adjacent road system. Access and exit points on one side is outward route north to south, on reverse names are inverted to show return route south to north.
Maps available :
100 L'Autostrada del Sole, 1966
101 Torino - Milano, Milano - Venezia, Milano - Genova, Bologna - Rimini, 1967
Each L 850

CARTA REGIONALE
Various scales
Firenze : Litografia a Artistica Cartografica
Regional road map series, relief shaded with touring information and places of interest.
Maps available :
Abruzzo e Molise
1:300, 000 58 x 74
Calabria
1:300, 000 55 x 86
Compania
1:300, 000 58 x 74
Emilia-Romagna
1:300, 000 70 x 100
Friuli-Venezia Giulia
1:200, 000 64 x 72
Lazio
1:300, 000 64 x 88
Liguria
1:350, 000 64 x 88
Lombardia
1:350, 000 64 x 88
Marche
1:200, 000 75 x 79
Molise
1:100, 000 80 x 120
Piemonte
1:350, 000 64 x 88
Puglie e Basilicata
1:350, 000 70 x 93
Sardegna
1:350, 000 64 x 88
Sicilia
1:350, 000 64 x 88
Toscana
1:350, 000 70 x 90
Tre Venezie
1:350, 000 70 x 90
Umbria
1:200, 000 58 x 74
Valle d'Aosta
1:150, 000 50 x 70

DOLOMITEN - ADRIA
1:250, 000
Munchen : Kompass
Regional road map, relief shaded, covering the area from the Dolomites to the Adriatic Coast. DM 4.90

CARTE STRADALE DELLE ZONE TOURISTICHE ITALIANE
1:250, 000
Novara : Ag
Tourist road maps, available for the following areas :
Riviera di Levante
Riviera di Ponente
Versilia
Riviera Adriatica
Laghi Prealpini I (Cusio, Verbano, Lario e Laghi minori)
Laghi Prealpini II (Iseo, Idro et Garda)
Laguna Veneta
Golfi di Napoli e Salerno
Each L 400

VALLE D'AOSTA
1:250, 000
Novara : Ag
Road map in Fr and It. L 120

GENERALKARTE
1:200, 000
Stuttgart : Mair
Various sizes
Showing all classes of roads, distances in km, route numbers, railways, car ferries, places of tourist interest, scenic routes, nature reserves, hotels, airports and state boundaries
Sheets published :
Sudtirol
Oberitalische Seen
Italische Riviera
Italische Adria
Gardasee-Venedig

OBERITALIEN
1:200, 000
Bern : Hallwag
94 x 47
Col. map showing all classes of roads and passes. Covers Lake Garda - Verona - Venice
Spot heights, relief shading.

SUISSE
1:200, 000
No 26
Paris : Michelin
108 x 48
Martigny to Morbegno and Bessans to Pandino. All classes of roads, road conditions and numbers, paths, distances in km, spot heights in metres, airports, scenic routes, state boundaries.
see also SWITZERLAND 494 A1

CARTA AUTOMOBILISTICA
Various scales
Bologna : Studio FMB
Series of col. tourist maps showing roads, relief shading and tourist details.
Maps available :

Adriatic Riviera	1:200, 000	100 x 70
Lake Como	1: 75, 000	70 x 50
Lake Maggiore	1: 75, 000	74 x 58
Lake Garda	1:120, 000	84 x 64
Lake Garda	1: 80, 000	100 x 70
La Maddalena	1: 25, 000	58 x 74
Costa Esmeralda	1:120, 000	100 x 70
Isola d'Elba	1: 40,000	58 x 74

Island of Elba, with Guide in English.

CARTA PROVINCIALI
Various Scales
Firenze : Litografia Artistica Cartografia
Series of large scale maps of the provinces showing all classes of roads with relief shading, boundaries and tourist information.
Maps available :

PIEMONTE		
Alessandria	1:150, 000	58 x 74
Asti	1:100, 000	58 x 74
Cuneo	1:150, 000	64 x 88
Novara	1:150, 000	64 x 88
Torino	1:150, 000	70 x 90
Vercelli	1:150, 000	58 x 74
VALLE D'AOSTA	1:150, 000	50 x 70
LOMBARDIA		
Bergamo	1:150, 000	50 x 70
Brescia	1:150, 000	64 x 88
Como	1:100, 000	58 x 74
Cremona	1:150, 000	50 x 70
Mantova	1:150, 000	58 x 74
Milano	1:150, 000	58 x 74
Pavia	1:150, 000	58 x 74
Sondrio	1:125, 000	70 x 100
Varese	1:100, 000	50 x 70
VENETO		
Belluno	1:150, 000	58 x 74
Padova	1:150, 000	50 x 70
Rovigo	1:150, 000	58 x 74
Treviso	1:100, 000	64 x 82
Venezia	1:150, 000	64 x 88
Verona	1:150, 000	58 x 74
Vicenza	1:100, 000	64 x 88
TRENTINO ALTO-ADIGE		
Bolzano	1:200, 000	64 x 88
Trento	1:150, 000	64 x 88
LIGURIA		
Genova	1:125, 000	53 x 80
Imperia	1:100, 000	50 x 70
La Spezia	1:100, 000	50 x 70
Savona	1:125, 000	50 x 70
EMILIA ROMAGNA		
Bologna	1:150, 000	58 x 74
Ferrara	1:150, 000	50 x 70
Forli	1:150, 000	50 x 70
Modena	1:150, 000	58 x 74
Parma	1:150, 000	58 x 74
Piacenza	1:100, 000	72 x 102
Ravenna	1:100, 000	64 x 88
Reggio Emilia	1:150, 000	50 x 70
TOSCANA		
Arezzo	1:150, 000	58 x 74
Firenze	1:150, 000	58 x 74
Grosseto	1:150, 000	64 x 73
Livorno	1:100, 000	64 x 88
Lucca	1:100, 000	58 x 74
Massa-Carrara	1:100, 000	50 x 70
Pisa	1:100, 000	64 x 88
Pistoia	1:100, 000	50 x 70
Siena	1:150, 000	58 x 74
MARCHE		
Ancona	1:150, 000	50 x 70
Ascoli P	1:150, 000	50 x 70
Macerata	1:150, 000	50 x 70
Pesaro	1:150, 000	50 x 70
LAZIO		
Frosinone	1:150, 000	58 x 74
Latina	1:150, 000	50 x 80
Rieti	1:100, 000	73 x 90
Roma	1:150, 000	64 x 88
Viterbo	1:100, 000	80 x 92
ABRUZZO		
Chieti	1:100, 000	64 x 88
L'Aquila	1:150, 000	66 x 80
Pescara	1:100, 000	52 x 70
Teramo	1:100, 000	58 x 74
MOLISE		
Campobasso	1:125, 000	58 x 74
Isernia	1:125, 000	50 x 70
CAMPANIA		
Avelino	1:100, 000	70 x 90
Benevento	1:100, 000	58 x 74
Caserta	1:100, 000	67 x 88
Napoli	1:100, 000	58 x 74
Salerno	1:150, 000	70 x 90
PUGLIE		
Bari	1:150, 000	64 x 88
Brindisi	1:100, 000	60 x 72
Foggia	1:150, 000	70 x 96
Lecce	1:100, 000	70 x 90
Taranto	1:100, 000	70 x 100
BASILICATA		
Matera	1:150, 000	50 x 70
Potenza	1:150, 000	63 x 96
CALABRIA		
Catanzaro	1:200, 000	64 x 82
Cosenza	1:200, 000	64 x 74
Reggio, Calabria	1:150, 000	58 x 74
SICILIA		
Agrigento	1:150, 000	58 x 74
Caltanissetta	1:150, 000	58 x 74
Catania	1:150, 000	58 x 74
Enna	1:150, 000	58 x 74
Messina	1:150, 000	64 x 88

Palermo
1:150, 000 64 x 88
Ragusa
1:150, 000 58 x 74
Siracusa
1:150, 000 58 x 74
Trapani
1:150, 000 58 x 74

CARTE TURISTICHE
Various scales
Firenze : Litografia Artistica Cartografica
Series of topog. regional maps of tourist areas.
Maps available :
Golfo di La Spezia e 5 Terre
1:40, 000 59 x 98
Golfo Tigullio
1:25, 000 50 x 70
Isola d'Elba
1:50, 000 44 x 64
Isola d'Ischia
1:20, 000 50 x 70
Lago di Garda
1:150, 000 37 x 58
Lunigiana
1:55, 000 70 x 100
Massa-Carrara e dint.
1:35, 000 58 x 74
Penisola Sorrentina
1:35, 000 64 x 88
Torino e dint.
1:35, 000 54 x 74
Versilia
1:35, 000 58 x 74

LAGO DI GARDA
1:120, 000
Novara : Ag
Tourist road map of Lake Garda and environs. L 400

WANDERKARTEN
1:100, 000
Wien : FB
see AUSTRIA 436 A2

CARTE DELLE ZONE TURISTICHE
1:50, 000
Milano : TCI
Various sizes
Topog. series showing ski-routes, hill shading, contours, spot heights, footpaths, tourist cabins and mountain huts. Legend in It.
Sheets available :
D54 Cortina d'Ampezzo e le Dolomiti Cadorine
D55 Il Cervino e il Monte Rosa
D56 Val Gardena, Marmolada, Catinaccio, Gruppe di Selle
D58 Il Golfo di Napoli I (Naples, Vesuvius, Ischia)
D59 Il Golfo di Napoli II (Sorrento, Salerno, Capri)
D60 San Martino di Castrozza e zone adiacenti
D61 Gruppo del Monte Bianco
D62 Gruppo Ortles-Cevedale
D63 Gruppo Adamello-Presanella
D64 Gruppo di Brenta
Gruppo delle Grigne, 1:20, 000
Dintorni di Roma, 1:100, 000 (L 750)
L 850

WANDERKARTEN
1:50, 000
München : Kompass
see AUSTRIA 436 A2.

LAGO MAGGIORE UND TESSIN
1:100, 000
No 682
München : JRO
40 x 85
Walking map covering Locarno, Ascona, Brissago, Pallanza, Stresa, Arona, Luino, Borrmeische Inseln. Relief shading. Shows roads, tourist information.
DM 2.50

LAGO MAGGIORE, LUGANER UND COMER SEE
1:100, 000
No 684
München : JRO
79 x 58
Covers Lugano, Collina d'Oro, Vedeggiotal, Tesserete, Como, Bellagio, Tremezzo, Cadenabbia, Gravedona, Lecco, Varenna
Walking map showing paths and various tourist details. DM 3.00

GARDASEE
1:150,000
No 783
München : JRO
55 x 60
Covers Lake Garda, Brescia, Verona, Trient. "Excursion" map, with roads, places of interest, relief shading.
DM 2.50

GARDASEE
No 546
München : JRO
41 x 60
Birds eye view map of Lake Garda. Land formation and relief, roads, settlements, water features.
DM 1.50

CARTE SENTIERI E RIFUGI
1:50, 000
In 7 sheets
Udine : Tabacco
Various sizes
Italian and German lang. maps showing roads, distances, paths, spot heights in metres, accommodation, vegetation colouring, relief contours. Available for :
1 Cortina - Cadore - Dolomiti di Sesto, 70 x 100 L 500
2 Val Gardena - Alpe di Siusi-Marmolada, 70 x 100
L 500
3 Bolzano - Mendola - Alpe di Siusi
4 Trento-Pale di S Martino-Belluno (in prep)
5 Catena del Monte Bianco
70 x 100 L 550
6 Alpi Italo - Franco-Suizzere
7 Monte Cervino - M Rosa

IL GRUPPO DEL BERNINA
Novara : Ag
Panoramic view map of the area, showing relief, roads and footpaths.
L 400

B TOWN PLANS

ITALY TOWN PLANS
Various scales
Bologna : FMB unless stated otherwise.
Col. plans with index to streets.
Maps available :
Ancona 1: 7, 500
Bari 1:10, 000
Bologna Commune 1:18, 000
Bologna 1:16, 000
Bologna 1:13, 000
Bolzana 1: 6, 000 Tabacco
Brescia 1:10, 000
Cagliari 1: 9, 000
Carpi 1: 6, 000
Cesana 1: 8, 000
Como 1:10, 000
Cremona 1: 6, 500
Ferrara 1: 8, 000
Firenze Commune 1:12, 500 LAC
100 x 70 - 2 sheets
Firenze 1:10, 000
Firenze 1: 9, 000 LAC
70 x 50
Firenze 1: 9, 000 LAC
100 x 70
Forli 1:15, 000
Genova 1:12, 000
Genova 1:10, 000
Visceglia 75 x 51
La Spezia 1: 8, 500
Livorno 1:10, 000
Lugo 1: 5, 000
Manitova 1: 7, 000
Mestre-Marghera 1:12, 000
Milano 1:20, 000
Milano 1:15, 000 Ag
Milano 1:13, 500 Hallwag
Milan (Mailand) 1:12, 000/1:40, 000
Falk
Modena 1:12, 000
Napoli 1:10, 000 Vincintorio
Napoli 1:10, 000 LAC
74 x 58
Napoli 1:10, 000 LAC
100 x 70
Napoli Commune 1:10, 000 LAC
105 x 75
Novara 1: 7, 500 Ag
Padova 1:13, 000
Parma 1: 8, 000 LAC
85 x 64
Perugia 1: 6, 500
Pesaro 1: 8, 000
Pescara 1: 8, 000
Piacenza 1:10, 000
Pisa 1: 9, 000
Pisa 1: 8, 000 LAC
90 x 70
Pompei 1: 4, 000 LAC
63 x 43
Pontedera 1: 5, 000
Prato 1:13, 500
Ravenna 1: 7, 000
Reggio-Emilia 1:12, 000
Riccione 1:10, 000
Rimini 1:10, 000
Rome and Vatican City
Foldex and Miniplan
Roma 1:18, 000
Vincintorio
Roma 1:13, 000 Tabacco
Roma 1:12, 000/1:20, 000
Polyglott
Roma 1:12, 500/1:35, 000
Falk
Roma 1:12, 500 Hallwag
Roma 1:12, 500 Ag
Roma 1:12, 000 Verdesi
80 x 102
Sassari 1: 5, 000
Savona 1: 6, 000
Siena 1: 7, 500
Sorrento 1: 6, 000 87 x 35
Torino 1:20, 000
Vincintorio
Torino 1:15, 000
Torino 1:15, 000 Ag
Treviso 1:10, 000
Trieste 1:30, 000
Vincintorio
Venezia 1: 6, 000 Tabacco
Verona 1:13, 000
Viareggio 1:10, 000

C OFFICIAL SURVEYS

KARTA MIRA
1:2, 500, 000
VVK
3 sheets to cover Italy
see WORLD 100C and index 100/2.

THE WORLD
1:1, 000, 000
DMS Series 1301
6 sheets needed for coverage
see WORLD 100C and index 100/1.

THE WORLD
1:500, 000
DMS Series 1404
18 sheets needed for complete coverage.
see WORLD 100C and index 100/7.

CARTA DELLE REGIONI D'ITALIA
1:250, 000
Firenze : IGM, 1935
Hypsometric tint maps available for: Calabria, Campania, Emilia, Lazio-Abruzzo, Liguria, Piemonte, Sardegna.
NB New editions have been issued for : Lombardia 1971, Sardegna 1963, Trentino - Alto Adige 1971, Friuli-Venezia Giulia 1971, Veneto 1971.

CARTA STRADALE D'ITALIA
1:200, 000
In 67 sheets, see index 45/3
Firenze : IGM
80 x 55 each
Topog. road series in 11 colours, not inc. Sardinia. Vegetation in green, roads classified by col, distances in km, spot heights in metres, relief shading, contours in grey, province boundaries.
Each L 600

CARTA TOPOGRAFICA D'ITALIA
1:100, 000
In 278 sheets, see index 45/4
Firenze : IGM
60 x 57 each
Official topog. series contoured with new sheets showing roads in red, available in 3 eds.
Contoured ed. with relief shading
Contoured ed.
Ed. with admin. boundaries overprinted in purple
Each L 800
Conventional sign sheet (1955)
L 1, 300

CARTA TOPOGRAFICA D'ITALIA
1:50, 000
See index 45/5
Firenze : IGM
72 x 61 each
Topog. series in progress, based on 1:25, 000 maps. Contoured at 25m intervals, relief shading, UTM grid.
Each sheet L 800

CARTA TOPOGRAFICA D'ITALIA
1:25, 000
In 3, 556 sheets
Firenze : IGM
Topog. series covering the whole country, sheets are 1/16th of standard 1:100, 000 map. Available in 3 eds :
Black and white, showing contours, topog. features, UTM grid in purple.
Old style lettering.
3 coloured ed: topog. detail black, water features blue, contours brown.
5 coloured : supersedes other 2 eds.
Vegetation in green, roads in red.
Each L 700
Conventional sign sheet (3 colour ed)
1960 L 650
Conventional sign sheet (5 colour ed)
1963 L 1, 100

CARTA DELLE VALANGHE
1:100, 000
In 24 sheets
Firenze : IGM
60 x 57 each
Special sheets from the 1:100, 000 Topog. Series, showing avalanche areas, their courses etc.
Each L 800

ROMA E DINTORNI
1:100, 000
Firenze : IGM, 1954
84 x 111
Coloured and contoured map of Rome and environs. L 1000

ZONA AD EST DI ROMA
1:100, 000
Firenze : IGM, 1954
84 x 111
Coloured map with contours.
L 1000

CARTE LOCALI
Various scales
Firenze : IGM
Various sizes
Pianta di Firenze, 1:8, 000, 1964
(1966 ed showing 1966 flood level)
L 700
Carta topografica della Calabria
1:10, 000, 1957, 54 x 46
L 290
Carta topografica dell'Isola di Capri
1:10, 000, 1957, 54 x 37
L 430
Carta topografica di Firenze e dintorni
1:250, 000, 1967, 72 x 52
L 800

REPUBLICA DI SAN MARINO
1:25, 000
Firenze : IGM, 1949
42 x 49
Shows roads, tracks, hill shading, contours, boundaries, railways. L 390

TURIN
1:25, 000
Firenze : IGM
79 x 74 each
2 maps : Torino e zona ouest (1950). Torino e zona est (1951). Coloured maps, with contours. L 750

MONTE BIANCO
1:25, 000
In 6 sheets
Firenze : IGM, 1948
40 x 45 each
Coloured topog. map series.
Complete L 2150

MONTE CERVINO
1:25, 000
Firenze : IGM, 1961
58 x 49
Coloured map, with contours.
L 700

CORTINA D'AMPEZZO E DINTORNI
1:25, 000
Firenze : IGM, 1955
80 x 59
Coloured map with relief shading.
Available till stocks exhausted.
L 860
With tourist overprint L 960

ISOLO DI PANTELLERIA
1:10, 000
In 4 sheets
Firenze : IGM, 1943
67 x 76 each
Black and white map, contoured.
L 500

D POLITICAL & ADMINISTRATIVE

ITALIA POLITICA
1:5, 000, 000
Novara : Ag
33 x 26
Moulded plastic relief map, with physical and geopolitical details on reverse.
L 450

UMRISSKARTE ITALIEN
1:3, 000, 000
No 0820
Bern : K & F
37 x 45
Outline map with rivers and boundaries.

ITALIA FISICO- POLITICO-ADMMINISTRATIVA
1:1, 250, 000
Novara : Ag
86 x 106
School wall map showing relief of land and sea, political and administrative boundaries.
L 1750
Mounted L 3500

CARTA D'ITALIA
1:1, 250, 000
Milano : TCI
87 x 100
Col. map showing provincial boundaries.
L 750
Mounted for hanging L 1200

ITALIA POLITICA
1:1, 000, 000
Novara : Ag
125 x 160
2 sheet wall map for schools, showing relief shading, admin. boundaries, rivers, major communications, spot heights in metres, towns graded by pop. 1st series.
L 3000
Mounted L 4500
Second series showing similar details at 1:700, 000 (In 4 sheets)
180 x 215 L 4000
Mounted L 8500
Third series 1:1, 000, 000, 100 x 140,
L 2200
Mounted L 5000

ITALIA
1:1,000, 000
Torino : Paravia
111 x 147
Col. by departments, cities graded by pop, mountains and communications shown.

ITALIA DIVISIONI AMMINISTRATIVE REGIONALI E PROVINCIAL
1:1, 000, 000
Milano : Elmo
100 x 119
Showing different types of administrative boundaries.

CARTA D'ITALIA, EDIZIONE "MUTA"
1:1, 000, 000
Firenze : IGM
107 x 146 complete
2 sheet map on Bonnes' projection, with subdued colouring.
Each L 800

ITALIA
1:600, 000
Torino : Paravia
172 x 208
Wall map col. by departments, relief indicated by hachures, communications.

ITALIA
1:5, 000, 000
Novara : Ag
Small hand outline map.
L 40

ITALIA
1:2, 000, 000
Novara : Ag
4 small regional outline maps.
Italia Settentrionale
Centrale
Meridionale
Insulare
Each L 40

ITALIA
Barcelona : Editorial Teide
25 x 33
Outline map for schools.
S.Ptas 1

E1 PHYSICAL:
RELIEF

L'ITALIA NEL MEDITERRANEO
1:3, 000, 000
Novara : Ag
170 x 100
School wall map showing physical relief, political boundaries, major communications, cities graded by pop. L 3000
L 6000

CARTA D'ITALIA
1:2, 000, 000
Firenze : IGM, 1956
54 x 70
Topog. map, contoured, communications and settlement. L 700

ITALIE
1:1, 500, 000
Groningen : Wolters Noordhoff
85 x 107
Physical wall map for schools; relief shading, boundaries, communications.
Fl. 44.75

ITALIE
1:1, 500, 000
Praha : Kart
Physical/political reference map, in series "Poznávame Svet" (Getting to know the world). With thematic text vol.
Kcs 16

ITALIE (PHYSIQUE)
1:1, 000, 000
No 1178 in French, 1179 in Italian
St Germain-en-Laye : Éditions MDI
92 x 126
Plastic coated physical wall map for schools. Economic map on reverse.

LES GRANDES PUISSANCES : ESPAGNE
1:1, 000, 000
Editions MDI
See SPAIN 460 E1

ITALIEN UND SUDOSTEUROPA
1:1, 000, 000
München : Wenschow
225 x 175
Inc. Italy, Greece etc. showing relief and elevation, boundaries, railways, cities graded by pop. DM 142

ITALIA
1:1, 000, 000
Torino : Paravia
99 x 139
Physical map showing elevations, regional boundaries.

ITALIA FISICA
1:1, 000, 000
Novara : Ag
125 x 156
2 sheet physical wall map for schools.
First series. L 3000
Mounted L 6500
Second series, 1:700, 000 (in 4 sheets)
180 x 215 L 4000
Mounted L 8500
Third series, 1:1, 000, 000. 100 x 140
L 2200
Mounted L 5000

ITALIA
1:900, 000
Braunschweig : Westermann
160 x 195
Physical wall map with legend etc. in It. Relief shown by layer col, cities graded by pop, communications.

ITALIEN
1:750, 000
Gotha : Haack, 1967
185 x 192
Physical wall map, inc. Italian Islands. Layer col, communications.
DM 128

ITALIA : FISICO-POLITICA
1:700, 000
In 4 sheets
Novara : Ag
180 x 215 complete
School wall map showing relief of land and sea, admin areas, water features, major communications, cities graded by pop.
L 4000
Mounted L 8500

ITALIA
1:600, 000
Torino : Paravia
167 x 203
Physical wall map, showing elevations in col, physical features, glaciers, rivers.

ITALIA FISICA
Barcelona : Editorial Teide
25 x 33
School hand map showing boundaries, major cities etc. S.Ptas 1

ITALIA FISICA
1:5, 000, 000
Novara : Ag
33 x 26
Plastic relief map, with physical details on reverse. L 350

ITALIA POLITICA
1:5, 000, 000
Ag
Moulded plastic relief map.
see ITALY 45 D

L'ITALIA E LE SUE REGIONI
1:2, 500, 000
Novara : Ag
10 x 15
Moulded plastic relief map of Italy in 16 sheets in box with magnifying glass.
L 1800

PLASTICO D'ITALIA
1:1, 250, 000
Firenze : IGM
93 x 133
Fully col. moulded plastic raised relief map in one sheet. Vertical exaggeration x 6¼.
L 15000

PLASTICI DELLE REGIONI D'ITALIA
1:1, 250, 000
Novara : Ag
28 x 21
Small scale regional moulded plastic relief maps; with physical, political, economic details on reverse.
Maps available :
Piemonte e Valle d'Aosta
Liguria
Lombardia
Venezie
Emilia Romagna
Toscana
Marche e Umbria
Arbruzzo e Molise
Lazio
Compania
Puglia e Basilicata
Calabria
Sicilia
Sardegna
Each L 450

ITALIA FISICO-POLITICO
1:1, 100, 000
Novara : Ag, 1969
136 x 100
Moulded plastic relief map, physical-political col. with communications, admin. boundaries. L 20, 000

PLASTICI GEOGRAFICI
1:350, 000
Novara : Ag
74 x 91 (91 x 74)
Plastic relief maps, with vertical scale 1:100, 000. With metal corners. Available in regions for:
Piemonte e Valle d'Aosta
Liguria
Lombardia
Trentino - Alto Adige e Venezie (103 x 84)
Emilia - Romagna
Toscana
Marche e Umbria
Arbruzzi e Molise
Lazio
Campania
Puglia e Basilicata (103 x 84)
Calabria
Sicilia (103 x 84)
Sardegna
Each L 15,000

PLASTICI E MINERALI
Various scales
Novara : Ag
37 x 32
Moulded plastic relief maps with minerals, specimens from areas shown. Political/ physical details on reverse.

Valle d'Aosta	1:300, 000
Dolomiti	1:250, 000
Isola d'Elba	1:250, 000
Roma e dintorni	1:250, 000
Golfo di Napoli	1:250, 000
Sardegna	1:1, 000, 000
Each	L 1000

LOMBARDIA
1:250, 000
Firenze : IGM, 1967
101 x 94
Plastic relief map of the Lombardy area.
L 15, 000

LAZIO
1:200, 000
Firenza : IGM
114 x 48
Moulded plastic relief map of the area.
L 21, 000

PLASTICI NORMALI
Various scales
see index 45/4 and 45/5
Firenze : IGM
Various sizes
Some sheets from the 1:50, 000 and 100, 000 topog. series and all the 200, 000 topog. series have been produced in plastic relief editions.

1:100, 000/200, 000	each	L 4, 600
1:50, 000	each	L 5, 500

ROMA E DINTORNI, PLASTICI
1:100, 000
Firenze : IGM
90 x 122
Moulded plastic relief map of parts of sheets 143, 144, 149, 150 and 158 of the topog. series. L 24, 300

ZONA AD EST DI ROMA, PLASTICI
1:100, 000
Firenze : IGM
90 x 122
Plastic relief map of parts of sheets 145, 146, 151, 152, 159 and 160.
L 24, 300

PLASTICI
1:25, 000
Firenze : IGM
Plastic relief maps of special regions:

Cortina d'Ampezzo 81 x 61	L 27, 200
Monte Bianco 49 x 52	L 24, 300
Monte Cervino 58 x 49	L 24, 300

E2 PHYSICAL: LAND FEATURES

CARTA DELLE IRRIGAZIONI D'ITALIA
by A Antonietti et al
1:750, 000
In 15 sheets
Roma : Inst. Nat di Economia Agraria, 1965
Various sizes
To accompany 351pp report. Base map contoured and layered with 3 major irrigation types and land affected 1:2, 500, 000 derived map of whole country.

CARTA DELLE IRRIGAZIONI
Roma : SII
In 5 parts :
Carta delle irrigazioni nella regione Calabro-Lucana
Carta della irrigazioni Marchigiane
Carta delle irrigazioni Siciliane
Carta delle irrigazioni nella Campania
Carta delle irrigazioni nella regione Umbro-Laziale

Parts 1-4	L 3, 500
Part 5	L 10, 000

SCHIZZO PLANIMETRICO DELLA ZONA DI TERRENO DEVASTATA DAL TERREMOTO DEL 17 GIUGNO 1879 (ACIREALE)
1:50, 000
Roma : SGI, 1879
Shows areas devastated by the 1879 earthquake. L 800

CARTA DELLA PARTE SETTENTRIONALE DELL'ETNA (ERUZIONE DEL 1879)
1:50, 000
Roma : SGI, 1879
Mt Etna's eruption in 1879.
L 1, 000

F GEOLOGY

CARTA GEOLOGICO D'ITALIA
1:1, 000, 000
In 2 sheets
Roma : SGI, 1961
107 x 65 each
Detailed geological map covering mainland Italy and all its islands, Corsica, the Dalmation coast and parts of Switzerland and France.

CARTE GEOLOGICO D'ITALIA
1:100, 000
See index 45/6
Roma : SGI, 1884+
40 x 37
Series of geol. maps on sheet lines of topog. 1:100, 000 series: various eds and dates. Series in progress. Memoirs pub. for some sheets.

CARTA GEOLOGICA DELL'UMBRIA
1:500, 000
Roma : SGI, 1926
Col. geol. map. L 2, 500

CARTA GEOLOGICA DELLE ALPI OCCIDENTALI
1:400, 000
Roma : SGI, 1908
Col. geol. map L 4, 500

ABBOZZO DI CARTA GEOLOGICA DELLA BASILICATA
1:400, 000
Roma : SGI, 1878
Sketch geol. map. L 2000

CARTA GEOLOGICA DELLA PROVINCIA DI LECCE
1:400, 000
by C de Giorgi
Rome : SGI, 1880
Col. geol. map. L 2000

CARTA GEOLOGICA DELLA PARTE CENTRALE DELLE ALPI GRAIE
1:250, 000
Roma : SGI, 1892
Col. geol. map. L 1500

CARTA GEOLOGICA DELLE ALPI APUANE E REGIONI LIMITROFE
1:250, 000
Rome : SGI, 1932
Col. geol. map. L 2500

CARTA GEOLOGICA DELLE RIVIERE LIGURI E DELLE ALPI MARITIME
1:200, 000
Roma : SGI, 1887
Col. geol. map. L 5000

CARTA GEOLOGICA DELLE REGIONE VULCANICA DEI COLLI ALBANI
1:100, 000
Roma : Consiglio Nazionale delle Ricerche, 1958
66 x 70
On card with relative vulcanic structure superimposed. L 5000

CARTA GEOLOGICA DEI VULCANI VULSINI
1:100, 000
Roma, 1904
Col. geol. map. L 2500

CARTA GEOLOGICA DEL VULCANO LAZIALE
1:75, 000
Roma : SGI, 1900
Col. geol. map.

CARTA GEOLOGICA DEI VULCANI CIMINI
1:75, 000
Roma : SGI, 1972
Col. geol. map.

GEOLOGISCHE KARTEN ITALIEN
1:75, 000
Wien : GB, 1903-20
Austrian geol. series.
Sheets available :
Borgo-Fiera di Primiero (1909)
Bormio - Passo del Tonale (1908)
Cles (1903)
Glurns - Ortler (1912)
Rovereto - Riva (1903)
Tolmein (1920)
Trient (1903)
Triest (1920)
Each A.Sch. 270

CARTA GEOLOGICA DEI DINTORNI DI MASSA MARITTIMA
1:50, 000
Roma : SGI, 1893
Col. geol. map. L 2500

CARTA GEOLOGICA DEL MONTE SUBASIO
1:50, 000
Roma : SGI, 1912
Col. geol. map L 1000

CARTA GEOLOGICA DELLE ALPI APUANE
1:50, 000
In 4 sheets
Roma : SGI, 1897
Col. geol. map.
Also available at 1:25, 000 in 17 sheets

(1:50, 000)	L 10 000
(1:25, 000)	L 30 000

CARTA GEOLOGICA DEL S GOTTARDO
1:50, 000
Roma : SGI, 1873
Col. geol. map. L 2200

GEOLOGY, GEOPHYSICS AND HYDROGEOLOGY OF THE MONTE AMIATA GEOTHERMAL FIELDS (TOSCANA)
1:50, 000
Roma : SGI, 1970
90 x 75
4 col. maps, 3 black and white, 1 cross section. In Eng. with 10pp text.

CARTA GEOLOGICO-MINERARIA DEL SARRABUS
1:50, 000
Roma : SGI, 1890
Col. geol. map showing location of minerals.
L 1500

CARTA GEOLOGICA DELLA VALLE DEL PESCARA
1:50, 000
Roma : SGI, 1926
Col. geol. map with separate sheet of sections. L 2500

CARTA GEOLOGICA DELLE ISOLE EOLIE
1:50, 000 - 1:500, 000
In 8 sheets
Roma : SGI, 1892
Col. geol. maps : 7 at 1:50, 000, 1 at 1:500, 000 L 500

CARTA GEOLOGICA DELLA PARTE ORIENTALE DELL'ISOLA D'ELBA
1:50, 000
Roma : SGI, 1871
Col. geol. map. L 1800

CARTA GEOLOGICA DELLE ISOLE PONTINE
1:50, 000
Roma : SGI, 1893
Col. geol. map. L 1000

CARTA GEOLOGICA DEI DINTORNI DI BRESCIA
1:40, 000
Roma : SGI, 1915
Col. geol. map with sheet of sections.
L 1500

CARTA GEOLOGICA DELL'ISOLA D'ELBA
1:25, 000
In 2 sheets
Roma : SGI, 1884
Col. geol. map with text.
L 5000
Also available at 1:50, 000, 1886,
L 2500

CARTA GEOLOGICA DI VALLE AURINA E REGIONI VICINE
1:25, 000
Roma : SGI, 1930
Col. geol. map. L 800

CARTA GEOLOGICO - MINERARIA DELL'IGLESIENTE
1:25, 000
In 10 sheets
Roma : SGI, 1928-1958
Col. geol. series on official topog. sheet lines of SW coast of Sardinia.
Sheets published :
217 III SO-NO Terralba, 1958
224 I SE - 225 IV SO Punta Acqua Durci-Montevecchio, 1955
II SE Buggerru, 1930
225 III SO Punta Campo Spina (gia Miniera di S Benedetto) 1928
IV SE Guspini, 1954
NO M Arcuentu, 1958
232 I NE Nebida, 1920
SE, Portoscuso, 1926
233 IV SO Barbusi, 1932
NO Iglesias, 1919
Each sheet L 2000

CARTA GEOLOGICA DEL TERRITORIO ERUTTIVO DI PREDAZZO E MONZONI, NELLE DOLOMITI DI FIEMME E FOSSA
1:25, 000
In 2 sheets
Padova/Roma : SGI, 1930
135 x 95 complete
Col. geol. map. L 2500

CARTA GEOLOGICA DELLE ISOLE PONZA, PALMAROLA E ZANNONE
1:20, 000
Roma : SGI, 1876
Col. geol. map. L 1500

CARTA GEOLOGICA DI ROMA
1:15, 000
Roma : SGI, 1915
Col. geol. map. L 2500

CARTA GEOLOGICA E PETROGRAFICA DELL'ADAMELLO MERIDIONALE
1:12, 500
Roma : SGI, 1937
Col. geol. map. L 1000

CARTA GEOLOGICA DEL MONTE CASTELLACCIO E DINTORNI PRESSO IMOLA
1:5, 000
Roma : SGI, 1881
Col. geol. map. L 1000

G EARTH RESOURCES

CARTA MAGNETICA D'ITALIA
1:2, 000, 000
Firenze : IGM
Map showing equal horizontal component of Earth's magnetic field. January 1959.
L 700

CARTA MAGNETICA D'ITALIA
1:2, 000, 000
Firenze : IGM
Map showing lines of equal magnetic declination as of January 1955.
L 700

PLASTICI E MINERALI
Various scales
Ag
see ITALY 45 E1

H BIOGEOGRAPHY

CARTE DELL'UTILIZZAZIONE DEL SUOLO D'ITALIA
1:200, 000
In 26 sheets, see index 45/7
Napoli : Consiglio Nazionale delle Richerche, 1956-68
119 x 49 each
Land use series showing rural land use with Memoirs. In Italian. L 1000

CARTA DELLA VEGETAZIONE DELL' ANFITEATRO MORENICO DI RIVOLI (TORINO)
1:50, 000
Editor Dr U Tosco
Grenoble : Univ. Scientifique et Médicale de Grenoble, 1975
64 x 37
Coloured vegetation map with legend in Italian.

J CLIMATE

CARTA DELLE PRECIPITAZIONI MEDIE ANNUE IN ITALIA
1:1, 500, 000
Rome : Consiglio Nazionale delle Richerche, 1964
70 x 91
Col. rainfall map of Italy 1921-50. with insets of rainfall intensity and frequency and rainfall profiles. L 1000

CARTA DEI REGIMI PLUVIO-METRICI D'ITALIA, TRENTENNIO 1921-50
1:1, 250, 000
Roma : Inst. Geog. Univ. Pisa, 1969
59 x 40
Map of rainfall during the 30 years from 1921-1950.

K HUMAN GEOGRAPHY

CARTA DELLA DISTRIBUZIONE DELLA POPOLAZIONE IN ITALIA
1:1, 000, 000
Roma : Consiglio Nazionale delle Richerche, 1964
126 x 132
Showing pop. distribution.
L 1500

L ECONOMIC

JUHOVYCHODNÁ EVROPA A TALIANSKO
1:2, 500, 000
1st edition
In 4 sheets
Praha : Kart, 1970
Economic wall map, covering S E Europe and Italy.

EKONOMICHESKAYA KARTA
1:1, 250, 000
Moskva : GUGK
Single sheet economic map.

ITALIE (PHYSIQUE)
1:1, 100, 000
Editions MDI
Economic map on reverse.
see ITALY 45 E1.

VERKEHRSKARTE ITALIEN
1:1, 000, 000
Berlin : Gea. Verlag
110 x 137
Col. map showing roads and rail networks.

M HISTORICAL

HISTORY MAPS
Indianapolis : Cram
School col. historical wall maps.
Maps available :
General Reference Map of Ancient Italy
The Roman World 14 AD
The Roman World 117 AD
Rise and Growth of Christianity to 325 AD
The Roman World 337 AD
The City of Rome About 350 AD
General Reference Map of the Roman World
Unification of Italy
Each US $13.75

HISTORIQUE WANDKARTEN
Darmstadt : Perthes
Series of large historical wall maps.
Maps available :
Deutschland und Italien im Zeitalter der Sächischen und salischen Kaiser 911-1125, 1:1, 000, 000
172 x 215 DM 142
Deutschland und Italien im Zeitalter der Hohenstaufen, 1125-1273
1:1, 000, 000, 172 x 215
DM 142
Das Römische Weltreich, 1:2, 000, 000
270 x 175 DM 160

RÖMISCHES REICH
1:2, 500, 000
Gotha : Haack, 1967
214 x 164
Historical wall map, showing "Development of the Roman Empire 264 BC - AD 117" with second map "The Decline of the Western Empire" at 1:5, 000, 000. Uses pictorial symbols.
Also by Haack :
Imperium Romanum 1:3, 000, 000, 1967, 199 x 175
Political map
Italia 1:750, 000, 1963, 149 x 175
Covers ancient Italy, with Latin names.

HISTORICAL WALL MAPS, LATIN TEXTS
Various scales
Novara : Ag
Various sizes :
Maps available :
Imperium Populi Romani ab anno CCXLI A. Chr. N.ad annum circiter CL P. Chr.N. (Roman Empire 241 BC - 150 AD) 1:3, 500, 000, 190 x 140
2 sheets, flat L 3500
Italia ante Bellum Social 1:800, 000
140 x 190, 2 sheets
L 3500
Italie Pars Media (Central Italy)
1:300, 000, 200 x 140, 2 sheets
L 3500
Italia Antiqua Imperatorum Romanorum aetate (Ancient Italy, time of Augustus)
1:800, 000, 140 x 190, 2 sheets
L 3500
Forma Urbis Romae Imperatorum aetate (Ancient Rome) 1:4, 000, 180 x 140,
2 sheets L 3500

DREVNYAYA ITALIYA (ANCIENT ITALY)
1:1, 500, 000
Moskva : GUGK, 1973
Historical wall map for schools.
kop 12
Also - Rost Rimskogo Gosudarstva v III v. do n.e. - II v.n.e. (Growth of the Roman State, 3rd C BC)
1973 kop 30
Rimskaya Imperiya v IV - V vv
Padenie Zapadnoi Rimskoi Imperii (Roman Empire in the 4th - 5th C. Decline of the Western Roman Empire),
1973 1:4, 000, 000

CARTE STORICHE
Various scales
Novara : Ag
Various sizes
Series of large col. historical wall maps.
Maps available :
L'Impero Romano dal 241 AC - al 150 circa DC, 1:3, 500, 000, 190 x 140, 2 sheets
L 3500
Italia intorno al Mille (about 1000)
1:1, 000, 000, 140 x 200, 2 sheets
L 3500
Itali a dopo la Pace di Lodi (After the Peace of Lodi, 1494), 1:1, 000, 000
140 x 200, 2 sheets L 3500
Le Grandi Scoperte Geografiche (Geog. Discoveries) 1:25, 000, 000, 180 x 140,
2 sheets L 3500
Italia nel 1559 : La Preponderanza Spagnola (Spanish Domination) 1:800, 000,
142 x 200, 2 sheets L 3500
Italia Napoleonica (1797) el del Congresso di Vienna (1815) 1:1, 500, 000 170 x 140,
2 sheets L 3000
Carta Storica dell' unità d'Italia dal Risorgimento al Compimento dell'unità
1:1, 000, 000, 140 x 195, 2 sheets
L 3500
Ex-Colonie Italiane Fisico-Politico (1939)
1:3, 000, 000, 140 x 100
L 2200

BREASTED-HUTH-HARDING HISTORICAL WALL MAPS
Chicago : Denoyer-Geppert
112 x 81
Historical series on manilla paper.
Maps available :

204111	Ancient Italy - 2 maps showing People and Tribes 500 BC Military Org. 90 BC
204121	Growth of Roman power in Italy 500 - 265 BC
204131	Rome - Republican and Imperial
204141	Conquests of the Mediterranean
204161	The Roman Empire in the Time of Augustus
204391	Unification of Italy, 1850-1870 and Central Europe population

PUTZGER HISTORISCHER WANDKARTEN
Bielefeld : Cornelsen-Velhagen and Klasing
Historical wall maps.
Maps available :
Rom und Karthago : Romisches Reich zur Zeit Caesars 1:1, 500, 000, 169 x 220
Das Romische Weltreich seit Kaiser Augustus 1:2, 500, 000, 197 x 154
Die Romer in Deutschland, 1:550, 000
138 x 193
Untergang des Romischen Weltreiches/ Germanische Volkerwanderung
1:4, 000, 000, 205 x 160

PALMER WORLD HISTORY MAPS
Various scales
Chicago : Rand McNally
50 x 46
Col. historical wall maps for :
Roman Empire and Republic about 120 AD
Roman Empire about 400 AD
Unification of Italy - 1866-1919.

IMPERIUM ROMANUM
1:3, 500, 000
Praha : Kart
100 x 84
Wall map showing the Roman Empire.
Kcs 165

L'ITALIE ANCIENNE - ROME
1:3, 850, 000
No 1504
St Germain-en-Laye : Éditions MDI
92 x 126
Plastic coated physical wall map for schools. "L'Empire Romain" at 1:4, 500, 000 on reverse.

A RÓMAI BIRODALOM
1:3, 750, 000
2nd edition
In 2 sheets
Budapest : Cart, 1970
Historical wall map of Roman Empire with inset of Rome at 1:20, 000.

DAS RÖMISCHE REICH
1:2, 500, 000
Braunschweig : Westermann
211 x 203
Col. historical wall map, with 3 insets of various areas.

DAS ALTE ROM
1:6, 000
Braunschweig : Westermann
102 x 140
Showing the city of Rome at the 4th C BC, with insets of Capitol and Forum, and Christian Rome, showing catacombs.

CARTA DELLE ZONE ARCHAEOLOGICHE D'ITALIA
1:200, 000
In 26 sheets, see index 45/8
Milano : TCI
Various sizes
Pub. in conjunction with the Ministero della Pubblica Instruzione. 30 maps on 26 sheets, showing the various archaeological sites. For study or general interest.
Per sheet L 500

CARTE ARCHEOLOGICA
1:100, 000
See index 45/4
Firenze : IGM
60 x 51 app. each sheet
Topog. series with sites of archaeological sites marked. Corresponds to sheet line of 100, 000 series. Text inc. legend, brief description of monument etc. Available in the following sheets :

17	Chiavenna
20	M Adamello
21	Trento
27/28	M Bianco-Aosta
29	M Rosa
32	Como
38	Conegliano
42	Ivrea
50	Padova
52/53	S Dona di Piave e Foce Tagliamento
82	Genoa
104	Pisa
105	Lucca

108 Mercato Saraceno
140 Teramo
204 Lecce
Each L 2000

CARTE ARCHEOLOGICHE DI ROMA
1:2, 500
In 9 sheets
Firenze : IGM
Set of large scale topog. plans on which are marked sites of archaeological interest. 2 sheets only published.

ATLASES
W3 WORLD LOCAL EDITION

IL NUOVO ATLANTE DELLA SCUOLA MEDIA
Ag
see WORLD 100 ATLASES W3

ATLASES
A1 GENERAL : ROADS

ITALIA - ATLANTE STRADALE
1:500, 000
Novara : Ag
14 x 24
Road atlas with legends in It, Ger, Eng, French, with table of distances.
L 1000

ATLANTE STRADALE D'ITALIA
1:250, 000
Novara : Ag, 1971
182 pp
16 x 26
Road atlas of Italy showing all classes of roads with distances and index.
L 3200

ATLANTE AUTOMOBILISTICO D'ITALIA
1:200, 000
Milano : TCI
In 3 vols.
25 x 32
Vol I Italia Settentriole, 124 pp
Vol 2 Italia Centrale e Sardegna, 97pp, 1970
Vol 3 Italia Meridionale e Sicilia, 88pp, 1971
Based on the 200, 000 series of road maps.
Each vol. L 4250

ATLASES
M HISTORICAL

ATLANTE AEROFOTOGRAFICO DELLE SEDI UMANE IN ITALIA
Firenze : IGM
53 x 42
Atlas of human settlemen, in 2 parts, showing archaeological sites, photographed from the air, and those reconstructed from research carried out. 163pp text available separately from the atlas, in 4 langs, 33 x 23.
Part I L'utilisatione delle fotografie aere nello studio degli in sediamenti (1964) L 25 000
Part II Le sedi antichi scomparse (1970) L 55 000

ATLASES
P REGIONAL

ATLANTE DELLA SARDEGNA
Ed R Pracchi and A Terrosu Asole
Cagliari : La Zattera, 1971
26 x 34
In 3 parts, inc. 120 col. plates, covering physical, social, economic, climatic, physiographical, biogeographic, aspects of the Island.
1st part, 34 maps, with 79p text.

458.2 Malta, Gozo, Comino

A1 GENERAL MAPS: ROADS

MALTA
1:50, 000
47 x 42
Valetta : Progress Press
With bus routes, hotels, places of interest, major beaches and general tourist information. Inset of Sliema.
20p

B TOWN PLANS

OFFICIAL TOWN PLAN OF VALLETTA
Valetta : Progress Press
57 x 36
Showing places of interest and also contains general tourist information.

C OFFICIAL SURVEYS

SURVEY MAP OF MALTA, GOZO AND COMINO
1:32, 000
Valetta : Allied Malta Newspapers Ltd, 1970
74 x 83
Main and secondary roads, footpaths, places of interest, contours at 25 foot intervals, spot heights in feet. Reduction of DOS 352. 55p

MALTA
1:25, 000
DOS 352 (m 898)
In 3 sheets, see index 458.2/1
Tolworth : DOS
Topog. series. All classes of roads, antiquities, contours at 25 foot intervals, spot heights in feet, ferries and rock outcrops.
Sheets available :
1 Gozo and Comino, 1962-63
84 x 60
2 Malta West, 1962-63
61 x 91
3 Malta East, 1969
64 x 86
Each 50p

MALTA DOS
1:2, 500
DOS 152
In 94 sheets, see index 458.2/1
Prepared by DOS
Valetta : Min. of Works
Large scale planning series covering Gozo and Comino in 44 sheets, Island of Malta in 150 sheets. Showing roads, tracks, footpaths, rock outcrops and antiquities. Contours on new series (in progress) at 10 foot intervals.
Each 20p

D POLITICAL & ADMINISTRATIVE

MALTA
1:750, 000
Edition 1, DOS 17/19
Tolworth : DOS, 1948
Small general map showing communications, boundaries and settlement.
15p

F GEOLOGY

GEOLOGICAL MAP OF MALTA
1:31, 680
Prepared by British Petroleum
Valetta : Min. of Works, 1957
Geol. map in 2 sheets, contoured at 25 ft intervals.
Sheet 1 Gozo, Comino
82 x 62
Sheet 2 Malta
91 x 84

G EARTH RESOURCES

MALTA AND GOZO - SOILS
1:31, 680
Edition 1, DOS (Misc) 258
Tolworth : DOS, 1960
Col. soil map. 65p

46 Iberian Peninsula

A1 GENERAL MAPS: ROADS

SPANIEN - PORTUGAL
1:1, 700, 000
No 205
Köln : Polyglott
Roads classified; distances in km.
DM 3.20

SPANELSKO A PORTUGALSKO
1:1, 500, 000
Warszawa : PPWK, 1971
84 x 68
Pol. text. In series "Przeglądowa Europy" (Review Maps of Europe)

SHELL REISEKARTE SPANIEN - PORTUGAL
1:1, 500, 000
Stuttgart : Mairs
82 x 49
Shows all types of roads with distances, much tourist information incl. camp sites and places and buildings of interest. Principal tourist areas inset at 1:750, 000 and plans of Madrid and Barcelona.
Double sided DM 4.80

WORLD TRAVEL SERIES MAP OF SPAIN AND PORTUGAL
1:1, 250, 000
Edinburgh : Bart
71 x 96
All classes of roads, road numbering and distances, spot heights in m, railways, airports, boundaries and hill shading. Madrid inset, scale 1 mile to 1".

SPANIEN — PORTUGAL
1:1, 250, 000
No 389
Hamburg : Falk
Col. road map, patent folding.
DM 5.60

SPANIEN UND PORTUGAL
1:1, 200, 000
No 883
Stuttgart : Ravenstein
80 x 100
Col. map; roads classified and numbered, distances in km, other communications, items of tourist interest.
DM 7.80

ESPANA Y PORTUGAL
1:1, 000, 000
Bilbao : FH
102 x 98
Roads classified, distances in km, railways, places of tourist interest and accommodation. Madrid and environs inset.
Also available in 2 sheet ed, North and South, 102 x 49 each.

SPANIEN - PORTUGAL
1:1, 000, 000
Ref 1144
Bern : K & F
109 x 90
All classes of roads with distances in km, hill shading, car ferries, scenic routes, railways, airports, camping sites and motels. Balearic Islands inset.

ESPAGNE PORTUGAL GRANDES ROUTES
1:1, 000, 000
Ref 990
Paris : Michelin, 1976
110 x 96
All classes of roads, conditions and road widths, picturesque routes, distances in km. Balearic Islands inset at 1:1, 300, 000.

SPAGNA E PORTOGALLO
1:1, 000, 000
Novara : Agostini
94 x 121
Coloured road and tourist map.
L 700

SPANIEN UND PORTUGAL
1:1, 000, 000
München : JRO
123 x 88
Green base map, with main roads in red, numbered, with distances in km, tourist information. DM 6.80

SPANIEN UND PORTUGAL
1:1, 000, 000
Bern : Hallwag
108 x 90
All classes of roads, distances in km, spot heights in metres, hill shading, car ferries, railways. Balearic Islands inset.

IBERIAN PENINSULA
1:1, 000, 000
London : Foldex
Shows roads classified, relief shading; patent fold. 45p

SPANIEN - PORTUGAL
1:800, 000
No 85
Stuttgart : RV
75 x 114
Double sided map showing all classes of roads, distances in km, hill shading, spot heights in metres, distances in km, airports, motels, camping sites. 12 through-town plans inset. Also Balearic Islands.
DM 8.80

SPAIN AND PORTUGAL
1:600, 000
In 6 sheets
London : Foldex
Shows roads classified; relief shading; patent fold.
Each 35p
3 double-sided maps,
Each 60p

MAPAS DE CARRETERAS
1:500, 000
In 9 sheets, see index 46/1
Bilbao : FH
112 x 50 each
Roads classified and numbered, distances in km, spot heights in metres, petrol and service stations, airports. Legend in Sp.
3 sheets for Portugal.

D POLITICAL & ADMINISTRATIVE

ISPANIYA I PORTUGALIYA
1:1, 750, 000
Moskva : GUGK
Reference map.

SPANELSKO A PORTUGALSKO
1:1, 250, 000
Praha : Kart, 1968
General wall map for schools.
Kcs 85

ISPANIYA I PORTUGALIYA
1:750, 000
Moskva : GUGK, 1973
Col. study map showing water features, settlements, admin. divisions and centres, communications, boundaries, economic details, pop, Geog. description.

PÉNINSULE IBÉRIQUE (ESPAGNE ET PORTUGAL)
No 65
Paris : Hatier
100 x 120
School wall map; political with economic map on reverse. In Sp. No 64.

PENISOLA IBERICA
1:4, 000, 000
Novara : Agostini
Small hand outline map.
L 40

PENÍNSULA IBÉRICA
Barcelona : Editorial Teide
25 x 33
School hand map without boundaries or cities. S.Ptas 1

E1 PHYSICAL

MAPA FÍSICO
1:2, 000, 000
Madrid : IGC
Physical map of Spain and Portugal, contoured, layer col.

TERRAIN MAP OF SPAIN AND PORTUGAL
1:2, 000, 000
Williamsburg : Robert Frank Collins, 1967
46 x 61
Physical map, showing relief by hachures.

SPANJE EN PORTUGAL
1:1, 500, 000
Groningen : Wolters-Noordhoff
107 x 85
Physical wall map for schools : relief shading, boundaries, communications.
In Dutch. Fl. 44.75

ŠPANĚLSKO A PORTUGALSKO
1:1, 500, 000
Praha : Kart
Physical/political reference map in series "Poznaváme Svět" (Getting to know the World). With thematic text volume.
Kcs 14

PENÍNSULA IBÉRICA
1:1, 000, 000
Madrid : Aguilar
100 x 130
Physical school wall map; hypsometric tints with altitudes indicated.
Paper S.Ptas 75
Cloth S.Ptas 250

PÉNINSULE IBÉRIQUE (PHYSIQUE)
1:1, 000, 000
No 1185
St Germain-en-Laye : Éditions MDI
126 x 92
Plastic coated physical wall map; for schools. Economic map on reverse.

SPANIEN UND PORTUGAL
1:1, 000, 000
2nd ed.
Munchen : List
175 x 130
Relief wall map, layer col, relief shaded, communications and settlement, inc. Islands and Coast of North Africa. In Sw and Ger. Wenschow wall map.
DM 128

ESPAÑA Y PORTUGAL
1:900, 000
Braunschweig : Westermann
175 x 172
Col. relief wall map in Sp, layer col. with relief shading.

SPANIEN UND PORTUGAL
1:750, 000
Darmstadt : Perthes, 1971
161 x 154
Physical wall map showing relief and elevation by hill shading, layer col, communications. DM 142

ESPAÑA Y PORTUGAL
Barcelona : Editorial Teide
33 x 50
Hand map showing physical features, main cities, boundaries. S.Ptas 2

PENISOLA IBERICA
1:5, 000, 000
Novara : Agostini
33 x 26
Plastic relief map for schools; physical, political and economic details on reverse.
L 450

E2 PHYSICAL: LAND FEATURES

MAP DE SÍNTESIS DE SISTEMAS ACUIFEROS DE ESPAÑA PENINSULAR, BALEARES Y CANARIAS
1:1, 650, 000 app
Madrid : IGM, 1971
82 x 63
Coloured map showing aquiferous and ground water areas.

F GEOLOGY

MAPA GEOLÓGICO DE LE PENÍNSULA IBÉRICA, BALEARES Y CANARIAS
1:4, 000, 000
Madrid : IGM, 1964
30 x 23
Col. geol. map.

MAPA GEOLÓGICO DE LA PENÍNSULA IBÉRICA
1:2, 500, 000
Madrid : IGM, 1967
48 x 37
Col. geological map of Spain in one sheet. Inc. Balearic and Canary Islands.
S.Ptas 100

MAPA SISMOTECTÓNICO DE ESPAÑA PENINSULAR Y BALEARES
1:2, 500, 000
Madrid : IGM, 1960
80 x 50
Showing structure and principal formations of Iberia, with seismic intensity curves.
S.Ptas 300

CARTE GÉOLOGIQUE INTERNATIONALE DE L'EUROPE
1:1, 500, 000
UNESCO - BB
Sheets available for Spain :
A6 Lisboa 1952
B6 Madrid 1952
Legend sheet
see also EUROPE 4 G.

MAPA GEOLÓGICO DE ESPAÑA Y PORTUGAL PENINSULARES, BALEARES Y CANARIAS
1:1, 250, 000
Madrid, IGM, 1965
100 x 80
General geol. map in col.

MAPA GEOLÓGICO DE LA PENÍNSULA IBÉRICA
1:1, 000, 000
In 2 sheets
Madrid : IGM, 1966
62 x 86 each
Col. geol. map inc. Balearic and Canary Islands. S.Ptas 300

MAPA SISMOESTRUCTURAL DE LA PENÍNSULA IBÉRICA, BALEARES Y CANARIAS
1:1, 000, 000
Madrid : IGM, 1966
120 x 91
Col. map. S.Ptas 300

CARTE GÉOLOGIQUE DU NORD-OUEST DE LA PÉNINSULE IBÉRIQUE
1:500, 000
Lisboa : SGP, 1969
103 x 84
Col. map showing Hercynian and Antehercynian in NW Spain and Portugal.

J CLIMATE

MAPA DE LLUVIA UTIL O ESCORRENTIA TOTAL DE LA ESPAÑA PENINSULAR E ISLA DE MALLORCA
1:1, 000, 000
Madrid : IGM, 1971
129 x 99
Coloured map showing useful rainfall, for Spain and Majorca.

L ECONOMIC

PÉNINSULE IBÉRIQUE (PHYSIQUE)
Editions MDI
Economic map on reverse
see IBERIAN PENINSULAR 46 E1

ATLASES
A1 GENERAL: ROADS

ATLAS DE ESPAÑA Y PORTUGAL
1:1, 000, 000
Bilbao : FH, 1969
12 x 27
80 pp
35pp maps; roads classified and numbered, distances in km, places of tourist interest. 33pp town plan guides showing stations etc, route planning maps, tourist guide.

EL LIBRO DE LA CARRETERA SELECCIONES DEL READER'S DIGEST
1:500, 000
Madrid : FH/Lisboa : Selecciones del Readers' Digest, 1968
17 x 29
Road atlas of Spain and Portugal with 157pp text, 36pp town and motorway maps. With index and other plates. In Spanish. Portuguese edition (slightly different) available as "O Livro da Estrada : Seleccoes do Readers' Digest".

460 Spain

See also :

46 IBERIAN PENINSULA

A1 GENERAL: ROADS

SPAIN AND BALEARIC ISLANDS
1:1, 000, 000
London : Foldex
Shows roads classified, relief shading; patent fold. 45p

ESPAÑA-MAPA GENERAL DE CARRETERAS
1:800, 000
2nd Edition
Madrid : Min de Obras Publicas, 1974
139 x 58
Detailed road map with brief notes.
S.Ptas 100.00

CARTA STRADALE D'EUROPA
1:500, 000
Milano : TCI, 1970
Various sizes
4 sheets needed for complete coverage : Nos 9, 10, 11 and 12
All classes of roads, distances in km, road conditions, railways, spot heights, car ferries and contour layer col.
see also EUROPE 4 A1.

A2 GENERAL MAPS: LOCAL

TURISMAP
1:400, 000
In 47 sheets
Ed L Regalado
Madrid : Ed. Hernando
44 x 56
Series of tourist road maps with roads classified.
Paper folded each S.Ptas 60

ROAD MAP OF NORTH EAST SPAIN
1:400, 000
In 2 sheets
Paris : Michelin
109 x 50 each
Covering Pyrénées. All classes of roads with distances in km, spot heights in metres, railways, scenic routes and airports. Legend in Sp. and Fr.
Sheets :
42 Santander - Gimont south to Huesca, 1971
43 Sanguesa - Argeles south to Tarragona with inset of the Balearic Islands, 1972

MAPAS TURÍSTICOS
1:200, 000
13 sheets, see index 460/1
Bilbao : FH
124 x 60
All classes of roads, road widths, distances in km, railways, airports, petrol and service stations, towns of interest, camping sites, spot heights and relief shading. Guide supplement.
Sheets :
T20 Rias Gallegas
T21 Costa Verde - Picos de Europa
T22 Cornisa Cantabrica
T23 Pirineo Occidental
T24 Pirineo Occidental
T25 Costa Brava - Costas de Cataluna
T26 Islas Baleares 1:175, 000
T27 Costa Dorada - Costa del Azahar
T28 Costa Blanca - Costa de Levante
T29 Costa del Sol
T30 Costa de la Luz - Costas Colombinas
T31 Madrid sus Alrededores (Madrid and Segovia inset 1:175, 000)
T32 Islas Canarias 1:150, 000/400, 000

SPANISCHE GENERALKARTE MITTELMEERKUSTE
1:200, 000
In 3 sheets
Stuttgart : Mair, 1973
Tourist maps for the Spanish coast, showing roads, scenic routes, shaded relief, tourist information by symbols.
Available for :
Costa Brava
Costa Blanca
Costa del Sol
Each DM 3.50

MAPA DE LOS TRES MACIZOS DE LOS PICOS DE EUROPA
1:50, 000
Madrid: Federacion Espanola de Montanismo
70 x 50
Los Lagos to Treviso and Las Arenas to Pollayo. Tourist map based on Spanish Official Survey maps with contours at 20 metre intervals and spot heights; tourist guide printed on reverse. Legend and text in Sp.

GUIAS CARTOGRAFICAS
1:25, 000
see index 460/2 and 3
Granollers : Editorial Alpina
Various sizes
Detailed series of maps suitable for walking and climbing, showing roads, tracks, boundaries, elevations and contour intervals at 20 metres.
Legend in Sp.
Sheets available :
Cordillera Cantabrica
36 Picos de Europa 1 Govadonga S.Ptas 45
60 Picos de Europa II - Naranjo de Bulnes S.Ptas 45
Cordillera Central
63 Guadarrama S.Ptas 45
Pyrenees
Valle de Ordesa - Vignemale S.Ptas 50
Posets - Benasque S.Ptas 45
La Maladeta - Aneto S.Ptas 50
La Vall d'Aran, 1:40, 000 (V Guide) S.Ptas 60
La Ribagorca S.Ptas 45
Montardo - Aigues Tortes S.Ptas 45
Sant Maurici - Els Encantats S.Ptas 45
Pica d:Estats - Vall Ferrera I de Cardos, 1:40, 000 S.Ptas 50
Andorra i sectors fronterers, 1:40, 000 S.Ptas 50
Pont de Suert - Escales, 1:40, 000 S.Ptas 50
Montsent de Pallars - Sort S.Ptas 45
Puigmal - Nuria - Caranca S.Ptas 45
Costabona - Coll d'Ares S. Ptas 45
Serra del Cadi - Pedraforca S.Ptas 45
Moixero - La Molina S.Ptas 45
Montgrony - Fonts del Llobregat S.Ptas 45
Taga - Valls de Ribes i de S Joan S.Ptas 45
Port del Comte - Serra del Verd S.Ptas 50
Rasos de Peguera - Serra d'Ensija S.Ptas 45
Puigsacalm - Bellmunt S.Ptas 45
El Montsec, 1:40, 000 S.Ptas 60
Garrotxa, 1:40, 000 S.Ptas 60
Costa Brava
Guilleries - Collsacabra, 1:40, 000 S.Ptas 50
Moianes S.Ptas 45
El Montseny, 1:40, 000 S.Ptas 50
Cingles de Berti i de Gallifa S.Ptas 45
Sant Lorenc del Munt - Serra de l'Obac S.Ptas 45
El Farell S.Ptas 45
Montserrat - Tossa de Montbui, 1:40, 000 - Alto Montserrat 1:10, 000 S.Ptas 50
S Salvador de les Espases-Terrassa S.Ptas 45
Ordal - Vallirana S.Ptas 45
Garraf - Castelldefels S.Ptas 45
Gran Barcelona S.Ptas 50
Sant Mateu - Cercanias de Barcelona S.Ptas 45
El Corredor S.Ptas 45
Montnegre S.Ptas 45
Costa Brava I - Tossa S.Ptas 45
Costa Brava II - Cadaques 1:80, 000 S.Ptas 35

CATALUÑA TURÍSTICA
Granollers : Editorial Alpina
65 x 80
Simplified map showing roads and panoramic views in 5 cols. S.Ptas 40

B TOWN PLANS

TOWN PLANS
Various scales
Col. plans with index to streets.
Maps available :
Barcelona (Falk) 1:12, 500 DM 4.80
Barcelona (Foldex), 1:10, 000 65p
Barcelona (Miniplan) 20p
Bilbao (Foldex) 65p
Gibralter (Miniplan) 17½p
Gran Bilbao (FH) 65p
Granada (Foldex) 65p
Madrid (Falk) 1:12, 500 DM 4.80
Madrid (IGM) 1:10, 000
Madrid (Miniplan) 20p
Madrid (Foldex) 65p
Madrid Monumental (Foldex) 65p
Santiago (Foldex) 65p

Seville (Foldex) 65p
Toledo (Foldex) 65p

C OFFICIAL SURVEYS

KARTA MIRA
1:2, 500, 000
VVK : Carti, Cart
4 sheets for complete coverage of Spain, inc. islands.
see WORLD 100C and index 100/2.

THE WORLD
1:1, 000, 000
DMS Series 1301
5 sheets for coverage of Spain
see WORLD 100C and index 100/1.

THE WORLD
1:500, 000
DMS Series 1404
15 sheets needed for complete coverage.
see WORLD 100C and index 100/7.

MAPA MILITAR DE ESPAÑA
1:800, 000
In 6 sheets, see index 460/4
Madrid : Servicio Geografico del Ejercito
Topog. series to be published.

MAPA MILITAR DE ESPAÑA (SERIES) 4CE)
1:400, 000
In 31 sheets, see index 460 /4
Madrid : Servicio Geografico del Ejercito
Topog. series including the Canary Isles. Contoured, layer col, with communications, boundaries and settlement.

MAPA MILITAR DE ESPAÑA (SERIES 2C)
1:200, 000
In 150 sheets (app), see index 460/4
Madrid : Servicio Geografico del Ejercito
55 x 37
Topog. series including the Canary Islands, contoured with layer col, road and rail communications, boundaries and settlement.

MAPA MILITAR DE ESPAÑA (SERIES C)
1:100, 000
See index 460/5
Madrid : Servicio Geografico del Ejercito
New topog. series in progress, contoured with roads, railways, boundaries, settlement.

MAPA MILITAR DE ESPAÑA (SERIES L)
1:50, 000
In 115 sheets, see index 460/6
Madrid : Servicio Geografico del Ejercito
59 x 37
New topog. series in progress, contoured with roads and railways marked also tracks, topographical features, vegetation and crop detail.

D POLITICAL & ADMINISTRATIVE

MAPA DE ESPAÑA
1:2, 000, 000
Barcelona : Editorial Teide
50 x 65
Contoured general map for classroom purposes. S.Ptas 10

PENINSULA IBÉRICA - MAPA ESPAÑA POLITÍCA
1:1, 200, 000
Barcelona: Editorial Vicens Vives, 1976
126 x 88
Physical political map in spanish on plasticised paper S.Ptas 500

ESPAÑA
1:1, 000, 000
Madrid : Aguilar
100 x 130
Politically coloured school wall map.
Paper S.Ptas 75
Cloth S.Ptas 250

ESPAÑA
1:1, 000, 000
Madrid : Seix-Barral
111 x 81
Political map col. by provinces.
Canary Isles inset.

ESPANA POLÍTICA
Barcelona : Editorial Teide
115 x 88
Political wall map for schools.
S.Ptas 275

MAPAS MURALES REGIONALES
1:500, 000
Aguilar
see SPAIN 460L.

MAPAS MURALES DE LAS PROVINCIAS ESPANOLAS
1:300, 000 - 1:200, 000
Aguilar
see SPAIN 460L

MAPA TOPOGRAFICO DE CATALUNA
1:250, 000
Granollers : Editorial Alpina
100 x 120
Contours, relief shading, with provincial, district, judicial and episcopal boundaries marked. S.Ptas 125

MAPA DE CATALUNYA
1:250, 000
Granollers : Editorial Alpina
110 x 120
Relief map showing former provincial, county, judicial and ecclesiastic boundaries.
S.Ptas 125

CATALUNA
Barcelona : Editorial Teide
115 x 88
General school wall map of the region.
S.Ptas 330

GENERAL MAPS
Barcelona : Editorial Teide
33 x 25
School hand maps, showing boundaries, principal cities.
Maps available :
España politica
Meseta Norte
Meseta Sur
Galicia, Asturias, Santander
Vasconia, Depresion del Ebro
Cataluna
Levante e Baleares
Andalucia
Canarias, Territ, africanos
Each S.Ptas 1

BARCELONA
1:200, 000
Granollers : Editorial Alpina
63 x 86
Col. relief map showing county and judicial boundaries. S.Ptas 60

GERONA
1:200, 000
Granollers : Editorial Alpina
63 x 86
Col. relief map showing county and legal boundaries. S.Ptas 60

LÉRIDA
1:250, 000
Granollers : Editorial Alpina
63 x 86
Col. relief map showing county and judicial areas. S.Ptas 60

TARRAGONA
1:200, 000
Granollers : Editorial Alpina
63 x 86
Col. relief map showing county and legal boundaries. S.Ptas 60

VALLES-MARESME
1:100, 000
Granollers : Editorial Alpina
Col. map showing all administrative districts, inc. municipal ones. Relief shading.
S.Ptas 60

UMRISSKARTE SPANIEN
1:3, 000, 000
No 0819
Bern : K & F
43 x 37
Outline map with rivers and boundaries.

MAPA MUDOS DE ESPAÑA
Madrid : Aguilar
Outline map of Spain. S.Ptas 150

E1 PHYSICAL: RELIEF

ESPAÑA FÍSICA
Barcelona : Editorial Teide
33 x 25
Contoured, physical hand map for schools.
S.Ptas 1

ESPAÑA
1:1, 187, 500
Madrid : Seix-Barral
111 x 81
Physical wall map, showing relief by hill shading and layer cols with ocean depths, principal cities.

ESPAÑA FÍSICA
1:1, 000, 000
Barcelona : Editorial Teide
115 x 88
Physical wall map for schools.
S.Ptas 275

ESPAGNE
1:1, 000, 000
TC 44 (No 1613)
St Germain-en-Laye : Éditions MDI
126 x 92
Plastic coated physical wall map for schools.
Italy on the reverse at 1:1, 100, 000.

E2 PHYSICAL: LAND FEATURES

MAPA VULCANOLÓGICO DE ESPAÑA
1:1, 000, 000
In 2 sheets
Madrid : IGM
62 x 86 each
Volcanic areas in red, referred to by key.
S.Ptas 75

F GEOLOGY

MAPA GEOLÓGICO DE ESPAÑA
1:2, 500, 000
Madrid : IGM
Col. geol. map. S.Ptas 75

MAPA RECONOCIMIENTO HIDROGEOLÓGICO DE LA ESPAÑA
1:1, 000, 000
Madrid : IGM, 1971
128 x 99
Coloured hydrogeological reconnaissance map.

MAPA LITOLÓGICO DE ESPAÑA
1:500, 000
In 4 sheets
Madrid : IGM, 1969
122 x 183 complete
Col. map showing lithologic strata, roads, towns, etc. In envelope, with legend sheet.
S.Ptas 700

MAPA GEOLÓGICO NACIONAL ESPAÑA
1:400, 000
5th edition
In 64 sheets, see index 460/7
Madrid : IGM, 1954+
43 x 35
New col. geol. series in progress which will replace earlier 4th ed. sheets.
Per sheet S.Ptas 200

MAPA PETROGRÁFICO Y ESTRUCTURAL DE GALICIA
1:400, 000
Madrid : IGM
Col. structural map. S.Ptas 250

MAPA GEÓLOGICO DE LA CUENCA DEL DUERO
1:250, 000
Madrid : IGM
Col. geol. map. S.Ptas 250

MAPA GEOLÓGICA DE SÍNTESIS
1:200, 000
In 87 sheets, see index 460/4
Madrid : IGM, 1971
Geological complete for the whole of the country series. With text.
S.Ptas 400

MAPAS GEOLÓGICOS PROVINCIALES
1:200, 000
Madrid : IGM
Col. geol. maps.
Available for the following provinces:
Barcelona
La Coruña (1964)
Salamanca
Murcia
Almería (1967)
Valencia (1968)
Cáceres (text 1971)
Madrid (1970)
Per sheet S.Ptas 300

MAPA GEOTÉCNICO GENERAL
1:200, 000
In 96 sheets
Madrid : IGM
Series of geotectonie maps now complete for the whole of Spain with descriptive notes.
each S.Ptas 200

MAPA DE ROCAS INDUSTRIALES
1:200, 000
In 93 sheets
Madrid : IGM
Series of maps depicting industrial rocks with descriptive notes.
Each S.Ptas 200

GEOLOGISCHE KARTE DES PYRENÄISCH - KANTABRISCHEN GRENZGEBIETES
1:200, 000
1st Edition
Editor. F Lotze, Akad. der Wissenschaften u.der Lit., Mainz.
Wiesbaden : Franz Steiner Verlag GmbH, 1973
Coloured map of the Pyrenean-Cantabrian border region with notes.
DM 12.50

MAPA GEOLÓGICO DE LA ISLA DE LANZAROTE
1:100, 000
Madrid : IGM
Col. geol. map. S.Ptas 250

MAPA GEOLÓGICO DE LA PROVINCIA DE GUIPÚZCOA
1:100, 000
Madrid : IGM
Col. geol. map. S.Ptas 300

MAPA GEOLÓGICO DE ESPAÑA
1:50, 000
In 1130 (2nd edition in progress) sheets
Madrid : IGM
Col. geol. series in progress.
Texts available for some sheets.
1st edition S.Ptas 300
2nd edition S.Ptas 400

MAPA GEOLÓGICO DE LA PROVINCIA DE GUIPÚZCOA
1:50, 000
Madrid : IGM
Col. geol. map, with memoir.
S.Ptas 600

MAPA GEOLÓGICO DE LA PROVINCIA DE ALAVA
1:50, 000
Madrid : IGM
Col. geol. map. with Memoir.
S.Ptas 600

GEOLOGICAL MAP OF THE FLAMISELT AND MANANET VALLEYS
1:25, 000
Ed K J Roberti
Leiden : Geol. Inst., Leiden Univ, 1970
Col. geol. map.

G EARTH RESOURCES

BOSQUEJO METALOGÉNETICO DE ESPAÑA PENINSULAR E INSULAR
1:2, 500, 000
Madrid : IGM, 1963
65 x 48
Col. sketch map of Spain, Balearic and Canary Is. showing locations and importance of formations containing mineral ores, excluding coal and iron. With text. S.Ptas 100

MAPA DE LOS CRIADEROS DE HIERRO DE ESPAÑA
1:2, 500, 000
Madrid : IGM, 1961
55 x 45
Map showing locations, type and production of deposits of iron ore in Spain. With text.
S.Ptas 100

MAPA DEL COBRE
1:2, 500, 000
Madrid : IGM, 1961
Showing copper deposits of Spain.
S.Ptas 100

MAPA METALOGENÉTICO DE ESPAÑA
1:1, 500, 000
In 17 sheets
Madrid : IGM
Series of maps showing locations of various minerals each with explanatory text.
1 Aluminium
2 Sulphur
3 Bismuth
4 Lead-Zinc
5 Copper
6 Strontium
7 Fluorite
8 Phosphates
9 Iron
10 Soft Coal
11 Manganese
12 Mercury
13 Nickel
14 Gold
15 Potassium
16 Titanium
17 Wolfram
Each S.Ptas 400

MAPA MINERO DE ESPAÑA
1:1, 000, 000
2nd edition
Madrid : IGM, 1964
121 x 90
Map of Spain, Balearic and Canary Islands, showing locations and products of working and disused mines, excluding coal and iron. With text. S.Ptas 300

ESPAÑA MINERA
Barcelona : Editorial Teide
115 x 88
School wall map showing Spain's mineral resources. S.Ptas 275

MAPA METALOGENÉTICO DE ESPAÑA
1:200, 000
In 87 sheets
Madrid : IGM
Series of metallogenetic maps with descriptive notes.
Each S.Ptas 400

H BIOGEOGRAPHY

MAPA DE CULTIVOS Y APROVECHAMIENTO DE ESPAÑA
1:1, 000, 000
Madrid : Dir. Gen. de Agricultura
1962
127 x 94
With text. Showing present land use and progress.

MAPA FORESTAL DE ESPAÑA
1:400, 000
Madrid : Dir. General de Montes
Casa y Pesca Fluvial, 1966
42 x 54
Folio containing Forest Map of Spain in 20 folded sheets, showing distribution of principal species of trees in Spain, Balearic and Canary Islands. Accompanied by text for each species, with colour photographs and location mao at 1:3, 600, 000.

L ECONOMIC

ESPAÑA AGRÍCOLA
Barcelona : Editorial Teide
115 x 88
Agricultural wall map for schools.
S.Ptas 275

MAPAS MURALES REGIONALES
1:500, 000
Madrid : Aguilar
125 x 98
Regional general maps, with densely populated zones inset at 1:250, 000. Thematic insets at 1:2, 000, 000 showing energy resources, minerals and industry; agriculture, cattle raising and fishing: population density and important cities.
Available for the following areas:
Andalucia
Cataluna - Valle del Ebro
La Meseta Norte - Atlantica
La Meseta Sur
Levante
Each S.Ptas 650

MAPAS MURALES DE LAS PROVINCIAS ESPAÑOLAS
1:300, 000 - 1:200, 000
Madrid : Aguilar
80 x 55
General maps of the individual provinces, showing towns, boundaries, economic statistics and population figures etc.
Maps available :
Alava
Albacete
Alicante
Almeria
Avila
Caceres
Cadiz
Castellon
Cordoba
Gerona
Granada
Guipuzcoa
La Coruna
Lerida
Lugo
Malaga
Orense
Oviedo
Pontevedra
Sevilla
Soria
Tarragona
Valencia
Each S.Ptas 30

M HISTORICAL

HISTORIA DE ESPAÑA
Barcelona : Editorial Teide
115 x 88
Historical wall map for schools.
S.Ptas 275

ESPAÑA
1:1, 250, 000
Madrid : Seix-Barral
119 x 86
Pictorial map showing transport systems.

ATLASES
A1 GENERAL: ROADS

ESPAÑA - MAPA OFFICIAL DE CARRETERAS
1:400, 000
11th edition
Madrid : Min. de Obras Públicas, 1975
42 x 31
90pp
45 fold out pages of col. maps, inc. Balearic and Canary Islands, with layer scale maps for tourist areas and town plans of major cities. All classes of road shown with route numbers and distances, also national parks, accommodation, and places of interest marked by symbols. 36pp motoring and tourist information. Spiral bound, no index.
S.Ptas 400

ATLASES
K HUMAN GEOGRAPHY

ATLAS LINGUISTIC DE CATALUNYA
Ed A Griera
Barcelona : Ediciones Poligrafa
In 10 vols
31 x 44
Study of Catalan language, with 1, 287 maps, covering the area Rousillon - Alghero and Ribagorza - Alicante. Inc. text vol.
17 x 25
36pp S.Ptas 250
Index vol. 12 x 25, 172pp
S.Ptas 825
Per vol. S.Ptas 3, 500

ATLASES
L ECONOMIC

ATLAS COMERCIAL DE ESPAÑA
Madrid: Camaras de Comerico
1963
48 x 36
Industrial and commercial atlas of Spain with 50 maps of economic features, trade and industry and statistical tables. In Sp.

ATLASES
M HISTORICAL

ATLAS DE HISTORIA DE ESPAÑA
J Vicens Vives
Barcelona : Editorial Teide
18 x 25
104pp
Covers the history of Spain to the 20th C, with 74 maps and text.
For schools. S.Ptas 125

ATLASES
O NATIONAL

ATLAS NACIONAL DE ESPAÑA
Madrid : IGC, 1965+
41 x 55 (Map size 75 x 52)
Official national atlas of Spain to contain over 100 col. map plates covering physical, cultural, economic and political matters together with 1:500, 000 physical map, transparent reference overlay, 2 bound booklets describing geography of Spain and a toponymic index of over 40, 000 names. Being issued in parts, the first 3 having been published.
First three parts S.Ptas 4, 000

NUEVO ATLAS DE ESPAÑA
Madrid : Aguilar, 1961
23 x 32
462pp
Comprehensive atlas of Spain: with maps of the whole country and of provinces, insets, photographs, descriptions, index, statistical tables. Special maps on pop, agriculture, industry, geol, vegetation, climate, administration. In Sp. Hard covers.
S.Ptas 500

467.2 Andorra

A1 GENERAL MAPS: ROADS

LA PRINCIPAUTÉ D'ANDORRE
1:80, 000
Paris : IGN, 1966
45 x 40
Col. map with historical and geog. info. Roads and distances, paths and other tourist details.
Folded F.Fr 5.00

THE VALLEYS OF ANDORRA
1:62, 000
Nottingham : Ray Palmer, 1968
55 x 47
Contoured map with roads and topographical detail. Legend in Eng and Sp. In folder.

ANDORRA I SECTORS FRONTERERS
1:40, 000
Granollers : Editorial Alpina, 1971
75 x 62
Topog. map, contoured with roads and tracks. S.Ptas 50

C OFFICIAL SURVEYS

CARTE DE FRANCE
1:50, 000
Paris : IGN
Sheet XXI-49 FONTARGENTE covers Andorra.
see FRANCE 44C and index 44/14.

467.5 Balearic Islands

A1 GENERAL MAPS: ROADS

GENERALKARTE MALLORCA (SHELL)
1:175, 000
Stuttgart : Mairs
112 x 47
Inc. Ibiza, Menorca, Formentera.
All classes of roads, distances in km, footpaths, relief shading and places of tourist interest.

ISLAS BALEARES
1:175, 000
T-26
Bilbao : FH
122 x 48
All classes of roads, road widths, distances in km, spot heights and relief shading, railways, petrol and service stations, airports and camping sites. Guide supplement inc. Plan of Mallorca on reverse.

A2 GENERAL MAPS: LOCAL

ISLAS DE IBIZA Y FORMENTERA
1:75, 000
Bilbao : FH
70 x 48
Col. map relief shaded, roads classified according to importance and width. Considerable tourist information shown including places of interest, camp sites, golf courses etc. Town plans of Ibiza and San Antonio Abad on reverse.

C OFFICIAL SURVEYS

MAPA MILITAR DE ESPAÑA
(Series 2C)
1:200, 000
Servicio Geografico del Ejercito
4 sheets to cover Balearic Islands:

9-8	Ibiza & Formentera	50p
10-7	Majorca	60p
10-8	Cabrera	50p
11-7	Minorca	50p

See SPAIN 460C and index 460/4.

ATLASES
A2 GENERAL: LOCAL

BARNETTS MAJORCA ATLAS
Barking : Barnett
48pp
Atlas with a fold out road map in colour and 28 sheet plans of principal resorts.
45p

468.2 Gibraltar

A1 GENERAL MAPS: ROADS

MINIPLAN OF GIBRALTAR
1:9, 400
London : Miniplans Ltd.
Col. plan of peninsular marking places of interest with index to features and brief guide on reverse. 25p

C OFFICIAL SURVEYS

TOPOGRAPHICAL PLAN OF GIBRALTAR
1:2, 500
In 6 sheets, see index 468.2/1
Gibraltar : Gibraltar Survey, 1970
80 x 56
2 colour plan, contours brown, base land details (roads, buildings, topog. features) in grey.
Each 50p

D POLITICAL & ADMINISTRATIVE

GIBRALTAR
1:40, 000
DOS 963, edition 2
Tolworth : DOS, 1948
Small general map showing communications and settlement. 10p

WORLD LECTURE MAPS - GIBRALTAR
1:12, 500
GSGS 4948 Map B 12
Feltham : DMS
Sketch planning map, principal contours and layer cols. communication and settlement. 50p

468.5 Canary Islands

A1 GENERAL MAPS: ROADS

ISLAS CANARIAS
1:150, 000
T-32
Bilbao : FH
121 x 72
All classes of roads, road widths and distances in km, petrol and service stations, towns of interest, camping sites, airports, relief shading and spot heights. Guide supplement to Eng, Fr, Sp and Ger; insets of Lanzarote and Fuerteventura, scale 1:400, 000. Plans of 4 major towns.

KANARISCHEN INSELN
1:150, 000
In 2 sheets
Stuttgart : Mair
Tourist maps, showing roads, footpaths, relief shading, places of tourist interest by symbols.
Sheets :
I Tenerife - La Palma - Gomera - Hierro
II Gran Canaria - Fuerteventura - Lanzarote

A2 GENERAL MAPS: LOCAL

GRAN CANARIA
1:150, 000
Bilbao : FH
70 x 48
Main and secondary roads, distances in km, airports and tourist attractions. Town plan of Las Palmas with street index on reverse.

TENERIFE, MAPA TURISTICO
1:150, 000
Bilbao : FH
50 x 48
Tourist map, showing main and secondary roads, distances in km, places of interest. Town plans of Santa Cruz and Puerto de la Cruz on reverse, with street index.

F GEOLOGY

MAPA GEOLÓGICO DE LA ISLA DE TENERIFE
1:200, 000
Madrid : IGM
Generalised geol. map of Tenerife.
S.Ptas 250

BOSQUEJO GEOLÓGICO DE HIERRO
1:200, 000
Madrid : IGM
Generalised geol. map of the island of Hierro. S.Ptas 75

MAPA GEOLÓGICO DE LA ISLA DE FUERTEVENTURA
1:100, 000
Madrid : IGM
Col. geol. map. S.Ptas 250

MAPA GEOLÓGICO DE LA ISLA DE GRAN CANARIA
1:100, 000
Madrid : IGM
Col. geol. map. S.Ptas 250

469 Portugal

See also: 46 IBERIAN PENINSULA

A1 GENERAL MAPS: ROADS

PORTUGAL
1:1, 000, 000
London : Foldex
Shows roads classified, relief shading: patent fold. 45p

PORTUGAL
1;700, 000
London : Foldex
Show roads classified, relief shading: patent fold. 45p

PORTUGAL
1:500, 000
Sheet 37
Paris : Michelin, 1975
49 x 109
All classes of roads, distances in km, road numbers, spot heights in m, picturesque routes, railways and state boundaries. Legend in Fr and Port. with easily understood sympols.

CARTA STRADALE D'EUROPA
1:500, 000
Sheet 13
Milano : TCI, 1965
63 x 112
All classes of roads, road conditions, distances in km, spot heights in m, car ferries, railways and layer col.
see also EUROPE 4 A1.

MAPAS DE CARRETARAS
1:500, 000
FH
3 sheets for Portugal - C1, 4, 7
see IBERIAN PENINSULAR 46 A1.

B TOWN PLANS

TOWN PLANS
Various scales
Col. plans with index to streets.
Plans available:

Lisbon		
1:13, 500	Hallwag	DM 4.50
Lisbon		
1:13, 500	Falk(209)	DM 4.80
Oporto		
1:10, 000	official	

C OFFICIAL SURVEYS

KARTA MIRA
1:2, 500, 000
VVK
1 sheet required for complete coverage of mainland Portugal - No 52
see WORLD 100C and index 100/2.

CARTA INTERNATIONAL DO MONDO
1:1, 000, 000
Lisboa : IGC
3 sheets published covering Portugal
NJ-29 Lisboa 1957
NI-28 Madeira, 1969
NJ-26 Acores, 1965
Each Esc. 15.00
see WORLD 100C and index 100/1.

CARTA DE PORTUGAL
1:1, 000, 000
Lisboa : IGC, 1971
Based on the International Map of the World sheets, with relief shading added, layer col. contours communications and settlement. Esc. 30.00

THE WORLD
1:1, 000, 000
DMS Series 1301
see WORLD 100C and index 100/1.

THE WORLD
1:500, 000
DMS Series 1404
see WORLD 100C and index 100/7.

CARTA COROGRÁFICA DE PORTUGAL
1:400, 000
In 3 sheets
Lisboa : IGC, 1968
98 x 69 each
Showing towns, communications and contours. Layer coloured.

Sheet 1	North
Sheet 2	Central
Sheet 3	South
Each	Esc. 25.00

CARTA DE PORTUGAL
1:200, 000
Series M585
In 8 sheets, see index 469/1
Lisboa : IGC, 1972+
64 x 80 each sheet
Col. series classifying roads with distances; contours, wooded areas in green, relief shading. Sheets 7 and 8, ie Baixo Alentefo and Algarve West and East, pub. 1972.

CARTA DE PORTUGAL
1:100, 000
In 53 sheets, see index 469/1
Lisboa : IGC
Topog. series in progress replacing earlier series, contoured with roads, paths, railways, boundaries, settlement and vegetation.
Esc. 15.00

ANTIGA CARTA DE PORTUGAL
1:100, 000
Lisboa : IGC
80 x 50
First topographic series of the country 1853-1892. Contoured. Available in 37 sheets.
Each Esc. 10.00

CARTA COROGRÁFICA DE PORTUGAL
1:50, 000
In 171 sheets, see index 469/1
Lisboa : IGC, 1941+
64 x 40 each
Col. maps showing topographic, hydrographic, orographic details. Footpaths, railways, provincial boundaries and contours.
Each Esc. 15.00

CARTA TOPOGRÁFICA DE PORTUGAL
1:10, 000
Lisboa : IGC 1948+
64 x 40
Large scale planimetric series in progress, published for central Lisbon area and also 1 sheet for Ponta da Sagnes.
Each Esc. 15.00

CARTA TOPOGRÁFICAS
1:5, 000
Lisboa : IGC
Large scale planimetric series in progress.
Sheets published :
34D/2-Ib Lisboa (Prazeres) 1960
26C/2-2c,d, 3-2a,b Berlenga 1967
Each Esc. 15.00

D POLITICAL & ADMINISTRATIVE

CARTA ADMINISTRATIVA DE PORTUGAL
1:600, 000
Lisboa : IGC, 1952
77 x 113
Administrative divisions in different cols, showing communes and districts.
Esc. 30.00

E1 PHYSICAL: RELIEF

CARTA DE PORTUGAL METROPOLITANO
1:2, 500, 000
Lisboa : IGC, 1972
111 x 80
Covering land and adjacent islands. Contours, relief shading, hypsometric and bathymetric colours. Azores and Madeira inset. Esc. 50.00

SPANIEN UND PORTUGAL
1:1,000, 000
2nd ed
Munchen : List
175 x 130
Relief wall map, inc. Spanish Islands and N African coast. DM 128

ESPANA Y PORTUGAL
1:900, 000
Braunschweig : Westermann
175 x 172
Col. physical wall map in Sp.

CARTA HIPSOMETRICA DE PORTUGAL
1:600, 000
Lisboa : IGC, 1955
Contours, relief shown by hypsometric cols.
Esc. 30.00

CARTA HIPSOMETRICA DE PORTUGAL
1:500, 000
In 2 sheets
Lisboa : SGP, 1906
Contoured with layer colours.
Esc. 200.00

MAPA ORO-HIDROGRAFIA DE PORTUGAL
1:200, 000
Lisboa : Livraria Portugal
In 38 sheets
44 x 34 each
Inc. 1 text sheet showing contours and water, without names.
In case.

F GEOLOGICAL

CARTA GEOLÓGICA DE PORTUGAL
1:1, 000, 000
Lisboa : SGP, 1968
52 x 75
Generalised geol. map with structural indications. With 15pp text.
Esc. 25.00

CARTA GEOLÓGICA DO QUATERNARIO DE PORTUGAL
1:1, 000, 000
Lisboa : GSGP, 1969
55 x 77
Quaternary map in cols.
Esc. 25.00

CARTA LITOLÓGICA DE PORTUGAL
1:1, 000, 000
Lisboa : SGP, 1967/8
52 x 68
Col. Lithological map: description in Port. With 89pp text.

CARTA HIDROGEOLÓGICA DE PORTUGAL
1:1, 000, 000
Lisboa : SGP, 1970
55 x 77
Hydrogeological map. Esc. 25.00

CARTE GÉOLOGIQUE DU NORD-OUEST DE LA PÉNINSULE IBÉRIQUE
1:500, 000
Lisboa : SGP, 1969
103 x 84
Col. map showing Hercynian and antehercynian rocks of NW Spain and Portugal.
Esc. 30.00

CARTA E CORTES GEOLÓGICAS DOS ARREDORES DE TORRES VEDRAS
Lisboa : SGP, 1928
Geological map and description of the geology of Torres Vedras and surroundings.
Esc. 50.00

CARTA GEOLÓGICA DE PORTUGAL
1:50, 000
In 76 sheets, see index 469/2
Lisbon : SGP, 1952+
63 x 41
Geol. series in progress.
Each Esc. 30.00

G EARTH RESOURCES

CARTA DAS NASCENTES MINERAIS DE PORTUGAL
1:1, 000, 000
Lisboa : SGP, 1970
55 x 77
Map of original minerals.
Esc. 25.00

CARTA MINEIRA DE PORTUGAL
1:500, 000
Lisboa : SGP, 1965
73 x 59 each
South and North sheets; mineral occurrences against geol. background. With text in French. Esc. 100.00

CARTA DOS SOLOS DE PORTUGAL
1:50, 000
In 260 sheets
Lisboa : Serv. de Recon. Agrario Col. series of soil maps in progress.

H BIOGEOGRAPHY

CARTA AGRÍCOLA E FLORESTAL DE PORTUGAL
1:250, 000
In 3 sheets
Lisboa; Serv. Rec. e Ord Agrario, 1960-65
115 x 87 each
Col. map showing agricultural and forest regions of Portugal and principal land usage.

CARTA AGRÍCOLA E FLORESTAL
1:50, 000
In 260 sheets, see index 469/3
Lisboa : Serv. de Recon. Agrario
Series showing agricultural and forest regions; in progress.

CARTE DE CAPACIDADE DE USO DO SOLOS
1:50, 000
In 60 sheets
Lisboa : Serv. de Recon. Agrario
Following standard 50, 000 sheet lines; showing land use. Series in progress.

K HUMAN GEOGRAPHY

DISTRIBUCAO DE POPULACÃO DE PORTUGAL
1:500, 000
In 2 sheets
Lisboa : Ministeria de Economia, 1940
88 x 130 complete
Population indicated by dot method.

469.8 Madeira

C OFFICIAL SURVEYS

ARQUIPELAGO DA MADEIRA
1:50, 000
In 3 sheets
Lisboa : IGC
Contoured topog. maps.
Sheets available:
Ilha da Madeira (2 sheets)
1971 140 x 81 complete
Esc. 30.00
Ilha do Porto Santo
1970 75 x 26 Esc. 15.00
Ilhas Desertas e Ilhas Selvagens
1970 82 x 60 Esc. 15.00

469.9 Azores

C OFFICIAL SURVEYS

INTERNATIONAL MAP OF THE WORLD
1:1, 000, 000
Sheet NJ 26 - Arquipelagos dos Acores
Lisboa : IGC, 1965
see WORLD 100C and index 100/1.

ARQUIPÉLAGO DOS ACORES
1:200, 000
In 2 sheets
Lisboa : IGC, 1969-71
Topog. map, contoured with roads, tracks and settlement.
Sheets :
Grupo Oriental (São Miguel - S Maria) 1969
Grupo Central (Faial, Pico, S Jorge, Graciosa, Terceira), 1971
Each Esc. 15.00

ARQUIPÉLAGO DOS AÇORES
1:50, 000
In 9 sheets
Lisboa : IGC
Topog. series contoured, in the following sheets :
Ilha de São Miguel (2 sheets) 1971
Ilha de Santa Maria, 1965
Ilha Terceira, 1965
Ilha Graciosa, 1968
Ilha de São Jorge (2 sheets), 1969
Ilha do Pico (East), 1969
Ilha do Faial e do Pico (West), 1969
Ilha das Flores e Corvo, 1969
Per sheet Esc. 15.00

ARQUIPÉLAGO DOS ACORES - ILHA DO FAIAL
1:25, 000
Lisboa : IGC, 1942
Topog. map, contoured with roads, paths and settlement. Esc. 20.00

F GEOLOGY

CARTA GEOLÓGICA DE ACORES
1:25, 000 - 1:50, 000
Lisboa : SGP
Series of col. geol maps.
Maps published:
Ilha do Corvo 1:25, 000, 1967 text
Ilha do Faial " 1959 text
Ilha do Flores " 1968 text
Ilha do Pico 1:50, 000 1963 2 sheets
Santa Maria " 1961 text
São Miguel " 1958
2 sheets, text
Each sheet Esc. 30.00

47 European USSR

See also:
57 USSR
4 EUROPE

A1 GENERAL MAPS: ROADS

OSTEUROPA
1:3, 000, 000
Bern : Hallwag
67 x 80
Oslo to Moscow, Genoa to Ankara.
Main and secondary roads, distances in km, road numbers, mountain passes with heights in metres, car and air ferries, frontiers.

EUROPE - EASTERN
1:2, 500, 000
Edinburgh : Bart
72 x 94
Main and secondary roads, with numbers. Distances. Relief shading, contours, railways. Legend in 4 langs.

OSTEUROPA
1:2, 000, 000
Wien : FB, 1971
82 x 115
Stockholm to Kostroma and Salonica to Ankara. Main and secondary roads, distances in km, route numbering, spot heights in metres, railways and state boundaries. DM 6.80

WESTLICHE SOWJETUNION
1:2, 000, 000
No 896
Frankfurt : Ravenstein
80 x 100
Physical, political road map of European Russia. DM 8.80

ROAD MAP OF EASTERN EUROPE
1:1, 950, 000
Budapest : Cart, 1971
76 x 108
Main and secondary roads, distances in km. European USSR inset at 1:7, 800, 000.

RUMÄNIEN-BULGARIEN
1:1, 000, 000
No 1175
Bern : K & F
90 x 127
Main and secondary roads, numbered and classified, distances in km, relief shading, tourist details. DM 6.80

A2 GENERAL MAPS: LOCAL

BALTIC STATES - EESTI, LATVIJA, LIETUVA
1:700, 000
Brussels : Mantniek
84 x 108
Shows all classes of roads, vegetation, hydrography in green. Estonia, Latvia, Lithuania.

ESTONSKAYA SSR - TURISTSKAYA SKHEMA
Moskva : GUGK, 1971
Contours map showing forests and tourist details.

B TOWN PLANS

MOSCOW
Hamburg : Falk/Prag : Cart
Col. plan of all principal streets with major buildings illustrated. Street index.
DM 4.80

TOWN PLAN OF RIGA
1:25, 000
70 x 62
Photographic map of older ed. Inset plan of Old City at 1:6, 300. Legend in Ger. With separate index.

C OFFICIAL SURVEYS

THE WORLD
1:1, 000, 000
AMS Series 1301
see WORLD 100C and index 100/1.

THE WORLD
1:500, 000
DMS Series 1404
see WORLD 100C and index 100/7.

UBERSICHTSKARTE VON MITTELEUROPA
1:300, 000
Frankfurt : Inst. fur Angewandte Geodasie
see GERMANY 430 C.

D POLITICAL & ADMINISTRATIVE

EVROPEISKAYA CHAST' SSSR - POLITIKO-ADMINISTRATIVNAYA KARTA
1:4, 000, 000
Moskva : GUGK, 1973
82 x 105
Political-admin. wall map.

WESTLICHER TEIL DER UdSSR
1:3, 000, 000
1st ed.
Gotha : Haack
72 x 88
Col. hand map of western USSR showing boundaries, communications, and 64pp text. M 7.00

SSSR - EVROPSKÁ CAST
1:2, 500, 000
Praha : Cart, 1971
General school wall map of the European USSR. Kcs 165

EVROPEISKAYA CASTSSSR
1:2, 500, 000
In 4 sheets
Moskva : GUGK, 1969
120 x 160 complete
Surface col. showing districts, communications network.

RUSIA EUROPEA
Barcelona : Editorial Teide
25 x 33
School hand map showing boundaries, major cities. S.Ptas 1

KAVKAZ - POLITIKO-ADMINISTRATIVNAYA KARTA
1:1, 000, 000
Moskva : GUGK, 1970
140 x 105 complete
2 sheet map showing the Caucasus.
Inc. communications. Legend in Rus.

EVROPEISKAYA CHASTV'SSSR
1:15, 000, 000
Moskva : GUGK, 1973
Outline map.

URSS PARTE EUROPEA
1:12, 000, 000
Novara : Ag
Small hand outline map for schools.
L 40

E1 PHYSICAL: RELIEF

ZSRR CZEŚĆ EUROPEJSKA
1:3, 000, 000
Warszawa : PPWK, 1969
102 x 69
Physical map with contours, communications. Double sided, north and south.

EUROPESKAJA SSR
1:2, 500, 000
In 4 sheets
Moskva : GUGK
120 x 160 complete
Shows contours, railways. In Rus.

REGIONE RUSSA (URSS EUROPEA)
1:13, 500, 000
Novara : Ag
33 x 26
Plastic relief map, with physical-political-economic details on reverse.
L 450

E2 PHYSICAL: LAND FEATURES

GEOMORFOLOGICHESKAYA KARTA EVROPEYSKOY CHASTI SSSR I KAVKAZA
1:2, 500, 000
In 4 sheets
Moskva : GUGK, 1970
140 x 156 complete
Covering USSR (European) and the Caucasus. Morphological map with descriptive text vol, 1966.

M HISTORICAL

RUSSIAN EMPIRE FROM THE EARLY 19th C - 1861 (EUROPEAN PART)
1:3, 000, 000
Moskva : GUGK, 1973
School historical wall map.
Kop 30

EXPANSION OF RUSSIA IN EUROPE AND EUROPEAN INVASIONS OF RUSSIA - PALMER WORLD HISTORY MAP
Chicago : Rand McNally
127 x 116
Shows Russian territory in 1533, 1598, 1914.

ARKHITEKTURNYE PAMYATNIKI EVROPEYSKOY CHASTI SSSR
Moskva : GUGK
Architectural memorials of European USSR.

ATLASES
A1 GENERAL: ROADS

ATLAS AVTOMOBIL'NYKH DOROG SSSR
1:1, 000, 000
Moskva : GUGK, 1973
17 x 21
166pp
Containing detailed col. road maps at scales from 1:4, 000, 000 covering whole of USSR, except Siberia. Strip diagrams of principal routes, maps of the approaches to Moscow, distance tables, index. Text in Russian.

TSENTR EVROPEYSKOY CHASTI SSSR ATLAS AUTOMOBIL'NYKH DOROG
Moskva : GUGK, 1973
17 x 27
40pp
Road atlas of Central European USSR.
Kop 50

SEVERO-ZAPAD EVROPEYSKOY CHASTI SSSR ATLAS AVTOMOBIL 'NYKH DOROG
Moskva : GUGK, 1973
17 x 27
32pp
Road atlas of N W part of European USSR.
Kop 50

48 Scandinavia

See also: 4 EUROPE

A1 GENERAL MAPS: ROADS

SKANDANAVIEN "POLAR"
1:3, 000, 000
Bern : Hallwag, 1975
52 x 80
Covers Norway, Sweden, Denmark, Finland. Main and secondary roads, distances in km. Road numbers, spot heights in metres, car ferries, state frontiers.
DM 5.80

WORLD TRAVEL MAP OF SCANDINAVIA
1:2, 500, 000
Edinburgh : Bart, 1975
50 x 79
Norway, Sweden and Denmark. Principal and secondary roads only. Railways, airports, state frontiers. Contoured and layer col.

SKANDINAVIEN
1:2, 000, 000
Wien : F & B
81 x 101
Norway, Sweden, Denmark and Iceland. All classes of roads numbered: distances in km, spot heights in metres, state frontiers. DM 6.80

NORDEN
1:1, 500, 000
Stockholm : GLA
89 x 130
Norway, Sweden, Denmark, Finland, Iceland, Faroe Islands. Main and secondary roads with numbers, railways, ferries and boats, hill shading, spot heights in metres, forests and cultivated lands, airports, national parks. Pop. indicated. Boundaries.
Flat or folded S.Kr. 22.50
Rollers S.Kr. 67.00
Boards S.Kr. 94.00

DANIMARCA, SVEZIA MERIDONALE E NORVEGIA MERIDIONALE
1:1, 000, 000
Novara : Ag
98 x 94
Coloured road and tourist map for Denmark, Southern Sweden and Norway.
L 700

SCANDINAVIA
1:1, 000, 000
In 2 sheets
London : Foldex
2 double-sided sheets, showing roads classified, relief shading: patent fold.
Each 45p

SKANDINAVIEN
1:1, 000, 000
No 1886
München : JRO
88 x 123
Green base, roads classified and numbered. Distances in km, tourist information, some relief shading. (N Scandinavia inset at 1:3, 000, 000) DM 6.80

A2 GENERAL MAPS: LOCAL

NORWEGEN UND SCHWEDEN
1:800, 000
No 887
Frankfurt : Ravenstein, 1976
135 x 96
Roads classified and numbered with distances in km. Covers Norway and Sweden. Relief shading, ferry routes, frontiers, places of interest, pop. indicated. Double-sided.
DM 9.80

POHJOISKALOTTI
1:1, 000, 000
Helsinki : Maan, 1972
Road map of Northern Scandinavia.
FMK 6.00

NORDKALOTTEN
1:1, 000, 000
Stockholm : GLA
83 x 65
Road map of Northern Scandinavia, roads numbered with distances, other tourist details. Legend in 6 langs.
S.Kr. 8.50

SÜDSKANDINAVIEN
1:1, 000, 000
No 1146
Bern : K & F
89 x 114
Sweden, Norway, Denmark, Trondheim south to Hamburg. All classes of roads numbered, with distances in km, spot heights in metres, railways, car ferries, airports, state frontiers, tourist details.
DM 6.80

SÜD-SKANDINAVIEN
1:800, 000
No 91
Stuttgart : RV, 1975
97 x 128
Main and secondary roads, with numbers and distances in km, tourist interest places, other communications. Covers S Norway, S Sweden, Denmark. Pop. indicated. Legend in 4 langs, inc. Eng.
DM 6.80

D POLITICAL & ADMINISTRATIVE

OSTSEELANDER
1:3, 000, 000
Gotha : Haack, 1969
60 x 88
Haack "hand-map" of Northern Europe. Political col, boundaries, railways. 55pp index.

NORTHERN EUROPE
1:2, 437, 500
Washington : NGS
73 x 91
Political col. wall map covering Scandinavia.
Paper US $2.00
Plastic US $3.00

SEVERNÍ EVROPA
1:1, 250, 000
Praha : Kart
General school wall map of Northern Europe. Kcs 150

POHJOLA (THE NORTH)
1:1, 000, 000
Helsinki : WSOY
104 x 230
School wall map. FMK 100

EUROPA SETTENTRIONALE
1:7, 500, 000
Novara : Ag
Small outline hand map of Scandinavia for schools. L 40

SKANDINAVIEN UMRISSKARTEN
1:5, 000, 000
No 0821
Bern : K & F
36 x 43
Outline map with rivers and boundaries.

E1 PHYSICAL: RELIEF

NOORDWEST-EUROPA
1:2, 500, 000
Groningen : Wolters-Noordhoff
85 x 107
Physical school wall map; relief shading, boundaries, communications.
Fl. 44.75

SCANDINAVIE (PHYSIQUE)
1:1, 750, 000
No 1173
St Germain-en-Laye : Éditions MDI
92 x 126
Plastic coated physical wall map for schools. Economic map on reverse.

NORDEN
1:1, 750, 000
Stockholm : GLA
44 x 132
Phys. with state boundaries.
S.Kr. 18.00

SKANDINAVIEN
1:1, 625, 000
Hamburg : Flemming
99 x 137
Physical col. wall map, layer col, relief shading, cities graded by pop, boundaries, railways.

LES ÉTATS SCANDINAVES, RELIEF
Map No 253
Eds. Vidal Lablache and H. Varon
Paris : Armand Colin
120 x 100
Relief wall map for schools. Economic map on reverse.

NORDEUROPA
1:1, 500, 000
Gotha : Haack
156 x 177
Physical school wall map, layer col, hachures, communications, internat. boundaries.

OSTSEELANDER
1:1, 200, 000
Braunschweig : Westermann
180 x 220
Covers Sweden, Denmark, Norway, Finland and the Baltic countries. Physical wall map, layer col, hill shading, cities graded by pop, communications, boundaries.

NORDEN
1:1, 000, 000
In 4 sheets
Stockholm : GLA
160 x 220
Wall map of Scandinavia, relief shading and communications.

Flat	S.Kr. 100.00
Rollers	S.Kr. 195.00
Board	S.Kr. 268.00

SKANDINAVIEN
1:1, 000, 000
München : List
170 x 220
Wenschow physical wall map for schools. Iceland and Faroe Islands inset.
Eds. in Ger. and Sw. 3rd ed.
DM 142.00

DANIA-SZWECJA
1:1, 000, 000
Warszawa : PPWK
General physical map with communications.

EUROPA SETTENTRIONALE
1:7, 500, 000
Novara : Ag
33 x 26
Moulded plastic relief map covering Scandinavia (including Iceland). Physical, political, economic details on reverse.
L 450

NORDEN RELIEFKARTA
1:7, 500, 000
Stockholm : SRA
25 x 34
Self-framed col. plastic relief map in Sw.

F GEOLOGY

NORDENS BERGGRUND ÖVERSIKTSKARTA
1:1, 000, 000
Stockholm : GLA, 1967
140 x 190
Col. geol. map of Scandinavia, inc. Iceland and Spitsbergen inset.

NORDEN GEOLOGISK ÖVERSIKTSKARTA
1:1, 000, 000
Stockholm : SGU
166 x 220
Col. geol. wall map.

L ECONOMIC

SCANDANAVIE (PHYSIQUE)
No 1173
Editions MDI
Economic map on reverse.
see SCANDINAVIA 48 E1.

LES ETATS SCANDINAVES - RELIEF
Armand Colin
Economic map on reverse.
see SCANDINAVIA 48 E1.

SEVERNÁ EUROPA, HOSPODARSKA MAPA
1:1, 250, 000
In 4 sheets
Praha : Kart, 1970
Economic wall map of Northern Europe, covering Denmark, Norway, Sweden, Finland, Island, Spitsbergen at 1:1, 500, 000, Faroe Island 1:1, 000, 000.

M HISTORICAL

SUOMEN JA POHJOISMAIDEN HISTORIALLINEN KOULUKARTTA
1:1, 000, 000
Helsinki : WSOY
172 x 225
Historical school wall map of Finland and the Northern countries.
FMK 90.00

SVECIA, DANIA ET NORVEGIA, 1662
Stockholm : GLA
33 x 43
Facsimile of Andreas Bureus and J Blaeus map.

Flat	S.Kr. 17.00

CARTA MARINA
Stockholm : GLA
117 x 90
Facsimile of Olaus Magnus map of 1539. Covers whole of Scandinavia inc. Iceland. Decorative facsimile map.

Flat	S.Kr. 29.00
Rollers	S.Kr. 79.00
Board	S.Kr. 73.00
Text also available	S.Kr. 6.00

ATLASES
A1 GENERAL: ROADS

DET BÄSTAS BILBOK
Stockholm : Reader's Digest AB, 1969
27 x 28
Swedish road atlas with 149pp text, 112pp maps, 80pp index, 47pp town plans and motorways maps.
Also available in Norwegian as "Det Bestes Bilbok", pub. Det Beste A/S, Oslo.

480 Finland

A1 GENERAL MAPS: ROADS

MAANTEIDEN YLEISKARTTA
OVERSIKTSKARTA ÖVER
LANDSVÄGARNA
1:1, 500, 000
Helsinki : Maan, 1970
39 x 78
Main and secondary roads of Finland, distances in km, roads with numbers, airports, ferries, park areas, traffic signs, with 62 through-town plans on reverse.
FMK 5.50

PIKKU TIEKARTTA
1:1, 500, 000
Helsinki : Maan, 1969
Pocket road map of Finland.
FMK 4.00

FINNLAND
1:1, 500, 000
No 220
Koln : Polyglott
Roads classified, with distances in km.
DM 3.20

SHELL REISEKARTE FINNLAND
1:1, 500, 000
Stuttgart : Mair
Roads classified and numbered, distances in km; tourist info. and details etc. Legend in 12 langs. DM 4.80

SUOMEN MAANTIEVERKKO
1:1, 000, 000
Helsinki : Maan, 1969
63 x 122
Showing motorway network.
FMK 7.00

FINNLAND
1:1, 000, 000
No 1147
Bern : K & F
65 x 115
Road map showing all classes of roads, distances, scenic routes, railways, places of interest.

FINNLAND
1:1, 000, 000
Bern : Hallwag
81 x 81
All classes of roads, distances in km, route numbers, spot heights in metres, hill shading, railways, ferries and state boundaries. Area north of Rovaniemi inset, scale 1:4, 000, 000
DM 5.80

FINLAND
1:1, 000, 000
London : Foldex
Shows roads classified, relief shading; patent folding. 30p

FINNLAND
1:800, 000
No 877
Stuttgart : Ravenstein, 1976
94 x 75
Double-sided map showing north on one side, south on the other. Roads classified showing route numbers and distances; camping sites, airports, ferries and sites of interest. DM 8.80

ETELA SUOMI AUTOILIJAN TIEKARTTA
1:750, 000
In 2 sheets
Helsinki : Maan, 1971
All classes of roads, road numbers and conditions, distances in km, spot heights in metres, ferries, airports, camping sites, youth hostels, motels and state frontiers. With index.
North - Nuogam to Oulu. Town plan insets of Tornio, Kemi, Oulu and Rovaniemi
58 x 80
South - Oulu to Hango. Town plan insets of Tampere, Helsinki and Turku.
86 x 79
Each FMK 9.00

AUTOILIJAN TIEKARTTA
1:750, 000
Helsinki : Maan, 1972
90 x 156
Motoring road map, mounted on cloth or fibre board. FMK 72.00

SUOMEN TIEVERKKO
1:600, 000
In 2 sheets
Helsinki : Maan, 1972
120 x 88 and 88 x 125
Boundaries, water, road network with numbers. FMK 9.00

SUOMEN TIEKARTTA VÄGKARTA
OVER FINLAND
1:200, 000 - 1:400, 000
In 13 sheets, see index 480/1
Helsinki : Maan, 1969-72
Various sizes
All clases of roads, distances in km, spot heights in metres, railways, ferries, camping sites, youth hostels, motels, airports and state boundaries, sketch town plans inset.
Sheets 12 and 13 at 1:400, 000.
Each FMK 8.00
GT eds. available for Sheets 2, 3, 4 and 7,
Each FMK 12.50

A2 GENERAL MAPS: LOCAL

ALAND (AHVENANMAA)
MATKAILUKARTTA
1:200, 000
Helsinki : Maan, 1972
Touring map of the island.
FMK 5.00

ÅLAND (AHVENANMAA)
MATKAILUKARTTA
1:100, 000
Helsinki : Maan, 1973
Touring map of the island of Åland.

ULKOILUKARTAT
1:100, 000
See index 480/1
Helsinki : Maan
Maps of environs of towns showing hiking, skiing and camping areas.
Available for :
Helsinki ympparistoineen, 1972
Hameenlinna " 1970
Tampere " 1972
Turku " 1971
Each FMK 8.00

ULKOILUKARTAT
1:50, 000
See index 480/1
Helsinki : Maan
Excursion maps, contoured and showing information for camping, hiking etc.
Available for :
Rukatunturi-Oulanka, 1972
Ylläs - Levi, 1971
Pallas - Keimio, 1972
Hetta - Outtakka, 1972
Halti - Kilpisjärvi, 1969
Lemmenjoki, 1972
Inari - Menesjärvi, 1972
Kaunispää - Kopsusjärvi, 1971
Sokosti - Suomujoki, 1972
Each FMK 7.00
In preparation :
Tekeilla
Hämeenlinna

ULKOILUKARTAT
1:25, 000
See index 480/1
Helsinki : Maan
Excursion maps based on topog. series, with details for walking and camping.
Available for :
Ostersundom, 1966
Helsinki, 1971 (without hiking information, FMK 8.00)
Nuuksio, 1965
Turku Abo, 1969
Jyvaskyla, 1967
Kajaani, 1971
Oulu, 1966
Rovaniemi, 1966
Pyhatunturi, 1967
Lahiti, 1966

B TOWN PLANS

ESPOO, YLEISKARTTA
1:50, 000
Helsinki : Maan, 1970
Town plan and guide.

HELSINKI - OPASKARTTA
1:20, 000
Helsinki : Helsingen KKK, 1973
124 x 83
Col. plan with legend in 6 languages incl. English. Street index.

TOURIST MAP OF TAMPERE
1:15, 000
Tampere : Tampereen Kaupungin
Mittansosasto, 1972
Tourist map in colour.

MAP OF TAMPERE CITY CENTRE
1:10, 000/50, 000
Tampere : Tampereen Kaupungin Mittausosasto, 1972
Coloured map.

TAMPERE : ADDRESS MAP
1:10, 000
In 6 sheets
Tempere : Tampereen Kaupungin Mittausosasto, 1971
Address map of the City, showing streets, public buildings, districts. In colour.

VIRASTOKARTTA TAMPERE
1:10, 000
In 21 sheets
Tampere : Tampereen Kaupungin Mittansosasto, 1971
Street map of the city, for office planning purposes.

C OFFICIAL SURVEYS

KARTA MIRA
1:2, 500, 000
VVK
1 sheet for complete coverage.
see WORLD 100C and index 100/2.

SUOMI
1:1, 000, 000
Helsinki : Maan, 1972
70 x 114
Topog. map with communications, towns and administrative boundaries and layer col. Administrative districts inset.
FMK 12.00

THE WORLD
1:1, 000, 000
AMS 1301
see WORLD 100C and index 100/1.

THE WORLD
1:500, 000
DMS Series 1404
see WORLD 100C and index 100/7.

YLEISKARTTA
1:400, 000
In 31 sheets, see index 480/3
Helsinki : Maan, 1962+
General, topographic map series, with contours (not all sheets) and relief shading.
Each FMK 6.00
Also available in atlas format.

SUOMEN YLEISKARTAN SUURENNOS
1:200, 000
In 76 sheets
Helsinki : Maan
Enlargement of 1:400, 000 Yleiskartta in 3-5 colours.
Complete sheet of 1:400, 000
FMK 8.00
½ sheet of 1:400, 000 FMK 6.00
¼ sheet of 1:400, 000 FMK 4.00
Available in old ed. at 1:100, 000
FMK 1.50

TALOUSALUEKARTAT
1:200, 000
Helsinki : Maan, 1965+
Maps of economic regions series based upon official topog. maps. Available for the following regions:
Uusimaa'Nyland, 1965
Tammermaa, 1969
Keski-Suomi, 1968
Etelä-Pohjammaa 1, Syd-Österbotten 1, 1969
Etelä-Pohjammaa 2, Syd-Österbotten 2, 1969
Etelä Savo, 1969
Pohjois - Savo, 1968
Etelä-Karjala, 1968
Pohjois-Karjalan laani, 1969
Varsinais-Suomi, Egentliga Finland, 1967
Kymenlaakso, Kymmenedalen, 1967
Etelä-Hame, 1967
Satakunta, 1967
Each FMK 7.00

TOPOGRAFINEN KARTTA
1:100, 000
See index 480/3
Helsinki : Maan, 1931+
30 x 40
Col. topog. series in progress based upon complete 1:20, 000 series.
Planimetric details, contours at 10 metre intervals. Sheets for N Finland fells have oblique grey hachuring. For outdoor purposes, also as base map.
Multicol. sheets FMK 5.00
Former eds. FMK 3.00

TALOUDELLINEN KARTTA
1:100, 000
Helsinki : Maan
Economic base map series and showing relief. No longer up-to-date, and no new eds. for areas where 100, 000 topog. is available.
Each FMK 3.00

VENALAINEN TOPOGRAFINEN KARTTA
1:21, 000, 1:42, 000, 1:84, 000
Helsinki : Maan
Series of Russian topog. maps of Southern Finland.
Each sheet FMK 3.00

TOPOGRAFINEN KARTTA
1:50, 000
Helsinki : Maan, 1951+
Topog. series in progress, contoured. Produced by photog. reproduction of 1:20, 000 series.
Quarter 1:100, 000 sheet
FMK 5.00
Half 1:100, 000 sheet
FMK 7.00

PERUSKARTTA
1:20, 000 (1:10, 000)
Helsinki : Maan, 1947+
Basic planimetric series of southern Finland surveyed at 1:10, 000 but available at same scale or 1:20, 000. They generally show : planimetric details, contours and cadastral boundaries.
Full ed. FMK 7.00
Other eds. FMK 6.00

TOPOGRAFINEN KARTTA
1:20, 000
Helsinki : Maan, 1958+
Planimetric series for northern Finland, surveyed at 1:20, 000 with contours and roads in brown, hydrography blue. Administrative and state forest boundaries.
Each FMK 6.00

D POLITICAL & ADMINISTRATIVE

FINLANDIYA
1:2, 000, 000
Moskva : GUGK, 1973
Col. study map showing water features, settlements, admin. boundaries, divisions and centres, communications, economic details, pop. Geog. description.
Kop 30

FINLANDIA
1:1, 500, 000
Warszawa : PPWK, 1972
60 x 91
General map with communications and administrative areas. Zl 12

TILASTON POHJAKARTTA
1:4, 000, 000
Helsinki : Maan, 1972
Statistical base map showing municipal boundaries and names.
FMK 0.90
Also available at :
1:3, 000, 000, 1972 FMK 1.50
1:2, 000, 000, 1972
(39 x 64) FMK 3.00
1:1, 000, 000, 1972
(74 x 122) FMK 5.00

SUOMEN TILASTOALUEET
1:400, 000
Helsinki : Maan, 1971
Statistical regions with municipal boundaries and areas. FMK 0.90
Also available at :
1:3, 000, 000, 1971 FMK 1.50

SUOMI : SEINÄKARTTA
by Caselius
1:750, 000
114 x 175
School wall map. FMK 146.00

SUUMMITTELUKARTTA
1:500, 000
In 4 sheets
Helsinki : Maan, 1972
87 x 106
Planning map in sheets A - D.
Roads, principal towns and hydrography.
Each FMK 12.50

LÄÄNINKARTAT
1:400, 000
Helsinki : Maan, 1969
Province map, based on Motoring map. Sheet for Oulun laani, Uleaborge lan.
FMK 7.00

KARTTALEHTIÖ UUDENMAAN LÄÄNI
1:100, 000
In 18 sheets
Helsinki : Maan, 1971
Topog. map of the Uusimaa province.
FMK 85.00

PITÄJÄNKARTTA
1:20, 000
Helsinki : Maan
Map of Parishes, series with or without surface information. Available on uniform sheet lines for SW of the country and certain other individual parishes.
Per sheet FMK 2.00

E1 PHYSICAL: RELIEF

SUOMI
1:4, 000, 000
Helsinki : Maan, 1972
23 x 33
Contoured with hypsometric layer cols.
FMK 1.50

SUOMI
1:3, 000, 000
Helsinki : Maan, 1972
33 x 57
Contoured with hypsometric layer col.
FMK 2.00

SUOMI
1:2,000 , 000
Helsinki : Maan, 1972
47 x 74
Multi-col, hypsometric tints with contours.
FMK 3.50

UUSI SUOMEN SEINÄKARTA
1:1, 000, 000
Helsinki : Maan, 1972
74 x 119
New Wall map of Finland, showing settlements, hypsometric layers communications etc. Inc. inset map of Europe.
FMK 12.00

FINLANDIA
1:1, 000, 000
Warszawa : PPWK, 1972
60 x 91
Physical map; contours, communications. Pol. text on reverse. In series "Przegladowa Mapa Europy" (Review maps of Europe)
ZI 12

F GEOLOGY

SUOMEN MAAPERÄKARTTA
1:2, 000, 000
Helsinki : Geog. Soc. Finland, 1969
43 x 62
Map of quaternary deposits.
FMK 7.00

KALLIOPERÄKARTTA
1:2, 000, 000
Helsinki : Geog. Soc. Finland, 1971
43 x 62
Pre-quaternary rocks. FMK 7.00

CARTE GÉOLOGIQUE INTERNATIONALE DE L'EUROPE
1:1, 500, 000
UNESCO - BB
3 sheets give complete coverage of Finland. see EUROPE 4G.

KIVILAJIKARTTA
1:400, 000
Helsinki : Geol. Survey, 1910+
Showing pre-quaternary rocks.
Each FMK 6.00
Descriptions FMK 4.00
Available for :
B1 Turku, 1958
B3 Vaasa, 1934
B4 Kokkola, 1932
B5-6 Tornio-Ylitornio, 1910
B7 Muonio, 1936
B8 Enontekiö, 1959
C3 Kuopio, 1935
C4 Kajaani, 1929
C5-B5 Oulu - Tornio, 1952
C7 Sodankylä, 1937, 1971
C8-C9 Inari - Utsjoki, 1965
D4 Nurmes, 1924
D5 Suomussalmi, 1954

MAAPERÄKARTTA
1:400, 000
Helsinki : Geol. Survey, 1906+
Showing quaternary deposits in cols.
Sheets available :
B2 Tampere, 1906
B3 Vaasa, 1953
B4 Kokkola, 1947
C3 Kuopio, 1934
C4 Kajaani, 1929
D4 Nurmes, 1931
18 Kilpisjärvi, 1967
27 Kittila, 1964
28 Enontekiö, 1966
37 Sodankylä, 1966
Each FMK 7.00
Description FMK 4.00

MAAPERÄKARTTA
1:100, 000
Helsinki : Geol. Surv. Finland, 1954+
Quaternary deposits, series of basic geology maps in col.
Each FMK 6.00
Text FMK 4.00

KALLIOPERÄKARTTA
1:100, 000
Helsinki : Geol. Surv. Finland, 1949
Series of col. maps showing pre-quaternary rocks.

SUOMEN MAAPERÄKARTTA
1:50, 000
Helsinki : Geol. Surv. Finland, 1949
Pre-quaternary deposits. Map-sheet for Helsinki and environs available.
FMK 6.00

G EARTH RESOURCES

CHEMICAL WOOD PULP MINES IN FINLAND, 1965
1:7, 000, 000/1:11, 000, 000
Helsinki : Finnicell (Finnish Cellulose Union)
36 x 56
Two maps, one being reduction of other. Smaller map 21 x 30. Classifies sulphate and sulphite mines with their capacity.

AGROGEOLOGIST KARTAT
Various scales
Helsinki : Agricultural Research Centre
Soil maps - early surveys.
Sheets available :
Etelä-Pohjanmaa, 4 sheets, 1:100, 000, 1927
Paimio, 1:50, 000, 1924
Loimaa, 4 sheets, 1:50, 000, 1933
Salo IV, 1:50, 000, 1938
Helsinki III, 1:50, 000, 1938
Nummi - Pusula, 1:50, 000, 1946
Nivala, 1:50, 000, 1938
Karjalohja, 1:25, 000, 1916

AGROGEOLOGISET KARTAT
1:20, 000
Helsinki : Agricultural Research Centre, 1947+
Series of maps in progress showing distribution of soils, following standard 20, 000 sheet lines.
Each FMK 6.00
Description FMK 4.00

H BIOGEOGRAPHY

SUOMEN VALTIONMETSÄ IN KARTA
1:1, 000, 000
Helsinki : Maan, 1969
61 x 120
Map of Finnish State Forests.
FMK 10.00

METSÄHALLITUKSEN METSÄT
1:200, 000/400, 000
Helsinki : Maan, 1969+
Forests belonging to the National Board of Forestry.
Sheets 2-11 at 200, 000, 1969-72
Sheets 12-13 at 400, 000, 1970
Each FMK 12.50

K HUMAN GEOGRAPHY

VÄESTÖN LEVINNEISYYS SUOMESSA 1967
1:400, 000
In 4 sheets
Helsinki : Nat. Planning Office, 1968
Various sizes
Showing pop. distribution 1967, white base map; population indicated by red dots. Various boundaries and communications also shown. With 48pp text, in plastic case.

LOMA-ASUNTOJEN SIJAINTI SUOMESSA
1:500, 000
In 4 sheets
Helsinki : Maan/National Planning Office, 1972
Map of recreational dwelling sites in Finland.

L ECONOMIC

SUOMEN POSTI-JA RAUTATIEKARTTA
1:1, 000, 000
Helsinki : Maan, 1969
126 x 89
Postal and railway wall map of Finland with index to towns surrounding map, and reference indicator. N Finland at 1:1, 750, 000.
Metal strip fittings FMK 60.00
Cloth backed FMK 86.00

M HISTORICAL

SUOMENMAAN KORKO-KARTTA
1:1, 000, 000
Helsinki : Maan, 1972
77 x 126
Facsimile map of Finland, from the original by C W Gylden in 1853.

ATLASES
A1 GENERAL MAPS: ROADS

SUOMI YLEISKARTTAKIRJA
Helsinki : Maan, 1968
Atlas of Finland based on the 1:400, 000 topog. maps. Contains map of whole country at 1:2, 000, 000, 84pp maps at 1:400, 000, 2 small maps of glacial features and a 28 page index.
Hard covers FMK 33.00

ATLASES
D PHYSICAL & ADMINISTRATIVE

KARLTALEHTIÖ UUDENMAAN LÄÄNI
1:100, 000
In 18 sheets
Helsinki : Maan, 1971
Topog. sheets for the Uusimaa Province bound in spiral atlas form.

ATLASES
L ECONOMIC

SAIMAAN KANAVAN KARTASTO
Helsinki : Nat. Board of Public Roads and Waterways, 1968
41 x 32
Regional atlas of the Saimaa Canal, from the Gulf of Finland to the Saimaa lake region, 27pp navigation charts inc. 7 general pages. FMK 60.00

ATLASES
M HISTORICAL

KANSOJEN HISTORIAN KARTASTO
Ed Pentti Papunen
Cartography Berit Lie
Helsinki : WSOY, 1962
163pp
Historical atlas for high schools, with compendium and chronology of rulers and kings. 108 maps. FMK 7.30

ATLASES
O NATIONAL

NYKY-SUOMI KUVIN JA KARTOIN
H Smeds and P Fogelberg
Helsinki : WSOY, 1967
136pp
School atlas "Modern Finland in pictures and maps". 61 illus. and 79 maps.
FMK 13.00

481 Norway

See also: 48 SCANDINAVIA

A1 GENERAL MAPS: ROADS

CAPPELENS BIL-OG TURIST- KART OVER HELE NORGE
1:1, 000, 000
No 13
Oslo : Cappelen, 1975
68 x 98
Roads classified and numbered, distances in km, ferry routes, relief shading, camping sites, spot heights in metres, other features, Oslo area inset at 1:150, 000. Legend in Eng. Nor, Ger.

SHELL REISEKARTE NORWEGEN
1:1, 500, 000
Stuttgart : Mair
48 x 83
Roads classified and numbered: places of interest for the tourist, camping sites, ferry routes. Inset of N Norway.
DM 4.80

NORWEGEN
1:1, 500, 000
No 217
Koln : Polyglott
Roads numbered and classified, distances in km, camping sites. DM 3.20

GYLDENDALS NORGES KART
1:1, 000, 000
Oslo : Gyldendal, 1973
72 x 106
Main and secondary roads, railways, state frontiers, hill shading. Inset maps of Oslofjord area at 1:500, 000 and Spitsbergen 1:3, 000, 000. Index and distance chart on reverse.

BILKART OVER NORGE
1:1, 000, 000
In 2 sheets
Oslo : KNA-Forlaget, 1976
25 x 13
Roads classified, distances in km, and route numbers.
North N.Kr 12.00
South N.Kr 15.00

NORWAY
1:1, 000, 000
In 4 sheets
London : Foldex
2 double-sided sheets, showing roads classified, relief shading : patent fold.
Each 45p

NORWEGEN UND SCHWEDEN
1:800, 000
No 887
Frankfurt : Ravenstein, 1976
135 x 96
Roads classified and numbered, distances in km. Covers Norway and Sweden. Relief shading, ferry routes, frontiers, places of interest, pop. indicated. Double sided.
DM 9.80

NORVEGIYA
Moskva : GUGK
Road map with geog. guide.

NORGE BIL- OG TURISTKART
1:325, 000-1:400, 000
See index 481/1
Oslo : Cappelen
All classes of roads, numbers, conditions, distances in km, car ferries, spot heights in metres, airports, tourist huts, camping sites and motels, youth hostels and state frontiers.
Sheet 1-2
1:325, 000 134 x 96 1976
Sheet 3-4
1:325, 000 135 x 95 1976
Sheet 5-6
1:325, 000 134 x 94 1973
Sheet 7-8
1:400, 000 70 x 137 1974
Sheet 9-10
1:400, 000 138 x 71 1974

A2 GENERAL MAPS: LOCAL

SOR-NORGE BILKART
1:1, 000, 000
Oslo : Cappelen, 1973
45 x 96
Mo i Rana south to Lindesnes. All classes of roads, distances in km, numbers, ferries, spot heights in metres, state frontiers. Inset of Oslo area at 1:150, 000. Index and 8 town plans.

BILKARTET
1:500, 000
Oslo : KNA-Forlaget
Regional road map series. All classes of roads.
Sheets available :
Sorlandet 1:250, 000
Oslofjord 1:200, 000
Ostandet 1:500, 000
Westlandet 1:500, 000

CAPPELEN REGIONAL MAPS
1:325, 000
Oslo : Cappelen, 1973
50 x 70
Mountain maps giving summer and winter information, roads classified, distances, surfaces and places of interest.
Sheets published :
40 Hardangervidda - Heiene (Hemsedal-Gol-Treungen-Voss)
41 Jotunheimen-Rondane (Hjerkinn-Lillehammer-Fagernes-Gudvangen)
42 Møre-Trollheimen (Lokken-Folldal-Olden-Ålesund)
43 Femundsmarka-Sylene (Trondheim-Femund-Koppang-Ulsberg)

TURISTKART
Various scales
See index 481/2
Oslo : NGO
Collection of special regional maps covering popular tourist areas. Maps based on official surveys, contoured and land detail, footpaths, etc. Some show ski-routes.
Maps available :
1 Andenes
1:25, 000 1970 N.Kr 8.65
2 Aust-Jotunheimen
1:50, 000 1933 N.Kr 8.65
3 Blåtind
1:50, 000 1972 N.Kr 8.65
4 Brattberget
1:25, 000 1956 N.Kr 8.65
5 Dombås omegn
1:50, 000 1972 N.Kr 5.40
6 Dovrefjell
1:100, 000 1962 N.Kr 9.70
7 Elvegårdsmoen
1:25, 000 1972 N.Kr 8.65
8 Evje
1:25, 000 1967 N.Kr 6.10
9 Gardermoen
1:25, 000 1970 N.Kr 6.10
10 Gullfjell
1:50, 000 1936 N.Kr 5.40
11 Hallingdal
1:250, 000 1954 N.Kr 15.30
12 Hamar og Hedm. vidda
1:100, 000 1966 N.Kr 8.65
13 Hardangervidda
1:200, 000 1966 N.Kr 11.40
14 Heistadmoen
1:25, 000 1968 N.Kr 8.65
15 Holtsjøen
1:25, 000 1956 N.Kr 8.65
16 Høybuktmoen
1:25, 000 1968 N.Kr 8.65
17 Jotunheimen
1:250, 000 1960 N.Kr 15.30
18 Jorstadmoen
1:50, 000 1967 N.Kr 8.65
19 Kampen
1:50, 000 1971 N.Kr 8.65
20 Kvamsskogen
1:25, 000 1969 N.Kr 8.65
21 Kirkenes med omegn
1:100, 000 1956 N.Kr 11.40
22 Midt-Jotunheimen
1:50, 000 1960 N.Kr 8.65
23 Mjølfjell
1:25, 000 1972 N.Kr 9.70
24 Nes i Hallingdal
1:50, 000 1973 N.Kr 8.65
25 Norefjell
1:50, 000 1963 N.Kr 8.65
26 Okstindan
1:100, 000 1952 N.Kr 7.20
27 Porsangmoen
1:25, 000 1957 N.Kr 8.65
28 Raundal-Flamsdal
1:50, 000 1936 N.Kr 8.65
29 Rondane
1:100, 000 1954 N.Kr 11.40
30 Skjold
1:50, 000 1966 N.Kr 8.65
31 Steinkjer
1:25, 000 1969 N.Kr 8.65
32 Sætermoen
1:25, 000 1971 N.Kr 6.10
33 Sætermoen
1:50, 000 1972 N.Kr 8.65
34 Telemark
1:250, 000 1960 N.Kr 15.30
35 Terningmoen
1:25, 000 1952 N.Kr 6.10
36 Vest-Jotunheimen
1:50, 000 1960 N.Kr 8.65
37 Vagsli
1:50, 000 1972 N.Kr 6.10
38 Våler
1:25, 000 1966 N.Kr 6.10
39 Molde
1:50, 000
40 Solnkletten
1:75, 000

OMLANDSKART
1:25, 000/1:50, 000
Oslo : NGO
Various sizes
Series of topog. environs maps for major towns.
Maps available :
Arendal Omland
1:25, 000 3 sheets N.Kr 7.20
Bergen Omland
1:25, 000 8 sheets N.Kr 7.20
Harstad Omland
1:50, 000 1960 N.Kr 8.65
Kristiansund Omland
1:25, 000 1955 N.Kr 8.65
Lillehammer skimap
1:50, 000 1972 N.Kr 7.20
Oslo Nordmark
1:50, 000 1972 N.Kr 14.00
Oslo Vestmark (ski-routes)
1:50, 000 1933 N.Kr 7.20
Oslo Østmark
1:50, 000 1972 N.Kr 11.40
Skien-Porsgrunn Brevik
1:25, 000 2 sheets
1952-6 N.Kr 7.20
Stavanger Omland
1:25, 000 6 sheets
1955-61 N.Kr 7.20
Tromsø Omegn
1:50, 000 1947 N.Kr 7.20
Trondheim Skikart
1:25, 000 4 sheets
1945 N.Kr 7.20

B TOWN PLANS

BERGEN IN A NUTSHELL
1:12, 500
Bergen : John Grieg, 1972
Street map of Central Bergen, with index and guide in English. N.Kr 9.50

NARVIK
1:5, 000
Narvik : Commune of Narvik
1971
125 x 90
Black and white map contoured showing parkland, private and commercial building. Street index. N.Kr 10.00

GREATER OSLO
1:13, 000-1:30, 000
Oslo : Cappelen, 1976
Double-sided plan of city centre and surroundings.

OSLO
1:17, 000-1:27, 000
Hamburg : Falk/Oslo : Aschehoug
Col. plan with street index.
DM 3.90

OSLO
London : Miniplans Ltd.
Small pocket size plan of city centre with index to streets. 20p

TRONDHEIM
1:12, 500
Trondheim : Brunn
Col. plan with street index.

C OFFICIAL SURVEYS

KARTA MIRA
1:2, 500, 000
VVK
2 sheets for complete coverage of Norway.
see WORLD 100C and index 100/2.

THE WORLD
1:1, 000, 000
AMS Series 1301
6 sheets needed for complete coverage.
see WORLD 100C and index 100/1.

THE WORLD
1:500, 000
DMS Series 1404
14 sheets needed for complete coverage.
see WORLD 100C and index 100/7.

NORGE SERIE 1501
1:250, 000
AMS Series M 1501
In 46 sheets, see index 481/3
Oslo : NGO
Various sizes
Topog. maps contoured at 100 metre intervals, spot heights, all classes of roads, footpaths, route numbering, railways, airports and state boundaries.
Paper folded, each N.Kr 13.00

TOPOGRAFISKE KART
1:100, 000
See index 481/4
Oslo: NGO
Various sizes
Topog. map series available in either Gradteigskart or Rektangelkart according to latitude and projection, contoured with spot heights, roads, footpaths, railways, ferries, airports, forest areas, state boundaries. Legend in Nor. N.Kr 8.15

TOPOGRAFISKE KART
1:50, 000
AMS Series M711
See index 481/5
Oslo : NGO, 1951+
Various sizes
Topog. series contoured with spot heights, roads, railways, airports, serial cableways, tourist shelters and state boundaries. Legend in Nor. In black and white with water in blue. New col. series in progress.
Each N.Kr 7.20

OKONOMISK KARTVERK
1:5, 000/1:10, 000
Oslo : NGO, 1964+
48 x 64
Aerial photographic maps for the various provinces of Norway, showing names and areas in black, contours brown, field boundaries in green, hydrography in blue.
Available for :
Østfold
Akershus
Hedmark
Oppland
Buskerud
Aust-Agder
Vest-Agder
Rogaland
Hordaland
Sogn og Fjordane
Møre og Romsdal
Sør-Trondelag
Nord-Trondelag
Nordland
Troms
Finnmark

D POLITICAL & ADMINISTRATIVE

KOMMUNEKART FOR NORGE
1:1, 000, 000
Oslo : Norges Communicationer, 1969
Showing commune boundaries as at 1st July 1969.

NORGES KOMMUNER
1:1, 000, 000
In 2 sheets
Oslo : NGO, 1971
73 x 90 North
88 x 54 South
Outline map with boundaries of State, Fylke and Kommune, with town classification and boundaries.
Each N.Kr 11.50

STANDARD FOR HANDELSOMRÅDER
1:1, 000, 000
In 2 sheets
Oslo : NGO, 1967
60 x 94 each
Planning regions overprinted on Norges Kommuner.
Each N.Kr 11.50

E1 PHYSICAL: RELIEF

KONTURKART OVER NORGE
1:1, 000, 000
In 2 sheets
Oslo : NGO, 1917
Physical map, contoured with layer cols.
Each N.Kr. 7.45

REFSDALS SKOLEREGGKART NORGE
1:400, 000
Oslo : Aschehoug
Wall map in layer col. hachuring and roads, railways, pop. by towns, bathymetric col.
In 3 maps :
I Sør-Norge, 2 sheets, 1965
122 x 181 complete
II Nordland, 2 sheets, 1965
105 x 175 complete
III Troms og Finnmark, 1962
177 x 114

F GEOLOGY

INTERNATIONAL QUATERNARY MAP OF EUROPE
1:2, 500, 000
UNESCO
3 sheets for coverage of Norway
see EUROPE 4 G.

CARTE GÉOLOGIQUE INTERNATIONALE DE L'EUROPE
1:1, 500, 000
UNESCO - BB
5 sheets for complete coverage, excluding Svalbard.
see EUROPE 4G.

KART OVER NORGE - BERGGRUNNSKART
1:1, 000, 000
Comp. Holtedahl and Dons
Oslo : NGU, 1960
86 x 122
Geol. map showing the structure and bedrock without quaternary deposits. In Nor. and Eng. N.Kr 25.00

KVARTAEGEOLOGISKE
LANDGENERALKART
1:250, 000
Ed G Holmsen
See index 481/6
Oslo : NGU
Col. geol. series.
Sheets available :

Hallingdal, 1954	N.Kr 8.00
Oppland, 1950	N.Kr 8.00
Oslo, 1949	N.Kr 8.00
Røros, 1956	N.Kr 8.00
Ljordalen, 1958	N.Kr 6.00
Østerdalen, 1960	N.Kr 12.00

LANDGENERALKART
1:250, 000
Ed J Rekstad
see index 481/6
Oslo : NGU
Geol. maps series.
Sheets available :

Hattfjelldal, 1925	N.Kr 8.00
Traena, 1925	N.Kr 8.00
Rana, 1932, Ed G Holmsen	N.Kr 8.00
Salta, 1930	N.Kr 8.00
Vega, 1917	N.Kr 8.00

OVERSIKTSKART OVER
KRISTIANIAFELLET
1:250, 000
Oslo : NGU, 1923
General. geol. map.

GEOLOGISKE KART
1:100, 000
See index 481/6
Oslo : NGO, 1915+
Col. geol. maps for certain parts of the country on the same sheet lines as the topog. 1:100, 000 series.
Each N.Kr 5.30

GEOLOGISK KART OVER OSLO OG
OMEGN
1:50, 000
Oslo : Universitetsforlaget, 1952
65 x 100
Coloured geol. map with legend in Nor. and Eng. contained in 117pp guide in English, 1966.

H BIOGEOGRAPHY

OVERSIKTSKART PRODUKSIONS-
GRUNNLAGET FOR LANDBRUKET
1:250, 000
Trondelag : Dept. of Ag. Devt.
General land use map in colours showing cultivated and reclaimable land and forests.
Sheets available :
Hordaland og Sogn og Fjordane, 1969
86 x 121
Trondelag Nordre, 1968,)
96 x 60) 96 x 136
Trondelag Sor, 1968) complete
96 x 80)
Salten, Nordre, 1967,
74 x 110
Colour key in Nor. and Eng.

AUSTLANDET : DYRKA JORD OG
DYRKINGSJORD
1:250, 000
Trondelag : Dept. of Ag. Devt, 1970
65 x 93
Showing cultivated and reclaimable land; principle roads marked; col. key.

PRODUKSJONSGRUNNLAGET FOR
LANDBRUKET
1:100, 000
Trondelag : Dept. of Ag. Devt.
Series based upon official topog. sheet lines showing cultivated, forest and reclaimable land, published for majority of country.

K HUMAN GEOGRAPHY

BOSETTINGSKART OVER NORGE
1:400, 000
In 15 sheets
Oslo : Stat. Sentralbyrå
62 x 48 sheet size
33 x 25 folder size
Showing population at the 1950 census by the dot method on a physical base map showing admin. boundaries. Contained in a folder with legend sheet.

N MATHEMATICAL

OVERSYNSKART OVER
TRIANGULERING
1:1, 600, 000
In 2 sheets
Oslo : NGO, 1970
Triangulation diagram.

OVERSYNSKART OVER
NIVELLEMENTER
1:1, 000, 000
In 2 sheets
Oslo : NGO, 1970
General levelling map, North and South sheets.
Each N.Kr 7.45

485 Sweden

See also: 48 SCANDINAVIA

A1 GENERAL MAPS: ROADS

SKANDINAVIEN
1:2, 000, 000
Wien : FB, 1971
81 x 101
Detailed road map showing main highways and secondary roads, route numbers and distances. Relief shown by shading and spot heights.

KAK - SVERIGEKARTA
1:1, 500, 000
Stockholm : GLA, 1971
General road map of Sweden from KAK Bilatlas. S.Kr 6.75

SCHWEDEN - SHELL REISEKARTE
1:1, 500, 000
Stuttgart : Mair
48 x 107
All classes of roads, numbers, distances in km, relief shading, ferry routes, places of tourist interest. Legend in 12 langs.
DM 4.80

BILISTENS VAGKARTA OVER SVERIGE
1:1, 000, 000
In 2 sheets
Stockholm : GLA, 1971
65 x 68 each
All classes of roads, distances in km, route numbers, ferries, railways, state boundaries. South sheet has insets of Malmo and Stockholm districts at 1:600, 000.
North sheet Osthammar northwards
South sheet Soderhamm southwards
S.Kr 5.75

SWEDEN
1:1, 000, 000
London : Foldex
Shows roads classified, relief shading: patent fold. 2 double sided sheets.
Each 45p

NORWEGEN/SCHWEDEN
1:800, 000
No 887, 888
Frankfurt : Ravenstein, 1976
135 x 96
Double sided road map covering 2 countries; all classes of roads, with route numbers and distances. Camp sites, places of interest, airports. DM 9.80
Southern sheet available separately
No 888 DM 7.80

SHVETSIYA
Moskva : GUGK, 1971
Tourist map of Sweden with geog. guide.

SVENSKA TURIST KARTAN
1:300, 000
In 10 sheets, see index 485/1
Stockholm : GLA
Various sizes
All classes of roads, numbers, distances in km, hill shading, contours, spot heights in metres, ferries, railways, airports, tourist details, state and provincial boundaries.
S.Kr 5.40

KAK BILKARTOR
1:200, 000/400, 000
Stockholm : GLA
Individual maps from the KAK Bilatlas.
Set S.Kr 24.50

A2 GENERAL MAPS: LOCAL

NORDISK
1:1, 000, 000
Bern : Hallwag
83 x 116
Road map of S Scandinavia inc. Trondheim-Ostersund-Sundsvall south to include all of Denmark.
All classes of roads, route numbers and distances, ferries, railways, camping sites and places of interest.

BIL- OCH TURISTKARTOR
1:250, 000
Stockholm : SRA
Various sizes
Road and tourist maps available for the following areas :

Skåne	70 x 78
Västra Gotaland	83 x 119
Östra Gotaland	80 x 119
Östra Svealand	81 x 99
Svealand	118 x 80
Dalarna	
Jamtland	80 x 118
Each	S.Kr 12.75

UTFLYKTSKARTA
1:200, 000
Stockholm : GLA
Excursion maps. Showing roads, footpaths etc, camping and rest areas.
Sheets available:

Stockholm	66 x 62
Goteborg	104 x 77
Each	S.Kr 9.50

SVENSKA FJÄLLKARTAN
Various scales
see index 485/2
Stockholm : SRA
Various sizes
Swedish mountain maps. Based on early topog. series in black and white relief shown by hachures. Footpaths and mountain huts shown in red.
Maps available :

1 Torneträsk-Treriksroset-Soppero
1:200, 000 59 x 80 S.Kr 8.50
2 Abisko-Saltokuokta
1:200, 000 58 x 75 S.Kr 8.00
3 Sitasjaure-Sarek-Sulitelma-Kvikkjokk
1:200, 000 48 x 75 S.Kr 8.00
4 Saltoloukta - Kvikkjokk
1:200, 000 36 x 49 S.Kr 5.25
5 Kvikkjokk-Nasafjall-Ammarna's-Arjeplog
1:200, 000 68 x 70 S.Kr 8.00
6 Nasafjäll-Ammarnas-Tarna-Vivisen
1:200, 000 61 x 70 S.Kr 8.00
7 Tarna - Vivisen - Kultsjon - Frostviken
1:200, 000 61 x 77 S.Kr 8.00
8 Hotagsfjällen och Kall-Offerdalsfjällen
1:200, 000 56 x 75 S.Kr 8.00
9 Torrön-Kolasen-Skalstugan
1:100, 00 73 x 72 S.Kr 8.50
10 Åre-Storlien-Sylarna-Lunn-dörren
1:100, 000 88 x 65 S.Kr 8.50
(winter and summer eds. available)
11 Undersåker-Lunndörrsfjällen-Anarisfjällen - Oviksfjällen
1:100, 000 69 x 68 S.Kr 8.50
12 Luundörrsfjällen-Helagsfjället-Fjallnäs-Ljusnedal
1:100, 000 84 x 70 S.Kr 8.50
(summer and winter editions)
13 Grövelsjön-Tanasjön
1:100, 000 84 x 62 S.Kr 8.50
14 Lofsdalen-Hede-Klövsjö-Sveg
1:100, 000 78 x 74 S.Kr 8.50
15 Fulufjället-Städjan-Särna
1:100, 000 84 x 61 S.Kr 8.50
16 Transtrandsfjallen
1:100, 000 50 x 66 S.Kr 5.25

Other mountain maps :
Fulufjället
1:100, 000 51 x 43 S.Kr 4.00
Idrefjällen
1:100, 000 39 x 40 S.Kr 3.50
Grövelsjön
1:100, 000 50 x 43 S.Kr 4.00
Harjedalen, 1971
1:100, 000 71 x 49
Abisko, Björkliden
1:25, 000 39 x 53 S.Kr 4.00
Valadalsfjällen
1:50, 000 66 x 63 S.Kr 9.50
Valadalen
1:50, 000 34 x 28 S.Kr 4.00

NYA FJÄLLKARTAN
1:100, 000
see index 485/3
Stockholm : SRA
Various sizes
Series of mountain maps in progress, giving summer and winter information, ie footpaths and ski-routes and facilities.
Available for :

BD5 Abisko, Bjorkliden, Riksgransen
60 x 49 S.Kr 8.00
BD6 Abisko, Kebnekajse
65 x 74 S.Kr 12.00
BD7 Akkajaure, Sitasjaure
65 x 74 S.Kr 12.00
BD8 Kebnekaise, Saltoluokta
65 x 74 S.Kr 12.00
BD9 Vaisaluokta, Staloluokta
65 x 68 S.Kr 12.00
BD10 Sareks national park
79 x 79 S.Kr 12.00
BD11 Saltoluokta, Kvikkjokk
S.Kr 12.00
BD12 Saltoluokta, Sulitelma, Kvikkjokk S.Kr 12.00

STORA FRITIDSKARTAN
1:100, 000
Stockholm : GLA
100 x 140
Large leisure map series covering tourist and recreation areas.
Maps available :
Stor-Stockholm (Greater Stockholm)
1971 S.Kr 21.50
Örestad S.Kr 21.50
Stockholms Skärgård
1:200, 000 S.Kr 12.00
Siljan runt, 1971
1:200, 000 S.Kr 9.50
Västkusten : Oslo-Goteborg
1:300, 000 S.Kr 8.50
Västkusten : Goteborg-Trelleborg
1:300, 000 S.Kr 6.75
Östkusten
1:300, 000 S.Kr 7.50
Öst Sverige S.Kr 10.00
Gotland-semesterkarta, 1971
1:150, 000 S.Kr 9.75
Öland-semesterkarta S.Kr 7.50

FJÄLLKARTOR
Various scales
Stockholm : GLA
Series of mountain maps, contoured with tourist detail.
Maps available :
Fjällen i v : a Harjedalen, 1971
1:100, 000 S.Kr 7.50
Fjällen kring Storlien
1:100, 000 S.Kr 5.75
Fjällen kring Storlien
1:50, 000 S.Kr 5.25
Fjällen kring Tarna
1:100, 000 S.Kr 7.50
Transtrandsfjällen
1:50, 000 S.Kr 5.00
Fjällen kring Are
1:100, 000 S.Kr 6.75
Kungsleden
1:300, 000 S.Kr 5.00
Vasaloppet (new edition)
S.Kr 6.50

TURISTKARTA ÖVER ÖLAND
1:100, 000
Stockholm : SRA
23 x 139
Tourist map showing roads, accommodation and places of interest.

B TOWN PLANS

TOWN PLANS
Various scales
Col. plans with index to streets.
Maps available :
Stockholm
1:15, 000-1:33, 000 Falk
DM 4.80
Uppsala
1:10, 000 Almqvist & Wiksell
Malmö
1:10, 000 GLA
Göteborg
1:10, 000 Official plan

STOCKHOLM PLANS
Various scales
Stockholm : GLA
Plans available :
Stockholm :
Gamla Staden (old town)
flat S.Kr 10.50
folded S.Kr 9.50
Gator - places and remains
S.Kr 20.00

Trafikkarta over Stockholm
1:10, 000/1:40, 000
S.Kr 4.95
Officiella Stockholmskartan
1:10, 000
Per sheet S.Kr 10.00
Stockholm
1:12, 000 S.Kr 4.00
Stockholm med förorter (suburbs)
1:12, 000 S.Kr 5.50
Stockholm - outer suburbs :
Brannkyrka-Hägersten S.Kr 6.50
Enskede-Farsta S.Kr 6.50
Bromma S.Kr 6.50
Solna - Sunbyberg S.Kr 6.50
Nacka S.Kr 6.50
Huddinge S.Kr 6.50
Saltsjöbaden S.Kr 6.50
Lidingö S.Kr 6.50
Boo S.Kr 6.50
Hasselby-Spanga S.Kr 6.50
Djursholm-Stocksund-Danderyd
S.Kr 6.50
Stor-Stockholm, 1972
1:17, 000 195 x 200
S.Kr 265.00
Boards S.Kr 365.00

TRAFIKANTKARTA ÖVER STOR-STOCKHOLMSREGIONEN
1:15, 000/33, 000
Stockholm : SRA
Satellite series map, based on Falk plan, showing Stockholm Central and suburbs, from Vendelso to Rotebro in the south, Akersberga Ska to Boo, Saltsjobaden in the East.

TRAFIKKARTA ÖVER STOCKHOLM
1:10, 000
Stockholm : SRA
88 x 67
Col. map of central area showing roads and other traffic information.
Reverse has larger area at 1:40, 000, covering motorways, tunnels etc.
Flat S.Kr 4.50
In case S.Kr 5.00

C OFFICIAL SERIES

KARTA MIRA
1:2, 500, 000
VVK
2 sheets available for Sweden.
see WORLD 100C and index 100/2.

INTERNATIONAL MAP OF THE WORLD
1:1, 000, 000
Stockholm : SRA
Sheets NO 32, 34
Stockholm, Ed 3, 1970
NP 33, 34
Sundsvall, Ed 2, 1970
NQ 32, 34
Kiruna, Ed 2, 1970
see WORLD 100C and index 100/1.

THE WORLD
1:1, 000, 000
DMS series 1301
6 sheets needed for complete coverage.
see WORLD 100C and index 100/1.

THE WORLD
1:500, 000
DMS series 1404
18 sheets needed for complete coverage.
see WORLD 100C and index 100/7.

OVERSIKTSKARTAN
1:400, 000
In 25 sheets
Stockholm : SRA, 1913-27
48 x 40
Col. general map, relief by col. hachures, communications, boundaries and settlement.

PROVISORISKA ÖVERSIKTSKARTEN OPERATIONSKARTA
1:250, 000
In 48 sheets, see index 485/4
Stockholm : SRA
Various sizes
Military series showing topog. detail including boundaries, communications and settlements with woodland col, bogland, spot heights, contours, hill shading and navigational features.

TOPOGRAFISKA KARTAN
1:100, 000 - 1:50, 000
See index 485/5
Stockholm : SRA
50 x 50 - standard
50 x 75 - large sheets
Detailed topog. series in progress, showing communications, boundaries, settlements etc, woodland and bog colouring, contours and spot heights, with hill shading on recent sheets. The quarter sheets in the south and east are at 1:50, 000 scale, the full sheets in the north at 1:100, 000 only.

GENERALSTABENS KARTA ÖVER SÖDRA SVERIGE
1:100, 000
In 97 sheets, see index 485/6
Stockholm : GLA
59 x 44
In black and white, relief by hachures; water in blue, roads in red, available in Grundversion - basic edition, Military ed - with UTM grid and Televersion and also Trafargsversionen 2 col. ed.
Flat S.Kr 5.00

GENERALSTABENS KARTA ÖVER NORRA SVERIGE
1:200, 000
In 84 sheets, see index 485/7
Stockholm : SRA
54 x 41
Topog. map of N Sweden, showing land and boundaries, communications etc. In 3 cols, relief by hachures. Sheets of this series go out of print on publication of new 1:100,000 topog. series
Each S.Kr 4.00
Also available enlarged to 1:100, 000 at S.Kr 6.00 per sheet.

GENERALSTABENS KARTA ÖVER NORRA SVERIGE
1:100, 000
In 85 sheets, see index 485/7
Stockholm : SRA
54 x 41
Relief by hachures, in black with water in blue, roads in red. Available in Basic, Military (with UTM grid) or Televersion edition. Available as quarter sheets.
Full sheet S.Kr 6.00
Large sheet (138 x 70) S.Kr 9.00

EKONOMISKA KARTAN (OFFICIAL ECONOMIC SERIES FOR SWEDEN)
1:10, 000 and 1:20, 000
Stockholm : SRA
50 x 50
Aerial photographic maps of Sweden, printed in green monochrome with yellow overprint of productive fields and gardens, detailed administrative and communication information, incl. routes of electricity, water supplies etc. and contours at 5 metre intervals - variations in some provinces - 1:10, 000 in the south, 1:20, 000 in the north; mountain areas will not be mapped. Series in progress, province by province.
Sheets printed in 3 styles :
Fully col. S.Kr 15.00
Black and green S.Kr 11.00
Black only S.Kr 9.00

RIKSFOTOKARTAN
1:10, 000
Stockholm : SRA
50 x 50
Series of photographic plans for Bohus, Göteborgs, Gotlands, Kalmar and Blekinge län. With contours for Blekinge (15.00 S.Kr each sheet)
Per sheet S.Kr 9.00

D POLITICAL & ADMINISTRATIVE

SVERIGE, PLANERINGSKARTA
1:2, 000, 000
Stockholm : GLA
Planning map in outline with boundaries.
S.Kr 5.00

KOMMUNER 1964
1:1, 000, 000
Stockholm : GLA, 1971
70 x 160
2 sheet map of communes, parishes and district boundaries.
Also available as "Kommuner och Kommunblock 1964" adding names and commune boundaries to basic map.
Flat S.Kr 17.00
Rollers S.Kr 55.00
Boards S.Kr 75.00

KOMMUNKARTA ÖVER SVERIGE
1:700, 000
In 2 sheets
Stockholm : GLA
96 x 126
Map of Sweden showing commune boundaries.

KOMMUNBLOCKSKARTA
1:500, 000
Stockholm : SRA, 1965
84 x 60
Map of administrative areas and divisions as at 1st January 1964.

INDELNINGSKARTEN ÖVER SVERIGE
1:400, 000
In 25 sheets
Stockholm : GLA
Showing in black and blue "lan" areas from 1st January 1953. Boundaries in red. Based on official 400, 000 series.

LANDKARTOR
1:200, 000/1:400, 000
In 24 sheets
Stockholm : GLA
Various sizes
Series of individual maps of the provinces, communications, settlement and commune boundaries shown.
Maps available :
Blekinge län
1:200, 000 62 x 38 S.Kr 18.00
Gotlands län 50 x 69 S.Kr 7.00
Gavelborgs län*, 1972
1:200, 000 44 x 66 S.Kr 21.00
Göteborgs och Bohus län
1:200, 000 55 x 96 S.Kr 18.00
Hallands län*
1:200, 000 55 x 76 S.Kr 14.00
Jamtlands län
1:400, 000 70 x 105
S.Kr 18.00
Jönköpings län*
1:200, 000 90 x 83 S.Kr 18.00
Kalmar län*
1:200, 000 60 x 127
S.Kr 16.00
Kopparbergs län*, 1971
1:400, 000 68 x 74 S.Kr 21.50
Kronobergs län*
1:200, 000 90 x 57 S.Kr 18.00
Norrbottens län
1:400, 000 109 x 118
S.Kr 17.00
Skaraborge län*
1:200, 000 83 x 75 S.Kr 18.00
Skåne
1:150, 000 100 x 110
S.Kr 16.00
Stockholms och Uppsala län*
1:200, 000 85 x 115
S.Kr 18.00
Sodermanlands län
1:200, 000 68 x 60 S.Kr 18.00
Värmlands län
1:400, 000 55 x 72 S.Kr 18.00
Västerbottens län S.Kr 16.00
Västernorrlands län*
1:400, 000 68 x 76 S.Kr 18.00
Västermanlands län*
1:200, 000 69 x 126
S.Kr 18.00
Örebro län*
1:200, 000 23 x 74 S.Kr 14.00
Ostergotlands län S.Kr 18.00

Maps marked * also available in old edition.

E1 PHYSICAL: RELIEF

WORLD TRAVEL MAP OF SCANDINAVIA
1:2, 500, 000
Wien : FB
81 x 101
Detailed road map showing main highways and secondary roads, route numbers and distances. Relief shown by shading and spot heights.

SVERIGE
1:3, 000, 000
Stockholm : GLA
26 x 56
Landscape in different cols. with boundaries, roads, towns and important places.
Folded S.Kr 3.00

SVERIGE - LANDSKAP
1:2, 000, 000
Stockholm : GLA, 1969
32 x 79
Col. physical map, showing roads, ferries, airports; pop. indicated.
Flat or folded S.Kr 7.50
Boards S.Kr 24.00

SVERIGE, TOPOGRAFI
1:2, 000, 000
Stockholm : GLA
Col. topog. wall map.
Flat or folded S.Kr 7.50
Boards S.Kr 24.00

SVERIGE
1:1, 500, 000
Stockholm : GLA
60 x 120
Physical map showing communications, boundaries. With index, or without.
Flat S.Kr 16.00
Laminated S.Kr 19.50
Rollers S.Kr 46.00
Boards S.Kr 58.00

GENERALKARTA SVERIGE, G5
1:1, 000, 000
In 3 sheets
Stockholm : GLA, 1969
72 x 55 each
Physical and general map, with topog. detail, woodland col. and hill shading. Also shows territorial waters.
S.Kr 39.00

SKANE RELIEFKARTE
1:600, 000
Stockholm : SRA
30 x 27
Plastic relief map of Southern part of Sweden.

E2 PHYSICAL: LAND FEATURES

KARTA OVER LANDISENS AVSMALTNING OCH HÖGSTA KUSTLINJEN I SVERIGE
1:1, 000, 000
In 3 sheets
Stockholm : SGU, 1961
76 x 162 complete
The de-glaciation and the highest shore-line in Sweden, with descriptive text in Swedish with English summary, by D Lundqvist.

ÖVERSIKTSKARTA ÖVER SÖDRA SVERIGES MYRMARKER
1:500, 000
Stockholm : SGU, 1923
Map of boggy ground in S Sweden, with description by L von Post, 1927.

FICKSTEREOSKOP OCH STEREO-BILDER
Stockholm : SRA
Series of stereoscopic pictures, covering glacial aspects, permafrost, active volcanoes, glacial valleys, craters etc. With stereoscope.
Set S.Kr 56.00

F GEOLOGY

CARTE GÉOLOGIQUE INTERNATIONALE DE L'EUROPE
1:1, 500, 000
UNESCO-BB.
see EUROPE 4F.

KARTA ÖVER SVERIGES BERGGRUND
1:1, 000, 000
In 3 sheets
Stockholm : SGU, 1957
76 x 112
Pre-quaternary rocks of Sweden col. geol. map showing solid geol. of Sweden. With descriptive text in English, by N H Magnusson, 1960.

KARTA ÖVER SVERIGES JORDARTER
1:1, 000, 000
In 3 sheets
Stockholm : SGU, 1958
76 x 162 complete
Quaternary deposits of Sweden. Col. map of superficial deposits.

SÖDRA SVERIGE I SENGLACIAL TID
1:500, 000
In 4 sheets
Stockholm : SGU, 1910
Map of South Sweden in late glacial times. Prepared by G de Geer, showing ridges, moraines, striae etc. Ger. ed. only available.

JORDARTSKARTA ÖVER SÖDRA OCH MELLERSTA SVERIGE
1:400, 000
By K E Sahlstrom
In 3 sheets
Stockholm : SGU, 1947-9
135 x 170
Quaternary deposits of South and Central Sweden.

ÖVERSIKT ÖVER NORRA NORRBOTTENSFJÄLLENS KALEDONBERGGRUND
1:400, 000-1:200, 000
Stockholm : SGU, 1965
89 x 148
Geol. of the Caledonian rocks of the N Norrbotten mts. 1 map at 1:400, 000, 2 at 1:200, 000.

KARTA ÖVER BERGGRUNDEN INOM VÄSTERBOTTENS FJÄLLOMRADE
1:200, 000
Stockholm : SGU
Geol. map of the Vasterbotten Mts.
Text by P Quensel, 1960. Also available in Ger.

GEOLOGISKA KARTBLAD
1:50, 000
See index 485/8
Stockholm : SGU, 1862-1956
A series of maps combining pre-quaternary and quaternary deposits, with descriptive texts for most sheets.

GEOLOGISKA KARTBLAD
1:50, 000
See index 485/8
Stockholm : SGU, 1964+
A new series combining the pre-quaternary and quaternary deposits, with texts. Series in progress.
Sheets published :
Stockholm NO, Ae 1
Stockholm NV, Ae 2
Stockholm SO, 1968
Stockholm SV, 1968
Örebro SV, 1970
Örebro NV, 1970
Uppsala SV, 1970

BERGGRUNDSKARTOR
1:50, 000
Stockholm : SGU, 1966+
Petrological maps, with text, new series.
Available for :
Nos 1-4 (29 J) Kiruna, text by J Offerberg, 1966
Nos 5-8 Tarendo, text 1970
Nos 9-12 Lainio, 1970

KVARTARGEOLOGISK KARTA ÖVER STOCKHOLMSTRAKTEN
1:50, 000
Stockholm : SGU, 1929
Geol. map of Stockholm area.
Description with Eng. summary, by G de Geer, 1932.

BERGGRUNDSKARTA ÖVER STOCKHOLMSTRAKTEN
1:50, 000
Stockholm : SGU, 1946
Pre-quaternary rocks of the Stockholm district. Text by N Sundius, 1948.

AGROGEOLOGISKA KARTBLAD
1:20, 000
Stockholm : SGU, 1947+
Agrogeological series, with descriptions.
Sheets available : ed: G Ekstrom

1	Hardeberga Map 1947	Text 1947
2	Lund Map 1953	Text 1953
3	Revinge Map 1951	Text 1961
4	Löberöd Map 1951	Text 1960
5	Öortofta Map 1952	Text 1961
6	Kävlinge Map 1966	Text 1966
7	Teckomatorp Map 1966	Text 1966
8	Trollenäs Map 1966	Text 1966
9	Bosjökloster Map 1966	Text 1966

AGRONOMISKT GEOLOGISK KARTA ÖFVER TORREBY I BOHUSLÄN
1:15, 000
Stockholm : SGU, 1892
Map of Torreby in the Bohuslan region.
Description by J Jonsson, 1892.

AGRONOMISKT - GEOLOGISK KARTA ÖFVER EGENDOMEN SVALNÄS I ROSLAGEN
1:10, 000
Stockholm : SGU, 1887
Agronomic geol. map of Svalnäs in the Roslagen area. Description by J Jonsson.

G EARTH RESOURCES

JORDARTSKARTA ÖVER GÖTAÄLVDALEN
1:20, 000
by B Jarnefors
In 3 sheets
Stockholm : SGU, 1959
Soil map of the Göta älv valley.

JORDARTSKARTA ÖVER UPPSALATRAKTEN
Stockholm : SGU, 1956
Soil map of the Uppsala area.
Description by B Jarnefors, 1958.

H BIOGEOGRAPHY

NATURSEVÄRDHETER SVERIGE
1:1, 500, 000
Stockholm : GLA
Map of the natural zones, with index.
S.Kr 30.00

KARTA ÖVER SVERIGES Å KER AREAL ENLIGT ABSOLUT METOD SAMMANSTÄLLD EFTER STATISTISKA CENTRALBYRÅNS OFFICIELLA PUBLIKATIONER
1913-20
by C J Annck
1:1, 000, 000
Stockholm : SGU, 1921
Area under cultivation in Sweden in agreement with the official publications 1913-20 of the Swedish Central bureau of statistics, mapped out by absolute method.
With text - Eng. summary.

K HUMAN GEOGRAPHY

BEFOLKNINGENS FÖRDELNING 1965
1:1, 000, 000
Stockholm : GLA, 1968
86 x 156
Pop. distribution in 1965. 2 sheets.
S.Kr 58.00

FOLKMÄNGDENS FÖRÄNDRING 1951-60 SAMT TÄTORTERNAS UTBREDNING
1:1, 000, 000
In 2 sheets
Stockholm : GLA, 1963
85 x 165
Map showing pop. changes during the period 1951-60.

NÄRINGSKARAKTAR OCH PENDLING 1960 I SVERIGE
1:1, 000, 000
Prod. by Central Bureau of Statistics, with Prof. Gerd. Enequist, Uppsala Univ.
In 2 sheets
Stockholm : GLA
70 x 160
Showing characteristics of industry and commuting.

INDUSTRINS LOKALISERING I SVERIGE
1:1, 000, 000
In 2 sheets
Stockholm : GLA/Sveriges Industriforbund, 1967
66 x 81
Industrial places in Sweden showing communications with pop. (indicated by circle areas) engaged in industry in 1964.
Legend in Eng. and Sw.
S.Kr 42.50

L ECONOMIC

POST- OCH JARNVAGSKARTA MED VISARE
1:1, 000, 000
Stockholm : GLA, 1972
140 x 100
Postal and railway map with index.
Mounted on board. S.Kr 139.00

M HISTORICAL

SVENSKA KRIGSMAKTENS ORGANISATION
Stockholm : GLA
Map of Swedish military organisation
Flat S.Kr 24.00

HISTORICAL MAPS
Stockholm : GLA
Collection of reproductions of interesting district maps of the last century (Dukedoms).
Maps available :
S G Hermelins karta över Göteborg och Bohus läns Höfdingadöme 1806 S.Kr 18.00
Stora Kopparbergs Höfdingadöme 1800 S.Kr 18.00
Karta över Upsala Höfdingadöme 1801 S.Kr 10.00
Carlstads Höfdingadöme, 1808 S.Kr 18.00
Stockholms Höfdingadöme, 1812 S.Kr 18.00
Gotlands eller Visby Höfdingadöme S.Kr 18.00
Östergotlands Höfdingadöme, 1810 S.Kr 18.00

GERHARD BUHRMANNS KARTA ÖVER SKÅNE
Stockholm : GLA
Reproduction of the 1684 map.
S.Kr 18.00

STOCKHOLM, 1733
Stockholm : GLA
89 x 72
Facsimile of city map by Petrus Tillaeus.
Folded S.Kr 5.75

STOCKHOLM PLANS
Stockholm : GLA
110 x 90
Facsimile maps of Stockholm.
Maps available :
Stockholm pa 1870-talet in cols.
Flat S.Kr 29.00
Boards S.Kr 68.00
Stockholm pa 1970-talet
Flat S.Kr 19.00
Boards S.Kr 54.00
Stockholm pa 1870-och, 1970-talet, by Neuhaus-Gerne. S.Kr 157.50

SVERIGE SOUVENIRKARTA
Stockholm : GLA
Souvenir pictorial wall map, showing features of interest.
Flat in roll S.Kr 15.00

ATLASES
A1 GENERAL: ROADS

KAK BILATLAS
1:200, 000/400, 000
Stockholm : GLA, 1973
19 x 31
296pp
46 fold out road maps, classified and numbered, other communications, places of tourist interest. Legend in Sw, Eng, Fr, Ger. Gazetteer 45, 000 names. Guide in Sw, tourist details of various towns. Complete road map of Sweden with plastic pointer in back of atlas.
S.Kr 48.00

ATLASES
B TOWN PLANS

TAXIKARTAN - ADRESSKARTEN ÖVER STOR-STOCKHOLM
Stockholm : GLA, 1971
20 x 28
51pp
Spiral bound road atlas of Greater Stockholm area; fold-out maps, information essential to taxi-drivers.
S.Kr 78.00

ATLASES
M HISTORICAL

ATLAS TILL HISTORIEN
Ed B Y Gustafson
Stockholm : Svenska Bokforlaget
Historical school atlas.

ATLASES
O NATIONAL

ATLAS ÖVER SVERIGE
Ed Svenska Sällskapet for Antropologi och Geografi
Stockholm : GLA, 1953-69
36 x 46 (case size)
Loose-leaf national atlas including approx. 1, 000 maps on the 150 plates, each with descriptive text. Legends Sw and Eng, text in Sw. Covers geol, climate, natural life, pop, agriculture, land use, social and economic aspects, history etc.
Loose sheets in carrying box
S.Kr 775.00
Clothbound S.Kr 1150.00

489 Denmark

See also: 48 SCANDINAVIA

A1 GENERAL MAPS: ROADS

SHELL REISEKARTE DANMARK
1:1, 000, 000
Stuttgart : Mair
59 x 48
Main and secondary roads, numbered, shipping and ferry routes, airports, distances in km, places of interest, camping sites etc. Legend in 12 langs.
DM 4.80

DENMARK
1:1, 000, 000
London : Foldex
Shows roads classified, relief shading; patent folding. 30p

DANMARK
1:750, 000
København : GI, 1970
44 x 50
Road map, with main and secondary roads numbered. Relief shading, vegetation in green. Bornholm Island inset. Table of distances on cover. D.Kr 5.00

POLITIKENS KORT OVER DANMARK
1:505, 000
København : Politikens
60 x 100
Roads classified and numbered, distances in km, spot heights in metres, places of tourist interest, ferries, railways. Bornholm inset.
D.Kr 4.75

DÄNEMARK
1:505, 000
No 214
Köln : Polyglott
57 x 77
Roads numbered and classified; distances in km, places of interest, camping sites.

DÄNEMARK
1:505, 000
No 396
Hamburg : Falk
60 x 94
All classes of roads, distances in km, road numbers, railways, ferries, airports, scenic routes, spot heights in metres, youth hostels, state frontiers and index. Inset of Bornholm. Falk patent folding. DM 4.80

KORT OVER DANMARK
1:500, 000
København : GI, 1969
99 x 76
All classes of roads, spot heights in metres, road numbers, railways, airports, state boundaries. Insets of Bornholm and Faroe Islands. Legend in Danish.
D.Kr 10.00

DÄNEMARK, FAERÖERNE, GRÖNLAND
1:500, 000
No 876
Frankfurt : Ravenstein, 1976
76 x 95
Main and secondary roads, numbered with distances in km, other communications, inc, shipping. Places of interest etc. Inc. Faroe Islands and Greenland on reverse.
DM 7.80

DÄNEMARK
1:400, 000
No 1484
München : JRO
86 x 122
Inc. Schleswig-Holstein. Roads numbered and classified, distances in km, other communications, airports, tourist details.
DM 6.80

DÄNEMARK
1:300, 000
No 1145
Bern : K & F
125 x 98
Road map showing all classes of roads, distances, scenic routes, railways and places of interest.

NYT FAERDSELSKORT
1:150, 000
In 10 sheets, see index 489/1
København : GI
Various sizes
Series of excursion maps covering the whole country. Roads classified and numbered. Distances in km, spot heights, tourist details.
Each D.Kr 9.00

A2 GENERAL MAPS: LOCAL

TURISTKORT-BORNHOLM
1:60, 000
København : GI
60 x 69
Topog. contoured map with spot heights, roads, footpaths, railways and inset map of Christians. District maps of Nordbornholm, Aldmindingen and Faradisbakkerne, scale 3" to 1 mile and 6 town plans on reverse.
Legend in Danish. D.Kr 7.00

TURISTKORT
1:20, 000
København : GI
Contoured, topographic maps showing roads, paths, land types etc.
Sheets available :
Hundested-Tisvrldeleje
Gilleleje og omegn
Helsingor og omegn
Dijrehaven - Hareskovene

B TOWN PLANS

TOWN PLANS
Various scales
Col. plans with index to streets
Maps available :
Aalborg
1:10, 000 Aalborg Stiftstidendes
Aarhus
1:18, 000 C Olsen
Kopenhagen, Central
1:16, 000 Falk
Kopenhagen
1:16, 000-1:36, 000 Falk
DM 4.80
København Monumental Kort
1:15, 000 Politiken

AARHUS
Braunschweig : Bollmann-Bildplan, 1970
Col. pictorial town plan, oblique view, showing individual buildings.
Decorative border. DM 5.50

KOPENHAGEN
NV 107
Braunschweig : Bollmann-Bildkarten, 1971
Col. pictorial town plan, oblique view, showing individual buildings.
Decorative border. DM 6.50
On hand made paper. DM 12.00

KØBENHAVN OG OMEGN
1:17, 500
København : GI
100 x 140
Sheet map of Copenhagen and environs.

C OFFICIAL SURVEYS

THE WORLD
1:1, 000, 000
DMS Series 1301
4 sheets needed for complete coverage
see WORLD 100C and index 100/1.

THE WORLD
1:500, 000
DMS Series 1404
5 sheets needed for complete coverage
see WORLD 100C and index 100/7.

KORT OVER DANMARK
1:300, 000
In 3 sheets, see index 489/2
København : GI, 1972
I, II - 63 x 62
III - 50 x 62
All classes of roads, route numbering, spot heights in metres, airports and state frontier.
Legend in Danish.

FAERDSELSKORT DANMARK
1:200, 000
In 4 sheets, see index 489/3
56 x 45
Contoured topog. series with roads, administrative districts and land detail.

KORT OVER DANMARK : 1cm KORT
1:100, 000
In 34 sheets, see index 459/4
København : GI
56 x 45 each
All classes of roads, paths, railways, contours, spot heights in metres, airports and state boundaries. The legend is in Danish.
D.Kr 9.00

OFFICIAL TOPOGRAPHICAL SERIES - 2cm KORT
1:50, 000
In 112 sheets, see index 489/5
København : GI
56 x 45
New col. series in progress, superseding 1:40, 000 series, contoured, roads, rivers, paths, woodland and land detail in col.
D.Kr 9.00

ATLASBLADE
1:40, 000
In 236 sheets, see index 489/6
København : GI
47 x 37
Topog. maps, showing roads, vegetation, contours, spot heights, hydrography. Now being replaced by 1:50, 000 series.
Each D.Kr 8.00

DANMARK - 4cm KORT
1:25, 000
In 410 sheets, see index 489/7
København : GI
56 x 45
Detailed contoured land maps in preparation, superseding the old 1:20, 000 series. Provisional ed. in black, blue and brown.
D.Kr 9.00

DANMARK
1:20, 000
In 835 sheets, see index 489/8, 10
København : GI
47 x 37 each
Topog. map showing contours, with spot heights, roads, paths. Inc. Faroe Islands. Very detailed series, being superseded by new 25, 000 series.
Each D.Kr 8.00

KORTMANUSKRIPTER
1:10, 000
København : GI
41 x 37
Manuscript copies of photogrammetric base maps for 4cm series. Black and white maps, with much topog. detail.

DANMARK FLYVEFOTOGRAFI
1:1, 000/25, 000
København : GI
25 x 25
Aerial photographs at various scales.

D POLITICAL & ADMINISTRATIVE

OVERSIGTSKORT
1:1, 000, 000
København : GI
31 x 38
General map showing roads, railways, towns, administrative district boundaries. In black and blue. D.Kr 3.00

KOMMUNE - OG SOGNEKORT
1:500, 000
København : GI, 1972
108 x 85
Map of communes and parishes, showing boundaries. Faroe Islands inset at 1:750, 000 and Greenland at 1:10, 000, 000. D.Kr 9.00

E1 PHYSICAL: RELIEF

DANMARK
1:1, 000, 000
København : GI
40 x 44
Relief map with roads, spot heights, topographic detail. Available as wall map 50 x 63.
Each D.Kr 8.00

DANIA - SZWECJA P.D.
1:1, 000, 000
Warszawa : PPWK, 1963
90 x 76
Physical map of Denmark and Sweden with contours, hydrography, communications. In the "Mapa Przegladowa Europy" (Review Maps of Europe) Series.

OVERSIGTSKORT OVER DANMARK
1:750, 000
København : GI, 1970
49 x 60
Small col. physical map with contours, vegetation, communications.

DÄNEMARK
1:312, 500
Berlin : Columbus
162 x 111
Physical school wall map, showing relief by layer col, boundaries, communications, land cover. Faroe Islands and Greenland inset.

DÄNEMARK
1:300, 000
Darmstadt : Perthes
196 x 184
Large scale physical wall map, with Faroe Islands and Greenland inset.
DM 142.00

DÄNEMARK
1:300, 000
Braunschweig : Westermann
209 x 194
Physical col. wall map, layer col, relief shading. Greenland and Faroe Islands inset. Communications, tourist sites, boundaries, location inset.

HØJDEKORT OVER DANMARK
1:250, 000
København : GI, 1964
196 x 155
14 col. relief map showing elevations and depth by col. variation. With or without names. School wall map. København and Greenland inset. D.Kr 100.00

OVERSIGTSKORT OVER DANMARK
1:250, 000
In 4 sheets
København : GI
155 x 196
Physical wall map - new edition in preparation.

E2 PHYSICAL: LAND FEATURES

LANDSKABSKORT OVER DANMARK
1:250, 000
In 4 sheets
København : GI, 1960
196 x 155
Geomorphological map in 13 cols.
Shows relief features, land types, moraines etc. D.Kr 100.00

TYPISKE LANDSKABER : HØJDEKORT OG BLOKDIA-GRAMMER
1:65, 000
København : GI
115 x 72 average
Series of maps with block diagrams, showing structure and nature of typical land forms.
Sheets available :
Odsherred (N W Zealand)
A Danish moraine landscape and its evolution
Vendysyssel (N Jutland)
Moraine landscape and coastal plains at different levels
Midtylland (Central Jutland)
A glacial lake district
Marsk og gest (S W Jutland)
Marsh plains and glacial landscape
Stevns (E Zealand)
Moraine flat limited by chalk cliffs, shore lines
Bornholm
A glaciated landscape
Each D.Kr 25.00

F GEOLOGY

GEOLOGISKE KORT OVER DANMARK
1:160, 000
København : DGU, 1916+
35 x 45 average
Col. geol. maps with descriptive text.
Available :
Nordøstjælland, 1935
Nordvestjælland, 1943

GEOLOGISK KORT OVER SØNDERJYLLAND
1:125, 000
Ed A Jessen
København : DGU, 1935
Geological map of South Jutland with 8pp text. D.Kr 41.90

GEOLOGISK KORT OVER DANMARK
1:100, 000
København : DGU, 1893+
Geol. series with descriptive texts, many sheets now out of print.
Sheets available :
Vissenbjærg, 1940
Sønderborg, 1945
Fåborg, 1959
Fredericia, 1958
Tinglev, 1970

G EARTH RESOURCES

JORDBUNDSKORT OVER DANMARK
1:500, 000
3rd series, No 24
København : DGU, 1935/70
68 x 78
Soil map, with text in Danish and English.
D.Kr 41.40

L ECONOMIC

ERHVERVSGEOGRAFISK KORT OVER DANMARK
1:300, 000
København : GI
109 x 153
2 sheet commercial geog. map, showing mining, fishing, industrial and agricultural areas etc. School wall map.
D.Kr 70.00

M HISTORICAL

DANIAE, 1629
København : GI
Col. reproduction of Johannes Janssonius map. D.Kr 30.00

KONGERIGET DANMARK MED HERTUGDOMMET SLESVIG (1846)
1:480, 000
In 2 sheets
København : GI
Facsimile in black and white.

JYLLAND (1820)
1:360, 000
København : GI
Copper print in black and white.

SJAELLAND OG MOEN (1813)
1:320, 000
København : GI
Copper print in black and white.

SONDER JYLLAND (1836)
1:240, 000
København : GI
Copper print in black and white.

SJAELLAND OG MØEN (1777)
1:240, 000
København : GI
Facsimile in black and white.

DANMARK
1:160, 000
In 24 sheets
København : GI (1909-1916)
Bornholm inset at 1:100, 000.
Reproduction in black and white.

SLESVIGS FASTLAND (1851-1854)
1:120, 000
In 6 sheets
København : GI
Facsimile in black and white.

HOLSTEN OG LAUENBURG (1855-1862)
1:120, 000
In 8 sheets + title sheet
København : GI
Facsimile in black and white.

DANMARK OG SLESVIG
1:120, 000
København : GI
Reproduction map of Denmark and Schleswig in 17 sheets, 1768-1826. Bornholm and Anholt at larger scale.

SJAELLAND OG FYN (1854-72)
1:80, 000
In 29 sheets
København : GI
Facsimile prints in black and white.

KJOBENHAVNS AMT (1766)
1:80, 000
København : GI
Map of the Copenhagen district.
Copper print facsimile.

ANHOLT (1792)
1:40, 000
København : GI
Copper facsimile print in black and white.

MONUMENTALKORT OVER DANMARK
København : Politikens
39 x 46
Col. pictorial map of monuments and important buildings.

ATLASES
W3 WORLD ATLAS: LOCAL EDITION

HAASES ATLAS FOR FOLKESKOLEN
2nd Edition
København : P Haase, 1975
19 x 25
104pp
High school atlas, 82pp mainly physical maps. D.Kr 39.00

ATLASES
A1 GENERAL: ROADS

BILISTENS STORE HÅNDBOG
1:320, 000
København : Det Bedste fra Reader's Digest A/S, 1969-70
17 x 28
Road atlas with 24 maps of Europe, 45pp town plans. 126 maps of Europe. In Danish, with 201pp index and preliminary text of touring information.

ATLASES
B TOWN PLANS

POLITIKENS BOGKORT, KØBENHAVN OG OMEGN
1:14, 500
13th edition
København : Politiken, 1973
304pp
89 double pp maps of København and environs in colour. Text in Dan. and Eng. Index to streets, hotel and other tourist details. D.Kr 19.00

ATLASES
C OFFICIAL SURVEYS

BOGEN DANMARK
1:200, 000
København : GI
17 x 28
118pp
Complete set of official 1:200, 000 topog. series with index of 12, 000 names.
D.Kr 45.00

ATLASES
L ECONOMIC

LILLE ERHVERVSGEOGRAFISK ATLAS
Ed Maps : J Humlum, Text : T Gregersen and T Holm
København : Gyldendal, 1972
39pp
Small industrial atlas for schools including coloured maps and descriptive text. Danish.
D.Kr 32.00

ATLASES
O NATIONAL

ATLAS OF DENMARK
Ed Prof. Dr N Nielsen
In 2 vols.
København : The Royal Danish Geog. Soc.
38 x 56
Each section is accompanied by a handbook in English. The maps have a legend in English and Danish.
Volumes :
I The Landscapes D.Kr 115.00
II The Population D.Kr 115.00

DANMARK ATLAS
2nd Edition
Ed J Humlum and K Nygård
København : Gyldendal, 1976
23 x 29
40pp
26 col. maps describing the physical nature, economy, pop, and communications etc. of the country, including Faroes and Greenland, explanatory text in Danish.
D.Kr 60.00

GYLDENDALS ATLAS - DANMARK
Eds. M Rentsch and K Werner Larsen
København : Gyldendal, 1972
14pp maps, 10pp text
School atlas of Denmark.
D.Kr 27.50

ATLASES
P REGIONAL

WATTENMEER
Karl Wachholtz, 1976
Atlas of offshore islands south of Esbjerg and the Friesian islands.
see EUROPE 5 ATLASES P

491.1 Iceland

A1 GENERAL MAPS : ROADS

TOURIST ROAD MAP OF ICELAND
1:750, 000
Reyjavik : Touring Club of Iceland, 1974
73 x 57
Showing roads, paths, mountain tracks, road conditions, spot heights in metres, hill shading with contours, official and other tourist huts. Is.K. 150.00

SHELL VEGAKORT ÍSLAND
1:600, 000
Stuttgart : Mair
46 x 71
Roads classified and numbered, distances in km, hill shading. Double sided map.
DM 3.00
Also available as BP Road Map of Iceland.

A2 GENERAL MAPS : LOCAL

SÉRKORT AF MYVATNI
1:50, 000
Reykjavík : LI 1973
48 x 42
Special map of Lake Myvatn contoured and relief shaded with roads.
Paper flat Is.Kr. 90.00
Paper folded Is.Kr. 100.00

SÉRKORT AF THINGVELLIR
1:25, 000
Reykjavík : LI, 1969
56 x 51
Special area map, contoured with roads, tracks, farms, churches, camp sites and car parks. On reverse side is 1:3, 500 plan of Parliament site with explanation in 4 languages, including English.
Paper flat Is.Kr. 100.00
Paper folded Is.Kr. 100.00

SÉRKORT AF SURTSEY I OKTOBER 1964
1:10, 000
Reykjavík : LI, 1964
25 x 25
Special map of the island, contoured with relief shading and including a brief history of the eruptions and location map of the Westmann Islands. Text in Icelandic and English.
Paper flat Is.Kr. 60.00

SÉRKORT AF VESTMANNAEYJAR
1 50, 000
Reykjavík : LI, 1973
44 x 40
Special edition of standard topog. sheet 49 NW with inset plan of the town of Vestmannaeyjakaupstadur and aerial photograph of volcanic fissure which erupted 23.1.73.

B TOWN PLANS

REYKJAVÍK - HAFNARFJORÐUR - KÓPAVOGUR - SELTJARNARNES - GARÐAHREPPUR - BESSASTAÐA - HREPPUR
1:15, 000
Reykjavík : Águst Bodvarsson, 1971
86 x 56
Double sided plan of the town and environs contoured with streets named also buildings marked and named. Inset of town centre. On reverse is the area to the south of the town including Hafnarfjordur and index to streets.
Paper flat Is.Kr. 140.00
Paper folded Is.Kr. 150.00

AKUREYRI
1:7, 500
Reykjavík : LI, 1957
32 x 54
Col. plan showing town and surroundings, with index to streets and farms and list of accommodation, public buildings, etc. on reverse.

C OFFICIAL SURVEYS

KARTA MIRA
1:2, 500, 000
Cart
Sheet 12 - Reykjavík
see WORLD 100C and index 100/2.

INTERNATIONAL MAP OF THE WORLD
1:1, 000, 000
Reykjavík : LI
Sheets : NP 27, 28
NQ 27, 28
see WORLD 100C and index 100/1.

THE WORLD
1:1, 000, 000
Iceland - Special sheet
AMS 1301
see WORLD 100C and index 100/1.

AÐALKORT YFIR ÍSLAND
1:250, 000
In 9 sheets, see index 491.1/1
Reykjavík : LI
70 x 48 each sheet
Topog. series with contours at 20 metre intervals, spot heights, roads, tracks, paths marked by cairns, indistinct paths, inns and farms.
Paper flat Is.Kr. 120.00
Paper folded Is.Kr. 130.00

AÐALKORT YFIR ÍSLAND - TURISTKORT
1:250, 000
see index 491.1/1
Reykjavík : LI
Combination sheets of the standard series showing same information.
Sheets available :
1 and 2 Western Iceland, 1969
3 and 6 Southern Iceland, 1969
4 and 7 Northern Iceland, 1970
8 and 9 Eastern Iceland, 1971
Paper flat Is.Kr. 180.00
Paper folded Is.Kr. 200.00

ATLAS BLOÐIN
1:100, 000
In 87 sheets, see index 491.1/1
Reykjavík : LI
44 x 40
Topog. series with contours at 20 metre intervals, spot heights, roads, tracks, paths marked by cairns, indistinct paths, inns and farms.
Paper flat Is.Kr. 105.00
Paper folded Is.Kr. 115.00

FJÓRÐUNGSBLOÐIN
1:50, 000
see index 491.1/1
Reykjavík : LI
44 x 40
Series covering 440 square km (170 square miles) of Western and Southern Iceland Contoured at 20 metre intervals, spot heights, roads, tracks, paths marked by cairns, indistinct paths, inns and farms.
Paper flat Is.Kr. 90.00
Paper folded Is.Kr. 100.00

FJÓRÐUNGSBLOÐIN - NÝ ÚTGÁFA
1:50, 000
AMS Kort C 761, see index 491.1/2
Reykjavík : LI
New series in preparation, contoured and marking roads, paths and tracks, also settlement, drainage and mountain huts.
Paper flat Is.Kr. 105.00
Paper folded Is.Kr. 115.00

D POLITICAL & ECONOMIC

ISLANDIYA
1:1, 000, 000
Moskva : GUGK, 1973
Col. study map showing water features, settlements, admin. centres and divisions, communications, boundaries, economic details, pop, Geog. description.
Kop. 30

E1 PHYSICAL : RELIEF

KORT TIL SKOLEBRUG
1:1, 000, 000
Reykjavík : LI
58 x 47
Physical wall map for schools, relief shaded, communications, boundaries and settlement. Kr. 75.00
Also available at 1:2, 000, 000 Kr. 60.00

ÍSLAND - STAÐFRAEÐILEGT YFIRLITSKORT
1:1, 000, 000
Reykjavík : LI, 1963
53 x 38
Topog. map, contoured with roads and towns graded according to pop.
Legend in 3 langs, incl. English.
Paper flat Is.Kr. 75.00
Paper folded Is.Kr. 90.00

ÍSLAND - LANDSLAGSKORT
1:500, 000
Reykjavík : LI
111 x 77
Coloured wall map, contoured with layer colouring showing main towns and settlement.
Mounted on linen with rollers top and bottom. Is.Kr. 450.00

ÍSLAND - LANDSLAGSKORT
1:350, 000
In 4 sheets
Reykjavík : LI
110 x 160 complete size
Physical wall map, contoured with layer colouring, showing settlement, farms, roads, water courses, mountains etc.
Mounted on linen with rollers top and bottom. Is.Kr. 1040.00

PLASTIC RELIEF KORT OVER ISLAND
1:1, 000, 000
Reykjavík : LI
Moulded plastic relief map with relief colouring. Kr. 600.00

E2 PHYSICAL : LAND FEATURES

BREIÐAMERKURJÖKULL, SE ICELAND
1:35, 000
In 2 sheets
Glasgow : Univ. of Glasgow, Geog. Dept, Sheet 1 1945, 2 1965
67 x 37
Col. glaciological map of South East Iceland.

F GEOLOGY

INTERNATIONAL QUATERNARY MAP OF EUROPE
1:2, 500, 000
Sheet 1 : Reykjavík
UNESCO - BB
see EUROPE 4F.

JARÐFRAEÐIKORT
1:250, 000
In 9 sheets, see index 491.1/1
Reykjavík : The Cultural Fund Press
70 x 48 each sheet
Coloured series showing lithology, structures, volcanic and glacial features with contours at 100 metre intervals.
Legend in Icelandic and English. Sheet lines the same as topog. series.
Sheets published : 1 Norðvesturland, 1969, 2 Vest Mið Island, 1968, 3 Suðvesturland, 1960, 5 Mið Island, 1965, 6 Mið Suðurland, 1962
with :
Supplementary notes to the legend of the Geological Map of Iceland.
Compiled by Guðmundur Kjartansson
10 pages.
Paper flat or folded Is.Kr. 120.00

JARÐFRAEÐIKORT AF REYKJAVÍK OG NÁGRENNI
1:40, 000
Reykjavik : City Council, 1958
72 x 48
Coloured geological map of the town and its neighbourhood.
Paper flat Is.Kr. 100.00

G EARTH RESOURCES

CARTE METALLOGÉNIQUE DE L'EUROPE
1:2, 500, 000
Sheet 1 - Europe Nord - Ouest (covering Iceland)
UNESCO/BRGM
see EUROPE 4G.

GEOMAGNETIC MAP
1:250, 000
In 9 sheets
Reykjavík : LI
Series following standard topog. sheet lines in 3 editions : with magnetic profiles, magnetic contours or magnetic profiles and contours combined.

H BIOGEOGRAPHY

GRÓÐURKORT AF ÍSLAND
1:40, 000
In 430 sheets, see index 491.1/3
Reykjavík : The Cultural Fund Press
74 x 57
Coloured map series in preparation classifying approximately 60 vegetation types and indicating the nature of the land surface according to drainage and vegetation cover.
Paper flat or folded Is.Kr. 80.00

L ECONOMIC

ÍSLAND LANDGRUNNID
1:3, 000, 000
Reykjavík : LI, 1971
36 x 31
Map of Icelandic fishing grounds showing sea boundaries and fishing banks.
Is.Kr. 60.00

491.2 Faroe Islands

C OFFICIAL SURVEYS

INTERNATIONAL MAP OF THE WORLD
1:1, 000, 000
Sheet NP 29 - Thorshavn
Kobenhavn : GI
see WORLD 100C and index 100/1.

FØRØYAR
1:200, 000
København : GI, 1971
50 x 72
Topographical contoured map, Roads, footpaths and spot heights in metres.
D.Kr. 8.00

FÆRØERNE
1:100, 000
In 4 sheets, see index 489/10
København : GI, 1962
39 x 60
Contoured topog. map.
Each D.Kr. 8.00

FÆRØERNE
1:20, 000
In 53 sheets, see index 489/10
København : GI
47 x 37
Topog. series, with contours, roads and paths and land detail. D.Kr. 8.00

FLYVEFOTOGRAFIER
1:12, 000-1:25, 000
København : GI
Series of black and white aerial photographs produced at 1:12, 000 from 1958 and 1:25, 000 after 1970.

E2 PHYSICAL : LAND FEATURES

TYPISKE LANDSKABER : HOJD KORT OG BLOKDIAGRAMMER - FÆRØKYSTER
København : GI
102 x 72
Diagram illustrating a basalt landscape and its coastal types in the Faroes with 2 block diagrams.

F GEOLOGY

GEOLOGISK KORT OVER FÆRØERNE
1:200, 000
Series No 25
København : DGU, 1970
40 x 63
Col. geol. map (prequaternary) with 140pp text in Eng. D.Kr. 97.75

GEOLOGISK KORT OVER FÆRØERNE
1:50, 000
Series No 24
In 6 sheets
København : DGU
Prequaternary geol. map with 370pp text (1969) in Danish, with Eng. summary.
D.Kr. 276.00

492 Benelux Countries

A1 GENERAL MAPS : ROADS

BELGIO, PAESI BASSI E LUSSEMBURGO
1:1, 000, 000
Novara : Ag
Tourist road map covering Belgium, the low countries and Luxembourg.
L. 700

BENELUX
1:585, 000
Bern : Hallwag
70 x 104
Showing all classes of roads, railways, ferries and camping sites.

BENELUX
1:500, 000
No 86
Stuttgart : RV - Bruxelles : Mantniek
75 x 110
Roads classified, route numbers, distances, places of interest.
DM 5.80

BENELUX-CHAMPAGNE
1:500, 000
No 1182
Bern : K & F
90 x 128
All classes of roads, route numbers, distances, scenic routes, railways and places of tourist interest.

CARTA STRADALE D'EUROPA
1:500, 000
Sheet 5 - Benelux
Milano : TCI, 1972
75 x 111
Contoured and layer col. with all classes of roads, road conditions and distances.
see also EUROPE 4 A1.

BELGIEN-LUXEMBURG
1:500, 000
Koln : Polyglott
Roads classified with distances.
DM 3.20

SHELL REISEKARTE : BENELUX
1:400, 000
Stuttgart : Mair, 1972
66 x 73
Roads classified and numbered, places of tourist interest, accommodation, motoring information. Legend in 12 langs.
DM 4.80

BENELUX
1:400, 000
No 1483
München : JRO
84 x 119
Col. map, roads classified and numbered, distances in km, places of interest, 6 through-town plans, boundaries, railways. DM 6.80

BENELUX
1:400, 000
London : Foldex
Shows roads classified, relief shading, patent folding. 45p

BELGIEN-LUXEMBURG
1:320, 000
No 381
Hamburg : Falk
Falk patent folded road map.
DM 3.60

D POLITICAL & ADMINISTRATIVE

BENELUX
No 59
Paris : Hatier
100 x 120
School wall map; political with economic map on reverse.

PAYS BAS, PHYSIQUE ET AGRICOLE
1:300, 000
Map No 29
Ed. Vidal Lablache and H Varon
Armand Colin
100 x 120
Physical and agricultural map with political and industrial map on reverse.

E1 PHYSICAL : RELIEF

BELGIA I HOLANDIA
1:1, 000, 000
Warszawa : PPWK, 1972
57 x 46
General, physical map, showing communications and administrative areas.
Zl. 12

NIEDERLANDE-BELGIEN-LUXEMBURG
1:300, 000
Braunschweig : Westermann
136 x 219
Physical wall map for schools, showing relief, layer col, communications, minerals, international boundaries.

BELGIE EN LUXEMBURG
1:300, 000
Groningen : Wolters-Nordhoff
107 x 85
Col. school wall map; physical, relief shading, communications, boundaries.
Fl. 44.75

PAYS-BAS, PHYSIQUE ET AGRICOLE
1:300, 000
Paris : Armand Colin
120 x 100
School wall map showing physical and agricultural details. With political and industrial map on reverse.

BENELUX
1:2, 000, 000
Novara : Ag
33 x 26
Moulded plastic relief map, covering Belgium, the Low Countries, Luxembourg, with physical, political and economic details on reverse.
L. 450

L ECONOMIC

BENELUX (PHYSIQUE)
Editions MDI
Economic map on reverse.
see BENELUX 492 E1

BENELUX
No 59
Hatier
Political-economic map.
see BENELUX 492 D

PAY BAS, PHYSIQUE ET AGRICOLE
1:300, 000
Armand Colin
Political and industrial map on reverse.
see BENELUX 492 E1.

ATLASES
A1 GENERAL : ROADS

BENELUX : AUTOATLAS AMSTERDAM - PARIS
1:500, 000
No 382
Hamburg : Falk
Falk patent fold plan : contains general map of Benelux, with motorways, main roads, distances: Amsterdam town, map of the Hague and Rotterdam, Brussels town, map of Antwerp, Dusseldorf, Paris city and Luxembourg city. DM 5.60

AUTOATLAS BELGIEN - LUXENBURG
1:250, 000
No 384
Hamburg : Falk
Sectional road atlas with patent folding.
DM 7.80

492.1 Netherlands

See also: 492 BENELUX

A1 GENERAL MAPS : ROADS

TOERISTISCHE AUTOKAART VAN NEDERLAND
1:500, 000
Delft : TD
52 x 64
Tourist map showing all classes of roads, recreation facilities, youth hostels, places of tourist interest etc.
Fl. 2.50

HOLLAND
1:500, 000
No 206
Koln : Polyglott
White base with roads classified, distances in km, places of interest, camping sites.
DM 3.20

NEDERLAND WEGENKAART
1:400, 000
Kaart No 29
3rd edition
Bruxelles : R De Rouck, 1970
66 x 82
Clear road map. Roads classified, with route numbers and distances in km. Railways, boundaries, ferries and principal places of interest marked, also towns graded according to population. 19 page index to places. B.Fr 50.00

NIEDERLANDE
1:400, 000
No 873
Frankfurt : Ravenstein, 1976
66 x 95
All classes of roads, distances in km, other communications, boundaries; town plans of Rotterdam, Amsterdam, Hague inset.
DM 7.80

HOLLAND
1:400, 000
London : Foldex
Shows roads classified; relief shading; patent fold.
45p

SHELL REISEKARTE : NIEDERLANDE
1:400, 000
Stuttgart : Mair
Coloured road map, roads classified and numbered, distances in km, places of tourist interest, accommodation, motoring details. Legend in 5 langs. DM 4.80

DIE NIEDERLANDE
1:300, 000
Bern : K & F
79 x 102
Roads classified and numbered, distances in km. Railways, crossings, boat services and ferries, frontiers, other details.
DM 5.80

TOURENKARTE DER NIEDERLANDE
1:250, 000
No 1209
Munchen : JRO
88 x 124
Roads classified and numbered, distances in km.
DM 6.80

AUTOKARTE DER NIEDERLANDE
1:250, 000
No 380
Hamburg : Falk
91 x 61
Patent folding. All classes of roads, distances in km, other communications, tourist details. DM 7.80

AUTOKAART VAN NEDERLAND
1:200, 000
In 3 sheets :
Autokaart Noord-Nederland
Autokaart Midden-Nederland
Autokaart Zuid-Nederland
Hague : ANWB
Coloured with roads numbered and classified, distances in km, places of interest etc.

NEDERLAND
1:200, 000
In 3 sheets, Nos 1, 5, 6, see index 492/1
Paris : Michelin, 1971
102 x 47 each
Roads classified and numbered, distances in km, spot heights, tourist attractions.
30p

TOERISTENKAART
1:100, 000
In 12 sheets
The Hague : ANWB
75 x 80 each
Regional road series ; distances in km, roads classified and numbered, places of interest, etc.
Sheets published :

1	Hollands-Noorden
2	Friesland
3	Groningen en Noord Drenthe
4	Drenthe
5	Westlÿke Randstad
6	Utrecht-Amsterdam
7	Veluwe
8	Twente-Achterhoek
9	Zeeland-Voome en Putten
10	Noord Brabant-West
11	Noord Brabant-Midden
12	Noord Brabant-Oost and Noord Limburg
13	Limburg Zuid

A2 GENERAL MAPS : LOCAL

SUD LIMBURG UND UMGEBUNG
1:350, 000
No 399
Hamburg : Falk Verlag
General route map of the region and area around. DM 3.00

SUD LIMBURG (NIEDERLANDE)
1:50, 000
No 398
Hamburg : Falk Verlag
Topographical route map of the region.
DM 2.50

B TOWN PLANS

TOWN PLANS
Various scales
Hamburg : Falk
Col. plans with index to streets.
Maps available :

Amsterdam	No 222
1:15, 000	DM 6.80
Amsterdam	No 223
1:14, 000/36, 000	DM 3.90
Arnhem	No 226
1:10, 000	DM 3.90
Eindhoven	No 233
1:12, 500	DM 3.90
Groningen	No 232
1:10, 000	DM 3.90
Haarlem	No 231
1:10, 000	DM 3.90
Hague (S'Gravenhage)	No 221
1:17, 500/28, 000	DM 3.90
Den Haag ('s Gravenhage)	No 220
1:15, 500/25, 000	DM 5.60
Maastricht	No 229
1:10, 000	DM 3.90
Rotterdam	No 224
1:15, 000	DM 6.80
Rotterdam	No 225
1:18, 000/25, 000	DM 3.90
Utrecht	No 228
1:12, 500	DM 3.90

AMSTERDAM
Nr 124
Braunschweig : Bollmann Bildkarten 1971
71 x 88
Coloured pictorial town plan; showing individual buildings, oblique view.
Decorate border.
Flat DM 6.80
On hand made paper DM 12.00

C OFFICIAL SURVEYS

THE WORLD
1:1, 000, 000
DMS Series 1301
4 sheets needed for complete coverage
see WORLD 100C and index 100/1.

THE WORLD
1:500, 000
DMS Series 1404
2 sheets needed for complete coverage
see WORLD 100C and index 100/7.

OVERZICHTSKAART VAN NEDERLAND
1:250, 000
In 6 sheets, see index 492.1/1
Delft : TD
69 x 58 each
Coloured topographical series, contours, communications, boundaries.
Each Fl. 700

TOPOGRAFISCHE KAART
1:100, 000
In 34 sheets, see index 492.1/2
Delft : TD, 1957-58
40 x 50 each
Coloured topographical series showing communications, vegetation and land detail.
Col. Fl. 5.20
Grey print Fl. 2.57

TOPOGRAFISCHE KAART
1:50, 000
In 110 sheets, see index 492.1/4
Delft : TD
40 x 50
Col. series showing roads classified, vegetation, relief shading, paths etc. Also available in grey printed edition with contours in brown.
Col. sheet Fl. 17.00
Grey print Fl. 9.90

TOPOGRAFISCHE KAART
1:25, 000
In 369 sheets, see index 492.1/3
Delft : TD
40 x 50
Topographical series showing land types, relief, roads, dwellings, water features etc. Available col. or grey print. Legend sheet available.
Coloured Fl. 7.70
Grey print Fl. 4.30

KAARTEN VAN DE NORDZEE-EILANDEN
1:25, 000
Delft : TD
Island maps based on official 25, 000 series. Available for :
Texel Fl. 10.00
Vlieland Fl. 8.30
Terschelling Fl. 8.30
Ameland Fl. 3.50
Schiermonnikoog Fl. 8.30
Walcheren Fl. 7.00

LUCHTFOTOS
1:20, 000
Delft : TD
18 x 18 or 23 x 23
Series of aerial photos covering the whole of the Netherlands, indicating land use, geology, archaeology, topographic details etc.
Available in following editions :
1 for loan (maximum 3 weeks) Fl. 2.00 & Postage
2 contact print Fl. 16.00
3 enlargement by 2 Fl. 27.00
4 enlargement by 4 Fl. 70.00
5 special printing

TOPOGRAFISCHE KAART
1:10, 000
Delft : TD
62 x 100
Topog. series in grey print. Shows roads, dwellings, field boundaries and other topographical features.
Uncontoured Fl. 12.30
Contoured Fl. 15.00

HOOGTEKAART VAN NEDERLAND
1:10, 000
Delft : TD
62 x 100 each
Multi sheet series showing land heights for water control, by contours and spot heights. On the same sheet lines as the 1:10, 000 Topografische Kaart. Fl. 22.40

KADASTRALE KAART VAN NEDERLAND
1:1, 250, 1:2, 500, 1:5, 000
In 2, 400 sheets
Delft : TD
100 x 70
Large scale cadastral series showing property boundaries, district divisions, houses and buildings etc. To be replaced by new metric series on scales of 1:1, 000 and 1:2, 000.
Available in following styles:
a as a negative on document paper Fl. 14.00
b as a positive on document paper Fl. 31.50
c as a positive on film or as a photocopy Fl. 59.50

D POLITICAL & ADMINISTRATIVE

GEMEENTENKAART VAN NEDERLAND
1:400, 000
Delft : TD, 1972
76 x 94
Black and white map showing province boundaries, chief towns, index to admin. districts. Fl. 12.00

KANTOORKAART VAN NEDERLAND
1:320, 000
Munchen : Kompass, 1969
88 x 120
Col. map with province boundaries, communications. Index on reverse.

GROTE WANDKAART VAN NEDERLAND
1:300, 000
Assen : Born
90 x 100
Shows province boundaries, communications network inc. canals. Index to places. Fl. 14.50

E1 PHYSICAL : RELIEF

BELGIA - HOLANDIA
1:1, 000, 000
2nd edition
Warszawa : PPWK
68 x 46
Contours, communications, hydrography. Legend and text on reverse in Polish. From the series "Przegladowa Mapa Europy" (Review Maps of Europe). Zl. 12

HOLLAND
1:350, 000
Series GSGS 4948, World Lecture Maps, Sheet B14
Feltham : DMS
Generalized base or display map showing international boundaries, capital cities and important large towns shown by symbol, principal road and rail communications and relief by contours and layer colours. 50p

E2 PHYSICAL : LAND FEATURES

AFWATERINGSGEBIEDEN
1:600, 000
's-Gravenhage : Rijkswaterstaat
50 x 60
Generalised map depicting drainage units in colour and including water control detail, polders, water levels etc. Fl. 6.00
Navigation ed. Fl. 2.30

HOOFDWATERKERINGEN
1:600, 000
's-Gravenhage : Rijkswaterstaat
50 x 60
Shows major dykes on sea and river areas with admin. agencies.

WATERSCHAPPEN DIE BIJZONDERE BELANGEN BEHARTIGEN
1:600, 000
's-Gravenhage : Rijkswaterstaat
50 x 60
Shows major polderboard regions.

WATERSCHAPPEN GROOTER DAN 500 HA
1:600, 000
's-Gravenhage : Rijkswaterstaat
50 x 60
Showing polderboards with an area of more than 500 hectares.

GEMALENKAART VAN NEDERLAND
1:600, 000
's-Gravenhage : Rijkswaterstaat
50 x 60
Shows pumping plants and windmills used for drainage.

WATERSTAATSKAART VAN NEDERLAND
1:50, 000
's-Gravenhage : Rijkswaterstaat, 1954+
50 x 60
Water management series showing by col. polders, catchment areas, drainage units, water levels, pumping facilities. On 1:50, 000 topog. series sheet lines. Provincial description books available and 2 transparent overlays : "Hydrologische waarnemingspunten" (hyd. observation points) and "Watervoorzienings-eenheden" (water supply units)
Each Fl. 8.50

PEILMERKEN VAN HET N.A.P.
1:25, 000
Delft : Meetkundige Dienst van de Rijkswaterstaat
Based on standard 1:25, 000 topog. series, in blueprint ed. Showing water levels based on the Amsterdam datum.
Each Fl. 3.85

IJSSELMEERGEBIET
1:100, 000
s'Gravenhage : Zuider Zee Projekt, 1967
82 x 112
Coloured map showing reclaimed land areas, drainage and further projections.

GEOMORPHOLOGICAL MAP OF THE NETHERLANDS
1:50, 000
Haarlem : Rijks Geologische Dienst, 1967+
62 x 58 app
Map based on sheet lines of 1:50, 000 Topog. series and showing 8 classifications of relief and 18 land-form types. Series provisional.
Sheets published :
5E, 6E and W, 17E and W, 25E, 26W, 29W, 31E and W, 32E and W, 39E, 40E, 41W.
Photocopies Fl. 50.00
The first standard sheets in colour have been published :
31 Utrecht 1975
32 Amersfoort 1975

F GEOLOGY

GEOLOGISCHE KAART VAN NEDERLAND
1:600, 000
Haarlem : Rijksgeologische Dienst, 1975
70 x 65
Coloured geological map with additional maps of sand and gravel, glacial features and tectonic origins at the same scale, also geological cross-section and 150pp explanatory text.
Set Fl. 25.00

HYDROGEOLOGISCHE KAART VAN NEDERLAND
1:1,500, 000
Haarlem : Rijksgeologische Dienst, 1975
36 x 26
Set of 2 maps in colours, one showing the geology of the country, the other hydrological information. Legend in Dutch and English.
Set Fl. 7.00

GEOLOGISCHE OVERZICHTSKAART VAN NEDERLAND
1:200, 000
In 23 sheets, including legend and title.
Delft : Koninklijk Nederlands Geologisch Mijnbouwkundig Genootschap, 1936-53
34 x 54 each
Col. geol. map. 4 sheets now out of print.
Each Fl. 9.90

ZUID-LIMBURG-GEOLOGISCHE OVERZICHTSKAART
1:100, 000
Haarlem : Rijks Geologische Dienst, 1972
34 x 51
Small geol. map of the West Maastricht district, showing pre-quaternary information.
Fl. 3.00

GEOLOGISCHE KAART VAN NEDERLAND
1:50, 000
1st edition
Haarlem : Rijks Geol. Dienst
55 x 43
Col. geol. series available as quarter sheets each with cross section in margin. Sheets going out of print and will be replaced by new 2nd ed. sheets. Fl. 1.60

GEOLOGISCHE KAART VAN NEDERLAND
1:50, 000
2nd edition
Haarlem : Rijks Geol. Dienst, 1964+
70 x 60
New col. geol. series in progress on sheet lines of topog. series including with each sheet single-value maps 1:100, 000, cross sections and explanatory note with diagrams, photographs and itinerary of geol. phenomena.
Sheets published :
16E, 38E, 42E pt 36E, 43E and W, 48W pt 47E, 52W, 54W pt 53E, 54E, 55W.
Each Fl. 16.75

G EARTH RESOURCES

BODEMKAART VAN NEDERLAND
1:200, 000
In 9 sheets
Wageningen : Stichting voor Bodemkartering, 1961
67 x 56
Detailed coloured soil map series, with 2 explanatory legend sheets in folder.

Set	Fl. 31.20
Each sheet	Fl. 3.65
Dutch legend	Fl. 1.05
Eng. legend	Fl. 2.60

BODEMKAART VAN NEDERLAND
1:50, 000
See index 492.1/4
Wageningen : Stichting voor Bodemkartering, 1964+
40 x 50 each
Col. soil map in progress. Texts available. Follows sheet lines of 1:50, 000 Topog. series.
Each Fl. 30.00

H BIOGEOGRAPHY

EERSTE WANDKART VAN NEDERLAND
1:250, 000
Groningen : Wolters-Noordhoff
117 x 150
Wall map of the Country, physical-land use col, relief shading, road, rail, river and canal communications, town sites indicated but no names. Fl. 121.75

TWEEDE WANDKAART VAN NEDERLAND
1:200, 000
Groningen : Wolters-Noordhoff, 1968
160 x 183
Large coloured wall map, with 13 classifications of land types, also roads, boundaries, airports, oil and gas deposits, some relief shading. Fl. 198.00

REGIOKAARTEN VAN NEDERLAND
1st editions
Groningen : Wolters-Noordhoff, 1972
100 x 140
Coloured to indicate predominant land use, also roads and railways, relief and items of economic and historical interest.
Sheets available :

1	Noord-Nederland	1:130, 000
2	Randstad Holland	1:100, 000
3	Deltagebied	1:100, 000
4	Ijsselmeergebied	1:80, 000
5	Rivierengebied	1:80, 000
6	Industriegebied	1:80, 000
7	Oost-Nederland	1:80, 000
8	Zuid-Limburg	1:80, 000
Each		Fl. 108.00

DERDE WANDKAART VAN NEDERLAND - GRONDGEBRUIK
1:200, 000
Groningen : Wolters-Noordhoff
160 x 183
Wall map showing by means of cols. the distribution of glass-house culture, grassland, woods, moorland, beaches and dunes. Mounted on linen with rollers top and bottom. Fl. 198.00

KAARTEN VAN DE NEDERLANDSE NATUURGEBIEDEN
1:50, 000
's-Gravenhage : Rijkswaterstaat
Map of natural regions for scientific and environment purposes, showing natural areas owned by private and state bodies, forestry areas, woodland etc. Follows sheet lines of TD series 1:50, 000.
Each Fl. 5.80

GRONDGEBRUIKSKAART VAN NEDERLAND
1:10, 000
Delft : TD on behalf of Centraal Bureau voor de Statistiek
Land use series showing by a series of 20 categories industry, agriculture, recreation land, water etc. in xerox-copy.

L ECONOMIC

SCHIPPERSKAART
1:400, 000
Assen : Born, 1975
66 x 79
Shows navigable waterways and those under construction, internat. waterway classification, state boundaries. Separate index to places. Fl. 9.35

BORN'S KAART MEER EN PLAS
1:100, 000
Assen : Born, 1976
64 x 68
Coloured waterway map of the Friesian lakes.
Fl. 5.50

BORN'S DELTAKAART
1:100, 000
Assen : Born, 1974
61 x 45
Coloured waterway map of the Zeeland Delta region. Fl. 5.50

WATERKAARTEN
Various scales
see index 492.1/5
Den Haag : ANWB
Series of large scale waterway maps for rivers and popular boating regions.
Each Fl. 6.50

M HISTORICAL

FACSIMILE UITGAVE VAN DE EERSTE TOPOGRAFISCHE EN MILITAIRE KAART VAN HET KONINKRIJK DER NEDERLANDEN
1:50, 000
In 62 sheets
Delft : TD
Facsimile edition of the first topographic and military map of the Netherlands originally published 1850-64.

Individual sheets	Fl. 22.50
Explanatory book	Fl. 12.50
Set	Fl. 995.00

ATLASES
W3 WORLD ATLASES : LOCAL EDITIONS

DE GROTE BOSATLAS
Prof. Dr F J Ormeling
Wolters-Noordhoff, NV, 1972
see WORLD ATLASES 100 W3

NEDERLAND EN DE WERELD
Meulenhof, 1967
see WORLD ATLASES W WORLD, LOCAL EDITION

ATLASES
A1 GENERAL : ROADS

HET BESTE BOEK VOOR DE WEG
1:250, 000/1:1, 000, 000
Edition 7
Amsterdam - Buitenveldert : Uitgeversmaatschappij The Readers Digest NV, 1975
32 x 27
Road Atlas of Netherlands and Europe comprising 256 pages of text, 174 pages of road maps, 88 pages of town plans and 110 page index. Legend in Dutch.
1:3, 000, 000 fold-out Road Map of Europe in pocket inside back cover.
D.Fl. 74.90

TOURISTENATLAS DER NIEDERLANDE
1:350, 000
No 383
Hamburg : Falk
69 x 89
Roads classified, distances, places of tourist interest. Patent folding.
DM 3.60

ATLASES
L ECONOMIC

ATLAS ZUIDERZEEPROJECT
1972-73
6th edition
Lelystad : Rijksdienst voor de Ijsselmeerpolders, 1972
32 x 22
167pp
Describes the development, public and social services, agriculture, housing, industry, future of the polder lands with text maps and photographs.

ATLASES
J CLIMATE

CLIMATOLOGICAL ATLAS OF THE NETHERLANDS
Compiled : Royal Netherlands Meteorological Institute
1st edition
The Hague : Government Publishing Office, 1972
40 x 27
34 double charts size 40 x 54 comprising 411 maps in total. Each sheet is divided into 12 separate charts for each month or season of the year. Information is shown in colour with climatological readings generally shown by isolines.
Fl. 130.00

ATLASES
O NATIONAL

ATLAS VAN NEDERLAND - ATLAS OF THE NETHERLANDS
Editorial Board : Prof. Dr A J Pannekoek, Prof. Dr H J Keuning, Prof. Dr J P Bakker, W F den Hengst, Prof. Dr A C de Vooys, Dr J Winsemius
1st edition
's-Gravenhage : Stattsuitgeverij, 1963-
38 x 64
Published in 98 maps grouped in the following sections :
I Cartography and Topography,
II Geology, Geophysics, Mineral Resources,
III Geomorphology,
IV Soils
V Climate
VI Biogeography
VII Water management
VIII Historical Geography
IX Settlements
X Anthropology, Language and Folk Life
XI Population, Demography, Social and Economic Structure
XII Public Utilities
XIII Agricultural Land Utilization
XIV Fisheries
XV Manufacturing Industries
XVI Transportation and Commerce
XVII Physical Planning
Each map, size 56 x 46, folds in half, with descriptive text to each on the reverse side in English and Dutch and is contained in a rigid filing box.

Per plate	Fl. 3.50
Binder	Fl. 35.00

ATLASES
P REGIONAL

WATTENMEER
Karl Wachholtz, 1976
Atlas of West Friesian (Wadden) and other offshore islands.
see EUROPE Atlases P

H

493 Belgium

See also: 492 BENELUX COUNTRIES

A1 GENERAL MAPS : ROADS

BELGIEN/LUXEMBURG
1:400, 000
No 874
Frankfurt : Ravenstein, 1976
61 x 81
Motorways, main and secondary roads, scenic routes, distances in km, railways, car ferries, airports, provincial and state boundaries. Town plan insets.
Paper folded DM 7.80

BELGIUM
1:400, 000
London : Foldex
Includes Luxemburg. Shows roads classified, relief shading. Patent folding.
45p

AUTOKARTE DER BELGIEN - LUXEMBOURG
1:320, 000
No 381
Hamburg : Falk Verlag
61 x 76
All classes of roads, road numbers, distances in km, railways, car ferries, airports, an index and a distance chart.
Paper folded DM 3.60

BELGIQUE ROUTIER
1:300, 000
No 44
Bruxelles : R de Rouck
114 x 82
Clear road map of Belgium and adjacent countries, roads classified with route numbers and distances in km. Airports, camping sites and places of interest also marked. Legend in 4 langs inc. Eng.
B.Fr 50

BELGIEN
1:300, 000
No 1192
Bern : K & F
98 x 78
Road map of Belgium and adjacent lands, roads classified, distances, scenic routes and places of interest.

AUTOKARTE BELGIE LUXEMBOURG
1:250, 000
No 384
2nd edition
Hamburg : Falk Verlag, 1970
115 x 94
Patent folded plan, detailed road information with town plans on reverse, with brief guide in 3 langs. Index to places.
DM 7.80

BELGIE-BELGIQUE
1:250, 000
Edition 3
Bruxelles : IGMB, 1975
118 x 50
All classes of roads, route numbers, distances in km, footpaths, hill shading, contours, spot heights in metres, other communications, places of tourist interest, state boundaries. Printed on both sides. Legend in 4 langs.
B.Fr 120.00
Also available in 2 paper flat sheets
Each B.Fr 60.00

CARTE ROUTIERE DE BELGIUM
1:200, 000
In 3 sheets, see index 492/1
Paris : Michelin
130 x 49
All classes of roads with road numbering, distances in km, scenic attractions and spot heights.

A2 GENERAL MAPS : LOCAL

CARTE DE LA FORÊT DE SOIGNES ET DU PARC DE TERVUEREN
1:25, 000
Bruxelles : IGMB, 1973
Detailed walking map of the region marking roads and tracks and extent of the park.
Folded B.Fr 100.00

B TOWN PLANS

TOWN PLANS
Various scales
Bruxelles : R de Rouck, unless otherwise stated
Col. plans with street indexes.
Maps available :

Alost/Aalst
No 80 1:6, 000
Anvers et faubourgs (Antwerp)
No 77 1:10, 000
Anvers et Grande Banlieue (Antwerp)
No 69 1:15, 000
Antwerpen (Falk)
No 227 1:16, 500-37, 000
DM 4.80
Audenarde
No 84 1:15, 000
Bruges et Environs (Brugge)
No 66 1:10, 000
Bruxelles-Centre
No 88 1:7, 500
Bruxelles-Monuments
No 72 1:10, 000
Plan and Guide of Brussels in Eng, Fr, Ger and Dutch eds
No 42 1:10, 000
Plan of Brussels and Suburbs in Eng, Fr, Ger and Dutch eds
No 4 1:15, 000
Plan de Bruxelles et de la Gde Banlieue
No 39 1:20, 000
Brussel (Falk)
No 210 1:12, 500-31, 500
DM 5.60
Brussels (Hallwag)
1:12, 500
50p
Brussels (Miniplans) 20p
Charleroi et Environs
No 61 1:15, 000
Gand et Environs (Ghent)
No 75 1:10, 000
Gand et Faubourgs (Ghent & Suburbs)
No 10 1:10, 000
Grammont
No 82 1:10, 000
Hasselt
No 92 1:7, 500
Knokke-le-Zoute
No 94 1:8, 000
Liège et faubourgs (Luik)
No 58 1:10, 000
Liège et Grande Banlieue (Gtr Liege)
No 76 1:15, 000
Lokeren
No 83 1:15, 000
Louvain et Environs (Leuven)
No 59 1:15, 000
Malines et Environs (Mechelen)
No 62 1:15, 000
Namur (Namen)
No 56 1:15, 000
Ostend
No 68 1:8, 500
La Panne
No 95 1:7, 500
Renaix (Ronse)
No 85 1:7, 500
St Nicholas
No 86 1:10, 000
Termonde
No 81 1:8, 000
Verviers
No 54 1:7, 500

C OFFICIAL SURVEYS

THE WORLD
1:1, 000, 000
AMS Series 1301
see WORLD 100C and index 100/1.

THE WORLD
1:500, 000
DMS Series 1404
see WORLD 100C and index 100/7.

CARTE DE BELGIQUE
1:100, 000
In 24 sheets, see index 493/1
Bruxelles : IGMB, 1955-65
74 x 57
Roads and railways classified with relief by contours at 5, 10 or 20 metre intervals according to region. Fords, ferries, rivers, canals, woods and boundaries also shown. Complete coverage in 24 sheets.
B.Fr 80.00

CARTE TOPOGRAPHIQUE DE BASE DE BELGIQUE
1:50, 000
Series M736
In 74 sheets, see index 493/1
Bruxelles : IGMB
74 x 57 each
Topog. series in progress. Available in 3 eds: 9 col. ed, brown ed, orohydrographic ed.
Each B.Fr 80.00
Former series, Type R (Series M735) also in 74 sheets, still available, 1955-65. 2 eds : 5 col. and orohydrographic.
Each B.Fr 80.00

CARTES TOPOGRAPHIQUES DE BELGIQUE - ANCIENNE FACTURE
1:40, 000
In 75 sheets
Bruxelles : IGMB, 1934-1940
87 x 64 each
Early topog. series in black and white.
B.Fr 30.00
Separate conventional sign sheet.
B.Fr 10.00

CARTE TOPOGRAPHIQUE DE BELGIQUE
1:25, 000
In 238 sheets, see index 493/1
Bruxelles : IGMB
74 x 57 each
New second series in progress to supersede 1st edition, contoured, communications, land detail. Published in 3 eds : 7 col, 3 col. and orohydrographic ed.
Each B.Fr 60.00

CARTE TOPOGRAPHIQUE DE BELGIQUE
1:10, 000
2nd edition
In 448 sheets, see index 493/1
Bruxelles : IGMB
114 x 89 each
Large scale planimetric series in progress available in 2 styles: 4 col. ed and 1 col. ed. Second edition in preparation, 88 sheets published.
Each B.Fr 80.00

D POLITICAL & ADMINISTRATIVE

BELGIYA
1:500, 000
Moskva : GUGK, 1973
Col. study map showing water features, settlements, admin. divisions and centres, communications, boundaries, capitals, economic details, pop. Geog description.
Kop. 30.00

CARTE ADMINISTRATIVE DE BELGIQUE AVEC FUSIONS DE COMMUNES
1:300, 000
Bruxelles : IGM, 1976
104 x 77
Provisional administrative map showing the new boundaries coming into operation Jan. 1977. With index to the old and new districts. B.Fr 60.00

CARTE ADMINISTRATIVE DE BELGIQUE
1:300, 000
Bruxelles : IGM 1973
104 x 77
Administrative map with list of communes. Also available at 1:500, 000 scale.
Each B.Fr 60.00

CARTES DES VOIES DE COMMUNICATION - ÉDITION TEINTEE PAR PROVINCES
1:300, 000
Bruxelles : IGMB, 1973
104 x 77
Base route map with administrative regions shown in colour and an index of communes inset. B.Fr 60.00

CARTE DES VOIES DE COMMUNICATION - ÉDITION SANS TEINTEE PLATES
1:300, 000
Bruxelles : IGMB, 1973
104 x 77
Monochrome planning map showing road pattern and boundaries.
B.Fr 60.00

BELGIQUE ADMINISTRATIVE
1:200, 000
Bruxelles : Mantnieks
160 x 120
School wall map, showing physical details and administrative areas.

E1 PHYSICAL : RELIEF

CARTE DES VOIES DE COMMUNICATION - ÉDITION AVEC TEINTES HYPSOMÉTRIQUES
1:300, 000
Bruxelles : IGMB, 1973
104 x 77
Base route map overprinted with contours and layer colouring. B Fr 60.00

BELGIUM
1:300, 000
Series GSGS 4948, Sheet B4
Feltham : DMS
Generalised base or display map showing international boundaries, capital cities and important large towns shown by symbols, principal road and rail communications and relief by contours and layer colours.
50p

BELGIE EN LUXEMBURG
1:300, 000
Groningen : Wolters - Noordhof
107 x 85
Physical wall map showing relief by layer colouring and with town pop. graded by symbols. Mounted on linen with rods.
Fl 44.75

BELGIQUE
1:270, 000
No 1183
St Germain-en-Laye : Éditions MDI
92 x 126
Plastic coated physical wall map for schools, with physical outline map on reverse.

BELGIQUE - CARTE SPECIALE
1:150, 000
Bruxelles : Mantnieks
250 x 180
Physical wall map showing relief of land and sea, cities graded by pop, communications, provincial boundaries, geol. inset at 1:320, 000. Fr text.
Also at 1:200, 000, 120 x 160

F GEOLOGY

CARTE GÉOLOGIQUE DE LA BELGIQUE
1:160, 000
In 12 sheets , see index 493/2
Bruxelles : IGMB, 1945
40 x 42 each
Coloured geological series with 2 legend sheets. Some sheets out of print available only in black and white edition.
Coloured B.Fr 80.00
Uncoloured B Fr 40.00

CARTE GÉOLOGIQUE ET HYPSOMÉTRIQUE DU SOCLE PALÉOZOÏQUE DE LA BELGIQUE
1:100, 000
R Legrand
In 10 sheets
Bruxelles : Service Geol. Belg, 1952
Showing geology and hypsometry, morphology of chalk areas.
Sheets published:
1 Bruges, 1948
2 Anvers, 1948
3 Turnhout, 1949
4 Turnai, 1948
5 Bruxelles, 1950
6 Liege, 1950
7 Mons, 1950
8 Dinant, 1950
9 Arlon, 1950
10 Malmedy, 1950
Each B.Fr 40.00
Complete B.Fr 325.00
With text (1951) B.Fr 420.00

CARTE GÉOLOGIQUE DETAILLÉE DE LA BELGIQUE
1:40, 000
In 226 sheets, see index 493/3
Bruxelles : Service Géol. de la Belgique
Col. geological series now available for the whole of the country.
Each B.Fr 150.00

CARTE GÉOLOGIQUE DETAILLÉE DE LA BELGIQUE
1:25, 000
Bruxelles : Service Géol. de la Belgique, 1958
76 x 58 each
Geological series in progress, with explanatory texts in French (Flemish summaries).
Per sheet B.Fr 185.00
Text B.Fr 90.00
Sheets published :
140 Jurbise-Obourg, 1964
148 Louveigne-Spa, 1958
150 Quievrain-St Ghislain, 1971
151 Mons-Givry, 1967
159 Harze-La Gleize, 1959
160 Stavelot-Malmedy, 1963
161 Roisin-Erquennes, 1972
233 St Vith-Schonberg, 1965

LE RELIEF DU SOCLE PALÉOZOÏQUE DU BASSIN DE LA HAINE
1:20, 000
J Cornet and Ch Stevens
In 2 parts
Bruxelles : Service Geol. Belg.
Part 1 (1921) out of print.
Part 2 (1923) in the following sheets:
Jurbise, Obourg, le Roeulx, Seneffe, Mons, Givry, Binche, Morlanwelz.
B.Fr 130.00

G EARTH RESOURCES

CARTE DES SOLS DE LA BELGIQUE
1:20, 000
In 450 sheets
Gent : Centre de Cartographie des Sols
Col. soil series in progress with texts in French and Flemish.

H BIOGEOGRAPHY

CARTE DE LA VÉGÉTATION DE LA BELGIQUE
1:20, 000
Bruxelles : Inst. pour l'Encouragement de la Recherche Sci. dans l'Industrie et l'Agric.
Coloured vegetation series. 27 sheets published representing each ecological region. Explanations in French and Flemish.
Each B.Fr 300.00

L ECONOMIC

CARTE DES CANAUX DE FRANCE ET BELGIQUE
1:1, 000, 000
Girard et Barrere
see FRANCE 44L.

KAART VAN BELGIE EN NOORD-FRANKRIJK
1:500, 000
Assen : Born, 1971
68 x 72
Waterways map with roads, railways and index. Fl. 12.65

CARTE RÉSEAUX ÉLECTRIQUE A HAUTE TENSION
1:400, 000
Bruxelles : IGM, 1976
86 x 85
Col. map showing high tension electricity cable network of 4 capacities together with those projected also thermal, hydraulic and nuclear power centres and transmission stations. Includes adjacent national networks and links. Available also in a reduced size edition - 22 x 18.

BELGIQUE ECONOMIQUE
1:150, 000
Bruxelles : Mantnieks
250 x 180
Wall map showing location of minerals and industrial and agricultural production.

BELGIQUE ECONOMIQUE
1:200, 000
Bruxelles : Mantnieks
160 x 120
Economic wall map showing heavy industries and traffic networks.

M HISTORICAL

CARTES MURALES D'HISTOIRE
Namur : Ad Wesmael Charlier
Series of col. historical wall maps.
Maps available :

I La Belgique a la période bourguignonne
F Quicke
80 x 120 - new ed in preparation

II La Belgique romaine au début du IVe siècle
H Swolfs-Polfliet
120 x 160 B.Fr 302.00

III Les Principautés belges au XIe siecle (suivant Bonenfant) et les circonscriptions ecclésiastiques dans les régions belges (suivant E de Moreau)
H Joosen
120 x 160 - new ed in preparation

IV Les Pays-Bas sous Charles-Quint
R Cazier
120 x 160 - new ed in preparation

V La Belgique au XVIIe siècle
G Gysels
120 x 160 B.Fr 330.00

VI La Belgique au XVIIIe siècle
F Quicke
120 x 160 B.Fr 302.00

VII Carte historique du Congo
J Stengers
115 x 155 B.Fr 302.00

L'HABITAT RURAL A L'ÉPOQUE ROMAINE
1:500, 000
Bruxelles : Service National des Fouilles, 1972
Map of rural settlements during the Roman period, with 51pp text.
B.Fr 150.00

LA BELGIQUE A L'EPOQUE ROMAINE
1:500, 000
Bruxelles : Service National des Fouilles, 1968
2 maps, showing Roman admin. divisions, cities, roads under the height and decline of the Roman Empire. With 28pp illus. text.
B.Fr 150.00

CHOROGRAFISCHE KAART DER OOSTENRIJKSE NEDERLANDEN
1789
(Carte Chorographique de Pays-Bas Autrichiens)
by de Bouge
1:214, 000 approx
In 16 sheets
Bruxelles : IGMB
60 x 40 each
Reproduction in black and white.
Each B.Fr 400.00

KAART VAN VLAANDEREN VAN 1540 VAN G MERCATOR (Carte des Flandres de Mercator annee 1540)
Edited by Van Raemdonck
1:200, 000
Bruxelles : IGMB, 1882
110 x 85
Specially prepared reprint in black and white. B.Fr 150.00

CARTE DES PAYS-BAS AUTRICHIENS
by Fricx
1:135, 000 app
In 15 sheets
Bruxelles : IGMB, c1744
55 x 80 each sheet
Set of black and white facsimile maps covering all except the extreme south eastern corner of Belgium.
Each B.Fr 150.00

KAART VAN BELGIE
(Carte Topographique de Belgique - type ancien)
1:100, 000
Bruxelles : IGMB
85 x 70 each
Early (pre 1940) topographic series now superseded by 1:100, 000 Type R.
Each B.Fr 250.00

TOPOGRAFISCHE EN MILITAIRE KAART VAN BELGIE 1836
(Carte Topographique et Militaire de la Belgique)
by Capitaine
1:86, 400
In 65 sheets, see index 493/3
Bruxelles : IGMB
60 x 40 each
Reproduction in black and white.
Each B.Fr 400.00

KAART VAN BELGIE c 1832
(Carte de la Belgique)
after Ferraris
by Établissement Géographique de Bruxelles
1:88, 000
In 42 sheets
Bruxelles : IGMB
65 x 54 each
Enlarged facsimile map with 6 plans of important towns and showing roads, canals and other information. Prepared 1777 to 1831.
Each B.Fr 400.00

CHOROGRAFISCHE KAART DER OOSTENRIJKSE NEDERLAND
c 1780
(Carte Chorographique des Pays-Bas Autrichiens)
by Comte de Ferrari
1:86, 400 approx
In 25 sheets
Bruxelles : IGMB
100 x 67 each
Reproduction in black and white.
Each B.Fr 150.00

KAART VAN BELGIE 1830
by Gerard and Vandermaelen
1:80, 000
In 24 sheets
Bruxelles : IGMB
80 x 60 each
Reproduction in black and white.
Each B.Fr 400.00

KAART VAN BELGIE
(Carte Topographique de Belgique - type ancien)
1:40, 000
Bruxelles : IGMB
90 x 65 each
Early (pre 1940) topographic series now superseded by 1:50, 000 Type R.
Photographic reproduction.
Each B.Fr 400.00

CARTE DE LA FORÊT DE SOIGNES
1:21, 600 approx.
Bruxelles : IGMB
Reproduction of an early map in black and white. B.Fr 150.00

KAART VAN BELGIE
(Carte Topographique de Belgique - type ancien)
1:20, 000
Bruxelles : IGMB
65 x 50 each
Original base topographic series now superseded by new 1:25, 000 series pre 1940 eds. Photographic reproductions.
Each B.Fr 400.00

KADASTRALE PLANS VAN BELGIE, 1850
1:20, 000
Bruxelles : IGMB
55 x 35 each
Series of maps produced by parishes - reproduced in black and white.
Each B.Fr. 400.00

KAART VAN BELGIE
by Vandermaelen
1:20, 000
In 24 sections each of 12 sheets
Bruxelles : IGMB
75 x 50 each
Reproduction in black and white, 19th century series.
Each B.Fr. 400.00

KAART DER OOSTENRIJKSE NEDERLAND c 1775
known as 'KABINETKART'
(Carte de Cabinet des Pays Bas Autrichiens)
by Comte de Ferrari
1:11, 520 approx.
In 275 sheets
Bruxelles : IGMB
140 x 95 or 70 x 42
Reproduction in black and white.
Quarter sheets B.Fr. 400.00

STADSPLANNEN
by Deventer
Bruxelles : IGMB
Reproductions of various town plans of Belgium. B.Fr. 400.00

ATLASES
W3 WORLD ATLAS : LOCAL EDITION

ATLAS DE GEOGRAPHIE
Ed J A Sporck et L Pierard
Asedi, 1968
see WORLD 100 ATLASES W 1 WORLD: REFERENCE

ATLASES
M HISTORICAL

ATLAS D'HISTOIRE UNIVERSELLE ET D'HISTOIRE DE LA BELGIQUE
Revised by F Hayt
Namur : Ad Wesmael Charlier, 1976
20 x 26
152pp
130 coloured maps of world history. 19 for Belgium. Index.
B.Fr. 266.00

ATLAS DER ALGEMENE GESCHIEDENIS EN DER BELGISCHE GESCHIEDENIS
Editors : F Hayt; H Haerens
Namur : Wesmael Charlier, 1976
152pp
Flemish historical atlas comprising 141 coloured maps with index of approx. 4, 000 names, depicting Belgium's place in world history. B.Fr. 266.00

CULTUURHISTORISCHE ATLAS - HET DOCUMENT IN KAART
Editors : Bradt, Cazier, De Roeck, Maes en van den Broeck
Namur : Ad Wesmael Charlier, 1976
54pp
Historical atlas for schools containing 133 coloured maps with index to places. Text in Flemish. B.Fr. 250.00

MANUEL-ATLAS D'HISTOIRE DE BELGIQUE
F. Hayt and R. Cousen
Namur : Wesmael-Charlier
112pp
Primary school historical atlas.
B.Fr. 198.00

ATLAS D'HISTOIRE
Editors : Maes, Pierard et Tellier
Namur : Ad Wesmael-Charlier
60 page historical school atlas including 130 maps together with index.
B.Fr. 156.00

L'ÉVOLUTION TERRITORIALE DE BRUXELLES - LA CARTOGRAPHIE DE 1550 a 1840
Editor : L Danckaert
Bruxelles : Arcade, 1968
26 x 18
168pp text
3 plans, 2 size 54 x 61 and 1 108 x 122 (in 4 sections). Reproductions of early maps which together depict the development of the city. Contained in the text volume are 133 plan sections arranged chronologically. Legend in French.

ATLASES
O1 NATIONAL : REFERENCE

ATLAS GÉNÉRALE DE BELGIQUE
Bruxelles : Academie Royale de Belgique
58 x 47
National Atlas arranged in the following sections : Belgium in Europe; Cartography and Geophysics; Physical Geography - geology, soils etc, climatology, hydrography and littoral; Biogeography; Regional Geography; and Administration. Comprising approx. 65 col. map plates on scales of 1:2, 000, 000, 1:1, 000, 000 and 1:500, 000. Explanatory commentaries cover each subject in French and Flemish. Individual plates available separately.

Binder	B.Fr. 550.00
52 published sheets	B.Fr. 2, 700.00
23 commentaries	B.Fr. 1, 622.00
Individual plates	B.Fr. 75.00

ATLASES
O2 NATIONAL : SCHOOL

ATLAS CLASSIQUE
Ed J Tilmont et M de Roeck
Namur : Wesmael-Charlier, 1976
25 x 40
32 pages, 220 map - physical and thematic for the whole country and for smaller areas.
B.Fr. 465.00

ATLAS ÉLÉMENTAIRE
Ed J Tilmont and M De Roeck
Namur : Ad Wesmael Charlier, 1976
25 x 32
32pp
Elementary school atlas containing 220 coloured maps B.Fr. 126.00

ATLASES
P REGIONAL

GENT. EEN STEDENAARDRIJKSKUNDIGE STUDIE
Maurice E Dumont
Brugge : De Tempel, 1951
In 2 vols
xii, 590pp
A study of the urban geography of Ghent. One text and one atlas vol. of maps and plans. B.Fr. 1300.00

493.1 Luxembourg

See also: 492 BENELUX COUNTRIES

A1 GENERAL MAPS : ROADS

LUXEMBOURG
1:400, 000
London : Foldex
Shows roads classified, relief shading; patent fold.

CARTE DU LUXEMBOURG
1:200, 000
No 8
Paris : Michelin, 1971
33 x 48
Roads classified with route numbers and distances and conditions, scenic routes.

CARTE ROUTIÈRE DU GRAND DUCHÉ DE LUXEMBOURG
1:100, 000
No 64
Bruxelles : de Rouck
71 x 104
All classes of road, with distances, footpaths and places of interest. Index and guide in French.

B TOWN PLANS

PLAN DE LUXEMBOURG VILLE
1:7, 000
No 89
Bruxelles : de Rouck
86 x 63
Col. plan of the city with street index.

LUXEMBURG
Nr 24
Braunschweig : Bollmann-Bildkarten, 1961
58 x 67
Pictorial town plan showing buildings drawn from an oblique view.
DM 4.10

C OFFICIAL SURVEYS

LUXEMBOURG
1:100, 000
Luxembourg : Admin. du Cadastre et de la Topog/IGN, 1972
71 x 99
Coloured topog. map, contoured with relief shading, admin. boundaries and roads.
L.Fr. 60.00

CARTE DE FRANCE
1:100, 000
Sheet P5 Longwy
IGN
see FRANCE 44C.

CARTE DE BELGIQUE
1:100, 000
Sheets :
C 22 Bastogne
C 24 Arlon
see BELGIUM 493C.

CARTE TOPOGRAPHIQUE DU GRAND DUCHÉ DE LUXEMBOURG
1:50, 000
In 10 sheets, see index 493.1/1
Luxembourg : Admin. du Cadastre et de la Topog./IGN, 1966
Coloured topog. series.
Each L.Fr. 50.00

CARTE DE LUXEMBOURG
1:25, 000
In 30 sheets, see index 493.1/1
Luxembourg : Admin. du Cadastre et de la Topog./IGN, 1952
66 x 55
Col. topog. map series showing contours, vegetation.
Each L.Fr. 40.00

CARTE TOPOGRAPHIQUE DU GRAND DUCHÉ DE LUXEMBOURG
1:20, 000
In 30 sheets, see index 493.1/1
Luxembourg : Admin. du Cadastre et de la Topog./IGN, 1963
Coloured topog. series.
Each L.Fr. 40.00

LUXEMBOURG
1:10, 000
In 97 sheets
Luxembourg : Admin. du Cadastre et de la Topog./IGN, 1963
Cadastral series showing land detail and field boundaries, available as photoprints.
Each L.Fr. 50.00

D POLITICAL & ADMINISTRATIVE

LUXEMBOURG CARTE POLITIQUE SCOLAIRE
1:250, 000
Luxembourg : Admin. du Cadastre et de la Topog, 1972
28 x 40
Col. map showing Communes and Communications. 3 insets. L.Fr. 25.00

LUXEMBOURG - CARTE ADMINISTRATIVE ET POLITIQUE
1:75, 000
Luxembourg : Admin. du Cadastre et de la Topog.
95 x 130
Communes, communications, col, with insets.

F GEOLOGY

CARTE GÉOLOGIQUE GENERALE DU GRAND DUCHÉ DE LUXEMBOURG
1:100, 000
Luxembourg : Service Geologique de Luxembourg, 1966
69 x 86
Col. geol. map in one sheet.

CARTE GÉOLOGIQUE DU LUXEMBOURG
1:25, 000
In 8 sheets, see index 493.1/2
Luxembourg : Service Geologique du Luxembourg
104 x 69 each sheet
Coloured geological maps with Stratigraphical sections on Sheets 1 and 7 and Tectonic sketch map of Luxembourg and the Eifel on Sheet 5. Legend in French and German.
Sheets :

1	Esch-s-Alzette	
	1:25, 000	1947
2	Remich	
	1:25, 000	1947
3	Luxembourg	
	1:25, 000	1948
4	Grevenmacher	
	1:25, 000	1948
5	Redange-s-Attert	
	1:25, 000	1948
6	Diekirch	
	1:25 000	1949
7	Echternach	
	1:25, 000	1949
8	Wiltz	
	1:50, 000	1949

K HUMAN GEOGRAPHY

RECENSEMENT DE LA POPULATION
1:200, 000
Luxembourg : Admin. du Cadastre et de la Topog.
30 x 44
Results of Census for 1960 and 1966.

ATLASES
K HUMAN GEOGRAPHY

LUXEMBURGISCHER SPRACHATLAS
Editor L E Schmitt
Part 2 of Deutscher Sprachatlas
Marburg : N G Elwert Verlag
Language atlas of Luxembourg
Vol I Sound and Form Atlas, 175 maps
1963 DM 170.00
II Word Atlas - in preparation

ATLASES
O NATIONAL

ATLAS DU LUXEMBOURG
Luxembourg : Min. de l'Education Nat, 1971
40 x 50
602pp
42 maps, mainly black and white, some col. at 1:400, 000 and 1:200, 000. Covers history, physical geog, demography, economy, admin. etc. Loose leaf. The 1st section 1971 of 42 maps is now out of print. The 2nd section 1973 of maps is available.
L.Fr. 500.00
The 3rd and last part is due at the end of 1976.

494 Switzerland

A1 GENERAL MAPS : ROADS

ITALIE ET SUISSE
1:1, 000, 000
No 988
Paris : Michelin, 1976
109 x 99
All classes of roads, conditions, distances in km, car ferries and scenic routes.

SCHWEIZ-NORDITALIEN
1:600, 000
Wien : FB, 1970
101 x 78
Basle to Innsbruck, Cannes to Ancona. All classes of roads, distances in km, route numbers, spot heights in metres, hill shading, railways, airports, camping sites, car ferries, state boundaries.

HALLWAG ALPINA III - CENTRAL ALPS
1:600, 000
Bern : Hallwag
112 x 84
Besancon to Salzburg and as far south as Florence. All classes of roads, route numbers, distances in km, spot heights, hill shading, airports, railways, ferries and the main camping sites.

SHELL REISEKARTE SCHWEIZ
1:500, 000
Stuttgart : Mair
Roads classified and numbered, distances in km, tourist details etc. Legend in 12 langs.
DM 4.80

SCHWEIZ
1:500, 000
No 872
Stuttgart : Ravenstein
100 x 80
Col. map; roads classified and numbered, distances in km, other communications, places of tourist interest.
DM 7.80

SCHWEIZ UND ANGRENZENDE LANDER
1:400, 000
No 1437
München : JRO
123 x 88
Roads classified and numbered, distances in km, places of tourist interest, boundaries, railways. Inc. Switzerland and bordering countries. DM 6.80

SCHWEIZ
1:400, 000
No 1441
München : JRO
85 x 59
Section from JRO Road Map No 1437 covering Bodensee, Schaffhausen, Basel, Genf, Como, Kempten, Lindau.
DM 2.90

STRASSENKARTE SCHWEIZ
1:400, 000
No 1025
Bern : K & F
94 x 63
Col. road map, with 12 town plans, roads classified with distances.
S.Fr. 3.50

SCHWEIZ-TIROL
1:400, 000
No 70
Stuttgart : RV
125 x 86
Colmar to Munich and Annecy to Venice. All classes of roads, distances in km, road numbers, railways, places of tourist interest, camp sites, youth hostels, motels and state boundaries. DM 8.80

SWITZERLAND
1:400, 000
London : Foldex
Shows roads classified, relief shading; patent fold. 45p

STRASSENKARTE SCHWEIZ
1:350, 000
Zürich : OF, 1976
119 x 81
Road map of Switzerland, relief shaded with legend in 4 languages.
S.Fr. 7.90

SCHWEIZ OFFIZIELLE
STRASSENKARTE TCS
1:300, 000
No 1013
Bern : K & F
125 x 90
All classes of roads, distances in km, spot heights, road conditions, rail and car ferries, state frontiers, airports, hill shading, camp sites and motels. Table of distances and Alpine passes. Official map of the Touring Club Suisse. S.Fr. 5.80

SCHWEIZ
1:300, 000
Bern : Hallwag
121 x 90
All classes of roads, distances in km, spot heights, hill shading, car ferries, route numbers, railways, state frontiers and car camping sites.

SCHWEIZ, FREIZEITKARTE
1:300, 000
No 0120
Bern : K & F
129 x 92
Leisure map, roads classified with distances and locations of places of interest.

SCHWEIZ OFFIZIELE
STRASSENKARTE ACS
1:250, 000
No 1001
Bern : K & F
126 x 89
All classes of roads, distances in km, route numbers, car ferries, railways, airports, hill shading, state frontiers. Official map of the Automobile Club of Switzerland.
S.Fr. 5.80

SCHWEIZ
STRASSEN- UND WANDERKARTEN
1:200, 000
In 4 sheets
Bern : Hallwag
90 x 58 each
Showing all classes of roads, distances in km, railways, hill shading, spot heights, ferries and state frontiers.

SUISSE
1:200, 000
In 4 sheets
Paris : Michélin
121 x 49 each
All classes of roads, road conditions and numbers, spot heights, distances in km, scenic routes, railways, car ferries and state boundaries.
Sheets :
21 North Basle to St Gallen
23 West Geneva to Berne
24 East Andermatt to Bolzano
26 South Martigny to Milan

A2 GENERAL MAPS : LOCAL

BODENSEE : WANDER- UND
AUSFLUGSKARTE
1:150, 000
No 717
München : JRO
84 x 50
Col. tourist and excursion map. Shows places of interest and natural beauty, roads, paths, tourist details. DM 3.00

BODENSEE : PANORAMAKARTE
No 521
München : JRO
82 x 42
Bird's-eye view map, showing physical features, relief land forms, roads, settlements etc. DM 1.90

SCHWEIZ TEILGEBIETE
Various scales
Bern : K & F
Series of large scale regional maps for various tourist areas. They are generally physical maps, relief shaded and showing roads, footpaths and places of interest.
Maps available :
0603 Adelboden
1:33, 333 42 x 61
0610 Arosa
1:25, 000
0612 Baden
1:25, 000
Reverse side
1:75, 000 62.5 x 54
0618 Beatenberg
1:33, 333 36 x 51
0628 Bern und Umgebung
1:25, 000
0630 Berner Oberland und Oberwallis
1:75, 000 96 x 78
0633 Berner Oberland und Wallis
1:150, 000 71 x 65
0634 Berner Oberland Ost.
1:50, 000 102 x 75
0635 Berner Oberland West
1:50, 000 102 x 75

0636 Bielersee-Chasseral-Seeland
1:25, 000 76 x 103
0639 Brünig-Hasliberg
1:20, 000 61 x 65
0645 Emmental-Napf-Entlebuch
1:50, 000 90 x 70
0648 Engelberg
1:33, 333 68 x 48
0651 Feldis
1:50, 000 34 x 47
0652 Fiesch
1:50, 000 41 x 52
0654 Flims
1:25, 000 44.5 x 52
0657 Fricktal
1:50, 000 64 x 46
0660 Frutigen
1:33, 333 38 x 49
0661 Furka-Oberalp Bahn
1:100, 000 73 x 56
0666 Glärnischgebiet
1:25, 000 61 x 49
0669 Glarnerland
1:50, 000 78 x 85
0673 Grächen
1:33, 333 40 x 42
0675 Graubünden
1:200, 000 81 x 64
0678 Grindelwald
1:35, 000 45 x 41
0679 Gruyère
1:50, 000 77 x 53
Jurakartenwerk
1:50, 000 91 x 76 each
1 Aargau
2 Basel-Olten
3 Solothurn-Delsberg
4 Biel-Neuenburg
5 Yverdon-Ste-Croix
6 Lausanne-St-Cergue
0700 Kandersteg und Umgebung
1:30, 000 62 x 56
0703 Kiental
1:50, 000 44.5 x 35
0706 Lauterbrunnen-Wengen-Mürren und Umgebung
1:33, 333 54 x 65
0709 Leukerbad
1:50, 000 67 x 39
0715 Maggiatal-Valle Maggia
1:50, 000 62 x 73.5
0718 Montana-Vermala
1:33, 333 53 x 53
0721 Mont-Blanc-Kette
1:50, 000 102 x 55
0645 Napf-Emmental-Entlebuch
1:50, 000 90 x 70
0724 Oberaargau
1:25, 000 71 x 101
0727 Oberengadin und Bernina
1:50, 000 59 x 72
0642 Oberhasli
1:50, 000 57 x 43
0730 Obertoggenburg (Wildhaus-Unterwasser-Alt St Johann)
1:25, 000 82 x 68
0731 Obertoggenburg (Nesslau-Neu St Johann)
1:25, 000 82 x 68
0737 Poschiavo
1:50, 000 38 x 51
0736 Prättigau
1:50, 000 90.5 x 63
Saas Fee
1:50, 000 47 x 61
0754 Tessin und Oberitalienische Seen
1:200, 000 62 x 72
0757 Thunersee
1:50, 000 80 x 55
0767 Val d'Anniviers
1:50, 000 28 x 65
0769 Vallée du Trient
1:40, 000 47.5 x 47.5
0772 Vierwaldstättersee-Zentralschweiz
1:100, 000 69 x 73
0781 Wallis
1:200, 000 37 x 57
0786 Zermatt und Umgebung
1:50, 000 78 x 57
0793 Zug
1:50, 000 77 x 63
0787 Zürcher Oberland-Tösstal
1:25, 000 90 x 72

NUOVA CARTA DEL CANTINO TICINO
1:150, 000
Zürich : OF, 1974
46 x 61
General map of the Ticino Canton.
In Italian. S.Fr. 5.00

REISEKARTE KANTON ZÜRICH
1:150, 000
Zürich : OF 1974
47 x 64
Road map of Zürich Canton.
S.Fr. 6.00

WANDERKARTE DES KANTON ZÜRICH
1:50, 000
Zürich : OF, 1976
99 x 70
Double-sided walking map - Zürich - Schaffhausen. On reverse Zürichsee-Zug
S.Fr. 25 00

B TOWN PLANS

TOWN PLANS
Various scales
Coloured plans with index to streets.

Basel	1:10, 00 - 1:20, 00		63 x 67
	OF	1976	S.Fr. 6.50
Bern	1:13, 000		
	Hallwag		
Berne	1:14, 00		90 x 62
	K & F		S.Fr. 5.90
Berne-centre			
	1:14, 000		36 x 33
	K & F		S.Fr. 2.60
Fribourg	1:10, 000		66 x 63
	OF	1974	S.Fr. 5.50
Lausanne	1:10, 000		83 x 51
	OF	1973	S.Fr. 6.50
Lausanne - small plan			
	K & F		S.Fr. 3.00
Luzern	1:10, 000		81 x 64
	OF	1973	S.Fr. 6.50
Montreux-Vevey			
	1:12, 000		94 x 49
	OF	1975	S.Fr. 5.50
Neuchâtel, Le Locle, La Chaux-de-Fonds			
	1:12, 000		94 x 49
	OF	1975	S.Fr. 6.50
St Gallen	1:12, 000		87 x 31
	OF	1973	S.Fr. 6.50
Locarno und Ascona			
	1:10, 000		72 x 48
	OF	1974	S.Fr. 5.50
Zug und Umgebung			
	1:12, 000		74 x 65
	OF	1975	S.Fr. 5.50
Zürich	1:20, 000		67 x 73
	OF	1976	S.Fr. 6.50
Zürich	1:10, 000		52 x 49
	OF (Ger., Eng. & Fr. eds.)		
	1974	Each	S.Fr. 3.00
Zürich	1:14, 000 - 1:35, 000		61 x 62
	Falk		

C OFFICIAL SURVEYS

INTERNATIONAL MAP OF THE WORLD
1:1, 000, 000
AMS Series 1301
see WORLD 100C and index 100/1.

THE WORLD
1:500, 000
DMS Series 1404
see WORLD 100C and index 100/7.

CARTE NATIONALE DE LA SUISSE
1:200, 000
In 4 sheets
Bern : ST
99 x 72
Topog. map, contoured with graphic relief shading, roads classified in colour with footpaths, railways, chairlifts and land information.
Sheets published :
1 NW, 1972 2 NE, 1973
3 SW, 1971 4 SE, 1976

LANDESKARTEN DER SCHWEIZ
1:100, 000
In 23 sheets, see index 494/1
Bern : ST
78 x 57 each
Fully contoured topographic maps with hill shading, spot heights and hachuring, roads, railways and footpaths, chair lifts, mountain railways, canton and state boundaries.
Each S.Fr. 5.80
Half sheets S.Fr. 4.60
Special area sheets (90 x 70)
102 Basel - Luzern
103 Zürich - St Gallen
104 Lausanne - Bern
Each S.Fr. 9.50

LANDESKARTEN DER SCHWEIZ
1:50, 000
In 76 sheets, see index 494/2
Bern : ST
70 x 49 each
Contoured topog. maps, hill shading, rock outcrops, spot heights, contours at 20 metre intervals, roads, railways, footpaths, ski-lifts, mountain railways, mountain huts, chair lifts, canton and state boundaries.
Each S.Fr. 5.50
Half sheets S.Fr. 4.60
Special area maps (100 x 70)
5001 Gotthard
*5002 Arosa-Lenzerheide
5003 Mont Blanc - Grand Combin
5004 Berner Oberland
5005 Seetal - Brugg
*5006 Zermatt u Umgebung
5007 Locarno - Lugano
5008 Vierwaldstättersee
5009 Gstaad-Adelboden
5010 Zürich-Schaffhausen
5011 Zürichsee-Zug
5012 Flumser Berge-Prättigau
5013 Oberengadin-Engiadin' Ota
5014 St Gallen - Appenzell
5015 Toggenburg - St Galler Oberland
Each S.Fr. 9.50
*Half sheets each S.Fr. 5.50

LANDESKARTEN DER SCHWEIZ
1:25, 000
In 250 sheets, see index 494/3
Bern : ST
77 x 56

New topog. series covering Switzerland and surrounding area. Boundaries, communications, settlements, water features, tracks, cable railways, woodland, spot heights, contours at 20 metre intervals and hill shading. Series in progress.
Each S.Fr. 5.20
Special area maps :
2501 St Gallen und Umgebung
2502 Bern und Umgebung
2503 Bière et environs
2504 Magglingen - Macolin
2505 Basel und Umgebung
2506 Säntisgebiet
2507 Lausanne et Environs
2508 Fribourg - Schwarzenburg
2509 Pizolgebiet
2510 Luzern und Umgebung
2511 Schaffhausen und Umgebung
2512 Flumserberg Walensee
Each S.Fr. 9.50

KARTE DES ALETSCHGLETSCHERS
1:10, 000
In 5 sheets
Bern : ST
114 x 84 (3 sheets)
61 x 84 (2 sheets)
Map of Aletsch (Rhone) glacier district in 1957. Col. map with settlements, tracks, hill shading, contours at 10 metre intervals, indications of former extent of glaciers. Contours continued over ice; crevasses, moraines, other ice features shown.

D POLITICAL & ADMINISTRATIVE

ÜBERSICHTSKARTE DER SCHWEIZ MIT IHREN GRENZGEBIETEN
1:1, 000, 000
Bern : ST
Hachured relief map with national boundary.

SCHULKARTE DER SCHWEIZ
1:600, 000
K & F
see SWITZERLAND 494 E1.

POLITISCHE SCHÜLERKARTE DER SCHWEIZ
1:500, 000
No 0156
Bern : K & F
77 x 62
School political map.

GEMEINDEKARTE DER SCHWEIZ
1:400, 000
Bern : ST
91 x 61
Administrative map showing commune boundaries only in black and white.

SCHWEIZ, BURO-UND ORGANISATIONSKARTE
1:300, 000
No 0105
Bern : K & F
129 x 92
White background map, with administrative boundaries, settlements, communications and index of places.

POSTLEITZAHLNEKARTE
1:300, 000
No 0100
Bern : K & F, 1966
115 x 75
Coloured map showing postal districts and numbers, with 3 inset maps.

GEMEINDEKARTE DER SCHWEIZ
1:200, 000
In 4 sheets
Bern : ST
Monochrome map showing commune boundaries.
Also available with sheet lines and numbers of official survey maps 1:25, 000 and 1:50, 000.

SCHÜLERKARTE DER KANTONS
Various scales
Bern : K & F
Series of school maps of the Kantons, relief shaded with communications, towns and villages.
Maps available :
0600* Aargau
1:100, 000 60 x 60
0621* Bern
1:250, 000 63 x 69
0663 Genève
1:50, 000 72 x 62
0672 Glarus
1:100, 000 44 x 58
0745* Schaffhausen
1:75, 000 65 x 57
0748 Schyx
1:100, 000 69 x 52
0751* Solothurn
1:100, 000 55 x 51
0760* Thurgau
1:100, 000 70 x 51
0778 Vaud
1:150, 000 63 x 67
0784* Wallis
1:250, 000 58 x 47
0790 Zug
1:50, 000 78 x 63
* available printed on Syntosil (plasticised paper)

BERN
1:200, 000
No 0627
Bern : K & F
64 x 83
Col. district map of the Kanton.

BERN
1:200, 000
No 0624
Bern : K & F
64 x 83
Planning map showing communications with district and parish boundaries.

SCHULKARTE DER SCHWEIZ
1:600, 000
Bern : K & F
65 x 68
School hand map of Switzerland.
Available in 3 editions :
0157 Ed C - monochrome relief map
0158 Ed D - political
0159 Ed E - col. physical relief map

SVIZZERA
1:1, 350, 000
Novara : Ag
Small outline hand map for schools.
L 40

UMRISSKARTE DER SCHWEIZ - POLITISCHER AUSGABE
1:1, 500, 000
N 0813
Bern : K & F
28 x 20
Base map showing routes and important towns.

UMRISSKARTE DER SCHWEIZ
1:1, 450, 000
No 0812
Bern : K & F
24 x 19
Base map showing hydrography and relief.

UMRISSKARTE DER SCHWIEZ
1:600, 000
No 0804
Bern : K & F
65 x 50
Col. relief map, with hydrography and boundaries.

UMRISSKARTE DER SCHWEIZ - STATISTISCHE AUSGABE
1:600, 000
No 0805
Bern : K & F
62 x 40
Statistical ed. showing hydrography, canton and district boundaries.

UMRISSKARTE DER SCHWEIZ
1:500, 000
No 0803
Bern : K & F
81 x 64
Base map showing hydrography, relief, boundaries.

UMRISSKARTE DER SCHWEIZ
1:300, 000
No 0800
Bern : K & F
127 x 90
Outline map showing boundaries and rivers.

POLITISCHE KARTE KANTON ZÜRICH
1:100, 000
Zürich : OF, 1973
66 x 59
Administrative map S.Fr. 14.00

E1 PHYSICAL : RELIEF

CARTE NATIONALE DE LA SUISSE
1:500, 000
Bern : ST
78 x 57
Map in cols, showing relief by contours and relief shading, roads classified, railways, towns and villages. S.Fr. 4.30

SCHWEIZ PHYSIKALISCHE UBERSICHTSKARTE
1:500, 000
Zurich : Orell Fussli, 1971
79 x 63
Physical map with contours, relief shading. Economic map on reverse, showing industry, agriculture, tourist trade.

SCHÜLERKARTE DER SCHWEIZ
1:500, 000
No 0154
Bern : K & F
77 x 62
Physical and political school wall map.

RELIEFKARTE SCHWEIZ
1:500, 000
Zurich : OF, 1971
76 x 57
Physical map with contours, relief shading. Economic map of Switzerland on reverse.
S.Fr. 6.00

ÜBERSICHTS-UND REISEKARTE SCHWEIZ
1:500, 000
Zürich : OF, 1974
76 x 57
Physical map, contoured with relief shading and communications. On reverse are 6 thematic maps - geology, population, climate, economy. Available in Ger., Fr., It. editions. S.Fr. 6.00

ZWITSERLAND
1:500, 000
Groningen : Wolters-Noordhoff
107 x 85
Physical school wall map; relief shading, communications, boundaries. Text in Dutch. Fl. 44.75

SUISSE : PHYSIQUE ET AGRICOLE
1:350, 000
Map No 26
Paris : Armand Colin
120 x 100
Physical and agricultural school wall map, with political and economic map on reverse.

CARTE MURALE DE LA SUISSE
1:300, 000
Bern : ST
121 x 80
Enlarged wall map ed. of the 1:500, 000 map 'Carte Nationale de la Suisse', contoured, relief shaded, major roads and railways.

OFFIZIELLE SCHULWANDKARTE DER SCHWEIZ
1:200, 000
No 2. 7025
In 4 sheets
Bern : K & F
210 x 144
School wall map showing topog. and physical details in col.

SCHWEIZ
1:185, 000
Gotha : Haack
220 x 167
Physical wall map, showing relief, roads etc.

SVIZZERA
1:1, 500, 000
Novara : Ag
33 x 26
Plastic relief map for schools, with physical, political and economic details on reverse. L 450

F GEOLOGY

GEOLOGISCHE KARTE DER SCHWEIZ
1:500, 000
Bern : CGS, 1972
76 x 48
Geological map in colour on topog. base. Legend in French and German in margins. Printed on Syntosil.

CARTE TECTONIQUE DE LA SUISSE
1:500, 000
Bern : CGS, 1972
76 x 48
Coloured tectonic map on topog. base. Legend in French and German in margins. Printed on Syntosil.

GEOLOGISCHE WANDKARTE
by Dr W Staub
1:200, 000
Bern : K & F
190 x 130
Geol. wall map showing strata in colour.

CARTE GÉOLOGIQUE GÉNÉRALE DE LA SUISSE
1:200, 000
In 8 sheets
Bern : CGS
Col. geol. map.
Sheets available :
1 Neuchatel
1944 - text 1956
2 Basle - Bern
1942 (out of print) Text 1951
3 Zurich - Glarus
1950 - text 1957
4 St Gallen - Chur
1959
5 Geneve - Lausanne
1948 - text 1955
6 Sion
1942 (out of print), text 1965
7 Ticino
1955
8 Engadin
1964
Flat S.Fr. 18.65
Text S.Fr. 3.00

CARTE GÉOTECHNIQUE DE LA SUISSE / GEOTECHNISCHE KARTE DER SCHWEIZ
1:200, 000
In 4 sheets
2nd rev. edition
Bern : CGS
94 x 66 each
Shows nature and properties of rocks at the surface and in sub-soil, the locations from which ores and minerals are extracted and their uses. Structure and age of rocks not indicated.
1 Neuchatel - Bern - Basel
1964
2 Luzern - Zurich - St Gallen - Chur,
1963
3 Genève - Lausanne - Sion
1965
4 Bellinzona - St Moritz, 1967
Each S.Fr. 24.85

GEOLOGISCHER ATLAS
1:25, 000
Bern : CGS
Col. geological maps based on sheet lines of the official 25, 000 topog. series, with descriptive texts.
Sheets published :
1032 1964
1047 1970
1052 1967
1054 1968
1065 1969
1066 1965
1075 1964
1085 1963
1090 1966
1093 1970
1133 1969
1144 1968
1145 1971
1202 1963
1235 1971
1264 1965
1281 1964
1301 1965
1305 1971
1333/pt 1334 1962

ATLAS GÉOLOGIQUE DE LA SUISSE
1:25, 000
Bern : CGS, 1930+
Series of geol. maps based on early topog. maps : Siegfriedkarte. Covering some parts of the country only. Each sheet has a descriptive text. Various styles and eds.
Sheets available :
56-59 Pfyn - Marstetten -Frauenfeld - Bussnang, 1943
142-145 Fraubrunnen - Wynigen - Hindelbank - Burgdorf, 1950
186-189 Beromünster - Hochdorf - Sempach - Eschenbach, 1945
202-205 Luzern, 1955
222-225 St Gallen - Appenzell, 1949
276-277 La Chaux - Les Verrières, 1930
304-307 Jorat, 1952
332-335 Neuenegg - Oberbalm - Schwarzenburg - Rueggisberg, 1953
336-339 Munsingen - Konolfingen - Gerzensee - Heimberg
348-351 Gurnigel, 1961

PHOTOGEOLOGISCHE KARTE DER TÖDIKETTE VOM BIFERTEN-STOCK BIS CALANDA
1:25, 000 - 1:100, 000
In 7 sheets
Zürich : Eidg Technische Hochschule, 1948
Photographic maps describing the geology and tectonics of the Tödi range. Eng/Ger legend.

TEKTONISCHE ÜBERSICHT DES WÜRZELGEBIETES DER HELVETISCHEN DECKEN AM OSTENDE VON AAR- UND GOTTHARD MASSIV
1:100, 000
by Fr Weber
Bern : CGS, 1922
With text.

DIE GRUNDWASSERVERHALTNISSE DES KANTONS ZÜRICH
1:100, 000
by J Hug and A Belik
Bern : CGS, 1934
Map of groundwater in Zurich canton with xx, 328pp text.

GEOLOGISCHE KARTE DES KANTONS ZÜRICH UND SEINER NACHBARGEBIETE
1:50, 000
Zurich : Kommissions Verlag Leeman, 1967
Geological map of Zurich and neighbouring areas. With 32pp text.

GEOLOGISCHE KARTE DER BERNINA-GRUPPE UND IHRER UMGEBUNG IN OBERENGADIN, BERGELL, VAL MALENCO, PUSCHLAV UND LIVIGNO
1:50, 000
by R Staub
Bern : CGS, 1946

GEOLOGISCHE KARTE DER LANDSCHAFT SCHAMS
1:50, 000
by O Wilhelm
Bern : CGS, 1929

GEOLOGISCHE KARTE DES SÜDOSTLICHEN RÄTIKON
1:25, 000
by W Hafner
Bern : CGS, 1926

GEOLOGISCHE KARTE DER ERR-JULIER-GRUPPE
1:25, 000
by H P Cornelius
Bern : CGS, 1932
2 sheet map.

GEOLOGISCHE KARTE DES WÄGGITALES UND SEINER UMGEBUNG
1:25, 000
by H Schardt et al
Bern : CGS, 1924
With 2 texts.

GEOLOGISCHE KARTE VON MITTELBUNDEN
1:25, 000
by P Arbenz
Bern : CGS, 1926
Two texts available.

GEOLOGISCHE KARTE VON WINTERTHUR UND UMGEBUNG
1:25, 000
by J Weber
Bern : CGS, 1924
Col. map with text.

QUATTERVALS
1:25, 000
No 0553
Editor W Hegwein
Bern : K & F
65 x 70
Col. geol. map of the National Park.
S.Fr. 7.30

PETROGRAPHISCHE DETAILKARTE DES GEBIETES VON PUNTEGLIAS-LA GONDA
1:20, 000
by Fr Weber
Bern : CGS, 1924
With text, and profile.

G EARTH RESOURCES

FUNDSTELLEN MINERALISCHER ROHSTOFFE IN DER SCHWEIZ
1:600, 000
by E Kundig & F de Quervain
Bern : CGS, 1953
Location of mineral ores in Switzerland.
Monograph with map. Fr. 8.00

ÜBERSICHTSKARTE DER URAN- UND THORIUMMINERALISATIONEN DER WESTALPEN
1:500, 000
Hugi and de Quervain
Bern : CGS, 1962
Map of uranium and thorium mineralisation of the Western Alps.

H BIOGEOGRAPHY

VEGETATIONSKARTE DER SCHWEIZ
1:200, 000
by E Schmid
No 0060
In 4 sheets
Bern : K & F
183 x 124 complete
Col. map showing distribution of vegetation types.

L ECONOMIC

SUISSE PHYSIQUE ET AGRICOLE
1:350, 000
Armand Colin
Political and economic on reverse.
see SWITZERLAND 494 E1

M HISTORICAL

SCHÜLERKARTE ZUR GESCHICHTE DER SCHWEIZ
1:500, 000
No 0075
Bern : K & F
77 x 62
Historical school wall map.

KARTE DER KULTURGÜTER/ CARTE DES BIENS CULTURELS
1:300, 000
3rd edition
Bern : ST, 1970
121 x 83
Showing buildings and sites of historic and cultural importance in Switzerland and Liechtenstein, with large scale plans of areas of importance on the reverse side.
Legend in 4 langs.

BURGENKARTE DER SCHWEIZ
1:200, 000
In 4 sheets
Official map of the Schweizerischen Burgenvereins
Bern : Eidgenössische Landestopographie
100 x 72
Locating and classifying chateaux, churches, towns, battlefields, roman and prehistoric remains. With handbook containing detail of local areas, a 88pp gazetteer describing each feature with grid references.
Sheets published :
1 North West 1976
2 South West 1974
Sheets 3 and 4 are in preparation.
Each S.Fr. 16.00

ALTER STADTPLAN VON BERN, 1623
by Bremgartenwald
Bern : K & F
70 x 84
Facsimile plan.

PANORAMAKARTE DER SCHWEIZ
No 532
Munchen : JRO
75 x 47
Pictorial relief map of Switzerland.

SCHWEIZ : PANORAMAKARTE
No 532
Munchen : JRO
75 x 47
Col. birds eye map showing land types, relief, settlements, roads etc.
DM 1.90

ATLASES
W3 WORLD ATLAS: LOCAL EDITION

SCHWEIZER SCHULATLAS
Bern : K & F
25 x 32
51pp
Atlas of Switzerland, Europe and the World.
In Ger. and Fr.

ATLASES
A1 GENERAL: ROADS

SCHWEIZ- MITTELEUROPA
1:300, 000/2, 500, 000
No 1515
Bern : K & F
13 x 23
60pp
Road atlas of Switzerland, scale 1:300, 000 with 16 town plans and road maps of the rest of Europe 1:2, 500 000.

ATLASES
B TOWN PLANS

29 STÄDTEPLÄNE DER SCHWEIZ
No 1521
Bern : K & F, 1971
13 x 20
121pp
Atlas of the 29 major towns, each with street index. Spiral bound.

PLAN DE VILLE GENÈVE
1:10, 000
Zürich : OF, 1976
17 x 21
32pp
Street atlas with index. In French.
S.Fr. 8.50

STADTPLAN ZÜRICH IN 13 TEILBLÄTTERN
1:20, 000
Zürich : OF, 1976
17 x 21
13pp street atlas in German with guide and index. S.Fr. 6.50

GEMEINDE-ATLAS REGION ZÜRICH
1:20, 000
Zürich : OF, 1974
21 x 16 or 10 x 16
25pp
Atlas of Zürich and environs including map sections, guide and index.
S.Fr. 15.00

ATLASES
K HUMAN GEOGRAPHY

ATLAS DER SCHWEIZERISCHEN VOLKSKUNDE/ATLAS DE FOLK-LORE SUISSE
Basel : Schweizerischen Gesellschaft fut Volkskunde, 1971
Ed : Paul Geiger
Folklore atlas in preparation - incl. an introductory vol. and 110 col. map plates at 1:1, 000, 000 and larger scales.

COMPUTER ATLAS DER SCHWEIZ
Ed A Kilchenmann, D Steiner, O Matt
Bern : K & F, 1972
72pp
A collection of 54 maps compiled from computer statistical records covering population, residency, earnings, agriculture.
S.Fr. 24.00

ATLASES
M HISTORICAL

HISTORISCHER ATLAS DER SCHWEIZ
Hektor Ammann and Karl Schib
Aaran : Verlag Sauerlandes, 1958
24 x 34
Historical atlas with 34pp text in Fr, Ger, It. 67 maps, mainly in colour. Covers Swiss history from earliest times.
S.Fr. 21.70

DIE SCHWEIZ AUF ALTEN KARTEN
Leo Weisz
2nd edition
Zürich : Buchverlag der Neuen Züricher Zeitung, 1969
247pp
Contains map reproductions and drawings, with some folded, coloured maps.
S.Fr. 62.00

500 JAHRE SCHWEIZER LAND-KARTEN
G Grosjean and M Cavelti
Zurich : OF, 1971
48 x 60
30 map facsimiles, spanning a period of 500 years. In case, with explanatory text.
S.Fr. 260.00

ATLASES
O NATIONAL

ATLAS DER SCHWEIZ/ATLAS DE LA SUISSE
Ed Prof Dr E Imhoff
Bern : ST, 1965+
In 9 parts
38 x 51 (76 x 51 map size)
Approx. 86 map plates, double size at 1:500, 000. Covering the following subjects : topographical, political, physical, geological, historical, biological, social, industrial, agricultural, economic etc. General map and regional ones. The first 8 sections have been issued.

ATLASES
P REGIONAL

STRUKTUR - ATLAS DER REGIO NORDWESTSCHWEIZ - OBERELSASS - SÜDSCHWARZWALD
1:250, 000
Basel : Geog. Inst. Univ.
Containing app. 80 col. maps covering topog, thematic subjects at scales of 1:250, 000 - 1:500, 000. In loose-leaf binder.

PLANUNGSATLAS - KANTON BERN
Bern : Kantonalen Planungsamt
Regional planning atlas of the Bern Canton in preparation.
Parts published :
Part 1 - Population, 1969
Part 2 - Economy, 1971.

494.9 Liechtenstein

A2 GENERAL MAPS : LOCAL

F & B WANDEKARTE
1:100, 000
Sheet 37
Wien : F & B
see AUSTRIA 436. A2.

KOMPASS WANDERKARTE
1:50, 000
Sheet 21
Wien : Kompass - Geografa
see AUSTRIA 436. A2.

C OFFICIAL SURVEY

LANDESKARTE DER SCHWEIZ
1:50, 000
Sheets : 227, 228, 237, 238
Bern : ST
see SWITZERLAND 494 C.

ÖSTERREICHISCHE KARTE
1:50, 000
Sheets 140, 141
Wien : BEV
see AUSTRIA 436 C.

FÜRSTENTUM LIECHTENSTEIN
1:25, 000
Vaduz : Amt. Lehrmittelverlag
58 x 106
Topographical map contoured, with relief shading, roads and footpaths. New edition in preparation.

LANDESKARTE DER SCHWEIZ
1:25, 000
In 6 sheets
Bern : ST
see SWITZERLAND 494 C.

FÜRSTENTUM LIECHTENSTEIN
1:10, 000
In 4 sheets
Vaduz : Amt Lehrmittelverlag
Physical wall map, contoured with relief shading.

F GEOLOGY

GEOLOGISCHE KARTE VON LIECHTENSTEIN
1:25, 000
Vaduz : Amt. Lehrmittelverlag
73 x 107
Coloured geological map.

M HISTORICAL

KULTURGÜTERKARTE SCHWEIZ - LIECHTENSTEIN
1:300, 000
Bern : ST
see SWITZERLAND 494 M.

495 Greece

A1 GENERAL MAPS : ROADS

KLEINASIEN, OSTLICHES MITTELMEER
1:2, 000, 000
Wien : FB
122 x 82
Covers Greece, Bulgaria, Turkey and south to the North African coast. Main highways and secondary routes, distances in km, road conditions and numbers, spot heights in metres, hill shading, railways and state boundaries.

REISEKARTE GRIECHENLAND
1:1, 700, 000
No 211
Koln : Polyglott
Roads classified and numbered, distances in km.

SHELL REISEKARTE GRIECHENLAND
1:1 500, 000
Stuttgart : Mair
83 x 48
Inc. Gk. Islands, with Crete inset. Roads classified and numbered, distances in km, spot heights in metres, relief shading, ferry routes, sites and other places of interest. 4 inset plans of sites. Legend in 12 langs.
DM 4.80

GRIECHENLAND
1:1, 000, 000
No 884
Frankfurt : Ravenstein, 1976
100 x 69
Col map. Roads classified and numbered, distances in km, other communications, places of tourist interest.
DM 7.80

GREECE
1:1, 000, 000
London : Foldex
Shows roads classified, relief shading; patent fold. 45p

GRIECHENLAND
1:1, 000, 000
Bern : Hallwag, 1972
95 x 82
All classes of roads, distances in km, spot heights, hill shading, car ferries, railways, airports, car camping sites and state boundaries. Crete inset. Inc. Aegean Is.

GRIECHENLAND - ÄGÄIS
1:1, 000, 000
No 1134
Bern : K & F, 1972
87 x 74
All classes of roads, road conditions, tracks, footpaths, distances in km, hill shading, route numbering, airports, car ferries, railways, camping sites, motels and state boundaries. Inset sketch plan of Athens.

GRIECHENLAND
1:800, 000
No 84
Stuttgart : RV
120 x 80
Inc. Crete and outer islands. All classes of roads, numbers, conditions, hill shading, distances in km, spot heights in metres, railways, car ferries, motels, camping sites, airports, tourist attractions and state boundaries. Inc. handbook of practical touring information for the motorist with text in Ger, 4 through-way town plans and 5 plans of historic sites.
DM 8.80

GRIECHENLAND
1:600, 000
Wien : FB
76 x 94
Covering mainland only. All classes of roads, route numbering, distances in km, spot heights in metres, car ferries, airports, camping sites, railways and state frontiers. Crete, Athens and Salonika inset. Guide map of Cultural Periods on reverse at 1:600, 000. Text in Ger.

CARTA STRADALE D'EUROPA
1:500, 000
No 31
Milano : TCI, 1972
74 x 112
Mainland only. All classes of roads, distances in km, spot heights, road conditions, layer col, car ferries and state frontiers. Insets of Crete, Corfu and Rhodes.
see also EUROPE 4 A1.

A2 GENERAL MAPS : LOCAL

MACEDONIA
1:500, 000
Athens : Al-Ma
70 x 50
General physical map in Greek, relief shading, communications.

PELOPPONESE
1:500, 000
Athens : Al-Ma
48 x 68
Physical map, with communications. Text in Greek.

ROAD MAP OF CRETE
1:300, 000
Athens : Mathloulakis, 1972
98 x 34
Main and secondary roads, distances in km, hill shading, archaeological sites and Byzantine monasteries. Inset sketch plans of Chania, Agios Nikolaos, Iraklion and Rethimnon and site plan of Knossos, Phaistos and Arkadi.

AL-MA DAY TRIPS FROM ATHENS
1:250 000
Athens : Al-Ma
69 x 47
Physical map of Athens and environs. All classes of roads, road conditions, distances in km, spot heights, archaeological sites, railways, hill shading and ferries.

GUIDE AND ROAD MAP OF RHODES
Athens : Al-Ma
45 x 64
All classes of roads, road conditions and distances, archaeological sites, airports and brief guide to the island. Also town plan of Rhodes showing places of interest and hotels.

CORFOU
1:200, 000
Athens : Al-Ma
Tourist map - distances in km, camping sites etc. Plan of Corfu City on reverse. Text in Eng and Fr.

ROAD AND TOURIST MAP OF CORFU
1:100, 000
Athens : Al-Ma, 1971
44 x 64
3 classes of roads with road conditions, distances in km, spot heights and archaeological sites. Guide in 4 langs. on reverse.

CORFU - FAIREY LEISURE MAP
1:100, 000
Maidenhead : Fairey Surveys Ltd, 1973
50 x 55
Col. map, relief shaded showing roads, places of interest, major hotels, restaurants, beaches etc. Inset of Corfu town, gazetteer of places and index to hotels and restaurants.

KERKIRA TRAVEL AND TOURIST MAP
1:100, 000
Athens : Paraskhoi L Kalfaki, 1965
70 x 49
Tourist map of Corfu in Greek.

GENERAL AND TRAVEL MAPS
Various scales
Athens : Loukopolous
Various sizes
Series of general physical maps for the provinces and Greek islands. Relief shaded with communications. Text in Greek.
Maps available :
Attica-Boeotia
1:150, 000
Dodecanese
1:120, 000 Island names in Eng. also
Epirus and Environ
1:170, 000
Euboea
1:200, 000
Kos
1:50, 000
Cyclades
1:120, 000
Macedonia
1:360, 000
Peloponnese
1:30, 000

Roumeli - Levkas - Kephallinia
1:250, 000
Samos
1:50, 000
Thessaly
1:250, 000
Thessalonica
1:100, 000
Thrace
1:250, 000

B TOWN PLANS

TOWN PLANS
Various scales
Col. maps with index to streets.
Maps available :

Athens	1:10, 000	Gouvoussis
Athens	1:8, 500	Hallwag
Salonica	1:10, 000	Loukopoulos

C OFFICIAL SURVEYS

KARTA MIRA
1:2, 500, 000
Carti
2 sheets required for complete coverage.
No's 54 and 74.
see WORLD 100C and index 100/2.

THE WORLD
1:1, 000, 000
DMS Series 1301
5 sheets needed for complete coverage.
see WORLD 100C and index 100/1.

THE WORLD
1:500, 000
DMS Series 1404
11 sheets needed for complete coverage.
see WORLD 100C and index 100/7.

MAPS OF THE NOMI (DEPARTMENTS) OF GREECE
1:200, 000
In 52 sheets, see index 495/1
Athens : NSSG
89 x 59 - large sheets
53 x 39 - small sheets
Showing roads, railways, layer col. with contours, spot heights and admin. boundaries. Each sheet contains an administrative district with full detail but the area shown outside of the administrative boundary has less detail. Text in Greek.

D POLITICAL & ADMINISTRATIVE

GRETSIYA, POLITIKO-ADMINISTRATIVNAYA KARTA
1:1, 500, 000
Moskva : GUGK, 1973
Political admin. map. Kop. 15

GRECIA
Barcelona : Editorial Teide
25 x 33
School outline hand map without boundaries or cities. Ptas. 1

E1 PHYSICAL : RELIEF

GRECJA, ALBANIA
1:1, 500, 000
Warszawa : PPWK, 1972
68 x 69
Col. physical map; contours, communications. Pol. text on reverse.
In series "Przegladowa Mapa Europy" (Review Maps of Europe).
Zl. 12

E2 PHYSICAL : LAND FEATURES

GROUND WATER POSSIBILITIES MAP OF GREECE
1:50, 000
Athens : IGSR
Col. hydrological map.
Sheet available : Platanias (Crete).

F GEOLOGY

CARTE GÉOLOGIQUE INTERNATIONALE DE L'EUROPE
1:1, 500, 000
UNESCO - BB
Sheets available for Greece :
D6 Athene, 1959
see EUROPE 4 F.

GEOLOGICAL MAP OF GREECE
1:500, 000
In 2 sheets
by C Renz et al
Athens : IGSR, 1976/77
87 x 124
Col. geol. map also showing mineral deposits and mines. Legend Greek and Eng.
New edition in preparation.

HALBINSEL CHALKIDIKI UND ANGRENZENDE GEBIETE
1:300, 000
Hannover : B-B, 1971
64 x 46
General geological map in colour of the Chalcidice peninsula. DM 5.00

GENERAL GEOLOGICAL MAP OF GREECE
1:200, 000
Athens : IGSR
Col. geol. series in Greek and English.
Sheet published : Euboea

CARTE GÉOLOGIQUE DE L'EPIRE
1:100, 000
Paris : Éditions Technip, 1966
North Sheet 105 x 82
South Sheet 118 x 89
2 sheet map showing stratigraphy, mineral resources. To accompany text vol. 320pp.
Map F.Fr. 87.50

KALAMBAKA BASIN (W THESSALY)
1:100, 000
Athens : IGSR, 1970
123 x 100
Col. hydrogeological map, with 197pp text in Greek and Eng.

GEOLOGICAL MAP OF GREECE
1:50, 000
Athens : IGSR, 1956+
Series of detailed col. geol. maps, in Greek with English, French or German legend.
Series in progress.
Sheets published :

D9	Kalambaka
D17	Sitochorion
F7	Nestorion
F8	Argos Orestikon
F14	Epanomi
G7	Pentalofon
G8	Grevena
H4	Tsamantas
H5	Doliana
H6	Tsepelovon
H7	Metsovon
I3	Sayiadha
I4	Filiates
I5	Klimatia
I6	Joannina
I7	Pramanda
I8	Kastanea
I10	Trikala
J3/4	Parga
J5	Paramythia
J6	Thesprotikon
J7	Agnanda
J10	Kardhitsa
J11	Sophadhes
J12	Farsalla
K4/5	Kanalakion
K6	Arta
K7	Petas
K8	Raftopoulon
K11	Leontarion
K12	Domokos
K13	Anavra
K14	Almyros
L10	Karpenision
L11	Sperchias
L12	Lamia
L13	Stylis
L14	Myli
M12	Amphissa
M13	Amphiklia
M14	Elatia
M15	Atalanti
N10	Nafpaktos
N12	Galaxidion
N13	Delfi
N14	Levadia
N15	Vagia
N16	Thivai
N19	Aliverion
O16	Erythrai
P7	Vartholomion
P13	Nemea
P14	Korinthos
Q11	Vytino
Q12	Tripolis
Q13	Argos
Q14	Nauplion
R11	Megalopolis
R12	Kollinai
R13	Astros
R14	Paralion-Astrous
S11	Kalamata
S12	Sparti
S14	Leonidion
T13	Yithion
VW26	Anaphi
YZ17	Kastelion
YZ18	Platanias
YZ19	Khania
Za18	Alikianos
Za27/28	Sitia
a26	Ierapetra
a27/28	Ziros

Special area maps :
1 Penins, Kassandras
2 Paxi
3 Kardamyli-Anoyia
4 Molaoi-Richea
5 Areopolis-Layia-Mavrovounion
6 Papadianika
7 Kythira
8 Antiparos
9 Siphnos
10 Karpathos North
11 Karpathos South
12 Lefkas
13 Korfu North
14 Korfu South
15 Laurium
16 Chios North
17 Chios South
21 Samothraki Island
Enesos
Mithymna
Hagia Paraskeri
Policnnitos
Plomarion-Mytilini
Kythnos
Alonisos

GROUND WATER GEOLOGICAL MAP OF GREECE
1:50, 000
Athens : MGMR-ex IGSR
Published sheet :
Erythrai

SOUTH MT. GHIONA REGION
1:50, 000
Athens : IGSR, 1968
70 x 100
Hydrogeological map with 395pp text in Greek and Eng.

STRATIGRAPHY AND TECTONICS OF THE MEGARA ISTHMUS
1:25, 000
Athens : IGSR, 1968
Geol. map with 23pp text.

G EARTH RESOURCES

METALLOGENETIC MAP OF GREECE
1:1, 000, 000
by K Zachos & G Maratos
Athens : IGSR, 1965
68 x 94
Text in French and Greek.

THE PEAT-LIGNITE DEPOSITS OF PHILIPPI
1:50, 000
Athens : IGSR, 1969
Mineral map, legend in Greek and Ger, 250pp text by H G Melidonis.

M HISTORICAL

CARTES MURALES ISSAC
Paris : Hachette
90 x 90
Series of col historical wall maps.
Maps available :
La Grece antique
La Grece au Ve siecle
L'Empire d'Alexandre

PALMER WORLD HISTORY MAPS
Various scales
Chicago : Rand McNally
50 x 46
Col. historical wall maps.
Maps available :
Classical Greece about 450 BC and Ancient Athens
Alexander's Empire and Hellenistic world, 3rd C BC

BREASTED-HUTH-HARDING HISTORICAL MAPS
Chicago : Denoyer-Geppert
112 x 81 each
Series of col. wall maps printed on stout manilla paper.
204041 The Achaean World
204051 Ancient Greece
204061 Greek and Phoenician Colonies and Commerce
204071 Boeotia and Attica
204081 Athens
204091 Sequence Map of Greece
204101 Alexander's Empire
204401 The Balkan States

DAS KLASSICHE GRIECHENLAND
1:500, 000
by Prof. Dr S Lauffer
Darmstadt : Perthes
210 x 195
Col. wall map depicting major political boundaries and towns of the 4th and 5th centuries BC on shaded relief base. Legend in Ger. Mounted CR

LA GRÈCE ANCIENNE
1:1, 000, 000
J Bouillon
No 1502
St Germain-en-Laye : Éditions MDI
92 x 126
Plastic coated historical wall map for schools.

GRAECIA
1:375, 000
Gotha : Haack, 1967
149 x 173
Historical wall map, covering period 8th-4th C BC. Shows main tribes, with relief indicated. In Latin

STAROVĚKÉ ŘECKO
Praha : Kart
Wall map of Ancient Greece in Czech. Kcs. 115

GENERAL REFERENCE MAP OF ANCIENT GREECE
Indianapolis : Cram
Shows states, towns and other sites. School wall map. US $13.75

DREVNYAYA GRETSIYA
1:1, 000, 000
Moskva : GUGK, 1973
Historical wall map of ancient Greece. Kop. 15

GRAECIA ANTIQUA CUM ORIS MARIS AEGAEI
1:700, 000
Novara : Ag
170 x 140
2 sheet historical wall map with Latin text, showing Ancient Greece and the Aegean coast. L. 3, 000

DAS REICH ALEXANDERS DES GROSSEN : DIADOCHENREICHE UM 301 UND 200 v CHRIST
1:3, 000, 000
Bielefeld : Cornelsen-Velhagen & Klasing
196 x 154
Historical wall map of the Empire of Alexander the Great.

ATLASES
A1 GENERAL : ROADS

ATCG ROAD MAPS AND TOURIST GUIDE TO GREECE
Athens : Automobile and Touring Club of Greece
16 x 22
186pp
Scale undefined. In English; 44pp of route strip maps showing first class and other roads with distances in km, road conditions, railways, spot heights, airports, hill shading, places of interest, ferries and archaeological sites. Text contains details of district shown on the map and its history, archaeological significance, sites worth visiting etc.
Main Gk. islands inc. Index.

ATLASES
L ECONOMIC

INDUSTRIAL ATLAS OF GREECE
Athens : Nat. Statistical Service, 1963
59 x 44 (map size)
48 coloured maps, covering industrial regions, comparative production; based on 1963 Census of industrial, handicraft and mining establishments. Text Greek, English, French.

ATLASES
O NATIONAL

ECONOMIC AND SOCIAL ATLAS OF GREECE
B Kayser and K Thompson
Athens : Nat. Statistical Service, 1964
48 x 43
73 plates in colour or monochrome at 1:2, 000, 000 or 1:4, 200, 000. Shows relief, geology, agriculture, industry, population. Each plate with text in Greek, English or French. Statistical supplement. In screw binder.

496.5 Albania

A1 GENERAL MAPS : ROADS

GENERALKARTE VON ALBANIEN
1:200, 000
In 2 sheets
Wien : BEV
84 x 93 each sheet
Contoured map. All classes of roads, footpaths, inns, forest areas, other surface features and state boundaries. Legend in Ger.

C OFFICIAL SURVEYS

THE WORLD
1:1, 000, 000
DMS Topographical Series 1301
2 sheets needed for complete coverage.
see WORLD 100C and index 100/1.

THE WORLD
1:500, 000
DMS Topographical Series 1404
3 sheets needed for complete coverage.
see WORLD 100C and index 100/7.

D POLITICAL & ADMINISTRATIVE

SHQIPËRIA - HARTË POLITIKO ADMINISTRATIVE
1:500, 000
Tiranë : "Hamid Shijaku", 1969
53 x 75
Col. by districts; roads classified and railways; towns graded by pop.
In Albanian.

E1 PHYSICAL : RELIEF

ALBANIA FISICO-POLITICA (1939)
1:275, 000
Novara : Ag
80 x 140
Col. physical wall map of 1939 period.
L 2, 000

SHQIPËRIA HARTË FIZIKE
1:500, 000
Tiranë : "Hamid Shijaku", 1970
45 x 68
Layer col, physical map, shaded relief; major towns and physical features. In Albanian.

SHQIPËRIA - HARTË FIZIKO-POLITIKE
1:200, 000
Tiranë : "Hamid Shijaku"
2 sheets joined
95 x 197
Physical col. wall map, contoured and layered; administrative boundaries, communications, towns graded. Inset of Balkans. In Albanian.

F GEOLOGY

CARTE TECTONIQUE DE L'ABANIE
1:500, 000
Tirane : Ministère de l'Industrie et des Mines, 1969
53 x 76
Col. tectonic map, Italy and Balkans inset. Based on 1967 Geol. map (1:200, 000). Index to structural zones etc. Map and legend sheet in paper envelope.

PASURITË E NËNTOKËS TË R.P. TË SHQIPËRISË
1:275, 000
In 2 sheets
Tiranë : N. I. Sh. Mjete Mesimore e Sportive "Hamid Shijaku", 1970
100 x 137
Col. geol. base showing mineral location; graph of production inset.

CARTE GÉOLOGIQUE D'ALBANIE
1:200, 000
In 3 sheets
Tirane : Ministère d'Industrie et des Mines, Institut de Recherches Industrielle et Minières, 1967
76 x 166
Detailed geol. map with contours at 200 metre intervals and legend in Fr.

H BIOGEOGRAPHY

GJITARET KAFSHET NË R. P. TË SHQIPËRISË
1:200, 000
Tiranë : "Hamid Shijaku", 1971
Zoological map of the Peoples' Republic of Albania.

LES OISEAUX DE LA R. P. D'ALBANIE
1:200, 000
Tirane : "Hamid Shijaku", 1971
Map of the birds of Albania in French.

L ECONOMIC

ELEKTRIFIKIMI I R. P. TË SHQIPËRISË
1:200, 000
In 3 sheets
Tiranë : "Hamid Shijaku", 1970
95 x 205
Shows electricity grid and production centres; classifies hydro-electric, diesel and thermal power.

M HISTORICAL

HISTORICAL MAPS
Various scales
Tirane : "Hamid Shijaku"
Series of historical wall maps. In Albanian.
Maps available :
Vëndbanimet Prehistorike të vëndit tonë (Map of prehistoric remains) 1:500, 000, 1971
Harta arkeologjike e Shqipërisë (archaeological map) 1:400, 000, 1971
Toka Shqiptare nga fundi i shek. IX deri në shek. XII (Defence lines from the end of the 9th C to the end of the 11th C), 1:500, 000, 1971
Shtegtime të Shqiptarvë ne Mesjetë (Pop. movement during the Middle Ages), 1:250, 000, 1971
Principate e Arberit fundi i shek XII deri në fillimin e shek. XIII (Duchy of Albania 12th - 13th C) 1:500, 000, 1971
Shqipëria fillim i shek. XVI - gjymsa e dytë e shek. XVIII (Resistance from the beginning of the 16th C to the 18th C)
RRitja e lëvizjës kombëtare Shqiptare në vitet 1882-1908 (Troop movement) 1:500, 000, 1971
Lëvizja kombëtare Shqiptare 1908-1912 (Insurrections), 1:500, 000, 1971
Lufta e Parë Ballkanike 1912-13 Shqipëria ahe Traktati i Bukureshtit (the Balkan War and after the peace of Bucharest) 1:1, 000, 000, 1971
Shqipëria gjatë Luftës se 1 Botevore 1914-1918 (1st World War), 1:500, 000, 1970
Shqipëria pas Luftës Irë Botevore, 1918-24, 1:500, 000, 1971
Reducconi i Qershorit 1924, 1:400, 000, 1971
Shqipëria në vitet 1925-1939 1:500, 000, 1971

HARTË HISTORIKE
Tiranë : "Hamid Shijaku
Small maps illustrating history of Albania. In Albanian.
Maps available :
1380-1443 Invazioni i Turqve dhe rezistenca e Populit Shqiptar 1970, 62 x 80
Shqipëria gjatë viteve 1443-1450
1450-1457 Shteti i Pavarur Shqiptar dhe Fitoret e Tij
Shqipëria Gjatë Viteve 1457-1468
1468-1506 Lufta për Liri dhe Lëvizjet e Armatosura.

497 Balkans

A1 GENERAL MAPS : ROADS

BALKANSKÉ STÁTY : PŘEHLEDNÁ AUTOMAPA
1:1, 500, 000
Praha : Kart, 1971
90 x 72
Road map of South East Europe, covering Yugoslavia, Hungary, Bulgaria, Rumania. Roads numbered with distances.
Kcs. 8

BALKANLÄNDER
1:1, 000, 000
No 1887
Munchen : JRO
137 x 98
Double-sided map in colour. Roads classified and numbered, distances in km, tourist details. DM 9.80

GRECIA, ALBANIA, BULGARIA
1:1, 000, 000
Novara : Ag
94 x 98
Coloured road and tourist map.
L 700

D POLITICAL & ADMINISTRATIVE

PRIDUNAYSKI YE STRANY
1:2, 000, 000
Moskva : GUGK
93 x 70
School wall map, political col, communications, description, place locations.

BALKANSKOG POLUSTRVA
1:1, 000, 000
In 4 sheets
135 x 136 complete
Political wall map in cyrillic and latin script, covering the Balkan Peninsula.
Cloth mounted Dn. 150

REGIONE BALCANICA
1:5, 000, 000
Novara : Ag
Small outline hand map for schools.
L 40

E1 PHYSICAL : RELIEF

BALKANSKIE STATY
1:1, 500, 000
Moskva : GUGK
92 x 110
Physical with contours, relief shading, communications, borders, 2 insets, tables and diagrams. Text vol. in Czech.

VENGRIYA, RUMINIYA, BOLGARIYA, ALBANIYA, YUGOSLAVIYA I GRETSIYA
1:1, 250, 000
In 2 sheets
Moskva : GUGK, 1973
115 x 140 complete
Physical wall map of Hungary, Romania, Bulgaria, Albania, Yugoslavia, Greece.
Kop. 32

DIE BALKAN
1:1, 000, 000
Berlin : Columbus
142 x 200
Covers Hungary, Romania, Bulgaria, Yugoslavia, Italy. Physical wall map, relief shading, railways, cities graded by pop.

REGIONE BALCANICA
1:5, 000, 000
Novara : Ag
33 x 26
Plastic relief map for schools covering Albania, Greece, Turkey in Europe. Physical, political and economic detail on reverse. L 450

L ECONOMIC

ÉTATS BALKANIQUES ; PHYSIQUE ET AGRICOLE
1:3, 400, 000
Armand Colin
Political and industrial map on reverse.
see BALKANS 497 E1

VENGRIYA, RUMINIYA, BOLGARIYA, ALBANIYA, YUGOSLAVIYA, I GRETSIYA, EKONOMICHESKAYA KARTA
1:1, 250, 000
In 2 sheets
Moskva : GUGK, 1973
Economic wall map in Russian.
Kop. 34

M HISTORICAL

THE BALKAN STATES - BREASTED-HUTH-HARDING HISTORICAL WALL MAP
Chicago : Denoyer-Geppert
From the height of the Ottoman Empire in 1683 until World War I.

SLOWANIE W IX WIEKU
1:3, 000, 000
PPWK, 1972
see EUROPE 4M

497.1 Yugoslavia

See also : 497 BALKANS

A1 GENERAL MAPS : ROADS

AUTOMAPA JUGOSLAVIE
1:1, 500, 000
Praha : Kart
Roads classified and numbered, distances in km, motoring and tourist information.
Kcs. 9

SHELL REISEKARTE - JUGOSLAWIEN, BULGARIEN, RUMANIEN, UNGARN
1:1, 500, 000
Stuttgart : Mair
87 x 48
Roads numbered and classified, distances in km, relief shading, spot heights in metres, places of tourist interest. S parts of Yugoslavia and Bulgaria not covered.
DM 4.80

JUGOSLAWIEN
1:1, 000, 000
Bern : Hallwag, 1972
81 x 81
All classes of roads, distances in km, hill shading, railways, ferries, spot heights in metres, important camping sites, airports and state boundaries.

JUGOSLAWIEN
1:1, 000, 000
No 1140
Bern : K & F
87 x 74
All classes of roads, route numbering and conditions, hill shading, spot heights in metres, picturesque roads, distances in km, railways, ferries, airports, camping sites, motels and state boundaries.

JUGOSLAWIEN
1:1, 000, 000
No 1859
München : JRO
88 x 95
Roads classified and numbered, distances in km, boundaries, places of tourist interest, with index. Inc. Italian Adriatic Coast.
DM 6.80

AUTOKARTA JUGOSLAVIJE
1:1, 000, 000
Beograd : Geokarta
Road map with distances.
Dn. 10

JUGOSLAWIEN
1:1, 000, 000
No 212
Koln : Polyglott
Roads classified and numbered, distances in km.

IUGOSLAVIA
1:1, 000, 000
Novara : Ag
81 x 72
Coloured road and tourist map.
L 700

YUGOSLAVIA
1:1, 000, 000
London : Foldex
Shows roads classified, relief shading, patent fold. 45p

JUGOSLAWIEN
1:800, 000
No 90
Stuttgart : RV
121 x 75
Main and secondary roads, numbers, conditions, hill shading, distances in km, spot heights in metres, car ferries, railways, petrol and service stations, mountain huts, motels, camping sites and places of tourist interest. Inc. handbook of motorist practical touring information, text in Ger, and 27 through-way town plans.
DM 6.80

JUGOSLAWIEN
1:800, 000
No 881
Frankfurt : Ravenstein, 1976
95 x 70
Roads classified and numbered, distances in km, ferry routes, relief shading, spot heights in metres, places of tourist interest. S E area inset. DM 7.80

AUTOKARTE JUGOSLAWIEN
1:600, 000
Wien : FB, 1975
78 x 104
Double sided (E & W); roads classified and numbered, distances in km, spot heights in metres, relief shading, other communications, places of tourist interest, state boundaries.

CARTA STRADALE D'EUROPA
1:500, 000
In 2 sheets, 29 and 30
Milano : TCI, 1971
All classes of roads, distances in km, road conditions, layer col, spot heights in metres, railways and car ferries.
see also EUROPE 4 A1

PUTNA KARTA JUGOSLAVIJA
1:500, 000
Beograd : Militargeog. Inst, 1968
Roads classified and numbered, distances in km, tourist information.

AUTOKARTA JUGOSLAVIJE
1:500, 000
In 4 sheets
Ljubljana : Držařna Založba
Slovenije
Series of road and tourist maps. Roads classified and numbered, distances in km, places of tourist interest etc. Legend in 5 langs.
Sheets :
1 Slovenia
2 Bosnia - Dalmatia
3 Montenegro - Macedonia
4 Serbia

A2 GENERAL MAPS : LOCAL

KARNTEN - NÖRDLICHE ADRIA
1:500, 000
München : Kompass
No 352
Road map covering Graz - Merano - Parma - Rimini - Zagreb. All classes of road with route numbers and distances.
DM 4.90

YUGOSLAVIAN ADRIATIC COAST
1:400, 000
Zagreb : Ucila
Tourist map, with guide on reverse.

JADRANSKA OBALA
1:400, 000
Zagreb : Jug. Leksikografiski Zavod
Tourist map of the Adriatic Coast area.
Dn. 5

GENERALKARTE DALMATINISCHE KUSTE
1:200, 000
In 3 sheets
Stuttgart : Mair, 1974/5
103 x 47 each
Roads classified and numbered, relief and vegetation, shading, national parks, places of tourist information, inc. beaches, swimming etc. Legend in 2 langs.
Also available in a Hallwag ed.
Sheets :
I Triest - Istria - Zadar
II Zadar - Split - Mostar
III Ston - Dubrovnik - Bar
Each DM 3.50

BELGRADE ENVIRONS
1:100, 000
Beograd : Geokarta, 1973
Elementary school map in Cyrillic.

WANDERKARTEN
1:100, 000
Wien : F & B
Sheets 14 Julische Alpen
47 Ostkarawanken und Steiner Alpen
see AUSTRIA 436 A2 and index 436/2

JULIJSKE ALPE
1:50, 000
Ljubljana : Slovak Mt Club, 1969
65 x 90
Col. touring map; contours, vegetation col, walking and hiking routes, mt. huts etc.

B TOWN PLANS

TOWN PLANS
Various scales
Col. plans with street index
Maps available :
Beograd, 1:20, 000, Stampa
Dubrovnik, 1:17, 000 (pictorial) Minceta
Rijeka, 1:10, 000, Mladost
Split, 1:7, 100, Geoprojekt
Zadar, 1:5, 000, Mladost
Zagreb, 1:12, 500, Grada

BEOGRADA
1:8, 000
In 6 sheets
Beograd : Geokarta
200 x 200 complete
Large scale wall plan of Belgrade.
Cloth mounted Dn. 250

C OFFICIAL SURVEYS

KARTA MIRA
1:2, 500, 000
Carti – VVK
2 sheets required for complete coverage.
No's 53 and 54.
see WORLD 100C and index 100/2.

THE WORLD
1:1, 000, 000
DMS Series 1301
4 sheets needed for complete coverage.
see WORLD 100C and index 100/1.

THE WORLD
1:500, 000
DMS Series 1404
11 sheets needed for complete coverage.
see WORLD 100C and index 100/7.

GENERALKARTE VON
MITTELEUROPA
1:200, 000
In 48 sheets, see index 436/1
Vienna : BEV
48 x 66
Topog. series with relief by hachures, all classes of roads, tracks and footpaths, railways, airports, hotels, youth hostels, shelters, mountain inns, state and provincial boundaries. Pre-war series with some post-war revision.

D POLITICAL & ADMINISTRATIVE

JUGOSLAVIJA KABINETSKA
1:600, 000
In 4 sheets
Beograd : Geokarta
164 x 138 complete
Office map, latin alphabet.
Mounted cloth Dn. 150

JUGOSLAVIJE
1:600, 000
In 4 sheets
Beograd : Geokarta, 1973

JUGOSLAVIJA
1:550, 000
Beograd : Geokarta
180 x 135
School map, in cyrillic and latin alphabets.
Cloth mounted Dn. 150

S. R. SRBIJE
1:1, 000, 000
Beograd : Geokarta
50 x 35
Small atlas plate map of Serbia.
Dn. 1.50

S. R. SRBIJE
1:300, 000
In 4 sheets
Beograd : Geokarta, 1973
School wall map in cyrillic.

KOSOVO
1:150, 000
Beograd : Geokarta, 1973
School map of the province to be published in Albanian.

E1 PHYSICAL : RELIEF

JUGOSLAWIA
1:1, 500, 000
Warszawa : PPWK, 1971
57 x 46
Physical hand map, with contours, layer col, communications, towns graded by pop.

JUGOSLAVIJA FIZIČKA
1:1, 250, 000
Beograd : Geokarta
67 x 84
Physical map in latin and cyrillic lettering.
Dn. 6

JUGOSLAVIJA
1:1, 250, 000
Beograd : Geokarta
67 x 84
Legend in cyrillic and latin alphabets, contours, communications, boundaries.
Dn. 5

YUGOSLAVIYA
1:1, 125, 000
3rd edition
Moskva : GUGK, 1972
Physical general map; industry and agriculture inset at 1:3, 500, 000.
Supp. in Rus.

SFR JUGOSLAVIJA
1:1, 000, 000
Zagreb : Ucila, 1972
70 x 100
Hand map showing relief, communications, boundaries; political maps and plans inset on reverse.

JUGOSLAVIJE
1:500, 000
In 6 sheets
Beograd : Mladost, 1972
184 x 170 complete
Physical map with communications, relief shading, boundaries.

DALMAZIA FISICO-POLITICA
(1943)
1:300, 000
Novara : Ag
135 x 140
Col. physical wall map of the period
1943. L 3, 000

F GEOLOGY

GEOLOŠKA KARTA F.N.R.
JUGOSLAVIJE
1:500, 000
In 4 sheets
Beograd : Energetika i Ekstvaktivna Industrija Vlade F.N.R, 1953
210 x 173 complete
Generalised geol. map, in Serbo-Croatian and French, compiled from pre-1939 documents. Covers Yugoslavia and parts of Italy, Hungary, Rumania, Bulgaria, Greece and Albania.

GEOLOŠKA KARTA SR SRBIJE/
CARTE GÉOLOGIQUE DE LA R. S.
DE SERBE
1:200, 000
In 10 sheets
Beograd : Inst. de Recherches Geol. et Géophysiques, 1968
Geol. map of Serbia, in Fr, and Serbo-Croatian, 8 map sheets, 1 legend sheet, 1 title sheet.

GEOLOGISCHE KARTE JUGOSLAWIEN
1:75, 000
Wien : GB, 1896-1920
Austrian geol. series.
Sheets available :
Bischoflack-Idria (1909)
Carlopago-Jablanac (1909)
Cherso - Arbe (1908)
Cilli - Ratschach (1907)
Görz - Gradisca (1920)
Haidenschaft - Adelsberg (1905)
Insel Busi (1914)
Insel Sant'Andrea (1914)
Insel Solta (1914)
Kistanje - Drniš (1896)
Knin - Ervenik (1920)
Lussin piccolo - Puntaloni (1908)
Medak - Sveti Rok (1909)
Novegrad - Benkovac (1908)
Pago (1912)
Pettau - Vinica (1898)
Pragerhof - Windisch Feistritz (1898)
Prassberg a. d. Sann (1898)
Rohitsch - Drachenburg (1907)
Sebenico Trau (1900)
Selve (1909)
Sinj - Spalato (1914)
Unie - Sansego (1914)
Veglia - Novi (1905)
Zapuntello (1914)
Zara (1920)
Zaravecchia - Stretto (1905)
Each A.Sch. 150 or 270

GEOLOGISCHE KARTE
SÜDDALMATIEN
1:25, 000
Wien : GB, 1903-9
Geol. maps of part of Austro-Hungarian Empire.
Sheets available :
Budua, 1903 A.Sch. 150
Spizza Nordhälfte, 1909
A.Sch. 100
Spizza Sudhälfte, 1909
A.Sch. 100
Set A.Sch. 300

K HUMAN GEOGRAPHY

KARTA RAZMJESTAJA
STANOVNIŠTVA SFRJ
1:1, 000, 000
Sarajevo : Geog. Soc. Bosnia and Herzegovina, 1969
90 x 68
Showing population distribution with statistics on topog. base map. Legend in Eng, Serbo-Croatian. From 1961 census figures.

L ECONOMIC

JUGOSLAVIJA INDUSTRIJSKA
1:550, 000
In 4 sheets
Beograd : Geokarta
180 x 135 complete
Industrial map in latin and cyrillic alphabets. Dn. 5

PRIVREDNA KARTA JUGOSLAVIJE
1:1, 500, 000
Beograd : Geokarta
Economic map of Jugoslavia.
Dn. 5

M HISTORICAL

BREASTED-HUTH-HARDING HISTORICAL MAP : THE BALKAN STATES
No 204411
112 x 81
Chicago : Denoyer-Geppert
Col. historical wall map.

ATLASES
A1 GENERAL : ROADS

AUTOATLAS JUGOSLAVIJA
1:750, 000
Zagreb : Jug. Leksikografski Zavod, 1973
15 x 24
32pp
22 maps showing roads classified and numbered, distances in km, other communications, motoring and tourist information. Legend in 12 langs.

AUTOATLAS JUGOSLAVIJE
1:600, 000
Zagreb : Ucila
54pp maps, roads classified, distances in km, through town plans, tourist information. Legend in 5 langs.

ATLASES
A2 GENERAL : LOCAL

JADRANSKA OBALA I OTOCI
1:300, 000
Zagreb : Jugoslavenski Leksikografski Zavod, 1971
Road atlas.
No 1 Trieste - Lukovo - Cres - Losinj - Krk

ATLASES
M HISTORICAL

HISTORIJSKI ATLAS
Beograd : Geokarta, 1973
To be pub. in cyrillic.

497.2 Bulgaria

See also : 497 BALKANS

A1 GENERAL MAPS : ROADS

AUTOMAPA BULHARSKO
1:1, 500, 000
Praha : Kart
Roads classified and numbered, distances in km, motoring and tourist information.
Kcs. 8

SHELL REISEKARTE - JUGOSLAVIEN - BULGARIEN - RUMANIEN - UNGARN
1:1, 500, 000
Mair
see YUGOSLAVIA 497.1 A1

ROMANIA - BULGARIA AUTOTÉRKÉPE
1:1, 000, 000
3rd rev. edition
Budapest : Kart, 1972
74 x 94
Roads classified and numbered, distances in km, relief shading, spot heights in metres, airports, car ferries, places of tourist interest. Legend in 3 langs. Explanation of signs in insets; town maps of Bucuresti, Sofia, Constanta, Varna.
Also published as Autokarte Rumanien-Bulgarien, F & B, 1972.

RUMÄNIEN-BULGARIEN
1:1, 000, 000
No 882
Frankfurt : Ravenstein, 1974
80 x 88
Roads classified and numbered, distances in km, relief shading, spot heights in metres, places of tourist interest, airports, ports, state boundaries, railways etc.
DM 7.80

RUMÄNIEN-BULGARIEN
1:1, 000, 000
No 1175
Bern : K& F
90 x 126
Main and secondary roads, distances in km, route numbering, airports, car ferries, railways, camping sites and state boundaries. Inc. 4 town plan insets.

ROAD MAP OF BULGARIA
1:800, 000
Sofia : Bulgarian Travel Office
78 x 96
Main and secondary roads, route numbering, railways, spot heights in metres, distances in km, camping sites, motels, airports, places of interest and tourist information. 5 town plans and motoring information on reverse.

A2 GENERAL MAPS : LOCAL

TOURIST MAP OF RILA
1:125, 000
Sofia : "Balkan-Tourist", 1969
67 x 46
Col. map with relief shading. Text Eng, Fr, Ger, on reverse.

B TOWN PLANS

TOWN PLANS
Sofia : Bulgarian Tourist Office
Col. plans with index to streets
Maps available :
PLOVDIV
SOFIA
VARNA

C OFFICIAL SURVEYS

THE WORLD
1:1, 000, 000
DMS Series 1301
4 sheets needed for complete coverage
see WORLD 100C and index 100/1.

THE WORLD
1:500, 000
DMS Series 1404
9 sheets needed for complete coverage
see WORLD 100C and index 100/7.

GENERALKARTE VON MITTELEUROPA
1:200, 000
Wien : BEV
25 sheets needed for complete coverage
see AUSTRIA 436C and index 436/1.

E1 PHYSICAL : RELIEF

BULGARIA
Washington : Govt Printing Office/ Central Intelligence Agency
60 x 58
Small map showing relief, urban areas, main admin. divisions, them. insets.
US $0.50

BALGARIJA
1:1, 500, 000
Milano : TCI
49 x 31
Plate from TCI world atlas, political and physical map with communications and inset of Sofia and environs at 1:250, 000.

BULHARSKO
1:1, 500, 000
Prague : USGK, 1968
Czech map with communications and province boundaries. 8pp text.

BULGARIA
1:1, 000, 000
Warszawa : PPWK, 1971
68 x 46
Contours, communications. Text in Pol. on reverse.

G EARTH RESOURCES

POCHVENA KARTA NA BŬLGARIYA
1:400, 000
Sofia : Academy of Sciences, 1968
139 x 100 complete
2 sheet soil map in colour. Title and legend in Bulgarian and Eng. Text vol, 23pp.

ATLASES
M HISTORICAL

ATLAS PO BŬLGARKA ISTORIYA
Sofia : Bulgarian Academy of Sciences, 1963
24 x 32
87pp
Historical atlas of Bulgaria and the Balkans with text and index.

ATLASES
P REGIONAL

ATLAS SLIVENSKI OKRAG
Sofia : Kartproekt, 1968
92pp
Atlas of the Sliven District. 74 maps covering economic and social aspects of the District after 9th September 1944. For educational and domestic needs.

498 Romania

See also: 497 BALKANS

A1 GENERAL MAPS : ROADS

AUTOMAPA RUMUNSKO
1:1, 500, 000
Praha : Kart
Road map in Czech. Roads classified and numbered, distances in km, motoring and tourist details. Kcs. 10

SHELL REISEKARTE - JUGOSLAWIEN - BULGARIEN - RUMANIEN - UNGARN
1:1, 500, 000
Mair
see YUGOSLAVIA 497.1 A1

TOURIST MAP OF ROMANIA
1:1, 000, 000
Bucureşti : Meridiane
Physical details, roads classified, places of tourist interest and accommodation.
Legend Rom, Eng, Fr, Ger.

RUMÄNIEN - BULGARIEN, AUTOKARTE
1:1, 000, 000
No 882
Frankfurt : Ravenstein, 1974
80 x 88
Col. map, roads classified and numbered, distances in km, other communications, places of tourist interest.
DM 7.80

RUMÄNIEN - BULGARIEN
1:1, 000, 000
No 1175
K & F
see BULGARIA 497.2 A1.

RUMANIA - BULGARIǍ AUTOTÉRKÉPE
1:1, 000, 000
Kart 1972
see BULGARIA 497.2 A1.

HARTA TURISTICǍ
1:850, 000
Bucureşti : Nat. Council for Physical Education and Sport, 1970
Roads classified with distances and road maps of 20 towns.

C OFFICIAL SURVEYS

THE WORLD
1:1, 000, 000
DMS Series 1301
5 sheets needed for complete coverage
see WORLD 100C and index 100/1.

THE WORLD
1:500, 000
DMS Series 1404
11 sheets needed for complete coverage.
see WORLD 100C and index 100/7.

GENERALKARTE VON MITTELEUROPA
1:200, 000
Wien : BEV
38 sheets needed for complete coverage.
see AUSTRIA 436C and index 436/1.

D POLITICAL & ADMINISTRATIVE

RSR HARTA FIZICǍ-ADMINISTRATIVǍ
1:1, 000, 000
Bucureşti : Ed. Didacticǎ i Pedagogicǎ, 1969
see ROMANIA 498 E1.

E1 PHYSICAL : RELIEF

RUMUNSKO
1:2, 250, 000
Praha : USGK
42 x 34
School physico-political map.

RSR HARTA FIZICA-ADMINISTRATIVA
1:1, 000, 000
Vasile Stefanescu
Bucureşti : Editura Didacticǎ şi Pedagogicǎ, 1969
74 x 54
Double sided map, physical and contoured with political map showing communications and boundaries on reverse.

RUMUNIA
1:1, 000, 000
Warszawa : PPWK, 1971
80 x 69
Col. physical map in series "Przegladowa Mapa Europy" (Review maps of Europe).

F GEOLOGY

GEOLOGICAL MAP OF ROMANIA
1:1, 000, 000
Bucureşti : Geol. Inst, 1967
With booklet and Eng. explanation.

CARTE DU QUATERNAIRE
1:1, 000, 000
Bucureşti : Geol. Inst, 1964
Map showing Quaternary deposits with explanation in Fr.

CARTE GÉOLOGIQUE DES FORMATIONS ANTEWESTPHALIENNES
1:1, 000, 000
Bucureşti : Geol. Inst, 1969

CARTE GÉOLOGIQUE DES FORMATIONS ANTETORTONIENNES
1:1, 000, 000
Bucureşti : Geol. Inst, 1969

CARTE GEOLOGIQUE DES FORMATIONS ANTEVRACONIENNES
1:1, 000, 000
Bucureşti : Geol. Inst, 1969

CARTE HYDROGÉOLOGIQUE
1:1, 000, 000
Bucureşti : Geol. Inst, 1969
With text in Fr.

GEOLOGICAL MAP OF ROMANIA
1:500, 000
In 12 sheets
Bucureşti : Geol. Inst, 1936-59
Col. geol. series.

ATLAS LITHOFACIAL DE LA R.S. DE ROUMANIE - NÉOGÈNE
1:500, 000
In 12 sheets
Bucureşti : Geol. Inst, 1963-65
Covering the strata of the Pliocene and Miocene.

GEOLOGICAL MAP OF ROMANIA
1:200, 000
In 50 sheets, see index 498/1
Bucureşti : Geol. Inst, 1966-7
Col. geol. series, with explanatory text in Fr.

HARTA HIDROGEOLOGICǍ RSR
1:100, 000
See index 498/1
Bucureşti : Geol. Inst, 1963-9
Hydrogeological map of Romania.
Sheets published :
36d, 37a, 37b, 42b, 42d, 44a, 44b, 44d, 45a, 45b, 45c, 50a-b, 37c, 37d.

GEOLOGICAL MAP OF ROMANIA
1:100, 000
See index 498/1
Bucureşti : Geol. Inst, 1963-5
Col. geol. series.
Sheets published :
3a, 3b, 3c, 3d, 17a, 17b.

G EARTH RESOURCES

CARTE MÉTALLOGENIQUE
1:1, 000 000
Bucureşti : Geol. Inst, 1970

CARTE DES SUBSTANCES MINÉRALES UTILES
1:1, 000, 000
Bucureşti : Geol. Inst, 1969
Mineral map with text in Fr.

HARTA SOLURILOR
1:1, 000, 000
1st edition
Bucureşti : Geol. Inst, 1964
72 x 56
Soil map in colour indicating parent material, with legend in Romanian, title Russian and French. Booklet also, with Eng. explanation.

HARTA SOLURILOR
1:200, 000
In 50 sheets, see index 498/1
Bucureşti : Geol. Inst, 1963-69
Soil series in progress.
Sheets published :
30, 37, 38, 39, 44, 45, 46, 47, 48, 49, 50.

CARTES GEOPHYSIQUES
1:200 000
In 2 sheets
Bucureşti : Geol. Inst, 1968
Geophysical map.

L ECONOMIC

REPUBLICA SOCIALISTǍ ROMÂNIA
HARTA GEOGRAFICO - ECONOMICǍ
1:500, 000
by I Velcea et al
In 4 sheets
Bucureşti : Inst. Geog, Academy of Romania, 1971
114 x 178
Economic map with 3 insets; population in 1970, physical map, animal map, all at 1:2, 500, 000.

ATLASES
O NATIONAL

ATLASUL REPUBLICII SOCIALISTE ROMÂNIA
Bucureşti : Editura Academiei Republicii Socialiste România, 1974-78
63 x 44 (binder)
In 76 plates
Atlas to be pub. during the period 1974-1978. Loose leaf, issued in parts. 350 maps (81 x 62) at 1:500, 000 and 1:1-6, 000, 000. In 13 Chapters : Introduction, Geology, Relief, Climate, Waters, Biogeography, History, Population, Settlements, Industry, Agriculture, Communications, Conclusions.

ATLAS GEOGRAFIC REPUBLICA SOCIALISTIKA ROMANIA
Ed Dr Tufescu Victor
Bucureşti : Ed Didactica si Pedagogica, 1965
24 x 34
141pp
110pp physical and them. maps, 31pp text, with graphs. Maps cover industry, agriculture, economy, climate, geology, communi-cations, physical and social aspects of Romania. Double page maps at 1:1, 750, 000 single pages at 1:2, 500, 000.

MIC ATLAS GEOGRAPHIC
by A Barsan
Bucureşti : Ed. Stiintifica, 1971
300pp
Small geographic atlas, 208pp text, 30pp atlas, 62pp index.

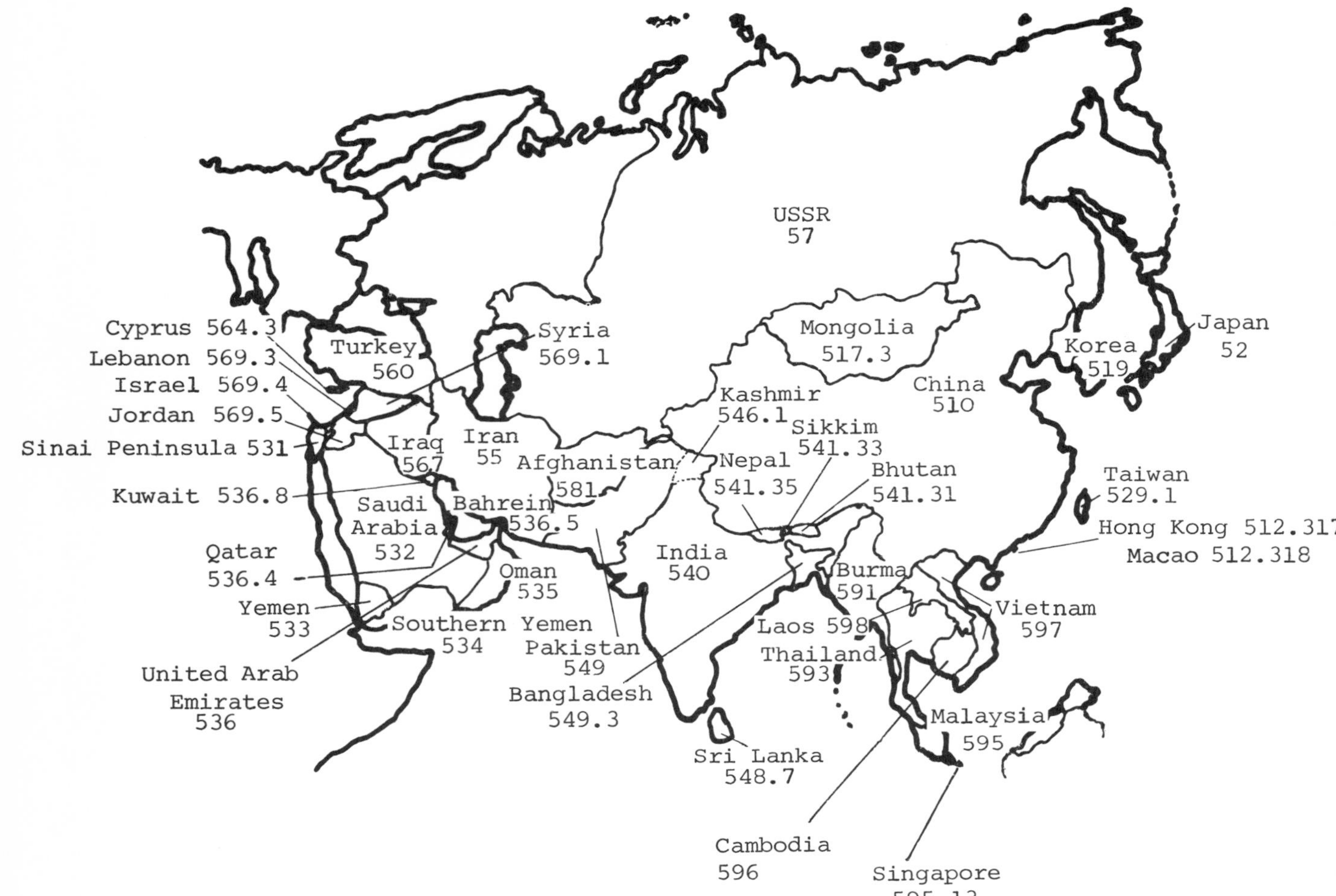

Regions

Asia 5

Near and
Middle East 53

Indian Subcontinent 54

South East Asia 59

Indo China 596/598

Asia

5 Asia

C OFFICIAL SURVEYS

THE WORLD
1:5,000,000
AGS
6 sheets to cover Asia
see WORLD 100C and index 100/3.

INTERNATIONAL MAP OF THE WORLD
1:1,000,000
Various series
see WORLD 100C and index 100/1

D POLITICAL & ADMINISTRATIVE

AZJA
1:30,000,000
Warszawa : PPWK
50 x 40
Small school political map.

AZJA, MAPA FIZYCZNA I POLITYCZNA
1:20,000,000
PPWK, 1972
see ASIA 5 E1

ASIA
Barcelona : Editorial Teide
50 x 33
School hand map showing boundaries and major cities. S. Ptas 2
Also : Asia Politica
(33 x 25) S. Ptas 1

ASIA
No PS 11
Tehran : Sahab
50 x 35
Political student map with physical and location insets and National Flags.
In Persian.

ASIA
1:16,000,000
Tehran : Sahab
60 x 90
Boundaries, settlements with physical, economical, pictorial insets. In Persian.

SUPERIOR WALL MAP OF ASIA
Maplewood : Hammond
97 x 66
Col. political map in folder.
US $2.00

ASIA
Barcelona : Editorial Teide
115 x 88
General school wall map. S. Ptas 275

GENERAL MAP OF ASIA
1:13,500,000
London : Stanford, 1970
91 x 79
Col. politically with road and rail communications and town symbols graded by pop, pictorial border of national crests.
45p

DIE STAATEN ASIENS
1:12,500,000
Darmstadt : Perthes
106 x 115
Haack political col. wall map.
Kleiner Geographischer Wandatlas series.

ASIEN
1:12,000,000
No 4123
Bern : K & F
93 x 72
Political col, relief shading, road and rail communications, airports, oases and pipelines, towns graded by pop. Inset of Australia on smaller scale, pictorial border of national flags.

POLITICAL SMALLER WALL MAP OF ASIA
1:12,000,000
London : Philip
101 x 79
Political col. with railways, shipping routes and towns graded by pop.
Paper flat £1.50
Mounted CR £5.50
Mounted on cloth dissected to fold £7.00

PHILIP'S COMPARATIVE WALL ATLAS OF ASIA – POLITICAL
1:12,000,000
Philip
see ASIA E1

ASIE PHYSIQUE
1:12,000,000
Armand Colin
see ASIA 5 E1

EXCELLO POLITICAL WALL MAP
1:10,625,000
Indianapolis : Cram
116 x 101
Political col. wall map. US $12.50

ASIE
No 22
Paris : Hatier
100 x 120
Political school wall map; with economic map on reverse.

AZJA
1:10,000,000
Warszawa : PPWK, 1972
176 x 119
Political wall map for schools, showing political boundaires, basic communications. Zl 130

POLITICAL MAPS OF ASIA
1:10,000,000
Indianapolis : Cram
129 x 122
Two school wall maps available at different levels and depths.
Level B simplified
Level C Political-physical US $23.00

ASIA : POLITICAL GEOGRAPHY WALL MAP
1:9,375,000
No 107031
Chicago : Denoyer-Geppert
111 x 137
Political col. school wall map, showing boundaries, communications, water features, pop.
CR US $19.25

MAP OF ASIA
1:8,785,000
Michigan : Hearne Bros.
167 x 122
Col. school wall map, political boundaries, relief shading, 'mechanical' tape index.
US $152.50

ASIA
1:8,500,000 app.
Chicago : Rand McNally
119 x 165
Politically col school wall map.

ASIE
1:8,400,000
Bruxelles : Mantnieks
163 x 119
Politically coloured wall map in French. Azimuthal equivalent projection. Available mounted in various styles.

ASIA
1:8,000,000
In 4 sheets
Moskva : GUGK
160 x 160 complete
Col. political map.

ASIA
1:8,000,000
Madrid : Aguilar
190 x 130
Political coloured school wall map.
Paper S. Ptas 100
Cloth S. Ptas 550

ASIE
1:8,000,000
Praha : Kart, 1970
General school wall map of Asia.
Kcs 150

POLITICAL LARGE WALL MAP OF ASIA
1:6,000,000
London : Philip
178 x 168
Col. politically with boundaries, railways, sea routes and towns graded by pop.
Mounted CR £15.00
Mounted on cloth dissected to fold £17.00

AASIA
1:6,000,000
Helsinki : WSOY
196 x 223
School wall map. FMK 100

DAILY TELEGRAPH MAP OF THE MIDDLE EAST, INDIA AND PAKISTAN
1:7,000,000
London : Gia
96 x 69
Political col, principal railways, canals, boundaries, pipelines, ports, points of interest on map. Insets of pop, economy, religion, distances. 45p

OST - UND SUDOSTASIEN
1:6,000,000
Gotha : Haack, 1969
72 x 110
Political col. "hand map" showing boundaries, communications : index separate. With 64pp text. M 7.30
(2nd ed. in prep.)

JIŽNI ASIE
1:5,000,000
Praha : Kart, 1970
General school wall map of Southern Asia
Kcs 150

JIHOZAPADNI ASIE
1:5,000,000
Praha : Kart, 1970
General school wall map of South West Asia. Kcs 98

INDOCHINA, INSULINDIA, JAPON
No scale given
Barcelona : Editorial Teide
33 x 25
School hand map showing major cities and boundaries. S. Ptas 1

ASIA
1:40,000,000
Novara : Agostini
Small hand outline map for schools.
L 40

OUTLINE MAP OF ASIA
1:40,000,000
Moskva : GUGK
In black and white.

ASIA FÍSICA-POLÍTICA MAPA MURAL
1:15,500,000
Barcelona : Ed. Vincens Vives, 1976
126 x 88
Physical, political map printed on plasticised paper. S. Ptas 500

LARGE OUTLINE MAP OF ASIA
1:12,000,000
London : Philip
101 x 79
Printed in black on white cartridge paper, showing contours. £1.25

MAP BUILDING SHEET ('BLACKBOARD MAP') OF ASIA
1:12,000,000
London : Philip
101 x 79
Same as Large Outline Map above but printed in yellow on blackboard paper.
Mounted CR £4.00

ASIE POLITIQUE
Ed. A. Gibert
Map No 11
Paris : Delagrave
125 x 105
Political wall map of Asia with political map of Africa on reverse. F. Fr. 45.00

POLITICAL OUTLINE MAPS OF ASIA
1:10,000,000
Indianapolis : Cram
129 x 122
Boundaries in black and white.
US $27.50
Desk edition available,
size 43 x 30 US $0.60

VITO-GRAPHIC CHALKBOARD OUTLINE MAP OF ASIA
1:7,000,000
Ref VS 5
Chicago : Weber Costello Co
152 x 137
Land areas in green, meridians, parallels and outlines in yellow, water areas in blue. On cloth — various mounted styles.

LERNKARTE VON ASIEN
1:6,000,000
Ed H Haack
Darmstadt : Perthes
185 x 190
Wall map with countries outlined. Chief mountain areas and principal cities indicated. DM 108
Available in "Schuler-handkarte" ed.
30 x 40 DM 1.50

ASIA
1:4,500,000 app.
Chicago : Denoyer-Geppert
102 x 127
Blackboard outline map.

ASIA, OUTLINE SLATED
1:9,375,000
No 165031
Chicago : Denoyer-Geppert
112 x 129
Blackboard map showing countries : blue and yellow on black. US $19.95

VISUAL CONTOUR MAP OF ASIA
London : Philip
28 x 23
Small outline map with principal contours.
25p for ten

E1 PHYSICAL: RELIEF

ASIA
1:40,000,000
Novara : Agostini
33 x 26
Relief map with political map including physical and economic information on the reverse. L 450

ASIA FISICA
Barcelona : Teide
33 x 25
School physical hand map. S. Ptas 1

ASIE
1:30,000,000
Praha : USGK
44 x 44
School physico-political map.

AZJA : MAPA FIZYCZNA I POLITYCZNA
1:20,000,000
Warszawa : PPWK, 1972
68 x 59
Small, school double-sided map: shows relief, hydrography, communications on physical map, political areas on reverse.
Zl 5

AZJA, MAPA FIZYCZNA
1:20,000,000
Warszawa : PPWK, 1972
54 x 52
Physical hand map with contours.
Zl 1

WORLD TRAVEL SERIES MAP OF EURASIA
1:15,000,000
Edinburgh : Bart
90 x 71
Contoured with layer col. showing principal road and rail communications and boundaries, covering the whole of Europe and Asia. 75p

ASIEN
1:12,500,000
Ed H Haack
Darmstadt : Perthes
106 x 115
Physical wall map, showing relief, bathymetry. DM 48

PHYSICAL SMALLER WALL MAP OF ASIA
1:12,000,000
London : Philip
101 x 79
Layer col, with political boundaries in red.
Also available in Arabic.
Paper flat £1.50
Mounted CR £5.50
Mounted on cloth dissected to fold £7.00

GRAPHIC RELIEF MAP OF ASIA
1:12,000,000
London : Philip, 1968
101 x 79
Col. to simulate predominant vegetation cover, producing a three dimensional effect. No town names.
Paper flat £1.50
Mounted CR £5.50
Mounted on cloth dissected to fold £7.00

PHILIP'S COMPARATIVE WALL ATLAS OF ASIA
1:12,000,000
London : Philip
101 x 79 each
A set of five maps for comparative study, comprising:
Relief of Land — Political and Communications
Climate — Summer Conditions, Winter Conditions, Rainfall, Isobars, Winds, Actual Temperature and Sea-Level Isotherms
Natural Vegetation
Political
Density of Population
Single sheets :
Paper flat £1.50
Mounted CR £5.50
Mounted on cloth dissected to fold £7.00
Set of five maps:
Mounted on cloth on split roller £20.00

ASIE (PHYSIQUE)
1:11,000,000
No 1229 Arabic; No 1234 English; No 1065 French
St Germain-en-Laye : Éditions MDI
126 x 92
Plastic coated physical wall map for schools. Agricultural and climate map on reverse.

ASIE PHYSIQUE
Ed. A. Gibert
Map No 10
Paris : Delagrave

125 x 105
Physical wall map of Asia with physical map of Africa on reverse.
F.Fr. 45.00

EXCELLO PHYSICAL WALL MAP
1:10,000,000
Indianapolis : Cram
137 x 100
Physical col. US $12.50

PHYSICAL MAPS OF ASIA
1:10,000,000
Indianapolis : Cram
129 x 129
Two col. school wall maps available at different levels and depths :
Level B simplified
Level C physical-political
US $23.00 each

AZIE
1:10,000,000
Groningen : Wolters-Noordhoff
120 x 90
Physical wall map showing relief and settlements.
Fl. 96.25

TRI-GRAPHIC MAP OF ASIA AND AUSTRALIA
1:10,000,000
Ref TR1-5
Chicago : Weber Costello Co
101 x 137
Physical layer colouring with graphic relief shading and political boundaries.
Available mounted in various styles.

ASIA
1:9,400,000 app.
Chicago : Rand McNally
127 x 173 app
Azimuthal projection, physical col.
Inc. Europe. Available in varying eds. for different age groups .

ASIA : VISUAL RELIEF
1:9,375,000
No 110031
Chicago : Denoyer-Geppert
147 x 111
Physical wall map for schools showing land and sea relief, boundaries etc.
US $18.75
Reduced size as Desk Map, No. 301531, 28 x 43 US $3.30 per 25 copies

ASIA
1:9,375,000
No 130031-10
Chicago : Denoyer-Geppert
147 x 111
Classroom physical-political map showing land detail, boundaries, pop.
Rollers US $15.50

ASIA
1:8,500,000
Chicago : Rand McNally
114 x 165
Merged relief school wall map, available in simplified or advanced eds. Azimuthal projection. Simplified version includes Arctic ocean, Greenland, unexplored ice-packs. Advanced ed. includes Kamchatka, Kuroshio and other currents.

ASIA – FIZICHESKAYA KARTA
1:8, 000, 000
In 4 sheets
Moskva : GUGK
160 x 160 complete

ASIA
1:8,000,000
Madrid : Aguilar
190 x 130
Physical school wall map with hypsometric tints and altitudes indicated.
Paper S. Ptas 100
Cloth S. Ptas 550

ASIE
1:8,000,000
In 4 sheets
Praha : KN, 1970
Physical school wall map.

ASIEN
1:8,000,000
In 4 sheets
København : GI
162 x 151
Elevation and depth indicated by 13 col. variations. Available with or without names.
D.Kr.100.00

AZSIA
1:8,000,000
In 4 sheets
Budapest : Cart
166 x 175
Physical col. school wall map.

ASIA : FISCO-POLITICA
1:8,000,000
Novara : Agostini
140 x 155
2 sheet school wall map, showing state boundaries, relief of land and sea, water features, cities graded by pop.
First series L 3,000
Mounted L 6,500
Second series:
1:7,000,000 (In 4 sheets) 160 x 214
L 4,000
Mounted L 8,500
Third series:
1:10,000,000 100 x 140
L 2,200
Mounted L 5,000

AZJA
1:7,000,000
Warszawa : PPWK, 1972
160 x 190
Physical school wall map, showing relief by contours, hypsometric tints, bathymetry, land resources, water features, communications, political boundaries. Zl 130

AZIJA
1:7,000,000
In 4 sheets
Beograd : Geokarta
145 x 138
Wall map with cyrillic and latin lettering.
Mounted cloth Dn 150.00

ASIE
1:6,500,000
Bruxelles : Mantnieks
183 x 180
Physical wall map for schools, showing relief by layer and bathymetric colouring, water features, ocean currents, political boundaries in red. Also available in English, Dutch and Spanish.

PHYSICAL LARGE WALL MAP OF ASIA
1:6,000,000
London : Philip
178 x 168
Physically col. with hill shading, political boundaries, railways and ocean routes.
Mounted CR £15.00
Mounted on cloth dissected to fold
£17.00

ASIA (EURASIA)
1:6,000,000
Braunschweig : Westermann
210 x 225
Physical col. wall map, showing major towns, communications, bathymetry, relief.
Available in Eng. Fr. Ger. eds.

ASIEN
1:6,000,000
Ed H Haack
Darmstadt : Perthes, 1967
180 x 217
Physical col. wall map for schools. Covering Asia and Europe. Relief shown by layer col., ocean depths, boundaries, main physical features. DM 132

ASIEN
1:6,000,000
No 9741
Munchen : JRO
200 x 180
School physical wall map with "Arbeitskarte" (work map). 2 col. base map with plastic writing surface on reverse. DM 148
No 9742, as above, without "Arbeitskarte"
DM 138

EURASIEN (MIT MEERESBODEN–RELIEF)
1:6,000,000
Munchen : List
210 x 215
Wenschow wall map, showing relief of land and sea in col, ocean currents, names etc., Shows land types and communications.
Eng and Fr eds. also available.

ASIEN
1:6,000,000
Munchen : List
200 x 220
Harms wall map showing relief of land and sea, ocean currents.

ASIE
1:6,000,000
Praha : USGK
77 x 106
Physical school wall map.

VISUAL RELIEF MAP OF ASIA
1:4,500,000 app.
Chicago : Denoyer-Geppert
102 x 127
Bold col. relief map. Also available in desk size map.

SOUTH ASIA AND THE MIDDLE EAST VISUAL RELIEF
1:5.000.000
No 123821-10
Chicago : Denoyer-Geppert
162 x 137
School wall map showing relief of land and sea, cities classified by pop, boundaries, etc.
Rollers US $22.25

JIŽNÍ, ASIE
1:5,000,000
In 2 sheets

Praha : KN, 1970
Physical wall map of South Asia.

SREDNYAYA AZIYA
1:5,000,000
Moskva : GUGK
Physical wall map of Central Asia

OST- UND SUDOST ASIEN
1:4,000,000
Braunschweig : Westermann
182 x 202
Col. physical wall map covering E and SE Asia; relief shading, political boundaries, cities graded by pop, communications. Eng, Fr, Ger, eds.

SUD-ASIEN
1:4,000,000
Munchen : List
233 x 172
Wenschow physical wall map of Southern Asia, showing relief, communications, boundaries.

EAST ASIA, VISUAL RELIEF
1:4,000,000
No 123801-10
Chicago : Denoyer-Geppert
162 x 137
Col. school wall map, showing relief of land and sea, cities graded by pop, boundaries.
Rollers US $21.75

SUDWESTASIEN
1:3,500,000
Eds Haack-Painke
Darmstadt : Perthes
210 x 175
Physical wall map, relief col. and shaded, communications. Including India, Arabia, N E Africa, Turkey and southern USSR.

SUDOSTASIEN, CHINA UND JAPAN
1:3,500,000
Eds Haack - Painke
Darmstadt : Perthes
210 x 230
Physical wall map, relief col. and shaded, communications. Including Indonesia.

CENTRAL ASIA
1:1,500,000
In 4 sheets
Moskva : GUGK
174 x 116
Russian physical map with contours.

RAISED RELIEF MAP OF ASIA
1:20,000,000
New York : Hagstrom
68 x 50
3-D plastic relief map US $2.95

RAISED RELIEF MAP OF ASIA
1:10,727,000
NR3
Chicago : Nystrom, 1975
112 x 98
Plastic moulded map, physical layer colouring, principal communications and boundaries.
Unframed US $46.00
Framed US $74.00

ASIA FISICO-POLITICA
1:10,000,000
Novara : Agostini
100 x 131
Plastic relief map, in frame with metal corners. L 20,000

PHYSICAL OUTLINE MAP OF ASIA
1:10,000,000
Indianapolis : Cram
129 x 129
Black and white map with contours.
US $27.50

F GEOLOGY

GEOLOGICAL MAP OF ASIA AND THE FAR EAST
1:5,000,000
2nd edition, in 4 sheets
Geneva : UN/ECAFE, 1971
97 x 69 each
Covers India, China, Japan, SE Asia - W. Irian. Shows age and composition of igneous and volcanic rocks. With legend and explanatory text (100pp).
Complete £5.63

G EARTH RESOURCES

MINERAL DISTRIBUTION MAP OF ASIA AND THE FAR EAST
1:5,000,000
In 4 sheets
Geneva : UN/ECAFE, 1963
97 x 69 each
Col. map showing location of minerals by symbols on col. geol. base map, covering Afghanistan, India, China, Japan and South East Asia, extending east to West Irian, with explanatory text.

OIL AND NATURAL GAS MAP OF ASIA AND THE FAR EAST
1:5,000,000
In 4 sheets
Geneva : UN/ECAFE, 1962
97 x 69 each
Col. to show simplified geol. emphasising sedimentary deposits with oil and gas fields classified according to production, wells, pipelines and refineries, covering Afghanistan, India, Pakistan, China, Japan and South East Asia east to include West Irian.

H BIOGEOGRAPHY

ASIA, VEGETATION AND LAND USE
1:16,000,000
No 70
Tehran : Sahab
60 x 90
Showing variety of vegetation and cultivation, irrigation, pasture, oases, forest.
In Persian and English Rls 80

PHILIP'S COMPARATIVE WALL ATLAS OF ASIA - NATURAL VEGETATION
1:12,000,000
Philip
see ASIA E1

AZIYA KARTA RASTITEL'NOSTI
1:8,000,000
In 4 sheets
Moskva : GUGK, 1970
160 x 160 complete
Vegetation map.

ASIEN - VEGETATIONSBILDKARTE
No 9913
Munchen : JRO
130 x 88
Picture wall map of vegetation.
DM 48

ASIEN BODENNUTZUNGBILDKARTE
No 9915
Munchen : JRO
130 x 88
Picture wall map of land use. DM 48

ASIEN : MENSCHEN, HAUSTIERE UND NUTZPFLANZEN
Westermann
see ASIA 5K

ASIEN : WILDTIERE UND WILDPFLANZEN
Braunschweig : Westermann
137 x 160
Pictorial wall map of wild animals and plants.
English edition published by Denoyer-Geppert.

TIERWELT
No 9914
Munchen : JRO
130 x 88
Picture wall map showing the animal world of Asia. DM 48

J CLIMATE

ASIA
1:17,500,000
No 110031
Chicago : Denoyer-Geppert
111 x 162
4 thematic maps on 1 sheet including two showing climate (13 types) and annual precipitation. US $15.50

ASIEN, KLIMA UND VEGETATION
1:15,000,000
Ed H Haack
Darmstadt : Perthes
254 x 158
Wall map showing January and July temperatures, annual rainfall, vegetation types. 4 maps on 1 sheet.

ASIEN, KLIMA UND VEGETATION
1:15,000,000
Braunschweig : Westermann
250 x 190
Col. wall map for schools showing climate and vegetation. DM 142

PHILIP'S COMPARATIVE WALL ATLAS OF ASIA - CLIMATE
1:12,000,000
Philip
see ASIA E1

ASIE (PHYSIQUE)
1:11, 000, 000
Editions MDI
Includes climatic information
see ASIA 5 E1

K HUMAN GEOGRAPHY

PHILIP'S COMPARATIVE WALL ATLAS OF ASIA - DENSITY OF POPULATION
1:12,000,000
Philip
see ASIA E1

AZIYA : KARTA NARODOV
1:8,000,000
In 4 sheets
Moskva : GUGK
160 x 160 complete
Pop. map

ASIA
No 109031
Chicago : Denoyer-Geppert
111 x 162
4 thematic maps on 1 sheet including one showing population density.
US $15.50

CARTE PERNET : ASIE, POPULATION, ETATS
Paris : Hachette
School political wall map with pop. indicated.

ASIEN : MENSCHEN, HAUSTIERE UND NUTZPFLANZEN
Braunschweig : Westermann
137 x 160
Pictorial wall map of peoples, domestic animals and cultivated plants.
English edition by Denoyer-Geppert
US $5.00

ASIA, ECONOMIC
Indianapolis : Cram
School wall map, showing population density, nat. langs, education, literacy, government, religion. US $13.75

BREASTED-HUTH-HARDING HISTORY MAP - ASIAN RELIGIONS
No 204581
Chicago : Denoyer-Geppert
Col. map showing origin and spread of religions also modern distribution.

AUSBREITUNG DES ISLAM
1:4,300,000
Bielefeld : Cornelsen, Velhagen and Klasing
194 x 138
Putzger historical wall map showing the spread of Islam.

L ECONOMIC

ASIEN - WIRTSCHAFT
1:8,000,000
Munchen : List
160 x 120
Harms wall map, showing economy by symbols.

HOSPODARSKA MAPA ASIE
1:6,000,000
Praha : USGK
114 x 76
School economic wall map.

CARTE PERNET : ASIE OCCIDENTALE : ÉCONOMIE
Paris : Hachette
Economic wall map of W Asia

ASIA
No 109031
Chicago : Denoyer-Geppert
111 x 162
4 thematic maps on 1 sheet including one showing economic activities.
US $15.50

ASIEN : WIRTSCHAFT UND VERKEHR
Braunschweig : Westermann
137 x 160
Pictorial wall map of economy and communications.
English edition by Denoyer-Geppert
US $5.00

ASIE (PHYSIQUE)
1:11,000,000
Editions MDI
Includes agricultural information.
see ASIA 5E1

ASIA, POLITICAL
Indianapolis : Cram
School wall map showing agriculture, trade, minerals and petroleum. US $13.75

ASIA - VERWALTUNG, WIRTSCHAFT UND VERKEHR
No 9916
Munchen : JRO
130 x 88
Picture wall map showing administration, economy and communications.
DM 48

M HISTORICAL

HISTORY MAPS
Indianapolis : Cram
School wall maps showing:
Palestine 1025-722 BC and time of Christ
Persian Empire about 500 BC
Campaign and Empire of Alexander
Mohammedan Conquests at their height 750 AD
Europe and the Near East in 1519
Christians and Mohammedans in 1600
Europe and the Near East, 1740
World War II, Pacific Theater
Each US $13.75

PALMER WORLD HISTORY MAPS
Chicago : Rand McNally
Maps available:
Eastern and Southern Asia about 750 AD
Asia at the death of Kublai Khan
Eastern and Southern Asia about 1775
Asia 1900
Asia after World War II

BREASTED-HUTH-HARDING HISTORICAL WALL MAPS - ASIA
No 204531
Chicago : Denoyer-Geppert
112 x 81
Shows new political states, cities, sea routes, railways etc.

HISTORICAL WALL MAPS
Moskva : GUGK
Drevneyi Vostok, Indiya i Kitai, (Ancient East India and China)
1:5,000,000
Drevneyi Vostok, Perednaya Asiya i Egepet (Ancient East, Asian Peninsula and Egypt), 1973
1:3,000,000

AZ ÓKORI KELET IDŐSZÁMITÁSUNK KEZDETÉIG (THE ANCIENT ORIENT UP TO THE BEGINNING OF OUR ERA)
Budapest : Kart, 1970
2 sheet historical wall map with inset of Egypt and Mesopotamia up to 4th C BC.

CARTES HISTORIQUES
J Bouillon
Various scales
St Germain-en-Laye : Éditions MDI
92 x 126
Series of plastic coated, double-sided historical wall maps for schools.
1500 L'Égypte des Pharaons - Le Proche-Orient (Near East) Ancien
1502 L'Empire d'Alexandre 1:4,680,000
1516 Les Croisades 1:5,000,000

BREASTED-HUTH-HARDING HISTORICAL MAP - FAR EAST IN 1895
No 204571
Chicago : Denoyer-Geppert
Col. map showing southern and eastern Asia during period of colonialism's greatest expansion.

ASIA - FACSIMILE MAPS
Wien : Editio Totius Mundi
Maps available:
No 3 Asia by W Blaeuw, 1636, 55 x 41
col. DM 35
uncol. DM 25
860 Near East, Persia, Armenia, Anatolia, Arabia, F de Wit, 1673, 56 x 48
col. DM 38
216 Arabia with Persia, P.v.d.Aa, 1729 15 x 10
col. DM 2

ATLASES
G EARTH RESOURCES

ENERGY ATLAS OF ASIA AND THE FAR EAST
New York : UN, 1970
46 x 37
Atlas of energy sources and supplies in Asia (excluding USSR), 25 map sheets in colour, 3pp text.

ATLASES
M HISTORICAL

HISTORICAL ATLAS OF THE FAR EAST IN MODERN TIMES
Michael P Onorato
Chicago : Denoyer-Geppert
22 x 28
32pp
Black and white maps covering history of India, China, Japan and S E Asia from 1500 to the present day. For schools.
US $1.50

HISTORICAL ATLAS OF ASIA
Tokyo : Heibonsha
18 x 26
320pp
Covers Africa and Asia from prehistoric times to the 1960s. 148pp col. maps. In Japanese. Y 7,000

SOUTH ASIA IN MAPS
R C Kingsbury
Chicago : Denoyer-Geppert
21 x 28
96pp
Black and white maps covering history, physical features, etc.
US $1.50

510 China

B TOWN PLANS

TOURIST MAP OF PEKING
Peking : People's Publishing House, 1972
Showing places of interest and principal streets named.

D POLITICAL & ADMINISTRATIVE

ZHONGHUA RENMIN GONGHEGUO DITU
1:6,000,000
Peking : Peoples' Publishing House, 1975
100 x 68
Political map of the Peoples' Republic of China, provinces in colour, principal roads and railways. Names in pinyin (latin script)

CHINA
1:5,500,000
Budapest : Cart, Stockholm, Esselte, 1967
106 x 78
Political map showing internal admin. divisions, cities graded by pop. Industry, population and nationality maps inset. With separate index of 6000 names, glossary in English, German, French, Russian.

CINA A MONGOLSKO
1:5,000,000
Praha : Kart, 1969
General wall map of China and Mongolia, Kcs 120

CHINE : PHYSIQUE ET AGRICOLE
1:5,000,000
Armand Colin
see CHINA 51 E1

CHINE No 2 (AGRICOLE)
1:4,500,000
Editions : MDI
see CHINA 51 L

ZHONGHAUREMINGONGHEGUO DITU (MAP OF PEOPLES' REPUBLIC OF CHINA)
1:4,000,000
Peking : Peoples' Publishing House, 1971
163 x 114
General political map, showing provinces in colour, communications network, major geog. places. Legend in Chinese.

CHINA COAST AND KOREA
1:3,437,500
Washington : NGS
64 x 107
Political col. wall map, boundaries in colour, towns and settlement in detail.
Paper US $2.00
Plastic US $3.00

CHINA
No scale given
Barcelona : Editorial Teide
33 x 25
School hand map, showing boundaries, major cities. S. Ptas 1

E1 PHYSICAL: RELIEF

CINA - MONGOLSKO
1:6,000,000
Praha : Kart, 1967
91 x 90
Physical with contours, boundaries, thematic insets and legend on reverse. With 53pp text, inc. index. In series "Poznavame Svet" (Getting to know the World) Kcs 16.50

CHINE, PHYSIQUE ET AGRICOLE
1:5,000,000
Map No 352
Paris : Armand Colin
120 x 100
Physical and agricultural school wall map with political and industrial map on reverse.

KITAI, MONGOL'SKAYA NARODNAYA RESPUBLIKA, KOREYA
1:5,000,000
Moskva : GUGK, 1968
124 x 100
2 sheet physical wall map of China, Mongolian Peoples' Republic, Korea. Contours, railways.

REGIONAL WALL MAP OF CHINA
1:5,000,000
London : Philip
117 x 91
Physically col. with communications, boundaries and towns graded by pop.
Paper £1.50
Mounted CR £5.50
Mounted on cloth dissected to fold £7.00

BARTHOLOMEW'S WORLD SERIES TRAVEL MAP OF CHINA
1:4,500,000
Edinburgh : Barts
91 x 71
Contoured with layer col, principal roads and rail communications, towns, villages, airports etc. 75p

CHINE No 1 (PHYSIQUE)
1:4,500,000
No 1190
St Germain-en-Laye : Éditions MDI
126 x 92
Plastic coated physical wall map for schools. Map of mines and industry on reverse.

CHINE
1:4,500,000
TC 42 (No 1611)
St Germain-en-Laye : Éditions MDI
126 x 92
Plastic coated physical wall map for schools. On reverse physical map of USA.

VOLKSREPUBLIK CHINA
1:3,000,000
Darmstadt : Perthes
217 x 163
Haack wall map; physical col, with boundaries, communications and settlements.
Mounted CR DM 142

F GEOLOGY

GEOLOGICAL MAP OF ASIA AND THE FAR EAST
1:5,000,000
UN (ECAFE), 1971
see ASIA 5F

GEOLOGIC MAP OF THE REPUBLIC OF CHINA
1:4,000,000
Taipei : Chinese Petroleum Corp, 1970
154 x 113
Coloured general geological map, with provinces marked. Text in Chinese and English in margin. US $10.00

GEOLOGICAL MAP OF CHINA
1:3,000,000
2nd edition
Peking : Min. of Geol, 1960
Col. geol. map.

GEOLOGIC MAP OF CHINA AND MANCHURIA
1:250,000
In 115 sheets approx.
Tokyo : Compilation Committee, Geol. Min. Resources Far East c/o Tokyo Geographical Society
Coloured geological series in progress covering Northern China and Manchuria only.

G EARTH RESOURCES

MINERAL DISTRIBUTION MAP OF ASIA AND THE FAR EAST
1:5,000,000
UN (ECAFE), 1963
see ASIA 5G

OIL AND NATURAL GAS MAP OF ASIA AND THE FAR EAST
1:5,000,000
UN (ECAFE), 1962
see ASIA 5G

L ECONOMIC

KITAI, MONGOL'SKAYA NARODNAYA RESPUBLIKA, KOREYA EKONOMICHESKAYA KARTA
1:5,000,000
Moskva : GUGK, 1968
125 x 98
2 sheet economic wall map of China, Mongolian Peoples' Republic, Korea.

CHINE No 1 (PHYSIQUE)
1:4,500,000
Editions MDI
see CHINA 51 E1

CHINA, BERGBAU UND INDUSTRIE
1:3,000,000
Gotha : Haack, 1968
217 x 163
Haack wall map showing mining and industry by symobls. Cities graded by pop.

M HISTORICAL

CHINA VOM MANDSCHUREICH ZUR VOLKSREPUBLIK
1:6,000,000
Hamburg : Flemming
188 x 142
Historical wall map showing China from the Manchu Empire to the Peoples' Republic. 4 maps on 1 sheet : Expansion and Decline of the Manchu Empire; Disintegration of the Manchu Empire; China and the Ascendancy of Japan in the Pacific Area (1910-1943); Peoples' Republic of China, 1934+.

CHINA (1945)
1:6,875,000
Washington : NGS
94 x 67
Political col. wall map
Paper US $2.00
Plastic US $3.00

BREASTED -HUTH-HARDING HISTORICAL WALL MAPS
Various scales
Chicago : Denoyer Geppert
112 x 81
204591 Expansion and Decline of Manchu Power, 1644-1864
204601 Disintegration of Manchu Power, 1865-1905
204611 China : Japanese Domination in the Pacific World, 1905-1945
204621 The Peoples' Republic of China

ATLASES
D POLITICAL AND ADMINISTRATIVE

COMMUNIST CHINA ADMINISTRATIVE ATLAS
Washington : US Central Intelligency Agency, 1969
22 coloured map plates, illustrating admin. data.

L'ATLAS POLITIQUE DE LA CHINE
Paris : Bordas
In preparation.

ATLASES
E1 PHYSICAL

ATLAS OF THE REPUBLIC OF CHINA
Ed Dr Chang Chi-yun
In 5 vols
Taiwan : The National War College
27 x 38
Arranged by administrative districts and covered by physical and political plate with many towns inset. Lettering in Chinese and English.
Vol. I Taiwan, 1972, 58pp maps
II Hsitsang (Tibet), Sinkiang and Mongolia, 1964, 22pp maps
III North China, 1966, 37pp maps
IV South China, 1964, 26pp maps
V General Maps of China, 1967, 23pp maps

SVEN HEDIN CENTRAL ASIA ATLAS
1:1,000,000-1:500,000
Sino-Swedish Expedition Pub'n.
47 (1.1)
Stockholm : Sven Hedins Stiftelse (Sven Hedin Foundation)
23 x 29
13 maps of Central Asia - AMS editions from data supplied by expedition and other sources, with additional 1:500,000 topog. map NK 47 VIII-XII d-h and 5 Reconnaissance Triangulation Charts. Contained in filing box.
S.Kr. 255.00
Memoirs
Vol. I Records on Surveys 1967
Paper S.Kr. 96.00
Bound S.Kr. 111.00
II Index of Geographic Names 1967
Paper S.Kr. 78.00
Bound S.Kr. 93.00
III Parts 1-3 in preparation

ATLASES
M HISTORICAL

AN HISTORICAL ATLAS OF CHINA
by A Herrmann
New edition by N Ginsburg and P Wheatley
Chicago : Aldine Pub. Co/Edinburgh UP, 1966
xxxii, 88pp
22 x 29
New ed. of 1935 atlas, 65pp col. maps, covering archaeology, anthropology, economics, culture, minerals, industry. Insets and plans of ancient cities, index of geog. and proper names. List of Chinese characters, bibliog.

HISTORICAL AND CULTURAL ATLAS OF CHINA
Special Publication No.1
1st edition
Ed Prof Chen Cheng-siang
Hong Kong. Int. Comm. for China Studies 1974-76
49 x 39
Collection of 150 black and white maps scale 1:900,000. In Chinese and English.
Each US $1.00

ATLASES
O NATIONAL

THE TIMES ATLAS OF CHINA
Editors: Prof D C Twitchett and P J M Geelan
London : Times Books, 1974
27 x 38
232pp
Includes 109pp of coloured maps and 67pp of explanatory text covering China's geography, history and socio-economic structure. Index of 20,000 names.
£25.00

RAND McNALLY ILLUSTRATED ATLAS OF CHINA
Chicago : Rand McNally, 1972
23 x 37
77pp
The country is divided into 6 geographical regions each illustrated by a 1:4,600,000 physical map with descriptive text and photographs. Followed by maps and text covering various subjects including cultural, economic and historical matters and a section on Peking. Indexed.
Paper covers US $4.95

CHINA IN MAPS
London : Philip, 1975
28 x 22
25pp
Aspects of the country's history and economy. Inc. a 4pp physical map of the country with separate plates on communications and world trade.
80p

ATLAS OF NEW CHINA
Special Publication No.4
1st edition
Ed Prof Chen Cheng-siang
Hong Kong : Int. Comm. for China Studies, 1976
33 x 45
Collection of approx. 120 thematic maps of China, generally scale 1:10.000,000. In Chinese and English. Publication in progress.
Each sheet US $0.50

PEOPLES' REPUBLIC OF CHINA ATLAS
Washington : US Central Intelligence Agency, 1971
82pp
51pp geog. economic, historical maps, also photos and diagrams, enables comparison of China with US.
US $5.25

COMMUNIST CHINA MAP FOLIO
Washington : Office Basic and Geog. Intelligence, 1967
17 regional maps at 1:4,500,000 with 12 explanatory texts, compiled from data 1949-1965 covering various economic and political aspects of the country.

HEIBONSHA ATLAS OF CHINA
Tokyo : Heibonsha
23 x 29
64pp
15pp of coloured maps including China as a whole at 1.16 million with principal districts at 1:4-10 million with detailed maps of urban areas. Names in western modern Chinese characters and their Japanese readings. Y 750

512.317 Hong Kong

A1 GENERAL MAPS

HONG KONG
1:300,000
DOS 965
Tolworth : DOS
General hand map depicting principal towns and communications. 10p

HONG KONG AND THE NEW TERRITORIES
1:50,000
HK1
2nd edition
Hong Kong: CLSO, 1972
Topog. map in col. Dual lang. ed, available in 2 sheets or printed both sides.
US $3.00

HONG KONG ISLAND
1:25,000
Countryside Series No 1
Hong Kong : CLSO, 1972
63 x 48
In Chi. and Eng. Insets of Peak area at 1:6,250, Aberdeen Reservoir area at 1:12,500 and Tai Tam Reservoir at 1:12,500 on reverse. All maps show roads and bus routes, notes on Island walks.
US $2.00

B TOWN PLANS

HONG KONG OFFICIAL GUIDE MAP
1:10,000
Hong Kong : CLSO, 1972
57 x 85
Coloured town plan, with street index in margin. Physical map on reverse. In Chinese and English. US $3.00

MOSAIC OF URBAN AREAS
1:6,000
In 12 sheets
Hong Kong : CLSO, 1963-4
Air photos.
Per set US $87.50

C OFFICIAL SURVEYS

HONG KONG AND NEW TERRITORIES
1:100,000
Prepared by DMS, Series L681
Hong Kong : CLSO, 1972
69 x 37
2 sheet map, contours, roads classified, railways, vegetation; covers Hong Kong, New Territories, Lema Is. US $3.00

HONG KONG AND THE NEW TERRITORIES
1:25,000
DOS 331 (L882)
In 20 sheets, see index 512. 317/1
Tolworth : DOS, 1969-70
Topog. series, contoured with roads, railways, boundaries and other land detail.

MOSAIC OF WHOLE COLONY
1:25,000
In 12 sheets
Hong Kong : CLSO, 1963-4
Air photos.
Per set US $120.00

HONG KONG TOPOGRAPHICAL SERIES
1:20,000
Series HM20C, In 16 Sheets, see index 512. 317/2
Hong Kong : CLSO
75 x 60
Coloured series, contoured, detailed topographical information. Names and legend in Chinese and English. Series in progress.

HONG KONG AND THE NEW TERRITORIES
1:10,000
DOS 231 (L884)
In 62 sheets, see index 512. 317/1
Hong Kong : CLSO, 1968-70
Topographical series, contoured, communications, land detail.

SURVEY PLANS OF THE NEW TERRITORIES AND ISLANDS
Various scales
Hong Kong : CLSO
Plans in black and white. Available in the following editions :

1:12,000	In 1200 sheets	US $3.00
1:48,000	In 46 sheets	US $3.00
1:96,000	In 11 sheets	US $3.00

SURVEY PLANS OF HONG KONG ISLAND, KOWLOON AND NEW TERRITORIES
Various scales
Hong Kong: CLSO
Topog. series in black and white. Available in the following editions :

1:600	In 700 sheets app.	US S3.00 ea.
1:2,400	In 60 sheets	US S3.00
1:4,800	In 14 sheets (highly developed Urban areas only)	US $3.00
1:7,920	In 7 sheets	US $3.00
1:15,840	In 2 sheets	US $3.00

D POLITICAL & ADMINISTRATIVE

APPROVED TOWN PLANNING DEVELOPMENT AND LAYOUT PLANS OF HONG KONG ISLAND, KOWLOON, NEW KOWLOON AND THE NEW TERRITORIES (INC. ISLANDS)
Various scales
Hong Kong : CLSO
Available : black and white and white plans US $3.00
Col. plans US $25.00
Col. plan and booklet US $8-12.00
Land Utilization in HK 31.3.66, 1:100,000 US $15.00
Density Zoning plans of HK and K - 2 sheets US $3.00 set
Height Restrictions HK Island US $3.00
Height Restrictions HK Island (in col.) US $20.00
Height Restrictions Kowloon US $3.00
Height Restrictions Kowloon (in col.) US $20.00

F GEOLOGY

INTERIM GEOLOGICAL MAPS
1:75,000
Hong Kong : CLSO
1 sheet geol. map US $3.00

INTERIM GEOLOGICAL MAPS
1:25,000
In 17 sheets
Hong Kong : CLSO US $3.00

H BIOGEOGRAPHY

LAND UTILISATION IN HONG KONG AS AT 31st MARCH 1966
1:80,000
by T R Tregear
Hong Kong : CLSO
Col. map with booklet. US $5.00
Separate gazetteer to this map is available, 108pp, 24 x 17, 1958.

FUNCTIONAL LAND USE IN THE URBAN AREA OF HONG KONG
1:27,500 app.
Hong Kong : CLSO, 1967
64 x 45
Coloured land use map.

K HUMAN GEOGRAPHY

DISTRIBUTION OF POPULATION IN HONG KONG, 1966
1:100,000 app.
Hong Kong : CLSO, 1967
64 x 45
Showing urban and rural pop. by coloured dots. Based on 1966 Census.

POPULATION DENSITY IN THE URBAN AREAS OF HONG KONG
1:32,000
Hong Kong : Govt. Publications, 1967
64 x 45
Black and white map showing pop.

POPULATION DISTRIBUTION IN THE URBAN AREAS OF HONG KONG
1:32,000 app.
Hong Kong : Govt. Publications, 1967
64 x 45
Black and white pop. map, based on 1966 Census.

LAND CENSUS PLAN, 1961
No scale given
In 2 sheets
Hong Kong : CLSO
Sheets available :
1 Hong Kong, Kowloon and New Kowloon
2 New Territories
US $0.50 each

MARINE CENSUS MAP
No scale given
Hong Kong : CLSO
Marine population plotted by col. dots.
Based on 1961 Census. US $0.50

M HISTORICAL

ARCHAEOLOGICAL MAP OF
HONG KONG
Hong Kong : CLSO
Sites of historical interest marked by
symbols. US $4.00

ATLASES
L ECONOMIC

A SOCIO-ECONOMIC ATLAS OF
HONG KONG
Research Report 20
1st edition
Ed Prof Chen Cheng-siang
Hong Kong : Geographical Research Centre,
1967
78 x 55
Collection of approx. 88 coloured thematic
maps. In Chinese and English.
Each US $0.60-1.85

512.318 Macao

C OFFICIAL SURVEYS

THE WORLD
1:500,000
DMS Series 1404
Sheet 614A covers Macao.
see WORLD 100C and index 100/7.

517.3 Mongolia

D POLITICAL & ADMINISTRATIVE

CINA A MONGOLSKO
1:5,000,000
Kart, 1969
see CHINA 51 D

E1 PHYSICAL: RELIEF

CINA A MONGOLSKO
1:6,000,000
Kart, 1967
see CHINA 51 E1

KITAI, MONGOL'SKAYA NARODNAYA RESPUBLIKA, KOREYA
1:5,000,000
GUGK
see also KOREA

A SZOVJETUNIO ES MONGOLIA (THE SOVIET UNION AND MONGOLIA)
1:5,000,000
Budapest : Kart, 1969
Geog. wall map.

WORLD TRAVEL SERIES MAP OF CHINA
1:4,500,000
Edinburgh : Barts
see also KOREA

MONGOL'SKAYA NARODNAYA RESP.
1:3,000,000
Moskva : GUGK, 1966
85 x 51
Contours, relief shading, communications. 2 insets of economy and climate at 1:12,000,000. In Russian.

G EARTH RESOURCES

MONGOLIA, MINERALS
1:5,000,000
Budapest : Kart, 1971
Wall map showing mineral distribution by symbols.

L ECONOMIC

KITAI, MONGOL'SKAYA NARODNAYA RESPUBLIKA, KOREYA
EKONOMICHESKAYA KARTA
1:5,000,000
GUGK
see also KOREA

ATLASES
E1 PHYSICAL

ATLAS OF THE REPUBLIC OF CHINA VOL II HSITSANG (TIBET), SINKIANG AND MONGOLIA
Ed Dr Chang Chi-yun
Taiwan : National War College, 1964
see CHINA ATLASES 51 E1

519 Korea

A1 GENERAL MAPS: ROADS

TOURIST MAP OF KOREA
1:800,000
Seoul : Bureau of Tourism
80 x 104
Roads and railways classified; sites of interest; large scale regional insets on reverse, with plan of Seoul.

KOREA ROAD MAP
1:700,000
Washington : Defense Mapping Agency
1970
88 x 112 each
2 sheet road map of N and S Korea. Contours, roads classified, railways, boundaries; also in Eng. US $1.00 each

B TOWN PLANS

OFFICIAL PLAN OF SEOUL
1:37,000
Seoul : Bureau of Tourism
Plan of the city naming principal streets and buildings.

D POLITICAL & ADMINISTRATIVE

CHINA COAST AND KOREA
1:3,437,500
Washington : NGS
see CHINA 51D

JAPONSKO A KOREA
1:2,500,000
Kart, 1969
see JAPAN 52D

JAPAN AND KOREA
1:1,375,000
Washington : NGS
see JAPAN 52D

KOREA
1:1,000,000
New York : Geographia
68 x 104
Political col. map, roads, railways, relief shown by hachures. Asia inset.

E1 PHYSICAL: RELIEF

KITAI, MONGOL'ESKAYA NARODNAYA RESPUBLIKA, KOREYA
1:5,000,000
GUGK, 1968
see CHINA 51 E1

WORLD TRAVEL SERIES MAP OF CHINA
1:4,500,000
Edinburgh : Bart
see CHINA 51 E1

JAPONSKO A KOREA
1:3,000,000
Kart, 1969
see JAPAN 52 E1

KOREA
1:1,500,000
Moskva : GUGK, 1973
Hand map with contours, communications, boundaries, legend in Russian.

F GEOLOGY

GEOLOGICAL MAP OF KOREA
1:1,000,000
Seoul : Geol. Survey Korea, 1956
90 x 122
Col. map in Eng and Korean.

GEOLOGIC MAP OF TAEBAEGSAN REGION
1:50,000
Geol. Investigation Corps of Taebaegsan
In 17 sheets
Seoul : Geol. Soc. Korea, 1962
Col. map showing ore deposits and sections. Accompanying "Report on the Geol. and Mineral Resources of the Taebaegsan Region for the Geol. Survey of Korea" by Y Choi et al. 89pp in English.

GEOLOGICAL ATLAS OF KOREA
1:50,000
Approx 817 sheets
Seoul : Geol. Survey of Korea, 1963+
46 x 38
Col. geol. series with sections and explanatory notes in Korean with English summaries. Mineral deposits also shown.

G EARTH RESOURCES

RECONNAISSANCE SOIL MAP OF KOREA
1:250,000
In 4 sheets
Seoul : Korea Soil Survey and Inst. of Plant Environment
75 x 108
Col. soil map in Korean and English.
W.605

GENERAL SOIL MAP OF CHUNG CHONG NAM DO
1:250,000
Seoul : Inst. of Plant Environment
78 x 83
Col. map with 4 insets. In Korean and English. Not on public sale.

GENERAL SOIL MAP OF CHE JU DO
1:100,000
Seoul: Inst. of Plant Environment, 1963
110 x 79
Col. map with 4 insets. In Korean and English. Not on public sale.

L ECONOMIC

KITAI, MONGOL'SKAYA NARODNAYA RESPUBLIKA, KOREYA EKONOMICHESKAYA KARTA
1:5,000,000
Moskva : GUGK, 1968
125 x 98
see CHINA 51 L

M HISTORICAL

DONG-KOOK-YU-JI-DO: A RECENTLY DISCOVERED MANUSCRIPT OF A MAP OF KOREA
Norman J Thrower and Young Il Kim
Amsterdam : N Israel, 1967
22 x 29
Photographs and text of original map by Sang-Ik Chung, 1786.

ATLASES
G EARTH RESOURCES

RECONNAISSANCE SOIL MAP OF KOREA
1:50,000
Seoul : Korea Soil Survey, 1971
29 x 46
Series of regional soil surveys comprising a number of coloured maps contained in a folder. In Korean and English.
Soil Surveys published:
1. City of Seoul and Gycong Gi Do 58 sheets 1971
2. Gangweon Do 58 sheets 1971
3. Chung Cheong Bug Do 33 sheets 1971
4. Chung Cheong Nam Do 45 sheets
5. Jeon La Bug Do 39 sheets
6. Jeon La Nam Do 75 sheets
7. Gyeong Sang Bug Do 68 sheets
8. Busan City and Gycong Sang Nam Do 52 sheets
9. Je Ju Do 10 sheets

each W 1,370

DETAILED SOIL MAP OF KOREA
1:25,000
Seoul : Korea Soil Survey and Inst. of Plant Environment
29 x 46 1-13; 53 x 38 14-25
Series of regional soil surveys comprising a number of coloured maps contained in a folder. In Korean and English.
Soil Surveys published:
1. Ulsansi and Uljn Gun 18 sheets 1971
2. Giang Jusi and Gwang San Gun 11 sheets 1971
3. Dae Gusi and Dal Seong Gun 18 sheets 1971
4. Gim Je Gun 11 sheets 1971
5. Bu Yeo Gun 14 sheets 1971
6. Dam Yang Gun 10 sheets 1971
7. Sang Ju Gun 24 sheets 1971
8. Pyeong Chang Gun 24 sheets 1971
9. Gim Hae Gun 14 sheets 1971
10. Gyeong San Gun 8 sheets 1970
11. Gim Po Pian 8 sheets 1970
12. Ye San Gun 10 sheets 1970
13. Amp Ye Cheon Gun 13 sheets 1970
14. Amp I Ri Si and Ig San Gun 7 sheets 1971
15. An Dong Si and And ong Gun 18 sheets 1971
    Ext.1 Miho River Basin 4 sheets 1971
    Ext.2 Anseong River Basin 8 sheets 1971
16. Pyeong Taeg Gun 8 sheets 1972

17. Cheong Jusi and Cheong Weon Gun
15 sheets 1972
18. Non San Gun 10 sheets 1972
19. Chil Gog Gun 8 sheets 1972
Inst. of Agric. Sciences:
20. Suweon Si and Hwa Seong Gun
14 sheets 1973
21. Na Ju Gun 8 sheets 1973
22. Daejeon Si and Daedeog Gun
8 sheets 1974
Honam Crops Exp. Stations and
Inst. of Agric. Sciences:
23. Jeon Jusi and Wanju Gun 11 sheets 1974
24. Gochang Gun 10 sheets 1975
Yeongnam Crops Exp. Station and
Inst. of Agric. Sciences:
25. Seonsan Gun 10 sheets 1975
each W 1,370

52 Japan

A1 GENERAL MAPS: ROADS

ROAD MAP OF JAPAN
1:1,200,000
Tokyo : Nippon Kokuseisha Co Ltd
107 x 40
Contours, roads classified, National Parks, tourist information. Through town plans of Tokyo, Nagoya, Osaka on reverse, with Hokkaido at 1:1,600,000. Index.

JAPAN ROAD MAP
1:1,000,000
AMS L302
In 3 sheets
Washington : Defense Mapping Agency
Various sizes
Topographic map, contoured, layer coloured, roads classified in detail.
US$1.00

JAPAN ROAD MAPS
1:250,000/500,000
In 9 sheets
Tokyo : Buyodo
Various sizes
Roads classified, contours, relief shading, much tourist information.
Legend Jap. and Eng. Maps at 1:250,000 double sided, mostly with through town plans.
Sheets available:

1	Hokkaido 1968	1:500,000 107 x 76
2	Tohoku 1969	1:500,000 63 x 93
3	Kanto 1968	1:250,000 91 x 63
4	Tokaido 1968	1:250,000 91 x 39
5	Chubu 1968	1:250,000 91 x 63
6	Kansai 1968	1:250,000 91 x 63
7	Chu-Shikoku 1968	1:500,000 91 x 63
8	Kyushu 1969	1:250,000 107 x 78
9	Kyushu 1969	1:500,000 62 x 93

GENERAL MAP OF JAPAN
1:250,000
In 23 sheets. see index 52/1
Tokyo : Buyodo
85 x 65 each
Roads classified and numbered, distances, topog. details, relief shading. Legend Jap, Eng.

A2 GENERAL MAPS: LOCAL

TRAVEL MAP OF KANSAY
1:180,000
Tokyo : Buyodo
Road map, with inset plans of Osaka, Koyoto, Nara.

EXPRESSWAY KOBE-TOKYO
1:300,000
Tokyo : Buyodo, 1970
109 x 39
Double sided map with relief shading.

B TOWN PLANS

STANDARD TYPE OSAKA PLAN
1:20,000
Tokyo : Buyodo
78 x 108
Town plan in Jap and Eng, with environs map on reverse.

GREAT TOKYO DETAILED MAP
1:15,000
Tokyo : Nippon Kokuseisha Co Ltd
79 x 109
Detailed col. plan with principal streets named, block address numbers, principal public buildings and transport systems. Inset at smaller scale indicates major hotels.

STANDARD TYPE TOKYO PLAN
1:10,000
Tokyo : Buyodo
With invirons map at 1:45,000. In Jap and Eng.

MINIPLAN OF TOKYO, OSAKA, KYOTO, KOBE, NARA
Various scales
London : Miniplans, 1969
56 x 34
General plans naming principal streets and public buildings with classified index to streets, buildings etc. Tokyo on one side, other plans on the reverse. 32½p

GUIDE MAP OF YOKOHAMA
1:15,000
Tokyo : Buyodo, 1968
62 x 88
Col. tourist plan with street index.

C OFFICIAL SURVEYS

INTERNATIONAL MAP OF THE WORLD
1:1,000,000
GSI
see WORLD 100C and index 100/1 and 52/2

TOPOGRAPHICAL MAP - DISTRICTS
1:500,000
In 8 sheets, see index 52/2
Chiba : GSI
100 x 70
Topographic series, contoured with considerable land detail. On sheets 1 and 2 green hachures show relief. Legend in Japanese.
Sheets published:

1	Hokkaido
2	Hokkaido
3	Tohoku District
4	Kanto Koshin - Etsu District
5	Chubu Kinki District
6	Chugoku Shikoku District
7	Kyushu District
8	Ogasawara and S W Islands

40p each

TOPOGRAPHICAL SERIES
1:200,000
In 124 sheets, see index 52/3
Chiba : GSI
45 x 37 each
Detailed 6-col. maps, contoured with relief shading, roads classified by width, railways, administrative boundaries and considerable topographic land detail shown. Paddy and cultivated land indicated by symbols.
Text Jap only.

TOPOGRAPHICAL SERIES
1:50,000
In 1258 sheets
Chiba : GSI
58 x 46 each
Contoured with major land use indicated by symbols, all classes of roads and railways also much land detail. Generally in black and white but some col. Text in Jap.

TOPOGRAPHICAL SERIES
1:25,000
In 2065 sheets
Chiba : GSI
58 x 46 each
Contoured with major land use indicated by symbols, all classes of roads and railways, also much land detail included. Generally in black and white but some in col. Series in progress, text in Jap only.

TOPOGRAPHICAL MAPS OF JAPAN
1:10,000
Chiba : GSI
Large scale topographic maps, contoured, published for most urban areas.

D POLITICAL & ADMINISTRATIVE

APONIYA
1:2,000,000
Moskva : GUGK, 1973
Political-admin. reference map.
15 kop

JAPAN AND KOREA
1:1,375,000
Washington : NGS
82 x 106
Political col. wall map
Paper US$2.00
Plastic US$3.00

JAPON
No scale given
No 34
Paris : Hatier
100 x 120
School political wall map; physical map on reverse.

E1 PHYSICAL: RELIEF

RELIEF FEATURES
1:4,000,000
Tokyo : Internat. Sco. for Educ. Info, 1969
48 x 33
Col. physical map with relief and bathymetric shading. In Maps of Japan series. Text in Eng, Fr, Sp, on reverse.

JAPANSKO A KOREA
1:3,000,000
Praha : Kart, 1964
91 x 78
Physical map with contours; insets of soil, economy and industry at 1:9,000,000. With 92pp text. Poznavame Svet series (getting to know the world)
Kcs 14

BARTHOLOMEW'S WORLD TRAVEL SERIES MAP OF JAPAN
1:2,500,000
Edinburgh : Barts
54 x 46
Contoured with layer col, roads, railways, airports, volcanoes and boundaries. Hokkaido and Tokyo Bay inset. Iwo Jima and Okinawa at larger scales.

JAPAN AND ITS ADJACENT AREAS
1:2,500,000
Chiba : GSI, 1969
110 x 115
2 sheet topog. map, contours, hydrog, communication lines.

WHOLE JAPAN GENERAL MAP
1:2,500,000
Tokyo : Buyodo
Col. map with relief, communications network, description Jap and Eng.

JAPONSKO A KOREA
1:2,500,000
Praha : Kart, 1969
General school wall map of Japan and Korea. Kcs 120

THE MAP OF JAPAN
1:2,000,000
Tokyo : Nichiesho
79 x 110
Contours, railways, roads classified. 5 insets and 3 district maps of Tokyo, Osaka, Nagoya at 1:500,000 Indexed.

REGIONAL WALL MAP OF JAPAN
1:1,750,000
London : Philip
119 x 94
Bold physical layer col, with road and rail communications, boundaries and towns graded by pop.
Paper flat £1.50
Mounted CR £5.50
Mounted on cloth dissected to fold £7.00

JAPON
1:1,540,000
No.1203
Ed R Moreau
St. Germain-en-Laye : Éditions MDI, 1976
92 x 126
Double sided wall map, physical map with economic map on the reverse.

NEW MAP OF JAPAN
1:1,500,000
Tokyo : Tokyo Chizu Co, 1971
94 x 66
Layer col. contoured with generalised layer col, communications, cities graded by pop, prefectures boundaries in red. Insets of Hokkaido, Nikko, Hakone and Izu also local maps of Kobe-Osaka-Kyoto, and Kanto area. Index to places in margin.
Y 250

JAPAN, PHYSICAL-POLITICAL
1:1,500,000
No 1131 31
Chicago : Denoyer-Geppert
111 x 147
School wall map showing physical features, communications, them. insets.
Rollers US$18.75

JAPAN
1:1,500,000
No 300252
Braunschweig : Westermann
110 x 154
Physical col. wall map for schools. Insets of annual rainfall, land use, pop, economy.

GREAT MAP OF JAPAN
1:1,200,000
Tokyo : NK, 1971
74 x 103
Contoured, clear layer col, roads and railways classified, towns graded according to status, shipping routes, parks, sites of interest and airports. Kyushu inset at same scale, Hokkaido at 1:1,600,000; other insets show air and sea communications of SE Asia and Pacific, air routes in Japan and enlargements of Tokyo, Osaka and Nagoya. Index on map cover. Y 300

JAPON
No scale given
No 34
Paris : Hatier
100 x 120
School physical wall map, political map on reverse.

E2 PHYSICAL: LAND FEATURES

DISTRIBUTION MAP OF HOT SPRINGS OF JAPAN
1:2,000,000
Kawasaki : Geol. Survey, 1957
78 x 108
In Eng and Jap.

DISTRIBUTION MAP OF GROUND WATER IN JAPAN
1:2,000,000
Kawasaki : Geol. Survey, 1957
70 x 98
In Eng and Jap.

VOLCANOES OF JAPAN
Comp. Isshiki, Matsui and Ono
1:2,000,000
Kawasaki : Geol. Survey
78 x 108
Legend and description and 78pp text in Jap and Eng. With bibliog.
US $5.00

LANDFORMS MAPS OF JAPAN
1:800,000
In 3 sheets
Chiba : GSI
2 col. map portraying and classifying dominant landforms.

MORPHOLOGICAL MAP OF JAPAN
1:500,000
In 6 sheets
Kawasaki : Geol. Survey
108 x 78 each
Col. map series indicating landforms and structural make up.

A GEOMORPHOLOGICAL SURVEY MAP OF THE KUZURYU RIVER BASIN INDICATING AREAS SUBJECT TO FLOODING
Dr Fumio Tada
1:50,000
Tokyo : Resources Bureau, Sci. & Tech. Agency, 1968
33 x 56
Map in English, French, Japanese.

MAP OF THE KUZURYU RIVER BASIN SHOWING THE INUNDATION OF 1965
Dr Fumio Tada
1:50,000
Tokyo : Resources Bureau, Sci. & Tech. Agency, 1968
33 x 56
Map in English, French and Japanese.

F GEOLOGY

GENERAL GEOLOGICAL MAP
1:2,000,000
Kawasaki : Geol. Survey, 1968
73 x 98
Col. map in Jap and Eng. Nansei Islands inset. US $12.00

TECTONIC MAP OF JAPAN
1:2,000,000
Kawasaki : Geol. Surv. 1968
78 x 108
Col. map in 2 sheets. Jap only.
I Showing distribution of elementary tectonic constituents
II Geol. provinces

GEOLOGICAL MAP OF HOKKAIDO
1:600,000
Kawasaki : Geol. Surv.
93 x 73
Col. map in Jap only.

TECTONIC MAP OF AKITA
1:500,000
Prepared by S Sato
Kawasaki : Geol. Surv, 1968
Col. map US $7.00

COMPILED GEOLOGICAL SHEET MAPS
1:500,000
In 17 sheets, see index 52/4
Kawasaki : Geol. Survey
79 x 55 each
Col. series in progress.

GEOLOGICAL MAP OF JAPAN
1:500,000
In 6 sheets
Tokyo : Geol. Surv, 1968
108 x 78 each
Col. detailed map, only in Jap. In case.

COMPILED GEOLOGICAL SHEET MAPS
1:200,000
see index 52/4
Kawasaki : Geol. Survey, 1957+
65 x 50 each
Col. series. In Eng and Jap.

HYDROGEOLOGICAL MAPS OF JAPAN
1:100,000

Kawasaki : Geol. Survey
Available with explanatory texts for:
1 The Kiso, Ya hagi and Toyo River Basins, 1961
2 Central Part of Kanto Plain, 1962
3 Southwestern Part of Kanto Plain, 1962
4 Kamanashi and Fuefuk; River Basins, Yamanash, 1:50,000 1963
5 Kato, Doki and Zaita River Basins, 1964
6 Kinsei, Kamo, Nakayama and Shigenobu River Basins, 1964
7 Western Part of Chiba, 1964
8 The Yamato River Basins, 1:50,000, 1965
9 The Tama, Sagami and Sakawa River Basins, 1965
10 The NW Part of Kanto Plain, 1966
11 The Matsumoto Basin, 1:50,000, 1966
12 The Southwestern District of Hyogo Prefecture, 1967
13 The Chikugo River Basin, 1:50,000, 1967
14 Mount Fuji, 1:50,000, 1967
15 The Miyakonojo Basin, 1968
16 The Sendai Port, 1968
Various prices

GEOLOGICAL SHEET MAPS
1:75,000
Kawasaki : Geol. Survey
Col. series with explanatory texts.
Sheets available for:
41 Onikobe
80 Nakoso
82 Shiobara
124 Numazu
225 Takamatsu
230 Tokushima
231 Wakimachi
258 Tsuwano

GEOLOGIC MAP OF MT FUJI
by Hiroomichi Tsuya
1:50,000
Kawasaki : Geol. Surv, 1968
110 x 135
Col. 2 sheet map with text. Sections on reverse. Legend in Eng and Jap.
US $10.00

GEOLOGICAL SHEET MAPS AND EXPLANATORY TEXTS
1:50,000
In 150 sheets app.
Kawasaki : Geol. Survey
Col. series in progress; in Jap and Eng, with explanatory text.

GEOLOGICAL MAPS OF THE COAL FIELDS OF JAPAN
Various scales
Kawasaki : Geol. Survey
Available with explanatory texts for:
1 Joban Coal Field, 1:50,000, 1957 US $20.00
2 Hokusho Coal Field, 1:25,000, 1959-60 US $30.00
5 Kushiro Coal Field (Shinnuibetsu District, Hokkaido) 1:10,000, 1961 US $5.00
6 Ishikari Coal Field (Higashiashibetsu Area, Sorachi District, Hokkaido), 1:10,000, 1961 US $10.00
8 Uryu-Rumoi Coal Field, 1:20,000 US $10.00
9 Sasebo SW Coal Field, 1:10,000 US $6.00
10 Niigata (Akaya) Coal Field, 1:5,000 US $6.00

GEOLOGICAL MAP OF NORTHERN SASEBO
1:25,000
Kawasaki : Geol. Survey, 1970
73 x 96
Geological map in Japanese and English.
With 2 sheets profiles. US $6.00

G EARTH RESOURCES

GEOLOGY AND MINERAL SOURCES OF JAPAN
1:3,000,000
Kawasaki : Geol. Survey, 1962
108 x 78
With 314pp text with maps and tables in Eng.

MAP OF COAL FIELDS IN JAPAN
1:2,000,000
Kawasaki : Geol. Survey, 1957
70 x 98
In Jap and Eng.

DISTRIBUTION MAP OF OIL AND GAS FIELDS IN JAPAN
1:2,000,000
Kawasaki : Geol. Survey, 1959
70 x 98
In Eng and Jap.

MINERAL PROVINCES OF JAPAN
1:2,000,000
Kawasaki : Geol. Survey
70 x 98
4 maps showing:
Mineralisation of Quaternary Period
Mineralisation of Neogene Period
Mineralisation of Mesozoic to Paleogene Period
Mineralisation of Paleozoic Period

MAPS OF METALLIC AND NON-METALLIC MINERAL DEPOSITS OF HOKKAIDO
1:800,000
Kawasaki : Geol. Survey
3 maps covering:
Mineralisation of Late Neogene Tertiary to Quaternary Period
Mineralisation of Neogene Tertiary Period
Mineralisation of Late Paleozoic to Early Tertiary Period

DISTRIBUTION MAPS OF THE OIL AND GAS FIELDS OF JAPAN
Various scales
Kawasaki : Geol. Survey
Available for the following areas:

Aoyamaoku	1:50,000	US $4.00
Yokohama	1:15,000	US $5.50
Yokosuka	1:20,000	US $4.00
Futtu-Otaki	1:50,000	US $3.50
Southern part of Gojyome	1:15,000	US $5.00
Miura Peninsula	1:25,000	US $5.00
Uonuma	1:50,000	US $10.00
Honjuku	1:25,000	US $7.00
Nanatani	1:25,000	US $5.00
Mobara	1:15,000 1:50,000	US $12.00

BOUGUER ANOMALIES IN JAPAN
1:2,000,000
Tokyo : Geol. Surv. Inst, 1970

FREE AIR ANOMALIES IN JAPAN
1:2,000,000
Tokyo : Geog. Surv. Inst. 1970

H BIOGEOGRAPHY

LAND USE MAPS
1:50,000
Chiba : GSI
Sheets published:
8 colour maps - small sheet edition
Matsumato, Okayama, Tamano, Kure, Onomichi, Toyoda, Nagoya (Main, South) Okazaki, Ogaki, Tsushima, Kuwana, Yokkaichi, Matsuzaka, Ise, Tsu.
8 colour maps, large sheet edition
Niigata, Fukuoka, Hyuga, Nobeoka, Hiroshima, Fukuyama, Tamashima, Handa, Gamagori, Toyohashi, Gifu, Wake, Kamigori, Banshu Ako, Subo, Tsuchioi, Imabari East, Saijo, Takehara, Mitsu, Imabari West, Kurahashijima, Matsuyama North, Matsuyama South, Mitohama, Gunchu

Small 8 col eds.	75p
Large 8 col eds.	£1.10

COMPOUNDED MAPS
1:50,000
Chiba : GSI
Col. maps illustrating land types.
Available for the following areas:

Oze	40p
Tokyo	35p
Zao	55p
Yari-Hodaka	
Tateyama, Nikko Daisen-Hiruzen	55p

LAND CONDITION MAPS
1:25,000
Chiba : GSI
Available in various eds. for different areas.
12 col. eds. Osaka (NE, SE, NW, SW)
13 col. eds. Gamagori, Tokyo (NE, SE, NW, SW), Chiba, Yokkaichi, Handa, Hachioji, Haramachida, Fujisawa, Matsuzaka, Toyohashi, Yokohama, Ogaki, Tsushima, Gifu, Ise, Hiroshima, Okazaki, Toyoda, Nagoya (N, S), Kuwana, Tsu, Kisarazu, Anegasaki
16 col. eds. Himeji, Kobe, Kyoto-S, Takasago

12 col maps	80p
16 col maps	90p

K HUMAN GEOGRAPHY

CITIES
1:4,000,000
Tokyo : Internat. Soc. for Educ. Info, 1969
48 x 33
Showing land relief, cities in red, pop. by circles. Text in Eng, Fr, Sp on reverse.

1970 POPULATION CENSUS MAPS OF JAPAN
1:1,500,000 unless otherwise stated
In 24 sheets
Tokyo : Bureau of Statistics, 1971-1974
Series of maps in Japanese with English translation.
Sheets published:
1. Population distribution by landforms 1:1,000,000 1973 Y2 200
2. Population density 1971 Y 800
3. Rate of population change 1971 Y1 600

4. Percent working age population 1973 Y2 100
5. Ratio of aged population 1973 Y2 100
6. Percent population moved after 1965 1973 Y2 100
7. Number of Persons per household 1973 Y2 100
8. Percent family nuclei 1973 Y1 700
9. Percent employed households 1973 Y1 700
10. Percent agricultural households 1973 Y1 700
11. Number of dwelling rooms per household 1973 Y1 700
12. Number of tatami per household member 1973 Y1 700
13. Percent owned houses 1973 Y1 700
14. Percent persons completed elementary school or junior high school by Shi, Ku, Machi and Mura 1973 Y1 500
15. Percent persons completed junior college or university by Shi, Ku, Machi and Mura 1973 Y1 500
16. Percent workers employed in primary industries by Shi, Ku, Machi and Mura 1973 Y1 800
17. Percent workers employed in secondary industries by Shi, Ku, Machi and Mura 1973 Y1 800
18. Percent workers employed in tertiary industries by Shi, Ku, Machi and Mura 1973 Y1 800
19. Percent workers in production and transport occupations by Shi, Ku, Machi and Mura 1973 Y1 800
20. Percent workers in sales and services occupations by Shi, Ku, Machi and Mura 1973 Y1 800
21. Percent workers in clerical, technical and managerial occupations by Shi, Ku, Machi and Mura 1973 Y1 800
22. Workers and students commuting to large cities 1974 Y2 100
23. Distribution of commuting persons by means of transportation 1974 Y1 800
24. Ratio of -day and night-time population 1974 Y1 800

POPULATION MAP OF JAPAN
1:500,000 – 1:1,500,000
Tokyo : Bureau of Statistics
78 x 102
Series of maps based on 1965 census.
Maps available:

1. Population distribution by Shi, Ku, Machi and Mura 1:1,000,000 in 3 sheets, 1968
2. Population change by Shi, Ku, Machi and Mura 1:1,000,000 in 3 sheets, 1967
3. Percentage of workers employed in industries for Shi, Ku, Machi and Mura 1:1,500,000 1968
    1. Percentage of workers employed in primary industry by Shi, Ku, Machi and Mura
    2. Percentage of workers employed in secondary industry by Shi, Ku, Machi and Mura
    3. Percentage of workers employed in tertiary industry by Shi, Ku, Machi and Mura
4. Workers and students commuting to large cities 1:500,000 in 8 sheets, 1968
5. Households and housing by Shi, Ku, Machi and Mura 1:1,500,000, 1969
    1. Percentage of owned houses by Shi, Ku, Machi and Mura.
    2. Number of persons by household by Shi, Ku, Machi and Mura.
    3. Number of dwelling rooms per household by Shi, Ku, Machi and Mura.
    4. Number of tatami per household member by Shi, Ku, Machi and Mura.
6. Sex and age compositions by Shi, Ku, Machi and Mura 1:1,500,000 1970.
    1. Sex ratio by Shi, Ku, Machi and Mura.
    2. Percent working age population by Shi, Ku, Machi and Mura
    3. Ratio of aged population by Shi, Ku, Machi and Mura.

STATISTICAL MAPS ON GRID SQUARE BASIS POPULATION CHANGE (1965-1970)
1:300,000
In 3 sheets
Tokyo : Bureau of Statistics, 1974
10 x 70
Population-change statistical maps for Tokyo, capital region, Chukyo and Kinki regions.
Y 3,500

TOKYO - STATISTICAL MAPS
1:300,000
In 20 sheets
Tokyo : Bureau of Statistics, 1970
72 x 102
Col. maps, statistics based on small grid squares.
Sheets:

Part 1 Population
1. Population
2. Sex Ratio
3. Percent Childhood Pop.
4. Percent Aged Pop.
5. Percent Foreign People

2 Activity and Occupation
6. Female Labour Force Participation Rate
7. Commutation Rate
8. Percent Professional, Managerial and Clerical Workers.
9. Percent Production Workers and Labourers
10. Percent sales and service workers

3 Industry
11. Percent Employed Persons in Primary Industry
12. Percent Employed Persons in Secondary Industry
13. Percent Employed Persons in Tertiary Industry
14. Percent Employees
15. Percent Agricultural Households.

4 Housing·
16. Percent Owned Houses
17. Percent Households Living in Rental Rooms
18. Number of Persons per Household
19. Number of Tatami per Household Member
20. Number of Rooms per Household.

L ECONOMIC

MANUFACTURING PLANTS
1:4,000,000
Tokyo : Internat. Soc. for Educ. Info, 1969
48 x 33
Various types of industry indicated by different col. circles. Insets of Hansin. Tyukyo and Keihin areas at 1:800,000
Text in Eng, Fr, Sp, on reverse.

JAPON ÉCONOMIQUE
1:1,540,000
Éditions MDI, 1976
see JAPAN 52 E1 (Japon 1:1,540,000)

ATLASES
W3 WORLD ATLAS : LOCAL EDITION

SHO GAKKO SHAKAIKA CHIZUCHO
Social study atlas for primary school pupils
2nd edition
Tokyo : Teikoku, 1976
66pp
18 x 26
Paperbound for schools. In Japanese.
Y 520

ATLASES
A1 GENERAL : ROADS

ROAD ATLAS OF JAPAN
1:250,000
Tokyo : Buyodo
18 x 24
In 4 vols:

I Kyushu, with Okinawa, 1968, 44pp
II West Japan, with Tokyo, 1968, 100pp
III East Japan, with Tokyo, 1967, 100pp
IV Hokkaido, 1969, 60pp

Roads classified, distances in km, many insets, national parks, shipping lines.
In Jap (large place names in Eng.)

ATLASES
B TOWN PLANS

TOKYO TONAI CHIZU
—Tokyo map for businessmen
1:22,000 – 1:45,000
2nd edition
Tokyo – Teikoku – Shoin, 1976
Atlas covering the whole 23 wards with enlarged maps of important areas, directory of government offices and principal companies with index.
Y 1300

ATLASES
J CLIMATE

CLIMATIC ATLAS OF JAPAN
Tokyo : Japanese Met. Agency
In 2 vols.
47 x 68

Vol. 1, 1971, 59 map sheets with maps at 1:3/6,000,000. Climatic diagrams, covering temperature, monthly rainfall etc.
Vol. 2, 1972, 90 map sheets covering maximum and minimum temperatures, snow, wind, tracks of typhoons etc.
2pp text in Eng.

ATLASES
K HUMAN GEOGRAPHY

STATISTICAL MAPS ON GRID SQUARE BASIS (1970 POPULATION CENSUS RESULTS) CAPITAL REGION
Tokyo : Bureau of Statistics, 1974
30 x 33
30pp
Series of computer printed maps of Tokyo region in Japanese with English translation.
Y 2,600

STATISTICAL MAPS ON GRID SQUARE BASIS (1970 POPULATION CENSUS RESULTS, KINKI AND CHUKYO REGIONS)
Tokyo : Bureau of Statistics, 1973
21 x 25
Series of computer printed maps of Kinki and Chukyo regions in Japanese with English translation. Y 6,200

ATLASES
L ECONOMIC

JAPAN RAILWAY ATLAS
1:1,500,000
Ed J R Yonge
Exeter : Quail Map Co. 1975
34 x 24½
6 Double sided, loose leaf sheets, classifying all types of railways with index and enlargements of congested areas. Legend in Eng, French, Ger, Jap. £1.50

ATLASES
M HISTORICAL

OLD MAPS IN JAPAN
Matsutaro Nanba and others
Osaka : Sogensha, 1971
160pp
26 x 38
93 maps in colour, with 4 folded; 18 maps of the world, 14 of Japan, 7 Kaido (highway) maps, 10 district maps, 9 prefectural, 26 city maps, 9 maps painted on ceramics etc. English text, translated by Hiromichi-Takeda and Peter Anton. US $55.00

SHIN SEN NIHONSHI SEIZU
Detailed Atlas of Japanese History for High School Students
4th Edition
Tokyo : Teikoku – Shoin, 1976
26 x 18
72 pp
Historical school atlas. In Japanese.
Y 320

ATLASES
O1 NATIONAL: REFERENCE

TEIKOKU'S COMPLETE ATLAS OF JAPAN
Tokyo : Teikoku–Shoin 1974
21 x 30
58pp
18pp cover general survey of the country as a whole, with col. maps, showing administration, national parks, geol, soils, climate, agriculture, industry, communications, population and history.
17pp of physical maps at 1:1,800,000 with many large scale insets of areas of interest. Supplement giving climate statistics, national park guide, glossary and index.
Y 900

REGIONAL STRUCTURE OF JAPANESE ARCHIPELAGO (ATLAS)
Eds Drs S Kirchi and K Tange
Tokyo : Jap. Centre for Area Devt. Research, 1967
30 x 30
Shows much data in graphic, tabular and cartographic form. Divided into 7 sections on Physical Features, pop, Tangible Fixed Assets, Industry, Transportation, Communications and Living Space. 26 maps, 61 graphs, 27 tables and 5 pp index to cities, towns and villages. In Eng. and Jap.

ATLAS OF JAPAN
Ed Drs. Akira Ebato and Kazuo Watanabe
Tokyo : Internat. Soc. Educ. Info, 1974
25 x 35
viii, 128pp
64pp coloured maps showing physical, economic, social factors. Text in Eng, Fr, Sp. US $33.00

THE POCKET ATLAS OF JAPAN
Tokyo : Heibonsha/Japanese Cartographic Inst, 1970
10 x 16
282 pp
76pp col. maps, 75pp text, 106pp index with 12,000 names. Political physical maps, social statistics, Hokkaido at 1:2,000,000. Individual prefectures at 1:1,000,000. 3 large areas at 1:350,000. In Japanese.
Y 1,250

THE NATIONAL ATLAS OF JAPAN
being prepared by the Committee for the National Atlas of Japan.
Chiba : GSI
42 x 59
300pp
In preparation.

ATLASES
O2 NATIONAL: SCHOOL

A SIMPLE ATLAS OF JAPAN
Ed Masahiko Oya and Nagao Kosaka
Tokyo : Internat. Soc. for Educ. Info.
1969
13pp
21 x 30
Children's atlas including 9 them. col. maps and 3 plates. English edition.

529.1 Taiwan

A1 GENERAL MAPS : ROADS

FORMOSA ROAD MAP (TAIWAN)
1:500,000
Washington : Defense Mapping Agency
75 x 108
Physical with contours, roads, railways, province and "Hsien" boundaries. In Chi and Eng. Hill shading inc. Pescadores.
US $1.00

MAP OF TAIWAN
1:500,000
Taipei : Nan Hua, 1971
78 x 55
Roads classified, tourist info, boundaries, political map. Also available in Chinese ed.

THE MINUTE TRAFFIC MAP OF TAIWAN
1:360,000
Taipei : Nan Hua
Road classified with distances.

B TOWN PLANS

TAIWAN CITY MAPS
Various scales
Taipei : Nan Hua
Maps available:
Taipei 1:16,500 (Eng and Chinese eds)
Keelung 1:10,000
Taichung 1:10,000 (Eng and Chinese eds)
Tainan 1:10,000
Kaohsiung 1:15,000
Sanchung 1:6,000
Pingtung 1:6,000
Chiayi 1:6,000

D POLITICAL & ADMINISTRATIVE

TAIWAN – DISTRICT MAPS (HSIEN)
Various scales
Taipei : Nan Hua
Relief map showing admin. boundaries.
Maps available by Hsien:

Taipei	1:100,000
Ilan	1:123,000
Taoyuan	1:100,000
Hsinchu	1:100,000
Miaoli	1:100,000
Taichung	1:130,000
Changwa	1:80,000
Nantow	1:150,000
Yunlin	1:100,000
Chiayi	1:100,000
Tainan	1:100,000
Kaohsiung	1:100,000
Pingtung	1:150,000
Hwalian	1:190,000
Taitung	1:180,000
Penghu	1:100,000

F GEOLOGY

GEOLOGICAL MAP OF TAIWAN
1:300,000
prepared by Li-Sho Chang
In 2 sheets
Taipei : Geol. Survey of Taiwan, 1953
Col. geological map.

GEOLOGICAL MAP OF TAIWAN
1:50,000
Taipei : Geol. Survey of Taiwan, 1953+
75 x 50 each
Series in progress, each map with text in Chi and Eng.
Available for :

5	Tatunshan	1953
9	Juifang	1953
10	Taipei	1953

K HUMAN GEOGRAPHY

TAIWAN POPULATION DISTRIBUTION
1:500,000
by Mei-Ling Hsu
Florida : AAG, 1969
70 x 108
Col. statistical map, showing rural and urban pop, 4 insets on reverse showing pop. growth, employment structure etc.
With text. US $3.00

ATLASES
E1 PHYSICAL

ATLAS OF THE REPUBLIC OF CHINA
Ed Dr Chang Chi-yun
Taiwan : National War College
Vol I Taiwan, 1966, 58pp maps.
see CHINA ATLASES 51 E1.

ATLASES
H BIOGEOGRAPHY

ATLAS OF LAND UTILISATION IN TAIWAN
by Cheng -Siang Chen
Research Report No. 15
Taipei : Fu-Min Geog. Inst. of Econ. Devt., 1950
174pp
27 x 38
164 col. maps at mostly 1:1,500,000 incl. 8 aerial photographs. Chinese text with Eng. translation (except index).
US $21.50

ATLASES
O NATIONAL

GEOGRAPHICAL ATLAS OF TAIWAN
Ed. Cheng-siang Chen
Research Report No 93,
Taipei : Fu-Min Geog. Inst. of Econ. Devt. 1959.
19 x 26
xx, 144pp
Collection of 200 thematic maps, covering admin, climate, economy, population transportation and geog. regions.
English ed. US $9.00
Chinese Ed. US $7.50

53 Near and Middle East

See also: 569.4 ISRAEL
(for Biblical maps)

A1 GENERAL MAPS: ROADS

MIDDLE EAST
1:5,000,000
No 128
Tehran : Sahab
96 x 74
Showing main and secondary roads, railways and including inset town plans of major cities. In Pers. and Eng.

TURKEI - NAHER OSTEN
1:3,000,000
Bern : Hallwag
67 x 57
Road map with distances and route numbers, railways, pipelines, boundaries. Relief shaded. Includes Turkey and eastern Mediterranean seaboard.

TURKEI, NAHER OSTEN, ÄGYPTEN
1:3,000,000
Bern : Hallwag
67 x 58
Roads classified with distances in km, relief shading, railways, pipelines and sites of interest. Includes Levant coast, Nile south to Aswan (inset) and North African coast west to Benghazi.

ROAD MAP SERIES
1:2,000,000
2 sheets
Wien : F - B
Main highways and secondary roads, route numbering, spot heights in metres, hill shading and state boundaries.
Sheets:
Kleinasien, Ostliches Mittelmeer
(Eastern Mediterranean and Asia Minor inc. Benghazi, Cairo, Jordan, Turkey and Greece)
1971 121 x 83
Naher Osten
(Near East - Istanbul, Cairo, Shiraz, Caspian Sea)
1968 101 x 80

A2 GENERAL MAPS: LOCAL

ARABIISKII POLUOSTROV
(ARABIAN PENINSULA)
1:2,500,000
Moskva : GUGK, 1973
Col. study map showing water features, settlements, admin. divisions and centres, communications, boundaries, capitals, economic details, pop. Geog. description.
Ro 0.30

PERSIAN GULF AND OMAN SEA
1:1,000,000
Tehran : Sahab
90 x 60
2 sided map including Bandar-e-Abbas, Bandar-e-Busheht, Kish Is,'Lavan Is, Bandar-e-Jask, Bandar-e-Languen, Farur Is, Borazjan, Larak Is, Persian Gulf, Kharg Is, Bahrein Is, Minab, Hormoz Is, Qeshm Is. Text in English and Persian.

SOUTHERN ARABIA
1:500,000
In 2 sheets
London : RGS, 1958
1 – 42 x 54 2 – 46 x 73
Showing part of Aden Prot. from Shuqra to al Shir and Baihan to Hadramaut. Physical, with contours, vegetation, roads, water courses, wadis. 4 insets at 1:250,000 of Pathinan, Wadi Jirdan, Wadi Hadramaut, Mouth of Wadi As-Kasar, from surveys by H von Wissman. £2.00 set

SOUTHERN ARABIA
1:1,250,000
RGS
see SAUDI ARABIA 532 A2

D POLITICAL & ADMINISTRATIVE

DAILY TELEGRAPH MAP OF THE MIDDLE EAST, INDIA AND PAKISTAN
1:7,000,000
Geographia
see ASIA 53 D

NAHER OSTEN
1:5,000,000
No 4320
Bern : K & F
100 x 75
Political col, releif shading, roads and caravan tracks, boundaries, railways, sea routes, pipelines and towns graded by pop. Legend in 5 langs, inc. English.

MIDDLE EAST
1:4,000,000 app.
Chicago : Rand McNally
165 x 104
Political col, pipelines, railways, major cities etc.

BRENNPUNKT NAHER OSTEN
1:4,000,000
No 503
Frankfurt : Ravenstein
80 x 50
General political map of the near east with road and rail communications.
DM 2.00

LANDS OF THE BIBLE TODAY
1:2,912,500
Washington : NGS
104 x 73
Modern col. map with notes. US $2.00

MOYEN-ORIENT
1:2,500,000
Paris : IGN, 1970
94 x 72
Political with relief shading, roads, pipelines, land shading. F.Fr. 14.17

MIDDLE EAST : POLITICAL GEOGRAPHY WALL MAP
1:2,500,000
No 107831
Chicago : Denoyer-Geppert
111 x 162
Political col. school wall map, showing boundaries, communications, water features, pop.
CR US $19.25

ASIE OCCIDENTALE (MOYEN-ORIENT)
No 16
Paris : Hatier
100 x 120
Political-economic school wall map.

SOYUZNYE RESPUBLIKI SREDNEI AZII
1:10,000,000
Moskva : GUGK
Outline maps of Middle and Near East.

UMRISSKARTE NAHER OSTEN
1:5,000,000
No 0837
Bern : K & F
103 x 75
Political col. outline map.

PROXIMO ORIENTE
Barcelona : Editorial Teide
33 x 25
School outline hand map without boundaries or cities. S.Ptas 1

E1 PHYSICAL: RELIEF

EUROPE AND THE MIDDLE EAST
1:11,000,000
RGS, 1940
see EUROPE 4 E1

BLÍZKÝ VÝCHOD (THE NEAR EAST)
1:6,000,000
Praha : Kart
74 x 84
Physical-political map in "Poznavame Svet" (Getting to know the world) series. With text vol. Kcs 12

SOUTH ASIA AND THE MIDDLE EAST, VISUAL RELIEF
1:5,000,000
No 123821-10
Chicago : Denoyer-Geppert
162 x 137
School wall map showing relief of land and sea, cities classified by pop, boundaries.

JUHOZAPADNA ASIE
1:5,000,000
In 2 sheets
Praha : KN, 1970
Physical wall map of S W Asia.

NEAR EAST
1:5,000,000
Tel Aviv : Surv. Israel, 1971
87 x 68
Physical map, contoured and layer col. with communications and boundaries. Including Turkey, Iran, Red Sea and Arabia. In Hebrew.

BARTHOLOMEW'S WORLD TRAVEL MAP SERIES : THE MIDDLE EAST
1:4,000,000

Edinburgh : Bart
93 x 71
Contours, layer col, road and rail communications, boundaries. South Yemen inset at same scale. 75p

REGIONAL WALL MAP OF THE NEAR EAST AND MIDDLE EAST
1:4,000,000
London : Philip
122 x 94
Physical col. with communications, boundaries and towns graded by pop. Covers Kiev to Berbera and Corfu to Muscat
Paper flat £1.50
CR £5.50
Cloth, dissected to fold £7.00

VORDERASIEN UND INDIEN
1:4,000,000
Braunschweig : Westermann
196 x 162
Physical wall map covering area Rangoon east to Athens. Layer col, cities graded by pop, communications, state boundaries. Eng, Fr, Ger, eds.

YUGO-ZAPADNAYA AZIYA
1:4,000,000
Moskva : GUGK, 1971
Physical wall map of Near East for schools.

PROCHE ORIENT
1:3,500,000
No 1375
Ed. F Le Meur
St. Germain-en-Laye : Éditions MDI, 1975
126 x 92
Physical wall map of the Near East with an economic map on the reverse. Also available in an Arabic edition.

SUDWESTASIEN
1:3,500,000
Eds Haack-Painke
Darmstadt : Perthes
210 x 175
Physical wall map, relief col. and shaded with communications. Inc. India - N W Africa - Black Sea - Arabian peninsula.

WENSCHOW WALL MAP - VORDERASIEN - ARABIEN
1:3,000,000
Munchen : List
165 x 175
Physical map covering Near and Middle East with relief of land and sea bottom.

MEDITERRANEO ORIENTALE
1:2,500,000
Novara : Agostini
140 x 100
School wall map of the Eastern Mediterranean, with physical colouring. L 2,200
Mounted L 5,000

NEAR EAST
1:2,500,000
In 4 sheets
Tel Aviv : Surv. Israel, 1962
Physical map, contoured, layer col, communications and boundaries.

MITTELMEERLANDER UND VORDERER ORIENT
1:2,000,000
Braunschweig : Westermann
262 x 138
Physical school wall map of the Mediterranean and the Near East. Relief shading, layer colouring, communications, cities graded by pop.

NAHER OSTEN
1:2,000,000
Darmstadt : Perthes
242 x 240
Bold physical col. with communications, boundaries, towns and villages. Includes N E Africa, Red Sea, Turkey and Iran. DM 142

MIDDLE EAST BRIEFING MAP
1:1,500,000
AMS 1308
Washington : Defense Mapping Agency
78 x 104
Contoured, layer col, communications US $ 1.00

ISRAEL UND SEINE ARABISCHEN NACHBARN
1:1,000,000
Eds Haack-Painke
Darmstadt : Perthes
210 x 140
Physical wall map covering S Turkey, Syria, Iraq, Jordan and Nile Delta.

F GEOLOGY

CARTE GÉOLOGIQUE DE L'AFRIQUE
1:5,000,000
UNESCO - ASGA
Sheet 3 covers Near East
see AFRICA 6 F

CARTE TECTONIQUE INTERNATIONALE DE L'AFRIQUE
1:5,000,000
UNESCO - ASGA
Sheet 3 covers Near East
see AFRICA 6 F

INTERNATIONAL GEOLOGICAL MAP OF EUROPE AND THE MEDITERRANEAN REGION
1:5,000,000
UNESCO
see EUROPE 4F

G EARTH RESOURCES

CARTE MINERALE DE L'AFRIQUE
1:10,000,000
UNESCO/AAGS
includes Middle East
see AFRICA 6 G

CARTE INTERNATIONALE DES GISEMENTS DE FER DE L'EUROPE
1:2,500,000
see EUROPE 4 G

L ECONOMIC

ECONOMIC GEOGRAPHIC MAP OF THE ARABIAN PENINSULA
1:4,000,000
Mecca : Saudi Arabia Min. Petroleum and Mineral Resources, 1970.
Physical map showing locations of mineral resources.

YUGO-ZAPADNAYA AZIYA EKONOMICHESKAYA KARTA
1:4,000,000
In 2 sheets
Moskva : GUGK, 1971
120 x 108
School economic wall map, covering Near East, Iran and Turkey particularly.

PROCHE ORIENT - ÉCONOMIQUE
1:3,500,000
Éditions : MDI, 1975
see NEAR AND MIDDLE EAST 53 E1

M HISTORICAL

ARABIE V VII-VI VV
1:5,000,000
Moskva : GUGK, 1973
Historical wall map of Arabia, in the 7th - 9th C. 30 kop

DER ALTE ORIENT
1:3,000,000
Braunschweig : Westermann
210 x 140
4 maps on one wall map, showing the ancient kingdoms of the Near East.

KARTE ZUR BIBLISCHEN ERDKUNDE (BIBLE LANDS)
1:2,500,000
Braunschweig : Westermann
184 x 152
School wall map, physical, insets of Sinai and Arabian Peninsula areas.

NOVA PERSIAE (ANATOLIA ET ARABIA)
by De Wit, 1688 AD
Tehran : Sahab
70 x 50
Black and white facsimile.

531 Sinai Peninsular

See also: 569.4 ISRAEL

SINAI
1:1,000,000
Tel Aviv : Surv. Israel, 1957,
rep. 1969
Contoured, layer col, topog. map, with roads, tracks and railways. Includes Nile Delta, Sinai, Jordan and N Arabia. In Hebrew ed. only.

SINAI
1:250,000
In 4 sheets
Tel Aviv : Surv. Israel, 1967
Detailed topog. map, contoured, layer coloured, being an extension of the 2 sheet map of Israel.
Only available in Hebrew.
Sheets available:
El-Arish (N Sinai) 1969
Gulf of Suez (SW Sinai) 1967
Gulf of Eilat (SE Sinai) 1971
Cairo (Nile Delta) 1967

532 Saudi Arabia

See also: 53 NEAR & MIDDLE EAST

A1 GENERAL MAPS

ARABIISKII POLUOSTROV
(ARABIAN PENINSULA)
1:2,500,000
GUGK, 1973
see NEAR & MIDDLE EAST 53 A2

A2 GENERAL MAPS : LOCAL

SOUTH WEST ARABIA
1:1,000,000
London : RGS, 1976
85 x 57
Showing relief, modern routes and pre-Islamic archaeological sites. Printed in 2 colours. Archaeological data compiled by N. St. J. Groom.
£4.00

SOUTHERN ARABIA
1:500,000
RGS, 1958
see SOUTHERN YEMEN 534 A2

SOUTHERN ARABIA
1:1,250,000
London : RGS
Various sizes
3 maps, reprinted from the Geographical Journal showing the journeys of W Thesiger.
A Journey through the southern Rub al Khali, Oct 1945 - Feb 1946 (G J Dec 1946) 64 x 44
A Journey through the eastern Rub al Khali, Oct 1946 - Feb 1947 (G J March 1948) 42 x 56
A Journey through the Mahra Country, Mar-April, 1947 (G J March 1948) 45 x 40
each £1.50

C OFFICIAL SURVEYS

GEOGRAPHIC MAP SERIES OF THE KINGDOM OF SAUDI ARABIA
1:500,000
In 21 sheets, see index 532/1
Washington : USGS - Min of Pet. and Min. Resources, S.A.
86 x 88
Topographic series showing detailed water information, generalised relief, spot heights with sand terrain types, roads classified, railways, airports, oil fields, wells and pipelines and date gardens. In Arabic and Eng. with glossary of terms.
S.Ri 10

E1 PHYSICAL : RELIEF

TOPOGRAPHIC MAP OF THE ARABIAN PENINSULA
1:4,000,000
Map AP-1
Riyadh : Min. of Petrol and Min. Resources, 1972
58 x 68
Coloured map, contoured with roads and tracks. Available in either English or Arabic editions.
S.Ri.10

JAZIRAT AL ARAB
1:4,000,000
Riyadh: Aerial Survey Dept., Min. of Petrol and Min. Resources, 1974
58 x 68
Contoured with hill. In Arabic.
S.Ri. 15

GENERAL MAP OF SAUDI ARABIA
1:4,000,000
Tehran : Sahab, 1962
60 x 90
Shows main and secondary roads, railways, airports, some relief hachuring. Mecca inset. In Eng. and Per.
S.Ri 100

WORLD TRAVEL SERIES MAP OF THE MIDDLE EAST
1:4,000,000
Edinburgh : Barts
93 x 71
Contoured with layer col, road and rail communications and boundaries, covering Turkey, Nile Valley through to Iran. South Yemen inset at same scale.
75p

ARABIAN PENINSULA
1:2,000,000
Misc. GI 1-270B-2
2nd edition
Washington : USGS - Min. of Pet. and Min Resources, S.A. 1963.
114 x 173
Detailed map with generalised relief and sand detail, roads classified, railways, towns, cities, wells, oil fields, pipelines, terminals, pumping stations and refineries, date gardens and cultivated areas. Available in English and Arabic editions.
S. Ri 20

F GEOLOGY

GEOLOGIC MAP OF THE ARABIAN PENINSULA
1:2,000,000
Misc GI 1-270A
Washington : USGS - Min. of Pet. and Min. Resources, S.A. 1963
114 x 173
Col. geol. map with notes on series overprinted on topographic base, mapping complete peninsula north to include southern Jordan.
S.Ri 20

GEOLOGIC MAP SERIES OF THE KINGDOM OF SAUDI ARABIA
1:500,000
In 21 sheets, see index 532/1
Washington : USGS - Min. of Pet. and Min. Resources, S.A. 1956-63
86 x 88
Col. geol. series with legend in Arabic and Eng. and glossary of terms.
S.Ri 20

G EARTH RESOURCES

SAUDI ARABIA AEROMAGNETIC SERIES
1:500,000
see index 532/3
Riyadh : DGMR/USGS
Total intensity aeromagnetic series with text

SAUDI ARABIA GEOLOGIC - MINERAL SERIES
1:25,000 – 1:100,000
see index 532/3
Riyadh : DGMR/USGS
Series of coloured geological and mineral maps.

M HISTORICAL

ARABIE U VII – XI UU
1:5,000,000
Moskva : GUGK, 1973
Historical wall map of Arabia in the 7th – 9th C.
Ro 0.30

NOVA PERSIAE (ANATOLIA ET ARABIA)
by De Wit, 1688 AD
Tehran : Sahab
70 x 50
Black and white facsimile.

533 Yemen

See also : 53 NEAR & MIDDLE EAST

C OFFICAL SURVEYS

INTERNATIONAL MAP OF THE WORLD
1:1,000,000
GSGS Series 1301
2 sheets needed : NE 38
ND 38
see WORLD 100C and index 100/1

WORLD
1:500,000
DMS Series 1404
6 sheets needed for complete coverage:
668 C, D
687 A, B, C, D
see WORLD 100C and index 100/7

GEOGRAPHIC MAP SERIES OF THE KINGDOM OF SAUDI ARABIA
1:500,000
USGS
Sheet I-217BASIR covers northern boundary.
see SAUDI ARABIA 532 C and index 532/1

534 Southern Yemen

See also : 53 NEAR & MIDDLE EAST
532 SAUDI ARABIA

A2 GENERAL MAPS : LOCAL

SOUTHERN ARABIA
1:500,000
In 2 sheets
London : RGS 1958
1 – 42 x 54 2 – 46 x 73
Showing part of Aden Protectorate from Shuqra to al Shir and Baihan to Hadramaut. Physical, with contours, vegetation, roads, water courses, wadis. 4 insets at 1:250,000 of Dathinah, Wadi Jirdan, Wadi Hadramaut, Mouth of Wadi As-Kasar. Based on surveys by H von Wissman. set £2.00

C OFFICIAL SURVEYS

INTERNATIONAL MAP OF THE WORLD
1:1,000,000
DMS Series 1301
see WORLD 100C and index 100/1

WORLD
1:500,000
DMS Series 1404
see WORLD 100C and index 100/7

ADEN PROTECTORATE
1:100,000
DOS 554 (K667)
In app. 115 sheets, see index 534/1
Tolworth : DOS, 1958
Photo-topographic series, without contours. each 50p

D POLITICAL & ADMINISTRATIVE

ADEN PROTECTORATE
1:3,000,000
DOS 953
Edition 4
Tolworth : DOS, 1964
40 x 32
Small political map with roads and inset of Aden and surroundings. 10p

F GEOLOGY

GEOLOGICAL MAP OF EAST ADEN PROTECTORATE
1:1,000,000
DOS (Geol) 1148
Tolworth : DOS, 1963
Coloured geological map. 65p

GEOLOGICAL MAP OF ADEN PROTECTORATE
1:500,000
In 3 sheets
DOS (Geol) 1147A
South Mahra
DOS (Geol) 1147B
S W Hadhramut
Tolworth : DOS, 1963
Col. geological maps.
each 50p

PHOTOGEOLOGICAL MAPS OF WESTERN ADEN PROTECTORATE
1:250,000
DOS (Geol) 1159 AB
In 2 sheets
Tolworth : DOS, 1967
120 x 80 each
Col. map. each 65p

GEOLOGICAL MAP OF COASTAL SOUTH YEMEN AND DHUFAR/ GULF OF ADEN
Report on the Red Sea Discussion Meeting
see INDIAN OCEAN 534 E1

K HUMAN GEOGRAPHY

HEALTH SERVICE INSTITUTIONS IN ADEN PROTECTORATE
1:3,200,000
DOS (Misc.) 265
Tolworth : DOS, 1959
Small hand map showing locations by symbols. 15p

535 Oman

See also : 53 NEAR & MIDDLE EAST
532 SAUDI ARABIA

A2 GENERAL MAPS : LOCAL

MUSANDAM PENINSULA
1:100,000
London : RGS 1973
58 x 48
Topographical map based on surveys of the RGS Musandam Expedition 1971-72
£1.00

C OFFICIAL SURVEYS

INTERNATIONAL MAP OF THE WORLD
1:1,000,000
DMS Series 1301
4 sheets for coverage of Muscat and Oman
see WORLD 100C and index 100/1

WORLD
1:500,000
DMS Series 1404
10 sheets for coverage of Muscat and Oman
see WORLD 100C and index 100/7

F GEOLOGY

TRUCIAL OMAN GEOLOGICAL MAP
1:100,000
DOS (Geol) 1168 AB
In 2 sheets
Tolworth : DOS, 1969
Coloured geological map 65p

G EARTH RESOURCES

TRUCIAL OMAN – GEOCHEMICAL MINERAL LOCATION MAP
1:100,000
DOS (Geol.) 1169 AB
In 2 sheets
Tolworth : DOS 1969
Coloured resources map 30p

536 United Arab Emirates

See also : 53 NEAR & MIDDLE EAST
532 SAUDI ARABIA

A2 GENERAL MAPS

PERSIAN GULF AND OMMAN SEA
1:1,000,000
Tehran : Sahab
90 x 60
2 sided map in Persian and Eng. Including Bandar-e-Abbas, Bandar-e-Bushehr, Kish Is, Lavan Is, Bandar-e-Jask, Bandar-e-Languen, Farur Is, Borazjan, Larak Is, Persian Gulf, Kharg Is, Bahrein Is, Minab, Hormoz, Queshm Is.
Rls 100

C OFFICIAL SURVEYS

INTERNATIONAL MAP OF THE WORLD
1:1,000,000
DMS series 1301
see WORLD 100C and index 100/1

WORLD
1:500,000
DMS Series 1404
see WORLD 100C and index 100/7

F GEOLOGY

PHOTOGEOLOGICAL MAP OF THE TRUCIAL OMAN
1:100,000
DOS (Geol) 1168 AB
Tolworth : DOS, 1969
96 x 74
2 sheet photogeological map in col.
50p each

G EARTH RESOURCES

GEOCHEMICAL AND MINERAL LOCATION MAP OF TRUCIAL OMAN
1:100,000
DOS (Geol) 1169A
Tolworth : DOS, 1969
84 x 56
2 sheet map set in col.

536.4 Qatar

C OFFICIAL SURVEYS

THE WORLD
1 : 1,000,000
DMS Series 1301
Sheet NG 39 covers Qatar
see WORLD 100C and index 100/1.

THE WORLD
1:500,000
DMS Series 1404
Sheets 547D and C cover Qatar
see WORLD 100C and index 100/7.

GEOGRAPHIC MAP SERIES OF THE KINGDOM OF SAUDI ARABIA
1:500,000
Washington : USGS
Sheets I 208 and I 209 cover Qatar.
see SAUDI ARABIA 532C and index 532/1.

536.5 Bahrein

A1 GENERAL MAPS

MAP OF BAHREIN
1:97,500
Tehran : Sahab, 1963
29 x 55
Col. sketch map showing roads, pipelines, relief by formlines. Insets of Mannameh, Maharreq with island's position and main features. In Eng. and Pers.
Rls 60

BAHREIN ISLANDS
1:63,360
Manama : Pub. Works Dept, 1968-9
74 x 106
Coloured map with contours, communications. Inset of Hawar Island. 1 sheet in Arabic (1969), 1 in English (1968).

B TOWN PLANS

MANAMA
1:4,000
DRG 353/4
Col. T D Lewis
Manama : Pub. Works Dept, 1967
61 x 38
Town plan.

536.8 Kuwait

A1 GENERAL MAPS

GENERAL MAP OF KUWAIT
1:500,000
Tehran : Sahab, 1965
55 x 65
Uncol. map showing land features—rivers, wadis, marshes, dunes etc, roads, railways, oil fields, pipelines. Inset of Kuwait town and environs. In Eng. and Pers.
Rls 100

F GEOLOGY

SYNOPTIC GEOLOGICAL MAP OF THE STATE OF KUWAIT
1:250,000
Wien : GB, 1967
121 x 88
Col. map inc. Neutral Zone, with sections and diagrams. Names in Eng. and Arabic. With 87pp text in Eng. 1968.
A Sch 200

54 Indian Subcontinent

D POLITICAL & ADMINISTRATIVE

INDIA AND ADJACENT COUNTRIES
1:12,000,000
1st edition
Dehra Dun : SI, 1964
53 x 47
Political col. by provinces, with hill shading. Ru 1.25

DAILY TELEGRAPH MAP OF THE MIDDLE EAST, INDIA AND PAKISTAN
1:7,000,000
see ASIA 5D

INDIA, PAKISTAN, BURMA AND CEYLON
1:4,506,250
Chicago : Denoyer—Geppert
111 x 99
Iran-Laos, China-Malaysia. Col. by states, cities graded by pop, railways, climatic maps inset. US $13.75

INDIA AND ADJACENT COUNTRIES
1:2,500,000
5th edition in 4 sheets
Dehra Dun : SI, 1969
152 x 121
Political wall map with communications and 7 them. insets, showing climate, geology, pop. and industry.

INDE
No 57
Paris : Hatier
100 x 120
School wall map; economic and political map on reverse.

AFGHANISTAN, PENNINSULA DEL INDOSTAN, BIRMANIA
No scale given
Barcelona : Editorial Teide
33 x 25
School hand map showing major cities and boundaries. S.Ptas 1

OUTLINE MAP OF INDIA AND ADJACENT COUNTRIES
1:16,000,000
3rd edition
Dehra Dun :SI, 1964
38 x 33
Map in black and white. Also available in Hindi edition. 1965.

INDIA AND ADJACENT COUNTRIES
1:12,000,000
1st edition
Dehra Dun : SI, 1964
53 x 47
Outline map showing political boundaries. Ru 0.50

E1 PHYSICAL : RELIEF

PŘEDNÍ INDIE
1:6,000,000
Praha : Kart
73 x 73
Physical reference map, with thematic text, covering politics, economy, geog. conditions. In series "Poznavame Svet" (Getting to know the world). Kcs 12

WORLD TRAVEL SERIES MAP OF INDIA, PAKISTAN AND CEYLON
1:4,000,000
Edinburgh : Bart, 1975
71 x 94
Contoured with layer col, roads classified, railways, canals, airports and boundaries. Inset plans of 5 main cities, Andaman and Nicobar Is. 75p

SUDASIEN
1:2,000,000
Ed Dr H Haack
Darmstadt : Perthes
195 x 196
Haack physical wall map of Indian Sub Cont, relief shading, layer col, communications, international and admin. boundaries.

H BIOGEOGRAPHY

CARTE DES BIOCLIMATS DU SOUS-CONTINENT INDIEN
by L Labrone, P Legris & M Viart
1:2,534,000
In 4 sheets
Pondichery : Inst. Fr, 1965
96 x 60 each
Col. map with diagrams and insets of rainfall and dry season on reverse. With 32pp text.

L ECONOMIC

INDIYA — PAKISTAN — ZEYLON
1:4,000,000
Moskva : GUGK, 1969
92 x 105
Showing economy and industry.

M HISTORICAL

BREASTED-HUTH HARDING HISTORICAL WALL MAPS — INDIA PAKISTAN, BURMA, CEYLON
No. 204561
Chicago : Denoyer—Geppert
Political map with states of India col. separately.

ATLASES
J CLIMATE

STUDIES IN THE CLIMATOLOGY OF SOUTH ASIA
U Schweinfurth and others
Heidelberg : Südasien—Institut/ Wiesbaden : Franz Steiner, 1970
viii, 16pp
15 maps in ring binder atlas, showing rainfall of the Indo-Pakistan subcontinent. DM 86.00

540 India

See also : 546.1 KASHMIR
54 INDIAN SUBCONTINENT

A1 GENERAL MAPS : ROADS

ROAD MAP OF INDIA
1:2,500,000
In 2 sheets
3rd edition
Dehra Dun : SI, 1973
120 x 150
Col. map showing all classes of road with distances. Insets of East and West Pakistan. Ru 3.00

B TOWN PLANS

CITY AND TOWN GUIDE MAPS
Various scales
Dehra Dun : SI
Maps available :

Abu	1:10,000	1968
Agra	1:15,840	1925
Agra City	1:5,280	1920
Allahabad	1:15,840	1936
Allahabad City	1:5,280	1922
Bangalore	1:21,120	1948
Benares	1:15,840	1933
Benares City	1:5,280	1920
Cawnpore	1:5,840	1933
Delhi	1:20,000	1969
Lashkar and Gwalior	1:21,120	1948
Lucknow	1:15,000	1933
Pachmarhi	1:10,560	1926
Secunderabad and Bolarum	1:21,120	1929
Seringapatam	1:21,000	1926
Simla	1:7.920	1939
Simla and extension	1:1,800	1928
Simla and extension	1:2,640	1928
Simla Mahasu	1:2,640	1920
Simla Mashobra	1:2,640	1919–20
Udaipur	1:15,840	1935

TOURIST GUIDE MAPS
Calcutta : Dipti
33 x 44 each
Small plans naming main streets and buildings for the following towns:

Bombay	50 x 68
Calcutta and Howran 1:4,000	54 x 85
Delhi	33 x 44
Madras	33 x 44

GUIDE MAP OF MADRAS
1:42,240
New Delhi : Tourist Devt. Corp, 1967
37 x 44
Col. plan showing principal streets with names, major buildings marked. Insets of Mount Road and Harbour areas.

D POLITICAL & ADMINISTRATIVE

POLITICAL MAP OF INDIA
1:15,000,000
Dehra Dun : SI, 1971
30 x 32
Political map, provinces in colour.
Ru 1.00

POLITICAL MAP OF INDIA
1:4,500,000
1st edition
Dehra Dun : SI, 1963, rev. 1968
91 x 90
Col. by states with internal district boundaries shown, also principal roads, railways and district and state headquarter towns. In Hindi. Ru 8.00

STATE MAPS
1:1,000,000
Dehra Dun :SI
Series of general col. maps.
Sheets available :
1 Andhra Pradesh, 1970, 90 x 86
4 Chandigarh, Delhi, Haryana, Himachal, Pradesh and Punjab 1968, 78 x 53
Other sheets in preparation.

STATE MAPS FOR PLANNED MARKETING
Bombay : Bureau of Commercial Intelligence and Statistics, 1972
Various sizes
Series of maps based on 1971 Census showing towns graded by population, admin. districts in red, quarter towns (listed in margin), road and rail communications. Available for:
1 Maharashtra and Gujarat 88 x 76
2 Madhya Pradesh 73 x 71
3 Andhra Pradesh, Mysore, Tamil Nadu and Kerala, 73 x 71
4 Kashmir, Himachal Pradesh Haryana, Punjab, Uttar Pradesh, Delhi and Rajasthan, 76 x 101
5 Bihar, Orissa, Bengal, Assam etc. 76 x 101

Each	Ru 19.00
Complete	Ru 95.00

MAP OF WEST BENGAL
No scale given
Calcutta : Dipti
46 x 72
Col. by districts, with principal roads, railways, main towns. Pop. table, with inset plan of Calcutta and suburbs.

ADMINISTRATIVE MAP OF BOMBAY METROPOLIS REGION
1:126, 720
Bombay : Town Planning Dept, 1968

HARYANA, POLITICAL MAP
1:506,880
Delhi : Vidya Chitr Prakashan
Col. wall map.

INDIA–PLAIN OUTLINE MAPS
Various scales
Dehra Dun : SI
Intended to be used as original base maps for private Publishers. In English and Hindi eds. Maps available.

1:35,000,000	14 x 17	Ru 0.15
1:17,500,000	26 x 29	Ru 0.25
1:8,500,000	43 x 62	Ru 0.50

INDIA OUTLINE MAPS
Various scales
Dehra Dun : SI
Intended to be used as base maps for private publishers. In English and Hindi eds. Maps available:

State Boundaries		
1:35,000,000	14 x 17	Ru 0.25
1:17,500,000	26 x 29	Ru 0.35
1:8,500,000	43 x 62	Ru 0.75
Major Rivers		
1:35,000,000	14 x 17	Ru 0.35
1:17,500,000	26 x 29	Ru 0.50
1:8,500,000	43 x 62	Ru 1.00

INDIA–PHYSICAL
1:15,000,000
1st edition
Dehra Dun : SI 1964
30 x 32
Contoured and layer coloured.
Ru 0.50

PHYSICAL MAP OF INDIA
1:4,500,000
Dehra Dun : SI, 1971
90 x 94
Contoured map inc. Nepal, Pakistan. Communications, boundaries.
Ru 2.00

WORLD TRAVEL SERIES MAP OF INDIA, PAKISTAN AND CEYLON
1:4,000,000
Edinburgh : Bart, 1975
71 x 94
Contoured with layer col, roads classified, railways, canals, airports and boundaries, inset plans of 5 main cities, and Andaman and Nicobar Islands.
75p

F GEOLOGICAL SURVEY

GEOLOGICAL MAP OF INDIA
1:5,000,000
Dehra Dun : SI, 1962
60 x 62
Col. geol. map.

GEOLOGICAL MAP OF INDIA
1:2,000,000
6th Edition
In 4 sheets
Dehra Dun : Geol. Surv. India, 1962
142 x 162
Col. map showing geol. on communications base map. With explanatory text, 1963.

TECTONIC MAP OF INDIA
1:2,000,000
In 4 sheets
Dehra Dun : Geol. Surv. India, 1963
142 x 162
Classifying by col. ages of folding and orogenic sub-divisions. With explanatory text.

GEOHYDROLOGICAL MAP OF INDIA
1:2,000,000
In 4 sheets
Calcutta : Geol. Surv. India, 1969
146 x 183 complete
In colours.

G EARTH RESOURCES

INDIA - SOILS
1:15,000,000
1st edition
Dehra Dun : SI, 1964
30 x 32
Soil map in col. Ru 0.50

METALLOGENETIC-MINEROGENETIC MAP
1:2,000,000
1st edition
In 4 sheets
Dehra Dun : Geol. Surv. India, 1963
142 x 162
Showing in col. on a geotectonic background mineral deposits, types and origins. With text in Eng.

H BIOGEOGRAPHY

INDIA - FOREST AND IRRIGATED AREAS
1:15,000,000
1st edition
Dehra Dun : SI, 1964
30 x 32
Map in col. Ru 0.50

CARTE INTERNATIONALE DU TAPIS VEGETAL
1:1,000,000
Pondichery : Fr. Inst.
Series of maps following international sheet lines, showing vegetation cover.
Sheets available :
No 2 Cape Comorih, 1961
NC 43,44 with text.
3 Madras, 1962
ND 44, Text 1963
5 Godavari, 1963
NE 43, 44 Text 1964
6 Jagannath, 1963
NE 44, 45 Text 1964
11 Mysore, 1965
ND 43 Text 1966
12 Bombay, 1965
NE 43 Text 1966
14 Kalkiawar, 1968
NF 42, 43 Text 1968
15 Satpura Mountains, 1968
NF 43, 44 Text 1970
17 Rajasthan, 1971
Ghardia, 1969, 1:500,000

L ECONOMIC

INDIA - RAILWAYS AND SEA ROUTES
1:15,000,000
1st edition
Dehra Dun : SI, 1964
30 x 32
Route map in cols. Ru 0.50

INDIA - ROADS AND AIR ROUTES
1:15,000,000
1st edition
Dehra Dun : SI, 1964
30 x 32
Map in colours. Rs 0.50

RAILWAY MAP OF INDIA
1:3,000,000
Dehra Dun : SI, 1968
89 x 114
Coloured map showing rail system.
Available in English or Hindi.
Ru 2.00 each

M HISTORICAL

INDIA - ARCHAEOLOGY AND TOURISM
1:15,000,000
1st edition
Dehra Dun : SI, 1964
30 x 32
Map in cols. Ru 0.50

PALMER WORLD HISTORY MAP - ANCIENT INDIA
Chicago : Rand McNally
Shows Mauryan and Gupta Empires, inc. other states. Also important archaeological sites.

C OFFICIAL SURVEYS

INTERNATIONAL MAP OF THE WORLD
1:1,000,000
SI
Many of these sheets were originally published as the HIND 5000 series, and they are now being re-converted to IMW style.
see WORLD 100C and index 100/1.

INDIA - TOPOGRAPHICAL SERIES
Dehra Dun : SI
New large scale surveys are being published on scales of 1:25,000, 1:50,000 and 1:250,000 in 7 colours. These will replace earlier series surveyed prior to 1905 on scales of 1:63,360, 1:126,720 and 1:253,440. NB The Government of India has imposed a ban on the export of these large scale maps.

ATLASES
A1 GENERAL : ROADS

MOTORISTS' INDIA GUIDE
Calcutta Dipti
In 2 vols.
Vol. I - 88pp
Motoring info, with sketch motoring maps, facing page of guide
Vol II - 74pp
Motoring maps, with guide
With separate folder containing black and white plans of Calcutta and Howran, Delhi, Bombay, Madras.

ATLASES
B TOWN PLANS

CALCUTTA ATLAS AND GUIDE
by A C Roy
Calcutta : A C Roy, 1965
20 x 23
384pp
41 maps of Calcutta and suburbs, streets, places of interest, bus and tram routes.

ATLASES
K HUMAN GEOGRAPHY

CENSUS ATLAS OF INDIA
Ed Dr P Sen Gupta
New Delhi : Registrar General & Ex-Officio Census Commissioner for India, 1970
51 x 41
423pp
Based on 1961 Census figures. Covers conditions, demography, economy, socio-economy, cultural aspects in 191 maps. Also physiographical maps. Arranged in separate parts for different regions of India.

ATLASES
L ECONOMIC

POWER ATLAS OF INDIA
New Delhi : Gov't of India, Publications Division, 1972
27 x 40
88pp
Presents growth of generating capacity, power utilisation, development of transmission system, and other factors concerning power growth by means of maps, charts and pictograms. £1.00

THE PLANNING ATLAS OF THE DAMODAR VALLEY REGION
Calcutta : Joint Committee for Diagnostic Survey of Damodar Valley Region, 1969
50 x 26
30pp
Atlas in 30 coloured map sheets, each with text on reverse by Prof. S P Chatterjee. Covers administrative, climatic, vegetation, geological, land use, agricultural and industrial factors.

ATLASES
M HISTORICAL

AN HISTORICAL ATLAS OF THE INDIAN PENINSULA
by C C Davies
2nd edition
London : OUP, 1959
40pp
47 black and white maps, with text.

ATLASES
O NATIONAL ATLAS

NATIONAL ATLAS OF INDIA
Prof. Chatterjee
Calcutta : Min. of Education and Scientific Research, 1959
English edition in preparation. A series of individual plates arranged under subjects. Sections A Population B Physical, C Transport and Tourism and I Adminstrative are to be mapped at 1:1,000,000 in 16 sheets plus other small scale maps. Other sections for which sheets have been published include F Agriculture and G Livestock. Further sheets in preparation.

541.31 Bhutan

E1 PHYSICAL : RELIEF

BHUTAN - WORLD LECTURE MAP
1:300,000
GSGS 4948 - E3
Feltham : DMS
122 x 91
Basic wall map with contours and communications.

THE KINGDOM OF BHUTAN
1:253,440
Florida : AAG, 1965
142 x 85
Shaded relief map, showing settlements, communications.

NORTH - WESTERN BHUTAN
1:250,000
reprinted from Geog. Journal Dec. 1966
London : RGS, 1966
51 x 35
Topographical map based on a traverse by M Ward, F Jackson and R Turner 1964-66 £1.50

541.33 Sikkim

E1 PHYSICAL MAPS

THE KINGDOM OF SIKKIM
by Pradyumna P Karan
1:150,000
Florida : AAG, 1969
78 x 97
Physical map with mountain shading, contours, glaciers, settlements of various types, roads. Plan of Gangtok on reverse. US$3.00

541.35 Nepal

A2 GENERAL MAPS: LOCAL

WESTERN NEPAL, KANJIROBA HIMAL
1:150,000
London : RGS
32 x 34
Reprinted from the Geog. Journal (Sept, 1967) from survey by the Kanjiroba Himal Expedition of 1964. Shows contours, hydrography, tracks and passes, spot heights in feet. Inset of whole country at 2,500,000, showing 1961 and 1964 routes. £1.50

THE MOUNT EVEREST REGION
1:100,000
London : RGS, 1975
73 x 64
Detailed topographical map, contoured with relief shading, moraine detail and rock drawing. Tracks, bridges, villages and huts are also shown £5.00

NEPAL
1:25,000 - 1:50,000
see index 541.35/1
Innsbruck : Univ. Verlag Wagner
Topographical series, contoured with roads, paths, towns, villages and settlements.
Sheets published :

Dudh Kosi	1:50,000
Everest-Chomolongma	1:25,000
Khumbu Himal	1:50,000
Tamba Kosi	1:50,000
Lapchi Kang	1:50,000
Rolwaling Himal	1:50,000

Sheets in preparation:

Kathmandu Valley	1:25,000
Khumbakarna Himal	1:50,000
Langtang/Jugal Himal	1:50,000

E1 PHYSICAL: RELIEF

RELIEFKARTE NEPAL
1:1,408,000
Bern : K & F
61 x 27
Relief shaded map, with main roads, mule tracks, airports, railways.
Legend Eng. Fr, Sp, Ger.

NEPAL
1:506,880
GSGS Series U 462
Feltham : DMS
184 x 85 complete
Map in 2 sheets, East and West, contoured with relief shading, roads, railways, district boundaries, bridges and towns classified according to administrative status. 30p each

F GEOLOGY

GEOLOGICAL MAP OF NEPAL
1:1,000,000
Basel : Swiss Nature Research Co, 1969
Map accompanying 2 vol. Report on Geol. Surv. of Nepal by Toni Hagen.

GEOLOGIC AND TECTONIC MAPS OF HIMALAYAN REGION
by A Gansser
A collection of maps, sketches and sections from "Geology of the Himalayas" 1964
Inc:
Plate 1A Geological map of the Himalayas 1:2,000,000 (col)
Plate 1B Tectonic map of the Himalayas 1:10,000,000 inset map (127 x 70)
Plate II Generalised sections through the Himalayas (in cols) (90 x 28)
Plate III Geological sections through the Eastern Kumaon Himalayas (160 x 28)
Plate IV Panorama of East & Central Kumaon and Eastern Nepal, Himalayas.
The above plates are folded and contained in a cardboard folder.

H BIOGEOGRAPHY

LA CARTE ÉCOLOGIQUE DU NÉPAL
1:250,000 - 1:50,000
Map in 8 sheets, see index 541.35/2
Editor J F Dobremez
Grenoble Univ. Scientifique et Médicale de Grenoble/Paris : CNRS
Series of ecological maps of Nepal each with a descriptive text.
Sheets published:

1. Région Annapurna-Dhaulagiri	1:250,000-197
2. Région Jiri-Thodung	1:50,000 - 197
3. Région Kathmandu-Everest	1:250,000-197
4. Région Terai Central	1:250,000-197
5. Region Ankhu Kola-Trisuli	1:50,000-1974
6. Région Biratnagar-Kangchenjunga	1:250,000-197

ATLASES
O NATIONAL

NEPAL IN MAPS
Prepared by Dept. of Publicity
1st edition
Katmandu: Ministry of Information, 1966
26 maps, 15pp statistical tables.

546.1 Kashmir

A2 GENERAL MAPS : LOCAL

HIMALAYA (HISPAR-BIAFO REGION)
1:253,440
London : RGS, 1940
58 x 39
Contoured, topog. map, surveyed by members of E E Shipton's Karakorum Expedition, 1939.
Reprinted from Geog. Journal
£1.50

N W KARAKORUM : MINAPIN (RAKAPOSHI RANGE)
1:50,000
W Berlin : Inst. fur Angewandte Geodasie, 1967
47 x 38
Col. map with contours, heights, snow, vegetation etc. indicated.
With 12pp booklet.

TOPOGRAPHICAL MAP OF KARAKORUM
1:12,500
Milano : Univ. di Milano
Col. map with contours.

E1 PHYSICAL RELIEF

KASHMIR - WORLD LECTURE MAP
1:750,000
GSGS 4948 - E11
Feltham, Middlesex : DMS
122 x 92
Basic military wall map, showing contours, main roads, rivers etc.

F GEOLOGY

WESTERN KARAKORUM, GEOLOGICAL TENTATIVE MAP
1:500,000
Milano : Univ. Geol. Inst. 1964
61 x 41
Col. map.

GEOLOGICAL MAP OF THE BALTORO BASIN (KARAKORUM) CENTRAL ASIA
1:100,000
Milano : Univ. Geol. Inst. 1969

548.7 Sri Lanka

A1 GENERAL MAPS: ROADS

SRI LANKA MOTOR MAP
1:506,880
Colombo : SDC, 1976
61 x 91
Coloured road map, with tourist details, distances in miles.

B TOWN PLANS

TOWN MAPS OF SRI LANKA
Various scales
Colombo : SDC
Various sizes
Available for :

Town	Scale	Size
Colombo	1:12,672	66 x 109
Colombo and surroundings	1:12,672	66 x 109
Colombo and surroundings with municipal wards and postal zones	1:12,672	66 x 109
Colombo showing wards	1:39,600	25 x 38
Colombo in sections	1:792	51 x 66 each
Colombo and surroundings in sections	1:3,168	50 x 71
Ambalangoda	1:6,336	46 x 53
Anuradhapura	1:9,504	84 x 78
Avissawella	1:6,336	61 x 53
Badulla	1:7,920	66 x 61
Bandarawela	1:3,960	63 x 61
Batticaloa	1:7,920	73 x 101
Chilaw	1:6,336	50 x 106
Dehiwala—Mt Lavina	1:9,504	53 x 96
Diyatalawa	1:4,952	73 x 94
Dondra	1:6,336	38 x 38
Galle	1:9,504	96 x 68
Gampola	1:4,952	61 x 71
Hambantota	1:6,336	81 x 66
Horana	1:6,336	61 x 86
Jaffna	1:7,920	99 x 76
Kalutara	1:6,336	53 x 101
Kandy	1:9,504	83 x 97
Kolonnawa	1:6,336	71 x 89
Kotte	1:9,504	71 x 99
Kurenegala	1:6,336	89 x 76
Madampe	1:3,960	78 x 50
Matale	1:6,336	48 x 76
Matara	1:6,336	101 x 66
Minuwangoda	1:4,952	40 x 30
Nawalpitiya	1:3,960	53 x 76
Negombo	1:7,920	81 x 91
Nuwara Eliya	1:1,584	78 x 76
Panadura	1:6,336	55 x 91
Puttalam	1:7,920	78 x 104
Ratnapura	1:6,336	101 x 73
Trincomalee	1:6,336	101 x 81
Weligama	1:12,672	38 x 35
Wattala-Mabole-Peliyagoda	1:6,336	63 x 106

C OFFICIAL SURVEYS

SRI LANKA TOPOGRAPHICAL SERIES
1:63,360
In 73 sheets, see index 548. 7/1
Colombo : SDC, 1960-70
69 x 44 each
Contoured, roads classified, paddy and cultivated land shown in col. with symbols indicating crops grown and considerable land detail. All sheets are pub. but many are frequently reprinted and not always immediately available.

D POLITICAL & ADMINISTRATIVE

CEYLON, ELECTORAL MAP
1:253,440
In 4 sheets
Colombo : SDC
122 x 185
Showing electoral and admin. boundaries.

E1 PHYSICAL: RELIEF

PHYSICAL MAP OF CEYLON
1:1,000,000
Colombo : SDC, 1970
37 x 50
General, physical map in colour, with contours, major roads and railways, district boundaries.

ZEYLON
1:750,000
Moskva : GUGK, 1971
52 x 67
Physical hand map, contours, communications, boundaries, 3 insets. In Country Map Series.

CEYLON GENERAL MAP
1:253,440
In 4 sheets
Colombo : SDC, 1969
122 x 185 complete
Col. and layered general map. Also available uncol. Contours, communications.

E2 PHYSICAL: LAND FEATURES

CEYLON SHOWING PLANNED RIVER BASIN DEVELOPMENT OF LAND, IRRIGATION & POWER
1:506,880
Colombo : SDC
60 x 91
Col. map indicating roads, water tanks, proposed and existing reservoirs, channels, power houses and tunnels, development schemes, paddy fields, reserves and plantations and a table of river effluences.

F GEOLOGY

PRELIMINARY TECTONIC MAP OF CEYLON
1:1,520,640
Colombo : SDC
18 x 30
Black and white map indicating principal anticlines, synclines and faults.

G EARTH RESOURCES

SET OF EIGHT THEMATIC MAPS OF CEYLON
1:1,500,000
i) Natural Resources
SDC
see CEYLON 548.7L

MAP SHOWING APPROXIMATE DISTRIBUTION OF GREAT SOIL GROUPS
1:500,000
Colombo : SDC
68 x 106
Col. map showing major soil groups.

H BIOGEOGRAPHY

LAND UTILISATION MAP
1:2,000,000
Colombo : SDC
16 x 25
Indicating dry and wet zones and land use product areas in col.

CARTE INTERNATIONALE DU TAPIS VEGETAL—CEYLON
1:1,000,000
Pondichery : Fr. Inst, 1964
Detailed col. map of vegetation, following international sheet lines, NC 44, NB 44, Text in Fr, 1965.

CEYLON LAND UTILISATION MAP
1:253,440
In 4 sheets
Colombo ' SDC
122 x 185
Col. map showing land use areas with indications of crops grown.

J CLIMATE

CLIMATIC MAP OF CEYLON
1:506, 880
Colombo : SDC, 1968
68 x 101
3 coloured climatic map, with temperature tables on reverse.

K HUMAN GEOGRAPHY

SET OF EIGHT THEMATIC MAPS OF CEYLON
1:1,500,000
ii) Population, 1953
vi) Technical Educational Facilities
vii) Craft Schools
viii) Craft Centres
SDC
see CEYLON 548.7 L

L ECONOMIC

SET OF EIGHT THEMATIC MAPS OF CEYLON
1:1,500,000
Colombo : SDC
22 x 34 each
Some in col, some in black and white, depicting various aspects of the country's life:
i) Natural Resources
ii) Population (1953)
iii) Agriculture
iv) Industries
v) Crop Distribution
vi) Technical Educational Facilities
vii) Craft Schools
viii) Craft Centres

CEYLON PLANTATION MAP
1:253,440
In 4 sheets
Colombo : SDC
135 x 122 complete
Plantations classified by colours, central area only.

549 Pakistan

See also:
54 INDIAN SUBCONTINENT

A1 **GENERAL MAPS: ROADS**

MAP OF PAKISTAN
1:6,250,000
Karachi : Surv. Pakistan, 1971
40 x 28
Roads, boundaries and communications.
PRu 1.00

PAKISTAN
1: 3,000,000
Tehran : Sahab
48 x 61
Road map in Eng and Persian.
Cities, boundaries, communications, Bangladesh, Junagadh, Manavadar inset. Pictorial border.

A2 **GENERAL MAPS: LOCAL**

MAP OF BALUCHISTAN
1:1,000,000
In 2 sheets
Karachi : Surv. Pakistan
General communication map.
PRu 2.00

C **OFFICIAL SURVEYS**

INTERNATIONAL MAP OF THE WORLD
1: 1,000,000
In 12 sheets
Karachi : Surv. Pakistan
see WORLD 100C and index 100/1

D **POLITICAL & ADMINISTRATIVE**

MAP OF PAKISTAN
1:3,125,000
Karachi : Surv. Pakistan, 1971
52 x 72
Map showing political divisions.
PRu 2.00

PAKISTAN
1:2,000,000
In 4 sheets
Karachi : Surv. of Pakistan, under revision 1972
118 x 106 complete
Political col, communications, insets of climate, economy etc.

MAP OF BOUNDARY BETWEEN CHINA'S SINKIANG AND THE CONTIGUOUS AREA, THE DEFENCE OF WHICH IS UNDER THE ACTUAL CONTROL OF PAKISTAN
1:1,500,000
Karachi : Surv. Pakistan, 1966
General Topog. map. P.Ru 2.00

MAP OF PUNJAB
1:1,000,000
Karachi: Surv. Pakistan, 1967
70 x 55
Map showing administrative divisions, including Bahawalpur, Lahore, Multan, Rawalpindi and Sargodha Divisions.
P.Ru 2.00

MAP OF NORTH WEST FRONTIER PROVINCE
1:1,000,000
Karachi : Surv. Pakistan, 1968
46 x 66
Showing political divisions D I Khan and Peshawar Divisions, Amb, Chitral, Div and Swat (now in Malakand Div). P. Ru 2.00

E1 **PHYSICAL: RELIEF**

WORLD TRAVEL SERIES MAP OF INDIA, PAKISTAN and CEYLON
1:4,000,000
Edinburgh : Bart, 1975
71 x 94
Contoured with layer col, roads, airports, boundaries. Inset plans of 5 main cities, Andaman and Nicobar Islands. 75p

F **GEOLOGY**

GEOLOGICAL MAP OF PAKISTAN
1:2,000,000
Quetta : Geol. Surv. Pak, 1964
112 x 91
Detailed col. map covering East and West Pakistan, W. Kashmir with sections and map sources.

RECONNAISSANCE GEOLOGY OF PARK OF WEST PAKISTAN
1:253,440
In 29 sheets
Toronto : Photo Surv. Corp.
Canada and Geol. Survey Pak, 1958
Col. geol series compiled 1953-56 covering southern region of the country west of 70°E.

G **EARTH RESOURCES**

MAP SHOWING THE LOCATION OF THE PRINCIPAL MINERAL DEPOSITS IN WEST PAKISTAN
1: 4,235,200
Karachi : Director of Mineral Devt, 1962
38 x 32

L **ECONOMIC**

MAP OF PAKISTAN AND SURROUNDING COUNTRIES
1:1,500,000
Karachi : Surv. Pakistan under revision 1972
Showing railway communications.

ATLASES

W3 **ATLASES WORLD ATLAS : LOCAL EDITION**

THE OXFORD SCHOOL ATLAS FOR PAKISTAN
OUP, 1966
see WORLD ATLASES 100 W 3

549.3 Bangladesh

See also : 549 PAKISTAN
54 INDIAN SUBCONTINENT

A1 GENERAL MAPS: ROADS

TRANSPORTATION MAP OF BANGLADESH
1: 1,000,000
Dacca : Surveyor General, 1967
Map showing transportation routes.

MAP OF EAST PAKISTAN
1: 1,000,000
Karachi : Surv. Pakistan, 1962
54 x 71
Col. general map with administrative boundaries, communications.
P. Ru 2.00

C OFFICIAL SURVEYS

INTERNATIONAL MAP OF THE WORLD
1:1,000,000
4 sheets cover Bangladesh:
NG 45, 46, NF 45, 46
Survey of Pakistan
see WORLD 100C and index 100/1.

D POLITICAL & ADMINISTRATIVE

POLITICAL MAP OF BANGLADESH
1:700,000
Calcutta : Society and Commerce Publications, 1972

K

55 Iran

See also: 53 NEAR & MIDDLE EAST

A1 GENERAL MAPS : ROADS

IRAN, GENERAL WITH COMPLETE DETAILS
1:3,500,000
No 43
Tehran : Sahab
100 x 70
Showing admin. divisions, roads, physical features, index of cities and inset maps showing—Mineral deposits, roads, handicrafts, industries and factories, flora, relief, forest regions, local costumes and airways.
In English Rls 200

IRAN HIGHWAY MAP
1:2,500,000
Tehran : Ministry Roads and Communications, 1970
92 x 68
In Per. and Eng. Col. road map, printed both sides, Eng. and Arabic; illus. col. photographs.
Shows roads of all classes, distances in km, settlements, flooded areas distance chart.

MAP OF IRAN
1:2,500,000
No 165
Tehran : Sahab, 1971
77 x 57
Roads classified according to type, relief shading, distances in km, railways, petrol stations, desert areas, airports, beaches, monuments etc. Legend Eng, Fr. Per. Inset plans on reverse.
Rls 150

IRAN ROAD MAP
1:2,500,000
AMS K201
Washington : Defense Mapping Agency
86 x 86
Boundaries, roads classified, railways, spot heights. U.S. $ 1.00

IRAN GENERAL, ROADS AND COMMUNICATIONS
1:2,250,000
No 108
Tehran : Sahab
100 x 70
Showing main and secondary roads, distances, list of historical sites.
In English. Rls 150

A2 GENERAL MAPS : LOCAL

NEW GUIDE MAPS OF PROVINCES
Various scales
see index 55/1
Tehran : Sahab
Double sided maps showing all classes roads, distances and filling stations, tourist and economic information, insets of town plans.
English and Persian text.
Maps available :

No	Map	Scale	Size
116	Azarbaijan (east)	1:500,000	58 x 57
126	Azarbaijan (west) & Rezaiyeh	1: 1,000,000 and 1:7,500	60 x 45
140	Chahar-Mahal & Bakhtiyari	1:250,000	90 x 60
96	Guilan	1:500,000	90 x 50
129	Isfahan	1:500,000	90 x 60
166	Fars	1:1,000,000	90 x 60
104	Kermanshahan	1:500,000	90 x 50
131	Kerman	1:500,000	90 x 60
120	Khorasan	1:1,000,000	90 x 60
97	Khuzestan	1:500,000	90 x 60
109	Khuzestan	1:500,000	90 x 60
89	Mazandaran	1:500,000	90 x 60
119	Persian Gulf and Oman Sea	1:1,000,000	90 x 60
176	Sistan and Baluchestan	1:1,000,000	90 x 60
127	Western Iran (Kurdestan, Hamedan, Zanjan) (single sided)	1:1,000,000	100 x 70

IRAN REGIONAL MAPS
Various scales
Tehran : Sahab
Showing roads, railways, boundaries
Maps available :

No	Map	Scale	Size
P3	Aligudarz and Borujerd Townships	1:300,000	90 x 60 (Per)
46	Arak and Tafresh Townhips (Per and Eng)	1:200,000	90 x 60
P4	Azarbaijan (west and east provinces)	1:500,000	95 x 90 (Per)
P7	Gorgan and Gonbad-E-Kavous Townships	1:400,000	70 x 60 (Per)
84	Bam and Narmashir Townships (Per and Eng)	1:100,000	90 x 60
P9	Iranshahr Township (Per and Eng)	1:200,000	90 x 60
P10	Kermanshah Township	1:200,000	90 x 60 (Per)
62	Khuzestan Province (North Section) (Per and Eng)	1:250,000	110 x 90
P12	Malayer, Nahavand and Tuyserkan Townships	1:250,000	80 x 60 (Per)
42	Northern Coasts of Iran (Per and Eng)	1:250,000	150 x 90
P14	Qazvin Township	1:250,000	60 x 50 (Per)
P15	Qom and Mahallat Townships	1:250,000	50 x 40 (Per)
88	Shahsavar and Nowshahr Townships (Per and Eng)	1:100,000	125 x 60
87	Sistan Township (Per and Eng)	1:200,000	90 x 60
2	Tehran and Environs	1:250,000	90 x 60 (Eng)

B TOWN PLANS

TOWN PLANS
Tehran : Sahab
In Eng and Per, available for :

No	Town	Scale	Size	Price
157	Abadan and Khorramshahr	1:6,000	70 x 50	Rls 100
138	Ahwaz	1:20,000	66 x 41	Rls 60
6	Isfahan	1:15,000	60 x 45	Rls 60
28	Kerman	1:10,000	60 x 45	Rls 60
159	Mash'had	1:10,000	90 x 60	Rls 100
125	Mash'had	1:20,000	70 x 50	Rls 60
126	Rezaiyeh	1:15,000	60 x 45	Rls 60
117	Shiraz, Persepolis and Environs	1:20,000	60 x 45	Rls 60
12	Tabriz	1:10,000	90 x 60	Rls 100
161	Tabriz	1:17,500	70 x 50	Rls 60
133	Tehran Central	1:20,000	43 x 70	Rls 50
P21	Tehran Central	1:20,000	60 x 45	(Per only)
164	Tehran Center and North	1:22,500	60 x 90	Rls 30
112	Tehran Mini Map	1:30,000	39 x 45	Rls 10
105/6	Tehran Complete	1:15,000	60 x 90	Rls 70
45	Tehran, Greater, City and Vicinity (3 sheets)	1:10,000	270 x 200	Rls 1500
92	Tehran and Shemiranat, complete	1:20,000	100 x 70	Rls 100
71	Torbate—Heydariyeh	1:6,000	45 x 60	Rls 70
91	Zahedan	1:7,500	60 x 45	Rls 70

C OFFICIAL SURVEYS

IRAN—REGIONAL PLANS
Various scales
Tehran : Natn'l Cart. Center
Large scale series of regional plans in black and white with contours, field boundaries and other land detail. Legend in Persian.
Maps available:

Map	Sheets	Size	Scale
Esfehan	32 sheets	99 x 69	1:2,500
Kordestan-Lorestan	9 sheets	99 x 79	1:50,000
Bandar-e-Bushehr			1:2,000

11 sheets 99 x 69
Bandar-e-Abbas Munab
1:50,000
6 sheets 89 x 79
Abadan 1:2,000
32 sheets 99 x 69
Dezful 1:2,500
5 sheets 99 x 69
Aghajari 1:2,000
4 sheets 69 x 99

D POLITICAL & ADMINISTRATIVE

IRAN
1:6,000,000
No PS18
Tehran : Sahab
50 x 35
Admin. divisions, prov. centres and governorships, rivers etc. Insets Economy, physical features, admin, div. chart.

IRAN
1:3,000,000
No PS8
Tehran : Sahab
90 x 60
Wall map showing admin. divisions, provincial centres and governorships, rivers etc. shaded relief, roads and railways. Insets : Physical and Economic Features. Population chart. In Persian text.

IRAN POLITICAL MAP
1:2,500,000
No 196
Tehran : Sahab
110 x 84
School wall map showing political divisions. In Persian only.

IRAN, ADMINISTRATIVE DIVISIONS
1:2,000,000
No 139
Tehran : Sahab
90 x 90
Showing boundaries of provinces and sub-provinces, including population chart (1966 census) Rls 100

E1 PHYSICAL : RELIEF

IRAN PHYSICAL
1:2,500,000
No 178
Tehran : Sahab
90 x 60
Contoured and layer coloured with inset showing physiographic divisions In Persian only.

IRAN GENERAL MAP
1: 2,500,000
No 179
Tehran : Sahab
80 x 57
Coloured road map with distances, contoured with map of physiographic divisions inset. Rls 150

PHYSICAL MAP OF IRAN
1:2,500,000
No 188
Tehran : Sahab
110 x 84
Contoured with communications, water in blue, roads in red, railways brown.

MAP OF IRAN
1:1,500,000
In 4 sheets
Tehran : Nat. Cart Centre, 1968
140 x 130 complete
Col. map, contours, roads classified, railways, boundaries.

E2 PHYSICAL : LAND FEATURES

PHYSIOGRAPHIC DIVISIONS OF IRAN
1:3,000,000
No 79
Tehran : Sahab
88 x 59
Shows many physiographic divisions, with cross section of the Iranian plateau Legend in English and Persian.
Rls 100

IRAN WATER OUTLINE MAP
1:2,500,000
Tehran : Min. Water Power Gen. Div. of Water Resources Hydrogeology Div. 1966
93 x 70

MAIN RIVER BASINS
by M Rabbani
1:2,500,000
Tehran : Min Water Power Gen. Div. of Water Resources Hydrogeology, 1965
93 x 70
Marginal notes on average discharge of the five water years, 1335 - 1340 Aban (1956-61)

F GEOLOGY

GEOLOGICAL MAP OF IRAN
1:4,000,000
No 135
Tehran : Sahab
65 x 45
Black and white geological map with 2 insets : Sketch map of known salt domes and, Structural Elements of Iran with 3 profiles. In English.
Rls 100

GEOLOGICAL MAP OF IRAN
1:2,500,000
Tehran : Natn'l Iranian Oil Co, 1969
76 x 72
Col. Map with 20pp explanation, incl. bibliography in English

PORTFOLIO OF GEOLOGICAL MAPS OF SOUTH WEST PERSIA
1: 1,000,000
In 6 sheets
London : British Petroleum Co, 1956
85 x 60 each
4 sheets with 24 geol. sections, 7 sheets showing stratigraphy. In plastic binder.
£12.00

CENTRAL LUT RECONNAISSANCE, EAST IRAN
1:500,000
Prepared by J Stocklin and others
Tehran : Geol. Surv.
Col. geol. map. Rls 200

GEOLOGICAL MAPS, COLUMNS AND SECTIONS OF THE HIGH ZAGROS OF SOUTH-WESTERN IRAN
1:250,000
In 16 sheets
London : British Petroleum Co, 1964
77 x 48
Col. series of geol. maps.
Set £6.00
Also available bound in volume
£12.00

GEOLOGICAL QUADRANGLE MAPS
1:250,000
Tehran : Geol. Surv. (UN Special Fund Project)
Series in prep. based on the Topographic quadrangle maps prep. by the Geographic Branch of the Iranian Imperial Army. Description in Latin lettering : each sheet has text vol. in Eng.
Sheets available :
Golpaygan Quad. 1963,
Zanjan Quad. 1969,
Boshruyeh Quad. 1971,

GEOLOGY AND PETROGRAPHY OF MOUNT DAMAVAND AND ITS ENVIRONMENT (CENTRAL ALBORZ)
1:100,000
Tehran : Geol. Surv, 1970
Col. map in Persian Text.
Rls 200

GEOLOGICAL MAP OF THE CENTRAL ALBORZ
1:100,000
Sheet : DEMAVAND
Tehran : Geol. Surv, 1972
Coloured geological map with text (153pp in Persian with English summary)
Rls 100

GEOLOGY AND PETROGRAPHY OF THE AREA NORTH OF NAIN, CENTRAL IRAN
1:100,000
Tehran : Geol. Surv, 1972
Col. map in text. Rls 200

GEOLOGY OF THE TAROM DISTRICT, WESTERN PART (ZANJAN AREA, NW IRAN)
1:100,000
Tehran : Geol. Surv, 1966
Col. map in text. Rls 100

GEOLOGY OF THE SHIRGESTH AREA (TABAS AREA, E IRAN)
1:100,000
Tehran : Geol. Surv, 1968
Col. geol. map in text. Rls 250

GEOLOGY AND MINERAL RESOURCES OF THE SOLTANIEH MOUNTAINS (NW IRAN)
1:100,000
Tehran : Geol. Surv, 1965
Col. geol. map in text. Rls 100

GEOLOGY OF SHOTORI RANGE (TABAS AREA, E IRAN)
1:100,000
Tehran : Geol. Surv, 1965
Col. map in text
Rls 150

GEOLOGICAL MAP OF UPPER DJADJERUD AND LAR VALLEYS, CENTRAL ELBURZ
1:50,000
Milano : Univ. di Milano, 1966
170 x 85
2 sheet map, with tectonic sketch map at 1:50,000. 86pp description.

G EARTH RESOURCES

COPPER DEPOSITS IN IRAN
1:3,000,000
Tehran : Geol. Surv, 1969
Col. Map in text. Rls 150

GEOLOGICAL ENVIRONMENT OF THE CHAHR-GONBAD COPPER MINE
1:5,000
Tehran : Geol. Surv, 1969
Col. map in text Rls 100

H BIOGEOGRAPHY

ZOOGEOGRAPHY OF IRAN
1:3,000,000
No 53
Tehran : Sahab, 1966
55 x 62
Animals, zoogeographic regions and classification of animals. Insets : hunting of birds at 1:9,220,000 and mammals at 1:7,575,000 4pp leaflet giving Eng. names of animals.
Rls 100

LIVESTOCK POULTRY AND AGRICULTURE
1:3,000,000
No 124
Tehran : Sahab
90 x 60
With English and Persian text. Showing animal varieties with 2 insets: distribution of sheep breeds and pasture lands. Rls 100

J CLIMATE

IRAN—CLIMATE
1:3,000,000
No 123
Tehran : Sahab, 1969
90 x 60
Climatic map in Per and Eng, showing temperature extremes. Insets : Average annual precipitation and climatic currents. Rls 100

L ECONOMIC

IRAN, ROADS
1:4,000,000
No P8
Tehran : Sahab
90 x 50
Showing main and secondary roads, railways and airways (inset). In Persian.
Rls 30

ECONOMIC MAP OF IRAN
1:3,000,000
Tehran : Sahab, 1970
58 x 88
Economy shown by pictorial symbols. 2 insets showing roads, agriculture, livestock, vegetation. Text Per and Eng.
Rls 100

AGRICULTURAL PRODUCTS
1:3,000,000
No 57
Tehran : Sahab, 1969
85 x 54
Orange and white base map, agricultural products indicated by symbols. Insets of industrial plants, fruit trees, vegetables, agricultural types. Legend in Eng and Per.
Rls 150

IRAN, POLITICAL—PHYSICAL—ECONOMICAL
1:1,000,000
No 93,
Tehran : Sahab
180 x 180
Main and secondary roads, distances, railways, ports. Inset maps—admin. divisions, physiographic divisions, livestock, agriculture and industries, list of dams.
Rls 1000

M HISTORICAL MAPS

HISTORICAL MAPS
Tehran : Sahab
Series of historical maps with text in English and Persian.
Maps available :
1000 Iran under Darius the Great, 500 BC 1:4,000,000app 1970 100 x 145 Rls 400
1001 Iran under the Seljuqs 1040-1457 1:4,000,000app 1970 100 x 70 Rls 200
1002 Iran under the Safavi Dynasty 1:3,500,000app 1970 100 x 70 Rls 200
1003 Alexander's Eastern Expeditions and Conquests 1:4,000,000 1970 100 x 70 Rls 200

FACSIMILES OF EARLY MAPS
Tehran : Sahab
Printed in black and white on tinted paper.
Maps available :
136 Carte de Perse en 1724 par G Delisle, 70 x 50
170 Same as above but 180 x 140
174 Nova Persiae (Anatolia et Arabia) by F de Wit, 1688 70 x 50
175 Map of Persia by Eman. Bowen, 1747, London, 70 x 50
180 Carte du Monde Connu en 1688 par le Sieur Jargeon 100 x 70
207 Persia sive Sophorum Regnum by Theodorous Tholing, 1634 70 x 50
208 The Kingdome of Persia with the Chief Cities and Habits described by John Speed, 1676, 70 x 50
209 A New Map of the Empire of Persia from Mons. R Danville, 1st Cartographer to the most Christian King—pub'd Laurie & Whittle, London, 1794 70 x 50
210 Persien nach seinem neuesten zustande oestliene und westuche Reich. Von C G Reichard, 1804, 70 x 50

ATLASES
W3 WORLD ATLASES: LOCAL EDITIONS

ATLAS-E-JAHAN DAR-ASR-E-FAZA (ATLAS OF THE WORLD IN THE SPACE AGE)
3rd edition
Tehran : Sahab
18 x 25
136pp
General physical-political world atlas incl. space illus, national flags, insets on maps of individual countries showing relief, climate, land use, population and economy and statistics. In Persian. Rls 120

ATLAS-E-NAKHOSTEEN (THE FIRST ATLAS)
3rd edition
Tehran : Sahab
25 x 35
50pp
Elementary school atlas of the world and heavens. In Persian. Rls 60

ATLAS-E-DANESH-AMUZ (STUDENTS' ATLAS)
Tehran : Sahab
18 x 25
48pp
General high school atlas. In Persian.
Rls 36

ATLASES
J CLIMATE

CLIMATIC ATLAS OF IRAN
By Dr A Mostofi, M H Ganji
Tehran : Sahab, 1967
42 x 35 (plate size)
In Per and Eng. 117 col. plates, inc. 215 maps and 108 windroses. Covers precipitation, temperature, pressure, humidity, cloud, thunderstorms, duststorms, windroses.

ATLASES
M HISTORICAL

ATLAS OF GEOGRAPHICAL MAPS AND HISTORICAL DOCUMENTS OF THE PERSIAN GULF
Ed A Sahab
Tehran : Sahab, 1971
302pp
25 x 35
Collection of black and white facsimile maps from clay tablets (2,500 BC) to modern school textbooks. Arranged chronologically in 8 chapters, including index and bibliography. With notes in Eng, and Pers. Rls 2000

ATLAS OF ANCIENT AND HISTORICAL MAPS OF IRAN
Tehran : Sahab, 1971
25 x 35
200pp
Containing 133 black and white reproductions of maps of Iran and 42 reproductions of topographical prints of Iran's cities through the ages. Notes in Eng. and Pers.

ATLASES
O NATIONAL

ATLAS OF IRAN : WHITE REVOLUTION, PROCEEDS AND PROGRESSES
Tehran : Sahab, 1971
192pp
25 x 35
Comprehensive atlas illustrating aspects of political, social, economic, agricultural subjects, also population, communications and future potential. In Persian and English.

560 Turkey

A1 GENERAL MAPS : ROADS

TURKEI
1:3,000,000
Bern : Hallwag
67 x 58
Covers Turkey, Egypt and the Eastern Mediterranean. Main and secondary roads, distances in km, hill shading, spot heights in metres, car ferries, railways, airports and state boundaries.

F & B AUTOKARTE
1:2,000,000
Wien : FB
116 x 88
Road map series covering Europe and Middle East, roads classified with conditions and distances, hill shading. Sheets covering Turkey : Kleinasien - Napoli - Erzurum - Suez
Naher Osten - Istanbul - Konya - Cairo - Shiraz
DM 6.80

EUROPÄISCHE STRASSENKARTE - TURKIYE
1:2,000,000
No 885
Frankfurt : Ravenstein, 1976
96 x 66
Relief shading, roads classified with distances in km, railways, ferries, camping sites, other tourist information.
DM 7.80

REISEKARTE TURKEI
1:2,000,000
No 229
Koln : Polyglott
Roads classified, distances in km, relief shading, road guide, camping sites.

KARAYOLLARI HARITASI TURKIYE
1:1,850,000
Ankara : General Directorate of Highways, 1969
93 x 50
Official road map, roads classified, places of interest. On reverse through plans of Ankara, Istanbul, Izmir.

ROAD MAP OF TURKEY
1:1,850,000
Ankara : Turkish Automobile Club
93 x 50
Roads classified and numbered, distances in km, boundaries, airports, ports, places of tourist interest. Tables and text in English on reverse.

TURKEY
1:1,000,000
London : Foldex
Shows roads classified, relief shading; patent fold.
45p

TURKEI
1:1,000.000
No. 1177
Bern : K & F
128 x 74
Road map showing all classes of roads, distances, scenic routes, railways and places of interest.

B TOWN PLANS

TOWN PLANS
Ankara : MSB Harita Genel Mudurlugu
Coloured plans naming streets and public buildings
Plans available :
Ankara 1:15,000 79 x 67 1972
Istanbul 1:20,000

HALLWAG PLAN OF ISTANBUL
1:12,500
Bern : Hallwag, 1973
63 x 58
Col. plan with index.

C OFFICIAL SURVEYS

KARTA MIRA
1:2,500,000
Carti : GUGK
2 sheets required
see WORLD 100C and index 100/2.

INTERNATIONAL MAP OF THE WORLD
1:1,000,000
DMS
8 sheets needed for complete coverage
see WORLD 100C and index 100/1.

WORLD
1:500,000
DMS Series 1404
21 sheets for coverage.
see WORLD 100C and index 100/7.

D POLITICAL & ADMINISTRATIVE

TURKIYE
1:2,000,000
Ankara : KY
120 x 78
Political col. map.

FAIK RESIT UNAT TURKIYE ILLER VE YOLLAR HARITASI
1:1,500,000
Ankara : KY
120 x 75
Col. admin. map, provinces in col, towns graded by pop, principal roads and railways.

E1 PHYSICAL : RELIEF

TURKIYE
1:2,000,000
Ankara : KY
120 x 78
Physical with contours, provinces.

FAİK REŞİT UNAT TÜRKİYE FIZINI HARİTASI
1:1,500,000
Ankara : KY
121 x 78
Contours, communications. Inset of administrative areas, towns graded by pop.

E2 PHYSICAL : LAND FEATURES

TÜRKİYE JEOMORFOGRAFİK HARİTA
Prof Dr Resat Izbirak
1:850,000
Ankara : Harita Genel Müdürlüğü Matbaasci Doner Sermayesi, 1968
Layer coloured map, with contours, hydrography, main mountain chains, hachuring. 2 insets (monochrome) of areas liable to earthquake and structural phenomena.

F GEOLOGY

TURKIYE JEOLOJİ HARİTASI
1:500,000
In 18 sheets
Ankara : Min. Res. and Exploration Inst, 1961-64
57 x 45 each
Col. geol. series, some with explanatory text.

G EARTH RESOURCES

DISTRIBUTION OF MINERAL RESOURCES
1:2,500,000
Ankara : Mining Res. and Exploration Inst, 1960
74 x 30
Col. map showing resources by symbol.

SOIL MAP OF THE QUMRA AREA (GUMRA BOLGESININ TOPRAK HARITASI)
1:100,000
Prepared for Soils and Fert. Research Inst, Ankara.
Wageningen : Centre for Agric. Pub & Doc 1969
45 x 26
Coloured map with legend in Turk. and Eng. with 105pp text.

SOILS OF THE GREAT KONYA BASIN
1:200,000
Prepared for Soils and Fert. Research Inst, Ankara.
Wageningen : Centre for Ag. Pub. & Doc. 1970
109 x 80
Coloured map in English and Turkish with 290pp text.

SOIL SURVEY OF THE KÖYCEĞIZ-DALAMAN AREA
1:50,000
Ed. L. J. Pows and C. H. Edelman
Ankara: Soil and Fertilizer Research Inst. 1964
56 x 80
Coloured soil and land suitability maps with 108pp explanatory text published in English and Turkish editions.

J CLIMATE

RAINFALL IN TURKEY
1:2,250,000
Istanbul : State Meteorological Service, 1962
88 x 48
Col. map showing rainfall by isohyets at 200m intervals.

K HUMAN GEOGRAPHY

TÜRKİYE NUFUS HARİTASI
1:1,000,000
Istanbul : Univ. of Instanbul, 1963
170 x 70
Pop. maps showing density by dots and land forms by contours. Legend and explanation in Turkish and English.

ATLASES
O NATIONAL

TÜRKİYE ATLASI
Istanbul : Univ. Faculty of Letters, 1961
35 x 49
Containing 45pp col. maps inc. 16pp physical map. Covers structural, climatic, social and economic subjects. Text in English and Turkish.

564.3 Cyprus

A2 GENERAL MAPS : LOCAL

TROODOS AND HILL RESORTS
1:25,000
3rd edition
Nicosia : Dept. Lands & Surv. 1969
58 x 85
Coloured topog. map of the area.

B TOWN PLANS

TOWN PLANS
Nicosia : Surv. of Cyprus
Col. plans naming principal streets and buildings.
Plans available :
Famagusta and Varosha Plan
1:5,000 1963
Limassol Official Plan
1:5,000 1962
Limassol and Environs
1:10,000 1962
Nicosia-within-the-walls
1:2,500 1966
Nicosia In 2 sheets
1:7,500 1964
Troodos and hill Resorts
1:2,500
Larnaca and Scala
1:5,000 1967
Ktima and Paphos
1:5,000 1967
Kyrenia
1:5,000 1967

C OFFICIAL SURVEYS

TOPOGRAPHICAL SERIES
1:31,680
In 60 sheets, see index 564.3/3
Nicosia : Govt. of Cyprus Printing Office
63 x 47
Series of planimetric maps, showing settlement and field boundaries.
Available as Sunprints only.

CYPRUS
1:25,000
In 59 sheets, see index 564.3/1
DOS 355 (K8110)
Tolworth : DOS, 1960-66
Showing contours, vegetation, archaeological sites. each 50p

CYPRUS
1:10,000
DOS 255 (K818), see index 564.3/1
Tolworth : DOS, 1960-66
Contours, vegetation, other topographical detail. each 50p

CADASTRAL PLANS
Various scales
Nicosia : Gov't of Cyprus Printing Office
Series of large scale plans showing field boundaries, available only as Sunprints.
1:5,000 for Nicosia, Limassol, Paphos, Larnaca (part), Districts
1:2,500 for Famagusta, Kyrenia, Nicosia (part), Larnaca (part) Districts
1:1,250 for Villages of Cyprus
1:1,000 for Limassol, Larnaca, Famagusta, Nicosia (part), Towns
1:500 for Kyrenia, Ktima, Nicosia (part) Towns

E1 PHYSICAL . RELIEF

ADMINISTRATION AND ROAD MAP OF CYPRUS
1:253,440
Nicosia : Survey of Cyprus, 1970
91 x 58
Contours, layer col, roads classified, railways, topographic detail, archaeological sites.

CYPRUS
1:250,000
Washington : AMS
93 x 65
Physical col. map with roads classified, railways, airports, boundaries.

TOPOGRAPHICAL MAP OF CYPRUS
1:126,720
Nicosia : Surv. of Cyprus, 1969
180 x 115
Contours, district boundaries, vegetation, historical areas.

LAND UTILISATION MAP OF CYPRUS
1:250,000
London : Geog. Pubs, 1956
82 x 51
Illustrating 11 categories of land use, by hachures and stipples in black and brown.

HYDROGEOLOGICAL MAP OF CYPRUS
by Tullstrom
1:250,000
Nicosia : Geol. Surv. of Cyprus, 1970
91 x 58
Col. map with 2 insets on reverse.

CYRPUS, GEOLOGICAL SERIES 1103
1:31,680
DOS (Geol) 1103
Tolworth : DOS/Nicosia : Geol. Surv. Cyprus, 1959-66
Various sizes
Col. geol. series to accompany explanatory memoirs.
Sheets available for:
Xeros-Troodos area, 1 & 2, 1959 65p each
Xeros-Troodos area, diagrammatic sections 30p each
Peristerona-Lagoudhera, 1960 65p each
Akaki-Lythrodonda area, 1960 65p each
Dhali area, 1960 65p each
Pano-Lefkara-Larnaca area, 1960 65p each
Agros-Apsiou area, 1960 65p each
Apsiou-Akrotiri area, 1960 65p each
Astromeritis-Kormakiti, 1960 65p each
Pharmakas-Kalavasos, 1966 65p each

GEOLOGICAL MAP OF THE CENTRAL KYRENIA RANGE
1:25,000
In 3 sheets
Nicosia : Geol. Surv. of Cyprus, 1969
75 x 50 each
Detailed map in cols.

G EARTH RESOURCES

RECONNAISSANCE SOIL SURVEY MAP OF CYPRUS
1:125,000
In 2 sheets
Nicosia : Min. of Ag. and Nat. Resources, 1961
91 x 120 complete
Detailed map in cols.

SOIL SERIES OF CYPRUS
1:25,000
In 59 sheets, see index 564.3/1
Nicosia : Min. of Ag. and Nat. Resources
105 x 75 each
Same sheet lines as Topographical Series. Sheets so far available :
No 20 Kokkinotrimithia, 1968
No 22 Kythrea, 1965
No 51 Paphos, 1967

H BIOGEOGRAPHY

FOREST MAP OF CYPRUS
1:253,440
Nicosia : Gov't of Cyprus Printing Office, 1964
93 x 60
Col. map showing forests designated as 'Prescribed Areas under the Goats Law'

PASTURE SURVEY OF CYPRUS
1:50,000
In 16 sheets, see index 564.3/2
Nicosia : Land Reg. and Surveys, 1958
110 x 85 each
Land use series with insets showing vegetation and geology.

LAND SUITABILITY MAP OF CYPRUS
1:25,000
In 59 sheets
Nicosia : Gov't of Cyprus Printing Office
100 x 68 each
Soil potential series following topographic series sheet lines.
Sheets available :
No 20 Kokkinotrimithia, 1968
No 51 Paphos, 1968

K HUMAN GEOGRAPHY

CYPRUS POPULATION
DISTRIBUTION 1960
1:253,440
Nicosia : Dept. Lands and Surveys,
1964
84 x 54
Outline map with district boundaries showing, by col. dots, distribution and nationalities of Island's pop.

K2

567 Iraq

See also : 53 NEAR AND MIDDLE EAST

A1 GENERAL MAPS : ROADS

GUIDE MAP OF IRAQ
1:2,000,000
No 1581
Tehran : Sahab, 1971
57 x 47
Shows main and secondary roads with distances in km. Photographs, distance table and town plans inset. Rls 100

TOURIST MAP OF IRAQ
1:1,650,000
Baghdad : Summer Resorts and Tourism Service
59 x 72
Roads classified, distances in km, numbers, land types, places of tourist interest, railways. Table of distances. Index.

ROAD MAP OF IRAQ
1:1,500,000
Baghdad : Survey Press
57 x 67
Col. road map; roads classified, places of interest marked.

B TOWN PLANS

BAGHDAD CITY
1:31,300
Baghdad : Summer Resorts and Tourist Service
48 x 40
Col. town plan, roads named, important buildings marked. Tourist camping site inset. Index on reverse.

MAP OF BAGHDAD
1:30,000
Baghdad : Survey Press
60 x 50
Street map, index on reverse, contained in guide book. Illus. col. photographs. In Arabic only.

MAP OF BAGHDAD
1:20,000
No 137
Tehran : Sahab
60 x 40
Col. town plan Rls 60

C OFFICIAL SURVEYS

INTERNATIONAL MAP OF THE WORLD
1:1,000,000
DMA Series 1301
6 sheets needed for complete coverage.
see WORLD 100C and index 100/1.

WORLD
1:500,000
DMS series 1404
13 sheets needed for complete coverage.
see WORLD 100C and index 100/7.

D POLITICAL & ADMINISTRATIVE

ADMINISTRATIVE MAP OF IRAQ
1:1,500,000
Baghdad : Director General Surv; 1971
Political map showing boundaries.

E1 PHYSICAL : RELIEF

PHYSICAL MAP OF IRAQ
1:1,000,000
In 2 sheets
Baghdad : Director Gen. Surv, 1964
Contoured and layer col.

F GEOLOGY

PROVISIONAL GEOLOGIC MAP OF IRAQ
1:2,000,000
Baghdad : Dir. Gen. Surv. 1957
Col. generalised map.

GEOLOGICAL MAP OF IRAQ
1:1,000,000
Baghdad : Ministry of Devt, 1960
87 x 102
Description in English. Inset of Physiographic Provinces on reverse.

M HISTORICAL

HISTORICAL MAP OF ALEXANDER'S EASTERN EXPEDITIONS AND CONQUESTS
1:5,000,000 app.
Tehran : Sahab
90 x 83
Map with description in English and Persian.

ARCHAEOLOGICAL MAP OF IRAQ
1.1,500,000
Baghdad : Survey Press, 1967
57 x 67
Map in col. marking roads, rivers and archaeological sites. Rock monuments named with ref. to chronological period shown in inset.
Also available in Arabic edition.

CARTE DE PERSE, DRESSEE POUR L'USAGE DU ROY PAR G DELISLE, 1724
Tehran : Sahab
70 x 50
Black and white facsimile map including Iraq.

NOVA PERSIAE (ANATOLIA ET ARABIA)
by F De Wit, 1688
Tehran ; Sahab
70 x 50
Black and white facsimile map.

569.1 Syria

See also : 53 NEAR AND MIDDLE EAST

A1 GENERAL MAPS : ROADS

SYRIA
1:1,500,000
Damascus : Tourist Organisation
63 x 43
Col. general map showing 1st and 2nd class and paved roads, railways and boundaries and tourist and archaeological sites. Legend in Arabic and English. Brief guide and table of distances on reverse.

WORLD ROAD MAP OF THE MIDDLE EAST
Sheet 2 - Syria - Lebanon - Israel
1:1,000,000
AMS 1304W
Washington : AMS, 1963
90 x 100
Physical with contours.

C OFFICIAL SURVEYS

INTERNATIONAL MAP OF THE WORLD
1:1,000,000
DMS series 1301
4 sheets for coverage.
see WORLD 100C and index 100/1.

WORLD
1:500,000
DMS series 1404
6 sheets for complete coverage
see WORLD 100C and index 100/7

SYRIA
1:500,000
In 6 sheets
Damascus : Serv. Geog. de Syrie, 1945
Topog. series, contours, layer colouring, communications, boundaries, land detail. Includes Lebanon. Legend in Arabic and French.

CARTE DU LEVANT
1:200,000
In 28 sheets, see index 469.1/2
Damascus : Serv. Geog. de Syrie
50 x 60 each
Topog. series, covering Syria and Lebanon, showing contours, railways, vegetation types, land detail. In Arabic with French legends for some sheets.

CARTE DU LEVANT
1:50,000
see index 569.1/1
Damascus : Serv. Geog. de Syrie, 1940-45
Old topog. series, covering coastal area of Syria and Lebanon.
Contoured. Legend in Arabic and French. Special area sheets :
Alep (Arabic only), Damas, Homs, Rastane - Mecherfeh.

D POLITICAL & ADMINISTRATIVE

SIRIYA
1:1,000,000
Moskva : GUGK, 1973
Col. study map showing water features, settlements, admin. centres and divisions, communications, boundaries, economic details, pop, Geog. description.
Ro 0.30

E1 PHYSICAL : RELIEF

SYRIE ET LIBAN
1:1,000,000
Damascus : Serv. Geog. de Syrie
1945
90 x 69
Contoured and layer col. road and rail communications, towns classified according to status and population. Legend in French.

SYRIA AND LEBANON
1:1,000,000
Tel Aviv : Surv. Israel, 1958
Contours, communications. In Hebrew.

F GEOLOGY

CARTE GÉOLOGIQUE LIBAN-SYRIE ET BORDURE DES PAYS VOISINS
1:1,000,000
Paris : CNRS, 1962
Contained in 'Lexique stratigraphique international' Vol III, fasc. c. I.
Liban, Syrie, Jordanie.
F fr 209.60

569.3 Lebanon

See also : 569.1 SYRIA
53 NEAR AND MIDDLE EAST

A1 GENERAL MAPS : ROADS

CARTE GÉNÉRALE DU LIBAN - ROUTIÈRE ET TECHNIQUE
1:200,000
Bayrouth : Dir. Geog. Affairs, 1966
69 x 95
Contours, relief shading, roads classified with distances in km, boundaries, woodland, railways, buildings of historical and religious importance indicated by symbols.

CARTE ROUTIÈRE ET TOURISTIQUE DU LIBAN
1:200,000
Bayrouth : Dir. Geog. Affairs, 1966
69 x 95
Roads, places of interest, contours, vegetation col.

CARTE ROUTIÈRE
1:100,000
Bayrouth : Nat. Office of Tourism, 1965
14 x 29
Col. map in bookform with fold-out pages, relief shading, roads and sites of interest.

B TOWN PLANS

BAYROUTH (BEIRUT)
Various scales
Bayrouth : Dir. Geog. Affairs
Maps available :
Beirut and suburbs (topog)
1:10,000 4 sheets 1969-70
Beirut City (Electricity)
1:7,500 1967
Beirut and suburbs (Forces of Sec)
1:2,500 8 sheets 1964
Beirut-Southern suburbs (Min. of Planning)
1:2,000 14 sheets 1963
Beirut City (GAL)
1:2,000 33 sheets 1964

C OFFICIAL SURVEYS

WORLD
1:500,000
DMS Series 1404
3 sheets for complete coverage.
see WORLD 100C and index 100/7.

CARTE DU LIBAN
1:100,000
In 6 sheets, see index 569.3/1
Bayrouth : Dir. Geog. Affairs, 1964
Various sizes
Contoured at 50m intervals, vegetation relief shading, roads classified, distances in km.

CARTE DU LIBAN - ANCIEN
1:50,000
In 27 sheets, see index 569.3/2
Bayrouth : Dir. Geog. Affairs
1962-66
42 x 56 each
Col. topographical series, contours at 10m intervals. A new 1:50,000 hypsometric series is in preparation which will replace this survey.

CARTE DU LIBAN - HYPSOMETRIQUE
1:50,000
In 12 sheets, see index 569.3/3
Bayrouth : Dir. Geog. Affairs
106 x 60
Col. topog. series in progress, contoured, with layer colours and relief shading, communications, boundaries and land detail. This series will replace earlier 1:50,000 series, type ancien in 27 sheets.

TOPOGRAPHICAL SERIES - CARTE DU LIBAN
1:20,000
In 119 sheets, see index 569.3/4
Bayrouth : Dir. Geog. Affairs
1964-68
58 x 47 each
Col. series in progress. Showing land detail, road and rail communications, contours at 10m intervals.

D POLITICAL & ADMINISTRATIVE

ADMINISTRATIVE MAP OF LEBANON
1:200,000
Bayrouth : Dir. Geog. Affairs, 1968
69 x 95
Col. by Caza districts with roads classified according to condition, railways, boundaries with municipality, police station, hospital and tourist locations.

G EARTH RESOURCES

CARTE DES RESOURCES EN SOLS DE LIBAN SUD-VERSANT OUEST
1:20,000
Bayrouth : Dir. Geog. Affairs, 1969
80 x 65 each
Soil series in progress, following 20,000 topog. series sheet lines.
In French.

H BIOGEOGRAPHY

CARTE FORESTIERE DU LIBAN
1:200,000
Bayrouth : Dir Geog. Affairs, 1965
69 x 95
Contours, detailed vegetation coverage. Legend Arabic and Eng.

CARTE FORESTIERE DU LIBAN
1:50,000
Bayrouth : Dir. Geog. Affairs, 1968
42 x 56
Series of maps showing forest types in progress following same sheet lines as topog - ancien series.

L ECONOMIC

CARTE AGRICOLE DU LIBAN
1:200,000
Bayrouth : Dir. Geog. Affairs, 1963
69 x 95
Map in colours illustrating areas of production together with aspects of meteorology, social life and administration. In French.

M HISTORICAL

PLAN DE BEYROUTH DÉDIÉ A SMJ LE SULTAN ABDUL HAMID II PAR JULIUS LOYT VED VICE CONSUL DE DANEMARK INTENDENT DES ÉCOLES ANGLO-SYRIENNES ETC.
1:12,000
Beirut : Dir. Geog. Affairs. 1970
33 x 58
Facsimile of the 1876 map.

ATLASES
J CLIMATE

ATLAS CLIMATIQUE DU LIBAN
Bayrouth : Min. des Travaux Publiques et des Transports
In 3 vols.
Vol i, 1966; Vol II, 1967; Vol III, 1969
Detailed collection of climate maps and data.

569.4 Israel

A1 GENERAL MAPS . ROADS

MAP OF ISRAEL
1:800,000
Tel Aviv : Graphic Productions, 1969
42 x 61
Layer col, relief shading, rail and road communications, boundaries, sites of tourist and historic interest. Pictorial border with biblical quotations.

ISRAEL UND ANGRENZENDE LANDER (ADJOINING COUNTRIES)
1:750,000
Bern : K & F
74 x 89
Roads classified and numbered, distances in km, railways, footpaths, places of interest, spot heights in metres, deserts, coral reefs, tourist accommodation. Covers Israel, Sinai Peninsula, parts of Egypt, Saudi Arabia. Relief shading, political inset of Near East Region.

TOURING MAP OF ISRAEL THROUGH 4000 YEARS OF HISTORY
1:260,000
Tel Aviv : Amir, 1973
58 x 86
Relief col. and shaded with roads and sites of historical importance shown pictorially also national parks, nature reserves and Kibbutz Inns (guest houses). Detailed index to places and sites with information on reverse.

HOLYLAND TOURING MAP
1:300,000
Jerusalem : Carta, 1972
93 x 31
Roads and rail, distances, old towns, reverse has town plans and inset of Sinai. In Eng.

B TOWN PLANS

TOWN MAPS AND PLANS
1:10,000 (unless stated otherwise)
Tel Aviv : Surv. Israel
Various sizes
Col. maps in Hebrew only unless otherwise stated.
Maps available :
Afula, Nazerat, Illit, 1966
Akko, 1968
Ashqelon, Ashdod, 1968
Be'er Sheva, 1968
Hadera, Pardes Hanna, Karkur, 1970
Haifa, 1:12, 500, 1970
Haifa, 1962
Haifa East, 1966
Herzliyya, 1963
Herzliyya, 1:12,500, 1970
Holon, Bat Yam, Azor, 1:12, 500 1970
Holon, Bat Yam, Azor, 1962
Jerusalem, 1:14,000, 1968 (Eng. ed)
Jerusalem, 1:12,500, 1970
Jerusalem, 1967
Kefar, Sava, Hod Hasharon, Ra' Ananna, 1968
Nahariyya, Qiryat Shemona, Zefat, Bet She'an, Hazor, 1969
Netanya, 1968
Or Yehuda, 1968
Petah Tiqwa, 1968
Qiryat Gat, 1968
Ramla, Lod. 1969
Rehovot, 1:16,000, 1968 (Also in Eng)
Rishon le Zion, 1968
Tel Aviv, 1:14,000, 1968 (Eng ed)
Tel Aviv, 1:12,500, 1970
Tel Aviv, South of River, 1966
Tel Aviv, 2 sheets, 1969 (Eng ed)
Tiberias, 1962
Tirat Karmel, 1970
Dimona, 1971
Elat, 1971
Yeroham, 1971
Arad, 1971
Mizpe Ramon, 1971
Nes Ziyyona, 1971
Karmiel, 1971
Qiryat Mal'Akhi, 1971
Bet Shemesh, 1971

TOWN PLANS
Tel Aviv : Amir
Various sizes
Small pictorial tourist plans, noting places of interest.
Tiberias, 1972, English and Hebrew
Netanya, 1973, Eng. Hebrew, Fr. Ger. Swedish
Haifa, 1972 (inc. Old Acre), English
Kfar Sava, 1969, English

JERUSALEM, THE OLD CITY
1:50,000
Jerusalem : Aharon Bier, 1971
26 x 32
Aerial photographic map, roads and principal buildings outlined in red. Index to places of tourist interest, map of Jerusalem on reverse. Eng or Hebrew eds.
Also at 1:25,000, 40 x 50

JERUSALEM AND SURROUNDINGS
1:10,000
In 6 sheets
Tel Aviv : Surv. of Israel, 1946
63 x 58 each
Col. topog. map, contoured.

PICTORIAL MAP OF JERUSALEM
1:7,000
5th edition
Tel Aviv : Amir, 1973
87 x 61
Streets named, places of interest illustrated, restaurants, hotels etc. shown. Reverse has index, tourist information. Map of the Old City at 1:38,000 with Ramot Eshkol at 1.9,000 and Kiryat Yovel at 1:13,000. Map diagrams in margin.
37p

JERUSALEM
Nr 100
Braunschweig: Bollman Bildkarten, 1970
Coloured pictorial plan from oblique view showing individual buildings.
DM 7.50
on hand made paper DM 32.00

OLD JERUSALEM
Nr 100a
Braunschweig: Bollman Bildkarten, 1970
Coloured pictorialplan from oblique view showing individual buildings.
DM 6.50
on hand made paper DM 12.00

JERUSALEM
by Hermann Bollman
1:5,000
Haifa : Van Leer, 1969
90 x 55
Graphic portrayal of the city illustrating individual buildings, oblique view. Street index on reverse. 16pp information Eng, Fr, Ger. Also available in standard and De luxe wall editions.

OLD JERUSALEM
Ed Hermann Bollman
1:3,000
Haifa : Van Leer, 1969
65 x 53
Large scale plan of the old city. Index illus. text, 16pp. Eng, Fr, Ger. Also available in standard and De luxe wall editions.

ACCO (ACRE)
Nr 105
Braunschweig : Bollmann-Bildkarten 1972
Coloured pictorial town plan, oblique view, showing individual buildings. Decorative border.
on hand made paper DM 12.00

BETHLEHEM
Nr 104
Braunschweig: Bollman Bildkarten 1970
Col. town plan, showing streets and individual buildings. Pictorial map, oblique view.
Flat DM 6.50
on hand made paper DM 12.00

HAIFA
1:12,500
Eds Friedlaender, Blustein
Kiryat Yam : B Blustein, 1976
56 x 64
Coloured plan marking public buildings, bus routes, places of tourist interest with street index.

HAIFA BAY
1:12,500
Eds Frielaender, Blustein
Kiryat Yam : B Blustein, 1976
30 x 60
Street map of residential and industrial area with Krayot and Kishon Harbour; index; available in Eng or Hebrew eds.

NAZARETH
Nr 103
Braunschweig : Bollman-Bildkarten
1972
Col. town plan, pictorial. Oblique view, decorative border.
Rollers DM 12.00

TEL AVIV - YAFO
1:18,000
Haifa : Zvi Friedlaender 1975
54 x 80
Inc. Ramat Gan, Givatayim, Bne Beraq, Holon, Bat Yam; Col. plan, roads named, bus routes, public buildings etc, with index.

TEL AVIV MAP
1:15,000
Jerusalem : Carta
46 x 62
Map of city, places of interest. Index. In Eng.

PICTORIAL MAP OF TEL AVIV
1:9,400
2nd edition
Tel Aviv : Amir, 1973
61 x 87
Col. map with streets named, buildings and places of interest drawn, restaurants, hotels etc. Reverse has index, list of institutions, inset of shopping centre. Old City of Jaffa. Tourist information.
37p

C OFFICIAL SURVEYS

ISRAEL-TOPOGRAPHIC
1:250,000
In 2 sheets, see index 569.4/1
Tel Aviv : Survey of Israel
69 x 100 each
Detailed col. map with separate list of settlements, localities and antiquity sites, 1970.
Available in the following editions:
With layer tints and shaded relief, 1969
With layer tints only, 1971
Without layer tints, 1971
All available in either Eng or Heb eds. With distances and road numbers, 1970, available in Heb only.
Adjacent sheets covering Sinai are published - see separate entry.

SINAI - NILE DELTA
1:250,000
5 sheets, see index 569.4/1
Tel Aviv : Surv. Israel
69 x 100
Topog. series, contoured, layer coloured, communications. In Heb. ed. only. Adjacent series to Israel 1:250,000 topog. map.
Sheets available :
El Arish (N Sinai), 1969
Gulf of Suez (SW Sinai), 1967
Gulf of Eilat (SE Sinai), 1971
Cairo (unlayered), 1967

TOPOGRAPHICAL SERIES - NEW DIVISION
1:100,000
In 24 sheets, see index 569.4/2
Tel Aviv : Surv. Israel. 1967/70
64 x 50 each
Covers whole country. Contoured with roads, railways, boundaries, important public buildings, indications of principal land types and plantations.
In Hebrew only, with legend also in English. This series replaces earlier pre-war survey on old division sheet lines (index 569.4/3) English edition.

VILLAGE BLOCK PLAN REDUCTION
1:10,000
Tel Aviv : Surv. Israel
Offset or diazo (sun) prints of large scale cadastral plans for urban areas.

URBAN ASSESSMENT BLOCK PLANS
Various scales
Tel Aviv : Surv. Israel
Large scale cadastral plans for urban areas. Available as diazo (sun) prints, in Eng.

REGISTRATION BLOCK PLANS
Various scales
Tel Aviv : Surv. Israel
Large scale urban plans available as diazo prints. In Hebrew and/or English.

D POLITICAL & ADMINISTRATIVE

ADMINISTRATIVE BOUNDARIES
1:250,000
Tel Aviv : Surv. Israel, 1967
64 x 84
2 sheet col. map in Hebrew only.

DEFENSIBLE BORDERS
Jerusalem : Carta
70 x 100
Col. wall map with 4 insets. Shows strategic position of Israel and Egypt and Israel's vulnerability of pre June 1967. In English.

JERUSALEM - MUNICIPAL JURISDICTION BOUNDARIES
1:50,000
Tel Aviv : Surv. Israel, 1970
Col. map showing admin. boundaries. In Hebrew only.

E1 PHYSICAL : RELIEF

ISRAEL
1:1,000,000
Tel Aviv : Surv. Israel. 1965
17 x 49
Col. physical map with relief shading in Hebrew or English.

ISRAEL UND SEINE ARABISCHEN NACHBARN
1:1,000,000
Darmstadt : Perthes
210 x 140
Physical wall map, roads, borders, pipelines. DM 142

ISRAEL
1:750,000
Tel Aviv : Surv. Israel, 1971
51 x 84
Contoured and layer coloured map, communications. Including Sinai and showing boundaries at the end of 1967 war.

ISRAEL
1:500,000
Tel Aviv : Surv. Israel, 1971
Available in 4 editions, with or without layer tints and contours, with or without layer tints and shaded relief (1971)
Contoured with roads classified, railways, historic sites and towns graded by population.
Available in the following editions; each in either Hebrew or English : With layer tints and shaded relief
With layer tints only
With shaded relief only
Without layer tints

BARTHOLOMEW'S WORLD TRAVEL MAP SERIES: ISRAEL WITH JORDAN
1:350,000
Edinburgh : Bart
60 x 79
Contoured with layer col, roads, railways, boundaries, airports and historic sites. Southern Negev region inset on smaller scale, also Sinai and Near East.
75p

ISRAEL
1:200,000
Munchen : List
87 x 208
Wenschow wall map, showing relief in col, roads, railways, settlements; Jerusalem inset.

E2 PHYSICAL : LAND FEATURES

ELAT - GEOMORPHOLOGICAL
1:100,000
Tel Aviv : Surv. Israel, 1966/72
64 x 50
Sheet 24 of old division, topog. series showing relief and landforms.

F GEOLOGY

GEOLOGICAL MAP
1:250,000
Tel Aviv : Surv. Israel, 1965
71 x 94 each
Detailed col. geol. map in 2 sheets with legend in Eng and Hebrew, covering adjacent areas east of the Jordan.

GEOLOGICAL MAP
1:500,000
Tel Aviv : Surv. Israel 1963
91 x 38
Col. geol. map covering adjacent areas east of the Jordan.

SOUTH ISRAEL
1:250,000
Tel Aviv : Surv. Israel, 1947
Col. geol. map with text in English.

GEOLOGICAL MAP OF ISRAEL
1:100,000
See index 569.4/3
Tel Aviv : Surv. Israel, 1955+

Sheets following old topographic division
1,2,3,4,5,6,8,9,11,20 1955/6
16 (Inc. structure map and sections), 1956
17 (Inc. structure map and sections), 1961
19 (structure map, cross sections, booklet), 1957
21 (structure map), 1954

GEOLOGICAL MAP OF GALILEE
1:50,000
In 6 sheets
Tel Aviv : Surv. Israel, 1958
Geol. map in Hebrew and English.

JERUSALEM, BET SHEMESH - GEOLOGICAL
1:50,000
In 3 sheets
Tel Aviv : Surv. Israel, 1964
Stratigraphical, structure map and cross sections.

GEOLOGICAL MAP OF WADI EL QUILT
1:50,000
Tel Aviv : Surv. Israel, 1971
40 x 40
Detailed, col. geol. map, with separate, structural contour map. Legend in Hebrew and English.

G EARTH RESOURCES

MINERAL RESOURCES OF ISRAEL
1:940,000
London : IGS
Shows principal mineral occurrences by means of symbols.

SOIL SALINITY
1:750,000
Tel Aviv : Surv. Israel, 1967
51 x 84
Col. map.

DISTRIBUTION OF SOILS AFFECTED BY SALINITY IN ISRAEL
1:500,000
2nd edition
Prepared by S Ravikovitch
Tel Aviv : Surv. Israel, 1969
32 x 85
Col. map on topog. base. II 6

SOIL - LAND USE SERIES
1:500,000
Tel Aviv : Surv. Israel, 1957
34 x 55
Series of 4 col. maps covering Israel pre June 1967. In Hebrew, legend also in English.
Soil Map
Soil Erosion
Land Use Capabilities for Dryland Farming
Land Use Capabilities for Irrigable Land

ISRAEL SOIL MAP
1:250,000
Prepared by S Ravikovitch
2nd edition
Jerusalem : Hebrew Univ, 1969
64 x 84
2 sheet map, with separate inset - map at 1:750,000. Distribution of soils affected by salinity in Israel. II 6

IRRIGATED AREAS, 1955
1:250,000
Tel Aviv : Surv. Israel, 1959
61 x 103
Showing irrigation projects, fish-ponds, orchards, vineyards.

MAP OF IRRIGATED AREAS, 1950/1
1:250,000
Tel Aviv : Surv. Israel, 1954
61 x 103
Illus. in col. on a black and white administrative base map, fish ponds, irrigated groves, orchards, vineyards and irrigated crop areas. Exc. southern Negev region.

WATER PROJECTS ON THE JORDAN - YARMUK RIVER SYSTEM
1:250,000
Jerusalem : Carta
89 x 124
Col. wall map, in English.

K HUMAN GEOGRAPHY

MAP OF THE KIBBUTZIM IN ISRAEL
1:360,000
Tel Aviv : Amir, 1972
41 x 120
Relief col. and shaded, roads, with kibbutz, natural settlement, kibbutz inn, historical sites. On reverse is list of Kibbutzim, Kibbutz Enterprises and Projects. Kibbutz Inns (Guest Houses) and background to the Fed. of the Kibbutz movements.

INDEX TO VILLAGES AND SETTLEMENTS
1:250,000
Tel Aviv : Surv. Israel, 1951
100 x 70
Topog. map in English with Hebrew overprint.

SETTLEMENTS OF ISRAEL (TYPE AND POPULATION ACCORDING TO THE 1961 CENSUS)
1:250,000
Tel Aviv : Surv. Israel, 1963
64 x 84
2 sheet map in Hebrew, classifying settlements with population information.

L ECONOMIC

A DEVELOPMENT PLAN OF ISRAEL, 1948-65
1:500,000 app.
Jerusalem : Carta
64 x 94
Shows 1948 settlements, communications etc. in black, 1965 in red. Oil and water lines, industry, land use. Statistical tables.

OUTLINE SCHEME OF ISRAEL COASTAL STRIP
1:20,000
In 24 sheets
Ed Prof Elisha Efrat
Jerusalem : Min. of the Interior, 1975
34 x 60
Development plan with text in Hebrew and English summary

PHYSICAL MASTER PLANS
Elisha Efrat and Ehud Gabrieli
Jerusalem : Min. of the Interior
34 x 64
Showing proposals for physical planning of the country; indicates land use by agriculture, residential buildings, industry, recreation.
Text in Hebrew with English summary.
Volumes Published:
Israel Coastal Strip 17 sheets 1966
Northern Negev 1:350,000 14 sheets 1966
Jerusalem - Ashdod Region 1:100,000 14 sheets 1967

FISHERMAN'S CHART
1:100,000
In 4 sheets
Tel Aviv : Surv. Israel, 1938
In Hebrew and English.

PAST AND PRESENT MAP
Jerusalem Carta
46 x 62
Set of maps, showing natural resources, industry, health and welfare services, immigration, foreign aid, large map showing 1967 Cease-Fire lines on reverse. With 5 charts (62 x 36). In English.

M HISTORICAL

PALESTINE OF THE OLD TESTAMENT
1:500,000
Tel Aviv : Surv. Israel, 1938
37 x 62
Physical map showing towns of the period with modern equivalents in brackets.

THE HOLY LAND TODAY
1:312,500
Washington : NGS
82 x 106
Col. map showing biblical events, archaeological digs. Crusades, walled City of Jerusalem.
Paper US $2.00
Plastic US $3.00

PALASTINA
1:250,000
Braunschweig : Westermann
120 x 163
Physical col. wall map of time of Christ, inset of old Jerusalem.

PALESTINA
1:250,000
Ed H Haack
Darmstadt : Perthes, 1962
92 x 125
Historical wall map, with relief shown. 2 maps of Jerusalem inset.

PALESTINA ANTIQUA, EIUSQUE DIVISIO AETATE JESU CHRISTI
1:250,000
Novara : Ag
100 x 140
Col. historical wall map in Latin text, showing ancient Palestine and its partition at the time of Christ.
L2,200

PALASTINA - LAND DER BIBEL
1:2,000,000
Darmstadt : Perthes
125 x 160
Physical wall map with certain inset maps suitable for lecture purposes.
In English.
CR DM 95

WALL ATLAS OF THE BIBLE LANDS
London : Philip
94 x 117
each map fully coloured :
1 The Distribution of the Nations illus. Book of Genesis
2 Egypt, the Sinai Peninsula and the Promised Land illus. Book of Exodus
3 Canaan as divided among the Twelve Tribes, illus, Book of Joshua and Judges
4 The Holy Land in the Time of Kings, illus. history of the Hebrew Kingdoms to the capture of Samaria by the Assyrians
5 Syria and Mesopotamia, illus. Jewish Captivities
6 Palestine in the Time of Christ
7 The Journeys of St Paul : The Roman Empire. Two maps on one sheet
8 Modern Palestine. Contoured map showing roads, railways and ancient sites.

Paper, flat, each £1.50
Mounted, CR £5.50
Cloth, dissected £7.00
Set of 8 maps :
Cloth, as wall atlas on one roller £30.00

PALESTINA : LOS VIAJES DE JESUS
Barcelona : Editorial Teide
99 x 137
School wall map showing 17 journeys of Christ, 31 coloured photographs, 2 supplementary maps, with city plans.
S.Ptas 600

BREASTED-HUTH-HARDING HISTORICAL MAPS
Chicago : Denoyer-Geppert
112 x 81
Series of col. wall maps suitable for lecture purposes, printed on manilla.
204021 Ancient Orient and Palestine
204231 Holy Roman Empire (10th and 11th C)

PALESTINE OF THE CRUSADERS
1:350,000
Tel Aviv : Surv. Israel, 1944
55 x 77
Physical map noting by symbols ecclesiastical centres, battlefields and castles with medieval place names, and modern equivalents.

PILGRIMS MAP OF THE HOLY LAND
No scale given
2nd edition
Tel Aviv : Amir, 1972
59 x 84
Col. map showing various stages in Israel's history, with sites of antiquity, cities etc. marked and described. Map of Holy Land today, with index and New Testament Story on reverse. 37p
Also available in smaller ed, in French, Spanish, English, Italian, Dutch.

HISTORICAL & ARCHAEOLOGICAL MAP OF GOLAN AND UPPER GALILEE
Tel Aviv : Amir
61 x 44
To be published, Autumn, 1973.

ISRAEL PAST AND PRESENT
Jerusalem : Carta, 1970
60 x 36
Shows Cease Fire lines of June 1967, historical sites; text on reverse.

THE HOLY LAND
London : Francis Chichester
76 x 101
Pictorial map in colour showing Bible scenes. 38p

MADABA MOSAIC MAP OF 565 AD
No scale given
Tel Aviv : Surv. Israel
Col. facsimile map.

ANCIENT MAPS OF THE HOLY LAND
Jerusalem : Carta
60 x 48
3 hand col. facsimile maps in case:
Description of the Lands of the Dispersion from Babylon (mid 16th C)
The Holy Land . . . The Land of Promise, 1569
The Holy City of Jerusalem, 1544

SONDERKARTE ISRAEL UND DIE KRISE IN NAHOST
No 28
Munchen : JRO
60 x 83
Double-sided map, showing Middle East crisis. In "Aktuelle JRO-Landkarte" series. DM 4.80

IDF ROUTES OF ADVANCE, 5-10 JUNE, 1967
1:1,000,000
Tel Aviv : Surv. Israel, 1967
77 x 53
Map in Hebrew or English, contoured, layer cols, communications.

ATLASES
A1 GENERAL : ROADS

ISRAEL ROAD GUIDE
Jerusalem : Carta
24 x 11
144pp
146 maps showing all types of roads and also historical sites, places of interest, petrol stations.
Descriptions of sites by maps. In Eng.

ISRAEL MOTOR ATLAS
Jerusalem : Carta, 1970
20 x 11
84pp
15 col. maps, 46 town maps. Index.
In English.

ATLASES
B TOWN PLANS

ATLAS OF JERUSALEM
Compiled by Geography Dept, Hebrew University
1st edition
Ramat Gan : Masada Press, 1973
33 x 48
54pp including 105 coloured computer based maps divided into 10 sections : The region, history, Quarters and Streets, Urban Morphology, Urban Land Use, Public Institutions, Transportation, Population, Town Planning Schemes, Recent Developments. Each map page is folded in half and contained in filing box with an 11 chapter explanantory booklet.

ATLASES
M HISTORICAL

ATLAS OF THE BIBLE
By Yohanan Aharon
Jerusalem : Carta
30 x 23
128pp
174 col. maps showing 4000 years of Bible history. Index. In Heb.
Available in English as The Macmillan Bible Atlas.

BIBLE ATLAS
by Emil G Kraeling, Rev. ed.
Chicago : Rand McNally
18 x 26
488pp
Places in Biblical history; over 400pp text. US $9.95

HISTORICAL ATLAS OF THE HOLY LAND
Chicago : Rand McNally
18 x 26
88pp
Locates places of Old and New Testaments, 40pp maps; 40 plates.
US $1.95

SCRIPTURE ATLAS
Ed H Fullard
London : Philip, 1970
23 x 28
36pp
Illus. Old and New Testaments, with physical, climatic and historical maps with descriptive notes. 40p
With 19pp photographic supplement
75p

ATLAS OF THE NEW TESTAMENT
by J F Stirling
London : Philip
22 x 14
Completely redrawn and revised, the journeys of Jesus and the Apostles are traced with the location of each incident marked. 44 full page coloured maps with 20 pages of descriptive and explanatory notes.
75p
The following sections are published separately:
An Atlas of the Life of Christ
An Atlas of the Acts of the Apostles and Epistles
each with 32pp of maps and notes
35p each

THE OXFORD BIBLE ATLAS
Ed H G May
2nd Edition
Oxford : OUP, 1974
19 x 25
144pp Series of 26 coloured maps with 92 illustrations, Gazetteer £3.00

CARTA'S ATLAS OF PALESTINE, FROM ZIONISM TO STATEHOOD
by Yehuda Wallach
Jerusalem : Carta
30 x 23
144pp
202 col. maps In Hebrew. English edition in prep.

CARTA'S ATLAS OF THE SECOND TEMPLE, THE MISHNAH AND THE TALMUD
by Michael Avi-Yonah
Jerusalem : Carta
30 x 23
112pp
162 col. maps covering the period. Available in English as the Macmillan Bible Atlas.

CARTA'S ATLAS OF PALESTINE FROM BETHTHR TO TEL-HAI
by Mordecai Gichon
Jerusalem : Carta
30 x 23
128pp
210 col. maps of military history through the ages. In Hebrew. Bibliog.

THE NEW ISRAEL ATLAS; BIBLE TO THE PRESENT DAY
by Zev Vilnay
Jerusalem : Israel UP, 1968
23 x 30
112pp
114 maps, 4pp gazetteer. English and Hebrew editions available (English edition McGraw Hill, New York, 1969). Covers Jewish settlement in Biblical times up to modern times, also political and thematic maps. With gazetteer.

JERUSALEM : MAPS AND VIEWS
by Herrmann M Meyer
In 11 sheets
Jerusalem : Univ. Booksellers, 1971
Portfolio of 12 facsimile maps and views.

CARTA'S HISTORICAL ATLAS OF JERUSALEM : A BRIEF ILLUSTRATED HISTORY
by Dan Bahat
Jerusalem : Carta
30 x 23
18pp
8 maps showing Jerusalem at various stages of history, with text and photos. In Hebrew. English edition in preparation.

ATLASES
O NATIONAL

ATLAS OF ISRAEL
Comp. Surv. Israel
Amsterdam : Elsevier, 1970
39 x 50
296pp
70 double-sided maps covering physical geography, geology, climate, biogeography, land use, history, population, industry, communications, agriculture, etc. With text, illustrations, bibliog. on reverse. In English.

FI 470

569.5 Jordan

See also : 53 NEAR AND MIDDLE EAST

A1 GENERAL MAPS : ROADS

WORLD ROAD MAPS
1:1,000,000
AMS 1304 W, Sheet 2
Washington : AMS, 1962
101 x 101
Contoured, layer coloured with roads classified.

THE HASHEMITE KINGDOM OF JORDAN
1:750,000
Amman : Min. of Tourism and Antiquities
32 x 40
Sketch map showing principal roads with highway numbers, also resthouses, petrol stations, rivers and railways.

JORDAN : THE HOLY LAND TOURISTIC MAP
1:700,000
Amman : Min. Tourism and Antiquities, 1968
30 x 38, 29 x 17
Double-sided map showing communications and places of interest.

C OFFICIAL SURVEYS

INTERNATIONAL MAP OF THE WORLD
1:1,000,000
DMS series GSGS 1301
3 sheets for complete coverage.
see WORLD 100C and index 100/1.

WORLD
1:500,000
DMS series 1404
6 sheets for complete coverage.
see WORLD 100C and index 100/7.

JORDAN
1:100,000
In 21 sheets
Amman : Dept. of Lands and Surveys
Topog. series, contoured, land detail.
In Arabic only.

E1 PHYSICAL : RELIEF

JORDAN
1:750,000
Series GSGS K332
Feltham : DMS
45 x 56
Topog. map, contours, layer tints, roads classified according to surface, railways, towns, settlements.
27p

WORLD TRAVEL MAP OF ISRAEL WITH JORDAN
1:350,000
Edinburgh : Bart
60 x 79
Covers W Central Jordan only, contoured with layer col, roads, railways, boundaries, airports and historic sites. Southern Negev - Ma'an region inset at smaller scale, also Sinai and Near East. 75p

F GEOLOGY

GEOLOGISCHE KARTE VON JORDANIEN
1:250,000
In 5 sheets
Hanover : B-B, 1968
101 x 95
Geological map in colour. With cross sections, stratigraphic sections, index map, reliability diagram. Title and scale also in Arabic. Explanatory text 230pp, 1968, Vol 7 in "Regional Geology of the Earth"

H BIOGEOGRAPHY

THE HASHEMITE KINGDOM OF JORDAN – AREAS CONTROLLED BY DEPT. OF FORESTS
1:250,000
In 2 sheets
Amman : Dept. of Lands and Surveys
1951
66 x 81 each sheet
Col. map showing 3 categories of Forest lands in Gov't, Private and scheduled forests.

57 USSR

A2 GENERAL MAPS : LOCAL

KARTA KURORTOV GRUZINSKOY SSR
1:600,000
Moskva : GUGK, 1965
Map of Georgian health resorts.

TOURIST PLANS
Various scales
Moscow : GUGK
Col. plans available for :
Altava-Teletskoe ozero (lake)
Gruzinskaya SSR
Istoriko-revolutsionnye Pamyatniki na territorii SSR (Historic and Revolutionary Monuments)
Krem
Latviyskaya SSR
Litovskaya SSR
Ozero Seliger (Seliger Lake)
Okrestnosti Leningrada (Leningrad and environs)
Orenburgskaya Oblast'
Po Kirovskoy Oblasti
Rayon Kavkazskykh Mineralenykh Vod (Caucasus Mineral Springs Region)
Stavropol'skiy Krai (district)
Chernomorskoe poberezh'e Kavkaza (Caucasus : Black Sea Coast)
Estonskaya SSR
Bol'shoe Kavkazskoe kol'tso (circle)
Valdayskaya vozveshennost' (heights)
Moskovskaya krugosvetka (Moscow and surroundings)
Moskva-Astrakhan-Rostov-na-Donu
Moskva-Kiev-Zakarpatie
Po Kaspitsskomu i Chernomorskomu poberezhu kavkaza
Po pyati respublikam na aytomobile (Through 5 Republics by Car)
Po reke Enisei (river) (Krasnoyarsk-Dikson)
Po reke (river) Enisei (Shushenskoe-Krasnoyarsk)
Po respublikam Yrednei Asii
Repino Priozersk-Vyborg
Leningrad-Kiev-Odessa
Kavkaz (Caucasus)
Krasnoyarskaya (Nature Park)
Ryazana krugosvetka
Gruzinskaya SSR
Lake Bayka
Po Lene
Po Moldavii
Architekturnye pamyatniki Moskovskoy Oblasti (architectural monuments of Moscow district)
Pushkinskiy zapovednik (Pushkin Nature park)

B TOWN PLANS

FALK PLAN MOSKVA (MOSCOW)
No scale given
1st edition
Hamburg : Falk Verlag, 1971
Patent fold
Coloured plan naming principal streets and illustrating public buildings, places of interest eg, cultural entertainments, hotels etc. marked by symbols.

TOWN PLANS
Moskva : GUGK
Plans available :
Literary Moscow
Musical and Theatrical Moscow
Historical Revolutionary Moscow
Perislavi-Zalesski
Rostov
Sysdale

C OFFICIAL SURVEYS

INTERNATIONAL MAP OF THE WORLD
1:1,000,000
AMS Series 1301
About 145 sheets needed for complete coverage.
see WORLD 100C and index 100/1.

D POLITICAL & ADMINISTRATIVE

POLITIKO-ADMINISTRATIVNAYA KARTA SSSR
at various scales
Moskva : GUGK, 1976
Political admin. wall map available at the following scales :

1:4,000,000	Kop 56
1:5,000,000	kop 45
1:8,000,000	kop 14
1:15,000,000	kop 9

ZWIAZEK SOCJALISTYCZNYCH REPUBLIK RADZIECKICH
1:15,000,000
see USSR 57 E1

UNION OF SOVIET SOCIALIST REPUBLICS
1:8,875,000
Washington : NGS
103 x 75
Political col. wall map.
Paper US $2.00
Plastic US $3.00

ADMINISTRATIVE AREAS OF THE USSR
1:8,000,000
GSGS 5103
Tolworth : MOD
113 x 85
Admin. divisions shown by col, symbols indicate town pop, railways classified and a glossary of admin. terms and abbreviations, divisions and capital towns.
63p

SSSR
1:8,000,000
Moskva : GUGK, 1971
Admin. map

NEUVOSTOLIITTO
1:7,500,000
Helsinki : Wsoy
244 x 181
School wall map of the USSR
FMK 100

URSS No 1 (PHYSIQUE)
1:7,000,000
Editions MDI
see USSR 57 E1

SSSR POLITCHESKAYA KARTA
1:5,000,000
In 4 sheets
Moskva : GUGK, 1976
190 x 130
Col. map showing states. Ko 0.45

SSSR : POLITIKO-ADMINISTRATIV-NAYA KARTA
1:5,000,000
In 2 sheets
Moskva : GUGK, 1973
Shows "oblasti" and other admin. area divisions. Ko 0.29

SOVIET UNION
1:5,000,000 app.
Chicago : Rand McNally
165 x 104
Political col. railways, major cities, etc. Inc. neighbouring countries and seas.

SSSR
1:5,000,000
Praha : Kart, 1970
General school wall map of the USSR
Kcs 165

UNION OF SOVIET SOCIALIST REPUBLICS
1:4,000,000
Chicago : Denoyer-Geppert
244 x 173
Shows 15 unions, various types of local govt, cities graded by pop, railways, mineral resources.
US $44.00

USSR
No 194102-14
Chicago : Denoyer-Geppert
218 x 147
Political col. wall map for schools.
Spring Rollers US $39.50

SOVIET UNION
1:6,000,000
Chicago : Denoyer-Geppert
No 108521
162 x 111
School wall map showing the 15 Republics. Cities graded by pop, political col.
CR US $18.00

POUVENNAYA KARTA SSSR
1:5,000,000
In 4 sheets
Moskva : GUGK
School wall map.

URSS
No scale given
No 56
Paris : Hatier
120 x 100
School wall map on double sheet; political and economic map on reverse.

PLAN MESTNOSTI I USLOVNYE ZNAKI
1:5,000,000
Moskva : GUGK
2 sheet map of districts.

WESTERN SOVIET UNION
1:3,937,500
Washington : NGS
82 x 103
Political col. wall map
Paper US $2.00
Plastic US $3.00

SOYUZNE RESPUBLIKI ZAKAVKAZ'YA
1:3,500,000
Moskva : GUGK
Outline map.

KARTY SOY UZNYKH RESPUBLIK (MAPS OF THE UNION REPUBLICS)
Moskva : GUGK
Administrative ref. maps.
Available for :

Armyanskaya SSR	1:600,000
Azerbaidzhanskaya SSR	1:600,000
Kasachskaya SSR	1:1,500,000
Kirgizskaya SSR	1:1,000,000
Litovskaya SSR	1:600,000
Tad Zhikskaya SSR	1:1,000,000
Turkmenskaya SSR	1:1,500,000
Ukrainskaya SSR and Moldavskaya SSR	1:1,500,000
Uzbekskaya SSR	1:1,000,000

POLITICAL MAPS OF ADMINISTRATIVE DISTRICTS
1:600,000 (unless given otherwise)
Moskva : GUGK
Maps available :

Altai-Kray	1:1,000,000
Armurskaya Oblast'	1:1,250,000
Azerbaidzhanskaya SSR	
Byelorusskaya SSR (White Russia)	
Brestskaya Oblast'	
Bryanskaya Oblast'	
Khabarovskiy-Kraj	1:1,500,000
Evreyskay Autonomnaya Oblast	
Gomel'skaya Oblast'	
Gruzinskaya SSR	
Irkutskaya Oblast'	
Ivano-Frankovskaya Oblast'	
Yaroslavskaya Oblast'	
Kamchatskaya Oblast'	1:2,000,000
Karagandinskaya Oblast'	1:1,000,000
Karel'skaya SSR	1:750,000
Kazakhskaya SSR	1:1,500,000
Kemerovskaya Oblast'	1:750,000
Komi ASSR	1:1,500,000
Kostromskaya Oblast'	
Latviyskaya SSR	
Lipetskskaya Oblast'	
Litovskaya SSR	
L'vovskaya Oblast'	
Mariyskaya ASSR	
Minskaya Oblast'	
Moldavskaya SSR	
Mordovskaya ASSR	
Murmanskaya Oblast'	1:750,000
Nakhichevanskaya ASSR	
Novosibirskaya Oblast'	
Orlovskaya Oblast'	
Psovskaya Oblast'	
Ryazanskaya Oblast	
Rostovskaya Oblast'	
Saratovskaya Oblast'	
Semipalatinskaya Oblast'	1:1,000,000
Stravropolskaya Oblast'	
Zhritomir-Kievskaya Oblasti	
Tambovskaya Oblast'	
Tyumenskaya Oblast'	1:2,500,000
Chetschenskaya-Ingushskaya ASSR	
Chitinskaya Oblast'	1:1,500,000
Chuvashskaya ASSR	
Ulyanovskaya Oblast'	
Vinnitsskaya Oblast'	
Vitebskaya Oblast'	
Volynskaya i Rovenskaya Oblast'	
Voronezhskaya Oblast'	

MAPS OF THE ASSR, AND "OBLASTI"
1:600,000 (unless stated otherwise)
Moskva : GUGK

Alma-Atinskaya Oblast'	1:750,000
Arkhangelskaya Oblast'	1:1,500,000
Astrakhanskaya Oblast'	
Bel'gorodskaya Oblast'	
Khar'kovskaya Oblast'	
Dnepropetrovskaya Oblast'	
Ivano-Frankovskaya Oblast'	
Kaluzhskaya Oblast'	
Karagandinskaya Oblast'	1:1,000,000
Karel'skaya ASSR	
Kirovogradskaya i Cherkasskaya Oblasti	
Krymskaya Oblast'	
L'vovskaya Oblast'	
Nikolaevskaya i Khersonskaya Oblasti	
Tulskaya Oblast'	
Tyumenskaya Oblast'	1:2,500,000
Vladimirskaya Oblast'	
Volvnskaya and Rovenskaya Oblast	
Vologodskaya Oblast'	
Vostochno-Kazakhstanskaya Oblast'	

KARTA SSR
1:25,000,000
Moskva : GUGK, 1976
Outline map. Ko 1

VOSTOCHNAYA SIBIR'
1:16,000,000
Moskva : GUGK
Outline map of E. Siberia

ZAPADNAYA SIBIR'
1:12,000,000
Moskva : GUGK
Outline map of W. Siberia.

UKRAINSKAYA SSR I MOLDAVSKAYA SSR
1:7,500,000
In 4 sheets
Moskva : GUGK, 1969
186 x 136 complete
Outline map of the areas.

Also available at :
1:10,000,000 1969 145 x 110
1:15,000,000 1969 96 x 72

TSENTRAL'NYE RAYONY (TSENTRAL' NO PROMYSHZENNYY, TSENTRAL' NOCHERNOZEMNYY I VOLGO-VYATSKIY)
1:6,000,000
Moskva : GUGK
Outline map of Central Ukraine, Central Industrial and Volga-Vyatka areas.

E1 PHYSICAL : RELIEF

ZWIAZEK SOCJALISTYCZNYCH REPUBLIK RADZIECKICH
1:15,000,000
Warszawa : PPWK, 1972
68 x 51
Double sided hand map of the USSR. Physical map has relief colouring, vegetation types, etc. Map of admin. areas on reverse. Zl 5

WORLD TRAVEL MAP SERIES : EURASIA
1:15,000,000
Edinburgh : Bart
90 x 71
Contoured with layer col. showing principal roads and rail communications and boundaries. Covering the whole of Europe and Asia. 75p

SOVETSKÝ SVAZ
1:10,000,000
Praha : Kart
92 x 65
Physical/political reference map of the USSR. In series "Poznavame Svet" (Getting to know the World), with text vol. Kcs 17.50

PHYSICAL MAP OF THE USSR
1:8,000,000
GSGS 5104
Tolworth : MOD
113 x 85
Roads classified by surface and importance; railways classified, topography by contours in metres with altitude tints, spot heights in metres, limits of unnavigable sea ice in average year, drainage pattern, international, interstate and provincial boundaries, towns symbolised by pop. 63p

WANDKAART VAN DE SOVJETUNIE
1:7,000,000
Groningen : Wolters-Noordhoff
140 x 100
General school base wall map with topographic details, agricultural and mineral areas; communications indicated
Fl 89.50

USSR (PHYSIQUE) (LES GRANDES PUISSANCES)
1:7,000,000
Editions MDI
see GREAT BRITAIN 410 E1

L'URSS
1:6,500,000
Bruxelles : Mantnieks
180 x 125
Physical wall map for schools, showing relief by layer and bathymetric colouring, ocean currents, political boundaries in red.

REGIONAL WALL MAP OF THE USSR
1:6,250,000
London : Philip
163 x 112
Col. relief map, layer col, principal communications, internal boundaries and main cities and towns.
Mounted CR £6.25
Mounted on cloth dissected to fold £6.75

SOVIET UNION
1:6,000,000
Chicago : Rand McNally
196 x 134
Physical school wall map. Inc. Mediterranean, Baltic, Black and Caspian Seas, Mongolia, Japan etc. Relief shading of land and sea, political boundaries, cities graded by population.

UNION OF SOVIET SOCIAL REPUBLICS
1:5,875,000
No 150521
Chicago : Denoyer-Geppert
162 x 111
Contour-layer col, boundaries, cities graded by pop, communications. School wall map. US $21.50

SSSR : PHIZICHESKAYA KARTA
1:5,000,000
In 4 sheets
Moskva : GUGK, 1976
190 x 130
Contours, industrial centres. Available at different school levels.
Ro 0.29

A SZOVJETUNIÓ ÉS MONGOLIA (THE SOVIET UNION AND MONGOLIA)
1:5,000,000
Budapest : Cart, 1976
Physical wall map for schools.

SOWJETUNION
1:4,000,000
Ed H Haack
Darmstadt : Perthes
234 x 165
Relief wall map, layer col; road and rail communications, boundaries, towns graded according to pop. Available in German or Russian.

NORDASIEN (UdSSR)
1:4,000,000
Braunschweig : Westermann
240 x 190
Col. physical wall map, relief shading, principal communications, spot heights in metres, major settlements.

WENSCHOW WANDKARTE DER SOWJETUNION
1:4,000,000
Munchen : List
245 x 170
Col. physical school wall map, relief shading, rivers etc. political units in red, resources indicated.

PHYSICAL MAPS OF THE UNION REPUBLICS, ASSR AND OBLASTI
Moskva : GUGK
Maps available :

Armyanskaya SSR	1:600,000
Aserbaidzhanskaya SSR	1:600,000
Bashkirskaya ASSR	1:600,000
Buryatskaya ASSR	1:1,000,000
Chuvashskaya ASSR	1:600,000
Gor'kovskaya Oblast' i Mordovskaya ASSR	1:600,000
Grodnenskaya Oblast'	1:600,000
Ivano-Frankovskaya Oblast'	1:600,000
Kabardino Balkarskaya ASSR	1:600,000
Kalmytskaya ASSR	1:600,000
Karel'skaya ASSR	1:600,000
Krasnoyarskie Kraj	1:2,000,000
Latviyskaya SSR	1:600,000
Litovskaya SSR	1:400,000
Magadanskaya Oblast'	1:2,000,000
Mariyskaya ASSR	1:600,000
Moskoyskaya Oblast'	1:600,000
Novosibirskaya Oblast'	1:800,000
Saratovskaya Oblast'	1:600,000
Tatarskaya ASSR	1:600,000
Ulyanovskaya Oblast'	1:600,000
Vinnitskaya Oblast'	1:600,000
Vologodskaya Oblast'	1:750,000
Volgogradskaya Oblast'	1:600,000
Zaporozhskaya Oblast	1:600,000

ZAPADNAYA SIBIR'
1:2,000,000
Moskva : GUGK
Physical wall map of West Siberia.

UKRAINSKAYA SSR I MOLDAVSKAYA SSR
1:1,000,000
Moskva : GUGK
148 x 108
Physical wall map in 2 sheets.

FIZICHESKAYA KARTA GRUZINSKOY SSR
1:600,000
Moskva : GUGK, 1969
Physical map of Georgian SSR.

E2 PHYSICAL : LAND FEATURES

CARTE GEOMORPHOLOGIQUE DE L'URSS
1:10,000,000
Paris : CNRS
To accompany series "Structure geologique de l'URSS", translated to Fr. from Rus.
F.Fr 5.40

F GEOLOGY

GEOLOGISCHESKAYA KARTA RUSSKOV PLATFORMY I EE OBRAMLENIYA
1:15,000,000
In 16 sheets
Moskva : Min. Geol, 1970
60 x 68 app.
Geol. map of the Russian platform and its surroundings.

CARTE GÉOLOGIQUE DE L'URSS
1:7,500,000
Paris : CNRS
126 x 81
Detailed 2 sheet map in col. with names and legend in Fr.
Folded in pocket to accompany series "Structure Geologique de l'URSS" translated from Rus.
F.Fr 51.40

GEOLOGICHESKAYA KARTA SSSR
1:5,000,000
In 4 sheets
Moskva : GUGK, 1976
180 x 130 complete
School geol, wall map, with 2 profiles on reverse.
Ro 0.54

KARTA CHETVERTICHNYKH OTLOZHENIY SSSR
1:5,000,000
In 4 sheets
Moskva : Min. Geol. 1969
58 x 88 each
Map of Quaternary deposits.

TEKTONICHESKAYA KARTA SSSR
1:5,000,000
Moskva : GUGK, 1973
180 x 115
2 sheet tectonic wall map for schools.
Ro 0.34

TEKTONICHESKAYA KARTA SSSR
1:2,500,000
In 19 sheets
Moskva : Min. Geol. 1971
60 x 150
Legend in Eng, place names Russian.
Covers following regions :
Russian Platform
Siberian Platform
Urals Folded System
Tien-Shan Folded System
Kazakhstan Folded System
Zaysan Folded System
Altay-Sayan Folded System
Baikal Folded System
Mongolo-Amur Folded System
Verkhoyansk Folded System
Chukota Folded System
Taymir Folded System
Alpine Folded System

TEKTONICHESKAYA KARTA NEFTEGAZONOSNYCH OBLASTEY
1:2,500,000
In 16 sheets
Moskva : GUGK, 1970
90 x 60 each
Tectonic map of petrol and natural gas areas. 148pp text in Rus.

INZHENERNO-GEOLOGICHESKAYA KARTA SSSR
1:2,500,000
In 16 sheets
Moskva : GUGK, 1971
Engineering geol. map.

KARTA MAGMATICHESKIKH FORMATSIY SSR
1:2,500,000
In 17 sheets
Moskva : GUGK, 1971
86 x 63 each sheet
Map of the Magmatic rock formations of USSR coloured, with legend and 85pp explanatory booklet in Russian. With legend sheet in English.

GIDROGEOLOGICHESKAYA KARTA SSSR
1:2,500,000
In 16 sheets
Moskva : GUGK, 1971
96 x 68 each sheet
Hydro-geological map of USSR, fully coloured with text and legend in Russian.

KARTA GEOLOGICHESKICH FORMATSIY VOSTOCHNOGO KAZAKHSTANA
1:1,500,000
In 4 sheets
Moskva : GUGK, 1971
59 x 68 each
Map of the Geol. Formation of E. Kazakhstan with title and legend sheet in Eng. Text vol. in Russian.

H BIOGEOGRAPHY

SOWJETUNION, WELTMACHT IN EUROPA UND ASIEN (LAND USE)
1:15,000,000
List
see USSR 57M

ZONY RASTITEL'NOSTI SSSR
1:5,000,000
In 4 sheets
Moskva : GUGK, 1973
180 x 115 complete
School wall map of vegetation areas. Ro 0.34

ZOOGEOGRAFICHESKAYA KARTA SSSR
Ed G P Feodorovskaya
1:5,000,000
In 4 sheets
Moskva : GUGK, 1973
Zoogeographic map. Ro 0.54

PRIRODNYE ZONY SSSR
1:5,000,000
In 4 sheets
Moskva : GUGK, 1973
190 x 130 complete
Map of natural zones and landscape.
School wall map. Ro 0.54

KARTA RASTITELNOSTI GRUZINSKOY SSR
1:600,000
Moskva : GUGK, 1970
Vegetation map of Georgia.

PRIRODNYE ZONY GRUZINSKOY SSR
1:600,000
Moskva : GUGK, 1967
Map of natural zones of Georgia.

J CLIMATE

KLIMATICHESKAYA KARTA GRUZINSKOY SSR
1:600,000
Moskva : GUGK, 1970
Map of climate in Georgia.

K HUMAN GEOGRAPHY

SOWJETUNION, WELTMACHT IN EUROPA UND ASIEN (POPULATION)
1:15,000,000
List
see USSR 57M

PLOTNOST' NASELENIYA SSSR
1:5,000,000
In 4 sheets
Moskva : GUGK
190 x 130
Col. wall map of pop. density.

L ECONOMIC

SOWJETUNION, WELTMACHT IN EUROPA UND ASIEN (INDUSTRY)
1:15,000,000
List
see USSR 57M

URSS No 2
1:7,000,000
No 1163
St Germain-en-Laye : Éditions MDI
126 x 92
Plastic coated agricultural wall map for schools, with industry and communications on reverse at 1:5,000,000

OSNOVNYE STROIKI PYATILETKI (1971-1975 gg)
1:6,000,000
Moskva : GUGK
Map of the basic Constructions of the 5 year plan.

SERIES OF INDUSTRIAL MAPS
1:6,000,000
Moskva : GUGK
146 x 87 complete
Series of 2 sheet col. maps. illus. various types of industry :
Chernaya i Zvetnaya Metallurgija SSSR (metal industry)
Toplivnaya promishlennost' SSSR (fuel industry)
Pishchevaya promishlennost' SSSR (food industries)
Khimicheskaya promishlennost' SSSR (chemical industries)
Mashinostroenie i Metalloobrabotka (engineering)
Tekstil'naya promishlennost' SSR (textile industries)
Lesnaya i Tsellyulono-bumazhnaja promishlennost' (wood and paper industry)

SOWJETUNION BERGBAU UND INDUSTRIE
1:4,000,000
Gotha : Haack
235 x 166
Col. wall map showing mining and industries by symbols.

SOWJETUNION, WIRTSCHAFT
1:4,000,000
Berlin : Velhagen & Klasing und Hermann Schroedel
232 x 166
Economic wall map.

EKONOMICHESKAYA KARTA ZAPADNAYA SIBIR'
1:2,500,000
Koskva : GUGK, 1969
93 x 128
Col. map of West Siberia, showing economy and industry by symbols.

EKONOMICHESKAYA KARTA GRUZINSKOY SSR
1:600,000
Moskva : GUGK, 1965
Economic map of Georgia.

ECONOMIC MAPS OF THE OBLASTI AND REGIONS
Moskva : GUGK

Atlayskiy Kray	1:1,000,000
Bashkirskaya ASSR	1:600,000
Belorusskaya SSR	1:600,000
Ivano-Frankovskaya Oblast'	1:600,000
Chelyabinskaya Oblast'	1:600,000
Kirovskaya Oblast'	1:600,000
Krasnoyarskiy Kray	1:2,000,000
Moskovskaya Oblast'	1:600,000
Orenburgskaya Oblast'	1:750,000
Permskaya Oblast'	1:700,000
Smolenskaya Oblast'	1:600,000
Ulyanovskaya Oblast'	1:600,000
The Urals	1:1,250,000

3 AGRICULTURAL MAPS
1:5,000,000
Moskva : GUGK
180 x 115
Each map in 2 sheets
1 Zernovye Kul'tury SSSR - cereal crops.
2 Tekhnicheskie Kul'tury SSSR - technical crops (sugar, tea, soya beans etc.)
3 Zhi votnovodstvo SSSR - map of stock breeding.

PUTI SOOBSHCHENIYA SSSR
1:5,000,000
In 4 sheets
Moskva : GUGK, 1970
180 x 130
Communications wall map showing roads, railways, air routes, shipping and canals.

M HISTORICAL

SCHOOL RUSSIAN HISTORY WALL MAPS
Moskva : GUGK
Col. historical maps in Russian :
For Primary Schools
Ancient Russian States from the 9th to early 12th C, 1973, 1:3,000,000
Formation and Expansion of Russian States in the 14th to 17th C 1:5,000,000
Russian Empire in the 18th C 1:3,000,000
The Great October Socialist Revolution and Civil War, 1973 1:5,000,000
For Middle Schools :
Ancient Tribes and States on our land and neighbouring countries 1:5,000,000
Primitive Systems and States on our territory and lands, 1973, 1:6,000,000
Feudal System 9th - first third 13th C, 1973, 1:3,000,000

Russian Principalities in the 12th to the beginning of the 13th C 1:3,000,000
Formation of Russian central multinational States 1:2,750,000
Russian States in the period of Christian Wars and struggle from intervention by Polish-Lithuanian and Swedish Feudal System in the early 7th C, 1973, 1:2,500,000
Russian States in the 17th C, 1973 1:3,000,000
Russian Empire in the second half of the 18th C. 1:3,000,000
National War 1812, 1973 1:2,000,000
Russian Empire from the early 19th C - 1861, European sector 1:3,000,000
Russo-Japanese War, 1904-5, 1973 1:2,500,000
Russian 1907 - 1914
Russian Territorial Position, 1700-1914, 1:5,000,000
Foreign Wars, Invasion and Civil War in the USSR, in 1918 1:4,000,000
Foreign Wars, Invasion and Civil War in the USSR, 1919-20 and 1918-19, 1:4,000,000
Industrial Development in the Pre War years, 1:5,000,000
Great Civil War of the Soviet Union, 1941-45, 1973, 1:3,000,000
Cultural Construction of the USSR in the years of Soviet power 1:5,000,000
Russia in the 19th - early 20th C, 1973, 1:4,000,000
Formation of the Russian Central States, 1973 1:3,000,000
Russian States in the first half of the 16th C, 1973, 1:3,000,000
Expansion of Russian States in the first half of the 16th - 17th C, 1973, 1:5,000,000
Russia - 17th C - 1860s, 1973, 1:3,000,000
Russia after Reforms (the Devt. of Capitalism 1861 - 1900), 1973 1:2,500,000
Growth of the Russian Territorial Empire, 1700-1914, 1973 1:5,000,000
First Russian Revolution, 1905-7,
Preparation for the Great October Revolution, 1973, 1:3,000,000
The Great October Socialist Revolution and the triumphant process of Soviet Rule (October 1917 - March 1918), 1973, 1:3,000,000
Great National Wars of the Soviet Union (1941-45), 1973, 1:3,000,000
Cultivation and Structure of the USSR in the years of Soviet Rule, 1973, 1:5,000,000

PIONERSKAYA ORGANIZATSIYA SSSR
1:8,000,000
Moskva : GUGK
Pictorial map of the early organisation of the USSR. Ro 0.27

LENIN O RAZVITII KAPITALIZMA V ROSSII K KONTSU XIX VEKA
1:8,000,000
Moskva : GUGK
Lenin and the development of Capitalism in Russia at the end of the 19th C.
Ro 0.27

BIRTH OF LENIN'S PARTY (1903)
1:8,000,000
Moskva : GUGK
Pictorial map.

PARTIYA V REVOLUTSII 1905-07 gg
Various scales
Moskva : GUGK
Pictorial map of the Party during the Revolution of 1905-07. Ro 0.27

ORGANIZATSIYA POBEDY V GRAZHDANSKOY VOINE I INOSTRAN-NOY VOENNOY INTERVENTSII (1918-22 gg)
1:8,000,000
Moskva : GUGK
Victory organisation in the Civil War and intervention of foreign wars 1918-22.
Ro 0.27

ORGANIZATSIYA STROITELSTRYA I UPROCHENIY SOTSIALIZMA (1926-1941)
1:8,000,000
Moskva : GUGK
Organisation, construction and consolidation of socialism, 1926-41. Pictorial map.
Ro 0.27

NATSIONAL'NO-GOSUDARSTVENNOE STROITEL'STVO SSSR (1922-1972)
1:8,000,000
Moskva : GUGK
Construction of the National State of the USSR. Pictorial map. Ro 0.27

PART - VOZHDI OKTYABR
Various scales
Moskva : GUGK
Pictorial map illustrating efforts of the October Party leaders. Ro 0.25

LENIN OB IMPERIALIZME
1:8,000,000
Moskva : GUGK
Covers pictorially Lenin on Imperialism.
Ro 0.27

LENIN VO GLAVE OBORONI SOTSIALISTICHESKOGO OTECHESTVA
1:8,000,000
Moskva : GUGK
Pictorial wall map of Lenin as defence head of socialist country. Ro 0.27

LENIN V MOSKVE I PODMOSKOVE V 1918-1924
Various scales
Moskva : GUGK
Pictorial map of Lenin in Moscow.
Ro 0.27

VELIKAYA BITVA POD MOSKVOY
1:650,000
Moskva : GUGK
Pictorial map of the Great Battle of Moscow. Ro 0.27

BITVA POD KURSKOM
Various scales
Moskva : GUGK
Pictorial map of the Battle of Kurskom.
Ro 0.27

VELIKAYA BITVA NA VOLGE
Various scales
Moskva : GUGK
Pictorial map of the Great Battle on the Volga. Ro 0.27

BREASTED-HUTH-HARDING HISTORICAL MAPS
204491
Growth of Russia 1462-1939
Chicago : Denoyer-Geppert
112 x 81
Col. wall map printed on manilla.

THE EXPANSION OF THE RUSSIAN EMPIRE, 1613 - 1914
No scale
Indianapolis : Cram
School historical wall map, showing Grand Principality of Moscow 1462, Acquisitions 1462-1613, 1615-1725, 1725-1796, 1796-1914.
US $13.75

EXPANSION OF RUSSIA IN ASIA - PALMER WORLD HISTORY MAP
Chicago : Rand McNally
127 x 116
Shows Russian territory in 1533, 1598, 1914.

GESCHICHTSWANDKARTEN
Ed Putzger
Bielefeld : Cornelsen, Velhagen & Klasing
Historical wall maps in German :
Vordringen Russlands nach Asien bis 1914 (Advance of Russia into Asia until 1914) 1:5,000,000 194 x 140
Die Sowjet union der Gegenwart (Present USSR) 1:5,000,000 194 x 140
DM 132

HAACK SCHOOL HISTORY MAPS
1:4,800,000
Darmstadt : Perthes
Die Sowjetunion 1917-39 206 x 182
Die Sowjetunion 1939-70 206 x 122

SOWJETUNION-WELTMACHT IN EUROPA UND ASIEN (WORLD POWER IN EUROPE AND ASIA)
1:15,000,000
Munchen : List
245 x 180
Harms wall map - 4 maps in one covering history, land use, pop, density, industry.
DM 142

ATLASES
A1 GENERAL : ROADS

ATLAS AUTOMOBIL'NYKH DOROG SSSR (ROAD ATLAS OF THE USSR)
Moskva : GUGK, 1976
17 x 27
171pp detailed col. road maps, 1:4,000,000. Covers whole USSR except Siberia. Strip diagrams of principal routes, maps of approaches to Moscow, distance tables, index. Text in Russian.
Ro 3

CHERNOMORSKOE POBEREZH'E (COAST) AND KAVKAZ (CAUCASUS) ATLAS AVTOMOBIL' NYKH DOROG
Moskva : GUGK, 1973
17 x 27
40pp
Road atlas of Black Sea coast of Caucasus in maps and plans. Ro 0.50

PRIBALTIKA. ATLAS AVTOMOBIL'-NYKH DOROG
Moskva : GUGK, 1973
17 x 27
16pp
Regional road atlas of the Baltic states.
Ro 0.40

KAZAKHSTAN I SREDNYAYA AZIYA. ATLAS AVTOMOBIL'NYKH DOROG
Moskva : GUGK, 1973
17 x 27
32pp
Road atlas of Kazakhstan and Central Asia.
Ro 0.50

ATLASES
B TOWN PLANS

PLAN MOSKVY
Moskva : Mysl', 1968
18 x 21
18 double pp col. town plans, principal roads named, parks, railways, stations, museums etc. 80pp index. With fold out map.

ATLASES
D POLITICAL & ADMINISTRATIVE

ATLAS "SSSR V DEVYATOY PYATILETKE"
Moskva : GUGK, 1972
21 x 28
Atlas of the ninth 5 year plan. 42pp maps.
Ro 0.50

ATLASES
F GEOLOGY

ATLAS OF THE LITHOLOGICAL-PALAEOGEOGRAPHICAL MAPS OF THE USSR
Ed A P Vinogradov
In 4 vols.
Moskva : GUGK
63 x 83
Covers geol. periods of sedimentary deposition. Col. maps show thickness of sediments, erosion and minerals of each individual period. Palaeotectonic maps mark stages of tectonic devt. and additional plates depict the accumulation of phosphorites, iron ores, oil and gas within the various regions of the USSR.

Vol I	Pre-Cambrian, Cambrian, Ordovician and Silurian periods.
Vol II	Devonian, Carboniferous and Permian periods
Vol III	Triassic, Jurassic and Cretaceous periods
Vol IV	Paleogene, Neogene and Quaternary periods.

ATLAS STRUKTURNYKH PALEO-TEKTONICHESKICH KART I GEOLOGICHESKICH KART DLYA TERRITORII ZAPADNO-SIBIRSKOY NIZMENNOSTI
Moskva : GUGK, 1969/70
28 x 34
Structural palaeotectonic and geol. maps for the West Siberian plains. 17 col. maps at 1:5,000,000, 53 x 64 and 175pp text in Russian.

ATLAS GRYAZEVYCH VULKANOV AZERBAIDZHANSKOY SSR
Baku : Academy of Sciences, Azerbaidzhan SSR, 1972
43 x 31
Atlas of mud volcanoes, with 400 plates and aerial photographs, 100 small scale maps. Text also in Eng.

ATLAS LITOLOGO - PALEOGEO-GRAFICHESKIKH KART ARMYANSKOY SSR
Moskva : Academy of Sciences, 1972
Palaeogeographic-lithological atlas of the Armenian USSR.

ATLASES
J CLIMATE

KLIMAT YAKUTSKOY ASSR
Leningrad : Gidrometeorologicheskoe Izdatel'stvo, 1968
29 x 34
32pp
Climatic Atlas of Yakutsk, 21 col. climatic maps, text in Russian.

KLIMATICHESKIY ATLAS UKRAINSKOY SSR
Leningrad : Hydrometeorological Research Inst. of the Ukraine, 1968
26 x 17
232pp
200pp climatic atlas of Ukraine.
30pp text in Russian.

ATLASES
L ECONOMIC

ECONOMIC ATLAS OF THE SOVIET UNION
by George Kish
2nd rev. edition
Michigan : Univ. Press, 1971
27 x 27
90pp
65pp maps, 4 general, 60 regional.
Covers agriculture, land use, mining, industry, transport. US $12.50

OXFORD REGIONAL ECONOMIC ATLAS OF THE USSR AND EASTERN EUROPE
Oxford : OUP, 1969
19 x 25
142pp
Reissue of 1956 ed. 69pp coloured maps. Covers East Germany to Hungary, Poland - Albania. General and economic distribution maps; 25pp gazetteer. 48pp notes, diagrams, statistics.

Boards	£3.15
Paper covers	£1.75

ATLAS SSSR DLYA SREDNEY SHKOLY KURS EKONOMICHESKOI GEOGRAFII
Moskva : GUGK, 1970
22 x 28
48pp
School atlas of economic geog. (for middle schools).

ATLAS SKHEM ZHELEZNYKH DOROG SSSR (DIAGRAMMATIC RAILWAY ATLAS)
Moskva : GUGK, 1976
11 x 16
62 railway plans, with list of stations.
Ro 0.40

ZHELEZNYE DOROG SSSR : NAPRAVLENIYA I STANTSII (USSR RAILWAYS : DIRECTIONS AND STATIONS)
Moskva : GUGK, 1966
11 x 16
150pp
94 plans, index.

ATLAS LENINGRADSKOY OBLASTI
Moskva : GUGK, 1967
21 x 29
vi, 82pp
Economic biased atlas for the Leningrad Oblast.

ATLASES
M HISTORICAL

RUSSIAN HISTORY ATLAS
by Martin Gilbert
London : Weidenfeld & Nicolson, 1972
146 maps covering history from 800 BC up to the present day. In black and white, with textual information.
£3.25

AN ATLAS OF RUSSIAN HISTORY: ELEVEN CENTURIES OF CHANGING BORDERS
by Allen F Chew
Yale : Yale Univ. Press, 1971
Rev. edition
21 x 27
127pp
37 maps extending from the Kievan Rus. state in the 9th C to the present day.
Spiral bound. US $4.95

ATLAS ISTORII SREDNIKH VEKOV DLYA VI KLASSA SREDNEY SHKOLY (HIST. ATLAS OF THE MIDDLE AGES FOR 6th CLASS OF MIDDLE SCHOOLS)
Moskva : GUGK
20 x 26
16pp
18 maps.

ATLAS "OBRAZOVANIE I RAZVITIE SSSR" (EDUCATION AND DEVT. USSR)
Moskva : GUGK, 1972
25 x 34
77pp maps, covering history of devt.
Ro 4.00

ATLAS NOVOY ISTORII (MOD. HIST. ATLAS)
Moskva : GUGK
20 x 26
16pp
17 maps, school atlas, in 2 editions for 8th, 9th and 10th classes.

ATLAS ISTORII SSSR
Moskva : GUGK
20 x 26
Russian school atlas available in different editions for 4th, 7th, 8th and 9th classes.

ATLAS ISTORII SSSR SO SVEDENIYAMI PO NOVOY I NOVEISHEY ISTORII ZARUBEZHNYKH
Moskva : GUGK
20 x 26
38pp
School history atlas of USSR and abroad.

LENIN - ISTORIKO-BIOGRAFI-CHESKIY ATLAS
Moskva : Inst. Marxism/Leninism, GUGK, 1970
Showing life of Lenin and spread of his ideas through maps.

PO LENINU ZHIVEM I STROIM - ATLAS NOVOSIBIRSKAYA OBLAST' (WE ARE LIVING AND CONSTRUCT-ING AS LENIN TAUGHT US - ATLAS OF NOVOSIBIRSK REGION)
Ed K L Provorov
Moskva : GUGK, 1970
Covers changing history of Siberia.

ATLASES
01 NATIONAL : REFERENCE

ATLAS SSSR
Moskva : GUGK, 1969
38 x 28
148pp
Covers general geog, pop. maps, transport, hydrography, relief, political-admin. divisions, specialised socio-economic maps. Scales generally 1:3M and 1:6M

SOVIET UNION IN MAPS
Ed H Fullard
London : Philip, 1975
28 x 22
33pp
Physical, political, economic, linguistic, racial and communication maps, with 8pp history with explanatory text.

ATLASES
02 NATIONAL : SCHOOL EDITIONS

GEOGRAFICHESKIY ATLAS DLYA UCHITELEY SREDNEY SHKOLY (ATLAS FOR MIDDLE SCHOOL TEACHERS)
Moskva : GUGK, 1968
27 x 37
164pp maps for USSR and World, 34pp index, text in Russian.

NASHA RODINA (OUR HOMELAND)
Moskva : GUGK
22 x 28
16pp
General geographical atlas of USSR in Russian.

GEOGRAFICHESKIY ATLAS DLYA 5-GO KLASSA
Moskva : GUGK, 1970
22 x 28
17pp
School atlas for the 5th Class.

GEOGRAFICHESKIY ATLAS DLYO 7-go — 8-go KLASSOV
Moskva : GUGK
22 x 28
36pp
School atlas for 7th, 8th Classes.

GEOGRAFICHESKIY ATLAS SSSR DLYA 7-go KLASSA
Moskva : GUGK, 1970
32pp
Atlas of USSR for the 7th Class.

MALYY ATLAS SSSR (SMALL ATLAS OF THE USSR)
Moskva : GUGK, 1973
12 x 19
136pp maps • Ro 2.00

ATLASES
P REGIONAL

ATLAS AZERBAIDZHANSKOY SSR
Baku : Academy of Sciences, 1963
23 x 33
213pp
Col. thematic maps, few pp text in Russian.

ATLAS SEVERNOGO KAZAKHSTANA
Moskva : GUGK
37 x 27
200pp

ATLAS LATVIYSKOY SSR
Moskva : GUGK
200pp

ATLAS TADZHIKSKOY SSR
Moskva : GUGK
25 x 35
208pp

UKRAINIAN AND MOLDAVIAN SSR
Moskva : GUGK, 1973
17 x 27
32pp Ro 0.50

ATLASES OF THE OBLASTI
Moskva : GUGK
Regional atlases.
Available for the following Oblasti :
Astrakhan
Vologda, 1968
Karagand, 1969
Kirov, 1960
Kuibyshev
Murmansk
Orenburg
Pskov
Stavropol'
Sakhalin
Tyumen'

581 Afghanistan

A1 GENERAL MAPS : ROADS

AFGHANISTAN
1:3,000,000
Kabul : Afghan Cart, Inst, 1967
45 x 32
Relief shaded, drainage in blue, main and secondary roads and provincial boundaries shown. Inset shows Afghanistan's position in Asia. On reverse is a guide to Afghan. language.

ROAD MAP OF AFGHANISTAN
1:3,000,000
Kabul : Af. Tourist Org.
Physical road map.

TOURIST MAP OF AFGHANISTAN
1:2,100,000
Kabul : Afghan Tourist Org, 1970
59 x 45
Shows roads, natural features, items of tourist interest. Reverse has table of distances. Legend also in English.

A2 GENERAL MAPS : LOCAL

NURISTAN
1:475,000
Reprinted from Geog. Journal, Dec. 1957
London : RGS
21 x 29
Topographical map based on a traverse by Wilfred Thesiger, 1956 £1.50

KOH-E-KESHNIKHAN/HOHER HINDUKUSCH
1:25,000
Innsbruck : Universitatsverlag Wagner, 1972
60 x 89
Contoured map of the Austrian scientific expedition of 1970, showing relief, glaciers, moraines, footpaths; 139pp text "Hindu Kusch : Osterreichische Forschungs - expedition in den Wakhan im Jahre 1970", ed Dr Karl Gratzh. Available separately.

B TOWN PLANS

KABUL CITY
1:25,000
Kabul : Afghan Tourist Org, 1972
51 x 55
Coloured town plan, with contours and list of places of interest.

TOWN PLAN OF KABUL
1:20,000
Kabul : Afghanistan Cartographic Inst.
56 x 47
Col. plan, contoured, index of principal buildings.

MAP OF KABUL
1:20,000
Tehran : Sahab
60 x 90
Town plan in Eng. and Persian.
Rls 70

C OFFICIAL SERIES

INTERNATIONAL MAP OF THE WORLD
1:1,000,000
DMS Series 1301
see WORLD 100C and index 100/1

OFFICIAL TOPOGRAPHIC SERIES
1:250,000
In 101 sheets
Kabul : Af. Cart, Inst.
Col. topog. series in progress, contoured with roads classified, woodland and land detail. Northern half of the country has been published.

OFFICIAL TOPOGRAPHIC SERIES
1:100,000
In 440 sheets
Kabul : Af. Cart. Inst.
Series in progress currently published for the northern part of the country. In black and white only, but will eventually be republished in colours.

OFFICIAL TOPOGRAPHIC SERIES
1:50,000
In 1,650 sheets
Kabul : Af. Cart. Inst.
Series in progress currently published for central and southern regions of the country. In black and white only, but will eventually be republished in colours.

D POLITICAL & ADMINISTRATIVE

GENERAL MAP OF AFGHANISTAN
1:2,000,000
Tehran : Sahab, 1969
90 x 60
Col. by provinces, roads marked with distances in km, railways, airports. Economic map and plan of Kabul inset. In Eng. and Persian. Rls 100

AFGHANISTAN
1:2,000,000
Moskva : GUGK, 1973
Col. study map showing water features, settlements, admin. centres and divisions, communications, boundaries, capitals, economic details, pop. Geog. description.
Ro 0.30

GENERAL MAP OF AFGHANISTAN
1:1,000,000
No 98
Tehran : Sahab, 1967
130 x 98
Wall map showing boundaries, roads etc. Text in Eng. and Persian. Rls 600

E1 PHYSICAL : RELIEF

PHYSICAL MAP OF AFGHANISTAN
1:2,000,000
1st edition
Kabul : Af. Cart. Inst. 1968
67 x 61
Relief col. with roads classified, distances, also tracks, railways; towns graded by admin. status, detailed place names, administrative boundaries. Guide to language on reverse. Af 20

PHYSICAL AND POLITICAL MAP OF AFGHANISTAN
1:1,500,000
1st edition
Kabul : Af. Cart. Inst, 1968
89 x 81
2 sheets joined as one, spot heights, sand dunes, roads, railways and boundaries. Black and white insets of Kabul, Qandahar, Herat and Mazar-i-Sharif. On reverse is a guide to Afghani pronunciation.
Af 80

PHYSICAL AND POLITICAL MAP OF AFGHANISTAN
1:1,300,000
Kabul : Af. Cart. Inst, 1968
110 x 100
Contours, hydrography, roads, province boundaries, railways.

MAP OF AFGHANISTAN
1:1,000,000
Kabul : Afghan Tourist Organisation, 1964
70 x 51
Physical col, relief shading, roads with distances, rivers, province boundaries.

F GEOLOGICAL

GEOLOGICAL MAP OF AFGHANISTAN
1:2,500,000
Kabul : Af. Geol. Surv. 1969
61 x 47
Coloured map, legend in English.

L ECONOMIC

ECONOMIC MAP OF AFGHANISTAN
1:3,000,000
Kabul : Af. Cart. Inst. 1967
56 x 40
Distribution of economic products indicated by pictorial symbols, also showing roads, principal towns and gas stations.

M HISTORICAL

ARCHAEOLOGICAL MAP OF
AFGHANISTAN
1:2,400,000
Kabul : Af. Cart, Inst, 1968
62 x 46
Shows roads and archaeological
features by symbols.

59 South East Asia

D POLITICAL & ADMINISTRATIVE

DAILY TELEGRAPH MAP OF THE FAR EAST
1:7,000,000
London : Gia
95 x 69
Political col, railways and factual notes, insets showing pop. and political groupings. 35p

SOUTH EAST ASIA
1:5,937,500
Washington : NGS
85 x 67
Political col. wall map.
Paper US $2.00
Plastic US $3.00

PHILIP'S WALL MAP OF SOUTH EAST ASIA
1:5,000,000
London : Philip
91 x 114
Political col, from Canton to Darwin and Andaman Islands to West Irian.
Paper flat £1.50
Mounted CR £5.50
Mounted on cloth dissected to fold £7.00

JIHOVYCHODNI ASIE
1:5,000,000
Praha : Kart, 1969
General school wall map of S E Asia. Kcs 150

VIETNAM, CAMBODIA, LAOS AND THAILAND
1:1,875,000
Washington : NGS
80 x 109
Political col. wall map.
Paper US $2.00
Plastic US $3.00

SOUTH-EAST ASIA
1:1,000,000
NZMS 241
1st edition
Wellington : NZMS, 1965
86 x 113 each sheet
2 sheet map showing communications, internat, external admin. boundaries. Shows Cambodia, Laos, N & S Vietnam. NZ $0.75

EAST ASIA ROAD MAPS
1:1,250,000
AMS 1306
In 5 sheets
Washington : AMS/Feltham : DMS
Various sizes
Contoured with layer colouring, roads classified, railways, boundaries, towns graded by population.
Sheets available :

1 Covering N Vietnam and northern Laos
2 Covering S Vietnam and southern Laos and Cambodia
3 Covering Thailand excluding extreme southern tip.

SOUTH EAST ASIA
No 105
Sydney : Gregory
76 x 50
Col. map showing S E Asia, Australia, Pacific Islands, Japan. Index. Air distances in miles, pop indicated. 60c

ASIA DEL SUDOESTE
No scale given
Barcelona : Editorial Teide
25 x 33
School hand map showing major cities and boundaries. S.Ptas 1

E1 PHYSICAL : RELIEF

OFFICIAL MAP OF SOUTHEASTERN ASIA
1:6,336,000
Chicago : Rand McNally, 1968
143 x 101
Land and submarine contours, layer col, relief shading, principal roads, railways and airports marked, national boundaries, towns graded by pop. Inc. India to Japan, Sumatra to New Guinea. US $1.00

AUSTRALIEN UND SUDOSTASIEN
1:6,000,000
Wien : F B
215 x 175
Physical wall map.

REGIONAL WALL MAP OF THE FAR EAST
1:6,500,000
London : Philip
94 x 119
Physical col, communications, boundaries and towns graded by pop; covers Irkutsk to Timor, Chittagong to Mariana Islands.
Paper flat £1.50
Mounted CR £5.50
Mounted on cloth dissected to fold £7.00

WORLD TRAVEL MAP OF SOUTH EAST ASIA
1:5,800,000
Edinburgh : Bart
95 x 68
Covers Mandalay to Hong Kong, Sumatra to West Irian. Physical col. with roads, railways, boundaries, airports and spot heights. Insets show North Burma, Papua and New Guinea and Malaya. 75p

SOUTH EAST ASIA
1:5,000,000
Moskva : GUGK, 1969
125 x 110
2 sheet physical map, contours, land use.

SOUTHEAST ASIA, VISUAL RELIEF
1:4,000,000
No 123811-10
Chicago : Denoyer-Geppert
162 x 137
Col. school wall map, showing relief of land and sea, cities classed by pop. boundaries.
Rollers US $21.75

OST-UND SUDOSTASIEN
1:4,000,000
Braunschweig : Westermann
185 x 201
Physical wall map. DM 128

CONTINENTAL SOUTH-EAST ASIA
1:2,500,000
AMS Series 1206
Washington : Defense Mapping Agency
78 x 104
Contoured and layer coloured, communications, boundaries. Covering Southern Burma, Laos, Vietnam, Cambodia, Thailand and W. Malaysia. US $1.00

SUDOSTASIEN
1:2,000,000
Ed Haack - Painke
Darmstadt : Perthes
230 x 210
Haack wall map, layer col, hill shading, boundaries, cities, railways.

SOUTHEAST ASIA BRIEFING CHART
1:2,000,000
AMS 5213
Washington : Defense Mapping Agency, 1968
85 x 61
Contoured with boundaries, communications and airfields, covering Vietnam, Laos, Cambodia and eastern Thailand. US $1.00

SOUTHEAST ASIA BRIEFING GRAPHIC
1:1,000,000
AMS L307
In 2 sheets
Washington : Defense Mapping Agency
116 x 96 each sheet.
Topog. map, contoured with boundaries, communications and airfields, covering Laos, Vietnam, Cambodia and eastern Thailand.

F GEOLOGY

SEDIMENTARY BASIN MAP OF S E ASIA
1:20,000,000
Kuala Lumpur : Surv. Dept, 1962
17 x 23
Col. geol. map, classifying sedimentary deposits, positions of oil and gas fields, potential sites shown by symbols. Covers Burma, Vietnam, Sumatra, Borneo.

J CLIMATE

BIOCLIMATS DU SUD-EST ASIATIQUE
1:2,534,000
Pondichery : Inst. Fr, 1967
96 x 60
Col. map with diagrams and insets, rainy seasons on reverse. 114pp text.

K HUMAN GEOGRAPHY

PEOPLES OF SOUTHEAST ASIA
1:13,625,000
Washington : NGS, 1971
95 x 82
Political col. wall map showing races.
Paper US $2.00
Plastic US $3.00

ETHNOLINGUISTIC GROUPS OF MAINLAND SOUTHEAST ASIA
Eds : LeBar, Hickey, Musgrave
1:3,000,000
Map in 2 sheets
New Haven, Conn : Human Relations Area Files Press, 1964
55 x 74 each sheet
Coloured map drawn to accompany 'Ethnic Groups of Mainland Southeast Asia' 1964. US $2.50

L ECONOMIC

OSTASIEN - WIRTSCHAFT UND VERKEHR
1:5,750,000
Hamburg : Ost-Asiatischen Verein, 1961
123 x 160
Physical col. map of East and South East Asia showing economic information and communications, also contours, ports etc. Legend in 8 langs. Many insets.

UGO-VOSTOCHNAYA ASIYA, EKONOMICHESKAYA KARTA
1:4,000,000 and 1:5,000,000
Moskva : GUGK, 1973
2 sheet economic school wall maps.
Each Ro 0.28

M HISTORICAL

BREASTED-HUTH-HARDING HISTORICAL WALL MAPS : THE FAR EAST IN 1895
No 204571
Chicago : Denoyer-Geppert
112 x 81
Col. wall map printed on manilla.

ATLASES
M HISTORICAL

SOUTHEAST ASIA IN MAPS
T F Barton and others
Chicago : Denoyer-Geppert
21 z 28
96pp
Black and white maps covering history, physical features etc. US $1.50

591 Burma

A1 GENERAL MAPS : ROADS

BURMA – ASIA TRANSPORTATION MAP
1:2,200,000
AMS 5201
Washington : Defense Mapping Agency
66 x 124
Roads classified, railways and boundaries. US $0.75

E1 PHYSICAL : RELIEF

BIRMA
1:2,000,000
Moskva : GUGK, 1970
55 x 110
Physical map with insets - climate, 1:8,000,000; economy, 1:6,000,000

BURMA
Washington : Govt. Printing Office/ Central Intelligence Agency
58 x 66
Showing relief, urban areas, main admin. divisions, them insets.
US $0.50

593 Thailand

See also : 59 SOUTHEAST ASIA
593 THAILAND ATLASES O - for thematic maps.

A1 GENERAL MAPS : ROADS

THAILAND HIGHWAY MAP
1:2,000,000
In 4 sheets
Bangkok : Thai Surv. Dept, 1972
52 x 67 complete
10 types of road classified, numbers and distances, contours etc. Legend and names in Siamese and English.
US $10.00

EAST ASIA ROAD MAP
1:1,500,000
AMS 1306
Washington : AMS, 1968
84 x 90
Contoured and layer col, roads classified, railways, airports, vegetation. 3 sheet series. Sheet 3 covers Thailand, except extreme southern tip.

THAILAND HIGHWAY MAP
1:1,000,000
In 4 sheets
Bangkok : TDH
59 x 73 each
13 road classifications of status, surfaces and condition. Highway numbers and distances in km, contours, town pop, rivers and provincial boundaries.

B TOWN PLANS

BANGKOK
1:30,000
Bangkok : Newman Lee
54 x 75
Sketch plan in red, principal roads named, hotels marked, places of interest, railways etc, index in margin. 45p

BANGKOK
1:25,000
Bangkok : Thai Surv. Dept.
Detailed col. plan naming principal streets, public buildings and open spaces.

BANGKOK AND CHIENGMAI
Bangkok : Tourist Office of Thailand.
Col. plan naming major streets and public buildings.

C OFFICIAL SURVEYS

INTERNATIONAL MAP OF THE WORLD
1:1,000,000
DMS Series 1301
7 sheets needed for complete coverage
see WORLD 100C and index 100/1.

THAILAND AMS SERIES L509
1:250,000
AMS Series L509
In 52 sheets, see index 593/1
Washington : AMS
Bangkok : Thai, Surv. Dept.
74 x 56 each
Detailed topog. series contoured, roads classified, distances in km, railways, airports, boundaries, tropical grassland, forests, rice paddy fields. Legend in Eng, and Fr. overprinted with UTM grid.
Each US $10.00

D POLITICAL & ADMINISTRATIVE

MAP OF THAILAND
1:2,500,000
Bangkok : Thai, Surv. Dept.
49 x 76
Map shows admin. divisions by Changwat (provinces) US $10.00

E1 PHYSICAL : RELIEF

MAP OF THAILAND
1:2,000,000
Bangkok : Thai, Surv. Dept.
82 x 144
Physical colouring, contours, communications, boundaries. 2 sheet map in Thai.
US $20.00

GEOGRAPHIC MAP OF THAILAND
In 4 sheets
Bangkok : Thai, Surv. Dept.
In 4 sheets
103 x 172
Main and secondary roads overprinted on brown photographic relief base.
Principal towns marked.

GEOGRAPHICAL MAP OF THAILAND
1:1,000,000
Bangkok : Thai, Surv. Dept, 1969/70
102 x 173
2 sheet map col. to indicate woodland and rice fields, roads classified, railways, boundaries, relief indicated by formlines. Names and legend in Thai and English.
US $15.00

F GEOLOGY

GEOLOGICAL MAP OF THAILAND
1:1,000,000
In 2 sheets
Bangkok : Dept. Nat. Resources, 1969
Col. geological map with 17pp explanatory text.

G EARTH RESOURCES

KINGDOM OF THAILAND : GENERAL SOIL MAP
F R Moormann and S Rojanasoonthon
Bangkok : Soil Survey Division
N - 71 x 78; S - 62 x 79
2 sheet soil map for north and south.

ATLASES
O NATIONAL

KHRONGKAN CHAT THAM SAMUT PHAENTHI SAPPHAYAKON (NATIONAL RESOURCES ATLAS)
1:2,500,000
Vol 4
Bangkok : Thai, Surv. Dept, 1969
54 x 78
110pp
17 them. maps, text in English. Some maps available separately without text.

Types of Climate, 1969	US $7.00
Types of Forests, National Parks and Wildlife Preserved areas, 1969	US $8.00
Water Resources Devt.	US $7.00
Mineral Resources of Thailand, 1969	US $8.00
Density of Population per square km. 1969	US $7.00
Education, 1969	US $10.00
Percentage of Land with Certificates, 1969	US $7.00
Industrial Establishment by Changwat 1969	US $9.00
Electric Generation and Transmission Systems	US $7.00
General Soil Conditions, 1969	US $10.00
Reconnaissance Geology, 1969	US $10.00
Inland Waterways, 1969	US $7.00
Telecommunications	US $8.00
Highways, Railways & Domestic Airlines, Roads, 1970 Text in English	US $10.00
Climatic Charts	US $7.00
Administrative Divisions	US $10.00
Set	US $170.00
Fisheries, 1969	US $8.00
Telecommunications	US $8.00
Highways, Railways & Domestic Airlines, Roads, 1970. Text in English	US $10.00

595 Malaysia

See also: 59 SOUTH EAST ASIA

A1 GENERAL MAPS : ROADS

West Malaysia

MALAYA AND SINGAPORE
1:1,800,000
DOS 17/18
Tolworth : DOS, 1948
Small hand map showing road and rail communications, boundaries and settlement.

PETA JALAN – MALAYSIA BARAT (ROAD MAP OF MALAYA)
1:1,140,480
Edition 2
Kuala Lumpur : Dir. of Natnl. Mapping, 1970
107 x 84
Double sided, roads classified, map of Singapore and environs; town plans and distances table on reverse.

East Malaysia

BRITISH TERRITORIES IN BORNEO
1:2,500,000
DOS (Misc) 85
Tolworth : DOS, 1953
Small hand map showing boundaries and principal communications.

ROAD MAP OF SARAWAK
1:1,000,000
In 2 sheets
Kuching : Surv. Dept. 1971
43 x 33
In black and white showing roads, divisional boundaries and District Headquarters.
Sheet 1 - Kuching - Sibu - Bintalu
2 - Bintalu - Miri - Limbang
Each M 0.25

SABAH
1:1,425,000
DOS 973
Edition 4
Tolworth : DOS, 1964
Small hand map showing roads, towns and boundaries. 10p

A2 GENERAL MAPS : LOCAL

West Malaysia

TAMAN NEGARA
1:380,160
Kuala Lumpur : Dir. of Natnl. Mapping
36 x 33
Uncoloured plan of the National Park area.

B TOWN PLANS

BANDAR KUCHING
1:10,000
Series No. RAMPN 83
Kuala Lumpur : Dir. of Natnl. Mapping, 1973
94 x 64
Coloured street plan of the city with inset of shopping centre. M $2.00

East Malaysia

TOWN MAP OF SANDAKAN
1:5,000
Series T 936
Kuala Lumpur : Dir. of Natnl. Mapping
55 x 55 M $1.00

C OFFICIAL SURVEYS

INTERNATIONAL MAP OF THE WORLD
1:1,000,000
AMS Series 1301
7 sheets needed for complete coverage.
see WORLD 100C and index 100/1.

MALAYSIA – TOPOGRAPHIC SERIES
1:250,000. 1:63,360, 1:25,000
Kuala Lumpur : Dir. of Natnl. Mapping
All large scale series are not on general public sale, but are subject to security control.

West Malaysia

MALAYSIAN MAP EXTRACTS
1:63,360
London : John Murray, 1973
2 series, each comprising a wallet with 8 large scale maps (Director of National Mapping, Malaysia). For school map study, topog. maps.
Series A: Alor Star, Parit Buntar, Kampar, Taiping, Kota Bharu, Sungei Lembing, Kukup, Bagan Datoh
Series B: Kuala Terengganu, Port Swettenham and Kelang, Kuala Lumpur, Johore (Yong Peng), Labis, Kuala Krai, Penang Island and Butterworth, Johore (Batu Pahat) 65p each

MALAYA BALIK PALAU
1:25,000
DOS (Misc) 409
Tolworth : DOS
Topog. map reproduced from Malayan Survey sheets 28a and 28c covering Penang. 10p

D POLITICAL & ADMINISTRATIVE

West Malaysia

PETA MALAYSIA - PEMERENTAHAN
1:1,140,480
Kuala Lumpur : DBP
210 x 90
2 sheet political col. wall map with communications.

MALAYSIA BARAT – WEST MALAYSIA
1:760,000
Kuala Lumpur : Dir. of Natnl. Mapping, 1968
69 x 85
Political map col. by states with district boundaries, roads classified, airports and railways. Insets show Malaya and adjacent territories.

STANFORD'S GENERAL MAP OF MALAYA
1:633,600
London : Stanford, 1968
89 x 105
Political col. by states, showing roads, railways, airports and towns graded by pop. Inset of Malaysia.

MALAYSIA BARAT – WEST MALAYSIA
1:500,000
Kuala Lumpur : Dir. of Natnl. Mapping, 1967
101 x 135 complete
Physical map in 2 sheets, contoured with layer col, roads classified, railways, boundaries and airports. Inset of Malaya and adjacent territories.

PHILIP'S MAP BUILDING SHEET (BLACKBOARD MAP) OF MALAYA
1:570,240
London : Philip
94 x 119
Coastlines and boundaries printed in yellow on blackboard paper.
Mounted CR £4.00

East Malaysia

SARAWAK
1:2,000,000
Sarawak Series No. 13
3rd edition
Kuching : Surv. Dept. 1974
38 x 30
Bahasa Malaysia political map showing Divisional boundaries and road communications. M $0.50

E1 PHYSICAL : RELIEF

West Malaysia

PETA MALAYSIA – MAKABUMI
1:1,140,480
Kuala Lumpur : DBP
114 x 88
2 sheet physical col. map of Malaysia, Singapore, Brunei, with contours.

MALAYSIA BARAT – WEST MALAYSIA
1:760,000
Kuala Lumpur : Dir. of Natnl. Mapping, 1968
69 x 85
Physical map, contoured with layer col, roads classified, railways, airports and boundaries. Insets show Malaya and adjacent territories.

REGIONAL WALL MAP OF MALAYA
1:570,240
London : Philip
94 x 119
Physical col, with principal road and rail communications, towns graded by pop, and boundaries.
Paper £1.50
Mounted CR £5.50
Mounted on cloth dissected to fold £7.00

SARAWAK
1:500,000
Sarawak series No. 8
Edition 3 PPNM
Kuala Lumpur : Dir. of Natnl. Mapping, 1974
135 x 101 complete
Physical map in 2 sheets, contoured with layer col, roads classified, railways, boundaries and airports. Inset of Malaya and adjacent territories.
Set M $10.00

East Malaysia

SARAWAK AND BRUNEI
1:1,670,000
Series DOS 979
2nd edition
Tolworth : DOS, 1964
41 x 31
Physical map with contours and layer colouring, district Divisional boundaries, roads, airports. M $0.50

REGIONAL WALL MAP OF NORTH BORNEO (SABAH), BRUNEI AND SARAWAK
1:1,000,000
London : Philip
117 x 91
Physical map, contoured with layer col, principal road and rail communications, boundaries and towns graded by pop.
Paper flat £1.50
Mounted CR £5.50
Mounted on cloth dissected to fold £7.00

BRITISH BORNEO
1:500,000
DOS (Geol) 1078
In 3 sheets
Tolworth : DOS, 1956-62
Black and white topographic base maps :
West Sarawak, 1956
East Sarawak and Brunei, 1956
North Borneo, 1962
20p

SARAWAK – BRUNEI
1:500,000
In 2 sheets
Kuching : Surv. Dept. 1969
137 x 91
Physical col, with contours, communications.

F GEOLOGY

West Malaysia

THAI-MALAY PENINSULA, GEOLOGICAL MAP
1:5,500,000
Ipoh : Geol. Surv, Malaya, 1958
23 x 30
Col. geol. map. M $0.30

THAI-MALAY PENINSULA TECTONIC MAP
1:5,500,000
Ipoh : Geol. Surv. Malaya, 1958
23 x 30
Generalised tectonic map.
M $0.30

MALAYSIA BARAT GEOLOGICAL MAP
1:2,000,000
Ipoh : Geol. Surv. Malaya, 1968
23 x 33
Col. geol. map showing rock types and faults. $2.00

GEOLOGICAL MAP OF MALAYA
1:500,000
In 2 sheets
Ipoh : Geol. Surv, 1963
113 x 144 complete
Col. geological map. M $8.00
Mounted M $10.00

GEOLOGICAL MAP OF NORTH EAST MALAYA
1:250,000
Ipoh : Geol. Surv.
Col. geological map. M $5.50

GEOLOGICAL MAP OF MALAYSIA
1:63,360
Ipoh : Geol. Surv, Malaya
Col. series, showing solid geol formations, some with separate cross sections.
Sheets available :
3/B/7 & part of 3/B/8 Fraser's Hill
3/D/1 & part of 3/D/5 Sungei Lembing
3/D/2 Kuantan
2/P/13 Bundi
2/P/14 Chukai
3/B/10 Kuala Selangor
3/B/11 Rasa
2/N/5 & part of 2/M/8 Ipoh
2/N/9 & part of 2/N/12 Batu Gajah
150 (new series) Palau Langkawi
3C:11-12 (part of) Sg. Bera - T. Chini
3C:15-16 (part of) Sg. Jeram - T. Bera
2/E/5 Kaki Bukit
2/E/6 Chuping
2/E/10 Jitra
2/E/9 Kangar
2/J/9 Grik
Geological sections across :
3/B/8 and 3/B/12
2/N/5, 2/N/9 and 2/N/8
150 (new series)
2/E/5 & 6, 2/E/9 & 10
2/J/9
Each M $3.00

WEST MALAYSIA – REGIONAL GEOLOGICAL MAPS
1:63,360 unless otherwise stated
Ipoh : Geol. Surv, Malaya
Geology and Mineral Resources Maps:
Neighbourhood of Chegar Perah and Merapoh, Pehang, Malaya (Mem 4) 1950
Frasers' Hill area, Selangor, Perak and Panang, Malaya (Mem 5) 1951
Neighbourhood of Kuantan, Pahang, Malaya (Mem 6) 1952
Neighbourhood of Kuala Selangor and Rasa, Selangor, Malaya (Mem 7) 1953
Neighbourhood of Bentang, Bahang, Malaya (Mem 8)
Kinta Valley, Perak, Malaysia (Mem 9)
North Kelanton and North Trengganu, W Malaysia (Mem 10) 1:250,000
Geology and Bauxite Map :
Pengerang Area, S E Johore (Mem 14)

East Malaysia

GEOLOGICAL MAP OF SARAWAK AND SABAH, E MALAYSIA
1:3,300,000
Kuching : Geol. Surv, 1968
M $0.50

GEOLOGICAL MAP OF SARAWAK, BRUNEI AND SABAH
1:2,000,000
2nd edition
In 2 sheets
Kuching : Geol. Survey. 1964
42 x 29 each sheet
Col. coded, detailed legend, location diagram inset, mountain and river areas named.
Each sheet M $1.50

GEOLOGICAL MAP OF SABAH
1:500,000
2nd edition
Kuching : Geol. Surv, 1972
108 x 89
Col. map showing main mineral occurrences. M $5.00

IGNEOUS ROCKS OF SABAH
1:500,000
Kuching : Geol. Surv, 1968
From Bull 5. M $3.00

IGNEOUS ROCKS OF W SARAWAK
1:500,000
Kuching : Geol. Surv, 1968
From Bull 5 M $3.00

EAST MALAYSIA – REGIONAL GEOLOGICAL MAPS
Various scales
Kuching : Geol. Surv.
Maps available accompanying Memoirs :
Strap and Sadong Valleys (W Sar) 1:125,000 Mem 1
Queen Seam, Silimpopon Coalfield (N Born) 1:15,000 Mem 2
Kuching – Lundu Area (W Sar) 1:125,000 Mem 3
Bau Mining District (W Sar) 1:50,000 Mem 3
Upper Segama Valley and Darvel Bay Area (Sabah) 1:125,000 Mem 4
Kota Belud and Kudat Area (N Born) 1:125,000 Mem 5
Taritipan Area, Marudu Bay (N Born) 1:50,000 Mem 5
Jesselton – Kinabalu Area 1:125,000 Mem 6
Lupar and Saribas Valleys (W Sar) 1:125,000 Mem 7
Upper Rajang & Adjacent Areas (Sar) Sheet 1 & 2 1:250,000 Mem 8
Hose Mountains and the Linau-Balui Plateau Area (Sar) 1:125,000 Mem 8
Usun Apau Area (E Sar) 1:125,000 Mem 8
Sandakan Area, and Parts of the Kinabatangan and Labuk Valleys (N Born) 1:125,000 Mem 9
Brunei Town Area 1:50,000 Mem 10
Lower Rajang Valley and Adjoining Areas (Sar) 1:250,000 Mem 11
Pensiangan and Upper Kinabatangan Area (N Born) 1:250,000 Mem 12
Suai-Baram Area (Sar) 1:250,000 Mem 13
Semporna Peninsula (N Born) 1:250,000 Mem 14
Banggi Island Area Sheet 1 (N Born) 1:125,000 Mem 15
Sugut River area, Sheet 2 (N Born) 1:125,000 Mem 15
Dent Peninsula (Sabah) 2 sheets 1:125,000 Mem 16
Labuan and Padas Valley (Sabah) 1:250,000 Mem 17
Labuan Island and Klias Peninsula 1:125,000 Mem 17
Maps available accompanying Reports :
Sematan Area (W Sar) 1:50,000 Rep 1
Lundu Area (W Sar) 1:50,000 Rep 1
Penrissen Area (W Sar) 1:50,000 Rep 2
Serian Area (W Sar) 1:50,000 Rep 3
Bidu-Bidu Hill Area (Sabah) 1:50,000 Rep 4
Bintulu Area (C Sar) 1:50,000 Rep 5
Sandakan Area (E Sabah) 1:50,000 Rep 6
Maps available accompanying Bulletins :
Bau Mining District (W Sar)
Sheet I Bau
Sheet II Krokong
1:10,000 Bull 7
Each M $3.00

G EARTH RESOURCES

West Malaysia

MINERAL DISTRIBUTION MAP OF MALAYA
1:4,000,000
Ipoh : Geol. Surv. Malaya, 1959
Location of minerals by symbols.
M $0.30

MALAYSIA MINERAL DEVELOPMENT POTENTIALITIES
1:4,000,000
Ipoh : Geol. Surv, Malaya, 1958
15 x 20
Classification in colours of established or potentially rich mining land, possible mining areas and those unlikely to be required for mining.
M $0.30

FEDERATION OF MALAYA, MINERAL DEVELOPMENT POTENTIALITIES MAP
1:762,320
Ipoh : Geol. Surv. Malaya, 1958
Col. geol. map indicating location of minerals.

MINERAL DISTRIBUTION MAP OF MALAYA
1:500,000
In 2 sheets
Ipoh : Geol. Surv, Malaya, 1966
Marking extent of granitic and intermediate intrusive rocks, locations of mineral occurrences, distinguished worked and known deposits. Enlargement of Kinta Valley area inset.
M $8.00
Mounted M $10.00

MINERAL DEVELOPMENT POTENTIALITIES MAPS
Differing scales
Ipoh : Geol. Surv. Malaya
Available for :
Johore 1:190,000 1958 M $6.00
Malacca (wallmap) 1:63,360 1956 M $7.00

SOIL MAP OF MALAYA
1:1,500,000 app.
Kuala Lumpur : Min. Ag. Coop, 1963
Col. soil map. M $2.50

KELANTAN SCHEMATIC RECONNAISSANCE SOIL MAP
1:500,000
Kuala Lumpur : Geol. Surv. & Div. Ag. Malaya, 1960
Map in colours. M $2.50

TRENGGANU DRAFT SCHEMATIC SOILS MAPS
1:500,000
Kuala Lumpur : Geol. Surv. & Ag. Div. Malaya, 1958
Col. map with 4pp report.
M $2.50

East Malaysia

MINERAL RESOURCES MAP OF SARAWAK AND SABAH, MALAYSIA
1:2,000,000
Kuching : Geol. Surv, 1965
54 x 37
Mineral occurrences and potential indicated by symbols on col. geol. map. Also summary of mineral resources.
M $2.00

MINERAL RESOURCES MAP OF SARAWAK, BRUNEI, AND NORTH BORNEO
1:2,000,000
Kuching : Geol. Surv, 1962
M $2.00

NORTH BORNEO – ROAD MAKING MATERIALS
1:1,000,000
DOS (Misc) 314
Tolworth : DOS, 1964
Col. map indicating soils and geology classified according to their potential use.

NORTH BORNEO SOIL SURVEY – MERUTAI BINUANG
1:50,000
In 8 sheets
DOS (Misc) 3007
Tolworth : DOS, 1960
Col. series accompanying the Report on the Soils of the Semperna Peninsula, N. Borneo, by T R Paton. 50p each

H BIOGEOGRAPHY

VEGETATION MAP OF MALAYSIA
1:5,000,000
Compiled by C G G J van Steenis for UNESCO Humid Tropics Research Project
Groningen : P Noordhof, 1958
127 x 71
Showing 18 classifications of vegetation depicted in colours covering Malaysia also Philippines, South Celebes, East Timor and New Guinea.

PHILIP'S LAND USE MAP OF MALAYSIA AND SINGAPORE
1:2,500,000
London : Philip
94 x 119
Land use regions indicated in colours Borneo, Brunei and Sarawak at 1:1,250,000
Paper flat £1.50
Mounted CR £5.50
Mounted on cloth dissected to fold £7.00

West Malaysia

MALAYA LAND UTILISATION MAP
1:760,720
Kuala Lumpur : Dir. of Natnl. Mapping
76 x 102
Producing areas of principal crops inc. rubber, rice, oil palm, coconut and pineapple; mining lands and forest reserves on detailed base map.

FOREST RESOURCES MAP OF MALAYA
1:760.720
Kuala Lumpur : Dir. of Natnl. Mapping, 1954
76 x 102
Shows in col. forest, game and mangrove reserves, areas of principal cultivations and mining land.

PENGGUNAAN TANAH-SEKARANG : MALAYSIA BARAT
1:500,000
In 2 sheets
Kuala Lumpur : Dir. of Natnl. Mapping, 1970
105 x 75 each
Showing present land use for West Malaysia, based on 1966 position, in colours.

East Malaysia

SARAWAK
1:1,500,000
Sarawak Series No. 11
4th edition
Kuching : Surv. Dept. 1970
51 x 41
Generalised map showing principal cultivation and forest areas to illustrate soil conditions and potential land use.
M $0.50

SABAH
1:1,425,000
Kuching : Surv. Dept. 1957
36 x 30
Land use map in cols.

J CLIMATE

West Malaysia

PETA MALAYSIA – HUJAN
1:1,140,000
Kuala Lumpur : DBP
114 x 88
2 sheet map showing annual rainfall.

East Malaysia

RAINFALL MAP OF SARAWAK
3:750,000
Sarawak Series No. 5
Kuching : Surv. Dept., 1949
20 x 15
Coloured distribution map. M $0.50

K HUMAN GEOGRAPHY

PETA MALAYSIA – PENDUDOK
1:1,140,000
Kuala Lumpur : DBP
114 x 88
2 sheet map of pop. in Malaysia, Singapore, Brunei.

West Malaysia

WEST MALAYSIA CENSUS 1947
1:1,013,760
Kuala Lumpur : Dir. of Natnl. Mapping
61 x 50
Col. map indicating population distribution. M $1.50

ATLASES
W3 WORLD ATLAS : LOCAL EDITION

SECONDARY ATLAS FOR MALAYSIA AND SINGAPORE
Ed J A Johnson
Brisbane : Jacaranda, 1971
22 x 28
106pp
Atlas for secondary schools, 30pp maps for S E Asia. Index. Bahasa-Malaysian ed, Atlas Sekolah Menegah Malaysia, 86 physical and thematic maps. Index.
A $2.50

ATLASES
B TOWN PLANS

West Malaysia

KUALA LUMPUR STREET DIRECTORY
1:10,560
Kuala Lumpur : Dir. of Natnl. Mapping
Street atlas with index. M $2.00

ATLASES
O NATIONAL ATLASES

ATLAS KEBANGSAAN MALAYSIA – NATIONAL ATLAS OF MALAYSIA
Kuala Lumpur : DBP, 1973
36 x 51
81 col. maps, text in Bahasa Malaysia with synopsis also in Eng. Arranged in 10 sections covering History, Administration, Physical nature, Population, Agriculture and Industries, Public services. Index,
approx. M $100.00

MAP BOOK OF MALAYSIA
by P G Collenette
Borneo : Literature Bureau, 1968
30 x 21
26pp
Describes geog. of the area, with political, physical thematic black and white sketch maps.

595.13 Singapore

See also: 595 MALAYSIA
59 SOUTH EAST ASIA

B TOWN PLANS

SINGAPORE CITY
1:15,000
Singapore : Tourist Promotion
Board, 1972

SINGAPORE CITY MAP
1:10,000
In 4 sheets
Singapore : Surv. Dept, 1959
86 x 56 each
Topog. map of city, showing water detail in blue, open spaces green, contours, roads (some named). The sheets are :
Bukit Timah
Kallang
Pasu Panjang
Singapore City

C OFFICIAL SURVEYS

TOPOGRAPHIC MAP OF SINGAPORE
1:75,000
Series SMU 075
Edition 1 SMU
Singapore : Mapping Branch MINDEF,
1974
74 x 57
Contoured map showing roads and vegetation cover, Cassini Soldner projection. S $5.00

ROAD MAP OF SINGAPORE
1:25,000
Series Misc. 1169
In 4 sheets
Edition 1 SMU
Singapore : Mapping Branch MINDEF,
1973
88 x 56
Roads and road names, important buildings. Rectified Skew Orthomorphic projection.
Each S $5.00

H BIOGEOGRAPHY

RURAL LAND USE SURVEY MAPS
1:6,336
In 346 sheets
Singapore : Singapore Improvement
Trust, 1958
44 x 31
Shows broad land use; with index and map notation sheets.

596/598 Indo-China

See also: 59 SOUTH EAST ASIA

A1 GENERAL MAPS: ROADS

PHYSICAL AND ROAD MAP OF VIETNAM, CAMBODIA AND LAOS
1:2,000,000
Dalat : NGD, 1966
72 x 97
Contours, roads, district boundaries.

EAST ASIA ROAD MAPS
1:1,250,000
AMS Series 1306
In 5 sheets
Washington : AMS, 1968
Various sizes
Col. maps with communications network classified, contours and layer cols.
Sheets available:
No 1 North Laos - North Vietnam
110 x 94
No 2 Cambodia - South Laos - South Vietnam
77 x 100
No 3 Thailand (excluding extreme southern tip)
81 x 73

D POLITICAL & ADMINISTRATIVE

ADMINISTRATIVE MAP OF VIETNAM, LAOS, CAMBODIA
1:2,000,000
Hanoi : Geodetic and Cart Office, 1971

OFFICIAL MAP OF VIETNAM, LAOS AND CAMBODIA
1:1,250,000
Chicago : Rand McNally, 1966
91 x 138
Political col, roads classified and numbered, railways, airfields, boundaries, towns and villages acc. pop. Facts in margin, with glossary of terms.

E1 PHYSICAL: RELIEF

ZADNI INDIE A INDONEZIE (INDO-CHINA AND INDONESIA)
1:6,000,000
Praha : Kart
Map in "Poznavame Svet" (Getting to know the world) series. Physical, pop, economic data with text.

VIETNAM, CAMBODIA, LAOS
1:4,000,000
Dalat : NGD, 1950
Physical map with relief shading.

HINTERINDIEN UND INDONESIEN
1:3,000,000
Ed H Haack
Darmstadt : Perthes
193 x 216
Physical wall map covering Indo-China to Indonesia, hill shading, layer col, state boundaries, cities, bathymetric col.

F GEOLOGY

GEOLOGICAL MAP OF VIETNAM, CAMBODIA, CHINA
1:2,000,000
Dalat : NGD, 1971
84 x 108
2 sheet col. geol. map.

GEOLOGICAL MAP OF VIETNAM, CAMBODIA, LAOS
1:500,000
In 22 sheets, see index 596/8/1
Dalat : NGD, 1962-3
72 x 60 each
With explanatory text.

K HUMAN GEOGRAPHY

ETHNOLINGUISTIC MAP OF VIETNAM, CAMBODIA, LAOS
1:2,000,000
Dalat : NGD, 1949 (1964 reprint)
68 x 92

L ECONOMIC

ECONOMIC MAP OF VIETNAM, CAMBODIA, LAOS
1:2,000,000
Dalat : NGD, 1956

596 Cambodia

See also: 596/598 INDO-CHINA
59 SOUTHEAST ASIA

A1 GENERAL MAPS: ROADS

CAMBODGE CARTE ROUTIÈRE ET ADMINISTRATIVE
1:2,000,000
Cambodia : Serv. Geog, 1966
29 x 24
Roads classified, railways, boundaries.

EAST ASIA ROAD MAPS : NO 2 CAMBODIA
1:1,250,000
AMS Series 1306
Washington : AMS, 1968
77 x 100
Physical col, roads classified, railways, airports.

ROYAUME DU CAMBODGE CARTE TOURISTIQUE
1:1,000,000
Cambodia : Serv. Geog, 1968
66 x 58
Roads classified, distances in km, railways, airports, tourist info. shown pictorially - buildings etc. Province boundaries, towns graded acc. pop.

CARTE ADMINISTRATIVE AND ROUTIÈRE DU CAMBODGE
1:500,000
Cambodia : Serv. Geog, 1966
2 sheet map with roads classified, railways and admin. districts.

C OFFICIAL SURVEYS

INTERNATIONAL MAP OF THE WORLD
1:1,000,000
AMS Series 1301
2 sheets needed for coverage :
ND 48, NC 48
see WORLD 100C and index 100/1

D POLITICAL & ADMINISTRATIVE

KAMBODZHA
1:5,000,000
Moskva : GUGK, 1973
Political-admin. map. Ro 0.15

E1 PHYSICAL: RELIEF

KAMBODZHA
1:1,000,000
Moskva : GUGK, 1971
78 x 55
Russian physical map with contours, communications, boundaries. 3 insets.

CAMBODIA
Washington : Govt. Printing Office/Central Intelligence Agency
45 x 60
Showing relief, urban areas, main admin. divisions, them. insets. US S0.40

H BIOGEOGRAPHY

CARTE INTERNATIONALE DU TAPIS VÉGÉTAL - CAMBODGE
1:1,000,000
Pondichery : Fr. Inst, 1971
Detailed col. vegetation map following internat. sheet lines, NC 48, ND 48.
With text. F. Fr. 60

597 Vietnam

See also: 596/598 INDO-CHINA
59 SOUTH EAST ASIA

A1 GENERAL: ROADS

BAN DO VIETNAM - VA DUONGSA
1:2,000,000
Dalat : NGD, 1969
70 x 100
Road map with physical colouring, province boundaries. Legend in Vietnamese.

EAST ASIA ROAD MAPS
Series 1306
1:1,250,000
AMS Series 1306
Washington : AMS, 1968
81 x 74 each
2 sheet road map, contours, layer tints, roads classified acc. surface, railways, vegetation, boundaries:
1 North Vietnam and adjacent territories
2 South Vietnam

REPUBLIC OF VIETNAM ROAD MAPS
1:250,000
In 9 sheets
Dalat : NGD, 1966
Road maps series covering South Vietnam only, available flat or folded in case. Roads classified, spot heights, railways, vegetation, distances in km. Restricted release.

B TOWN PLANS

CITY MAPS
Series L909
1:15,000
Dalat : NGD
Restricted release maps available for:
Saigon, 1968
Kontum, 1961

CITY MAPS
Series L909
1:12,500
Dalat : NGD, 1963+
Series of 1 sheet maps, on restircted release.
Available for:
Khanh Hung
Rach Gia
Long Xuyen
Chau Doc
Yung Tau
Phan Thiet
Phan Rhang
Dalat
Nha Trang
Ban Me Thuot
Qui Nhon
Pleiku
An Khe (An Tuc)
Quang Ngai
Chu Lai
Da Nang
Hue
Quang Tri

CITY PICTO MAPS
Series L909
1:12,500
Dalat : NGD, 1969+
Restricted release maps available for:
Can Tho
Cu Chi
Phu Bai
Quang Tri
Gio Linh
Dong Ha

CITY MAPS
1:10,000
Dalat : NGD
Restricted release maps available for:
Can Tho, 1967, 2 sheets
Vinh Long, 1969
My Tho, 1966
Do Thanah Saigon, 1959, 2 sheets
Saigon - Tan Son Nhut - Gia Dinh, 1966, 6 sheets
Tay Ninh, 1967, 2 sheets
Bien Hoa, 1968, 4 sheets
Dalat, 1960
Dalat, 1967, 4 sheets

TOPOGRAPHIC CITY MAPS
1:5,000
Dalat : NGD
Plans available:Dalat City, 1952
Ban Me Thuot City, 1951

C OFFICIAL SURVEYS

INTERNATIONAL MAP OF THE WORLD
1:1,000,000
AMS Series 1301
7 sheets needed for complete coverage.
see WORLD 100C and index 100/1.

VIETNAM ADMINISTRATIVE AND ROAD MAP
1:500,000
In 12 sheets, see index 597/1
Dalat : NGD, 1965-6
100 x 60
Col. maps, relief shading, communications, vegetation, land use.

TOPOGRAPHIC SERIES L701
1:50,000
In 418 sheets
Dalat : NGD, 1965+
Restricted release series, contoured in cols.

TOPOGRAPHIC MAP SERIES L8015
1:25,000
In 51 sheets
Dalat : NGD, 1967+
Restricted release series.

PICTOMAPS - Series L8020
1:25,000
In 527 sheets,
Dalat, NGD, 1966
Restricted release maps covering South Vietnam.

ORTHOPICTOMAPS
Series L8023
1:25,000
Dalat : NGD, 1970+
Restricted release series.

TOPOGRAPHIC MAPS
Series L8021
1:10,000
Dalat : NGD
Available on restricted release for:
My Tho - Tan An, 23 sheets
Tau, 9 sheets, 1970
Tay Ninh, 9 sheets, 1969

TOPOGRAPHIC MAPS
1:5,000
In 24 sheets
Dalat : NGD
Series available for various areas, still being printed. Restricted release.

D POLITICAL & ADMINISTRATIVE

V'ETNAM
1:2,000,000
Moskva : GUGK, 1973
Col. study map, showing water features, settlements, admin. centres and divisions, communications, boundaries, economic details, pop, Geog. description.
Ro 0.30

REPUBLIC OF VIETNAM ADMINISTRATIVE MAP
1:1,000,000
Dalat : NGD, 1967
78 x 105
Shows admin. divisions of South Vietnam and pop. figures. List of admin. areas on reverse.

ADMINISTRATIVE AND ROAD PROVINCE MAPS
Various scales
In 44 sheets
Dalat : NGD, 1971
Showing admin. boundaries and roads classified. 1 sheet for each province at scales of 1:100,000, 1:150,000, 1:200,000, 1:250,000

E1 PHYSICAL: RELIEF

WIETNAM
1:4,000,000
Warszawa : PPWK, 1968
43 x 46
Relief shading, communications, vegetation. Text in Polish.

V'ETNAM - SPRAVOCHNAYA KARTA
1:2,000,000
Moskva : GUGK, 1968
58 x 90
Reference map with physical col. contours, communications, boundaries. 5 thematic insets, 20pp text and index in Russian.

VIET NAM
1:1,000,000
Washington : US Air Force
91 x 172
Physical - political map, contours, 3-D relief shading; for identifying war areas.

E2 PHYSICAL: LAND FEATURES

MEKONG DELTA - SURFACE CONFIGURATION
1:500,000
Washington : Dept. of the Army, 1969
61 x 69
Topographical map with booklet.

MAP OF THE MEKONG RIVER BASIN (VIENTIANE, NONK KHAI AND THE SURROUNDING AREA STIUATED IMMEDIATELY DOWNSTREAM FROM PAMONG) SHOWING THE INUNDATION OF 1966
1:50,000
Bangkok : UN Economic Commission for Asia and the Far East
85 x 60
Map with 4pp booklet.

A GEOMORPHOLOGICAL SURVEY MAP OF THE MEKONG RIVER BASIN (VIENTIANE NONG KHAI AND THE SURROUNDING AREA SITUATED IMMEDIATELY DOWNSTREAM FROM PAMONG)
1:50,000
Bangkok : UN Economic Commission for Asia and the Far East, 1969
85 x 60
Map of areas subject to flooding with 44pp booklet.

G EARTH RESOURCES

REPUBLIC OF VIETNAM (SOUTH) GENERAL SOIL MAP
1:10,000,000
Dalat : NGD, 1961
72 x 104
Col. map with 66pp text in Eng. and Fr. showing major soils in relation to agricultural use and potential.

SOIL MAP OF PHAN RANG AREA
1:50,000
Dalat : NGD, 1969
99 x 70
Col. general semi-detailed soil map.

H BIOGEOGRAPHY

VEGETATION MAP OF THE REPUBLIC OF VIETNAM
1:1,000,000
Dalat : NGD, 1969
72 x 104
Col. map of South Vietnam with legend in Vietnamese and English.

J CLIMATE

MEKONG DELTA, CLIMATE, ANNUAL PRECIPITATION (MM)
1:500,000
Washington : Dept. of the Army, 1969
61 x 69

L ECONOMIC

ECONOMIC MAP OF VIETNAM
1:2,000,000
Dalat : NGD, 1962
61 x 85
Economic distribution shown by symbols.

INLAND WATERWAYS IN THE SOUTH PART
In 2 sheets
Dalat : NGD, 1965
120 x 103
Col. map. Index to waterways on reverse in Vietnamese.

AN GIANG PROVINCE
1:100,000
Washington : Dept. of the Army, 1969
61 x 69 each
Series of thematic maps, covering:
3 Geology and Construction Materials
5 Surface water resources
6 Soil Series
7 Agricultural soil capability groups
9 Land Use
10 Population Density - 1966
11 Administrative boundaries
12 Self-help projects
13 Settlements
15 Industries
16 Specialised agricultural farms and co-operatives
17 Transportation
18 Electric power
19 Elementary schools - 1967
20 Medical facilities
21 Land Ownership

M HISTORICAL

VIETNAM 1653
by Alexandre de Rhodes
Dalat : NGD
Facsimile reproduction.

HANOI 1873
by Phan dinh Bach
Dalat : NGD
Map of Hanoi City.

ATLASES
P REGIONAL

ATLAS OF PHYSICAL, ECONOMIC AND SOCIAL RESOURCES OF THE LOWER MEKONG BASIN
Prepared by US Engineer Agency for Resources Inventories
Bangkok : UN Economic Commission for Asia and the Far East, 1968
32 x 46
257pp
Maps and text.

598 Laos

See also: 596/598 INDO-CHINA
59 SOUTH EAST ASIA

B TOWN PLANS

TOWN PLANS
Various scales
Vientiane : Serv. Geog. Nat.
Plans available:

Luang-Prabang	1:10,000
Pakse	1:10,000
Savannakhet	1:10,000
Vientiane	1:10,000 1970

C OFFICIAL SURVEYS

INTERNATIONAL MAP OF THE WORLD
1:1,000,000
AMS Series 1301
4 sheets needed for complete coverage
see WORLD 100C and index 100/1

CARTE DU LAOS
1:250,000
Series L509
In 29 sheets, see index 598/1
Washington : AMS, 1963-7
72 x 55 each
Col. topog. series.

CARTE GÉNÉRALE DU LAOS
1:100,000
In app. 150 sheets
Vientiane : Serv. Geog. Nat.
New series, not yet complete, contoured.

D POLITICAL & ADMINISTRATIVE

CARTE ADMINISTRATIVE DU LAOS
1:2,000,000
Vientiane : Serv. Geog. Nat, 1964
54 x 69
Col. by provinces and districts.

E1 PHYSICAL: RELIEF

LAOS
1:1,250,000
Moskva : GUGK, 1971
68 x 82
Physical col. with contours, communications, boundaries. 3 insets.
In Russian.

CARTE GÉNÉRALE DU LAOS
1:1,250,000
1st edition
Vientiane : Serv. Geog. Nat, 1968
65 x 88
Physical col, rivers, railways, roads, land type, state boundaries, towns named.

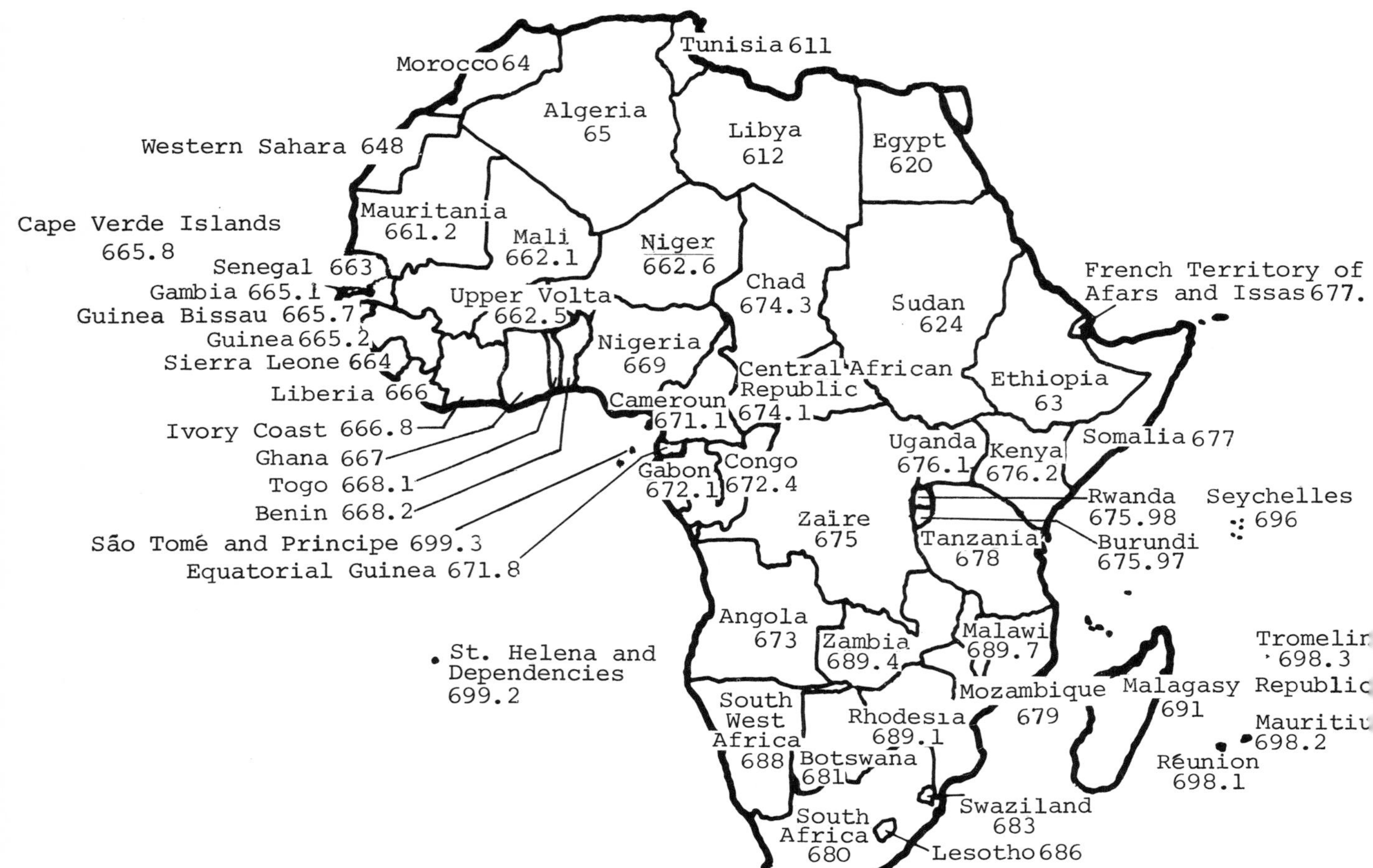

Regions

Africa 6
North Africa 61
West Africa 66
Southern Africa 68
Equatorial Africa 672
East Africa 676

Africa

6 Africa

A1 GENERAL MAPS: ROADS

MICHELIN ROAD MAPS OF AFRICA
1:4,000,000
In 3 sheets, see index 6/1
153 Africa North and West 120 x 97
154 Africa North-East 86 x 96
155 Africa, Central and South, and Madagascar 97 x 119
Paris : Michelin, 1971
Series of road maps covering Africa, showing political boundaries, settlements, forests, mines, motoring and tourist features, petrol stations, hotels and National Parks. Roads graded by condition, numbered with distances in km and miles. In French and English.

C OFFICIAL SURVEYS

MEYERS DEUTSCHE WELTKARTE
1:5,000,000
Bibliog. Inst.
In 6 sheets - No's 3-8 cover Africa.
see WORLD 100C and index 100/9

KARTA MIRA
1:2,500,000
Carti, GUGK (Bulg) : PPWK
Africa covered on 23 sheets
see WORLD 100C and index 100/2

AFRICA - AMS SERIES 2201
1:2,000,000
In 36 sheets, see index 6/2
Washington : AMS/Tolworth : MOD
76 x 58
Topog. series, showing international, provincial, district boundaries, layer tints, communications, vegetation, surface features. 37p each

INTERNATIONAL MAP OF THE WORLD
1:1,000,000
Various publishers
see WORLD 100C and index 100/1

CARTE DE L'AFRIQUE
1:1.000,000
see index 6/4
Paris : IGN
75 x 50
Series of topog. maps on ICAO sheet lines, contoured, hill shaded with layer colouring and road distances. Series being replaced by French International Map of the World editions but following sheets are still available:

NC 30/31	Bobo Dioulasso
NC 31/32	Parakou
ND 28	Dakar
ND 33	Fort Lamy
NE 28	St Louis - Novakchott
NE 31	Kidal
NE 32	Agades
NE 33	Bilma
NE 34	Largeau
NF 28	Port Etienne
NF 30	Taoudenni
NF 31	Fort Laperrine
NF 32	In Azaoua
NF 33	Djado
NG 29	Tindouf
NG 31	In Salah
SB 33/32	Brazzaville

Each F.Fr. 6.50

WORLD
1:500,000
DMS Series 1404
see WORLD 100C and index 100/7

D POLITICAL & ADMINISTRATIVE

AFRICA POLITICAL
1:25,000,000
Accra : Surv. Ghana
Shows political states of May 1969.
C 1.00

AFRYKA, MAPA FIZYCZNA I POLITYCZNA
1:20,000,000
PPWK
see AFRICA 6 E1

AFRICA
Barcelona : Editorial Teide
33 x 50
General school hand map showing major cities and boundaries. S.Ptas 2
Also : Africa Politica
(25 x 33) S.Ptas 1

AFRIQUE - POLITIQUE ET ECONOMIQUE
1:12.500,000
Bern : K & F, 1965
67 x 80
Countries in col. with roads, railways and shipping routes. Inset map of vegetation and economy. Legend in Fr and Ger. English ed. available.

DAILY TELEGRAPH MAP OF AFRICA
1:11,500,000
London : Gia
69 x 94
Political map regularly revised to show latest changes in communications and economic information shown. Many insets.
45p

AFRICA SUPERIOR WALL MAP
Maplewood : Hammond
63 x 96
Political col. map in folder.
US $2.00

AFRICA
Barcelona : Editorial Teide
88 x 115
General wall map for schools.
S.Ptas 275

WALL MAP OF AFRICA
Pretoria : Af. Inst, 1971
Shows positions of states, details on their admin. status, statistical diagrams, insets of educational statistics. R. 0.75

CARTE POLITIQUE DE L'AFRIQUE
1:10,000,000
Paris : IGN, 1972
105 x 115
Showing state boundaries, major places, surface colouring, major communications, multi-lingual description. F.Fr. 16.67

THE AFRICA MAGAZINE MAP OF THE CONTINENT
1:10,000,000
Chicago : Rand McNally, 1969
80 x 91
Political col. map showing boundaries, capitals (national and divisional), railways. Relief indicated. In folder, containing index.

AFRIQUE POLITIQUE
1:10,000,000
Map No 17
Eds Vidal Lablache and H Varon
Paris : Armand Colin
120 x 100
Political wall map for schools with blank outline map on reverse

DIE STAATEN AFRIKAS - HAACK KLEINER GEOGRAPHISHER WANDATLAS
1:10,000,000
Darmstadt : Perthes
106 x 125
Political col. wall map. DM 48

AFRIQUE POLITIQUE
Ed. A Gibert
Map No 13
Paris : Delagrave
105 x 125
Political wall map of Africa with a political map of Asia on the reverse. F.Fr. 45.00

AFRIQUE
No 21
Paris : Hatier
100 x 120
School wall map; political and economic map on reverse.

AFRICA
1:9,875,000
Washington : NGS
82 x 106
Political col. wall map.
Paper US $2.00
Plastic US $3.00

PHILIP'S POLITICAL SMALLER WALL MAP OF AFRICA
1:9,000,000
London : Philip
84 x 109
Politcal col. with railways and shipping routes.
Paper £1.50
Mounted CR £5.50
Mounted on cloth dissected to fold £7.00

PHILIP'S COMPARATIVE WALL ATLAS - POLITICAL
1:9,000,000
Philip
see AFRICA 6 E1

AFRIKA
1:9,000,000
Gotha : Haack, 1972
84 x 110
Coloured hand map with 84pp text vol. Shows relief shading, state boundaries.
Text M 7.80

AFRICA
Indianapolis : Cram
Various col. political school wall maps for different levels.
Level B Africa (simplified)
1:8,000,000 129 x 144
US $23.00
Level C Africa Political-Physical
1:8,000,000 129 x 124
US $23.00
Africa – Excello Wall Map
1:9,063,500 111 x 116
US $16.50

AFRIKA
1:8,000,000
Praha : Kart, 1970
2 sheet political wall map. Kcs 120

AFRIKA, POLITICHESKAYA KARTA
1:8,000,000
Moskva : GUGK, 1973
2 sheet pol. wall map. Ro 0.28

PHILIP'S POLITICAL LARGE WALL MAP OF AFRICA
1:7,500,000
London : Philip
119 x 173
Political col. with boundaries and communications.
Mounted CRV £15.00
Mounted on cloth dissected to fold with eyelets £17.00

AFRIKA, STAATEN (HARMS WALL MAP)
1:7,500,000
Munchen : List
155 x 140
Harms school political wall map with inset of Africa in 1914. DM 92

AFRICA : POLITICAL GEOGRAPHY WALL MAP
1:7,187,500
No 107041
Chicago : Denoyer-Geppert
111 x 147
Political col. school wall map, showing boundaries, communications, water features, pop.
CR US $19.25

AFRICA
1:7,000,000
Detroit : Hearne Bros.
122 x 167
Col. political wall map, showing state boundaries, relief shading, mechanical strip index.
US $152.50

AFRIKA
1:7,000,000
In 4 sheets
Beograd : Geokarta
136 x 140 complete
Political map with cyrillic and latin lettering.
Cloth mounted Dn 150

AFRIQUE
1:6,400,000
Bruxelles : Mantnieks
119 x 163
Political col. wall map in French or English ed. Lambert projection, some relief shading. Available mounted in various styles.

LERNKARTE VON AFRIKA
1:6,000,000
Darmstadt : Perthes
172 x 205
School wall map showing political boundaries, rivers, land type, ocean currents. Inset of States and their capitals.
DM 108
With school hand map
40 x 30 DM 1.50

AFRICA
1:6,000,000
Madrid : Aguilar
125 x 170
Political col. school wall map.
Paper S. Ptas 100
Cloth S. Ptas 550

AFRIKKA
1:5,000,000
Helsinki : Wsoy
182 x 206
Political school wall map in Finnish.
FMK 100

AFRIKA
1:40,000,000
Moskva : GUGK, 1973
Outline map. Ro 0.1

AFRICA
1:40,000,000
Novara : Agostini
Small hand outline map for schools.
L 40

AFRICA FÍSICA-POLÍTICA MAPA MURAL
1:15,500,000
Barcelona: Ed. Vicens Vives, 1976
126 x 88
Physical, political map printed on plasticised paper.
S Ptas 500

GEOGRAPHIA PLANNING AND RECORD MAP OF AFRICA
1:15,000,000
London : Gia
46 x 75
Black and white outline map showing countries. 30p
Also available in reduced size edition
30 x 40 folded
set of 10 75p

UMRISSKARTE DER AFRIKA
1:12,000,000
No 0840
Bern : K & F
78 x 87
Political col. outline map.

PHILIP'S LARGE OUTLINE MAP OF AFRICA
1:10,500,000
London : Philip, 1968
102 x 80
Printed in black on white cartridge paper with contours. 50p

PHILIP'S MAP BUILDING SHEET OF AFRICA (BLACKBOARD MAP)
1:10,500,000
London : Philip, 1968
102 x 80
Printed in yellow on blackboard paper. Information can be added in chalk and removed.
CR £4.00

POLITICAL OUTLINE MAP OF AFRICA
1:8,000,000
Indianapolis : Cram
129 x 144
Boundaries marked in colour.
US $27.50
Small outline desk map available
28 x 40 US $0.10

PHYSICAL OUTLINE MAP OF AFRICA
1:8,000,000
Indianapolis : Cram
129 x 129
Outline map with relief indicated.

AFRICA, OUTLINE SLATED
1:7,187,500
No 165041
Chicago : Denoyer-Geppert
111 x 129
Blackboard map for schools, showing countries; blue and yellow on black.
US $19.95

VITO-GRAPHIC CHALKBOARD OUTLINE MAP OF AFRICA
1:7,000,000
Ref VS6
Chicago : Weber Costello Co
117 x 150
Land areas in green, meridians, parallels and outlines in yellow, water areas in blue. On cloth – various mounted styles.

AFRIKA, ARBEITSKARTE
1:6,000,000
No 9733
Munchen : JRO
135 x 173
2 colour base map with plastic working surface. DM 108

E1 PHYSICAL : RELIEF

AFRICA
1:40,000,000
Novara : Agostini
33 x 26
Physical map with political map, physical and economic details on reverse.
L 450

AFRICA FISICA
1:40,000,000
Barcelona : Editorial Teide
25 x 33
Physical hand map for schools.
S. Ptas 1

AFRYKA, MAPA FIXYCZNA I POLITYCZNA
1:20,000,000
Warzsawa : PPWK, 1972
57 x 43
Double sided map, showing hydrographic and topog. detail on physical map,

political boundaries and communications on reverse. Zl 5

AFRYKA, MAPA FIZYCZNA
1:20,000,000
Warszawa : PPWK, 1972
57 x 43
Contoured physical hand map. Zl 1

FEDERAL ATLAS PLATE NO 1
AFRICA PHYSICAL
1:15,000,000
Dept. of Trig. and Topo. Surveys, Federation of Rhodesia and Nyasaland, 1962
52 x 61
Physical map, layer col, main topog. features.

AFRIKA
1:12,000,000
Praha : Kart
74 x 78
Physical/political reference map in series "Poznavame Svet" (Getting to know the World). With thematic text volume.
Kcs 10,50

WORLD TRAVEL MAP SERIES OF AFRICA
1:10,000,000
Edinburgh : Bart
73 x 90
Physical map showing political boundaries, communications, settlements and topog. features, contours and layer col. 75p

HAACK'S "KLEINER GEOGRAPHISCHER WANDATLAS"
1:10,000,000
Darmstadt : Perthes
106 x 125
Col. physical wall map, with political boundaries. DM 48

AFRICA
1:10,000,000
London : Collins-Longman, 1973
83 x 99
Physical wall map for schools with political detail. 40p

PHILIP'S PHYSICAL SMALLER WALL MAP OF AFRICA
1:9,000,000
London : Philip
84 x 109
Layer col. without hill shading, showing political boundaries.
Paper £1.50
Mounted CR £5.50
Mounted on cloth dissected to fold £7.00
Also available in Arabic edition.

PHILIP'S GRAPHIC RELIEF WALL MAP OF AFRICA
1:9,000,000
London : Philip
86 x 107
Col. to simulate predominant vegetation cover in 3-D way. No town names.
Paper £1.50
Mounted CR £5.50
Mounted on cloth dissected to fold £7.00

PHILIP'S COMPARATIVE WALL ATLAS OF AFRICA
1:9,000,000
London : Philip
84 x 109
Set of 5 maps providing geog. background to the continent.
Relief of Land : Political and communications.
Climate: Summer conditions, Winter conditions, Rainfall, Isobars, Winds, Actual Temperature and Sea-level Isotherms
Natural Vegetation
Political
Density of Population
Individual sheets, each:
Paper £1.50
Mounted CR £5.50
Mounted on cloth dissected to fold £7.00
Set of 5 maps :
Mounted on cloth as wall atlas on one (split) roller £20.00

AFRICA
Indianapolis : Cram
2 col. physical school wall maps for different levels
Level B Simplified
1:8,000,000 129 x 129
US $23.00
Level C Physical-Political
1:8,000,000 129 x 129
US $23.00

AFRICA FISICO-POLITICA
1:8,000,000
Novara : Agostini
120 x 135
2 sheet school wall map, showing relief shading of land and sea, political boundaries, towns graded by pop, water features.
First series: L 3,000
Mounted L 6,000
Second series :
1:7,000,000 (In 2 sheets)
138 x 190 L 3,500
Mounted L 7,500
Third series :
1:10,000,000
100 x 140 L 2,200
Mounted L 5,000

AFRIQUE (PHYSIQUE)
1:8,000,000
No 1050 French, 1239 English, 1220 Arabic
St. Germain-en-Laye : Editions MDI
92 x 126
Plastic coated physical wall map for schools. Economic map on reverse.

AFRIKA
1:8,000,000
3rd edition
Groningen : Wolters-Noordhoff
90 x 120
Physical wall map, relief shaded, marking principal towns and location of minerals. Inset of Suez-Sinai region. Fl 98.75

AFRIKA
1:8,000,000
Moskva : GUGK, 1973
2 sheet physical wall map. Ro 0.28

PHILIP'S PHYSICAL LARGE WALL MAP OF AFRICA
1:7,500,000
London : Philip
119 x 173
Orographical col, hill shading, boundaries, railways and ocean routes.
Mounted CR £15.00
Mounted on cloth dissected to fold with eyelets £17.00

TRI-GRAPHIC MAP OF AFRICA
1:7,500,000
TRI-6
Chicago : Weber Costello Co
101 x 137
Physical layer colouring with graphic relief shading and political boundaries
Available mounted in various styles.

AFRIQUE PHYSIQUE
Ed. A. Gibert
Map No. 12
Paris : Delagrave
105 x 125
Physical wall map of Africa with a physical map of Asia on the reverse. F.Fr 45.00

EXCELLO WALL MAP OF AFRICA
1:7,500,000
Indianapolis : Cram
111 x 137
Physical school wall map. US $16.50

AFRICA
1:7,187,500
No 130041-10
Chicago : Denoyer-Geppert
111 x 147
Classroom physical-political map showing land detail, boundaries, pop.
Rollers US $15.50

AFRICA, VISUAL RELIEF
1:7,187,500
No 1 10041
Chicago : Denoyer-Geppert
111 x 147
Physical school wall map showing relief of land and sea, boundaries etc. Reduced size as Desk Map, No 301541, 29 x 43, $3.30 per 25 copies US $18.75

AFRYKA
1:7,000,000
Warszawa : PPWK, 1972
115 x 170
Physical wall map for schools, showing relief of land and sea, hypsometric tints, land resources. Zl 150

AFRIQUE
1:6,500,000
Bruxelles : Mantnieks
125 x 180
Physical wall map for schools showing relief of land and sea by layer and bathymetric colouring, political boundaries in red. In French. Also available in English.

AFRIKA, PHYSISCHE KARTE
1:6,000,000
Ed Dr H Haack
Darmstadt : Perthes
172 x 205
Physical, relief shown by layer tints, boundaries and communications. Legend in English.
Mounted CR DM 142

AFRIKA
1:6,000,000
Munchen : List

160 x 185
Wenschow wall map; physical, bathymetric col, relief of land and sea, ocean currents, political boundaries. DM 142
Also in Eng. and Fr. editions.

AFRIKA
1:6,000,000
Braunschweig : Westermann
154 x 170
Col. physical school wall map with relief shading and political boundaries.

AFRIKA
1:6,000,000
No 9731
Munchen : JRO
135 x 173
Physical wall map showing relief of land and sea with "Arbeitskarte" (2 col. base map with plastic writing surface) on reverse.
DM 138
No 9732, as above without Arbeitskarte DM 128

AFRICA
1:6,000,000
No 42007
Madrid : Aguilar
130 x 170
Physical col. wall map, hypsometric tints.

MAP SERIES OF AFRICA
1:6,000,000
Praha : Kart
Various sizes
In the series "Posnavame Svet" 4 sheets:
Blizky vychod (Near East and N E Africa) Kcs 12
Severni a Zapadni Afrika (N & W Africa) 1965 Kcs 15
Jizni Afrika (S Africa) 1964 Kcs 14
Stredni Afrika (Central) 1966 Kcs 18
Physical/political reference maps, with thematic text volumes.

WORLD TRAVEL MAP SERIES
1:5,000,000
In 3 sheets
Africa North West
Africa North East
Africa Central and Southern
Edinburgh : Bart
72 x 94
Shows political boundaries with communications, settlements and topog. features, contoured with layer col.
75p

THE WORLD
1:5,000,000
Washington : AGS
3 sheets cover Africa :
North Western Africa Sheet 2
North Eastern Africa Sheet 3
Southern Africa Sheet 4
see WORLD 100C and index 100/3

HARMS "AFRIKA"
1:5,000,000
Munchen : List
185 x 210
Physical col, wall map, with relief, political boundaries, shipping routes, ocean currents, bathymetric col. DM 142

AFRIKA, PHYSISCH
1:5,000,000
Berlin : Velhagen & Klasing und Hermann Schroedel
162 x 218
Physical wall map, inc. most of Europe.
DM 114

AFRICA FISICO-POLITICA
1:10,000,000
Novara : Agostini
100 x 131
Plastic relief map in frame with metal corners. L 20,000

RAISED RELIEF MAP OF AFRICA
1:8,000,000
NR4, 1975
Chicago : Nystrom
104 x 114
Plastic moulded map, physical layer colouring, principal communications and boundaries.
Unframed US $46.00
framed US $74.00

F GEOLOGY

AFRIQUE TERRAINS AQUIFERE
1:16,000,000 app
No 2033
New York : UN, 1971
Map of aquiferous land, on equivalent sinusoidal proj. In Fr.

CARTE TECTONIQUE DE L'AFRIQUE
1:15,000,000
Paris : Comm. for Geol. Map of the World – UNESCO, 1968
59 x 58
Simplified tectonic map, showing principal structural features and depth of sedimentary cover of Africa.

ESQUISSE STRUCTURALE PROVISOIRE DE L'AFRIQUE
1:10,000,000
Paris : AAGS, 1958
95 x 99
General geol. map in col. with 16pp text.
F.Fr. 30

GEOLOGICHESKAYA KARTA I KARTA POLEZNYKH ISKOPAEMYKH AFRIKI
1:10,000,000
In 2 sheets
Moskva : GUGK, 1969
92 x 117 complete
2 maps (2 sheets each) showing geology and useful mineral deposits of Africa in colour. Legend Eng. and Russian. 44pp text in Russian.

AFRICA - GEOLOGIC BACKGROUND MAPS
1:10,000,000
Paris : UNESCO – AAGS, 1967
89 x 88
Designed to 'serve as a basis for various syntheses or thematic maps' geol. information printed in brown monochrome.

GEOLOGICAL MAP OF AFRICA (CARTE GEOLOGIQUE INTERNATIONALE DE L'AFRIQUE)
1:5,000,000
In 8 sheets (+ legend) see index 6/3
Paris : UNESCO/ASGA, 1964
96 x 55 each
Includes Arabian Peninsula and Near East. Shows in 20 colours igneous rock types, ages and main structural features of other rocks. With text, bibliog. maps in English and French. Special legend sheet.
Each £2.30
Complete with text £19.65

INTERNATIONAL TECTONIC MAP OF AFRICA (CARTE TECTONIQUE INTERNATIONALE DE L'AFRIQUE)
1:5,000,000
In 8 sheets (+ legend) see index 6/3
Paris : UNESCO/ASGA, 1968
96 x 55 each
Includes Arabian Peninsula and Near East. Shows age and distribution of orogenic belts, folds, faults and other tectonic features coloured by age. Structure and bathymetric contours etc. Legend sheet (7) In English and French.
Each £2.25
Complete with text £15.00

G EARTH RESOURCES

CARTE MINERALE DE L'AFRIQUE
1:10,000,000
Paris : UNESCO -AAGS, 1969
92 x 120
Subdued geol. base map with mineral distribution, each symbol graded by size, indicating percentage of world production. Legend in Fr. and Eng. with explanatory brochure. F.Fr. 40

CARTE DES GISEMENTS DE FER DE L'AFRIQUE
by J Lombard and P Rouveyrol
1:10,000,000
Paris : AAGS, 1970
Map of iron-bearing strata. F.Fr. 25

CARTE DES DÉPOTS HOUILLERS DE L'AFRIQUE
1:10,000,000
Paris : AAGS, 1966
88 x 89 each
Col. map in 2 sheets, showing coal-bearing strata against geol. background. With text.
Set F.Fr. 10

SOILS MAP OF AFRICA
1:5,000,000
In 7 sheets
Lagos : Comm. for Tech. Co-operation in Africa
Col. map in folder with 205pp explanatory monograph by D L D'Hoore.

H BIOGEOGRAPHY

THE GRASS COVER OF AFRICA
1:10,000,000
Paris : FAO, 1968
81 x 89
Shows vegetation types. With 168pp text.

PHILIP'S COMPARATIVE WALL ATLAS OF AFRICA – NATURAL VEGETATION
1:9,000,000
Philip
see AFRICA 6 E1

AFRIKA - KARTA RASTITELNOSTI
1:8,000,000
Moskva : GUGK
2 sheet vegetation wall map.

AFRIKA : KARTA PRIRODNYE ZONY
1:8,000,000
Moskva : GUGK, 1969
118 x 140
2 sheet wall map of natural zones.

AFRICA, VEGETATION AND LAND USE
1:15,000,000
Tehran : Sahab
60 x 90
Map in Eng and Persian showing vegetation types, cultivation, irrigation and forests etc. With inset showing Rainfall.
Rls 80

AFRIKA — VEGETATION
No 9909
Munchen : JRO
96 x 120
School pictorial wall map of vegetation zones. DM 48

AFRIKA : WILDTIERE UND WILDPFLANZEN
Braunschweig : Westermann
96 x 127
Pictorial wall map of wild animals and plants. English ed. published Chicago : Denoyer-Geppert
US $5.00

AFRIKA — BODENNUTZUNG
No 9911
Munchen : JRO
96 x 120
Pictorial school wall map of land use.
DM 48

DISTRIBUTION OF THE TSETSE SPECIES IN AFRICA
1:5,000,000
1205 (misc) 48AB
In 3 sheets
Tolworth : DOS 1953, 4
Various sizes
Col. map covering Africa south of the Sahara, classifying species and indicating their distribution.
each 65p

AFRIKA — TIERWELT
No 9910
Munchen : JRO
96 x 120
Pictorial school wall map of the animal world.
DM 48

J CLIMATE

AFRIKA : KLIMA UND VEGETATION
1:12,000,000
Braunschweig : Westermann
205 x 190
School wall map of climate and vegetation.
DM 142

AFRIKA : KLIMA UND VEGETATION
1:12,000,000
Gotha : Haack, 1969
215 x 168
4 maps on 1 sheet (wall map). Shows Mean Temperature in January;
Mean Temperature in July;
Mean Annual Rainfall and Ocean Currents; Natural Zones of Vegetation and Cultivated Land.

PHILIP'S COMPARATIVE WALL ATLAS OF AFRICA — CLIMATE
1:9,000,000
Philip
see AFRICA 6 E1

AFRIKA, KLIMATICHESKAYA KARTA
1:8,000,000
In 2 sheets
Moskva : GUGK, 1973
Climatic school wall map. Ro 0.28

AFRICA
1:6,562, 500
No 130041
Chicago : Denoyer-Geppert
111 x 162
4 thematic maps on 1 sheet including climate map. US $15.50

K HUMAN GEOGRAPHY

AFRICA
1:14,375,000
No 130041
Chicago : Denoyer-Geppert
111 x 162
4 thematic maps on 1 sheet including pop. density map. US $15.50

AFRIKA, MENSCHEN, HAUSTIERE UND NUTZPFLANZEN
Braunschweig : Westermann
96 x 127
Pictorial wall map of people, domestic animals and useful plants. Eng. ed. Rand McNally. US $5.00

TIMES MAP OF THE TRIBES, PEOPLES AND NATIONS OF MODERN AFRICA
1:10,000,000
Edinburgh : Bart, 1972
72 x 91
Shows national boundaries in white, tribal ones in brown, with brief description.
£1.50

BEVOLKERUNGSDICHTE IN AFRIKA, 1960
1:10,000,000
Braunschweig : Westermann, 1966
84 x 86
Map of pop. density with 12pp text.
DM 5

PHILIP'S COMPARATIVE WALL ATLAS - DENSITY OF POPULATION
1:9,000,000
Philip
see AFRICA 6 E1

AFRIKA - PLOTNOST' NASELENIYA
1:8,000,000
Moskva : GUGK, 1968
90 x 102
Pop. density map, with insets of the Nile Delta, S W Nigeria and Johannesburg.

KARTA NARODOV AFRIKI
1:8,000,000
In 2 sheets
Moskva : GUGK, 1970
118 x 140
Ethnographic map of Africa.

THE CATHOLIC CHURCH IN AFRICA
Washington : Afr. Research and Information Centre, 1965
Map with 2 insets.

L ECONOMIC

AFRICA, ECONOMY
1:15,000,000
Tehran : Sahab
90 x 60
Map in English and Persian covering agriculture, livestock, fisheries and mineral deposits. Inset map showing Industries and Factories. Rls 100

AFRIKA, ECONOMICHESKAYA KARTA
1:8,000,000
Moskva : GUGK, 1973
118 x 130
2 sheet school economic wall map, covering agricultural land use, minerals, industry. Ro 0.28

AFRIKA - WIRTSCHAFT (HARMS WALL MAP)
1:7,500,000
Munchen : List
100 x 140
School wall map showing economy by pictorial symbols. DM 54

AFRYKA : MAPA GOSPODARCZA
1:7,000,000
Warszawa : PPWK, 1972
170 x 115
Economic wall map for schools, showing industry, mineral resources, transport, etc. Zl 130

HOSPODARSKÁ MAPA AFRIKY
1:6,000,000
Praha, Kart
81 x 91
Economic wall map for schools, showing agriculture, minerals, industry, cities graded by pop.

AFRIKA, BERGBAU UND INDUSTRIE
1:6,000,000
Gotha : Haack, 1968
162 x 180
Haack wall map showing mining and industry by areas. Cities graded by pop.

AFRIKA, WIRTSCHAFT
1:5,000,000
Berlin : Velhagen & Klasing und Hermann Schroedel
162 x 218
Economic wall map.

AFRIKA : WIRTSCHAFT UND VERKEHR
Braunschweig : Westermann
96 x 127
Pictorial wall map of economy and communications. English ed. Denoyer-Geppert at US $5.00

AFRICA, ECONOMIC AND POLITICAL
Indianapolis : Cram
School wall map, showing foreign trade, ag, transport, minerals, petroleum, education. US $13.75

AFRIQUE (PHYSIQUE)
Editions MDI
Economic map on reverse
see AFRICA 6 E1

AFRIKA – VERWALTUNG, WIRTSCHAFT UND VERKEHR
No 9912
Munchen : JRO
96 x 120
Pictorial school wall map of admin. areas, economy and communications.
DM 48

AFRICA
No 130041
Chicago : Denoyer-Geppert
111 x 162
4 thematic maps on 1 sheet. Shows Economic Activities. US $ 15.50

M HISTORICAL

AFRICA ABOUT 1815 AND PARTITIONS OF AFRICA – PALMER WORLD HISTORY MAP
Chicago : Rand McNally
127 x 116
2 wall maps, showing Africa before European supremacy, 1815 with Port, Brit, Fr. territories, partition of Africa 1895.

BREASTED-HUTH-HARDING HISTORICAL MAPS
204511 Partition of Africa to 1935
204541 Africa in 1940 and 1966
Chicago : Denoyer-Geppert
112 x 81
Series of col. wall maps printed on stout manilla paper.

AFRIKA IN 19 UND 20 JAHRHUNDERT
1:5,000,000
Bielefeld : Cornelsen, Velhagen & Klasing
177 x 220
Putzger historical wall map.

AFRIKA VON DER KOLONISATION BIS ZUR UNABHANGIGKEIT (COLONIAL DEVT. TO SELF GOVT)
1:6,000,000
Braunschweig : Westermann
200 x 180
Political wall map of Africa, 1961 with 4 insets covering the periods up till 1824, 1824-1914, and till 1950, and 1961.

L'AFRIQUE HISTORIQUE
No 1560
St Germain-en-Laye : Éditions MDI
92 x 126
Plastic-coated, double-sided historical wall map for schools, showing Africa to the 18th C. Reverse covers period 18th C – 1972.

AFRICA
No 130041
Chicago : Denoyer-Geppert
111 x 162
4 thematic maps on 1 sheet including Independence, a chronological study.
US $15.50

DIE KOLONIALE AUFTEILUNG BIS 1939 (COLONIAL DIVISIONS) DIE NEUEN STAATEN NACH 1945 (NEW STATES AFTER 1945)
1:7,000,000
Darmstadt : Perthes
146 x 193
Two historical school wall maps.
Each DM 94

THE HERITAGE OF AFRICA
1:14,572,800
Washington : NGS, 1971
Background map to Africa's History and Culture.

AUSBREITUNG DES ISLAM
1:4,300,000
Bielefeld : Cornelsen, Velhagen & Klasing
194 x 138
Puzger historical wall map showing spread of Islam.

ATLASES
E1 PHYSICAL

ATLAS AFRIKI
Moskva : GUGK, 1968
26 x 32
118pp
64pp mainly physical maps, some thematic, 45pp index, 39pp Appendix of data translated into English.

ATLASES
H BIOGEOGRAPHY

AN ATLAS OF SPECIATION IN AFRICAN PASSERINE BIRDS
B P Hall and R E Moreau
London : Natural History Museum, 1970
27 x 39
Shows evolutionary process by plotting of species on 439 maps; indicated vegetation pattern. Text on ecology and character of species, introduction, table of species, bibliog. £15.00

ATLASES
L ECONOMIC

AFRICA, MAPS AND STATISTICS
1:30,000,000/60,000,000
Pretoria : Af. Inst
28 x 28/15 x 15
Series of folio volumes containing thematic plates on particular subjects. In Afrikaans and English.
Parts available:
1 Population, 1962
2 Vital and Medical Aspects, 1962
3 Cultural and Educational Aspects, 1963
4 Transport and Communication, 1963
5 Energy Resources, Production and Consumption, 1963
6 Agriculture and Forestry, 1963
7 Livestock, Farming and Fishing 1964
8 Mining, Industry and Labour, 1964
9* Trade, Income and Aid, 1964
10* Political Development, 1965
*sold out 75c each

ATLASES
M HISTORICAL

THE HISTORY OF AFRICA IN MAPS
H A Gailey, Jr
Chicago : Denoyer-Geppert, 1971
21 x 27
96pp
46 col. maps with text. Black and white maps in two sections; physical geog. and historical development.
US $2.50

THE SOURCES OF THE NILE: EXPLORERS' MAPS
London : RGS
53 x 40
Reproductions of 10 maps, 1856-1891, with notes and reproductions of drawings contained in a folder. £5.00

AFRIKA AUF KARTEN DES XII-XVIII JAHRHUNDERTS
Ed Egon Klemp
Leipzig : Edition Leipzig, 1968
21 x 30
57pp
77 reproduction maps of Africa in the 12th-18th C, col. and black and white. 64pp text, also available in Eng. Bibliog.
M 600

61 North Africa

See also: 6 AFRICA

A1 GENERAL MAPS : ROADS

MICHELIN MAPS OF AFRICA
1:4,000,000
Sheets 153 N W Africa, 120 x 97
154 N E Africa, 86 x 96
See Index 6/1
Paris : Michelin
Road maps showing political boundaries, settlements, forests and mines, motoring and tourist features, hotels and National Parks. Roads graded by condition, numbered with distances in km and miles. In Eng and Fr.

NORDAFRIKA – STRASSENKARTE
1:2,000,000
Wien : FB
124 x 82
Main and secondary roads, route numbers, spot heights in metres, hill shading, state boundaries. Includes Tunisia, Northern Algeria and Morocco.

CARTE DES VOIES DE COMMUNICATIONS DE L'AFRIQUE DU NORD
1:2,000,000
In 2 sheets
Paris : IGN
100 x 112
Showing communications, especially roads and tracks, classified by usability; distances in km, contours.
each F.Fr. 14.17

CARTE ROUTIERE MAROC ET AFRIQUE DU NORD
1:2,000,000
Paris : Blondel
Esso road map with insets at various scales of Casablanca, Marrakesh, Fes - Ville Ancienne and Nouvelle, Rabat, Canary Isles, Mediterranean Basin

C OFFICIAL SURVEYS

THE WORLD
1:5,000,000
2 Sheets
Sheet 2 North Western Africa
Sheet 3 North Eastern Africa
Washington : AGS
Physical-political map contoured with layer col.
see WORLD 100C and index 100/3

CARTE DE L'EUROPE ET DE L'AFRIQUE
1:5,000,000
Sheets 3, 4, 5, 6, cover Africa north of the Equator.
see EUROPE 4C

D POLITICAL & ADMINISTRATIVE

AFRIQUE DU NORD
No 18
Paris : Hatier
100 x 120
School wall map; political with economic map on reverse.

AFRICA DEL NORDESTE
AFRICA DEL NOROESTE
Barcelona : Editorial Teide
33 x 25 each
2 general school hand maps, showing major cities and boundaries.
each S.Ptas 1

STANFORD'S GENERAL MAP OF NORTH EAST AFRICA
1:5,500,000
London : Stanford, 1968
72 x 98
Political col, boundaries, roads, railways, canals, airports, pipelines, spot heights, settlements graded by pop. Pictorial border.

E1 PHYSICAL : RELIEF

THE NILE BASIN
1:10,000,000
No 5843
Khartoum : Surv. Dept.
32 x 46
Simple map showing basic physical features of the area. General or hydrographic eds. available.

WORLD TRAVEL MAP SERIES
1:5,000,000
2 sheets
Africa N W, 73 x 95, 1970
Africa N E, 97 x 74, 1972
Edinburgh : Bart
Physical map showing political boundaries, communications, settlements and topog. features, contoured with layer col.
40p

DALLA CIRENAICA ALL'ETIOPIA
1:4,000,000
Novara : Agostini
70 x 100
School wall map covering area from Cyrenaica (Libya) to Ethiopia.
Shows relief of land and sea, water features, major communications, cities graded by pop. L 1,500

NORDAFRIKA
1:3,000,000
Gotha : Haack, 1970
280 x 170
Physical wall map, layer col, hill shading. Covers area North of the Equator and Mediterranean. M 150

NORDAFRIKA
1:3,000,000
Braunschweig : Westermann
264 x 162
Physical col. wall map, political boundaries, relief shading, communications, cities graded by pop.

CIRENAICA E BASSO EGITTO
1:2,500,000
Novara : Agostini
70 x 50
School wall map covering the area from Cyrenaica (Libya) to Lower Egypt. Shows relief of land and sea, major communications, political boundaries, towns graded by pop.
L 1,000

CARTE EN RELIEF – EUROPE – AFRIQUE
1:5,000,000
Paris : IGN
61 x 87
Raised plastic relief map covering Western Europe from the British Isles southwards and the northwestern part of Africa. Vertical scale decreasing with height, self framed. F.Fr 83.33

F GEOLOGY

CARTE GEOLOGIQUE DU NORD-OUEST DE L'AFRIQUE
1:2,000,000
In 4 Sheets
Paris : CNRS, 1962
Geological map of North West Africa, 2 sheets available, covering the Sahara zone of North West Africa:-
3 Sahara Central
4 Sahara Occidental (West Sahara)

HYDROGEOLOGICAL MAP OF THE ARID ZONES OF AFRICA NORTH OF THE EQUATOR
Paris : UNESCO/BB
In Preparation.

H BIOGEOGRAPHY

VEGETATION MAP OF THE MEDITERRANEAN REGION
1:5,000,000
UNESCO – FAO
see SEAS AND OCEANS – MEDITERRANEAN 262 H

BIOCLIMATIC MAP OF THE MEDITERRANEAN REGION
1:5,000,000
UNESCO – FAO
see SEAS AND OCEANS – MEDITERRANEAN 262 H

K HUMAN GEOGRAPHY

THE MAGHREB POPULATION DENSITY
by Paul F Mattingly and Elsa Schmidt
1:2,000,000
Florida : AAG, 1971
110 x 76
Showing Density with insets of Average Annual Precipitation and Agricultural Land Use. US $3.00

M HISTORICAL

NORTHERN AFRICA, 1954
1:7,375,000
Washington : NGS
104 x 73
Political col. wall map

Paper	US $2.00
Plastic	US $3.00

ATLASES
L ECONOMIC

OXFORD REGIONAL ECONOMIC ATLAS OF THE MIDDLE EAST AND NORTH AFRICA
OUP
see NEAR AND MIDDLE EAST — ATLASES 53L

611 Tunisia

A1 GENERAL MAPS : ROADS

ALGÉRIE – TUNISIE
1:1,000,000
No 172
Michelin 1972
see ALGERIA 65 A1

TUNISIE PHYSIQUE ET ROUTIÈRE
1:1,000,000
Tunis : Dir. Topog. et Cart
51 x 70
Col. map, roads classified, distances in km, relief shaded.

CARTE ROUTIÈRE ET PHYSIQUE DE TUNISIE
1:500,000
In 2 sheets
Tunis : Secretariat d'Etat aux Travaux Publics et a l' Habitat Showing roads, railways, topog. features, contours and woodland col.

B TOWN PLANS

PLAN DE TUNIS
1:25,000
Tunis : Dir. Topog. et Cart
Monochrome town plan.

REGION DE BIZERTE
1:20,000
In 30 sheets
Tunis : Dir. Topog. et Cart and Paris : IGN
40 x 50 each
Topog. plan of Bizerte and regions, in col. with contours.

TUNIS
1:10,000
Tunis : Dir. Topog. et Cart
Monochrome town plan.

TOWN PLANS
1:5,000
Tunis : Dir. Topog. et Cart
Available for :
Kelibia
Korba
Mzel Bourguiba
Sfax
Sousse
Tunis
Zarzis

TOWN PLANS
1:2,000
Tunis : Dir.Topog. et Cart.
Monochrome plans available for:
Ain-Draham
Ariana
Beja
Bekalta
Bizerte
Bou-Ficha
Degache
Djebiniana
Djederda
Djemmal
El Alio
El Aroussa
El Djem
Enfidaville
Gabes
Gafsa
Galaat-el-Andleuss
Hammamet
Mammam Sousse
Hara-Sghira
Houmt-Souk
Kairouan
Kalaa-Kebira
Kalaa-Sghira
Kasserine
Kelibia
Korba
Ksour-Essaf
Le Kef
Mahares
Mahdia
Maknine
Massicault
Mateur
Medenine
Medjez-el-Bab
Metline
Monastir
Mzel Bou-Zelfa
Mzel Djemil
Mzel Temime
Nabeul
Nefta
Pont du Fahs
Porto Farina
Ras-el-Djebel
Sbeitla
Sidi-Bou-Zid
Sk el Arba
Sk El Khemis
Soliman
Sousse
Tabarka
Teboulba
Tebourba
Teboursouk
Testour
Tozeur
Tunis
Zaghouan

PLAN DU GRAND TUNIS
1:1,000
Tunis : Dir. Topog. et Cart.
80 x 50
Monochrome cadastral series with contours at 1 metre intervals.

TOWN PLANS
1:1,000
Tunis : Dir. Topog. et cart.
Available for :
Kebili
Medenine
Sbeitla

TOWN PLAN OF TUNIS
1:500
Tunis : Dir. Topog. et Cart
Monochrome plan.

C OFFICIAL SURVEYS

AFRICA
1:2,000,000
AMS Series 2201
Sheet 3 covers Tunisia.
see AFRICA 6C

INTERNATIONAL MAP OF THE WORLD (AFRICA)
1:1,000,000
IGN
3 sheets required for coverage:
Tunis, Sfax, Hassi-Messaoud
see WORLD 100C and Index 100/1

WORLD
1:500,000
DMS Series 1404
Sheet 345C covers northern part of country.
see WORLD 100C and index 100/7

CARTE DE TUNISIE
1:500,000
In 7 sheets
see index 611/1
Tunis : Dir. Topog. et Cart and Paris : IGN, 1958
57 x 44
Topog. series with woodland col, contours and hill shading

CARTE DE TUNISIE
1:500,000
In 2 sheets, North and South
Tunis : Dir. Topog. et Cart, and Paris : IGN
92 x 62
Topog. detail, woodland col, contours and hill shading, with road distances. Excludes extreme southern region.

CARTE DE TUNISIE
1:200,000
In 46 sheets, see index 611/2
Tunis : Dir. Topog. et Cart. and Paris : IGN
96 x 60
Topog. series contoured with hill shading. See index.
Table of conventional signs in 1 sheet available.

CARTE DE TUNISIE
1:100,000
see index 611/3
Tunis : Dir. Topog. et Cart. and Paris : IGN
48 x 30
Topographical series in progress, contoured with hill shading, covering central Tunisia. Table of conventional signs available.

CARTE DE TUNISIE
1:50,000
See index 611/4
Tunis: Dir. de la Topog. et Cart
64 x 40
Topog. series in progress covering northern half of Tunisia. Sheets published in 1 of 2 eds:
Type Algerie-Tunisie - 7 col, before 1942
Type 1922 - 5 col, after 1942
Both showing topog. detail with hill shading and contours.
Table of conventional signs available.

CARTE TOPOGRAPHIQUE DE LA TUNISIE
1:25,000
Tunis : Dir. de la Topog. et Cart.
64 x 40
Col. topog. series in preparation with contours, vegetation col.

COUVERTURE AERIENNES
Various scales
Tunis : Dir. Topog. et Cart, 1963-71
18 x 18/24 x 24
Aerial photo cover available for various areas at the following scales:
1:4,000
1:7,000
1:7,500
1:15,000
1:15,500
1:16,000
1:25,000
1:30,000
1:90,000

D POLITICAL & ADMINISTRATIVE

TUNIS
1:1,000,000
Moskva : GUGK, 1973
47 x 87
Col. study map showing water features, settlements, admin. centres and divisions, communications, boundaries, economic details, pop. Geog. description. Ro 0.30

CARTE ADMINISTRATIVE DE LA TUNISIE
1:750,000
Tunis : Secretariat d'Etat aux Travaux Publics et a l'Habitat
77 x 126
Surface col. by governates, boundaries, description.

F GEOLOGY

CARTE GÉOLOGIQUE DE LA TUNISIE
1:50,000
see index 611/4
Tunis : Serv. Géol.
45 x 30
Multi-sheet series on same sheet lines as topog. series with explanatory notes.
Sheets published:
7 Porto Farina, 1952
13 Ariana, 1970
17 Zaouiet-Medien, 1956
21 La Goulette, 1971
24 Fernana, 1956
28 Bir M'Charga, 1957
29 Grombalia 1970
31 Ghardimaou, 1952
35 Zaghouan – in prep.
36 Bouficha, 1969
38 Ouargha, 1951
41 Djebel Mansour, 1960
42 Djebel Fkirine, 1974
44 Le Kef, 1956
51 Tadjerouine, 1956
53 Maktar, 1959
63 Kairouan, 1950
69 Sbiba, 1952
77 Djebel Mrhila, 1949
78 Hadjeb El Aïoun, 1947
84 Kasserine, 1946

CARTE HYDROGÉOLOGIQUE DE LA TUNISIE
1:50,000
See index 611/4
Tunis : Serv. Géol.
45 x 30
Col. series in preparation on same sheet lines as topog. series. One sheet currently published:
84 Kasserine, 1946

G EARTH RESOURCES

CARTE DES GÎTES MINÉRAUX DE LA TUNISIE
1:500,000
Ed P Nicolini and others
Tunis : Div. de la Prod. Industrielle, 1968
107 x 80
2 sheet col. mineral map with Fr. text.
T.Din. 1,500

ÉTUDE PÉDOLOGIQUE DE SIDI MEHEDEB SUD
by M Sourdat
1:100,000
Paris : ORSTOM, 1963
3 maps : soil; soil aptitude for dry farming; soil aptitude for irrigated farming.
F.Fr. 12

ÉTUDE PÉDOLOGIQUE DES SOLS DE LA PLAINE DE BOU ARADA
1:50,000
by A Lobert
Paris : ORSTOM, 1962
3 maps : pedologique; vocation des sols en fonction de leurs aptitudes vis-a-vis des cultures seches; vocation des sols en fonction de leurs aptitudes vis-a-vis des cultures iriguees. (Shows soil potentiality for dry and irrigated farming).
F.Fr. 12

ÉTUDE PÉDOLOGIQUE DU PÉRIMÈTRE DE GROMBALIA
1:50,000
By A Chauval
Paris : ORSTOM, 1963
4 maps covering : speed of filtration; pedology; soil aptitude for dry farming; soil aptitude for irrigated farming.
F.Fr 12

ENFIDAVILLE
1:50,000
By R Sabathe
Paris : ORSTOM, 1962
2 maps : 1 pedogenetic; 1 map of soil classification by function of aptitude for irrigated farming. F.Fr. 12

CARTE PÉDOLOGIQUE DE TUNISIE
1:50,000
By A Chauval
Paris : ORSTOM, 1966
Soil map in 5 sheets, inc. legend sheet.
Areas : Perimetre Bir El Hafey
Sidi Bou Zid
Jebel El Meloussi
Sidi Al Ben Aoun
F.Fr. 12

CARTE DES APTITUDES DES SOLS AUX CULTURES SÈCHES
1:50,000
By A Chauval
In 5 sheets
Paris : ORSTOM, 1965
Col. map showing soil aptitude to dry farming. Sheets cover :
Perimetre Bir El Hafey
Sidi Bou Zid
Jebel El Meloussi
Sidi Ali Ben Aoun,
and legend.

H BIOGEOGRAPHY

CARTE INTERNATIONALE DU TAPIS VÉGÉTAL – TUNIS-SFAX
1:1,000,000
Pondichery : Fr. Inst., 1958
100 x 73
Detailed col. map, 6 thematic insets on reverse. Fr. text. Covering IMW. Sheets NJ 32-NI 32.

CARTE PHYTO - ÉCOLOGIQUE DE LA TUNISIE CENTRALE ET MÉRIDIONALE
1:500,000
by H N le Houerou
Tunis : Inst. Nat. de la Recherche Agronomique de Tunisie Col. map showing plant and vegetation types. With text.

CARTE PHYTO-ÉCOLOGIQUE DE LA TUNISIE SEPTENTRIONALE
1:200,000
by H N le Houerou
Tunis : Inst. Nat. de la Recherche Agronomique de Tunisie, 1969
98 x 153
Col. map showing plant and vegetation types, climate, thematic insets. With Fr. text, 622pp.

612 Libya

C OFFICIAL SURVEYS

KARTA MIRA
1:2,500,000
Cartimex
4 sheets for complete coverage.
see WORLD 100C and index 100/2.

AFRICA
1:2,000,000
AMS Series 2201
4 sheets for coverage — 3, 4, 8, 9.
see AFRICA 6C

INTERNATIONAL MAP OF THE WORLD
1:1,000,000
Various editions
12 sheets needed for complete coverage.
see WORLD 100C and index 100/1.

CARTA DIMOSTRATIVA DELLA LIBIA
1:1,000,000
In 11 sheets, see index 612/1
Firenze : IGM, 1934-41
58 x 45
Contoured series derived from
1:400,000 series L600 each

CARTA DIMOSTRATIVA DELLA LIBIA
1:400,000
In 45 sheets, see index 612/2
Firenze : IGM, 1934-41
48 x 56
Policentrical proj, contours, relief shading.
L600 each

WORLD
1:500,000
DMS Series 1404
see WORLD 100C and index 100/7.

E1 PHYSICAL : RELIEF

LIVIYA — SPRAVOCHNAYA KARTA
1:2,500,000
Moska : GUGK, 1968
72 x 66
Reference map — physical with contours and insets.

TOPOGRAPHICAL MAP OF THE UNITED KINGDOM OF LIBYA
1:2,000,000
Misc. Geol. Inv. 1-350-B
Washington : USGS
82 x 79
Relief indicated by occasional contours and escarpment lines, desert types and stipples, vegetation and oases in green, communications marked and classified, also oil wells and pipelines. Names in Eng. and Arabic.

F GEOLOGY

GEOLOGIC MAP OF THE UNITED KINGDOM OF LIBYA
1:2,000,000
Misc. Geol. Inv. 1-350-A
Washington : USGS, 1964
82 x 79
Col. geol. map with map legend and text in English and Arabic.

M HISTORICAL

TABULA IMPERII ROMANI
(IMPERIAL ROMAN EMPIRE)
1:1,000,000
See index 100/8
London : Society of Antiquaries
Series of maps depicting evidence of Roman occupation and settlement together with boundaries and place names of the period. Map folded in cover with descriptive text.
Sheets available for Libya :
NH 33, pt NI 33 Lepcis Magna
NH 34, pt NI 34 Cyrene

ATLASES
F GEOLOGY

GEMINI SPACE PHOTOGRAPHS OF LIBYA AND TIBESTI
A Geological and Geographical Analysis
by Angelo Pesce
Editor Angus S Campbell
Tripoli : Petroleum Exploration Soc. of Libya, 1968
24 x 31
81pp
Containing 34 col. illustrations including 11 space photographs with facing page a geol. interpretation map together with transparent overlay giving geographical names and features for use with either map. Includes other ground and air photographs and text describing photographs, references, and technical data.

620 Egypt

A1 GENERAL MAPS : ROADS

PRINCIPAL DESERT ROADS OF EGYPT
1:2,720,000
Cairo : Auto Club of Egypt, 1968
53 x 60
Outline map showing roads, desert roads, railways, towns and wells. In English and Arabic.

ROAD MAP OF THE MIDDLE EAST
1:1,000,000
AMS 1304W
Sheet 1 — UAR
Washington : AMS, 1962
101 x 101
Physical detail, with roads classified and numbered, distances in km, other communications, through town plans. Extends south to Aswan.

EGYPT
1:750,000
London : Foldex
Shows roads classified, relief shading, patent folding. 30p

ROAD MAP OF UAR, EGYPT REGION
1:500,000
Cairo : Drafting Office, 1968
71 x 100
Col. map showing roads and railways of Nile Valley and Delta and adjacent areas, with index to towns and table of distances. Political col. by provinces, text in English.

ROAD MAP OF EGYPT
1:300,000
Cairo : Auto Club of Egypt
84 x 112
Road map of Egypt (Nile Valley) in 2 sheets : Lower Egypt (Nile Delta to Ben Suef) and Upper Egypt (Beni Snef-Assuan) with Egypt as a whole inset.

ROAD MAP OF UPPER EGYPT
1:1,330,000
Cairo : Auto Club of Egypt, 1966
31 x 40
Roads classified in black and red. Legend in Arabic and English. Covering southern half of country.

ROAD MAP OF LOWER EGYPT
1:633,600
Cairo : Auto Club of Egypt, 1968
36 x 30
Black and white map showing road types towns, railways, airports. Legend Egyptian and English. Covering northern part of the country and Nile Delta.

B TOWN PLANS

TOWN PLANS
Various scales
Plans available :
Cairo — Southern Main Entrance
1:25,000
Cairo : Auto & Touring Club d'Egypte
Plan of Alexandria
1:17,000
Cairo : Cairo Drafting Office

C OFFICIAL SURVEYS

KARTA MIRA
1:2,500,000
Carti
2 sheets for coverage.
see WORLD 100C and index 100/2.

AFRICA
1:2,000,000
AMS Series 2201
4 sheets required for coverage
see AFRICA 6C

INTERNATIONAL MAP OF THE WORLD
1:1,000,000
AMS Series 1301
6 sheets for coverage.
see WORLD 100C and index 100/1.

WORLD
1:500,000
DMS Series 1404
22 sheets for coverage
see WORLD 100C and index 100/7.

SINAI-NILE DELTA
1:250,000
5 sheets, see index 569.4/1
Tel Aviv : Survey of Israel
69 x 100
Topog. series, contoured, layer col, communications; adjacent series to Israel 1:250,000 topog. map. In Hebrew only.
Sheets available :
El Arish (N Sinai) 1969
Gulf of Suez (S W Sinai) 1967
Gulf of Eilat (S E Sinai) 1971
Cairo unlayered 1967

D POLITICAL & ADMINISTRATIVE

ARABSKAYA RESPUBLIKA EGIPET
1:2,000,000
Moskva : GUGK, 1973
Col. study map showing water features, settlements, admin. divisions and centres, communications, boundaries, capitals, economic details, pop. Geog. description. Ro 0.30

E1 PHYSICAL : RELIEF

SINAI — EGYPT
1:1,000,000
Tel Aviv : Surv. Israel
83 x 64
Physical map, contoured, layered, covering the area Alexandria — Amman including lower Nile basin, Sinai, southern Israel and Jordan. In Hebrew.

F GEOLOGY

TECTONIC MAP OF EGYPT
1:2,000,000
Cairo : Geol. Surv. 1959
72 x 72
3 col. geol. map with 26pp text.

GEOLOGICAL MAP OF GEBEL GATTAR AND GEBEL DOKHAN AREAS
1:50,000
Cairo : Geol. Surv, 1967
60 x 74
Black and white map with 26pp text.

M HISTORICAL

DREVNII VOSTOK - PEREDN YAYA AZIYA I EGIPET
1:3,000,000
Moskva : GUGK, 1969
82 x 105
Coloured school historical wall map with Babylon inset.

NILE VALLEY — LAND OF THE PHAROAHS
1:1,270,000 app.
Washington : NGS
48 x 63
Inc. description of Ancient Egypt. US $1.00

L'EGITTO GRECO—ROMANO : CARTINE SCHEMATICHE
Mariangela Vandari
Milano : La Goliardica, 1970
8 maps showing Egypt in Classical times. L800

TABULA IMPERII ROMANI — MAP OF THE IMPERIAL ROMAN EMPIRE
1:1,000,000
See Index 100/8
London : Soc. Antiquaries, 1958
Series based on sheet lines of International World Map, depicting evidence of Roman occupation and settlement together with place names and boundaries, with an accompanying descriptive text.
1 sheet available for Egypt
Coptos NG 36
Paper folded with text.

ATLASES
A1 GENERAL

UAR TOURIST ATLAS
Cairo : Automobile and Touring Club d'Egypte
21 x 30
69pp
Contains a general touring map with locations of principal tourist and economic features and also a town plan of principal city of each of the 25 Governates of the country. Maps in colour many folding out. A brief description of each region follows together with Glossary, Governate Badges and photographs. Paper covers.

ATLASES
L ECONOMIC

STATISTICAL ATLAS OF THE UAR
1952-1966
Cairo : Central Agency for Public Mobilisation and Statistics, 1968
123pp
Showing present day life in ARE by statistics and maps — economic, social, cultural — since July Revolution, 1952.

ATLASES
M HISTORICAL

THE SOURCES OF THE NILE'
1856-91
London : RGS
53 x 40
10 collotype reproductions (2 colour) of manuscript maps made by British explorers, belonging to the Society. With notes by G R Crone.
£5.00

624 Sudan

A1 GENERAL MAPS : ROADS

BASIC MAP
1:8,000,000
Khartoum : Surv. Dept. 1954/5
28 x 42
Showing roads and rivers.
In English or Arabic edition.

SUDAN ROADS
1:4,000,000
Khartoum : Surv. Dept. 1964
49 x 58
Outline map showing all-weather and seasonal roads.

BASIC MAP OF SUDAN
1:2,000,000
In 3 sheets
Khartoum : Surv. Dept, 1953/4
57 x 76
5 colour map showing towns, communications, boundaries and rivers.
3 sheets:
NORTH EASTERN,
NORTHWESTERN,
AND SOUTHERN (57 x 85)

A2 GENERAL MAPS : LOCAL

BAHR EL GHAZAL AND EQUATORIA PROVINCES
1:3,000,000
Khartoum : Surv. Dept., 1956
55 x 36
Outline map in 1 colour.

BLUE NILE PROVINCE
1:3,000,000
Khartoum : Surv. Dept, 1956
25 x 35
Outline map in 1 colour.

DARFUR PROVINCE
1:3,000,000
Khartoum : Surv. Dept, 1954
35 x 50
1 colour outline map.

KASSALA PROVINCE
1:3,000,000
Khartoum : Surv. Dept, 1956
35 x 50
1 colour outline map.

KORDOFAN PROVINCE
1:3,000,000
Khartoum : Surv. Dept. 1956
35 x 45
1 colour outline map.

NORTHERN PROVINCE
1:3,000,000
Khartoum : Surv. Dept, 1956
55 x 35
1 colour outline map.

UPPER NILE PROVINCE
1:3,000,000
Khartoum : Surv. Dept, 1956
37 x 36
1 colour outline map.

KHARTOUM PROVINCE
1:1,000,000
Khartoum : Surv. Dept, 1956
35 x 32
1 colour outline map.

EASTERN KHARTOUM PROVINCE (BASIC)
1:250,000
Khartoum : Surv. Dept, 1953
60 x 80
1 colour map.

DONGOTONA HILLS
1:100,000
Khartoum : Surv. Dept, 1954
58 x 85
Coloured map.

YEI AREA
1:100,000
Khartoum : Surv. Dept, 1955
61 x 90
2 sheet map in colour.

KARARI TRAINING AREA
!:50,000
Khartoum : Surv. Dept, 1954
60 x 80
Coloured map.

KHARTOUM – THE 3 TOWNS
1:50,000
Khartoum : Surv. Dept, 1952
80 x 60
Plan of Khartoum, Khartoum North and Omdurman.

RIVER ATBARA DIVERSION SCHEME
1:25,000
In 5 sheets
Khartoum : Surv. Dept, 1954
58 x 75
2 colour map, contoured.

ROSEIRES RESERVOIR
1:15,000
In 18 sheets
Khartoum : Surv. Dept, 1954
58 x 100 each
Topog. map, contoured.

B TOWN PLANS

TOWN PLANS
Various scales
Khartoum : Surv. Dept.
Plans available:

Atbara	
1:2,500	12 sheets
Aweil	
1:2,500	2 sheets
Berber	
1:2,500	5 sheets
Ed Dueim	
1:2,500	2 sheets
Ed Damer	
1:2,500	2 sheets
El Fasher	
1:2,500	5 sheets
El Fasher (Basic)	
1:10,000	1 sheet
El Fasher (Contour	
1:10,000	1 sheet
Gedaref	
1:2,500	12 sheets
Geneina (Aerodrome)	
1:2,500	4 sheets
Juba	
1:2,500	6 sheets
Hasaheisha	
1:2,500	3 sheets
Kassala	
1:2,500	7 sheets
Kassala	
1:5,000	9 sheets
Kassala	
1:20,000	1 sheet
Khartoum	
1:5,000	16 sheets
Khartoum	
1:20,000	1 sheet
Khartoum (Contour)	
1:20,000	1 sheet
Khartoum	
1:17,000	1 sheet
Khartoum North	
1:5,000	12 sheets
Khartoum North (Contour)	
1:10,000	2 sheets
Khartoum North	
1:20,000	1 sheet
Karima	
1:2,500	2 sheets
Kosti	
1:2,500	9 sheets
Malakal	
1:2,500	5 sheets
Merowe	
1:2,500	2 sheets
Nahud	
1:2,500	4 sheets
El Obeid	
1:2,500	20 sheets
Omdurman	
1:3,000	9 sheets
Omdurman	
1:10,000	1 sheet
Omdurman	
1:20,000	1 sheet
Port Sudan	
1:2,500	13 sheets
Port Sudan (Contour)	
1:2,500	6 sheets
Port Sudan	
1:10,000	3 sheets
Rufa'a	
1:2,500	5 sheets
Roseires	
1:2,500	4 sheets
Roseires (Contour)	
1:2,500	4 sheets
Rumbek	
1:2,500	1 sheet
Shendi	
1:2,500	4 sheets
Sennar	
1:2,500	6 sheets
Wad Medani	
1:2,500	8 sheets
Wad Medani	
1:2,500	2 sheets
Wau	
1:2,500	6 sheets
Wau	
1:5,000	2 sheets

C OFFICIAL SURVEYS

CARTE DES CONTINENTS
1:5,000,000 IGN
Bande 1, Sheet 8 covers Sudan.
see WORLD 100C and index 100/5

SUDAN AIR PHOTO
1:4,000,000
Khartoum : Surv. Dept.
55 x 75
Shows air photo cover and 1:100,000 mapping.

KARTA MIRA
1:2,500,000
Cartimex : GUGK (Bulg)
3 sheets for coverage.
see WORLD 100C and index 100/2

INTERNATIONAL MAP OF THE WORLD
1:1,000,000
Various editions
14 sheets required for coverage.
see WORLD 100C and index 100/1.

WORLD
1:500,000
DMS Series 1404
see WORLD 100C and index 100/7.

SUDAN
1:250,000
In app. 178 sheets, see index 624/1
Khartoum : Surv. Dept.
63 x 45
Topog. series covering country, mostly uncontoured.

SUDAN
1:100,000
Khartoum : Surv. Dept.
Topog. series in progress, contoured, land detail.

D POLITICAL & ADMINISTRATIVE

POLITICAL MAP OF SUDAN
1:8,000,000
Khartoum : Surv. Dept, 1950
28 x 42
Col. map.

SUDAN LOCAL GOVERNMENT
1:8,000,000
Khartoum : Surv. Dept. 1949
28 x 42
Col. admin. map.

ADMINISTRATIVE BOUNDARIES
1:4,000,000
Khartoum : Surv. Dept, 1954
55 x 75
Col. map showing admin. districts.
60p

SUDAN LOCAL GOVERNMENT
1:4,000,000
Khartoum : Surv. Dept, 1961
49 x 58
Outline map with admin. districts.

SUDAN : PARLIAMENTARY CONSTITUENCIES
1:2,000,000
In 3 sheets
Khartoum : Surv. Dept, 1953
57 x 76
Col. admin. map.
3 sheets :
NORTH EASTERN
NORTH WESTERN
AND SOUTHERN (57 x 85)

SUDAN OUTLINE MAP
1:4,000,000
Khartoum : Surv. Dept, 1961
50 x 59
Monochrome map showing towns, admin. boundaries, railways and rivers.

E1 PHYSICAL : RELIEF

SUDAN PHYSICAL
1:8,000,000
Khartoum : Surv. Dept, 1950
28 x 42
Col. map, contours.

SUDAN
1:4,000,000
Moskva : GUGK
Physical map with them. insets.

SUDAN – LAYERED MAP
1:2,000,000
In 3 sheets
Khartoum : Surv. Dept, 1955
57 x 76
Contoured with layer colours, communications.
3 sheets
NORTH EASTERN
NORTH WESTERN
AND SOUTHERN (57 x 85)

NORTH EASTERN SUDAN – CONTOUR COVER
1:2,000,000
Khartoum : Surv. Dept. 1955
57 x 76

F GEOLOGY

GEOLOGICAL MAP OF SUDAN
1:4,000,000
3rd edition
Khartoum : Geol. Surv. 1963
91 x 61
Generalised geological map showing bedrock with some superficial deposits.
£50.50

SOUTHERN SUDAN GEOLOGICAL MAP
!:2,000,000
Khartoum : Geol. Surv.
£50.50

GEOLOGICAL MAP OF KHARTOUM PROVINCE
1:1,000,000
Khartoum : Surv. Dept, 1952
55 x 80
Coloured geol map.

SUDAN GEOLOGICAL SERIES
1:250,000
Khartoum : Geol. Surv.
66 x 46
Col. geological series in progress.
Sheets published:

36M	Muhammad Qol 1962
46I	Derudeb 1956
66A	Rashad 1957
66E	Talodi 1957

KORDOFAN – LAND AND WATER USE SURVEY – GEOLOGY
1:250,000
Surv. Dept. 1964
see SUDAN 624 H

G EARTH RESOURCES

KORDOFAN – LAND AND WATER USE SURVEY – GEOMORPHOLOGY AND SOIL
1:250,000
Surv. Dept, 1964
see SUDAN 624 H

SOIL MAPS
1:100,000
Khartoum : Geol. Surv.
Maps in "Rainland Series", available for:

55-I-4	El Obeid	
55-I-5	Rofa	
55-I-6	Yassin	
55-E-2	Er Rahad	
55-M-3	Umm Ruivaba	
66A	Rashad	
66E	Talodi	
each		£S 0.25

H BIOGEOGRAPHY

SUDAN ECOLOGICAL
1:8,000,000
Khartoum : Surv. Dept. 1953
28 x 42
Col. map.

MAIN GAME HABITATS
1:8,000,000
Khartoum : Surv. Dept. 1955
28 x 42
Col. map.

SUDAN FAUNAL
1:8,000,000
Khartoum : Surv. Dept. 1954
28 x 42
Col. map.

SUDAN ANIMAL DENSITY
1:4,000,000
Khartoum : Surv. Dept.
55 x 75
4 maps showing density of :
Camels
Cattle
Goats
Sheep

SOUTHERN SUDAN, SEASONAL CATTLE MOVEMENT
1:2,000,000
Khartoum : Surv. Dept.
57 x 85
Map showing migration and grazing of cattle.

VEGETATION OF SUDAN
1:4,000,000
Khartoum : Surv. Dept.
Col. map showing vegetation zones.

UPPER NILE BASIN VEGETATION TYPES
1:2,000,000
Khartoum : Surv. Dept.
61 x 65
App. distribution of predominant vegetation

types within area directly affected by Upper Nile Project.

KORDOFAN - LAND AND WATER USE SURVEY
1:250,000
Khartoum : Surv. Dept. and FAO, 1964
Series of maps, each in 4 sheets, covering:
Topography
Geomorphology and Soil
Vegetation
Geology
Present Land Use

MONGALLA - GEMMEIZA SUGAR SCHEME
1:50,000
In 12 sheets
Khartoum : Surv. Dept.
60 x 60
Coloured map showing vegetation and soil pattern.

J CLIMATE

RAINFALL MAPS
1:8,000,000
Khartoum : Surv. Dept.
28 x 42
Maps available:
Average Annual Rainfall (1921-1950)
2 sheets, 1954
Average Monthly Rainfall (Jan-Dec)
1921-1950, 12 sheets, 1954
Average Probable Error of Annual Rainfall,
1954

K HUMAN GEOGRAPHY

PILOT POPULATION CENSUS 1953
1:8,000,000
Khartoum : Surv. Dept. 1953
28 x 42
Col. map.

TRIBAL
1:8,000,000
Khartoum : Surv. Dept. 1949
28 x 42
Col. map.

SUDAN - TRIBES
1:2,000,000
In 3 sheets
Khartoum : Surv. Dept. 1962
57 x 76
Coloured map marking tribal boundaries.
3 sheets:
NORTH EASTERN
NORTH WESTERN
AND SOUTHERN (57 x 85)

SUDAN CENSUS AREAS
1:4,000,000
Khartoum : Surv. Dept.
55 x 75
Coloured map of census areas.

EQUATORIA PROVINCE : SCHOOLS
1:3,000,000
Khartoum : Surv. Dept, 1951
55 x 36
2 colour map.

EQUATORIA PROVINCE : MISSION SPHERE
1:3,000,000
Khartoum : Surv. Dept, 1951
55 x 36
2 colour map.

EQUATORIA PROVINCE : ENDEMIC DISEASES
1:3,000,000
Khartoum : Surv. Dept, 1951
55 x 36
Maps I and II.

EQUATORIA PROVINCE : TRIBAL AND ADMINISTRATION
1:3,000,000
Khartoum : Surv. Dept. 1951
55 x 36
2 colour map.

SOUTHERN SUDAN, DISTRIBUTION OF POPULATION DURING THE WET SEASON
1:2,000,000
Khartoum : Surv. Dept.
57 x 85
Outline map showing pop. distribution and seasonal navigability of rivers.

L ECONOMIC

AGRICULTURAL REGIONS
1:8,000,000
Khartoum : Surv. Dept. 1954
28 x 42
Col. map.

PRINCIPAL AGRICULTURAL PRODUCTS
1:8,000,000
Khartoum : Surv. Dept. 1954
28 x 42
Col. map.

ROADS AND AERODROMES
1:8,000,000
Khartoum : Surv. Dept. 1954
28 x 42
Col. map.

SOUTHERN SUDAN INVESTIGATION TEAM MAPS
1:6,000,000
Khartoum : Surv. Dept. 1954
23 x 34
Series showing the following factors:
Fig D Ecological Map
Fig E Hydrological Map
Fig F Areas of Potential Crop Production
Fig G Cattle Types and Cattle Trade
Fig H Areas of Potential Development and Proposed Railway Extension.

UPPER NILE BASIN MAPS : JONGLEI INVESTIGATION TEAM
Various scales
Khartoum : Surv. Dept, 1954
Various Sizes
Series of maps showing the following factors:
2 Ground Survey
1:3,000,000 35 x 47
3 Isohyets
1:3,000,000 35 x 47
4 Communication
1:3,000,000 35 x 47
5 Equatorial Nile Project Engineering Works
1:3,000,000 35 x 47
6 Areas occupied by peoples directly affected by the Equatorial Nile Project
1:2,000,000 61 x 64
7 App. Distribution of the Predominant Vegetation Types
1:2,000,000 61 x 64
8 App. Distribution of the Soil Types
1:2,000,000 61 x 64

SUDAN LANDING GROUNDS
1:4,000,000
Khartoum : Surv. Dept. 1950
55 x 75
2 colour map.

SUDAN RAILWAYS
1:2,500,000
Khartoum : Surv. Dept. 1959
40 x 50
Coloured railway map.

NORTH AND SOUTH GEZIRA
1:250,000
In 2 sheets
Khartoum : Surv. Dept. 1951
61 x 85
Showing SGB blocks and SID boundaries and extent of irrigated land.

MONGALLA - GEMMEIZA SUGAR SCHEME
1:50,000
In 12 sheets
Khartoum : Surv. Dept. 1955
60 x 60 each
Coloured map. Also available showing proposed Canalization.

M HISTORICAL

ANTIQUITY SITES OF THE SUDAN
1:2,000,000
Khartoum : Surv. Dept.
Indicating historic sites by symbols.
£S 0.25

N MATHEMATICAL

SUDAN TRIANGULATION (1st and 2nd ORDER) AND PRECISE LEVELLING
1:4,000,000
Khartoum : Surv. Dept. 1955
55 x 75
In colour.

NORTH EASTERN SUDAN - TRIANGULATION FIRST AND SECOND ORDER
1:2,000,000
Khartoum : Surv. Dept.
60 x 95

63 Ethiopia

A1 GENERAL MAPS : ROADS

HIGHWAY MAP OF ETHIOPIA
1:2,000,000
Addis Ababa : Imp. Highway Authority 1970
92 x 91
Road map with tourist information.
Legend etc. in English.

A2 GENERAL MAPS : LOCAL

SIMEN NATIONAL PARK
1:50,000
Addis Ababa : IEGMLRA, 1970
E $1.00

SOUTHERN BEGEMIDIR – LOCATION MAP
No scale given
Addis Ababa : IEGMLRA, 1957

B TOWN PLANS

MAPS OF ADDIS ABABA
Addis Ababa : IEGMLRA
1:10,000, 1969 E $2.50
1:20,000 4 col. ed. 1964 E $1.50
1:40,000 City Limit (in Amharic) 1965 E $1.00
1:20,000 Govt. offices, 1962 E $1.00
1:500,000 Hospitals, Clinics, Pharmacies, 1962 E $1.75
1:20,000 Places of Worship, 1962 E $1.75
1:20,000 Schools, 1962 E $1.75
Rainfall and Temperature 1962 E $2.50
1:12,500 2 sheet map with insets 1962 E $4.50

URBAN MAPS
Addis Ababa : IEGMLRA
Plans available:
Arba Minch, 1955, 1:10,000 (Amharic & Eng) E$1.25
Aseb, 1965 1:12,500 E$0.40
Asela, 1965 1:5,000 E$1.00
Asmera (Central) 1965, 1:40,000 E$0.40
Debre Birhan, 1961 1:10,000 (Amharic & Eng) E$0.70
Debre Markos, 1961, 1:10,000 (Amharic & Eng) E$1.75
Debre Zeyit, 1961 1:10,000 E$1.75
Debre Zeyit, 1962 1:4,000 E$1.80
Dessie, 1961 1:10,000 (Amharic & Eng) E$1.30
Fiche, 1961 1:5,000 E$0.60
Giyon (Woliso), 1962 1:4,000 2 sheets (Amharic) E$1.75
Harer, 1970 1:25,000 E$1.25
Jibuti (Djibuti), 1965 1:10,000 E$0.50
Jima, 1961 1:5,000 (Amharic & Eng) E$2.00
Messewa, 1965 1:12,000 E$0.50
Nazret, 1961 1:5,000 (Amharic & Eng) E$1.75
Nekemte, 1961 1:10,000 (Amharic & Eng) E$0.80
Shambu, 1961 (Amharic & Eng) E$0.25

C OFFICIAL SURVEYS

KARTA MIRA
1:2,500,000
GUGK (Bulg)
3 sheets for coverage
see WORLD 100C and index 100/2

AFRICA
1:2,000,000
AMS/DMS Series 2201
4 sheets for coverage
see AFRICA 6C

WORLD
1:500,000
DMS Series 1404
see WORLD 100C and index 100/7

CARTA DIMOSTRATIVA DELL' ERITREA E DELLE REGIONI ADJACENTI
1:400,000
In 14 sheets, see index 63/1
Firenze : IGM, 1934
54 x 55
Policentrical proj. contours, relief shading.
L 500 each

TOPOGRAPHICAL MAP SERIES
1:250,000
AMS Series 1501
Addis Ababa : IEGMLRA
Topog. map in 5 cols; contoured.
The following sheets available :
NC 37-8
ND 36-16
ND 37-8
NC 37-4
ND 38-9
ND 38-13
NC 37-10
ND 37-12 E $2.00 each

D POLITICAL & ADMINISTRATIVE

ADMINISTRATION ETHIOPIA
1:4,000,000
Addis Ababa : IEGMLRA, 1971
Admin. districts. E **$0.60**

ETHIOPIA TRANSPORT AND ADMINISTRATION MAP
1:2,800,000
Addis Ababa : IEGMLRA, 1966
61 x 59
Political col. showing Governates, with roads, railways, towns and airports.

EFIOPIYA
1:2,500,000
Moskva : GUGK, 1973
Col. study map showing water features, settlements, admin. divisions and centres, communications, boundaries, economic details, pop. Geog. description.
Ro 0.30

GOVERNORATE GENERAL AND AWRAJAS
1:2,000,000
Addis Ababa : IEGMLRA, 1967 and 1968
Admin. district map in colours. In Amharic. E $1.75

EMPIRE SCHOOL MAPS
1:2,000,000
3rd edition
Addis Ababa : IEGMLRA, 1962
General col. maps for school use.
E $1.75

ETHIOPIA : LOCATION MAP
1:1,000,000
Addis Ababa : IEGMLRA, 1968
E $5.00

ADMINISTRATIVE MAPS OF THE PROVINCES
Addis Ababa : IEGMLRA, 1971
Arusi – Administrative Divisions 1:500,000 E $0.50
Shewa – Administrative Divisions and location map 1:500,000 E $1.50
(also available in Amharic)

GENERAL MAPS OF PROVINCES
Various scales
Addis Ababa, 1971
Maps available :
Arusi - Relief 1:500,000 E $0.50
Arusi – Governorate General 1:500,000 E $50
Eritrea – Governorate General 1:200,000 E $1.50
Bale – Governorate General 1:500,000 E $1.75
Gojam – Governorate General 1:250,000 E $2.00
Gojam – Governorate General 1:500,000 (1962) E $2.00
Wellega – Location 1:1,000,000 E $0.40
Wellega — Water Resource and Drainage Basin 1:1,000,000 E $0.40
Wellega – Governorate General 1:250,000 (1962) E $2.00
Welo – Governorate General 1:500,000 E $1.75

AWRAJA (SUB-PROVINCE) MAPS
Addis Ababa : IEGMLRA
Maps available :
Borena, 1963 (Amharic) 1:500,000 E $1.25
Chilalo, 1967 1:100,000 E $1.75
Gambela, 1969 1:250,000 E $1.50
Gofa, 1965 (Amharic) 1:500,000 E $0.25
Harer Zuria, 1955 1:100,000 E $1.50
Haykoch and Butajira, 1971 1:100,000 E $2.75

Jemjem, 1955
1:100,000 E $1.25
Jibat and Mecha, 1961 (Amharic)
1:250,000 E $1.50
Jibat and Mecha, 1966 (English)
1:250,000 E $1.50
Jima, 1955
1:500,000 E $1.25
Kembata, 1971
1:100,000 E $1.50
Menagesha, 1971 (Amharic)
1:100,000 E $1.00
Menz and Gishe, 1962, location
1:100,000 E $1.75
Menz and Gishe, 1971 (English)
1:100,000 E $1.00
Nekemte, Arjo & Guduru, 1961
1:10,000 E $0.80
Tegulet and Bulga E $1.75
Welamo, 1964 (Amharic)
1:100,000 E $1.40
Welamo, 1957, (English)
1:100,000 E $1.40
Yerer and Kereyu, 1957
1:50,000 E $1.00
Yerer and Kereyu, Church owned land, 1957
1:50,000 E $1.75
Debre Zeyit, 1957
1:50,000 E $1.75
Lume Wereda, 1957
1:100,000 E $0.50

WEREDA MAPS
Addis Ababa : IEGMLRA
District maps available:
Alemgena Wereda
1:10,000 In Amharic and Eng.
Location map, 1966, E $1.75
Alemgena Wereda
1:500,000 In Amharic
Location map, 1965, E $1.00
Sululta Wereda
1:50,000, 1953, E $1.75
Kutaye Mikitil Wereda
1:250,000, 1966 E $1.50

E1 PHYSICAL : RELIEF

EFIOPIJA
1:2,500,000
Moskva : GUGK, 1968
75 x 70
Reference map in physical ed.

ETHIOPIA : GENERAL RELIEF MAP
1:2,000,000
Addis Ababa : IEGMLRA, 1960
Contoured and layer col.
E $1.79

E2 PHYSICAL : LAND FEATURES

MAJOR RIVERS OF ETHIOPIA
1:1,000,000
Addis Ababa : IEGMLRA, 1960
E $1.75

NORTHERN AFAR – TOPOMORPHIC MAP
1:250,000
In 4 sheets
Firenze : IGM, 1968
176 x 140 complete
Col. map with spot heights, springs, water sources, volcanic regions. The 4 sheets are : Edd, Assab, Guilietti Lake, Mersa Fatma.

F GEOLOGY

GEOLOGY OF ETHIOPIA
1:2,000,000
Addis Ababa : IEGMLRA, 1960
Col. map. E $1.75

WELLEGA : GEOLOGY AND MINERAL RESOURCES
1:1,000,000
Addis Ababa : IEGMLRA, 1971
E $0.40

GEOLOGICAL MAP OF THE DANAKIL DEPRESSION (NORTHERN AFAR)
F Barberi and others
1:500,000
Paris : CNRS/Roma : Consiglio Nat. delle Richerche, 1971
77 x 75
Map in French or English.

DANAKIL-SENKE
1:250,000
In 4 sheets
Bad Godesberg : BB, 1970
108 x 162
Col. geol. map on topog. base.
DM 40

G EARTH RESOURCES

NON METALS MAP
1:4,000,000
Addis Ababa : IEGMLRA, 1970
Distribution of non-metallic minerals.

MINERAL DEPOSITS IN ETHIOPIA
1:4,000,000
Addis Ababa : IEGMLRA, 1970
Distribution indicated by symbols.
E $0.35

H BIOGEOGRAPHY

BIOGEOGRAPHIC MAPS OF ETHIOPIA
Addis Ababa : IEGMLRA
Locust Breeding Areas
1:2,000,000 1955 E $1.75
Major soil groups
1:4,000,000 1967 E $0.35
Malaria Distribution
1:2,000,000 1961 E $1.75
Malaria Incidence
1:2,000,000 1961 E $1.75
Malaria Intensity in periods of Transmission
1:2,000,000 1961 E $1.75
Natural Vegetation
1:4,000,000 1967 E $0.35

CEREAL DISTRIBUTION IN ETHIOPIA
1:2,000,000
Addis Ababa : IEGMLRA, 1962
E $1.75

LAND USE MAPS OF THE PROVINCES
Addis Ababa : IEGMLRA, 1971
Arusi :
General Land Use Pattern
1:500,000 E $0.50
Land Utilization
1:500,000 E $0.50
Percentage of Cultivated Land to total area
1:500,000 E $0.50
Gojam : Land Use, 1962
1:500,000 E $2.00
Wellega :
Agricultural Regions
1:1,000,000 E $0.40
Land Use
1:1,000,000 E $0.40
Land Use
1:500,000 E $0.40

MENZ AND GISHE AWRAJA – LAND USE
1:100,000
Addis Ababa : IEGMLRA, 1962
E $1.75

YERER AND KEREYA SUB PROVINCE - FERTILE LAND
1:50,000
Addis Ababa : IEGMLRA, 1957
E $1.75

A LEMGENA WEREDA, PLANT PESTS
1:10,000
Addis Ababa : IEGMLRA, 1965
E $1.00

J CLIMATE

PROVINCE CLIMATE MAPS
1:500,000
Addis Ababa : IEGMLRA, 1971
Maps available :
Arusi :
Mean Annual Rainfall
Monthly Average Rainfall
Mean Annual Temperature
E $0.50
Wellega :
Physio-Climatic Divisions E $0.40
Average Annual and Monthly Rainfall
1:100,000 E $0.40

K HUMAN GEOGRAPHY

POPULATION DENSITY
1:4,000,000
Addis Ababa : IEGMLRA, 1967
E $0.35
Also : Population Distribution, 1967

MEDICAL SERVICES IN ETHIOPIA
Addis Ababa : IEGMLRA
Maps available :
Medical Services 1:1,000,000
1970 E $1.75
Ethiopian School Clinics
1962 E $1.75

PROVINCE MAPS DEALING WITH SOCIAL FACTORS
1:500,000 (unless stated otherwise)
Addis Ababa : IEGMLRA, 1971
Maps available :
Arusi :
Distribution of Public Services
E $0.50
Distribution of Churches and Mosques
E $0.50
Ratio of School-going children to schools
E $0.50
Percentage of Students in each Wereda as of Arusi total E $0.50
Shewa :
Government Schools (Names and Location)
1970 E $1.75
Non Govt. Schools (Mission, private, Church), 1970 E $1.75

Wellega :
Medical Services , 1:1,000,000 E $0.40
Educational Centres, 1:1,000,000 E $0.40
Ethnic Groups, 1:1,000,000 E $0.40
Religion, 1:1,000,000 E $0.40

POPULATION MAPS OF THE PROVINCES
Addis Ababa : IEGMLRA, 1971
Maps available :
Arusi :
Rural Population Density
1:500,000 E $0.50
Crude Density of Rural Pop
1:500,000 E $0.50
Density of Pop. on Cultivated Land
1:500,000 E $0.50
Sex Ratio of Rural Pop.
1:500,000 E $0.50
Number of Land Owners and Tenants
1:500,000 E $0.50

YERER AND KEREYU SUB PROVINCE, POPULATION DENSITY
1:50,000
Addis Ababa : IEGMLRA, 1957
E $1.75

ALEMGENA WEREDA, DENSITY OF POPULATION
1:10,000
Addis Ababa : IEGMLRA
Map in Amharic and English. E $1.00

L ECONOMIC

COFFEE DIVERSIFICATION OF ETHIOPIA
1:4,000,000
Addis Ababa : IEGMLRA, 1967
E $0.35

COFFEE AREAS AND HIGHWAY DEVELOPMENT OF ETHIOPIA
1:2,000,000
Addis Ababa : IEGMLRA, 1967
E $1.75

ECONOMIC MAPS
Addis Ababa : IEGMLRA
Fibre Distribution
1:2,000,000 1962 E $1.75
Forestry
1:2,000,000 1956 E $1.75
Fruit, Honey and Sugar Cane Distribution
1:2,000,000 1962 E $1.75
Legume Distribution
1:2,000,000 1955 E $1.75
Major Cotton Production Areas
1:2,000,000 1955 E $1.75
Oil Seeds Distribution
1:4,000,000 1967 E $0.35
Power Plants
1:4,000,000 1967 E $0.35
Precious Metals
1:4,000,000 1967 E $0.35
Tourism
1:4,000,000 1967 E $0.35

COTTON DEVELOPMENT IN ETHIOPIA
1:2,000,000
Addis Ababa : IEGMLRA, 1957
E $1.75

TRANSPORT MAPS
Addis Ababa : IEGMLRA
Maps Available :
Transportation Pattern
1:2,000,000 1962 E $1.75
Transportation Pattern (In Amharic)
1:2,000,000 1962 E $1.75
Transportation and Administration
1:2,800,000 1966 E $2.00
Transportation and Administration (In Amharic)
1:2,800,000 61 x 89 E $2.00

ECONOMIC MAPS OF THE PROVINCES
Addis Ababa, 1971
Arusi :
Distribution of Markets
1:500,000 E $0.50
Number of Flour Mills
1:500,000 E $0.50
Accessibility
1:500,000 E $0.50
Distribution of Cattle
1:500,000 E $0.50
Distribution of Sheep and Goats
1:500,000 E $0.50
Distribution of Pack Animals
1:500,000 E $0.50
Density of Livestock
1:500,000 E $0.50
Density of Cattle
1:500,000 E $0.50
Density of Sheep and Goats
1:500,000 E $0.50
Density of Pack Animals
1:500,000 E $0.50
Number of Livestock per Household
1:500,000 E $0.50
Number of cattle vaccinated against rinderpes and bovine pleuro-pneumonia
1:500,000 E $0.50
Eritrea :
Economic Crops, 1964
1:2,000,000 E $1.00
Coffee and Cotton Growing Areas
1:1,000,000 E $0.40
Transportation and Communications
1:1,000,000 E $0.40

YERER AND KEREYU SUB PROVINCE, AGRICULTURAL TYPES
1:50,000
Addis Ababa : IEGMLRA, 1957
E $1.75

YERER AND KEREYU SUB PROVINCE
1:50,000
Addis Ababa : IEGMLRA, 1957
Number of maps, showing:
Market Centres and Areas
Grain Marketing Structure
Grain Mills
Weekly Markets E $1.75 each

ALEMGENA WEREDA, AGRICULTURAL PRODUCTS
1:10,000
Addis Ababa : IEGMLRA, 1965
E $1.00

64 Morocco

A1 GENERAL MAPS : ROADS

CARTE DU MAROC AVEC SAHARA
1:4,000,000
Rabat : Dir. de la Cons. Foncière et des Travaux Topog
49 x 46
General communications map of Morocco and adjacent Sahara territory.

NORDAFRIKA STRASSENKARTE
1:2,000,000
Wien : FB
115 x 88
Road map covering Morocco south to Tiznit also Spain, S Italy, Tunisia and N Algeria. Sheet from European series. DM 6.80

CARTE ROUTIERE MAROC ET AFRIQUE DU NORD
1:2,000,000
Paris : Blondel
Esso road map with insets at various scales of Casablanca, Marrakesh, Fes-Ville Ancienne and Nouvelle, Rabat, Canary Isles. Mediterranean Basin.

MAROC
1:1,250,000
Paris : Blondel
General road map in colours.

MAROC AGRANDISSEMENTS
1:1,000,000
No 169
Paris : Michelin, 1971
107 x 96
Roads numbered and classified by col. according to importance and condition, distances, road widths and gradients shown, woodland in green, principal landmarks and locations of minerals and 5 insets.

MAROKKO – KANARISCHE INSELN
1:1,000,000
Bern : Hallwag, 1973
123 x 80
Roads classified with route numbers and distances, places of interest and tourist services indicated by symbols. Relief shaded. Legend in 6 languages.

A2 GENERAL MAPS : LOCAL

REGIONAL SCHOOL MAPS
1:50,000/1:100,000
Rabat : Comite Nat. de Geog. du Maroc, 1972
2 simplified map sheets for school use.
Agdz (South) 1:100,000 showing relief
Argana (North) 1:50,000 Triasic depression of the High Atlas Dh 2

LOCAL PLANS
1:20,000
Rabat: Dir. de la Cons. Foncière et des Travaux Topog. Series of coloured plans of local regions and firing ranges.
Maps available:

Camp d'El Hajeb	3 sheets	124 x 80 45 x 84
Camp de Mediouna		60 x 77
Champ de Tir de Sefrou		54 x 69
Champ de Tir Dito		48 x 70
Champ de Tir Jbel Ram Ram		76 x 93
Carte du Massif du Toubkal	2 sheets	68 x 100
Rabat-Salé		67 x 84
Tafilalet	2 sheets	63 x 90

B TOWN PLANS

TOWN PLANS
1:10,000
Paris : IGN. Rabat : Dir. de la Cons. Foncière et des Travaux Topog.
Each plan is contoured with streets named and principal buildings listed.
Available for :

Marrakesh	2 sheets	99 x 70
Casablanca	2 sheets	99 x 70
Fes	New ed, in prep.	73 x 66
Meknes	In prep.	92 x 65
Oujda	New ed. in prep.	82 x 70
Kenitra	New ed. in prep.	68 x 52
Taza		63 x 45
Tanger		99 x 68

PLANS – GUIDES – POL
Lyon : Francis Bererd
Town plans with tourist guide information.
Available for :
Casablanca 1:12,500
1971 (14th Ed) F.Fr 8
Marrakech et region 1:12,000
1973 (7th ed) F.Fr. 5
Rabat 1:12,000
1973 (10th ed) F.Fr. 6

C OFFICIAL SURVEYS

KARTA MIRA
1:2,500,000
Cartimex
Sheet 72 covers Morrocco
see WORLD 100C and index 100/2.

AFRICA
1:2,000,000
AMS series 2201
3 sheets for coverage, No's 1, 2, 6.
see AFRICA 6C

INTERNATIONAL MAP OF THE WORLD
1:1,000,000
IGN
4 sheets for coverage.
see WORLD 100C and index 100/1.

WORLD
1:500,000
DMS Series 1404
see WORLD 100C and index 100/7

CARTE DU MAROC
1:500,000
In 6 sheets, see index 64/1
Paris : IGN - Rabat : Service Topographique
66 x 88
Contoured, layer col, forests in green. See index.
each F.Fr. 16.67

CARTE DU MAROC
1:250,000
In 34 sheets
Rabat : Dir. de la Cons. Foncières et des Travaux Topog, 1975.
62 x 48
New 6 colour topographical series in progress.
First sheet published — Tiznit.

CARTE DE RECONNAISSANCE DU MAROC
1:200,000
see index 64/2
Paris : IGN - Rabat : Service Topographique
48 x 30
Series providing almost complete coverage of the country, with water in blue, vegetation green, contours brown. Conventional sign sheet also available.
each F.Fr 14.17

CARTE DU MAROC : PROVINCE DE TARFAYA
1:200,000
In 9 sheets
Paris : IGN - Rabat: Service Topographique 1964-5
3 colour map, showing planimetry and writing in black, hydrography blue, contours brown.
each F.Fr. 14.17

CARTE DU MAROC (TYPE 1922)
1:100,000
see index 64/3
Paris : IGN - Rabat: Serv. Topographique
47 x 55
New series in progress showing settlements in red, water blue, vegetation green, contours brown with relief shading. Some sheets available in Provisional ed. only. Table of conventional signs available.
F.Fr. 14.17

CARTE DE RECONNAISSANCE DU MAROC
1:100,000
see index 64/4
Paris : IGN - Rabat : Service Topographique 1954
48 x 30
Series in old and new ed. showing principal and secondary roads in red. water blue, vegetation green, contours brown. Sheets in early ed. have no red overprint. Incomplete. Available in either full or half sheets. Sheet of conventional signs available
each F.Fr. 14.17

CARTE DU MAROC (TYPE 1922)
1:50,000
see index 64/5
Paris : IGN - Rabat : Service Topographique
47 x 55
Series in progress: contours in brown, vegetation green, water blue, relief shading. A few sheets pub. in provisional ed. with reduced information.
each F.Fr. 14.17

MAPA DEL NORTE DE MARRUECOS
1:500,000, 1:200,000, 1:100,000, 1:50,000
Madrid : IGM
Early topog. series, contoured with communications covering the old Spanish Protectorate.

D POLITICAL & ADMINISTRATIVE

MAROKKO
1:7,500,000
Moskva : GUGK, 1973
72 x 60
Col. study map showing water features, settlements, boundaries, admin. divisions and centres, communications, economic details, pop. Geog. description.
Ro 0.30

FOND DE CARTE
1:1,500,000
Rabat : Comite Geog. du Maroc
71 x 55
Base map showing hydrography in blue, towns in black.

CARTE ADMINISTRATIVE DU MAROC
1:1,000,000
Rabat: Dir de la Cons. Foncière et des Travaux Topog.
90 x 65
Three colour administrative map — in preparation.

E1 PHYSICAL : RELIEF

CARTE DU MAROC EN RELIEF
1:5,000,000
Rabat : Dir. de la Cons. Foncière et des Travaux Topog.
28 x 23
Plastic relief map in French and Arab editions.

CARTE DU MAROC EN RELIEF
1:1,200,000
Rabat : Dir de la Cons. Foncière et des Travaux Topog.
100 x 80
Moulded plastic relief map in colours — in preparation.

CARTE GENERALE DU MAROC
1:1,000,000
Paris : IGN - Rabat Service Topographique 1972
122 x 95
Map in 2 sheets showing roads in red, forests green and relief by hypsometric tints. F.Fr 27.50

F GEOLOGY

CARTE GÉOLOGIQUE DU MAROC
1:500,000
In 6 sheets
Rabat : Dir. des Mines et de la Geol, 1955
75 x 107 each
Col. map. Sheet 6 'Hammada du Guir' not available. Showing detailed geol. and some mineral information.

CARTE GEOLOGIQUE DE L'ANTI-ATLAS
1:200,000
Rabat : Dir. Mines et Geol.
Detailed sheets from the 'Anti-Atlas'
Col. geol. maps with legend on reverse.
Available in the following sheets:

138	Quarzazate — Alougoum et Telouet Sud, 1970	107 x 79
159	Foum el Hassane-Assa, 1969	79 x 73
163	Akka — Tafagount — Tata 1970	73 x 93
90	Plage Blance - Goulimine-Cap Dra et Taidalt, 1956	
219	Plaines du Dra au Sud, 1971	

CARTES GÉOLOGIQUES DU MAROC
1:100,000
Rabat : Direction des Mines et de la Geologie
74 x 90 each
Coloured geological map series in progress, with profiles and legend in margin.

CARTE GÉOLOGIQUE DU MAROC
1:100,000, 1:50,000, 1:20,000
Rabat : Service Carte Geol.
Col. series in progress.

CARTE GÉOTECHNIQUE DE FES
1:20,000
In 2 sheets
Rabat : Serv. Mines et Geol, 1967
2 sheet map showing lithology, stratigraphy, morphology, hydrogeology, structure. With text.

G EARTH RESOURCES

MAROC : CARTE DES MINERALISATIONS PLOMBO-ZINCIFÈRES
1:2,000,000
Prepared by A Emberger
Rabat : Dir. Min. et Geol, 1969
96 x 68
Coloured mineral map of lead and zinc bearing strata, with 8 thematic insets. Legend in French.

CARTE GRAVIMÉTRIQUE DU MAROC
1:500,000
In 7 sheets
Rabat : Serv. Mines et Geol.
76 x 106 each
Bouguer Anomaly map in French. Text in preparation.

CARTES DES GÎTES MINERAUX DU MAROC
1:500,000
In 6 sheets
Orleans : BRGM, 1969
87 x 106
Col. map of mineral bearing straits.
1st sheet — Oujda — available.

CARTE PÉDOLOGIQUE DE LA ZONE DE L'OUED N'FIS
by P Mahler and J Concaret
1:50,000
Paris : ORSTOM, 1960
Col. soil map. F.Fr. 12

CARTE PÉDOLOGIQUE DE LA PLAINE DE ZEBRA
by A Ruellan
1:20,000
Paris : ORSTOM, 1961
Col. soil map. F.Fr. 12

H BIOGEOGRAPHY

CARTE DE LA VÉGÉTATION
1:200,000
Toulouse : Inst. de la Carte Internat. du Tapis Végétal, 1960
Depicting vegetation types by colours and hatchings.
Published : Sheet for Rabat-Casablanca
F.Fr. 25

J CLIMATE

CARTE DES PRÉCIPITATION
1:1,600,000
Rabat : Dir. de la Cons. Foncière et des Travaux Topog.
100 x 69
Twelve colour rainfall map.

CARTE DES PRÉCIPITATIONS
1:1,500,000
Rabat : Comité Geog. du Maroc
71 x 55
Showing average rainfall 1926-40.

CARTE DES PRÉCIPITATIONS DU MAROC
1:500,000
In 6 sheets
Toulouse : Inst. de la Carte Internat. du Tapis Végétal
Map series showing precipitation.

K HUMAN GEOGRAPHY

CARTE DES DENSITÉS DE POPULATION
1:1,500,000
Rabat. Dir. de la Cons. Foncière et des Travaux Topog.
90 x 65
Coloured population density map.

CARTE DES TRIBUS
1:1,500,000
Rabat : Comite Geog. du Maroc, 1958
71 x 55
Shows tribes of Morocco and areas they inhabit. New edition in preparation.

L ECONOMIC

LES TRANSPORTS ROUTIERS DE MARCHANDISES
J P Charrie
1:2,000,000
Rabat : Comite Nat. de Geog. du Maroc, 1973
Coloured map showing goods transportation by road. With inset at 1:5,000,000 of Road Traffic Density in 1969. With 74pp illus. text. Dh 10

CARTE DES VOIES DE COMMUNICATION DU MAROC
1:1,500,000
Rabat : Comite Geog. du Maroc, 1958
71 x 55
Col. map showing communications of all types, contours and woodland.

CARTE ÉCONOMIQUE
1:1,500,000
Rabat : Comite Geog. du Maroc, 1958
71 x 55
Col. economic map.

ATLASES
O NATIONAL

ATLAS DU MAROC
1:2,000,000
Rabat : Comite Geog. du Maroc
In 54 plates
64 x 50 (plates)
Atlas in progress (18 plates available), with plates to cover physical, social, economic, agricultural, historical, geog. aspects. Each plate consists of 1 or more sheets, and has accompanying text. (14 x 22)
Complete (1st part) Dh 210

ATLASES
P REGIONAL

ATLAS DU BASSIN DU SÉBOU
Rabat : Min. de l'Agriculture, 1970
65 x 55
143pp
51 col. sheets of physical, social and economic devt. maps of the Rabat, Mèknes and Fèz basin areas. 143pp text vol. in Fr. and Eng. Dh 100.00

648 Western Sahara

A1 GENERAL MAPS: ROADS

IFNI Y SAHARA Y ARCHIPELAGO DE CANARIAS
1:2, 000, 000
Madrid : IGM, 1960
53 x 56
General map showing communications, relief by hachures.

C OFFICIAL SURVEYS

KARTA MIRA
1:2, 500, 000
Cartimex
2 sheets for coverage, No's 72, 92
see WORLD 100C and index 100/2.

AFRICA
1:2, 000, 000
AMS Series 2201
Sheet 6 gives coverage.

INTERNATIONAL MAP OF THE WORLD
1:1, 000, 000
IGN
Sheets for Western Sahara :
NG 28, 29
NF 28
see WORLD 100C and index 100/1.

AFRICA OCCIDENTAL ESPAÑOLA
1:500, 000
In 14 sheets
Madrid : IGM, 1958
Topographical series with communications.

AIT-BA-AMARAN (IFNI)
1:50, 000
In 7 sheets
Madrid : IGM
Topog. map in colours.

F GEOLOGY

CARTES GÉOLOGIQUES DU NORD-OUEST DE L'AFRIQUE
1:2, 000, 000
CNRS
Sheet SAHARA OCCIDENTAL covers Western Sahara.
see NORTH AFRICA F.Fr 6.00

MAPA GEOLÓGICO DEL SAHARA
1:1, 500, 000
Madrid : IGM, 1958
68 x 81
General geol. map.

65 Algeria

A1 GENERAL MAPS: ROADS

PRINCIPALES VOIES DE COMMUNICATION DE L'AFRIQUE DU NORD
1:2, 000, 000
Paris : IGN - Alger : INC
100 x 56 each
2 sheet map covering most of Algeria and adjacent countries. Roads and tracks classified by condition, contours, shading.

ALGÉRIE-TUNISIE
1:1, 000, 000
No 172, 5th edition
Paris : Michelin, 1976
143 x 100
Roads classified and numbered, distances in km, other communications, tourist details. N Algerian Coast inset at 1:500, 000. Alger at 1:50, 000, Tunis at 1:35, 000. With other insets.

A2 GENERAL MAPS: LOCAL

B TOWN PLANS

TOWN PLANS
Various scales
Alger : INC
Detailed plans with contours.
Plans available :
Alger 1:10, 000, 91 x 64
Alger et ses environs, 1:10, 000, 4 sheets, 140 x 220 complete

GUIDES POL - ORAN
1:8, 000
Lyon : F Bererd
51 x 42
Detailed col. plan with street index and list of post independence name changes.

C OFFICIAL SURVEYS

KARTA MIRA
1:2, 500, 000
Cartimex - VVK
5 sheets required for coverage.
see WORLD 100C and index 100/2.

AFRICA
1:2, 000, 000
AMS series 2201
7 sheets for coverage.
see AFRICA 6C.

INTERNATIONAL MAP OF THE WORLD
1:1, 000, 000
Paris : IGN
13 sheets for coverage.
see WORLD 100C and index 100/1.

WORLD
1:500, 000
DMS series 1404
see WORLD 100C and index 100/7.

CARTE D'AFRIQUE (ALGÉRIE)
1:500, 000
see index 65/2
Paris : IGN - Alger : INC
57 x 43
7-col. series in progress, replacing 'Carte d'Algérie' series. Contours, hill shading, roads classified, tracks and oases.
Currently pub. for central area only.
Each F.Fr 16.67

CARTE DES RÉGIONS SAHARIENNES
1:200, 000
see index 65/3
Paris : IGN - Alger : INC
50 x 55
Topog. series in progress covering most of the Algerian Sahara, pub. in 3 eds :
Edition Provisoire - old ed. inc. sketch maps
Fond - New planimetric ed. in 3/4 col, no contours
Edition Normale - New contoured ed. in 4 to 5 col. F.Fr 14.17

CARTE D'ALGÉRIE TYPE 1960
1:200, 000
see index 65/4
Paris : IGN - Alger : INC
64 x 40 each
Topog. series covering Northern Algeria.
7 col, hill shading, contours at 50m intervals, road distances and classifications.
Each F.Fr 14.17

ALGÉRIE-SAHARA
1:100, 000
see index 65/5
Paris : IGN - Alger : INC
64 x 40
New topog. series in progress, covering the northern part of Algerian Sahara. Contoured at 40 metre intervals and hill shaded.
F.Fr 14.17

CARTE D'ALGÉRIE
1:50, 000
In 491 sheets, see index 65/6
Paris : IGN - Alger : INC
64 x 40 each
Topographical series in progress covering Northern Algeria. In 3 eds:
Type "Algérie - Tunisie" pre 1942, In col, showing roads, hydrography, planimetric detail, vegetation.
Type 1922. After 1942, in 5 cols, with relief.
Edition Provisoire. Preliminary ed, without relief.
List of conventional signs for Algérie-Tunisie type available. F.Fr 14.17

CARTE D'ALGÉRIE
1:25, 000
see index 65/1
Paris : IGN, 1960 + Alger : INC
64 x 40 each
Multi-sheet series in progress, type 1960. Covers Northern Algeria, topog. details, contoured at 5 and 10 metre intervals.
F.Fr 14.17

E1 PHYSICAL - RELIEF

ALGÉRIE SAHARA (PHYSIQUE)
No 1360 French, 1211 Arabic
St Germain-en-Laye : Editions MDI
92 x 126
Plastic coated physical wall map for schools. Economic map on reverse.

F GEOLOGY

CARTES GÉOLOGIQUES DU NORD-OUEST DE L'AFRIQUE
1:2, 000, 000
CNRS
see NORTH AFRICA F.Fr 6.00

CARTE GÉOLOGIQUE DE L'ALGÉRIE
1:500, 000
In 6 sheets
Alger : Service de la Carte Geol.
228 x 224
Detailed geol. map with legend.

CARTE GÉOLOGIQUE DU HOGGAR
1:500, 000
In 9 sheets
Orléans : BRGM
Geol. map with title and legend sheet.
Text by P-C Reboul et al, 1961. In the following sheets :
Fort Laperrine
Tazrouk
Amguid-Arak
Ti-M-Misaou
In Ouzzal
Fort-Polignac - Fort Gardel
Ouallen - Bidon 5
Fort-Charlet - In Ezzane
In Azaoua
Each F.Fr 26.00
Set F.Fr 200.00

CARTE GÉOLOGIQUE DE L'ALGÉRIE
1:200, 000, 1:100, 000, 1:50, 000
Alger : Serv. de la Carte Geol. de l'Algérie.
Col. geol. series in progress.

LE MASSIF VOLCANIQUE DE L'ATAKOR (HOGGAR, SAHARA ALGERIEN)
1:50, 000
Paris : CNRS, 1971
Col. geological map with handbook, 176pp. F.Fr 79.60

H BIOGEOGRAPHY

CARTE DE LA VÉGÉTATION DE L'ALGÉRIE
1:500, 000
Toulouse : Inst. de la Carte Internat. du Tapis Vegetal
90 x 68
Multi-sheet vegetation map series in progress.
Sheet published :
N1 31 SW GHARDIA F.Fr 20.00

CARTE DE LA VÉGÉTATION; GUELT-ES-STEL-DJELFA
Toulouse : Inst. de la Carte Internat. du Tapis Vegetal, 1960
Vegetation map with text.
F.Fr 30.00

L ECONOMIC

ALGÉRIE SAHARA (PHYSIQUE)
Editions : MDI
(Economic map on reverse side)
see ALGERIA 65 E1

66 West Africa

A1 GENERAL MAPS: ROADS

AFRIQUE NORD ET OUEST
1:4, 000, 000
Paris : Michelin, 1976
120 x 97
Roads classified by condition, numbered, distances in km and miles. Political boundaries, forests, mines, motoring and tourist features, National Parks.

C OFFICIAL SURVEYS

CARTE DES CONTINENTS
1:5, 000, 000
IGN
For W Africa - Sheet 7 :
Dakar - Yaounde
see WORLD 100 and index 100/5.

THE WORLD
1:5, 000, 000
AGS
Sheet 2 North Western Africa
see WORLD 100C and index 100/3.

KARTA MIRA
1:2, 500, 000
Cartimex - GUGK (Bulg)
Sheets 92, 93, 112, 113
see WORLD 100C and index 100/2.

INTERNATIONAL MAP OF THE WORLD
1:1, 000, 000
IGN
see WORLD 100C and index 100/1.

CARTE DE L'AFRIQUE
1:1, 000, 000
IGN
see AFRICA 6C and index 6/4.

CARTE DU MONDE OACI - version terrestre
1:1, 000, 000
see index 6/4
Paris : IGN
75 x 50
Topog. series on ICAO sheet lines without air information. In 5 - 9 colours, contoured and layered. To be replaced by new Int. Map of the World series.
F.Fr 14.17

CARTE DE L'AFRIQUE DE L'OUEST
1:500, 000
see index 66/1
Paris : IGN
64 x 44 app.
Topog. series
Nouvelle ed: 5 cols, superseding other eds. Road distances, contours brown, water detail blue, vegetation green.
2 special
sheets cover northwest Mauritania (inc. Novakchott) and the south of Western Sahara.

CROQUIS DE RECONNAISSANCE
1:500, 000
see index 66/1
Paris : IGN
64 x 44 each
1 colour map series, formline contours brown, with a few sheets pub. in 2 or 3 colours. F.Fr 16.67

CARTE DE L'AFRIQUE DE L'OUEST
1:200, 000
see index 66/2
Paris : IGN
55 x 55 app.
Topog. series in progress. 3 eds. available, each varying according to whether desert or other landscapes are covered.
"Carte" - contoured
"Fond" - 6 colours (uncontoured)
"Fond" - 1 - 4 cols. F.Fr 14.17

CARTE DE L'AFRIQUE DE L'OUEST
1:50, 000
see index 66/3
Paris : IGN
55 x 55 app.
Type "Outre-Mer" multi-sheet topog. series in progress. Water detail in blue, contours brown, vegetation green, with some variation. Available in standard ed, or planimetric base.
F.Fr 14.17

D POLITICAL & ADMINISTRATIVE

CARTE DE L'AFRIQUE DE L'OUEST
1:7, 500, 000
Paris : IGN, 1959
51 x 32
Base map of West Africa available in 2 eds :
Fond planimetrique - In 4 cols.
Fond d'etude - In 2 cols.
F.Fr 7.50

ZAPADNAYA AFRIKA (W AFRICA)
1:5, 000, 000
Moskva : GUGK, 1973
105 x 70
Col. study map showing water features, settlements, admin. boundaries, divisions and centres, communications, economic details, pop, Geog. description.
RO 0.30

CARTE DE L'AFRIQUE DE L'OUEST
1:5, 000, 000
Paris : IGN, 1959
76 x 48
Edition - Fond d'étude - 2 colour base map allowing for additional information to be overprinted. Also available in col. editions with or without layer colouring.
"Fond" - 2 colours F.Fr 11.67
"Carte" - 6 colours F.Fr 16.67

AFRIQUE OCCIDENTALE ET ÉQUATORIALE
No 51
Paris : Hatier
100 x 120
Political school wall map, with economic map on reverse.

CARTE ADMINISTRATIVE ET ROUTIÈRE DE L'AFRIQUE DE L'OUEST
1:2, 500, 000
In 4 sheets
Paris : IGN, 1955
75 x 54 each
Map showing political and admin. boundaries, communications.
Available in édition normale and édition d'étude in 3 cols.
Set F.Fr 45.83

WALL MAP OF WEST AFRICA
1:2, 000, 000
Accra : Surv. Ghana, 1960
183 x 81 complete
3 sheet map showing communications and boundaries. Covers area from Dakar to Fort Lamy. C 5.00
Mounted CR C 6.00

E1 PHYSICAL AND ECONOMIC

BARTHOLOMEW, TRAVEL MAP SERIES - NORTH WEST AFRICA
1:5, 000, 000
Edinburgh: Bart
74 x 95
Political boundaries with communications, settlements, topog. features, contours, layer col. 75p

AFRIQUE NOIRE NO 1 (PHYSIQUE)
1:5, 000, 000
No 1361
St Germain-en-Laye : Éditions MDI
126 x 92
Plastic coated physical wall map for schools. Map of vegetation and fauna on reverse.

SAHARA : FEUILLE OUEST
1:4, 000, 000
Novara : Agostini
100 x 83
Physical school wall map of the Western Sahara, showing political boundaries and major settlements. L 1, 750

F GEOLOGY

CARTE GÉOLOGIQUE DE L'AFRIQUE
1:5, 000, 000
AAGS - UNESCO
Sheets 1,2,4,5 cover West Africa
see AFRICA 6F.

CARTE TECTONIQUE INTERNATIONALE DE L'AFRIQUE
1:5, 000, 000
AAGS - UNESCO
Sheets 1,2,4,5 cover West Africa
see AFRICA 6F

CARTE GÉOLOGIQUE DE L'AFRIQUE OCCIDENTALE
1:2, 000, 000
In 9 sheets, see index 66/4
Orléans : BRGM, 1960
75 x 54 each
Col. geological series covering French West Africa, with text in French by J Barrene and M. Slansky. F.Fr 200.00

CARTE GÉOLOGIQUE DE L'AFRIQUE OCCIDENTALE
1:500, 000
see index 66/5
Orléans : BRGM, 1950-60
55 x 65 app.
Col. geol. sheets with text. 25 sheets available.
Per sheet F.Fr 24.00

G EARTH RESOURCES

CARTE DE LA DÉCLINAISON MAGNÉTIQUE EN AFRIQUE DE L'OUEST AU 1.1.57
1:5, 000, 000
Paris : IGN
76 x 48
3 colour, showing magnetic declination of 1st January 1957, on planimetric base, and annual variation.
Each F.Fr 11.67

H BIOGEOGRAPHY

CARTE DE RÉPARTITION DES GLOSSINES EN AFRIQUE OCCIDENTALE D'EXPRESSION FRANCAISE
by A Rickenbach
1:10, 000, 000
Paris : ORSTOM, 1961
Col. map in 2 sheets showing distribution of the Glossina genus of tsetse fly.
F.Fr 5.00

AFRIQUE NOIRE NO 1 (PHYSIQUE)
1:5, 000, 000
Vegetation and fauna map on reverse
see WEST AFRICA 66 E1.

CARTE DE RÉPARTITION DES ANOPHÉLÈS DE L'AFRIQUE OCCIDENTALE
by J Hamon
1:2, 000, 000
Paris : ORSTOM, 1957
3 sheet map showing distribution of Anopheles genus of mosquito, in black and white.
Complete F.Fr 20.00

CARTE DE LA VÉGÉTATION DE L'AFRIQUE TROPICALE OCCIDENTALE
1:1, 000, 000
by G Roberty
see index 66/6
Paris : ORSTOM
Coloured series showing vegetation types.
Sheets published :
NB 28 Bonthe (including legend sheet not repeated on other sheets), 1963
F.Fr 30.00
NC 28 Conakry, 1962 F.Fr 36.00
ND 28 Dakar, 1962 F.Fr 36.00
Glossary and Introduction to Series, 108pp
F.Fr 50.00
Notes on sheets NB 28, NC 28, 129pp
F.Fr 50.00
Notes on sheets ND 28, 213pp
F.Fr 50.00

CARTE DE LA VÉGÉTATION DE L'AFRIQUE OCCIDENTALE FRANCAIS
by G Roberty et al
1:200, 000
Paris : ORSTOM, 1950
Col. series showing vegetation types.
Sheet published :
Thies (Senegal) with 4pp text, 1951
F.Fr 10.00

ATLASES
W3 WORLD ATLAS: LOCAL EDITION

WHEATON NEW WEST AFRICA ATLAS
Ed S Knight
Oxford : Pergamon Press, 1967
(Rev ed. 1972)
21 x 27
51pp
For West African schools. 24pp for Africa, covering physical and human geog. of individual countries, with other thematic maps, including the World. Separate indexes for Africa and the World.
70p

ATLASES
O NATIONAL

INTERNATIONAL ATLAS OF WEST AFRICA (ATLAS INTERNATIONAL DE L'OUEST AFRICAIN)
Lagos : Organisation for African Unity, Scientific, Technical Research Commission, 1971
18 x 53
Large national atlas in progress, col. maps with descriptive text; index, bibliog. Covers relief, geology, pedology, sources of energy, administrative and political boundaries, health facilities.
Unbound, in case. Text Eng, Fr.
The first 2 sections have been issued.

ATLASES
P REGIONAL

ATLAS DES STRUCTURES AGRAIRES AU SUD DU SAHARA
Paris : ORSTOM, 1968+
21 x 27
Series of local land use, and cultural studies illustrated by maps and text. Available in the following parts :

1 Yobri (Haute Volta) - Etude geographique d'un village gourmantche
2 Tiogo (Haute Volta) - Etude geographique d'un terroir lela
3 Zengoaga (Cameroun)
4 Pina (Haute Volta) - Etude d'un terroir de front pionnier en pays dagiri
5 Adiamprikofikro - Douakankro (Cote d'Ivoire) - Etude geographique d'un terroir bauste.

661.2 Mauritania

See also: 66 WEST AFRICA

A2 GENERAL MAPS: LOCAL

CAP BLANC
1:100, 000
Paris : IGN, 1952
30 x 40 each
2 sheet map on planimetric base, without contours. UTM proj.
Set F.Fr 27.50

ER RICHAT - ESQUISSE TOPOGRAPHIQUE
1:80, 000
Paris : IGN, 1952
59 x 59
3 col. topog. map, contoured, based on aerial photographs. F.Fr 11.67

RÉGION DE KEDITE IJIL
1:20, 000
In 5 sheets
Paris : IGN, 1953
Various sizes
Provisional edition in 2 cols, contours at 10m intervals. Topog. base.
Set F.Fr 50.00

PORT-ETIENNE ET ENVIRONS
1:20, 000
Paris : IGN, 1957
50 x 70
3 col. map with contours at 5m intervals.
F.Fr 11.67

C OFFICIAL SURVEYS

CARTE ET CROQUIS DE RECONNAISANCE DE L'AFRIQUE DE L'OUEST
1:500, 000
IGN
see WEST AFRICA 66C

CARTE DE L'AFRIQUE DE L'OUEST
1:200, 000
IGN
see WEST AFRICA 66C.

CARTE DE L'AFRIQUE DE L'OUEST
1:50, 000
IGN
see WEST AFRICA 66C.

D POLITICAL & ADMINISTRATIVE

MAVRITANIYA
1:2, 500, 000
Moskva : GUGK, 1973
56 x 65
Col. study map, showing water features, settlements, admin. boundaries, divisions and centres, communications, economic details, pop. Geog. description.
RO 0.30

F GEOLOGY

RÉPUBLIQUE ISLAMIQUE DE MAURITANIE - CARTE GEOLOGIQUE
1:1, 000, 000
Orléans : BRGM, 1968
Col. geological map.

G EARTH RESOURCES

CARTE GRAVIMÉTRIQUE ET DU MAGNÉTISME DER NORD MAURITANIE
1:1, 000, 000
Paris : ORSTOM, 1961-4
2 sheets in black and white. Magnetic map showing "Z" anomalies. With 4pp text, 1971. F.Fr 15.00

CARTE PÉDOLOGIQUE DU GUIDIMAKA
by P Audry and S Pereira-Barreto
1:200, 000
Paris : ORSTOM, 1961
Local soil map of the region.
F.Fr 12.00

ATLASES
L ECONOMIC

ATLAS PASTORAL POUR LA MAURITANIE ET LE SÉNÉGAL
by F Bonnet-Dupeyron
Paris : ORSTOM, 1950
15 x 23 (text)
11 sheets of economic and social maps - 37pp text. Maps comprise :

1a/b Déplacements saisonniers des éleveurs en Basse et Moyenne Mauritanie
1:500, 000

1c Aspect général de la nomadisation en Moyenne Mauritanie
1:2, 000, 000

2a/b Déplacements saisonniers des éleveurs en Sénégal
1:500, 000

3 Carte sommaire des principaux groupes ethniques du Sénégal et de la Mauritanie Sud
1:1, 000, 000

4 Cartes démographiques de la Mauritanie (1:1, 300, 000) et du Sénégal (1:1, 000, 000)

5 Densité des bovins et des caprins au km²
1:2, 000, 000

6 Rapports numériques bovins-caprins aux 100 habitants
1:2, 000, 000

7 Races et variétés bovines (1:2,000,000); rapports numériques chevaux, ânes chameaux au 1,000 habitants (1:3,000,000); viande consommable par habitant et par an (1:5,000,000)

8 Principaux itinéraires et centres commerciaux
1:1, 300, 000

F.Fr 48.00

662.1 Mali

See also: 66 WEST AFRICA

A1 GENERAL MAPS: ROADS

CARTE GÉNÉRALE DE LA RÉPUBLIQUE DE MALI
1:2, 500, 000
Paris : IGN, 1971
89 x 57
Roads classified according to condition, distances, contours at 200m and relief shading. F.Fr 20.83

B TOWN PLANS

BAMAKO ET SES ENVIRONS
1:20, 000
Paris : IGN, 1960
77 x 50
Contours, relief shading, in colour.
F.Fr 20.83

NIAMEY, ZINDER ET MARADI
1:15, 000
Paris : IGN, 1960
78 x 28
3 plans. 2 colour map, with street names and alphabetical index to principal buildings and streets.
Each F.Fr 16.65

C OFFICIAL SURVEYS

KARTA MIRA
1:2, 500, 000
Carti - GUGK (Bulg)
4 sheets to cover Mali :
72, 92, 93, 112
see WORLD 100C and index 100/2.

INTERNATIONAL MAP OF THE WORLD
1:1, 000, 000
IGN
see WORLD 100C and index 100/1.

CARTE ET CROQUIS DE RECONNAISSANCE DE L'AFRIQUE DE L'OUEST
1:500, 000
IGN
see WEST AFRICA 66C

CARTE DE L'AFRIQUE OUEST
1:200, 000
IGN
see WEST AFRICA 66C.

CARTE DE L'AFRIQUE
1:1, 000, 000
IGN
see AFRICA 6C and index 6/4.

E1 PHYSICAL: RELIEF

MALI
1:4, 000, 000
Moskva : GUGK, 1971
Physical hand map with them. insets.

F GEOLOGICAL

CARTE GÉOLOGIQUE DU GOURMA - RÉPUBLIQUE DU MALI, DE HAUTE VOLTA ET DU NIGER
1:500, 000
Orléans : BRGM, 1967
103 x 73
Col. geol. F.Fr 39.00

CARTE GÉOLOGIQUE DU L'ADRAR DES IFORAS
by R Karpoff
1:1, 000, 000
Orléans : BRGM, 1960
Col. map with text, 270pp.
Map F.Fr 39.00

G EARTH RESOURCES

CARTE PÉDOLOGIQUE DU MALI
by S Pereira-Barreto and M Gavaud
1:50, 000
Paris : ORSTOM, 1961
Col. soil map - Sombasso sheet.
F.Fr 12.00

CARTE PÉDOLOGIQUE DU MALI, SEGALA
by S Pereira-Barreto and M Gavaud
1:10, 000
Paris : ORSTOM, 1961
2 sheet col. soil map. F.Fr 12.00

662.5 Upper Volta

See also: 66 WEST AFRICA

C OFFICIAL SURVEYS

KARTA MIRA
1:2, 500, 000
Carti - GUGK (Bulg)
4 sheets to cover Upper Volta :
92, 93, 112, 113
see WORLD 100C and index 100/2.

INTERNATIONAL MAP OF THE WORLD (AFRICA)
1:1, 000, 000
IGN
see WORLD 100C and index 100/1.

CARTE ET CROQUIS DE RECONNAISANCE DE L'AFRIQUE DE L'OUEST
1:500, 000
IGN
see WEST AFRICA 66C

CARTE DE L'AFRIQUE DE L'OUEST
1:200, 000
IGN
see WEST AFRICA 66C

E1 PHYSICAL: RELIEF

HAUTE-VOLTA (PHYSIQUE)
No 1364
St Germain-en-Laye : Éditions MDI
92 x 126
Plastic coated physical wall map for schools, economic map on reverse.

F GEOLOGY

CARTE GÉOLOGIQUE DU GOURMA - Républiques du Mali, de Haute Volta et du Niger
1:500, 000
BRGM
see MALI 662. 1 F.

G EARTH RESOURCES

CARTE PÉDOLOGIQUE DE HAUTE VOLTA
by M Gavaud
1:50, 000
Paris : ORSTOM, 1961
Col. map sheet for Bereba.
F.Fr 12.00

CARTE PÉDOLOGIQUE DE HAUTE - VOLTA, SHEET KATANA
by M Gavaud et al
1:20, 000
Paris : ORSTOM, 1961
Col. soil map with 133pp text.
F.Fr 12.00

CARTE PÉDOLOGIQUE DE HAUTE-VOLTA
by M Gavaud and A Sakho
1:10, 000
Paris : ORMSTOM, 1961
Soil maps in colour;
Maps available :
Lantaogo
Manga
Kougny
Each F.Fr 12.00

CARTE PÉDOLOGIQUE DE HAUTE-VOLTA
by M Gavaud and S Pereira-Barreto
1:5, 000
Paris : ORSTOM, 1961
Soil maps available for :
Dakiri (2 sheets)
Dori-Marie (3 sheets)
Louda (2 sheets)
Mogtedo (4 sheets)
Each F.Fr 12.00

L ECONOMIC

HAUTE VOLTA (PHYSIQUE)
Éditions MDI
Economic
see UPPER VOLTA 662. 5m E1

ATLASES
P REGIONAL

ATLAS DES STRUCTURES AGRAIRES AU SUD DU SAHARA
ORSTOM, 1968
see WEST AFRICA 66 ATLASES P.

M2

662.6 Niger

See also: 66 WEST AFRICA

A1 GENERAL: ROADS

CARTE GÉNÉRALE DE LA RÉPUBLIQUE DU NIGER
1:2, 500, 000
Paris : IGN, 1965
86 x 59
General map with contours, relief shading, communications, road details, distances in km. F.Fr 20.83

B TOWN PLANS

NIAMEY, ZINDER AND MARADI
1:15, 000
Paris : IGN, 1966
78 x 28
Plan with index to principal roads and buildings. F.Fr 16.67

C OFFICIAL SURVEYS

KARTA MIRA
1:2, 500, 000
Carti - GUGK (Bulg)
2 sheets to cover Niger :
93 Niamey
113 Lagos
see WORLD 100C and index 100/2.

AFRICA
1:2, 000, 000
AMS Series 2201
3 sheets needed for Niger : 8, 12, 13
see AFRICA 6C and index 6/2.

INTERNATIONAL MAP OF THE WORLD
1:1, 000, 000
IGN
8 sheets needed for Niger.
see WORLD 100C and index 100/1.

CARTE DE L'AFRIQUE
1:1, 000, 000
IGN
see AFRICA 6C and index 6/4.

CARTE DE L'AFRIQUE DE L'OUEST
1:500, 000
IGN
see WEST AFRICA 6C and index 66/1.

AFRIQUE DE L'OUEST
1:200, 000
IGN
see WEST AFRICA 6C and index 66/2.

AFRIQUE DE L'OUEST
1:50, 000
IGN
see WEST AFRICA 6C and index 66/3.

D POLITICAL & ADMINISTRATIVE

CARTE ADMINISTRATIVE DE LA RÉPUBLIQUE DU NIGER
1:5, 000, 000
Paris : IGN, 1962
37 x 24
5 colour map of admin. areas.
F.Fr 11.67

FOND D'ÉTUDE
1:5, 000, 000
Paris : IGN, 1962
37 x 26
Black and white map of Niger, for use as study base, showing main geog. features.
F.Fr 5.00

F GEOLOGY

CARTE GÉOLOGIQUE DU NIGER
1:2, 000, 000
Orléans : BRGM, 1967
by J Greigert and R Pougnet
Col. geol. map with explanatory text.
F.Fr 39.00

CARTE DE RECONNAISSANCE GÉOLOGIQUE DU MANGA
F Piraud
1:500, 000
Orléans : BRGM, 1967
125 x 95
Col. geol. map with text vol.
F.Fr 24.00

CARTE GÉOLOGIQUE DU GOURMA - Rép. du Mali, Haute Volta et Niger
1:500, 000
BRGM, 1967
see MALI 662. 1 F.

CARTE GÉOLOGIQUE DU NIGER OCCIDENTAL
E Machens
1:200, 000
In 2 sheets
Orléans : BRGM, 1967
108 x 75
Coloured map, covering area West of Niamey and River Niger. With text.
F.Fr 39.00

G EARTH RESOURCES

CARTES GRAVIMÉTRIQUES DU NIGER
1:1, 000, 000
Paris : ORSTOM, 1967
Map with 11pp text by J Rechenmann, 1969. F.Fr 15.00

CARTE PÉDOLOGIQUE DU NIGER - LOCALISATION DES OBSERVATIONS PÉDOLOGIQUES
by M Gavaud and R Boulet
1:500, 000
In 4 sheets
Paris : ORSTOM, 1963
Covers :
Central Niger, 1963
black and white F.Fr 12.00
Zinder, 1964, 120 x 74,
colour F.Fr 12.00
Maradi, 1965, 98 x 68,
colour F.Fr 12.00
Niamey, 1967, 90 x 111,
colour F.Fr 12.00

LOCALISATION DES OBSERVATIONS PÉDOLOGIQUES DE LA REGION DE L'ADER DOUTCHI
1:200, 000
Paris : ORSTOM, 1963
Also by G Bocquier and M Gavaud at 1:100, 000, 1964. Black and white map.
F.Fr 12.00

CARTE PÉDOLOGIQUE DU BASSIN DU GOROUOL-BELI
by M Gavaud
1:100, 000
Paris : ORSTOM, 1965
Col. soil map in 1 sheet.
F.Fr 12.00

CARTE PÉDOLOGIQUE DES ALLUVIONS DU BASSIN DU GOROUL-BELI
by M Gavaud
1:50, 000
Paris : ORSTOM, 1965
Coloured soil map of alluvial drift.
F.Fr 12.00

CARTE PÉDOLOGIQUE DE LA PLAINE DE KOULOU
by B Dabin and A Perraud
1:10, 000
Paris : ORSTOM, 1961
Col. soil map with 43pp text.
F.Fr 12.00

CARTE PÉDOLOGIQUE DU PÉRIMÈTRE D'IRRIGATION D'ADOUNA, DE KEITA, DE TABOYE
by G Bocquier and M Gavaud
1:5, 000
Paris : ORSTOM, 1962
Col. soil map in 3 sheets.
F.Fr 12.00

CARTE PÉDOLOGIQUE RÉPUBLIQUE DU NIGER, PLAINE DE SAY
by B Dabin and A Perraud
1:5, 000
Paris : ORSTOM, 1961
2 sheet black and white soil map with 43pp text. F.Fr 12.00

H BIOGEOGRAPHY

CARTE INTERNATIONALE DU TAPIS VÉGETAL - SHEET DJADO
1:1, 000, 000
Pondichery : French Inst, 1968
Detailed vegetation map in colour, following international sheet lines.

CARTE D'UTILISATION DES TERRES
M Gavaud and R Boulet
1:500, 000
Paris : ORSTOM
Land use map, black and white outline.
Sheets for :
Zinder, 1965
Maradi, 1965
Each F.Fr 12.00

663 Senegal

See also: 66 WEST AFRICA

A1 GENERAL MAPS: ROADS

CARTE ROUTIÈRE DU SÉNÉGAL
1:1, 000, 000
Paris : IGN, 1973 F.Fr 20.83

A2 GENERAL MAPS: LOCAL

CARTE TOURISTIQUE DU PARC NATIONAL DU NIOKOLOKOBA
1:200, 000
Paris : IGN, 1966
Roads and distances overprinted in red, reserves of park in yellow and beige. Tourist details with centre of park enlarged on reverse with text. F.Fr 14.17

CARTE DE LA PRESQ'ÎLE DE CAP VERT
1:50, 000
In 4 sheets
Paris : IGN, 1956
Covering peninsula and immediate hinterland, showing topog. detail with contours at 10 metre intervals.
Each F.Fr 16.67

CARTE DE LA PRESQU'ÎLE DE CAP VERT
1:20, 000
In 15 sheets
Paris : IGN
Covering peninsula and parts of hinterland, showing topog. detail with woodland col. and contours at 5 metre intervals.
F.Fr 11.67

B TOWN PLANS

PLAN DE DAKAR
1:10, 000
Paris : IGN, 1964
100 x 70
Town plan with street names and important places related to a grid. F.Fr 11.67

C OFFICIAL SURVEYS

KARTA MIRA
1:2, 500, 000
Cartimex
Sheet 92 Dakar covers Senegal
see WORLD 100C and index 100/2.

AFRICA
1:2, 000, 000
AMS Series 2201
Sheet 11 covers Senegal
see AFRICA 6C and index 6/2.

INTERNATIONAL MAP OF THE WORLD - AFRICA (CARTE INTERNATIONAL DU MONDE EN AFRIQUE)
1:1, 000, 000
IGN
see WORLD 100C and index 100/1.

CARTE DE L'AFRIQUE
1:1, 000, 000
IGN
see AFRICA 6C and index 6/4.

CARTE DE L'AFRIQUE DE L'OUEST
1:500, 000
IGN
see WEST AFRICA 66C and index 66/1.

AFRIQUE DE L'OUEST
1:200, 000
IGN
see WEST AFRICA 66C and index 66/2.

AFRIQUE DE L'OUEST
1:50, 000
IGN
see WEST AFRICA 66C and index 66/3.

D POLITICAL & ADMINISTRATIVE

CARTE ADMINISTRATIVE DU SÉNÉGAL
1:2, 000, 000
Paris : IGN, 1968
34 x 24
Col. map showing admin. boundaries.
1965 edition available in monochrome.
F.Fr 11.67

CARTE ADMINISTRATIVE DU SÉNÉGAL
1:1, 000, 000
Paris : IGN, 1966
Col. map showing admin. boundaries.
F.Fr 11.67

F GEOLOGY

SÉNÉGAL ET GAMBIA - CARTE GÉOLOGIQUE
1:500, 000
In 4 sheets
Dakar : Dir. Mines et Géol, 1962
144 x 104 complete
Col. general geol. map with 36pp text.

SÉNÉGAL - CARTE GÉOTECHNIQUE DU SÉNÉGAL
1:500, 000
In 4 sheets
Dakar : Dir. Mines et Géol.
142 x 103 complete
Col. general tectonic map with 43pp text.

CARTE GÉOLOGIQUE DU SÉNÉGAL ORIENTAL
1:200, 000
In 7 sheets
Dakar : Dir. Mines et Géol, 1963
Col. series following same sheet lines as topog. series of West Africa with explanatory notes.
Sheets published :
Kédougou
Kossanto
Bakel
Kenieba
Dalafi
Youkounkoun
Tambacounda
Each Fr.CFA 3, 000

CARTE GÉOLOGIQUE DE LA RÉGION DU FLEUVE SÉNÉGAL
1:200, 000
In 7 sheets
Dakar : Dir. Mines et Géol, 1967-68
Col. series of geol. maps following same sheet lines as West Africa topog. series.

CARTE GÉOLOGIQUE DU SÉNÉGAL ORIENTAL
By F Witschard
1:100, 000
Orléans : BRGM, 1965
With Memoir No 44. F.Fr 165.00

CARTE GÉOLOGIQUE DE LA PRESQU' ÎLE DE CAP VERT
1:20, 000
Orléans : BRGM
Geological map in 2 sheets, Dakar and Ouakam with text.

G EARTH RESOURCES

CARTE PÉDOLOGIQUE DU SÉNÉGAL
R Maignien
1:1, 000, 000
Paris : ORSTOM, 1965
Col. soil map with 63pp text.
F.Fr 34.00

CARTE PÉDOLOGIQUE DE RECONNAISSANCE DU SÉNÉGAL
1:200, 000
Paris : ORSTOM, 1966
Coloured reconnaissance soil map series.
Sheets available :
Bakel S Pereira-Barretu, 1966
Tambakounda S Pereira-Barretu, 1966
Oriental Kadougou and Kossanto
Kenieba Campagne, 1964-5, 28 sheets
A Chauvel, 1967. with 48pp text.
Each F.Fr 12.00

CARTE PÉDOLOGIQUE DE MOYENNE - CASAMANCE
by J Baldensperger et al
1:200, 000
Paris : ORSTOM, 1968
Col. soil map. F.Fr 12.00

CARTE PÉDOLOGIQUE DE HAUTE - CASAMANCE
by J F Turenne and J F Vizier
1:200, 000
Paris : ORSTOM, 1963
Col. soil map. F.Fr 12.00

CARTE PÉDOLOGIQUE DE LA PRESQU'ÎLE DU CAP VERT
by R Maignien
1:50, 000
In 3 sheets
Paris : ORSTOM, 1959
Col. soil map. F.Fr 36.00

CARTE PÉDOLOGIQUE DE DAHRA DJOLOFF
by P Audry
1:20, 000
Paris : ORSTOM, 1962
Col. soil map. F.Fr 12.00

CARTE PÉDOLOGIQUE DES NIAYES
by S Pereira-Barreto
1:10, 000
In 6 sheets
Paris : ORSTOM, 1962
Col. soil map in the following sheets :
Lac de Mekhe
M'Boro
Balgaye
Diambalo
Niaye N
Tanha
with index sheet and legend.
Each F.Fr 12.00

CARTE DES GÎTES MINÉRAUX DE LA RÉPUBLIQUE DU SÉNÉGAL
by F Permingeat and J Sagatsky
1:500, 000
In 4 sheets
Orléans : BRGM, 1966
Mineral-bearing strata. F.Fr 75.00

H BIOGEOGRAPHY

CARTE DE LA VÉGÉTATION DE L'AFRIQUE OCCIDENTALE FRANÇAISE
1:200, 000
by G Roberty et al
Paris : ORSTOM, 1950
Col. series showing vegetation types.
Sheet published : Thies (Sénégal) with 4pp text. F.Fr 10.00

ATLASES
L ECONOMIC

ATLAS PASTORAL POUR LA MAURITANIE ET LE SÉNÉGAL
by F Bonnet-Dupeyron
Paris : ORSTOM, 1950
see MAURITANIA 661. 2
ATLASES L ECONOMIC

ATLASES
O NATIONAL

RÉPUBLIQUE DU SÉNÉGAL - CARTES
Dakar : l'Aménagement du Territoire, 1965
39 x 28. 40 maps in black and white covering physical, administrative, population and economic aspects with separate population overlay. No text or index.

664 Sierra Leone

See also: 66 WEST AFRICA

B TOWN PLANS

FREETOWN ROAD MAP
1:6, 250
In 6 sheets
Freetown: Surveys and Lands Divisions, 1959
95 x 66 each
Road map with street names, buildings and contours.

SIERRA LEONE - TOWN PLANS
1:2, 500
DOS 119
Tolworth : DOS
Large scale planning series showing streets and buildings.
Plans available :

Bo	15 sheets	1964+
Kenema	8 sheets	1965+
Makeni	13 sheets	1966+
Kailahun	6 sheets	1967+
Pujehun	4 sheets	1958+
Moyamba	15 sheets	1968+

SIERRA LEONE - TOWN PLANS
1:2, 500
DOS 019
Tolworth : DOS
Large scale planning series showing streets and buildings.
Plans available :

Port Loko	10 sheets	1969+
Western Area	111 sheets	1969-73
Kambia	10 sheets	1974
Kabala	9 sheets	1976

C OFFICIAL SURVEYS

AFRICA
1:2, 000, 000
AMS Series 2201
Sheet No 16 covers Sierra Leone
see AFRICA 6C and index 6/2.

SIERRA LEONE
1:50, 000
DOS 419 (G 742)
In 111 sheets, see index 664/1
Tolworth : DOS, 1960-1973
76 x 84 each
Topog. series showing communications, boundaries, settlements, vegetation types, contours. 50p

FREETOWN - SPECIAL SHEET
1:50, 000
DOS 419 (G 742)
Edition 1
Tolworth : DOS, 1968
55 x 55 each
Special coloured sheet showing land and sea areas, roads classified, forest areas, vegetation shown by symbols, hill shading and contours. Insets of the Banana Islands and Central Freetown. 65p

SIERRA LEONE, FREETOWN PENINSULA
1:10, 000
DOS 219 (G 841)
In 22 sheets, see index 664/1
Tolworth : DOS, 1958-67
76 x 84 each
Topog. map of Freetown Peninsula, contoured. 35p

D POLITICAL & ADMINISTRATIVE

SIERRA LEONE
1:1, 000, 000
DOS 981
Edition 7
Tolworth : DOS, 1968
Small map showing boundaries, roads and towns. 15p

E1 PHYSICAL: RELIEF

SIERRA LEONE
1:500, 000
DMS Series G 442
Tolworth: MOD,
79 x 74
Topog. map showing boundaries, settlements, communications, road distances, contours and layer col. 33p

SIERRA LEONE
1:250, 000
DOS 619
Edition 1
In 4 sheets
Tolworth : DOS, 1972-3
142 x 140 complete
Contoured, layer colouring, road and rail communications classified, mines, historic sites and services shown by symbols.
Each 65p

F GEOLOGY

SIERRA LEONE - GEOLOGICAL
1:1, 000, 000
DOS 1120 Geol.
Tolworth : DOS, 1960
40 x 40
Col. geol. sketch map of Sierra Leone with index to DOS (Geol) 1081.
30p

SIERRA LEONE - GEOLOGY OF THE SULA MOUNTAINS AND THE KANGARI HILLS
1:50, 000
DOS 1081 (Geol)
In 5 sheets
Tolworth : DOS, 1958+
89 x 64 each
Geol. maps with some tectonic and mineral information. 65p
with :
SIERRA LEONE - SULA MOUNTAINS SECTION
DOS (Geol) 1081/a
Geological sections of Schist Belt to accompany DOS (Geol) 1081.
30p

SIERRA LEONE - GEOLOGY OF THE GBANGBAMA AREA
1:50, 000
DOS 1139 (Geol)
In 3 sheets
Tolworth : DOS
Provisional geol. map of parts of the areas covered by DOS 419, topog. sheets 87, 98 and 99. Each 30p

SIERRA LEONE - GEOLOGY OF THE GOLA FOREST AREA
1:50, 000
DOS 1152 (Geol)
In 5 sheets
Tolworth : DOS, 1966-7
Geol. map of part of the area covered by DOS 419, sheets 103, 104, 112 and 92.
50p

G EARTH RESOURCES

SIERRA LEONE - SOILS SKETCH MAP
1:1, 000, 000
DOS (Misc.) 310
Tolworth : DOS, 1963
Coloured soil map. 30p

SIERRA LEONE - BOLILANDS SOIL MAP
1:50, 000
DOS (LU) 3015
In 4 sheets
Tolworth : DOS, 1962
Map in colours.
Each 65p

H BIOGEOGRAPHY

SIERRA LEONE - THE FOREST ESTATE AT 31.6.61
1:1, 000, 000
DOS 981 (For)
Tolworth : DOS, 1962
40 x 40
Map showing location of forests.
15p

SIERRA LEONE LAND USE AND SKETCH MAP SERIES
see index 664/1
Tolworth : DOS
Various sizes
Pairs of maps for 3 areas, one sketch map and one land use map. See index to DOS 419 (10 sketch maps and 10 land use maps):
DOS (misc) 255 Little Scarcies sketch map, 2 sheets, 1:40, 000, 1959
DOS 3004 Little Scarcies Land Use map, 2 sheets, 1:40, 000, 1960
DOS (misc) 256 Riba Bumpe sketch map, 2 sheets, 1:40, 000, 1959
DOS 3005 Riba Bumpe land use map, 2 sheets, 1:40, 000, 1960
DOS (misc) 254 Rhombe sketch map, 6 sheets, 1:16, 000, 1959
DOS 3003 Rhombe land use map, 6 sheets, 1:16, 000, 1960
Each 30p

L ECONOMIC

SIERRA LEONE - CHIEFDOM BOUNDARIES, AGRICULTURAL PRODUCTION AND TRADE
1:500, 000
DOS (Misc.) 7AB
Tolworth : DOS, 1948
Coloured distribution map.
50p

ATLASES

O NATIONAL ATLASES

ATLAS OF SIERRA LEONE
Freetown : Surveys and Lands Division, 1966
27 x 39
Small national atlas containing maps at 1:1, 000, 000 and 1:3, 000, 000 depicting physical features, vegetation, climate, soils, geol, pop, minerals, agriculture etc. Inc. town plans, statistical data and gazetteer. 2nd edition.
Limp covers £1.15

SIERRA LEONE IN MAPS
Edition 2
by J I Clark
London : Hodder and Stoughton
22 x 28
120pp
Physical and them. maps with descriptive text. £2.75

665.1 Gambia

A1 GENERAL MAPS: ROADS

GAMBIA - ROAD MAP
1:500, 000
6th edition
Bathurst : Surv. Dept.
Road maps classified with admin. divisions.
82p

A2 GENERAL MAPS: LOCAL

COASTAL STRIP CONTOURED (GAMBIA RIVIERA)
1:10, 000
DOS 215 (G824)
In 3 sheets
Tolworth : DOS, 1972
89 x 65 each
Covers 8 x 50 km. Coastal strip facing Atlantic Ocean. Contours, vegetation, roads, settlement. Sheets 1 and 2 only published.
Each 50p

CONTOUR MAP OF MAC CARTHY ISLAND
1:6, 250
Bathurst : Surv. Dept.
Topographical map. 35p

B TOWN PLANS

BATHURST GUIDE PLAN
1:14, 000
DOS Misc. 383
Tolworth : DOS
Tourist plan.

BATHURST STREET PLAN AND PUBLIC BUILDINGS
1:5, 000
Bathurst : Surv. Dept.
Large scale plan. 36p

GAMBIA - TOWN PLANS
1:2, 500
DOS 115
Edition 1
Tolworth : DOS, 1966/70
Large scale series of plans available for :
Bathurst - 5 sheets, 1966
Farjar and Bakau - 5 sheets, 1966
Sere Kunda - 11 sheets, 1968-
Each 30p

LARGE SCALE PLANS COVERING PRINCIPAL TOWNS AND VILLAGES
1:2, 500
Bathurst : Surv. Dept.
Plans available :
Bakau
Bansang
Barra
Basse Wharf Town and environs
Bathurst
Bintang
Brikama
Brufut
Bwiam
Fajara
Farafenni
Fatoto Wharf Town
Georgetown
Gunjur
Illiassa
Jambanjah
Jappeni
Jowara
Kaur
Kerewan
Kuntaur
Lamin
Mansakonko
Pakali Nding
Salikene
Serekunda and environs
Sibanor
Sukuta
Yundum Airport and environs
Each 38p

C OFFICIAL SURVEYS

KARTA MIRA
1:2, 500, 000
Cartimex
1 sheet to cover Gambia :
92 Dakar
see WORLD 100C and index 100/2.

THE WORLD
1:2, 000, 000
AMS Series 2201
Sheet 11 for Gambia
see AFRICA 6C and index 6/2.

CARTE DE L'AFRIQUE
1:1, 000, 000
IGN
1 sheet to cover Gambia :
Sheet ND 28
see AFRICA 6C and index 6/4.

GAMBIA
1:125, 000
DOS 515 (G 624)
3rd Edition
In 3 sheets, see index 665. 1/1
Tolworth : DOS, 1966
Various sizes
Topog. map showing roads and vegetation.
Each 50p

GAMBIA
1:50, 000
DOS 415 (G 724)
2nd Edition
In 30 sheets, see index 665. 1/1
Tolworth : DOS, 1964-65
Various sizes
Topog. series in progress, uncontoured.
Each 50p

D POLITICAL & ADMINISTRATIVE

GAMBIA
1:1, 000, 000
DOS 962
Edition 4
Tolworth : DOS, 1964
35 x 18 app.
Admin. boundaries, road and rail communications. Bathurst and environs inset. 15p

ELECTORAL CONSTITUENCY MAP OF THE GAMBIA
1:250, 000
Bathurst : Surv. Dept.
Boundaries in colour. £1.00

F GEOLOGY

SÉNÉGAL ET GAMBIA - CARTE GÉOLOGIQUE
1:500, 000
Dir. of Mines Sénégal, 1962
see SENEGAL 663 F

GEOLOGICAL MAP OF THE GAMBIA
1:500, 000
Bathurst : Surv. Dept.
Map in colours. £1.00

H BIOGEOGRAPHY

GAMBIA - OIL PALM AREAS
1:50, 000
DOS (LR) 3058
Tolworth : DOS
Showing distribution of oil palms in colours.
5 sheets currently published.
Each 35p

GAMBIA LAND USE
1:25, 000
DOS 3001 (G 823)
In 35 sheets, see index 665. 1/1
Tolworth : DOS, 1958
Various sizes
Coloured series depicting land use areas.
Each 65p

VEGETATION MAP OF MAC CARTHY ISLAND
1:6, 250
Bathurst : Surv. Dept.
Vegetation types shown in colour.
35p

665.2 Guinea

See also: 66 WEST AFRICA

C OFFICIAL SURVEYS

AFRICA
1:2, 000, 000
AMS Series 2201
Sheet 16 for Guinea
see AFRICA 6C and index 6/2.

INTERNATIONAL MAP OF THE WORLD
1:1, 000, 000
IGN
see WORLD 100C and index 100/1.

CARTE DE L'AFRIQUE
1:1, 000, 000
IGN
see AFRICA 6C and index 6/4.

CARTE DE L'AFRIQUE DE L'OUEST
1:500, 000
IGN
see WEST AFRICA 66C and index 66/1.

CARTE DE L'AFRIQUE DE L'OUEST
1:200, 000
IGN
see WEST AFRICA 66C and index 66/2.

CARTE DE L'AFRIQUE DE L'OUEST
1:50, 000
IGN
see WEST AFRICA 66C and index 66/3.

D POLITICAL & ADMINISTRATIVE

GUINEA/PORTUGUESE GUINEA
1:1, 660, 000 app
No 1389
New York : UN, 1970
General administrative and planning map.

E1 PHYSICAL: RELIEF

GVINEYA
1:1, 250, 000
Moskva : GUGK, 1971
74 x 60
Physical hand map with contours, communications.

F GEOLOGY

CARTE GÉOLOGIQUE DE L'AFRIQUE OCCIDENTALE FRANÇAISE
1:500, 000
see index 66/5
Dakar : Dir. Géol. Prosp. Min. AOF
Col. geological series with accompanying explanatory notes.

665.7 Guinea Bissau

See also: 66 WEST AFRICA

A1 GENERAL MAPS: ROADS

CARTA DA PROVÍNCIA DA GUINÉ
1:500, 000
Lisboa : PUP, 1962
56 x 50
Rivers and water features in blue, roads red, towns graded by pop. General map.

C OFFICIAL SURVEYS

KARTA MIRA
1:2, 500, 000
Carti - GUGK (Bulg)
2 sheets required for Portuguese Guinea :
92 Dakar
112 Accra
see WORLD 100C and index 100/2.

AFRICA
1:2, 000, 000
AMS Series 2201
Sheet 16 for Portuguese Guinea
see AFRICA 6C and index 6/2.

CARTE DE L'AFRIQUE
1:1, 000, 000
IGN
see AFRICA 6C and index 6/4.

GUINÉ
1:50, 000
Series in 72 sheets, see index 665. 7/1
Lisboa : PUP, 1953-1963
Topographical series, contoured.

D POLITICAL & ADMINISTRATIVE

GUINEA - PORTUGUESE GUINEA
1:1, 584, 000
No 1389
New York : UN, 1969
General administrative and planning map.

E1 PHYSICAL: RELIEF

GVINEYA PORTUGALSKAYA
1:500, 000
Moskva : GUGK, 1970
72 x 47
Physical map with contours, communications, insets.

F GEOLOGY

CARTA GEOLÓGICA DA GUINÉ
1:500, 000
Lisboa: Junta Investig. Ultramar, 1968
Col. geological map. P.Esc. 40.00

665.8 Cape Verde Islands

See also: 469 PORTUGAL

C OFFICIAL SURVEYS

KARTA MIRA
1:2, 500, 000
Carti
Sheet 91 Cape Verde Islands
see WORLD 100C and index 100/2.

CABO VERDE
Various scales
Lisboa : PUP
Topog. maps, contoured, available for the following islands :

Boa Vista	1:100, 000	1937
Fogo	1:100, 000	1929
Maio	1:100, 000	1928
Sal	1:100, 000	1930
S Nicolau	1:100, 000	1929
S Tiago	1:100, 000	1932
Santa Luzia	1: 75, 000	1930
Brava	1: 50, 000	1930

E1 PHYSICAL: RELIEF

ARQUIPÉLAGO DE CABO VERDE
1:500, 000
Lisboa : JIU, 1962
64 x 59
Covers all the islands, showing roads, contours, spot heights.

666 Liberia

C OFFICIAL SURVEYS

AFRICA
1:2, 000, 000
AMS Series 2201
Sheet 16 covers Liberia
see AFRICA 6C and index 6/2.

CARTE DU MONDE OACI
édition terrestre
1:1, 000, 000
IGN
Sheets required :
2781 Haut Niger
2818 Ile Sherbro
also Abidjan Carte de l'Afrique
see AFRICA 6C and index 6/4.

CARTE DE L'AFRIQUE
1:1, 000, 000
IGN
Sheet required :
Abidjan
also Carte du Monde ICAO
sheets 2781, 2818
see AFRICA 6C and index 6/4.

LIBERIA - GEOGRAPHIC SERIES
1:250, 000
see index 666/1
Miscellaneous Geologic Investigations
Washington : USGS (and Liberian Geol. Survey)
53 x 74
Series of topographic maps covering the whole country.
Each US $0.75

D POLITICAL & ADMINISTRATIVE

PLANIMETRIC MAP OF LIBERIA
1:1, 000, 000
Washington : Coast and Geodetic Survey, 1958
60 x 64
Col. map, roads classified, vegetation etc.

PLANIMETRIC MAP OF LIBERIA
1:500, 000
Washington : Coast and Geodetic Survey, 1957
100 x 100
2 sheet map showing communications, boundaries.

E1 PHYSICAL: RELIEF

CARTE D'ASSEMBLAGE DES SONDAGES DU LIBERIA
by P Rancurel
In 3 sheets
Paris : ORSTOM, 1967
Index sheet of sea depths, with map of 'Topographie du plateau continental Liberien'. With text.

ATLASES
O NATIONAL

LIBERIA IN MAPS
Ed. Stefan von Gnielinski
1st edition
London : Hodder and Stoughton, 1972
22 x 28
112pp
Physical, social, economic and cultural data shown on black and white maps each with explanatory text. Bibliography.
£2.50

666.8 Ivory Coast

See also 66 WEST AFRICA

A1 GENERAL MAPS: ROADS

RÉPUBLIQUE DE CÔTE D'IVOIRE
1:1, 000, 000
Paris : IGN, 1972
New road map with distances and route numbers. F.Fr 20.83

CÔTE D'IVOIRE - ENVIRONS D'ABIDJAN
1:800, 000
No 175
Paris : Michelin, 1971
97 x 96
Roads classified according to condition, distances in km, tourist information inc. petrol stations, game reserves, hotels, places of interest, principal mines. Inset plan of Abidjan. Legend in Fr.

C OFFICIAL SURVEYS

KARTA MIRA
1:2, 500, 000
GUGK (Bulg)
Sheet 112 - Accra - covers the Ivory Coast
see WORLD 100C and index 100/2.

AFRICA
1:2, 000, 000
AMS Series 2201
Sheet 17 covers Ivory Coast
see AFRICA 6C and index 6/2.

INTERNATIONAL MAP OF THE WORLD
1:1, 000, 000
IGN
Sheet required :
Abidjan
also 2781 Carte de Monde OACI
NC 30/31 Carte de l'Afrique
see WORLD 100C and index 100/1.

CARTE DE L'AFRIQUE
1:1, 000, 000
IGN
Sheet required :
NC 30/31
also 2781 Carte du Monde OACI
Abidjan
see AFRICA 6C and index 6/4.

CARTE DU MONDE OACI ÉDITION TERRESTRE
1:1, 000, 000
IGN
Sheet required :
2781 Haut Niger
also NC 30/31 Carte de l'Afrique
Abidjan Int. Map of World
see AFRICA 6C and index 6/4.

CARTE DE L'AFRIQUE DE L'OUEST
1:500, 000
IGN
see WEST AFRICA 66C and index 66/1.

CARTE DE L'AFRIQUE DE L'OUEST
1:200, 000
IGN
see WEST AFRICA 66C and index 66/2.

CARTE DE L'AFRIQUE DE L'OUEST
1:50, 000, Type Outre-Mer
IGN
see WEST AFRICA 66C and index 66/3.

F GEOLOGY

CARTE GÉOLOGIQUE DE LA CÔTE D'IVOIRE
1:1, 000, 000
Abidjan : Dir. Mines et Geol, 1965
Col. geol. map.

G EARTH RESOURCES

CARTE SÉDIMENTOLOGIQUE DU PLATEAU CONTINENTAL DE CÔTE D:IVOIRE
1:200, 000
In 3 sheets
by L. Martin
Paris : ORSTOM, 1973
Col. map depicting superficial underwater deposits with Notice No 48.
F.Fr 40.00

CARTE D'ASSEMBLAGE DES SONDAGES DE CÔTE D'IVOIRE (1 sheet)
TOPOGRAPHIE DU PLATEAU CONTINENTAL IVOIRIEN (2 sheets)
by P Rancurel
Paris : ORSTOM, 1967
Set of 3 sheets, an index of depth sounding and relief map of continental plateau off Ivory Coast with Notice No 35.
F.Fr 24.00

CARTE PÉDOLOGIQUE DE LA RÉPUBLIQUE DE LA CÔTE D'IVOIRE
1:2, 000, 000
by B Dabin et al
Paris : ORSTOM, 1960
Col. soil map with 31pp text.
F.Fr 12.00

CARTE PÉDOLOGIQUE DE LA RÉGION DE BEREBY
by A Perraud
1:50, 000
Paris : ORSTOM, 1963
Col. soil map, with Land Use Map for the same region in black and white.
F.Fr 12.00

CARTE PÉDOLOGIQUE DE LA RÉGION DE SASSANDRA-SAN-PEDRO
by A Perraud
1:50, 000
Paris : ORSTOM, 1964
2 sheet col. soil map; with Land Use Map for the same region, in black and white.
F.Fr 12.00

CARTE PÉDOLOGIQUE DU SECTEUR TABOU - OLODIO - NIDIA
1:50, 000
by P de la Souchere
Paris : ORSTOM, 1963
Col. soil map, with 'Carte de vocation culturale Tabou-Olodio-Nidia' (potential land yield). F.Fr 12.00

H BIOGEOGRAPHY

CARTE DE LA VÉGÉTATION DE LA RÉGION DE BEREBY
by A Perraud
1:50, 000
Paris : ORSTOM, 1963
Col. vegetation map. F.Fr 12.00

ATLASES
L ECONOMIC

ATLAS DES STRUCTURES AGRAIRES AU SUD DU SAHARA
Part 5 - Adiamprikofiko - Douakankro
Etude geographique d'un terroir baoule
ORSTOM, 1968
see WEST AFRICA 66

ATLASES
O NATIONAL

ATLAS DE CÔTE D'IVOIRE
Part 1
Ministère du Plan - Université d'Abidjan
1st edition
Paris : ORSTOM, 1971
58 x 43
15pp coloured maps, 18pp descriptive text. Contained in loose leaf binder, maps accompanied by descriptive text in French.

667 Ghana

See also: 66 WEST AFRICA

Thematic maps :
see also GHANA ATLASES
O NATIONAL (The Ghana Atlas)

A1 GENERAL MAPS: ROADS

GHANA ROAD MAP
1:500, 000
6th edition
Accra : Surv. Ghana, 1970
94 x 71 each section
Map in 2 sections - North and South, each 2 sheets, roads classified with official numbering and distances in miles, admin. boundaries etc.
each C 1.80
Mounted C 2.00
Mounted CR C 3.80

A2 GENERAL MAPS: LOCAL

SPECIALIST PROJECT MAPS
Accra : Surv. Ghana
Various sizes
Available for dam and river projects.
Sunprints if no printed copy available.
Accra-Weijer (water supply)
1:5, 000 17 sheets 65 pesewas
Bui Dam Project
1:25, 000 20 sheets 65 pesewas
Mpaitri
1:2, 000 4 sheets 60 pesewas
Offin River Project
1:2, 500 41 sheets 65 pesewas
Offin River Project
1:12, 500 10 sheets 65 pesewas
Pakro Dam Site
1:5, 000 11 sheets C 1.30
Pra River Project
1:10, 000 32 sheets C 1.00
Tanoso (Tano River Project)
1:2, 000 18 sheets C 1.00

THE SOUTHERN SAVANNAH AREA
1:16, 000
Accra : Surv. Ghana
Uncontoured series, based on aerial photographs.
Each 60 pesewas

THE LOWER VOLTA FLOOD PLAIN AREA
1:16, 000
Accra : Surv. Ghana
Contoured series, based on aerial photographs.
Each 60 pesewas

THE VOLTA RIVER AREA
1:5, 000
DOS 13 (G 851)
Edition 1
In 22 sheets
Tolworth : DOS, 1948
Maps compiled from air photographs.
Each 40 pesewas (30p)

VOLTA DELTA
1:5, 000
DOS 12 (G 852)
Edition 1
In 8 sheets
Tolworth : DOS, 1947
Large scale series of topog. plans.
Each 30p

B TOWN PLANS

A GUIDE MAP OF ACCRA
1:20, 000
Accra : Surv. Ghana
Tourist map in col. naming principal roads and public buildings.
50 pesewas
Mounted CR C 1.00

NAVRONGO AND ENVIRONS
1:12, 500
Accra : Surv. Ghana
Map based on aerial photographs.
60 pesewas

CITY OF ACCRA
1:10, 000
In 6 sheets
Accra : Surv. Ghana
142 x 162 complete
Plan showing roads with names, govt. and public buildings.
Each 60 pesewas

TOWN MAPS
1:6, 250
Accra : Surv. Ghana
Covering principal towns of Ghana showing road patterns, contours, ward boundaries.
Available for :
Akropong and Abiriu
Asamankese
Atuabo
Axim
Beyin
Cape Coast
Dunkwa
Elmina
Essiama
Half Assini
Ho (4 sheets)
Keta
Kibi
Koforidua
Kumasi (3 sheets)
Nsawam
Oda (2 sheets)
Salaga
Saltpond
Sekondi-Takoradi (6 sheets)
Sunyani
Swedru (Agona)
Tamale
Tarkwa
Winneba
Each C 1.00

CITY OF KUMASI
1:5, 000
Accra : Surv. Ghana
2 sheets covering the City centre.
Each C 1.50
Mounted each C 2.00

TOWN PLANS
1:2, 500
Accra : Surv. Ghana
Large scale plans for most towns.
Contours brown, buildings grey, some named. Some sheets only available as sunprints.
Plans available :

Accra	240 sheets
Achiase	3 sheets
Agogo	4 sheets
Agona Junction	2 sheets
Akuse	19 sheets
Anomabu	1 sheet
Asakraka	1 sheet
Asankrangwa	4 sheets
Bawku	26 sheets
Bechem	8 sheets
Begoro	3 sheets
Bekwai	6 sheets
Bepong	1 sheet
Berekum	3 sheets
Bibiani	9 sheets
Bimbila	4 sheets
Bole	9 sheets
Bolgatanga	2 sheets
Bunsu Plantation	5 sheets
Cape Coast	38 sheets
Chereponi	14 sheets
Damongo	10 sheets
Dodowa	6 sheets
Dunkwa	7 sheets
Efiduase and Asokori	4 sheets
Elmina	9 sheets
Essiama	1 sheet
Foso	12 sheets
Gambaga	2 sheets
Gambaga Escarpment	12 sheets
Gushiegu	15 sheets
Half Assini	2 sheets
Ho	12 sheets
Hohoe	11 sheets
Inchaban	1 sheet
Jasikan	4 sheets
Keta	10 sheets
Kete Krachi	8 sheets
Kikam	1 sheet
Kintampo	1 sheet
Koforidua	8 sheets
Kokofu	1 sheet
Komenda	1 sheet
Konongo-Odumasi	6 sheets
Kpandai	9 sheets
Kpong	11 sheets
Kotoku	1 sheet
Kokurantumi	8 sheets
Kumasi	165 sheets
Kumbungu	9 sheets
Kwahu Tafo	1 sheet
Langbinsi	16 sheets
Lawra	1 sheet
Mampong (Ashanti)	6 sheets
Mankessim	1 sheet
Nakpanduri	9 sheets
Nalerigu	15 sheets
Navrongo	15 sheets
New Drobo	1 sheet
Nkawkaw	6 sheets

Nkoranza	1 sheet
Nkrofro	2 sheets
Nkwatia	2 sheets
Nsawam	11 sheets
Nsuta	1 sheet
Nteso	1 sheet
Nyakrom	9 sheets
Nyankpala	14 sheets
Obenemasi	1 sheet
Odumasi-Somanya	16 sheets
Pokoasi	4 sheets
Pong-Tamale	12 sheets
Pramkese	1 sheet
Saboba	16 sheets
Sakogu	12 sheets
Salaga	2 sheets
Saltpond	6 sheets
Savelugu	18 sheets
Senchi-Ogoli	9 sheets
Senya-Breku	6 sheets
Shama	2 sheets
Shama Junction	1 sheet
Sogakofe	6 sheets
Sunyani	4 sheets
Swedru (Agona)	5 sheets
Tamale	125 sheets
Tarkwa	7 sheets
Tema	149 sheets
Tolon	13 sheets
Wa	15 sheets
Wanchi	2 sheets
Wenchi	3 sheets
Wiawso	8 sheets
Winneba	28 sheets
Yendi	2 sheets
Each	65 pesewas

TOWN PLANS
1:1, 250
Accra : Surv. Ghana
Cadastral series, for important towns, showing buildings in grey, contours in brown at 5 foot intervals. Many plans on this scale now superseded by 1:2, 500 series.
Plans available :

Abetifi	2 sheets
Abodum	4 sheets
Aburi	4 sheets
Accra	230 sheets
Ada	9 sheets
Adaiso	5 sheets
Adukrom	3 sheets
Agogo	2 sheets
Akropong and Abiriu	5 sheets
Akwatia	4 sheets
Anomabu	3 sheets
Anwiawso	2 sheets
Asamankese	7 sheets
Asankrangwa	3 sheets
Atuabo	10 sheets
Axim	4 sheets
Begro	6 sheets
Bekwai	16 sheets
Berekum	6 sheets
Beyin	3 sheets
Bebiani	6 sheets
Big Ada	8 sheets
Bisa	8 sheets
Bolgatanga	2 sheets
Duakwa	9 sheets
Dunkwa	13 sheets
Elmina	10 sheets
Enchi	6 sheets
Esiama	4 sheets
Goaso	4 sheets
Half Assini	6 sheets
Insu	5 sheets
Kibi	13 sheets
Kikam	1 sheet
Koforidua	19 sheets
Komenda	16 sheets
Kukurantumi	2 sheets
Kumasi	136 sheets
Kumawu	1 sheet
Kwanyaku	4 sheets
Larteh	8 sheets
Mampong (Akwapim)	8 sheets
Mampong (Ashanti)	3 sheets
Mamfe & Amanokrom	7 sheets
Mangoasi	9 sheets
Manso-Nkwanta	1 sheet
Mpraeso	6 sheets
Nkawkaw	13 sheets
Nsawam	13 sheets
Obo	3 sheets
Obomen	4 sheets
Odumasi	15 sheets
Prampram	4 sheets
Salaga	26 sheets
Saltpond	20 sheets
Savelugu	10 sheets
Sefwi Bekwai	2 sheets
Sekondi-Takoradi	107 sheets
Shama	2 sheets
Suhum	5 sheets
Swedru (Agona)	15 sheets
Swedru (Akim)	7 sheets
Tafo	29 sheets
Tamale	32 sheets
Teshi	6 sheets
Tema	133 sheets
Walewale	7 sheets
Wenchi	4 sheets
Wiawso	4 sheets
Winneba	16 sheets
Each	40 pesewas

AKOSOMBO TOWN
1:500
Accra : Surv. Ghana
Large scale plans produced for the development of the town. Contoured at 2 foot intervals.
Each 60 pesewas

C OFFICIAL SURVEYS

AFRICA
1:2, 000, 000
AMS Series 2201
Sheet 17 covers Ghana
see AFRICA 6C and index 6/2.

CARTE DU MONDE OACI ÉDITION TERRESTRE
1:1, 000, 000
IGN
see AFRICA 6C and index 6/4.

CARTE DE L'AFRIQUE
1:1, 000, 000
IGN
see AFRICA 6C and index 6/4.

GHANA
1:250, 000
In 23 sheets, see index 667/1.
Accra : Surv. Ghana
34 x 44 each
Text in black, contours and principal roads in brown, water in blue and admin. boundaries in red.
Each 40 pesewas

GHANA
1:125, 000
In 88 sheets (approx) see index 667/2
Accra : Surv. Ghana
34 x 44 each
Series in progress. Text in black, contours and principal roads in brown, water in blue and admin. boundaries in red.

GHANA
1:62, 500
see index 667/3
Accra : Surv. Ghana
74 x 56
Topographical series based on ground surveys of 1923-42 with occasional revision. Contours, regional and district boundaries. 40 pesewas

GHANA
1:50, 000
DOS 414 (G 751)
Editions 1 and 2
see index 667/3
Tolworth : DOS, 1952-53
Topographical series available in either contoured or uncontoured editions.
Each 30p

GHANA
1:50, 000
see index 667/3
Accra : Surv. Ghana, 1966
New topographical series constructed by DOS but published Surv. Ghana, currently available for northern part of the country.

AERIAL PHOTOGRAPHS
Various scales
Accra : Surv. Ghana
Available at various scales covering towns, villages and other specific areas.

CADASTRAL PLANS
Accra : Surv. Ghana
Plans at various scales, showing plans of sites, lease plots, stool land boundaries, concessions etc.

D POLITICAL & ADMINISTRATIVE

GHANA
1:2, 000, 000
DOS 17/13
Tolworth : DOS, 1947
Admin. boundaries, road and rail communications. 10p

GHANA - LOCAL COUNCILS
1:1, 000, 000
Accra : Surv. Ghana, 1969
59 x 82
Admin. boundaries on white background, with communications.

ELECTORAL DISTRICTS MAP
1:1, 000, 000
Accra : Surv. Ghana
Shows 140 electoral districts established in 1967. C 1.00

GREY BASE MAPS
Accra : Surv. Ghana

1:500, 000 (4 sheets)	15 pesewas each
1:1, 000, 000	20 pesewas
1:1, 500, 000	15 pesewas
1:2, 000, 000	10 pesewas

Outline maps of Ghana for planning and lecture purposes.

E1 PHYSICAL: RELIEF

GANA
1:1, 250, 000
Moskva : GUGK, 1970
52 x 68
Physical map, contoured with communications and them. insets.

REGIONAL WALL MAP OF GHANA
1:1, 000, 000
London : Philip
86 x 56
Political col. with communications and boundaries.
Paper flat £1.50
Mounted CR £5.50
Mounted on cloth dissected to fold £7.00

THE WALL MAP OF GHANA
1:400, 000
Accra : Surv. Ghana, 1960
183 x 142
Relief wall map for schools or offices. Contours, boundaries, communications.
C 4.40
Mounted CR C 5.00

F GEOLOGY

GHANA - GEOLOGICAL MAP
1:1, 000, 000
Accra : Surv. Ghana, 1955/8
Illus. geol. structure in col.

H BIOGEOGRAPHY

GHANA - FORESTRY
1:500, 000
In 4 sheets
Accra : Surv. Ghana
94 x 71 each section (2 sheets joined) north and south.
Ghana road map overprinted in green with existing and proposed forest reserves and centres, land planning areas and game reserves. In 2 sections North and South, each comprising 2 joined sheets.
Each section C 1.05

N MATHEMATICAL

FRAMEWORK DIAGRAMS
1:1, 000, 000
Accra : Surv. Ghana
Shows primary and secondary triangulation, primary, secondary, tertiary traverses, primary and secondary levels.
60 pesewas

ATLASES
O NATIONAL

THE GHANA ATLAS
1:2, 000, 000
Accra : Surv. Ghana
24 x 36 each
Includes the following plates which are also available separately :
Administrative, 1969 40 pesewas
Physical, 1969 40 pesewas
Vegetation Zones, 1969 40 pesewas
Agricultural Products, 1969 40 pesewas
Mineral Deposits, 1969 40 pesewas
Annual Rainfall, 1968 40 pesewas
Isogonic 40 pesewas
Great Soil Groups, 1969 50 pesewas
Geological, 1969 60 pesewas
Volta River Project (Flood Limits) 40 pesewas
Population (1960) 40 pesewas
Also available : Portfolio of Ghana Maps, containing 9 of the above maps, with 3 city plans : Accra, Kumasi, Sekondi-Takoradi. C 3.50

PORTFOLIO OF GHANA MAPS
1:2, 000, 000
Accra : Surv. Ghana
see THE GHANA ATLAS

ATLASES
K HUMAN GEOGRAPHY

POPULATION ATLAS OF GHANA
Edited by T E Hilton
London : Nelson, 1960
30 x 41
40pp
Maps showing comparative distribution, density, increase and decrease of pop. for significant years with maps illus. social and economic factors. £2.50

668.1 Togo

See also: 66 WEST AFRICA

A1 GENERAL MAPS: ROADS

CARTE ROUTIÈRE ET TOURISTIQUE DE LA RÉPUBLIQUE DU TOGO
1:500, 000
Paris : IGN, 1960
50 x 111
Col. road and tourist map, with distances, contours, hill shading. F.Fr 29.83

B TOWN PLANS

PLAN DE LOME
1:15, 000
Paris : IGN, 1960
72 x 28
Col. town plan with street index and guide.
F.Fr 16.67

C OFFICIAL SURVEYS

CARTE DE L'AFRIQUE
1:1, 000, 000
IGN
Sheets required :
NC 30/31, NC 31/32
also 2816 Volta - Carte du Monde OACI
see AFRICA 6C and index 6/4.

CARTE DU MONDE OACI ÉDITION TERRESTRE
1:1, 000, 000
IGN
Sheet required :
2816 Volta
also NC 30/31, NC 31/32
Carte de l'Afrique
see AFRICA 6C and index 6/4.

CARTE DE L'AFRIQUE DE L'OUEST
1:500, 000
IGN
see WEST AFRICA 66C and index 66/1.

CARTE DE L'AFRIQUE DE L'OUEST
1:200, 000
IGN
see WEST AFRICA 66C and index 66/2.

CARTE DE L'AFRIQUE DE L'OUEST
1:50, 000
IGN
see WEST AFRICA 66C and index 66/3.

G EARTH RESOURCES

CARTE PÉDOLOGIQUE DU TOGO
by M Lamouroux
1:1, 000, 000
Paris : ORSTOM, 1967
46 x 69
Col. soil map with 92pp text, 1969.
F.Fr 35.00

LAND USE POTENTIAL MAPS
by J Vieillejon
1:50, 000
Paris : ORSTOM
Maps available :
Carte des aptitudes culturales des sols de la région des Savanes. In 5 sheets, showing actual productivity, 1965 and potential, 1966.
Carte des aptitudes culturales des sols de la région maritime. In 5 sheets, showing actual productivity, 1965 and potential, 1966.
Carte pédologique de la région maritime. In 5 sheets, 1966.
Carte pédologique de la région des Savanes. In 5 sheets, 1966.
Each F.Fr 12.00

L ECONOMIC

TOGO (PHYSIQUE)
Editions MDI
Economic map on reverse
see TOGO 668 E1

668.2 Benin

See also: 66 WEST AFRICA

A1 GENERAL MAPS: ROADS

CARTE TOURISTIQUE ET ROUTIÉRE
DE LA RÉPUBLIQUE DU DAHOMEY
1:500, 000
Paris : IGN, 1968
70 x 184
2 sheet road and tourist map, with distances, topog. detail.

C OFFICIAL SURVEYS

AFRICA
1:2, 000, 000
AMS Series 2201
Sheet 17 covers Dahomey
see AFRICA 6C and index 6/2.

CARTE DE L'AFRIQUE
1:1, 000, 000
IGN
Sheets required :
NC 30/31, NC 31/32
also ND 31 Niamey, Int. Map of World
and 2816 Volta, Carte du Monde OACI.
see AFRICA 6C and index 6/4.

INTERNATIONAL MAP OF THE WORLD
1:1, 000, 000
IGN
Sheet required :
ND 31 Niamey
also NC 30/31, NC 31/32 Carte de l'Afrique
and 2816 Carte du Monde OACI.
see WORLD 100C and index 100/1.

CARTE DU MONDE OACI ÉDITION
TERRESTRE
1:1, 000, 000
IGN
Sheet required :
2816 Volta
also ND 31 Niamey, Int. Map of the World
and NC 30/31, NC 31/32 Carte de l'Afrique.
see AFRICA 6C and index 6/4.

CARTE DE L'AFRIQUE DE L'OUEST
1:500, 000
IGN
see WEST AFRICA 66C and index 66/1.

CARTE DE L'AFRIQUE DE L'OUEST
1:200, 000
IGN
see WEST AFRICA 66C and index 66/2.

CARTE DE L'AFRIQUE DE L'OUEST
1:50, 000
IGN
see WEST AFRICA 66C and index 66/3.

F GEOLOGY

CARTE GÉOLOGIQUE DE L'AFRIQUE
OCCIDENTALE FRANÇAISE
1:500, 000
Dakar : Dir. Geol. Prosp. Min.
Col. geol. series with explanatory texts.
see WEST AFRICA 66F and index 66/5.

G EARTH RESOURCES

CARTE PÉDOLOGIQUE DU DAHOMEY
by P Williame and B Volkoff
1:1, 000, 000
Paris : ORSTOM, 1967
63 x 86
Col. soil map, text in preparation.
F.Fr 15.00

CARTE PÉDOLOGIQUE DE LA RÉGION
D'AGONVY
by R Fauck
1:20, 000
Paris : ORSTOM, 1961
Col. soil map, also land use map 'Carte d'utilisation des terres de la région d'Angovy' in black and white. F.Fr 12.00

CARTE PÉDOLOGIQUE DU SECTEUR DE
BOUKOMBE
by P Williame
1:20, 000
Paris : ORMSTOM, 1963
Col. soil map with land use map 'Carte d'utilisation des terres du secteur de Boukombe'. F.Fr 12.00

CARTE PÉDOLOGIQUE D'AGAME
by P Williame
1:10, 000
In 3 sheets
Paris : ORSTOM, 1962
Col. soil map with black and white land use map 'Carte d'utilisation des terres d'Agame'.
F.Fr 12.00

669 Nigeria

See also: 66 WEST AFRICA

for Thematic Maps
see also 669 NIGERIA, ATLASES 01
Nigeria Atlas
Plates available individually

A1 GENERAL MAPS: ROADS

ROAD MAP OF NIGERIA
1:1, 585, 000
Lagos : Fed. Surv. 1972
92 x 75
Roads classified by col, numbered, mileages, railways, boundaries, ferries.

ROADS OF THE NORTHERN PROVINCES
1:2, 000, 000
Lagos : Fed. Surv.
General road map.

ROAD MAP OF THE WESTERN PROVINCES
1:750, 000
Lagos : Fed. Surv.
General road map.

B TOWN PLANS

THE NATION'S CAPITAL - A STREET GUIDE TO LAGOS
1:20, 000
Lagos : Fed. Surv. 1975
57 x 79
Coloured plan of town and environs with index to streets and public buildings. 5 large scale inset plans.

TOWN WALL MAPS
1:15, 000
Lagos : Fed. Surv.
Available for Ikoyi and Lagos.

LAGOS
1:12, 500
In 7 sheets
Lagos : Fed. Surv.
Various sizes
Naming roads and principal buildings.

NIGERIA - TOWNSHIP MAPS
1:12, 500 unless otherwise stated
Lagos : Fed. Surv.
Plans available :
Aba
Argungu
Bama
Bauchi
Bida
Birnin Kebbi
Calabar
Enugu
Enugu 1:10, 000 (Photomosaic)
Funtua
Gboko
Gboko (Photomosaic)
Gombe
Gusau
Hadejia
Ibi (Photomosaic)
Idah
Ikot Ekpene
Ilorin
Jimeta
Jos
Kabba
Kaduna
Kaduna SW
Kano
Kano Township
Kano Airport
Katsina
Keffi
Kontagora
Lokoja
Lokoja (Photomosaic)
Maiduguri
Makurdi
Minna
Mubi
Nguru
Nsukka
Onitsha
Oturkpo
Port Harcourt
Samuru
Sokoto
Umuahia - Ibeku 1:10, 000
Uyo
Uzuakoli 1:10, 000 (Photomosaic)
Wusasa
Yola
Zaria
Zungeru

NIGERIA TOWN PLANS
Various scales
DOS 130
Tolworth : DOS
Plans available :
Ikeja and Environs
1:1, 200 1965 29 shts pub'd
Port Harcourt
1:4, 800 1966 26 shts pub'd
Enugu
1:4, 800 1966 13 shts pub'd
Each sheet 30p

NIGERIA TOWN PLANS - LAGOS
1:1, 200
DOS 0030
Tolworth : DOS, 1970
Large scale plan, 4 sheets published.
Each 30p

C OFFICIAL SURVEYS

KARTA MIRA
1:2, 500, 000
Carti - GUGK (Bulg)
2 sheets to cover Nigeria :
93 Niamey
112 Lagos
see WORLD 100C and index 100/2

AFRICA
1:2, 000, 000
AMS Series 2201
Sheets 13, 17, 18 for Nigeria.
see AFRICA 6C and index 6/2.

INTERNATIONAL MAP OF THE WORLD
1:1, 000, 000
IGN
see WORLD 100C and index 100/1.

CARTE DE L'AFRIQUE
1:1, 000, 000
IGN
see AFRICA 6C and index 6/4.

CARTE DU MONDE OACI ÉDITION TERRESTRE
1:1, 000, 000
IGN
see AFRICA 6C and index 6/4.

NIGERIA
1:500, 000
In 33 sheets, see index 669/2
Lagos : Fed. Surv, 1970
New topog. series in progress to replace the earlier 16 sheet edition. Contoured with communications, towns and villages.

NIGERIA
1:500, 000
In 16 sheets, see index 669/1
Lagos : Fed. Surv, 1960-65
68 x 58 each
General road map series, roads classified, relief by contours, railways, boundaries, other topog. information. Sheet 16 legend sheet.

NIGERIA
1:250, 000
See index 669/3
Lagos : Fed. Surv.
44 x 55
Topog. series, not all sheets contoured, with roads, railways, boundaries and predominant vegetation types.

NIGERIA
1:100, 000 - 1:125, 000
See index 669/4
Lagos : Fed. Surv.
55 x 55
Topog. series in progress; some sheets contoured, some uncontoured. More recent 1:100, 000 series to eventually replace older 1:125, 000 series. Varying sizes.

NIGERIA
1:100, 000
DOS 44 (G662), Edition 1
See index 669/5
Tolworth : DOS, 1953-56
Topog. series in progress, uncontoured.
Each 30p

NIGERIA
1:50, 000
See index 669/6
Lagos : Fed. Surv.
60 x 83
Topog. series in progress, available in either planimetric (uncontoured) or contoured edition. Some sheets have been prepared by DOS but are published by Fed. Surv.

NIGERIA
1:50, 000
DOS 430 (G762)
See index 669/5
Tolworth : DOS, 1954-69
60 x 83
Topog. series in progress;
Uncontoured edition each 30p
Contoured edition each 50p

CONTOUR MAP OF THE ESCARPMENT AREA (RIVERS STATE)
1:5, 000
In 54 sheets
Lagos : Fed. Surv.
Topog. series. 4/-

D POLITICAL & ADMINISTRATIVE

STATES MAP OF NIGERIA
1:3, 000, 000
Lagos : Fed. Surv.
50 x 46
Administrative map. 5/-

STATES MAP OF NIGERIA
1:2, 000, 000
Lagos : Fed. Surv.
68 x 56
Showing political boundaries in colour.
7/6

ADMINISTRATIVE WALL MAP
1:1, 000, 000
In 4 sheets
Lagos : Fed. Surv, 1968
139 x 112 complete
Each state illus. in col. showing roads, boundaries, towns and villages.

LOCAL GOVERNMENT OF THE EASTERN PROVINCES
1:750, 000
Lagos : Fed. Surv.
Local government boundaries in colour.

OUTLINE MAP OF THE EASTERN PROVINCES
1:750, 000
Lagos : Fed. Surv.
Black and white map, showing rivers, principal road and rail communications.

OUTLINE MAP OF THE WESTERN PROVINCES
1:1, 500, 000
Lagos : Fed. Surv. 5/-

NIGERIA - PROVINCIAL MAPS
Various scales
Lagos : Fed. Surv.
Boundaries, principal roads and towns.
Maps available :
Bauchi 1:500, 000
Benin 1:500, 000
Benue (2 sheets)
1:500, 000
Bornu 1:750, 000
Delta 1:500, 000
Egba 1:250, 000
Egbado 1:250, 000
Ibadan 1:250, 000
Ife Ilesha 1:250, 000
Ilorin 1:750, 000
Kano 1:500, 000
Katsina 1:500, 000
Okitipupa 1:125, 000
Ondo (W State)
1:500, 000
Ondo (M W State)
1:500, 000
Oshun 1:250, 000
Owo 1:250, 000
Oyo 1:250, 000
Rivers 1:500, 000
Sokoto (2 sheets)
1:500, 000
Zaria 1:500, 000

NIGERIA - STATE MAPS
Various scales
Lagos : Fed. Surv.
Maps available :
Benue Plateau State
1:1, 000, 000 General
Lagos State 1968 96 x 64
1:250, 000 Topog.
Mid-Western State
1:500, 000 General
North Central State
1:250, 000 Admin.
North Eastern State
1:100, 000 General
North Western State
1:2, 000, 000 Admin.
North Western State
1:1, 000, 000 General
Rivers State 1968 98 x 74
1:250, 000 Topog.
Rivers State 4 sheets
1:250, 000 Outline
South Eastern State 4 sheets
1964 102 x 123
1:250, 000 Topog.

NIGERIA - DIVISIONAL MAPS
Various scales
Lagos : Fed. Surv.
Boundaries and principal roads and towns.
Maps available :
Aboh 1:250, 000
Afenmai 1:250, 000
Ahoada 1:250, 000
Asaba 1:125, 000
Calabar 1:250, 000
Eket 1: 63, 360
Ishan 1:125, 000
Midwest 1:500, 000
Obubra 1:100, 000
Udi 1:125, 000
Urhobo 1:250, 000
Warri 1:250, 000
Western Ijo 1:250, 000
Zaria 1:500, 000

E1 PHYSICAL: RELIEF

NIGERIA
1:2, 000, 000
Moskva : GUGK, 1970
68 x 75
Physical map, contoured with them. insets.

REGIONAL WALL MAP OF NIGERIA
1:1, 400, 000
London : Philip
107 x 84
Physical col. with communications.
Paper flat £1.50
Mounted CR £5.50
Mounted on cloth dissected to fold £7.00

PHYSICAL WALL MAP
1:1, 000, 000
In 4 sheets
5th edition
Lagos : Fed. Surv, 1965
139 x 112
Relief by contours at 1, 000 ft. intervals, layer col, roads, boundaries, towns and villages.

F GEOLOGY

GEOLOGICAL AND MINERAL MAP
1:5, 000, 000
Lagos : Fed. Surv.
Col. map showing location of minerals by symbols.

GEOLOGICAL MAP OF NIGERIA
1:2, 000, 000
Lagos : Fed. Surv, 1964
68 x 56
Coloured geol. map with reliability diagram.

BENUE VALLEY
1:500, 000
DOS (Geol) 1137-A
Tolworth : DOS, 1963
2 maps covering the region :
(Geol) 1137 Base geol. map
(Geol) 1137A Bouguer Gravity Contours
Each 30p

CHAD BASIN SW
1:500, 000
DOS (Geol) 1136-A
Tolworth : DOS, 1963
2 maps covering the region :
(Geol) 1136 Base geol. map
(Geol) 1136A Bouguer Gravity Contours
Each 30p

GEOLOGICAL MAP SERIES OF NIGERIA
1:250, 000
In 85 sheets, see index 669/3
Lagos : Federal Survey
44 x 44
Col. geol. series on same sheet lines as 200, 000 topog. series.

NIGERIA GEOLOGICAL SERIES
1:100, 000
Lagos : Geol. Survey
55 x 55
Series of col. geol. maps in progress on same sheet lines as topog. editions with explanation in Geol. Bulletin 32.
Sheets published :
147 Lere 1962
148 Toro 1963
168 Naraguta 1963
169 Maijuju 1962
190 Pankshin 1962
189 Kurra 1964
DOS 65p

G EARTH RESOURCES

SOIL MAPS OF NIGERIA
1:250, 000
See index 669/3
Tolworth : DOS, 1970
54 x 84 each
Col. soil map series, following sheet lines of 250, 000 Topog. series.
Sheets published :
(LR) 3070 Maiduguri Sheet 27
(LR) 3039 AB Biu Sheets 37 & 38
Each 65p

NIGERIA - SOILS
1:100, 000
Tolworth : DOS, 1970
Col. soil maps generally following topog. sheet lines.
Sheets available :
Bui Plateau, sheets 37, 38
DOS (LR) 3038 AB
DOS (LR) 3039 AB, in 2 sheets
113 pt, 134 and 154 pt, 155
Each 65p

KANO PLAINS - SOIL SURVEY
1:50, 000
Prepared by V da Costs
Nairobi : Univ. of Nairobi, 1972
71 x 68
Coloured soil map. K.Sh. 70

H BIOGEOGRAPHY

FORESTRY RESERVES OF THE EASTERN PROVINCES
1:750, 000
Lagos : Fed. Surv.
Forest reserves in green.

FOREST MAP OF THE NORTHERN PROVINCES
1:3, 000, 000
Lagos : Fed. Surv.
Forest areas in green.

SOUTHERN CAMEROONS - BAMENDA
1:250, 000
DOS (Misc) 298 A-D
Tolworth : DOS, 1961
A 5-map study of the Bamenda region:
(Misc) 298 Sketch Map
(Misc) 298A Map 1 - Forest Reserves, Watersheds, Tsete Fly Limits
(Misc) 298B Map 2 - Land Form
(Misc) 298C Map 3 - Vegetation and Agricultural Use
(Misc) 298D Map 4 - Agricultural Potential
Each 30p

SOUTHERN SARDAUNA AND SOUTHERN ADAMAWA
1:50, 000
DOS (LR) 3028 AB
Tolworth : DOS, 1966
72 x 88 each
2 maps covering the region :
Land Systems
Agricultural Potential
Each 65p

FARM SETTLEMENT AREA MAPS
1:10, 000
DOS (Misc) 365 A-C
Tolworth : DOS, 1963
Large scale plans of farm areas.
Plans available :
(Misc) 365A Omasi In 2 sheets
(Misc) 365B Igbarium In 2 sheets
(Misc) 365C Chaji In 4 sheets
Each 30p

K HUMAN GEOGRAPHY

REST HOUSES
1:1, 750, 000
Lagos : Fed. Surv.
Base map with rest houses marked by col. symbols.

POPULATION MAP OF THE EASTERN PROVINCES
1:750, 000
Lagos : Fed. Surv.
Black and white map indicating pop. by dots. Based on 1953 Census.

POPULATION OF THE NORTHERN PROVINCES, 1952
1:2, 000, 000
Lagos : Fed. Surv.
Black and white map, showing relative pop. by dots.

NORTHERN NIGERIA - POPULATION DISTRIBUTION
1:1, 000, 000
DOS (Misc) 237, Edition 1
In 4 sheets
Tolworth : DOS, 1959
Distribution indicated by dot method.
Each 30p

NORTHERN NIGERIA - POPULATION DENSITY
1:1, 000, 000
DOS (Misc) 237A, Edition 1
In 4 sheets
Tolworth : DOS, 1961
Density shown by shading.
Each 50p

ATLASES
W3 WORLD ATLAS: LOCAL EDITION

OXFORD ATLAS FOR NIGERIA
OUP, 1968
see 100 W3 WORLD ATLASES

ATLASES
01 NATIONAL: REFERENCE

NIGERIA - ATLAS PLATES
1:3, 000, 000
Lagos : Fed. Surv, 1965+
50 x 46 each
Series of col. thematic maps covering various aspects of country. Available as sets or individually.
Plates available :
Administrative Map
Agricultural Products
Capital Cities - Maiduguri, Kaduna, Kano, 1:50, 000
Capital Cities - Ilorin, Ibadan, Benin City, 1:50, 000
Capital Cities - Lagos - the Nations Capital
Capital Cities - Jos-Sokoto
Capital Cities - Enugu - Port Harcourt, Calabar
Communications, Internal
Communications, Rail Road and River
Educational Facilities
Forest Reserves
Geology and Mineral Deposits
Health Facilities
Humidity, Mean Daily Relative 10.00 hours
Humidity, Mean Daily Relative 16.00 hours
Industries, Main Agricultural Exports and Locations of Mineral Deposits
Languages and Dialects
Mineral Deposits and Power Resources
Physical Map
Railways and Principal Commodities
Rain Days, Mean Annual Number
Rain Days for Twelve Months, Mean Number of (12 small scale maps)
Rainfall, Mean Annual
Rainfall, Mean Monthly (12 small scale maps)
Rest House and Hotels
Soil Map
Telecommunications, Internal (Exchanges & Telephone Routes System)
Telecommunications, Internal (Telegraph & Radio Trunk Routes)
Temperature, Mean Annual Maximum
Temperature, Mean Annual Minimum
Temperature, Mean Annual Range
Temperature, Mean Daily Minimum
Trade, Internal
Tribal
Vegetation Map
Vegetational Zone

ATLASES
O2 NATIONAL: SCHOOL EDITION

A SKETCH MAP ATLAS OF NIGERIA
H O N Oboli
2nd edition
London : George Harrap, 1962
24 x 19
47pp
Revised edition for schools; shows major geographical facts in simplified map form. With brief text and exercises.
22½p

671.1 Cameroon

See also: 672 EQUATORIAL AFRICA

A1 GENERAL MAPS: ROADS

CARTE ROUTIÈRE DU CAMEROUN
1:1, 500, 000
3rd edition
Paris : IGN 1975
65 x 90
Roads in colour, classified, distances in km, relief shading, other communications. Environs of Yaounde and Plan of Douala on reverse. F.Fr 20.83

B TOWN PLANS

TOWN PLANS
1:5, 000 ; 1:10, 000
Paris : IGN
Contoured plans with names of principal streets.
Available for :
Douala, 1965 11 sheets
Each F.Fr 41.67
Garoua, 1965 9 sheets
Each F.Fr 41.67
Nkongsamba, 1966
9 sheets Each F.Fr 41.67
Maroua, 1966 8 sheets
Each F.Fr 41.67
Ngaoundere 1:10, 000,
1964 Each F.Fr 16.67
2 sheets
Yaounde 1:10, 000,
1971 1 sheet
Each F.Fr 16.67

C OFFICIAL SURVEYS

AFRICA
1:2, 000, 000
AMS Series 2201
Sheets 18 and 21 cover Cameroun
see AFRICA 6C and index 6/2.

INTERNATIONAL MAP OF THE WORLD - CARTE DE L'AFRIQUE CENTRALE
1:1, 000, 000
IGN
see Equatorial and Central Africa 672C and indexes 672/1 and 100/1.

CARTE DU CAMEROUN OCCIDENTAL
1:500, 000
In 10 sheets, see index 672/2
Paris : IGN, 1965
64 x 79 each
Topog. sheet. Provisional ed. without contours, covering the ex-territory of Southern Cameroun
Each F.Fr 20.83

CARTE DE L'AFRIQUE CENTRALE
1:500, 000
IGN
see Equatorial and Central Africa 672C and Index 672/2.

CARTE DE L'AFRIQUE CENTRALE
1:200, 000
IGN
see Equatorial and Central Africa 672C and index 672/3.

CARTE DE L'AFRIQUE CENTRALE
1:50, 000
IGN
see Equatorial and Central Africa 672C and index 672/4.

D POLITICAL & ADMINISTRATIVE

CARTE DE L'ORGANISATION ADMINISTRATIVE
1:3, 666, 666
Paris : IGN, 1965
42 x 27
Principal admin. divisions in black and white.
F.Fr 5.00

CARTE DU CAMEROUN
1:5, 000, 000
Paris : IGN, 1964
27 x 21
Col. map showing hydrography and communications, hunting reserves etc.
F.Fr 5.00

CARTE ADMINISTRATIVE
1:2, 000, 000
Paris : IGN, 1966
39 x 64
Divided by admin. regions - departments, arrondissements. In colour.
F.Fr 11.67

CARTE D'ÉTUDE
1:2, 000, 000
Paris : IGN, 1961
39 x 64
Hydrography, communications, topog. details, admin. divisions in grey, allowing addition of further information.
F.Fr 11.67

CARTE ADMINISTRATIVE ET ROUTIÈRE
1:1, 000, 000
Paris : IGN, 1965
83 x 133
2 sheet map showing admin. boundaries, road classification with distances in km, ethnic and climatic maps inset.
F.Fr 33.33

E1 PHYSICAL: RELIEF

CAMEROUN - CARTE EN RELIEF
1:2, 000, 000
Paris : IGN, 1972
74 x 54
Self-framed moulded plastic relief map. Contours, communications, towns and villages. F.Fr 104.17

F GEOLOGY

ÇARTE GÉOLOGIQUE DE L'AFRIQUE EQUATORIALE ET DU CAMEROUN
1:2, 000, 000
BRGM, 1952
see Equatorial and Central Africa 67 F

CARTE GÉOLOGIQUE DU CAMEROUN
by J Gazel et al
1:1, 000, 000
In 2 sheets
Orléans : BRGM
Col. geol. map with text.

CARTE GÉOLOGIQUE DU CAMEROUN
1:500, 000
Orléans : BRGM, 1953-9
Col. maps with explanatory notes.
Sheets available :
Banyo, by P Koch 1953
Batouri-Est by J Gazel and G.Gerard 1954
Batouri-Ouest by J Gazel 1954
Douala-Est by G Weecksteen 1957
Garoua-Ouest by P Koch 1959
Ngaoundére-Ouest by Ch Guiraudie 1955
Yaoundé-Ouest by G Champetier de Ribes and M Aubague 1956
Yaoundé-Ouest by G Champetier de Ribes and D Reyre 1959
Each F.Fr 24.00

G EARTH RESOURCES

CARTE PÉDOLOGIQUE DE LA CAMEROUN OCCIDENTAL
1:1, 000, 000
Yaoundé : ORSTOM, 1970
49 x 48
Coloured soil map of W Cameroun, with 48pp text, 1971.

CARTE PÉDOLOGIQUE DU CAMEROUN ORIENTAL
by P Segalen and D Martin
1:1, 000, 000
Yaounde : ORSTOM, 1965
90 x 148
2 sheet soil map in col. with 125pp text, 1966. F.Fr 46.00

LES SOLS DU MUNGO ET LEUR UTILISATION
1:500, 000
Yaoundé : ORSTOM, 1965
With 27pp text by D Martin.

ETUDES PÉDOLOGIQUE DANS LE CENTRE-CAMEROUN
Various scales
Yaoundé : ORSTOM, 1965
1 soil map, 1:200, 000, 6 at 1:400, 000, 9 at 1:50, 000, 2 at 1:20, 000, 2 at 1:50, 000 with analytical tables and 162 pp text by D Martin, covering the area Nango-Eboko to Bertona.

LES SOLS DE LA PLAINE DE KOZA MOZOGO
1:200, 000
Yaoundé : ORSTOM, 1954
6pp text by A Combeau et al.

KRIBI : RAPPORT ET CARTE DE LA PROSPECTION
1:200, 000
Yaoundé : ORSTOM, 1951
15pp text by B Lepoutre

ÉTUDE PÉDOLOGIQUE DE LA VALLÉE DU MAYO LOUTI (RÉGION MARBAK-GAOUAR)
1:200, 000
Yaoundé : ORSTOM, 1954
With 10pp text by M Curis.

OBSERVATIONS COMPLÉMENTAIRES DANS LA VALLÉE DU MAYO LOUTI
1:200, 000
Yaoundé : ORSTOM, 1954
2 sheet map, 4pp explanation.

PROSPECTION DE LA RÉGION SISE ENTRE LA ROUTE NKAPA-MBANGA ET LE MUNGO
1:200, 000
Yaoundé : ORSTOM, 1951
7pp text by G Bachelier

OBSERVATIONS SUR LES SOLS VOLCANIQUES DANS LA RÉGION DE NKONGSAMBA
1:100, 000 and 1:200, 000
Yaoundé : ORSTOM, 1954
2 maps with 21pp text by G Combeau.

INTRODUCTION A L'ÉTUDE PÉDOLOGIQUE DE LA VALLÉE DU NOUN
1:200, 000
Yaoundé ' ORSTOM, 1957
1 soil map, 1 soil use map with 12pp text by G Bachelier et al.

CARTE PÉDOLOGIQUE DU NORD-CAMEROUN
1:100, 000
Yaoundé : ORSTOM
The following sheets available :
Kaele by D Martin, 1963, with 100pp text F.Fr 12.00
Yagoua by G Sieffermann and M Vallerie, 1963 F.Fr 12.00
Mousgoy by D Martin and G Sieffermann, 1963, 102pp text F.Fr 12.00
Maroua by P Segalen, 1962 F.Fr 12.00
Mokolo by P Segalen and M Vallerie, 1963 F.Fr 12.00
Kalfou by G Sieffermann, 1963 F.Fr 12.00
Mora by D Martin, 1961, 100pp text.

RECONNAISSANCES PÉDOLOGIQUES DANS LE DÉPARTEMENT DE LA BENQUE
1:100, 000
Yaoundé : ORSTOM, 1962
1 map, List of analysis, 46pp text by D Martin.

CARTE PÉDOLOGIQUE DU CANTON DE LAM
1:100, 000
Yaoundé : ORSTOM, 1957
With 12pp text by M Curis and D Martin.

PROSPECTION PÉDOLOGIQUE DE LA RIVE CAMEROUNAISE AU LOGONE EN VUE DE LA RIZICULTURE
1:100, 000
Yaoundé : ORSTOM, 1951
24pp text by A Laplante et al.

CARTE DE RECONNAISSANCE DE LA RÉGION COMPRISE ENTRE LA DÉPRESSION DE FIANGA ET LE COURS DU LOGONE
1:100, 000
Yaoundé : ORSTOM, 1954
With explanation.

RAPPORT DE TOURNÉE DE LA RÉGION COMPRISE ENTRE MEME ET MAKILINGAI
1:100, 000
Yaoundé : ORSTOM, 1954
With 3pp explanation.

ÉTUDES PÉDOLOGIQUES DANS LE CENTRE-CAMEROUN : NANGA-EBOKO A BETOUA
1:100, 000 and 1:50, 000
Yaoundé : ORSTOM, 1963
4 maps, 35pp text by D Martin.

LES SOLS DE L'OUEST-CAMEROUN
1:50, 000
Yaoundé : ORSTOM, 1957
1 soil map, 1 soil use map for Mbouda-Bamendjida, 53pp text by G Bachelier et al.

RECONNAISSANCE PÉDOLOGIQUE DANS LA VALLÉE DE LA METCHIE
1:50, 000
Yaoundé : ORSTOM, 1956
With 8pp text by G Bachelier and D Martin.

PROSPECTION PÉDOLOGIQUE DE LA PLAINE DES MBO
1:50, 000
Yaoundé : ORSTOM, 1952
22pp text by G Bachelier.

CARTE PÉDOLOGIQUE DE NGAOUNDÉRE
1:50, 000
Paris : ORSTOM, 1968
Coloured soil map; text out of print. F.Fr 12.00

CARTE PÉDOLOGIQUE DU NORD-CAMEROUN
1:50, 000
Yaoundé : ORSTOM
The following sheets available with soil use and analysis sheets :
Bidzar and Guider by M Vallerie, 1964, 70pp text
Pitoa by G Sieffermann, 1964, 51pp text
Boula Ibib by G Sieffermann, 1964, 55pp text.

RECONNAISSANCE PÉDOLOGIQUE DU BASSIN VERSANT DU RISSO A NDOK (NORD-CAMEROUN)
1:50, 000
Yaoundé : ORSTOM, 1970
Col. map with 30pp text by P Brabant.

ÉTUDE PÉDOLOGIQUE DU BASSIN VERSANT DU BOME PRÈS DE TOUBORG (BÉNOUÉ)
1:50, 000
Yaoundé : ORSTOM, 1965
Soil map with 27pp text by F X Humbel.

CARTE PÉDOLOGIQUE DE NGAOUNDERE
by F X Hambel and J Barbery
1:50, 000
Yaoundé : ORSTOM, 1968
Col. soil map.

ÉTUDE PÉDOLOGIQUE DE LA PLAINE DE LA VINA
1:50, 000
Yaoundé : ORSTOM, 1954
With 12pp text by G Bachelier
In same series :
Études pédologiques dans la vallée du Djerem, 14pp text.
Études pédologiques diverses dans la région de Ngaoundére et de Meiganga, 33pp text.

ÉTUDE PÉDOLOGIQUE DU MUNGO
1:20, 000 and 1:50, 000
Yaoundé : ORSTOM, 1960
5 maps, 70pp text by G Sieffermann.

INTRODUCTION A LA PÉDOLOGIE DE L'ADAMAOUA
1:25, 000
Yaoundé : ORSTOM, 1953
40pp text by A Laplante and G Bachelier.

ÉTUDE PÉDOLOGIQUE DE LA PLAINE DE KARTOA
1:25, 000
Yaoundé : ORSTOM, 1954
With 9pp text by A Combeau et al.

ÉTUDES PÉDOLOGIQUES DES BASSES TERRASSES ALLUVIATES DU WOURI ENTRE DOUALA ET YABASSI
1:20, 000
Yaoundé : ORSTOM, 1951
22pp text by B Lepoutre.

ÉTUDE PÉDOLOGIQUE DE PLAINE BANANIERE
1:20, 000
Yaoundé : ORSTOM, 1956
With 30pp text.

CARTE PÉDOLOGIQUE DU PLATEAU DES KAPSIKIS AU SUD DU MOGODE AND RECONNAISSANCE PÉDOLOGIQUE DE DEUX TERRAINS SITUÉS AU SUD DE MAROUA
1:20, 000
Yaoundé : ORSTOM, 1957
2 maps with 20pp text by G Bachelier.

ÉTUDE PÉDOLOGIQUE DU SOUS-SECTEUR DE MODERNISATION DE MOUSGOY
1:20, 000
Yaoundé : ORSTOM, 1957
2 maps, Mousgoy-Belli and Yapere-Libe, with 16pp text, by G Bachelier.

ÉTUDE DE SOLS HALOMORPHES DU NORD-CAMEROUN
1:20, 000
Yaoundé : ORSTOM, 1965
Map for Maroua area, with 63pp text by F X Humbel.

PROSPECTION PÉDOLOGIQUE DES PALMERAIES NATURELLES DU SUD CAMEROUN
1:20, 000
Yaoundé : ORSTOM, 1950
21pp text.

ÉTUDE PÉDOLOGIQUE DE PIEDMONT SUD DU PESKE-BORI
1:20, 000
Yaoundé : ORSTOM, 1967
With 44pp text. 1 soil map and 1 map of agricultural yield.

ÉTUDE PÉDOLOGIQUE DU SECTEUR D'EXTENSION DE LA PALMERAIE DE KOMPINA (MUNGO)
1:20, 000
Yaoundé : ORSTOM, 1966
Col. map with 65pp text by F X Humbel.

ÉTUDE PÉDOLOGIQUE DE LA STATION AGRICOLE DE GUETALE
1:10, 000
Yaoundé : ORSTOM, 1960
17pp text by D Martin

ÉTUDE PÉDOLOGIQUE DU POST DE PAYSANNAT DO MOKIO
1:10, 000
Yaoundé : ORSTOM, 1960
With 19pp text by D Martin.

ÉTUDE PÉDOLOGIQUE DE LA PLAINE DE LOGONE
1:10, 000
Yaoundé : ORSTOM, 1958
Maps available :
No 1 for Secteur Tagoua-Kartoa, 39pp text by D Martin and P Segalen
No 2 for Secteur Kartoa-Merigne, 8 maps, 35pp text by G Sieffermann and D Martin
No 3 for Secteur Djafga-Pouss, 35pp text by D Martin
No 4 Out of print
No 5 for Secteur Nord-Pouss, 1960, 26pp text

RAPPORT DE PROSPECTION DE LA PARTIE NORD-OUEST DE LA FEUILLE DE MAROUA
1:100, 000
Yaoundé : ORSTOM, 1955
With 5pp text by G Claisse.

CARTE PÉDOLOGIQUE DU PÉRIMÈTRE DE REBOISEMENT DU MELAP (FOUMBAN)
1:10, 000
Yaoundé : ORSTOM, 1960
With 11pp text by P Segalen.

ÉTUDE PÉDOLOGIQUE DU SOUS-SECTEUR DE MODERNISATION DE MOUSGOY
1:10, 000
Yaoundé : ORSTOM, 1955
Laboratory study with 11pp text by G Claisse.

ÉTUDE PÉDOLOGIQUE DE LA STATION DU QUINQUINA, DSCHANG BANSOA, NGOUNGE
1:10, 000 and 1:4, 000
Yaoundé : ORSTOM, 1961
2 maps with 27pp text by D Martin.

LES SOLS DU SOUS-SECTEUR DE MODERNISATION DE GOLOMPOUI
1:5, 000
Yaoundé : ORSTOM, 1955
With 13pp text by A Combeau.

ÉTUDE PÉDOLOGIQUE DU SECTEUR DE MODERNISATION DE LARA
1:5, 000
Yaoundé : ORSTOM, 1954
11pp text by G Claisse.

ÉTUDES PÉDOLOGIQUES DANS LE MARGUI - WANDALA
1:5, 000
In 14 sheets
Yaoundé : ORSTOM, 1964
With 30pp text by M Vallerie.

ÉTUDE PÉDOLOGIQUE DANS LE BASSIN DE LA MOYENNE SANAGA
1:5, 000
Yaoundé : ORSTOM, 1950
18pp text by A Laplante.

ATLASES
W3 WORLD: LOCAL EDITION

ATLAS FOR WEST CAMEROON
Collins-Longman, 1971
see WORLD 100 ATLASES W3

ATLASES
L ECONOMIC

ATLAS DES STRUCTURES AGRAIRES DU SAHARA
Part 3 Zengoaga (Cameroons)
ORSTOM
see WEST AFRICA 66 ATLASES L

ATLAS DÉPARTEMENTAUX
Various scales
Yaoundé : ORSTOM, 1960
Series of Departmental atlases illustrating national economic plan.

Atlas du Mbam (2 parts)	1:400, 000
Atlas du Haut Nyong	1:600, 000
Atlas du Lom et Kadei	1:600, 000
Atlas de la Boumba Ngoko	1:600, 000
Atlas du Dja et Lobo	1:500, 000
Atlas du Ntem	1:500, 000

ATLASES
O NATIONAL

ATLAS DU CAMEROUN
Ed F Bonnet-Dupeyron
Paris : ORSTOM, 1960+
36 x 45
Comprehensive national atlas providing complete background to the country. Issued in sections, each containing folded col. maps, explanatory text and diagrams. Covers physical, social, economic and other geographical matters. The first section containing 7 map plates and 34 pages of text has been issued.

671.8 Equatorial Guinea

See also: 672 EQUATORIAL AFRICA

A1 GENERAL MAPS: ROADS

MAPA MILITAR DE LA GUINEA ESPAÑOLA
1:400, 000
Madrid : SGE
General map, contoured, communications and vegetation cover.

C OFFICIAL SURVEYS

MAPA ITINERARIO (TOPOGRÁFICO Y FORESTAL) DE LA GUINEA ESPAÑOLA
1:200, 000
In 4 sheets, see index 671.8/1
Madrid : SGE
Communications with distances, layer colours and forest areas.

ADVANCE DEL MAPA TOPOGRÁFICO FORESTAL DE GUINEA
1:100, 000
In 16 sheets, see index 671.8/1.
Madrid : SGE
Topog. series, contoured, communications and vegetation cover.

MAPA MILITAR DE LA ISLA DE FERNANDO POO
1:100, 000
Madrid : SGE
76 x 94
Topog. map; vegetation col, contours at 100m intervals.

MAPA DE LA ISLA DE FERNANDO POO
1:50, 000
In 4 sheets
Madrid : SGE
135 x 165
Topog. map : roads, settlements, vegetation col, contours at 100m intervals.

672 Equatorial Africa

A1 GENERAL MAPS: ROADS

AFRIQUE CENTRE ET SUD MADAGASCAR
1:4, 000, 000
No 155
Paris : Michelin, 1971
96 x 119
Political boundaries, settlements, forests, tourist features. Roads graded by condition, distances in km and miles. Eng. and Fr.

CARTE DE L'AFRIQUE CENTRALE
1:2, 500, 000
In 2 sheets
Paris : IGN, 1969
Col. communications map, available with or without vegetation cover overprint.
Each F.Fr 27.50

C OFFICIAL SURVEYS

CARTE DE L'AFRIQUE CENTRALE
1:1, 000, 000
In 16 sheets, see index 672/1 and 100/1
Paris : IGN
Coverage of equatorial Africa in Int. Map of the World and Carte de l'Afrique (on ICAO sheet lines) editions. Also 3 special sheets in 6 cols, contoured with layer tints sheets - Yaoundé, Pointe Noire and Franceville-Brazzaville.
Each F.Fr 14.17

CARTE DE L'AFRIQUE CENTRALE
1:500, 000
See index 672/2
Paris : IGN
Topog. series in progress : 2 eds. Normal and Special. Covers Cameroon Republic and surrounding area. Contoured and hill shaded.
Each F.Fr 16.67

CARTE DE L'AFRIQUE CENTRALE
1:200, 000
See index 672/3
Paris : IGN
55 x 55
Topog. series in progress; complete coverage except Northern Chad; varying eds. according to terrain covered. 'Carte Regulière - standard edition, Carte Provisoire - provisional edition. Contours on some sheets only.
Each F.Fr 14.17

CARTE DE L'AFRIQUE CENTRALE
1:50, 000
See index 672/4
Paris : IGN
55 x 55
Topog. series in progress, names black, water blue, contours brown, vegetation green.
Each F.Fr 14.17

D POLITICAL & ADMINISTRATIVE

GENERAL MAP OF CENTRAL AND SOUTH AFRICA
1:5, 500, 000
London : Stanford
79 x 104
Political col, communications, boundaries, spot heights, settlements graded by pop. Pictorial border.
Paper flat or folded 45p
Mounted CRV £3.50

EK VATORIAL'NAYA I YUZHNAYA AFRIKA
Moskva : GUGK, 1971
Map of Central and S Africa showing communications and boundaries.

AFRICA ECUATORIAL Y AUSTRAL
Barcelona : Editorial Teide
25 x 33
General school hand map of Equatorial and Southern Africa, showing major cities and boundaries. Pta. 1

E1 PHYSICAL: RELIEF

STŘEDNÍ AFRIKA
1:6, 000, 000
Praha : USGK, 1966
92 x 78
Physical map of Central Africa, communications, statistics and index on reverse.

WORLD TRAVEL MAP SERIES : CENTRAL AND SOUTHERN AFRICA
1:5, 000, 000
Edinburgh : Bart
72 x 94
Physical map, political boundaries, communications, settlements, topog. detail, contoured, layer col.
Paper flat or folded 75p

MITTEL- UND SÜDLICHES AFRIKA
1:3, 000, 000
Braunschweig : Westermann
235 x 182
Physical col. wall map, political boundaries, relief shading, cities graded by pop.

F GEOLOGY

CARTE GÉOLOGIQUE DE L'AFRIQUE ÉQUATORIALE
1:2, 000, 000
by G Ge
In 4 sheets
Orléans : BRGM, 1956-8
114 x 164 complete
General geol. map of Central African Republic, Chad, Congo and Gabon. Structural sketch map and text.
F.Fr 60.00

CARTE GÉOLOGIQUE DE L'AFRIQUE ÉQUATORIALE ET DU CAMEROUN
by M Nickles
1:2, 000, 000
In 3 sheets
Orléans : BRGM, 1952
Col. geol. map with 109pp text.
F.Fr 50.00

CARTE GÉOLOGIQUE DE RECONNAISSANCE : AFRIQUE ÉQUATORIALE
1:500, 000
See index 672/5
Orléans : BRGM, 1953-63
In 22 coloured sheets with text.
Each sheet F.Fr 24.00

H BIOGEOGRAPHY

CARTE DE RÉPARTITION DES GLOSSINES DE L'AFRIQUE ÉQUATORIALE
by L Maillot
1:2, 000, 000
In 3 sheets
Paris : ORSTOM, 1957
Showing distribution of glossina tsetse fly, with 'Carte de répartition probable des sous-espèces de Glossina palpalis and Glossina fuscipes'. With 23pp text, 1960.
F.Fr 30.00

K HUMAN GEOGRAPHY

ESQUISSE ÉTHNIQUE GÉNÉRALE
1:5, 000, 000
by M M Soret
Paris : IGN, 1962
44 x 67
25 ethnic groups in Central African, Congo, Gabon and Chad republics.
F.Fr 16.67

CARTE ÉTHNIQUE DE L'AFRIQUE ÉQUATORIALE
M Soret
1:1, 000, 000
Paris : ORSTOM
Col. map illustrating ethnic and tribal types and their distribution, on similar sheets to Int. Map of the World.
Maps published :
1 Brazzaville, 1955
2 Pointe Noire, 1955
5 Bangassou, 1962
4 Ouesso, 1962
Each F.Fr 16.00

672.1 Gabon

See also: 672 EQUATORIAL AFRICA

A1 GENERAL MAPS: ROADS

CARTE GÉNÉRALE ET ROUTIÈRE DU GABON
1:1, 000, 000
Edition 2
Paris : IGN, 1975
73 x 86
Classified roads with distances. Railways, airports, reserves and hotels, hospitals, telephones, petrol etc. marked. Plan of Libreville inset.

A2 GENERAL MAPS: LOCAL

LIBREVILLE
1:100, 000
Paris : IGN, 1960
Map in 2 sheets - covering town and vicinity.
Each F.Fr 11.67

B TOWN PLANS

LIBREVILLE ET ENVIRONS
1:20, 000
In 3 sheets
Paris : IGN, 1962
Various sizes
Contoured.
Set F.Fr 27.50

LIBREVILLE
1:10, 000
Paris : IGN, 1970
Col. town plan, contoured.
F.Fr 16.67

PORT GENTIL
1:100, 000
Paris : IGN
4 colour map of the area. UTM grid.
F.Fr 11.67

C OFFICIAL SURVEYS

AFRICA
1:2, 000, 000
AMS Series 2201
Sheet 22 for Gabon.
see AFRICA 6C and index 6/2.

INTERNATIONAL MAP OF THE WORLD - CARTE DE L'AFRIQUE CENTRALE
1:1, 000, 000
IGN
see Equatorial Africa 672C and index 672/1.

CARTE DE L'AFRIQUE CENTRALE
1:200, 000
IGN
see Equatorial Africa 672C and index 672/3.

CARTE DE L'AFRIQUE CENTRALE
1:50, 000
IGN
see Equatorial Africa 672C and index 672/4.

E1 PHYSICAL: RELIEF

GABON
1:1, 000, 000
Libreville : Service de l'Information et de Tourisme, 1971
68 x 75
Physical with tourist details, relief shading.

F GEOLOGY

CARTE GÉOLOGIQUE DE LA RÉPUBLIQUE DU GABON
by H Hudeley
1:1, 000, 000
Orléans : BRGM, 1966
106 x 86
Col. map with Memoir, 192pp, 1970.
F.Fr 130.00

G EARTH RESOURCES

CARTE PÉDOLOGIQUE DE RECONNAISSANCE; LIBREVILLE-KANGO
M Delhumeau
1:200, 000
Paris : ORSTOM, 1969
Coloured soil map with 51pp text.
F.Fr 12.00

672.4 Congo

See also: 672 EQUATORIAL AFRICA

A1 GENERAL MAPS: ROADS

CARTE DU CONGO
1:5, 000, 000
Paris : IGN, 1961
27 x 21
Water features blue, roads red, woodland green. Admin. districts overprinted in magenta. F.Fr 5.00

CARTE ROUTIÈRE DU CONGO ET DE LA REPUBLIQUE GABONAISE
1:1, 500, 000
IGN
see GABON 672.1 A1

CARTE ROUTIÈRE DU CONGO
1:1, 000, 000
Paris : IGN, 1973
87 x 109
Road map of Congo. F.Fr 20.83

A2 GENERAL MAPS: LOCAL

CARTE DU STANLEY POOL
1:50, 000
Paris : IGN, 1964
Shows vegetation, hydrography of the area, planimetric detail. F.Fr 5.83

BRAZZAVILLE ET SES ENVIRONS
1:20, 000
Paris : IGN, 1970
103 x 104
1 sheet map, contoured.
F.Fr 27.50

POINTE NOIRE ET ENVIRONS
1:20, 000
In 4 sheets
Paris : IGN, 1960
Contoured map of the town and environs.
Set F.Fr 23.50

B TOWN PLANS

PLAN DE BRAZZAVILLE
1:10, 000
Paris : IGN, 1964
99 x 63
Map in 6 col, roads named.
F.Fr 16.67

PLAN DE POINTE NOIRE
1:10, 000
Paris : IGN, 1965
99 x 66
2 col. map,contoured with road names.
F.Fr 16.67

C OFFICIAL SURVEYS

KARTA MIRA
1:2, 500, 000
GUGK (Bulg), PPWK
3 sheets to cover Congo (Brazzaville):
113 Lagos
114 Kisangani (Stanleyville)
133 Kinshasa (Leopoldville)
see WORLD 100C and index 100/2.

AFRICA
1:2, 000, 000
AMS Series 2201
Sheets 22, 26 cover Congo.
see AFRICA 6C and index 6/2.

INTERNATIONAL MAP OF THE WORLD - CARTE DE L'AFRIQUE CENTRALE
1:1, 000, 000
IGN
see Equatorial Africa 672C and index 672/1.

CARTE DE L'AFRIQUE CENTRALE
1:500, 000
IGN
see Equatorial Africa 672C and index 672/2.

CARTE DE L'AFRIQUE CENTRALE
1:200, 000
IGN
see Equatorial Africa 672C and index 672/3.

CARTE DE L'AFRIQUE CENTRALE
1:50, 000
IGN
see Equatorial Africa 672C and index 672/4.

D POLITICAL & ADMINISTRATIVE

CARTE DE L'ORGANISATION ADMINISTRATIVE
1:5, 000, 000
Paris : IGN, 1961
21 x 27
Admin. map in monochrome.
F.Fr 5.00

CARTE ADMINISTRATIVE
1:3, 125, 000
Paris : IGN, 1963
28 x 26
Map in 5 col. showing admin. areas.
F.Fr 5.83

E1 PHYSICAL: RELIEF

CARTE PHYSIQUE
1:3, 125, 000
Paris : IGN, 1963
27 x 31
Contoured, layer col. F.Fr 5.83

KONGO-BRAZZAVILLE
1:2, 000, 000
Moskva : GUGK, 1971
50 x 60
Physical map, contoured, 3 them. insets.

F GEOLOGY

CARTE GÉOLOGIQUE DE LA RÉPUBLIQUE DU CONGO
by G Gerard
1:2, 000, 000
Orléans : BRGM, 1962
69 x 53
Geol. map in brown and black.

CARTE GÉOLOGIQUE DE L'AFRIQUE EQUATORIALE FRANÇAISE
1:2, 000, 000
In 4 sheets
Orléans: BRGM, 1958
114 x 164
General geol. of Central African Republic, Chad, Congo and Gabon. Incl. structural sketch map and text 1958.

CARTE GÉOLOGIQUE DE LA RÉPUBLIQUE DU CONGO
by P Dadet
1:500, 000
Orléans : BRGM, 1966
112 x 82
Col. map with Memoir. F.Fr 110, 000

G EARTH RESOURCES

CARTE PÉDOLOGIQUE DU CONGO
P de Boissezon and F Gras
1:500, 000
Paris : ORSTOM, 1970
57 x 65
Coloured soil map.
Sheets available : Sibiti-Est with 144pp text. F.Fr 50.00

ATLASES
O NATIONAL

ATLAS DU CONGO
1:2, 000, 000
Paris : ORSTOM, 1969
50 x 62 (sheet size)
Detailed thematic atlas containing large col. plates and descriptive text. 1st part is published and contains following maps :
I Éléments climatologiques et océanographiques
II,III,IV Eléments climatiques mensuels
V Éléments climatiques annuels
VI Éléments climatiques divers
VII Oro-hydrographie
VIII Géologie
IX Pédologie
X Phytogéographie

673 Angola

A1 GENERAL MAPS: ROADS

MAPA DE ESTRADAS DE ANGOLA
1:2, 000, 000
Porto : Lello
69 x 98
Road and other communication details; plan Luanda on reverse.

MAPA RODOVIARO DE ANGOLA
1:1, 500, 000
Luanda : Junta Autonoma de Estrados de Angola, 1969/70
91 x 52
Double-sided road map; road and tourist details, contoured.

C OFFICIAL SURVEYS

KARTA MIRA
1:2, 500, 000
PPWK
4 sheets to cover Angola :
133 Kinshasa (Leopoldville)
134 Lubumbashi (Elisabethville)
153 Windhoek
154 Salisbury
see WORLD 100C and index 100/2.

AFRICA
1:2, 000, 000
AMS Series 2201
Sheets needed for Angola :
26, 27, 29, 30
see AFRICA 6C and index 6/2.

INTERNATIONAL MAP OF THE WORLD
1:1, 000, 000
7 sheets needed for Angloa.
see WORLD 100C and index 100/1.

ANGOLA
1:250, 000
In 57 sheets, see index 673/1
Lisboa : PUP
Topog. series in progress, covering the whole country, but excluding Cabinda.

ANGOLA
1:100, 000
See index 673/2
Lisboa : PUP, 1959
Topog. series in progress, contoured covering the whole country, but excluding Cabinda.

D POLITICAL & ADMINISTRATIVE

ANGOLA
1:6, 600, 000 app.
No 2066
New York : UN, 1972
General admin. map with place names.

PROVINCIA DE ANGOLA
1:5, 000, 000
Lisboa : PUP, 1968
Col. general map showing boundaries, principal communications and settlement.

ANGOLA
1:2, 500, 000
Moskva : GUGK, 1973
59 x 80
Col. study map showing water features, settlements, admin. divisions and centres, communications, boundaries, capitals, economic details, pop. Geog. description.
30 kop

CARTA DE ANGOLA
1:2, 000, 000
Lisboa : PUP, 1966
78 x 88
Political col. by districts, roads, railways and principal contours.

F GEOLOGY

CARTA GEOLÓGICAS DE ANGOLA
1:2, 000, 000
Lisboa : Serv. Geologicos de Portugal
79 x 90
Col. geological map.

ANGOLA : CARTA GEOLÓGICA
1:250, 000
Lisboa : Serv. Geologicos de Portugal, 1961+
72 x 60 each
Multi-sheet geological series in progress, each sheet having own text in Port.

ANGOLA : CARTA GEOLÓGICA
1:100, 000
Lisboa : Serv. Geologicos de Portugal, 1971
New geological series in progress. Each sheet has text vol. in Port.

G EARTH RESOURCES

OCORRÊNCIAS MINERAIS ANGOLA
1:2, 000, 000
Lisboa : Serv. Geologicas de Portugal, 1966
72 x 82
Col. geol. showing minerals by symbols, with 58pp Port. text.

674.1 Central African Republic

See also: 672 EQUATORIAL AFRICA

A1 GENERAL MAPS: ROADS

CARTE ROUTIÈRE
1:1, 500, 000
Paris : IGN, 1965
97 x 65
Road communications, distances in km and items of tourist interest.
F.Fr 20.83

B TOWN PLANS

PLAN DE BANGUI
1:10, 000
Paris : IGN, 1972
Topog. plan with street names and contours.
F.Fr 16.67

C OFFICIAL SURVEYS

AFRICA
1:2, 000, 000
AMS Series 2201
Sheets 18 and 19 cover Central African Republic
see AFRICA 6C and index 6/2.

INTERNATIONAL MAP OF THE WORLD - CARTE DE L'AFRIQUE CENTRALE
1:1, 000, 000
IGN
see Equatorial Africa 672C and index 672/1 and 100/1.

CARTE DE L'AFRIQUE CENTRALE
1:500, 000
IGN
see Equatorial Africa 672C and index 672/2.

CARTE DE L'AFRIQUE CENTRALE
1:200, 000
IGN
see Equatorial Africa 672C and index 672/3.

CARTE DE L'AFRIQUE CENTRALE
1:50, 000
IGN
see Equatorial Africa 672C and index 672/4.

E1 PHYSICAL: RELIEF

RÉPUBLIQUE CENTRAFRICAINE (PHYSIQUE)
No 1366
St Germain-en-Laye : Éditions MDI
126 x 92
Plastic coated physical wall map for schools. Economic map on reverse.

F GEOLOGY

CARTE GÉOLOGIQUE DE LA RÉPUBLIQUE CENTRAFRICAINE
1:1, 500, 000
Orléans : BRGM, 1964
98 x 67
Col. geol. map, insets of reconnaissance mapping and structural tectonic map.
F.Fr 24.00

G EARTH RESOURCES

ESQUISSE PÉDOLOGIQUE DE GRIMARI
1:50, 000
ORSTOM
see CENTRAL AFRICAN REPUBLIC H

H BIOGEOGRAPHY

TOPOGRAPHIE ET VÉGÉTATION DE GRIMARI
1:50, 000
by P Quantin
Paris : ORSTOM, 1963
Col. map; also "Esquisse pédologique de Grimari" (soil sketch) by P Quantin and A Forget. With 46pp text, 1965.
F.Fr 12.00

L ECONOMIC

RÉPUBLIQUE CENTRAFRICAINE (PHYSIQUE)
Editions MDI
Economic map on reverse.
see CENTRAL AFRICAN REPUBLIC E1

674.3 Chad

See also: 672 EQUATORIAL AFRICA

A1 GENERAL MAPS: ROADS

CARTE ROUTIÈRE DE LA RÉPUBLIQUE DU TCHAD
1:1, 500, 000
Paris : IGN, 1968
83 x 125
2 sheet map, with roads classified, distances in km, physical map inset.
F.Fr 27.50

A2 GENERAL MAPS: LOCAL

EMI-KOUSSI
1:25, 000
München : Arbeitsgemeinschaft fur Vergleichende Hochgebirgsforschung, 1969
60 x 75
Topog. map of part of Tibesti-Sahara region; contours, relief etc. DM 14.70

B TOWN PLANS

PLAN DE FORT LAMY
1:10, 000
Paris : IGN, 1965
6-col. map, contoured with roads named.
F.Fr 16.67

C OFFICIAL SURVEYS

KARTA MIRA
1:2, 500, 000
Carti - GUGK (Bulg)
4 sheets to cover Chad :
93 Niamey
94 Khartoum
113 Lagos
114 Kisangani (Stanleyville)
see WORLD 100C and index 100/2.

AFRICA
1:2, 000, 000
AMS Series 2201
Sheets 8, 9, 13, 14, 18, 19 cover Chad.
see AFRICA 6C and index 6/2.

INTERNATIONAL MAP OF THE WORLD - CARTE DE L'AFRIQUE CENTRALE
1:1, 000, 000
IGN
see Equatorial Africa 672C and index 672/1 and 100/1.

CARTE DE L'AFRIQUE CENTRALE
1:500, 000
IGN
see Equatorial Africa 672C and index 672/2.

CARTE DE L'AFRIQUE CENTRAL
1:200, 000
IGN
see Equatorial Africa 672C and index 672/3.

E2 PHYSICAL: LAND FEATURES

LAKE CHAD BASIN
1:5, 000, 000
Paris : Lake Chad Basin Commission/UN Devt. Project/UNESCO, 1969
44 x 37
Set of maps, with 2 legend sheets in French and English. Maps show various elements and rainfall, hydrography, soil, vegetation, geology, etc.

STUDY OF WATER RESOURCES IN THE LAKE CHAD BASIN
1:1, 000, 000
Paris : Lake Chad Basin Commission/UN Devt. Project/UNESCO, 1969
In 3 sheets
Sheets : Geology; Surface hydrology, rainfall and infiltration capacities; hydrogeology. With sheet of hydrogeological sections, at vertical scale of 1:10, 000.

ESQUISSE HYDROLOGIQUE DE LA RÉPUBLIQUE DU TCHAD
1:1, 500, 000
Paris : ORSTOM, 1966
Coloured hydrological sketch map.
F.Fr 12.00

F GEOLOGY

CARTE GÉOLOGIQUE DE LA RÉPUBLIQUE DU TCHAD
1:1, 500, 000
by J P Wolff
In 2 sheets
Orléans : BRGM, 1964
Col. geol. map. F.Fr 39.00

CARTE GÉOLOGIQUE DE RECONNAISSANCE DE LA RÉPUBLIQUE DU TCHAD
1:1, 000, 000
Orléans : BRGM
Col. geol. series in progress.
Sheets available :
Fort-Lamy by J Barbeau, 1956
Borkou-Ennedi-Tibesti by Ph Wacrenier et al, 1958
With explanatory text.
Each F.Fr 24.00

G EARTH RESOURCES

CARTE PÉDOLOGIQUE DU TCHAD
by J Pias
1:1, 000, 000
Paris : ORSTOM, 1968
68 x 105 each
2 sheet col. soil map with text, 1970.
F.Fr 100.00

CARTE PÉDOLOGIQUE
1:200, 000
Paris : ORSTOM
Col. soil maps with explanatory notes.
The following sheets available :
Mogroum, by J Pias and J Barbery, 1963
Fort-Lamy, by J Pias et al, 1963
Massenya, by J Pias and P Poisot, 1963
Abeche, Biltine, Oum Hadjer, 3 sheets, 1962

CARTE PÉDOLOGIQUE DE RECONNAISSANCE DU TCHAD
1:200, 000
Paris : ORSTOM
The following sheets available :
Melfi, Centre de Fort Lamy by E Guichard & P Poisot, 1964
Dagela, Centre de Fort Lamy, 1964
Fort-Archambault, Centre de Fort Lamy by C Marius & J Barbery, 1964
Moussafoyo, Centre de Fort Lamy, by C Marius and J Barbery, in 2 sheets, 1964
Lac Iro Djouna, by J Pias & J Barbery, in 2 sheets, 1964
Am Timam, by P Audry, 1967
Niellim by P Audry & P Poisot, 1967, text 1969
Moundou by J Barbery & G Bouteyre, 1967
Koumra by G Bouteyre, 1967
Am Dam by G Bouquier et al, 1967
Singako by G Bouquier & J Barbery, 1967
Abou Deia, Mangalme by J Pias & P Poisot, 1967
Fiang, Lai by J F Vizier & M Fromaget, 1969
Léré, by C Cheverry & M Fromaget, 1969
Bousso by G Clavaud & R Sayol, 1969
Bongor by J F Vizier & R Sayol, 1970

CARTE PÉDOLOGIQUE DE LA ZONE ERE-LOKA
by J Barbery and E Guichard
1:50, 000
Paris : ORSTOM, 1960
Coloured soil map with 176pp text and 3 black and white sketches.
F.Fr 12.00

CARTE PÉDOLOGIQUE DE LA ZONE LOKA-KABIA
by E Guichard
1:50, 000
Paris : ORSTOM, 1961
Coloured soil map with 104pp text and 2 black sketch maps at 1:100, 000.
F.Fr 12.00

CARTE PÉDOLOGIQUE DE LA ZONE SATEGUI-DERESSIA
by E Guichard and P Poisot
1:50, 000
Paris : ORSTOM, 1962
2 sheet col. map, with 3 black sketches at 1:100, 000. F.Fr 12.00

CARTE PÉDOLOGIQUE DU CASIER "A" NORD-BONGOR
by B Lepoutre and G Bouteyre
1:20, 000
In 5 sheets
Paris : ORSTOM, 1958
Coloured soil map for : Migou, Bedem, Billiam-Oursi, Magao, Fressou.
F.Fr 12.00

H BIOGEOGRAPHY

ESQUISSE DE LA COUVERTURE VÉGÉTALE DU TCHAD
by J Pias
1:1, 500, 000
Paris : ORSTOM, 1970
106 x 70
Col. vegetation map with 47pp text.

CARTE INTERNATIONALE DU TAPIS VÉGÉTALE - LARGEAU
1:1, 000, 000
Pondichery : Fr. Inst, 1964
Detailed col. map following International Sheet lines, covers sheet NE 34.

ATLASES
M HISTORICAL

CARTE ARCHÉOLOGIQUE DES ABORDS DU LAC TCHAD
1:500, 000
Paris : CNRS, 1970
1 vol. of 172pp with wallet containing 5 sketches and 3 col. maps in 5 sheets.
F.Fr 107.50

675 Zaïre

A1 GENERAL MAPS

CARTE ROUTIÈRE DE LA RÉPUBLIQUE DÉMOCRATIQUE DU CONGO
1:8, 000, 000
Kinshasa : Inst. Geog.
Col. road map indicating route numbers and distances.

DEMOCRATIC REPUBLIC OF THE CONGO ROAD MAP
1:2, 000, 000
Washington : Defense Mapping Agency
114 x 105
General communications map.
$1.00

CARTE GÉOGRAPHIQUE DU CONGO, RWANDA ET BURUNDI
1:3, 000, 000
Bruxelles : IGMB, 1961
84 x 94
Admin. boundaries, road and rail communications shown.
Ozalid print B.Fr 150.00

CARTE ROUTIÈRE DE LA PROVINCE DU CONGO CENTRALE
1:1, 000, 000
Kinshasa : Inst. Geog.
Roads classified, distances in km.

CARTES ROUTIÈRES ET ADMINISTR-ATIVES DES PROVINCES
1:1, 000, 000
Kinshasa : Inst. Geog.
Various sizes
Road details, province boundaries with inset plan of capital town at 1:100, 000. The following sheets available :

Congo Central et Bandundu, 1968	110 x 95
Ecuateur, 1968	102 x 95
Kasai Occidental and Oriental, 1968	92 x 82
Katanga, 1966	112 x 100
Kivu, 1968	85 x 75
Orientale, 1968	110 x 94

IGMB editions (1959) available in ozalid print reproduction.
Each B.Fr 100

A2 GENERAL MAPS: LOCAL

CARTE DU DOMAINE DU CSK
1:2, 000, 000
Tervuren : Pat. du Musée Royal de l'Afrique Centrale
Black and white planning map of Shaba.
B.Fr 160

CARTE DU DOMAINE DU CSK
1:1, 000, 000
Tervuren : Pat. du Musée Royal de l'Afrique Centrale, 1940
Single col. map of Shaba.
B.Fr 160

CARTE DU DOMAINE DU CSK
1:1, 000, 000
Tervuren : Pat. du Musée Royal de l'Afrique Centrale, 1958
Black and white general map of Shaba.
B.Fr 160

CARTE DU KATANGA MÉRIDIONAL
1:1, 000, 000
Tervuren : Pat. du Musée Royal de l'Afrique Centrale, 1948
Black and white planning map of southern Shaba. B.Fr 160

CARTE DU KATANGA MÉRIDIONAL
1:500, 000
Tervuren : Pat. du Musée Royal de l'Afrique Centrale, Comité Spécial du Katanga, 1932
Col. map with form lines.
B.Fr 160

CARTE DE TERRAINS SUPERFICIELS DU KATANGA MÉRIDIONAL
1:500, 000
Tervuren : Pat. du Musée Royal de l'Afrique Centrale, 1932
Col. land map of southern Shaba.
B.Fr 160

CARTES RÉGIONALES
1:200, 000 - 1:100, 000
Kinshasa : Inst. Geog.
District maps of the town and environs.
Maps available :
Leopoldville (Kinshasa) Official Plan
1:200, 000
Stanleyville (Kisangani) Official Plan
1:200, 000
Luluabourg 1:100, 000

B TOWN PLANS

KINSHASA (LEOPOLDVILLE)
Various scales
Kinshasa : Inst. Geog.
Plans available :
Plan officiel de Kinshasa
1:10, 000 6 sheets
Plan officiel des Communes de la Ville de Kinshasa et environs
1:20, 000
Plan officiel de Ville de Kinshasa et environs
1:40, 000

C OFFICIAL SURVEYS

KARTA MIRA
1:2, 500, 000
GUGK (Bulg) PPWK
5 sheets to cover Zaire : 113, 114, 133, 134, 154
see WORLD 100C and index 100/2.

AFRICA
1:2, 000, 000
AMS Series 2201
Sheets 23 and 27 cover Zaïre
see AFRICA 6C and index 6/2.

INTERNATIONAL MAP OF THE WORLD
1:1, 000, 000
11 sheets cover Zaïre
see WORLD 100C and index 100/1.

CARTES PLANIMÉTRIQUES (KATANGA)
1:500, 000
Tervuren : Pat. du Musée Royal de l'Afrique Centrale - Comité Spécial du Katanga
Planimetric series, communications, settle-ment and rivers published for the Shaba region only.
Printed sheets B.Fr 160
Ozalid prints B.Fr 75

CARTE DU ZAÏRE (CONGO)
1:200, 000
Kinshasa : Inst. Geog.
Planimetric series in progress based on aerial surveys. Generally 2 colour editions but some in 6 colours. Currently published for South West and northern regions only.

CARTES GÉOGRAPHIQUES (KATANGA)
1:200, 000
Tervuren : Pat. du Musée Royal de l'Afrique Centrale
Topog. series available in varying editions on both paper and blueprint, published for the Shaba region only in 37 sheets.

CARTES TOPOGRAPHIQUES DU ZAÏRE (CONGO)
1:100, 000
Tervuren : Pat. du Musée Royal de l'Afrique Centrale - Comité Spécial du Katanga
Topographical series published by ¼ degree sheets published by CSK for the Katanga region only. B.Fr. 160

CARTES TOPOGRAPHIQUES DU CONGO
1:50, 000
Kinshasa : Inst. Geog.
New series in progress, col, contoured, to be published for only the economically develop-ed areas. At present covering the Bas Congo (Lower Congo) and some mining areas. This series will replace the earlier black and white edition.

CARTE DU CONGO
1:25, 000
Kinshasa : Inst. Geog.
Series in progress; available in planimetric and topographic eds, publication planned for areas of economic interest or urban areas.

D POLITICAL & ADMINISTRATIVE

RÉPUBLIQUE DU CONGO (ZAÏRE)
1:3, 000, 000
Bruxelles : IGMB, 1961
74 x 74
Shows admin. boundaries, roads in red, rivers and water features blue.
Ozalid print B.Fr 150

RÉPUBLIQUE DÉMOCRATIQUE DU CONGO ORGANISATION TERRITORIALE ET ADMINISTRATIVE AU 12 JANVIER 1968
1:3, 000, 000
Kinshasa : Inst. Geog. du Congo, 1968
Contoured, state, provincial, district and territory boundaries, roads, railways, principal land features, table of admin. districts.

CARTES DES TERRITOIRES
1:200, 000
Bruxelles : IGMB, 1958-60
Maps of the individual admin. districts of the Congo showing communications, spot heights and settlement.
Various prices.
Each B.Fr 150

RÉPUBLIQUE DU CONGO (MUETTE)
1:4, 000, 000
Bruxelles : IGMB
Outline map in monochrome.
B.Fr 10

E1 PHYSICAL: RELIEF

KONGO
1:2, 500, 000
Moskva : GUGK
Physical, with contours and them. insets.
In Russian.

CARTE HYPSOMÉTRIQUE DU KATANGA MÉRIDIONAL
1:1, 000, 000
Tervuren : Pat. du Musée Royal de l'Afrique Centrale, 1948
Col. map, contoured with layer colours of southern Katanga. B.Fr 160

F GEOLOGY

CARTE GÉOLOGIQUE DU ZAÏRE
1:2, 000, 000
Tervuren : Pat. du Musée Royal de l'Afrique Centrale, 1974
120 x 65
2 sheet coloured geological map, North and South with Legend. B.Fr 450
Explanatory notes, 67pp in French.
B.Fr 150

CARTE GÉOLOGIQUE DU CONGO : RÉGIONS DE L'ARUWIMI-ITURI ET DU BAS-UELE
1:500, 000
Tervuren : Pat. du Musée Royal de l'Afrique Centrale, 1970
148 x 97 complete
2 sheet geol. map with explanation in French. Cross sections and legend in margin.
Each sheet B.Fr 150
Text B.Fr 40

CARTE GÉOLOGIQUE DU ZAÏRE (CONGO)
1:200, 000
See index 675/1
Tervuren : Pat. du Musée Royal de l'Afrique Centrale
Col. geol. series in progress, each sheet with legend.
Available in the following sheets :
Inkisi, 1970
Léopoldville, 1963
Luozi-Kai Mbaku, 1963
Luiza-Musodi, 1963
Dibaya, 1966
Kinshasa, 1963
Ngungu (Thysville), 1972
Each B.Fr 240
Explanatory notes - in French
Each B.Fr 50
Other sheets published by Comité Spécial du Katanga :
Haut-Lomami
Mitwaba
Sokele
Mokabe
Sampwe
Lukafu
Sakabinda Tenike
Each B.Fr 160

CARTE GÉOLOGIQUE DU BAS-ZAÏRE
1:50, 000
Tervuren : Pat. du Musée Royal de l'Afrique Centrale, 1958-62
The following sheets available :
Thysville - 7 sheets
S6/14, NW2, NW4, SW2, SW4, NE1 NE2, NE3
Inkisi - 8 sheets
S6/15, NW1, NW2, NW3, NW4, SW1, SW2, SW3, SW4
Léopoldville - 3 sheets
S5/15, SW3, SW4, SE3
Each B.Fr 140

G EARTH RESOURCES

CARTE DES SOLS ET DE LA VÉGÉTATION DU CONGO, DU RWANDA ET DU BURUNDI
Various scales
Bruxelles : SERDAT
Series of reports covering soil and vegetation. Each report is illustrated by maps and diagrams. Reports available :
Carte des sols du Congo belge et du Ruanda-Urundi, 1960
Carte des sols du Rwanda et du Burundi, 1963
1* Kaniama (Haut Lomami), 1955
2* Mvuazi (Bas Congo), 1954
3* Vallée de la Ruzizi, 1955
4* Nioka (Ituri), 1954
5* Mosso (Urundi), 1955
6 Yangambi
1* Weko, 1954
2* Yangambi, 1956
3* Lilanda, 1957
4 Yambaw, 1957
7* Bugesera-Mayaga (Ruanda) 1956
8* Vallée de la Lufira, 1956
9* Région d'Élisabethville (Haut Katanga), 1959
10* Kwango, 1958
11 Ubangi, 1960
12 Bengamisa, 1958
13 Région du Lac Albert, 1959
14 Uele, 1960
15 Kasai, 1960
16 Dorsale du Kivu, 1960
17 Région de Yanonge-Yatolema, 1960
18 Bassin de la Karuzi, 1962
19 Maniema, 1965
20 Région Tshuapa-Équateur, 1960
21 Paysannat Babua, 1967
22 Ubangi, 1968
23 Haute-Lulua, 1969
24 Région Mahagi, 1969
25 Bas Congo (Vegetation), 1970
26 Nord Kivu et Région Lac Édouard, 1970
* Out of print.

H BIOGEOGRAPHY

CARTE DES SOLS ET DE LA VÉGÉTATION DU CONGO DU RWANDA ET DU BURUNDI
Various scales
Inst. Nat. pour l'Étude agronomique du Congo
see ZAÏRE G

J CLIMATE

RÉGIMES NORMAUX ET CARTES DES PRÉCIPITATIONS DANS L'EST DU CONGO BELGE POUR LA PÉRIODE 1930 A 1946
Communication No. 1 : Bureau Climatologique
Ed F Bultot
Brussels : SERDAT, 1950
56pp Report containing 13 rainfall maps for the former eastern Congo (Long. 26° to 31° E, Lat.4N to 5S)
B.Fr 300

SUR LE CARACTÈRE ORGANISÉ DE LA PLUIE AU CONGO BELGE
Communication No. 6 : Bureau Climatologique
Ed F Bultot
Brussels : SERDAT, 1952
16pp report containing 8 rainfall maps of the former Belgian Congo.
B.Fr 80

RISQUES D'ANNÉES SÈCHES ET PLUVIEUSES AU CONGO BELGE ET AU RUANDA-URUNDI
Communication No 13 : Bureau Climatologique
Ed F Bultot
Brussels : SERDAT, 1957
22pp report including 5 rainfall maps of the former Belgian Congo.
B.Fr 80

ESTIMATION, A PARTIR D'UN NOMBRE LIMITÉ DE MESURES, DES MOYENNES VRAIES JOURNALIÈRES, DIURNES ET NOCTURNES DE LA TEMPÉRATURE ET DE L'HUMIDITÉ DE L'AIR AU CONGO, AU RUANDA ET AU BURUNDI
Communication No. 20 : Bureau Climatologique
Ed F Bultot
Brussels : SERDAT, 1961
97pp analysis of a selection of average actual day and night temperature and humidity figures including 8 maps for the former Belgian Congo.
B.Fr 300

K HUMAN GEOGRAPHY

CARTE ETHNOGRAPHIQUE
1:3, 000, 000
Kinshasa : Inst. Geog, 1961
84 x 80
Col. pop. map.

CARTES DE LA DENSITÉ ET DE LA LOCALISATION DE LA POPULATION
1:1, 000, 000
Ed Roger-Ernest de Smet
Bruxelles : Universite Libre de Bruxelles en Afrique Centrale
105 x 90 each
Divided by Provinces. 3 maps, with text, for each, comprising :
Limites Administratives, Densite de la Population, Localisation de la Population.
Available for :
Province Orientale, 1962, 49pp text, B.Fr 750
Ancienne Province de Leopoldville, 1966, 46pp text B.Fr 750
Province du Katanga, 1971, 38pp text B.Fr 750

L ECONOMIC

CARTE ÉCONOMIQUE
1:3, 000, 000
Kinshasa : Inst. Geog, 1968
82 x 83
Col. economic map, indicating location of products.

CARTE DES MINES ET DES INDUSTRIES
1:3, 000, 000
Kinshasa : Inst. Geog, 1969
84 x 80
Col. map depicting location and product industries.

CARTE DES TRANSPORTS DE SURFACE EN RÉPUBLIQUE DU ZAÏRE
Bruxelles : Académie Royale des Sciences d'Outre Mer
Map to show road, rail and water communications. In preparation.

M HISTORICAL

CARTE HISTORIQUE DU CONGO
J Strengers
Namur : Wesmael-Charlier
115 x 155
Historical wall map for schools.
B.Fr 302

ATLASES
J CLIMATE

ATLAS CLIMATIQUE DU BASSIN CONGOLAIS
by F Bultot
1:10, 000, 000/20, 000, 000
Bruxelles : SERDAT, 1971
32 x 33
In 4 parts :
I Les Composantes du bilan de rayonnement, 1971, 178pp maps and diagrams
II Les Composantes du bilan d'eau, 1971, 149pp maps and diagrams
III Température et humidité de l'air, rosée, température du sol 1973. 150pp maps and diagrams
IV La pression atmosphérique, la nébulosité, la visibillté et le brouillard. In preparation.
Each B.Fr 1500

ATLASES
P REGIONAL

ATLAS DU KATANGA
Comité Spécial du Katanga
In 5 parts
Tervuren : Pat. du Musée Royal de l'Afrique Centrale
Atlas containing 12 maps, scale 1:200, 000 depicting topography and geology with photographs and text.
Part 1 (no date)
Sheets Elisabethville (Lubumbashi) and Tshinsenda. Small scale maps of Africa and the Congo. Out of print.
Part 2 (no date)
Sheets Kambove and Tenke B.Fr 400
Part 3 (1932)
Sheet Ruwe B.Fr 400
Part 4 (1940)
Sheets Sakabinda and Lukafu B.Fr 400
Part 5 (1952)
Sheets Mokabe and Sampwe B.Fr 800
Complete set B.Fr 2,000

675.97 Burundi

See also: 675 ZAÏRE

C OFFICIAL SURVEYS

CARTE DU RUANDA-URUNDI
1:200, 000
In 6 sheets
Ed 1937 (Ministère des Colonies)
Bruxelles : IGMB
Monochrome series. B.Fr 25

CARTE TOPOGRAPHIQUE DU RUANDA-URUNDI
1:100, 000
In 30 sheets, see index 675.97/1
Tervuren : Pat. des Musée Royal l'Afrique centrale, 1938
Topog. series, contoured, published by Ministère des Colonies, 1938.
Ozalid prints. B.Fr 75

CARTE PLANIMÉTRIQUE DU BURUNDI
1:100, 000
In 13 sheets, see index 675.97/2
Tervuren : Pat. du Musée Royal de l'Afrique Centrale
Planimetric series.
Ozalid prints. B.Fr 75

CARTE PLANIMÉTRIQUE DU BURUNDI
1:50, 000
In 55 sheets, see index 675.97/3
Tervuren : Pat. du Musée Royal de l'Afrique Centrale
Topog. series based on aerial photographs showing settlement and water pattern.
Ozalid prints B.Fr 75
Film B.Fr 250

D POLITICAL & ADMINISTRATIVE

CARTE ADMINISTRATIVE RWANDA-BURUNDI
1:500, 000
Bruxelles : IGMB, 1961
7 coloured topog. map showing boundaries and communications, available in either French or Flemish edition.
Ozalid print B.Fr 150

F GEOLOGY

CARTE GÉOLOGIQUE DES RÉGIONS DU MOSSO ET DU NKOMA
1:200, 000
Tervuren : Pat. du Musée Royal de l'Afrique Centrale
Col. geol. map in French with text (1965).
312pp. B.Fr 675

675.98 Rwanda

See also: 675 ZAÏRE

C OFFICIAL SURVEYS

CARTE DU RWANDA
1:250, 000
Bruxelles : IGMB
Compilation from the 1:50, 000 sheets.
Monochrome Ozalid ed.
B.Fr 150

CARTE PLANIMÉTRIQUE DE LA RÉPUBLIQUE RWANDAISE
1:250, 000
Tervuren : Pat. du Musée Royal de l'Afrique Centrale, 1963
Showing settlement and rivers, available as Ozalid print. B.Fr 75

CARTE DU RUANDA-URUNDI
1:200, 000
Ed 1937 (Ministère des Colonies)
In 6 sheets
Bruxelles : IGMB
Monochrome series
Each B.Fr 25

CARTE TOPOGRAPHIQUE DU RUANDA-URUNDI
1:100, 000
In 30 sheets, see index 675. 97/1
Tervuren : Pat. du Musée Royal de l'Afrique Centrale, 1938
Topog. series, contoured, ed. Ministère Colonies, 1938.
Ozalid prints. B.Fr 75
Film prints. B.Fr 250

CARTE PLANIMÉTRIQUE DU RWANDA
1:100, 000
In 14 sheets, see index 675. 98/1
Tervuren : Pat. du Musée Royal de L'Afrique Centrale
Series in progress, showing planimetric detail. Available as Ozalid or black and magenta printed.
Printed B.Fr. 140
Ozalid prints. B.Fr 75

CARTE PLANIMÉTRIQUE DU RWANDA
1:50, 000
In 47 sheets, see index 675. 98/2
Tervuren : Pat. du Musée Royal de l'Afrique Centrale
Planimetric series showing settlement and rivers, available as Ozalid prints.
B.Fr 75
Film prints B.Fr 250

D POLITICAL & ADMINISTRATIVE

CARTE ADMINISTRATIVE RWANDA-BURUNDI
1:500, 000
Bruxelles : IGMB, 1961
7 colour topog. map showing boundaries and communications available in either French or Flemish eds.
Ozalid print B.Fr 150

F GEOLOGY

CARTE GÉOLOGIQUE DU RWANDA
1:100, 000
In 12 sheets, see index 675, 98/1
Tervuren : Pat. du Musée Royal de l'Afrique Centrale
100 x 75
Col. geol. maps with explanatory notes. The following sheets are available :
Kagitumba, 1964
Kigali, 1967
Rwinkwavu, 1967
Kibungo, 1967
Bugesera, 1970
Ruhengeri-Nord, 1971
B.Fr 190

676 East Africa

A1 GENERAL MAPS: ROADS

MICHELIN AFRICA SERIES
1:4, 000, 000
Paris : Michelin
Road maps showing political boundaries, settlements, motoring and tourist features. Roads graded by condition, numbered, distances in km and miles. Eng and Fr.
Maps available :
154 Africa North-East - south to Nairobi
86 x 96
155 Africa, Central and Southern, Madagascar - north to Lake Rudolf
97 x 119

C OFFICIAL SURVEYS

AFRICA
1:2, 000, 000
AMS Series 2201
5 sheets for coverage.
see AFRICA 6C and index 6/2.

EAST AFRICA SERIES Y 503
1:250, 000
Surveys of Kenya, Uganda and Tanzania
65 x 45
Topog. series, showing boundaries, settlements etc. UTM grid. For index, see individual countries. 7/50 sh

D POLITICAL & ADMINISTRATIVE

STANFORD GENERAL MAP SERIES
1:5, 500, 000
London : Stanford
79 x 104 each
Political col; boundaries, communications, spot heights, settlements graded by pop. Pictorial border.
Sheets available :
N E Africa - south to Dar es Salaam
37p
CRV £6.50

EAST AFRICA
1:4, 000, 000
DOS (Misc) 299A
Tolworth : DOS, 1961
39 x 60
General communication map with boundaries. 30p

EAST AFRICA - OUTLINE MAP
1:4, 000, 000
DOS (Misc) 299H
Tolworth : DOS, 1961
39 x 60
Outline map in black 30p

EAST AFRICA
1:3, 000, 000
DOS (Misc) 203A
Tolworth : DOS, 1960
General map with boundaries, towns and communications. 50p

E1 PHYSICAL: RELIEF

STREDNI AFRIKA
1:6, 000, 000
Praha : Kart, 1967
92 x 78
Contours, communications, index in Czech.

WORLD TRAVEL MAP SERIES
1:5, 000, 000
Edinburgh : Bart
Political boundaries, communications, settlements and topog. features, contoured, layer col.
Maps available :
Africa N E - south to Lake Albert, 1970
97 x 74
Africa Central and Southern - north to Lake Rudolf, 1972
72 x 94 75p

OBLIQUE MAP OF EAST AFRICA
1:4, 000, 000
Nairobi : SK
66 x 46
Col. map as viewed obliquely from above, showing main topog. features, communications, National Parks, etc.
3/-

EAST AFRICA-PHYSICAL MAP
1:4, 000, 000
DOS (Misc) 299B
Tolworth : DOS, 1961
39 x 60
Contoured with layer colouring
50p

EAST AFRICA
1:4, 000, 000
No SK 53
Nairobi : SK
46 x 35
Col. relief map showing main communications 4/-

EAST AFRICA
1:2, 500, 000
No SK 80
Nairobi : SK, 1972
76 x 57
Col. map, with layer tints, covering all of Kenya, Uganda and Tanzania.
7/50sh

PHILIP'S REGIONAL WALL MAP OF EAST AFRICA
1:2, 000, 000
London : Philip
91 x 122
Physical col, communications and boundaries.
Paper £1.50
Mounted CR £5.50
Mounted on cloth dissected to fold £7.00

E2 PHYSICAL: LAND FEATURES

MBARARA AREA - GEOMORPHOLOGICAL MAP
1:250, 000
Nottingham : Univ. Geog.Dept/Entebbe : Geol. Surv, 1969/70
91 x 62
Col. map, with 78pp report.

F GEOLOGY

EAST AFRICA - GEOLOGY
1:4, 000, 000
DOS (Misc) 299F
Tolworth : DOS, 1961
39 x 60
Coloured geological map
65p

GEOLOGICAL MAP OF EAST AFRICA
1:2, 000, 000
Dodoma : Geol. Surv. Tanzania, 1954
76 x 105
General geol. map of Kenya, Uganda and Tanzania.

G EARTH RESOURCES

EAST AFRICA-MINERALS-FOREST AND GAME RESERVES
1:4, 000, 000
DOS, 1961
See EAST AFRICA 676 H

EAST AFRICA - SOILS
1:4, 000, 000
DOS (Misc) 299G
Tolworth : DOS, 1961
39 x 60
Coloured soil map. 65p

H BIOGEOGRAPHY

EAST AFRICA-RAINFALL-POPULATION-TSETSE FLY
1:3, 000, 000
DOS, 1961, 1954
see EAST AFRICA 676 J

J CLIMATE

EAST AFRICA RAINFALL-POPULATION-TSETSE FLY
1:3, 000, 000
DOS (Misc) 203 B & C
In 2 sheets
Tolworth : DOS, 1961, 1954
Each sheet includes the 3 distribution maps in colour.
Each 65p

MEAN ANNUAL RAINFALL OF EAST AFRICA
1:2, 000, 000
Nairobi : E Af. Meteorol. Dept.
71 x 92
Rainfall map of Kenya, Tanzania and Uganda in 2 sheets with overlap.
7/50 sh

EAST AFRICA, MEAN MONTHLY RAINFALL
1:2, 000, 000
Nairobi : E Af. Meteorol. Dept.
71 x 92
12 2-sheet maps
Per sheet 7/50 sh

EAST AFRICA, RAINFALL PROBABILITY
1:2, 000, 000
Nairobi : E Af. Meteorol. Dept.
71 x 92
Two 2-sheet maps showing 5 year or 20% probability and 10 year or 10% probability.
Per sheet 7/50 sh

K HUMAN GEOGRAPHY

EAST AFRICA-RAINFALL-POPULATION-TSETSE FLY
1:3, 000, 000
DOS, 1961, 1954
see EAST AFRICA 676 J

EAST AFRICA - POPULATION DISTRIBUTION, AUGUST 1962
1:2, 000, 000
by Philip W Porter
Florida : AAG, 1966
83 x 119
Black and white base map showing population density by coloured symbols.
$2.50

L ECONOMIC

EAST AFRICA-MINERALS-FOREST AND GAME RESERVES
1:4, 000, 000
DOS (Misc) 299 C
Tolworth : DOS, 1961
39 x 60
Coloured distribution map.
50p

AFRIQUE ORIENTALE (PHYSIQUE)
1 : 3.000, 000
Economic map on reverse.
see EAST AFRICA 676E1

ATLASES
W3 WORLD ATLASES: LOCAL EDITIONS

OXFORD ATLAS FOR EAST AFRICA
OUP
see WORLD ATLASES 100W3

NELSON'S SCHOOL ATLAS FOR KENYA, MALAWI, UGANDA, ZAMBIA
Ed Simeon H Ominde and P J H Clarke
London : Nelson, 1968
76pp
64pp coloured maps.

SCHOOL ATLAS FOR EAST AFRICA
London : Philip
23 x 28
32pp
World atlas for E African schools.
25p

EAST AFRICAN MODERN SCHOOL ATLAS
London : Philip
23 x 28
Secondary school atlas for E African schools. 80p

ATLASES
P REGIONAL

ACCOMPANYING MAPS TO THE 'HANDBOOK OF NATURAL RESOURCES OF EAST AFRICA'
1:4, 000, 000
DOS (Misc) 299
Tolworth : DOS, 1969
39 x 60
Set of maps of Kenya, Tanzania and Uganda :
A General
B Physical Features
C Mineral Resources, Forests and Game
F Geology
G Soils
H Outline

676.1 Uganda

A2 GENERAL MAPS: LOCAL

MOUNT ELGON
1:125, 000
Kampala : Dept. Lands and Surveys, 1967
92 x 65
Topog. map, contours, relief shading, spot heights in feet, hunting details.

NATIONAL PARK MAPS
1:125, 000
Series USD 11
Kampala : Dept. of Lands and Surv.
Series showing topog. features of Parks, contours.
Published sheets :
Queen Elizabeth National Park
Murchison Falls National Park
Kigezi
Elgon
Kidepo National Park - in preparation.
5/- and 7/50 sh

CENTRAL RUWENZORI
1:25, 000
Kampala : Dept. Lands and Surv, 1970
55 x 80
Topog. map of central Ruwenzori Mountains, contoured at 100ft intervals, hill shaded; some mountaineering information. 7/50 sh

B TOWN PLANS

KAMPALA AND ENVIRONS
1:25, 000
Kampala : Dept of Lands and Surv, 1958
70 x 55
Col. contoured map.

TOWN SERIES
1:10, 000
USD 2
Kampala : Dept. Lands and Surv
Various sizes
Col. town maps; buildings, streets, boundaries, contoured at 10 ft intervals; inc. street gazetteer. In progress. Published sheets :
Entebbe
Fort Portal
Jinja
Kampala
Masaka
Mbale
Tororo 7/50 sh

TOWN SERIES
1:2, 500
USD 6
Kampala : Dept. Lands and Surv.
55 x 55
Col. maps, contoured at 5ft intervals, cadastral boundaries.
Plans available :
Arua - 9 sheets
Bombo - 12 sheets
Bugiri
Busembatia
Bushenyi
Entebbe - 28 sheets
Fort Portal - 24 sheets
Gulu - 27 sheets
Hima - 10 sheets
Hoima - 7 sheets
Iganga - 6 sheets
Jinja and Environs - 83 sheets (45 published)
Kabale - 11 sheets
Kaberamaido
Kaliro
Kalisizo - 3 sheets
Kampala - 126 sheets (99 published)
Kamuzi
Kapchorwa - 4 sheets
Kasese - 14 sheets
Kumi - 3 sheets
Lake Katwe - 6 sheets
Lira - 5 sheets
Lugazi - 4 sheets
Luwero - 2 sheets
Masaka - 15 sheets
Masindi - 5 sheets
Mbale - 30 sheets
Mbarara - 9 sheets
Mutyana
Moroto - 7 sheets
Moyo - 5 sheets
Mpigi - 4 sheets
Mubende - 10 sheets
Mukono - 4 sheets
Pakwach - 4 sheets
Pallisa
Soroti - 17 sheets
Tororo - 28 sheets
Wobulenzi - 2 sheets

C OFFICIAL SURVEYS

KARTA MIRA
1:2, 500, 000
GUGK : (Bulg) PPWK
2 sheets to cover Uganda : 114, 134
see WORLD 100C and index 100/2.

AFRICA
1:2, 000, 000
AMS Series 2201
Sheet 24 covers Uganda
see AFRICA 6C and index 6/2.

KENYA AND UGANDA
1:2, 000, 000
Series GSGS 2201
Kampala : Dept. Lands and Surv.
65 x 50
Col. map, contoured with layer tints.
5/- sh

INTERNATIONAL MAP OF THE WORLD
1:1, 000, 000
AMS Series 1301
see WORLD 100C and index 100/1.

UGANDA
1:1, 000, 000
Kampala : Dept. Lands and Surv, 1963
70 x 60
Special centralised sheet of Series 1301, covering whole of Uganda. Topog. map with UTM grid. 7/50 sh

EAST AFRICA
1:250, 000
Series Y 503
See index 676. 1/1
Kampala : Dept. Lands and Surv.
75 x 60
Topog. series covering Kenya, Tanzania and Uganda in a common style, showing national, district, county and National Park boundaries, communications with roads graded by surface, relief features, settlements, rivers and lakes, contours or form lines and hill shading on most sheets. Includes UTM grid with admin. diagram. 18 sheets to cover Uganda.

UGANDA
1:50, 000
DOS 426 (Y 732)
see index 676. 1/2
Kampala : Dept. Lands and Surv.
Tolworth : DOS
Topog. series in progress covering the country. Uncontoured, contoured or form lined.

D POLITICAL & ADMINISTRATIVE

UGANDA
1:2, 000, 000
DOS 986
Edition 1
Tolworth : DOS, 1958
Admin. boundaries, communications and settlement. 10p

PHILIP'S LARGE OUTLINE MAP OF UGANDA
1:750, 000
London : Philip
104 x 83
Printed in black on white cartridge paper with contours. £1.25

E1 PHYSICAL: RELIEF

PHILIP'S REGIONAL WALL MAP OF UGANDA
1:750, 000
London : Philip
91 x 117
Physical col. with communications and boundaries.
Paper £1.50
Mounted CR £5.50
Mounted on cloth dissected to fold £7.00

UGANDA
1:500, 000
2nd edition
In 4 sheets
Kampala : Dept. of Lands and Surv, 1963
118 x 127
Physical map with topog. features, boundaries, roads classified by surface, towns by importance, layer col.
30/-

F GEOLOGY

UGANDA GEOLOGY
1:1, 500, 000
2nd edition
Entebbe : Geol. Survey, 1969
40 x 40
Coloured geological map with text on the reverse. Extract from the Atlas of Uganda.
U.Sh. 10.00

GEOLOGICAL MAP OF UGANDA
1:1, 250, 000
Entebbe : Geol. Surv, 1960
52 x 51
Generalised geol. map. U.Sh 10.00

Also available with Bouguer contour overprint. U.Sh 12.00

UGANDA GEOLOGICAL SERIES
1:250, 000
See index 676. 1/3
Entebbe : Geol. Surv.
65 x 45
Geol. series in progress, showing structure, mines, mineral occurrences, water boreholes. Also available with Bouguer contours.
U.Sh 10.00

MBARARA GEOMORPHOLOGY
1:250, 000
Entebbe : Geol. Survey, 1969
86 x 44
Geomorphologic map in colours.
U.Sh 10.00

GEOLOGICAL MAP OF UGANDA
1:100, 000
Entebbe : Geol. Surv.
55 x 55
Geol. series in progress, shows geol. mines, boreholes etc.
Each U.Sh 10.00

G EARTH RESOURCES

UGANDA SOILS SERIES
1:250, 000
See index 676. 1/3
Kampala : Dept. Lands and Surv.
65 x 45
Series in progress showing soil type, source rock and productivity rating. Sheet lines as for 1:250, 000 topog. series.

H BIOGEOGRAPHY

CURRENT LAND USE
1:1, 500, 000
Kampala : Dept. Lands & Surv.
Depicting land use districts in col.
3/- sh

RANGE RESOURCES
1:1, 500, 000
Kampala : Dept. Lands and Surv.
Portraying potential pasture and land usage.
3/- sh

ECOLOGICAL ZONES
1:1, 500, 000
Kampala : Dept. Lands and Surv.
Land type boundaries shown in cols.
3/- sh

VEGETATION MAP OF UGANDA
1:500, 000
In 4 sheets
Kampala : Dept. Lands and Surv, 1964
120 x 125 complete
Showing principal vegetation types.
Complete 30/-

UGANDA VEGETATION SERIES
1:250, 000
See index 676. 1/3
Kampala : Dept.Lands and Surv.
65 x 45
Series in progress showing vegetation types and zones in detail. Sheet lines as for 1:250, 000 topog. series.
Each 7/50 sh

J CLIMATE

UGANDA MEAN MONTHLY RAINFALL
1:4, 000, 000
Kampala : Dept. Lands & Surv, 1958
55 x 80
12 monthly diagrams on 1 sheet.
5/- sh

K HUMAN GEOGRAPHY

UGANDA POPULATION DENSITIES 1959
1:1, 250, 000
Kampala : Dept. Lands and Surv, 1960
50 x 50
Col. map showing pop. by gombololas (sub-counties), 1959 Census.

L ECONOMIC

UGANDA
1:2, 000, 000
Kampala : Dept. Lands and Surv, 1964 (rev. ed.)
35 x 35
Col. map showing road, rail and air communications. 2/- sh

UGANDA : GINNERIES AND COTTON BUYING POSTS
1:1, 250, 000
Kampala : Dept. Lands and Surv, 1961
50 x 50
With gazetteer of ginnery names.
3/- sh

ATLASES
E2 PHYSICAL: LAND FEATURES

LAND SYSTEM OF UGANDA : TERRAIN CLASSIFICATION AND DATA STORAGE
Christchurch : MVEE, 1969
66 x 67
233pp
Loose leaf atlas containing 1:1, 000, 000 land system map with descriptions of each represented by an annotated air photograph, block diagram and tables of soils, landforms and vegetation. Bibliog.
£8.00

ATLASES
G EARTH RESOURCES

GEOCHEMICAL ATLAS OF UGANDA
1:2, 000, 000 - 1:4, 000, 000
Entebbe : Geol. Survey, 1973
30 x 38
32pp
Shows rock, regoloith and stream sediment samples maps including the following trace elements : Cu, Pb, Zn, Co, Ni, Cr, Nb, Be, Mn, Sr, As, Sn. Preliminary maps showing generalised geology, soils, vegetation and climate.
Limp covers U.Sh 125.00
Hard covers U.Sh 150.00

ATLASES
O NATIONAL

ATLAS OF UGANDA
1:1, 500, 000
Kampala : Dept. Lands and Surv, 1967
50 x 50
Containing 38 col. plates depicting aspects of geog, geol, economy. Each plate has an accompanying text; additional pp of text, photographs, diagrams and a gazetteer of the country. 75/- sh
The following plates are available separately:
Relief
Geology
Soils
Forest Reserves
Education Facilities
Tribal & Ethnic groups
Population Densities
Tsetse Control
Geomorphology
Archaeological & Historical sites
Geophysics & Seismology
Mean Monthly Rainfall
Vegetation
Game Conservation
Political
Malaria
Distribution of Cattle by sub-counties
Internal Communications
Each 3/- sh

676.2 Kenya

A1 GENERAL MAPS: ROADS

TOURIST MAP OF KENYA
1:2, 000, 000
SK 72
Nairobi : SK, 1968
47 x 60
Places of tourist interest, indicated by col. pictorial symbols. Information and insets on reverse - list of animals, climate and mileage charts. 5/-

ROUTE MAP OF KENYA
1:1, 000, 000
SK 81
Nairobi : SK, 1971
91 x 64
Double sided map, contoured with layer col, boundaries and communications. For motorists and those on safari.
7/-

A2 GENERAL MAPS: LOCAL

THE KENYA COAST
1:250, 000 and 1:1, 000, 000
SK 79
Nairobi : SK, 1972
Tourist map in col. with layer tints.
5/-

TSAVO WEST NATIONAL PARK
1:250, 000
SK 78
Nairobi : SK
Col. map with layer tints.
5/-

MOUNT KENYA
1:125, 000
DOS 2657
1st edition
Tolworth : DOS, 1975
Topographical map, contoured with relief shading.

MERU NATIONAL PARK
1:100, 000
SK 65
Nairobi : SK
55 x 55
Col. tourist map. 5/-

PART OF MASAI - MARA GAME RESERVE
1:50, 000
SK 69
Nairobi : SK
85 x 58
Col. map showing Keekorok Lodge Area.
5/-

MAP OF NAIROBI NATIONAL PARK
1:25, 000
SK 71
Nairobi : SK, 1971
87 x 53
Map and guide to park with list of game animals. 5/-

NAIROBI AND ENVIRONS
1:100, 000
SK 58
Nairobi : SK
66 x 50
Col. topog. map with layer tints and relief shading. 7/50

MOUNT KENYA
1:25, 000
SK 75
3rd edition
Nairobi : SK
59 x 53
Relief map, hill shading, contours at 50 ft vertical intervals; shows main peaks and glaciers. 5/-

MOUNT KENYA
1:5, 000
München : Forschungsunternehmen Nepal-Himalaya (Wien : FB)
54 x 63
Contours at 20m intervals, glaciers, snow fields, footpaths. DM 16.80
Also available at 1:10, 000, 31 x 36.
DM 8.40

B TOWN PLANS

MOMBASA ISLAND AND ENVIRONS
1:14, 000
SK 54
Nairobi : SK
Col. map showing principal roads and buildings. 5/-

MAP AND GUIDE TO MOMBASA, MALINDI AND THE COAST
1:14, 000
Nairobi : Univ. Af. Press
Text in Eng, Fr, Ger. on reverse.
Also available : Map and Guide to Nairobi, 1:20, 000.

MUNICIPAL AREAS
1:10, 000
Nairobi : SK
Various sizes
Cadastral maps in dyeline print form, showing surveyed boundaries, registered plot numbers. With some topog. detail, contoured at 10 ft vertical intervals.
Available for :
Eldoret, 85 x 58, SK 6
Nairobi (3 sheets) 88 x 55, SK 7
Nakum, 77 x 55, SK 16
Kitale, 71 x 54, SK 17
Kisumu, 67 x 60, SK 18
Each 6/-
Nairobi and Environs, 1:25, 000, 55 x 55, SK 20 6/-
Eldoret, SK 43 (Special), 1:250, 000
Nanyuki, SK 43
Kericho, SK 43
Nairobi, SK 43
Mombasa, SK 43

MUNICIPAL AREAS
1:10, 000
SK 21
Nairobi : SK
Various sizes
Cadastral series, monochrome, uncontoured, available for the Mombasa, Malindi and Settlement Scheme Areas. Available as dyeline prints.
Each 6/-

CITY OF NAIROBI
1:20, 000
SK 46
Nairobi : SK, 1971
79 x 49
Detailed plan covering town and suburbs; index to streets and principal buildings.
Paper folded 7/50

NAIROBI CITY CENTRE
1:5, 000 app
SK 59
Nairobi : SK
Photographic mosaic map, names over-printed in red. 1/-

NAIROBI CITY
1:5, 000
SK 66
Nairobi : SK
55 x 55
Topog. - Cadastral series in progress. Based on recent airphotos, in 4 colours.
5/-

NAIROBI AND DISTRICT
1:5, 000
SK 14
Nairobi : SK
76 x 46
Topog. series covering the city and suburbs. Each 5/-

NAIROBI AND DISTRICT
1:2, 500
SK 13
Nairobi : SK
76 x 46
Nairobi within 1962 city boundary, plus area to the NE. Topog. map series with contours, cadastral overprint.
Each 5/-

TOWN MAPS
1:2, 500
Nairobi : SK
79 x 47
Contoured maps, with cadastral overprint.
Available for :
Eldoret (4 sheets) SK 24
Kericho SK 25
Fort Hall SK 29
Naivasha SK 31
Gilgil SK 32
Embu SK 38
Nyeri SK 67
Each 5/-

C OFFICIAL SURVEYS

KARTA MIRA
1:2, 500, 000
GUGK (Bulg) PPWK
4 sheets to cover Kenya :
114, 115, 134, 135
see WORLD 100C and index 100/2.

AFRICA
1:2, 000, 000
AMS Series 2201
Sheets 20 and 24 cover Kenya
see AFRICA 6C and index 6/2.

KENYA AND UGANDA
1:2, 000, 000
GSGS 2871
Nairobi : SK, 1961
65 x 44
Special sheet, contoured with layer colours.

INTERNATIONAL MAP OF THE WORLD
1:1, 000, 000
Series 1301
see WORLD 100C and index 100/1.

EAST AFRICA
1:250, 000
Series Y 503
In 46 sheets, see index 676, 2/1
Nairobi : SK
75 x 60
Topog. series to cover Kenya, Tanzania and Uganda in a common style. National, District, county and National Park boundaries, communications with roads graded by surface, principal buildings, settlements, rivers and lakes, relief features, contours or form lines and hill shading. The UTM grid is also shown with administrative diagram.

KENYA
1:100, 000
Y 633
See index 676. 2/2
Nairobi : SK
Topographical series covering the north and south east of the cojntry, contoured.
Each 7/50

KENYA
1:100, 000
DOS 523 (Y633)
See index 676. 2/3
Tolworth : DOS, 1964
Topographical series available in contoured or uncontoured editions.
Each 50p

EAST AFRICA (KENYA)
1:50, 000
DOS 423 (Y731)
See index 676, 2/3
Nairobi : SK/Tolworth : DOS
55 x 55
Jointly published topog. map series in progress, available in either contoured, form lined or uncontoured editions.

AIR PHOTOGRAPHIC COVER
1:1, 000, 000
Nairobi : SK
91 x 64
Two maps : SK 57E shows large scale cover, 57F small scale cover. Overprinted on Kenya Route Map. Each 7/50

AERIAL PHOTOGRAPHS
1:80, 000/1:10, 000
Nairobi : SK
Coverage available for most of Kenya.

REGISTRY INDEX SHEETS
1:2, 500
Nairobi : SK
Dyeline print maps :
SK 49 1:50, 000 Covers areas of settled pop. and agriculture 6/-
SK 50 Settlement Towns
SK 64 Nairobi Blocks
SK 62 Mombasa (Island) Blocks

D POLITICAL & ADMINISTRATIVE

PHILIP'S LARGE OUTLINE MAP OF KENYA
1:1, 250, 000
London : Philip
104 x 83
Printed in black on white cartridge paper with contours. £1.25

ADMINISTRATIVE BOUNDARIES
1:1, 000, 000
SK 57C
Nairobi : SK, 1968
87 x 100
2 sheet provisional ed; all types of admin. boundaries overprinted on base route map.
Set 10/-

KENYA ADMINISTRATIVE MAP
1:1, 000, 000
SK 41 H
Nairobi : SK
87 x 106
2 sheet map showing admin. boundaries in col. on subdued base map.

PARLIAMENTARY CONSTITUENCIES
1:1, 000, 000
SK 57D
Nairobi : SK
2 sheet map also showing province, district and county boundaries.
Set 10/-

KENYA
1:50, 000
SK 61
Nairobi : SK
Violet overprint on Y731 topog. series, showing location and sub location boundaries (limited availability).

E1 PHYSICAL AND GENERAL

KENYA PHYSICAL AND GENERAL
1:3, 000, 000
SK 10
Nairobi : SK
50 x 60
Contoured, layer col, communications and boundaries. (Also available subdued monochrome as base map) 4/-

KENJA
1:2, 000, 000
Moskva : GUGK, 1971
52 x 70
Physical map, contoured with 3 them. insets.

PHILIP'S REGIONAL WALL MAP OF KENYA
1:1, 250, 000
London : Philip
91 x 117
Physical col. with communications and boundaries.
Paper £1.50
Mounted CR £5.50
Mounted on cloth dissected to fold £7.00

KENYA TOPOGRAPHICAL MAP
1:1, 000, 000
SK 57
Nairobi : SK
87 x 106
Map in 2 sheets, contoured, layer col, boundaries, communications.
12/50

F GEOLOGY

GEOLOGICAL MAP OF KENYA
1:3, 000, 000
Nairobi : Geol. Survey, 1962
Showing geol. structure in colour and major faults.

KENYA, GEOLOGY
1:125, 000
See index 676. 2/4
Nairobi : Mines and Geology Dept.
45 x 44
Coloured geological series with text.

G EARTH RESOURCES

MINERAL MAPS OF KENYA
1:3, 000, 000
Nairobi : Geol, Surv, 1962
Marking locations of minerals by symbols.

NAIROBI-MACHAKOS SOIL SURVEY
1:100, 000
DOS (LU) 3014
Edition 1
Tolworth : DOS, 1963
2 colour sheets on topog. sheet lines
West (sheets 148, 149), East (sheets 149, 150) depicting soils and land use.
Each 65p

NAIROBI-MACHAKOS SOIL SURVEY
1:50, 000
DOS (LU) 3013
Edition 1
In 8 sheets
Tolworth : DOS, 1962
Monochrome set of maps on topog. sheet lines depicting soils and land use.
Sheets included : 148/2, 4; 149/1,2,3 and 4; 150/1,3.
Each 50p

KENYA SOIL SURVEY
1:50, 000
Tolworth : DOS
Series of col. soil maps indicating their potential.
Maps available :
DOS (Misc) 3009A Songhor, sheets 117/1 and 103/3 (part) 1960
- A Soil Survey 65p
- B Soil Groups significant to management 50p
- C Areas suitable for sugar cane 65p

DOS (Misc) 3010 East Konyanga, sheet 129/2,4 and 130/1,3 (part) 1961
- A Soil Survey 65p
- B Areas suitable for sugar cane 50p

DOS (LU) 3013 Soil Survey, sheets 148/2,4, 149/1,2,3,4, 150/1,3, 1962, 1:100, 000
DOS (LU) 3014 Soil Survey, West Sheet: pts. 148, 149. East Sheet: pts 149, 150

H BIOGEOGRAPHY

KENYA-BOUNDARIES-RAINFALL-POPULATION-TSETSE FLY-LAND UNITS
1:2, 000, 000
DOS, 1961
see KENYA 676.2 J

KENYA HUNTING MAP
1:1, 000, 000
SK 57B
Nairobi : SK, 1965
91 x 64
Overprinted on base Route Map, showing numbered Hunting Blocks, National Parks, Game Reserves, Controlled Areas etc. Double sided. 7.50

KENYA - VEGETATION
1:250, 000
DOS (LR) 3006
Tolworth : DOS
93 x 55
4 sheets covering SW Kenya showing vegetation types and zones. 2 sheets published : sheet 1, 1966; sheet 3, 1970.
65p

SOUTH WESTERN KENYA, CLIMATE AND VEGETATION
1:250, 000
DOS (LR) 3059
In 4 sheets
Tolworth : DOS, 1969
108 x 95 each
Vegetation zones on physical base map, with rainfall and temperature diagrams. Sheets 1, 1969 and 3, 1970 only are available.
Each 65p

J CLIMATE

KENYA-BOUNDARIES-RAINFALL-POPULATION-TSETSE FLY-LAND UNITS
1:2, 000, 000
DOS (Misc) 203D
Tolworth : DOS, 1961
Coloured distribution map.
65p

K HUMAN GEOGRAPHY

KENYA-BOUNDARIES-RAINFALL-POPULATION-TSETSE FLY-LAND UNITS
1:2, 000, 000
DOS, 1961
see KENYA 676.2 J

POPULATION OF KENYA, DENSITY AND DISTRIBUTION
1:1, 000, 000
by Morgan & Shaffer
Nairobi : OUP
91 x 63 each
2 maps, each of 2 sheets, enclosed in text, based on Census of 1962.
Density Map - col. by districts, Locations and Wards
Distribution Map - dot method

KENYA, DISTRIBUTION OF POPULATION
1:1, 000, 000
Compiled under the direction of Prof. S H Ominde
Nairobi : Univ. of Nairobi, 1969
87 x 106
Coloured population map based on 1969 census. 25/00

KENYA, DENSITY OF POPULATION
1:1, 000, 000
Compiled under the direction of Prof. S H Ominde
Nairobi : Univ. of Nairobi, 1969
87 x 106
Coloured population map based on 1969 census. 25/00

DOT DISTRIBUTION MAP OF KENYA
1:1, 000, 000
Nairobi : Univ. College Kenya, 1969
87 x 106
2 sheet population density map based on 1962 Census.

THE ETHNIC MAP OF THE REPUBLIC OF KENYA
Prof S H Ominde
1:1, 000, 000
Nairobi : Univ. College, Kenya, 1965
87 x 106
2 sheet map showing distribution of peoples - Bantu, Nilotic, Nilo-Hamitic and Others - by district. With 12pp Memoir.
40/00

N MATHEMATICAL

PRIMARY AND SECONDARY TRI-ANGULATION AND TRILATERATION
1:1, 000, 000
SK 57G
Nairobi : SK
91 x 64
Overprinted on road map base (SK 57).
7/50

ATLASES
E2 PHYSICAL : LAND FEATURES

LAND SYSTEM ATLAS OF WESTERN KENYA
Christchurch : MVEE, 1971
95 x 77
Two sheet land system map scale 1:500, 000 with descriptions of each system represented by an annotated air photograph, block diagram and tables of soils, landforms and vegetation.

ATLASES
L ECONOMIC

A COMPUTER ATLAS OF KENYA
by D R F Taylor
Ottawa : Georg. Dept, Carleton Univ, 1971
21 x 28
121pp
Example of computer mapping systems; synthesised planning information about an area. Bibliog. of computer mapping. 64pp maps, 56pp text. $4.95

ATLASES
O NATIONAL

NATIONAL ATLAS OF KENYA
1:3, 000, 000 (standard scale)
3rd edition
Nairobi : SK, 1970
40 x 38
103pp
43 col. maps, 5 in black and white, covering physical features, agriculture, geology, climate, vegetation, economy, population, industry, history. With text and gazetteer.
120/-

677 Somalia

A2 GENERAL MAPS: LOCAL

MOGADISCIO
1:50, 000
Firenze : IGM, 1935
44 x 40
Col. physical map of the town and environs.
Each L 500

C OFFICIAL SURVEYS

KARTA MIRA
1:2, 500, 000
GUGK (Bulg) - PPWK
2 sheets to cover Somalia : 115, 135
see WORLD 100C and index 100/2.

AFRICA
1:2, 000, 000
AMS Series 2201
Sheets 21, 24, 25 cover Somalia
see AFRICA 6C and index 6/2.

INTERNATIONAL MAP OF THE WORLD
1:1, 000, 000
6 sheets cover Somalia.
see WORLD 100C and index 100/1.

CARTA DIMOSTRATIVA DELLA SOMALIA
1:1, 000, 000
In 8 sheets, see index 677/1
Firenze : IGM, 1935
67 x 44
Col. map on modified policonical proj, covering former Italian and British Somaliland.
Each L 500

WORLD
1:500, 000
DMS 1404
see WORLD 100C and index 100/7.

CARTA DIMOSTRATIVA DELLA SOMALIA
1:200, 000
In 12 sheets, see index 677/2
Firenze : IGM, 1910
56 x 37
Black and white land series covering the coastal region around Mogadishu.
Each L 500

CARTA DELLA SOMALIA (MEDIA E BASSA GOSCIA)
1:50, 000
In 9 sheets, see index 677/3
Firenze : IGM, 1910-12
55 x 37
Black and white topog. series covering the Juba River.
Each L 500

SOMALILAND PROTECTORATE
1:125, 000
DOS 539 (Y 625)
In 68 sheets, see index 677/4
Tolworth : DOS, 1952-57
Series showing basic topog. detail, uncontoured, black and white.
30p

SOMALILAND PROTECTORATE
1:50, 000
DOS 427 (Y 721)
See index 677/4
Tolworth : DOS, 1952-54
Topographical series, uncontoured; 4 sheets published. 30p

SOMALILAND PROTECTORATE
1:25, 000
DOS 339 (Y 823)
See index 677/4
Tolworth : DOS, 1959
Series giving basic topog. detail, uncontoured, contoured or form-lined. Published for 2 local areas only, 9 sheets available.
30p

D POLITICAL & ADMINISTRATIVE

SOMALILAND PROTECTORATE
1:2, 500, 000
DOS 983
Tolworth : DOS
Small map showing boundaries, roads and towns.

E1 PHYSICAL: RELIEF

SOMALI
1:2, 500, 000
Moskva : GUGK
Physical map, contoured with them. insets.

F GEOLOGY

GEOLOGICAL MAP OF NORTHERN SOMALIA AND SOCOTRA/GULF OF ADEN - REPORT ON THE RED SEA DISCUSSION MEETING
1:2, 000, 000
RGS
see INDIAN OCEAN 267 ATLASES E1

GEOLOGICAL MAPS OF THE SOMALI DEMOCRATIC REPUBLIC
1:125, 000
DOS (Geol) 1076
See index 677/4
Tolworth : DOS, 1959-71
Coloured geological series, in progress, covering the former British Somaliland Protectorate. Each 65p

677.1 French Territory of the Afars and Issas

B TOWN PLANS

DJIBOUTI ET ENVIRONS
1:20, 000
In 4 sheets
Paris : IGN
60 x 75 each
In 3 colours, topog. detail in black, water in blue, contours in brown. Based on information 1939-42. F.Fr 11.67

DJIBOUTI
1:10, 000
Paris : IGN, 1945
52 x 70
Provisional edition in black and white, with contours. F.Fr 11.67

DIKHIL ET ENVIRONS
1:10, 000
Paris : IGN
63 x 42
Black and white plan with contours.
F.Fr 16.67

C OFFICIAL SURVEYS

WORLD
1:500, 000
DMS 1404
3 sheets for coverage
see WORLD 100C and index 100/7.

CARTE GÉNÉRALE DE LA CÔTE FRANÇAISE DES SOMALIS
1:200, 000
In 4 sheets
Paris : IGN
118 x 105 complete
General topog. map in colours, contoured with relief shading. F.Fr 11.67

CARTE DE LA CÔTE FRANÇAISE DES SOMALIS
1:100, 000
In 12 sheets, see index 677.1/1
Paris : IGN
55 x 55
Col. topog. series. Planimetric detail black, water features blue, vegetation green, contours brown. With UTM grid.
F.Fr 11.67

F GEOLOGY

CARTE GEOLOGIQUE DE LA CÔTE FRANÇAISE DES SOMALIS
1:400, 000
Paris : Imprimerie Nationale, 1939-46
Geological map, with 4pp notice by H Besaire.

678 Tanzania

A2 GENERAL MAPS: LOCAL

TANZANIA - SPECIAL MAPS
Various scales
Dar es Salaam
Series of tourist or technical maps.
Sheets available :

S1 Kilimanjaro 1:100, 000 with hill shading (DOS 552) 1965
S2 Ngorongo Conservation Area 1:250, 000
S3 Zanzibar Sheet 1 1:63, 360 (DOS 8 (Y 744)) 1953
S4 Zanzibar Sheet 2 1:63, 360 (DOS 8 (Y 44)) 1953
S5 Pemba Island (Weti) 1:63, 360
S6 Pemba Island (Chake Chake) 1:63, 360
S7 Pemba Island 1:125, 000
S8 Mafia Island North 1:50, 000 Y 743
S9 Mafia Island South 1:50, 000 Y 743
S11 Guide Map of Dar es Salaam 1:25, 000, 1968
S14 Dar es Salaam - Behen Marks, 1:25, 000

B TOWN PLANS

TOWNSHIP MAPS
Various scales
Dar es Salaam
Series of large scale plans covering the legally defined Townships, each is, or will be, covered by a composite map and also by series of large scale plans scale 1:2, 500 or 1:5, 000. Based on aerial photography with contours and plot boundaries. Maps available:

Arusha :
1:10, 000
1: 2, 500 in 5 sheets, 1966
Bukoba :
1: 5, 000
1: 2, 500 in 5 sheets, 1962
Dar es Salaam :
1:25, 000
1: 5, 000 in 11 sheets
1: 2, 500 in 6 sheets, 1957/59
Dodoma :
1: 2, 500 in 16 sheets, 1962/63
Iringa :
1: 2, 500 in 6 sheets, 1957
Kigoma - Ujiji
1: 2, 500 in 4 sheets, 1964
1: 2, 500 in 4 sheets, 1961
Lindi :
1:2, 500 in 3 sheets, 1960
Mbeya :
1: 5, 000
1: 2, 500 in 4 sheets, 1965
Morogoro :
1:10, 000
1: 2, 500 in 6 sheets, 1963
Moshi :
1:10, 000
1: 2, 500 in 10 sheets, 1962
Mtwara-Mikindani :
1: 2, 500 in 10 sheets, 1964
Musoma :
1: 2, 500 in 5 sheets, 1960
Mwanza :
1: 2, 500 in 9 sheets, 1963
Tabora :
1:10, 000
1: 2, 500 in 7 sheets, 1957/65
Tanga :
1:10, 000
1: 2, 500 in 17 sheets, 1958/59

URBAN MAPS
1:5, 000 - 1:1, 000
Dar es Salaam : Surv. Div.
Series of maps covering the developed extent of certain urban areas, generally based on aerial photography with contours and plot boundaries. Maps available in either coloured 'C' or monochrome 'M' editions :

Town	Scale	Year	Sheets	Edition
Bagamoyo	1:5, 000	1953		M
	1:2, 500	1968		C
Biharamulo	1:2, 500	1962	2 sheets	C
Geita	1:5, 000	1966		C
Ifakara	1:5, 000	1961		M
Kilosa	1:2, 500	1958		M
Kilwa Kivinje	1:2, 500	1963		C
Kissessa	1:1, 000	1961		M
Kondoa	1:5, 000	1957		C
Korogwe (old)	1:2, 500	1951		M
Kyela	1:2, 500	1965	2 sheets	C
Lushoto	1:2, 500	1963	3 sheets	C
Malya	1:2, 500	1967		C
Manyoni	1:2, 500	1967		C
Mbulu	1:5, 000	1966		C
Misungwi	1:2, 500	1957		M
Mpwapwa	1:2, 500	1964	4 sheets	C
Mufindi	1:2, 500	1964		C
Nansio	1:2, 500	1962		C
Njombe	1:2, 500	1962	2 sheets	C
Nyakata	1:1, 000	1960		M
Pangani	1:2, 500	1965		C
Shinyanga	1:2, 500	1961	4 sheets	C
Singida	1:2, 500	1962	4 sheets	C
Songea	1:5, 000	1963		C
Sumbawanga	1:2, 500	1967	2 sheets	C
Tarime	1:2, 500	1965		C
Tukuyu	1:2, 500	1963	2 sheets	C
Usagara	1:2, 500	1957		M
Vwawa	1:2, 500	1967		C

C OFFICIAL SURVEYS

KARTA MIRA
1:2, 500, 000
PPWK
Sheets 134, 135 for Tanzania.
see WORLD 100C and index 100/2.

AFRICA
1:2, 000, 000
AMS Series 2201
Sheets 24, 28 cover Tanzania.
see AFRICA 6C and index 6/2.

INTERNATIONAL MAP OF THE WORLD
1:1, 000, 000
Series 1301
DOS edition Tanzania
6 sheets to cover Tanzania
see WORLD 100C and index 100/1.

LAKE PROVINCE MAP
1:500, 000
In 4 sheets
Dar es Salaam : Surv. Div.
Topographical map of the region surrounding southern Lake Victoria.

TANZANIA
1:250, 000
Dar es Salaam : Surv. Div.
Series of special area topog. maps which will be superseded by the new Y 503 series.
Sheets still available :
Masailand, sheets 1-11
Dodoma
Ukimbu
Kaliua
Mpanda
Sumbawanga
Manda
Lindi
Shinyanga

EAST AFRICA
1:250, 000
Series Y 503
See index 678/1
Dar es Salaam : Surv. Div.
75 x 60
Topog. series showing national, district, county and National Park boundaries, communications, roads graded by surface, settlements, principal buildings, rivers, lakes, relief features, contours or form-lines and hill shading. The UTM grid is shown with grid data and admin. diagram. 22 sheets available for Tanzania, some in preliminary unlayered edition. Series in progress.

TANZANIA
1:50, 000
DOS 422 (Y 742)
See index 678/2
Dar es Salaam : Surv. Div./
Tolworth : DOS
55 x 55 each
Topog. series in progress to cover Tanzania; uncontoured, contoured, or form-lined.

D POLITICAL & ADMINISTRATIVE

TANZANIA BASE MAP
1:4, 000, 000
S 10
Dar es Salaam
Small hand map in grey monochrome, base map editions also available :
S 16 1:3, 000, 000 and
S 17 1:2, 000, 000

PHILIP'S LARGE OUTLINE MAP OF TANGANYIKA
1:1, 500, 000
London : Philip
104 x 83
Printed in black on white cartridge paper with contours. £1.25

TANZANIA - DISTRICT SERIES
1:500, 000 - 1:100, 000
Dar es Salaam : Surv. Div.
Various sizes
Series of administrative maps covering individual Districts on separate sheets. Showing roads, settlement and admin. information; forest reserves and large estates appear on later editions.

E1 PHYSICAL: RELIEF

TANZANIA
1:2, 000, 000
Dar es Salaam : Surv. Div.
76 x 84
General map of Tanzania showing boundaries, communications, settlements, physical features, contours, layer col.

TANZANIYA
1:2, 000, 000
Moskva : GUGK
86 x 66
Physical, contoured, them. insets.

PHILIP'S REGIONAL WALL MAP OF TANZANIA
1:1, 500, 000
London : Philip
111 x 91
Physical col, communications and boundaries.
Paper £1.50
Mounted CR £5.50
Mounted on cloth dissected to fold £7.00

F GEOLOGY

GEOLOGICAL MAP OF TANZANIA
1:3, 000, 000
Dar es Salaam : Surv. Div.
54 x 42
Col. geol. map with text on reverse.

TANZANIA - GEOLOGICAL SURVEY
1:125, 000
In 97 sheets,
Dodoma : Mineral Resources Division
44 x 44
Col. geological series in progress.

G EARTH RESOURCES

TANGANYIKA - ISOGONIC CHART
1:4, 000, 000
S 15
Dar es Salaam : Surv. Div.

N MATHEMATICAL

TANZANIA - PRIMARY LEVELLING DIAGRAM
1:4, 000, 000
S 13
Dar es Salaam : Surv. Div.

TANZANIA - TRIANGULATION DIAGRAM
1:2, 000, 000
S 12
Dar es Salaam : Surv. Div.
76 x 84
Triangulation network shown in colour.

ATLASES
O NATIONAL

ATLAS OF TANZANIA
Dar es Salaam : Surv. Div, 1968
55 x 46
Maps at basic scale 1:3, 000, 000
incl. plates on geol, soils, climate, vegetation, pop. admin, industry, commerce; gazetteer. Each map has accompanying text. 3rd edition.

TANZANIA IN MAPS
1st Edition
Ed L Berry
London : Hodder & Stoughton, 1971
22 x 28
176pp
65 black and white maps covering physical and them. subjects with facing descriptive text and statistical data of human and natural resources. £3.50

679 Mozambique

A1 GENERAL MAPS: ROADS

MAPA RODOVIARIO DE MOÇAMBIQUE
1:2, 000, 000
2nd edition
Lourenco Marques : Junta Autonoma de Estradas de Moçambique, 1972
64 x 92
Roads classified, numbered, distances in km, other communications etc. 3 enlargements of important areas, distance table. On reverse side are 5 sketch town plans.
Paper folded.

C OFFICIAL SURVEYS

KARTA MIRA
1:2, 500, 000
PPWK
5 sheets to cover Mozambique :
134, 135, 154, 155, 174
see WORLD 100C and index 100/2.

AFRICA
1:2, 000, 000
AMS 2201
Sheets 28, 31, 34 to cover.
see AFRICA 6C and index 6/2.

INTERNATIONAL MAP OF THE WORLD
1:1, 000, 000
see WORLD 100C and index 100/1.

MOÇAMBIQUE
1:500, 000
In 18 sheets, see index 679/1
Lisboa : PUP, 1939-1956
Topographical series, contoured.
The 10 sheets covering the northern half of the country are now out of print.

CARTA DE PORTUGAL - PROVÍNCIA DE MOÇAMBIQUE
1:250, 000
In 102 sheets, see index 679/2
Lisboa : PUP
New topog. series in progress, contoured, which will replace earlier series.

MOÇAMBIQUE
1:250, 000
In 61 sheets, see index 679/3
Lisboa : PUP, 1936-1955
Detailed topog. series, contoured. A large number of sheets are now out of print. To be replaced by new series : Carta de Portugal - Provincia de Moçambique.

CARTA DE PORTUGAL - PROVINCIA DE MOÇAMBIQUE
1:50, 000
In 1207 sheets, see index 679/4
Lisboa : PUP
Detailed topog. series in progress, contoured, based upon aerial photography. Southern coastal areas only published.

D POLITICAL & ADMINISTRATIVE

MOZAMBIQUE
1:8, 300, 000 app
No 1388
New York : UN, 1971
General administrative map.

CARTA DE PORTUGAL - PROVÍNCIA DE MOÇAMBIQUE
1:5, 000, 000
Lisboa : PUP, 1970
General map showing communications, settlement and administrative boundaries.

CARTA DE MOÇAMBIQUE
1:2, 000, 000
4th edition
Lisboa : PUP, 1971
66 x 93
Col. by districts, all classes of roads, railways, aerodromes, rivers, towns graded acc. admin. status.

E1 PHYSICAL: RELIEF

MOZAMBIK
1:2, 000, 000
Moskva : GUGK
Physical, contours, them. insets.

F GEOLOGY

CARTA GEOLÓGICA DE MOÇAMBIQUE
1:2, 000, 000
Lourenço Marques : Dir. Serv. Geol. e Minas, 1968
73 x 102
Col. geol. map.

CARTA GEOLÓGICA PROVISORIA
1:250, 000
Lourenço Marques : Serv. Geol. e Minas
Multi-sheet col. geol. series in progress.

68 Southern Africa

A1 GENERAL MAPS: ROADS

AFRICA, CENTRAL AND SOUTH, MADAGASCAR
1:4, 000, 000
No 155
Paris : Michelin, 1975
97 x 119
Road map; political boundaries, settlements, motoring and tourist features. Roads graded by condition, numbered, distances in km and miles. Fr and Eng.

ROAD MAP OF MALAWI, RHODESIA AND ZAMBIA
1:2, 600, 000 app
Kitwe : Automobile Association of Zambia, 1971
Road map giving route numbers and distances.

C OFFICIAL SURVEYS

GENERAL REFERENCE MAP OF THE WORLD
1:5, 000, 000
AGS
Sheet 4 to cover Southern Africa.
see WORLD 100C and index 100/3.

AFRICA
1:2, 000, 000
AMS 2201
see AFRICA 6C and index 6/2.

WORLD AERONAUTICAL CHART ICAO SOUTH AFRICAN TOPOGRAPHICAL EDITION
1:1, 000, 000
See index 68/1
Pretoria : Govt. Printer
72 x 47
Topog. series on ICAO sheet lines, without air information, showing basic topog. detail, contours, layer col.

D POLITICAL & ADMINISTRATIVE

AFRICA SOUTH OF THE SAHARA
1:7, 500, 000
Pretoria : Govt. Printer, 1971
78 x 100
Political col. map.

STANFORD'S GENERAL MAP OF CENTRAL AND SOUTH AFRICA
1:5, 500, 000
London : Stanford, 1968
73 x 98
Political col, boundaries, roads, railways, canals, airports, pipelines, spot heights, settlements graded by pop. Pictorial border.

GEOGRAPHIA INTERNATIONAL SERIES: SOUTHERN AFRICA (SUIDELIKE AFRIKA)
1:2, 700, 000
London : Gia
107 x 81
Political col, principal towns, roads, railways, shipping routes and national parks. Eng and Afrikaans. In slip cover, containing maps of Africa and description.
40p

PHILIP'S POLITICAL SMALLER WALL MAP OF SOUTH AFRICA
1:2, 500, 000
London : Philip
109 x 84
Political col, railways and shipping routes.
Paper £1.50
Mounted CR £5.50
Mounted on cloth dissected to fold £7.00

E1 PHYSICAL: RELIEF

AFRICA SOUTH OF THE SAHARA
1:7, 500, 000
Pretoria : Govt. Printer, 1971
78 x 100
Topographic map, physical colouring.

JIŽNÍ AFRIKA
1:6, 000, 000
Praha : USGK, 1964
92 x 68
Physical, contours, communications, them. insets. In series "Poznavame Svet" (know the World). 44pp text.

WORLD TRAVEL MAP SERIES : CENTRAL AND SOUTHERN AFRICA
1:5, 000, 000
Edinburgh : Bart, 1975
72 x 94
Physical; political boundaries, communications, settlements, topog. features, contoured, layer col. 75p

EKVATORIAL'NAYA I YUZHNAYA AFRIKA
1:5, 000, 000
Moskva : GUGK, 1971
Map of Central and S Africa; physical, contours, them. insets.

MITTEL- UND SUDAFRIKA
1:3, 000, 000
Braunschweig : Westermann
212 x 176
Physical wall map, also in Eng. ed.
DM 142

SOUTHERN AFRICA
1:2, 500, 000
TSO Misc. 2223
2nd edition
Pretoria : Govt. Printer, 1965
113 x 88
Physical map covering Republic of S Africa, S W Africa, Botswana, most of Rhodesia and Mozambique. Communications, water features, settlements, contoured, layer col.

PHILIP'S PHYSICAL SMALLER WALL MAP OF SOUTH AFRICA
1:2, 500, 000
London : Philip
109 x 84
Layer col, political boundaries, town stamps indicated by initial letter only.
Paper £1.50
Mounted CR £5.50
Mounted on cloth dissected to fold £7.00

PHILIP'S PHYSICAL LARGE WALL MAP OF SOUTH AFRICA
1:1, 500, 000
London : Philip
178 x 122
Orographical col, hill shading, boundaries, railways and ocean routes.
Mounted CRV £15.00
Mounted on cloth dissected to fold with eyelets £17.00

L ECONOMIC

STANDARD SPOORWEGKAART VAN SUID AFRIKA EN AANGRENSEND-GEBIEDE
1:3, 500, 000
TSO Misc. 3735
Pretoria : S African Railways, 1968
97 x 71
'Standard Railway map of South Africa and Neighbouring Territories' col. by states, showing railway lines and stations. 5 insets.

ATLASES

W3 WORLD ATLASES: LOCAL EDITIONS

VENTURE ATLAS FOR SOUTHERN AFRICA
London : Philip
22 x 28
Middle school atlas, 36pp maps.

JUNIOR SCHOOL ATLAS FOR SOUTHERN AFRICA
London : Philip
19 x 23
24pp maps, 6pp economic maps, 9pp index.

LARGE-PRINT ATLAS FOR SOUTHERN AFRICA
London : Philip, 1976
23 x 28
48pp maps
(Also available as Juta Springbok Large Print Atlas for Southern Africa)

PHILIP'S STUDENTS' ATLAS FOR SOUTHERN AFRICA
London : Philip
23 x 28
88pp maps.

PHILIP'S COLLEGE ATLAS FOR SOUTHERN AFRICA
London : Philip
23 x 28
116 coloured plates, 16pp special maps covering Southern Africa.

ATLASES
A1 GENERAL: ROADS

ROAD ATLAS AND TOURING GUIDE OF SOUTHERN AFRICA
Johannesburg : Automobile Assoc.
4th Edition
S Africa, 1972
19 x 25
232pp
Road maps, through town plans, tourist and motoring details covering Zambia, Rhodesia, Malawi, Lesotho, Botswana and South West Africa.

ATLASES
P REGIONAL

ATLAS OF THE FEDERATION OF RHODESIA AND NYASALAND
1:2, 500, 000
Salisbury : Dept. Trig. & Topog. Surv, 1960-64
67 x 79
24 col. plates covering :
1 Africa physical 1:15, 000, 000
2 Southern Africa, communications 1:6, 000, 000
Rhodesia & Nyasaland
3 Physical, general map
4 Geology
5 Mineralogy
6a Hunting Areas
6b Tsetse Fly Areas
7 Administrative Areas
8 African Tribes and Languages
9 Population Distribution
10 Vegetation
11 Soil
12a Rainfall
12b Rainfall Utilisation
13a Agricultural Production
13b Natural Farming Regions
14 Temperature
15 Humidity
16 Sunshine
17a Winds - July
17b Winds - January
18 Routes of early European Travellers
19 Electric Power Distribution
20 Tobacco Production
Plates available separately.

680 South Africa

See also: 68 SOUTHERN AFRICA

A1 GENERAL MAPS: ROADS

TOURISTENKARTE REPUBLIK SUDAFRIKA
1:2, 400, 000
Johannesburg : Map Studio Prod.
Road map of South Africa with insets of S Coast of Natal, Cape Peninsula.

SOUTH AFRICA
1:1, 750, 000
Johannesburg : Map Centre, 1964
132 x 122
2 sheet wall map : communications, boundaries etc.

A2 GENERAL MAPS: LOCAL

MAP OF THE ORANGE FREE STATE GOLDFIELDS
1:125, 000
Pretoria : Govt. Printer
88 x 108
Admin. and property boundaries, roads graded by class, settlements, mines, quarries, water features, other topog. detail, contours at 100 ft intervals.

B TOWN PLANS

HOLMDEN'S STREET MAP OF GREATER JOHANNESBURG
1:28, 160
Johannesburg : Map Office (Pty) Ltd, 1975
71 x 129
Includes Randburg and Sandton naming streets with distance radius circles from centre. Index to streets.
S.A.Ra 1.85

C OFFICIAL SURVEYS

KARTA MIRA
1:2, 500, 000
PPWK
4 sheets to cover South Africa :
153, 154, 173, 174
see WORLD 100C and index 100/2.

AFRICA
1:2, 000, 000
AMS Series 2201
Sheets 33, 34, 35, 36 give coverage.
see AFRICA 6C and index 6/2.

WORLD AERONAUTICAL CHART ICAO SOUTH AFRICAN TOPOGRAPHICAL EDITION
1:1, 000, 000
See index 68/1
Pretoria : Govt. Printer
72 x 47
Series on ICAO sheet lines without air information showing basic topographical detail, contours and layer colouring.

SOUTH AFRICA TOPOGRAPHICAL SERIES
1:500, 000
See index 680/1
2nd edition
Pretoria : Govt. Printer
61 x 66
Basic topog. detail, contours, layer col.
Also available in Aeronautical and admin. eds.

SOUTH AFRICA TOPOGRAPHICAL SERIES
1:250, 000
See index 680/2
Pretoria : Govt. Printer
76 x 44
Series showing detailed topog. info, woodland col, contours, layer col.

SOUTH AFRICA TOPO-CADASTRAL SERIES
1:250, 000
See index 680/3
Pretoria : Govt. Printer
Topographic base series, brown contours, blue water features, red roads with mines and magisterial district boundaries in purple.

SOUTH AFRICA TOPOGRAPHICAL SERIES
1:50, 000
See index 680/4
Pretoria : Govt. Printer
50 x 55
Col. topog. series; boundaries, settlements, communications, water features, vegetation types, contours. Second ed. in progress.

EXPERIMENTAL PHOTOMAPS
1:10, 000/50, 000
Mowbray : Trig survey
Various sizes
Experimental orthophoto and photo-maps, available for :

Ca Mier, 1967	
1:50, 000	55 x 51
Leonardville, 1967	
1:50, 000	55 x 51
Rondesbosch, 1966	
1:10, 000	48 x 66
Honeydew Area, 1969	
1:10, 000	55 x 50

D POLITICAL & ADMINISTRATIVE

PHILIP'S POLITICAL SMALLER WALL MAP OF SOUTH AFRICA
1:2, 500, 000
London : Philip
109 x 84
Political col, railways and shipping routes.
Also available in Afrikaans.

Paper	£1.50
Mounted CR	£5.50
Mounted on cloth dissected to fold	£7.00

USHNO-AFRIKANSKAYA RESPUBLIKA
1:2, 500, 000
Moskva : GUGK, 1973
83 x 66
Col. study map showing water features, settlements, admin. centres and divisions, communications, boundaries, economic details, pop. Geog. description.
30 kop

MAGISTERIAL BOUNDARIES - MAP G - WATER AFFAIRS MAP SET
1:1, 500, 000
Govt. Printer
see SOUTH AFRICA 680 E2

E1 PHYSICAL: RELIEF

SOUTHERN AFRICA
1:2, 500, 000
TSO Misc. 2223
Pretoria : Govt. Printer
Physical map with topographical detail, contours and layer colouring.

PHILIP'S PHYSICAL SMALLER WALL MAP OF SOUTH AFRICA
1:2, 500, 000
London : Philip
109 x 84
Layer col, political boundaries.
Town stamps indicated by initial letter only. Also available in Afrikaans.

Paper	£1.50
Mounted CR	£5.50
Mounted on cloth dissected to fold	£7.00

PHILIP'S PHYSICAL LARGE WALL MAP OF SOUTH AFRICA
1:1, 500, 000
London : Philip
178 x 122
Orographical col, hill shading, boundaries, railways and ocean routes.

CRV	£15.00
On cloth dissected to fold	£17.00

E2 PHYSICAL: LAND FEATURES

WATER AFFAIRS
1:1, 500, 000
Pretoria : Govt. Printer (Secretary for Water Affairs)
Series of 12 maps, each in 2 sheets:

A	Basic Map
B	River System
C	Perennial river areas
D	Irrigation in S Africa
E*	Main Drainage Regions
F*	Minor Drainage Regions
G	Magisterial district boundaries
H	Rainfall Map
I	Evaporation

* out of print.
Each 60 c

F GEOLOGY

GEOLOGICAL MAP OF THE REPUBLIC OF SOUTH AFRICA AND THE KINGDOMS OF LESOTHO AND SWAZILAND
1:1, 000, 000
In 4 sheets
3rd edition
Pretoria : Geol. Surv, 1970
190 x 145 complete
Coloured map with list of working mines. Shows boundaries, roads and rivers.
R 2.40
Also available in Gravity Ed, showing Bouguer Anomalies overprinted.

GEOLOGICAL MAP OF THE REPUBLIC OF S AFRICA
1:250, 000
In 71 sheets, see index 680/5
Pretoria : Geol. Surv.
76 x 44
Col. geol. series in progress.

SOUTH AFRICA - GEOLOGICAL SERIES
1:148, 750
See index 680/6
Pretoria : Geol. Survey
Col. geol. series to be replaced by the new 1:125, 000 series.

MAP OF THE REPUBLIC OF S AFRICA
1:125, 000
See index 680/6
Pretoria : Geol. Surv.
Col. geol. series incl. parts of S W Africa, with explanations.

GEOLOGICAL MAP OF THE KLERKSDORP-VENTERSDORP AREA
1:60, 000
Pretoria : Geol. Surv, 1955
With explanation by L T Nel.
R 1.05

GEOLOGICAL MAP OF THE COUNTRY AROUND HEIDELBERG
1:60, 000
Pretoria : Geol. Surv, 1922
With explanation by A W Rogers.
85 c

GEOLOGICAL MAP OF THE BARBERTON AREA
1:50, 000
Pretoria : Geol. Surv, 1956
With explanation by O R van Eeden et al.
R 3.50

GEOLOGICAL MAP OF PIETER-MARITZBURG & ENVIRONS
1:50, 000
Pretoria : Geol. Surv, 1948
With explanation by L C King.
50 c

G EARTH RESOURCES

SOUTH AFRICAN MAIN MINERAL RESOURCES
1:7, 500, 000
No 1764
New York : UN, 1967
17 x 20
Monochrome map showing gold, copper, manganese, asbestos, coal and diamonds.

GRAVITY MAP OF THE UNION OF SOUTH AFRICA ON GEOLOGICAL BASE
1:1, 000, 000
In 4 sheets
2nd edition
Pretoria : Dept. Geol. & Mines, 1970
188 x 140
Col. geol. map with overprint of Bouguer anomalies. R 2.40

AEROMAGNETIC MAPS
1:50, 000 - 1:250, 000
Pretoria : Govt. Printer, 1971
Maps published for two areas :
Transvaal - Louis Trichard - Bandelierkop
1:250, 000 in 1 sheet
1: 50, 000 in 16 sheets
N W Cape - Gamoep
1:250, 000 in 1 sheet
1: 50, 000 in 15 sheets

H BIOGEOGRAPHY

STATE FORESTRY MAP OF SOUTH AFRICA
1:2, 000, 000
Pretoria : Govt. Printer, 1953
109 x 88
Silvicultural zones with basic topog. features.

J CLIMATE

RAINFALL - MAP H EVAPORATION - MAP I - WATER AFFAIRS MAP SET
1:1, 500, 000
Govt. Printer
see SOUTH AFRICA 680 E2

AVERAGE RAINFALL MAP
1:250, 000
In 71 sheets
Pretoria : Govt. Printer
Col. series in progress following sheet lines of topog. series.

L ECONOMIC

STANDARD SPOORWEGKAART VAN SUID AFRIKA EN AANGRENSEND GEBIEDE
1:3, 500, 000
TSO Misc 3735
Pretoria : Govt. Printer, 1968
97 x 71
Coloured "Standard Railway Map of South Africa and Neighbouring Territories". With names of operating railway companies. 5 insets.

AGRICULTURAL ECONOMIC MAP OF SOUTH AFRICA, 1965
1:2, 000, 000
Pretoria : Govt. Printer, 1967
101 x 77
Agricultural land use indicated by col. Diagram inset.

REPUBLIC OF SOUTH AFRICA
1:1, 124, 000
Johannesburg : Map Centre, 1965
200 x 134
2 sheet wall map; communications, railway stations, admin. districts on white base map.

M HISTORICAL

PHILIP'S HISTORICAL WALL MAPS OF SOUTH AFRICA
by A N Boyce
London : Philip
119 x 96 each
Available in Eng or Afrikaans
1 The Expansion of the Cape Colony 1652-1806
2 South Africa during the Great Trek
3 Boer Republics and Adjacent Territories 1852-99
4 The Extension of the Cape Colony and Battles fought in Natal and Zululand 1819-99
5 South Africa in the Age of British Imperialism 1870-1902
6 Economic and Transportation Development to 1910
7 Bantu Areas within the Republic of South Africa

Each CR £2.25

ATLASES
W3 WORLD ATLASES: LOCAL EDITIONS

WORLD ATLAS FOR THE REPUBLIC OF SOUTH AFRICA
Salisbury : M O Collins (Pvt) Ltd.
22 x 30
Atlas for Primary schools. In a number of eds : Afrikaans, Venda, Zulu, Tswana, S Sotho, N Sotho, Xhosa, Transkei.
Each US $2.00

THE NEW JUNIOR ATLAS FOR SOUTH AFRICA
Salisbury : M O Collins (Pvt) Ltd.
22 x 30
A 32pp World Atlas for lower Secondary Schools. US $2.40

ATLASES
B TOWN PLANS

HOLMDEN'S REGISTER OF JOHANNES-BURG-RANDBURG AND STANDTON
Vol 10
Johannesburg : Map Office (Pty) Ltd, 1975
16 x 27
Street Atlas to Johannesburg region with index to streets. S.A.Rs 2.35

ATLASES
O NATIONAL

ONTWIKKELINGSATLAS (DEVELOP-MENT ATLAS)
Pretoria : Govt. Printer (Dept. Planning), 1966
56 x 48
Atlas in Afrikaans and Eng with text. The first section contains the following plates :

1.1 Topography, 1965 R 1.10
1.2 Climate, 1966 R 1.60
2.1 Administration, 1966 R 1.10
2.2 Population (3 maps) R 2.80
2.3 Educational and Research Facilities, 1970
2.4 Health Services & Facilities, 1968 R 1.60
2.5 Outdoor Recreation and Tourism, 1968 R 1.10
3.1 Water Resources & Utilisation, 1968 R 1.60
4.1 Materials used in the Iron and Steel Industry, 1966 R 1.10

4.2 Precious Metals & Minerals, 1966
R 1.10
4.3 Base, Radio-Active and Rare Metals, 1966 R 1.10
4.4 Other Minerals, 1966
R 1.10
5.3 Fishing Industry, 1969
6.1 Communications & Transport, 1968
10.1 Gross Geographical Product per capita (2 maps) 1967 R 1.70

681 Botswana

A1 GENERAL MAPS: ROADS

LEFATSHE LA BOTSWANA
(REPUBLIC OF BOTSWANA)
1:1, 000, 000
Gaborone : Surv. Dept, 1971
108 x 106
Coloured map showing roads, railways, district boundaries. R 1.00

A2 GENERAL MAPS: LOCAL

NGAMILAND AND NORTHERN AREAS
1:1, 250, 000
DOS (Misc) 214
Tolworth : DOS/Gaborone : Surv. Dept, 1954
Regional topog. map in black and white.
30p

OKAVANGO SWAMPS
1:500, 000
DOS (Misc) 215
Tolworth : DOS, 1954
General topog. map. 30p

OKAVANGO RIVER DELTA
1:400, 000
DOS (Misc) 216
Tolworth : DOS, 1954
General topog. map 30p

B TOWN PLANS

BOTSWANA TOWN PLANS
1:2, 400
Tolworth : DOS, 1966-70
Series of large scale plans also included in the Gaborone Surv. Dept. list of Township Mapping.
Plans available :
DOS 147 Lobatse in 19 sheets
Serowe in 24 sheets
DOS 947 Gaborone in 30 sheets
Moshupa in 16 sheets
Each 30p

LARGE SCALE TOWNSHIP MAPPING
Various scales
Gaborone : Surv. Dept.
Series of large scale plans compiled from aerial photographs available in either Dyeline "D" or Printed "P" form. Plans published :

Francistown		
1:10, 000	1970	1 sheet D
1: 5, 000		10 sheets D
1: 2, 500		36 sheets D
Gaborone		
1: 5, 000	1970	14 sheets P
1: 2, 500		12 sheets P
Ghanzi		
1: 4, 800	1968	1 sheet P
1: 2, 400	1968	3 sheets D
Kanye		
1: 6, 000	1967	1 sheet D
1: 2, 400	1967	16 sheets D
Kanye (Mining Area)		
1: 2, 500	1970	10 sheets D
Kasane		
1: 5, 000	1966	3 sheets D
1: 2, 400	1967	6 sheets D
Lobatse		
1: 5, 000	1970	12 sheets P
1: 2, 400	1966	19 sheets P
Mahalapye		
1:2, 400	1969	8 sheets P
	1969	5 sheets D
Maun		
1:4, 800	1968	1 sheet D
1:2, 400	1968	13 sheets D
Mochudi		
1:6, 000	1968	1 sheet D
1:2, 400	1968	9 sheets D
Molepolole		
1:6, 000	1967	1 sheet D
1:2, 400	1967	17 sheets D
Moshupa		
1:2, 400	1966	16 sheets P
Palapye		
1:4, 800	1966	1 sheet D
1:2, 400	1966	9 sheets D
Ramotswa		
1:4, 800	1968	1 sheet D
1:2, 400	1968	6 sheets D
Shashe-Tonota		
1:5, 000	1969	20 sheets P
Selebi-Pikwe		
1:4, 800	1969	6 sheets D
1:2, 500	1969	6 sheets P
1:2, 400	1969	24 sheets D
Serowe		
1:6, 000	1967	5 sheets D
1:2, 400	1967	24 sheets P
Thamaga		
1:5, 000	1969	4 sheets D

Extra maps available :

Francistown		
1:2, 400	1969	32 sheets D
Francistown		
1:2, 500	1963	9 sheets D
Kasane		
1:4, 800	1967	2 sheets D
Mahalapye		
1:4, 800 (1)	1967	1 sheet D
1:4, 800 (II)	1969	1 sheet D
Francistown		
1:4, 800	1969	9 sheets D
Kanye		
1:5, 000	1970	1 sheet D
Gaborone		
1:2, 400	1970	30 sheets P

C OFFICIAL SURVEYS

KARTA MIRA
1:2, 500, 000
PPWK
2 sheets to cover Botswana : 154, 174
see WORLD 100C and index 100/2.

AFRICA
1:2, 000, 000
AMS Series 2201
Sheets 30, 33, 34 cover Botswana
see AFRICA 6C and index 6/2.

INTERNATIONAL MAP OF THE WORLD
1:1, 000, 000
6 sheets for coverage.
see WORLD 100C and index 100/1.

WORLD AERONAUTICAL CHART ICAO, SOUTH AFRICAN TOPOGRAPHICAL EDITION
1:1, 000, 000
Gov't Printer
see SOUTHERN AFRICA 68C and index 68/1.

BOTSWANA (BECHUANALAND)
1:500, 000
DOS 847 (Z 462)
In 11 sheets, see index 681/1
Gaborone : Surv. Dept/Tolworth : DOS 1965-
66 x 40, 44 x 61
Topographic series with land detail, admin. boundaries, water features, in black and white.
Each 30p

BOTSWANA
1:125, 000
DOS 547 (Z 661)
See index 681/1
Tolworth : DOS/Gaborone : Surv. Dept.
Topog. series in progress.
Available in contoured or uncontoured editions.
Each 30p

BOTSWANA
1:50, 000
DOS 447 (Z 761)
See index 681/1
Tolworth : DOS/Gaborone : Surv. Dept, 1967-
55 x 55 each
Topog. series in progress.
Available in contoured or uncontoured editions.
Each 50p

BOTSWANA - PHOTOMAP
1:50, 000
DOS 447P (Z 761)
see index 681/1
Tolworth : DOS/Gaborone : Surv. Dept.
55 x 55
Photomap series, compiled from aerial photographs.
Each 50p

D POLITICAL & ADMINISTRATIVE

BOTSWANA
1:3, 000, 000
DOS (Misc) 448
Tolworth : DOS, 1967
38 x 41
Roads, railways with Tribal Area and Northern State Lands boundaries. In black and white. 30p

BOTSVANA
1:1, 000, 000
Moskva : GUGK, 1973
Col. study map showing water features, settlements, admin, centres and divisions, communications, boundaries, economic details, pop. Geog. description.
30 kop

BECHUANALAND PROTECTORATE
1:1, 700, 000
DOS (Misc) 282
Tolworth : DOS, 1960
64 x 73
Road and rail communications in black and white, water bore holes in blue.
30p

F GEOLOGY

GEOLOGICAL MAP OF BOTSWANA
1:1, 000, 000
Lobatse : Geol. Surv. of Botswana, 1973
108 x 106
Col. geol. map. S.A.Ra 4.00

GEOLOGICAL MAP OF BOTSWANA
1:2, 000, 000
Lobatse : Geol. Surv. of Botswana, 1971
Two colour geol. map. S.A.Ra 0.50

DISTRIBUTION OF THE KARROO SYSTEM IN BOTSWANA
1:2, 000, 000
Lobatse : Geol. Surv. of Botswana
Col. printed map. S.A.Ra 0.75

THE TECTONO-METAMORPHIC COMPLEX OF EASTERN BOTSWANA
1:500, 000
Lobatse : Geol. Surv. of Botswana
Col. map.
Each S.A.Ra 3.00

GEOLOGICAL MAPS OF BOTSWANA
1:250, 000
Lobatse : Geol. Surv. of Botswana
Coloured geological maps
Sheets published :
The Pre-Cambrian Geology of North-Eastern Botswana 1974
North Ghanziland 1974
Each S.A.Ra 2.00

GEOLOGICAL MAP OF THE COUNTRY AROUND MAHALAPYE AND MACHANENG
1:200, 000
Lobatse : Geol. Surv. of Botswana.
S.A.Ra 0.30

BOTSWANA - GEOLOGICAL SERIES
1:125, 000
See index 681/2
Lobatse : Geol. Surv. of Botswana
Quarter degree sheets series in progress.
Available in colour printed form or as dyeline prints.

GEOLOGICAL MAP OF THE MOKORO HILLS
1:29, 500
Lobatse : Geol. Surv. of Botswana.
S.A.Ra 0.30

G EARTH RESOURCES

THE INDUSTRIAL MINERALS OF BOTSWANA
1:1, 000, 000
1st edition
Lobatse : Geol. Surv. of Botswana, 1973
Two colour map which accompanies Mineral Resources Report No 3 Industrial Rocks and Minerals. S.A.Ra 2.00

H BIOGEOGRAPHY

VEGETATION MAP
1:3, 000, 000
Gaborone : Surv. Dept, 1970
Rev. ed. S.A.Ra 0.40

L ECONOMIC

EASTERN BECHUANALAND
1:500, 000
DOS (LU) 3016 AB
Tolworth : DOS/Gaborone : Surv. Dept, 1963
Covering sheets 5, 8, 11 of topog. series, available in 2 editions :
A Land Systems each 30p
B Agricultural Potential each 65p

IRRIGATION POTENTIAL TATIMOT-LOUTSE
1:500, 000
Gaborone : Surv. Dept, 1970
General topog. map indicating rivers.
S.A.Ra 0.45

683 Swaziland

See also: 680 SOUTH AFRICA

A1 GENERAL MAPS: ROADS

TOURIST MAP OF SWAZILAND
1:250, 000
Mbabane : Air Survey Company, 1966
67 x 85
Tourist and general map, communications, tourist features, road distances, settlements, relief by hill shading, inset town plans of Mbabane and Manzini.

C OFFICIAL SURVEYS

AFRICA
1:2, 000, 000
AMS Series 2201
Sheet 34 covers Swaziland.
see AFRICA 6C and index 6/2.

SWAZILAND
1:500, 000
DOS (Misc 408)
Edition 1
Tolworth : DOS, 1965
38 x 44
Communications, settlement and boundaries. 30p

SWAZILAND
1:50, 000
DOS 435 (Z 771)
In 31 sheets, see index 683/1
Mbabane : Pub, Works Dept/
Tolworth : DOS, 1954-71
55 x 57, 73 x 49
Basic topog. detail, contours.
Series in progress.
Each 50p

F GEOLOGY

GEOLOGICAL MAP OF SWAZILAND
1:250, 000
Mbabane : Geol. Surv, 1970
68 x 83
General geol. map. R 1.00

GEOLOGICAL MAP OF SWAZILAND
1:125, 000
Mbabane : Geol. Surv. & Mines Dept, 1959
109 x 150
Geol. map in 2 sheets. R 6.30
Text by D R Hunter, 1960
R 1.00'

SWAZILAND GEOLOGICAL
1:50, 000
DOS (Geol) 1089
See index 683/1
Mbabane : Geol. Surv. & Mines Dept./
Tolworth : DOS, 1961/67
Geological series on topog. sheet lines (DOS 435). In progress. With explanatory notes.
Coloured Each 65p
Uncoloured Each 50p

GEOLOGICAL MAP SERIES OF SWAZILAND
1:25, 000
Mbabane : Geol. Surv. & Mines Dept, 1968+
Available for :
1 Hhohho, 1968
2 Pigg's Peak, 1969
3 Forbes Reef, 1970
4 Motjane, 1971
Each R 1.50

G EARTH RESOURCES

SWAZILAND - MINERALS
1:500, 000
DOS (Geol) 1143
Tolworth : DOS, 1963
Indicating location of minerals by symbols.
30p

GRAVITY ANOMALIES IN SWAZILAND
1:250, 000
Mbabane : Geol. Surv. & Mines Dept, 1970
76 x 91 each
5 maps to accompany Bulletin No 7.
1 Bouguer Anomaly Map
2 Isostatic Anomaly Map
3 Residual Isostatic Anomaly Map
4 Aeromagnetic Trend Map
5 Airborne Geophysical Survey - Magnetic Intensity (total field)

SOIL MAP OF SWAZILAND
1:125, 000
Mbabne : Min. Agriculture, 1967
117 x 163
2 sheet coloured soil map with text.
R 2.00

SWAZILAND SOIL
1:50, 000
DOS 3002
See index 683/1
Tolworth : DOS, 1961
Soil survey on same sheet lines as DOS 435. 3 sheets covering Lower Usutu Basin (South) have been published.
Each 65p

H BIOGEOGRAPHY

LAND CAPABILITY MAP OF SWAZILAND
1:125, 000
In 2 sheets
Mbabane : Min. Agriculture
117 x 163
Coloured potential land use map.
S.A.Ra 2.00

K HUMAN GEOGRAPHY

POPULATION DISTRIBUTION, 1966
1:250, 000
Mbabane : Census Commissioners, 1967
61 x 92
Pop. indicated on white base by red dots.
S.A.Ra 1.00

ATLASES
E2 PHYSICAL: LAND FEATURES

ATLAS OF LAND SYSTEMS IN SWAZILAND
Christchurch : MVEE, 1971
29 x 40
A 1:500, 000 land systems map with full descriptions of each, represented by an annotated air photograph, block diagram and tables of soils, landforms and vegetation.

686 Lesotho

See also: 680 SOUTH AFRICA

B TOWN PLANS

MASERU TOURIST MAP
1:12, 500
DOS 221
Tolworth : DOS, 1975
Coloured town plan.
65p

C OFFICIAL SURVEYS

LESOTHO
1:250, 000
DOS 621 (Z 582)
Edition 1
Tolworth : DOS, 1969
101 x 61 each
2 sheet physical map, contoured with layer colours, communications.
Each 65p

TOPOGRAPHICAL SERIES OF LESOTHO
1:50, 000
In 60 sheets, see index 686/1
DOS 421 (Z 782)
Tolworth : DOS, 1953+
Contoured series.
Each 50p

D POLITICAL & ADMINISTRATIVE

BASUTOLAND
1:750, 000
DOS (Misc) 280
Tolworth : DOS, 1960
General boundaries and communication map. 30p

G EARTH RESOURCES

LESOTHO WATER RESOURCES
1:750, 000
DOS (Misc) 281
Tolworth : DOS, 1960
Coloured distribution map.
30p

LESOTHO - SOILS
1:250, 000
DOS (LR) 3031A
Tolworth : DOS, 1967
101 x 61 each
2 sheet map in cols.
Each 65p

L ECONOMIC

LESOTHO - LAND SYSTEMS
1:250, 000
DOS (LR) 3031B
Tolworth : DOS 1967
101 x 61 each
2 sheet map in cols.
Each 65p

LESOTHO - AGRICULTURAL POTENTIAL
1:250, 000
DOS (LR) 3031C
Tolworth : DOS, 1967
101 x 61 each
2 sheet map in cols.
Each 65p

688 South West Africa

See also: 68 SOUTHERN AFRICA

C OFFICIAL SURVEYS

KARTA MIRA
1:2, 500, 000
PPWK
Sheets 153, 154, 173, 174 cover South West Africa.
see WORLD 100C and index 100/2.

AFRICA
1:2, 000, 000
AMS Series 2201
Sheets 29, 30, 33 cover South West Africa.
see AFRICA 6C and index 6/2.

INTERNATIONAL MAP OF THE WORLD
1:1, 000, 000
see WORLD 100C and index 100/1.

E1 PHYSICAL: RELIEF

SOUTH WEST AFRICA
1:1, 000, 000
Johannesburg : Surveyor General, 1972
101 x 145
Topo-cadastral map, also available in Afrikaans. S.A.Ra 4.00

F GEOLOGY

GEOLOGICAL MAP OF SOUTH WEST AFRICA
1:1, 000, 000
In 4 sheets
Pretoria : Geol. Surv, 1963
Col. map showing mineral occurrences and Bouguer anomalies. S.A.Ra 2.40

689.1 Rhodesia

A2 GENERAL MAPS: LOCAL

TOURIST MAPS
Salisbury : Surv. Dept.
Col. maps showing relief and communications with tourist facilities marked.
Maps available :
Lake McIlwaine Tourist Map, 1:25, 000
Inyonga Tourist Map, 1:63, 360

LARGE SCALE REGIONAL MAPPING
Various scales
Salisbury : Surv. Dept.
Series of maps, generally contoured for various local areas.
Maps available :

1 Bindura Area
1:5, 000 1949 18 sheets
2 Glendale Area
1:5, 000 1949 25 sheets
3 Bulawayo Area
1:5, 000 1949/55 34 sheets
4 Sebakwe River Area
1:5, 000 1950 37 sheets
5 Hartley Area (Umfuli River)
1:20, 000 1951 7 sheets
6 Norton
1:5, 000 1951 4 sheets
7 Mtilikwe River Project
1:20, 000 1951/64 9 sheets
8 Wankie Coal Fields
1:20, 000 1951 6 sheets
9 Erin & Placefell Forest Reserve
1:10, 000 1952 4 sheets
10 Martin Forest Reserve
1:10, 000 1952 4 sheets
11 Cashel Forest Reserve
1:10, 000 1952 5 sheets
12 Border Farms North
1:10, 000 1952 2 sheets
13 Vumba (Umtali)
1:5, 000 1952/53 6 sheets
14 Tarka Forest Reserve
1:10, 000 1952 7 sheets
15 Triangle Ranch
1:20, 000 1952 5 sheets
16 Sabi Native Division
1:20, 000 1952 8 sheets
17 Que Que Area (Township)
1:5, 000 1952 6 sheets
18 Lundi River Area
1:20, 000 1952 7 sheets
19 Stapleford Forest Reserve
1:10, 000 1952 2 sheets
20 Sabi East Bank Pilot Scheme
1:5, 000 1952 40 sheets
21 Sabi Left Bank
1:5, 000 1952 5 sheets
22 Gungunyana Forest Reserve
1:10, 000 1952 1 sheet
23 Hunyani Area
1:20, 000 1952 10 sheets
23a Toronto
1:5, 000 1953 1 sheet
24 Gwelo Area
1:5, 000 1953/56 36 sheets
25 Gatooma Area
1:20, 000 1953 8 sheets
26 Hartley (Township)
1:5, 000 1953 4 sheets
27 Nyamaropa & Lucan Forest Reserve
1:10, 000 1953 10 sheets
28 Odzi Area
1:5, 000 1953 1 sheet
29 Penhalonga Area
1:5, 000 1953/59 2 sheets
30 Sabi West Bank
1:20, 000 1953 22 sheets
31 Concession
1:5, 000 1953 1 sheet
32 Zambezi Valley Area E (Kariba Dam and Gorge)
1:5, 000 1954 20 sheets
33 Zambezi Valley (lake area west of Chirundu)
1:25, 000 1955 43 sheets
34 Archie Henderson Research Stn
1:5, 000 1955 4 sheets
34a St Marys
1:5, 000 1955 2 sheets
35 Inyanga Area
1:5, 000 1955 2 sheets
36 Hartley Area (Duchess Hill)
1:20, 000 1955/56 2 sheets
37 Belingwe
1:25, 000 1955/56 2 sheets
38 Nyamaropa Reserve North East
1:25, 000 1955/56 1 sheet
39 Umzingwane River
1:25, 000 1955/56 1 sheet
40 Marandellas Area
1:5, 000 1956 17 sheets
41 Karoi
1:5, 000 1956 1 sheet
42 Sinoia
1:5, 000 1956 2 sheets
43 Odzi (River)
1:25, 000 1957 2 sheets
44 Bembezi
1:25, 000 1957 3 sheets
45 Kyle Dam Project
1:25, 000 1957 5 sheets
46 Zambesi Valley (east of Chirundu)
1:25, 000 1958 27 sheets
47 Rusape
1:5, 000 1959 6 sheets
48 Shabani
1:5, 000 1959 10 sheets
49 Bangala Dam Basin
1:10, 000 1960 4 sheets
50 Nuanetsi-Manyoshi
1:5, 000 1963 26 sheets
51 Manjirenje Dam
1:20, 000 1963 1 sheet
52 Dotts Drift Dam Basin
1:20, 000 1963 6 sheets
53 Sabi-Chiredzi Irrigable Area
1:10, 000 1963 23 sheets
54 Ingwesi Dam Basin 1, 2 and 3
1:20, 000 1963 2 sheets
55 Lundi-Munaka Dam Basin
1:10, 000 1963/65 2 sheets
56 Tokwe-Mukorsi Dam Basin
1:10, 000 1963 6 sheets
57 Lukosi Irrigable Area
1:5, 000 1963 5 sheets
58 Kazungula
1:4, 000 1964 1 sheet
59 Turgwe-Siya Mapping
1:20, 000 1964 1 sheet
60 Chisumbanje Irrigable Area
1:10, 000 1964 12 sheets
61 Lundi-Tende Dam Basin
1:20, 000 1964 2 sheets
62 Devure-Chirorgwe Dam Basin
1:20, 000 1964 1 sheet
63 Lundi-Mtilikwe Mapping TR45 (Nuanetsi-Manyoshi East TR56)
1:20, 000 1965 35 sheets
64 Ingesi-Buchwa Dam Basin TR51
1:20, 000 1965 1 sheet
65 Sabi Dotts Drift TR58
1:10, 000 1966 21 sheets
66 Nuanetsi-Manyoshi (Extension) TR53
1:20, 000 1966 6 sheets
67 Hunyani-Dande Irrigable Area TR73
1:10, 000 1966 12 sheets
68 Dande Dam Basin TR68
1:20, 000 1966 2 sheets
69 Hunyani-Glyn-a-Mel Dam Basin TR70
1:20, 000 1966 5 sheets
70 Wengi TR57
1:5, 000 1966 8 sheets
71 Mkwasini-Muzaki Dam Basin TR60
1:20, 000 1966 1 sheet
72 Limpopo River Development
1:6, 000 1967 23 sheets
73 Hunyani-Darwendale Dam Basin
1:20, 000 1967 5 sheets
74 Hunyani-Nyakapupu Dam Basin TR69
1:20, 000 1967 7 sheets
75 Hunyani-Nyakapupu Gorge TR69
1:5, 000 1967 9 sheets
76 Insiza-Mayfair Project TR79
1:20, 000 1967 5 sheets
77 Sabi-Condo Dam Basin TR74
1:20, 000 1967 7 sheets
78 Mkwasini Irrigable area TR78
1:20, 000 1967 5 sheets
79 Kana Dam Basin TR98
1:20, 000 1968 2 sheets
80 The Range Dam Basin TR91
1:10, 000 1968 1 sheet
81 Sherwood Irrigation Scheme TR96
1:5, 000 1968 16 sheets
82 Sabi Odzi TR84
1:5, 000 1968 40 sheets
83 Nyazwidzi Dam Basin TR89
1:20, 000 1968 2 sheets
84 Umzingwani-Shobi Basin TR95
1:20, 000 1968 2 sheets
85 Devure-Pembezi TR90
1:20, 000 1968 1 sheet
86 Ingezi-Mzowe TR92
1:10, 000 1968 1 sheet
87 Mondi-Mataga TR93
1:20, 000 1968 1 sheet
88 Maizana Dam Basin and Canal TR94
1:20, 000 1968 2 sheets
89 Bembezaan-Nyabongwe Dam Basin TR97
1:10, 000 1968 1 sheet
90 Hozori Dam Basin TR99
1:20, 000 1968 5 sheets
91 Gwai-Shangani TR108
1:10, 000 1969 5 sheets
92 Upper Umfuli TR103
1:5, 000 1969 26 sheets
93 Musengezi-Mkumbura
1:5, 000 1969 11 sheets
94 Matibi TR106
1:5, 000 1969 18 sheets
95 Nuangadzi Dam Basin TR118
1:10, 000 1969 1 sheet
96 Lower Umfuli TR110
1:20, 000 1969 9 sheets
97 Lower Umsweswe Dam Basin TR117B
1:10, 000 1969 4 sheets
98 Devure TR119
1:5, 000 1969 5 sheets
99 Musengesi TR104
1:10, 000 1969 5 sheets
100 Nyagui-Shavanhohwe TR122
1:20, 000 1970 1 sheet
101 Umsweswe Dam Basin TR117
1:10, 000 1970 4 sheets

102 Nyamukwarara Valley TR125
1:10, 000 1970 13 sheets
103 Insiza-Ncema TR116
1:20, 000 1970 2 sheets
104 Grootvlei TR126
1:5, 000 1970 13 sheets
105 Odzi Diversion TR123
1:5, 000 1970 5 sheets
106 Rasa Dam Basin TR121
1:10, 000 1970 1 sheet
107 Gwai-Umgusa TR124
1:20, 000 1970 3 sheets
108 Upper Umsweswe Dam Basin
1:10, 000 1970 11 sheets
109 Rusape-Inyazura TR131
1:5, 000 1970 37 sheets
110 Insiza-Mayfair Dam Basin TR132
1:20, 000 1970 1 sheet
111 Mkwasini Mukazi Left Bank TR105
1:5, 000 1970 17 sheets
112 Shangani-Tiyabenzi Dam Basin TR153
1:10, 000 1971 1 sheet
113 Gwai Shangani Dam Basin TR158
1:10, 000 1972 4 sheets
114 Gwai Dahlia Dam Basin TR159
1:10, 000 1972 9 sheets
115 Nyashanu Dam Basin TR166
1:10, 000 1972 1 sheet

B TOWN PLANS

TOWN MAPS
Salisbury : Surv. Dept.
Series of detailed large scale plans.
Maps available :
Salisbury :
Highfield Township 1:7, 500
Harari Township 1:7, 500
Bulawayo :
Njube 1:10, 000
Mzilikazi 1:10, 000
Luveve 1:10, 000
Westgate 1:10, 000
Salisbury : street map 1:33, 333
Bulawayo : street map 1:33, 333
Each S.A.Ra 0.60

TOPO - CADASTRAL SERIES
1:5, 000
Salisbury : Surv. Dept.
Contoured topog. series with land boundaries with UTM grid. Some sheets "Consequential" ie photographic reduction of 2, 500 series, uncontoured. Not all sheets pub. The following urban areas are in progress :
Salisbury app. 630 sheets
Gatooma 28 sheets
Gwelo 35 sheets
Chipinga 6 sheets
Bulawayo 176 sheets
Fort Victoria-Kyle Dam
66 sheets
Umtali 57 sheets
Que Que 31 sheets
Sinoia 30 sheets
Marandellas 18 sheets
Gutu 3 sheets (none pub)
Victoria Falls
9 sheets (none pub)
Melsetter 4 sheets
Binga 11 sheets
Msango Range
5 sheets
Each S.A.Ra 0.60

SALISBURY
1:2, 500
Salisbury : Surv. Dept.
Large scale series on UTM projection. Uncontoured, black and white. In progress. Published for central area only and Highlands region to the NE.

C OFFICIAL SURVEYS

KARTA MIRA
1:2, 500, 000
PPWK
Sheet 154 covers Rhodesia
see WORLD 100C and index 100/2.

AFRICA
1:2, 000, 000
AMS Series 2201
Sheets 30, 31 and 34 cover Rhodesia.
see AFRICA 6C and index 6/2.

INTERNATIONAL MAP OF THE WORLD
1:1, 000, 000
see WORLD 100C and index 100/1.

RHODESIA
1:500, 000
In 4 sheets
Salisbury : Surv. Dept, 1975
Contoured, layer coloured with boundaries, towns and villages, railways and road communications classified in detail.

TOPOGRAPHICAL SERIES
1:250, 000
In 33 sheets, see index 689.1/1
Salisbury : Surv. Dept.
Multi-sheet series : UTM grid lines overprinted, topog. or topo-cadastral sheets. Layered and unlayered.
Each S.A.Ra 0.60

TOPOG. SERIES
1:100, 000
See index 689.1/2
Salisbury : Surv. Dept.
Topo-cadastral series on linen or paper. Some sheets superseded by 50, 000 series and these will not be reprinted.
Each S.A.Ra 0.60

CADASTRAL SERIES
1:50, 000
See index 689.1/2
Salisbury : Surv. Dept.
60 x 80 app.
Large scale series showing property boundaries. Some sheets monochrome, others col; topog. detail.
Each S.A.Ra 0.60

D POLITICAL & ADMINISTRATIVE

RHODESIA - SKETCH MAP
1:2, 000, 000
Salisbury : Surv. Dept.
Outline map in grey monochrome. Also at 1:3, 000, 000.
Each S.A.Ra 0.50

E1 PHYSICAL: RELIEF

RELIEF MAP
1:2, 500, 000
Salisbury : Surv. Dept.
Available layered or unlayered with communications and settlement.
Each S.A.Ra 0.50

RELIEF MAP
1:1, 000, 000
Salisbury : Surv. Dept, 1967
88 x 76
Topog. centralised edition of ICAO map - land edition; contours at 1000 ft intervals. With or without hypsometric tinting layers.
Each S.A.Ra 0.60

E2 PHYSICAL: LAND FEATURES

HYDROLOGICAL MAP OF RHODESIA
1:1, 000, 000
Salisbury : Surv. Dept, 1970
95 x 78
Showing water systems.
S.A.Ra 0.60

F GEOLOGY

GEOLOGICAL MAP OF RHODESIA
1:1, 000, 000
Salisbury : Geol. Surv. Dept, 1971
95 x 84
Col. geol. map.

PROVISIONAL GEOLOGICAL MAP OF SOUTHERN RHODESIA
1:1, 000, 000
Salisbury : Geol. Surv. Dept, 1961
Col. geol. map with explanatory notes.

G EARTH RESOURCES

PROVISIONAL MINERAL MAP OF SOUTHERN RHODESIA
1:2, 000, 000
Salisbury : Geol. Surv. Dept, 1960
Map in cols. with explanatory notes.
Bull. No 42.

SOIL MAP OF RHODESIA
1:1, 000, 000
Salisbury : Surv. Dept, 1957
112 x 85
Col. soil map. S.A.Ra 0.60

H BIOGEOGRAPHY

LAND TENURE MAP OF RHODESIA
1:1, 000, 000
Salisbury : Surv. Dept, 1970
88 x 76
Details of forest, parkland, tribal areas etc.
S.A.Ra 0.60

AGRO-ECOLOGICAL MAP OF RHODESIA
1:1, 000, 000
Salisbury : Surv. Dept.
112 x 95
Col. map showing ag. land use.
S.A.Ra 0.60

J CLIMATE

MEAN ANNUAL RAINFALL MAP
1:2, 500, 000
Salisbury : Surv. Dept, 1968
64 x 45
Col. map. S.A.Ra 0.50

AVERAGE RAINFALL MAPS FOR THE MONTHS OF JANUARY - DECEMBER, 1968
1:2, 500, 000
Salisbury : Surv. Dept, 1969
64 x 45
Col. map. S.A.Ra 0.50

HIGHEST 24 HOUR RAINFALL TOTALS ON RECORD
1:2, 500, 000
Salisbury : Surv. Dept, 1968
56 x 45 S.A.Ra 0.50

AVERAGE RAINFALL MAP OF RHODESIA
1:2, 000, 000
Salisbury : Surv. Dept.
55 x 44
Col. map. S.A.Ra 0.50

K HUMAN GEOGRAPHY

AFRICAN POPULATION DISTRIBUTION MAP
1:1, 250, 000
Salisbury : Surv. Dept, 1971
83 x 73
As at April/May 1969. European pop. inset. S.A.Ra 0.60

AFRICAN POPULATION DENSITY MAP
1:1, 250, 000
Salisbury : Surv. Dept, 1971
83 x 73
As at April/May 1969. Statistical indication of pop. density, showing rural pop. change 1962-9 in Rhodesia. S.A.Ra 0.60

L ECONOMIC

NATURAL FARMING REGIONS - AGRO-ECOLOGICAL MAP
1:3, 000, 000
Salisbury : Surv. Dept, 1971
34 x 32
Gen. economic and ag. map.
S.A.Ra 0.50

ATLASES
W WORLD ATLAS - LOCAL EDITIONS

THE RHODESIAN PLACE IN THE WORLD
Salisbury : M O Collins (PVT) Ltd
22 x 30
World atlas for primary schools.
US $1.60

ATLASES
A1 ROADS

THE RHODESIAN BOOK OF THE ROAD
Salisbury : M O Collins (PVT) Ltd
22 x 29
13pp of road maps on 1:1, 000, 000 scale, with 2pp of town plans, 6pp on road history and road signs and 39pp of text, illustrations and inset maps describing touring areas and gazetteer. US $12.00

ATLASES
B TOWN PLANS

GUIDE TO GREATER SALISBURY
Salisbury : M O Collins (PVT) Ltd
64pp
41pp of detailed street maps, scale 1:33, 333 together with index to streets, districts and buildings. US $1.80

GUIDE TO BULAWAYO
Salisbury : M O Collins (PVT) Ltd
13 x 16
39pp
20pp of detailed street maps, scale 1:25, 000 with index to streets, districts and buildings. US $1.50

ATLASES
O NATIONAL

ATLAS OF THE FEDERATION OF RHODESIA AND NYASALAND
1:2, 500, 000
Dept. of Trig. and Topo. Survey, 1960-64
see SOUTHERN AFRICA ATLASES 68P REGIONAL

RHODESIA - ITS ECOLOGY AND ECONOMY
Salisbury : M O Collins (Pvt) Ltd, 1965
44 x 38
42 maps, general scale 1:2, 500, 000, grouped into subject groups, ie Topography, Natural subjects, climate, agriculture, minerals and industry with 24pp of descriptive text. US $14.00

689.4 Zambia

A1 GENERAL MAPS : ROADS

ZAMBIA ROAD MAP
1:1, 500, 000
Lusaka : Surveys Dept.
89 x 73
Outline map prepared by the Roads Dept. showing distances in km with distance chart.
K 0.60

ZAMBIA DESIGNATED ROADS
1:1, 000, 000
In 2 sheets
Lusaka : Surveys Dept. 1968
Map prepared by Roads Dept.
K 0.60

A2 GENERAL MAPS : LOCAL

LAKE KARIBA AREA
1:500, 000
Lusaka : Surv. Gen.
78 x 74
Uncontoured map.
Ngwee 50

BANGWEULU SWAMPS
1:350, 000
DOS (Misc) 64
Tolworth : DOS, 1952
Shaded relief topog. map of the area.
50p

TOURIST MAP, LIVINGSTONE-VICTORIA FALLS AREA
1:10, 000, 1:20, 000, 1:50, 000
DOS (Misc) 572
Lusaka : Surveys Dept./Tolworth : DOS, 1970
Composite map of Falls Area and environs with plan of Livingstone and descriptive notes. 65p

B TOWN PLANS

ZAMBIA - STREET MAPS OF PRINCIPAL TOWNS
1:20, 000
Lusaka : Surveys Dept.
Series of printed plans, some with street index
Plans available :

Chingola-Nchanga	1960	K 0.50
Kabwe	1960	K 0.50
Kitwe	1974	K 0.80
Kitwe-Chingola-Mufulira	1961	K 0.50
Kitwe-Nkana	1960	K 0.50
Livingstone-Victoria Falls	1961	K 0.50
Luanshya-Ndola	1961	K 0.50
Luanshya-Rokana	1960	K 0.50
Lusaka	1972	K 0.80
1:10, 000		
Kalulushi	1960	K 0.50

TOWNSHIP SERIES
1:5, 000
Lusaka : Surveys Dept.
Series of large scale contoured plans
Dyeline prints unless otherwise stated.
Plans published with number of sheets :

Chililabombwe & District	40 sheets
Chozi	1 sheet
Feira printed	3 sheets
Kabompo	6 sheets
Kafue	7 sheets
Kalomo	4 sheets
Kaoma	7 sheets
Kapiri-Mposhi	4 sheets
Kasama	7 sheets
Kasempa	7 sheets
Kitwe-Nkana-Kalulushi K 0.80	53 sheets
Livingstone printed K 0.80	14 sheets
Livingstone, Peri Urban 1967-70	53 sheets
Lubombo	1 sheet
Lusaka	78 sheets
Luwingu	12 sheets
Mazabuka	4 sheets
Mufulire uncontoured 1959 K 0.80	14 sheets
Mwense	2 sheets
Mwinilunga	10 sheets
Nyimba	2 sheets
Rufunsa	2 sheets
Siavonga printed, 1967 K 0.80	9 sheets
Zambezi	4 sheets

Unless stated otherwise each K 0.50

TOWNSHIP SERIES
1:2, 500
Lusaka : Surveys Dept.
Detailed series of plans with 2m contours, plotted from aerial photography, available as dyeline prints.
Plans published with number :

Batoka	6 sheets
Chiengi	4 sheets
Chisamba	3 sheets
Chisekeshi	4 sheets
Choma	12 sheets
Kapalala	5 sheets
Magoye	4 sheets
Mansa	6 sheets
Mbala	4 sheets
Mkushi	12 sheets
Mumbwa	8 sheets
Mungwi	14 sheets
Namwala	8 sheets
Nchelenge	12 sheets
Old Mkushi	6 sheets
Pemba	6 sheets
Puta	5 sheets
Solwezi	6 sheets
Each K 0.50	

C OFFICIAL SURVEYS

KARTA MIRA
1:2, 500, 000
PPWK
2 sheets to cover Zambia : 134, 154
see WORLD 100C and index 100/2.

AFRICA
1:2, 000, 000
AMS Series 2201
Sheets 27, 28, 30 cover Zambia.
see AFRICA 6C and index 6/2.

INTERNATIONAL MAP OF THE WORLD
1:1, 000, 000
see WORLD 100C and index 100/1.

MAP OF ZAMBIA
1:1, 000, 000
In 5 sheets
Lusaka : Surveys Dept. 1955
Coloured and contoured series with road and rail communications.
K 1.20
Sheet 3055 Lubumbashi
Dyeline only K 0.80

ZAMBIA- RHODESIA SERIES
1:500, 000
In 4 sheets
Lusaka : Surveys Dept. 1964
Outline map with contours, covering Zambia.
Kafue Basin South
Copperbelt-Kafue Basin North
Lusaka - Salisbury
Mbala - Northern Malawi
Each Ngwee 75

ZAMBIA
1:500, 000
In 17 sheets
Lusaka : Surveys Dept. 1962
76 x 56 each
Uncontoured, provisional ed. in col.
Ngwee 75

ZAMBIA AND MALAWI
1:250, 000
In 58 sheets, see index 689.4/1
Lusaka : Surveys Dept. 65 x 44
Topog. series (2nd ed. in progress).
Admin. areas, reserves, roads graded by condition and weight limit, railways, settlements, relief by hill shading.

1st ed. layered	K 1.00
unlayered	K 0.60
2nd ed.	K 1.00

REPUBLIC OF ZAMBIA
1:50, 000
DOS 424 (Z 741), see index 689.4/2
Lusaka : Surveys Dept./Tolworth : DOS, 1949-
59 x 65
Topog. series in progress. Some early sheets out of print. Available contoured or uncontoured. Zambian Official revision, 1970+

Uncol.	K 0.60 (30p)
Col.	K 1.00 (50p)

D POLITICAL & ADMINISTRATIVE

NORTHERN RHODESIA
1:3, 500, 000
DOS 974
Tolworth : DOS, 1964
Communications, boundaries and settlement.

ZAMBIYA
1:2, 000, 000
Moskva : GUGK, 1973
Col. study map showing water features, settlements, admin. centres and divisions, communications, boundaries, economic details, pop, Geog. description
Kop. 30

OUTLINE MAP OF ZAMBIA
1:4, 000, 000
Lusaka : Dept. Lands
In black and white.

ZAMBIA
1:1, 500, 000
No SDT 324/1
Lusaka : Surv. Gen.
Outline map; district and Province boundaries. KO. 70

PROVINCIAL AND DISTRICT MAPS
1:500, 000
Lusaka : Surv. Gen.
Various sizes
Outline maps of each Province showing Province, District and Ward boundaries with communications.
Price varies acc. to map size.

PROVINCIAL SERIES
1:750, 000
In 4 sheets
Lusaka : Surveys Dept. 1976
New coloured map showing communications, settlements, and boundaries.
Each K 1.50

PROVINCIAL SERIES
1:500, 000
In 17 sheets
Lusaka : Surveys Dept. 1962
Series of coloured maps of the provinces showing communications and boundaries.
Each KO. 80
Also available in Outline edition showing District and Ward boundaries.
Each KO. 60

ZAMBIA - DISTRICT SERIES
1:250, 000
Lusaka : Surveys Dept.
Series of outline maps for each District showing ward boundaries in red.
Each KO. 70

E1 PHYSICAL : RELIEF

ZAMBIYA
1:2, 000, 000
Moskva : GUGK, 1968
69 x 66
Col. map showing physical detail, communications, admin. boundaries.

THE REPUBLIC OF ZAMBIA
1:1, 500, 000
Lusaka : Surv. Gen, 1975
89 x 73
Col. topog. map, contours and layer col, communications. K1.50

F GEOLOGY

GEOLOGICAL MAP OF NORTHERN RHODESIA
1:1, 000, 000
In 4 sheets
Lusaka : Geol. Surv, 1963
Col. map. Description in Geol. Bull. No 3. K. 3.00

GEOLOGICAL MAP OF THE COPPERBELT
1:500, 000
Lusaka : Geol. Surv.
Col. geol. map.

KARROO SYSTEM AND COAL RESOURCES OF THE GWEMBLE DISTRICT
1:125, 000
Lusaka : Geol. Surv.
North East section in 2 sheets contained in Geol. Bull. No 1
Each 50 n
South West section in 2 sheets from Geol. Bull. No 4, 1960.

ZAMBIA GEOLOGICAL SERIES
1:100, 000
see index 689.4/2
Lusaka : Geol. Surv.
Series of col. maps contained in Reports or Bulletins, often with supplementary maps and diagrams.

GEOLOGICAL MAP OF THE BIG CONCESSION, MUMBWA DISTRICT, NORTHERN RHODESIA
1:75, 000
Lusaka : Geol. Surv.
From Bulletin No 2. 50 n

GEOLOGICAL MAP OF THE CARBONATITE AREA, RUFUNSA VALLEY, FEIRA DISTRICT
1:75, 000
Lusaka : Geol. Surv, 1960
Part of 1529 NE and 1530 NW from Bulletin 5. 50 n

GEOLOGY AND FOSSIL LOCALITIES OF PART OF THE UPPER LUAWANGA VALLEY
1:66, 500 app.
Lusaka : Geol. Surv, 1963
From memoir No 1. 50 n

GEOLOGICAL MAP OF THE LUSAKA AREA
1:50, 000
Lusaka : Geol. Surv, 1958
Available for solid and superficial eds, for sheet 1528 NW. From Records 1958.
Each 50 n

DETAILED GEOLOGICAL MAP OF PART OF KARIBA AREA
1:10, 000
Lusaka : Geol. Surv.
Area 1628 SE, from Report No 3.

G EARTH RESOURCES

MINERAL MAP OF NORTHERN RHODESIA
1:3, 000, 000
Lusaka : Geol. Surv, 1959
76 x 43
Outline map of mineral deposits and working mines with output statistics.

MAP OF THE PROSPECTING, EXPLORATION AND MINING AREAS
Lusaka : Geol. Surv, 1972
Location map indicating areas of mining activity. 50 n

H BIOGEOGRAPHY

ZAMBIA, NATIONAL PARKS AND GAME MANAGEMENT
1:1, 500, 000
Lusaka : Surv. Gen.
104 x 79
Game reserves, hunting areas marked on base map.

ZAMBIA - TSETSE FLY DISTRIBUTION
1:1, 500, 000
Lusaka : Surveys Dept.
89 x 73
Showing areas affected by tsetse fly.
KO.70

VEGETATION-SOIL MAP OF NORTHERN RHODESIA
1:1, 000, 000
DOS 3012
Tolworth : DOS
70 x 100
2 sheet map showing woodland col, other vegetation types related to the types of soil.
Each 65p

K HUMAN GEOGRAPHY

POPULATION MAPS OF ZAMBIA
1:2, 500, 000
Lusaka : Nat. Council Sci. Research, 1969
60 x 50 each
2 maps showing pop. density and distribution. Based on 1969 Census Returns, from Atlas of the Population of Zambia.

MEDICAL FACILITIES MAP OF ZAMBIA
1:1, 500, 000
Lusaka : Surv. Gen.
104 x 79
Hospitals, mission and industrial etc. overprinted in red on outline map.
KO. 80

ATLASES
K HUMAN GEOGRAPHY

ATLAS OF THE POPULATION OF ZAMBIA
Mary E Jackman and D Hywel Davies
Lusaka : Nat. Council for Sci. Research, 1971+
53 x 43
Atlas in progress.
Part I, 1971, 2 maps showing distribution and density; 8pp text.

ATLASES
O NATIONAL

THE ATLAS OF ZAMBIA
Lusaka : Surv. Gen.
National Atlas in progress designed to cover aspects of the country's nature and economy.
Pub. sheets available separately :
(1:2, 500, 000)

1 Africa Political (1:18, 000, 000) 1969
1a Africa Physical, 1967
2 Central Africa communications (1:4, 500, 000) 1966
5 Minerals 1968
7 Tsetse Fly distribution 1966
7a Livestock 1966
7b Cattle diseases 1966
9 Languages 1974
10 Population (1963) 1967
12 Soils (1:1, 500, 000) 1969
13 Mean Annual Rainfall 1968
13a Rainfall - exceeded one year in five 1968
13b Rainfall - exceeded four years out of five 1968
13c Rainfall 1975
13d Mean Annual Rain Days 1975
14 Medical Facilities 1967
17 Annual Temperature, Range 1974
17a July Mean Temperature 1974
17g Average Number of Days of frost per year. 1974
18 Humidity 1968
19 Sunshine 1975
20 Winds (January and July) 1967
21 Winds (April and October) 1967
26 Educational facilities 1967

Each K 0.70

ATLAS OF THE FEDERATION OF RHODESIA AND NYASALAND
Dept. of Trig. and Topog. Survey, 1960-64
see SOUTHERN AFRICA ATLASES
68p

ZAMBIA IN MAPS
Ed D Hywel Davies
London : Hodder and Stoughton, 1971
22 x 28
128pp Black and white thematic and physical maps with descriptive text and statistical section. £3.00

689.7 Malawi

B TOWN PLANS

TOWNSHIP SERIES
Various scales
Blantyre : Dept. of Surv. 1968-
Large scale series of plans contoured - many still in progress. Available as diazo prints only.
Plans available :
Balaka
1:2,500, 9 sheets
Blantyre :
1:16, 000 Col. street plan K. 0.75
1:2, 500, 150 sheets
Cape Maclear
1:2, 500, 7 sheets
Chileka Airport
1:2, 500, 4 sheets
Chilumba
1:2, 500, 5 sheets
Chintheche
1:2, 500, 6 sheets
Chitipa
1:2, 500, 4 sheets
Dedza
1:2, 500, 12 sheets
Dowa
1:2, 500, 24 sheets
Karonga
1:5, 000, 5 sheets
Kasungu
1:2, 500, 7 sheets
Lilongwe
1:2, 500, 176 sheets
Liwonde
1:2, 500, 26 sheets
Mangochi
1:2, 500, 7 sheets
Mchinjl
1:2, 500, 8 sheets
Monkey Bay
1:2, 500, 8 sheets
Mponela
1:2, 500, 3 sheets
Mulanje
1:10, 000, 17 sheets
Mwanza
1:2, 500, 10 sheets
Mzimba
1:2, 500, 2 sheets
Mzuzu
1:2, 500, 8 sheets
Nkhata Bay
1:2, 500, 4 sheets
Nkhota Bay
1:2, 500, 9 sheets
Ntcheu
1:2, 500, 4 sheets
Ntchisi
1:2, 500, 5 sheets
Salima
1:2, 500, 2 sheets
Salima Lakeshore
1:5, 000, 14 sheets
Thyolo
1:10, 000, 24 sheets
Zomba
1:5, 000, 9 sheets
Each K. 0.75-K. 1.00

C OFFICIAL SURVEYS

KARTA MIRA
1:2, 500, 000
PPWK
2 sheets cover Malawi : 134, 154
see WORLD 100C and index 100/2.

AFRICA
1:2, 000, 000
AMS 2201
Sheets 28, 31 cover Malawi.
see AFRICA 6C and index 6/2.

INTERNATIONAL MAP OF THE WORLD
1:1, 000, 000
see WORLD 100C and index 100/1.

MALAWI NATIONAL SERIES
1:250, 000
In 10 sheets, see index 689.7/1
Blantyre : Dept. of Surv. 1974-76
93 x 64 each
New series with road and rail communications, contoured, available with or without layer colours, topog. features and boundaries, UTM grid.
Each K. 1.00

MALAWI NATIONAL SERIES
1:50, 000
DOS 425 (Z742)
See index 689.7/2
In 159 sheets
Blantyre : Surv. Dept./Tolworth : DOS, 1972-76
Series in progress, contoured with topog. detail, roads and cadastral boundaries

Each K. 0.75
DOS 50p

D POLITICAL & ADMINISTRATIVE

MALAWI
1:2, 500, 000
DOS 975, 7th edition
Tolworth : DOS, 1971
Small hand map, communications and boundaries. 15p

MALAWI BASE MAP
1:2, 000, 000
Blantyre : Dept. of Surv.
Monochrome. K. 0.15

BASE MAP OF MALAWI
1:1, 000, 000
DOS 825
Blantyre : Dept. of Surv. 1970
86 x 48
Monochrome map, marking roads, boundaries, etc. K. 0.50

E1 PHYSICAL : RELIEF

MALAWI
1:1, 000, 000
(DOS 825/1)
Ed. 2
Blantyre : Dept. of Surv. 1974
50 x 89
Contoured, layer cols, communications and towns shown. K. 1.00

F GEOLOGY

NYASALAND - GEOLOGY
1:2, 000, 000
DOS (Geol) 1071A
Tolworth : DOS, 1955
Col. geol. map. 50p

GEOLOGICAL MAP OF MALAŴI
1:1, 000, 000
Ed K Bloomfield
Zomba : Geol. Surv, 1966
44 x 88
Col. geol. map with table of radiometric age determinations.
K. 1.00

PROVISIONAL GEOLOGICAL MAP OF MALAŴI
1:1, 000, 000
Ed J D Bennett
Zomba : Geol. Survey 1973
54 x 87
Uncoloured geological map.
K. 0.50

GEOLOGICAL MAPS OF MALAŴI
1:250, 000
see index 689.7/3
F Habgood
DOS (Geol) 1175
Zomba : Geol. Surv./Tolworth : DOS, 1971
65 x 45 each
Coloured geological series, with text.
Sheet I Nsanje 1971
II Zomba 1971
IV Dedza 1972
VIII Nkhata Bay 1973

MALAŴI, GEOLOGIC MAPPING
1:100, 000
DOS (Geol) 1083-1204
See index 689.7/4
Coloured geological maps with legend in English and accompanying Bulletin.
Bull. 9-1083 Port Herald, 1957 50p
10-1086 Middle Shire, 1958
12-1098 Lake Chilwa Area, 1959 50p
14-1106 W of Shire River between Chikwawa and Chiromo shts 1 and 2, 1960
13-1107 Tambani-Salambidwe, 1960 50p
16-1142 Zomba, 1964
17-1146 Kirk Range-Lisongwe Valley Area, 1964
18-1149 Shire Highlands, 1964
19-1160 Ncheu-Balaka, 1966

22-1161 Cholo, 1967
23-1165 Lilongwe South, 1967
21-1170 Mlanje, 1969
24-1171 Mchinji - Upper Bua, 1969
28-1172 C Maclear Penn : and L Bwanje Valley, 1970
29-1173 Dedza, 1969
30-1178 Salima - Mvera Mission 1970
25-1179 Kasungu NW, 1971
25-1180 Kasungu SW, 1971
34-1183 Lake Chiuta, 1972
27-1188 Ntchisi-Middle Bua, 1973
26-1189 Lilongwe-Dowa, 1975
38-1190 Nkhata Bay-South, 1973
38-1191 Nkhata Bay-North, 1974
31-1193 Dwanga, 1975
39-1194 Rumphi, 1975
37-1195 Mzimba, 1975
36-1201 South Viphya East, 1975
36-1204 South Viphya West, 1975

Unless marked otherwise each 65p

GEOLOGICAL MAPS OF MALAŴI
Various scales
Zomba : Geol. Survey/Tolworth : DOS
Coloured geological maps with legend in English.
Sheets available :

1:80, 000
(Geol) 1134 Alkaline Dykes, Tundulu Area Map No 2, 1961 65p

1:50, 000
(Geol) 1102 Livingstonia Coalfield, Rumpi District, 1959 50p
1141 Geology of the Kangankunde Carbonate Complex, Map No 2, 1963 65p

1:36, 000 Nkana Coalfield, 1958

1:20, 000
(Geol) 1008 Chambe Plateau, Mlanje Mts. 1952 50p
1140 Vents and Dykes of the Chilwa Alkaline Province in the Western Shire Valley, Map No 1, 1963 50p

1:10, 000
(Geol) 1080 Chilwa Island, 1957 50p
1132 Tundulu Carbonate Ringcomplex Map No 1, 1961 65p

1:2, 500
(Geol) 1118 Nathace Hill, 1960 15p

H BIOGEOGRAPHY

MALAWI - NATURAL REGIONS AND AREAS
1:500, 000
DOS (LU) 3024 A.B.C.
In 3 sheets
Blantyre : Surv. Dept/Tolworth : DOS, 1965
Showing agricultural and land use.
K. 0.75 (65p)

J CLIMATE

CLIMATIC REGIONS OF MALAWI
1:1, 000, 000
Blantyre : Surv. Dept, 1961
34 x 86
Col. according to comparative regions of associated rainfall and temperature.
K. 0.75

L ECONOMIC

MAPS ILLUSTRATING DEVELOPMENT PROJECTS
1:2, 000, 000
Blantyre : Surv. Dept.
Series of maps covering education, health, local government, agriculture, forestry, surveys, water resources, Veterinary Services, transport and communications, Public Works and supplies, fisheries, Central and Regional Development Projects eg Lilongwe and Karonga projects.
1976/77-1978/79
1:3, 000, 000 32 maps, monochrome to 4 colours 1976.
Each K. 0.15
Set K. 4.50

ATLASES
W3 WORLD ATLAS: LOCAL EDITION

ATLAS FOR MALAWI
Ed A MacGregor Hutcheson
Glasgow : Collins-Longman
Physical and topog. maps.

ATLASES
O NATIONAL

ATLAS OF THE FEDERATION OF RHODESIA AND NYASALAND
Dept. of Trig. and Topog. Survey, 1960-64
see SOUTHERN AFRICA ATLASES
68p

MALAWI IN MAPS
Ed Prof. Swanzie Agnew and Dr Michael Stubbs
1st edition
London : Hodder and Stoughton, 1972
21 x 38, 144pp
Black and white maps covering political, physical, climatic, economic, social and industrial aspects, with text and bibliography. £2.95

691 Malagasy Republic

See also : 68 SOUTHERN AFRICA

A1 GENERAL MAPS : ROADS

MADAGASCAR ET COMORES
1:4, 000, 000
Paris : IGN - Inst. Cart. Madagascar, 1970
48 x 43
Roads and tourist info. La Réunion and Mauritius inset at 1:500, 000
F.Fr. 9,17

CARTE ROUTIÈRE ET TOURISTIQUE
1:2, 000, 000
Paris : IGN, Inst. Cart. Madagascar, 1966
56 x 81
Roads classified by surface conditions, relief shading, forest areas green, tourist info. Tananarive and environs inset.
F.Fr. 20, 83

CARTE GÉNÉRALE
1:1, 000, 000
In 3 sheets
Paris : IGN - Inst. Cart. Madagascar, 1960
88 x 167 complete
Incl. the Comores; roads in red, classified acc. condition, vegetation, contours, relief shading. Insets of islands of Mauritius and Reunion at 1:500, 000.
Each F.Fr. 55,00

A2 GENERAL MAPS : LOCAL

REGIONAL MAPS
Paris : IGN, Inst. Cart. Madagascar
Alaotra (Region du Lac)
1:20, 000 1942-44 11 sheets
Alaotra (Region du Lac)
1:50, 000 1945 10 sheets
Ambatolampy (Region du Champ de Tir)
1:20, 000 1932 1 sheet
Ankazobe (Champ de Tir)
1:20, 000 1960 2 sheets
Antsirabe et environs
1:20, 000 1928-29 10 sheets
Antsirabe et ses environs
1:150, 000 1972
(town plan at 1:10, 000)
Behenjy et environs
1:20, 000 1955 2 sheets
Brickaville-Ambila-Lemaitso et environs
1:20, 000 1944
Plaine de la Demoka
1:20, 000 1954-57 35 sheets
(4 published)
Diego-Suarez et environs
1:20, 000 1934-40 14 sheets
Diego-Suarez et environs
1:50, 000 1926 2 sheets
Itongafeno (Champ de Tir)
1:20, 000 1963
Mahabo
1:20, 000 1972 3 sheets
Mahitsy et environs
1:10, 000 1943 2 sheets
Majunga et environs
1:50, 000 1935-40 5 sheets
Mangoky (Vallee du Bas)
1:20, 000 1954-57
Mantasao (Lac)
1:20, 000 1972 Tourist plan
Moramanga (Camp de)
1:20, 000 1958 2 sheets
Nossi-Be (Ile de)
1:50, 000 1958 Tourist map
Tamatave et environs
1:50, 000 1935-44 3 sheets
Tananarive et environs
1:10, 000 New ed. in prep. 1952
20 sheets
Tananarive et environs
1:20, 000 2 sheets
Tananarive et environs
1:50, 000 1950 4 sheets
Tananarive et environs - coup speciale
1:50, 000 1958 1 sheet

B TOWN PLANS

TOWN PLANS
Various scales
Paris : IGN, Inst. Cart. Madagascar
Large scale series of plans, generally contoured
Plans available :
Antsirabe et ses environs
1:10, 000 1972
(environs at 1:150, 000)
Each F.Fr. 11,67
Diego-Suarez (Ville)
1:2, 000 1935 4 sheets
Each F.Fr. 11,67
Fianarantsoa
1:10, 000 1970 2 sheets
Each F.Fr. 18,33
Tamatave (Ville)
1:2, 000 1949 10 sheets
Each F.Fr. 11,67
Tamatave (Ville)
1:10, 000 1951 1 sheet
Each F.Fr. 11,67
Tananarive
1:10, 000 1961 1 sheet
Each F.Fr. 11,67

C OFFICIAL SURVEYS

KARTA MIRA
1:2, 500, 000
PPWK
3 sheets available for the Malagasy Republic : 135, 155, 175
see WORLD 100C and index 100/2.

AFRICA
1:2, 000, 000
AMS 2201
Sheet 32 covers Madagascar
see AFRICA 6C and index 6/2.

INTERNATIONAL MAP OF THE WORLD
1:1, 000, 000
IGN
5 sheets to cover Madagascar.
see WORLD 100C and index 100/1.

RÉPUBLIQUE MALGACHE
1:500, 000
In 12 sheets, see index 691/1
Paris : IGN, Inst. Cart. Madagascar, 1963
91 x 56
Roads classified acc. condition, numbered, distances in km, contours, relief shading, vegetation, town pop. F.Fr. 20,83

RÉPUBLIQUE MALGACHE
1:100, 000
See index 691/2
Paris : IGN, Inst. Cart. Madagascar
32 x 44
Complete coverage in differing eds. Most of island is in Normal ed, contoured, relief shaded, showing water, communications, boundaries, vegetation and settlement. Provisional series have less detail and are uncontoured.
F.Fr. 11,67

RÉPUBLIQUE MALGACHE
1:50, 000
See index 691/2
Paris : IGN, Inst. Cart. Madagascar
64 x 44
Series in progress; contoured, relief shading, water, vegetation, settlements, communications, boundaries. 2 eds. Definitive and Simplified.
F.Fr. 16,67

ARCHIPEL DES COMORES
1:50, 000
In 7 sheets
Paris : IGN, Inst. Cart. Madagascar
Various sizes
Legend black, water blue, contours brown and vegetation green.
Sheets available :
Grand Comore 2 sheets
Moheli 1 sheet
Anjouan 2 sheets
Mayotte 2 sheets
F.Fr. 11,67

D POLITICAL & ADMINISTRATIVE

CARTE ADMINISTRATIVE ET DE DENSITÉ DE POPULATION
1:2, 000, 000
Paris : IGN, Inst. Cart. Madagascar, 1967
67 x 95
Pop. densities by canton and prefecture in col, with index to cantons inset. Environs de Tamatave and Fianarantsoa at 1:750, 000. F.Fr. 20,83

E1 PHYSICAL : RELIEF

CARTE PHYSIQUE DE MADAGASCAR
1:4, 000, 000
Paris : IGN, 1970, Inst. Cart. Madagascar
32 x 40
Physical and bathymetric col.
F.Fr. 9,17

CARTE PHYSIQUE
1:2, 500, 000
Paris : IGN, 1960, Inst. Cart. Madagascar
39 x 66
7 col. map showing relief by contours and hypsometric tints. F.Fr. 14,17

MALAGASIYSKAYA RESPUBLIKA
1:2, 000, 000
Moskva : GUGK, 1971
59 x 83
Physical, contours, them. insets.

RÉPUBLIQUE MALGACHE
1:1, 000, 000
Paris : IGN, 1951
52 x 80
Col. map with relief overprint.

MADAGASCAR
1:250, 000
Paris : Forest
91 x 129
Physical col. wall map; relief col. communications, cities graded by pop, admin. boundaries.

CARTE EN RELIEF RÉPUBLIQUE MALGACHE
1:2, 000, 000
Paris : IGN - Inst. Cart. Madagascar, 1960
57 x 86
General route map in moulded plastic form, col. with plastic frame.
F.Fr. 83,33

E2 PHYSICAL : LAND FEATURES

CARTE GÉOMORPHOLOGIQUE DE MADAGASCAR
1:1, 000, 000
1st edition
In 3 sheets
Tananarive: Serv. Geol, 1964
82 x 163
Geomorphological map available as an Ozalid print.
Per set Fmg. 900

F GEOLOGY

CARTE DES GROTTES D'ANDIANOBOKA
by J de Saint-Ours and A Ramahalimby
1:1, 000 - 1:2, 000
Paris : ORSTOM, 1952
53 x 88
Geol. map of the caves.

CARTE TECTONIQUE DE MADAGASCAR
1:3, 000, 000
Tananarive : Serv. Géol, 1957
82 x 163
Map in 3 col. Depicting structural regions and features. Fmg. 450

CARTE GÉOLOGIQUE SCHÉMATIQUE DE MADAGASCAR
1:2, 500, 000
Tananarive : Serv. Géol, 1960
22 x 33
Black and white geol. sketch map.
Fmg. 150

CARTE DES PRINCIPALES MINERALISATIONS ÉCONOMIQUES DE MADAGASCAR
1:2, 500, 000
1st edition
Tananarive : Serv. Géol, 1972
21 x 27
Location of mineral industry.

CARTE GÉOLOGIQUE DE LA RÉPUBLIQUE DU MALGACHE
1:1, 000, 000
In 3 sheets
Tananarive : Serv. Géol
85 x 60 each
Col. geol. map inc. locations of principal minerals.

CARTE DES CARRIÈRES
1:1, 000, 000
In 3 sheets
Tananarive : Serv. Géol, 1957
82 x 163 complete
Showing location of quarries available as Ozalid print. Fmg. 900

CARTE GÉOLOGIQUE
1:500, 000
2nd edition
In 8 sheets, see index 691/3
Tananarive : Serv. Géol, 1969
159 x 347 complete
Set of col. geol. maps.
Each Fmg. 800

CARTE HYDROGÉOLOGIQUE DU SUD DE MADAGASCAR
1:500, 000
Tananarive : Serv. Géol, 1957
62 x 75
Col. hydrogeologic map.
Fmg. 450

CARTE GÉOLOGIQUE BASSIN DE MAJUNGA
1:500, 000
In 2 sheets
Tananarive : Serv. Géol, 1966
94 x 144 complete
Col. geol. map.
Per set Fmg. 600

CARTE GÉOLOGIQUE
1:200, 000
See index 691/4
Tananarive : Serv. Géol, 1931+
Series of col. geol. maps in progress.

RÉGION AURIFÈRE DE MANANJARY
1:200, 000
Tananarive : Serv. Geol, 1952
56 x 76
Col. geol. map. Fmg. 300

CARTE GÉOLOGIQUE
1:100, 000
See index 691/5
Tananarive : Serv. Géol, 1952
Series of col. geol. maps in progress.

BASSIN CHARBONNIER DE L'ONILAHY
1:50, 000
Tananarive : Serv. Géol, 1953
63 x 85
Map of the coal producing area.
Fmg. 300

PEGMATITES DE BERERE
1:20, 000
Tananarive : Serv. Géol, 1956
50 x 66
Regional geological map.
Fmg. 150

G EARTH RESOURCES

CARTE GRAVIMÉTRIQUE DE MADAGASCAR
1:2, 500, 000
Paris : ORSTOM, 1953
Fr. 6

CARTE DE LA DÉCLINAISON MAGNÉTIQUE
1:2, 500, 000
Paris : IGN, 1955, Inst. Cart. Madagascar
40 x 66
Monochrome map showing magnetic declination; annual variations from 1938-1955 and supplementary sketch map.
F.Fr. 7,50

CARTE MINIÈRE
1:2, 500, 000
2nd edition
Tananarive : Serv. Géol, 1964
46 x 64
3 col. map marking extent of principal mineral-bearing beds with locations and potential. Fmg. 450

CARTE PÉDOLOGIQUE DE MADAGASCAR
1:1, 000, 000
In 3 sheets
Paris : ORSTOM, 1968
100 x 180 complete
Col. soil map; North, South and Centre.
Text in preparation. Fr. 45

CARTE PÉDOLOGIQUE ET D'UTILISATION DES SOLS
1:200, 000
Paris : ORSTOM
Available for the following regions :
Bas-Mandrare, 1951 Fr. 10
Basse Menarandra, 1951
Fr. 10
Bas-Mangoky, 1951 Fr. 10
Manja - Mahabo - Morondava, 1952
2 sheets Fr. 20
Mitsinjo - Majunga, 1954
Fr. 10
Maevatanana, 1954 Fr. 10
Marovoay - Mahajamba, 1955
Fr. 10
Diego-Suarez Fr. 10
Moramanga - Brickaville, 1956
69pp text Fr. 10
Ambovombe, 1957
70pp text 1958 Fr. 10
Ampanihy - Beloha, 1959
113pp text Fr. 10
Fort-Dauphin, 1960
51pp text Fr. 10
Antonibe, 1961,
58pp text Fr. 10
Antsohihy, 1960
text 1962 Fr. 10
Ambilobe, 1965
54pp text Fr. 12

CARTE PÉDOLOGIQUE ET D'UTILISATION DES SOLS
Various scales
Paris : ORSTOM
1:100, 000
Anjouan (Comores), 1952
1:50, 000

Lac Alaotra, 1949	5 sheets
Ankaizinana, 1951	4 sheets
Mananjeba, Mahavavy, 1955	2 sheets
Basse Vallée du Mandrare, 1955	2 sheets
Ambilobe, 1955	2 sheets
Île de Saint-Marie, 1961	1 sheet
Haute Vallée d'Ifasy, 1965	1 sheet
Île de Nosy-Bé, 1965	1 sheet
1:40, 000	
Andilamena, 1954	1 sheet
Région Saint-Pierre - Étang Sale 1959	1 sheet
1:20, 000	
Kianjasoa, 1952	1 sheet
Bealanana, 1953	1 sheet
Ambohimandroso, 1954	1 sheet
Ankadimondry et Babetville, 1954	1 sheet
Marovoay, 1956	6 sheets
Ambohijanahary - Alaotra, Morarano-Amparafaravda, 1958	7 sheets
La Plaine de Vohipeno, 1958	1 sheet
Anjiafia, 1959	1 sheet
La Plaine de Morondava, 1959	1 sheet
Manandrotsy, 1959	1 sheet
Ambalabe, 1960	1 sheet
La Plaine du Kamoro, 1963	3 sheets
Vallée de la Manambato, 1964	1 sheet
Delta du Mangoky, 1964	1 sheet
Soalala, 1964	1 sheet
1:10, 000	
Andranoerefina (Lac Alaotra) 1953	2 sheets
Vallée de l'Onive, 1958	2 sheets
Vallée de l'Imady, 1958	2 sheets
La Plaine d'Anosibe, 1959	1 sheet
Station Agronomique d'Ilaka, 1959	1 sheet
Vallée de la Mananantanana, 1959	1 sheet
Ankona, 1959	1 sheet
Menarahaka, 1960	1 sheet
Delta du Mangoky, 1961 and 1963	2 sheets
1:5, 000	
Anosivelo, 1961	1 sheet

H BIOGEOGRAPHY

CARTE INTERNATIONALE DU TAPIS VÉGÉTAL
1:1, 000, 000
Pondichery : Fr. Inst.
Detailed col. vegetation map following international sheet lines.
Sheets available :

Cap St André - Alaotra, 1964	SE 38, 39
Mangoky - Cap Ste Marie, 1965	SF, SG 38
Baie d'Ampasindava, 1965	SD 38, 39

Text in Fr "Madagascar" available 1965.
Complete Fr. 60

CARTE DE RÉPARTITION DES ANOPHÉLÈS DE MADAGASCAR
by A Grjebine
1:500, 000
In 10 sheets
Paris : ORSTOM, 1958
Showing distribution of Anopheles genus of mosquitoes. Fr. 90

CARTE DE RÉPARTITION DES ANOPHÉLÈS, PROVINCE DE TANANARIVE
by A Grjebine and A Lacan
1:450, 000
Paris : ORSTOM, 1953
Showing distribution of Anopheles genus of mosquito. Fr. 10

K HUMAN GEOGRAPHY

MADAGASCAR, CARTE DE DENSITÉ ET DE LOCALISATION DE POPULATION
by P Gourou
1:2, 000, 000
Paris : ORSTOM/Bruxelles:Universite de Bruxelles en Afrique Centrale, 1967
3 maps showing admin. areas at 1:2, 000, 000; 2 sheet map at 1:1, 000, 000 of localisation of pop; col. map at 1:2, 000, 000 showing pop. density. With 28pp text.
B.Fr. 540
F.Fr. 54

L ECONOMIC

ATLASES
O NATIONAL

ATLAS DE MADAGASCAR
Tananarive : Assoc. des Geographes de Madagascar, 1969 and 1971
In 60 plates
33 x 42
Loose-leaf atlas, with plates covering economic, social, physical, climatic etc. features of the country. With explanatory text.

696 Seychelles

B TOWN PLANS

MAHÉ-VICTORIA
1:2, 500
DOS 004 (7854)
Tolworth : DOS, 1972
Series of large scale plans, 10 sheets published.
Each 30p

MAHÉ-VICTORIA
1:1, 250
DOS 0004
Tolworth : DOS, 1972-
Series of large scale plans. 11 sheets published.
Each 30p

C OFFICIAL SURVEYS

MAHÉ
1:50, 000
DOS 404 (Y752)
Tolworth : DOS, 1966
64 x 85
Map of the island, showing topog. features, communications, settlements, contours, hill shading. Inset of Victoria at 1:12, 500.
65p

ALDABRA
1:25, 000
DOS 6001
Tolworth : DOS, 1969
Photo-map of the island in 2 sheets.
Each 65p

ALDABRA
1:25, 000
DOS 304 (Y852)
Tolworth : DOS, 1964
94 x 83 each
Topog. map in 2 sheets.

SEYCHELLES
1:10, 000
DOS 204 (Y851), see index 696/1
In 11 sheets
Tolworth : DOS, 1963-67
Various sizes
Topographical series.
Sheets available :
Mahé 11 sheets, contoured
Each 50p

MAHÉ
1:2, 500
In 9 sheets
DOS (Misc) 396
Tolworth : DOS
Detailed planimetric series in black and white.
Each 20p

D POLITICAL & ADMINISTRATIVE

SEYCHELLES
1:3, 000, 000
DOS 980
Edition 3
Tolworth : DOS, 1969
Small map of the island group with inset of Mahé at 1:175, 000.
15p

SEYCHELLES
Washington : Govt. Printing Office/ Central Intelligence Agency
22 x 27
Small relief map, showing urban areas, main admin. divisions, them. insets.
35¢

F GEOLOGY

GEOLOGY AND MINERAL RESOURCES OF THE SEYCHELLES ARCHIPELAGO
Nairobi : Geol. Surv, 1963
4 col. maps from Kenya Geological Survey Memoir No 3 with text.

G EARTH RESOURCES

SEYCHELLES - SOILS
1:50, 000
DOS (LR) 3023 A-D
In 4 sheets
Tolworth : DOS, 1966
Col. soil maps.
Each 65p

698.1 Reunion

A1 GENERAL MAPS : ROADS

CARTE ROUTIÈRE ET TOURISTIQUE DE LA RÉUNION
1:100, 000
Paris : IGN, 1972
80 x 65
Roads classified in colour, distances in km, spot heights, relief shading, vegetation, tourist details. In French and English.
F.Fr. 10,00

C OFFICIAL SURVEYS

CARTE GÉNÉRALE DE LA RÉUNION
1:50, 000
In 4 sheets
Paris : IGN, 1954
142 x 128 complete
Topog. map in 4 sheets, indicating relief by contours and relief shading.
F.Fr. 11,67

E1 PHYSICAL : RELIEF

LA RÉUNION - CARTE EN RELIEF
1:100, 000
Paris : IGN
85 x 64
Moulded relief ed. of Tourist Map.
Vertical scale 1/1.
F.Fr. 104,17

F GEOLOGY

CARTE GÉOLOGIQUE DE LA RÉUNION
1:100, 000
Orléans : BRGM, 1967
80 x 65
1 sheet geol. map with text. Flat or folded.
Fr. 24,00

CARTE GÉOLOGIQUE EN RELIEF DE RÉUNION
1:100, 000
Orléans : BRGM/Paris : IGN
88 x 68
Raised relief map showing outcrops of geol. formations by relief and col. Copy of paper flat geol. map and descriptive text.

CARTE GÉOLOGIQUE DE LA RÉUNION
1:50, 000
In 4 sheets
Orléans : BRGM, 1969
145 x 140 complete
Col. geol. map in the following sheets :
Saint-Denis
Saint-Benoit
Saint-Pierre
Saint-Joseph
No text. Fr. 42,00

G EARTH RESOURCES

CARTE DES SOLS DE LA RÉUNION
by J Riquier
1:100, 000
Paris : ORSTOM, 1960
Col. soil map with 72pp text.
Fr. 10

CARTE DE RECONNAISSANCE DES SOLS
1:40, 000
by J Riquier
Paris : ORSTOM, 1959
Soil map, available for the following regions :
Région de Saint-Paul Fr. 10
Région de Saint-Pierre - Étang - Sale Fr. 10

698.2 Mauritius

A1 GENERAL MAPS : ROADS

CARTE TOURISTIQUE ET ROUTIÈRE - ÎLE MAURICE
1:100, 000
Paris : IGN, 1972
64 x 86
Relief shaded, roads and tracks in detail, settlement and places of interest. Insets of Port Louis, Curepipe, admin. divisions and climate and brief history in French and English. F.Fr. 10,00

B TOWN PLANS

PORT LOUIS
1:2, 500
DOS 029
Edition 1
Tolworth : DOS, 1969+
Detailed series of plans to cover town and environs, in progress.
67 sheets published.

PORT LOUIS
1:1, 250
DOS 0029
Edition 1
Tolworth : DOS, 1969+
Detailed series of plans to cover the town and environs, in progress. 18 sheets published.
Each 30p

ROSE BELLE, CUREPIPE
1:2, 500
DOS 029
Tolworth : DOS 1973
Detailed town plans series. In progress, 14 sheets published.
Each 30p

C OFFICIAL SURVEYS

MAURITIUS
1:25, 000
DOS 329 (Y881)
In 13 sheets, see index 698.2/1
Tolworth : DOS, 1957-58
Topog. series, contoured with land detail.
Each 50p

D POLITICAL & ADMINISTRATIVE

MAURITIUS
1:500, 000
DOS 971
Edition 4
Tolworth : DOS, 1962
Small map of island, showing principal boundaries, communications and settlement.
15p

MAURITIUS
Washington : Govt. Printing Office/ Central Intelligence Agency
38 x 27
Showing relief, urban areas, main admin. divisions, them. insets.
35¢

E1 PHYSICAL : RELIEF

MAURITIUS
1:100, 000
GSGS (Y682)
2nd edition
London : D Survey, MOD, 1971
64 x 57
Col. relief shaded with communications and settlement.

G EARTH RESOURCES

MAURITIUS SOIL MAP
1:100, 000
DOS (Misc) 317
Tolworth : DOS, 1962
64 x 79
Provisional classification soil map.
50p

H BIOGEOGRAPHY

MAURITIUS LAND USE
1:300, 000
DOS (Misc) 293
Tolworth : DOS, 1960
Small land use map.
20p

J CLIMATE

MAURITIUS AGROCLIMATIC
1:100, 000
DOS (Misc) 446
Tolworth : DOS, 1967
64 x 79
Coloured map showing zones of Thermal Efficiency Index and Moisture Efficiency Index. 50p

ATLASES
W3 WORLD ATLAS : LOCAL EDITION

ATLAS FOR MAURITIUS
London : MacMillan
22 x 29
33pp coloured maps of Mauritius and the World. No index.

698.3 Tromelin

ÎLE DE TROMELIN
1:10, 000
Paris : IGN, 1956
24 x 26
2 col. map based on aerial photo.
F.Fr. 11,67

699.2 St Helena and Dependencies

A2 **GENERAL MAPS : LOCAL**

ASCENSION ISLAND
1:200, 000
DOS 977
Tolworth : DOS, 1962
Small map in black and white.
15p

SAINT HELENA
1:164, 500
DOS 976
3rd edition
Tolworth : DOS, 1972
15 x 22
Small coloured hand map with relief shading and paths. 15p

TRISTAN DA CUNHA
1:140, 000
DOS 978
2nd edition
Tolworth : DOS, 1972
17 x 25
Small hand map with hill shading and paths.
15p

GOUGH ISLAND, SOUTH ATLANTIC OCEAN
1:40, 000
reprinted from Geog. Journal Mar. 1957
London : RGS
33 x 29
Topographical map from a survey by J B Heaney and M W Holdgate 1955-6.
£1.50

ASCENSION ISLAND
1:25, 000
DOS 327 (G892)
Edition 2
Tolworth : DOS, 1967
Contoured with relief shading, land detail.
50p

F **GEOLOGY**

GOUGH ISLAND GEOLOGY
1:40, 000
DOS (Geol) 1095
Tolworth : DOS, 1958
Small contoured geol. map.
30p

H **BIOGEOGRAPHY**

ST HELENA AGRICULTURE AND FORESTRY
1:50, 000
DOS (Misc) 234
Tolworth : DOS, 1957
44 x 34
Monochrome map with overprint of land use information. 15p

699.3 São Tomé and Principe

C **OFFICIAL SURVEYS**

ILHA DE S TOMÉ
1:75, 000
Lisboa : PUP, 1961
Contoured with communications and settlement.

ILHA DE S TOMÉ
1:25, 000
In 6 sheets
Lisboa : PUP, 1961-62
Contoured series with communications and settlement.

ILHA DO PRINCIPE
1:25, 000
In 2 sheets
Lisboa : PUP, 1964
Contoured map with communications, and settlement.

The Americas

7/8 The Americas

D POLITICAL & ADMINISTRATIVE

CONTINENT AMÉRICAIN POLITIQUE
1:15, 000, 000
Map No 318
Eds Vidal Lablache and H Varon
Paris : Armand Colin
120 x 100
Political col. wall map for schools, with a physical map on reverse.

ATLASES : NATIONAL ATLAS SCHOOL EDITION

COLORATLAS CONTINENTE AMERICANO
2nd Edition
Buenos Aires : Ed. Kapelusz, 1974
23 x 32
Physical, political school atlas of the Americas US $ 1.00

E1 PHYSICAL : RELIEF

CONTINENT AMÉRICAIN PHYSIQUE
Ed A Gibert
Map No 14
Paris : Delagrave
105 x 125
Physical wall map of the Americas with map of Oceania on reverse.
F.Fr. 45.00
Americas map only, on paper
F.Fr. 17.80

AMERICA FÍSICA
1:15, 500, 000
prepared by Inst. Cart. Latino
Barcelona : Editorial Vicens-Vives, 1976
88 x 126
Physical wall map of the Americas with inset of Antarctica. Principal towns and geographical regions marked. Printed on plastic paper with metal hanging strips. On reverse side is a political map of the Americas. S.Ptas. 500

CONTINENT AMÉRICAIN PHYSIQUE
1:15, 000, 000
Map No 318
Eds Vidal Lablache and H Varon
Paris : Armand Colin
120 x 100
Physical wall map of the Americas for schools, with political map on reverse.

THE AMERICAS
1:12, 500, 000
New York : AGS, 1953
85 x 127
Physical, contoured, layer col, thematic insets.
Flat $3.00
Rolled $3.50

AMERIKA
1:10, 000, 000
Gotha : Haack, 1967
117 x 164
Col. wall map for schools. Shows relief of land, ocean depths, boundaries, main physical features, towns graded by pop.

THE WORLD : AMERICAS
1:5, 000, 000
In 5 sheets, see index 100/3
New York : AGS
117 x 89 each sheet
Physical and political map, contoured, layer col, principal communications, admin. boundaries, towns graded by pop.
Sheets include :
1A Mexico, Central America and the West Indies
1B South America (North)
1C South America (South)
1D Northern Canada, Alaska and Greenland
1E United States and Southern Canada
Several of these sheets are currently unavailable, or in black and white edition only.

M HISTORICAL MAPS

EARLY MAP REPRODUCTIONS
- From Joan Blaeu's Theatrum Orbis Terrarum - Atlas Novus
Plate : The Americas 1635
Edinburgh : Bart.
61 x 52
Colour reproduction from the 1648 atlas.
£1.50

AMERICAS - FACSIMILE MAPS
Wien : Editio Totius Mundi
Maps available :
6 America
A. Ortelius 1570 50 x 36
col. 35DM uncol. 25DM
23 America
W. Blaeuw 1636 55 x 41
col. 35DM uncol. 25DM
30 America
J. Hondius 1631 50 x 37
col. 35DM uncol. 25DM
31 America
N. Visscher 1648 54 x 43
col. 35DM uncol. 25DM
39 America
"Nie Nuw Welt" S. Munster 1538 34 x 25
col. 30DM uncol 25DM
43 America
Th. de Bry 1596 39 x 32
col. 30DM uncol. 25DM
1146 America
L'America (after Cook) 1778 46 x 34
col. 25DM uncol. 18DM
136 America
'America of Nieuw Ontekte Weereld' P.v.d. Aa 1729 30 x 20
col. 10DM uncol. 4DM
157 America
'Neuholland' P.v.d. Aa 1729 30 x 20
col. 10DM uncol. 5DM
160 America
'Nieuw Weereld' P.v.d. Aa. 1729 30 x 20
col. 10DM uncol. 5DM

AMERICA POLÍTICA
1:15, 500, 000
Editorial Vicens - Vives, 1976
see THE AMERICAS 7/8 EI

ATLASES
M HISTORICAL

GRAPHIC HISTORY OF THE AMERICAS - PREHISTORY TO THE PRESENT
Theodore R Miller
New York : John Wiley, 1969
28 x 37
61pp
Black and white maps, covering Western hemisphere. The Americas shown on each page, with insets. Paper covers, spiral bound.
$7.95

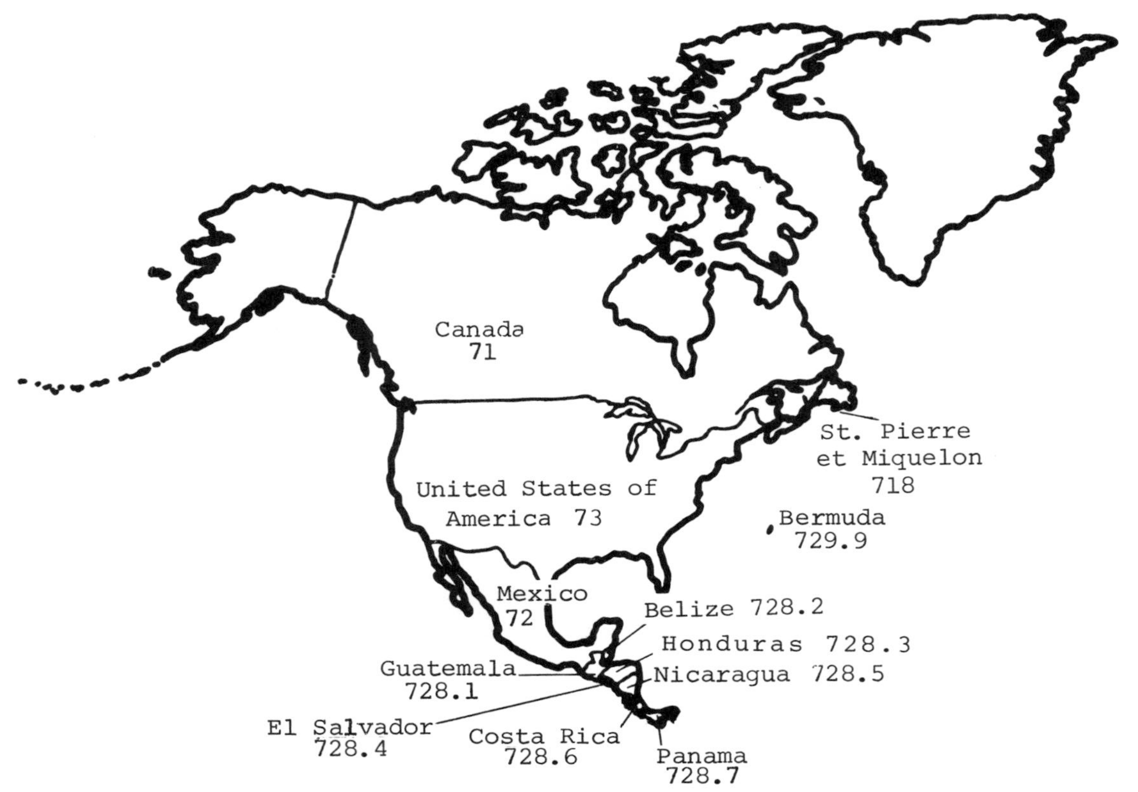

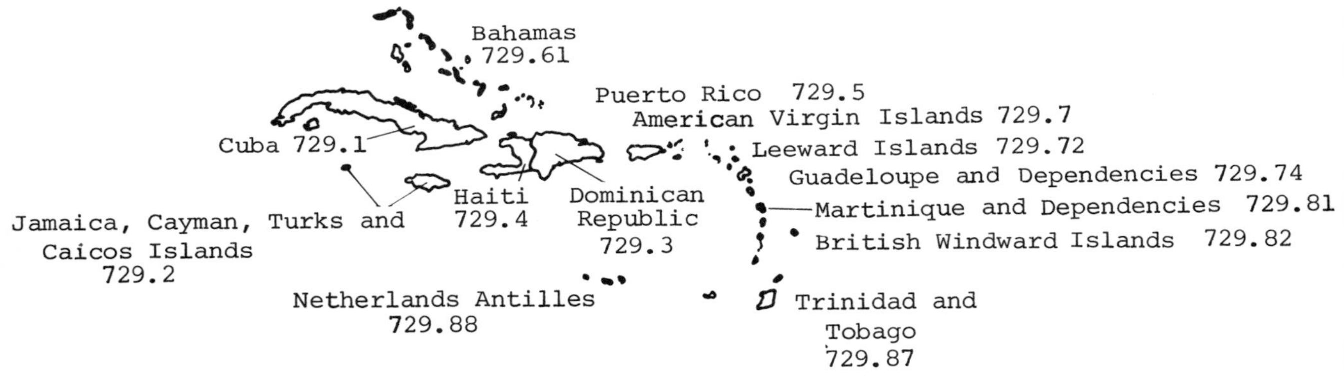

Regions

North America 7
Central America 728
West Indies 729
Lesser Antilles 729.7/8

North and Central America

7 North America

A1 GENERAL MAPS

VACATIONLANDS - US AND SOUTHERN CANADA
1:5, 062, 375
Washington : NGS
96 x 66
Scenic and historic sites, index, insets of popular recreation areas on reverse.
Plastic $3.00

D POLITICAL & ADMINISTRATIVE

AMERICA DEL NORTE
1:25, 000, 000 approx.
Barcelona : Editorial Teide
33 x 50
School hand map showing major cities and state boundaries.
2 ptas
Also : America del Norte politica
25 x 33 1 pta

AMERYKA PÓLNOCNA, MAPA FIZYCZNA I POLITYCZNA
1:20, 000, 000
Warszawa : PPWK, 1972
54 x 43
Double sided map, on one side a layer coloured, relief shaded physical map and on the reverse a map politically coloured by departments. Each map shows towns and communications. zl 1.00

NORTH AMERICA
1:10, 000, 000
MCR 31
Ottawa : DEMR, 1971
82 x 100
Azimuthal proj, centred on Prince Albert, coloured by provinces with roads and railways. In English and French editions.

SUPERIOR MAP OF NORTH AMERICA
1:10, 000, 000 app.
Maplewood : Hammond
83 x 127
Col. political map in folder showing principal towns, road and rail communications. $2.00

NORDAMERIKA
1:10, 000, 000
No. 894
Frankfurt : Ravenstein
76 x 91
Political map of North America with principal road and rail communications.
DM 8. 80

DIE STAATEN NORDAMERIKAS
1:10, 000, 000
Darmstadt : Perthes
106 x 125
Col. political wall map in series "Kleiner Geographischer Wandatlas"
48 DM

SEVERNAYA AMERIKA
1:10, 000, 000
Moskva : GUGK, 1973
Political admin. reference map.
15 kop

NORTH AMERICA
1:9, 504, 000
Washington : NGS, 1969
82 x 106
Boundaries in colour, road and rail communications, detailed place names, airports. Chamberlain Trimetric projection.
Paper $2.00
Plastic $3 00

PHILIP'S POLITICAL SMALL WALL MAP OF NORTH AMERICA
1:9, 000, 000
London : Philip, 1968
85 x 101
Political. col. showing railways, shipping routes and towns graded by population.
Paper flat £1.50
Mounted CR £5.50
Mounted cloth dissected to fold £7.00

PHILIP'S COMPARATIVE WALL ATLAS OF NORTH AMERICA - POLITICAL
1:9, 000, 000
Philip
see NORTH AMERICA 7 E 1

AMÉRIQUE DU NORD POLITIQUE
1:8, 500, 000
Map No. 319
Eds. Vidal Lablache and H. Varon
Paris : Armand Colin
120 x 100
Political wall map for schools with blank outline map on reverse.

EXCELLO POLITICAL WALL MAP
1:8, 125, 000
Indianapolis : Cram
111 x 116
Political coloured wall map, showing communications, boundaries and principal towns. Mounted on linen.
$12.50

NORTH AMERICA
1:8, 000, 000
No 4243
Bern : K & F
89 x 118
Political col, principal road, rail and sea communications, boundaries, towns graded by pop. New York region inset.

AMERIQUE DU NORD
1:8, 000, 000
No 19
Paris : Hatier
100 x 120
School wall map, political and economic map on reverse.

UMRISSKARTE NORDAMERIKA
1:8, 000, 000
No 0838
Bern : K & F
99 x 120
Political col. outline map.

SEVERNÍ AMERIKA
1:8, 000, 000
Praha : Kart, 1969
General school wall map of North America. Political colouring.
kcs 150

SEVERNA AMERIKA
1:8, 000, 000
Beograd : Geokarta
98 x 138
2 sheet map with latin and cyrillic lettering.
Cloth mounted 100 dn

NORTH AMERICA : POLITICAL GEOGRAPHY WALL MAP
1:7, 187, 500
No 107051
Chicago : Denoyer-Geppert
111 x 147
Political col, school wall map showing boundaries, communications, water features, pop.
CR $19.25

POLITICAL MAPS OF NORTH AMERICA
Various scales
Indianapolis : Cram
Coloured political school wall maps, available at different levels and depths :
Level B Simplified 1:7, 062, 500
129 x 144 $23.00
Level C Detailed 1:7, 062, 500
129 x 144 $23.00

NORTH AMERICA AND THE ARCTIC
1:6, 900, 000
Michigan : Hearne Bros.
122 x 167
Political boundaries, relief shading, mechanical index. Col. school wall map, inc. Central America.
$152.50

PHILIP'S POLITICAL LARGE WALL MAP OF NORTH AMERICA
1:6, 500, 000
London : Philip
122 x 150
Political col, boundaries, railways, sea routes, towns graded by pop.
Mounted CR £15.00
Mounted on cloth dissected to fold £17.00

NORDAMERIKA, POLITISCHE WANDKARTE
1:6, 000, 000
Braunschweig : Westermann
216 x 207
Col. political school wall map.

NORDAMERIKA
1:6, 000, 000
No 9713
Munchen : JRO
135 x 173
2 col. map, plastic surface for working on.
108 DM

AMÉRIQUE DU NORD
1:6, 000, 000
Bruxelles : Mantnieks
119 x 160
Politically coloured wall map with names and available in French and English editions. Azimuthal Equidistant projection.

AMERICA DEL NORTE
1:5, 000, 000
Madrid : Aguilar
130 x 200
Politically col. wall map for schools.
Paper 100 ptas
Cloth 550 ptas

POHJOIS - AMERIKKA
1:5, 000, 000
Helsinki : Wsoy
194 x 217
School wall map 100 FMK

SEVERNAYA AMERIKA
1:40, 000, 000
Moskva : GUGK, 1973
Outline map 1 kop

AMERICA SETTENTRIONALE E CENTRALE
1:40, 000, 000
Novara : Agostini
33 x 26
Small hand outline map for schools L 40

NORTH AMERICA
1:20, 000, 000
MCR 60
Ottawa : DEMR
55 x 63
Outline map

PHILIP'S LARGE OUTLINE MAP OF NORTH AMERICA
1:9, 000, 000
London : Philip
85 x 101
Black on white cartridge paper, contours.
£1.25

PHILIP'S MAP BUILDING SHEET ('BLACKBOARD MAP') OF NORTH AMERICA
1:9, 000, 000
London : Philip, 1967
85 x 101
As Large Outline map but in yellow on blackboard paper and rollers £4.00

NORTH AMERICA, OUTLINE SLATED
1:7, 187, 500
No 165051
Chicago : Denoyer-Geppert
111 x 129
Blackboard map for schools showing countries; blue and yellow on black.
$19.95

OUTLINE MAP OF NORTH AMERICA
1:7, 062, 500
Indianapolis : Cram
129 x 144
In black and white, showing international and state boundaries.
Mounted on linen $27.50
Also available : Desk Outline map
30 x 43 60c

VITO-GRAPHIC CHALKBOARD OUTLINE MAP OF NORTH AMERICA
1:7, 000, 000
Ref VS 3
Chicago : Weber Costello Co
117 x 158
Land areas in green, meridians, parallels and outlines in yellow, water areas in blue. On cloth - various mounted styles.

LERNKARTE VON NORDAMERIKA
1:6, 000, 000
Darmstadt : Perthes
138 x 160
School wall map, showing basic geog. features, with symbols, info to be added.
94 DM
With "Schuler-Lernkarte von Nordamerika"
1: 30, 000, 000 for pupil use 1,50 DM

MAPA MUDOS
Barcelona : Editorial Vicens-Vives
33 x 24
Series of outline maps in 2 colours. Maps available:
America del Norte — física
America del Norte — política
Alaska y Canada
Estados Unidos
Mejico y America central
50 copies S Ptas 100

E 1 PHYSICAL : RELIEF

AMERICA SETTENTRIONALE
1:40, 000, 000
Novara : Agostini
33 x 26
Physical map with political map, including some economic detail on reverse.
L 450

AMERICA DEL NORTE FISICA
1:40, 000, 000
Barcelona : Editorial Teide
25 x 33
Physical hand map for schools. 1 pta

AMERYKA POLNOCNA, MAPA FIZYCZNA I POLITYCZNA
1:20, 000, 000
PPWK, 1972
see NORTH AMERICA D

BARTHOLOMEW'S WORLD TRAVEL MAP SERIES : NORTH AMERICA
1:10, 000, 000
Edinburgh : Bart
69 x 90
Contoured, layer col, road and rail communications, boundaries. Lesser Antilles and Aleutian Islands inset at same scale. 75p

NORDAMERIKA
1:10, 000, 000
Darmstradt : Perthes
106 x 125
Col. physical map in "Kleiner Geographischer Wandatlas" series.
48 DM

CARTE GÉNÉRALE DU MONDE
1:10, 000, 000
IGN
Sheets 3, 4, 7, 8 cover N. America
see WORLD 100 E1 and index 100/4

PHILIP'S PHYSICAL SMALLER WALL MAP OF NORTH AMERICA
1:9, 000, 000
London : Philip
85 x 101
Layer col, political boundaries in red.
Paper flat £1.50
Mounted CR £5.50
Mounted on cloth dissected to fold £7.00

PHILIP'S COMPARATIVE WALL ATLAS OF NORTH AMERICA
1:9, 000, 000
London : Philip
85 x 101 each
A set of 5 maps for comparative study :
Relief of Land - Political and communications
Climate - Summer conditions, Winter conditions, Rainfall, Isobars, Winds, Actual Temperature and Sea Level Isotherms.
Natural Vegetation
Political
Density of Population
supplementary map :
Commercial Development
single sheets,
Paper flat £1.50
Mounted CR £5.50
Mounted on cloth dissected to fold £7.00

PHILIP'S GRAPHIC RELIEF WALL MAP OF NORTH AMERICA
1:8, 750, 000
London : Philip
86 x 107
Col. to simulate predominant vegetation cover, producing a 3-D effect. No town names.
Paper flat £1.50
Mounted CR £5.50
Mounted on cloth dissected to fold £7.00

NOORD-AMERICA
1:8, 000, 000
Groningen : Wolters - Noordhoff
90 x 120
Physical wall map showing relief and settlements.
Fl. 101.50

AMÉRIQUE DU NORD (PHYSIQUE)
1:8, 000, 000
No 1058 French, 1232 English
St Germain-en-Laye : Editions MDI
92 x 126
Plastic coated physical wall map for schools. Agricultural and climatic map on reverse.

SEVERNAYA AMERIKA FIZICHESKAYA KARTA
1:8, 000, 000
Moskva : GUGK, 1973
2 sheet physical school wall map.
Cyrillic. 28 kop

AMERICA SETTENTRIONALE FISICO-POLITICA
1:8, 000, 000
Novara : Agostini
120 x 135
2 sheet school wall map showing relief of land and sea, political boundaries, cities graded by pop. First series.
L 3,000
Mounted L 6,000
Second series 1:7, 000, 000 (2 sheets)
138 x 190 L 3,500
Mounted L 7,500
Third series 1:10, 000, 000
100 x 140 L 2,200
Mounted L 5,000

NORDAMERIKA
1:7, 500, 000
W 747
München : List
100 x 140
Wenschow coloured physical wall map printed on 'Antihydro' plasticised paper, showing land and sea relief, major towns, communications, boundaries. 54 DM

TRI-GRAPHIC MAP OF NORTH AMERICA
1:7, 500, 000
Ref TRI-3
Chicago : Weber Costello Co
101 x 137
Physical layer colouring with graphic relief shading and political boundaries.
Available mounted in various styles.

PHYSICAL MAPS OF NORTH AMERICA
Various scales
Indianapolis : Cram
Col. school wall maps, available for different levels and depths:
Level B Simplified Physical-Political
1:7, 062, 500 129 x 129 $23.00
Level C Detailed Physical-Political
1:7, 062, 500 129 x 129 $23.00
Physical Outline
1:7, 062,000 129 x 129 $27.50
Excello Physical Wall Map
1:7, 500, 000 111 x 137 $12.50

NORTH AMERICA
1:7, 187, 500
No 130061-10
Chicago : Denoyer-Geppert
111 x 147
Classroom map, physical-political, showing land detail, boundaries, pop.
Rollers $15.50

NORTH AMERICA, VISUAL RELIEF
1:7, 187, 500
No 110051
Chicago : Denoyer-Geppert
111 x 147
Physical school wall map showing land and sea relief, boundaries etc. Reduced size as Desk Map No 301551 29 x 43, $3.50 per 25 copies.
$18.75

PHILIP'S PHYSICAL LARGE WALL MAP OF NORTH AMERICA
1:6, 500, 000
London : Philip
120 x 150
Physical col, hill shading, political boundaries, railways, ocean routes.
Mounted CR £15.00
Mounted on cloth dissected to fold £17.00

NORDAMERIKA
1:6, 000, 000
Darmstadt : Perthes
172 x 205
Haack Wall Map, physical, layer col, boundaries and communications.
Mounted CR 142 DM

NORDAMERIKA
1:6. 000, 000
Braunschweig : Westermann
157 x 177
Col. physical wall map, with relief shading, boundaries, railways, cities graded by pop.

AMÉRIQUE DU NORD
1:6, 000, 000
Bruxelles : Mantnieks
125 x 180
Physical wall map for schools showing relief of land and sea, direction of ocean currents, political boundaries. Also available in English.

NORDAMERIKA
1:6, 000, 000
Gotha : Haack, 1967
162 x 186
Physical wall map, layer col, international boundaries, cities, railways, ocean depths, other physical features.

NORDAMERIKA
1:6, 000, 000
No 9711
München : JRO
135 x 173
Physical col. wall map, land and sea relief. Work map on reverse, plastic surface.
138 DM

NORDAMERIKA
1:6, 000, 000
No 9712
München : JRO
135 x 173
Physical wall map on linen. Inc. Central America 128 DM

NORDAMERIKA, MIT MEERESBODENRELIEF
1:6, 000, 000
W 713
München : List
155 x 185
Wenschow col. wall map, physical with relief of sea bottom. 164 DM

AMERICA DEL NORTE
1:5, 000, 000
Madrid : Aguilar
130 x 200
Physical col. wall map, hypsometric tints.
Paper 100 ptas
Cloth 550 ptas

NORDAMERIKA
1:5, 000, 000
H 208
München : List
190 x 215
Harms wall map showing in col. land and sea relief, ocean currents. 164 DM

CARTE DES CONTINENTS
1:5, 000, 000
IGN
Bande 2, Sheets 1, 2, 3, 4 cover N. America
see WORLD 100 E1 and index 100/5

ÉTATS-UNIS ET MÉXIQUE
1:3, 700, 000
Bruxelles : Mantnieks
180 x 125
Physical wall map for schools showing relief by bathy metric and layer colouring, political boundaries in red, ocean currents. Also available in English.

VEREINIGTE STAATEN UND MITTELAMERIKA
1:3, 000, 000
W734
München : List
240 x 175
Wenschow physical wall map, layer coloured with hachures, communications and settlement. DM 164

SEVERNAYA AMERIKA
1:3, 000, 000
Moskva : GUGK, 1973
School map in 1 sheet 17 kop

AMERICA SETTENTRIONALE FISICO-POLITICO
1:10, 000, 000
Novara : Agostini
131 x 100
Plastic moulded relief map in frame with metal corners. L 20,000

RAISED RELIEF MAP OF NORTH AMERICA
1:5, 000, 000
NR 5
Chicago : Nystrom, 1975
95 x 128
Plastic moulded map, physical layer colouring, principal communications and boundaries.
Unframed US $46.00
Framed US $74.00

E 2 PHYSICAL : LAND FEATURES

RETREAT OF WISCONSIN AND RECENT ICE IN NORTH AMERICA
1:5, 000, 000
by V. K. Prest
GSC Map No 1257A
Ottawa : GSC, 1969
Coloured map C $2.00

NINE GLACIER MAPS - NORTH-WESTERN NORTH AMERICA
1:10, 000
New York : AGS 1960
9 maps in case, with 22pp text. Contours over ice surfaces. Results of programme for International Geophysical Year 1957-58.
$4.00

F GEOLOGICAL

GENERALIZED TECTONIC MAP OF NORTH AMERICA
1:15, 000, 000
Misc. Geologic Investigations Map
1 - 688
1st Edition
Washington : USGS, 1972
51 x 61
Coloured map with legend in margin.
$1.00

GEOLOGIC MAP OF NORTH AMERICA
1:5, 000, 000
Washington : USGS, 1965
99 x 142 each
2 sheet geological map by the North American Geologic Map Committee
set $5.00

BASEMENT MAP OF NORTH AMERICA
1:5, 000, 000
Washington : USGS, 1967
101 x 134
Coloured geological map indicating base rocks between lats 24° and 60° prepared in assoc with AAPG $1.00

TECTONIC MAP OF NORTH AMERICA
1:5, 000, 000
Washington : USGS, 1969
162 x 193
2 sheet map comp. with Geol. Surveys of Canada, Mexico, Greenland (Denmark). Shows foldings, chemical composition, platform deposits, faults, volcanic deposits etc. set $5.00

RETREAT OF WISCONSIN AND RECENT ICE IN NORTH AMERICA
by V K Prest
1:5, 000, 000
Map No 1257A
Ottawa : GSC, 1969
Shows speculative ice-marginal positions during retreat of last ice-sheet complex.
$2.00

G EARTH RESOURCES

SOIL MAP OF THE WORLD
1:5, 000, 000
Paris : UNESCO, 1972
106 x 74
2 sheets to cover North America II - 1, 2 including explanatory volume II
see WORLD G and index 100/6

NORTH AMERICAN PETROLEUM MAP SERIES
1:5, 000, 000
In 4 sheets.
Oklahoma : Petroleum Publishing Co. 1976
137 x 102
Set of 4 maps covering the whole of North America. Base map shows basement rock outcrop, boundaries and towns.
Maps in series :

1. Oil and gas production
2. Crude pipelines with oilfields
3. Gas pipelines with gas fields
4. Products pipelines with refineries

set. US $80.00

1976 PRODUCTS PIPELINE MAP OF USA AND CANADA
1:5, 000, 000
Oklahoma : Petroleum Publishing Co. 1976
145 x 102
Six colour wall map showing over 100 product pipelines including pump stations, terminals, interconnections and refineries.
folded US $8.00
flat US $10.00

1973 CRUDE PIPELINE WALL MAP OF USA AND CANADA
1:5, 000, 000
Oklahoma : Petroleum Publishing Co.1973
145 x 102
Six colour wall map showing pipelines and producing oil fields.
folded US $8.00
flat US $10.00

1974 NATURAL GAS PIPELINE WALL MAP
1:5, 000, 000
Oklahoma : Petroleum Publishing Co. 1974
145 x 102
Six colour wall map showing pipelines and producing gas fields.
folded US $7.50
flat US $9.50

H BIOGEOGRAPHY

NORTH AMERICA VEGETATION
1:12, 000, 000
Tehran : Sahab
60 x 90
Map in Eng. and Persian showing vegetation types, cultivation, irrigation and forests.
80 Rls

NORDAMERIKA KLIMA UND VEGETATION
1:12, 000, 000
Haack, 1967
see NORTH AMERICA 7J

PHILIP'S COMPARATIVE WALL ATLAS OF NORTH AMERICA NATURAL VEGETATION
1:9, 000, 000
Philip
see NORTH AMERICA 7 E1

SEVERNAYA AMERIKA, PRIRODNYE ZONY
1:8, 000, 000
Moskva : GUGK, 1973
2 sheet school wall map showing natural zones 34 kop

NORDAMERIKA : WILDTIERE UND WILDPLFANZEN
Scale not given
Braunschweig : Westermann
96 x 127
Pictorial col. wall map showing Wild Animals and Natural Vegetation for schools.

NORD - UND MITTELAMERIKA
Scale not given
No 9902
München : JRO
96 x 120
Col. pictorial wall map of land use, and useful animals. 48 DM

NORD - UND MITTELAMERIKA - VEGETATION UND TIERWELT
No 9901
München : JRO
96 x 120
Pictorial wall map showing main vegetation types and animals. 48 DM

J CLIMATE

NORTH AMERICA
1:14, 375, 000
No 109051
Chicago : Denoyer-Geppert
111 x 162
4 thematic maps on 1 sheet. Shows Climate Types (12 zones) and Frost Free Days.
$15.50

NORDAMERIKA KLIMA UND VEGETATION
1:12, 000, 000
Braunschweig : Westermann
205 x 166
Col. school wall map showing vegetation and climate. 142 DM

NORDAMERIKA : KLIMA UND VEGETATION
1:12, 000, 000
Gotha : Haack, 1967
205 x 166
4 maps on one sheet, showing Jan. and July temperatures, average annual rainfall, and vegetation types.

PHILIP'S COMPARATIVE WALL ATLAS OF NORTH AMERICA - CLIMATE
1:9, 000, 000
Philip
see NORTH AMERICA 7E1

AMERIQUE DU NORD PHYSIQUE-AGRICOLE (CLIMAT)
1:8, 000, 000
Éditions MDI
see NORTH AMERICA 7 E1

SEVERNA AMERIKA - KLIMATICHESKAYA KARTA
1:8, 000, 000
Moskva : GUGK
115 x 140 each
Climatic wall map in 2 sheets, showing rainfall, isotherms, wind direction etc.

K HUMAN GEOGRAPHY

NORTH AMERICA
1:14, 375, 000
No 109051
Chicago : Denoyer-Geppert
111 x 162
4 thematic maps on 1 sheet
Population Density. $15.50

PHILIP'S COMPARATIVE WALL ATLAS OF NORTH AMERICA - DENSITY OF POPULATION
1:9, 000, 000
Philip
see NORTH AMERICA 7 E1

L ECONOMIC

NORTH AMERICA
1:13, 375, 000
No 109051
Chicago : Denoyer-Geppert
111 x 162
4 thematic maps on 1 sheet. Shows Economic Activities, mining, land use.
$15.50

PHILIP'S COMPARATIVE WALL ATLAS OF NORTH AMERICA - COMMERCIAL DEVELOPMENT
1:9, 000, 000
Philip
see NORTH AMERICA 7 E1

NORD - UND MITTELAMERIKA - VERWALTUNG, WIRTSCHAFT UND VERKEHR
1:8, 000, 000 approx.
No 9904
München : JRO
96 x 120
Col. pictorial wall map showing admin, economy, communications. 48 DM

NORD - UND MITTELAMERIKA - BODENSCHÄTZE UND INDUSTRIE
1:8, 000, 000 approx.
No 9903
München : JRO
96 x 120
Col. pictorial wall map of soil yield and industry. 48 DM

SEVERNAYA AMERIKA - EKONOMICHESKAYA KARTA
1:8, 000, 000
Moskva : GUGK, 1973
Economic wall map in 2 sheets.
28 kop

NORDAMERIKA : WIRTSCHAFT UND VERKEHR
1:8, 000, 000 approx.
Braunschweig : Westermann
96 x 127
Col. pictorial wall map showing economy and transport in symbols.

AMÉRIQUE DU NORD (PHYSIQUE-AGRICOLE (CLIMAT))
1:8, 000, 000
Éditions MDI
see NORTH AMERICA 7 E1

NORD AMERIKA : WIRTSCHAFT
1:7, 500, 000
München : List
100 x 140
Harms col. wall map showing economy by pictorial symbols. 54 DM
Also available as double wall map with "Nordamerika" physical map
see NORTH AMERICA 7 E1 92 DM

TRANSPORTATION FACILITIES OF NORTH AMERICA
1:7, 187, 500
No 109551
Chicago : Denoyer-Geppert
111 x 162
Shows roads, railways, airports, ports; inland waterways inset. Spring rollers $19.25

FOREST INDUSTRIES MILL MAP OF NORTH AMERICA
1:6, 250, 000
2nd edition
San Francisco : Miller Freeman Pubns, 1976
127 x 91
Shows the precise location of 2,933 sawmills, plywood, particle-board, hardboard and insulation board mills in the USA and Canada. Background colours indicate major forest areas. Insets of congested areas. US $15.50

PULP AND PAPER MILLS IN THE UNITED STATES AND CANADA
1:6, 250, 000
6th edition
San Francisco : Miller Freeman Pubn's.1976
107 x 74
Showing location of every pulp, paper and paperboard mill and also those under construction. Insets of congested areas, index to mills and major forests indicated in colour US $12.50

NORTH AMERICA, ECONOMIC AND POLITICAL
No scale given
Indianapolis : Cram
Shows trade, agriculture, wealth, pop. School wall map. $13.75

M HISTORICAL

ELEMENTARY HISTORY MAPS
Indianapolis : Cram
132 x 100
Large scale historical wall maps, showing :
Early Grants and Origin of the 13 Colonies
European Claims and Possessions 1754-1763
European Settlements to about 1760
The Thirteen Colonies 1760-1775
Western Land Claims and Ordinance 1787
The United States in 1810
Mexican War and Compromise of 1850
Territorial Expansion to 1854
United States in 1861
Continental United States
For 12 maps S106.00

HISTORY MAPS
Indianapolis : Cram
Coloured school maps available for :
Spanish Exploration and Settlement to 1580 AD
Indians during Early Exploration and Settlement
Hispanic America - Discovery and Settlement and Colonial Administration
Claims of the Nations in North America 1689-1713
Early Grants and Origin of the Thirteen Colonies
European Claims and Possessions 1754-1763
European Settlements to about 1760
The Thirteen Colonies, 1760-1775
The Revolution in the Middle and Northern Colonies
The Revolution in the South and West
Western Land Claims and the Ordinance of 1787
The United States in 1790 and about 1802
The United States in 1810
Elections of 1812, 1828, 1840 and 1856
The United States in 1840
Transportation– River and Canal Period 1816-1840
Hispanic America, Inter-American Relations
The Mexican War and Compromise of 1850
Territorial Expansion to 1854
The United States in 1861
The Civil War 1861-1865
The Westward Movement of the Population to 1870
Transportation - Early Railroad Period, 1840-80
Transportation, Principal Railroads since 1880
The United States in 1890, Physical, Political, Economic
Four Important Elections since the Civil War
The World War 1914-1918
Continental United States each $13.75

"OUR AMERICA"
Ed Edgar B Wesley
Chicago : Denoyer-Geppert
111 x 96
Series of 38 school historical wall maps:
BACKGROUNDS AND DISCOVERY
Spread of Western Civilization 200011
Beginnings of Civilization 200021
Early Mediterranean Cultures 200031
Later Mediterranean Cultures 200041
Europe in Middle Ages 200051
Age of Discovery, 1492-1580 200061
Spanish Exploration, 1492-1610 200071
Early Indians and their Culture 200081
Exploration and Colonization, 1580-1750 200091
Colonial Grants 200101
Colonial Development, 1690-1774 200111
Struggle for a Continent, 1680-1800 200121
FORMATION AND GROWTH OF THE NATION
War for Independence 1775-83 200131
Union and Unity 200141
National Expansion to 1819 200151
Early Westward Movement, 1763-1829 200161
The United States in 1821 200171
Latin America, 1830;
Monroe Doctrine 200181
Growth of the US, 1776-1853 200191
Mexican War, Territorial Adjustments 200201
Development of Transportation 1829-60 200211
Secession, 1860-1861 200221
War Between the States, 1861-65 200231
National Recovery and Growth, 1865-76 200241
CONTEMPORARY UNITED STATES
The United States in 1959 200251
Overseas America, 1867-1940 200261
European Area in World War I 200271
Growth of Population, 1790-1940 200281
Transportation Systems 200291
Land Use and Conservation 200301
Farming and Grazing 200311
Manufacturing and Minerals 200321
European Area in World War II 200331
Pacific Area in World War II 200341
The Air Age World 200351
The World in 1965 200361
The 50 United States :
Their Geographic Extent 200371
Population Density, 1960 200381
CR each $13.75
Set CR $472.74

HART BOLTON AMERICAN HISTORY MAPS
Chicago : Denoyer-Geppert
111 x 81
Series of col. school history wall maps :
World of Columbus 201011
World Exploration, 1492-1580 201021
Caribbean Settlement, 1492-1543 201031
Internation Rivalries 201041
English Colonial Grants 201051
Partition of America 201061
Colonial Commerce, Industries 201071
The Revolution 201081
State Claims and Ratification 201091
Westward Movement 201101

Louisiana Purchase	201111
Historic Oregon Country	201651
Historic Pacific Northwest	201661
Territorial Acquisitions	201121
Land and Water Routes	201131
Mexican War; Compromise of 1850	201141
Secession	201151
Civil War	201161
Abolition and Reconstruction	201171
Western Statehood; Land Grants to Railroads	201181
Lines of Transportation	201191
Resources and Conservation	201201
Industrial United States	201211
Agricultural United States	201221
United States in the Caribbean	201231
European Area in World War I	200271
European Area in World War II	200331
Pacific Area in World War II	200341
Greater United States	201241
Population Density, 1960	200381

Set $152.00
Each CR $10.00

NORD - UND MITTELAMERIKA IM 19 UND 20 JAHRHUNDERT
1:6, 200, 000
Bielefeld : Cornelsen, Velhagen und Klasing
195 x 138
Putzger historical wall map. DM 145.00

NORDAMERIKA VON DER ENTDECKUNG BIS HEUTE
1:6, 000, 000
Braunschweig : Westermann
216 x 207
From the discovery of North America to the present. Col. historical wall map with insets of North America and the USA. Inc. Central America. 6 maps on 1 sheet.

HISTORICAL WALL MAPS
1:3, 000, 000
Moskva : GUGK
Voyna za Nezavisimost i Obrazovadne SSA
Historical wall map of the Wars of Independence and the Formation of the USA, 1775-1783
Grazdanskaya Voyna v SSA (1861-1865) (Civil War USA) 1973

COLONIAL-REVOLUTIONARY AMERICAN LITERATURE
1585-1789
No 161711-14
Chicago : Denoyer-Geppert
162 x 137
Pictorial wall map for schools.
Spring rollers $24.00

NORDAMERIKA : ENTDECKUNG UND BESIEDLUNG
No scale given
Braunschweig : Westermann
96 x 127
North America : Discovery and Settlement - col. pictorial wall map for schools.

NORTH AMERICA - FACSIMILE MAPS
Wien : Editio Totius Mundi
Maps available:

193	America Borealis C de Jode 1593 col. 30 DM	50 x 36 uncol.	25 DM
983	America Settentrionale M V Coronelli 1691 col. 35 DM	44 x 60 uncol.	25 DM
1145	America Borealis anon 1699 col. 22 DM	35 x 22 uncol.	15 DM

NORTH AMERICA - FACSIMILE MAPS
Ottawa : DEMR
Maps available :
MCR 300 America Septentrionalis
54 x 61 (reproduced from a plate from 'Nouveau Theatre du Monde ou Nouvel Atlas' by Jansson, Amsterdam)
MCR 2302 Amerique Septentrionale
62 x 91 prepared by Alexis Hubert Jaillot c 1696
MCR 2304 British North America
61 x 48 by Arrowsmith pub'd 15 Feb 1834
each C$1.00

A MAP OF THE BRITISH EMPIRE IN AMERICA WITH THE FRENCH AND SPANISH SETTLEMENTS ADJACENT THERETO, BY HENRY POPPLE, 1733
1:3, 168, 000 app.
In 23 sheets
Lympne Castle (Kent) : Harry Margary 1972
76 x 57 each
Facsimile map; 20 map sheets, key, title and introduction sheets.

NORTH AMERICA
Maplewood : Hammond
62 x 41
Set of reproduction maps :
Virginia and Florida by Hondius, 1606
New England and New York, John Speed Atlas, c 1676
North America by Valk and Schenk, c 1683
New France, with Quebec City view, 1719 $3.95

ATLASES
A1 GENERAL : ROADS

ROAD ATLAS OF THE UNITED STATES, CANADA AND MEXICO
Chicago : Rand McNally
28 x 38
132 pp
Col. detailed road maps covering each State, Canada and Mexico inc. city and National Park plans, ill. section on National Forests and Parks, trip planner guide, index of 24,000 place names
Annual ed. $2.95

ATLASES
L ECONOMIC

OXFORD REGIONAL ECONOMIC ATLAS OF THE UNITED STATES AND CANADA
2nd edition
Oxford : OUP, 1975
178pp
19 x 25
80pp coloured maps (including 17 urban plans, 48pp topog. maps) covering population growth, geology, agriculture, industry and mining.

Boards £8.00
Paper covers £8.75

ATLAS OF NORTH AMERICAN AFFAIRS
by D K Adams and H B Rodgers
London : Methuen, 1969
144 pp
15 x 21
57 thematic maps - economy, agriculture, industry, pop, etc. covers present-day North America and its sociological problems. £2.50
Paperback £1.00

ATLASES
M HISTORICAL

ATLAS OF AMERICAN HISTORY
Chicago : Denoyer-Geppert
32pp
22 x 28
inc. 28 maps from the Wesley "Our America" series of wall maps (q.v.)
Covers : History and Development; Internal Development and Expansion; Development and Position of the US as a world power. For schools. $1.00

ATLAS OF AMERICAN HISTORY
Maplewood NJ : Hammond
40pp
24 x 31
Covering major events and periods from the Voyages of Discovery to the Present Day $2.50
Paper $1.28

ATLAS OF AMERICAN HISTORY
Ed. Cole
Lexington, Mass : Ginn
22 x 30
Outstanding events in American history with maps. Paperboard. $2.88

THE BLATHWAYT ATLAS
Ed. Jeanette D Black
Providence : Brown UP, 1970
48 maps
Facsimile copy of the atlas bound for William Blathwayt, Foreign Secretary, c 1683 for purposes of colonial admin. 34 printed, 14 manuscript maps covering the various American colonies (with 1 for Bombay Harbour, India) $500
Vol. II Commentary 245pp. 1975 $25.00

AMERICA SETTENTRIONALE, COLLE NUOVE SCOPERTE FIN'AL L'ANNO 1688 (ATLANTE VENETO VOL I)
Vincenzo Maria Coronelli, 1695
Chicago : Rand McNally, 1971
51 x 76
Facsimile edition of original atlas.

BRITISH MAPS OF COLONIAL AMERICA
Ed. W.P. Cumming
Chicago : Univ. of Chicago Press, 1974.
21 x 26
114 pp
Containing a series of map reproductions describing the development of British cartography in colonial North America and offering new information on the history of significant maps and individual mapmakers.
US $10.95

71 Canada

See also:
7 NORTH AMERICA

A1 GENERAL MAPS : ROADS

KANADA
1:7, 500, 000
Moskva : GUGK, 1973
Col. study map, showing water features, settlements, admin. centres and divisions, communications, boundaries, economic details, pop. Geog. description.
Text in Russian. 30kop

IMPERIAL MAP OF CANADA
1:6, 000, 000
Chicago : Rand McNally
107 x 69
Political colouring, showing railways, airports and generalised relief by hachuring. Index in margin.

VACATION LANDS U.S. AND SOUTHERN CANADA
1:5, 062, 375
N.G.S.
see
7 NORTH AMERICA

NORTHWEST CANADA — TRANSPORTATION
1:3, 168,000
MCR 35
Ottawa : DEMR, 1974
86 x 61
Col. map showing communications — road, rail, airports etc.

CANADA AND NORTHERN UNITED STATES HIGHWAY MAP
1:2, 825, 000
Ottawa : Canadian Govt. Travel Bureau
Road map with insets of W. United States and Canada at 1:9, 375, 000, Eastern US & Canada at 1:9, 375, 000, Yukon and Northwest Territories at 1:6, 875, 000

GREAT LAKES REGION OF US AND CANADA
1: 2, 000, 000
N.G.S.
see
73 USA D

TOURIST ROAD MAPS
Published by the Provincial Tourist Boards
Official Road Map of Alberta
1:1, 700, 000 Alberta T.B.
Road Map of British Columbia
1:1, 900, 000 BCTB
Official Highway Map of Nova Scotia
1:633, 600 NSTB
Official Road Map of Ontario
1:1, 000, 000 OTB
New Brunswick
1:700, 000 NBTB
Prince Edward Island Road Map and Tourist Guide
1:360, 000 PEITB

MAPS OF THE PROVINCES AND TERRITORIES
Various scales
Ottawa : DEMR
Series of general maps showing road and rail communications, boundaries etc.
MCR
36 North-West Territories & Yukon Territory
1:4, 000, 000 1974 93 x 119
47 Yukon Territory
1:2, 000, 000 1972 66 x 55
3 British Columbia
1:2, 000, 000 1973 100 x 78
27 Prairie Provinces
1:2, 000, 000 1973 106 x 78
39 Ontario
1:2, 000, 000 1973 105 x 91
42 Quebec
1:2, 000, 000 1973 114 x 101
77 Atlantic Provinces
1:2, 000, 000 1973 106 x 78
40 Ontario South (outline map)
1:1, 000, 000 1965 86 x 61
83 Alberta (2 sheets)
1:750, 000 1972 106 x 172
45 Saskatchewan (2 sheets)
1:760, 000 1963 183 x 99
26 Manitoba (2 sheets)
1:760, 000 1964 177 x 101
30 Newfoundland
1:633, 600 1969 109 x 91
38 Maritime Provinces
1:633, 600 1968 129 x 94
29 New Brunswick
1:500, 000 1972 102 x 92
37 Nova Scotia and Prince Edward Island
1:500, 000 1962 127 x 96
41 Prince Edward Island
1:250, 000 1973 91 x 63
Various prices.

British Columbia

BRITISH COLUMBIA
1:1, 900, 000
No 1J
Victoria : DLFWR, 1970
76 x 96
Road, other communications, some topog. detail, uncontoured. Inset of Victoria and Vancouver and road mileage table. $1.50

WALL MAP OF BRITISH COLUMBIA
1:1, 000, 000
No. 1A
Victoria : DLFWR, 1958
144 x 180
2 sheet wall-map showing road, railways etc. $2.00

New Brunswick

HIGHWAY MAP OF NEW BRUNSWICK
1:731, 000
Chicago : Rand McNally, 1971
Coloured map marking route numbers and distances.

Ontario

PROVINCE OF ONTARIO
1:2, 000, 000
No. 20
Toronto : Dept. Lands & Surv, 1956
102 x 92
Showing communications, boundaries and settlement.

PROVINCE OF ONTARIO showing geog. townships
1:1, 250, 000
No. 28
Toronto : Dept. Lands and Surv, 1959
Townships in black and blue, list of geog. names.

Quebec

CARTE GÉNÉRALE DU QUÉBEC
1:4, 000, 000
Quebec : Min. des Terres et Forêts, 1970
58 x 50
General map showing principal communications, boundaries and settlement. $0.50

PROVINCE DE QUÉBEC
1:2, 500, 000
Quebec : Min. des Terres et Forêts, 1970
91 x 76
With inset of Montreal and Quebec and suburbs. Communications, boundaries and settlement. $1.00

QUÉBEC
1:1, 250, 000
Quebec : Min. des Terres et Forêts, 1969
150 x 95 each sheet
2 sheet map. South and North (New Quebec). South sheet col. showing admin. areas, communications, insets of Montreal and Quebec. North sheet showing hydrog. settlements, boundaries. $1.00 each

LES ROUTES DU QUÉBEC
1:700, 000 app.
Quebec : Min de la Voirie, 1972
Road map for the province of Quebec. In a number of sheets.

A2 GENERAL MAPS : LOCAL

NATIONAL PARK MAPS
Various scales
Ottawa : DEMR
Available for:
Banff Park, Alberta
1:199, 000 1974 86 x 61 MCR 200
Glacier Park, BC
1:126, 720 1955 61 x 86 MCR 202
Jasper Park, Alberta
1:250, 000 1974 MCR 217
Kootenay Park, Alberta BC
1:126, 720 1974 85 x 49 MCR 206
Riding Mountain Park, Man.
1:199, 000 1954 61 x 76 MCR 207
Mount Revelstoke Nat. Park, BC
1:50, 000 1971 106 x 78 MCR 208

Cape Breton Highlands Park, NS
1:126, 720 1970 61 x 76 MCR 209
Prince Albert Park, Saskatchewan
1:126, 720 1973 76 x 61 MCR 210
Waterton Lakes Park, Alberta BC
1:63, 360 1973 61 x 86 MCR 211
Yoho Park, Alberta, BC
1:126, 720 1961 61 x 76 MCR 213
Terra Nova Park, Newfoundland
1:50, 000 1966 96 x 78 MCR 214
Fundy National Park, NB
1:50, 000 1962 68 x 57 MCR 215
Gatineau Park, Quebec
1:50, 000 1970 111 x 43 MCR 216
(Kingsmere Camp Fortune Area on reverse)
Wood Buffalo Park, (See 125, 000 topog series : 74L, 74M, 841, 840, 84P, 85A, 85B)
Parks of the Canadian Rockies
1:500, 000 1970 95 x 59

PROVINCIAL PARK MAPS OF BRITISH COLUMBIA
Various scales
Victoria : DLFWR
Available for:

Mt. Assiniboine (contours)		
1:31, 000	PSA2	$0.40
Bowron Lake, (contours)		
1:63, 360	PSB2	.75
Garibaldi (contours)		
1:120, 000	PSG2	.75
Garibaldi W (contours)		
1:63, 360	PSG3	.75
Kokanee Glacier (contours)		
1:31, 000	PSK2	.75
Mt. Robson (contours)		
1:120, 000	PSR2	.75
Tweedsmuir (planimetric)		
1:500, 000	PST1	.40
Tweedsmuir (planimetric)		
1:250, 000	PST2	.75
Wells Gray (planimetric)		
1:250, 000	PSW1	.40
Wells Gray (contours)		
1:120, 000	PSW2	.75

B TOWN PLANS

CITY MAPS OF THE FEDERAL RIDINGS
Varying scales
Ottawa : DEMR
Available for:

MCR 265 St. John's Newfoundland	1:12, 000
MCR 266 Halifax and Dartmouth	1:25, 000
MCR 267 Montreal and Laval	1:36, 000
MCR 268 Quebec	1:25, 000
MCR 269 Hamilton	1:25, 000
MCR 270 London	1:25, 000
MCR 271 Ottawa	1:25, 000
MCR 272 St. Catherines	1:25, 000
MCR 273 Toronto	1:30, 000
MCR 274 Windsor	1:25, 000
MCR 275 Winnipeg	1:25, 000
MCR 276 Calgary	1:28, 000
MCR 277 Edmonton	1:20, 000
MCR 278 Vancouver	1:25, 000
MCR 279 Victoria	1:25, 000
MCR 280 Saskatoon	1:25, 000
MCR 281 Regina	1:20, 000

TOWN PLANS — various

AMC Plan of Edmonton	
Arrow City Plan of Edmonton	
Marshall Plan of Halifax — Dartmouth	1:5, 000
Arrow City Plan of Hamilton	1:19, 000
AMC Plan of Montreal	1:24, 000
Arrow City Map of Montreal	1:26, 000
Might Plan of Ottawa	
OTCB Plan of Ottawa	
Ottawa — Map of National Capital Region DEMR	1:25, 000
'Pathfinder' Map of Port Arthur	1:13, 200
Arrow City Plan of Quebec	1:23, 000
OMT Plan of Quebec	
Might Plan of Toronto	
AMC Plan of Vancouver	
Arrow City Plan of Winnipeg	1:37, 000

C OFFICIAL SURVEYS

INTERNATIONAL MAP OF THE WORLD
1:1, 000, 000
DEMR
see World 100 C and index 100/1
Sheets for Canada:

NK/NL 20	Halifax
NL/12, 22	St Johns
NL 17	Sudbury
NL 18	Ottawa
NM 8, 9	Prince Rupert
NM 9, 10	Vancouver
NM 10	Prince George
NM 11	Kootenay Lake
NM 13	Regina
NM 14	Winnipeg
NM 15	Lake of the Woods
NM 18	Lac Chibougamau
NM 19	Chicoutimi
NM 20	Anticosti Island
NM 21, 22	Cornerbrook
NN 11	Lesser Slave Lake
NN 13	Prince Albert
NN 15	Gods Lake
NN 16	Winisk Lake
NN 17	James Bay
NN 18	Lac Bienville
NN 21	Cartwright
NO 9	Dease Lake

WORLD AERONAUTICAL CHART ICAO
1:1, 000, 000
Series in 68 sheets, see index 71/1
Ottawa : DEMR
91 x 65
Covering whole of Canada, contoured and layered at 1,000' intervals, spot heights, road and rail communication. C $1.50

NATIONAL TOPOGRAPHIC SERIES
1:500, 000
In 218 sheets — see index 71/2
Ottawa : DEMR
76 x 65
Complete series, contoured with layer colouring, spot heights, road and rail communications and topographical information. Each C $1.50

NATIONAL TOPOGRAPHIC SERIES
1:250, 000
In 218 sheets — see index 71/2
Ottawa : DEMR
74 x 57
Detailed land series printed in 9 colours, contoured with roads classified, woodland, water detail and urban areas shown
Each C $1.50

NATIONAL TOPOGRAPHIC SERIES
1:125, 000
See index 71/2
Ottawa : DEMR
Detailed topographic series in progress, contoured with communications, woodland areas and land detail. Certain sheets available in standard or shaded relief edition. To replace earlier 1:126, 720 editions
Each C $1.50

NATIONAL TOPOGRAPHIC SERIES
1:50, 000
Ottawa : DEMR
35 x 58
Detailed series in progress.
Standard series have relief shown by contours at 50' intervals, communications and land detail. Certain sheets are only available in a provisional or photomap edition often without colour. Most urban areas published. A set of index sheets are available showing extent of publication.
Each C $1.50

PHOTOMAPS
1:50, 000
Ottawa : DEMR
Topog. sheets not following standard 50, 000 sheet lines. Available for:

Tracadie, NB	1962
Hardwicke, NB	1962
Blackville NE, NB	1962
Blackville NW, NB	1962
Blackville SE, NB	1962
Blackville SW, NB	1962
Paquetville, NB	1962
Brantville, NB	1963
Kent Junction, NB	1963
Camp Fortune Skiing Area	
1:10, 000	1967

(experimental Orthophoto Map)
Maps prepared from a mosaic of true scale rectified aerial photographs.

NATIONAL TOPOGRAPHIC SERIES
1:25, 000
Ottawa : DEMR
Large scale series published principally for urban areas, showing all roads, contours and other topog. details. Index sheets available.

British Columbia

VANCOUVER ISLAND
1:370, 000
Victoria : DLFWR, 1971
No. SGS 1
76 x 106
Shows relief and roads $2.00

PLANIMETRIC MAPS OF BRITISH COLUMBIA
1:63, 360
Victoria : DLFWR
Showing water features, place-names and communications. Available for:

IB	N.W. British Columbia	
	1962	76 x 96
ID	N. E. British Columbia	
	1971	76 x 96
IE	S.E. British Columbia	
	1962	71 x 96
IF	W. Central British Columbia	
	1968	76 x 96
IG	E. Central British Columbia	
	1968	76 x 96
IK	S.W. British Columbia	
	1963	76 x 96

Also available in landform ed. showing relief in grey. $1.50

SPECIAL MAPS OF BRITISH COLUMBIA
1:63, 360
Victoria : DLFWR
76 x 96 each
Showing water features and relief in brown.
Available for:

IBLS	N.W. British Columbia	1962
IDLS	N.E. British Columbia	1961
IELS	S.E. British Columbia (71 x 96)	1962
IFLS	W. Central British Columbia	1968
IGLS	E. Central British Columbia	1959
IKLS	S.W. British Columbia	1963

$1.50 each

LOCAL TOPOGRAPHICAL MAPS
Victoria : DLFWR
Available for:
Howe Sound — Burrard Inlet (contoured) South 1:31, 000
1929 71 x 106 5BS
Howe Sound — Burrard Inlet (contoured) North 1:31, 000
1929 71 x 106 5BN
Lower Squamish Valley (contoured) 1:15, 000
1952 63 x 101 5E
$1.00 each

COLUMBIA RIVER BASIN
1:30, 000
Ottawa : DEMR
In 97 sheets
Topog. series:
sheets 1 — 6 at 1:12, 000

Quebec

CARTES PLANIMÉTRIQUES DU QUÉBEC
1:31, 680, 1:20, 000, 1:15, 840
Quebec : Min des Terres et Forêts
Various editions and sizes
Series of large scale planning maps based upon aerial surveys. There are also other local maps on differing scales.

CARTES TOPOGRAPHIQUES DU QUÉBEC
1:48, 000, 1:31, 680, 1:24, 000
1:20, 000, 1:15, 840, 1:12, 000,
1:10, 000.
Quebec : Min. des Terres et Forêts
Various editions and sizes
Topographical map series each covering a small local region.

QUÉBEC — CARTES RÉGIONALES
1:190, 080, 1:380, 160
Quebec : Min. des Terres et Forêts
Various sizes and editions
Series of maps covering southern Quebec. 20 sheets scale 3 mile : 1". 3 sheets covering western Quebec at 6 miles to 1". To be replaced by the new 1:200, 000 regional series.

QUÉBEC — CARTES RÉGIONALES
1:200, 000
Quebec — Min. des Terres et Forêts
1970—72.
89 x 71
New regular series of maps in preparation showing communications, settlement and land detail. 10 sheets published. $1.00

QUÉBEC — PARCS ET RESÉRVES
Quebec : Min. des Terres et Forêts
1. Réserve de chasse et de pêche de Kipawa 1:126, 720
2. Réserve de chasse et de pêche de Chibougamau 1:190, 080
3. Parc de la Verendrye 1:190, 080
4. Parc provinciale de la Gaspesie et réserve de chasse et de pêche des Chic-Chocs 1:126, 720

$1.00 each

CARTE TOPONYMIQUE DE LA RÉGION DE MONTRÉAL
1:63, 360
Quebec : Min. des Terres et Forêts, 1968
96 x 76
Depicting place names in detail and regional names. $0.50

D POLITICAL & ADMINISTRATIVE

CANADA
1:15, 840, 000
MCR 18 English Edition
MCR 19 French Edition
Ottawa : DEMR, 1970
43 x 36
7 colour political map available in either English or French editions. $0.50 each

CANADA
1:8, 800, 000
MCR 15 English Edition
MCR 16 French Edition
Ottawa : DEMR, 1970
76 x 68
Political col. map in 2 editions.

CANADA
1:6, 336, 000
MCR 10 English Edition
MCR 11 French Edition
Ottawa : DEMR, 1970
102 x 91
Col. political map with communications. Available in 2 editions.

RAND McNALLY IMPERIAL MAP OF CANADA
1:6, 000, 000
Chicago : Rand McNally
94 x 62
Political colouring with principal roads and railroads, airports and major towns $1.00

CANADA — PHYSIQUE — ADMINISTRATIVE
1:5, 000, 000
Ref. 1236
Éditions MD1
see CANADA MAPS E1

CANADA
1:5, 000, 000
Maplewood : Hammond
126 x 83
'Superior Wall Map' Series. Political col. communications. $2.00

CANADA, POLITICAL
1:4, 000, 000
No. 108111-14
Chicago : Denoyer Geppert
162 x 137
School political wall map showing provinces, settlement, communications, mounted on cloth with rollers. $24.00

CANADA
1:4, 000, 000
MCR 8 English Edition
MCR 8F French Edition
Ottawa : DEMR, 1966
157 x 149
2 Sheet wall map available 2 editions. Political col. with communications and insets. $3.00

CANADA
1:4, 000 000
Montreal : Geo-Carto of Canada (Mantniek)
180 x 124
Politically coloured wall map which is available in either French or English editions. Principal railways.
Azimuthal equidistant projection.
Available mounted in various styles.

POLITICAL MAPS OF CANADA
Indianapolis : Cram
School col. wall maps available for different levels

Level B simplified	1:4, 375, 000
129 x 122	$23.00
Political outline	1:4, 375, 000
129 x 122	$27.50
Desk outline map	no scale
43 x 30	60c

PHILIPS POLITICAL LARGE WALL MAP OF CANADA
1:3, 000, 000
London : G. Philip
183 x 122
Politically coloured wall map marking boundaries and railways, sea routes and principal towns.
Available mounted on cloth with rollers £15.00
or mounted on cloth, dissected £17.00

CANADA
1:2, 000, 000
MCR 5 English Edition
MCR 82 French Edition
Ottawa : DEMR, 1971
In 6 sheets
152 x 106 each
Political col. wall map, communications, admin. districts etc.
Available in 2 editions.

CANADA
1:15, 000, 000
MCR 64
Ottawa : DEMR, 1965
43 x 35
Outline map in 2 cols. $0.10

CANADA
1:15, 000 000
MCR 22
Ottawa : DEMR, 1962
43 x 35
Black and white outline map with no names given.

CANADA
1:13, 500, 000
MCR 80
Ottawa : DEMR
53 x 45
Outline map in black and white

CANADA
1:6, 700, 000
MCR 78
Ottawa : DEMR
106 x 78
Outline map in black and white

CANADA
1:6, 650, 000
MCR 78
Ottawa : DEMR, 1968
106 x 78
Outline map with no names given

VITO-GRAPHIC CHALKBOARD OUTLINE MAP OF CANADA
1:5, 000, 000
Ref VS9
Toronto : Weber Costello of Canada Ltd
125 x 117
Land areas in green, meridians, parallels and outlines in yellow, water areas in blue. On cloth — various mounted styles.
Also available with the World (VS1-9) on reverse.

CANADA
1:4, 000, 000
MCR 8B
Ottawa : DEMR
152 x 106
Outline map in black and white

CANADA — OUTLINE SLATED
1:4, 000, 000
No. 165111
Chicago : Denoyer Geppert
152 x 129
Blackboard school map, blue and yellow on black. $28.50

MILITARY BRIEFING MAP OF CANADA
1:3, 000, 000
MCE 119
Ottawa : DEMR
123 x 92 each
4 sheet map, clearly but roughly drawn. $4.00 set

VITO-GRAPHIC PROVINCIAL CHALKBOARD OUTLINE MAPS OF CANADA
VS10 Atlantic Provinces (NS, NB, PE1, Nfld)
VS11 Newfoundland
VS12 Quebec
VS13 Ontario, Southern Ontario (Reversible)
VS14 Prairie Provinces (Man., Sask., Alta)
VS15 British Columbia
VS16 South Western British Columbia
Toronto : Weber Costello of Canada Limited
Land areas in green, meridians, parallels and outlines in yellow, water areas in blue. On cloth — various mounted styles

MAPA MUDOS — ALASKA Y CANADA
Barcelona : Editorial Vicens Vives
33 x 24
Outline map in 2 colours
50 copies 100 S. Ptas

CENSUS DIVISIONS
1:15, 000, 000
MCR 43
Ottawa : DEMR
54 x 37
1961 Census Divisions $0.50

RESULTS, FEDERAL ELECTIONS OCT 30, 1972
1:7, 500, 000
Ottawa : DEMR, 1972
107 x 71
Electoral districts col-coded to show successful candidates. In Fr. or Eng. $1.00

ELECTORAL DISTRICTS OF CANADA
1:4, 000, 000
MCR 250
Ottawa : DEMR
157 x 149
Large map depicting Districts and Federal Ridings.

ENUMERATION AREA SETS
1:500, 000
Ottawa : DEMR
Map sets showing how to apply Census statistical data: consist of
1 outline map with electoral districts boundaries marked, with enumeration areas
2 transparent overlay, keyed to outline map, showing Census divisions and subdivisions and
3 standard 1:500, 000 NTS sheet
Available for:
INW Avalon — Burin
2SW Notre Dame — Bonavista
11NE La Poile — Burges
12SE St Georges — White Bay
12NE Harrington — Belle Isle (Newfoundland Island only)
31SE Ottawa — Montreal
41NE Chapleau — Sudbury
Regional indexes showing Census Divisions for:
Prairie Provinces
1:2, 000, 000/4, 000, 000
Ontario
1:2, 000, 000/4, 000, 000
Atlantic Provinces
1:2, 000, 000/4, 000, 000

PROVINCIAL MAPS OF FEDERAL RIDINGS
Various scales
Ottawa : DEMR
Showing electoral districts etc.
Available for:

Newfoundland	1:630, 000
Prince Edward Island	1:250, 000
Nova Scotia	1:500, 000
New Brunswick	1:500, 000
Quebec	1:1,200, 000
Ontario North	app 1:2,000, 000
Ontario South	1:1,000, 000
Manitoba	1:760, 000
Saskatchewan	1:760, 000
Alberta North	1:760, 000
Alberta South	1:760, 000
British Columbia	1:1, 260, 000
Yukon Territory	1:2, 000, 000
Northwest Territory	1:6, 000, 000

British Columbia

BRITISH COLUMBIA ADMINISTRATIVE BOUNDARY MAPS
1:6, 750, 000
Victoria : DLFWR, 1968
28 x 38 each
Set inc.

Land Districts	No. 1SB
Land Recording Districts (amended 1972)	1SC
Mining Divisions (amended 1958)	1SD
Assessment & Collection Districts (amended 1960)	1SE
Provincial Elecotral Districts (redistribution 1966)	1SF
Counties and Sheriffs Districts (amended 1965)	1SG
Forest and Grazing Districts (gazetted 1972)	1SJ
Bills of Sale Registration Districts (rev. 1960)	1SK
Land Registration Districts	1SL
Regional Districts (1971)	1SR
Census Divisions (revised 1957)	1SS
Water Disctricts	1SW

$1.00

B.C. SCHOOL DISTRICTS
1:1, 900, 000
No. 1JH
Victoria : DLFWR, 1957
76 x 96
Red. ed. 1971. Only available as a photo-print. 90c

B.C. ELECTORAL DISTRICTS (REDISTRIBUTION 1966)
1:1, 900, 000
No. 1JF
Victoria : DLFWR, 1964
76 x 96 90c

Ontario

ELECTORAL MAP OF THE PROVINCE OF ONTARIO (PROVINCIAL RIDINGS)
1:500, 000
No. 33A
Toronto : Dept. Lands and Surv.
1964-5

ELECTORAL MAP OF METROPOLITAN TORONTO (PROVINCIAL RIDINGS)
1:10, 000
33A Sup.
Toronto : Dept. Lands and Surv, 1966

Quebec

QUEBEC - CARTE DES DISTRICTS JUDICAIRES
1:1, 267, 800
Quebec : Min. des Terres et Forêts 1967
153 x 101
Black and white Ozalid photo copy showing judicial districts of Quebec $2.00

CARTES DES DIVISIONS D'ENREGISTREMENT
1:1, 267, 800
Quebec : Min. des Terres et Forêts 1965
153 x 101
Black and white Ozalid photo copy showing registration districts $2.00

E1 PHYSICAL : RELIEF

CANADA
1:15, 000, 000
MCR 81
Ottawa : DEMR, 1961
43 x 35
Col shaded relief map. $0.25

TRI-GRAPHIC MAP OF CANADA
1:5, 700, 000
TRI-0
Toronto : Weber Costello of Canada
137 x 101
Physical layer colouring with graphic relief shading and political boundaries. Available mounted in various styles.

PHILIPS GRAPHIC RELIEF MAP OF CANADA
1:5, 500, 000
London : G. Philip
102 x 82
Coloured to simulate predominant vegetation cover and relief shaded producing a 3D effect. No town names.
Mounted on cloth with rollers £5.50
Mounted on cloth, dissected to fold £7.00

PHILIPS PHYSICAL SMALLER WALL MAP OF CANADA
1:5, 000, 000
London : G. Philip
109 x 84
Physical layer colouring with political boundaries in red.
Mounted on cloth with rollers £5.50
Mounted on cloth, dissected to fold £7.00

CANADA – PHYSIQUE – ADMINISTRATIVE
1:5, 000, 000
Ref. 1236
Ed. R. Brunet
St. Germain en Laye : Éditions MDI
127 x 94
Coloured wall map in French, double sided – physical map and a political map on the reverse.
Also available in English edition – agent Moyer Vico Ltd., Toronto.

RAISED RELIEF MAP OF CANADA
1:3, 168, 000
Chicago : Nystrom, 1975
114 x 104
Plastic moulded map, physical layer colouring, principal communications and boundaries.
unframed US $ 46.00
framed US $ 74.00

CANADA
1:3, 700, 000
Bruxelles : Mantniek
180 x 125
Physically coloured wall map on azimuthal equidistant projection. Available in French or English edition.

PHILIPS PHYSICAL LARGE WALL MAP OF CANADA
1:3, 000, 000
London : G. Philip
185 x 122
Physical layer colouring, hill shaded, political boundaries, railways and ocean routes.
Mounted on cloth with rollers £15.00
Mounted on cloth, dissected to fold £17.00

CARTES MURALES GÉOGRAPHIQUES
No. 251 Canada Économique – reverse: Brésil Physique
No. 252 Canada Physique – reverse: Brésil Economique
Ed. Vidal-Lablache et H. Varon
Paris : Armand Colin
120 x 100
2 reversibel maps in French with a map on each side mounted on rigid card.

CANADA
1:3, 125, 000
131101 10 East Canada
131111 10 West Canada
Chicago : Denoyer-Geppert
111 x 147
Classroom maps, physical, political, showing land detail, boundaries, pop. etc.
Rollers $15.50 each

KANADA
1:3, 000, 000
Braunschweig : Westermann
210 x 195
Col. physical wall map, showing relief, settlements, communications, physical features. German text. Also available in French edition.

MOYER PHYSICAL WALL MAPS OF CANADIAN PROVINCES
The Prairie Provinces
1:1, 300, 000 167 x 121
Saskatchewan
1:750, 000 121 x 191
Alberta
1:1, 000, 000 76 x 132
Ontario (with insets) 1970
1:1, 000, 000 182 x 121
Atlantic Provinces 1970
153 x 116
Quebec (French ed.) 1970
157 x 116
Toronto : Moyer Vico Ltd.
Series of coloured relief wall maps showing communications and settlement. Available mounted in various styles.

British Columbia

BRITISH COLUMBIA RELIEF MAP
1:1, 900, 800
Victoria : DLFWR, 1967-68
89 x 72
Contoured and layer coloured showing road and railways. Insets of physiographic sub-divisions and annual precipitation. $2.00

Quebec

TOPONYMIE DES PRINCIPAUX RELIEFS DU QUÉBEC
1:2, 500, 000
Quebec : Min. des Terres et Forêts 1972
114 x 76
Coloured relief map of Quebec with all major natural features named. $1.00

QUÉBEC
1:1, 100, 000
Bruxelles : Mantniek
160 x 120
Physically coloured wall on azimuthal equivalent projection.
French text.

E2 PHYSICAL : LAND FEATURES

PERMAFROST IN CANADA
1:7, 603, 200
Map 1246A
Ottawa : GSC, 1967, Rep. 1969
73 x 72
In col. showing physiographic and permafrost regions, climatic temperature zones. Notes on map. C$0.50

CANADA : LAKES, RIVERS AND GLACIERS
1:7, 500, 000
MCR 50
Ottawa : DEMR
86 x 78
Map showing locations of water features $1.50

LANDFORMS MAP OF CANADA
1:6, 336, 000
Washington : Quartermaster General, Environmental Protection Section, 1965
Shows land types and hydrography with text. Arctic inset.

PHYSIOGRAPHIC REGIONS OF CANADA
1:5, 000, 000
Map 1254 A
Ottawa : GSC, 1972
84 x 85 .
Physiog. sub-divisions, inc. those of Canadian Shield. $2.00

GLACIAL MAP OF CANADA
1:5, 000, 000
Ref. 1253A
Ottawa : GSC, 1970
84 x 85
Glacier formation in col, ice-flow features, moraines, major ice areas.
Inset 1:10, 000, 000 of continental shelf extension off Newfoundland. $2.00

RETREAT OF WISCONSIN AND RECENT ICE IN NORTH AMERICA
1:5, 000, 000
GSC Map No. 1257A
by V.K. Prest
Ottawa : GSC, 1969
Map in colours C $2.00

GLACIER MAPS OF CANADA SERIES
1:1, 000, 000
Ottawa : DEMR
Available for:
1WB 1000 South. BC and Alberta
1WB 1001 North. BC and SE Alaska
1WB 1002 Yukon Terr. and District of Mackenzie each size 123 x 76
1WB 1003 N.Queen Elizabeth Is.
1WB 1004 S. Queen Elizabeth Is.
1WB 1005 N. Baffin Is.
1WB 1006 S. Baffin Is.
each size 119 x 78
Showing the location of glaciers with listing of large scale glacier mapping and NTS maps on reverse.

PHYSIOGRAPHY OF SOUTHERN ONTARIO
1:253, 440
In 5 sheets.
Toronto : Univ. of Toronto Press, 1972
Coloured map series.

ALPINE AND GLACIER MAPS
Various scales
Ottawa : DEMR
Available for:
Woolsey Glacier
1:10, 000 72 x 58
Meighen Island North
1:50, 000 94 x 91
Meighen Island South
1:50, 000 94 x 91
Meighen Ice Cap
1:25, 000 94 x 78
Thompson Glacier Region
1:50, 000 91 x 76
Thompson Glacier Snout
1:5, 000 91 x 76
White Glacier
1:5, 000 91 x 76
Centennial Glacier
1:125, 000 86 x 76
Cockburn Land Glacial Features
1:500, 000 88 x 58
Isortoa River Glacial Features
1:250, 000 88 x 58
Foxe Basin North Glacial Features
1:500, 000 88 x 58
Foxe Basin North Surface Materials
1:500, 000 88 x 58
Ram River Glacier
1:10, 000 55 x 48
Sentinel Glacier
1:10, 000 73 x 55
Peyto Glacier, Banff National Park, Al.
1:10, 000 1970 114 x 86
Place Glacier
1:10, 000 73 x 55
The above include special glacier mapping and also standard NTS sheets.

Quebec

CARTE DES PRINCIPAUX BASSINS HYDROGRAPHIQUES DU QUÉBEC
1:4, 000, 000
Quebec : Min. des Terres et Forêts 1970
58 x 50
Depicting hydrographic basins and watersheds. $0.50

Nova Scotia

TRURO – GROUNDWATER PROBABILITY – NOVA SCOTIA
1:250, 000
Ottawa : GSC, 1966 50c

Ontario

LOCATION OF DAMS ON PRINCIPAL WATERSHEDS
Southern Ontario (No. D166)
1:1, 000, 000
Northern Ontario (No. D266)
1:2, 000, 000
Toronto : Dept. lands and surv. 1966

PHYSIOGRAPHY – SOUTHERN ONTARIO
1:1, 000, 000
Ottawa : DEMR
Shows 14 physiographic aspects.

Saskatchewan

PHYSIOGRAPHY – WYNYARD SASKATCHEWAN
1:250, 000
Ottawa : DEMR
Shows over 25 physiographic aspects.

F GEOLOGY

GEOLOGICAL MAP OF CANADA
1:5, 000, 000
Map 1250A
Ottawa : GSC
1969
84 x 85
Coloured geological map. $2.00

TECTONIC MAP OF CANADA
1:5, 000, 000
Map 1251A
Ottawa : GSC, 1969
84 x 85
Col. tectonic map with notes. $2.00

TECTONIC MAP OF THE CANADIAN SHIELD
1:5, 000, 000
Map No. 4 1965
Ottawa : GSC
1965
84 x 85
Coloured by orogenic regions with boundaries of affected areas by respective eons, eras and sub-eras within each. C $1.00

REGIONAL GEOLOGICAL CROSS-SECTION OF WESTERN CANADA SEDIMENTARY COVER
1:1, 000, 000 (horizontal)
1:2, 000ft (vertical)
Toronto : Geol. Assoc. Canada
Series of stratigraphic cross sections in colour $2.85

GEOLOGICAL MAP OF CANADA
1:250, 000
Ottawa : GSC
Various editions
Full sheet 74 x 57 Half sheet 37 x 57
Series of coloured geol. maps following the same sheet lines as the standard NTS topo series. Published for certain areas only. $0.50

CANADA – GEOLOGICAL SURVEY SERIES
1:500, 000. 1:126, 720, 1:63, 360
1:50, 000
Ottawa : GSC
Various editions and sizes.
Many maps on these scales are published intermittently for varying areas generally on standard NTS sheet lines. Index sheets showing current state of publication for any particular area are published annually.

GEOLOGICAL MAP OF ALBERTA
1:1, 267, 000
Edmonton : Research Council of Alberta, 1972.
Coloured geological map.

GEOLOGICAL MAP OF LABRADOR
1:1, 000, 000
by B.A. Greene
St. Johns : Dept. of Mines and Energy, 1972
Coloured geological map C $3.00

GEOLOGICAL MAP OF THE DISTRICT OF MACKENZIE
1:1, 267, 200
Map No. 1055A
Ottawa : GSE, 1958.
Coloured geological map C $0.50

GEOLOGICAL MAP OF NEW BRUNSWICK
1:500, 000
Ref. NR-1
1968
94 x 91
Coloured geological map with legend in English and French.

GEOLOGIC MAP OF THE ISLAND OF NEWFOUNDLAND
1:1, 000, 000
Map 1231A
Ottawa : GSC, 1967
63 x 56
Geology in colours of those areas mapped, indicating minerals. C $1.00

PRELIMINARY GEOLOGICAL MAP OF NORTHWEST TERRITORIES AND YUKON TERRITORY
1:3, 000, 000
Map No. 30
Ottawa : GSC 1963
Coloured geological map. C $0.50

GEOLOGICAL MAP OF ONTARIO
1:1, 013, 760
In 6 sheets
Ottawa : DEMR, 1971
92 x 62
Series of coloured maps in wrapper including the following maps:
2196 Legend incl. 2 inset maps
2197 Southern
2198 East Central
2199 West Central
2200 Northeast
2201 Northwest

SURFICIAL DEPOSITS OF PRINCE EDWARD ISLAND
1:126, 720
GSC Map No. 1366A
by V.K. Prest
Ottawa : GSC, 1973
Coloured map. On reverse is a map of glacial indicators and date of postglacial marine overlap and past development. Extensive descriptive notes. C $2.00

GEOLOGICAL MAP OF SASKATCHEWAN
1:1, 267, 000
Regina : Sas. Dept. of Min. Resources, 1972
Coloured geological map.

GEOLOGICAL MAP OF THE PROVINCE OF ONTARIO
1:1, 267, 200
Map No. 1958B
Toronto : Ontario, Dept. of Mines
1958
124 x 100
Coloured map of the Province.

G EARTH RESOURCES

METALLOGENIC MAP – IRON IN CANADA
1:7, 603, 200
Map No. 1187A
Ottawa : GSC
1965
75 x 73
Contained in Economic Geology Report No 22 Vol 1 – map available separately.
C $1.00

METALLOGENIC MAP – LITHIUM IN CANADA
1:7, 603, 200
Map No 1207A
Ottawa : GSC 1965
75 x 73
Supplements Economic Geology Report No 21 – map available separately.

PRINCIPAL MINERAL AREAS OF CANADA
1:7, 603, 200
Map 900A
25th Edition
Ottawa : GSC, 1975
75 x 73
Coloured map with notes. 50c

ISOTOPIC AGE MAP OF CANADA
1:5, 000, 000
Map No. 1256A
Ottawa : GSC, 1970
84 x 85
Isotopic ages of minerals and rocks. $2.00

NICKEL IN CANADA
1:5, 000, 000
Ottawa : GSC, 1970
84 x 85
Nickel occurence shown on uncoloured geol. base map, with notes. $2.00

VANADIUM IN CANADA
1:5, 000, 000
Map No. 1321A
Ottawa : GSC 1973
84 x 85
Illustrating the types of ore, deposits, size, age and grade of vanadiferrous deposits in Canada. C $2.00

LEAD CONTENT OF STREAM AND SPRING SEDIMENTS, KENO HILL AREA, YUKON TERRITORY
1:126, 720
Ottawa : GSC, 1966
Shows value of lead samples. 50c

For the same area:
SILVER CONTENT OF STREAM AND SPRING SEDIMENTS
ZINC CONTENT OF STREAM AND SPRING SEDIMENTS
ARSENIC CONTENT OF STREAM AND SPRING SEDIMENTS 50c each

MINERAL REFERENCE MAPS
1:63, 360
Victoria : DLFWR
Available for:
Trout Lake, Lardeau and Ainsworth
1928 71 x 109 MRM2
Ainsworth, Trout Lake and Slocan
1928 55 x 81 MRM3
Nelson and Trail (Ymir)
1929 61 x 106 MRM4
Trail Creek and Nelson (Rossland)
1929 55 x 106 MRM5
Grand Forks, Greenwood and Trail Creek
1932 55 x 109 MRM6
Greenwood and Osoyoos
1934 55 x 106 MRM7
Bakerville and Lightning Creek
1935 81 x 111 MRM8 $1.00 each

CARTES DES ANOMALIES AÉROMAGNÉTIQUES DU CANADA
1:5, 000, 000
Ottawa : GSC, 1971
84 x 85
Showing aeromagnetic anomalies. $2.00

BOUGUER GRAVITY ANOMALY MAP OF CANADA
1:5, 000, 000
GMC 69-1
Ottawa : DEMR
1969
125 x 110
Showing Bouguer Gravity Anomaly field, coloured at 20 miligal intervals.

GRAVITY MAP OF CANADA
1:2, 500, 000
GMC 671-4
Ottawa : DEMR. 1967
In 4 sheets
129 x 106 each
Shows a Bouguer anomaly field, col. at 20 miligal intervals.

ISOGONIC MAPS
MCR706 Northwest Territories and Yukon
1:5, 068, 800 1957 77 x 98
MCR707 Alberta
1:1, 267, 200 1957 111 x 73
MCR708 Saskatchewan
1:1, 267, 200 1957 111 x 67
MCR709 Manitoba
1:1, 267, 200 1957 111 x 78
Ottawa : DEMR C $1.00 each

GEOPHYSICAL AND MAGNETIC MAPS
1:6, 336, 000
Ottawa : DEMR, 1965
101 x 91
The following maps available:
Canada, Isogenic
Canada, H – Isodynamic
Canada, F – Isodynamic
Canada, Isoclinic
Canada, Z – Isodynamic

CANADA – AEROMAGNETIC SERIES
1:250, 000, 1:63, 360, 1:50, 000, 1:31, 680
Ottawa : GSC
Various editions and sizes
Series in progress generally in accordance with NTS sheet lines – published intermittently.

GEOPHYSICAL SERIES (ELECTROMAGNETIC)
1:50, 000
Ottawa : GSC
Series in progress based on NTS sheet lines published for certain areas only.

CANADA NATURAL RESOURCE SERIES
1:250, 000
Ottawa : Canadian Hydrog. Service.
Series of coloured maps in progress designed as a basis for the exploration of natural resources in Canadian offshore waters.
Each sheet is to be published in 3 editions:
A Bathymetry
B Gravity (Free Air Anomaly)
C Magnetic (Total Field)
Also available: Plotting base, which is a print of the bathymetric edition in grey.
each C $2.00

GREAT LAKES WATER USE
1:1, 580, 000
Ottawa : DEMR, 1971
144 x 86
Shows relationship between Great Lakes' water resources and human inhabitants.

H BIOGEOGRAPHY

LAND USE MAPS OF CANADA
Ottawa : DEMR

1:1, 000, 000
Sheet published :
Southern Ontario
91 x 65

1:500, 000
Sheets published:
72NE Moose Jaw – Watrous (Sask)
72NW Hanna – Kindersley (Alb-Sask)
76 x 65

1:250, 000
Sheets published :

11D	Halifax	(NS)
11E	Truro	(NS)
11F-C	Canso	(NS)
11K-J-N	Sydney	(NS)
200-P	Shelburne	(NS)
21A	Annapolis	(NS)
21B	Eastport	(NS)
21G	Fredericton	(NS)
21H	Amherst	(NS)

74 x 57

1:126, 720
Sheets published :

11L/SE	Kings County	(PEI)
11L/SW	Prince County	(PEI)
11L/NW,SW	Queens County	(PEI)

1:50, 000
Sheets published:

30L/13E	Dunville	(Ont)
30L/13W	Dunville	(Ont)
30L/14E	Welland	(Ont)
30L/14W	Welland	(Ont)
30L/15W	Fort Erie	(Ont)
30M/3W	Niagara	(Ont)
30M/4E	Grimsby	(Ont)
30M/4W	Grimsby	(Ont)
30M/3E & 6E	Niagara	(Ont)
40G/15E & 10E	Pelee	(Ont)
401/9W	Long Point	(Ont)
401/16E	Simcoe	(Ont)
401/16W	Simcoe	(Ont)
40J/2E	Essex	(Ont)
40P/1E	Brantford	(Ont)
92B/5E	Sooke	(BC)
92B/6W	Victoria	(BC)
92B/11W	Sidney	(BC)
92B/12E	Shawnigan	(BC)
92G/2E	New Westminster	(BC)
92G/2W	New Westminster	(BC)
92G/3E	Vancouver South	(BC)
92H/4W	Chilliwack	(BC)
37 x 56		each $0.50

ARCTIC ECOLOGY MAP SERIES
CRITICAL WILDLIFE AREAS
1:500, 000
In 34 sheets
Canadian Wild Life Service
Ottawa: DEMR, 1972
Series of coloured maps with 324pp text.

CANADA LAND INVENTORY, LAND CAPABILITY SERIES
1:250, 000
Ottawa : Canada Land Inventory, Dept. of the Environment
74 x 57
Series of maps based on N.T.S. sheet lines each depicting distributions of a particular subject i.e. Wildlife — waterfowl, ungulates, red deer, Agriculture, Soil, Recreation. Series in progress.

LAND STATUS — REGIONAL MAP
Sheets published:
3C Stuart Lake
1:190, 000 1963 71 x 106
3E Peace River
1:240, 000 1965 73 x 101
(revised status 1969)
Victoria : DLFWR
Showing lot surveys and vacant Crown land. $1.00 each

CARTE DES TENURES FORESTIÉRES DU QUÉBEC
1:1, 250, 000
Quebec : Min. des Terres et Forêts 1970
153 x 107
Showing boundaries of forest regions and ownership in colours. $1.00

K HUMAN GEOGRAPHY

CANADA — DENSITY OF POPULATION 1961
1:7, 500, 000
Ottawa : DEMR, 1972
Coloured population map.

CANADA — DISTRIBUTION OF POPULATION 1961
1:7, 500, 000
Ottawa : DEMR, 1972
Coloured population map.

BRITISH COLUMBIA — POPULATION DISTRIBUTION, 1961
1:2, 000, 000
Vancouver : Univ. B.C. 1961
89 x 72
Urban and dispersed pop. shown in col. on black and white map. SE British Columbia inset. $1.25

RÉPARTITION DE LA POPULATION DU QUÉBEC, 1961
1:500, 000
Maps prepared by: l'Institute de Géographie de l'Université Laval
Quebec : Conseil d'Orientation Économique du Québec
In 4 sheets each 99 x 67
Showing distribution of population in southern Quebec by dots and proportional circles. Provincial and census division boundaries marked also extent of wooded area.
4 maps contained in card folder.

L ECONOMIC

CARTES MURALES GÉOGRAPHIQUES
No. 251 Canada Économique - reverse Brésil Physique
No. 252 Canada Physique — reverse Brésil Économique
Ed. Vidal Lablache et H. Varon
Armand Colin
See Canada 71 E1

PRINCIPAL HIGH VOLTAGE TRANSMISSION LINES
1:4, 000, 000
Ottawa : DEMR, 1972
127 x 106
Principal transmission lines and electric generating plants.

PRINCIPAL OIL AND PRODUCTS PIPE LINES IN CANADA
1:4. 000, 000
Ottawa: DEMR, 1967
127 x 112
Pipe lines col-coded to indicate operating company. Insets of S. Alberta and S. Ontario.

PRINCIPAL GAS PIPE LINES IN CANADA
1:4, 000, 000
Ottawa : DEMR
1967
127 x 112
Showing pipe lines col. coded to indicate operating company with insets of S. Alberta and S. Ontario.

OIL AND GAS POOLS OF WESTERN CANADA
1:760, 320
Ottawa : GSC, 1970
3 maps:
1316A S. Alberta
1317A N. Alberta and NE BC
1318A S. Sask, SW Manitoba with Yukon Terr, and part NW Terr.
Showing oil and gas distribution by col. $1.50 set

WESTERN CANADA
1:2, 375, 000
Vancouver : Mundy Map Co.
132 x 137
Shows industry, natural resources, geol., communications.

TORONTO — WINDSOR AREA, ONTARIO — GAS AND OIL FIELDS, PIPELINES, COMPRESSOR STATIONS AND REFINERIES
1:250, 000
Ottawa : GSC, 1970
Gas and oil data, with notes 50c

ATLANTIC PROVINCES RESOURCES AND ECONOMIC ACTIVITY
1:1, 800, 000
Ottawa : DEMR, 1967
111 x 84
Showing economic devt. with 6 insets, also communications, power resources etc.

URBAN ANALYSIS SERIES OF MAPS
1:25, 000
Ottawa : DEMR
123 x 91
Showing various urban characteristics of Toronto and Vancouver.
Toronto East:
- Existing land use
- Land slope and elevation
- Density of coverage of land by buildings
- Distribution of broadcasting facilities
- Population distribution, 1961
- Population distribution, updated
- Estimate of daytime population distribution
- Distribution of children under 5 and adults over 70
- Distribution of dwelling units
- Distribution of schools
- Distribution of hospitals and doctor's offices
- Port facilities
- Distribution of retail and wholesale automotive sales and services

Toronto West:
- Same maps as above

Vancouver:
- Existing land use
- Land slope and elevation
- Density of coverage of land by buildings
- Structural material of buildings
- Height of buildings
- Electric power, trunk system
- Gas, trunk main system
- Distribution of broadcasting facilities
- Population distribution, 1961
- Population distribution, updated
- Estimate of daytime population distribution
- Distribution of children under 5 and adults over 70
- Distribution of dwelling units
- Distribution of schools
- Distribution of hospitals and doctors' offices
- Land transportation facilities
- Port facilities
- Distribution of retail and wholesale automotive sales and services

M HISTORICAL

CANADIAN HISTORY SERIES
Chicago : Denoyer-Geppert
111 x 104
Series of col. historical wall maps for schools:
202011 Original Inhabitants and Routes of Explorers to 1650

202021 Colonial Settlements and the Seven Years War
202031 Struggle for Continent, 1689-1800
202041 US War for Independence, 1775-1783
202051 The US – Union and Unity
202061 British North America 1800
202071 US Expansion to 1819
202081 Growth of US, 1776-1853
202091 British North America, 1865
202101 War between the States, 1861-65
202111 The Political Evolution of Canada, 1867-1898
202121 Canada, 1905
202131 Canada, 1967
202141 Growth of Population
202151 Land Use
202161 Manufacturing and Minerals
Set of 16 maps $79.50

TERRITORIAL EVOLUTION OF CANADA
MCR 2306
Ottawa: DEMR,
76 x 60
23 small-scale maps, showing formation of Canadian boundaries from Treaty of Breda, 1667 to the entry of Newfoundland, 1949

BRITISH NORTH AMERICA
MCR 2304
Ottawa : DEMR
by J. Arrowsmith, published 15th February 1834
Facsimile
48 x 60
Copy of original map in black and white.
$1.00 each

AN ACCURATE MAP OF CANADA
Published by J. Hinton, London, c1761
MCR 2303
Ottawa : DEMR
Facsimile
38 x 30
Copy of original map in black and white.
$1.00

AMÉRIQUE SEPTENTRIONALE
Prep. by Alexis Hubert Jaillot, c 1696
MCR 2302
Ottawa : DEMR
Facsimile
91 x 62
Reproduction in black and white $1.00

LE CANADA, OU NOUVELLE FRANCE
Prep. in Paris by Nicolas Sanson, 1656
MCR 2301
Ottawa : DEMR
Facsimile
61 x 48
Reproduction in black and white. $1.00

AMERICA SEPTENTRIONALIS
Reproduction plate from Jansonius' "Nouveau Theatre du Monde ou Nouvel Atlas" pub. Amsterdam, 1639
MCR 2300
Ottawa: DEMR
Facsimile
61 x 54
Reproduction in black and white. $1.00

BIRD'S EYE VIEW OF OTTAWA
No scale given
MCR 2305
Ottawa : DEMR
71 x 55
Sketch of Ottawa as it was in 1876. $0.50

ATLASES
W3 WORLD ATLASES : LOCAL EDITIONS

NELSON'S CANADIAN SCHOOL ATLAS
Ed. J. Wreford Watson
Nelson, 1968
See World section 100

PHILIP'S SENIOR ATLAS FOR CANADA
Ed. H. Fullard
G. Philip
See World Atlas section 100 W3

LARROUSSE ATLAS CANADIEN
B. Brouillette
Larrousse, 1971
See World – School Atlases 100

ATLASES
A GENERAL : ROADS

ROAD ATLAS OF THE UNITED STATES, CANADA AND MEXICO
Rand McNally, 1976
See North America 7

ROAD ATLAS OF CANADA
Chicago : Rand McNally, 1976
28 x 37
48 pp
Covering Canada from coast to coast with general road maps and detailed town plans.
C $3.95

ATLASES
B TOWN PLANS

A COMPUTER ATLAS OF OTTAWA: HULL
by D.R.F. Taylor and D.H.Douglas
Ottawa : Carleton Univ, 1970
71pp
32 maps, covering socio-economic aspects of the Ottawa-Hull metropolitan area, with 18 maps for Ontario. Bibliog. of computer mapping

ATLASES
C OFFICIAL SURVEYS

LANDFORMS ATLAS – GEOLOGY AND LANDFORMS AS ILLUSTRATED BY SELECTED CANADIAN TOPOGRAPHIC MAPS
Ed. D.M. Baird
Ottawa : DEMR
Set of 42 topographic maps in folder together with Geol. Survey of Canada Paper 64-21, 59pp 1972 describing them. Maps taken from standard NTS series to illustrate geomorphological and geological features.
$11.50 map folder
$0.75 Paper 62-21

ATLASES
E2 PHYSICAL : LAND FEATURES

ICE ATLAS OF ARCTIC CANADA
Ottawa : DEMR
86 x 50
67 pp
34 sheets showing sea ice and its effect on shipping, the results of surveys from 1900-56.
$7.50

ATLASES
L ECONOMIC

OXFORD REGIONAL ECONOMIC ATLAS OF THE UNITED STATES AND CANADA
2nd Edition
Oxford : OUP, 1975
19 x 25
178 pp
80 pp of detailed economic and thematic maps and a 48 pp section of topographical maps and urban town plans. Gazetteer of over 10,000 names.
£8.00
Paper covers £3.75

ATLASES
M HISTORICAL

HISTORICAL ATLAS OF CANADA
D.G.G. Kerr
3rd revised edition
Ontario : Nelson, 1975
24 x 31
100 pp
112 col. maps and 117 graphs with text. Sponsored by the Canadian Historical Association.

PHILIPS' HISTORICAL ATLAS OF CANADA
Eds. J.W. Chalmers, W.J. Eccles, H. Fullard.
London : G. Philip
22 x 28
60 pp
48 pp coloured maps showing main historical events from early colonisation to the present day economy. Index. 90p

ATLASES
O NATIONAL

THE NATIONAL ATLAS OF CANADA
4th Edition
Ottawa : DEMR
1970 –
Folio size 27 x 38
Map size 52 x 37
It is planned to contain 131 double folding plates covering Physical, Human and Economic Geography subjects, including detailed colour maps, explanatory text and statistical tables. Issued in folios of loose plates. Folio A 1970 30 double plates, Folio B 1972 32 double plates.

ATLAS AND GAZETTEER OF CANADA
prepared by DEMR
1st Edition
Ottawa : Queens Printer
1969

26 x 37
104 pp
General atlas containing col. maps scale 1:2, 000, 000 of southern half only (south of 60°N), general maps of the country and 8 pages of town area maps scale 1:250, 000;
Extensive gazetteer of place names.
Clothbound S7.50
Paperbound $5.00

ATLASES
P REGIONAL

ATLAS OF THE PRAIRIE PROVINCES
Ed. T.R. Weir and G. Matthews
Cartography G. Matthews
Toronto : Toronto UP, 1971
54 x 38
31 pp of Maps 55 pp of text
Limited ed. (500). Coloured maps generally 1:4, 000, 000 and explanatory text describe the three basic sections; resource base, settlement and population and resource use. Looseleaf.
£35.00

ATLAS OF ALBERTA
Toronto : UTP/Alberta UP, 1969
34 x 44
172 pp
Detailed atlas containing 158 pp of coloured maps + 4 pp gazetteer. Thematic maps double (1:2, 000, 000) or single (1:3, 300, 000) page spread or at smaller scales several to the page. Grouped by subject : Relief and Geology, Climate, Water, Vegetation, Soil, Wildlife, History, Population, Land Use, Agriculture, Forestry, Fishing & Trapping, Minerals, Power, Manufacturing, Services, Settlement Patterns and Administration.

BRITISH COLUMBIA : ATLAS OF RESOURCES
Prepared by B.C. Natural Resources Conference
Victoria : DLFWR
56 x 44
Containing 48 coloured map plates describing the locations and distributions of the state's resources.

ECONOMIC ATLAS OF ONTARIO
Ed. W. G. Dean & G. J. Matthews
Toronto : Univ. of Toronto Press 1969
26 x 34
113 plates
Comprehensive atlas comprising 385 maps, 149 insets and 49 graphs of statistical analysis of economic quantitative data. In 10 main divisions : Aggregate economy, Population, Manufacturing, Resource industries, Wholesale and consumer trade, Agriculture, Recreation, Transportation and communication, Administration, Reference maps.

ATLAS OF SASKATCHEWAN
Ed. J. H. Richards
Saskatoon : Sask, UP, 1969
26 x 34
236 pp
Covering physical, historical, social and economic aspects with explanatory text, statistical section and gazeteer.

PHYSCIAL ENVIRONMENT OF SASKATOON – CANADA
N.R.C. Pub. No. 11378
Ed. E. A. Christiansen
1st edition
Ottawa : Saskatchewan Research Council and The National Research Council of Canada
1970
33 x 39
A pioneer study of a local region presenting the basic geology in a detailed way together with associated information. 54 map plates with explanatory text covering, beside geology: soils, climate, geo-technology (hydrogology, seismicity and engineering properties), land use, outdoor recreation and agricultural potential. Spiral bound, board covers.
$15.00

GEORGIA STRAIT URBAN REGION
Ed. Louis Skoda
Ottawa : Urban Affairs Canada and Environment Canada, 1975
A single sheet containing maps and text. Comprises 4 sections: Description, population analysis map, land use patterns and changes map (½ page) and movement and traffic patterns. In either English or French
C $3.00

ATLAS RÉGIONAL DU BAS SAINT-LAURENT, DE LA GASPESIE ET DES ÎLES DE LA MADELEINE
Quebec – l'Editeur Officiel du Quêbec, 1966.
Containing 68 coloured thematic maps.
F. Fr. 58.00

718 St Pierre et Miquelon

C OFFICAL SURVEYS

CARTE GÉNÉRALE DE ST PIERRE ET MIQUELON
1:50, 000
Paris : IGN, 1957
71 x 92
Based upon 1:20, 000 series. Contours at 10 metre intervals with relief shading. Map in 5 colours.
F. Fr. 11,67

CARTE GÉNÉRALE DE ST PIERRE ET MIQUELON
1:20, 000
Paris : IGN, 1952
in 6 sheets, see index 718/1
76 x 46 each
Coloured topog. series; planimetry black, water features blue, vegetation green, contours at 5m intervals in brown.
F. Fr. 11.67

72 Mexico

See also:
728 CENTRAL AMERICA

A1 GENERAL MAPS : ROADS

REPÚBLICA MEXICANA (CARRETERAS)
1:4, 000, 000
Mexico City : Lib. Patria
Roads classified and numbered, distances in km. Political col. $12.80

MAPA TURISTÍCO DE CARRETERAS
1:3, 500, 000
Mexico City : Secretaria de Obras Publicas/ Dept. de Turismo y Petroleos Mexicanos, 1973
94 x 67
Roads classified in colour with route numbers and distances in km. Insets of driving times, central Mexico City, Monterrey, Acapulco, Guadalcjave.

CARTA GEOGRÁFICA DE MÉXICO
1:3, 000, 000
Mexico D.F. : Asociación Nacional Automovilística
1970
Detailed map showing relief and all classes of roads. Inset of Mexico City region scale 1:63, 360. Map contained in folder with separate index to places.

CARTA GEOGRÁFICA DE MÉXICO
1:2, 500, 000
6th ed.
Mexico City : Asociación Nacional Automovilística
1974
119 x 89
All classes of roads, boundaries, land information. Separate index to towns. Mexico City and environs inset.

MÉXICO, MAPA TURÍSTICO DE CARRETERAS
1:1, 750, 000
Mexico City : Secretaria de Obras Publicas/Dept. de Turismo y Petroleos Mexicanos, 1971
All classes of roads, distances in km.

A2 GENERAL MAPS : LOCAL

CARTAS DE ESTADOS

Jalisco		
1:500, 000	1956	
2 sheets	89 x 95	$45.00
San Luis Potosi		
1:500, 000	1930	
2 sheets	118 x 98	$25.00
Sonora		
1:500, 000	1957	
4 sheets	128 x 162	$25.00
Tamaulipas		
No scale	1946	
3 sheets	137 x 179	$25.00
Tlaxcala		
1:100, 000	1930	
4 sheets	120 x 160	$25.00
Yucatan		
1:200, 000	1944	
4 sheets	137 x 179	$25.00
Nayarit		
1:500, 000	1957	
	137 x 179	$15.00
Serrania de Zacatecas		
No scale	1943	
	94 x 69	$25.00
Zacatecas		
1:500, 000	1961	
2 sheets	118 x 98	$30.00

Tacubaya : DGGM
Large coloured official State wall maps.

MAPAS DE LOS ESTADOS "SERIE PATRIA" SERIE AZUL
Various scales
Mexico City : Libreria Patria
New series of state maps, superseding old series (q.v.) Contains plans of capitals, communications, tourist and historic details, admin divisions. Availbale for:

1 Aguascalientes	
2 Baja California, State	1:800, 000
3 Baja California, Territory	
4 Campeche	
5 Coahuila	
6 Colima	
7 Chiapas	
8 Chihuahua	1:1. 300, 000
9 Durango	
10 Guanajuato	1:400, 000
11 Guerrero	1:800, 000
12 Hidalgo	
13 Jalisco	1:1, 000, 000
14 Mexico, Estado	1:400, 000
15 Michoacan	
16 Morelos	1:200, 000
17 Nayarit	1:500, 000
18 Nuevo León	1:800, 000
19 Oaxaca	
20 Puebla	
21 Queretaro	1:400, 000
22 Quintana Roo	
23 San Luis Potosi	1:800, 000
24 Sina Loa	1:900, 000
25 Sonora	1:1, 400, 000
26 Tabasco	1:600, 000
27 Tamaulipas	
28 Tlaxcala	
29 Veracruz	1:1, 000, 000
30 Yucatan	
31 Zacatecas	$12.00 each

MAPAS DE LOS ESTADOS DE LA REPÚBLICA MEXICANA (SERIE ROJA)
1:500, 000
Mexico City : Libreria Patria, 1958
64 x 45
Col. map series of States showing roads, contours, admin. regions, other communications. Old series. still available for:
Aguascalientes
Baja California
Campeche
Colima Chiapas
Durango
Hidalgo
Puebla
Quintana Roo
Tamaulipas
Yucatan
Zocatecas $10.00 each

B TOWN PLANS

PLAN OF MEXICO CITY
1:36, 000
Mexico City : Asociación Nacional de Automovilística
Double sided plan in colour with index to streets.

MEXICO CITY
1: 27, 000
Mexico City : Asociación Nacional de Automovilística
92 x 132
Large coloured wall map with streets and principal buildings named. Index to streets.

C OFFICAL SURVEYS

KARTA MIRA
1:2, 500, 000
Budapest : Cartographia
see World 100 C

INTERNATIONAL MAP OF THE WORLD
1:1, 000, 000
Hispanic America Series
Washington : AGS
14 sheets required to cover Mexico of which 3 sheets are out of print –
See index World 100/1
See South America 8 C

CARTA GENERAL DE LA REPUBLICA MEXICANA
1:500, 000
In 47 sheets See index 72/2
México, D.F. : DGGM, 1958
Topog. series, contoured, vegetation col., communications, relief shading etc.
$25.00 each
Set $1,000.00

CARTA DE LA REPÚBLICA MEXICANA
1:500, 000
In 51 sheets See index 72/1
Tacubaya : DGGM, 1949
Col. topog. series with contours.
$25.00 each
Set $1,000.00

CARTA DEL GOLFO DE MÉXICO
1:100, 000
In 14 sheets
Tacubaya : DGGM, 1952
61 x 58 each
4 col. map showing communications, settlements. Available in the following sheets:
Laguna de Tamiahua
Alvarado
Roca Partida
Barra de Santa Ana
Chiltepec
Bunta de San Juan
Coatzacoalcos
Grijalva
San Pedro
Tlaliscoyan
Tamiahua
Las Flores
Misantla
Nautla $15.00 each

D POLITICAL & ADMINISTRATIVE

CARTA GENERAL DE LA REPUBLICA MEXICANA
1:3, 500, 000
Mexico City : Libreria Patria, 1964
86 x 62
Roads classified, other communications, political col. Inset of Mexico City.

MEXICO AND CENTRAL AMERICA
1:3, 447, 500
Washington : NGS
94 x 69
Detailed political wall map, boundaries in colour, communications.
$2.00 paper
$3.00 plastic

MEXICO
1:3, 125, 000
No. 203111
Chicago : Denoyer-Geppert
111 x 86
Political col. school wall map, showing spot heights, railways, Pan American Highway. Text in Spanish and English.
$10.00

RAND McNALLY IMPERIAL MAP OF MEXICO
1:3, 000, 000
Chicago : Rand McNally
116 x 80
States shown by col., roads, railways, national and divisional capitals. Inset of Mexico City and environs, index to towns on border.
$1.00

POLITICAL-PHYSICAL MAP OF MEXICO
1:2, 187, 500
Indianapolis : Cram
129 x 124
Col. school wall map, countries politically coloured with some relief hachures. Various styles of mounting.
Linen mounted,spring roller. $23.00

CARTA GENERAL DE LA REPÚBLICA MEXICANA
1:2, 000, 000
In 2 sheets
Tacubaya : DGGM, 1970
166 x 112
Coloured by provinces with communications and a table of administrative district inset.

E1 PHYSICAL : RELIEF

MEXICO, VISUAL RELIEF
1:2, 187, 500
Ed. J. Granville Jensen
Chicago : Denoyer-Geppert
No. 120671
162 x 137
Physical wall map, states named, communications, cities classed by pop. Text English and Spanish.
Rollers $21.50

REPUBLICA MEXICANA
1:2, 000, 000
In 4 sheets
Tacubaya : DGGM
137 x 179
Political col. wall map, states shown in different colours, communications.
$150.00 set

CARTA ALTIMÉTRICA DE LA REPÚBLICA MEXICANA
1:2, 000, 000
In 4 sheets
Tacubaya : DGGM
137 x 179
Col. political map with contours. Also black and white ed.

MEXICO
No scale
No. 198472
Chicago : Denoyer-Geppert
43 x 55
3-D vinyl moulded, natural colour relief map. $4.95

F GEOLOGY

MAPA GEOLÓGICO DE LA REPÚBLICA MEXICANA
1:5, 000, 000
Tacubaya : DGGM
80 x 60
Col. plate from the "Atlas Geografico de la Republica Mexicana"

TECTONIC MAP OF MEXICO
1:2, 500, 000
Comp. Zoltan de Cserna
Boulder, Col. : GSA, 1961
88 x 103
Tectonic map in Spanish and English. Water depths in metres. $6.50

CARTA GEOLÓGICA DE LA REPÚBLICA MEXICANA
1:2, 000, 000
Tacubaya : DGGM, 1960
162 x 120
Col. geol. map showing distribution of rock structure, geologic age; ocean depths with contours in metres.

CARTA GEOLÓGICA DE LA REPÚBLICA MEXICANA
1:2, 000, 000
Washington D.C. : Williams and Heintz Map Corp. (for Comite de la Carta Geologica de Mexico) 1968
Coloured geological map.

G EARTH RESOURCES

APROVECHAMIENTO DEL AGUA Y DEL SUELO EN MEXICO
1:100, 000
Ed. Jorge L. Tamayo
Mexico City : Secretaria de Recursos Hidraulicos
1958
Large scale series in 706 sheets illustrating values of water and soil in Mexico. Accompanied by handbook containing generalised map scale 1:1, 000, 000.

J CLIMATE

CARTA ALTIMÉTRICA DE LOS UNIDOS MEXICANOS CON HUMEDAO RELATIVA
1:2, 000, 000
In 4 sheets
Tacubaya : DGGM, 1971
160 x 112
Col. Map showing contours, isohytes, isotherms, mid-year temperature.

K HUMAN GEOGRAPHY

DESARROLLO Y DISTRIBUCIÓN DE LA POBLACIÓN URBANA EN MÉXICO
1:4, 000, 000
Mexico City : Univ. Nacional Autónoma de México, 1965
Showing the increase and distribution of the urban population of Mexico.

ZONAS ECONÓMICAS PARA LA FIJACIÓN DE LOS SALARIOS MÍNIMOS 1972-1973, DIVISIÓN MUNICIPAL DEL CENSO GENERAL DE POBLACIÓN DE 1970, ACTUALIZADA AL 31 DE ENERO DE 1971
1:2, 000, 000
2 sheets
Mexico DF : Comisión Nacional de los Salarios Mínimos
1971
Showing zone boundaries with index to districts.

ATLASES:
A1 ROADS

ROAD ATLAS OF THE UNITED STATES, CANADA AND MEXICO
Chicago : Rand McNally, 1976
See
North America 7A

ATLAS RUTAS DE MEXICO
1:2, 500, 000
Mexico City : Asociacion Nacional Automovilística, 1968
160 pp app.
34pp road maps inc. through town plans with 126 pp guide in Spanish and English.

ATLASES
D POLITICAL

ATLAS GEOGRÁFICO DE LA REPUBLICA MEXICANA POR ESTADOS
Mexico City : Dir. Gral. de Geog. y Met. 1959-72
55 x 44 cm
A collection of 94 maps of each state on scales varying from 1:150, 000 to 1:1, 400, 000 according to size. They show towns, communications with an indication of relief. Each map has a transparent overlay marking the administrative districts and map sketching the relief and water features. 29 pages of index to places shown.
Complete P600.00
Atlas económico, containing 32 political state maps only P350.00
Maps separately P15.00

ATLASES
M HISTORICAL

HISTORIA DE MÉXICO
Diego Lopez Rosado
Mexico City : Universidad Nacional Autonoma de Mexico, 1959
27 x 21
63 pp
Ring bound atlas of black and white historical maps.

ATLAS ARQUEÓLOGICO DE LA REPÚBLICA MEXICANA
Volumes:
Quintana Roo by F. Muller 1959
74 pp with map $20.00
Campeche by F. Muller 1960
54 pp map $20.00
Chiapas by R.P. Chan 1968
98 pp with 4 maps and photographs $20.00

ATLAS GÉOGRAPHIQUE ET PHYSIQUE DU ROYAUME DE LA NOUVELLE-ESPAGNE
Stuttgart : Brockhaus, 1969
31 x 47
Facsimile of atlas printed in Paris 1811 by Alexander von Humboldt. 126 pp text.
DM170
Also pub. Mexico City : Editorial Porrua $1,200.00

ATLASES
O NATIONAL

ATLAS GEOGRÁFICO GENERAL DE MÉXICO
Prepared by Jorge L. Tamayo (atlas volume from: 'Geografía General de Mexico')
2nd Edition
Mexico
Mexico City : Inst. Mex. de Investigaciones Economicas
1962
38 x 47
66 pages of maps including facsimiles, physical background, climate, social, cultural and economic matters.

ATLAS OF MEXICO
2nd Edition
By S.A. Arbingost and others
Austin : Univ. Texas, Bureau of Business Research, 1975
23 x 30
164 pp
152 pp of thematic and physical maps, including new historical section text in English. Spiral binding. $15.00

NUEVO ATLAS PORRUA DE LA REPUBLICA MEXICANA
E. Garcia de Miranda and Z. Falcon de Gyves
Mexico City : Editorial Porrua S.A.
1972
197 pp
Atlas in 3 sections : historic maps showing political divisions; general geog. of each country; thematic maps
$60.00
Linen $85.00

728 Central America

D POLITICAL

MITTELAMERIKA
1:6, 000, 000
Gotha : Haack, 1971
96 x 66
Haack hand map, boundaries, communications, 55 pp text.
6.80 complete

THE GULF AND THE CARIBBEAN
1:5, 000, 000
Maplewood : Hammond
96 x 63
Political col, communications.
Covers West Indies, Gulf of Mexico, Atlantic Coast Area. Not West Mexico
$2.00

TSENTRALNAYA AMERIKA I VEST INDIYA
1:5, 000, 000
Moskva : GUGK, 1973
Col. study map showing water features, settlements, admin. centres and divisions, communications, boundaries, economic details, pop. Geog. description. 30 kop

WEST INDIES AND CENTRAL AMERICA
1:4, 750, 000
Washington : NGS, 1970
75 x 46
Political col. wall map.
Paper $2.00
Plastic $3.00

POLITICAL MAP OF MIDDLE AMERICA
1:4, 687, 500
Indianapolis : Cram
129 x 122
Col. school wall map, simplified. $23.00

IMPERIAL MAP OF WEST INDIES AND THE CARIBBEAN
1:3, 500, 000
Chicago : Rand McNally
115 x 80
Political col, roads, railways, towns, villages. Inc. Guatemala south to Colombia and Venezuela; large scale insets of principal islands. Index with pop.
Paper folded $1.00

MEXICO AND CENTRAL AMERICA
1:3, 447, 500
NGS
See MEXICO 72D

MAPA DE AMERICA CENTRAL
1:2000, 000
Guatemala : IGN, 1972
95 x 76
Political map in 2 sheets of central America, excluding Mexico. Coloured by states with main communications.

AMERICA CENTRAL
No scale given
Barcelona : Editorial Teide
115 x 88
General wall map for schools, political
275 ptas

AMERICAS CENTRAL Y ANTILLAS
No scale given
Barcelona : Editorial Teide
25 x 33
General school hand map, showing major cities and state boundaries. 1 pta

MAPA MUDOS – MEXICO Y AMERICA CENTRAL
Barcelona : Editorial Vicens-Vives
33 x 24
Outline map in 2 colours.
50 copies S Ptas 100

AMERICA CENTRAL Y MERIDIONAL
No scale given
Barcelona : Editorial Teide
33 x 25
School outline hand map, without boundaries or cities. 1 pta

E1 PHYSICAL : RELIEF

CENTRAL AMERICA, WEST INDIES AND NORTH SOUTH AMERICA, VISUAL RELIEF
1:7, 187, 560
No. 125671-10
Chicago : Denoyer-Geppert
137 x 111
Physical school wall map. Canal Zone and Puerto Rico inset. Text Eng. Sp.
Rollers $18.75

STŘEDNÍ AMERIKA (CENTRAL AMERICA)
1:6, 000, 000
Praha : Kart
Physical/political reference map in series "Poznavame Svet" (Getting to know the world) Kcs 14.50

MITTELAMERIKA UND WESTINDIEN
1:5, 000, 000
Wien : FB
111 x 76
Covering Caribbean and neighbouring countries. Physical wall map, with boundaries, communications.

MIDDLE AMERICA, VISUAL RELIEF
1:4, 375, 000
No 126771-10
Chicago : Denoyer-Geppert
162 x 111
School wall map showing relief of land and sea; transport and political divisions inset.
Rollers $21.50

CENTRALINAYA AMERIKA
1:4, 000, 000
Moskva : GUGK, 1973
2 sheet physical wall map. 14 kop

MITTELAMERIKA UND NORDLICHES SUDAMERIKA
1:3, 000, 000
Braunschweig : Westermann
245 x 160
Physical wall map, showing relief, settlements, boundarles etc..

VEREINIGTE STAATEN UND MITTELAMERIKA
1:3, 000, 000
See USA 73E1

CENTRAL AMERICA
1:1, 000, 000
Stuttgart : Rubasmen
152 x 132
3rd. edition of old map. Relief shading by Alfredo Vischer; settlements. Canal Zone excavations inset.

G EARTH RESOURCES

MAPA METALOGENÉTICO DE AMERICA CENTRAL
1:2, 000, 000
In 2 sheets
Guatemala : Inst. Centroamericano de Investigacion y Technologia Industrial (ICAITI), 1969
90 x 70
Col. map showing geol. divisions and minerals. Legend in English and Spanish.
US $20.00

M HISTORICAL

ARCHAEOLOGICAL MAP OF MIDDLE AMERICA
1:2, 250, 000
Washington : NGS, 1968
63 x 48
Archaeological sites, insets, historical notes. Printed both sides.
$1.00

EARLY MAP REPRODUCTIONS FROM BLAEUS ATLAS NOVUS' 1662 – INSULAE AMERICANAE
Edinburgh : Bart
61 x 57
Coloured reproduction map of the West Indies. £1.50

CENTRAL AMERICA FACSIMILE MAPS
Wien : Editio Totius Mundi
Maps available:

13 Insulae Americanae
W Blaeuw 1636 52 x 37
col. 22 DM uncol. 15DM

40 Florida (incl. Cuba)
Th de Bry 1585 45 x 36
col. 26 DM

17 'Granatense' Panama (incl. Columbia and Venezuela)
W. Blaeuw 1636 52 x 37
col. 22 DM uncol. 15 DM

212 Gulf von Mexico "Tamaica Panuco" P. v.d. Aa 1729
col. 2 DM 15 x 10

211 Honduras, Costa Rica "Guatimala" P. v.d. Aa 1729
col. 2 DM 15 x 10

180 Central America 'Terre Ferme' (Columbia, Panama, Venezuela)
anon. 1650 18 x 13
col. 5 DM uncol. 3 DM

ATLASES
G EARTH RESOURCES

MUNGER MAP BOOK (SOUTH AND CENTRAL AMERICA AND WEST INDIES)
Munger Map Service, 1968
See SOUTH AMERICA ATLASES G

ATLASES
P REGIONAL

COLORATLAS AMERICA CENTRAL Y ANTILLES
2nd edition
Buenos Aires : Ed. Kapelusz, 1975
23 x 32
Physical, political atlas of central America and the Caribbean. US $1.85

728.1 Guatemala

A1 GENERAL MAPS : ROADS

MAPA PRELIMINAR DE LA REPUBLICA DE GUATEMALA
1:1, 000, 000
Guatemala : IGN, 1971
57 x 57
Col. general map with communications and boundaries.
Q. 0.50

B TOWN PLANS

CIUDAD DE GUATEMALA
1:25, 000
Guatemala : IGN, 1971
48 x 48
Coloured plan with roads named and classified, public buildings and places of tourist interest.

PICTOMAPA DE LA CIUDAD DE ANTIGUA GUATEMALA
1:7, 500
Guatemala : IGN, 1968
48 x 61
Aerial map showing buildings of historic significance. Q. 0.50

C OFFICIAL SURVEYS

INTERNATIONAL MAP OF THE WORLD
1:1, 000, 000
Hispanic America Series
AGS
4 sheets required
See World 100 and index 100/1

MAPA BASICO DE GUATEMALA
1:250, 000
Series E 503. In 13 sheets, see index 728.1/1
Washington : (Dir. Gen. de Cart. de Guatemala) DGC – AMS
Topographic series contoured with detailed land information.

MAPA TOPOGRAFICO DE LA REPUBLICA DE GUATEMALA
1:50, 000
In 200 sheets app. – see index 728.1/2
Guatemala : IGN
Topog. series in progress.
Q. 1.00 each

E1 PHYSICAL : RELIEF

MAPA HIPSOMETRICO DE LA REPUBLICA DE GUATEMALA
1:500, 000
Guatemala : IGN, 1970
In 4 sheets
113 x 116
Physical details, roads, boundaries.

GUATEMALA – FORMAS DE LA TIERRA
1:1, 000, 000
Guatemala : IGN
73 x 58
Morphological map showing land relief, hydrography. Physiographical regional maps on reverse. (from Atlas Nacional de Guatemala) Q. 1.00

E2 PHYSICAL : LAND FEATURES

MAPAS DE CUENCAS DE LA REPÚBLICA
1:500, 000
Guatemala : IGN
In 4 sheets
112 x 136
Maps of river basins, showing hydrography, contours, boundaries.

F GEOLOGY

MAPA GEOLÓGICO DE LA REPÚBLICA DE GUATEMALA
1:500, 000
Guatemala : IGN, 1970
In 4 sheets
110 x 114 complete
Col. geol. map. Explanation in English and Spanish.
Q. 5.00 set

MAPA GEOLÓGICO GENERAL DE GUATEMALA
1:250, 000
See index 728. 1/1
Guatemala : Direccion General de Cartografia
65 x 44
Col. geol. series in progress.

MAPA DE RECONOCIEMENTO GEOLÓGICO DE LA REGIÓN DE ALTA VERAPAZ
1:125, 000
Guatemala : IGN, 1967
74 x 58
Col. geol. map. Q. 1.00

MAPA GEOLÓGICO DE LA REPÚBLICA DE GUATEMALA
1:50, 000
See index 728.1/2 for sheets published
Guatemala : IGN
71 x 54
Coloured geological series in progress, contoured. Q. 1.00 each

H BIOGEOGRAPHY

MAPA FORESTAL DE LA REPÚBLICA DE GUATEMALA
1:250, 000
See index 728.1/1 for sheets published
Guatemala : IGN
Multi-sheet series in progress. Q. 1.00 each

MAPA DE USO DE TIERRA DE LA REPÚBLICA DE GUATEMALA
1:50, 000
See index 728. 1/2
Guatemala : IGN
71 x 54
Multi-sheet series, contoured at 20 metre intervals with form lines at every 10 metres, showing in 8 cols. the land use for an area of approx. 500 sq. km. Q. 1.00 each

J CLIMATE

MAPA CLIMATOLÓGICO PRELIMINAR DE LA REPÚBLICA DE GUATEMALA
1:1, 000, 000
Guatemala : IGN
57 x 57
Coloured map indicating precipitation and temperatures.

ATLASES
O NATIONAL ATLASES

ATLAS PRELIMINAR DE GUATEMALA
3rd Edition
Guatemala : IGN
1966
33 x 38
Including 23 maps 1:1, 500, 000 with facing page of explanation – physical, communications, natural sciences, demography, industry and mapping.

728.2 Belize

A1 **GENERAL MAPS : ROADS**

BRITISH HONDURAS
1:800, 000
DOS 958
Ed. 3
Tolworth : DOS, 1974
38 x 31
Layer col., rail and road communications.
15p

B **TOWN PLANS**

DIAGRAM OF BELIZE CITY
1:10, 800
Belize City : Lands and Surv. Dept, 1962
22 x 33
Central town area, principal streets and buildings marked
35p

C **OFFICIAL SURVEYS**

BRITISH HONDURAS
1:250, 000
DOS 649 (E 552), Ed. 3.
In 3 sheets
See index 728. 2/1
Tolworth : DOS, 1974
81 x 44
Topog. map, contoured, layer col., boundaries, communications, other land detail. 65p

BRITISH HONDURAS
1:50, 000
DOS 4499, (E 755)
In 45 sheets
See index 728. 2/1
Tolworth : DOS
53 x 55
Topog. series, relief shown by form lines, prep. jointly by DOS and MOD
50p

F **GEOLOGY**

GEOLOGICAL MAP OF SOUTHERN BRITISH HONDURAS
1:275, 000
Belize City : Lands and Surv. Dept. 1955
45 x 60
Col. map showing basic land information faults in red. 2 cross sections.
£1.50

G **EARTH RESOURCES**

BRITISH HONDURAS : OIL EXPLORATION AND PROSPECTING LICENCES DIAGRAM
1:900, 000
Belize City : Lands and Surv. Dept.
26 x 33
Shows company licence areas ; key handwritten.

H **BIOGEOGRAPHY**

LAND USE MAPS FROM "LAND IN BRITISH HONDURAS : REPORT OF THE BRITISH HONDURAS LAND USE SURVEY TEAM" HMSO
Tolworth : DOS, 1954

Misc. 241J Land Formation
1:1, 750, 000 35p
Misc. 241L Environmental Zones
1:625, 500 10p
Misc. 241D Distribution of Crown and Private lands showing Forest Reserves and Distribution of Fertile soils
1:1, 000, 000 10p
Misc. 241H Land Slops Classes
1:1, 000, 000 35p
Misc. 241K Soil Forming Parent Materials
1:1, 000, 000 20p
Misc. 241M Farming Population
1:1, 000, 000 10p
Misc. 241N Ancient Mayan Sites
1:1, 000, 000 10p
Misc. 241A Provincial Soil Map sheets 1&2
1:250, 000 65p each
Misc. 241B 1 & 2 Natural Vegetation Map sheets
1:250, 000 65p each
Misc. 241C 1 & 2 Potential Land Use Map sheets
1:250, 000 65p each

J **CLIMATE**

CLIMATIC MAPS AND DIAGRAMS FROM "LAND IN BRITISH HONDURAS : REPORT OF THE BRITISH HONDURAS LAND USE SURVEY TEAM" HMSO
Tolworth : DOS, 1954

Misc. 241F Histograms showing rainfall distribution 10p
Misc. 241G Monthly Rainfall
1:1, 750, 000 35p
Misc. 241E Mean Annual Rainfall
1:1, 000, 000 10p

728.3 Honduras

B TOWN PLANS

MAPA TURÍSTICO DE TEGUCIGALPA
1:10, 000
Tegucigalpa : IGN, 1969
76 x 55
Principal roads named, some buildings indexed, history of town, oblique sketch of central area on reverse.

C OFFICIAL SURVEYS

INTERNATIONAL MAP OF THE WORLD
Hispanic America Series
1:1, 000, 000
AGS
Sheet ND 16 Tegucigalpa for Honduras
See World section and index 100/1

REPÚBLICA DE HONDURAS
1:50, 000
AMS E. 572 See index 728. 3/1
In 250 sheets app.
Tegucigalpa : IGN
New series in progress, showing communications, vegetation etc.

D POLITICAL & ADMINISTRATIVE

MAPA GENERAL DE LA REPÚBLICA DE HONDURAS
1:1, 000, 000
3rd Ed.
Tegucigalpa : IGN, 1970
83 x 56
Coloured by provinces with contours and communications.

F GEOLOGY

HONDURAS – MAPA GEOLÓGICA
1:50, 000
Follows 1:50, 000 series sheet lines, with geol. overprint.

728.4 El Salvador

A1 GENERAL MAPS : ROADS

MAPA OFICIAL DE LA REPUBLICA DE EL SALVADOR
1:300, 000
San Salvador : IGN, 1966
96 x 52
Contoured with communications, boundaries and towns classified according to status and population.
₡ 3.00

B TOWN PLANS

PLANO DE LA CIUDAD DE SAN SALVADOR
1:15, 000
San Salvador : IGN, 1968
105 x 70
Coloured plan with streets named and principal buildings and admin. districts indexed, contours at 25 metre intervals.
₡ 3.00

PICTOMAPAS DE CIUDADES DEL PAIS
San Salvador : IGN
Maps available:
San Salvador
1:15, 000 ₡ 3.00
Nueva San Salvador
1:5, 000
Santa Ana
San Vicente
Sonsonate
San Miguel
Zacatecoluca
Ahuachapan
Usulutan
Cojutepeque
Semi-pictorial plans illustrating principal buildings with main streets names.
each ₡ 2.00

INTERNATIONAL MAP OF THE WORLD: HISPANIC AMERICA SERIES
1:1, 000, 000
Sheet ND16 Tegucigalpa, for El Salvador
See World 100, Index 100/1

EL SALVADOR – MAPA BASICO
1:50, 000
In 54 sheets, see index 728/4
San Salvador : IGN, 1955+
73 x 56 each app.
Col. topog. series with contours.
₡ 5.00 each

MAPA TOPOGRÁFICO DE LA REPÚBLICA DE EL SALVADOR
1:20, 000
See index 728. 4/1
San Salvador : IGN
75 x 55
Topog. series, contoured at 10m intervals. 4 sheets to each 1:50, 000 map. Available as blue prints only. ₡ 3.00 each

D POLITICAL & ADMINISTRATIVE

MAPA OFICIAL DE LA REPUBLICA DE EL SALVADOR
1:500, 000
San Salvador : IGN, 1968
62 x 42
Political col, communications. ₡ 1.00

MAPAS DEPARTMENTALES DEL PAIS
1:100, 000
In 14 sheets
San Salvador : IGN, 1964-9
Series covering the 14 Departments – physical with communications and boundaries
San Salvador
Santa Ana
Sonsonate
Ahuachapan
Cuscatlan
La Libertad
Usulutan
La Paz
Cabanas
Chalatenango
San Vicente
Morazan
La Union
San Miguel
₡ 2.00 each

ATLASES
L ECONOMIC

ATLAS ECONOMICO DE EL SALVADOR
San Salvador : Dir. Gen. de Estadistica y Census, 1975
Thematic atlas covering: demography, industry, commerce, social matters, agriculture, trade, finance, education with economic indicators for Central America and Panama.
US $5.00

ATLASES
O NATIONAL

EL SALVADOR – ATLAS DE RECURSOS FÍSICOS
1:500, 000
San Salvador : IGN 1969
76 x 46
34 col. map sheets of physical and them. maps, 58 pp text in Spanish.
49 x 72
Paper Cover ₡ 100.00
Luxury Board Cover ₡ 125.00

728.5 Nicaragua

A1 GENERAL MAPS : ROADS

RED VIAL CARRETERAS
1:1, 000, 000
Managua : Dir. Gen. Cart, 1967
Showing highway network with roads classified and distances in km.
Cs 2.00

MAPA OFICIAL DE NICARAGUA : EDICION PRELIMINAR
1:500, 000
Managua : Dir. Gen. Cart, 1968
100 x 115
Physical col. maps, contours, communications, province boundaries.

A2 GENERAL MAPS : LOCAL

REGIONAL TOPOGRAPHIC MAPS
Managua : Dir. Gen. Cart.
Sheets :

Corn Island	1:10, 000	1969
Little Corn Island	1:10, 000	1968
Isletas de Granada	1:10, 000	1969

Cs 10.00 each

B TOWN PLANS

TOWN PLANS
Managua : Dir. Gen. Cart.
Plans available:

Puerto Cabezas	1:10, 000	1969
Puerto Corinto e Vecindad	1:5, 000	1969
Mapa Granada y Vecindad	1:5, 000	1968
Cuidad de Leon	1:10, 000	1970
Mapa Managua y Vecindad	1:10, 000	1964
Mapa Masaya y Vecindad	1:5, 000	1966
Pictomapa de Masaya	1:5, 000	1967
Puerto Somoza	1:5, 000	1968

Cs 10.00 each

C OFFICIAL SURVEYS

INTERNATIONAL MAP OF THE WORLD
Hispanic America Series
1:1, 000, 000
3 sheets required for coverage:
ND 16 Tegucigalpa
NC 16 Lago de Nicaragua
NC 17 Panama
AGS
See World Section, index 100/1

SERIE TOPOGRÁFICA – ZONA DEL PACÍFICO
1:250, 000
Series E503. See index 728. 5/1
Managua : Dir. Gen. Cart.
4 col. sheets pub. 1965-68
Cs 8.00
3 relief sheets 1968 Cs 50.00
Topographic series in progress covering western half of country, contoured at 100m intervals with some hachures.

SERIE PLANIMÉTRICA – ZONA DEL ATLÁNTICO
1:250, 000
Series E503. See index 728. 5/1
Managua : Dir. Gen. Cart.
4 one col. sheets 1962-67 Cs 4.00
4 col. sheets 1968 Cs 8.00
Topographic series covering eastern half of country contoured at 100m intervals with some hachures.

SERIE PLANIMÉTRICA – ZONA DEL PACÍFICO
1:100, 000
Series E651. See index 728. 5/2
Managua : Dir. Gen. Cart.
Available in 3 eds :
1a 1956-8 16 sheets published
Cs 2.00 each
2a 1963-5 8 sheets published
Cs 3.00 each
2a 1968 3 sheets published (col)
Cs 5.00 each
Planimetric series in progress, uncontoured with some relief hachures.

NICARAGUA – SERIE TOPOGRAFÍA
1:50, 000
Series E751. In 300 sheets app.
See index 728. 5/3
Managua : Dir. Gen. Cart, 1956-69
Topographical series in progress contoured at 20m intervals.
Cs 5.00 each

SERIE TOPOGRAFÍA DE LOS CAYOS DEL ATLANTICO
1:25, 000
Series E857
Managua : Dir. Gen. Cart, 1965-7
4 sheets covering Atlantic offshore islands, contoured at 10m intervals.
Cs 5.00 each

D POLITICAL & ADMINISTRATIVE

REPUBLICA DE NICARAGUA MAPA POLITICO
1:1, 000, 000
Managua : Dir. Gen. Cart.
1966
60 x 51
Coloured by departments and showing rivers and principal towns. Cs 5.00

NICARAGUA : DIVISION POLITICA – MUNICIPIOS
1:1, 000, 000
Managua : Dir. Gen. Cart, 1965
70 x 56
Marking administrative boundaries.
Cs 2.00

CARTA DEPARTMENTO
Managua : Dir. Gen. Cart.
Maps available:
Departmental Chinandega – Planimetrico
1:150, 000 1967 Cs 10.00
Departmento Masaya – Topografico
1:50, 000 1967 Cs 10.00
Coloured district maps indicating administrative divisions and communications

E1 PHYSICAL : RELIEF

NICARAGUA – MAPA HIPSOGRÁFICO
1:1, 000, 000
Managua : Dir. Gen. Cart. 1966
70 x 56
Physical map, contoured and layer coloured with rivers and principal towns.
Cs 5.00

E2 PHYSICAL : LAND FEATURES

NICARAGUA – MAPA HIDROGRÁFICO
1:1, 000, 000
Managua : Dir. Gen. Cart, 1966
70 x 56
Shows lakes and rivers in blue on white base. Cs 5.00

G EARTH RESOURCES

NICARAGUA – MAPA ISOGONICO
1:1, 000, 000
Managua : Dir. Gen. Cart, 1965
70 x 56
Showing lines of magnetic variation, graded in colour. Cs 5.00

H BIOGEOGRAPHY

MAPAS FORESTALES
1:100, 000
Managua : Dir. Gen. Cart/FAO, 1967
56 x 70 each
Forestry maps for the following regions:
Puerto Cabezas – Awastigni – Wounta – Cabo Gracias a Dios – Waspan – Alamicamba – Bambana – Prinzapolka – Mapa de Caminos (Coco-Wawa)
1:250, 000 1966
Cs 4.00 each

728.6 Costa Rica

A1 GENERAL MAPS : ROADS

MAPAS DE COSTA RICA Y SAN JOSE
1:800, 000
San José : Inst. Costarricense de Turismo, 1972
Road map with inset of capital region and plan of San José on reverse.

B TOWN PLANS

CIUDAD DE SAN JOSÉ
1:10, 000
2nd edition
San José : Inst. Geog. Costa Rica
Coloured plan naming principal roads and buildings.

C OFFICIAL SURVEYS

INTERNATIONAL MAP OF THE WORLD
Hispanic America Series
1:1, 000, 000
AGS
Sheets :
NC 16 Lago de Nicaragua
NC 17 Panama
See World 100 and index 100/1

COSTA RICA
1:200, 000
Series 2 CM (E 561) Ed. 1
In 9 sheets, see index 728.6
San José : Inst. Geog. Costa Rica, 1968-70
Col. series showing contours, wood col, communications, province boundaries.

MAPA BÁSICO DE COSTA RICA
1:50, 000
In 138 sheets – see Index 728.6/2
San José : Inst. Geog. Costa Rica
55 x 36
Multi-sheet series in progress, contoured at 100m intervals and showing details and information.

COSTA RICA
1:25, 000
In 552 sheets – see Index 728.6/2
San José : Inst. Geog. Costa Rica
55 x 36
Multi-sheet series in progress, contoured at 10m intervals with formlines at 5m.

D POLITICAL & ADMINISTRATIVE

MAPA DE COSTA RICA
1:1, 500, 000
Edicion Escolar Provisional
San José : Inst. Geog. de Costa Rica
1961
29 x 24
Coloured by provinces and marking rail, road and river communications. Isla del Coco inset. ₡ 0.50

MAPA POLÍTICO DE COSTA RICA
1:1, 000, 000
San José : Inst. Geog. Costa Rica
53 x 42
Coloured by provinces with road and rail communications and towns classified by status. Insets of Isla del Coco and provincial statistics.

COSTA RICA, DIVISION TERRITORIAL ADMINISTRATIVA
1:600, 000
San José : Dir. Gen. de Estadistica y Censos, 1971
Coloured map indicating provincial and divisional boundaries.

MAPA MURAL ESCOLAR DE COSTA RICA
1:350, 000
San José : Inst. Geog. Cost Rica
School wall map, contours, communications, boundaries.

E1 PHYSICAL : RELIEF

MAPA FÍSICO
1:1, 500, 000
San José : Inst. Geog. Costa Rica
29 x 24
Contoured and layer coloured and marking rail, road and river communications. Isla del Coco inset ₡ 0.50

MAPA ESCOLAR DE COSTA RICA
1:1, 000, 000
Edicion Provisional
San José : Inst. Geog. Nacional, 1967
38 x 36
Contoured and layer coloured, communications, boundaries and towns. Isla del Coco inset. Scale 1:200, 000 ₡ 1.00

MAPA DE COSTA RICA
1:750, 000
Edicion Escolar Provisional
3rd Edition
San José : Inst. Geog. de Costa Rica, 1962
58 x 47
Layer coloured showing boundaries, road and rail communications.

COSTA RICA MAPA FÍSICO-POLITICO
1:500, 000
Edicion Provisional
San José : Inst. Geog. de Costa Rica, 1971
77 x 72
Contoured and layer coloured, showing road and rail communications, towns and settlements. Zona Central (San Jose and environs) inset, scale 1:250, 000, also inset Isla del Coco.

PROVINCIA DE GUANCASTE
1:250, 000
San José : Inst. Geog. Costa Rica
2 sheet physical map, contoured with boundaries, communications and land detail.

F GEOLOGY

MAPA GEOLÓGICO DE COSTA RICA
1:700, 000
Edicion Preliminar
55 x 51
San José : Dir. de Geología, Minas y Petroleo, 1968
Coloured geological map compiled in co-operation with ICAITI with inset showing sources of information.

G EARTH RESOURCES

MAPA DE RECURSOS MINERALES DE COSTA RICA
1:750, 000
San José : Dir. de Geol. Minas y Petroleo
1971
58 x 48
Black and white map showing location of minerals by symbols.

H BIOGEOGRAPHY

MAPA ECOLOGICO DE COSTA RICA
1:750, 000
San José : Centro Científico Tropical
1969
53 x 50
Coloured map indicating principal natural regions, with key to zones in Spanish and English. Inset Isla del Coco and explanatory diagram of natural zones according to world system by L. R. Holdridge.

728.7 Panama

A1 GENERAL MAPS : ROADS

PANAMÁ
1:1, 000, 000
Panamá : IGN, 1968
69 x 33
Col. map showing contours, water features, roads, province boundaries.

PANAMÁ CARRETERAS
1:1, 000, 000
Panama : IGN
69 x 33
Roads classified, contours, boundaries.

B TOWN PLAN

CIUDAD DE PANAMÁ
1:5, 000
Panama : IGN
Series in 11 sheets

C OFFICIAL SURVEYS

INTERNATIONAL MAP OF THE WORLD
Hispanic America Series
1:1, 000, 000
AGS
3 sheets needed to cover Panama;

NB, NC 17	Panama
NB 18	Bogota
NC 18	Barranquilla

See World 100 and index 100/1

PANAMÁ (ESPECIAL)
1:250, 000
In 12 sheets – see index 728. 7/1
Panamá : IGN, 1967
71 x 55 each
Topog. maps, legend in Spanish. Contours, layer col. towns classified accor. pop and status, boundaries, railways.

PANAMÁ
1:50, 000
Series E 762 – see index 728. 7/2
Panamá : IGN
Topographical series in progress, contoured at 20m, with formlines at 10m. boundaries, communications and land features.

PANAMÁ – CARTA BÁSICO GENERAL
1:25, 000
Series E 866
Panama : IGN
Topographical series in progress, currently published for the Panama Canal Zone and vicinity.

PANAMÁ – CARTA CATASTRAL
1:10, 000
Panamá : IGN
Large scale planimetric series currently published for the coastal region of Golfo de Parita (107 sheets) and David (2 sheets).

D POLITICAL & ADMINISTRATIVE

REPÚBLICA DE PANAMÁ – MAPA POLÍTICO
1:500, 000
Panamá : IGN, 1970
142 x 58 complete
2 sheet map; providing col, district boundaries, some topog. detail. Inc. Panama Canal Zone.

E1 PHYSICAL : RELIEF

REPÚBLICA DE PANAMÁ – MAPA FISICO
1:500, 000
Panamá : IGN, 1970
142 x 58 complete
2 sheet map, contours, layer col. roads, railways, boundaries.

E GEOLOGY

MAPA GEOLÓGICO DE LA REPÚBLICA DE PANAMÁ
1:1, 000, 000
Prepared by Min. de Comercio e Industrias
Panamá : IGN, T. Guardia, 1975
65 x 38
Coloured geological map in Spanish.
US $4.00

MAPA GEOLÓGICO – PROYECTO MINERO DE AZUERO
1:250, 000
In 2 sheets
Prepared by Min. de Comercio e Industrias,
Panamá : IGN T. Guardia, 1969
48 x 66
Coloured geological map of Azuero in Spanish each US $2.50

MAPA GEOLÓGICO – PROYECTO MINERO – FASE II
1:250, 000
In 4 sheets
Prepared by Min. de Comercio e Industrias
Panama : IGN T. Guardia
Four geological maps in course of preparation for UN Development Programme.

Region	'A'	Bocas de Toro
	'B'	Majé
	'C'	San Blas
	'D'	Darién-Pirre

GEOLOGIC MAP OF CANAL ZONE AND ADJOINING PARTS OF PANAMA
1:75, 000
Misc. Geol. Inv. 1-1
Compiled by W.P. Wooding
Washington : USGS, 1965 $1.00

MAPA GEOLÓGICO – AREA GENERAL – RIO PITO
1:40, 000
Prepared by Min. de Comercio e Industrias
Panamá : IGN T. Guardia
56 x 42
Coloured geological map for UN Development Programme. US $2.50

MAPA GEOLÓGICO AREA 65 – CERRO PETAQUILLA
1:15, 000
Prepared by Min. de Comercio e Industrias
Panamá: IGN T. Guardia
57 x 48
Coloured geological map for UN Development Programme. US $2.50

MAPA GEOLÓGICO – AREA 101-1 – RIO PITO
1:8, 000
Prepared by Min. de Comercio e Industrias
Panamá : IGN T. Guardia, 1972
39 x 51
Coloured geological map for UN Development Programme. US $2.50

G EARTH RESOURCES

MAPA DE INFORMACIÓN DE PROSPECTOS MINEROS
1:1, 000, 000
Panamá : Min. de Comercio e Industrias
68 x 33
Map of potential mineral deposits.
Blueprint US $1.50

MAPA DE CONCESIONES Y SOLICITUDES DE MATERIALES DE CONSTRUCCIÓN
1:500, 000
Panamá : Min. de Comercio e Industrias
133 x 55
Concession map for construction minerals
Blueprint US $1.75

ATLASES
O NATIONAL

ATLAS DE PANAMÁ
Panamá : IGN
46 x 30
193 pp
92 col. maps in 18 major sections, including historical, physical, climatic, vegetation, geology, social, economic, industrial and political subjects. Each section has explanatory text in Spanish. Illustrated by photographs.

729 West Indies

See also : 728 CENTRAL AMERICA

D POLITICAL & ADMINISTRATIVE

WEST INDIA COMMITTEE MAP OF THE WEST INDIES AND CARIBBEAN
1:3, 500, 000
London : G. Philip
122 x 94
Boldly coloured political map showing principal towns and communications.
Paper 85p
Cloth with rollers £2.30
Cloth dissected £2.70

CARIBBEAN AND CENTRAL AMERICA
1:1, 250, 000
Madrid : Seix Barral
121 x 83
Political col. map, communications; Physical map of the Caribbean and Panama Canal Zone inset.

E1 PHYSICAL : RELIEF

PHILIPS REGIONAL WALL MAP OF THE WEST INDIES
1:2, 500, 000
London : G. Philip
117 x 91
Physical map, contoured and layer coloured, communications, boundaries and towns.
Paper £1.50
Cloth with rollers £5.50
Cloth dissected £7.00

CARIBBEAN AREA – VISUAL RELIEF
1:1, 562, 500
No. 120771
Chicago : Denoyer-Geppert
162 x 111
Physical school wall map. Canal Zone and Puerto Rico inset. Text English and Spanish.
Rollers $21.50

ATLASES
W3 WORLD ATLASES : LOCAL EDITIONS

ATLAS FOR BARBADOS, WINDWARDS AND LEEWARDS
London : Macmillan Educational Ltd., 1974
22 x 29
32 pp
Includes 16 pp of large scale topo. and thematic maps of the Caribbean area with maps of the Continent and World.
Illustrated.

ATLAS FOR THE EASTERN CARIBBEAN
Collins – Longman, 1971
See World 100

ATLAS FOR JAMAICA AND THE WESTERN CARIBBEAN
Collins – Longman, 1971
See World 100

COLLINS CARIBBEAN SCHOOL ATLAS
Collins
See World 100

729.1 Cuba

A1 GENERAL MAPS : ROAD

MAPA TURÍSTICO CUBA
1:300, 000
Habana : Inst. Cubana de Geodesia y Cart, 1972
Road map with route numbers and distances. With inset plans of 10 cities.

A2 GENERAL MAPS : LOCAL

PROVINCIA DE ORIENTE
1:350, 000
Habana : Inst. Cubana de Geodesia y Cart, 1971
Coloured map showing communications and boundaries.

C OFFICIAL SURVEYS

INTERNATIONAL MAP OF THE WORLD-
Hispanic America Series
1:1, 000, 000
AGS
4 sheets to cover Cuba:

NF 15, 16,	Yucatan
NF 17	Habana
NF 18	Santiago de Cuba
NE 17, 18	Kingston — Port au Prince

See World 100 and index 100/1.

CUBA
1:250, 000
Habana : Inst. Cubana Cart y Catastro
Maps of single provinces, coloured and showing communications and boundaries.

CUBA
1:100, 000
Habana : Inst. Cubana Cart. y Catastro
Topog. series in progress, contoured, communications, boundaries and land detail.

D POLITICAL & ADMINISTRATIVE

KUBA — SPRAVOCHNAYA KARTA
1:1, 000, 000
Moskva : GUGK, 1973
Reference map — political and admin.
15 kop

REPUBLICA DE CUBA
1:750, 000
2nd Edition
Habana : Inst. Cubana de Geodesia y Cart, 1971
School wall map, coloured by provinces showing towns and principal communications.

E1 PHYSICAL : RELIEF

CUBA AND THE BAHAMAS
1:1, 500, 000
GSGS 4948, World Lecture Map
No. F9
Tolworth : MOD
122 x 92
Sketch planning map showing contours, communications, boundaries and major towns.

CUBA
1:1, 000, 000
Washington : USAF
121 x 91
Layer col. map. contours, cities; industry indicated by pictorial symbols.

F GEOLOGY

MAPA GEOLOGICO DE CUBA
Ed. A. Núñez Jiménez et al
1:1, 000, 000
Habana : Inst. Cubana de Recursos Minerales, 1962
132 x 58
Col. geol. map, note on principal rock types. Legend in Spanish.

CARTE HYDROGRAPHIQUE DE LA BAYE DE LA HAVANE AVEC LE PLAN DE SES FORTS POUR JOINDRE A LA CARTE DE L'ISLE DE CUBE
S Bellin
Ithaca, NY : Historic Urban Plans, 1971
Facsimile of the 1762 map produced by order of the Duc de Choiseul.
$10.00

ATLASES
O NATIONAL

ATLAS NACIONAL DE CUBA
Chief. Ed. Antonio Núñez Jiménez
La Habana : Geog. Inst. of Academy Sci. & GUGK, Moskva, 1970
150 pp
38 x 49
132 pp col. physical them. maps and description, covering climate, economy, vegetation etc. Index, geog. data and statistics. Russian ed. also available.

729.2 Jamaica, Cayman Islands, Turks and Caicos Islands

A1 GENERAL MAPS : ROADS

TURKS AND CAICOS
1:1, 250, 000
DOS 901
Tolworth : DOS
Black and white sketch map.
15p

JAMAICA
1:720, 000
DOS 966
Ed. 1
Tolworth : DOS
1956
Small hand map showing communications, boundaries and settlements.
15p

JAMAICA – A FAIREY LEISURE MAP
1:550, 000
Maidenhead : Fairey Surveys Ltd., 1974
85 x 37
Relief shaded, classifying roads and tracks with distances in miles. Railways, country boundaries, vegetation, beaches and 28 classifications of tourist interests and recreational facilities shown by symbols. Insets of Montego Bay and Kingston.
60p

TURKS AND CAICOS ISLANDS
1:200, 000
DOS 609
Tolworth : DOS, 1971
88 x 68
Map of Island group, roads, vegetation, airfields, contoured with layer colouring.
65p

A2 GENERAL MAPS : LOCAL

REGIONAL TOPOGRAPHICAL MAPS
Various scales
Kingston : Surv. Dept.

Pedro Plains	1:5, 000	
18 sheets		$1.50 each
Annotto Bay	1:5, 000	
2 sheets		$1.50 each
Yallahs Valley	1:5, 000	
40 sheets		25c per sq. ft.
Water Commission		
Hope Catchment	1:5, 000	
18 sheets		25c per sq. ft.
Highgate	1:5, 000	
15 sheets		$1.50 each
East St. Catherine		
Plains	1:5, 000	
29 sheets		$1.50 each
Hellshire Hills	1:5, 000	
12 sheets		$1.50 each
Santa Cruz	1:2, 500	
8 sheets		$2.50 each
Ocho Rios	1:2, 500	
8 sheets		$2.50 each
Porus	1:2, 500	
6 sheets		$2.50 each
Long Mountain –		
Wareika	1:2, 500	
5 sheets		$2.50 each
Port Royal – Palisades –		
Harbour View	1:1, 250	
20 sheets		$1.00 each
Montego Bay	1:25, 000	
1 sheet		S1.50
Rio Pedro	1:10, 000	
2 sheets		S1.50
Cane River	1:10, 000	
2 sheets		S1.50
St. Dorothy Plains	1:5, 000	
12 sheets		$1.50 each
Outram Watershed	1:5, 000	
4 sheets		S1.50 each
Mid Clarendon Plains	1:5, 000	
11 sheets		S1.50 each
Cave Valley Watershed	1:5, 000	
6 sheets		S1.50 each

B TOWN PLANS

KINGSTON
1:10, 000
DOS 201 series E922 in 6 sheets
see Index 729. 2/1
Ed. 1
Tolworth : DOS 1962-65
Map of town and vicinity.
30p each

COCKBURN HARBOUR – CAICOS ISLANDS
1:2, 500
DOS 109
Tolworth : DOS
Topographical plan, contoured 30p

PLANIMETRIC MAPS OF PRINCIPAL TOWNSHIPS
1:1, 250
Kingston : Surv. Dept.
Available for the following areas:
a) Kingston and St. Andrew 44 sheets and 72 sheets 1:2, 500
b) Spanish Town 24 sheets
c) May Pen 16 sheets
d) Mandeville 32 sheets
e) Black River 8 sheets
f) Savanna-la-mar 8 sheets
g) Lucea 7 sheets
h) Montego Bay 38 sheets
i) Falmouth 8 sheets
j) St. Ann's Bay 7 sheets
k) Port Maria 6 sheets
l) Port Antonio 15 sheets
m) Morant Bay 14 sheets

Detailed plans in black and white showing buildings and property boundaries
50c each

C OFFICIAL SURVEYS

JAMAICA
1:170, 946
Kingston : Surv. Dept. 1880
152 x 76
Photographic prints $1.00 per sq. ft.
Ozalid prints
203 x 91 25c per sq. ft.
Reproduction of an early survey of the island.

JAMAICA – TOPO. SERIES (PHOTOGRAPHIC PRINTS)
1:100, 000
Kingston : Surv. Dept.
Reduction of 50, 000 Topog. Series in 12 sheets.
Photographic prints $1.00 per sq. ft.
Ozalid prints 25c per sq. ft.

TOPOGRAPHICAL MAP OF JAMAICA
1:50, 000
DOS 410 (E 721) in 12 sheets, see index 729. 2/1
Tolworth : DOS, 1952
Topographical series, contoured with considerable land detail. 50p each

TURKS AND CAICOS ISLANDS
1:25, 000
DOS 309 (E 8112) in 15 sheets, see index 729. 2/3
Edition 1
Tolworth : DOS 1969
Topog. series, contoured. 50p each

UNITED NATIONS DEVELOPMENT PROJECT : ALL ISLAND MAPPING
1:12, 500
In 240 sheets app., see index 729. 2/2
Kingston : Survey Dept.
Topographical series, contoured with considerable land detail.
Preliminary edition,
Black Ozalid 75c
Preliminary edition,
Black and brown litho $1.00

TURKS AND CAICOS ISLANDS
1:10, 000
DOS 209 (E 8113)
In 59 sheets See index 729. 2/3
Tolworth : DOS, 1967
Edition 1
Contoured topographical series. 20p each

JAMAICA – CADASTRAL MAPS
1:7, 900 app. (20 chains to 1 inch)
Kingston : Surv. Dept.
Early survey depicting settlement and property boundaries.
As photographic prints – $1.00 per sq. ft.
Ozalid prints 25c per sq. ft.

CAYMAN ISLANDS
1:150, 000
DOS 928
Edition 3
Tolworth : DOS, 1975
Col. topog. hand map. 15p

CAYMAN ISLANDS
1:25, 000
DOS 328 (E 821) In 4 sheets
Edition 1
Tolworth : DOS, 1965-66
1 Grand Cayman
2 Grand Cayman
3 Little Cayman
4 Cayman Brac
Topog. map, contours, land details
50p each

CAYMAN ISLANDS
1:2, 500
DOS 128 (E 823)
Edition 1
Tolworth : DOS
1965
Topographical series in progress.
19 compilation plots completed for western coastal area. 30p each

D POLITICAL & ADMINISTRATIVE

PARISH MAPS
1:63, 360
In 13 sheets
Kingston : Surv. Dept.
Coloured map series showing settlement and parish boundaries. S3.00 each

E1 RELIEF : PHYSICAL

PHILIP'S REGIONAL WALL MAP OF JAMAICA
1:260, 000
London : G. Philip
102 x 79
Physical layer col. boundaries, towns graded by pop.

Paper	£1.50
Mounted CR	£5.50
Mounted on cloth dissected to fold	£7.00

JAMAICA
1:250, 000
DOS 602 (Series E 523)
Edition 4
Tolworth : DOS, 1966
104 x 69
Topog. map, contours, layer col. communications, boundaries
50p

F GEOLOGY

JAMAICA
1:250, 000
DOS, Geol, 1099
Tolworth : DOS, 1959
104 x 69
Geol. map in col. 65p

JAMAICA GEOLOGY
1:50, 000
DOS 1177
Tolwroth : DOS
New coloured series of geological maps in progress.
Sheets published:
25 Kingston 1975

L ECONOMIC

TURKS AND CAICOS ISLANDS BASIC DEVELOPMENT MAP
1:125, 720
DOS (Misc.) 431
Tolworth : DOS, 1966
Coloured map indicating constructional development projects.
65p

M HISTORICAL

EARLY MAP REPRODUCTIONS — JAMAICA by John Ogilby 1671
Edinburgh : Bart
61 x 51
Coloured facsimile map.
£1.50

ATLASES
W3 WORLD ATLAS : LOCAL EDITION

ATLAS FOR JAMAICA AND THE WESTERN CARIBBEAN
Collins — Longman, 1971
See World 100

ATLASES
O NATIONAL

JAMAICA IN MAPS
Ed. C. G. Clarke and A. G. Hodgkiss
London : Hodder & Stoughton, 1975
22 x 28
Collection of black and white maps covering physical, economic, social and industrial aspects each with descriptive text. Bibliography
£2.50

729.3 Dominican Republic

C OFFICAL SERIES

INTERNATIONAL MAP OF THE WORLD-
Hispanic America Series
1:1, 000, 000
AGS
1 sheet required for coverage
NE 19 Santo Domingo – San Juan
See World 100 and index 100/1

DOMINICAN REPUBLIC
TOPOGRAPHIC SERIES
1:50, 000
Series F 733
Santo Domingo : Inst. Cart. Militar
Topographical series in progress, contoured at 20m intervals.

729.4 Haiti

B TOWN PLANS

PORT-AU-PRINCE ET ENVIRONS
1:12, 500
Port-au-Prince : Service de Géol.
et de Cart.
Coloured plan of the city and surroundings, contoured.

C OFFICIAL SURVEYS

INTERNATIONAL MAP OF THE WORLD-
Hispanic America Series
1:1, 000, 000
AGS
2 sheets for coverage :
NE 17,18 Kingston — Port-au-Prince
NE 19 Santo Domingo — San Juan
See World 100 and index 100/1

HAITI — CARTE TOPOGRAPHIQUE
1:100, 000
Series in 28 sheets
Port-au-Prince : Service de Géol.
et de Cart.
Topographical series contoured at 40m intervals with communications, boundaries.

HAITI — CARTE TOPOGRAPHIQUE
1:50, 000
Series in 78 sheets
Port-au-Prince : Service de Géol.
et de Cart.
Topographical series in progress currently published for the area west of 72° 45′.

HAITI — CARTE TOPOGRAPHIQUE
1:25, 000
Series in 270 sheets
Port-au-Prince : Service de Géol.
at de Cart.
Topographical series in progress currently published for the North, North East, Artibonite, Central and West and South West Departments and the island of La Tortue.

HAITI — CARTE PLANIMÉTRIQUE
1:10, 000
Port-au-Prince : Service de Géol.
et de Cart.
Areas published :
Vallée des Trois Rivières
Plaines des Moustiques
Plaine de la Coma
Plaine de Jean Rabel
2 colour series, uncontoured showing land boundaries.

HAITI — CARTE PLANIMÉTRIQUE
1:5, 000
Port-au-Prince : Service de Géol.
et de Cart.
Areas published :
Plaine des Cayres et de Torbeck
black and white 75 sheets.
Plaine des Gonaives
in 2 colours 32 sheets.
Preliminary series of plans contoured at 2m intervals.

729.5 Puerto Rico

B TOWN PLANS

MAP OF SAN JUAN AND VICINITY
1:20, 000
Washington : USGS, 1964
175 x 121
Topog. map, contoured with land detail.
$2.00

SAN JUAN
Detroit : Hearne Brothers
127 x 172
Shows all streets, principal public and social buildings, house numbering system. Mounted with mechanical index.
$152.50

C OFFICIAL SURVEYS

PUERTO RICO
1:20, 000
In 65 sheets see index 729. 5/1
Washington : USGS
Topog. series, contoured and considerable land detail. Some sheets show woodland in green.

ISLAND OF VICQUES, P.R.
1:30, 000
Washington : USGS, 1943-49
119 x 49
Topographical map with contours.
$1.00

CULEBRA AND ADJACENT ISLANDS, P.R.
1:30, 000
Washington : USGS, 1948
71 x 55
Topographical map with contours.
50c

D POLITICAL & ADMINISTRATIVE

PUERTO RICO AND ADJACENT ISLANDS BASE MAP
1:120, 000
Washington : USGS, 1951
167 x 81
Showing communications and settlements in black and water features in blue. Legend in Spanish.

PUERTO RICO AND ADJACENT ISLANDS BASE MAP
1:240, 000
Washington : USGS, 1951
137 x 55
Showing communications and settlements in black and water features in blue. Legend in Spanish.

E1 PHYSICAL : RELIEF

PLASTIC RELIEF MAP OF PUERTO RICO
1:250, 000
Washington : Defense Mapping Agency
52 x 73 each
Moulded relief map in 2 sheets, showing communications, boundaries and settlement.
$8.75

PUERTO RICO AND ADJACENT ISLANDS RELIEF MAP
1:240, 000
Washington : USGS, 1951
137 x 55
Graphic relief shading is superimposed on the topographical map.

PUERTO RICO AND ADJACENT ISLANDS TOPOGRAPHICAL MAP
1:240, 000
Washington : USGS, 1951
137 x 55
Contours overprinted on Base Map. Legend in Spanish.

PUERTO RICO AND ADJACENT ISLANDS TOPOGRAPHICAL MAP
1:120, 000
Washington : USGS, 1951
167 x 81
Contours overprinted on Base Map. Legend in Spanish.

F GEOLOGICAL

PROVISIONAL GEOLOGICAL MAP OF PUERTO RICO AND ADJACENT ISLANDS
1:240, 000
Misc. Geol. Inv. 1-392
Washington : USGS, 1964
140 x 81
Geol. shown in black and white. $1.00

PRELIMINARY TECTONIC MAP OF THE EASTERN GREATER ANTILLES REGION
1:500, 000
Misc. Geol. Inv. 1-732
by T. E. Garrison and others.
Washington : USGS, 1972
124 x 102
A preliminary tectonic map of Puerto Rico, the Virgin Islands and surrounding sub-sea areas. A residual magnetic anomaly map and a summary map of shipboard geophysical and bathymetric tracklines of the N.E. Caribbean region one inset.
US $0.75

GEOLOGIC MAP OF PUERTO RICO
1:20, 000
Misc. Geol. Inv. Series in 65 sheets see index 729. 5/1
Washington : USGS
Various sizes
Coloured geological series in progress.
$1.25 each

G EARTH RESOURCES

PUERTO RICO METALLOGENIC MAP
1:240, 000
Misc. Geol. Inv. 1-721
Washington : USGS, 1973
140 x 85
Coloured map showing mineral locations on a generalised geologic base.

729.61 Bahamas

A1 GENERAL MAPS

BAHAMA ISLANDS
1:2, 300, 000
DOS 954
Edition 1
Tolworth : DOS
Small hand map showing principal communications, boundaries, towns, villages 15p

B TOWN PLANS

NASSAU – NEW PROVIDENCE
1:2, 500
DOS 158 (E 819) in 12 sheets
Edition 1
Tolworth : DOS, 1963
Series of contoured plans covering the town and environs. 30p each

C OFFICIAL SURVEYS

BAHAMA ISLAND
1:25, 000
DOS 358 See indexed 729. 61/1
Edition 1
Tolworth : DOS, 1962
Various sizes
Topog. series, contours, land detail

E 815	New Providence Island	sheets 1 & 2
E 818	Cat Island	sheets 1-8
E 817	Eleuthera Island	sheets 1-8
E 811	Grand Bahama and Abaco	sheets 1-33

(uncontoured) 50p each

729.71 American Virgin Islands

See also : 729. 5 PUERTO RICO

C OFFICIAL SURVEYS

VIRGIN ISLANDS (US)
1:24, 000
Washington : USGS
Topographical series in col. with contours and land detail
St Croix — 3 sheets
St John — 2 sheets (East & West)
St Thomas — 3 sheets (East, Central, West)

F GEOLOGY

PRELIMINARY TECTONIC MAP OF THE EASTERN GREATER ANTILLES REGION
(Including Virgin Islands)
1:500, 000
USGS 1972
See PUERTO RICO 729.5 F

729.72 Leeward Islands

A1 GENERAL MAPS

LEEWARD ISLANDS
1:1. 000, 000
DOS 17/17
Tolworth : DOS
1948
Small hand map showing location of islands. 15p

C OFFICIAL SURVEYS

BRITISH VIRGIN ISLANDS
1:200, 000
DOS 997
Edition 2
Tolworth : DOS
1967
Col. hand map with layering 15p

VIRGIN ISLANDS
1:100, 000
DOS 546 (E633)
Edition 1
Tolworth : DOS, 1963
Contoured map in black and white. 50p

BRITISH VIRGIN ISLANDS
1:25, 000
DOS 346 (E837)
Edition 1
Tolworth : DOS
1959-74
Various sizes
1 Jost van Dyke
2 Tortola
3 Beef Island
4 Peter Island
5 Virgin Gorda
6 Anegada
Topog. series, contours, roads, boundaries, land detail. 50p each

RECONNAISSANCE GEOLOGY OF ANEGADA ISLAND
1:25, 000
Special Pub'n. No. 1
St. Thomas (U.S.V.I.) : Caribbean Research Inst., 1970
Coloured map with 19 pp text.

BEEF ISLAND (BRITISH VIRGIN ISLANDS)
1:5, 000
DOS (Misc) 67
Edition 1
Tolworth : DOS
1963
Topog. map of the island with contours. Black and white 20p

VIRGIN ISLANDS – TORTOLA
1:2, 500
DOS 146
Tolworth : DOS
1964
Black and white plans:
East End 2 sheets
Road Town 4 sheets
20p each

ANTIGUA
1:125, 000
DOS 993
Edition 2
Tolworth : DOS
1967
Small hand map showing principal communications, boundaries and settlements. 10p

ANTIGUA TOURIST MAP
1:50, 000
DOS 406 (E703)
Edition 3
Tolworth : DOS, 1975
Contoured map with communications and settlement. 65p

ANTIGUA
1:25, 000
DOS 306 (E843)
Edition 3
Tolworth : DOS
1961
Topog. map in 2 sheets, contours, communications, boundaries and land detail. 35p each

ANTIGUA
1:5, 000
DOS 106
Tolworth : DOS
1971
Contoured, topog. series in progress; covers Northern part of the island. 20p each

ANTIGUA
1:2, 500
DOS 006
Tolworth : DOS, 1970
Topog. series in progress covering Northern part of the island. 30p each

BARBUDA
1:25, 000
DOS 357 (E803) in 2 sheets
Tolworth : DOS
1970-71
Topographical map, contoured. 50p each

BARBUDA
1:10, 000
DOS 257 in 9 sheets
Tolworth : DOS
1970
Topog. map, contoured. 30p each

MONTSERRAT
1:50, 000
DOS 999
Edition 2
Tolworth : DOS, 1967
Small hand map showing roads, principal land detail. 15p

MONTSERRAT
1:25, 000
DOS 359 (E803)
Edition 2
Tolworth : DOS
1967
Topog. map, contours, roads, tracks. 50p

MONTSERRAT
1:2, 500
DOS 059
Edition 1
Tolworth : DOS
1970
Contoured series in progress, eastern side of the island only. 30p each

ST KITTS–NEVIS–ANGUILLA
1:127, 000
DOS 1000
Edition 1
Tolworth : DOS
1963
Col. hand map with hypsometric tinting. 15p

LESSER ANTILLES – ANGUILLA
1:50, 000
DOS 443
Tolworth : DOS
1974 50p
Contoured map.

ST KITTS–NEVIS–ANGUILLA
1:25, 000
DOS 343 (E848)
In 3 sheets
Edition 3 (Ed. 4 was UTM grid)
Tolworth : DOS
Various sizes.
Sheets:
1 Anguilla 1003 803 1973
2 St Christopher 1975
3 Nevis 1975
Topog, col, communications, boundaries, land detail. 50p each

ST CHRISTOPHER
1:2, 500
DOS 043
Tolworth : DOS
Contoured topo. series available as dyeline prints.
Sheets published:
Basseterre sheets 1, 2, 3, 4.
Paper dyeline, each 20p
Stable base dyeline, each 50p

NEVIS
1:2, 500
Tolworth : DOS, 1975
Topo. series, currently published for the Charleston area. Available as dyeline prints only.

F GEOLOGY

PRELIMINARY TECTONIC MAP OF THE EASTERN GREATER ANTILLES REGION
(Including Virgin Islands)
1:500, 000
USGS 1972
See PUERTO RICO 729.5 F

729.74 Guadeloupe and Dependencies

A1 GENERAL MAPS

CARTE TOURISTIQUE ET ROUTIÈRE DE LA GUADELOUPE
1:100, 000
Paris : IGN
1971
98 x 88
Relief shading, roads classified, distances in km. Topog. and tourist detail; inc. Iles des Saintes, Marie Galant, La Desirade, insets of St Martin (inc. Southern Dutch half) and Saint Barthelemy.
F. Fr. 10,00

C OFFICIAL SURVEYS

CARTE GÉNÉRALE DE LA GUADELOUPE
1:50, 000
In 6 sheets
See index 729. 74/1
Paris : IGN, 1969
71 x 81 each
Contoured, relief shading, roads classified, vegetation in green.
F. Fr. 11,67

CARTE GÉNÉRALE DE LA GUADELOUPE
1:20, 000
In 36 sheets
See index 729. 74/1
Paris : IGN, 1969
44 x 46 each
Contoured, vegetation detail in green, roads, railways, other land detail.
F. Fr. 11,67

D POLITICAL & ADMINISTRATIVE

GUADELOUPE ET DÉPENDANCES
1:117, 500
Paris : Forest
109 x 99
Wall map showing internal divisions, communications, settlements. Relief shown by hill shading.

E1 PHYSICAL : RELIEF

GUADELOUPE – CARTE EN RELIEF
1:100, 000
Paris : IGN, 1964
97 x 75
Raised plastic relief map based on Tourist Road map. Vertical scale 1. 5/1 with plastic frame.
F. Fr. 104.17

F GEOLOGY

CARTE GÉOLOGIQUE DE LA GUADELOUPE
1:50, 000
Orléans : BRGM
Geol. map with text, available in the following sheets:
La Guadeloupe – Grande Terre
1963 F.Fr. 30.00
La Guadeloupe – Basse Terre
(N & S sheets on 1 map)
1965 F.Fr. 50.00
Saint Martin and Saint Barthélemy
1965 F.Fr. 30.00
Marie-Galante et la Desirade
1965 F.Fr. 30.00

729.81 Martinique

A1 GENERAL MAPS

CARTE TOURISTIQUE
1:100, 000
Paris : IGN
1972
53 x 64
Relief shown by shading, spot heights, roads classified, distances in km. vegetation, topog. and tourist detail.
F. Fr. 10,00

B TOWN PLANS

FORT DE FRANCE ET ENVIRONS
1:10, 000
Paris : IGN
1955
80 x 65
Plan of the town, contours, inset of town centre, index to streets.
F. Fr. 11,67

C OFFICIAL SURVEYS

CARTE GÉNÉRALE DE LA MARTINIQUE
1:50, 000
In 4 sheets
See index 729. 81/1
Paris : IGN , 1957
108 x 70
Contours, relief shading, roads classified, woodland, other topog. detail.
F. Fr. 11,67

CARTE GÉNÉRALE DE LA MARTINIQUE
1:20, 000
In 23 sheets
See index 729. 81/1
Paris : IGN, 1951-54
48 x 46
Contoured, roads classified, woodland, other topog. detail F. Fr. 11,67

E1 PHYSICAL MAPS : RELIEF

MARTINIQUE
1:100, 000
Paris : IGN, 1957
69 x 59
Raised plastic relief map based on tourist map mentioned above. Vertical scale 1.5/1. with plastic frame.
F. Fr. 104,17

F GEOLOGY

CARTE GÉOLOGIQUE DE LA MARTINIQUE
1:50, 000
by H. Grunevald
Orléans : BRGM, 1962
Col. geological map in 2 sheets with text.
Flat. F.Fr. 50.00

729.82 British Windward Islands

A1 GENERAL MAPS

WINDWARD ISLANDS
1:2, 500, 000
DOS 17/36
Edition 1
Tolworth : DOS
1948
Small hand map showing relative locations of islands in group.
15p

B TOWN PLANS

DOMINICA – ROSEAU AND ENVIRONS
1:5, 000
DOS 151
Tolworth : DOS 1974
Contoured plan of the town.
65p

C OFFICIAL SURVEYS

Barbados

BARBADOS
1:250, 000
DOS 955
Edition 2
Tolworth : DOS
1956
Small hand map showing principal communications and settlements.
15p

BARBADOS
1:50, 000
DOS 418 (E749)
Edition 2
Tolworth : DOS
1974
Topog. map contoured, roads, boundaries, other land detail.
50p

BARBADOS
1:10, 000
DOS 18 (E8412)
In 18 sheets
See index 729. 82/1
Edition 1
Tolworth : DOS
1954-56
Various sizes
Relief shown by contours, boundaries, roads, other land detail.
50p each

BARBADOS – BRIDGETOWN
1:1, 250
DOS 0018
Tolworth : DOS
Large scale planimetric series with contours, available as dyeline copies only.
Paper 20p
Stable base 50p

Dominica

DOMINICA
1:122, 500
DOS 998
Edition 1
Tolworth : DOS
1964
Hand map showing communications, boundaries and settlement. 15p

DOMINICA
1:50, 000
DOS 451 (E703)
Edition 1
Tolworth : DOS
1963
Topog. map, contoured, hill shaded, roads, other land detail. 65p

DOMINICA
1:50, 000
DOS (Misc.) 228
Edition 1
Tolworth : DOS
1957
Black and white base map. 30p

DOMINICA
1:25, 000
DOS 351 (E847)
In 3 sheets
Edition 1
Tolworth : DOS
1960
Topog. map showing roads, boundaries, other land detail. 50p

DOMINICA
1:2, 500
DOS 051
Tolworth : DOS, 1974 –
Contoured series for urban areas. Available as dyeline prints only.

Grenada

GRENADA
1:100, 000
DOS 995
Edition 2
Tolworth : DOS
1965
Small hand map showing principal communications, boundaries and settlement. 15p

GRENADA
1:50, 000
DOS 442 (E703)
Edition 1
Tolworth : DOS
1966
Topog. map, contours, hill shaded, roads and other land detail. 65p

GRENADA
1:25, 000
DOS 342 (E844)
Edition 2
Tolworth : DOS
1962
Topog. map in 2 sheets, contoured, roads and other land detail. 50p each

GRENADINES
1:25, 000
DOS 344 (E802)
In 6 sheets
Edition 1
Tolworth : DOS
1968-69
Topog. series contoured 50p each

GRENADINES
1:10, 000
DOS 244 (E802)
In 16 sheets
Edition 1
Tolworth : DOS
1967-69
Topog. series, contoured 50p each

Saint Lucia

SAINT LUCIA
1:120, 000
DOS 945
Edition 1
Tolworth : DOS
1967
Small hand map showing principal communications, boundaries and settlement, layer coloured. 15p

SAINT LUCIA
1:50, 000
DOS 445
Edition 1
Tolworth : DOS
1964
Topog. map, contoured, hill shaded, roads and other land detail. 50p

SAINT LUCIA
1:25, 000
DOS 345 (E803)
In 3 sheets
Edition 3
Tolworth : DOS
1972
Topog. map, contoured, roads, boundaries and other land detail. 50p each

Saint Vincent

SAINT VINCENT
1:40, 000
DOS 994
Edition 1
Tolworth : DOS
1960
Small hand map in black and white. 15p

SAINT VINCENT
1:50, 000
DOS 417 (E 703)
Edition 4
Tolworth : DOS
1968
Topog. map, contoured, roads and other land detail.
65p

SAINT VINCENT
1:25, 000
DOS 317 (E803)
Edition 3
Tolworth : DOS
1973
Topog. map in 2 sheets, contoured, hill shaded, roads, boundaries and other land detail. 50p each

ST VINCENT
1:2, 500
DOS 017
Tolworth : DOS, 1975 –
Large scale planimetric series in progress. Available as dyeline prints.

G EARTH RESOURCES

DOMINICA
1:25, 000
DOS 3140
Tolworth : DOS 1972
Series of 3 maps each in 3 sheets.
A Soils
B Interim Land Capability
C Forest Management

729.87 Trinidad and Tobago

A1 GENERAL MAPS

TRINIDAD
1:500. 000
DOS 17/33
Edition 1
Tolworth : DOS
1948
Small hand map showing principal communications, boundaries and settlement. 15p

TRINIDAD
1:150, 000
Port of Spain : Land & Surveys Dept., 1973
Contoured, layer coloured.

B TOWN PLANS

PORT OF SPAIN
1:10, 000
Port of Spain : Lands & Surveys Dept., 1973
Coloured plan of the town.

C OFFICIAL SURVEYS

TRINIDAD
1:25, 000
DOS 316 (E803)
In 27 sheets
See index 729. 87/1
Edition 1
Tolworth : DOS
1964-66
84 x 60 each
Topog. series of which 4 sheets covering central part of the island are published, contoured, boundaries, land detail. To be replaced by series DOS 316/1. 50p

TRINIDAD
1:25, 000
DOS 316/1 (E804)
See index 729. 87/1
Edition 1
Tolworth : DOS
1970 –
86 x 68 average
Topog. series in progress, contoured, land detail, UTM grid. To replace DOS series 316. 50p each

TRINIDAD
1:10, 000
76 sheets
See index 729. 87/1
Port of Spain : Land and Surveys Dept.
Cadastral series showing land boundaries and settlement. Covering northern half of the country only.
Available as dyeline copies only.

TRINIDAD
1:10, 000
DOS 216 (E8413)
See index 729. 87/1
Edition 1
Tolworth : DOS
1964-66
Planimetric series in progress currently published for central region only. 50p

TOBAGO
1:50, 000
Port of Spain : Land & Surveys Dept., 1973
Contoured and layer coloured.

TOBAGO
1:25, 000
DOS 307 (E8410)
In 3 sheets
See index 729. 87/1
Edition 1
Tolworth : DOS
1962-63
Topog. map, contoured, boundaries, land detail. 50p each

TOBAGO
1:10, 000
DOS 207
In 19 sheets
See index 729. 87/1
Edition 1
Tolworth : DOS
1962-63
Topog. map covering the island. 50p

F GEOLOGY

GEOLOGICAL MAP OF TRINIDAD
1:100, 000
Prep. H. G. Kugler
Pointe-a-Pierre : Texaco Trinidad Inc.
118 x 91
Geol. map in col, indicating mud, volcano and asphalt flows with separate sheet showing 7 col, geol. sections through Trinidad (90 x 77). set £2.00

G EARTH RESOURCES

SOIL MAP OF CENTRAL TRINIDAD
1:50, 000
DOS (Misc) 55
In 4 sheets
Edition 1
Tolworth : DOS
1954
Map in col. showing locations of principal soil groups. 50p

729.88 Netherlands Antilles

C OFFICIAL SURVEYS

ARUBA
1:25, 000
In 4 sheets
Delft : TD, 1960-61
48 x 48 each
Topographical map, contoured and land detail. set Fl. 21.00

SABA
1:10, 000
Delft : TD, 1963
50 x 60
Topographical map, contoured and land detail. Fl. 7.55

ST EUSTATIUS
1:10, 000
Delft : TD, 1963
70 x 80
Topographical map, contoured and land detail. Fl. 7.55

ST MAARTEN
1:25, 000
Delft : TD, 1966
60 x 80
Relief, communications, boundaries, land detail. Also covering the French portion of the island. Legend in English and Dutch. Fl. 7.55

ÎLE ST MARTIN
1:50, 000 and 1:20, 000
IGN
see 729. 74 Guadeloupe

729.9 Bermuda

A1 GENERAL MAPS

BERMUDA
1:150, 000
DOS 956
Edition 4
Tolworth : DOS
1971
20 x 17
General map showing boundaries, roads, railways and principal landmarks. 15p

BERMUDA TOURIST MAP
1:31, 680
DOS 411
Tolworth : DOS, 1970
92 x 70
Col. map showing relief, hill shading, feaures of tourist interest, parish boundaries. 65p

C OFFICIAL SURVEYS

BERMUDA
1:10, 560
DOS 311 (E8110)
In 6 sheets
See index 729. 9/1
Edition 1
Tolworth : DOS
1975
104 x 74 each
Detailed topog. plan of islands, field boundaries, sketch contours inc. in black and white 50p each

BERMUDA
1:2, 500
DOS 111 (E811)
In 74 sheets
See index 729. 9/1
Edition 1
Tolworth : DOS
1975
Large scale topog. series, contoured, land boundaries. 50p each

M HISTORICAL

EARLY MAP REPRODUCTIONS FROM BLAEU'S ATLAS NOVUS
– BERMUDA 1635
Edinburgh : Bart
61 x 51
Coloured reproduction £1.50

73 United States of America

See also : 7 NORTH AMERICA

A1 GENERAL MAPS : ROADS

VACATION LANDS – US AND SOUTHERN CANADA
1:5, 062, 375
NGS
See NORTH AMERICA 7 A1

CHAMPION MAP OF THE UNITED STATES
1:3, 400, 000
Charlotte : Champion Map Corpn, 1969
145 x 94
Map showing US and Interstate highways, with Alaska, Hawaii, Canal Zone, Puerto Rico and Virgin Islands inset.

UNITED STATES OF AMERICA – FEDERAL AID HIGHWAYS
1:3, 168, 000
Washington : Govt. Printing Office, 1970
162 x 106
Shows : National System of Interstate and Defense Highways, the Federal-Aid Primary Highway System and the US numbered Highway System. In col. with park areas. Inset of Alaska, Canal Zone, Hawaii, Puerto Rico and Virgin Islands. S1.50

CANADA AND NORTHERN UNITED STATES HIGHWAY MAP
1:2, 875, 000
Canadian Government Travel Bureau, 1971
see CANADA 73 A1

POCKET REFERENCE MAPS
1: 880, 000
Chicago : Rand McNally
Various sizes
Showing main and other roads, parks, airports, places of interest, mileage chart,
Available for individual states :
Alabama
Alaska
Arizona
Arkansas
California
Colorado
Connecticut and Rhode Island
Florida
Georgia
Hawaii
Idaho
Illinois
Indiana
Iowa
Kansas
Kentucky
Louisiana
Maine
Maryland and Delaware
Massachusetts
Michigan
Minnesota
Mississippi
Missouri
Montana
Nebraska
Nevada
New Hampshire
New Jersey
New Mexico
New York
North Carolina
North Dakota
Ohio
Oklahoma
Oregon
Pennsylvania
South Carolina
South Dakota
Tennessee
Texas
Utah
Vermont
Virginia
Washington
West Virginia
Wisconsin
Wyoming

NORTHERN AND SOUTHERN CALIFORNIA
1:1, 637, 500
Washington : NGS
50 x 38
Tourist map printed on both sides.
Insets of principal city and park areas. $1.00

ROAD MAP OF FAIRFIELD COUNTY
New York : Hagstrom
Coloured road map with distances and route numbers.

ROAD MAP OF LONG ISLAND
New York : Hagstrom
81 x 81
Col. road map with distances and route numbers. $0.95

ROAD MAP OF NEW JERSEY
New York : Hagstrom
61 x 111
Col. road map with distances and route numbers. $0.95

ROAD MAP OF WESTCHESTER COUNTY
New York : Hagstrom
55 x 86
Col. road map with distances and route numbers. $1.25

A2 GENERAL MAPS : LOCAL

ROUND ABOUT THE NATION'S CAPITAL
1:562, 500
Washington : NGS
86 x 73
Col. wall map, boundaries in colour.
Paper $2.00
Plastic $3.00

NEW YORK AND ENVIRONS
No scale given
No. 140591-14
Chicago : Denoyer-Geppert
111 x 142
Spring rollers $27.00

APOLLO & PHOTOMAPS OF THE WEST-EAST CORRIDOR FROM THE PACIFIC OCEAN TO NORTHERN LOUISIANA
1:500, 000 app.
In 4 sheets
Washington : USGS, 1970
130 x 48 each
Set $1.50

GREAT SALT LAKE, UTAH
by Deon C Creer
1:125, 000
Florida : AAG, 1971
With inset of fluctuations in lake level from 1851 – 1970.
$3.00

NATIONAL MONUMENTS
Various scales
Washington : USGS
Topog. maps, contoured. Other National Monument sites are shown on standard topog. series sheets.
Maps available:
Bandelier NM (N Mex)
1:24, 000 1953 107 x 134
contoured or shaded relief edition
$1.50
Badlands N M (S Dak)
1:62, 500 1960 121 x 111
Black Canyon of the Gunnison N M (Colo)
1:24, 000 1934-50 58 x 76
contoured or shaded relief edition
50c each
Canyon de Chelley N M (Ariz)
1:48, 000 1938 76 x 91
Grand Canyon N M (Ariz)
1:48, 000 1936 83 x 106
Cedar Breaks N M (Utah)
1:15, 840 1936 43 x 53
contoured or relief edition 50c
Colonial N M (Yorktown Battlefield)
1:9, 600 1931 73 x 76 $1.00
Craters of the Moon NM (Idaho)
1:31, 680 1925-57 61 x 84 $1.00
Custer Battlefield N M (Mont)
1:24, 000 1891 48 x 55
Devils Tower N M (Wyo)
1:4, 800 1933-49 55 x 55
contoured or shaded relief edition
50c each
Dinosaur N M (Utah-Colo)
1:62, 500 1973 76 x 129
contoured or relief edition. $1.75
Great Sand Dunes N M (Colo)
1:24, 000 1972 71 x 83
contoured or shaded relief edition
$1.50 each
Scotts Bluff N M (Nebr)
1:15, 840 1939 43 x 53
contoured or shaded relief edition 50c

MOUNT McKINLEY – A RECONNAISSANCE TOPOGRAPHIC MAP
1:50, 000
Zurich : Swiss Foundation for Alpine Research, 1960
76 x 77
Graphically presented relief map of this glacial region, contoured, relief shaded with spot heights, also showing moss or grassland in green.

MT KENNEDY
1:31, 650
Washington : NGS
Topog. chart showing vertical data, mean sea level, contours at 100ft intervals.

B TOWN PLANS

TOWN PLANS
Various scales Boston : Arrow Maps inc.
Plans available:

Alabama
 Gadsden, Hamilton, Huntsville, Mobile, Muscle, Shoals, Tuscaloosa, Birmingham
Alaska
 Anchorage
Arizona
 Phoenix, Tucson
California
 Bakersfield, Carmichael/Fair Oaks, Eureka, Lake Tahoe, Lancaster/Palmdale, Los Angeles, Merced, Monterey/Salinas, Oakland/San Francisco, Ontario/Pomona, Redding/Red Buff, Roseville/Orangeville, Sacramento, San Bernardino/Riverside, San Francisco, Santa Barbara, Stockton, Vallejo, Ventura, Visalia and Tulare
Colorado
 Boulder, Colorado Springs, Denver, Atlas
Connecticut
 Berlin, Branford, Bristol, Hamden, Hartford, Hartford Atlas, Manchester, Middleton, New Haven, New London, Newtown, Waterbury, Westport
Delaware
 Dover, Wilmington
Florida
 Daytona Beach, Florida East Coast, Fort Myers, Jacksonville, Key West, Manhattan, Miami, Naples, Orlando, Panama City, Pensacola, Port Charlotte
Georgia
 Albany, Athens, Atlanta, Augusta, Columbus, Rome, Savannah, Deklab
Hawaii
 Hawaii
Illinois
 Aurora, Bloomington, Carbondale, Champaign-Urbana, Chicago North Suburban, Chicago West Suburban, Danville, Decatur, East Lake County, Elgin, Freeport, Hinsdale, Quad Cities, Rockford, Springfield
Indiana
 Anderson, Bloomington, Elkhart, Evansville, Fort Wayne, Gary, Hammond, Kokomo, Lafayette, La Porte, Muncie, Porter, Richmond, South Bend/Mishawaka, South Bend/Elkhart Atlas, Indianapolis Atlas
Iowa
 Cedar Rapids, Davenport/Quad Cities, Des Moines, Dubuque, Fort Dodge, Sioux City, Waterloo, West Union, Iowa City.
Kansas
 Hutchinson, Wichita
Kentucky
 Ashland, Hopkinsville, Lexington, Murray, Paducan, Princetown, Winchester
Louisiana
 Baton Rouge, New Orleans
Maine
 Portland
Maryland
 Annapolis, Baltimore Atlas, Frederick
Massachusetts
 Attleboro, Boston, Boston Atlas Boston Souvenir, Boston Transit, Brockton, Danvers, Fan River, Framingham, Lowell, Lynn, Lynnfield, Newton, Salem, South Shore, Springfield, Taunton, Waltham, Wellesley, Western Massachusetts Atlas, Worcester, Worcester Atlas
Michigan
 Ann Arbor, Bray City, Detroit, Flint, Jackson, Kalamazoo, Lansing, Midland, Saginaw
Minnesota
 Duluth, Rochester
Mississippi
 Belzoni, Gulfport, Jackson
Missouri
 Joplin, Poplar Bluff, St Joseph
Montana
 Kalispell
Nebraska
 Beatrice, Grand Island, Lincoln, Omaha
Nevada
 Lake Tahoe, Las Vegas, Reno
New Hampshire
 Manchester, Nashua, Newmarket, Plaistow
New Jersey
 Asbury Park, Caldwell, Livingston, Middletown, Red Bank, Trenton, New Brunswick
New Mexico
 Albuquerque
New York
 Albany, Auburn, Beacon, Buffalo, Buffalo Atlas, Catskill, Goshen, Poughkeepsie, Rochester, Rochester Atlas, Rockland, Syracuse, Syracuse Atlas, Utika, Watertown
North Carolina
 Asheville, Charlotte, Durham, Fayetteville, Greensboro, Rocky Mount, Winston, Salem
Ohio
 Akron, Canton, Canton Atlas, Cincinnati, Cincinnati Atlas,Cleveland, Cleveland Atlas, Columbus, Columbus Atlas, Dayton, Lima, Mansfield, Middletown, Portsmouth, Sandusky, Springfield, Stevbenville
Oklahoma
 Oklahoma City, Tulsa
Oregon
 Coos Bay, Eugene, Medford, Portland, Salem, Springfield
Pennsylvania
 Allentown, Easton, Harrisburg, Hazelton, Johnstown, Lancaster, Lebanon, McKeesport, Meadville, Monesson, Norristown, Oil City, Pittsburgh, Reading, Scranton, Wilkes Barre, Williamsport, York, Erie
Rhode Island
 Pawtucket, Providence, Rhode Island Cities Atlas
South Carolina
 Charleston, Columbia, Greensville, Spartanburg
Tennessee
 Crossville, Knoxville, Maryville, Murfreesboro, Nashville
Texas
 Abilene, Austin, Beaumont, Bryan, Dallas, El Paso, Fort Worth, Galveston, Harlingen, Houston, Orange, San Angelo, San Antonio, Temple, Wichita Falls
Virginia
 Charlottesville, Danville, Richmond
Washington
 Everett, Longview, Olympia, Pasco, Seattle, Spokane, Walla Walla, Wenatchee
West Virginia
 Charleston, Clarksburg, Parkersburg, Wheeling
Wisconsin
 Appleton, Kenosha, Milwaukee, Racine, Wausau

STREET MAPS
New York : Hagstrom
Coloured plans with street index.
Maps available:

Connecticut	
Bridgeport	$1.25
Greenwich	$1.25
Norwalk, Darien and New Canaan	.95
New Haven County (upper)	$1.50
New Haven County (lower)	$1.50
Stamford	.95
Upper Fairfield County	$1.95
Westport, Fairfield and Sections Weston, Wilton	.95
Long Island	
Babylon	$1.00
Brookhaven	$1.50
Nassau County	$1.50
New Jersey	
Bergen County	$1.95
Elizabeth — Linden — Roselle — Roselle Pk.	.95
Essex County	$1.95
Hudson County	$1.95
Jersey City & Hoboken	$1.25
Mercer County	$1.95
Middlesex County	$1.95
Monmouth County	$1.95
Morris County	$1.95
Newark	$1.25
New Brunswick	.95
Ocean County	$1.95
Passaic County	$1.95
Paterson, Clifton and Passaic	.95
Somerset County	$1.95
Union County	$1.95
New York City	
Bronx	.95
Brooklyn	$1.00

Five Boros (unmounted)	$39.25
Five Boros (mounted)	$70.00
New York City (Manhattan)	.95
Midtown	.75
New York Bus Routes	.95
New York Subways	.95
Queens	$1.00
Richmond(Staten Is)	.95
25 Mile Radius	.95
50 Mile Radius	.95
Philadelphia	
Philadelphia-Camden	$1.50
Westchester & Rockland	
Rockland County	$1.95
Westchester, Upper	$1.95
Lower	$1.50
White Plains	.95
Yonkers	.95

TOWN PLANS
Various scales
Fort Lauderdale : Dolph Map Co.
Plans available:
Alabama
- Anniston
- Birmingham
- Decatur
- Gadsden
- Hunstville
- Montgomery
- Phoenix City
- Tuscaloosa

Arkansas
- El Dorado
- Fayetteville
- Fort Smith
- Little Rock
- Pine Bluff

Florida
- Bradenton
- Broward County
- Cocoa
- Daytona Beach
- Fort Lauderdale
- Fort Myers
- Fort Pierce
- Gainesville
- Hollywood
- Jacksonville
- Lakeland
- Miami & Miami Beach
- Ocala
- Orlando
- Naples
- Palm Beaches & Lake Worth
- Panama City
- Sarasota
- Sebring
- St Petersburg & Clearwater
- Tallahassee
- Tampa & Environs

Georgia
- Albany
- Atlanta
- Augusta
- Brunswick
- Columbus
- Decatur
- De Kalb County
- Macon
- Savannah
- Valdosta
- Waycross

Kansas
- Wichita

Louisiana
- Alexandria & Pineville
- Baton Rouge
- Lake Charles
- Leesville & DeRidder
- Shreveport

Maryland
- Baltimore

Mississippi
- Gulfport & Biloxi
- Jackson

Oklahoma
- Tulsa

Pennsylvania
- New Kensington

South Carolina
- Aiken
- Charleston
- Columbia
- Florence
- Greenville
- Spartanburg

Tennessee
- Knoxville

Texas
- Amarillo
- Arlington
- Austin
- Beaumont & Pt Arthur
- Big Spring
- Fort Worth
- Galveston
- Houston
- Lubbock
- Midland
- Odessa
- Waco

Virginia
- Danville
- Lynchburg
- Newport News
- Norfolk & Virginia Beach
- Petersburg
- Richmond
- Roanoke
- Williamsburg

Washington DC

TOURIST MANHATTAN, GREATER NY
Washington : NGS
50 x 38
Tourist map with index, printed on both sides. $1.00

FALK TOWN PLANS
Various scales
Hamburg : Falk Verlag
Col. plans with patent folding system.
Plans available:

New York & 5 Boroughs	
1:7, 500 – 17, 800	9.80 DM
St. Louis	
1:24, 000 – 28, 000	9.80 DM

METROGRID GUIDE TO NEW YORK (MINIPLANS)
1:15, 000 approx.
London : Miniplans
56 x 34
Col. plan with index of Southern Manhattan 27½p

NEW YORK
Nr. 40
Braunschweig : Bollmann
Bildkarten, 1962
54 x 68
Pictorial city plan in col. Shows roads with individual buildings drawn from an oblique view.

Folded	5.50 DM
On Hand Made Paper	12.00 DM

BOROUGH MAP OF NEW YORK CITY
No scale
No 107591-14
Chicago : Denoyer-Geppert
101 x 137
Wall map showing roads and admin. boundaries.
Spring Rollers $19.25

NEW YORK
1:40, 000
Braunschweig : Westermann
110 x 140
Col. wall plan of New York, with Manhattan inset.

THE NATION'S CAPITAL – WASHINGTON DC
1:36, 000
Washington : D.C. Dept., of Highways & Traffic, 1973
Street plan of District of Columbia with central Washington on reverse.

C OFFICIAL SURVEYS

KARTA MIRA
1:2, 500, 000
Cart.
9 sheets required for full coverage
See WORLD 100C and index 100/2.

USA TOPOGRAPHIC SERIES
1:1, 000, 000
See index 73/1
Washington : USGS
71 x 81 each
Topog. series showing main and secondary roads, railways, canals, contours, and altitude tints. Some sheets in International Map of the World edition, others in AMS editions not fully meeting IMW specifications.

USA TOPOGRAPHIC SERIES
1:250, 000
In 472 sheets, See index 73/2
Washington : USGS
66 x 44 each
Topog. series showing main and other roads, railways, airfields, spot heights in ft, contours at 100ft intervals, and international and state boundaries.

USA TOPOGRAPHIC SERIES
1:125, 000
Washington : USGS
Pub. for certain areas only and are to be replaced by the larger scale 7½' and 15' series. Contoured, communications, boundaries, topog. detail. Shown on topographic map index diagrams for individual states.

USA TOPOGRAPHIC SERIES
1:62, 500
Washington : USGS
44 x 58
Quadrangles covering 15 minutes of latitude and longitude covering certain areas only. Printed in 3 colours with roads, railroads, cities and towns in black, water features in blue, and relief features and contours in brown. Detailed index diagrams are available for each individual state.

USA TOPOGRAPHIC SERIES
1:24, 000
Washington : USGS
44 x 58 each
Quadrangles covering 7½ minutes of latitude and longitude covering certain areas only. Printed in 3 colours with roads, railroads, cities and towns in black, water detail in blue and relief features and contours in brown. Detailed index diagrams are available for each individual state.

SPECIAL MAPS
Various scales
Washington : USGS
Individual topog. maps, supplementary to standard topog. series covering river basins, damsites, reservoirs etc, many with profile diagrams.
Maps available:

ALASKA

Anchor River and Halibut Creek
1:4, 800 – 1:2, 400 – 1:24, 000
55 x 76 1971

Baranof Lake and Carbon Lake
1:24, 000 55 x 71 1956
2 sheets

Bradley River and Bradley Lake
1:24, 000 55 x 71 1955
2 sheets

Cascade Creek and vicinity
1:24, 000 76 x 101 1950

Chakachatna River and Chakachamna Lake
1:24, 000 55 x 71 1960
2 sheets

Chilkoot Lake
1:24, 000 55 x 71 1956

Cooper Lake
1:24, 000 55 x 71 1950

Crater Lake & Long Lake
1:24, 000 – 1:4, 800
2 sheets 55 x 71 1951

Crescent Lake
1:24, 000 55 x 71 1951

Deer Lake
1:24, 000 55 x 71 1957

Duck River and Silver Lake
1:24, 000 55 x 71 1957

Eagle River
1:24, 000 55 x 71 1949

Eklutna Lake
1:12, 000 55 x 71 1947
3 sheets

Grant Creek and Lake
1:24, 000 55 x 71 1950

Juneau Lake
1:24, 000 55 x 71 1953

Kasilof River
1:24, 000 55 x 71 1953

Kashyku Lake
1:24, 000 55 x 71 1957

Kenai River (Moose River – Skilak Lake)
1:24, 000 55 x 71 1954

Kenai River (Skilak Lake – Kenai Lake and damsite)
1:24, 000 55 x 71 1953
2 sheets

Lost Lake
1:24, 000 55 x 71 1955

Lowe River
1:24, 000 55 x 71 1957

Misc. damsites including Tanana River, Chackaloon River and Carter Lake
1:9, 600 – 1:4, 800
55 x 71 1956

Nellie Juan Lake
1:24, 000
2 sheets 55 x 73 1964

Nenana River reservoir site
1:24, 000 55 x 71 1949

Olive Kunk and Anita Lakes
1:12, 000 55 x 73 1960

Power Creek
1:24, 000 55 x 71 1948

Ptarmigan Lake
1:24, 000 55 x 71 1951

Scenery Creek and Lake
1:24, 000 55 x 71 1949

Seldoria River and Lake
1:24, 000 55 x 71 1953

Sheep Creek and Carlson Creek
1:24, 000 55 x 71 1952

Ship Creek
1:24, 000 55 x 71 1949

Snow River
1:24, 000 55 x 71 1956
2 sheets

Spiridon Lake
1:24, 000 55 x 71 1961

Sweetheart Lakes
1:24, 000 55 x 71 1958

Takatz Creek and Lake
1:24, 000 55 x 71 1957

Tazlina River and Klutina River
1:4, 800 – 1:2, 400
55 x 76 1971

Terror Lake
1:24, 000 55 x 71 1961

Umiat Special
1:62, 500 43 x 68 1946

Valdez and vicinity No 29
1:62, 500 71 x 81 1911-16
(contoured or relief editions)

Virginia Lake
1:24, 000 55 x 71 1958

ARIZONA

Black Creek
1:24, 000 55 x 71 1937
2 sheets

Bright Angel
1:62, 500 43 x 53 1937
(contoured or relief editions)

Colorado & San Juan Rivers
1:31, 680 53 x 68 1921
22 sheets

Gila River (Butter damsite to Coolidge Dam)
1:31, 680 55 x 71 1935
3 sheets

Gila River (Brown Canal Intake to Virden)
1:31, 680 55 x 71 1935-41
2 sheets

Little Colorado River (Mouth to Tolchio damsite)
1:31, 680 53 x 68 1926
5 sheets

Little Colorado River (Tolchio damsite to Lyman Res.)
1:31, 680 55 x 71 1934
18 sheets

Phoenix Space Photo Map (experimental)
1:250, 000 61 x 86 1969

Salt River
1:31, 680 53 x 63 1916-32
10 sheets

Williams River
1:31, 680 53 x 68 1934
9 sheets

CALIFORNIA

Cache Creek
1:31, 680 55 x 71 1936
3 sheets

Carson River
1:31, 680 55 x 71 1934
10 sheets

Central Valley
1:250, 000 101 x 121 1957
2 sheets

Deer Creek
1:31, 680 53 x 68 1932
3 sheets

Fresno River
1:24, 000 55 x 71 1947
3 sheets

Kaweah River
1:24, 000 55 x 66 1957
4 sheets

Kern River
1:31, 680 55 x 71 1934
7 sheets

Kings River
1:24, 000 55 x 71 1936-52
12 sheets

Klamatu River
1:24, 000 55 x 71 1955
18 sheets

McCloud River
1:24, 000 55 x 71 1954
6 sheets

Naval Petroleum Reserve No. 1
1:31, 680 50 x 94 1927

New River
1:24, 000 55 x 71 1951

North Fork Trinity River
1:24, 000 55 x 71 1951
3 sheets

North Yuba River
1:24, 000 55 x 71 1955
2 sheets

Sacramento River
1:24, 000 55 x 71 1954

San Francisco Bay Region
1:125, 000 91 x 106 & 106 x 119
3 sheets 1970

San Francisco Bay region slope map
1:125, 000 91 x 111 1972
(cont. overprint on map above)

Smith River
1:2, 400 55 x 73 1960
2 sheets

South Fork Trinity River
1:24, 000 55 x 66 1951
10 sheets

Stanislaus River
1:24, 000 55 x 71 1958
10 sheets

Trinity River
1:31, 680 55 x 73 1936-46
9 sheets

Yosemite Valley
1:24,000 48 x 106 1958-70
(cont. or relief)
Yuba River
1:31,680 55 x 71 1935
12 sheets
COLORADO
Alta Basin and vicinity
1:12,000 63 x 89 1936
Arkansas River
1:24,000 55 x 73 1955
10 sheets
Colorado River
1:24,000 55 x 71 1950
2 sheets
Colorado River (from mile 987-1076)
1:24,000 55 x 71 1944
14 sheets
Eagle River
1:24,000 55 x 71 1949
7 sheets
Elk River & Middle Fork Little Snake River
1:12,000 55 x 71 1963
Fryingpan Creek
1:31,680 55 x 71 1934
sheets
Henson Creek
1:24,000 55 x 71 1950
King Solomon Creek
1:12,000 55 x 71 1963
Miscellaneous damsites, Colorado River drainage basin (Buford, Red Wash, Mt Sopris, Redstone, Camp Hale, Iron Mt)
1:9,600 – 1:4,800
55 x 71 1959
Navajo River
1:24,000 55 x 71 1955-57
6 sheets
Owens Creek reservoir site
1:24,000 50 x 55 1936
San Juan River
1:31,680 55 x 71 1934
3 sheets
Tenmile district
1:31,680 46 x 53 1882
Tenmile mining district
1:12,000 83 x 101 1927-40
2 sheets
Whitewater Reservoir site
1:24,000 55 x 71 1947
2 sheets
Yampa River (mouth to Elk River)
1:31,680 55 x 68 1939
5 sheets
Yampa River (Green River to Morgan Gulch)
1:31,680 53 x 68 1922
5 sheets
DISTRICT OF COLUMBIA
Washington and vicinity
1:24,000 127 x 170 1965
GEORGIA
Cartersville Mining District
1:62,500 30 x 51 1941
HAWAII
Kauai (Island)
1:62,500 109 x 83 1910
Lanai (Island)
1:62,500 58 x 50 1923
Maui (Island)
1:62,500 143 x 101 1957
(cont. or relief eds)
Molokai (Island)
1:62,500 119 x 53 1952
(cont. or relief eds)

Niihau (Island)
1:62,500 55 x 48 1926
Oahu (Island)
1:62,500 94 x 121 1954
(cont. or relief eds)
IDAHO
Bear Creek
1:24,000
incl. damsite
1:2,400 56 x 71 1962 50c
Bennett Creek
1:24,000 56 x 71 1939 50c
Clark Fort
1:31,680 56 x 71 1912
5 sheets 50c each
Coeur d'Alene River
1:31,680 56 x 71 1939
6 sheets 50c each
Devil and Deep Creeks
1:31,680 56 x 71 1939
3 sheets 50c each
Dry Creek area
1:24,000 43 x 51 1946
East Fork, Salmon River (damsites)
1:2,400 56 x 71 1960
East Fork and Yankee Fork, Salmon River (damsites)
1:2,400 56 x 71 1960 50c
King Hill Area
1:24,000 56 x 71 1946 50c
Kootenai River (lower)
1:12,000 56 x 71 1928
9 sheets 50c each
Kootenai River (upper)
1:31,680 56 x 71 1934
9 sheets 50c each
Lemhi River
1:24,000 56 x 74 1958
5 sheets 50c each
Little Eightmile Mining District
1:48,000 33 x 53 50c
Little Weiser River
1:12,000 56 x 71 1963
(damsite 1:2,400) 50c
Mann Creek
1:31,680 56 x 71 1936 50c
Mission Creek
1:24,000 56 x 71 1939 50c
Moyie River
1:31,680 56 x 71 1935
3 sheets 50c each
Payette River
1:31,680 53 x 69 1925
7 sheets 50c
Pend Orielle River
1:31,680 56 x 71 1934 50c
Priest River
1:31,680 56 x 71 1934
5 sheets 50c each
Rush Creek
1:31,680 56 x 71 1939 50c
Salmon River
1:31,680 48 x 51 1919
7 sheets 50c each
Snake River (middle)
1:31,680 56 x 71 1936
19 sheets 50c each
Spokane River
1:12,000 56 x 71 1938
4 sheets 50c each
Warm Creek
1:12,000 56 x 71 1939 50c
LOUISIANA
Red River
1:31,680 56 x 71 1944
19 sheets 50c each

MONTANA
Badger Creek
1:24,000 55 x 71 1957
Blackfoot River
1:31,680 55 x 71 1934
10 sheets
Clark Fork
1:24,000 55 x 71 1964
10 sheets
Clark Fork (damsites)
1:7,200 55 x 76 1969
2 sheets
Elk Basin
1:15,840 86 x 109 1944
Flathead River
1:31,680 55 x 71 1928
10 sheets
Flathead River (middle fork)
1:31,680 55 x 71 1939
3 sheets
Flathead River (south fork)
1:31,680 55 x 71 1935
4 sheets
Flathead River (Knowles and Perma damsites)
1:9,600 55 x 71 1957
Flathead River (Sloan Bridge damsite)
1:12,000 55 x 71 1955
Grinnell Glacier (Glacier N P)
1:6,000 55 x 86 1950-60
Hinsdale special
1:62,500 41 x 50 1904
Kootenai River (upper)
1:31,680 55 x 71 1934
9 sheets
Little Missouri River
1:24,000 55 x 71 1946
11 sheets
Lonesome Special
1:62,500 41 x 50
Moorhead Reservoir
1:12,000 55 x 71 1947
6 sheets
National Bison Range
1:31,680 28 x 31 1929
Powder River
1:24,000 55 x 71 1946
Rock Creek
1:24,000 55 x 71 1956
2 sheets
Ruby River
1:31,680 55 x 71 1934
3 sheets
Saco Special
1:62,500 43 x 50 1903
Sperry Glacier (Glacier N P)
1:6,000 55 x 71 1950-60
Yaak River
1:31,680 55 x 71 1948
4 sheets
NEVADA
Austin Area. Reese River Mining district
1:4,800 89 x 89 1937 50c
Carson River (plans and profiles)
1:31,680 56 x 71 1934
10 sheets 50c each
Ely
1:30,000 41 x 51 1910 50c
Ely Range
1:48,000 56 x 71 1916 50c
Eureka mining district
1:24,000 41 x 61 1931 50c
Fort McDermitt Reservoir Site
1:12,000 56 x 74 1962 50c

Keese River
1:31,680 53 x 69 1935 50c
Little Humboldt River
1:31,680 56 x 71 1935
4 sheets 50c each
McDermitt Creek Reservoir
1:12,000 56 x 74 1962 50c
Muddy River
1:31,680 53 x 64 1934
2 sheets 50c each
Quinn River
1:31,680 69 x 69 1959 50c
Rochester mining district
1:24,000 41 x 51 1916 50c
NEW MEXICO
Gallinas River
1:31,680 56 x 71 1939
4 sheets 50c each
Gila River
1:31,680 56 x 71 1935-41
2 sheets 50c each
Magdalen district
1:12,000 41 x 92 1910-29 50c
Navajo River
1:24,000 56 x 71 1955-57
6 sheets 50c each
Pecos River
1:31,680 56 x 71 1937
25 sheets 50c each
Rio Chama
1:31,680 56 x 71 1935
8 sheets 50c each
Rio Grande
1:31,680 56 x 71 1935
2 sheets 50c each
Rio Penasco
1:31,680 56 x 71 1936
3 sheets 50c each
NORTH DAKOTA
Heart River
1:24,000 53 x 99 1941
4 sheets 50c each
Little Missouri River (Medora-Marmarth)
1:24,000 56 x 71 1946
11 sheets 50c each
Little Missouri River (Marmarth-North Fork)
1:24,000 56 x 71 1946
11 sheets 50c each
OREGON
Bradley Creek Reservoir & Damsite
1:24,000 55 x 71 1962
Catherine Creek
1:31,680 53 x 71 1933
Chewaucan River
1:31,680 55 x 71 1936
3 sheets
Coos River (South Fork)
1:24,000 2 sheets 1955
Cow Creek
1:24,000 55 x 71 1936
Deep Creek and Camas Creek
1:24,000 55 x 71 1936
4 sheets
Donner und Blitzen River
1:24,000 55 x 71 1961
Evans Creek
1:31,680 55 x 71 1936
2 sheets
Fishawk Creek
1:24,000 55 x 71 1957
Gales Creek
1:31,680 53 x 71 1934
Grave Creek
1:31,680 55 x 71 1936
Hood River
1:31,680 55 x 71 1913-33
4 sheets
Imnana River
1:24,000 55 x 71 1957
Indian Creek Reservoir & Damsite
1:12,000
1:24,000 55 x 71
Jumpoff Joe Creek
1:31,680 1936
Kiger Creek
1:12,000 55 x 68 1965
Klamath River
1:24,000 55 x 71 1955
18 sheets
Little Butte Creek
1:31,680 53 x 71 1936
3 sheets
Lookout Point Reservoir Site
1:12,000 53 x 71 1935
4 sheets
Luckieamute River
1:31,680 55 x 71 1935
Miscellaneous Damsites, Coasts and Streams (incl. Nehalem R. Alsea R, Siuslaw R and Lake Creek)
1:4,800 55 x 71 1957
Nehalem River
1:31,680 55 x 71 1936
7 sheets
Nestucca River
1:24,000 55 x 71 1955
2 sheets
Nestucca River
1:4,800 and 1:12,000
2 sheets 55 x 68 1969
Rogue River
1:31,680 53 x 68 1923
14 sheets
Rondowa Reservoir Site
1:4,800 46 x 63 1948
2 sheets
Siletz River and West Olalla Creek
1:2,400 55 x 71 1959-60
Silvies River
1:24,000 55 x 71 1958
Siuslaw River
1:2,400 – 1:4,800
2 sheets 55 x 73 1964
Smith River
1:2,400 55 x 73 1960
2 sheets
Smith River Damsites
1:2,400 46 x 63 1963
South Santiam River
1:31,680 55 x 71 1931-35
5 sheets
South Umpqua River
1:24,000 55 x 71 1936
3 sheets
South Yamhill River
1:31,680 53 x 71 1934
2 sheets
Squaw Butte Ranch
1:24,000 51 x 68 1936
Squaw Creek
1:2,400 46 x 63 1969
Trask River
1:24,000 55 x 71 1955
Trask and McKenzie Rivers
1:2,400 1959-60
Umatilla River
1:12,000 53 x 71 1936
3 sheets
Walla Walla River
1:31,680 53 x 63 1932
4 sheets
Wallowa and Lostine Rivers
1:2,400 55 x 71 1959
White River
1:31,680 53 x 63 1914-32
3 sheets
Willamina Creek
1:31,680 53 x 71 1934
Wilson River
1:24,000 55 x 71 1955
3 sheets
PENNSYLVANIA
Greater Pittsburgh Region
1:125,000 119x121 1971
SOUTH DAKOTA
Little Missouri River
1:24,000 55 x 71 1946
11 sheets
TEXAS
Land Use Houston, Area Test Site
1:500,000 53 x 61
(9 land use categories)
1:250,000 53 x 73 21 sheets
(20 land use categories)
1:125,000 53 x 73 4 sheets
Terlingua District
1:50,000 41 x 50 1902
UTAH
Bear River
1:31,680 55 x 71 1936
13 sheets
Bull Valley District
1:48,000 46 x 66 1938
Colorado and San Juan Rivers
1:31,680 53 x 68 1921
22 sheets
Colorado River
1:24,000 55 x 71 1944
14 sheets
Cottonwood and Pleasant Creeks
1:31,680 53 x 68 1933
2 sheets
Duchesne River
1:31,680 53 x 68 1924
6 sheets
Ephraim Creek
1:31,680 53 x 68 1934
Glen Canyon Recreation Area
1:250,000 81 x 91 1969
Huntington Creek
1:31,680 53 x 68 1933
3 sheets
Jordan River Tributaries
1:31,680 48 x 53 1920
4 sheets
Manti Creek
1:31,680 53 x 68 1934
Provo River
1:31,680 48 x 53 1920
10 sheets
Weber River
1:31,680 48 x 53 1920
6 sheets
Willard Creek
1:12,000 53 x 68 1936
WASHINGTON
Calligan Creek and Lake
1:12,000 55 x 71 1954

Carbon River
1:24,000 55 x 71 1942
3 sheets
Cavanargh Lake and Location of Conduit from Deer Creek
1:15,840 55 x 71 1925
Chehalis River
1:24,000 55 x 71 1940
2 sheets
Chewack Creek
1:31,680 55 x 71 1934
2 sheets
Columbia River
1:24,000 55 x 71 1944
11 sheets
Cowemau River
1:24,000 55 x 71 1962
Dosewallips River
1:31,680 55 x 71 1932
2 sheets
Duckabush River
1:31,680 55 x 71 1932
Dungeness
1:24,000 55 x 71 1945
Entiat River
1:24,000 55 x 73 1959
Faber Damsites
1:4,800 55 x 71 1936
Green River (Cowlitz & Lewis Co's)
1:4,800 – 1:24,000
55 x 73 1963
Green River (Upper)
1:24,000 55 x 71 1943
2 sheets
Hamma Hamma River
1:31,680 55 x 71 1932-36
2 sheets
Hancock Creek & Lake
1:12,000 55 x 71 1953
Humptulips
1:31,680 55 x 71 1934
5 sheets
Kalama River
1:24,000 2 sheets 1960
Kettle River
1:24,000 55 x 71 1950
5 sheets
Klickitat River
1:24,000 55 x 71 1957
3 sheets
Lake Isabel & Dorothy Lake
1:12,000 55 x 71 1955
Lewis River
1:31,680 55 x 71 1935
10 sheets
Nisqually Glacier
1:12,000 71 x 86 1951, 1956&1961
Nisqually Glacier
1:12,000 55 x 73 1966
Nooksack River
1:31,680 55 x 71 1934
8 sheets
Nooksack River
1:9,600 55 x 71 1948
Nooksack River (Lower)
1:24,000 55 x 71 1938
5 sheets
North Cascades
1:250,000 66 x 89 1955-72
Okanogan River & Osoyoos Lake (downstream)
1:4,800 55 x 71 1944-49
Patterson Ridge
1:24,000–1:9,600
63 x 91 1970

Pend Orielle River
1:31,680 55 x 71 1934
5 sheets
Queets River
1:31,680 53 x 68 1933
5 sheets
Quinault River (East Fork)
1:31,680 55 x 71 1934
Salmon Creek
1:24,000 55 x 71 1943
Satsop River
1:31,680 55 x 71 1934
3 sheets
Sauk River Reservoir site
1:24,000 55 x 71 1936
4 sheets
Sheep Creek
1:31,680 55 x 71 1934
2 sheets
Similkameen River
1:31,680 55 x 71 1934
2 sheets
Skagit River
1:24,000 55 x 71 1952
5 sheets
Skookumchuck River
1:24,000 55 x 71 1939
Skykomish River (South Fork)
1:24,000 55 x 71 1955
Spokane River
1:12,000 55 x 71 1938
4 sheets
Stilagaumish River
1:31,680 55 x 71 1925
2 sheets
Tolt River
1:31,680 55 x 71 1938
3 sheets
Touchet River
1:24,000 55 x 71 1941
3 sheets
Toutle River
1:31,680 55 x 71 1936
5 sheets
Wenas Creek
1:12,000 55 x 71 1951
White Salmon River
1:24,000 55 x 73 1958
2 sheets
Wind River
1:24,000 55 x 71 1957
2 sheets
Wynoochee River
1:24,000 55 x 71 1955
5 sheets

WYOMING

Bear River
1:31,680 55 x 71 1936
13 sheets
Elk Basin
1:15,840 86 x 109 1944
Laramie River
1:31,680 55 x 71 1934
10 sheets
Little Missouri River
1:24,000 55 x 71 1946
11 sheets
Moorhead Reservoir
1:12,000 55 x 71 1947
6 sheets
Powder River
1:24,000 55 x 71 1946
7 sheets
Rock Creek
1:24,000 55 x 71 1956
2 sheets

Savery Creek
1:31,680 55 x 71 1936
2 sheets
Superior Coal District
1:24,000 50 x 91 1940
Willow Creek district
1:24,000 53 x 99 1943

USA STATE MAPS – BASE
1:500,000 unless otherwise stated
Washington; USGS
Counties, cities, towns and railroads in black, rivers and water features in blue.
Maps available:

Alabama	81 x 117	1964
Arizona	119 x 144	1955
Arkansas	89 x 99	1965
California 2 sheets	121 x 165	1968
Colorado	111 x 134	1968
Connecticut 1:125,000 (highways in red)	114 x 142	1965
Georgia	99 x 109	1963
Idaho	112 x 168	1964
Illinois	81 x 135	1948
Indiana	69 x 107	1950
Iowa	84 x 117	1965
Kansas	81 x 143	1963
Kentucky	69 x 145	1956
Louisiana	102 x 112	1966
Maine	76 x 112	1958
Maryland and Delaware	56 x 92	1948
Massachusetts, Rhode Is, and Connecticut	61 x 76	1948
Michigan 2 sheets	132 x 168	1970
Minnesota	124 x 142	1963
Mississippi	78 x 132	1972
Missouri	129 x 111	1972
Montana 2 sheets	119 x 200	1965
Nebraska	81 x 158	1962
Nevada	114 x 165	1962
New Hampshire and Vermont	56 x 71	1950
New Jersey	58 x 71	1948
New Mexico	127 x 142	1967
New York	112 x 147	1953
North Carolina	74 x 168	1957
North Dakota	84 x 102	1961
Ohio	86 x 94	1951
Oklahoma	89 x 137	1948
Oregon	111 x 143	1965
Pennsylvania	73 x 111	1953
South Carolina	81 x 101	1970
South Dakota	99 x 83	1961
Tennessee	48 x 165	1957
Texas 4 sheets	208 x 259	1962
Utah	99 x 121	1958
Virginia	76 x 162	1955
Washington	94 x 132	1961
West Virginia	91 x 101	1963
Wisconsin	106 x 116	1966
Wyoming	104 x 132	1964

USA STATE MAPS – BASE
Reduced edition
1:1,000,000
Washington; USGS
Reduced edition of State Base Maps described above. Maps available:

Alabama	41 x 61	1964
Arizona	61 x 73	1955

Arkansas	46 x 53	1965
California	106 x 121	1968
Colorado	55 x 71	1968
Georgia	53 x 58	1963
Idaho	58 x 86	1964
Illinois	43 x 69	1948
Indiana	36 x 53	1950
Iowa	43 x 58	1965
Kansas	43 x 73	1963
Kentucky	38 x 76	1956
Louisiana	51 x 56	1966
Maine	41 x 56	1958
Maryland and Delaware	30 x 48	1948
Massachusetts,Rhode Is. and Connecticut	33 x 46	1948
Michigan	71 x 86	1970
Minnesota	66 x 74	1963
Mississippi	43 x 64	1972
Missouri	61 x 66	1969
Montana	61 x 101	1965
Nebraska	43 x 79	1962
Nevada	59 x 86	1962
New Hampshire and Vermont	31 x 38	1950
New Jersey	30 x 38	1948
New Mexico	64 x 74	1967
New York	58 x 74	1953
North Carolina	35 x 84	1957
North Dakota	46 x 64	1961
Ohio	46 x 51	1961
Oklahoma	46 x 73	1948
Oregon	55 x 71	1965
Pennsylvania	41 x 56	1953
South Carolina	43 x 53	1970
South Dakota	50 x 68	1961
Tennessee	28 x 89	1957
Texas	106 x 134	1962
Utah	50 x 63	1958
Virginia	41 x 81	1955
Washington	48 x 68	1961
West Virginia	46 x 50	1963
Wisconsin	58 x 61	1966
Wyoming	53 x 66	1964

50c each

USA STATE MAPS – TOPOGRAPHIC
1:500, 000
Washington : USGS
Overprint on State Base Maps with highways in purple and contours in brown. National monuments, forests and wildlife refuges shown in colour.
Maps available:

Alabama	81 x 117	1964
Arizona	119 x 144	1955
Arkansas	89 x 99	1965
California 2 sheets	121 x 165	1968
Colorado	111 x 134	1968
Connecticut (also in woodland ed.) 1:125, 000	114 x 142	1965
Georgia	99 x 109	1963
Idaho	112 x 168	1964
Illinois	81 x 135	1948
Indiana (uncontoured)	69 x 107	1950
Iowa	84 x 117	1965
Kansas	81 x 143	1963
Kentucky	69 x 145	1956
Louisiana	102 x 112	1966
Maine	76 x 112	1958
Maryland and Delaware	56 x 92	1948
Massachusetts, Rhode Is. and Connecticut	61 x 76	1948 $1.50
Michigan 2 sheets	132 x 168	1970
Minnesota	124 x 142	1963
Mississippi	78 x 132	1972
Missouri	129 x 111	1972
Montana 2 sheets	119 x 200	1965
Nebraska	81 x 158	1962
Nevada	114 x 165	1962
New Hampshire and Vermont	56 x 71	1950
New Jersey	58 x 71	1948
New Mexico	127 x 142	1967
New York	112 x 147	1953
North Carolina	74 x 168	1957
North Dakota	84 x 102	1961
Ohio	86 x 94	1961
Oregon	111 x 143	1965
Pennsylvania	73 x 111	1953
South Carolina	43 x 53	1970
South Dakota	99 x 83	1961
Tennessee	48 x 165	1957
Texas (4 sheets)	208 x 259	1962
Utah	99 x 121	1958
Virginia	76 x 162	1955
Washington	94 x 132	1961
West Virginia	91 x 101	1963
Wisconsin	106 x 116	1966
Wyoming	104 x 132	1964

$2.00 each

USA MAPS – RELIEF
1:500, 000 except where otherwise stated
Washington : USGS
Overprinted on modified State Base Map. Physical features emphasised by shaded relief in colour (uncontoured)

Alabama	71 x 109	1964
Arizona	119 x 144	1955
Arkansas	83 x 94	1968
California 1:1, 000, 000	109 x 116	1968
Colorado	111 x 134	1968
Connecticut 1:125, 000	114 x 142	1965
Georgia	71 x 109	1964
Idaho	112 x 168	1964
Kentucky	69 x 148	1956
Maine	76 x 112	1958
Maryland and Delaware	58 x 92	1948
Missouri	119 x 137	1950
Montana (2 sheets)	119 x 200	1965
Nevada	114 x 165	1962
New Hampshire and Vermont	56 x 71	1950
New Jersey	58 x 71	1971
New Mexico	127 x 142	1967
New York	112 x 147	1953
North Carolina	74 x 168	1957
North Dakota	84 x 102	1961
Ohio	86 x 94	1961
Oklahoma	89 x 137	1948
Oregon	111 x 143	1965
Pennsylvania	73 x 111	1953
South Carolina	81 x 102	1970
Tennessee	48 x 165	1957
Texas 1:1, 000, 000	106 x 134	1962
Utah	99 x 121	1958
Virginia	76 x 162	1955
Washington	94 x 132	1961
West Virginia	91 x 101	1963
Wyoming	104 x 132	1964

$2.00 each

ALASKA STATE MAPS
Various scales
Washington : USGS
Series of maps of differing styles:

Map A
In black and blue only, uncontoured
1:1, 500, 000
46 x 63 1969

Map B
Base edition, railroads, highways, settlement etc. Uncontoured. 2 sheets
1:1, 584, 000
91 x 129 1969

Map B
Contour edition, as above, with contours.
1969

Map E
Base edition, as Map B above,
1:2, 500, 000 1969

Map E
Shaded relief edition
1:2, 500, 000 1969

D POLITICAL & ADMINISTRATIVE

SPOJENÉ STÁTY AMERICKÉ
1:5, 000, 000
Praha : Kart, 1969
General school wall map of the USA in Czech. Kcs 115

ESTADOS UNIDOS
Barcelona : Editorial Teide
33 x 25
General hand map for schools, showing major cities and state boundaries. 1 pta

STANFORD'S GENERAL MAP OF THE USA
1:5, 000, 000
London : Stanford
98 x 72
Political col. by states, road and rail communications, principal airports. Alaska and Hawaii inset. Pictorial border of state seals.
Paper folded 75p
Mounted CRV £6.50

ÉTATS-UNIS ET MÉXIQUE
1:4, 000, 000
Bruxelles : Mantniek
119 x 160
Politically coloured wall map in French or English editions.
Azimuthal equidistant projection.
Available mounted in various styles.

SUPERIOR WALL MAP OF THE UNITED STATES
1:4, 400, 000
Maplewood : Hammond
127 x 83
Political map showing state boundaries
$2.00

UNITED STATES
1:3, 500, 000
Washington : NGS
108 x 70
Political col. wall map.
Paper $2.00
Plastic $3.00
Enlarged ed. 172 x 109 $5.00

POLITICAL MAP OF THE UNITED STATES
Various scales
Chicago : Denoyer-Geppert
100061-14 United States Beginners
1:3, 125, 000 162 x 205 $30.00
100001-14 US Geographical Extent
1:6, 250, 000 162 x 111 $24.00
101061-14 Beginners Geog. Terms
1:3, 135, 000 162 x 205 $30.00
108061-14 50 States
1:3, 135, 000 162 x 172 $27.00
108031-14 US 48 States
1:3, 135, 000 162 x 111 $24.00
107011 US (50 States), Mexico
1:4, 687, 500 $19.25

UNITED STATES : POLITICAL MAPS
Indianapolis : Cram
Series of col. school wall maps at 4 different levels, with increasing detail.
Level A Beginners Map
1:3, 070, 000 162 x 132 $26.25
Level B US (50 States)
1:3, 750, 000 129 x 124 $23.00
US (50 States)
1:3, 000, 000 162 x 132 $27.25
Level C US (50 States)
1:3, 750, 000 129 x 124 $23.00
Political Outline (all levels)
1:3, 750, 000 129 x 124 $27.50
1:3, 000, 000 162 x 132 $31.75
Coloured Outline Desk Map
No scale 43 x 31 50c
Slated Outline (blackboard)
No scale $16.00
Excello Wall Map
No scale 101 x 116 $12.50

ÉTATS-UNIS NO 1 (PHYSIQUE)
Editions MDI
Political map on the reverse
See USA 73 E1

ÉTATS-UNIS D'AMÉRIQUE
No. 33
Paris : Hatier
120 x 100
School wall map; political and economic map on reverse.

POLITICAL MAPS OF STATES
Various scales
Chicago : Denoyer-Geppert
Political maps, available for:

108021	Alaska-Hawaii	162 x 71
107162	Kentucky	127 x 127
107182	Maine	101 x 162
107232	Mississippi	101 x 142
107252	Montana	127 x 122
107272	Nevada	101 x 147
107282	New Hampshire	91 x 106
107292	New Jersey	101 x 160
107352	Pennsylvania	111 x 81
107442	Vermont	91 x 106
107492	Wyoming	127 x 127
107722	New England	101 x 162

Spring Rollers (14) $21.75

EXCELLO POLITICAL WALL MAP OF THE STATES
Various scales
Indianapolis : Cram
111 x 116
Political col. wall maps for schools, available for the following states:
Georgia
Illinois
Indiana
Iowa
Kansas
Missouri
Nebraska
North Dakota
Oklahoma
South Dakota
Texas $12.50 each

USA MAP SERIES
Various scales
Detroit : Hearne Bros.
122 x 167
Series of col. wall maps showing communications, admin. boundaries, rivers, park areas, with many inset maps.
Maps available :

SM2	Alabama
SM4	Alaska
SM6	Arizona
SM8	Arkansas
SM10	California
SM12	Colorado
SM14	Connecticut
SM16	Delaware
SM18	Florida
SM20	Georgia
SM22	Hawaii
SM24	Idaho
SM26	Illinois
SM28	Indiana
SM30	Inland Empire
SM32	Iowa
SM34	Kansas
SM36	Kentucky
SM38	Louisana
SM40	Maine
SM42	Maryland
SM44	Massachusetts
SM46	Michigan
SM48	Minnesota
SM50	Mississippi
SM52	Missouri
SM54	Montana
SM56	Nebraska
SM58	Nevada
SM60	New England States
SM62	New Hampshire
SM64	New Jersey
SM66	New Mexico
SM68	New York
SM70	North Carolina
SM72	North Dakota
SM74	Ohio
SM76	Oklahoma
SM78	Oregon
SM80	Pennsylvania
SM82	Rhode Island
SM84	South Carolina
SM86	South Dakota
SM88	Tennessee
SM90	Texas
SM92	The Five Northwestern States
SM94	Utah
SM96	Vermont
SM98	Virginia
SM100	Washington
SM102	West Virginia
SM104	Wisconsin
SM106	Wyoming

GREAT LAKES REGION OF US AND CANADA (NORTH EASTERN US)
1:2, 000, 000
Washington : NGS
106 x 71
General wall map.
Paper $2.00
Plastic $3.00

NORTH CENTRAL US
1:2, 437, 500
Washington : NGS
71 x 67
Political col. wall map.
Paper $2.00
Plastic $3.00

SOUTH CENTRAL US
1:2, 437, 500
Washington : NGS
74 x 61
Political col. wall map.
Paper $2.00
Plastic $3.00

STATE MAPS
Various scales
Indianapolis : Cram
Various sizes
Series of maps for individual states, showing county divisions in col.
Also available in col. outline ed. without names, and desk outline maps. 30 x 43, 60c each.
Each $23.00

ALASKA
1:5, 000, 000
Washington : USGS
111 x 71
Political base map: shows national and international boundaries, principal communications, drainage detail.

ALASKA
1:2, 937, 500
Washington : NGS
89 x 73
Political col. wall map.
Paper $2.00
Plastic $3.00

CALIFORNIA
1:1, 312, 500
Washington : NGS
73 x 94
Political pol. wall map.
Paper $2.00
Plastic $3.00

NEW ENGLAND
1:750, 000
Washington : NGS
73 x 106
Political col. wall map.
Paper $2.00
Plastic $3.00

USA COUNTY WALL MAPS
Various scales
Detroit : Hearne Bros.
122 x 167
Series of col. wall maps of counties and urban

areas showing road and rail communications, admin. boundaries, rivers, park areas with brief history of the area and many inset maps. Index to places by pivoted tape. Mounted on cloth with cellulose acetate finish on a spring roller with mounting rail and brackets.
Maps available:

ALABAMA
A2 Birmingham & Jefferson County
A4 Gadsden & Etowah County
A6 Huntsville & Madison County
A8 Mobile & Mobile County
A10 Montgomery & Montgomery County
A12 Tuscaloosa & Tuscaloosa County

ARIZONA
A14 Flagstaff & Coconino County
A16 Phoenix & Maricopa County
A18 Tucson & Pima County
A20 Yuma & Yuma County

ARKANSAS
A22 Fort Smith & Sebastian County
A24 Little Rock & Pulaski County
A26 Pine Bluff & Jefferson County

CALIFORNIA
A28 Alameda County (Southern Portion)
A30 Anaheim-Santa Ana & Northern Half of Orange County
A32 Antelope Valley (N.L.A. Co.)
A34 Bakersfield & Kern County
A36 Central Coast Counties Area
A38 Chico & Butte County
A40 Contra Costa County (Central Portion)
A42 El Centro & Imperial County
A44 Eureka & Humboldt County
A46 Fresno & Fresno County
A48 Hanford-Tulare, Kings & Tulare Counties
A50 Lake Tahoe & Vicinity
A52 Los Angeles Metropolitan Area
A54 Los Angeles County (East Central Portion)
A56 Los Angeles County (Eastern Portion)
A58 Los Angeles County (Southern Portion)
A60 Los Angeles County (South-western Portion)
A62 Los Angeles County (Western Portion)
A64 Madera & Merced Counties
A66 Mid-Peninsular Area (Portions of San Mateo & Santa Clara Counties)
A68 Modesto & Stanislaus County
A70 Monterey & Monterey County
A72 Napa & Napa County
A74 Newport Beach & Southern Half of Orange County
A76 Oakland & Alameda County
A78 Redding & Shasta County
A80 Redwood City & San Mateo County
A82 Richmond & Contra Costa County
A84 Riverside & Riverside County
A86 Roseville & Placer County
A88 Sacramento & Sacramento County
A90 Sacramento Valley Area
A92 San Bernardino & San Bernardino County
A94 San Diego Metropolitan Area
A96 San Diego, Northern Portion (Oceanside-Escondido)
A98 San Fernando Valley (L.A.Co)
A100 San Francisco Metropolitan Area
A102 San Francisco-Oakland Metropolitan Bay Area Co's
A104 San Gabriel Valley (L.A.Co)
A106 San Joaquin Valley Area
A108 San Jose & Santa Clara County
A110 San Luis Obispo City & County
A112 San Rafael & Marin County
A114 Santa Barbara & Santa Barbara County
A116 Santa Cruz & Santa Cruz County
A118 Santa Rosa & Sonoma County
A120 Southern California Counties
A122 Stockton & San Joaquin County
A124 Vallejo & Solano County
A126 Ventura County (Trading Area)
A128 Woodland & Yolo County
A130 Yreka & Siskiyou County
A132 Yuba & Sutter Counties

COLORADO
A134 Boulder & Boulder County
A136 Colorado Springs & El Paso County
A138 Denver Metropilitan Area
A140 Fort Collins & Larimer County
A142 Greeley & Weld County
A144 Pueblo & Pueblo County

CONNECTICUT
A146 Bridgeport & Eastern Fairfield County
A148 Hartford & Hartford County
A150 Middletown & Middlesex County
A152 New Haven & New Haven County
A154 New London & New London County (Shore Line)
A156 Rockville & Tolland County
A158 Stamford & Western Fairfield County
A160 Torrington & Litchfield County
A162 Willimantic & Windham County

DELAWARE
A164 Dover & Kent County
A166 Wilmington & New Castle County

DISTRICT OF COLUMBIA
A168 Washington, DC & Environs

FLORIDA
A170 Daytona Beach with Volusia & Brevard Counties
A172 Fort Lauderdale & Broward County
A174 Fort Myers & Lee County
A176 Gainesville & Alachua County
A178 Jacksonville & Duval County
A180 Key West & Monroe County
A182 Lakeland & Polk County
A184 Miami & Dade County
A186 Orlando & Orange County
A188 Panama City & Bay County
A190 Pensacola with Escambia & Santa Rosa Counties
A192 St Petersburg & Pinellas County
A194 Sarasota-Bradenton, Sarasota & Manatee Counties
A196 Tallahassee & Leon County
A198 Tampa & Hillsborough County
A200 West Palm Beach & Palm Beach County

GEORGIA
A202 Albany & Dougherty County
A204 Atlanta with De Kalb & Fulton Counties
A206 Augusta & Richmond County with Aiken County, SC
A208 Columbus & Muscogee County with Phenix City, Ala.
A210 Macon & Bibb County
A212 Marietta & Cobb County
A214 Savannah & Chartham County

HAWAII
A216 Hilo & Hawaii County
A218 Honolulu & Honolulu County

IDAHO
A220 Boise with Ada & Canyon Counties
A222 Idaho Falls & Bonneville County
A924 Inland Empire
A224 Pocatello & Bannock County
A226 The Five Northwestern States

ILLINOIS
A228 Alton & Madison County
A230 Aurora & Kane County (Fox River Valley)
A232 Bloomington & McLean County
A234 Champaign-Danville, Champaign & Vermillion Counties
A236 Chicago & Southern Cook County
A238 Decatur & Macon County
A240 East St Luis & St Clair County
A242 Elmhurst with DuPage & Western Cook Counties
A244 Joilet & Will County
A246 Kankakee & Kankakee County
A248 Ottawa & La Salle County
A250 Peoria & Peoria County
A252 Quincy & Adams County
A254 Rock Island & Rock Island County with Davenport, Iowa
A256 Rockford & Winnebago County with Beloit, Wisc.
A258 Springfield & Sangamon County
A260 Waukegan with Lake & Northern Cook Counties (North Shore)
A262 Woodstock & McHenry County

INDIANA
A264 Anderson & Madison County
A266 Bloomington & Monroe County
A268 Elkhart & Elkhart County
A270 Evansville & Vanderburgh County
A272 Fort Wayne & Allen County
A274 Gary-Hammond & Lake County with Southern Cook County, Ill.
A276 Indianapolis & Marion County
A278 Kokomo & Howard County
A280 Marion & Grant County
A282 Michigan City — La Porte & La Porte County
A284 Muncie & Delaware County
A286 New Albany-Jeffersonville, Floyd & Clark Counties
A288 Richmond—New Castle, Wayne & Henry Counties

A290 South Bend & St Joseph County
A292 Terre Haute & Vigo County

IOWA
A294 Cedar Rapids & Linn County
A296 Council Bluffs with Omaha & Douglas County, Nebraska
A298 Davenport & Scott County with Rock Island, Illinois
A300 Des Moines & Polk County
A302 Dubuque & Dubuque County
A304 Marshalltown & Marshall County
A306 Sioux City & Woodbury County
A308 Waterloo & Black Hawk County

KANSAS
A310 Kansas City, Kansas & Missouri (Twin Cities)
A312 Salina & Salina County
A314 Topeka & Shawnee County
A316 Wichita & Sedgwick County

KENTUCKY
A318 Ashland & Boyd County
A320 Covington with Kenton & Campbell Counties
A322 Lexington & Fayette County
A324 Louisville & Jefferson County
A326 Owensboro & Davies County
A328 Paducah & McCracken County

LOUISIANA
A330 Alexandria & Rapides Parish
A332 Baton Rouge & East Baton Rouge Parish
A334 Lafayette & Lafayette Parish
A336 Lake Charles & Calcasieu Parish
A338 Monroe & Ouachita Parish
A340 New Orleans with Orleans & Jefferson Parishes
A342 Shreveport & Caddo Parish

MAINE
A344 Augusta & Kennebec County
A346 Bangor & Penobscot County
A348 Lewiston & Androscoggin County
A350 Portland Metropolitan Area

MARYLAND
A352 Aberdeen & Harford County
A354 Annapolis & Anne Arundel County
A356 Baltimore & Baltimore County
A358 Cumberland & Allegany County
A360 Ellicott City & Howard County
A362 Frederick & Frederick County
A364 Hagerstown & Washington County
A366 La Plata & Charles County
A368 Lexington Park & St Marys County
A370 Rockville & Montgomery County
A372 Upper Marlboro & Prince Georges County

MASSACHUSETTS
A374 Boston & Vicinity
A376 Brockton & Plymouth County
A378 Fall River-New Bedford & Bristol County
A380 Framingham-Natick Metropolitan Area
A382 Greenfield & Franklin County
A384 Hyannis with Branstable, Dukes, & Nantucket Counties
A386 Lawrence & Essex County
A388 Lowell & North Half of Middlesex County
A390 Northampton & (So) Hampshire County (see Springfield)
A392 Pittsfield & Berkshire County
A374 Quincy & Norfolk County (see Boston)
A380 Southern Half of Middlesex County (See Framingham)
A390 Springfield & Hampden County (Connecticut River Valley Area)
A394 Worcester Metropolitan Area

MICHIGAN
A396 Adrian & Lenawee County
A398 Ann Arbor & Washtenaw County
A400 Battle Creek & Calhoun County
A402 Bay City — Saginaw, Bay & Saginaw Counties
A404 Benton Harbor & Berrien County
A406 Dearborn & Western Wayne County
A408 Detroit & Eastern Wayne County
A410 Flint & Genesee County
A412 Grand Rapids and Kent County
A414 Jackson & Jackson County
A416 Kalamazoo & Kalamazoo County
A418 Lansing & Ingham County
A420 Lapeer & Lapeer County
A422 Marquette & Marquette County
A424 Midland & Midland County
A426 Monroe & Monroe County
A428 Mount Clemens & Macomb County
A430 Muskegon & Muskegon County with Northern Ottawa County
A432 Pontiac & Oakland County
A434 Port Huron & St Clair County
A436 Sandusky & Sanilac County

MINNESOTA
A438 Anoka & Anoka County
A440 Daluth-Superior Metropolitan Area with Two Harbors
A442 Mankato & Blue Earth County
A444 Mesabi Iron Range
A446 Minneapolis & Hennepin County
A448 Moorhead & Clay County with Fargo & Cass County, ND
A450 Rochester & Olmsted County
A452 St Cloud with Stearns, Benton, & Sherburne Counties
A454 St Paul & Ramsey County

MISSISSIPPI
A456 Biloxi & Harrison County
A458 Greenville & Washington County
A460 Hattiesburg & Forrest County
A462 Jackson & Hinds County

MISSOURI
A464 Columbia & Boone County
A466 Jefferson City & Cole County
A468 Joplin & Jasper County
A470 Kansas Cit, Missouri & Kansas (Twin Cities)
A472 St Joseph & Buchanan County
A474 St Louis & St Louis County
A476 Springfield & Greene County

MONTANA
A478 Billings & Yellowstone County
A480 Butte & Silver Bow County
A482 Great Falls & Cascade County
A484 Helena & Lewis & Clark County
A924 Inland Empire
A486 Missoula & Missoula County
A226 The Five Northwestern States

NEBRASKA
A488 Grand Island-Hastings, Hall & Adams Counties
A490 Lincoln & Lancaster County
A492 North Platte & Lincoln County
A494 Omaha & Douglas County with Council Bluffs, Iowa
A496 Scottsbluff & Scotts Bluff County

NEVADA
A498 Lake Tahoe & Vicinity
A500 Las Vegas & Clark County
A502 Reno & Washoe County with Lake Tahoe

NEW HAMPSHIRE
A504 Concord & Merrimack County
A506 Dover-Rochester & Strafford County
A508 Manchester & Hillsborough County
A510 Portsmouth & Rockingham County

NEW JERSEY
A512 Asbury Park & Monmouth County
A514 Atlantic City & Atlantic County
A516 Bridgeton & Cumberland County
A518 Burlington & Burlington County
A520 Camden & Camden County
A522 Camden-Trenton-Philadelphia Metropolitan Trading Area
A524 Elizabeth & Union County
A526 Flemington & Hunterdon County
A528 Hackensack & Bergen County
A530 Jersey City & Hudson County
A532 Morristown & Morris County
A534 New Brunswick & Middlesex County
A536 New Jersey — New York Metropolitan Trading Area
A538 Newark & Essex County
A540 Newton & Sussex County
A542 Paterson & Passaic County
A544 Phillipsburg & Warren County
A546 Point Pleasant & Ocean County
A548 Salem & Salem County
A550 Somerville & Somerset County
A552 Trenton & Mercer County
A554 Wildwood & Cape May County
A556 Woodbury & Gloucester County

NEW MEXICO
A558 Albuquerque & Bernalillo County
A560 Carlsbad & Eddy County
A562 Farmington & San Juan County
A564 Hobbs & Lea County
A566 Las Cruces & Dona Ana County
A568 Roswell & Chaves County
A570 Santa Fe & Santa Fe County

NEW YORK
A572 Albany-Troy, Albany & Renssalaer Counties
A574 Binghampton & Broome County
A576 Brooklyn-Queens, Kings & Queens Counties
A578 Buffalo & Erie County
A580 Carmel & Putnam County
A582 Elmira & Chemung County

A584 Jamestown & Chautauqua County
A586 Kingston & Ulster County
A588 Manhattan-Bronx, New York & Bronx Counties
A590 Nassau County (Northern Portion)
A592 Nassau County (Southern Portion)
A594 New City & Rockland County
A596 New York City (Five Boros)
A598 New York — New Jersey Metropolitan Trading Area
A600 Newburgh & Orange County
A602 Niagara Falls & Niagara County
A604 Ogdensburg & St Lawrence County
A606 Olean & Cattaraugus County
A608 Patchogue-Riverhead & Suffolk County
A610 Poughkeepsie & Dutchess County
A612 Rochester & Monroe County
A614 Schenectady & Schenectady County
A616 States Island & Richmond County
A618 Syracuse & Onondaga County
A620 Utica-Rome & Oneida County
A622 Watertown & Jefferson County
A624 Westchester County (Lower Portion)
A626 Westchester County (Upper Portion)

NORTH CAROLINA
A628 Asherville & Burncombe County
A630 Burlington & Alamance County
A632 Charlotte & Mecklenburg County
A634 Concord-Salisbury, Cabarrus & Rowan Counties
A636 Durham & Durham County
A638 Fayetteville & Cumberland County
A640 Gastonia-Shelby, Gaston & Cleveland Counties
A642 Greensboro & Guildford County
A644 Hendersonville & Henderson County
A646 Lexington & Davidson County
A648 Lamberton & Robeson County
A650 Raleigh & Wake County
A652 Wilmington with New Hanover & Brunswick Counties
A654 Winston-Salem & Forsyth County

NORTH DAKOTA
A656 Bismarck-Mandan, Burleigh & Morton Counties
A658 Fargo & Cass County with Moorhead, Minn.
A660 Grand Forks and Grand Forks County
A662 Minot & Ward County

OHIO
A664 Akron & Summit County
A666 Ashtabula & Ashtabula County
A668 Batavia & Clermont County
A670 Bowling Green & Wood County
A672 Canton & Stark County
A674 Cincinnati & Hamilton County
A676 Cleveland & Cuyahoga County
A678 Columbus & Franklin County
A680 Dayton & Montgomery County
A682 East Liverpool & Columbiana County
A684 Hamilton & Butler County
A686 Ironton & Lawrence County
A688 Kent-Ravenna & Portage County
A690 Lima & Allen County
A692 Lorain & Lorain County
A694 Mansfield & Richland County
A696 Painesville with Lake & Geauga Counties
A698 Portsmouth & Scioto County
A700 Sandusky & Erie County
A702 Springfield & Clark County
A704 Steubenville & Jefferson County with Weirton, W.Va.
A706 Toledo & Lucas County
A708 Troy & Miami County
A710 Wadsworth & Medina County
A712 Xenia & Green County
A714 Youngstown-Warren, Mahoning & Trumbull Counties
A716 Zanesville & Muskingum County

OKLAHOMA
A718 Enid & Garfield County
A720 Lawton & Comanche County
A722 Muskogee & Muskogee County
A724 Norman & Cleveland County
A726 Oklahoma City & Oklahoma County
A728 Tulsa & Tulsa County

OREGON
A730 Eugene & Lane County
A732 Hillsboro & Washington County
A924 Inland Empire
A734 Medford-Klamath Falls, Jackson & Klamath Counties
A736 Oregon City & Clackamas County
A738 Portland & Multnomah County
A740 Roseburg with Douglas & Coos Counties
A742 Salem & Marion County
A226 The Five Northwestern States

PENNSYLVANIA
A744 Aliquippa & Beaver County
A746 Allegheny County (Northern Portion)
A748 Allentown-Bethlehem, Lehigh & Northamton Counties
A750 Altoona & Blair County
A752 Bristol & Bucks County
A754 Butler & Butler County
A756 Chambersburg & Franklin County
A758 Chester & Delaware County
A760 Erie & Erie County
A762 Gettysburg-Mechanicsburg, Adams & Cumberland Counties
A764 Greensburg & Westmoreland County
A766 Harrisburg & Dauphin County
A768 Indiana & Indiana County
A770 Johnstown & Cambria County
A772 Kittanning & Armstrong County
A774 Lancaster & Lancaster County
A776 Lebanon & Lebanon County
A778 New Castle & Lawrence County
A780 Norristown & Montgomery County
A782 Oil City & Venango County
A784 Philadelphia-Camden-Trenton Metropolitan Trading Area
A786 Philadelphia Metropolitan Area
A788 Pittsburgh & Vicinity (Southern Portion of Allegheny County)
A790 Pottsville & Schuylkill County
A792 Reading & Berks County
A794 Scranton & Lackawanna County
A796 Shamokin & Northumberland County
A798 Sharon & Mercer County
A800 Uniontown & Fayette County
A802 Washington & Washington County
A804 West Chester & Chester County
A806 Wilkes-Barre & Luzerne County
A808 Williamsport & Lycoming County
A810 York & York County

RHODE ISLAND
A812 Newport & Newport County
A814 Providence-Pawtucket Metropolitan Area
A816 Woonsocket Metropolitan Area

SOUTH CAROLINA
A818 Aiken-Augusta with Aiken County, S C & Richmond County, Ga
A820 Anderson & Anderson County
A822 Charleston & Charleston County
A824 Columbia & Richland County
A826 Greenville & Greenville County
A828 Rock Hill & York County
A830 Spartanburg & Spartanburg County

SOUTH DAKOTA
A832 Pierre with Hughes & Stanley Counties
A834 Rapid City & Pennington County
A836 Sioux Falls & Minnehaha County

TENNESSEE
A838 Chatanooga & Hamilton County
A840 Jackson & Madison County
A842 Johnson City — Kingsport, Washington & Sullivan Counties
A844 Knoxville & Knox County
A846 Memphis & Shelby County
A848 Nashville & Davidson County
A850 Oak Ridge with Anderson & Roane Counties

TEXAS
A852 Abilene with Taylor & Jones Counties
A854 Amarillo & Potter County
A856 Austin & Travis County
A858 Beaumont & Jefferson County
A860 Brownsville-McAllen, Cameron & Hidalgo Counties
A862 Corpus Christi & Nueces County
A864 Dallas & Dallas County
A866 El Paso & El Paso County
A868 Fort Worth & Tarrant County
A870 Houston-Galveston Bay Area
A872 Houston & Harris County
A874 Laredo & Webb County
A876 Lubbock & Lubbock County
A878 Odessa-Midland, Ector & Midland Counties
A880 San Antonio & Bexar County
A882 Waco & McLennan County
A884 Wichita Falls & Wichita County

UTAH
A886 Ogden & Weber County
A888 Provo & Utah County
A890 Salt Lake City with Salt Lake & Davis Counties

VERMONT
A892 Barre-Montpelier & Washington County

A894 Burlington & Chittenden County
A896 Rutland & Rutland County

VIRGINIA
A898 Arlington & Fairfax Counties with Alexandria
A900 Bluefield & Tazewell County
A902 Charlottesville & Albemarle County
A904 Danville & Pittsylvania County
A906 Lynchburg & Campbell County
A908 Newport News with all of the Lower Peninsula
A910 Norfolk Metropolitan Area
A912 Petersburg Metropolitan Area
A914 Richmond & Vicinity with all of Henrico County
A916 Roanoke & Roanoke County

WASHINGTON
A918 Bellingham & Whatcom County
A920 Bremerton & Kitsap County
A922 Everett & Snohomish County
A924 Inland Empire
A926 Olympia & Thurston County
A928 Seattle & King County
A930 Spokane & Spokane County
A932 Tacoma & Pierce County
A226 The Five Northwestern States
A934 Vancouver & Clark County
A936 Yakima-Richland-Walla Walla Valley Area

WEST VIRGINIA
A938 Charleston & Kanawha County
A940 Clarksburg & Harrison County
A942 Huntington & Cabell County with Tri-States Area
A944 Parkersburg & Wood County
A946 Wheeling with Ohio & Marshall Counties

WISCONSIN
A948 Appleton & Outagamie County
A950 Beloit-Janesville with Rock County, Wisc. & Winnebago County, Ill.
A952 Eau Claire & Eau Claire County
A954 Fond du Lac & Fond du Lac County
A956 Green Bay & Brown County
A958 La Crosse & La Crosse County
A960 Madison & Dane County
A962 Manitowoc & Manitowoc County
A964 Milwaukee & Milwaukee County
A966 Oshkosh & Winnebago County
A968 Racine-Kenosha, Racine & Kenosha Counties
A970 Sheboygan & Sheboygan County
A972 Superior-Duluth Metropolitan Area with Two Harbors
A974 Waukesha & Waukesha County
A976 Wausau & Marathon County

WYOMING
A978 Casper & Natrona County
A980 Cheyenne & Laramie County
A982 Laramie & Albany County
A226 The Five Northwestern States

each $152.00

GE-50 MAPS
1:5, 000, 000
Washington : US Dept. Commerce, Bureau of the Census
106 x 76
Showing county, district, township boundaries.

11 Congressional Districts for the 90th Congress (1967-8) 50c

35 Congressional Districts for the 92nd Congress (1970) 50c

46 Congressional Districts for the 93rd Congress (1972)

APPALACHIAN REGION, AS DESIGNATED BY THE REGIONAL COMMISSION
1:2, 500, 000
Washington : USGS, 1967
66 x 79
State and county boundaries, App. region and its counties in red with national parks, monuments, national forests, wildlife refuges and Indian reservations. $1.00

US-MEXICO BORDER AREA – ZONA FRONTERIZA MEXICO – EEUU
1:2, 500, 000
Washington : US-Mexico Commission for Border Devt. and Friendship, 1969
53 x 85
With insets of Tijuana-Mexicala and Gulf of Mexico – Rio Grande City at 1:1, 000, 000. In Spanish and English.

STATE POSTAL MAPS
Various scales
Washington : Govt. Printing Office
Postal boundaries in colour.
Maps available:

Alabama, 1.1.69
1:793, 750 1969 55 x 81
Alaska, 1.10.70
1:3, 125, 000 1970 53 x 81
Arizona, 1.8.70
1:937, 500 1970 81 x 63
Arkansas, 1.12.69
1:793, 750 1969 63 x 68
California-Nevada (N), 1.2.69
1:1, 000, 000 app. 1969 55 x 81
Colorado, 1.6.70
1:937, 500 1970 55 x 81
Florida, 1.3.68
1:812, 500 app. 1969 81 x 63
Georgia, 1.1.70
1:812, 500 app 1970 78 x 63
Hawaii, 1.10.70
1:793, 750 1970 50 x 78
Idaho, 1.2.70
1:1, 000, 000 app 1970 81 x 59
Illinois, 1.7.69
1:812, 500 app 1969 81 x 55
Indiana, 1.9.69
1:625, 000 1969 81 x 53
Iowa, 1.3.70
1:625, 000 1970 55 x 81
Kansas, 1.5.70
1:1, 250, 000 1970 45 x 81
Kentucky, 1.7.70
1:937, 500 1970 40 x 86
Louisiana, 1.12.68
1:812, 500 app 1968 63 x 73
Maine, 1.5.70
1:625, 000 1970 81 x 55
Minnesota, 1.5.69
1:812, 500 app 1969 81 x 66
Mississippi, 1.6.69
1:812, 500 app 1969 81 x 55
Missouri, 1.7.70
1:812, 500 app 1970 63 x 81
Montana, 1.6.70
1:1, 937, 500 1970 50 x 81
Nebraska, 1.1.69
1:1, 250, 000 1969 45 x 81
New Hampshire-Vermont, 1.4.70
1:390, 625 1970 81 x 63
New Mexico, 1.10.69
1:937, 500 1969 78 x 66
North Carolina, 1.3.68
1:781, 350 1968 55 x 81
North Dakota, 1.3.70
1:781, 350 1970 58 x 81
Oklahoma, 1.8.70
1:781, 350 1970 76 x 63
Oregon, 1.5.69
1:812, 500 app 1969 63 x 81
Pennsylvania (E), 1.8.69
1:400, 000 app 1969 73 x 63
Pennsylvania (W), 1.8.69
1:400, 000 app 1969 73 x 63
Puerto Rico and Virgin Islands, 1.9.70
1:312, 500 1970 43 x 81
South Carolina, 1.9.70
1:625, 000 1970 63 x 81
South Dakota, 1.3.69
1:781, 350 1969 58 x 81
Tennessee, 1.3.69
1:937, 500 1969 30 x 81
Texas (E), 1.4.69
1:1, 300, 000 app 1961 81 x 55
Texas (W), 1.4.69
1:1, 300, 000 app 1969 81 x 55
Utah, 1.1.70
1:781, 350 1970 81 x 58
Virginia, 1.9.69
1:625, 000 1969 50 x 81
Washington, 1.12.69
1:812, 500 app 1969 60 x 81
West Virginia, 1.2.70
1:625, 000 1970 55 x 81
Wisconsin, 1.10.69
1:812, 500 app 1969 76 x 63
Wyoming, 1.4.70
1:1, 300, 000 app 1970 55 x 81

Each 35c

STATE-COUNTY SUBDIVISION MAPS
1:750, 000 (generally)
Washington : US Dept. Commerce Bureau of the Census, 1970
91 x 121
Shows county census divisions (townships, districts) for 1970 census. Available for each state including these combinations:

Massachusetts, Connecticut, Rhode Island;
Vermont, New Hampshire;
Maryland and Delaware
Each 20c

BASE MAP OF THE UNITED STATES
1:7, 000, 000
Map 7A
Washington : USGS, 1916
50 x 76
Map shows states boundaries, principal cities in black and water features in blue. Excludes Alaska and non-conterminous territories. 50c
Similar maps at reduced sizes available:

Map 11A
1:11, 875, 000 33 x 48 1906 20c

Map 16A
1:16, 500, 000 24 x 33 1911 10c

OUTLINE MAP OF THE USA
1:5, 000, 000
Washington : USGS
68 x 106
Available in 4 editions each with insets of Alaska, Hawaii, Canal Zone, Puerto Rico and Virgin Is.
Map 5A
State and County Boundaries and names 1933 50c
Map 5B
State and County Boundaries and names with counties and water features in blue, 1933 75c
Map 5C
State Boundaries and names in black, water features blue, 1933 75c
Map 5D
State Boundaries and names only 1940 75c

UNITED STATES COUNTY OUTLINE MAP
1:5, 000, 000
Washington : US Dept. Commerce, Bureau of the Census, 1970
104 x 66
Map showing boundaries; 2 editions — boundaries and names in black and state boundaries black, County boundaries and names in blue. 20c and 25c

PHILIPS MAP BUILDING SHEET ('BLACKBOARD MAP') OF THE UNITED STATES
1:4, 500, 000
London : Philip
104 x 83
Outline map printed in yellow on black-board paper.
Mounted CR £4.00

VITO-GRAPHIC CHALKBOARD OUTLINE MAP OF THE UNITED STATES
1:3, 500, 000
Ref: VS 2
Chicago : Weber Costello Co
158 x 119
Land areas in green, meridians, parallels and outlines in yellow, water areas in blue. On cloth — various mounted styles.
Also available with WORLD VS1-2 on reverse side.

BASE MAP OF THE UNITED STATES OF AMERICA
1:3, 168, 000
Map No 3A
Washington : USGS, 1965
165 x 107
Wall map, showing state boundaries and names, principal cities, with national forests, parks and monuments, Indian reservations and wildlife refuges marked. Puerto Rico, Panama Canal Zone, Alaska, Hawaii, Guan, American Samoa, Manua Islands inset.
$1.50

UNITED STATES, SLATED OUTLINE
1:3, 125, 000
No 165011
Chicago : Denoyer-Geppert
152 x 129
Black board outline map, yellow and blue on black, 48 states.
$28.50

Available also as individual states :
165251 California
1:875, 000 111 x 129 $19.95
165291 New Jersey
1:250, 000 111 x 129 $19.95
165591 New York City
1:62, 500 111 x 129 $19.95
165341 Ohio
1:375, 000 152 x 129 $28.50
Yellow on black :
166131 Inidana
1:375, 000 111 x 129 $19.50
166321 N Carolina
1:500, 000 152 x 129 $25.00
166481 Wisconsin
1:500, 000 111 x 129 $19.50

BASE MAP OF THE UNITED STATES
1:2, 500, 000
Washington : USGS, 1972
137 x 202 complete
2 sheet wall map showing State and County boundaries, capitals, water features, on a buff tinted background. Alaska, Hawaii, Canal Zone, Puerto Rico, Virgin Islands inset.
Per set $2.00
Also available :
Map 2B, as above without buff tinted background.
Per set $1.50

E1 PHYSICAL : RELIEF

STATI UNITI D'AMERICA
1:15, 000, 000
Novara : Ag
33 x 26
Physical map with political map and economic details on reverse. L450

CONTOUR MAP OF THE UNITED STATES
1:7, 000, 000
Map No 7B
Washington : USGS, 1916
106 x 68
State boundaries and pirncipal cities in black, water features in blue, contours in brown. Alaska and non-conterminous territories not shown. 50c

SPOJENÉ STÁTY AMERICKÉ
1:6, 000, 000
Praha : Kart
87 x 58
Physical/political reference map, in series "Poznavame Svet" (getting to know the world). With text vol. Kcs 17.50

SOEDINENNYE SHTATY AMERIKI
1:6, 000, 000
Moskva : GUGK, 1973
Col. study map showing water features, settlements, admin. centres and divisions, communications, boundaries, economic details, pop. Geog. description.
30 kop

STATI UNITI
1:5, 000, 000
Novara : Ag
140 x 100
School wall map showing relief of land and sea, political boundaries, water features, major communications, towns graded by pop. L2,200

Mounted L5,000
(Also available in English edition)

THE UNITED STATES
1:5, 000, 000
New York : AGS, 1968
97 x 64
Contoured, láyer col. cities classified acc. pop, roads, railways etc.
Alaska and Hawaii inset $2.50

THE WORLD
1:5, 000, 000
AGS
Sheet 1E United States and Southern Canada
See WORLD 100C and index 100/3.

TRIGRAPHIC MAPS OF THE UNITED STATES
1:5, 000, 000
Ref. TR1-2

Chicago : Weber Costello Co
101 x 137
Physical layer colouring with graphic relief shading and political boundaries. Includes the 50 states and possessions.
Available mounted in various styles.

PHILIP'S GRAPHIC RELIEF MAP OF THE UNITED STATES
1:4, 500, 000
London : Philip
86 x 107
Col. to simulate predominant vegetation cover, relief shading producing a 3-D effect. No town names.
Paper flat £1.50
Mounted CR £5.50
Mounted on cloth dissected to fold £7.00

ÉTATS-UNIS NO 1 (PHYSIQUE)
1:4, 000, 000
No 1200 French 1235 English
St Germain-en-Laye : Éditions MDI
126 x 92
Plastic coated physcial wall map for schools. Political and population map on reverse

LES GRANDES PUISSANCES : USA
1:4, 000, 000
TC 42 (No 1611)
St Germain-en-Laye : Éditions MDI
126 x 92
Plastic coated physical wall map for schools. China on reverse at
1:4, 500, 000

VEREINIGTE STAATEN UND MITTELAMERIKA
1:3, 500, 000
Gotha : Haack
202 x 168
Physical wall map showing USA and Central America. Layer col. and hachuring, boundaries, major cities and communications.

VEREINIGTE STAATEN
1:3, 500, 000
Ed H Haack
Darmstadt : Perthes
146 x 100
Layer col. wall map with principal communications, towns graded by pop.
48 DM

PHYSICAL MAPS OF THE USA
Various scales
Chicago : Denoyer-Geppert
School wall maps, available at different levels and depths.
102011-14 US, Mexico Simplified
1:3, 125, 000 162 x 205 $30.00
102061-14 US, Simplified
1:3, 125, 000 162 x 205 $30.00
102051-14 US, Simplified
1:3, 125, 000 162 x 205 $27.00
(Above inc. Alaska and Hawaii)
102041-14 US, Mexico
1:3, 125, 000 162 x 205 $27.00
102031-14 US
1:3, 125, 000 162 x 205 $24.00
120011-14 US (50 States) Mexico Visual Relief
1:3, 125, 000 162 x 205 $32.00
120061-14 US (50 States) Visual Relief
1:3, 125, 000 162 x 205 $32.00
120041-14 US (48 States) Mexico Visual Relief
1:3, 125, 000 162 x 205 $27.50
120031-14 US (48 States) Visual Relief
1:3, 125, 000 162 x 205 $27.50
110011 US (50 States) Mexico Visual Relief
1:4, 687, 500 147 x 111 $18.75
301511 US (50 States) Desk Relief Map
No scale 42 x 28 for 25 $3.50
129011-10 Extra Large US (48 States) Visual Relief
1:2, 175, 000 218 x 147 $42.50
129811-10 Giant Size Visual Relief
1:1, 562, 500 342 x 216 $99.50
135061-14 Large Physical-Political
1:2, 125, 000 162 x 203 $30.00
130011-10 Classroom Physical Political, Mexico
1:4, 687, 500 111 x 147 $15.50
131711-10 Classroom Physical Political, East US
1:2, 187, 500 111 x 147 $15.50
131771-10 Classroom Physical Political, Western US
1:2, 187, 500 111 x 147 $15.50
198011 Tactual Raised Relief in Steel Frame
1:5, 000, 000 121 x 91 $49.50
198412 3-D Vinyl Relief Map
No scale 86 x 55 $7.95
198512 3-D Vinyl Relief Map
No scale 66 x 43 $4.95

UNITED STATES — PHYSICAL — POLITICAL MAPS
Indianapolis : Cram
Col. wall maps for schools at 4 different levels; Hawaii and Alaska inset.
Level A Primary Map
1:3, 070, 000 162 x 132 $26.25
Level B USA
1:3, 750, 000 129 x 129 $23.00
USA
1:3, 000, 000 162 x 132 $27.25
Level C USA
1:3, 750, 000 129 x 129 $23.00
USA
1:3, 000, 000 162 x 132 $27.75
Level D Astro-vue
1:3, 000, 000 162 x 132 $30.50
Physical Outline (all levels)
1:3, 750, 000 129 x 129 $27.50
Excello Wall Map
1:5, 000, 000 137 x 101 $12.50

MAGNA-GRAPHIC MAP OF THE UNITED STATES — CONTOUR — RELIEF MAP
1:3, 000, 000
Ed E Putnam Parker
Chicago : Weber Costello Co
167 x 114
Physical-political map with relief shades to produce 3-D effect. Alaska, Hawaii, US possessions inset.
Available mounted in various styles.

THE UNITED STATES — PHYSICAL MAP
1:3, 000, 000
No 3060C
Washington : Coast & Geodetic Surv.
175 x 120 complete
Physical map in 2 sheets, contours at 1,000ft intervals, layer col, principal towns.

VEREINIGTE STAATEN VON AMERIKA UND SUDLICHES KANADA
1:3, 000, 000
Braunschweig : Westermann
Physical wall map showing relief, settlements, boundaries etc.

VEREINIGTE STAATEN UND MITTELAMERIKA
1:3, 000, 000
Munchen : List
240 x 175
Wenschow wall map showing relief of land and sea bottom, individual states indicated.
164 DM

VEREINIGTE STAATEN
1:2, 500, 000
Darmstadt : Perthes
210 x 140
Haack physical wall map, showing relief of land and sea. 128 DM

SECTIONAL MAPS OF THE USA
1:1, 562, 500
Chicago : Denoyer-Geppert
162 x 137
Series of col. visual wall maps for schools. Cities graded by pop, communications etc.
N121701-10 Northeastern US
$21.50
121731-10 Southeastern US
$21.50
121751-10 North Central US
$21.50
121771-10 Western US
162 x 195 $38.50
121791-10 South Central US
$21.50
121841-10 Southwestern US
$21.50
121851-10 Northwestern US
$21.50
Available as set, mounted on 1 roller
$154.00
Also as desk maps,
43 x 38 per 25 copies $3.30

STATE AND REGIONAL MAPS
Various scales
Chicago : Denoyer-Geppert
Topog. and physical school wall maps in various styles mounted on cloth with rollers: VR — Visual Relief; RL Relief-like; RP Physical-Political; NC Natural Colour; SC Simplified Col.
131021 Alabama
1:570, 680 96 x 142 $21.75
120021 Alaska and Hawaii VR
1:3, 125, 000 162 x 76 $19.25
150021 Alaska and Hawaii RL
1:3, 125, 000 162 x 76 $19.25
135021 Alaska and Hawaii RP
1:3, 125, 000 162 x 76 $19.25
131031 Arizona RP
111 x 162 $29.00

131041 Arkansas RP
101 x 142 $29.00
131511 British Columbia RP
1:1, 250, 000 111 x 147 $19.25
111051 California VR
1:875, 000 111 x 147 $21.75
131062 Colorado (Jeppesen) NC
1:500, 000 142 x 129 $25.00
111191 *Chesapeake Bay Area VR
1:411, 840 111 x 162 $21.75
111191 Delaware (Ches. Bay) VR
1:411, 840 111 x 162 $21.75
121091 Florida VR
1:625, 000 162 x 137 $27.50
131161 Georgia RP
129 x 172 $29.00
111111 Idaho VR
1:625, 000 111 x 162 $21.75
111121 Illinois VR
1:500, 000 111 x 162 $21.75
131121 Illinois RP
1:500, 000 111 x 147 $19.25
111131 Indiana VR
1:375, 000 111 x 162 $21.75
131141 Iowa RP
1:500, 000 101 x 127 $19.25
131152 Kansas RP
1:625, 000 132 x 114 $21.75
131171 Louisiana RP
1:500, 000 111 x 162 $19.25
111191 Maryland (Ches. Bay) VR
1:411, 840 111 x 162 $21.75
111211 Michigan VR
1:625, 000 111 x 162 $21.75
131221 Minnesota RP
1:531, 250 111 x 147 $19.25
131241 Missouri RP
1:562, 500 111 x 147 $19.25
131261 Nebraska RP
1:687, 500 111 x 147 $19.25
121721 New England VR
1:375, 000 137 x 162 $27.50
131302 New Mexico NC
1:625, 000 104 x 116 $25.00
121311 New York VR
1:500, 000 162 x 137 $27.50
121321 North Carolina VR
1:531, 250 162 x 111 $27.50
139101 North Carolina Phy-Pol. RP
1:150, 000 111 x 162 $19.25
131331 North Dakota RP
101 x 106 $25.00
111341 Ohio VR
1:375, 000 111 x 162 $21.75
131351 Oklahoma VR
1:750, 000 111 x 147 $19.25
121561 Ontario VR
1:1, 250, 000 162 x 111 $27.50
111361 Oregon VR
1:625, 000 111 x 162 $21.75
121651 +Pacific Northwest VR
1:625, 000 183 x 162 $32.00
131651 +Pacific Northwest RP
1:1, 125, 000 111 x 147 $19.25
121371 Pennsylvania VR
1:343, 750 162 x 111 $27.50
131371 Pennsylvania RP
1:500, 000 111 x 147 $19.25
130891 South Carolina RP
1:500, 000 111 x 162 $19.25
131401 South Dakota RP
1:625, 000 111 x 147 $19.25
130781 Tennessee RP
1:725, 000 111 x 147 $19.25
121421 Texas VR
1:1,000, 000 137 x 162 $27.50
131411 Simplified Texas SC
1:1, 125, 000 111 x 147 $19.25
131431 Utah RP
1:500, 000 111 x 147 $19.25
121451 Virginia VR
1: 500, 000 162 x 111 $27.50
111461 Washington VR
1:625, 000 111 x 162 $21.75
131471 West Virginia RP
1:411, 840 111 x 147 $19.25
111481 Wisconsin VR
1:500, 000 111 x 162 $21.75

* Includes all of Md, Del, and portions of Va, W. Va, NJ and Penna.
\+ Includes all of Washington, Oregon and Idaho.

IMPERIAL MAP OF ALASKA
1:2, 500, 000
Chicago : Rand McNally, 1972
122 x 89
Detailed ref. map showing highways, railways, mts, and valley in shaded relief.
$1.00

USA FISICO-POLITICA
1:5, 000, 000
Novara : Agostini
131 x 100
Moulded plastic relief map in frame with metal corners. L20,000

RAISED RELIEF MAP OF THE UNITED STATES OF AMERICA
1:3, 168, 000
Chicago : Nystrom, 1975
NRI
153 x 97
Plastic moulded map, physical layer colouring, principal communications and boundaries.
Unframed $46.00
Framed $74.00

RAISED RELIEF MAP OF THE US
New York : Hagstrom
68 x 50
3-D plastic raised relief map. $2.95

3-D VINYL NATURAL COLOR RELIEF MAPS
Various scales
Chicago : Denoyer-Geppert
Raised relief maps available for the following states :

198402	Alaska	53 x 61	$7.95
198432	Arizona	43 x 53	$4.95
198452	California	55 x 63	$7.95
198462	Colorado	43 x 55	$4.95
198502	Hawaii	43 x 55	$4.95
198422	New England	43 x 55	$4.95
198702	New Mexico	43 x 50	$4.95
198562	Oregon	43 x 55	$4.95
198522	Texas	53 x 53	$5.95
198532	Utah	43 x 55	$4.95
198582	Washington	43 x 55	$4.95
198592	Wyoming	43 x 55	$4.95

ALASKA IN 3-D
1:4, 752, 000 (horizontal)
1:16, 000ft app. (vertical)
1st edition
Denver : Kistler Graphics, 1970
137 x 152
Coloured, moulded plastic relief map.
Aleutian Islands (not 3-D) inset. $7.95

NEW ENGLAND IN 3-D
1:1, 774, 000 (horizontal)
1:8, 000 (vertical)
Denver : Kistler Graphics, 1969
56 x 49
Coloured moulded plastic relief map, with cultural overlays.

OHIO
No scale given
No 198341
Chicago : Denoyer-Geppert
83 x 91
Tactual raised relief map showing physiographic divisions, cities graded by pop.
In steel frame.
$40.00

RAISED RELIEF TOPOGRAPHIC MAPS
1:250, 000
Philadelphia : Panoramic Studios
56 x 84 (average size)
Plastic moulded relief maps. following USGS 1:25, 000 series sheet lines. Show relief at vertical exaggeration of 3:1, and 2:1, boundaries, settlement, communications, woodland detail etc. $9.95 each

GRAND CANYON NATIONAL PARK
1:253, 440
Grand Canyon : G C Natural History Assoc/National Park Service, 1967
Plastic relief model of the park.

E2 PHYSICAL : LAND FEATURES

PHYSICAL DIVISIONS OF THE UNITED STATES
1:7, 000, 000
Map 7C
Washington : USGS, 1946
106 x 68
Physical divisions outlined in red on base map (Map 7A). Subdivisions and characteristics of each division are listed in the margin.
50c

RETREAT OF WISCONSIN AND RECENT ICE IN NORTH AMERICA
1:5, 000, 000
GSC No 1257A
by V.K. Prest
Ottawa : GSC, 1969
Coloured map. $2.00

LANDFORMS OF MICHIGAN
Erwin Raisz and Christopher Mills
1:2, 260, 000 app.
Boston : Erwin Raisz, 1968
17 x 20
Physical landforms map with insets of regions, successive ice fronts and moraines, generalised section.

TEXAS – GEOGRAPHIC REGIONS
1:2, 600, 000
Austin : Univ. of Texas, Bureau of Business Research, 1976
56 x 45
Base map with main highways and county boundaries. State classified into 12 geographic regions.
$1.00

MAP SHOWING EXTENT OF GLACIATIONS IN ALASKA
1:2, 500, 000
Misc. Inv. 1-415
Washington : USGS 1965 rep. 1974
132 x 89
Showing contour on inferred surfaces of glaciers of late Pleistocene age.
$1.00

GLACIAL MAP OF THE UNITED STATES EAST OF THE ROCKY MOUNTAINS
1:1, 750, 000
Boulder, Col. : GSA, 1959
92 x 109 each
2 sheet col. glacial map showing moraines, age drifts, drift sheets etc. $8.00

BATHYMETRIC MAPS, EASTERN CONTINENTAL MARGIN USA
1:1, 000, 000
In 3 sheets
Tulsa : Am. Assoc. Petroleum Geologists, 1970
Sheet 1 covers Atlantic Ocean N of Cape Hatteras 109 x 152
Sheet 2 Atlantic S of Cape Hatteras 109 x 152
Sheet 3 Northern Gulf of Mexico 81 x 175
$10.00

GEOTHERMAL RESOURCES OF NEW MEXICO
1:1, 000, 000
Resource Map 1
Compiled by W.K. Summers
Sante Fe : New Mexico Bureau of Mines and Mineral Resources 1972

HYDROLOGIC INVESTIGATION ATLASES
Various scales
Washington : USGS
Series of local and regional maps depicting availability of ground water, descriptions of flood areas, river drainage and alluvial deposits.

OHIO – PRINCIPAL STREAMS AND THEIR DRAINAGE AREAS
1:650, 000
Columbus : Ohio Dept. of Natural Resources, 1973
Hydrological map.

WASHINGTON URBAN AREA – ANNOTATED ORTHOPHOTO MAP 1970
1:100, 000
Misc. Inv. 1-858-B
Washington : USGS, 1974
72 x 77
$0.75

NATION'S CAPITAL AREA
1:250, 000
Washington : USGS, 1973
Earth Resources Technology Satellite, National Aeronautics and Space Admin. Image. In 2 sheets.

F GEOLOGY

GEOLOGIC MAP OF THE UNITED STATES
1:2, 500, 000
In 4 sheets
Washington : USGS
227 x 130
Col. geol. map excluding Alaska and Hawaii.

TECTONIC MAP OF THE UNITED STATES – EXCLUSIVE OF ALASKA AND HAWAII
1:2, 500, 000
Washington : USGS, 1962
194 x 120 complete
Map in 2 sheets, showing metamorphic, intrusive, volcanic and certain sedimentary rocks in col. structural contours, faults, folds, salt domes etc.
$4.50 set

GEOLOGICAL MAP OF ALASKA
1:2, 500, 000
Washington : USGS
147 x 91
Detailed geol. map in col. with details of sources inset.

TECTONIC MAP OF THE UNITED STATES
1:2, 500, 000
Tulsa : Am. Assoc. Petroleum Geologists, 1962
101 x 127
Wall map showing analysis of principal rocks, faults and foldings. In col.
$4.50

BASEMENT ROCK MAP OF THE UNITED STATES
1:2, 500, 000
Washington : USGS, 1968
194 x 120 complete
2 sheet map showing configuration of metamorphosed basement rocks, rock systems in col. contours, fault types, folds, drill holes. Hawaii and Alaska not included.
$3.00

METAMORPHIC MAP OF THE APPALACHIANS
1:2, 500, 000
Misc. Geol. Inv. 1-724
Washington : USGS, 1972
72 x 99
Coloured map showing major metamorphic belts and the degree of metamorphism by isograds, mineral facies and mineral facies series. With 10 page text.
$1.00

GEOLOGICAL HIGHWAY MAPS
1:1, 875, 000
See index 73/4
Tulsa : AAPG
91 x 70 each
Series of road maps combined with general geol. map; text, diagrams on reverse
Sheets published :

1 Mid Continent Region, 1966
2 Southern Rocky Mountains Region, 1967
3 Pacific Southwest Region, 1968
4 Mid Atlantic Region, 1970
5 Northern Rockies, 1972
6 Pacific Northwest Region, 1973
7 Texas
8 Alaska and Hawaii 1:3½m and ½m, 1974

each $1.75

TECTONIC MAP OF GULF COAST REGION, USA
1:1, 000, 000
Tulsa : Am. Assoc. Petroleum Geologists, 1972
101 x 193
Col. tectonic map. $9.00

GENERALISED PRE-PLEISTOCENE GEOLOGIC MAP OF THE NORTHERN UNITED STATES ATLANTIC CONTINENTAL MARGIN
1:1, 000, 000
Misc. Inv. 1-861
Washington : USGS 1974
Sheet 1 77 x 98 Sheet 2 79 x 91
Map in 2 sheets depicting pre-Pleistocene surface for the Northern Atlantic Coastal Plain, continental Shelf and slope, bore-holes and sea bed samples are located and tabulated. Cross section showing geology.
set $1.25

SUBSURFACE CAMBRIAN AND ORDOVICIAN STRATIGRAPHY OF THE TRENTON GROUP – PRECAMBRIAN INTERVAL IN NY STATE
by D W Flagler
Albany : NY State Museum, 1966
Col. geol. map.
$2.75

TECTONIC MAP OF THE ALASKA PENINSULA AND ADJACENT AREAS
by C A Burk
1:1, 000, 000
Boulder, Co. : GSA, 1965
79 x 97
Col. map as part 3 of Memoir 99.
$3.25

GEOLOGIC MAP OF THE ALASKA PENINSULA SOUTHWEST OF WIDE BAY
by C A Burk
1:250, 000
Boulder, Col. : GSA, 1965
103 x 125 each
2 sheet col. map, part 2 of Memoir 99.
Contoured at 200 and 1000ft intervals
$8.00

GEOLOGIC MAP OF YELLOWSTONE NATIONAL PARK
1:125, 000
Misc. Geol. Inv. 1-711
Washington : USGS, 1971
99 x 124
Col. geol. map.
Also available : Surficial edition 1-710 1972.

LIMESTONES OF JEFFERSON CITY, NY
by John H Johnsen
Albany : NY State Museum
Col. geol. map. $2.50

PRECAMBRIAN GEOLOGY OF POPOTOPEN LAKE QUADRANGLE, SOUTHEASTERN NEW YORK
by R T Dodd, Jr
Albany : New York State Museum, 1965
Col. geol. map. $2.00

GLACIAL GEOLOGY OF TROY, NY QUADRANGLE
by Robert La Fleur
Albany : NY State Museum
Col. geol. map. $2.50

BEDROCK GEOLOGY OF THE ST REGIS QUADRANGLE, NY
by Brian T C Davis
Albany : NY State Museum, 1971
Col. geol. map.

GEOLOGY OF THE PLATTSBURGH AND ROUSES POINT, NY-VERMONT QUADRANGLES
by Donald W Fisher
Albany : NY Stare Museum, 1968
Col. geol. map.

BEDROCK GEOLOGY OF THE GOSHEN-GREENWOOD LAKE AREA, NY-VERMONT QUADRANGLES
by T W Offield
Albany : NY State Museum
Col. geol. map $5.00

STRATIGRAPHIC CROSS SECTION OF PALEOZOIC ROCKS, WEST TEXAS TO NORTHERN MONTANA
Ed John C Maher
Tulsa : AAPG, 1960
6 Cross sections, 15 pp text.
$7.00

CORRELATIONS OF SUBSURFACE MESOZOIC AND CENZOIC ROCKS ALONG THE ATLANTIC COAST
John C Maher
Tulsa : AAPG, 1965
18 pp text, physiographic diagram, 8 correlation charts, Florida Keys to Long Island.
$7.00

CROSS SECTION NO 4 STRATIGRAPHIC CROSS SECTION OF PALEOZOIC ROCKS, COLORADO TO NEW YORK
Ed W C Adkison
Tulsa : AAPG, 1966
7 cross sections, 58 pp text.
$7.00

CROSS SECTION NO 5 STRATIGRAPHIC CROSS SECTION OF PALEOZOIC ROCKS, OKLAHOMA–SASKATCHEWAN
Ed Russell Smith
Tulsa : AAPG, 1967
6 cross sections, 23 pp text.
$7.00

CROSS SECTION NO 6 CORRELATION OF SUBSURFACE MESOZOIC AND CENOZOIC ROCKS ALONG THE EASTERN GULF COAST
Tulsa : AAPG, 1968
Text with 5 charts, 1 physiographic diagram.
$9.00

GEOLOGIC MAP OF ARIZONA
1:500, 000
E D Wilson and Richard T Moore
Washington : USGS/Arizona Bureau of Mines, 1969
178 x 121
Base map with col. geol. overprint $2.50

GEOLOGIC MAP OF CALIFORNIA
1:2, 500, 000
Misc. Geol. Inv. I-512
Washington : USGS, 1966
43 x 52 25c

GEOLOGIC MAP OF GEORGIA
1:2, 500, 000
Atlanta : Dept. of Mines, Mining and Geology, 1968
Coloured geological map.

BEDROCK OF IOWA
1:2, 000, 000
Iowa City : Geol. Survey 1969
Coloured map of basic rocks with stratigraphic column of Iowa.

GEOLOGIC MAP OF IOWA
1:500, 000
Iowa City : Iowa Geol. Soc, 1969
127 x 79
Coloured geological map.

GEOLOGIC MAP OF MISSISSIPPI
1:500, 000
Jackson : Mississippi Geol. Survey, 1969
Coloured geological map.

GEOLOGIC MAP OF NEW MEXICO
1:500, 000
Washington : USGS, 1965
124 x 160
1 sheet geol. map, 1 sheet explanation.
$2.50 set

GEOLOGIC MAP OF NEW YORK
by D W Fisher, Y W Isachsen, L V Richard
In 5 sheets
Albany : N Y State Museum, 1970
Col. geol. map for Niagara, Finger Lakes, Hudson-Mohawk, Adirondack, Lower Hudson.
each $2.00
set, inc. legend sheet $12.00

BEDROCK GEOLOGIC MAP OF NORTH DAKOTA
Clarence G Carlson
1:1, 000, 000
Bismarck : N D Geol. Surv. 1969
58 x 72
Coloured geological map with generalised glacial map inset at 1:2, 500, 000 app.

GEOLOGICAL MAP OF OREGON
1:2, 000, 000
Misc. Geol. Inv. I-595
Washington : USGS, 1969
35 x 66
General geol. map. 25c

BEDROCK GEOLOGIC MAP OF RHODE ISLAND
by A W Quinn
Washington : USGS, 1971
85 x 110
Col. geol. map with 68 pp text, 1971

GENERALISED GEOLOGIC MAP OF TENNESSEE
1:2, 900, 000
Nashville : Dept. Conservation, Geology Division, 1970

GEOLOGIC MAP OF WASHINGTON
1:2, 000, 000
Misc. Geol. Inv. I-583
Washington : USGS, 1969
28 x 73
General geol. map in colour. 25c

WISCONSIN
C E Dutton and R E Bradley
1:500, 000
Misc. Geol. Inv. I-631
Washington : USGS
55 x 58
Lithographic, geophysical and mineral commodity maps of Precambrian Rocks; 5 maps with details on: Lithologic Data, Magnetic and Bouguer Gravity Curves, Areal Geology, Mineral Commodity Localities of N Wisconsin and Part of Michigan. With text.

USA – GEOLOGIC MAPPING
Washington : USGS
Large scale geologic mapping is generally produced at scales of 1:24, 000 and 1:62, 500 as geologic quadrangle maps with other special maps at varying scales. Details of sheets published are given on individual state indexes to geological mapping which are available at a small charge. New publications are listed in the USGS "Monthly list of New Publications".

MISCELLANEOUS GEOLOGIC INVESTIGATIONS
Various scales
Washington : USGS
Maps published at various scales for many differnt areas including local districts of the USA and other countries. Many of these maps have been listed individually in their appropriate positions.

G EARTH RESOURCES

MINERAL RESOURCES MAPS
Washington : USGS
Maps available :
USA 1:5, 000, 000(x) and 1:3, 168, 000
MR2x Uranium deposits 1955
3x Potash occurrences 1955
13 Copper 1962
14 Borates 1962
15 Lead 1962
16 Vanadium 1962
17 Asbestos 1962
18 Pyrophyllite and Kyanite and related minerals 1962
19 Zinc 1962
20 Antimony 1962
21 Epigenetic uranium deposits 1962
22 Bismuth 1962
23 Manganese 1962
24 Gold 1962
25 Tungsten 1962
26 Chromite 1962
27 Magnesite and brucite 1962
28 Thorium and rare earths 1962
29 Titanium 1962
30 Mercury 1962

MR31 Talc and soapstone 1962
33 Gypsum and anhydrite 1962
35 Beryllium 1962
36 Niobium and tantalum 1963
37 High Alumina kaolinitic clay 1963
43 Barite 1965
44 Tin 1965
51 Iron 1967
55 Molybdenum 1970

ALASKA 1:2, 500, 000
10 Molybdenum, tin and tungsten 1960
11 Antimony, bismuth, mercury 1960
32 Lode gold, silver 1962
38 Placer gold 1964
40 Iron 54°–68°N; 130°–170°W; 1:250, 000
41 Industrial minerals and construction materials 1964
52 Antimony 1970
53 Bismuth 1970
54 Mercury 1970
56 Uranium, thorium and rare earth elements 1970

ARIZONA 1:500, 000 2 sheets
46 Selected minerals 1967

CALIFORNIA AND NEVADA
39 Oxidised zinc districts in Cal. and Nev. 1:750, 000 2 sheets 1964
47 Selected minerals in northern third of Cal. 1:500, 000 1967
48 Selected minerals in central third of Cal. 1:500, 000 1971

COLORADO
57 Selected minerals 1:500, 000 1971

CONNECTICUT
7 Mineral deposits 1:500, 000 1957

MARYLAND
12 Mineral deposits 1:250, 000 1961

MASSACHUSETTS AND RHODE ISLAND
4 Mineral deposits 1:500, 000 1956

MONTANA
50 Selected minerals 1:500, 000 2 sheets 1967

NEW HAMPSHIRE
6 Mineral deposits 1:500, 000 1957

NEW MEXICO
45 Selected minerals 1:500, 000 2 sheets 1965

VERMONT
5 Mineral deposits 1:500, 000 1957

WASHINGTON – OREGON
1 Geologic environment of aluminia resources of the Columbia Basin 1:1, 500, 000 1952

WYOMING
42 Selected minerals 1:500, 000 1964

MINERAL MAP OF OKLAHOMA
K S Johnson
1:750, 000
Norman : Univ. Oklahoma, 1969
60 x 105
Coloured mineral map, excluding oil and gas fields. In envelope with text, bibliog. and "Index to Mountain Systems of Oklahoma" at 1:4, 500, 000
$1.00

MINES AND MINERALS OF WYOMING
1:500, 000
Laramie : Geological Survey, 1970
Coloured distribution map.

MINERAL RESOURCE MAPS AND CHARTS
Various scales
Washington : USGS
Series of large scale maps and diagrams depicting the geology and mineral resources of local areas of economic importance.
They are published in the following series:
Coal Investigation Maps
Oil and Gas Investigations – Maps and Charts
Mineral Investigations – Field Studies Maps
Resource Maps – see separate list.

NATURAL GAS
1:12, 500, 000 app
Washington : Govt. Printing Office, 1971
33 x 48
Shows major natural gas pipelines at June 30, 1971, in col.
15c

COAL FIELDS OF THE UNITED STATES
1:5, 000, 000
Washington : USGS
Sheet 1 USA (Inc. 4 inset maps and 2 charts) 89 x 132 1959 $1.50
Sheet 2 Alaska 70 x 88 1961 $1.00

MAP OF SOUTHWESTERN INDIANA SHOWING LOCATIONS OF ACTIVE COAL MINES
Harold C. Hutchinson
Bloomington : Geol. Surv. Indiana, 1962 (1968)
Misc. Publication No 7
91 x 56

OIL AND GAS FIELDS OF THE UNITED STATES
1:2, 500, 000
Washington : USGS, 1964
194 x 120 complete
2 sheet map, not inc. Hawaii and Alaska
$2.00 set

EXECUTIVES REFERENCE MAPS
Dallas : Geomap
Col. maps showing drilling and oil producing areas. Sheets available:
303 Southwest Louisiana 1:316, 800 1973
304 Southeast Louisiana 1:316, 800 1973 each $45.00
305 Mississippi 1:380, 160 1967
306 Permian Basin (2 sheets) 1:277, 200 1963 each $35.00
311 Western Oklahoma – Texas Panhandle 1:443, 520 1976
312 Northeast Texas Gulf Coast 1:443, 520 1975
313 Southwest Texas Gulf Coast 1:443, 520 1975
322 Powder River Basin 1:443, 520 1976
326 Western Wyoming 1:443, 520 1975 each $47.50

JURASSIC DRILLING MAPS
Dallas : Geomap
Col. Maps available for the following areas:
301 Texas 1:297, 000 1972 $35.00
307 Mississippi and W. Alabama and Florida 1:380, 160 1975 $97.50
309 Arkansas – N Louisiana 1:277, 200 1972 $35.00

MISSOURI BASIN STUDIES
Various scales
Washington : USGS
Various sizes
1 Mineral Resources of the Missouri Valley region, 1945-6 1:250, 000, 4 sheets, Rep. 1957 $1.50 set
2 Preliminary may showing sand and gravel deposits of Colorado 1:500, 000 1946 50c
3 Preliminary map showing sand and gravel deposits of North Dakota 1:500, 000 1946 35c
4 Preliminary map showing sand and gravel deposits of Wyoming 1:500, 000 1946 50c
5 Preliminary map showing sand and gravel deposits of Montana 1:500, 000 1946 2 sheets 70c set
7 Preliminary map showing sand and gravel deposits of Nebraska 1:750, 000 1948 55c
9 Map showing construction materials and non metallic mineral resources of Wyoming 1:500, 000 1946 70c
10 Map showing construction materials and non metallic mineral resources of Colorado 1:500, 000 1946 80c
11 Map showing construction materials and non metallic mineral resources of Montana 1:750, 000 1948 2 sheets 90c set
12 Map showing construction materials and non metallic mineral resources of South Dakota 1:500, 000 1947 60c
13 Map showing metallic mineral deposits of South Dakota 1:1, 000, 000 1947 60c
14 Map showing construction materials and non metallic mineral resources of North Dakota 1:500, 000 1947 60c
15 Map showing construction materials and non metallic mineral resources of Nebraska 1:750, 000 1948 40c
16 Map showing metallic mineral deposits of Montana 1:1, 000, 000 1947 30c
17 Map showing metallic mineral deposits of Wyoming 1:1, 000, 000 20c
18 Map showing mineral deposits of Missouri 1:1, 000, 000 1948 20c
20 Reconnaissance map showing locations of possible sources of riprap in Western North Dakota and in northwestern South Dakota 1:500, 000 1947 50c

OIL AND GAS FIELDS OF THE STATE OF LOUISIANA
1:500, 000
Washington : USGS, 1939
50c

PERMAFROST MAP OF ALASKA
1:2, 500, 000
Misc. Geol. Inv. I-445
Washington : USGS, 1965
124 x 95
Col. map of distribution and thickness of permafrost, with grades of superficial deposits. $1.00

SOIL SURVEY MAPS
1:20, 000
or 1:15, 840
Washington : US Dept. Agriculture, 1899–
In addition to soil maps these surveys contain general information about the agriculture and climate and descriptions of each kind of soil and also a discussion of the formation and classification of soils with soil laboratory data when available. Surveys published since 1957 include more detailed descriptions and contain soil maps printed on a photo-mosaic base. Most soil surveys cover one or more counties and where only part of a county is covered the word 'Area' is used.
Maps available :

ALABAMA
1964 Baldwin
1961 Calhoun
1959 Chambers
1972 Chilton
1939 Colbert
1929 Coosa
1921 Crenshaw
1962 Cullman
1960 Dale
1938 Dallas
1958 De Kalb
1955 Elmore
1965 Fayette
1927 Franklin
1965 Franklin
1971 Greene
1939 Hale
1968 Houston
1954 Jackson
1931 Lauderdale
1959 Lawrence
1950 Lee
1953 Limestone
1944 Macon
1958 Madison
1959 Marshall
1916 Monroe
1960 Montgomery
1944 Morgan
1902 Perry
1930 Perry
1967 Randolph
1916 Wilcox
1937 Winston

ALASKA
1963 Fairbanks Area
1971 Homer-Ninilchik Area
1962 Kenai-Kasilof Area
1916 Kenai Peninsula
1968 Matanuska Valley Area
1960 Northeastern Kodiak Island Area

ARIZONA
1967 Beaver Creek Area
1927 Buckeye-Beardsley Area
1941 Casa Grande Area
1928 Gila Bend Area
1964 Holbrook Show-Low Area
1930 Nogales Area
1970 Safford Area
1926 Salt River Valley Area
1921 San Simon Area
1954 Sulphur Springs Valley Area
1941 The Duncan Area
1931 Tucson Area
1938 Upper Gila Valley Area
1942 Virgin River Valley Area
1941 Yuma Desert Area

ARKANSAS
1972 Arkansas
1961 Bradley
1967 Chicot
1968 Cleveland
1916 Craighead
1968 Cross
1972 Decker
1972 Desna
1971 Franklin
1969 Greene
1916 Hempstead
1971 Mississippi
1973 Ouacuita
1966 St Francis
1969 Washington
1968 Woodruff

CALIFORNIA
1966 Alameda Area
1931 Alturas Area
1965 Amador Area
1969 Antelope Valley Area
1945 Bakersfield Area
1937 Barstow Area
1920 Brawley Area
1971 Carson Valley Area
1923 Coachella Valley Area
1952 Coalinga Area
1939 Contra Costa
1971 Eastern Fresno
1964 Eastern Stanislaus Area
1930 El Cajon Area
1918 El Centro Area
1968 Glenn
1918 Grass Valley Area
1946 Kings
1937 Lodi Area
1952 Los Banos Area
1962 Madera Area
1956 Mendota Area
1962 Merced Area
1938 Napa Area
1948 Newman Area
1922 Palo Verde Area
1942 Pixley Area
1927 Placerville Area
1954 Sacramento Area
1941 Sacramento San Joaquin Delta Area
1925 Salinas Area
1969 San Benito
1973 San Diego
1961 San Mateo Area
1958 Santa Barbara Area
1972 Santa Barbara Area – North
1958 Santa Clara Area
1944 Santa Cruz Area
1927 Santa Ynez Area
1919 Shasta Valley Area
1951 Stockton Area
1930 Suisan Area
1967 Tehama
1943 Tracy Area
1970 Ventura Area
1940 Visalia Area
1942 Wasco Area
1971 Western Riverside
1972 Yolo

COLORADO
1947 Akron Area
1971 Arapahoe
1926 Arkansas Valley Area
1971 Bent
1932 Brighton Area
1968 Crowley
1967 Delta-Montrose Area
1966 Elbert (eastern part)
1927 Fort Collins Area
1962 Fraser-Alpine Area
1955 Grand Junction Area
1929 Greeley Area
1930 Longmont Area
1968 Morgan
1971 Phillips
1966 Prowers
1970 Sedgwich
1961 Trout Creek Watershed

CONNECTICUT
1962 Hartford
1970 Litchfield
1966 Tolland

DELAWARE
1971 Kent
1970 New Castle

FLORIDA
1954 Collier
1958 Dade
1960 Escambia
1962 Gadsden
1958 Hillsborough
1923 Lake
1958 Manatee
1971 Okeechobee
1960 Orange
1927 Polk
1959 Sarasota
1966 Seminole
1965 Suwannee
1965 Washington

GEORGIA
1971 Barker
1941 Bartow
1969 Ben Hill-Irwin
1922 Bibb
1916 Brooks
1968 Bulloch
1925 Calhoun
1948 Candler
1971 Carroll and Harelson
1941 Catoosa
1927 Clarke
1968 Clarke-Oconee
1914 Clay
1914 Colquitt
1919 Coweta and Fayette
1916 Crisp
1942 Dade
1972 Dawson Lumkin and White
1939 Decatur
1923 Dooly

1968 Dougherty
1961 Douglas
1928 Elbert
1917 Floyd
1960 Forsyth
1903 Fort Valley Area
1958 Fulton
1965 Gordon
1967 Gwinnett
1963 Habersham
1941 Hall
1929 Hart
1963 Hart
1967 Houston and Peach
1914 Jackson
1916 Jasper
1930 Jefferson
1968 Jenkins
1927 Lee
1937 McDuffie
1961 McIntosh
1918 Madison
1916 Meriwether
1965 Meriwether
1965 Morgan
1922 Muscogee
1968 Pierce
1914 Polk
1926 Quitman
1971 Steven
1914 Tattnall
1914 Terrell
1959 Tift
1939 Toombs
1954 Towns
1964 Treutlen
1950 Union
1964 Walton
1965 Wayne
1929 Worth

HAWAII
1955 The Territory of Hawaii
1972 Kauai, Ochu, Mani, Molokai and Lanai

IDAHO
1930 Benewah
1943 Blackfoot-Aberdeen Area
1939 Bonner
1972 Canyon
1965 Gem County Area
1929 Gooding Area
1950 Idaho Falls Area
1971 Kooskia
1969 Teton Area Idaho-Wyoming
1921 Twin Falls Area

ILLINOIS
1971 Douglas
1969 Gallatin
1966 Jersey (State)
1964 Johnson (State)
1970 Lake
1969 Montgomery
1968 Pulaski and Alexander
1964 Wabash

INDIANA
1969 Allen
1947 Bartholomew
1916 Benton
1928 Blackford
1946 Brown
1958 Carroll
1955 Cass
1922 Clay
1937 Dubois
1960 Fayette and Union
1966 Fountain
1950 Franklin
1946 Fulton
1922 Gibson
1925 Hancock
1971 Howard
1940 Jennings
1948 Johnson
1943 Knox
1922 Kosciusko
1944 La Porte
1972 Lake
1967 Madison
1946 Martin
1927 Miami
1950 Morgan
1955 Newton
1953 Noble
1930 Ohio and Switzerland
1964 Owen
1967 Parke
1969 Perry
1938 Pike
1968 Pulaski
1925 Putnam
1931 Randolph
1937 Rush
1950 St Joseph
1962 Scott
1940 Steuben
1971 Sullivan
1964 Spalding
1971 Steven
1914 Tattnall
1959 Tippecanoe
1944 Vanderburgh
1930 Vermillion
1939 Washington
1925 Wayne

IOWA
1963 Adams
1958 Allamakee
1940 Audubon
1967 Bremer
1930 Calhoun
1969 Cass
1919 Cedar
1940 Cerro Gordo
1923 Clarke
1916 Clay
1969 Clay
1925 Clayton
1928 Crawford
1940 Davis
1939 Decatur
1922 Delaware
1938 Franklin
1921 Greene
1929 Guthrie
1930 Hancock
1935 Howard
1961 Humboldt
1939 Ida
1967 Iowa
1941 Jackson
1921 Jasper
1960 Jefferson
1971 Keokuk
1917 Linn
1960 Lucas
1927 Lyon
1939 Marion
1920 Mills
1916 Mitchell
1959 Monona
1931 Monroe
1940 Osceola
1928 Pocahontas
1960 Polk
1914 Pottawattamie
1929 Poweshiek
1916 Ringgold
1924 Sac
1961 Shelby
1941 Story
1950 Tama
1954 Taylor
1961 Van Buren
1930 Washington
1918 Wayne
1971 Wayne
1922 Winneshiek
1968 Winneshiek
1972 Woodberry
1922 Worth

KANSAS
1938 Allen
1931 Bourbon
1960 Brown
1926 Clay
1915 Cowley
1973 Edwards
1965 Finney
1965 Ford
1960 Geary
1969 Grant
1968 Gray
1961 Greeley
1961 Hamilton
1971 Harper
1968 Haskell
1973 Hodgeman
1928 Johnson
1963 Kearny
1938 Kingman
1972 Lane County
1964 Logan
1930 Marion
1913 Montgomery
1963 Morton
1930 Neosho
1968 Pratt
1966 Reno
1967 Republic
1959 Saline
1965 Scott
1965 Seward
1970 Shawnee
1961 Stanton
1961 Stevens
1965 Wichita
1931 Woodson

KENTUCKY
1964 Adair
1969 Barren
1963 Bath
1966 Caldwell
1945 Calloway
1964 Clark
1965 Elliott
1968 Fayette
1965 Fourteen Co Eastern Ky Reconnaissance

1964 Fulton
1921 Garrard
1953 Graves
1972 Grayson
1968 Harrison
1967 Henderson
1966 Jefferson
1915 Jessamine
1919 Logan
1970 McCreary-Whitley Area
1973 Madison
1950 Marshall
1930 Mercer
1967 Metcalfe
1920 Muhlenberg
1971 Nelson
1916 Shelby

LOUISIANA
1962 Acadia
1928 Beauregard
1962 Bossier
1968 East Baton Rouge
1918 La Salle
1931 Livingston
1921 Natchitoches
1919 Sabine
1973 St James and St John the Baptist Parishes
1959 St Mary
1968 Tensas
1960 Terrebonne
1922 Washington

MAINE
1970 Androscoggin and Sagadahoc
1964 Aroostook Northeastern Part
1964 Aroostook Southern Part
1963 Penobscott
1972 Somerset
1955 Waldo
1952 York

MARYLAND
1973 Anne Arundel
1928 Calvert
1971 Calvert
1929 Caroline
1964 Caroline
1969 Carroll
1960 Frederick
1968 Howard
1930 Kent
1961 Montgomery
1967 Prince Georges
1931 Queen Annes
1966 Queen Annes
1966 Somerset
1970 Talbot
1962 Washington
1970 Wicomico
1924 Worcester

MASSACHUSETTS
1925 Dukes and Nantucket
1925 Essex
1929 Franklin
1967 Franklin
1924 Middlesex
1969 Plymouth
1922 Worcester

MICHIGAN
1929 Alger
1924 Alpena
1967 Arenac
1931 Bay
1929 Branch
1939 Cheboygan
1927 Chippewa
1942 Clinton
1927 Crawford
1972 Gladwin
1966 Grand Traverse
1941 Ingham
1967 Ionia
1937 Iron
1926 Jackson
1926 Kent
1972 Lapeer
1961 Lenawee
1929 Luce
1971 Macomb
1922 Manistee
1939 Mason
1925 Menominee
1950 Midland
1960 Montcalm
1930 Montmorency
1968 Muskegon
1951 Newaygo
1938 Oceana
1969 Osceola
1931 Oscoda
1921 Ontonagon (Reconnaissance)
1972 Ottawa
1924 Roscommon
1938 Saginaw
1929 St Clair
1961 Sanilac
1939 Schoolcraft
1926 Tuscola
1930 Washtenaw

MINNESOTA
1968 Carver
1965 Crow Wing
1960 Dakota
1961 Dodge
1957 Faribault
1958 Fillmore
1929 Hennepin
1929 Houston
1930 Hubbard
1958 Isanti
1939 Kanabec
1926 Lake of the Woods (Reconnaissance)
1954 Le Sueur
1970 Lincoln
1955 McLeod
1927 Mille Lacs
1958 Nicollet
1941 Pine
1972 Pope
1939 Red River Valley Area
1949 Rock
1942 Roseau
1959 Scott
1968 Sherburne
1971 Stevens
1972 Swift
1965 Wabasha
1965 Waseca
1968 Wright

MISSISSIPPI
1970 Adams
1971 Alcorn
1958 Bolivar
1965 Calhoun
1926 Claiborne
1963 Claiborne
1965 Clarke
1959 Coahoma
1965 Covington
1959 De Soto
1932 Greene
1967 Grenada
1930 Hancock
1924 Harrison
1916 Hinds
1959 Humphreys
1961 Issaquena
1927 Jackson
1964 Jackson
1973 Lee
1959 Leflore
1963 Lincoln
1938 Marion
1972 Marshall
1966 Monroe
1916 Newton
1960 Newton
1963 Panola
1922 Perry
1968 Pike
1957 Prentiss
1958 Quitman
1962 Sharkey
1959 Sunflower
1970 Tallahatchie
1967 Tate
1966 Tippah
1944 Tishomingo
1956 Tunica
1968 Walthall
1964 Warren
1961 Washington

MISSOURI
1962 Boone
1964 Daviess
1914 De Kalb
1971 Dent
1914 Harrison
1953 Holt
1954 Jasper
1914 Johnson
1911 Laclede
1945 Linn
1956 Livingston
1964 Moniteau
1971 Pemiscot
1914 Pettis
1922 Ray
1956 St Charles
1917 Texas
1968 Worth

MONTANA
1944 Big Horn Valley Area
1914 Bitterroot Valley Area
1959 Bitterroot Valley Area
1953 Central Montana (Reconnaissance)
1931 Gallatin Valley Area
1967 Judith Basin Area
1929 Lower Flathead Valley Area
1939 Lower Yellowstone Valley Area
1940 Middle Yellowstone Valley Area
1929 Northern Plains of Montana (Reconnaissance)
1971 Powder River Area

1967 Treasure
1960 Upper Flathead Valley Area
1943 Upper Musselshell Valley Area
1958 Wibaux
1972 Yellowstone

NEBRASKA
1954 Blaine
1972 Boone
1937 Boyd
1938 Brown
1941 Cass
1956 Cherry
1922 Cuming
1915 Dawes
1921 Deuel
1965 Deuel
1929 Dixon
1931 Dundy
1963 Dundy
1939 Frontier
1930 Furnas
1964 Gage
1924 Garden
1938 Garfield
1938 Gosper
1937 Greeley
1962 Hall
1930 Harlan
1938 Hayes
1930 Hitchcock
1970 Hitchcock
1938 Holt
1964 Hooker
1937 Keya Paha
1962 Kimball
1930 Knox
1948 Lancaster
1937 Loup
1969 McPherson
1917 Morrill
1922 Nance
1960 Nance
1950 Otoe
1921 Perkins
1973 Phelps
1967 Red Willow
1937 Rock
1939 Sarpy
1965 Saunders
1968 Scotts Bluff
1931 Sherman
1929 Stanton
1968 Thayer
1965 Thomas
1972 Thurston
1932 Valley
1964 Washington
1923 Webster
1937 Wheeler

NEVADA
1967 Las Vegas and Eldorado Valley Area
1965 Lovelock Area
1968 Pahranagat-Penoyer Area

NEW HAMPSHIRE
1968 Belknap
1949 Cheshire and Sullivan
1943 Coos
1939 Grafton
1953 Hillsboro
1965 Merrimack
1959 Rockingham
1973 Strafford

NEW JERSEY
1925 Bergen Area
1971 Burlington
1926 Camden Area
1966 Camden
1927 Freehold Area
1862 Gloucester
1972 Mercer
1969 Salem

NEW MEXICO
1958 Bluewater Area
1968 Cabezon Area
1958 Curry
1928 Deming Area
1971 Eddy Area
1930 Fort Summer Area
1932 Lovington Area
1959 Portales Area
1930 Rincon Area
1967 Roosevelt
1933 Roswell Area
1960 Southwest Quay Area
1970 Torrance Area
1967 Zuni Mountain Area

NEW YORK
1942 Albany and Schenectady
1956 Allegany
1932 Broome
1971 Broome
1940 Cattagaugus
1932 Chemung
1914 Clinton
1961 Cortland
1955 Dutchess
1929 Erie
1958 Franklin
1969 Genesee
1960 Lewis
1956 Livingston
1973 Monroe
1972 Niagara
1938 Onondaga
1958 Ontario and Yates
1939 Orleans
1940 Otsego
1937 Rensselaer
1925 St Lawrence
1969 Schoharie
1942 Seneca
1946 Sullivan
1953 Tioga
1965 Tompkins
1940 Ulster
1938 Wyoming

NORTH CAROLINA
1960 Alamance
1955 Avery
1937 Brunswick
1920 Buncombe
1954 Buncombe
1937 Chatham
1951 Cherokee
1941 Clay
1929 Craven
1922 Cumberland
1927 Davie
1959 Duplin
1931 Franklin
1953 Graham
1954 Haywood
1943 Henderson
1964 Iredell
1948 Jackson
1938 Jones
1933 Lee
1927 Lenoir
1914 Lincoln
1929 Macon
1956 Macon
1942 Madison
1952 Mitchell
1930 Montgomery
1921 Onslow
1937 Pamlico
1957 Pasquotank
1905 Perquimans and Pasquotank
1926 Rockingham
1967 Scotland
1940 Stokes
1937 Surry
1947 Swain
1948 Transylvania
1970 Wake
1942 Warren
1932 Washington
1958 Watauga
1962 Yadkin
1952 Yancey

NORTH DAKOTA
1944 Billings
1914 La Moure
1971 La Moure and Parts of James River Valley
1942 McKenzie
1951 Morton
1964 Sargent
1968 Stark
1918 Traill
1966 Tri-county Area
1972 Walsh
1970 Wells

OHIO
1938 Adams
1965 Allen
1930 Brown
1927 Butler
1971 Champaign
1958 Clark
1962 Clinton
1968 Columbiana
1969 Delaware
1971 Erie
1960 Fairfield
1955 Huron
1925 Lake
1938 Licking
1939 Logan
1943 Lucas
1971 Mahoning
1916 Miami
1925 Muskingum
1928 Ottawa
1960 Paulding
1969 Preble
1930 Putnam
1967 Ross
1940 Scioto
1913 Stark
1954 Tuscarawas
1972 Van Wert
1938 Vinton
1973 Warren
1926 Washington
1966 Wood

OKLAHOMA
1965 Adair
1939 Alfalfa
1962 Beaver
1968 Blaine
1938 Carter
1970 Cherokee and Delaware
1943 Choctaw
1960 Cimarron
1954 Cleveland
1967 Comanche
1963 Cotton
1973 Craig
1959 Creek
1963 Dewey
1966 Ellis
1939 Garfield
1967 Garfield
1931 Grant
1937 Greer
1967 Greer
1960 Harper
1968 Hughes
1961 Jackson
1967 Kay
1962 Kingfisher
1931 Kiowa
1931 Le Flore
1970 Lincoln
1960 Logan
1966 Love
1938 McIntosh
1940 Major
1969 Major
1937 Mayes
1939 Murray
1956 Noble
1952 Okfuskee
1969 Oklahoma
1968 Okmulgee
1964 Ottawa
1959 Pawnee
1937 Pittsburg
1971 Pittsburg
1941 Pontotoc
1963 Roger Mills
1966 Rogers
1970 Sequoyah
1964 Stephens
1930 Texas
1961 Texas
1930 Tillman
1942 Tulsa
1968 Washington
1941 Washita
1950 Woods
1938 Woodward
1963 Woodward

OREGON
1949 Astoria Area
1954 Baker Area
1920 Benton
1921 Clackamas
1929 Columbia
1970 Curry Area
1958 Deschutes Area
1972 Marion
1966 Prineville Area
1964 Sherman
1964 Tillamook Area
1948 Umatilla Area

PENNSYLVANIA
1967 Adams
1939 Armstrong
1970 Berks
1962 Carbon
1963 Chester and Delaware
1958 Clarion
1916 Clearfield
1966 Clinton
1967 Columbia
1954 Crawford
1972 Dauphin
1960 Erie
1973 Fayette
1938 Franklin
1969 Fulton
1944 Huntingdon
1931 Indiana
1968 Indiana
1964 Jefferson
1959 Lancaster
1963 Lehigh
1971 Mercer
1967 Montgomery
1955 Montour and Northumberland
1969 Pike
1958 Potter
1973 Susquehenna
1929 Tioga
1946 Union
1938 Wayne
1968 Westmoreland
1929 Wyoming
1963 York

PUERTO RICO
1965 Lajas Valley Area
1942 Puerto Rico

RHODE ISLAND
1939 Kent and Washington
1942 Newport and Bristol
1943 Providence

SOUTH CAROLINA
1937 Abbeville
1966 Bamberg
1963 Calhoun
1971 Charleston
1962 Cherokee
1960 Darlington
1931 Dillon
1938 Edgefield
1929 Greenwood
1915 Hampton
1919 Kershaw
1963 Lee
1922 Lexington
1965 Marlboro
1960 Newberry
1963 Oconee
1943 Pickens
1962 Saluda
1968 Spartanburg
1943 Sumter
1928 Williamsburg
1965 York

SOUTH DAKOTA
1971 Bennett
1959 Brookings
1966 Codington
1922 Grant
1963 Hand
1921 McCook
1964 Minnehaha
1971 Shannon
1921 Union
1969 Washabaugh

TENNESSEE
1947 Bedford
1953 Benton
1959 Blount
1958 Bradley
1953 Carter
1948 Claiborne
1955 Cocke
1959 Coffee
1950 Cumberland
1955 Decatur
1972 Dekalb
1965 Dyer
1964 Fayette
1958 Franklin
1968 Giles
1948 Grainger
1958 Greene
1946 Hamblen
1947 Hamilton
1926 Hardin
1960 Henderson
1958 Henry
1958 Houston
1946 Humphreys
1941 Jefferson
1956 Johnson
1955 Knox
1969 Lake
1959 Lawrence
1946 Lincoln
1961 Loudon
1957 McMinn
1958 Marion
1959 Maury
1953 Norris Area
1973 Obion
1953 Perry
1963 Putnam
1948 Rhea
1942 Roane
1968 Robertson
1956 Sevier
1916 Shelby
1970 Shelby
1953 Sullivan
1967 Warren
1958 Washington
1964 Williamson

TEXAS
1965 Armstrong
1963 Bailey
1938 Bee
1966 Bexar
1958 Brazos
1948 Brown
1941 Cameron
1962 Carson
1937 Cass
1959 Cherokee
1963 Childress
1964 Cockran
1930 Collin
1969 Collin
1966 Crosby
1960 Dawson
1968 Deaf Smith
1922 Dickens
1970 Dickens
1943 Dimmit
1964 Ellis

1971 El Paso
1973 Erath
1932 Falls
1946 Fannin
1966 Fisher
1964 Foard
1960 Fort Bend
1929 Frio
1965 Gaines
1930 Galveston
1966 Gray
1967 Hall
1960 Handsford
1972 Hardeman
1922 Harris
1961 Haskell
1925 Hidalgo
1965 Hockley
1969 Howard
1939 Hunt
1965 Jefferson
1940 Kaufman
1967 Kinney
1962 Lamb
1959 Lynn
1958 McLennan
1942 Maverick
1967 Menard
1928 Midland
1969 Mitchell
1972 Montgomery
1965 Nueces
1973 Ochiltree
1930 Polk
1970 Randall
1919 Reconnaissance Northwest
1922 Reconnaissance West Central
1919 Red River
1970 Runnels
1931 Scurry
1972 Starr
1968 Sutton
1962 Terry
1932 Wheeler
1962 Wilbarger
1926 Willacy
1938 Williamson
1964 Yoakum
1940 Zavala

UTAH
1920 Ashley Valley Area
1960 Beryl-Enterprise Area
1970 Carbon-Emery Area
1968 Davis-Weber
1959 East Millard Area
1939 Price Area
1958 Richfield Area
1959 Roosevelt-Duchesne Area
1946 Salt Lake Area
1962 San Juan Area
1921 Uinta River Valley Area
1971 Utah (Central Part)
1942 Virgin River Valley Area

VERMONT
1971 Addison
1959 Grand Isle
1937 Reconnaissance of Entire State

VIRGINIA
1917 Accomack and Northampton
1940 Albemarle
1937 Augusta
1954 Bland
1967 Carroll
1952 Culpeper
1963 Fairfax
1956 Fauquier
1958 Fluvanna
1930 Grayson
1938 Halifax
1941 Isle of Wight
1953 Lee
1960 Loudoun
1962 Mathews
1956 Mecklenburg
1932 Nansemond
1959 Norfolk Area
1963 Northumberland and Lancaster
1960 Nottoway
1971 Orange
1958 Prince Edward
1945 Princess Anne Area
1961 Rappahannock
1931 Rockbridge
1945 Russell
1951 Scott.
1948 Smyth
1937 Southampton
1948 Tazewell
1945 Washington
1954 Wise

VIRGIN ISLANDS
1932 Reconnaissance of St Croix Island
1970 Virgin Islands of the US

WASHINGTON
1967 Adams
1916 Benton
1971 Benton
1951 Clallam
1972 Clark
1958 Island
1952 King
1939 Kitsap
1945 Kittitas
1954 Lewis
1960 Mason
1955 Pierce
1962 San Juan
1960 Skagit
1956 Skamania
1947 Snohomish
1917 Spokane
1968 Spokane
1958 Thurston
1964 Walla Walla
1953 Whatcom
1958 Yakima

WEST VIRGINIA
1968 Barbour
1966 Berkeley
1918 Braxton and Clay
1941 Greenbrier
1961 Jackson and Mason
1915 Lewis and Gilmer
1960 Marshall
1923 Mercer
1925 Monroe
1965 Monroe
1959 Preston
1914 Raleigh
1931 Randolph
1921 Tucker
1967 Tucker-Randolph
1970 Wood and Wirt

WISCONSIN
1958 Barron
1961 Bayfield
1962 Buffalo
1925 Calumet
1930 Crawford
1961 Crawford
1916 Door
1961 Grant
1922 Green
1922 Green Lake
1962 Iowa
1918 Jackson
1970 Kenosha and Racine
1960 La Crosse
1966 Lafayette
1916 Milwaukee
1971 Milwaukee and Waukesha
1970 Ozaukee
1964 Peppin
1923 Pierce
1968 Pierce
1915 Portage
1915 Reconnaissance South Part of North Central
1959 Richland
1927 Trempealeau
1928 Vernon
1969 Vernon
1971 Walworth
1971 Washington
1921 Washington and Ozaukee
1917 Waupaca
1927 Winnebago
1915 Wood

WYOMING
1928 Basin Area
1955 Campbell
1972 Gashen
1939 Johnson
1969 Teton Area Idaho-Wyoming
1940 Uinta

ISOGONIC CHART OF THE UNITED STATES
1:5,000,000
No 3079
Washington : US Coast & Geodetic Serv, 1970
Shows lines of equal magnetic declination and equal annual change. Alaska on reverse at same scale, with Hawaii inset at 1:7,500,000.

BOUGUER GRAVITY ANOMALY MAP OF THE UNITED STATES
1:2,500,000
Washington : USGS, 1964
194 x 120 complete
2 sheet map with contours. Not showing Alaska and Hawaii 75c set

RESIDUAL AEROMAGNETIC MAP OF ARIZONA
1:1,000,000
Tucson : Dept. Geosciences Univ. Arizona, 1971

AEROMAGNETIC MAP OF MICHIGAN AND THE ADJACENT GREAT LAKES
1:1,000,000
Geophysical Inv. GP. 894
Washington : USGS, 1974
104 x 93
Map showing magnetic contours of region. $1.00

AEROMAGNETIC MAP OF MINNESOTA
Isidore Zieta & John R Kirby
GP-725
Washington : USGS, 1970
66 x 58
Coloured map. 75c

SIMPLE BOUGER GRAVITY ANOMALY MAP OF NEW YORK
1:250, 000
Map & Chart Series 17—17C in 4 sheets
by Frank A Ravetta and William Diment
Albany — NY State Museum, 1971
In black and white.
Folded 50c

USA — GEOPHYSICAL INVESTIGATION MAPS
Various scales
Washington : USGS
Maps published at various scales generally following topog. sheet lines showing aeromagnetic Bouguer anomally, radioactivity information.

H BIOGEOGRAPHY

POTENTIAL NATURAL VEGETATION OF THE CONTERMINOUS UNITED STATES
1:3, 168, 000
New York : AGS, 1964
165 x 101
Shows 116 vegetation types by coloured symbols. With 156 pp manual containing 44 pp text. 116 plates showing the vegetation types.
Map in roll $8.00
Map in case $12.00

LAND USE IN THE SOUTHWESTERN UNITED STATES FROM GEMINI AND APOLLO PHOTOGRAPHS
by Norman J W Thrower
1:1, 000, 000
Flórida : AAG, 1970
78 x 88
Shows unimproved land, roads, railways etc. on generalised photo map. $3.00

ALASKA GAME MANAGEMENT UNITS
1:4, 500, 000 app
Douglas : Alaska Dept. Highways, 1971
Showing management areas for game, with inset map on reverse.

UNITED STATES OF AMERICA : SHOWING THE EXTENT OF PUBLIC LAND SURVEYS, REMAINING PUBLIC LAND, HISTORIC BOUNDARIES, NATIONAL FORESTS, INDIAN RESERVATIONS, WILDLIFE REFUGES, NATIONAL PARKS AND MONUMENTS
1:2, 500, 000
Washington : USGS, 1965
206 x 132
States with Public Land Surveys have grey grid overprint. Inset of principal meridians and base lines.
In 2 sheets.
$3.00 set

UNITED STATES OF AMERICA : NATIONAL PARKS AND MONUMENTS, INDIAN RESERVATIONS, WILDLIFE REFUGES, PUBLIC LANDS AND HISTORICAL BOUNDARIES
1:3, 168, 000
Washington : USGS, 1964
140 x 107
Inc. present boundaries and settlements.

NATIONAL PARKS OF THE UNITED STATES
Various scales
Washington : Govt. Printing Office
8 maps in 1 packet, showing over 250 parks, other tourist items, roads, accommodation etc.
1 National Parks of the United States 20c
2 National Parks of the Midwest
1:7, 500, 000, 1968
4 maps 15c
3 New York City (inc. Long Island)
1:34, 000 1968
3 maps 10c
4 The Northeast 15c
5 The Southeast 15c
6 The Southwest 15c
7 Washington DC (inc. Maryland, Virginia) 15c
8 The West 15c

NATIONAL PARKS
Various scales
Washington : USGS
Topog. maps, contoured, some also available in shaded relief edition.
All other National Parks are shown on standard topog. series maps.
Maps available:
Acadia NP (Maine)
1:62, 500 58 x 63 $1.25
Bryce Canyon NP (Utah)
1:31, 680 1932 81 x 111
contoured or relief eds. $1.00 ea.
Canyonlands NP (Utah)
1:62, 500 1969 116 x 154
Carlsbad Caverns NP (N Mex)
1:24, 000 1934 48 x 51
Crater Lake NP and Vicinity (Oreg)
1:62, 500 1888-1956 63 x 89
contoured or relief eds $1.00 ea.
Denver Mountain Area (Col.) (Incl. Rocky Mountains and Denver NPs
1938-48 66 x 96
contoured or relief eds. $1.00 ea.
Glacier NP (Mon)
1:125, 000 1900-38 78 x 91
$1.00
Glen Canyon Recreation Area
1:250, 000 1969 81 x 91
$1.00
Grand Canyon NP (Ariz)
1:62, 500 1962 96 x 153
$1.50
Grand Teton NP (Wyo)
1:62, 500 1968 86 x 117
contoured or relief eds. $2.50 ea.
Great Smoky Mountains NP and Vicinity (NC Tenn)
1:125, 000 1961 71 x 97
contoured of relief eds. $1.00 ea.
Great Smoky Mountains NP (NC Tenn)
1:62, 500 1931 71 x 81
2 sheets $1.00 ea.
Isle Royale (Mich)
1:62, 500 1957-70 99 x 137
contoured or relief eds. $1.50
Lassen Volcanic NP (Calif)
1:62, 500 1957 61 x 76
contoured or relief eds 50c ea.
Mammoth Cave (Ky)
1:31, 680 1930 61 x 81
Mesa Verde NP (Col)
1:24, 000 1973 116 x 137
contoured or relief eds
Mount McKinley NP
1:250, 000 1898-1951 63 x 81
contoured or relief eds 50c
Mt Rainier NP (Wash)
1:62, 500 1910-55 55 x 66
50c
North Cascades (Wash) (Incl. NP Lake Chelan Natn'l Rec. Area. Glacier Peak Wilderness Area, Russ Lake Natn'l Rec. Area)
1:250, 000 1955-72 76 x 101
$1.25
Olympic NP (Wash)
1:125, 000 1972 83 x 119
contoured or relief eds $1.00 ea.
Petrified Forest NP (Ariz)
1:62, 500 1967 43 x 81
50c
Rocky Mountains NP (Col)
1:62, 500 1961 71 x 99
contoured or relief eds.
Sequoia and Kings Canyon NP (Cal)
1:125, 000 1942-67 76 x 104
contoured or relief eds. $1.00
Shenandoah NP (Va)
1:62, 500 1969 53 x 96
3 sheets $1.00
Vicksburg Nat. Military Park (Miss)
1:9, 600 1935 89 x 119
Yellowstone (Wyo-Mont-Idaho)
1:125, 000 1961 97 x 104
contoured or relief eds $1.00 ea.
Yosemite NP (Cal)
1:125, 000 1958 73 x 78
contoured or relief eds $1.00 ea.
Zion NP (Kolob Section) (Utah)
1:31, 680 1938-57 78 x 86
contoured or relief eds $1.00 ea.
Zion NP (Zion Canyon Section)
1:31, 680 1932-57 99 x 119
contoured or relief eds $1.50 ea.

NATIONAL FOREST MAPS
Various scales
Washington : US Forest Service
Available for:
Apache Ariz.
1972 1:126, 720
Apalachicola
1970 1:126, 720
Bitterfoot, Mon + 1d
1972 1:126. 720
Black Kettle .N. Grassland, Ok
1972 1:125, 000
Clark, Mo
1971 1:265, 440
Coronado — south, Ariz.
1972 1:125, 000

Hiawatha
1969 2 sheets 1:250, 000
Klamath, Recreation Map
1968 1:126, 720
Manistee, Mich
1967 (1971) 1:253, 440
Ocala
1971 1:125, 000 app
Ottawa, Mich
1964 (1971) 1:253, 400
San Isabel, Col.
1972 1:125, 000
Shawnee, Ill.
1973 1:125, 000
Shoshone, Wy.
1971 1:126, 720
The South
1970 1:2, 407, 680
Toiyabe
1968 1:126, 720
Wayne (3 maps)
1970 1:250, 000
White Mountain
1970 1:250, 000
Winema, Oreg.
1971 1:125, 000

J CLIMATE

SELECTED CLIMATIC MAPS OF THE UNITED STATES
1:10, 000, 000
In 32 sheets
Washington : US Environmental Data Service
Illus. maps showing :
Mean annual number of days maximum temperature 90°F and above, except 70°F and above in Alaska.
Mean annual total snowfall (inches)

K HUMAN GEOGRAPHY

ÉTATS-UNIS NO 1 (PHYSIQUE)
Éditions MDI
With political and population map on reverse.
See USA 73 E1

GE-50 MAPS
1:5, 000, 000
Washington : US Dept. Commerce, Bureau of the Census
106 x 76
Series of col. data statistical maps, shown by Counties.

6 Familes with Incomes under S3, 000 in 1959-1960 50c
7 Older Americans in the US 1960 50c
9 Population with High School Eduction or More, 1960 50c
10 Youths of 16 and 17 Years of Age in School, 1960 50c
16 Negro Population as Per Cent of Total Population, 1960 50c
28 Housing Construction Authorized in Permit Issuing Places by Selected Metropolitan Statistical Areas of the US 1964-7 50c
36 Older Americans, 1970 30c
37 Year of Maximum Population (variable) 30c
38 Population Density by Counties 1970 30c
39 Percent of Population Urban 1970 50c
41 Percent Change in Pop. by Counties of the US and Puerto Rico, 1960-70 25c
42 Population Trends, 1940-70 25c
43 1970 Population as a Percent of Maximum Pop. 1970 30c
47 Number of Negro persons by counties of the US: 1970, 1973
48 Negro population as Percent of total population by counties of the US, 1973
49 Number of American Indians by counties of the US: 1970,1973
50 Number of Chinese by counties of the US: 1970, 1973
51 Number of Japanese by counties of the US: 1970, 1973

DOMESTIC AGRICULTURAL MIGRANTS IN THE UNITED STATES : COUNTIES IN WHICH AN ESTIMATED 100 OR MORE SEASONAL AGRICULTURAL WORKERS MIGRATED INTO THE AREA TO WORK DURING THE PEAK SEASON IN 1965
1:1, 584, 000 app
Washington : Public Health Serv. 1966
92 x 53
With insets of location, travel patterns.
Statistical tables on reverse.

SERIES OF POPULATION MAPS OF THE COLONIES OF THE UNITED STATES, 1625-1970
by Hermans R Friis
New York : AGS, 1968
21 x 28
52 pp
Text, with sheet 43 x 86 of 10 maps of pop. at different periods.
$3.00

CALIFORNIA POPULATION DISTRIBUTION in 1970
1:1, 000, 000
by Norman J W Thrower
Long Beach : California State Univ. 1974
97 x 125
3 col. maps indicating pop. by dots; 3 insets at 1:250, 000. Reverse has table of pop. $2.50

MINNESOTA – POPULATION DISTRIBUTION, 1970
1:1, 370, 000
Minnesota : Center for Urban and Regional Affairs, 1973.
In colours.

TEXAS URBANIZATION & POPULATION DENSITY
1:2, 600, 000
Austin : The Univ. of Texas, Bureau of Business Research, 1976
56 x 45
Coloured map showing population density of counties in colours and classifying towns by population. Separate City and County Location and Population Tables $1.00

POPULATION ORIGIN GROUPS IN RURAL TEXAS
by Terry G Jordan
1:1, 500, 000
Florida : AAG, 1970
90 x 85
Pop. map of immigrants and their descendents $3.50

LITERARY DEVELOPMENT OF THE UNITED STATES
No 161011-14
Chicago : Denoyer-Geppert
162 x 111
School wall map in col.
Spring Rollers $24.00

L ECONOMIC

ECONOMIC WALL MAPS OF USA
Indianapolis : Cram
Col. school wall maps, showing :
Agricultural regions of the US Agricultural Products of the US Coal, Iron, Petroleum, Gas Regions of the US.
Mineral Production of the US
Manufacturing Industries of the US
Trade Routes and the Pacific Ocean
Each $13.75

ECONOMIC DEVELOPMENT DISTRICTS AND FUNDED REDEVELOPMENT AREAS
1:6, 200, 000 app
Washington : Office Devt. Organisations, 1969
50 x 69
Development map in colour, with 5 insets.

USA, INDUSTRIE
1:6, 000, 000
Gotha : Haack
202 x 168
Col. wall map for schools

GE-50 MAPS
1:5, 000, 000
Washington : US Dept. Commerce, Bureau of the Census
106 x 76
Series of col. statistical data maps, shown by counties.

12 Employment in Manufacturing, 1960 50c
22 Manufacturing in the United States, 1963 50c
23 Mineral Industries in the United States, 1963 50c
29 Size of Farms, 1964 50c
30 Percent Change in Size of Farms, 1940-64 50c
31 Value of Farm Products Sold Per Acre of Land in Farms, 1964 50c
32 Percent Change in the Value of Farm Products Sold per Acre of Land in Farms, 1939-64 50c
33 Corn Yield per Acre, 1964 50c
34 Percent Change in Corn Yield per Acre, 1939-64 50c

HOSPODARSKA MAPA SPOJENÉ STÁTY AMERICKÉ
1:5, 000, 000
Praha : Kart
Economic school wall map of the USA.
Kcs 115

SOEDINENNEJE STATE AMERIKI
1:4, 000, 000
Moskva : GUGK, 1973
130 x 95
2 sheet economic wall map of USA 28 kop

VEREINIGTE STAATEN VON AMERIKA, WIRTSCHAFT
1:3, 000, 000
Berlin : Velhagen & Klasing und Hermann Schroedel
232 x 166
Economic wall map.

WIRTSCHAFT DER USA
1:2, 500, 000
Darmstadt : Perthes
210 x 140
Col. wall map, illus. principal industries by symbols. 128 DM

USA : BERGBAU, INDUSTRIE, VERKEHR
Braunschweig : Westermann
127 x 96
Pictorial wall map in col. of mining, industry, and communications.

USA – LANDWIRTSCHAFT UND FISCHEREI
No scale given
Braunschweig : Westermann
127 x 96
Pictorial wall map of agriculture and fishing areas.

UMRISSKARTE DER USA
No 0841
Bern : K & F
29 x 31
Outline map of industrial areas of USA.

RAILROAD MAP OF THE UNITED STATES
1:2, 500, 000
In 4 sheets
Washington : Defense Mapping Agency
106 x 111 each $0.60 each

FLORIDA'S GROWTH MARKETS
1:1, 500, 000 app
Tampa : Trend Publications Inc, 1969
62 x 54
Coloured marketing map with tables: edited by "Florida Trend".

ECONOMIC VIABILITY OF FARM AREAS IN NEW YORK STATE
Howard E Conklin and R E Linton
1:500, 000
Albany : Office Planning Coordination, 1969
95 x 110
Planning map on Lambert conformal conic projection. On USGS base map.

ENERGY RESOURCES OF WYOMING
1:500, 000
Laramie : Geological Survey, 1972
Coloured distribution map.

PRINICPAL ELECTRIC FACILITIES IN UNITED STATES, 1966
1:3, 437, 500
Washington : Govt. Printing Office, 1966
162 x 111 $1.25

PRINCIPAL ELECTRICAL FACILITIES, 1970
1:2, 000, 000 app
In 8 sheets
Washington : Govt. Printing Office
Various sizes
Show generating stations, transmission lines, ownership,

1	North Eastern	66 x 111
2	Great Lakes	66 x 111
3	North Central Region	111 x 76
4	Northwestern Region	66 x 111
5	Southwestern Region	66 x 137
6	South Central	66 x 111
7	Southeastern Region	66 x 109
8	Alaska, Hawaii, Puerto Rico and Virgin Islands	66 x 114

50c each

M HISTORICAL

USA – A PICTORIAL AND HISTORICAL MAP
1:5, 000, 000
Edinburgh : Bart
94 x 61
Coloured by states with their badges illustrated together with characters and events from history. 40p

HISTORICAL MAP OF THE US
1:4, 837, 500
Washington : NGS
104 x 67
Col. map from early exploration to present time.
Paper $2.00
Plastic $3.00
Enlarged ed. 170 x 110 $5.00

DAS WERDEN DER VEREINIGTEN STAATEN BIS 1783
1:2, 500, 000
Darmstadt : Perthes
210 x 140
Historical wall map showing the growth of the US until 1783, settlements, colonies, etc. 128 DM

DIE ENTWICKLUNG DER VEREINIGTEN STAATEN IM 19 UND 20 JAHRHUNDERT
1:2, 500, 000
Darmstadt : Perthes
210 x 140
Historical wall map of the devt. USA in 19th and 20th C.
128 DM

INDIAN HISTORY MAPS
Various scales
Detroit : Hearne Bros.
122 x 167
Col. mounted wall maps available by state:

SIM 202	Alabama
SIM 204	Alaska
SIM 206	Arizona
SIM 208	Arkansas
SIM 210	California
SIM 212	Colorado
SIM 214	Connecticut
SIM 216	Delaware
SIM 218	Florida
SIM 220	Georgia
SIM 222	Hawaii
SIM 224	Idaho
SIM 226	Illinois
SIM 228	Indiana
SIM 230	Iowa
SIM 232	Kansas
SIM 234	Kentucky
SIM 236	Louisiana
SIM 238	Maine
SIM 240	Maryland
SIM 242	Massachusetts
SIM 244	Michigan
SIM 246	Minnesota
SIM 248	Mississippi
SIM 250	Missouri
SIM 252	Montana
SIM 254	Nebraska
SIM 256	Nevada
SIM 258	New Hampshire
SIM 260	New Jersey
SIM 262	New Mexico
SIM 264	New York
SIM 266	North Carolina
SIM 268	North Dakota
SIM 270	Ohio
SIM 272	Oklahoma
SIM 274	Oregon
SIM 276	Pennsylvania
SIM 278	Rhode Island
SIM 280	South Carolina
SIM 282	South Dakota
SIM 284	Tennessee
SIM 286	Texas
SIM 288	Utah
SIM 290	Vermont
SIM 292	Virginia
SIM 294	Washington
SIM 296	West Virginia
SIM 298	Wisconsin
SIM 300	Wyoming

Each $152.50

NATIONAL HISTORIC SITES
Various scales
Washington : USGS
Maps available:
Home of Franklin D Roosevelt, NHS (NY)
1:960 1946 48 x 76 50c
Vanderbilt Mansions, NHS (NY)
1:3, 600 1946 33 x 64 50c

SELECTED CIVIL WAR MAPS
Various scales
Washington : Govt. Printing Office
60 x 77
US Coast Survey Maps, 1861 - 65
20 maps.
per set $5.00

HYDROGRAPHICAL BASIN OF THE UPPER MISSISSIPPI RIVER, 1843
1:1, 200, 000
J N Nicollett
Engraved W J Stone
Detroit : US Corps of Engineers, 1969

OREGON TRAIL WALL MAP
by W F McIlwraith
Oregon : Binfords and Mort
43 x 82
Map showing pioneering trails with pictorial border. $2.50

CARTE DES ÉTATS-UNIS DE L'AMÉRIQUE SUIVANT LE TRAITÉ DE PAIX DE 1783. DÉDIÉE ET PRESENTÉE À S. EXCELLENCE MR. BENJAMIN FRANKLIN, SERVITEUR LATTRÉ. 1784
Chicago : Donnelley Deeptone, 1973.
A facsimile from the original in the Newberry Library, Chicago.

USA REGIONS – FACSIMILE MAPS
Wien : Editio Totius Mundi
Maps available:

No.	Map	Date	Size		Price
40	Florida with Cuba, Th de Bry,	1585	45 x 36	col.	26 DM
				uncol.	18 DM
12	Virginia and Florida, W Blaeuw	1636	50 x 38	col.	26 DM
				uncol.	15 DM
41	Virginia , Th de Bry,	1585	41 x 30	col.	30 DM
				uncol.	25 DM
14	Nova Virginia, W Blaeuw	1636	50 x 38	col.	22 DM
				uncol.	15 DM

R

15	Nova Belgica (Inc. New York State) W de Baleuw			
	1636	50 x 38	col.	22 DM
			uncol.	15 DM
42	Neobelgii Tabula (with view of early NY) J Ottens			
	1673	54 x 46	col.	30 DM
			uncol.	25 DM

MAP OF STATEN ISLAND
1:35, 000 app
New York : Staten Island Inst. Arts and Sciences, 1968
Facsimile of the 1896 map by Charles W Leng, with 'Ye Olde Names and Nicknames' by William T Davis.

CHICAGO
Jas S Wright
1:7, 800 app
Ithaca, NY : Historic Urban Plans, 1969
45 x 35
Facsimile reproduction of 1834 map.
$10.00

PLAN OF DETROIT
John Mullett
1:3, 000
Ithaca, NY : Historic Urban Plans, 1969
47 x 35
Facsimile of 1830 map published by Bowen & Cos., Philadelphia. $7.50

PLAN DE LA NOUVELLE ORLÉANS, CELLE QU'ELLE ESTOIT AU MOIS DE DEXEMBRE, 1731
by Conichon
New Orleans : Louisiana State Museum, 196-
Facsimile of French original. $20.00

ATLASES
A1 GENERAL : ROADS

RAND McNALLY ROAD ATLAS OF THE UNITED STATES, CANADA AND MEXICO
Rand McNally
See NORTH AMERICA ATLASES 7A1

ROAD ATLAS AND VACATION GUIDE
Maplewood, NJ : Hammond, 1976
21 x 28
48 pp
Road atlas for 50 States; double-page maps, town indexes, mileage charts, city maps.
$1.00

INTERSTATE ROAD ATLAS
Chicago : Rand McNally, 1976
21 x 28
100 pp app
70 pp maps, 25 pp text.

US – ROAD ATLAS
1:3, 800, 000
No 395
Hamburg : Falk
120 x 79
Falk patent fold; roads classified and numbered, distances in miles, index, land types $9.80 DM

ATLASES
A2 GENERAL : LOCAL

THE ROCKFORD SNOW TRAIL ATLAS FOR MICHIGAN
Rockford : Rockford Map Publishers, 1971
86 pp
68 maps. $1.95

ATLASES
B TOWN PLANS

URBAN ATLAS : 20 AMERICAN CITIES
A communications study notating Selected Urban Data, by
J R Passoneau and R. S. Wurman
Cambridge, Ma : Massachusetts Inst. Tech. (MIT)
44 x 44
160 pp
For Atlanta, Boston, Chicago, Cincinnati, Cleveland, Denver, Detroit, Houston, Miami, Los Angeles, Milwaukee, Minneapolis-St Paul, New Orleans, New York, Philadelphia, Pittsburgh, St Louis, San Francisco, Seattle and Washington DC.
The maps illus. distributions of population densities, land uses, income distribution, housing, by col. symbols. $25.00

NORTHERN CALIFORNIA COUNTY POPULAR STREET ATLASES
San Francisco : Thomas Bros. 1974
Series of spiral bound county street atlases.
Atlases available:

101	Alameda	$5.25
102	Alameda – Contra Costa	$9.75
105	Contra Costa	$5.25
114	Marin	$4.00
122	Sacramento	$5.50
128	Golden Gate counties – Marin – San Francisco – San Mateo – Santa Clara	$14.50
130	Santa Clara	$5.00
131	Sonoma	$5.00
132	San Mateo	$6.00

STREET ATLASES
New York : Hagstrom

Connecticut :	
Fairfield County Atlas	$6.95
New Haven County	$6.95
Long Island :	
Huntington Twp	$1.50
Nassau County	$4.95
Suffolk County	$7.95
New Jersey :	
Bergen-Rockland Counties	$7.95
Mercer County	$5.95
Middlesex County	$6.95
Monmouth County	$6.95
Morris-Somerset Counties	$7.95
Ocean County	$6.95
Passaic County	$7.95
Union-Hudson-Essex Counties	$7.95
New York City :	
New York City Atlas (5 boros)	$4.95
Pocket Atlas (5 boros)	$1.95
Philadelphia :	
Philadelphia-Camden Atlas	$5.95
New York State	
Westchester County Atlas	$6.95
Rochester Atlas	$5.95
Texas:	
Dallas Atlas	$6.95

ATLASES
C OFFICIAL SURVEYS

SET OF 100 TOPOGRAPHIC MAPS ILLUSTRATING SPECIFIED PHYSIOGRAPHIC FEATURES
Washington : USGS
Folder 61 x 76
Set of maps to demonstrate principal landforms in USA. Folder of 100 maps, location diagram, list, brief description of each feature shown.
Maps are selected from those pub. by USGS. $75.00
Also available as selection : Set of 25 Topographic Maps $18.75

ATLAS OF LANDFORMS
2nd rev. edition
Compiled by the Dept. Earth, Space and Graphic Sciences, US Military Academy, West Point 1965.
New York : Wiley, 1974
37 x 30
144 pp
Compiled from USGS set of 100 topog. maps (qv) with aerial photographs, geol. and structural sketch maps, diagrams and descriptive text.
Extracts from the maps not complete sheets; aerial photographs in stereo pairs or triplets. Incl. index map, bibliog.
Spiral bound, soft covers.

ATLASES
D POLITICAL & ADMINISTRATIVE

CONGRESSIONAL DISTRICT ATLAS
Washington : US Dept. Commerce, 1970
23 x 29
Set of Maps showing boundaries of the Districts of the 92nd Congress, of Jan 1971, with indexes to each state:
List A Counties, selected districts and identifying congressional districts, List B Counties by congressional districts. Cross-reference between lists and maps.
$1.75

ATLASES
E2 LAND FEATURES

COLOR AERIAL STEREOGRAMS OF SELECTED COASTAL AREAS OF THE UNITED STATES
Harland R Cravat and Raymond Glaser
Washington : US National Ocean Survey, 1971
iii, 93 pp
Paired colour aerial photographs, location maps, glossary, stereo viewer. $4.75

ATLAS OF RIVER BASINS OF THE UNITED STATES
Prepared by US Soil Conservation Services
2nd edition
Washington : Govt. Printing Office, 1970
57 x 43
8 pp
Shows also drainage areas, land resource regions. 84 maps, 8 pp text. $13.00

THE LOOK OF OUR LAND
– An Airphoto of the Rural United States
Washington : US Dept. of Agriculture
29 x 24
A set of 5 handbooks containing airphoto mosaics of selected regions with a facing stereo pair and notes describing land use, topography, climate and soils.
Handbooks published:
The Far West
North Central
The East and South
The Mountains and Deserts
The Plains and Prairies

WATER ATLAS OF THE UNITED STATES
Eds. J J Gregory and others
Fort Washington, NY : Water Information Center Inc., 1973
35 x 24
122 plates, 198 pp
Covering climate, precipitation, water network, watershed run off, groundwater, irrigation, high tides, water reserves, springs, drinking water and chemical constituents.

ATLAS OF INDUSTRIAL WATER USE
Barry R Lawson
Ithaca, NY : Cornell Univ. Water Resources Center, 1967
47 pp
Report to the Water Resources Council, including 21 maps with loose county outline overlay.
$5.00

ATLASES
F GEOLOGY

GEOLOGIC ATLAS OF THE ROCKY MOUNTAIN REGION
Denver : Rocky Mountain Assoc. Geologists., 1972
45 x 55
331 pp
Coloured atlas covering physical, economic and historical geology in maps, mainly at 1:5, 500, 000. With profiles, sketch maps, tables, illus. description.

ENVIRONMENTAL GEOLOGIC ATLAS OF THE TEXAS COASTAL ZONE – GALVESTON – HOUSTON AREA
Austin Univ. of Texas, 1972
91 pp
Contents: Environmental geology, physical properties, environments and biologic assemblies, current land use, mineral and energy resources, active processes, man-made features and water systems, rainfall, discharge and surface salinity, topography and bathymetry.

ATLASES
G EARTH RESOURCES

ATLAS OF PENNSYLVANIA'S MINERAL RESOURCES
Bernard J O'Neill
Harrisburg : Penn. Geol. Surv.
Part 1 : Limestones and Dolomites of Pennsylvania.

ATLAS
H BIOGEOGRAPHY

ATLAS OF UNITED STATES TREES
Washington : US Forest Service
30 x 28 (map size)
326 pp
Vol. 1, 1971 by Elbert L Little, Jr.
Shows in 200 maps natural distribution and range of native tree species in USA, inc. Alaska. $16.75

A FOREST ATLAS OF THE NORTHEAST
by Howard W Lull
Upper Darby, Pa : US Dept. Ag, NE Forest Experiment Station, 1968
26 x 33
46 pp
Type and extent of forest, soil, climate, people. 16 maps, text and tables. $3.00

A FOREST ATLAS OF THE SOUTH
Thomas C Nelson and Walter M Zilgitt
New Orleans : Southern Forest Experiment Station, 1969
26 x 33
21 pp maps with 6 pp text. Southern Counties admin. map at 1:3, 155, 000

ATLAS OF SOUTHERN FOREST GAME
Lowell K Halls and John J Stransky
New Orleans : US Southern Forest Experiment Station, 1971
21 x 27
24 pp
Set of maps illustrating the distribution of game.

ATLASES
J CLIMATE

CLIMATIC ATLAS OF THE UNITED STATES
1:25, 000, 000 / 1:5, 000, 000
Washington : US Experimental Data Service, 1968
56 x 41
80 climatic maps, diagrams, tables in Ring Binder. $4.25

WORKBOOK OF WEATHER MAPS
John J Hidore
Dubuque : Iowa, 1968
28 x 21
Set of 25 weather maps covering the conterminous US and Southern Canada.

GREAT LAKES ICE ATLAS
Donald R Rondy
Detroit : US Lake Survey, 1969
iii, 11 pp
35 maps Research Report 5-6.

ATLASES
K HUMAN GEOGRAPHY

ATLAS OF MICHIGAN'S FOREIGN BORN POPULATION
Anthony V Rizzo
Dearborn : Free World Press, 1968
27 x 37
iv, 31 pp
24 population distribution maps.

LINGUISTIC ATLAS OF TEXAS GERMAN
Glenn G Gilbert
Marburg : N.G. Elwart Verlag
Austin : Univ. Texas Press, 1972
14 2-colour maps and 6 special maps
222.00 DM

ATLAS OF 19th AND EARLY 20th CENTURY GERMAN/AMERICAN SETTLEMENTS
Editor H Kloss
Marburg : N.G. Elwert Verlag, 1974
45 x 64
18 pp text, 96 double page maps
Cartographic presentation of the settlement of German speaking peoples in the United States. Text in English and German.
190.00 DM

ATLASES
L ECONOMIC

OXFORD REGIONAL ECONOMIC ATLAS OF THE UNITED STATES AND CANADA
2nd Edition
Oxford : OUP, 1975
19 x 25
178 pp
80 pp of detailed economic and thematic maps and a 48 pp section of typographical maps and urban town plans.
Gazetteer of over 10,000 names.
£8.00
Paper Cover £3.75

RAND McNALLY COMMERCIAL ATLAS AND MARKETING GUIDE
102nd edition
Chicago : Rand McNally, 1971
38 x 53
Including double page maps of each state showing populated places, railroads, county names and boundaries, townships and range lines and an index to each of cities, towns, counties, transportation lines, banks and post offices.
General and thematic introductory map section.
Rental Fee : $75.00

CLEARTYPE BUSINESS CONTROL ATLAS OF THE UNITED STATES AND CANADA
3rd edition
New York : American Map Co., 1969
22 x 29
120 pp
Contains black and white maps of each state and province showing county names and boundaries plus populated areas of 1,000 inhabitants or more.

SALES PLANNING ATLAS OF THE UNITED STATES AND CANADA
Maplewood, NJ : Hammond (with Sales Management Magazine) 1968
21 x 28
160 pp
Contains city county outline maps of each state accompanied by individual indexes to cities and towns and a table giving County Retail Sales and Income by households, with fold-out outline map of USA showing counties.
73 x 48 $4.95

RAND McNALLY ZIP CODE ATLAS
Ed R L Forstall
Chicago : Rand McNally, 1970
22 x 28
136 pp
'State Maps and Marketing Data for the Newest System of Marketing Units — the 561 ZIP Code Sectional Areas'
$12.50

THE APPALACHIAN REGION OF NEW YORK STATE
"ATLAS OF NATURAL AND CULTURAL RESOURCES"
Albany, NY : State Office of Planning Coordination, 1969
70 x 54
42 maps
Showing devt. programme in geog, economic and social factors.

AN ECONOMIC ATLAS OF ARKANSAS
Little Rock : Arkansas Industrial Devt. Commission, 1961
Ref Atlas for industrial exective.

ECONOMIC ATLAS OF IDAHO
by H H Caldwell
Moscow (Idaho) : Bureau Mines & Geology, 1970
22 x 28
82 pp maps in col.and black and white, with text on reverse: economic maps, physical environment, culture, land resources, climate.
$2.00

MARYLAND ECONOMIC ATLAS
Annapolis : Dept. Economic Devt. (Maryland), 1967
37 x 25
64 pp
Maps in black and white showing features of economic interest, agriculture, industry, social aspects, communications.
$2.50

NORTH DAKOTA ECONOMIC ATLAS
Arthur Leno
2nd edition
Bismarck : ND State Planning Agency, 1969
26 x 36
51 pp
30 maps in black and white covering economy, demography, natural resources, climate. With numerous graphs.
$1.00

INDUSTRIAL ATLAS OF TENNESSEE
by Sue J Magargel
Memphis : Univ. Bureau Business and Economic Research
vi, 50 pp app
Distribution of industrial plants in each county with maps for major industry groups, admin. offices etc. 20 maps, 20 pp tables.

ATLAS OF WASHINGTON AGRICULTURE
Seattle : US Dept. Ag (Wash)/Washington Crop and Livestock Reporting Service, 1963
28 x 22
137 pp
Arranged in 6 parts covering agricultural, history, regions and current pattern, crops, fruits and berries and livestock with statistical appendix and index.

ATLASES
M HISTORICAL

THE AMERICAN HERITAGE PICTORIAL ATLAS OF UNITED STATES HISTORY
New York : American Heritage Publishing Co, Inc., 1966
22 x 29
424 pp
Comprehensive series of historical maps and narrative text including portfolios of pictorial maps depicting battles and other matters.
$16.50

AMERICAN HISTORY ATLAS
Martin Gilbert
New York : Macmillan Co. / London: Weidenfeld and Nicolson, 1968
18 x 24
112 black and white historical maps.

ATLAS OF AMERICAN HISTORY
Maplewood, NJ : Hammond, 1969
24 x 31
64 pp
Shows economic, social, demographic, ecological factors of Am. history in chronological order.
Indexed. $2.50
Paper $1.28

OUR UNITED STATES : ITS HISTORY IN MAPS
Edgar R Wesley
Chicago : Denoyer-Geppert
22 x 28
96 pp
39 col. maps of nation's history, devt. natural resources and economy. Each map separate legend with sketches, maps and diagrams.
Indexed $2.50

ATLAS OF THE UNITED STATES, 1795 -1800
by Joseph Scott
Chardon, Ohio : Bloch
Collections of facsimile maps of the USA covering this period.
$12.50

THE AMERICAN REVOLUTION, 1775-1783; AND ATLAS OF 18th CENTURY MAPS AND CHARTS, THEATERS OF OPERATIONS.
compiled by W B Greenwood
Washington : Haval History Division, Dept. of the Navy, 1972
61 x 48
93 pp including text and 20 maps.
$8.50

PIONEER ATLAS OF THE AMERICAN WEST
Chicago : Rand McNally
29 x 35
80 pp
Facsimile ed. of maps and indexes of the West from Rand McNally's Business Atlas of 1876. Historical text on each date by Dale L Morgan.

HISTORICAL ATLAS OF CALIFORNIA
Eds. W A Beck and Y D Haase
Oklahoma City : Univ. of Oklahoma Press, 1974
23 x 30
Geog. and historic data from prehistoric to modern times shown in 101 monochrome maps with bibliography and index.
Cloth $9.95
Paper $4.95

MAPS OF INDIANA COUNTIES IN 1876 TOGETHER WITH THE PLAT OF INDIANAPOLIS AND A SAMPLING OF ILLUSTRATIONS
Alfred Theodore Andreas
Indianapolis : Indiana Historical Socy, 1968
96 pp
Reprinted from the illustrated historical Atlas of the State of Indiana, pub. Baskin; Forster & Co. Chicago 1876.

A SERIES OF COUNTY OUTLINE MAPS OF THE SOUTHEASTERN UNITED STATES FOR THE PERIOD 1790-1860
Map Study No 2
prepared by S S Birdsall & J W Florin
Chapel Hill, NC : Univ. of N Carolina, Geog. Dept. 1973
61 x 51
8 maps contained on 6 sheets, showing growth of counties in southeastern US for 10 year intervals between 1790-1860.

HISTORICAL ATLAS OF ALABAMA
by D B Dodd
Tuscaloosa : Univ. of Alabama Press
157 pp
History of the state in 136 maps and text covering physical, structure, agriculture, industry, population and political allegiances.
$10.00

ILLUSTRATED HISTORICAL ATLAS OF THE STATE OF IOWA
Alfred Theodore Andreas
Iowa City : State Historical Society, 1970
579 pp
Reproduction of the 1875 atlas published by Andreas Atlas Co., Chicago,
88 pp county maps, 44 pp city plans, 231 pp views.

HISTORICAL ATLAS OF KANSAS
Ed H E Socoolfsky and H Self
Norman : Univ. of Oklahoma Press, 1972
172 pp including 70 maps.

HISTORICAL ATLAS OF NEW MEXICO
Warren A Beck and Ynez D Haase
Norman : Oklahoma UP, 1969
30 x 23
Geog. and historic data from prehistoric to modern civilisation depicted in 65 monochrome maps with bibliography and index.
Hardbound $4.95
Paperbound $2.95

AN HISTORICAL ATLAS OF EARLY OREGON
by J A Farmer and K L Holmes
Portland : Historical Cartographic Pubns.
State historical atlas.

ATLAS OF JEFFERSON AND OLDHAM COUNTIES AND KENTUCKY
Louisville : Historic Reprints
34 x 42
Facsimile reprint of 'New and Actual Surveys compiled and published by Beers and Lanagan, Philadelphia 1879. Has maps of each parish and town plan of Louisville at 1:90, 000 app.

THE EXPEDITIONS OF JOHN CHARLES FREMONT
Ed D Jackson and M Lee Spence
Urbana : Univ. Illinois Press, 1970
Map portfolio, 5 maps; 1843 map of hydrographical basin of the Upper Mississippi River; Exploration of Country between Missouri River and Rocky Mountains; Mountain Exploration, 1843-4; Topog. map of the Road from Missouri to Oregon, 1846; Map of Oregon and Upper California, 1848. To accompany 3 vol. account.
Maps $10.00
Vol. 1 and Maps $22.50

ATLASES
O NATIONAL

NATIONAL ATLAS OF THE UNITED STATES OF AMERICA
Ed Aven C Gerlach
Washington : USGS, 1970
38 x 51
417 pp of maps, scales 1:500, 000 / 1:34, 000, 000 also diagrams and index. Covering various characteristics of the country. Sections include :
Physical—relief, geol, climate, water resources
Historical—discovery, exploration, territorial growth
Economic—agriculture, minerals and mining, trade, industry, transportation
Sociocultural—population, income, education
Admin—counties, statistical areas, judicial districts, congressional districts.
Complete $100.00

THESE UNITED STATES; OUR NATION'S GEOGRAPHY, HISTORY AND PEOPLE
Pleasantville, NY : Readers Digest Association 1968
28 x 40
236 pp
174 pp coloured maps with descriptive text and index. Part 1 'The 50 State' maps of each state and possession with brief notes and gazetteer to places. Part 2 'The People of America' history and growth of America. Part 3 'The American Land' natural and physical resources.

ATLAS SOEDINENNEX STATOV AMERIKI
Moskva : GUGK, 1966
25 x 34
80 pp
Them. atlas, about 90 maps, diagrams and tables.

ATLASES
P REGIONAL

ATLAS OF THE PACIFIC NORTHWEST
Ed R M Highsmith Jnr
Corvallis : Oregon State College, 1968
30 x 24
176 pp
Outline of resources and devt. with col. maps, explanatory text, incl. Washington, Oregon, Idaho and Western Montana.
$8.00

ATLAS OF ALABAMA
Ed N G Linebeck
Tuscaloosa : Univ. of Alabama Press, 1973
x : 134 pp
Arranged into 3 sections; Physical Landscape, Cultural and Social Patterns, Economic Characteristics. Includes numerous cartograms, 19 coloured maps, graphs, tables and photographs.

ENVIRONMENTAL ATLAS OF ALASKA
Philip R Johnson and Charles W Hartman
Fairbanks : Geophysical Inst., Univ., of Alaska, 1969
32 x 26
111 pp
Black and white maps, some with blue overprint, explanatory text. In 5 sections; Physical Description; Alaskan Waters; Light and Climate; Engineering information.
$7.00

PATTERNS ON THE LAND : GEOGRAPHICAL, HISTORICAL AND POLITICAL MAPS OF CALIFORNIA
R W Durrenberger
3rd edition
Palo Alto; Nat. Press Books, 1967
23 x 30
109 pp
5 Sections; Physical Geog; Explorations and Settlement; Population and Urban Growth; Utilization of Resources; Commerce and Industry. With text and index.

THE NEW FLORIDA ATLAS : PATTERNS OF THE SUNSHINE STATE
by R Wood and E A Fernald
Tallahassee : Trend Pubns. 1974
119 pp
Contains over 260 2-colour maps, physical, historical, cultural and economic with statistical text matter, photographs and bibliography.
$14.95

ATLAS OF HAWAII
developed and compiled by the Dept. pf Geog. Univ. of Hawaii
Honolulu : The Univ. Press of Hawaii, 1973
23 x 31
232 pages
Includes 130 coloured maps, 82 photographs (50 col.) arranged into 5 parts;
1 reference maps; 2 natural environments;
3 the people (language, religion, culture);
4 the economy; 5 bibliography, place names and gazetteer.
app. $20.00

AN ATLAS OF INDIANA
by Robert C Kingsbury
Occasional Paper No 5
Bloomington : Univ. Dept. Geog, 1970
21 x 28
94 pp
Them, atlas of natural conditions and human activity. 109 black and white maps inc. computer plans.
$2.00

LAKE COUNTY, INDIANA, IN MAPS
Daniel F Dull
Bloomington : Dept. Geography, Univ. Indiana, 1971
52 pp
40 black and white maps showing historical, cultural and physical features. 8 pp text including contents, tables, list of sources.
$1.50

AN ECONOMIC AND SOCIAL ATLAS OF MARYLAND
by D Thompson and J W Wiedel
Occasional Papers in Geog. No 3
Univ. of Maryland, Dept. of Geog. 1974
126 pp
Includes 102 pp of coloured maps (1:1, 500, 000), 70 charts and tables with descriptive text and bibliography.
$5.00

ATLAS OF MICHIGAN
by Earl J Senninger Jr.
3rd edition
Flint (Mich) : Flint Geographical Press,
28 x 22
103 pp
98 maps covering physical, industrial, economic, political and social geography.
$5.60

ATLAS OF MINNESOTA RESOURCES AND SETTLEMENT
John R Borchert and Donald P Yaeger
St Paul : Minnesota State Planning Agency 1968 (1969)
26 x 21
262 pp
Showing geographical analysis of the State; trade, population. With transparent overlay with minor civil divisions and water features
$3.50

ENVIRONMENTAL CONDITIONS AND RESOURCES OF SOUTHWESTERN MISSISSIPPI
Washington : USGS, 1970
58 pp
26 pp maps — aerial and space photography.
$2.25

ATLAS OF MISSOURI
Ed M D Rafferty, R L Gerlach, D J Hrebec
Springfield : Aux-Arc Research Associates, 1970
35 x 28
92 pp
Black and white sketch maps with text, covering physical, social, climatic, economic factors. $5.80

RICHARDS' ATLAS OF NEW YORK STATE
by Robert J Raybach, Rev. Edward L Towle
Phoenix (NY) : F E Richards, 1965
57 x 44
92 pp
School atlas covering history, geog, pop, economy. 86 pp maps, 92 pp text, separate vol.
$121.5

ATLAS OF NORTH CAROLINA
Richard E Lonsdale
Chapel Hill : North Carolina UP/OUP, 1967
24 x 32
168 pp
Physical, economic, social aspects, with maps, diagrams, photographs and descriptive text; covers regional variations in agriculture and industry.
$7.50

METROLINA ATLAS
Ed J W Clay and D M Orr Jr.
Chapel Hill NC : Univ. of N. Carolina Press, 1972
22 x 29
Regional atlas of the town of Charlotte, North Carolina, and its neighbourhood covering various aspects as a basis for planning. $13.95

THE PUGET SOUND REGION : A PORTFOLIO OF THEMATIC COMPUTER MAPS
Occasional Paper No 3
Ed J W Mairs and E A Hoerauf
Corvallis : Center for Pacific Northwest Studies, 1974
35 x 25
41 pp
Portfolio containing 37 maps covering the 12 counties adjacent to Puget Sound, analysing 1970 population census data. A two-dimensional choropleth map and a three-dimensional isoline diagram with brief explanations for 18 topics.
$2.95

ATLAS OF SOUTH DAKOTA
Ed Edward P Hogan et al
Dubuque : Kendall/Hunt Publishing Co. 1970
28 x 21
137 pp
137 coloured maps, text on reverse: showing physical, climatic, agricultural, mineral and industrial features.
$7.50

ATLAS OF TEXAS
5th edition
S A Arbingast, L G Kennamer and M E Bonine
Austin : Texas UP/Bureau of Business Research, 1976
23 x 30
158 pp
Outline maps with information superimposed. In 5 sections: Physical Setting; Population, Transportation, Education and Recreation; Agriculture; Mining and Manufacturing; Culture and History. Two foldout maps included in pocket.
Spiral bound $10.00

AN ATLAS OF WISCONSIN
2nd edition
Charles W Collins
Madison : American Printing & Publishing Inc., 1972
187 pp
22 x 28
Portraying statistical data on population, physical geography, climate, agriculture, industry, conservation and tourism.

THE ATLAS OF WISCONSIN
1st edition
Ed A H Robinson and J B Culver
Madison : Univ. of Wisconsin Press, 1974
26 x 33
Collection of 15 1:1, 500, 000 maps, contoured with roads, parks etc, 19 town maps 1:125, 000 and general physical-political maps of the state. 81 pp gazetteer of 14,000 entires.
Paper binding $5.95
Cloth Binding $20.00

Venezuela
87
Guyana 881
Colombia
861
French Guiana
882
Ecuador
866
Surinam
883
Brazil
81
Peru
85
Bolivia
84
Paraguay
892
Chile
83
Argentina
82
Uruguay
899

South America

R2

8 South America

C OFFICIAL SURVEYS

HISPANIC AMERICA SERIES
1:1, 000, 000, 000
In 107 sheets, see index 8/1
Washington : AGS, 1922-45
67 x 44
Series covering Central and South America in conformity with International Map of the World. Contoured, layer col, boundaries, road and rail communications, towns graded by status and population, other land features.
Per sheet $3.00

D POLITICAL & ADMINISTRATIVE

AMERYKA POLUDNIOWA, MAPA FIZYCZNA I POLITYCZNA
1:20, 000, 000
PPWK, 1972
see SOUTH AMERICA 8 E1

DIE STAATEN SUDAMERIKAS
1:10, 000, 000
Darmstadt : Perthes
106 x 125
Political col, wall map in Haack "Kleiner Geographischer Wandatlas" series.
48DM

SÜDAMERIKA
1:10, 000, 000
Frankfurt : Ravenstein
76 x 97
Physical, political map with principal road and rail communications. 8.80 DM

LATINSKAYA AMERIKA
1:10, 000, 000
Moskva : GUGK, 1973
Political-admin. reference map.
15 kop

PHILIP'S POLITICAL SMALLER WALL MAP OF SOUTH AMERICA
1:9, 000, 000
London : Philip
83 x 102
Political col, railways, shipping routes, towns graded by pop.
Paper flat £1.50
Mounted CR £5.50
Mounted on cloth dissected to fold £7.00

SOUTH AMERICA
1:8, 000, 000
No 4253
Bern : K & F
73 x 112
Political col, main roads, railways, shipping routes, canals, airports etc.

USHNAYA AMERIKA, POLITICHES-KAYA KARTA
1:8, 000, 000
Moskva : GUGK, 1972
2 sheet school political wall map.
22 kop

AMERICA DEL SUR
No scale given
Barcelona : Editorial Teide
88 x 115
General wall map for schools. 275 ptas

SUPERIOR WALL MAP OF SOUTH AMERICA
1:8, 000, 000
Maplewood, NJ : Hammond
80 x 115
Political col. wall map.
Flat or folded $2.00

IMPERIAL MAP OF SOUTH AMERICA
1:8, 000, 000
Chicago : Rand McNally
66 x 113
Political col. by states, railways etc. Index on reverse.

JIZNI AMERIKA
1:8, 000, 000
Praha : Kart, 1969
General school wall map of South America.
kcs 145

SOUTH AMERICA
1:7, 500, 000
Washington : NGS, 1969
92 x 106
Political wall map inc. all South American islands with boundaries in colour, detailed place names.
Paper $2.00
Plastic $3.00

SOUTH AMERICA : POLITICAL GEOGRAPHY WALL MAP
1:7, 187, 500
No 107061
Chicago : Denoyer-Geppert
111 x 147
Political col. school wall map, showing boundaries, communications, water features, pop.
CR $19.25
Also available in Spanish edition (No 107661)

JUZNA AMERIKA
1:7, 000, 000
Beograd : Geokarta
98 x 136
2 sheet map with latin and cyrillic lettering.
Cloth mounted 100 dn

EXCELLO POLITICAL WALL MAP
1:6, 875, 000
Indianapolis : Cram
111 x 116
Political coloured wall map, mounted on linen. $12.50

POLITICAL WALL MAPS OF SOUTH AMERICA
Various scales
Indianapolis : Cram
Col. school wall maps available at different levels and depths:
Level B Simplified 1:6, 250, 000
129 x 144 $23.00
Level C Detailed 1:6, 250, 000
129 x 144 $23.00

PHILIP'S POLITICAL LARGE WALL MAP OF SOUTH AMERICA
1:6, 000, 000
London : Philip
119 x 178
Political col. boundaries, railways, sea routes, towns graded by pop.
Mounted CR £15.00
Mounted on cloth dissected to fold £17.00

SÜDAMERIKA
1:6, 000, 000
Gotha : Haack, 1972
60 x 83
Col. hand map, showing boundaries, communications etc. With 56pp text.
6.80 DM

AMÉRIQUE DU SUD
1:5, 000, 000
Bruxelles : Mantniek
119 x 163
Politically coloured wall map in French and English editions. Azimuthal equivalent projection. Available mounted in various styles.

AMERICA DEL SUR
1:5, 000, 000
Madrid : Aguilar
130 x 200
Political coloured wall map for schools. Cloth map

ETELA - AMERIKKA
1:5, 000, 000
Helsinki : Wsoy
171 x 125
School wall map, political colouring.
100 FMK

AMÉRIQUE DU SUD
No scale given
No 20
Paris : Hatier
100 x 120
Political school wall map; with economic map on reverse.

SUPERIOR WALL MAP OF LATIN AMERICA
No scale given
Maplewood, NJ : Hammond
63 x 71
Political col. wall map in Spanish.
Flat or folded $2.00

AMERICA DEL SUR
No scale given
Barcelona : Editorial Teide
33 x 50
General hand map for schools showing major cities, boundaries.
2 ptas
Also : America del Sur Politica (25 x 33) 1 pta

PAISES ANDINOS SEPTENTRIONALES
PAISES DEL PLATA Y CHILE
Scales indicated
Barcelona : Editorial Teide
25 x 33
2 general school hand maps showing major rivers and state boundaries. Each 1 pta

AMERICA MERIDONALE
1:40, 000, 000
Novara: Agostini
Small hand outline map for schools. L 40

UZHNAYA AMERIKA
1:40, 000, 000
Moskva : GUGK, 1973
Outline map. 1 kop

PHILIP'S MAP BUILDING SHEET ('BLACKBOARD MAP') OF SOUTH AMERICA
1:9, 000, 000
London : Philip
83 x 102
As Large Outline Map but in yellow on blackboard paper
Mounted CR £4.00

SÜDAMERIKA
1:8, 000, 000
No 0839
Bern : K & F
80 x 117
Political col. outline map.

SOUTH AMERICA, OUTLINE SLATED
1:7, 187, 500
No 165061
Chicago : Denoyer-Geppert
111 x 129
Blackboard map for schools showing countries; blue and yellow on black.
$19.95

VITO-GRAPHIC CHALKBOARD OUTLINE MAP OF SOUTH AMERICA
1:7, 000, 000
Ref VS 4
Chicago : Weber Costello Co
117 x 150
Land areas in green, meridians, parallels and outlines in yellow, water areas in blue. On cloth - various mounted styles.

POLITICAL OUTLINE MAP OF SOUTH AMERICA
1:6, 250, 000
Indianapolis : Cram
129 x 144
Political boundaries, rivers and principal towns in black and white.
Mounted on linen with rollers $27.50
Also available Physical Outline Map
1:6, 250, 000
129 x 129 $27.50
Reduced edition : Desk Outline Map (Political) 30 x 43 60c

ARBEITSKARTE : SÜDAMERIKA
1:6, 000, 000
No 9723
München : JRO
135 x 173
2 col. map on plastic surface, suitable for working on. 108 DM

LERNKARTE VON SÜDAMERIKA
1:6, 000, 000
Darmstadt : Perthes
138 x 160
Base map showing basic relief, political boundaries, ocean current directions. Economy etc. can be shown by symbols. No names. 94 DM
Schuler-Lernkarte 30 x 42 available
1.50 DM

EASTERN SOUTH AMERICA (1955)
1:4, 937, 500
Washington : NGS
73 x 103
Political col. wall map.
Paper $2.00
Plastic $3.00

E1 PHYSICAL : RELIEF

AMERICA MERIDIONALE
1:40, 000, 000
Novara : Agostini
33 x 26
Physical map, with political map and physical and economic detail on reverse.
L 450

AMERYKA POLUDNIOWA MAPA FIZYCZNA I POLITYCZNA
1:20, 000, 000
2nd edition
Warzawa : PPWK, 1972
59 x 43
Double sided map; physical side shows hydrographic and topog. detail with communications; reverse has political boundaries, with admin. map of Brazil.
zl 5

BARTHOLOMEW'S WORLD TRAVEL MAP SERIES : SOUTH AMERICA
1:10, 000, 000
Edinburgh : Bart
59 x 84
Contoured, layer col. road and rail communications, boundaries 75p

SÜDAMERIKA
1:10, 000, 000
Darmstadt : Perthes
106 x 125
Wall map in "Haack Kleiner Geographischer Wandatlas". Physical, bathymetric col. boundaries, names. 48 DM

PHILIP'S PHYSICAL SMALLER WALL MAP OF SOUTH AMERICA
1:9, 000, 000
London : Philip, 1972
83 x 102
Physical layer col, political boundaries in red.
Paper flat £1.50
Mounted CR £5.50
Mounted on cloth dissected to fold £7.00

PHILIP'S GRAPHIC RELIEF WALL MAP OF SOUTH AMERICA
1:9, 000, 000
London : Philip
83 x 102
Col. to simulate predominant vegetation cover, relief shading, producing a 3-D effect. No town names.
Paper flat £1.50
Mounted CR £5.50
Mounted on cloth dissected to fold £7.00

PHILIP'S COMPARATIVE WALL ATLAS OF SOUTH AMERICA
1:9, 000, 000
London : Philip
83 x 102 each
Set of 5 maps for comparative study :
Relief of Land - Political and Communications.
Climate - Summer Conditions, Winter Conditions, Rainfall, Isobars, Winds, Actual Temperature and Sea Level Isotherms
Natural Vegetation
Political
Density of Population
Mounted CR £5.50
5 maps mounted on one roller £9.50

AMERICA MERIDIONALE FISICO-POLITICO
1:8, 000, 000
Novara : Agostini
100 x 140
School wall map showing relief of land and sea, political boundaries, cities graded by pop. First series. L 2,200
Mounted L 5,000
Second series : 1:7, 000, 000 (2 sheets)
138 x 190 L 3,500
Mounted L 7,500
Third series : 1:10, 000, 000
100 x 140 L 2,200
Mounted L 5,000

ZUID-AMERIKA
1:8, 000, 000
Groningen : Wolters-Noordhoff
90 x 120
Physical wall map showing relief and settlements Fl. 96.25

YUZHNAYA AMERIKA
1:8, 000, 000
Moskva : GUGK, 1973
2 sheet physical wall map. 22 kop

SÜDAMERIKA
1:7, 500, 000
W 706
München : List
90 x 130
Wenschow wall map; physical col, relief of land and sea, names, international boundaries, main railways. 54 DM
Also available as double map with "Südamerika : Wirtschaft" 8 G No H 279 (q.v.) 92 DM

EXCELLO PHYSICAL WALL MAP
1:7, 500, 000
Indianapolis : Cram
111 x 137
Physical wall map of South America mounted on linen $12.50

TRI-GRAPHIC MAP OF SOUTH AMERICA
1:7, 500, 000
Ref: TRI-4
Chicago : Weber Costello Co.
101 x 137
Physical layer colouring with graphic relief shading, political and boundaries. Available mounted in various styles.

LATIN AMERICA
1:7, 187, 500
No 126761
Chicago : Denoyer-Geppert
137 x 177
Visual-relief col. school wall map, covering the area from Chicago to Cape Horn. Text English and Spanish
Spring rollers $27.50

SOUTH AMERICA
1:7, 187, 500
No 130061
Chicago : Denoyer-Geppert
111 x 147
Classroom physical-political map, showing land detail, boundaries, pop, communications.
Rollers $15.50

SOUTH AMERICA, VISUAL RELIEF
1:7, 187, 500
No 110061
Chicago : Denoyer-Geppert
111 x 147
Physical school wall map, showing land and sea relief, boundaries etc. Reduced size as Desk Map, No 301561, 29 x 43, $3.30 per 25 copies. $18.75

AMÉRIQUE DU SUD (PHYSIQUE)
1:6, 500, 000
No 1059 French, 1233 English, 1228 Arabic
St Germain-en-Laye : Editions MDI
92 x 126
Plastic coated physical wall map for schools. Economic map on reverse.

PHYSICAL MAPS OF SOUTH AMERICA
Various scales
Indianapolis : Cram
Col. school wall maps available at different levels and depths.
Level B Simplified Physical-Political
1:6, 250, 000 129 x 129 $23.00
Level C Detailed Physical-Political
1:6, 250, 000 129 x 129 $23.00

PHILIP'S PHYSICAL LARGE WALL MAP OF SOUTH AMERICA
1:6, 000, 000
London : Philip
119 x 178
Physical col, hill shading, ocean routes, railways, political boundaries.
Mounted CR £15.00
Mounted on cloth dissected to fold with eyelets £17.00

SÜDAMERIKA
1:6, 000, 000
Darmstadt : Perthes
172 x 205
Haack Wall Map. Physical col, relief shown by layer col, boundaries, communications.
Mounted CR 142 DM

SÜDAMERIKA, MIT MEERESBODEN-RELIEF
1:6, 000, 000
W 714
München : List
150 x 190
Wenschow col. wall map showing relief of land and sea, ocean currents, boundaries.
142 DM

SÜDAMERIKA
1:6, 000, 000
Gotha : Haack, 1967
118 x 194
Physical col. wall map for schools. Shows relief by layer col, ocean depths, boundaries, main physical features.

SÜDAMERIKA
1:6. 000, 000
Braunschweig : Westermann
146 x 184
Physical col. school wall map showing relief of land and sea, land types, cities graded by pop, internat. boundaries, Subdivisions of Brazil.

PHYSIKALISCHE KARTE
1:6, 000, 000
No 9721
München : JRO
135 x 175
Physical col. school wall map showing relief of land and sea, names, boundaries. "Arbeitskarte" (plastic 2 col. map) on reverse. 128 DM
Physical map on rollers No 9762 118 DM

THE WORLD
1:5, 000, 000
AGS
2 sheets required to cover South America:
IB South America (sheet north)
IC South America (sheet north) currently out of print
see WORLD 100C and index 100/3

AMERICA DEL SUR
1:5, 000, 000
Madrid : Aguilar
130 x 300
Physical wall map for schools. Hypsometric colouring, altitudes indicated. Cloth.

SÜDAMERIKA
1:5, 000, 000
H 209
München : List
180 x 215
Harms col. school map. Relief of land and sea indicated, boundaries. 142 DM

AMÉRIQUE DU SUD
1:5, 000, 000
Bruxelles : Mantnieks
125 x 180
Physical wall map for schools, showing relief of land and sea, direction of ocean currents, political boundaries. Available in French or English edition.

AMÉRICA DEL SUR FÍSICA
No scale indicated
Barcelona : Editorial Teide
25 x 33
Physical hand map for schools. 1 pta

JIŽNÍ AMERIKA — VRCHLÍK
1:18, 000, 000
Praha : Kart, 1968
Relief — globe section of South America
Kcs 85

AMERICA MERIDIONALE FISICO-POLITICA
1:10, 000, 000
Novara : Agostini
100 x 131
Plastic moulded relief map in frame with metal corners. L 20,000

RAISED RELIEF MAP OF SOUTH AMERICA
1:5, 000, 000
Chicago : Nystrom, 1974
95 x 128
Plastic moulded map, physical layer colouring, principal communications and boundaries.
Unframed US $46.00
Framed US $74.00

PHOTO IMAGE MAP OF PARTS OF PERU BOLIVIA AND CHILE
Washington : USGS, 1967
46 x 112
Air photo-map from Gemini 9.

ECUADOR, GUYANA, KOLUMBIE, PERU A VENEZUELA
1:6, 000, 000
Praha : Kart
74 x 73
Czech physical col. wall map; contours, boundaries. In series "Poznavame Svet".

ARGENTINA, CHILE, PARAGUAY A URUGUAY
1:6, 000, 000
Praha : Kart, 1968
Col. physical wall map in "Poznavame Svet" series.

F GEOLOGY

GEOLOGICAL MAP OF SOUTH AMERICA
1:5, 000, 000
Boulder, Col. : GSA, 1964
81 x 116
2 sheet map in col; legend French, Spanish, Portuguese. $8.25

TECTONIC MAP OF SOUTH AMERICA
1:5, 000, 000
Paris : UNESCO
2 sheet map with brochure in preparation.

G EARTH RESOURCES

SOUTH AMERICA : MAGNETIC INTENSITY, HORIZONTAL AND VERTICAL
1:15, 000, 000
Valparaiso : Chilean Navy, 1955
80 x 64
2 sheets, showing vertical and horizontal magnetism.

SOIL MAP OF THE WORLD
1:5, 000, 000
Paris : UNESCO, 1970
106 x 74
2 sheets to cover South America, ie IV 1 and 2 including explanatory volume IV.
see WORLD G and index 100/6

H BIOGEOGRAPHY

SOUTH AMERICA, VEGETATION AND LAND USE
1:12, 000, 000
Tehran : Sahab
60 x 90
Map in English and Persian showing vegetation types, cultivation, irrigation with inset rainfall. 80 Rls

SÜDAMERIKA : VEGETATION
1:10, 000, 000 approx.
No 9905 München : JRO
96 x 120
Col. pictorial map for schools, showing vegetation types. 48 DM

SÜDAMERIKA : TIERWELT
1:10, 000, 000
No 9906
München : JRO
96 x 120
Pictorial school wall map showing animal species. 48 DM

SÜDAMERIKA : BODENNUTZUNG
1:10, 000, 000 approx.
No 9907
München : JRO
96 x 120
Pictorial school wall map showing land use. 48 DM

PHILIP'S COMPARATIVE WALL ATLAS OF SOUTH AMERICA – NATURAL VEGETATION
1:9, 000, 000
Philip
see SOUTH AMERICA 8 E1

SÜDAMERIKA : MENSCHEN, HAUSTIERE UND NUTZPFLANZEN
No scale given
Braunschweig : Westermann
95 x 125
Pictorial wall map for schools, showing tribes, domestic animals, natural vegetation.

SÜDAMERIKA : WILDTIERE UND WILDPFLANZEN
No scale given
Braunschweig : Westermann
95 x 125
Pictorial wall map for schools, showing wild animals and plants.

J CLIMATE

SOUTH AMERICA – CLIMATE
1:14, 375, 000
No 109061
Chicago : Denoyer-Geppert
111 x 162
4 thematic maps on 1 sheet, showing various aspects of climate. $15.50

SÜDAMERIKA : KLIMA UND VEGETATION
1:9, 000, 000
Gotha : Haack
189 x 197
4 maps on 1 sheet, showing January and July average temperatures and atmospheric pressure, mean annual precipitation and ocean currents, vegetation areas.

SUDAMERIKA : KLIMA UND VEGETATION
1:9, 000, 000
Braunschweig : Westermann
189 x 197
School col. wall map showing climate and vegetation. 148 DM

PHILIP'S COMPARATIVE WALL ATLAS OF SOUTH AMERICA – CLIMATE
1:9, 000, 000
Philip
see SOUTH AMERICA 8 E1

YUZHNAYA AMERIKA, KLIMATICHESKAYA KARTA
1:8, 000, 000
Moskva : GUGK, 1973
2 sheet climatic wall map for schools. 34 kop

K HUMAN GEOGRAPHY

SOUTH AMERICA – POPULATION
1:14, 375, 000
No 109061
Chicago : Denoyer-Geppert
111 x 162
4 thematic maps on 1 sheet. Shows population density. $15.50

PHILIP'S COMPARATIVE WALL ATLAS OF SOUTH AMERICA – DENSITY OF POPULATION
1:9, 000, 000
Philip
see SOUTH AMERICA 8 E1

ETHNO-LINGUISTIC DISTRIBUTION OF SOUTH AMERICAN INDIANS
by Cestmir Loukotta
1:8, 500, 000
Florida : AAG, 1967
67 x 110
Col. map showing distribution. $3.00

L ECONOMIC

SOUTH AMERICA – TRANSPORTATION
1:14, 375, 000
No 109061
Chicago : Denoyer-Geppert
111 x 162
4 thematic maps on 1 sheet, showing aspects of transportation, inc. air travel. $15.50

SOUTH AMERICA – ECONOMY
1:14, 375, 000
No 109061
Chicago : Denoyer-Geppert
111 x 162
4 thematic maps on 1 sheet showing economic activities. $15.50

SOUTH AMERICA – ECONOMY
1:12, 000, 000
Tehran : Sahab
60 x 90
Map in Persian and English showing agriculture, livestock, fishing, mineral deposits with inset industries and factories. 100 Rls

SÜDAMERIKA : WIRTSCHAFT UND VERKEHR
No scale given
Braunschweig : Westermann
95 x 125
Pictorial wall map for schools, showing economy and transport.

SÜDAMERIKA : VERWALTUNG, WIRTSCHAFT UND VERKEHR
No 9908
Munchen : JRO
96 x 120
Pictorial school wall map showing admin. economy and transport. 48 DM

LATINSKAYA AMERIKA
1:8, 000, 000
Moskva : GUGK, 1972
115 x 145
2 sheet school wall map showing economy by symbols. 34 kop

SÜDAMERIKA : WIRTSCHAFT
1:7, 500, 000
H 279
München : List
100 x 140
Harms wall map showing economy by col. symbols. 54 DM
Also as double wall map with physical map No W 706 (q.v.) as No 269 92 DM

TRANSPORTATION FACILITIES OF SOUTH AMERICA
1:7, 187, 500
No 109561
Chicago : Denoyer-Geppert
111 x 162
Wall map showing roads, railways, airports, ports, inland waterways inset.
Spring rollers. $19.25

AMÉRIQUE DU SUD (PHYSIQUE-ÉCONOMIQUE)
1:6, 500, 000
Éditions MDI
see SOUTH AMERICA 8E1

SÜDAMERIKA, WIRTSCHAFT
1:5, 000, 000
Berlin : Velhagen und Klasing und Hermann Schroedel
162 x 218
Economic wall map.

SOUTH AMERICA, ECONOMIC AND POLITICAL
Indianapolis : Cram
School col. wall map, showing trade, pop, etc. $13.75

M HISTORICAL

HISPANIC AMERICA SERIES
Chicago : Denoyer-Geppert
111 x 81
Set of 16 historical wall maps for schools:
203011 Relief and Cultures
203021 Discovery of America
203031 The Caribbean 1492-1543
203041 European Expansion to 1580
203051 Hispanic America in 16th Century
203061 Colonial Trade and Government
203071 Colonial Expansion 1700 and 1763
203081 Spain's Northern Frontier, 1763-1800
203091 The Struggle for Independence
203101 Hemisphere Solidarity, 1945
203111 Mexico
203121 The Caribbean Region in 1960
203131 Brazil and Columbia in 1940
203141 Argentina and Chile 1960
203151 Population, 1960
203161 Economic, Communications, 1960
CR (each) $10.00
Set $79.50

OBRAZOVANIE NEZAVISIMYKH GOSUDARSTV V LATINOSKOY AMERIKE V NACHALE XIX V
(Formation of Independent States of Latin America in the early 19th C)
1:10, 000, 000
Moskva : GUGK, 1973
Historical wall map. 24 kop

SÜDAMERIKA VON DER INKAZEIT BIS HEUTE
1:6, 000, 000
Braunschweig : Westermann, 1966
188 x 204
Col. historical wall map, with insets, covering the history of the continent from the 'Incas to today'.

SOUTH AMERICA - FACSIMILE MAPS
Wien : Editio Totius Mundi
Maps available :

29 South America 'America Meridionalis' G Mercator
1585 43 x 28
col. 35 DM uncol. 25 DM

21 South America, A Langren
1595 56 x 39
col. 35 DM uncol. 25 DM

367 South America, G. Mercator
1585 18 x 13
col. 4 DM

10 Argentina and Uruguay 'Paraguay', W. Blaeuw
1636 47 x 37
col. 22 DM uncol. 15 DM

17 'Granatense' (Panama, Venezuela, Columbia), W Blaeuw
1636 48 x 37
col. 22 DM uncol. 15 DM

A1 GENERAL ATLASES

ATLAS LATINSKOY AMERIKI
Moskva : GUGK, 1968
54pp maps
24 x 32
Covering countries of South and Central America; physical and them. maps; text in Russian, 34pp supp. in Spanish

G EARTH RESOURCES ATLASES

MUNGER MAP BOOK (SOUTH AND CENTRAL AMERICA AND WEST INDIES)
Los Angeles : Munger Map Service, 1968
32 x 48
Loose-leaf bound book showing petroleum development with generalised geol. of South, Central America and the West Indies.

M HISTORICAL ATLASES

HISTORICAL ATLAS OF LATIN AMERICA
by A Curtis Wilgus
2nd edition
New York : Cooper Square Publishers, 1967
365pp
15 x 23
Cultural and historical atlas; geog. and economic 19th C background to Latin America shown in maps and text (illus.).

81 Brazil

A1 GENERAL MAPS : ROADS

PLANO NACIONAL DE VIAÇÃO—
SECTOR RODOVIÁRIO
1:10, 000, 000
Rio de Janeiro : IBGE, 1971
50 x 50
Road map in col. showing basic communication network.

REGIONAL ROAD MAPS
Various scales
Rio de Janeiro : IBGE
In 5 sheets
Series of road map in 2 col. for planning purposes.

Regiao Sul	1:2, 750, 000
Regiao Norte	1:3, 000, 000
Regiao Sudeste	1:3, 125, 000
Regiao Nordeste	1:4, 500, 000
Regiao Centro-Queste	1:5, 200, 000

MAPAS RODOVIÁRIO DE ESTADOS
E TERRITÓRIOS
1:2, 000, 000/3, 250, 000
Rio de Janeiro : Dept. Nac. de Estradas de Rodagem
In 26 sheets
Col. map series, roads classified, projected roads, distances

MAPA CARTOGRAMA (RODOVIÁRIO)
DOS ESTRADOS DO SUL DE BRASIL
1:1, 250, 000
Curitiba : Sociedade Comercial e Representacões Gráficas, 1973
91 x 152
General political col. map, with roads, distances in km, boundaries. Covering Sao Paulo, Parana, Santa Catarina, Rio Grande do Sul. B$ 10.00

MAPA RODOVIÁRIO DO ESTADO
DE SÃO PAULO
1:1, 000, 000 app.
São Paulo : Depto. de Estradas de Rodagem, 1970
Road map for Sao Paulo state.

NOVO MAPA RODOVIÁRIO DO
ESTADO DO PARANÂ
1:1, 000, 000
Curitiba : Soc. Comercial e Representacões Gráficas, 1972
65 x 95
Col. road map with route number and distances. B$ 8.00

A2 GENERAL MAPS : LOCAL

MUNICIPIO CURITIBA
1:100, 000
Curitiba : Sociedade Comercial e Representacões Gráficas, 1968
69 x 105
Map of admin. area of Curitiba
B$ 10.00

MAPA DO DISTRITO FEDERAL
1:100, 000
Rio de Janeiro : IBGE, 1961
Showing roads and rivers with contours at 50 metre intervals.

SÃO PAULO MUNICIPIO E REGIOES
1:100, 000
São Paulo : Depto. de Estradas de Rodagem, 1970
115 x 90
Map of city and environs; col. roads, railways, water features, admin. boundaries on white background.

B TOWN PLANS

BRASILIA
No scale
Curitiba : Sociedade Comercial e Representacões Gráficas, 1973
81 x 102
New edition of town plan; illustrated, decorated. B$ 12.00

CURITIBA, TOWN PLAN
1:20,000
Curitiba : Sociedade Comercial e Representacões Gráficas, 1972
89 x 119 B$ 10.00

FALK PLAN OF RIO DE JANEIRO
1:20, 000/40, 000
No 262
Hamburg : Falk
Patent folding
Plan with local insets and index.
9.80 DM

ESTADO DA GUANABARA CIDADE
DO RIO DE JANEIRO
Jose Ricardo Bartolo
1:16, 000
Paulistano : Informador Geografico, 1971
Plan of the city naming principal roads and buildings.

RIO DE JANEIRO : MAPA TURÍSTICO
1:25, 000
Rio de Janeiro : Secretaria de Turismo, 1968
88 x 98
Coloured tourist map showing reliefs with insets and index. Bird's-eye-view map of buildings on reverse at 1:4, 000

SÃO PAULO
1:21, 500/34, 400
Hamburg : Falk
Patent folding system
Detailed town plan of town centre and suburbs. 9.80 DM

C OFFICIAL SURVEYS

KARTA MIRA
1:2, 500, 000
for index see 100/2
V,V.K.
10 sheets required for coverage :

109	Caracas
110	Cayenne
128	Quito
129	Manaus
130	Belem
131	Recife
149	La Paz
150	Rio de Janeiro
169	Buenos Aires
170	Porto Alegre

CARTA DO BRASIL
1:1, 000, 000
In 46 sheets
see index 81/1
Rio de Janeiro : IBGE
67 x 44
Topog. series, contoured, layer col. classified communications, mineral workings, towns graded by pop.
For areas not published in this series, AGS eds. are available - see South America 8C

CARTA DO BRASIL
1:500, 000
see index 81/1
Rio de Janeiro : IBGE
62 x 45
Col. contoured series in progress.
See index.

CARTA DO BRASIL
1:250, 000
Rio de Janeiro : IBGE
66 x 44
Topog. series in progress; contours, roads, water features, settlements.

CARTA DO BRASIL
1:100, 000
Rio de Janeiro : IBGE
51 x 55
Series in progress, showing vegetation, water features, contours.

CARTA DO BRASIL
1:50, 000
Rio de Janeiro : IBGE
Topog. series in progress, contoured with water and vegetation detail, communication and settlement.

D POLITICAL & ADMINISTRATIVE

BRAZILIYA, GAYANA, SURINAM,
GVIANA
Moskva : GUGK, 1971
Political wall map, showing admin. divisions, communications, water features.

MAPA POLÍTICO DO BRASIL
1:5, 000, 000
Rio de Janeiro : IBGE
1968
105 x 95
Col. by states, towns graded by status.
Brasilia inset.

BRASIL DIVISÃO MUNICIPAL
1:5, 000, 000
Rio de Janeiro : IBGE, 1968
114 x 114
Shows admin. divisions as at 30. 7. 67. with index to names on reverse.

BRASIL - MAPA POLÍTICO
1:4, 500, 000
Rio de Janeiro : IBGE, 1972
100 x 120
Col. map, political col. by states, communications and towns.

BRASIL
1:4, 500, 000
Curitiba : Soc. Comercial e Representacões Gráficas, 1972
103 x 122
Political col. map with insets, communications. B$ 12.50

BRAZIL
1:4, 000, 000
Paris : Forest
129 x 129
Political map in Portuguese with legend in 5 languages. Shows boundaries, communications, cities graded by pop.

MAPA DO BRASIL DIVISÂO ADMINISTRATIVA
1:2, 500, 000
Rio de Janeiro : IBGE, 1967
In 4 sheets
190 x 192 complete
Map showing all types of regional and district admin. areas, with index to districts.

MAPA DO BRASIL POLÍTICO
1:2, 500, 000
In 4 sheets
Rio de Janeiro : IBGE, 1969
200 x 200
Coloured by states with communications and towns graded according to population and admin. status.

STATE MAPS
Curitiba : Soc. Comercial e Representacões Gráficas
Coloured maps showing communications and settlement.
Maps available :

Estado de Bahia	1:1, 250, 000
1971	104 x 120
Estado de Ceara	1:500, 000
1972	105 x 131
Estado de Goias	1:1, 500, 000
1971	97 x 138
Estado de Mato Grosso	1:1, 600, 000
1972	90 x 129
Estado de Minas Gerais	1:1, 250, 000
1972	98 x 120
Espirito Santo	1:400, 000
1971	72 x 112
Estado Para	1:1, 500, 000
1973	106 x 112
Noite de Estado do Paraná	1:500, 000
1968	95 x 128
Estado do Paraná	1:600, 000
1973	119 x 86
Estado Rio de Janeiro	1:400, 000
1971	90 x 120
Estado de Rio Grande do Sul	1:750, 000
1972	106 x 129
Estado de Santa Catarina	1:500, 000
1973	90 x 125
	1:1, 000, 000
1971	62 x 45
Estado de São Paulo	1:1, 000, 000
	74 x 103

In Preparation:
Estado Pernambuco 1:400, 000
Estado Guanabara (Rio)
Parana/Santa Catarina
Estado Amazonas

Crs 10,00

MAPAS DOS ESTADOS
Various scales
Rio de Janeiro : IBGE
Various sizes
Physico political general maps of the States; contours, hydrography, communications, boundaries.
Available for :

Acre	1:1, 000, 000
1970	94 x 64
Amazonas	1:2, 000, 000
1966	
Ceara	1:500, 000
1972	105 x 130
Espirito Santo	1:400, 000
1967	77 x 108
Estado de Guanabara	1:75, 000
1969	106 x 61
Goias	1:1, 500, 000
1969	70 x 112
Paraiba	1:500, 000
1970	105 x 68
Piaui	1:1, 000, 000
1970	74 x 104
Territorio de Reraima	1:1, 000, 000
1970	75 x 87
Rio Grande do Norte	1:500, 000
1968	

NORDESTE-NORTE DO BRASIL
1:1, 500, 000
Curitiba : Sociedade Comercial e Representacões Gráficas, 1972
105 x 121
General political map of the region, showing towns and communications
B$ 12.00

MAPA DO NORDESTE DO BRASIL
1:1, 500, 000
Rio de Janeiro : IBGE, 1972
121 x 105
Political map, coloured by provinces, with communications.

TERRITORIO DO AMAPA
1:1, 000, 000
Rio de Janeiro : IBGE, 2965
Political map showing communications and settlement.

E1 PHYSICAL : RELIEF

BOLIVIE A BRAZILIE
1:6, 000, 000
Kart 1969
see BOLIVIA 84E

MAPA FISICO DO BRASIL
1:5, 000, 000
Rio de Janeiro : IBGE, 1965
105 x 95
Contoured, layer col. towns graded by pop. and status. Brasilia, Federal District and Sudeste (Rio de Janeiro region) inset.

BRASIL - MAPA FISICO
1:4, 500, 000
Rio de Janeiro : IBGE, 1972
103 x 108
New ed. col. with contours, water features, boundaries.

BRASIL
1:4, 500, 000
Curitiba : Sociedade Comercial e Representacões Gráficas, 1972
94 x 101
Hysometric and balthy metric col. roads, towns, railways indicated; international and internal boundaries. Insets of ocean islands, federal district of Brasilia and 4 thematic maps of Brazil.
B$ 15.00

CARTES MURALES GÉOGRAPHIQUES
No 251 Brésil Physique - reverse Canada Économique
252 Brésil Économique - reverse : Canada Physique
Ed. Vidal—Lablache et H. Varon
Paris : Armand Colin
120 x 100
2 reversible maps in French with a map on each side mounted on rigid card.

MAPA DA BACIA AMAZÓNICA
1:1, 500, 000
In 4 sheets
Rio de Janeiro : IBGE, 1971
225 x 182 complete
General wall map of the Amazon Basin. Contoured, hill shading, water features, communications.

E2 RELIEF : LAND FEATURES

MAPA GEOMORFOLÓGICO DO BRASIL
1:5, 000, 000
Rio de Janeiro : IBGE, 1968
89 x 91
Col. by basic geol. divisions, landform types, hatchings, black and white. Island territories inset at 1:100, 000

MAPA GEOLOGICO DO BRASIL
1:5, 000, 000
Prepared by A. R. Larnego
Rio de Janeiro : IBGE, 1960
91 x 90
Col. geol. map.

MAPA GEOLÓGICO DO ESTADO DE PERNAMBUCO
1:1, 000, 000
Prepared by J. D. O. Dias
Recife : Univ. Rural de Pernambuco
1957
Fully coloured map contained in 'Estudos Geologicos de Pernambuco' Monografias No. 2.

MAPA GEOLÓGICO DO TERRITORIO FEDERAL DE RONDONIA : PESQUISA DE CASSITERA
1:1, 000, 000
Rio de Janeiro : Dep. Nac da Prod. Min, 1966
91 x 75
Coloured geological map of the province - tin investigation, Shows location of principal mineral deposits. Contained in Div. Formento Prod. Minero Anex Bol. No. 125

MAPA GEOLÓGICO DO ESTADO DE SÃO PAULO
1:1, 000, 000
São Paulo : Inst. Geog. e Geol, 1963
Fully coloured map with legend in Portuguese.

MAPA GEOLÓGICO DO ESTADO DE PARANA
1:750, 000
Prepared by R. Maack
Rio de Janeiro : Inst. Biol. e Pesq. Tec. 1953
120 x 85
Coloured geol. map.

MAPA GEOLÓGICO DA REGIÃO DO MEDIO TAPAJOS
1:500, 000
Rio de Janeiro : Dep. Nac. da Prod. Min., 1968
98 x 58
Coloured geological map covering the area 4°30' - 7°00' S and 59°00' 55°00' W approx.

MAPA GEOLÓGICOS DA QUADRICULA DE BRASIL
1:250, 000
Series in 760 sheets
Rio de Janeiro : Dep. Nac. da Prod. Min. 1966
Coloured geological series in progress, also showing principal mineral deposits and accompanied by descriptive 'Boletins'.

RECONHECIMENTO FOTOGEOLÓGICO DA REGIÃO NORDESTE BRASIL
1:250, 000
Series in 34 sheets
Rio de Janeiro : Dep. Nac. da Prod. Min. 1960
Series of coloured geological maps in progress.

CARTA GEOLÓGICA DO BRASIL
1:100, 000
Rio de Janeiro : Dep. Nac. da Prod. Min. 1946 +
Coloured geological series in progress with accompanying descriptive 'Boletins'.

PARANÁ GEOLOGICAL SERIES
1:70,000
Curitiba : Commissao da Carta Geol. do Paraná
39 x 36
Geological map series in Portuguese and English.

MAPA GEOLÓGICO DO ESTADO DA GUANABARA
1:50, 000
Prepared : R Hembold, J G Valenca, O H Leonardos
In 3 sheets :
Santa Cruz - Restinga da Marambala
SF 23-Q-III-4, SF 23-W-I-2
Vila Militar - Pontal de Sernambetiba
SF 23-Q-IV-3, SF 23-W-II-1
Baia de Guanabara - Ilha Rosa
SF 23-Q-IV-4, SF 23-W-II-2
Rio de Janeiro : Dep. Nac. da Prod. Min 1964-65
77 x 22
Fully coloured maps.

G EARTH RESOURCES

APTIDAO AGRÍCOLA DOS SOLOS
1:5, 000, 000
Rio de Janeiro : Dep. Ped. e Agri, 1966
106 x 95
Map showing agricultural soil aptitude, in Portuguese and English.

MAPA ESQUEMATICO DOS SOLOS
1:5, 000, 000
Rio de Janeiro : Dep. Ped. e Agr. 1966
106 x 95
Diagrammatic soil map in English or Portuguese

H BIOGEOGRAPHY

BRASIL - VEGETAÇÃO
1:5, 000, 000
Min. do Plan. e Coord. Gerd
Rio de Janeiro : IBGE, 1970
107 x 100
Coloured map showing chief vegetation areas of Brazil.

K HUMAN GEOGRAPHY

MAPA DE POPULAÇÃO RIO GRANDE DO SUL
1:1, 000, 000
Rio de Janeiro : IBGE, 1969
110 x 74
Population indicated by administrative district and urban areas by relative sized circles.

I ECONOMIC

CARTES MURALES GÉOGRAPHIQUES
No 251 Brésil Physique - reverse : Canada Économique
252 Brésil Économique - reverse : Canada Physique
Ed. Vidal—Lablache et H Varon
Armand Colin
see Brazil E1

ATLASES
W2 WORLD ATLAS : SCHOOL EDITION

ATLAS DO BRASIL
Porte Alegre : Globo, 1966
96pp
33 x 44
30 pp general and thematic maps.
66 pp index and text.

ATLASES
W3 WORLD ATLAS : LOCAL EDITION

ATLAS GEOGRAFICO ESCOLAR
Fundacao Nacional de Material Escolar, 1970
see WORLD-ATLASES 100 W2

ATLASES
J CLIMATE

ATLAS CLIMATOLÓGICO DO BRASIL (REEDICÃO DE MAPAS SELECIONADOS)
1:17, 000, 000
Rio de Janeiro : Escritorio de Meterologia, 1969
100 maps
31 x 36
Selected maps showing various climatic features. Each map has the Sao Paulo region inset at 1:10, 000, 000 and Rio de Janeiro and Federal district at 1:3, 300, 000

ATLASES
O NATIONAL

ATLAS NACIONAL DO BRASIL
Rio de Janeiro : IBGE, 1966
57 x 48
50 map plates with statistical data and explanatory text; in 5 sections :

I	Political and Administrative	(5 plates)
II	Physical	(11 plates)
III	Demographic	(6 plates)
IV	Economic	(22 plates)
V	Socio-Cultural	(6 plates)

82 Argentina

A1 GENERAL MAPS : ROADS

REPÚBLICA ARGENTINA, RED CAMINERA PRINCIPAL
1:4, 500, 000
Buenos Aires : IGM, 1970
Main road map.

MAPA VIAL DEL REPÚBLICA ARGENTINA
1:4, 000, 000
Buenos Aires : Automobil Club Argentino, 1968
65 x 104
Col. road map, distances, boundaries, index.

CARTA TURÍSTICA
1:1, 000, 000
Buenos Aires : Automobil Club Argentino
In 8 sheets, see index 82/1
70 x 80 each
1 North West
2 North East
3 Mendoza - Cordoba
4 Buenos Aires - Corrientes
5 Neuquen - Rio Negro - Santa Ro
6 Buenos Aires
7 Cubut - Santa Cruz
8 Santa Cruz - Tierra del Fuego - Islas Malvinas
Roads classified, distances in km, tourist details, through-town plans, index.

A2 GENERAL MAPS : LOCAL

CARTA CAMINOS DE ACCESSO A BUENOS AIRES
1:350, 000
Buenos Aires : Automobil Club Argentino
Coloured road map of the town and suburbs.

B TOWN PLANS

GRANO BUENOS AIRES: PLANO DE LA ZONA URBANA
1:40, 000
Buenos Aires : Editorial Mapa
116 x 82
Col. town plan, inc. suburbs. Roads named and classified, railways, underground, 9th ed.

PLANO DE LA CIUDAD DE BUENOS AIRES Y ALREDORES
1:25, 000
Buenos Aires : Oficina Cartografica "Ludwig"
Coloured plan of the town and environs. Also available, plan of wider environs, scale 1:35, 000.

C OFFICIAL SURVEYS

KARTA MIRA
1:2, 500, 000
Berlin : VVK
6 sheets for full coverage :
149 La Paz
169 Buenos Aires
170 Porto Alegre
188 Concepcion
189 Mar del Plata
207 Tierra del Fuego
see World 100C and index 100/2

INTERNATIONAL MAP OF THE WORLD — HISPANIC AMERICA EDITION
1:1, 000, 000
AGS
20 sheets required for full coverage.
see World 100C and index 100/1

CARTA DE LA REPÚBLICA ARGENTINA
1:500, 000
Series in 111 sheets, see index 82/2
Buenos Aires : IGM, 1950
70 x 53
Topog. series in progress. each $6.00

CARTA PROVISIONAL DE LA REPÚBLICA ARGENTINA
1:500, 000
Buenos Aires : IGM
Topographical series, contoured, covering western and northern areas of the country being superseded by the new 'Carta Topografica' series.
$6.00

CARTA TOPOGRÁFICA DE LA REPÚBLICA ARGENTINA
1:250, 000
In 246 sheets, see index 82/3
Buenos Aires : IGM
75 x 57
Topog. series in progress, contoured with hypsometric tints. each $6.00

ARGENTINA : CARTA TOPOGRÁFICA
1:100, 000
Buenos Aires
46 x 37
Multi-sheet series in progress.
3-5 col. on white background, contours.
each $6.00

CARTA DE LA REPÚBLICA ARGENTINA
1:50, 000
Buenos Aires : IGM
46 x 37
Multi-sheet series in progress..
3-5 col. on white background, contours.
each $6.00

ARGENTINA
1:25, 000
Buenos Aires : IGM
46 x 37
Multi-sheet series covering certain urban areas only. Col. on white background, contours. each $6.00

D POLITICAL & ADMINISTRATIVE

REPÚBLICA ARGENTINA : MAPA FÍSICO POLÍTICO
1:10, 000, 000
Buenos Aires : IGM, 1971
46 x 81
Political map coloured by states, with communications and subdued relief shading. $5.50

MAPA FÍSICO-POLÍTICO DE LA REPÚBLICA ARGENTINA
1:5, 000, 000
Buenos Aires : IGM, 1965
60 x 94
Each province col. separately showing communications, towns graded by status. Buenos Aires and Argentina's claim to Antarctica inset $5.50

MAPA POLÍTICO DE LA REPÚBLICA ARGENTINA
1:5, 000, 000
Buenos Aires : IGM, 1972
83 x 62
Black and white map showing departmental divisions overprinted; key to places in margin. $5.50

MAPA GENERAL DE LA REPÚBLICA ARGENTINA
1:3, 000, 000
Buenos Aires : Peuser
95 x 130
Political col. map, provincial boundaries.

REPÚBLICA ARGENTINA : MAPA PARCIALMENTE ACTUALIZADO
1:2, 500, 000
Buenos Aires : IGM, 1970
2 sheet general map.

E1 PHYSICAL : RELIEF

MAPA FÍSICO POLÍTICO DE LA REPÚBLICA ARGENTINA
1:2, 500, 000
Buenos Aires : IGM, 1969
106 x 173
Contoured, layer col. relief shading, inter-provincial boundaries, communications, towns graded by pop. Insets inc. Buenos Aires and environs, Argentina's claim to Antarctica. $12.00

MAPA GENERAL DE LA REPÚBLICA ARGENTINA
1:3, 000, 000
Buenos Aires : Peuser
93 x 130
Physical col. map.

F GEOLOGY

MAPA GEOLÓGICO DE LA REPÚBLICA ARGENTINA
1:5, 000, 000
Buenos Aires : Dir. Gen. de Geol. y Mineria, 1964
62 x 88
Col. geol. map with 18 pp text.

MAPA HIDROGEOLÓGICO DE LA REPÚBLICA ARGENTINA
1:5, 000, 000
Buenos Aires : Dir. Gen. de Geol. y Mineria, 1963
50 x 88
Coloured preliminary map with 46 pp text in Spanish.

MAPA GEOLÓGICO DE LA REPÚBLICA ARGENTINA
1:2, 500, 000
In 3 sheets
Buenos Aires : Direccion Nacional de Geol. y Mineria, 1964
80 x 120
Coloured geological map with insets of South Orkney, Tierra del Fuego, Antarctic and southern Atlantic islands. Explanatory text.

CARTAS GEOLÓGICO-ECONÓMICAS DE LA REPÚBLICA ARGENTINA
1:200, 000
Buenos Aires : Dir. Gen. de Geol. y Mineria
Series in progress; text in Spanish on reverse, with bulletin.

G EARTH RESOURCES

MAPA MINERO DE LA REPÚBLICA ARGENTINA
1:4, 500, 000
Buenos Aires : Dir.Gen.de Geol. y Mineria, 1957
45 x 88
Col. map showing mineral types by symbol.

ATLAS MINERO DE LAS PROVINCIAS
1:750, 000
Buenos Aires : Dir. Gen de Geol. y Mineria, 1966
64 x 93
Series in progress, comprising individual mineral maps for each province.
Plates available :
San Juan, 1966
Catamarca-Tucuman, 1966
La Rioja, 1966
Mendoza, 1966

M HISTORICAL

MAPA HISTÓRICO DE LA ARGENTINA
1:4, 000, 000
Buenos Aires : IGM, 1968
107 x 168
2 sheet map, covering all of southern South America, depicting Argentina's history, inset of Antarctic claimed territory and Argentinian expeditions there. $8.00

ATLASES
D POLITICAL

ATLAS DE LA REPÚBLICA ARGENTINA I PARTE POLÍTICA
Buenos Aires : IGM, 1965
24 x 32
Preliminary section contains political maps of the World, Americas and Argentina followed by sections on each of the country's provinces, including col. photos, population and political map, statistical tables and list of towns. Text in Spanish.
$8.50

ATLASES
G EARTH RESOURCES

ATLAS MINERO DE LA PROVINCIAS
1:750, 000
Dir. Gen. de Geol. y Mineria, 1966
For plates published see MAPS 82G

ATLASES
L ECONOMIC

ATLAS DEL POTENCIAL ARGENTINO
J Quargnolo
Buenos Aires : Estrada, 1972
1st edition
25 x 33
160pp
Coloured maps, mostly at 1:8, 800, 000 showing agriculture, cattle breeding, communications routes. Illustrated text on reverse of maps, with 32pp statistical text.

ATLASES
O NATIONAL

ATLAS DE LA REPÚBLICA ARGENTINA
Buenos Aires : IGM
20pp
39 x 39
7 preliminary pp general maps, description and data, separate map of each province showing communications and towns. Text in Spanish.

COLORATLAS REGIONAL ARGENTINA
Buenos Aires : Ed. Kapelusz, 1975
23 x 32
62pp
School atlas containing physical, political and economic maps. US $2.58

NUEVO ATLAS GEOGRÁFICO DE LA ARGENTINA
by J Ares
Buenos Aires : Peuser, 1970
22 x 37
31pp maps
School atlas with 100 pp. physical, political, them. maps for Argentina.

ATLAS ESCOLAR FISÍCO POLÍTICO DE LA REPÚBLICA ARGENTINA
Buenos Aires : IGM, 1970
28 x 40
20pp
School atlas, 29 maps - physical and political, mostly at 1:2, 500, 000
$8.50

83 Chile

A1 GENERAL MAPS : ROADS

TURÍSTICO CAMINERO DE CHILE
1:3, 000, 000
Santiago : IGM
63 x 53
Road map with pictorial information.

B TOWN PLANS

AVANCE TOPOGRÁFICO DEL GRAN SANTIAGO
1:20, 000
In 9 sheets
Santiago : IGM
Topographic plan of the town and environs.

C OFFICIAL SURVEYS

KARTA MIRA
1:2, 500, 000
Berlin, VVK
6 sheets required for coverage :
149 La Paz
168 Juan Fernandez Is.
169 Buenos Aires
188 Concepcion
189 Mar del Plata
207 Tierra del Fuego
see WORLD 100C and index 100/2

INTERNATIONAL MAP OF THE WORLD – HISPANIC AMERICA SERIES
1:1, 000, 000
AGS
14 sheets required for coverage.
see WORLD 100C and index 100/1

CARTA NACIONAL DE CHILE
1:500, 000
In 36 sheets, see index 83/1
Santiago : IGM, 1971
New topog. series, contoured and coloured which will replace the earlier 'Carta Nacional de Chile'.

CHILE-LEVANTAMIENTO AEROFOTOGRAMETRICO - NUEVA CARTA
1:500, 000
See index 83/3
Santiago : IGM, 1973
76 x 55
New topog. series in progress based on aero-photogrametric plots

CARTA PRELIMINAR CHILE
1:250, 000
In 104 sheets, see index 83/2
Santiago : IGM
77 x 55
Contours, roads classified, in col.
Also available as atlas.

CARTA NACIONAL - LEVANTAMIENTO AEROFOTOGRAMETRICO
1:100, 000
ZONA NORTE covering northern region in 116 sheets, see index 83/4
Santiago : IGM
Topographical series in progress, coloured.

CARTA DE CAMPAÑA
1:100, 000
In 22 sheets, see index 83/4
Santiago : IGM
60 x 37
Topographic series, contoured.
Covering Valparaiso - Santiago region including La Ligua, San Antonio and Licanten. Available as a set mounted on linen and folded.

CARTA TOPOGRÁFICO DE CHILE - LEVANTAMIENTO AEROFOTO-GRAMETRICO
1:50, 000
Series 1225/a/b/c
Santiago : IGM, 1963
Topographical series in progress designed to cover the central and southern part of the country.

CARTA TOPOGRÁFICO DE CHILE - SECTORES ESPECIALES
1:50, 000
Santiago,: IGM
Series of special topographical local area maps. Sheets available :
1223 1 Junquillar - Constitucion
2 Carrizal - Maquegua
3 Pullallao - Las Canas
4 Coinco
5 Tunca - Quinta de Tilcoco
6 Laguna de Cauquernes - Chanqueative
7 Morza
8 Tinguiririca - El Perejil
9 Chimbarongo Sur
10 Huemul
11 Guaico Arriba
12 Guaico
1224 Punta Arenas y alrededores

CARTA TOPOGRÁFICO DE CHILE - LEVANTAMIENTO ANTIGUO
1:25, 000
See index 83
Santiago : IGM
Large scale topographical series in progress, contoured, black and white. Approx 500 sheets published in the central part of the country.

D POLITICAL & ADMINISTRATIVE

MAPA POLÍTICO ESCOLAR DE CHILE
1:3, 000, 000
Santiago : IGM
63 x 53
School map col. by provinces, communications, in 3 sheets.

ESQUICIO DE CHILE
1:3, 000, 000
Santiago : IGM
63 x 53
1 col. outline and work map, showing boundaries.

E1 PHYSICAL : RELIEF

MAPA FISICO DE CHILE
1:1, 000, 000
In 8 sheets
Santiago : IGM, 1970
211 x 170
Contoured, layer col. for land and sea, roads, railways, mines, towns graded according to admin. status. Inc. Chilean claim to Antarctica.

MAPA DE CHILE
1:3, 000, 000
Santiago : IGM, 1971
54 x 183
Physical col. map, land and sea relief, communications, Chile's Antarctic Claim. Inset of Magellan Straits. Also available at 1:6, 000, 000

RELIEF MAP OF CHILE
1:1, 000, 000
In 6 sheets
Santiago : IGM, 1971
75 x 93 each
Relief shaded map with contours and hachures, communications and towns.

E2 PHYSICAL : LAND FEATURES

MAPA GEOMORFOLÓGICO DE CHILE
1:3, 500, 000
Santiago : IGM, 1965
40 x 30
Geomorphological map in 110 pp text, coloured.

F GEOLOGICAL

MAPA GEOLÓGICO DE CHILE
1:1, 000, 000
In 7 sheets
Santiago : Inst. de Investigaciones Geologicas, 1968
Various sizes
Coloured geological map. US $25

GEOLOGÍA DE LA CORDILLERA DE LOS ANDES DE LAS PROVINCIAS DE CAUTIN, VALDIVIA, OSORNO Y LLANQUIHUE
1:500, 000
Santiago : Inst. de Investigaciones Geol, 1964
Col. geological map contained in Boletin No 17, 37 pp.

RECONOCIMIENTO GEOLÓGICO EN LAS PROVINCIAS DE LLANQUIHUE Y CHILOE
1:500, 000
Santiago : Inst. de Investigaciones Geol. 1966
Col. geological map contained in Boletin No 19, 45 pp.

GEOLOGÍA Y RECORSOS MINERALES DEL DEPARTMENTO DE ARICA
1:300, 000
Santiago : Inst. de Investigaciones Geol. 1966
Geological map contained in Boletin No 21, 114 pp.

GEOLOGÍA DE LAS HOJAS COPIAPO Y OJOS DEL SALADO, PROVINCIA DE ATACAMA
1:250, 000
Santiago : Inst. de Investigaciones Geol. 1968
Geological map contained in Boletin No 24, 58 pp.

GEOLOGÍA DE LA HOJA OVALLE, PROVINCIA DE COQUIMBO
1:250, 000
Santiago : Inst. de Investigaciones Geol. 1967
Geological map contained in Boletin No 23, 58pp.

GEOLOGÍA DE LA CORDILLERA DE LOS ANDES DE CHILE CENTRAL, PROVINCIAS DE SANTIAGO, O'HIGGINS, COLCHAGUA Y CURICO
1:150, 000
Santiago : Inst. de Investigaciones Geol. 1960
Coloured geological map contained in Boletin No 8, 95pp.

GEOLOGÍA DE LOS ANDES DE CHILE CENTRAL, PROVINCIA DE ACONAGUA
1:100, 000
Santiago : Inst. de Investigaciones Geol. 1960
Col. geological map contained in Boletin No 9, 70 pp.

CARTA GEOLÓGICA DE CHILE
1:50, 000
Santiago : Inst. de Investigaciones Geol.
In 22 maps
Geological quadrangle sheets for various areas in preparation, each in accompanying volume.
Sheets published :

1 Los Loros (Prov. de Atacama) 1959
2 Cerrillos (Prov. de Atacama) 1959
3 Quebrada Paipote (Prov. de Atacama) 1960
4 Llampos (Prov. de Atacama) 1960
5 Chamonate (Prov. de Atacama) 1960
6 Copiapo (Prov. de Atacama) 1962
7/10 Pica, Alca, Matilla y Chacarilla (Prov. de Tarapaca) 1962
11 Tulor (Prov. de Antofagasta) 1963
12 Pintadas (Prov. de Atacama) 1963
13 Chanarcillo (Prov. de Atacama) 1964
14 San Pedro de Atacama (Prov. de Antofagasta) 1965
15 Quebrada Marquesa (Prov. de Coquimbo) 1965
16 Vicuna (Prov. de Coquimbo) 1967
17 Mamina (Prov. de Tarapaca) 1967
18 Juan de Morales (Prov. de Tarapaca) 1968
19/20 Camaraca y Azapa (Prov. de Tarapaca) 1968
21/22 Iquique y Caleta Molle (Prov. de Tarapaca) 1970

U$ S5.00

G EARTH RESOURCES

MAPA METALLOGENÉTICO DE CHILE
1:1, 500, 000
Santiago : Inst. de Investigaciones Geol, 1962
124 x 100
Gives locations of principal minerals in relation to structure of locality.

H BIOGEOGRAPHY

MAPA TEMÁTICO PARQUES NACIONALES
1:3, 000, 000
Santiago : IGM
Map of national park areas inc. forests.

PLANO DE LAS PLANTACIONES FORESTALE DE LA ZONA CENTRO-NORTE DE CHILE
1:500, 000
In 3 sheets
Santiago : Instituto Forestal, 1970
110 x 77
Showing forest plantations of the central region of Chile classifying principal species of trees. In Spanish Sheets available:
Zona Centro-Norte: Aconcagua, Valparíso Santiago, O'Higgins, Colchagua, Curicó, Talca, 1970
Zona Centro – sur : Maule, Linares, Nũble, Concepción, Arauco, Bío-Bío, Malleco, Cautín, 1965
Zone Sur : Valdivia, Osorno, Llanquihue, 1970. each US $15.00

MAPA PRELIMINAR DE TIPOS FORESTALES
1:500, 000
Santiago : Instituto Forestal, 1964
110 x 77
Showing location and extent of forest resources, indicating principal species and forest types. In Spanish.
Maps available :

1. Bío-Bío, Malleco, Arauco, Cautín, Valdivia
2. Osorno, Llaniquihue, Chiloé

each US $15.00

PROVINCE DE ARAUCO : PLANTILLA DE LAS PLANTACIONES FORESTALES
1:250, 000
Santiago : Instituto Foresta, 1963
Indicating the location and extent of forest plantations within the province and the principal woodland species : In Spanish.
US $10.00

K HUMAN GEOGRAPHY

DISTRIBUCION DE LA POBLACION URBANA Y RURAL CHILE
1:1, 000, 000
Washington : Organisacion de los Estados Americanos, 1969
2 sheet map showing rural and urban population distribution. $3.00

L ECONOMIC

MAPA ECONÓMICO DE CHILE
1:1, 000, 000
In 5 sheets
Santiago : IGM, 1963
55 x 76 each
Indicating by col. blocks and symbols, agricultural, industrial distribution and productions. Map in 5 sheets (southern sheet 1:3, 000, 000) with explanatory text. Legend in Spanish.

ATLASES
A1 GENERAL : ROADS

ATLAS CAMINERO DE CHILE
1st edition
Santiago : Automovil Club de Chile, 1971
12 x 17
31pp
Small road atlas, arranged by province; roads classified, towns graded by admin. status, distances in km.

ATLASES
O NATIONAL

ATLAS DE LA REPÚBLICA DE CHILE
Editor : Pedro Medina Arriaza
2nd edition
Santiago : IGM, 1970
31 x 41
249 pp
In Sp. in 3 distinct sections

I Preliminary plates showing basic physical and political information
II Physical map of the country, 1:1, 000, 000 layer col, roads, railways etc., interleaved with photographs, some in col, captions in 3 langs, inc. Eng.
III Thematic maps covering physical and economic subjects.

84 Bolivia

A1 GENERAL MAPS : ROADS

MAPA ITINERARIO BOLIVIO
1:1, 000, 000
In 6 sheets
La Paz : IGM
Photoprint map, contours, roads classified.

B TOWN PLANS

GUIA MARVAL DE LA CIUDAD DE LA PAZ
1:17, 500
La Paz : Univ. Mayor de San Andres
150 pp guide with fold-out plan of the city.

PLANO DE LA PAZ
1:15, 000
La Paz : IGM
Coloured plan of the town and suburbs.

C OFFICIAL SURVEYS

KARTA MIRA
1:2, 500, 000
VVK
2 sheets to cover Bolivia
129 Manaus
149 La Paz
see WORLD 100C and index 100/2

INTERNATIONAL MAP OF THE WORLD - HISPANIC AMERICA SERIES
1:1, 000, 000
AGS
9 sheets to cover Bolivia
see WORLD 100C and index 100/1

MAPA DE BOLIVIA
1:250, 000
In 58 sheets
La Paz : IGM, 1939-51
92 x 60
Topog. series, available in blue print edition, communications and spot heights.

CARTA NACIONAL DE BOLIVIA
1:250, 000
In 84 sheets, see index 84/1
La Paz : IGM
New topographic series in progress, coloured and contoured, prepared in collaboration with AMS.

CARTA NACIONAL DE BOLIVIA
1:50, 000
In 2,357 sheets, see index 84/1
La Paz : IGM
70 x 56
Topog. series in progress; contours in brown at 25m intervals, vegetation green, etc.

BOLIVIA - CARTA NACIONAL
1:25, 000
La Paz : IGM
50 x 50
Multi-sheet topog. series on blue-prints, currently published for La Paz and Cochabamba departments.

D POLITICAL & ADMINISTRATIVE

MAPA DE LA REPÚBLICA DE BOLIVIA
1:3, 000, 000
Cochabamba : Los Amigos del Libro, 1958
55 x 63
Political map col. by depts. showing roads, railways classified, boundaries, towns graded by admin. status, relief shading.

MAPA DE LA REPÚBLICA DE BOLIVIA
1:2, 000, 000
La Paz : Giskert
81 x 103
Map col. by Departments; communications.

E1 PHYSICAL : RELIEF

BOLIVIE A BRAZILIE
1:6, 000, 000
Praha : Kart, 1969
92 x 78
Physical map, contours, 2 insets, them. maps and diagrams on reverse.
Czech text, 48 pp. "Poznavame Svet" series (Getting to know the world)
Kcs 19.50

F GEOLOGY

MAPA GEOLÓGICO DE LA REPÚBLICA DE BOLIVIA
1:2, 500, 000
La Paz : Serv. Geol. de Bolivia, 1968
57 x 67
Col. geol. map with 39 pp text in Sp.

MAPA GEOLÓGICO DE BOLIVIA
1:100, 000
La Paz : Serv. Geol. de Bolivia Geol. series in progress.

G EARTH RESOURCES

RESERVAS MINERALÓGICAS DE BOLIVIA
La Paz : Corporacio Minera de Bolivia, 1968
50 pp
Pamphlet on the mining industry, with map supp.
Mapa Geologico de Bolivia, 1:1, 500, 000
Yacimientos Minerales (min. deposits) de Bolivia, 1:1, 500, 000
Estadististica de Poblacion y Desarollo Socio-Economico (shows Pop. statistics)
53 x 73 each

K HUMAN GEOGRAPHY

ESTADÍSTIC DE POBLACIÓN Y DESAROLLO SOCIOECONOMICO
Contained in Reservas Mineralogicas de Bolivia
see BOLIVIA G

L ECONOMIC

MAPA DE COMUNICACIONES DE REPÚBLICA DE BOLIVIA
1:3, 000, 000
La Paz : IGM, 1969
55 x 74
Communications on white background, with 3 distancetables.

M HISTORICAL

MAPA ARQUEOLÓGICO DE BOLIVIA
1:3, 000, 000
La Paz : Univ. Mayor de San Andres
55 x 74
Col. map with archaeological information.

MAPA FOLKLÓRICO DE BOLIVIA
Prepared by Eberhardt
Cochabamba : Los Amigos del Libro
Col. pictorial map depicting principal figures in the history and folklore of the country. U$ S2.50

ATLASES
O NATIONAL

ATLAS ESCOLAR DE BOLIVIA I & II
La Paz : Univ. Mayor de San Andres, 1958
24 x 31
I - 18 pp. II - 11 pp col. maps for the country and its provinces, with text, Italian edition.

85 Peru

A1 GENERAL MAPS : ROADS

CARRETERAS DEL PERÚ - GUIA TURISTICA
1:3, 000, 000
Lima : IGM
50 x 60
Map in 3 parts; roads classified, distances in km, boundaries. Plan of Lima and environs on reverse, with general map of Peru.

CARRETERAS DEL PERÚ
1:2, 500, 000
Lima : Touring Automovil Club del Peru
Roads classified, distances in km. boundaries, relief shading.

MAPA TURÍSTICO DEL PERÚ
1:2, 500, 000
Lima : Editoriales Didacticas, 1970
Coloured road map with route numbers and distances in km.

MAPA VIAL DEL PERÚ
1:2, 200, 000
Lima : Petróleos del Perú/Min. de Transportes y Comunicaciones 1976
68 x 80
Roads classified, distances, airports, dept. boundaries. Plans of 16 major towns on reverse.

A2 GENERAL MAPS : LOCAL

LEVANTAMIENTO REGULAR DE LAS PROVINCIAS DE LIMA Y CANTA
1: 100, 000
In 2 sheets
Lima : IGM
Topographical map, contoured and coloured.

LEVANTAMIENTO EXPEDITIVO DE LURIN - CHILCA - MALA
1: 50, 000
In 2 sheets
Lima : IGM
Topographical map, contoured.

LEVANTAMIENTO AEROFOTO-GRAMÉTRICO DE PIURA
1:50, 000
Lima : IGM
Topographical map of the town and region.

CENTRAL ANDES OF PERU
1:500, 000
London : RGS
43 x 49
Map reprinted from the Geog. Journal (March 1957), from surveys by J. V. Harrison, 1939-54 £1.50p

CORDILLERA BLANCA
1:200, 000
Innsbruck : Qsterreichen Alpenverein
1939 (app) /1969/
50 x 86
Contours, relief shading, spot heights, rock hachuring, names, roads and tracks.
45 Sch.

MAP OF THE NORTHERN CORDILLERA BLANCA, PERU, ALPAMAYO REGION
G Holdsworth and J Ricker
1:56, 340
Ottawa : Inland Waters Branch DEMR, 1970
21 x 19
Topographical map, contoured.

HUASCARAN CORDILLERA BLANCA
1:25, 000
München : Forschungsunternehmen Nepal-Himalaya, 1967
66 x 100
Col. map with contours, relief shading, glaciers, vegetation.

CORDILLERA CARABAYA
A Parton and A Chinn
1:15, 840
New Zealand Andean Expedition, 1967
39 x 47
Relief map, with insets of Southern Peru at 1:6, 336, 000. Surrounding Cordillera area at 1:96, 000
Information from Keele Univ. expedition, 1965.

NEVADO HUASCARAN
1:15, 000
München : Forschungsunternehmen Nepal-Himalaya, 1967
52 x 116
Col. map showing Glacier shift at 10. 1. 62.

B TOWN PLANS

PLANO DE LA CUIDAD DE LIMA METROPOLITANA
1:250, 000 app.
Lima : Cart. Nacional, 1969
88 x 62
Street plan col. by districts, principal buildings and open spaces.

PLANO DE LIMA Y ALREDEDORES
1:20, 000
In 36 sheets
Lima : IGM, 1954-64
Topographical series of Lima and environs, contoured, coloured and showing roads and land detail.

PLANO DE LA CIUDAD DE LIMA METROPOLITANA
1:15, 000
Lima : Cart. Nacional, 1968
150 x 108
Large col. wall map of the town and environs.

LEVANTAMIENTO REGULAR DE AREQUIPA Y ALREDODORES
1:20, 000
In 9 sheets
Lima : IGM
Topographical series covering the town and environs.

LEVANTAMIENTO AEROFOTO-GRAMÉTRICO DE MANCORA - LOS ORGANOS
1:20, 000
In 13 sheets
Lima : IGM
Topographical series, contoured and coloured.

PLANO DE TALARA Y ALREDEDORES
1:20, 000
In 4 sheets
Lima : IGM
Topographical series covering the town and environs.

LEVANTAMIENTO AEROFOTO-GRAMÉTRICO DEL VALLE DEL MANTARO
1:10, 000
In 19 sheets
Lima : IGM
Topographical series covering the towns of Concepcion, Jauja and Huancayo.

C OFFICIAL SURVEYS

KARTA MIRA
1:2, 500, 000
VVK
4 sheets required for coverage :
128 Quito
129 Manaus
148 Lima
149 La Paz
see WORLD 100C and index 100/2

INTERNATIONAL MAP OF THE WORLD - HISPANIC AMERICA SERIES
1:1, 000, 000
AGS
12 sheets required for coverage
see WORLD 100C and index 100/1

CARTA NACIONAL DEL PERÚ
1:200, 000
In 280 sheets, see index 85/1
Lima : IGM
38 x 60
Topog. series, contours, water features, vegetation etc. Some border areas on restricted sale. No further sheets will be published in this series.

CARTA NACIONAL DEL PERÚ
1:100, 000
In 504 sheets, see index 85/2
Lima : IGM, 1933-54
60 x 75
Topog. series in progress, contours, vegetation etc. New series in preparation to replace this edition begun 1960.

D POLITICAL & ADMINISTRATIVE

MAPA POLÍTICO Y FÍSICO DEL PERÚ
1:2, 500, 000
Lima : Lascano
64 x 95
Political map col. by provinces, communications, with relief shading.

REPÚBLICA DEL PERÚ - MAPA POLÍTICO
1:1, 000, 000
In 8 sheets
Lima : IGM, 1971
160 x 215 complete
Col. by departments, roads classified, railways, airports, harbours and towns graded by status.

MAPAS DEPARTMENTALES
Various scales
Lima : IGM
Various sizes
Map series covering the provinces; physico-political detail - contours, communications, water features, admin. areas overprinted. Available for:

Lima	1:500, 000 65 x 91	1968
Loreto	1:800, 000 65 x 88	1970
Puno	1:670, 000 65 x 88	1971

E1 PHYSICAL : RELIEF

REPÚBLICA DEL PERÚ : MAPA FÍSICO POLÍTICO
1:2, 000, 000
Lima : IGM, 1970
77 x 110
Col. map. contours, roads, railways, other communications, boundaries, settlements marked and named.

F GEOLOGY

MAPA GEOLÓGICO DEL PERÚ
1:2, 000, 000
Lima : Soc. Geol. de Peru, 1956
84 x 118
Col. geol. map in 2 sheets.

CARTA GEOLÓGICA NACIONAL
1:100, 000
Lima : Soc. Geol. de Peru
Multi-sheet geol. seriés on topog. sheet lines.
Sheets published :

16-h	Pataz 1964
17-g	Santiago de Chuco 1964
18-g	Santa Rosa 1964
33-o	Atico 1960
33-p	Ocona 1960
35-s	Bombon 1963
35-t	Clemesi 1963
35-v	Tarata 1965
35-x	Maure 1965
35-y	Antajave 1965
36-t	Ilo 1964
36-u	Locumba 1964
36-v	Pachia 1962
36-x	Palca 1962
37-u	La Parada 1963
37-v	Tarna 1963
37-x	Huayjillas 1963

MAPA GEOLÓGICO DE LA PROVINCIA DE LIMA Y SUS ALREDEDORES
1:100, 000
Lima : Inst. Nac. de Invest. y Fomento Mineros, 1958
Coloured geological map of Lima and environs.

G EARTH RESOURCES

PERU : MAPA METALOGENÉTICO
1:1, 000, 000
Lima : Soc. Nac. de Mineria y Petroleo, 1969
In 8 sheets
61 x 82 each
Coloured metallogenic map overprinted on topographic base showing mineral strata by coloured symbols. Political map of Peru in S America inset. 128 pp text and description in Spanish.

ATLASES
O NATIONAL

ATLAS HISTORICO-GEOGRÁFICO Y DE PAISAJES PERUANOS
Lima : Inst. Nac. Planification, 1969
738 pp
143 x 58
App. 200 pp maps - geog. historical, them. In 5 sections; thematic cart; depts. of Peru; boundary lands; cartographic history; countryside details - photos etc. Text in Spanish, indexed.

ATLAS OF PERU
Lima : Lascanos, 1965/6
80 pp app.
Inc. sketch maps of each of 24 depts. showing towns, roads, railways, boundaries with facing page giving transport, pop. data etc: general maps of the country showing agricultural, mineral and livestock information. Index to towns.

MAPAS DE TIERRAS ARIDAS Y SEMIARIDAS DEL PERÚ
1:3, 000, 000
Lima : IGM
13 maps covering geology, vegetation, soil, land use etc.

861 Colombia

A2 GENERAL MAPS : LOCAL

VILLAVICENCIO Y ALREDEDORES (DEPARTAMENTO DEL META)
1:50, 000
Bogotá : IGM, 1965
104 x 94
Coloured general map with contours, vegetation colouring and communications.

B TOWN PLANS

COLOMBIA - TOWN PLANS
Bogotá : Inst. Geog. "Agustin Codazzi"
Plans available :

Bogotá	1:25, 000
Cali	1:25, 000
Cucuta	1:25, 000
Medellín	1:25, 000
Medellín y Alrededores	1:50, 000
Villavienco	1:5, 000
Villavienco y Alrededores	1:50, 000

C OFFICIAL SURVEYS

KARTA MIRA
1:2, 500, 000
VVK
4 sheets required for coverage :

108	Bogota
109	Caracas
128	Quito
129	Manaus

see WORLD 100C and index 100/2

INTERNATIONAL MAP OF THE WORLD - HISPANIC AMERICA SERIES
AGS
10 sheets required for coverage :
see WORLD 100C and index 100/1

CARTA GENERAL DE COLOMBIA
1:250, 000
Series E504, in 104 sheets
Washington : AMS
Topog. series in progress, contoured, vegetation cover, roads and land detail.
Prepared by AMS in association with Colombian Geog. Inst.

CARTA GENERAL COLOMBIA
1:100, 000
In 360 sheets, see index 861/1
Bogotá : Inst. Geog. "Agustin Codazzi"
63 x 43
Topog. series in progress, contoured and coloured.

CARTA GENERAL COLOMBIA
1:50, 000
Series E772
Washington : AMS
Monochrome map showing contours, roads and tracks of all types.
Prepared by AMS in association with Colombian Geog. Inst.

CARTA PRELIMINAR COLOMBIA
1:25, 000
Bogotá : Inst. Geog. "Agustin Codazzi"
Topog. series in progress, contoured and coloured, published for northern and central areas only.

D POLITICAL & ADMINISTRATIVE

COLOMBIA:
MAPA FÍSICO-POLÍTICO
1:1, 500, 000
Bogotá : IGM, 1972
99 x 140
Map coloured by departments, showing roads and distances, contours, major cultural and commercial sites.

COLOMBIA
1:693, 750
Madrid : Seix–Barral
86 x 119
Political wall map showing internal divisions, communications, cities graded by pop.

DEPARTMENTAL MAPS
1:250, 000
Bogotá : Inst. Geog. "Agustin Codazzi"

Aranca	1962	65 x 140
Atlantico		110 x 72
Bolivar (2 sheets)		180 x 94
Caldas	1970	73 x 59
El Cesar (2 sheets)	1970	77 x 162
Choco (1:500, 000)	1970	58 x 112
Magdalena	1969	78 x 118
Cundinamarca	1965	92 x 108

F GEOLOGY

MAPA GEOLÓGICO DE COLOMBIA
1:1, 500, 000
Bogotá : Inst. Nac. de Invest. Geol. - Mineras, 1962
91 x 130
Col. geol. map, topog. base.
Insets of Island of San Andres, Providencia, Santa Catalina and Malpelo with location sketch. US $1.00

MAPA FOTOGEÓLOGIÇO DE CALDAS RISARALDA Y QUINDÍO
1:250, 000
Bogotá : Inst. Nac. de Invest. Geol. - Mineras
Coloured geological map US $3.50

MAPA GEOLÓGICO DEL DEPARTAMENTO DEL TOLIMA
1:250, 000
Bogotá : Inst. Nac. de Invest. Geol. - Mineras
Coloured geological map. US $3.50

MAPA GEÓLOGICO DE RECONOCIMIENTO SIERRA NEVADA DE SANTA MARTA
1:100, 000
Bogotá : Inst. Nac. de Invest. Geol. - Mineras, 1969
Coloured geological map. US $5.00

GEOLÓGICO DE COLOMBIA
1:200, 000
See index 861/2
Bogotá : Inst. Nac. de Invest. Geol. - Mineras
30 x 40 each
Col. geol. series in progress. US $2.70

GEOLÓGICO DE COLOMBIA
1:100, 000
See index 861/2
Bogotá : Inst. Nac. de Invest. Geol. - Mineras
80 x 100 (average)
Col. geological series in progress on same sheet lines as the 1:200, 000 series.
US $5.00

G EARTH RESOURCES

APTITUDES DE EXPLOTACIÓN DE LOS SUELOS (MAPA PRELIMINAR)
1:1, 000, 000
Bogotá : Inst. Geog. "Agustin Codazzi", 1966
122 x 152
Coloured map in 2 sheets, grading soil types and their suitability for agriculture and forestry. Text in Spanish.

COLOMBIA : MAPA DE SUELOS
Bogotá : Inst. Geog. "Agustin Codazzi"
Maps published :

Ubate - Chiquirienda	1964	1:1, 000, 000
Llanos Orientales (7 sheets)	1964	1:250, 000
Región de Uraba	1961	1:250, 000
Cafetera Central (Assoc. de suelos)	1962	1:100, 000
Región del Rio Mira	1960	1:100, 000
Hoya, hidrografia alta del Rio Bogotá		1:100, 000
Atlantico dep. (4 sheets)	1959	1:50, 000
Valle del Río Risaralda	1959	1:30, 000
Cafetera Central (29 sheets)	1960	1:25, 000
Saldana, del dist. de Irrigacion	1960	1:20, 000

MAPA MINERALÓGICO DE CALDAS RISARALDAS Y QUINDÍO
1:250, 000
Bogotá : Inst. Nac. de Invest. Geol. - Mineras
Coloured Mineralogical map. US $3.50

MAPA MINERALÓGICO DEL DEPARTAMENTO DEL TOLIMA
1:250, 000
Bogotá : Inst. Nac. de Invest. Geol. - Mineras
Coloured mineralogical map. US $3.50

H BIOGEOGRAPHY

MAPA ECOLÓGICO
1:1, 000, 000
In 4 sheets
Bogotá : Inst. Geog. "Agustin Codazzi", 1962
79 x 105 each
Illus. by col. various vegetable types based on L R Holdridge's classification system.
202 p handbook 'Formaciones Vegetates de Colombia' inc. photographs, statistical inf. in Spanish, English summary.

REPÚBLICA DE COLOMBIA :
MAPA GENERAL DE BOSQUES
1:1, 000, 000
Bogotá : Inst. Geog. "Agustin Codazzi",
1967
99 x 146 complete
2 sheet map in col. classifying 8 woodland types; also roads, railways, towns graded by pop. With brief text, 1967.

M HISTORICAL

REPÚBLICA DE COLOMBIA :
MAPA HISTÓRICO POLÍTICO
1:1, 500, 000
Bogotá : Inst. Geo. "Agustin Codazzi",
1960
116 x 165
2 sheet map, political col. by provinces with routes of explorers, battles, foundation of cities etc; list of important historical sites, covers conquest and independence, portraits of explorers in margin.

ATLASES
L ECONOMIC

ATLAS DE ECONOMÍA
COLOMBIANA
Ed. E A Latorre
Bogotá : Banca de la Republica, 1959-64
40 x 29
In 4 vols.
Part 1
Aspectos físico y geográfico 1959
Part 2
Aspectos político, humano y administrativo, 1960
Part 3
Fuentes de energia - recursos mineros y forestales - sistemas de comunicaciones, 1962
Part 4
Aspectos agropecuarios y su fundamento ecológico 1964
Economic atlas containing 63 full colour map plates with many small maps, diagrams, photographs and descriptive text. $ Col. 200.00 set

ATLASES
M HISTORICAL

ATLAS DE MAPAS ANTIGUOS DE
COLOMBIA
Bogotá : Academia Colombiana de Hist.
32 x 45
169 pp
Covers the 16th - 19th C. 59 plates - col. and black and white maps.
$ Col 750

ATLASES
O NATIONAL

ATLAS DE COLOMBIA
Ed. E A Latorre
Bogotá : Inst. Geog. "Agustin Codazzi",
1969
32 x 45
216 pp
Col. maps, photos, illus. text. Divided into historical, topog, climate, admin, physical, human and economic sections, and by Depts. each with physical map, town plan, photos. Indexed. Also available in reduced edition for schools as "Atlas Escolar de Colombia".

866 Ecuador

A1 GENERAL MAPS: ROADS

MAPA VIAL TURÍSTICO DE LAS REGIÓNES DEL ECUADOR
1:2,000,000
Quito: IGM – CETURIS
56 x 71
Roads classified, distances in km, through town plans. Galapagos Islands inset.

B TOWN PLANS

OFFICIAL TOWN PLANS
Quito: IGM
Various sizes
Detailed plans in colour naming principal streets
Plans published:
Plano de la Cuidadde Guayaquil 1964
1:10,000 $15.00
Plano de Quito 1975
1:10,000 $30.00

C OFFICIAL SURVEYS

KARTA MIRA
1:2,500,000
VVK
2 sheets required for full coverage:
108 Bogotá
128 Quito
see WORLD 100C and index 100/2

INTERNATIONAL MAP OF THE WORLD – HISPANIC AMERICA SERIES
1:1,000,000
AGS
5 sheets required for full coverage.
see WORLD 100C and index 100/1

CARTA TOPOGRÁFICA DEL ECUADOR
1:100,000
Series J621 See index 866/1
Quito: IGM
56 x 37
Topog. series in progress.
each $10.00

CARTA TOPOGRÁFICA DEL ECUADOR
1:50,000
Series J721 See index 866/1
Quito: IGM, 1962
56 x 37
Col. topog. series in progress.
each $10.00

CARTA CROQUIS PLANIMETRICA
1:50,000
In 240 sheets
1st edition
Quito: IGM, 1973
55 x 37
Provisional Planimetric survey providing coverage for areas not yet published in topographical series
$20.00

CARTA TOPOGRAFICA DEL ECUADOR
1:25,000
Series J821
Quito: IGM See index 866/1
56 x 37
New topog. series in progress, superseding old 25,000 series, in 3 col. covering the Provinces of Pichincha, Cotopaxi, Tungurohua and Loja.
each $10.00

D POLITICAL AND ADMINISTRATIVE

MAPA POLÍTICO DEL ECUADOR
1:1,000,000
2nd edition
Quito: IGM, 1975
83 x 111
Politically coloured map.
$40.00

E1 PHYSICAL: RELIEF

MAPA FÍSICO DEL ECUADOR
1:2,000,000
Quito: IGM, 1974
48 x 62
Physical map with contours, roads classified.
$10.00

MAPA FÍSICO DEL ECUADOR
1:1,000,000
2nd edition
Quito: IGM, 1974
83 x 111
Contoured and layer coloured map, with roads classified and railways.
$35.00

SOUTH PACIFIC OCEAN – ARCHIPELAGO DE COLON – GALAPAGOS ISLANDS
1:600,000
Washington: USGS
Contours, depths.

MAPA GEOGRÁFICO DE LA REPÚBLICA DEL ECUADOR
1:500,000
In 4 sheets
Quito: IGM, 1976
194 x 273 complete
Contoured, layer col, relief shading, towns graded according to pop and status, roads classified. Insets of South America political, Galapagos Islands, compilation sources and statistical tables.

F GEOLOGICAL SERIES

MAPA GEOLÓGICO DE LA REPÚBLICA DEL ECUADOR
1:1,000,000
Quito: Serv. Nac. de Geol. y Mineria, 1969
68 x 96
2 sheet coloured geological map with cross-section. Insets of Colon Archipelago, Galapagos Islands at 1:5,000,000. With list of sources used.

ECUADOR: MAPA GEOLÓGICO DETALLADO
1:100,000
Quito: Serv. Nac. de Geol. y Mineria
1968
56 x 69 each
New geological series in colour on topog. base. Monochrome sketch maps and profiles on reverse. Legend sheet in Spanish.

G EARTH RESOURCES

MAPA INDICE MINERALÓGICO REPÚBLICA DEL ECUADOR
P M Fozzard & Carlos Mosquera
1:1,000,000
Quito: Serv. Nat. Geol. y Mineria
1969
76 x 109
Work done during UN Devt. Project. Contours, geol. col. mineral detail.
2 sheet map in Eng. and Sp.

ATLASES
02 NATIONAL ATLAS; SCHOOL EDITION

ATLAS GEOGRÁFICO ESCOLAR DEL ECUADOR
Editor: Francisco Sampedro V
Quito: Offset Editorial Colon
1963-64
22 x 31
39pp
Includes general coloured maps of the country and the provinces.

87 Venezuela

A1 GENERAL MAPS: ROADS

MAPA VIAL CON OTRES DATOS DE COMUNICACIONES TERRESTRES, MARITIMAS Y AEREAS DE LA REPÚBLICA DE VENEZUELA
1:1,000,000
In 4 sheets
Caracas: Dir. de Cart. Nac, 1970
200 x 140 complete
Road map with rail, sea and air communications also, relief shading, boundaries, index on margin.

B TOWN PLANS

PLANOS DE CIUDADES
Caracas: Dir. de Cart. Nac.

Altagracia de Orituco	1:5,000	1963
Barcelona	1:10,000	1948
Barinas	1:10,000	1948
Barquisimeto	1:10,000	1950
Bocono	1:5,000	1963
Cagua	1:5,000	1962
Caracas, Area Metropolitana		
6 sheets	1:20,000	1957
Caracas y Alrededores	1:20,000	1971
Casanay	1:5,000	1965
Ciudad Bolivar	1:10,000	1948
Ciudad Bolivar	1:10,000	1964
Coro	1:10,000	1948
Cumana	1:10,000	1965
Cumanacoa	1:5,000	1965
Duaca	1:5,000	1966
El Sombrero	1:5,000	1963
Guanare	1:10,000	1948
La Guaira y Maiquetia	1:10,000	1936
Maracay	1:10,000	1948
Puerto Cabello	1:10,000	1948
San Casimiro	1:5,000	1964
San Cristobal	1:5,000	1961
San Felipe	1:10,000	1948
San Felipe	1:5,000	1962
San Juan de los Morros	1:10,000	1948
San Sebastian	1:5,000	1966
Turmero	1:5,000	1960
Valencia	1:10,000	1938

CARACAS – PLANO DIRECTORIO
1:20,000
Caracas: Interamericana Tecnica
64 x 94
Double sided plan of town and suburbs with index.

C OFFICIAL SURVEYS

KARTA MIRA
1:2,500,000
VVK
2 sheets required for full coverage:
108 Bogota
109 Caracas
see WORLD 100C and index 100/2

INTERNATIONAL MAP OF THE WORLD – HISPANIC AMERICA SERIES
1:1,000,000
AGS
7 sheets required for full coverage:
see WORLD 100C and index 100/1

CARTA AERONAÚTICA
1:500,000
In 25 sheets
Caracas: Dir. de Cart. Nac. 1954
Principally designed for flying but showing detailed relief information, contoured series in progress.

VENEZUELA: CARTAS GEOGRÁFICAS
1:250,000
In 44 sheets
Caracas: Dir. Cart. Nac.
74 x 58
New topog. series in progress, contoured with road information and land detail.

VENEZUELA: CARTAS GEOGRÁFICAS NACIONAL
1:100,000
See index 87/1
Caracas: Dir. Cart. Nac.
70 x 55
Old 4-col. topog. series, not complete. Superseded by the "Nuevas Cartas" 1962-, still in progress.

VENEZUELA
1:25,000
Caracas: Dir. Cart. Nac.
97 x 69
Topog. series in progress, contoured and coloured.

D POLITICAL & ADMINISTRATIVE

MAPA FÍSICO-POLÍTICO DE LA REPÚBLICA DE VENEZUELA
1:4,000,000
Caracas: Dir. Cart. Nac, 1965
44 x 37
Political col. by states, communications and relief shading.

MAPA FÍSICO Y POLÍTICO DE LA REPÚBLICA DE VENEZUELA
1:2,000,000
Caracas: Dir. Cart. Nac, 1967
89 x 72
Col. politically by states, relief shading, roads classified, railways, boundaries, towns graded by status and pop.

MAPA FÍSICO Y POLÍTICO DE LA REPÚBLICA DE VENEZUELA
1:1,000,000
In 6 sheets
Caracas: Dir. Cart. Nac, 1955
186 x 180 complete
Col. by states, showing relief by contours and some hachuring, roads classified, railways, airports.

MAPA DEL DESAROLLO REGIONAL
1:2,000,000
Caracas: Dir. Cart. Nac, 1969
100 x 82
Col. map showing regional devt. and admin. at 11.6.69.

MAPA INDICE DE ESTADOS Y DISTRITOS DE VENEZUELA
1:2,000,000
Caracas: Min. de Minas e Hidrocarburos
Indicates states and territorial district boundaries with list of names.

REGIONES ADMINISTRATIVAS; MAPA DE LA REGIONALISACION DE VENEZUELA
1:2,000,000
Caracas: Dir. Cart. Nac.
Showing admin. divisional boundaries.

MAPAS DE ESTADOS
Various scales
Caracas: Dir. Cart Nac. 1969
65 x 48
A new series of state maps, coloured with boundaries, towns and villages.
Maps published:

Anzoategui	1:750,000
Apure	1:1,150,000
Aragua	1:360,000
Barinas	1:800,000
Bolivar	1:1,375,000
Carabobo	1:262,500
Cojedes	1:360,000
Falcon	1:650,000
Guarico	1:800,000
Lara	1:420,000
Merida	1:400,000
Miranda	1:480,000
Monagas	1:550,000
Nueva Esparta	1:140,000
Portuguesa	1:500,000
Sucra	1:500,000
Tachira	1:280,000
Trujillo	1:320,000
Yaracuy	1:260,000
Zulia	1:650,000

MAPAS DEL TERRITORIO FEDERAL
Various scales
Caracas: Dir. Cart. Nac. 1969
65 x 48
A new series covering the territorial districts coloured with boundaries, towns and villages.
Maps published:

Distrito Federal	1:210,000
Territoria Federal Amacuro	1:800,000
Territoria Federal Amazonas	1:1,400,000

E1 PHYSICAL: RELIEF

MAPA FISIOGRÁFICO REPÚBLICA DE VENEZUELA
1:4,000,000
Caracas: Min. de Mines e Hidrocarburos
Physiographic map of Venezuela.
US $3.00

BATIMÉTRICO DE VENEZUELA
1:2,000,000
Caracas: Min. de Minas e Hidrocarburos
Map showing sea depths around the coast of Venezuela.
Bs 1.50

E2 PHYSICAL: LAND FEATURES

TIPOS DE TERRENOS REGIÓN NORTE DE VENEZUELA
1:1,500,000
Caracas: Min. de Minas e Hidrocarburos
Geomorphological map of northern Venezuela.
Bs 1.50

F GEOLOGY

MAPA TECTÓNICO DE VENEZUELA
1:5,555,555
Caracas: Min. de Mines e Hidrocarburos.
Tectonic map
US $1.00

MAPA GEOLÓGICO DE VENEZUELA
1:3,333,333
Caracas: Min. de Mines e Hidrocarburos.
Geological map.
US $1.00

GEOLÓGICO Y TIPOS DE ROCAS DE VENEZUELA
1:2,500,000
Caracas: Min. de Mines e Hidrocarburos
Geological map of Venezuela
US $3.00

GEOLÓGICO DE VENEZUELA
1:2,000,000
Caracas: Min. de Minas e Hidrocarburos
Geological map
US $3.00

GEOLÓGICO DE VENEZUELA – CAOLÍN
1:2,000,000
Caracas: Min. de Minas e Hidrocarburos
Showing location of kaolin clay deposits.
US $3.00

GEOLÓGICO DE VENEZUELA – ARENAS
1:1,500,000
Caracas: Min. de Minas e Hidrocarburos
Showing location of sand deposits.
US $3.00

GEOLÓGICO DE VENEZUELA – CALIZAS
1:1,500,000
Caracas: Min. de Minas e Hidrocarburos
Showing location of calcareous beds.
US $3.00

MAPA GEOLÓGICO – TECTÓNICO DEL NORTE DE VENEZUELA
1:1,000,000
Caracas: Soc. Ven. de Ingenieros de Petroleo, 1962
189 x 82
Prep. for 1st Venezuelan Petroleum Congress March 1962. 2 sheet in col. Legend Sp, Eng.

MAPA HIDROGEOLOGICO DE VENEZUELA
1:500,000
In 13 sheets.
Caracas: Min. de Mines e Hidrocarburos.
Hydro-geologic series covering the northern half of the country.
each Bs. 25.00
set Bs. 250.00

GEOLÓGICO TECTÓNICO GENERALIZADO DE LA PARTE OCCIDENTAL DE LA REGIÓN CENTRAL DE LA CORDILLERA DE LA COSTA
1:250,000
In 2 sheets
Caracas: Min. de Mines e Hidrocarburos
Generalised geological – tectonic map of the western part of central region of Coastal Range.
US $3.00

MAPA GEOLÓGICO DE LA CORDILLERA CENTRALES DE VENEZUELA
1:100,000
Caracas: Min. de Mines e Hidrocarburos.
Geological map of the Central Andes with separate sheets of cross sections and legend.
each US $3.00

MAPA GEOLÓGICO DE LA CORDILLERA DE LA COSTA
1:100,000
Caracas: Min. de Mines e Hidrocarburos.
Geological map of the coastal range.
US $3.00

REGIONAL GEOLOGICAL MAPS
Caracas: Min. de Mines e Hidrocarburos
Maps published:
ESTADO ANZOATEGUI
00024 Cuenca Carbonifera de Naricual
1:10,000
Geológico de Soledad, carta No. 3,608
00411 Estados Amoátegui y Bolivar
1:100,000
00463 Geológico y Recursos Minerales del E stado Amoátegui
1:500,000
00014 Mapa Topográfico Geológico zona Puerto La Cruz Pertigalene
1:10,000
00019 Region de Barcelona y Puerto La Cruz
1:10,000
00449 Mapa geológico Cuenca Carbonĩfera de Naricual
1:10,000
ESTADO ARAGUA
00694 Geológico y Recursos Minerales del Estado Aragua
1:250,000
00705 Mapa Geológico de Aragua Central
1:50,000
00706 Mapa Geológico del Area de La Victoria
1:50,000
00692 Mapa y Cortes Geológicos de la Región de Camatagua
1:100,000
00402 Mapa geológico Choroni Colonia Tovar
1:100,000
00710 Mapa Geológico zona de Pardillal
1:2,500
ESTADO BARINAS
00892 Mapa Geológico y Recursos Minerales del Estado Barinas
1:500,000
00910 Mapa Geológico Región de Barinitas Santo Domingo
1:50,000
ESTADO BOLIVAR
01943 Mapa Geológico y de Recursos Minerales del Estado Bolivar
1:1,000,000
01940 Mapa Geológico de la Región de la Gran Sabana
1:500,000
01796 Mapa Geológico de la Región de Guasipati – El Dorado
1:200,000
01995 Mapa Geológico del Cuadrilátero de Upata
1:100,000
01794 Mapa Geológico del Cuadrilátero Las Adjuntas – Panamo
1:100,000
01947 Geológia de la parte norte Central del Escudo de Guayana. Estado Bolĩvar (hojas Este y Oeste)
1:500,000
00114 Mapa Geológico de la zona de Guasipati – El Callao El Dorado
1:100,000
01936 Mapa Geológico de la Regĩon de Caicara
1:200,000
01942 Mapa Geológico de la Regĩon de Botanamo
1:200,000
01999 Mapa Geológico de la Regĩon de los Indios El Pilar
1:50,000
03474 Mapa Geológico del Cerro San Isidro
1:50,000
ESTADO CARABOBO
02138 Mapa Geológico y de Recursos Minerales del Estado Carabobo
1:250,000
02140 Mapa Geológico de la Regĩon Este del Estado Carabobo
1:50,000
02145 Mapa geológico del área de las Trincheras El Cambur
1:500,000
ESTADO COJEDES
00179 Mapa Geológico del Macizo de El Baul
1:60,000
02147 Mapa Geológico de la Regĩon Norcentral del Estado Cojedes
1:100,000
02153 Mapa Geológico de la Regĩon Rio Pao – Rio Tiznados
1:100,000
02146 Mapa Geológico de San Carlos. Carta No. 2,309
1:100,000
DISTRITO FEDERAL
02256 Secciones Estructurales de la Region de Caracas
1:25,000
02238 Mapa Geológico de la Carta No. 240,321 Carayaca
1:25,000
ESTADO FALCON
02484 Mapa Geológico y de Recursos Minerales del Estado Falcón
1:1,000,000
02459 Plano Geológico del área Pueblo Nuevo Peninsula de Paraguaná
1:25,000
02310 Mapa Geológico Adicura Pueblo Nuevo (5 hojas)
1:200,000

02311 Mapa Geológico La Concepción-Casigua-Rio Machango (hoja 2)
1:200,000
02312 Mapa Geológico Capatarida-Paraguaná-Puerto Cumarebo-Rio Tocuyo-Rio Maticora (hoja 3)
1:200,000
02313 Mapa Geológico Punta Gavalán-Valencia-San Carlos Chivacoa (hoja 4)
1:200,000
02314 Mapa Geológico Campo Mene Grande-Barquisimeto-Acarigua-Valera (hoja 5)
1:200,000
ESTADO GUARICO
02518 Localización de los Depósitos de Yeso del área de El Portachuelo (Distrito Monagas, Estado Guárico)
1:25,000
02518 Mapa Geológico Estructural de San Juan de los Morros
1:25,000
02520 Mapa Geológico y de Recursos del Estado Guárico
1:1,000,000
02524 Cuenca Carboñifera de Guárico y Miranda
1:100,000
02527 Mapa Geológico del Noroeste de Gúarico-Lago de Valencia
1:100.000
02519 Mapa Geológico de la Región de San Juan de Los Morros
1:100,000
ESTADO LARA
02553 Mapa Geológico y de Localidades Carboniferas del Estado Lara
1:500,000
02557 Mapa Geológico de la Regíon de Barquisimeto
1:100,000
00188 Plano de Localización de Arenas en la Región de Aguide
1:4,000
02547 Mapa Geológico región Barquisimeto Urachiche Rio Tocuyo
1:200,000
ESTADO MERIDA
02633 Mapa Geológico y de Recursos Minerales del Estado Mérida
1:500,000
02650 Mapa Geológico y de Recursos Minerales de Los Andes
1:500,000
02664 Mapa Geológico de Tovar
1:50,000
02667 Mapa Geológico de la Azulita
1:100,000
02669 Mapa Geológico de la Región de Timotes
1:50,000
02675 Mapa Geológico y Cortes Estructurales Flanco Oriental de la Culata
1:50,000
ESTADO MIRANDA
02693 Mapa Geológico de Los Teques – Cúa
1:50,000
02698 Mapa Geológico de la Región Central del Estado Miranda
1:50,000
02244 Mapa Geológico de la Región Colonia Tovar-Guatire
1:100,000
02691 Mapa Geológico Araira Cabo Codera
1:100,000

02695 Mapa Geológico de la Cuenca de Santa Lucia Ocumare
1:100,000
ESTADO MONAGAS
02708 Mapa Geológico y de Recursos Minerales del Estado Monagas
1:500,000
ESTADO NUEVA ESPARTA
02777 Mapa Geológico del Estado Nueva Esparta
1:100,000
02746 Mapa Geológico de la Región Oriental de Margarita
1:50,000
02736 Mapa Geológico y de Recursos Naturales Estado Nueva Esparta
1:133,000
ESTADO SUCRE
02852 Geologia de la Región de la Bahia de Sante Fé
1:25,000
02843 Mapa Geológico y de Recurses Minerales de los Estados Sucre y Nueva Esparta
1:300,000
02793 Mapa Geológico de la Peninsula de Araya
1:25,000
02786 Mapa Geológio de la Peninsula de Paria (5 hojas)
1:50,000
02801 Mapa Geológico de la Region Nor-Central del Estado Sucre
1:200,000
02821 Mapa Geológico Ocurrencias de Cianita al Este de la Peninsula de Araya
1:25,000
02797 Mapa Geologico de la zona de Falas de El Pilar
1:100,000
02820 Mapa Geológico de la Región de Carupano
1:100,000
02804 Mapa Geológico de la Peninsula de Arava (3 hojas)
1:117,000
ESTADO TACHIRA
02869 Mapa Geológico y de Recursos Minerales del Estado Táchira
1:500,000
02863 Mapa Geológico de la Región de Pregonero
1:50,000
02862 Cortes de Pregonero
1:50,000
02878 Mapa Geológico de la Región de La Grita – San Cristóbal
1:50,000
02879 Mapa Geológico de Seboruco
1:50,000
03054 Mapa Geológico de la Región del Rio Momboy zona Occidental
1:50,000
ESTADO TRUJILLO
03033 Mapa Geológico y de Recursos Minerales del Estado Trujillo
1:500,000
TERRITORIO FEDERAL DELTA AMACURO
03302 Mapa Geológico y de Recursos Minerales del Territorio Delta Amacuro
1:500,000
ESTADO YARACUY
03242 Mapa Geológico y de Recursos Minerales del Estado Yaracuy
1:250,000
03152 Mapa Geológico del Yaracuy Occidental
1:250,000

03254 Mapa Geológico del Estado Yaracuy
1:100,000
ESTADO ZULIA
03262 Cuenca Carboniffera del Estado Zulia
1:100,000
03264 Mapa Geológico y de Recursos Minerales del Estado Zulia
1:500,000
03265 Mapa Geológico de la Goajira Venezolana
1:250,000
DEPENDENCIAS FEDERALES
00267 Mapa Geológico y Topografico de las Islas Los Frailes
H1:5,000 V1:2,500
03322 Mapa Geológico del Archipiélago de los Hermanos
1:25,000
03323 Mapa Geológico del Archipiélago de Los Testigos
1:25,000
03324 Mapa Geológico de la Isla La Blanquilla
1:25,000
03325 Mapa Geológico de la Isla de La Tortuga
1:20,000
03330 Mapa Geológico de la Isla La Orchila
1:25,000
03333 Mapa Geológico de la Isla Gran Roque
1:5,000
03335 Reconchniento Geológico de los Islotes Monjes dal Sur, Norte y Este
1:4,000
03336 Mapa de Localización del Archipielago de los Monjes
1:1,000,000

G EARTH RESOURCES

MAPA DE RECURSOS MINERALES DE VENEZUELA
1:6,000,000
Caracas: Min. de Mines e Hidrocarburos
Mineral resources of Venezuela
US $3.00

MAPA DE SUELOS DE VENEZUELA
1:2,000,000
Caracas: Min. de Minas e Hidrocarburos
Black and white map indicating distribution of soil types.
Bs 1.50

MAPA DEL ORIENTE DE VENEZUELA EN RELACIÓN CON LA INDUSTRIA DEL HIERRO
1:2,000,000
Caracas: Min. de Minas e Hidrocarburos
Map of eastern Venezuela illustrating the locations and working of the iron industry.
Bs 1.50

CARTA ISOGÓNICA
1:2,000,000
Caracas: Dir. de Cart. Nac, 1970
100 x 84
Col. isogonic mao.

GEOLÓGICO Y DE RECURSOS MINERALES DE VENEZUELA
1:1,500,000
Caracas: Min. de Minas e Hidrocarburos
On a simplified geological base map location of minerals are indicated by symbols.
Bs 1.50

MAPA METALOGÉNICO PRONÓSTICO DE LOS ANDES VENEZOLANOS
1:500,000
Caracas: Min. de Mines e Hidrocarburos
Metallogenetic prognosis of the Venezuelan Andes.
US $3.00

H BIOGEOGRAPHY

REPÚBLICA DE VENEZUELA: MAPA ECOLÓGICO
1:2,000,000
Caracas: Min. de Agricultura y Cira
1968
89 x 72
Col. map divided by ecological zones. With 265pp text "Zonas de Vida de Venezuela".

ATLASES
H BIOGEOGRAPHY

ATLAS FORESTAL DE VENEZUELA
Caracas: Min. de Ag. y Cira, 1961
43 x 35
44pp
39 col. maps showing principal forest types, national parks and reserves, use and potential; text and statistics.

ATLASES
J CLIMATE

ATLAS CLIMATALÓGICO DE LA CUENCA HIDROGRÁFICA DEL VALLE DE CARACAS
Caracas: Serv. de Meterologia, 1968
31 x 46
Atlas of the Caracas Valley River Basin.
156pp col. maps.

ATLASES
L ECONOMIC

ATLAS AGRÍCOLA DE VENEZUELA
Caracas: Min. de Ag. y Cria, 1960
43 x 35
107 col. maps covering natural resources, agriculture, economy, social aspects; with statistics and explanatory text.

VENEZUELA: INVENTARIO NACIONAL DE RECURSOS
AID/EAR I Atlas No 8
Washington: US Engineer Agency for Resources Inventories, 1968
iii, 120pp app.
54 x 62
38pp maps showing national resources, 80 plates, text.

ATLASES
M HISTORICAL

CONTRIBUCIÓN AL ESTUDIO DE LOS PLANOS DE CARACAS – LA CIUDAD Y LA PROVINCIA 1567-1967
by Irma de Sola Ricardo
Caracas: Ediciones del Cuatricentenano de Caracas/Direccion de Cart. Nacional, 1967
52 x 38
278pp
Collection of plans and maps from earliest times, in chronological order. Covers City, Province, Country. Text in Port.

ATLASES
O NATIONAL

ATLAS DE VENEZUELA
Caracas: Dir. Cart. Nac, 1969
32 x 45
216pp comprising 280 maps
Maps, photographs, text; each Federal District described separately, thematic maps – social, economic, cultural, physical aspects.

881 Guyana

A1 GENERAL MAPS

BRITISH GUIANA
1:2,250,000
Edition 6
DOS 957
Tolworth: DOS, 1963
35 x 38
Shows roads, railways, admin. boundaries; principal relief indicated by hachures.
10p

MAP OF GUYANA
1:1,000,000
Georgetown: Surv. Dept, 1964
62 x 90
Reduction of DMS E491, showing roads, railways, water features, in black and white.
$1.00

A2 GENERAL MAPS: LOCAL

SOUTHERN GUYANA
1:700,000
reprinted from Geog. Journal March 1972
London: RGS
31 x 46
Topographic — 1 map from a photo-mosaic and interpretation by Jevan P. Berrangé and R.L. Johnson, 1969.
£1.50

B TOWN PLANS

OFFICIAL PLANS OF GEORGETOWN
Georgetown: Min. of Ag. & Nat. Res.
detailed plans in black and white showing all principal roads and buildings.
Maps available:
Plan of Georgetown and environs, 1:9,600, 1967, (reduction of plan DOS (Misc.) 301) G$.50
Street plan of Georgetown and environs, 1:11,850 G$.50

GREATER GEORGETOWN
1:4,800
Edition 2 in 2 sheets DOS (Misc.)301
Tolworth: DOS, 1967
Detailed plan in black and white showing all principal streets and buildings.

C OFFICIAL SURVEYS

KARTA MIRA
1:2,500,000
VVK
1 sheet provides coverage:
109 Caracas
see WORLD 100C and index 100/2

INTERNATIONAL MAP OF THE WORLD — HISPANIC AMERICA SERIES
1:1,000,000
AGS
4 sheets required for coverage:
NA 21 Alto Trombetas
NB 20 Roraima
NB 21 Georgetown
NC 20/21 Boca del Orinoco
see WORLD 100C and index 100/1

GUYANA
1:500,000
DOS (Misc.) 17 a,b,c,d
Tolworth: DOS, 1954
4 sheet general map indicating road and river communications and settlement. New edition in prep.
NE section 1972 currently published.
30p 1954 each
50p new edition 1972 each

GUYANA
1:500,000
DMS series E491
Feltham: DMS
Special edition of DOS (Misc.) 17 a-d map showing same information.
13p each

PLANIMETRIC MAP OF GUYANA
1:50,000
DOS 440, see index 88/1
Tolworth: DOS 1953
Topog. series available in uncontoured edition, showing roads, tracks, railways etc. 30p
Also editions published by Min. of Ag. and Nat. Res. Georgetown
Printed G$.50 each
Ozalid prints G$.2 00 "

D POLITICAL & ADMINISTRATIVE

BRAZILIYA, GAYANA, SURINAM, GVIANA
GUGK, 1971
see BRAZIL 81D

F GEOLOGY

PROVISIONAL GEOLOGICAL MAP OF BRITISH GUIANA
1:1,000,000
Georgetown: Geol. Surv, BG, 1962
55 x 84
Col. geol. map covering those areas for which reliable information exists.
£1.00

GEOLOGICAL ATLAS OF GUYANA
1:200,000
see index 881/2
Georgetown: Geol. Survey Dept. 1961
Detailed series of coloured geological maps in progress.

MISCELLANEOUS PRINTED GEOLOGICAL MAPS
Georgetown: Geol. Survey Dept.
Maps published:
Issano — Semang — Karanang Mazaroni District
1:100,000 1939
Towakaima District, Barima, Barama and Iroma Rivers
1:127,000 1939
Kariaku area, Barama River (sheet C4)
1:125,000 1949
Aurora district, Cuyoni River (sheet D4)
1:125,000 1948
Issineru — Enachu district, Mazaroni River (sheet E3)
1:125,000 1955
Map of the coastal plain of British Guiana
1:134,000 1955

G EARTH RESOURCES

GUYANA — ROAD MAKING MATERIALS
1:1,000,000
DOS (Misc.) 442
Tolworth: DOS, 1967
65 x 90
Indicating with col. locations of rock types of economic importance.
65p

MINERAL EXPLORATION MAP OF GUYANA
1:1,000,000
Georgetown: Geol. Survey Dept, 1966
55 x 84
Showing location and extent of mineral fields by col, mines, gas and oil wells, diagrams of principal mineral production. Base map shows roads, trails, railways and airports.
£1.00

MINERAL EXPLORATION MAP OF GUYANA
1:1,000,000
Georgetown: Geol. Survey Dept, 1966
Coloured map indicating location of minerals by symbols.

GUYANA — ENGINEERING SOILS
1:250,000
DOS (Misc.) 441
Tolworth: DOS, 1967
90 x 80
Col. map indicating soils of economic importance.
65p

AEROMAGNETIC MAPS OF GUYANA
1:50,000
Georgetown: Geol. Survey Dept. 1963
Series of dyeline prints in progress.

ELECTROMAGNETIC MAPS OF GUYANA
1:50,000
Georgetown: Geol. Survey Dept. 1964
Series of dyeline prints in progress.

L ECONOMIC

MAP OF GUYANA
1:1,500,000
Georgetown: Surv. Dept, 1968
41 x 59
Col. map showing major regions land use, communication economic details, historical sites, pop details.

$0.50

S

882 French Guiana

A1 GENERAL MAPS: ROADS

CARTE DE LA GUYANE
1:1,500,000
Paris: IGN, 1964
25 x 31
General map with roads in red, relief shown by brown hachures, vegetation in green.
F.Fr. 11,67

A2 GENERAL MAPS: LOCAL

COURS SUPÉRIEUR DE L'OYAPOCK
1:40,000
Paris: IGN, 1947
50 x 60
Monochrome provisional map, after the journeys of the Oyapock mission, 1947.
F.Fr. 5,83

B TOWN PLANS

ISLE DE CAYENNE (VILLE ET ENVIRONS)
1:20,000
Paris: IGN, 1957
84 x 65
Coloured topog. map of town and environs; contoured, roads, vegetation etc. Inset of Cayenne – Rochambeau airport.
F.Fr. 11,67

ST LAURENT DU MARONI ET ENVIRONS
1:10,000
Paris: IGN, 1948
42 x 55
Coloured topog. plan with contours at 5m intervals.
F.Fr. 11.67

ST JEAN DU MARONI
1: 5,000
Paris: IGN, 1946
25 x 34
Monochrome topog. map with contours at 5m intervals.
F.Fr. 5,83

ST LAURENT DU MARONI
1:5,000
Paris: IGN, 1948
46 x 40
Monochrome topographic map with contours at 5m intervals.
F.Fr. 5,83

C OFFICIAL SERIES

INTERNATIONAL MAP OF THE WORLD – HISPANIC AMERICA SERIES
1:1,000,000
AGS
4 sheets required for full coverage:
NA 21 Alto Trombetas
NA 22 Amapa
NB 21 Georgetown
NB 22 Cayenne
see WORLD 100C and index 100/1

CARTE DE LA GUYANE
1:500,000
Paris: IGN, 1963
89 x 110
Map in 2 sheets, contoured with roads in red and vegetation in green.
F.Fr. 5,83

CARTE DE LA GUYANE
1:200,000
In 11 sheets
see index 882/1
Paris: IGN
55 x 55
Topog. series, each sheet available in one of the following eds:
a) Esquisse photogrammetrique – in 3 col. showing contours, water detail and settlement.
b) Fond planimetrique monochrome – uncontoured with index of aerial surveys.
F.Fr. 11,67

CARTE DE LA GUYANE
1:100,000
See index 882/2
Paris: IGN
55 x 55 each
Topog. series in progress, available in one of the following eds:
a) Esquisse photogrammetrique – in 3/4 colours showing contours, water detail, settlement.
b) Esquisse photogrammetrique provisoire – in black and white with contours
F.Fr. 11,67

CARTE DE LA GUYANE FRANCAISE
1:50,000
see index 882/2
Paris: IGN
55 x 55
Series "type outre-mer". Contoured topog. series in progress, water features blue, vegetation green.
F.Fr. 11,67

D POLITICAL & ADMINISTRATIVE

BRAZILIYA, GAYANA, SURINAM, GVIANA
GUGK, 1971
see BRAZIL 81D

F GEOLOGY

GUYANE: CARTE GÉOLOGIQUE
1:500,000
Orleans: BRGM, 1960
55 x 78
2 sheet map (North and South). In colour.
F. Fr. 42.00

ESQUISSE GÉOLOGIQUE DE LA GUYANE SEPTENTRIONALE
1:200,000
In 3 sheets
Orleans: BRGM, 1956 (Provisional)
69 x 90
Provisional sketch map of Northern part of country, in colour.
F. Fr. 42.00

CARTE GÉOLOGIQUE DE LA GUYANE
1:100,000
Orleans: BRGM, 1956
Coloured geol. map series (on same sheet lines as topog. ed.) in folder with explanatory text. The following sheets published:
Cayenne, 1956
Kourou, 1959
Haut-Kourou, 1960
Iracoubo, 1961
Regina, 1961
Mana-Saint-Laurent, 1961
Saint-Jean, 1962
Basse-Mana, 1962
Baie de l'Oyapock – Pointe Behague, 1963
Saint-Elie-Adieu Vat, 1963
Arouany, 1964
Paul-Isnard, 1964
Lawa-Abounamy, 1965
Haute-Comte, 1966
Haute-Sinnamary, 1966
Haute-Mana, 1967
Maripasoula, 1967 F. Fr. 24.00 each

G EARTH RESOURCES

CARTE PÉDOLOGIQUE DE LA GUYANE FRANÇAISE
1:50,000
see index 882/3
C Marius et al
Paris: ORSTOM, 1968
Coloured soil map, with 60p text, 1969
F. Fr. 32

883 Surinam

A1 GENERAL MAPS

KAART VAN SURINAME
1:1,000,000
Ed. H Dahlberg
Paramaribo: C Kersten & Co, NV, 1966
53 x 80
Layer coloured, predominant land types indicated, towns and villages graded according to admin. status, also roads and minerals.

KAART VAN SURINAME
1:500,000
In 4 sheets
Paramaribo: Central Bureau Luchtkartering, 1966
110 x 120 complete
Photoprint map showing roads, rivers and settlements, topog. detail shown by symbols.

B TOWN PLANS

PARAMARIBO
1:12,500
Paramaribo: Central Bureau Luchtkartering
77 x 89
Photoprint street plan, principal roads named, religious buildings, petrol pumps, bridges and dykes.

WEGWIJZER VOOR PARAMARIBO EN OMGERING MET PLATTEGROUD EN STRAATNAMENREGISTER
1:10,000
Paramaribo: NV Varekamp
85 x 74
Road index of Paramaribo and surroundings, with buildings and street index. With col. plan.

OMGEVING PARAMARIBO
1:10,000
In 43 sheets
Paramaribo: Central Bureau Luchtkartering, 1959-60
50 x 63
Black and light print covering the town and environs.

KAARTERING VAN PARAMARIBO EN OMGEVING
In 169 sheets
1:1,000
Paramaribo: Central Bureau Luchtkartering
50 x 63
Series of large scale plans in a blue-print edition. Scale reductions of areas can be supplied at 1:5,000 and 1:12,500.

C OFFICIAL SERIES

INTERNATIONAL MAP OF THE WORLD – HISPANIC AMERICA SERIES
1:1,000,000
AGS
2 sheets required for coverage:
NA 21 Alto Trombetas
NB 21 Georgetown
see WORLD 100C and index 100/1

SURINAME TOPOGRAFISCHE KAARTEN
1:200,000
In 29 sheets, see index 883/1
Paramaribo: Central Bureau Luchtkartering
53 x 42
Topog. series; black and white contours.

SURINAME TOPOGRAFISCHE KAARTEN
1:100,000
In 108 sheets, see index 883/2
Paramaribo: Central Bureau Luchtkartering
53 x 46 (average)
Topog. series in progress; in various editions, with or without contours, in colour or blueprints.

SURINAME
1:40,000
See index 883/3
Paramaribo: Central Bureau Luchtkartering
50 x 63
Topog. series in progress, available in various editions, black and white, colours, with or without contours.

SURINAME HOOGTELINIJMEN KAARTEN
1:20,000
See index 883/4
Paramaribo: Central Bureau Luchtkartering
50 x 63
Topog. series in progress, contoured, available in various black and white photoprint editions.

SURINAME
1:10,000
Paramaribo: Central Bureau Luchtkartering
50 x 63
Available for coastal towns and other areas on the Suriname River. Published with or without contours in black and white.

D POLITICAL & ADMINISTRATIVE

BRAZILIYA, GAYANA, SURINAM, GVIANA
GUGK, 1971
see BRAZIL 8D

F GEOLOGY

FOTOGEOLOGISCHE KAART VAN SURINAME
Ed. Min van Opbouw Suriname
Vol. 27 of the Verhandelingen van het Kon. Ned. Geol. Mijnbouwkundig Genootschap.
The Hague: M. Nijhoff's Buekhandel.
51 x 53
Col. map legend also in Eng.
175pp text.
D.A. 36.50

ATLASES
0 NATIONAL ATLAS; SCHOOL EDITION

ATLAS VAN SURINAME
by Duif and Schalken
Paramaribo: Leo Victor, 1968
24pp
25 x 28
School atlas, mainly physical maps, 5pp index.

892 Paraguay

A1 GENERAL MAPS: ROADS

MAPA DE LA REPÚBLICA DEL PARAGUAY
1:2,000,000
Asuncion: IGM
63 x 90
Col. by provinces with roads classified.

B TOWN PLANS

PLANO DE ASUNCIÓN
1:20,000
Asuncion: IGM
Coloured plan with principal streets and buildings marked.

C OFFICIAL SURVEYS

KARTA MIRA
1:2,500,000
VVK
2 sheets required for coverage:
149 La Paz
169 Buenos Aires
see WORLD 100C and index 100/2

INTERNATIONAL MAP OF THE WORLD – HISPANIC AMERICA SERIES
1:1,000,000
AGS
5 sheets required for coverage:
see WORLD 100C and index 100/1

PARAGUAY: CARTA NACIONAL
1:50,000
Series H 741
Washington: AMS
58 x 76
Topog. series in progress, contoured.

D POLITICAL & ADMINISTRATIVE

MAPA FÍSICO POLÍTICO DEL PARAGUAY
1:1,600,000
Buenos Aires: Peuser
82 x 118
Political col. map with communications and relief shading.

PARAGUAY
1:1,000,000
Asuncion: IGM, 1970
94 x 110
Political map col. by admin. units; communications, location inset.

F GEOLOGY

MAPA GEOLÓGICO Y SECCIONES DE PARAGUAY
1:1,000,000
Washington: USGS, 1952
93 x 125
Col. geological map with 3 cross-sections and bibliography of map sources. Available separate from Handbook 'Geology and Mineral Resources of Paraguay – A Reconnaissance'.

GEOLOGY AND MINERAL RESOURCES OF PARAGUAY – A RECONNAISSANCE
by E B Eckel
P327
Washington: USGS, 1959
110p
Handbook containing two maps:
Mapa Geologico y Secciones de Paraguay
1:1,000,000 1952
Un Reconocimiento de Suelos y de Clasificacion de Tierras del Paraguay by P T Sulsona
1:2,000,000 1954

G EARTH RESOURCES

UN RECONOCIMIENTO DE SUELOS Y DE CLASIFICACIÓN DE TIERRAS DEL PARAGUAY
1:2,000,000
prepared by P T Sulsona
Contained in: 'Geology and Mineral Resources of Paraguay – A Reconnaissance
Washington: USGS, 1959

899 Uruguay

C OFFICIAL SURVEYS

KARTA MIRA
1:2,500,000
VVK
2 sheets for coverage:
149 La Paz
169 Buenos Aires
see WORLD 100C and index 100/2

INTERNATIONAL MAP OF THE WORLD – HISPANIC AMERICA SERIES
1:1,000,000
AGS
5 sheets required for coverage
see WORLD 100C and index 100/1

CARTAS TOPOGRÁFICAS URUGUAY
1:100,000
see index 899/1
Montevideo: SGM
Coloured topographical series in progress.

CARTAS TOPOGRÁFICAS URUGUAY
1:50,000
see index 899/2
Montevideo: SGM
Col. topog. series in progress, contoured.

D POLITICAL & ADMINISTRATIVE

MAPA POLÍTICO-FÍSICO DE URUGUAY
1:645,000
Buenos Aires: Peuser
78 x 107
Political map, col. by Departments; relief indicated, communications, settlements graded by pop.

CARTAS DEPARTMENTALES
1:100,000
Montevideo: IGM
Available for each Department in blue print edition. Also some Departments available at 1:200,000.

E1 PHYSICAL: RELIEF

CARTA GEOGRÁFICA DE LA REPÚBLICA URUGUAY
1:500,000
Montevideo: IGM.
Contoured, layer coloured with road and rail communications and towns graded by population.

F GEOLOGY

MAPA GEOLÓGICO DE LA REPÚBLICA ORIENTAL DE URUGUAY
1:500,000
In 2 sheets
Montevideo: Inst. Geol. de Uruguay
1957
100 x 130
Coloured geological map of the country.

URUGUAY: CARTA GEOLÓGICA
1:100,000
Montevideo: Inst. Geol. de Uruguay
1969
New coloured geological series in progress. Each sheet with text vol. in Spanish.

G EARTH RESOURCES

REPÚBLICA ORIENTAL DEL URUGUAY: RECONOCIMIENTO
1:2,000,000
Montevideo: Prog. de Estudio y Levantamiento de Suelos
Soil reconnaissance map.

LOS SEULOS DEL URUGUAY, SU USO Y MENEJO
1:500,000
Montevideo: Dir. de Agronomia, 1963
Handbook containing 3 maps:
Suelos agrupados de acuerdo con tipos predominantes (soils grouped according to predominant types)
Zonas de uso y manejo (Zones of use and management)
Regions de uso agricola de la Tierra (agricultural land use).

H BIOGEOGRAPHY

REPÚBLICA ORIENTAL DEL URUGUAY: USO Y OCUPACIÓN ACTUAL DE LA TIERRA
1:2,000,000
Montevideo: Prog. de Estudio y Levantamiento de Suelos
Land use and occupation map.

J CLIMATE

CUENCA DEL RIÓ DE LA PLATA: ESTUDIO PARA SU (PLANIFICACIÓN Y DESARROLLO)
1:3,000,000
Washington: Pan American Union, 1969
100 x 104 each
17 hydrographic and rainfall maps of the River Plate Basin, for planning study purposes. With 272pp text.

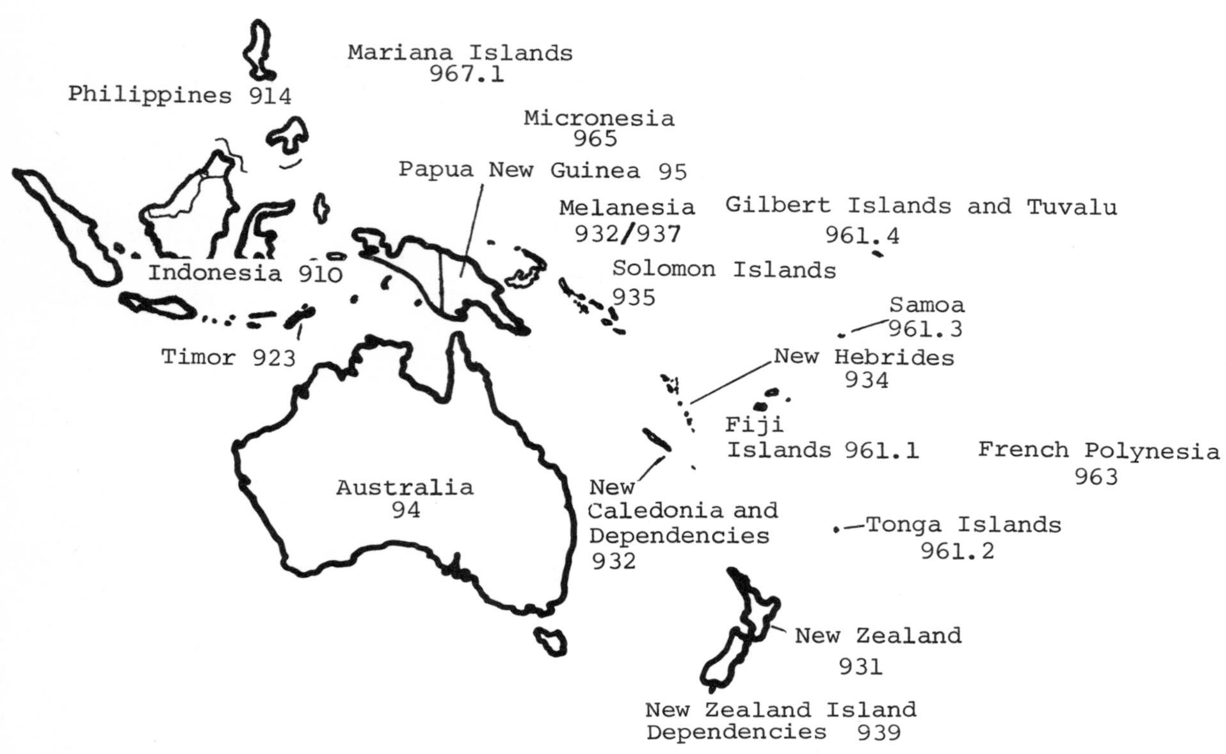

Australia and Oceania 9

Australia and Oceania

9 Australia and Oceania

D POLITICAL & ADMINISTRATIVE

PACIFIC OCEAN AND MAIN ISLAND GROUP
1:28,187,500
Gregory
see OCEANS: PACIFIC 265 A1

OCEANIA
1:12,500,000
Madrid: Aguilar
130 x 100
Politically coloured wall map for schools.
Paper 75 ptas
Cloth 250 ptas

OCÉANIE
1:12,500,000
No 23
Paris: Hatier
100 x 120
School wall map; political with economic map on reverse.

OCÉANIE
1:9,000,000
No. 1062
St. Germain-en-Laye: Éditions MDI, 1970
125 x 92
Double sided wall map. Physical map of Oceania with economic Map of Australia and N.Z. on reverse. Available in french, english and arabic editions.

AUSTRALIE ET OCÉANIE
1:6,000,000
Bruxelles: Mantnieks
160 x 120
Political wall map for schools, showing relief by layer and bathy-metric colouring.

OCÉANIE
Ed. A. Gibert
Map No. 17
Paris: Delagrave
125 x 105
General wall map of Oceania with physical map of the Americas on the reverse.
F.Fr. 45.00

AUSTRALIA AND THE PACIFIC: SUPERIOR WALL MAP
1:5,500,000 app.
Maplewood, NJ: Hammond
86 x 126
Political col. wall map showing states.
Flat or folded $2.00

OCEANIA
No scale given
Barcelona: Editorial Teide
115 x 88
Genral wall map for schools.
275 ptas

OCEANIA
No scale given
Barcelona: Editorial Teide
33 x 25
School hand map showing major cities and state boundaries.
1 pta

AUSTRALIA E OCEANIA
1:40,000,000
Novara: Agostini
Small hand outline map for schools.
L 40

WESTERN PACIFIC
1:6,300,000
DOS 1948
see OCEANS: PACIFIC 265 E1

E1 PHYSICAL: RELIEF

AUSTRALIA E OCEANIA
1:30,000,000
Novara: Ag
33 x 26
Physical with political map on reverse side.

AUSTRALIA I OCEANIA
1:20,000,000
Warszawa: PPWK, 1972
60 x 43
Physical map showing relief, hydrography, political boundaries and communications.
Zl 3

THE PACIFIC AND ADJACENT AREAS
1:20,000,000
NZMS, 1969
see OCEANS: PACIFIC 265 E1

OCEANIA
1:12,500,000
Madrid: Aguilar
130 x 100
Physical school wall map showing hypsometric tints and altitude.
Paper 75 ptas
Cloth 250 ptas

OCÉANIE
1:9,000,000
Map No. 2
by P Vidal Lablache
Paris: Armand Colin
120 x 100
School wall map with outline base map on the reverse.

AUSTRALASIA
Indianapolis: Cram
Various col. school wall maps.
Level B Simplified Physical-Political
1:8,437,500 129 x 129 $23.00
Level C Physical-Political
1:8,437,500 129 x 129 $23.00
Physical Outline
1:8,437,500 129 x 129 $22.50

AUSTRALIA E OCEANIA FISICO-POLITICO
1:8,000,000
Novara: Ag
145 x 115
2 sheet school wall map, showing relief of land and sea, political boundaries, towns graded by pop.
First series L 3,000
Mounted L 6,000
Second series 1:7,000,000 (4 sheets)
175 x 200 L 4,000
Mounted L 8,500
Third series 1:10,000,000
100 x 140 L 2,200
Mounted L 5,000

AUSTRALIEN UND POLYNESIEN
1:6,000,000
Gotha: Haack
236 x 177
Physical school wall map, showing sea depths; relief shading of land, boundaries.

AUSTRALIEN UND OZEANIEN
1:6,000,000
Braunschweig: Westermann
206 x 176
Physical wall map, layer col, hachures, political boundaries, towns etc.

AUSTRALIEN UND OZEANIEN
1:6,000,000
No 9751
München: JRO
185 x 123
Physical wall map, with relief of land and sea. "Arbeitskarte" (2 colour base map with plastic writing surface) on reverse.
138 DM
No 9752 As above, without Arbeitskarte
128 DM

AUSTRALIEN UND OZEANIEN MIT MEERESBODENRELIEF
1:6,000,000
W715
München: List
240 x 170
Wenschow school wall map showing relief of land and sea in col, ocean currents; covers Australia, NZ, Indonesia, Indo-China, Pacific Island Groups.
164 DM

AUSTRALIE ET NOUVELLE ZÉLANDE
1:6,000,000
Bruxelles: Mantnieks
180 x 125
Physical wall map for schools showing relief by layer and bathy-metric colouring, direction of ocean currents, political boundaries in red. Also available in English.

AUSTRALIEN, INDONESIEN, OZEANIEN
1:5,000,000
H211
München: List
220 x 195

Harms school wall map, showing relief of land, ocean current directions, state boundaries. Sea depths indicated.
164 DM

AUSTRALIA AND THE PHILIPPINES
1:4,687,500
No 1301 01
Chicago: Denoyer-Geppert
111 x 147
Classroom map, physical-political, showing land detail, boundaries, pop. etc.
Rollers $15.50

AUSTRALIA E OCEANIA FISICO-POLITICO
1:10,000,000
Novara: Agostini
131 x 100
Moulded plastic relief map in frame with metal corners.
L 20,000

F GEOLOGY

TECTONIC MAP OF THE SOUTH WEST PACIFIC
1:10,000,000
NZMS, 1970
see OCEANS: PACIFIC 265 F

INTERNATIONAL GEOLOGICAL MAP OF THE WORLD – AUSTRALIA AND OCEANIA
1:5,000,000
In 14 sheets (incl. 1 reference sheet)
see index 9/1
Paris: Comm. for the Geol. Map of the World
44 x 55
Coloured geol. series in progress, each sheet containing legend.
Aus or NZ $1.00

H BIOGEOGRAPHY

AUSTRALIA AND NEW ZEALAND – VEGETATION
1:9,375,000
No 109061
Chicago: Denoyer-Geppert
111 x 162
4 thematic maps on 1 sheet. Shows Natural Vegetation.
$15.50

AUSTRALIEN UND OZEANIEN: WILDTIERE, WILDPFLANZEN, KULTUR
No scale given
Braunschweig: Westermann
127 x 96
Col. school pictorial wall map, showing wild plants and animals life styles. American edition by Denoyer-Geppert
at $5.00

AUSTRALIEN-INDONESIEN: VEGETATION UND TIERWELT
No scale given
No 9917
München: JRO
130 x 88
Pictorial wall map of vegetation and the animal kingdom. For schools.
48 DM

J CLIMATE

AUSTRALIA AND NEW ZEALAND
1:9,375,000
No 109101
Chicago: Denoyer-Geppert
111 x 162
4 thematic maps on 1 sheet. Shows climate – 9 climatic regions
$15.50

K HUMAN GEOGRAPHY

STILLEHAV-OMRADET
1:12,000,000
GI, 1970
see OCEANS: PACIFIC 265 K

AUSTRALIA AND NEW ZEALAND – POPULATION
1:9,375,000
No 109101
Chicago: Denoyer-Geppert
111 x 162
4 thematic maps on 1 sheet. Pop. density
$15.50

L ECONOMIC

AUSTRALIA AND NEW ZEALAND
1:9,375,000
No 109101
Chicago: Denoyer-Geppert
111 x 162
4 thematic maps on 1 sheet. Shows Economic Activities – land use, energy sources, mineral deposits.
$15.50

AUSTRALASIA
1:9,375,000
Brisbane: Dept. Lands
Showing railway systems and main telegraph lines.
60c

AVSTRALYA I NOVAYA ZELANDIYA, EKONOMICHESKAYA KARTA
1:6,000,000
Moskva: GUGK, 1973
2 sheet economic map Australia and New Zealand
28 kop

AUSTRALIEN-INDONESIEN: VERWALTUNG, WIRTSCHAFT UND VERKEHR
No scale given
No 9918
München: JRO
130 x 88
Pictorial wall map of admin, economy and communications.
48 DM

AUSTRALIEN UND OZEANIEN: WIRTSCHAFT UND VERKEHR
No scale given
Braunschweig: Westermann
127 x 96
Col. school pictorial wall map showing economy and communications American edition by Denoyer-Geppert
at $5.00

ATLASES
A1 GENERAL

DESCRIPTIVE ATLAS OF THE PACIFIC ISLANDS
T F Kennedy
Wellington: Reed, 1968
64pp
19 x 23
Covers Australia, New Zealand, Polynesia, Micronesia, Melanesia, Philippines; black and white maps with descriptions of pop, vegetation, economy, etc. Index. For use in schools in Pacific Is. Rev. ed.

910 Indonesia

A1 GENERAL MAPS: ROADS

INDONESIA
1:6,000,000
Tehran: Sahab
88 x 58
Sketch map showing boundaries bordered with col, relief by hachures, principal roads, railways, rivers, airports and airfields. Text and names in Eng. and Arabic.
100 Rls

KILOMETER AND TOURIST MAPS – DJAWA BALI
1:830,000 app.
Djakarta: Pembina, 1968/9
In 4 sheets
Road and general map of Java and Bali; roads classified, other communications, settlements, places of tourist interest, layer col, hill shading.

B TOWN PLANS

INDONESIA TOWN PLANS
Various scales
Djakarta: Pembina
Plans published:

Djakarta	1:20,000
Kebajoran	1:15,000
Surabaya	1:13,000

C OFFICIAL SURVEYS

INTERNATIONAL MAP OF THE WORLD
1:1,000,000
GSGS – AMS
About 30 sheets needed for complete coverage.
see WORLD 100 and index 100/1

PETA ICHTISAR TOPOGRAFI
1:250,000
In 270 sheets
Djakarta: Direktorat Topografi
General topografic series in progress, contours, road and rail communications, boundaries.

PETA TOPOGRAFI DASAR
1:100,000
1,600 sheets approx.
Djakarta: Direktorat Topografi
Basic topographic map series in progress, contours at 50m intervals.

PETA TOPOGRAFI DASAR
1:50,000
6,400 sheets approx.
Djakarta: Direktorat Topografi
Basic topographic map series in progress, contours at 25m intervals.

D POLITICAL & ADMINISTRATIVE

INDONESIYA
1:5,000,000
Moskva: GUGK, 1973
Political-admin. map. 15 kop

E1 PHYSICAL: RELIEF

ZADNI INDIE A INDONEZIE (INDO CHINA AND INDONESIA)
1:6,000,000
Kart
see INDO-CHINA 59 E1

THE WORLD
1:5,000,000
Sheet 9 – Indonesia
AGS
see WORLD 100 and index 100/3

INDONESIA, MALAYSIA, SINGAPURA
1:4,500,000
Djakarta: Pembina, 1968/9
116 x 76
Physical, layered, hill shading, boundaries, principal towns and communications.

HINTERINDIEN UND INDONESIEN
1:3,000,000
Perthes
see INDO-CHINA 596 E1

PETA DJAVA-MADURA
1:500,000
Djakarta: Pembina
245 x 117
Physical wall map of Java including the island of Madura.

E2 PHYSICAL: LAND FEATURES

A GEOMORPHOLOGICAL RECONNAISSANCE OF SUMATRA AND ADJACENT ISLANDS
by H. Th. Verstappen
Amsterdam: Royal Dutch Geog.Soc.
182pp.
Handbook containing coloured map – 1:2,500,000
Geomorphological Map.
73 x 34 with illustrations & diagrams.
Text in English.

F GEOLOGY

PETA GEOLOGI INDONESIA
1:2,000,000
USGS MGI-414
Bandung: Geol. Surv./USGS
292 x 108
Col. geol. map in 2 sheets, covering all the islands of Indonesian territory.
Per set $5.00

GEOLOGICAL MAP OF SOUTHEAST KALIMANTAN
1:500,000
Jakarta: Geol. Survey of Indonesia, 1970
Coloured geological map.

GEOLOGICAL MAP OF DJAWA AND MADURA
1:500,000
Bandung: Geol. Surv. Indonesia, 1963
215 x 80
2 sheet geological map in colour.

GEOLOGICAL MAP OF BALI
1:250,000
compiled by M M Purbo – Hadiwidjojo
Jakarta: Geol. Survey of Indonesia, 1971
Coloured geological map.

PETA HIDROGEOLOGI TINDJAU – RECONNAISANCE HYDRO-GEOLOGIC MAP OF BALI
1:250,000
Compiled by M M Purbo – Hadiwidjojo
Bandung: Geol. Survey of Indonesia, 1972.

H BIOGEOGRAPHY

VEGETATION MAP OF MALAYSIA
1:5,000,000
Compiled by C G G van Steenis
Groningen: E P Noordhoff and UNESCO, 1958
127 x 71
18 classifications of vegetation depicted in col. covering Malaya, Sarawak, Brunei, North Borneo, Philippines, South Celebes, East Timor and New Guinea.
For UNESCO Humid Tropics Research Project.

BANDUNG – LAND USE
1:250,000
Djakarta: Direktorat Land Use, 1971
46 x 63
Col. land use map.

LAND USE MAP OF BALI
1:250,000
Djakarta: Direktorat Land Use, 1971
61 x 58
Col. map, legend in Indonesian.

PENGGUNAAN TANAH (LAND USE)
1:50,000/100,000
Djakarta: Direktorat Land Use, 1969
Multi-sheet series for:

Bali	1:50,000
Java	1:50,000
Kalimantan	1:100,000
Sulawesi	1:50,000
Sumatra	1:50,000
Sumba	1:50,000
Timor	1:100,000

ATLASES
W3 WORLD ATLASES: LOCAL EDITIONS

ATLAS INDONESIA AND DUNIA
Eds. E. Latif and M J Ridway
Jakarta: Pembina, 1974
24 x 32
28pp
School atlas including 14pp of shaded relief maps of Indonesia showing towns and provincial boundaries and two plans and photographs (b & w) of Jakarta. Remainder of atlas, maps of World and continents with some photographs. No index, list of provinces.

ATLAS NASIONAL SELURUH DUMA UNTUK SEKOLAH LANDJUTAN (ATLAS NASIONAL TENTANG INDONESIA DAN SELURUH DUMA)
Ed J E Romein
Djakarta: Ganaco, 1960
24 x 38
72pp maps, inc. 29 world maps, showing rainfall, pop, ethnography etc. 22pp maps of Indonesia, also technical maps of other countries covering geol, economy, pop, vegetation. In Indonesian.

ATLASES
L ECONOMIC

ATLAS SUMBER KEMAKMURAN INDONESIA
1:5,000,000/10,000,000
Djakarta: Badan Atlas Nacional, 1965
112 x 53 (map size)
Atlas of Indonesian Resources. Series of 30 coloured maps including climate, economy, geol, agriculture, pop.

ATLAS INDONESIA BUKU KEDUA EKONOMI
Djakarta: Direktorat Land Use, 1971
24pp
35 x 35
33 economic maps for Indonesia. Text Indonesian. 3pp subject index.
Rp 900

914 Philippines

A1 GENERAL MAPS: ROADS

PHILIPPINE ROAD MAP
1:1,000,000
Washington: Defense Mapping Agency
76 x 102
2 sheet map; roads in red on white ground, railways, boundaries.
$1.00

B TOWN PLANS

MANILA AND SUBURBS
1:20,000
Manila: Bur. of Coast and Geodetic Surv, 1968
2nd edition
89 x 100
Shows and names principal sheets.

CITY OF MANILA
1:10,000
Manila: Div. of Drafting and Surveys.
Plan of the city streets.

C OFFICIAL SURVEYS

INTERNATIONAL MAP OF THE WORLD
1:1,000,000
GSGS – AMS
9 sheets cover country.
see WORLD 100C and index 100/1.

PHILIPPINES
1:250,000
In 55 sheets, see index 914/1
2nd edition
Washington: AMS/Manila: Bur. of Coast and Geodetic Surv.
Various sizes
New series, relief shading, contours, roads, other communications.
each P 2.50

TOPOGRAPHIC MAPS OF THE PHILIPPINES
1:200,000
Manila: Bur. of Coast and Geodetic Survey
Various sizes
Coloured topographic series:
Sheets published:

3 Northern Luzon – northern sheet 73 x 116 P 5.00
4 Northern Luzon – southern sheet 78 x 124 P 6.00
5 Central Luzon – western sheet 81 x 127 P 7.00
6 Central Luzon – eastern sheet 78 x 114 P 4.00
7 Southern Luzon – western sheet 89 x 111 P 7.00
8 Southern Luzon – central sheet 86 x 109 P 7.00
9 Southern Luzon –southern sheet 91 x 104 P 5.00
10 Mindoro 81 x 101 P 5.00
11 Romblon, Tablas and Sibuyan 76 x 81 P 3.00
12 Masbate 73 x 89 P 4.00
13 Samar 91 x 101 P 5.00
14 Leyte 61 x 111 P 5.00
15 Cebu and Bohol 83 x 109 P 7.00
16 Negros 81 x 116 P 7.00
17 Panay 89 x 96 P 4.00
50 Mindanao (1:600,000) 89 x 99 P 7.00

D POLITICAL & ADMINISTRATIVE

REPUBLIC OF THE PHILIPPINES
1:3,651,400
No 25
2nd edition
Manila: Bur. of Coast and Geodetic Surv. 1966 (1967)
43 x 56
Political map coloured by provinces, communications and boundaries.
P 1.00
Also available (No 26) in outline edition P 0.50

REPUBLIC OF THE PHILIPPINES
1:1,380,000
Manila: Juan, 1971
96 x 127
Political col. map US $10.00

PHILIPPINES
1:1,000,000
No 100
Manila: Bur. of Coast & Geodetic Surv.
127 x 198
Political map in 2 sheets, admin. boundaries, communications, relief shown by hachuring, place names list.
P 14.00
Also available in mounted form.
Black and white edition available
P 11.00

PROVINCIAL MAP OF THE PHILIPPINES
Various scales
Manila: Bureau of the Census
Shows municipal boundaries and districts, provincial roads.
P 15.00 ea.

CONGRESSIONAL DISTRICT MAP
Various scales
Manila: Bureau of the Census
Various sizes
Shows limits of congressional provincial districts, cities and municipalities in each, roads.
P 15.00 ea.

REGIONAL MAP
Various scales
In 10 sheets
Manila: Bureau of the Census
Various sizes
Map produced at different scales, showing the 10 census regions of the country.
P 15.00 ea.

MUNICIPAL ENUMERATION DISTRICT MAP
No scale given
Manila: Bureau of the Census
45 x 53
Shows extent of municipalities, enumeration districts, sheets marked and named. Series.
P 10.00 ea.

Enlarged edition also available, showing individual buildings.
26 x 40 P 5.00 ea.

MUNICIPAL DISTRICT, MUNICIPAL CITY MAPS
Various scales
Manila: Bureau of the Census
45 x 53
Shows barrios and cities within municipal districts; city maps show streets etc.
P 10.00 ea.

BARRIO MAP
No scale
Manila: Bureau of the Census
20 x 33
Sketch map of barrios, municipal districts with location and names of cities within each. Roads marked, buildings shown by symbols. Pop. data, etc.
Per sheet P 3.00

OUTLINE MAPS OF THE PHILIPPINES
Various scales
Manila: Bur. of Coast and Geodetic Survey
Maps published:

1:5,000,000 No 3083)
(Mercator proj)
28 x 43 P 0.50
1:2,500,000 No 3082
(Polyconic proj)
50 x 76 P 1.50
1:1,600,000 No 104
83 x 127 P 2.00

E1 PHYSICAL: RELIEF

FILIPPINI
1:3,000,000
Moskva: GUGK, 1973
60 x 71
Physical, col. study map showing water features, settlements, admin. centres and divisions, communications, boundaries, economic details, pop. Geog. description.
30 kop

PHILIPPINES
1:1,500,000
No 150
Manila: Bur. of Coast and Geodetic Survey, 1968
81 x 116
Physical map, contours, layer col, roads, railways, topog. details.
$1.00

F GEOLOGY

GEOLOGICAL MAP OF THE PHILIPPINES
1:1,000,000
In 8 sheets
Manila: Phil. Bureau Mines, 1963
66 x 44 each
Showing geol. of various islands in col.

G EARTH RESOURCES

MINERAL DISTRIBUTION MAP OF THE PHILIPPINES
1:2,500,000
Manila: Phil. Bureau Mines, 1973
68 x 74
Coloured map, classifying rock types in colour and minerals by col. symbols with Explanation: Information Circular No. 22 on Philippine Mineral Resources. 60pp. listing mines with details.

H BIOGEOGRAPHY

VEGETATION MAP OF MALAYSIA
1:5,000,000
E P Noordhoff and UNESCO, 1958
see MALAYSIA 595H

M HISTORICAL

PHILIPPINES 1945
1:2,937, 500
Washington: NGS
44 x 66
Political col. wall map, detailed place names.
Paper $2.00
Plastic $3.00

ATLASES
A1 GENERAL

DESCRIPTIVE ATLAS OF THE PACIFIC ISLANDS
T F Kennedy
see AUSTRALASIA, OCEANIA ATLASES 9 A1

ATLASES
K HUMAN GEOGRAPHY

ETHNOGRAPHIC ATLAS OF IFUAGO
Harold C Conklin
New York: AGS
76 x 86
First issue, 1972; 8 maps showing land drainage, relief, vegetation, types of cultivation, settlements, agricultural areas, etc.
$32.00

ATLASES
O NATIONAL

THE PHILIPPINE ATLAS
In 2 volumes
Makati: Fund for Assistance to Private Education, 1975
30 x 38
490pp.
A comprehensive survey of the geography, history, culture, education and economy of the Philippines in 105 coloured maps. 243 photographs. 145 graphs, charts, tables and 28 overlays.
US $110.00

ATLAS OF THE PHILIPPINES
R S Hendry
Manila: Phil-Asian Publishers Inc.
Basic Books, 1959
228pp.
32 x 49
Detailed national atlas with 28pp of maps devoted to the economy, resources, climate and social life of the country followed by 200pp devoted to detailed political maps of the 50 provinces each with description, gazetteer and photographs.
US $75.00

CENSUS ATLAS OF THE PHILIPPINES
Manila: Bureau of Census and Statistics
In preparation 1973
Collection of political and topographic maps, statistical data and information on economic activities, agriculture, fisheries and population for each region of the country.

923 Timor

F GEOLOGY

GEOLOGICAL MAP OF
PORTUGUESE TIMOR
1:250,000
London: Geol. Soc. 1968
114 x 63
Col. geol map with Memoir, 76pp.

931 New Zealand

See also: 94 AUSTRALIA

A1 GENERAL MAPS

NEW ZEALAND IN THE SOUTH PACIFIC (INCLUDING NZ ISLAND TERRITORY)
1:10,000,000
NZMS 231
2nd edition
Wellington: NZMS, 1970
60 x 75
Outline map of New Zealand and Ocean environs with 28 large scale island insets including New Hebrides, Tokelau Group, Ellice Islands, Fiji and Cook Islands.
60c

NEW ZEALAND
1:4,000,000
NZMS 134
Wellington: NZMS, 1969
5th edition
45 x 38
Towns, railways, mt. ranges in black, main roads red, water features blue, hypsometric tinting brown.
30c

NEW ZEALAND
1:4,000,000
NZMS 145
Wellington: NZMS, 1957
Towns, roads, rivers in black, relief indicated.
20c

NEW ZEALAND (WITH STEAMER ROUTES AND ISLAND TERRITORIES)
1:2,000,000
NZMS 84A
6th edition
Wellington: NZMS, 1969
60 x 79
Railways, steamer routes, roads, drainage features, boundaries; New Zealand and Island Territories inset.
60c

NOVAYA ZELANDIYA
1:2,000,000
Moskva: GUGK, 1973
Col. study map showing water features, settlements, communications, admin. centres and divisions, boundaries, economic detail, pop. Geog. description.
30 kop

A2 GENERAL MAPS: LOCAL

OTOROHANGA COUNTY
1:300,000
NZMS 191
2nd edition
Wellington: NZMS, 1965
Names, towns, boundaries, roads classified.

TOURIST MAPS OF NEW ZEALAND
Various scales
Wellington: NZMS
Maps published:
THERMAL REGIONS OF NEW ZEALAND (Rotorua-Taupo areas)
1:380,160
NZMS 50
1968 60c
TARARUA MOUNTAIN SYSTEM
1:100,000
NZMS 57
6th edition, 1972 40c
MARLBOROUGH SOUNDS
1:100,000
NZMS 236
1st edition
1969 70c
RUAPEHU SKI FIELDS
1:12,500
NZMS 221
1969 50c
LAKE TAUPO AND ENVIRONS
1:80,000
NZMS 116
1967 70c
BAY OF ISLANDS
1:80,000
NZMS 151
3rd edition, 1972 50c
LAKE WAIKAREMOANA
1:40,000
NZMS 239
1968 45c
ROTORUA LAKES
1:63,360
NZMS 152
3rd edition, 1972 70c
STEWART ISLAND
1:126,720
NZMS 219
2nd edition, 1968 60c
LAKE TE ANAU AND ENVIRONS
1:200,000
NZMS 155
4th edition, 1972 70c
LAKE WAKATIPU AND ENVIRONS
1:200,000
NZMS 156
3rd edition, 1972 70c
WANGANUI RIVER
1:190,080
NZMS 258
1st edition
Wellington: NZMS 1973
76 x 41
A perspective view of the Wanganui River showing place names, tourist and historic information, huts and hill shading. NZ$ 0.50
WANGAPEKA TRACK
1:126,720
NZMS 233
2nd edition, 1971 50c

NATIONAL PARK MAPS
Various scales
Wellington: NZMS
Maps published:
FIORDLAND NATIONAL PARK
1:300,000
NZMS 122
4th edition, 1968 70c
WALKS IN THE CHATEAU AREA, TONGARIRO NATIONAL PARK
1:13,850
NZMS 186
1968 30c
TONGARIRO NATIONAL PARK
1:80,000
NZMS 150
3rd edition, 1969 70c
HEAPHY TRACK
1:63,360
NZMS 245
1st edition, 1971 40c
NELSON LAKES NATIONAL PARK
1:100,000
NZMS 164
3rd edition, 1972 60c
EGMONT NATIONAL PARK
1:40,000
NZMS 169
1968 70c
UREWERA NATIONAL PARK
1:100,000
NZMS 170
3rd edition, 1971 70c
WESTLAND AND MT COOK NATIONAL PARKS
1:100,000
NZMS 180
1964 50c
KAIMANAWA FOREST PARK
1:63,360
Wellington: NZ Forest Service
FSMS 3
1971 $1.50
ARTHURS PASS NATIONAL PARK
1:100,000
NZMS 194
4th edition, 1971 60c
ABEL TASMAN NATIONAL PARK
1:40,000
NZMS 183
1969 70c

B TOWN PLANS

TOWN PLANS
NZMS 17
Wellington: NZMS
NORTH ISLAND
Auckland
1:20,000 1968 50c
Auckland South
1:20,000 1969 45c
Auckland West
1:20,000 1972 45c
Dannevirke
1:7,920 1959 45c
Gisborne and Wairoa
1:12,500 1970 45c
Hamilton, Ngaruawahia, Te Awamutu, Cambridge, Huntly
1:20,000 1968 45c
Hastings, Havelock North, Waipukurau
1:15,000 1973 45c
Hawera, Stratford, Eltham, Patea
1:12,500 1968 45c
Hutt Valley
1:20,000 1973 50c
Manurewa and Papakura
1:20,000 1972 45c
Masterton, Carterton, Greytown, Featherston, Martinborough
1:10,000 1972 45c

Napier and Taradale
1:12,500 1970 45c
New Plymouth, Waitara, Inglewood, Oakura
1:12,500 1969 45c
North Shore (Auckland)
1:20,000 1972 50c
Palmerston North
1:12,500 1973 45c
Paraparaumu
1:15,000 1972 45c
Porirua
1:12,500 1972 45c
Rotorua
1:12,500 1970 45c
Tokoroa and Taupo
1:12,500 1966 45c
Tauranga and Mt Maunganui
1:17,500 1971 45c
Wanganui and Marton
1:15,000 1970 45c
Wellington
1:20,000 1960 50c
Whakatante, Kawerau, Murupara, Opotiki, Edgecumbe, Ohope
1:15,000 1970 45c
Whangarei
1:12,500 1968 45c
SOUTH ISLAND
Ashburton 1966
1:12,500 45c
Blenheim and Picton
1:10,000 1973 45c
Christchurch
1:20,000 1972 50c
Dunedin
1:20,000 1972 50c
Greymouth
1:12,500 1969 45c
Invercargill, Bluff, Gore, Mataura, and Riverton
1:17,500 1970 45c
Nelson
1:20,000 1970 45c
Oamaru
1:12,500 1971 45c
Queenstown, Frankton, Arrowtown
1:12,000 1972 45c
Timaru
1:12,500 1971 45c

TOWN MAP SERIES
1:1,584/7,920
NZMS 16
Wellington: NZMS
Show land subdivisions, boundaries in detail, topog. features, streets, buildings etc. Some gridded for ref. purposes.
app. $1.00 each

NORTH ISLAND

Ashhurst	1:3168
Athenree	1:3960
Atiamuri	1:3960
Bulls	1:7920
Cambridge	1:7920
Coromandel	1:4752
Edgecumbe	1:7920
Featherston	1:4752
Horopito	1:1584
Horopito West	1:3168
Hunterville	1:3960
Huntly	1:6336
Karewarewa Village	1:3960
Kawerau	1:7920
Kiwitea	1:4752
Kuaotunu	1:1584
Leamington	1:7920
Maketu	1:7920
Makohine Village	1:3960
Mamaku	1:3960
Mangakino	1:4752
Mangaweka	1:3960
Matamata	1:7920
Matata	1:3960
Morrinsville	1:7920
Mount Maunganui	1:7920
Murupara	1:4752
Ngaruawahia	1:7920
Ngatea	1:6336
Ninia	1:2376
Ohope	1:3960
Omokoroa Beach	1:3960
Opunake	1:3960
Otorohanga	1:7920
Owhango	1:1584
Paeroa	1:7920
Piopio	1:3960
Pipiroa	1:3960
Pirongia	1:3960
Putaruru	1:7920
Rongotea	1:2376
Rotowaro	1:3960
Taneatua	1:3960
Tangimoana	1:1584
Taupiri	1:3960
Taupo	1:7920
Tauranga	1:7920
Te Aroha	1:7920
Thames	1:7920
Tokoroa	1:7920
Turua	1:3960
Waharoa	1:3960
Waihi	1:7920
Waihi Beach	1:7920
Waikino	1:3960
Waimarino	1:2376
Waiouru	1:2376
Waverley	1:3960
Whakatane	1:7920
Whangamata	1:7920
Whitianga	1:7920

SOUTH ISLAND

Akaroa	1:1584
Albury	1:1584
Allanton	1:3168
Amberley	1:3960
Ahaura	1:1584
Arahura Pa	1:2376
Arawhata (Jackson Bay)	1:1584
Arthur's Pass	1:1584
Arundel	1:3168
Ashburton	1:1584
Ashley	1:1584
Barrys Bay	1:1584
Belfast	1:3960
Berwick	1:3960
Blackball	1:3168
Blueskin (Waitati)	1:3168
Brunner (Dobson and Taylorville)	1:1584
Camerons	1:2376
Cave	1:2376
Chertsey	1:1584
Cheviot	1:3960
Christchurch (part)	1:1584
Christchurch (New Brighton, Riccarton, Sumner)	1:7920
Clinton	1:6336
Coalgate	1:2376
Culverden	1:3960
Cust	1:2376
Darfield	1:1584
Diamond Harbour	1:1584
Dobson	1:1584
Domett	1:3960
Dunkeld (Beaumont)	1:6336
Duvauchelle	1:3960
Fairlie	1:1584
Geraldine	1:3960
Gladstone	1:1584
Glenavy	1:2376
Gore Bay	1:1584
Governors Bay	1:2376
Halswell (see Christchurch)	1:1584
Hampden	1:6336
Hanmer	1:2376
Harihari	1:3960
Harwarden	1:2376
Havelock	1:3960
Hermitage	1:1584
Hinds	1:7920
Hornby (see Christchurch)	1:2376
Hororata	1:1584
Hurunui	1:7920
Kaiata and Omoto	1:2376
Kaitangata	1:7920
Kaniere	1:2376
Kirwee	1:3960
Kokatahi	1:3960
Kumara	1:3168
Lawrence	1:3960
Leeston	1:2376
Leithfield	1:1584
Lincoln	1:1584
Little Akaloa	1:1584
Little River	1:3960
Lyttelton (part only)	1:1584
Mayfield	1:2376
Methven	1:2376
Mina	1:1980
Moana	1:3960
Moeraki	1:3960
Morven	1:1584
Motunau Beach	1:1584
Motunau and Environs	1:3960
Mount Somers	1:2376
Nelson Creek (Hatters Terrace)	1:1584
New Brighton (see Christchurch)	1:7920
Ngahere	1:2376
Okarito	1:1908
Orari	1:2376
Otira	1:2376
Outram	1:6336
Oxford	1:1584
Palmerston	1:6336
Pareora	1:1584
Paroa	1:1584
Pleasant Point	1:3960
Prebbleton	1:2376
Pukaki	1:2376
Punakaiki	1:3960
Purakanui	1:3960
Rakaia	1:3168
Rakaia Village	1:3960
Rapahoe	1:1584
Riccarton (see Christchurch)	1:7920
Roa	1:1584
Rolleston	1:2376
Ross	1:2376
Rotherham	1:7920
Runanga	1:3960
Scargill	1:3960
Seddon	1:3168
Sefton	1:1584
Sheffield	1:3960
Sockburn (see Christchurch)	1:2376
Southbridge	1:1584
Spotswood	1:2376
Springfield	1:3960
St Andrews	1:1584
Sumner (see Christchurch)	1:7920
Taitapu	1:1584
Taylorville	1:1584
Tekapo	1:3960
Templeton (see Christchurch)	1:2376
Timaru	1:1584
Waiau	1:1584
Waiho Gorge (Franz Josef Glacier)	1:1960
Waikari	1:2376
Waikouaiti (Hawkesbury)	1:6336
Waikouaiti (Karitane)	1:7920
Wainui	1:2376
Weheka (Fox Glacier)	1:2376
Weld (Bruce Bay)	1:7920
Whataroa (including Matainui)	1:1584

Winchester	1:2376
Winslow	1:3168

NZ CADASTRAL MAP – TOWN SERIES
1:4752/6336
NZMS 189
Wellington: NZMS
76 x 101
Land subdivisions, roads, railways, streets named, buildings, local authority boundaries etc. Not all sheets published yet in multi-sheet series. Available in the following sheets:

NORTH ISLAND

Ashhurst	1:4752
Auckland (58 sheets)	1:6336
Bulls	1:4752
Carterton	1:6336
Dannevirke	1:6336
Dargaville (2 sheets)	1:6336
Eketahuna	1:6336
Eltham	1:6336
Featherston	1:6336
Feilding (2 sheets)	1:6336
Foxton	1:6336
Gisborne (2 sheets)	1:6336
Greytown (6 sheets)	1:6336
Hamilton Series (6 sheets)	1:6336
Hawera	1:6336
Helensville	1:4752
Hunterville	1:4752
Inglewood	1:3168
Kaikohe	1:4752
Kaitaia	1:4752
Katikati	1:4752
Kawhia	1:4752
Kihikihi	1:4752
Levin	1:6336
Mangakino (2 sheets)	1:4752
Mangaweka	1:4752
Martinborough	1:6336
Marton	1:6336
Masterton (2 sheets)	1:6336
Murupara	1:4752
Napier Series (25 sheets)	1:6336
New Plymouth Series (14 sheets)	1:6336
Ohakune	1:6336
Ohaupo (2 sheets)	1:4752
Omokoroa Beach	1:4752
Opotiki	1:6336
Orewa	1:4752
Otaki	1:6336
Pahiatua	1:6336
Palmerston North (4 sheets)	1:6336
Pukekohe	1:6336
Raetihi	1:6336
Raglan (2 sheets)	1:4752
Rotorua Series (10 sheets)	1:6336
Ruatoria	1:4752
Shannon	1:6336
Stratford	1:4752
Taihape	1:6336
Taumarunui (2 sheets)	1:6336
Tauranga Series (13 sheets)	1:6336
Te Awamutu	1:4752
Te Kauwhata	1:4752
Te Kuiti	1:6336
Te Puke (2 sheets)	1:4752
Tirau	1:4752
Tuakau	1:6336
Turangi	1:4752
Waipawa	1:6336
Waipukurau	1:6336
Wairoa	1:6336
Waiuku	1:6336
Wanganui (4 sheets)	1:6336
Wellington Series (47 sheets)	1:6336
Whangamata (2 sheets)	1:4752
Whitianga (3 sheets)	1:4752
Woodville	1:6336
Whangarei (4 sheets)	1:6336

SOUTH ISLAND

Akaroa	1:4752
Albertown	1:4752
Alexandra	1:6336
Arrowtown	1:4752
Balclutha	1:6336
Balfour	1:4752
Blenheim (2 sheets)	1:6336
Bluff	1:6336
Christchurch Series (23 sheets)	1:6336
Clyde	1:6336
Cromwell	1:6336
Dipton	1:4752
Dunedin (17 sheets)	1:6336
Edendale	1:4752
Fairlie	1:4752
Frankton	1:4752
Geraldine	1:6336
Glenorchy	1:4752
Gore (5 sheets)	1:4752
Greymouth (including Karoro and South beach)	1:6336
Hanmer Springs	1:6336
Hokitika	1:6336
Hull	1:4752
Invercargill Series (15 sheets)	1:6336
Kaiapoi	1:6336
Kaitangata	1:4752
Kaikoura	1:6336
Kingston	1:4752
Kurow	1:4752
Lincoln	1:4752
Lumsden (2 sheets)	1:4752
Maheno	1:4752
Mataura	1:4752
Mossburn	1:4752
Motueka (2 sheets)	1:6336
Naseby	1:4752
Nelson (7 sheets)	1:6336
Nightcaps	1:4752
Oamaru (2 sheets)	1:6336
Ohai	1:4752
Otautau	1:4752
Picton	1:6336
Queenstown	1:6336
Rangiora	1:6336
Reefton	1:6336
Riverdale	1:4752
Riverton (3 sheets)	1:4752
Saint Bathams	1:4752
Takaka	1:6336
Te Anau	1:4752
Temuka	1:6336
Tuatapere	1:4752
Waihola	1:6336
Waimate	1:6336
Wanaka	1:6336
Westport	1:6336
Winton	1:6336
Wyndham	1:4752

C OFFICIAL SURVEYS

INTERNATIONAL MAP OF THE WORLD
1:1,000,000
3 sheets for coverage of New Zealand:

SK 59	Christchurch
SL 58	Fiords
SL 59	Dunedin

see WORLD 100C and index 100/1.

NEW ZEALAND
1:500,000
NZMS 19
2nd edition
In 7 sheets, see index 931/1
Wellington: NZMS
80 x 48
Contours, layer col, roads and railways classified, towns and villages, mines, plantations etc.
75c

REGIONAL PLANNING MAPS
1:253,440
NZMS 51
In 8 sheets
Wellington: NZMS, 1947
Black and white base map showing topog. and water features, contours, roads, with paper overlays for (1) vegetation and pop. density from 1945 census and (2) areas of land slope classified.
4 sheets published: Auckland, Wellington, Canterbury, Southland.

NEW ZEALAND TERRITORIAL SERIES
1:253,440
NZMS 10
In 35 sheets, see index 931/3
Wellington: NZMS
76 x 55
Black and white, showing topog. features, railways, roads, water features, trigonometric heights, uncontoured.
50c each
With County Boundaries overprinted in red, NZMS 10A.

NEW ZEALAND
1:250,000
NZMS 18
In 26 sheets, see index 931/2
Wellington: NZMS
84 x 43
Contoured, relief shading, detailed land information.
75c

NEW ZEALAND TERRITORIAL SERIES
1:250,000
NZMS 159
In 26 sheets, see index 931/2
Wellington: NZMS
New series in preparation. Black and white, topog. details, railways, roads, water features, coast and fathom lines, graticule cuts. Available with County Overprint, NZMS 159A.

NEW ZEALAND
1:63,300
NZMS 1
see index 931/1
Wellington: NZMS
65 x 43
Detailed series in progress, contoured, col. with land information, relief shading on some sheets.
70c

NEW ZEALAND CADASTRAL MAP
1:63,360
NZMS 177
Wellington: NZMS
71 x 55
Large scale series in col. showing land section areas, districts, boundaries, Maori areas, roads, railways, land cover, water features. Overprint showing registration districts and boundaries.
75c

NEW ZEALAND
1:25,000
NZMS 2
Wellington: NZMS
65 x 43

Detailed topographical series in progress, contoured, coloured showing roads, railways, admin. and land boundaries and land information.
60c

TOPOGRAPHICAL SERIES
1:15,840
NZMS 86
Wellington: NZMS
76 x 101
Col. topog. series; roads, names, vegetation, contours at 50ft intervals. 25 sheets published for area between Lake Tarpo and Rotorua and Bay of Plenty.

NEW ZEALAND MOSAIC MAP SERIES
1:15,840
NZMS 3
Wellington: NZMS
91 x 66
Photog. prints showing topog. features with names in white. Based on 1:25,000 sheet lines. Most urban areas are published.
$6.00

NEW ZEALAND – TOPOGRAPHIC MAP EXTRACTS SET 4
Selected A M Winter
Christchurch: Whitcomb and Tombs, 1968
32 x 37 each
Series of map extracts for school exercise purposes:
1 Ngaruawahia, North Is. 1:63,360 1965
2 Ngauruhoe, North Is. 1:25,000 1963
3 Wellington, North Is. 1:63,360 1962
4 Christchurch and Banks Peninsula, South Is. 1:250,000 1958
5 Lake Tekapo, South Is. 1:63,360 1965
6 Mt Cook, South Is. 1:100,000 1964
7 Mosgiel, South Is. 1:63,360 1965

D POLITICAL & ADMINISTRATIVE

NEW ZEALAND
1:8,000,000
NZMS 176
Wellington: NZMS, 1964
25 x 20
Outline map showing main cities, roads, railways in black.
10c

PHILIP'S LARGE OUTLINE MAP OF AUSTRALIA AND NEW ZEALAND
1:6,350,000
London: Philip
108 x 83
Coastlines and inter-state boundaries printed in black on white cartridge paper.
£1.25

PHILIP'S MAP BUILDING SHEET ('BLACKBOARD MAP') OF AUSTRALIA AND NEW ZEALAND
1:6,350,000
London: Philip
104 x 83
Same information as map above but printed in yellow on blackboard paper.
Mounted CR £4.00

NEW ZEALAND SKELETON MAP
1:4,000,000
NZMS 140
Wellington: NZMS, 1966
33 x 40
County boundaries in black.
10c

NEW ZEALAND
1:2,000,000
NZMS 146
Wellington: NZMS, 1958
70 x 91
Outline map showing principal topog. features in black, pop. indicated. Black and white.
40c

NEW ZEALAND
1:2,000,000
NZMS 216
2nd edition
Wellington: NZMS, 1970
48 x 55
2 sheets, North and South Islands. Topog. features, black and white.
30c each

NEW ZEALAND SKELETON MAP
1:2,000,000
NZMS 139
Wellington: NZMS, 1968
60 x 86
2 sheet map showing boundaries in 1 col.
30c each

PHILIP'S POLITICAL SMALLER WALL MAP OF NEW ZEALAND
1:1,500,000
London: Philip
82 x 102
Countries in differing col, showing railways, shipping routes, towns graded by pop.
Paper £1.50
Mounted CR £5.50
Mounted on cloth dissected to fold £7.00

NEW ZEALAND: LANDS TENURE MAP
1:1,013,760
NZMS 187
2nd edition
Wellington: NZMS, 1962
73 x 88
Shows land tenures in 1950 – Maori land yellow, Crown leasehold grey, state forest blue, reserves red, freehold green, Crown land white.

NEW ZEALAND
1:1,000,000
NZMS 138
Wellington: NZMS, 1957
101 x 76
Outline map showing towns, main communications, spot heights. 2 sheet map. Black and white.
40c
Also available with red County overprint, NZMS 138A, 5th edition, 1970
50c

E1 PHYSICAL: RELIEF

MAP OF NEW ZEALAND
1:2,000,000
NZMS 84
Wellington: NZMS, 1966
60 x 79
Contoured, layer col, relief shading, communications, towns graded by pop.
Paper flat or folded 60c

BARTHOLOMEW'S WORLD TRAVEL MAP SERIES: NEW ZEALAND
1:2,000,000
Edinburgh: Bart. 1971
52 x 71
Contoured, layer col, communications, airports. Insets of Auckland, Wellington, Christchurch, Dunedin and their environs; Kermadec, Auckland, Campbell, Chatham, Bounty and Antipodes Islands and the Snares.
75p

NEW ZEALAND
1:2,000,000
AMS 9201
Washington: Defense Mapping Agency
81 x 111
Topographic map, contoured and layer coloured based upon NZMS 84 survey map.
$1.00

PHYSICAL MAP OF NEW ZEALAND
1:1,637,000
NZMS 232
Wellington: NZMS, 1966
50 x 81
Hill shading, roads, railways, settlements, indicating pop.
50c

PHILIP'S PHYSICAL SMALLER WALL MAP OF NEW ZEALAND
1:1,500,000
London: Philip, 1968
82 x 102
Physical layer col, boundaries, principal communications.
Paper £1.50
Mounted CR £5.50
Mounted on cloth dissected to fold £7.00

PHILIP'S PHYSICAL SMALLER WALL MAP OF NEW ZEALAND
1:1,000,000
Sheets: North Island, South Island
London: Philip
84 x 109 each sheet
2 separate physically coloured maps with layer colouring, boundaries and principal communications.
Paper £1.50
Mounted CR £5.50
Mounted on cloth dissected to fold £7.00

F GEOLOGY

TECTONIC MAP OF THE SOUTH WEST PACIFIC
1:10,000,000
Dept. of Scientific and Industrial Research, 1971
see PACIFIC 265 F

INTERNATIONAL GEOLOGICAL MAP OF THE WORLD – AUSTRALIA AND OCEANIA
1:5,000,000
Sheet 13 covers New Zealand
Compiled: Lower Hutt: Geol. Surv. NZ, 1971
Paris: Comm. for the Geol. Map of the World.
NZ $1.00 each
see AUSTRALIA AND OCEANIA 9 F

GEOLOGICAL MAP OF NEW ZEALAND
1:2,000,000
Wellington: NZ Geol. Surv, 1958
64 x 80
Detailed col. map with separate sheet of cross sections.
Paper folded in cover $1.50

NEW ZEALAND – GEOLOGICAL SURVEY MAPS
1:250,000
In 28 sheets, see index 931/4
Wellington: Geol. Survey, 1959+ Col. geol. series. Each sheet has explanatory text.
NZ $2.00 each

GEOLOGICAL SERIES OF NEW ZEALAND
1:63,360
see index 931/1
Wellington: Geol. Surv, 1959+
65 x 43 each
Geol. series on topog, sheet lines. Each sheet has text. The following sheets are available:
N52 – 1968, N55 – 1966, N56 – 1966, N65 – 1965, N134, 135 and N141, 142 – 1971, S1, 3 and pt. 4 – 1971, S2 – 1968, S8 – 1971, S105 – 1961, S159 – 1965, S169 – 1968, S184 – 1961
NZ $0.50 each

LATE QUATERNARY TECTONIC MAPS
1:63,360
see index 931/1
Wellington: Department Sci. and Indust. Research, 1969+
65 x 43
Series showing late quaternary information on same sheet lines as topog. series. Sheets available:

1970	N153	Eketahuna
1969	N158	Masterton

NZ $0.50 each

W N BENSON MAP OF DUNEDIN DISTRICT
1:50,000
New Zealand Geol. Survey Miscellaneous Series
Wellington: NZGS, 1969
93 x 70
Geol. map with booklet covering sheets S164 and parts of S155 and S163.
NZ $1.00

INDUSTRIAL MAP SERIES
1:25,000
see index 931/1
Wellington: NZGS, 1965+
Series in progress. Showing geol. on aerial mosaic bases. Text with each sheet. On same sheet lines as topog. series. Sheets available:
N42/2, 4, 5, 8, N65/2.
NZ $0.50 each

G EARTH RESOURCES

SOIL MAP OF NEW ZEALAND
1:2,000,000
Wellington: Dept. Sci. and Indust. Research, 1948
Coloured soil map.
NZ $0.30

SOIL MAP OF NEW ZEALAND
1:1,000,000
In 2 sheets – North and South
Wellington: NZGS, 1965
North Is. 65 x 96
South Is. 76 x 91
Coloured, showing detailed soil classifications.

SOIL MAP OF NEW ZEALAND
1:250,000
In 21 sheets
Wellington: Dept. of Sci. and Indust. Research
Col. series. Of the 8 sheets covering North Is. sheets 1 – 5 only are available. South Is. is available in 13 sheets with legend.
North Is. 1945 NZ $0.30 each
South Is. 1965 NZ $0.50 each

SEDIMENTS OF COASTAL AREAS
1:200,000
Wellington: Oceanographic Inst, 1966+
Series in progress, covering coastal areas. Sheets available:

Foveaux	1966
Pegasus	1966
Mahia	1968
Patea	1970
Turnagain	1970

NZ $0.50 each

SOIL BUREAU MAPS
Various scales
Wellington: Dept. Sci. Indust. Research
Available for the following areas:
Heretaunga Plains (2 sheets)
1:25160 1938
Wairau Plains
1:63360 1938
Part Waipa County (5 sheets)
1:63360 1939
Erosion and Soil Map of High County – South Is. (2 sheets)
1:500,000 1944
Green Island, Kaitangata District
1:63360 1946
Awatere, Kaikoura and Marlborough Counties (Provisional)
1:250,000 1948
Whangarei County (4 sheets)
1:63360 1948
Lower Clutha Plains
1:31680 1954
Part Geraldine County (4 sheets)
1:31680 1954
Matakoa County
1:126,720 1954
Downs and Plains, Canterbury and North Otago (6 sheets)
1:126,720 1954
Oroua Downs and Part Glen Oroua
1:15,840 1954
Ellesmere County (2 sheets)
1:32,680 1957
Gisborne Plains (7 sheets)
1:15,840 1959
Kaingaroa State Forest
1:63,360 1961
Alexandra District (2 sheets)
1:15,840 1963
Waimea County
1:126,720 1965
Part Maniototo Plains (2 sheets)
1:32,680 1965
Flock House Farm, Rangitikei County
1:15,840 1965
Whareama Catchment, Wairarapa (Provisional)
1:126,720 1965
Heathcote County
1:63,360 1965
Greytown District
1:15,840 1966
Taita Experimental Station
1:2,476 1967
Ida Valley (2 sheets)
1:32,680 1967
Upper Clutha Valley (3 sheets)
1:32,680 1967
Manawatu-Rangitikei Sand County (2 sheets)
1:63360 1967

SOIL FOLDERS
1:31,680
Wellington: Dept. Sci and Indust. Research, 1971
Sets published:
Soil, Agriculture, Horticultural Maps, legend of part Paparua County, Canterbury, New Zealand. With text.

Set	$2.00
Map, legend, notes	$1.10
Map	$0.60

Soil Maps and Extended legend of mid Manu-Hereika Valley, Central Otago, New Zealand. With notes.

Set	$2.00
Map, legend, notes	$1.40
Map	$0.60

SINGLE FACTOR SOIL MAPS
Wellington: Dept. Sci. and Indust. Research
24 x 27
Maps printed in colour and 3 hole punched for use in ring binder.
Abbreviations: N for North Island, S for South Island, SV for Sweet Vernal Composition.
Sheets available:

1 pH in Topsoils (N)
2 pH in Topsoils (S)
3 pH in Subsoils (N)
4 pH in Subsoils (S)
5 Base Saturation in Topsoils (N)
6 Base Saturation in Topsoils (S)
7 Base Saturation in Subsoils (N)
8 Base Saturation in Subsoils (S)
9 Cation-exchange Capacity of Topsoils (N)
10 Cation-exchange Capacity of Topsoils (S)
11 Cation-exchange Capacity of Subsoils (N)
12 Cation-exchange Capacity of Subsoils (S)
13 Citric-soluble Phosphorus in Topsoils (N)
14 Citric-soluble Phosphorus in Topsoils (S)
15 Citric-soluble Phosphorus in Subsoils (N)
16 Citric-soluble Phosphorus in Subsoils (S)
17 Exchangeable Calcium in Topsoils (N)

18 Exchangeable Calcium in Topsoils (S)
19 Exchangeable Calcium in Subsoils (N)
20 Exchangeable Calcium in Subsoils (S)
21 Exchangeable Magnesium in Topsoils (N)
22 Exchangeable Magnesium in Topsoils (S)
23 Exchangeable Magnesium in Subsoils (N)
24 Exchangeable Magnesium in Subsoils (S)
25 Total Potassium in Topsoils (N)
26 Total Potassium in Topsoils (S)
27 Exchangeable Potassium in Topsoils (N)
28 Exchangeable Potassium in Topsoils (S)
29 Exchangeable Potassium in Subsoils (B horizons) (N)
30 Exchangeable Potassium in Subsoils (B horizons) (S)
31 Potassium-supplying Power of Topsoils (N)
32 Potassium-supplying Power of Topsoils (S)
33 Total Molybdenum in Topsoils (N)
34 Total Molybdenum in Topsoils (S)
35 Available (SV) Molybdenum in Soils (N)
36 Available (SV) Molybdenum in Soils (S)
37 Total Boron in Topsoils (N)
38 Total Boron in Topsoils (S)
41 Total Copper in Topsoils (N)
42 Total Copper in Topsoils (S)
45 Total Strontium in Topsoils (N)
46 Total Strontium in Topsoils (S)
49 Organic Matter in Topsoils (N)
50 Organic Matter in Topsoils (S)
51 Total Nitrogen in Topsoils (N)
52 Total Nitrogen in Topsoils (S)
53 Carbon/Nitrogen Ratio in Topsoils (N)
54 Carbon/Nitrogen Ratio in Topsoils (S)
55 Phosphate Extracted by nH_2SO_4 from Topsoils (N)
56 Phosphate Extracted by nH_2SO_4 from Topsoils (S)
57 Growth of Sweet Vernal Grass on Untopdressed Soils (N)
58 Growth of Sweet Vernal Grass on Untopdressed Soils (S)
59 Available (SV) Sodium in Soils (N)
60 Available (SV) Sodium in Soils (S)
61 Total Cobalt in Topsoils (N)
62 Total Cobalt in Topsoils (S)
65 Total Manganese in Topsoils (N)
66 Total Manganese in Topsoils (S)
69 Total Titanium in Topsoils (N)
70 Total Titanium in Topsoils (S)
71 Total Chromium in Topsoils (N)
72 Total Chromium in Topsoils (S)
73 Total Phosphorus in Untopdressed Topsoils (N)
74 Total Phosphorus in Untopdressed Topsoils (S)
75 Phosphate Retention by Topsoils (N)
76 Phosphate Retention by Topsoils (S)
77 Phosphorus in Sweet Vernal Grass on Untopdressed Topsoils (N)
78 Phosphorus in Sweet Vernal Grass on Untopdressed Topsoils (S)
81 Exchangeable Potassium in Subsoils (C horizons) (N)
82 Exchangeable Potassium in Subsoils (C horizons) (S)
89 Total Selenium in Topsoils (N)
90 Total Selenium in Topsoils (S)

10c each

GRAVITY MAP OF NEW ZEALAND
1:4,000,000
Comp. W I Reilly
Wellington: Geol. Surv.

NZ $1.00

GRAVITY MAPS OF NEW ZEALAND
1:250,000
Wellington: NZMS, 1965+
Shows Bouguer and Isostatic anomalies.
The following sheets are available:

1	North Cape	1965
2A	Whangarei	1965
3	Auckland	1971
4	Hamilton	1971
25	Dunedin	1969
26	Stewart Is.	1971
27	Christchurch	1966

NZ $1.00

MAGNETIC MAPS OF NEW ZEALAND
1:250,000
Wellington: Geol. Surv, 1969+
Series in progress showing Total Force Anomalies. Sheets available:

1	North Cape	1969
13	Golden Bay	1971
14	Marlborough Sounds	
15	Buller	1970
16	Kaikoura	1970
18	Hurunui	1970

NZ $0.50 each

H BIOGEOGRAPHY

LAND UTILISATION, WEST COAST (SOUTH ISLAND)
1:253,440
NZMS 154
1st edition
In 11 sheets
Wellington: NZMS, 1959
66 x 61
Boundaries, developed and undeveloped land, indexed with insets.

SOIL BUREAU MAPS
Various scales
Wellington: Dept. of Sci. and Indust. Research
Maps available:
Whangarei County: Land Use (1940-41)
1:63,360 1948
Potential Pastoral Uses, Matakaoa County
1:126,720 1954
Botanical Survey of the Taita Catchment (4 sheets)
1:1,584 1957

L ECONOMIC

GREAT CIRCLE DISTANCES AND AZIMUTHS FROM WELLINGTON TO ALL PARTS OF THE WORLD
1:90,000,000
see WORLD 100M

ATLASES
W3 WORLD ATLASES: LOCAL EDITIONS:

OXFORD ATLAS FOR NEW ZEALAND
OUP, 1966
see ATLASES 100 W WORLD

JACARANDA ATLAS FOR NEW ZEALAND
1st edition
Brisbane: Jacaranda Press, 1971
22 x 28
144pp
Secondary school atlas, covering physical geog, land use in 124pp maps. Index and col. photographs.

$2.95

ATLASES
A1 GENERAL

AA ROAD ATLAS OF NEW ZEALAND
Auckland: Paul Hamlyn Ltd, 1974
21 x 29
124pp
Including 39pp of 1:500,000 road maps showing road classifications, route numbers and distances. Double page plans of Auckland, Wellington, Christchurch and Dunedin with text. Supplementary information on car maintenance, road signs, trees, flowers, birds, fish, sheep and cattle, National Parks etc. Gazetteer.

SHELL ROAD MAPS OF NEW ZEALAND
Hastings: N.Z. Aerial Mapping Ltd
23 x 28
45pp
Containing 6 double page road maps scale 1:830,000 covering New Zealand together with enlargements of some areas of interest. Also included are 5 aerial photographs of major towns with main routes and names marked, plus 15 other plans. Distance chart, illustrations and index.

DESCRIPTIVE ATLAS OF THE PACIFIC ISLANDS
by T F Kennedy
A H and A W Reed
see ATLASES 9 A1 AUSTRALIA AND OCEANIA

ATLASES
M HISTORICAL

EARLY CHARTS OF NEW ZEALAND 1542-1851
Peter Bromley Maling
Wellington: A H and A W Reed, 1969
134pp
59 reproduction maps in colour or black and white facing page of text and bibliog. Limited edition of 500 copies.

ATLASES
01 NATIONAL ATLAS (SCHOOL)

ATLAS OF NEW ZEALAND GEOGRAPHY
by Linge and Frazer

Wellington: A H and A W Reed, 1966
64pp
30 double page maps with text on physical and economic geog: for secondary schools. With bibliog.

THE OXFORD SOCIAL STUDIES ATLAS FOR NEW ZEALAND
Ed R G Lister
Wellington: OUP, 1963
19 x 26
38pp of col. maps.
33p

NEW ZEALAND SOCIAL STUDIES RESOURCE AT LAS
Ed E R Bloomfield and C A Watson
Brisbane: Jacaranda Press 1972
22 x 28
92pp
For social studies courses in schools; inc. town plans, land use, urban functions etc.

932/937 Melanesia

E1 PHYSICAL: RELIEF

MELANESIA
1:500,000
In 17 sheets
Washington: Defense Mapping
Agency
60 x 60 each
Covering Solomon Is, New Hebrides.
Topog. series in col.
$0.50 each

ATLASES
A1 GENERAL

DESCRIPTIVE ATLAS OF THE
PACIFIC ISLANDS
by T F Kennedy
A H and A W Reed
see AUSTRALIA AND OCEANIA
ATLASES A1 GENERAL

932 New Caledonia and Dependencies

A1 GENERAL MAPS

OCÉANIE
1:2,000,000
Sheet: NOUVELLE HEBRIDES – NOUVELLE CALÉDONIE
Paris: IGN, 1971
Topographical planning map available with or without ICAO Air information overprint.
F.Fr. 14.17

C OFFICIAL SURVEYS

INTERNATIONAL MAP OF THE WORLD
1:1,000,000
IGN
Sheets SF 58 and parts 57 and 59 Noumea covering New Caledonia and Loyalty Islands.
see WORLD 100C and index 100/1

CARTE GÉNÉRALE DE LA NOUVELLE CALÉDONIE
1:200,000
In 5 sheets, see index 932/1
Paris: IGN, 1966
77 x 55
Covering New Caledonia and Loyalty Islands, contoured, hill shading, roads classified, distances in km, vegetation cover, towns and villages.
F.Fr. 11.67

CARTE DE LA NOUVELLE CALÉDONIE
1:50,000
In 46 sheets, see index 932/2
Paris: IGN
52 x 55 each
Topog. series inc. Loyalty Islands, Ile des Pins and Iles Belep, contoured, hill shading, water and vegetation detail.
F.Fr. 11.67

E1 PHYSICAL: RELIEF

NOUVELLE CALÉDONIE
1:406,562 app.
Paris: Forest
129 x 101
Physical wall map, contours, internat. boundaries, communications, cities.

CARTE DE LA NOUVELLE CALÉDONIE
1:500,000
Paris: IGN, 1967
100 x 78
Coloured map showing water features in blue, with ocean depth colouring, vegetation in green, roads classified with distances in km.
F.Fr. 11.67

F GEOLOGY

CARTE GÉOLOGIQUE DE LA NOUVELLE CALÉDONIE
1:50,000
see index 932/3
Orleans: BRGM
Geol. series in progress on the same sheet lines as topog. series. Each sheet folded in plastic wallet with explanatory note.
30.00 F. Fr. each

G EARTH RESOURCES

CARTE PÉDOLOGIQUE DE LA NOUVELLE CALÉDONIE: BOURAIL – MOINDOU
G Tercinier
1:40,000
Paris: ORSTOM, 1969
Coloured soil map of the Bourail-Moindou area.
F.Fr. 12

J CLIMATE

NOUVELLE – CALÉDONIE: CARTE DES PRÉCIPITATIONS ANNUELLES
F Moniod
1:400,000
Paris: ORSTOM, 1966
Coloured map, with 11pp text.
F.Fr. 12

934 New Hebrides

A1 GENERAL MAPS

NEW HEBRIDES
1:5,000,000
Edition 1
DOS 989
Tolworth: DOS, 1951
Small hand map showing island positions, settlement and communications.
15p

NEW HEBRIDES
1:4,000,000
DOS (Misc) 429
4th edition
Tolworth: DOS, 1970
Small hand map showing island positions.
15p

OCÉANIE
1:2,000,000
Sheet: NOUVELLE HÉBRIDES – NOUVELLE CALÉDONIE
Paris: IGN, 1971
Topographic planning map available with or without ICAO Air information overprint.
F.Fr. 14,17

NEW HEBRIDES – ADMINISTRATIVE AND GENERAL MAP
1:1,000,000
DOS 865 1st ed.
Tolworth: DOS, 1975
Hill shaded map showing boundaries, settlement and communications.
65p

C OFFICIAL SURVEYS

CARTE GÉNÉRALE DES NOUVELLES HÉBRIDES
1:500,000
In 2 sheets, see index 934/1
Paris: IGN, 1949
Sheet 1: 67 x 95
Sheet 2: 80 x 65
Relief shaded with communications. Inset on southern sheet shows geog. position of the group.
F.Fr. 11,67

CARTE GÉNÉRALE DES NOUVELLES HÉBRIDES
1:100,000
In 15 sheets, see index 934/1
Paris: IGN
90 x 66 each
Series in progress, contoured, hill shading, vegetation cover, communications, towns and villages. UTM grid.
Sheets published:
Ambrym-Pentecote
Aneytioum-Foutouna
Aoba
Efate
Epi-Shepherd
Erromango
Îles Banks – Nord
Îles Banks – Sud
Îles Torres
Lamap
Maevo
Matakova
Santo
Tanna
F.Fr. 11.67

CARTE GÉNÉRALE DES NOUVELLES HÉBRIDES
1:50,000
see index 934/1
Paris: IGN
Topographical series, contoured, showing communications, boundaries, woodland and settlement.
Sheets published:
Aneytioum-Foutouna
Aoba
Îles Bank – Nord
Îles Banks – Sud
Îles Torres
Maevo (2 sheets)
Malakova (3 sheets)
Île Efate (4 sheets)
F.Fr. 11.67

E1 PHYSICAL: RELIEF

NEW HEBRIDES
1:1,000,000
AMS X321
Washington: Defense Mapping Agency
60 x 101
Topographic map in colours, contoured with inset scale 1:4,000,000 of surrounding area incl. New Caledonia.
$1.00

F GEOLOGY

NEW HEBRIDES GEOLOGICAL SURVEY
1:100,000
(Geol) 1181
In 11 sheets
Tolworth: DOS, 1972+
100 x 85
Detailed coloured maps on topog. base.
Sheets available:
7 Malekula
8 Central Islands
9 Efate and Offshore Islands
each 65p

G EARTH RESOURCES

ARCHIPEL DES NOUVELLES HÉBRIDES, SOLS ET QUELQUES DONNÉES DU MILIEU NATUREL
Ed P Quantin
Paris: ORSTOM, 1973
Collection of maps scale 1:50,000–1:250,000 with explanatory text covering soils with data on the natural environment.
Parts published:
1 VATÉ 4 soil maps 1:100,000–1:250,000 F.Fr. 45.00
2 EPI-SHEPHERD 2 soil maps 1:100,000–1:50,000
F.Fr. 95.00

935 Solomon Islands

See also: 95 PAPUA NEW GUINEA

A1 GENERAL MAPS

BRITISH SOLOMON ISLANDS PROTECTORATE
1:2,750,000
DOS 988
Edition 4
Tolworth: DOS, 1968
Small hand map of the group showing principal towns and communications.
15p

B TOWN PLANS

HONIARA – GUADALCANAL
1:2,500
DOS 056
In 22 sheets
Edition 1
Tolworth: DOS, 1969
Cadastral plan showing streets, buildings, land boundaries.
30p each

C OFFICIAL SURVEYS

GUADALCANAL, BRITISH SOLOMON ISLANDS
1:150,000
Honiara: Dept. Lands & Survey
1968
101 x 52
Contours brown, water features blue, settlements, airfield, roads, topog. features black. Honiara and Savo Is. inset at 1:50,000.
$A1.50

BRITISH SOLOMON ISLANDS PROTECTORATE
1:50,000
DOS 456 (X711), see index 935/1
Tolworth: DOS 1965
55 x 59
Topographical series in progress, contoured. All principal islands published except Guadalcanal.
50p each

FLORIDA GROUP
1:40,000
DOS (Misc) 224 AB
In 8 sheets
Tolworth: DOS
Uncoloured provisional series in 8 sheets, showing basic topographic detail.
30p each

E1 PHYSICAL MAPS: RELIEF

BRITISH SOLOMON ISLANDS
1:1,000,000
DOS (Misc) 347A
In 2 sheets
Tolworth: DOS, 1969
85 x 106 each
Topog. wall map, layer col, hill shading, settlement and communications.
65p each

GEOLOGICAL MAP OF BRITISH SOLOMON ISLANDS PROTECTORATE
1:1,000,000
DOS (Geol) 1145
Edition 2
Tolworth: DOS, 1970
Col. geol. map.
65p

GEOLOGICAL SKETCH MAP OF NORTH CENTRAL GUADALCANAL
1:170,000
DOS (Geol) 1087
Tolworth: DOS, 1959
Map in colours.
50p

CHOISEUL GEOLOGICAL SKETCH MAP
1:150,000
DOS (Geol) 1117
Tolworth: DOS, 1960
2 sheet map in col.
30p each

GEOLOGICAL SURVEY OF THE BRITISH SOLOMON ISLANDS
Memoir No 2
Tolworth: DOS
4 col. maps to illustrate:
British Solomon Islands showing known field data and Bathymetry, also main folding and structure patterns.
1:1,000,000 Fig. 16 50p
Geology of San Cristobal
1:250,000 Fig. 51 50p
Geology of Western Guadalcanal
1:150,000 Fig. 21 50p
Geology of the Florida Group
1:125,000 Fig. 55 15p

GUADALCANAL – BETILONGA GEOLOGICAL SKETCH MAPS
2 maps
Geol: Sketch Map of Betilonga Basin Area
1:95,000 1960
Geol: Sketch Map of Betilonga Area
1:60,000 1960
Tolworth: DOS
15p each

G EARTH RESOURCES

ISOMAGNETIC MAP OF BRITISH SOLOMON ISLANDS PROTECTORATE
1:1,000,000
DOS (Geol) 1145AB
Edition 2
Tolworth: DOS, 1970
Overprinted on 'First Geological Map of BSIP' 1963
65p

939 New Zealand Island Dependencies

A1 GENERAL MAPS

NEW ZEALAND IN THE SOUTH PACIFIC (INCLUDING NZ ISLAND TERRITORY)
1:10,000,000
NZMS, 1970
see 931 A1 NEW ZEALAND

A2 GENERAL MAPS: LOCAL

AUCKLAND ISLANDS
1:95,520
NZMS 220
1st edition
Wellington: NZMS, 1962
56 x 43
Shows place names, tracks and relief by form lines and spot heights in feet.
$0.40

CHATHAM ISLANDS
1:63,360
NZMS 240
Wellington: NZMS, 1969
106 x 81
Topog. features, roads of all classes, reefs, shoals, grid lines at 5,000 yards, water features, vegetation, relief shading. Insets of Pitt Is, Waitangi Township; location diagram of is. and reefs. 1st ed. provisional. 70c
Also available with violet cadastral overprint, NZMS 240A

GENERAL MAP OF TOKELAU ISLANDS
1:750,000
NZMS 254
Wellington: NZMS, 1969
43 x 31
General map with insets locating individual islands – Atafu, Nukunonu, Fakaofo at 1:100,000.

MAP OF NIUE
1:50,000
NZMS 250
1st edition
Wellington: NZMS, 1970
61 x 71
Physical map of the island with communications, vegetation and reefs. Reliability diagram and Alofi inset at 1:12,500. Index on reverse.

G EARTH RESOURCES

SOIL MAP OF CHATHAM ISLANDS
1:100,000
Wellington: Dept. of Sci. and Indust. Research, 1959
Coloured Soil Bureau map.

SOIL BUREAU MAPS
Various scales
Wellington
Maps available:
Soil Map of Niue Is.
1:63,360 1958
Soil Map of Ranoul or Sunday Is.
1:15,840 1959

94 Australia

See also: 9 AUSTRALIA AND OCEANIA

A1 GENERAL MAPS: ROADS

AUSTRALIA
1:8,000,000 approx.
No 4
Sydney: Gregory
83 x 63
Col. map with boundaries, towns, and principal communications.
Folded in plastic bag 40 c

AUSTRALIEN
1:6,000,000
No 897
Frankfurt: Ravenstein
100 x 70
Physical, political road map.
DM 8.80

AUSTRALIA
1:4,500,000
Map No 0506
Sydney: Paul Hamlyn Ltd
102 x 89
Physical layer colouring with detailed road information indicating all categories of highways, also railways, airports, homesteads, route numbers and distances.

AUSTRALIA: ROAD AND REFERENCE MAP
1:5,000,000 app.
No 150
Sydney: Gregory
114 x 88
Road and rail communications, with insets showing climate, pop, mileages, etc. In col.
$1.00

AUSTRALIA
1:4,500,000 app.
No 500
Sydney: Robinson
99 x 72
Col. by states, roads classified with numbers and mileages, railways, reserves, Tasmania and Australian them. maps inset.
A$0.70

AUSTRALIA
1:4,000,000 approx.
No 526 Broadsheet Maps
Sydney: Robinson
Coloured road map with route numbers and distances and town plans inset.
A$1.00

ROBINSON'S POPULAR SERIES — SHEET MAPS
AUSTRALIA Ref 1501 A$0.65
AUSTRALIA AND NEW GUINEA Ref 573 A$0.70
S E ASIA AND AUSTRALIA Ref 1803 A$0.70
Sydney: Robinson
Various sizes
Series of general maps, coloured and showing boundaries, towns and principal communications.

A2 GENERAL MAPS: LOCAL

HIGHWAY AND HOLIDAY MAP OF AUSTRALIA
Various scales
Sydney: Gregory
Includes highway map of area between Brisbane and Adelaide; holiday insets of Snowy Mts. and New South Wales Coast and Street Maps of Sydney, Melbourne, Adelaide, Brisbane.
50c

ROBINSON'S REGIONAL ROAD MAPS
Sydney: Robinson
Various sizes
Series of large road maps of regions and localities.
Maps available:

Blue Mountain 432	90c
Central Eastern NSW 226	60c
Central North Coast NSW and Lake Macquarie	70c
Coastal NSW — Let's Go Fishing 434	A$1.00
Gold Coast 715	50c
100 Miles Around Bega 431	65c
100 Miles ARound Grafton 429	65c
100 Miles Around Kempsey 428	65c
100 Miles Around Nowra 430	65c
Upper Hawkesbury 155	60c

BROADBENT'S BROADSHEET MAPS
Sydney: Broadbent
Various sizes
Series of local and regional maps, coloured. Maps available:

Eastern Half Victoria	70c
Western Half Victoria	70c
100 Miles Around Melbourne	70c
Melbourne To and Fro	70c
Melbourne Metropolitan (Shire)	A$1.00
Melbourne North East Hill Country	50c
Mornington Peninsula	50c
Dandenongs	50c
South Gippsland	50c
Port Philip (Anglers Chart)	A$1.00
Lake Eucumbene	30c
Lake Eppalock	30c
Snowy Mountains	30c
South East South Australia	50c

BROADBENT'S FOOLSCAP SERIES
Sydney: Broadbent
20 x 33
Series of small local maps for various regions and settlements in Australia. Maps available:
Acheron Valley & Eildon
Across the Alps (Omeo — Bright District)
Adelaide — Murray Bridge District
Albury — Upper Murray District
Albury — Wangaratta District
Appollo Bay District (Lorne — Pt Campbell)
Ararat
Australian Capital Territory
Bairnsdale
Bairnsdale — Lakes Entrance District
Balcombe — Mt Martha District
Ballarat District
Batemans Bay — Canberra District
Bellarine Peninsula
Benalla
Bendigo — Daylesford District
Blairgowrie
Bordertown — Kingston — Mt Gambier District
Bright District and the Bogong High Plains
(Bright — Omeo District) Across the Alps
Buchan Caves — Lakes Entrance District
Canberra — Near NSW Coast District
Castlemaine
Castlemaine — Macedon — Kyneton District
Colac
Colac — Lorne — Geelong District
Colac — Terang District
Darwin
Daylesford — Bendigo District
Daylesford — Hepburn Springs
Deniliquin — Echuca District
Dromana
Drouin
East Gippsland
Echuca
Echuca — Deniliquin District
Eildon & Acheron Valley
(Flinders — Hastings) Western Port District
Frankston — Hastings District
Frankston — Mt Martha District
Geelong — Lorne — Colac District
Goulburn Valley (Shepparton District)
Hastings — Frankston District
(Hastings — Flinders) Western Port District
Healesville District
Hepburn Springs — Daylesford
Horsham
Jervis Bay — Nowra District
Kerang Lakes District
Kingslake — Yea District
Kingston — Bordertown — Mt Gambier District
Korumburra
Kyneton — Macedon — Castlemaine District
Lakes Entrance
Lakes Entrance — Bairnsdale District
Lakes Entrance — Buchan Caves District
Lakes Entrance — Orbost District
Leongatha
Licola — Noojee — Walhalla District
Lorne and District
Lorne — Colac — Geelong District
(Lorne — Pt Campbell) Apollo Bay District
Macedon — Kyneton — Castlemaine District
McCrae
Mallacotta Inlet
Mansfield — Seymour District
Marysville and District
Melbourne City and South

Merimbula — Mt Kosciusko District
Mildura
Mornington
Mt Buffalo National Park
Mt Eliza
Mt Gambier — Kingston — Bordertown District
Mt Gambier — Portland District
Mt Kosciusko — Merimbula District
Mt Martha — Balcombe District
Mt Martha — Frankston District
Murray Bridge — Adelaide District
Myrtleford — Alps and High Plains District
Narooma and District
Near NSW Coast — Canberra District
New South Wales
Noojee — Walhalla — Licola District
Northern Territory
Orbost — Lakes Entrance District
(Pt Campbell — Lorne) Apollo Bay District
Port Fairy — Warnambool
Pt Campbell — Warnambool District
Portland
Portland and District
Portland — Mt Gambier District
Portland — Warrnambool District
Portsea — Sorrento
Queensland
Rosebud
Rye
Sale
Seymour — Mansfield District
(Shepparton Dist) Goulburn Valley
Spa Country The (Daylesford District)
Stawell
Swan Hill
Tarra Valley District
Tasmania
Tasmania North Coast
Tasmania East Coast
Tasmania South East Coast
Terang — Colac District
Terang — Pt. Campbell District
Tootgarook
Upper Murray — Albury District
Upper Yarra Hill Country
Victoria
Walhalla — Noojee — Licola District
Wangaratta — Albury District
Warburton District
Warragul
Warragul District
Warrandyte District
Warrnambool — Pt Campbell District
Warrnambool — Port Fairy District
Western Australia
Yallourn
Yarra Hill
Yea — Kingslake District

A$0.30 each

BROADBENT'S CROWN SERIES
Sydney: Broadbent
38 x 51
Series of folded maps covering local areas in Australia.
Maps available:
Bendigo
Flinders Island
Grampians
Kangaroo Island
King Island
Lake Eildon
Mt Gambier
Phillip Island
Shepparton
Traralgon
Victor Harbor
Wagga Wagga
Wangaratta
Warrnambool
Wilson's Promontory
Moe-Newborough
Morwell

A$0.40 each

New South Wales

NEW SOUTH WALES
1:1,875,000
No 27
Sydney: Gregory
91 x 55
Black and blue showing roads. For planning purposes.

60c

NEW SOUTH WALES ROAD MAP
1:1,500,000
No 422
Sydney: Robinson
102 x 76
Roads classified, mileages, towns, villages, rivers, lighthouses and aerodromes shown. Index to places and mileage chart in margin.

75c

NEW SOUTH WALES
1:1,437,500
No 20
Sydney: Gregory
101 x 76
Shows roads, railways, rivers, mountains, distances. Sydney, Canberra, Newcastle, North Coast inset. Index.

85c

NEW SOUTH WALES
1:1,000,000
In 4 sheets
Sydney: Dept. Lands, 1969
138 x 116 complete
General map, no contours, relief shading, roads classified inc. surface, railways, water detail.

AUSTRALIA SNOWFIELDS
1:109,300 app
No 521
Sydney: Gregory
76 x 50
Shows main skiing areas New South Wales and Victoria, mountains, roads, tourist details.

50c

NEW SOUTH WALES, REGIONAL TOURIST MAPS
Various scales
Sydney: Dept. Lands
Various sizes
Road and tourist maps available for the following regions:

Dorrigo State Park	
1:12,375	50 x 76
Hawkesbury River	
1:63,360	97 x 74
Kosciusko State Park	
1:100,000	39 x 30
Port Hacking District	
1:47,520	

WYONG, GOSFORD, WOY WOY
1:63,360
Sydney: Gregory
76 x 50
Touring map in colour.

50c

SYDNEY COASTAL WATERWAYS MAP
1:14,700 app.
No 522
Sydney: Gregory
76 x 101
Boating information covering Sydney Harbor, Broken Bay, Hawkesbury River, George's River, Port Hacking, Botany Bay. In col.

70c

Northern Territory

NORTHERN TERRITORY
1:2,500,000
Canberra: DND 1974
Physical map with relief shading, towns and communications.

NORTHERN TERRITORY ROAD MAP
1:2,000,000
No 1105
Sydney: Robinson
49 x 87
Roads classified with route numbers and distances, also railways, airports, homesteads and places of interest. Insets of Darwin and Alice Springs. Index to localities in margins.

A$0.75

NORTHERN TERRITORY ROAD MAP
No 506
Sydney: Gregory
50 x 76
Road map, highways classified, with Alice Springs, Darwin, Nightcliff town maps inset, also Ayers Rock.

60c

Queensland

QUEENSLAND AND PAPUA
1:6,250,000
No 4a
Brisbane: Dept. Lands
33 x 48
General map showing communications and boundaries.

40c

QUEENSLAND AND PAPUA
1:5,000,000
No 4b
Brisbane: Dept. Lands
48 x 66
Coloured general map showing communications and boundaries.

60c

QUEENSLAND: BARRIER REEF AND COASTAL DISTRICTS
1:2,500,000
Brisbane: Dept. Lands
Col. general map of the region.

40c

QUEENSLAND
1:2,375,000
No 70
Sydney: Gregory
101 x 76
Col. map showing main highways, road and rail systems. Tablelands and Gold Coast inset. 70c
Also Queensland 70a in 6 col.

$1.00

QUEENSLAND ROAD MAP
1:2,000,000
No 710
Sydney: Robinson
76 x 102
Classifying highways, roads, tracks, showing railways, airports, places of interest, homesteads and towns. Index to places and Brisbane locality map inset.
75c

QUEENSLAND SCHOOL MAPS
1:2,000,000
Brisbane: Dept. Lands
2 sheet map in col. showing cities, towns, homesteads, road, rail and air communications, spot heights.
A$1.50 each

QUEENSLAND
1:1,875,000
No 6
Brisbane: Dept. Lands
71 x 97
2 sheet map showing railways, towns, physical features, head stations of pastoral properties, pastoral districts, roads, stock routes.
90c each
Also as 6a with stock routes and stock trucking facilities in red
$1.50 each
6b as no 6 at 1:2,500,000
$1.20

QUEENSLAND
1:1,875,000
No 6c
Brisbane: Dept. Lands
71 x 97
2 sheet map showing pastoral districts, railways, principal towns, physical features.
60c each
6d – reduced size edition
1:2,500,000
74 x 97
60c

BARRIER REEF AND COASTAL DISTRICTS
1:1,000,000
In 3 sheets
Brisbane: Dept. Lands
Coloured general map showing communications, boundaries and settlement.
60c each

TORRES STRAIT AND ISLANDS
1:750,000
Brisbane: Dept. Lands
General map showing position of islands.
60c

MORETON DISTRICT MAP
1:375,000
Brisbane: Dept. Lands
Map showing main roads, boundaries and settlement.
Coloured A$1.00
In black and white A$0.90
Also at 1:250,000 2 sheets 60c each

CAIRNS AND HINTERLAND (QUEENSLAND)
1:250,000
Brisbane: Dept. Lands
Col. map of the town and environs showing roads and topographical detail.
A$0.60

MORETON BAY AND ADJACENT AREAS
1:130,020
Brisbane: Dept. Lands
Col. tourist map
A$0.75
Waterproof edition A$1.20

MOUNT ISA
1:31,680
Brisbane: Dept. Lands
Shown mineral surveys and tenure details.
60c

South Australia

SOUTH AUSTRALIA
1:1,750,000
No 50
Sydney: Gregory
101 x 76
Col. map showing main and secondary roads, railways. Indexed. Adelaide and Intercity routes inset.
85c

SOUTH AUSTRALIA
1:1,700,000
No 0811
Sydney: Robinson
72 x 97
Road map indicating surface conditions, route numbers and distances also airports, homesteads, and places of interest. Insets of Adelaide and index to places.
A$0.75

SOUTH AUSTRALIA
1:1,267,200
Adelaide: Dept. Lands
General map in black and white with pastoral runs, stock routes, reserves, isohyets. Goyders Line Artesian basins in col.

SOUTH AUSTRALIA
1:1,267,200
Adelaide: Dept. Lands
2 sheet map showing major towns, railways, roads, dog fence, physical features in black.

SOUTH AUSTRALIA
1:1,013,760
In 4 sheets
Adelaide: Dept. Lands
Black and white map showing communications, settlements, admin. areas.

SOUTH AUSTRALIA
1:760,320
Adelaide: Dept. Lands
2 sheet map in black and white showing settlements, communications, physical features.

Tasmania

TASMANIA ROAD MAP
1:633,600
No 1002
Sydney: Robinson
55 x 56
Roads classified with route numbers and distances, also railways, parks and places of interest. Insets of Central North Coast, Hobart district and suburbs and plans of Burnie, Devonport, Launceston, and King and Flinders Is. Index to places.
A$0.75

TASMANIA
1:633,600
No 508
Sydney: Gregory
101 x 76
Col. map showing road and rail systems, King Island Group inset. Street maps of Hobart, Launceston, Burnie and Devonport on reverse.
65c

CRADLE MOUNTAIN – LAKE ST CLAIR NATIONAL PARK
1:100,000
Hobart: Natnl. Parks and Wildlife Service, 1974
43 x 67
Contoured with relief shading, showing roads, paths, huts, campsites and wooded areas with notes on reverse side.

TOURING MAP OF TASMANIA
1:600,000
Hobart: Royal Automobile Club of Tasmania, 1975
54 x 70
Relief shaded, roads classified, mileages given, railways, tourist sights and index to towns. King and Flinders Islands inset and 5 town plans on reverse.

HOBART AND ENVIRONS
1:63,360
2nd edition
Hobart: Lands and Surveys Dept, 1967
71 x 86
General map: relief shading, woodland areas in green, roads classified, railways etc. Covers Snug – Mangalore – Malbina – Bally Park.

Victoria

VICTORIA 1
1:1,077,120
No 45
Sydney: Gregory
86 x 55
Col. map showing railways, rivers, mountains, distances, Melbourne and suburbs inset. Index.
75c
Also Victoria 2 No 40, black and white.
60c

TOPOGRAPHIC MAP OF VICTORIA
1:1,000,000
Melbourne: DCLS
Contoured map with communications, boundaries and topographic information.
$1.00

VICTORIA
1:950,000
No 400
Sydney: Broadbent/Robinson
98 x 61
Roads classified, route numbers, mileages, railways, national parks and principal features. Index to towns and localities.
75c

TOPOGRAPHIC MAP OF VICTORIA
1:500,000
In 4 sheets
Melbourne: DCLS
Contoured map, communications, boundaries and land detail.
$1.00 each

Western Australia

WESTERN AUSTRALIA
1:4,612,500
No 60
Sydney: Gregory
91 x 58
Col. map. South-West section at 1:1,125,000. Shows roads, railways, mileages. Perth and suburbs inset. Index.
85c

ROAD MAP OF WESTERN AUSTRALIA
1:3,125,000
Perth: DCLS
Coloured road map. 75c
Also black and white. 50c

WESTERN AUSTRALIA, SHOWING MAIN AND IMPORTANT SECONDARY ROADS
1:3,000,000
Perth: W. Aust. Main Roads Dept., 1972
69 x 97
Showing road position as at 17 August, 1972.

WESTERN AUSTRALIA
1:3,000,000 approx.
No 0910
Sydney: Robinson
61 x 98
Road map indicating surface conditions and facilities also railways, airports, homesteads and places of interest. Insets of South West Districts and Perth. Index to places in margin.
A$0.75

ROAD MAP OF WESTERN AUSTRALIA
1:1,875,000
Perth: DCLS
Col. road map in 2 sheets.
75c each
Black and white. 50c each

WESTERN AUSTRALIA: MAP OF THE SOUTH WEST
1:1,000,000
Perth: DCLS
Col. general map showing towns, communications, boundaries and settlement, with gazetteer of names.
75c

WESTERN AUSTRALIA: MAP OF THE SOUTH WEST
1:1,000,000
In 2 sheets
Perth: DCLS, 1962
99 x 145
Black and white map, towns, communications, gazetteer of names, app. hill shading.
50c

PERTH METROPOLITAN REGIONAL ROAD MAP
1:50,000
Perth: DCLS
2 sheet road map in 2 editions.
Plain or with Shire boundaries.
50c each

PERTH METROPOLITAN REGIONAL ROAD MAP
1:25,000
In 12 sheets
Perth: DCLS
Available in col. or black and white ed. In the following sheets:
Perth North
Swan
Perth
Darling Range
Cockburn
Armadale
Rockingham
Serpentine
Wanneroo
Bullsbrook
Peel
Keysbrook
Col. 75c each
Plain 50c each
Also available, showing index to State Large Scale series:
Perth North
Swan
Perth
Darling Range
Cockburn
Armadale
Rockingham
Serpentine
Wanneroo 75c each

REGIONAL ROAD MAPS OF WESTERN AUSTRALIA
1:25,000
Perth: DCLS
Available for:
Albany
Mandurah
Geraldton
Kalgoorlie
Bunbury 50c each

Australian Island Territories

CHRISTMAS ISLAND
1:50,000
x 782. Edition 5
Canberra: DNM, 1972
47 x 41
Contoured, relief shaded with roads, railways and topo. features.

COCOS (KEELING) ISLANDS
1:50,000
T 726 Edition 1
Canberra: DNM, 1973
54 x 43
Coloured map of the atoll.

NORFOLK ISLAND
1:25,000
R 873
Canberra: DNM, 1971
39 x 64
Contoured, relief shaded with road, settlement and topo. detail. Includes Philip Is.

B TOWN PLANS

see also AUSTRALIA ATLASES 94 B

BROADBENT'S TOWN PLANS
Sydney: Broadbent
Various sizes
Series of town plans, coloured.
Maps available:
Ballarat and Suburbs
Geelong and Suburbs
Melbourne and Adjacent Suburbs
No 612 1:11,880
A$0.50 each

GREGORY TOWN PLANS
Various scales
Sydney: Gregory
Coloured plans, each with street index.
Plans available:
Adelaide and Environs
1:63,360 No 55 70c
Blue Mountains Street Map
1:18,800 No 57 80c
Central Coast Area, NSW
1:25,000 No 503 80c
(Covers Gosford, Woy Woy, Toukley, Budgewoi, Terigal Avoca, The Entrance, Umina)
Brisbane and Environs
1:31,680 No 78 70c
Melbourne Metropolitan (3 sheets)
1:1,975 $1.50 each
Melbourne and Suburbs
1:95,040 No 35 60c
City of Sydney
1:6,336 No 10 70c
City of Sydney
1:10,296 No 11 40c
Sydney and Environs
1:95,040 No 15 70c
Sydney and Suburbs
1:95,040 No 18 40c
Metropolitan Sydney
In 7 sheets $1.50 each
Metropolitan Sydney
(black and white) No 9 $2.50
Metropolitan Sydney
(with postcode overprint)
No 9A $3.00
Metropolitan Wollongong
1:31,680 80c

ROBINSONS TOWN PLANS
Sydney: Robinson
Various sizes
Series of coloured plans naming streets and indexed.
Plans available:
Canberra Official Tourist Map 5001 25c
Newcastle City and Suburbs 054 70c
Sydney City 004
1:8,500 50c
Sydney and Suburbs 5006 60c
Sydney Harbour 5007 80c
Wollongong and Suburbs 5008 50c

CITY AND TOWN MAPS OF QUEENSLAND
1:6,336 and 1:9,504
Brisbane: Dept. Lands
Series of plans for majority of urban areas. Showing allotments, divisions, streets and buildings.
$1.20 each

QUEENSLAND: COMPOSITE CITY AND TOWN MAPS
1:3,960/7,920/15,840
Brisbane: Dept. Lands

Series of large scale plans in black and white published for majority of urban areas.
$1.50 each

GOVERNMENT TOWN PLANS FOR SOUTH AUSTRALIA
1:792/1, 584/3, 168/3,960
Adelaide: Dept. Lands
Series of plans available as dyeline prints for all major urban areas.

CADASTRAL MAPS OF SOUTH AUSTRALIA
1:2,500 and 1:10,000
Adelaide: Dept. Lands
Col. maps showing street and area details, admin. groupings, physical features, contours. Various maps available as line maps, orthophotomaps or orthophotographs.

TOWNSHIP PLANS OF VICTORIA
Various scales
Melbourne: DCLS
Series of large scale plans published for all principal townships.
$1.00 per sheet

BASE MAPS OF VICTORIA
Various scales
Melbourne: DCLS
Contoured subdivision plans, available for:
Outer Melbourne Area 1:4,800
Mornington Peninsula and Philip Island 1:4,800
Ballarat 1:4,800
Geelong, Bendigo, Ararat 1:5,000
Printed $1.00 per sheet
Dyeline copy 80c per sheet

METROPOLITAN ADELAIDE
1:47,520
In 3 sheets
Adelaide: Dept. Lands
96 x 190
Roads and watercourse pattern in black, suburbs red, postcode green. Also at 1:63,360 with municipal and district Council boundaries and names in red, and 1:63,360 in black with contours brown.

METROPOLITAN ADELAIDE
1:10,000
Adelaide: Dept. Lands
Dyeline prints of one part of the city only, showing sections, sheets, suburbs. In 2 formats: 1–1 18 sheets and 1–2 in 35 sheets.
$1.00 each

ADELAIDE AND ENVIRONS MAP SERIES
1:7,920
In 40 sheets
Adelaide: Dept. Lands
Showing section boundaries and numbers, allotment boundaries, sheets, reserves, contours.
$1.00 each

CITY OF BRISBANE
1:63,360
Brisbane: Dept. Lands
Plans of the city and environs, showing State electorates etc.
60c

CITY OF BRISBANE
1:25,324
In 4 sheets
Brisbane: Dept. Lands
Wall map of suburbs, with street names, railways and tram routes.
$1.20 each

BRISBANE AND SUBURBS STREET MAP
1:23,760
Brisbane: Dept. Lands
Shows postal facilities, street names, railways, bus routes, places of interest.
Flat 70c
Folded 90c
Also in black without bus routes 60c
Black and white, no bus routes, contours and radial lines in col.
Flat 70c
Folded 90c

BRISBANE, CENTRAL MAP
1:13,072
Brisbane: Dept. Lands
Plan of the main business area of the city showing location of streets and buildings.
40c

CITY OF BRISBANE
1:1,584
Brisbane: Dept. Lands
In 12 sheets
Shows suburbs, street names, railways, and tram routes.
60c each

ENVIRONS OF GLADSTONE
1:7,920
Brisbane: Dept. Lands
Plan in black and white showing streets, buildings and boundaries.
60c

MELBOURNE AND SUBURBS
Various scales
Melbourne: DCLS
Central City Area
1:6,336 1956 20c
Melbourne and Suburbs (12 sheets)
1:15,840 1957 50c each
Melbourne and Suburbs (2 sheets)
1:31,680 1956 $1.00 each
Melbourne and Environs (22 sheets)
1:25,000 1971 $1.00 each
Set in folder $25.00
Melbourne Municipalities
1:6,000 1968 $1.00 each

CITY OF TOWNSVILLE STREET MAP
1:15,840
Brisbane: Dept. Lands
Postal facilities, street names, railways, places of interest.
Pallarenda, Partington and towns on Magnetic Island inset.
Flat – coloured 70c
Folded – coloured 90c
Black/white, street index 60c

C OFFICIAL SURVEYS

INTERNATIONAL MAP OF THE WORLD
1:1,000,000
In 47 sheets, see index 94/1
Canberra: Sydney
In progress available in standard (metric contours) or provisional editions. Where these sheets are not yet available World Aeronautical Charts are available.
see also WORLD 100 and index 100/1

AUSTRALIA (R 502) SERIES
1:250,000
See index 94/2
Canberra: DND
61 x 44
National topog. series showing roads, vegetation types, land detail, available in 2 eds – standard ed, fully col. and contoured, and provisional ed, showing relief by hill shading.
A$0.75 each

TOPOGRAPHIC MAP OF AUSTRALIA
1:100,000
See index 94/3
Canberra: DND
National series in progress, showing topog. features. Preliminary compilation copies also available. This new series is based on the Australian Map Grid and supersedes earlier series on the Australian National Yard Grid.
A$0.75

AIR PHOTOGRAPHS OF AUSTRALIA
1:80,000
Canberra: DND, 1960+
National series of photographs covering nearly the whole country replacing State produced series and other material at varying scales. Col. or black and white. Various prices.

TOPOGRAPHIC MAP OF AUSTRALIA
1:50,000
see index 94/3
Canberra: DND
National series in progress, showing topog. features. This new series is based on the Australian Map Grid and supersedes earlier series on the Australian National Yard Grid.
A$0.75

NORTHERN TERRITORY: PASTORAL MAP
1:2,000,000
66 x 97
Canberra: DND, 1973
Showing pastoral boundaries, settlement and pastoral runs, and aboriginal reserves
75c

PASTORAL SERIES OF THE NORTHERN TERRITORY OF AUSTRALIA
1:500,000
In 30 sheets
Darwin: L & S N T
56 x 54 each

Series available in temporary or provisional eds. in dyeline print form. Showing reserves, roads, holdings, pastoral boundaries.
Sheets available:
Cobourg Peninsula
Darwin
Arnhem
Caledon Bay
Fitzmaurice
Roper River
Pellew
Victoria River Downs
Newcastle Waters
McArthur River
Barrow Creek
Avon Downs
Alice Springs
Huckitta
Finke

QUEENSLAND
1:1,000,000
No 1b In 15 sheets
Brisbane: Dept. Lands
61 x 53
Series showing towns, railways, physical features, counties and pastoral districts.
60c each

SOUTH AUSTRALIA
1:500,000
In 15 sheets
Adelaide: Dept. Lands
Shows settlements, communications, admin. areas, physical features in black.

PASTORAL MAPS OF SOUTH AUSTRALIA
1:506,880
In 15 sheets
Adelaide: Dept. Lands
Covering portion of State pastoral areas, with pastoral run boundaries, names, physical features.

PASTORAL MAP OF SOUTH AUSTRALIA
1:253,440
In 17 sheets
Adelaide: Dept. Lands
Covering State pastoral areas; each sheet in Northern and Southern part. Dyeline print maps showing pastoral run boundaries, names, physical features.

PASTORAL MAP OF SOUTH AUSTRALIA
1:250,000
In 59 sheets
Adelaide: Dept. Lands
New series in progress, covering pastoral areas, available in dyeline prints. Shows pastoral run boundaries, names etc. Transverse Mercator Proj.

CADASTRAL MAPS OF SOUTH AUSTRALIA
1:50,000 and 1:100,000
Adelaide: Dept. Lands
Dyeline prints showing roads, reserves, hundred boundaries.

TASMANIA
1:250,000
In 8 sheets
Hobart: Land Surv. Dept. 1963
141 x 198 complete
Showing drainage pattern, relief shading, no contours. Roads classified and numbered, railways graded, airports, airfields and outpost radio. Bass Strait, King Island, Furneaux Group and Macquarie Island inset.

MAP OF WESTERN AUSTRALIA
1:500,000
In 25 sheets
Perth: DCLS
Showing basic topographic features, communications and boundaries.
Available in the following sheets:
Albany
Balladonia — Eyre
Bonaparte
Broome
Bunbury
Canning
Carnarvon — Exmouth
Carnegie
Cundeelee
De Grey
Derby
Esperance
Forrest
Gascoyne
Halls Creek
Kalgoorlie
Ninghan
Nullagine
Onslow
Peak Hill
Perth
Rawlinson
Wells
Wiluna
Wyndham 75c each

AUSTRALIA: TOPOGRAPHIC MAP EXTRACTS
Various scales
Christchurch: Whitcombe & Tombs
Sets extracted from official topog. series.
Set I selected by Geog. Teachers Assoc. of Victoria
30 x 25 each

1	Monbulk Sheet (Vic)	1:50,000
2	Humpty Doo Sheet (NT)	1:50,000
3	Darwin Sheet (NT)	1:50,000
4	Wyndham Sheet (WA)	1:50,000
5	Corunna and Iron Baron Sheet (SA)	1:50,000
6	Nagambie Sheet (Vic)	1:100,000
7	Mildura Sheet (Vic)	1:250,000
8	Legends and scales for all abstracts	

Set II selected by Geog. Teachers Assoc. of NSW
37 x 32 each

1	Ingham (Qu)	1:250,000
2	Newcastle Waters (NT)	1:1,000,000
3	Finke (NT)	1:250,000
4	Freemantle (WA)	1:63,360
5	Scone (NSW)	1:31,680
6	Sydney and Wollongong (NSW)	1:250,000
7	Canberra (ACT)	1:50,000

Set III selected by Geog. Teachers Assoc. of Queensland
25 x 36 each

1	Weipa (Q)	1:250,000
2	Innisfail (Q)	1:250,000
3	Townsville (Q)	1:100,000
4	Longreach (Q)	1:250,000
5	Ridgelands (Q)	1:63,360
6	Birdsville (Q)	1:250,000
7	Brisbane (Q)	1:253,440

With notes for each extract.

D POLITICAL & ADMINISTRATIVE

AUSTRALJA
1:8,500,000
In 4 sheets
Beograd: Geokarta
140 x 122
Map in cyrillic and latin lettering.
Cloth mounted 150 dn

AUSTRALIA
1:8,000,000
No 4143
Bern: K & F
101 x 74
Political col, by states, relief shading, road, rail and air communications, National Parks and Reserves, mines. Indonesia and New Zealand inset. In Ger. legend also Eng.

PHILIP'S COMPARATIVE WALL ATLAS OF AUSTRALIA AND NEW ZEALAND — POLITICAL
1:6,000,000
Philip
see AUSTRALIA 94 E1

STANFORD'S GENERAL MAP OF AUSTRALIA
1:5,000,000
London: Stanford, 1975
109 x 83
Col. by states, showing principal roads, railways and airports, pipelines, towns graded by pop. Pictorial borders.
Paper flat £1.00
Mounted CR £6.50

PHILIP'S POLITICAL SMALLER WALL MAP OF AUSTRALIA
1:5,000,000
London: Philip, 1967
103 x 82
States shown in different col. with railways, shipping routes and towns graded by pop.
Paper £1.50
Mounted CR £5.50
Mounted on cloth dissected to fold £7.00

AUSTRALIA
1:5,000,000
Helsinki: Wsoy
217 x 198
School wall map, political.
FMK 100

GEOGRAPHIA INTERNATIONAL SERIES: AUSTRALIA
1:4,750,000
London: Gia, 1969
107 x 84
Col. by states, showing major roads, railways, shipping lines, ports, places of interest. Insets of communications, physical map, resources. In wallet with information and maps on reverse.
40p

AUSTRALIA
1:4,312,500
Washington: NGS
106 x 82
Political wall map, boundaries in colour, detailed place names, communications.
Paper $2.00
Plastic $3.00

PHILIP'S POLITICAL LARGE WALL MAP OF AUSTRALIA
1:3,000,000
London: Philip
175 x 122
Political col. showing railways and shipping routes with towns graded by pop.
Mounted CR £15.00
Mounted on cloth dissected to fold with eyelets £17.00

AUSTRALIA
No scale given
Barcelona: Editorial Teide
33 x 25
School hand map, showing boundaries and major cities.
1 pta

VITO-GRAPHIC CHALKBOARD OUTLINE MAP OF AUSTRALIA
1:7,000,000
Ref: VS 8
Chicago: Weber Costello Co
117 x 160
Land areas in green, meridians, parallels and outlines in yellow, water areas in blue. On cloth – various mounted styles.

PHILIP'S LARGE OUTLINE MAP OF AUSTRALIA AND NEW ZEALAND
1:6,350,000
London: Philip
104 x 83
Coastline and inter-state boundaries printed in black on white cartridge paper.
£1.25

PHILIP'S MAP BUILDING SHEET ('BLACKBOARD MAP') OF AUSTRALIA AND NEW ZEALAND
1:6,350,000
London: Philip
104 x 83
Coastline and boundaries in yellow on blackboard paper.
Mounted CR £4.00

AUSTRALIA, OUTLINE SLATED
1:4,687,500
No 165101
Chicago: Denoyer-Geppert
111 x 129
Blackboard map for schools, showing countries; blue and yellow on black.
$19.95

AUSTRALIA PROJECT MAP
Sydney: Gregory
86 x 60
For junior schools, relief, mts, cities, historical details, 9 project cards on bottom.
30c

PARISH MAPS OF NEW SOUTH WALES
Various scales
Sydney: Lands Dept.
Showing mining leases and parish boundaries.
60c

QUEENSLAND
1:7,500,000
No 2
Brisbane: Dept. Lands
25 x 36
Administrative map showing shire and regional boundaries only
40c

QUEENSLAND
1:2,500,000
No 6e
Brisbane: Dept. Lands
74 x 97
Regional and local govt. boundaries in red. Overprinted on map 6b.
$2.40

QUEENSLAND TENURE MAP
1:1,000,000
No Q2 in 4 sheets
Brisbane: Dept. Lands
Shows towns, railways, physical features, land tenure, pastoral districts.
$2.00 each
Also available:
5a 1:2,000,000 $2.40
5b 1:2,000,000 with addition of District Boundaries in red. $2.40
5c 1:2,000,000 with Local Govt. Boundaries in red $2.40 (replaced by Q4c)
5d 1:2,000,000 Magistrates Courts Districts, Boundaries
5e 1:1,000,000 In 8 sheets, with the addition of Local Govt. Boundaries, stock trucking facilities and Stock Routes with mileages and water facilities.
$1.20 each

QUEENSLAND STATE ELECTORAL DISTRICT MAPS
Various scales
Brisbane: Dept. Lands
Series of maps showing electoral district boundaries.
60c each

ADMINISTRATIVE MAPS SERIES OF QUEENSLAND
Brisbane: Dept. Lands
Four Mile Series
1:250,000 All of Queensland except settled area in East. Details of surveys and tenure.
60c each
Two Mile Series
1:125,000 Covering closely settled area, details of surveys and tenure. 60c each
Parish Maps
1:31,680 Shows greater detail of surveys and tenure in closely settled areas. 60c each
Twenty Chain Series
1:15,840 Surveys and tenures in Brisbane, Ipswich and Bundaberg areas. 60c each
Forty Chain Series
1:31,680 As above. 90c each
Queensland Cadastral
1:100,000 To replace Two Mile Series.

SOUTH AUSTRALIA: SOUTHERN PORTION
1:1,013,760
Adelaide: Dept. Lands, 1968
75 x 95
Shows settlements, communications, admin. divisions in black and white. Also available showing counties in col.

ANNUAL REPORT PLAN No 1 (SOUTH AUSTRALIA)
1:1,013,760
Adelaide: Dept. Lands
Black and white general map with areas of state sold, leased etc. in col. Rev. annually.

SOUTH AUSTRALIA
1:760,320
Adelaide: Dept. Lands
General map in black and white with Municipalities in green and District councils in red.

COUNTY PLANS OF SOUTH AUSTRALIA
1:126,720
Adelaide: Dept. Lands
Individual countries in 1 or 2 sheets, showing hundreds and sections, black and white.

HUNDRED PLANS OF SOUTH AUSTRALIA
1:31,680
Adelaide: Dept. Lands
Show sections, reserves, roads. Dyeline prints.

SHIRE BOUNDARIES MAP OF VICTORIA
1:1,000,000
Melbourne: DCLS
State administrative map.
$1.00
Also at 1:500,000 in 4 sheets
$1.00 each

COUNTY AND PARISH BOUNDARIES OF VICTORIA
1:500,000
In 4 sheets
1:500,000
State administrative map.
$1.00 each

COUNTY, PARISH AND SHIRE BOUNDARIES OF VICTORIA
1:500,000
In 4 sheets
Melbourne: DCLS
State administrative map.
$1.00 each

ELECTORAL PROVINCES OF VICTORIA – UPPER HOUSE
Various scales
Melbourne: DCLS
Electoral boundaries in colour.
Per sheet $1.00
Skeleton sheets 20c each

ELECTORAL DISTRICTS OF VICTORIA – LOWER HOUSE
Various scales
Melbourne: DCLS
Electoral boundaries in colour.
Per sheet $1.00
Skeleton sheets 20c each

T

COUNTY PLANS OF VICTORIA
1:126,720
Melbourne: DCLS
Administrative map series in black and white.
Per sheet $1.00

PARISH PLANS OF VICTORIA
1:15,840/31,680
Melbourne: DCLS
Black and white maps of parish districts.
Per sheet $1.00

WESTERN AUSTRALIA: LOCAL AUTHORITY BOUNDARIES
1:3,125,000
Perth: DCLS
Administrative boundaries in black and white.
50c

WESTERN AUSTRALIA: PASTORAL STATION BOUNDARIES
1:1,375,000
In 2 sheets
Perth: DCLS
District map in black and white.
$1.00 each

WESTERN AUSTRALIA: THE SOUTH WEST WITH LOCAL AUTHORITY BOUNDARIES
1:1,000,000
Perth: DCLS
Black and white map.
50c

E1 PHYSICAL: RELIEF

AUSTRALIA
1:10,000,000
Canberra: DND, 1969
48 x 43
General map; relief shading, major roads and railways, water detail, towns and settlements.
10c

PHILIP'S REGIONAL WALL MAP OF AUSTRALIA AND EASTERN ASIA
1:10,000,000
London: Philip, 1966
89 x 112
Physical layer col, showing boundaries, principal communications and towns graded by pop.
Paper £1.50
Mounted CR £5.50
Mounted on cloth dissected to fold £7.00

TRI-GRAPHIC MAP OF ASIA AND AUSTRALIA
1:10,000,000
Ref: TRI-5
Chicago: Weber Costello Co
101 x 137
Physical layer colouring with graphic relief shading and political boundaries. Available mounted in various styles.

AUSTRALIEN
1:7,500,000
München: List
96 x 130
Wenschow wall map, layer col, relief shading, ocean depths. State and International boundaries, cities graded by pop.

PHYSICAL SMALLER WALL MAP OF AUSTRALIA AND NEW ZEALAND
1:6,000,000
London: Philip
108 x 83
Physical, layer col, with boundaries, railways and shipping routes.
Paper £1.50
Mounted CR £5.50
Mounted on cloth dissected to fold with eyelets £7.00

PHILIP'S COMPARATIVE WALL ATLAS OF AUSTRALIA AND NEW ZEALAND
1:6,000,000
London: Philip
108 x 83 each
Set of 5 maps describing geog. background of the country. The maps comprise:
Relief of Land: Political and Communications
Climate: Summer conditions, Winter conditions, Rainfall, Isobars, Wind, Actual Temperature and Sea Level Isotherms
Natural Vegetation
Political
Density of Population
Supplementary map:
Commercial Development
Single maps, each
Paper £1.50
Mounted CR £5.50
Mounted on cloth dissected to fold £7.00
Set of 5 maps.
Mounted on cloth on one (split) roller £20.00

AUSTRALIE
1:6,000,000
Groningen: Wolters-Noordhoff
120 x 90
Physical wall map showing relief and settlements.
Fl 109.00

AUSTRALIE A NOVY ZELAND
1:6,000,000
Praha: Kart
110 x 78
Physical map, with them. maps inset at 1:18,000.000 – geology, land use, pop. Index. 48pp text.

AUSTRALIJA – SPRAVOCHAYA KARTA
1:6,000,000
Moskva: GUGK
1 sheet reference map. Cyrillic text.

AUSTRALIJA
1:6,000,000
Moskva: GUGK
Physical wall map in 2 sheets. Cyrillic text.

AUSTRALIA
1:5,000,000
Canberra: DND, 1969
102 x 86
Physical, contoured and layer col, communications.
75c

BARTHOLOMEW'S WORLD TRAVEL MAP SERIES: AUSTRALIA
1:5,000,000
Edinburgh: Bart
94 x 71
Contoured, layer col, roads classified, railways and airports shown. Tasmania inset at same scale.
Paper flat or folded 75p

THE WORLD
Sheet 10
1:5,000,000
AGS:
see WORLD 100 and index 100/3

PHILIP'S GRAPHIC RELIEF WALL MAP OF AUSTRALIA
1:5,000,000
London: Philip
103 x 82
Col. to simulate predominant vegetation cover with hill shading, presenting a graphic impression. New Zealand inset.
Paper £1.50
Mounted CR £5.50
Mounted on cloth dissected to fold £7.00

AUSTRALIA, VISUAL RELIEF
1:4,675,000
No 10101
Chicago: Denoyer-Geppert
111 x 147
Physical school wall map showing land and sea relief, boundaries etc. Reduced size as Desk Map No 301101, 29 x 43, $3.30 per 25 copies.
$18.75

PHILIP'S PHYSICAL LARGE WALL MAP OF AUSTRALIA
1:3,000,000
London: Philip
178 x 122
Physical layer col, with hill shading, boundaries, communications and towns graded by pop.
Mounted CR £15.00
Mounted on cloth dissected to fold with eyelets £17.00

GAZETTEER MAP OF AUSTRALIA
1:2,500,000
In 4 sheets
Canberra: DND, 1970
190 x 162 complete
Contoured, layer col, hill shading, roads and railways classified, tunnels, boundaries, water detail, bathymetric tints. With separate 100pp gazetteer to places.
$3.00

NEW SOUTH WALES
1:1,000,000
In 4 sheets
Sydney: Dept. Lands, 1969
138 x 117
Physical map in col. showing topog. features, roads, etc.

E2 PHYSICAL: LAND FEATURES

IRRIGATION AREAS OF SOUTH AUSTRALIA: ANNUAL REPORT PLAN No 3
1:506,880
Adelaide: Dept. Lands

Showing roads, railways, hundreds, locks, barrages in black, hydrography blue, irrigation areas red. Annual revision.

A GEOMORPHIC MAP OF THE RIVERINE PLAIN OF SOUTH-EASTERN AUSTRALIA
Ed. B E Butler and others.
Canberra: Aust. Natn'l Press, 1973.
Physiographic map with text.
A$1.50

BERRI IRRIGATION AREAS
1:7,920
In 6 sheets
Adelaide: Dept. lands
Showing sections, reserves, roads in black.

COBDOGLA IRRIGATION AREAS
1:7,920
Adelaide: Dept. Lands
Showing sections, reserves, roads in black.
Available for the following divisions:

Cobdogla Division	1 sheet
Loveday Division	6 sheets
Nookamka Division	2 sheets
Weigall Division 1:31,680	1 sheet

LOXTON IRRIGATION AREAS
1:7,920
In 4 sheets
Adelaide: Dept. Lands
Showing sections, reserves, road pattern in black.
Also at 1:15,840 in 1 sheet.

WAIKERIE IRRIGATION AREAS
1:7,920
Adelaide: Dept. Lands
Showing sections, reserves, road patterns in black. For the following divisions:
Ho.der Division
Ramco Division
Waikerie Division

LONG FLAT IRRIGATION AREAS
1:3,960
Adelaide: Dept. Lands
Showing sections, reserves, road pattern in black.

POMPOOTA IRRIGATION AREAS
1:3,960
Adelaide: Dept. Lands
Showing sections, reserves, road pattern in black.

IRRIGATION AREA MAP – BARMERA AND ENVIRONS
1:3,168
Adelaide: Dept. Lands
2 sheet dyeline print map.

IRRIGATION AREA MAPS – BERRI AND ENVIRONS
1:3,168
Adelaide: Dept. Lands
Dyeline print map.

IRRIGATION AREA PLANS – CADELL CHAFFEY COWIRRA, JERVOIS, KINGSTON, LYRUP VILLAGE DISTRICT, MONTEITH, MOOROCK, MURRAY BRIDGE, MYPOLONGA, NEETA AND WALL
Various scales
Adelaide: Dept. Lands
Available as dyeline prints only.

F GEOLOGY

ATLAS OF AUSTRALIAN RESOURCES
1:6,000,000
Plate: Geology
DND
see AUSTRALIA ATLASES 94 0

GEOLOGICAL MAP OF THE WORLD: AUSTRALIA AND OCEANIA
1:5,000,000
BMR, 1966-8
Sheets 6, 7, 11, 12 cover Australia.
see AUSTRALIA AND OCEANIA 9F and index 9/1.

TECTONIC MAP OF AUSTRALIA AND NEW GUINEA
1:5,000,000
Sydney: Geol. Soc. of Australia, 1971
Coloured tectonic map.

GEOLOGICAL MAP OF FITZROY REGION, WA
1:500,000
Canberra: BMR, 1957
Coloured geol. map
AUS $3.00

AMADEUS BASIN, EAST AND WEST NT AND WA
1:500,000
Canberra: BMR, 1970
2 sheet geol, map.
each AUS $3.00

ARNHEIM LAND, NT
1:500,000
Canberra: BMR, 1967
Coloured geological map.
AUS $3.00

GEOLOGICAL MAP OF THE BOWEN BASIN, NORTH AND SOUTH QLD.
1:500,000
Canberra: BMR, 1967
2 sheet geol. map
Each sheet AUS $3.00

CARNARVON BASIN, WA
1:500,000
Canberra: BMR, 1963
2 sheet geol. map.
Each sheet AUS $3.00

GEOLOGICAL MAP OF THE EAST KIMBERLEY REGION, WA
1:500,000
Canberra: BMR, 1967
2 sheet geol. map
Each sheet AUS $3.00

GEOLOGICAL MAP OF GEORGETOWN – CLARKE RIVER AREA, QLD.
1:500,000
Canberra: BMR, 1963
Coloured map geol.
AUS $3.00

GEORGINA BASIN, NT AND QLD.
1:500,000
In 4 sheets
Canberra: BMR, 1966
Coloured geol. map.
Each sheet AUS $3.00

McARTHUR RIVER, NT, GEOLOGICAL MAP
1:500,000
Canberra: BMR, 1966
Col. geol. map.
AUS $3.00

STANDARD GEOLOGICAL MAPS OF AUSTRALIA
1:250,000
see index 94/4
Canberra: BMR
Coloured geological series in progress on national topog. series sheet lines. With explanatory notes and sheet bibliography. each AUS $3.00
Photogeological maps of certain areas also available. $1.00 each

GEOLOGICAL MAP OF NEW SOUTH WALES
1:3,000,000
Sydney: Geol. Surv. NSW
45 x 38
Small col. map showing 15 geol. classes represented in the State. 32pp Explanatory Notes, 1967.

GEOLOGICAL MAP OF NEW SOUTH WALES
1:1,000,000
Sydney: Geol. Surv, NSW, 1973
2 sheet geol. map with Reference in 2 sheets.
A$4.00

TECTONIC MAP OF NEW SOUTH WALES
1:1,000,000
1st edition
Sydney: Geol. Survey of NSW
New map in preparation expected early 1974.

GEOLOGICAL MAP OF NEW SOUTH WALES
1:500,000
In 10 sheets
Sydney: Geol. Survey of NSW
Coloured series in preparation, 6 sheets published, remaining 4 in black and white. Prov. Ed. Coloured A$1.00 each
B. & W. A$0.50 each

GEOLOGICAL MAP OF NEW ENGLAND, NSW
1:500,000
Sydney: NSW, Dept. of Mines, 1974
Coloured map in 2 sheets.
A$1.00

GEOLOGICAL MAP SERIES OF NEW SOUTH WALES
1:250,000
See index 94/4
Sydney: Geol. Survey of NSW
Col. geological series in progress.

GEOLOGICAL MAP OF NEW ENGLAND
1:250,000
Armidale (NSW): Univ. New England School of Geol, 1967
68 x 77
Detailed geol. map in outline in black and white. Text on reverse.

GEOLOGICAL MAP OF NEW SOUTH WALES
1:100,000
Sydney: Geol. Survey of NSW
Coloured geol. series in preparation.
Sheets available in black and white
Provisional Edition:
Port Hacking
Sydney
A$0.50 each

GEOLOGICAL MAP OF NEW SOUTH WALES
1:50,000
Sydney: Geol. Survey of NSW
Coloured geol. series in progress.
Sheets published:
New col. edition A$1.00
Windsor
Provisional ed. A$0.50 each
Coricudgy
Glen Alice
Glen Davis
Mellong
Olinda
Yerranderie

PARISH COBAR, COUNTY ROBINSON
1:15,840
Sydney: Geol. Surv. NSW
Col. geol. map. $1.00

GEOLOGICAL MAP OF QUEENSLAND
1:2,500,000
Brisbane: Dept. Lands, 1953
75 x 99
Col. geol. map $1.20

UPPER PALAEOZOIC IGNEOUS ROCKS OF NORTHWEST QUEENSLAND
1:500,000
Canberra: BMR, 1967
Coloured geol. map
AUS $3.00

GEOLOGICAL MAP OF MORETON DISTRICT
1:375,000
Brisbane: Dept. Lands
Coloured geol. map.
60c

GEOLOGICAL MAP OF QUEENSLAND
1:250,000
see index 94/4
Brisbane: Geol. Surv. Q
Col. sheets published by State Geol. Surv. In progress.
75c each

GEOLOGICAL MAPS OF BRISBANE
1:31,680
In 6 sheets
Brisbane: Dept. Lands
Available in 3 editions. Geol, Economic Geol, Contours.
60c each
Per set $3.00

GEOLOGICAL MAP OF SOUTH AUSTRALIA
1:2,000,000
Adelaide: Dept. Mines & Geol. Surv. 1953
50 x 66
Col. geol. map showing sedimentary, metamorphic and igneous + rock boundaries, faults, synclines, anticlines.
$1.00

GEOLOGICAL MAP OF SOUTH AUSTRALIA
1:250,000
see index 94/4
Adelaide: Geol. Surv. SA
Col. geological series in progress.

GEOLOGICAL MAPS OF SOUTH AUSTRALIA
1:63,360
Adelaide: Dept. Mines & Geol. Surv.
Col. geol. series in progress, showing topog. and geol. information.
$1.00 each

GEOLOGICAL MAP OF TASMANIA
1:500,000
Hobart: Geol. Surv. Tasmania
75 x 100
Col. map of the island.

GEOLOGICAL MAP OF VICTORIA
1:1,000,000
Melbourne: Geol. Surv. Vic, 1955
91 x 76
Col. map.

GEOLOGICAL MAP OF VICTORIA
1:250,000
see index 94/4
Melbourne: Geol. Surv. Vic.
Col. geological series in progress.
75c each

GEOLOGICAL MAP OF WESTERN AUSTRALIA
Comp. R C Horwitz
1:2,500,000
East Perth: Geol; Surv. W. Aust, 1966
76 x 102
Coloured geological map.
$1.50

WESTERN AUSTRALIA – GEOLOGICAL SERIES
1:250,000
see index 94/4
Perth: Geol. Surv. W. Aust/ Bureau Mineral Resources, 1955
Col. geol. series in progress, each with explanatory text.
75c each

THE REGIONAL SURVEY OF THE METROPOLITAN AREA (PERTH AND ENVIRONS)
1:63,360
J C McMath and others
In 3 sheets
East Perth: Geol. Surv. W. Aust, 1952
Sheets numbered 1-3, in 7 sets:
Geology, Silica; Clays, loams and shales; Dimension stone and aggregate; Limestone, limesands and bog limestone; Water; Land utilisation. Geol. Sheet 2 out of print.
50c each

GEOLOGICAL SERIES
1:50,000
Perth: Geol. Surv. W. Aust
Individual series comprising the following separate sheets, no systematic series is contemplated:

Nanson 1964	H/50-1-1840-I
Wokatherra 1964	H/50-1-1840-IV
Northampton 1968	H/50-1-1841-III
Hutt 1968	H/50-1-1841-IV
Mongeragarry 1968	H/50-1-1841-I
Ajana 1968	G/50-13–1842-III
Pencell 1968	G/50-13-1842-II
Naraling 1968	H/50-1-1841-11

50c each

PERTH AND ENVIRONS GEOLOGICAL MAPS
1:50,000
G H Low and others
In 4 sheets
Perth: Geol. Surv. W Aust, 1970
104 x 75 each
Detailed col. geol. map
$1.00 each

G EARTH RESOURCES

METALLOGENIC MAP OF AUSTRALIA AND PAPUA NEW GUINEA
1:5,000,000
Canberra: BMR, 1972
Coloured map showing the location of minerals. Accompanies BMR Bull. 145
A$3.00

ATLAS OF AUSTRALIAN RESOURCES
1:6,000,000
Plates: Mineral Deposits
Mineral Industry
DND
see AUSTRALIA – ATLASES 94 0

PETROLEUM EXPLORATION AND DEVELOPMENT TITLES MAP
1:5,000,000
Canberra: BMR, 1974.
94 x 78
Map showing exploration and titles up to 30.6.73 with accompanying key.
A$1.00

ATLAS OF AUSTRALIAN SOILS
1:2,000,000
Melbourne: MUP/Commonwealth Scientific and Indust. Research Org, 1960
see AUSTRALIA – ATLASES 94 G

MARINE GEOPHYSICAL MAPS
1:500,000
Canberra: BMR
Gravity, magnetic and seismic profiles covering offshore areas.
each AUS $1.00

GRAVITY MAPS
1:500,000
Canberra: BMR
Maps available for the States of Queensland, Western Australia, New South Wales and ACT, Northern Territory and various offshore regions.
each AUS $1.00

MAGNETIC MAPS
1:50,000–1:250,000
Canberra: BMR
Series of maps at varying scales, some sheets also containing radiometric or gravity information.
Dyeline prints $1.00

RADIOMETRIC MAPS
1:50,000–1:500,000
Canberra: BMR
Series of maps at varying scales, in progress. Mainly available as dyeline prints.
each AUS $1.00

COALFIELDS MAPS
1:32,680
Sydney: Geol. Surv. NSW
Maps available in black and white for:
Burragorang Coalfields
1 sheet $1.00 each
Capertree Rylstone Coalfield
4 sheets $1.00 each
Lithgow Coalfields
4 sheets $1.00 each
Maitland – Cessnock – Greta Coalfields
3 sheets $1.50 each
Newcastle Coalfields
3 sheets $1.00 each
Singleton Coalfields
1 sheet $1.00
Southern Coalfields
4 sheets $1.00

MINERAL MAP OF NEW SOUTH WALES
1:3,000,000
Sydney: Geol. Surv. NSW
Mineral occurrence, mining fields shown by col. symbols.
20c

MINES SUBSIDENCE DISTRICT MAPS
Various scales
Sydney: Geol. Surv. NSW
60c each

OFFSHORE GRATICULE MAPS
No scale given
Sydney: Geol. Surv. NSW
For the purpose of the Petroleum (Submerged Lands) Act.
60c

PETROLEUM EXPLORATION LICENCE MAP OF NEW SOUTH WALES
No scale given
Sydney: Geol. Surv. NSW
With schedule. $3.00

EXPLORATION LICENCE MAP OF NEW SOUTH WALES
No scale given
Sydney: Geol. Surv. NSW
With schedule $5.00

BROKEN HILL MINES
1:32,680
Sydney: Geol. Surv. NSW
2 sheet map in black and white with reference sheet.
Per sheet $1.00

QUEENSLAND: RESOURCES SERIES – BURDEKIN – TOWNSVILLE REGION
1:1,000,000
Canberra: DND, 1970
66 x 44
Maps for climate and soils with commentary.
$0.75 each

MAP OF WESTERN AUSTRALIA
1:2,500,000
Perth: Mines Dept. WA
Shows roads, railways, settlements, mining centres, goldfield boundaries, water features, contours. $1.00
Gazetteer of names 50c

H BIOGEOGRAPHY

AUSTRALIA – STATE FORESTS, TIMBER RESERVES AND FOREST ADMINISTRATIVE REGIONS
1:6,000,000
Canberra: Div. of Forest Res., CSIRO, 1964
70 x 64
Coloured distribution map.
AUS $1.00

AUSTRALIA – FORESTS
1:5,000,000
Canberra: Div. of Forest Res., CSIRO, 1974
94 x 78
Showing distribution of forests including native forest, plantations, and cypress pine. Prepared for 'FORWOOD' Conference April 1974
AUS $1.00

PHILIP'S COMPARATIVE WALL ATLAS OF AUSTRALIA AND NEW ZEALAND – NATURAL VEGETATION
1:6,000,000
Philip
see AUSTRALIA 94 E1

QUEENSLAND
1:2,500,000
No 6K
Brisbane: Dept. Lands, 1970
74 x 97
Land use map – broad vegetation, soil groups, devt. potential. Overprinted on map 6b.
$2.50

FITZROY REGION RESOURCES SERIES MAP
1:1,000,000
Brisbane: Dept. Lands
Series of col. map with booklet. Shows economy, pop, land detail, mineral details, climate. 75c

SOUTH AUSTRALIA: ANNUAL REPORT PLAN No 2
1:2,534,400
Adelaide: Dept. Lands
56 x 61
General map in black and white with land use areas in col: shows Goydon's line, national parks, artesian basins. Annual revision.

CROWN LANDS, STATE FORESTS AND NATIONAL PARKS OF VICTORIA
1:500,000
In 4 sheets
Melbourne: DCLS
Overprint on 4 sheet Map of Victoria.
$5.00 each

MAP OF WESTERN AUSTRALIA
1:3,168,000
Perth: Govt. Printer, 1968
84 x 57
Map showing natural resources regions in colour. Overprinted on 1962 base map.

LAND USAGE MAP OF WESTERN AUSTRALIA
1:3,125,000
Perth: DCLS, 1967
67 x 93
Col. vegetation map.
$1.00

VEGETATION SURVEY OF WESTERN AUSTRALIA: THE VEGETATION OF THE NEWDEGATE AND BREMER BAY AREAS, WESTERN AUSTRALIA
1:250,000
Sydney: Vegmap Publications, 1972
Maps and 32pp explanatory memoir.

WESTERN AUSTRALIA: LAND USAGE MAP OF THE SOUTH WEST
1:1,000,000
Perth: DCLS
$1.00

MARIA ISLAND NATIONAL PARK
1:50,000
Hobart: National Parks and Wildlife Service, 1973
35 x 50
Contoured with relief shading, marking tracks, wooded areas, land detail and names. Inset of Darlington and historical notes. Guide on reverse.
Paper folded.

J CLIMATE

MAP OF AUSTRALIA
1:12,672,000
Canberra: Forestry & Timber Bureau
36 x 32
Map showing a mean annual rainfall and temperature.
10c

PHILIPS COMPARATIVE WALL ATLAS OF AUSTRALIA AND NEW ZEALAND – CLIMATE
1:6,000,000
Philip
see AUSTRALIA 94 E1

RAINFALL MAP OF QUEENSLAND
1:5,068,000
Melbourne: Commonwealth Bureau Meteorology, 1971
Rainfall shown by isohyets.

QUEENSLAND: RESOURCES SERIES – BURDEKIN – TOWNSVILLE REGION
1:1,000,000
DND: 1970
see AUSTRALIA 94G

K HUMAN GEOGRAPHY

PHILIP'S COMPARATIVE WALL ATLAS OF AUSTRALIA AND NEW ZEALAND – DENSITY OF POPULATION
1:6,000,000
Philip
see AUSTRALIA 94 E1

POPULATION DISTRIBUTION MAPS OF AUSTRALIA
1:2,027,000
In 7 sheets
Canberra: Bureau of the Census, 1969
72 x 58
1 sheet for each state. Pop indicated on physical base map. Based on 1966 Census.

L ECONOMIC

AUSTRALIEN, WIRTSCHAFT
1:7,500,000
H280
Munchen: List
100 x 140
Col. economic wall map for schools.
DM 70.00

PHILIP'S COMPARATIVE WALL ATLAS OF AUSTRALIA AND NEW ZEALAND – COMMERCIAL DEVELOPMENT
1:6,000,000
Philip
see AUSTRALIA 94 E1

AUSTRALIE – NOUVELLE ZELANDE – ECONOMIQUE
1:6,000,000
Éditions MDI, 1970
see AUSTRALIA AND OCEANIA 9 D.

QUEENSLAND
1:5,000,000
No 4c
Brisbane: Dept. Lands
48 x 76
Col. map showing Primary Industries areas, isohyets, list of towns with pop. (1970)
60c

ESTUARY OF BRISBANE RIVER
1:15,840
Brisbane: Dept. Lands
Industrial devt. map in col.
70c

M HISTORICAL

SYDNEY
by J Blaschke, 1780
No 1302
Wien: Editio Totius Mundi
32 x 20
Facsimile plan.
Col. 18 DM
Uncol. 8 DM

SYDNEY
by S Calvert, 1872
No 1200
Wien: Editio Totius Mundi
118 x 63
Large facsimile plan of the city.
Col. 75 DM
Uncol. 45 DM

SYDNEY AND SUBURBS HISTORICAL MAP
No scale given
No 121
Sydney: Robinson
Coloured plan of the city, noting all places of historical interest.
A$0.80

ATLASES
W3 WORLD ATLAS: LOCAL EDITION

AUSTRALASIAN SCHOOL ATLAS
John Bartholomew and K R Cramp
OUP 1966
see WORLD ATLASES 100W

ATLASES
A1 GENERAL

DESCRIPTIVE ATLAS OF THE PACIFIC ISLANDS
by T F Kennedy
A H and A W Reed
see ATLASES AUSTRALIA 9 A1

ATLASES
B TOWN PLANS

100 MILES AROUND SYDNEY
1:95,040/285,120
Sydney: Gregory
128pp
21 x 12
60 maps showing road systems with tourist information, special trip maps. Index.
$1.00

GREGORY'S STREET DIRECTORIES
Sydney: Gregory
15 x 24 each
Large scale map books, index to streets etc. Annually revised.
Titles published:

Sydney	333pp	
(key map 60c)		$2.50
Melbourne	256pp	$2.25
Brisbane	150pp	$1.90
Adelaide	150pp	$1.80
Newcastle	96pp	$1.35
Wollongong	64pp	$1.20

ATLASES
G EARTH RESOURCES

ATLAS AND HANDBOOK OF AUSTRALIAN SOILS
1:2,000,000
Prepared for the IXth International Soil Science Congress in Adelaide.
In 13 sheets
Melbourne: Commonwealth Sci. and Indust. Research Org/Melbourne UP, 1967
72 x 56
Maps show soil categories, profiles, texture, organic profiles etc. Each has reliability diagram and 2 legend – colour key and literal symbols. With accompanying text.
each A$3.75
set A$33.00

ATLASES
H BIOGEOGRAPHY

THE DISTRIBUTION OF THE MORE IMPORTANT TREES OF THE GENUS EUCALYPTUS
C E Carter
Canberra: Forestry and Timber Bureau, 1945
38 x 53
Series of maps, showing natural habitat of 55 commercial timber species of eucalyptus, also forests, rainfall and climatic factors.
AUS $12.00

FOREST TREES OF AUSTRALIA
Ed N Hall, R D Johnston, G M Chippendale
Canberra: Aust. Gov't. Pub. Service, 1975
71 x 50
Collection of 133 one-page descriptions of individual species with illustrations and distribution map.
(Replaces Carter's Atlas, 1945).
AUS $12.95
This collection is complemented by a series of Forest Tree Leaflets with additional eucalypt species and a series on Australian Acacias.

EUCALYPTS OF THE WESTERN AUSTRALIAN GOLDFIELDS
Ed G M Chippendale
Canberra: Aust. Gov't Pub. Service, 1973.
71 x 50
Collection of 113 descriptions of individual species with 113 small distribution maps (1:63m), 96 colour plates, 201 b & w photographs.
AUS $3.75

ATLASES
01 NATIONAL

THE READER'S DIGEST COMPLETE ATLAS OF AUSTRALIA
Ed P J Devery
Sydney: Readers Digest Assoc. Pty, 1968
161pp
25 x 35
Inc. Papua, New Guinea, 82pp them. maps, 12pp geog. maps. Inc. specialised information, bibliog, index of 12,200 place names.

ATLAS OF AUSTRALIAN RESOURCES
Canberra: DND
1952-60 (1st series)
1962+ (2nd series)
71 x 65 (plate)
National Atlas of Australia; 30 col. sheets each with comprehensive commentary. Show distribution of physical resources, industries, pop. and services: commentaries inc. statistics, photographs, diagrams, additional maps. At present being progressively revised.
Plates:
Landforms 2nd series 1974
Geology 2nd series 1966
Mineral Deposits 2nd series 1965
Climate 2nd series 1974
Temperatures 2nd series 1974
Rainfall 2nd series 1970
Surface Water Resources 2nd series 1967
Conservation of Surface Water 1954
Groundwater 2nd series 1973
Soils 2nd series 1963
Vegetation Regions 1955
Land Use 2nd series 1974
Croplands 2nd series 1970
Crop Production 2nd series 1968
Livestock 2nd series 1970
Sheep and Wool 2nd series 1968
Forest Resources 2nd series 1967
Fish and Fisheries 2nd Series 1965
Mineral Industry 2nd series 1969
Electricity 2nd series 1962
Manufacturing Industries 1960
Population Distribution and Growth 2nd series 1964
Population Increase and Decrease, 1947-1954 1957
Grasslands 2nd series 1970
Immigration 2nd series 1970
Railways 1954
Roads and Aerodromes 2nd series 1967
Ports and Shipping 2nd series 1971
Educational Facilities 1956
Health Services 1957
State and Local Government Areas 1953
unfolded with commentary
75c
linen strip-mounted to file in Atlas binder, with commentary
75c
complete binder set: 30 linen strip-mounted maps with commentaries in box. $21.00

ATLASES
02 NATIONAL ATLAS: SCHOOL EDITION

ILLUSTRATED ATLAS OF AUSTRALIA
Australian Govt. Printing Service, 1971
16pp
5 continental maps, showing states, economic aspects.
$0.30

ATLASES
P REGIONAL

ATLAS OF TASMANIA
Ed J L Davies
1st Edition
Hobart: Lands and Surveys Dept.
1965
24 x 31cm
128pp incl. 15pp col. thematic maps, 15pp of topographical maps, scale 1:500,000 town environs maps, 106 black and white maps and diagrams, 16 black and white photographs. Each subject has commentary and includes a gazetteer and index.
A$2.00

95 Papua New Guinea

A1 GENERAL MAPS

NEW GUINEA – PAPUA
1:3,425,000
No 520
Sydney: Gregory
76 x 50
Col. map showing Papua, New Guinea, Bismarck Archipelago, British Solomon Islands. Mt. relief, distances from Australia. Insets of New Guinea Highland district with 6 sheet maps.
50c

A2 GENERAL MAPS: LOCAL

ROAD SYSTEM MAP OF PAPUA AND NEW GUINEA
1:1,000,000
In 4 sheets
Canberra: DND, 1969
181 x 121 complete
Topog. details, roads classified, relief shading, contours. Inc. Aust. islands, boundaries etc.

QUEENSLAND AND PAPUA
1:6,250,000 and 1:5,000,000
see AUSTRALIA 94 A2

C OFFICIAL SURVEYS

AUSTRALIAN GEOGRAPHICAL SERIES
1:1,000,000
Canberra: DND
Col. topog. series covering the Territory in 11 sheets, contoured and layer coloured, communications and settlement. Woodlark Is. sheet not yet published but is available in a World Aeronautical Chart edition. This series will eventually be replaced by the new Australian edition of the International Map of the World series.

NEW GUINEA
1:250,000
Series T504, see index 955/1
Canberra: DND
Col topog. series in progress, contoured, coloured.
75c each

TOPOGRAPHICAL SERIES OF NEW GUINEA
1:100,000
see index 955/2
Canberra: DND
Topographical series in progress, contoured.

PAPUA AND NEW GUINEA
1:50,000
see index 955/2
Canberra: DND
Col. topog. series in progress. Superseding 1:63,360 series. Available in coloured, published map edition or as a dyeline print.

BOUGAINVILLE TOPOGRAPHICAL SERIES (THE SOLOMON ISLANDS)
1:50,000
Series X713, in 37 sheets
Canberra: DND
Topographical series prepared by Royal Australian Survey Corp.

TOPOGRAPHICAL SERIES OF NEW BRITAIN
1:63,360
In 81 sheets
Canberra: DND
Planimetric series, uncontoured.
$0.75 each

TOPOGRAPHICAL SERIES OF NEW IRELAND
1:50,000
Series T795, in 33 sheets
Canberra: DND
Topographical series prepared by Royal Australian Survey Corp.
$0.75 each

D POLITICAL & ADMINISTRATIVE

PAPUA AND NEW GUINEA
1:875,000
Sydney: Robinson
96 x 73
Political col. map showing territory, district boundaries, capital cities, settlements, airports.

E1 PHYSICAL: RELIEF

PAPUA AND NEW GUINEA
1:5,000,000
Canberra: DND, 1970
48 x 33
Physical map with communications, contoured, layer coloured.
$0.75

PAPUA AND NEW GUINEA
1:2,500,000
Canberra: DND, 1973
97 x 71
Topog. map, relief shading, communications, settlements, in col.
$0.75

F GEOLOGY

GEOLOGICAL MAP OF PAPUA NEW GUINEA
1:1,000,000
In 4 sheets
Canberra: DMR, 1972
184 x 145
Coloured geological wall map with legend and cross-section.

G EARTH RESOURCES

METALLOGENIC MAP OF AUSTRALIA AND PAPUA, NEW GUINEA
1:5,000,000
see AUSTRALIA – 94 G

TERRITORY OF PAPUA AND NEW GUINEA: GEOPHYSICAL MAGNETIC MAPS
1:50,000 and 1:250,000
Canberra: BMR
Series in progress.
each A$1.00

K HUMAN GEOGRAPHY

LANGUAGES OF THE EASTERN, WESTERN AND SOUTHERN HIGHLANDS (NEW GUINEA)
Stefan A Wurm
1:1,000,000
Series D No 4
Canberra: (Pacific Linguistics), 1960

ATLASES
0 NATIONAL ATLAS

PAPUA NEW GUINEA RESOURCE ATLAS
Editor Edgar Ford
1st Edition
Brisbane: Jacaranda Press, 1974
60 x 42
58pp
Contains detailed coloured maps with facing page of descriptive text. Subjects covered include physical nature, climate, vegetation, land use, industry, communications, trade, administration and culture. Gazetteer of places. Contained in looseleaf screw binder.
A$42.00

961.1 Fiji Islands

A1 GENERAL MAPS

FIJI ISLANDS
1:1,500,000
DOS 961
Edition 5
Tolworth: DOS, 1967
55 x 43
Small map showing principal towns and island positions. 15p

A2 GENERAL MAPS: LOCAL

FIJI ISLANDS – VITI AND VANUA LEVU
1:500,000
DOS (Misc) 271 AB in 2 sheets
Tolworth : DOS, 1960
2 general maps showing communications, boundaries and settlement – one sheet for each island.
each 30p

CICIA ISLAND (LAU)
1:31,680
Suva : DLMS, 1958
30 x 45
Topog. map, dyeline print. 20c

CIKOBIA ISLAND (MACUATA)
1:31,680
Suva : DLMS, 1958
48 x 30
Topog. map in dyeline print. 20c

MAGO ISLAND (LAU)
1:31,680
Suva : DLMS, 1958
43 x 27
Topog. map in dyeline print. 20c

MOALA ISLAND (LAU)
1:31,680
Suva : DLMS, 1958
81 x 63
Topog. map in dyeline print. 60c

RABI ISLAND (E. VANUA LEVU)
1:31,680
Suva : DLMS, 1958
96 x 76
Topog. map in dyeline print. 90c

TOTOYA ISLAND (LAU)
1:31,680
Suva : DLMS, 1958
86 x 55
Topog. map in dyeline print. 60c

MATUKU ISLAND (LAU)
1:24,000
Suva : DLMS, 1958
53 x 40
Topog. map in dyeline print. 25c

KORO ISLAND (LOMAIVITI)
1:15,480
Suva : DLMS, 1964
101 x 76
Topog. map in dyeline print. 90c

VIWA AND ADJACENT ISLANDS (YASAWAS)
1:12,672
Suva : DLMS, 1961
101 x 76
Dyeline print, topog. map with NLC Survey data. 90c

ROTUMA ISLAND (N GROUP)
1:7,920
In 3 sheets
Suva : DLMS, 1964
Various sizes
Topog. map in dyeline print. set $2.70

VIWA ISLAND (YASAWAS)
1:6,336
Suva : DLMS, 1961
101 x 76
Dyeline print : topog. map with NLC Survey data. 90c

VATOA ISLAND (LAU)
1:4,800
Suva : DLMS, 1957
99 x 55
Topog. map in dyeline print. 65c

B TOWN PLANS

TOWNSHIP MAPS
1:1,584
Suva : DLMS
101 x 68
Showing admin. and street details. Dyeline prints available for the following areas:

Ba Township	(6 sheets)	1959
Sigatoka Township	(2 sheets)	1959
Nadi Township	(6 sheets)	1960
Labasa Township	(2 sheets)	1960
Nausori Township	(5 sheets)	1961
Lautoka Town	(10 sheets)	1965

each 80c

NADI – NADI AIRPORT
1:3,168
In 12 sheets
Suva : DLMS, 1969
101 x 68
Dyeline print map showing admin. areas.
each 80c

NADI AIRPORT
1:1,584
In 3 sheets
Suva : DLMS, 1965
101 x 68
Dyeline print map, showing admin. areas.
80c

SUVA AND SUBURBS
1:12,000
Suva : DLMS
66 x 51
Col. street map, streets named, principal buildings marked. 40c

CITY OF SUVA
1:1,584
In 26 sheets
Suva : DLMS, 1960
101 x 68
Admin. details and boundaries.
Dyeline print. 80c each

TAVUA
1:1,584
Suva : DLMS, 1965
101 x 68
Admin. areas shown : 2 sheet map, dyeline print. 80c

C OFFICIAL SURVEYS

FIJI ISLANDS
1:250,000
DOS 648 (X552)
In 7 sheets
See index 961.1/1
Tolworth : DOS
Topog. series in progress: contoured, layer col, communications, boundaries and towns. Sheets published:

1	Yasawa Group	1966	71 x 55
2	Vanua Levu	1963	101 x 73
4	Viti Levu	1963	88 x 60
6	Kandavu	1966	71 x 55

NB Sheets 3, 5, and 7 can be supplied from DLMS in Dyeline edition.
each 65p

LAU/LOMAIVITI GROUP
1:250,000
In 32 sheets
Suva : DLMS, 1969
101 x 76
Topog. map (dyeline print) with admin. details. 90c set

FIJI ISLANDS
1:50,000
DOS 448 (X754) see index 961.1/1
Editions 1960-69
Tolworth : DOS
Topog. series, contours or form lines : land detail. See index.
Sheets for :
Viti Levu (22 sheets)
1960 83 x 63
Vanua Levu (16 sheets) Series (X755)
1960 91 x 63
Yasawa Group (3 sheets)
1963 106 x 76
Kandavu (3 sheets)
1963 83 x 71
Lomaiviti (4 sheets)
1964,
1968 88 x 60
each 50p

D POLITICAL & ADMINISTRATIVE

FIJI ISLANDS
1:500,000
Suva : DLMS, 1965
101 x 76
Admin. map, dyeline print, boundaries in colour, communications and relief by hachures. 90c

VITI LEVU
1:126,720
In 4 sheets
Suva : DLMS, 1953
170 x 109 complete
Col. by provinces, showing communications, rivers and settlement. $2.50

FIJI ISLAND SKETCH MAP
1:1,250,000 and 1:2,375,000
DOS 914
Tolworth : DOS, 1960
45 x 33
General geog. map in black and white. 15p

F GEOLOGY

FIJI FIRST GEOLOGICAL MAP (PROVISIONAL)
1:500,000
DOS (Geol) 1158
Tolworth : DOS, 1966
Single sheet map in col. 65p

FIJI, – VITI LEVU GEOLOGICAL SERIES
1:50,000
DOS (Geol) 1101
See index 961.1/1
Tolworth : DOS
Col. geol. series in progress, on same sheet lines as Topog. DOS 448.
Sheets published:
3, 4, 7, 8, 13, 14, 20 65p each

H BIOGEOGRAPHY

VANUA LEVU – LAND USE
1:250,000
DOS 3022
Tolworth : DOS, 1964
101 x 73
Showing land use and admin. areas. 65p

VITI LEVU – LAND USE
1:250,000
DOS 3022
Edition 1
Tolworth : DOS 1964
88 x 73
Shows land use and admin. areas. 65p

ATLASES
A1 GENERAL

DESCRIPTIVE ATLAS OF THE PACIFIC ISLANDS
by T F Kennedy
A H and A W Reed
see AUSTRALIA AND OCEANIA 9 ATLASES A1

961.2 Tonga Islands

A1 GENERAL MAPS: ROADS

TONGA ISLANDS
1:2,000,000
DOS 990
Edition 2
Tolworth : DOS, 1960
Small map showing communications and principal towns. 15p

A2 GENERAL MAPS: LOCAL

NUKUALOFA
1:145,000
DOS (Misc) 94A
Tolworth : DOS, 1953
General map of the island. 15p

NUKUALOFA
1:20,000
DOS (Misc) 94B
Tolworth : DOS, 1953
General map of the island. 15p

KINGDOM OF TONGA – TONGATAPU ISLAND
1:50,000
DOS 6005 (X773)
Tolworth : DOS, 1971
65 x 83
Black and white photo map showing roads, tracks, settlement, other land detail. 65p

ATLASES
A1 GENERAL

DESCRIPTIVE ATLAS OF THE PACIFIC ISLANDS
by T F Kennedy
A H and A W Reed
see AUSTRALIA AND OCEANIA 9 ATLASES A1

961.3 Samoa

ATLASES
A1 GENERAL

DESCRIPTIVE ATLAS OF THE PACIFIC ISLANDS
by T F Kennedy
A H and A W Reed
see AUSTRALIA AND OCEANIA 9 ATLASES A1

B TOWN PLANS

Western Samoa

APIA AND ENVIRONS
1:10,000
1st edition
Apia: Lands and Surv. Dept, 1969
95 x 75
Col. plan of the town and suburbs.

APIA (TOWN)
1:2,000
NZMS 70
Wellington : NZMS, 1924
61 x 101
2 sheet map showing roads and streets (named), buildings, places of interest, natural features. Large scale.

C OFFICIAL SURVEYS

Western Samoa

WESTERN SAMOA
1:20,000
NZMS 174
Wellington : NZMS, 1959-65
80 x 65 each
Col. series showing vegetation, contours, UTM grid.

American Samoa

MANUA ISLANDS
1:24,000
Washington : USGS, 1963
76 x 142
Covers Tau, Ofu, Oloseega Is.
Contoured topog. map. 50¢

TUTUILA ISLAND, AMERICAN SAMOA
1:24,000
Washington : USGS, 1963
88 x 154
Col. map with contours. $1.00

E1 PHYSICAL: RELIEF

WESTERN SAMOA
1:200,000
2nd edition
Apia : Lands & Surv. Dept. 1966
80 x 62
Col. physical map with contours.
Apia and Environs inset.

G EARTH RESOURCES

SOIL BUREAU MAPS
1:100,000
Wellington : Dept. Sci. and Indust. Research, 1962
106 x 75
Maps available:
Soil maps of Savai'i
Soil map of Upolu NZ$0.35

H BIOGEOGRAPHY

SOIL BUREAU MAPS
1:100,000
Wellington : Dept. of Sci. and Indust. Research
106 x 75
Maps available:
Land Classification Map of Savai'i 1962
Land Classification Map of Upolu 1962
NZ$0.35

961.4 Gilbert Islands and Tuvalu

A1 GENERAL MAPS

GILBERT AND ELLICE ISLANDS
LOCATION OF GOVERNMENT DEPT. – TARAWA ATOLL
1:120,000
DOS (Misc) 515
Tolworth : DOS
Small hand map showing location of islands and gov't dept. 20p

CHRISTMAS ISLAND
1:50,000
DOS 436 (X782)
Edition 4
Tolworth : DOS, 1970
100 x 92
Planimetric map showing vegetation, island products, principal features. 50p

C OFFICIAL SURVEYS

GILBERT AND ELLICE ISLANDS CONDOMINIUM – MARAKEI ISLAND
1:12,500
DOS 6007 (X844)
Detailed plan of the island. 50p

GILBERT AND ELLICE ISLAND CONDOMINIUM
1:10,000
DOS 238P (X041)
Tolworth: DOS
Photomap series available either with or without UTM grid overprint.
Sheets published:
Vaitupu Island 1975. 50p

GILBERT AND ELLICE ISLAND CONDOMINIUM
1:2,500
DOS 038
Tolworth : DOS 1971
Detailed series of plans in progress, covering Tarawa Atoll.

GILBERT AND ELLICE ISLANDS – BETIO
1:1,250
DOS 0038 in 4 sheets
Tolworth : DOS, 1971
Detailed plan of the islet near Tarawa.

H BIOGEOGRAPHY

CHRISTMAS ISLAND – LAND USE MAPS
1:50,000 and 1:25,000
Tolworth : DOS, 1968
Maps available:
(LR) 3034A Map 2 1:50,000
Land use 50p
3034B Map 3 1:50,000
Soil and Ground Water 65p
3034C Map 4A 1:25,000
Vegetation 50p
3034C Map 4B 1:25,000
Vegetation 65p
3034C Map 4C 1:25,000
Vegetation 65p
3034D Map 5B 1:25,000
Coconut Plantations 50p
3034D Map 5C 1:25.000
Coconut Plantations 50p

ATLASES
A1 GENERAL

DESCRIPTIVE ATLAS OF THE PACIFIC ISLANDS
T F Kennedy
A H and A W Reed
see AUSTRALIA AND OCEANIA 9 – ATLASES A1

963 French Polynesia

C OFFICIAL SURVEYS

TAHITI – OFFICIAL INTERNATIONAL MAP OF THE WORLD ICAO EDITION
1:1,000,000
Sheet 3208 – 3209 Tahiti
Paris : IGN
45 x 65 app.
Contoured, layer col. communications, settlement, other land detail.
F.Fr. 14.17

CARTE TOURISTIQUE DES ÎLES DE LA SOCIÉTÉ
1:100,000
Paris : IGN, 1974
49 x 64
Inc. Tahiti and Moorea with Society Archipelago inset. Roads classified, distances in km, relief shading, tourist features. UTM grid. F.Fr. 10.00

ÎLES DE LA SOCIÉTÉ – CARTE GÉNÉRALE
1:40,000
In 10 sheets
Paris : IGN, 1955
Various sizes
Provisional series, contoured, detailed land information. 3 or 4 col. eds.
Sheets available:
1 Île de Bora-Bora
2 Île de Huahine
3 Île de Mooréa
4 Île de Raiatea
5 Tahaa
6 Île de Tahiti, inc. Presqu'île de Taiarapu (5 sheets) F.Fr. 11.67

ARCHIPEL TUAMOTO
1:50,000
In 11 sheets
Paris : IGN, 1962
Various sizes
Contoured, detailed land information.
Sheets available:
Fakarava (2 sheets)
Makemo (3 sheets)
Rangiroa (5 sheets)
Tikehau (1 sheet)
F.Fr. 11.67

ARCHIPEL TUAMOTU
1:20,000
In 4 sheets
Paris : IGN, 1962
Various sizes
Contoured, detailed land information.
Sheets available:
Anaa (2 sheets)
Haraiki (1 sheet)
Hikueru (1 sheet)
F.Fr. 11.67

E1 PHYSICAL: RELIEF

CARTE TOPOGRAPHIQUE DES ÎLES DE LA SOCIÉTÉ ET MAKATEA
1:200,000
Toulouse : Inst. de la Carte Internat. du Tapis Vegetal.
Physical map, contours, spot heights etc.
F.Fr. 6

TAHITI – CARTE EN RELIEF
1:100,000
Paris : IGN, 1974
74 x 59
Moulded plastic relief map, physical col, contoured, vegetation, communications, other land detail.
F.Fr. 104.17

F GEOLOGY

CARTE GÉOLOGIQUE DES ARCHIPELS POLYNÉSIENS
1:40,000
Orléans: BRGM
Coloured geol. map series with explanatory text by G Deneufbourg, 1965. Available sheets:
Bora-Bora
Huahine
Tahaa
Raiatea
Mooréa
Tahiti
each F.Fr. 30

ATLASES
A1 GENERAL

DESCRIPTIVE ATLAS OF THE PACIFIC ISLANDS
by T F Kennedy
A H and A W Reed
see AUSTRALIA AND OCEANIA 9 ATLASES A1

965 Micronesia

See also : 265 PACIFIC OCEAN
967.1 MARIANA ISLANDS

C OFFICIAL SURVEYS

KARTA MIRA
1:2,500,000
GUGK
Sheets 100, 101, 102, 120, 121, 123
cover Micronesia.
see WORLD 100C and index 100/2.

ATLASES
A1 GENERAL

DESCRIPTIVE ATLAS OF THE
PACIFIC ISLANDS
T F Kennedy
A H and A W Reed
see AUSTRALIA AND OCEANIA 9
ATLASES A1.

967.1 Mariana Islands

C OFFICIAL SURVEYS

GUAM. MARIANA ISLANDS
1:62,500
Washington : USGS, 1953
73 x 88
Contoured Topog. map. 50¢

ATLASES
A1 GENERAL

DESCRIPTIVE ATLAS OF THE
PACIFIC ISLANDS
T F Kennedy
A H and A W Reed
see AUSTRALIA AND OCEANIA 9
ATLASES A1

Polar Regions 98/99

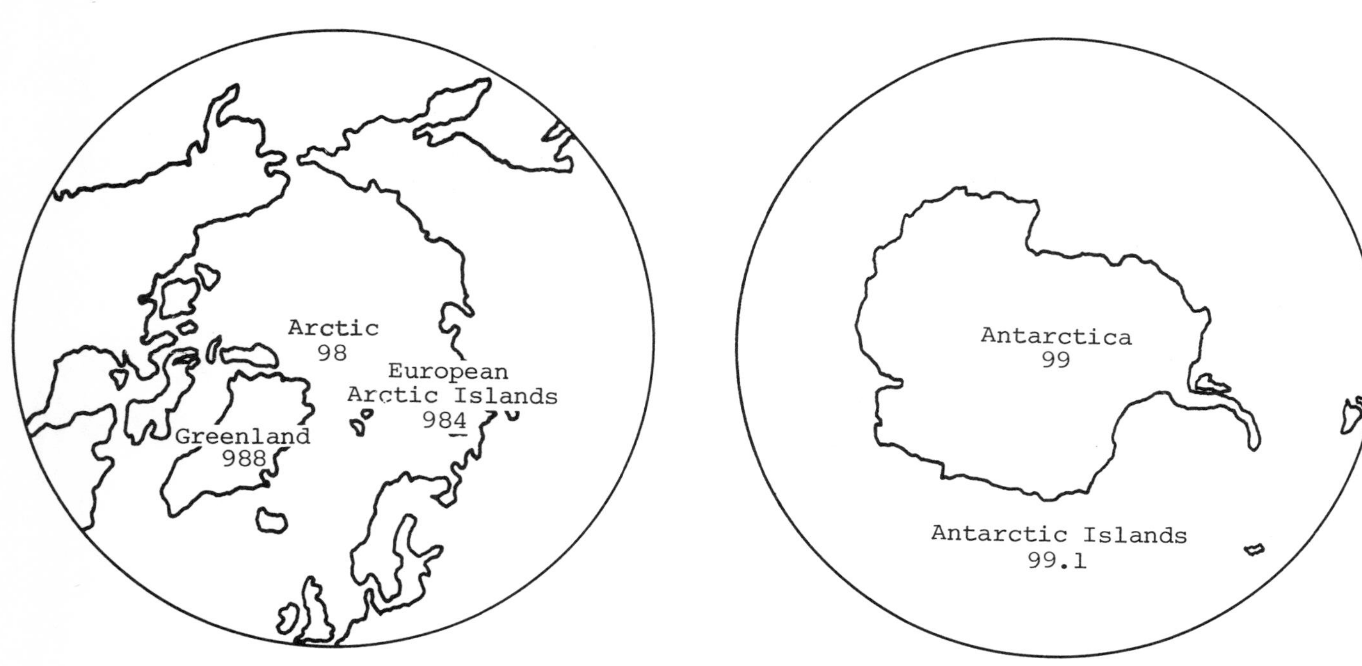

Polar Regions

98/99 Polar Regions

D POLITICAL & ADMINISTRATIVE

JRO-POLAR WELTKARTE
1:18,000,000
JRO
see WORLD 100D

TERRE POLAR
1:40,000,000
Novara : Agostini
Small outline map of the polar areas. L40

MAPAS MUDOS – REGIONES POLARES
Barcelona : Editoria Vicens-Vives
33 x 24
Outline map of the polar regions in 2 colours
50 copies S.Ptas 100

E1 PHYSICAL: RELIEF

NORD- UND SÜDPOLARGEBIETE
1:10,000,000
W719
München: List
190 x 130
Wenschow wall map of N and S Polar regions. Shows relief, limits of polar ice, major expeditions traced.
DM142

ATLASES
E1 PHYSICAL

OCEANOGRAPHIC ATLAS OF THE POLAR SEAS
Washington : US Naval Oceanographic Office
Part 1 – Antarctic 1957 (1970 reprint)
In 7 sections; Tides and currents; physical properties (temperature, salinity); ice; wind, sea and swell; marine geology; marine biology; distribution of oceanog. observations. Bibliog. fold-out relief map. 70pp.
$2.50

98 Arctic

A1 GENERAL MAPS

THE ARCTIC : PHYSICAL, EXPLORATION
No scale given
Chicago : Denoyer-Geppert
96 x 127
Col. pictorial wall map for schools.
$5.00

C OFFICIAL SURVEYS

CARTE DES CONTINENTS
1:5,000,000
IGN
Sheets 1, 2, 3, 4, cover North Pole
see WORLD 100C

KARTA MIRA
1:2,500,000
GUGK and Carti
17 sheets cover Arctic area.
see WORLD 100C and index 100/2.

D POLITICAL & ADMINISTRATIVE

THE TOP OF THE WORLD
1:13,750,000
Washington : NGS
72 x 75
Political col. wall map, boundaries in colour.
Paper $2.00
Plastic $3.00

E1 PHYSICAL:RELIEF

POLAR AIR AGE WORLD
1:25,000,000
Denoyer-Geppert
see WORLD 100 E1.

ARCTIC OCEAN, DOUBLE PORTRAIT MAP
1:9,062,500
Washington : NGS, 1971
63 x 48
Graphically shows relief of Arctic Ocean floor on one side, with detailed conventional map on the other.
$1.00

ARKTIKA - FIZICHESKAYA UCHEBNAYA KARTA
1:8,000,000
Moskva : GUGK, 1970
112 x 90
Physical school map showing summer and winter ice boundaries.

NORDPOLARGEBIET
1:6,000,000
Eds: Haack - Painke
No 165
Darmstadt : Perthes
230 x 210
Physical school wall map, layer col, communications and currents etc. Covers North Pole, Europe, N Asia and Canada.
Editions in German, French and Dutch language.
Cloth mounted.

MAP OF THE ARCTIC REGION
1:5,000,000
Washington : AGS, 1974
152 x 127
Contoured with layer colours and showing water detail, boundaries, roads, railways, airports etc. Also includes locations of major research stations, archaeological sites and weather stations.
US $12.00

ARCTIC BATHYMETRY MAPS
1:2,000,000
Ottawa : Canadian Hydrog. Service
2 coloured charts covering the Canadian segment of the Arctic.
896 Area north of $72^o - 0^o$ to 90^oW
897 Area north of $72^o - 90^o$ to 180^oW
each $2.00

OCEAN ATLANTIQUE ET POLE NORD
Hatier
see ATLANTIC 261 E1

F GEOLOGY

GEOLOGICAL MAP OF THE ARCTIC
1:7,500,000
Tulsa : Am. Soc. Petroleum Geographers, 1960
118 x 103
Col. geol. map : bathymetric contours of land areas adjacent to Pole.
Tectonic maps of Arctic and variations of Magnetic Compass (1955) inset.

GEOLOGICHESKAYA KARTA ARKTIKI I SUBARKTIKI
1:5,000,000
In 6 sheets
Moskva : Ministry for Geol, 1966
70 x 80 each
4 sheet geol. map with 2 legend sheets in Eng and Rus.

TEKTONICHESKAYA KARTA ARKTIKI I SUBARKTIKI
1:5,000,000
In 6 sheets
Moskva : Ministry for Geol, 1971
84 x 68 each
4 sheet map with 2 legen sheets.
Descriptions in Eng. and Rus.

G EARTH RESOURCES

ARCTIC OIL AND GAS MAP
1:3,800,000 app.
Calgary: Royal Bank of Canada, 1971
102 x 65
Col. map of Arctic Canada showing existing and potential oil and gas areas — fields, pipe lines, wells; towns and villages, air fields, all weather roads.

J CLIMATE

ICE LIMIT NORMALS
1:87,500,000
Bracknell : Met. Office, 1969
30 x 45
12 charts showing normal ice cover for each month, 1 showing ice symbols.
On reverse, satellite picture example.

EXTENT OF ICE
1:21,597,000
Bracknell : Met. Office, 1971
3 sheets
46 x 34
Showing ice at the end of January, February, March 1971. Sea temperatures on reverse. With sheet of notes.

ATLASES
A1 GENERAL

PICTURE ATLAS OF THE ARCTIC
R Thoren
Amsterdam : Elsevier, 1969
20 x 30
vii, 449pp
Eng. text with maps, illus. diagrams.
Aerial photographs covering Arctic areas of Canada, Iceland, Scandinavia, Greenland, Alaska, USSR.
D fl. 165.00

984 European Arctic Islands

C OFFICIAL SURVEYS

ICAO FLYKART
1:1,000,000
Oslo : NGO
Flying charts without overprint of air information, contoured, layer coloured.
Sheets published :

2016	Spitzbergen	1964
2042	Bjørnøya	1952
2054	Jan Mayen	1963

each kr 10.40

SVALBARD
1:500,000
In 4 sheets
Oslo : NP, 1964-70
54 x 62 each
Topog. series showing weather and radio stations, huts etc. with contours and moraines. Sheets for:
1 (SW) Vestspitsbergen, Søredel (southern part) 1964, 1968
2 (SE) Edgeøya, 1970
3 (NW) Vestspitsbergen, nordre del (northern part) 1964, 1968
4 (NE) Nordaustlandet, 1970
each kr 14.40

SVALBARD
1:100,000
see index 984/1
Oslo : NP, 1941+
68 x 55
Topog. series in progress. Contours, glacier features etc. Some sheets in preliminary edition.
Sheets published :
A7 Kongsfjorden, 1962
A8 Prins Karls Forland 1959
B9 Isfjorden, 1955
B10 Van Mijenfjorden — new. ed in preparation
B11 Van Keulenfjorden
B12 Torellbreen, 1953
C9 Adventdalen, 1950
C12 Markhambreen, 1957
C13 Sørkapp, 1947
G14 Hopen Prelim. Ed, 1949
Special sheet : Adventfjorden — Braganzavagen — Prelim. Ed, 1941
each kr 14.40
Prelim. ed. kr 7.20

SVALBARD
1:50,000
see index 984/2
Oslo : NP, 1949+
Topographic series, contoured in black and white, based upon 100,000 survey.
each kr 12.00

BJØRNØYA (BEAR ISLAND)
1:25,000
3rd edition
Oslo : NP, 1955
General map in colour. Supplement to Skrifter Nr 86. kr 12.00

BJØRNØYA
1:25,000
De Norske Svalbardekspedisjoner
Oslo : NP, 1925
Contoured, topographical map of Bear Island.
D.kr 12.00

BJØRNØYA (BEAR ISLAND)
1:10,000
In 6 sheets
Oslo : NP, 1925
Sheets published:
I Flavatna
II Tunheim (out of print)
III Røyevatnet
IV Miseryfjellet
V Ellasjøen
VI Sørhamna (out of print)
each kr 12.00

JAN MAYEN
1:100,000
Oslo : NP, 1955
64 x 50
Preliminary ed. Topog. map in black and white. kr 6.00

JAN MAYEN
1:50,000
Oslo : NP, 1959
60 x 62 each
2 sheet topog. map in col. Supp. to Skrifter Nr 120. each kr 14.40

JAN MAYEN
1:20,000
In 6 sheets
Oslo : NP
Topog. series in monochrome.
each kr 6.00

D POLITICAL & ADMINISTRATIVE

GRENSEKART FOR GODKJENDE OKKUPASJONAR
De Norske Svalbardekspedisjoner
1:50,000
Oslo : NP, 1927
Series of boundary maps of Western Svalbord for each recognised claim. Accompanying text in 2 parts out of print.
each D.kr 6.00

E1 PHYSICAL: RELIEF

SVALBARD
1:1,000,000
Oslo : NP, 1967
75 x 67
General map in col. with relief shading and contours.
kr 14.40

SPITZBERGEN, SOUTHERN NY FRIESLAND, CENTRAL VESTPITZBERGEN
1:125,000
London : RGS, 1962
58 x 87
Coloured map. from surveys by Cambridge Expeditions between 1940 and 1959. £1.00

F GEOLOGY

SVALBARD GEOLOGISK KART
1:1,000,000
prepared by A K Orvin
Oslo : NP, 1940
59 x 75
Col. map showing generalised geology with detail of folding, rock formation, types and features. 4 cross sections. Includes complete group, King Karls Land and Hopen. To accompany Norges Svalbard — og Ishavs — undersøkelser Skrifter Nr 78. Outline of the Geological History of Spitzbergen. 2nd edition, 1969, 60pp.
N.kr 20.00

SVALBARD — GEOLOGICAL MAP
1:500,000
In 4 sheets
Oslo : NP
83 x 60
General geol. map in preparation, col. Legend Norw. and Eng. Sheet 1G Spitzbergen — Southern Part, 1971.

NORDAUSTLANDET : SVALBARD
1:250,000
Oslo : NP, 1969
70 x 55
Col. geol. map of Northern and Central part. Accompanying Skrifter Nr 146, The Geology of Nordaustlandet, northern and central parts. 141pp by B Flood and others, in English.

988 Greenland

See also: **489 DENMARK**

A2 GENERAL MAPS: LOCAL

GREENLAND, NORTH-EAST
DRONNING LOUISE LAND
1:50,000
London : RGS
56 x 56
Map reprinted from the Geog. Journal (June 1956), from surveys of the British North Greenland Expedition, 1954. £1.50

C OFFICIAL SERIES

GREENLAND (ICAO)
1:1,000,000
In 14 sheets, see index 988/1
København : GI
70 x 50
ICAO flying charts without aeronautical information, contoured, layer coloured.
each kr 9.00

GRØNLAND
1:300,000
see index 988/1
In 19 sheets
København : GI
Various sizes
Lauge Kochs map of North Greenland, based on survey of 1917-23. 18 sheets + supp. sheet. each kr 12.00

GRØNLAND
1:250,000
see index 988/1
København : GI
Various sizes
Topog. series in col. Contours, spot heights, etc. each kr 12.00

AUST-GRØNLAND – ERIK RAUDES LAND FRA SOFIASUND
1:200,000
by Youngsund
Oslo : NP, 1932
Topographic map. kr 6.00

AUST-GRØNLAND – KARTE VON NORDOSTGRØNLAND
1:100,000
In 3 sheets
Oslo : NP, 1937 (in co-operation with Luftbild-Abteilung der Deutschen Versuchsanstalt fur Luftfahrt, Berlin-Adlershof and Hansa Luftbild GmbH, Berlin)
Sheets available:
Claveringøya
Jordan Hill
Geographical Society-oya kr 30.00

E1 PHYSICAL: RELIEF

GRØNLAND
1:5,000,000
København : GI
57 x 70
Sea and ice contours, spot heights, regional boundaries, mines, meteorlogical stations, towns, ports and outposts. kr 9.00

GRØNLAND
1:2,500,000
København : GI
85 x 120
Sea and ice contours, spot heights, regional boundaries, towns, outposts and telegraph stations. kr 15.00

GRØNLAND
1:2,000,000
København : GI, 1969
151 x 112
2 sheet wall map for schools in col. Showing elevations and depths, airports etc. kr 80.00

F GEOLOGY

QUATERNARY MAP OF GREENLAND
1:2,500,000
København : Grønlands Geol. Undersøgelse, 1971
85 x 115
Coloured quaternary map showing ice cap, surface and bedrock contours, holocene (postglacial) deposits, rock features classified, submarine topography. D.kr 30.00

TECTONIC/GEOLOGICAL MAP OF GREENLAND
1:2,500,000
København : Grønlands Geol. Undersøgelse, 1970
85 x 115
Coloured map. kr 30.00

GEOLOGISK KORT OVER GRØNLAND
1:500,000
see index 988/2
København : Grønlands Geologiske Undersøgelse
50 x 94cm
Series in progress covering the whole of Greenland in approx 14 sheets. Coloured with legend in English.
Sheets available:
SØNDRE STRØMFJORD-NUGSSUAQ, 1971
SYDGRØNLAND
1975 each D.kr 30.00

WEST GREENLAND : GEOLOGICAL RECONNAISSANCE MAP
1:500,000
København : Grønlands Geol. Undersøgelse, 1961
46 x 76
2 sheet map in col. with 9pp text.
kr 24.00

QUATERNARY MAPS OF GREENLAND
1:500,000
København : Grønlands Geologiske Undersøgelse
50 x 94
Series in progress, coloured with legend in English.
Sheet available:
Søndre Strømfjord – Nugssuaq 1974
D.kr 30.00

TECTONIC MAP OF EAST GREENLAND
1:500,000
In 3 sheets
København : Meddelelser om Grønland 1965
94 x 62 each
2 coloured tectonic maps folded in book, 286pp. D.kr 165.00
Maps separately D.kr 37.00

GEOLOGICAL MAP OF EAST GREENLAND 72° – 76°N
1:250,000
København : Meddelelser om Grønland.
195 x 160
Geological map in 13 sheets which can be assembled into a wall map measuring 195 x 160.
Available as separate sheets or in book form (26pp) both editions. D.kr 206.00

GEOLOGISK KORT OVER GRØNLANDS
1:100,000
see index 988
København : Grønlands Geol. Undersøgelse
82 x 56cm
Series in progress, coloured, with legend in English. Sheets available:

60 V1	Nord	Nunarssuit	1967
60 V1	Syd	Nanortalik	1973
60 V2	Nord	Julianehab	1972
61 V1	Nord	Neria	1975
61 V1	Syd	Ivigtut	1968
61 V2	Nord	Midternaes	1974
61 V3	Syd	Narssarssuaq	1973
70 V1	Nord	Agatdal	1974
71 Ø3	Nord	Frederiksdal	1975
71 Ø4	Nord	Charcot Land	1975
71 Ø4	Syd	Krummedal	1975
71 V2	Nord	Nugatsiaq	1971
71 V2	Syd	Marmorilik	1970
72 V2	Syd	Pangnertoq	1971

ATLASES
O NATIONAL

DANMARK ATLAS (INC. GREENLAND)
J Humlum and K Nygard
Gyldendal
see DENMARK 489 O

99 Antarctica

A1 GENERAL MAPS

ANTARCTICA
1:20,000,000
Canberra : DND, 1965
49 x 35
Small general map naming principal features. $0.10

MAP OF THE ANTARCTIC REGIONS
1:16,000,000
NZMS 94
Wellington : NZMS, 1963
69 x 69
General map showing accepted dependencies and territories with regions and principal features only named, relationships with adjacent continents. 3rd edition.
$0.50

ANTARCTICA
1:15,000,000
DOS (Misc) 135 (3101) Edition 1,
Tolworth : DOS, 1964
General map in colours, showing traverses and naming principal features. 50p

ANTARKTIKA, FISICHESKAYA KARTA
1:15,000,000
Moskva : GUGK, 1973
84 x 106
Physical map, relief shading, national bases, expedition routes etc.

ANTARCTIC
1:10,000,000
Washington : US Hydrographic Office
127 x 83
Shows water depths, land areas, mountain elevations in feet. Based on American exploration 1829-1956.

ANTARCTICA
1:10,000,000
Canberra : DND, 1970
77 x 77
Contoured map in col. showing traverse routes, ice and rock features.

ANTARCTICA
1:9,800,000
Tokyo : Japan Polar Research Assoc.
1970
47 x 69
General col. map

ANTARCTICA
1:6,062,500
Washington : NGS
106 x 82
Political col. wall map, naming ice and rock features and bases.
Paper $2.00
Plastic $3.00

SUDPOLARGEBIET
1:6,000,000
Ed Dr. Hans-Peter Kosack
No 106
Darmstadt : Perthes
230 x 210
Physical school wall map, layer coloured, relief shaded, ocean depths.
Mounted on cloth.
Editions in German, French and Dutch language.

L'ANTARCTIQUE
1:5,000,000
Paris : IGN, 1969
118 x 145
Col. map showing ice cover, relief by contours. Layer col. for outcropping rocks; spot heights, natural features etc. Special edition of the Carte des Continents.
F.Fr 25.00

ANTARCTICA
1:5,000,000
Washington : AGS
142 x 108
All known features and bases, traverses named with heights, bathymetric and ice contours etc. Inset of McMurdo Sound and 'Antarctic in relation to the World Ocean' with surface temperature and 'Antarctica and adjacent Seas Subglacial and Submarine relief'.

ANTARKTIKA
1:3,000,000
In 9 sheets
Moskva : Min. of the Navy, 1968
67 x 67 each
Map in Russian with some English-Russian text.

OCÉAN INDIEN ET POLE SUD
Hatier
see INDIAN OCEAN 267m A1

SÜDPOLARGEBEIT: TIERLEBEN UND FORSCHUNG
No scale given
Braunschweig : Westermann
96 x 127
Pictoral wall map of the South Pole area, showing animal life and exploration.

SÜDPOLARGEBIET: NATUR, FORSCHUNG UND WIRTSCHAFT
No scale given
Braunschweig : Westermann
96 x 127
Pictorial wall map showing natural life, discovery and exploration and economy.

C OFFICIAL SURVEYS

CARTE DES CONTINENTS
1:5,000,000
IGN
Sheets 5, 6, 7, 8 cover the Antarctic.
Also special sheet
see WORLD 100C.

Argentine Surveys

MAPA DEL TERRITORIO NACIONAL DE LA TIERRA DEL FUEGO, ANTARTIDA E ISLAS DEL ATLANTICO SUR
1:5,000,000
Buenos Aires : IGM, 1968
115 x 80
Physical map of Tierra del Fuego and Argentine claim to British Antarctic Territory and South Atlantic Islands. $7.00

Australian Surveys

INTERNATIONAL MAP OF THE WORLD
1:1,000,000
See index 99/1
Canberra : DND
60 x 55
Official series on IMW lines, covering Australian Antarctic territory. 2 col. series, contours, land detail etc. Base compilation prepared for coastal areas, standard edition in preparation.

AUSTRALIAN ANTARCTIC TERRITORY
1:250,000
See index 99/1
Canberra : DND
Topographical series in 4 or 5 cols. showing ice and rock features, traverse routes and other details, contoured shaded relief. Transverse Mercator Projection.
each $0.75

FRAMNES MOUNTAINS
1:100,000
Canberra : DND, 1963
104 x 89
Special topographical map, contoured.
$0.75

Belgian Surveys

EXPÉDITION ANTARCTIQUE BELGE, 1957-58
Various scales
Bruxelles : IGMB
Various sizes
3 maps showing:
Monts Belgica
1:50,000 94 x 78
Coloured map. B.Fr 60
Côte Princesse Ragnhild
1:200,000 67 x 46
2 Colour Map B.Fr 60
Terre de la Reine Maud
1:500,000 115 x 88
Monochrome map B.Fr 60

EXPÉDITION ANTARCTIQUE BELGE 1959-60
Various scales
Bruxelles : IGMB
Various sizes
3 maps showing:
Monts Belgica
1:25,000 90 x 98
3 colour map B.Fr 60
Côte Princesse Ragnhild
1:250,000 104 x 65
2 sheet map each B.Fr 60
Côte Princesse Astrid
1:250,000 104 x 65
2 colour map B.Fr 60

British Surveys

FALKLAND ISLANDS, SOUTH GEORGIA, SOUTH SANDWICK IS AND BRITISH ANTARCTIC TERRITORY
1:9,200,000
DOS 960
Edition 4
Tolworth : DOS, 1972
Small hand map showing locations of islands and principal features. 15p

ANTARCTIC PENINSULA – TRI-ANGULATION AND AIR PHOTOGRAPHY
1:3,100,000
DOS (Misc) 233
Edition 2
Tolworth : DOS, 1968
Including peninsula and S. Georgia and S. Sandwich Is. 15p

BRITISH ANTARCTIC TERRITORY
1:3,000,000
DOS 813 (3203)
Edition 1
Tolworth : DOS, 1963
58 x 70
Survey map inc. South Orkney, South Georgia and South Sandwich Is.
50p

GRAHAMLAND
1:3,000,000
DOS (Misc) 233 FIDS
Tolworth : DOS, 1959
General map in colours showing British Antarctic Survey Bases. 50p
Base map only available 15p

TRANS-ANTARCTIC CROSSING OF 1957-58
1:2,000,000
DOS 812
Edition 1
Tolworth : DOS, 1963
Black and white map depicting the traverse to the pole. 30p

QUEEN MAUD RANGE AND AXEL HEIBERG GLACIER
1:1,267,200 – 1:316,800
reprinted from Geog. Journal Dec. 1963
London: RGS.
29 x 21 and 29 x 33 on one sheet.
Topographical map from photographs and ground survey by W W Herbert, 1962.
£1.50

ALEXANDER ISLAND
1:1,000,000
reprinted from Geog. Journal June 1963.
London: RGS
34 x 47
Topographical map compiled by D J H Searle from trimetrogen air photography and various ground surveys. 1959-60.
£1.50

GRAHAM LAND
1:1,000,000
London : RGS
40 x 57
Map reprinted from the Geog. Journal (September 1940), from surveys by A Stephenson, during British Graham Land Expedition of 1936-7, showing sledge journeys and flights from the southern base.
£1.50

BRITISH ANTARCTIC TERRITORY
1:500,000
DOS 710 (D401)
see index 99/4
Tolworth : DOS, 1959 +
New topog. series in progress superseding pre 1951 series (DOS 701). 50p

BRITISH ANTARCTIC TERRITORY
1:500,000
DOS 701
Edition 1
Tolworth: DOS, 1948-50
Old series, uncontoured of Grahamland, Antarctic peninsula being replaced by new series DOS 710 (D401). each 30p

BRITISH ANTARCTIC TERRITORY
1:200,000
DOS 610 (D 510), see index 99/4
Tolworth : DOS, 1965 +
Topog. series in progress, inc. separate sheet for South Georgia,
Uncontoured. 30p
Contoured 50p

BRITISH ANTARCTIC TERRITORY
1:250,000
DOS-BAS 250, see index 99/5
Tolworth: DOS, 1972-
66 x 85
New topographical series in progress. This map will eventually replace the 1:200,000 DOS 610 (Series D 501). 50p

GRAHAM LAND – HORSESHOE ISLAND
1:25,000
DOS 310, see index 99/4
Edition 1
Tolworth : DOS, 1960
Topog. map, contoured with relief shading. 65p

GRAHAM LAND – HOPE BAY
1:25,000
DOS 310, see index 99/4
Edition 1
Tolworth: DOS 1960
Topog. map, contoured with relief shading. 65p

ANVERS ISLAND – SOUTH COAST
1:25,000
DOS 310 (D811)
Edition 2
In 2 sheets – see index 99/4
Tolworth : DOS, 1966
Topog. map, form lined and with relief shading. each 65p

ARTHUR HARBOUR (ANVERS IS) BRITISH ANTARCTIC TERRITORY
1:10,000
DOS 210
Edition 1
Tolworth : DOS, 1963
Detailed plan in black and white. 30p

ARGENTINE ISLAND (WITH ANAGRAM ISLAND)
1:10,000
DOS 210 (D812)
Edition 1
Tolworth : DOS, 1964
Topog. map in colours. 50p

Chilean Surveys

MAPA DE LA ANTARTICA
1:500,000
In 25 sheets
Santiago : IGM
Col. topog. series in progress to cover Chilean claim to British Antarctic Territory.

New Zealand Surveys

ROSS SEA REGION
1:4,000,000
NZMS 135
2nd Edition
Wellington : NZMS, 1970
72 x 91
Col. map, relief shading, contours, glaciers, ice shelves, stations etc. with inset of McMurdo Sound,
1:1,000,000 $0.70

ANTARCTIC TOPOGRAPHICAL SERIES (ROSS DEPENDENCY)
1:250,000
NZMS 166, see index 99/2
Wellington : NZMS, 1960+
87 x 64
Category A
Names, spot heights, graticules, relief shading, glaciers col, stations, mts, trigonometry in metres, US aerial photography and flight lines indicated. Crevassed areas, glacier flow lines, ice-free land and hydrographic information in blue.
Category B
As for Category A except that hydrographic detail in brown.
Category C
As for Category A but names in black and topography shown by relief shading.
Category D NZMS 175/3
Part of Victoria Land — all information in brown monochrome — no field party routes or US photo flight lines.

NEW ZEALAND ANTARCTIC MAPS
NZMS 175
Wellington : NZMS
28 x 45
Show names, ice-free areas, heights, sea areas, relief by contours or shading. Available for:

Beaufort Is.		
1:25,000	1960	NZMS 175/1
Cape Bird		
1:25,000	1961	NZMS 175/4
Cape Crozier		
1:50,000	1962	NZMS 175/16

Also: Facilitates in the Region of Scott Base 1:6,250 1966 L & S 37/10
3rd edition, Inset of Scott Base Area 1:2,000

Norwegian Surveys

DRONNING MAUD LAND
1:1,000,000
In 4 sheets
Oslo : NP, 1962
Topog. map based on oblique air photography covering coastal region.
each kr 6.00

KRONPRINSESSE MARTHA KYST-MAUDHEIMVIDDA
1:1,000,000
Oslo : NP, 1963
Topog. map showing air photography routes. Supp. to 'Norwegian-British-Swedish Antarctic Expedition', 1949-52.
kr 6.00

MAUDHEIMVIDDA AUST
1:500,000
Oslo : NP, 1963
Topog. map showing routes of field parties. Supp. to 'Norwegian-British-Swedish Antarctic Expedition', 1949-52.
kr 6.00

DRONNING MAUD LAND
1:250,000
See index 99/3
Oslo : NP, 1961+
Topog. series in progress.
Per sheet kr 9.60
NB 1:500,000 series in preparation.

United States Surveys

ANTARCTIC RECONNAISSANCE SERIES
1:500,000
Washington : USGS
83 x 63
Topographic series with shaded relief and contours covering coastal areas of Wilkes Land and Enderby Land.

ANTARCTICA SKETCH MAP SERIES
1:500,000
Washington : USGS
89 x 94
Relief shaded, but with no contours. These will eventually be republished in the topographic (reconnaissance) style but are at the present the best coverage for the area. Covering coast of Marie Byrd, Ellsworth and Northern Victoria Lands.

ANTARCTIC RECONNAISSANCE SERIES
1:250,000
Washington : USGS
Series with contours and relief shading published for Victoria Land and eastern side of Ross Ice Shelf, Horlick Mts, Guest Peninsula, Executive Committee Range, Ellsworth Mts. and Pensacola Mts.

USSR Surveys

ANTARKTIDA — ZEMLYA KOROLEVY MOD (QUEEN MAUD LAND)
1:100,000
Moskva: Ministry of Navy, 1966-7
37 x 35
Map series in preparation.

E2 PHYSICAL: LAND FEATURES

ANTARCTICA: RADIO ECHO SOUNDING MAP
1:5,000,000
Ed. D J Drewry
Cambridge: Scott Polar Research Inst.
Map in 3 sheets indicating thickness of surface ice cover.
each £1.25

F GEOLOGY

GEOLOGIC MAP OF ANTARCTICA
1:5,000,000
New York: AGS, 1972
104 x 121
Synthesis of information contained in Folio 12 of Antarctic Map Folio Series. Bathymetric and ice-sheet surface contours. $6.00

ANTARCTIC RECONNAISSANCE GEOLOGIC MAPS
1:250,000
Washington : USGS
86 x 76
Col. series based on topog. sheet lines. In progress. Sheet published:
Mount Rabot Quadrangle 1970
A-2 Mt. Elizabeth and Mt. Kathleen Quad. 1973
each $1.00

ANTARCTIC GEOLOGICAL MAP SERIES
1:5,000 — 1:250,000
Tokyo: National Institute of Polar Research
Series of 14 coloured maps with separate explanatory texts. In English.
Sheets published:
1. East Ongul Island 1:5,000
1974 13pp. text, 15 refs
2. West Ongul Island 1:5,000
1974 5pp. text, 9 refs

ATLASES
E1 PHYSICAL

ATLAS ANTARKTIKI
Ed Ye Tolstikov Bakayen
Moskva: Academy of Sciences, (GUGK) 1966
In 2 vols.
61 x 39
Covering physical, seismological, geol, magnetic, glaciological, climate aspects, history of explorations, biology.
Vol. 1 xxiii 300pp—maps 1966
Vol. 2 598pp—1969
text, photos, etc.

ANTARCTIC MAP FOLIO SERIES
1:1,000,000
Washington : AGS
Series of maps and texts, covering the following subjects:
1 Aeronautical Maps for the Antarctic
R Penndorf et al, 1964
6pp text, 9 maps US $3.00
2 Physical Characteristics of the Antarctic Ice Sheet
C R Bentley et al, 1964
10pp text, 10 maps US$4.00
3 Antarctic Maps and Surveys 1900-1964
AGS/USGS, 1965
4pp text, 11 maps US $5.00
4 The Antarctic Atmosphere: Climatology of the Troposphere and Lower Stratosphere. Nat. Weather Records Center, 1966
4pp text, 8 maps US $3.50
5 Terrestrial Life of Antarctica
S W Greene et al
24pp text, 11 maps US $7.50
6 Structure of Antarctic Waters between 20°W and 170°W
Arnold L Gordon, 1967
10pp text, 14 maps US $6.00
7 Glaciers of the Antarctic
John Mercer 1967
10pp text, 4 maps US $3.50
8 The Antarctic Atmosphere: Climatology of the Surface Environment. Nat Weather Records Center and W S Weynant
4pp text, 13 maps US $4.50

9 Magnetic and Gravity Maps of the Antarctic
J C Behrendt and C R Bentley
1968
4pp text, 9 maps US $4.00

10 Primary Productivity and Benthic Marine Algae of the Antarctic and Subantarctic
E Balech et al, 1968
12pp text, 15 maps US $6.00

11 Distribution of Selected Groups of Marine Invertebrates in Waters South of Latitude 35°S,
A W H Be et al, 1969
4pp text, 29 maps US $10.00

12 Geologic Map of Antarctica
Campbell Craddock et al, 1970
18 maps at 1:1,000,000 US $12.00

13 Circumpolar Characteristics of Antarctic Waters
A L Gordon, R D Goldberg
US $6.00

14 Birds of the Antarctic and Sub-antarctic
G E Watson et al
39 maps, text US $10.00

15 Coastal and Deep Water Benthic Fishes of the Antarctic
Hugh de Witt
31 maps, text US $6.00

16 Morphology of the Earth in the Antarctic and Subantarctic
B C Heezen, M Tharp,
C R Bentley, 1972
8 map plates and text. US $13.00

17 Marine sediments of the Southern Oceans
H G Goodell and others 1973
18pp, 9 plates and text US $11.00

18 Antarctic Mammals
S G Brown and others US $14.00

19 History of Antarctic Exploration and Scientific Investigation
H M Dater US $15.00

99.1 Antarctic Islands

AMSTERDAM AND ST. PAUL ISLANDS

CARTE DE RECONNAISSANCE DE L'ÎLE AMSTERDAM
1:25,000
Paris: IGN, 1968
50 x 42
Contoured at 10 metre intervals.

CARTE DE RECONNAISSANCE DE L'ÎLE ST PAUL
1:25,000
Paris: IGN, 1973
40 x 38
Coloured with contours and relief shading.
F.Fr 11.67

CROZET ISLANDS

CARTE DE RECONNAISSANCE DES ÎLES CROZET
1:200,000
Paris, IGN, 1971
100 x 60
Single sheet map contoured, relief shading in col. F.Fr 11.67

CARTE DE RECONNAISSANCE DE L'ÎLE DE LA POSSESSION
1:50,000
Paris: IGN, 1965
Provisional ed. F.Fr 11.67

FALKLAND ISLANDS

See also 82 ARGENTINA
83 CHILE

FALKLAND ISLANDS, SOUTH GEORGIA, SOUTH SANDWICH ISLANDS
1:9,200,000
DOS 960
Edition 4
Tolworth: DOS
Planimetric Report Map.

FALKLAND ISLANDS
1:1,500,000
DOS 30/1
Edition 3
Tolworth: DOS, 1961
Black and white sketch map.
10p

FALKLAND ISLANDS
1:800,000
DOS 30/1 (Prov)
Edition 1
Tolworth : DOS, 1964
Black and white sketch map. 10p

FALKLAND ISLANDS
1:643,000
DOS 906
Edition 1
Tolworth: DOS, 1966
50 x 36
Layer col, roads, tracks, principal geog. locations named. 15p

ISLAS MALVINAS (FALKLAND ISLANDS) TERRITORIO NACIONAL DE LA TIERRA DEL FUEGA, ANTARTIDA E ISLAS DE ATLANTICO SUR
1:500,000
Buenos Aires: IGM, 1940
78 x 61
Sheet 96 — 100 of the 500,000 Topog. series; coastal features named, slight relief shading.

GEOLOGICAL MAP OF THE FALKLAND ISLANDS
1:250,000
DOS 1185A & B
Tolworth: DOS, 1972
Coloured map in 2 sheets. East and West. 65p

FALKLAND ISLANDS
1:250,000
DOS 653 (H591)
In 2 sheets, see index 99.1/1
Tolworth : DOS, 1964/5
West Sheet 64 x 86
East Sheet 60 x 84
Contoured, layer col, roads, tracks, names etc. Property boundary diagram inset.
each 50p

FALKLAND ISLANDS
1:50,000
DOS 453 (H791)
In 29 sheets, see index 99.1/1
Edition 1
Tolworth : DOS
Various sizes
Topog. series, contours, spot heights, roads, tracks, etc. See index.
each 50p

STANLEY, FALKLAND ISLANDS
1:2,500
DOS 153
Tolworth : DOS
2 sheet town plan; roads, principal buildings named, property boundaries.
Sheets : Stanley 109 x 79
Stanley West 64 x 73
each 30p

FALKLAND ISLANDS DEPENDENCIES SURVEY : SOUTH ORKNEY ISLANDS – SIGNY ISLAND GEOLOGY
Comp. Univ. College of Swansea
1:12,500
Tolworth : DOS, 1959
Coloured geological map.

HEARD ISLAND

HEARD ISLAND
1:50,000
Canberra : DND
Coloured topog. map. $0.75

KERGUELEN ISLANDS

CARTE DES ÎLES KERGUELEN
1:200,000
Paris : IGN, 1973
105 x 90
Contoured map in one sheet covering islands; relief shading, contours.
F.Fr 11.67

CARTE DE RECONNAISSANCE DES ÎLES KERGUELEN
1:100,000
In 3 sheets
Paris : IGN, 1967
102 x 84 each
Contours, relief shading, in col.
F.Fr 11.67

LES GLACIERS DE L'ÎLE KERGUELEN
In 5 sheets
Paris: IGN
24 x 31
Collection of 5 maps folded in a pocket comprising: 1 general map and 4 col. maps:
Presqu'île de la Societe de Geographie
Glacier Cook
Presqu'île Rallier du Baty
Presqu'île Gallenieni
F.Fr 14.17

MACQUARIE ISLAND

MACQUARIE ISLAND
1:50,000
Canberra : DND, 1971
58 x 82
Topog. map in colour with contours and relief shading. $.0.75

SOUTH GEORGIA ISLANDS

SOUTH GEORGIA ISLANDS
1:500,000
DOS 701
Tolworth : DOS, 1948-50
Topog. map in colours uncontoured.
30p

SOUTH GEORGIA
1:200,000
DOS 610 (D501)
Edition 1
Tolworth : DOS
Topographical map, contoured with translucent travel overlay.
Map 50p
Overlay 30p

SOUTH ORKNEY ISLANDS

SOUTH ORKNEY ISLANDS
1:500,000
DOS 701
Tolworth : DOS 1948-50
Topog. map in colours, uncontoured.
30p

SOUTH ORKNEY ISLANDS
1:100,000
DOS 510 (D601)
Edition 1
In 2 sheets
Tolworth : DOS, 1964
Topog. map in colours, contoured.
WEST sheet only published. 50p

SIGNY ISLAND
1:10,000
2nd edition
DOS 210
Tolworth : DOS, 1975
Contoured map. 50p

SOUTH SANDWICH ISLANDS

SOUTH SANDWICH ISLANDS
1:500,000
DOS 701
Tolworth : DOS, 1948-50
Topog. series in colours,
uncontoured. 30p

SOUTH SHETLAND ISLANDS

BRITISH ANTARCTIC TERRITORY
1:500,000
DOS 701, sheets 6 and 7
1:200,000
DOS 610 (D510) 4 sheets
see ANTARCTICA 99C

ELEPHANT ISLAND
1:133,000
reprinted from Geog. Journal Sept. 1972
London : RGS
37 x 21
Topographical map from a survey by
the Joint Services Expedition 1970.
£1.50

FALKLAND ISLANDS DEPENDENCIES
SURVEY: SOUTH SHETLAND
ISLANDS – DECEPTION ISLAND
1:50,000
DOS (Misc) 217
Edition 1
Tolworth : DOS, 1954
Topog. map, contoured. 50p

FALKLAND ISLANDS DEPENDENCIES
SURVEY : SOUTH SHETLAND
ISLANDS – DECEPTION ISLAND
1:25,000
DOS 310
Edition 1
Tolworth : DOS, 1960
Topog. map, contoured with relief
shading. 65p

DECEPTION ISLAND – GEOLOGY
1:25,000
DOS (Geol) 1108
Edition 1
Tolworth : DOS, 1961
Coloured geological map. 50p

Space

S523.1 Space

A1 GENERAL MAPS

UNIVERS No.2
St. Germain-en-Laye: Éditions MDI
96 x 126
Double sided plastic surfaced school wall map with the Solar System on one side and the Moon Map on the reverse.

DIE EROBERUNG DES WELTRAUMS (CONQUEST OF SPACE)
No scale given
Bern : Hallwag
112 x 84
Double sided chart showing flight paths of space flights, and information on individual flights on reverse.

ATLASES
A1 GENERAL

STUDENT ATLAS OF EARTH SCIENCE AND OUTER SPACE
Indianapolis : Cram
32pp
22 x 30
Earth science, moon, solar system, earth satellites. School atlas.
$1.00

THE ATLAS OF THE UNIVERSE
Patrick Moore
London: Mitchell Beazley
28 x 78
272pp
Describes Earth as seen from space, the Moon, Stars etc. in detail. 160 col. pp. Illus. maps, charts, sketches, tables.
In slip case £11.75

THE MITCHELL BEAZLEY CONCISE ATLAS OF THE UNIVERSE
Ed. Patrick Moore
London : Mitchell Beazley, 1974
27 x 37
192 pp
Completely revised and updated concise edition of the original work, incorporating discoveries of the last 2 years.
£8.50

ATLAS DES SPECTRES DANS LE PROCHE INFRAROUGE DE VENUS, MARS, JUPITER ET SATURNE
by J and P Connes, J P Maillard
Paris : CRNS, 1969
32 x 55
476pp
Infrared photographs of the planets.

ATLAS ZUR HIMMELSKUNDE
Ed Dr Karl Schaifers
Mannheim : Bibliog. Inst. Meyers, 1969
32pp
21 x 30
Text in Eng, Fr, Ger, It, Russ.
Covers space, planets, comets, stars, etc. DM 48

S523.3 Moon

E1 PHYSICAL: RELIEF

MAPPE LUNARE
1:18,500,000
Novara : Agostini
22 x 30
Relief map of the moon with table of names and magnifying glass. L 450

MAPA KSIĘŻYCA
1:14,000,000
Warszawa : PPWK, 1971
95 x 125 each
Showing features of both faces of the moon in 2 sheets, col.

MAPA KSIĘŻYCA (THE EARTH'S MOON)
1:12,000,000
Warszawa : PPWK
40 x 60
Small general map of the moon naming principal features. zl 3

ERDMOND – VORDERSETTE/ RÜCKSEITE
1:12,000,000
Gothna: Haack
110 x 66
A map of both sides of the moon with 76pp text. DM 9.80

THE EARTH'S MOON
1:11,620,000
Washington : NGS, 1969
106 x 71
Col. map of Near Side and Far Side; index, notes, lunar flight data.
Paper $2.00
Plastic $3.00

CARTE DE LA LUNE
1:10,000,000 app.
Paris : IGN, 1969
130 x 79
Visible and hidden faces together. Surface features shown by relief shading, depressed sea areas in grey. Lat. and long. grid, names, phase diagrams. F.Fr 15.00

MAPPA LUNARE
1:6,000,000
Novara : Agostini
70 x 70
Moulded plastic relief map in frame. L 13,000

MONDKARTE
1:5,000,000
Bern : Hallwag, 1970
84 x 84
Col. map based on recent information from missiles and observatories. Near side on one side, Far side on reverse, separate text in 4 languages.

LUNAR PICTORIAL MAP
1:5,000,000
Washington : Defense Mapping Agency
91 x 91
Orthographic Proj. $1.00

MONDKARTE
1:4,000,000
No 450
Hamburg : Falk
86 x 104
Col. map showing relief, crater shading, names; moon phases indicated. DM 4.80

MANEKORT
1:4,000,000
Kobenhavn : Scanglobes
104 x 85
Map of the near side of the moon, showing mountains, craters etc.

DER MOND, VORDER-UND RUCKSEITE
1:4,000,000
W736
Munchen : List, 1970
198 x 140
Wenschow school wall map, showing both sides of the moon.
DM 192

LUNAR TOPOGRAPHIC CENTER SECTION
1:2,500,000
Washington : Defense Mapping Agency
137 x 81
Shaded relief map, modified stereographic proj. $2.50

LUNAR TOPOGRAPHIC
1:2,000,000
In 6 sheets
Washington : Defense Mapping Agency
137 x 81 each
Available in 3 styles : Relief, Gradient, Tint and Shaded Relief. Modified stereographic proj.
Relief set $6.00
Gradient set $15.00
Shaded Relief set $15.00

PHILIP'S MOON MAP
No scale given
London : Philip, 1971
70 x 50
Col. map of the nearside showing relief; shows landing sites of aircraft up to Apollo 14. Index hidden side inset. 45p

OFFICIAL MOON MAP
No scale given
Chicago : Rand McNally, 1969
135 x 121
Wall map showing 2,000 lunar features – oceans, craters, peaks, valleys, etc. Available cloth mounted.

MAPA MĚSIČNÍCH POLOKOULI – SESTIDILNY SOUBOR
1:10,000,000
Praha : Kart
Map of the Moon's hemispheres in 6 parts. Kcs 31,50

LUNAR TOPOGRAPHIC EASTERN SECTION
LUNAR TOPOGRAPHIC WESTERN SECTION
1:5,000,000
Washington : Defense Mapping Agency
137 x 96 each
Relief shown; modified stereographic proj. Also available in Gradient Tint and Shaded Relief Styles.
Each set $5.00

LUNAR TOPOGRAPHIC MAP
1:250,000
In 4 sheets
Washington : Defense Mapping Agency
137 x 81 each
Topog. series covering central region, modified stereographic proj.
set $4.00

F GEOLOGY

TEKTONICHESKAVA KARTA LUNY
1:7,500,000
Moskva : GUGK, 1969
69 x 103 each
2 sheet tectonic map showing visible and invisible faces of the moon. Explanation on reverse in Rus, Eng, Fr. 44pp text in Russian.

GEOLOGIC MAP OF THE NEAR SIDE OF THE MOON
1:5,000,000
Misc. Geol. Inv. 1-703
Washington : USGS, 1971
134 x 90
Coloured geological map with 7 pages text. $1.00

ENGINEER SPECIAL STUDY OF THE SURFACE OF THE MOON
1:3,800,000
No MGI 1-351
Washington : USGS, 1961
Folder with 3 maps and legend sheet. Showing : Generalised Photogeologic Map of the Moon; Lunar Rays; Physiographic Divisions of the Moon.

GEOLOGICAL MAP SERIES OF THE MOON
1:1,000,000
In 44 sheets, see index S 523.3/1
Washington : USGS
74 x 130
Series in progress. Showing distribution, relative age of geologic units, major structural features on base chart with app. contours and relief shading.

MISCELLANEOUS GEOLOGICAL MAPS OF THE MOON
Various scales
Washington : USGS
Various sizes
Col. maps, usually with text, in folder.

1-586 (RLC 15)
Alphonsus GA region
1:50,000 1969

1-594 (RCL 9)
Sabine DM region
1:50,000 1969

1-599 (RLC 14)
Alphonsus Region
1:250,000 1969

1-616 (ORB II - 2 (100)
Maskelyne DA region (inc. Apollo landing site 1)
1:100,000 1970

1-617 (ORB II - 2(25))
Geologic Map of Apollo landing site 1, part of Maskelyne DA region, southeastern Mare Tranquilitatis
1:250,000 1970

1-618 (ORB II 6)
Sabine D region
1:100,000 app. 1970

1-619 (ORB II - 6 (25))
Geologic Map of Apollo landing site 2 (Apollo II), part of Sabine D Region, southwestern Mare Tranquilitatis
1:25,000 1970

1-620 (ORB II-8 (100))
Oppolzer A region of the Moon, Lunar Orbiter sites 11 P-8, Sinus Medii, inc. Apollo landing sites 3 and 3R
1:100,000 1971

1-621 (ORB II - 8 (25))
Apollo landing sites 3 and 3R
1:25,000 1970

1-622 (ORB !! - 13 (100))
Maestlin G Region
1:100,000 1970

1-623 (ORB II - 13 (25))
Apollo landing site 5, part of Mastlin G region
1:25,000 1970

1-624 (ORB III - II (100))
Wichmann CA region
1:100,000 1971

1-625 (ORB III - II (25))
Geologic map of Apollo landing sites 4 and 4R, part of Wichmann CA region Oceanus Procellarum
1:25,000 1971

1-626 (ORB III - 12 (100))
Flamstead K region
1:100,000 1972

1-627 (ORB III-9 (100))
Lansberg P region
Apollo landing site 7
1:100,000 1972

1-678 (RLC-4)
Geologic Map of the Bonpland PQC region of the Moon
1:10,000 1971

1-679 (RLC-11)
Geologic Map of the Sabine EB region of the Moon
1:5,000 1971

1-693 (RLC-3)
Bonpland H region
1:100,000 1971

1-708
Fra Mauro region
1:25,000 and 250,000
1970

1-723
Geologic Maps of the Apennine Hadley region of the Moon, Apollo 15 pre-mission maps
1:250,000 and 1:500,000
1971

1-748
Geologic maps of the Descartes regions of the Moon, Apollo 16 pre-mission maps
1:250,000 and 1:50,000
1972

1-800
Taurus – Littrow region, Apollo 17
1:250,000 and 1:50,000
1972

ATLASES
E1 PHYSICAL

ATLAS OBRATNOI STORONOI LUNY
Moskva : Academy of Sciences
In 2 vols.
23 x 30
Vol. 1 1960 : Automatic Interplanetary Stations 7.10.59
Text, tables, diagrams, maps.
Vol. 2 1967 : Automatic Interplanetary Station, Probe 3, Photos, maps, tables, 236pp text.

ATLAS DE LA LUNE – ASTRONOMIE – ATLAS – ASTRONAUTIQUE
Ed V de Callatay
Bruxelles : Albert de Visscher & Cie
24 x 32
Arranged in 3 sections, Atlas section contains 22 double pages of photographs. The other 2 textual sections illustrated by photographs and diagrams. FB 600

LUNAR ATLAS
Ed. Dinsmore Alter
New York : Dover, 1968
154 plates of photos of the moon's surface with explanatory text. $6.00

S523.4 Planets

E1 PHYSICAL: RELIEF

THE RED PLANET MARS
1:31,770,000
Washington : NGS, 1973
Physical map with all principal features marked.

SHADED RELIEF MAP OF MARS
1:25,000,000 (at 0° latitude)
Misc. Geol. Inv. 1-810
Washington : USGS, 1972
102 x 92
Coloured map with insets of North and South Polar regions.
US $0.75

MARS PICTORIAL
1:10,000,000
Washington : Defense Mapping Agency
80 x 86
4 maps centred on 90°
180°
220°
270°
each $1.00

MARS CHART, MERIDIANI SINUS AND ENVIRONS
1:10,000,000
Santa Monica (Calif) : Rand Corporation for Nat. Aeronautics and Space Admin. 1971

F GEOLOGY

MAP OF MARS
Ed Alden A Loomis
1:35,000,000
Boulder, Col : GSA, 1965
78 x 59
Geol. base map of Mars. $2.50

ATLASES
A1 GENERAL

ATLAS DES PLANETES
V de Callatay and A Dollfus
Bruxelles : Albert de Visscher
168pp
24 x 32
Atlas of the planetary system with 130 plates, in black and white and colour and descriptive text in French. B.Fr 600

S523.8 Stars

A1 GENERAL MAPS

CARTE DU CIEL (Établie pour le 1.1.1980)
In 2 sheets:
HÉMISPHÈRE NORD
HÉMISPHÈRE SUD
Paris : IGN 1974
80 x 71 (diameter 64)
Map of the sky on stereographic projection showing stars listed in Catalogue FK4 up to 6th magnitude and naming those up to 2nd magnitude also constellations, ecliptic path of the sun. Editions in red and black for observers outside the celestial horizon. Also edition in green and red and Northern hemisphere only for observers within celestial horizon (amateur astronomers) 12 pages descriptive brochure in French.
F.Fr 8.33

CARTE DU CIEL (Établie pour le 1.1.1955) – HÉMISPHÈRE NORD
Paris : IGN
50 x 57
Depicting ¾ of the celestial sphere with descriptions and annual time-table indicated. Stars are shown in blue on a black background.
F.Fr 8.33

PHILIPS CHART OF THE STARS
London : Philip
117 x 91
Black and white : shows chief stars and constellations, Northern and Southern polar stars inset. Brief notes.
£1.00

STJARNKARTA
Stockholm : GLA
99 x 69
Map of the stars with Sw. text.
Flat or folded. kr 8.50

DIE STERNE (THE STARS)
Bern : Hallwag, 1969
126 x 84
2 hemispheres in col. showing visible stars: double and variable, nebulae, galaxies, clusters indicated. 26pp booklet. Legend in Eng. Fr. Ger.

MAPA SEVERNI A JIZNI HVEZDNE OBLOHY
Praha : Kart
Map of the Northern and Southern sky.
Kcs 20.50

DER NORDLICHE STERNHIMMEL
Gotha : Haack, 1965
156 x 162
School wall map of prominent constellations. Some clusters and nebulae also.

ATLASES
A1 GENERAL

ATLAS COELI
Antonin Bečvář
In 16 sheets
Praha : Czech Academy of Sciences, 1962
58 x 42
Map folio in colour, showing the heavens – various star types, nebulae, clusters etc. Introduction in 4 languages, grid overlay sheet.

ATLAS DU CIEL
Ed V de Callatay
2nd edition
Bruxelles : Albert de Visscher & Cie, 1962
24 x 32
81 maps covering the sky as a whole, with detailed sections on the constellations and congested areas.
With full commentary and photographs.
B.fr 600

POPULAR STAR ATLAS (Epoch 1950)
Edinburgh : Gall and Inglis, 1972
16 maps covering the whole Heavens; with lists of interesting objects for each, and notes. £1.00

NORTONS STAR ATLAS AND REFERENCE HANDBOOK
Edinburgh : Gall and Inglis, 1973 £3.75

COLOUR STAR ATLAS
Ed. Patrick Moore
London : Lutterworth
112p.
Contains extensive astronomical data, full lists of constellations major stars and star groups, their positions in the sky and periods of maximum visibility.
£2.95

Index Diagrams for Multi-sheet Maps

World

 INTERNATIONAL MAP OF THE WORLD

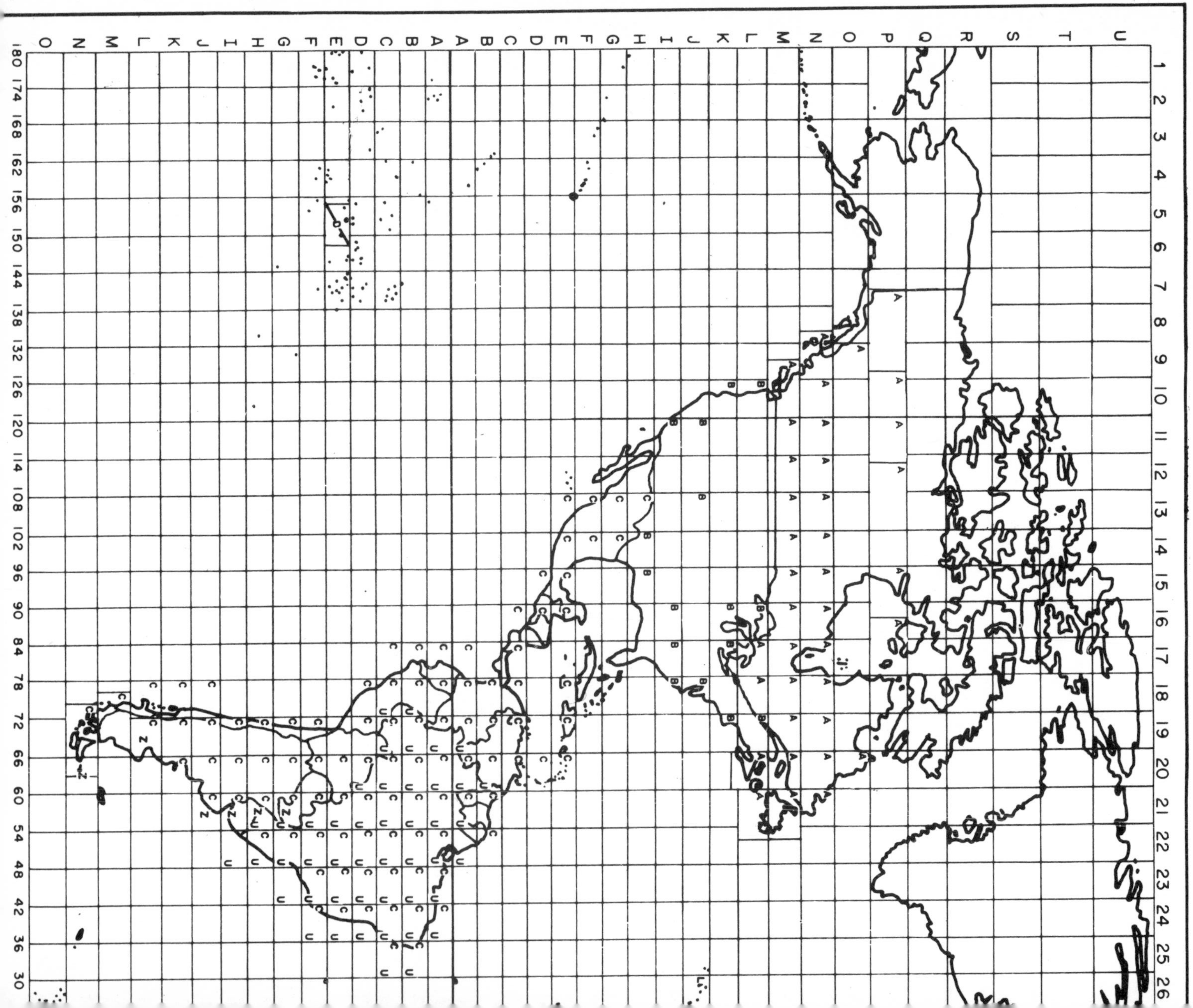

1:1,000,000

Topographical map series published at a uniform scale and style by each national survey department for their own territory.

Key to Publishers :

A	DEMR-Ottawa
B	USGS-Washington
C	AGS-New York
D	IGN-Paris
E	DND-Canberra
F	SI-Dehra Dun, India
G	NZMS-Wellington
H	DOS Series 900-Tolworth, UK
I	IGM-Firenze
J	Survey of Pakistan -Karachi
K	GSI-Tokyo
L	IGC-Lisbon
M	OS-Southampton
N	SRA-Stockholm
O	NGO-Oslo
P	Geo. Inst.-København
Q	Maan.-Helsinki
R	OS of Rep. of Ireland -Dublin
S	Inst. Angewandte Geodäsie-Frankfurt a/M
T	Survey Dept., Sudan -Khartoum
U	IBGE-Rio de Janeiro
V	Survey of Kenya-Nairobi
W	Surveyor General, Rhodesia-Salisbury
X	Dept. of Lands and Surveys, Uganda-Entebbe
Y	Surveys and Mapping Div.

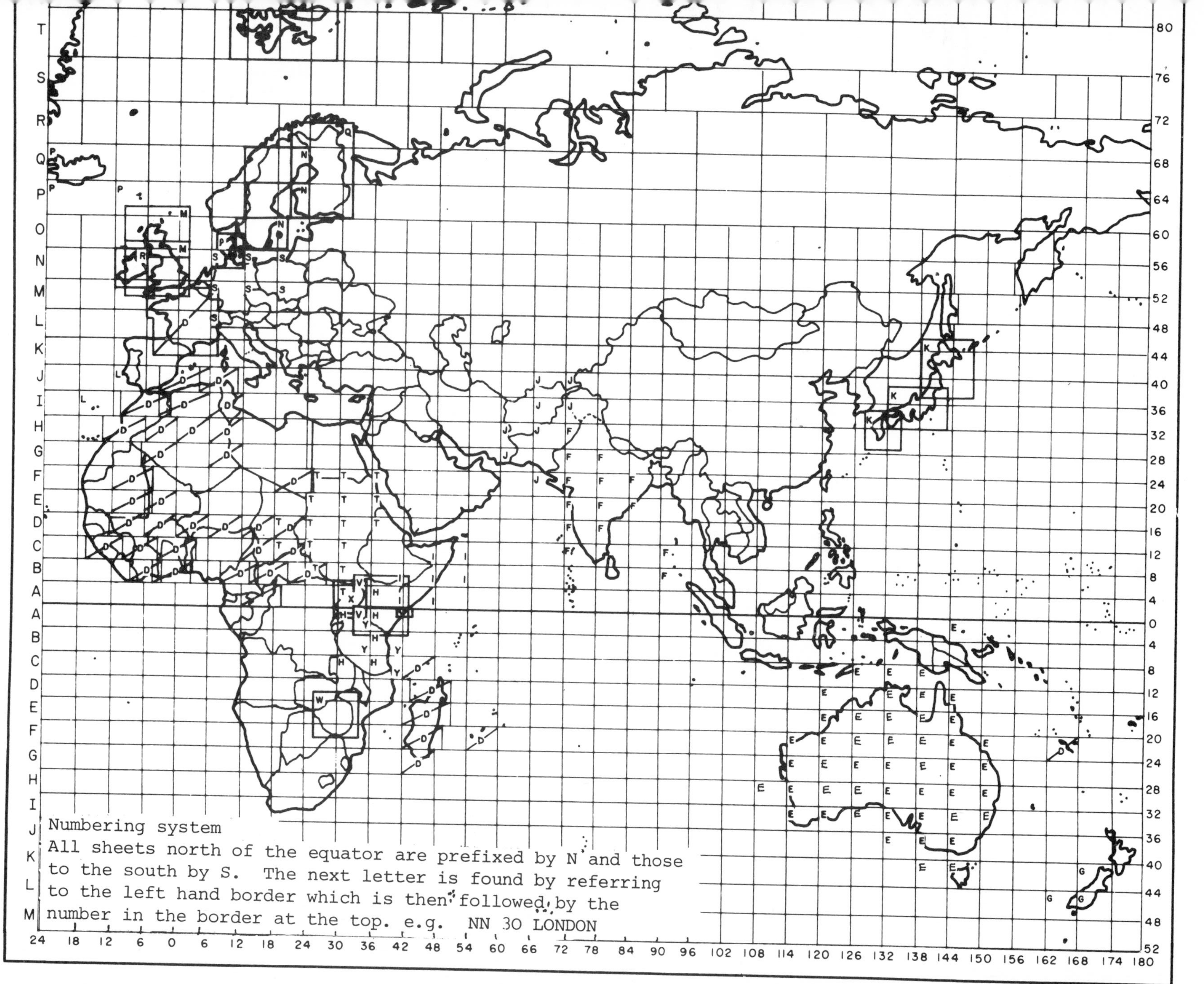
T
S
R
Q
P
O
N
M
L
K
J
I
H
G
F
E
D
C
B
A
A
B
C
D
E
F
G
H
I
J
K
L
M
80
76
72
68
64
60
56
52
48
44
40
36
32
28
24
20
16
12
8
4
0
4
8
12
16
20
24
28
32
36
40
44
48
52
24 18 12 6 0 6 12 18 24 30 36 42 48 54 60 66 72 78 84 90 96 102 108 114 120 126 132 138 144 150 156 162 168 174 180
Numbering system
All sheets north of the equator are prefixed by N and those to the south by S. The next letter is found by referring to the left hand border which is then followed by the number in the border at the top. e.g. NN 30 LONDON

.100/1B *INTERNATIONAL MAP OF THE WORLD*

1:1,000,000 Series 1301

Published by AMS and DMS

Topographical series conforming closely to I.

sheet lines and style

Sheets published by AMS

Sheets available from DMS including GSGS and AMS editions

AMS sheets available in Plastic Relief Editio

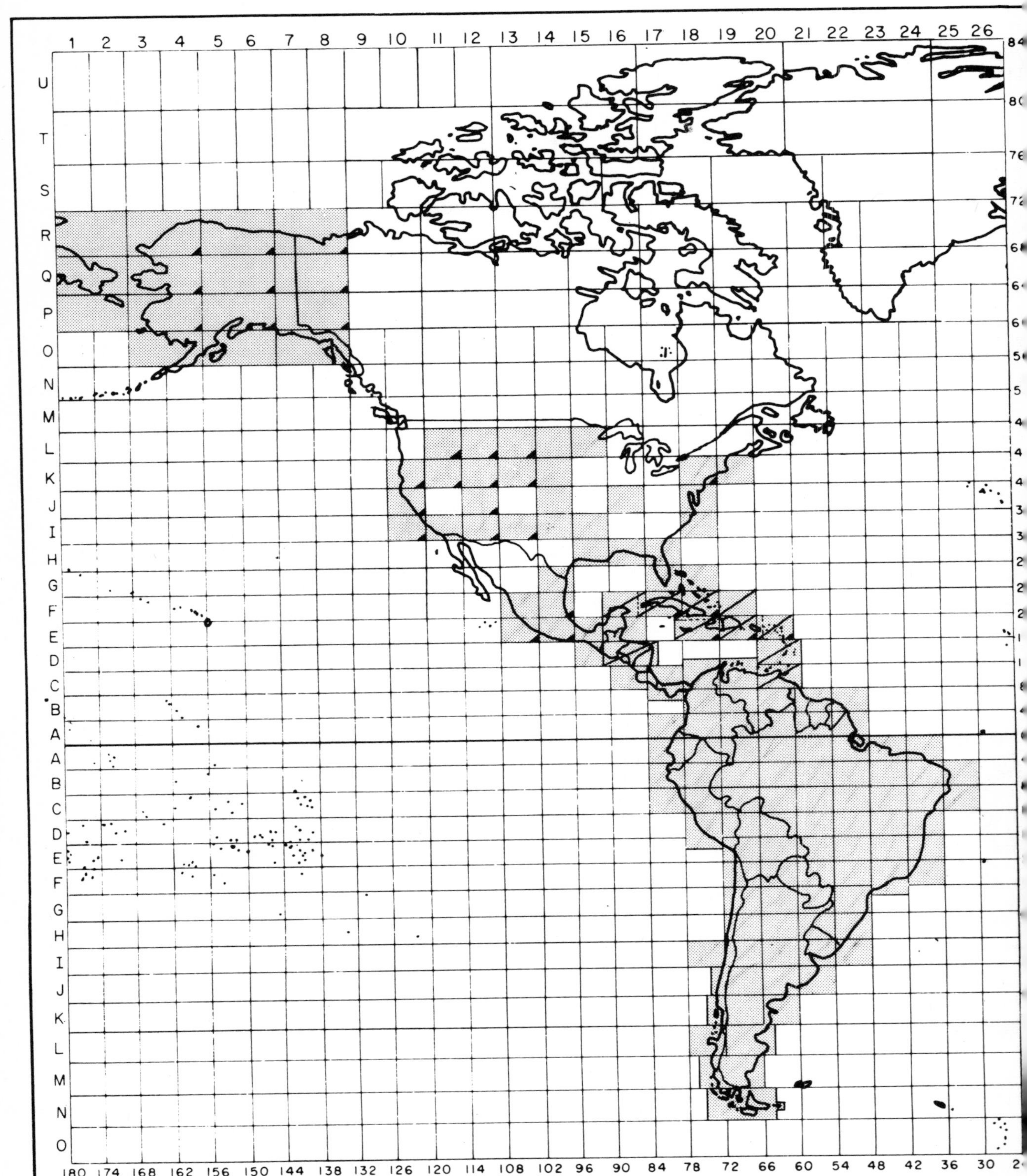

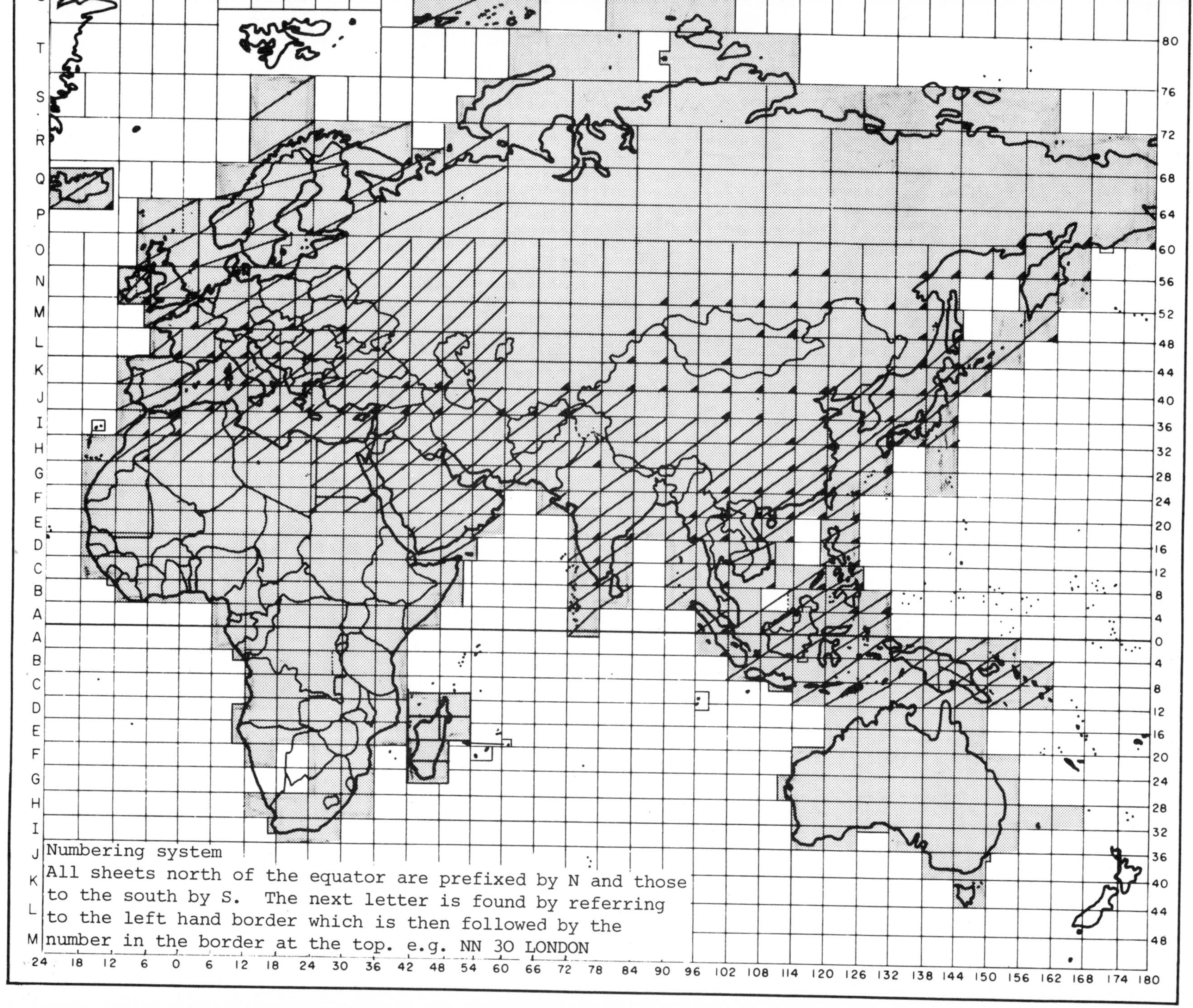

T
S
R
Q
P
O
N
M
L
K
J
I
H
G
F
E
D
C
B
A
A
B
C
D
E
F
G
H
I
J
K
L
M
80
76
72
68
64
60
56
52
48
44
40
36
32
28
24
20
16
12
8
4
0
4
8
12
16
20
24
28
32
36
40
44
48
24 18 12 6 0 6 12 18 24 30 36 42 48 54 60 66 72 78 84 90 96 102 108 114 120 126 132 138 144 150 156 162 168 174 180
Numbering system
All sheets north of the equator are prefixed by N and those to the south by S. The next letter is found by referring to the left hand border which is then followed by the number in the border at the top. e.g. NN 30 LONDON

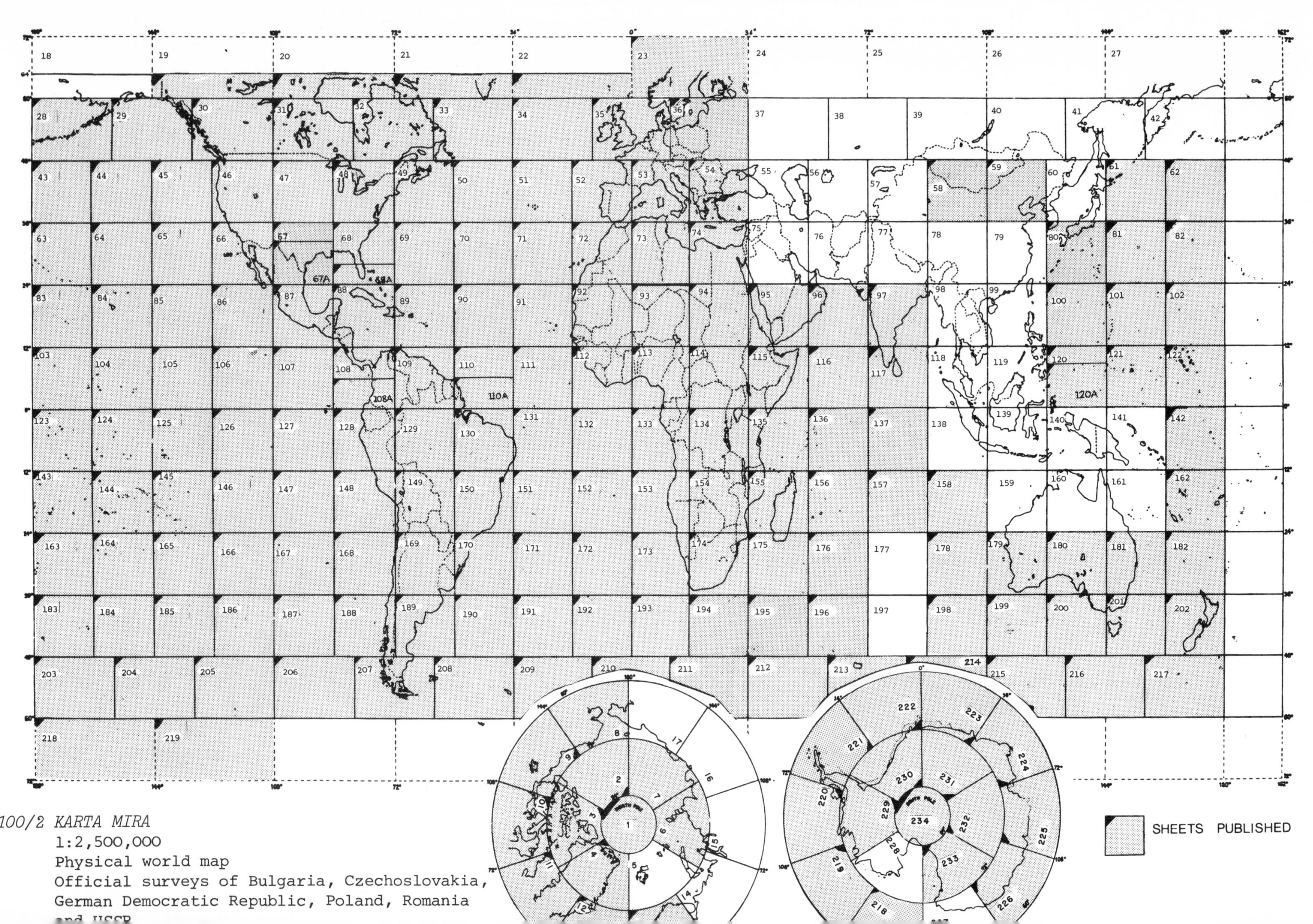

100/2 KARTA MIRA

1:2,500,000

Physical world map

Official surveys of Bulgaria, Czechoslovakia, German Democratic Republic, Poland, Romania and USSR

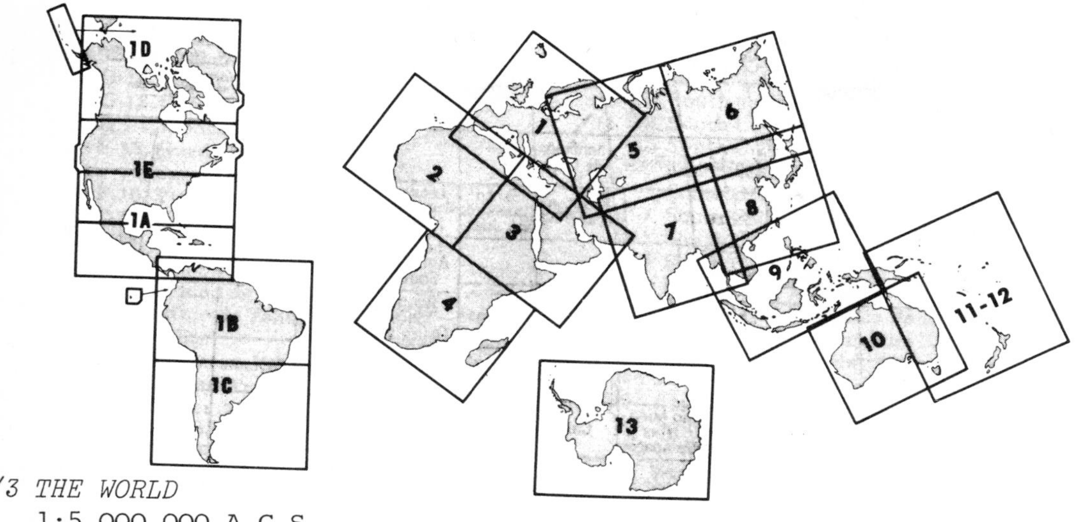

/3 *THE WORLD*

1:5,000,000 A.G.S.

Physical map in 18 sheets

The following sheets are currently out of print:

1C South America - south sheet

1D Northern Canada, Alaska and Greenland

1E United States and Southern Canada

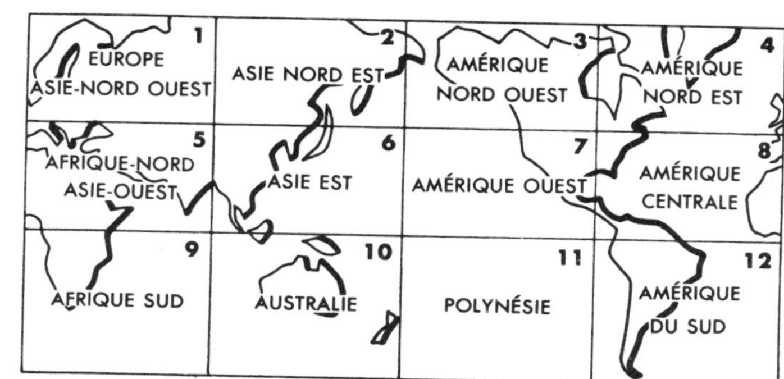

100/4 *CARTE GÉNÉRALE DU MONDE*

1:10,000,000 I.G.N.

General physical wall map of the world in 12 sheets

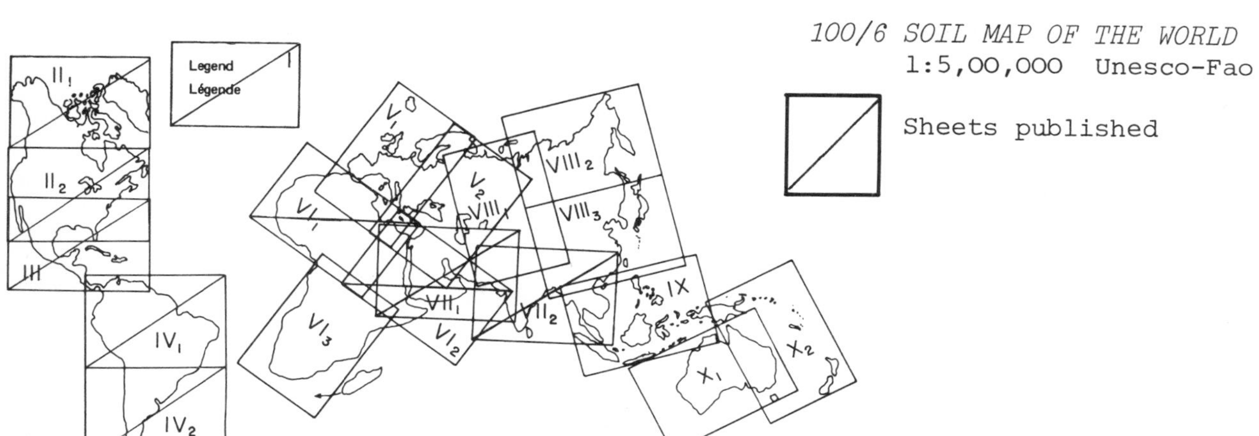

100/6 *SOIL MAP OF THE WORLD*

1:5,00,000 Unesco-Fao

Sheets published

AMÉRIQUE DU NORD

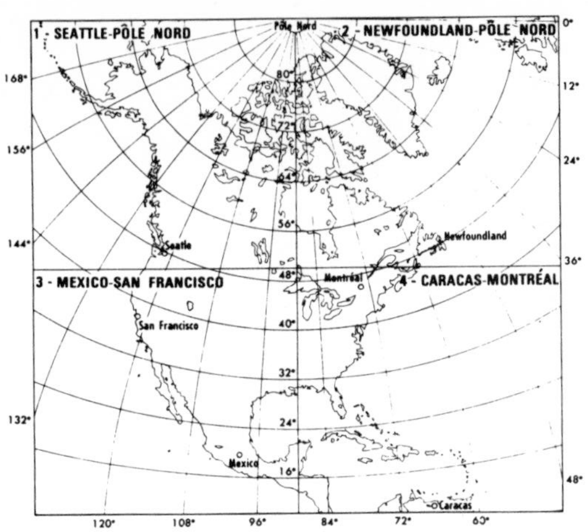
1 - SEATTLE-PÔLE NORD
2 - NEWFOUNDLAND-PÔLE NORD
3 - MEXICO-SAN FRANCISCO
4 - CARACAS-MONTRÉAL

ARCTIQUE-EUROPE-AFRIQUE

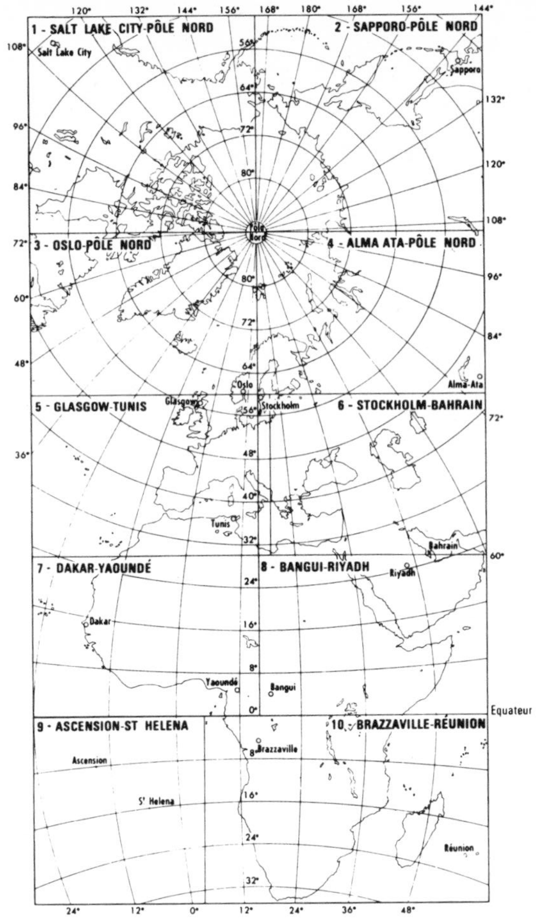
1 - SALT LAKE CITY-PÔLE NORD
2 - SAPPORO-PÔLE NORD
3 - OSLO-PÔLE NORD
4 - ALMA ATA-PÔLE NORD
5 - GLASGOW-TUNIS
6 - STOCKHOLM-BAHRAIN
7 - DAKAR-YAOUNDÉ
8 - BANGUI-RIYADH
9 - ASCENSION-ST HELENA
10 - BRAZZAVILLE-RÉUNION
Equateur

ASIE

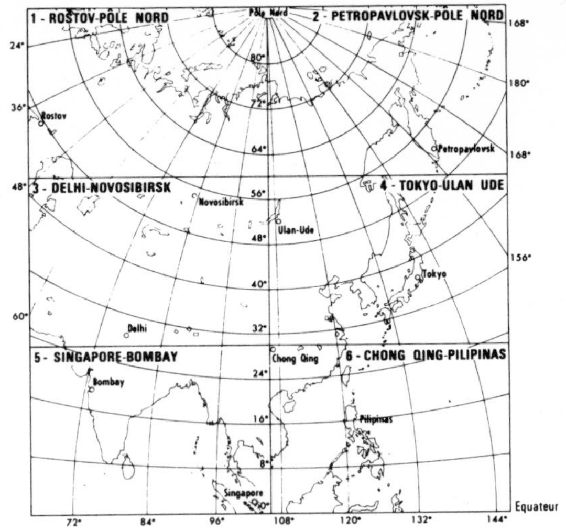
1 - ROSTOV-PÔLE NORD
2 - PETROPAVLOVSK-PÔLE NORD
3 - DELHI-NOVOSIBIRSK
4 - TOKYO-ULAN UDE
5 - SINGAPORE-BOMBAY
6 - CHONG QING-PILIPINAS
Equateur

AMÉRIQUE DU SUD-ANTARCTIQUE

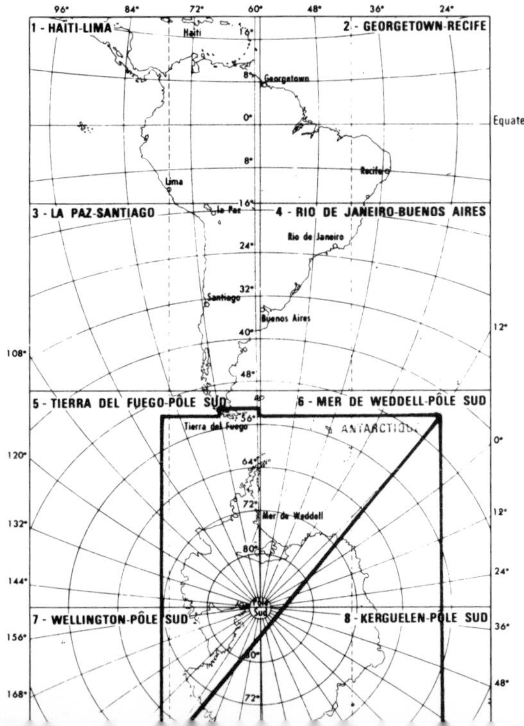
1 - HAÏTI-LIMA
2 - GEORGETOWN-RECIFE
3 - LA PAZ-SANTIAGO
4 - RIO DE JANEIRO-BUENOS AIRES
5 - TIERRA DEL FUEGO-PÔLE SUD
6 - MER DE WEDDELL-PÔLE SUD
7 - WELLINGTON-PÔLE SUD
8 - KERGUELEN-PÔLE SUD
ANTARCTIQUE
Equateur

INDONÉSIE-AUSTRALIE

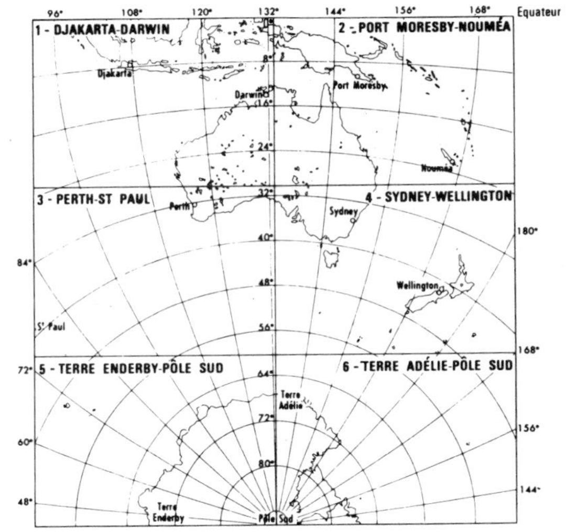
1 - DJAKARTA-DARWIN
2 - PORT MORESBY-NOUMÉA
3 - PERTH-ST PAUL
4 - SYDNEY-WELLINGTON
5 - TERRE ENDERBY-PÔLE SUD
6 - TERRE ADÉLIE-PÔLE SUD
Equateur

CARTE GÉNÉRALE DES CONTINENTS

AU 1 : 5 000 000

1 mm sur la carte représente 5 km.
Double projection de Mercator Transverse.
Ellipsoïde international.
Réseau géographique en degrés.
34 feuilles de format 93 × 64 à 93 × 85 cm (sauf pour les feuilles 5, 9 et 10 de la bande Arctique-Europe-Afrique) assemblables en 5 bandes.
1 feuille spéciale " Antarctique " de format 113 × 137 cm.
Toponymie internationale.
Edition en 7 à 11 couleurs, à plat.

100/5 *CARTE GÉNÉRALE DES CONTINENTS*
1:5,000,000 IGN
Physical sectional wall map of

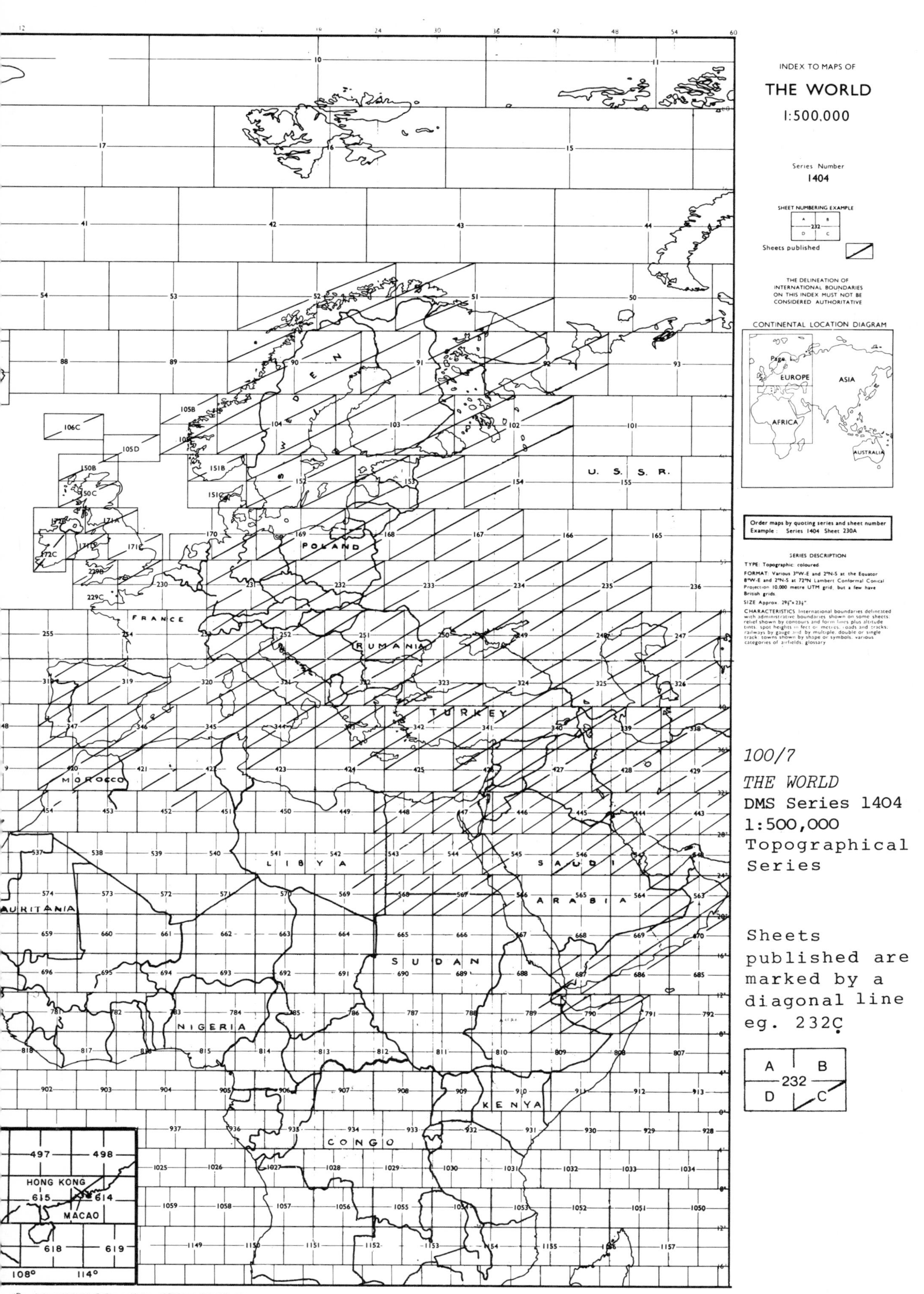
INDEX TO MAPS OF
THE WORLD
1:500,000
Series Number
1404
SHEET NUMBERING EXAMPLE
Sheets published
THE DELINEATION OF INTERNATIONAL BOUNDARIES ON THIS INDEX MUST NOT BE CONSIDERED AUTHORITATIVE
CONTINENTAL LOCATION DIAGRAM
EUROPE
ASIA
AFRICA
AUSTRALIA
Order maps by quoting series and sheet number
Example : Series 1404 Sheet 230A
SERIES DESCRIPTION
TYPE: Topographic: coloured
FORMAT: Various 3°W-E and 2°N-S at the Equator 8°W-E and 2°N-S at 72°N Lambert Conformal Conical Projection 10,000 metre UTM grid, but a few have British grids.
SIZE Approx. 29½"x 23½"
CHARACTERISTICS International boundaries delineated with administrative boundaries shown on some sheets: relief shown by contours and form lines plus altitude tints: spot heights in feet or metres: roads and tracks: railways by gauge and by multiple, double or single track: towns shown by shape or symbols: various categories of airfields: glossary
U. S. S. R.
POLAND
FRANCE
RUMANIA
TURKEY
MOROCCO
LIBYA
SAUDI ARABIA
MAURITANIA
SUDAN
NIGERIA
KENYA
CONGO
HONG KONG
MACAO
108°
114°
100/7
THE WORLD
DMS Series 1404
1:500,000
Topographical
Series
Sheets published are marked by a diagonal line eg. 232C
A
B
232
D
C
Index published by D. Survey, Ministry of Defence, United Kingdom

100/8 TABULA IMPERII ROMANI

1:1,000,000

International map of the Roman Empire

Sheets available

In preparation

Previously published but now out of print

100/9 DEUTSCHE WELTKARTE

1:5,000,000 Biblio. Inst. Meyer Verlag.

Physical world map with transparant overlay index diagram

Sheets published

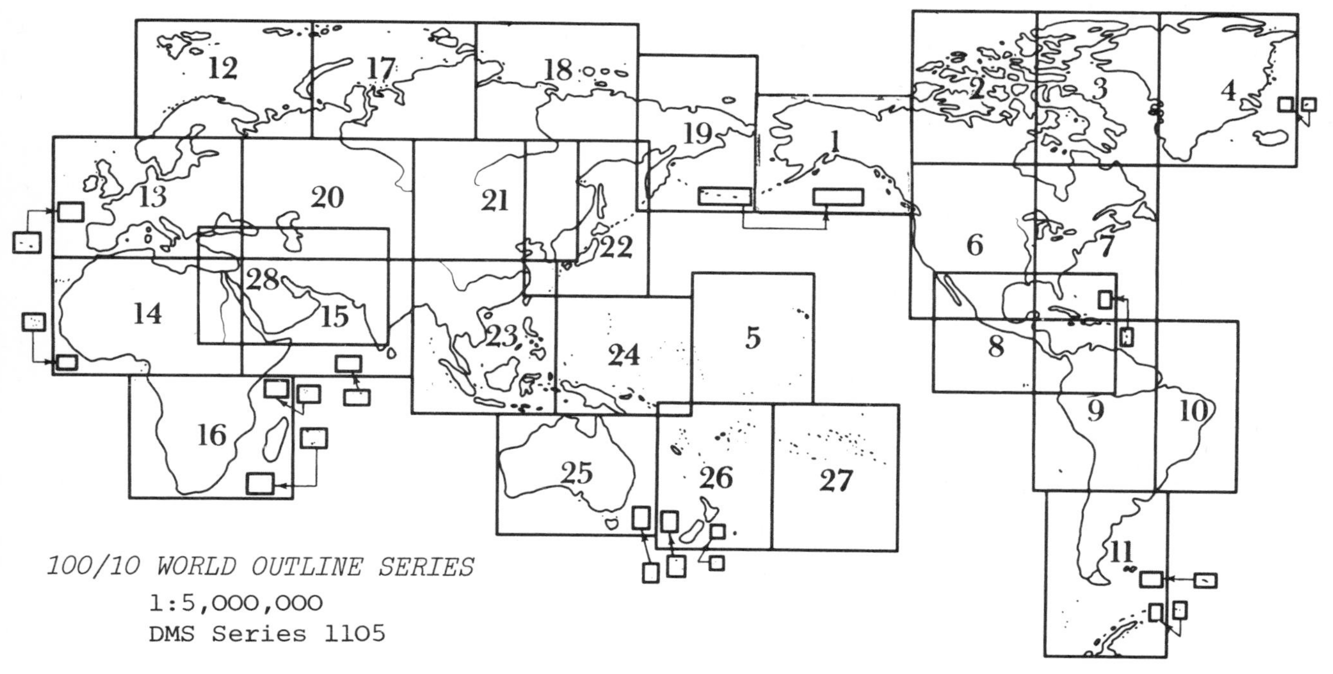

100/10 WORLD OUTLINE SERIES
1:5,000,000
DMS Series 1105

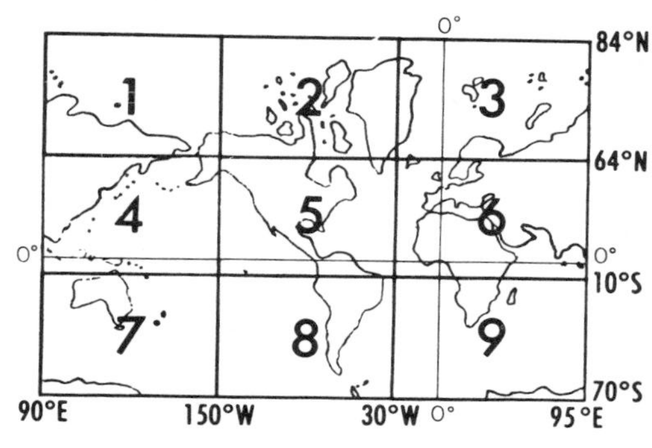

100/11 PHYSICAL MAP OF THE WORLD
1:11,000,000
AMS Series 1101

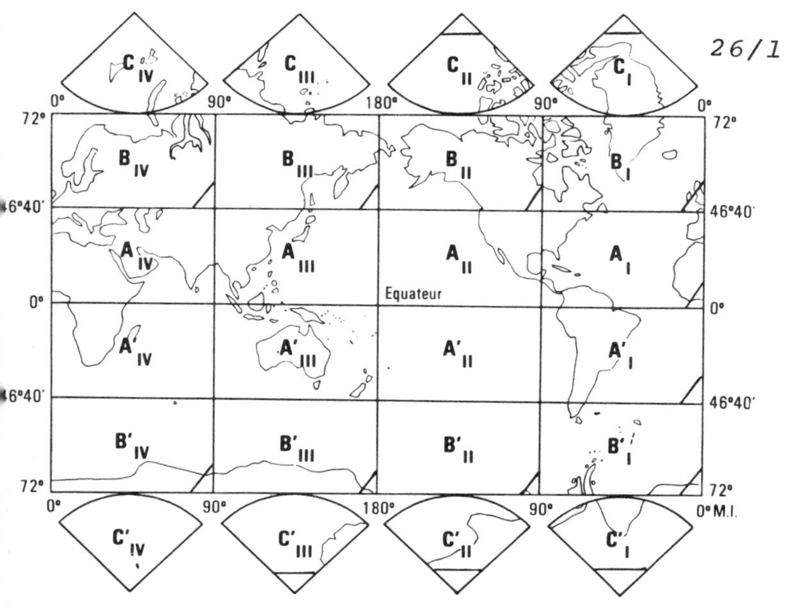

26/1 *CARTE GÉNÉRALE BATHYMETRIQUE DES OCEANS*
1:10,000,000 IGN
Bathymetric map of the Oceans

Sheets published

Europe

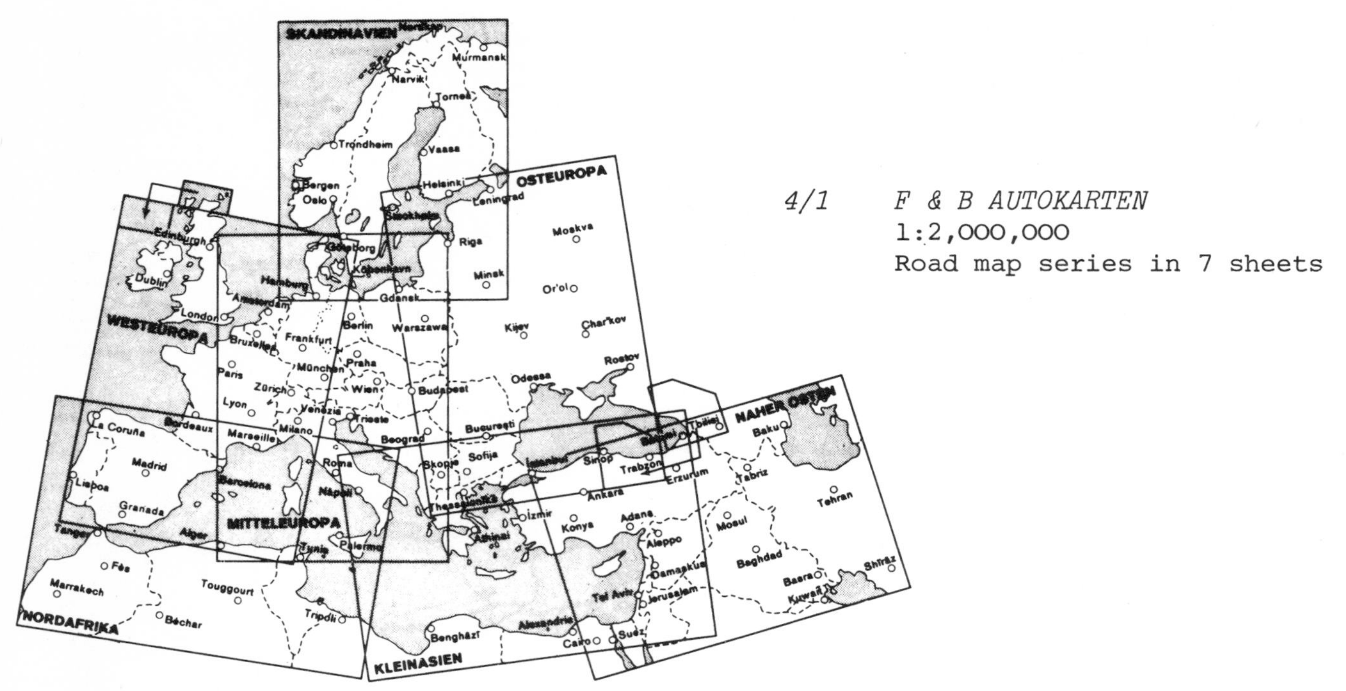

4/1 *F & B AUTOKARTEN*
1:2,000,000
Road map series in 7 sheets

4/2 *K & F AUTOKARTEN*
1:1,000,000
Road map series

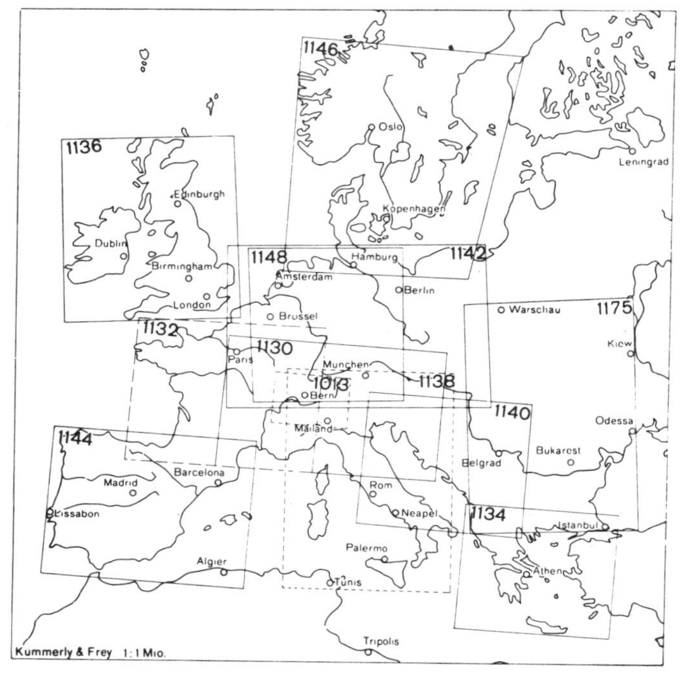

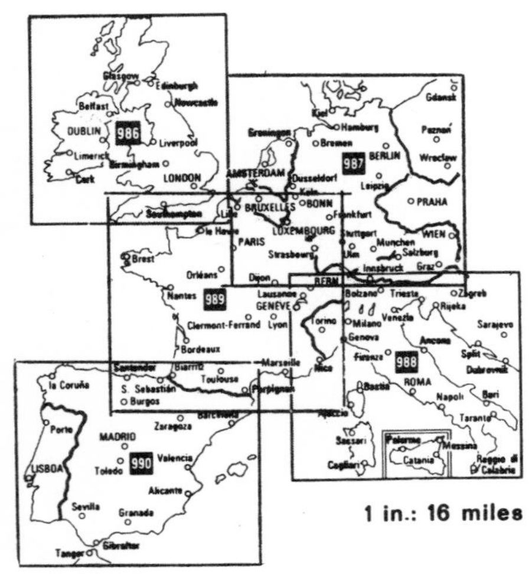

4/3 *CARTE MICHELIN*
1:1,000,000
Road map series

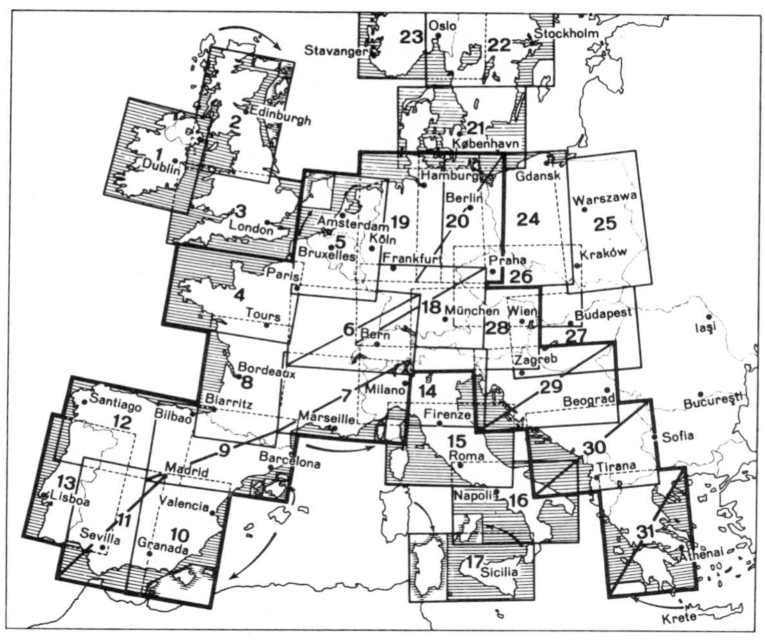

4/4 *CARTA STRADALE D'EUROPE*
1:500,000 T.C.I.
Road map series

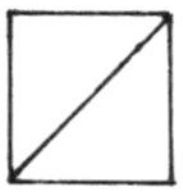

Sheets published

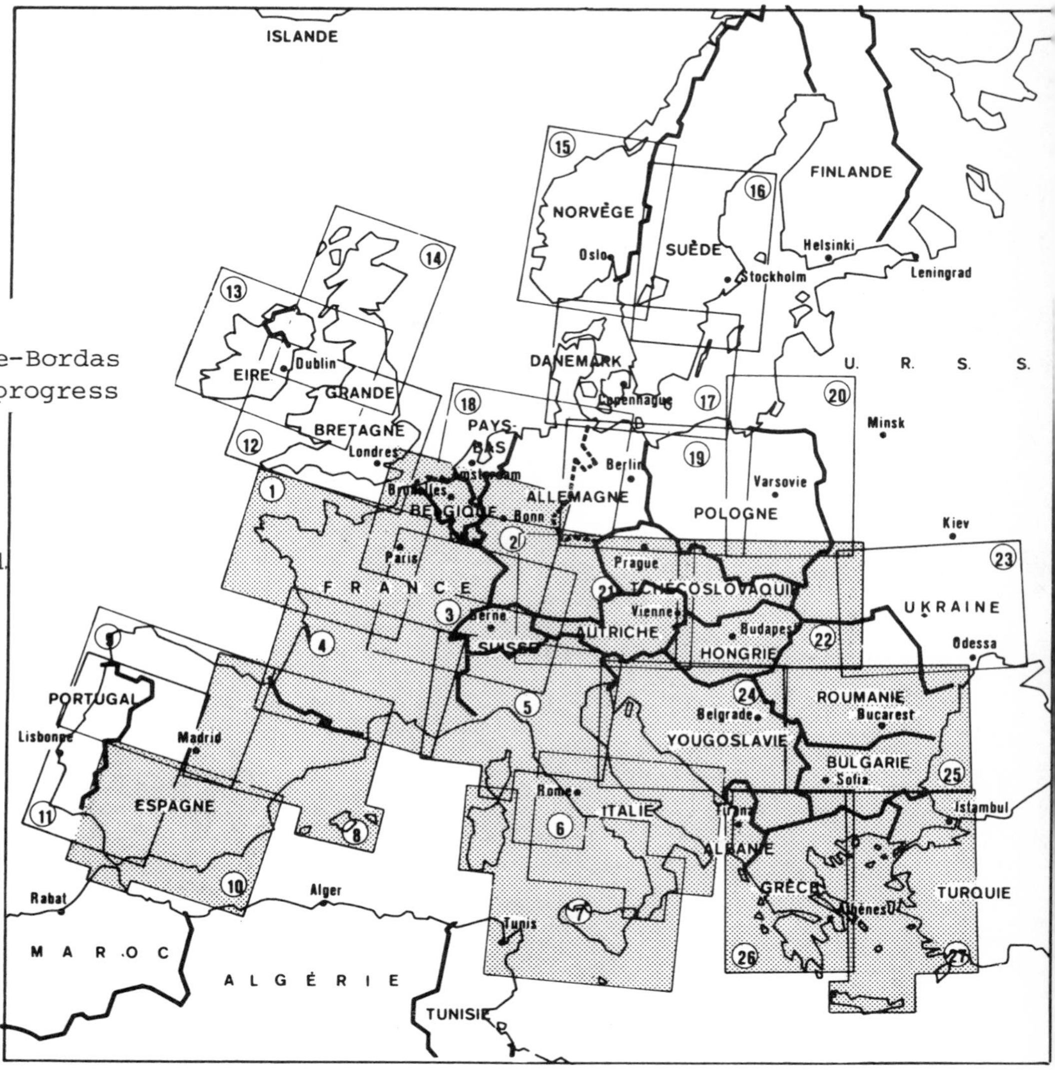

5 *LES CARTES BLEUES*
1:500,000 Hachette-Bordas
Road map series in progress

Sheets published

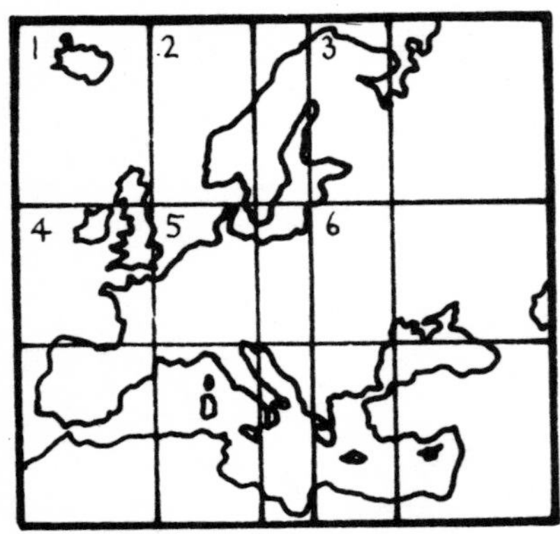

4/6 *EUROPE*

1:2,000,000 GSGS 1209
Physical wall map series

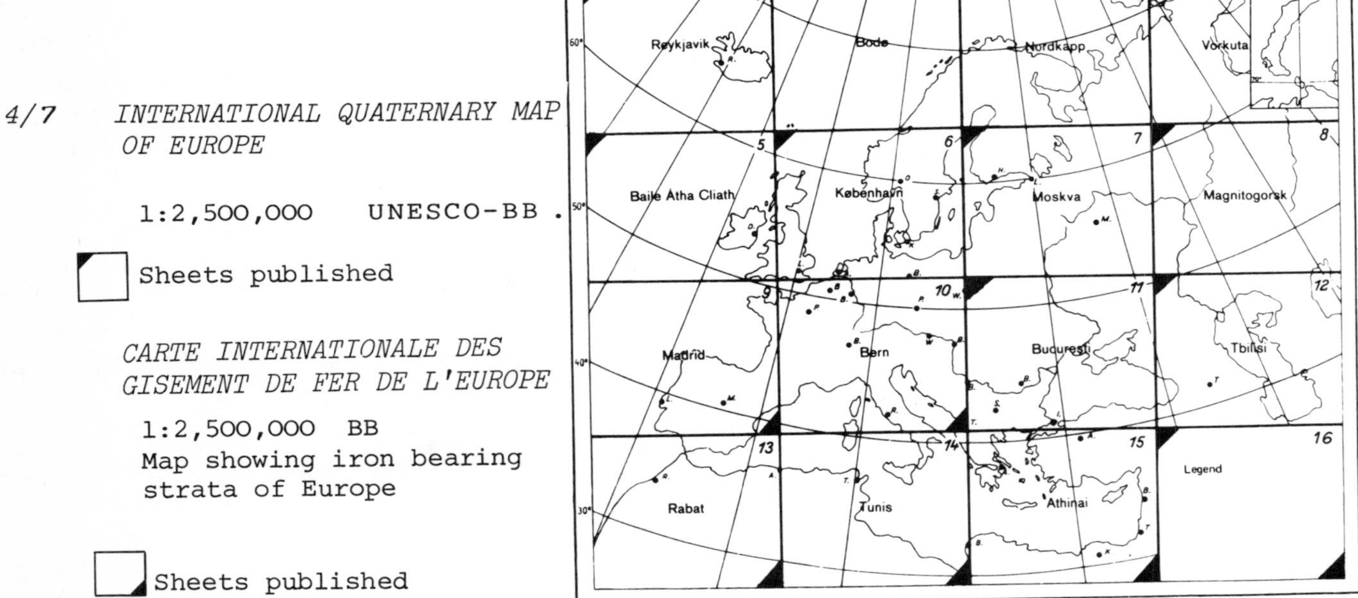

4/7 *INTERNATIONAL QUATERNARY MAP OF EUROPE*

1:2,500,000 UNESCO-BB .

Sheets published

CARTE INTERNATIONALE DES GISEMENT DE FER DE L'EUROPE

1:2,500,000 BB
Map showing iron bearing strata of Europe

Sheets published

NB. Sheet 16 is mapped and legend will be included on parts of sheets 1 and 5

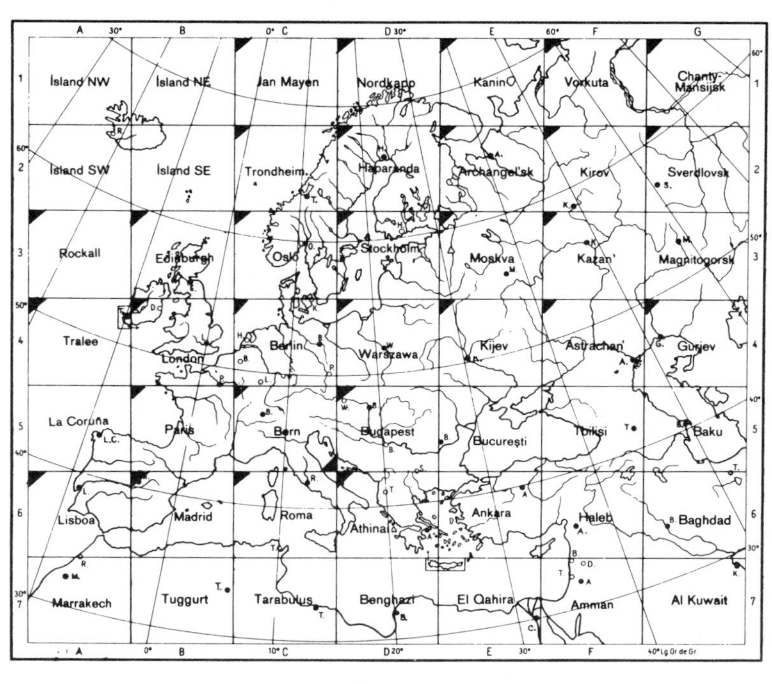

4/8 *CARTE INTERNATIONALE GÉOLOGIQUE D'EUROPE*
1:1,500,000 UNESCO-BB
International geological map of Europe

Sheets published

CARTE HYDROGÉOLOGIQUE INTERNATIONALE DE L'EUROPE
1:1,500,000 UNESCO-BB
International hydrogeological map of Europe

Sheets published

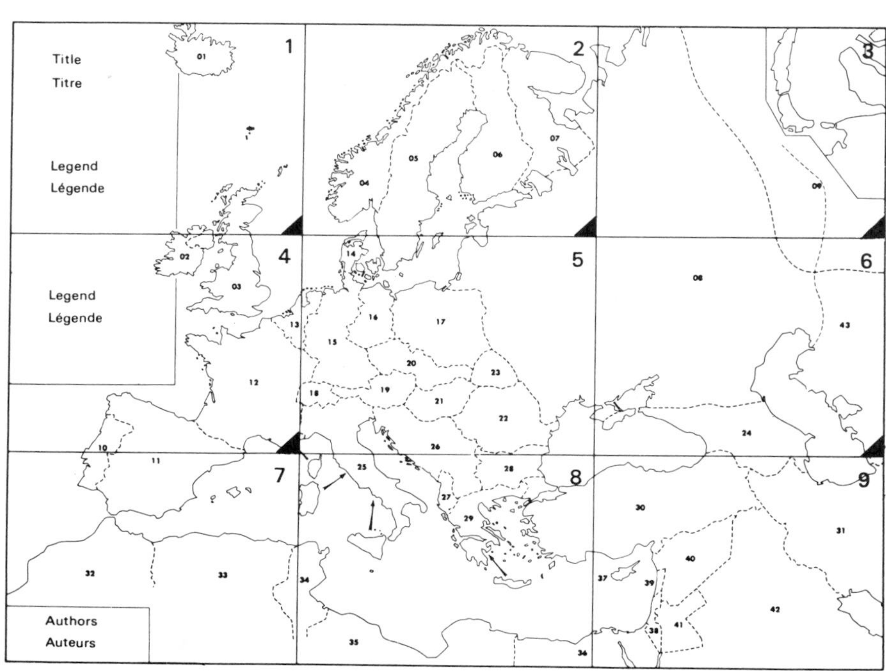

4/9 *CARTE MÉTALLOGÉNIQUE DE L'EUROPE*
1:2,500,000 UNESCO-BRGM
International Metallogenetic map of Europe

Sheets published

410/1 *A to Z GREAT BRITAIN ROAD MAP SERIES*
1:316,800 Geographers

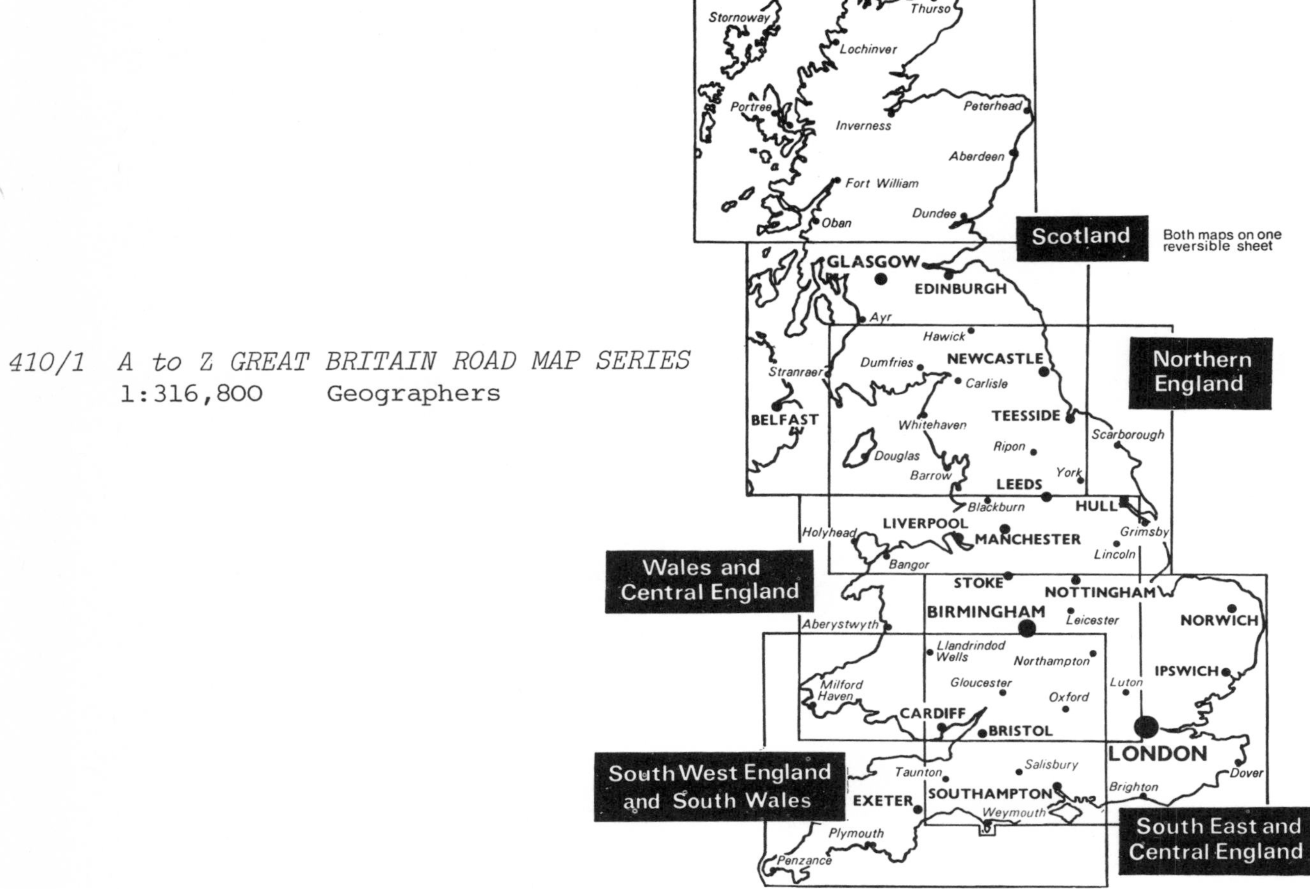

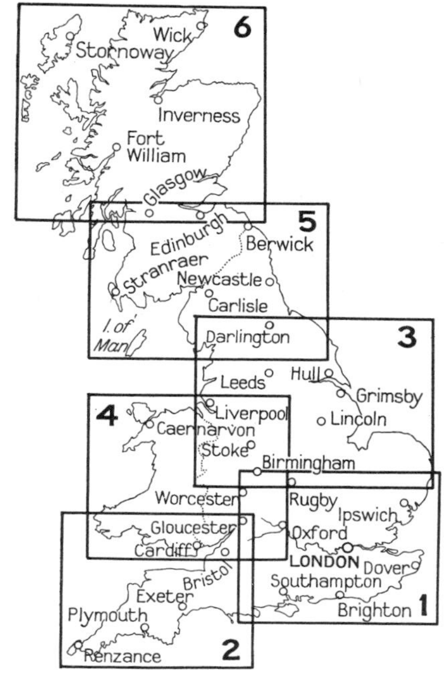

410/2 *DUNLOP WIDTH OF ROAD MAPS OF GREAT BRITAIN*
1:316,800 Geographia

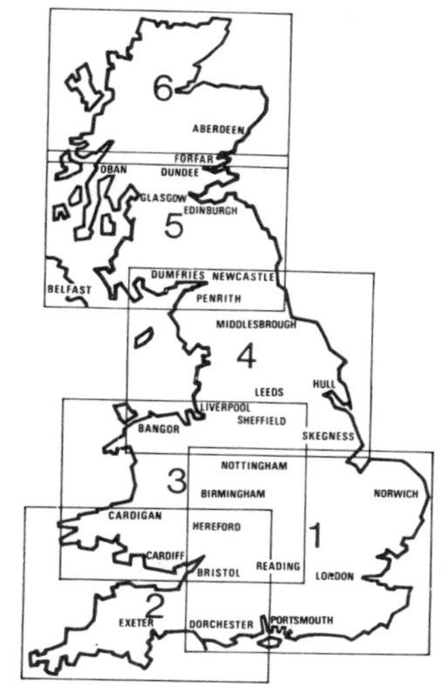

410/3 *PRIMARY ROUTES MAP*
1:300,000 Geographia

410/5 *RAC MOTORING MAPS OF GREAT BRITAIN*
1:190,080 England
1:253,440 Scotland Map Productions

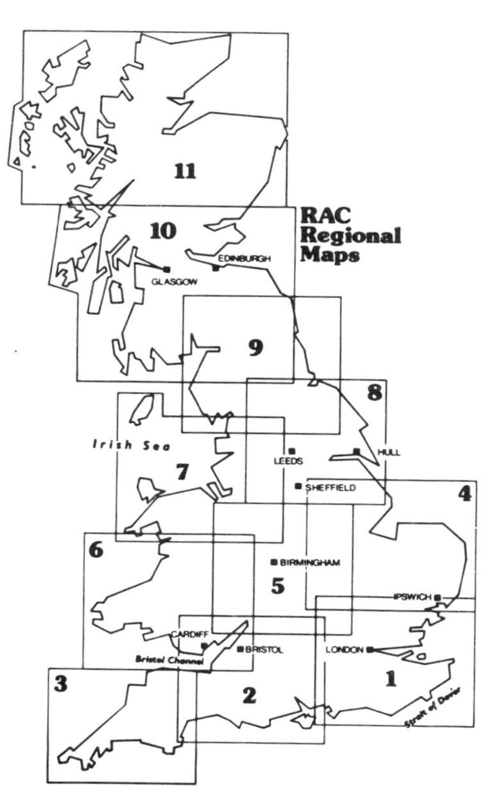

410/4 *G.T. MAP OF BRITAIN*
1:250,000 Bartholomew
Road map series

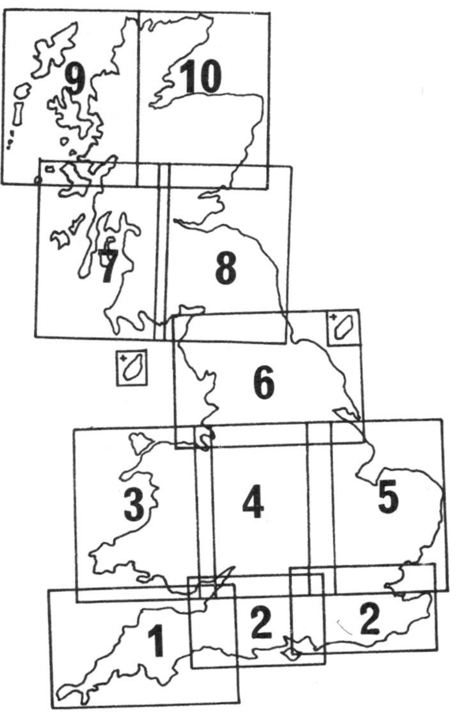

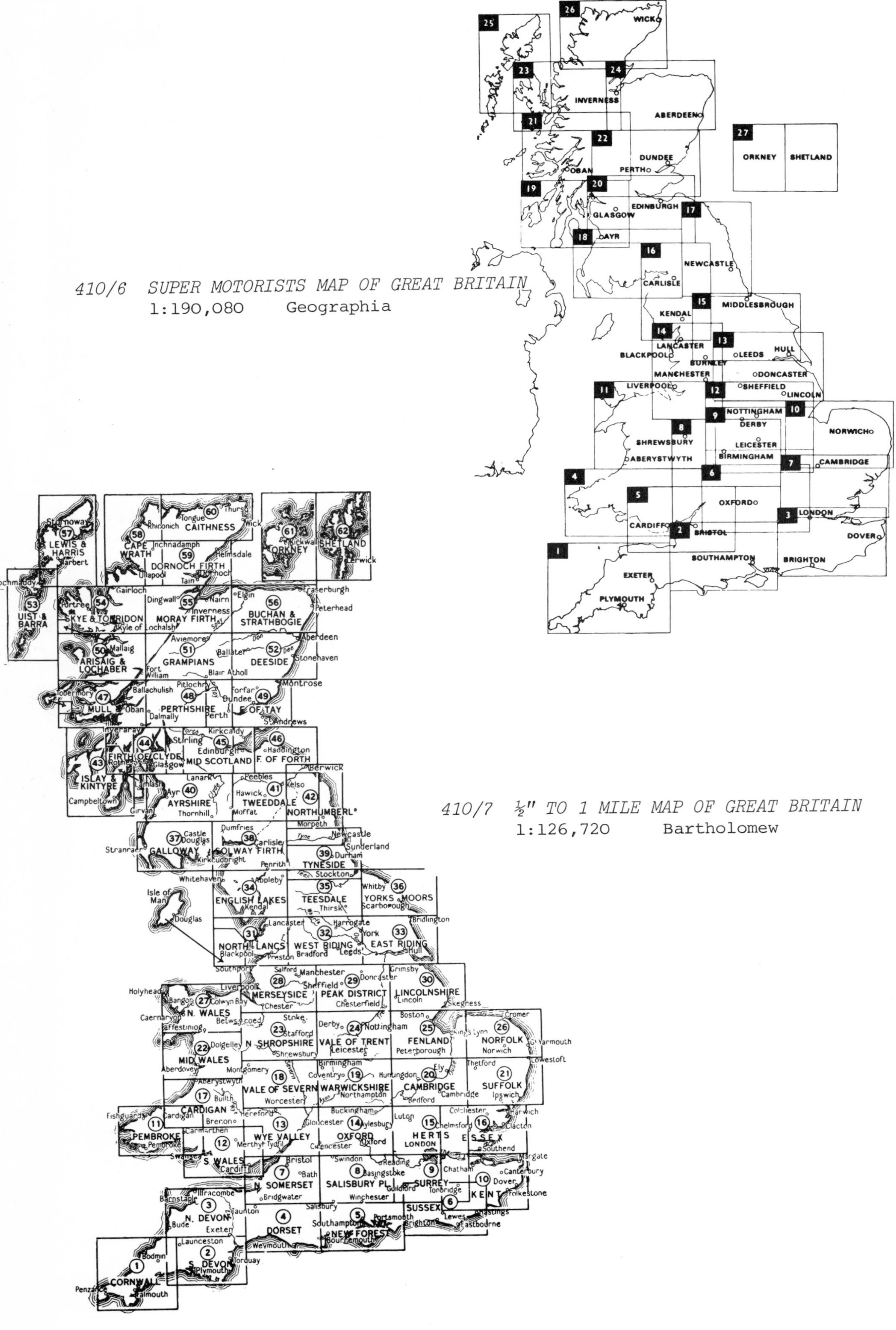

410/6 SUPER MOTORISTS MAP OF GREAT BRITAIN
1:190,080 Geographia

410/7 ½" TO 1 MILE MAP OF GREAT BRITAIN
1:126,720 Bartholomew

410/8 ORDNANCE SURVEY 1/4" MAP OF GREAT BRITAIN-
FIFTH SERIES
1:250,000 O.S.

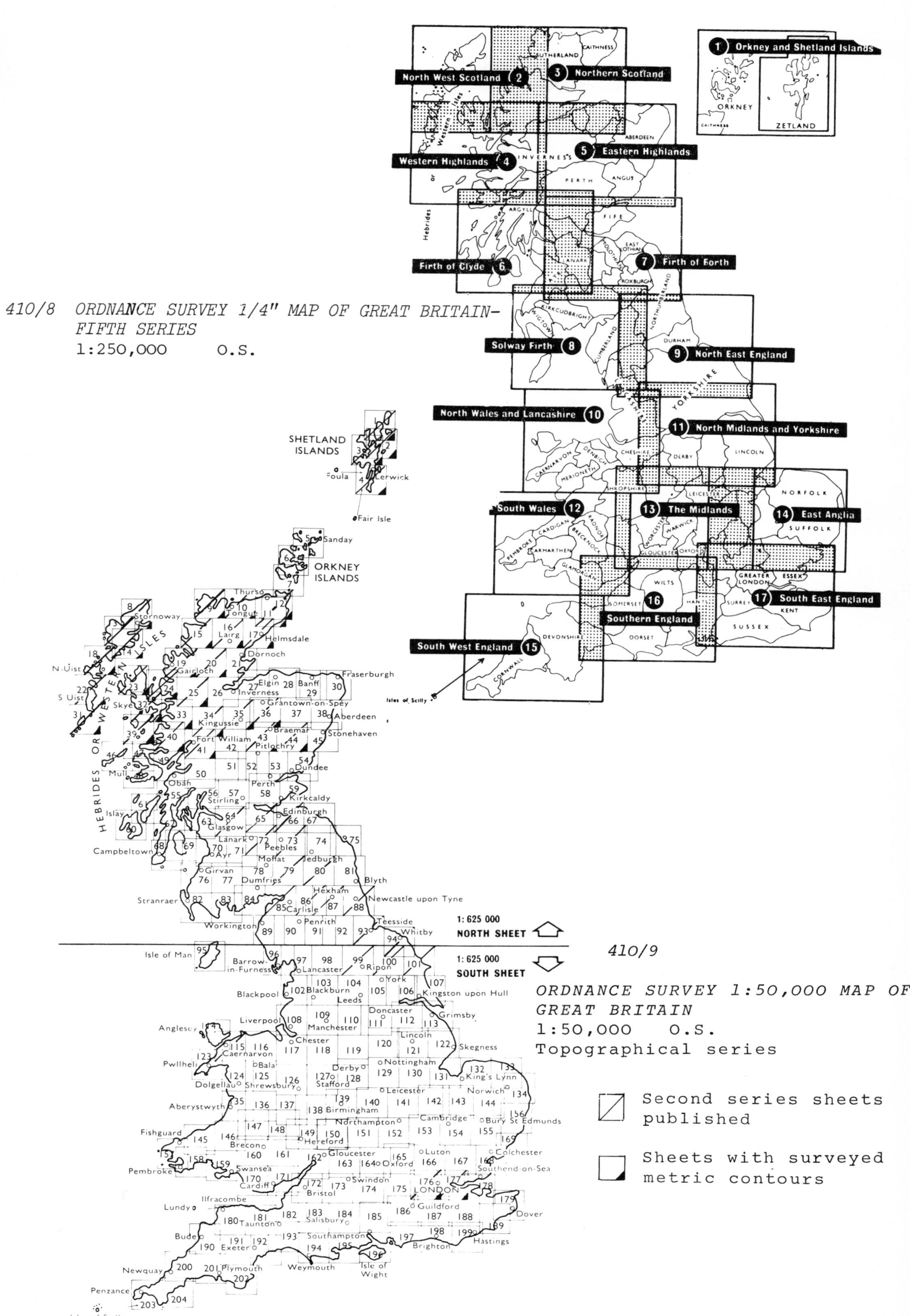

410/9

ORDNANCE SURVEY 1:50,000 MAP OF GREAT BRITAIN
1:50,000 O.S.
Topographical series

Second series sheets published

Sheets with surveyed metric contours

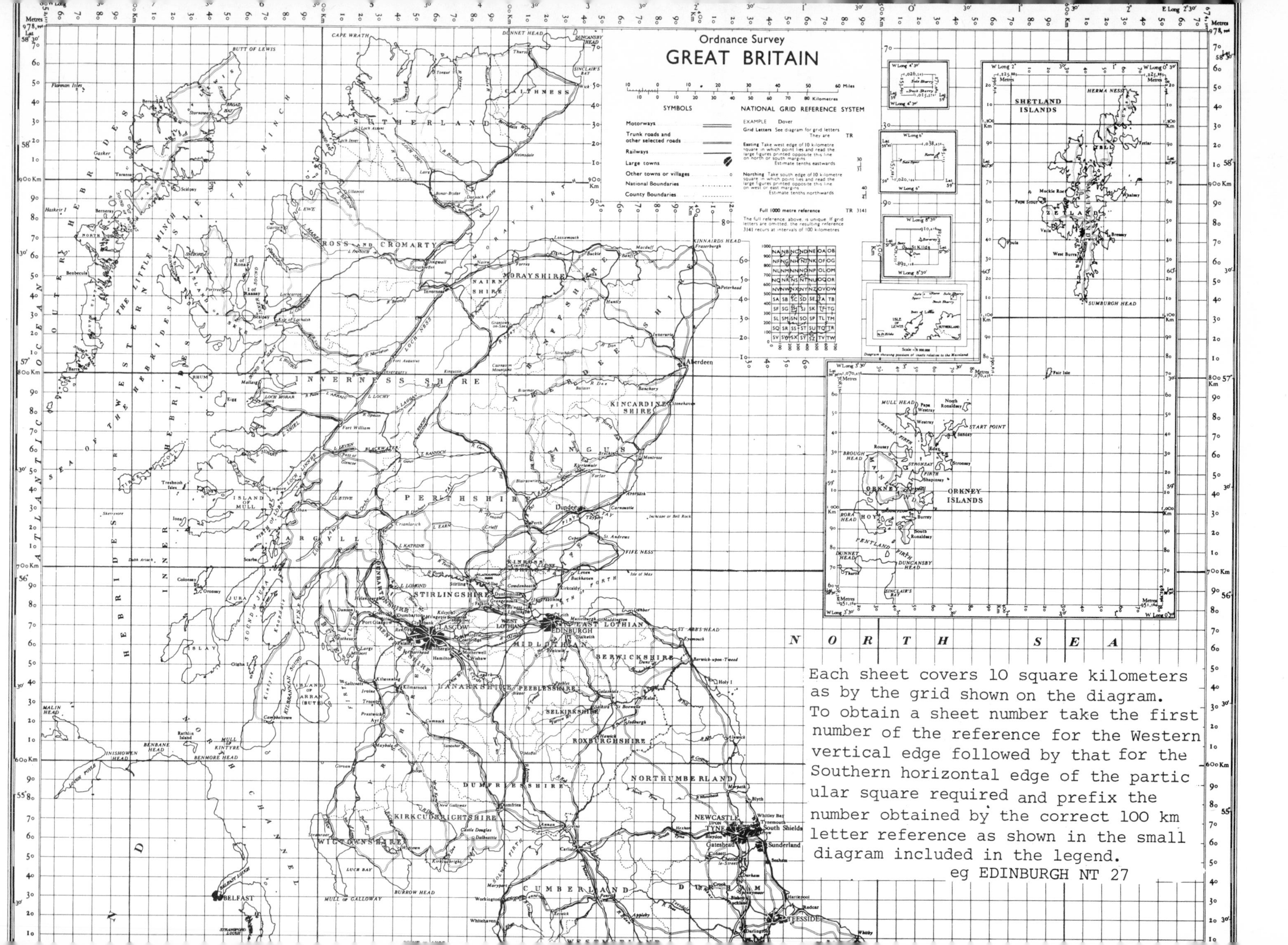

Ordnance Survey
GREAT BRITAIN
SYMBOLS
Motorways
Trunk roads and other selected roads
Railways
Large towns
Other towns or villages
National Boundaries
County Boundaries
NATIONAL GRID REFERENCE SYSTEM
EXAMPLE Dover
Grid Letters See diagram for grid letters They are TR
Easting Take west edge of 10 kilometre square in which point lies and read the large figures printed opposite this line on north or south margins. Estimate tenths eastwards
Northing Take south edge of 10 kilometre square in which point lies and read the large figures printed opposite this line on west or east margins. Estimate tenths northwards
Full 1000 metre reference TR 3141
The full reference, above, is unique. If grid letters are omitted, the resulting reference 3141 recurs at intervals of 100 kilometres
60 Miles
80 Kilometres
SHETLAND ISLANDS
ZETLAND
HERMA NESS
SUMBURGH HEAD
Fair Isle
ORKNEY ISLANDS
START POINT
MULL HEAD
PENTLAND FIRTH
DUNCANSBY HEAD
NORTH SEA
ATLANTIC OCEAN
OUTER HEBRIDES
INNER HEBRIDES
THE MINCH
THE LITTLE MINCH
SEA OF THE HEBRIDES
NORTH CHANNEL
BUTT OF LEWIS
CAPE WRATH
DUNNET HEAD
SUTHERLAND
CAITHNESS
ROSS AND CROMARTY
INVERNESS SHIRE
MORAYSHIRE
NAIRN SHIRE
ABERDEENSHIRE
KINCARDINE SHIRE
ANGUS
PERTHSHIRE
ARGYLL
STIRLINGSHIRE
DUNBARTONSHIRE
RENFREWSHIRE
LANARKSHIRE
WEST LOTHIAN
MIDLOTHIAN
EAST LOTHIAN
BERWICKSHIRE
PEEBLESSHIRE
SELKIRKSHIRE
ROXBURGHSHIRE
DUMFRIESSHIRE
KIRKCUDBRIGHTSHIRE
WIGTOWNSHIRE
NORTHUMBERLAND
CUMBERLAND
DURHAM
MORAY FIRTH
FIRTH OF FORTH
FIRTH OF TAY
SOLWAY FIRTH
Aberdeen
Dundee
EDINBURGH
GLASGOW
NEWCASTLE UPON TYNE
Gateshead
South Shields
Sunderland
TEESSIDE
BELFAST
ISLAND OF MULL
ISLAND OF ARRAN (BUTE)
ISLAY
JURA
SKYE
RHUM
MULL OF GALLOWAY
MULL OF KINTYRE
MALIN HEAD
Each sheet covers 10 square kilometers
as by the grid shown on the diagram.
To obtain a sheet number take the first
number of the reference for the Western
vertical edge followed by that for the
Southern horizontal edge of the partic
ular square required and prefix the
number obtained by the correct 100 km
letter reference as shown in the small
diagram included in the legend.
eg EDINBURGH NT 27

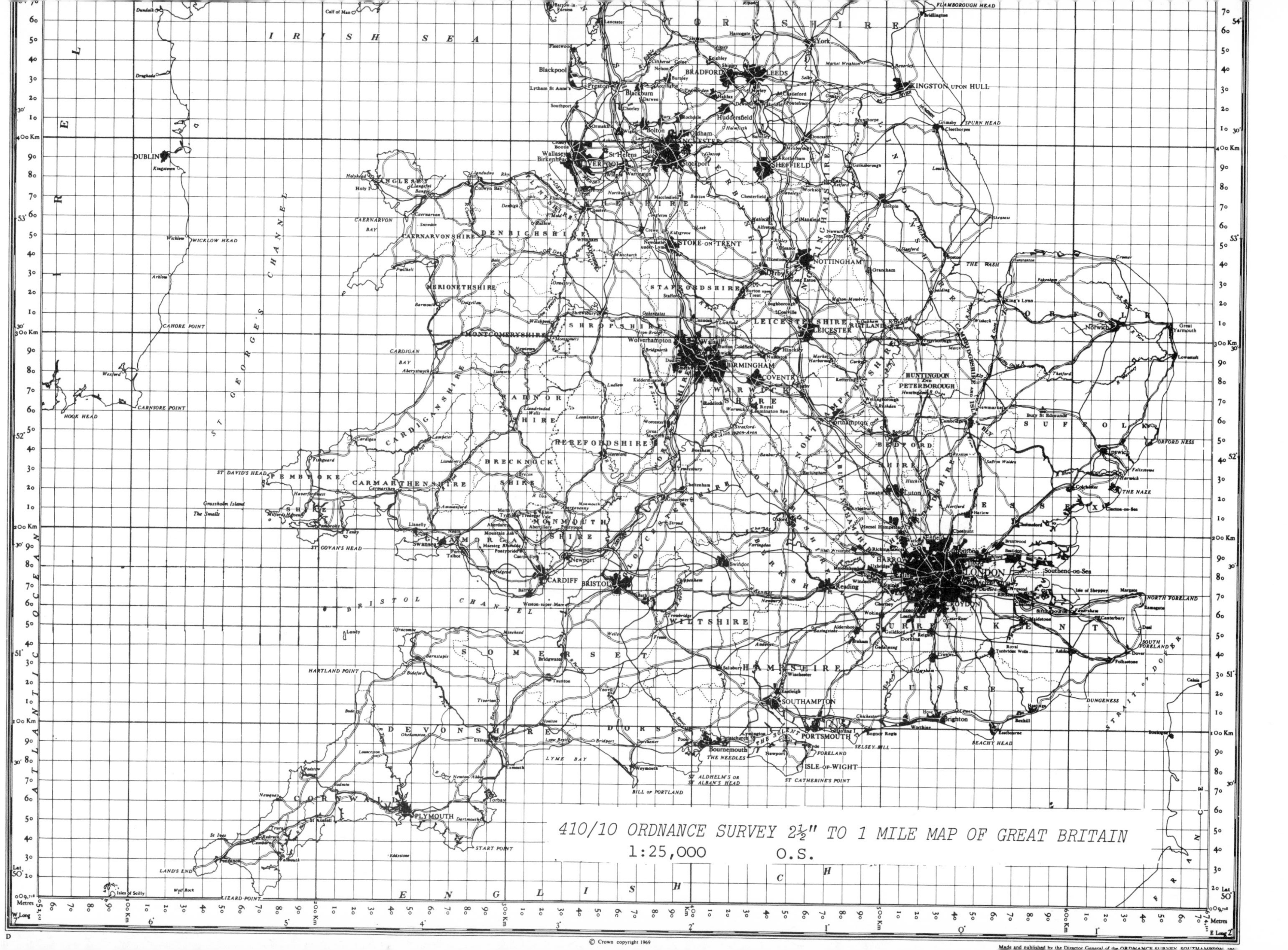
410/10 ORDNANCE SURVEY 2½" TO 1 MILE MAP OF GREAT BRITAIN
1:25,000 O.S.
IRISH SEA
ST GEORGE'S CHANNEL
BRISTOL CHANNEL
ENGLISH CHANNEL
ATLANTIC OCEAN
STRAIT OF DOVER
YORKSHIRE
LINCOLNSHIRE
NORFOLK
SUFFOLK
ESSEX
KENT
SUSSEX
SURREY
HAMPSHIRE
DORSET
DEVONSHIRE
CORNWALL
SOMERSET
WILTSHIRE
BERKSHIRE
OXFORDSHIRE
BUCKINGHAMSHIRE
BEDFORDSHIRE
HERTFORDSHIRE
CAMBRIDGESHIRE AND ISLE OF ELY
HUNTINGDON AND PETERBOROUGH
NORTHAMPTONSHIRE
RUTLAND
LEICESTERSHIRE
NOTTINGHAMSHIRE
DERBYSHIRE
CHESHIRE
STAFFORDSHIRE
SHROPSHIRE
WARWICKSHIRE
WORCESTERSHIRE
HEREFORDSHIRE
GLOUCESTERSHIRE
MONMOUTHSHIRE
GLAMORGAN
BRECKNOCKSHIRE
RADNORSHIRE
CARMARTHENSHIRE
PEMBROKESHIRE
CARDIGANSHIRE
MONTGOMERYSHIRE
MERIONETHSHIRE
CAERNARVONSHIRE
DENBIGHSHIRE
FLINTSHIRE
ANGLESEY
LONDON
BIRMINGHAM
MANCHESTER
LIVERPOOL
LEEDS
BRADFORD
SHEFFIELD
NOTTINGHAM
LEICESTER
COVENTRY
STOKE-ON-TRENT
KINGSTON UPON HULL
BRISTOL
CARDIFF
SOUTHAMPTON
PORTSMOUTH
PLYMOUTH
DUBLIN
FLAMBOROUGH HEAD
SPURN HEAD
THE WASH
ORFORD NESS
THE NAZE
NORTH FORELAND
SOUTH FORELAND
DUNGENESS
BEACHY HEAD
SELSEY BILL
ISLE OF WIGHT
ST CATHERINE'S POINT
THE NEEDLES
ST ALDHELM'S OR ST ALBAN'S HEAD
BILL OF PORTLAND
LYME BAY
START POINT
LIZARD POINT
LAND'S END
HARTLAND POINT
ST GOVAN'S HEAD
ST DAVID'S HEAD
CARDIGAN BAY
CAERNARVON BAY
WICKLOW HEAD
CAHORE POINT
CARNSORE POINT
HOOK HEAD
© Crown copyright 1969
Made and published by the Director General of the ORDNANCE SURVEY, SOUTHAMPTON

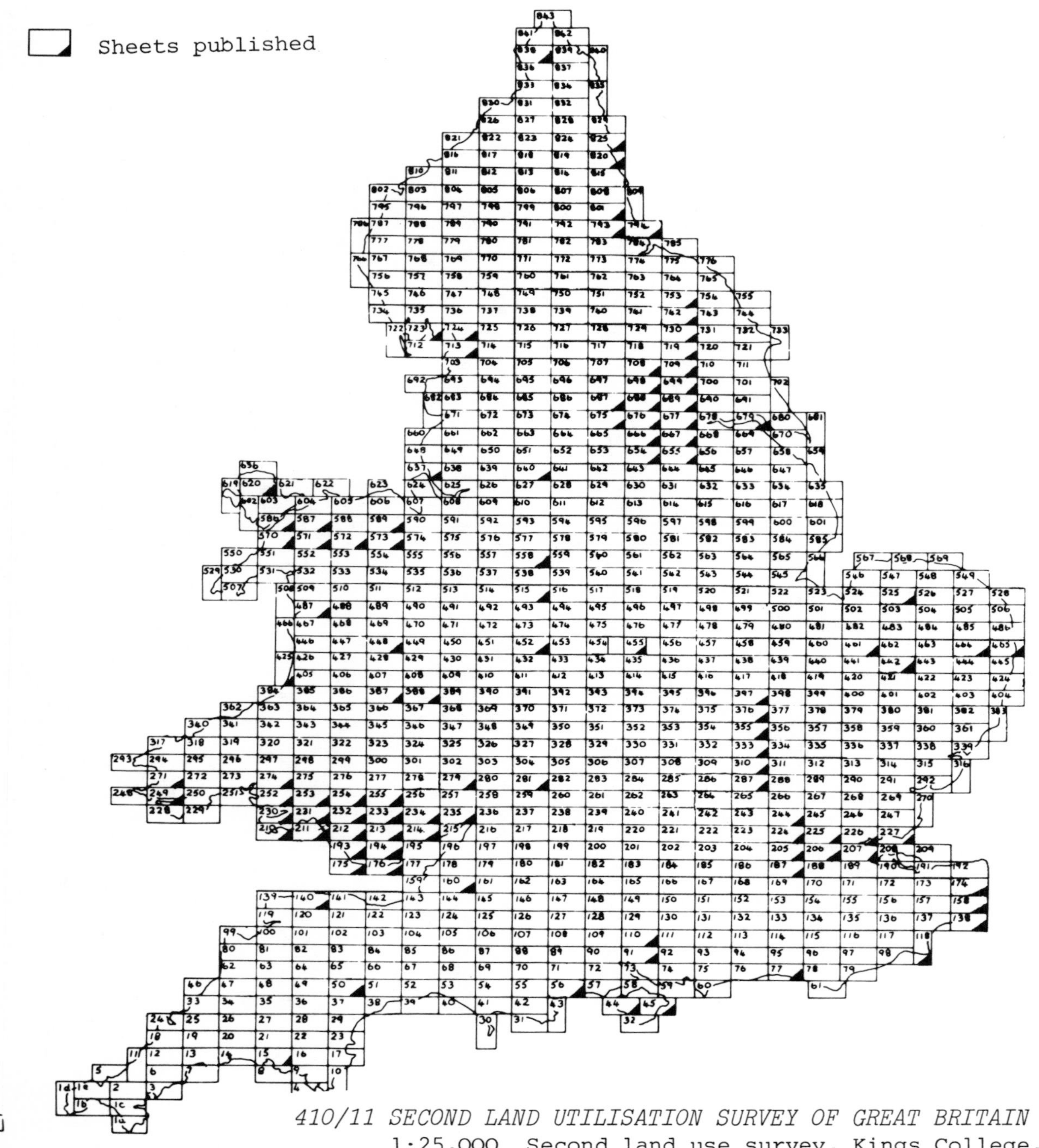

410/11 SECOND LAND UTILISATION SURVEY OF GREAT BRITAIN

1:25,000 Second land use survey, Kings College, London

NB. Sheets 13, 192, 263, 264, 278, 481, 486, 499, 757, 815 have been published but are out of print

411/1 **INDEX TO THE ONE-INCH AND QUARTER-INCH GEOLOGICAL MAPS OF SCOTLAND**

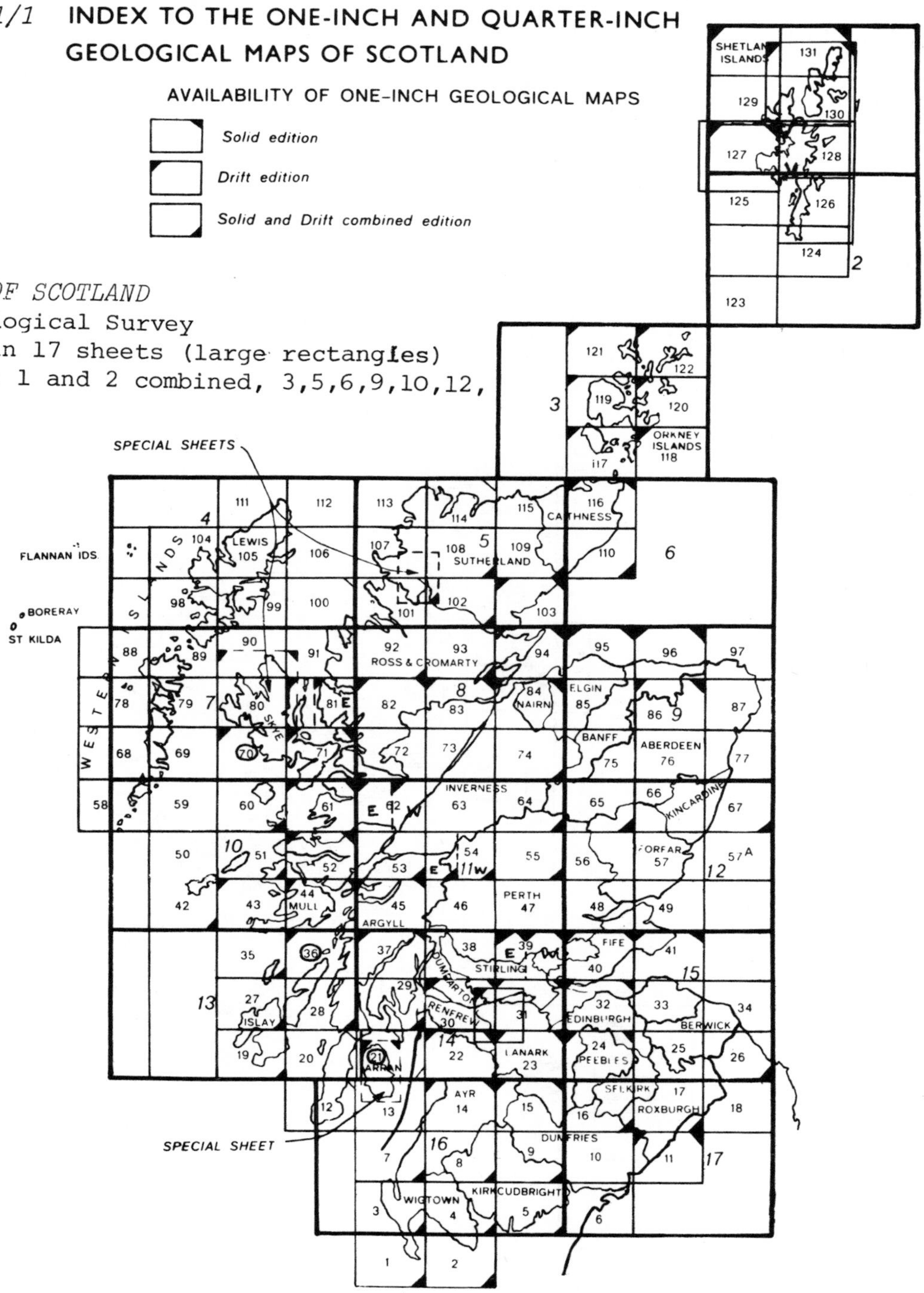

AVAILABILITY OF ONE-INCH GEOLOGICAL MAPS

Solid edition

Drift edition

Solid and Drift combined edition

GEOLOGICAL MAPS OF SCOTLAND
1:253,440 Geological Survey
Coloured series in 17 sheets (large rectangles)
Sheets published: 1 and 2 combined, 3,5,6,9,10,12,
13,14,15,16,17

SPECIAL SHEETS

SPECIAL SHEET

GEOLOGICAL MAPS OF SCOTLAND
1:63,360 and 1:50,000
When reprinted, one inch sheets are generally divided into two 1:50,000 sheets (western and eastern halves)

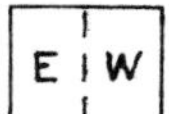

1:50,000

Full sheets at 1:50,000

ONE INCH TO ONE MILE
SPECIAL SHEETS OF SCOTLAND
1:63,360

Arran (S) and (D) 1:50,000
Assynt District (S & D)
Glasgow District (D)
Northern Shetland (S) and (D)
Western Shetland (S) and (D)
Northern Skye (S) and (D)

411/2 SOIL SURVEY OF SCOTLAND

1:63,360 Soil Survey, Macaulay Inst. for Soil Research - O.S.

Sheets published

Also available in Land Use Capability edition.

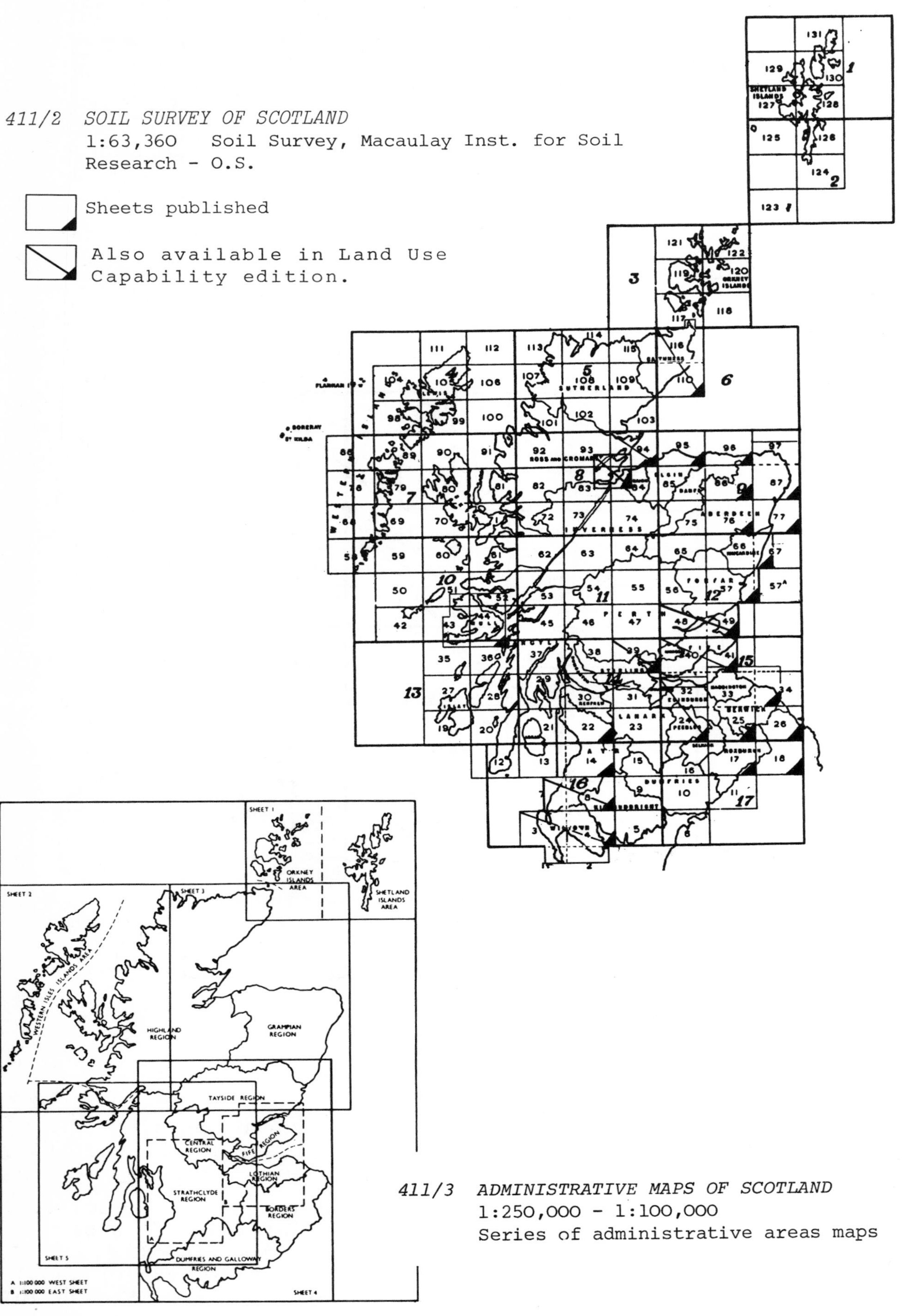

411/3 ADMINISTRATIVE MAPS OF SCOTLAND

1:250,000 - 1:100,000

Series of administrative areas maps

415/1 ORDNANCE SURVEY 1/4" MAP OF IRELAND
1:250,000 O.S. Rep. of Ireland
Topographical map in 5 sheets

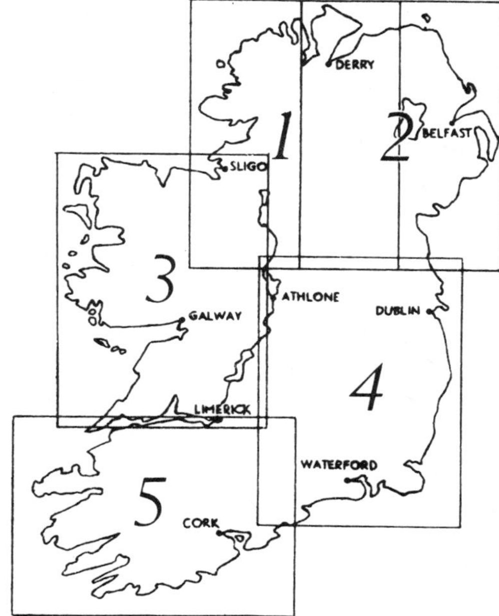

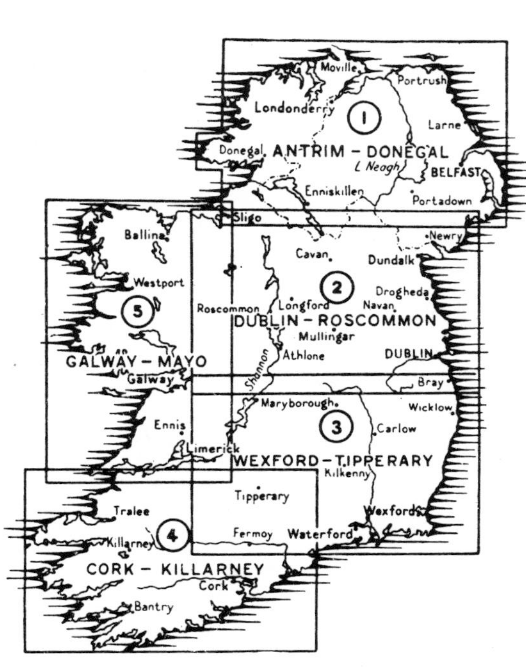

415/2 IRELAND TRAVEL MAP
1:250,000 , Bartholomew
Physical coloured touring map series

415/3 ORDNANCE SURVEY ½" MAP OF IRELAND
1:126,720 O.S. Rep of Ireland
Topographical series in 25 sheets

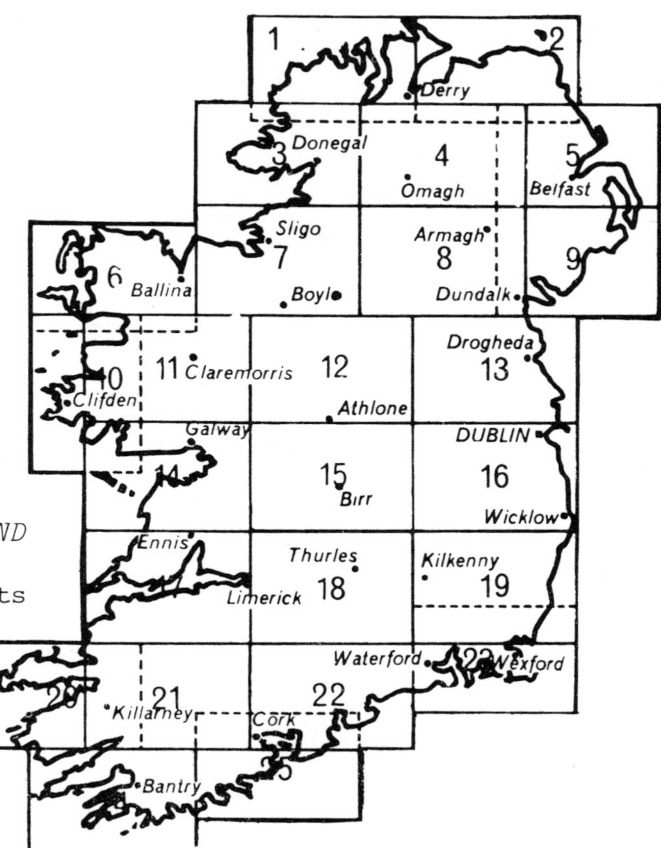

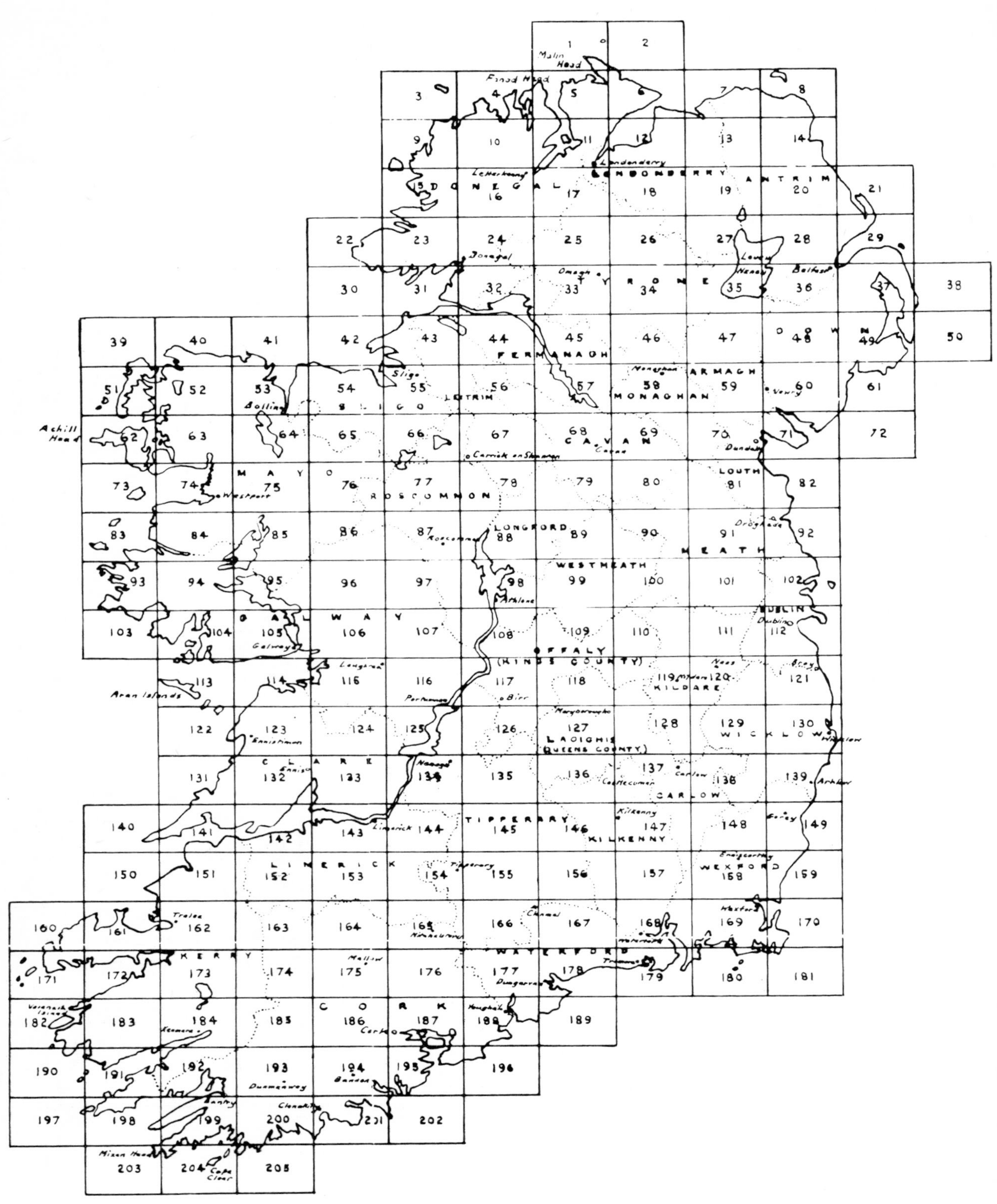

415/4 GEOLOGICAL MAPS OF IRELAND

1:63,360 Geol. Survey, Eire - O.S. of N

Series in black and white with some sheet

in colour

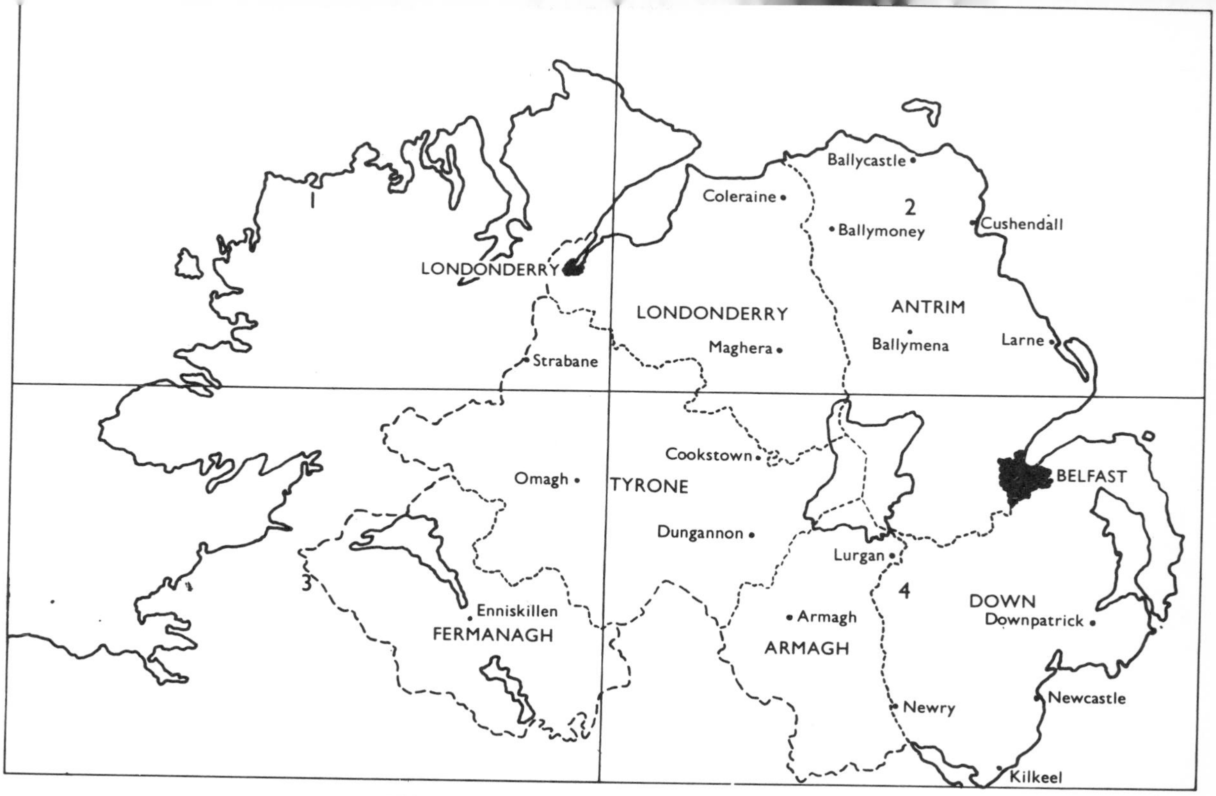

1
2
3
4
Ballycastle
Coleraine
Ballymoney
Cushendall
LONDONDERRY
LONDONDERRY
ANTRIM
Ballymena
Maghera
Larne
Strabane
Cookstown
Omagh
TYRONE
BELFAST
Dungannon
Lurgan
Enniskillen
FERMANAGH
Armagh
ARMAGH
DOWN
Downpatrick
Newry
Newcastle
Kilkeel

416/1 *THE HALF-INCH MAP OF NORTHERN IRELAND*
1:126,720 O.S. of N.I.
Topographical map in 4 sheets

/2
ONE-INCH MAP OF NORTHERN IRELAND
,360 O.S. of N.I.
graphical map in 9 sheets

1
Ballycastle
Coleraine
Cushendall
Ballymoney
Londonderry
Garvagh
2
LONDONDERRY
Maghera
3
ANTRIM
Larne
Strabane
Antrim
Castlederg
TYRONE
Cookstown
Belfast
4
Omagh
5
6
Kesh
Lurgan
Clogher
Portaferry
Enniskillen
Armagh
ARMAGH
DOWN
FERMANAGH
Downpatrick
Lisnaskea
Poyntz Pass
7
8
9
Newry
Kilkeel

N
6
7
8
BALLYCASTLE
11
12
13
2
14
LONDONDERRY
17
18
19
20
21
BALLYMENA
24
25
26
27
LOUGH NEAGH
28
29
OMAGH
33
32
34
35
36
BELFAST
37
38
5
44
45
46
47
48
49
50
ENNISKILLEN
ARMAGH
56
57
58
59
60
61
NEWRY
70
71
72

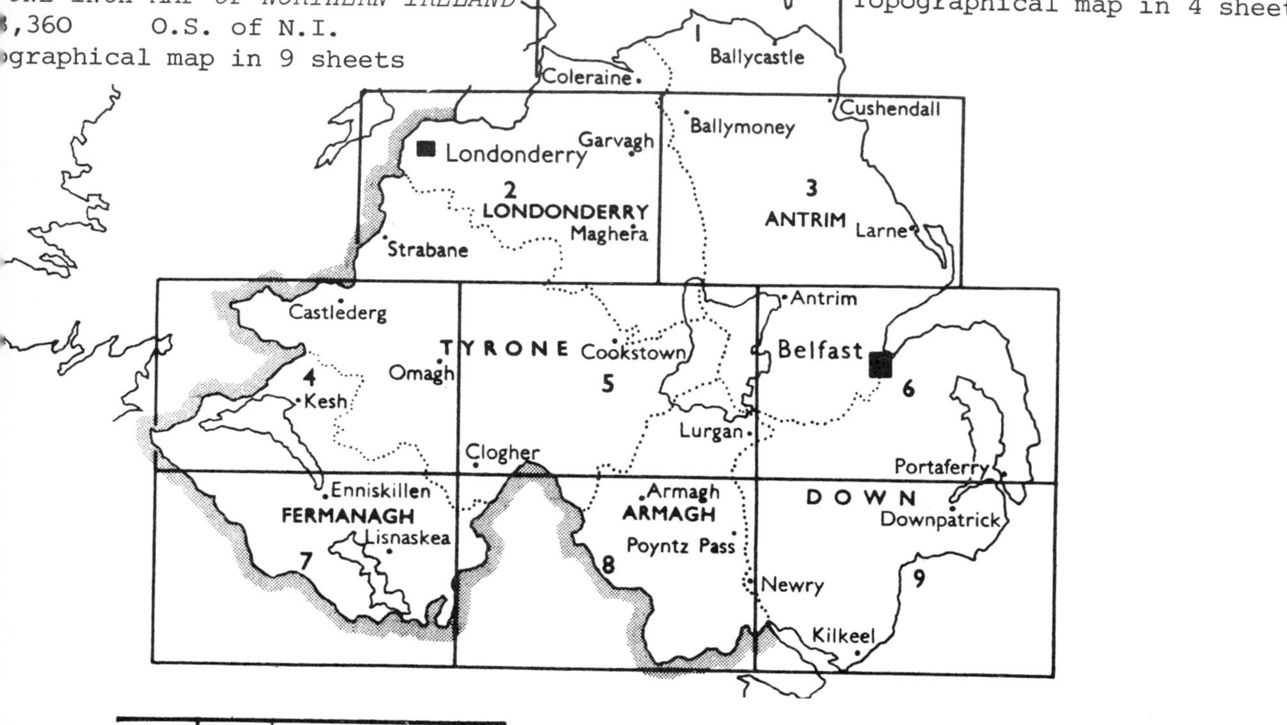

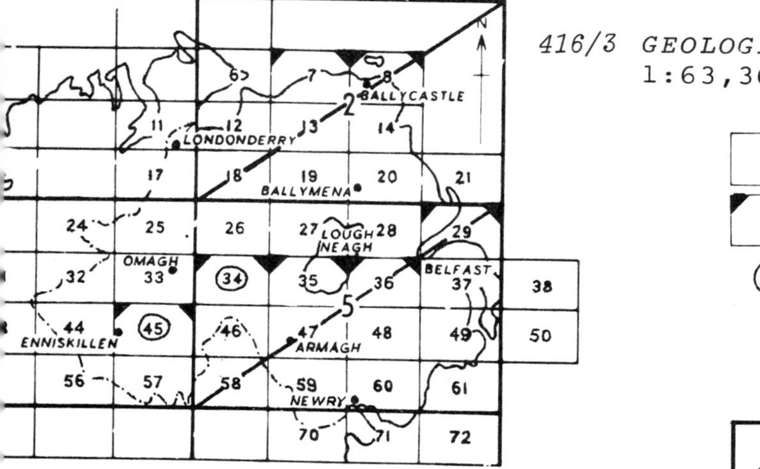

416/3 *GEOLOGICAL MAPS OF NORTHERN IRELAND*
1:63,360 and 1:50,000 Geol. Survey N.I.

Solid edition, sheets published

Drift edition, sheets published

(34) Published at 1:50,000

GEOLOGICAL MAPS OF NORTHERN IRELAND
1:253,440 Geol. Survey N.I.

Sheets published

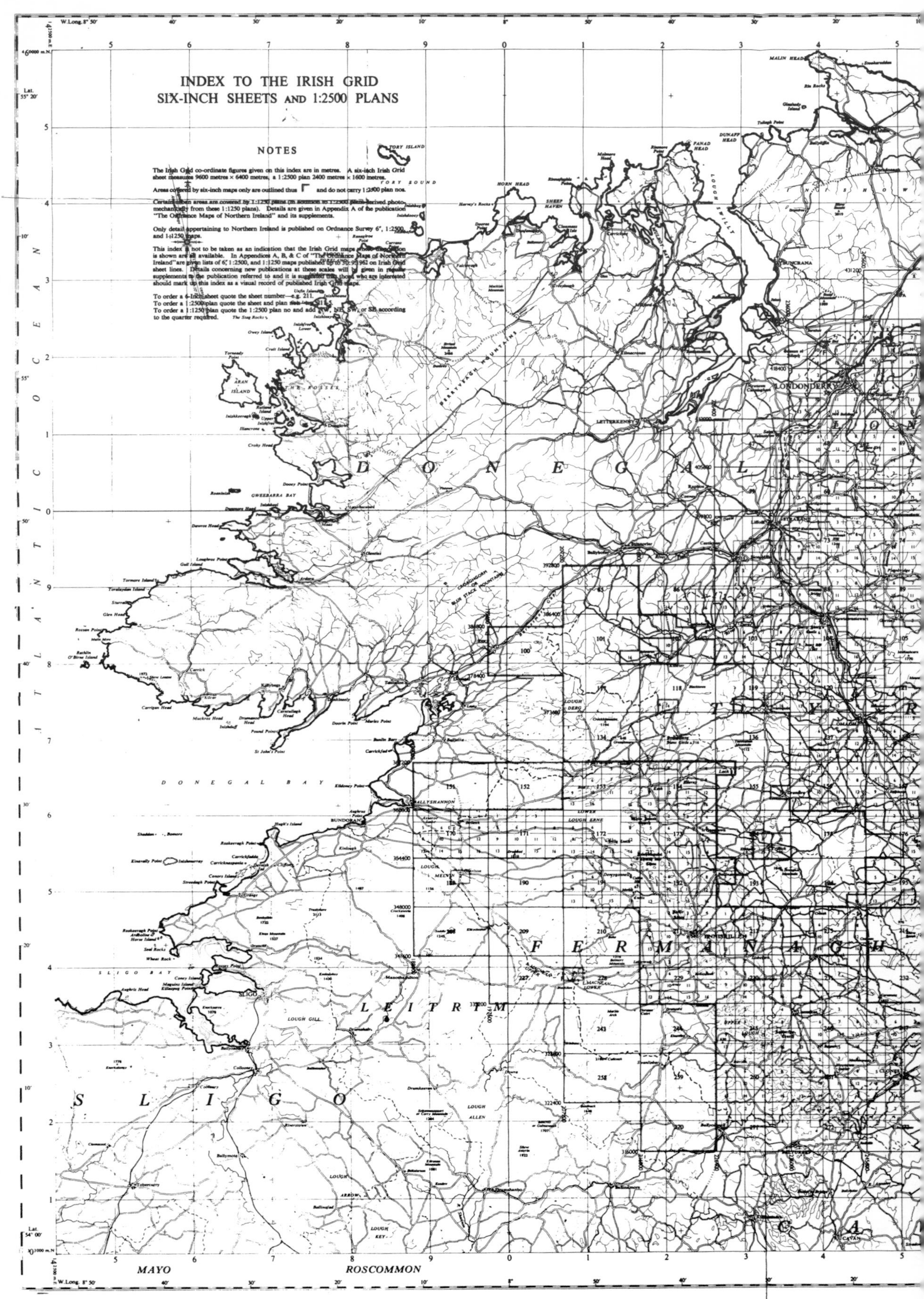

416/4 ORDNANCE SURVEY OF NORTHERN IRELAND IRISH GRID
1:10,560, 1:2,500, 1:1,250 O.S. of N.I.
Topographical series in progress replacing
earlier County series

RELAND

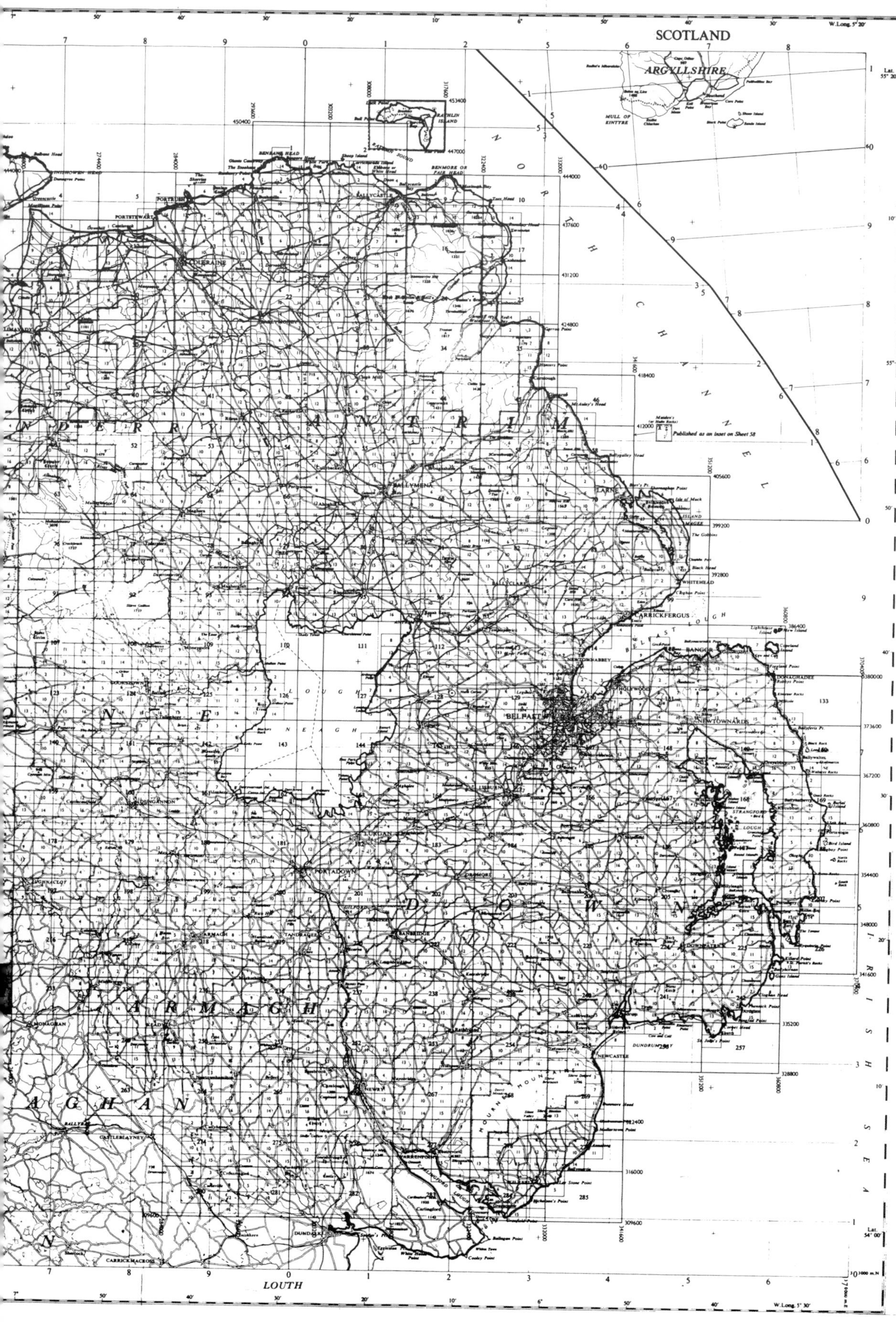

et numbering:
0,560 e.g. BELFAST 130
2,500 e.g. HOLYWOOD 130-4
1,250 e.g. HOLYWOOD 130-4 NW

NB: Where sheets are not yet published in this series coverage can be obtained from old 'County' editions on different sheet lines

NW
N
NE
W
Centre
E
SW
S
SE
LONDON
CHORLEYWOOD
WATFORD
POTTERS BAR
BARNET
CHINGFORD
EPPING
BRENTWOOD
HARROW
HENDON
TOTTENHAM
WANSTEAD
REDBRIDGE
ILFORD
BARKING
HILLINGDON
WEMBLEY
WILLESDEN
ISLINGTON
HACKNEY
HAYES
R. Thames
GRAYS
HOUNSLOW
RICHMOND
LAMBETH
LEE
LEWISHAM
BEXLEY
DARTFORD
STAINES
KINGSTON UPON THAMES
WIMBLEDON
EGHAM
MITCHAM
PENGE
BROMLEY
SWANLEY
CHERTSEY
ESHER
ORPINGTON
WEYBRIDGE
CROYDON
EPSOM
BANSTEAD
WROTHAM
WOKING
COULSDON
SEVENOAKS
RIPLEY
LEATHERHEAD
CATERHAM

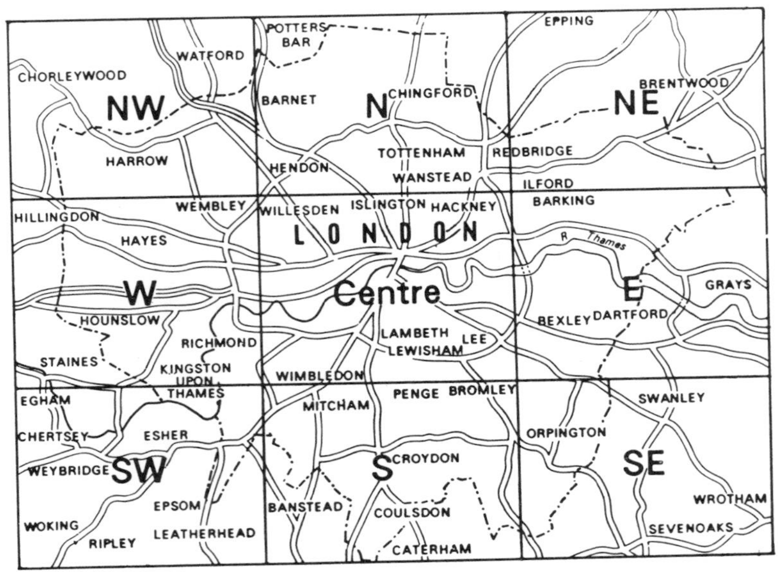

420/1 *MASTER MAP OF GREATER LONDON*
1:21,120 Geographers
Large scale street plan in 9 sheets

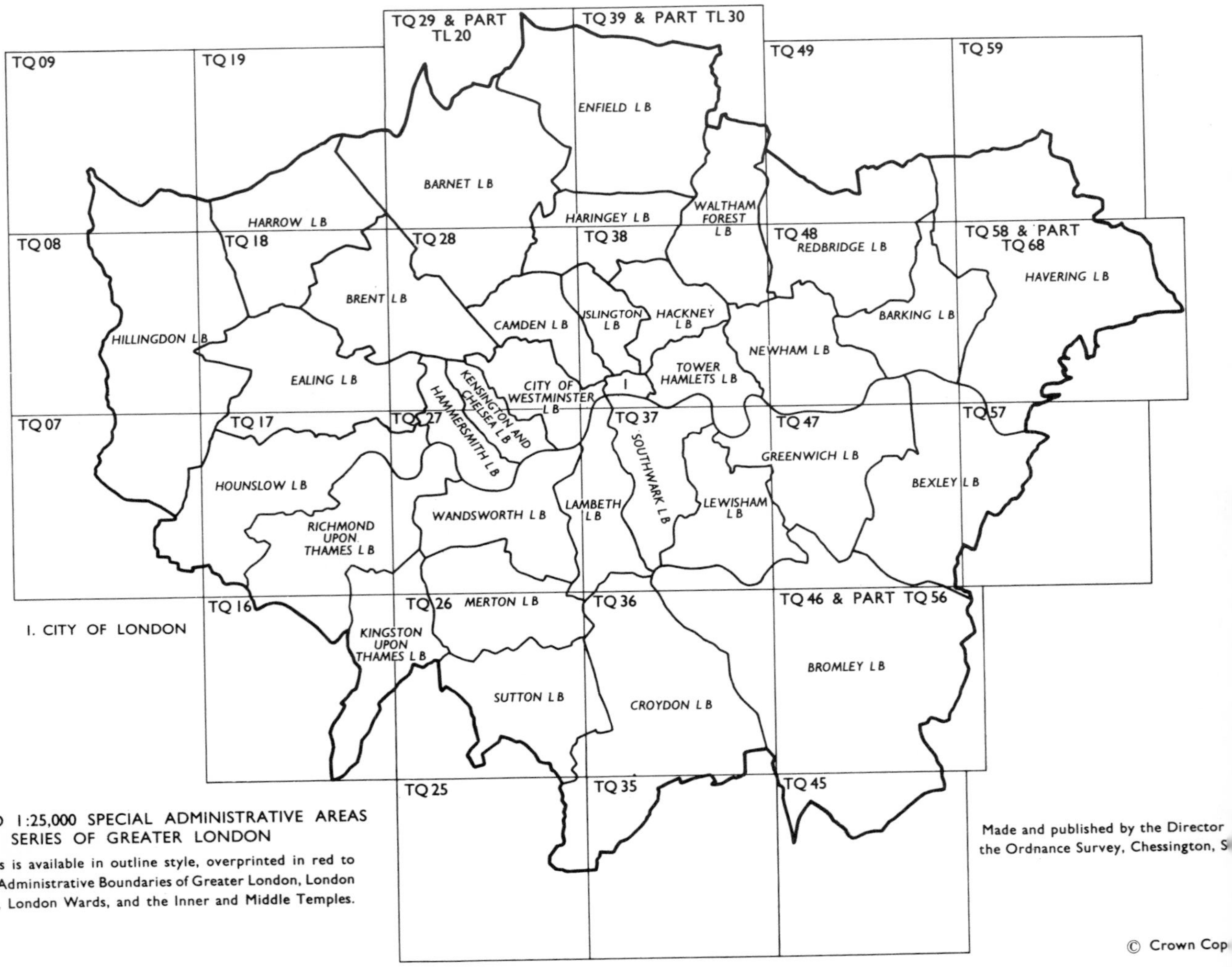

TQ 29 & PART TL 20
TQ 39 & PART TL 30
TQ 09
TQ 19
TQ 49
TQ 59
ENFIELD L B
BARNET L B
HARROW L B
HARINGEY L B
WALTHAM FOREST L B
TQ 08
TQ 18
TQ 28
TQ 38
TQ 48
REDBRIDGE L B
TQ 58 & PART TQ 68
HAVERING L B
BRENT L B
CAMDEN L B
ISLINGTON L B
HACKNEY L B
BARKING L B
HILLINGDON L B
NEWHAM L B
EALING L B
KENSINGTON AND CHELSEA L B
CITY OF WESTMINSTER L B
1
TOWER HAMLETS L B
HAMMERSMITH L B
TQ 07
TQ 17
TQ 27
TQ 37
TQ 47
TQ 57
SOUTHWARK L B
GREENWICH L B
HOUNSLOW L B
BEXLEY L B
LAMBETH L B
LEWISHAM L B
WANDSWORTH L B
RICHMOND UPON THAMES L B
TQ 16
TQ 26
MERTON L B
TQ 36
TQ 46 & PART TQ 56
1. CITY OF LONDON
KINGSTON UPON THAMES L B
BROMLEY L B
SUTTON L B
CROYDON L B
TQ 25
TQ 35
TQ 45

INDEX TO 1:25,000 SPECIAL ADMINISTRATIVE AREAS SERIES OF GREATER LONDON

This series is available in outline style, overprinted in red to show the Administrative Boundaries of Greater London, London Boroughs, London Wards, and the Inner and Middle Temples.

Made and published by the Director the Ordnance Survey, Chessington, S

420/2 *ADMINISTRATIVE AREAS SERIES OF GREATER LONDON*
1:25,000 O.S.

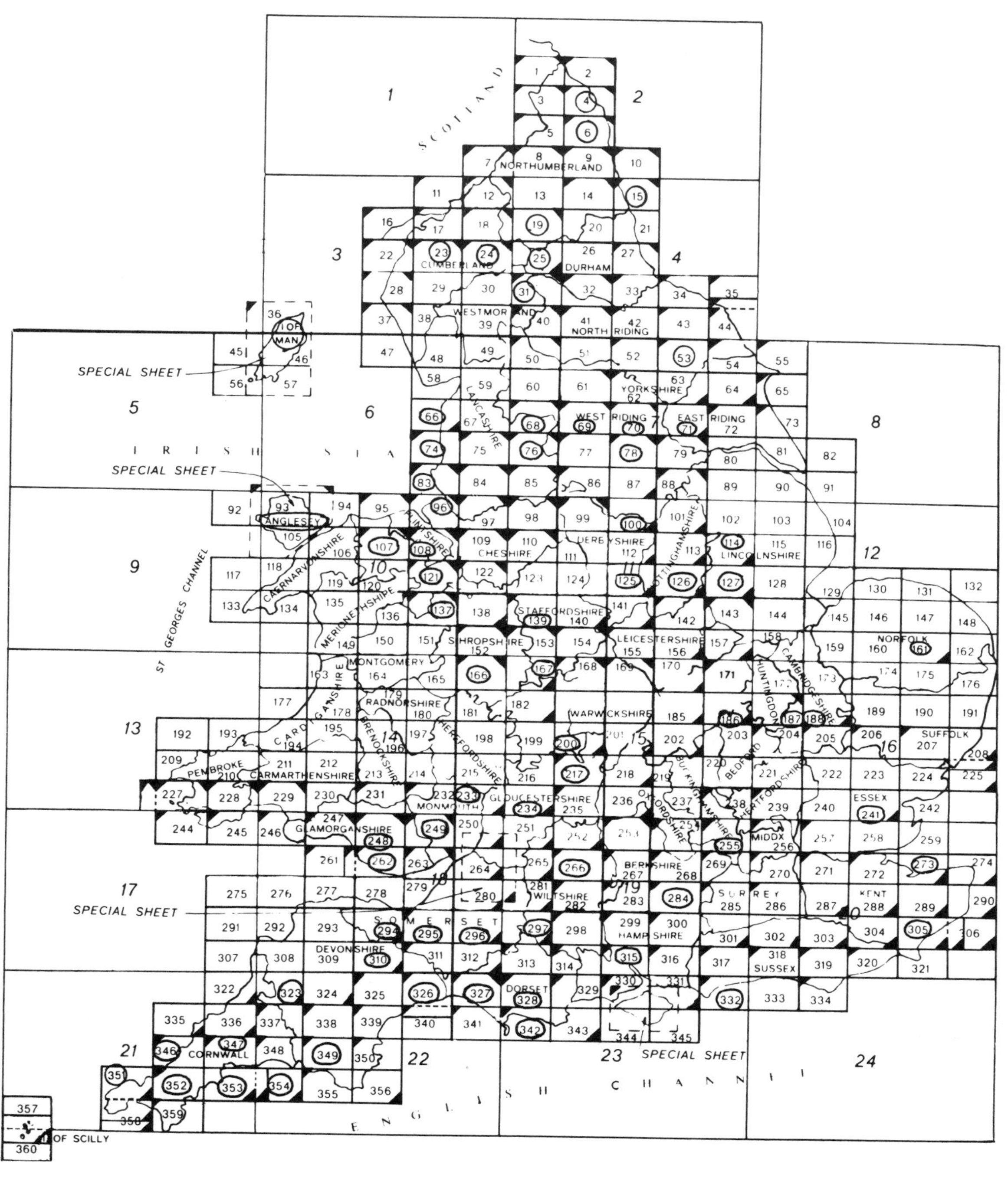

420/3 *GEOLOGICAL MAPS OF ENGLAND AND WALES*
1:63,360 and 1:50,000

Solid edition

Drift edition

Solid and Drift edition combined

(340) Sheets published at 1:50,000 with National Grid

SPECIAL SHEETS OF ENGLAND AND WALES
1:63,360

Anglesey (D) and (S) 1:50,000
Bristol District (S & D)
Isle of Man (D)
Isle of Wight (D)

GEOLOGICAL MAPS OF ENGLAND AND WALES
1:253,440 Geological Survey
Coloured series in 24 sheets (large rectangles)
Sheets published: 1 and 2 combined, 3, 4, 9, and 10 combined, 12, 21 and 25 combined, 22.

SOIL SURVEY OF ENGLAND AND WALES

1/63,360 series

265 *Published*

1/63,360 reconnaissance surveys

Published

Field work completed

Other reconnaissance surveys

Published

Field work completed

Soil Survey regional boundar

0 50 100 150 Kilometres

0 50 100 Miles

12/1975

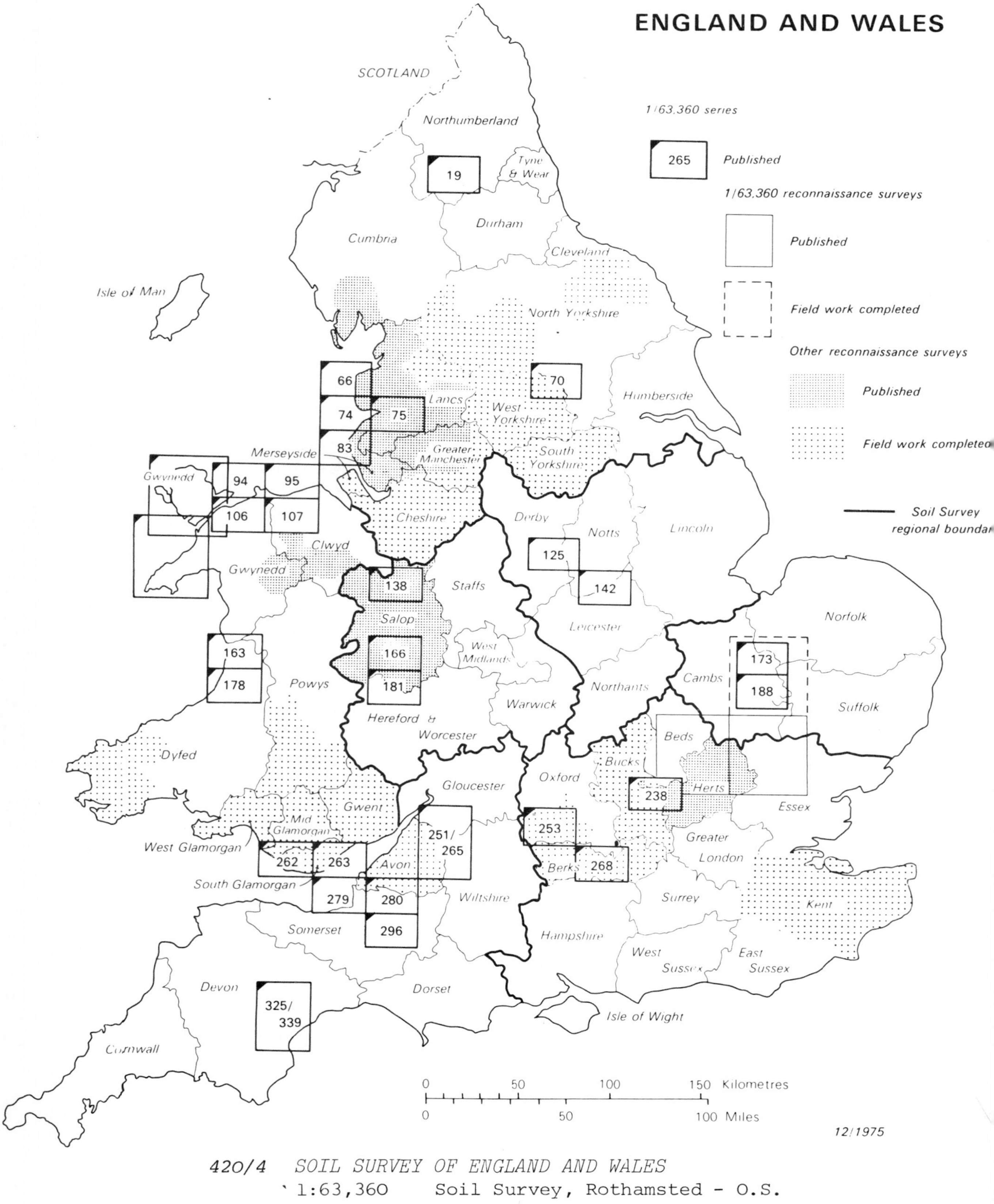

420/4 SOIL SURVEY OF ENGLAND AND WALES

1:63,360 Soil Survey, Rothamsted - O.S.

420/7 *AGRICULTURAL LAND CLASSIFICATION MAPS OF ENGLAND AND WALES*

1:63,360 Ministry of Agriculture, Fisheries and Food

420/8

AGRICULTURAL LAND CLASSIFICATION MAPS

1:250,000 Ministry of Agriculture Fisheries and Food

420/6 *TYPES OF FARM MAPS*

1:250,000 Ministry of Agriculture Fisheries and Food

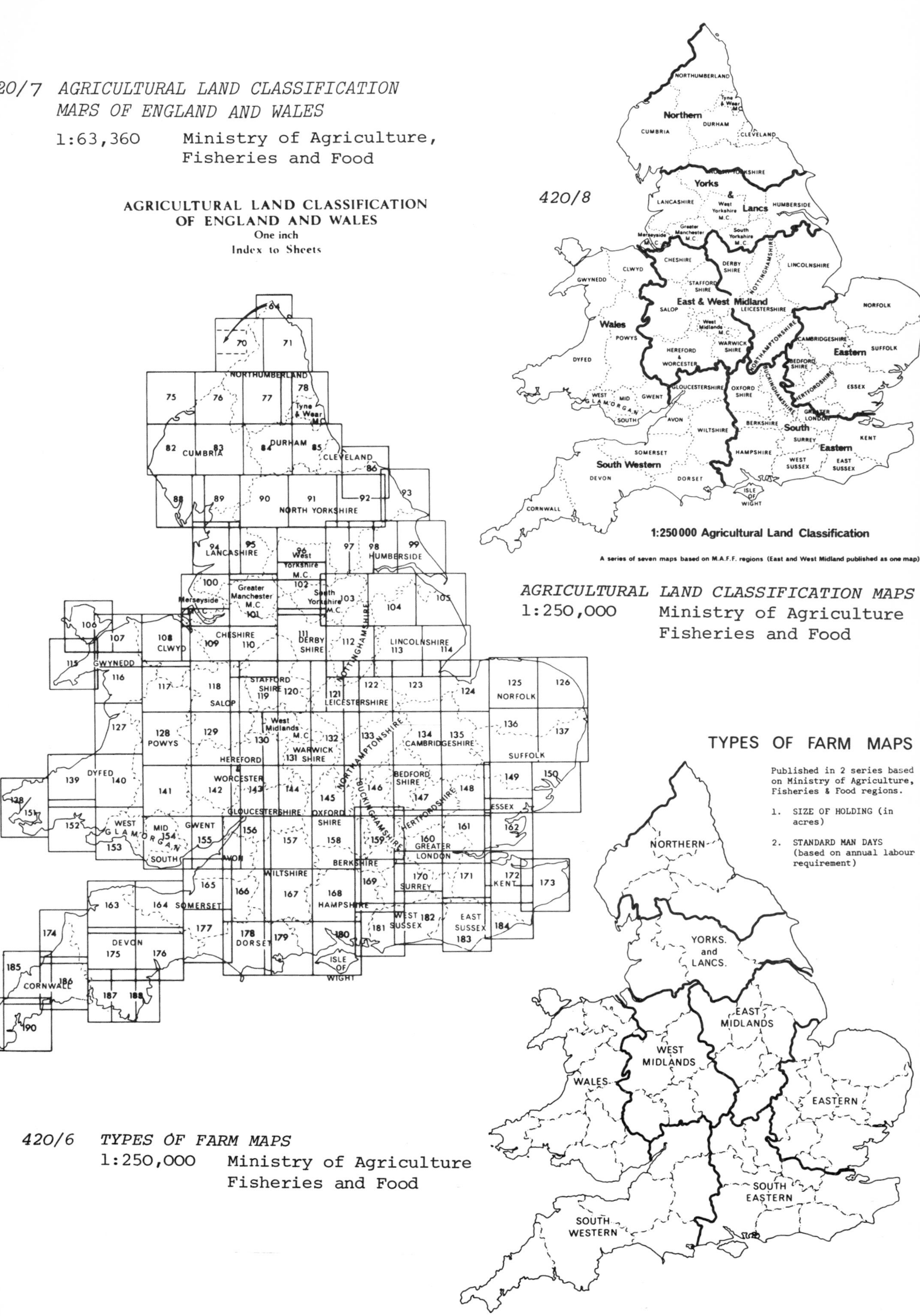

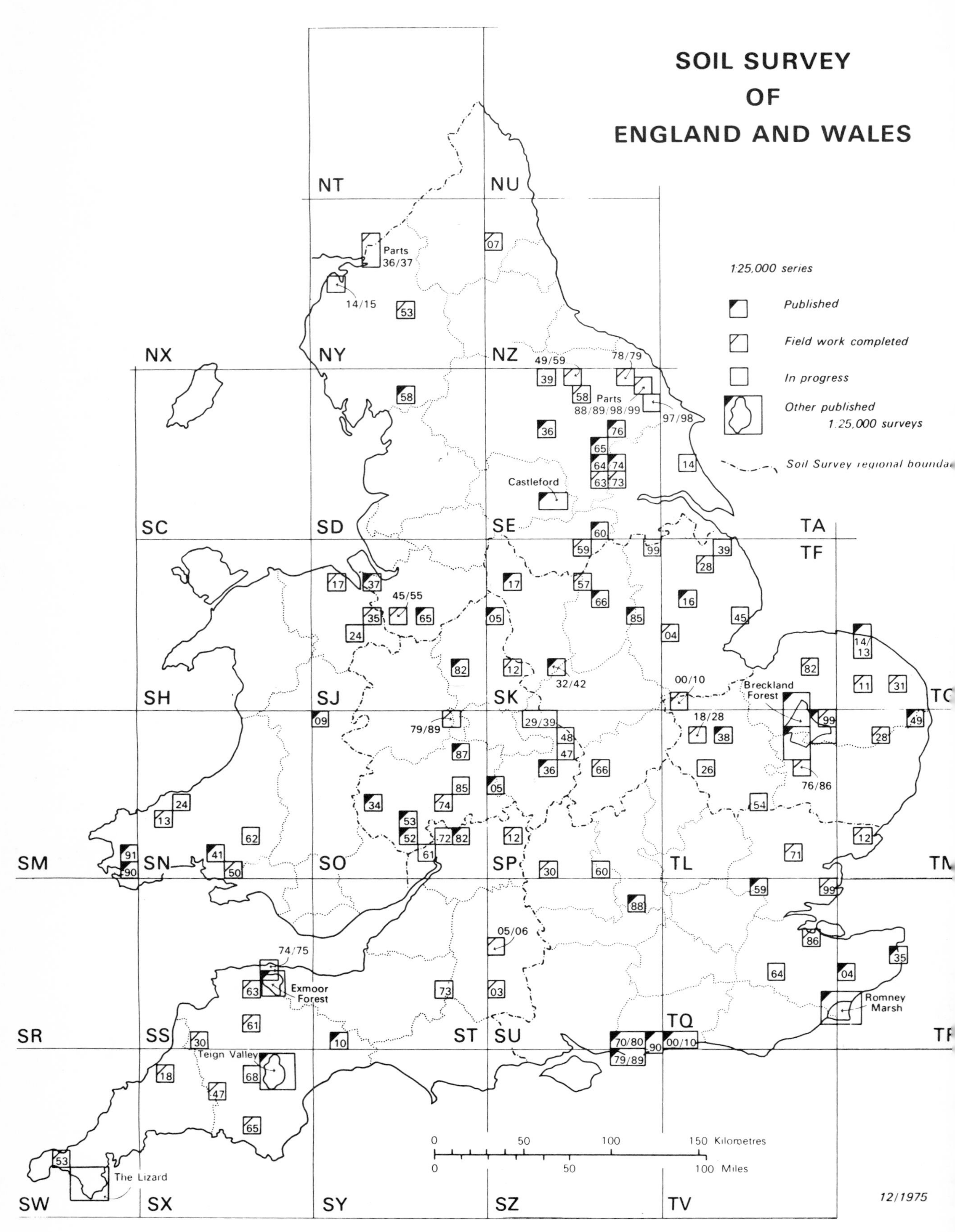

SOIL SURVEY OF ENGLAND AND WALES

420/5 1:25,000 Soil Survey, Rothamsted - O.S.
Soil map series on O.S. National grid sheet lines

0/9

E FIRST EDITION OF THE ONE-INCH ORDNANCE SURVEY

63,360 David and Charles

csimile reproduction on new sheet lines

lack and white)

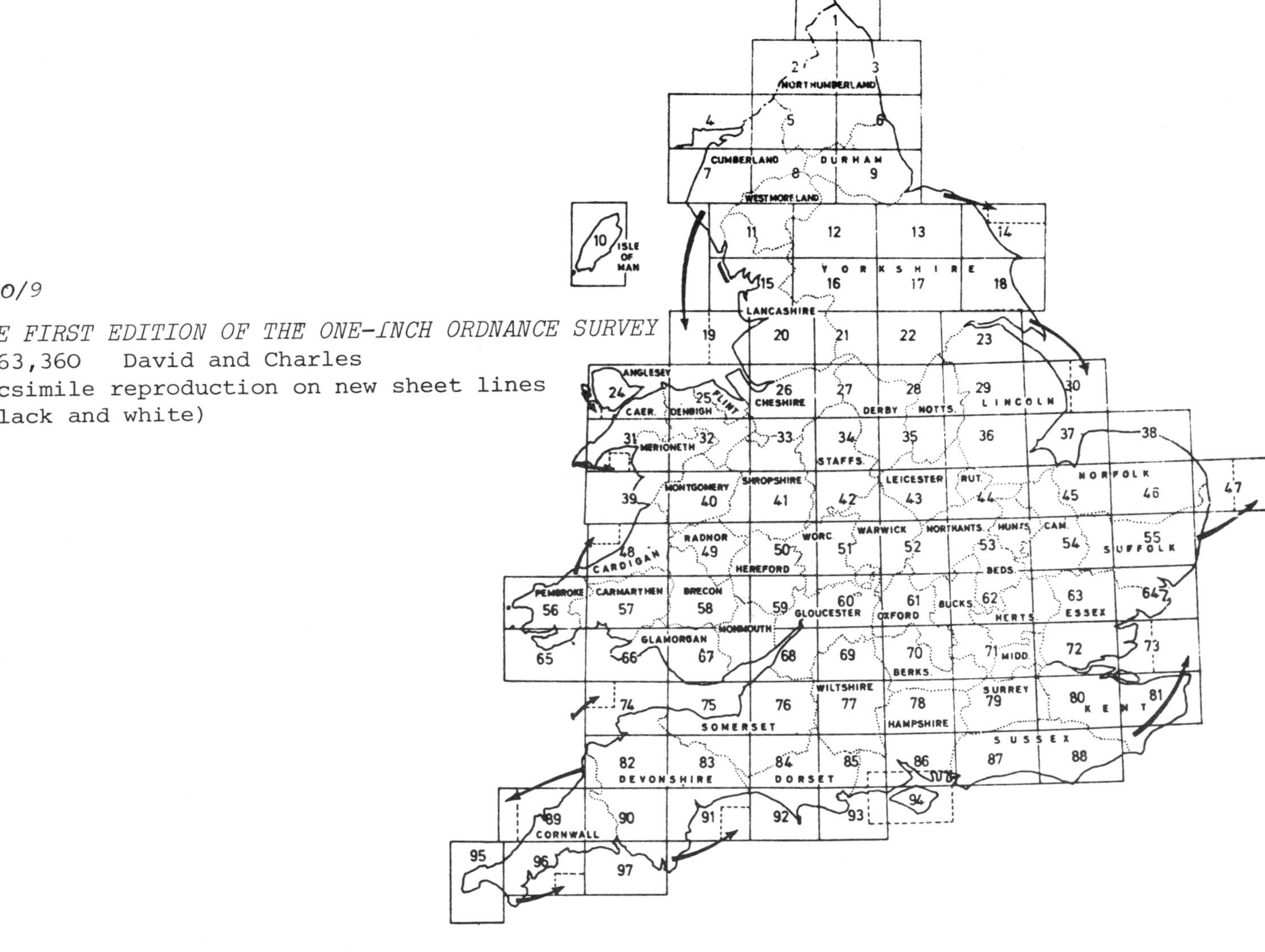

430/1 *ÜBERSICHTSKARTE VON MITTELEUROPA*
1:300,000 Inst. Angewandte Geodäsie
Topographical series, stocks limited

Edition A Black and White

Edition B Coloured

→ Fringe areas included in adjacent sheet
Numbering example: N53 BERLIN

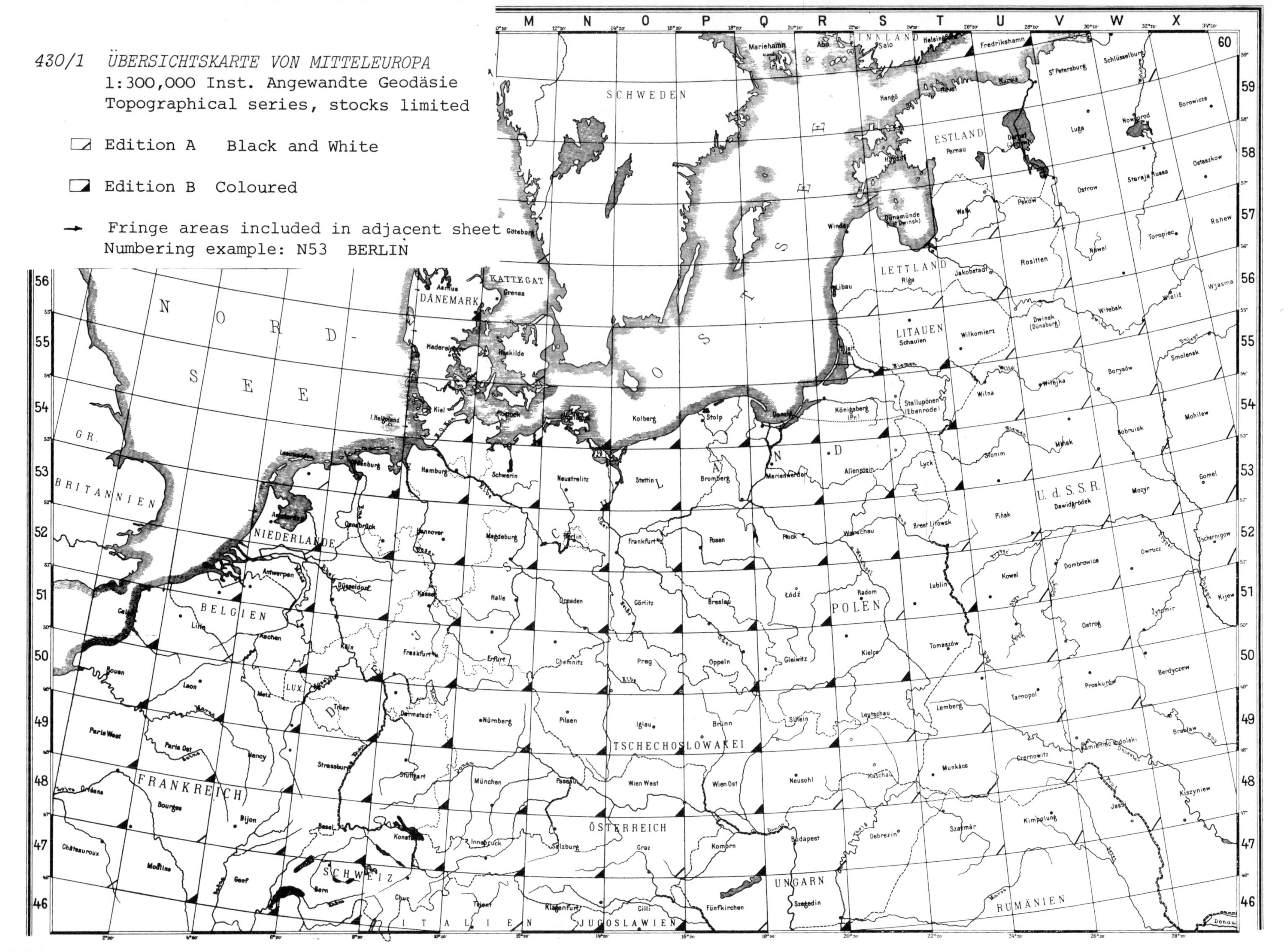

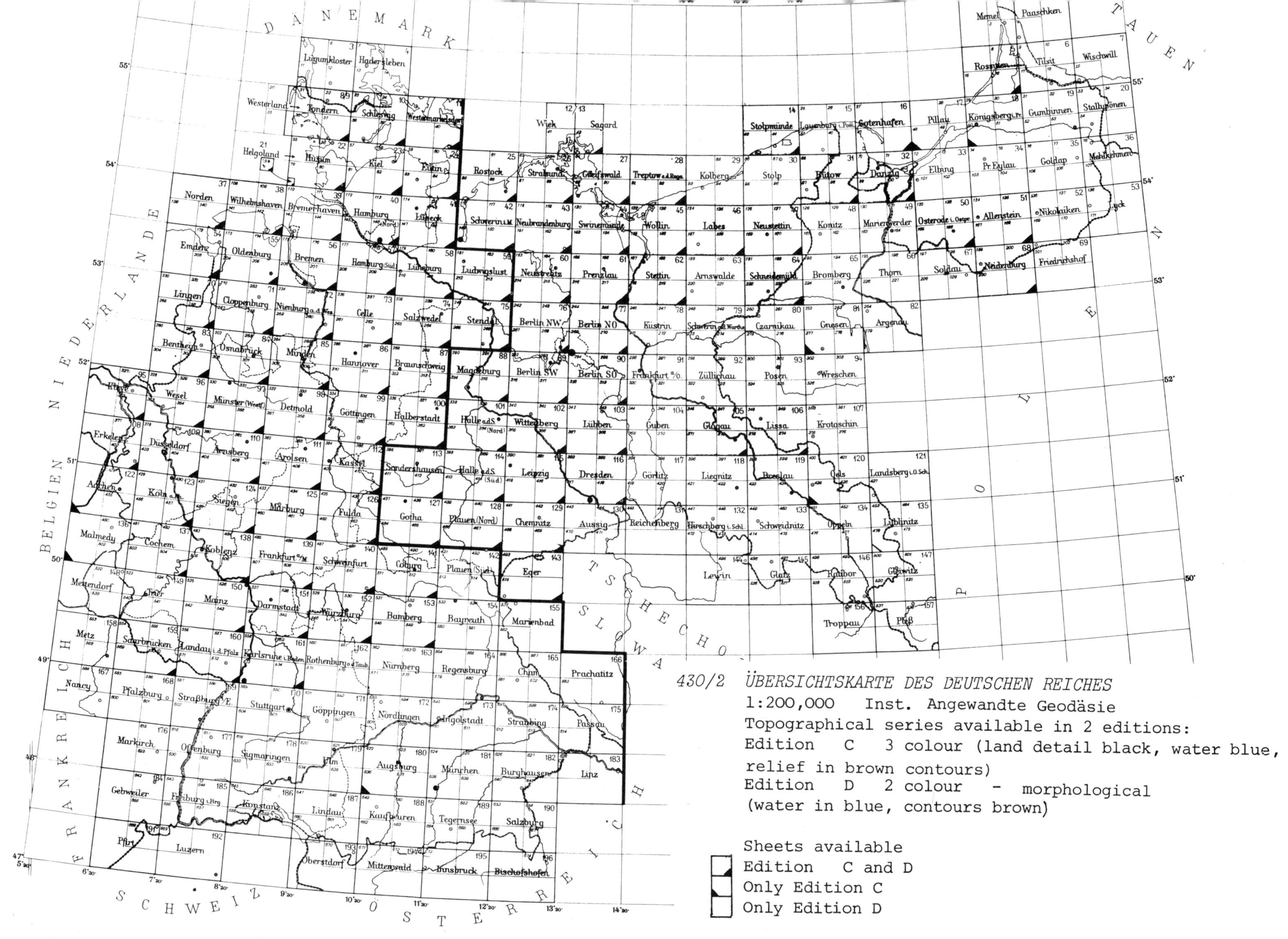

430/2 *ÜBERSICHTSKARTE DES DEUTSCHEN REICHES*

1:200,000 Inst. Angewandte Geodäsie

Topographical series available in 2 editions:

Edition C 3 colour (land detail black, water blue, relief in brown contours)

Edition D 2 colour - morphological (water in blue, contours brown)

Sheets available

- Edition C and D
- Only Edition C
- Only Edition D

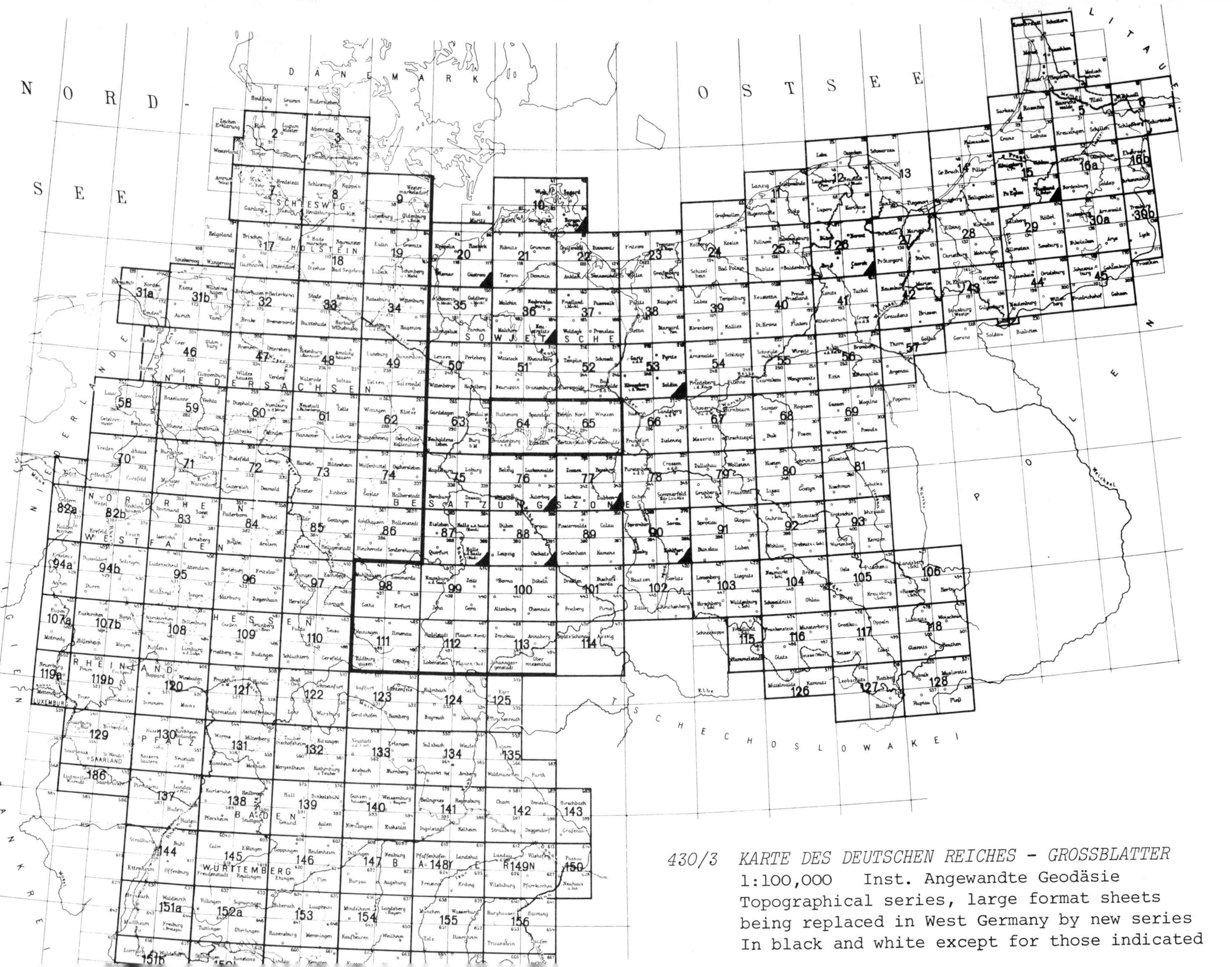

430/3 *KARTE DES DEUTSCHEN REICHES - GROSSBLATTER*

1:100,000 Inst. Angewandte Geodäsie

Topographical series, large format sheets being replaced in West Germany by new series

In black and white except for those indicated

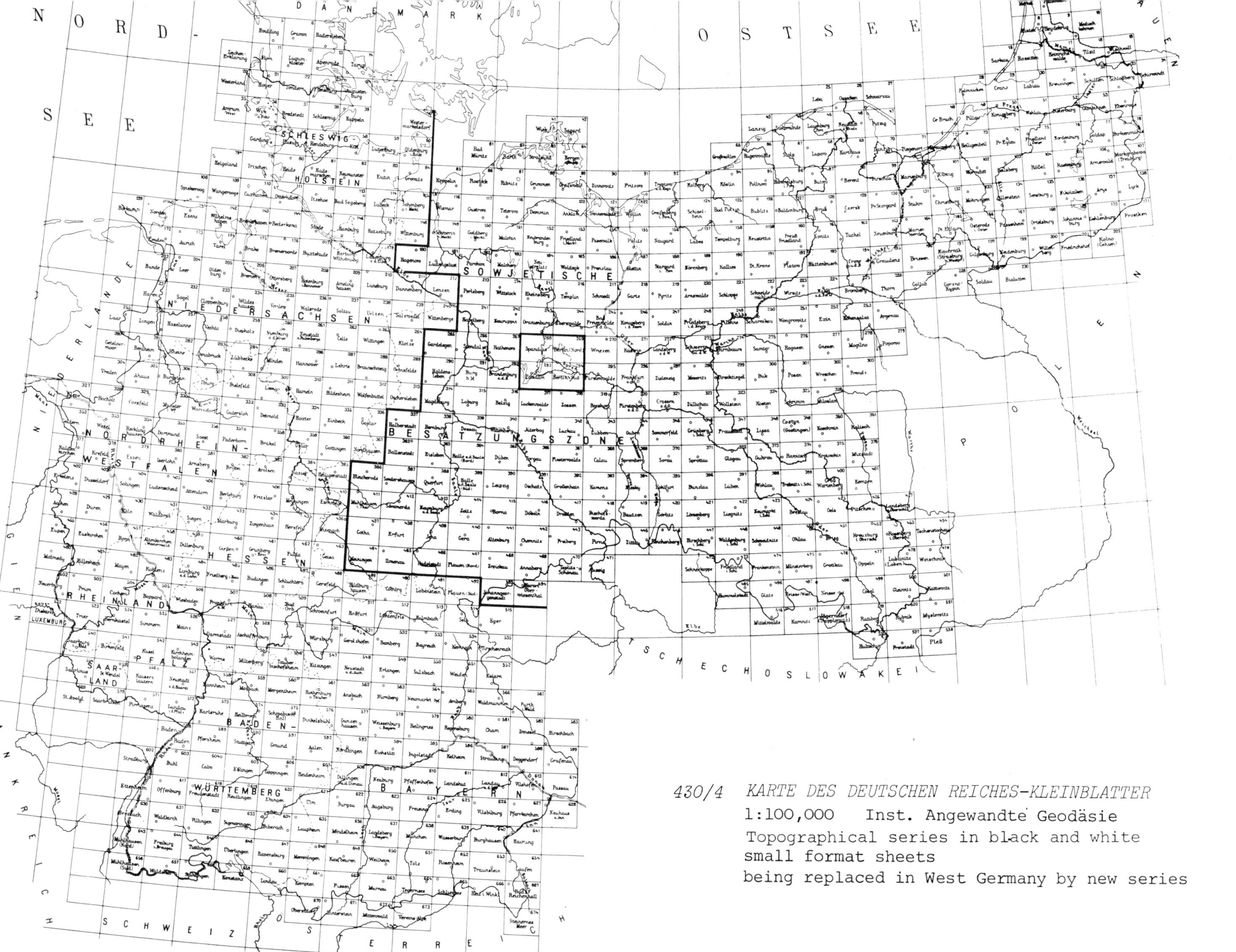

430/4 *KARTE DES DEUTSCHEN REICHES-KLEINBLATTER*

1:100,000 Inst. Angewandte Geodäsie

Topographical series in black and white small format sheets being replaced in West Germany by new series

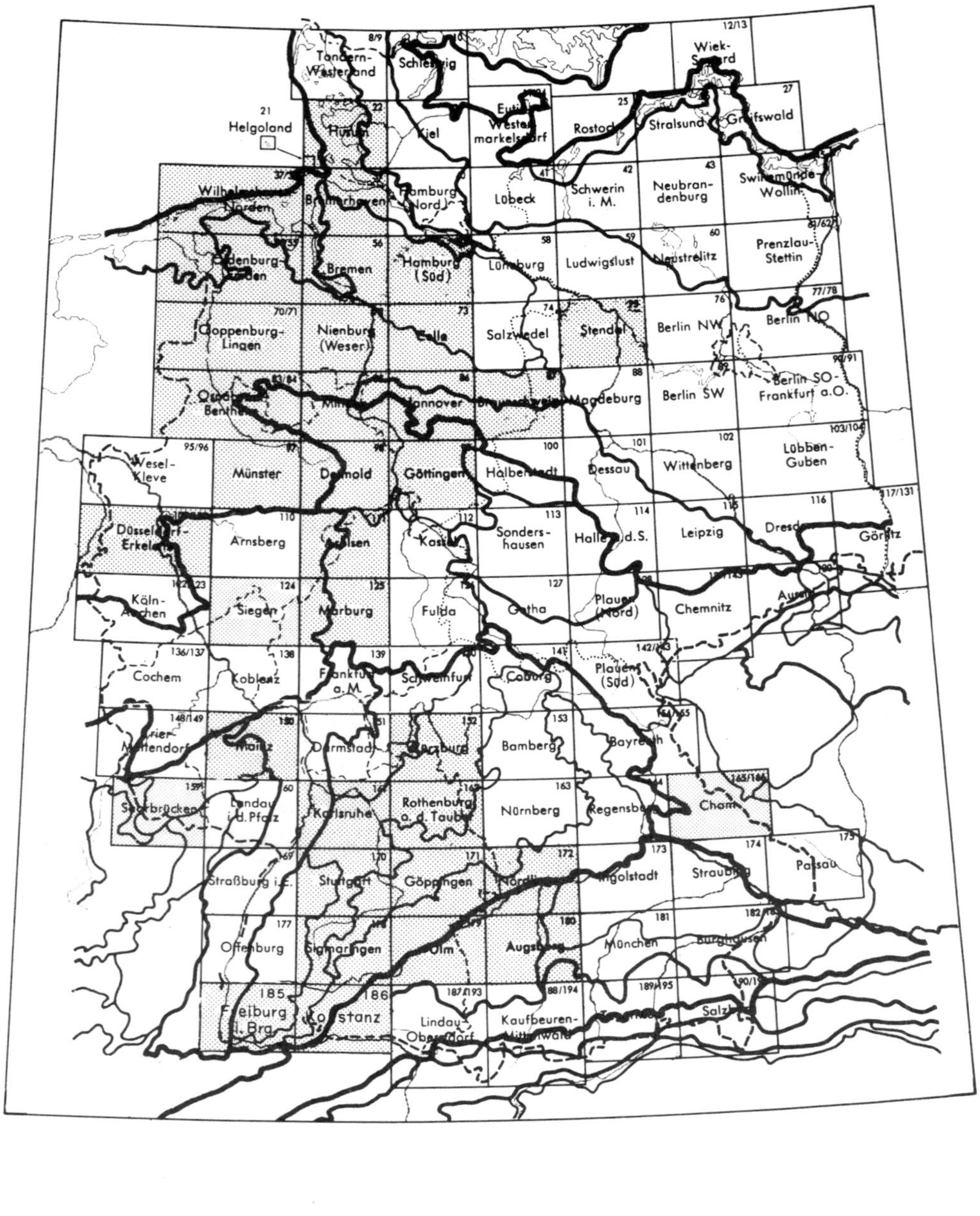

430/5 NATURRÄUMLICHE GLIEDERUNG DEUTSCHLAND

1:200,000 Inst. für Landeskunde

Land type series in progress

▨ Sheets published

430.1/1 JRO STRASSENKARTEN

1:300,000 JRO

Road map series in 7 sheets

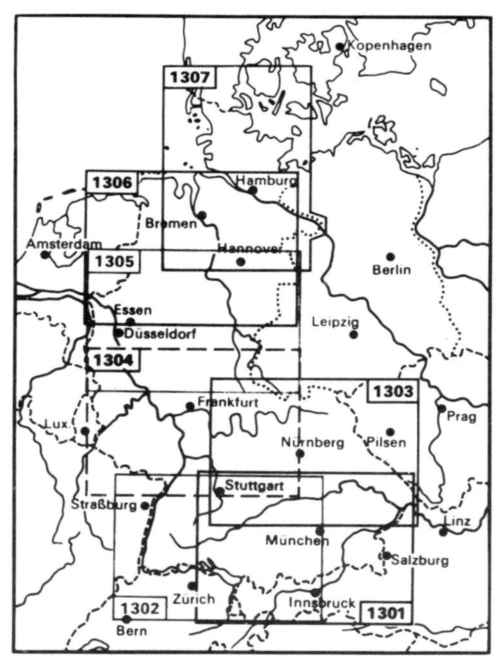

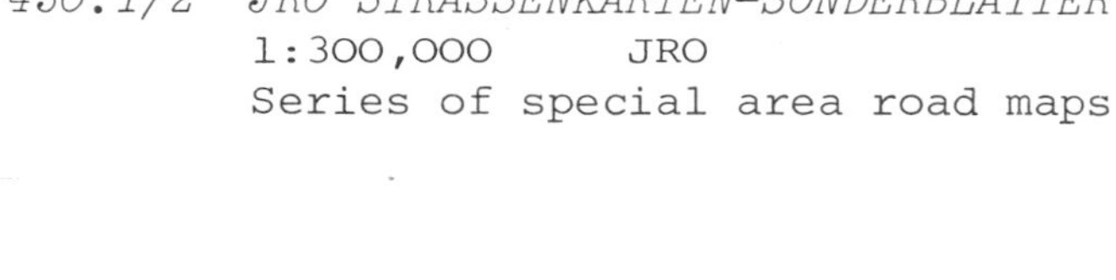

430.1/2 JRO STRASSENKARTEN-SONDERBLÄTTER

1:300,000 JRO

Series of special area road maps

430.1/3 DEUTSCHE STRASSENKARTE

1:250,000 Ravenstein

Road map series in 9 sheets

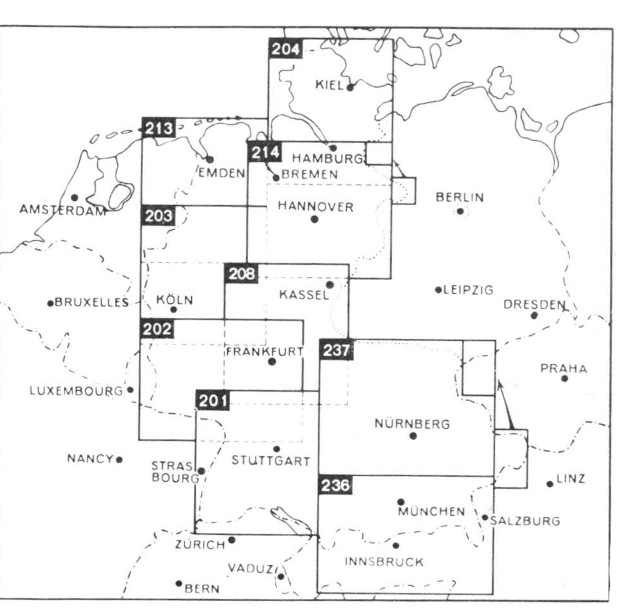

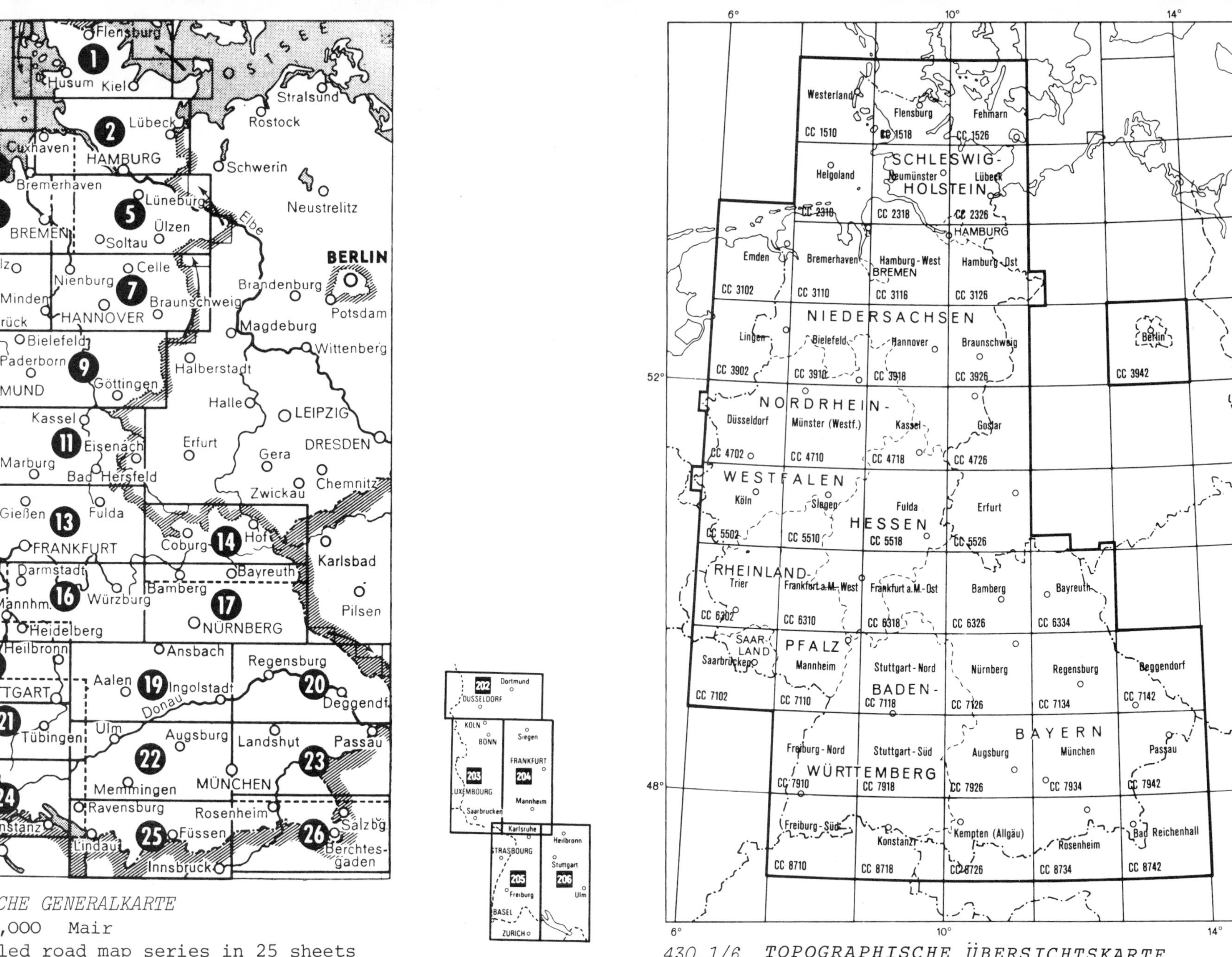

430.1/4 *DEUTSCHE GENERALKARTE*
1:200,000 Mair
Detailed road map series in 25 sheets

430.1/5 *CARTE MICHELIN*
1:200,000
Road map series covering

430.1/6 *TOPOGRAPHISCHE ÜBERSICHTSKARTE*
1:200,000 Inst. Angewandte Geodäsie
Official topographical series

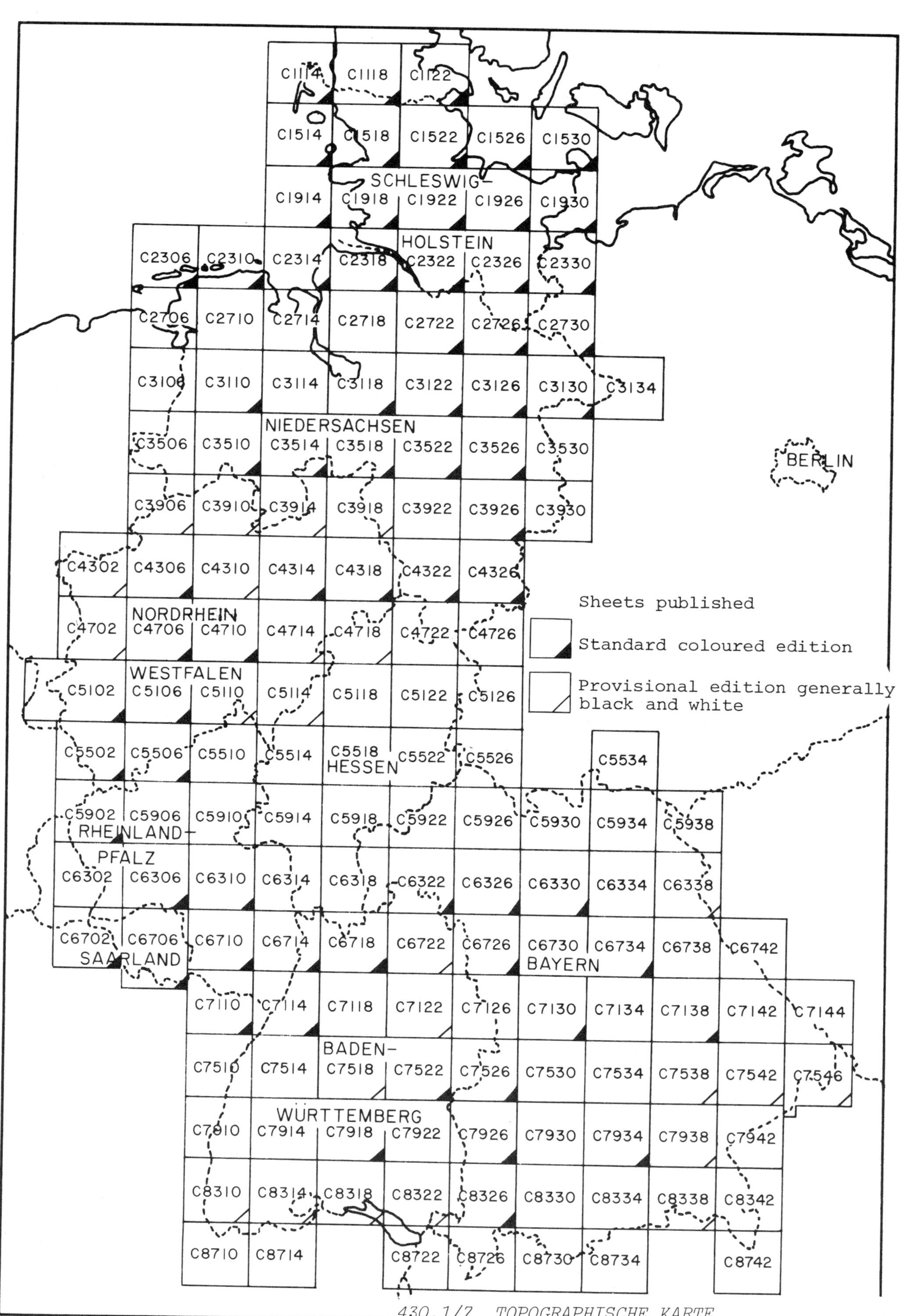

430.1/7 TOPOGRAPHISCHE KARTE

1:100,000 State Survey Offices (Lv)

Official topographical series

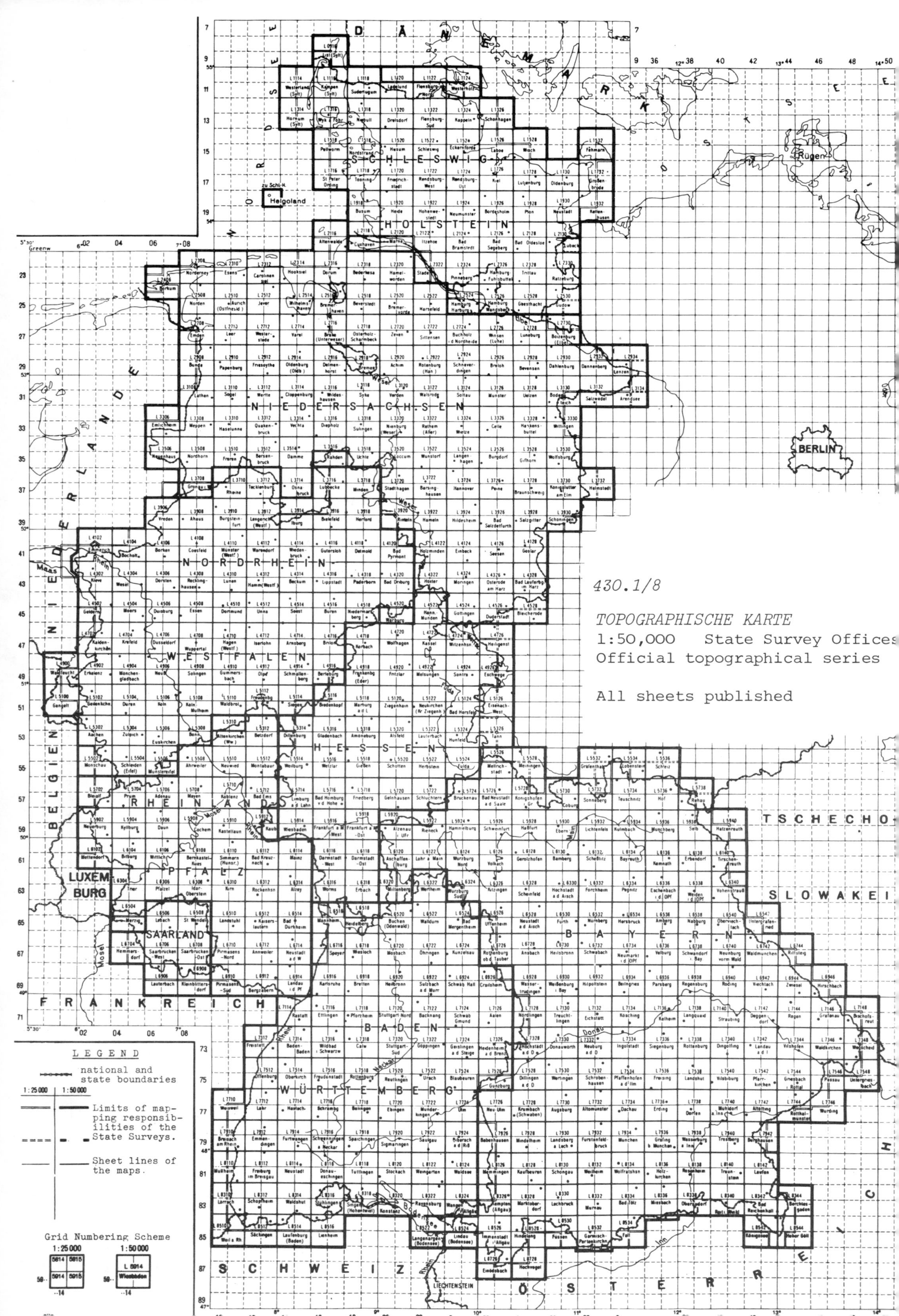

430.1/8
TOPOGRAPHISCHE KARTE
1:50,000 State Survey Offices
Official topographical series
All sheets published
D Ä N E M A R K
NORDSEE
SCHLESWIG
HOLSTEIN
NIEDERSACHSEN
NORDRHEIN
WESTFALEN
HESSEN
RHEINLAND
PFALZ
SAARLAND
LUXEMBURG
BADEN
WÜRTTEMBERG
BAYERN
NIEDERLANDE
BELGIEN
FRANKREICH
SCHWEIZ
ÖSTERREICH
TSCHECHO
SLOWAKEI
BERLIN
Rügen
Helgoland
zu Schl.-H.
LIECHTENSTEIN
Greenw
LEGEND
national and state boundaries
1:25000
1:50000
Limits of mapping responsibilities of the State Surveys.
Sheet lines of the maps.
Grid Numbering Scheme
1:25000
1:50000
5814
5815
5914
5915
L 5914
Wiesbaden

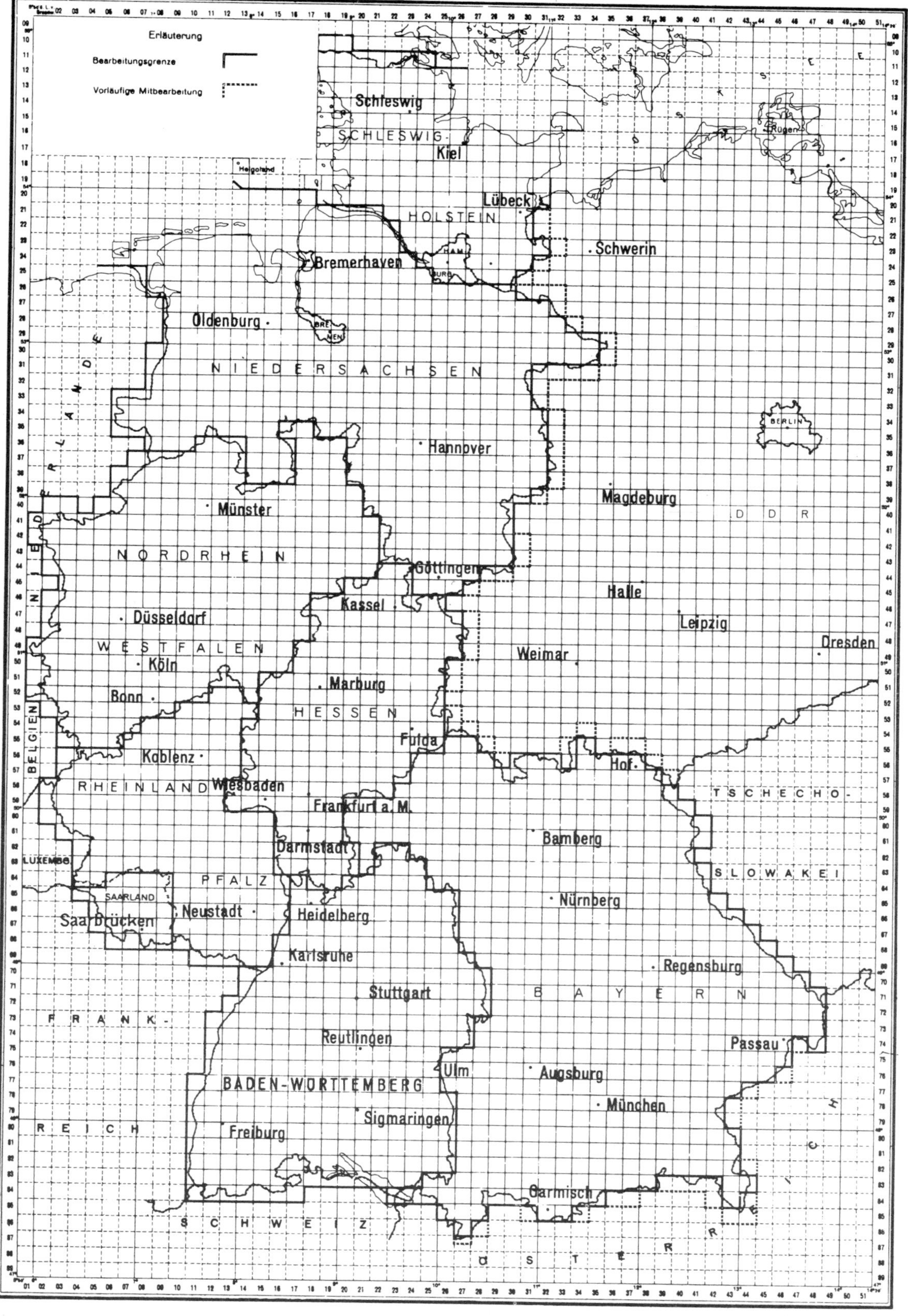

430.1/9 TOPOGRAPHISCHE KARTE
1:25,000 State Survey Offices (Lv)

Official topographical series.
All sheets published, majority in colour.
To obtain sheet number read off number in either side margin, level with the square required followed by the correct number in either the top or bottom margin e.g. BONN 5208

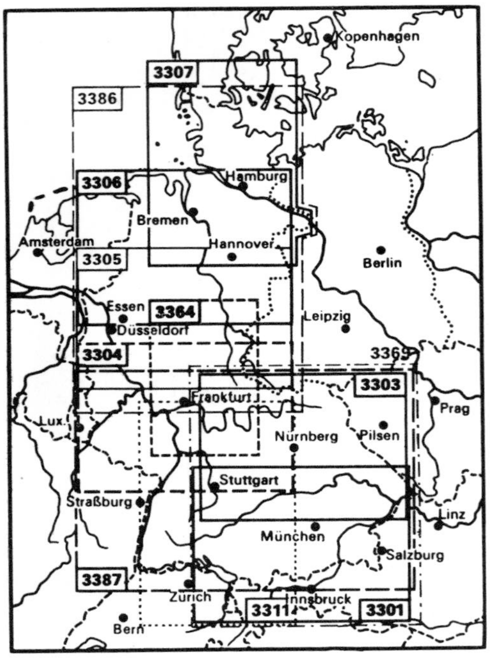

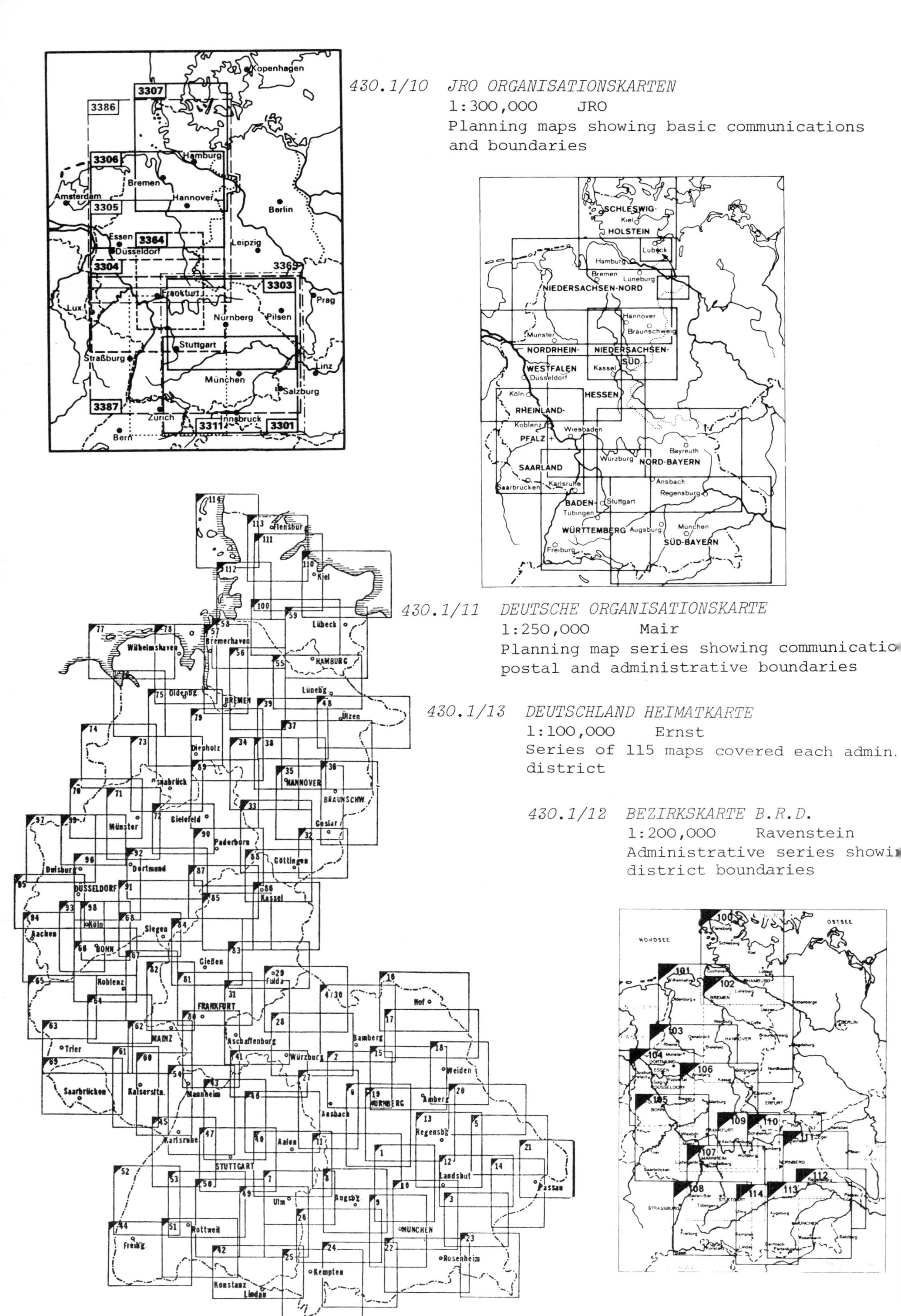

430.1/10 *JRO ORGANISATIONSKARTEN*
1:300,000 JRO
Planning maps showing basic communications and boundaries

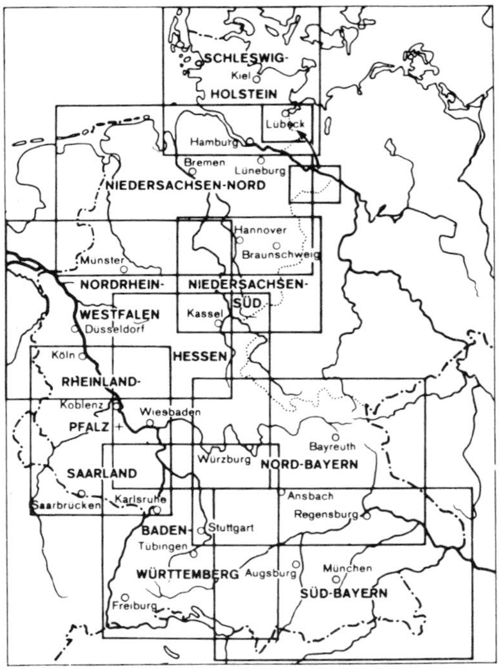

430.1/11 *DEUTSCHE ORGANISATIONSKARTE*
1:250,000 Mair
Planning map series showing communicatio
postal and administrative boundaries

430.1/13 *DEUTSCHLAND HEIMATKARTE*
1:100,000 Ernst
Series of 115 maps covered each admin. district

430.1/12 *BEZIRKSKARTE B.R.D.*
1:200,000 Ravenstein
Administrative series showi
district boundaries

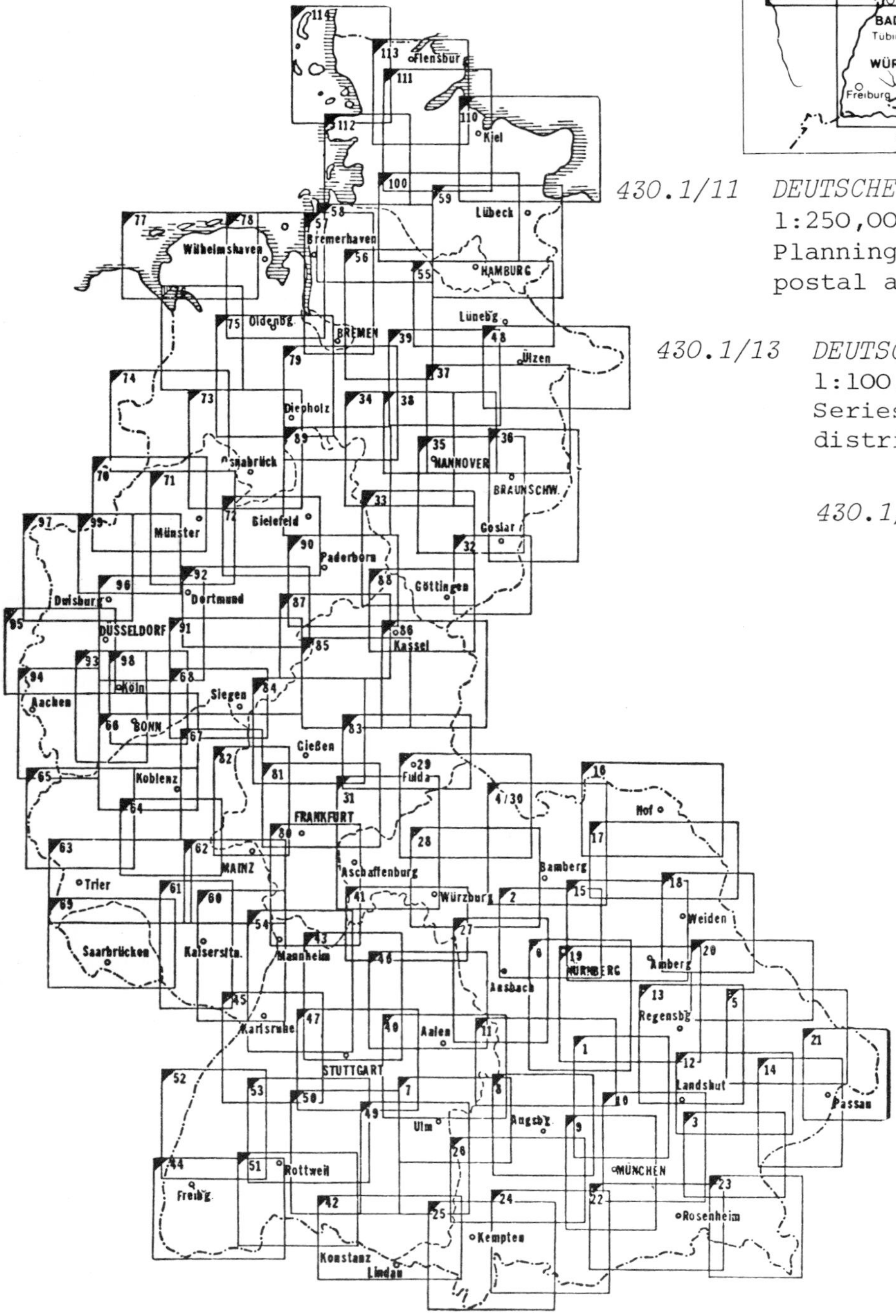

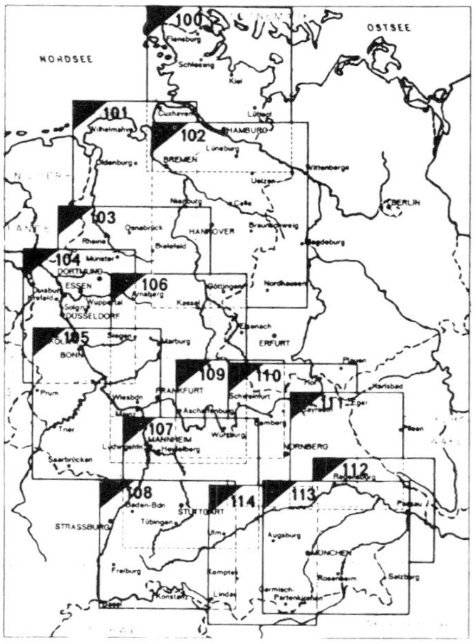

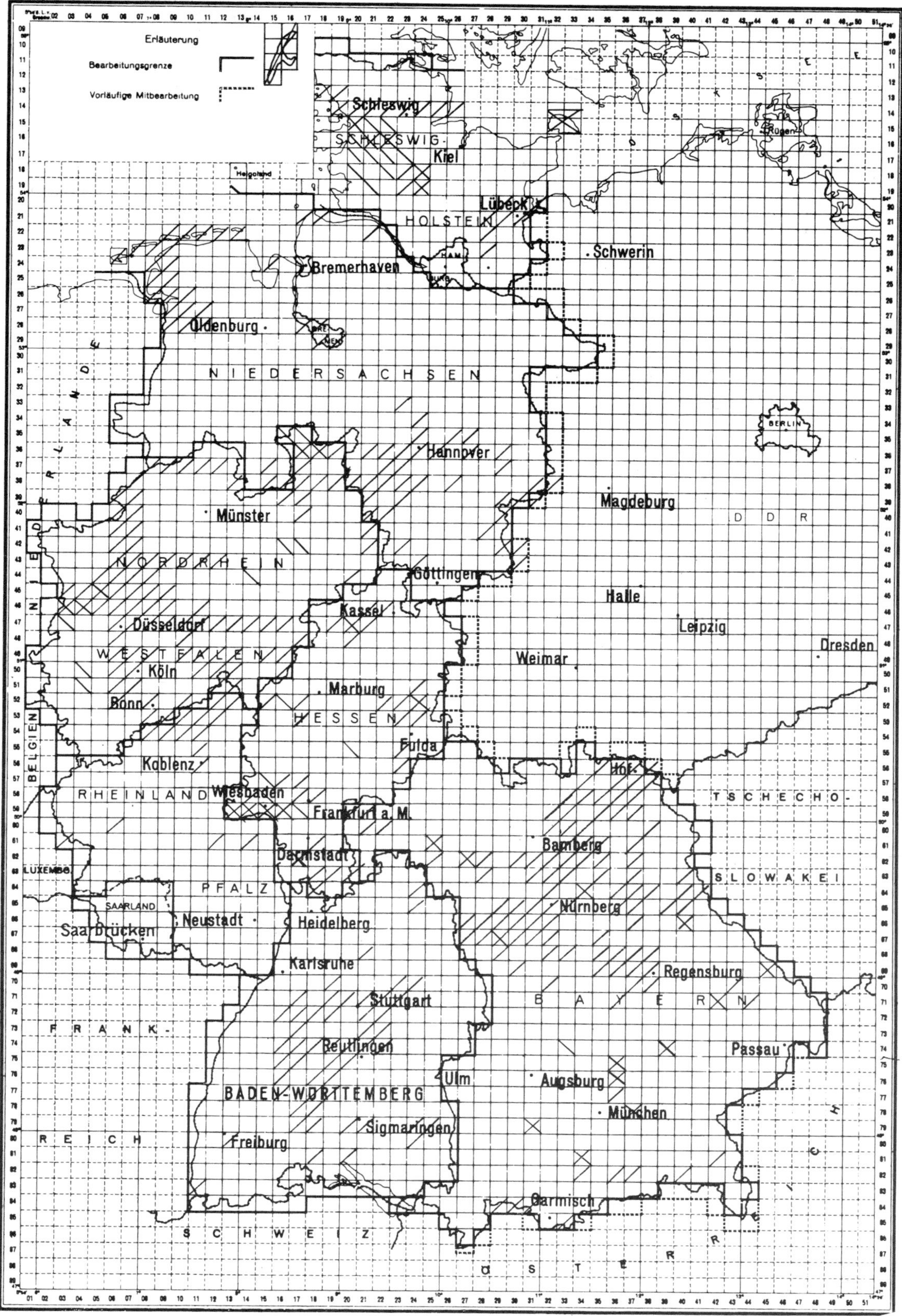

430.1/14 GEOLOGISCHE KARTE VON DEUTSCHLAND
BODENKARTE VON DEUTSCHLAND

1:25,000 State Geol. Surveys
Geological and Soil map series

Sheets published

Geological

Soil

430.2/1 VERKEHRSKARTE DER DDR

1:200,000 LV

Road map series of Germ.Democratic Republic

1 ROSTOCK
2 STRALSUND
3 STENDAL
4 BERLIN Hauptst. d. DDR
WB
5 HALBERSTADT
6 LEIPZIG
7 COTTBUS-DRESDEN
8 ERFURT
9 KARL-MARX-STADT

430.2/2

DDR - TOURING AND WALKING MAPS

1:5,000 - 1:120,000 LV

Series of local area road and footpath maps

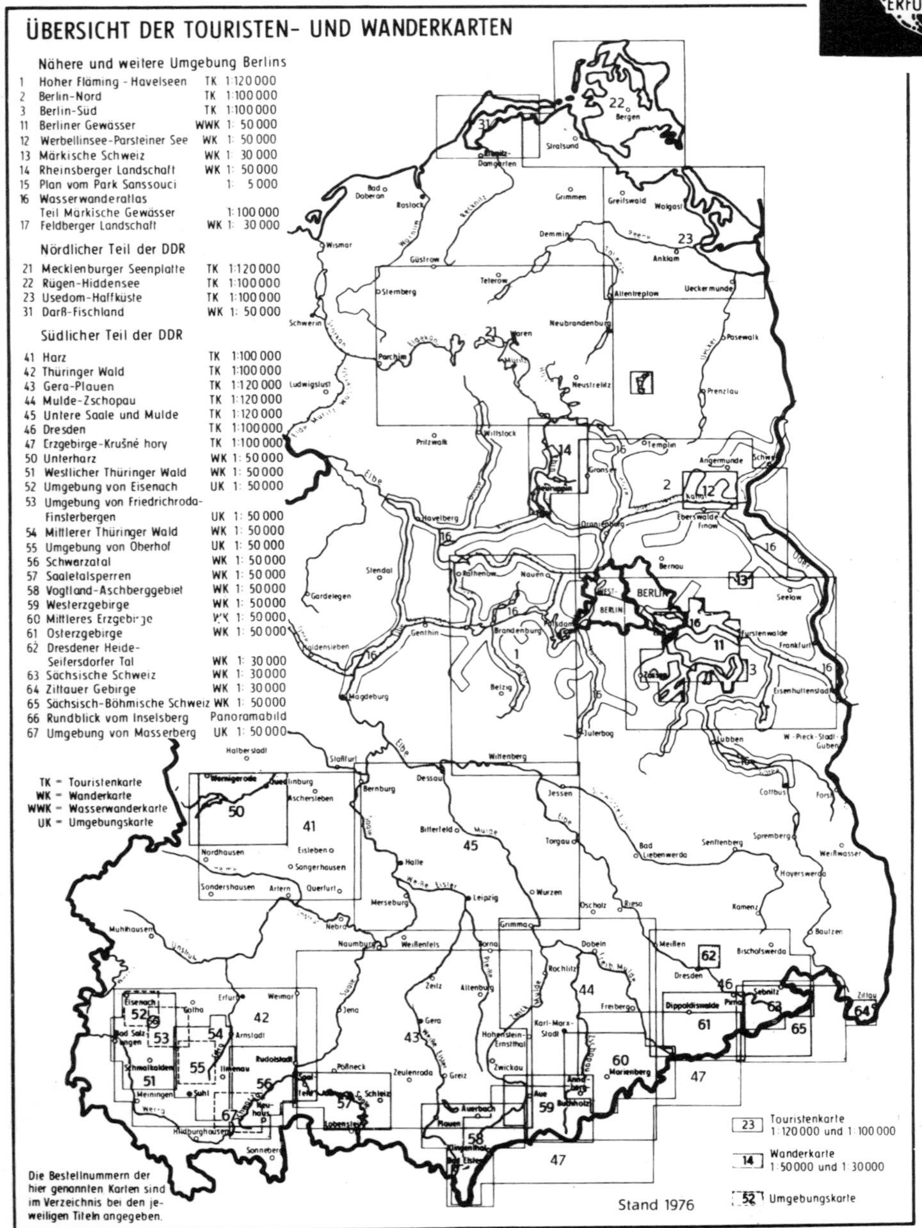

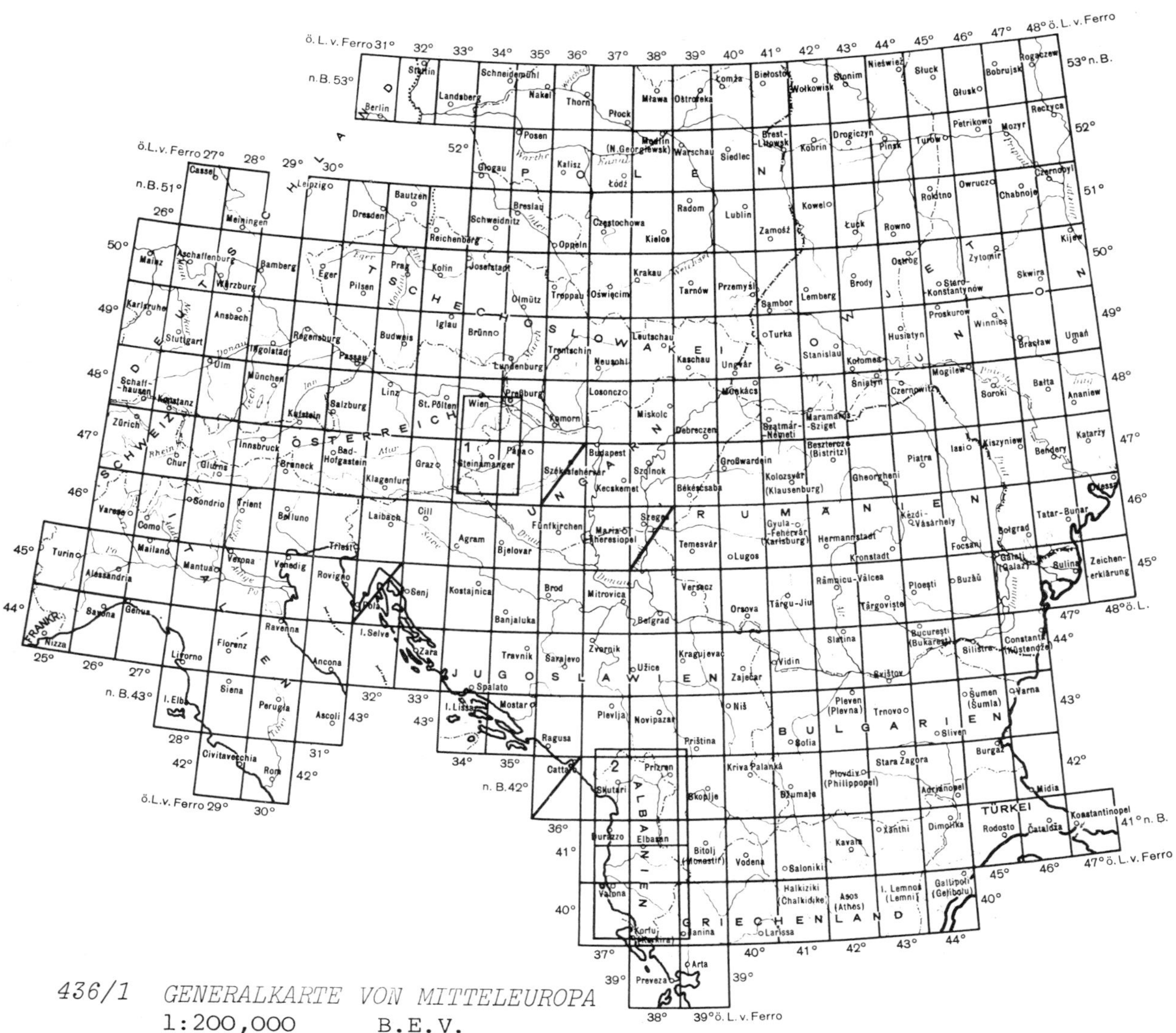

436/1 *GENERALKARTE VON MITTELEUROPA*

1:200,000 B.E.V.

Official Austrian topographical series covering Austria and central Europe. Relief by hachures

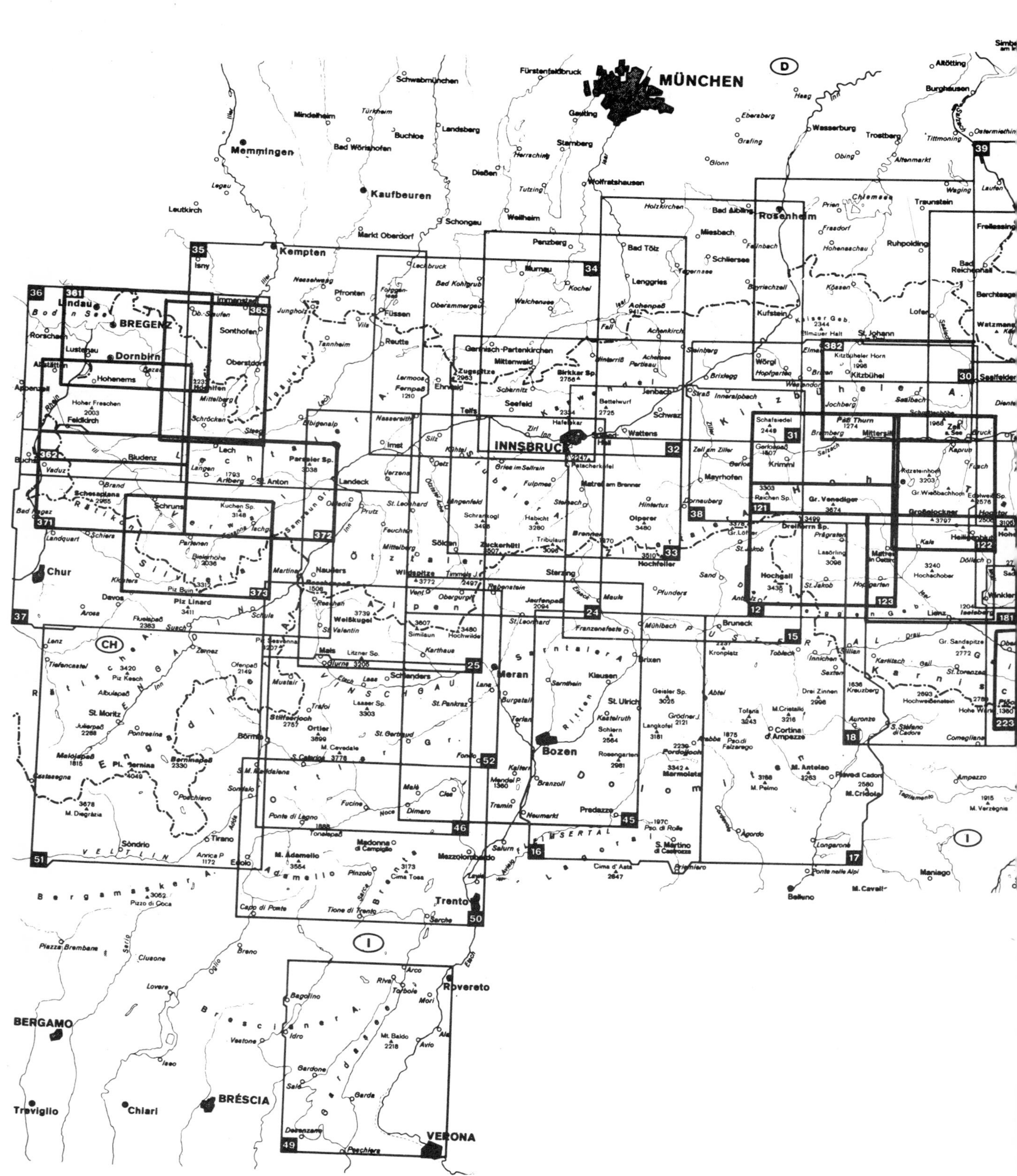

MÜNCHEN
D
Fürstenfeldbruck
Schwabmünchen
Mindelheim
Türkheim
Buchloe
Landsberg
Bad Wörishofen
Memmingen
Kaufbeuren
Leutkirch
Schongau
Markt Oberdorf
Kempten
Isny
Gauting
Starnberg
Herrsching
Dießen
Tutzing
Weilheim
Wolfratshausen
Ebersberg
Grafing
Glonn
Haag
Wasserburg
Trostberg
Obing
Altötting
Burghausen
Tittmoning
Altenmarkt
Waging
Laufen
Holzkirchen
Bad Aibling
Rosenheim
Miesbach
Schliersee
Tegernsee
Bad Tölz
Lenggries
Penzberg
Murnau
Kochel
Walchensee
Chiemsee
Prien
Traunstein
Frasdorf
Hohenaschau
Ruhpolding
Freilassing
Bad Reichenhall
Berchtesgaden
Watzmann
Kössen
Lofer
Kufstein
St. Johann
Kitzbühel
Kitzbüheler Horn
Wörgl
Hopfgarten
Pfronten
Füssen
Reutte
Tannheim
Vils
Jungholz
Nesselwang
Lechbruck
Bad Kohlgrub
Oberammergau
Garmisch-Partenkirchen
Mittenwald
Zugspitze 2963
Ehrwald
Lermoos
Fernpaß 1210
Scharnitz
Seefeld
Telfs
Achenpaß
Achenkirch
Achensee
Pertisau
Hinterriß
Birkkar Sp. 2756
Jenbach
Schwaz
Wattens
Hall
INNSBRUCK
Zirl
Inn
Hafelekar
Bettelwurf 2725
Patscherkofel
Brixlegg
Inneralpbach
Kitzbühel
Zell am Ziller
Gerlos
Krimml
Mayrhofen
Dornauberg
Hintertux
Olperer 3480
Hochfeiler 3510
Matrei am Brenner
Steinach
Brenner
Fulpmes
Habicht 3280
Tribulaun 3096
Zuckerhütl 3507
Schrankogl 3496
Längenfeld
Sölden
Vent
Obergurgl
Wildspitze 3772
Timmels J.
Rabenstein
Jaufenpaß 2094
Sterzing
Franzensfeste
Mühlbach
Brixen
Klausen
Sarnthein
Meran
Lana
Burgstall
Terlan
Bozen
Kaltern
Branzoll
Neumarkt
Tramin
Mendel P. 1360
Predazzo
St. Ulrich
Kastelruth
Schlern 2564
Rosengarten 2981
Langkofel 3181
Geisler Sp. 3025
Grödner J. 2121
Sella
Marmolata
Pordoijoch
Bruneck
Toblach
Innichen
Sexten
Drei Zinnen 2998
Tofana 3243
Cortina d'Ampezzo
M. Cristallo 3216
Falzarego
M. Antelao 3263
M. Pelmo 3168
Pieve di Cadore
M. Cridola
Auronzo
Comelico
S. Stefano di Cadore
Agordo
Longarone
Belluno
Ponte nelle Alpi
Maniago
M. Cavallo
I
Lienz
Matrei in Osttirol
Großglockner 3797
Heiligenblut
Kals
Hochschober 3240
Dölsach
Großvenediger 3674
Dreiherrn Sp. 3499
Prägraten
St. Jakob
Hochgall 3436
Lasörling 3098
Gr. Wiesbachhorn 3564
Kitzsteinhorn 3203
Kaprun
Zell a. See
Mittersill
Paß Thurn 1274
Saalbach
Jochberg
Bramberg
Krimml
Gerlospaß 1507
Schafsiedel 2449
Reichen Sp. 3303
Gr. Löffler
Sand
Pfunders
Kronplatz
Abtei
Karnische Alpen
Kartitsch
Gail
Kreuzberg 1636
Gr. Sandspitze 2772
Hochweißstein
Tagliamento
Ampezzo
M. Verzegnis
Lindau
BREGENZ
Bodensee
Rorschach
Lustenau
Dornbirn
Hohenems
Altstätten
Appenzell
Feldkirch
Hoher Freschen 2003
Rhein
Buchs
Vaduz
Bludenz
Brand
Schesaplana 2965
Rätikon
Bad Ragaz
Landquart
Schiers
Chur
Klosters
Davos
Arosa
Schruns
Partenen
Bielerhöhe 2036
Silvretta
Piz Buin 3312
Piz Linard 3411
Lech
Lechtaler Alpen
Langen
Arlberg 1793
St. Anton
Kuchen Sp. 3148
Parseier Sp. 3036
Landeck
Imst
Nassereith
Elbigenalp
Immenstadt
Sonthofen
Oberstdorf
Oberstaufen
Mittelberg
Schröcken
Steeg
Allgäuer Alpen
Hochifen
Samnaun
Ischgl
Prutz
Pfunds
St. Leonhard
Ötztaler Alpen
Feuchten
Mittelberg
Nauders
Martina
Reschenpaß 1508
Reschen
Weißkugel 3739
St. Valentin
Similaun 3607
Hochwilde 3480
Mals
Glurns
Schlanders
Laas
Vinschgau
Karthaus
Lana
St. Pankraz
Trafoi
Stilfserjoch 2757
Ortler 3899
Laaser Sp. 3303
M. Cevedale 3778
St. Gertraud
S. Caterina
Bormio
Mustair
Ofenpaß 2149
Zernez
Schuls
Süsch
Flüelapaß 2383
CH
Lenz
Tiefencastel
Piz Kesch 3420
Albulapaß
St. Moritz
Julierpaß 2268
Pontresina
Engadin
Maloja 1815
Piz Bernina 4049
Berninapaß 2330
Castasegna
Poschiavo
M. Disgrazia 3678
Sondrio
Tirano
Veltlin
Aprica P. 1172
Edolo
S.M. Maddalena
Sondalo
Ponte di Legno
Tonalepaß 1883
Fucine
Noce
Malè
Dimaro
Cles
Fondo
Madonna di Campiglio
M. Adamello 3554
Adamello
Pinzolo
Brenta
Cima Tosa 3173
Mezzolombardo
Lavis
Salurn
Trento
Fleimstal
Cima d'Asta 2847
S. Martino di Castrozza
Pso. di Rolle 1970
Primiero
Bergamasker A.
Pizzo di Coca 3052
Capo di Ponte
Tione di Trento
Sarche
Sarca
Breno
Oglio
Serio
Piazza Brembana
Clusone
Lovere
BERGAMO
Iseo
Vestone
Bresciane
BRESCIA
Chiari
Treviglio
Arco
Riva
Torbole
Rovereto
Mori
Bagolino
Idro
Mt. Baldo 2218
Avio
Ala
Gardone
Salò
Garda
Gardasee
Desenzano
Peschiera
VERONA
Etsch
Isar
Iller
Lech
Inn
Salzach

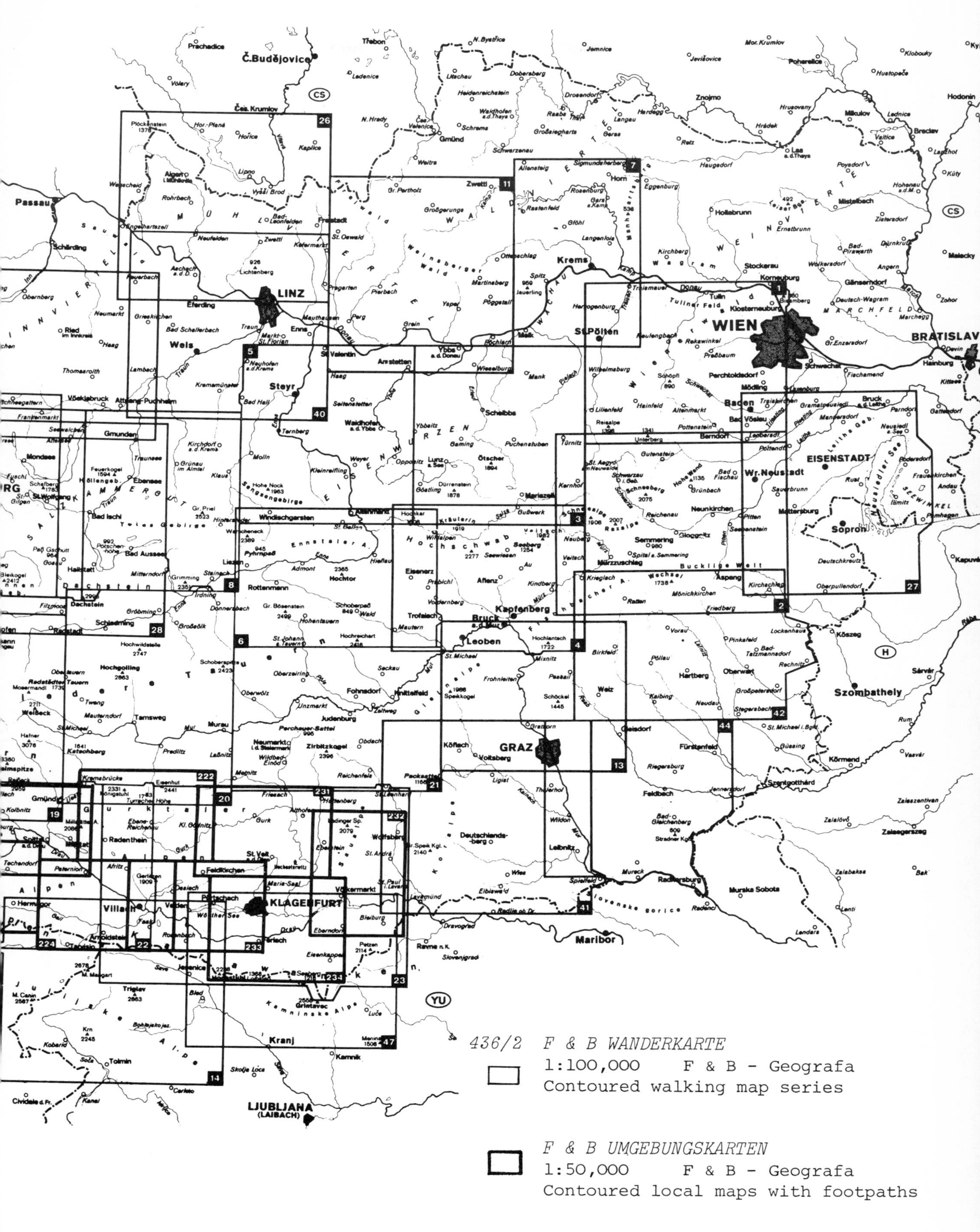

436/2 F & B WANDERKARTE

1:100,000 F & B - Geografa

Contoured walking map series

F & B UMGEBUNGSKARTEN

1:50,000 F & B - Geografa

Contoured local maps with footpaths

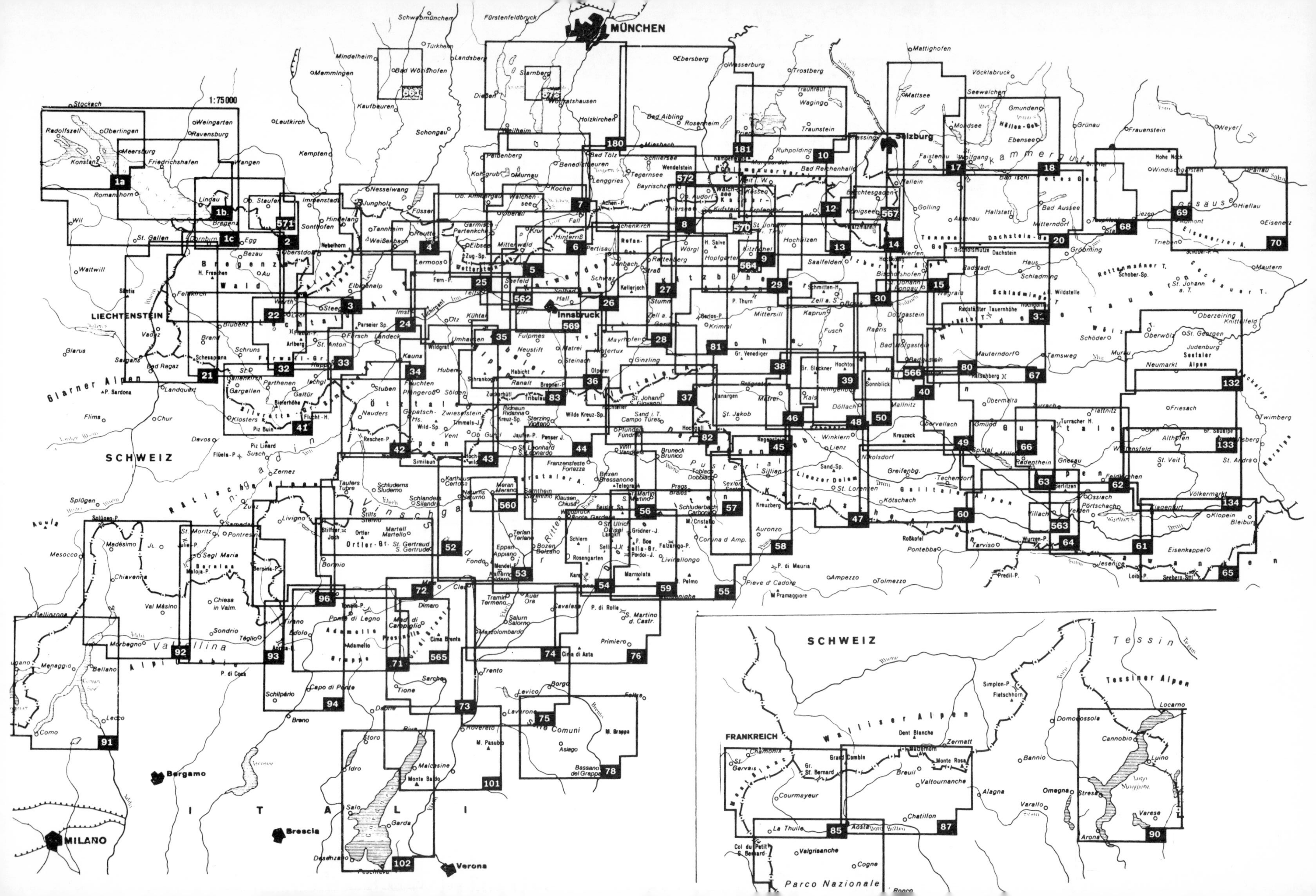
1:75000
MÜNCHEN
Salzburg
Innsbruck
LIECHTENSTEIN
SCHWEIZ
FRANKREICH
Tessiner Alpen
Walliser Alpen
Parco Nazionale
Verona
Brescia
Bergamo
MILANO

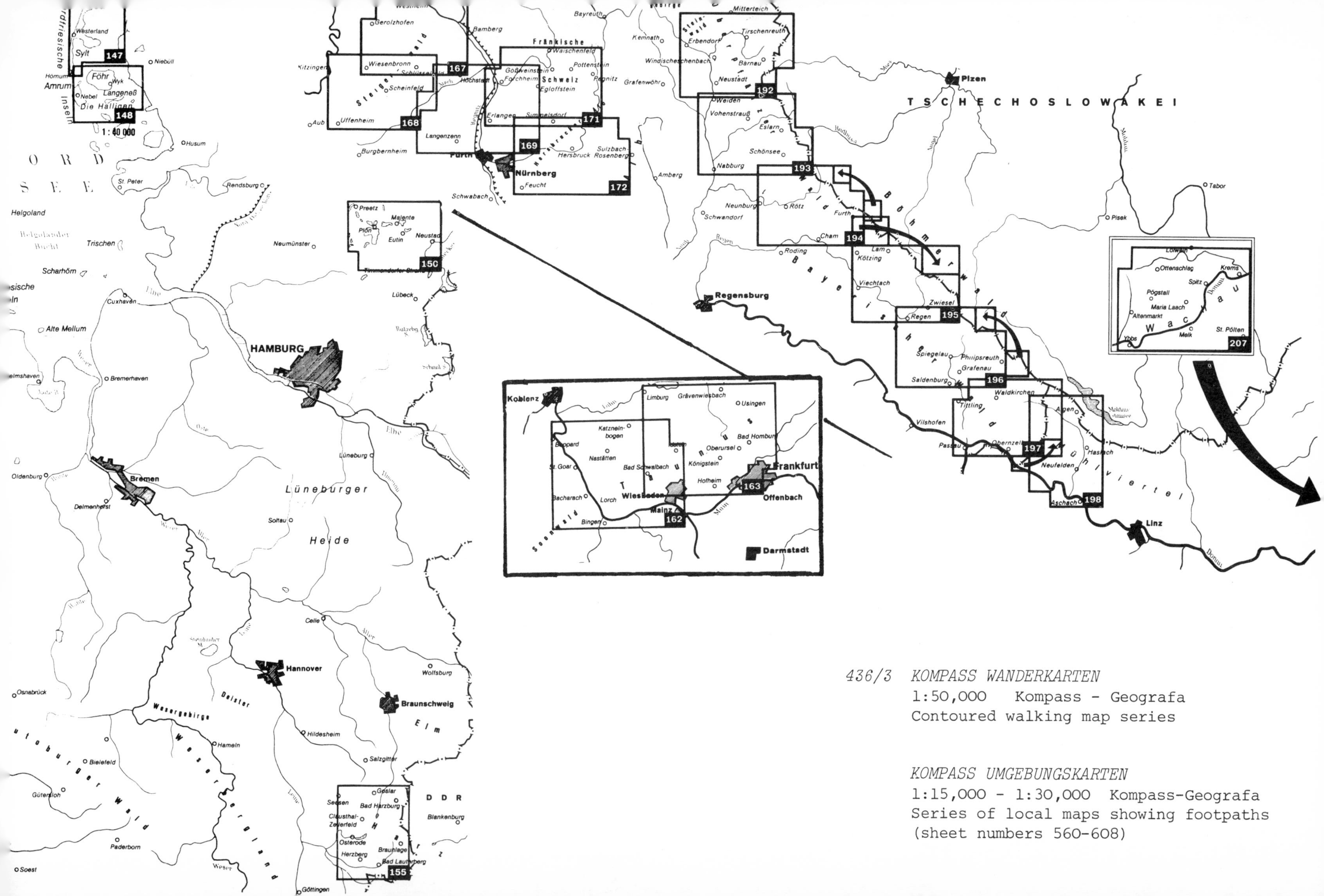

436/3 *KOMPASS WANDERKARTEN*
1:50,000 Kompass - Geografa
Contoured walking map series

KOMPASS UMGEBUNGSKARTEN
1:15,000 - 1:30,000 Kompass-Geografa
Series of local maps showing footpaths
(sheet numbers 560-608)

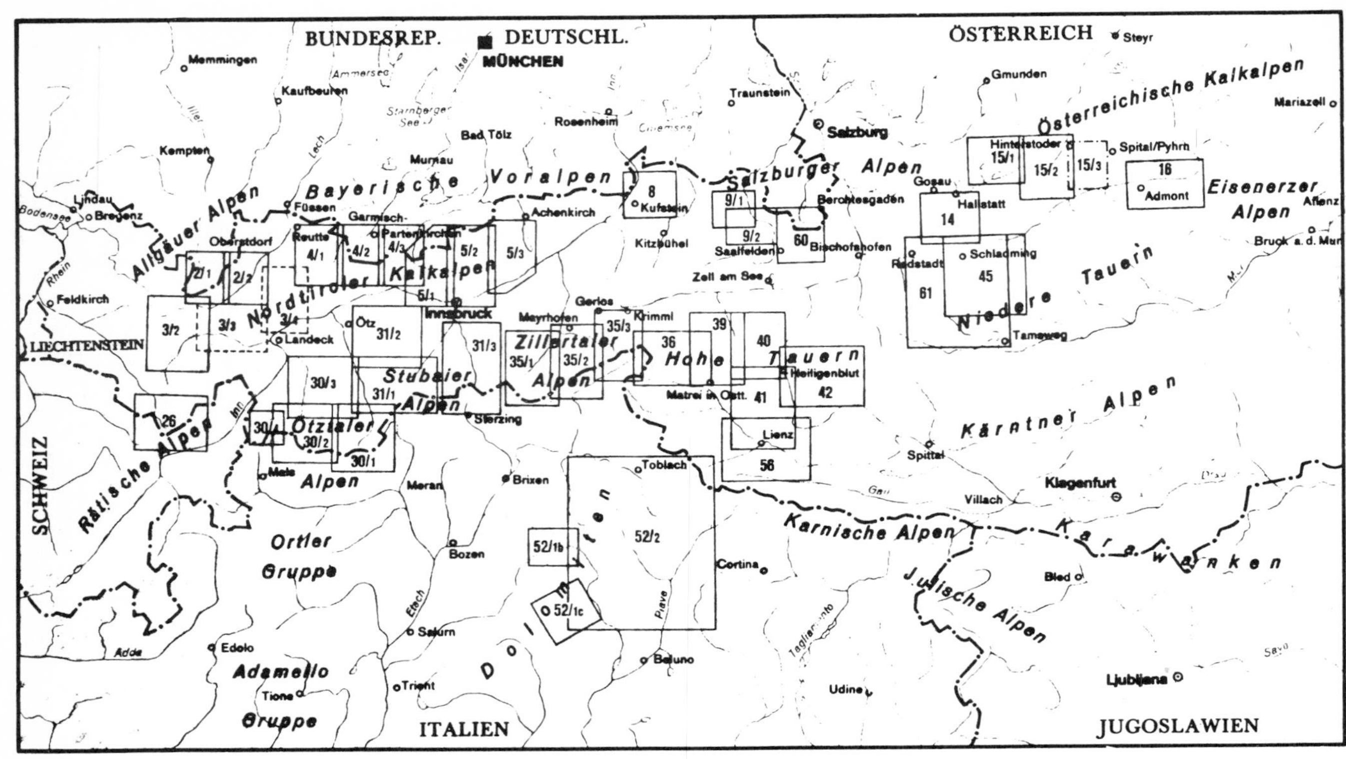

436/4 ALPENVEREINSKARTEN
1:25,000 O.A.V.
Large scale walking map series, contoured

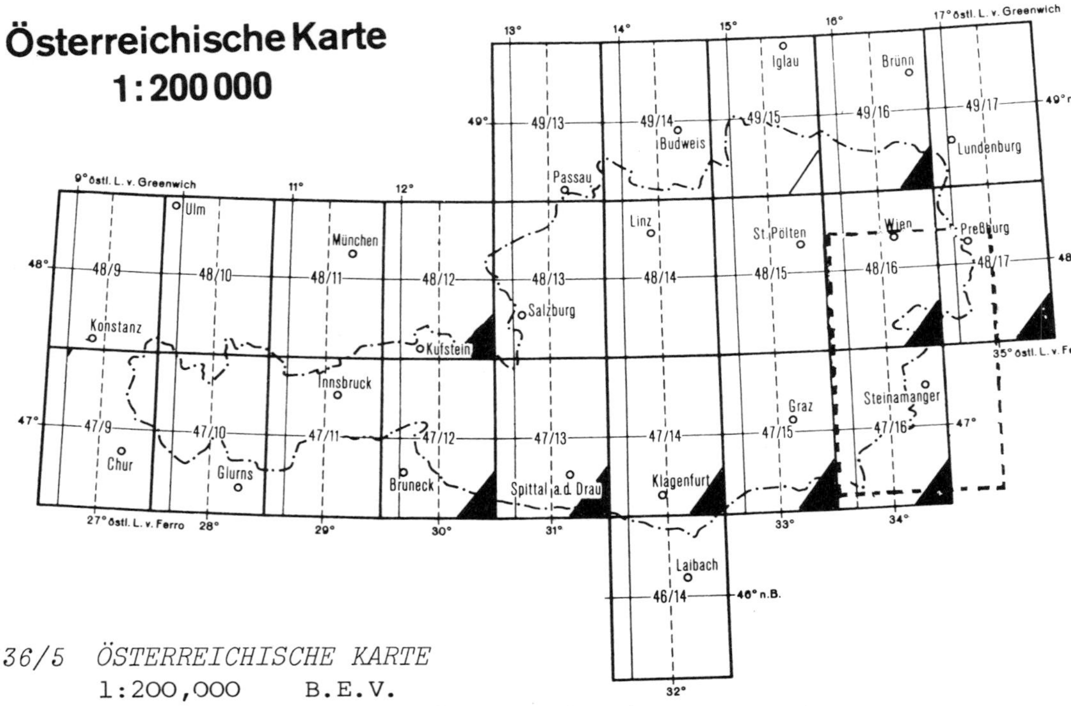

Österreichische Karte 1:200 000

436/5 ÖSTERREICHISCHE KARTE
1:200,000 B.E.V.
New offical topographical series in preparation

Sheets published

Sheets in preparation

Special Sheet
Burgenland 1:200,000

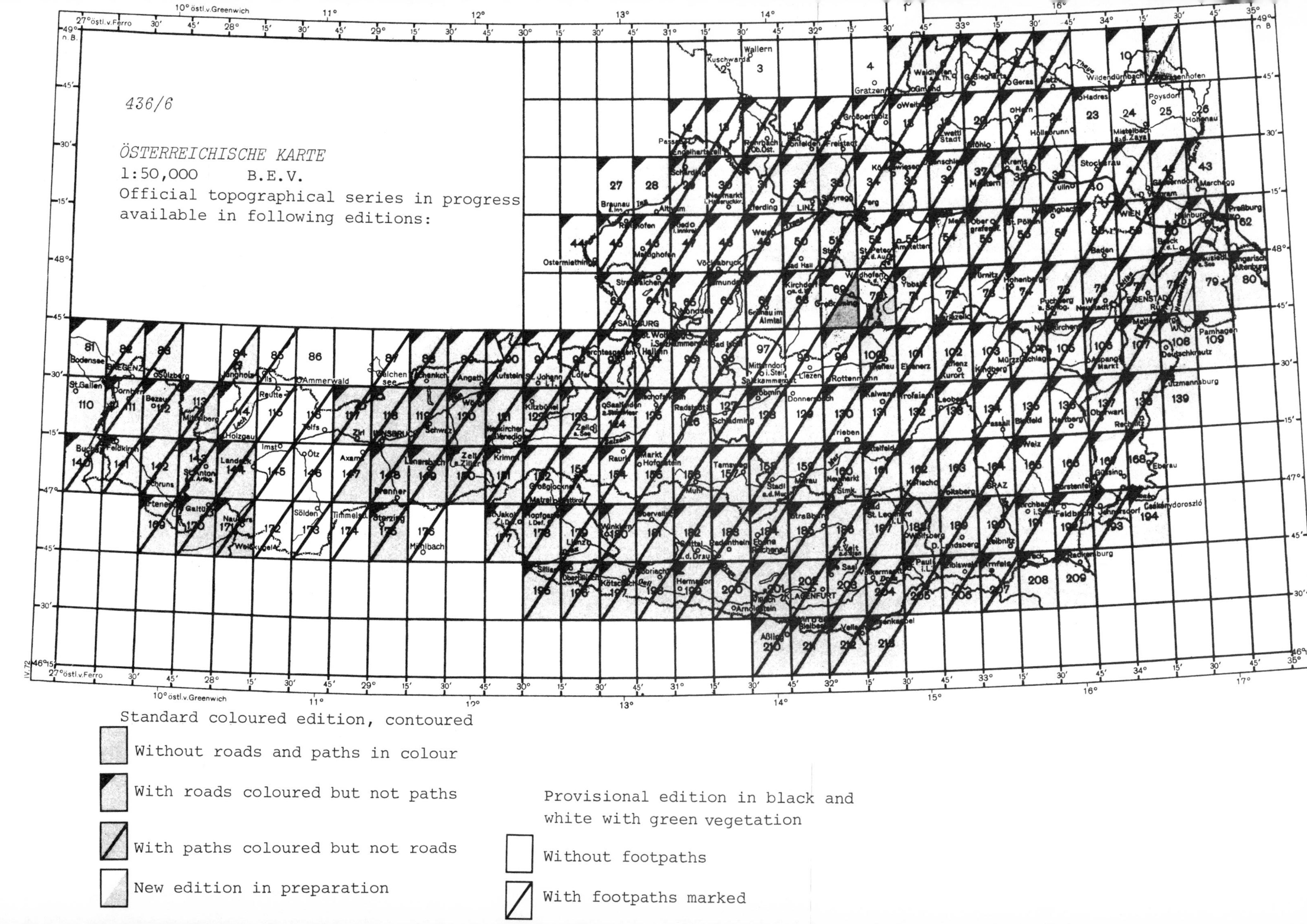
436/6
ÖSTERREICHISCHE KARTE
1:50,000 B.E.V.
Official topographical series in progress available in following editions:
Standard coloured edition, contoured
Without roads and paths in colour
With roads coloured but not paths
With paths coloured but not roads
New edition in preparation
Provisional edition in black and white with green vegetation
Without footpaths
With footpaths marked

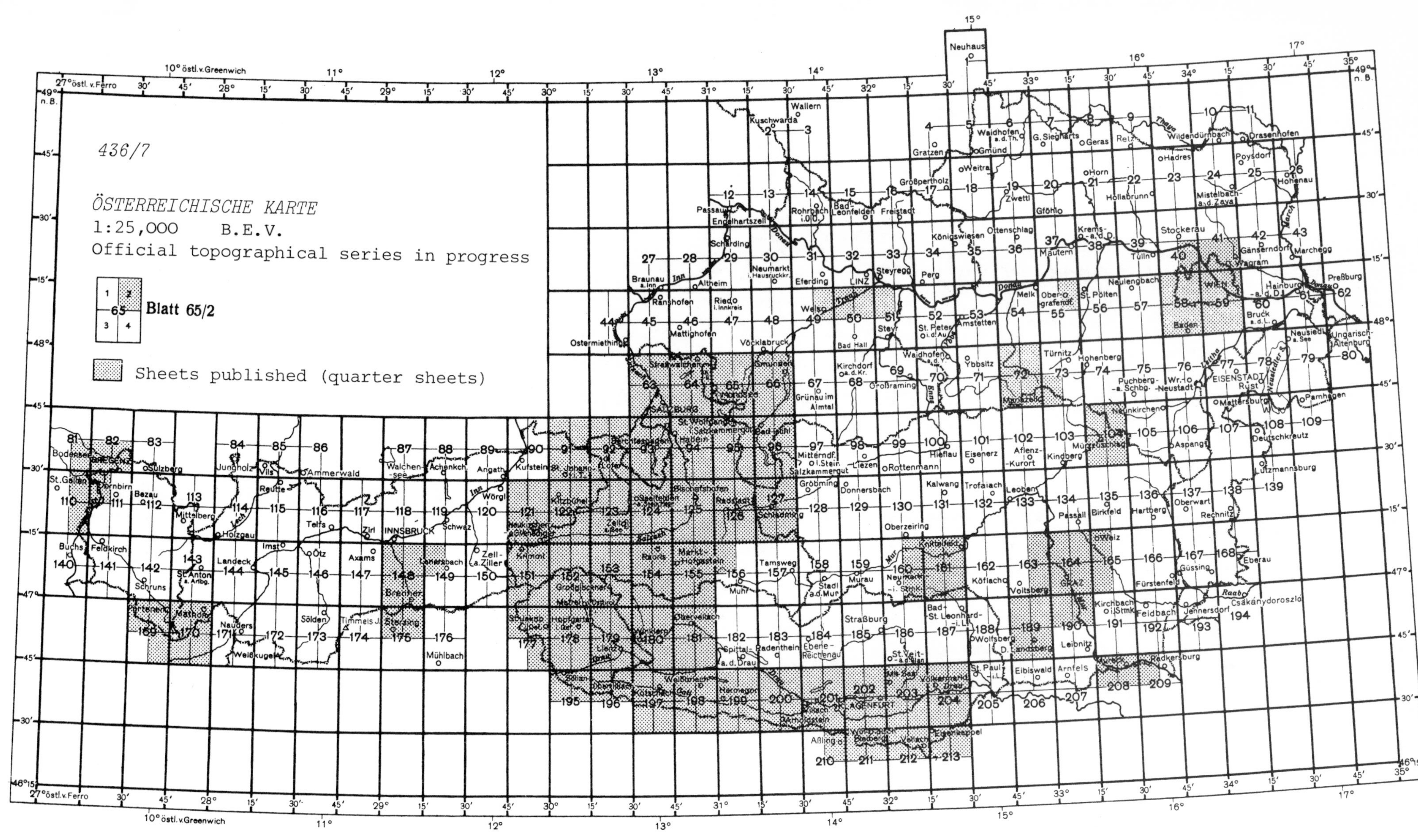
436/7
ÖSTERREICHISCHE KARTE
1:25,000 B.E.V.
Official topographical series in progress
Blatt 65/2
Sheets published (quarter sheets)

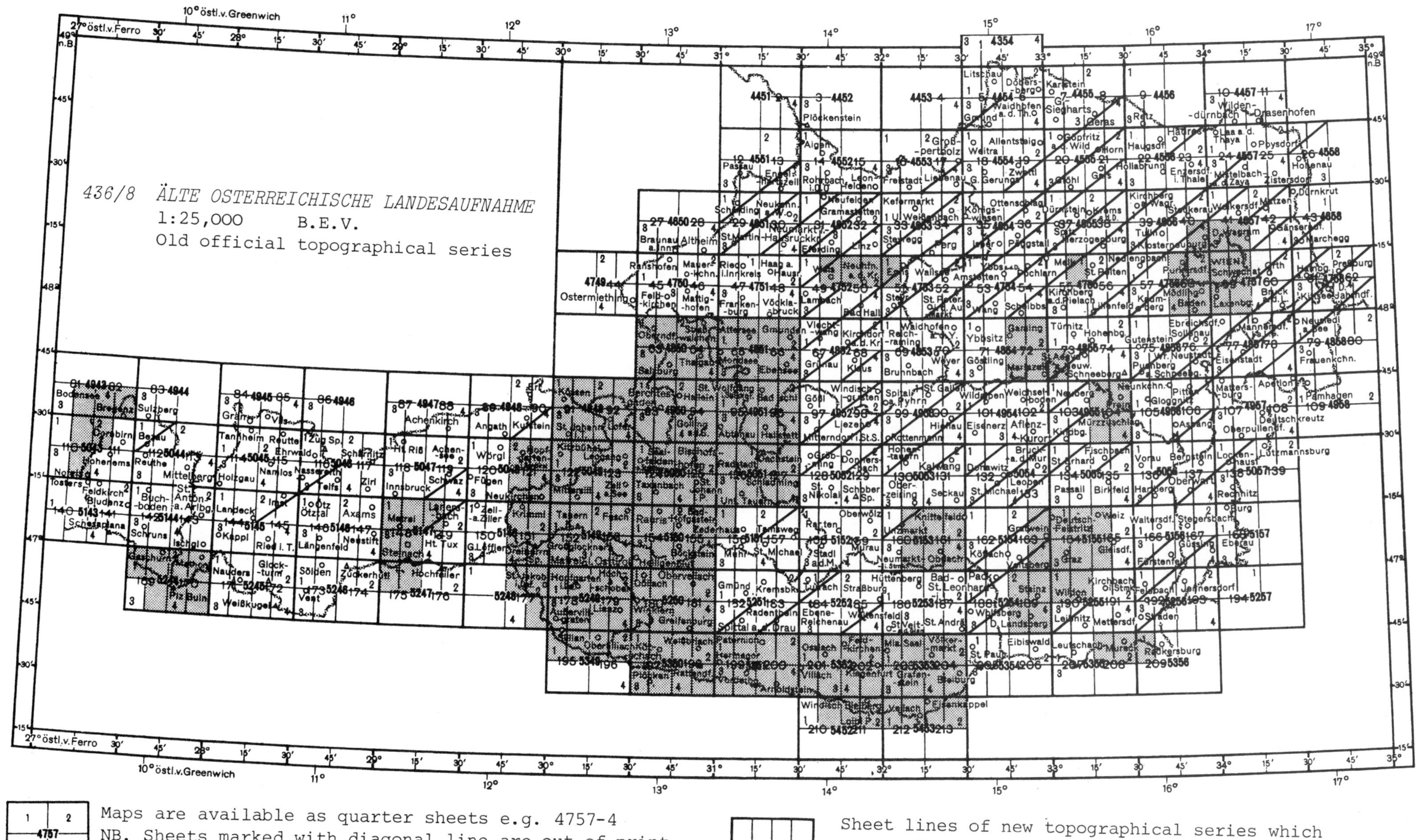

Maps are available as quarter sheets e.g. 4757-4
NB. Sheets marked with diagonal line are out of print

Sheet lines of new topographical series which supersede old sereies. Stippled areas indicate sheets published. (see index 436/7)

436/9 *GEOLOGISCHE KARTEN DER REPUBLIK ÖSTERREICH*

1:75,000 Geol. Bundesanstalt

Coloured geological series in progress

Sheets published
(sheets with corners marked include text)

Out of print

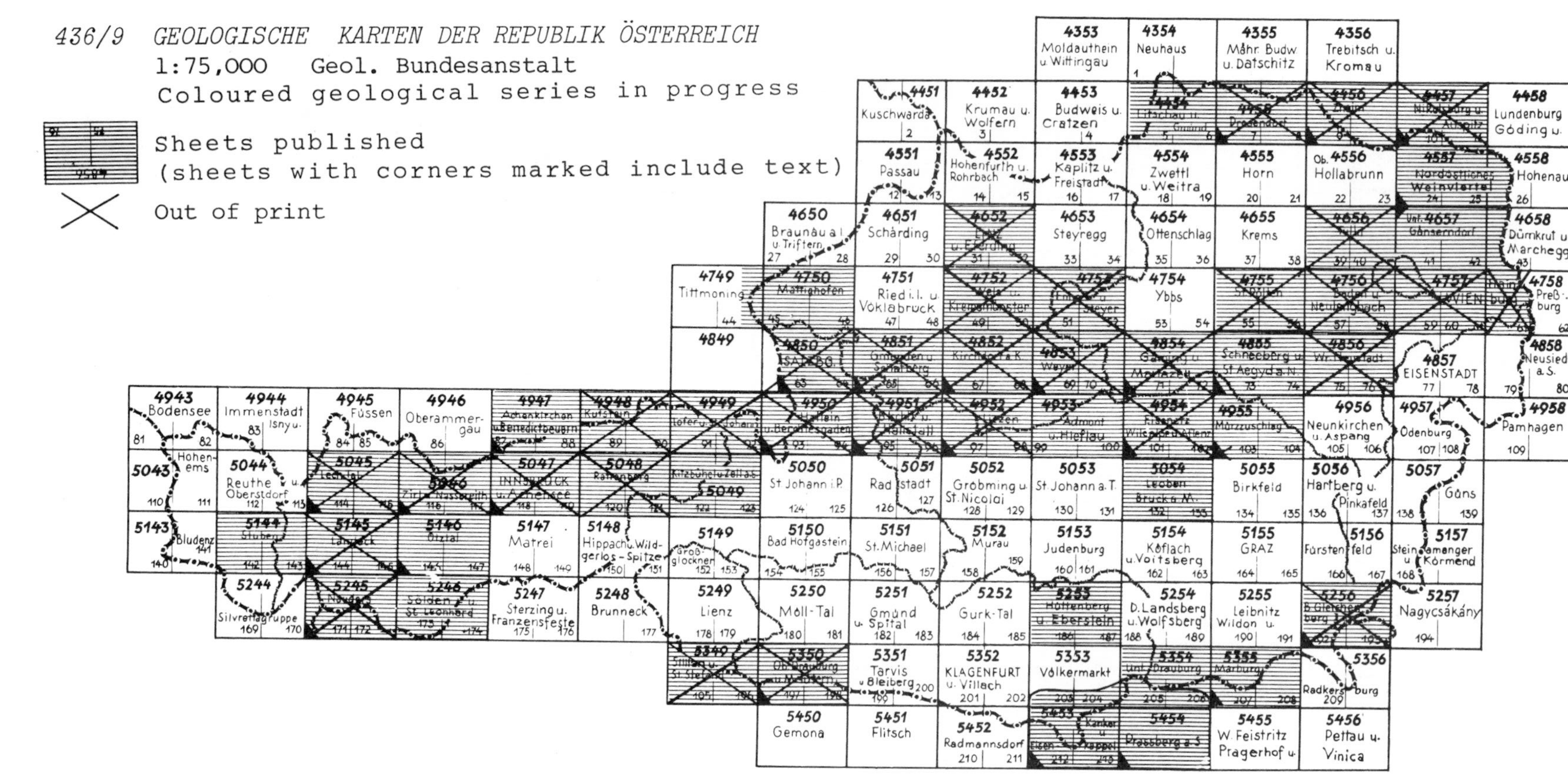

436/10 GEOLOGISCHE KARTEN DER REPUBLIK ÖSTERREICH

Various scales. Geol. Bundesanstalt

Series of special area geological maps with text

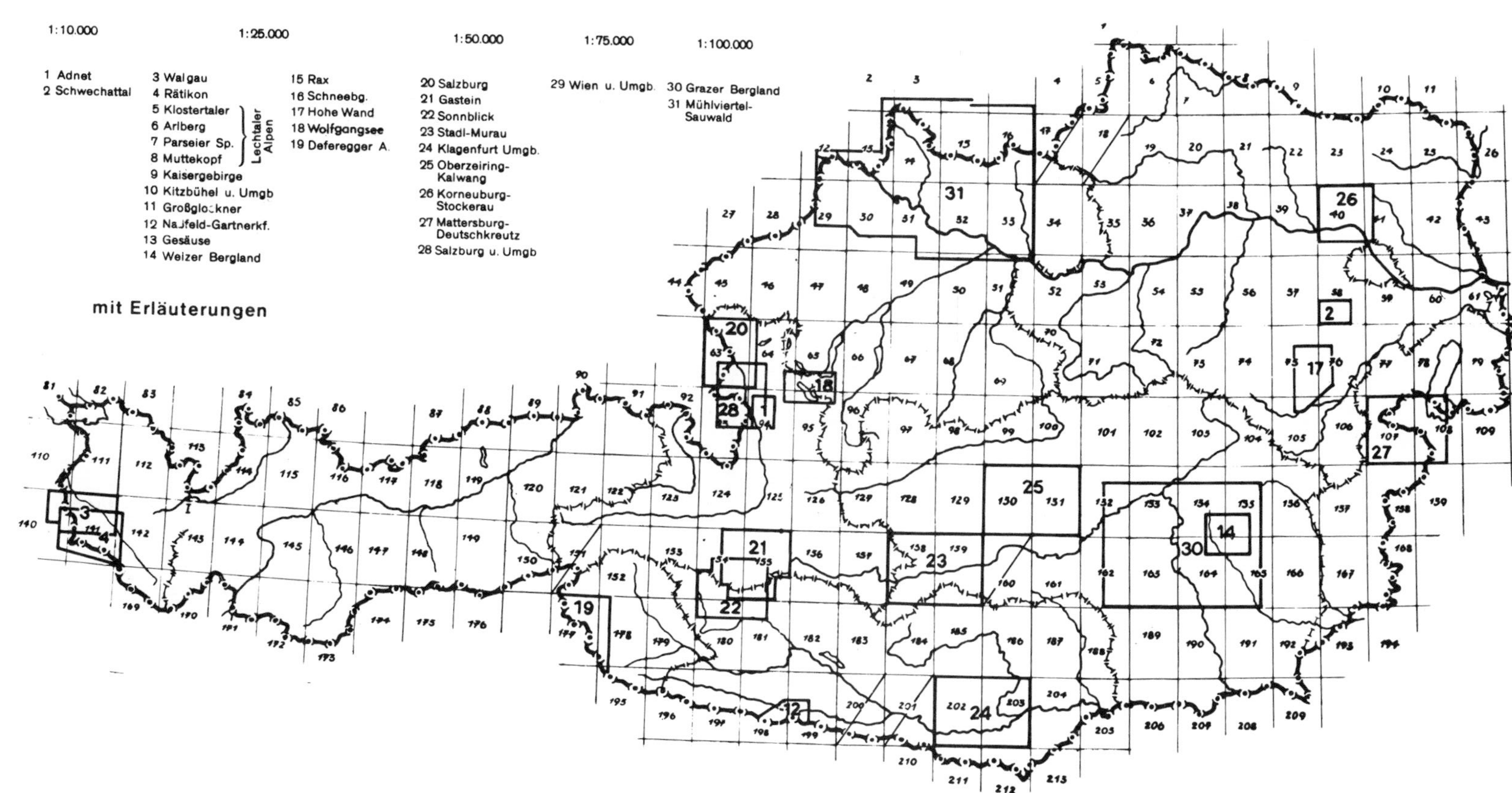

436/11 GENERALKARTE ÖSTERREICH
1:200,000 Mair
Road map series

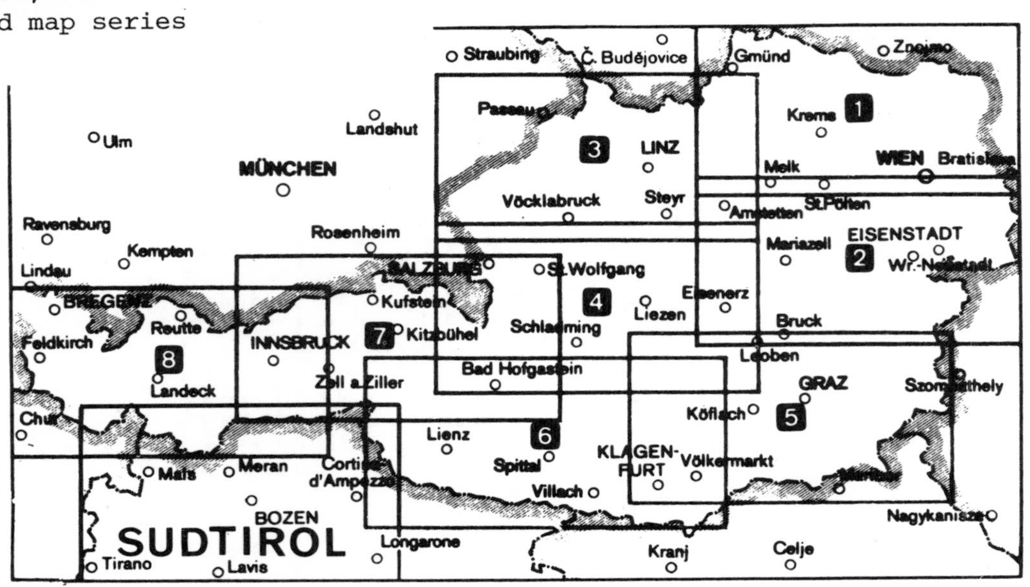

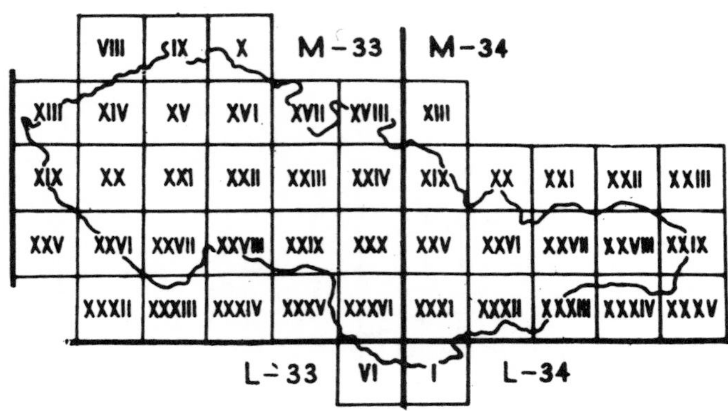

437/1 GEOLOGICKÁ MAPA ČSSR
1:200,000
Coloured geological series
Sheet numbers: quote number in roman numerals
preceded by large square reference
e.g. M33-XV PRAHA

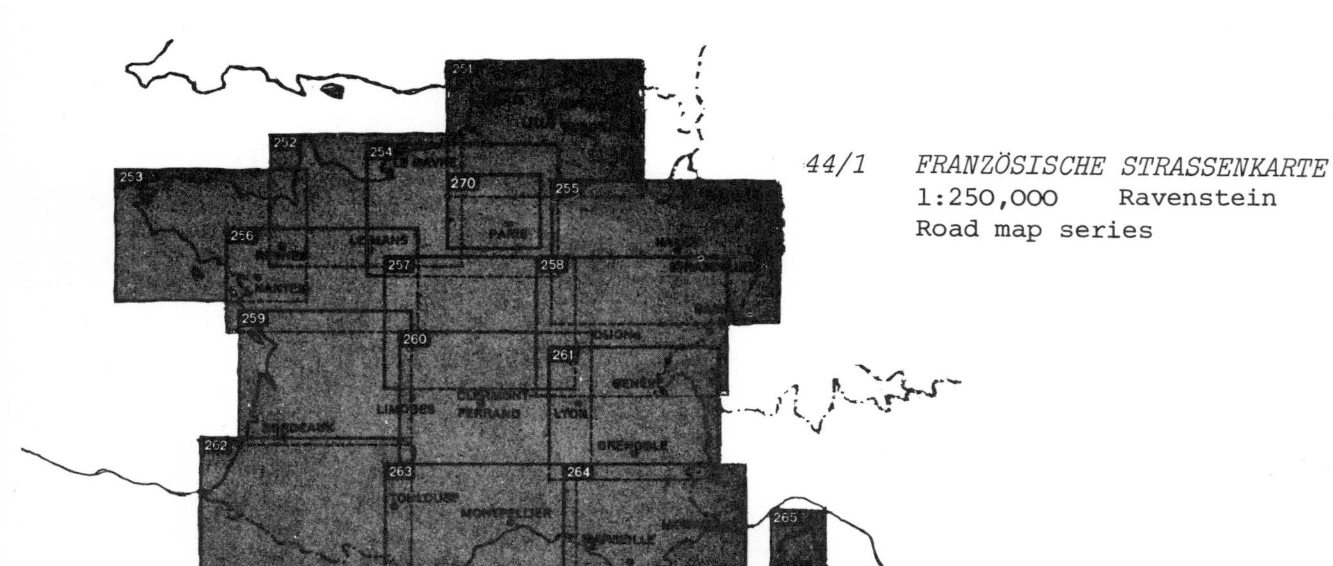

44/1 FRANZÖSISCHE STRASSENKARTE
1:250,000 Ravenstein
Road map series

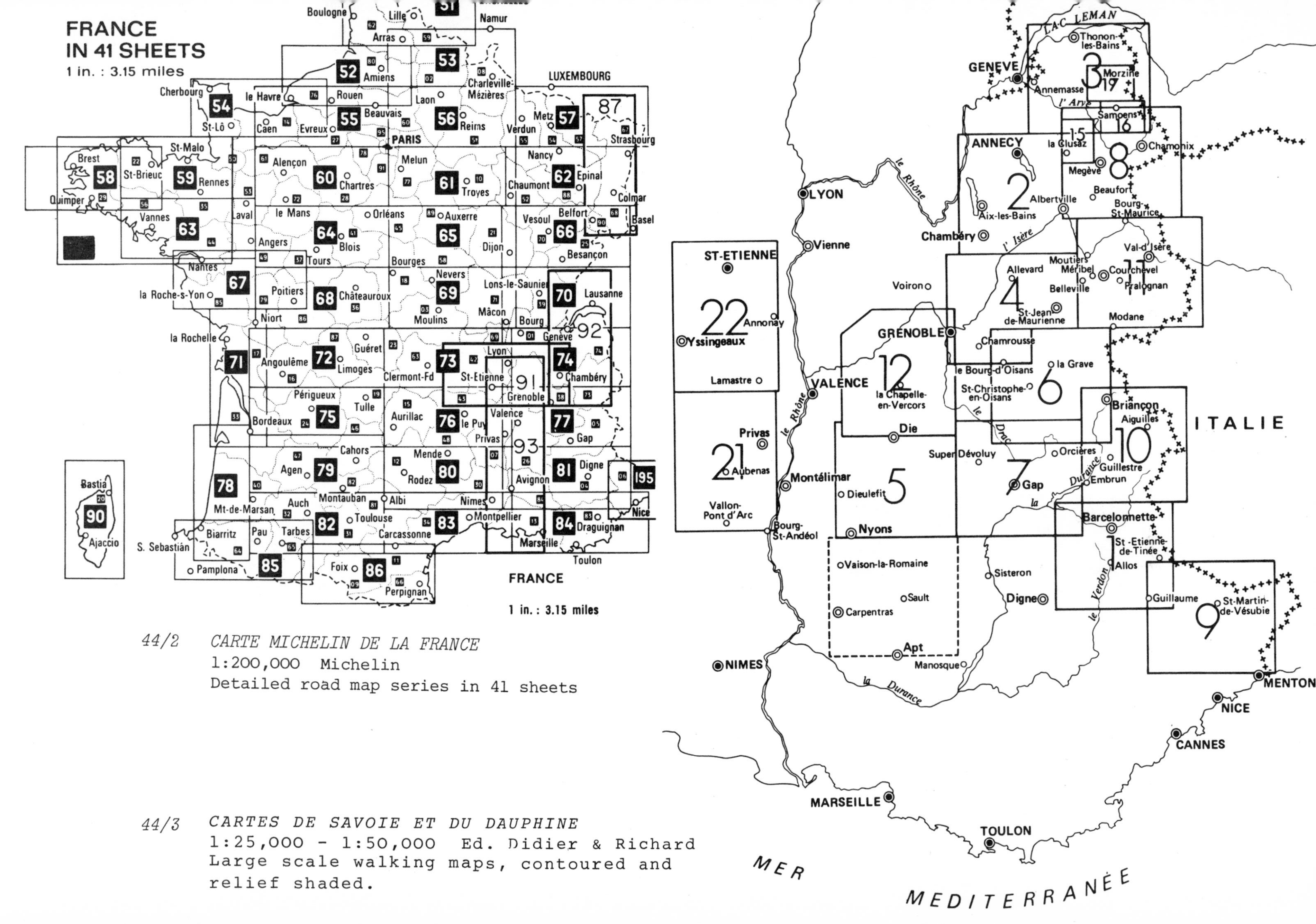

44/2 *CARTE MICHELIN DE LA FRANCE*
1:200,000 Michelin
Detailed road map series in 41 sheets

44/3 *CARTES DE SAVOIE ET DU DAUPHINE*
1:25,000 - 1:50,000 Ed. Didier & Richard
Large scale walking maps, contoured and relief shaded.

44/5 *PARIS - SERIE BANLIEUE ORIENTATION*
1:11,200 Ed. Ponchet
Large scale plan of Paris and its environs

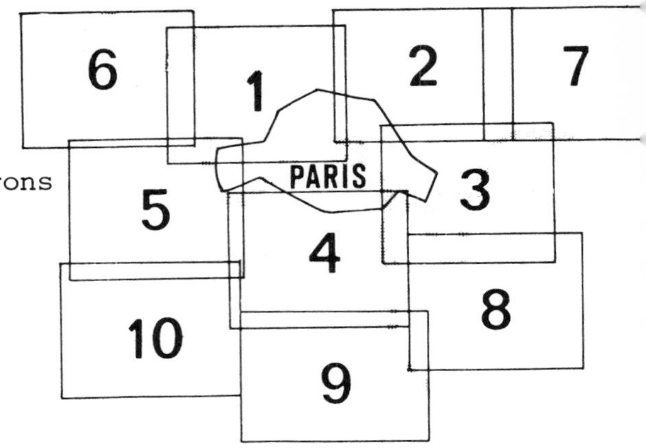

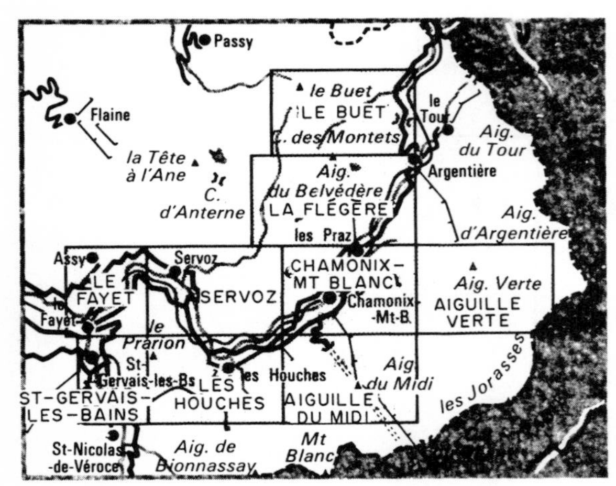

44/4 *CARTE DE LA RÉGION DU MONT BLANC*
1:10,000 IGN
Large scale detailed walking maps, contour relief shaded

44/6

CARTE DE FRANCE
1:250,000 IGN
Topographical series, all sheets published

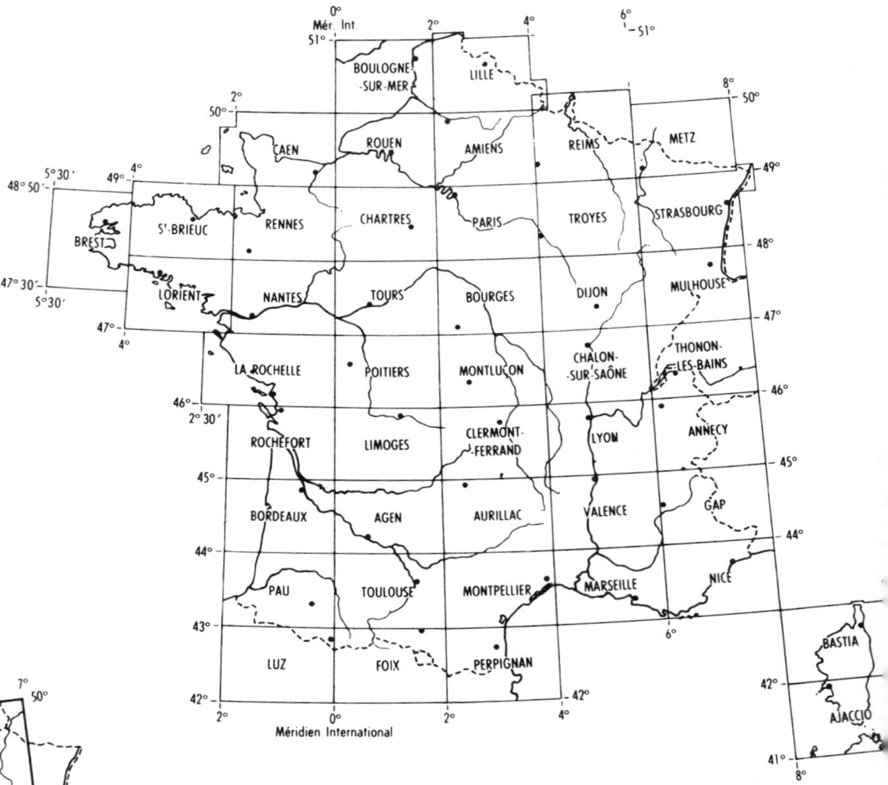

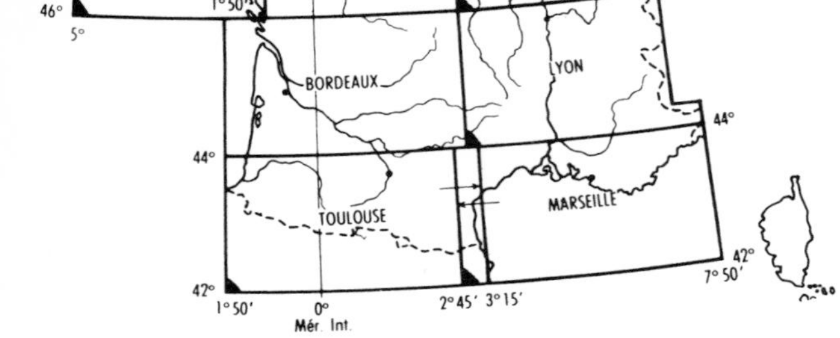

44/7

CARTE DE FRANCE
1:500,000 IGN
Topographical series in progress

Sheets published

44/8 *CARTE DE LA RÉGION PARISIENNE*

1:5,000 IGN

Planimetric series covering Paris and suburbs

Sheet numbering system of LAGNY X11-16 SE

Sheets published

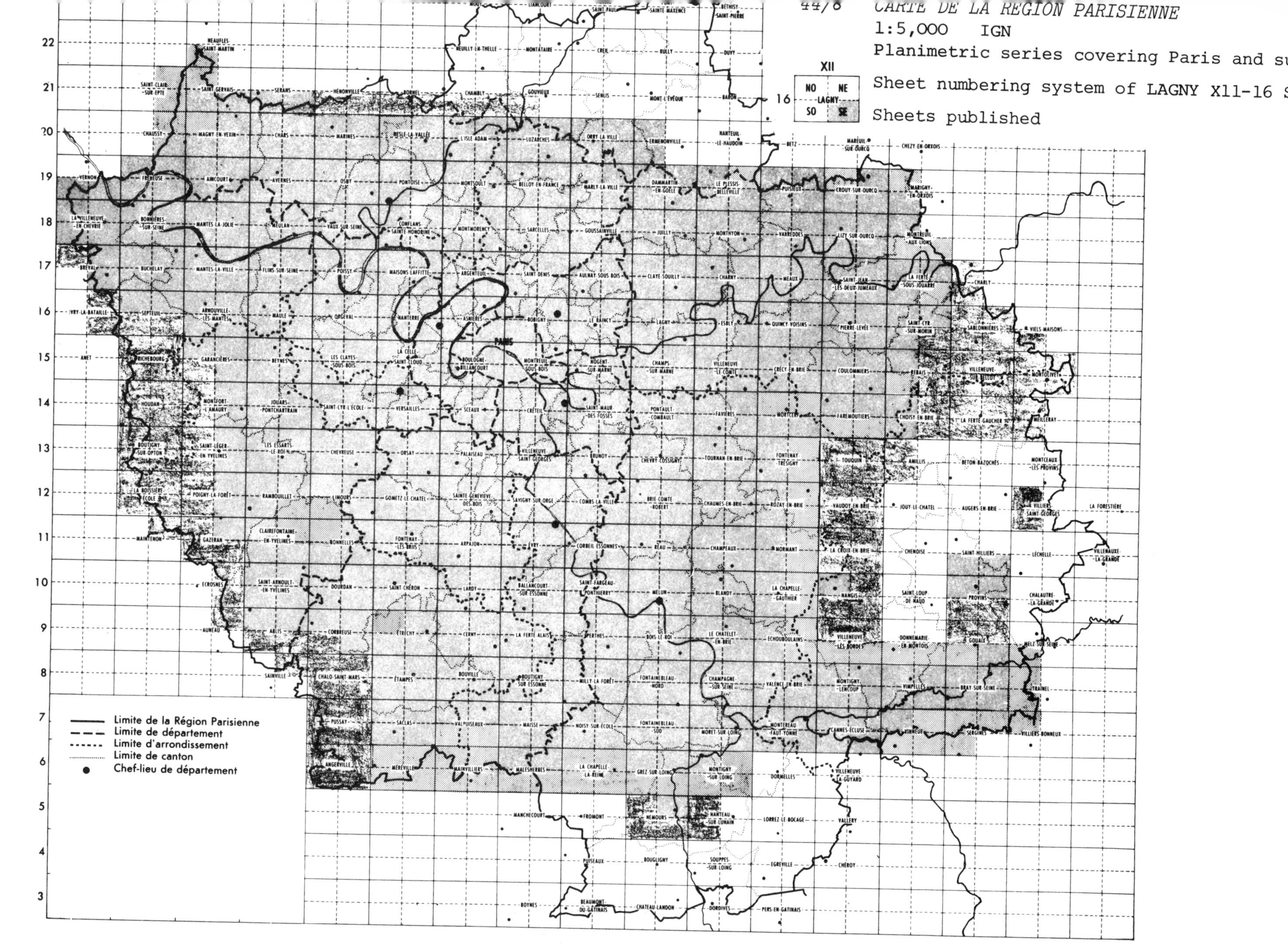

44/9 *CARTE DE L'ENVIRONMENT CULTUREL ET TOURISTIQUE (SÉRIE ROUGE)*

1:250,000 IGN

Tourist series showing roads and places of interest.

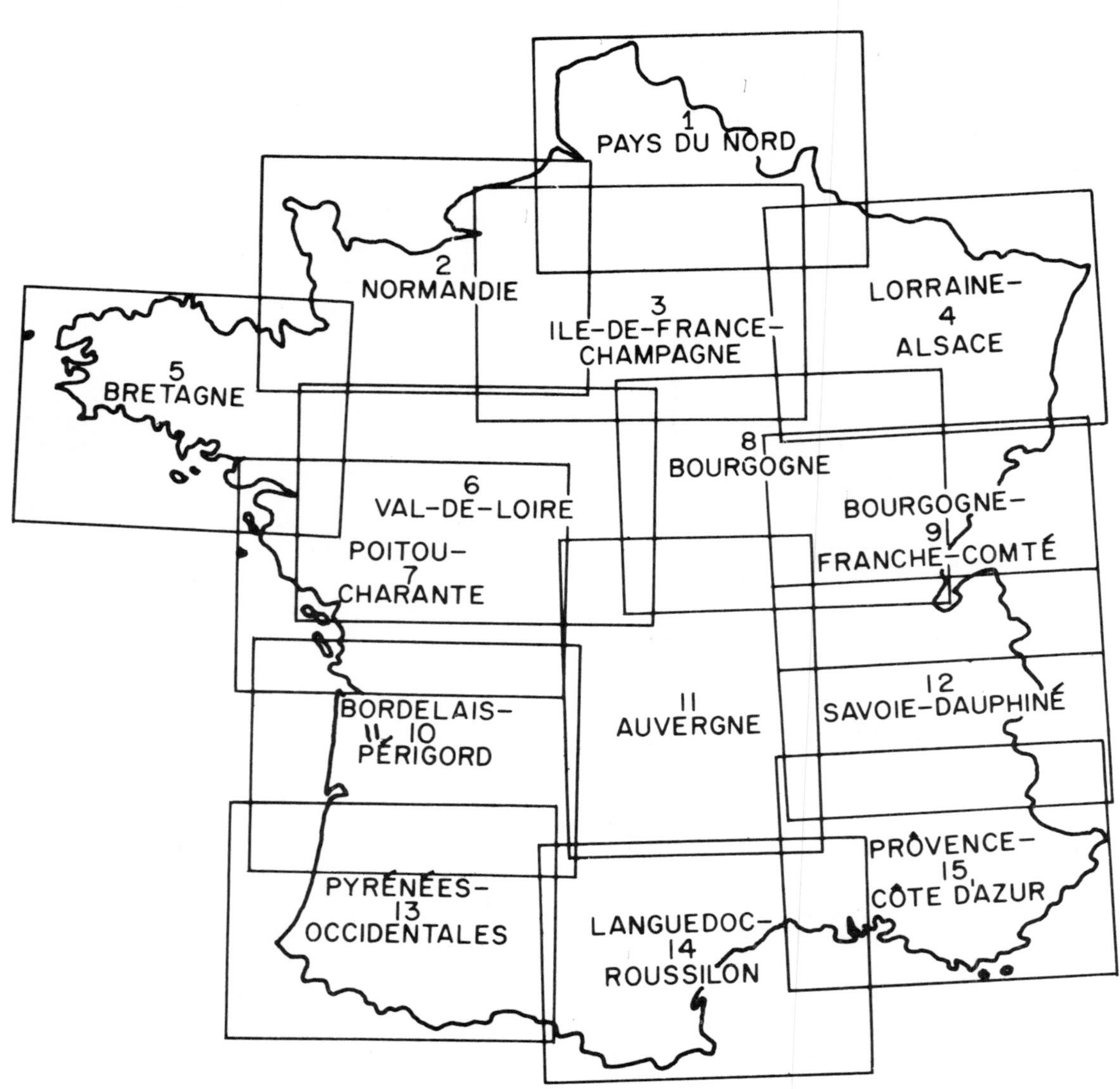

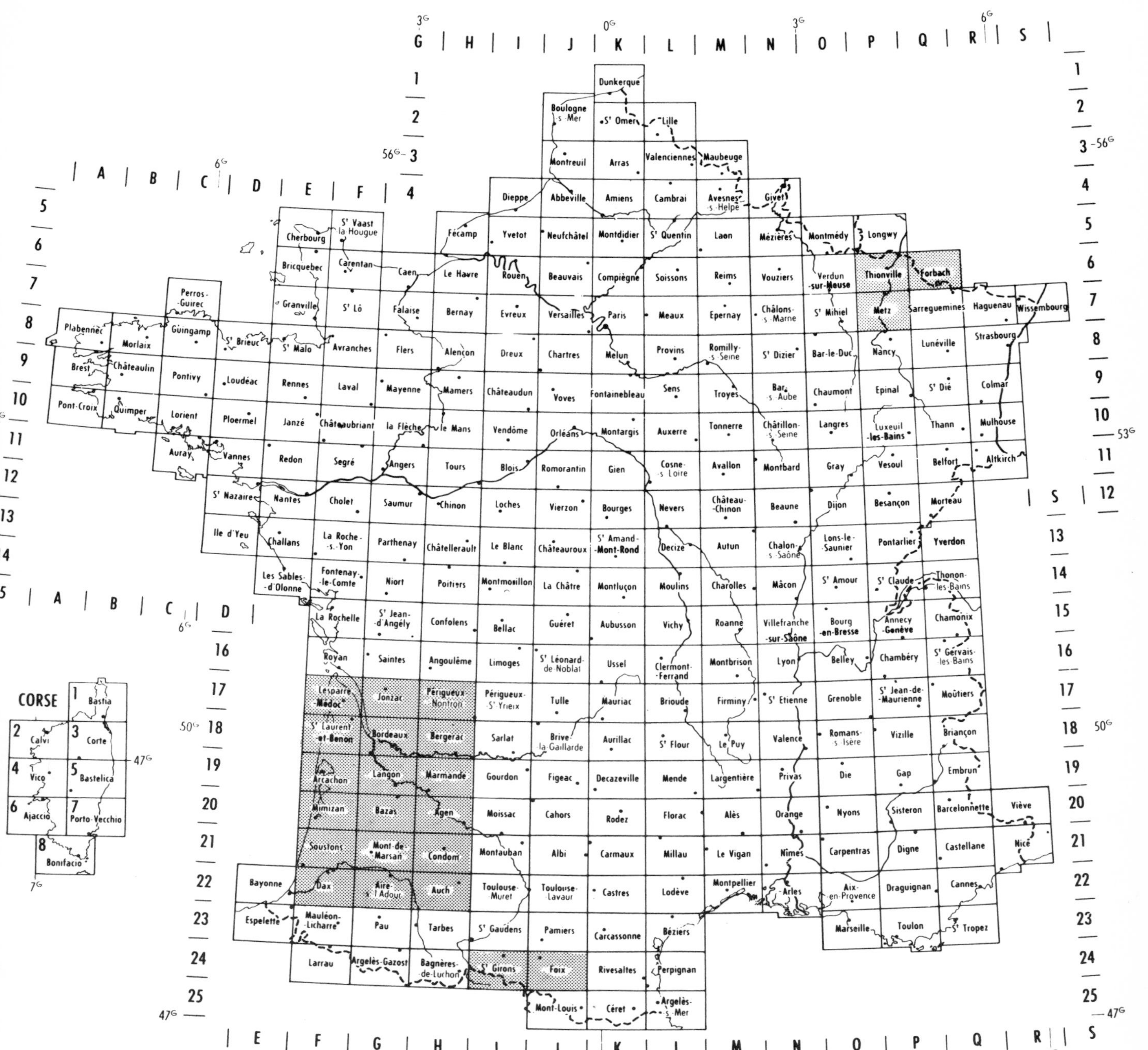

44/10 *CARTE DE FRANCE*

1:100,000 IGN

Official topographical series, being replaced by new large sheet series (see index 44/11)

CARTE FORESTIERE DE LA FRANCE

1:100,000 IGN-Serv. de l'inventaire Forestier Nat.

Series of forestry maps in progress

▒ Sheets published

Sheet numbering: Paris K7

44/11 *CARTE POUR LE TOURISME (SÉRIE VERTE)*

1:100,000 IGN

Official'Large sheet' topographical series. All sheets published.

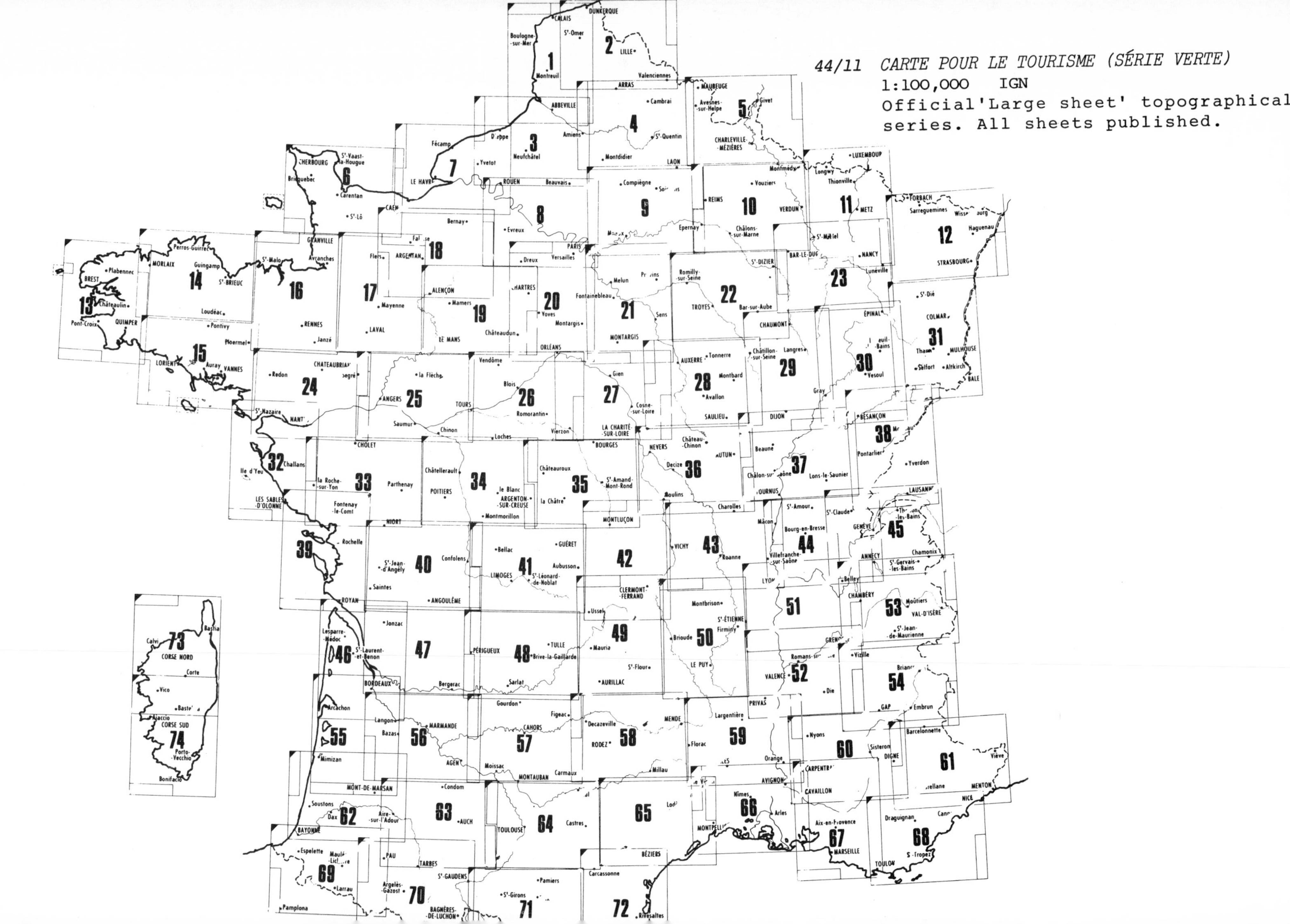

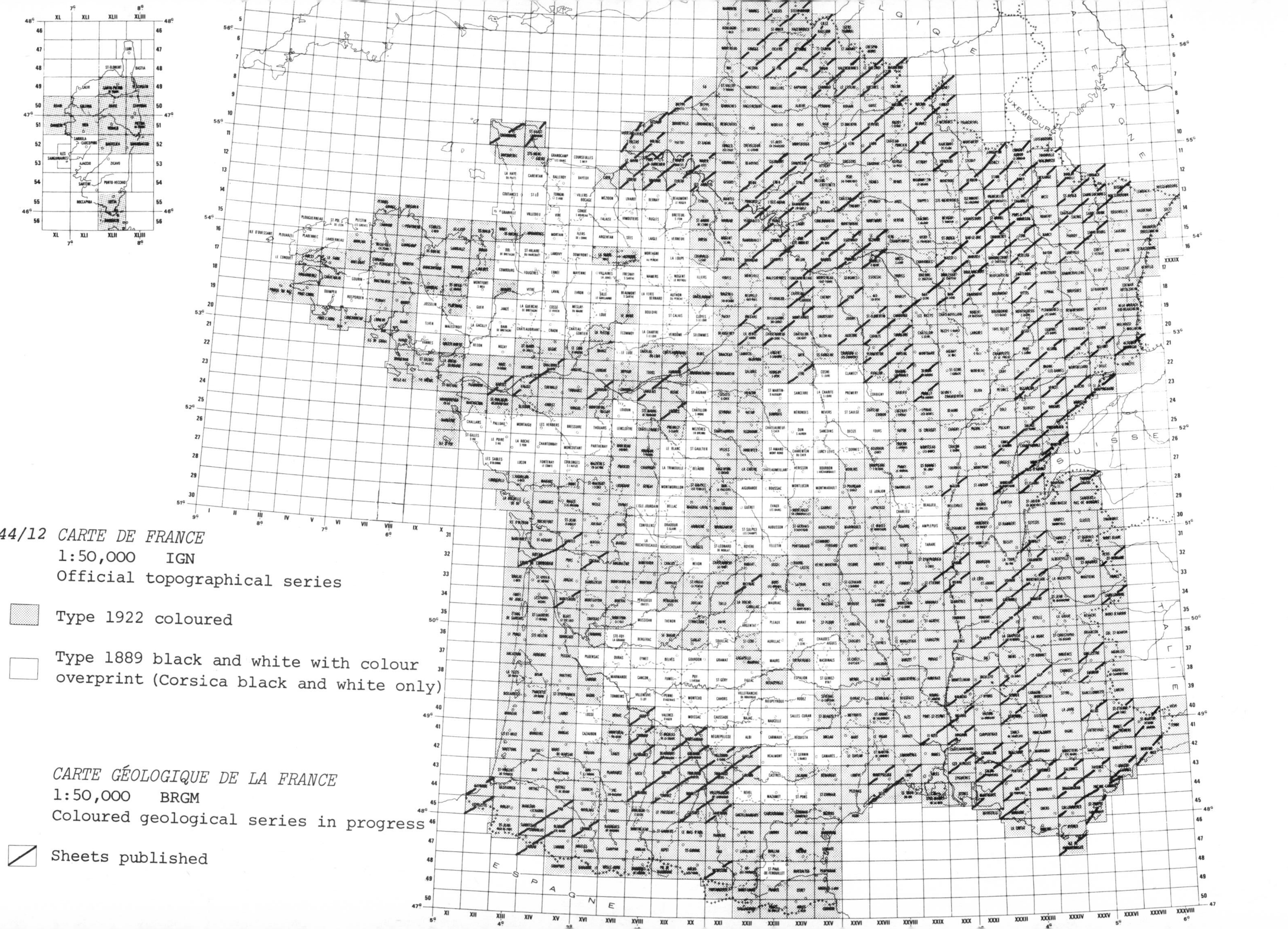

44/12 *CARTE DE FRANCE*
1:50,000 IGN
Official topographical series

Type 1922 coloured

Type 1889 black and white with colour overprint (Corsica black and white only)

CARTE GÉOLOGIQUE DE LA FRANCE
1:50,000 BRGM
Coloured geological series in progress

Sheets published

44/13 *CARTE DE FRANCE*

1:25,000 - 1:20,000 IGN

Official topographical series.

The 1:25,000 series are replacing the older 1:20,000 editions.

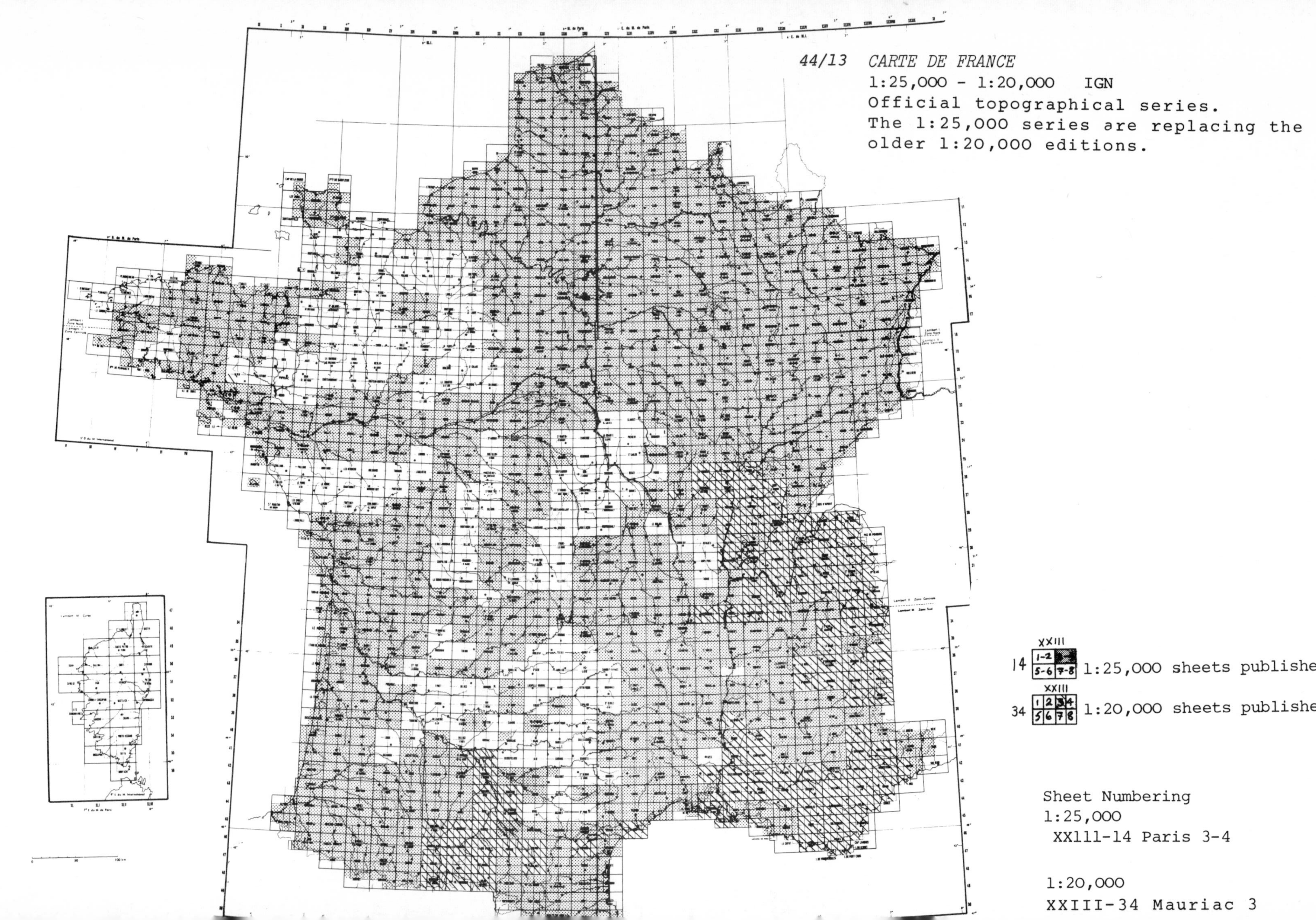

Sheet Numbering

1:25,000

XXIII-14 Paris 3-4

1:20,000

XXIII-34 Mauriac 3

44/14

CARTE GEOLOGIQUE DE FRANCE

1:80,000 BRGM

Coloured geological series in progress

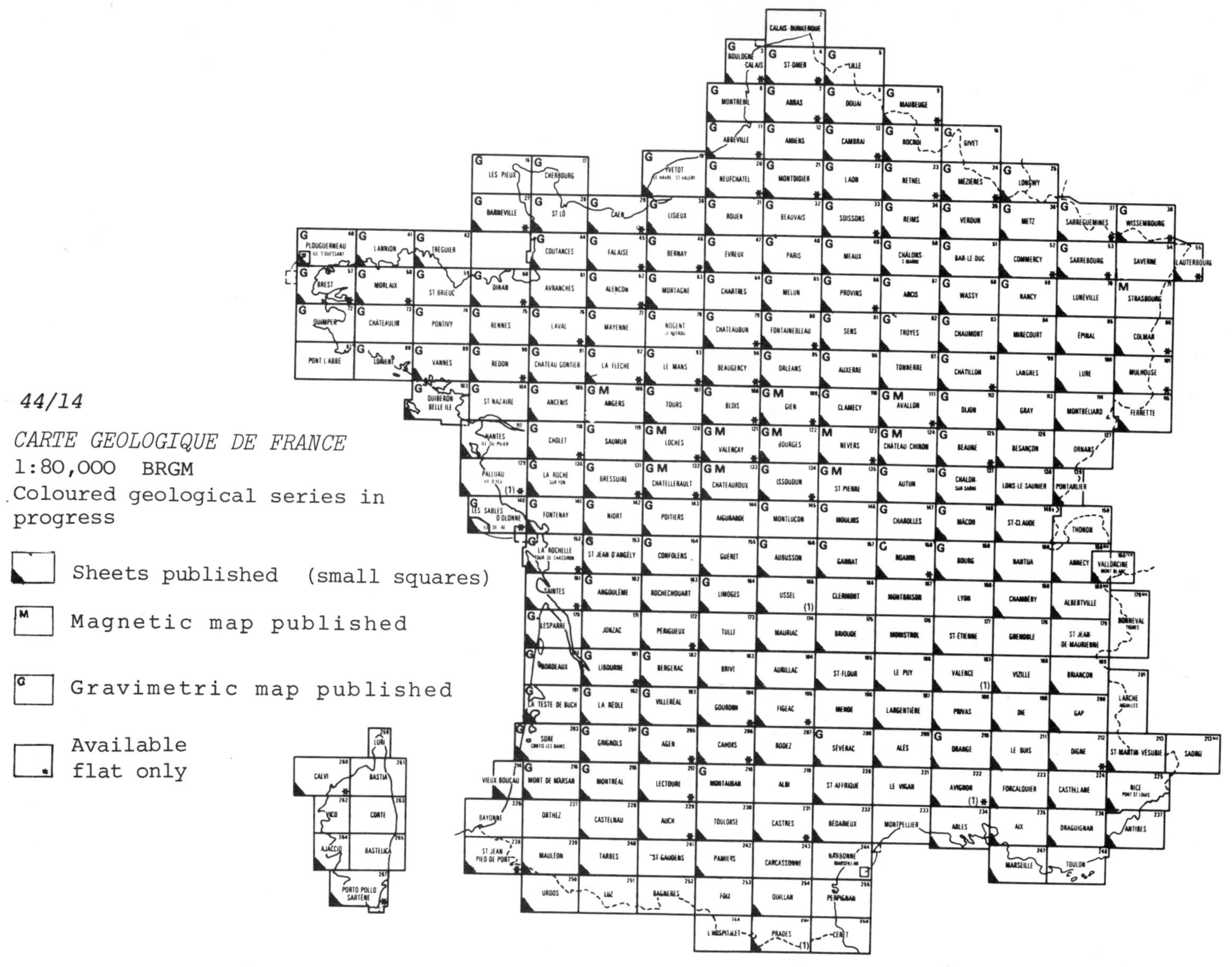

- Sheets published (small squares)
- Magnetic map published
- Gravimetric map published
- Available flat only

44/15

CARTE GÉOLOGIQUE DE LA FRANCE
1:320,000 BRGM
Coloured geological series

Sheets published

Only available paper flat

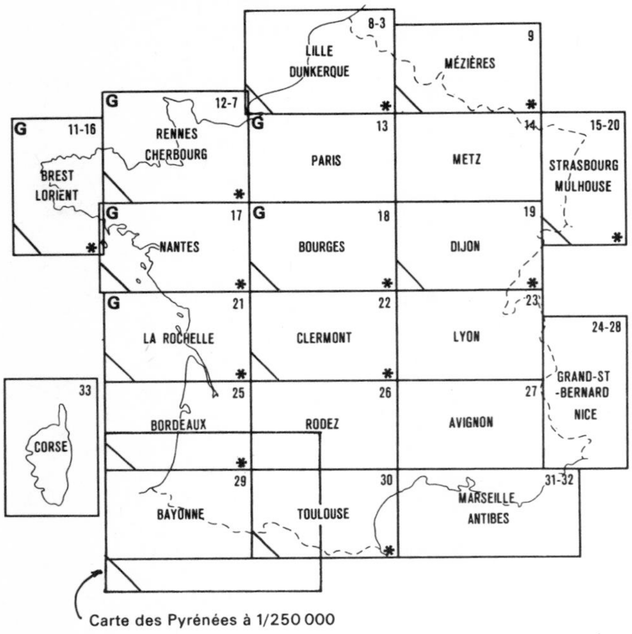

Carte des Pyrénées à 1/250 000

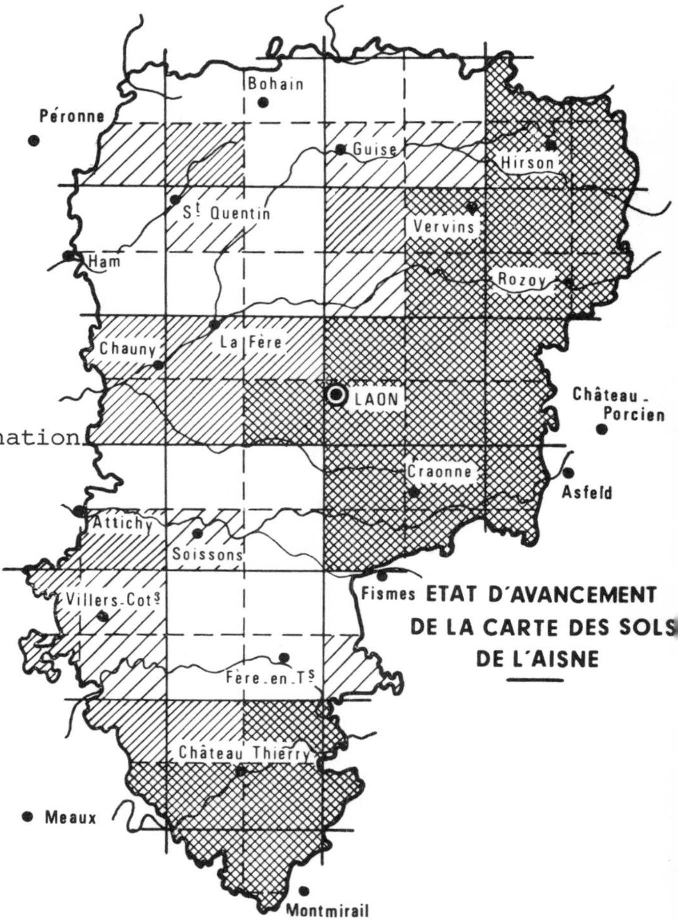

44/16 *CARTE DES SOLS DE L'AISNE*
1:25,000 Serv. Cart. des Sols-Aisne
Series of coloured soil maps with explanation

Sheets published

Maps in preparation

Maps in prospect

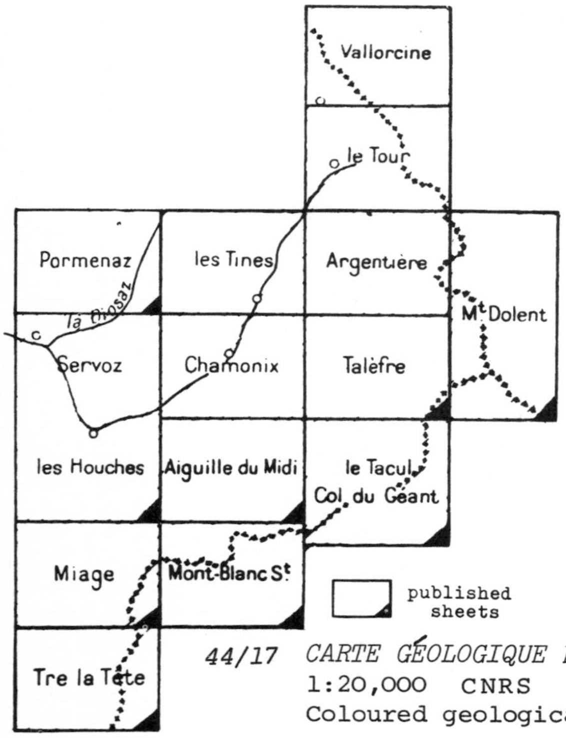

ETAT D'AVANCEMENT DE LA CARTE DES SOLS DE L'AISNE

published sheets

44/17 *CARTE GÉOLOGIQUE DU MASSIF DU MONT BLANC*
1:20,000 CNRS
Coloured geological series

44/18 *CARTE GÉOLOGIQUE DE LA MARGE CONTINENTALE- NATURE DES DÉPÔTS MEUBLES*
1:100,000 BRGM
Geological series showing submarine deposits.

sheets published

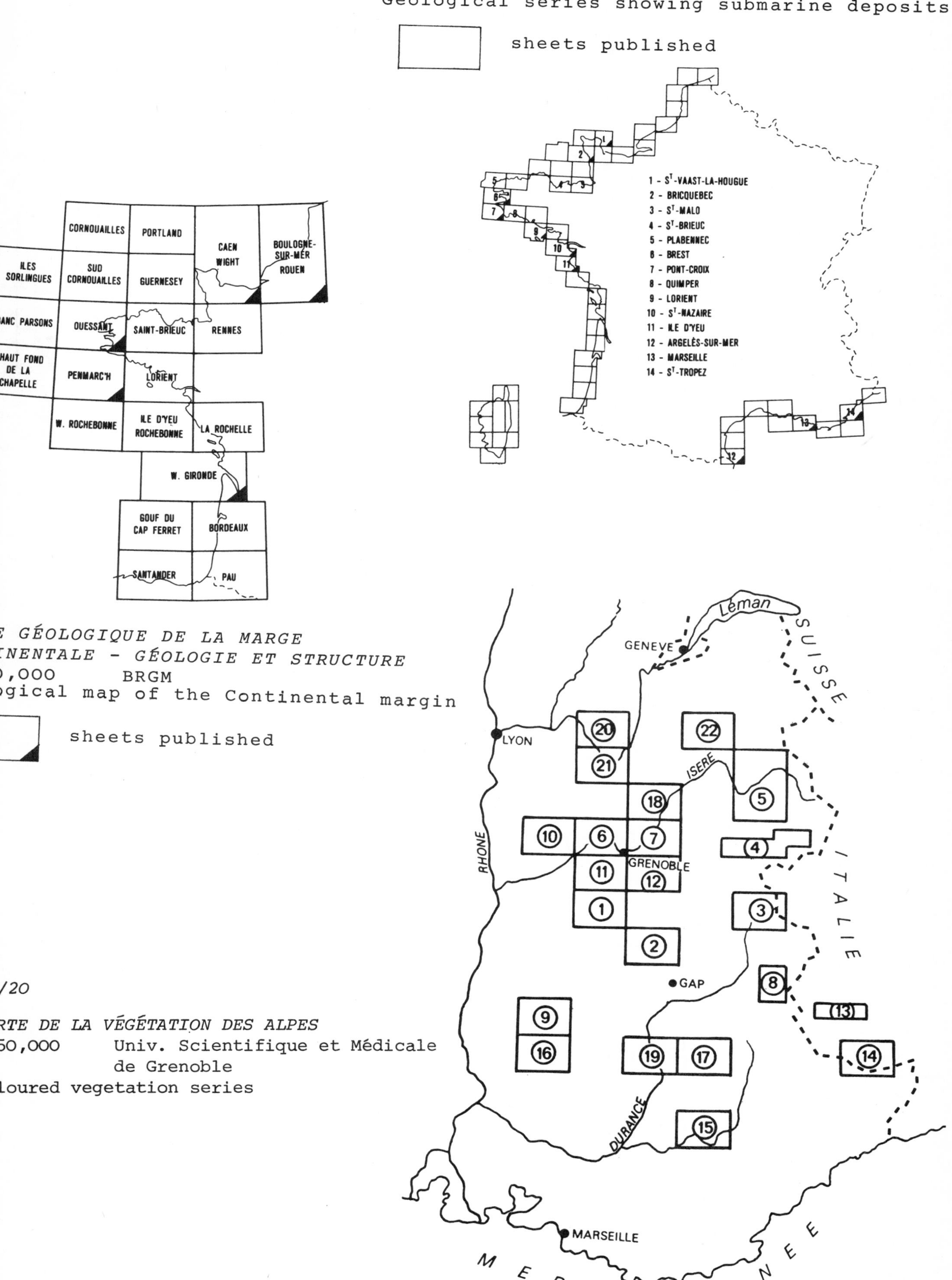

E GÉOLOGIQUE DE LA MARGE
INENTALE - GÉOLOGIE ET STRUCTURE
),000 BRGM
ogical map of the Continental margin

sheets published

/20

RTE DE LA VÉGÉTATION DES ALPES
50,000 Univ. Scientifique et Médicale de Grenoble
loured vegetation series

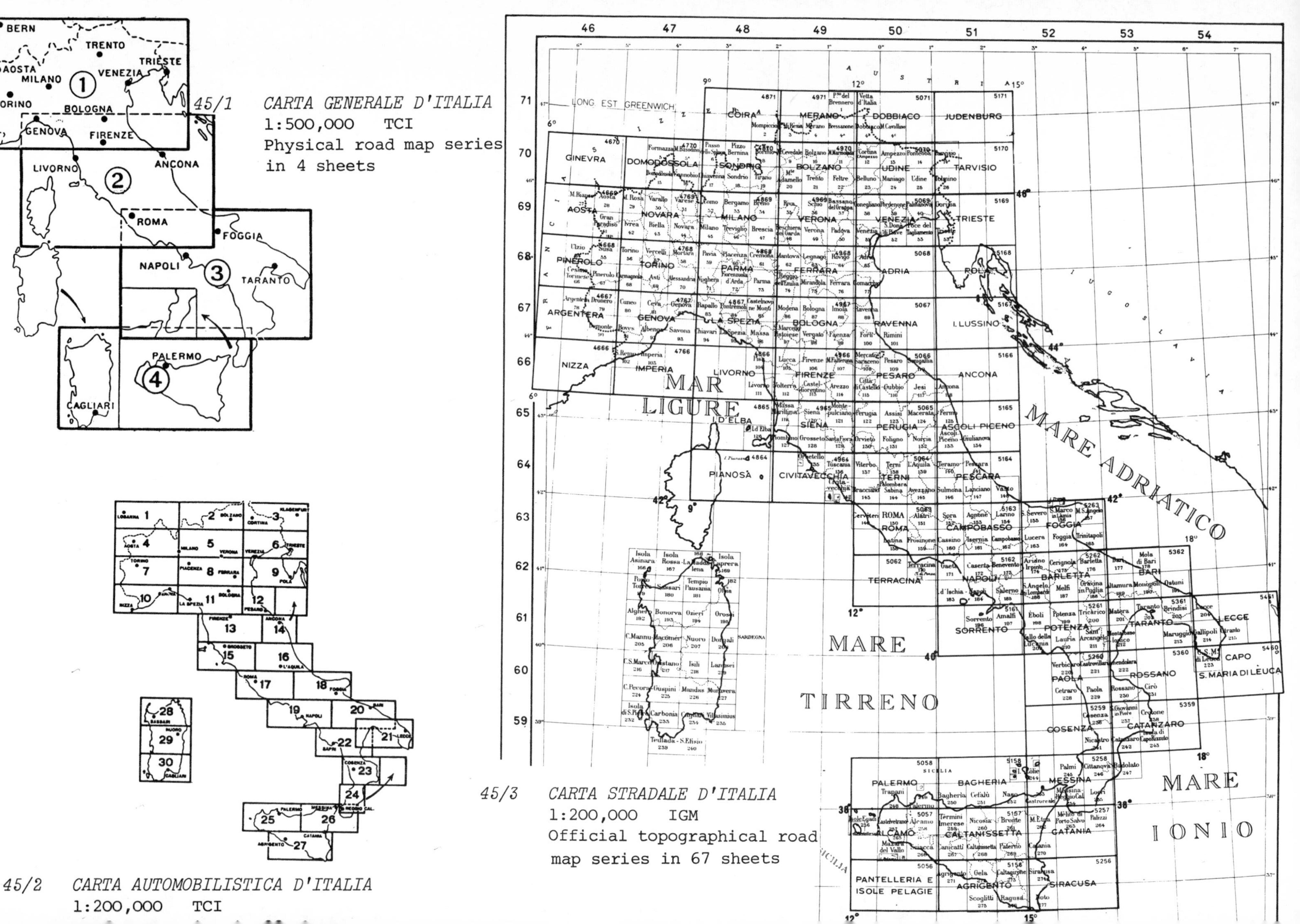

45/1 *CARTA GENERALE D'ITALIA*
1:500,000 TCI
Physical road map series in 4 sheets

45/2 *CARTA AUTOMOBILISTICA D'ITALIA*
1:200,000 TCI

45/3 *CARTA STRADALE D'ITALIA*
1:200,000 IGM
Official topographical road map series in 67 sheets

45/4 *CARTA TOPOGRAFICA D'ITALIA*

1:100,000 IGM

Official topographical series. All sheets published

Vynilite relief maps published

CARTA ARCHEOLOGICA

1:100,000 IGM

Archeological series in progress

Sheets published

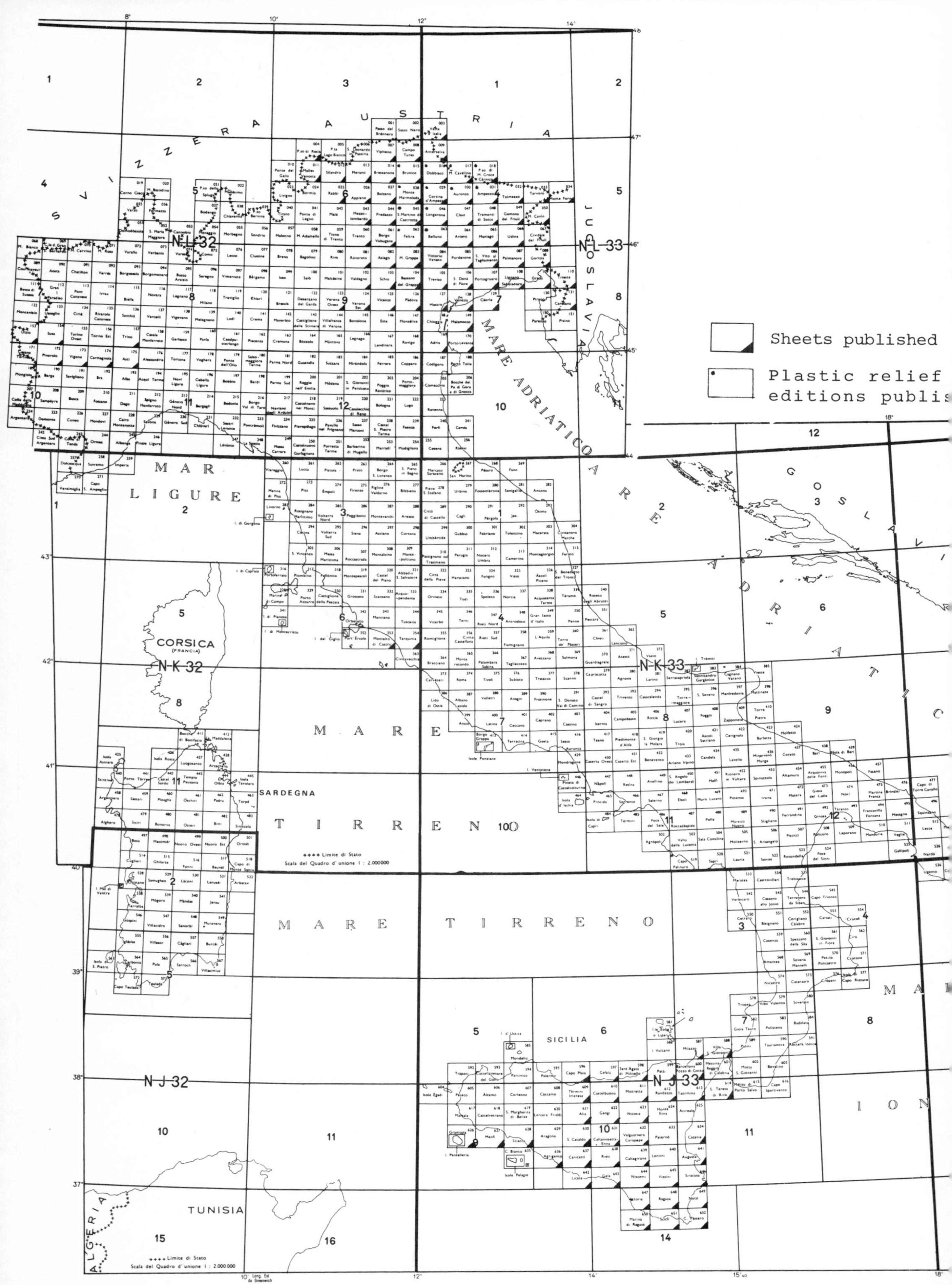

45/5 *CARTA TOPOGRAFICA D'ITALIA*

1:50,000 IGM

New official topographical series in prepara

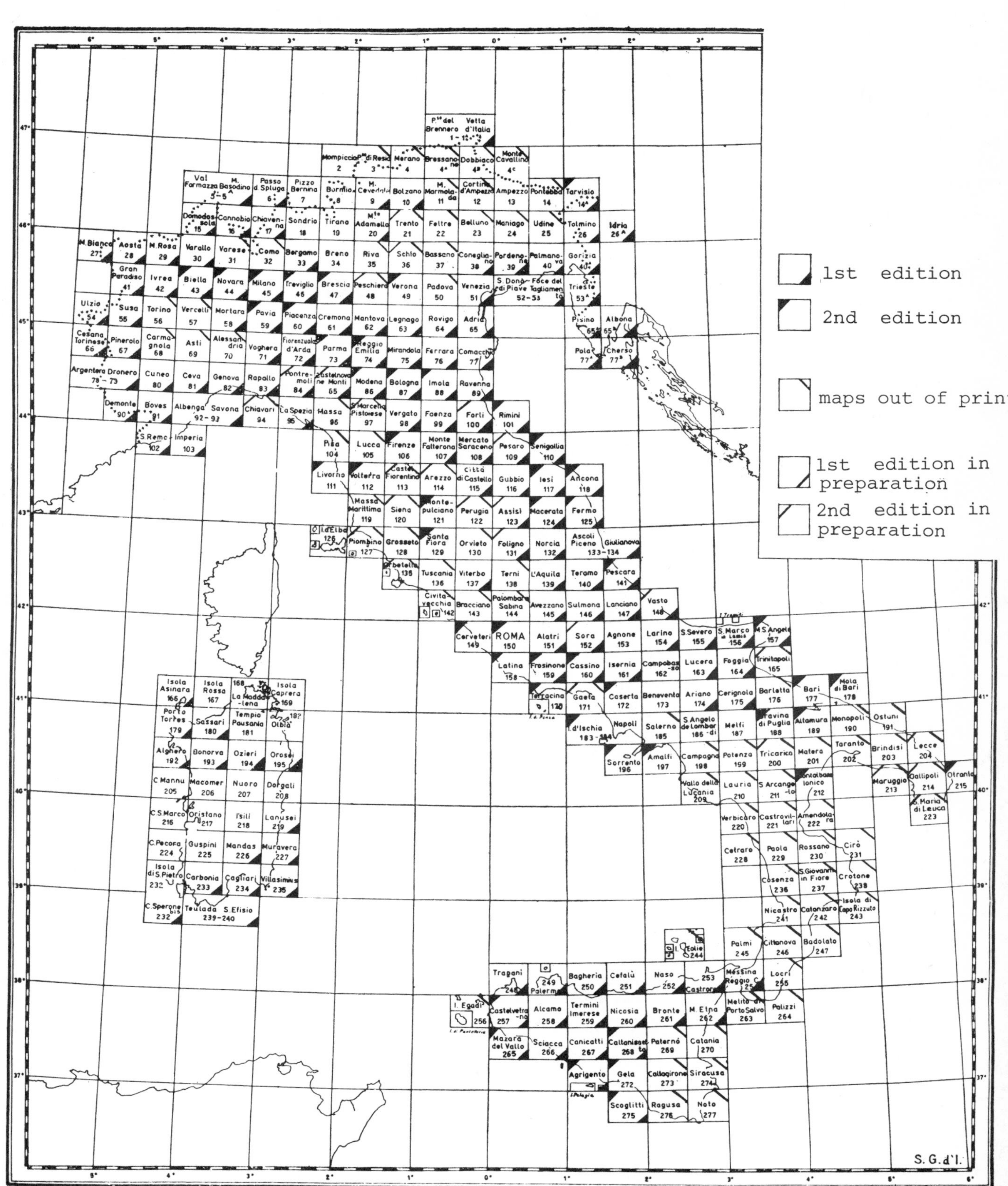

45/6 CARTA GEOLOGICA D'ITALIA

1:100,000

Coloured geological series

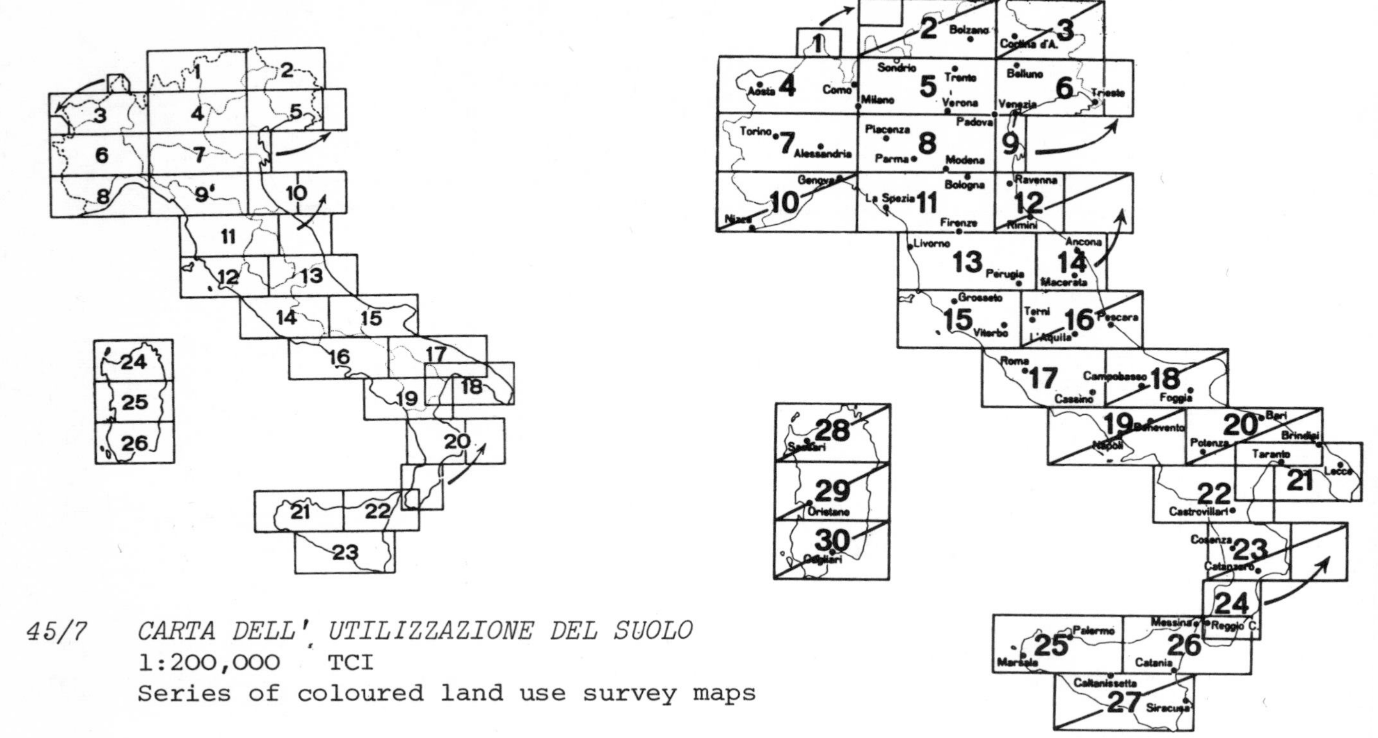

45/7 *CARTA DELL' UTILIZZAZIONE DEL SUOLO*
1:200,000 TCI
Series of coloured land use survey maps

45/8 *CARTA DELLE ZONE ARCHEOLOGICHE D'ITALIA*
1:200,000 TCI
Series of archaeological maps

Sheets published

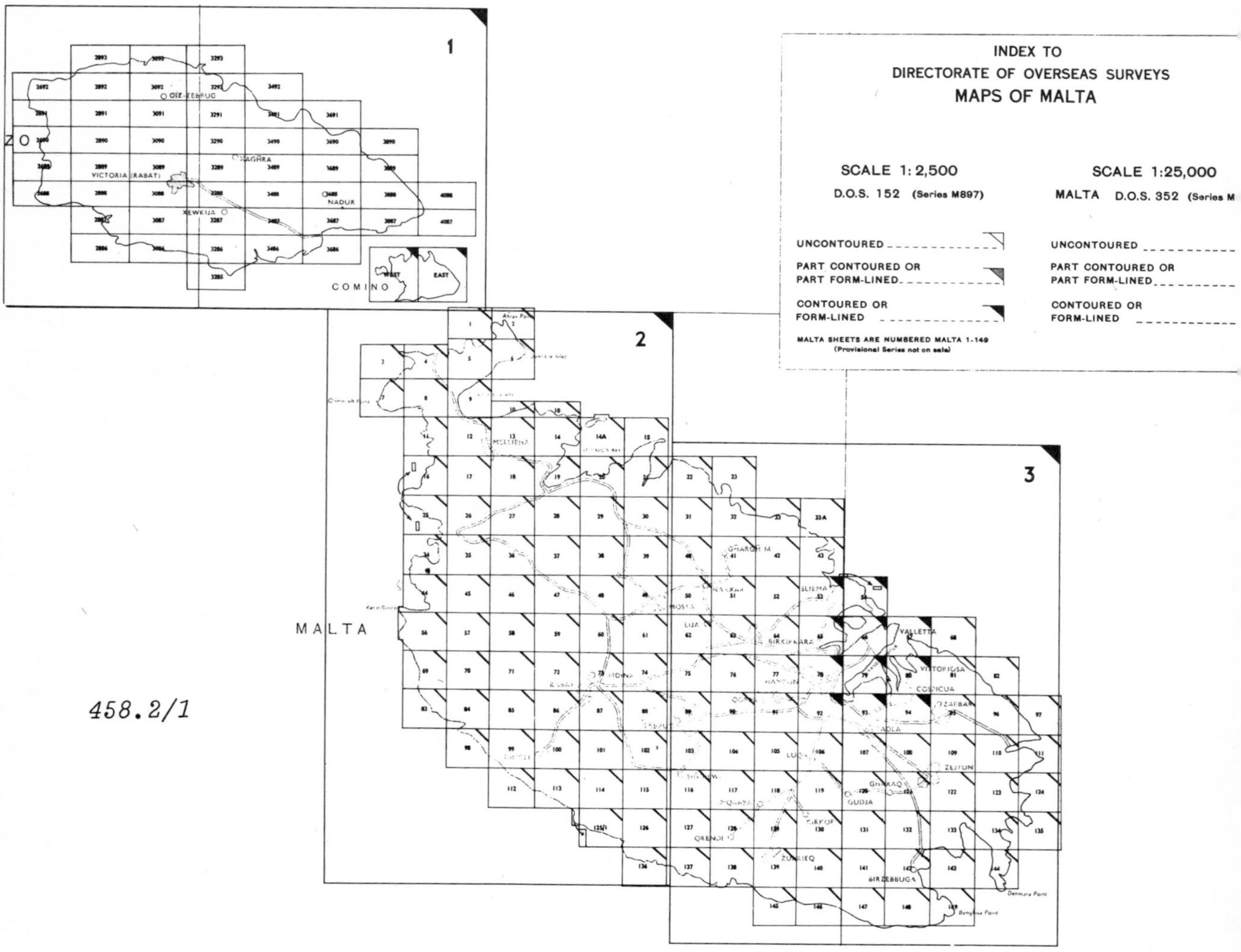

INDEX TO
DIRECTORATE OF OVERSEAS SURVEYS
MAPS OF MALTA

SCALE 1:2,500 D.O.S. 152 (Series M897)	SCALE 1:25,000 MALTA D.O.S. 352 (Series M
UNCONTOURED	UNCONTOURED
PART CONTOURED OR PART FORM-LINED	PART CONTOURED OR PART FORM-LINED
CONTOURED OR FORM-LINED	CONTOURED OR FORM-LINED

MALTA SHEETS ARE NUMBERED MALTA 1-149
(Provisional Series not on sale)

GOZO
VICTORIA (RABAT)
XAGHRA
NADUR
XEWKIJA
COMINO
MALTA
VALLETTA
SLIEMA
BIRKIRKARA
MOSTA
COSPICUA
ZURRIEQ
BIRZEBBUGA

458.2/1

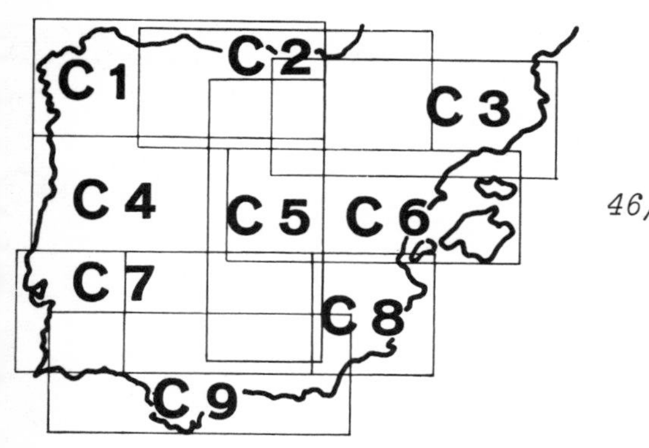

46/1 *FIRESTONE HISPANIA - MAPAS DE CARRETERAS*
1:500,000 Firestone
Road map series covering Spain and Portugal

460/1

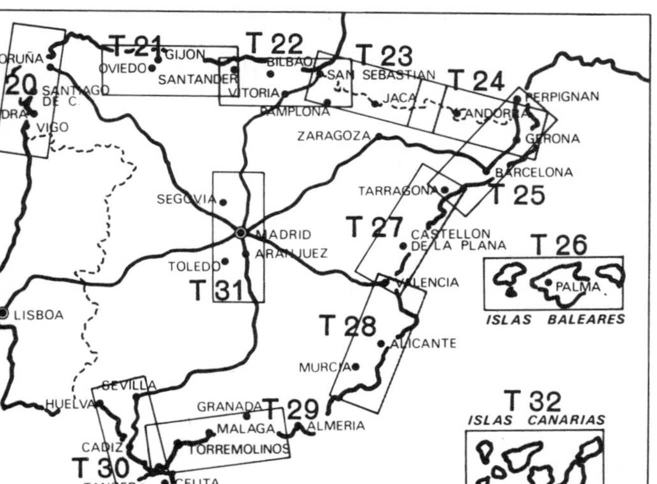

FIRESTONE HISPANIA - MAPAS TURISTICOS
1:200,000 - 1:175,000 Firestone
Series of tourist road maps with brief guide sheets available:

T-20	RIAS GALLEGAS
T-21	COSTA VERDE-PICOS DE EUROPA
T-22	CORNISA CANTABRICA
T-23	PIRINEO OCCIDENTAL
T-24	PIRINEO ORIENTAL
T-25	COSTA BRAVA
T-26	ISLAS BALEARES (1:175,000)
T-27	COSTA DORADA-COSTA DEL AZAHAR
T-28	COSTA BLANCA-COSTA DE LEVANTE
T-29	COSTA DEL SOL
T-30	COSTA DE LA LUZ-COSTA COLOMBINAS
T-31	MADRID Y ALREDEDORES (1:175,000)
T-32	ISLAS CANARIAS (1:150,000-1:400,000)

460/2 *MAPA TOPOGRAFICO DE LAS CORDILLERAS PIRENAICA, CENTRAL*
1:25,000-1:40,000
Series of large scale walking maps of the central Pyrenees

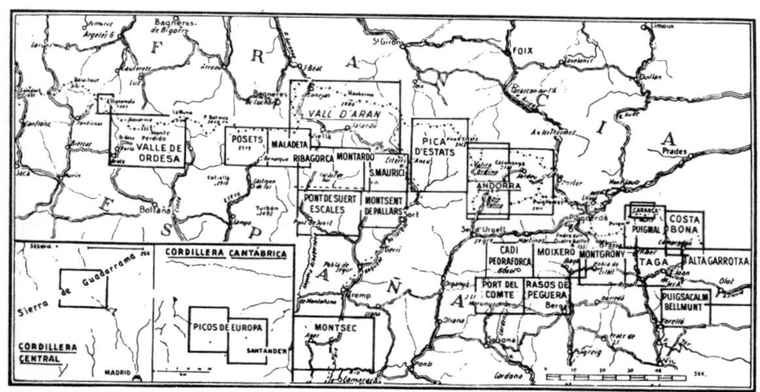

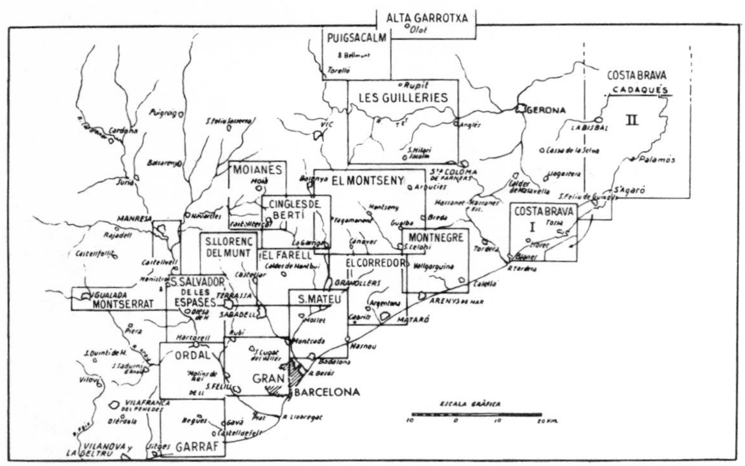

460/3 MAPA TOPOGRÁFICO DE CATALUÑA
1:25,000-1:40,000   Ed. Alpina
Series of large scale walking maps of the Catalonian coast

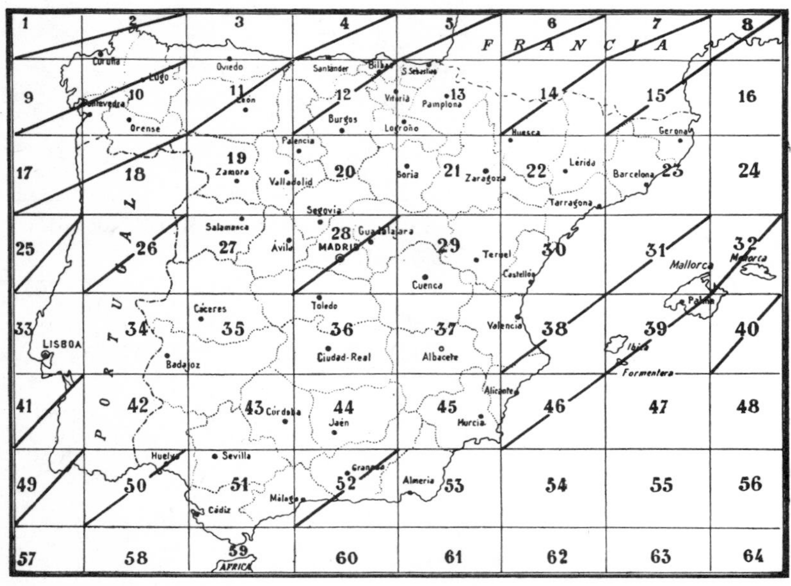

460/7 MAPA GEOLOGICO DE ESPAÑA
1:400,000
Coloured geological series in progress

Sheets published (5th edition)

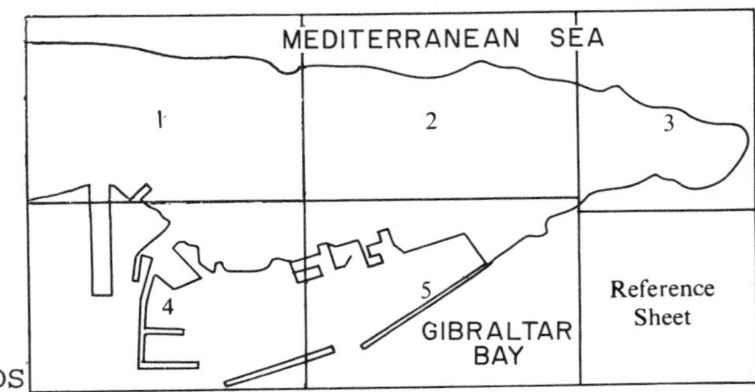

468.2/1 GIBRALTAR
1:2,500   Gib. Gov't - DOS
Large scale planimetric series in 6 sheets including legend

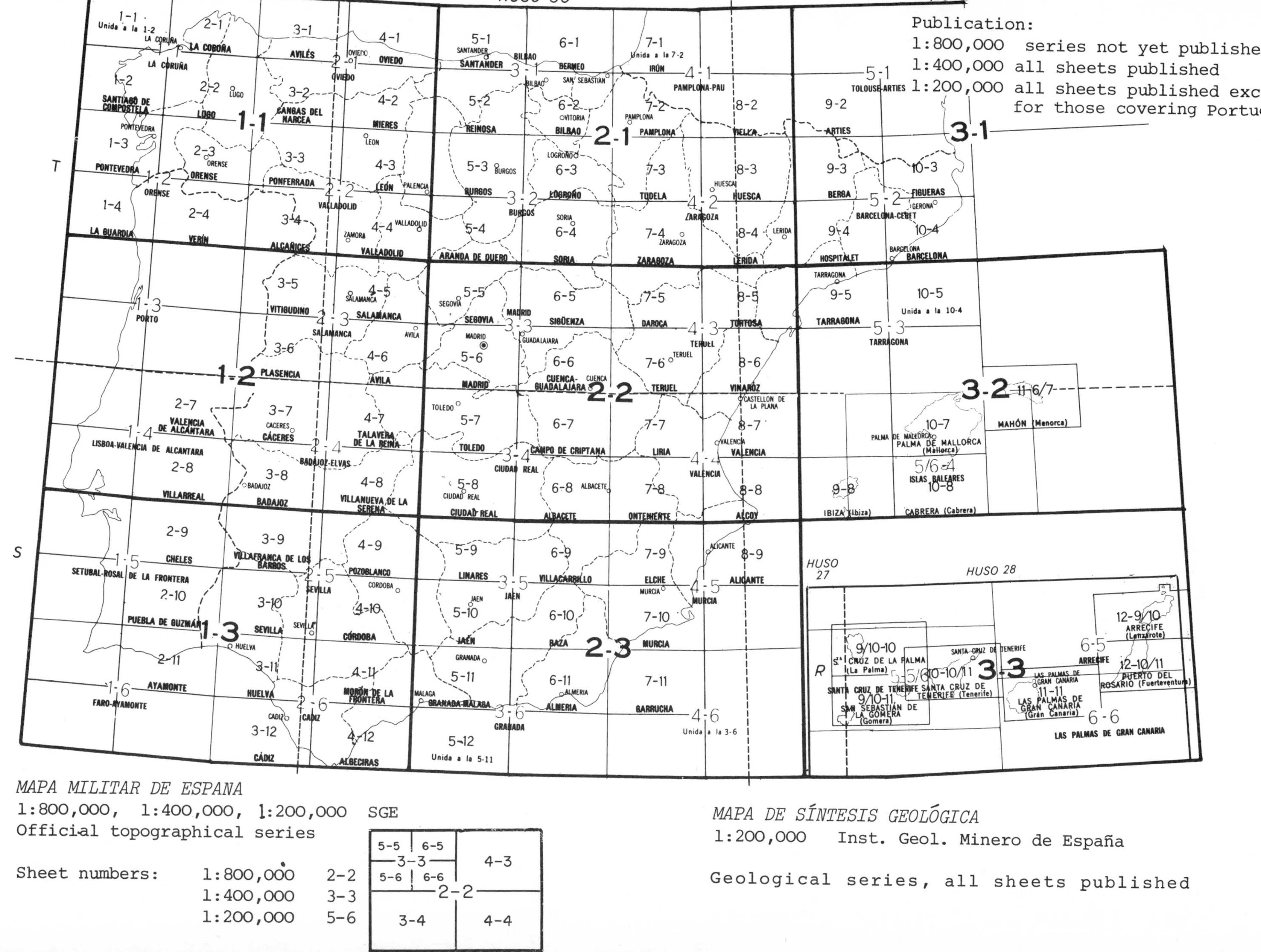

460/4 *MAPA MILITAR DE ESPANA*

1:800,000, 1:400,000, 1:200,000 SGE

Official topographical series

Sheet numbers:

1:800,000	2-2
1:400,000	3-3
1:200,000	5-6

MAPA DE SÍNTESIS GEOLÓGICA

1:200,000 Inst. Geol. Minero de España

Geological series, all sheets published

460/5 *MAPA MILITAR DE ESPAÑA, SERIE C*

1:100,000 SGE

Official topographical series

Sheets published

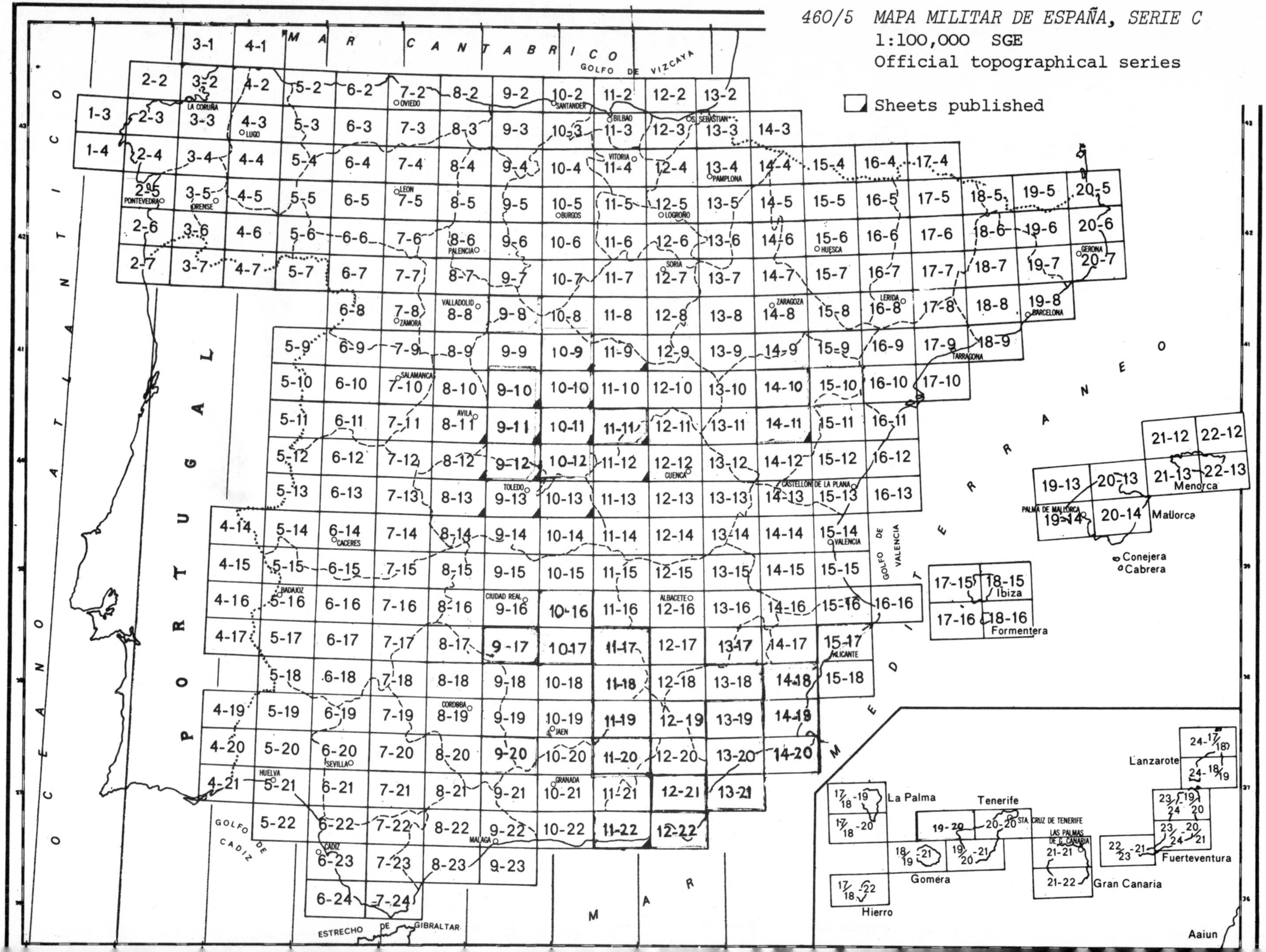

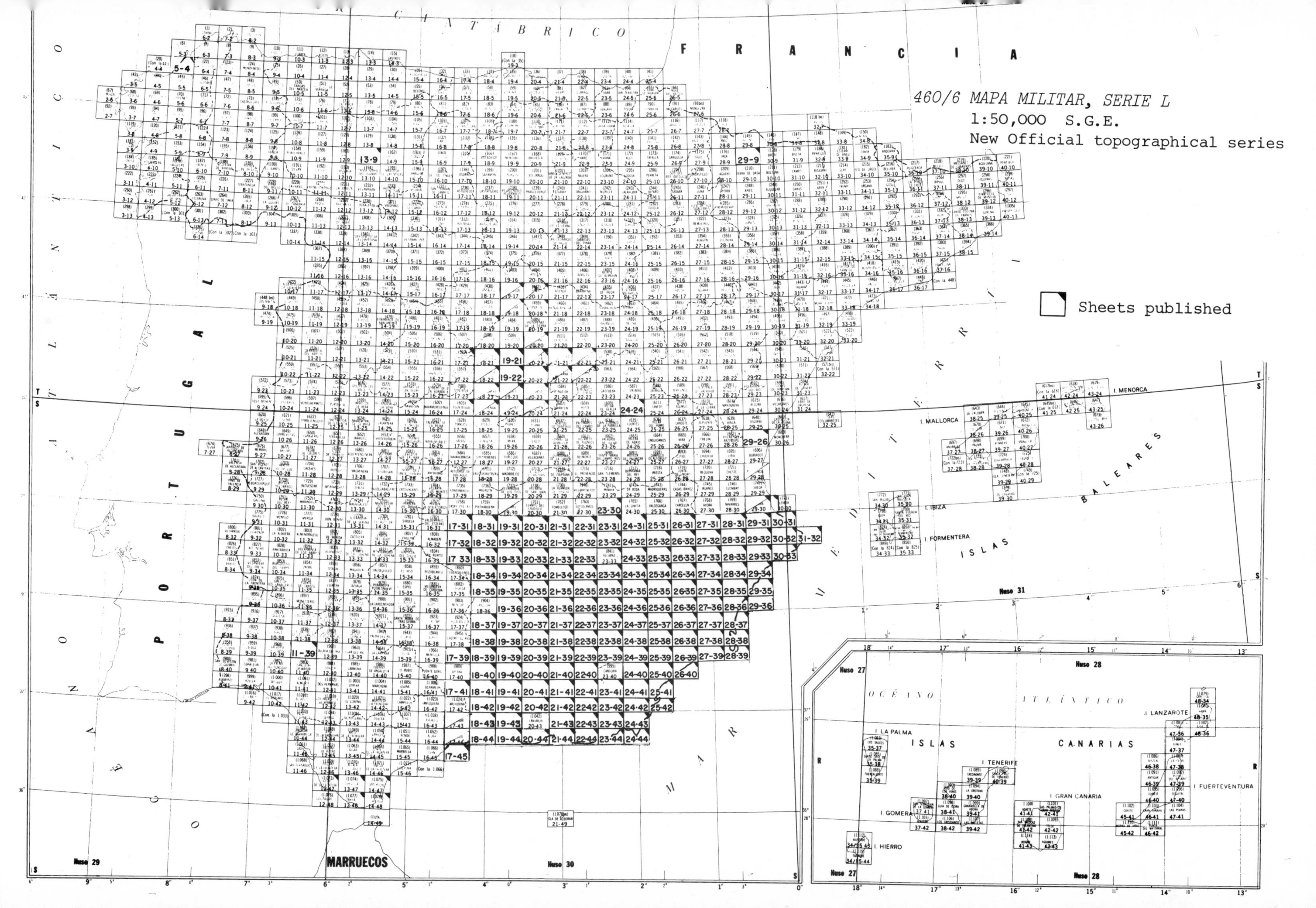

460/6 MAPA MILITAR, SERIE L
1:50,000 S.G.E.
New Official topographical series
Sheets published
FRANCIA
PORTUGAL
MARRUECOS
ISLAS BALEARES
I. MENORCA
I. MALLORCA
I. IBIZA
I. FORMENTERA
ISLAS CANARIAS
I. LANZAROTE
I. FUERTEVENTURA
I. GRAN CANARIA
I. TENERIFE
I. LA PALMA
I. GOMERA
I. HIERRO
Huso 27
Huso 28
Huso 29
Huso 30
Huso 31

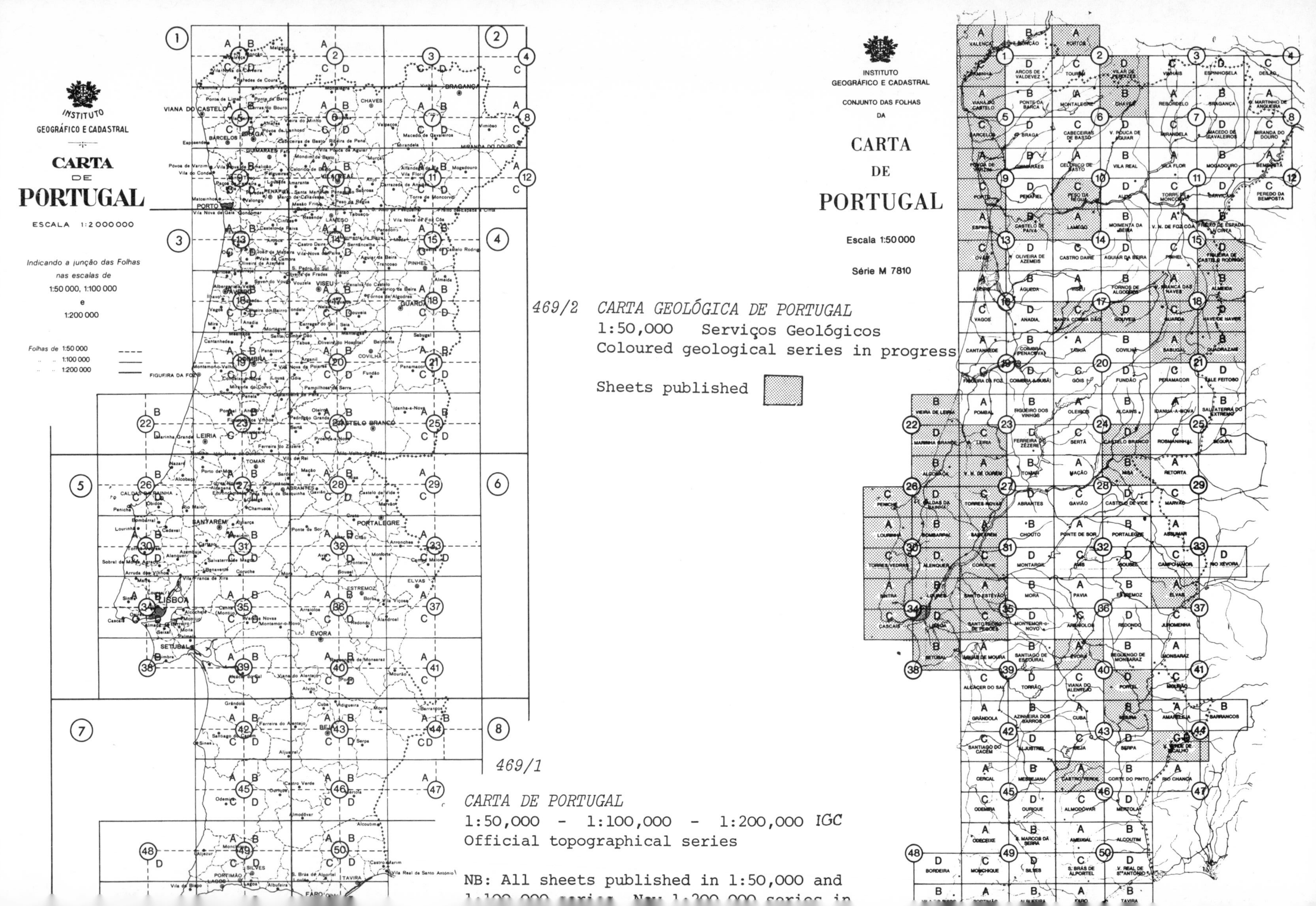

469/2

CARTA GEOLÓGICA DE PORTUGAL
1:50,000 Serviços Geológicos
Coloured geological series in progress

Sheets published

469/1

CARTA DE PORTUGAL
1:50,000 - 1:100,000 - 1:200,000 *IGC*
Official topographical series

NB: All sheets published in 1:50,000 and 1:100,000 series. New 1:200,000 series in

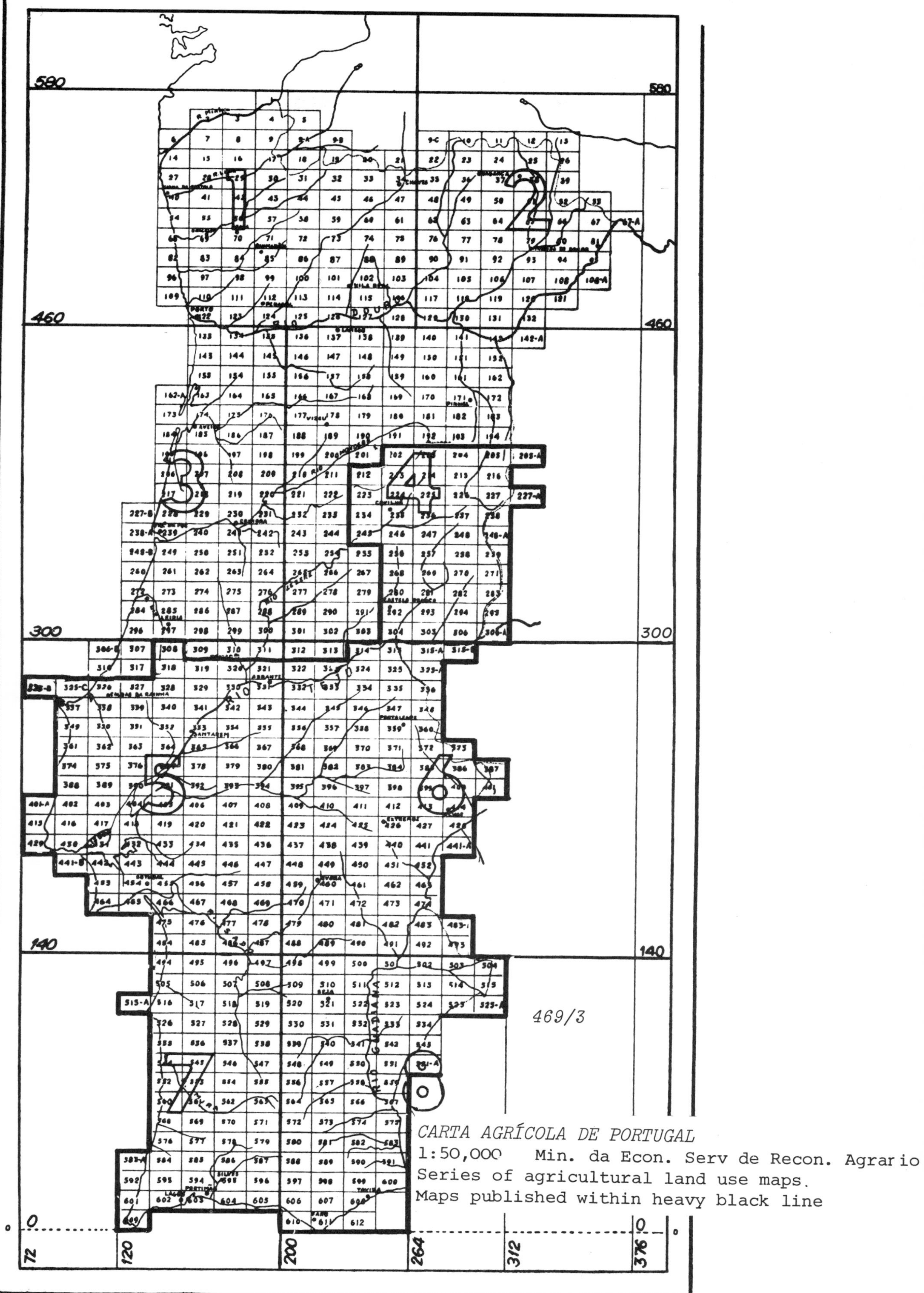

CARTA AGRÍCOLA DE PORTUGAL
1:50,000 Min. da Econ. Serv de Recon. Agrario
Series of agricultural land use maps.
Maps published within heavy black line

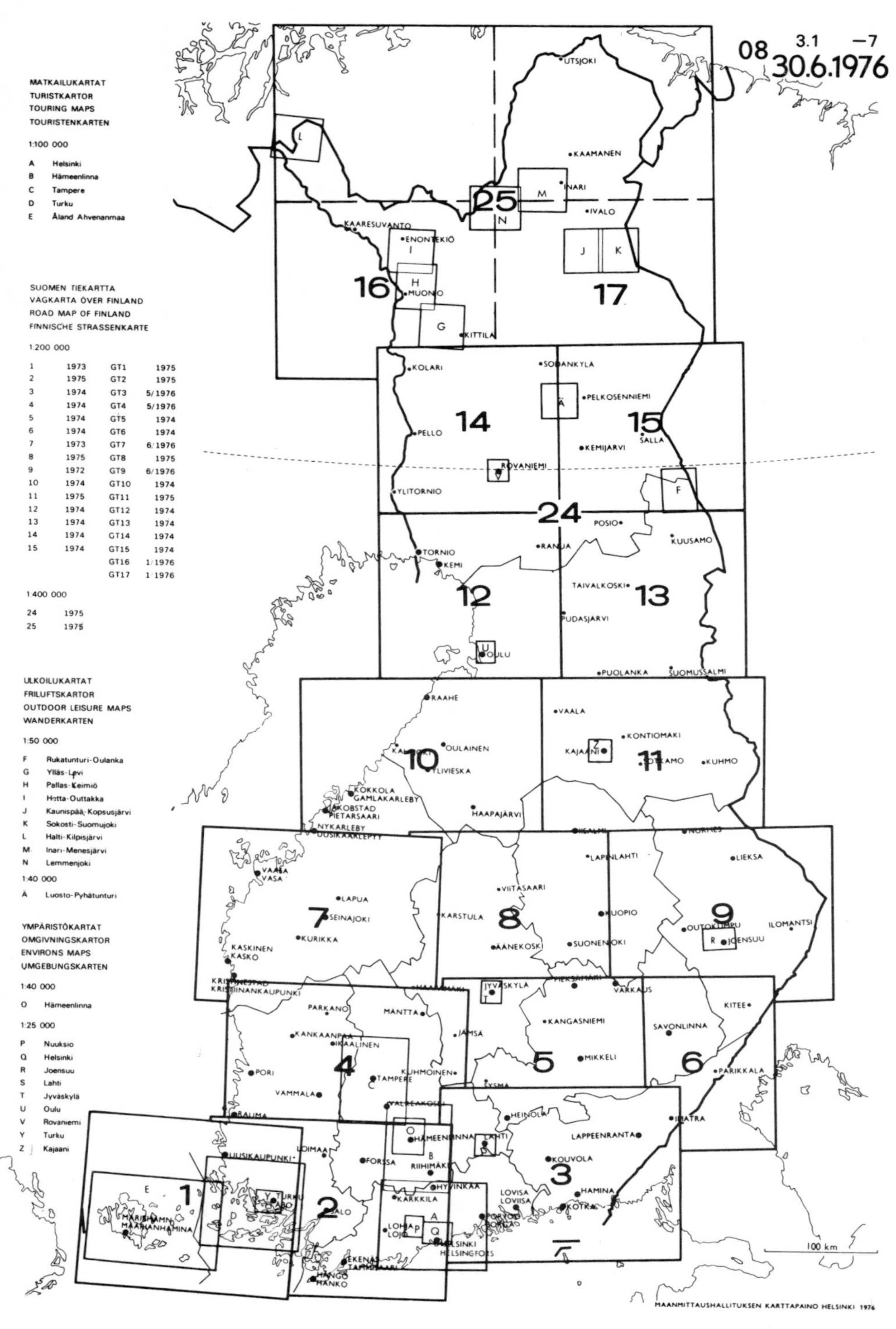

480/1 FINLAND *SUOMEN TIEKARTTA*
1:200,000 - 1:400,000
Road map series

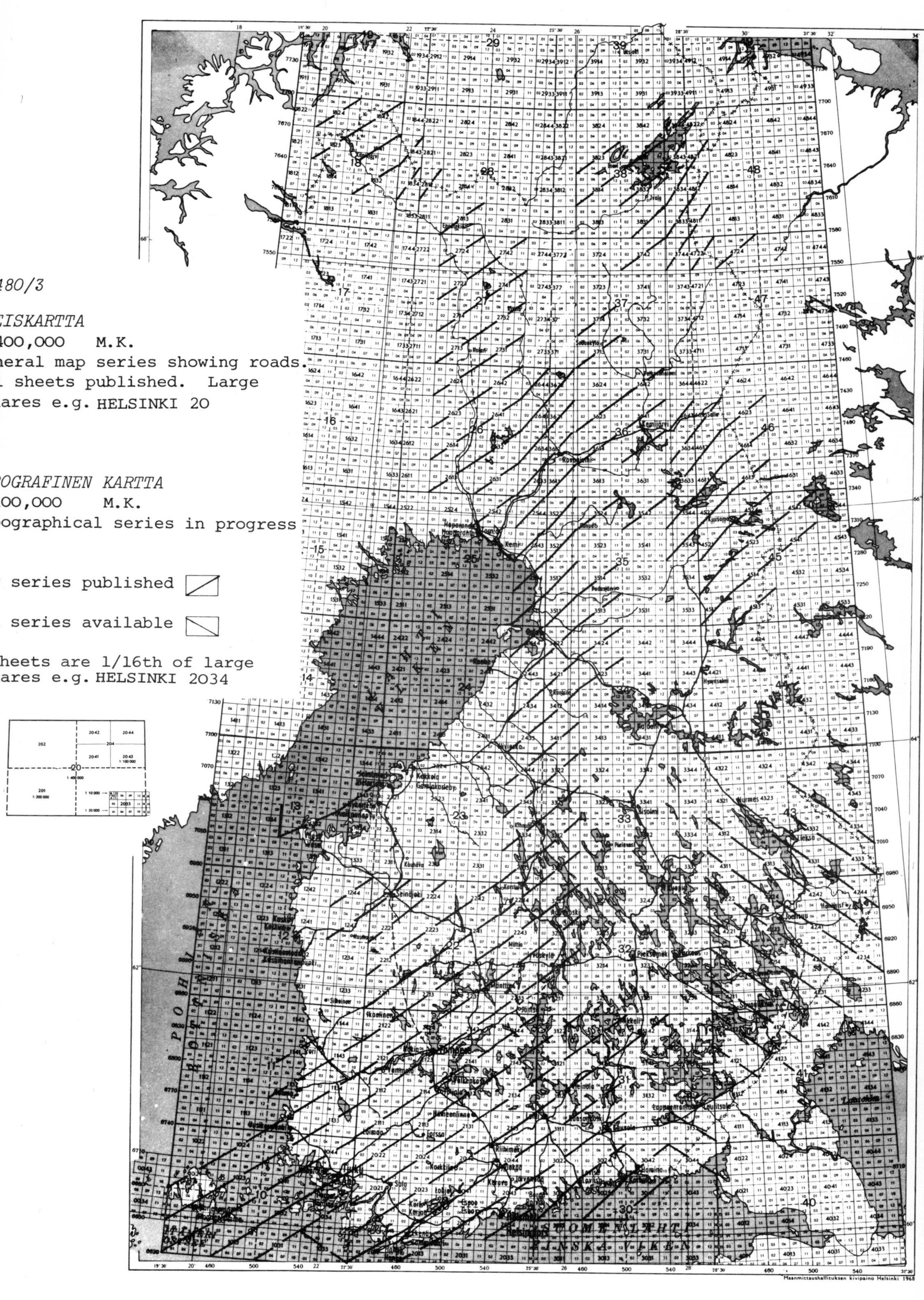

180/3
ISKARTTA
400,000 M.K.
ieral map series showing roads.
sheets published. Large
ares e.g. HELSINKI 20
OGRAFINEN KARTTA
00,000 M.K.
ographical series in progress
series published
series available
heets are 1/16th of large
ares e.g. HELSINKI 2034
Maanmittaushallituksen kivipaino Helsinki 1968

481/1 NORGE - BIL OG TURISTKART
1:325,000 - 1:400,000 Cappelen
Detailed tourist road map series

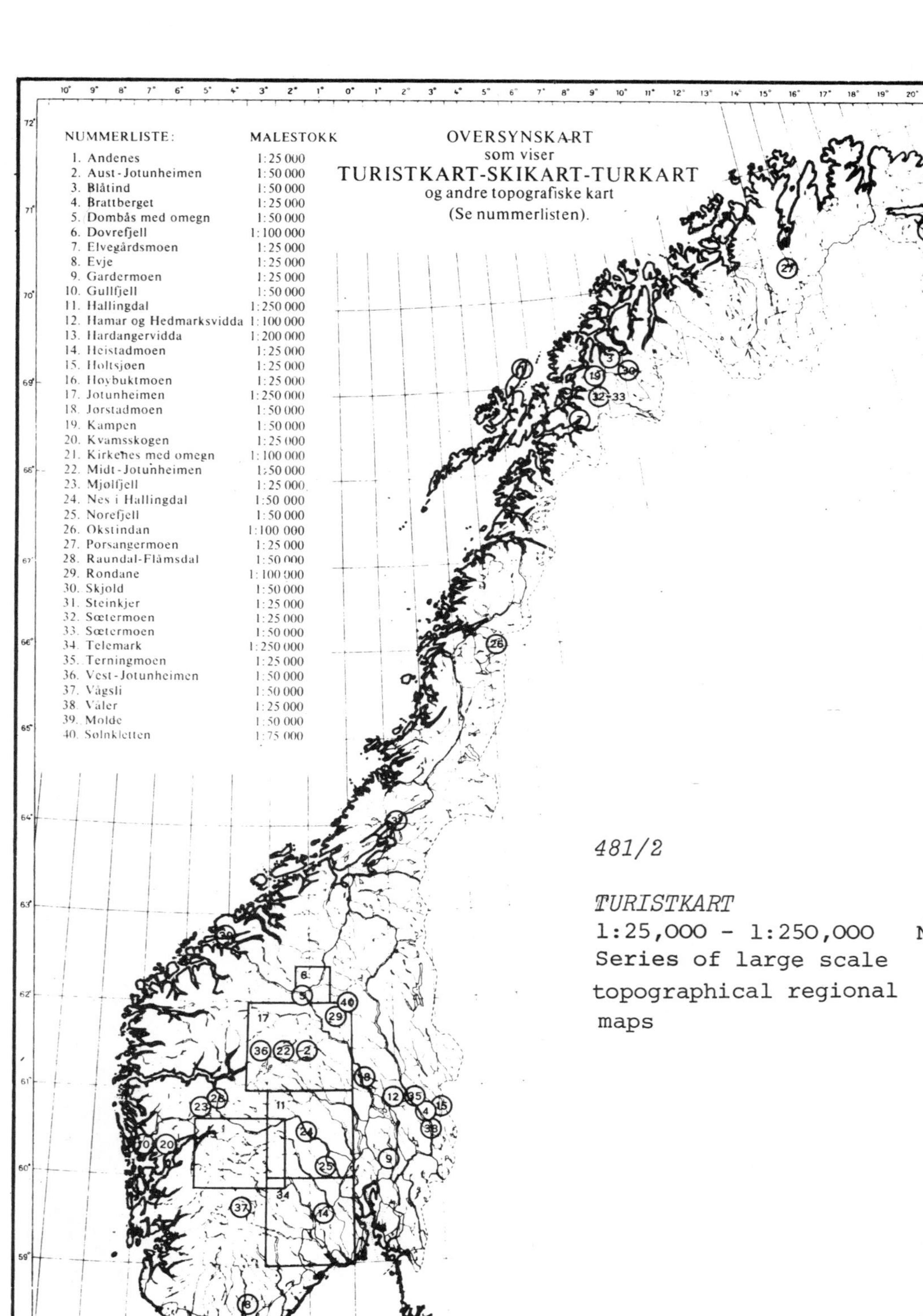

481/2

TURISTKART
1:25,000 - 1:250,000
Series of large scale topographical regional maps

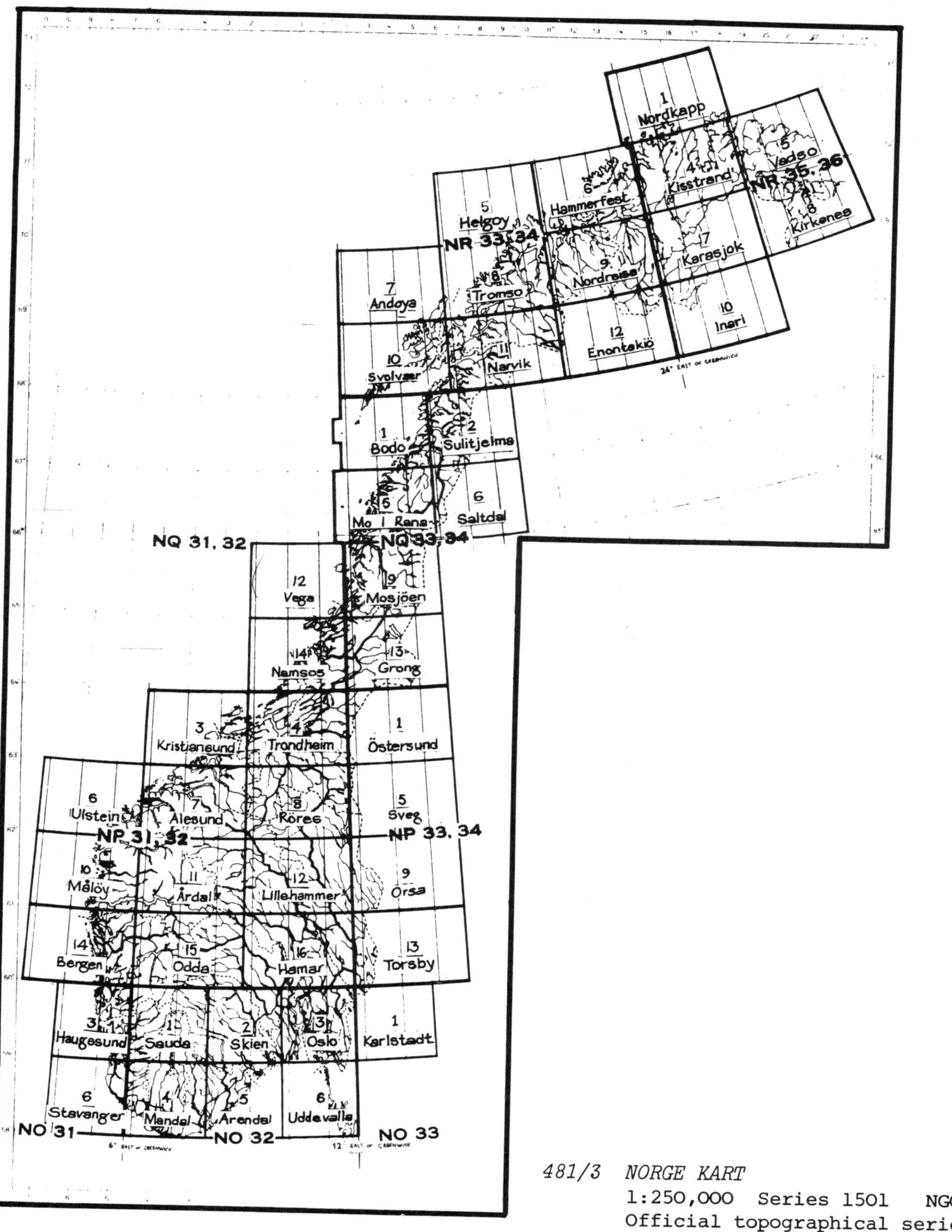

481/3 NORGE KART

1:250,000 Series 1501 NGO

Official topographical series

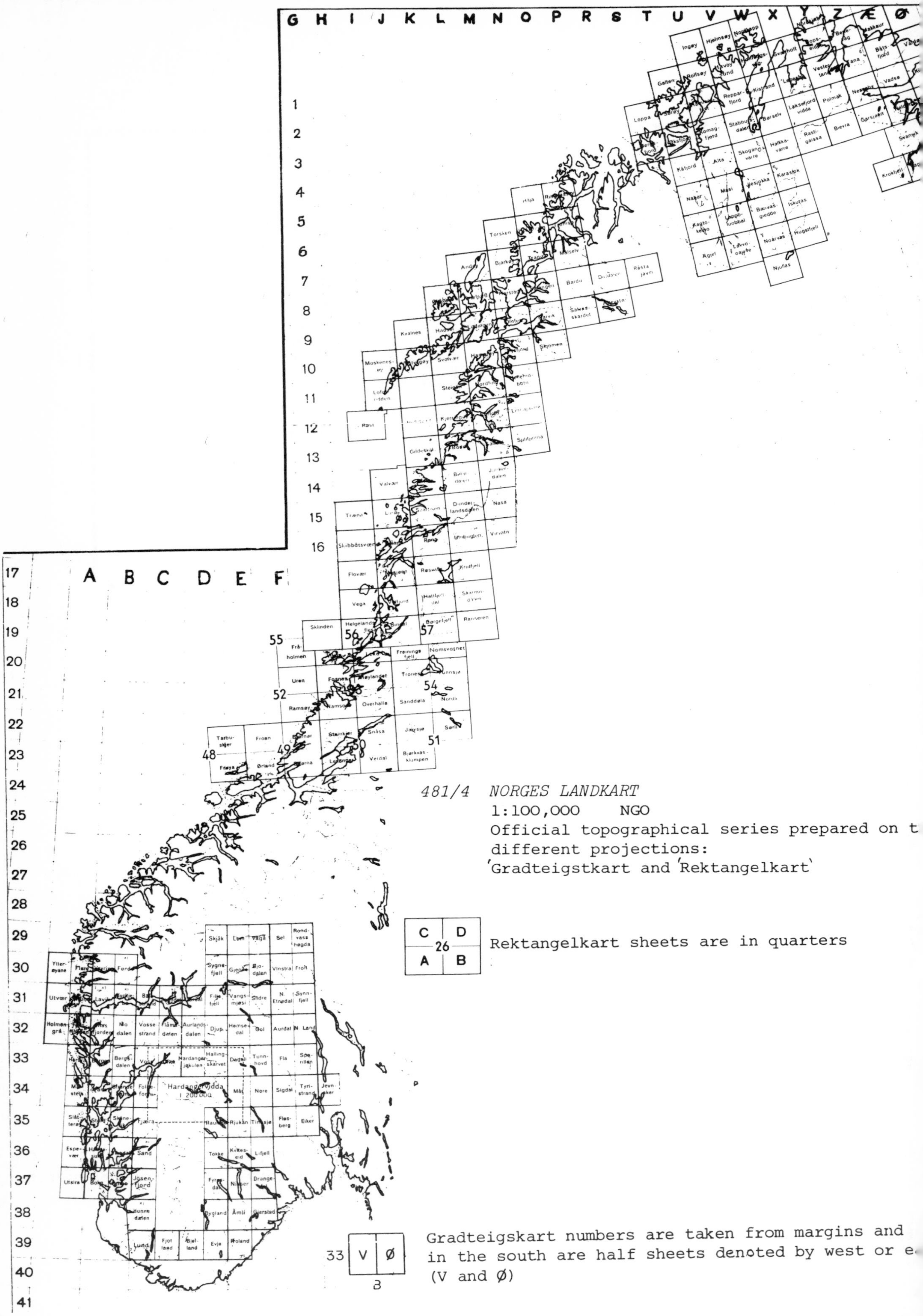

481/4 NORGES LANDKART
1:100,000 NGO
Official topographical series prepared on t
different projections:
'Gradteigstkart and 'Rektangelkart'

C	D
A	B

26

Rektangelkart sheets are in quarters

33 | V | Ø | 3

Gradteigskart numbers are taken from margins and
in the south are half sheets denoted by west or e
(V and Ø)

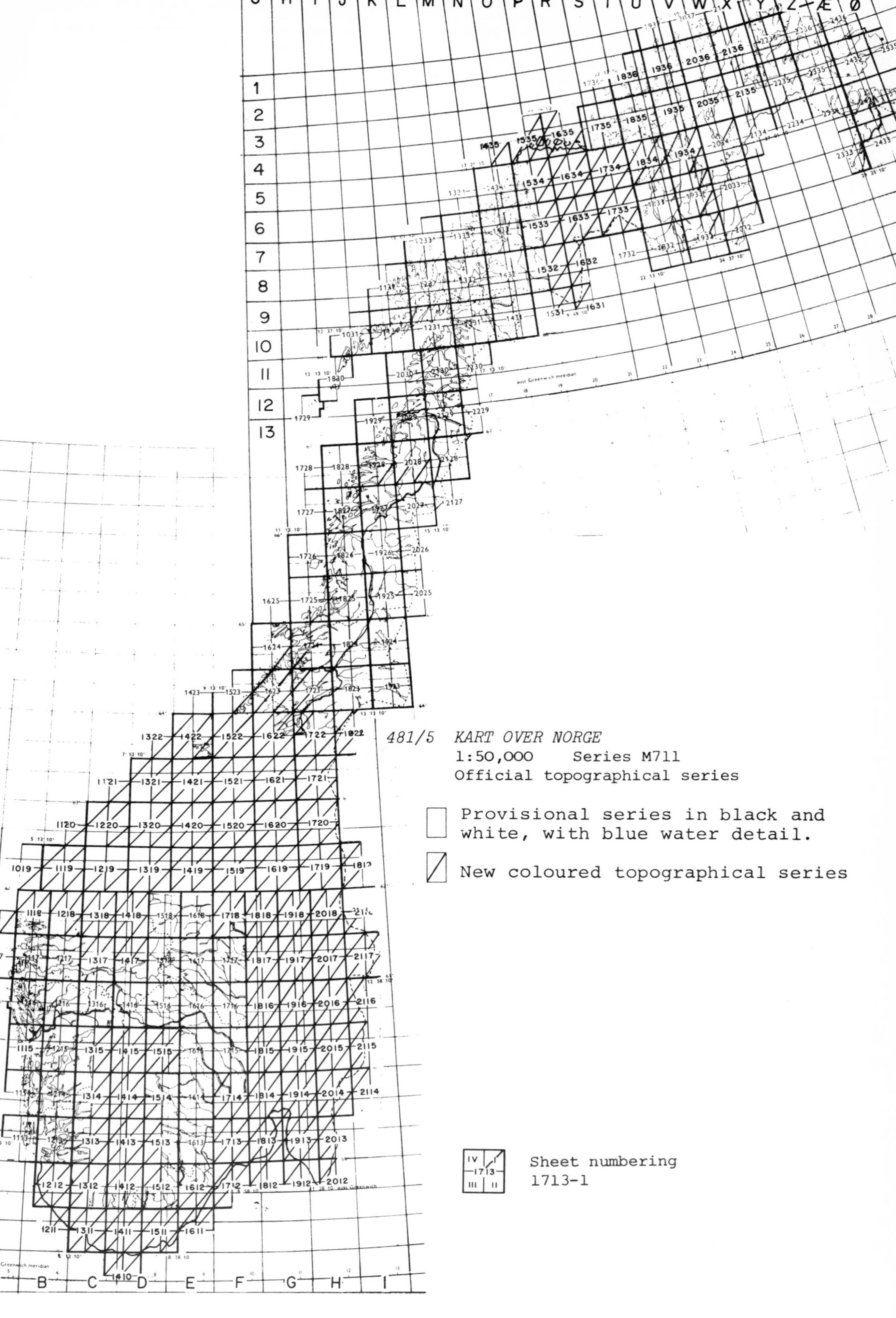
481/5 KART OVER NORGE
1:50,000 Series M711
Official topographical series
Provisional series in black and white, with blue water detail.
New coloured topographical series
Sheet numbering
1713-1
IV I
1713
III II

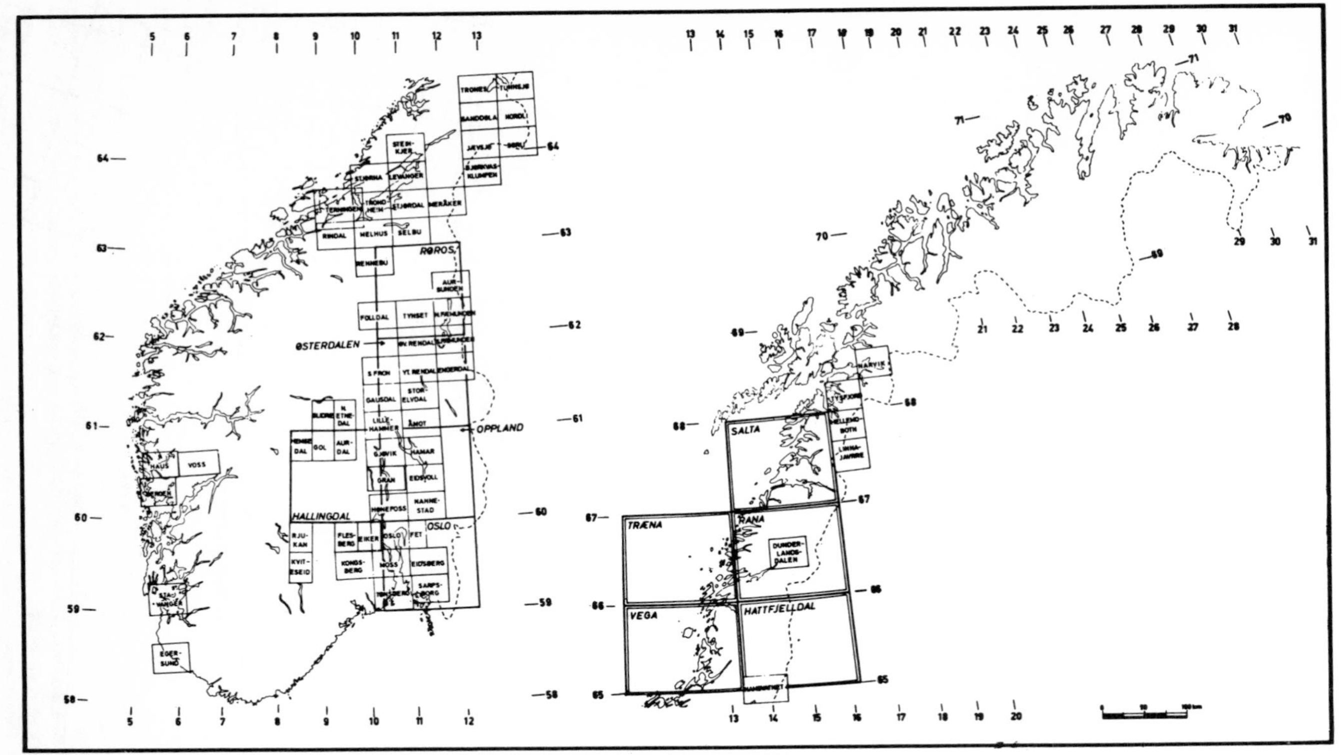

481/6 *GEOLOKISK KART*
1:250,000 - 1:100,000
Coloured geological series
Berggrunskart

Berggrunnskart 1:100,000	Pre-Quaternary Rocks
Kvartærgeologisk kart 1:250 000	Quaternary Rocks
Berggrunnskart (gammel serie) 1:250 000 (old series)	Pre-Quaternary Rocks—old series

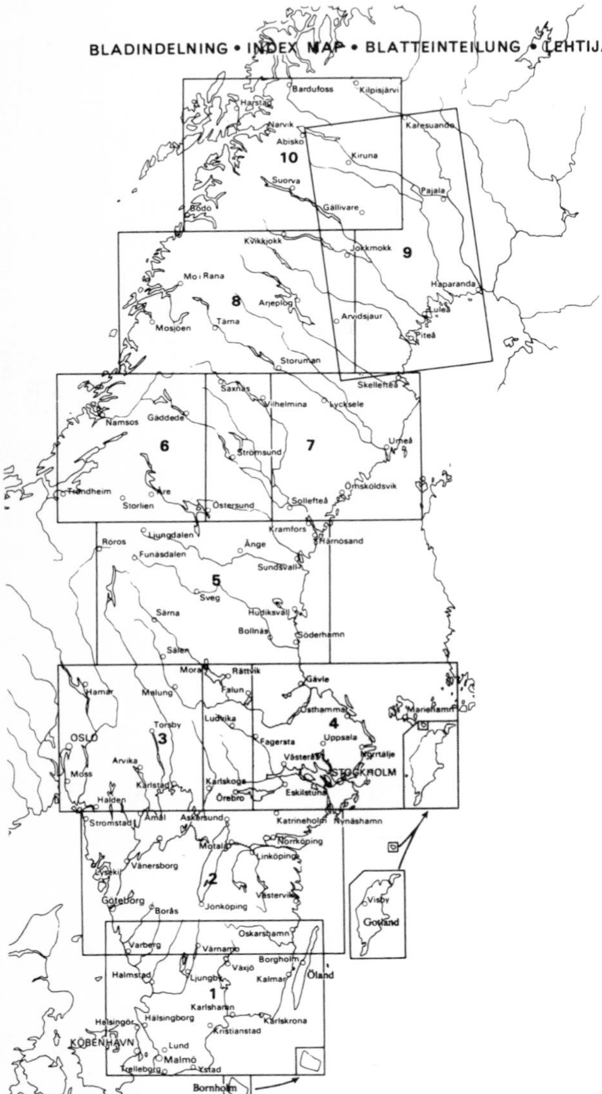

BLADINDELNING • INDEX MAP • BLATTEINTEILUNG • LEHTIJAKO

485/1 *SVENSKA TURISTKARTAN*
1:300,000 G.L.A.
Tourist road map series

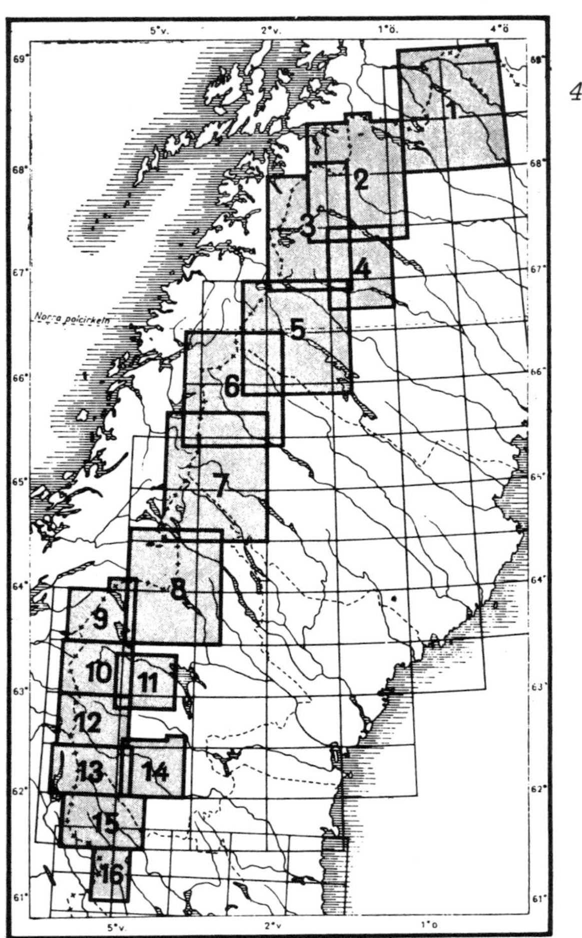

485/2 *SVENSKA FJÄLLKARTAN*
1:200,000 S.R.A.
Swedish mountain maps black and white with footpaths in red

485/3 *SVENSKA NYA FJÄLLKARTAN*
1:100,000 S.R.A.
Swedish mountain maps in colour, contoured with footpaths marked

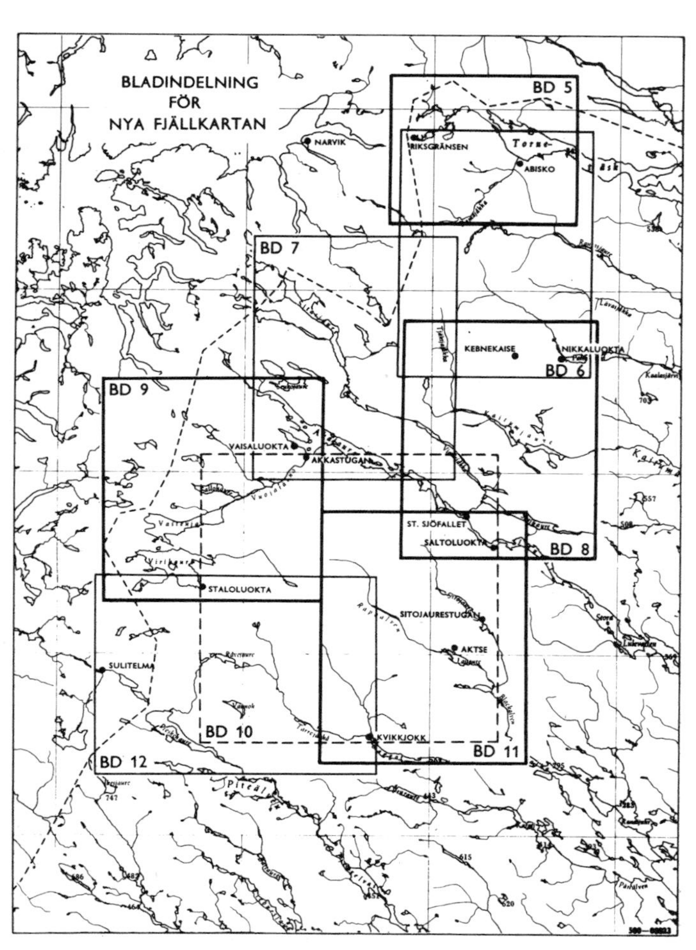

485/4 *PROVISORISKA ÖVERSIKTSKARTAN*
1:250,000 SRA
Provisional planning series

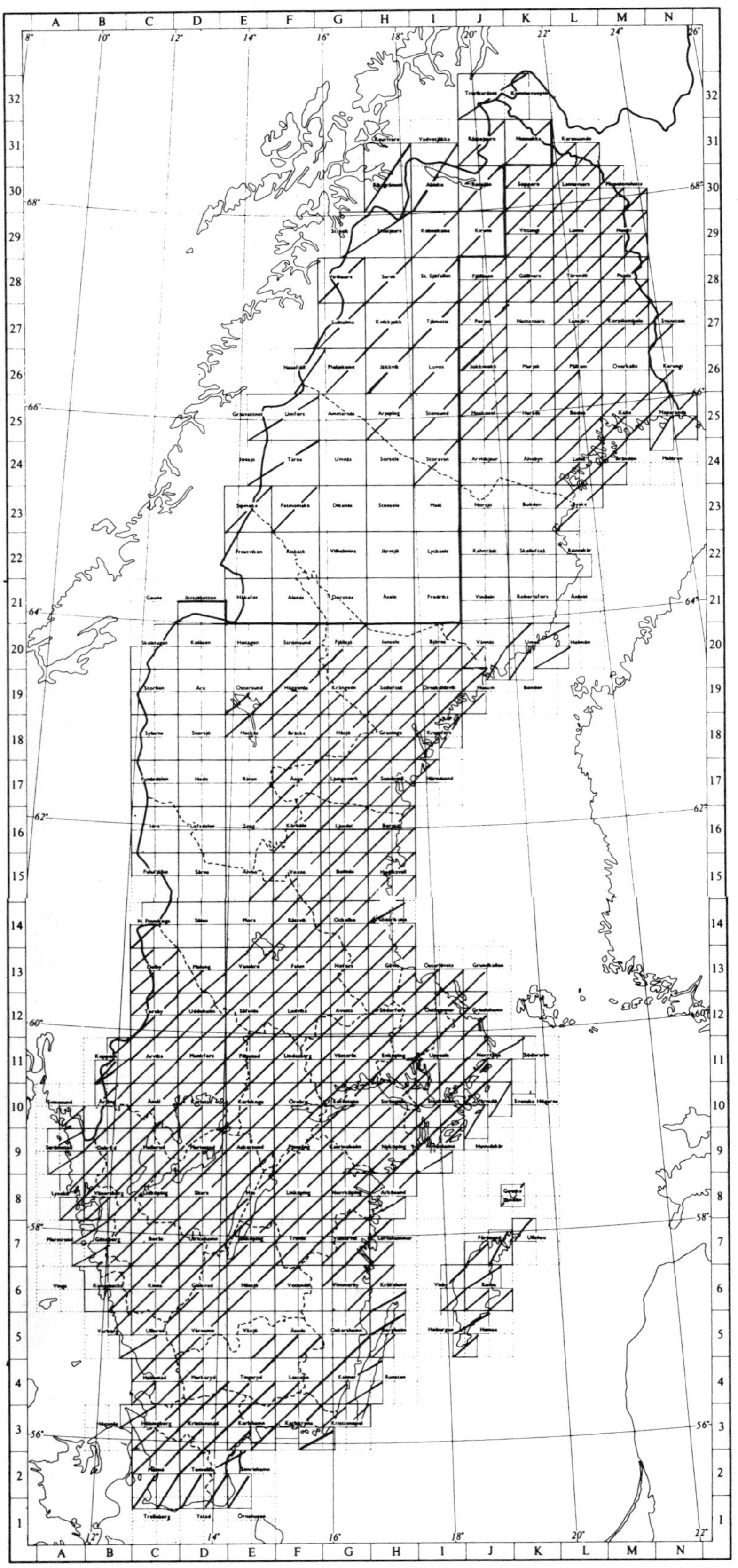

485/5 *TOPOGRAFISKA KARTAN*
1:50,000 - 1:100,000 SRA
Official topographical series

▱ Sheets published

N.B. Maps north of heavy black line on index are published only at 1:100,000

Sheet numbering
1:50,000

I10 NE STOCKHOLM

1:100,000

J29 KIRUNA

485/7 *GENERALSTABENS KARTA OVER NORRA SVERIGE*

1:100,000 SRA

Old topographical series covering northern Sweden

485/8

GEOLOGISKA KARTBLAD

1:50,000 - 1:100,000 - 1:200,000

Coloured geological series, combined quaternary and petrological maps with explanation

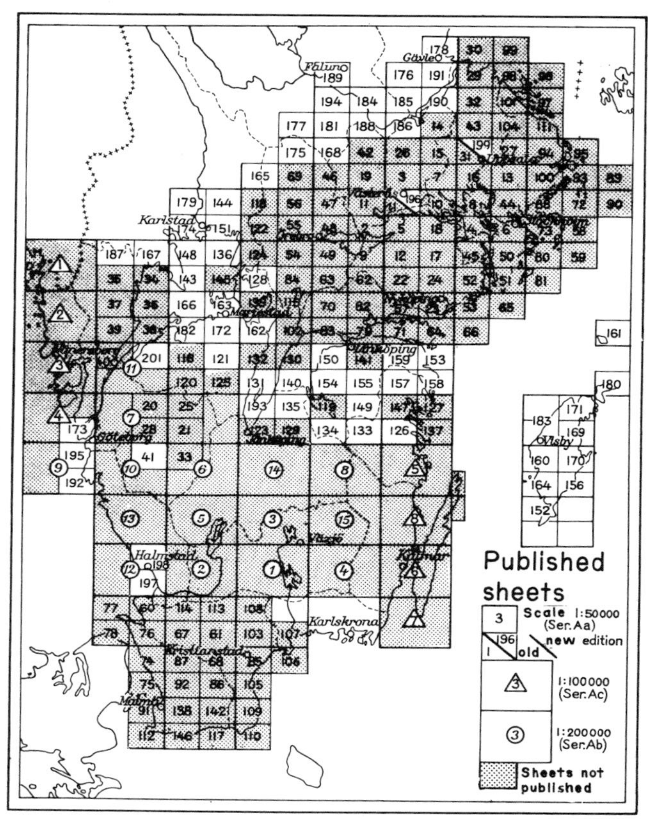

485/6

GENERALSTABENS KARTA OVER SODRA SVERIGE

1:100,000 SRA

Old topographical series covering southern Sweden Black and white with water detail in blue.

DANMARK 1:150 000 NYT FÆRDSELSKORT (Touring Map)

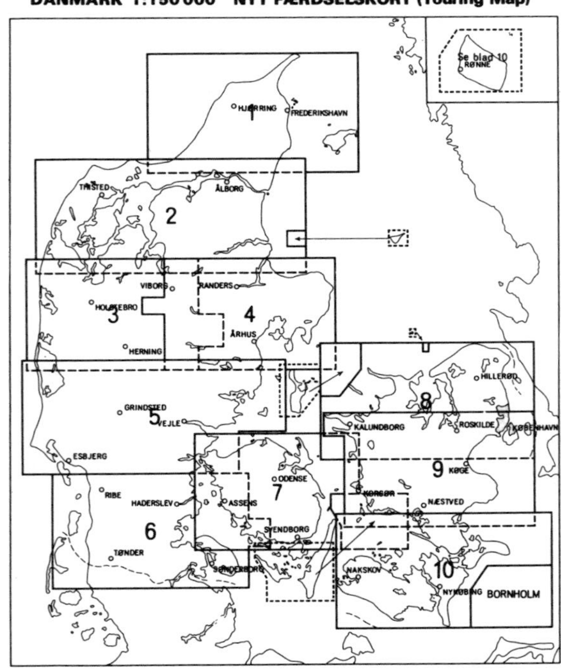

489/1 *NYT FAERDSELSKORT*
1:150,000 G.I.
Official touring map series

489/2 *DANMARK*
1:300,000 G.I.
Official general map in 4 sheets, uncontoured.
NØ sheet available paper flat only, the others can be supplied flat or folded

489/4 *DANMARK 1CM KORT*
1:100,000 G.I.
Official topographical series, contoured

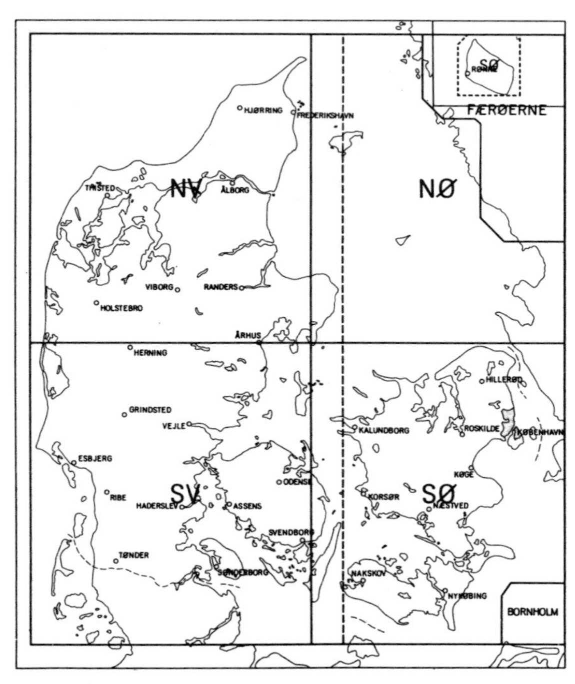

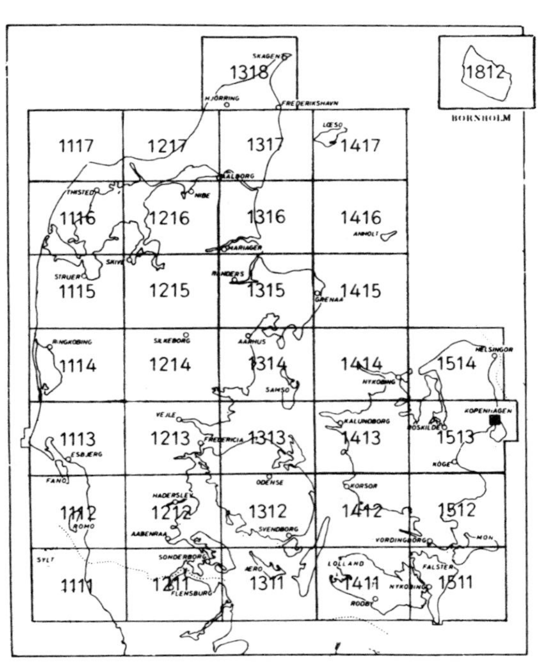

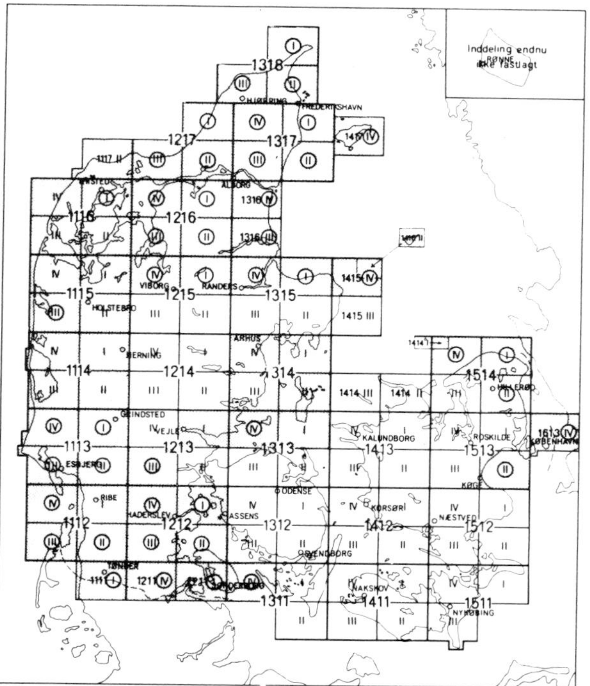

489/5 *DANMARK 2CM KORT*
1:50,000 G.I.
Official topographical series, contoured, in progress

published sheets / without UTM grid

published sheets / with UTM grid

489/7 *DANMARK 4CM MAPS*
1:25,000 G.I.
Official topographical series in progress

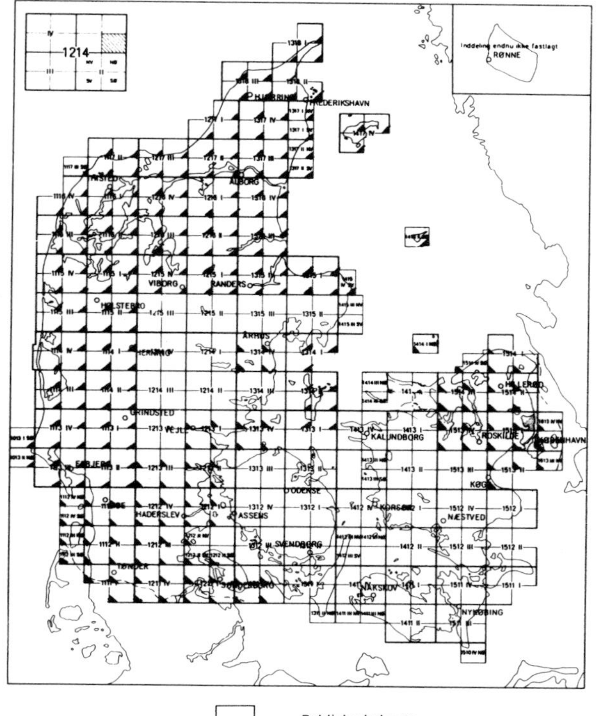

Published sheets

Sheets available in an interim edition

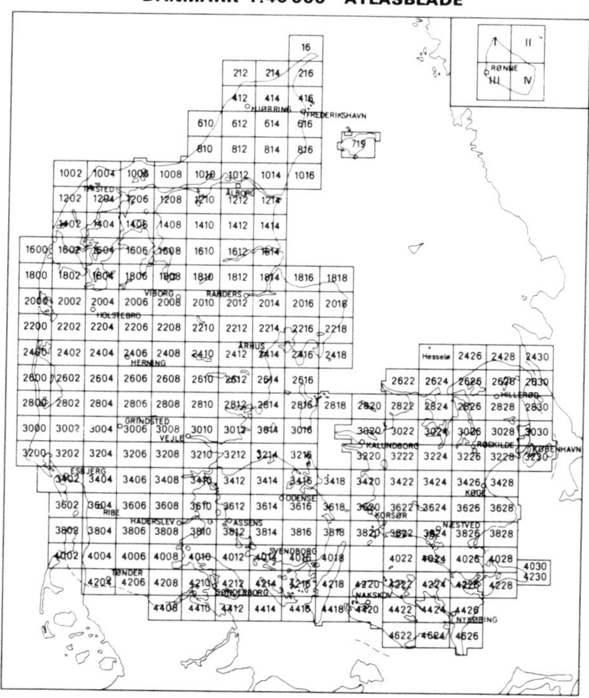

489/6 *DANMARK ATLASBLADE*
1:40,000 G.I.
Official topographical series to be replaced by new 1:50,000 edition

489/8 *DANMARK MÅLEBORDSBLADE*
1:20,000 G.I.
Official topographical series to be replaced by new 1:25,000 edition

DANMARK 1:20 000 MÅLEBORDSBLADE

The sheets are designated by the letter »M« and a number. The first or two first figures of the number refer to the horizontal row of map sheets and appear in the column to the left of the index map. The two last figures refer to the vertical column and appear in the row at the bottom of the map. E.g. Hjørring is situated on M 513, Grindsted on M 3006, and Nakskov on M 4421.

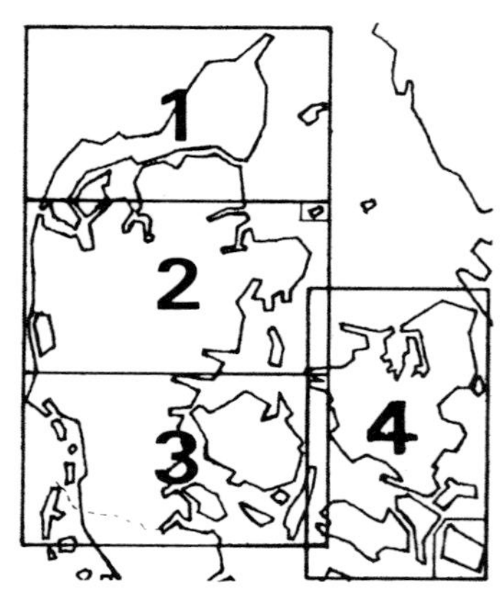

489/9

FAERDSELSKORT DANMARK
1:200,000 G.I.
Road map of Denmark

1:20 000

1:100 000

1:200 000

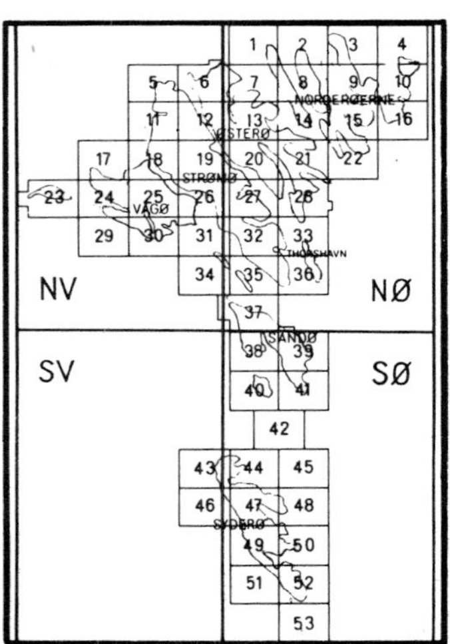

489/10 FAERØERNE
1:20,000 - 1:100,000 - 1:200,000 G.I.
Official topographical series

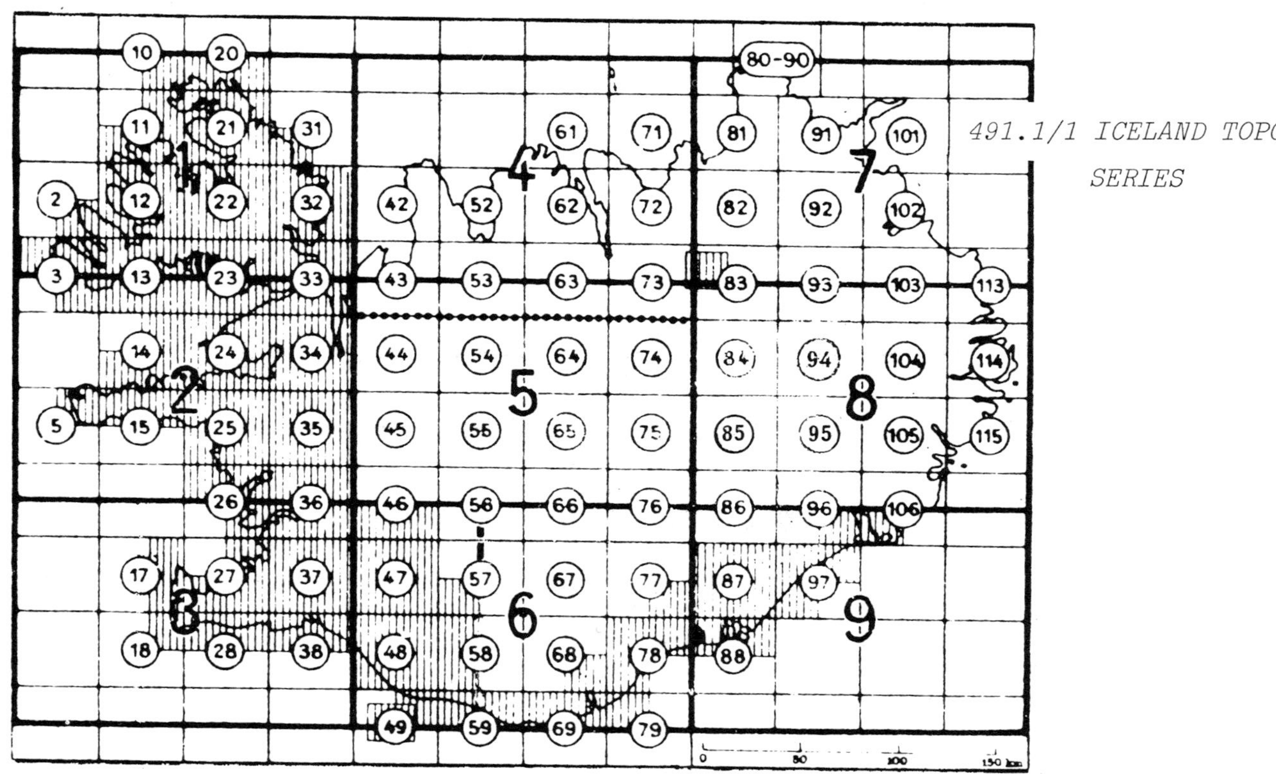

491.1/1 ICELAND TOPOGRAPHICAL SERIES

ATLASBLÖÐ
1:100,000 Landmaelingar Íslands
Topographical series in 87 sheets, complete

FJÓRDUNGSBLÖÐ
1:50,000 Landmaelingar Íslands
Topographical series for western and southern regions only.
4 sheets NW, SW, NE, SE.

AÐALKORT YFIR ÍSLAND
1:250,000 Landmaelingar Íslands
Topographical map in 9 sheets
also special combination sheets
1 & 2, 3 & 6, 8 & 9

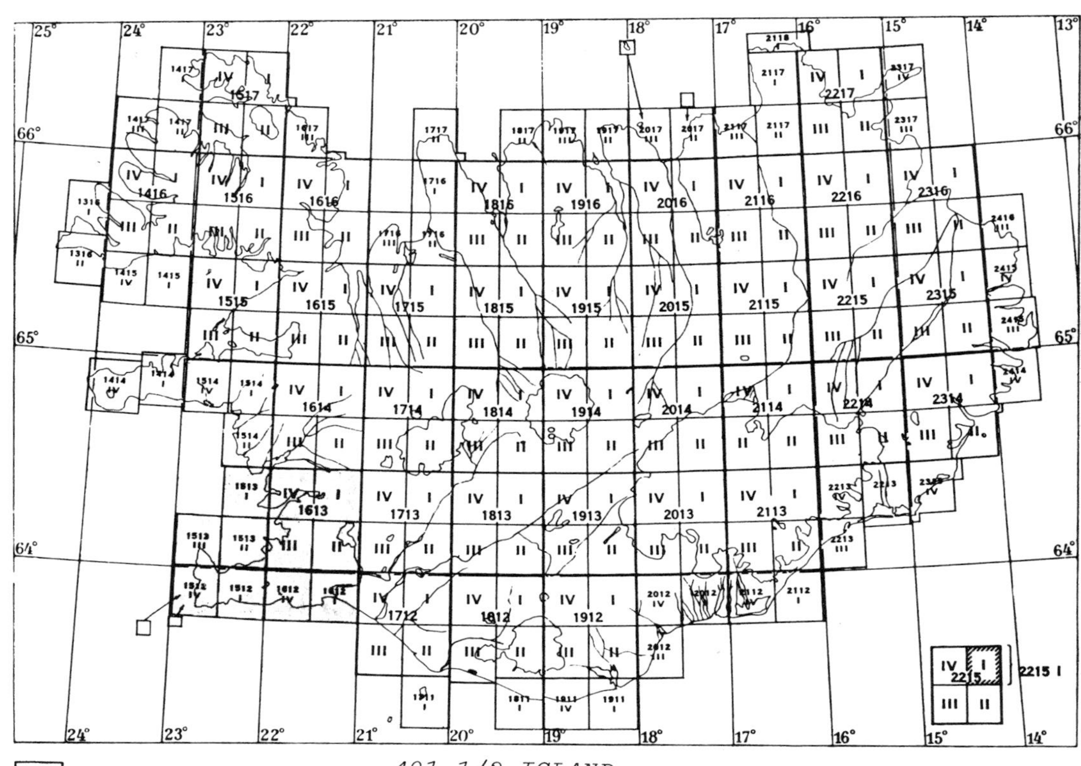

Sheets published

491.1/2 ISLAND
1:50,000 Landmaelingar Íslands
New topographical series in progress

ÍSLAND

GRÓÐURKORT

SKIPTING

NORÐUR ÍSHAF (ATLANTSHAF)

ATLANTSHAF

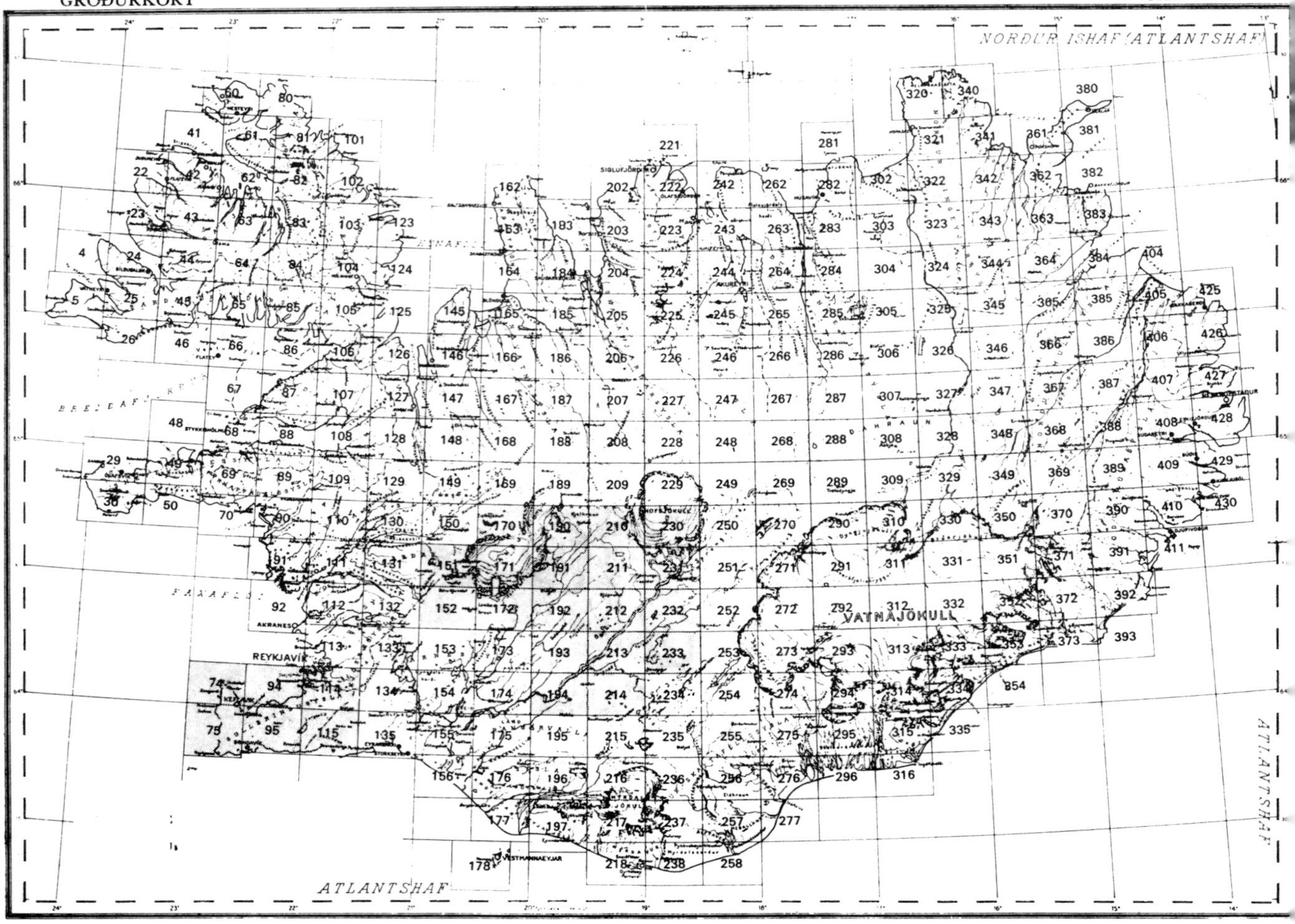

491.1/3 GRÓÐURKORT AF ÍSLANDI
1:40,000 Landmaelingar Íslands
Vegetation series in progress

Sheets published

492/1 CARTE MICHELIN
1:200,000 Michelin
Detailed road map series

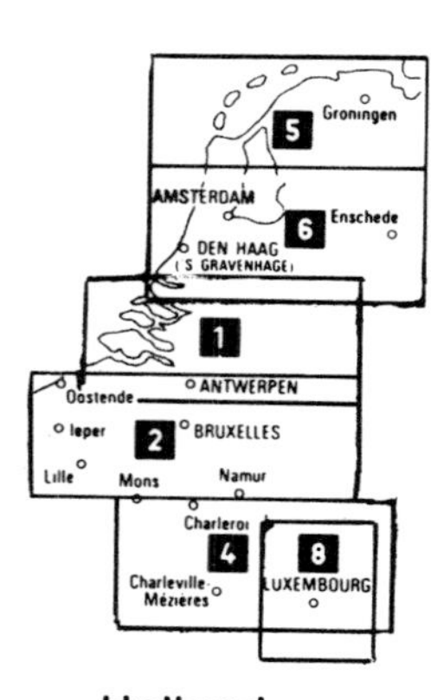

Holland
Belgium
Luxembourg

492.1/1 *OVERZICHTSKAART VAN NEDERLAND*

1:250,000 T.D.

Official topographical series, showing roads

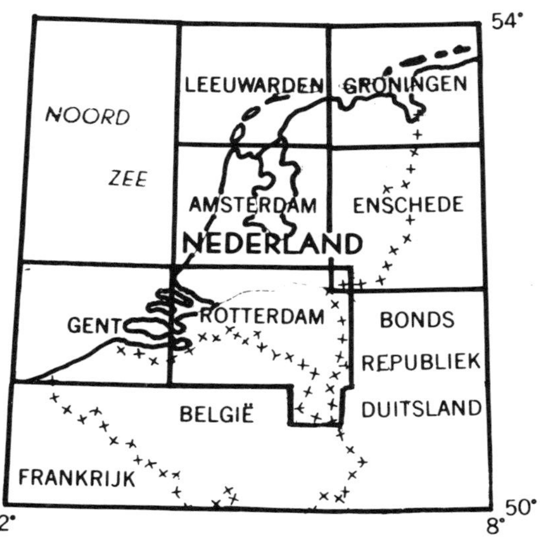

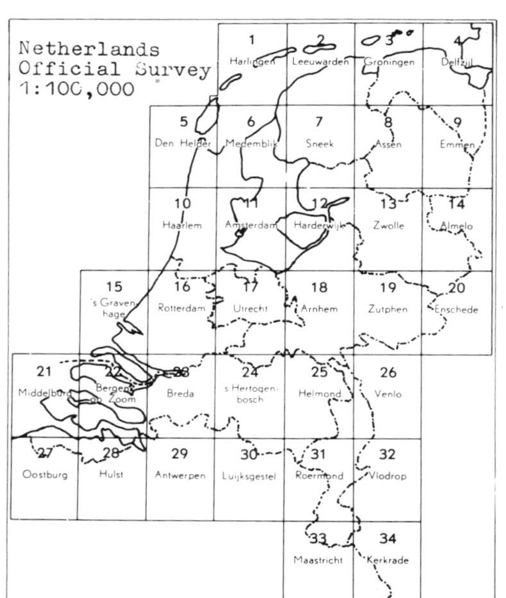

92.1/2 *TOPOGRAFISCHE KAART*

1:100,000 T.D.

Official topographical series

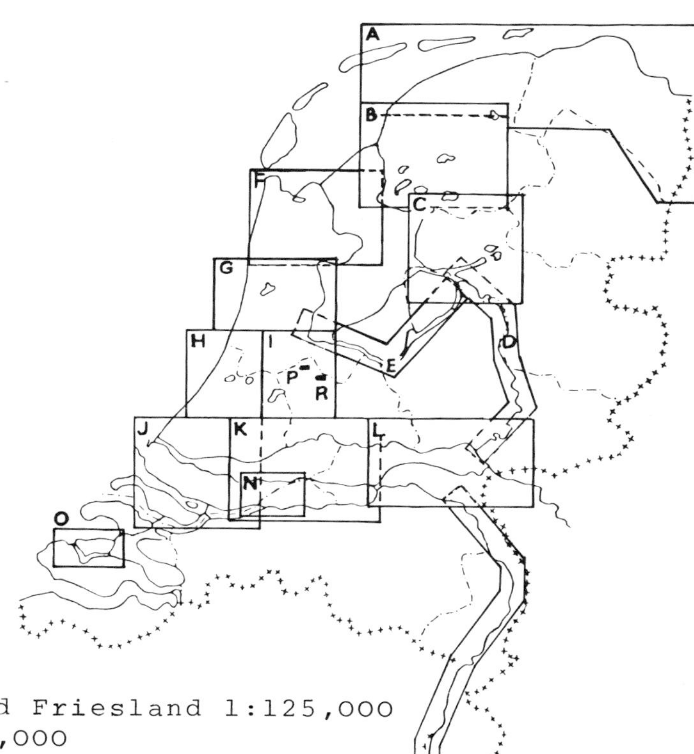

492.1/5 *WATERKAARTEN* *ANWB*

A Groningen en Noord Friesland 1:125,000
B Friese meren 1:50,000
C Noordwest - Overijssel 1:50,000
D Gelderse IJssel 1:25,000
E Randmeren 1:50,000
F Alkmaar - Den Helder 1:50,000
G Amsterdam - Alkmaar (with inset- Alkmaar - Den Helder) 1:50,000
H Hollandse plassen 1:50,000
I Vechtplassen 1:50,000
J Grote rivieren - west 1:50,000
K Grote rivieren - midden 1:50,000
L Grote rivieren - oost 1:50,000
M Limburgse Maas 1:25,000
N Biesbosch 1:25,000
O Veerse Meer 1:25,000
P Vinkeveense plassen 1:10,000
R Loosdrechtse plassen 1:15,000

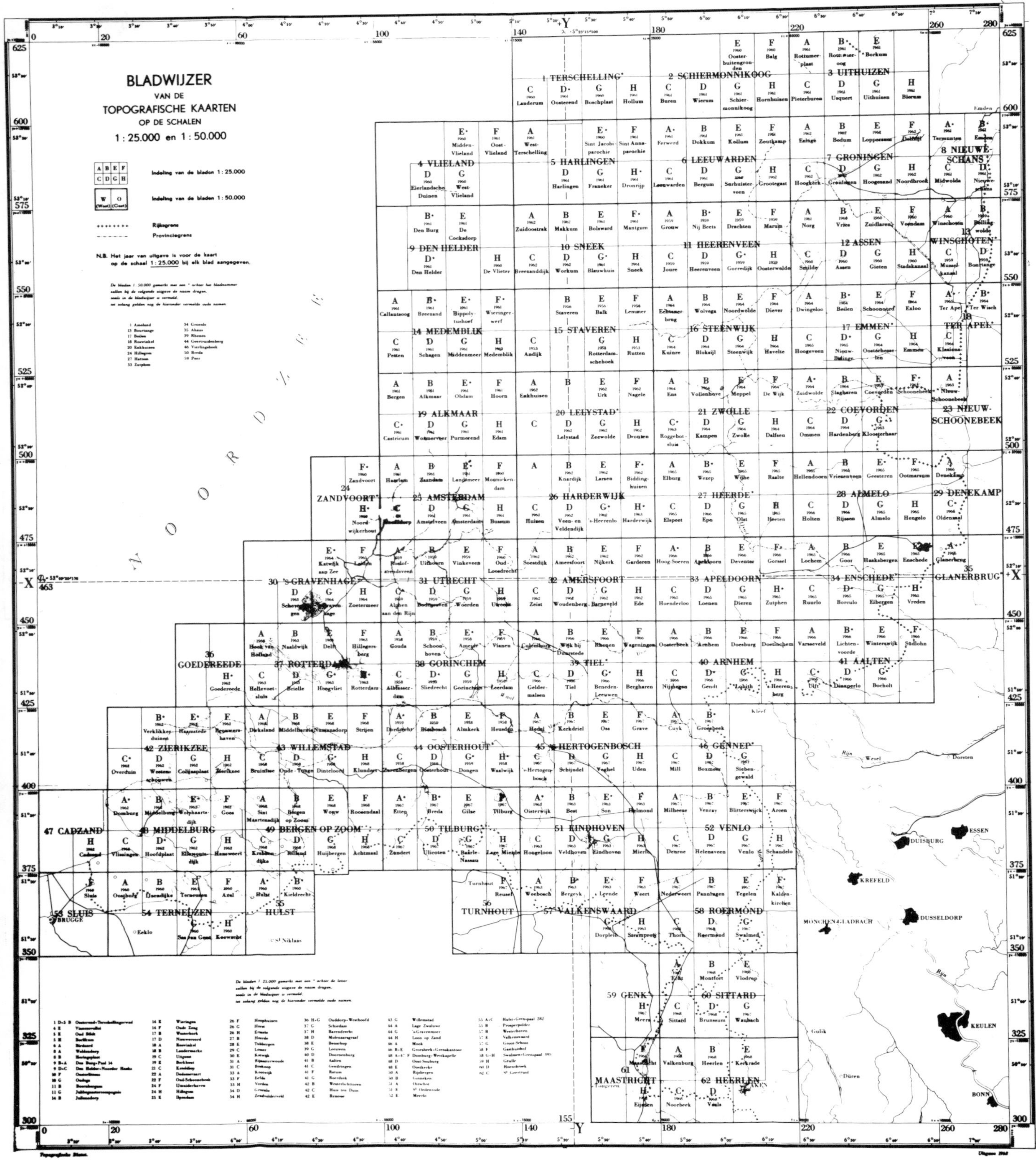

492.1/3 *TOPOGRAFISCHE KAART*

1:25,000 T.D.

Official topographical series

Sheets are 1/8th of large squares

numbering example: 25C AMSTERDAM

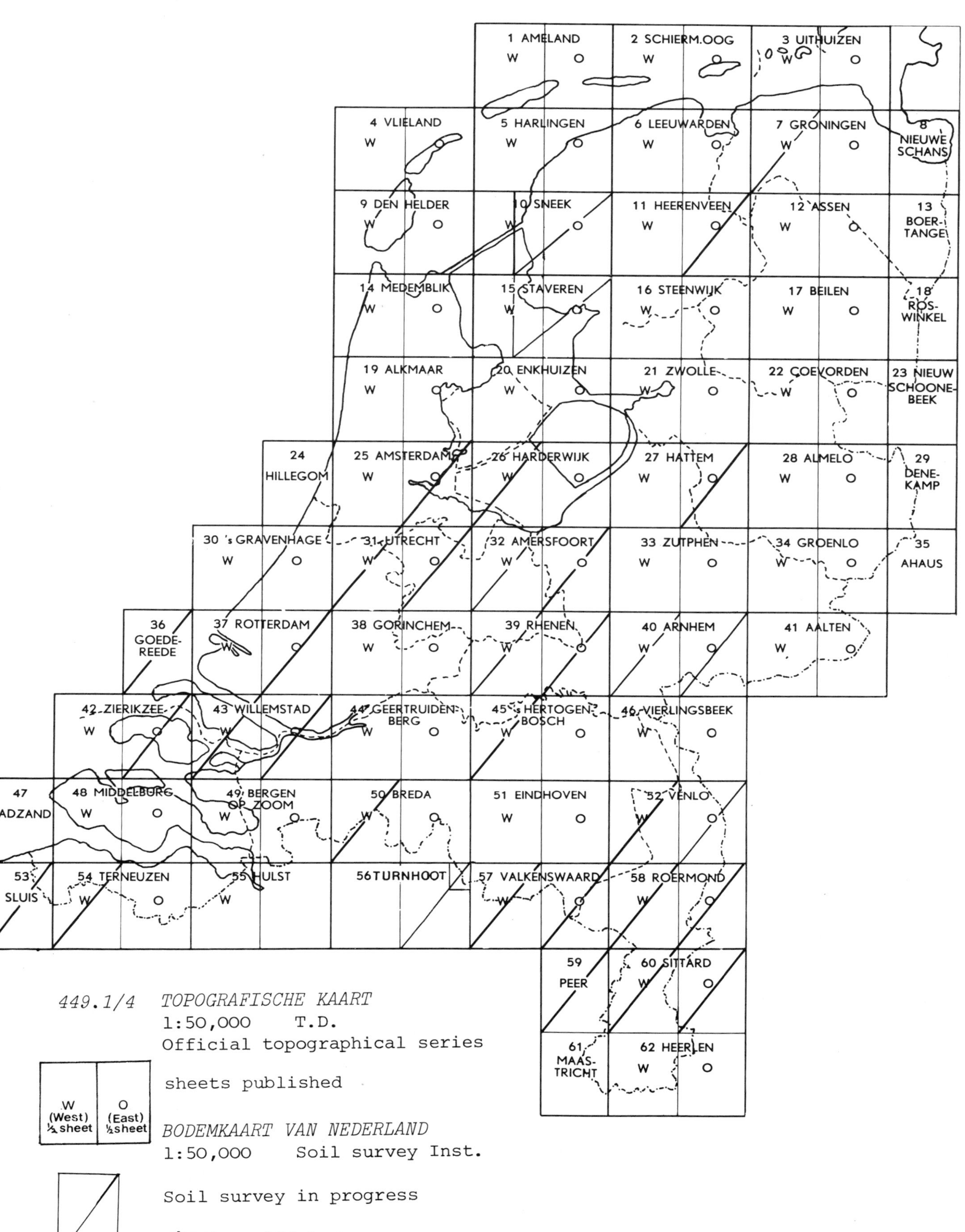

449.1/4 *TOPOGRAFISCHE KAART*
1:50,000 T.D.
Official topographical series

sheets published

BODEMKAART VAN NEDERLAND
1:50,000 Soil survey Inst.

Soil survey in progress

sheets published

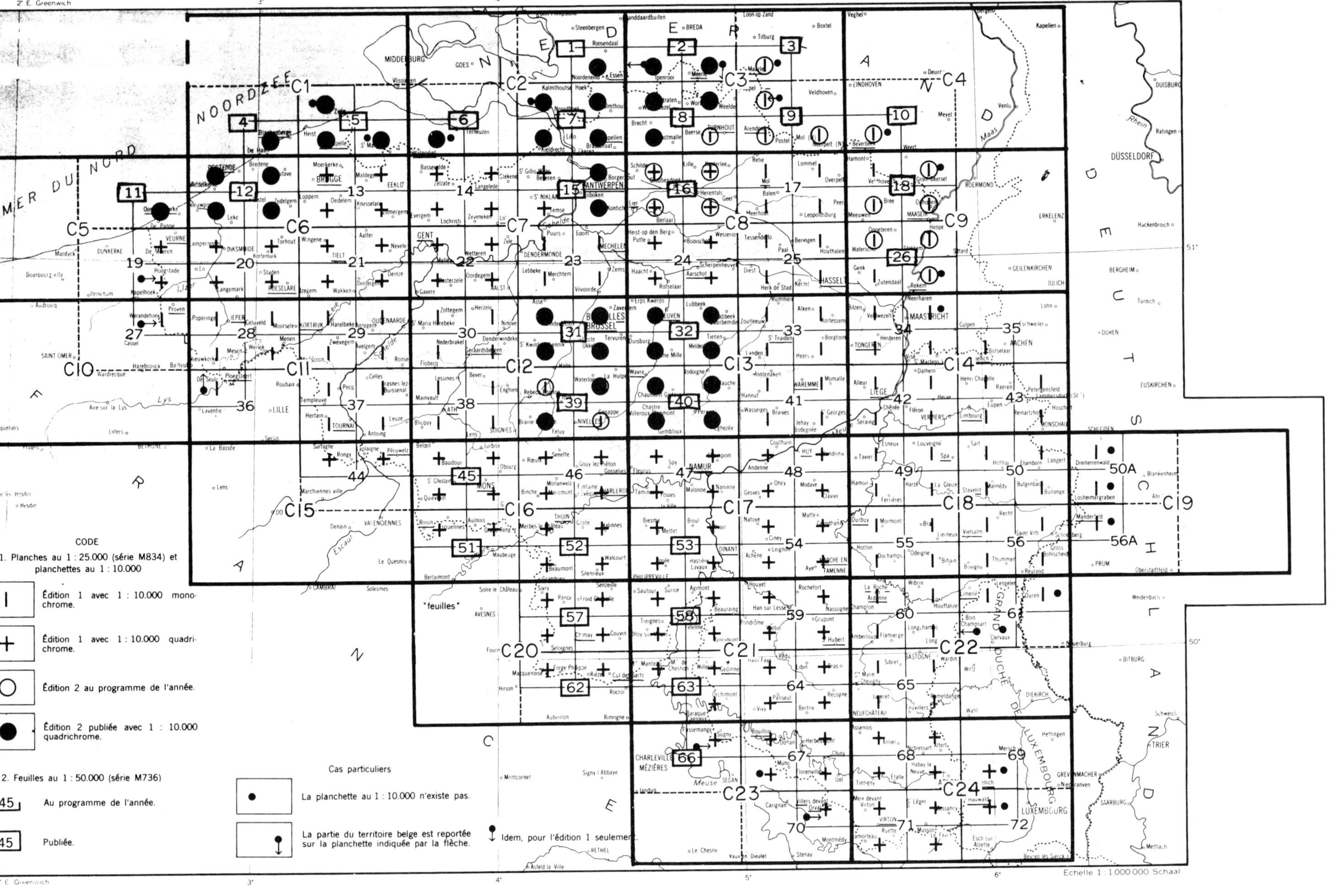

30	1-2	3-4
	31	
C12	5-6	7-8
	1 2	3 4

Sheet numbering system

1:100,000 - C12
1:50,000 - 30

493/1 *CARTES TOPOGRAPHIQUES DE LA BELGIQUE*
1:10,000 - 1:25,000 - 1:50,000 - 1:100,000 IGM
Official topographical series

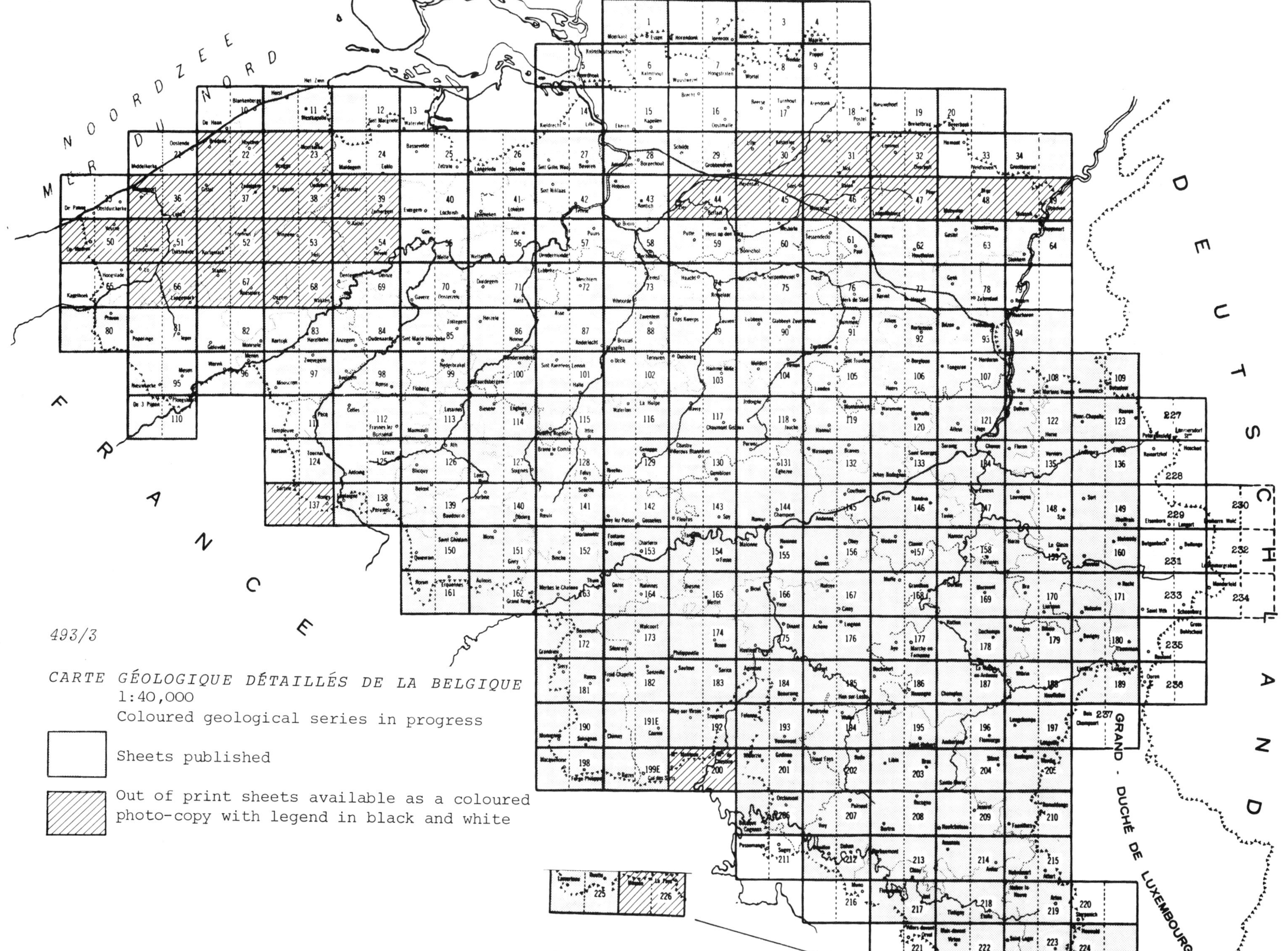

493/3

CARTE GÉOLOGIQUE DÉTAILLÉS DE LA BELGIQUE
1:40,000
Coloured geological series in progress

Sheets published

Out of print sheets available as a coloured photo-copy with legend in black and white

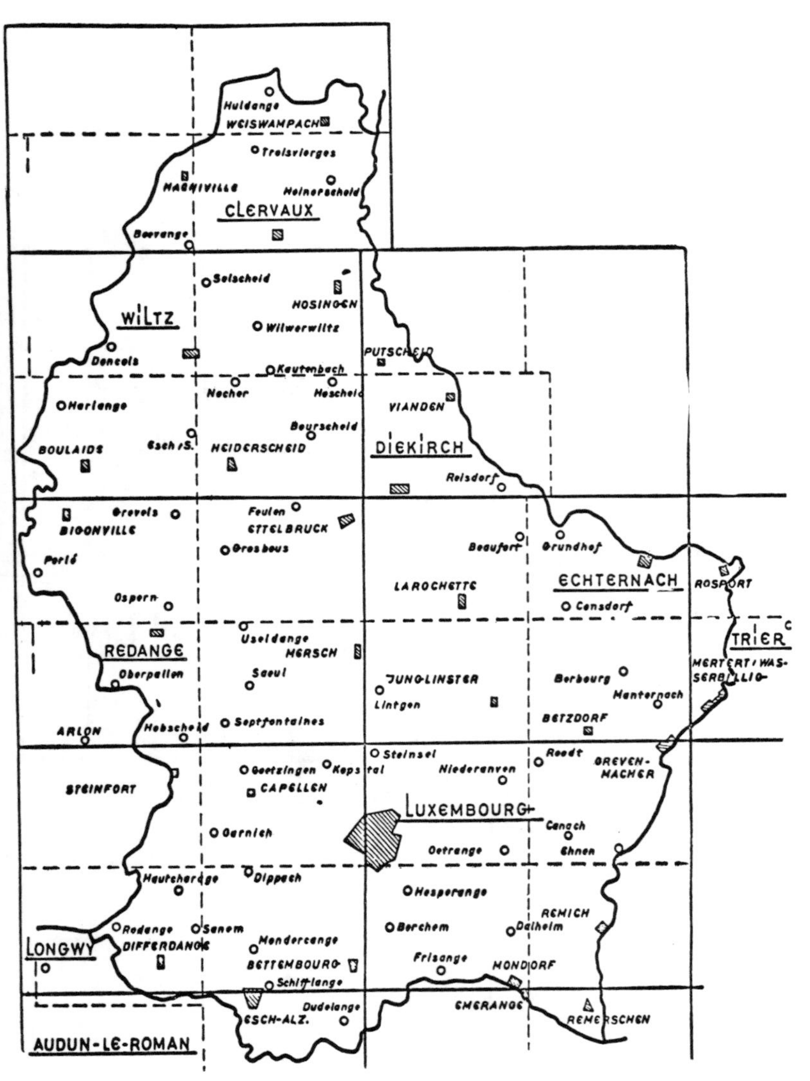

493.1/1 *CARTE DE LUXEMBOURG*
1:50,000 - 1:25,000/1:20,000 Admin. Cadastre et d
Topographie
Topographical series

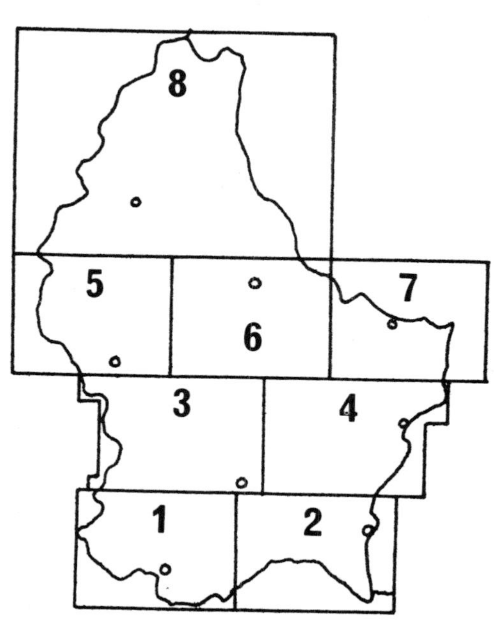

493.1/2

CARTE GEOLOGIQUE DU LUXEMBOURG
1:25,000 - 1:50,000 (Sheet 8 only)
Serv. Geol. de Luxembourg
Coloured geological series

I
II
III
IV
V
VI
VII
VIII
IX
X
XI
XII
OSTENDE
Bruges
GAND
ANVERS
Malines
MAESEYCK
Alost
Hasselt
Ypres
Courtrai
Louvain
BRUXELLES
Maastricht
Aix-la-Chapelle
Lille
TOURNAI
LIÉGE
Verviers
Nivelles
Huy
Malmedy
Douai
VALENCIENNES
Mons
Charleroi
NAMUR
Maubeuge
MARCHE
Cambrai
Givet
Bastogne
Hirson
MÉZIÈRES
Sedan
ARLON
Rethel
Longwy

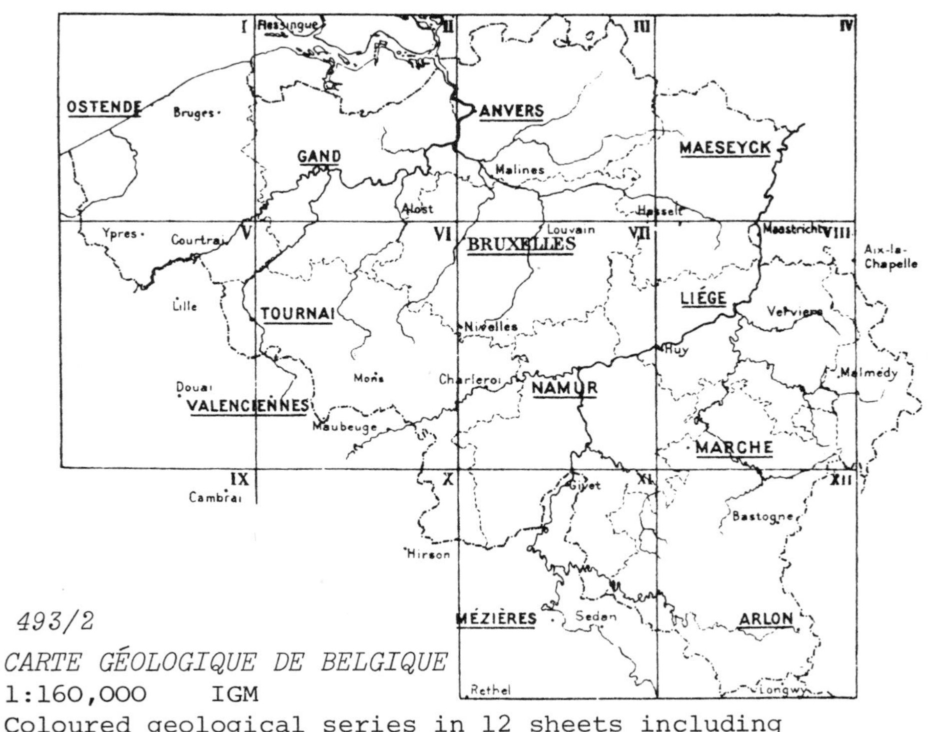

493/2

CARTE GÉOLOGIQUE DE BELGIQUE

1:160,000 IGM

Coloured geological series in 12 sheets including legend

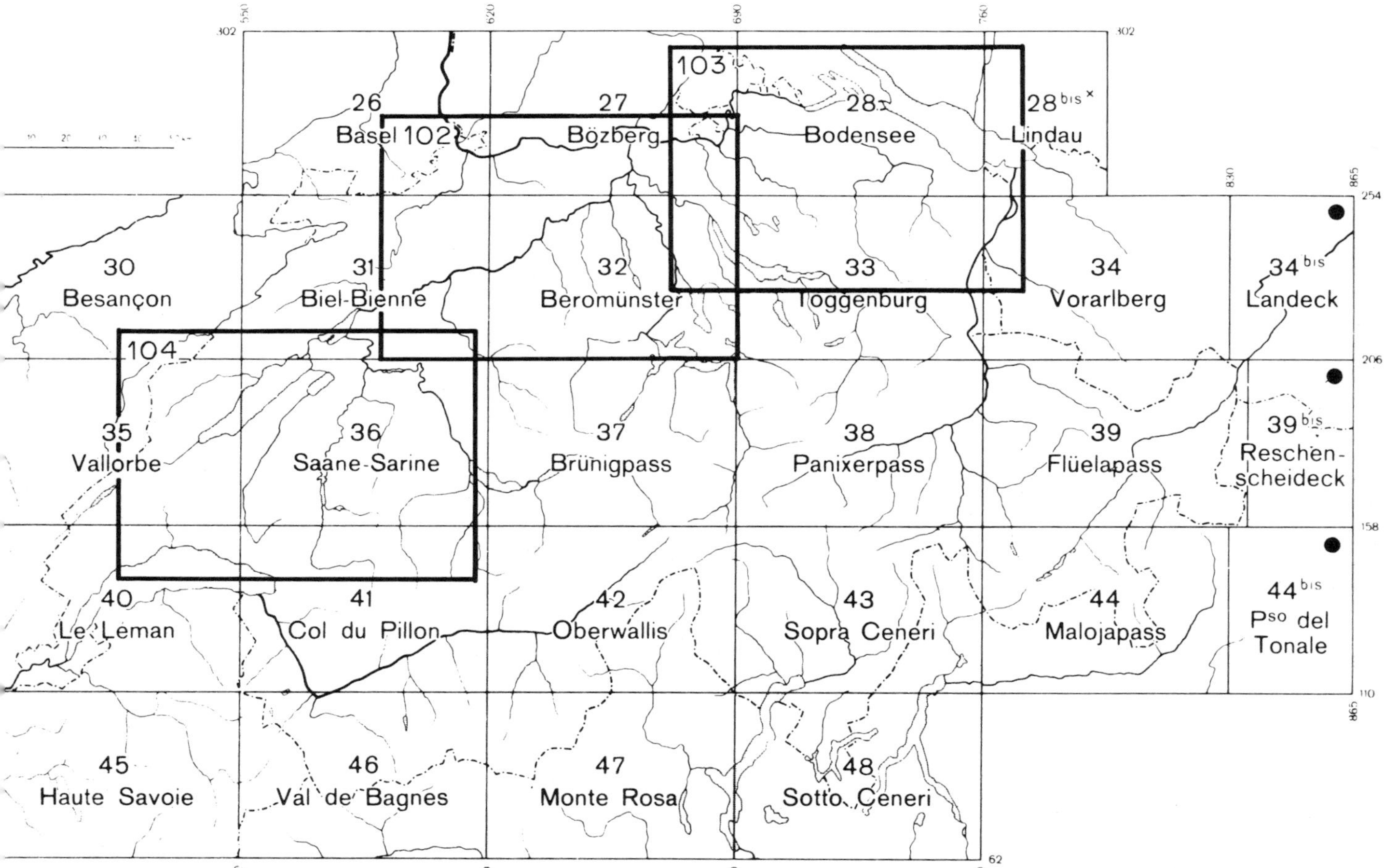

26 Basel
27 Bözberg
28 Bodensee
28 bis × Lindau
102
103
104
30 Besançon
31 Biel-Bienne
32 Beromünster
33 Toggenburg
34 Vorarlberg
34 bis Landeck
35 Vallorbe
36 Saane-Sarine
37 Brünigpass
38 Panixerpass
39 Flüelapass
39 bis Reschen-scheideck
40 Le Leman
41 Col du Pillon
42 Oberwallis
43 Sopra Ceneri
44 Malojapass
44 bis Pso del Tonale
45 Haute Savoie
46 Val de Bagnes
47 Monte Rosa
48 Sotto Ceneri

Special area maps

Half sheets, not published

Sheets published

494/1 LANDESKARTEN DER SCHWEIZ

1:100,000

Official topographical series

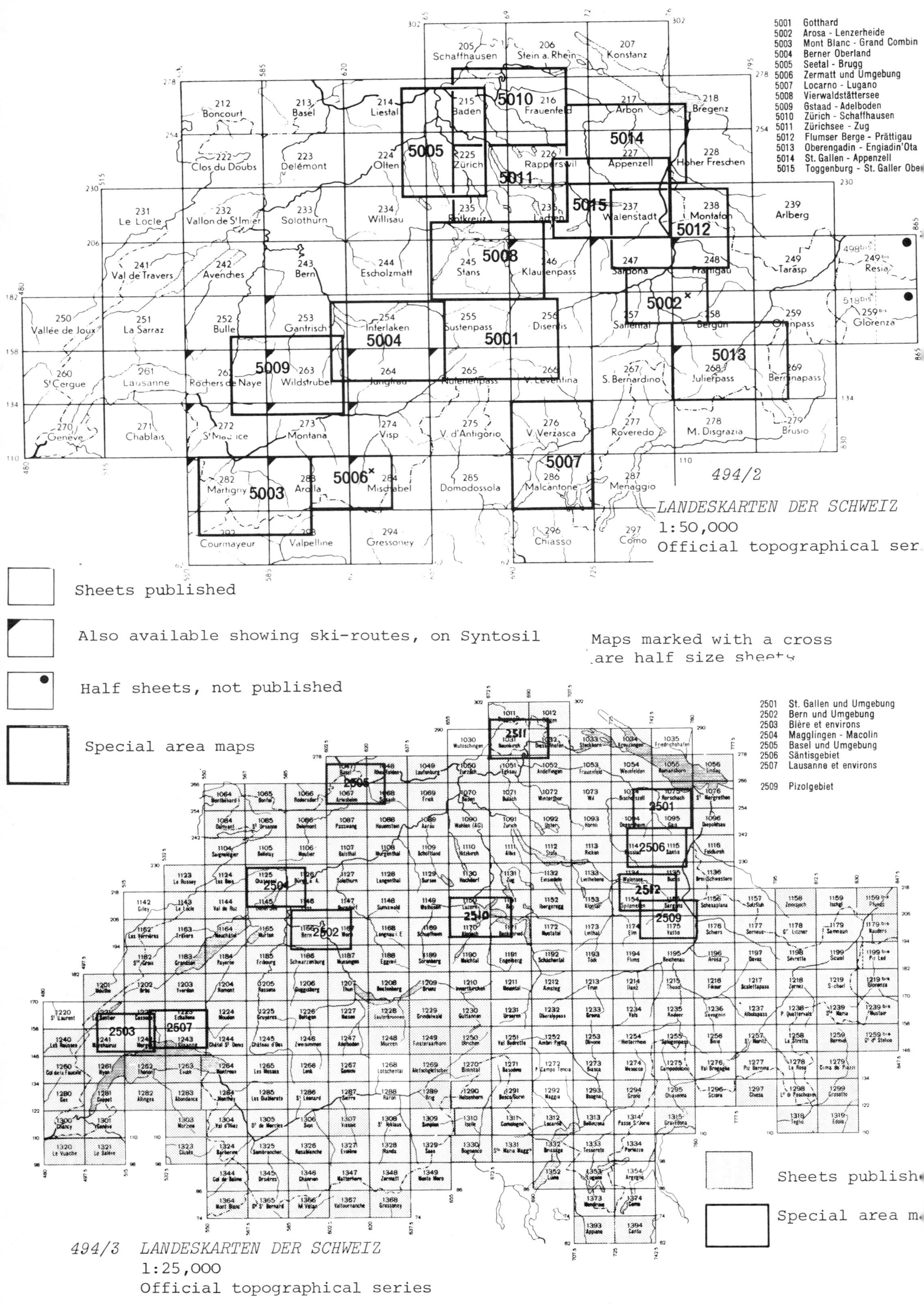

5001 Gotthard
5002 Arosa - Lenzerheide
5003 Mont Blanc - Grand Combin
5004 Berner Oberland
5005 Seetal - Brugg
5006 Zermatt und Umgebung
5007 Locarno - Lugano
5008 Vierwaldstättersee
5009 Gstaad - Adelboden
5010 Zürich - Schaffhausen
5011 Zürichsee - Zug
5012 Flumser Berge - Prättigau
5013 Oberengadin - Engiadin'Ota
5014 St. Gallen - Appenzell
5015 Toggenburg - St. Galler Obe
205 Schaffhausen
206 Stein a. Rhein
207 Konstanz
212 Boncourt
213 Basel
214 Liestal
215 Baden
216 Frauenfeld
217 Arbon
218 Bregenz
222 Clos du Doubs
223 Delémont
224 Olten
225 Zürich
226 Rapperswil
227 Appenzell
228 Hoher Freschen
231 Le Locle
232 Vallon de St Imier
233 Solothurn
234 Willisau
235 Rotkreuz
236 Lachen
237 Walenstadt
238 Montafon
239 Arlberg
241 Val de Travers
242 Avenches
243 Bern
244 Escholzmatt
245 Stans
246 Klausenpass
247 Sardona
248 Prättigau
249 Tarasp
498bis
249bis Resia
250 Vallée de Joux
251 La Sarraz
252 Bulle
253 Gantrisch
254 Interlaken
255 Sustenpass
256 Disentis
257 Safiental
258 Bergün
259 Ofenpass
518bis
259bis Glorenza
260 St Cergue
261 Lausanne
262 Rochers de Naye
263 Wildstrubel
264 Jungfrau
265 Nufenenpass
266 V. Leventina
267 S. Bernardino
268 Julierpass
269 Berninapass
270 Genève
271 Chablais
272 St Maurice
273 Montana
274 Visp
275 V. d'Antigorio
276 V. Verzasca
277 Roveredo
278 M. Disgrazia
279 Brusio
282 Martigny
283 Arolla
284 Mischabel
285 Domodossola
286 Malcantone
287 Menaggio
292 Courmayeur
293 Valpelline
294 Gressoney
296 Chiasso
297 Como
494/2
LANDESKARTEN DER SCHWEIZ
1:50,000
Official topographical ser
Sheets published
Also available showing ski-routes, on Syntosil
Maps marked with a cross are half size sheets
Half sheets, not published
Special area maps
2501 St. Gallen und Umgebung
2502 Bern und Umgebung
2503 Bière et environs
2504 Magglingen - Macolin
2505 Basel und Umgebung
2506 Säntisgebiet
2507 Lausanne et environs
2509 Pizolgebiet
Sheets publish
Special area m
494/3 LANDESKARTEN DER SCHWEIZ
1:25,000
Official topographical series

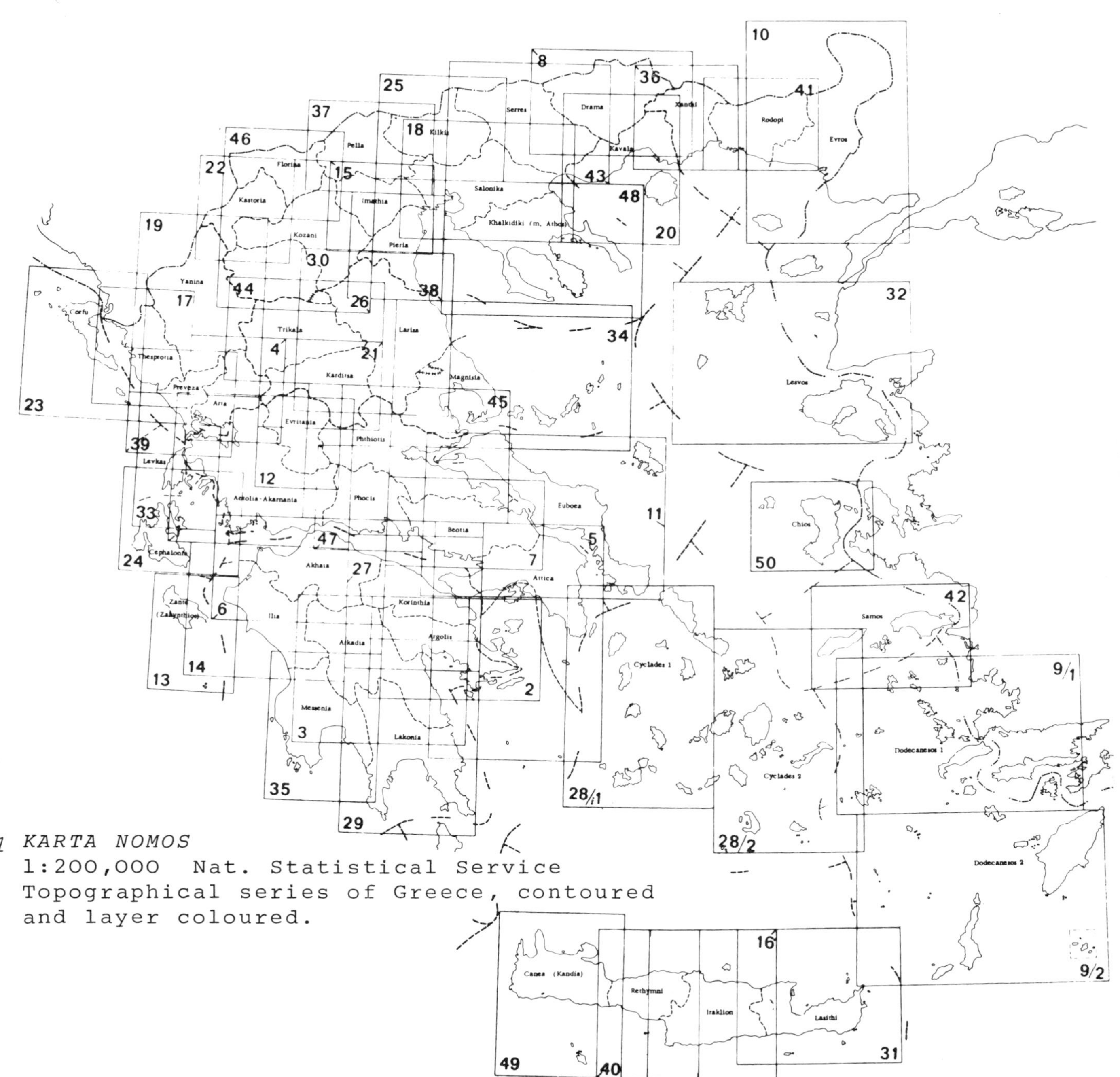

495/1 KARTA NOMOS

1:200,000 Nat. Statistical Service
Topographical series of Greece, contoured and layer coloured.

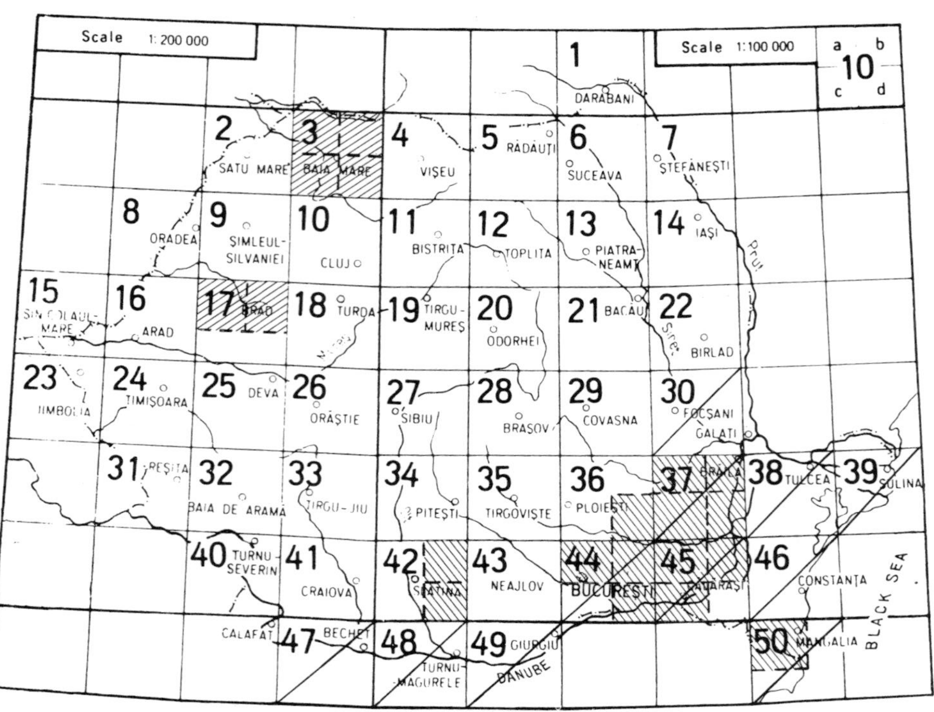

498/1

CARTES GÉOLOGIQUES ET CARTES DES SOLS
1:200,000 - 1:100,000 Inst. Geol.
Geological and soil map series of Romania

- ☐ Geological series 1:200,000, all sheets published
- ◿ Soil series 1:200,000 published
- Geological 1:100,000 sheets published
- Hydrogeological 1:100,000 sheets published

Asia

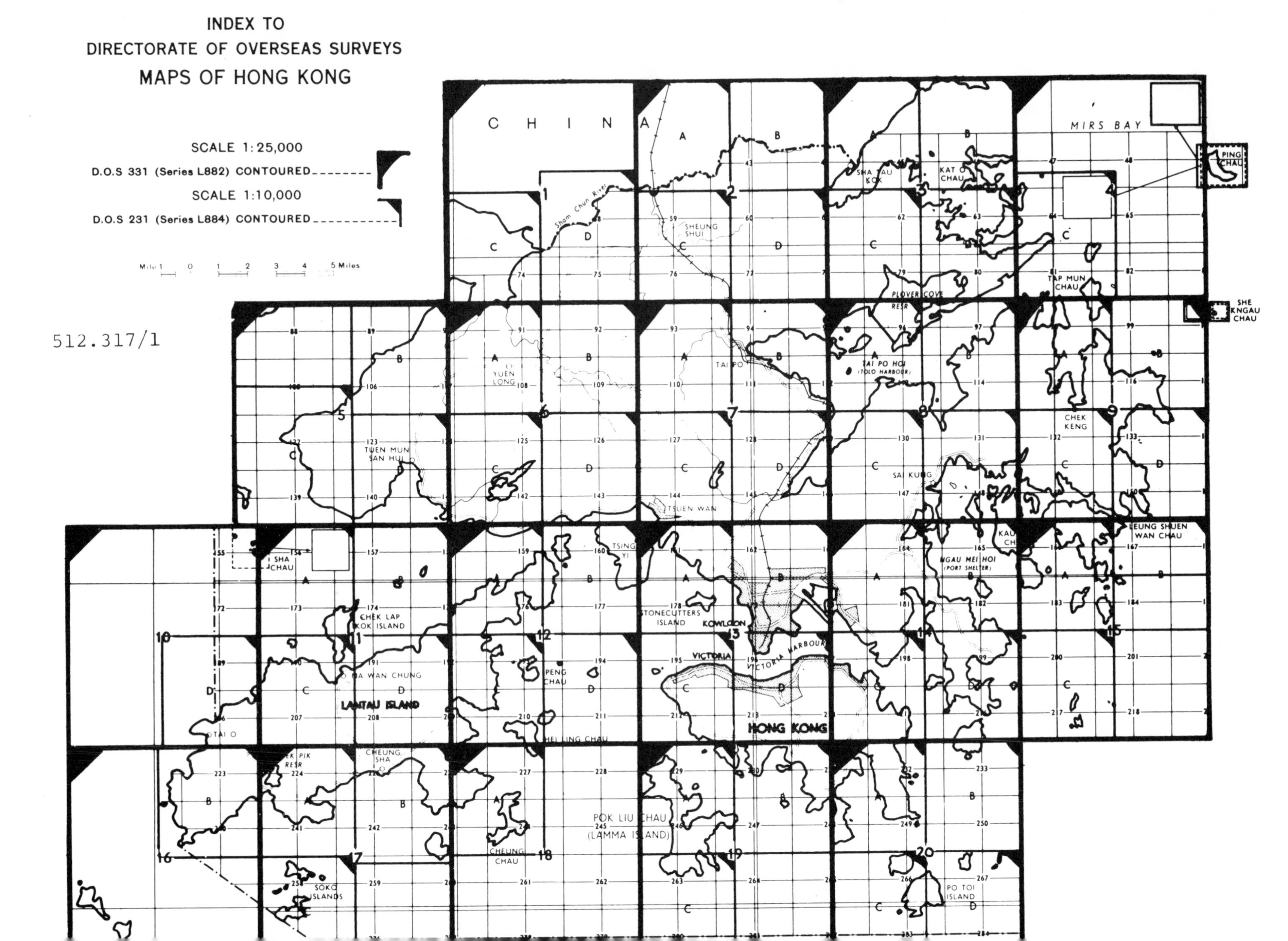

INDEX TO
DIRECTORATE OF OVERSEAS SURVEYS
MAPS OF HONG KONG
SCALE 1:25,000
D.O.S 331 (Series L882) CONTOURED
SCALE 1:10,000
D.O.S 231 (Series L884) CONTOURED
Mile 1 0 1 2 3 4 5 Miles
CHINA
MIRS BAY
PING CHAU
SHE KNGAU CHAU
Sham Chun River
SHEUNG SHUI
SHA TAU KOK
KAT O CHAU
TAP MUN CHAU
PLOVER COVE RESR
YUEN LONG
TAI PO
TAI PO HOI (TOLO HARBOUR)
CHEK KENG
TUEN MUN SAN HUI
SAI KUNG
TSUEN WAN
LEUNG SHUEN WAN CHAU
SHA CHAU
TSING YI
NGAU MEI HOI (PORT SHELTER)
CHEK LAP KOK ISLAND
STONECUTTERS ISLAND
KOWLOON
VICTORIA
VICTORIA HARBOUR
PENG CHAU
SHA WAN CHUNG
LANTAU ISLAND
HONG KONG
TAI O
HEI LING CHAU
SHEK PIK RESR
CHEUNG SHA
POK LIU CHAU (LAMMA ISLAND)
CHEUNG CHAU
SOKO ISLANDS
PO TOI ISLAND

Dotted lines indicate the 3 sheets covering Japan of International Map of the World 1:1,000,000.

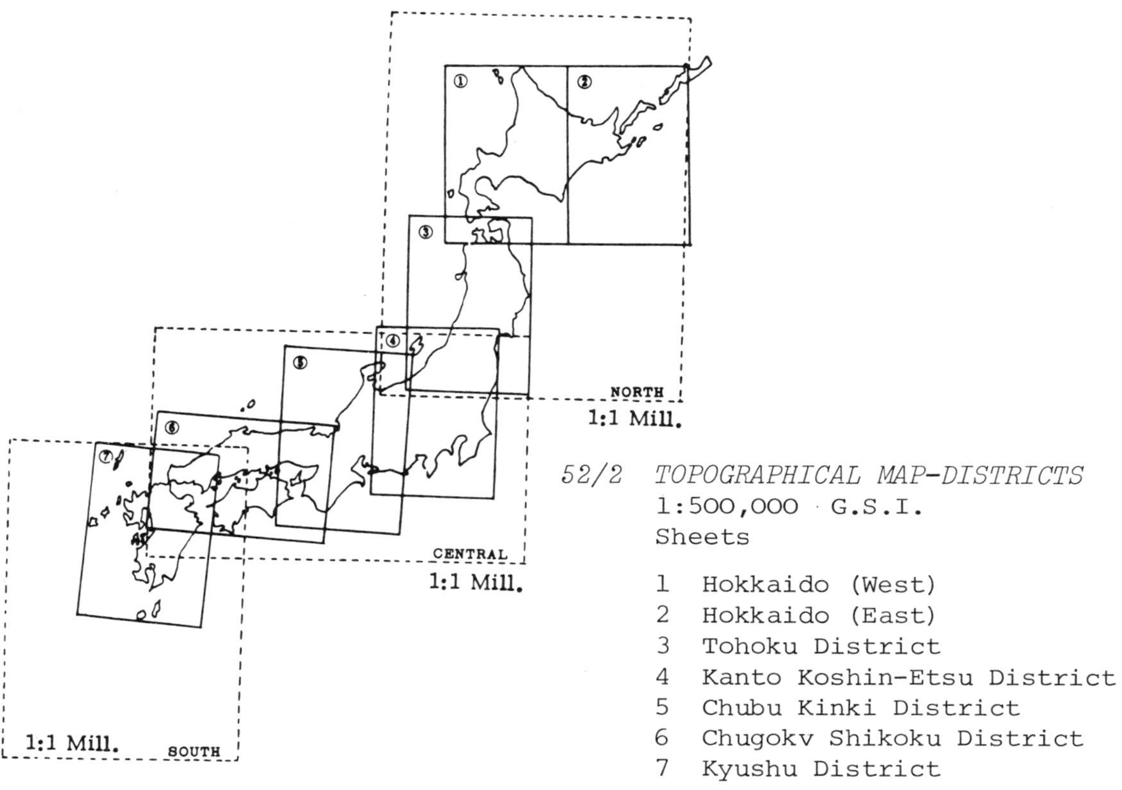

52/2 *TOPOGRAPHICAL MAP-DISTRICTS*
1:500,000 G.S.I.
Sheets

1 Hokkaido (West)
2 Hokkaido (East)
3 Tohoku District
4 Kanto Koshin-Etsu District
5 Chubu Kinki District
6 Chugokv Shikoku District
7 Kyushu District

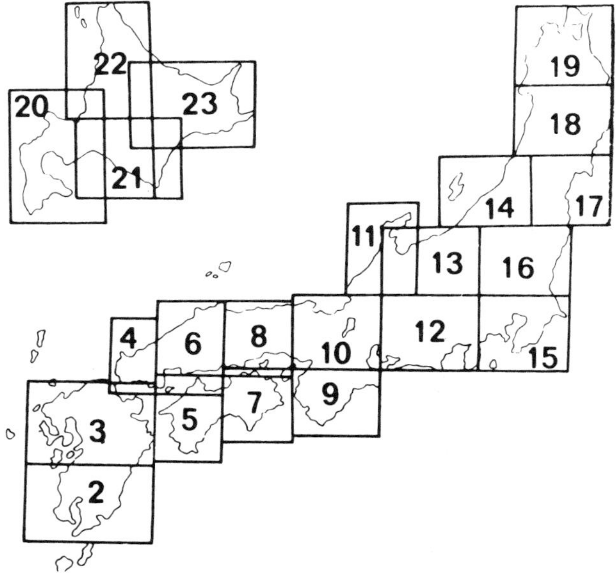

52/1 *GENERAL MAP OF JAPAN*
1:250,000 Buyodo
General road map in 23 sheets

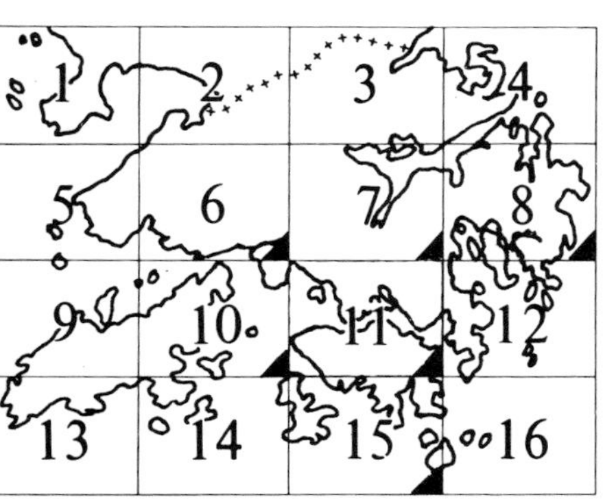

512.317/2
HONG KONG TOPOGRAPHICAL SERIES
1:20,000 CLSO
Contoured, topographical series in progress

 Sheets published

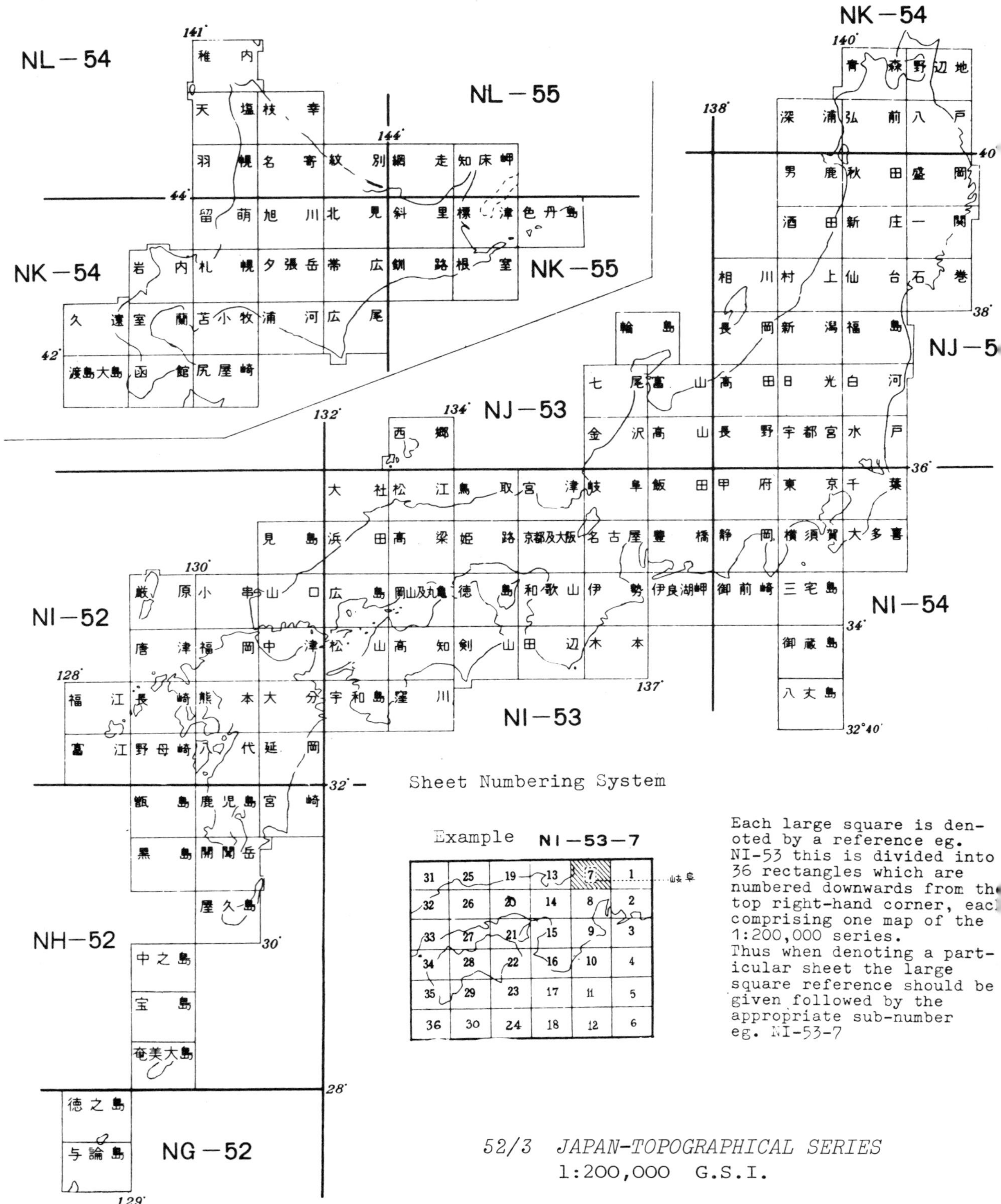

52/3 JAPAN-TOPOGRAPHICAL SERIES

1:200,000 G.S.I.

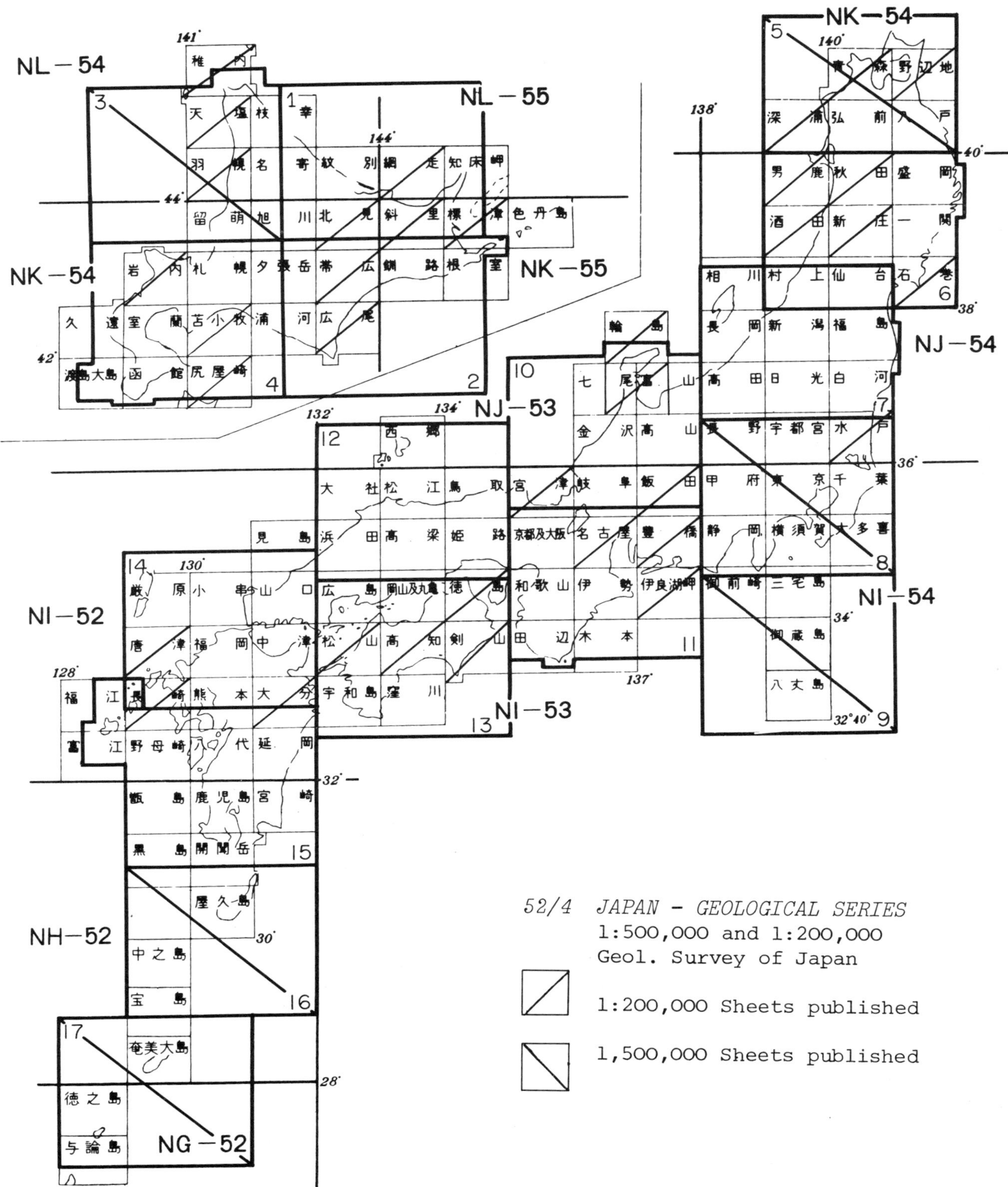
NL-54
NL-55
NK-54
NK-55
NK-54
NJ-54
NJ-53
NI-52
NI-53
NI-54
NH-52
NG-52
1
2
3
4
5
6
7
8
9
10
11
12
13
14
15
16
17
141°
144°
44°
42°
140°
138°
40°
38°
36°
34°
32°40'
137°
134°
132°
130°
128°
32°
30°
28°
129°
52/4 JAPAN - GEOLOGICAL SERIES
1:500,000 and 1:200,000
Geol. Survey of Japan
1:200,000 Sheets published
1,500,000 Sheets published

532/1 GEOGRAPHIC-GEOLOGIC MAP SERIES OF THE KINGDOM OF SAUDI ARABIA

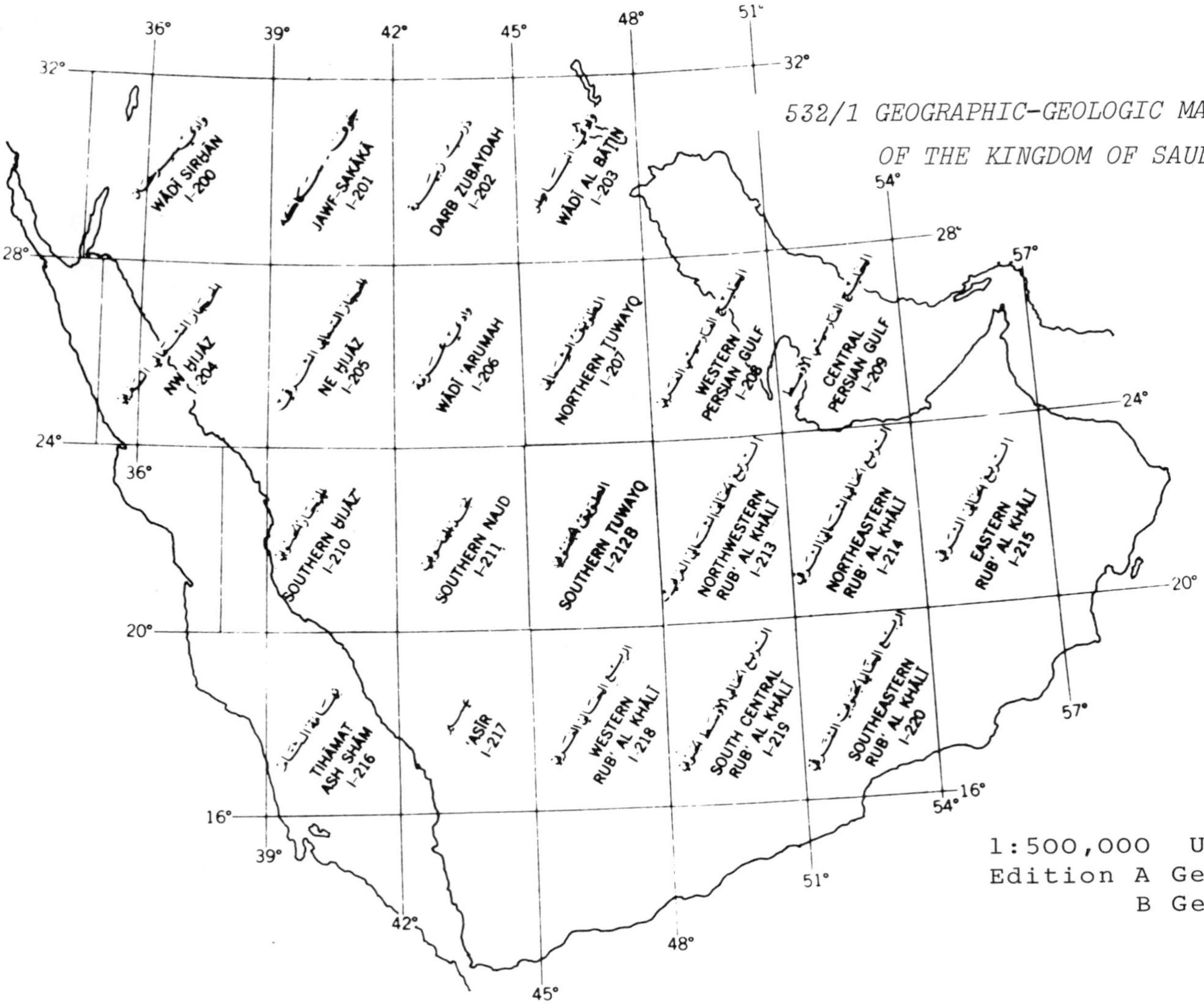

WĀDĪ SIRḤĀN I-200
JAWF-SAKĀKĀ I-201
DARB ZUBAYDAH I-202
WĀDĪ AL BĀṬIN I-203
NW ḤIJĀZ I-204
NE ḤIJĀZ I-205
WĀDĪ 'ARUMAH I-206
NORTHERN ṬUWAYQ I-207
WESTERN PERSIAN GULF I-208
CENTRAL PERSIAN GULF I-209
SOUTHERN ḤIJĀZ I-210
SOUTHERN NAJD I-211
SOUTHERN ṬUWAYQ I-212B
NORTHWESTERN RUB' AL KHĀLĪ I-213
NORTHEASTERN RUB' AL KHĀLĪ I-214
EASTERN RUB' AL KHĀLĪ I-215
TIHĀMAT ASH SHĀM I-216
'ASĪR I-217
WESTERN RUB' AL KHĀLĪ I-218
SOUTH CENTRAL RUB' AL KHĀLĪ I-219
SOUTHEASTERN RUB' AL KHĀLĪ I-220

1:500,000 USGS/DGMR
Edition A Geologic
B Geographic

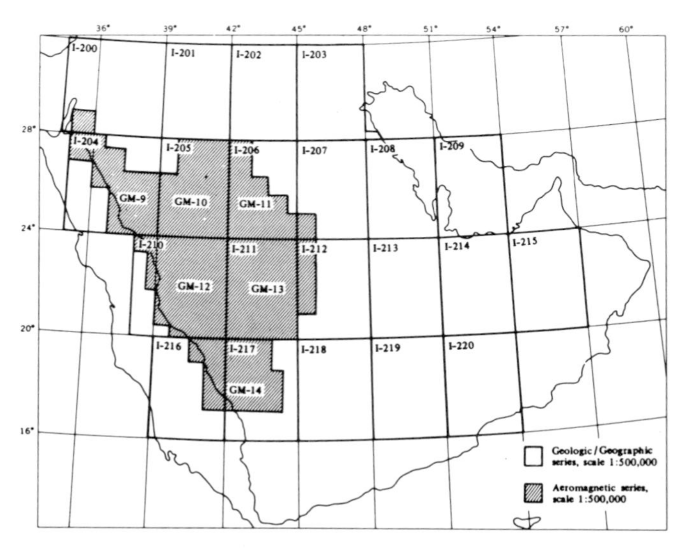

532/2 SAUDI ARABIA AEROMAGNETIC SERIES
1:500,000 DGMR/USGS
Total intensity aeromagnetic maps with text

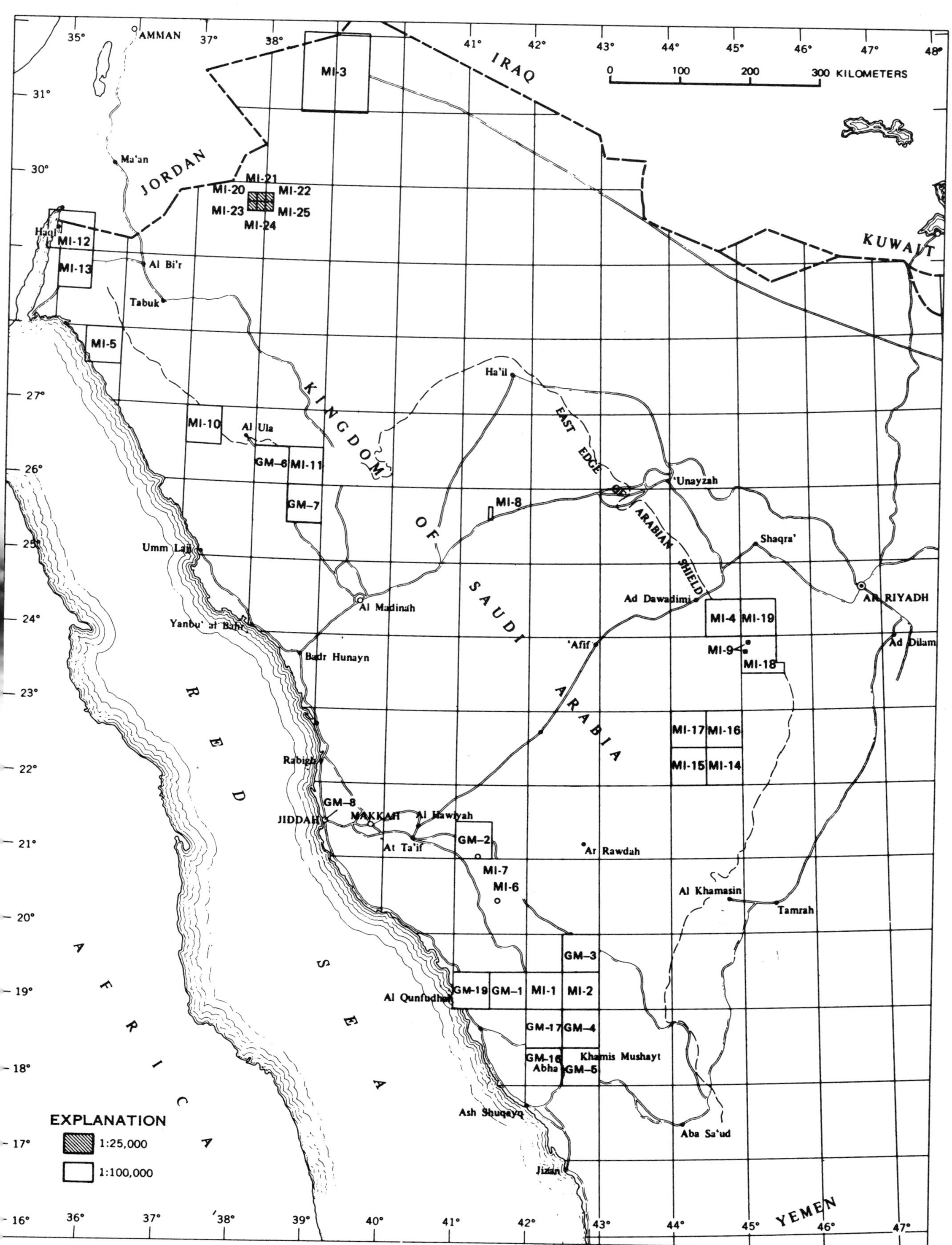

32/3 *SAUDI ARABIA GEOLOGICAL AND MINERAL MAPS*
1:25,000 - 1:100,000 DGMR/USGS
Series of coloured maps with texts, in progress

MI - Mineral Investigation Maps

GM - Geological maps

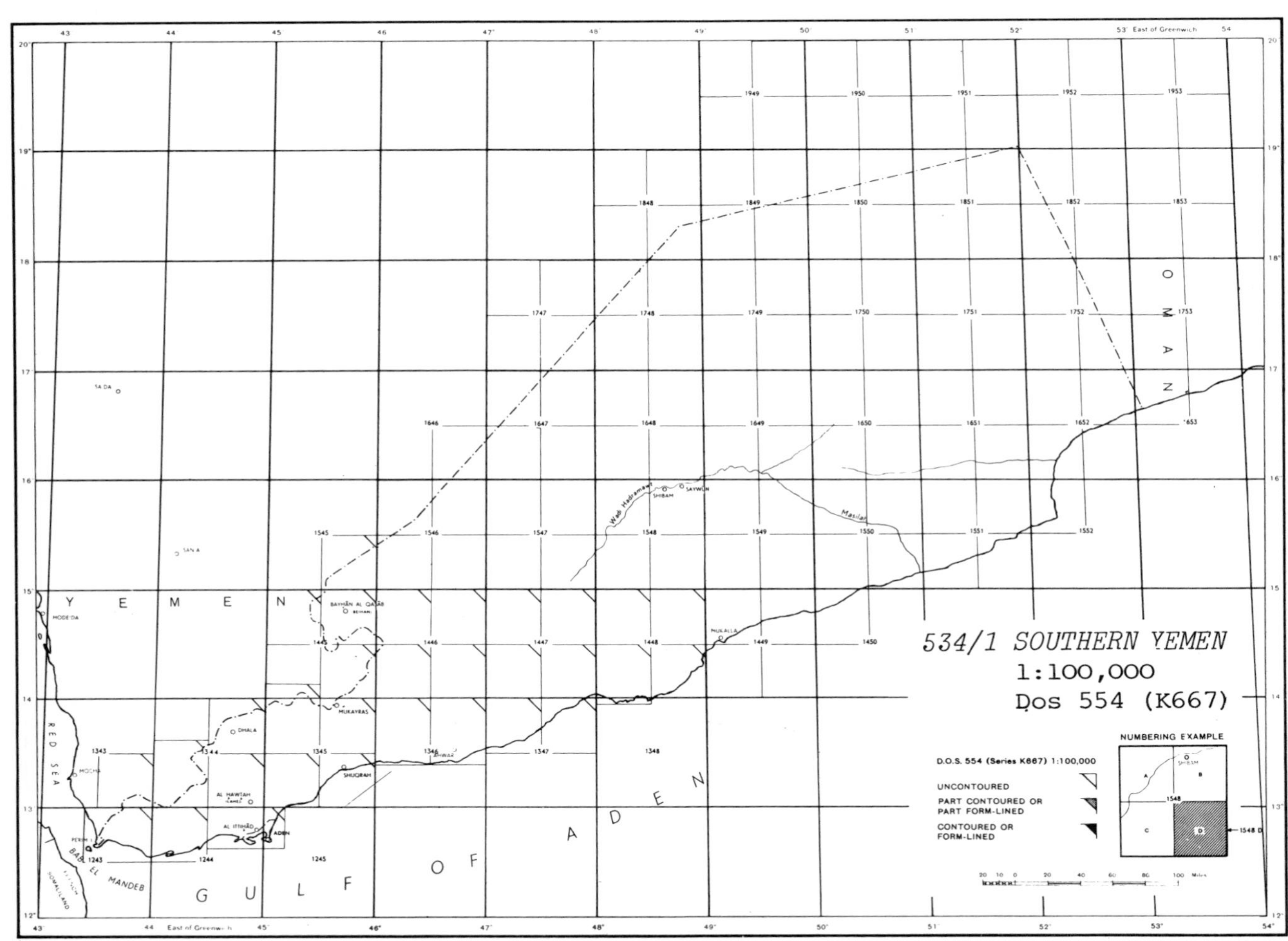

534/1 SOUTHERN YEMEN
1:100,000
Dos 554 (K667)
D.O.S. 554 (Series K667) 1:100,000
UNCONTOURED
PART CONTOURED OR PART FORM-LINED
CONTOURED OR FORM-LINED
NUMBERING EXAMPLE
SHIBAM
A
B
1548
C
D
1548 D
20 10 0 20 40 60 80 100 Miles
East of Greenwich
YEMEN
OMAN
GULF OF ADEN
RED SEA
BAB EL MANDEB
SOMALILAND
HODE'DA
SAN'A
SA'DA
BAYHĀN AL QAṢĀB
MUKAYRAS
DHALA
MOCHA
AL HAWTAH
AL ITTIHĀD
ADEN
PERIM I.
SHUQRAH
MUKALLA
SHIBAM
SAYWUN
Wadi Hadramawt
Masilah
1949 1950 1951 1952 1953
1848 1849 1850 1851 1852 1853
1747 1748 1749 1750 1751 1752 1753
1646 1647 1648 1649 1650 1651 1652 1653
1545 1546 1547 1548 1549 1550 1551 1552
1445 1446 1447 1448 1449 1450
1343 1344 1345 1346 1347 1348
1243 1244 1245

541.35/1 *NEPAL*
1:25,000 - 1:50,000 Univ. Verlag Wagner
Topographical map series

Maps published

Maps in preparation

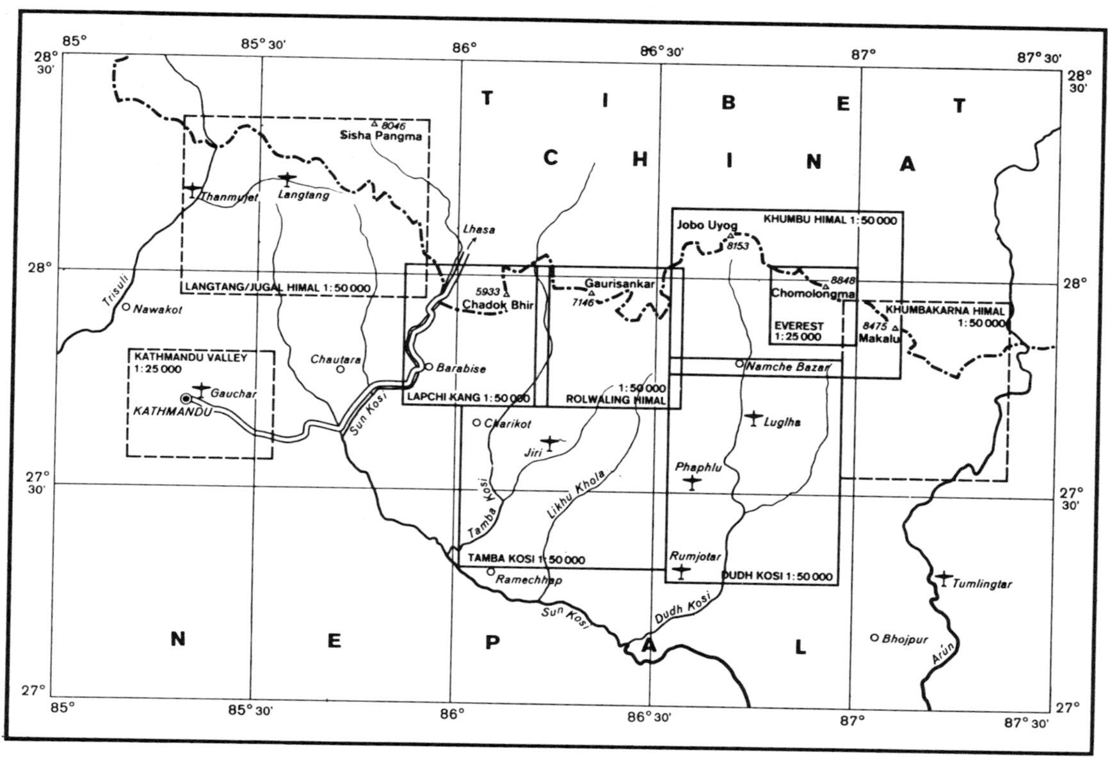

541.35/2 *LA CARTE ÉCOLOGIQUE DU NÉPAL*
1:250,000 - 1:50,000
Coloured series of ecological maps

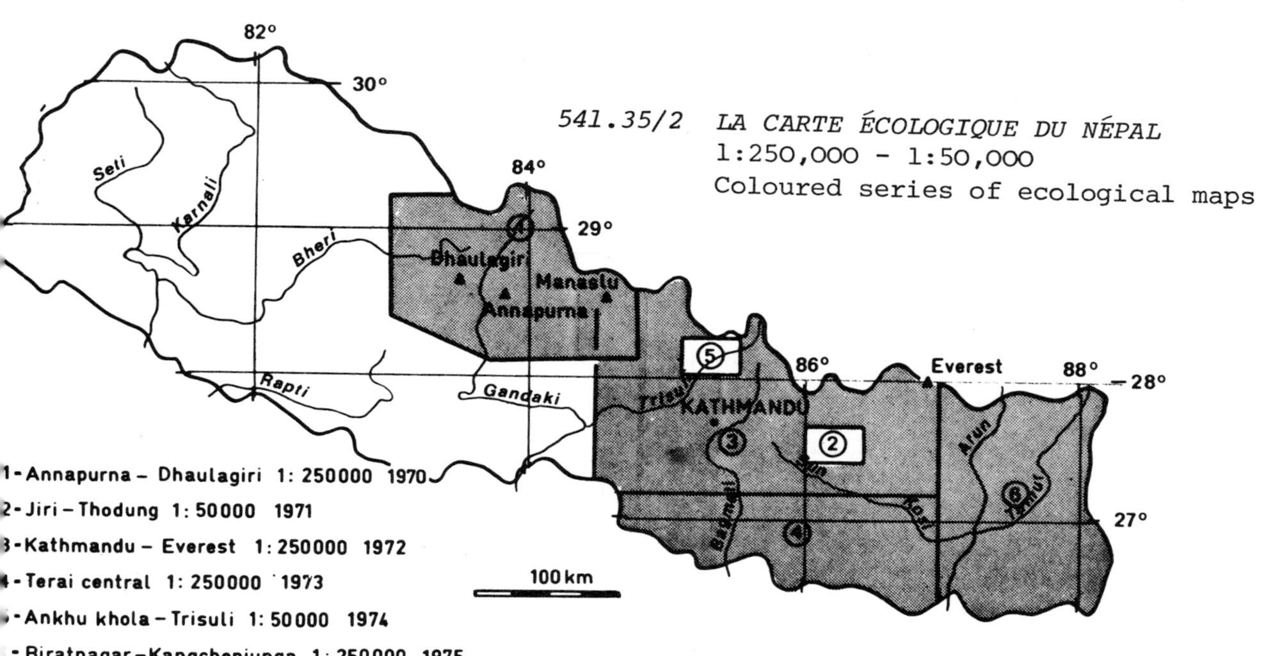

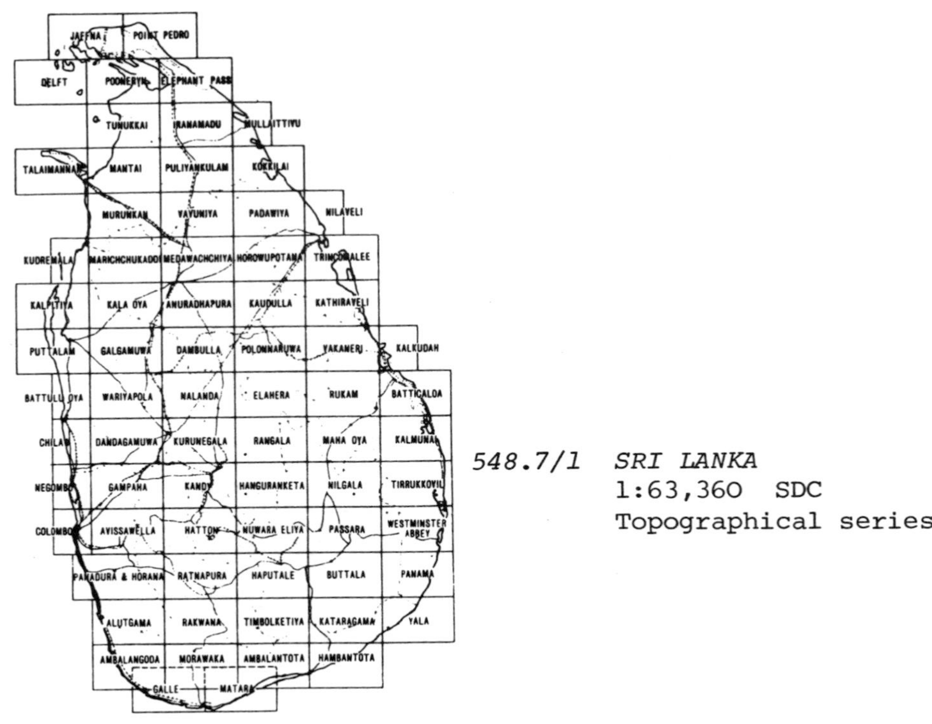

548.7/1 *SRI LANKA*
1:63,360 SDC
Topographical series

Guide to: New Guide Maps of the Provinces

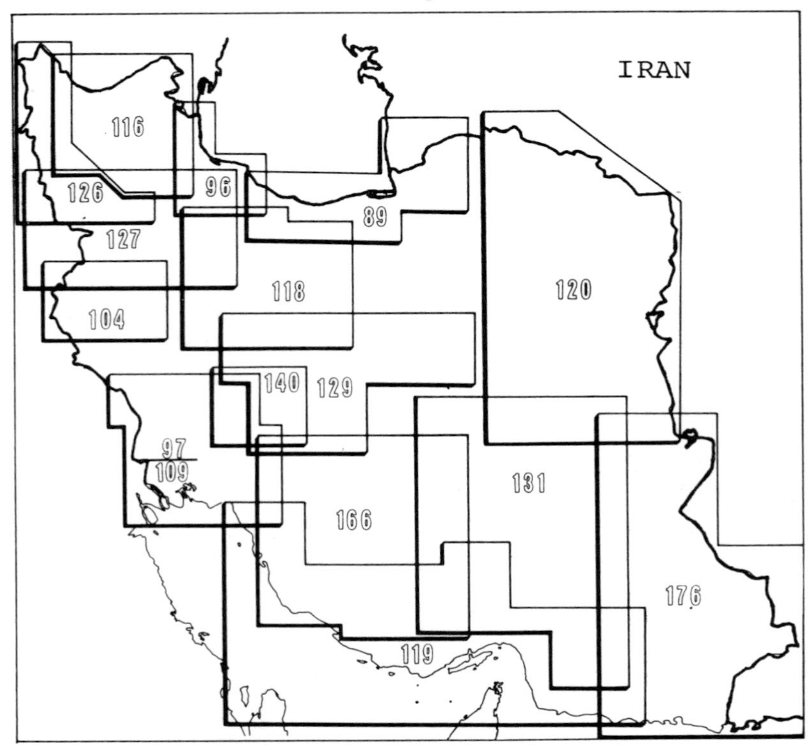

55/1 *NEW GUIDE MAPS OF THE PROVINCES*
Various scales Sahab

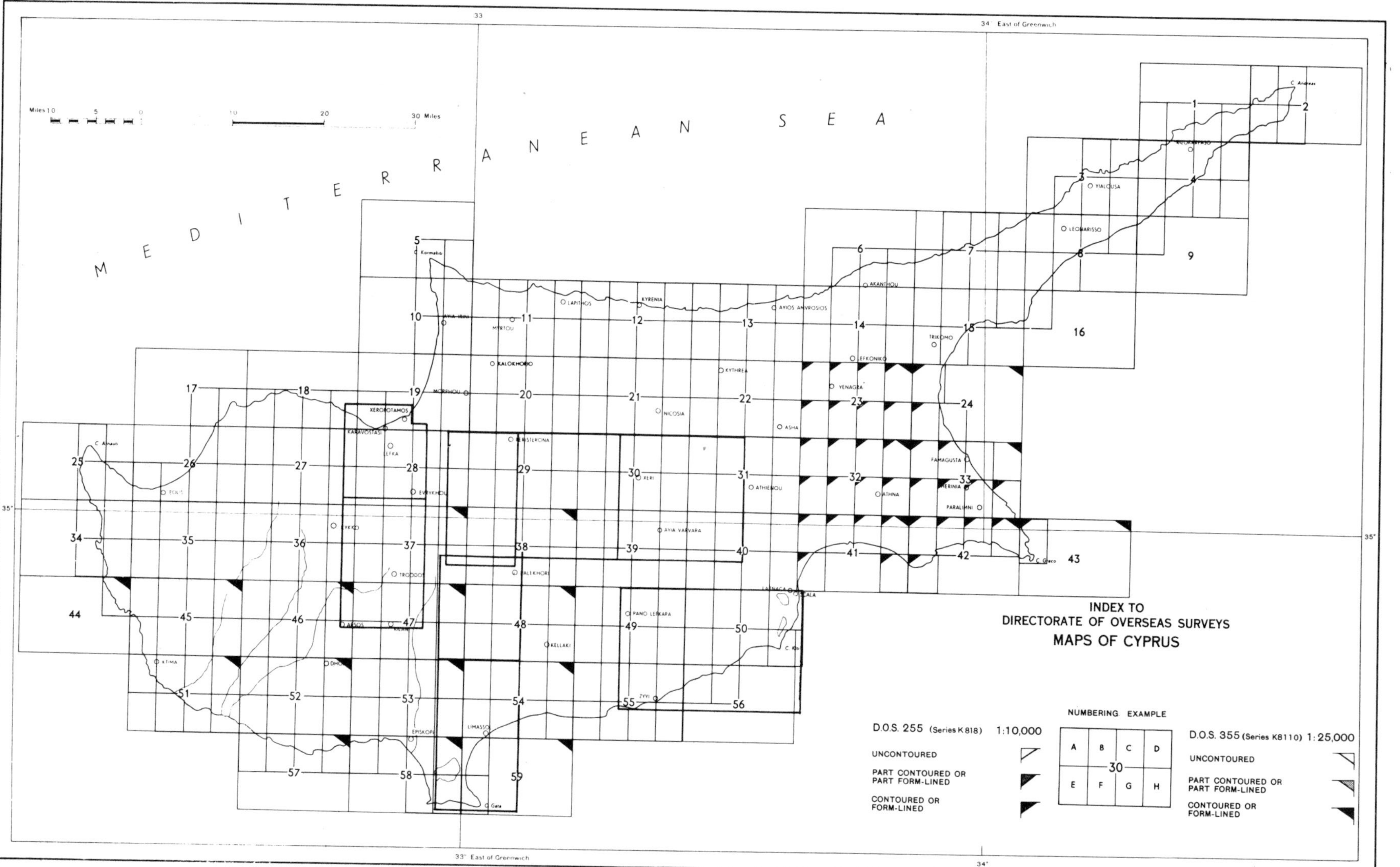

564.3/1 *CYPRUS*

1:10,000 DOS 255 (K818)

1:25,000 DOS 355 (K8110)

Topographical Series

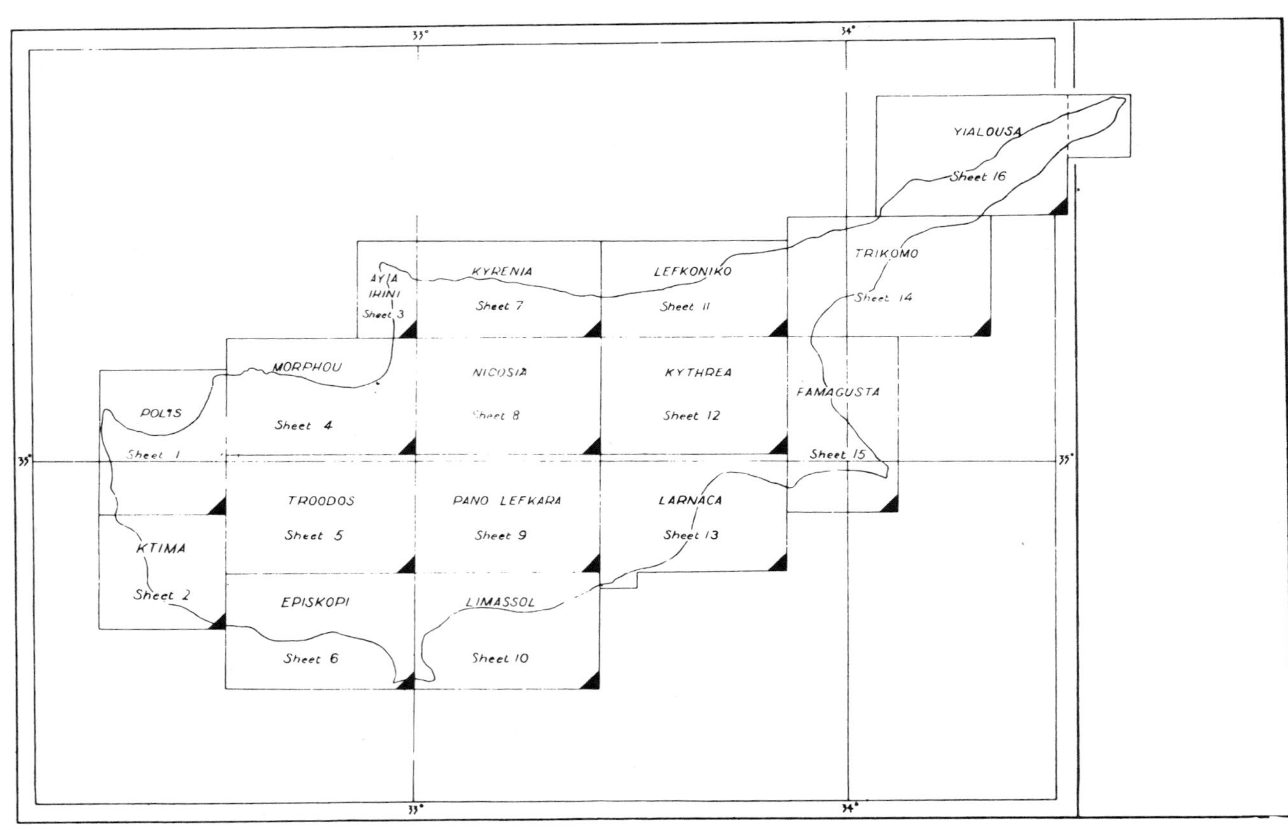

564.3/2 PASTURE SURVEY OF CYPRUS
1:50,000 Land Reg. and Surveys

564.3/3 CYPRUS-TOPOGRAPHICAL SERIES
1:31,680
Gov't of Cyprus Printing Office

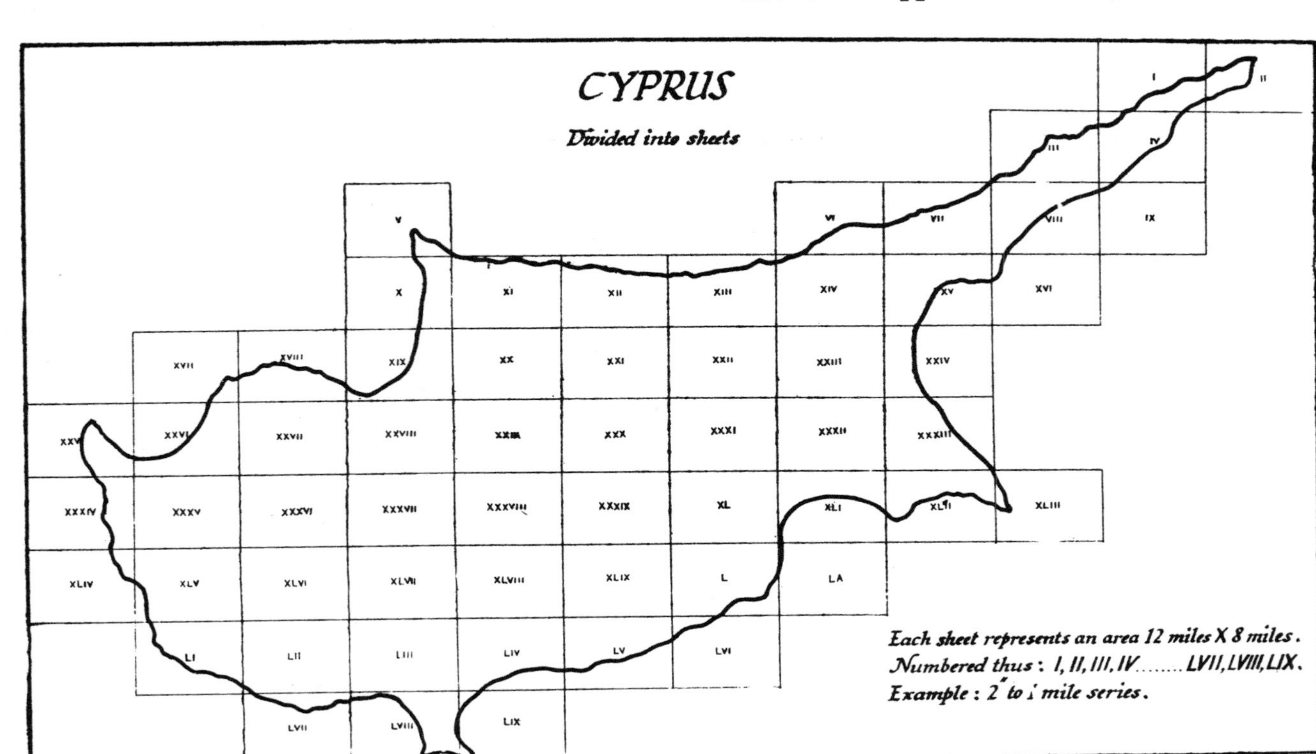

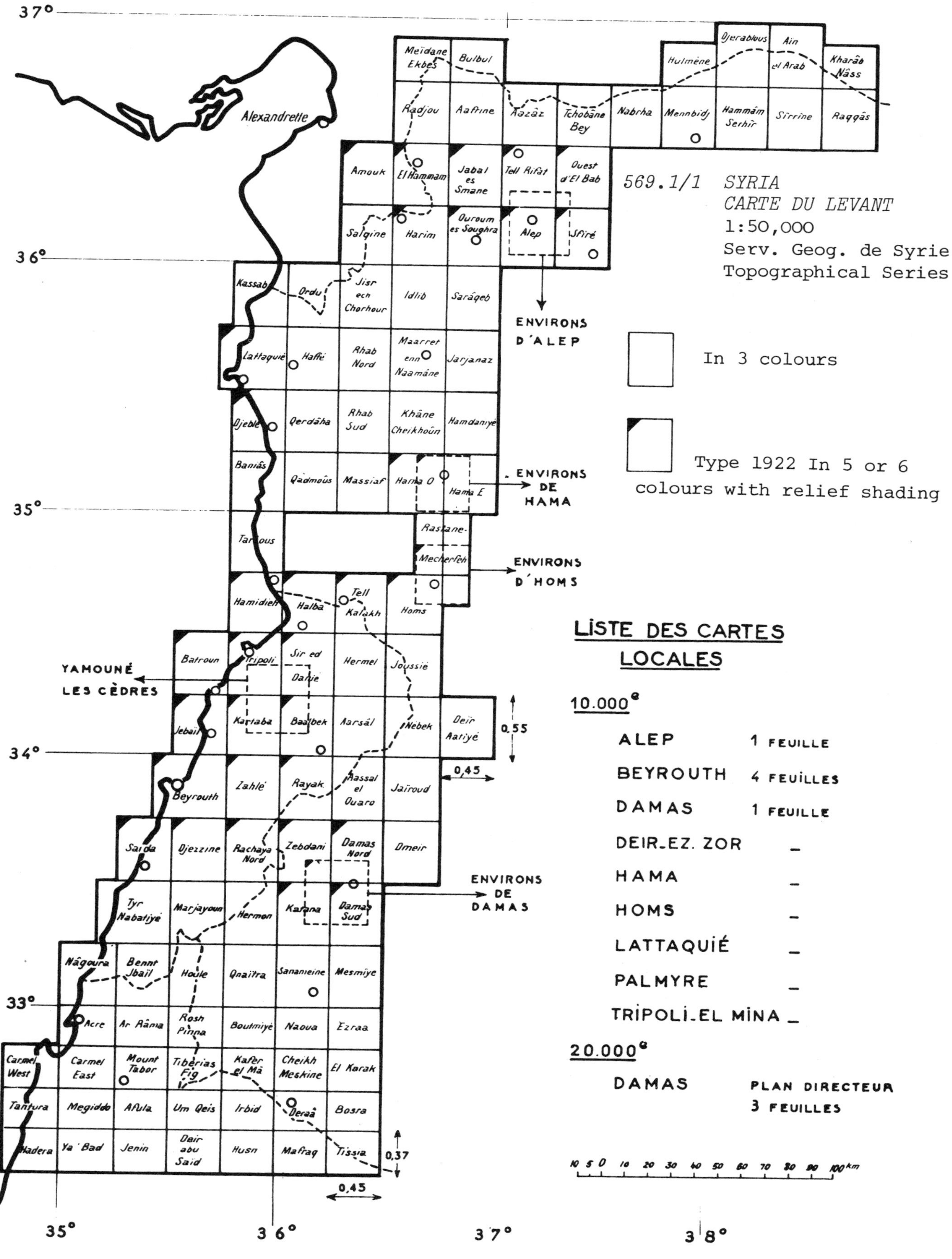
569.1/1 SYRIA
CARTE DU LEVANT
1:50,000
Serv. Geog. de Syrie
Topographical Series
In 3 colours
Type 1922 In 5 or 6 colours with relief shading
LISTE DES CARTES LOCALES
10.000e
ALEP 1 FEUILLE
BEYROUTH 4 FEUILLES
DAMAS 1 FEUILLE
DEIR-EZ. ZOR –
HAMA –
HOMS –
LATTAQUIÉ –
PALMYRE –
TRIPOLI-EL MINA –
20.000e
DAMAS PLAN DIRECTEUR 3 FEUILLES
ENVIRONS D'ALEP
ENVIRONS DE HAMA
ENVIRONS D'HOMS
ENVIRONS DE DAMAS
YAMOUNÉ
LES CÈDRES
Alexandrette
37°
36°
35°
34°
33°
35°
36°
37°
38°
0,55
0,45
0,37
0,45
10 5 0 10 20 30 40 50 60 70 80 90 100 km
Meïdane Ekbes
Bulbul
Djerablous
Aïn el Arab
Hulmène
Kharâb Nâss
Radjou
Aafrine
Aazâz
Tchobâne Bey
Nabrha
Mennbidj
Hammâm Serhîr
Sîrrine
Raqqâs
Amouk
El Hammam
Jabal es Smane
Tell Rifât
Ouest d'El Bab
Salqine
Harim
Ouroum es Soughra
Alep
Sfiré
Kassab
Ordu
Jisr ech Chorhour
Idlib
Sarâqeb
Lattaquié
Haffé
Rhab Nord
Maarret enn Naamâne
Jarjanaz
Djeblé
Qerdâha
Rhab Sud
Khâne Cheikhoûn
Hamdaniyé
Baniâs
Qadmoûs
Massiaf
Hama O
Hama E
Rastane
Tartous
Mecherfeh
Hamidieh
Halba
Tell Kalakh
Homs
Batroun
Tripoli
Sir ed Danie
Hermel
Joussié
Jebaïl
Kartaba
Baalbek
Aarsâl
Nebek
Deir Aatiyé
Beyrouth
Zahlé
Rayak
Assal el Ouaro
Jaïroud
Saïda
Djezzine
Rachaya Nord
Zebdani
Damas Nord
Omeir
Tyr Nabatiyé
Marjayoun
Hermon
Katana
Damas Sud
Nâqoura
Bennt Jbaïl
Houle
Qnaïtra
Sanameine
Mesmiyé
Acre
Ar Râma
Rosh Pinna
Boutmiyé
Naoua
Ezraa
Carmel West
Carmel East
Mount Tabor
Tiberias Fig
Kafer el Mâ
Cheikh Meskine
El Karak
Tantura
Megiddo
Afula
Um Qeis
Irbid
Deraâ
Bosra
Hadera
Ya' Bad
Jenin
Deir abu Said
Husn
Mafraq
Tissia

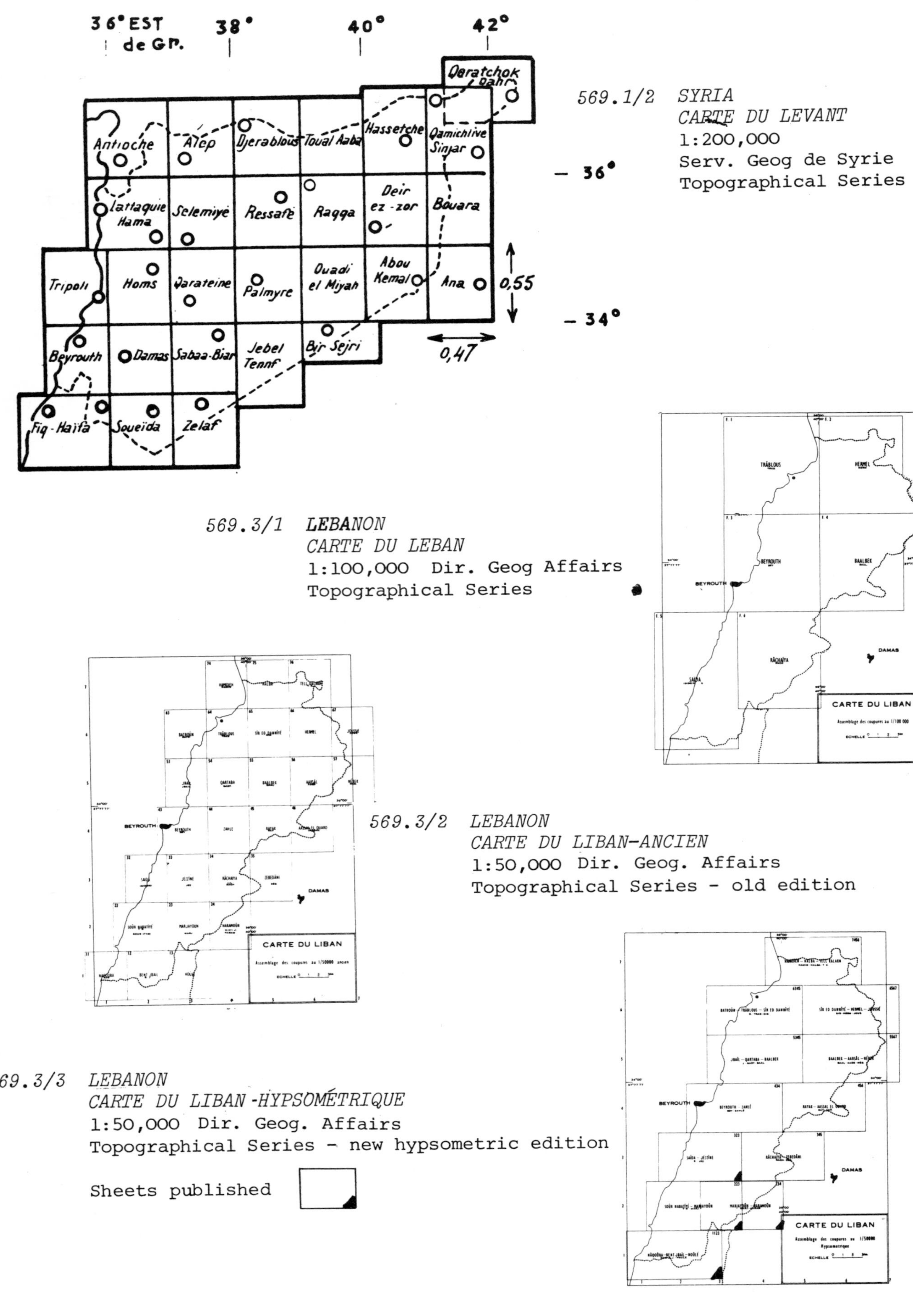

569.1/2 *SYRIA*
CARTE DU LEVANT
1:200,000
Serv. Geog de Syrie
Topographical Series

569.3/1 **LEBANON**
CARTE DU LEBAN
1:100,000 Dir. Geog Affairs
Topographical Series

569.3/2 *LEBANON*
CARTE DU LIBAN-ANCIEN
1:50,000 Dir. Geog. Affairs
Topographical Series - old edition

569.3/3 *LEBANON*
CARTE DU LIBAN-HYPSOMÉTRIQUE
1:50,000 Dir. Geog. Affairs
Topographical Series - new hypsometric edition

Sheets published

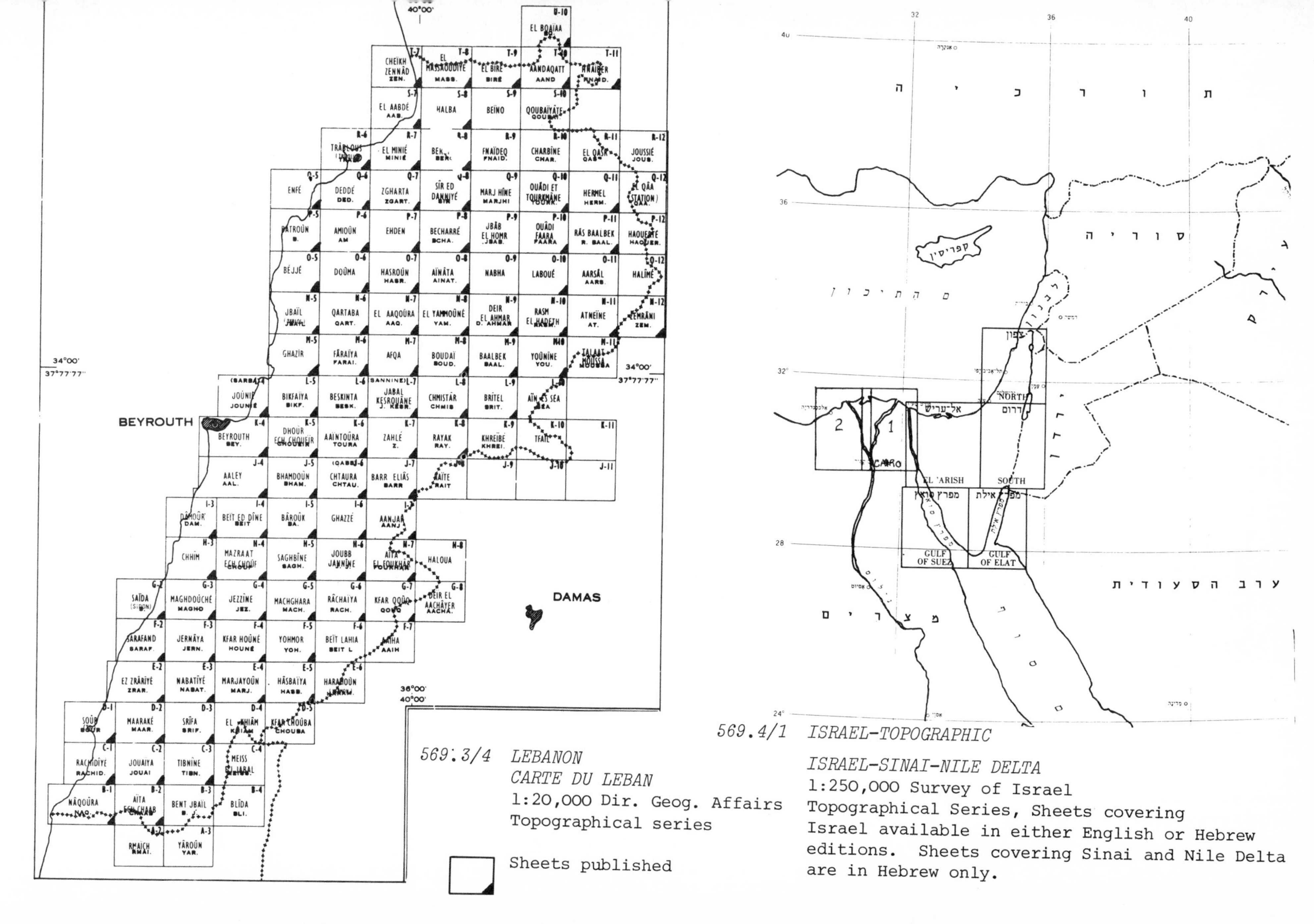

569.3/4 *LEBANON*
CARTE DU LEBAN
1:20,000 Dir. Geog. Affairs
Topographical series

Sheets published

569.4/1 *ISRAEL–TOPOGRAPHIC*

ISRAEL–SINAI–NILE DELTA
1:250,000 Survey of Israel
Topographical Series, Sheets covering
Israel available in either English or Hebrew
editions. Sheets covering Sinai and Nile Delta
are in Hebrew only.

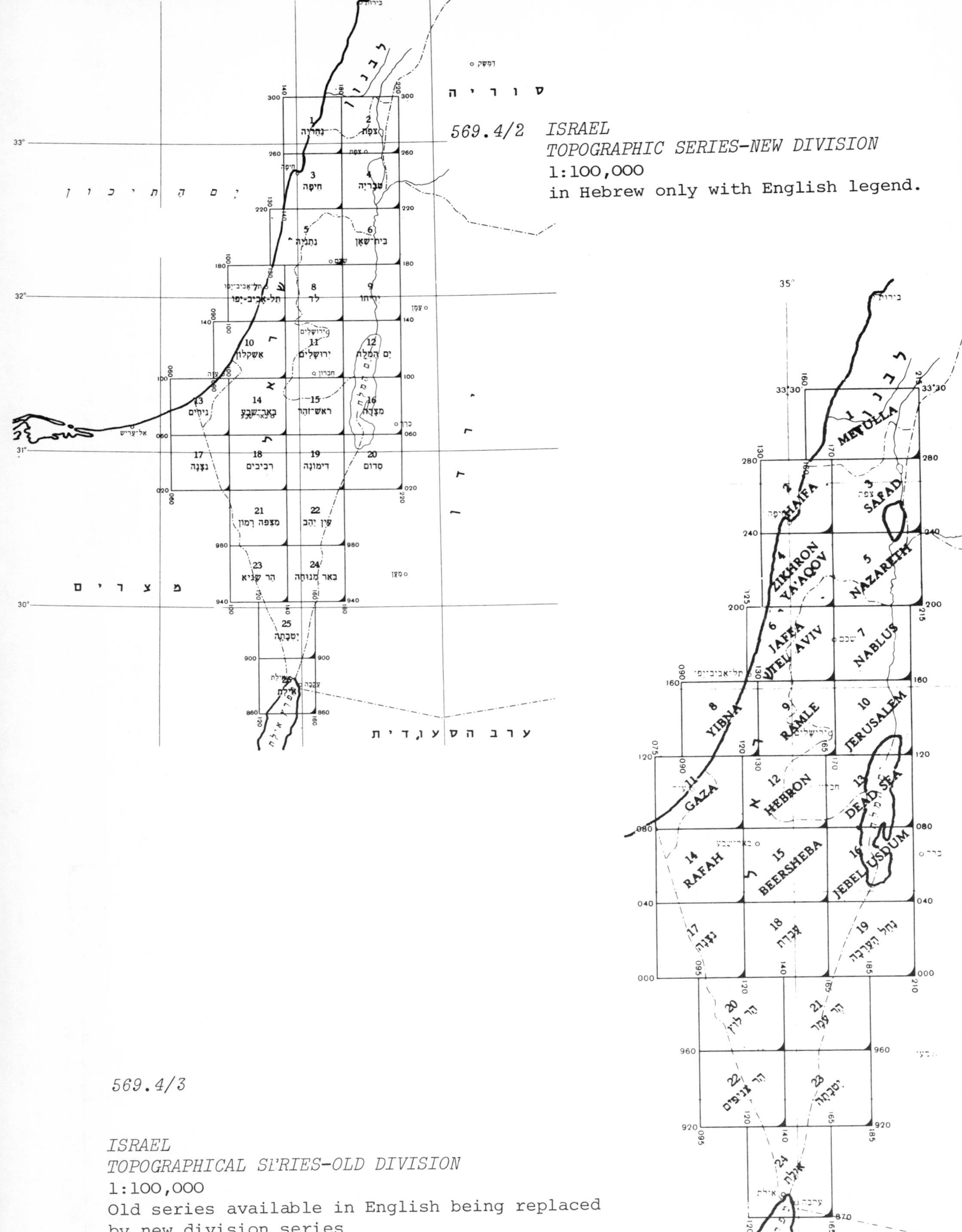

569.4/2 *ISRAEL*
TOPOGRAPHIC SERIES-NEW DIVISION
1:100,000
in Hebrew only with English legend.

569.4/3

ISRAEL
TOPOGRAPHICAL SERIES-OLD DIVISION
1:100,000
Old series available in English being replaced by new division series

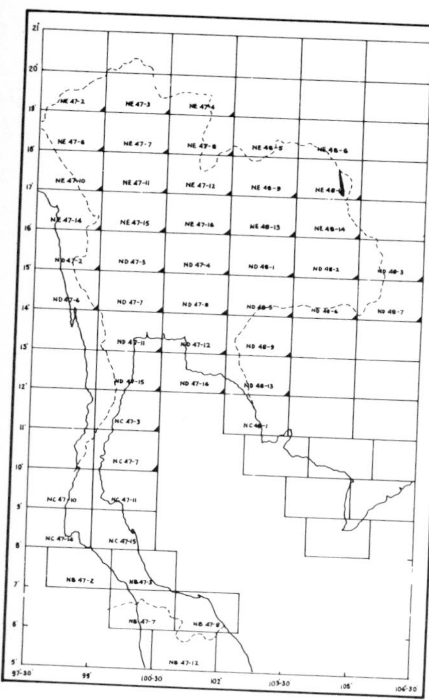

593/1 *THAILAND AMS SERIES* L509
1:250,000
Topographical series with legend in English and French

Sheets available

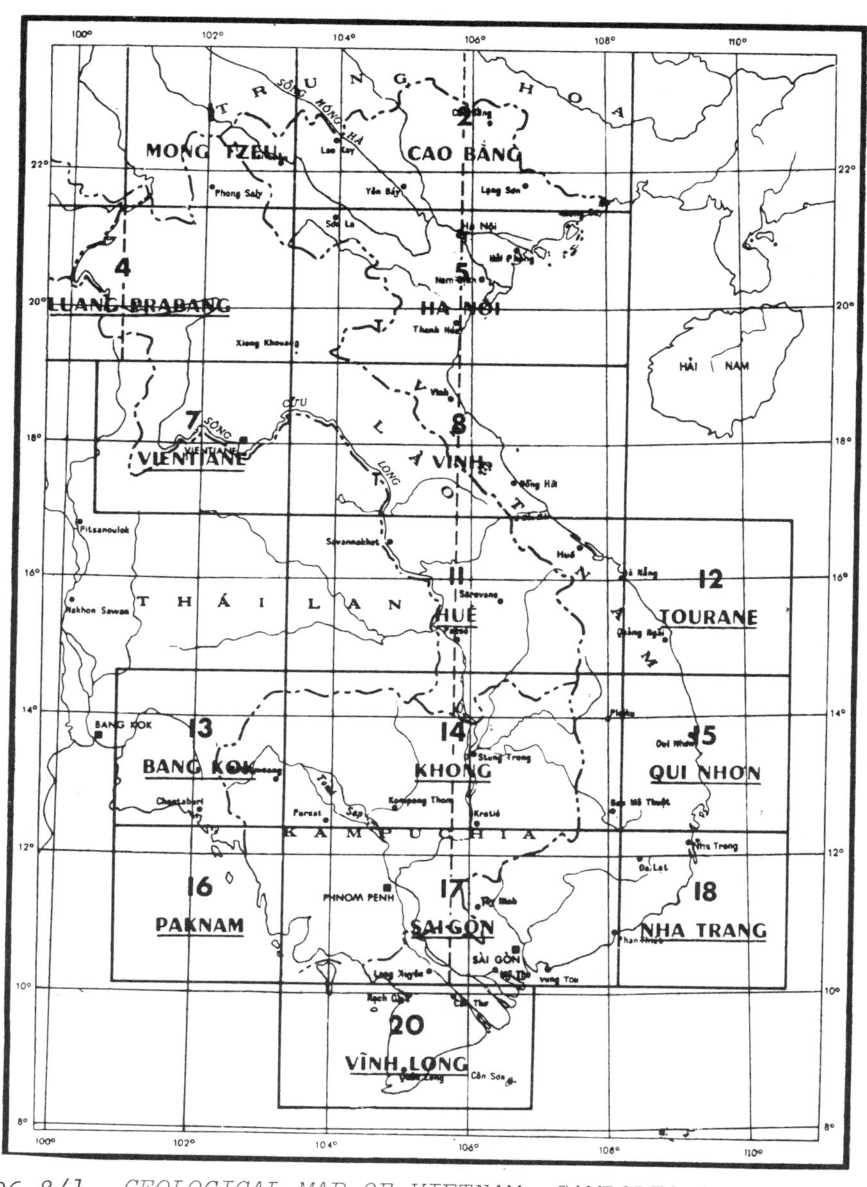

596-8/1 *GEOLOGICAL MAP OF VIETNAM, CAMBODIA AND LAOS*
1:500,000 NGD
Coloured series in 15 sheets.

NB Sheets with names underlined have an explanatory text.

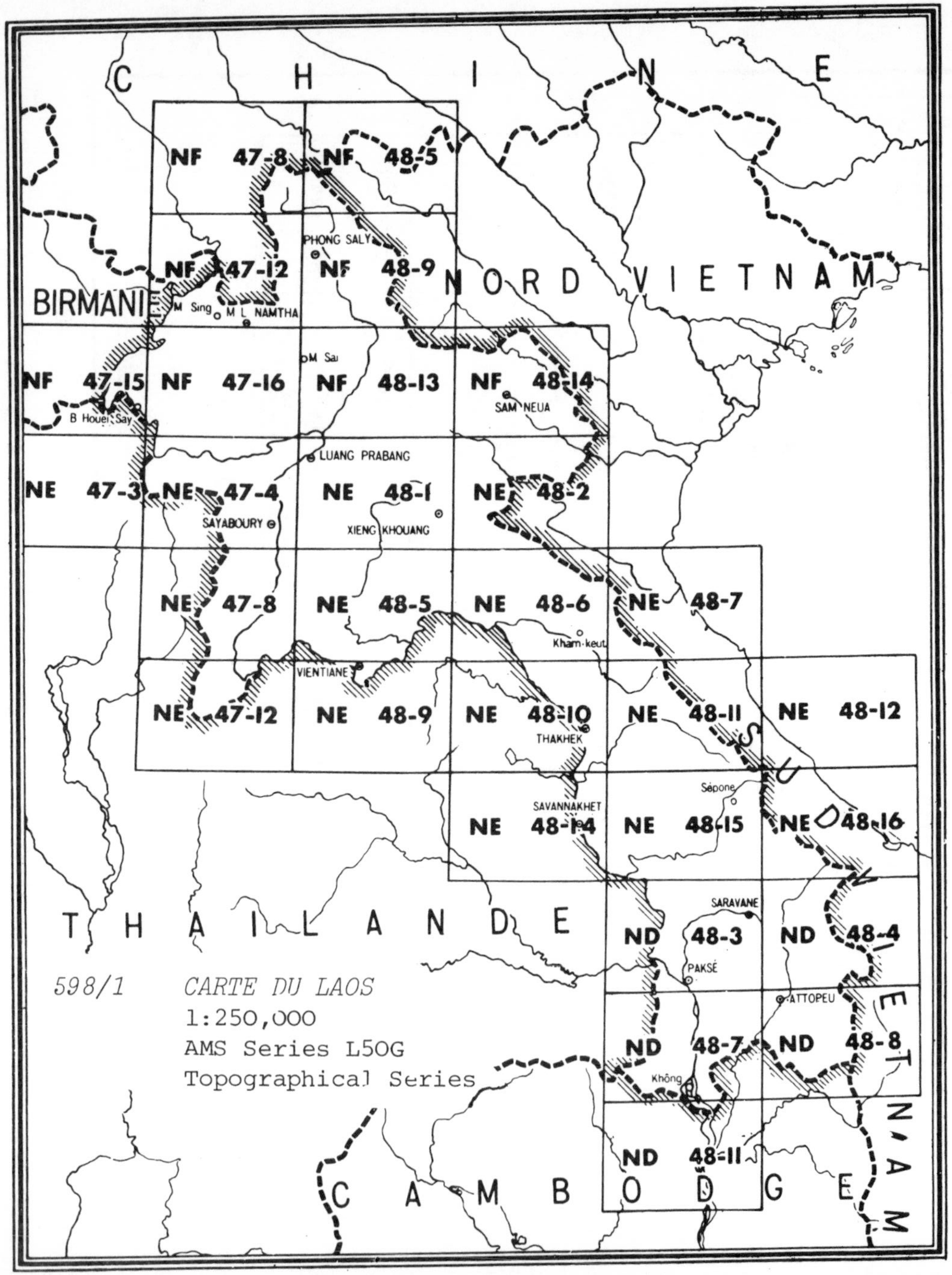

598/1 *CARTE DU LAOS*
1:250,000
AMS Series L50G
Topographical Series

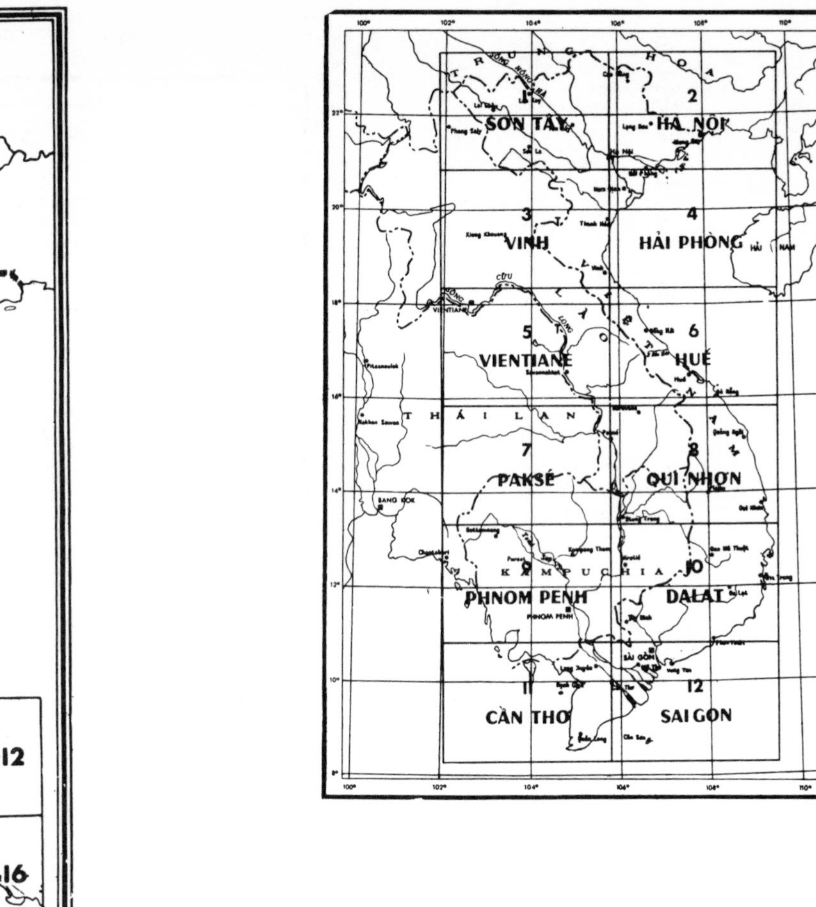

597/1 *VIETNAM ADMINISTRATIVE AND ROAD MAP*
1:500,000 NGD
Series in 12 sheets

Africa

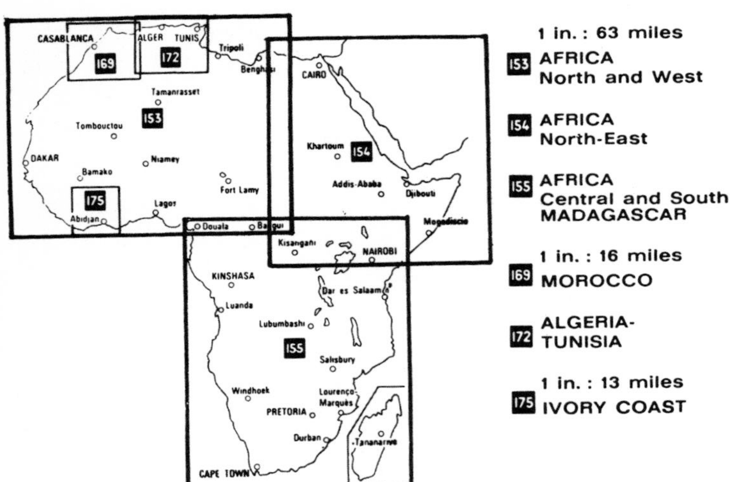

6/1 *MICHELIN ROAD MAPS OF AFRICA*
1:4,000,000

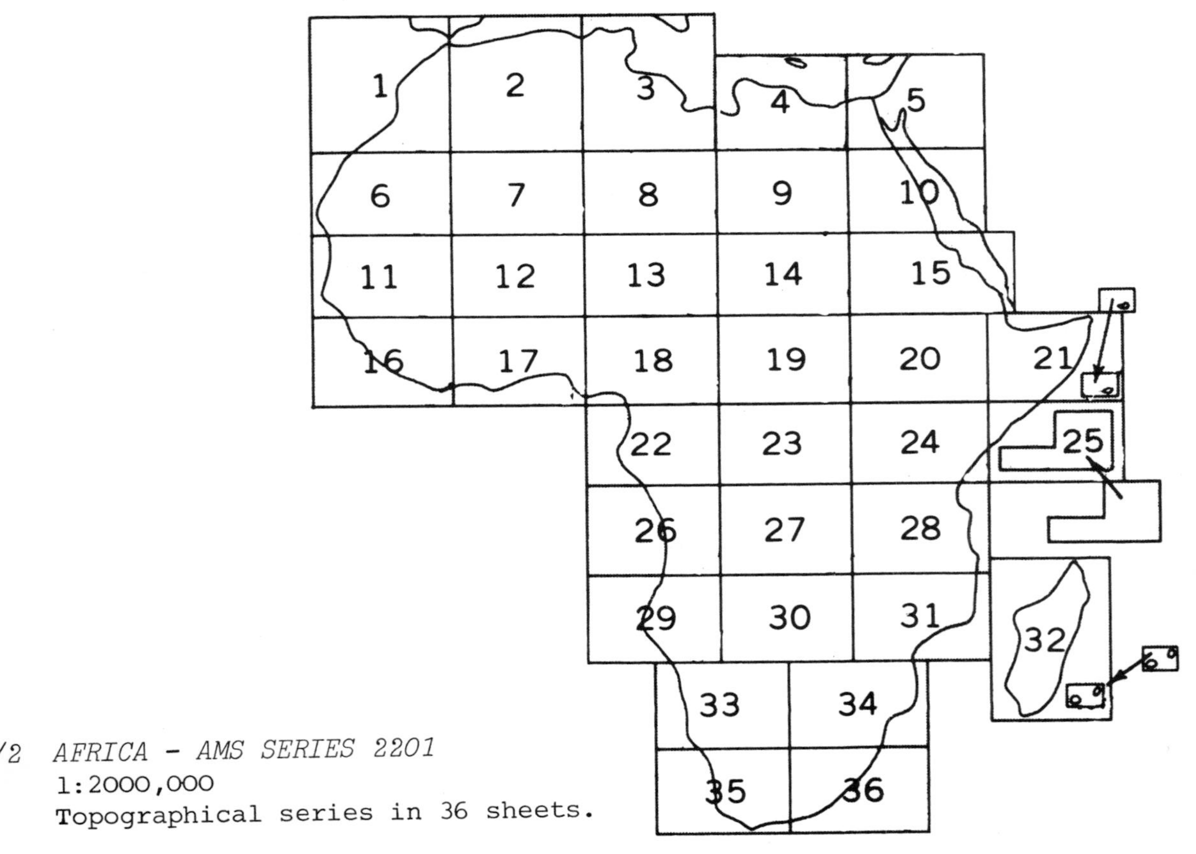

6/2 *AFRICA - AMS SERIES 2201*
1:2000,000
Topographical series in 36 sheets.

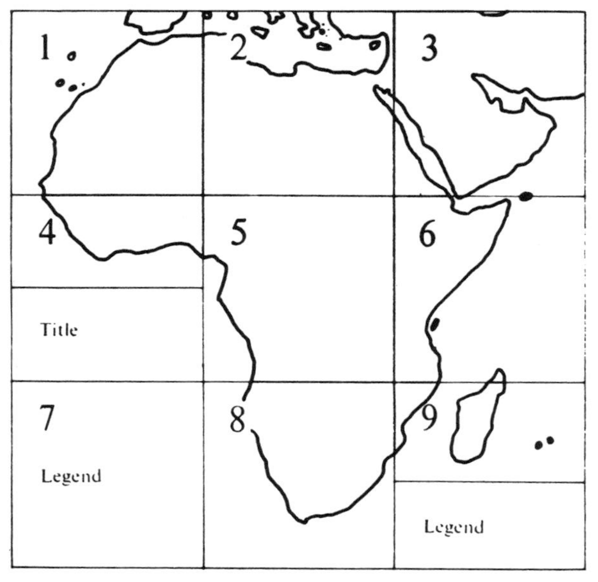

6/3 *INTERNATIONAL GEOLOGICAL MAP OF AFRICA*
(CARTE GÉOLOGIQUE INTERNATIONALE DE L'AFRIQUE)
1:5,000,000 Unesco/Asga
INTERNATIONAL TECTONIC MAP OF AFRICA
(CARTE TECTONIQUE INTERNATIONALE DE L'AFRIQUE)
1:5000,000 Unesco/Asga

2 maps each in 9 sheets including legend both on same sheet lines.

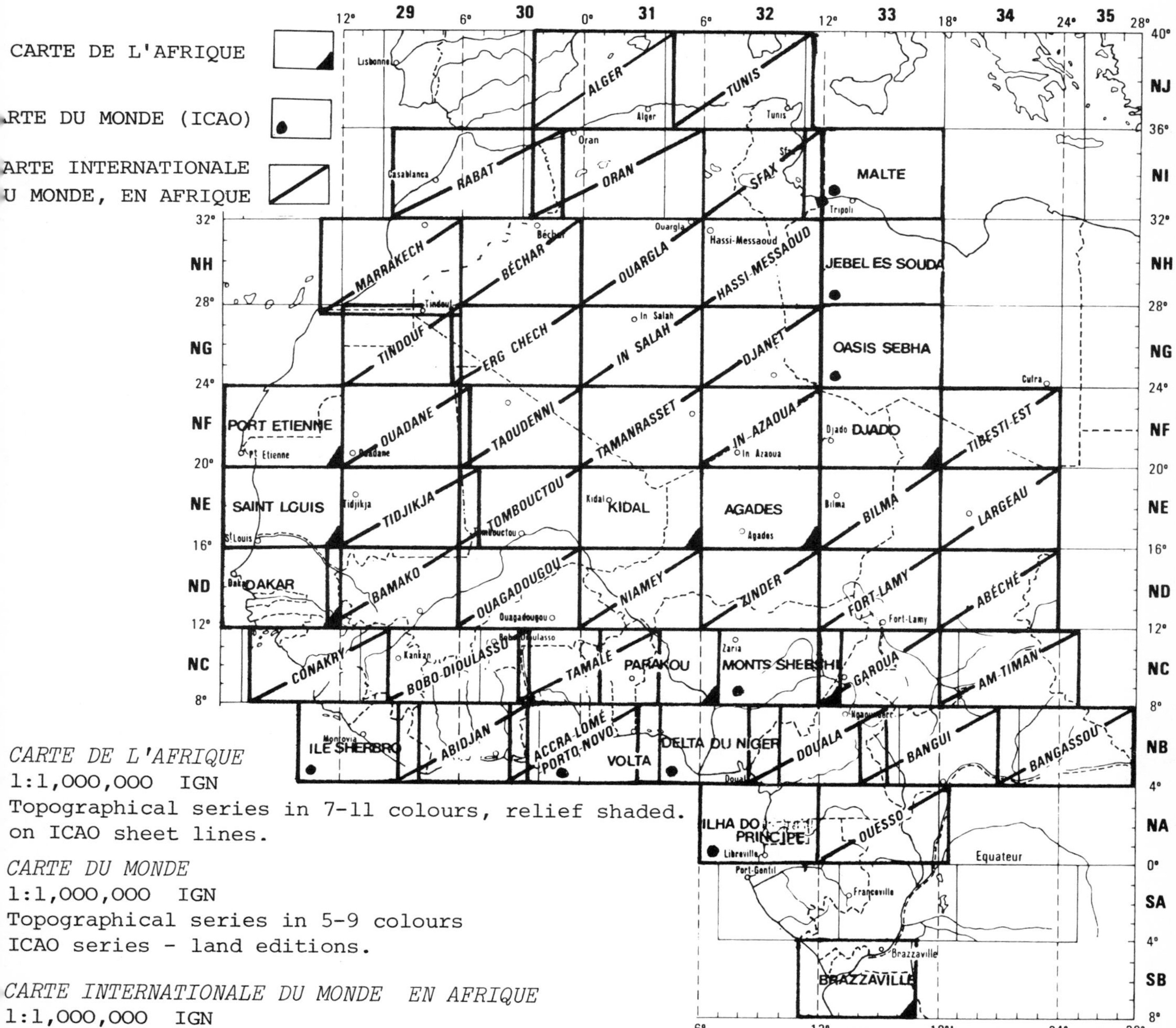

CARTE DE L'AFRIQUE
.RTE DU MONDE (ICAO)
ARTE INTERNATIONALE
U MONDE, EN AFRIQUE

CARTE DE L'AFRIQUE
1:1,000,000 IGN
Topographical series in 7-11 colours, relief shaded. on ICAO sheet lines.

CARTE DU MONDE
1:1,000,000 IGN
Topographical series in 5-9 colours
ICAO series - land editions.

CARTE INTERNATIONALE DU MONDE EN AFRIQUE
1:1,000,000 IGN
International map of the world editions which will eventually supersede the above two editions

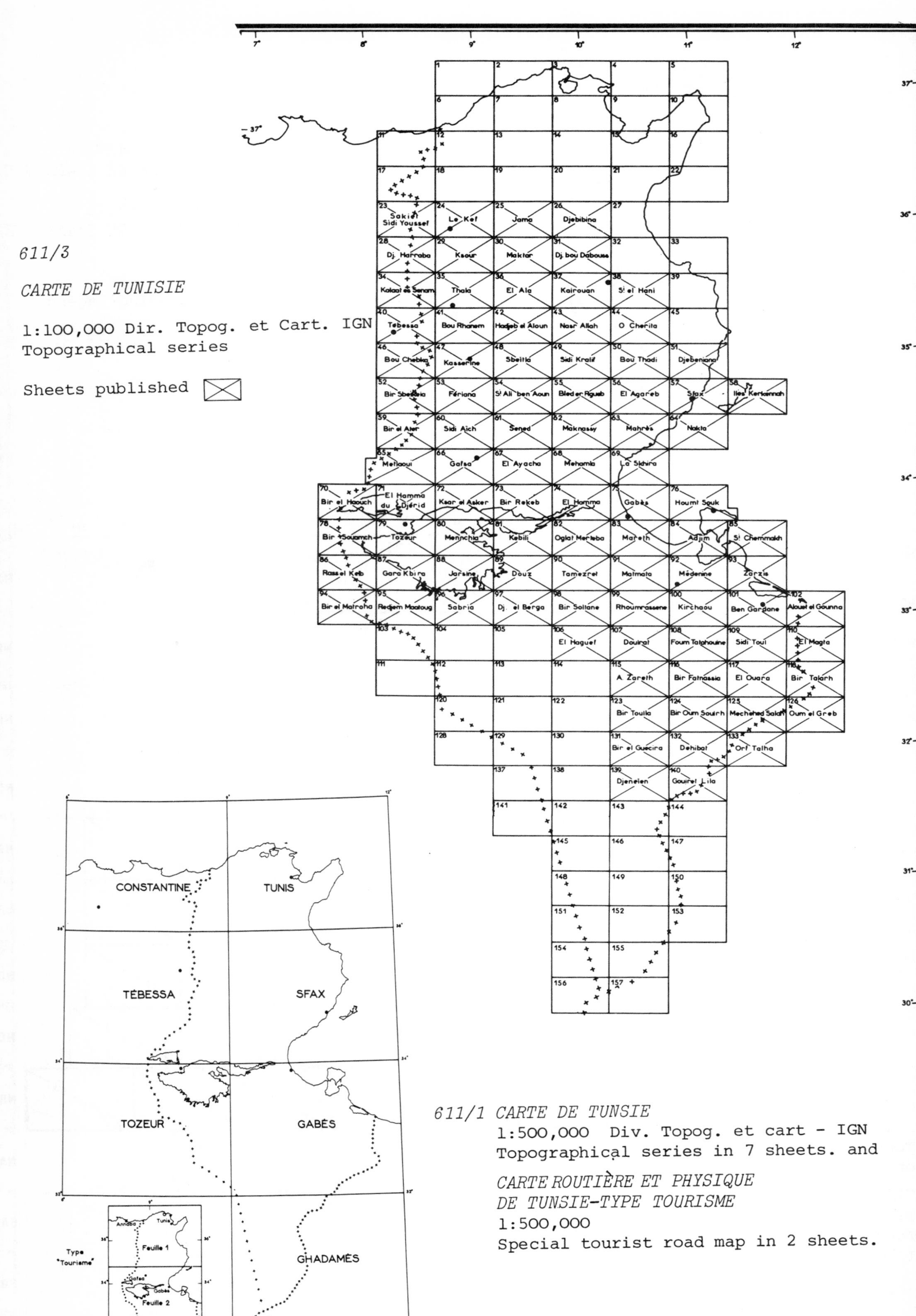

611/3

CARTE DE TUNISIE

1:100,000 Dir. Topog. et Cart. IGN
Topographical series

Sheets published ☒

611/1 CARTE DE TUNSIE
1:500,000 Div. Topog. et cart - IGN
Topographical series in 7 sheets. and

CARTE ROUTIÈRE ET PHYSIQUE
DE TUNSIE-TYPE TOURISME
1:500,000
Special tourist road map in 2 sheets.

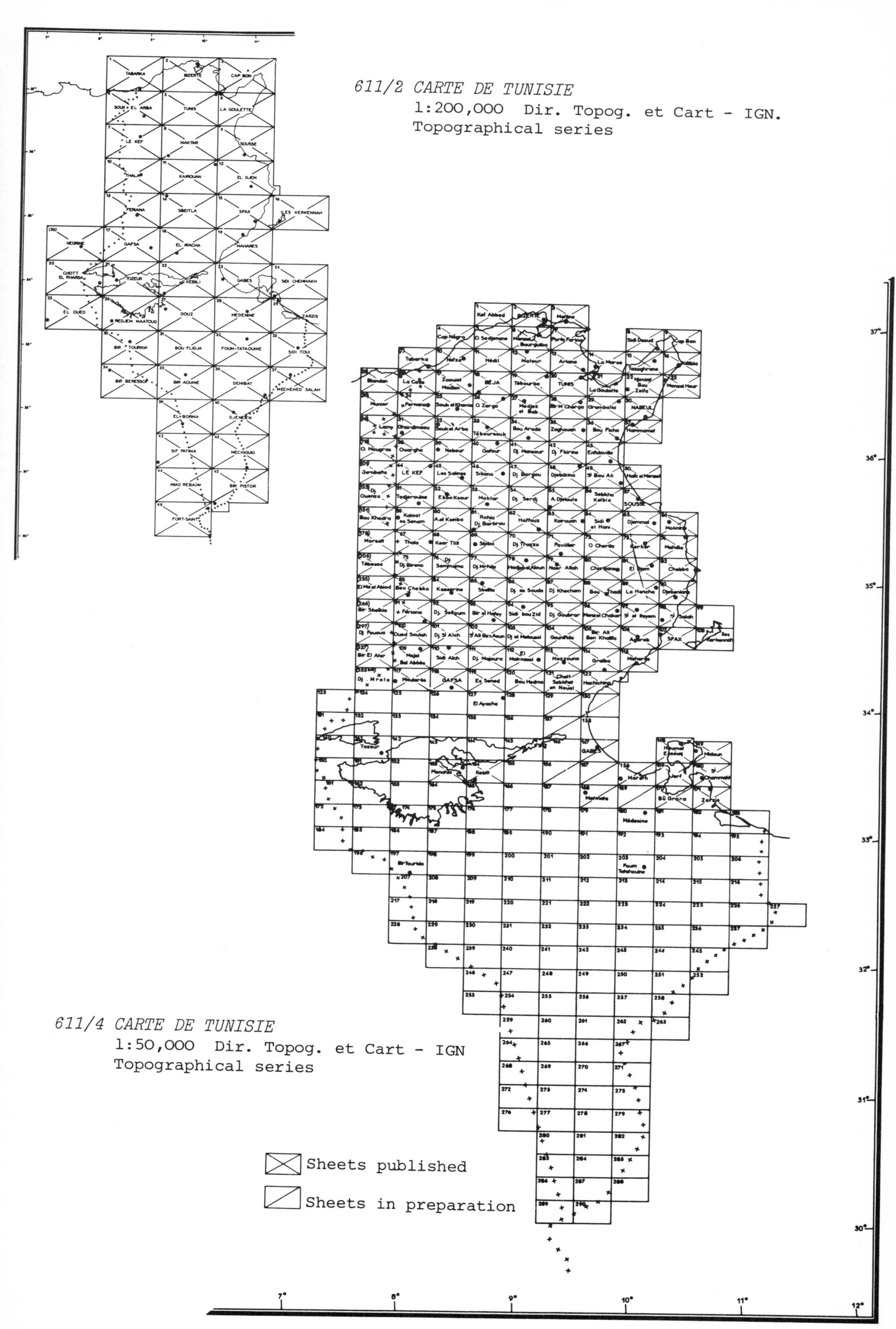
611/2 CARTE DE TUNISIE
1:200,000 Dir. Topog. et Cart - IGN.
Topographical series
611/4 CARTE DE TUNISIE
1:50,000 Dir. Topog. et Cart - IGN
Topographical series
Sheets published
Sheets in preparation

612/1
CARTA DIMOSTRATIVA DELLA LIBIA
1:1,000,000 IGM
Topographical Series in 11 sheets

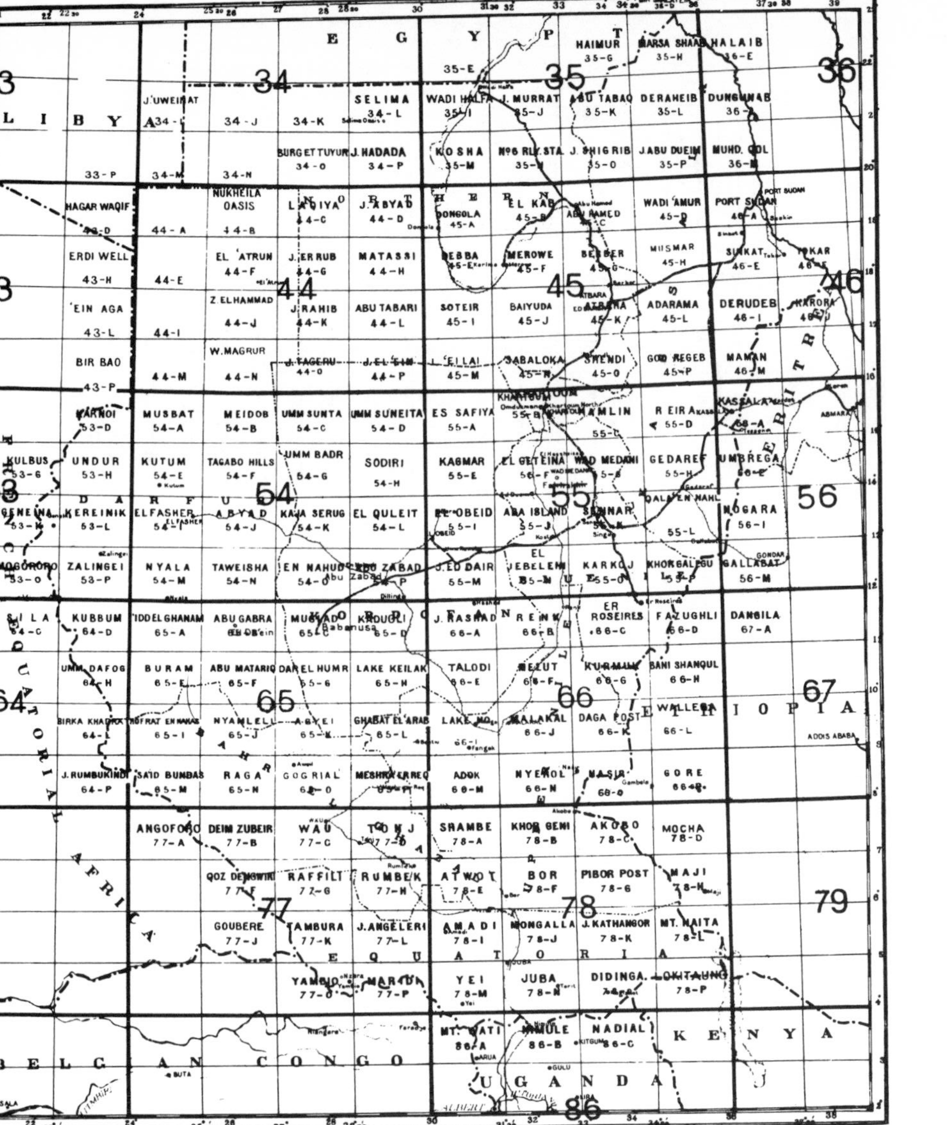

624/1 SUDAN
1:250,000 Sudan Survey Dept.
Topographical series in 178 sheets.

612/2 *CARTA DIMOSTRATIVA DELLA LIBIA*
1:400,000 IGM

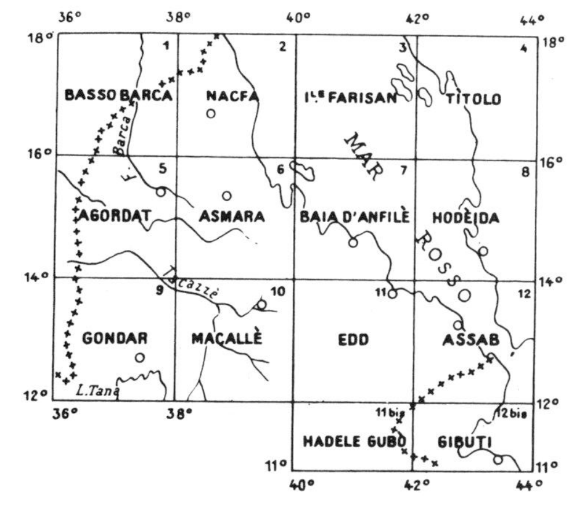

63/1 *CARTA DIMOSTRATIVA DELL ERITREA E DELLE REGIONI ADJACENTI*
1:400,000 1GM
Topographical series of Eritrea and adjacent area.

64/1 *CARTE DU MAROC*
1:500,000 1GN
Topographical series in 6 sheets.

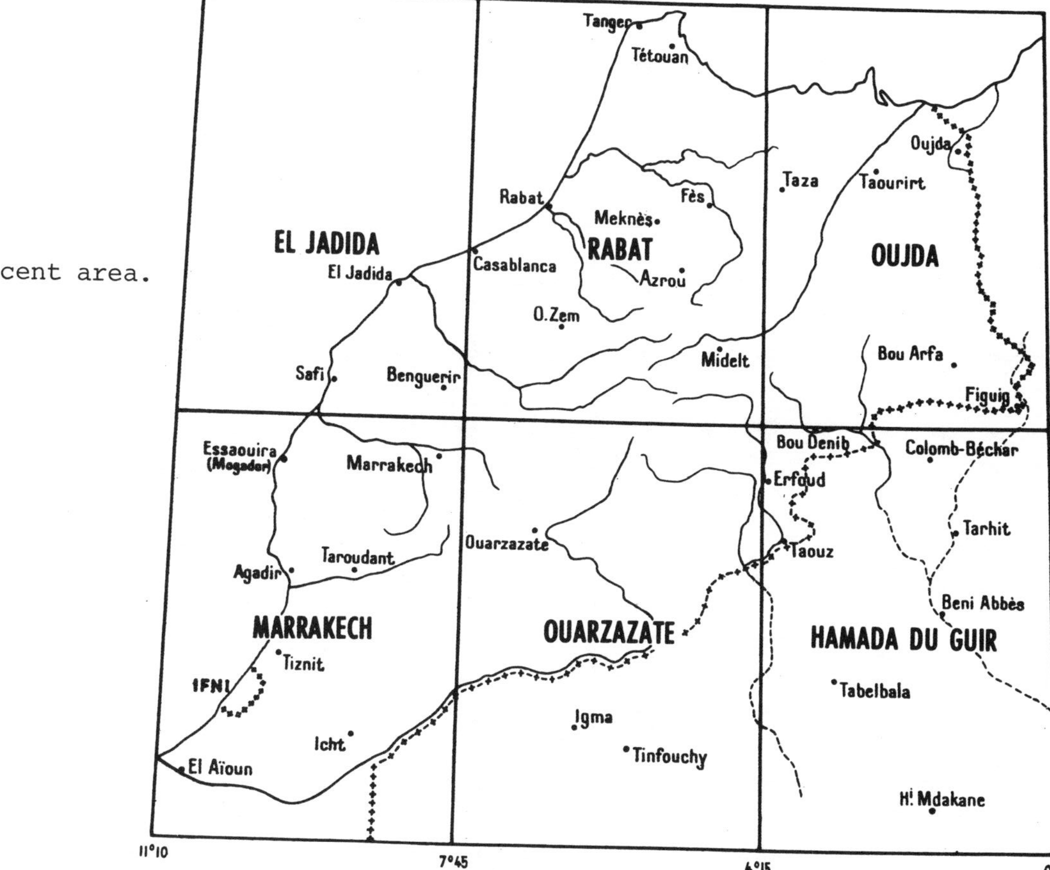

64/3 *CARTE DU MAROC*
1:100,000 1GN - Service Topographique
Topographical series in progress

Carte reguliere
contoured with relief shading

Edition provisiore
provisional edition - uncontoured
published in half sheets.

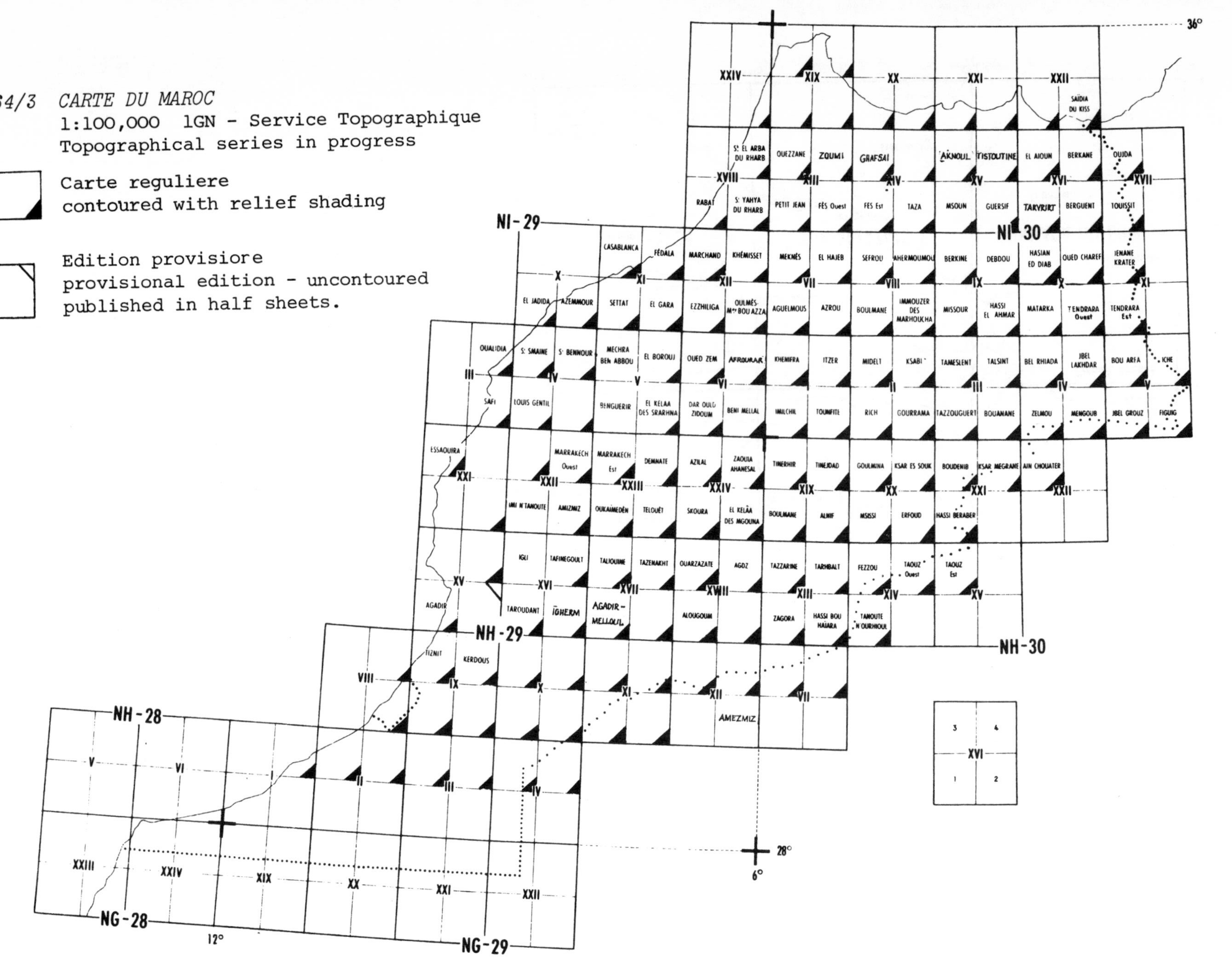

64/2 *CARTE DE RECONNAISSANCE DU MAROC*
1:200,000 IGN
Provisional Topographic series.

64/4 *CARTE DE RECONNAISSANCE DU MAROC*
1:100,000 IGN
Provisional topographical series

- Type 1954 in 5 colours - contoured
- Old series in 4 colours - uncontoured
- Sheets not published

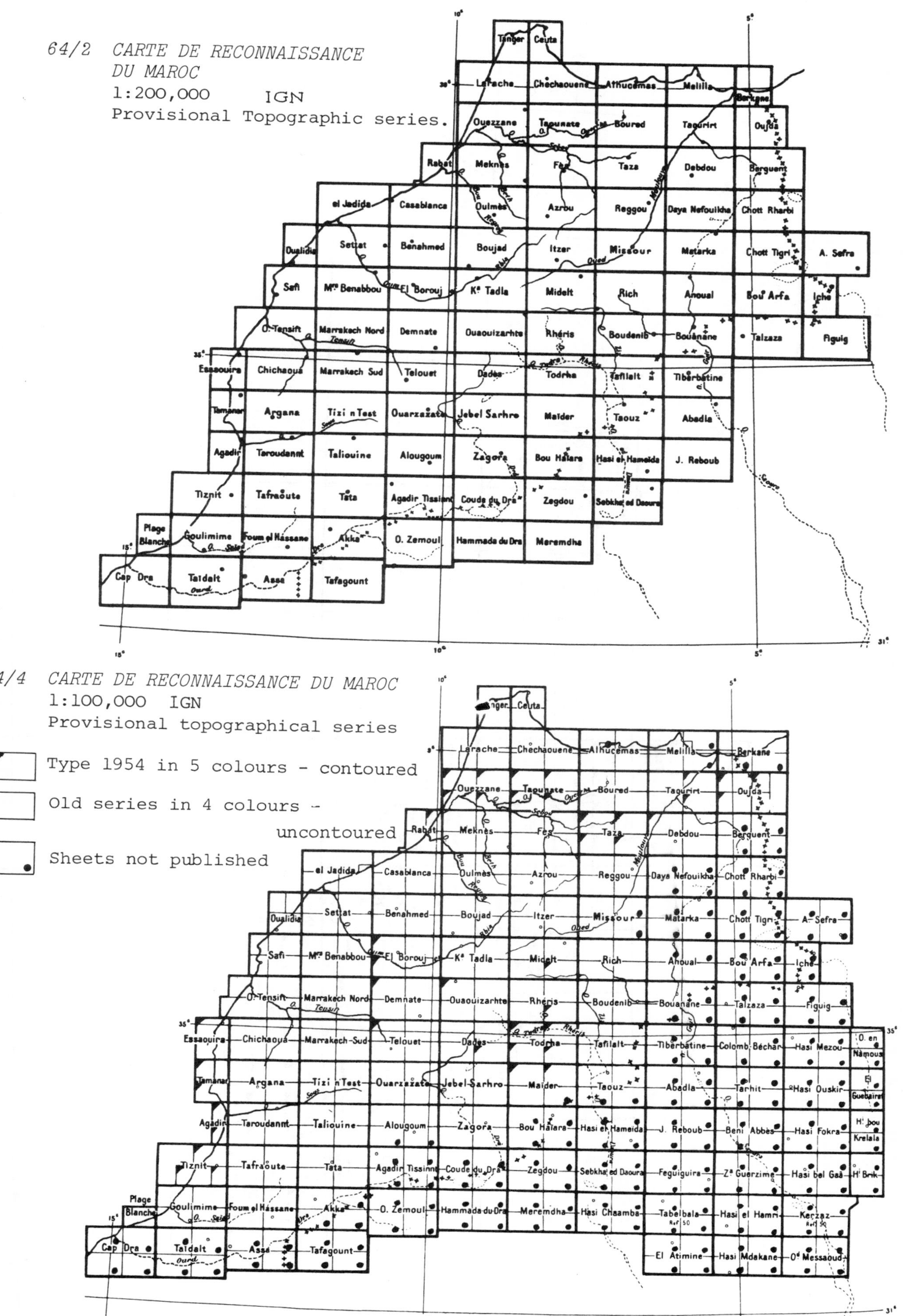

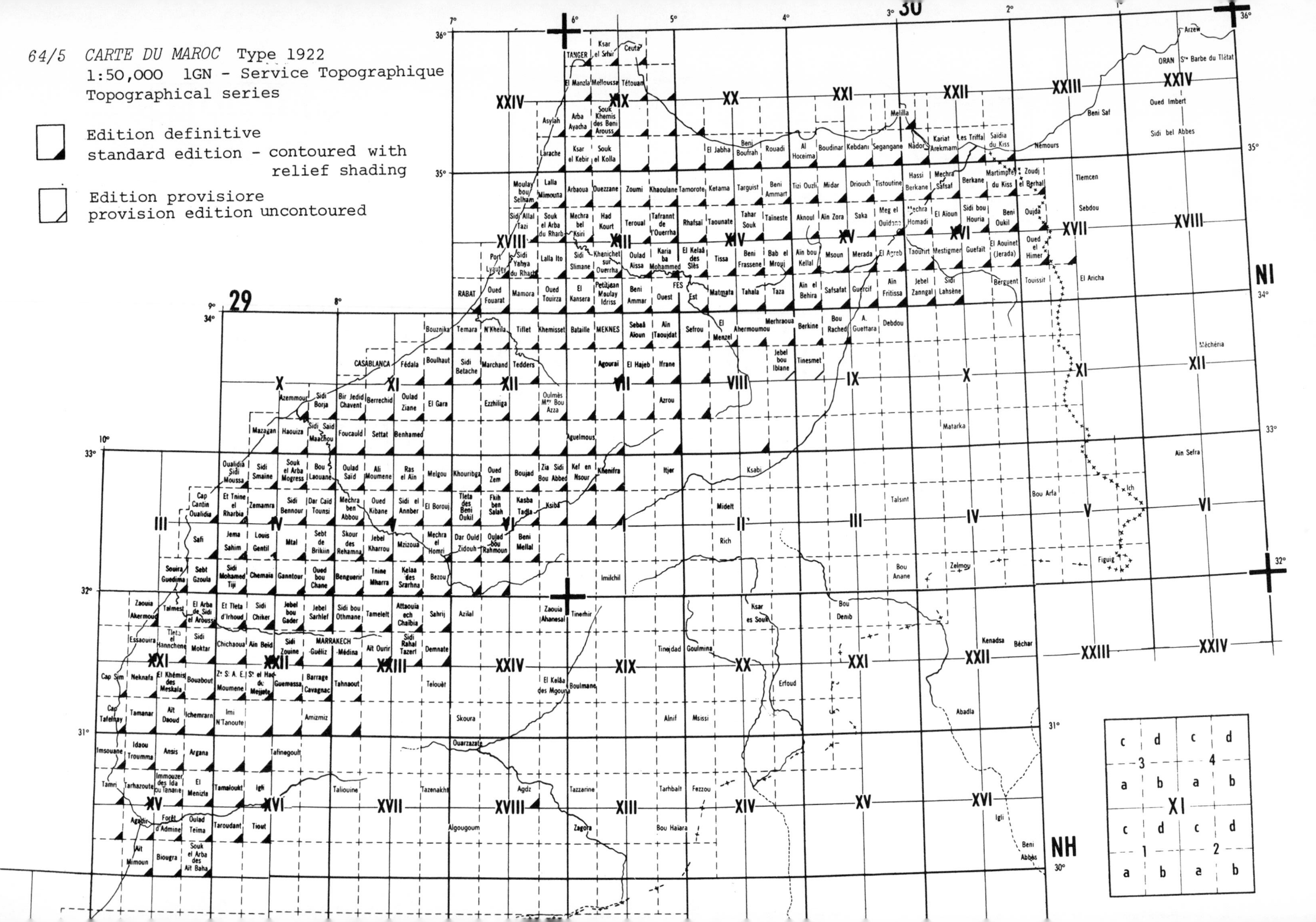
64/5 CARTE DU MAROC Type 1922
1:50,000 IGN - Service Topographique
Topographical series
Edition definitive
standard edition - contoured with relief shading
Edition provisiore
provision edition uncontoured
NI
NH
29
30
TANGER
Ksar el Srhir
Ceuta
Tétouan
El Manzla
Melloussa
Asylah
Arba Ayacha
Souk Khemis des Beni Arouss
Larache
Ksar el Kebir
Souk el Kolla
El Jabha
Beni Boufrah
Rouadi
Al Hoceima
Boudinar
Kebdani
Segangane
Melilla
Nador
Kariat Arekmam
Les Triffal
Saidia du Kiss
Nemours
Beni Saf
Oued Imbert
Sidi bel Abbes
ORAN
Ste Barbe du Tlétat
Arzew
Tlemcen
Sebdou
El Aricha
Méchéria
Ain Sefra
Moulay bou Selham
Lalla Mimouna
Arbaoua
Ouezzane
Zoumi
Khaoulane
Tamorot
Ketama
Targuist
Beni Ammart
Tizi Ouzli
Midar
Driouch
Tistoutine
Hassi Berkane
Mechra Safsaf
Berkane
Martimprey du Kiss
Zoudj el Berhal
Oujda
Sidi Allal Tazi
Souk el Arba du Rharb
Mechra bel Ksiri
Had Kourt
Teroual
Tafrannt de l'Ouerrha
Rhafsai
Taounate
Tahar Souk
Taineste
Aknoul
Ain Zora
Saka
Meg el Ouidane
Mechra Homadi
El Aioun
Sidi bou Houria
Beni Oukil
Oued el Himer
Port Lyautey
Sidi Yahya du Rharb
Lalla Ito
Sidi Slimane
Khenichet sur Ouerrha
Oulad Aissa
Karia ba Mohammed
El Kelaâ des Slès
Tissa
Beni Frassene
Bab el Mrouj
Ain bou Kellal
Msoun
Merada
El Agreb
Taourirt
Mestigmer
Guefait
El Aouinet (Jerada)
Touissit
RABAT
Oued Fouarat
Mamora
Oued Touirza
El Kansera
Petitjean Moulay Idriss
Beni Ammar
FES
Ouest
Est
Matmata
Tahala
Taza
Ain el Behira
Safsafat
Guercif
Ain Fritissa
Jebel Zanngal
Sidi Lahsène
Berguent
Bouznika
Temara
N'Khella
Tiflet
Khemisset
Bataille
MEKNES
Sebaâ Aioun
Ain Taoujdat
Sefrou
El Menzel
Ahermoumou
Merhraoua
Berkine
Bou Rached
A. Guettara
Debdou
CASABLANCA
Fédala
Boulhaut
Sidi Betache
Marchand
Tedders
Agourai
El Hajeb
Ifrane
Jebel bou Iblane
Tinesmet
Azemmour
Sidi Borja
Bir Jedid Chavent
Berrechid
Oulad Ziane
El Gara
Ezzhiliga
Oulmès Mey Bou Azza
Azrou
Mazagan
Haouiza
Sidi Said Maachou
Foucauld
Settat
Benhamed
Aguelmous
Matarka
Oualidia Sidi Moussa
Sidi Smaine
Souk el Arba Mogress
Bou Laouane
Oulad Saïd
Ali Moumene
Ras el Ain
Melgou
Khouribga
Oued Zem
Boujad
Zia Sidi Bou Abbed
Kef en Nsour
Khenifra
Itjer
Ksabi
Talsint
Bou Arfa
Ich
Cap Cantin Oualidia
Et Tnine el Rharbia
Zemamra
Sidi Bennour
Dar Caid Tounsi
Mechra ben Abbou
Oued Kibane
Sidi el Annber
El Borouj
Tleta des Beni Oukil
Fkih ben Salah
Kasba Tadla
Ksiba
Midelt
Safi
Jema Sahim
Louis Gentil
Mtal
Sebt de Brikiin
Skour des Rehamna
Jebel Kharrou
Mzizoua
Mechra el Homri
Dar Ould Zidouh
Oulad bou Rahmoun
Beni Mellal
Rich
Souira Guedima
Sebt Gzoula
Sidi Mohamed Tiji
Chemaia
Ganntour
Oued bou Chane
Benguerir
Tnine Mharra
Kelaa des Srarhna
Bezou
Imilchil
Bou Anane
Zelmou
Figuig
Zaouia Akermoud
Talmest
El Arba de Sidi el Arouss
Et Tleta d'Irhoud
Sidi Chiker
Jebel bou Gader
Jebel Sarhlef
Sidi bou Othmane
Tamelelt
Attaouia ech Chaibia
Sahrij
Azilal
Zaouia Ahanesal
Tinerhir
Ksar es Souk
Bou Denib
Kenadsa
Béchar
Essaouira
Tleta el Hannchene
Sidi Moktar
Chichaoua
Ain Beid
Sidi Zouine
MARRAKECH
Guéliz
Médina
Ait Ourir
Sidi Rahal Tazert
Demnate
Tinejdad
Goulmina
Cap Sim
Neknafa
El Khémis des Meskala
Bouabout
Moumene
Guemessa
Barrage Cavagnac
Tahnaout
Telouèt
El Kelâa des Mgouna
Boulmane
Erfoud
Abadla
Cap Tafelnay
Tamanar
Ait Daoud
Ichemrarn
Imi N'Tanoute
Amizmiz
Skoura
Alnif
Msissi
Imsouane
Idaou Troumma
Ansis
Argana
Tafinegoult
Ouarzazate
Tamri
Tarhazoute
Immouzer des Ida ou Tanane
El Menizla
Tamaloukt
Igli
Taliouine
Tazenakht
Agdz
Tazzarine
Tarhbalt
Fezzou
Agadir
Forêt d'Admine
Oulad Teima
Taroudant
Tiout
Algougoum
Zagora
Bou Haiara
Beni Abbès
Ait Mimoun
Biougra
Souk el Arba des Ait Baha
c d c d
3 4
a b a b
XI
c d c d
1 2
a b a b

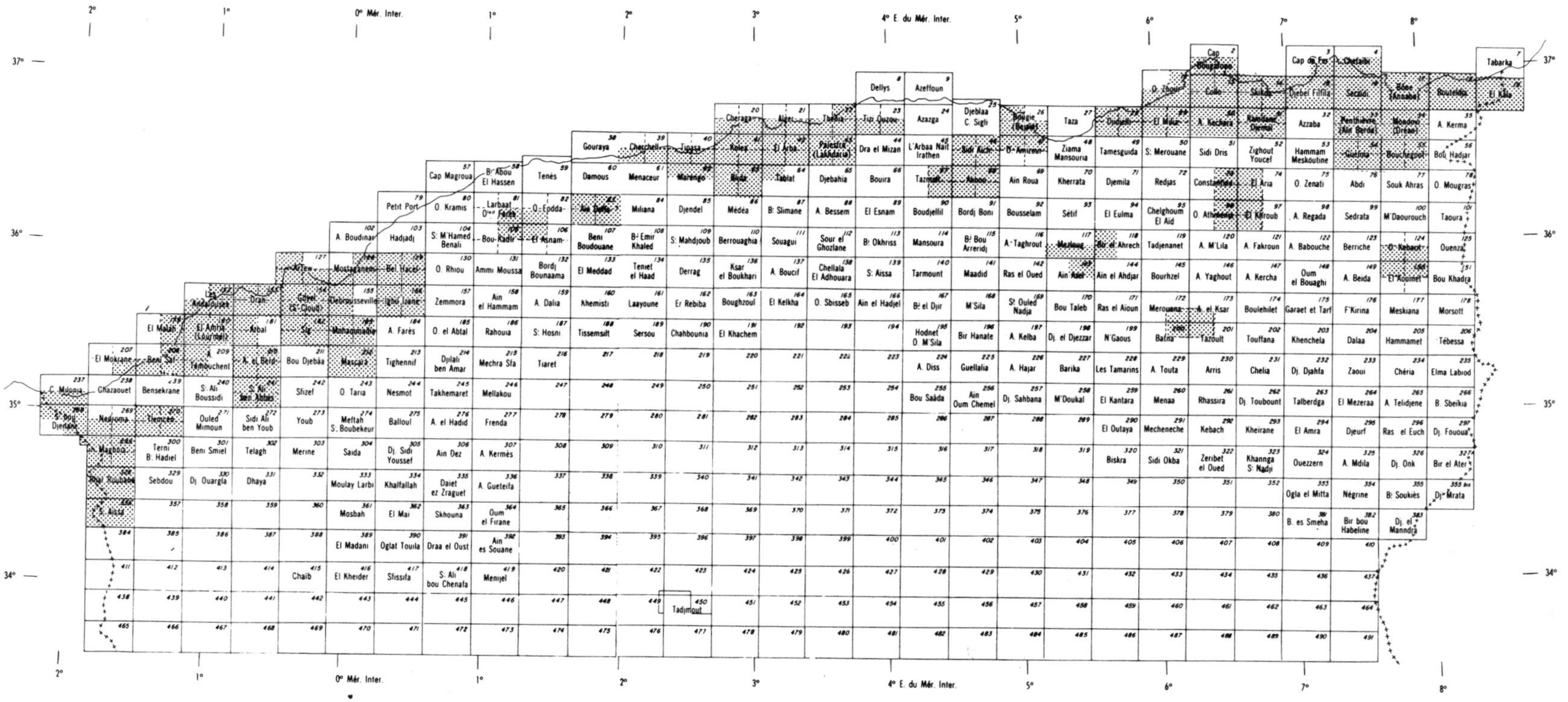

65/1 CARTE D'ALGÉRIE
1:25,000 IGN
Topographical series

Sheets published

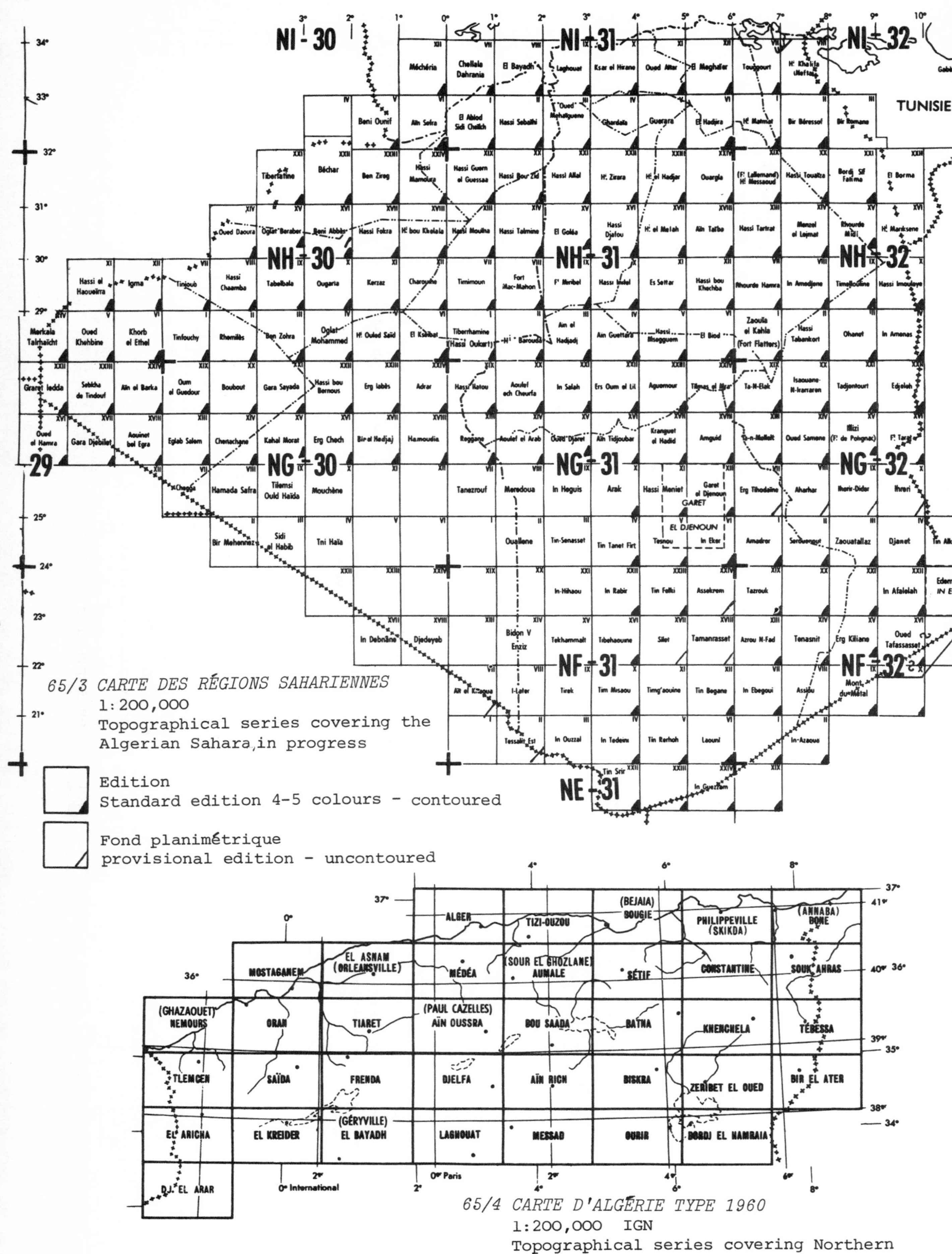

65/3 CARTE DES RÉGIONS SAHARIENNES

1: 200,000

Topographical series covering the Algerian Sahara, in progress

Edition
Standard edition 4-5 colours - contoured

Fond planimétrique
provisional edition - uncontoured

65/4 CARTE D'ALGÉRIE TYPE 1960

1:200,000 IGN

Topographical series covering Northern Algeria

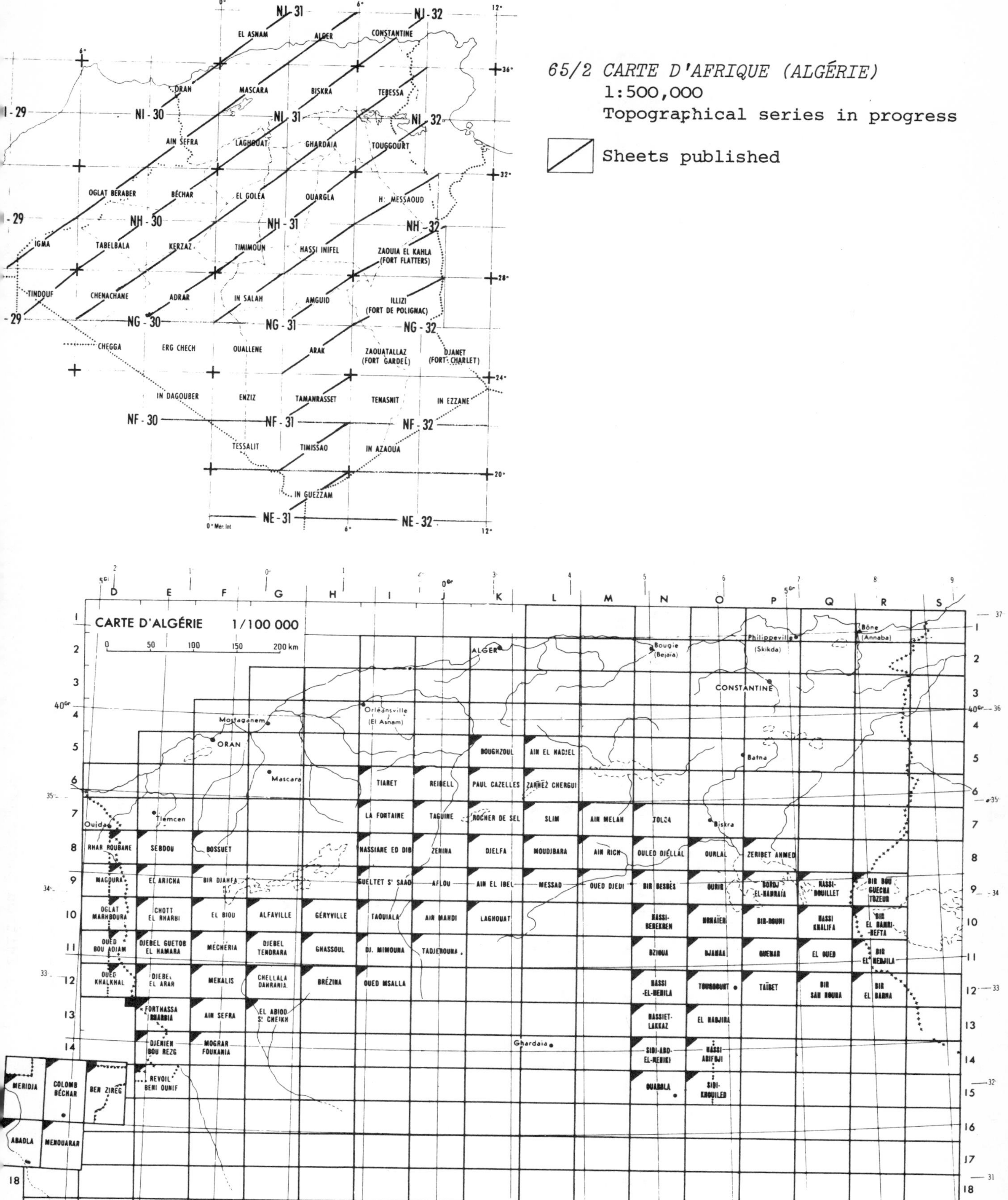

65/2 CARTE D'AFRIQUE (ALGÉRIE)

1:500,000

Topographical series in progress

Sheets published

65/5 ALGÉRIE-SAHARA

1:100,000 IGN

Topographical series in progress

Sheets published

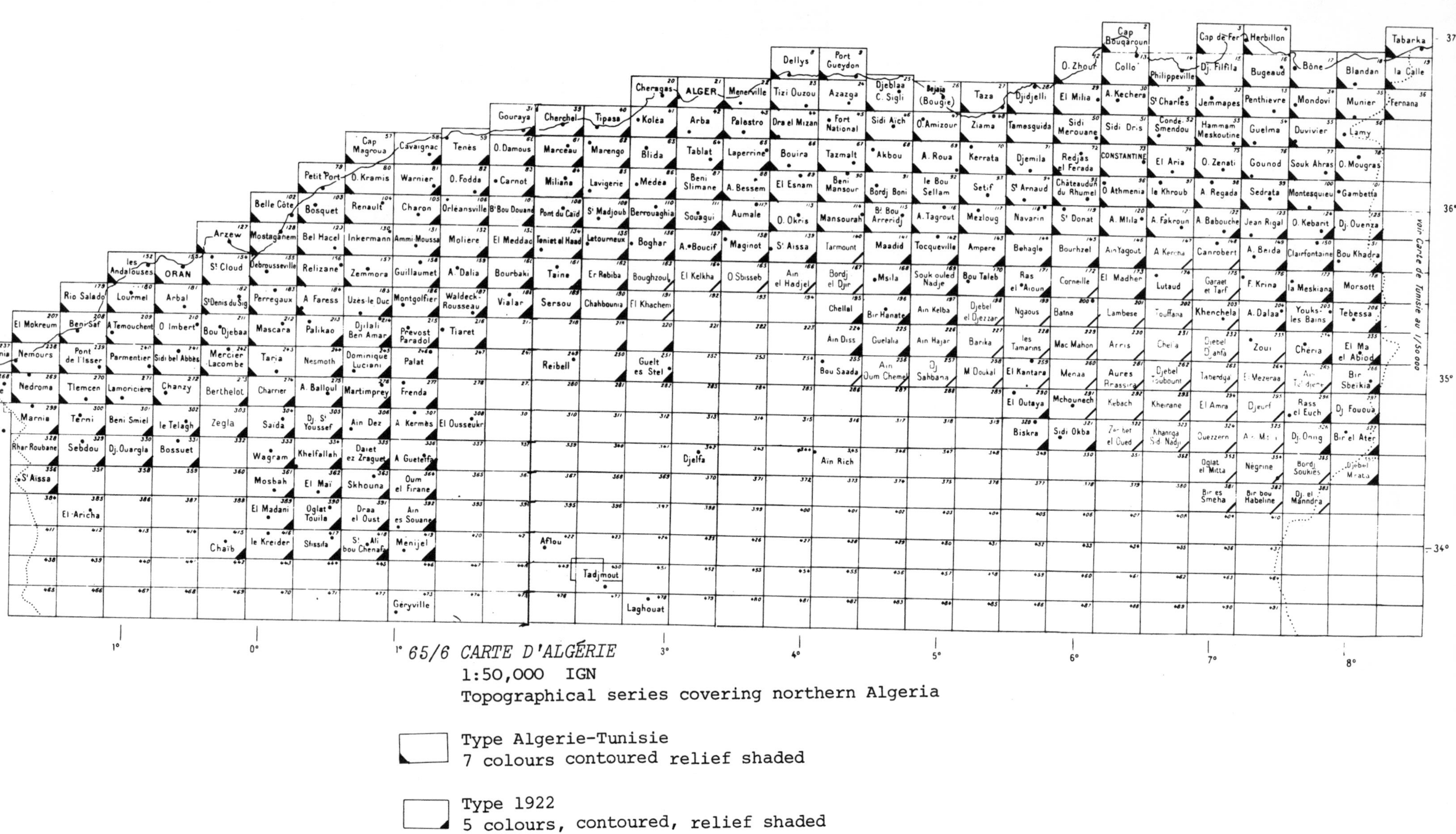

1° 65/6 *CARTE D'ALGÉRIE*
1:50,000 IGN
Topographical series covering northern Algeria

Type Algerie-Tunisie
7 colours contoured relief shaded

Type 1922
5 colours, contoured, relief shaded

Edition provisiore

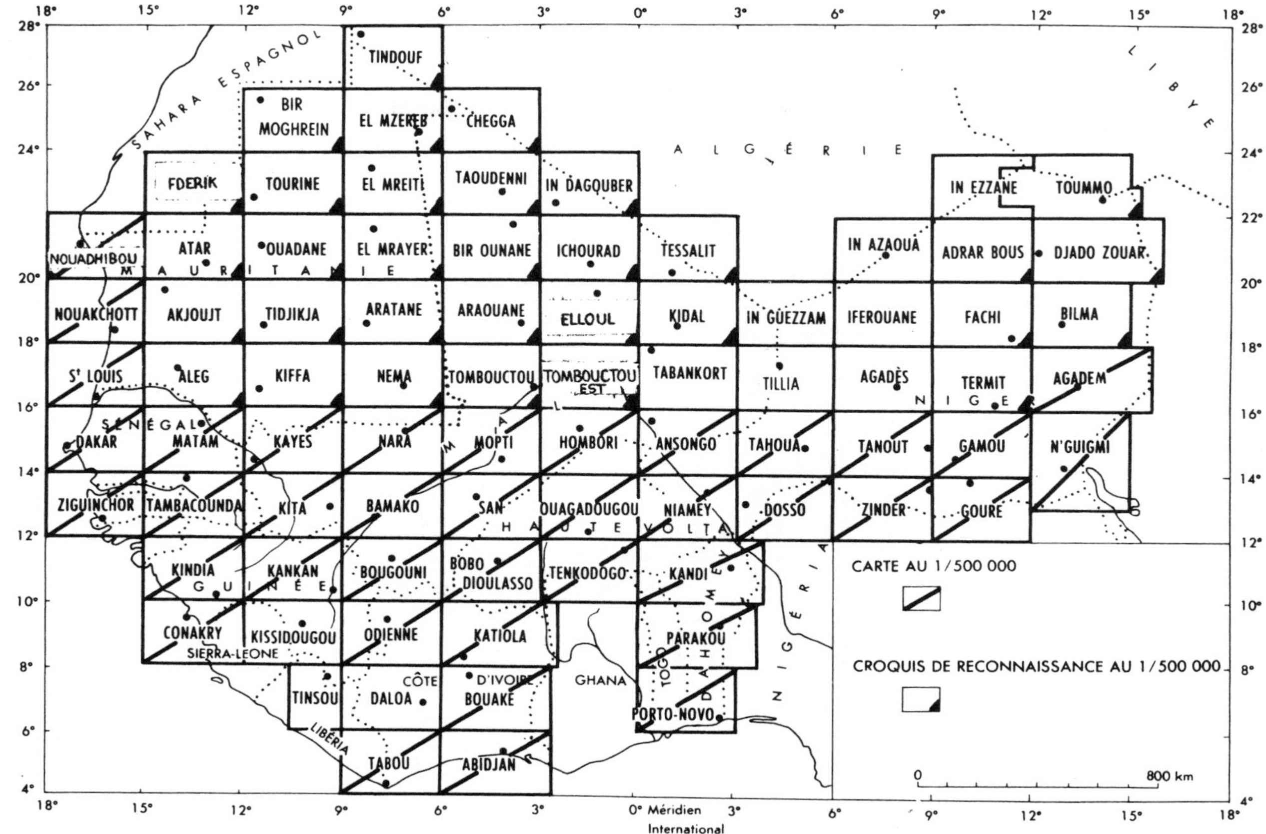

66/1 *CARTE DE L'AFRIQUE DE L'OUEST*
1:500,000 IGN
Topographical series

CROQUIS DE RECONNAISSANCE
1:500,000 IGN
Topographical series - provisional edition

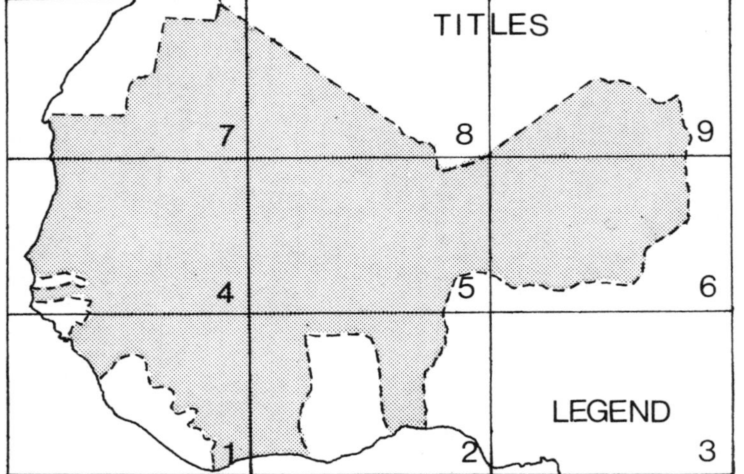

66/4 *CARTE GÉOLOGIQUE DE L'AFRIQUE OCCIDENTALE*
1:2,000,000 BRGM
Geological map of West Africa in 9 sheets.

ND 28 DAKAR
ND 29 BAMAKO
ND 30 OUAGADOUGOU
NC 28 CONAKRY
NC 29 KANKAN
NC 30 BOBO-DIOULASSO
NB 28 BONTHÉ (LÉGENDE)
NB 29 TABOU
NB 30 ABIDJAN

66/6 *CARTE DE LA VÉGÉTATION DE L'AFRIQUE TROPICALE OCCIDENTALE*
1:1,000,000 ORSTOM
Vegetation map of western tropical Africa.

Sheets published

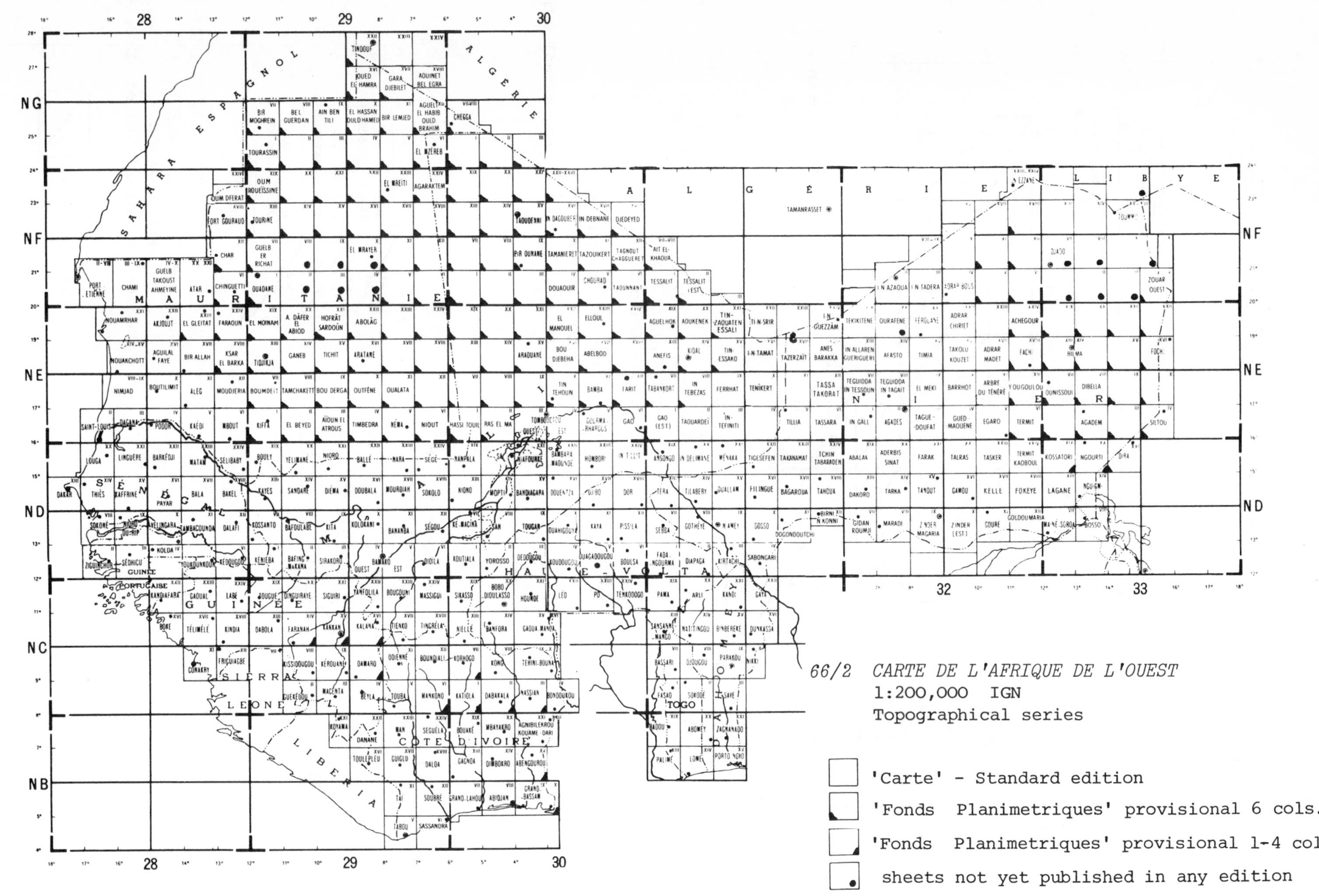

66/2 *CARTE DE L'AFRIQUE DE L'OUEST*

1:200,000 IGN

Topographical series

- 'Carte' - Standard edition
- 'Fonds Planimetriques' provisional 6 cols.
- 'Fonds Planimetriques' provisional 1-4 cols.
- sheets not yet published in any edition

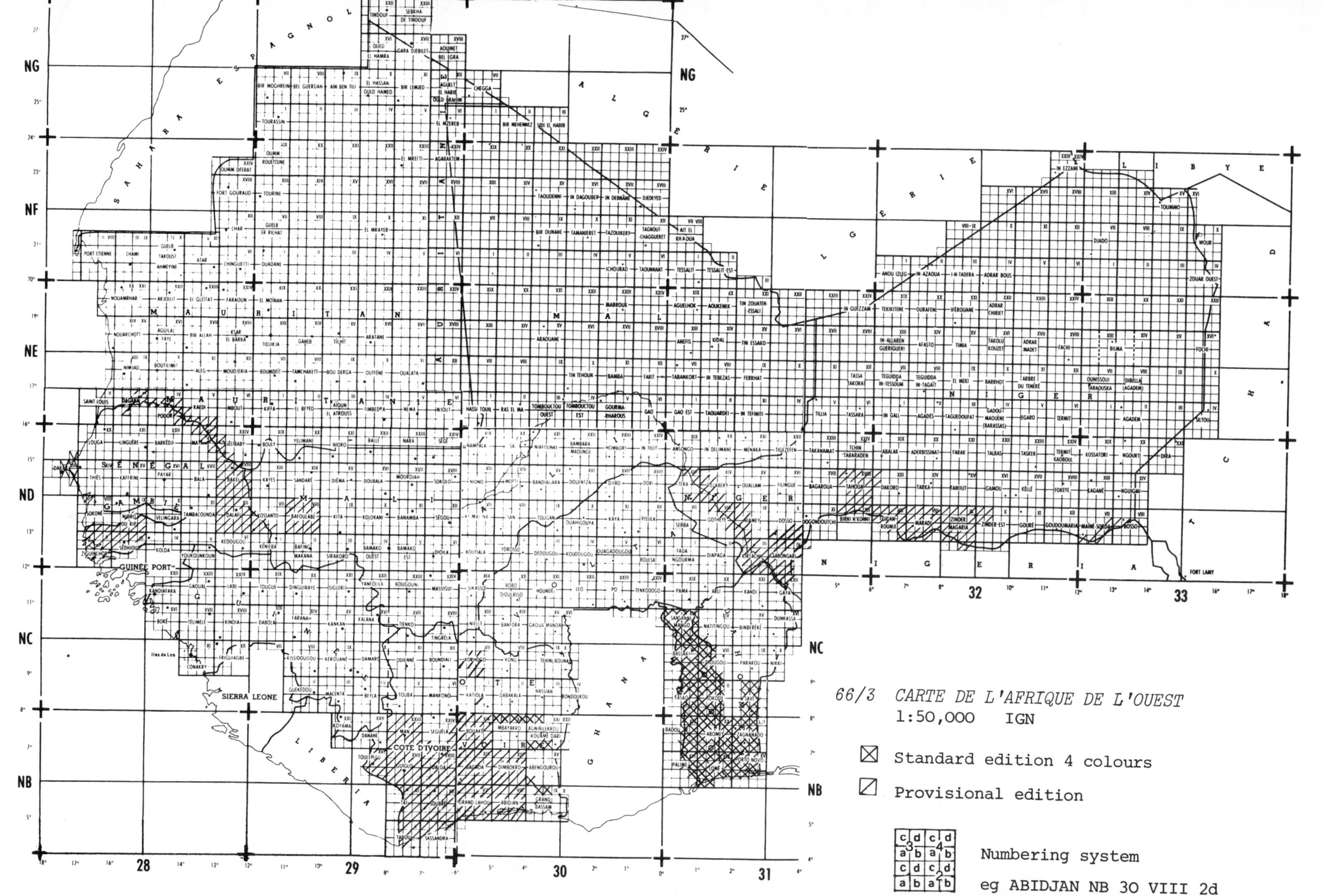
66/3 CARTE DE L'AFRIQUE DE L'OUEST
1:50,000 IGN
Standard edition 4 colours
Provisional edition
Numbering system
eg ABIDJAN NB 30 VIII 2d
NG
NF
NE
ND
NC
NB
28
29
30
31
32
33
SAHARA ESPAGNOL
ALGERIE
LIBYE
MAURITANIE
MALI
NIGER
TCHAD
SÉNÉGAL
GAMBIE
GUINÉE PORT
SIERRA LEONE
LIBERIA
COTE D'IVOIRE
GHANA
NIGERIA

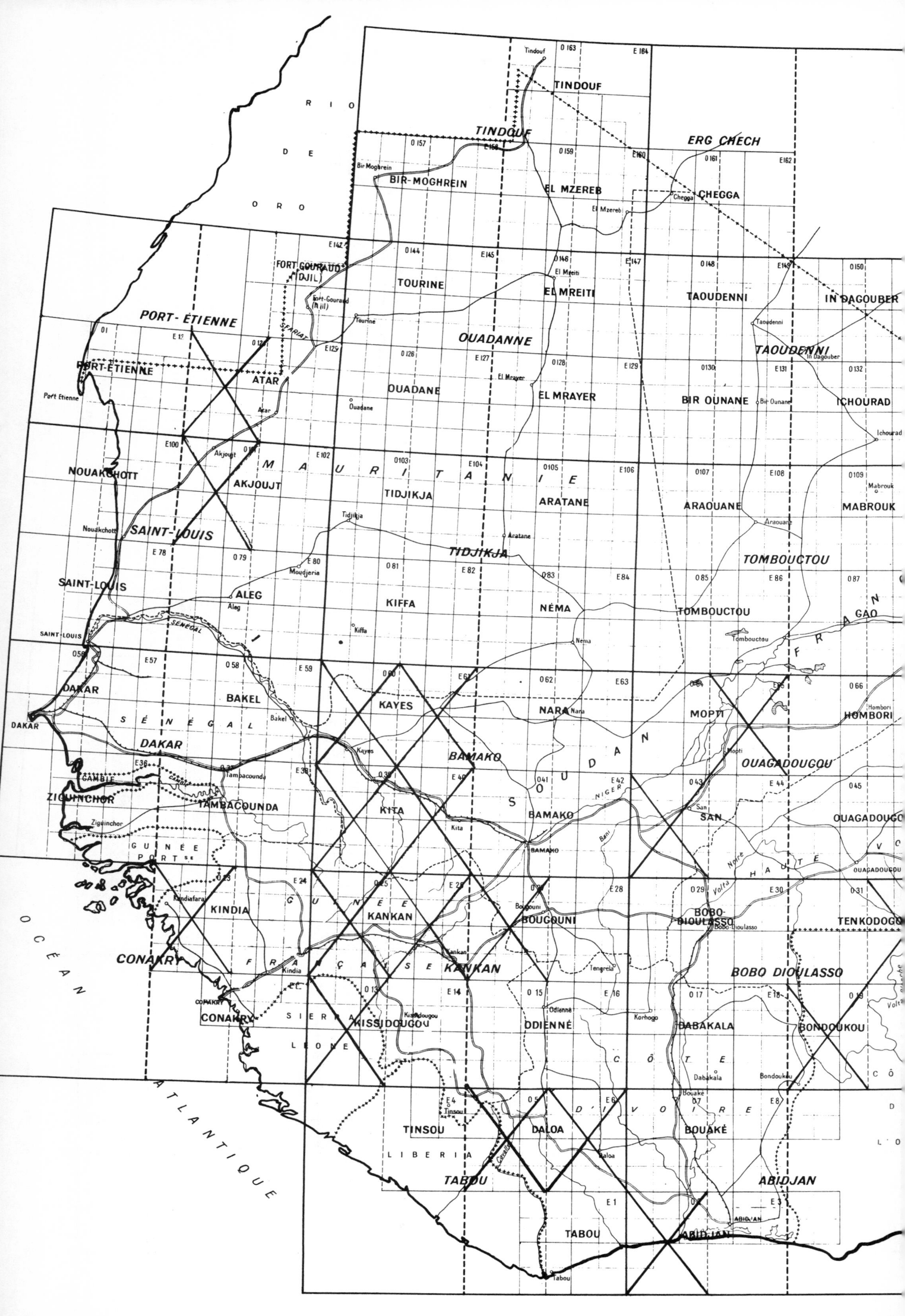

SYSTÈME CARTE INTERNATIONALE DU MONDE

Les feuilles géologiques au 1/1.000.000 et au 1/500.000 sont toujours des demi-coupures géographiques

Recouvrement d'une feuille géologique au 1/200.000

Recouvrement d'une ½ feuille géologique au 1/1.000.000

NIAMEY

DOSSO

Recouvrement d'une ½ feuille géologique au 1/500.000

Recouvrement d'une feuille géologique au 1/100.000

Demi-feuille au 1/500.000

fin de levé 51 | 027 N° de feuille

Année d'édition 52 | 49 Année début de levé

Frontière

Limite entre Fédérations

Limite entre Territoires

Routes, pistes

Voies ferrées

Rivières, fleuves importants

66/5 CARTE GÉOLOGIQUE DE L'AFRIQUE OCCIDENTALE

1:500,000 BRGM

Geological series of West Africa

Sheets published.

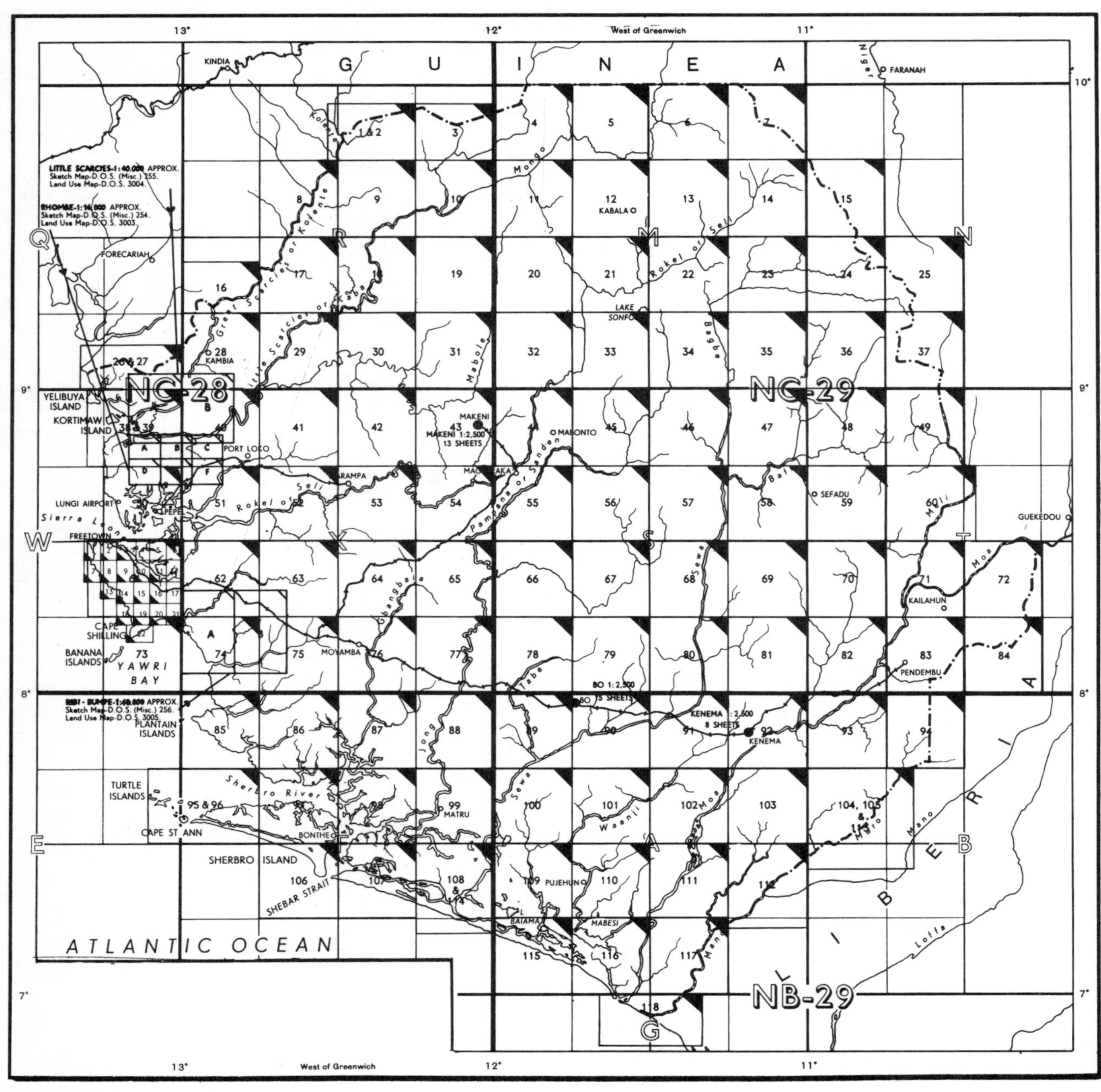

664/1 *SIERRA LEONE*
1:50,000
Dos 419 (G742)
Topographical series

Sheets published

SIERRA LEONE, FREETOWN PENINSULA
1:10,000
Dos 219 (G841)
Plan in 22 sheets

Sheets published

SIERRA LEONE-LAND USE AND SKETCH MAP SERIES
1:16,000 - 1:40,000 Dos

Sheets published

THE GAMBIA

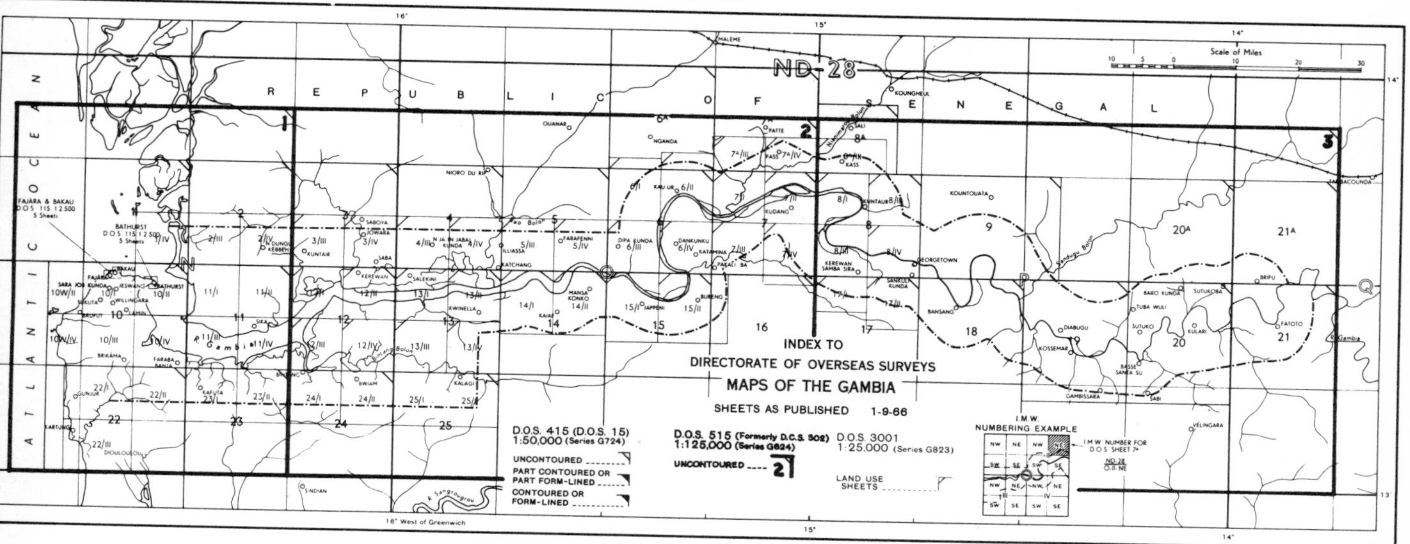

665.1/1 *GAMBIA*
1:125,000 Dos 515(G624)
Topographical series in 3 sheets

GAMBIA
1:50,000 Dos 415 (G724)
Topographical series

GAMBIA-LAND USE
1:25,000 Dos 3001

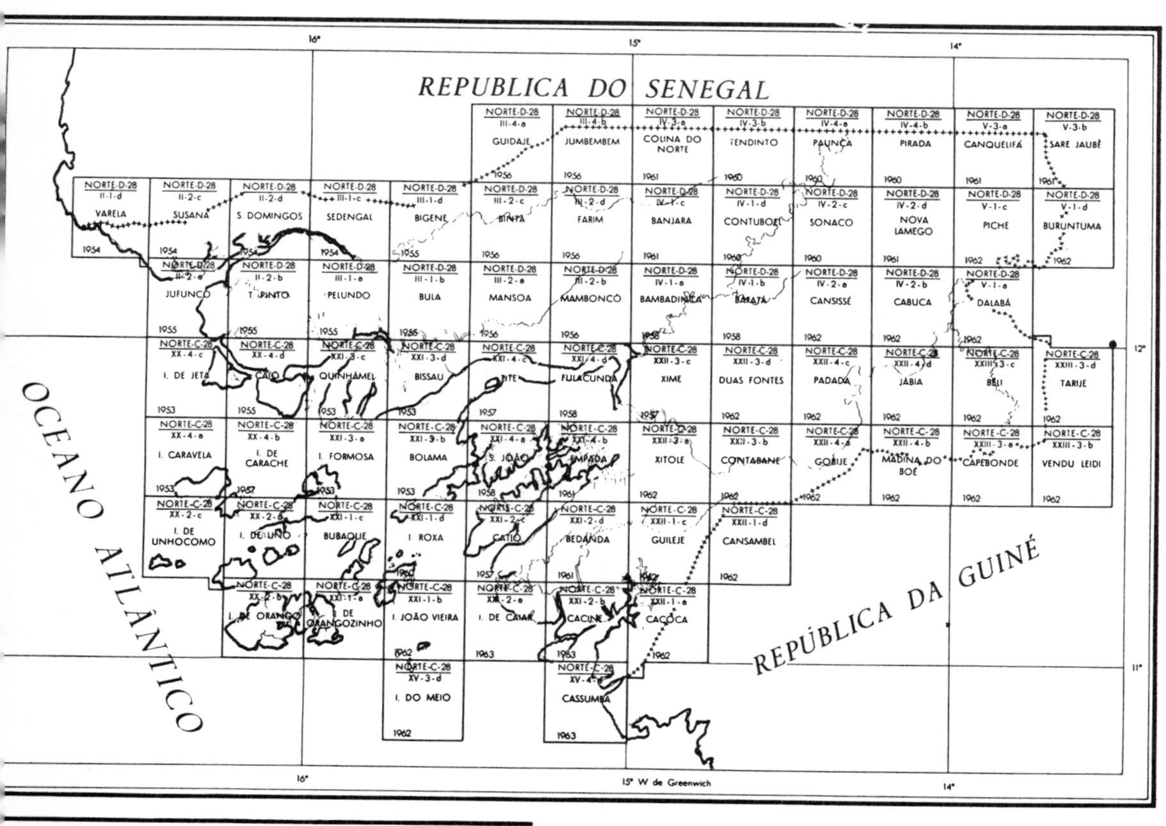

LOCALIZAÇÃO CONTINENTAL

FOLHAS PUBLICADAS

NORTE-C-28 XX-4-d — Número da folha
CAIÓ — Nome da folha
1955 — Ano da publicação

Publicação iniciada em 1953
N.° total de folhas da cobertura da Província: 72

665.7/1 *GUINEA*
1:50,000 P.U.P.
Topographical Series in 72 sheets

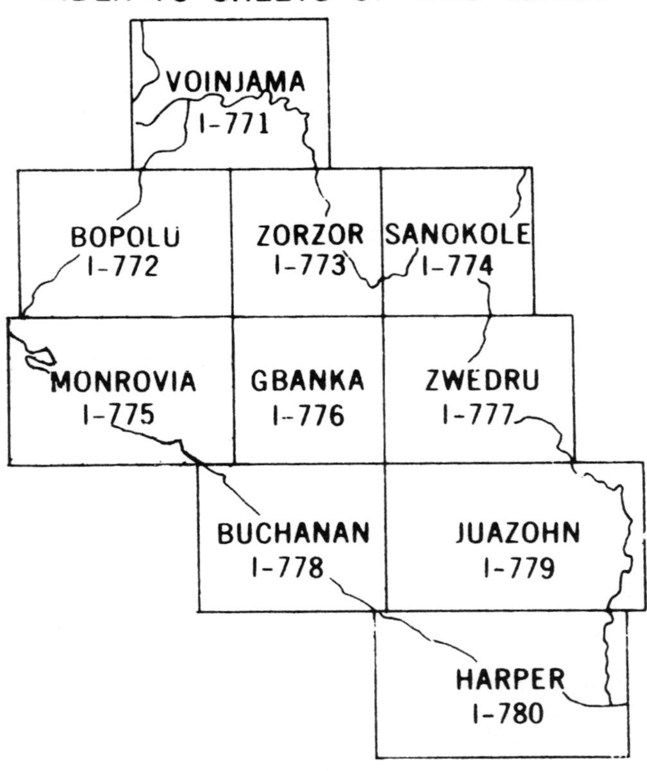

666/1 *LIBERIA*
1:250,000 USGS/LGS
Geographic series with shaded relief

667/1 *GHANA*
1:250,000 Surv. of Ghana
Topographical Series

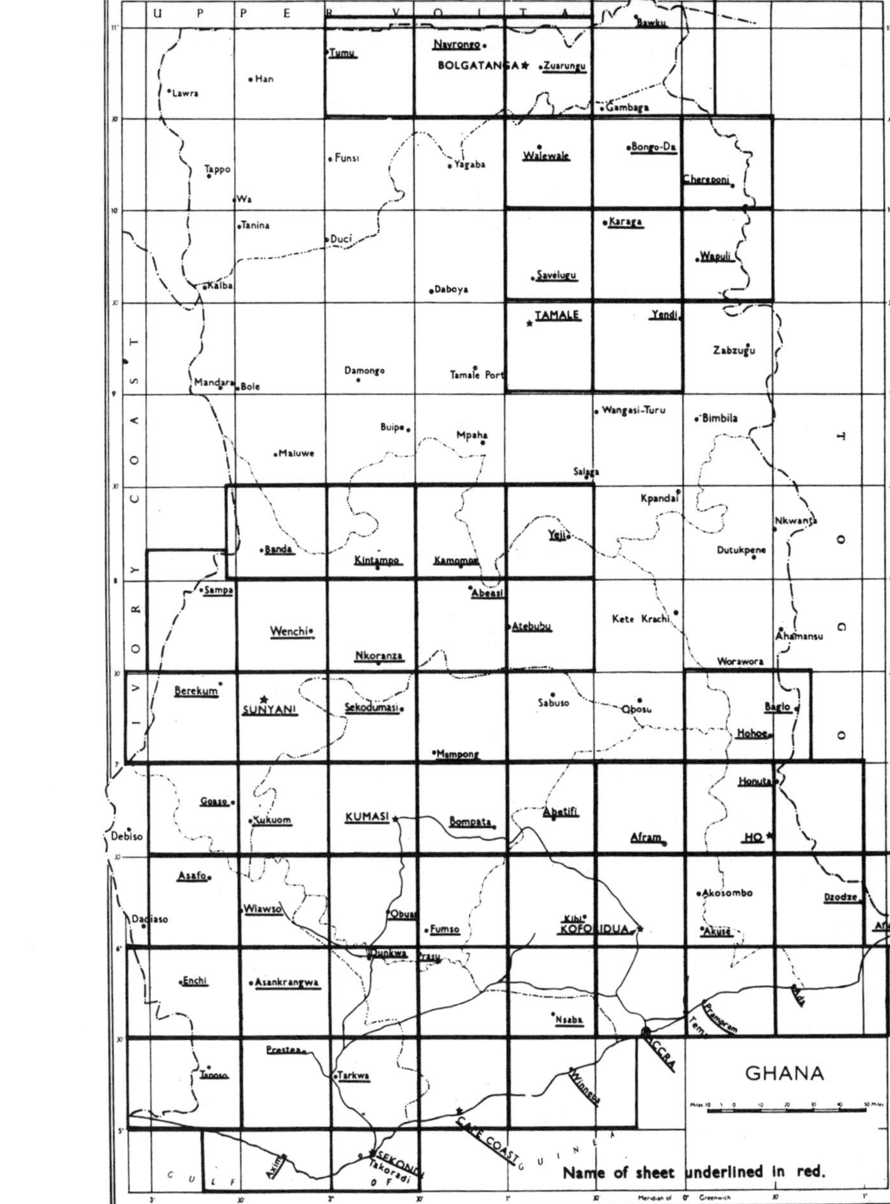

667/2 *GHANA*
1:125,000 Surv. of Ghana
Topographical Series

Sheets published are outlined in black

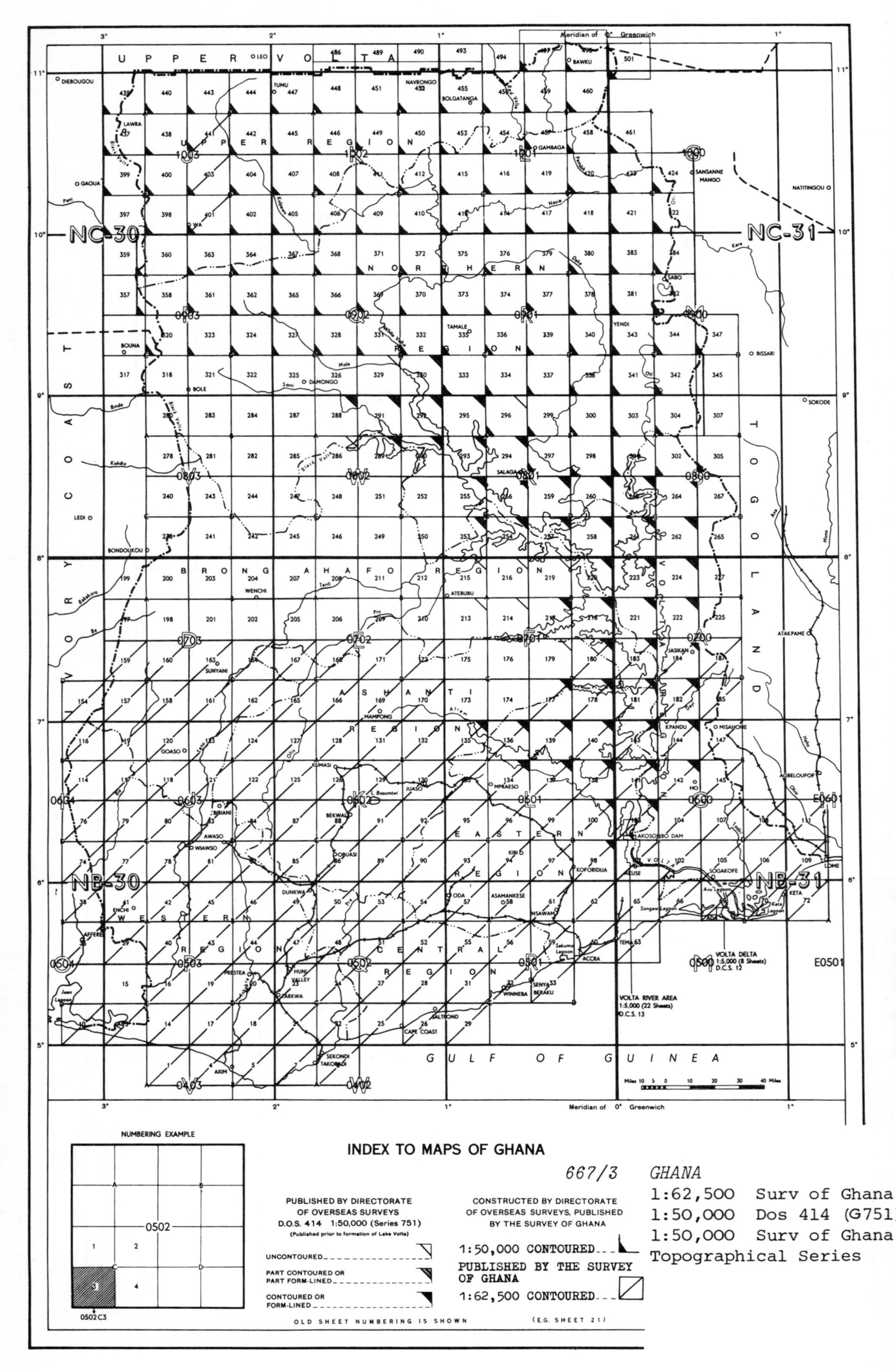

667/3 GHANA

1:62,500 Surv of Ghana
1:50,000 Dos 414 (G751)
1:50,000 Surv of Ghana
Topographical Series

669/1 NIGERIA

1:500,000 Fed. Surv.

Road map series in 16 sheets

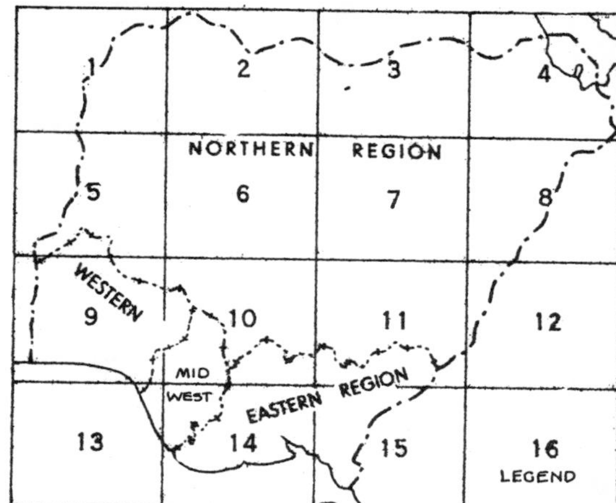

669/2 NIGERIA

1:500,000 Fed. Surv.

New topographical series in progress

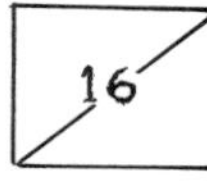

Sheets published

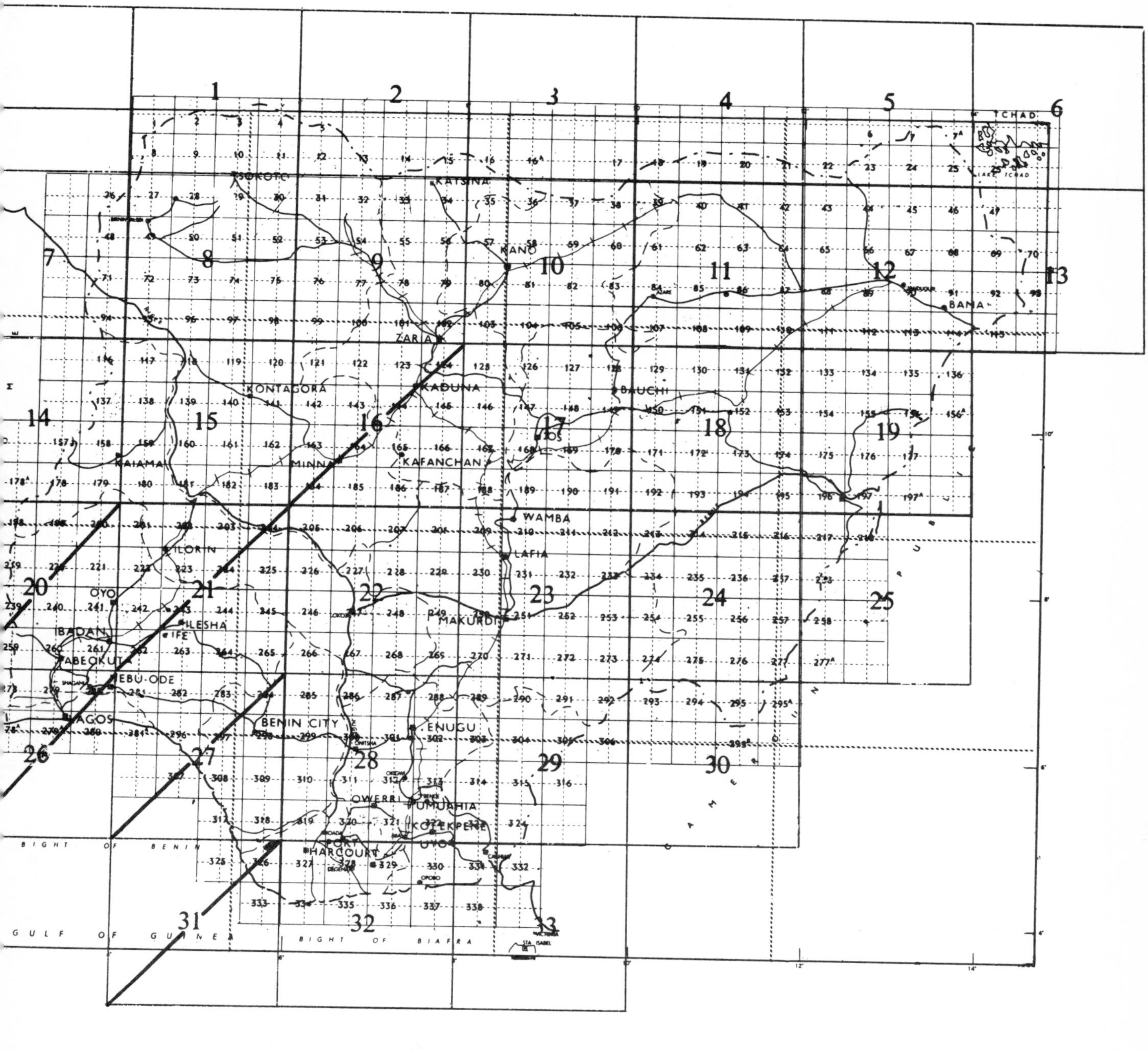

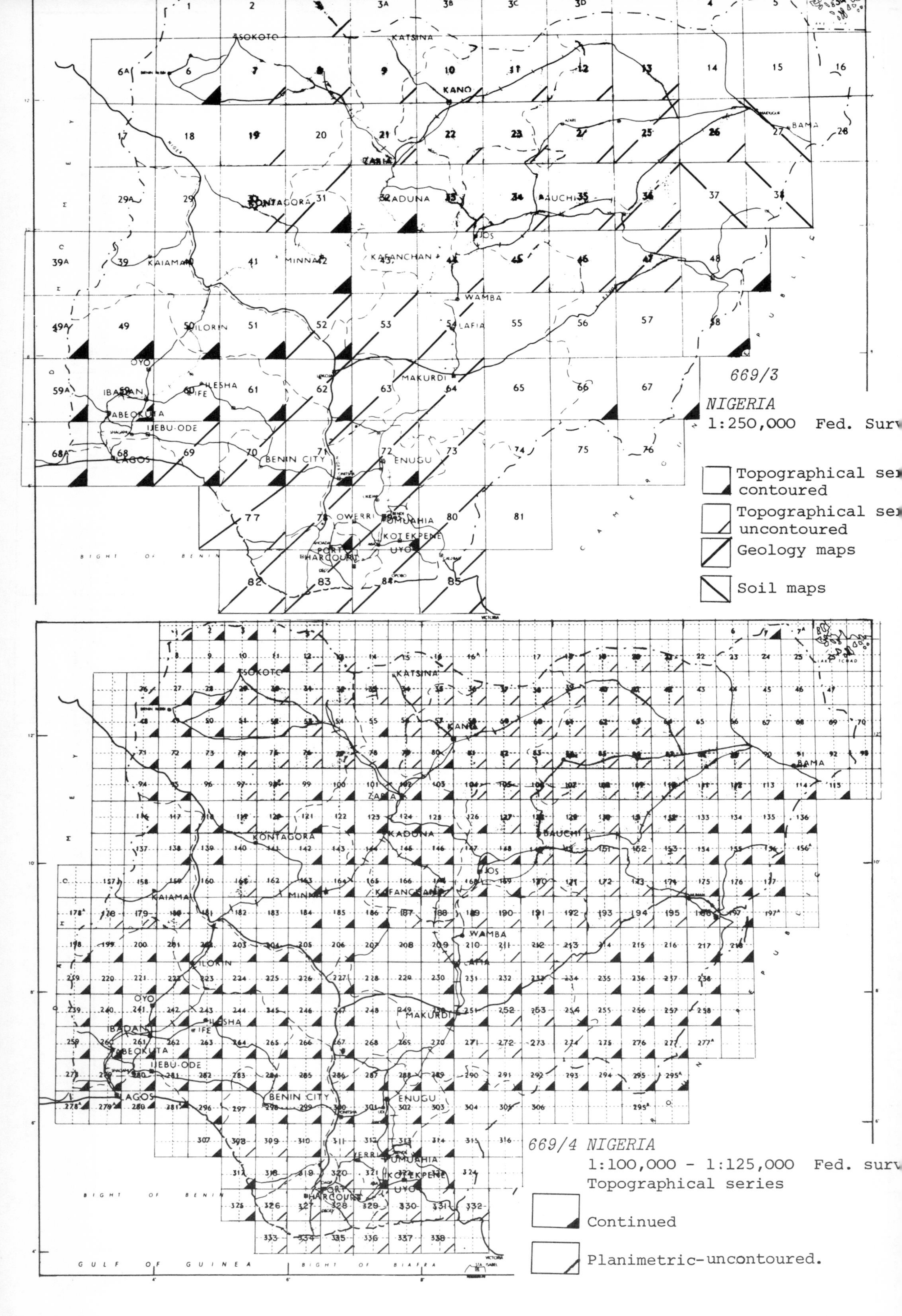

669/3
NIGERIA
1:250,000 Fed. Surv
Topographical ser contoured
Topographical ser uncontoured
Geology maps
Soil maps
669/4 NIGERIA
1:100,000 - 1:125,000 Fed. surv
Topographical series
Continued
Planimetric-uncontoured.
SOKOTO
KATSINA
KANO
ZARIA
KONTAGORA
KADUNA
BAUCHI
JOS
KAIAMA
MINNA
KAFANCHAN
WAMBA
ILORIN
LAFIA
BAMA
OYO
IBADAN
ILESHA
IFE
ABEOKUTA
IJEBU-ODE
MAKURDI
LAGOS
BENIN CITY
ENUGU
OWERRI
UMUAHIA
IKOT EKPENE
UYO
PORT HARCOURT
BIGHT OF BENIN
GULF OF GUINEA
BIGHT OF BIAFRA

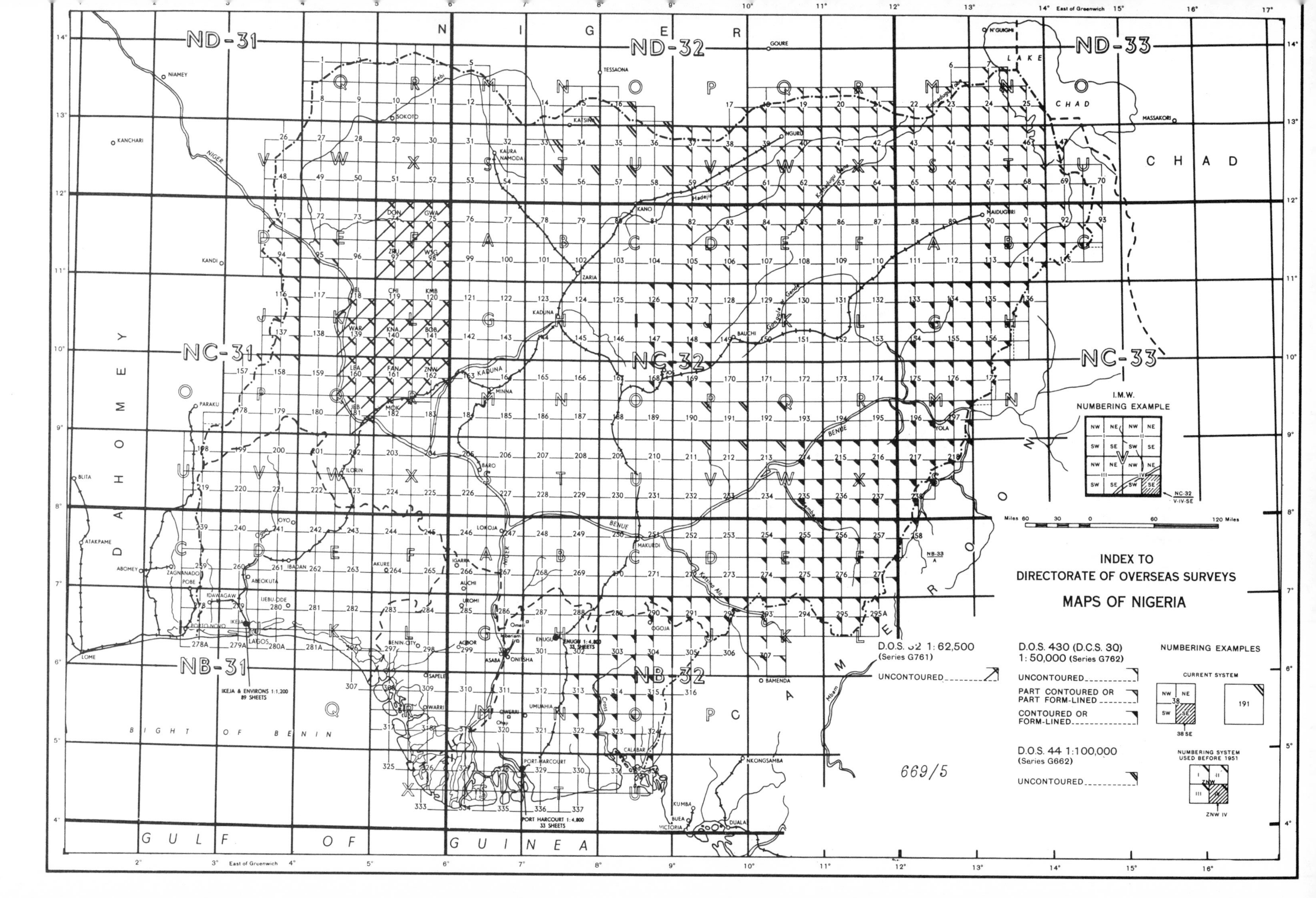
INDEX TO
DIRECTORATE OF OVERSEAS SURVEYS
MAPS OF NIGERIA
D.O.S. 430 (D.C.S. 30)
1: 50,000 (Series G762)
UNCONTOURED
PART CONTOURED OR
PART FORM-LINED
CONTOURED OR
FORM-LINED
D.O.S. 44 1:100,000
(Series G662)
UNCONTOURED
D.O.S. 32 1: 62,500
(Series G761)
UNCONTOURED
NUMBERING EXAMPLES
CURRENT SYSTEM
38 SE
191
NUMBERING SYSTEM
USED BEFORE 1951
ZNW IV
I.M.W.
NUMBERING EXAMPLE
NC-32
V-IV-SE
Miles 60 30 0 60 120 Miles
IKEJA & ENVIRONS 1:1,200
89 SHEETS
PORT HARCOURT 1:4,800
33 SHEETS
ENUGU 1:4,800
33 SHEETS
ND-31
ND-32
ND-33
NC-31
NC-32
NC-33
NB-31
NB-32
NB-33
NIGER
CHAD
LAKE CHAD
DAHOMEY
CAMEROON
BIGHT OF BENIN
GULF OF GUINEA
East of Greenwich
669/5

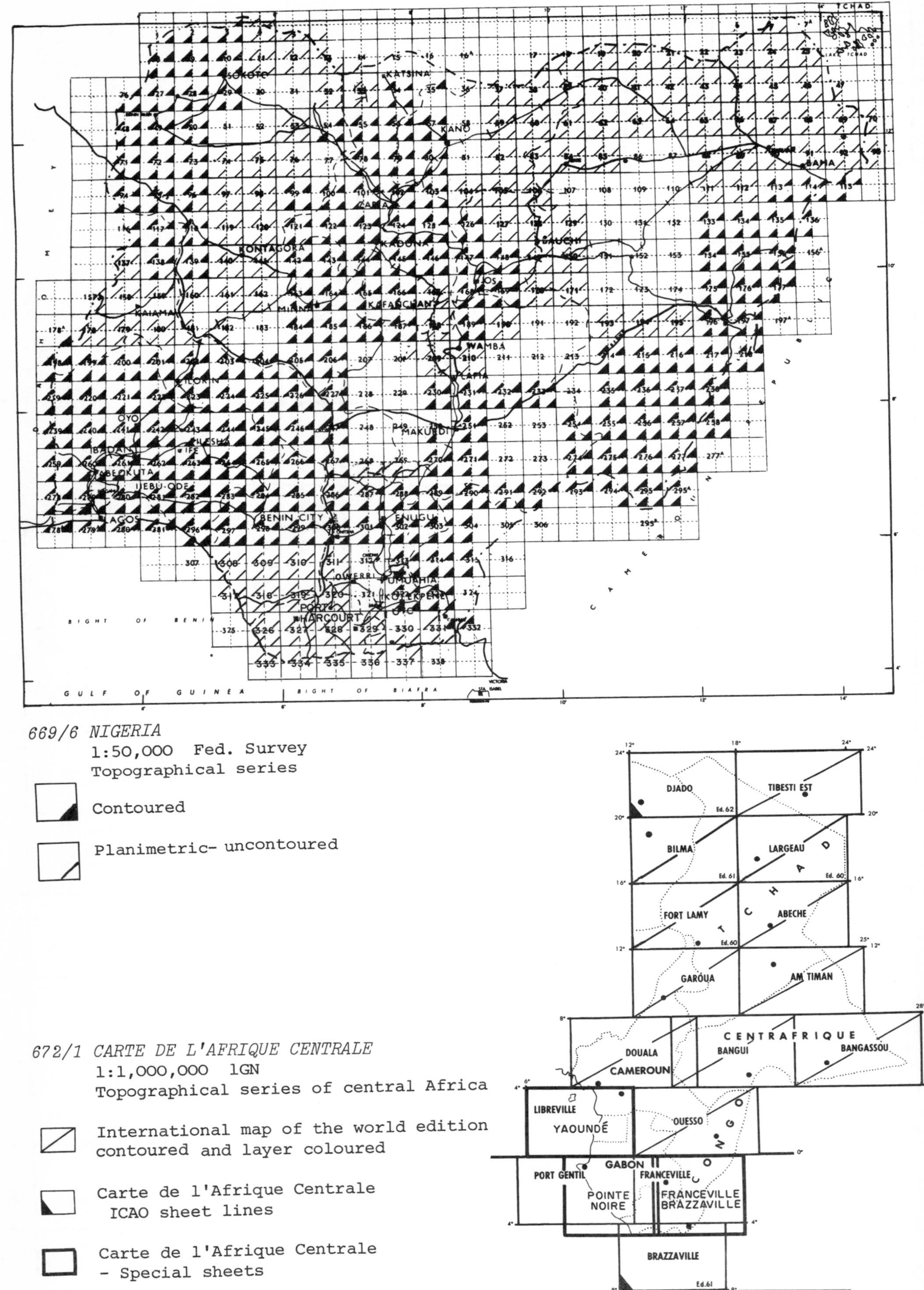

669/6 NIGERIA
1:50,000 Fed. Survey
Topographical series
Contoured
Planimetric- uncontoured
672/1 CARTE DE L'AFRIQUE CENTRALE
1:1,000,000 lGN
Topographical series of central Africa
International map of the world edition
contoured and layer coloured
Carte de l'Afrique Centrale
ICAO sheet lines
Carte de l'Afrique Centrale
- Special sheets
GULF OF GUINEA
BIGHT OF BENIN
BIGHT OF BIAFRA
CAMEROUN
SOKOTO
KATSINA
KANO
BAMA
ZARIA
KONTAGORA
KADUNA
BAUCHI
JOS
KAIAMA
MINNA
KAFANCHAN
WAMBA
LAFIA
ILORIN
OYO
MAKURDI
IBADAN
IFE
ILESHA
ABEOKUTA
IJEBU-ODE
LAGOS
BENIN CITY
ENUGU
OWERRI
UMUAHIA
PORT HARCOURT
DJADO
TIBESTI EST
BILMA
LARGEAU
FORT LAMY
ABECHE
GAROUA
AM TIMAN
TCHAD
CENTRAFRIQUE
DOUALA
BANGUI
BANGASSOU
LIBREVILLE
YAOUNDE
OUESSO
GABON
PORT GENTIL
FRANCEVILLE
POINTE NOIRE
FRANCEVILLE BRAZZAVILLE
BRAZZAVILLE
CONGO

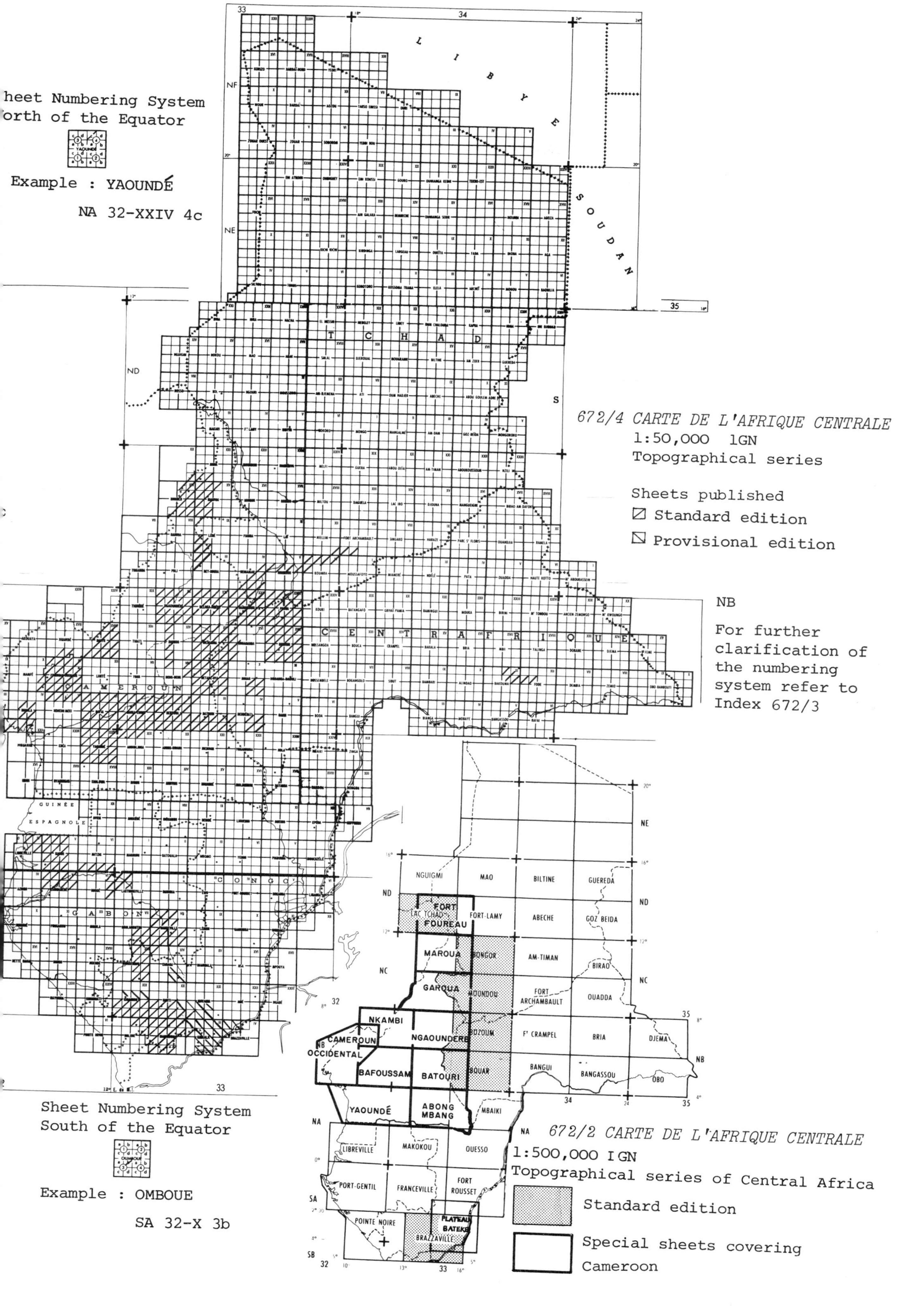
Sheet Numbering System
North of the Equator
Example : YAOUNDÉ
NA 32-XXIV 4c
L I B Y E
S O U D A N
T C H A D
C E N T R A F R I Q U E
C A M E R O U N
C O N G O
G A B O N
GUINÉE ESPAGNOLE
672/4 CARTE DE L'AFRIQUE CENTRALE
1:50,000 IGN
Topographical series
Sheets published
Standard edition
Provisional edition
NB
For further clarification of the numbering system refer to Index 672/3
Sheet Numbering System
South of the Equator
Example : OMBOUE
SA 32-X 3b
NGUIGMI
MAO
BILTINE
GUEREDA
FORT FOUREAU
LAC TCHAD
FORT-LAMY
ABECHE
GOZ BEIDA
MAROUA
BONGOR
AM-TIMAN
BIRAO
GAROUA
MOUNDOU
FORT ARCHAMBAULT
OUADDA
NKAMBI
NGAOUNDERE
BOZOUM
Ft CRAMPEL
BRIA
DJEMA
CAMEROUN OCCIDENTAL
BAFOUSSAM
BATOURI
BOUAR
BANGUI
BANGASSOU
OBO
YAOUNDÉ
ABONG MBANG
MBAIKI
LIBREVILLE
MAKOKOU
OUESSO
PORT-GENTIL
FRANCEVILLE
FORT ROUSSET
POINTE NOIRE
BRAZZAVILLE
PLATEAU BATEKE
672/2 CARTE DE L'AFRIQUE CENTRALE
1:500,000 IGN
Topographical series of Central Africa
Standard edition
Special sheets covering Cameroon

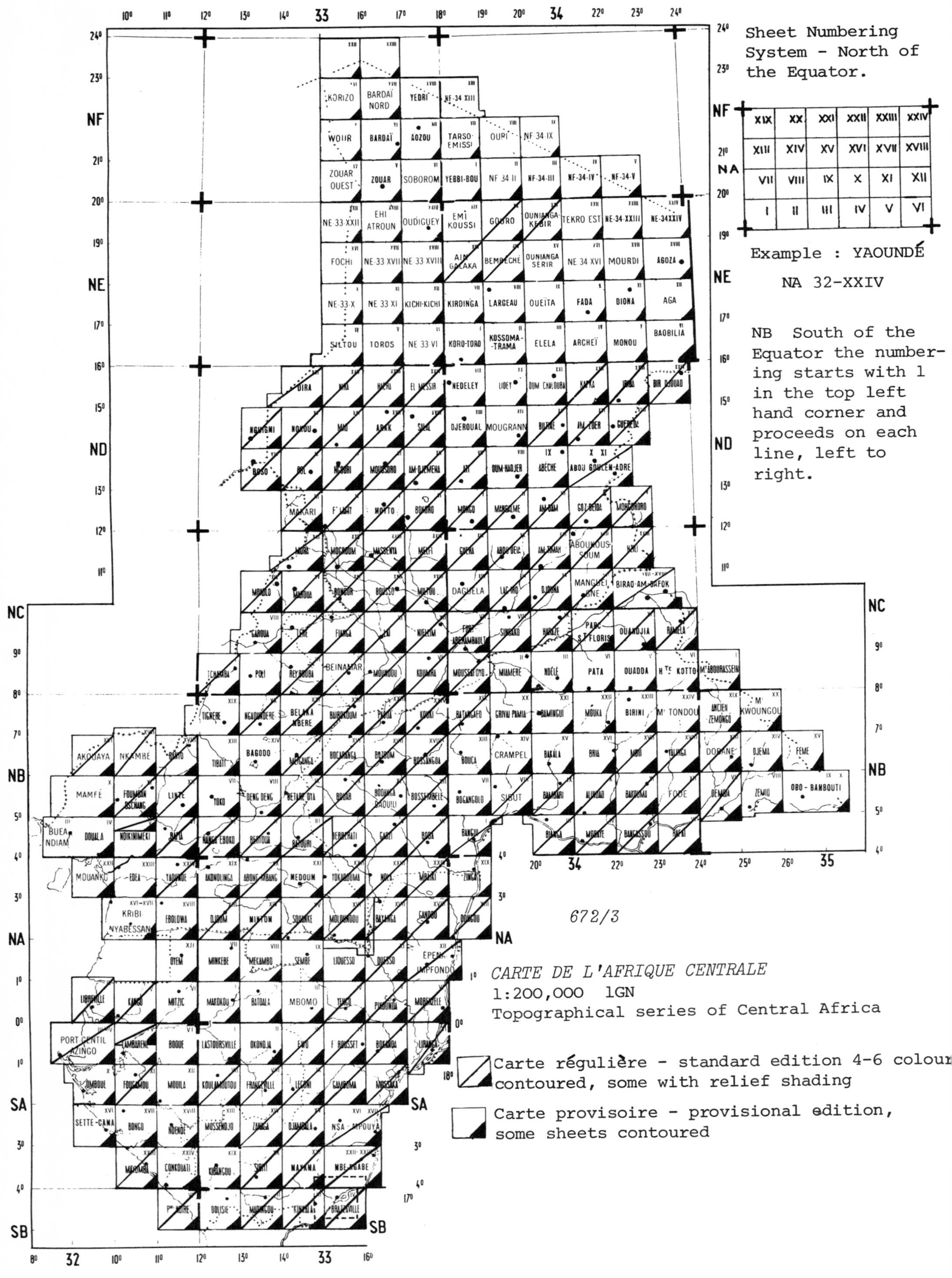

Sheet Numbering System - North of the Equator.
NF
NA
XIX XX XXI XXII XXIII XXIV
XIII XIV XV XVI XVII XVIII
VII VIII IX X XI XII
I II III IV V VI
Example : YAOUNDÉ
NA 32-XXIV
NB South of the Equator the numbering starts with 1 in the top left hand corner and proceeds on each line, left to right.
672/3
CARTE DE L'AFRIQUE CENTRALE
1:200,000 lGN
Topographical series of Central Africa
Carte régulière - standard edition 4-6 colour contoured, some with relief shading
Carte provisoire - provisional edition, some sheets contoured

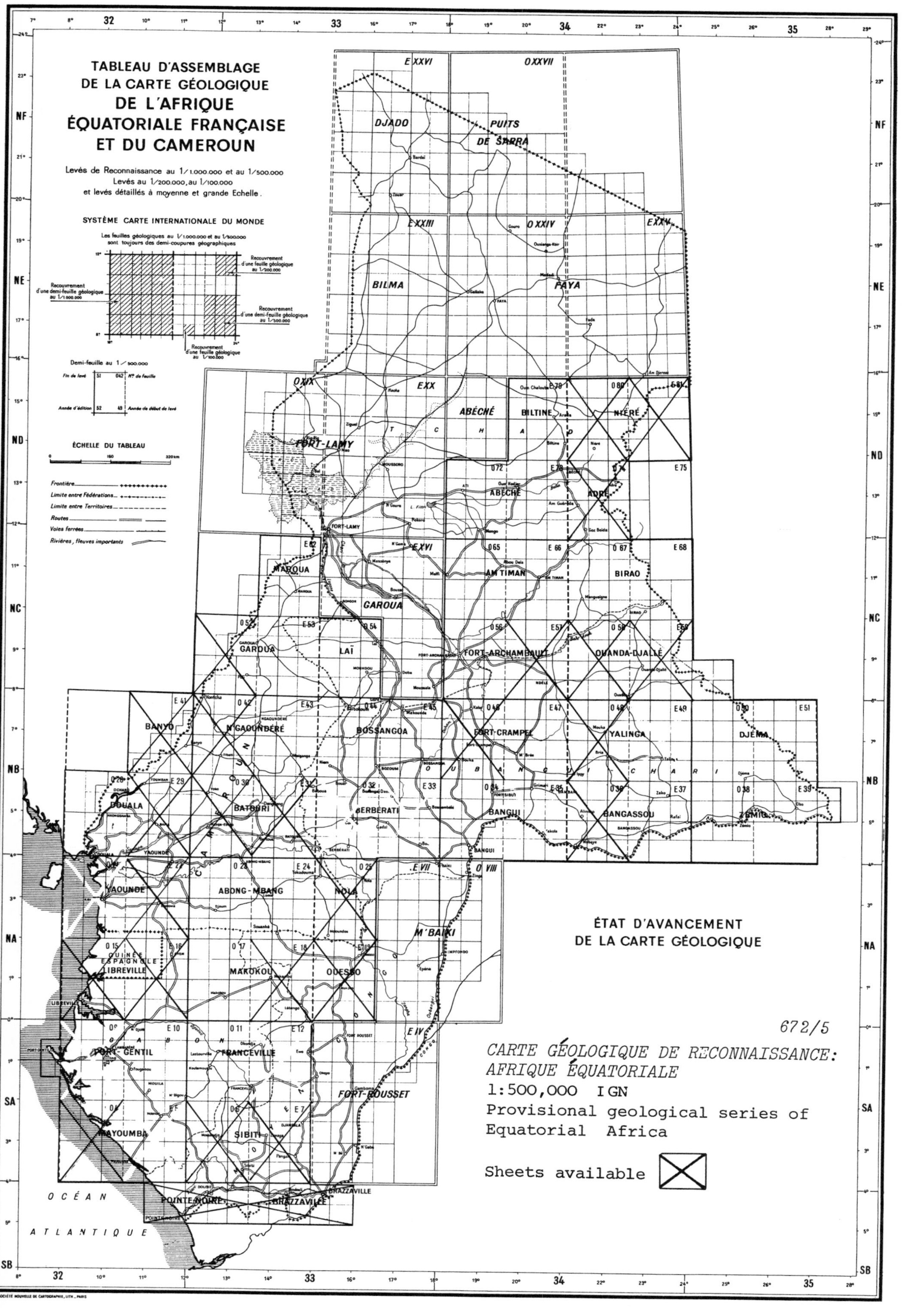

672/5

CARTE GÉOLOGIQUE DE RECONNAISSANCE: AFRIQUE ÉQUATORIALE
1:500,000 IGN
Provisional geological series of Equatorial Africa

Sheets available

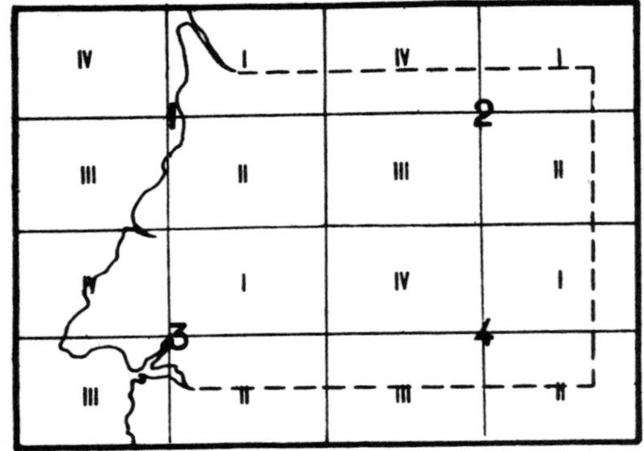

671.8/1 *EQUATORIAL GUINEA*
MAPA ITINERARIO (TOPOGRÁFICO & FORESTAL) DE LA GUINEA ESPAÑOLA
1:200,000 S.G.E.
Topographical map in 4 sheets

ADVANCE DEL MAPA TOPOGRÁFICO FORESTAL DE GUINEA
1:100,000 S.G.E.
Topographical map in 16 sheets

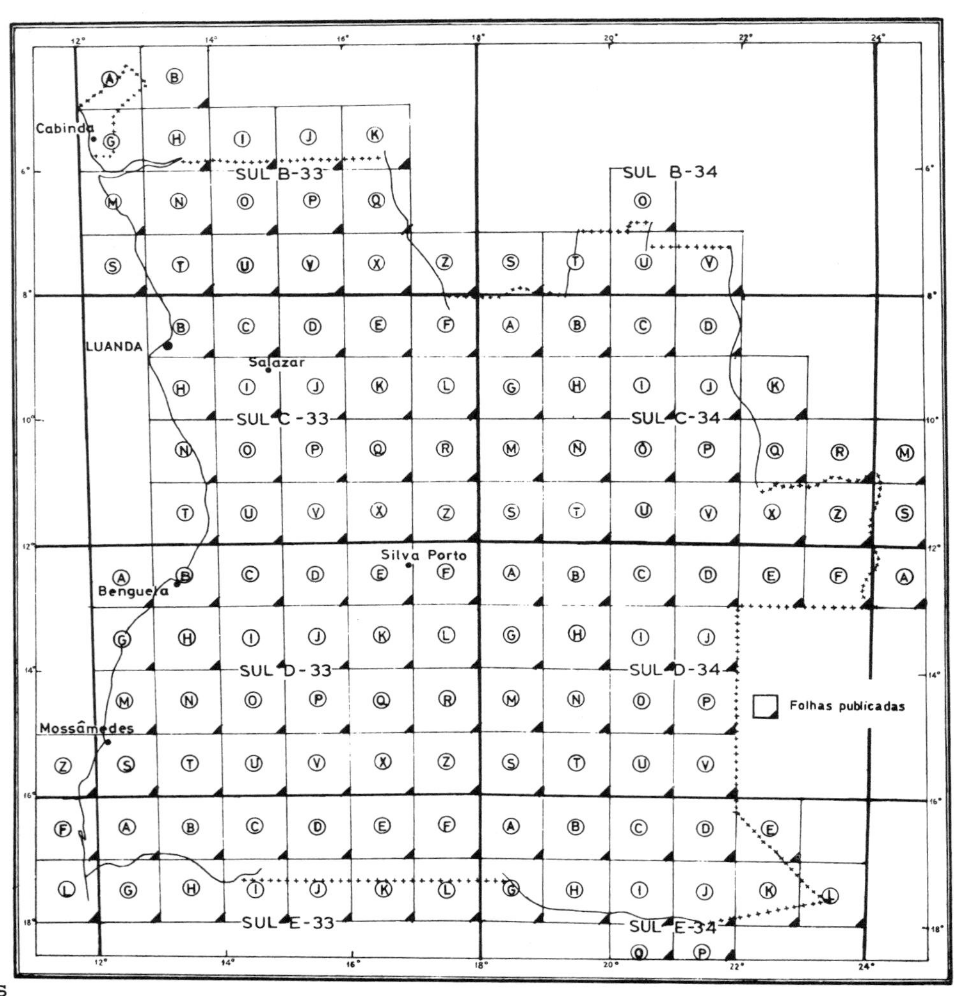

673/1 *ANGOLA*
1:250,000 P.U.P.
Topographical series

Sheets published

ANGOLA

SÉRIE NA ESCALA DE 1:100 000, EM EXECUÇÃO

Publicação dos Serviços Geográficos e Cadastrais de Angola e da Junta de Investigações do Ultramar

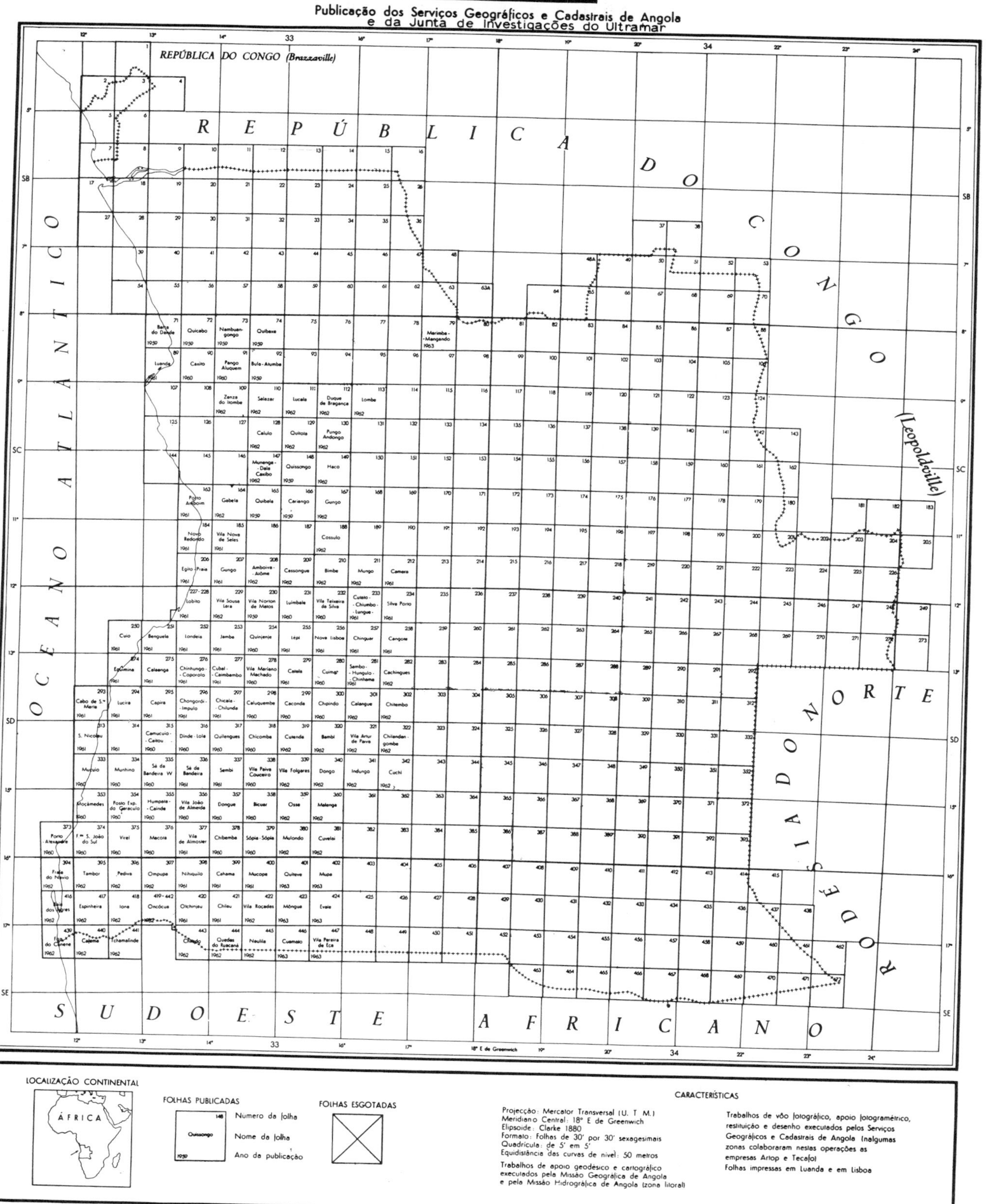

673/2 ANGOLA

1:100,000 P.U.P.

Topographical series

NB All sheets published except Nos 1-8 covering Cabinda

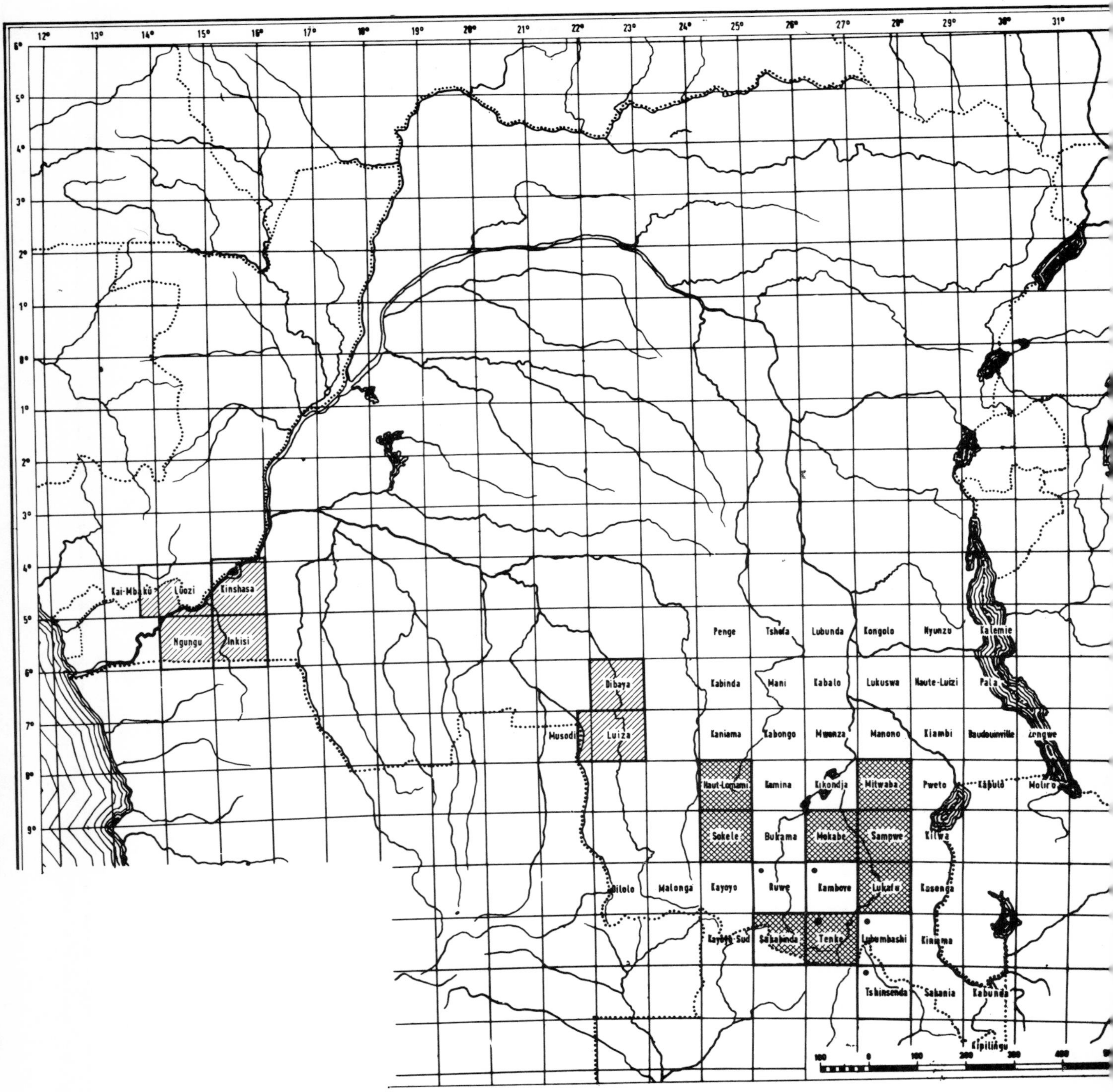

675/1 CARTE GÉOLOGIQUE DU ZAÏRE (CONGO)

1:200,000 KMMA

Geological series in progress

 Sheets published

 Sheets published in the Atlas of Katanga

675.97/1 CARTE TOPOGRAPHIQUE DU RUANDA URUNDI
1:100,000 KMMA
Topographical series in 28 sheets

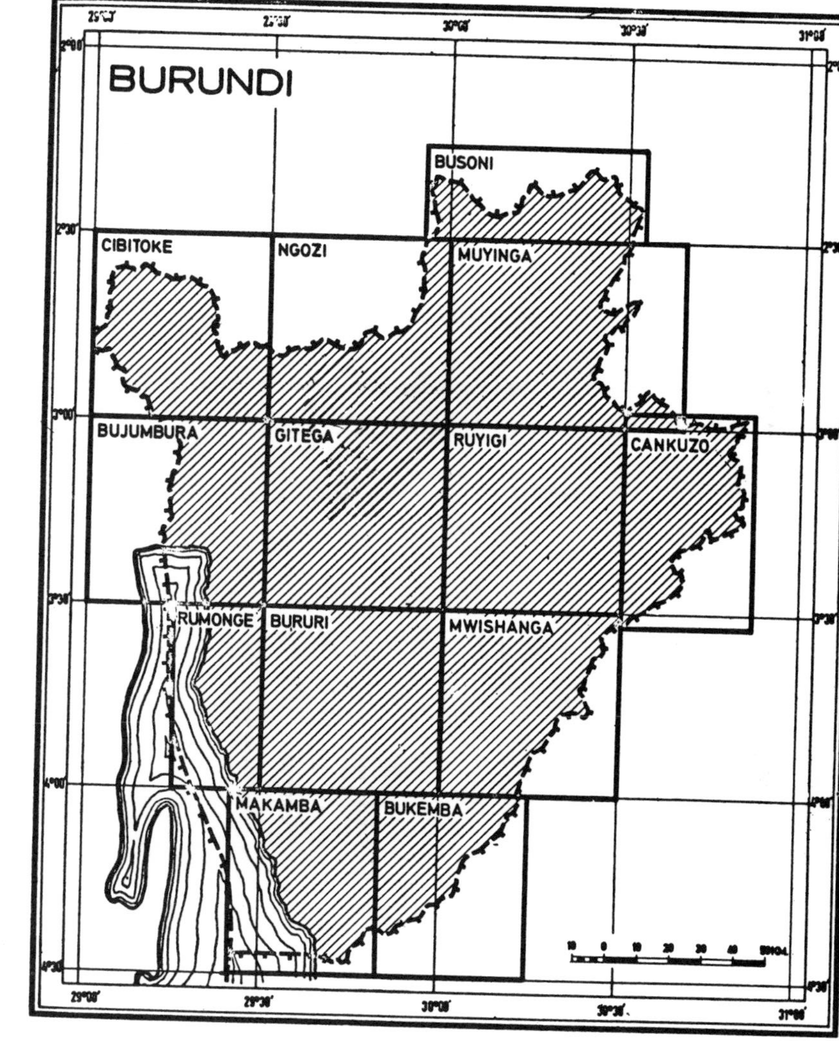

675.97/2 CARTE PLANIMÉTRIC DU BURUNDI
1:100,000 KMMA
Planimetric series uncontoured

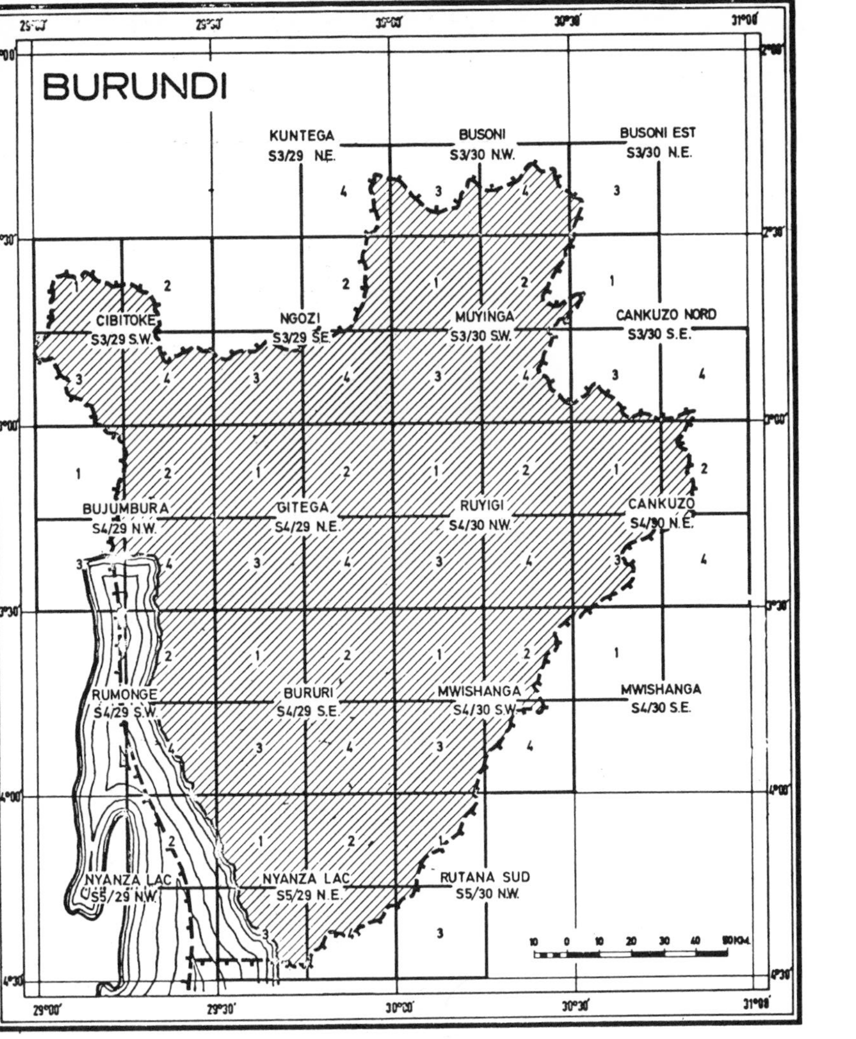

675.97/3 CARTE PLANIMÉTRIQUE DU BURUNDI
1:50,000 KMMA
Planimetric series uncontoured

NB Sheets S3/29SE 3,4, S4/2GNE
do not include place names

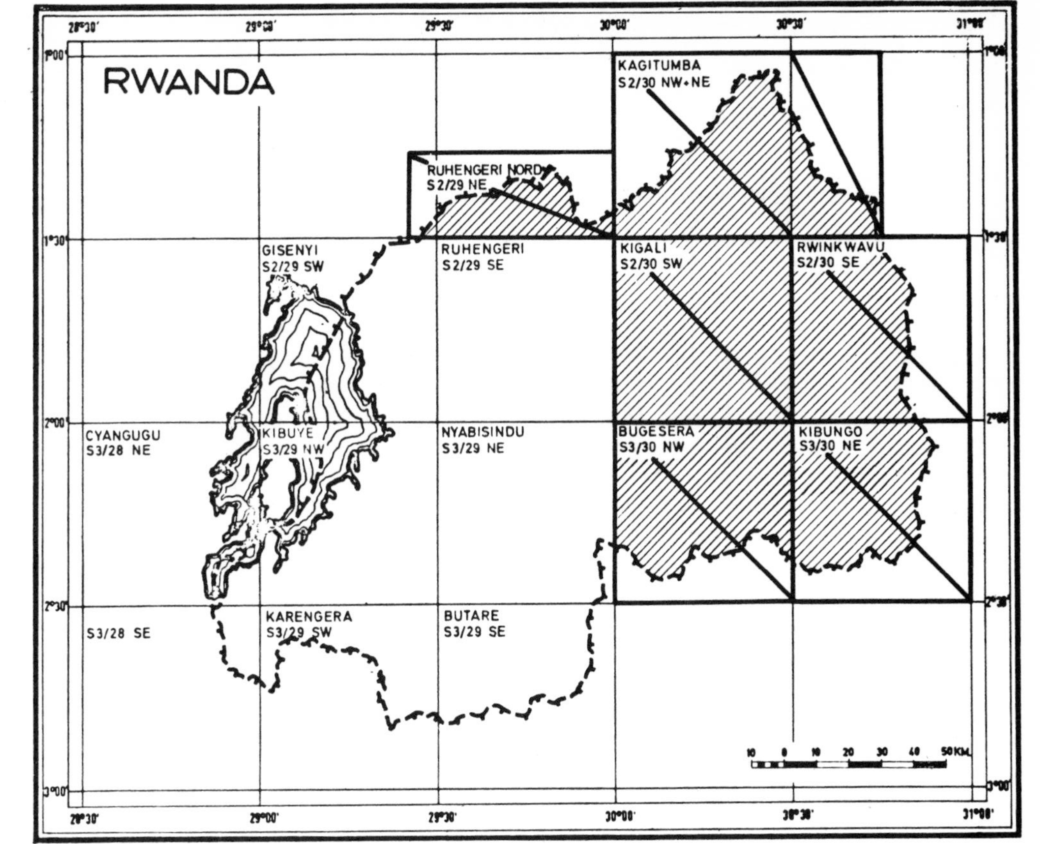

675.98/1 CARTE PLANIMÉTRIQUE DU RWANDA
1:100,000 KMMA
Planimetric series uncontoured

 Planimetric sheets published.

 Geological sheets published.

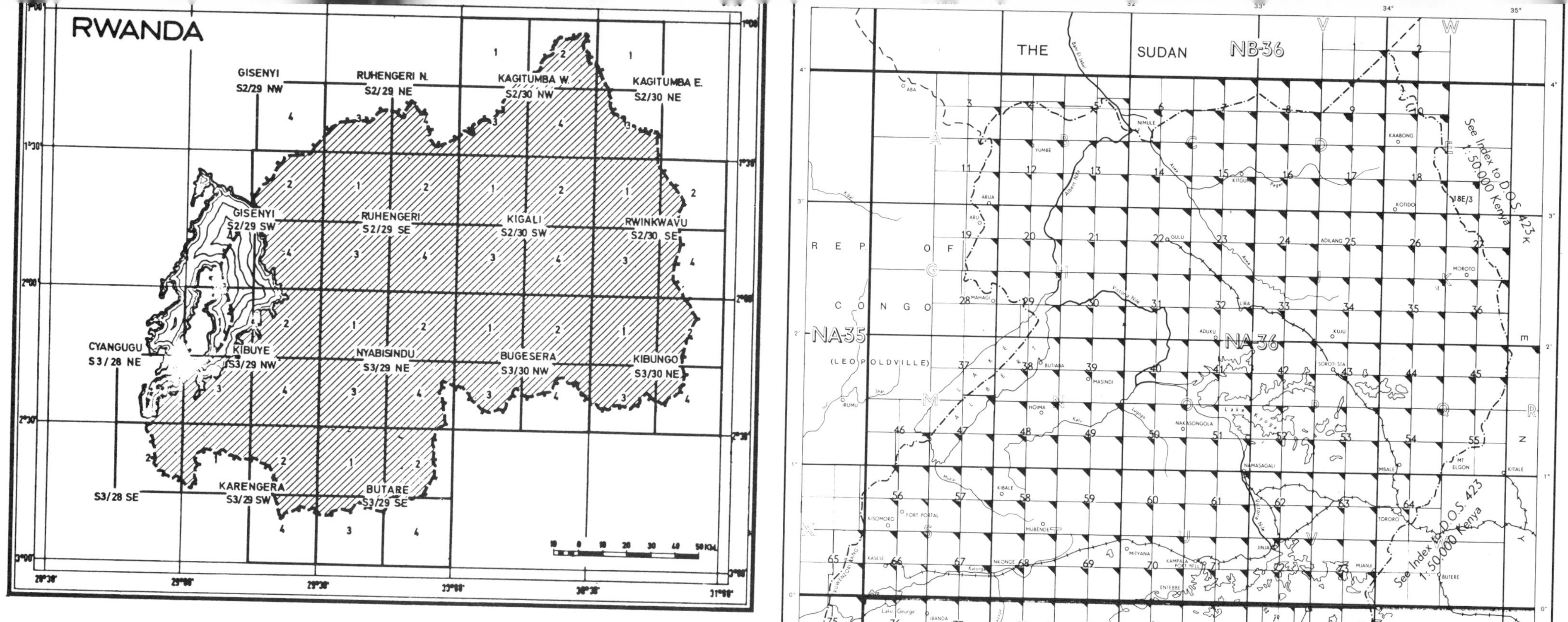

675.98/2 *CARTE PLANIMÉTRIQUE DU RWANDA*
1:50,000 KMMA
Planimetric series uncontoured.

676.1/2 *UGANDA SERIES DOS 426 (Y732)*
1:50,000 DOS
Topographical series

EAST AFRICA 1:250,000 TOPOGRAPHY

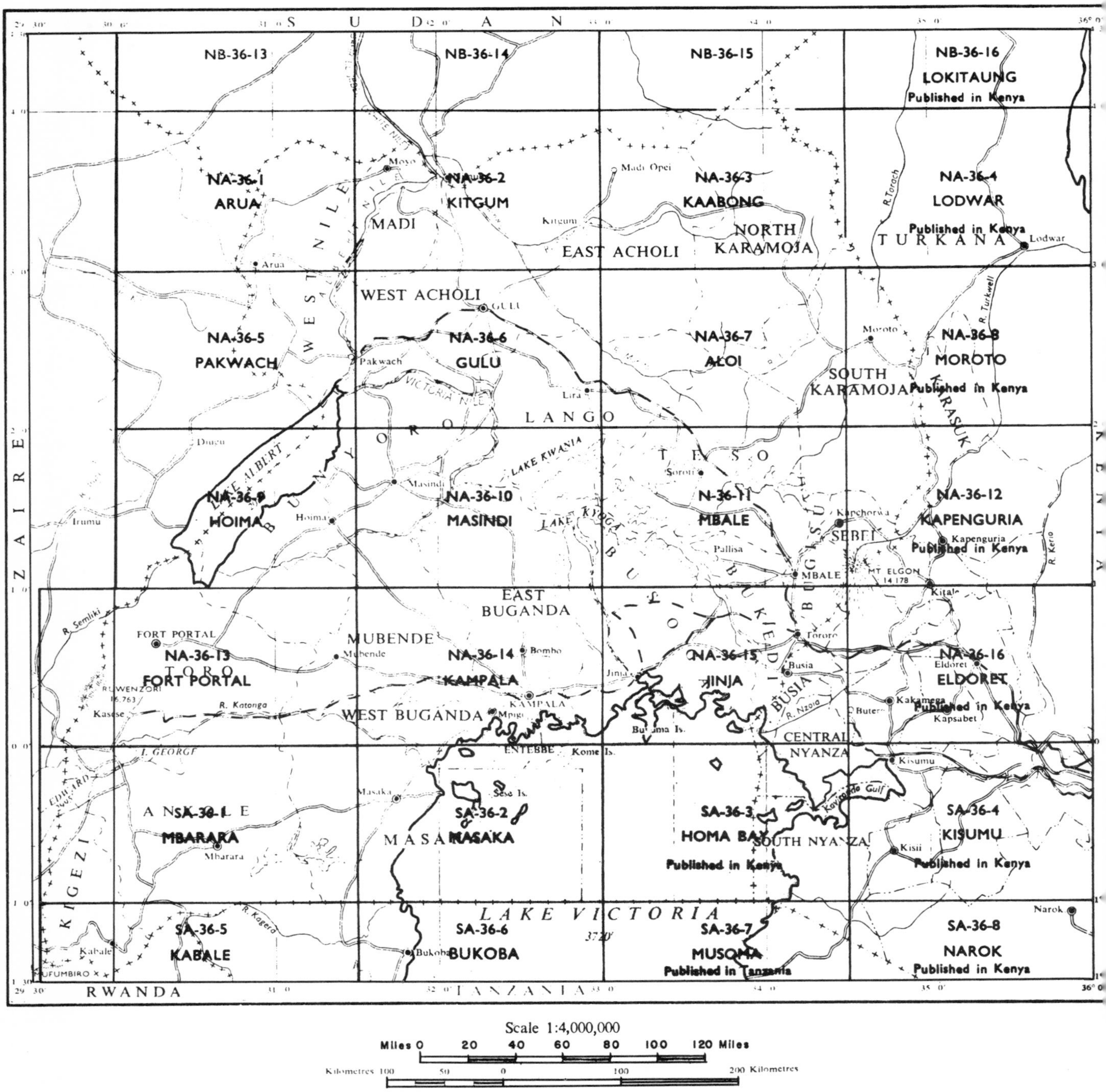

Scale 1:4,000,000

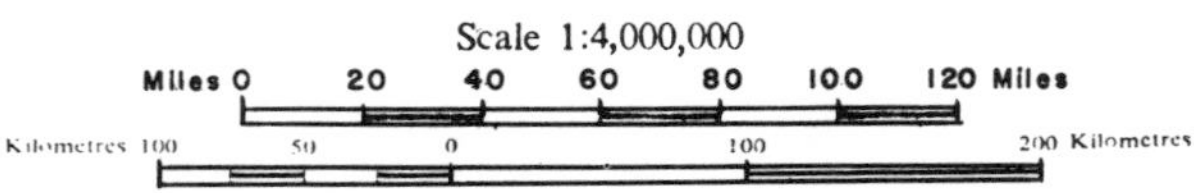

676.1/1 *UGANDA*
EAST AFRICA Series Y503
1:250,000 Dept. of Lands & Surveys
Topographical series, all sheets published

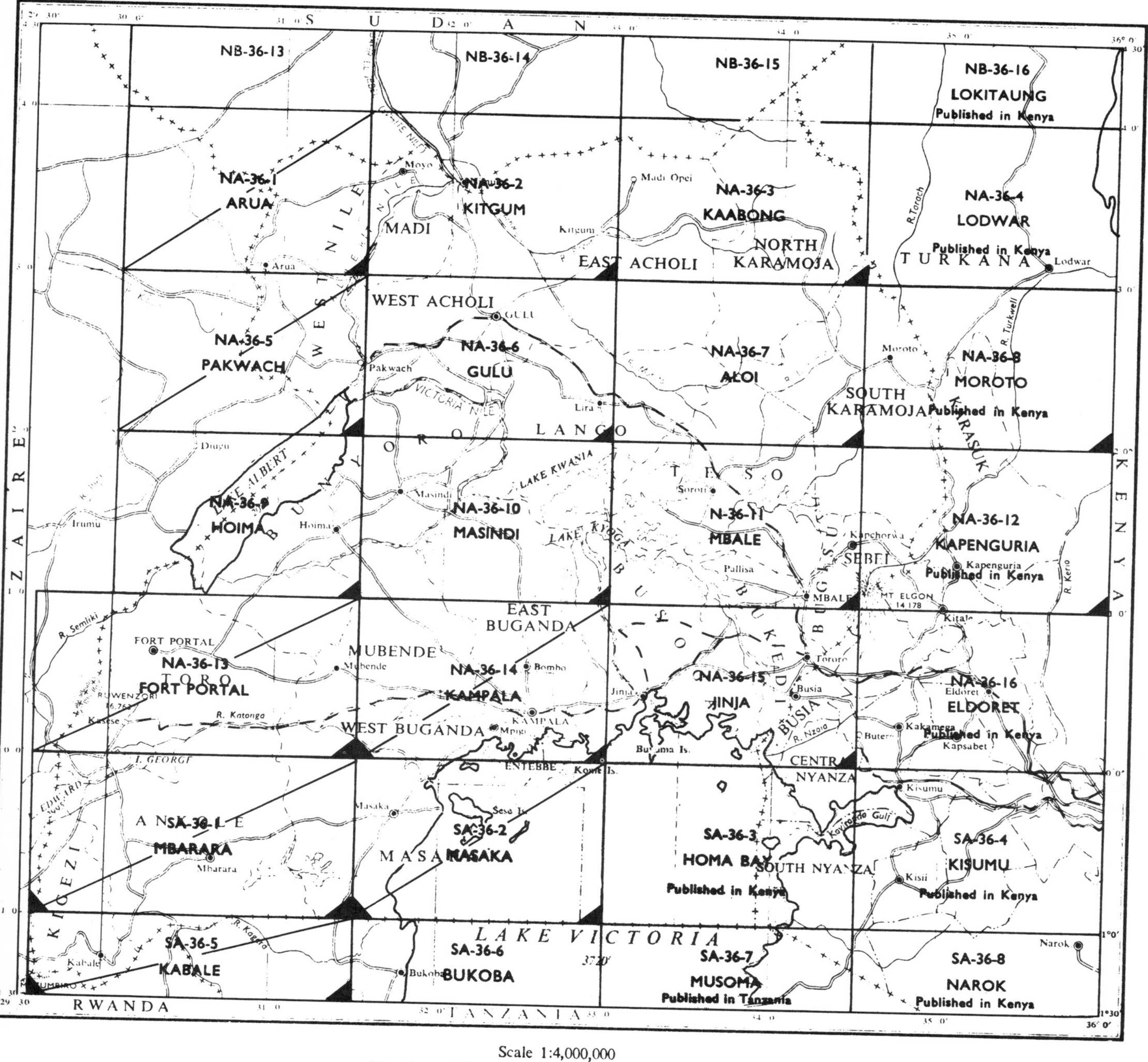

676.1/3 UGANDA

1:250,000 Dept. of Lands and Surveys.

Geology

Soils

Vegetation

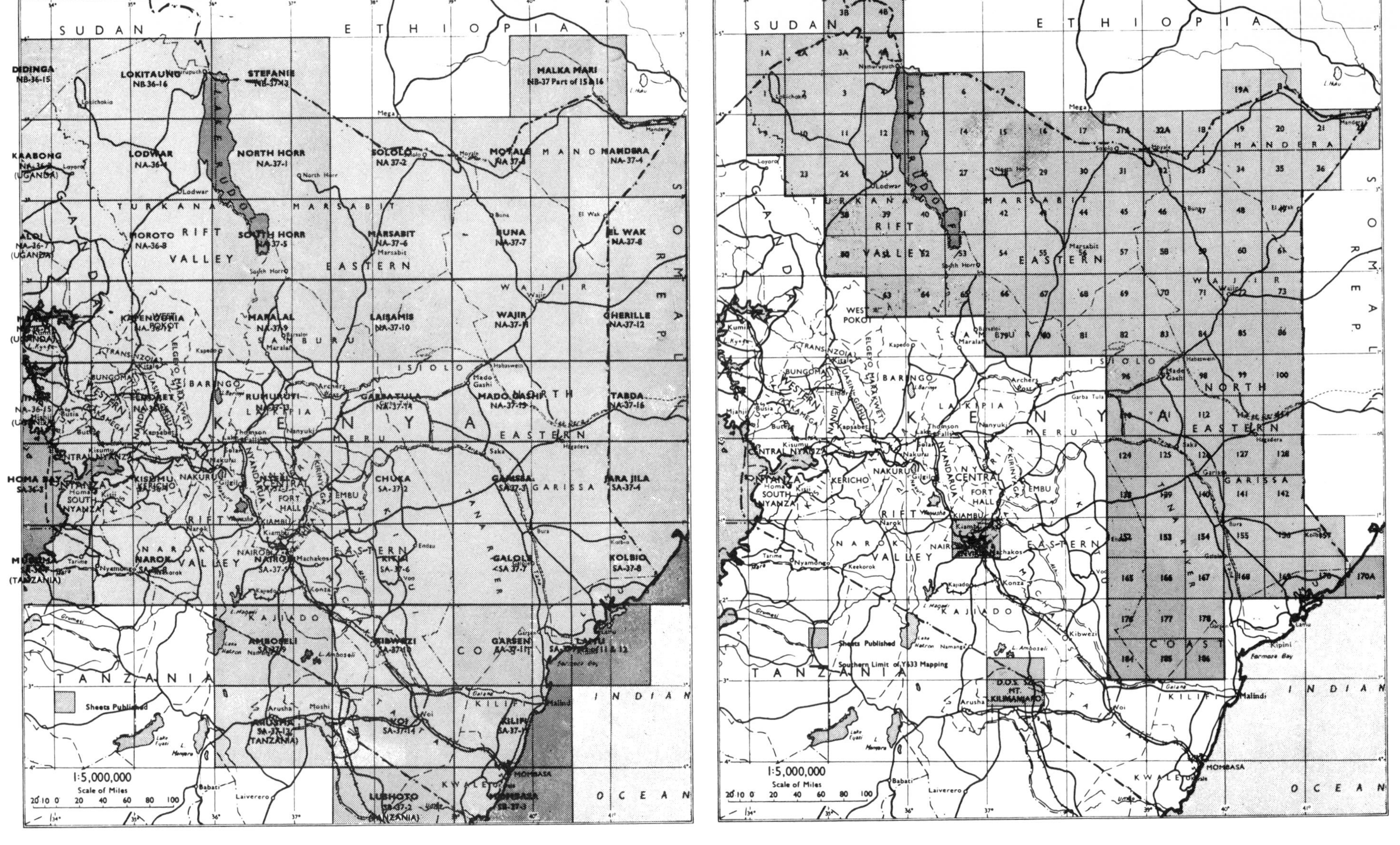

676.2/1 *EAST AFRICA Series 4503*
1:250,000 SK
Topographical series in 46 Sheets to cover Kenya

676.2/2 *KENYA Series 4633*
1:100,000
Topographical series

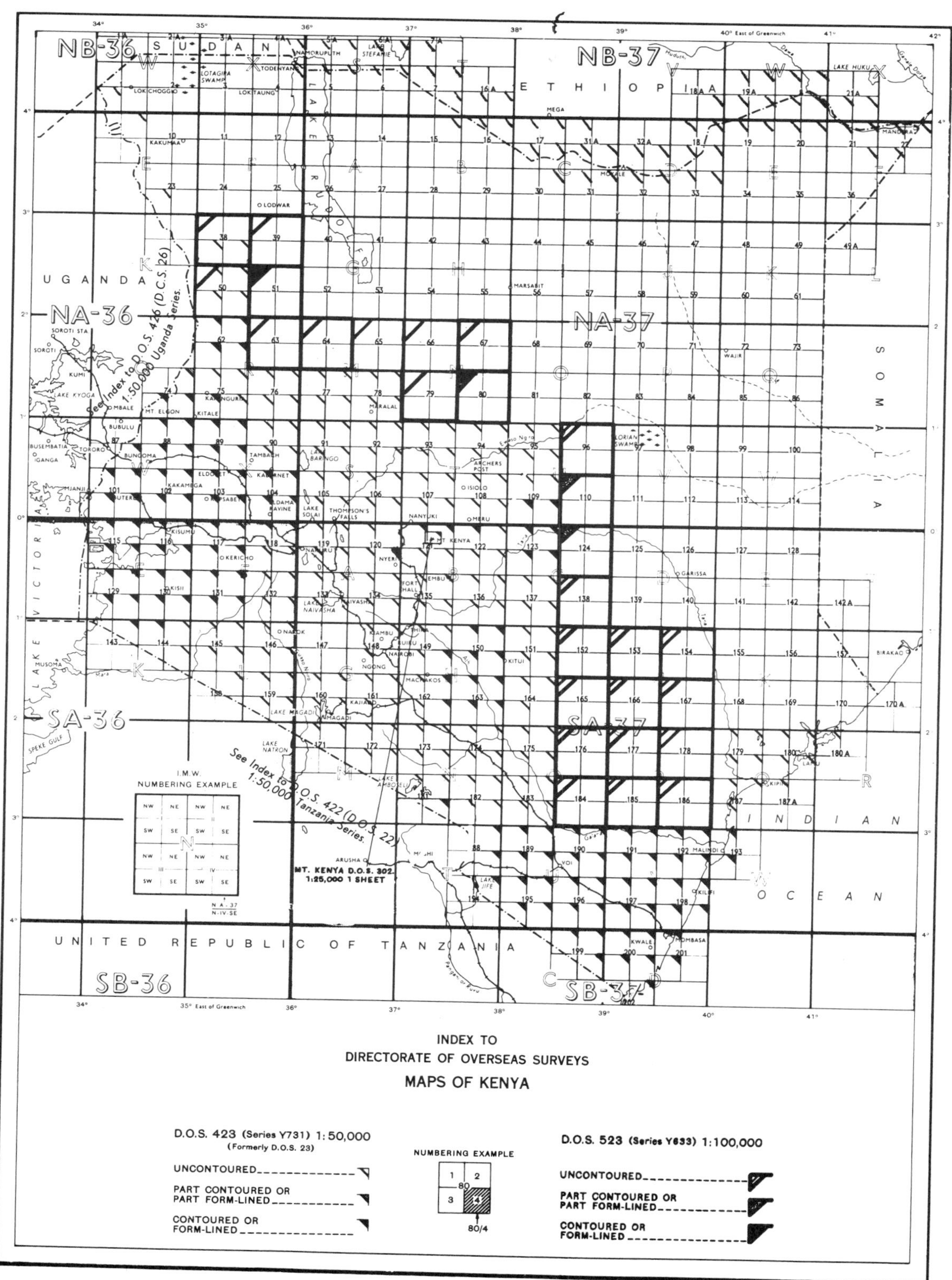

INDEX TO
DIRECTORATE OF OVERSEAS SURVEYS
MAPS OF KENYA
D.O.S. 423 (Series Y731) 1:50,000
(Formerly D.O.S. 23)
UNCONTOURED
PART CONTOURED OR PART FORM-LINED
CONTOURED OR FORM-LINED
NUMBERING EXAMPLE
80/4
D.O.S. 523 (Series Y633) 1:100,000
UNCONTOURED
PART CONTOURED OR PART FORM-LINED
CONTOURED OR FORM-LINED
NB-36
NB-37
NA-36
NA-37
SA-36
SA-37
SB-36
SB-37
S U D A N
E T H I O P I A
U G A N D A
S O M A L I A
U N I T E D R E P U B L I C O F T A N Z A N I A
I N D I A N O C E A N
L A K E V I C T O R I A
L A K E R U D O L F
See Index to D.O.S. 426 (D.C.S. 26) 1:50,000 Uganda Series.
See Index to D.O.S. 422 (D.O.S. 22) 1:50,000 Tanzania Series.
MT. KENYA D.O.S. 302 1:25,000 1 SHEET
I.M.W. NUMBERING EXAMPLE
N.A.-37 N-IV-SE
40° East of Greenwich
35° East of Greenwich

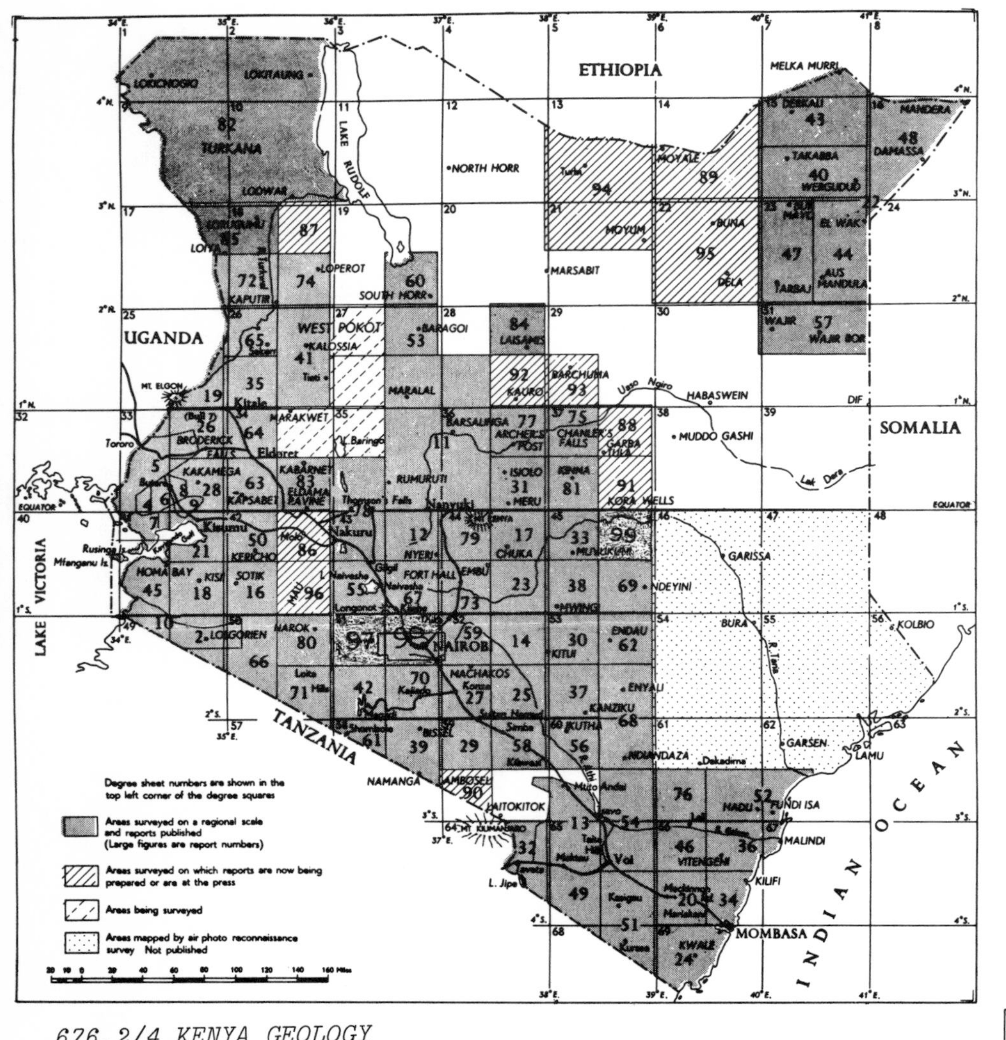

676.2/4 KENYA GEOLOGY
1:125,000 Mines and Geology Dept.

677/3 CARTA DELLA SOMALIA (MEDIA & BASSA GOSCIA)
1:50,000
Topographical series of South West Somalia

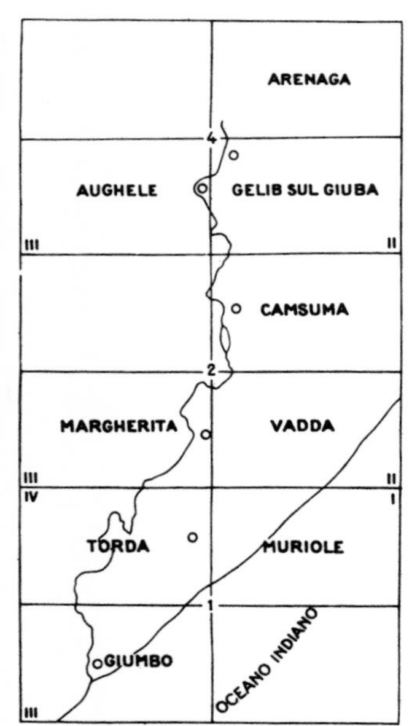

19 SCIDIE
20 ÌTALA
13 BARIRE
14 MOGADISCIO
15 EL ARACAI
9 MERCA
10 DANANE
5 PASSO DI COMIA
6 BRAVA
2 GELIB (GIUBA)
3 POZZI DI MACASI
1 GIUMBO

677/2 CARTA DIMOSTRATIVA DELLA SOMALIA
1:200,000 IGM
Topographical series

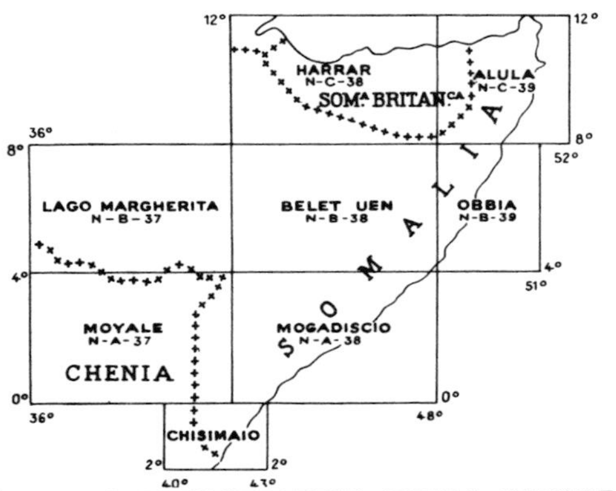

677/1 CARTA DIMOSTRATIVA DELLA SOMALIA
1:1,000,000 IGM
Topographical series

SOMALIA, PART OF
(FORMER SOMALILAND PROTECTORATE)

INDEX TO
DIRECTORATE OF OVERSEAS SURVEYS
MAPS OF SOMALILAND PROTECTORATE

1:50,000 DOS 427

I.M.W. NUMBERING EXAMPLE

D.O.S. NUMBERING EXAMPLE

DOS 539 (DCS 39) 1:125,000 (Series Y625)
UNCONTOURED

DOS 427 (DCS 27) 1:50,000 (Series Y721)
UNCONTOURED
PART CONTOURED OR PART FORM-LINED

DOS 339 1:25,000 (Series Y823)
UNCONTOURED
PART CONTOURED OR PART FORM-LINED
CONTOURED OR FORM-LINED

677/4 *GEOLOGICAL MAPS OF THE SOMALI DEMOCRATIC REPUBLIC*

1:125,000 DOS

Coloured maps - Series DOS(Geol) 1076

 Sheets published

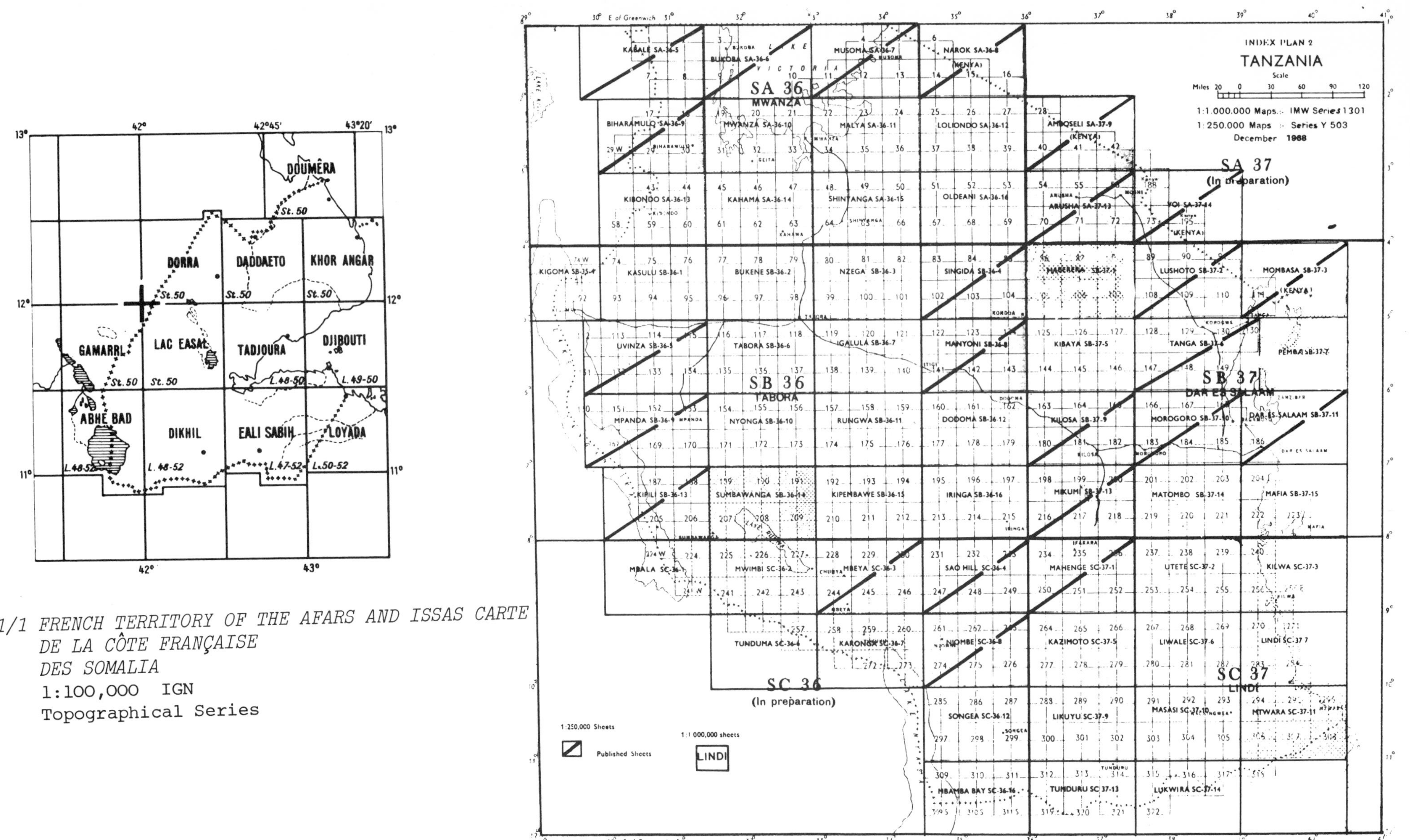

677.1/1 *FRENCH TERRITORY OF THE AFARS AND ISSAS CARTE DE LA CÔTE FRANÇAISE DES SOMALIA*
1:100,000 IGN
Topographical Series

678/1 *TANZANIA EAST AFRICA Series Y503*
1:250,000 Survey Division
Topographical series

Tanzania

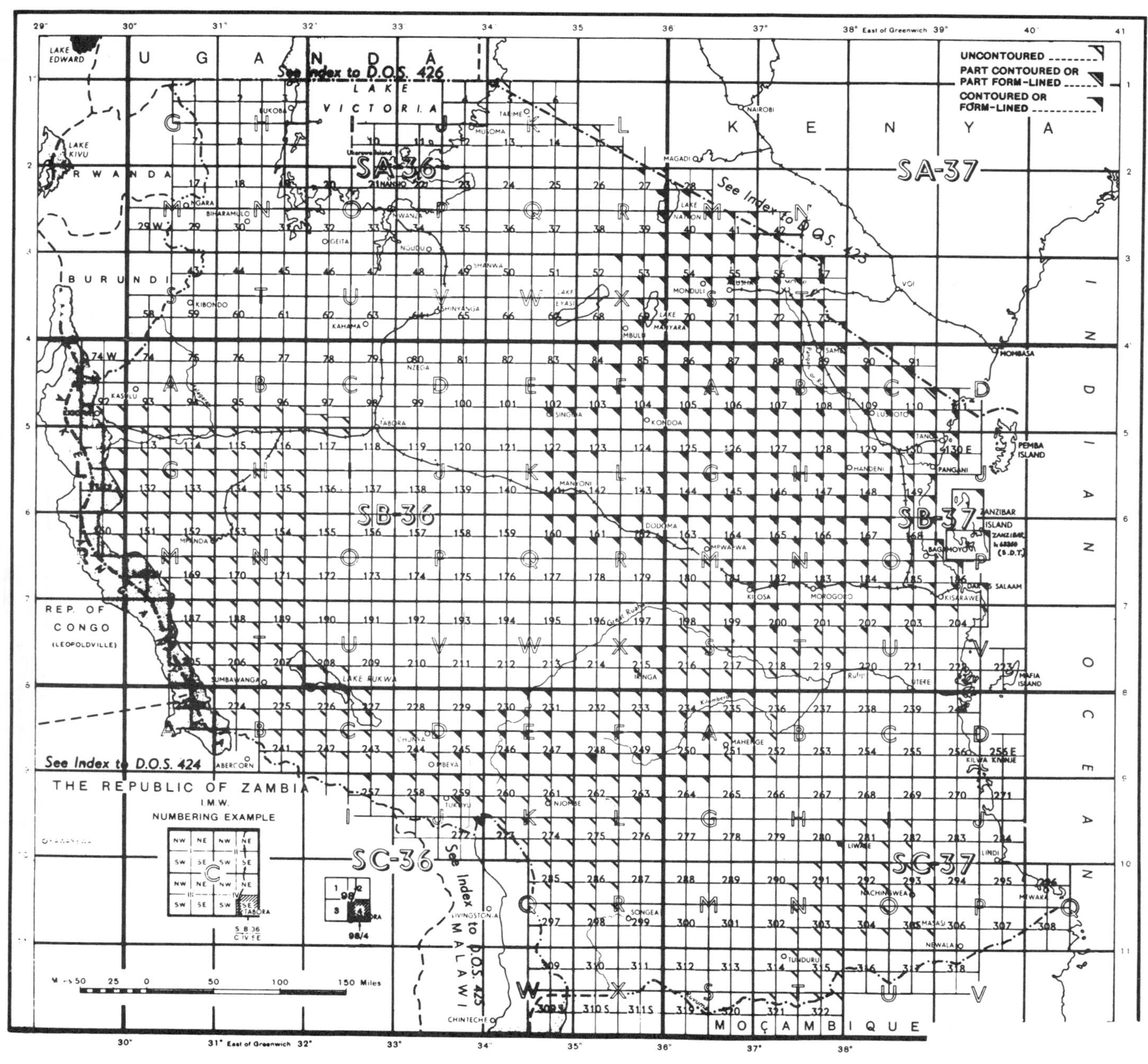

678/2 TANZANIA

1:50,000 DOS 422 (Z742)

Tanzania Survey Division - DOS.

Topographical series

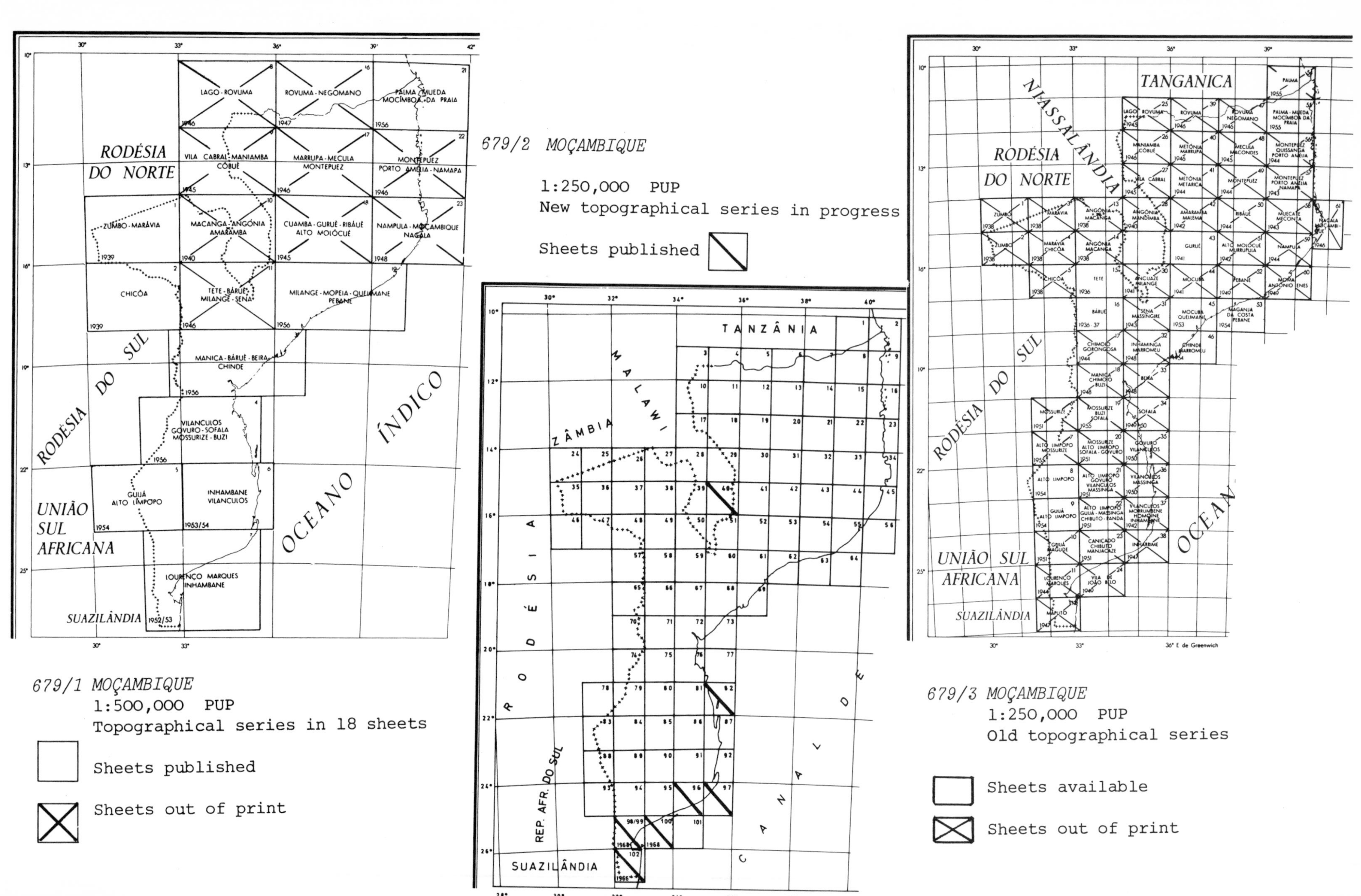

679/1 *MOÇAMBIQUE*

1:500,000 PUP

Topographical series in 18 sheets

Sheets published

Sheets out of print

679/2 *MOÇAMBIQUE*

1:250,000 PUP

New topographical series in progress

Sheets published

679/3 *MOÇAMBIQUE*

1:250,000 PUP

Old topographical series

Sheets available

Sheets out of print

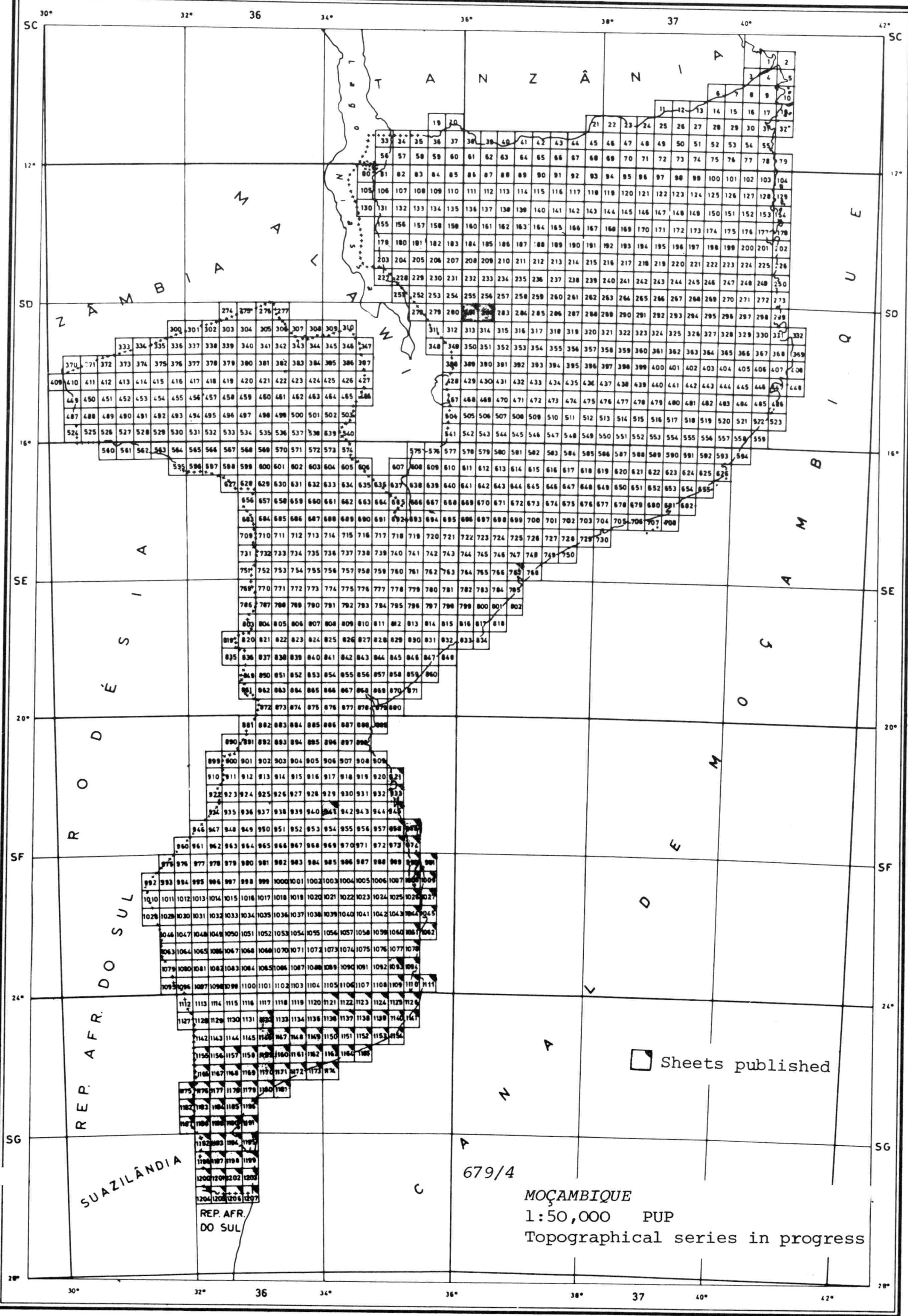

679/4

MOÇAMBIQUE
1:50,000 PUP
Topographical series in progress

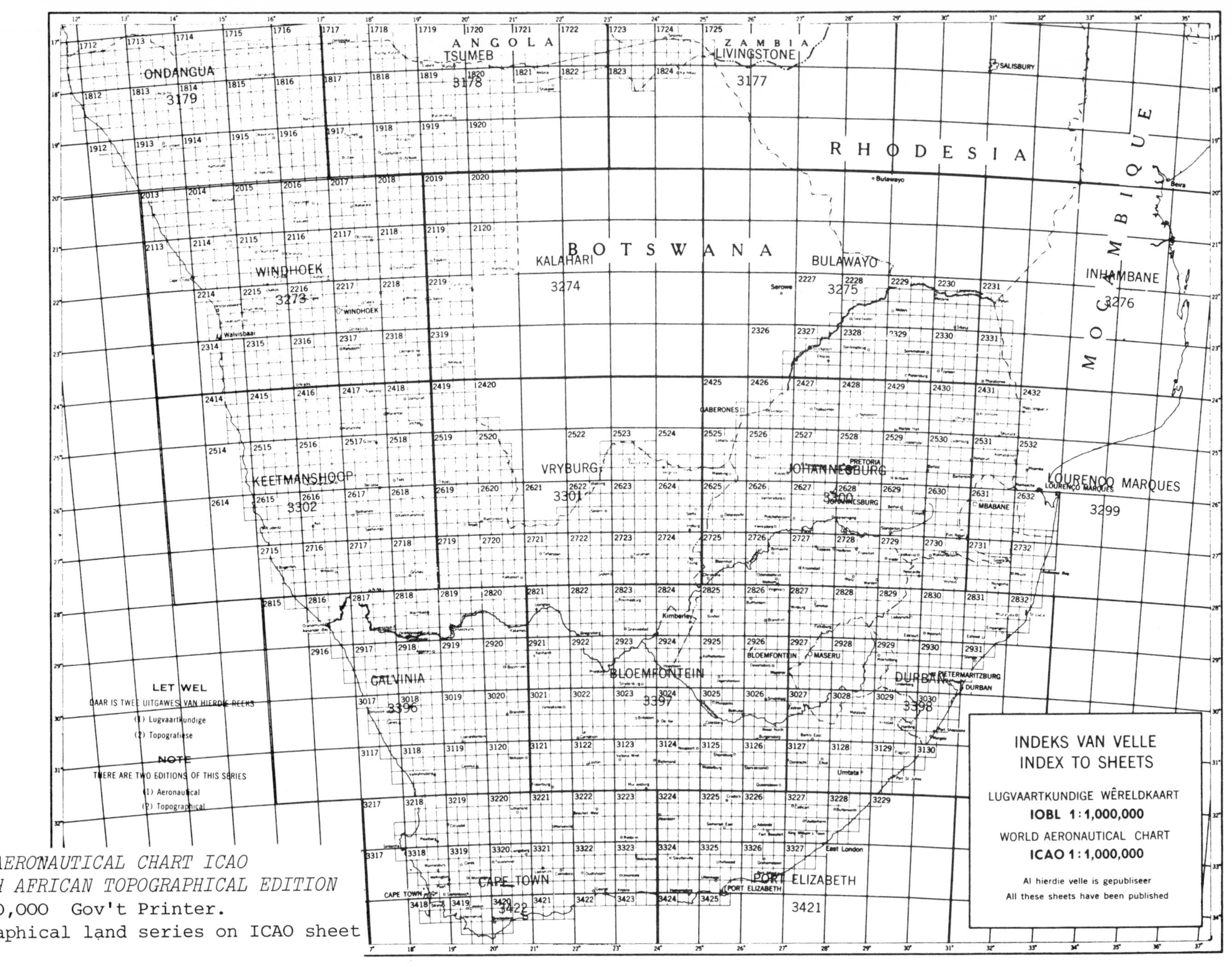

68/1

WORLD AERONAUTICAL CHART ICAO
- SOUTH AFRICAN TOPOGRAPHICAL EDITION
1:1,000,000 Gov't Printer.
Topographical land series on ICAO sheet lines

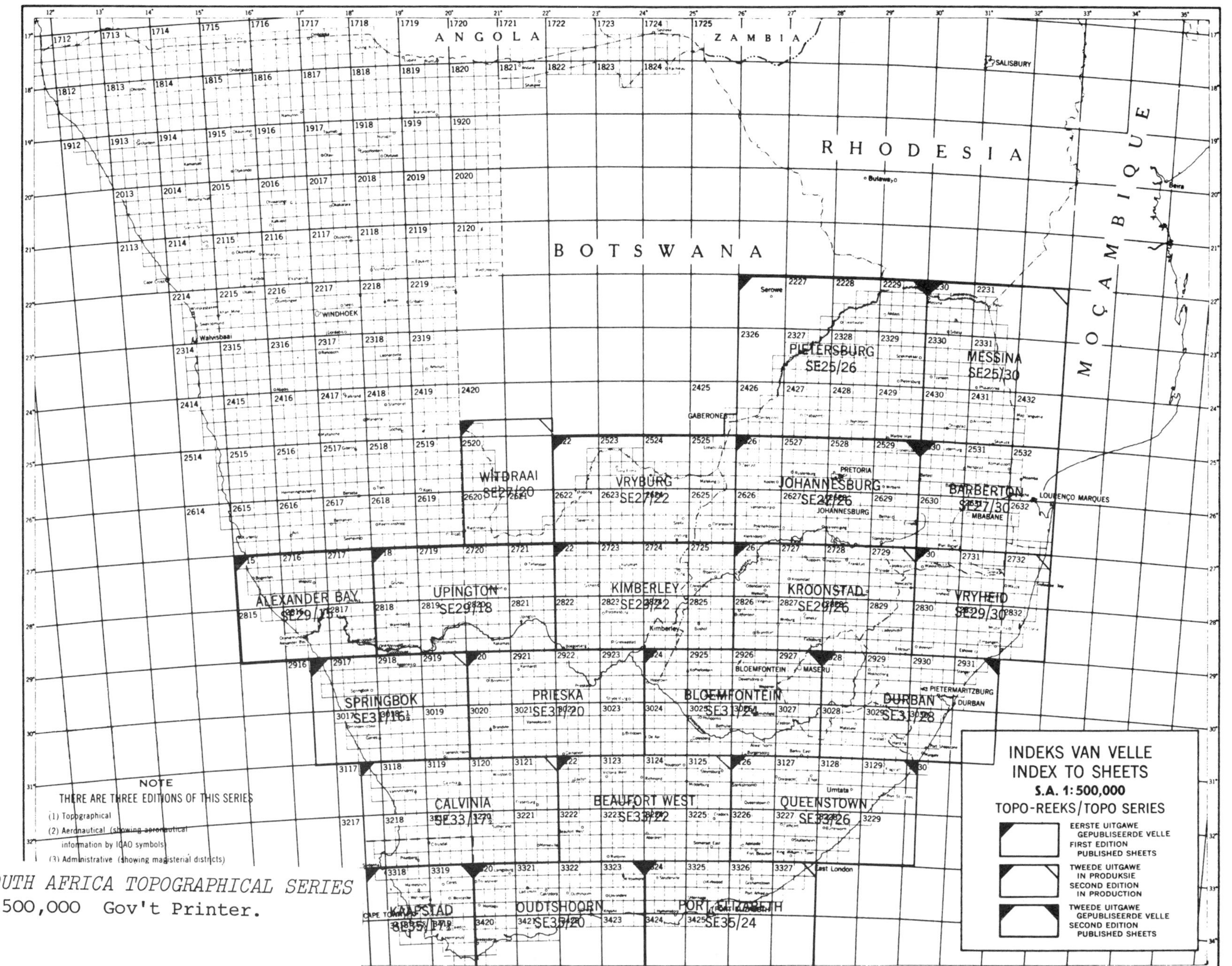

680/1 SOUTH AFRICA TOPOGRAPHICAL SERIES

1:500,000 Gov't Printer.

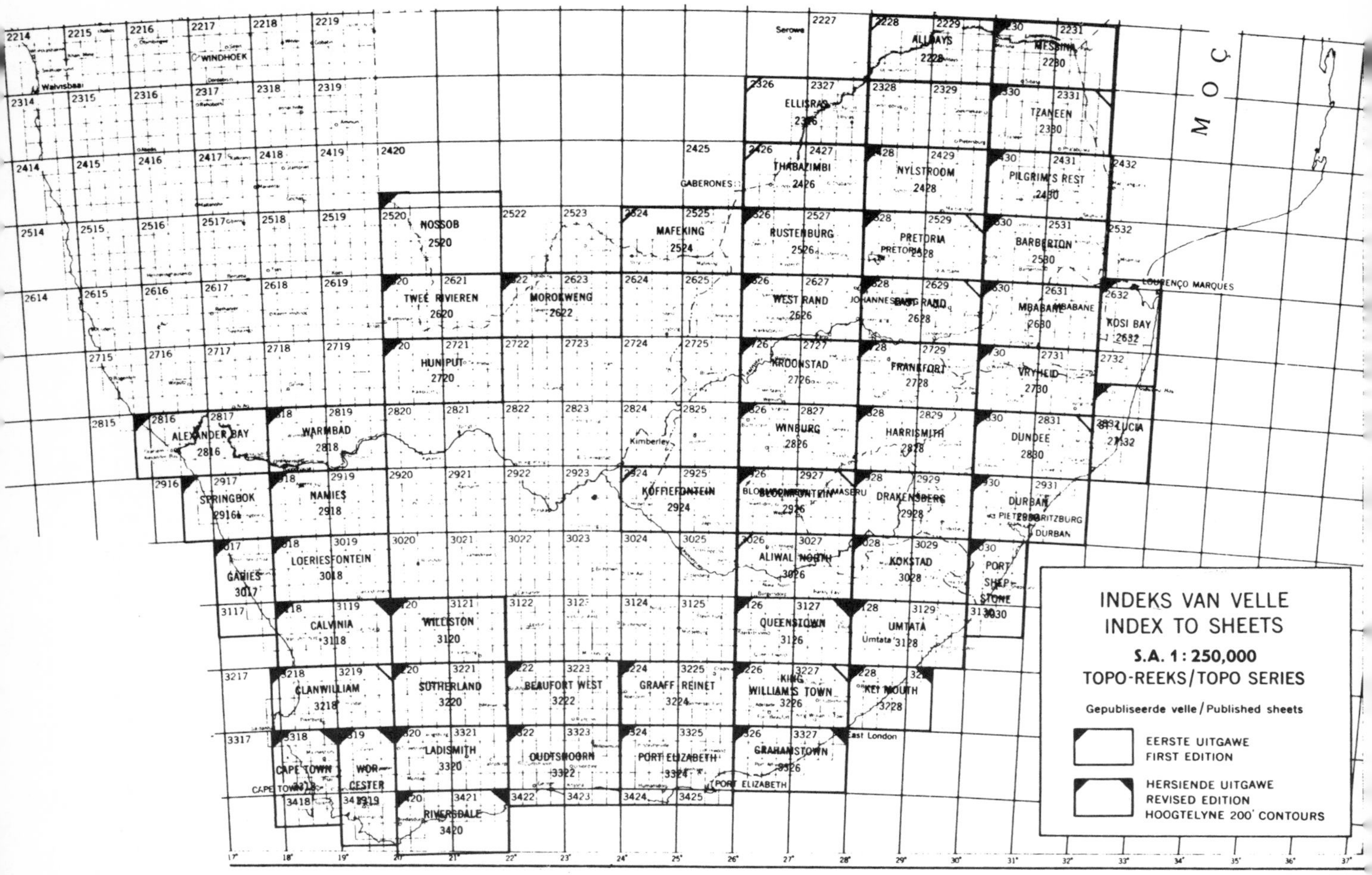

INDEKS VAN VELLE
INDEX TO SHEETS

S.A. 1 : 250,000
TOPO-REEKS/TOPO SERIES

Gepubliseerde velle/Published sheets

EERSTE UITGAWE
FIRST EDITION

HERSIENDE UITGAWE
REVISED EDITION
HOOGTELYNE 200' CONTOURS

680/2 SOUTH AFRICA TOPOGRAPHICAL SERIES
1:250,000 Gov't Printer.

680/3 SOUTH AFRICA TOPO-CADASTRA
1:250,000 Gov't Printer.

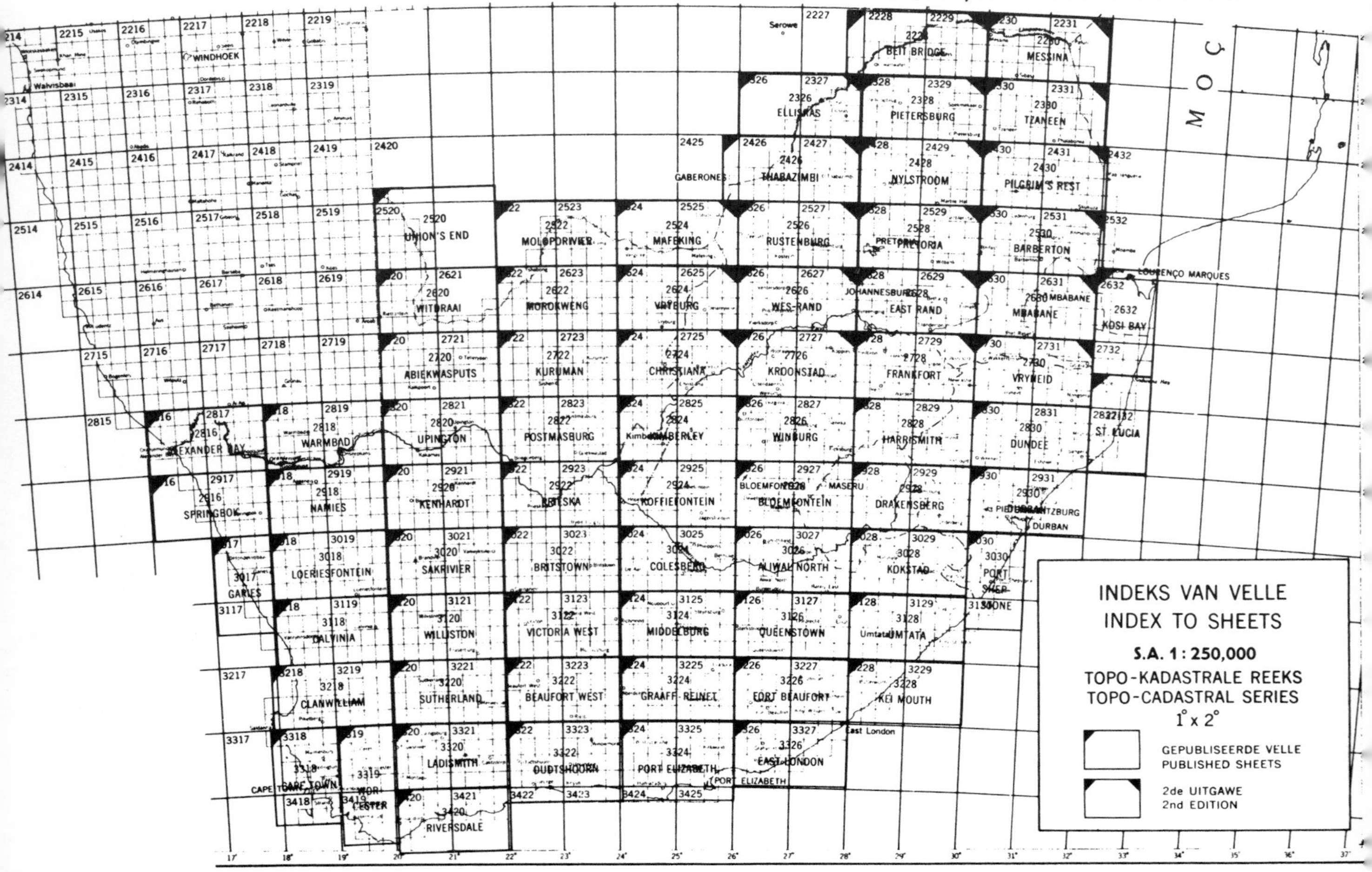

INDEKS VAN VELLE
INDEX TO SHEETS

S.A. 1 : 250,000
TOPO-KADASTRALE REEKS
TOPO-CADASTRAL SERIES
1° x 2°

GEPUBLISEERDE VELLE
PUBLISHED SHEETS

2de UITGAWE
2nd EDITION

INDEKS KAART VAN SUID-AFRIKA / INDEX MAP OF SOUTH AFRICA

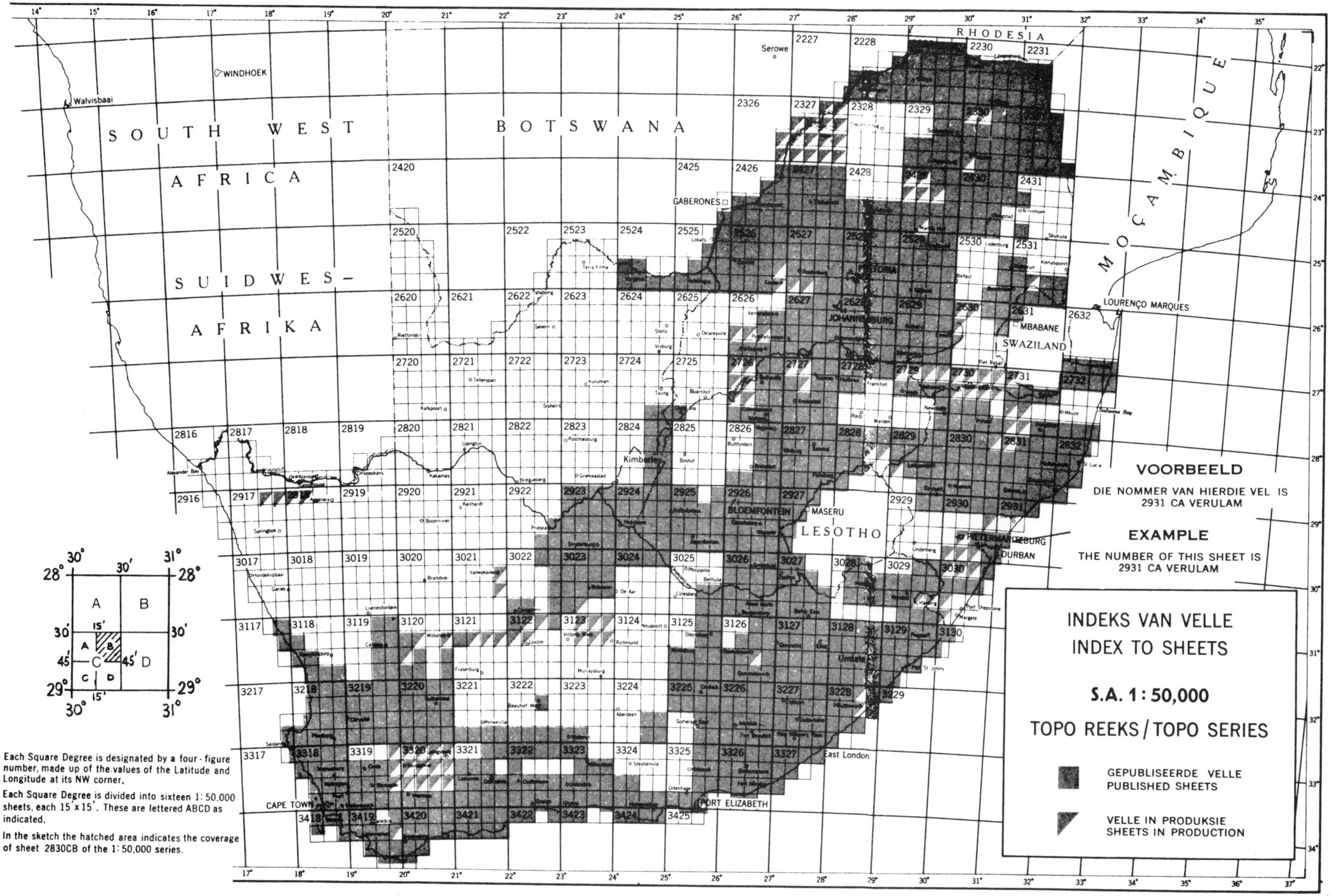

VOORBEELD

DIE NOMMER VAN HIERDIE VEL IS
2931 CA VERULAM

EXAMPLE

THE NUMBER OF THIS SHEET IS
2931 CA VERULAM

INDEKS VAN VELLE
INDEX TO SHEETS

S.A. 1 : 50,000

TOPO REEKS / TOPO SERIES

GEPUBLISEERDE VELLE
PUBLISHED SHEETS

VELLE IN PRODUKSIE
SHEETS IN PRODUCTION

a.) Each Square Degree is designated by a four-figure number, made up of the values of the Latitude and Longitude at its NW corner.

b.) Each Square Degree is divided into sixteen 1: 50,000 sheets, each 15′x 15′. These are lettered ABCD as indicated.

c.) In the sketch the hatched area indicates the coverage of sheet 2830CB of the 1: 50,000 series.

680/4 SOUTH AFRICA TOPOGRAPHICAL SERIES
1:50,000 Gov't Printer.

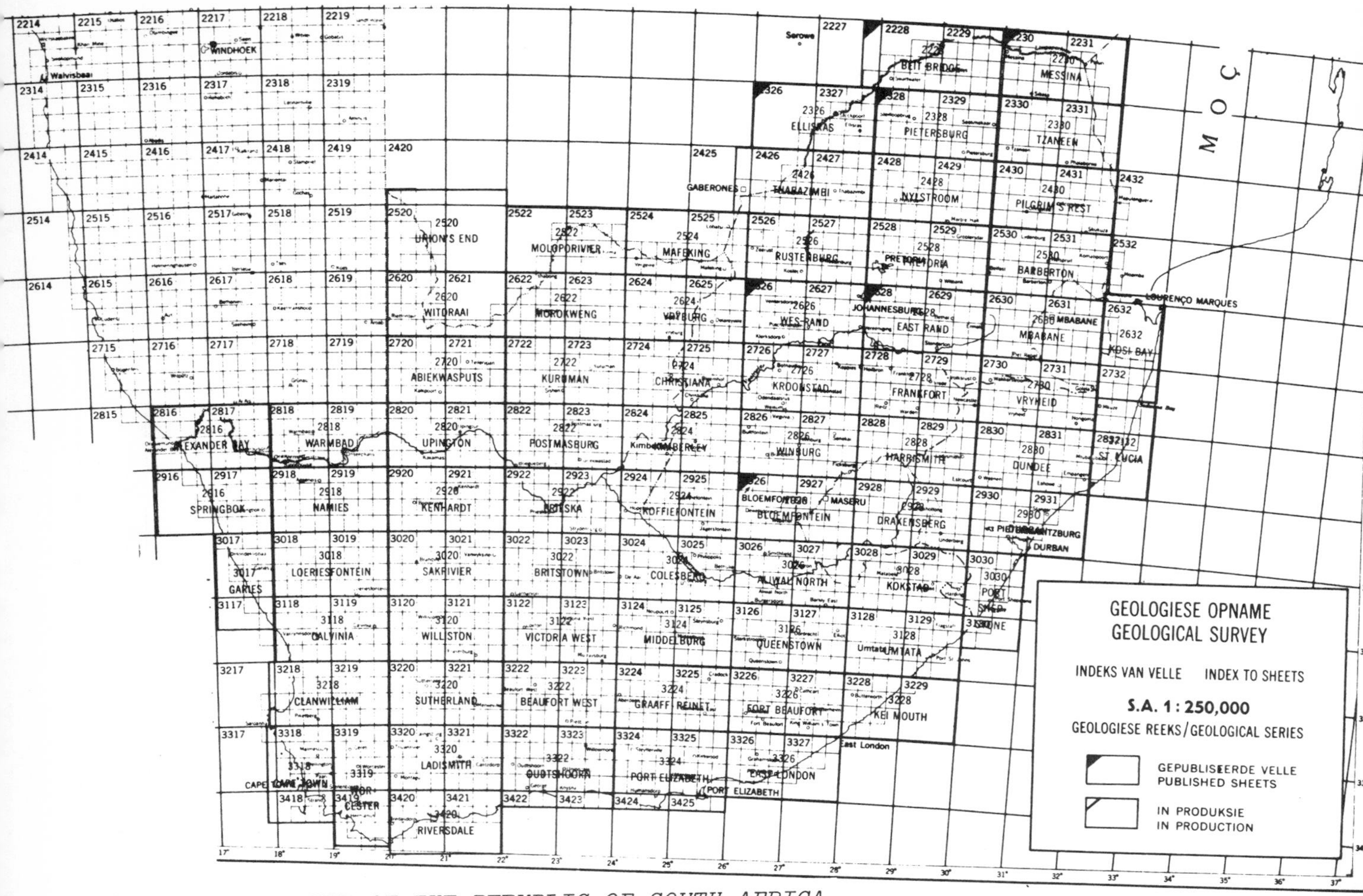

GEOLOGIESE OPNAME
GEOLOGICAL SURVEY

INDEKS VAN VELLE — INDEX TO SHEETS

S.A. 1 : 250,000
GEOLOGIESE REEKS/GEOLOGICAL SERIES

GEPUBLISEERDE VELLE
PUBLISHED SHEETS

IN PRODUKSIE
IN PRODUCTION

680/5 GEOLOGICAL MAP OF THE REPUBLIC OF SOUTH AFRICA
1:250,000 Geol. Survey.

680/6 SOUTH AFRICA - GEOLOGICAL SERIES
1:148,750 Geol Survey.

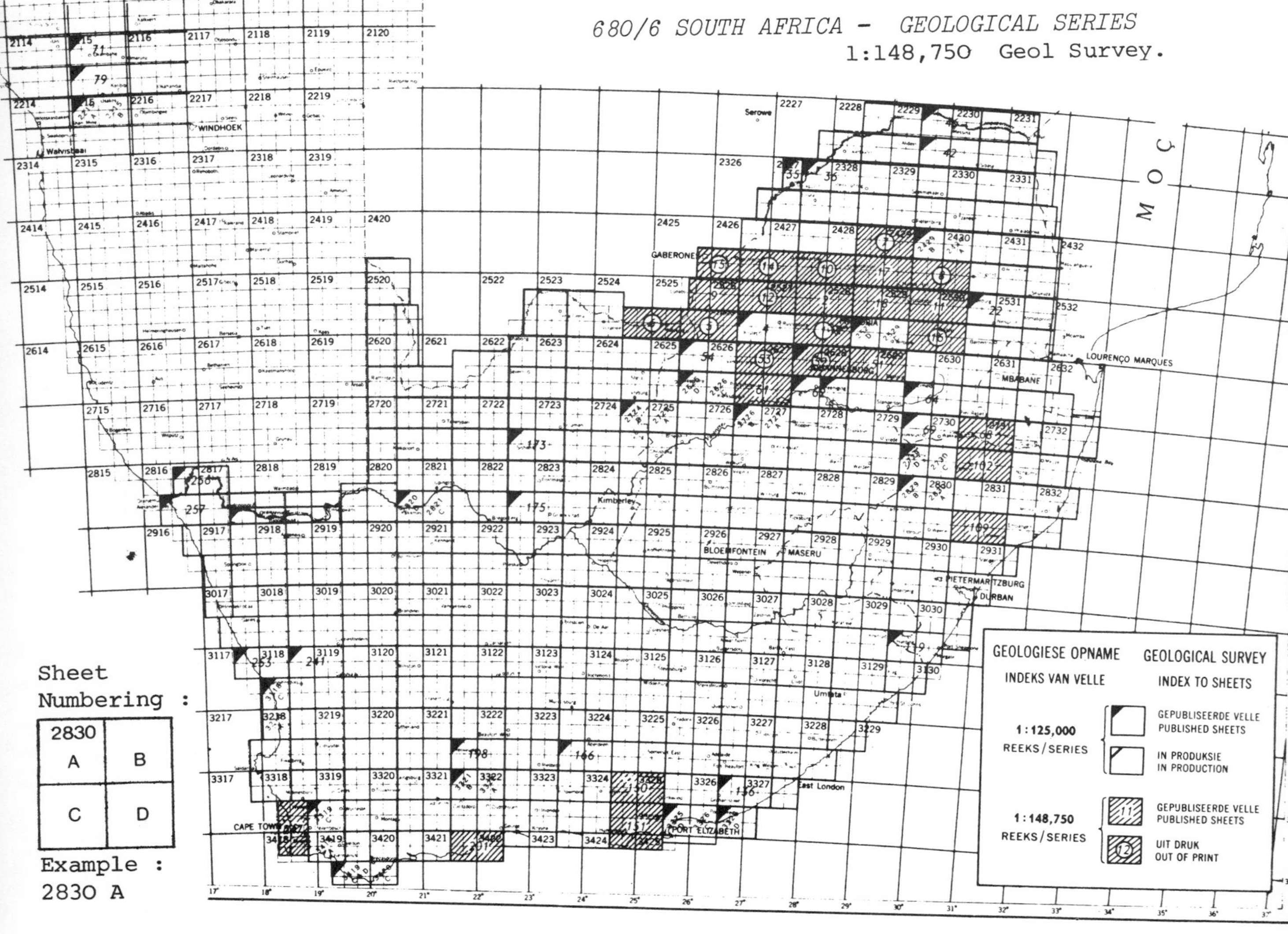

GEOLOGIESE OPNAME — GEOLOGICAL SURVEY

INDEKS VAN VELLE — INDEX TO SHEETS

1:125,000
REEKS/SERIES

GEPUBLISEERDE VELLE
PUBLISHED SHEETS

IN PRODUKSIE
IN PRODUCTION

1:148,750
REEKS/SERIES

GEPUBLISEERDE VELLE
PUBLISHED SHEETS

UIT DRUK
OUT OF PRINT

Sheet Numbering :

2830 A	B
C	D

Example :
2830 A

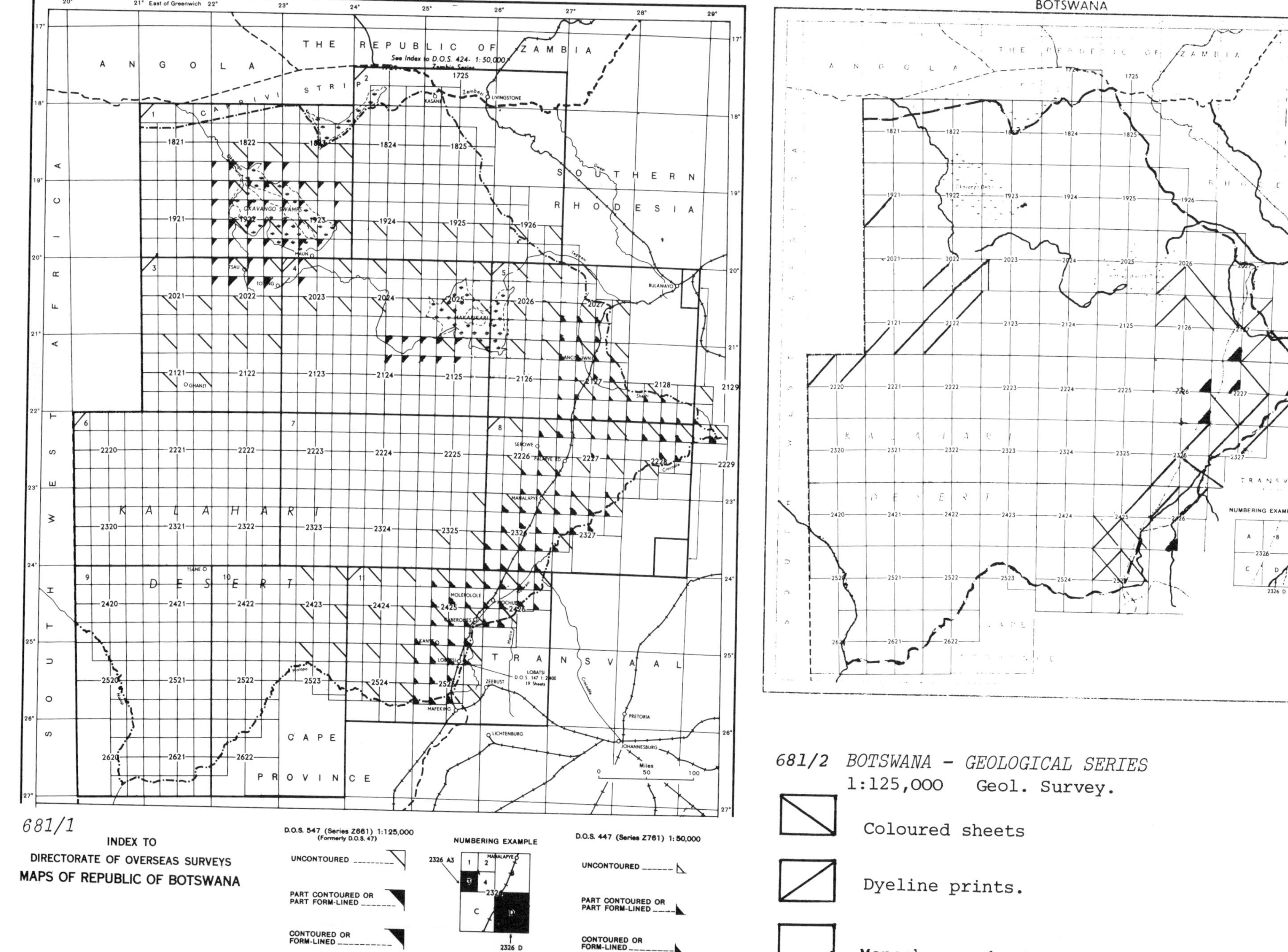

681/1

INDEX TO
DIRECTORATE OF OVERSEAS SURVEYS
MAPS OF REPUBLIC OF BOTSWANA

D.O.S. 547 (Series Z661) 1:125,000 (Formerly D.O.S. 47)

UNCONTOURED

PART CONTOURED OR PART FORM-LINED

CONTOURED OR FORM-LINED

NUMBERING EXAMPLE

2326 A3

2326 D

D.O.S. 447 (Series Z761) 1:50,000

UNCONTOURED

PART CONTOURED OR PART FORM-LINED

CONTOURED OR FORM-LINED

681/2 *BOTSWANA - GEOLOGICAL SERIES*
1:125,000 Geol. Survey.

Coloured sheets

Dyeline prints.

Monochrome sheets

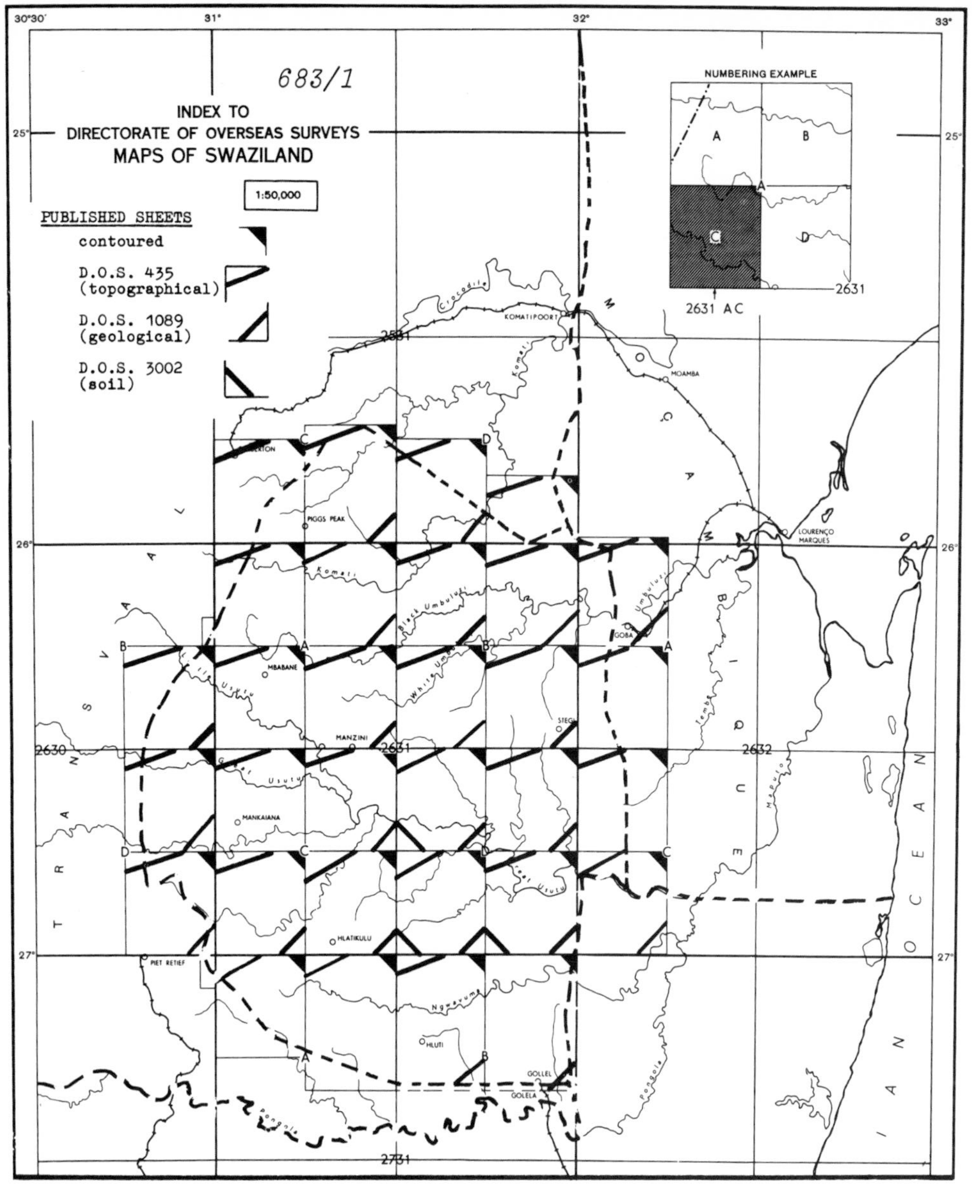

683/1
INDEX TO
DIRECTORATE OF OVERSEAS SURVEYS
MAPS OF SWAZILAND
1:50,000
PUBLISHED SHEETS
contoured
D.O.S. 435
(topographical)
D.O.S. 1089
(geological)
D.O.S. 3002
(soil)
NUMBERING EXAMPLE
2631 AC
2631
KOMATIPOORT
MOAMBA
LOURENÇO MARQUES
PIGGS PEAK
MBABANE
MANZINI
GOBA
STEGI
MANKAIANA
HLATIKULU
PIET RETIEF
HLUTI
GOLLEL
GOLELA
TRANSVAAL
MOÇAMBIQUE
INDIAN OCEAN
2531
2630
2631
2632
2731
30°30'
31°
32°
33°
25°
26°
27°

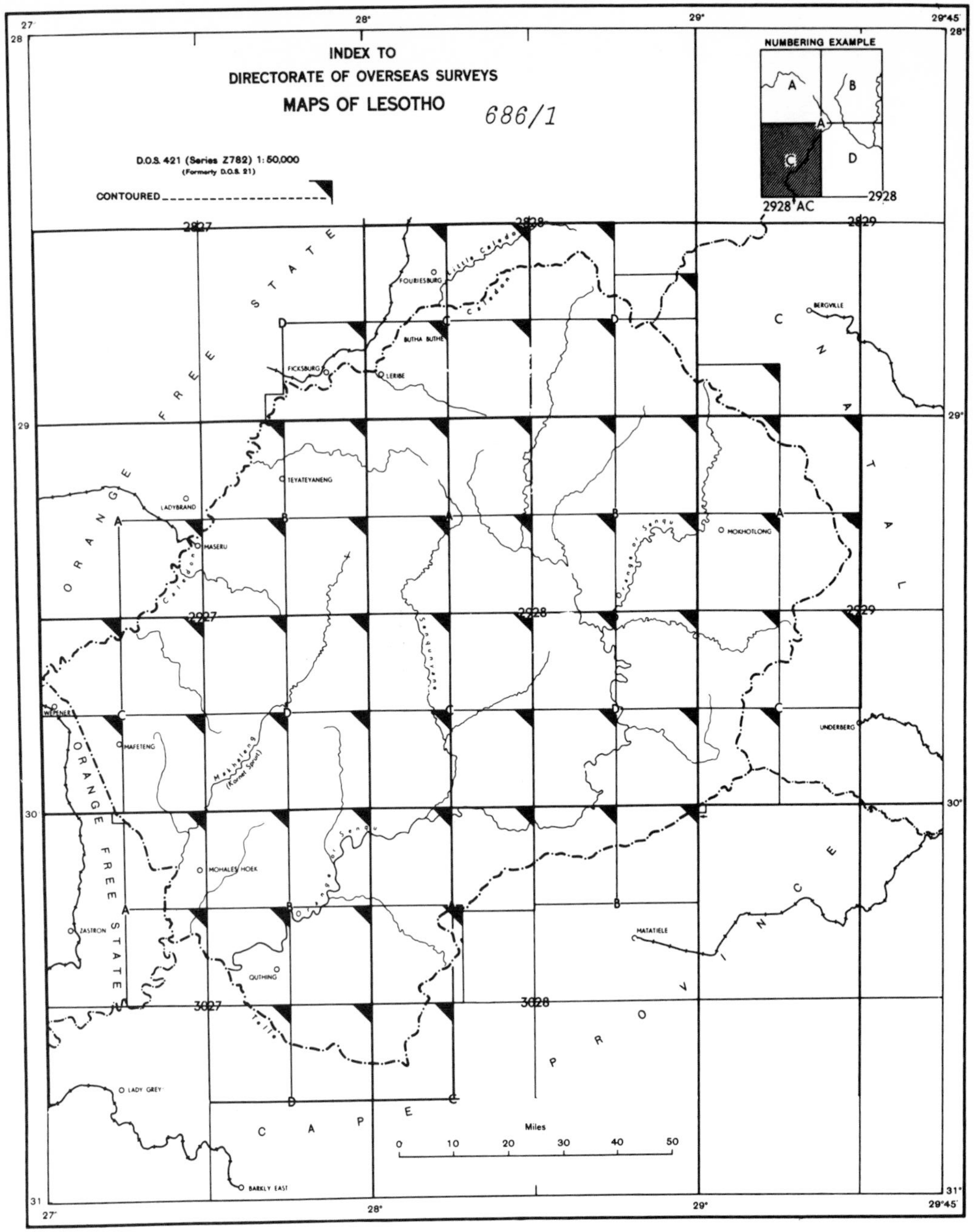

INDEX TO
DIRECTORATE OF OVERSEAS SURVEYS
MAPS OF LESOTHO
686/1
D.O.S. 421 (Series Z782) 1:50,000
(Formerly D.O.S. 21)
CONTOURED
NUMBERING EXAMPLE
2928 AC
2928
FOURIESBURG
BUTHA BUTHE
FICKSBURG
LERIBE
TEYATEYANENG
LADYBRAND
MASERU
MOKHOTLONG
BERGVILLE
UNDERBERG
WEPENER
MAFETENG
MOHALES HOEK
ZASTRON
QUTHING
MATATIELE
LADY GREY
BARKLY EAST
ORANGE FREE STATE
NATAL
CAPE PROVINCE
Miles
0 10 20 30 40 50
2827
2828
2829
2927
2929
3027
3028
27°
28°
29°
29°45'
30
31

689.1/1 RHODESIA

TOPOGRAPHICAL SERIES

1:250,000 Survey Dept.

Topographical or Topo-cadastral editions

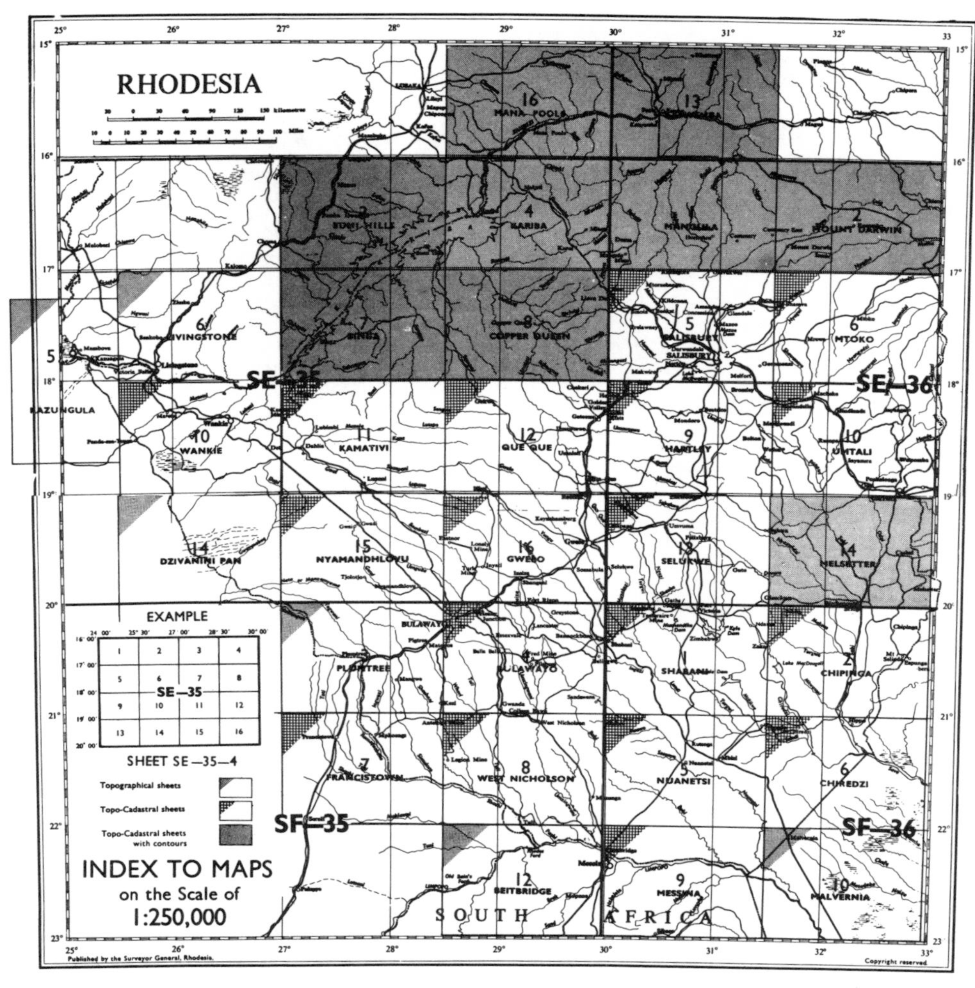

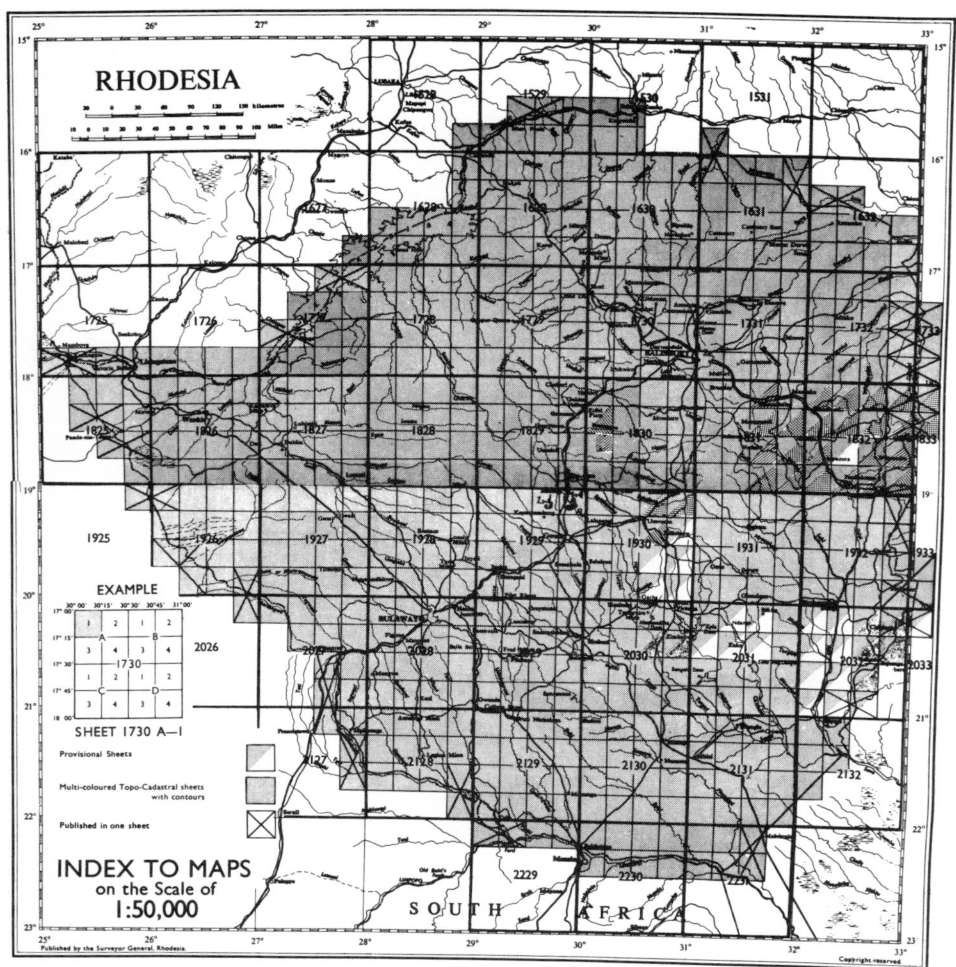

689.1/2 *RHODESIA*
CADASTRAL SERIES
1:50,000 Survey Dept.
Topo-cadastral editions

NB Topographical Series 1:100,000
Sheets available: 1730 A,B, 1831 D, 1829 B,D
1830 A,B,C, 1831 A,D, 1832 A, 1929 B,D.
1930 C, 1931 B, 1932 A,C, 2029 A,B.
2030 B, 2032 A,B,C.

689.4/1

ZAMBIA
1:250,000 Surveys Dept.
Topographical series

1st. edition sheets published
2nd. edition sheets published

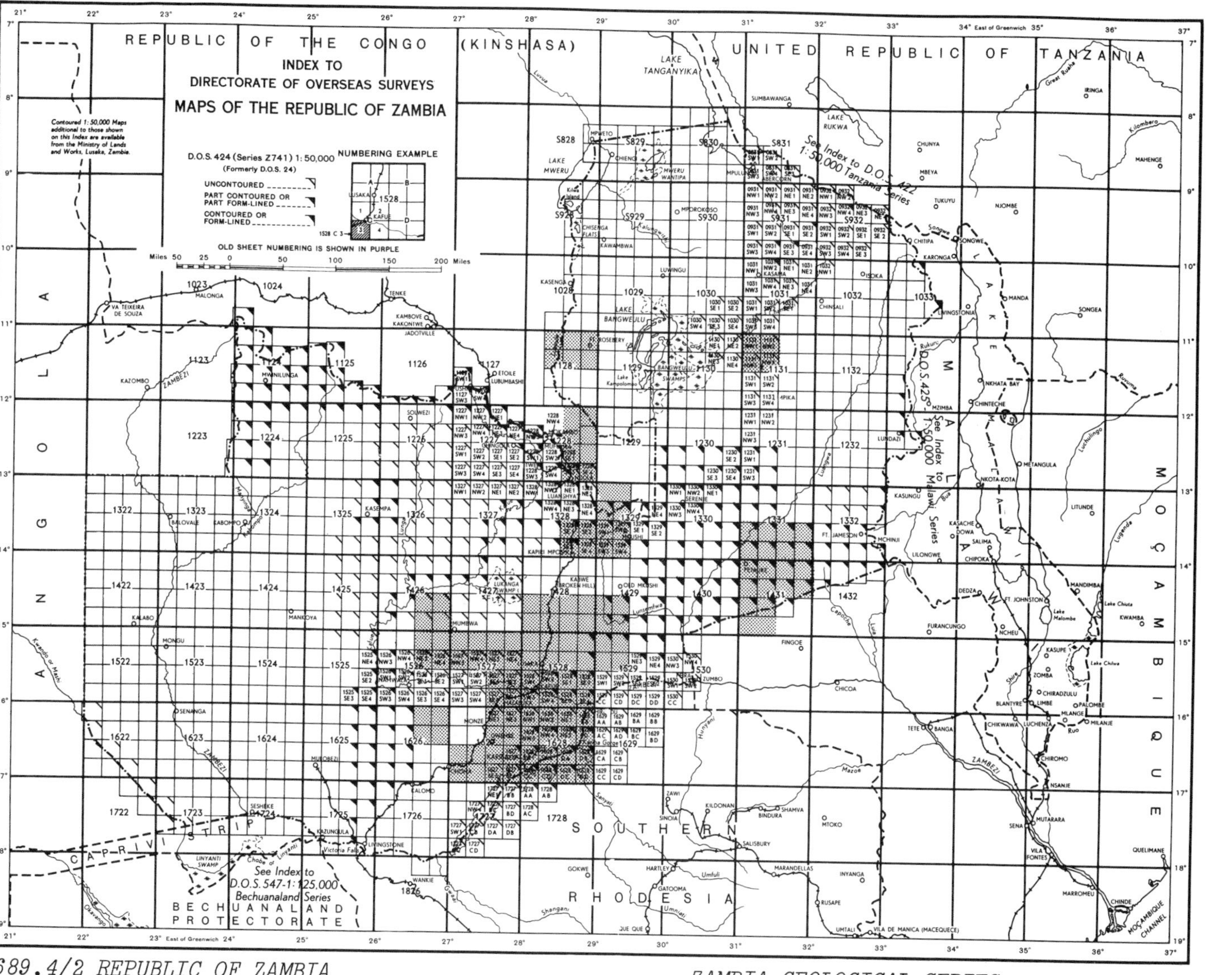

689.4/2 REPUBLIC OF ZAMBIA

1:50,000 Surveyor General-DOS.

Dos 424 (Z741)

Topographical Series

ZAMBIA GEOLOGICAL SERIES

1:100,000 Geological Survey

Sheets published.

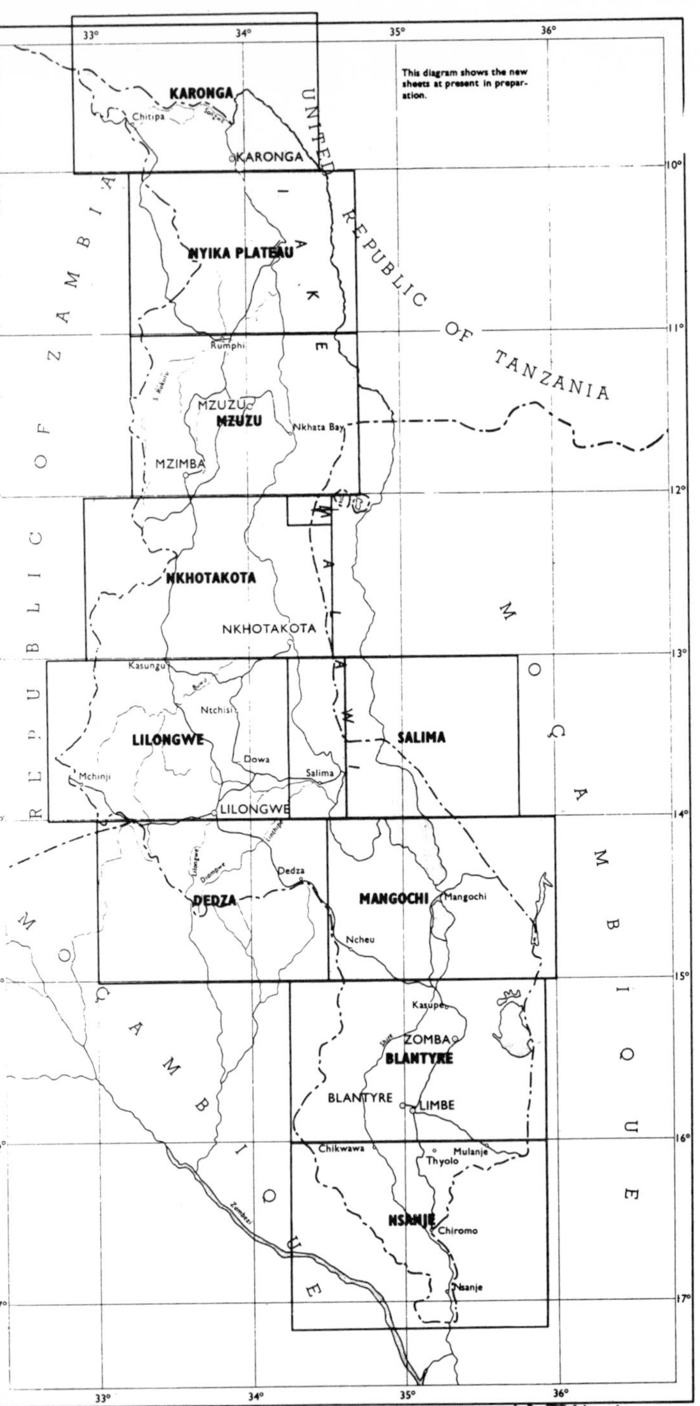

689.7/1 MALAWI NATIONAL SERIES

1:250,000 Survey Dept.

New topographical series in preparation.

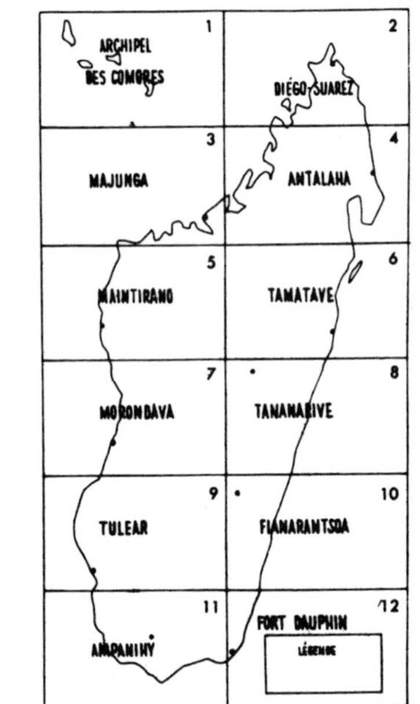

691/1 RÉPUBLIC MALGACHE

1:500,000 IGN

Physical road map series in 12 sheets

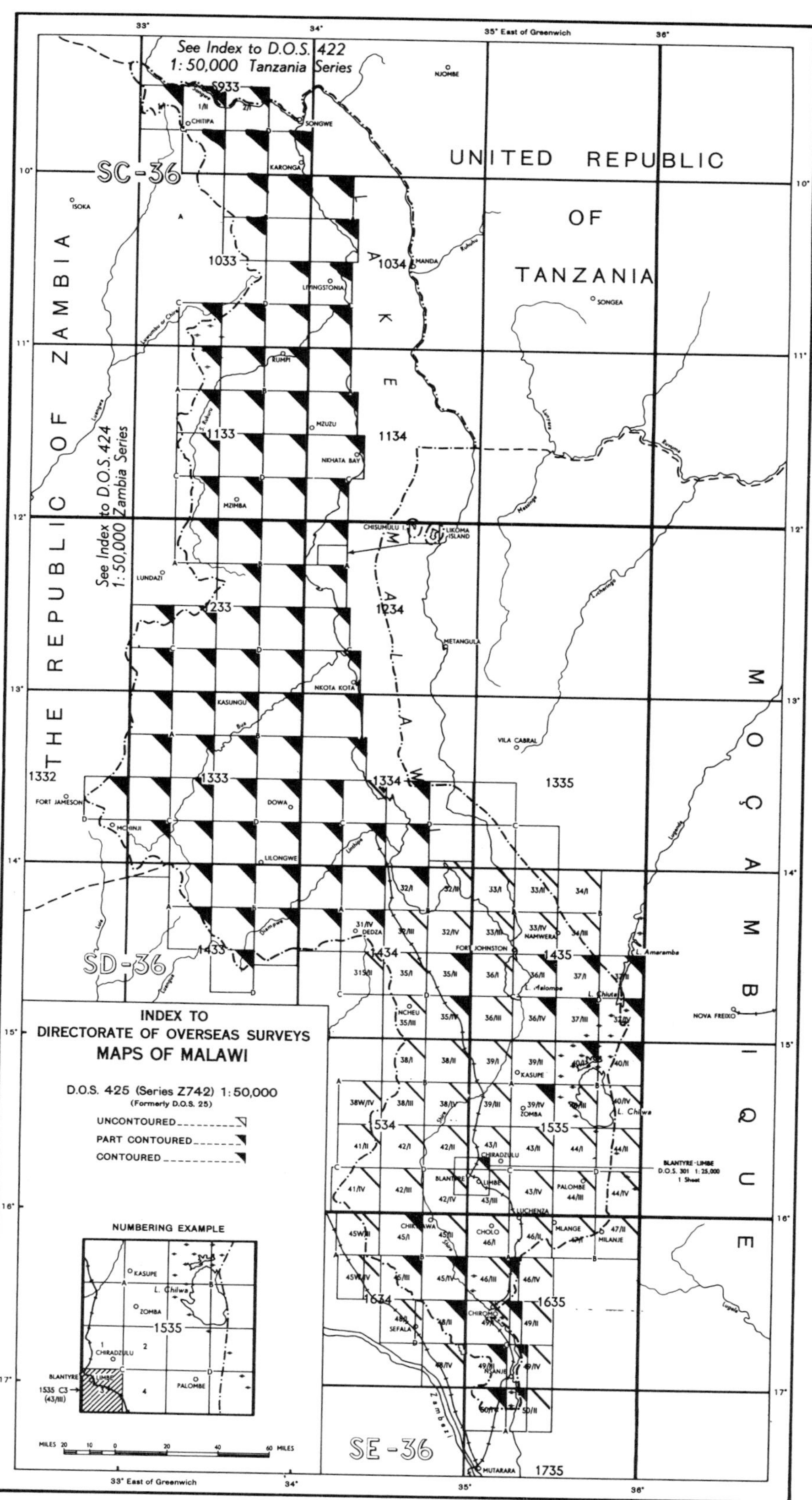
INDEX TO
DIRECTORATE OF OVERSEAS SURVEYS
MAPS OF MALAWI
D.O.S. 425 (Series Z742) 1:50,000
(Formerly D.O.S. 25)
UNCONTOURED
PART CONTOURED
CONTOURED
NUMBERING EXAMPLE
See Index to D.O.S. 422
1:50,000 Tanzania Series
See Index to D.O.S. 424
1:50,000 Zambia Series
UNITED REPUBLIC OF TANZANIA
THE REPUBLIC OF ZAMBIA
MOÇAMBIQUE
LAKE MALAWI
SC-36
SD-36
SE-36
BLANTYRE-LIMBE
D.O.S. 301 1:25,000
1 Sheet
33° East of Greenwich
35° East of Greenwich

689.7/2

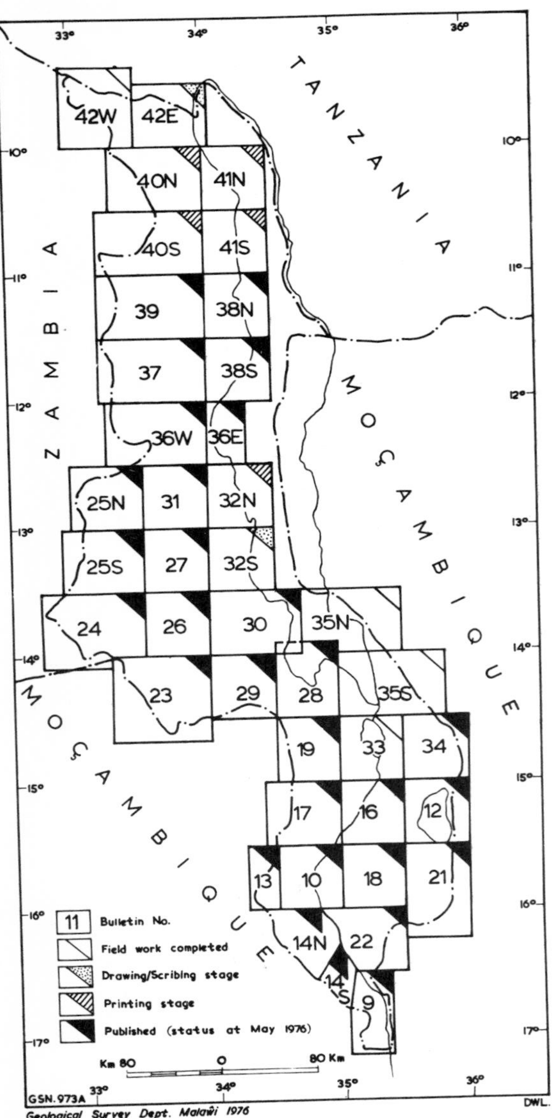

689.7/4 *MALAWI, GEOLOGIC MAPPING*
1:100,000 Geol. Survey
Coloured geological maps with an accompanying Bulletin

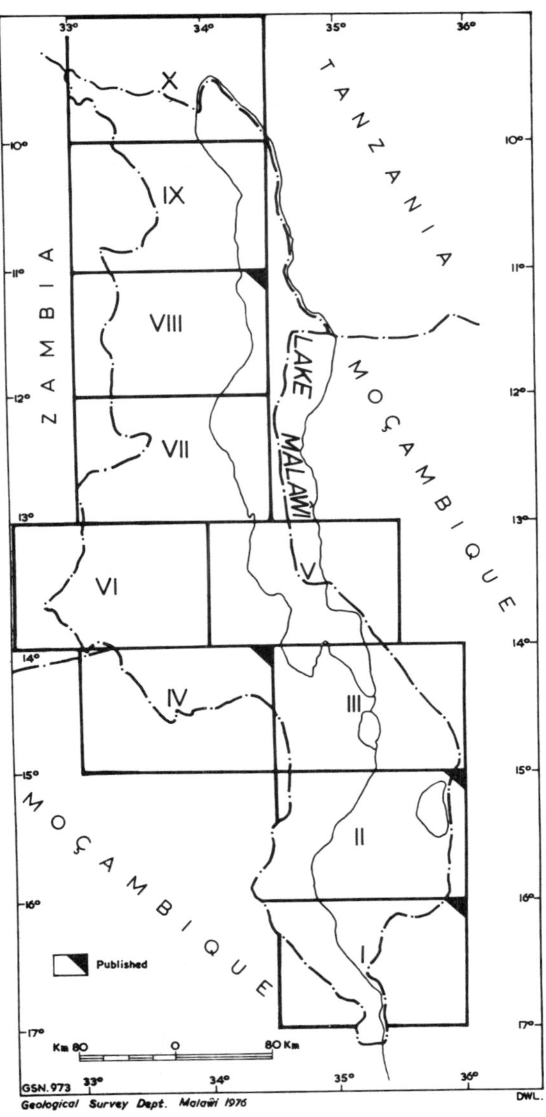

689.7/3 *GEOLOGICAL MAPS OF MALAWI*
1:250,000 Geol. Survey
Coloured geological series in progress

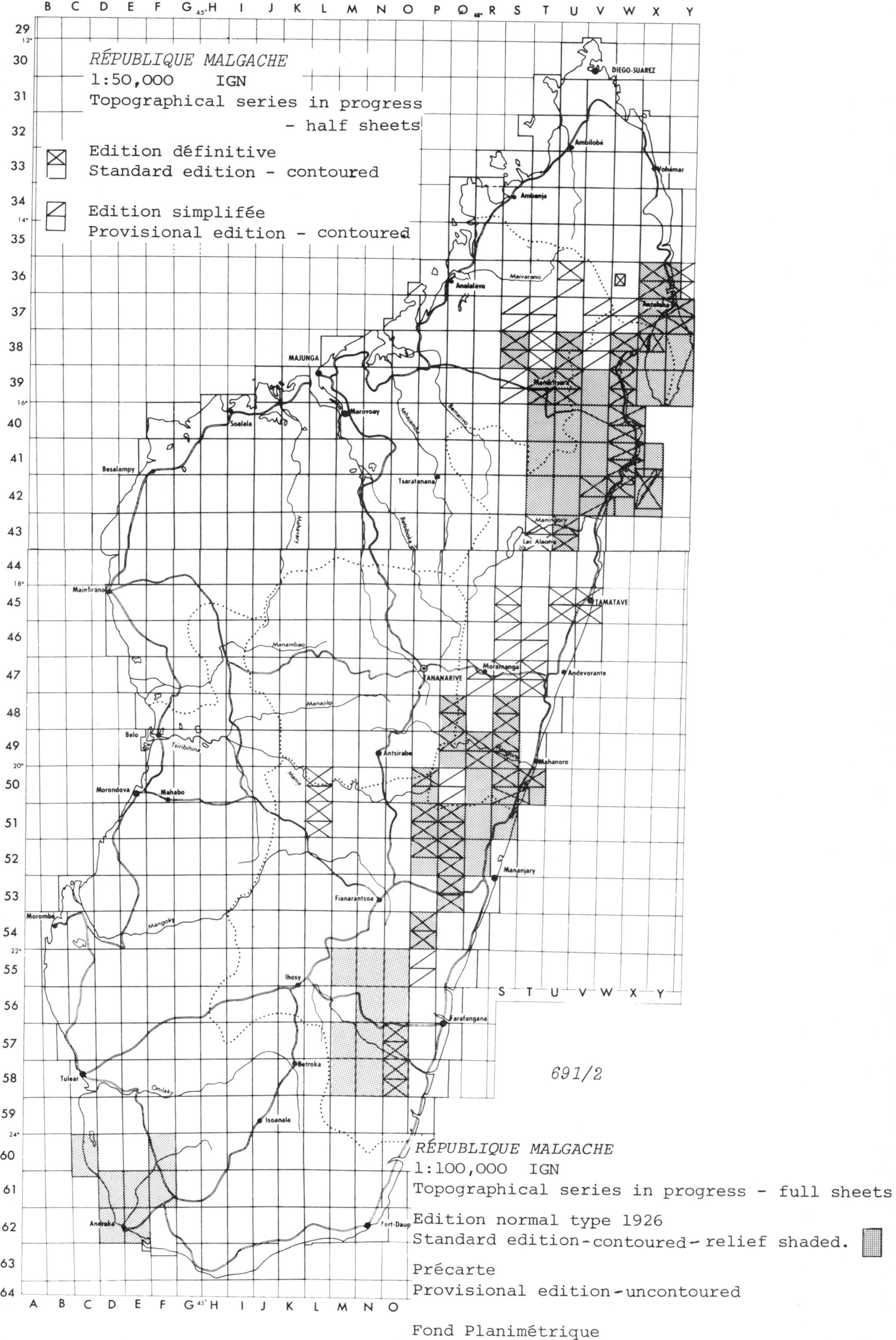

RÉPUBLIQUE MALGACHE
1:50,000 IGN
Topographical series in progress - half sheets
Edition définitive
Standard edition - contoured
Edition simplifée
Provisional edition - contoured
DIEGO-SUAREZ
Ambilobé
Vohémar
Ambanja
Analalava
MAJUNGA
Soalala
Marovoay
Besalampy
Tsaratanana
Maintirano
TAMATAVE
TANANARIVE
Moramanga
Andevorante
Belo
Antsirabe
Mahanoro
Morondova
Mahabo
Mananjary
Fianarantsoa
Morombé
Ihosy
Farafangana
Betroka
Tulear
Isoanala
Androka
Fort-Daup
691/2
RÉPUBLIQUE MALGACHE
1:100,000 IGN
Topographical series in progress - full sheets
Edition normal type 1926
Standard edition-contoured-relief shaded.
Précarte
Provisional edition-uncontoured
Fond Planimétrique
Planimetric base map series - uncontoured

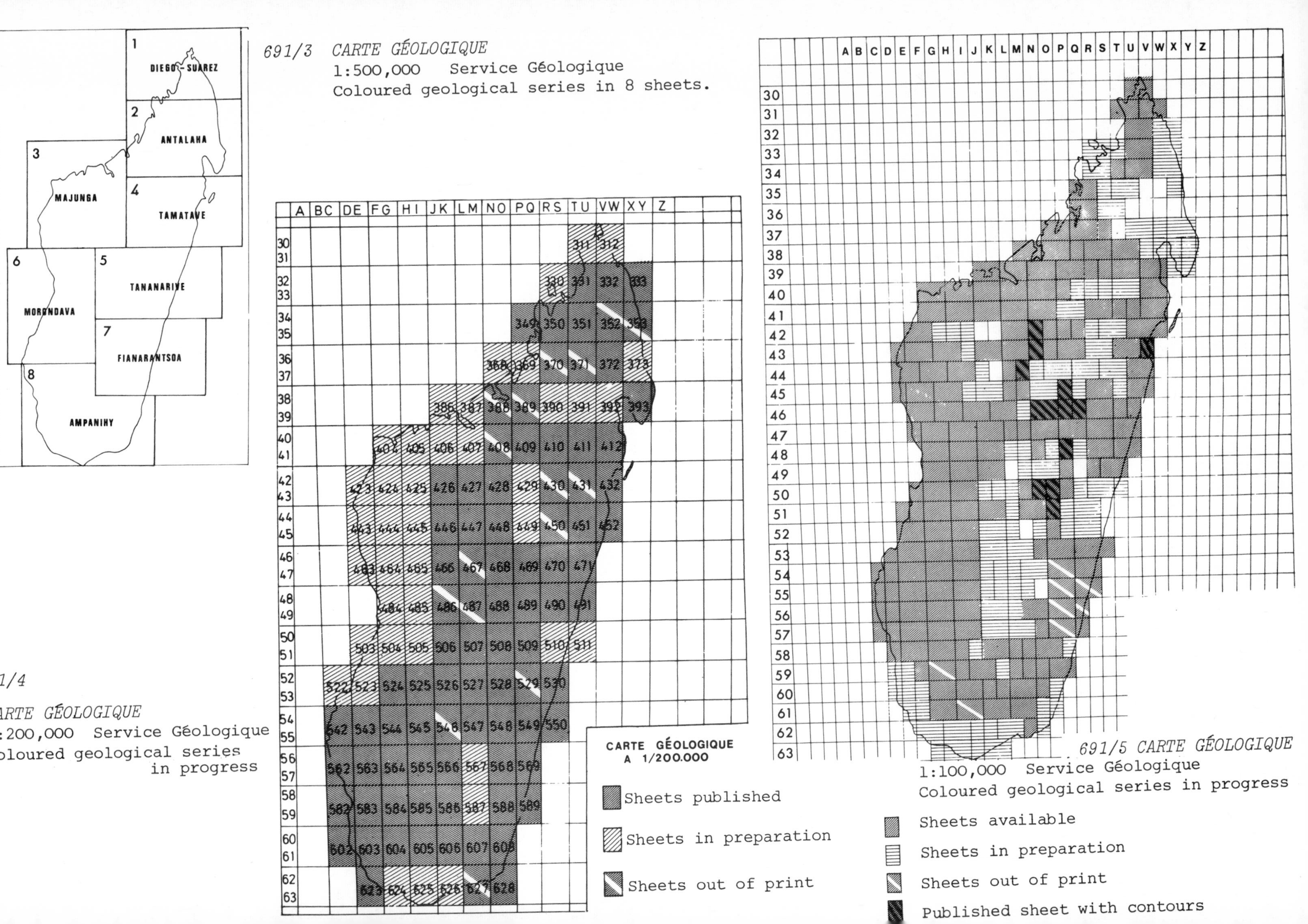

691/3 *CARTE GÉOLOGIQUE*
1:500,000 Service Géologique
Coloured geological series in 8 sheets.

691/4

CARTE GÉOLOGIQUE
1:200,000 Service Géologique
Coloured geological series in progress

691/5 *CARTE GÉOLOGIQUE*
1:100,000 Service Géologique
Coloured geological series in progress

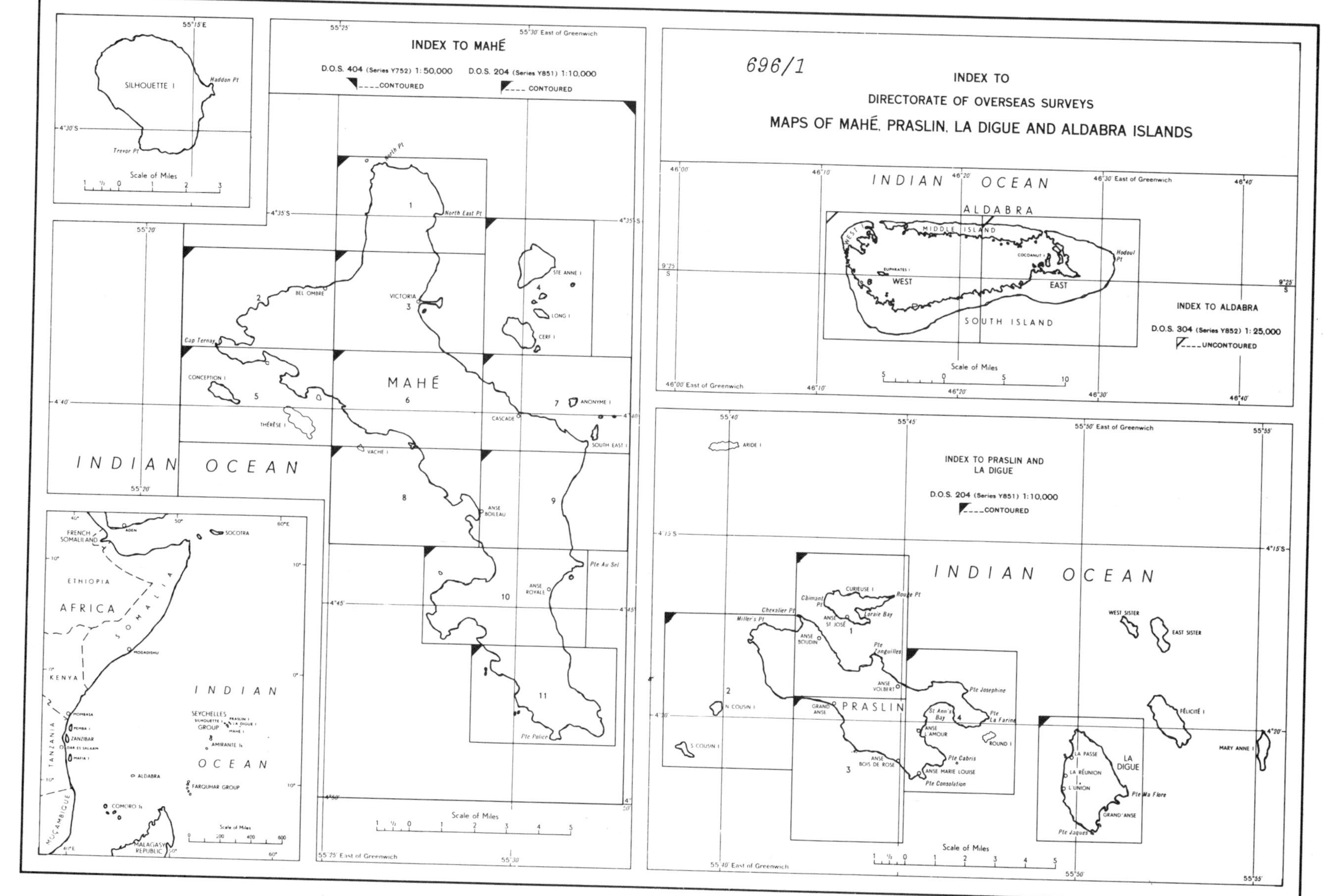
696/1
INDEX TO
DIRECTORATE OF OVERSEAS SURVEYS
MAPS OF MAHÉ, PRASLIN, LA DIGUE AND ALDABRA ISLANDS
INDEX TO MAHÉ
D.O.S. 404 (Series Y752) 1:50,000
CONTOURED
D.O.S. 204 (Series Y851) 1:10,000
CONTOURED
MAHÉ
VICTORIA
North Pt
North East Pt
BEL OMBRE
Cap Ternay
CONCEPTION I
THÉRÈSE I
VACHE I
CASCADE
ANSE BOILEAU
ANSE ROYALE
Pte Au Sel
Pte Police
STE ANNE I
LONG I
CERF I
ANONYME I
SOUTH EAST I
INDIAN OCEAN
Scale of Miles
55°25' East of Greenwich
55°30' East of Greenwich
SILHOUETTE I
Haddon Pt
Trevor Pt
55°15'E
4°30'S
INDEX TO ALDABRA
D.O.S. 304 (Series Y852) 1:25,000
UNCONTOURED
ALDABRA
WEST I
MIDDLE ISLAND
COCOANUT I
EUPHRATES I
WEST
EAST
SOUTH ISLAND
Hodoul Pt
46°00' East of Greenwich
46°30' East of Greenwich
INDEX TO PRASLIN AND LA DIGUE
D.O.S. 204 (Series Y851) 1:10,000
CONTOURED
PRASLIN
LA DIGUE
ARIDE I
CURIEUSE I
Rouge Pt
Câimant Pt
Laraie Bay
ANSE ST JOSÉ
ANSE BOUDIN
Chevalier Pt
Miller's Pt
Pte Zanguilles
ANSE VOLBERT
Pte Josephine
GRAND ANSE
St Ann's Bay
ANSE L'AMOUR
Pte La Farine
ROUND I
Pte Cabris
ANSE MARIE LOUISE
Pte Consolation
ANSE BOIS DE ROSE
N COUSIN I
S COUSIN I
WEST SISTER
EAST SISTER
FÉLICITÉ I
MARY ANNE I
LA PASSE
LA RÉUNION
L'UNION
Pte Ma Flore
GRAND'ANSE
Pte Jaques
55°40' East of Greenwich
55°50' East of Greenwich
FRENCH SOMALILAND
ADEN
SOCOTRA
ETHIOPIA
AFRICA
SOMALIA
MOGADISHU
KENYA
MOMBASA
PEMBA I
ZANZIBAR
DAR ES SALAAM
MAFIA I
TANZANIA
MOÇAMBIQUE
ALDABRA
COMORO Is
MALAGASY REPUBLIC
SEYCHELLES
SILHOUETTE I
PRASLIN I
LA DIGUE I
MAHÉ I
GROUP
AMIRANTE Is
FARQUHAR GROUP
INDIAN OCEAN

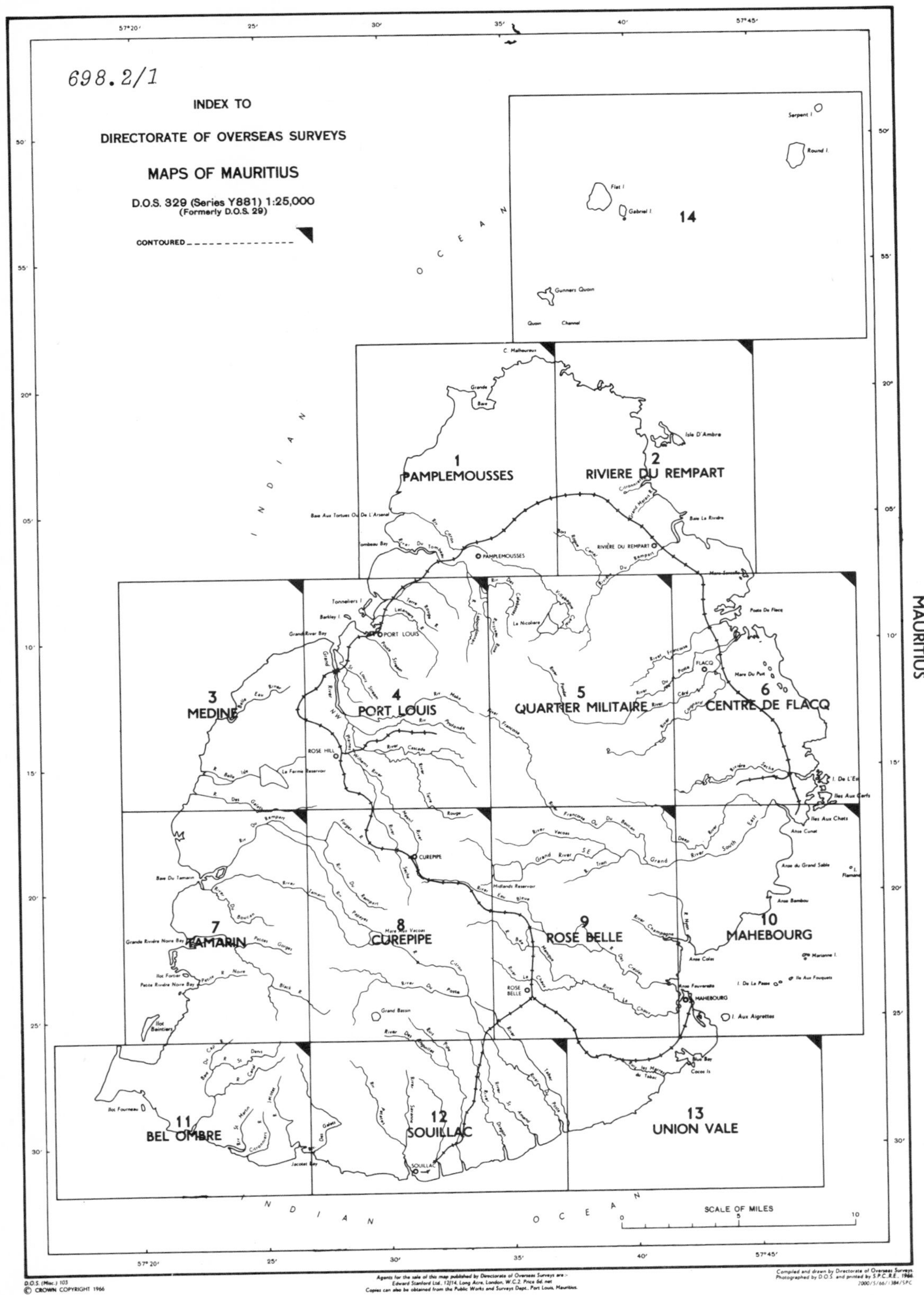

D.O.S. (Misc.) 105

Agents for the sale of this map published by Directorate of Overseas Surveys are:-
Edward Stanford Ltd., 12/14, Long Acre, London, W.C.2. Price 6d. net
Copies can also be obtained from the Public Works and Surveys Dept., Port Louis, Mauritius.

Compiled and drawn by Directorate of Overseas Surveys.
Photographed by D.O.S. and printed by S.P.C.R.E. 1966
2000/5/66/1384/SPC

North and Central America

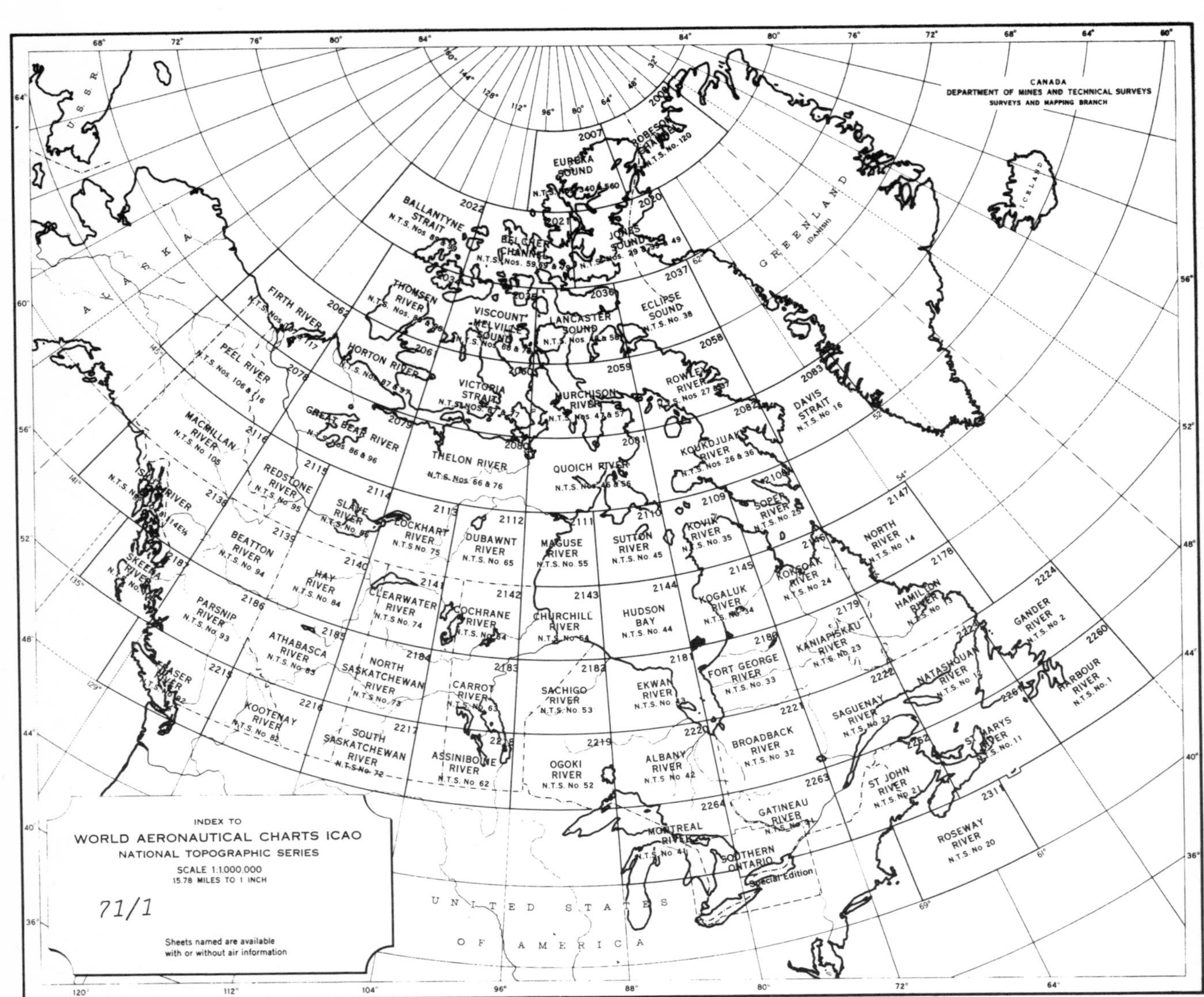

CANADA
DEPARTMENT OF MINES AND TECHNICAL SURVEYS
SURVEYS AND MAPPING BRANCH
INDEX TO
WORLD AERONAUTICAL CHARTS ICAO
NATIONAL TOPOGRAPHIC SERIES
SCALE 1:1,000,000
15.78 MILES TO 1 INCH
71/1
Sheets named are available
with or without air information
GREENLAND
ICELAND
ALASKA
U.S.S.R.
UNITED STATES OF AMERICA
EUREKA SOUND
BALLANTYNE STRAIT
BELCHER CHANNEL
JONES SOUND
THOMSEN RIVER
VISCOUNT MELVILLE SOUND
LANCASTER SOUND
ECLIPSE SOUND
FIRTH RIVER
HORTON RIVER
VICTORIA STRAIT
MURCHISON RIVER
ROWLEY RIVER
DAVIS STRAIT
N.T.S. No. 16
PEEL RIVER
GREAT BEAR RIVER
THELON RIVER
N.T.S. Nos. 66 & 76
QUOICH RIVER
KOUKDJUAK RIVER
MACMILLAN RIVER
N.T.S. No. 105
REDSTONE RIVER
SLAVE RIVER
LOCKHART RIVER
N.T.S. No. 75
DUBAWNT RIVER
N.T.S. No. 65
MAGUSE RIVER
N.T.S. No. 55
SUTTON RIVER
N.T.S. No. 45
KOVIK RIVER
N.T.S. No. 35
SOPER RIVER
NORTH RIVER
N.T.S. No. 14
BEATTON RIVER
N.T.S. No. 94
HAY RIVER
N.T.S. No. 84
CLEARWATER RIVER
N.T.S. No. 74
COCHRANE RIVER
CHURCHILL RIVER
HUDSON BAY
N.T.S. No. 44
KOGALUK RIVER
KOKSOAK RIVER
N.T.S. No. 24
HAMILTON RIVER
GANDER RIVER
N.T.S. No. 2
SKEENA RIVER
PARSNIP RIVER
N.T.S. No. 93
ATHABASCA RIVER
NORTH SASKATCHEWAN RIVER
CARROT RIVER
SACHIGO RIVER
N.T.S. No. 53
EKWAN RIVER
FORT GEORGE RIVER
N.T.S. No. 33
KANIAPISKAU RIVER
NATASHQUAN RIVER
HARBOUR RIVER
N.T.S. No. 1
FRASER RIVER
KOOTENAY RIVER
N.T.S. No. 82
SOUTH SASKATCHEWAN RIVER
N.T.S. No. 72
ASSINIBOINE RIVER
N.T.S. No. 62
OGOKI RIVER
N.T.S. No. 52
ALBANY RIVER
N.T.S. No. 42
BROADBACK RIVER
N.T.S. No. 32
SAGUENAY RIVER
ST MARYS RIVER
N.T.S. No. 11
ST JOHN RIVER
GATINEAU RIVER
MONTREAL RIVER
N.T.S. No. 41
SOUTHERN ONTARIO
Special Edition
ROSEWAY RIVER
N.T.S. No. 20

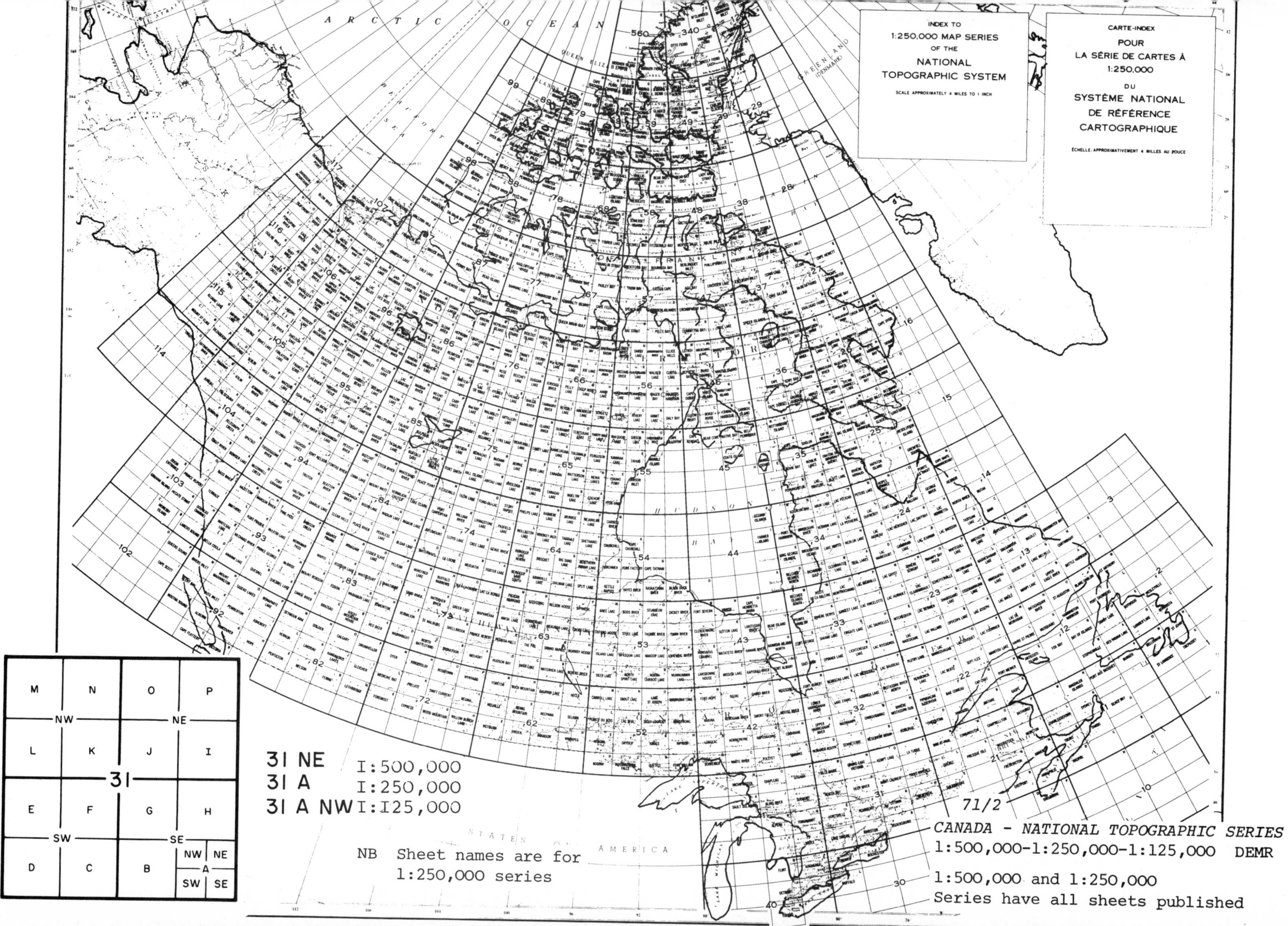
INDEX TO
1:250,000 MAP SERIES
OF THE
NATIONAL
TOPOGRAPHIC SYSTEM
SCALE APPROXIMATELY 4 MILES TO 1 INCH
CARTE-INDEX
POUR
LA SÉRIE DE CARTES À
1:250,000
DU
SYSTÈME NATIONAL
DE RÉFÉRENCE
CARTOGRAPHIQUE
ÉCHELLE: APPROXIMATIVEMENT 4 MILLES AU POUCE
ARCTIC OCEAN
GREENLAND (DENMARK)
BEAUFORT SEA
HUDSON BAY
STATES OF AMERICA
M N O P
NW NE
L K J I
31
E F G H
SW SE
D C B
NW NE A SW SE
31 NE I:500,000
31 A I:250,000
31 A NW I:125,000
NB Sheet names are for
1:250,000 series
71/2
CANADA - NATIONAL TOPOGRAPHIC SERIES
1:500,000-1:250,000-1:125,000 DEMR
1:500,000 and 1:250,000
Series have all sheets published

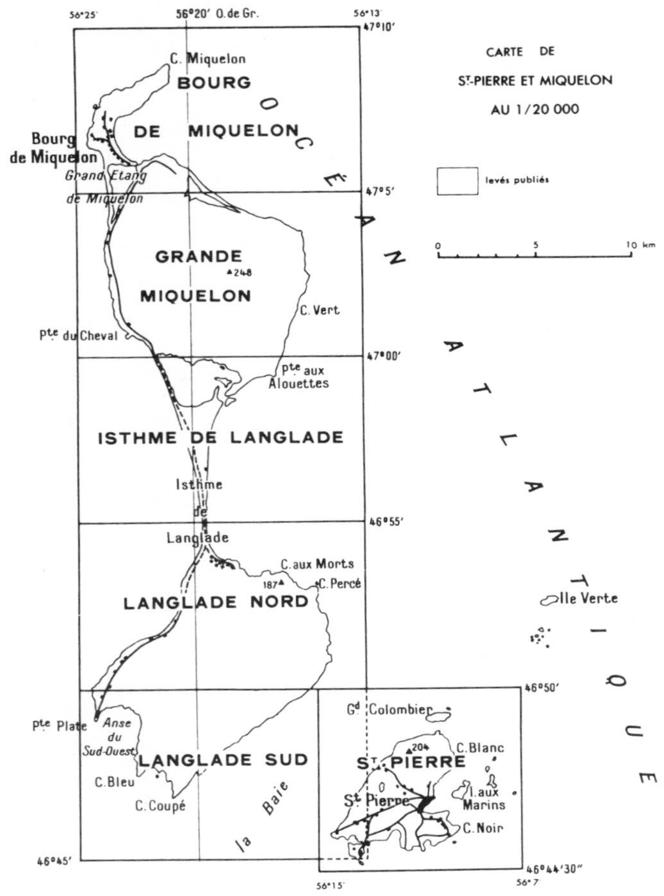

718/1 *ST.PIERRE ET MIQUELON*
1:20,000 IGN
Topographical series

72/1 *CARTA DE LA REPÚBLICA MEXICANA*
1:500,000 DGGM
Topographical series. 1944 Edition.

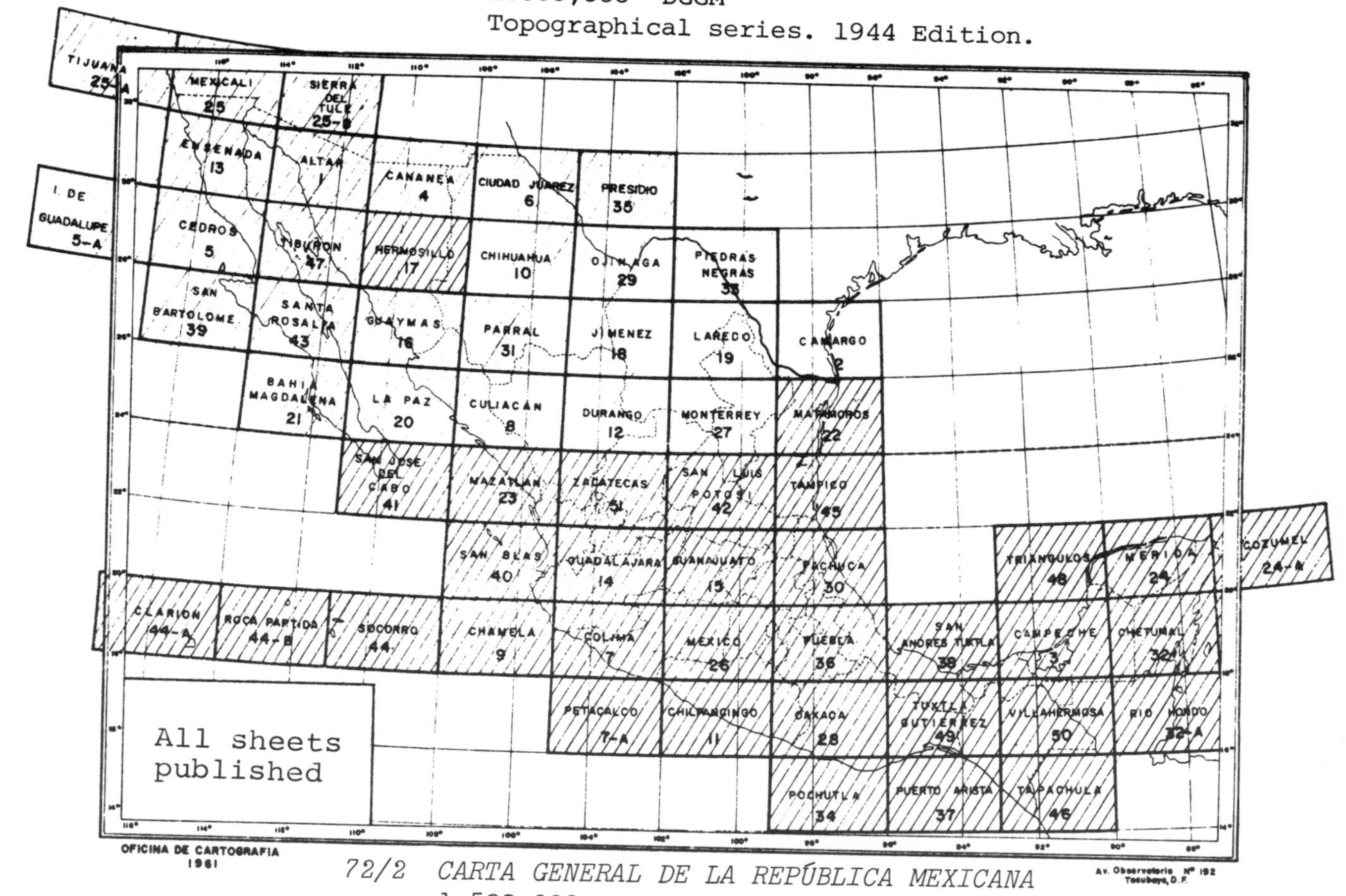

72/2 *CARTA GENERAL DE LA REPÚBLICA MEXICANA*
1:500,000 DGGM
Topographical series.

1 TIJUANA MEXICALI 11-S-VIII
2 ENSENADA 11-R-II
3 CABORCA 12-R-I SIERRA DEL TULE 12-S-VIII
4 NOGALES 12-R-II
5 CIUDAD JUAREZ 13-R-I BARRANCO DE GUADALUPE 13-R-II
6 CEDROS 11-R-IV I. DE GUADALUPE 11-R-III
7 ISLA TIBURON 12-R-III
8 HERMOSILLO 12-R-IV
9 CHIHUAHUA 13-R-III
10 OJINAGA 13-R-IV
11 PIEDRAS NEGRAS 14-R-III
12 PUNTA EUGENIA 11-R-VI
13 SANTA ROSALIA 12-R-V
14 CIUDAD OBREGON 12-R-VI
15 HIDALGO DEL PARRAL 13-R-V
16 JIMENEZ 13-R-VI
17 NUEVO LAREDO 14-R-V
18 BAHIA MAGDALENA 12-R-VII
19 LA PAZ 12-R-VIII
20 CULIACAN 13-R-VII
21 DURANGO 13-R-VIII
22 MONTERREY 14-R-VII
23 MATAMOROS 14-R-VIII REYNOSA 14-R-VI
24 SAN JOSE DEL CABO 12-Q-II
25 MAZATLAN 13-Q-I
26 ZACATECAS 13-Q-II
27 SAN LUIS POTOSI 14-Q-I
28 TAMPICO 14-Q-II
29 SAN BLAS 13-Q-III
30 GUADALAJARA 13-Q-IV
31 QUERETARO 14-Q-III
32 PACHUCA 14-Q-IV
33 TRIANGULOS 15-Q-IV
34 MERIDA 16-Q-III COZUMEL 16-Q-IV
35 COLIMA 13-Q-VI ZACATULA 13-Q-VIII IS. REVILLAGIGEDO
36 MEXICO 14-Q-V
37 VERACRUZ 14-Q-VI
38 COATZACOALCOS 15-Q-V
39 CAMPECHE 15-Q-VI
40 CHETUMAL 16-Q-V RIO AZUL 16-Q-VII
41 ACAPULCO 14-Q-VII
42 OAXACA 14-Q-VIII
43 TUXTLA GUTIERREZ 15-Q-VII
44 VILLAHERMOSA 15-Q-VIII
45 SAN PEDRO POCHUTLA 14-P-II
46 PIJIJIAPAN 15-P-I
47 TAPACHULA 15-P-II

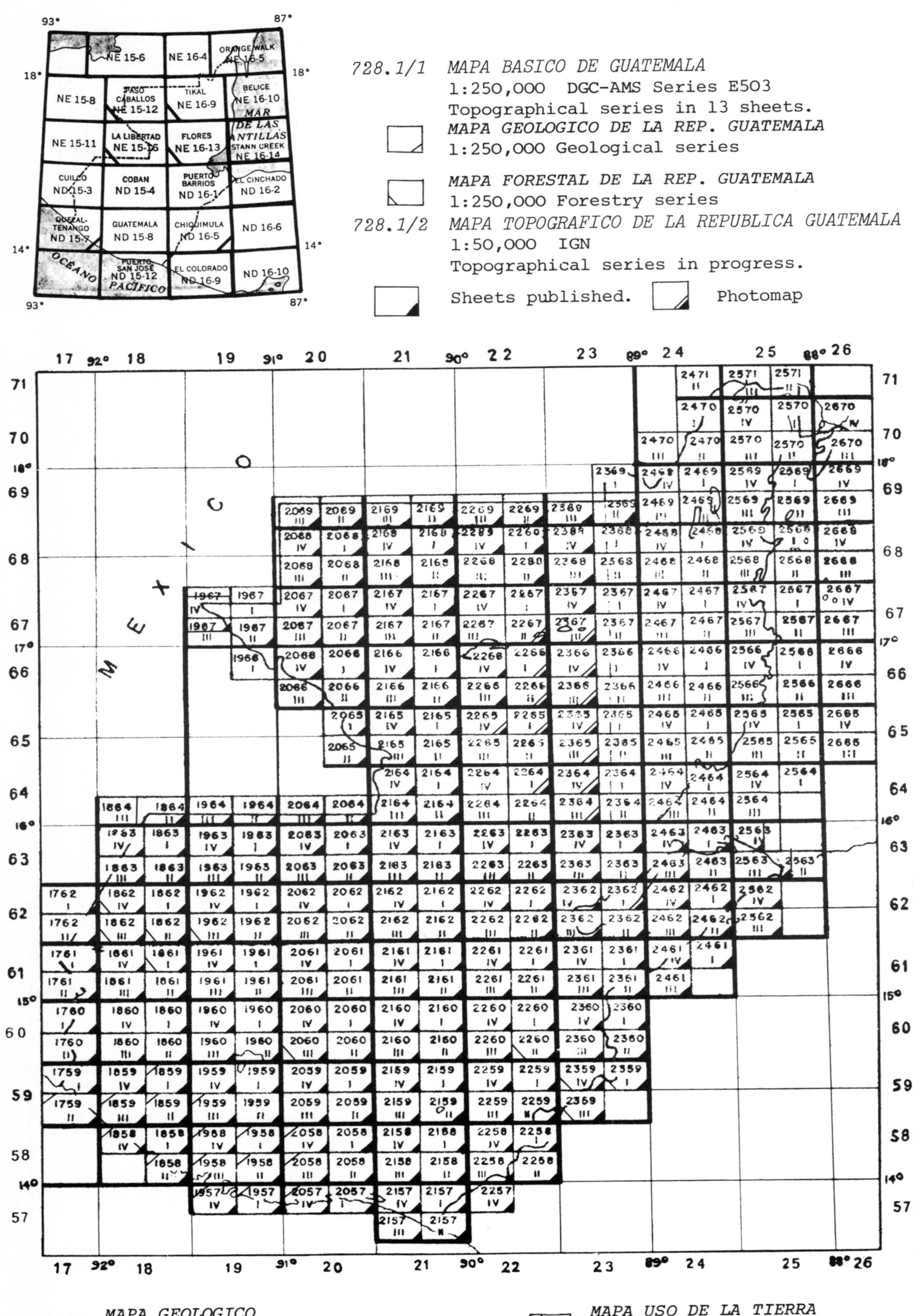

728.1/1 MAPA BASICO DE GUATEMALA
1:250,000 DGC-AMS Series E503
Topographical series in 13 sheets.
MAPA GEOLOGICO DE LA REP. GUATEMALA
1:250,000 Geological series
MAPA FORESTAL DE LA REP. GUATEMALA
1:250,000 Forestry series
728.1/2 MAPA TOPOGRAFICO DE LA REPUBLICA GUATEMALA
1:50,000 IGN
Topographical series in progress.
Sheets published.
Photomap
NE 15-6
NE 16-4
ORANGE WALK NE 16-5
NE 15-8
PASO CABALLOS NE 15-12
TIKAL NE 16-9
BELICE NE 16-10
NE 15-11
LA LIBERTAD NE 15-16
FLORES NE 16-13
STANN CREEK NE 16-14
MAR DE LAS ANTILLAS
CUILCO ND 15-3
COBAN ND 15-4
PUERTO BARRIOS ND 16-1
EL CINCHADO ND 16-2
QUEZALTENANGO ND 15-7
GUATEMALA ND 15-8
CHIQUIMULA ND 16-5
ND 16-6
PUERTO SAN JOSE ND 15-12
EL COLORADO ND 16-9
ND 16-10
OCEANO PACIFICO
MEXICO
MAPA GEOLOGICO DE LA REP. GUATEMALA
Geological Series 1:50,000 IGN
MAPA USO DE LA TIERRA DE LA REP. GUATEMALA
Land Use Series 1:50,000 IGN

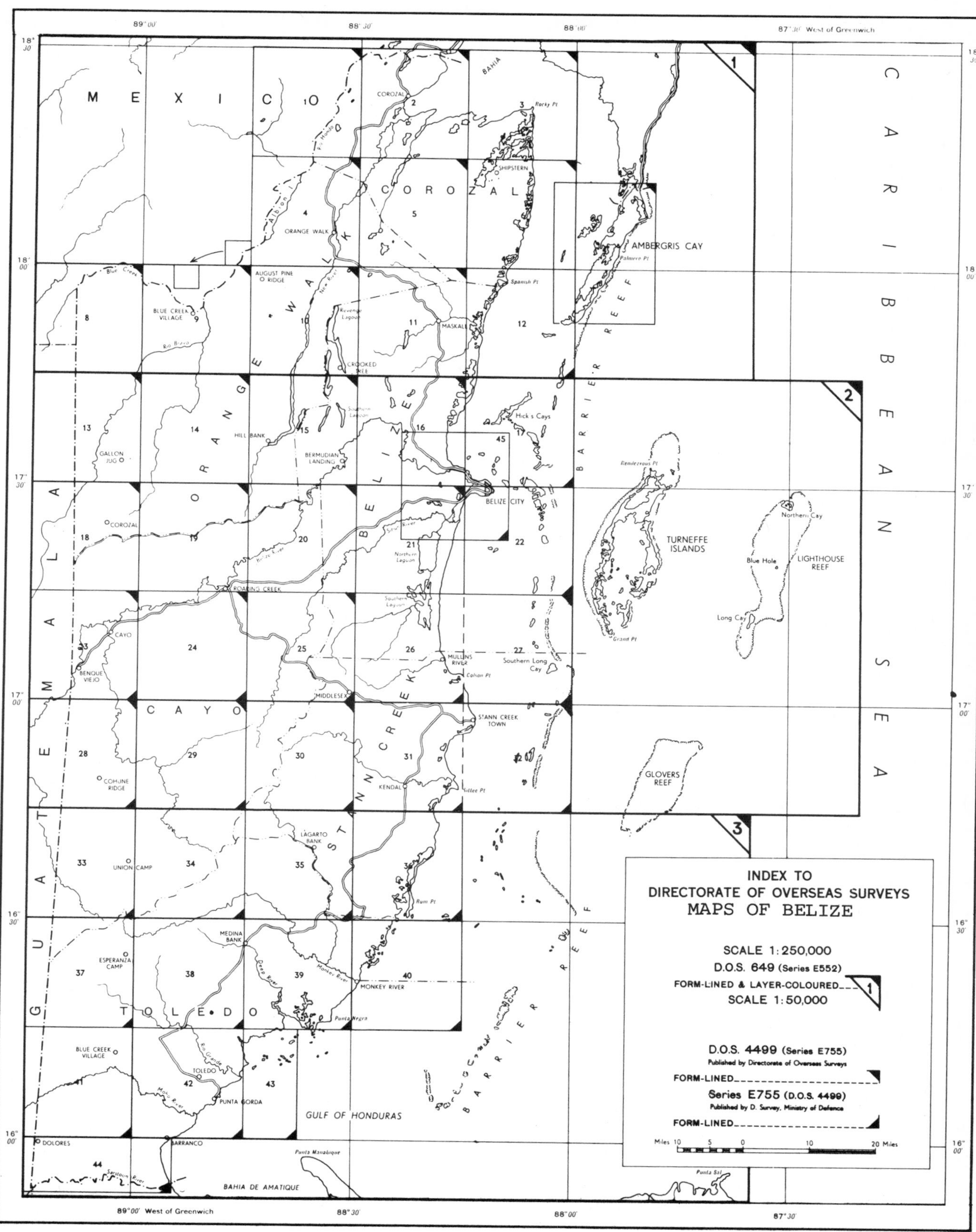
INDEX TO
DIRECTORATE OF OVERSEAS SURVEYS
MAPS OF BELIZE
SCALE 1:250,000
D.O.S. 649 (Series E552)
FORM-LINED & LAYER-COLOURED
SCALE 1:50,000
D.O.S. 4499 (Series E755)
Published by Directorate of Overseas Surveys
FORM-LINED
Series E755 (D.O.S. 4499)
Published by D. Survey, Ministry of Defence
FORM-LINED
Miles 10 5 0 10 20 Miles
89°00′ West of Greenwich
88°30′
88°00′
87°30′
87°30′ West of Greenwich
18° 30′
18° 00′
17° 30′
17° 00′
16° 30′
16° 00′
MEXICO
CARIBBEAN SEA
GUATEMALA
COROZAL
ORANGE WALK
BELIZE
CAYO
STANN CREEK
TOLEDO
BARRIER REEF
AMBERGRIS CAY
TURNEFFE ISLANDS
LIGHTHOUSE REEF
GLOVERS REEF
GULF OF HONDURAS
BAHIA DE AMATIQUE
BELIZE CITY
STANN CREEK TOWN
PUNTA GORDA
ORANGE WALK
COROZAL
SHIPSTERN
AUGUST PINE RIDGE
BLUE CREEK VILLAGE
MASKALL
CROOKED TREE
HILL BANK
BERMUDIAN LANDING
GALLON JUG
ROARING CREEK
CAYO
BENQUE VIEJO
MIDDLESEX
MULLINS RIVER
Southern Long Cay
Hick's Cays
Northern Cay
Blue Hole
Long Cay
COHUNE RIDGE
KENDAL
LAGARTO BANK
UNION CAMP
ESPERANZA CAMP
MEDINA BANK
MONKEY RIVER
TOLEDO
DOLORES
BARRANCO
Punta Manabique
Punta Sal
1
2
3

728.2/1

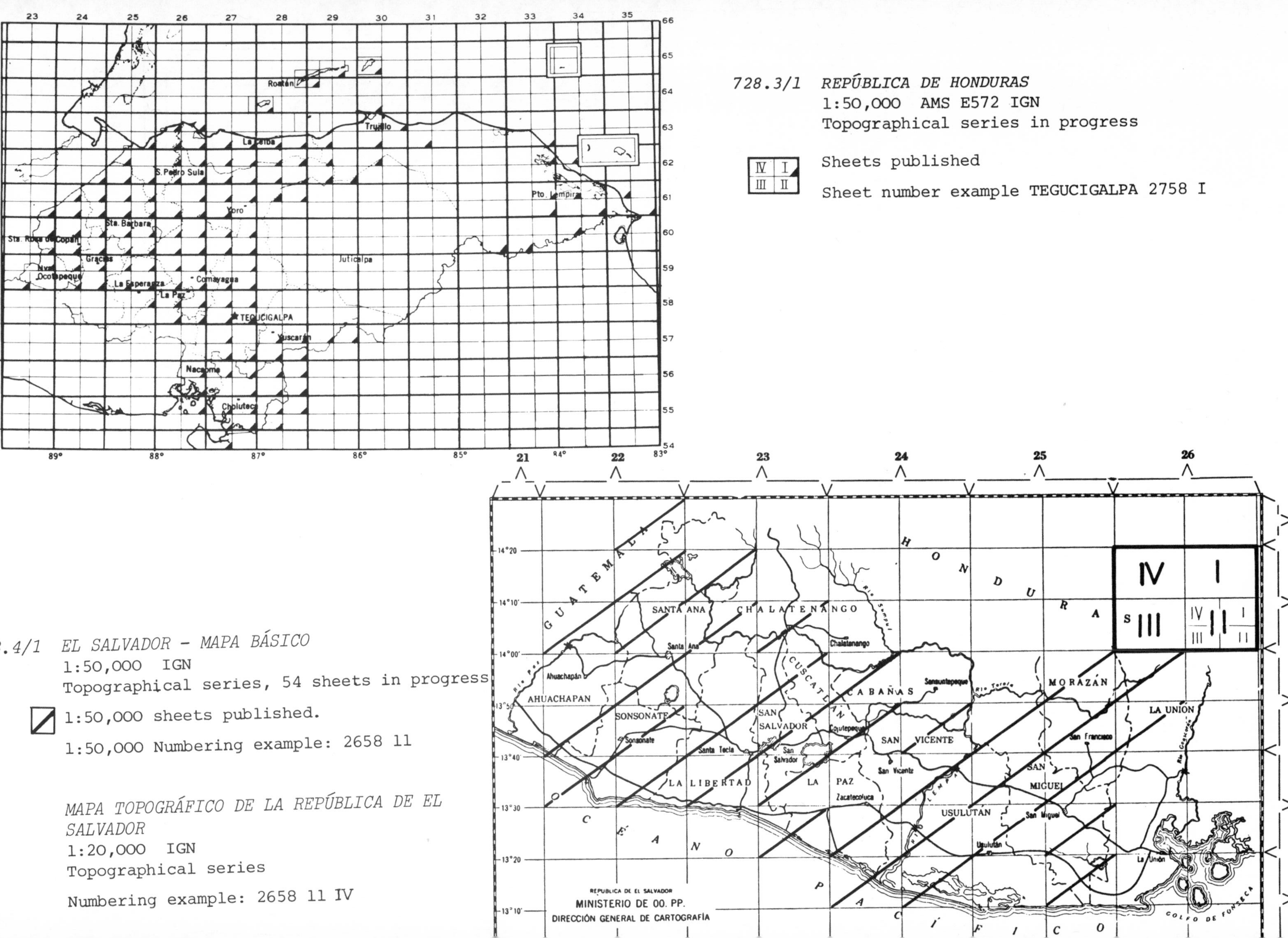

728.3/1 *REPÚBLICA DE HONDURAS*
1:50,000 AMS E572 IGN
Topographical series in progress

Sheets published

Sheet number example TEGUCIGALPA 2758 I

728.4/1 *EL SALVADOR - MAPA BÁSICO*
1:50,000 IGN
Topographical series, 54 sheets in progress

1:50,000 sheets published.

1:50,000 Numbering example: 2658 11

MAPA TOPOGRÁFICO DE LA REPÚBLICA DE EL SALVADOR
1:20,000 IGN
Topographical series

Numbering example: 2658 11 IV

728.5/1 NICARAGUA

1:250,000 Div. General de Cartografia
Topographical-Planimetric maps. Series E503

◪ Série Topográfica Zona Del Pacífico
◪ Série Planimétrica " " Atlántico

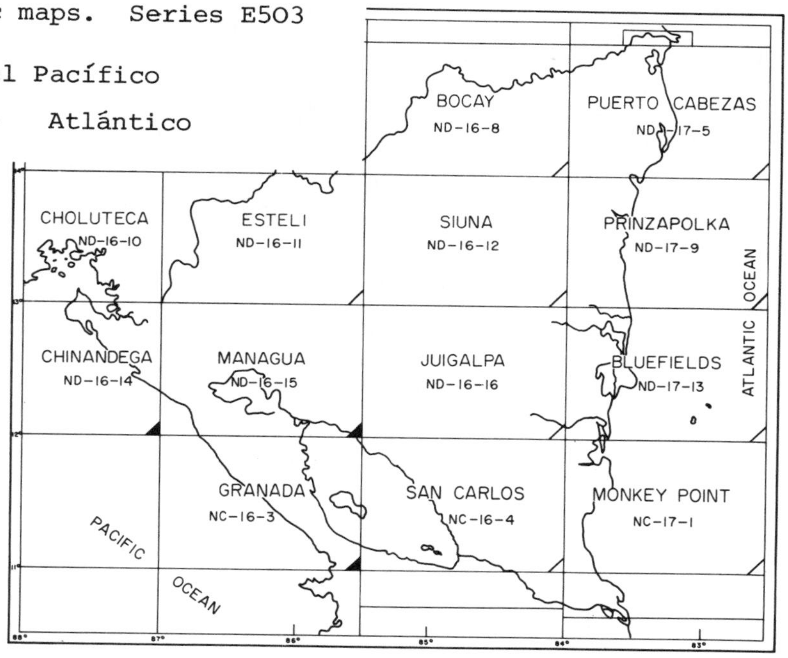

728.6/1 MAPA DE COSTA RICA
1:200,000 IGN
Topographical series

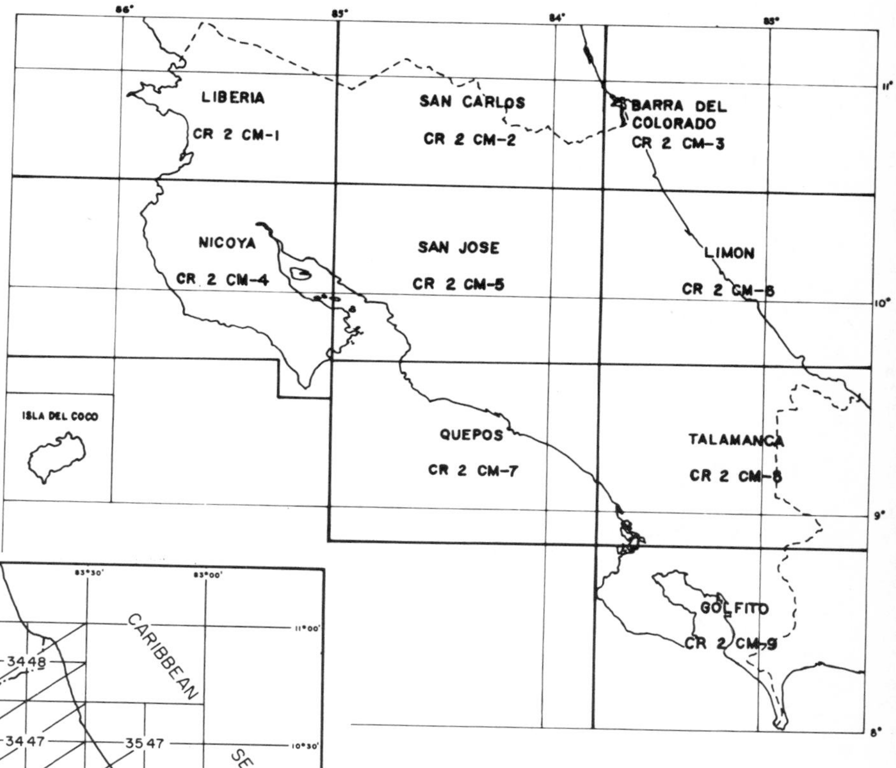

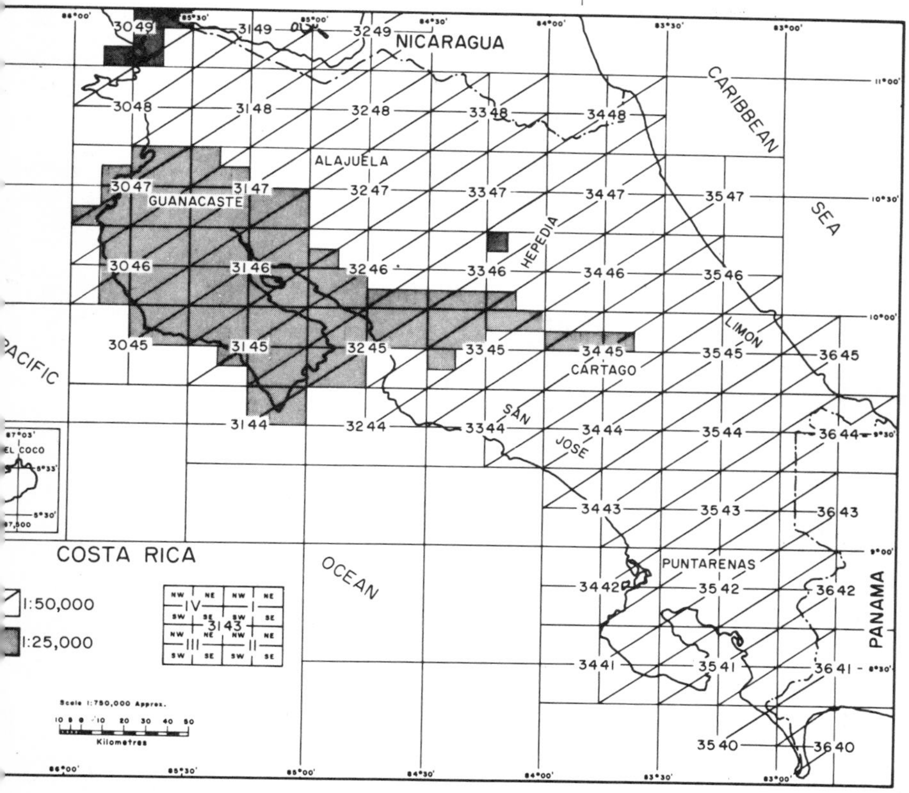

728.6/2

MAPA BÁSICO DE COSTA RICA
1:50,000 Inst. Geog. Costa Rica
Topographical series in progress.

COSTA RICA
1:25,000 Inst. Geog. Costa Rica
Topographical Series in progress

Sheet numbering
3143 lV 1:50,000
3143 lVSE 1:25,000

728.5/2 *NICARAGUA*
1:100,000 Dir. General de Cartografia
Series E651
Planimetric Series

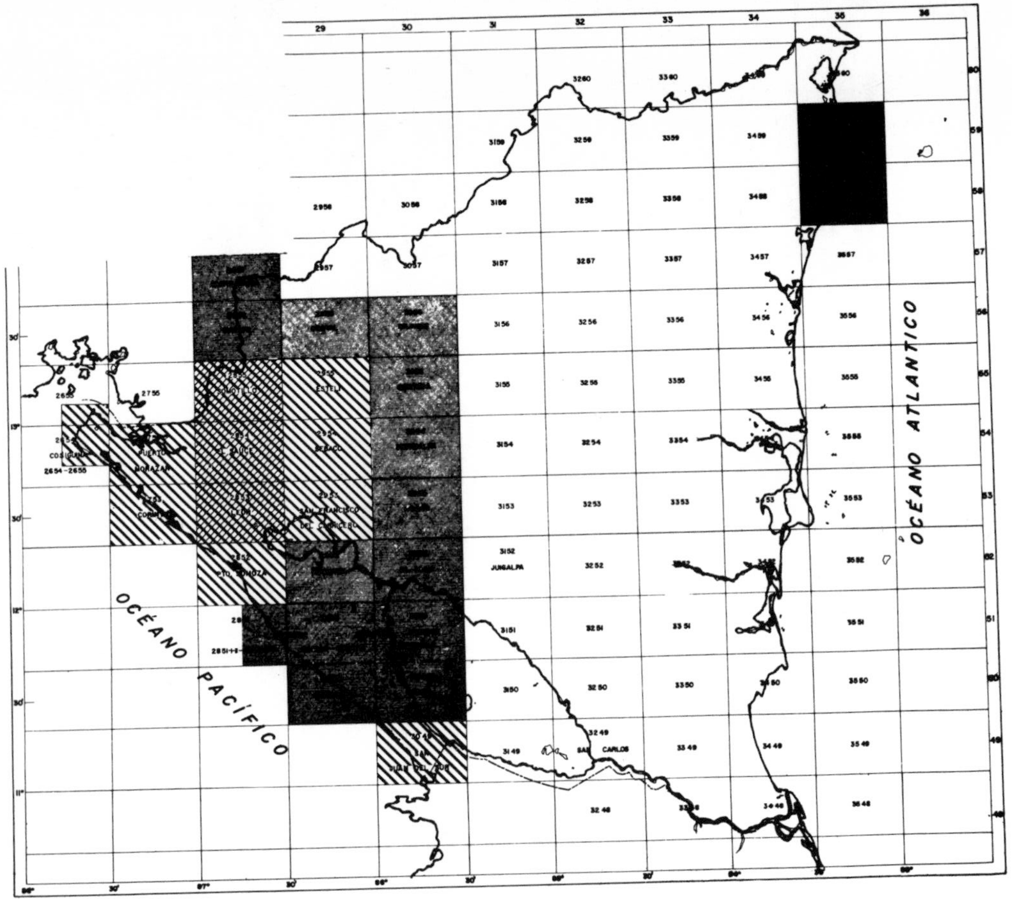

- 1st Edition
- 2nd Edition
- 5 colour edition (2a)

728.5/3 *NICARAGUA - SERIE TOPOGRAFICA*
1:50,000 Div. General de Cartografia
Series E751
Topographical series

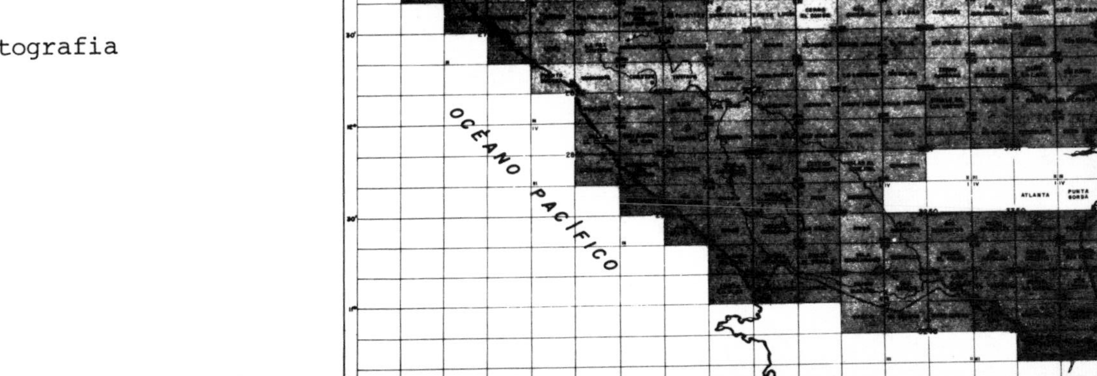

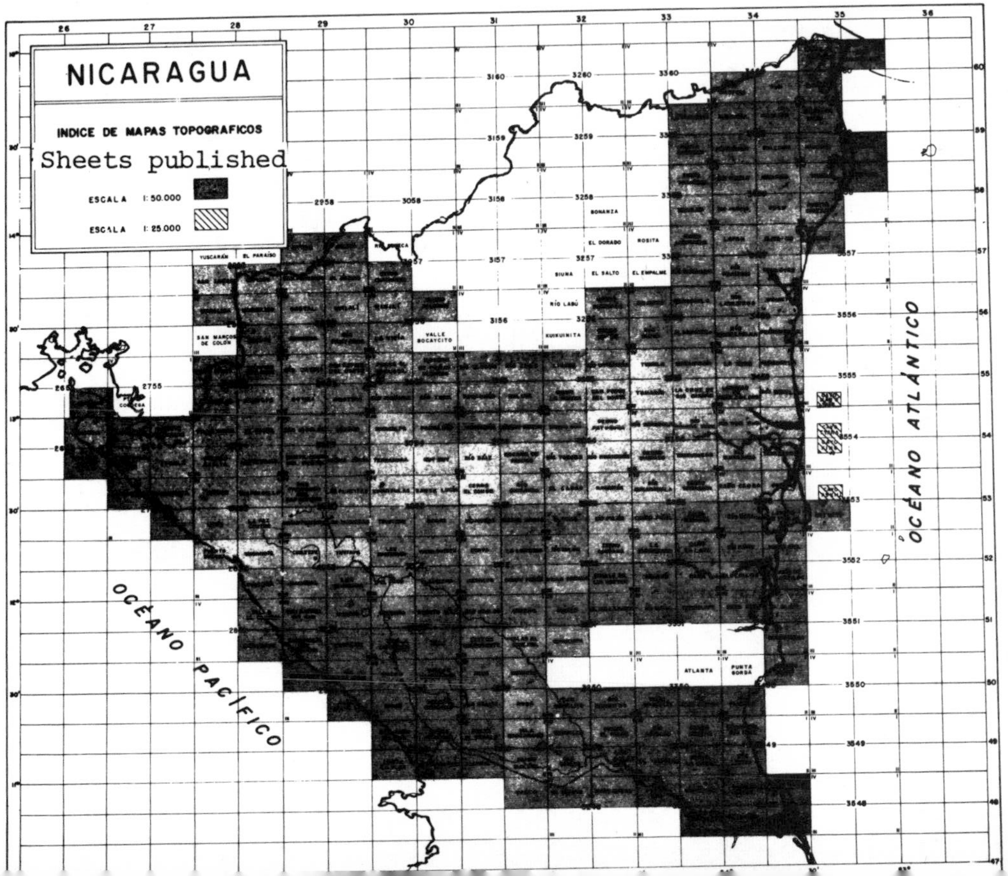

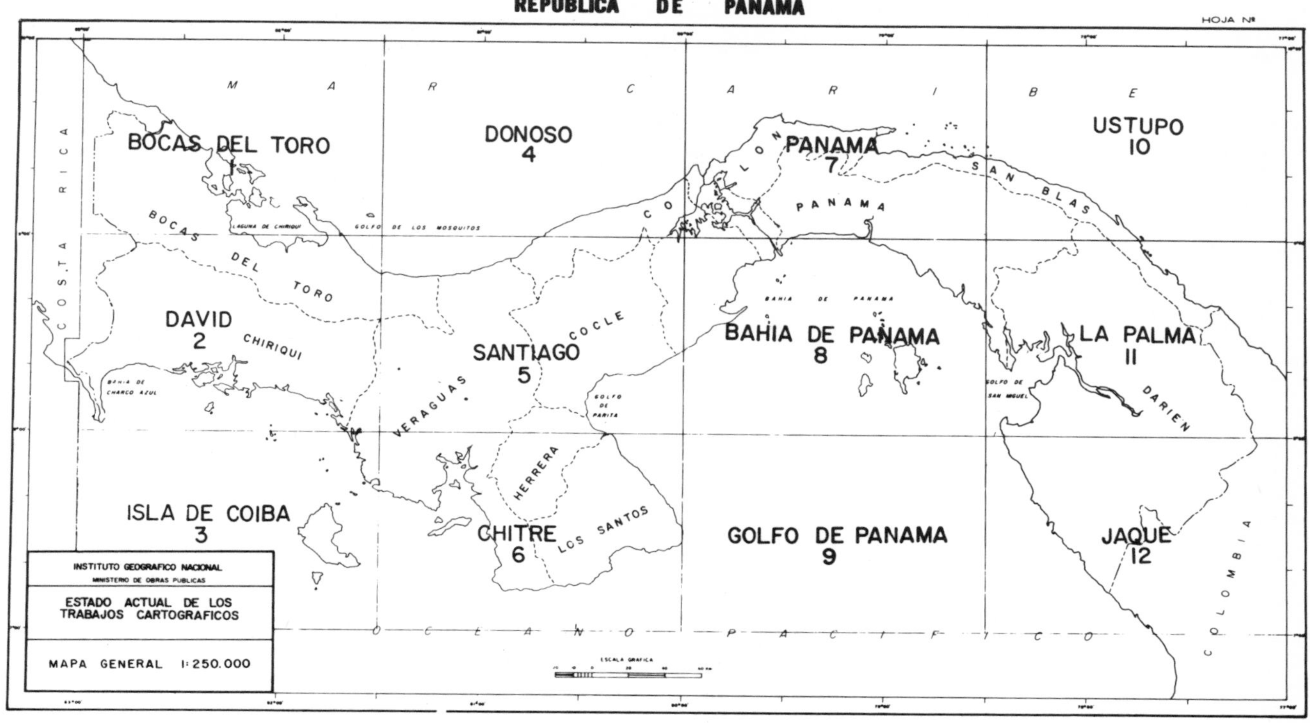

728.7/1 PANAMA (ESPECIAL)
1:250,000 IGN
Topographical map in 12 sheets.

728.7/2 PANAMA
1:50,000 Series E762 IGN
Topographical series in progress

▢ Sheets published.

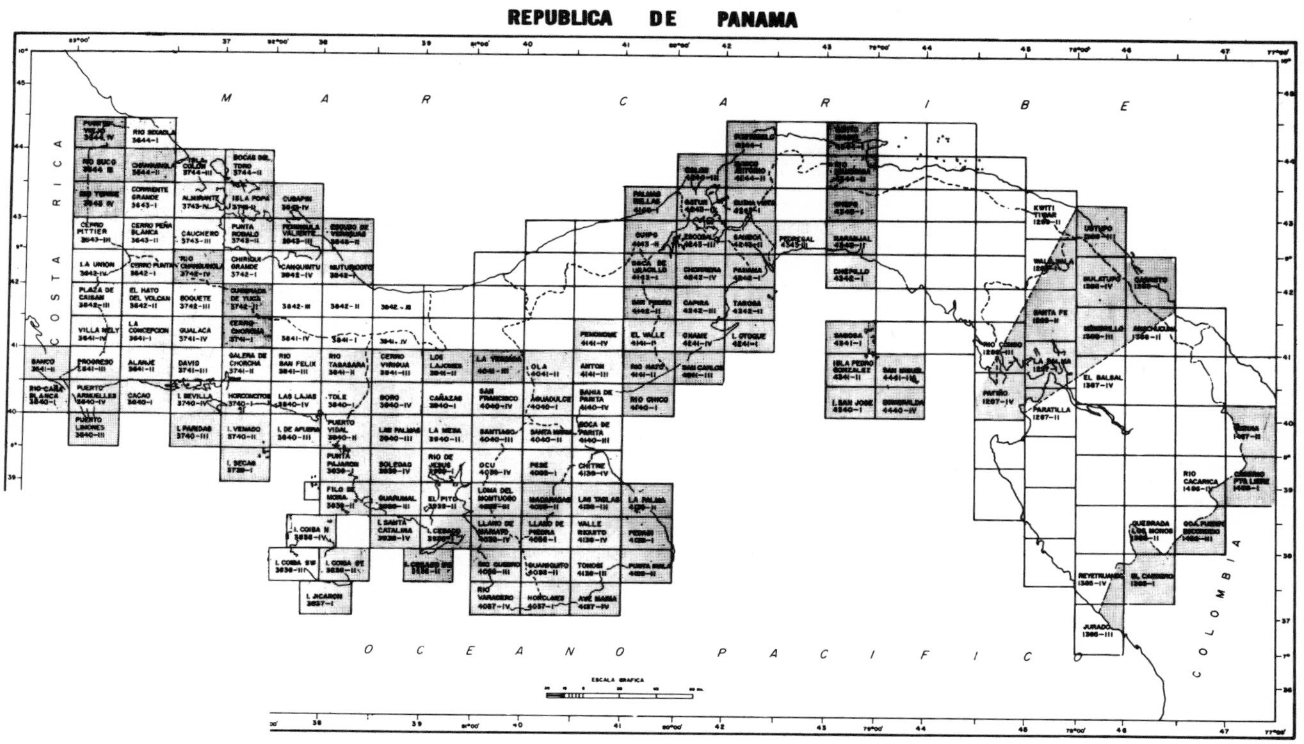

729.2/1

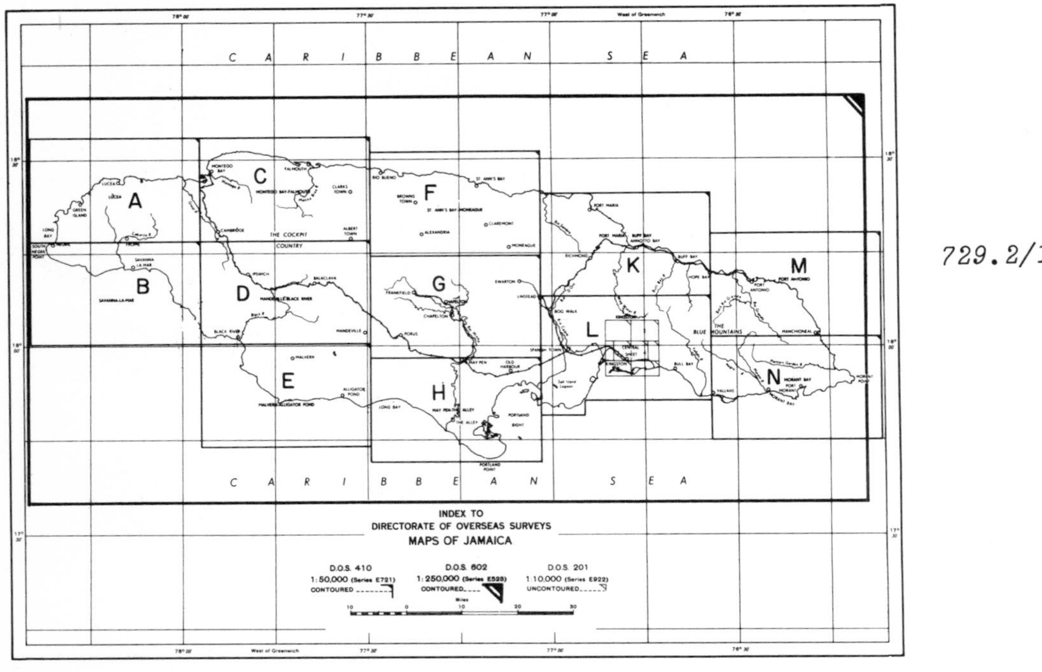
CARIBBEAN SEA
INDEX TO
DIRECTORATE OF OVERSEAS SURVEYS
MAPS OF JAMAICA
D.O.S. 410
1:50,000 (Series E721)
CONTOURED
D.O.S. 602
1:250,000 (Series E523)
CONTOURED
D.O.S. 201
1:10,000 (Series E922)
UNCONTOURED

729.2/3

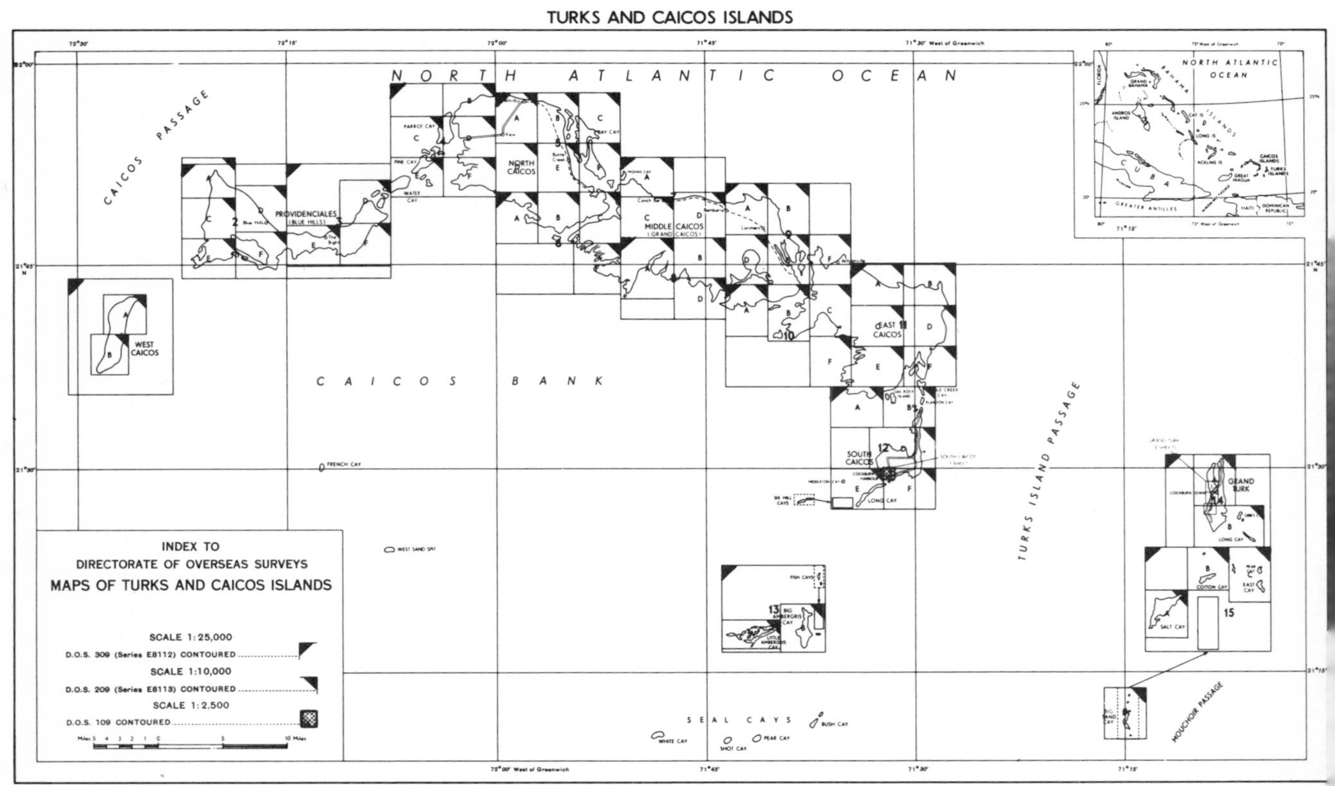
TURKS AND CAICOS ISLANDS
NORTH ATLANTIC OCEAN
CAICOS PASSAGE
CAICOS BANK
TURKS ISLAND PASSAGE
SEAL CAYS
MOUCHOIR PASSAGE
INDEX TO
DIRECTORATE OF OVERSEAS SURVEYS
MAPS OF TURKS AND CAICOS ISLANDS
SCALE 1:25,000
D.O.S. 309 (Series E8112) CONTOURED
SCALE 1:10,000
D.O.S. 209 (Series E8113) CONTOURED
SCALE 1:2,500
D.O.S. 109 CONTOURED

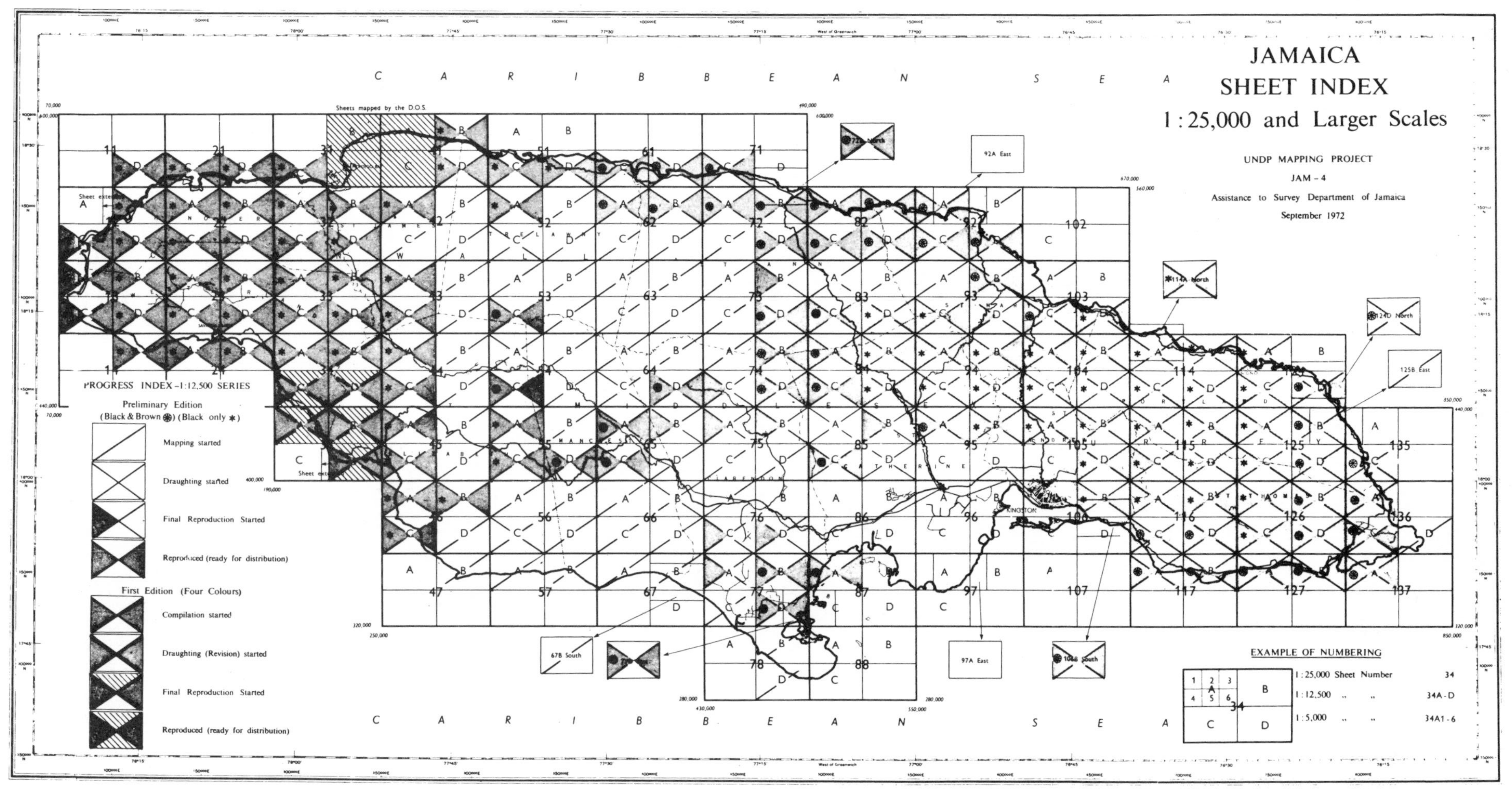

729.2/2 JAMAICA
UNITED NATIONS DEVELOPMENT PROJECT: ALL ISLAND MAPPING
1:12,500 Survey Dept. Kingston
Topographical series in progress

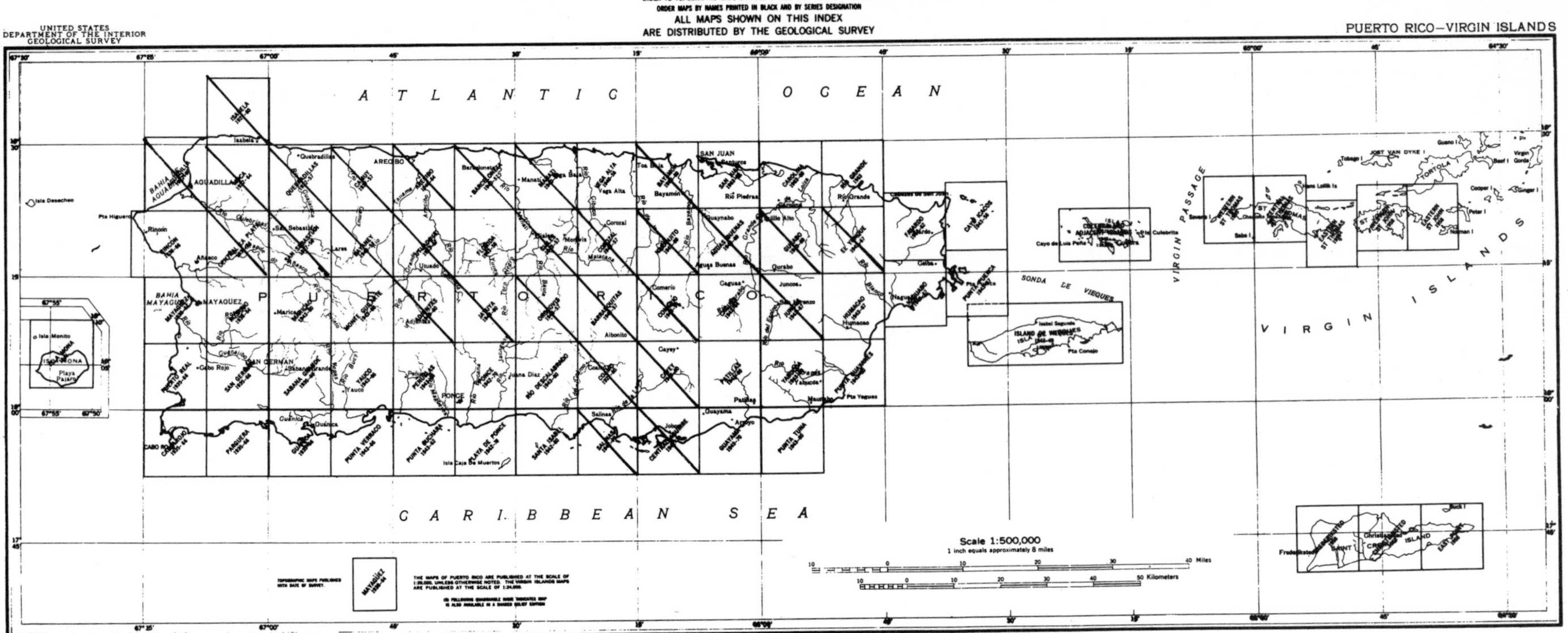

729.5/1 *PUERTO RICO*

1:20,000 USGS

Topographical series in 65 sheets: complete

Geological editions published (USGS)

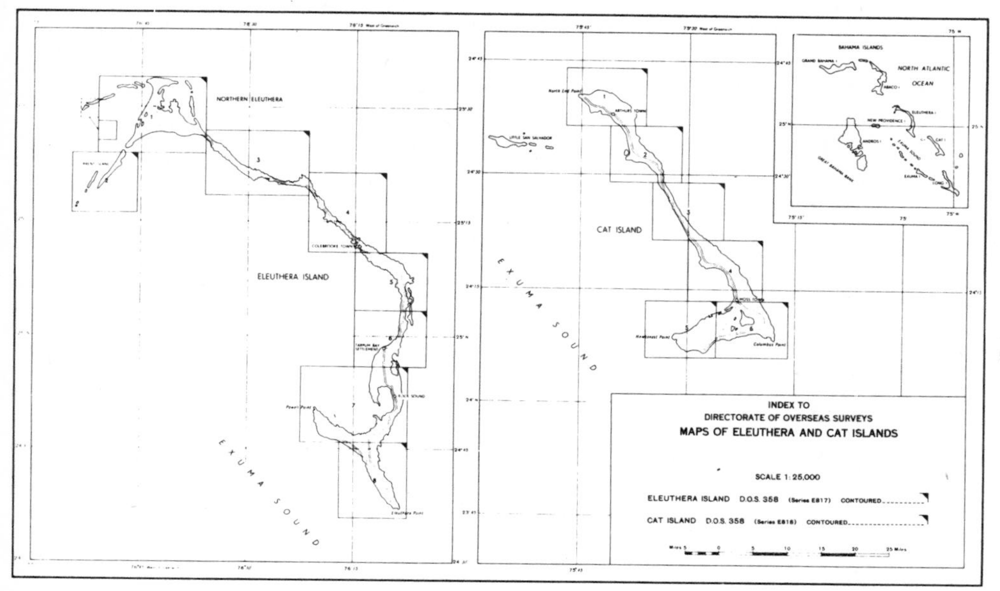

729.61/1
BAHAMA ISLANDS
1:25,000 DOS
Topographical series

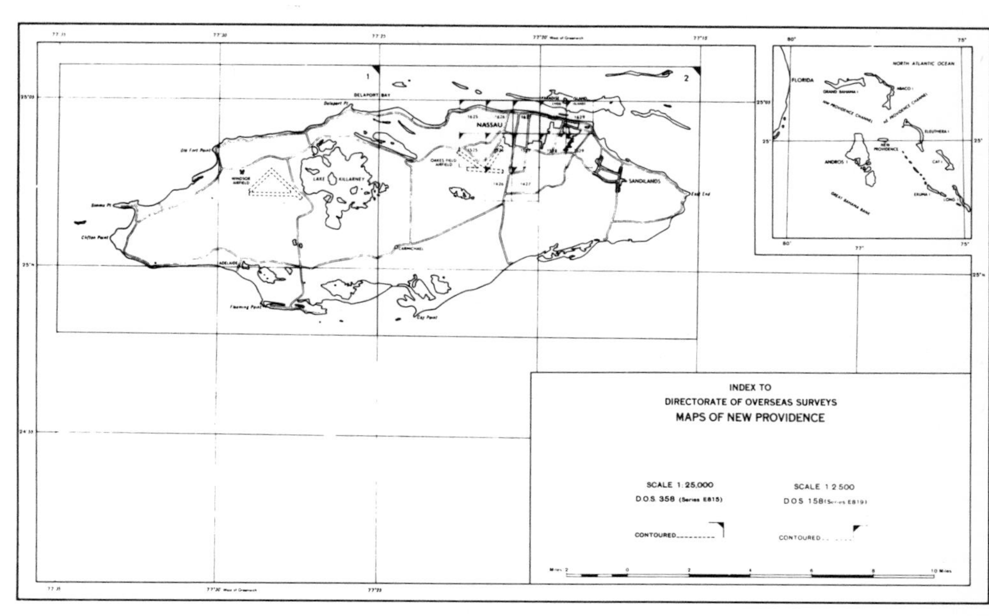

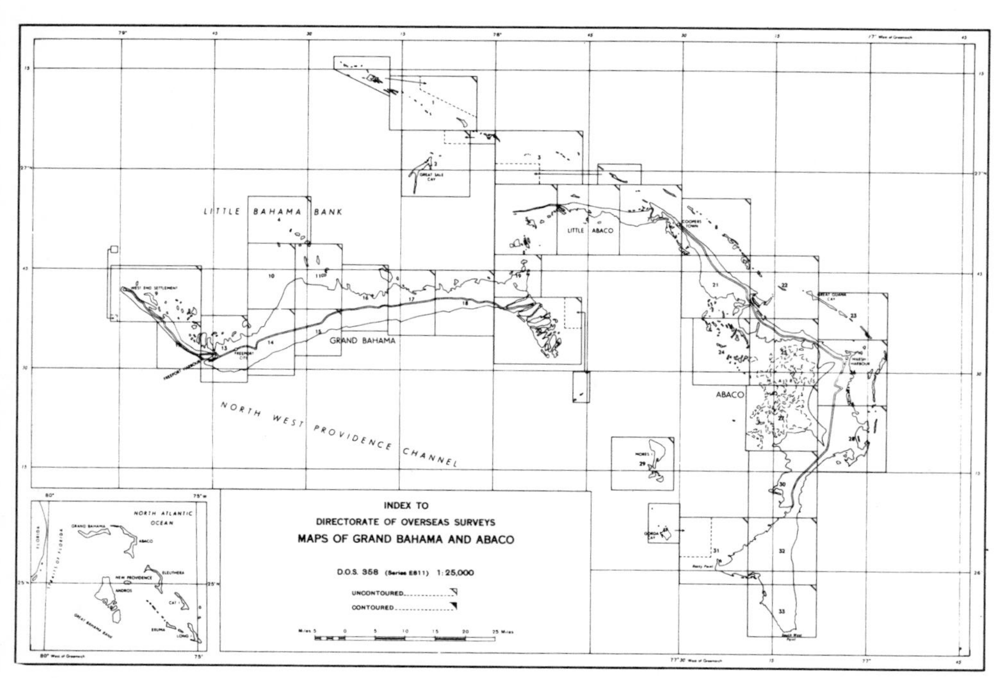

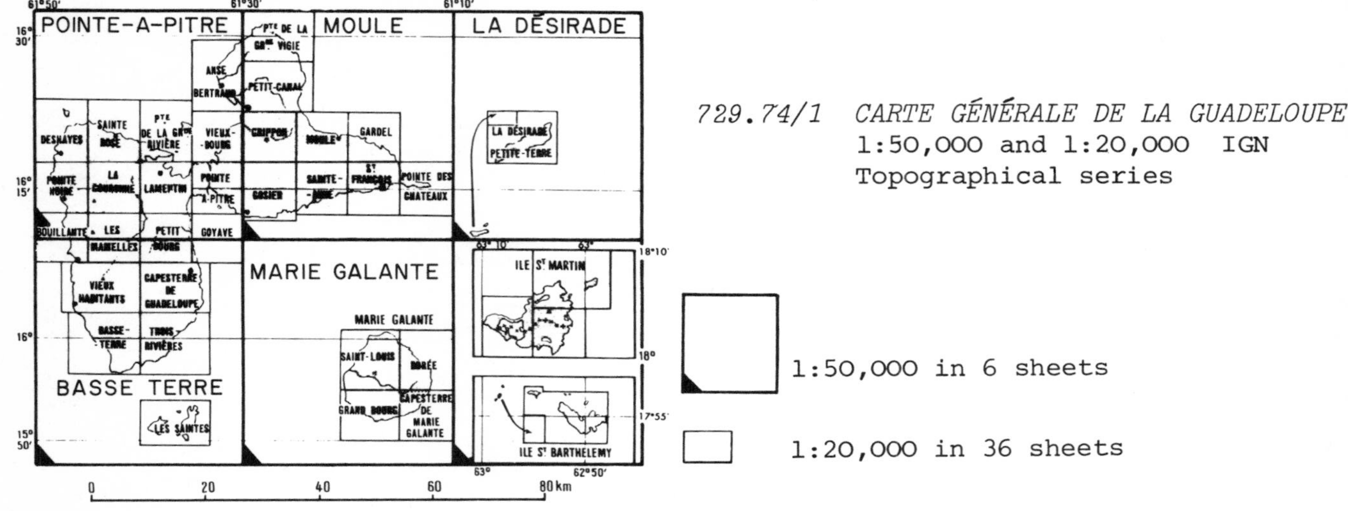

729.74/1 *CARTE GÉNÉRALE DE LA GUADELOUPE*
1:50,000 and 1:20,000 IGN
Topographical series

1:50,000 in 6 sheets

1:20,000 in 36 sheets

729.9/1

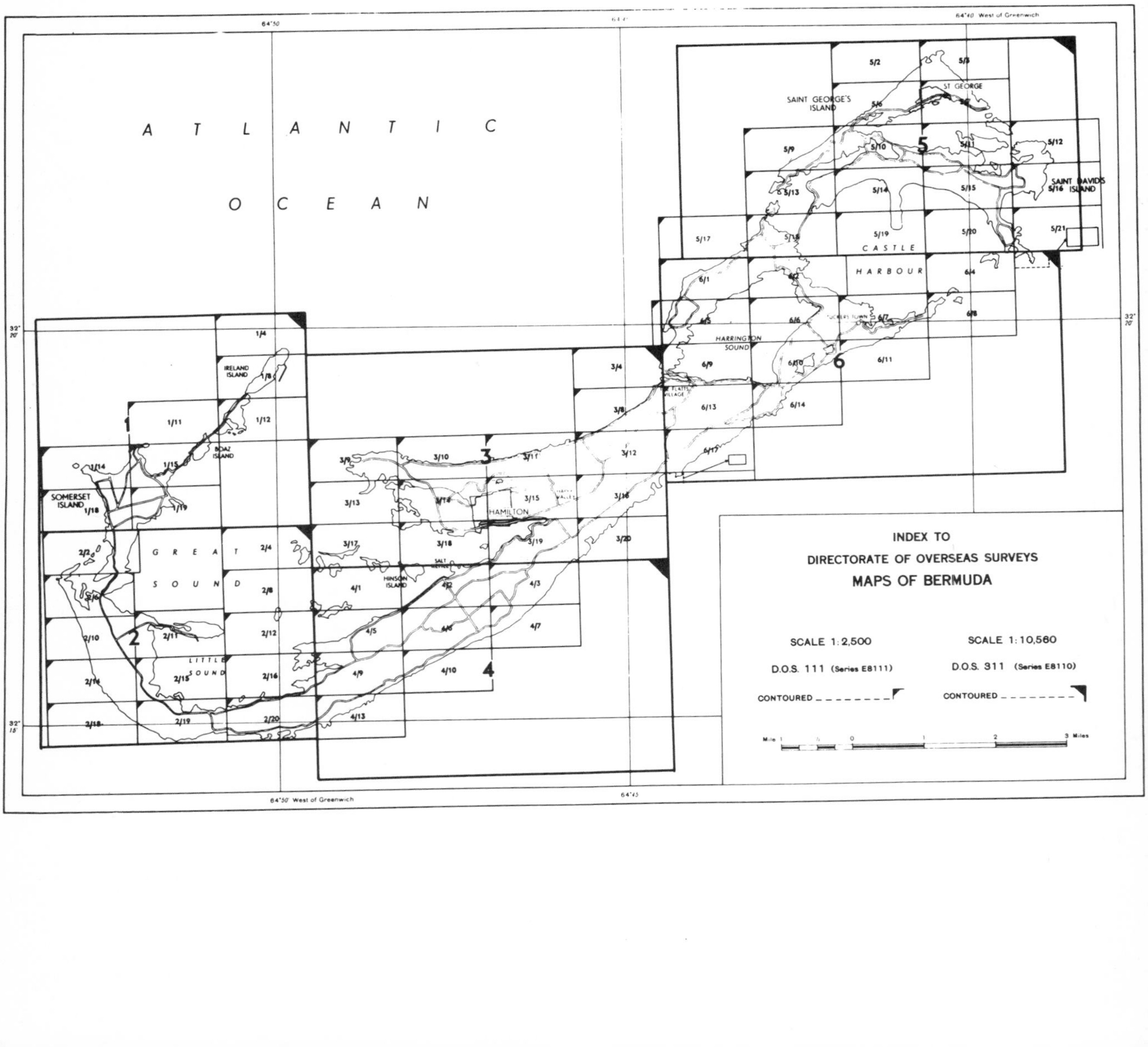

ATLANTIC OCEAN

INDEX TO
DIRECTORATE OF OVERSEAS SURVEYS
MAPS OF BERMUDA

SCALE 1:2,500
D.O.S. 111 (Series E8111)
CONTOURED

SCALE 1:10,560
D.O.S. 311 (Series E8110)
CONTOURED

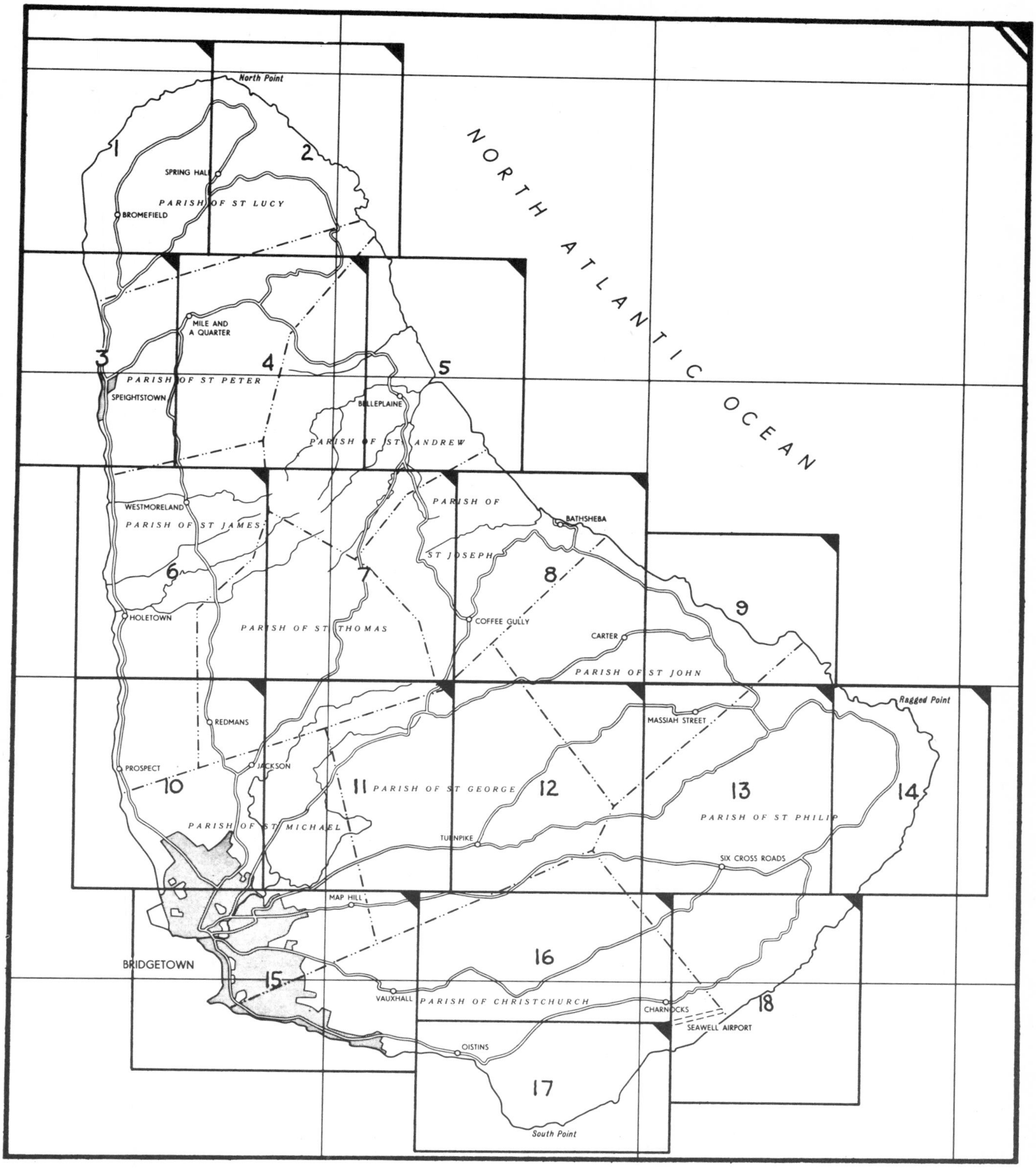

North Point

1

2

SPRING HALL

PARISH OF ST LUCY

BROMEFIELD

NORTH ATLANTIC OCEAN

MILE AND A QUARTER

3

4

5

PARISH OF ST PETER

SPEIGHTSTOWN

BELLEPLAINE

PARISH OF ST ANDREW

WESTMORELAND

PARISH OF ST JAMES

PARISH OF ST JOSEPH

BATHSHEBA

6

7

8

9

HOLETOWN

COFFEE GULLY

PARISH OF ST THOMAS

CARTER

PARISH OF ST JOHN

Ragged Point

REDMANS

MASSIAH STREET

PROSPECT

JACKSON

10

11

PARISH OF ST GEORGE

12

13

14

PARISH OF ST PHILIP

PARISH OF ST MICHAEL

TURNPIKE

SIX CROSS ROADS

MAP HILL

16

BRIDGETOWN

15

VAUXHALL

PARISH OF CHRISTCHURCH

CHARNOCKS

18

SEAWELL AIRPORT

OISTINS

17

South Point

INDEX TO DIRECTORATE OF OVERSEAS SURVEYS MAPS OF BARBADOS

SCALE 1:10,000

D.C.S. 18 (Series E8412)

SCALE 1:50,000

D.O.S. 418 (Series E749)

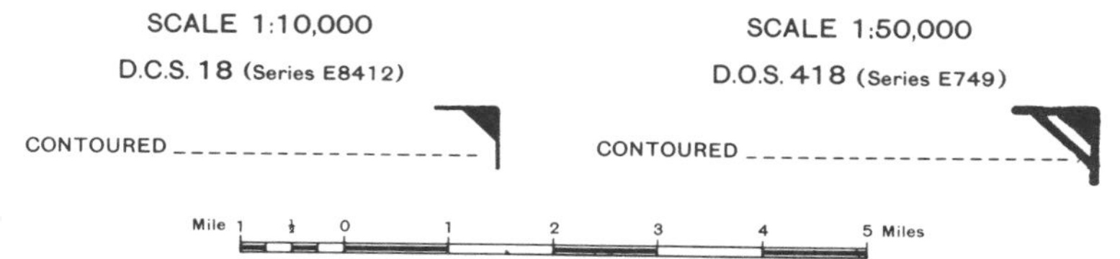

CARTE GÉNÉRALE DE LA MARTINIQUE AU 1/20 000

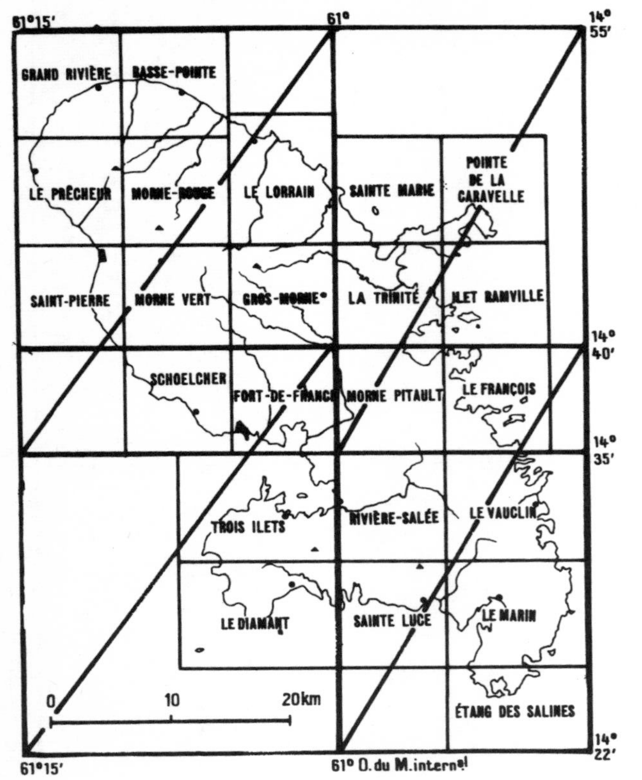

729.81/1 *CARTE GÉNÉRALE DE LA MARTINIQUE*
1:50,000 and 1:20,000 IGN
Topographical series

1:50,000 in 4 sheets

1:20,000 in 23 sheets

729.87/1

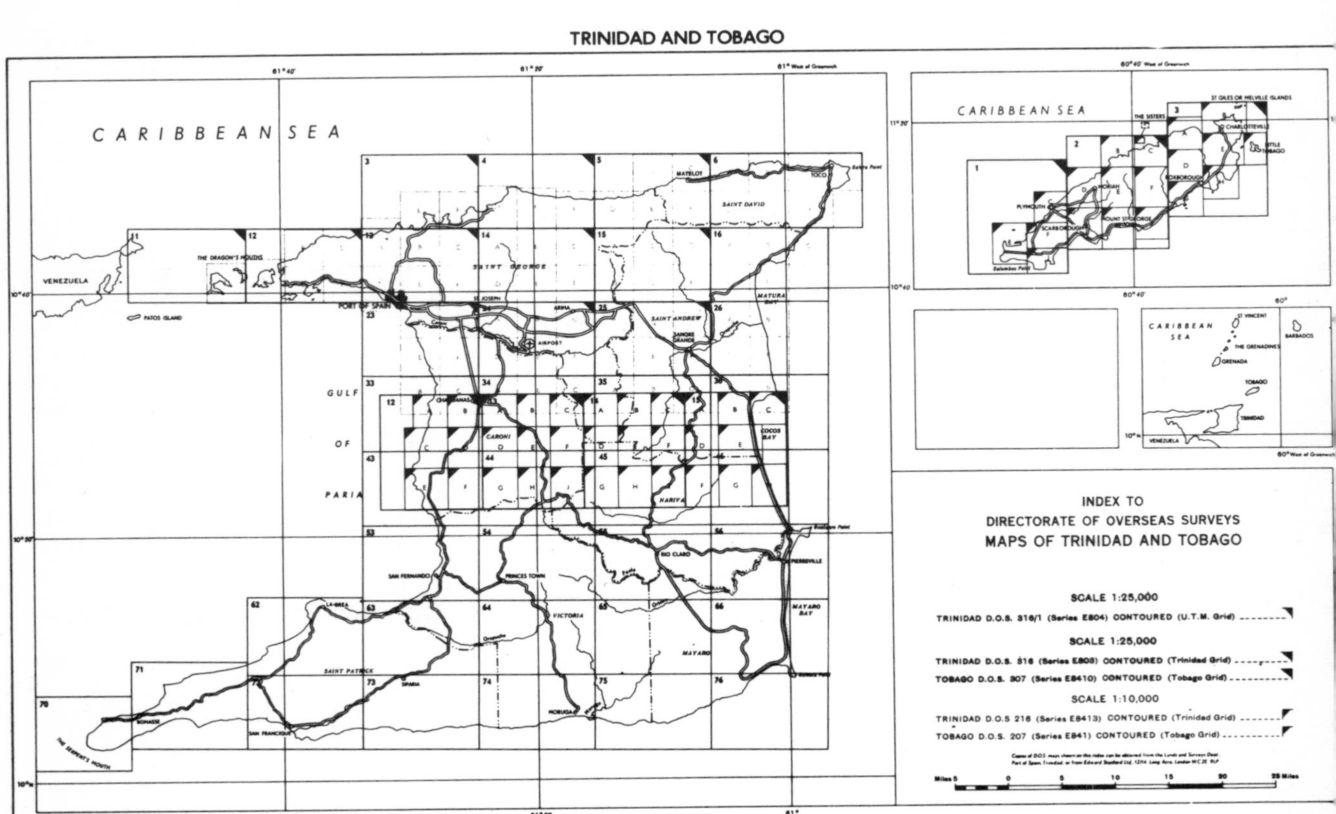

NL-10 CASCADE RANGE IMW 1945
NL-11 SNAKE RIVER 1960
NL-12 YELLOWSTONE 1955
NL-13 BIG HORN MTS 1955
NL-14 DAKOTAS 1956
NK-10 MT SHASTA IMW 1954 1959
NK-11 OWYHEE RIVER 1959
NK-12 GREAT SALT LAKE 1955
NK-13 CHEYENNE 1955
NK-14 PLATTE RIVER 1959
NJ-10 SAN FRANCISCO BAY 1959
NJ-11 MOUNT WHITNEY IMW 1966
NJ-12 GRAND CANYON 1959
NJ-13 PIKES PEAK IMW 1966
NJ-14 WICHITA 1953
NI-10 POINT CONCEPTION 1959
NI-11 LOS ANGELES IMW 1947
NI-12 GILA RIVER 1959
NI-13 SANTA FE 1955
NI-14 DALLAS 1954
NH-14 AUSTIN IMW 1945
WASHINGTON
OREGON
IDAHO
MONTANA
NORTH DAKOTA
SOUTH DAKOTA
WYOMING
NEVADA
UTAH
COLORADO
KANSAS
NEBRASKA
CALIFORNIA
ARIZONA
NEW MEXICO
TEXAS
OKLAHOMA
PACIFIC OCEAN
ALASKA
HAWAII

...ERS PRINTED IN BLACK.

UNITED STATES
DEPARTMENT OF THE INTERIOR
GEOLOGICAL SURVEY

INDEX TO TOPOGRAPHIC MAPS OF THE UNITED STATES

PUBLISHED AT THE SCALE OF 1:1,000,000

NH 14 AUSTIN IMW 1945 — INTERNATIONAL MAP OF THE WORLD AND DATE OF COMPILATION

NJ 14 WICHITA 1955 — NEW 1:1,000,000-SCALE SERIES MAP AND DATE OF COMPILATION

NOTES: SHEET NUMBER WITHOUT MAP NAME INDICATES MAP IN PREPARATION

WHEN BOTH THE IMW AND NEW 1:1,000,000-SCALE DATES ARE SHOWN, IT INDICATES THAT THE AREA IS COVERED BY MAPS OF BOTH SERIES. THE NEW 1:1,000,000-SCALE SERIES MAP WILL BE SUPPLIED UNLESS THE OLDER IMW MAP IS SPECIFICALLY REQUESTED.

73/1 U.S.A.
1:1,000,000 USGS
Topographical series

NL-15 MINNEAPOLIS 1955
NL-16 LAKE SUPERIOR IMW 1966
NL-19 QUEBEC IMW 1968
NK-15
NK-16 CHICAGO IMW 1942
NK-17 LAKE ERIE IMW 1944
NK-18 HUDSON RIVER 1955
NK-19 BOSTON IMW 1912 1955
NJ-15 OZARK PLATEAU 1971
NJ-16 LOUISVILLE 1959
NJ-17
NJ-18 CHESAPEAKE BAY IMW 1940 1955
NI-15 VICKSBURG 1956
NI-16 LOOKOUT MTN IMW 1968
NI-17 SAVANNAH IMW 1946
NI-18 HATTERAS IMW 1944 1955
NH-15 MISSISSIPPI DELTA IMW 1945 WHITE LAKE 1955
NH-16 MOBILE 1959
NH-17 JACKSONVILLE 1956
NG-17 FLORIDA KEYS 1959

GULF OF MEXICO
ATLANTIC OCEAN

CANAL ZONE
PUERTO RICO AND VIRGIN ISLANDS

U. S. DEPARTMENT OF THE INTERIOR
GEOLOGICAL SURVEY

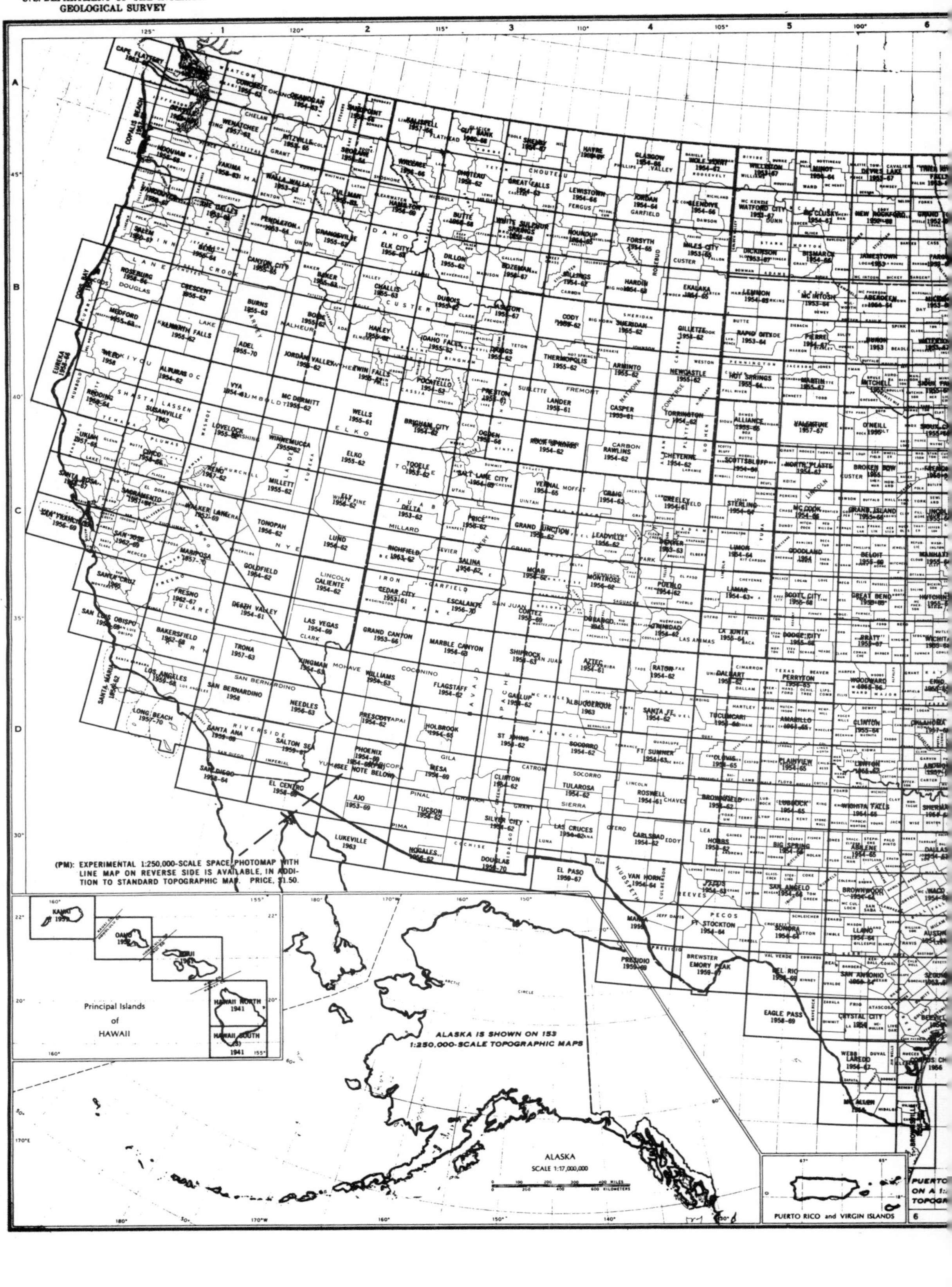

(PM): EXPERIMENTAL 1:250,000-SCALE SPACE PHOTOMAP WITH LINE MAP ON REVERSE SIDE IS AVAILABLE, IN ADDITION TO STANDARD TOPOGRAPHIC MAP. PRICE, $1.50.

Principal Islands of HAWAII

ALASKA IS SHOWN ON 153 1:250,000-SCALE TOPOGRAPHIC MAPS

ALASKA
SCALE 1:17,000,000

PUERTO RICO and VIRGIN ISLANDS

UNITED STATES 1:250,000

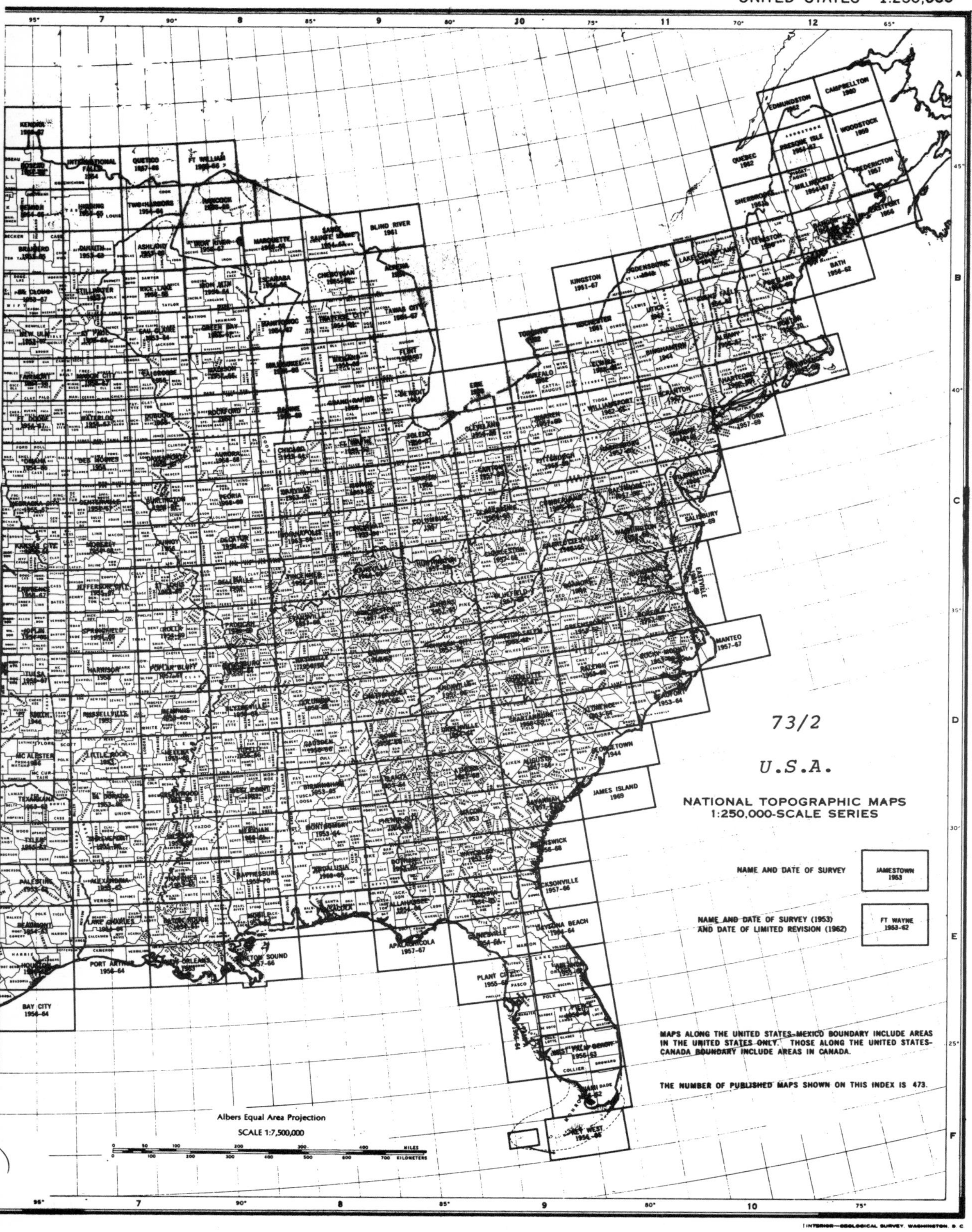

NEW GEOLOGICAL HIGHWAY MAPS

(Prepared with the cooperation of the U.S. Geological Survey)

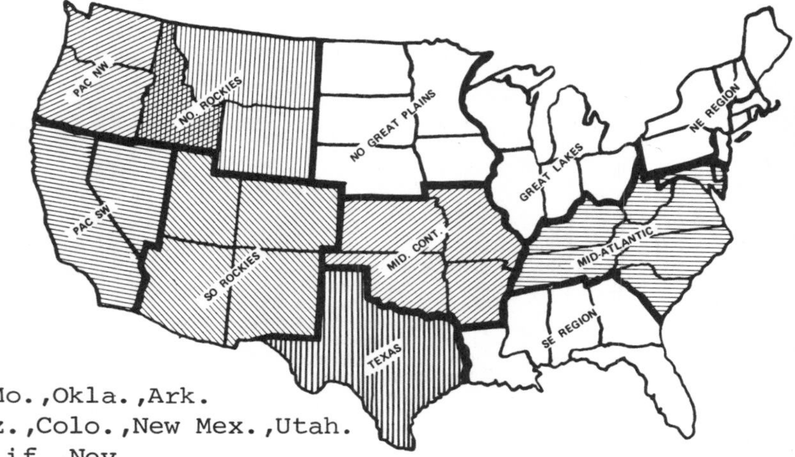

73/4 *GEOLOGICAL HIGHWAY MAPS*

1:875,000 AARG

Maps published:

1. Mid Continent - Kans.,Mo.,Okla.,Ark.
2. Southern Rockies - Ariz.,Colo.,New Mex.,Utah.
3. Pacific Southwest - Calif.,Nev.
4. Mid-Atlantic,Region - Ky.,W.Va.,Va.,Md.,Del., Tenn.,N.Car.,S.Car.
5. Northern Rockies - Ida.,Mont.,Wyo.
6. Pacific Northwest - Wash.,Or.
7. Texas
8. Alaska and Hawaii

South America

INDEX TO MILLIONTH MAP

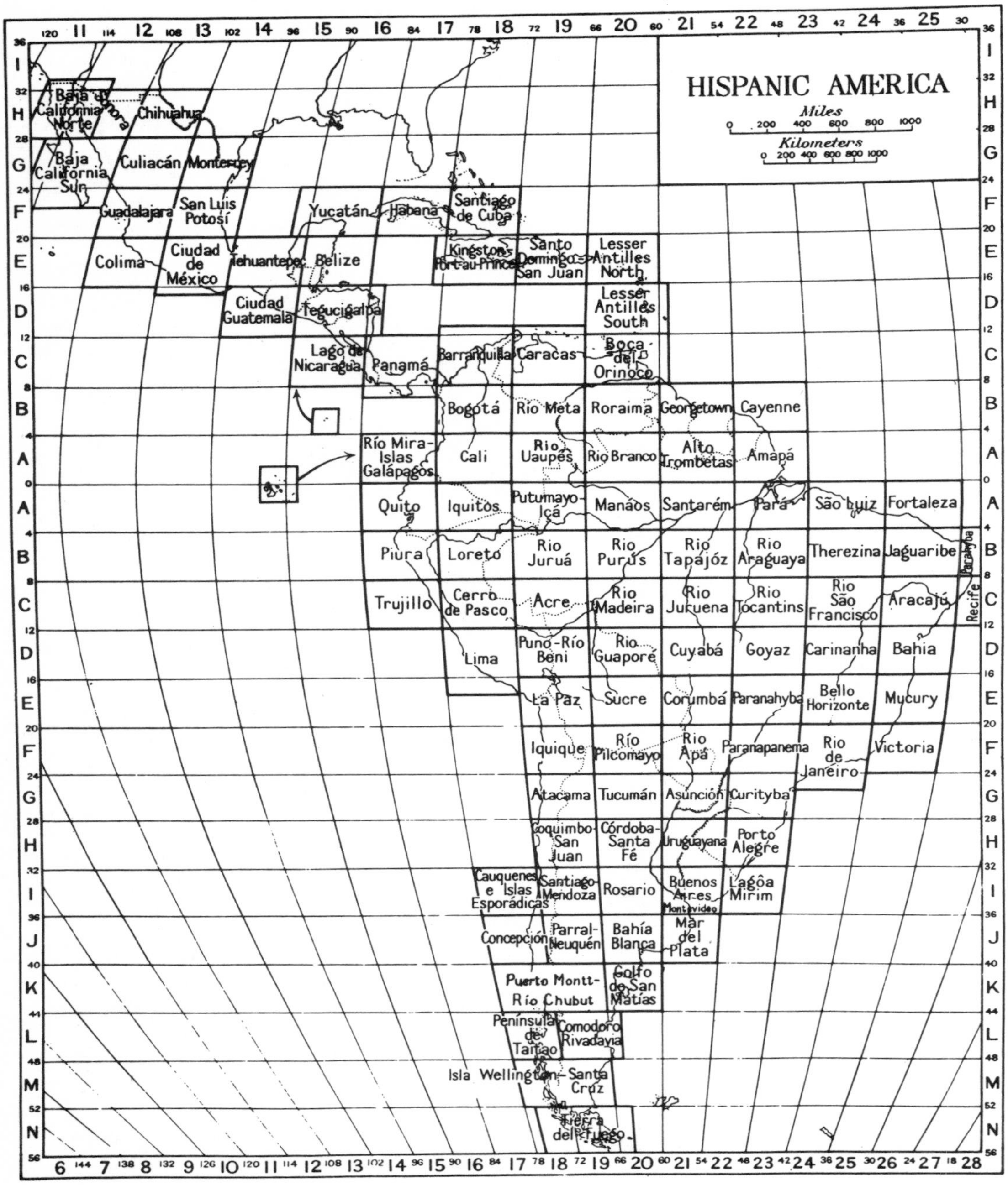

HISPANIC AMERICA

8/1 HISPANIC AMERICA SERIES

1:1,000,000 A.G.S.

Topographical series

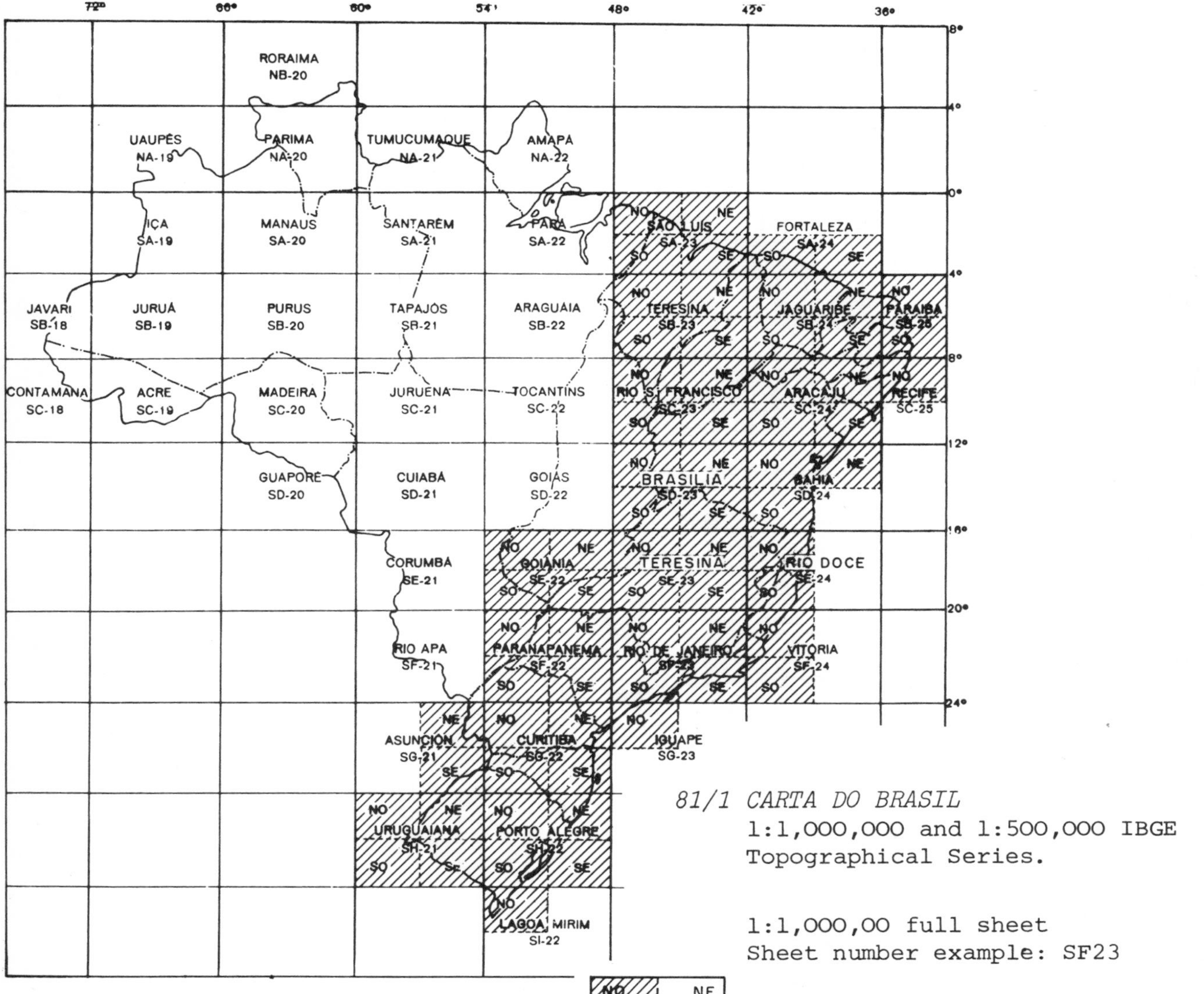

81/1 CARTA DO BRASIL

1:1,000,000 and 1:500,000 IBGE Topographical Series.

1:1,000,00 full sheet
Sheet number example: SF23

1:500,000 Series quarter sheet
Sheet number example: ARACAJU SC24 NO

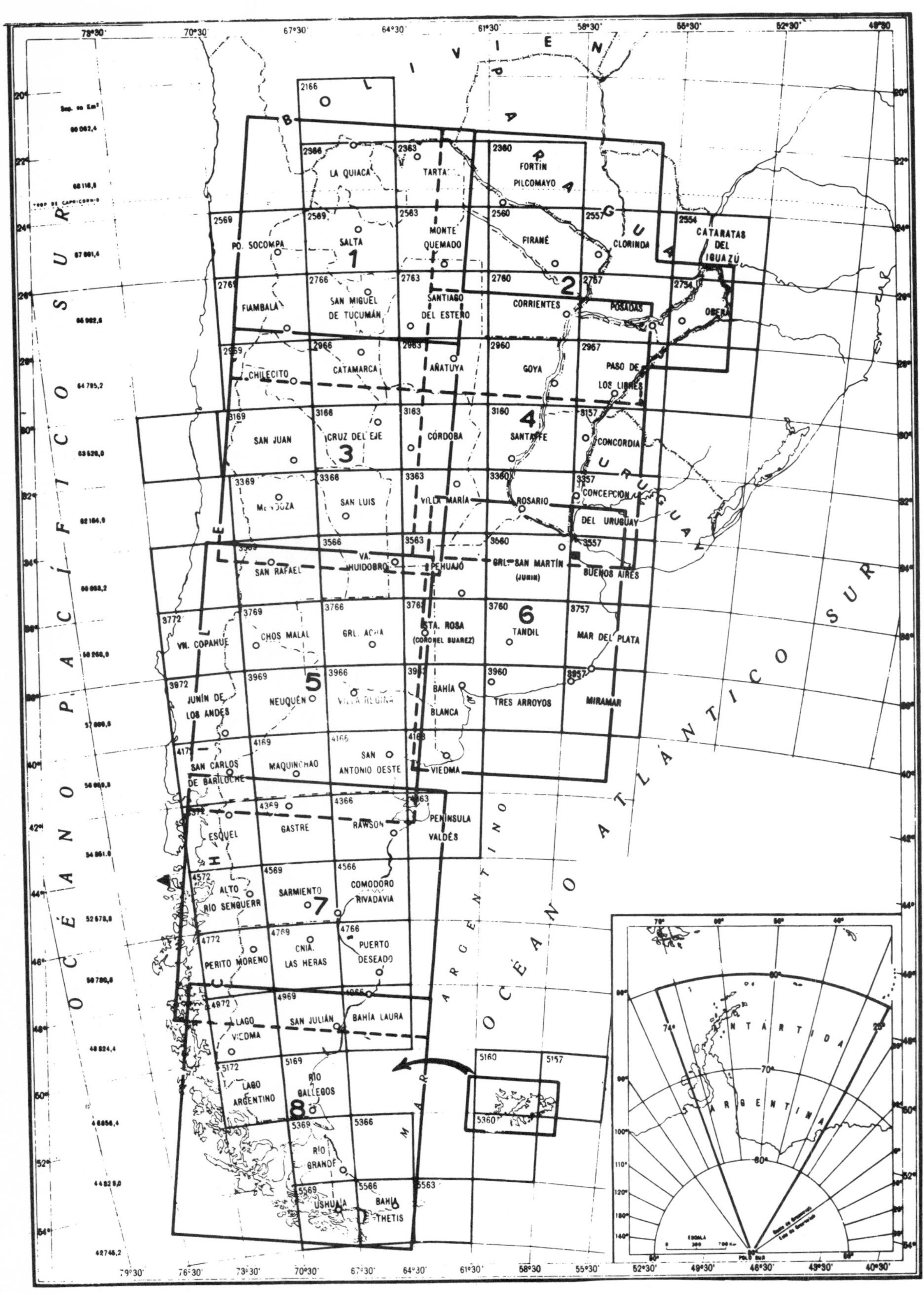

82/1 ARGENTINA CARTA TURÍSTICA
1:1,000,000
Automobil Club Argentina (Regional Tourist Series)

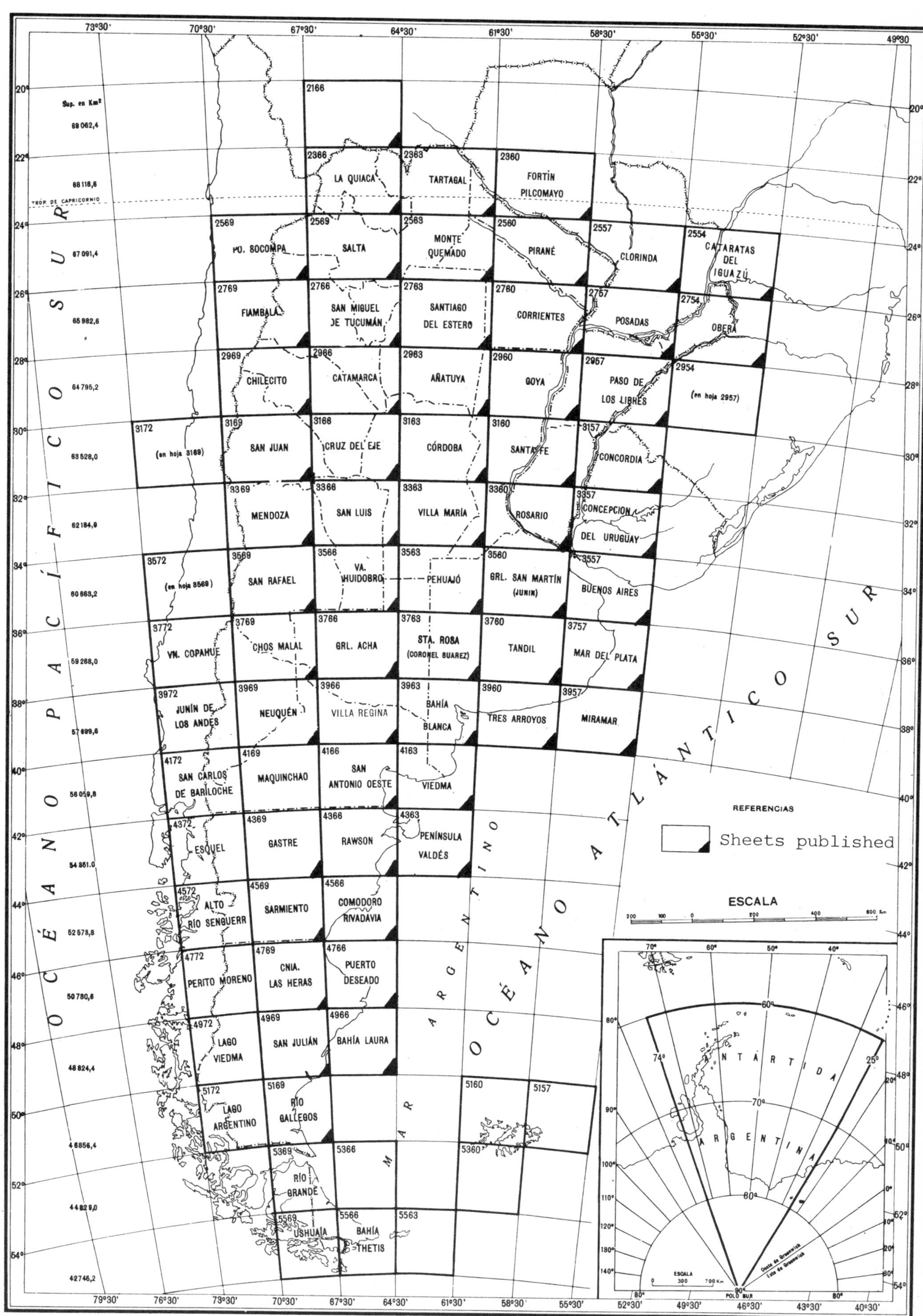

82/2 *CARTA DE LA REPÚBLICA ARGENTINA*
1:500,000 IGM
Topographical series

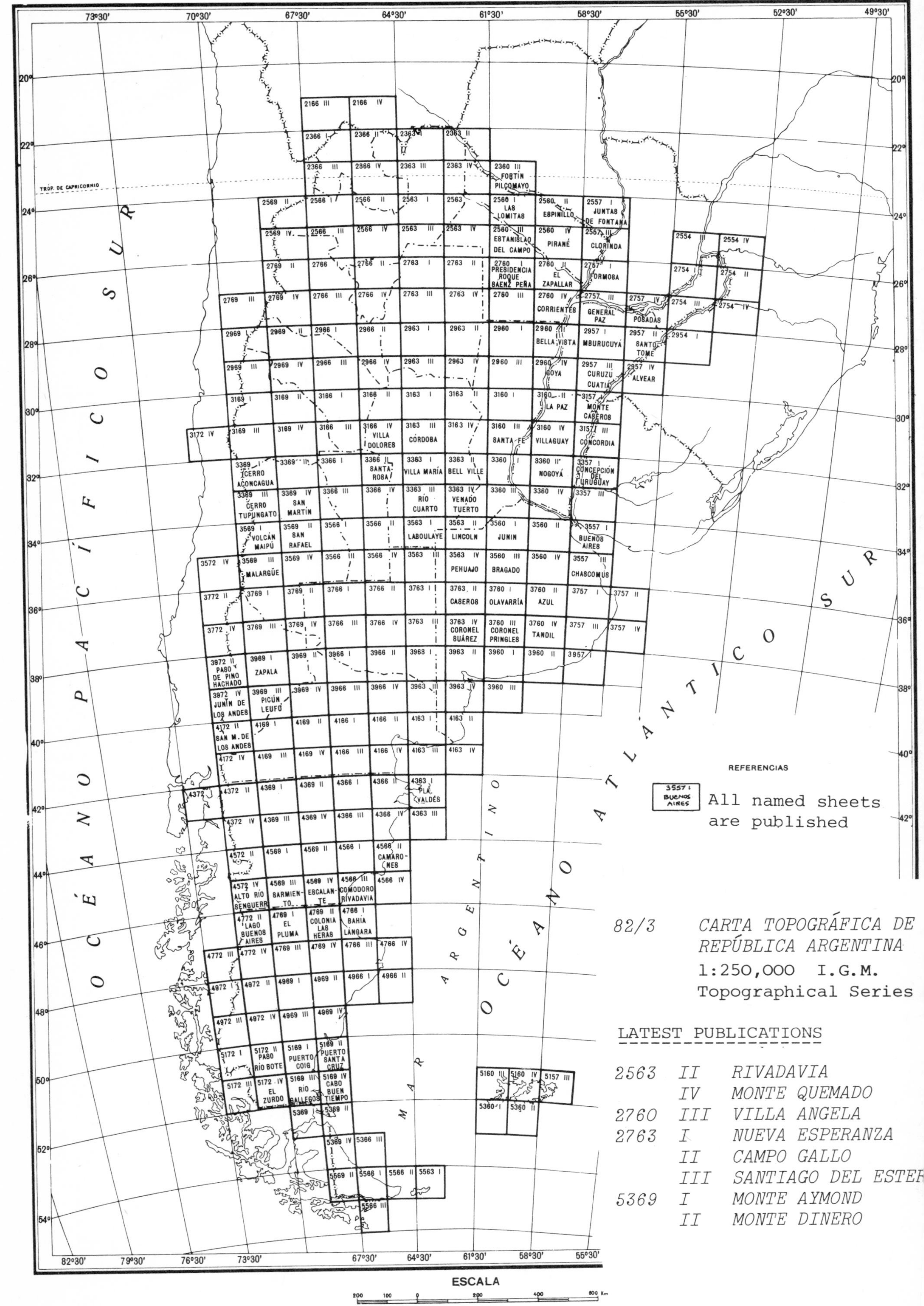

82/3 *CARTA TOPOGRÁFICA DE REPÚBLICA ARGENTINA*
1:250,000 I.G.M.
Topographical Series

LATEST PUBLICATIONS

2563	II	RIVADAVIA
	IV	MONTE QUEMADO
2760	III	VILLA ANGELA
2763	I	NUEVA ESPERANZA
	II	CAMPO GALLO
	III	SANTIAGO DEL ESTER
5369	I	MONTE AYMOND
	II	MONTE DINERO

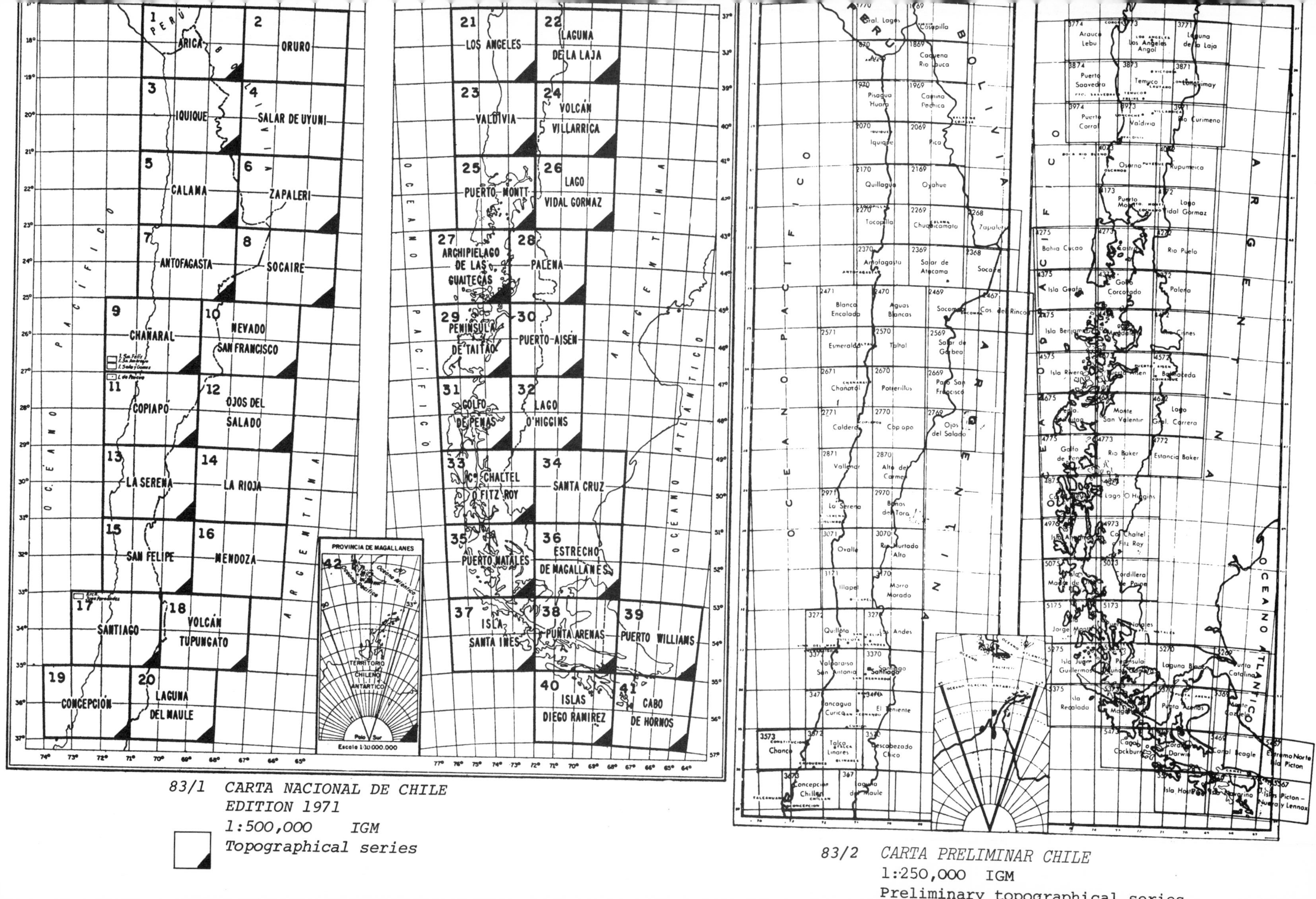

83/1 CARTA NACIONAL DE CHILE
EDITION 1971
1:500,000 IGM
Topographical series

83/2 CARTA PRELIMINAR CHILE
1:250,000 IGM
Preliminary topographical series

83/3

CHILE - LEVANTAMIENTO AEROFOTOGRAMETRICO
NUEVA CARTA (EDITION 1973)
1:500,000 IGM
New topographical series in preparation

Sheets published

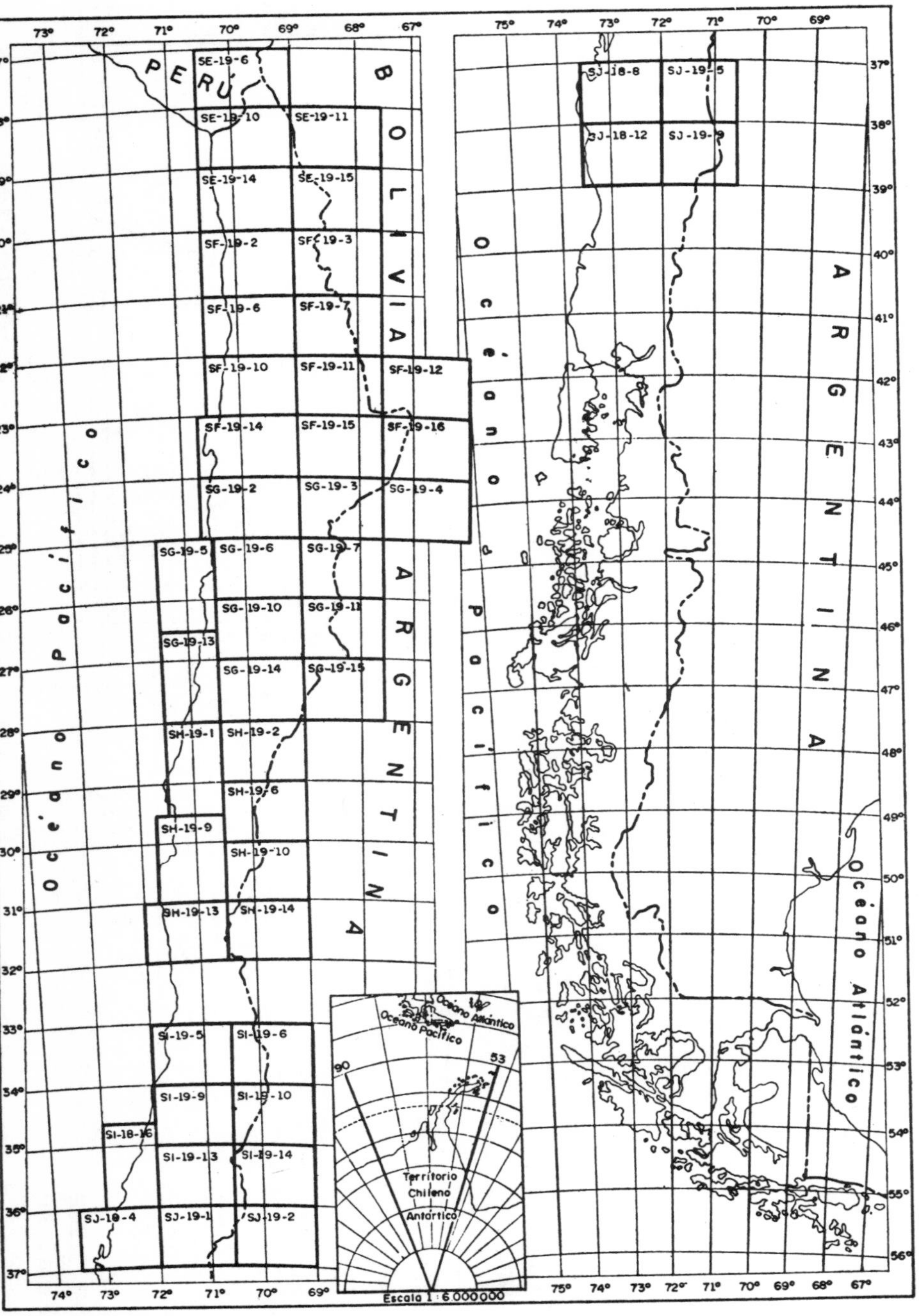

83/4 CARTA DE CAMPAÑA
1:100,000 IGM
Topographic series covering Valparaiso-Santiago region in 22 sheets.

Sheets published.

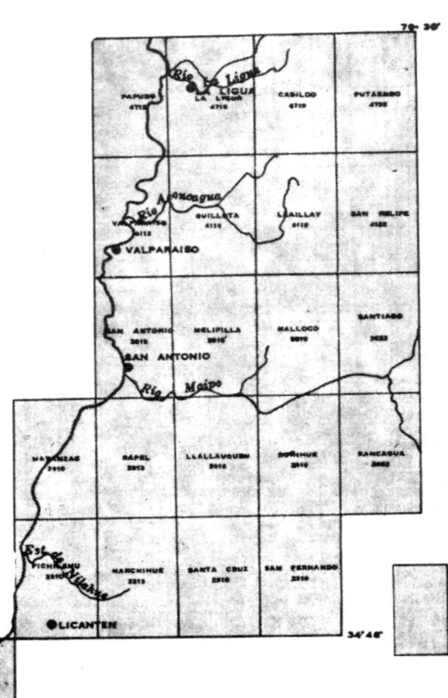

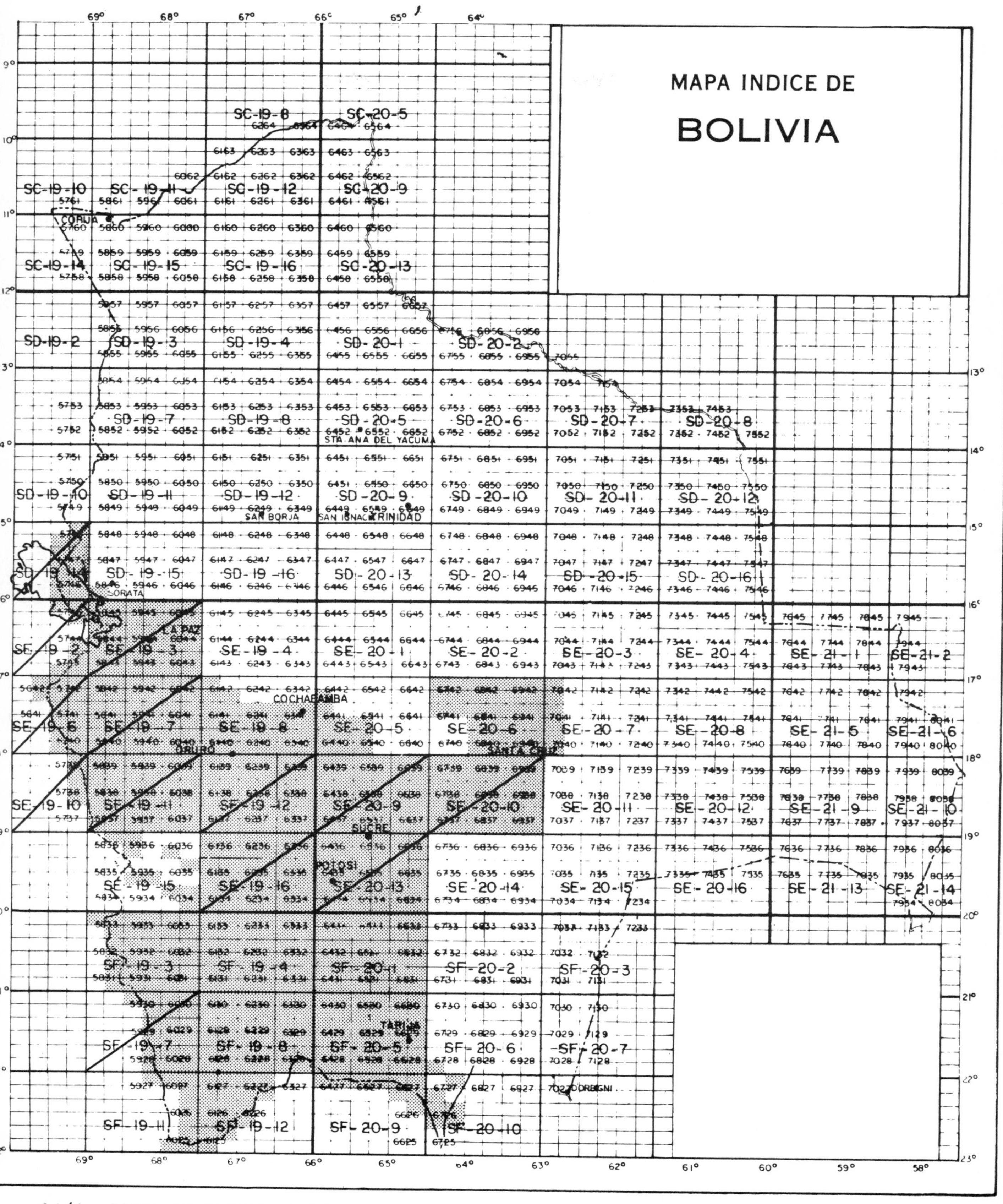

84/1 *CARTA NACIONAL DE BOLIVIA*
1:250,000 IGM
Topographical series in progress

Sheets published

Sheet number example SE19-3

CARTA NACIONAL DE BOLIVIA
1:50,000 IGM
Topographical series in progress

Sheets published

Sheet number example 5944 1

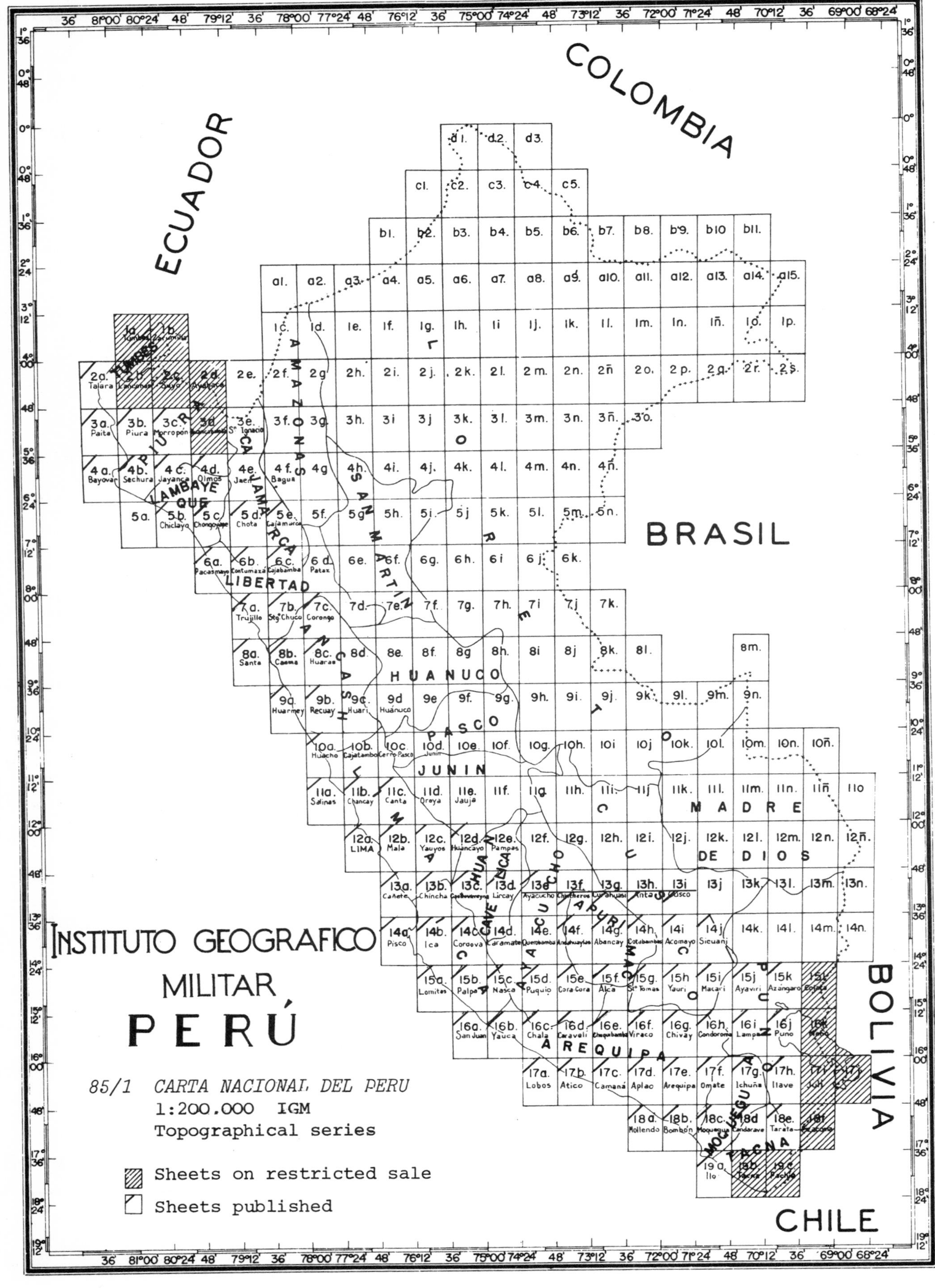
ECUADOR
COLOMBIA
BRASIL
BOLIVIA
CHILE
INSTITUTO GEOGRAFICO MILITAR
PERÚ
85/1 CARTA NACIONAL DEL PERU
1:200.000 IGM
Topographical series
Sheets on restricted sale
Sheets published

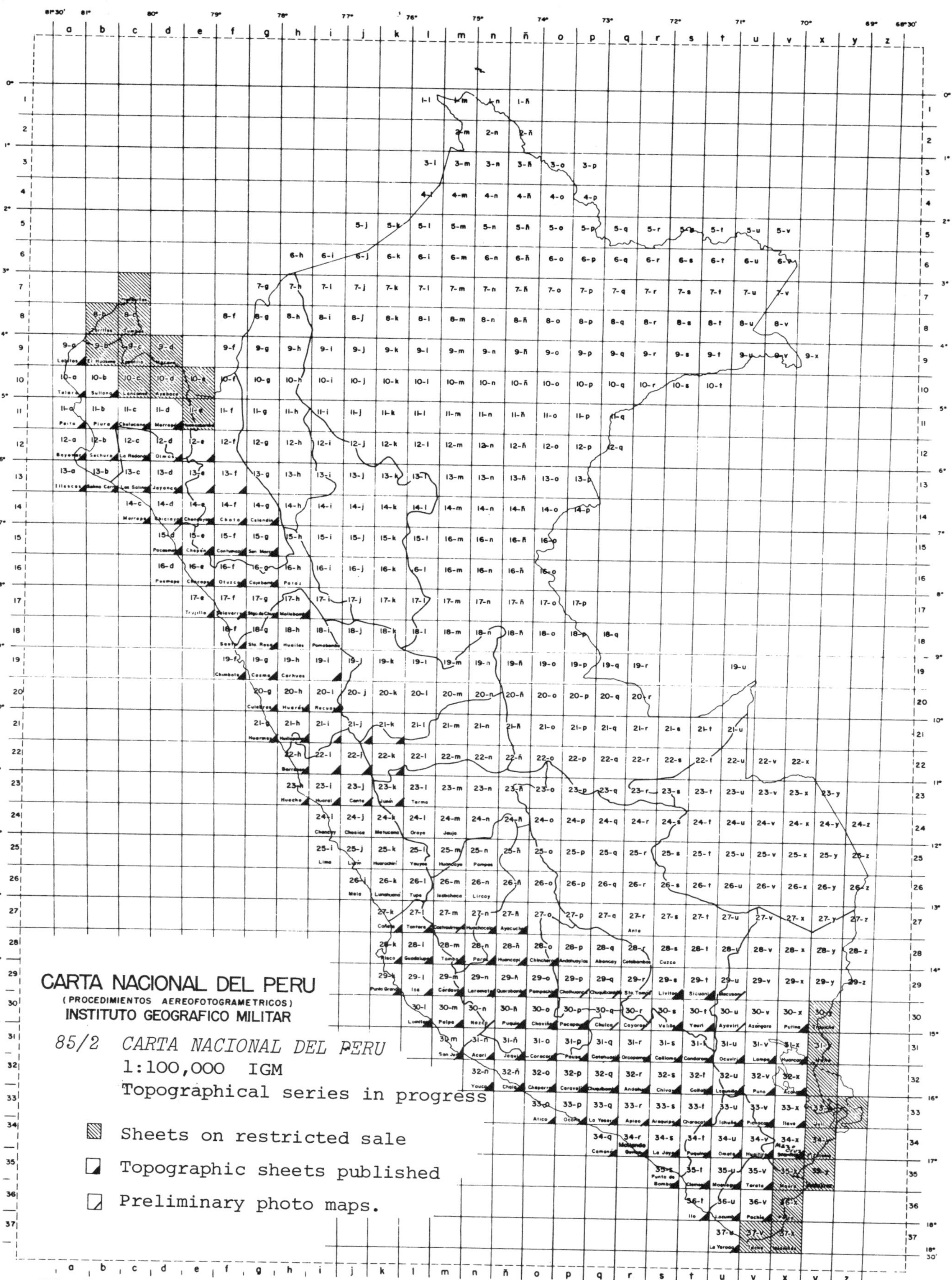
CARTA NACIONAL DEL PERU
(PROCEDIMIENTOS AEREOFOTOGRAMETRICOS)
INSTITUTO GEOGRAFICO MILITAR
85/2 CARTA NACIONAL DEL PERU
1:100,000 IGM
Topographical series in progress
Sheets on restricted sale
Topographic sheets published
Preliminary photo maps.

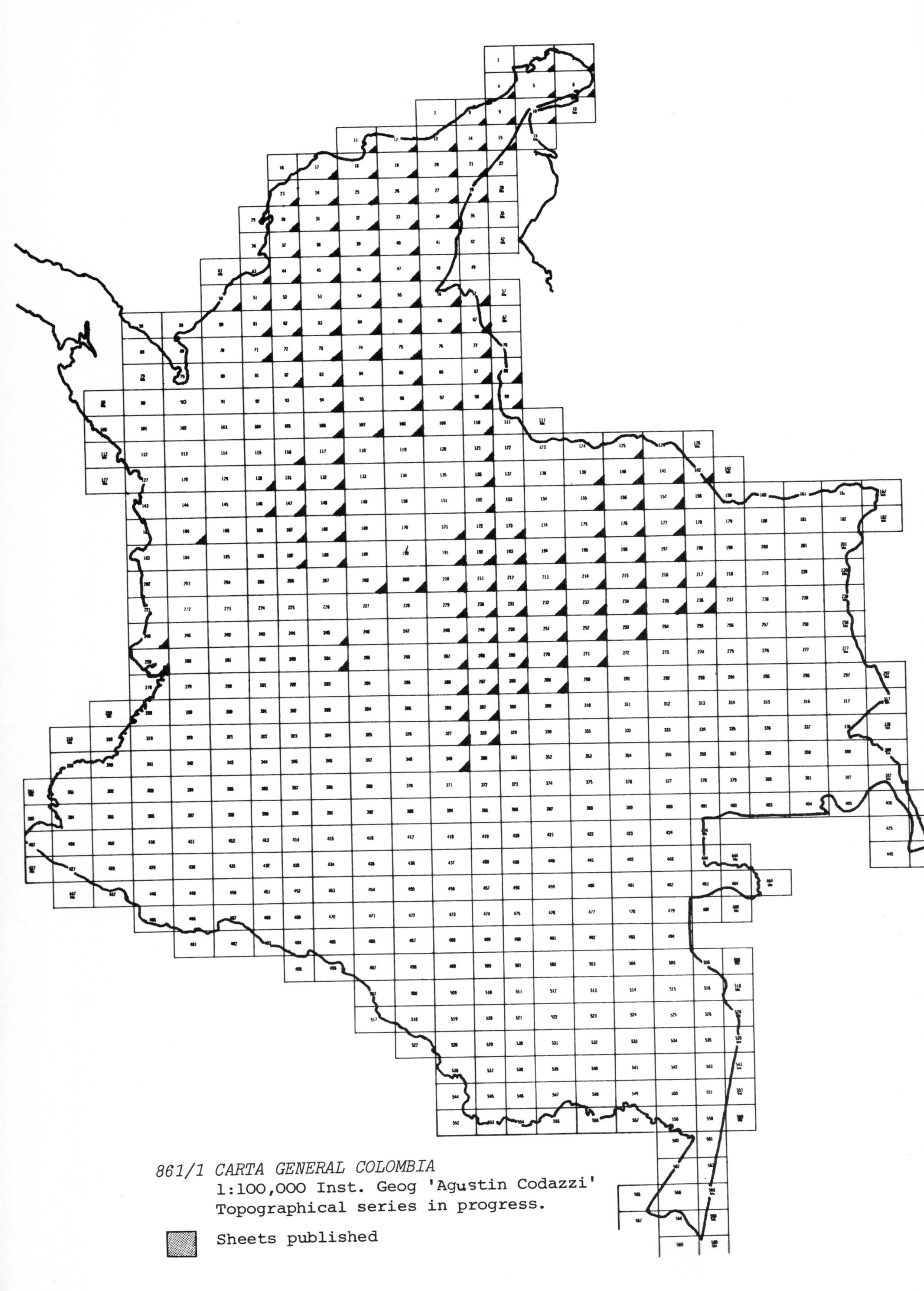
861/1 CARTA GENERAL COLOMBIA
1:100,000 Inst. Geog 'Agustin Codazzi'
Topographical series in progress.
Sheets published

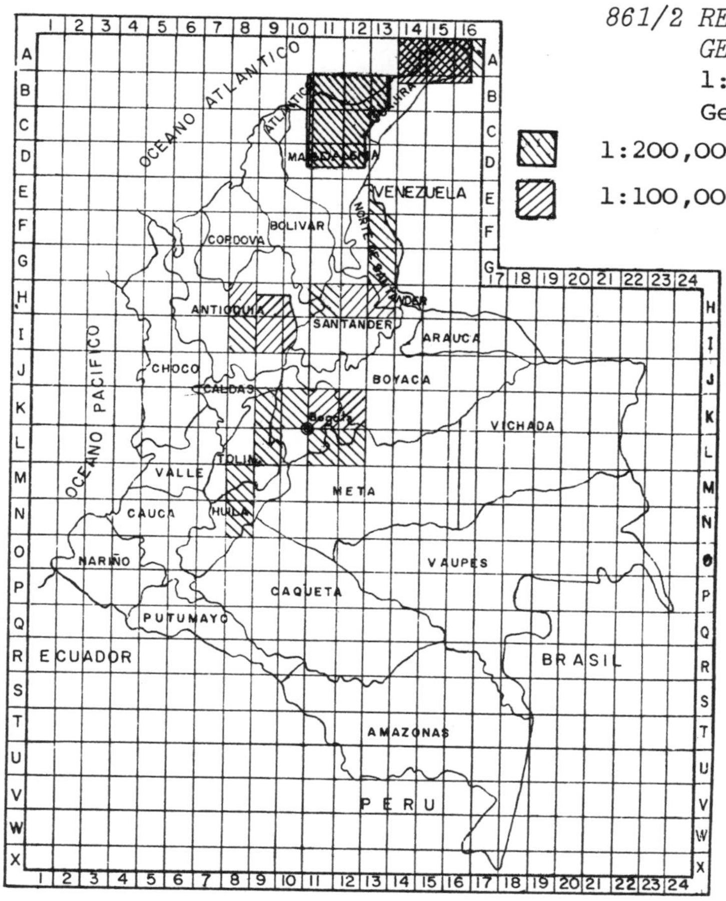

861/2 REPUBLICA DE COLOMBIA: GEOLOGIA DE CUADRANGULO

1:200,000 1:100,000 Serv. Geol Nat.

Geological series in progress

1:200,000 Sheets published

1:100,000 Sheets published

866/1 CARTA TOPOGRAFICA DEL ECUADOR

1:100,000 ; 1:50,000 IGM

Topographical series

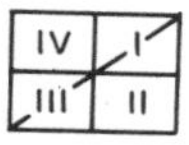

1:100,000 series J621

Sheets published

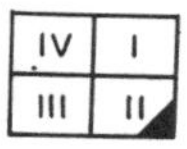

1:50,000 series J721

Sheets published

CARTA TOPOGRAFICA DEL ECUADOR

1:25,000 IGM

Topographical series

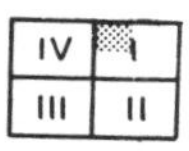

Sheets published.

Sheet numbering example :

QUITO-WEST

,000 Ñ III A 4b

,000 Ñ III A 4

00,000 Ñ III A

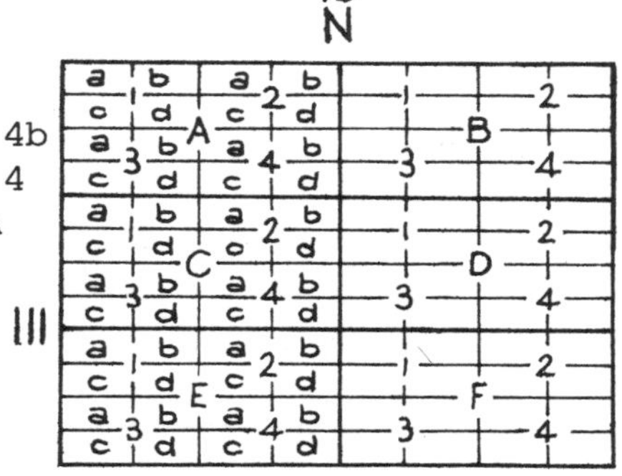

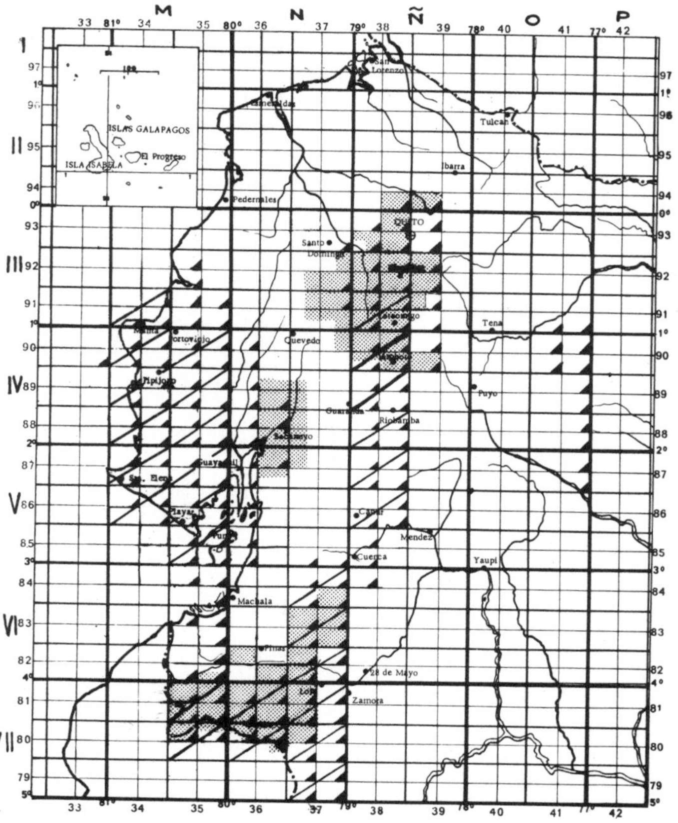

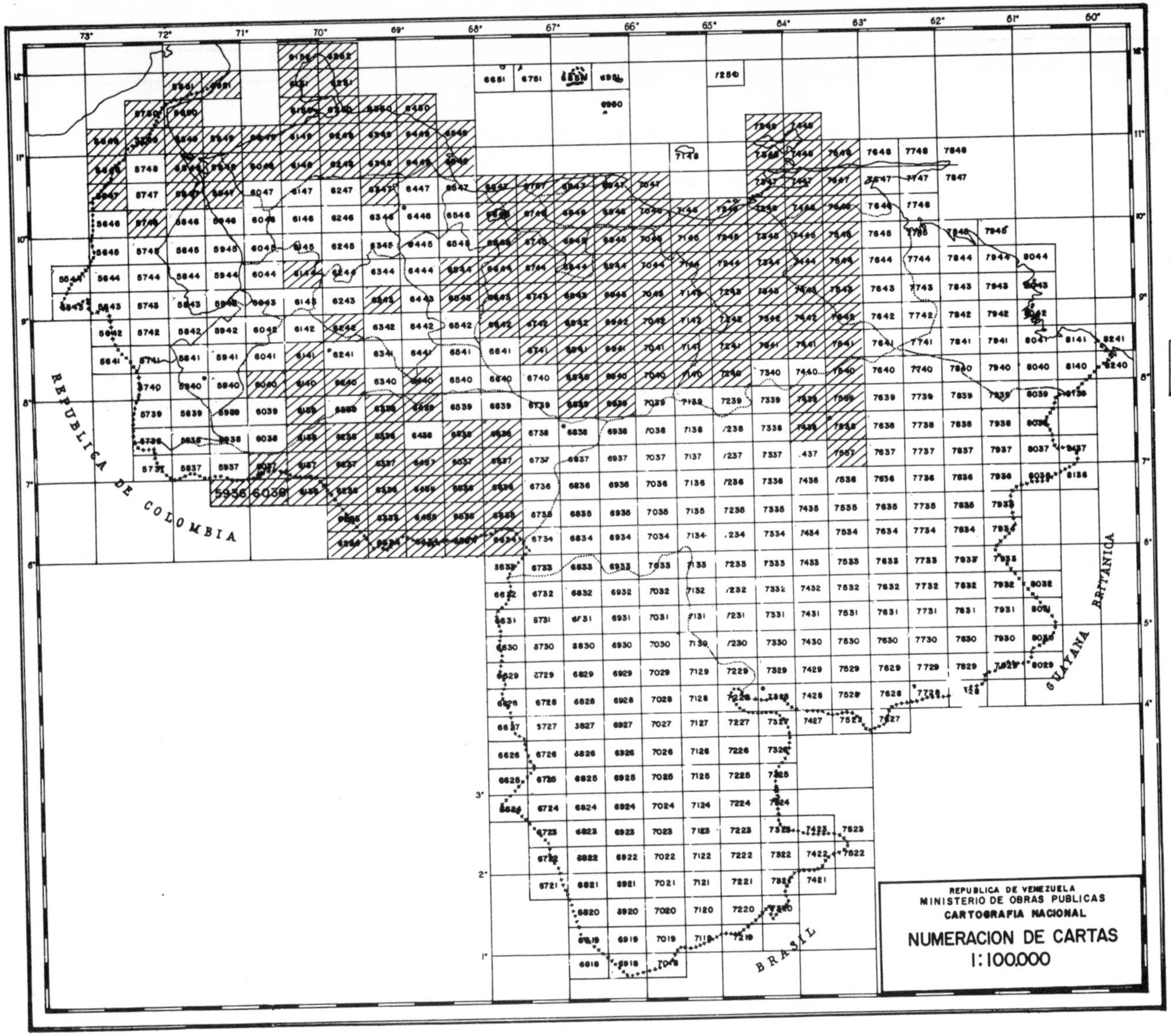

REPUBLICA DE VENEZUELA
MINISTERIO DE OBRAS PUBLICAS
CARTOGRAFIA NACIONAL
NUMERACION DE CARTAS
1:100,000

87/1 VENEZUELA: CARTAS GEOGRAFICAS NACIONAL
1:100,000 Dir. Cart. Nacional
Topographical series in progress

 Sheets published

881/2 GEOLOGICAL ATLAS OF GUYANA
1:200,000 Geol. Survey Dept.

Quarter sheets published denoted by name and NWSW, NE.SE

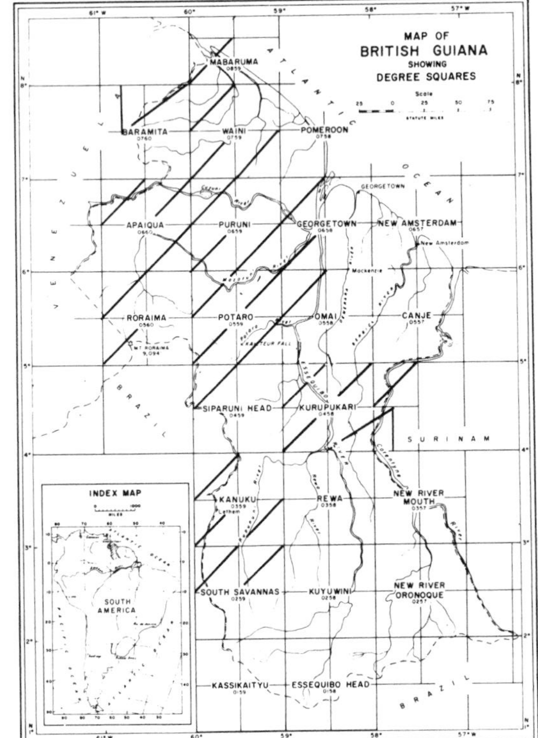

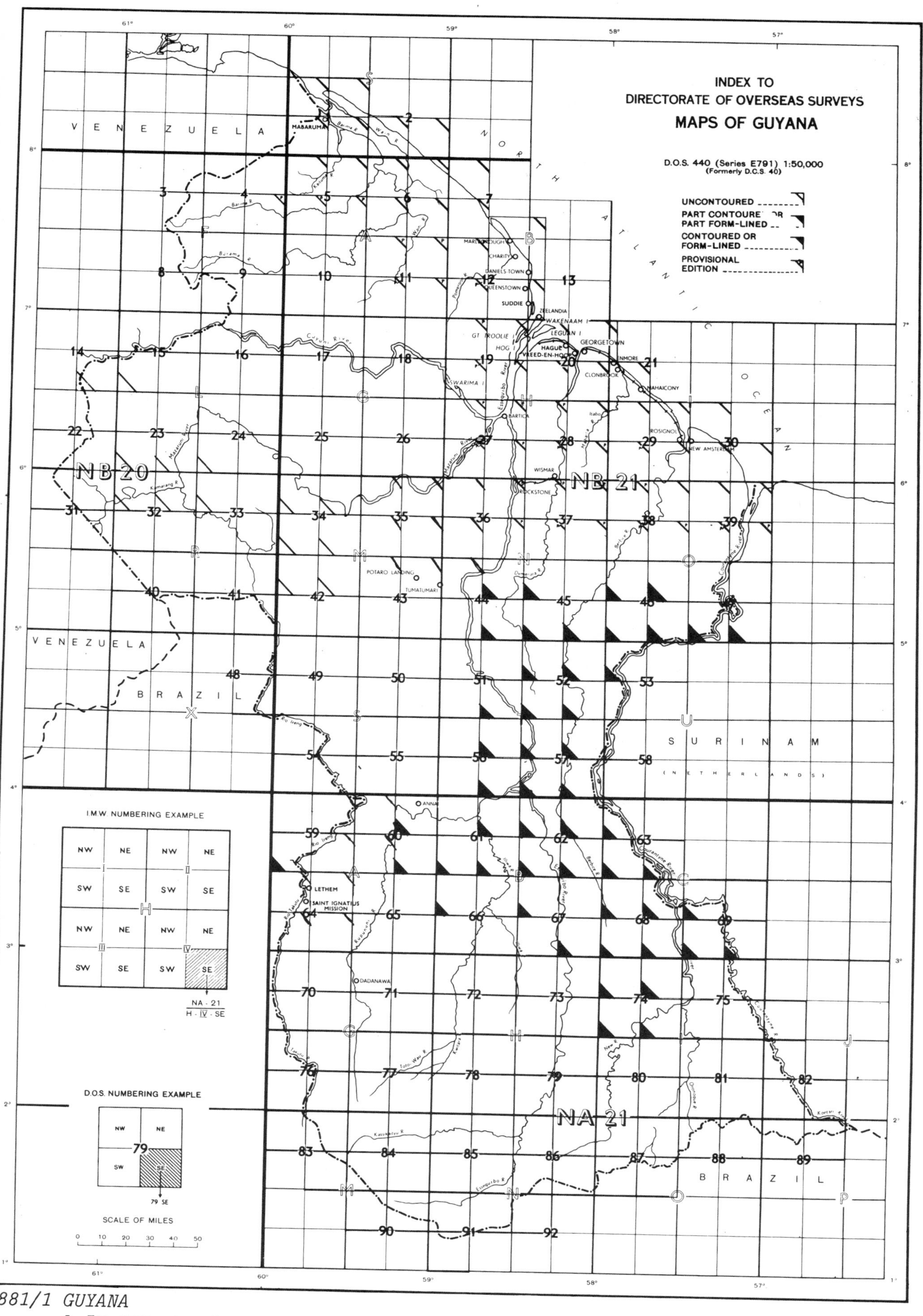

881/1 GUYANA

1:50,000 Lands Dept. Georgetown

Local series published in addition to DOS editions

Planimetric series

Topographical series

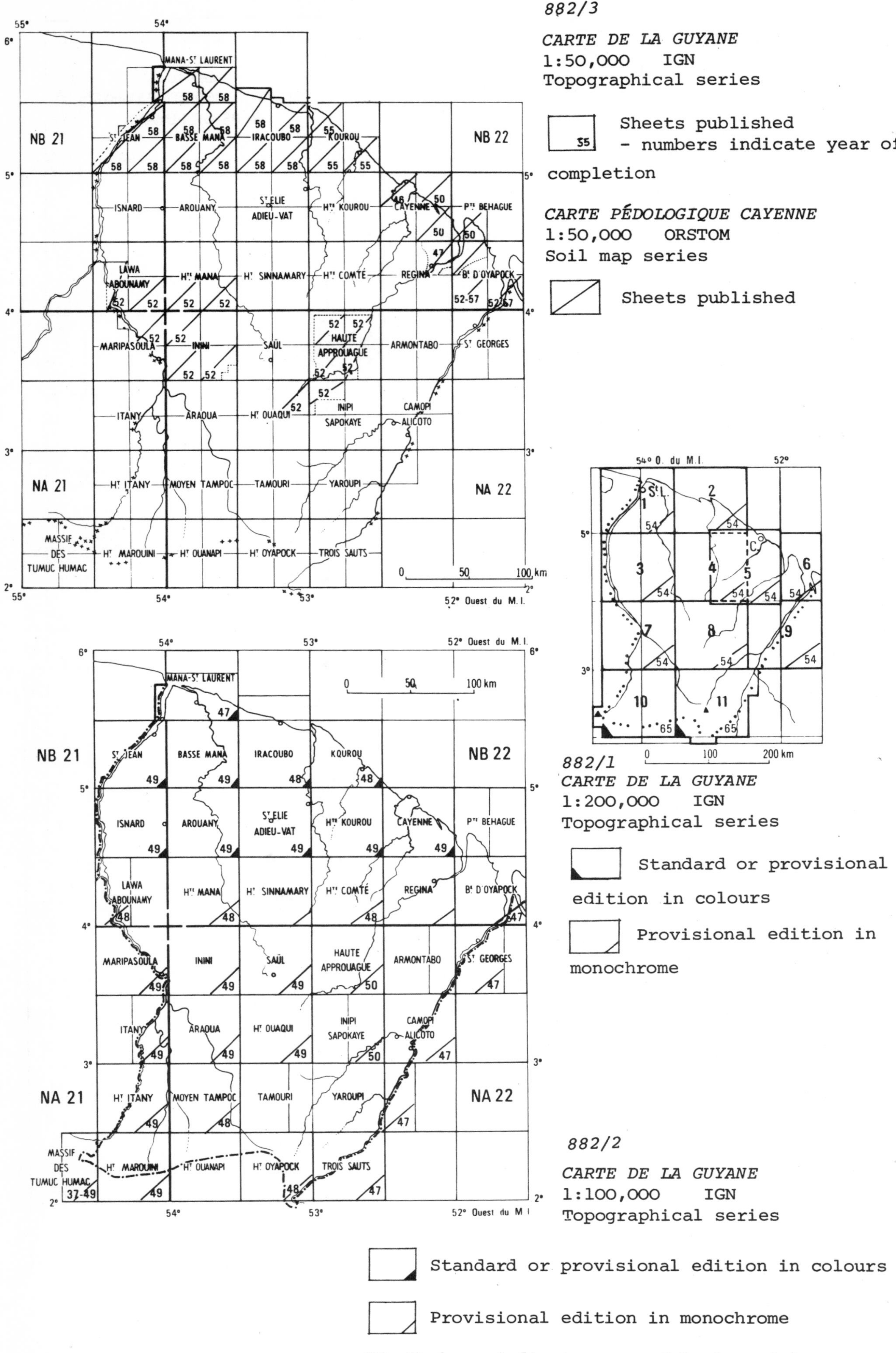

882/3
CARTE DE LA GUYANE
1:50,000 IGN
Topographical series
Sheets published - numbers indicate year of completion
CARTE PÉDOLOGIQUE CAYENNE
1:50,000 ORSTOM
Soil map series
Sheets published
882/1
CARTE DE LA GUYANE
1:200,000 IGN
Topographical series
Standard or provisional edition in colours
Provisional edition in monochrome
882/2
CARTE DE LA GUYANE
1:100,000 IGN
Topographical series
Standard or provisional edition in colours
Provisional edition in monochrome
NB Numbers indicate year of last revision
NB 21
NB 22
NA 21
NA 22
MANA-ST LAURENT
ST JEAN
BASSE MANA
IRACOUBO
KOUROU
ISNARD
AROUANY
ST ELIE ADIEU-VAT
HTS KOUROU
CAYENNE
PTE BEHAGUE
LAWA ABOUNAMY
HTS MANA
HT SINNAMARY
HT COMTÉ
REGINA
BT D'OYAPOCK
MARIPASOULA
ININI
SAÜL
HAUTE APPROUAGUE
ARMONTABO
ST GEORGES
ITANY
ARAOUA
HT OUAQUI
INIPI SAPOKAYE
CAMOPI ALICOTO
HT ITANY
MOYEN TAMPOC
TAMOURI
YAROUPI
MASSIF DES TUMUC HUMAC
HT MAROUINI
HT OUANAPI
HT OYAPOCK
TROIS SAUTS
52° Ouest du M.I.
54° O. du M.I.

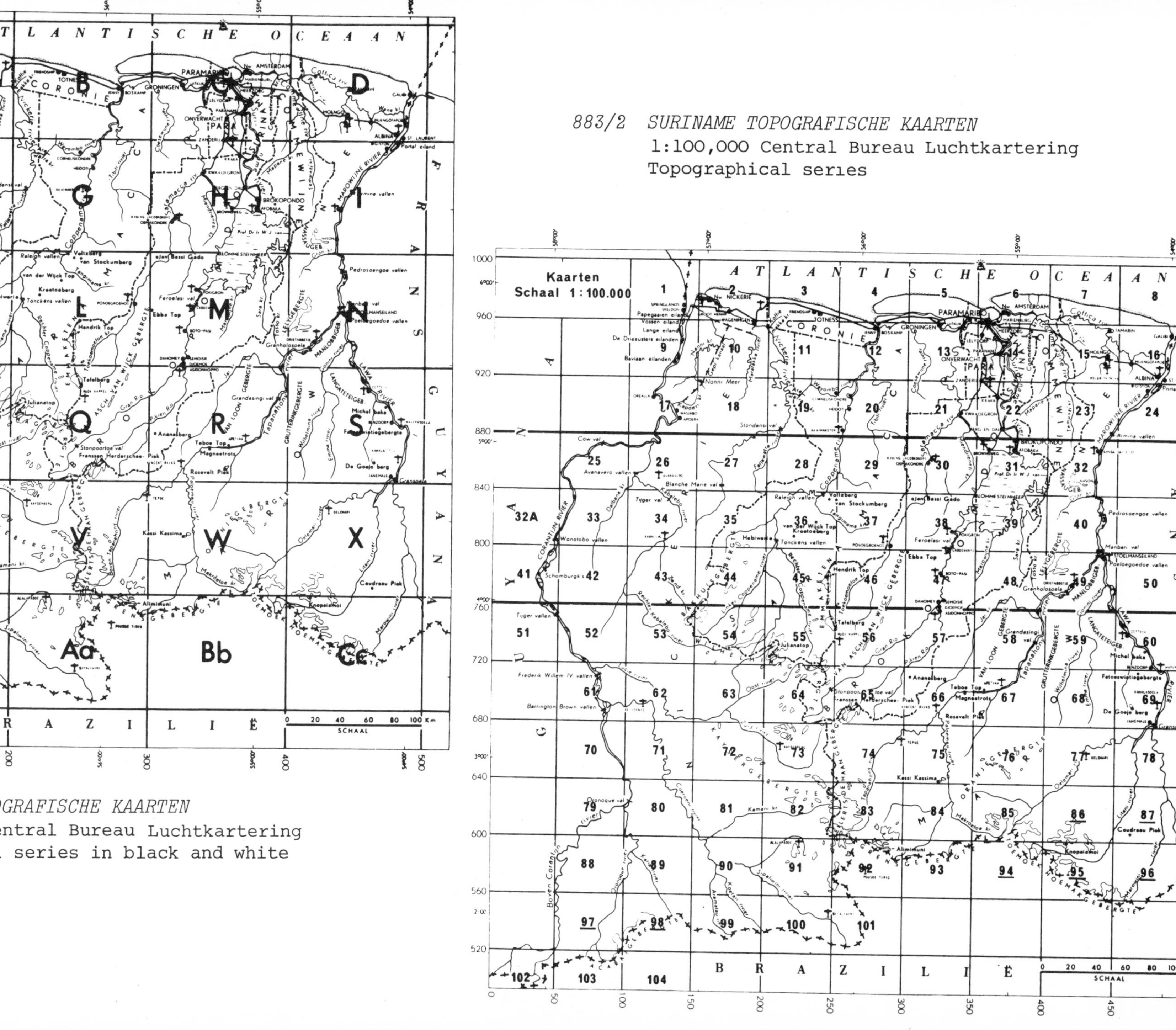

883/2 *SURINAME TOPOGRAFISCHE KAARTEN*
1:100,000 Central Bureau Luchtkartering
Topographical series

883/1 *SURINAME TOPOGRAFISCHE KAARTEN*
1:200,000 Central Bureau Luchtkartering
Topographical series in black and white

883/3 SURINAME

1:40,000 Central Bureau Luchtkartering

Topographical series in progress

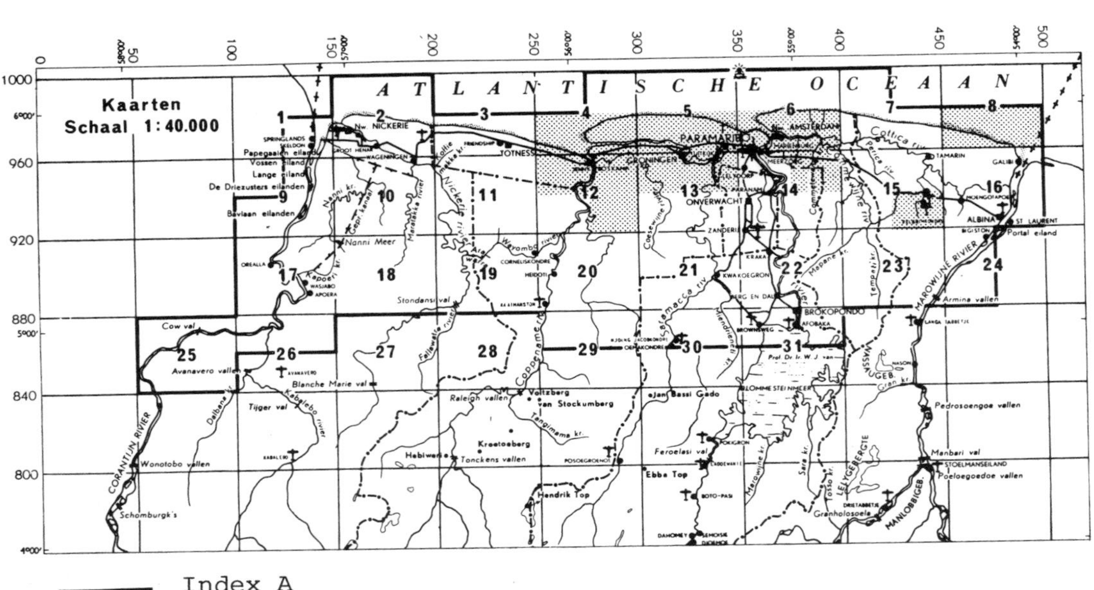

Index A
Uncontoured series
maps in colour edition

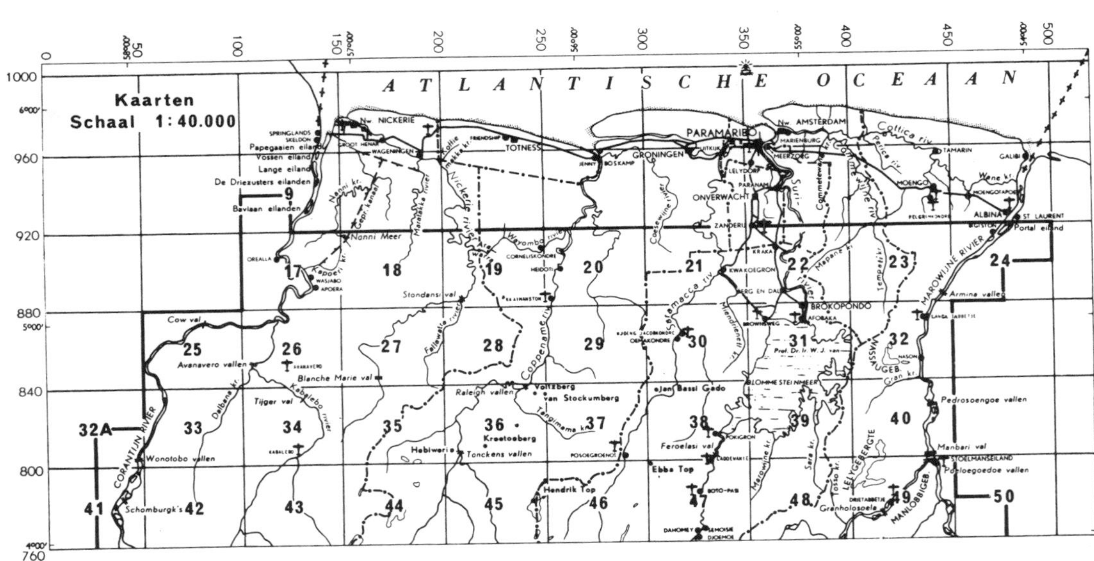

Index B
Contoured series

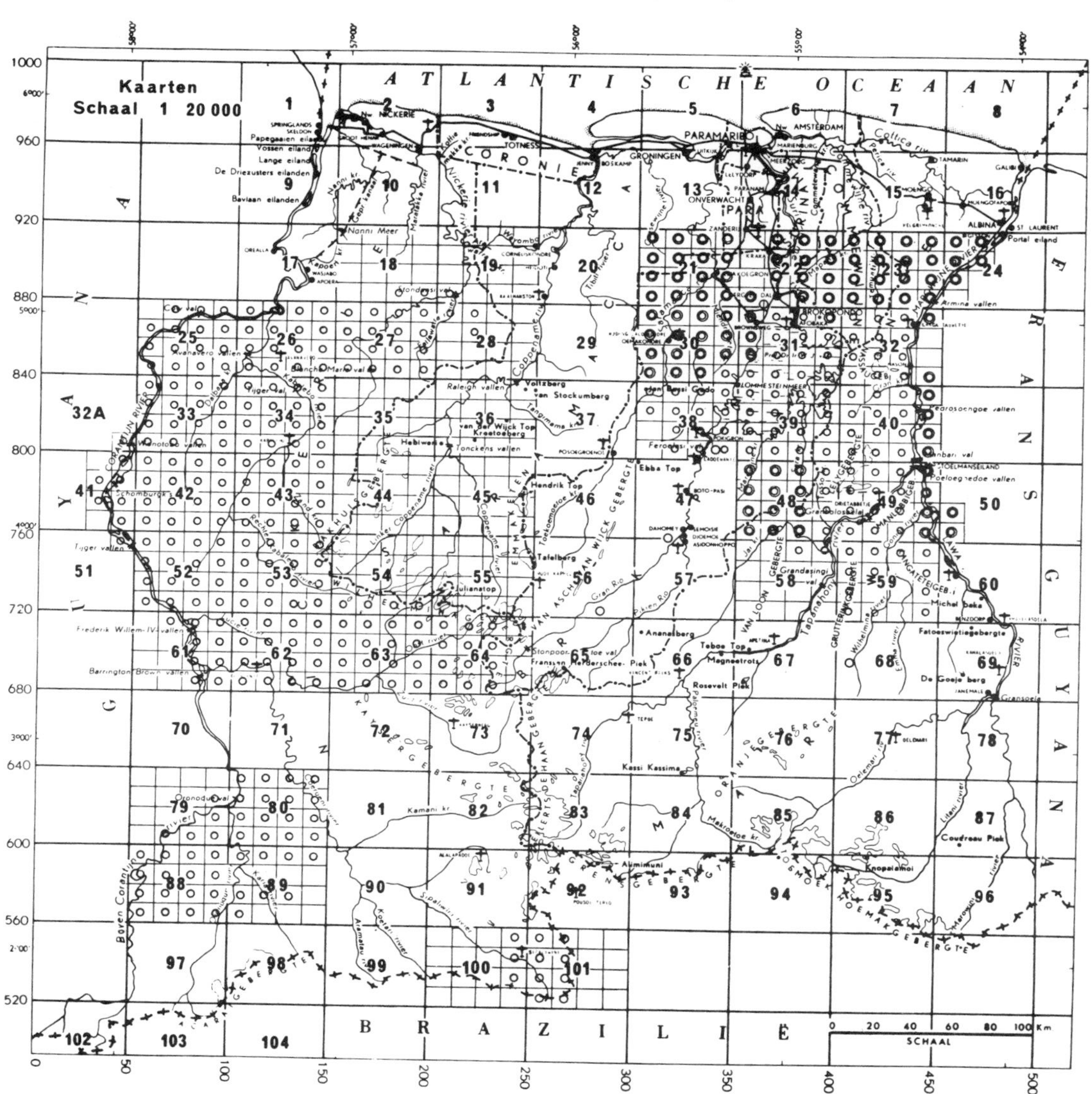

883/4 SURINAME HOOGTELINIJMEN KAARTEN
1:20,000 Central Bureau Luchtkartering
Topographical series in progress, contoured

◎ Blackprint edition

○ Phototype edition

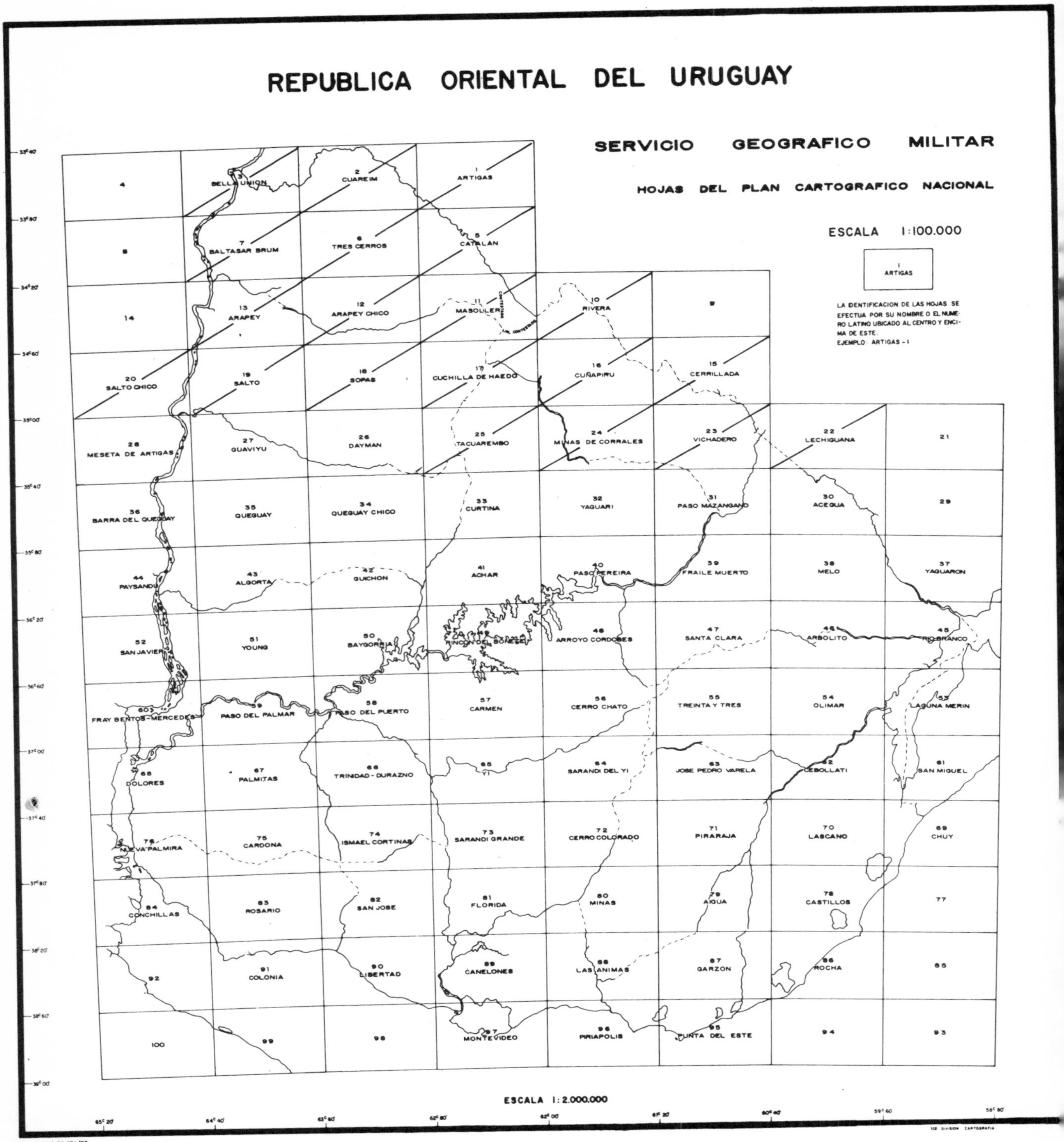

REPUBLICA ORIENTAL DEL URUGUAY

SERVICIO GEOGRAFICO MILITAR

HOJAS DEL PLAN CARTOGRAFICO NACIONAL

ESCALA 1:100.000

1
ARTIGAS

LA IDENTIFICACION DE LAS HOJAS SE EFECTUA POR SU NOMBRE O EL NUMERO LATINO UBICADO AL CENTRO Y ENCIMA DE ESTE.
EJEMPLO: ARTIGAS - I

4
3 BELLA UNION
2 CUAREIM
1 ARTIGAS
8
7 BALTASAR BRUM
6 TRES CERROS
5 CATALAN
14
13 ARAPEY
12 ARAPEY CHICO
11 MASOLLER
10 RIVERA
9
20 SALTO CHICO
19 SALTO
18 SOPAS
17 CUCHILLA DE HAEDO
16 CUÑAPIRU
15 CERRILLADA
28 MESETA DE ARTIGAS
27 GUAVIYU
26 DAYMAN
25 TACUAREMBO
24 MINAS DE CORRALES
23 VICHADERO
22 LECHIGUANA
21
36 BARRA DEL QUEGUAY
35 QUEGUAY
34 QUEGUAY CHICO
33 CURTINA
32 YAGUARI
31 PASO MAZANGANO
30 ACEGUA
29
44 PAYSANDU
43 ALGORTA
42 GUICHON
41 ACHAR
40 PASO PEREIRA
39 FRAILE MUERTO
38 MELO
37 YAGUARON
52 SAN JAVIER
51 YOUNG
50 BAYGORRIA
49 RINCON DEL BONETE
48 ARROYO CORDOBES
47 SANTA CLARA
46 ARBOLITO
45 RIO BRANCO
60 FRAY BENTOS-MERCEDES
59 PASO DEL PALMAR
58 PASO DEL PUERTO
57 CARMEN
56 CERRO CHATO
55 TREINTA Y TRES
54 OLIMAR
53 LAGUNA MERIN
68 DOLORES
67 PALMITAS
66 TRINIDAD - DURAZNO
65 YI
64 SARANDI DEL YI
63 JOSE PEDRO VARELA
62 CEBOLLATI
61 SAN MIGUEL
76 NUEVA PALMIRA
75 CARDONA
74 ISMAEL CORTINAS
73 SARANDI GRANDE
72 CERRO COLORADO
71 PIRARAJA
70 LASCANO
69 CHUY
84 CONCHILLAS
83 ROSARIO
82 SAN JOSE
81 FLORIDA
80 MINAS
79 AIGUA
78 CASTILLOS
77
92
91 COLONIA
90 LIBERTAD
89 CANELONES
88 LAS ANIMAS
87 GARZON
86 ROCHA
85
100
99
98
97 MONTEVIDEO
96 PIRIAPOLIS
95 PUNTA DEL ESTE
94
93

ESCALA 1:2.000.000

Dep. Legal 30.571/75

899/1 *CARTAS TOPOGRAFICAS URUGUAY*
1:100,000 SGM
Topographical series

Sheets published

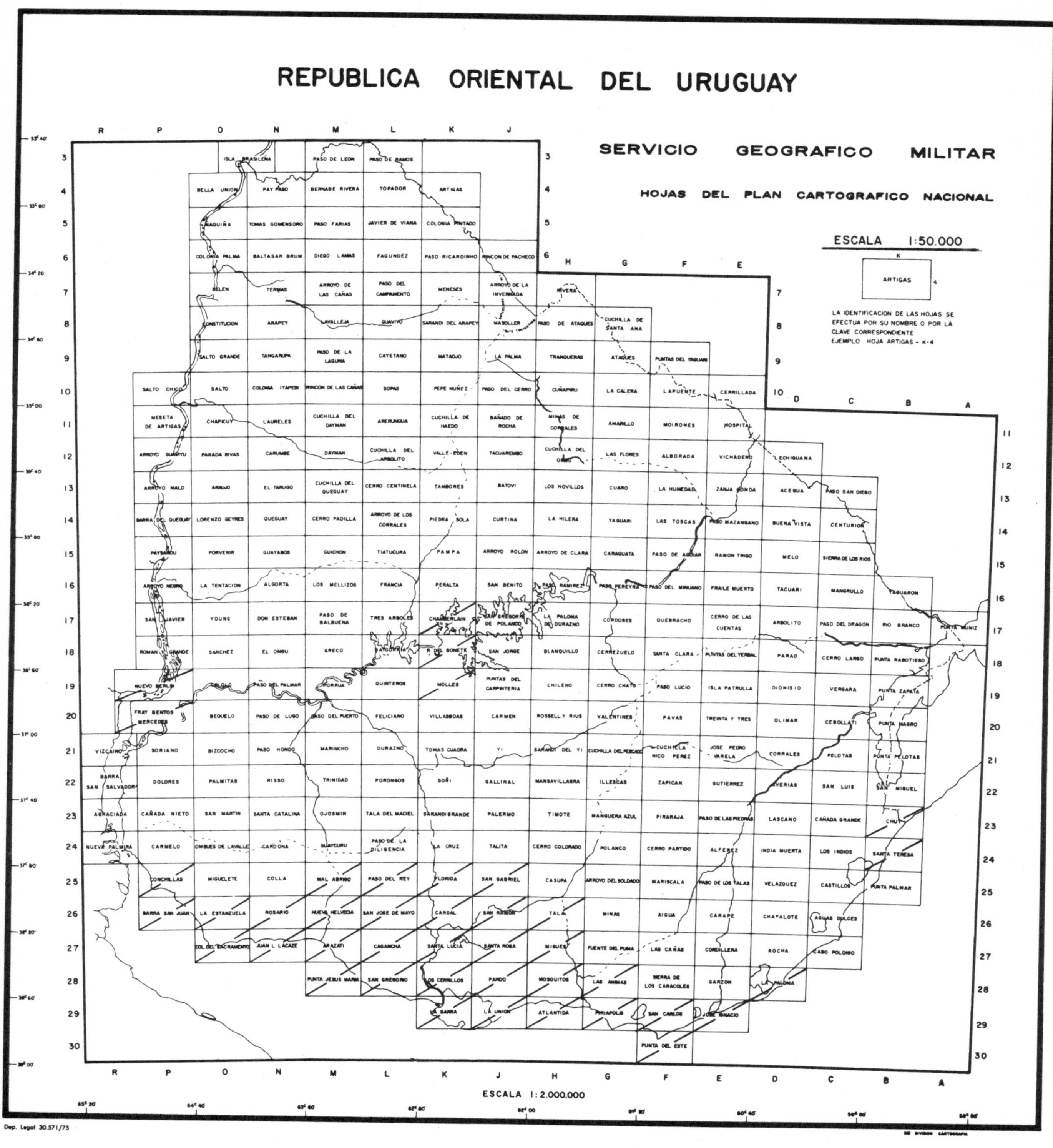

899/2 CARTAS TOPOGRAFICAS URUGUAY
1:50,000 SGM
Topographical series

Sheets published

Australia and Oceania

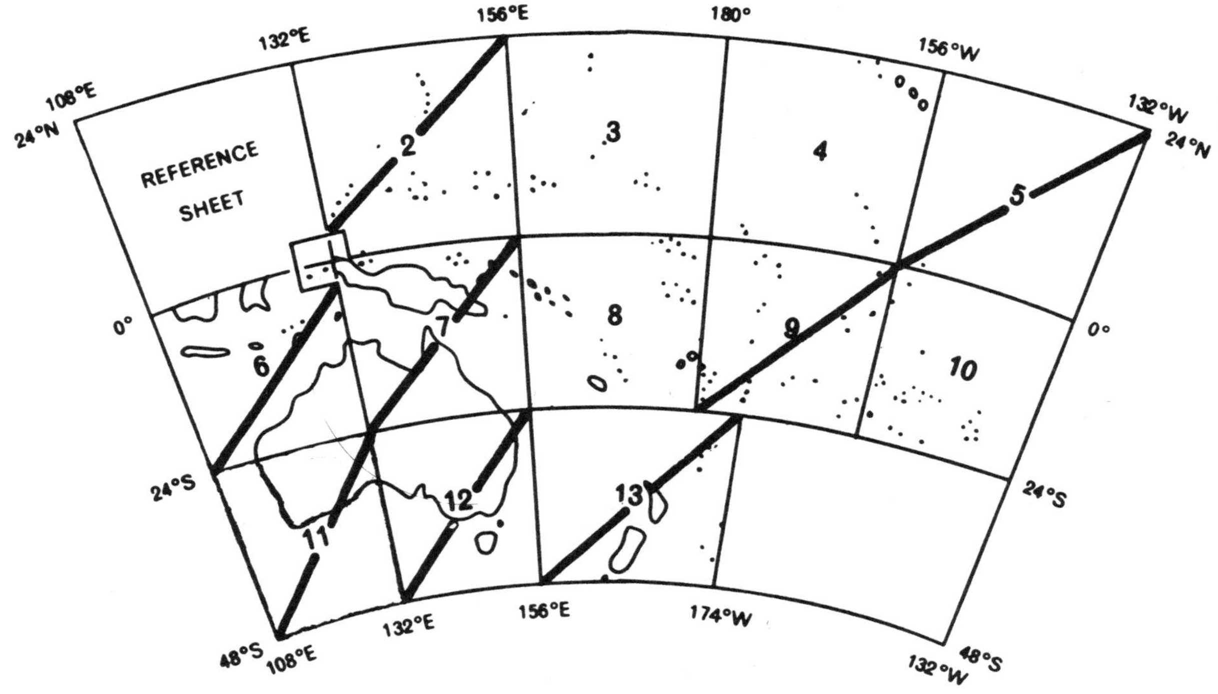

9/1 *INTERNATIONAL GEOLOGICAL MAP OF THE WORLD - AUSTRALIA AND OCEANIA*
1:5,000,000 DND
Commission for the Geological Map of the World
Coloured geological series in progress

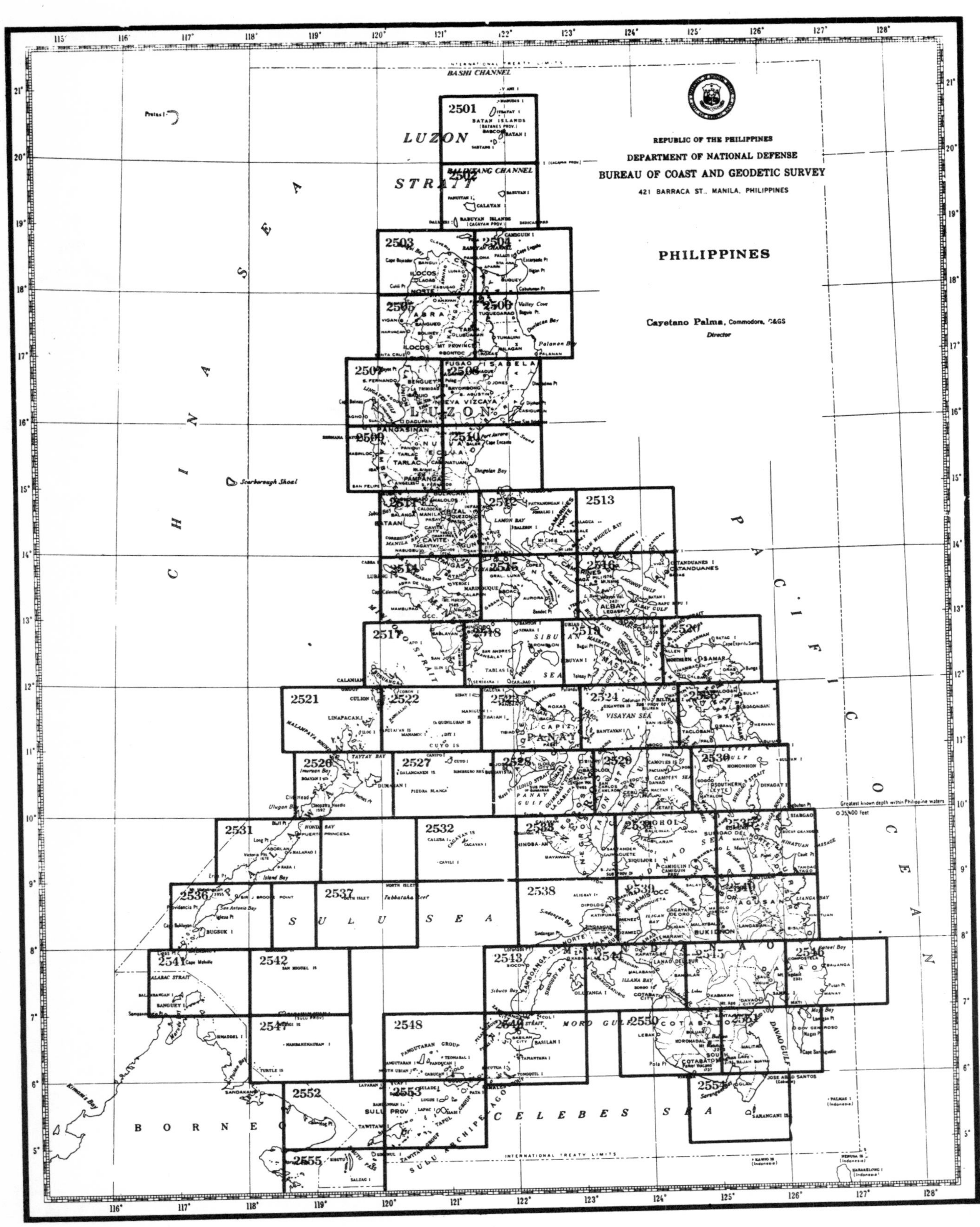

914/1 PHILIPPINES
1:250,000 AMS-Philippine Bureau
of Coast and Geodetic Survey
Topographical series in 55 sheets

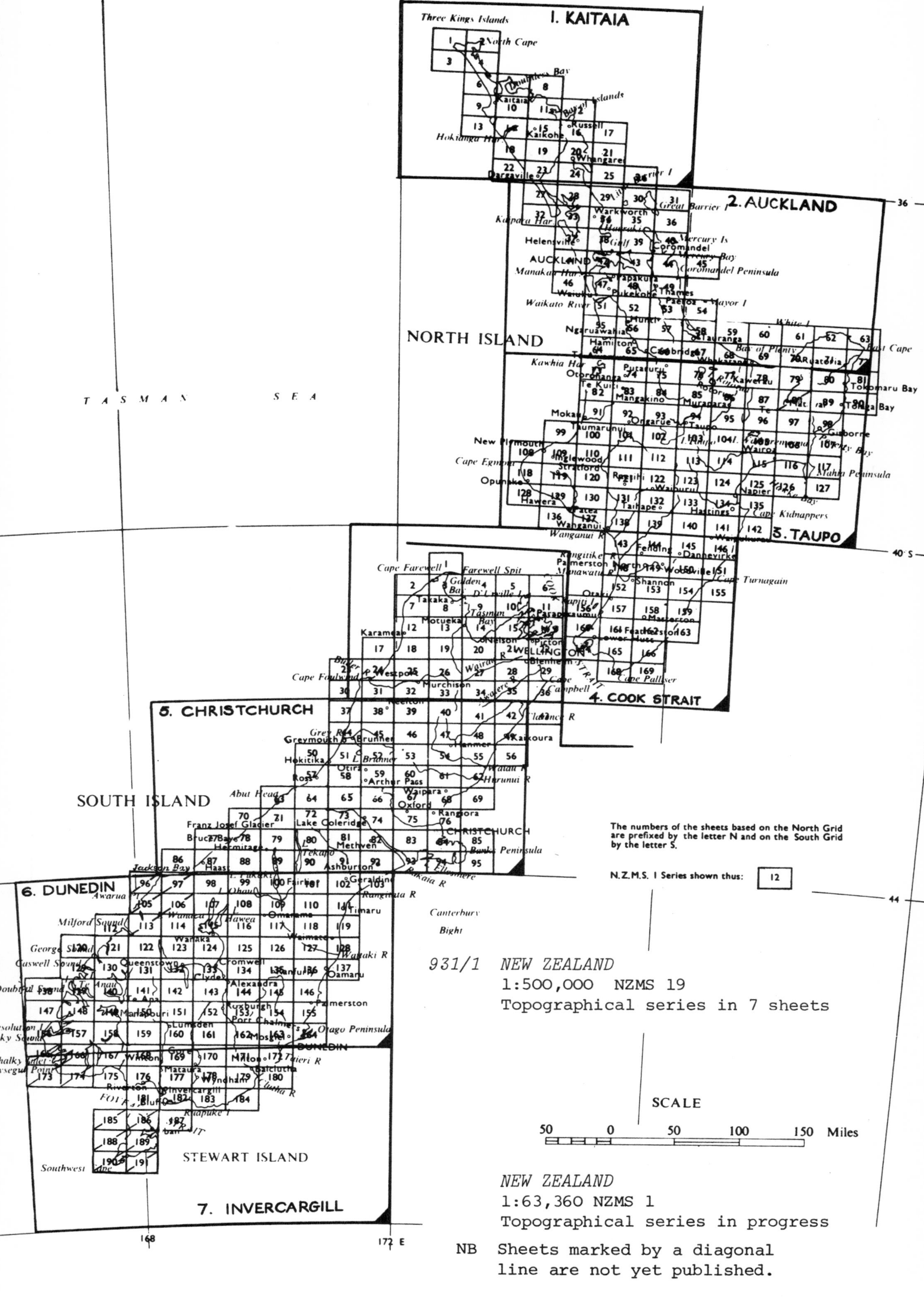

931/1 *NEW ZEALAND*
1:500,000 NZMS 19
Topographical series in 7 sheets

NEW ZEALAND
1:63,360 NZMS 1
Topographical series in progress

NB Sheets marked by a diagonal line are not yet published.

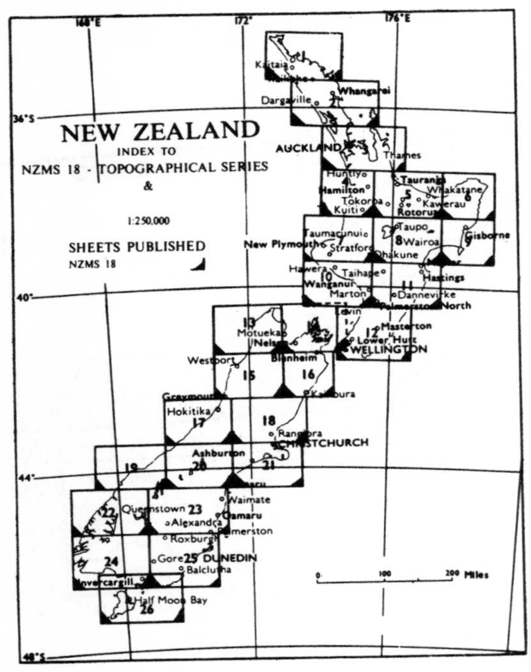

931/2 NEW ZEALAND
1:250,000 NZMS 18
Topographical series in 26 sheets.

 Sheets published

NEW ZEALAND TERRITORIAL SERIES
1:250,000 NZMS 159 and 159A
Black and White planning series in progress

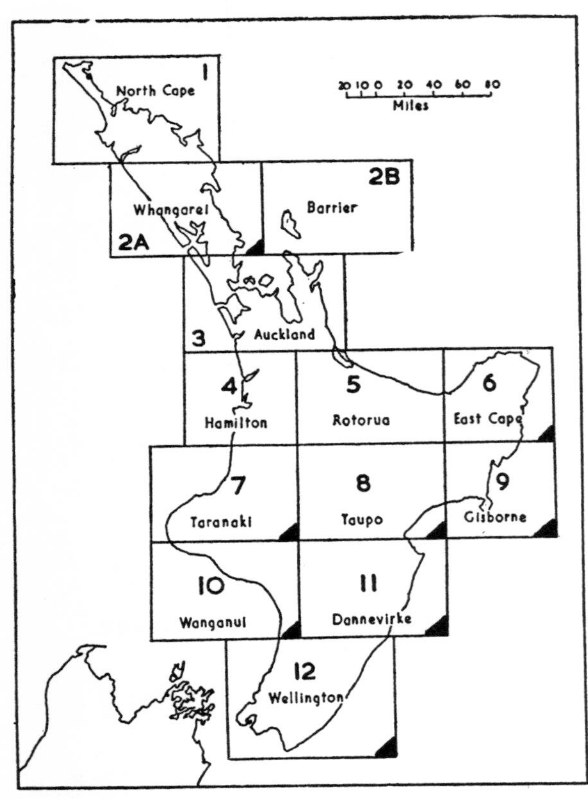

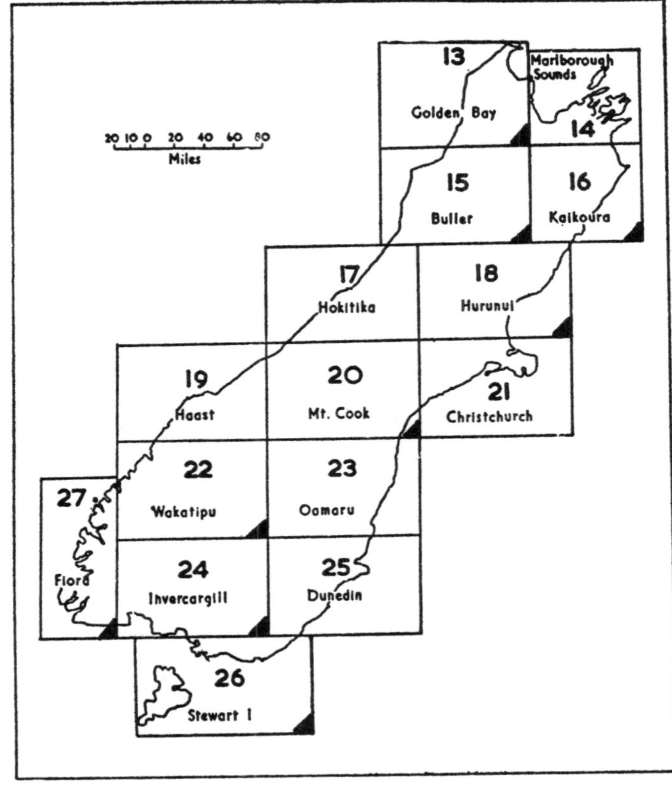

931/4 NEW ZEALAND-GEOLOGICAL SURVEY MAPS
1:250,000 Geological Survey

Coloured geological series each with explanatory text.

Sheets available (remainder out of print).

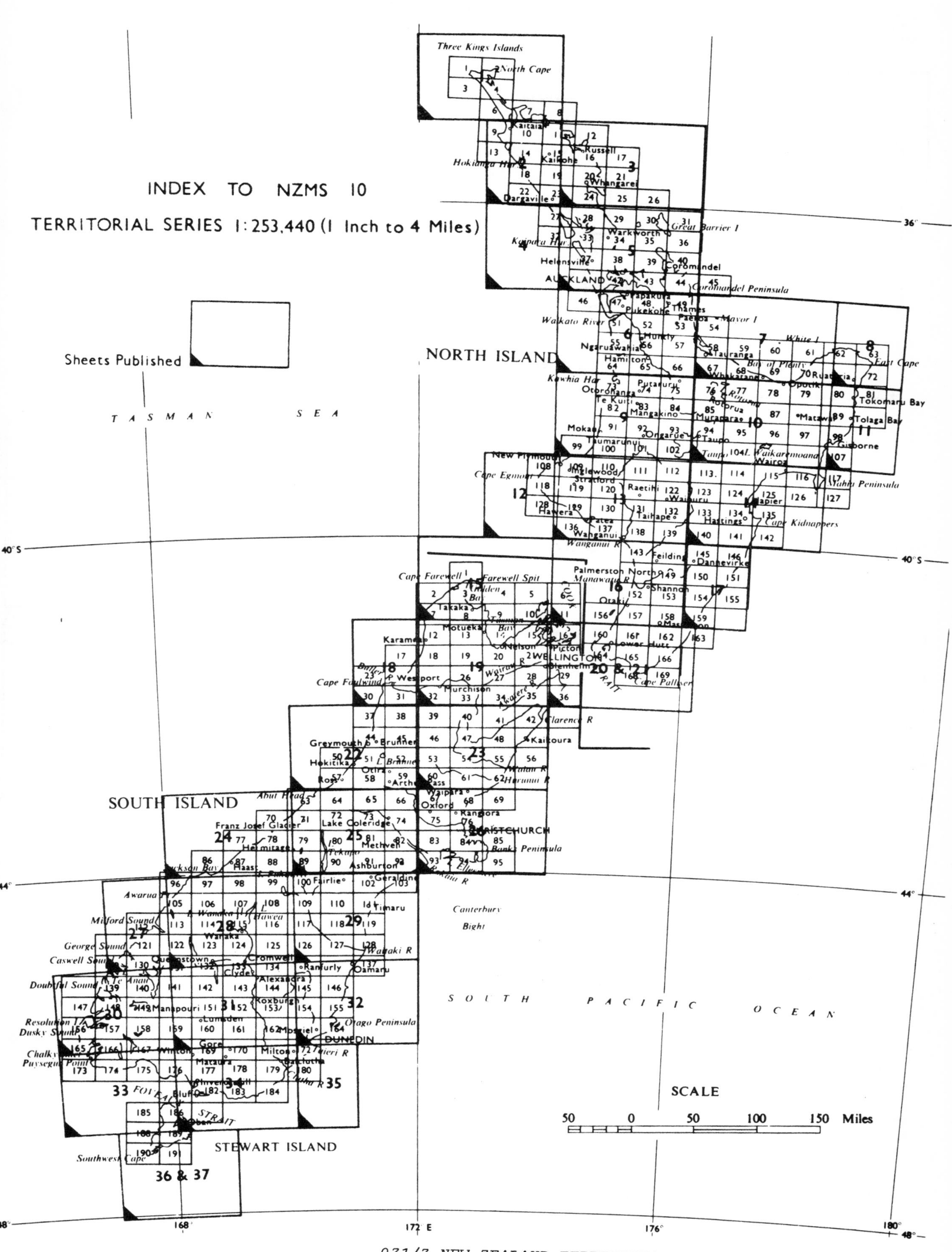

931/3 NEW ZEALAND TERRITORIAL SERIES
1:253 440 NZMS 10 and 10A
Black and White planning series in 35 sheets

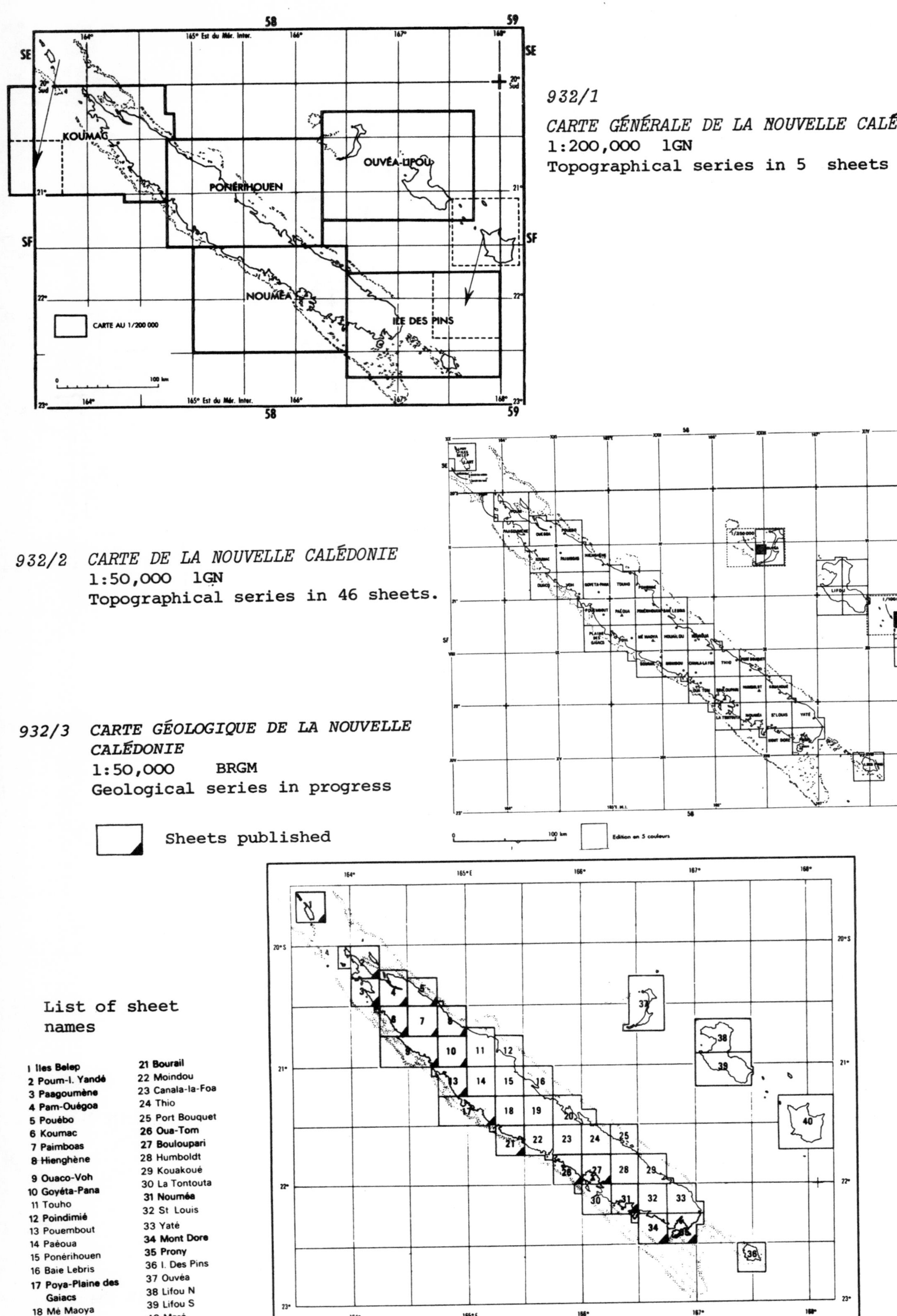

932/1

CARTE GÉNÉRALE DE LA NOUVELLE CALÉDONIE
1:200,000 IGN
Topographical series in 5 sheets

932/2 *CARTE DE LA NOUVELLE CALÉDONIE*
1:50,000 IGN
Topographical series in 46 sheets.

932/3 *CARTE GÉOLOGIQUE DE LA NOUVELLE CALÉDONIE*
1:50,000 BRGM
Geological series in progress

Sheets published

List of sheet names

1 **Iles Belep**
2 **Poum-I. Yandé**
3 **Paagoumène**
4 **Pam-Ouégoa**
5 **Pouébo**
6 **Koumac**
7 **Paimboas**
8 **Hienghène**
9 **Ouaco-Voh**
10 **Goyéta-Pana**
11 Touho
12 **Poindimié**
13 Pouembout
14 Paéoua
15 Ponérihouen
16 Baie Lebris
17 **Poya-Plaine des Gaiacs**
18 Mé Maoya
19 Houaïlou
20 Kouaoua
21 **Bourail**
22 Moindou
23 Canala-la-Foa
24 Thio
25 Port Bouquet
26 **Oua-Tom**
27 **Bouloupari**
28 Humboldt
29 Kouakoué
30 La Tontouta
31 **Nouméa**
32 St Louis
33 Yaté
34 **Mont Dore**
35 **Prony**
36 I. Des Pins
37 Ouvéa
38 Lifou N
39 Lifou S
40 Maré

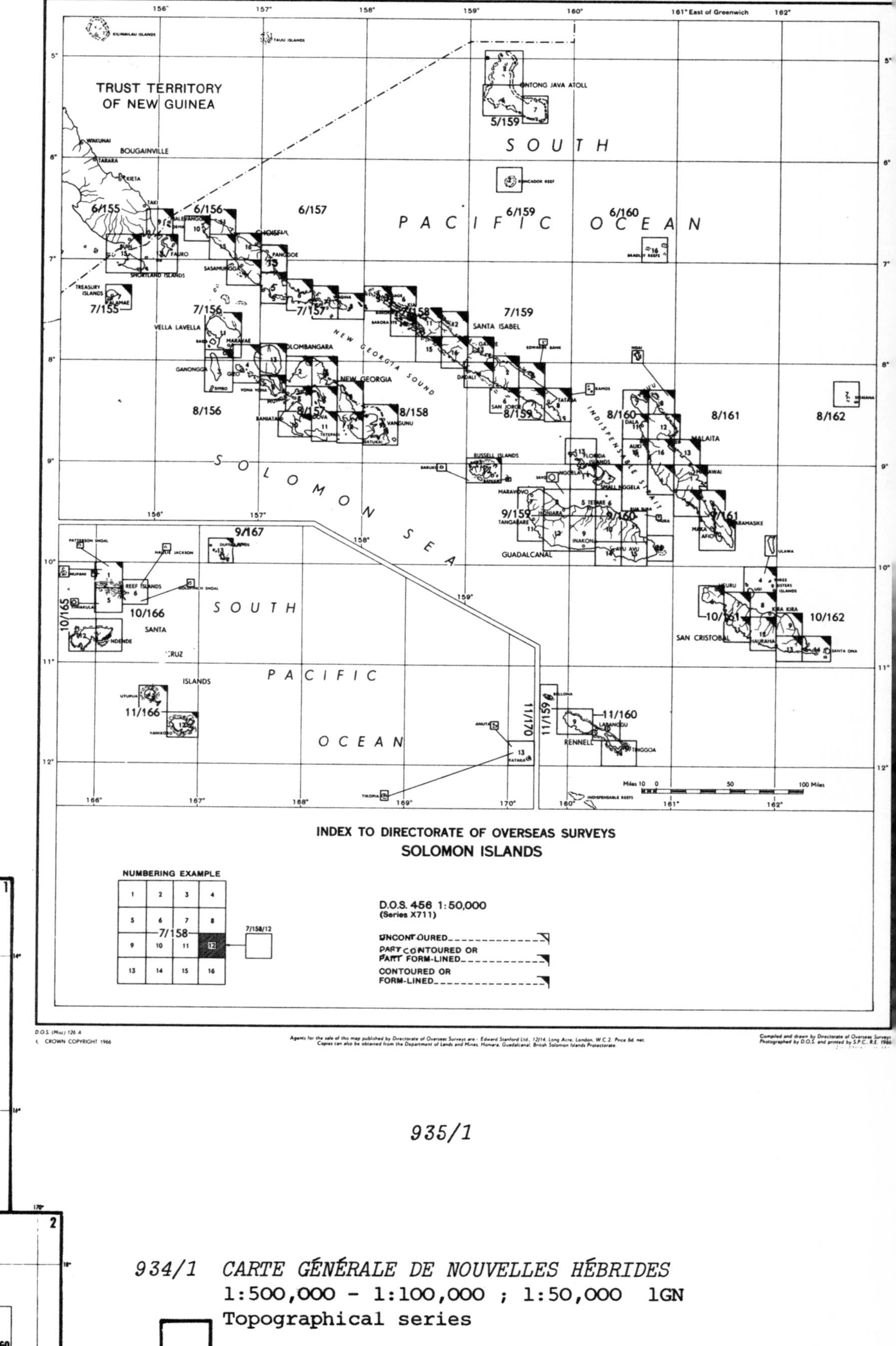

935/1

934/1 CARTE GÉNÉRALE DE NOUVELLES HÉBRIDES

1:500,000 - 1:100,000 ; 1:50,000 IGN

Topographical series

1:500,000 map in 2 sheets

1:100,000 sheets published

1:50,000 sheets published

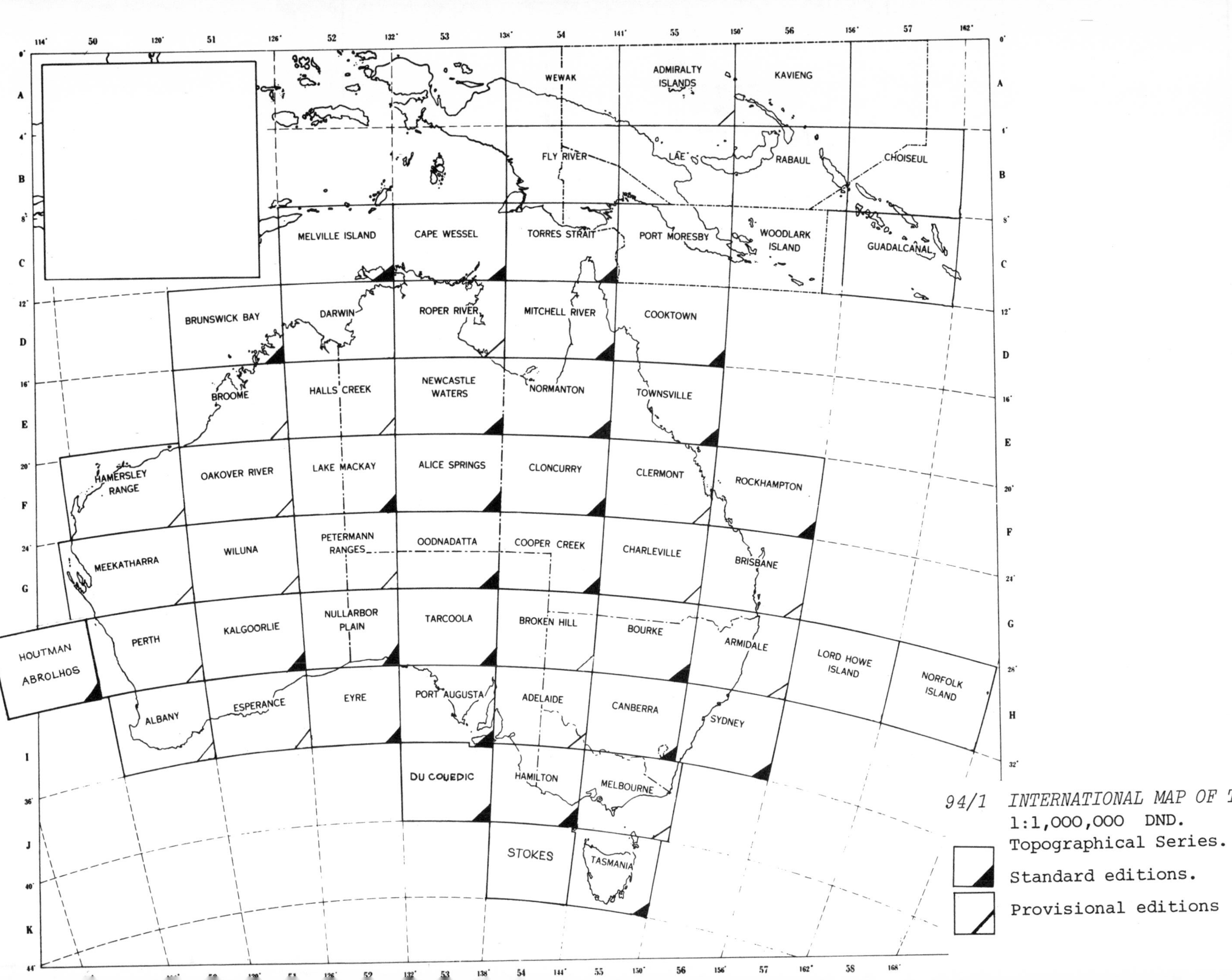
WEWAK
ADMIRALTY ISLANDS
KAVIENG
FLY RIVER
LAE
RABAUL
CHOISEUL
MELVILLE ISLAND
CAPE WESSEL
TORRES STRAIT
PORT MORESBY
WOODLARK ISLAND
GUADALCANAL
BRUNSWICK BAY
DARWIN
ROPER RIVER
MITCHELL RIVER
COOKTOWN
BROOME
HALLS CREEK
NEWCASTLE WATERS
NORMANTON
TOWNSVILLE
HAMERSLEY RANGE
OAKOVER RIVER
LAKE MACKAY
ALICE SPRINGS
CLONCURRY
CLERMONT
ROCKHAMPTON
MEEKATHARRA
WILUNA
PETERMANN RANGES
OODNADATTA
COOPER CREEK
CHARLEVILLE
BRISBANE
HOUTMAN ABROLHOS
PERTH
KALGOORLIE
NULLARBOR PLAIN
TARCOOLA
BROKEN HILL
BOURKE
ARMIDALE
LORD HOWE ISLAND
NORFOLK ISLAND
ALBANY
ESPERANCE
EYRE
PORT AUGUSTA
ADELAIDE
CANBERRA
SYDNEY
DU COUEDIC
HAMILTON
MELBOURNE
STOKES
TASMANIA
94/1
INTERNATIONAL MAP OF THE WORLD
1:1,000,000 DND.
Topographical Series.
Standard editions.
Provisional editions

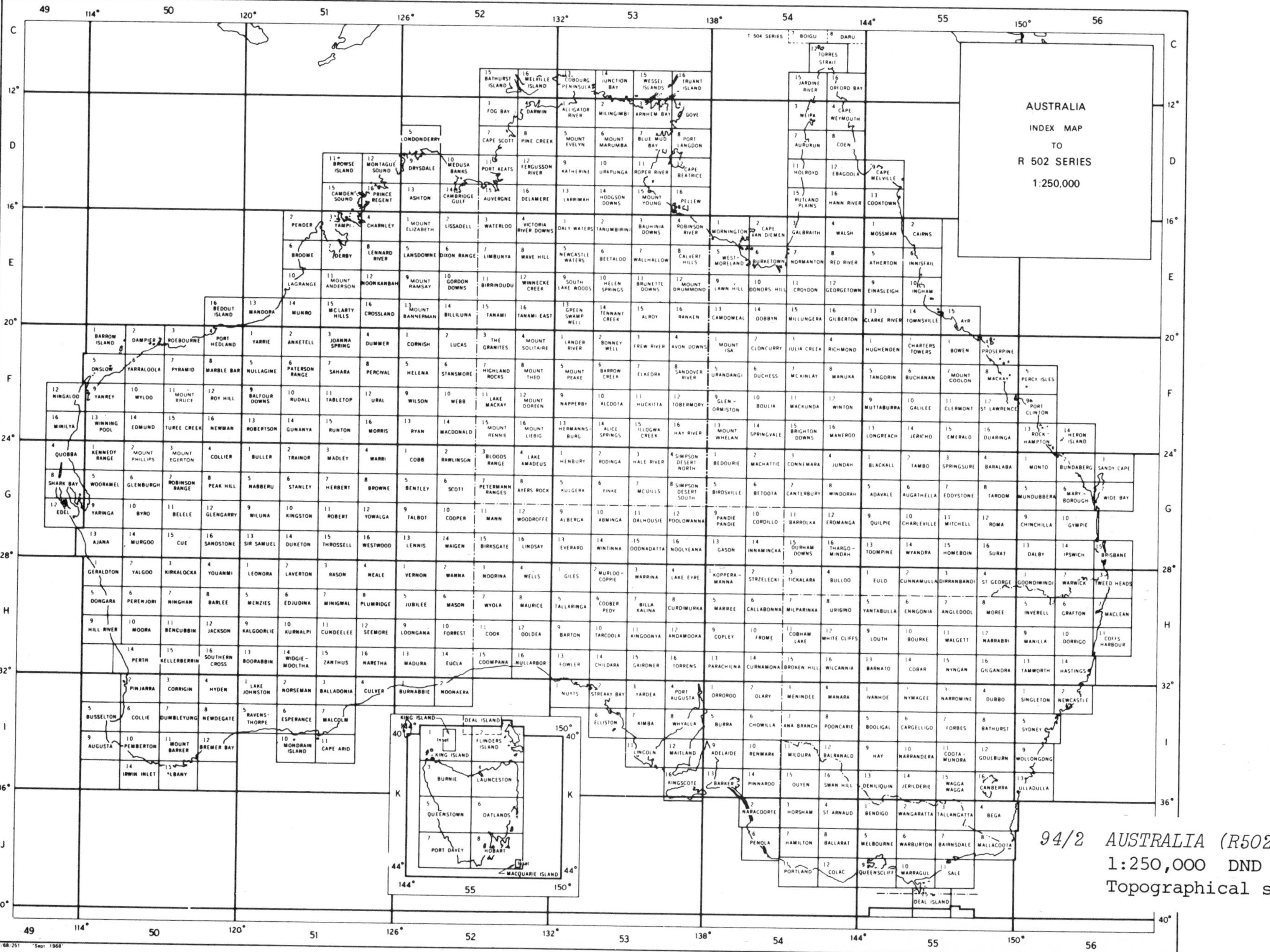

94/2 *AUSTRALIA (R502) SERIES*
1:250,000 DND
Topographical series

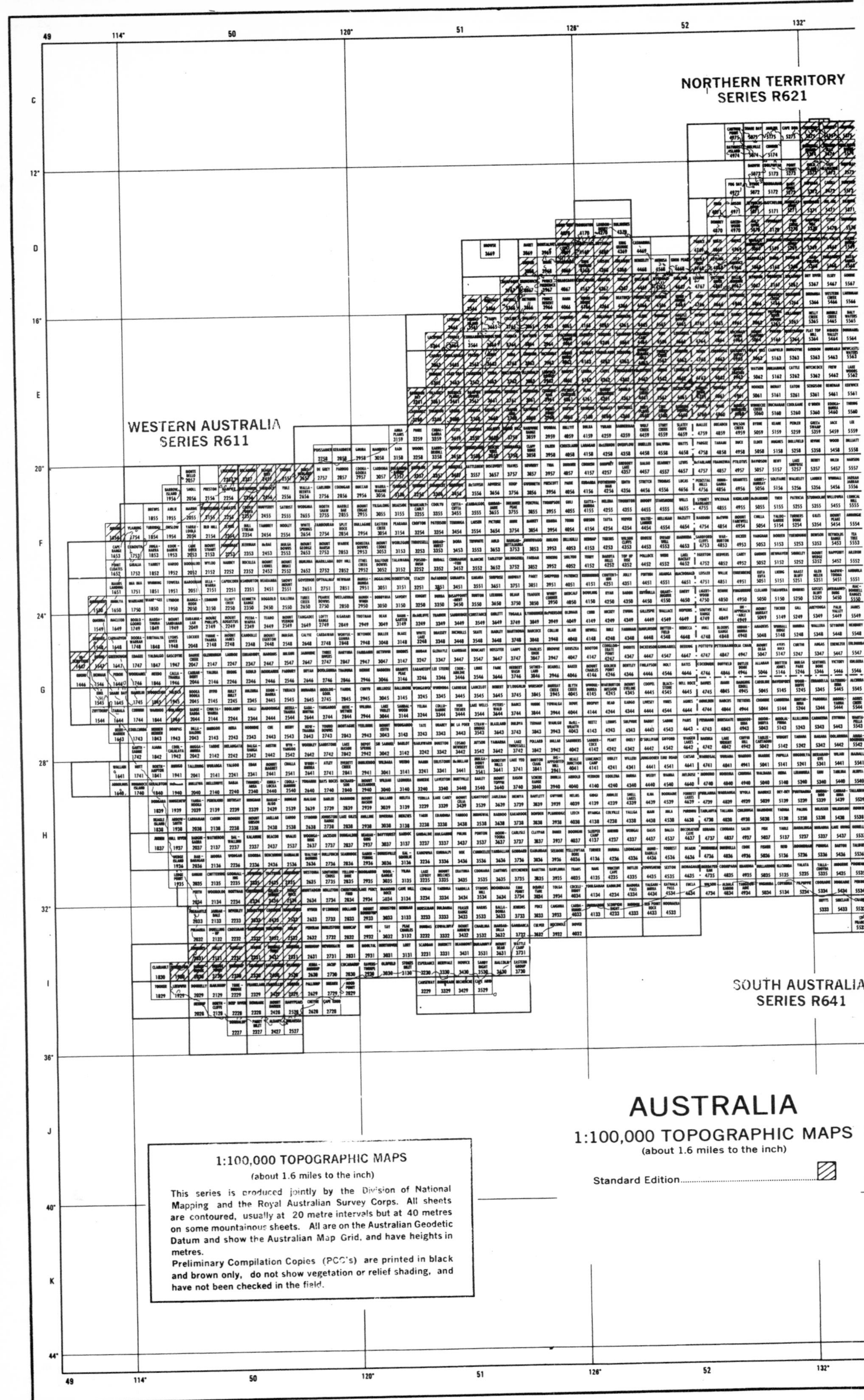

NORTHERN TERRITORY
SERIES R621
WESTERN AUSTRALIA
SERIES R611
SOUTH AUSTRALIA
SERIES R641
AUSTRALIA
1:100,000 TOPOGRAPHIC MAPS
(about 1.6 miles to the inch)
Standard Edition
1:100,000 TOPOGRAPHIC MAPS
(about 1.6 miles to the inch)
This series is produced jointly by the Division of National Mapping and the Royal Australian Survey Corps. All sheets are contoured, usually at 20 metre intervals but at 40 metres on some mountainous sheets. All are on the Australian Geodetic Datum and show the Australian Map Grid, and have heights in metres.
Preliminary Compilation Copies (PCC's) are printed in black and brown only, do not show vegetation or relief shading, and have not been checked in the field.

MP 69 125

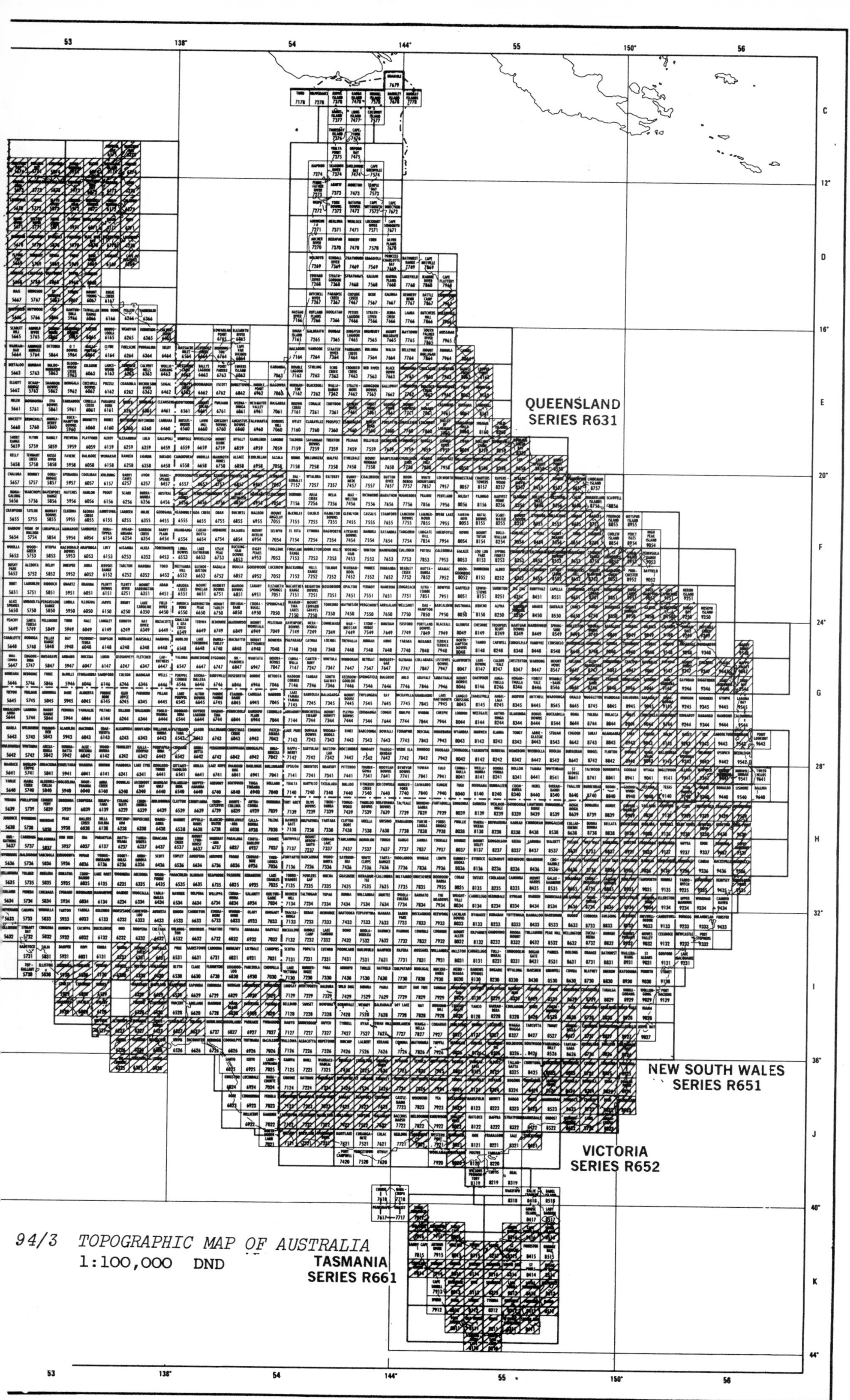

QUEENSLAND
SERIES R631
NEW SOUTH WALES
SERIES R651
VICTORIA
SERIES R652
TASMANIA
SERIES R661
94/3 TOPOGRAPHIC MAP OF AUSTRALIA
1:100,000 DND
53
138°
54
144°
55
150°
56
C
12°
D
16°
E
20°
F
24°
G
28°
H
32°
I
36°
J
40°
K
44°

94/4 *AUSTRALIA GEOLOGICAL SURVEYS*
1:250,000 - 1:253, 440

Standard Geological map of Australia (BMP)

1:250,000

1:253,440

State survey geological series 1:250,000

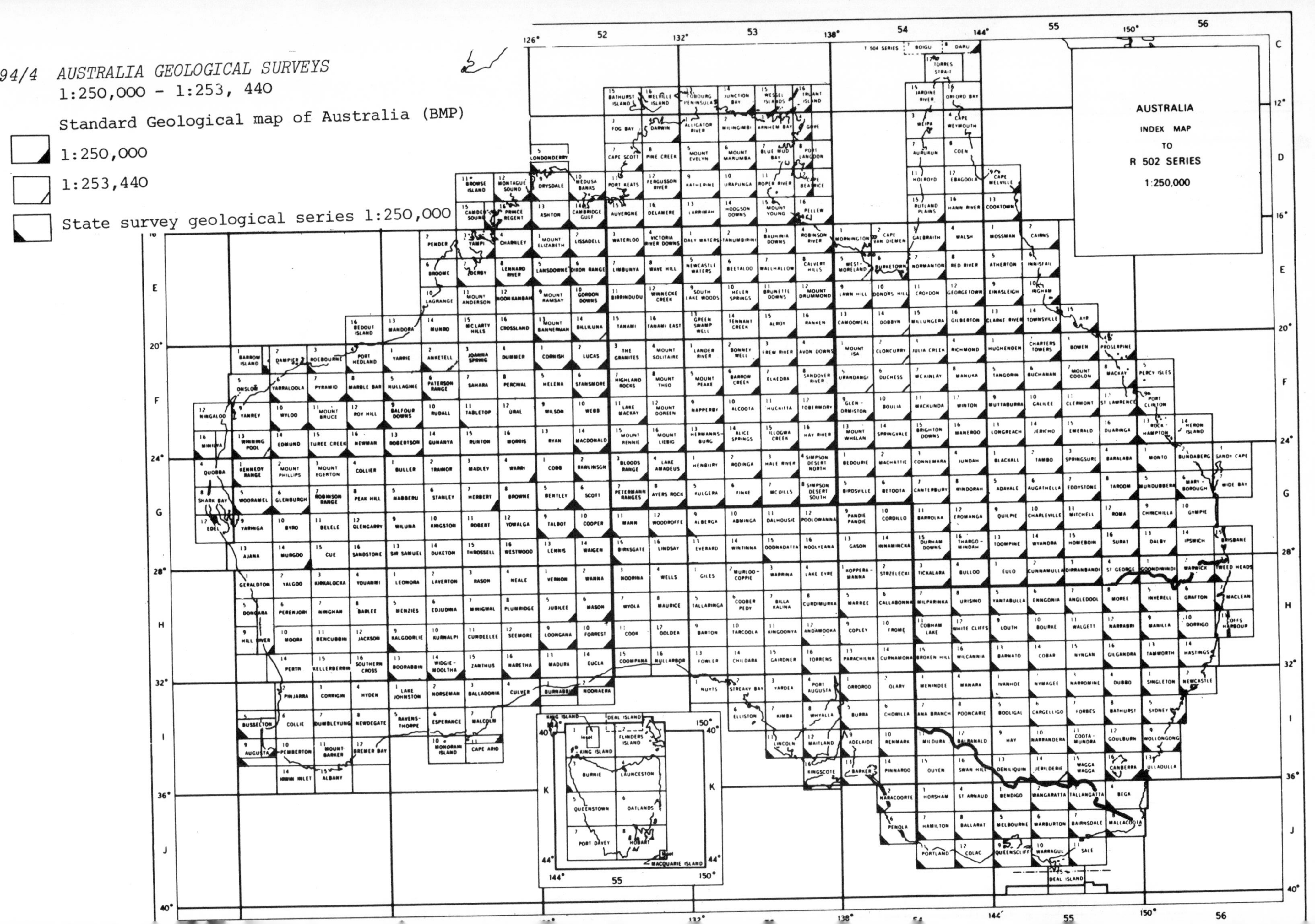

955/1 *PAPUA NEW GUINEA*

1:250,000 Series T504 DND

Topographical series

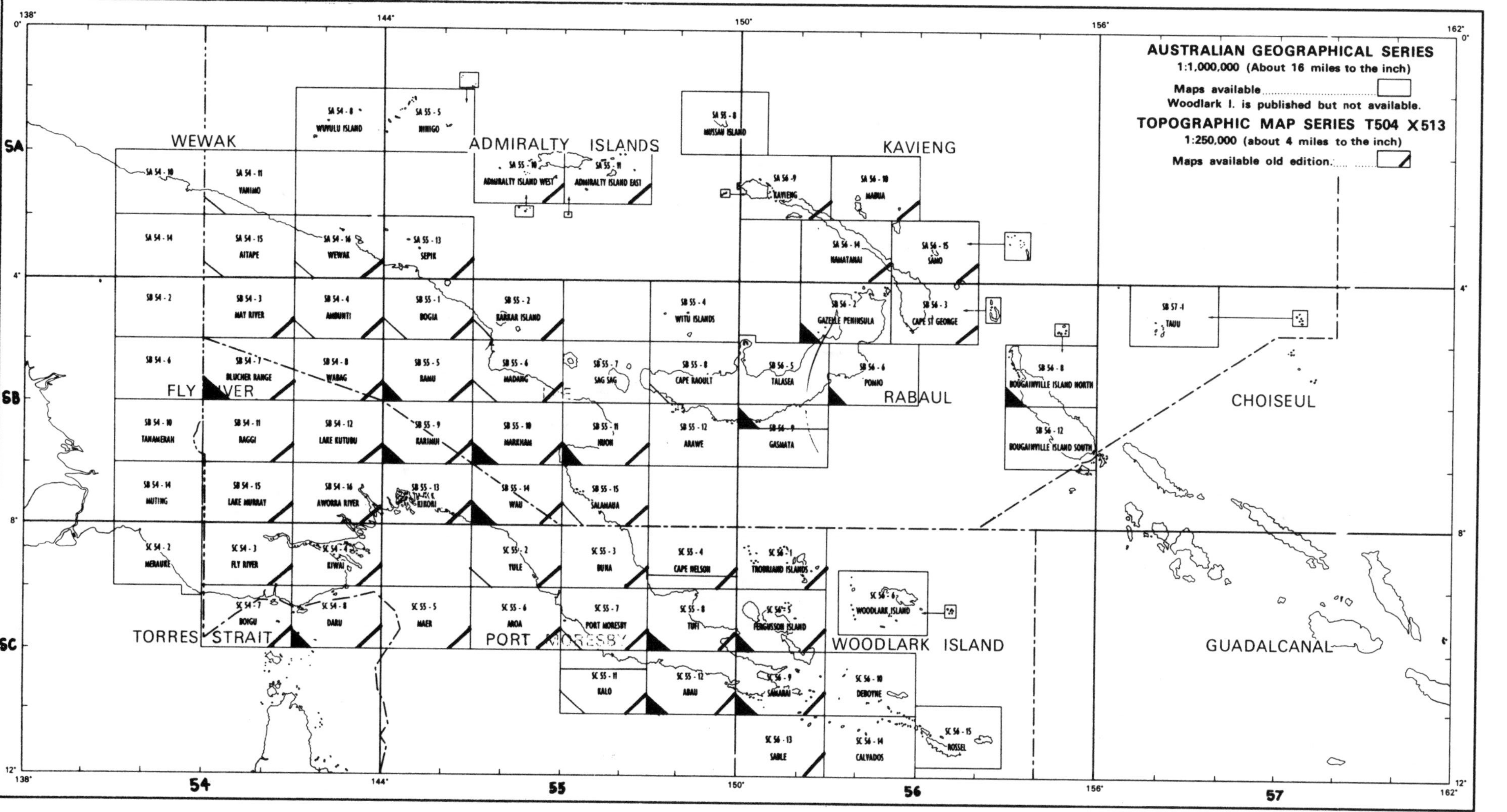

PAPUA NEW GUINEA GEOLOGICAL SERIES

1:250,000 DMR

Geological series

Standard series

Preliminary series

NB

The following sheets are combined as one in the geological edition only.

SB 55-7/11	SC 54-8/SC 55-5
SB 55-8/12	SC 55-4/8
SB 56-5/9	SC 55-7/11

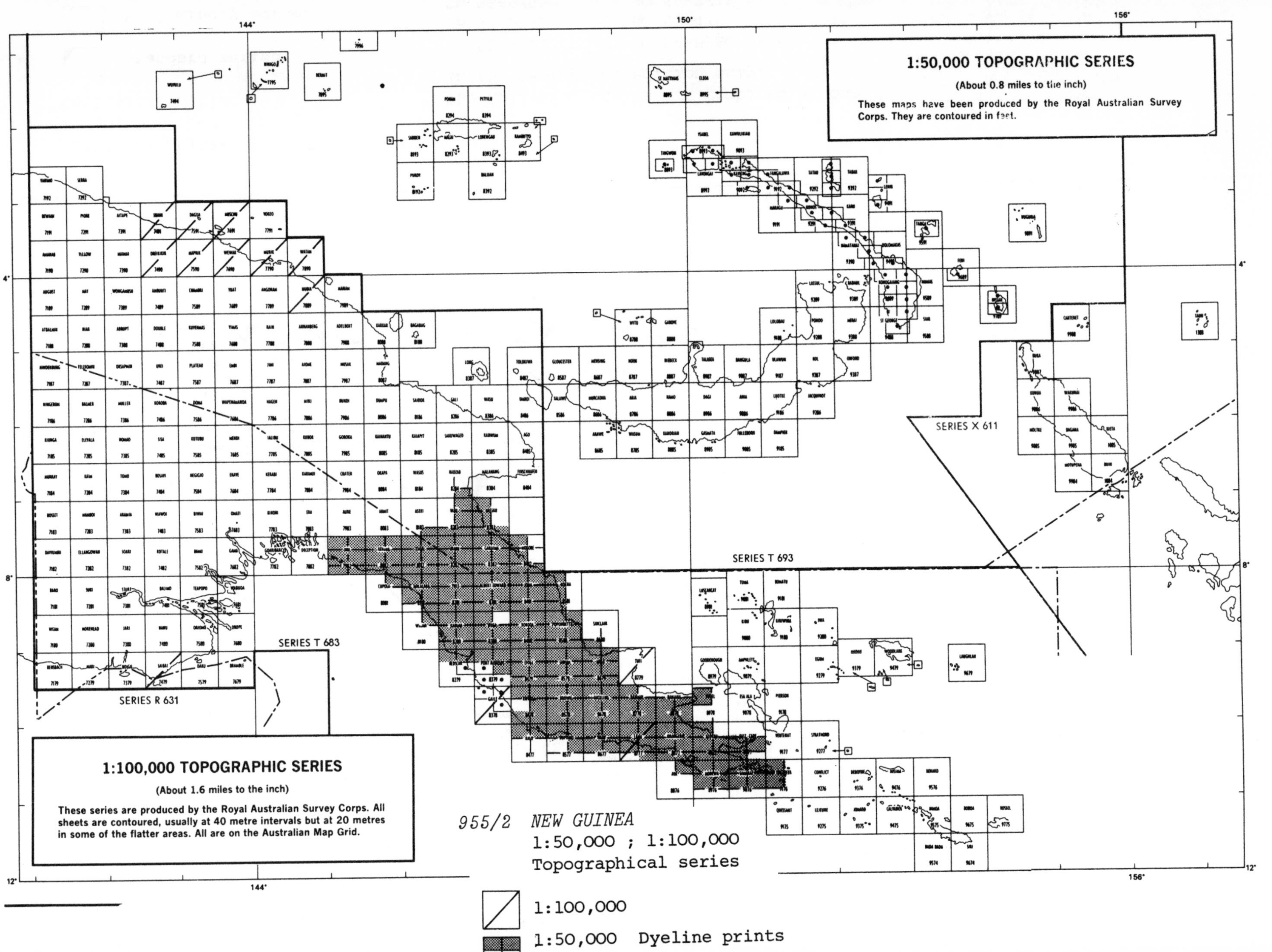
1:50,000 TOPOGRAPHIC SERIES
(About 0.8 miles to the inch)
These maps have been produced by the Royal Australian Survey Corps. They are contoured in feet.
1:100,000 TOPOGRAPHIC SERIES
(About 1.6 miles to the inch)
These series are produced by the Royal Australian Survey Corps. All sheets are contoured, usually at 40 metre intervals but at 20 metres in some of the flatter areas. All are on the Australian Map Grid.
SERIES X 611
SERIES T 693
SERIES T 683
SERIES R 631
144°
150°
156°
4°
8°
12°
955/2 NEW GUINEA
1:50,000 ; 1:100,000
Topographical series
1:100,000
1:50,000 Dyeline prints

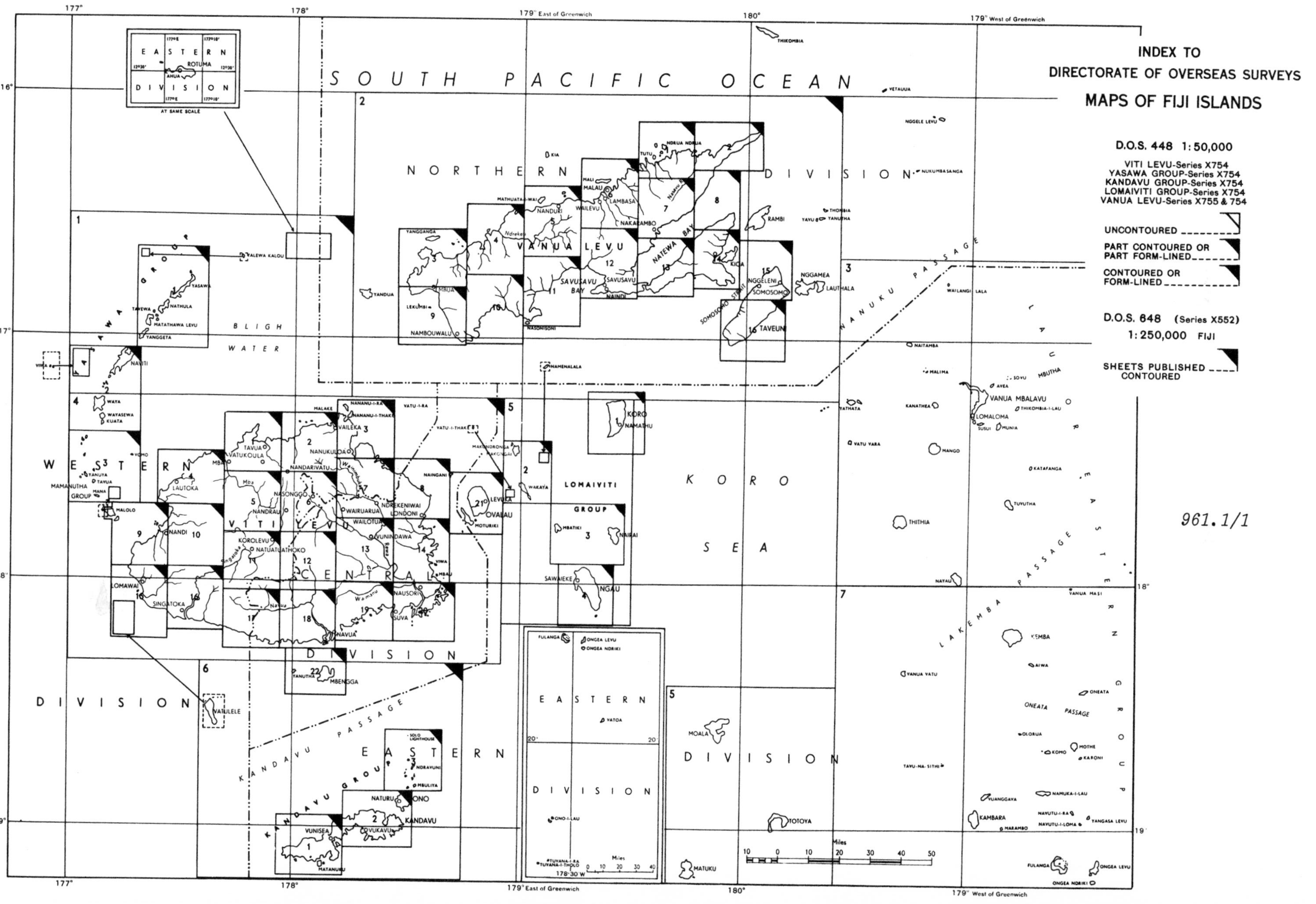

INDEX TO
DIRECTORATE OF OVERSEAS SURVEYS
MAPS OF FIJI ISLANDS
D.O.S. 448 1:50,000
VITI LEVU-Series X754
YASAWA GROUP-Series X754
KANDAVU GROUP-Series X754
LOMAIVITI GROUP-Series X754
VANUA LEVU-Series X755 & 754
UNCONTOURED
PART CONTOURED OR PART FORM-LINED
CONTOURED OR FORM-LINED
D.O.S. 648 (Series X552)
1:250,000 FIJI
SHEETS PUBLISHED CONTOURED
961.1/1
SOUTH PACIFIC OCEAN
NORTHERN DIVISION
VANUA LEVU
WESTERN DIVISION
CENTRAL DIVISION
EASTERN DIVISION
VITI LEVU
BLIGH WATER
KORO SEA
LOMAIVITI GROUP
NANUKU PASSAGE
KANDAVU PASSAGE
KANDAVU GROUP
LAKEMBA PASSAGE
ONEATA PASSAGE
EASTERN GROUP
YASAWA GROUP
ROTUMA
177°
178°
179° East of Greenwich
180°
179° West of Greenwich
16°
17°
18°
19°
Miles
10 0 10 20 30 40 50
SUVA
LAUTOKA
NANDI
TAVEUNI
KORO
NGAU
MOALA
MATUKU
TOTOYA
KANDAVU

Polar Regions

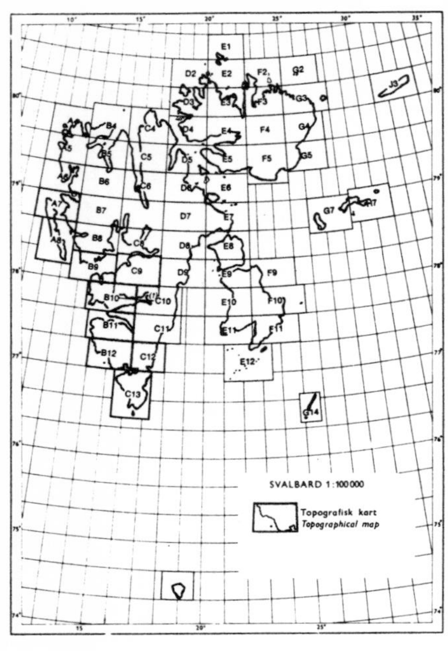

984/1 *SVALBARD*
1:100,000 NP
Topographical Series

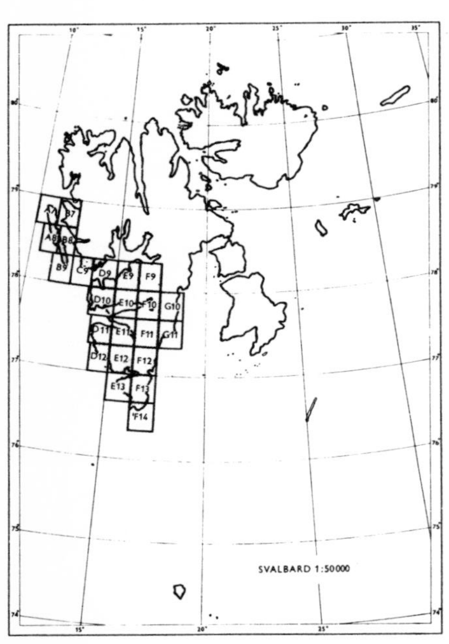

984/2 *SVALBARD*
1:50,000
Topographical Series

Sheets published

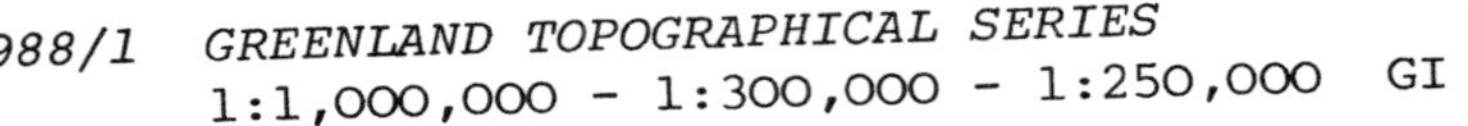

988/1 *GREENLAND TOPOGRAPHICAL SERIES*
1:1,000,000 - 1:300,000 - 1:250,000 GI

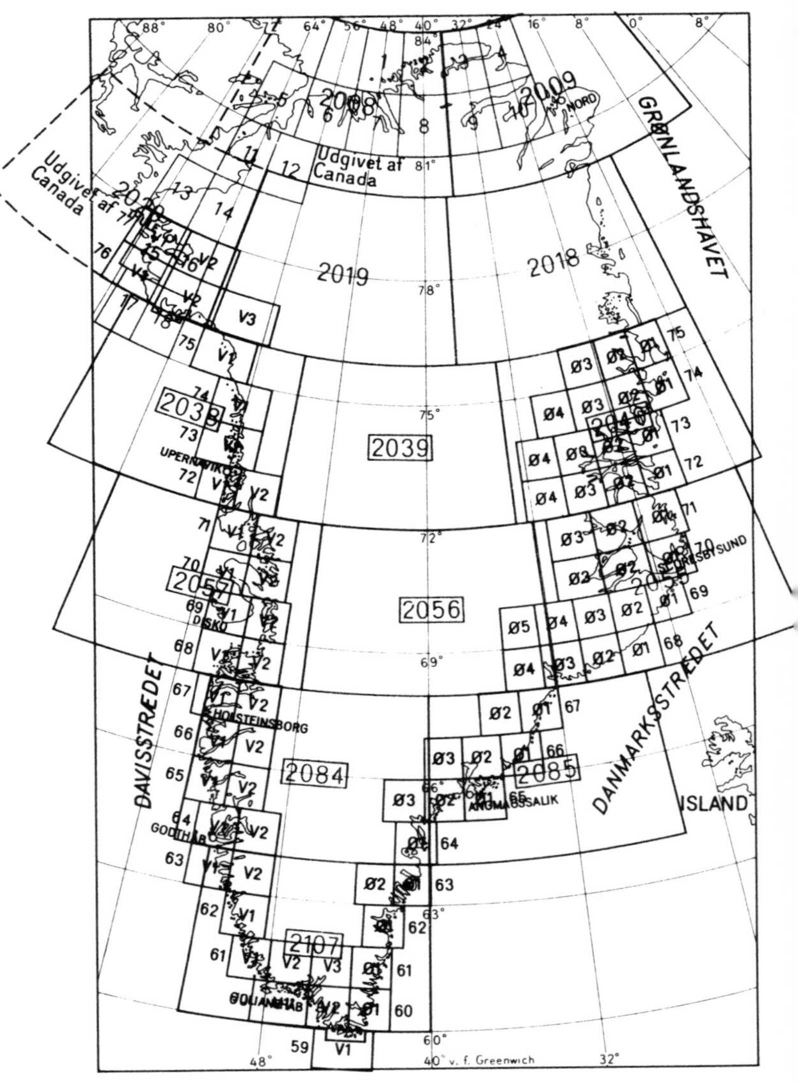

V2 Published sheets 1:250 000

4 Published sheets (Lauge Ko
1:300 000

2057 Published International Maps (ICAO)
1:1000000

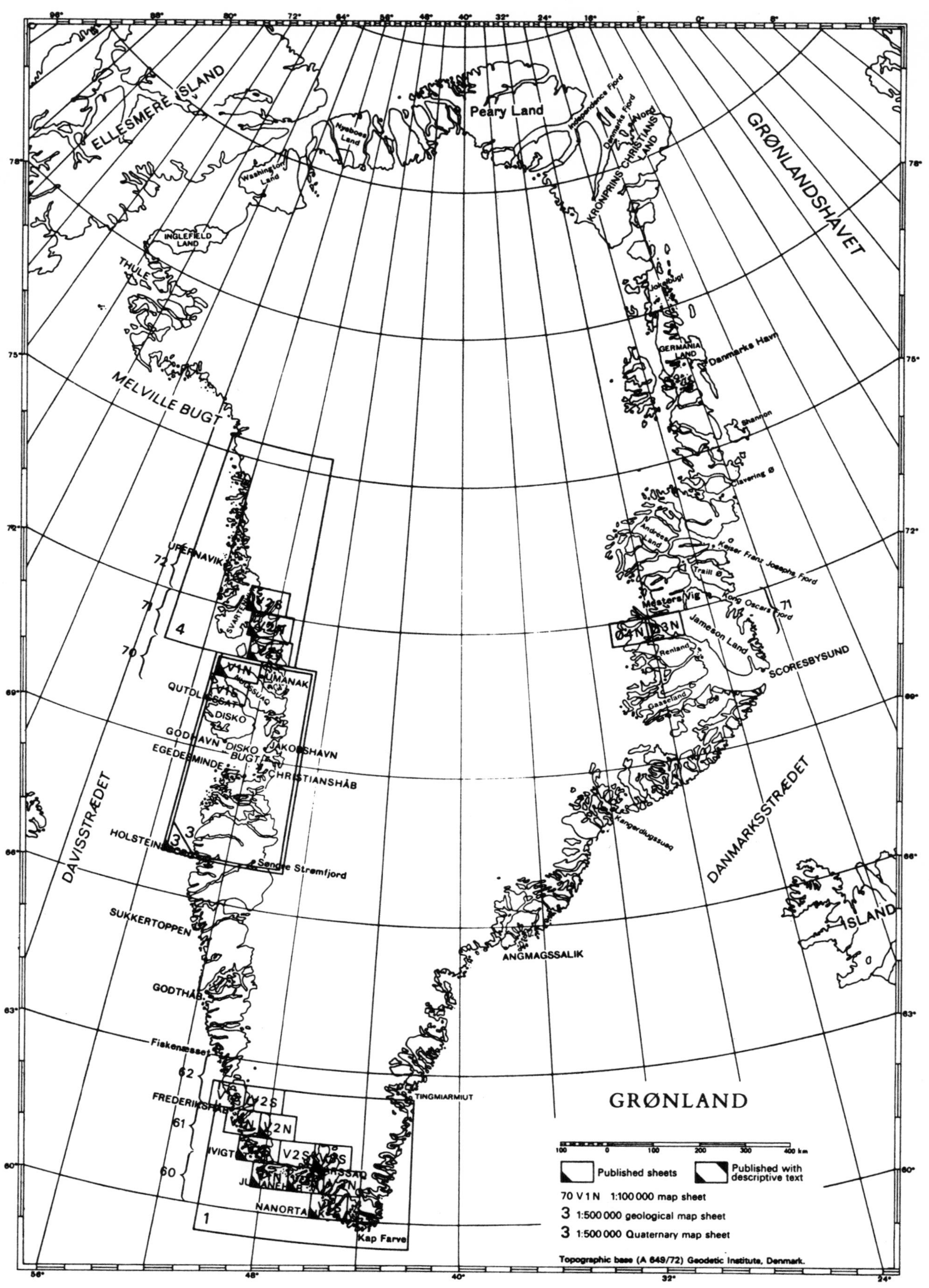

988/2 GREENLAND GEOLOGICAL SERIES
1:100,000 - 1:500,000 GGU

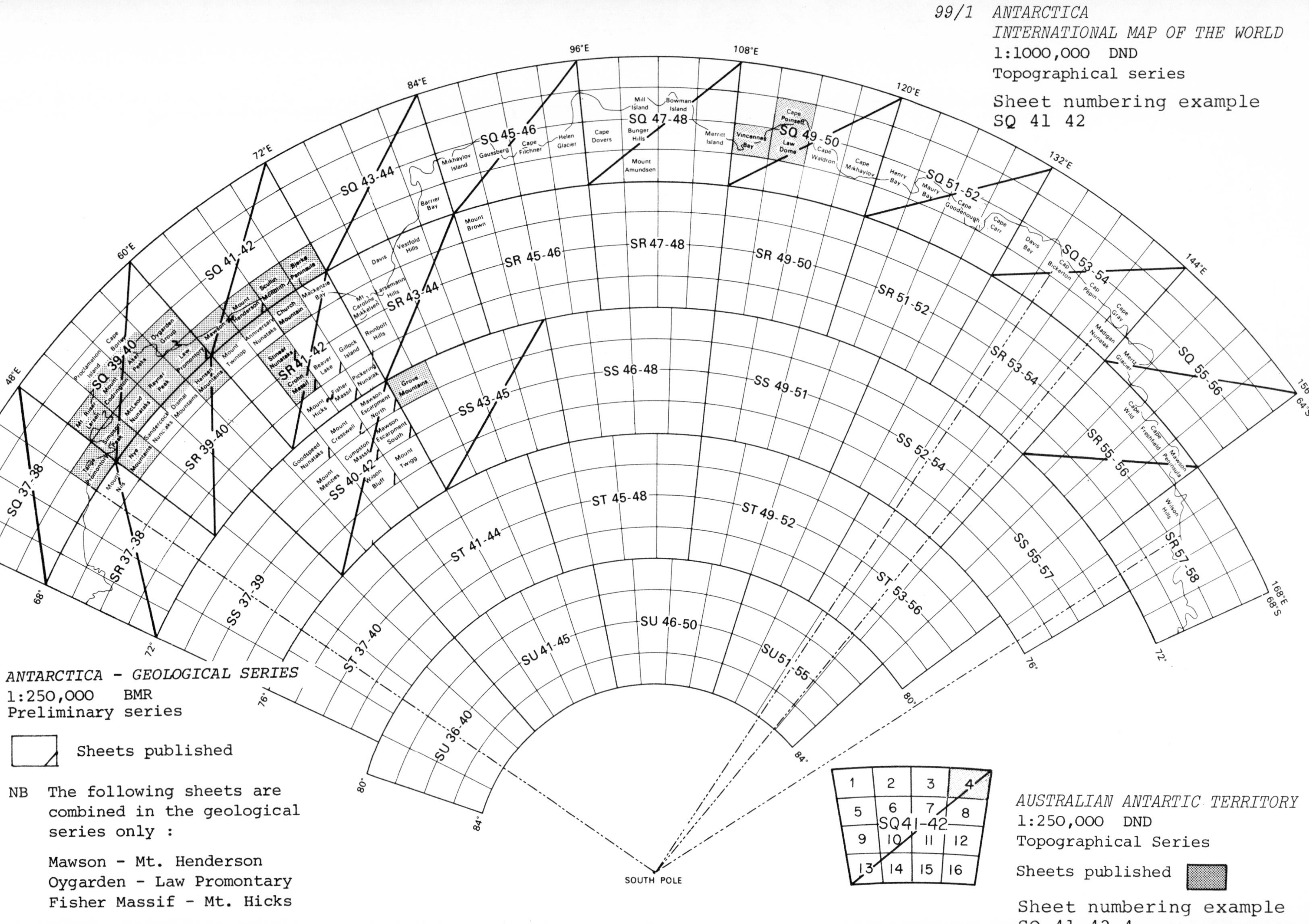
99/1 ANTARCTICA
INTERNATIONAL MAP OF THE WORLD
1:1000,000 DND
Topographical series
Sheet numbering example
SQ 41 42
ANTARCTICA - GEOLOGICAL SERIES
1:250,000 BMR
Preliminary series
Sheets published
NB The following sheets are combined in the geological series only :
Mawson - Mt. Henderson
Oygarden - Law Promontary
Fisher Massif - Mt. Hicks
AUSTRALIAN ANTARTIC TERRITORY
1:250,000 DND
Topographical Series
Sheets published
Sheet numbering example
SQ41-42
SOUTH POLE
48°E
60°E
72°E
84°E
96°E
108°E
120°E
132°E
144°E
156°E 64°S
168°E 68°S
SQ 37-38
SQ 39-40
SQ 41-42
SQ 43-44
SQ 45-46
SQ 47-48
SQ 49-50
SQ 51-52
SQ 53-54
SQ 55-56
SR 37-38
SR 39-40
SR 41-42
SR 43-44
SR 45-46
SR 47-48
SR 49-50
SR 51-52
SR 53-54
SR 55-56
SR 57-58
SS 37-39
SS 40-42
SS 43-45
SS 46-48
SS 49-51
SS 52-54
SS 55-57
ST 37-40
ST 41-44
ST 45-48
ST 49-52
ST 53-56
SU 36-40
SU 41-45
SU 46-50
SU 51-55

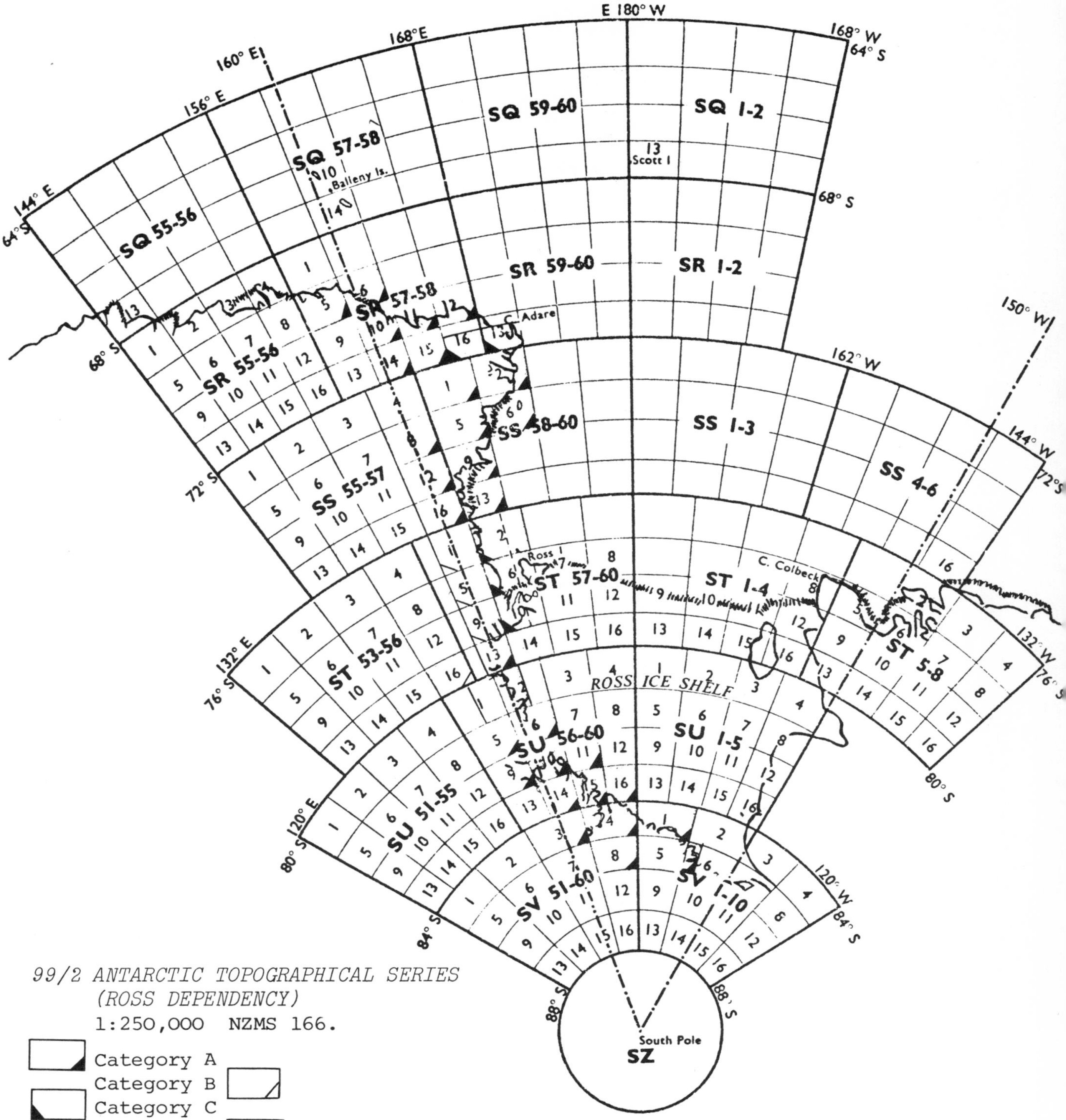

99/2 ANTARCTIC TOPOGRAPHICAL SERIES (ROSS DEPENDENCY)

1:250,000 NZMS 166.

Category A

Category B

Category C

Category D

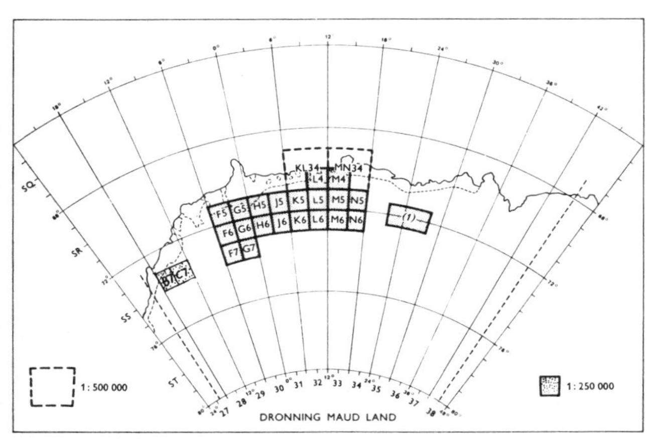

99/3 ANTARCTICA DRONNING MAUD LAND

1:250,000 NP

Topographical series

NB 1:500,000 series in preparation.

(1) Sør Rondane 1:250,000 1957

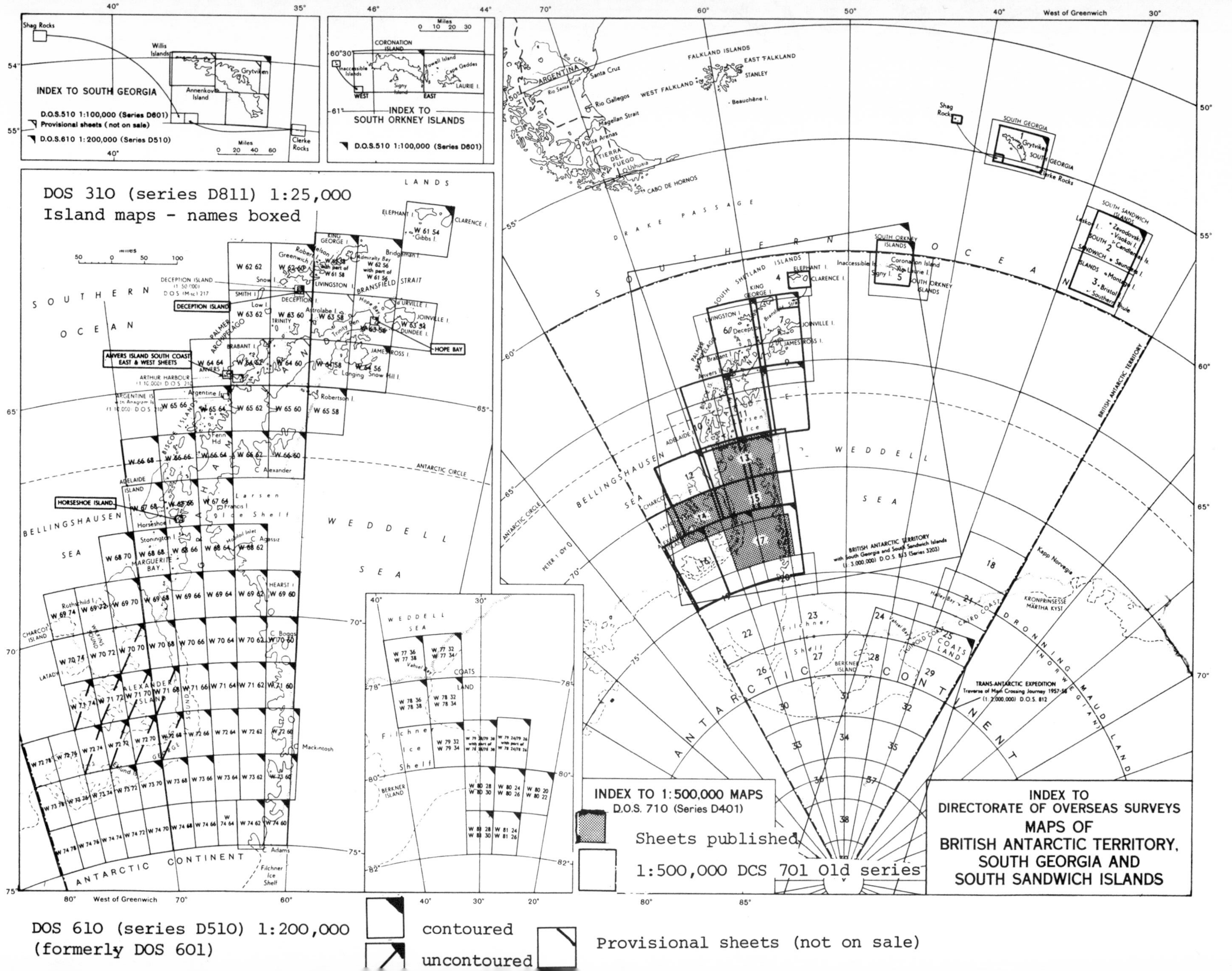
INDEX TO SOUTH GEORGIA
D.O.S.510 1:100,000 (Series D601)
Provisional sheets (not on sale)
D.O.S.610 1:200,000 (Series D510)
INDEX TO SOUTH ORKNEY ISLANDS
D.O.S.510 1:100,000 (Series D601)
DOS 310 (series D811) 1:25,000
Island maps - names boxed
DECEPTION ISLAND
ANVERS ISLAND SOUTH COAST EAST & WEST SHEETS
HOPE BAY
HORSESHOE ISLAND
INDEX TO 1:500,000 MAPS
D.O.S. 710 (Series D401)
Sheets published
1:500,000 DCS 701 Old series
INDEX TO
DIRECTORATE OF OVERSEAS SURVEYS
MAPS OF
BRITISH ANTARCTIC TERRITORY,
SOUTH GEORGIA AND
SOUTH SANDWICH ISLANDS
BRITISH ANTARCTIC TERRITORY with South Georgia and South Sandwich Islands (1:3,000,000) D.O.S. 813 (Series 3203)
TRANS-ANTARCTIC EXPEDITION Traverse of Main Crossing Journey 1957-58 (1:2,000,000) D.O.S. 812
DOS 610 (series D510) 1:200,000
(formerly DOS 601)
contoured
uncontoured
Provisional sheets (not on sale)

99/4

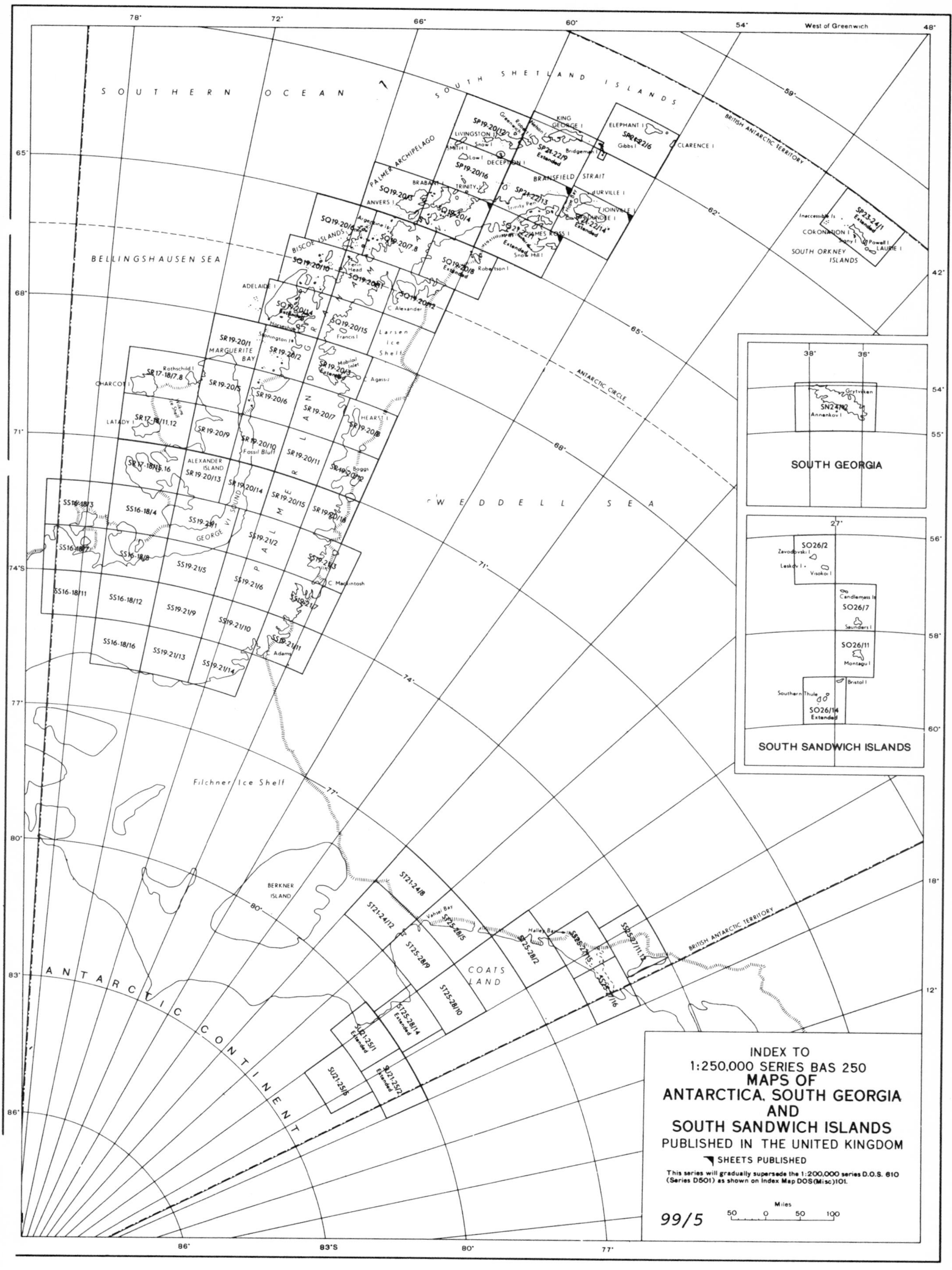
INDEX TO
1:250,000 SERIES BAS 250
MAPS OF
ANTARCTICA, SOUTH GEORGIA
AND
SOUTH SANDWICH ISLANDS
PUBLISHED IN THE UNITED KINGDOM
SHEETS PUBLISHED
This series will gradually supersede the 1:200,000 series D.O.S. 610 (Series D501) as shown on Index Map DOS(Misc)101.
99/5
Miles
50 0 50 100
West of Greenwich
SOUTHERN OCEAN
SOUTH SHETLAND ISLANDS
BRITISH ANTARCTIC TERRITORY
PALMER ARCHIPELAGO
BELLINGSHAUSEN SEA
WEDDELL SEA
ANTARCTIC CIRCLE
Filchner Ice Shelf
BERKNER ISLAND
COATS LAND
ANTARCTIC CONTINENT
SOUTH ORKNEY ISLANDS
SOUTH GEORGIA
SOUTH SANDWICH ISLANDS
ALEXANDER ISLAND
MARGUERITE BAY
GEORGE VI SOUND
BRANSFIELD STRAIT
Larsen Ice Shelf
Fossil Bluff
Vahsel Bay
Halley Bay
C Mackintosh
C Alexander
ELEPHANT I
CLARENCE I
KING GEORGE I
LIVINGSTON I
DECEPTION I
ANVERS I
ADELAIDE I
CHARCOT I
LATADY I
JOINVILLE I
CORONATION I
LAURIE I
Grytviken
Annenkov I
Zavodovski I
Leskov I
Visokoi I
Candlemass Is
Saunders I
Montagu I
Bristol I
Southern Thule
SN24/12
SO26/2
SO26/7
SO26/11
SO26/14 Extended
SP23-24/1 Extended
SP21-22/6
SP19-20/12
SP21-22/9 Extended
SP19-20/16
SP21-22/13
SP21-22/14 Extended
SQ19-20/3
SQ19-20/4
SQ19-20/7,8
SQ19-20/8 Extended
SQ19-20/10
SQ19-20/11
SQ19-20/12
SQ19-20/14 Extended
SQ19-20/15
SR19-20/1
SR19-20/2
SR19-20/3 Extended
SR17-18/7,8
SR19-20/5
SR19-20/6
SR19-20/7
SR19-20/8
SR17-18/11,12
SR19-20/9
SR19-20/10
SR19-20/11
SR19-20/12
SR17-18/15,16
SR19-20/13
SR19-20/14
SR19-20/15
SR19-20/16
SS16-18/3
SS16-18/4
SS19-21/1
SS19-21/2
SS19-21/3
SS16-18/7
SS16-18/8
SS19-21/5
SS19-21/6
SS19-21/7
SS16-18/11
SS16-18/12
SS19-21/9
SS19-21/10
SS19-21/11
SS16-18/16
SS19-21/13
SS19-21/14
ST21-24/8
ST21-24/12
ST25-28/5
ST25-28/9
ST25-28/10
ST25-28/14 Extended
ST25-28/2
SU21-25/1 Extended
SU21-25/2 Extended
SU21-25/6
83°S
74°S

FALKLAND ISLANDS

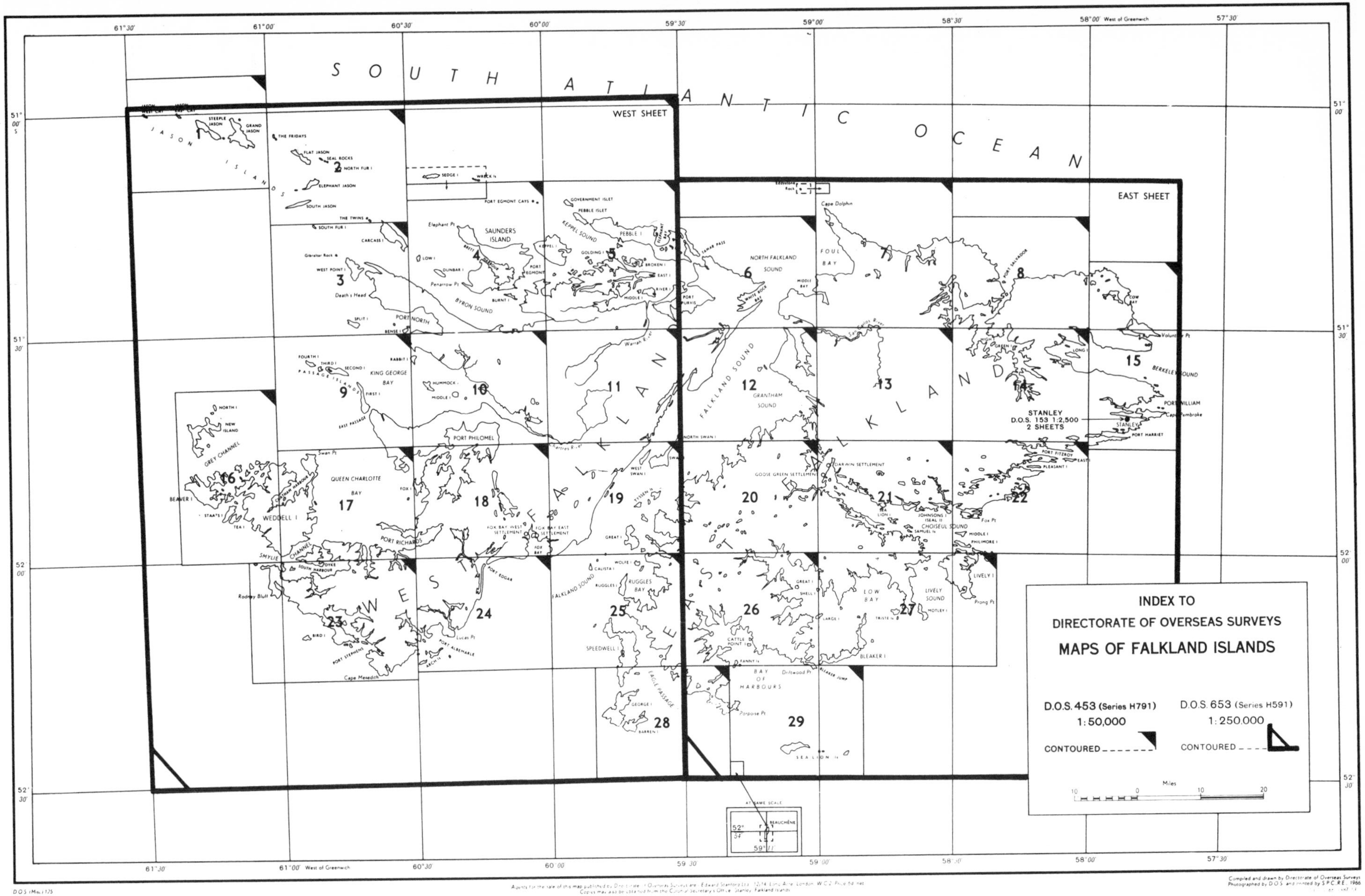

INDEX TO
DIRECTORATE OF OVERSEAS SURVEYS
MAPS OF FALKLAND ISLANDS

D.O.S. 453 (Series H791)
1:50,000
CONTOURED

D.O.S. 653 (Series H591)
1:250,000
CONTOURED

Miles 10 0 10 20

STANLEY
D.O.S. 153 1:2,500
2 SHEETS

WEST SHEET

EAST SHEET

SOUTH ATLANTIC OCEAN

WEST FALKLAND

EAST FALKLAND

D.O.S. (Misc.) 175

Agents for the sale of this map published by Directorate of Overseas Surveys are: Edward Stanford Ltd. 12-14 Long Acre, London W.C.2 [illegible]
Copies may also be obtained from the Colonial Secretary's Office, Stanley, Falkland Islands

Compiled and drawn by Directorate of Overseas Surveys
Photographed by D.O.S. and printed by S.P.C.R.E. 1966 [illegible]

99.1/1

Space.

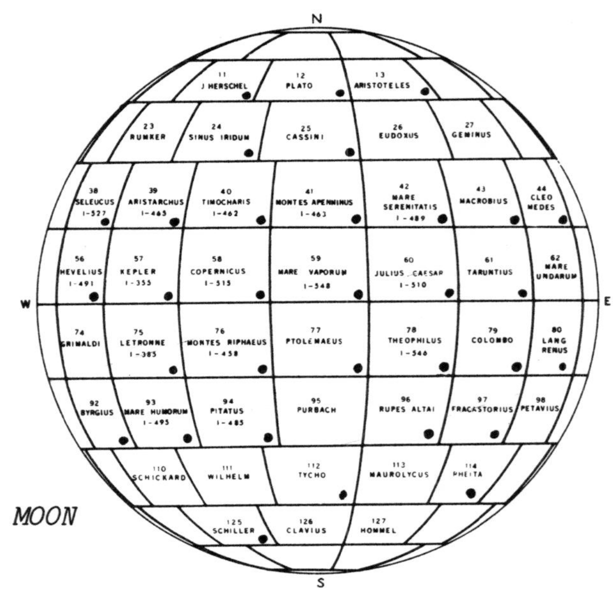

S523.3/1 GEOLOGICAL MAP SERIES OF THE MOON
1:1,000,000 USGS.

Sheets published.

Index of Geographical Names

Figures in parentheses are UDC numbers (see Introduction on page *X*); figures not in parentheses are page numbers.